AN ENCYCLOPEDIA OF
WORLD HISTORY

AN ENCYCLOPEDIA OF
WORLD HISTORY

ANCIENT, MEDIEVAL,
AND *MODERN*
CHRONOLOGICALLY ARRANGED

Compiled and Edited by

WILLIAM L. LANGER

Coolidge Professor of History, Emeritus
Harvard University

Fifth Edition
Revised and Enlarged
with Maps and
Genealogical Tables

HOUGHTON MIFFLIN COMPANY BOSTON

w 10 9 8 7 6 5 4

ISBN: 0-395-13592-3

Library of Congress Catalog Card Number: 68-14147
Printed in the United States of America

CONTRIBUTORS TO THE FOURTH AND FIFTH EDITIONS

Geoffrey Bruun

George Busalla

Carleton Coon

Frank M. Cross, Jr.

Sterling Dow

Robert H. Dyson, Jr.

Marija Gimbutas

Madeleine Gleason

Carol R. Harting

Stephen N. Hay

Halil Inalcik

Melvin Kranzberg

Dwight E. Lee

Derwood Lockard

J. A. B. Van Buitenen

CONTRIBUTORS TO EARLIER EDITIONS

* Crane Brinton
  Geoffrey Bruun
  Robert S. Chamberlain
* Paul P. Cram
  John K. Fairbank
* Charles S. Gardner
  Hans W. Gatzke
  Mason Hammond
* James B. Hedges
* Michael Karpovich
* Donald C. McKay
* Robert H. Pfeiffer
  Edwin O. Reischauer
* Penfield Roberts
  Robert O. Schlaifer
* William Thomson
* Lauriston Ward

* Since deceased.

PREFACE TO THE FIRST EDITION

This *Epitome of History* itself has a long and interesting history. More than seventy years ago Dr. Karl Ploetz, in his time a well-known German teacher, published an *Auszug aus der alten, mittleren und neueren Geschichte,* intended as a factual handbook for the use of students and for the convenience of the general reader. That his compilation filled a real need is attested by the fact that within a few years it went through seven editions, and by the further fact that to date more than twenty editions have appeared in Germany, revised and edited by noted scholars. The book has easily held its own despite competition of numerous similar works.

Ploetz's *Epitome* was translated into English by William H. Tillinghast and published by Houghton Mifflin Company in this country in 1883. The translator, recognizing that the original was designed particularly to meet the needs of the German student and that therefore the history of central Europe was weighted as against the history of France, England, and America, took the opportunity to enlarge a number of sections and to add others. No less a scholar than Edward Channing contributed the new sections on modern England and the United States. Furthermore, Tillinghast first added brief sections on the Middle and Far Eastern countries, which had been completely omitted from the German version. The book appeared under the title *An Epitome of Ancient, Medieval, and Modern History,* and proved so popular that no less than twenty-four printings were necessary before 1905. Occasional revisions were made and in 1915 the title was changed to *A Handbook of Universal History.*

Since historical knowledge and historical conceptions are notoriously fluid, it is not to be wondered at that even so sound and reliable a book as the old Ploetz-Tillinghast *Epitome* should ultimately have fallen behind the times. After the First World War the publishers therefore commissioned Dr. Harry Elmer Barnes to overhaul the book and bring it up to date. The new editor, with a number of collaborators, left the kernel of the old work (the Greek and Roman history, the medieval sections, and the early modern parts) as it was, judging quite rightly that in the large it was not so badly out of line as to justify rewriting and resetting. But the sections dealing with the early Near East, of which little was known in Ploetz's day, were completely redone, and a great deal of material on the period from 1883 to 1923 was added. The *Epitome,* thus revised, was published in 1925 as *A Manual of Universal History*. Like the preceding versions it has been widely used by students and laymen alike.

But despite revisions of one kind or another, it became increasingly clear that sooner or later the original book would require drastic changes if it were to keep abreast of modern knowledge and meet contemporary requirements. It stands to reason that in seventy years our command of the facts and our views of even those subjects best treated by Ploetz and Tillinghast have changed substantially. Above all, the past fifty years have witnessed the expansion of western influence over the entire globe and, as a result, there is now a much greater need to know something of the past of non-European countries and cultures, and a much livelier interest in formerly neglected fields. To fill the new requirements no amount of revision of the old book would do, for the original author wrote as a German and treated European history primarily as it touched his own country's development. Tillinghast attempted to give the English translation a somewhat more Anglo-American slant, and Dr. Barnes did what was humanly possible to adapt the old text to a more world-wide approach. But the point had been definitely reached where adaptations and adjustments would no longer suffice. The publishers therefore invited me to undertake a complete rewriting of the entire book, securing the aid of collaborators qualified to treat of special fields where it seemed desirable. It was my great good fortune to be able to interest fifteen of my colleagues to take over particular sections and to secure from them the most whole-hearted co-operation in what, after all, was an enterprise of some magnitude. Their names, with the sections for which they made themselves responsible, are listed above.

When embarking upon this project I still had hope that considerable parts of the old book might yet be salvaged and that a thoroughgoing revision would prove adequate for the ancient, medieval, and early modern sections. But it soon became apparent to all of us engaged in the work that the whole plan and approach required rethinking and that, consequently, there was but little use in trying to adhere to the old text. Here and there a few pages (thoroughly emended) have been retained, but they are relatively so few in number as to be hardly worth mentioning. Almost nothing of the substance of the old book remains; every single section has been gone over in thorough fashion, reduced or expanded and, above all, brought into line with present-day knowledge. Many other sections, naturally, have been newly written, so that I think we can honestly say that the book is no longer a manual of European history with some perfunctory reference to other countries, but genuine world history, in which the geographical divisions are dealt with on their merits.

In the course of rewriting we have, however, stuck by Ploetz's original conception. That is, we have tried to compile a handbook of historical facts, so arranged that the dates stand out while the material itself flows in a reasonably smooth narrative. Individual judgments have been kept in the background and divergent interpretations have been adduced only where they seemed to be indispensable. The great diversity of type which had crept into the old book has been done away with and we have broken the uniformity of the print only by the use of small and capital boldface and very occasional employment of italics. The number of genealogical charts has been much increased: new tables have been added for some of the non-European dynasties and all charts have been brought up to date. Furthermore, a considerable number of maps has been included, not with the idea of supplying a complete historical atlas, but simply for the convenience of the user who, when he is checking one event or another, cannot be expected to have always at hand the necessary map material.

In the preface to the 1925 edition Dr. Barnes referred to the growing interest in non-political aspects of history and to his attempt to expand sections dealing with economic and cultural developments. Though deeply interested in these phases of history, Dr. Barnes felt obliged to recognize that the majority of those who would use the book would come seeking information on political, military, and diplomatic history and that therefore those angles would have to be primarily considered. I subscribe entirely to this view, but I take this opportunity to point out further that cultural history does not lend itself readily to the method of treatment upon which this particular work is based. The backbone of this book is chronology which, in the case of general economic trends, religious and artistic movements, and intellectual currents, is both hard to define and of relatively less significance. For methodological reasons, if for no other, we could therefore give but slight emphasis to these aspects of history. In addition we had to consider the further difficulties presented by space limitation: obviously anything like adequate treatment of literature, art, science, and economics would have taken us so far afield that the results could not possibly have been enclosed within two covers. In some sections the reader will find brief summaries of cultural activities, in others not; but in any case we offer them only for what they may be worth, as a matter of convenience, without any thought of sufficiency, much less exhaustiveness. And these remarks apply equally to the special sections at the beginning of the nineteenth century, entitled *Social Thought and Social Movements, Scientific Thought and Progress,* and *Mechanical Inventions and Technical Achievements.** The material we adduce in these sections appeared to us indispensable for an understanding of nineteenth-century development. It cannot be suitably included under any one country, for its application is general. We could not aim or hope for completeness; hence our only objective in these sections has been to bring together an irreducible minimum of pertinent information.

Each successive editor of this *Handbook* has come away from his task impressed with the difficulties of attaining accuracy in dealing with so vast a number of dates covering so wide a range of time and territory. I am no exception to the rule and am far from being arrogant enough to suppose that this new book is even more free from error than the old. There is some consolation, however, in the thought that we collaborators have all done what we reasonably

*In the present edition these sections are entitled *Philosophical, Religious, and Social Thought; Science and Learning; Technological Achievements.*

could to guard against blunders and that, as a matter of fact, many dates are so uncertain or disputed that they will probably never be satisfactorily fixed.

The success of the *Epitome of History* over a period of more than two generations is ample proof of the need for a manual of this type. In the revised and extended form here presented, it ought to be more valuable than ever. Its use for students of history is obvious enough, but it ought to prove as helpful to many others. Students of the history of literature and of art should find a concise guide to political history a great boon and all readers of historical novels or biographies should welcome a book of reference to events of the past, to genealogical relationships, and so on. My own experience with the old book was that I used it more as I became better acquainted with it. Nothing would please me more than to have the new edition find a secure place on the shelves of all book-lovers.

In presenting the new *Epitome* I cannot refrain from expressing my profound gratitude to all the contributors and also to Professors Walter Clark and Vincent Scramuzza, to Professor Sterling Dow, Mr. Eugene Boardman, and to Miss Katharine Irwin for the ready help they gave in reading proof. My secretaries, Mrs. Elizabeth Fox and Mrs. Rosamund Chapman, took care of countless loose ends and deserve more than a little credit for whatever merit the book may have.

PREFACE TO THE FIFTH EDITION

Less than a decade has passed since the publication of the fourth edition of the present work, which was a basic redoing of the earlier editions and incorporated a great deal of new subject matter. Such drastic changes are necessary perhaps once in a generation, but in our fast-moving world important events are constantly occurring. For that reason it has seemed to the editor and the publisher desirable to bring the fourth edition chronologically up-to-date in a fifth edition which covers developments throughout the world through the year 1970.

In recent years important advances have been made in the fields of prehistory and early civilizations, and these have required some rewriting by experts in those matters. But most importantly, account has had to be taken of the events of the past seven years. During that time numerous states, former colonies of the European powers, have attained their independence and become members of the United Nations. Furthermore, dangerous conflicts have developed that are not even yet concluded. In the Middle East there has been a third round in the duel between the Israelis and the Arabs, while in Southeast Asia the war in Vietnam has grown to the point where it not only threatens to produce a world crisis, but has shaken the domestic politics of the United States to their foundations. Communist China has been racked by the so-called Cultural Revolution, and the antagonism between the two Communist giants, Soviet Russia and Communist China, has become steadily aggravated. Japan has risen to the rank of a prime industrial power, while in the midst of general affluence almost all nations have been confronted with a revolt of youth which has culminated in student upheavals and drastic changes in the educational systems. Race conflict, too, has become a major factor in political and social development. Yet these recent years have witnessed also the rapid development of the space age, vividly symbolized by the first landings of men on the moon and the initiation of explorations that will broaden and deepen our understanding of the entire universe.

Merely to catalogue a few major changes of the past decade suffices to indicate the extensive alterations and additions required by the fifth edition of this world-renowned historical handbook. As on previous occasions, I have called upon friends and colleagues for expert help and have benefited greatly from their continued interest and knowledge. Like former editions, this one also has gained from the correspondence of readers throughout the world who have discovered inconsistencies or errors. In short, no effort has been spared to make this one of the really indispensable reference books for all the innumerable readers who continue in the hectic present to find counsel and comfort from the study of man's past.

WILLIAM L. LANGER

CONTENTS

I. THE PREHISTORIC PERIOD

II. ANCIENT HISTORY

III. THE MIDDLE AGES

IV. THE EARLY MODERN PERIOD

V. THE MODERN PERIOD

VI. THE FIRST WORLD WAR AND THE INTER-WAR PERIOD, 1914–1939

VII. THE SECOND WORLD WAR
AND ITS AFTERMATH, 1939–1970

VIII. THE RECENT PERIOD

APPENDIX

MAPS

GENEALOGICAL TABLES

I. THE PREHISTORIC PERIOD

I. THE PREHISTORIC PERIOD

A. INTRODUCTION

1. DEFINITION, DATA, AND METHODS

HISTORY in its broadest sense should be a record of Man and his accomplishments from the time when he ceased being merely an animal and became a human being. The efforts to reconstruct this record may be classed under two heads: (1) **History** (in the stricter sense), which is based on written documents and covers part of the last five thousand years of Man's activities, and (2) **Prehistory,** which is based largely on archaeological evidence and covers all the long preceding period, which probably amounts to more than one million years.

The prehistoric period is important, not only by reason of its vast length, but also because during this time Man made almost all his major discoveries and adaptations to environment and group-life (except those connected with the recent machine age) and evolved physically into our living species and its races. Hence at least a brief summary of the prehistoric period is a necessary introduction to any account of the recorded history of Man.

The main body of material upon which the work of prehistoric reconstruction is based comprises: first, remains left by early peoples, largely in the form of tools, other artifacts, and animal bones found by excavation in old habitation sites or burials; secondly, other traces of their activities, such as buildings and rock-carvings or rock-paintings; and lastly, the bones of the people themselves. This material gives good evidence of the physical type of prehistoric peoples and their material culture, very slight evidence of their social, intellectual, and religious life and no evidence of their language. It can be supplemented to some extent—and with great caution—by a comparative study of the physical types, blood groups, languages, and material culture of modern peoples.

The time when prehistory ends and true history begins varies greatly in different parts of the world. Traditional history often covers the borderline between the two and can sometimes be successfully correlated with the archaeological evidence.

2. THE ORIGIN OF MAN

MAN'S PLACE AMONG THE ANIMALS. The various living and extinct species of Man are assigned by zoologists to the super-family *Hominoidea,* which belongs to the sub-order *Catarrhinae* (containing Old World monkeys, apes, and baboons), of the order Primates (containing also the *Platyrrhinae* [South American monkeys], *Tarsius,* the lemurs, and *Tupaia* [the tree shrew]), of the class **Mammalia.** His nearest living relatives are the three genera of the super-family *Pongidae* (the so-called Anthropoid Apes): the gorilla and chimpanzee of equatorial Africa and the orang-utan of southeastern Asia and the East Indies. Man is distinguished from the higher apes by the greater size of his brain (especially the forebrain), his fully erect position in walking, the better adaptation of his hands for grasping and holding, and his use of language for communication.

MAN'S ANIMAL ANCESTORS. All living men belong to the species *Homo sapiens,* in some regions 250,000 years old. Specimens of its ancestral species, *Homo erectus,* have been found in Java, China, and Africa from about 1,100,000 years onward. A third species, *Homo habilis,* has also been identified from bones found in Olduvai Gorge, Tanganyika, dated at 1,750,000 years by Argon-40 tests. A related genus, *Australopithecus,* lived in Africa and possibly South Asia at the same time. Although related to *Homo, Australopithecus* was not our ancestor.

Proconsul, a 24,000,000-year-old Early Miocene primate from East Africa, may have been ancestral to apes, *Australopithecenes,* and Man. Three 14,000,000-year-old primates (late Miocene or Early Pliocene) have been considered as our ancestors—*Ramapithecus* from India, *Kenyapithecus* from East Africa, and (the least likely) *Oreopithecus* from Italy.

DATE OF MAN'S ORIGIN. This has not yet been definitely established. The ancestors of the great apes and the ancestor of Man probably diverged from one another as early as the Miocene period, and Man acquired certain essentially human characteristics probably in the Pliocene period. The earliest known skeletal remains that are accepted as human are believed to date from near the end of the Lower Pleistocene. For the purposes of the prehistorian, who has to rely largely on archaeological evidence, the record of Man may be said to begin at the moment when he was able to fashion the first stone tools that can be unmistakably recognized to be of human workmanship. This was late in the Lower Pleistocene, or possibly in the very late Pliocene.

PLACE OF MAN'S ORIGIN. This is still uncertain. The old theory of Central Asia as the "Cradle of Mankind" was based on false premises, which have been abandoned. From the distribution of the living and fossil great apes, Australopithecenes, and men, it is thought that Man's divergence from the general anthropoid stem probably occurred somewhere in Africa.

3. CULTURES AND THEIR DATING

a. CULTURES AND PERIODS

Archaeological investigation of the material remains of prehistoric Man has shown that a wide variety of cultures flourished in different parts of the world and at different times. For convenience these have been grouped into a series of major cultures based primarily on the nature of the principal material used for implements (whether stone or one of the metals), and sometimes on the technique used in fashioning these implements. The oldest culture in the world was characterized by the use of chipped stone for implements and has been named Paleolithic culture. Neolithic culture, on the other hand, was characterized by the use of polished stone implements; Bronze culture, by the use of bronze implements, and so forth.

In most parts of the world the discovery and use of these different materials and techniques took place in a regular sequence in time. In the absence of fixed dates, it was thus found convenient to use these cultural terms in a chronological sense. Accordingly prehistoric times have usually been divided into the following series of periods or ages (beginning with the oldest): **Paleolithic** (Old Stone), characterized by chipped stone implements; **Mesolithic** (Intermediate Stone), a transitional period; **Neolithic** (New Stone), with polished stone implements; **Chalcolithic** (Stone and Copper), characterized by the first tentative use of copper implements; **Bronze Age,** with full development of copper and bronze implements; and **Iron Age,** with iron implements.

These names are excellent to identify cultures, but their use to designate periods of time has led to much inaccuracy and confusion, as the dates of the cultures to which they refer differ widely in different parts of the world. It is proper, for example, to speak of the Bronze Age of Hungary or some other limited area, where the beginning and end of the bronze culture can be fairly accurately dated. But it is quite impossible to speak with any meaning of the Bronze Age of the Old World, for this period began some thousand or fifteen hundred years earlier in Mesopotamia, for instance, than it did in western Europe, and it gave way to the Iron Age one or two thousand years earlier in Asia Minor than it did in some parts of Siberia; while in Japan there was no true Bronze Age and in Australia no Bronze Age at all. The names of these periods are, however, too well established to be abandoned and are often useful, if employed with caution.

DATING. As there are no written documents, a variety of other means have been employed to determine the duration and dates of prehistoric cultures.

b. RELATIVE DATING

This is established by the following methods:

(1) **Stratigraphy.** When there is accurate excavation of a site, the undisturbed remains in any given level may fairly safely be assumed to be earlier than the remains in the levels that overlie it.

(2) **Typology.** The age of a given culture may sometimes be determined approximately when most of the objects representing it appear to be identical in type with objects found elsewhere in a culture that has been dated by other means.

(3) **Geology.** The relative age of different remains can often be ascertained by finding the relative age of the geological strata in which the remains occur, as in the case of a series of sedimentary deposits, or river terraces and raised beaches, marking former shorelines or flood levels in valleys at times when the mutual relation of land and water was different from that of the present.

(4) **Paleontology.** The presence (with the human remains) of extinct or still existing species of animals (including marine and lacustrine fauna) frequently provides a fairly exact basis for dating the human remains, in terms of geological periods. **K. P. Oakley** has developed a method of comparing the fluorine content of

associated human and animal bones to test their contemporaneity.

(5) **Paleobotany.** The presence of plant remains furnishes a further basis for assigning associated human remains to certain geological periods.

(6) **Climatic evidence.** When the past record of major climatic sequences in an area is known, human remains can often be dated in terms of glacial advances and retreats or pluvial and dry periods, if the remains are found in deposits characteristic of such periods. The kinds of animals and plants found in association with the human remains frequently show whether the climate of the period in question was wet or dry or warm or cold. Thanks to the great progress that has recently been made in paleobotany it is now possible to trace climatic fluctuations (as reflected by the immigration of new forest forms) through microscopic examination of pollen grains preserved intact for thousands of years in peat beds and elsewhere. Associated archaeological remains can thus often be referred with great accuracy to a given climatic phase.

There is considerable room for error in the use of each of these methods, unless the greatest care is exercised, but they are all sound in principle and in general they may be relied upon, particularly when one confirms another. The ideal system would make use of all the methods listed above, establishing for any area the sequence of climatic changes, earth movements, and deposits, and using this as a chronological framework into which to fit the successive cultures, reconstructed on the basis of the stratigraphy of the archaeological remains. For very few regions has this been done.

c. ABSOLUTE DATING

This is more difficult, but several methods have been used.

(1) **Estimate of the time needed to produce observed changes in culture.** There is no exact basis for such estimates, and this method, though often the only one available, is extremely inaccurate and inadequate.

(2) **Estimate of the time necessary for the performance of certain geological work.** This is used to date geological horizons in which human remains occur. For example, the date of a high river terrace may be given if it is estimated that it must have taken the river at least one hundred thousand years to cut down its bed to the present level. Such estimates are almost equally uncertain and inadequate for the purposes of the prehistorian.

(3) **Geochronology;** that is, the counting of the annual layers (varves) of sediment deposited by the melt-waters of a retreating ice-sheet.

This method, first devised by the Swedish scientist, Baron **G. J. de Geer,** has been applied to the Scandinavian region as the basis of an absolute system of chronology covering the last twelve thousand years. Owing to the scarcity of archaeological remains found *in situ* in dated varves, this system is of value principally in correlating and dating the different stages of the retreat of the last ice-sheet and the major fluctuations in sea-level in the Baltic area. These in turn serve to date many deposits which, by pollen analysis, can be assigned to the various postglacial climatic cycles. Thus indirectly the archaeological remains found in these deposits can be tentatively dated.

(4) **Dendrochronology.** This method, devised by **Andrew E. Douglass** and applied first in the southwestern United States, is based on the fact that certain species of trees, especially in arid regions, show by the thickness of their annual rings of growth the alternation of relatively wet or dry years. By matching many specimens from trees of various ages it has been possible to construct a time scale by which to date timbers found in prehistoric ruins.

(5) **Historical evidence.** Late prehistoric cultures in backward areas can sometimes be dated in a general way by the presence of imported objects from a known historical culture in some more advanced area, where written documents already exist.

The foregoing methods of dating archaeological sites have been greatly supplemented by advances in chemistry and atomic physics. In addition to the fluorine test, Oakley has also used a nitrogen test, which gives some measure of absolute age in bones. The Carbon–14 test, invented by **Willard F. Libby,** determines the amount of C–14 remaining in charcoal, wood, and a few other organic substances, and calculates a date based on the half-life of this element of 5,760 years, with a probable error of no more than 2,000 years, depending on the size of the sample and its age. The oldest C–14 date yet obtained is 64,000 ± 1,100 years (GRO–1379). Thousands of such dates have been determined in many laboratories, each designated by a symbol for the laboratory (e.g. GRO = Groningen) and a number (GRO–1379). The Argon–40 test takes us back much farther. It depends on the measurement of the amount of Ar–40 gas formed by the decay of Potassium–40 into Ar–40 and Calcium–40 in material which had been subjected to great heat, after it had cooled. Our most recent Ar–40 date is 230,000 years, leaving a gap of 160,000 years between it and the oldest C–14 determination.

The study of cores of sediment cut from the bottom of the ocean, which includes a whole battery of tests and observations, fills in this

YEARS

			← B.C.	A.D. →			
	Jan. 1 to Dec. 31	Jan. 1 to Dec. 31	Jan. 1 to Dec. 31	Jan. 1 to Dec. 31			
Year 3	Year 2	Year 1	Year 1	Year 2	Year 3		

CENTURIES

← B.C.			A.D. →		
300 B.C. to 201 B.C.	200 B.C. to 101 B.C.	100 B.C. to 1 B.C.	1 A.D. to 100 A.D.	101 A.D. to 200 A.D.	201 A.D. to 300 A.D.
Third Century	Second Century	First Century	First Century	Second Century	Third Century

gap and confirms the accuracy of the Ar–40 method.

(6) **Centuries and years before and after Christ (B.C. and A.D.).** In civilizations of the past many and various schemes of designating and counting years have been used, starting from specific "era" dates. Thus the Greeks came to reckon from the year of the first Olympic Games, which they put at a year corresponding to our 776 B.C. The Romans settled on 753 B.C. as the year of the traditional founding of Rome, and called that 1 A.U.C. (*ab urbe condita*).

These and other schemes are reduced in modern histories to dates reckoned from the year (actually only approximate) of the birth of Christ, both backward and forward. Years of Our Lord (*Anno Domini*) are reckoned forward beginning with the year 1 A.D. Years before Christ begin with the year 1 B.C. The year before 1 B.C. was 2 B.C. and so on. But in counting days B.C., the months and days run forward: the first day of 3 B.C. was January 1, and the last day December 31, which was followed at once by January 1 of the year 2 B.C.

The same procedure applies to centuries. The 1st Century A.D. runs from 1 A.D. through 100 A.D.; the 2nd from 101 A.D. through 200 A.D., etc. Similarly the 1st Century B.C. runs from 100 B.C. (January 1) through 1 B.C. (December 31); the 2nd Century B.C. includes the years 200 B.C.—101 B.C., etc.

Millennia (thousands of years) are reckoned in the same way. Thus the span of recorded history extends from the 3rd millennium B.C. (when the Bronze Age began) into the 2nd millennium A.D., which began in 1001 A.D. and will end in 2000 A.D.

(7) **The Julian and Gregorian Calendars.** Until the 16th century the Christian world used the **Julian Calendar,** introduced in 46 B.C. by Julius Caesar. This calendar provided for a year of 365 days plus, every fourth (leap) year, an additional day. This system is generally referred to as **Old Style** (O.S.).

In 1582 Pope Gregory XIII introduced the **Gregorian Calendar** to correct the error in the Julian Calendar, which had fallen ten days behind, astronomically. Thenceforth dates were advanced ten days and, in order to forestall future error, it was provided that only those centesimal years (such as 1600, 1700, etc.) that could be divided by 400 should be leap years. This calendar is referred to as **New Style** (N.S.). It was not adopted by Great Britain, which was Protestant, until 1752, nor by Russia and other Greek Orthodox countries until 1917. The difference in the 19th century was twelve days, and thirteen days in the 20th. By 1950 the adoption of the Gregorian Calendar was worldwide.

In this Encyclopedia all dates have been reduced to New Style unless otherwise indicated.

B. THE PALEOLITHIC PERIOD

1. CULTURE AND INDUSTRIES

THE WORD *Paleolithic* is used to describe a stage of human culture, the earliest of which we have sure evidence. Although this culture persisted longer in some parts of the world than in others, we can use the term with reasonable accuracy to characterize a period of time. This period includes probably 99 per cent of Man's life on earth (at least since he became a tool-using animal), all the other periods down to the present covering the remaining 1 per cent.

Our knowledge of Paleolithic culture is based principally on implements and animal and human bones found in the gravels of old river terraces, in open camp sites, and in caves. Disregarding the variations of time and place, one may say in general that Paleolithic men knew the use of fire and lived by hunting and collecting vegetable foods, as the Australian natives and the Bushmen of South Africa do today. They had no agriculture and no domestic animals, excepting possibly the dog. For shelter they probably made wind-breaks and crude huts of branches, occasionally occupying caves. Their clothing was undoubtedly of skins (no textiles). Their tools and utensils were of stone, bone, and undoubtedly also of wood and basketry (no metal and no pottery). We know almost nothing of their social organization, religion, and intellectual life, except that late cave paintings and burials indicate belief in magic (in connection with hunting) and in some kind of existence of the individual after death.

It is fairly safe to assume, however, that a large part of the fundamental institutions and beliefs of modern primitive peoples and of our own early historical ancestors had their origin and first development in this period.

The **stone tools,** which are such important criteria for this period, were usually made of flint or other hard rock by a process of chipping. They are classified as **core tools,** when the basis of the implement was a piece of rock, improved by chipping, or **flake tools,** when one of the flakes knocked off from a core (which is then termed a nucleus) was used as the basis for the implement, or **blade tools,** when the core was carefully prepared for striking off long, parallel-edged blades. In the manufacture of **Levallois flakes** and of blades, the core was first made ready by creating a flat surface or striking platform. Chips were then removed by striking it, preferably through the intermediacy of a wooden or horn dowel. Sometimes the edges of a flake were improved by secondary chipping or flaking (retouching). The principal types of implements were hand-axes or *coups de poing* (large pear-shaped or almond-shaped cores, chipped on both sides); scrapers of various shapes; points; awls (borers); and, in late times, long blades with roughly parallel edges, and gravers (small tools of many shapes improved for use as chisels or gouges by striking a special blow near the point).

2. EUROPE

The **Pleistocene epoch,** or Ice Age, in the last two-thirds of which Paleolithic culture developed and flourished, is divided into Lower, Middle, and Upper. According to the conventional chronology, the **Lower Pleistocene** began about 1,000,000 years ago when cold-adapted mollusks appeared in previously warm waters and modern genera of horses, cattle, elephants, and camels appeared in North America, Eurasia, and Africa. Toward the end of the Lower Pleistocene the first of four mountain glaciers arose in the Alps (Günz), and in the Himalayas, and in North America the first of four successive icecaps, the Nebraskan, was formed. The **Middle Pleistocene** began about one half million years ago with the first continental icecap in Europe (the Elster), the second Alpine glaciation (Mindel), and the second

North American icecap, the Kansan. Then followed the Second or **Great Interglacial,** succeeded by the Saal icecap and Riss mountain glaciation, and the Illinoisan icecap in North America. The **Late Pleistocene** includes the **Third Interglacial,** beginning about 150,000 years ago and the two Würm glaciations, with the Weichsel icecap. Würm I lasted from about 75,000 to 40,000 years ago, Würm II from about 30,000 to 10,000. In between was a cool period, or Interstadial.

The new chronology, based on sea-cores, Ar–40 and C–14 tests, and other methods, extends the base of the Middle Pleistocene to 1,500,000 years ago, and returns the Lower Pleistocene or Villafranchian to the Pliocene where it was before being shifted to the Pleistocene by an international geological congress in 1948.

The new dating is as follows:*

Günz (Nebraskan) glaciation	1,500,000–1,375,000 years ago
First (Aftonian) interglacial	1,375,000–1,205,000
Mindel (Kansan) glaciation	1,205,000–1,060,000
Second (Yarmouth) interglacial	1,060,000– 420,000
Riss (Illinoisan) glaciation	420,000– 340,000
Third (Sangoan) interglacial	340,000– 115,000
Early Würm glaciation	115,000– 95,000
Interstadial	95,000– 65,000
Main Würm glaciation	65,000– 11,000

*From D. Ericson and G. Wollin, *The Deep and the Past* (New York: Alfred A. Knopf, 1964).

LOWER PALEOLITHIC. This period covers the greater part of the Pleistocene. Almost our only information about the peoples and movements of this time consists of what may be inferred from the stone implements, which show, according to Abbé **Henri Breuil,** the contemporary but more or less independent development and mutual inter-influence in western Europe of four separate techniques of manufacture (industries): (1) **Hand-axe** industry (French *biface*), developing through Pre-Chellean (Abbevillian) to Acheulean types; (2) **Clactonian** industry, characterized by rough flakes with an unfaceted striking-platform inclined at a high angle to the main flake surface; (3) **Levalloisean** industry, characterized by large flakes struck from a previously prepared core (tortoise core) and retaining a faceted striking-platform; and (4) **Mousterian** industry, consisting of smaller flakes of various forms, usually exhibiting a characteristic technique of retouching the edges (stepped retouch). These industries are found both separate and mixed, and there are additional intermediate forms. Chronologically they have been grouped into four periods: (1) **Pre-Chellean** (Abbevillian) period, characterized by extremely crude hand-axes; (2) **Chellean** period (now usually included with Acheulean), having hand-axes somewhat less crude than the Abbevillian, as well as some Clactonian tools; (3) **Acheulean** period, marked by more highly evolved hand-axes and, particularly in its later stages, by Levallois flakes; and (4) **Mousterian** period (sometimes designated as Middle Paleolithic), with typical flake tools (points and scrapers) and a continuation in some places of Levallois flakes. The Mousterian industry proper (which has Pre-Mousterian or Proto-Mousterian forerunners in northern and eastern Europe) is found particularly in the caves of central France, associated with bones of mammoth and reindeer and of Neanderthal Man.

UPPER PALEOLITHIC. This is a relatively short period, coinciding with the last part of the Ice Age from the **Göttweig Interstadial** to the retreat of the Scandinavian icecap. Modern European men replaced the Neanderthals and blade tools appeared, along with an extensive use of bone and ivory for spearheads and harpoons. The Upper Paleolithic Europeans left a priceless heritage of art including engraving, carving in the round, and cave paintings. Four principal cultures have been noted: (1) **Perigordian,** the earliest in France, characterized especially by "backed" blades, blunted on one edge for holding or hafting. (2) **Aurignacian,** marked by great use of the blade and including a variety of characteristic scrapers, gravers, points (Châtelperron, Gravette, Font Robert types), and beginning of very small tools (*microliths*); also bone implements and ornaments of shell and bone. Aurignacian remains are found widely through central and western Europe and the Mediterranean region. (3) **Solutrean,** distributed from eastern and central Europe as far as France, intruding on the Aurignacian. The climate was cold. The Solutreans lived in open camps and rock shelters, were great hunters of horses, and introduced the technique of pressure flaking (willow-leaf and laurel-leaf points). (4) **Magdalenian,** the latest to develop, flourished in northern and central Europe and southern France.

The Paleolithic period in Europe ended with the great changes in climate, fauna, and flora that marked the termination of the Pleistocene or Ice Age.

3. AFRICA

The Paleolithic period of Africa is characterized by a variety of stone industries, some of which are purely local, while others are similar to or practically identical with certain of the industries of Europe. Geological investigation, which has only recently been undertaken on an adequate basis, indicates that owing to fluctuations in rainfall the Pleistocene period throughout most of Africa can perhaps be divided into a succession of pluvial and interpluvial periods, which it is hoped may eventually be correlated in some way with the glacial and interglacial periods of Europe. The succession of cultures is well established for certain areas, but not yet for the continent as a whole.

NORTHWEST AFRICA. Heavily patinated hand-axes of definitely Chellean and Acheulean types together with an early fauna have been found, usually without stratigraphy, in Tunisia, Algeria, Morocco, and to the south in the Sahara region, which was apparently once less arid than now. A so-called Mousterian industry (accompanied by a later fauna) is also represented, and excavations show an evolution from Levalloisean types, without typical Mousterian, to a special development known as the Aterian industry, characterized by small, tanged, leaf-shaped points, delicately trimmed all over both faces. This was succeeded by the overlapping cultures, the Mouillian and the Capsian, and the Oranian, which were terminal Upper Paleolithic and Mesolithic in date and marked by blades, gravers, and microlithic forms, the earliest phases of which bear a fundamental though distant relationship to the early Aurignacian of Europe and western Asia.

EGYPT. The presence of Paleolithic Man is shown by discoveries of the following succession of industries, all *in situ,* in the terraces of the Nile Valley: Chellean, a primitive Acheulean and an Egyptian form of the Clactonian, in the 100-foot terrace (no human implements were found in the 150-foot terrace); developed Acheulean in the 50-foot terrace; Levalloisean (first reported as Early Mousterian) in the 30-foot terrace; and developed Levalloisean (reported as Egyptian Mousterian) in the 15- to 10-foot terrace. These were followed, in deposits of later age, by an Egyptian version of the Aterian and a local industry, the Sebilian.

EAST AFRICA. According to Louis and Mary Leakey and others, there is a Lower Pleistocene industry in Kenya, Uganda, and Tanganyika, which consisted of simple pebbles and unrolled stones, roughly chipped on one side to make a cutting edge (choppers) or on both sides (chopping-tools). These constitute the Oldowan industry, found in stratification in Oldovai Gorge, below true hand-axe types (Chellean and Acheulean industries). In higher geological horizons are found Levalloisian implements followed by the Stillbay—pressure-flaked bifacial points similar to the Aterian of North Africa. The Oldowan tools are believed to have been mostly Lower Pleistocene, the Chellean and Acheulean mostly Middle and early Upper Pleistocene, and the Levalloisean and Stillbay late Upper Pleistocene. The so-called "Aurignacian" of East Africa is now known to be Capsian and post-Pleistocene.

SOUTH AFRICA. Pebble tools have been found in the late Lower Pleistocene of the Vaal Valley. The Middle Pleistocene contains Chellean and Acheulian hand-axes and cleavers and the so-called Victoria West core-tools, all lumped under the term *Stellenbosch.* These continued through the early Upper Pleistocene and were gradually replaced by the Fauresmith culture (hand-axes and also flakes with faceted striking-platform, suggesting Levalloisian influence). The so-called Middle Stone Age, which was late Upper Pleistocene and even post-Pleistocene in date, was marked by a series of more or less contemporary flake industries (Mossel-bay, Glen Grey Falls, Howieson's Poort, Bambata Cave, Stillbay, etc.), suggesting by the shapes and technique of their implements a combination of Levalloisean and Capsian influences, together with pressure-flaking in one case (Stillbay).

OTHER AREAS. Ethiopia and Somaliland go with East Africa, and the Rhodesias form a transition to South Africa. In the forested regions of the Congo and West Africa are found so-called Sangoan or Tumbian core-tools, crude and picklike, derived from the hand-axe tradition, and lasting until the end of the Pleistocene if not later. The sequence of West Africa outside the forest has not been fully worked out.

4. ASIA AND OCEANIA

WESTERN ASIA. A remarkably complete sequence of stone industries, paralleling quite closely those of Europe, has been established for the Palestine-Syria region. Surface finds of Chellean implements are supplemented (in three caves in the Wady-el-Mughara, near Mt. Carmel) by the following stratigraphic series: Tayacian, Upper Acheulean, Levalloiseo-Mousterian (with skeletons of Neanderthaloid type), Aurignacian, and Natufian (a Mesolithic industry). Occasional sites with implements of one or another of these or similar types have been reported from northern Arabia, Asia Minor, Armenia, Transcaucasia, Mesopotamia, and Iran.

INDIA. Many implements of Chellean type, as well as Acheulean hand-axes and cleavers, have been reported in northern, central, and southern India. In the Punjab, Hellmut de Terra found Acheulean hand-axes in a deposit contemporary with the second Himalayan glaciation or somewhat later. These were succeeded by a crude pebble industry (Soan industry) in strata contemporary with the third Himalayan glaciation. A few Upper Paleolithic types, with some suggestions of Aurignacian, have also been found in central and northwestern India, as well as cave sites with rock paintings of uncertain age.

AFGHANISTAN. North of the Hindu Kush Mountains Levalloiseo-Mousterian implements have been found in the Haibak Valley, and an Upper Paleolithic blade culture was discovered in the cave of Kara Kamar and dated by Carbon–14 as over 34,000 years, probably during the local equivalent of the Göttweig Interstadial.

CHINA AND JAPAN. With the skeletal material found at Chou-kou-tien, southwest of Peking, were also discovered stone tools, dated at around 360,000 years, and thus of Second Glacial (Mindel–Elster) age. They include choppers and chopping-tools and bipolar flakes (struck on a stone anvil so that the blow comes, in effect, from both ends). From then on in China these tools were gradually refined until the end of the Pleistocene, and also, in northwest China, flake tools resembling Mousterian implements were made in Upper Pleistocene times. Tools similar to those of China have been found in Japan. In northern Hokkaido a number of sites have yielded large obsidian blade tools resembling the European Upper Paleolithic, but still of undetermined age.

SIBERIA AND RUSSIAN TURKESTAN. Mousterian tools have been excavated in Turkmenistan and Uzbekistan, particularly with the Neanderthal boy of Teshik Tash, and hearth sites. Paleolithic implements and remains of extinct animals have been found in southwestern and central Siberia, especially in the basin of the Ob River and its tributaries, the valleys of the Upper Yenisei (Minusinsk region) and Angara Rivers and around Lake Baikal. Some of the implements resemble quite closely certain Mousterian, Aurignacian, and Magdalenian forms of western Europe. The deposits in which they occur and the fauna suggest that they are probably mostly, if not entirely, post-glacial.

SOUTHEASTERN ASIA AND OCEANIA. Paleolithic implements have been found in Burma, Thailand, Indo-China, Java, Borneo, and the Philippines. They are essentially similar to those of China in that they consist of choppers, chopping-tools, and flakes of varying degrees of crudity. The oldest tools from Australia are probably about 16,000 years old, or late Upper Pleistocene, and they resemble the southeast Asian and Indonesian industries. No Paleolithic implements have been found in Oceania.

5. AMERICA

During the latter part of the Würm or Wisconsian glaciation the ancestors of the **American Indians** first crossed from Asia to Alaska over a wide corridor of dry land, now submerged. The earliest Carbon–14 date so far recovered is 16,375 ± 400 B.C. (O–999), from Venezuela, where a chopper-chopping tool industry of Chou-kou-tien facies is associated with clumsy extinct animals, including mastodon, glyptodon, megatherium, and macrauchenia, which could not long have survived the presence of Man. The remains of some of these animals, with similar artifacts, have also been found at the Strait of Magellan, at 8,760 ± 300 B.C. (W–915). If it took 8,000 years for Man to get from Venezuela to the Strait of Magellan, it is reason-able to postulate an initial entry over Bering Strait in the neighborhood of 20,000 years ago. So far the earliest date for a similar culture in North America is 9,580 ± 600 B.C. (C–609) at Danger Cave, Utah. Similar tools were made in the California Desert in modern times.

Well-made projectile points, pressure flaked on both sides, and in some sites fluted, go back to 9,330 ± 500 B.C. (M–811) at the Lehner Mammoth Site, Arizona (Clovis Points); 8,820 ± 375 B.C. (I [UW]–141) at Lindenmeier, Colorado; and about 7,000 B.C. (M–807, 808, 809, 810) at Bull Brook, Ipswich, Mass. (Folsom Points). These points, used in killing mammoths, seem not to have been made after the extinction of that animal.

6. INTERRELATIONSHIP OF PALEOLITHIC CULTURES

It should be clear from the foregoing that at present we know a great deal more about Paleolithic stone implements than we do about the Paleolithic people who made them. Our data are still too insufficient to warrant any sure account of the way in which the various ele-ments of Paleolithic culture were developed by different groups of mankind and spread by them throughout the world. However, three fundamental facts relating to this problem may be regarded as reasonably well established:

First, some of the more highly evolved implements and groups of implements found in widely different areas are so similar in shape and technique that we are forced to infer that the cultures in which they occur bear some time-relationship to one another, i.e. the art of making the typical implements in question (such as the hand-axe, the Levallois flake and the Aurignacian blade, to name three fundamental examples) was not evolved independently at different times and in different places but was spread from some original center, either by actual migrations of people or by cultural diffusion.

Second, the geographical distribution of these various type implements, although very wide, is not haphazard, but each one of the fundamental industries has its own distinct area of major development, with outliers along natural routes of migration. For example, the industry characterized by core implements of hand-axe type is found in one continuous area, comprising southwestern Asia, eastern and northern Africa, and southern and western Europe, with outliers in South Africa and India. A less sharply definable industry, characterized by the use of flake implements in preference to cores and (in its most developed form) by the use of flake imple-

ments of Levalloisean type with a faceted striking-platform, has its home in the same area, with addition of a broad belt stretching through central and eastern Europe and northern Asia. Finally the blade industry has a distribution which is practically identical with that last described, though with a less characteristic development in South Africa and India. The southeastern part of Asia, from the North China plain to Indonesia, seems to form a separate culture province, with an almost entirely independent development throughout Paleolithic times.

Third, the three major industries just referred to had their principal development at different periods of time, as is shown by the fact that wherever there is stratigraphic evidence they occur in the same order of succession, with the hand-axe industry the earliest, succeeded in turn by the Levalloisean flake industry and that by the blade industry, the latest of all. The foregoing outline is, of course, oversimplified and disregards many problems of local development and relations, but it is based on a mass of evidence, it represents the best opinion of archaeologists today, and it may be accepted provisionally as a true interpretation of the facts.

7. DATES OF PALEOLITHIC CULTURES

The Paleolithic period of Man's development is considered to be roughly contemporary, in some places, with most of the Pleistocene period of the earth's history and may best be dated in geological terms. The Pleistocene may be broadly divided, on the basis of faunal remains, into Lower, Middle, and Upper or (in Europe at least), on the basis of Alpine glacial deposits, into four major periods of glacial advance (Günz, Mindel, Riss, and Würm) with three corresponding interglacial periods. The dating of Paleolithic industries in terms of Alpine glacial and interglacial periods is still, however, a highly speculative affair, owing to the fact, which is not always properly appreciated, that almost no archaeological remains have yet been found in actual glacial deposits of the Alpine region. Attempts have been made to correlate glaciations in Asia and Africa with these Alpine glaciations and to correlate with both the series of implement-bearing river terraces (especially of the Thames, Somme, and Nile) and implement-bearing deposits of so-called Pluvial periods in non-glaciated regions (notably in East Africa), but only preliminary work has yet been done on this large and complicated problem. Hence statements of experts regarding the age of the earlier Paleolithic cultures differ greatly and should be regarded as opinions or

theories only, which require further evidence before they can be accepted as established fact.

That tool-making man existed as early as the Lower Pleistocene period has been contended by a number of authorities. **Teilhard de Chardin** has dated the Sinanthropus finds at Chou-kou-tien as Lower Pleistocene, and **Breuil** considers that deposits containing his Abbevillian (Pre-Chellean) industry and the earliest Clactonian industry belong to the First (Günz-Mindel) Interglacial period. Various alleged implements of a very primitive nature (including the so-called *eoliths*) found in Europe and Africa have been ascribed to this period and **Reid Moir** claims to have found tools of primitive types in deposits that are presumably of pre-Günz age. Such early dates are not yet universally accepted by archaeologists and geologists.

When we come to the Middle Pleistocene, however, there is a more general agreement that the early phases of the hand-axe and flake industries (Chellean, Clactonian, etc.) in Europe and Africa probably existed in the Second (Mindel-Riss) Interglacial period. De Terra has found similar implements in India in deposits contemporary with the end of his Second Himalayan Glacial Advance or the following interglacial period (which may be contemporary respectively with the Second or Mindel Glaciation of

Europe and the Mindel-Riss Interglacial).

Furthermore, it is thought very probable that in Europe the fully developed Acheulean and associated Levalloisean industries belong to the Third (Riss-Würm) Interglacial period, the typical Mousterian to the end of this period and the first maximum of the Fourth Glacial period (Würm I), the Perigordian and early Aurigna-cian to the time of the Göttweig Interstadial, while various phases of the Aurignacian, Solu-trean, and Magdalenian take up the rest of the Pleistocene. African and Asiatic implements that show relationship to some of the above industries are probably roughly contemporary with them.

8. SPECIES AND SUB-SPECIES OF FOSSIL MAN

The remains of Pleistocene men so far dis-covered total about 230 individuals complete enough to enable useful study. Of these, three come possibly from the Lower or earliest Mid-dle, 40 probably from the Middle, and the rest from the Upper Pleistocene. In the past these specimens were given many individual generic and specific names which will be used here for identification only, because modern workers assign them all to two successive species, *Homo erectus* and *Homo sapiens*. This classification does not include the so-called *Homo habilis* who was definitely from the Lower Pleistocene. While the transition between the two species was gradual, they may be distinguished by a combination of criteria, including the ratio between arcs and chords in the sagittal line of the frontal, parietal, and occipital bones, brow-ridge size, form of the tracks of the mid-men-ingeal blood vessels on the inside of the parietal bone, relative flatness of the base of the skull, ratios between palate size and tooth size versus brain size, the size of the seat of the pituitary (*Sella turcica*), and, to a lesser extent, cranial capacity itself, ranging from 750 cc. to 1280 cc. in *Homo erectus* and from 1175 cc. to at least 1710 cc. in fossil *Homo sapiens*.

Specimens of both species may be divided spatially into five geographical races or sub-species: the Australoid, Mongoloid, Caucasoid, Capoid, and Congoid, evolving respectively in southeast Asia and Indonesia, China, western Asia and Europe, North Africa, and Sub-Sa-haran Africa.

The **Australoid** line begins with four speci-mens from the Djetis Beds of Java, of late Lower Pleistocene Age; two lower jaws named *Meganthropus* variously called *Australopithecine* and *Homo erectus*, an adult *erectus* skull called *Pithecanthropus* No. 4, and an infant skull of the same type, *Homo modjokertensis*. From the Middle Pleistocene beds of Central Java (the Trinil Beds) come three other *Pithecanthropus* skulls, Nos. 1, 2, and 3. This line carries on through the 11 skulls of *Homo soloensis* found at Ngangdong in the Notopuro Beds of the Upper Pleistocene. All these form an evolution-ary progression within *Homo erectus*. An ado-lescent skull from the Niah Cave, North Borneo, dated at about 40,000 years by Carbon-14, is *sapiens*, and so are two very late Pleistocene skulls from Wadjak in Java. Australoid skulls have heavy, straight browridges, steeply sloping frontal bones, keeled vaults, flattish upper faces, broad nasal openings, great alveolar progna-thism, and large teeth with particularly large molars.

The **Mongoloid** line begins with 14 skulls and 12 lower jaws and a total of 147 teeth (in and out of jaws) from Chou-kou-tien, dated in the early to middle Middle Pleistocene, followed by three teeth from Ting-tsin (Shansi), a maxilla from Changyang (Hupei), a skull from Mapa (Kwangtung), all in the Middle Pleistocene. The Upper Pleistocene contains Mongoloid skulls from Tze-yang (Sze-chuan) and Lin-kiang (Kwang-si), one tooth from Sjara-Osso-Gol (Ordos), and an as yet racially unidentified skull from Aichi, Honshu, Japan. Three skulls from the Upper Cave of Chou-kou-tien date from the very end of the Pleistocene.

The transition from *Homo erectus* to *Homo sapiens* in the Mongoloid line came probably at the level of Mapa or Ting-tsin, in the late Mid-dle or early Upper Pleistocene, but all are Mongoloid. Mongoloid skulls have straight browridges, steeply rising, curved frontal bones, flat faces, protruding lower orbital rims, guttered nasal sills, alveolar prognathism, mandibular torus, and teeth noted for heavy shoveling of the incisors and canines.

The oldest **Caucasoid** specimen is the Mauer or Heidelberg mandible, from the early Middle Pleistocene. Two skulls from the Second or Great Interglacial, Steinheim and Swanscombe, bring the Middle Pleistocene roster to three. Twenty-six early Upper Pleistocene (pre-Würm) individuals are represented by specimens from France, Germany, Czechoslovakia, and Yugo-slavia, and one from Israel. Würm I Caucasoids include remains of 55 individuals from western and central Europe, four from the U.S.S.R., and 39 from western Asia. All but eight from Pales-tine and Lebanon are considered to be Nean-derthals. The Upper Paleolithic (Göttweig Inter-stadial and Würm II) include individuals from

161 sites in Europe and western Asia, of which 25 have been more or less adequately described.

With the possible exception of the Heidelberg jaw, which is in doubt because it has no cranium, all the Caucasoid skulls are *Homo sapiens* in the sense that they are all as fully evolved as those of living Australian aborigines, but in them an evolutionary progression may be seen, more or less, through time. Fully modern Caucasoids appear first in Würm I in Palestine and Lebanon and during the Göttweig Interstadial in Europe.

Caucasoid criteria are: a projecting nasal skeleton, laterally curved browridges, prognathism midfacial or absent, relatively narrow jaws, and relatively small teeth with little or no shoveling. The Neanderthals, who were not as aberrent as usually stated, had particularly prow-like faces, large noses, long faces, and relatively broad, low braincases. While the exact relationship between the Neanderthals and their predecessors and followers remains to be determined they were, in any case, Caucasoids, and probably cold-adapted. Although the Upper Paleolithic specimens have been assigned to several races on the basis of individual skulls (Crô-Magnon, Grimaldi, Chancelade, etc.) they were a single subspecific population no more variable than living Europeans.

The racial situation in Africa during the Pleistocene is more obscure. In North Africa a series of three mandibles and one parietal from Ternefine, Algeria, resemble those of Sinanthropus, and are of about the same age. Two Upper Pleistocene skulls from Jebel Ighoud, Morocco, three mandibles from the Moroccan Atlantic coast, and a child's maxilla from Tangier, carry this line at least into Würm I. With large, straight browridges, a curved frontal bone, flat upper facial skeleton, great prognathism, and large teeth with shoveling, this line resembles the Mongoloid in many respects and also the prehistoric skeletons of full-sized African Bushmen; Carleton Coon designates it as **Capoid.** At the end of the Pleistocene this race was displaced by an invasion of Mouillian Caucasoids.

Before the southward migration of the Bushman ancestors, Africa south of the Sahara was, apparently, Negro country **(Congoid),** although the evidence is limited to one early Middle Pleistocene skullcap from Olduvai Gorge (Chellian-3 Man) and Upper Pleistocene skulls and fragments thereof from Broken Hill (N. Rhodesia), Saldanha Bay (Cape Province), and Kanjera (Kenya). All but the last are *Homo erectus,* who seems to have lasted in South Africa until late in the Pleistocene, and all are racially Negro, as far as we can tell. The date of the Kanjera specimens is in doubt, but they may be as much as 50,000 years old. No material of any antiquity has yet been found in West Africa, the historic center of Negro differentiation.

C. THE POST-PALEOLITHIC PERIOD

1. NATURE AND SEQUENCE OF POST-PALEOLITHIC CULTURES

IN THE absence of exact dates, archaeologists have divided the time from the end of the Paleolithic to the present into the following major periods: Mesolithic period, Neolithic period, Chalcolithic period, Bronze Age, Iron Age, and Modern Age. As has been previously pointed out, this nomenclature has many disadvantages, since the names refer really to cultural stages rather than to periods of time. The words were first employed in the description of cultures as observed in Europe and the order of succession is not always the same for other continents. Furthermore, it is impossible to assign even estimated dates to these so-called periods, for each one began and ended at a different time in different parts of the world. On the whole, however, this chronological division does represent the general progress of culture, in the Old World at least, and although it often leads to confusion, unless applied with the greatest care, still it has the advantage of convenience and almost universal usage. The dividing line between prehistory and history comes at no particular place in this series, but varies in different areas. Following is a brief definition of the different periods, after which the Post-Paleolithic cultures of the world will be described by geographical areas.

a. MESOLITHIC PERIOD

The disappearance of the last ice-sheet, which marked the end of the Pleistocene period and, with it, the end of the Paleolithic, led to the rise of a new culture, generally referred to as the Mesolithic, in which the Paleolithic economy of food-gathering, though basically unchanged, was partly modified in some parts of the world under the influence of new climatic conditions. The big animals of the Pleistocene, on which the Paleolithic hunters had largely depended for their food, disappeared everywhere except in Africa and south Asia, and their place was taken by the present-day fauna. Also with the ice retreat new regions were opened to settlement. The stone implements of the Mesolithic cultures were still produced by chipping, but a preference was shown for extremely small forms (*microliths*), often of geometric shapes. Some of these forms had a wide distribution in Asia, Africa, and Europe, showing that there were certain cultural relations and also actual movements of peoples—the latter probably connected to some extent with the drying up of the Sahara and central Asiatic regions. The Mesolithic period is usually considered to have begun (in northern Europe at least) c. 8000 B.C., and Mesolithic cultures lasted for several thousand years until supplanted (at different dates in different areas) by the food-producing economy of the Neolithic peoples.

b. NEOLITHIC PERIOD

The next stage of development, the Neolithic, is marked by the invention and almost universal adoption of techniques for **producing food, grinding stone,** and **making pottery.** These new techniques and the results which flowed from them were revolutionary. Man ceased being a nomad, eternally following his food supply, and became a sedentary being, residing and growing his food in one spot. He now had an assured food supply to carry over lean seasons and this led to a great increase in the population in most of the formerly inhabited areas, and the opening up to settlement of new areas, such as loess lands of Asia and Europe. The altered conditions likewise made possible the accumulation of possessions, the creation and satisfaction of new needs, the leisure for invention and speculation, the growth of large communities and cities, the development of more complex social organization, and in fact all the progress that has taken place since that time.

The new techniques that characterized the Neolithic did not all originate in the same place at the same time. The grinding of stone began during late Mesolithic times while the first domestication of plants and animals occurred before the invention of pottery. This division has been partly formalized in the terms *Prepottery* and *Pottery Neolithic*. However, there is good reason to believe that these developments followed one another in a limited area and spread from there in successive waves to the ends of Asia, Africa, and Europe, but not in any significant sense to the New World. This original center was probably southwestern Asia, for the wild relatives of the cereals and animals that were first domesticated have their home there, and it was the region in which the higher culture or civilization which the Neolithic discoveries made possible was first developed. The earliest remains of **Prepottery Neolithic** culture which have yet been found occur in an arc from the southwest corner of Iran through northern Mesopotamia and Syria into the Jordan valley of Palestine. The earliest **Pottery Neolithic** appears to have been localized in the highlands of northern Mesopotamia, Iran, Syria and the southwestern Anatolian plateau. By about 6000 B.C. it was distributed from both Aegean shores to the western border of Iran, with a major development in the Konya Plain of the southern Anatolian plateau. The Neolithic economy is fully developed with wheat and barley in cultivation and sheep, goats, pigs, and possibly cattle as domesticated animals.

Neolithic remains of primitive character have been found in other parts of the Old World, but they are all apparently later than this in date. The first traces of the Neolithic that have been found in western Europe are not older than 5000 B.C., and Neolithic culture did not begin in many parts of Asia and Africa until much later still.

c. CHALCOLITHIC PERIOD

In a strict sense this is not a true period at all. The word *Chalcolithic* is a term conveniently but loosely used to describe a culture that is still essentially Neolithic in character, but in which the metal copper is just beginning to be used, without, however, replacing stone as the principal material for implements. It is a time during which villages began to develop into towns, and oxen and plow agriculture began largely to replace hoe cultivation. Chalcolithic cultures are thus transitional to urban civilization. People in many areas of the world did not pass through this intermediate stage, but obtained their first knowledge of copper directly from other peoples who had already fully developed the art of copper metallurgy. The dates of Chalcolithic cultures differ everywhere, depending upon the time it took for the knowledge of metal-working to spread. The earliest cultures in which copper has been found are in the Near East, and their estimated date is somewhere between 4500 and 3500 B.C. Copper did not appear in Europe much before 2500 B.C.

d. BRONZE AGE

In most regions of the Old World (but not in all of them) there was a period in which copper or bronze came into general use as a material for tools and weapons, but iron was still practically unknown. Because the ores required for the making of bronze and other alloys had a limited distribution, their increase in use led to the breakdown of the self-sufficiency of local Neolithic economies with a resultant growth of international trade and eventually the establishment of political units larger than the traditional city-state. This period is for convenience termed the **Bronze Age** (although strictly speaking the word *bronze* should refer only to true bronze, a mixed metal composed of copper alloyed with a certain percentage of tin). The date and duration of the Bronze Age in various parts of the Old World vary greatly. As already has been stated, the earliest known use of copper was in the Near East—in Mesopotamia and Egypt—in the early 4th millennium B.C. Considerable evidence points to the mountainous ore-bearing regions of Anatolia, Armenia, and Caucasia as the probable area in which copper metallurgy was first discovered and developed. Copper was in widespread use in the Near East by 3000 B.C. and this may be considered a good rough date for the beginning of the Bronze Age in southwestern Asia, although the general use of true bronze itself did not begin until five or six centuries later.

The Bronze Age in Europe did not begin until 2000 B.C. or later, and it was more retarded or entirely absent in parts of Asia, most of Africa, and all of Oceania. In the Near East iron began to be used extensively around 1000 B.C. The first use of iron for implements, even at considerably later dates, is considered in any area to bring the Bronze Age to a close.

e. IRON AGE

The **Iron Age** is usually considered by archaeologists to be the period of some centuries immediately following the time when iron began to replace bronze as the principal material for implements and weapons. In one sense, we are still living in the Iron Age, but the term is actually seldom used in connection with any specific culture that is later in date than the beginning of the Christian Era, except in referring to primitive peoples living in remote regions. Rare examples of early ornaments made of meteoric iron are known, and at least two cases of objects made of iron that was not meteoric (and hence may have been smelted) have been reported in Mesopotamia from levels dating before 2200 B.C. The first certain development of iron metallurgy on any scale, however, began in Asia Minor about the 14th century B.C. and in Europe in the Hallstatt region of Austria in the 11th or 10th century B.C. Iron did not penetrate to large parts of Asia and Africa until many centuries later and did not form part of any culture in the New World until introduced from Europe in the 15th and 16th centuries A.D.

2. MODERN RACES OF MAN

Although we know from the skeletal evidence that the five living subspecies of Man existed as far back as we can trace them in the Pleistocene, we have no evidence of soft-part morphology or pigmentation before the Upper Paleolithic cave paintings and sculptures, nor any of blood groups before modern times. But because the American Indians are as **Mongoloid** as the eastern Asiatics, we may assume that Mongoloid soft-part peculiarities go back at least to the late Upper Pleistocene.

These include straight, coarse, black head hair which grays late in life if at all, and rarely falls out; scanty beard and body hair; somewhat protuberant, relatively small eyeballs: brown iris color; a high frequency of epicanthic (inner) eye folds; skin ranging from a yellowing brunet white to a rich brown, according to latitude; and a scarcity of apocrine glands with a consequent paucity or absence of body odor. Characteristically, Mongoloids have relatively long bodies and short extremities, with small hands and feet, and little lumbar curve. Differences between the sexes in size, shape, and hair development are less than in Australoids or Caucasoids. Two face forms, one flattish nosed and the other aquiline, are found in many Mongoloid populations, with aquilinity commonest in American Indians and the Nagas of Burma and Upper Assam.

Although the **Australoids** evolved in southeastern Asia and Indonesia, at the end of the Pleistocene these lands began to be invaded by Mongoloids, leaving only dwarfed remnant populations in forested mountains and on offshore islands, and at about the same time the ancestors of the Australian aborigines, Papuans, and Melanesians moved to their previously uninhabited new homes. Other Australoids, with or without Mongoloid admixture, went to India at a time unknown. Some authorities consider it likely that the **Ainu** of northern Japan, Sakhalin Island, and the Kuriles may be the mixed, relatively depigmented descendants of an early Australoid movement up the chain of islands fringing the Pacific coast of Asia.

Australoid characteristics are skin varying from black to light brown; hair ranging from woolly to straight, and, in some areas, often blond (central Australia); full beards, body hair ranging from scant to very heavy, hair graying early in life and sometimes balding; brown eyes, large browridges, relatively flat nasal profiles, large, broad nasal tips, large teeth, and in most regions slender body build. Australoid trunk and limb proportions resemble the Caucasoid.

The **Caucasoids** invaded India postglacially on several occasions, and now they form the predominant population element in the subcontinent. They also invaded North Africa and the Sahara, siring the Berbers. Caucasoid Arabs came later. Caucasoids include Europeans and most of the western Asiatic peoples from the Mediterranean through Iran, Afghanistan, and West Pakistan to India, as well as the modern white inhabitants of the Americas, South Africa, Australia, New Zealand, and Siberia.

They resemble the Australoids most closely in body build, hair cover, graying and balding, but have a smaller frequency of curly hair. In skin color they range from virtually unpigmented to almost black, in hair color from blond to black, and in eye color from blue to brown. Their most distinctive characteristics are a relatively pointed, narrow face with little or no flattening, a narrow nose, relatively small teeth with small lateral incisors, and a reduced molar cusp formula.

The **Capoids,** represented today by the Bushmen and a few remnant tribes in Tanganyika, differ from their full-sized ancestors, whose skeletons have been found in North Africa, the Sudan, Kenya, and the Rhodesias, in being small of stature, relatively infantile in face and jaw development, and in certain aberrant features of the genitalia. They have very flat faces, often with an epicanthic fold, yellowish skin which wrinkles in mature adulthood, tightly spiraled black hair, and brown eyes.

The **Congoids,** like the Australoids, include both full-sized and dwarfed populations, Negro and Pygmy. Negroes have relatively long forearms and lower limbs, muscles with short bellies and long tendons, narrow hips, considerable lumbar curvature, black or dark brown skins, often bulbous foreheads, large, heavily pigmented eyes, broad noses, thick, everted lips, alveolar prognathism, and large teeth. Their hair is spiral, their head hair and beards full, and their body hair usually scant. They gray relatively late. The Pygmies are short, with relatively short extremities, usually lighter in skin color and hairier. Both have a relative abundance of apocrine glands and a body odor at the opposite extreme from the Mongoloids'.

Modern studies of blood group frequencies and fingerprints confirm the division of living man into the five subspecies listed, except that they fail to show as great a difference between Congoids and Capoids as between the others. This may perhaps be explained by the history of the Capoids, who moved from one end of Africa to the other over previously Negro territory.

3. REGIONAL DISTRIBUTION OF POST-PALEOLITHIC CULTURES

a. ASIA

SOUTHERN MESOPOTAMIA. Excavations at Eridu, Hajji Mohammad, Warka, Ur, Kish, Tello, Fara, Nippur, and other sites reveal the existence of a Late Neolithic or Chalcolithic culture in southern Mesopotamia during the late 5th and 4th millennia B.C. This culture has been divided into four broad periods:

c. 4500 B.C. The **Al Ubaid** period began with the appearance of painted pottery and a simple agricultural economy in the area. It is subdivided into three stylistic pottery phases: the Eridu, the Hajji Mohammad, and the Classic Ubaid. Monumental temple architecture had its inception in this period. The **Uruk** period, which followed, saw the decline of pottery painting as a craft with the first appearance of copper, cylinder seals, and writing. Monumental architecture was further developed.

c. 3000–2850 B.C. The **Jamdat Nasr** period marked the culmination of the prehistoric culture of southern Mesopotamia and led up to the **Early Dynastic** (Sumerian) period and the beginning of recorded history.

NORTHERN MESOPOTAMIA. A similar progress can be traced in northern Mesopotamia, beginning with the Prepottery Neolithic culture of Jarmo and continuing through the later levels at sites like Matarrah, Hassuna, Nineveh, Gawra, and Arpachiyah. In many respects the northern culture differs from the southern. It is particularly marked by the appearance of the brilliant Tell Halaf pottery of about 5000 B.C.   (*Cont. p. 27.*)

PALESTINE AND SYRIA. A Mesolithic culture, the **Natufian,** followed the end of the Upper Paleolithic in Palestine and lasted until about 7000 B.C. At Jericho it was succeeded by Prepottery Neolithic cultures with relationships to Syro-Cilicia and southern Anatolia. A town of unique size with stone fortification walls grew up at Jericho. The people made houses of mudbrick with polished plaster floors, and practiced a cult that made use of human skulls plastered over with clay modeled to represent human features. Around 5500 B.C. a Pottery Neolithic culture became widespread in the area.

c. 3000-2000 B.C. With the Early Bronze Age recorded history begins in this area, although our information for many centuries comes from Egyptian sources, supplemented by excavations at Bisan, Megiddo, Jericho, etc. An Early Bronze Age culture in Phoenicia has been revealed at Ras Shamra and Byblos, while Neolithic and Chalcolithic levels have been unearthed at Sakje-Geuzi, Carchemish, Tell Judeideh, Tabbat al-Hammam, and Chagar Bazar in northern Syria. *(Cont. p. 41.)*

ARABIA. With the exception of settlements connected with the Persian Gulf trade in the late 2nd millennium B.C. on Bahrein Island and nearby Qatar, and the historical Minaean and Sabaean kingdoms of southwestern Arabia in the 1st millennium B.C., practically nothing is known of this area.

ANATOLIA. A Pottery Neolithic culture flourished at Çatal Hüyük in the Konya Plain around 7000 B.C. Remains of textiles, clay figurines, wooden vessels, stone statuettes, shrines and private houses with beautiful wall paintings show a high level of cultural achievement. The later development of the Neolithic, Chalcolithic (3000–2600 B.C.), and Early Bronze Age (2600–1900 B.C.) is known from excavations at Haçilar, Troy, Alaça and Alishar Hüyük. The historical period begins with the founding of the first **Hittite** kingdom about 1900 B.C. *(Cont. p. 49.)*

ARMENIA AND TRANSCAUCASIA. Almost nothing is known of this region before the founding of the kingdom of **Urartu** in the 1st millennium B.C., and the beginning of history. A Chalcolithic culture has been discovered at Shamiramalti, on Lake Van, and there are dubious Neolithic and Bronze Age finds from the late 3rd and 2nd millennia B.C. south of the Caucasus. During the Early Iron Age (1000 B.C. and later) Georgia and Soviet Armenia were occupied by people who buried their dead in tumuli and who practiced an advanced metallurgy. *(Cont. p. 51.)*

IRAN AND SOVIET TURKMENISTAN. A little before 6000 B.C. Prepottery Neolithic people had begun to settle along the western edge of the Zagros Mountains at sites like Ali Kosh. By 6000 B.C. Pottery Neolithic cultures had been established in the higher valleys around Kermanshah (Tepe Sarab) and at the southern end of Lake Urmia (Hajji Firuz Tepe). By 5000 B.C. related agricultural cultures had become established along the Caspian shore (at Belt and Hotu Caves) and in Turkmenistan at Djeitun. Chalcolithic cultures characterized by fine painted pottery flourished widely in the 4th millennium B.C., notably at Anau, Namazga Tepe, Tepe Hissar, Rayy, and Tepe Sialk in the north, at Tepe Giyan (Nihavand) in the west, and at Susa, and Persepolis in the southwest. During the 3rd millennium B.C. a Bronze Age culture using much copper, and making burnished gray pottery, spread slowly over the northern part of the country, appearing first in the east at Tepe Hissar. At the end of the 2nd and the beginning of the 1st millennia B.C. new people, who buried their dead in stone cist graves with quantities of bronze weapons, spread through the mountains of northwestern Iran. A remarkable craftsmanship in gold is also evidenced for this period in the royal tombs of Marlik Tepe near Rudbar. The ancestors of the Medes and Persians probably entered Iran at about this time. The Early Iron Age is known from excavations at Tepe Sialk and Hasanlu. *(Cont. p. 52.)*

PAKISTAN AND INDIA. Excavations and scattered finds of microlithic implements and polished stone celts attest the existence of a Mesolithic and Neolithic culture in India as early as the 4th millennium B.C., but little is known of them. At the end of the 3rd millennium B.C. a copper-using Bronze Age culture, the **Harappa culture,** flourished in the northwest at such sites as Mohenjo Daro, Chanhu Daro, Kot Diji, and Harappa. The Harappa culture occupied the Indus Valley from the Punjab to the Indian Ocean, with outposts as far west as the Iranian border (Sutkagen-dor), and as far south as Bombay (Lothal). Material remains show a civilization that rivaled that of Mesopotamia and Egypt. Toward the middle of the 2nd millennium B.C. the Harappa culture declined and was replaced in the Indus Valley by local cultures such as the **Jhukar, Jhangar,** and **Harappa Cemetery H** cultures. Traditional history begins for northern India shortly after the invasion of the Indo-Aryans toward the end of the 2nd millennium B.C., but no archaeological remains have as yet been satisfactorily identified with this event. In the 1st millennium B.C. iron was introduced, probably from Iran, and a new Iron Age civilization arose in the Ganges Valley. Many of the cities famous in later history became important during this period, which was also marked by the use of a beautiful lustrous black pottery. In central and southern India local Chalcolithic cultures persisted until the late 2nd millennium B.C. Early in the 1st millennium B.C. a southern Iron Age culture characterized by cemeteries of megalithic tombs appeared. This culture overlapped the historic

Andhra period and the beginning of Roman trade around the time of Christ. (*Cont. p. 53.*)

SIBERIA AND MANCHURIA. This is a marginal area, which apparently retained a Mesolithic and later a Neolithic culture longer than other parts of the continent. The Bronze Age is represented in a few places, particularly the Minusinsk region of the Upper Yenisei Valley and the region from the western slopes of the Altai Mountains to the upper courses of the Ob and Irtish Rivers. Iron was introduced late in most parts of Siberia and in the extreme north and east many of the tribes were living in a Neolithic stage of culture until the Russian explorations and colonization in the 17th century A.D.

CENTRAL ASIA. Mesolithic and Neolithic cultures existed in Mongolia, but archaeologically we know little about them and practically nothing about Chinese Turkestan and Tibet before the opening centuries of the Christian Era. Such information as we have from Chinese records does not run much before the beginning of Han times (3rd century B.C.).

CHINA. Implements of Neolithic type but of uncertain date have been found in many parts of China. The **Yang-Shao culture,** characterized by the absence of metal and the presence of painted pottery suggesting that of western Asia, existed in Honan and neighboring provinces of northern China by at least 2000 B.C. This culture partially overlapped and was succeeded by a black ware culture, the **Lung-shan,** located further east in the lacustrine lowlands. Around 1400 B.C. followed the rich Bronze Age culture of the **Shang Dynasty** and the first written documents in the Far East (as found at An-yang). Numerous other remains, variously assigned to Neolithic or Bronze Ages, have been found in western Kansu, and central and south China, but are not yet well known.

JAPAN AND KOREA. The **Jomonshiki culture** (Neolithic) flourished in the northern half of the Main Island of Japan (Earliest, 4500–3700 B.C.; Early, 3700–3000 B.C.; Middle, 3000–2000 B.C.; Late, 2000–1000 B.C.; Latest 1000–250 B.C.). In the southern half of the Main Island and Kyushu there was a somewhat different Neolithic culture, represented by scattered finds dating before 250 B.C. This culture was followed by the Bronze Age **Yaiyoishiki culture** (250 B.C.–A.D. 200), with its nearest relationships with Korea, from which there were imports of bronze and, occasionally, even iron implements. Last of all was the Iron Age **Yamato,** or **Tomb, culture** (A.D. 200–A.D. 600) of the protohistoric period in central Japan, characterized by the gradual spread of iron implements and burial mounds through the whole of the Main Island. (*Cont. p. 149.*)

SOUTHEASTERN ASIA. A series of prehistoric cultures has been reported from Indo-China, especially from the Hoabinhian and Bacsonian areas in Tonkin. The earliest are Mesolithic, with Paleolithic survivals (Archaic period and Intermediate period of Hoabinhian and Keo-Phay period of Bacsonian), and possibly belong to the 3rd millennium B.C. They were followed by certain Proto-Neolithic cultures (Latest period of Hoabinhian and Early and Late Bacsonian). The full Neolithic is represented by the **Somrong-Sen culture,** which spread through all parts of Indo-China in the 2nd millennium B.C. and lasted until the beginning of the Bronze Age, about 500 B.C. Cultures somewhat similar to those of Indo-China have been reported from Burma and the Malay Peninsula.

b. EUROPE

In its broad outlines the prehistory of Europe from the close of the Paleolithic Age is a record of (1) a series of profound climatic changes, producing modifications of culture and the settlement of new areas; (2) a series of cultural influences coming in from Asia and Africa; (3) a series of invasions of new peoples from Asia and Africa; and (4) the formation of new peoples and the development of new cultures as a result of the interaction of these major factors.

(1) Climatic Changes and Time-Scale

By counting and comparing the varves, or annual layers of gravel and clay laid down in post-glacial lakes in many parts of the Baltic area, archaeologists have been able tentatively to tell the year in which each layer was formed over a period covering the past 10,000 years. The thickness of the varves and an analysis of the pollen contained in them and other deposits furnish a record of the progressive climatic changes year by year and date with reasonable accuracy typical archaeological remains found in some clear relation to these deposits. This gives a basic time-scale for northern Europe, which can be applied (in a general way and with modifications) to the rest of Europe, and can be checked, for the later periods, against tentative dates determined archaeologically on the basis of contacts with the historical cultures of Mesopotamia, Egypt, Greece, and Rome.

Following is the sequence of climatic periods in the Baltic region:

–8300 B.C. Sub-Arctic period. Contemporary with the Götiglacial stage of the ice retreat and end of the Paleolithic period. Very cold and characterized by *Dryas* flora, dwarf birch, willow, and tundra and steppe types of animals.

8300–7500. Pre-Boreal period. Contemporary

with the Finiglacial stage of the ice retreat, the Yoldia Sea and first half of the Ancylus Lake phase of the Baltic and the beginning of the Mesolithic period. Less cold, and characterized by birch, pine, and willow trees and mixed tundra and forest types of animals.

7500–5500. Boreal period. Post-glacial and contemporary with the last half of the Ancylus Lake phase of the Baltic. Rise in sea-level. Cool, dry "continental" climate, with birch and pine dominant, but alder and oak-mixed forest coming in and animals mostly of forest and lake type.

5500–3000. Atlantic period. Contemporary with the transgression of the Litorina Sea in the Baltic. Sea-level still high. Warm and moist "oceanic" climate (the so-called *period of climatic optimum*), with alder and oak-mixed forest (oak, elm, and lime) dominant, and forest, lake, and sea types of animals.

3000–400. Sub-Boreal period. Land relatively stable with relation to the sea and the Baltic Sea largely landlocked as at present. Dry, warm climate.

400– Sub-Atlantic period. Wet, cold climate.

(2) Cultural Changes and Periods

The principal outside cultural influences that came into Europe at different times followed four main routes: (1) from western Asia through Russia to central and western Europe; (2) from Asia Minor through the Aegean to Greece and also through Thrace to central Europe; (3) from the Near East and the Aegean by sea to the western Mediterranean; and (4) from North Africa to Spain and western Europe. Thus the general direction of cultural movement was from south to north and from east to west; hence at any given moment in time the southern and eastern areas were apt to be enjoying a more advanced form of culture than were the more peripheral regions to the northwest. This is well illustrated by the course developments took in each of the principal periods.

c. 8000– In the Mesolithic period, lasting for several thousand years, the **Tardenoisian culture,** which was most closely related to cultures in Africa and Spain and which was characterized by microlithic implements, spread from the south over most of Europe. At the same time, with the amelioration of the climate, there was a northward movement of peoples following the forests that gradually occupied the steppes and tundras of the North European plain and a forest culture was developed, characterized by the use of the chipped stone axe (Maglemosean and Ertebolle cultures).

c. 7th millennium to 3rd millennium. The full-fledged Neolithic culture in Europe appeared in the Aegean area in the 7th millennium B.C. The earliest villages are known from Thessaly and Macedonia. From Greece the food-producing economy spread to the Balkans, Bulgaria, Roumania, and Yugoslavia not later than the 6th millennium, and gradually into central Europe along the Danube.

The earliest Danubian villages in Czechoslovakia have been dated by Carbon-14 means to the first half of the 5th millennium B.C. Soon after, the Danubian farmers occupied the whole of central Europe between the Netherlands on the west and Moldavia and the western Ukraine on the east. Another wave of Neolithic diffusion was along the Mediterranean and Adriatic coasts, possibly from southeastern Anatolia, and very likely in the 6th millennium. In the west it reached the southern parts of the Iberian peninsula. In Crete the earliest Neolithic settlement is also dated by Carbon-14 to the 6th millennium B.C. North of the Black Sea local Mesolithic people were converted to a food-producing economy in the course of the 6th and 5th millennia B.C. Northern and western Europe entered the Neolithic stage around 3000 B.C.

c. 3000– The Bronze Age culture began, for Europe, in the Aegean and Greece shortly after 3000 B.C. and copper axes appeared in Hungary a little before 2000 B.C.—in both cases due to Asiatic influence. Other copper influences came into Europe by way of Spain about 2000 B.C. and diffused widely, apparently in association with the Bell Beaker culture. At the same time there were further developments of the Megalithic culture throughout its area. The Bronze Age for Europe as a whole is usually considered to cover the period from about 1800 to 750 B.C. and is divided into three sub-periods: Early, Middle, and Late Bronze Age.

c. 750– The Iron Age began not long after 1000 B.C. with the development of iron metallurgy in Austria and its spread through the rest of Europe. The first part of the Iron Age is usually referred to as the **Hallstatt period** (about 750 B.C. to 450 B.C.), the second part of the **La Tène period** (450 B.C. to 1 A.D.).

(3) Movements of Peoples

It is still uncertain to what extent the spread of all the various cultures was due to trade and borrowing, and to what extent it involved wholesale movements of peoples. The population of Europe in the early part of the Mesolithic period probably consisted largely of the descendants of the food-gathering Upper Paleolithic peoples and was predominantly of the long-headed, white or European stock, sometimes called Atlanto-Mediterranean. Round-headed peoples began to crowd in early in Mesolithic and Neolithic times, from the east (as shown at the site of Offnet in Bavaria) and possibly from Africa (as shown in certain sites in Portugal and Spain). During the succeeding millennia the three fundamental modern European types became established in their respective areas: the Mediterraneans in southern Europe, the Alpines in central and western Europe, and the Nordics in northern Europe. During the latter part of the Bronze Age and especially in the Iron Age we have further witness to great movements of peoples in the **spread of Indo-European languages** over the larger part of Europe. Greek-speaking and Illyrian-speaking peoples came down through the Balkans into Greece, and Italic-speaking peoples into Italy; Celtic-speaking peoples moved west through central and northern Europe as far as France and the British Isles, and were followed over much the same route by Teutonic-speaking and, for part of the way, by Slavic-speaking peoples. We know these groups were of mixed types, but information about their physical characteristics is inadequate.

(4) Regional Distribution of Cultures

AEGEAN AREA AND GREECE. In Crete a Neolithic culture flourished for at least several millennia. This was followed by a high Bronze Age civilization (with its center at Knossos), which has been divided into three major periods: **Early Minoan,** 2500–2200 B.C.; **Middle Minoan,** 2200–1550 B.C.; and **Late Minoan,** 1550–1100 B.C. Similar Bronze Age cultures have been reported from Melos and other islands of the Cyclades, namely: **Early Cycladic,** 2800–2200 B.C.; **Middle Cycladic,** 2200–1650 B.C.; and **Late Cycladic,** 1650–1300 B.C. On the mainland of Greece a third series of related cultures flourished in central Greece and the Peloponnesus: Neolithic, before 2800 B.C.; **Early Helladic,** 2800–2100 B.C.; **Middle Helladic,** 2100–1550 B.C.; and **Late Helladic,** 1550–1100 B.C. In Thessaly were two Neolithic cultures, with northern affinities: **Thessalian I,** before 2600 B.C., and **Thessalian II,** 2600–2400 B.C., followed by two of the Bronze Age cultures: **Thessalian III,** 2400–1800 B.C.; and **Thessalian IV,** 1800–1200 B.C. In Cyprus the Neolithic began at least in the 6th millennium, after which developed a series of Bronze Age cultures. During the latter half of the 2nd millennium B.C. the so-called **Mycenaean culture** (Late Helladic), with its center in Mycenae in the Peloponnesus, spread throughout Greece and the whole Aegean area, with extensions to western Asia Minor, Cyprus, and Syria. The Iron Age in Greece began about 1000 B.C. with the Geometric period, the close of which marked the beginning of history in this area.

RUSSIA. North of the Black Sea a local Neolithic culture lasted up to about the middle of the 3rd millennium when it was disturbed by the invasion of the steppe or Kurgan (Barrow) people from beyond the lower Volga. Subsequently, in the whole northern Pontic region and the northern Caucasus, the **Kurgan culture** (also called Ochre-Grave or Pit-Grave) firmly established itself and later spread further to the Caucasus, Anatolia, the Aegean, central, and northern Europe. The enormous Kurgan expansion may have brought the Indo-European language to Europe. During the Bronze Age, the offshoots of the Kurgan culture differentiated into the north Pontic or Cimmerian, the lower Volga or Timber-Grave, and the Fat'janovo in central Russia, the latter closely related to the culture in the East Baltic area and Poland. The most aggressive was the **Timber-Grave** or **Proto-Scythian culture** which gradually advanced to the Black Sea coasts and ultimately, in the 8th century B.C., to central Europe. The heirs of the Timber-Grave and its sister branch in Siberia, the **Andronovo culture,** are called by the general name Scythians. The Scythian culture, north of the Black Sea, flourished from the 7th to the 4th centuries B.C. Later the Scythians were replaced by another kindred group of eastern origin, the Sarmatians.

In northern Russia and the northern East Baltic area, a large Neolithic or Sub-Neolithic cultural bloc characterized by a primitive pit and comb impressed pottery differentiated during the Bronze Age into the **Turbino culture** in the east, the **Textile Pottery** in northern central Russia, and the **Asbestos Pottery** in Carelia and northwestern Russia. Many local variants emerged from these during the Early Iron Age and continued into history. These northern groups belonged to the Finno-Ugrian and Lapp families.

THE BALKANS AND CENTRAL EUROPE. Throughout the Neolithic period the Balkan peninsula remained intimately related with and was continually influenced by the Anatolian cultures. The basic characteristics are: large stratified tells (mounds), female figurines, and noteworthy pottery, usually painted. Throughout the millennia many local cultural groups formed, flourished, and declined and new cultural variants arose. The following groups, dating from the 6th to the 4th millennia B.C., can be treated as separate cultures: **Proto-Sesklo** and **Sesklo** in Greece; **Starčevo** in western Bulgaria, eastern Yugoslavia, southern and western Roumania (the earliest full-fledged Neolithic culture in this area); **Veselinovo** in eastern Bulgaria, with strong Anatolian elements, which replaced Starčevo in central Bulgaria and southern Roumania; **Boian** in Roumania, which partly supplanted Starčevo; **Hamangia,** a recently discovered cultural group along the Black Sea coast, mainly in Dobruja; **Gumelnita,** a later Neolithic-Chalcolithic culture, probably derived from Hamangia or Boian, which replaced both Hamangia and Boian; **Vadastra,** a sister branch of Boian in western Roumania, and its later development; **Pre-Tripolye** (c. 5th millennium B.C.), between the Dniester and Dnieper, which developed into the **Tripolye Painted Pottery culture** in the 4th and 3rd millennia B.C.

From the end of the 5th and during the 4th millennium B.C. new Anatolian influences caused remarkable changes in the peninsula resulting in the appearance of the Vinca-Tisza-Lengyel bloc in the central Balkans and the middle Danube basin. The Sesklo culture developed in this period into a **Dimini culture.**

In central Europe the so-called **Danubian culture** is held to be an outpost of the Balkan Starčevo culture, but developed its local character due to different climatic and soil conditions. Its eastern part was disturbed by the coming of the Lengyel people. The rest of the culture continued into the beginning of the 3rd millennium B.C. when it was rivaled by the northern European peoples known as **Funnel Beakers** and **Michelsberg.**

These long-lasting cultural groups were disturbed or conquered by the invasion of the Kurgan steppe peoples, very probably Indo-European speaking, around 2300–2200 B.C. This brought the beginning of a new era in Europe characterized by a mixture of cultural elements and the formation of new cultural groups.

The European Bronze Age had its beginnings in the mountainous regions, chiefly in the Carpathians. During the early 2nd millennium remarkable bronze cultures arose, such as the **Unĕtice** in central Europe followed by the Middle Bronze Age Tumulus and Late Bronze Age Urnfield periods, and the **Otomani** in Transylvania, both of Kurgan origin. The growth and expansions of the Únĕtice-Tumulus-Urnfield culture brought changes in ethnic configurations, bringing an end, towards the close of the 13th and the 12th centuries B.C., to the Mycenaean period in Greece, to the Hittite empire in Anatolia, and to local cultures in Italy, the Balkans, and eastern France. The central European Bronze Age culture was a cradle of the Celtic, Italic, Venetic, Illyrian, Phrygian, and the Armenian speaking peoples. In eastern Roumania (Moldavia) a distinctive culture called **Monteoru** formed and developed throughout the Bronze Age. South of it on the lower Danube the **Tei culture** flourished. Both of these may have been created by ancient Thracians. The first iron artifacts in central Europe appeared in the last centuries of the

2nd millennium B.C., but a true Iron Age started only near the end of the 8th and in the 7th centuries with the beginning of the **Hallstatt culture,** created by the Celts and Illyrians in the Alpine zone and north of the Adriatic Sea. Hallstatt was followed by the Celtic **La Tène,** which continued to Roman times.

ITALY. The earliest Neolithic culture in southern Italy, Sicily, and Liguria is represented by the **Impressed Pottery culture,** called Molfetta, Stentinello, and Arene Candide. It is of east Mediterranean origin and dates back to the 6th or 5th millennia B.C. This was followed by the **Painted Pottery culture** in southern Italy and Sicily with affinities in the east Adriatic area and Greece. The Copper Age started c. 3000 B.C. in Sicily. In eastern Sicily the sequence of Copper Age cultures is characterized by changing painted pottery styles: Conzo, Serraferlicchio, and Malpasso, followed by the Early Bronze Age Castellucio, Middle Bronze Age Thapsos, and Late Bronze Age Pantalica complexes. The local culture of central Italy was interrupted by the appearance of eastern (Kurgan) elements at c. 2000 B.C., which created a hybrid culture called Rinaldone. In the rest of the southern part of the peninsula a local culture called Apennine persisted throughout the greater part of the 2nd millennium B.C.

The Neolithic in northern Italy is little known except for Liguria. Around 2000 B.C. it was reached by the western Bell Beaker people under whose influence the Bronze Age Remedello culture in the Po Valley was formed, succeeded by the Terramare culture which lasted up to the infiltration of central European elements in Italy in the 13th and 12th centuries B.C. After the formative Previllanovian period of the 2nd millennium's last centuries **Villanova culture** (1000–600 B.C.) arose, which maintained intimate relations with central Europe.

ISLANDS OF THE WESTERN MEDITERRANEAN. A remarkable Neolithic development, characterized by massive stone temples and underground structures, took place in Malta. In Sardinia there was a distinctive Chalcolithic culture (Anghelu Ruju) shortly after 2000 B.C., followed by various phases of Megalithic (Giants' Tombs, dolmens, and Nuraghis), much of which dates to the early half of the 1st millennium B.C. There was a related Bronze Age culture, with stone constructions (Navetas and Talayots) in the Balearic Islands.

SPAIN. There were several cultures in the Iberian Peninsula in the Mesolithic period: Final Capsian in the south and center, Tardenoisian and Azilian in the north, and two special developments, the Portuguese Kitchen Middens in the west and the Asturian culture in the northwest. Some of these lasted well into the

3rd millennium B.C. and were succeeded by various Neolithic cultures of which the most important developments were in the southeast (Almerian culture) and in Portugal and Galicia (Megalithic). New trends in the development of the culture in the Iberian Peninsula started with the appearance of eastern Mediterranean colonists in the early 3rd millennium. The **Bell Beaker culture** (about 2000 B.C.) ushered in the Bronze Age, which was marked by a continuation of the Megalithic and, in the southeast, by the development of the **El Argar culture** (middle of 2nd millennium B.C.) in southeastern Spain. In the early part of the 1st millennium B.C. there was a local Iron Age culture, with Hallstatt affinities, which lasted until the time of the first Punic and Greek colonies (about 500 B.C.).

WESTERN EUROPE. Two cultures, the Tardenoisian and the Azilian, were dominant in western Europe during the Early Mesolithic period, with the Asturian (Late Mesolithic) partially represented in southern France and the Maglemosean (Early Mesolithic) in northern France and Belgium. Neolithic influences were late in arriving, but by the middle of the 4th millennium B.C., or earlier, there was a Neolithic culture, of Mediterranean origin, in the south. The Bell Beaker culture appeared here shortly after 2000 B.C., while the Megalithic culture spread through the coastal region (especially in Brittany), and influences from central Europe and the Rhine contributed to the development of the Bronze Age in France. Well along in the 1st millennium B.C. this gave way to a western version of the Hallstatt culture, which was followed, as elsewhere in Europe, by the La Tène.

The **British Isles** had a somewhat similar but still more retarded development. In the Mesolithic period a survival of the Upper Paleolithic Creswellian culture was modified in certain areas by the introduction of Azilian influences into southwestern Scotland, Maglemosean in southern and eastern England, and Tardenoisian more or less generally. About 3000 B.C., Neolithic features first appeared, in connection with the Windmill Hill culture and the Long Barrows. Bronze came into England some time after 2000 B.C. (Beaker culture, Long Barrows, and Round Barrows). About the end of the 8th century new bronze-using peoples from the continent invaded England, bringing some iron with them. The true Iron Age began about 400 B.C. with an invasion of continental peoples enjoying a predominantly Hallstatt culture (Iron Age A). They were followed, in the 1st century B.C., by La Tène peoples (Iron Age B), the Belgae (Iron Age C), and the Romans. Modified forms of some of these cultures reached Scotland and Ireland but at considerably later dates.

BALTIC REGION. In the early part of the Mesolithic, which corresponds to the Pre-Boreal period (8300–7500 B.C.), tanged-point cultures (Remouchamps, Ahrensburg-Lavenstadt, and Swiderian) occupied the north European plain from Belgium to Poland, with outliers in northern and western Norway (Komsa and Fosna cultures), but there were traces of an early Tardenoisian and the beginning of the new forest or axe cultures (Lyngby). In the Boreal period (7500–5500 B.C.), a Mesolithic axe culture, the Maglemosean, with many local variants, spread widely over the whole area from Yorkshire to Estonia. The Komsa and Fosna cultures continued in Norway, and Tardenoisian developed further at various points on the North German plain. In the Atlantic period (5500–3000 B.C.) the Ertebolle culture developed out of the Maglemosean, while the Komsa, Fosna, Tardenoisian, and a late version of Maglemosean survived in marginal areas. The beginning of the Neolithic period is synchronous with the beginning of the Sub-Boreal phase, c. 3000 B.C. At about 2500 B.C. the Early Neolithic elements were profoundly modified by the introduction of the Megalithic civilization, which had spread along the Atlantic seaboard, and the eastern Kurgan elements which spread via central Europe. Several distinct but contemporary cultures developed, viz.: Megalithic Battle-Axe or Separate Graves of Kurgan origin, Arctic, and Dwelling-Place cultures. In 1500 B.C. or thereabouts the Scandinavian and Baltic Bronze Age began, which was followed later by the Iron Age.

c. AFRICA

EGYPT. The Mesolithic period witnessed the final stages of the Sebilian culture. The Neolithic period began early in the Nile Valley (probably before 4000 B.C.) and is represented by the Fayum, Merimdean, Tasian, and Badarian cultures. During the 4th millennium B.C., under combined African and Asiatic influences, the important **predynastic culture** developed (Amratian, Gerzean, and Semainian phases), and ended about 3000 B.C. with the establishment of the First Dynasty and the beginning of the historical period.

NORTHWESTERN AFRICA. Mesolithic cultures (final stages of the Mouillian and Capsian) were, at dates as yet undetermined, modified and transformed by the infiltration of Neolithic influences, which spread gradually through Tunisia, Algeria, and Morocco and south across the Sahara. Bronze was late in reaching the Mediterranean coastal regions of this area, and did not penetrate the interior; generally stone did not give way to metal until the Punic Iron Age in the 1st millennium B.C.

EAST AFRICA. Following the close of the Pleistocene in this area the Capsian (formerly called the Aurignacian) penetrated the highlands from the north and two other Microlithic cultures developed (Wilton A and B) and another culture (Elmenteitan), but the dates of all three may be somewhat late as pottery was already present in Elmenteitan. The succeeding cultures (Gumban A and B, Njoroan, Wilton C, and Tumbian) were clearly Early Neolithic in character but not necessarily in date. There was apparently no true Bronze Age in this part of Africa and iron gradually replaced stone during the Christian Era.

SOUTH AFRICA. In what is termed the Later Stone Age of this area, two Mesolithic cultures, Wilton and Smithfield, spread through the greater part of South Africa, beginning at some time after the close of the Pleistocene and continuing with modifications until the Bantu invasions brought iron to the region at a comparatively recent date. South Africa had no true Neolithic period or Bronze Age, although some traces of agriculture and occasional polished stone implements have been found.

CENTRAL AND WEST AFRICA. This also was a marginal region. Mesolithic implements have been found in parts of the Sudan. The Tumbian culture (Mesolithic) was represented in the Congo Basin and persisted after the introduction of polished stone. Various other Neolithic cultures of more fully developed form but uncertain date have been reported from the Sudan and Nigeria. A true Bronze Age is not found here, and iron was late in arriving, but during the Christian Era bronze casting received a special development, notably in Benin.

d. OCEANIA

Australia, New Guinea, and the islands of Melanesia, Micronesia, and Polynesia were uninhabited before the end of the Pleistocene, when Australia and New Guinea were first occupied. The outer islands were reached much later. The first movement of peoples concerned was that of the Australoids from Indonesia along the Lesser Sundas to the Sahul Shelf, which was then out of water, and which connected Australia with New Guinea and Tasmania. This migration required short sea voyages in canoes or rafts.

Australian archaeologists have found various stone tool industries with choppers, chopping-tools, and flakes, and the living aborigines make all of these, plus blades and microliths in a few places. Some had learned to grind chopping tools into axes.

At an unknown time Australoids of Papuan type occupied the Melanesian island chain, perhaps as far as New Caledonia and Fiji. Later, probably not long before the time of Christ, predominantly Mongoloid peoples from Indonesia and Southeast Asia introduced garden agriculture, pigs, poultry, and polished stone axes to most of these islands, as well as Melanesian languages, although in the interior and south of New Guinea and the interiors of some of the other islands Papuan is still spoken.

The Polynesians and Micronesians are peoples of largely Mongoloid origin with some Australoid features. This condition is probably due to the fact their ancestors came from the coast of South China, which was a Mongoloid-Australoid frontier before the Chinese expansion forced various coastal peoples out to sea, the Polynesians apparently for the most part passing by the already occupied regions and pressing east across the Pacific to Micronesia and Polynesia. The date of these movements was comparatively recent. Navigation received its real development in this part of the world in the 1st millennium B.C. The first long voyages into Micronesia and Polynesia probably did not begin until the 4th century A.D., and the farther islands were not settled until some centuries later.

The majority of the peoples who took part in the settlement of Oceania were in a Neolithic stage of culture like that of southeast Asia and Indonesia. There is no concrete evidence to support the view that Polynesia was settled from South America.

e. AMERICA

Studies of the physical characteristics of **American Indians** show these to be predominantly Mongoloid, while there seems to be in both continents a marginal distribution of a stock that may represent the descendants of a group of very early arrivals possibly related in part to the Ainu.

At the time of the first European contact with America in the 16th and 17th centuries A.D., some Indians were still hunters and food-gatherers, like their Paleolithic ancestors, but the great majority were in a Neolithic stage of culture. The fact that they had no cereals that were cultivated in the Old World and no Old World domestic animals except the dog has led to the general opinion that agriculture and the domestication of animals were in this case independent developments after arrival in the New World. Certain polished stone tools, however, and even certain types of pottery show relationship to forms found in northeastern Asia. So two of the four main elements of

Neolithic culture may show some evidence of a continuation of Asiatic tradition. In a few cases American Indian groups passed beyond the Neolithic stage, as is indicated by the use of metal.

The first advanced culture in the western hemisphere is believed to have had its origin over two thousand years ago in the Andean region of South America and in the highland region of Central America and Mexico. Here grew up a high civilization, parallel in many striking ways to that of the Old World but probably entirely independent of it. The cultivation of Indian corn (*Zea mais*) was the basis of the new economy. Rich textiles, fine pottery, and magnificent ornaments of gold, silver, and copper were produced. Great city centers arose, with canals and gardens and monumental temples on lofty pyramids. A highly complex social organization was developed, with priest-emperors, standing armies, schools, courts, and systematized religions. Intellectual progress was marked by astronomical research, the invention of accurate calendars, and—in Yucatan and Mexico—an elaborate hieroglyphic writing.

In the Peruvian area the early Nasca and Chimu cultures were followed by Tiahuanacan and, in immediately pre-Columbian times, by the **Inca civilization.** Influences spread from this center across the Andes into the Amazon Basin and down the Andes to the Argentine region. Farther north, the Chibchan and Chorotegan cultures occupied the intervening area between Peru and Yucatan, where the **Maya civilization,** the climax of native American achievement, developed during the 1st millennium B.C. and reached its culmination shortly before the Spanish Conquest. Similarly, in the Valley of Mexico the Archaic and Toltec cultures culminated in the **Aztec civilization,** discovered by the Spaniards. The effect of these powerful centers of influence must have been felt in lessening degree throughout much of North America, especially in the advanced cultures of the Pueblo area of the southwest, the southeast, and the Mound Builder area in the Mississippi drainage. Simpler cultures occupied the woodlands area of the northeastern United States and Canada and the Central Plains. California was a marginal region, occupied largely by food-gatherers of a low stage of culture, while the Indians of the northwest coast and the Eskimos of Alaska and northern Canada had, each in their own way, developed highly specialized cultures, which suggest to some extent Asiatic relationships.

II. ANCIENT HISTORY

II. ANCIENT HISTORY

A. EARLY KINGDOMS OF ASIA AND AFRICA

1. MESOPOTAMIA, TO 333 B.C.

a. THE LAND AND THE PEOPLE

MESOPOTAMIA as a geographical term in its widest sense applies to the lands bordering and lying between the Euphrates and Tigris rivers, reaching from the foothills of the Armenian Taurus range in the northwest to the ancient shore of the Persian Gulf, on the west bounded by the steppes of the Great Syrian Desert, on the east by the barrier of the Zagros Mountains. The lands naturally divide into two sections, Upper Mesopotamia—the Mesopotamia proper of the Greeks, called today the **Jezireh** —and Lower Mesopotamia or Babylonia, the black alluvial plain south of modern Baghdad. In antiquity Upper Mesopotamia had two primary centers of civilization. One was in the country of the Upper Euphrates and included such ancient cities as Carchemish on the Euphrates, Harran on the Balikh and Gozan on the Khabur tributaries of the Euphrates, and further south on the Euphrates, Mari. In this territory arose the Hurrian **kingdom of Mitanni** (15th century) and the Amorite power at **Mari** (18th century). Another center was on the Upper Tigris near the confluences of the Greater and Lesser Zab. This was the country of ancient **Assyria** whose chief cities were Assur, Ninevah, Calah (modern Nimrud), and Dur Sharrukin (modern Khorsabad).

Lower Mesopotamia, the site of ancient **Sumer** and **Akkad,** also falls naturally into northern and southern sections. The northern part centered around **Babylon,** and included such additional cities as Eshnunna on the Diyala, and Sippar, Kutha, Kish, Borsippa, and Isin on the ancient Euphrates or its canals. In the deep south were the old Sumerian cities of **Eridu** and **Ur** with access to the Persian Gulf. The shoreline of the ancient gulf may have reached farther north than at present, or the cities may have been situated on a lagoon; there is conflicting evidence. Farther north were the cities of **Larsa, Uruk** (biblical Erech), **Lagash** and **Umma. Nippur,** in the middle of the country, was the religious center of Sumer and Akkad. These southern lands were marshy, capable of sustaining a significant population only when elaborate drainage canals and irriga-tion works were installed in the course of the 4th millennium.

The population of both Upper and Lower Mesopotamia in prehistoric times belonged to the brown, or Mediterranean, race. While this basic stock persisted in historical times, espe-cially in the south, it became increasingly mixed, especially with broad-headed Arme-noid peoples from the northeastern mountains, owing to recurrent incursions of mountain tribes into the plain.

The earliest settlers in Mesopotamia known to the historian were the **Sumerians,** who prob-ably created the irrigation culture of Mesopota-mia in Chalcolithic (Obeidian) times, beginning not long after 4000 (p. 16). The Sumerians are of unknown origin. They spoke an aggluti-native language which has no clear or close relationship to any known family of languages. **Semitic peoples,** presumably from the edges of the desert, and perhaps from the more arid areas of Upper Mesopotamia, were found living side by side with the Sumerians in apparent harmony in earliest historical times. As early as Protodynastic times (2850–2360), dynasts with Semitic names are found in northern Lower Mesopotamia, and the **Akkadians,** as these Semitic-speaking folk came to be called, had become dominant in this district before the rise of the Akkadian dynasty of Sargon (c. 2360–2180). Their Semitic dialect is called Akkadian. From the Old Akkadian of the 3rd millennium developed two major East Semitic dialects, **Assyrian,** spoken on the Upper Tigris, and **Babylonian.** In the course of the 2nd mil-lennium Babylonian became the *lingua franca* of the ancient world, in use in both the Egyp-tian and Hittite empires.

In addition to the Sumerians and Akkadians, Mesopotamia was occupied by a series of non-Semitic invaders from the northeastern moun-tains, and by West Semitic tribes from the adja-cent deserts. The former include the **Gutians,** who brought to an end the dynasty of Akkad toward 2180 B.C., the **Hurrians** (biblical Ho-rites), whose main movement beginning about 1700 overwhelmed Upper Mesopotamia, and the **Kashshu** (Cossaeans), whose incursions into Babylonia began in the 17th century, and who ruled Babylonia for nearly a half millennium. West Semitic peoples who successfully invaded Mesopotamia include the **Amorites,** who founded the 1st dynasty of Babylon in the 19th century, the **Aramaeans,** whose incursions began toward the end of the 12th century, and the **Chaldeans,** founders of the Neo-Babylonian empire in the 7th century. In Late Assyrian and Babylonian times, Babylonian gave way to **Aramaic** as the dominant spoken language of Mesopotamia. Aramaic served also as the *lingua franca* of the successive Assyrian, Neo-Babylonian, and Persian empires. Sumerian and Babylonian survived only as learned or religious tongues, dying out finally in Seleucid times.

b. CHRONOLOGY

The chronology of Mesopotamia rests on an extraordinary complex of sources and data which is constantly growing, thanks to archaeological activity. Among the major sources are classical authors, notably the **Canon of Ptolemy** (2nd century A.D.) and fragments of **Berossus** (3rd century B.C.), cuneiform documents including the great Assyrian, Babylonian, and Sumerian king lists, the eponym lists, the Synchronistic Chronicle, building inscriptions; and as well, astronomical data, literary and archaeological synchronisms tying Mesopotamia to Egypt, Syria-Palestine, and Anatolia; and in the early period, Carbon–14 dates.

The major framework of Mesopotamian history is fixed back into the 12th century B.C. within a year or two. Problems or lacunae disturbing calculation exist in the king lists in the 12th, 15th, and 17th centuries especially, and by the 18th century the range of possible error has mounted to more than a half century. Astronomical observations (the **Venus Tablets** of Ammisaduqa) exist for this era and, when sufficient data are in hand, promise to fix the chronology of the 2nd and late 3rd millennia. At present we must choose between two solutions yielded by astronomical calculation, 64 years apart. One gives the *Middle Chronology,* which places Hammurapi's reign in the years 1792–1750; the alternate, the *Low Chronology,* fixes his dates at 1728–1686. Babylonian records are more easily fitted, perhaps, to the Middle Chronology. Carbon–14 dates exclude neither chronology, but tend to favor later dates. The strongest evidence for the Lower Chronology consists of indirect archaeological synchronisms with Egypt, where the chronology is astronomically fixed. For example, the great Middle Bronze Age city at Hazor in Palestine, founded about 1750 following the fall of the Middle Kingdom in Egypt, is well known at Mari in the age brought to an end by the conquests of Hammurapi. Egypt on the other hand goes without mention in the Mari correspondence, a silence that seems incredible if the imperial power of the Middle Kingdom were at its zenith. The Low Chronology appears best at this time and is followed here in giving dates in the 2nd and 3rd millennia.

c. THE RISE OF MESOPOTAMIAN CIVILIZATION

The first great civilization of mankind was created by the Sumerians in Lower Mesopotamia. The formation of the basic lines of this culture took place early, in the **Protoliterate period** (3200–2850 B.C.). As its name suggests this era was marked by the **invention of writing.** The earliest known inscriptions, clay tablets in a pictographic forebear of cuneiform, were found in a temple of Uruk dating from shortly before 3000. The earliest tablets that can be interpreted fully are the archaic texts of Ur, from about 2800. The Protoliterate age witnessed the emergence of the highly organized city state, with its complex of irrigation works elaborated from earlier canal systems. True **ziqqurats,** the towers that dominated the Sumerian temple complex, began to rise from the plain. In much later times the "Tower of Babel," a structure of seven stages topped by a temple, would reach nearly 300 feet into the heavens. The influence of Protoliterate Mesopotamia spread as far as Egypt, stimulating the nascent civilization of the Nile Valley into a burst of energetic growth. This age and the subsequent period of classical Sumer and Akkad created a cultural world of myth and literature, polity, art, and science that dominated ancient Mesopotamia until the demise of the ancient Oriental world, and that ultimately bequeathed a legacy of legal and religious tradition to Israel, and of magical, astronomical, and mathematical lore to Greece.

The city state in earliest Mesopotamia was organized economically and religiously into **temple communities** headed by a priestly representative of the patron deity or deities of the city. A political assembly of citizens or elders also ruled. Later this primitive combination of theocracy and democracy in the cities gave way to rule by an **ensi,** a "governor," holding sway over both the religious and political establishment, or to rule by a **lugal,** "king," a superior title often used by sovereigns claiming wider dominion. In imperial times, highly centralized forms of monarchy emerged.

The **Sumerian gods** in earliest times were closely bound to natural phenomena, the powers of creativity, fertility, and forces confronted in the cosmos. Even at the dawn of history, however, these gods were conceived for the most part in human form and were organized in a cosmic state reflecting the social forms of pre-monarchical Sumer. The world of the gods was a macrocosm of Sumer where earthly temples, counterparts of cosmic abodes of the gods, forged links between the two realms. The assembly of the gods included four pre-eminent deities, **Anu,** the old god of the sky, titular head of the assembly; **Enlil,** young "Lord Storm," the violent as well as life-giving air; **Ninkhursag** or Ninmakh, the great mother, personification of the fertility of the earth; and **Enki,** god of underground waters, the source of the "masculine" powers of creativity in the earth. Another important triad consisted of **Nanna** (moon), **Utu** (sun), and **Inanna** (Venus). The chief cult-dramas included the cosmogonic battle enacted in the New Year's festival, in which Enlil, later Marduk of Babylon, established order by defeating the powers of chaos, and assumed kingship. Another important cycle of rites had to do with Dumuzi (Tammuz), with laments over his death, celebration of the return to life of the young god and his union (*heiros gamos*) with Inanna (Semitic Ishtar) which assured spring's resurgent life.

d. LOWER MESOPOTAMIA, 3200–1025 B.C.

3200–2850. THE PROTOLITERATE PERIOD. A system of city states dominated by temples emerged. Semitic tribes speaking Akkadian began to settle on the fringes of Sumer, especially in the north. Writing was invented. **2850–2360. THE EARLY DYNASTIC OR CLASSICAL SUMERIAN AGE.** The legendary **1st Dynasty of Uruk** may date from the first phase of this period if not earlier. Included in it are the divine or deified heroes of later epic tradition, Enmerkar, Lugalbanda, Tammuz, and Gilgamesh. The Archaic Tablets of Ur also come from early in the era. In the era called **Early Dynastic II,** beginning about 2600, the Akkadians grew increasingly powerful in the north. Several of the dynasts of Kish, for example, bore Semitic names. In the building arts the plano-convex brick was introduced and the great wall of Uruk, some $5\frac{1}{2}$ miles in circumference, was constructed. The Shuruppak Tablets, among them the earliest list of the gods, come from the 26th century. To the same century we probably must assign **Mesilim,** called king of Kish, known both from contemporary and later sources. The last phase of the Early Dynastic period begins about 2500. The **1st Dynasty of Ur** appears to have gained hegemony. Its best

known rulers are **Mesannepadda** and **Aannepadda,** and it may be that the rich "Royal Tombs of Ur" are to be attributed to this dynasty. Much more is known of the city state of **Lagash.** **Urnanshe** founded a vigorous dynasty at Lagash, contemporary with the 1st Dynasty of Ur. His grandson **Eannatum** (c. 2460) was a great warrior, defeating Sumerian cities including Ur in the south and Kish in the north, and extending his power into Elam and as far as Mari. His victory over Umma is recorded on the celebrated **Stele of Vultures.** Lagash's overlordship of Sumer was short-lived, however, and was passed over unmentioned in the canonical king list. At the close of the Early Dynastic Era, **Urukagina** took power in Lagash, instituting the first known social reforms in history. **Lugalzaggisi** (c. 2360), ensi of Umma, defeated Lagash, however, and went on to subdue all of Sumer, ruling as king of Uruk.

2360–2180. THE DYNASTY OF AKKAD. **Sargon the Great** (2360–2305) rose from mean origins in the service of Urzababa, king of Kish. The details of his revolt and achievement of royal rank are not clear. In any case, he built Akkad (Agade) as the new seat of his dynasty, fell on Uruk, defeating and capturing Lugalzaggisi, and in a series of battles reduced the last of the independent states of Sumer. Sargon the Akkadian was able to achieve what no Sumerian of classical times had done: he placed the city states of north and south, Akkad and Sumer, under a highly organized central government. On this base he built the **first world empire.** He gained control of the Persian Gulf, conquered Elam, the mountain lands of Iran, Upper Mesopotamia, and Syria, ruling from "sea to sea." Later legends, including those of the epic tale *King of Battle,* describe Sargon as extending his conquests into Anatolia and even across the sea to Crete. Rimush (2304–2296) and Manishtushu (2295–2281), the sons of Sargon, consolidated the empire. **Naramsin** (2280–2244), Sargon's grandson, brought Akkad to the zenith of its power and peaceful accomplishment. He was the first of the Mesopotamian kings to claim divinity, and to style himself "king of the four quarters" (of the world). The names of Sargon and Naramsin lived on in Babylonian, Hurrian, and Hittite legends as the greatest of Mesopotamian rulers. In the Akkadian era the arts flourished. The Sumerian script was adapted to Akkadian and perfected. Inscriptions and buildings of the dynasty were spread from the Mediterranean to Susa. Trade flourished even with the distant Indus Valley. **Sharkalisharri** (2243–2219), the last of Sargon's line, reigned in a time of troubles, defending his narrowing borders against the blows of surrounding barbarians. After him ephemeral kings held Akkad for some years longer, but the city fell about 2180 to Guti hordes from the Zagros.

c. 2180–2082. The Gutian Dynasty. During the dark interlude of Gutian rule, the Sumerians of the south revived. Utukhegal of Uruk drove out the Guti and re-established the Sumerian kingdom. Urbaba of Lagash flourished.

c. 2060–1950.   3RD DYNASTY OF UR: The Sumerian Renaissance. Urnammu of Ur (c. 2060–2043) seized power from his suzerain Utukhegal, and founded a new Sumerian dynasty. He was a vigorous ruler dedicated to restoring the glories of the Sumerian past. The oldest law code, a forerunner of later Sumerian law and the great code of Hammurapi, comes from his reign. Under the long reign of his son **Shulgi** (2042–1995), the feudal empire of Ur became most highly developed. He governed Elam, Assyria, and northwestern Mesopotamia, and like his Akkadian predecessors, proclaimed himself a god, king of the four quarters of the world. Bursin (1994–1986) and Shusin (1985–1977) maintained the empire. The vast program of temple building and refurbishing initiated by their fathers continued, adding to the brilliance of the Sumerian revival. In the time of Shusin, however, we hear of the building of a line of fortifications on the west to hold at bay the Amorites of the steppe. Fairly early in the reign of **Ibbisin** (1976–1952), the last of the emperors of Ur, the West Semitic Amorite tribesmen swept over Sumer and Akkad, devastating the land. The empire tottered. Later in Ibbisin's reign vassals took advantage of mounting difficulty to proclaim their independence of Ur. Ishbierra, governor of Mari, rebelled, established a kingdom at Isin, and controlled the north. Elam asserted its independence and at last furnished the coup de grâce. Ur was destroyed, an event remembered in a famous lament, and Ibbisin taken prisoner to Elam.

The imperial age of Ur was a golden age of **Sumerian literature.** Most of the surviving myth, epic, and gnomic literature of the Sumerians probably came into final form in this period, to be fixed in writing by copyists of the succeeding Old Babylonian period. **Gudea,** ensi of Lagash (c. 2000), a vassal of Ur, is one of the most brilliant figures of the period. His building inscriptions contain the most extensive and important texts we possess of the Sumerian renaissance.

During this period **Babylonian mathematics** reached its high level with a numbering system based upon the developed sexagesimal system with a place-value notation for both whole numbers and fractions. Also surviving are tables of squares and square roots, of cubes and cube roots, and of the sums of squares and cubes needed for numerical evaluation of cubic equations and exponential functions. Tables of Pythagorean numbers are also extant, showing that Pythagoras's equation was used many years before its formal solution.

The buildings were of mud-brick and although impressive have not survived like those of the Egyptian civilization. The **Hanging Gardens of Babylon** (one of the seven wonders of the Ancient World) was a stepped pyramid structure.

1960–1700.   THE   ISIN-LARSA   PERIOD. The Isin Dynasty (1953–1730) and Larsa Dynasty (1961–1699) struggled for hegemony following the fall of the 3rd Dynasty of Ur. Both were to give way to Babylon. **Ishbierra,** king of Isin (1953–1921), claimed the crown of the four regions of the world as early as 1953, shortly before the final fall of Ur, and held Nippur, Babylonia's central shrine, as early as 1963. He also imitated his Ur predecessors in using titles of divinity. He drove the Elamites from Ur late in his reign and secured the trade routes to Bahrein and the south. Naplanum, the Amorite usurper in Larsa (1961–1941), probably became a vassal of Ishbierra early in the latter's consolidation of the south. Ishbierra was succeeded by Shuilishu (1920–1911), Iddindagan (1910–1890), and Ishmedagan (1889–1871). About this time Larsa began to gain strength under its king **Samium** (1912–1878). However, Ishmedagan is remembered in the great *Ishmedagan Hymn* as a reformer and advocate of justice, and his son, Lipiteshtar (1870–1860), left behind a code of laws. In the time of Ishmedagan, Assyria first gave warning of imperial ambitions. Ilushuma raided Babylonia and is probably responsible for the destruction of Nippur celebrated in a lament of this period.

In the late Isin-Larsa period, Babylonia increasingly fell apart into small independent city states. The succeeding **kings of Isin** were Urninurta (1859–1832), Bursin (1831–1810), Lipitenlil (1809–1805), Erraimitti (1804–1797), Enlilbani (1796–1773), Zambija (1772–1770), Iterpisha (1769–1767), Urdukuga (1766–1764), Sinmagir (1763–1753), and Damiqilishu (1753–1730). **Rulers of the Larsa Dynasty** were Gungunum (1868–1842), Abishare (1841–1837), Sumuel (1830–1802), Nuradad (1801–1786), Sinidinnam (1785–1779), Sineribani (1778–1777), Siniqisham (1776–1772), Silliadad (1771), Waradsin (1770–1759), and Rimsin (1758–1699).

1830-1531. Ist DYNASTY OF BABYLON.
In the last years of the Isin-Larsa period Babylon gained independence and began a remarkable climb to power. The 1st Dynasty was founded by the Amorite **Sumuabum** (1830-1817), a contemporary of Sumuel of Larsa. His successors were Sumulael (1816-1781), Sabium (1780-1767), Apilsin (1766-1749), Sinnuballit (1748-1729) and **Hammurapi the Great** (1728-1686). **Rimsin,** scion of the ruling family of Yamutbal, ruled as the last king of Larsa. He brought Larsa to its fullest bloom and, conquering Damiqilishu of Isin, unified south and central Babylonia. He prepared the way of Hammurapi, who, upon his enthronement over the city state of Babylon in 1728, began a series of campaigns of conquest. Isin, Elam, and finally Larsa itself fell to Hammurapi in 1699. One great power, the **Kingdom of Mari,** lay between Hammurapi and the achievement of a new Mesopotamian empire. In 1697 Hammurapi defeated Zimrilim of Mari, and in 1695 razed the city. The **Hammurapi Age** is one of the best known periods of Oriental antiquity, thanks to many thousands of texts from this time, including some 20,000 tablets from Mari alone. Babylonian letters flourished. Akkadian became the common language of the land, Sumerian dying out. **Hammurapi's code** of laws is justly the most famous work of the period. Marduk, god of Babylon, replaced Enlil as king in the Babylonian pantheon. But while Babylonian religion and culture flourished in a new creative period, they remained fundamentally shaped by the mythology and institutions developed by the Sumerians. Shamshuiluna (1685-1648), Hammurapi's son, was unable to hold the empire in unity. The "sea lands" on the Persian Gulf broke free of his rule, and Ilumailu established the **1st Sea-Land Dynasty** which included twelve kings. Under Abieshu (1647-1620) the decline continued, but Ammiditana (1619-1583), Ammisaduqa (1582-1562), and Shamshuditana (1561-1531) strengthened the empire, forced the rulers of the Sea-Lands back, and controlled the people of Kashshu (the Kassites or Cossaeans), who were streaming into Babylon from the northeast. Disaster struck from an unexpected quarter. **Mursilis,** fourth king of the rising Hittite kingdom in Asia Minor, marched eastward and about 1531 or slightly earlier destroyed Babylon to the ground. He returned home with booty, apparently making little attempt to control the land. The barbarians from the mountains, the Kassites, seized power.

c. 1600-1150. THE KASSITE DYNASTY.
The 450 years of Kassite rule in Babylonia

was a period of little creative energy or military power. Agum II consolidated Kassite rule upon the fall of the 1st Dynasty of Babylon, but it was not until the time of Ulamburiash (c. 1450) that the Sea-Lands were conquered and Babylonia unified again. **Kurigalzu I,** contemporary of Amenophis III of Egypt (1417-1379), perhaps was the strongest of the Kassites. He conquered Susa, and entered into **alliance with Egypt.** Burnaburiash II (died c. 1350) protected his realm also by diplomatic marriages with the Egyptian royal house and with the family of Assuruballit I (1366-1331), the monarch of expanding Assyria. Babylonia fell to Tukulti-Ninurta I (1246-1209) and recovered independence only to be reduced again by the Elamites about 1150.

c. 1150-1025. 2ND DYNASTY OF ISIN. A native dynasty arose in the place of the Kassites but had only intermittent life. **Nabukadurriuşur I** (Nebuchadrezzar) (c. 1125-1104) was the only important king of the dynasty. He conquered Elam and held Assyria at bay for a time. Babylon then fell to Tiglathpileser I. Aramaean and Chaldean tribes from the Syrian Desert began to sweep into Upper and Lower Mesopotamia in this period breaking Assyrian power and bringing the collapse of Babylonia. Babylon played no significant rôle again in world politics until the appearance of Chaldean kings in the 7th century B.C.

e. UPPER MESOPOTAMIA, 1700-609 B.C.

1700-1500. THE HURRIAN INVASIONS.
The Hurrians, biblical **Horites,** began to drift south from the Caucasus as early as the Akkadian period. However, only small numbers entered northern Mesopotamia and the East Tigris country in the late 3rd millennium. Major invasions of these people began about 1700, and by 1500 they had penetrated into the whole of Mesopotamia, into Syria and eastern Anatolia, and into Palestine. Their language is imperfectly known, but is related to later Urartian. The earliest Hurrian texts are from Mari (18th century). Other texts come from the Hittite archives of Boghazköy (14th-13th centuries), from Ugarit (14th century), and from Egypt (an Amarna letter of the 14th century). Strange to say, the ruling class of the Hurrians bore not Hurrian but Indo-Aryan names. Evidently the Aryans drove both the Hurrians and Kassites before them in the 17th century, overrunning the former and establishing themselves as an aristocracy. Probably they won their position as chariot warriors, since it seems likely that the

horse-drawn chariot, introduced in the 18th century, and widely used in the 17th century, originated among Aryan peoples. The symbiosis of Hurrian and Indo-Aryan elements at all events is characteristic of Hurrian society wherever we come upon it. The Hurrians rather quickly assimilated Sumero-Akkadian religion and culture. They adopted the cuneiform script both for their own tongue and also for Babylonian, the chief language of diplomatic texts. They seem also to have played a special rôle in transmitting Sumero-Akkadian literature and religion to the Hittites, albeit in highly syncretistic, Hurrian guise.

1500–1380. THE KINGDOM OF MITANNI. Small Hurrian principalities were united toward 1500 into the Kingdom of Mitanni with its capital at Washukkani on the Khabur. At its widest extent it controlled Alalakh and Qatna in Syria on the west, and Nuzu and Arapkha, as well as Assyria, on the east. The earliest of the great kings of Mitanni was Sudarna I (c. 1500). His grandson **Saushsatar** (c. 1475) probably is to be credited with the consolidation of the kingdom. He established a feudal regime that gave a considerable amount of autonomy to vassal kings of Alalakh, Assyria, etc. In 1475 Tuthmosis III conquered northern Syria and pillaged Mitanni. However, **Egyptian control** did not extend east of the Euphrates, and Saushsatar remained strong. His son Artadama I gave his daughter in marriage to Tuthmosis IV (1425–1417), and apparently by this alliance, held Aleppo and part of northern Syria. Sudarna II (c. 1400) gave his daughter to Amenophis III (1417–1379), and, as we learn from the Amarna correspondence, Sudarna's successor, Tuishrata (c. 1390), also sent a daughter to Amenophis.

1380–1250.   THE DECADENCE OF THE HURRIAN STATE. Tuishrata mounted a disputed throne after the murder of his brother, Artasumara. Artadama II, another brother, also claimed kingship, and **Suppiluliumas** (c. 1380), the king of the Hittites, concluded a treaty with him. Tuishrata was forced thereby into a war with the Hittites. Suppiluliumas captured the western holdings of Mitanni and plundered the capital, Washukkani. Egypt, Mitanni's southern ally, made no move to come to Tuishrata's aid. At this point in his war with the Hittites, Tuishrata was killed by one of his sons, perhaps with the connivance of Suppiluliumas. In any case, Sudarna III, son of Tuishrata's rival Artadama, attempted to take power. Suppiluliumas abruptly changed sides, and supported Matiwaza, son of Tuishrata, and succeeded in securing his throne. After Suppiluliumas's death, Assu-

ruballit I of Assyria, an ally of Sudarna III, struck at Mitanni and pillaged it.

1356–1078.   THE MIDDLE ASSYRIAN EMPIRE.

1356–1199.   The Rise of Assyria. The fall of Mitanni freed Assyria to develop. Under **Assuruballit I** (1366–1331) Assyria swiftly became a great military power. Its culture was essentially Babylonian, though reflecting some elements of Hurrian and Hittite influence. Enlilnirari I (1330–1321) defeated Kurigalzu II of Babylon. His son, Arikdenilu (1320–1309), fought campaigns in the north and west and built up his royal city, Assur. He is the first of the Assyrian kings to leave military annals. He was succeeded by Adadnirari I (1308–1276) who, after defeating the Kassites, conquered the old cities of Mitanni (now called Hanigalbat in our sources), and finally reached the Euphrates about the time of the clash of the Hittites and the Egyptians at Qadesh in 1298. He now took the title "king of everything." In Assyria he built fortifications in Assur, and built new temples and restored old ones to glorify his capital.

Shalmaneser I (1275–1246) continued the energetic campaigns of conquest. He fought in the far north against Urartu (which appears now as a power for the first time), again crushed the Hurrians and their Hittite auxiliaries, and annexed their lands. He continued west as far as Carchemish. Shalmaneser I made no attempt to expand farther; no doubt the policy was imposed by the new treaty of Khattusilis III and Ramesses II formed in 1283 which divided Syria between the Egyptian and Hittite empires. His son, Tukultininurta I (1245–1209), attacked Kassite Babylon and conquered it, becoming the first Assyrian to be called "king of Babylonia" (*Karduniash*) in his official titulary. Tukultininurta fell victim to his son in 1209 and Assyria entered upon a time of weakness.

1209–1117.   Decline of Assyrian Might. The first half of the 12th century was a time of troubles throughout the Ancient World. Confusion reigned in Assur. The Hittite empire fell to Sea Peoples. In Babylon, the 2nd Dynasty of Isin succeeded the moribund Kassite regime. Nebuchadrezzar I brought about a brief Babylonian renaissance. Assurreshishi I (1134–1117) halted Babylonia's growing power, and Assyria stirred again, securing its borders.

1116–1078.   THE EMPIRE OF TIGLATHPILESER I. Tiglathpileser I brought the Middle Assyrian empire to its highest level of ascendancy. He was a fierce and clever warrior, and insatiable huntsman. Year after year he led his troops out, conquering the Mushqi,

Thraco-Phrygian invaders from Anatolia, the Nairi mountain country north and northeast of Assyria, the Aramaeans who were invading Syria and the lands of the Middle Euphrates, and finally Babylon. The Phoenician city states paid him tribute, and none dared oppose him from sea to sea. His policy of shifting populations, and the ruthlessness of his warfare made him, and Assyria after him, uniquely hated and feared.

1078–935. The Aramaean and Chaldean Invasions. A dark age when Upper Mesopotamia including Assyria was overrun by Aramaeans, Babylonia by Aramaeans and Chaldeans.

935–612. THE NEW ASSYRIAN EMPIRE.

935–860. THE RESURGENCE OF ASSYRIA. Assyrian annals commence again after a century and a half of silence, in the reign of Assurdan II (935–913). Assurdan, his son Adadnirari (912–892), Tukultininurta II (891–885), and Assurnasirapli II (884–860) reestablished the Assyrian empire, fighting repeated campaigns in the west, north, and northwest. Adadnirari II, after defeating the Babylonians, established boundaries and fixed a friendship treaty with the ancient land. A highly centralized bureaucracy emerged in Assyria, and the practices of exchange of population and mass execution became regular policy. Assurnasirapli II was the chief architect of this early phase of the empire. Like Tiglathpileser I he marched to the sea. He built Calah (Kalakh) anew as his capital. Most important, he handed on to his successor a compact, highly organized state.

859–825. THE REIGN OF SHALMANESER III. Shalmaneser was more ambitious, if possible, than his father Assurnasirapli. He proposed to annex conquered peoples and integrate them into the empire, and to establish regular, annual tribute from other vassals who by reason of their strength or distance could not yet be subjugated wholly. The Assyrian armies marched in annual campaigns. Their chief efforts were directed against the far west. In 858 Shalmaneser met a coalition of Aramaean kings (Sam'al, Hattina, Carchemish, and Bît Adini) at Lutibu near Sam'al (modern Zinjirli). Shalmaneser claimed victory, perhaps correctly, though he did not break the power of the allies. In the campaigns of 857–855 he conquered Bît Adini, captured its prince, and annexed the country to Assyria. The west again united against Shalmaneser in 854. The chiefs of the alliance were Irkhuleni of Hamath, Ben Hadad I (Hadadezer) of Damascus, and Ahab of Israel. The forces of Assyria and the west clashed at Qarqar on the Orontes. Despite Shalmaneser's usual claim

of victory, it is clear that he was stopped, if not seriously defeated, by the allies. In 850, 849, 846, and 842, Shalmaneser continued pounding against the western forces, finally breaking their power in 842. He then made conquests in Cilicia, and fought against Sardur I, king of Urartu. His reign ended in revolution.

824–746. Assyria and Urartu. Shalmaneser's son, Shamshiadad V (824–812), put down the revolt in Assyria with Babylonian aid, but lost parts of the empire. He was in turn succeeded by Adadnirari III (811–784), who came to the throne as a minor. For four years the queen-mother ruled. Her name was Sammuramat, the **Semiramis** of Greek legend. Adadnirari briefly reimposed tribute on the western states, but increasingly Assyria retreated before the Urarteans. Shalmaneser IV (783–774), Assurdan III (773–756), and Assurnirari V (755–746) were all weak. Urartu expanded under Argishti I (780–756) and Sarduri II (755–735). Under the latter, Commagene, Melitene, and even Carchemish came under Urartian domination.

745–728. THE REIGN OF TIGLATHPILESER III. Tiglathpileser III, a usurper, began a new era, the last and greatest period of the New Assyrian empire. He consolidated his regime at home and pacified Babylonia, leaving Nabunasir (Nabonassar, 747–735) on the throne of Babylon. Then in the years 743–738 Tiglathpileser made his first great western campaign. The Urartian allies were defeated at Arpad, and after a long siege Arpad taken. A coalition of Hamath and coastal cities of north Syria under the leadership of Azariah (Uzziah) of Judah was crushed, and in 738 Tiglathpileser received tribute from the important states of Syria-Palestine including Israel and Damascus. In 735 he stormed Urartu, and in 734–732 launched a second western series of campaigns against Rezin of Damascus, Pekah of Israel, and their allies. Gilead, Galilee, and Damascus were turned into provinces of Assyria. In 731 revolution broke out in Babylon and Tiglathpileser hastened back to stamp it out, naming himself king of Babylon in 729.

726–706. SHALMANESER V AND SARGON II. Shalmaneser V was faced with new rebellion in the west at the beginning of his reign. In 725 he invested Samaria, capital of Israel, and Tyre. Samaria fell in 722 to Shalmaneser (though Sargon later claimed credit for the victory). Sargon II (722–706) mounted his father's throne later in the same year. He turned first to Babylon, meeting Merodach-baladan, pretender to the Babylonian crown, and his Elamite allies in an indecisive battle at Der. He then moved west reconquering Hamath, Samaria, Ekron, and Gaza. Tyre, under siege five years, fell during this campaign, and Judah paid tribute (720). In 717-716, Sargon overthrew and annexed Carchemish, and defeated the Egyptian Pharoah Osorkon at Raphia. In 712 his armies crushed Ashdod, breaking up a conspiracy of Egypt and the southern states of Palestine. In 709 Sargon assumed the kingship of Babylon. Merodach-baladan went into exile, to return to cause mischief in the time of Sennacherib.

705-682. THE REIGN OF SENNACHERIB. In his first years Sennacherib devoted himself to peaceful pursuits, transforming Nineveh, his chosen capital, into a city of unparalleled splendor. Meanwhile Merodach-baladan developed a worldwide conspiracy, and in 703 seized power in Babylon. Sennacherib put down the revolt and subdued the Chaldeans, but for 13 years trouble seethed in Babylonia, leading finally to the **sacking of Babylon** in 689. In the western part of the empire, **Hezekiah of Judah** was a leader in a conspiracy which included Phoenicia, Egypt, and Philistia. In 701 Sennacherib marched west, pacified Phoenicia and Philistia without difficulty, and defeated Egyptian troops of Shabaka at Elteqeh. He then turned on Hezekiah. All of Judah was reduced except Jerusalem. At this point Hezekiah sued for peace. The Assyrians broke off the siege on this occasion. There is some evidence, much disputed, that later in Sennacherib's reign, Jerusalem was again besieged by the Assyrians and escaped intact. Despite these wars, Sennacherib's reign was a relatively peaceful period. No new provinces were added to the realm, and the arts and literature flourished. During this period the domestic water supply was improved and cotton introduced as a supplementary crop.

681-670. The Reign of Esarhaddon. Sennacherib was murdered by one of his sons. **Esarhaddon,** the designated heir, quelled the rebellion. Babylon was gloriously rebuilt and placed under the rule of Shamashshumukin, a son of Esarhaddon. Scythian and Cimmerian hordes appeared on Assyria's northern border and made some inroads into the empire. Esarhaddon was preoccupied, however, with grandiose plans to conquer Egypt. Sidon, an ally of Egypt, was taken in 677. Esarhaddon's first raids into Egypt in 675-674 were indecisive. In 671, Esarhaddon struck with full force, routed Tirhaqah, and took Memphis. Esarhaddon died in the course of another march on Egypt.

669-c. 627. THE REIGN OF ASSURBANA- **PAL.** The last great king of Assyria was an extraordinary figure, a great general, a sportsman, and a patron of arts and letters. His palace reliefs are the finest examples of Assyrian art. He was a master of cuneiform and gathered a great library of tablets which remains one of our chief sources for knowledge of Babylonian literature. In 667 the Assyrians again ousted Tirhaqah from Memphis, and in 663 destroyed the Ethiopian power in Egypt, capturing Thebes. In the years immediately preceding 652, Shamashshumukin, Assurbanapal's brother, who ruled as king of Babylon, became involved in a gigantic conspiracy to overthrow the kingdom. His allies included the Chaldeans and Aramaeans, Egypt and Elam. Civil war raged from 652 to 648 when Shamashshumukin finally surrendered in Babylon. Susa was sacked in 639. The strife, however, drained away the energies of Assyria.

626-609. The Last Days of Assyria. The Assyrian empire collapsed with extraordinary speed. Assuretililani (626-623?) and the usurper Sinshumlishir (623?) followed Assurbanapal. There was general revolt. Nabopolassar declared himself king of Babylon in 626. Sinsharishkun (622?-612), another son of Assurbanapal, took power. Cyaxares of Media and Nabopolassar joined forces to bring down Assyria. Nineveh fell to the allies in 612, an event celebrated by the *Book of Nahum.* Assuruballit II (611-609) attempted to regroup Assyrian forces in Harran. Harran fell in 610 to the Babylonians. An attempt of Assyrian remnants and Egyptian forces to retake Harran in 609 failed.

f. THE NEO-BABYLONIAN EMPIRE, 626-333 B.C.

626-605. THE RISE OF THE CHALDEAN DYNASTY OF BABYLON. Babylonia had become dominantly Chaldean during Neo-Assyrian times. **Nabopolassar** (626-605) finally organized Chaldean power, taking the diadem of Babylon in 626. He spent his energies as we have seen finishing off Assyria. In 605 **Nebuchadrezzar** the crown prince commanded the armies of Babylon in the battle of Carchemish against the Egyptian army of Necho. The battle ended in an overwhelming defeat for Necho, and Nebuchadrezzar fell heir to the western empire of Assyria. Shortly after Nabopolassar died. Nebuchadrezzar was crowned king on September 7, 605.

605-561. THE REIGN OF NEBUCHADREZZAR (II) THE GREAT. In the years following his accession, Nebuchadrezzar campaigned in Syria-Palestine pacifying his newly won territories. In 601 he marched against

Egypt. The clash near the Egyptian border was bloody but indecisive, each side retiring. In 598, Nebuchadrezzar again came west. Judah was crushed and **Jerusalem taken** in 597. After quelling a revolt at home, Nebuchadrezzar came west to put down a rebellion centering in Tyre and Judah. Nebuchadrezzar invested Jerusalem in 588. Hophra sallied out briefly from Egypt but retired in disarray when faced by Nebuchadrezzar's full strength. Jerusalem finally fell in July, 586. The city and its temple were laid waste, and many **Jews taken captive** to Babylon. Tyre, besieged for 13 years, according to Menander, was never taken. Nebuchadrezzar lavished wealth upon Babylon. The city, newly built by Esarhaddon, now became a wonder of the Ancient World.

561–539. THE END OF THE CHALDEAN EMPIRE. Nebuchadrezzar's death in reality was the end of Babylon as a world power.

Evil-merodach (Awil-Marduk) ruled two years (561–560) before he was killed by Neriglissar (Nergalsharusur, 559–556). His son Labashi-Marduk (556) was a weakling, shortly replaced by a usurper, Nabonidus (555–539). Nabonidus rallied the country briefly. He was a devotee of the gods, especially Sin of Harran, and an archaeologist and scholar. In his last years he spent much of his time at the Oasis of Teima, leaving his son Belshazzar regent. Meanwhile **Cyrus the Great** had united the Medes and Persians, and defeated the Lydians (547). In 539 he marched on Babylonia. The country fell almost without struggle. Babylon itself opened its gates to Gobryas, Cyrus's general, and on October 29, 539 Cyrus entered the city.

539–332. Mesopotamia under Persian rule.

332–323. Mesopotamia under Alexander the Great.

2. EGYPT, TO 332 B.C.

a. THE LAND AND THE PEOPLE

The name **Egypt,** from Homeric Greek *Aiguptos,* applied in antiquity to the lands of the Nile Valley, from the Delta on the Mediterranean southward to the First Cataract of the Nile above Suene (modern Aswan). The Egyptians applied the epithet *Keme* (*kmt*), the Black Land, to their country in reference to the strip of black alluvial soil laid down by the Nile along its banks. The valley extends for about 550 miles in a straight line, 750 miles as the river flows, never exceeding 13 miles in width, comprising only about 12,500 square miles of cultivable land. Egypt is a land of scant rainfall in the Delta, virtually no rainfall upstream. Cultivation is made possible by the annual inundation of the Nile, which rises late in June, crests in late September, and slowly subsides. The inundation both renews the extraordinary fertility of the soil and supplies water for irrigation. From earliest times life in Egypt has been dependent on the flood of the Nile and its elaborate control in irrigation works. The river also made possible easy communication, by either oared or square-sailed boats. Egypt is thus appropriately described as the "gift of the Nile" (Herodotus).

In predynastic times (before 2850 B.C.), **Lower Egypt** (the Delta) and **Upper Egypt** seem to have been organized as distinct kingdoms; in any case an ideology of the duality of "the Two Lands" persisted after the permanent unification of Egypt under Na'rmer until the end of the ancient state. Egypt was further divided into **nomes.** In the fully developed system

there were 42 such districts, 20 in Lower Egypt, 22 in Upper Egypt. The principal ancient cities of Lower Egypt included Avaris (later Tanis, biblical Zoan), Sais, Bubastis, Heliopolis (biblical On), and Memphis (biblical Mof or Nof). Those of Upper Egypt, south of the Fayyum, the great depression containing the Lake of Moeris, were Heracleopolis, Hermopolis (Egyptian Khmun), Akhetaten (modern Egyptian 'Amarna), Thinis, Abydos, Thebes (biblical No), and near the First Cataract, Yeb (Greek Elephantine). Egypt's culture was based more on village, agrarian life, than on the city. Capital cities were fixed simply by the residency of the king. While Thebes in Upper Egypt, Memphis-Hikuptah in Middle Egypt, and Tanis in the Delta were the most important of the capital cities, actually at one time or another, the capital rested in most of the above-named cities.

The **population** of ancient Egypt has been set by scholarly reckoning at about 5,000,000. This figure is little more than a guess, but is to be preferred to the high numbers of Diodorus (7,000,000) and Josephus (7,500,000). The predynastic people of Egypt were slight if well-muscled, long-headed, with little facial hair, a stock sharing many characteristics with the early Semitic folk. While this old strain may be traced throughout dynastic times in Egypt, it became mixed as early as the beginning of the historical period (29th century B.C.) with other stocks, notably with an Armenoid or broad-headed racial strain presumably from the north.

The **language** of ancient Egypt belongs to the rather ill-defined group of Hamitic tongues.

It is closely related to Semitic—particularly one stratum of Egyptian—to Berber, and more remotely to the Cushitic family of languages. Egyptian survived into the Middle Ages in late dialects known as Coptic.

b. THE RISE OF EGYPTIAN CIVILIZATION

Toward 3000 B.C. in the last, so-called late Gerzean phase of predynastic times, and in the beginning of dynastic times, Egyptian civilization, its art, architecture, and perhaps even its hieroglyphic system of writing, took vast strides ahead under the stimulus of the first great civilization of the Near East then developing in Mesopotamia. While the impact of this old Sumerian culture is quite palpable, it must also be said that the influence of Mesopotamia was ephemeral, serving primarily as an impetus to native Egyptian cultural forms and institutions. The early evolution of Egyptian civilization was swift. In the **Old Kingdom,** in most parts by the 3rd and 4th Dynasties (c. 2615–2440 B.C.), Egyptian cultural patterns reached maturity: the system of divine kingship, the canons of art and architecture, the organization of the funerary cultus, the classical forms of monumental (hieroglyphic) and cursive (hieratic) scripts, and the principal development of mathematics and of certain of the applied sciences. In medicine diagnostic techniques and systematic treatment were established. This classical culture of the Old Kingdom persisted with remarkably slight change through the next two millennia.

c. RELIGION

The origins of Egyptian religion remain relatively obscure. In earliest times we confront a bewildering host of gods in human form, in animal form, and in mixed human and animal form, not to mention deified abstractions and inanimate objects of nature. Attempts to trace the historic religion to a prehistoric totemism have wholly failed. No simple evolutionary picture can be drawn. We can say only that the gods easily alter form, in many instances between anthropomorphic and theriomorphic representation or symbolism. Each town or nome had its patron deity or deities, its cult, and "religious community." At the same time the Egyptian was tolerant, quick to identify gods with parallel functions (whether Egyptian or foreign), and saw all of nature, gods, men, and beasts as a continuum. The object of his religion was to find (or establish) the order of the powers manifest in nature, specifically the created order, and in piety and statecraft, in the present and in the world of the dead, to conform to or participate in this order of reality.

Already in the time of the Old Kingdom, one finds basic myths of creation, of divine kingship, of cosmic order. The "Memphite Theology" which can be no later than the beginning of the Old Kingdom, describes the process of creation in which the gods stem from Ptah, patron of Memphis. The pantheon was thus organized in effect as immanations or manifestations of one divine substance according to the order of creation, and can be described as tending toward a nature monotheism, or better, pantheism. The Egyptian state was an integral part of the divine order in the Memphite Theology (which was actually both a cosmology and political program). The king was identified with the god Horus, and Horus, the power of the sky, was fully incarnate in the king. The king's predecessor similarly "became" the dead god Osiris, lord of the Underworld. In Heliopolis the "sun god" Re' became the father of the gods, being identified with Atum, a creator god, and Harakhti, "Horus of The Horizon," as Re'-atum and Re'-harakhti respectively. The sun god in turn was head of the Ennead, which included in its system a series of generations of pairs: Shu and Tefnut, Geb (Earth) and Nut (Heaven), Osiris (god of death and fertility) and Isis (mother goddess, originally the deified throne of the king), Seth (the "storm god," Osiris' enemy) and Nephthys. By the 5th Dynasty the cult of Heliopolitan Re' was officially adopted by the king, now entitled "the son of Re'," the father ruling the heavens, his counterpart the earth. In the Middle Kingdom, Amun, god of Thebes, emerged as king of the gods. In origin the power in air, he was identified with Re', and in the New Kingdom his cult threatened to absorb all rivals. Egyptians tended, however, to keep both early and late myths and a variety of cosmologies, rituals, and symbols side by side in a rich mass, incompletely unified, perhaps even consciously contradictory. Religious truth for the Egyptian was manifold, arrived at by complementary myths and religious acts. The most rigorous attempt to systematize Egyptian religion was that of **Akhenaten** (and his advisers) in the 18th Dynasty who, as a devotee of the solar disk, suppressed alternate names, cults, and symbols of the sun god, as well as those of other deities. Even the Akhenaten revolution, however, did not discard the traditional centrality of sun worship, its use in the ideology of kingship and in the funerary cult. At all events his innovations in the direction of solar monotheism shortly died out, and Egyptian religion to the end remained a complex and archaic polytheism.

d. CHRONOLOGY

Manetho, an Egyptian priest (c. 280 B.C.), wrote a history of his country in Greek of which fragments have been preserved in Josephus, Sextus Julius Africanus, Eusebius, and Syncellus. He grouped the kings of Egypt into 30 dynasties beginning with Menes, founder of Dynasty I, ending with the conquest of Egypt by Artaxerxes III in 343 B.C. Despite all its defects, his dynastic arrangement is still used. Valuable ancient sources include the **Palermo Stone,** a chronicle inscribed in Dynasty V, the **Turin Canon,** a hieratic papyrus of Dynasty XIX, and the **Tables of Abydos** (Dynasty XIX), **Saqqarah** (Dynasty XIX), and **Karnak** (Dynasty XVIII).

The earliest fixed date in Egyptian chronology is based on an astronomical observation of the Middle Kingdom in c. 1872 B.C. in the seventh year of Sesostris III (Senwosre). It is a record of the date of the so-called heliacal rising of Sothis (Sirius) which was roughly coeval with the annual rising of the Nile, and hence determined the Egyptian New Year. The civil calendar of 365 days slowly rotated through the year coinciding with the solar calendar each 1460 years. While scholars at one time argued that the Sothic cycle had been recognized during the protodynastic period, or even in predynastic times, it appears likely now that the oldest Egyptian calendar was regulated by the rise of the Nile, and that the device of astronomical observation of Sirius was secondary, perhaps discovered as early as the end of the Old Kingdom.

The **chronology of Egypt,** thanks to annals, monuments, and astronomical observation, is fairly well fixed for the 12th Dynasty, c. 1991–1786 B.C. Even so an error of up to a decade is still possible in the 2nd and early 1st millennia. For the 3rd millennium the chronology becomes highly uncertain, reaching a margin of error of almost a century at the beginning of the historic period. Datings of the early dynasties are projected on the basis of king lists and monuments, certain crucial synchronisms with Mesopotamia, and so-called Carbon–14 datings. While Mesopotamian chronology is fixed by astronomical observations, multiple solutions, 64 years apart, must be further controlled by other less accurate data. This has given rise to several chronologies for the ancient Near East. Of them, the so-called *Middle Chronology* and *Low Chronology* remain the only probable alternates. We follow here the Low Chronology which sets the first regnal year of Hammurapi in 1728 B.C. Whether one selects the Low Chronology or the alternate chronology 64 years higher (1792 B.C.), the reckoning of early dates in Egypt and elsewhere in the ancient Near East must be raised or lowered together.

c. 3200–2850. THE GERZEAN CULTURE. Mesopotamian influences stimulated the development of Egyptian civilization in Late Gerzean times (after c. 3000 B.C.).

c. 2850–2615. THE PROTODYNASTIC PERIOD. Dynasties I–II. **Menes,** no doubt to be identified with Na'rmer, founded the 1st Dynasty uniting Egypt under his single rule. While Manetho termed these dynasties "Thinite," Na'rmer founded his new capital at Memphis.

e. THE OLD KINGDOM, c. 2615–1991 B.C.

c. 2615–2175. THE OLD KINGDOM. Dynasties III–VII (capital: Memphis). Djoser (Tosorthros), the founder of Dynasty III (c. 2615–2565 B.C.) built the step **pyramid of Saqqarah.** His architect Imhotep (Greek Imouthes) was later deified. With Dynasty IV (2565–2440 B.C.) the Old Kingdom reached its zenith. Snofru (Soris), the founder, fought successful wars with the Nubians and Libyans, and developed a brisk sea trade in cedar with Byblos. His greatest monuments are the two limestone pyramids of Dahshur, each more than 310 feet in height. He was succeeded by Cheops (Khufwey), Chephren (Kha'fre'), and Mycerinus (Menkaure'), who erected the colossal **pyramids of Gizeh,** which involved use of the plumb-lines and A-frame, as well as unlimited manpower. The great pyramid of Cheops originally rose to a height of 481.4 feet. Its base covered an area of about 13 acres. The pyramid of Chephren is only slightly smaller, and to Chephren is probably to be attributed the Sphinx. In the 4th Dynasty, kingship in Egypt reached the apogee of power and centralized authority. The 5th Dynasty (2440–2315 B.C.) witnessed the rise to power of the Heliopolitan priesthood. The kings regularly assumed the title "son of Re'," and built obelisk temples to the sun. The best-known kings are Userkaf (Usercheves), Sahure' (Sephres), Niuserre' (Rathures), and Unis. Under the last-named the first **Pyramid Texts** appear. The power of the king began to dissipate in the 5th Dynasty, a process which accelerated in the 6th Dynasty (c. 2315–2175 B.C.), especially under the long reign of Pepi II (Phiops, Piopi) (c. 2270–2180 B.C.). In turn the rulers of the nomes assumed independence and power as feudal lords. Dynasty VII, to which Manetho assigned 70 kings reigning 70 days, while evidently fictitious, is symbolic of the decay of the Old Kingdom.

c. 2175–1991. FIRST INTERMEDIATE PE-RIOD. Dynasties VIII–XI. For much of the period there was strife between competing dynasties, especially between nobles of Heracleopolis in Middle Egypt, and Thebes in Upper Egypt. The victory of Thebes permitted the **reunion of Egypt** under Menthotpe II, the fifth ruler of the 11th Dynasty (2133–1992 B.C.). In this era, the hope of a transfigured life after death was democratized to include non-royal persons. Literature flourished despite civil troubles. Notable are the *Coffin Texts,* the *Instruction for King Merykare',* and the *Admonitions of Ipuwer.*

of declining power of the king. Contemporary with it was the 14th Dynasty, hereditary lords of Xois in the Delta. Dynasty XV (c. 1678–1570) was made up of the **Hyksos** (from Egyptian *hiq-khase,* "chief of a foreign hill country"), invaders from Syria-Palestine. Where their Semitic names are known, they are chiefly Amorite. The Hyksos introduced the horse and chariot into Egypt. Their chief power was in the Delta, their capital at Avaris. Dynasty XVI (Hyksos) apparently was contemporary either with Dynasty XIII or XV. In Dynasty XVII (c. 1600–1570) the native rulers of Thebes regained power and, especially under **Kamose,** began wars against the Hyksos.

f. THE MIDDLE KINGDOM, c. 1991–1570 B.C.

c. 1991–1786. THE MIDDLE KINGDOM. Dynasty XII (capital: Lisht near Memphis). Ammenemes I (Amenemhe) (1991–1962) reorganized the country, reduced the power of the nobles, laying the basis again for a strong, stable, and prosperous Egypt. Building, art, literature, and international commerce flourished under him and his successors Sesostris I (Senwosre) (1971–1928), Ammenemes II (1929–1895), Sesostris II (1897–1879), Sesostris III (1878–1843), Ammenemes III (1842–1797), Ammenemes IV (1798–1790), and Sebeknofru (Scemiophris), daughter of Ammenemes III (1789–1786). The **practice of co-regency** was introduced by Ammenemes I and persisted through much of the dynasty. Already in Ammenemes's reign military action began to secure or extend Egypt's boundaries. Lower Nubia was taken, and a punitive campaign carried out against Asiatic nomads. By the reign of Sesostris III the southern border at the Second Cataract had been made secure. The same monarch also marched into Palestine as far north as Shechem. Apparently he made no attempt to set up an Asiatic empire but was content to keep open the routes of Egyptian trade. Under **Ammenemes III** national prosperity reached its peak. He developed the irrigation and land reclamation operations in the Fayyum, probably begun by Sesostris II. Turquoise mining in Sinai was expanded. At Hawara, Ammenemes III built one of his two pyramids and a great funerary temple known later as the *Labyrinth.* One of Egypt's great literary works, the *Story of Sinuhe* was composed in the Middle Kingdom.

c. 1785–1570. SECOND INTERMEDIATE PERIOD. Dynasties XIII–XVII. The 13th (Theban) Dynasty (c. 1785–1647) was a period

g. THE NEW KINGDOM, c. 1570–332 B.C.

c. 1570–1304. THE NEW KINGDOM. Dynasty XVIII (capital: Thebes). Amosis captured Avaris and drove the alien Hyksos out of Egypt. Under Amosis and his son **Amenophis I** ('Amenhotpe) (c. 1545–1525), the Nubian and Libyan borders were secured, and the power of the central government in Thebes re-established over the nobles of the land. Egypt was re-organized primarily as a military state, dedicated to imperial expansion, headed by a soldier-king. **Tuthmosis I** (Dhutmose) (1525–c. 1512) and **Tuthmosis II** (1512–1504) both fought successful campaigns in Nubia and Syria-Palestine. Tuthmosis II associated his queen **Hashepsowe** (Hatshepsut) with him in his reign, and when he died at a youthful age, Hashepsowe seized power, first as regent of **Tuthmosis II** (1504–1450), later as queen (1503–1482). Meanwhile Tuthmosis grew to manhood in the army, and in 1483 became sole ruler. In the same year he launched his first campaign of **conquest in Syria-Palestine,** and at the **battle of Megiddo** decisively defeated the allies under the king of Qadesh-on-the-Orontes. In 16 campaigns into Asia he succeeded in establishing an empire stretching to the Euphrates. Qadesh, the center of opposition, was destroyed in his sixth campaign (1474); in his eighth campaign (1471) he crossed the Euphrates and pillaged the Hurrian state of Mitanni. In his 42nd year (1462) he ended his Syrian campaigns. In the south he moved the Egyptian banner south to the Fourth Cataract, appointing a viceroy over Nubia. Egypt expanded to its greatest imperial scope and to its greatest power under Tuthmosis. It is in this period that a new title of the king came into use: *per-'o,* literally, "Great House," biblical *pharaoh.* Tuthmosis' son, **Amenophis**

II (c. 1450–1424), a great sportsman and warrior, vigorously maintained the Egyptian empire. After the short reign of Tuthmosis IV (c. 1424–1417), **Amenophis III** "the Magnificent" (c. 1417–1379) ruled over a period of unparalleled luxury and peace. He preserved his Syro-Palestinian possessions by diplomacy, among other things by marrying daughters of Sudarna and Tuishrata, kings of Mitanni. He was a fabulous builder whose projects included the great temple of Amun in Luxor, and two statues of himself nearly 70 feet high, the so-called **Colossi of Memnon.** The first signs of trouble in the empire and decadence at home appear in the late reign of Amenophis III, and mount in the reign of Amenophis IV (1379–1362), **Akhenaten.** The disintegration of the empire is graphically reflected in the international correspondence written in Akkadian found at Akhenaten's capital at El-ʿAmarna. Revolution and revolt spread through Palestine and Phoenicia. The Hittites under Suppiluliumas absorbed parts of the empire in Syria. Egypt under Akhenaten took no action. The king's limited energies were given to **religious innovation** at home. His court officially espoused the worship of Aten, the solar disk, and advocated a doctrine of "truth" (*maʿe*). Under his patronage new naturalistic styles in art and literature matured. The religious revolution was short-lived owing to the disintegration of the dynasty, and the implacable opposition of the priesthood of Amun, supreme god of Egypt under Akhenaten's imperial forbears. A male heir failing, Amenophis IV was succeeded by two sons-in-law, **Smenkhkareʿ** (c. 1361), and **Tutʿankhamun** (c. 1361–1351). The latter is known chiefly for his richly furnished tomb discovered by Howard Carter in 1922. Ay, an official of the court, seized power, probably before Tutʿankhamun's death, and reigned briefly (1351–1347). He was succeeded by Haremhab (Harmaïs) (c. 1347–1319), general of the armies, who undertook to restore the priesthoods and temples of Amun and the other traditional gods, and re-establish strong government.

c. 1319–1200. **Dynasty XIX** (capitals: Memphis and especially Tanis, rebuilt by Ramesses II). **Ramesses I** (Raʿmesse) (c. 1319), a general and later vizier, founded a vigorous new dynasty stemming from Tanis, city of the god Seth. His son **Sethos I** (Seti) (c. 1319–1304) set out to reconquer the lands of the Asiatic empire lost by Akhenaten. He was successful in Palestine and southern Syria extending his list of victories north to Qadesh-on-the-Orontes. Sethos built a great temple at Abydos, and continued work on the famous Hypostyle Hall in Karnak, completed by his son **Ramesses II,** the Great (1304–1237). Ramesses II had more difficulties in maintaining the empire. In his fifth year, 1298, he marched against the Hittites under Muwatallis. A great battle was fought at Qadesh. Ramesses boasted of his prowess in escaping an ambush and gaining victory. The Hittites, no doubt with more justification, claimed victory. After years of indecisive conflict, Ramesses and Khattusilis III (who had succeeded his brother Muwatallis) made a treaty of peace in 1283. Probably the boundary between the two powers was fixed at the Eleutherus Valley, the traditional northern boundary of "Canaan." Ramesses built prodigiously from Abu Simbel in Nubia to the Delta. In the northeastern Delta he rebuilt Tanis, renamed Pi-Raʿamesse, "House of Ramesses," as his capital, and Pi-Tum (Tell Retabeh). The latter two cities are identical with biblical Raamses and Pithom, the cities where the Israelites were corvée workers (Exodus, 1:11). The **flight of Israelites** from Egypt under Moses must be placed most probably in the reign of Ramesses II. By the fifth year of Merneptah (Ammenephthes) (1237–1225), the son of Ramesses, the Israelites were in Palestine where they suffered defeat at the hand of Merneptah. In the same year, Merneptah defeated a coalition of Libyans and Aegean peoples: Achaeans' (Aqiyawasha), Tyrrhenians (Turusha), Lycians (Luku), Sardinians (Shardina), and Shakrusha. The 19th Dynasty ended in a series of short, confused reigns about 1200, followed by an interregnum.

c. 1190–1065. **Dynasty XX** (capital: Tanis). **Ramesses III** (c. 1188–1156) rallied Egypt to face the deadly menace of another **confederation of Sea Peoples:** Pelast (Philistines), Tjikar (Sicilians?), Danuna (Greek Danaoi), Shardina (Sardinians), Washasha, and Shakrusha. Scenes of his victorious fighting are preserved on the walls of Ramesses's great temple at Medinet Habu. Egypt was saved and the empire held briefly. Some of the Sea Peoples, notably the Philistines and Tjikar, settled the Palestinian coast. Egypt sank into feebleness again under successive Ramessides, Ramesses IV–XI (1156–1065). Her commercial and political empire ceased to function. The priesthood of Amun-reʿ, controlling much of Egypt's land, grew increasingly powerful and arrogant. Hrihor, high priest in Karnak, became effective ruler in Thebes in the time of Ramesses XI. Imperial Egypt's force and spirit were spent. Reflecting these times is the *Tale of Wenamun.*

c. 1065–332. **LATE DYNASTIC PERIOD.** Dynasties XXI–XXXI.

c. 1065–935. **Dynasty XXI** (capitals: in Lower Egypt, Tanis, in Upper Egypt, Thebes). **Smendes** (Nesbanebded), a merchant prince, claimed the kingship on the death of Ramesses XI. He and his successors ruled in Tanis, and the theocratic dynasty of Hrihor governed in Thebes.

c. 935–725. Dynasty XXII (capital: Bubastis). Shoshenq I (Sesonchis) (935–914), founder of the dynasty, succeeded in appointing one of his sons high priest of Amun-re', reunifying the land. He is better known as biblical **Shishak.** He stormed Palestine, robbing the Temple in Jerusalem, laying waste many cities of the land (c. 918). His successors were Osorkon I (Osorthon) (c. 914–874), Takelot I (Takelothis) (c. 874–860), and Osorkon II (c. 860–832?), who sent soldiers to fight with the Syro-Palestinian allies against Shalmaneser III at Qarqar in 854. The remaining dynasts were Takelot II (c. 837–823), Shoshenq III (822–770?), Pami (c. 770–765) and Shoshenq IV (c. 765–725?). We know little of Dynasty XXIII (c. 759–715?) and Dynasty XXIV (c. 725–709).

c. 715–656. Dynasty XXV (Ethiopian). **Pi'-ankhi** (c. 751–710) about 715 invaded Egypt from Napata, his capital at the Fourth Cataract. He easily defeated Tefnakhte, Technactis, a princelet of the 24th Dynasty, and subdued Egypt. His brother and successor was Shabaka (Sabacon) (c. 710–698) who chose to become pharaoh and rule from Thebes. He was succeeded by **Shebteko** (Sebichos) (c. 696–685) and **Taharqo** (Tarcos) (co-regent 689–685; sole ruler 685–663). The power of imperial Assyria now made itself felt in Egypt. **Esarhaddon** (681–670), king of Assyria, attacked Taharqo in 671, conquering Memphis. Taharqo returned, only to be driven out again by **Assurbanapal** (669–627) in 667. Finally in 663, Assurbanapal sacked Thebes and defeated Tanuatamun (663–656).

663–525. Dynasty XXVI (capital: Sais). **Neko I** (Nechao, Necho), a governor of Sais, was named king of Egypt first by Esarhaddon and later by Assurbanapal. He was father of **Psammetichus I** (Psamtek, 663–609), real founder of the independent **Saite Dynasty.** Allying himself with Gyges of Lydia, he rebelled successfully against failing Assyria. He began the so-called **Saite revival** in art, painting and architecture, literature, and religion, a nostalgic attempt to re-create the forms and styles of the Old Kingdom. He was followed on the throne by **Neko II** (609–594). In 609 **Neko** marched north, ostensibly to aid Assyria, then being finished off by the founder of the Neo-Babylonian Empire, Nabopolassar. In fact he sought to restore Egypt's ancient empire. On his way northward he was opposed at Megiddo by **Josiah of Judah.** Judah was defeated and Josiah killed. However, Neko was delayed

long enough to prevent his giving aid to the Assyrians. In several campaigns he consolidated his power far north into Syria. However, at Carchemish in 605 he was crushingly defeated by **Nebuchadrezzar,** who succeeded Nabopolassar in the same year. Neko was driven from Syria-Palestine, but lived to defeat Nebuchadrezzar in 601 on Egypt's border. Herodotus records Neko's unsuccessful attempt to link the Nile with the Red Sea by a canal, and tells of a successful exploit, an expedition of Phoenician ships sent to circumnavigate Africa. Neko was succeeded by **Psammetichus II** (594–588), who was in turn followed by **Apries** (Wahibves') (588–568), the biblical Pharaoh Hophra (Jeremiah, 44:30). Apries apparently encouraged Syria-Palestine to revolt against Babylon by promising aid. He proved to be a poor ally. He sallied out briefly against Nebuchadrezzar during the latter's siege of Jerusalem, but when faced by Nebuchadrezzar's armies retired into Egypt in disarray. Similarly he was defeated by the Greeks of Cyrene when he went to the aid of Libyan allies at the end of his reign. Egypt had become a "broken reed." **Amasis** ('Ahmose-si-neit) (568–526) overthrew Apries. He was a peaceful man and a lover of Greek culture. His son **Psammetichus III** (526–525) mounted the throne only to face the **invasion of Cambyses.** After a hard-fought battle at Pelusium, the Egyptians surrendered.

525–404. Egypt under Persian rule (Dynasty XXVII).

404–399. Dynasty XXVIII consisting of a single king, Amyrtaeus of Sais.

399–380. Dynasty XXIX (capital: Mendes). **Achoris** (Hakor) (393–380), strongest of the kings of this dynasty, formed an alliance with Evagoras of Salamis against Artaxerxes II and fought off Persian attack with surprising vigor.

380–343. Dynasty XXX (capital: Sebennytus). The **last native dynasty** of Egypt numbers three kings, Nekhtnebef (Nectanebes) (380–363), Takhos (Djeho) (362–361), and Nekhtharehbe (Nectanebos) (360–343). The first and last enjoyed prosperous reigns and built widely in Egypt. In 373 Artaxerxes II sent a great Persian host against Egypt with no success, and in 350 **Artaxerxes III** sent an expedition against Egypt which failed scandalously, leading to a wave of revolts in the western empire. Artaxerxes himself led his armies against Egypt in 343, and in a brilliant campaign finally reduced Egypt.

343–332. Egypt again under Persian rule.

332. Egypt conquered by Alexander the Great.

(Cont. p. 96.)

3. SYRIA-PALESTINE, TO 332 B.C.

a. THE LAND AND THE PEOPLE

Syria, or Syria-Palestine, lay along the eastern Mediterranean coast, south of Mount Amanus, north of the River of Egypt (Wadi 'Arish). In the north its eastern frontier was the Euphrates, in the south the Syrian desert. This region, especially the coastal lands and hill country, was settled by West Semitic peoples speaking an Old Canaanite tongue. The time of their settlement can be no later than the Egyptian Old Kingdom, when Canaanite names are first attested, and probably goes back into the late 4th millennium. Racially these early settlers were Mediterranean with some mixture of other stocks. In the 16th and 15th centuries, the Hurrian invasions added a large element of Alpine traits.

After 1200 the Old Canaanite area was divided into three parts: Palestine, Aram, and Phoenicia. (1) In the south the **tribes of Israel** and associated peoples conquered the area later known as **Palestine.** It comprised Syrian territory south of Mount Hermon. In the course of the 12th century the Sea Peoples, notably the Philistines, took the coastal plain south of Mount Carmel, north of the River of Egypt, pressing Israel's border back into the low hill country (*Shephelah*). (2) The **Aramaean invasions** created a second division, **Aram.** This was the area of the Aramaean city states and later Aramaean empire. Its southern boundary lay below Damascus in the Hauran. Its northern limit was in the district of the Late Hittite city states between the Amanus and the Euphrates. The western border of Aram lay on the eastern side of the coastal range, Mount Bargylus (Jebel Nuseiriyeh) and Mount Lebanon. (3) The name of the third division, **Phoenicia,** is applied to the long narrow strip of land along the Mediterranean Sea from Arvad, north of the Eleutherus River, to Mount Carmel in the south. This was the remnant of the old Canaanite domain into which the Canaanites were eventually squeezed. By an arbitrary change of terminology, the Canaanites after 1200 are called Phoenicians. Actually "Phoenicia" is merely the Greek translation of "Canaan," "the land of purple (merchants)."

b. THE OLD CANAANITES, TO c. 900 B.C.

33rd to 29th centuries. Early Bronze Age I. City states developed in Syria-Palestine. The Canaanites served as mediators between the Protoliterate culture of Mesopotamia and the Gerzean culture of Egypt.

29th to 27th centuries. Early Bronze Age II. Syria-Palestine developed swiftly in urbanization and in size of population. There is indirect evidence for an Egyptian campaign into Palestine in this period. Egyptian inscriptions begin at Byblos with Nebka (Khasekhemwi).

27th to 22nd centuries. Early Bronze Age IIIA and IIIB. Egypt seems to have exercised commercial if not political control of Palestine in the Old Kingdom (2615–2175). We have direct evidence of military campaigns into Palestine in the 5th Dynasty (2440–2315), and in the 6th Dynasty, Weni, the general of Phiops I (c. 2300), left a report of his Syrian wars. **Sargon the Great** (2360–2305) conquered lands in northern Syria. At the end of this period the Canaanites developed their first indigenous writing system, a syllabary of pictographs based indirectly on Egyptian hieroglyphics.

21st to 19th centuries. Middle Bronze Age I. This era witnessed the great **Amorite movements** into Syria-Palestine, as well as into Babylonia, bringing the end of the Ur Empire (c. 1952). The *Execration Texts* (c. 1925–1825) from the Middle Kingdom in Egypt establish that Egypt claimed suzerainty over southern Syria-Palestine. The latter part of this period has been identified with the Patriarchal ("Abrahamic") age. Transjordan and much of the Syrian hinterland became nomadic in the 20th century.

1850–1500. Middle Bronze Age II. The first phase of this period (IIA, 1850–1750) was a time of settlement of the nomadic Amorites. Egyptian power in Syria-Palestine collapsed in the early 18th century. In many ways, Middle Bronze Age IIB–C (1750–1500) was the **golden age of Palestine.** The early Hyksos (for the most part Syro-Palestinian princes) built enormous fortifications of earthen-work (*terre pisée*), and began building an empire in the west. Hazor, Qatna, and Aleppo were the great centers of power contemporary with the Mari age in Mesopotamia. Yantin'ammu ruled in Byblos. The 15th Dynasty in Egypt (c. 1678–1590), the "Great Hyksos," exercised feudal authority in both Palestine and Egypt. Late in phase IIC of this period (1650–1500), the **Hurrians** streamed into Palestine.

1500–1400. Late Bronze Age I. Syria-Palestine fell under the power of the militant kings of the New Kingdom. Tuthmosis III (1504–1450) established full political control over the whole of Syria. The first extensive epigraphs in the

Proto-Canaanite alphabet made their appearance.

1400-1200.   Late Bronze Age II. Syria-Palestine continued under **Egyptian control** during the reign of Amenophis III (1417-1379), but the administration of the empire decayed steadily in the time of Akhenaten (1379-1362). This era, the **'Amarna Age,** is vividly illuminated by international correspondence, especially the letters of greater and lesser vassal kings of Syria to Egypt. The population of Syria was mixed, Canaanite, Amorite, and Hurrian. The society was feudal, stratified with a nobility of chariot warriors, serfs beneath, and little or no middle class. One segment of the population became freebooters and mercenaries, the so-called **'Apiru.** Their condottieri often seized towns or ravaged the countryside. **Ugarit** was one of the great cities of Canaan in the 14th and 13th centuries, alternating under Egyptian and Hittite suzerainty. We possess both Egyptian and Hittite diplomatic correspondence with the Ugaritic kings Ammishtamru I (c. 1380) and Niqmadda II (c. 1365-1325). From the 14th century come the epic and mythological **texts from Ugarit** written in a cuneiform adaptation of the Canaanite alphabet. These include the Ba'al and 'Anat cycle, and the Keret and Dan'el or Aqhat texts. At Ugarit and throughout Canaan in this period, the chief gods of the pantheon were **'El,** creator of heaven and earth, and patriarch in the council of the gods; **Ba'al-Haddu,** the young storm god and effective king of the gods; **Asherah-Elat,** 'El's consort and mother goddess; and **'Anat,** bloody war goddess and heavenly courtesan. International trade flourished in the Late Bronze Age. The Canaanites developed their **purple dye industry** and became famous for it throughout the Ancient World. The Mycenaean Greeks exported pottery to the Levant especially between about 1375 and 1225. In 1283, Ramesses the Great and Khattusilis III divided Syria between themselves, the boundary at the Eleutherus River (Nahr el-Kebir), a boundary line that persisted in early biblical traditions of the "Promised Land."

Late 13th to 11th centuries.   Invasions of Syria-Palestine. Elements of the tribal peoples that were to make up the later nation of Israel left the eastern Delta of Egypt and the southern desert and stormed Palestine in the third quarter of the 13th century. Their presence in Palestine is recorded in the stele of Merneptah (1232). They were joined evidently by kindred folk, as well as by rebellious or dispossessed elements in Palestine's feudal society, in the formation of the early **Israelite league.** About 1180, Sea Peoples, notably the Philistines and Tjikar, settled in the coastal plain of Palestine from Gaza to Mount Carmel. In the early period of their occupation they formed a loose league of five city states governed by "tyrants" (*seranim*): Gaza, Gath, Ashkelon, Ashdod, and Ekron. With the fall of the Hittite Empire, the Hittites, especially Luwian elements, moved into north Syria and formed the **Late Hittite principalities:** a northern group under the hegemony of Carchemish, and a southern group: Ya'diya, Khattina, Arpad, Til Barsip, and Hamath. The southern group became Aramaean states in the course of the late 11th and 10th centuries for the most part: Bit Agusi (Arpad) c. 900 or slightly later, Sam'al (Ya'diya) c. 920, and Bit Adini (Til Barsip) about 1000. As early as the late 12th century the Aramaeans had moved into southern Syria *en masse,* and in the course of the 11th century became dominant in the region of Damascus and Zobah (the valleys of the Anti-Lebanon, south of modern Homs). The Canaanites receded before the blows of these invasions to the narrow strip of coastal land from Tyre northward to Arvad, Phoenicia. Later they expanded south to Carmel, and a number of large Canaanite enclaves remained behind in Israelite, Philistine, and Aramaean country. Sidon and Byblos were the chief city states of the Phoenician coast at the beginning of the 12th century. Ugarit and Tyre had been destroyed by invaders. However, Tyre was refounded in the 12th century by the Sidonians, and shortly became the capital of the Sidonian state.

c. THE ISRAELITES,
c. 2000-722 B.C.

2000-1200.   ISRAELITE ORIGINS. The beginnings of Israel's religion and historical traditions may be traced back into the Patriarchal period, in the Middle Bronze Age (20th-16th centuries). The sagas preserved in the so-called epic **traditions of the Pentateuch** recall events and persons and in part the religious and social color of this ancient time. We come onto firmer historical ground in the era of **Moses,** contemporary of Ramesses II (1304-1237), though even here our sources derive from religious epic, much of it transmitted orally for longer or shorter periods. Elements of the tribes of Israel escaped from serfdom in the eastern delta of Egypt under the leadership of Moses and his Levitic clansmen. A **Proto-Israelite league** was formed in the wilderness south of Canaan, the clans and disparate peoples being bound into a legal community by a covenant with the god **Yahweh,** mediated by Moses. The new religion had many traits in common with Patriarchal religion: its covenantal form, the conception of Yahweh as leader in war, and the character of Yahweh as creator and judge. In fact, it has been argued plausibly that Yahweh is a cultic name of the old Canaanite and Amorite god 'El. At the same time, the religion of Moses differs from past religious tradition in significant ways from its beginnings. Its cult centered in historical remembrance of Israel's past: the exodus from Egypt and the conquest of Canaan. In memory and re-enactment, the community's covenant was forged anew. In contrast, the Canaanite cults centered in re-enactment of "primordial" events: the battle of creation, the *heiros gamos,* etc. Moreover, there appears to be no trace in our received traditions of a divine consort of Yahweh, the *sine qua non* of the Canaanite nature cults.

The conquest of the land was well advanced when Merneptah in 1232 recorded his defeat of Israel in Palestine, an event not remembered in biblical sources. Once established in Palestine, the league grew rapidly by covenant with new clans and by conquest. A number of Canaanite cities fell to Israelite arms including Hazor, the "head of the kingdom" in the land.

1200-1020. THE PERIOD OF THE JUDGES. While Israel had been successful in her first wave of conquest, a number of large Canaanite cities remained unconquered, and some that had been defeated regained power. Settlement and consolidation was imperiled also by the invasions of other peoples: the Philistines, Moabites, and Midianites in the 12th century, the Ammonites about 1100. Israel's full control of the land was not established until the time of David. The **Judges** of the pre-monarchic period responded to these threats to Israel's life, rallying as many tribes of the loosely knit league as would react to a specific danger. The office of the "judge" in Israel was primarily military and impermanent. In the 12th century **Gideon of Manasseh** led the northern tribes against the Midianites, camel-riding nomads from the Arabian desert. This is the first historical notice of the extensive use of camels, which evidently were domesticated about this time. Perhaps the most serious threat of the 12th century came from a coalition of Canaanite kings in the days of Deborah. The Israelite league was victorious in a battle fought in the Esdraelon Valley about 1125, celebrated in the *Song of Deborah* (Judges 5). The Philistines were not a serious menace to Israel for most of the 12th century. However, border strife intensified in the late 12th and early 11th century, a condition reflected in the legendary cycle of Samson tales. In the course of the 11th century the Philistines united under the king of Gath, and

became aggressive. Israel was conquered by the Philistines about 1050. The central shrine of the league at Shiloh was destroyed, and the Ark taken as booty. The last of the judges, **Samuel,** failed largely to free Israel from the Philistine yoke. He was forced finally to institute kingship in Israel to bring the tribes under a stronger central authority. **Saul** was annointed king in c. 1020.

1020-961. SAUL AND DAVID. Saul's kingship was sharply limited. The primary title in use by both Saul and David was *nagid,* "military commander." Moreover the rise of a new class of charismatics, the *nabi'im,* "prophets," served as a check on the king, preventing at least for a time the emergence of full-blown Canaanite kingship. Saul's capital was a modest fortress built at Gibeah. He was successful for a time in his wars with the Philistines, but fell at the catastrophic battle of Gilboa. He was succeeded by David (1000-961), Israel's greatest king. David was elected king of Judah upon Saul's death, and shortly gained power also over the northern tribes. He conquered **Jerusalem** and made the neutral city his capital. He carefully preserved the old religious institutions of the league by bringing the Ark to Jerusalem and housing it in a tabernacle, giving his new national shrine the nimbus of the old league sanctuary. He conquered the Philistines and made them a vassal state. He subjugated also the surrounding nations, including the early Aramaean power to the north, Aram Zobah. David did not conquer Phoenicia, but entered into a treaty with **Hiram of Tyre,** king of the Sidonians (969-936). When he died his kingdom stretched from the Euphrates in the northeast to the Gulf of Aqabah in the southeast. The era of David was also a time of literary activity in Israel. The religious and literary traditions of the era of the Judges were collected at this time and transformed into an epic (the so-called *Yahwistic source),* a major stage in the history of Pentateuchal tradition.

961-922. THE REIGN OF SOLOMON. While David had eschewed outright innovations which seriously violated traditional religious and social institutions, his son Solomon sought to transform Israel into a full-fledged Oriental monarchy. He built a dynastic temple, identical in plan and decoration with Canaanite temples of the period, except that the usual cult statue was replaced in the cella by the Ark. His building operations included a magnificent palace and citadel in Jerusalem, the fortifications of Gezer and Megiddo, and a copper refinery at Ezion-geber. To facilitate tax gathering and the imposition of the corvée, he centralized his control of the state by breaking up the traditional tribal boundaries into arbitrary administrative districts. The standing army was vastly expanded and equipped with chariots. His reign was kept peaceful by treaties and diplomatic marriages with other dynasties. In partnership with Hiram of Tyre he organized a great fleet of ships for trade in the Mediterranean, and on the Red Sea and Indian Ocean. With Cilicia and Egypt he developed a cartel in horses and chariots, and with the South Arabian kings arranged control of the caravan routes for trade in incense and aromatics.

922. The Disruption of the Monarchy. Rebellion followed immediately upon Solomon's death and the accession of his son **Rehoboam**. Solomon's breach of Yahwistic tradition, and the oppressive tactics of the king and the new nobility, were sorely resented, especially among the northern tribes. **Jeroboam I** became king in the north (Israel), Rehoboam remained king in the south (Judah).

922–722. The (Northern) Kingdom of Israel.

922–900. The Dynasty of Jeroboam I. Civil war between Rehoboam (c. 922–915) and Jeroboam I (c. 922–901) was broken off by the raid of Shishak (Shoshenq I, 935–914) in 918. He devastated Edom, Judah, and much of the Israelite north. Jeroboam organized a new national cult at the Patriarchal sanctuary of Bethel in an attempt to break ties of loyalty of the northern tribes to the sanctuary in Jerusalem. This disruption of the religious unity of Israel was viewed as a grave sin both by traditionalist circles in Shiloh, and, of course, by Judaeans including **Amos** (c. 750) and the Deuteronomistic historian (compiler of Deuteronomy, Joshua, Judges, Samuel, and Kings). Jeroboam's son Nadab (901–900) was murdered by Baasha.

900–876. The Dynasty of Baasha. Baasha attempted to re-ignite the smouldering civil war with Judah. Asa of Judah (913–873), however, called upon Ben Hadad I, king of Aram-Damascus (880–842). The latter attacked Baasha, laying waste part of Galilee and annexing territory northeast of the Yarmuk River (878). Baasha's son Elah (877–876) was assassinated by Zimri (876), who in turn was burnt to death in his palace in Tirzah by Omri.

876–842. The Omride Dynasty. Omri established a long-lived dynasty. He built a new capital at Samaria, and renewed alliances with Tyre by the marriage of Jezebel, daughter of Ittoba'al, king of Tyre (887–856) to Ahab, the crown prince. He also reconquered Moab as we learn from the Mesha inscription. Omri was evidently a strong king. The Assyrians called Israel after his name, Bît 'Omri

(Khumri). Ahab (869–850) fought defensive wars with Ben Hadad, but when the menace of Shalmaneser III (859–825) became clear after the subjugation of Bît Adini, the two joined against Assyria. In the **battle of Qarqar** in 854, Ahab of Israel, Ben Hadad of Damascus, and Irkhuleni of Hamath headed the coalition that stopped Shalmaneser's march of conquest. Ahab met his end in Transjordan fighting again against Ben Hadad. One of the most vivid figures in Israelite history flourished in this time, **Elijah the prophet.** He battled against the cult of Tyrian Ba'al sponsored by Jezebel, and began a religious revolution against economic injustice that ultimately brought down the house of Omri. Ahab was succeeded by Ahaziah (850–849) and by Joram (849–842).

842–748. The Dynasty of Jehu. In 842, the soldier Jehu at the instigation of Elisha led an open rebellion against the king and his oppressive and pagan nobility. Ahaziah of Judah was killed in the blood purge. In the same year Shalmaneser attacked and defeated Hazael of Damascus (842–806), who had just come to the throne. Jehu weakly paid tribute. Assyrian power was on the wane, however, and Hazael recovered and set out to win an empire. In Jehu's reign he took Transjordan. In the time of Joahaz (814–798), he reduced Israel to a dependency, conquered Philistia, and put Judah under enormous tribute. Meanwhile he had unified the Aramaean states. Hazael died in c. 806, shortly before Assyria returned to fight against Damascus. The campaign of Adadnirari III in 806 left Aram too weak to hold together its empire. Joash (798–782) led Israel in wars against Ben Hadad II (c. 806–750) in which he recovered Israel's lost territories. Later he turned against Judah and defeated Amaziah (797–769), taking Jerusalem and reducing the southern kingdom to vassalage. During the long reign of Amaziah's son **Jeroboam II** (783–748) Israel grew wealthy and powerful. Damascus and Hamath came under Israelite suzerainty for the first time since the days of Solomon. **Amos** and **Hosea** prophesied against the decadence and corruption of the times of Jeroboam. Zechariah (748), the last of the dynasty, was assassinated by Shallum.

748–722. The Last Days of Israel. Shallum (748) was killed in continued civil strife by Menahem (748–738). In his last year Menahem paid tribute to Tiglathpileser III (745–728). Pekahiah (738–736) was killed by the anti-Assyrian party led by Pekah (736–732). Rezin, king of Aram (750–732) and Pekah entered into a league against Assyria, and when Ahaz of Judah refused to join the conspiracy, declared war on Judah. Ahaz appealed to

Assyria for aid. Tiglathpileser came west in 734–732, laying waste both Israel and Damascus (732). Much of Israel and the whole of Aram were turned into provinces of Assyria. Hoshea (732–723) was appointed king in Samaria by the Assyrians. About 725 he rebelled, hoping to receive aid from Tefnakhte, an Egyptian ruler of the 24th Dynasty. He was shortly captured by the Assyrians, and in 722 Samaria fell after a three year siege. Sargon II (722–706) claimed to have taken captive 27,290 Israelites.

d. THE KINGDOM OF JUDAH, 922–586 B.C.

922–842. Rehoboam (922–915) died shortly after Shishak's raid. Civil war continued intermittently through the reigns of Abijah (915–913) and Asa (913–873). **Jehoshaphat** made peace with Ahab of Israel, and joined him in wars against Damascus. Judicial reforms are attributed to Jehoshaphat by the Chronicler. Jehoshaphat was succeeded by his son Jehoram (849–842) and by his grandson Ahaziah (842), who was killed in the Jehu revolution.

842–836. Athaliah, the dowager queen, seized power and tried to secure her throne by destroying the Davidic house. A small son of Ahaziah escaped, however, and in 836 with the backing of the high priest, Jehoash was enthroned and Athaliah killed.

836–769. Jehoash (836–797) came to the throne coeval with Hazael's rise to great power. He was forced to pay a heavy tribute to Aram. His son Amaziah (797–769) did not improve Judah's lot but lost his independence in a war against Joash of Israel.

769–734. THE REIGN OF UZZIAH (Azariah). The fortunes of Judah changed in the course of the rule of Uzziah. His military ventures in Philistia, Edom, and northern Arabia placed important caravan traffic in Judaean control. After the death of Jeroboam, his powerful rival in Israel, Uzziah became head of the western **coalition against Assyria.** He was defeated by Tiglathpileser shortly before 738, but unlike Hamath and his northern allies, escaped with little harm. In his later years Uzziah became a leper and lived in isolation from his court. His son Jotham served as regent (749–734). Jotham survived his father's death only a short while (734).

734–715. Ahaz came to the throne in 734 in time to face attack from the Syro-Ephraimite coalition: Pekah of Israel and Rezin of Aram. Against the prophet Isaiah's advice he appealed to Assyria. The Assyrian destruction of Damascus and Israel followed.

715–687. THE REIGN OF HEZEKIAH. Religious and political reforms were enacted by Hezekiah as part of a general plan to revive the glory of the days of David. Hezekiah entered into a far-flung coalition against the new king of Assyria, **Sennacherib** (705–682). In 701 Sennacherib marched westward to meet Hezekiah and his Phoenician, Philistine, and Egyptian allies. King Luli of the Sidonians fled in terror to Cyprus. Egyptian forces under Shabaka were easily defeated at Elteqeh, and Philistia fell. Sennacherib then reduced 46 walled cities of Judah according to his own report, and left Hezekiah shut up in Jerusalem "like a bird in a cage." Hezekiah capitulated, paying heavy tribute. Some confusion exists in the biblical sources dealing with Sennacherib's campaign. There is evidence, sharply disputed, that two separate campaigns of Sennacherib, one in the time of Shabaka, one in Taharqo's reign (after 689), are telescoped in the biblical account, and that at the end of Sennacherib's reign, Jerusalem was again besieged by the Assyrians but once more escaped destruction.

687–640. Manasseh (687–642) and his son Amon (642–640) ruled as puppets of Assyria during the brilliant reigns of Esarhaddon (681–670) and Assurbanapal (669–627). Manasseh is particularly remembered in biblical tradition for his syncretistic cults, including, no doubt, the official Assyrian cult, and for child sacrifice.

640–609. The Reign of Josiah. The progressive decay of Assyrian authority in the last years of Assurbanapal and during the reigns of his weak successors is sensitively reflected in Judaean politics. In the eighth year of his reign Josiah, under the guidance of his elders, "began to seek the God of David his father," that is to say, repudiated the gods of his Assyrian overlords. In 627, about the time of Assurbanapal's death, Josiah moved into the old territory of Israel, annexing the Assyrian provinces of Samaria, Gilead, and Galilee. About the same time he established garrisons along the *via maris* in Philistia. In 622 Josiah launched a full-scale politico-religious program for the re-establishment of the Davidic kingdom. A forgotten law book, the nucleus of Deuteronomy, was republished and made the basis of the religious reform. Foreign and syncretistic cults were extirpated. Worship was centralized in Jerusalem. Unfortunately the reign of Josiah and the new golden age of Judah were cut short. In 609 Josiah met his death at Megiddo fighting a delaying action against Neko II, who was hastening to Assyria's aid.

609–586. The Fall of Judah. Jehoahaz II (609)

ruled briefly before being removed from the throne by Neko and replaced by Jehoiakim (609–598). Jehoiakim transferred his allegiance to Nebuchadrezzar after the defeat of the Egyptians at Carchemish (605), but rebelled about 601, presumably after Necho's defeat of Nebuchadrezzar on the Egyptian border (601). In 598 Nebuchadrezzar led his forces against Judah. Jehoiakim died (perhaps by violence), leaving his son to pay for his folly. Jehoichin reigned three months (598–597) before Jerusalem fell. He and large numbers of his people were carried captive to Babylonia. Nebuchadrezzar replaced Jehoichin with Zedekiah (597–587). Despite the eloquent protests of Jeremiah, Zedekiah was tempted into revolt in league with Egypt. Nebuchadrezzar laid siege to Jerusalem in January, 588. The city fell and its temple was razed in July, 586. A second group of captives was taken to Babylon.

586–539. THE JEWS UNDER BABYLONIAN RULE. Judah was left a desolate land stripped of its leadership. Nevertheless, after the murder of Gedaliah, the governor of the province, the Chaldeans carried out a third deportation (582). In Babylon the Jewish community was treated well. Strange to say the captivity was an extremely creative period in Israel's religious life and literature. The oracles of Ezekiel and Second Isaiah were composed in this period. The Deuteronomic history, first compiled in the time of Josiah, was edited and brought up to date. The so-called Priestly edition of the Pentateuch was also prepared during the Exile.

539–332. Judah under Persian Rule. Babylon fell to Cyrus in 539. The Persian king released the Jews, those who wished, to return to Zion. Many returned in the 6th and 5th centuries. In the years 520–515 the temple was rebuilt at the urging of Haggai the prophet. Nehemiah, a high official of Artaxerxes I (Longimanus, 464–424) took leave of his office to come to the aid of the Jerusalem community. In 445 he came as governor to Jerusalem. He rebuilt the ancient walls of the city in 439, overcoming the opposition of Sanballat, governor of Samaria, and Tobiah, the Jewish governor of Ammon. The date of **Ezra's mission** is disputed. Evidently he was a younger contemporary of Nehemiah, and perhaps his mission is best dated in 438. Ezra instituted cultic and legal reforms with far-reaching effects on the development of Post-exilic Judaism.

332. Palestine conquered by Alexander the Great.

e. THE ARAMAEANS IN SYRIA-PALESTINE, 1300–732 B.C.

1300–1000. Early Aramaean Movements. In the late 14th century cuneiform records begin to mention a new group of nomadic peoples entering Mesopotamia and Syria called the Akhlamu. In the time of Tiglathpileser I (1116–1078) there is specific mention of the *akhlame armaya*, against whom Assyria directed military actions in the region of Palmyra. The relation between the Akhlamu and the later Aramaeans is not wholly clear; the Aramaeans at least replaced the Akhlamu, if they are not to be identified with them. In the course of the 11th century Aramaean bands flooded the Fertile Crescent. One major movement was directed west into Syria, others into Upper Mesopotamia and Babylonia.

1000–900. Early Aram and Israel. The earliest Aramaic states to form, so far as we know, were Zobah (Subatu) and Damascus. Already in the time of Saul (1020–1000) Israel came into conflict with the kings of Aram Zobah. About 970 Hadadezer of Beth Rehob, king of Zobah, headed a league of lesser states including Maacah, Beth Rehob, Tob, and perhaps Geshur and Damascus. On the pretext of aiding Ammon, Hadadezer attacked Davidic territory far south in Transjordan, probably with designs on the trade routes from the south. He was defeated by David in an initial engagement. Later, despite reinforcements from Damascus and farther east, Hadadezer was overcome by Israelite arms. David extended his border north to Hamath, northeast to the Euphrates. Rezon, a captain of Hadadezer, went with troops to Damascus and set himself up as king. Presumably this was shortly after David's death (c. 961), since Rezon is identified as an enemy of Solomon. In the course of the 10th century a number of the Late Hittite city states became Aramaean: Bît Agusi (Arpad), Sam'al (Ya'diya), and Bît Adini (Til Barsip). Carchemish and other northern Hittite states in league with Carchemish were heavily infiltrated by Aramaeans, but kept Hittite dynasties until their incorporation into the Assyrian Empire.

900–842. THE RISE OF DAMASCUS. Ben Hadad I (Hadadezer, 880–842), was the grandson of Hezyon, the son of Tabrimmon (Tabraman). We know little beside the names of Hezyon and Tabraman, and that they ruled in Damascus. Ben Hadad in 878 attacked Baasha at the request of Asa, king of Judah. He ravaged Naphtali and probably at this time annexed the territory of Bashan north of the Yarmuk. The campaigns of Assurna sirapli II (884–860) warned the Aramaean states of the danger of resurgent Assyria. Shalmaneser III (859–825) set out early in his reign to break the power of the Aramaean states. In 858 he engaged a coalition of northern Aramaean and Hittite states at Lutibu in Sam'al. Khayan, son of Gabbar, king of Sam'al, Akhuni of Bît Adini, together with the Hittite kings of Carchemish and Khattina, were defeated but not broken. Shalmaneser returned to the wars against the northern league, finally splitting it up. In the years 857–855 he attacked Akhuni of Bît Adini, the strongest of these princes, and conquered the state. Akhuni was taken captive, and Bît Adini turned into a province of Assyria. About this same time Ben Hadad and Ahab were engaged in warfare. Ben Hadad besieged Samaria with the aid of 32 kings under his hegemony. Apparently Ahab finally fought off the Aramaeans. In the following year after a severe defeat at Aphek, Ben Hadad settled happily for a treaty with Israel.

With the northern coalition broken, Shalmaneser turned against the southern states. Ben Hadad led the coalition of twelve city states which included Ahab of Israel and Irkhuleni of Hamath. At Qarqar in the territory of Hamath the armies met. Shalmaneser was forced to retire to Assyria. The swift growth of Damascene power is illustrated by a stele set up by Ben Hadad about 850 in the vicinity of Aleppo. By the time of the battle of Qarqar, Damascus appears to have been virtually the sole Aramaean power in the south. Evidently all the small Aramaean states of southern Syria were absorbed by Ben Hadad. Shalmaneser returned in four additional campaigns against Aram, finally succeeding in breaking the coalition's power in 842. Ben Hadad was murdered in 842 by Hazael, a commoner, who mounted the throne.

842–806. The Reign of Hazael. After a perfunctory campaign against Damascus in 839, Assyria ceased to intervene in the west for more than 30 years. Hazael was left free to pursue Aram's imperial ambitions. He subjugated Israel, and Philistia in good part, and placed a heavy tribute on Judah. He died in c. 806, shortly before the raid of Adadnirari III on Damascus in the same year.

806–732. The Decline of Aram. Ben Hadad II (Mari, c. 806–750) was unable to hold together the Aramaean empire of Hazael. Early in his reign he led a coalition of north Syrian kings against Zakir, king of Hamath, but failed to subdue him. Joash of Israel fought free of Damascene control, and under Jeroboam II (783–748) Damascus as well as Hamath actually became tributary to Israel. With the decline of Damascus, a northern Aramaean state came to the fore: **Arpad** or Bît Agusi. Matiel, after becoming a vassal of Assurnirari V in 755, broke faith and led the Aramaean states into a treaty with Ketek, an ally of Urartu, Assyria's most powerful enemy. Tiglathpileser III (745–727) defeated the Urartean allies at Arpad in 743. After a three-year siege Arpad fell. Azariah of Judah, the strongest king left in Syria-Palestine, became leader of the coalition. He was defeated shortly before 738. In 734 Pekah of Israel and Rezin, son of Ben Hadad II, attempted to rally Syria's failing Aramaic states once more. Ahaz, a faithful vassal of Assyria, refused to join the coalition, and when attacked by the two kings, called for aid from Assyria. Tiglathpileser laid waste Israel and Damascus. The whole of Aram-Damascus was divided into Assyrian provinces (732). This was the effective end of Aram as a political entity.

f. THE PHOENICIANS, 1100–332 B.C.

1100–888. The Rise of the Sidonian State. The Phoenicians did not fully recover from the blows that had ravaged their cities and robbed them of nine-tenths of their territory until the beginning of the 10th century. They turned more than ever to the sea, extending their trade routes and establishing trading colonies. Their expansion into the Mediterranean probably began after David broke the power of the Philistine Empire at the beginning of the 10th century. Colonization proceeded swiftly, evidently to Cyprus first, to Sicily and Sardinia, to Utica on the African coast, and finally to Spain. There is archaeological evidence that Spain was reached no later than the 9th century, and perhaps was colonized as early as 950. This extraordinary development of the Phoenicians as a maritime people must be attributed to **Hiram I of Tyre** (969–936) and his father Abiba'al. Tyre, built on an island, was a superbly defended harbor. After its refounding by Sidonians in the 12th century, it quickly became the capital of the Sidonian state. Hiram ruled the Sidonians in the most brilliant period of Phoenician history. He was a younger contemporary of David (1000–961), with whom he entered into league. His covenant with Israel persisted in the time of Solomon, when Phoenician influence on Israel reached its height. Hiram's workmen designed and built the temple of Solomon. Hiram's and Solomon's joint fleets sailed the Mediterranean Sea and the Indian Ocean. Of particular importance were the Tarshish fleets, ships linking distant mining and refining centers with Levantine ports. In the reign of Hiram the Sidonian state spread southward to Mount Carmel, northward to Arvad, unifying Phoenicia. However, vassal dynasties continued to rule at Byblos and Arvad. From the **kings of Byblos** in this period come a regular series of inscriptions: the sarcophogus inscription of Ahiram (c. 1000) prepared by his son Ittoba'al (c. 975), and dedicatory inscriptions of Yehimilk (c. 950), Abiba'al (c. 930), Eliba'al (c. 920), and Shipitba'al (c. 900). We know little of Hiram's successors: Ba'almazzer I (935–919), Abd'ashtart (918–910), Ashtart (909–898), 'Astartrom (897–889), and Pilles (888).

887–856. Ittoba'al was a priest of Astarte, according to tradition, who, having killed Pilles, initiated a new dynasty. Omri of Israel arranged a marriage between Jezebel, Ittoba'al's daughter, and his own son Ahab. It may be that Ittoba'al was also linked by marriage with the house of Ben Hadad I. Phoenician religious and cultural influence became powerful both in Samaria and in Damascus.

855–774. Ba'al'azor (855–850) succeeded Ittoba'al and in turn was followed by Ba'almazzer II (849–830) who paid tribute to Shalmaneser III in 842. He was succeeded by Mittin (829–821) and by Pu'myaton (Pygmalion, 820–774). Tradition relates that Pygmalion's sister Elissa fled from Tyre and founded the city of Carthage in the king's seventh year (814). The founding date, if not the legend, is almost certainly accurate.

774–701. Hiram II paid tribute to Tiglath-pileser in 738. Luli (c. 730?–701) conspired with Hezekiah and the Egyptians to rebel against Sennacherib (705–682). In 701 Sennacherib forced Luli to flee for his life to Cyprus, an event portrayed in Sennacherib's reliefs. Sennacherib set up separate vassal kings in Sidon and in Tyre.

701–627. Ittoba'al II, the appointee of Sennacherib, was at length replaced by 'Abdmilkot, who rebelled against Esarhaddon. In 677 the Assyrian suzerain razed Sidon to the ground and built for himself a new city opposite the old site which he named Kar-Esarhaddon. He caught 'Abdmilkot escaping by sea and cut off his head. Sidon became a province of Assyria. Ba'al, king of Tyre, also rebelled in the reign of Esarhaddon, but soon capitulated.

His mainland territories were taken from him and he paid tribute. However, he was still king of Tyre in the reign of Assurbanapal.

627–539. After the death of Assurbanapal, the Phoenicians enjoyed a brief period of independence. However, the Phoenicians were unable to recover fully. Greek colonization had ended their near monopoly in the Mediterranean.

The Chaldean rulers did not leave Phoenicia free of oppressors for long. Nebuchadrezzar the Great invested Tyre in the reign of Ittoba'al III in 587, the year Jerusalem fell. After thirteen years of siege, Tyre surrendered in 573. Ba'al II succeeded Ittoba'al III. Tyre then was ruled by judges for a short time after which the monarchy was restored.

539–332. Phoenicia under Persian Rule. In the fourteenth year of the reign of Hiram III, Cyrus the Great came to power in Babylon. Phoenicia became a part of the fifth satrapy. Nevertheless vassal kings still continued to rule in Sidon, Tyre, Arvad, and Byblos. The celebrated inscriptions of Tabnit and Eshmun'azor, kings of Sidon, come from the later part of the 5th century. Phoenician fleets played an important part in Persia's wars with Greece. In c. 350 Tennes led a revolt against the Persians in Sidon. He was crushed by Artaxerxes III with great loss of life.

332.   The Conquest of Phoenicia by Alexander. With the exception of Tyre, the Phoenician vassals of Persia attempted no resistance to Alexander. Still confident in his city's protected perch in the sea, **Azemilkos,** the last king of Tyre, refused Alexander entrance. The city was besieged by the Macedonians from January to July/August 332. Alexander threw a mole across from the mainland to the island and finally breached the city's defenses. The siege of Tyre was notorious for the atrocities committed by the Tyrians against Macedonian prisoners, and for the fierce vengeance exacted by Alexander when the city fell. A reported 8,000 were slain and 30,000 sold into slavery.

The main industries of Phoenicia were the manufacture of purple dye, weaving, glass, and metal working. Iron and copper were mined in Cyprus and worked by the Phoenicians, using techniques which originated in Egypt and Babylon.

(Cont. p. 88.)

4. ANATOLIA, TO 547 B.C.

a. THE LAND AND THE PEOPLE

The peninsula of Anatolia or Asia Minor stretches westward from the Armenian mountains to the Aegean Sea. It is separated from Syria by the Taurus range on the south, and from Upper Mesopotamia by the Anti-Taurus, a chain running northeastward to the Armenian massif. The central highland or plateau is ringed about with mountains, and near its center sinks into a basin which traps drainage waters in a salt lake (Tuz Göl). The people of ancient Anatolia were dominantly broad-headed Armenoids, but owing to repeated invasions became mixed, especially with people of Mediterranean affinities.

b. THE HITTITES, TO c. 1200 B.C.

The founders of the great Hittite state are called after the name of their land Khattu, "Hittites." Actually this designation more appropriately applies to one stratum of the Hittite population, no doubt the predecessors of the Hittites, now called "Proto-Khattians." The **Proto-Khattic language,** known from religious texts, is without affinities to other known language groups. The Hittites themselves spoke a language which belongs to the Indo-European family. They called it **Nesian** after the city of Nesa. Other languages closely affiliated include **Luwian,** the language of southeastern and southwestern Anatolia (ancient Kizzuwatna and Arzawa) and **Palaic,** a northern dialect. A form of Luwian is recorded in the Hittite hieroglyphic script used in inscriptions of the later kings and especially in the monuments of Late Hittite city states. A large part of our knowledge of Hittite history and religion stems from the many thousands of documents found in Khattusas (modern **Boghazkoy**), the capital of the Hittite state located in the bend of the Halys River.

The mixture of peoples in the Hittite homeland was ruled by an Indo-European aristocracy. The great king, called the "Sun" in the later titulary, was military leader, high priest, and judge. The nobility and the state were extensions of his person. **Hittite religion** is peculiarly syncretistic. Proto-Khattic, Hurrian, and Akkado-Sumerian gods and myths are mixed with Luwian and Hittite counterparts in a bewildering fashion. The state cult centered about the sun goddess of Arinna. Her Proto-Khattic name was Wurusemu. In the Empire she was identified with Hurrian Khepat. Her consort was the storm-god, Luwian Tarkhunt,

Proto-Khattic Taru, the equivalent of Hurrian Teshup. The chief event of the official cult was the *purulli festival,* evidently a New Year's festival, celebrating the combat of the storm-god with the dragon Illuyankas.

c. 1800–1700. The Cappadocian Texts. Our earliest real historical knowledge of the Anatolian plateau stems from the Assyrian merchant colonies in Cappadocia. At the end of the age of the colonies, contemporary with Shamshi-Adad I of Assyria (1748–1716), we learn of a certain Pitkhana and his son Anittas, kings of Kussar. They destroyed Hattusas, and established their capital at Nesa (possibly Kanish, modern Kultepe).

c. 1600–1500. The Old Hittite Kingdom. Tudkhaliyas I and Pusarma, who flourished in the late 17th century, are little more than names. **Labarnas I** (c. 1600) was credited with founding the Hittite kingdom, and his boundaries were said to reach the sea. His name and that of his queen Tawannannas were borne by his successors and their queens as if they were titles. **Khattusilis I** (Labarnas II, c. 1580) evidently shifted the capital to Khattusas. He continued the Hittite expansion, conquering Alalakh and attacking Arzawa. His successor **Mursilis I** (c. 1550–1530) subjugated northern Syria, destroying Aleppo. He then boldly marched on Babylon, pillaged it and brought down the 1st Dynasty of Babylon (c. 1531). He returned home to be assassinated. A time of troubles followed, petty king following petty king: Khantilis, Zidantas, Ammunas, and Khuzzias. **Telepinus** came to the throne about 1500 and halted the decline. He pushed back the Hurrians and made a treaty with Kizzuwatna. Telepinus composed an edict proclaiming a law of succession that stabilized the crown. The Hittite law code also dates from this general period.

c. 1450–1200. THE HITTITE EMPIRE.

c. 1450–1380. The Early Kings. Tudkhaliyas II established a new dynasty destined to build an empire. The reigns of the early kings gave no promise of this. In the reigns of Khattusilis II, Tudkhaliyas III, and Arnuwandas I, the state came into a time of grave danger. It was threatened by the Kingdom of Mitanni on the east, Arzawa on the west, and the hordes of Kashka people on the north. The Kashka actually reached Khattusas and sacked it.

c. 1380–1346. The Reign of Suppiluliumas. Suppiluliumas, a younger son of Tudkhaliyas, took the throne. He fortified and rebuilt his capital and reorganized the home territories. Then he marched into Syria. His first encounter with Tuishrata of Mitanni resulted in a severe defeat. By adding allies, including Artadama II, a rival of Tuishrata, who also claimed the kingship of Mitanni, Suppiluliumas later was able to conquer Washukkani, the Mitanni capital. The little kingdoms of northern Syria now easily fell into his hands. Aleppo and Carchemish became vassal kingdoms under sons of Suppiluliumas. Ugarit paid tribute. Suppiluliumas fell a victim to plague, and shortly after his son, Arnuwandas II, also died.

c. 1344–1316. The Reign of Mursilis II. In his early reign young Mursilis marched against Arzawa in the southwest, crushed a revolt there and killed Arzawa's king. For many years he fought almost annual campaigns against the Kashka. A revolt in Carchemish was pacified. Mursilis' annals are the most extensive historical work from Boghazkoy.

c. 1315–1295? The Reign of Muwatallis. Muwatallis inherited a powerful, well-organized empire from his father. Egypt, however, under Ramesses II, was ambitious to regain her empire. The inevitable clash between the two for the control of Syria came at Qadesh-on-the-Orontes in 1298. Both sides claimed victory. Ramesses when he returned home filled the walls of his temples with boasts of his valor in the battle. But Muwatallis' claim had more justification in view of the fact that he remained firmly in control of northern Syria.

c. 1295–1260. The Reigns of Urkhiteshup and Khattusilis III. Urkhiteshup (c. 1295–1289), Muwatallis' weak son, was shortly deposed by Khattusilis, Muwatallis' brother. Khattusilis III (c. 1289–1260) made treaties with the Kassites and in 1283 made his famous treaty with Ramesses II, setting a boundary favorable to the Hittites between their empires. Evidently these moves were made to counter the growing threat of Assyria under Shalmaneser I (1275–1246).

c. 1260–1200. The Decline and Fall of the Hittite Empire. Tudkhaliyas IV (c. 1260–1240) turned to western Anatolia to meet disturbances caused by the Achaeans (Akhkhiyawa), a portent of the future. A good part of his reign was peaceful, however, given to cultic reforms and the arts. Probably the celebrated **reliefs of Yazilikaya** are to be attributed to Tudkhaliyas. In the reign of Arnuwandas III (c. 1240), the situation in the western provinces abruptly worsened. The final waves of **Sea Peoples** and Phrygians which inundated and destroyed the empire probably came in the succeeding short reign of Suppiluliumas II (c. 1230). The Hittites spread through Syria and Palestine. In northern Syria, Hittite culture survived in a series of Late Hittite city states: Melid (Malatya), Kummukh (Commagene), Gur-

gum, Carchemish, Unqi, Arpad, Ya'diya (Sam'al), Aleppo, Til Barsip, and Hamath. The southernmost of these became Aramaean in the late 11th and 10th centuries.

c. THE PHRYGIANS, TO 547 B.C.

Civilization. The Phrygians (as well as the Mysians) came from Thrace with the great Aegean migrations, about 1200 B.C., and occupied central Anatolia, west of the Halys. Their language belonged to the Indo-European group. Their capital was **Gordion.** Tumuli (sepulchral mounds) are typical of the Phrygians, although graves cut into the rock also occur.

Religion. The chief deities of the Phrygians were **Cybele** (*Ma,* the Great Mother riding in a chariot drawn by lions), whose orgiastic cult was introduced into Rome in 191 B.C., and **Attis,** the god who died as a result of castration but came back to life; his priests, Galli, were eunuchs.

c. 1000–700. The **Kingdom of Phrygia,** the history of which is not known, was organized and grew in power. **Midas** (*Mita* of Mushku in the inscriptions of Sargon II of Assyria) ruled about 715.

690. The **Cimmerian invasion** devastated the kingdom; somehow the Phrygian nation survived until the time of Cyrus (547).

d. THE LYDIANS, TO 547 B.C.

Geography. Lydia, whose capital was Sardis, lies in western Asia Minor, between the Ionian cities on the coast and Phrygia; it borders on Mysia in the north and Caria in the south.

Civilization and Religion. Whereas Phrygia constituted a barrier between Greece and the Orient, Lydia became the link between east and west, culturally and commercially. If the Etruscans, or at least their nobility, came from Lydia (according to a classical tradition going back to Herodotus which modern scholarship is inclined to accept), the Lydians contributed materially to the civilization of ancient Italy. The Lydians were great merchants and expert craftsmen; they probably invented coinage. They were fond of horsemanship in the early period, and later contributed to the development of music and the dance; according to Greek tradition, **Aesop** was a Lydian. Little is known about the religion of the Lydians: the gods **Santas** (*Sandon*) and **Baki** (*Bacchus, Dionysos*) were named in their inscriptions.

680–652. Gyges, founder of the dynasty of the Mermnadae, in alliance with Asshurbanapal of Assyria, defeated the Cimmerians and extended the borders of the kingdom. But after sending Carian and Ionian mercenaries to the help of Psamtik, who drove the Assyrians out of Egypt, Gyges fell in battle against the Cimmerians.

652–547. Dynasty of the Mermnadae: Ardys, Sadyattes, Alyattes, Croesus. After overcoming the Cimmerian menace, Ardys and his successors carried out the conquest of the Greek cities on the coast (begun by Gyges), except Miletus, and of the interior of Asia Minor as far as the Halys, with the exception of Lycia. Lydia reached the zenith of her power under **Croesus,** who attacked the Persian Empire, but was defeated and taken prisoner by Cyrus in 547.

547–333. Asia Minor under Persian rule.

5. ARMENIA, TO 56 B.C.

a. THE KINGDOM OF VAN (URARTU)

Geography. The borders of Urartu (Ararat) cannot be fixed exactly: in a general way the kingdom was located between the Caucasus and Lake Van.

Population. The basic population seems to have been Hurrian; the Hurrian and Vannic languages seem to be related.

Civilization and Religion. The *Vannic inscriptions,* written in Assyrian cuneiform characters but still very obscure, were chiefly annals recording wars and building operations, particularly hydraulic works (the irrigation canal of Menuas is still in use). The Vannic people showed special aptitude in industrial arts, particularly metallurgy. At the head of the pantheon, which included numerous deities, stood a triad: **Haldi,** the national god, **Tesheba** (the Hurrian storm-god Teshub), and **Ardini** (a god or goddess of the sun). The temple of Haldi and his consort Bagbartu at Musasir, pictured on a bas-relief of Sargon II of Assyria at Khorsabad, is surprisingly similar to the Greek temples in the Doric style.

c. 1270–850. The Assyrian name for the **Kingdom of Van** (*Uruatri,* later *Urartu*) occurs for the first time in the inscriptions of Shalmaneser I (c. 1275–1246). The lands of the Nairi (east and north of Lake Van) were divided into numerous Hurrian principalities and subject to repeated attacks by the Assyrian kings, particularly by Tukulti-Ninurta I (c. 1245–1209), Tiglathpileser I (c. 1100), Ashurbelkala (c. 1070), Adadnirari II (c. 900), Tukulti-Ninurta II (c. 890), and Assurnasirapli II (884–860).

c. 860–843. Arame, first known king of Urartu, was defeated by Shalmaneser III (859–825), who captured his capital Arzashkun.

c. 832–820. Sarduri I, son of Lutipri, was probably a usurper; he chose Tushpa (Assyrian *Turushpa,* the present Van) as his capital and fortified it. He founded the principal dynasty.

c. 820–800. Ispuini conquered Musasir, appointing his son Sarduri II viceroy there, and was attacked by Shamshiadad V of Assyria.

c. 800–785. Menua, who was at first co-regent with his father Ispuini, enlarged the kingdom considerably, leaving inscriptions over a vast area.

c. 785–760. Argishti I (780–756) annexed the territory along the Araxes and around the Lake of Erivan. Shalmaneser IV of Assyria had no success in his campaigns against Urartu.

c. 760–733. Sarduri III preserved the integrity of the kingdom.

c. 733–612. The last kings of Urartu, Rusas I (c. 733–714) (probably the founder of a new dynasty), Argishti II (c. 714–685), Rusas II (c. 685–650), Sarduri IV (c. 650–625), and Rusas III (c. 625–612), ruled over a much restricted territory. The Cimmerian invasion and the raid of Sargon II of Assyria (714) weakened the kingdom, which met its doom after the Scythian invasion, when the Medes conquered the country (612). The Vannic nation ceased to exist.

b. ARMENIA

The Armenians are mentioned for the first time by Darius (519). They were probably a Phrygian tribe and they gradually occupied the territory of Urartu after 612. They adopted the religion of the Persians.

612–549. Armenia under the kings of Media.

549–331. Under the Persian kings, Armenia was a satrapy administered by a member of the royal family.

331–317. Under Alexander and his immediate successors, Armenia continued to be ruled by Persian satraps.

317–211. Ardvates (317–284), one of these Persian satraps, made the country independent of the Seleucids and founded a dynasty that ruled until 211.

211–190. Antiochus III, after removing Xerxes, the Armenian king, by treachery, divided the country into two satrapies, giving the western one (*Armenia Minor*) to Zadriades and the eastern one (*Armenia Major*) to Artaxias.

190–94. After Antiochus was defeated at Magnesia (190), Zadriades and Artaxias made themselves independent rulers, founding two separate dynasties.

94-56. TIGRANES I, a descendant of Artaxias, deposed Artanes, the last king of Armenia Minor, and united the two countries under his rule. From 83 to 69 he was the most powerful king in Asia, ruling over northern Mesopotamia, Syria, and parts of Asia Minor. Defeated by Lucullus in 69, he was stripped of his conquests, but was allowed by Pompey to rule over Armenia as a vassal of Rome.

6. IRAN, TO 330 B.C.

Geography. The Iranian plateau extends from the mountains east of the Tigris to the Indus Valley, and from the Persian Gulf and the Indian Ocean to the Caspian Sea and the Jaxartes River. Media (capitals: Ecbatana and Rhagae), Elam (capital: Susa), and Persia (capital: Persepolis) in the west played a much more important historical rôle than Sogdiana, Bactria, Aria, Drangiana, and Arachosia in the east. In the north-central region, the Parthians became Rome's rivals in the Near East.

Population. In the 4th and possibly the 5th millennia B.C., a population of unknown race living at Susa used copper and made pottery decorated with realistic and conventionalized animals. The mountaineers of the Zagros range (Gutium, Lullubu) and the Elamites predominated in the 3rd millennium. The Kassites, who ruled Babylonia from 1550 to 1180, were quite distinct from the Elamites. The Aryans, the Indo-European ancestors of the Indo-Iranians, invaded Iran from the northeast (probably about 1800) and became its basic population.

Religion. The religion of the early Iranians was similar to that of Vedic Indians: the worship of **Mithra** and **Varuna,** of the Asuras (Iranian *Ahura*), and of the Devas (degraded to demons by Zarathustra), the myths about the first man Yama (Iranian *Yima*) and about the killing of the dragon, and the conception of *rita* (Iranian *asha* or *urta*) or the inflexible order of the world, and the preparation, offering, and divinization of the sacred drink *soma* (Iranian *haoma*) are common to the Aryans of India and Iran and must date back to the time preceding their separation. **Zoroastrianism** was a reform of this ancient Aryan religion and preserved some of its elements even though it took issue with its naturalistic polytheism. **Zarathustra** (Zoroaster: "rich in camels") may have been born in Media about 660 B.C., but seems to have been active in Bactria, where according to tradition he converted King Vishtasp (Hystaspes). His teaching is preserved in the Gathas, the oldest hymns in the **Avesta.** The *Avesta* is divided into five parts: the *Yasna* (liturgical hymns including the *Gathas*), the *Vispered* (another liturgical book), the *Vendidad* (a code of ritual and ethical laws), the *Yasht* (mythological hymns in praise of the gods), and the *Khorda Avesta* (a prayer book for private devotions). The great doctrines of the finished Zoroastrian system: monotheism, dualism, individual and universal salvation, are present in the germ in the *Gathas*. In the cosmic battle between good and evil each person should contribute to his own salvation and to that of the world by obeying the will of the good god Ahura Mazda (Ormuzed: "Lord Wisdom"). In the later parts of the *Avesta* the god of evil or supreme devil is called Angro-mainyu or **Ahriman** (the evil spirit). After death the pious cross the Cinvat bridge to their reward, whereas the wicked fall from it and suffer in the "House of Lies."

a. THE ELAMITES, TO 640 B.C.

c. 2850-2180. Sumerians and Akkadians frequently defeated and subjected the Elamites, whose civilization was fundamentally Sumerian. **Dynasty of Awan** (c. 2500-2180).

2180-1830. Dynasty of Simash.

1770-1699. Kudur-mabug of Elam placed his son, Waradsin, on the throne of Larsa. The latter's brother and successor, Rimsin, was deposed by Hammurapi.

1176. Shutruk-nahunte raided Babylonia, taking to Susa the stele of Hammurapi and other monuments.

1150. Kudur-nahunte plundered the Temple of Akkad.

1128-1105. Nebuchadrezzar I of Babylon defeated the Elamites.

721-640. Merodach-baladan of Babylon and Humbanigash of Elam joined forces against Sargon of Assyria, who was defeated at Der by the Elamites (721). Shutruk-nahunte II allowed Sargon to depose Merodach-baladan (709). Hallushu (699-693) carried into captivity Sennacherib's son, who was ruling Babylonia (694). Umman-menanu (693-689), who succeeded Kudur-nahunte, fought at Halule against Sennacherib (691). Umman-haldash I (689-681). Umman-haldash II (681-674) raided Sippar during Esarhaddon's Egyptian campaign. Urtaku (674-664) ruled peacefully. Teumman (664-655) was defeated by Asshurbanapal and his kingdom was occupied by the Assyrians. Ummanigash (655-651) sent his forces to the help of Shamashshumukin, king of Babylon, who had rebelled against his brother Assurbanapal. Ummanigash was assassinated by his cousin Tammaritu. Tammaritu (651–649) was deposed by Indabigash and sought refuge in Nineveh. Ummanhaldash III (648–646) was defeated by Assurbanapal, who conquered Susa, and was deposed by Tammaritu II. Tammaritu II was taken prisoner by the Assyrians (646). Umman-haldash III (646–640) returned to the throne, but was taken prisoner by Assurbanapal, who completely devastated the land of Elam and destroyed Susa. The elimination of the Kingdom of Elam facilitated the task of Cyrus, who a century later founded the Persian Empire, with Susa as one of its capitals.

b. THE MEDES, TO 550 B.C.

835–705. **Media,** divided into small principalities, was attacked successively by Assyrian kings, from Shalmaneser III (in whose inscriptions the Medes are mentioned for the first time) to Sargon II.

705–625. Media under **Assyrian rule.** The two kings Dejoces (700–647) and Phraortes (647–625) mentioned by Herodotus were probably local chieftains.

625–585. **Cyaxares** was the founder of the Median Empire and of its dynasty. In alliance with Nabopolassar of Babylon (a daughter of Cyaxares was given in marriage to Nebuchadrezzar), Cyaxares destroyed Nineveh (612) and conquered the Assyrian territory east of the Tigris, as also Urartu (Armenia) and eastern Iran.

585–550. **Astyages** was deposed by Cyrus and Media became part of the Persian Empire (550).

c. THE PERSIANS, TO 330 B.C.

c. 600–550. Achaemenian kings of Anzan (in Elam): Teispes, Cyrus (I), Cambyses, Cyrus (II) the Great.

550–530. **CYRUS THE GREAT** deposed his sovereign Astyages of Media (559), conquered Lydia (546) and Babylonia (539), and founded the Persian Empire, which extended from the Indus to the Mediterranean, from the Caucasus to the Indian Ocean.

530–521. **Cambyses,** son of Cyrus, conquered Egypt (525).

521–486. **DARIUS I,** son of Hystaspes, after pacifying the empire torn by revolts, notably that of Gaumata or Smerdis, and extending its borders beyond the Indus (521–519), divided it into 20 satrapies. His royal residences were Susa, Persepolis, Ecbatana (Hamadan), and Babylon. Darius was a Zoroastrian. Good roads, with stations for royal messengers, made possible regular communications within the empire. A canal was dug from the Nile to the Red Sea. A general revolt of the Ionian Greeks in Asia ended with the fall of Miletus (500–494), but the war against the European Greeks was unsuccessful (**battle of Marathon, 490**).

486–465. After **Xerxes I** (Ahasuerus) was defeated by the Greeks on the sea at Salamis (480), and on land at Plataea and Mycale (479), Persia abandoned her plans for conquering Greece.

465–424. Athens took the offensive against **Artaxerxes I Longimanus,** by sending troops to aid a revolt in Egypt (456–454) and by attacking Cyprus (450), but finally signed a peace treaty (446). The Persian Empire began to decline.

424–404. **Xerxes II** was assassinated by his brother Sogdianus (424), who in turn fell at the hands of his brother Ochus or Darius II Nothus (424–404).

404–358. **Artaxerxes II Mnemon** defeated his rebellious brother Cyrus, the satrap of Anatolia, near Babylon at Cunaxa (401); Cyrus lost his life in the battle and his "ten thousand" Greek mercenaries, after great hardships, reached the Black Sea (Xenophon's *Anabasis*) in March of the year 400. Another insurrection broke out in Asia Minor under the leadership of Datames, the governor of Cappadocia, and spread to the western satrapies (366–360). Egypt became more or less independent after 404.

358–338. **Artaxerxes III Ochus** succeeded, through energetic measures, in asserting the royal authority over the satraps. He was followed by Arses (338–336).

336–330. **Darius III Codomannus** was killed after Alexander the Great, through the victories at Granicus (334), Issus (333), and Gaugamela, near Arbela (331), conquered the Persian Empire.

7. INDIA, TO 72 B.C.

An early urban civilization in the Indus Valley produced the polished stone, metals, incised seals, and pictographs excavated since 1920 at Harappa and Mohenjo Daro. Indian history begins much later with invasion from the Iranian plateau by **Aryans** of uncertain antecedents, who gradually conquered, pushed back, or absorbed the earlier black **Dravidian** and

Austro-Asiatic **Munda** populations. The conquest is variously placed at 2000–1200 B.C.

1200–c. 800 B.C. The Indian Aryans worshiped nature-gods. The chief were **Indra,** god of the air and of the storm, **Agni,** the sacrificial fire, and **Soma,** the intoxicant used for libations. **Varuna** was worshiped as guardian of cosmic regularity, including individual human acts. The oldest sacrificial hymns, composed in northern India west of the Ganges (perhaps 1200), are contained in the *Rigveda,* which dates from c. 1000 B.C., possibly two centuries prior to the related *Gathas* in the *Avesta* of Iran; the *Samaveda* which contains antiphonal selections from the *Rig;* the *Yajurveda,* hymns and sacrificial prose; and the *Atharvaveda,* a repertory of magical formulae. The *Rigveda* reveals an Indo-European hieratic literary language remarkable for clarity of structure and wealth of inflection, which was originally transmitted orally. It depicts a patriarchal society, engaged in cattle-raising and agriculture, characterized by usual monogamy, adult marriage, and normal widowhood. The Aryan tribes were frequently at war among themselves and with indigenous tribes. Their attitude toward life was vigorous and objective; the doctrine of reincarnation and the correlated aspiration to release are absent.

800–c. 550 B.C. A transition period during which the Aryans expanded eastward through Magadha (modern Bihar) is known chiefly from the *Brahmanas,* prose commentaries upon the *Vedas* (c. 800–600), and the earlier *Upanishads* or confidential teachings (c. 600–300). Beginning of the Vedic division of Aryan society into three honorable classes: priests (*brahman*), noble warriors (*kshatriya*), and commonalty (*vaisya*), including both farmers and artisans, augmented by a fourth group, the slaves (*sudra*) consisting of non-Aryans with whom the twice-born classes had no ritual community. Progressive **evolution of caste** may be traced to desire of priest and noble to perpetuate supremacy, to diversification of specialized occupation, and to indigenous rules of endogamy and to absorption of the sudras, many of whom improved their servile status. Continual elaboration by the priesthood of an already laborious ritual had become devoid of religious significance. The doctrine of continuous rebirth (*samsara*), conditioned by the inescapable results of former acts (*karma*), was first expressed in the early *Upanishads* (c. 600–550). The *Upanishads,* too, teach that the soul may escape from the suffering inherent in individual existence only by the realization of its identity with an impersonal cosmic soul. Union with the latter is possible through knowledge, but not through Brahman ritual.

550–321. The northern Indian area was divided among many petty states. Sixteen are enumerated in an early list. **Kosala** (King Prasenajit, contemporary of the Buddha) was the largest, extending from Nepal to the Ganges, including modern Oudh. **Magadha** was its small neighbor on the east, south of the Ganges. The King of Avanti ruled at Ujjain. The capital of the Vamsas (King Sedayama) was at Kosambi (on the Jumna below Agra). Ten tribal republics are named in the oldest Pali records.

Dissent from Brahmanism, to abolish authority of its scriptures and rites, was found in many schools, among them the **Jains,** followers of the Jina ("Victorious"), Vardhamana Mahavira (?540–468?), who elaborated the doctrines of an earlier prophet **Parsya,** and in Magadha under Kings Bimbisara (?543–491?) and his parricide son Ajatasatru (?491–459?). Parsya had enjoined four vows: to injure no life, to be truthful, not to steal, to possess no property. **Mahavira** added chastity and rigid asceticism as means to free man's immortal soul from bondage to the material world.

BUDDHISM was founded in the same period and region by **Siddhartha** (?563–483?) of the clan of Gautama and the hill tribe of Sakya, who attained "illumination" (*bodhi*) at Bodh-Gaya after he had convinced himself that Brahman doctrine and asceticism were alike ineffective. He taught the means of escape from the world of suffering and rebirth to **Nirvana,** a state of peaceful release from rebirth, through a twofold way of life, withdrawal for meditation and personal religious experience, combined with strict morality and self-sacrificial altruism. Shortly after the Buddha's death, 500 disciples met at Rajagriha to rehearse together his doctrine (*dharma*) and his code of discipline (*vinaya*) for the monastic community (*sangha*) which he founded. That community served as the instrument for propagation of his religion, which, like Christianity, offers salvation to all who accept the simple doctrine and ethics and seek for personal religious experience. A second **council at Vaisali** a century after the Buddha's death was concerned with the *vinaya*. About this time were formed the four *Nikayas,* earliest extant anthologies from more primitive collections (*Pratimoksa,* etc.).

517–509 B.C. **Darius I** of Achaemenid Persia seized Gandhara from the disunited Aryans and sent his Greek admiral Skylax to explore the Indus. *Kharoshthi* script, used in northwestern India (5th century), is based on Aramaic of the Persian scribes. It remained confined to the northwest.

The *Sutras* (c. 6th–2nd century B.C.),

"Threads" through the **Brahmanas,** compendious manuals designed to be learned by heart, prescribe rules of conduct of various Vedic schools, regions, and periods, for sacrifice and incidentally, for daily life, describe a society in which plural marriage is permitted, child marriage recommended, while numerous taboos mark the beginning of an elaborate theory of caste defilement. **Panini** (c. 400) gives in his *Sutra* the earliest extant Sanskrit grammar, with a wealth of illustration which is augmented by the *Varttikas* or supplementary rules of Katyayana (c. 180) and the rich *Mahabhashya* (Great Commentary) of Patanjali (c. 150 B.C.).

327–325. Alexander the Great invaded the Punjab, crossed the Indus (Feb. 326), was welcomed to the rich and cultured city of Takshasila (Taxila), won a battle on the banks of the Jhelum, and withdrew on demand of his troops, sending Nearchus with a fleet by sea.

c. 321–c. 184. The **MAURYA DYNASTY** was founded by **Chandragupta** (c. 321–c. 297), who first united northern India from Herat to the Ganges delta, with his capital at Pataliputra (Patna), and who defended it against Seleucus Nicator (c. 305). The emperor ruled with aid of a privy council and an elaborate official hierarchy, paid army, and secret service. Administration of public works embraced highways and irrigation.

A Jain high-priest **Bhadrabahu** led a portion of his community south into the Carnatic to escape a 12-year famine in Bengal. On their return (c. 300) the still resident monks in church council at Pataliputra undertook to collect the Jain scriptures, but were unable to record some of the older *purvas.* The canon of the Svetambara sect, the *Siddhanta,* written in its present form at the council of Valabhi (5th or early 6th century A.D.), is consequently incomplete. The returning monks maintained a stricter rule, avoided the council, and, as the **Digambara sect,** have steadily maintained that the true canon is lost. The Jain community had then already begun a westward migration to Ujjain and Mathura.

c. 274–c. 236. ASOKA'S EMPIRE, extended by conquest of Kalinga (Orissa with the Circars, c. 262), embraced two-thirds of the peninsula. As a devout convert he ruled at home and abroad in accordance with Buddhist law. Besides many pious foundations, he engraved on rocks and pillars throughout his empire in true Achaemenid style edicts in vernacular Prakrit exhorting respect for animal life, reverence, and truth, and appointed censors to enforce these injunctions. He sent Buddhist missions to Syria, Egypt, Cyrene, Macedonia, and Epirus, and with much greater success to Burma and Ceylon (c. 251–246; Aryan conquest of Ceylon, traditional date 485 B.C.). The Punjab and Gandhara became a stronghold of the liberal Mahasanghikas, who developed a canonical tradition enriched by legends to bring the life of the Buddha into that region. The canon was then or in the 2nd century in Kausambhi, Sanchi, and Malwa expanded and fixed in Pali to form the *Tripitaka* ("Three Baskets"): *sutra* (doctrine), *vinaya* (monastic code), and *abhidharma* (philosophical discussion). The Pali tradition, which was carried to Ceylon and there preserved intact, says a third church council was held at Pataliputra under Asoka.

The west remained the chief stronghold of **Brahman doctrine** which now reasserted itself. The gradual absorption of substratum cults within the formal brahmanistic framework under the tutelage of the Brahmans gave rise to the complex system of beliefs and practices known as **Hinduism.** As major gods arose **Siva,** personification of cosmic forces of destruction and reproduction implicit in all change; **Vishnu,** god of the sacrifice who was recognized as incarnate in **Krishna,** a hero presented by popular legend at Mathura as romantic lover of cowherd-girls, and on the west coast as a somber warrior. A second avatar or reincarnation of Vishnu was **Rama,** symbol of conjugal devotion. To Vishnu as Preserver and Siva as Destroyer was added **Brahma** the Creator, a personification of the Brahman principle of the *Upanishads.*

The *Mahabharata,* an epic poem composed by several generations of bards, seems to have taken form about the 4th century B.C., although probably revised early in our era. The original 9000 verses were swelled to 100,000 by later accretions, including myths, legends, popular philosophy, and moralizing narratives. It recounts a feud between the wily Kurus and the fierce Pandus. Krishna takes prominent part in the struggle as counselor of Arjuna, the Pandu chief. Noteworthy within the epic is the *Bhagavadgita* ("Song of the Lord"), which first urges personal love and devotion (*bhakti*) to Krishna. The *Ramayana,* although traditionally ascribed to Valmiki (?6th century B.C.), is, in its present form, later than the *Mahabharata.* It recounts the trials of Rama in rescuing, with an army of apes, his wife, Sita, from a fiend. Both epics are composed in a popular form of Sanskrit.

206. Antiochus III of Syria occupied Gandhara, but shortly lost it to the Greek (Yavana) King Demetrius of Bactria, who (c. 185) seized the Punjab also. Eastward expansion of the Yavanas was halted (after c. 162) by civil war between the houses of Euthydemus, represented especially by the warrior-philosopher Menander, and Eucratides.

c. 184–c. 72. The **SUNGA DYNASTY** was founded in the Ganges Valley and in Malwa by **Pushyamitra,** who overthrew the Maurya, repulsed the Yavanas under Menander, and by a Brahman reaction may have stimulated Buddhist emigration to Bharhut, Sanchi, and Mathura. The dynasty in its later years was overshadowed if not actually displaced by its line of Brahman advisers, the **Kanvas.**

At the same time (c. 100 B.C.–50 A.D.) flourished in Gandhara a school of sculpture which created a Buddha image based on the Greek Apollo. Only a few decadent monuments (mostly 1st century A.D.) bear dates (318, 356, 384 with coin of Kadphises, 399) by reference to a Mauryan era (?322 B.C.) or more probably the Seleucid era of 312 B.C. Stylistic influence of the art of Gandhara was exerted chiefly in Afghanistan (frescoes of Bamiyan and Dukhtar-i-Nushirwan), where it was fused with Sassanian influences, eastern Turkestan, China of the North Wei dynasty, and Japan. But its iconographic formulae were accepted by the entire Buddhist world. Meanwhile, in western India (near Bombay) were cut in rocky cliffs Buddhist *chaityas* or temple halls, of which the earliest (c. 125–100 B.C.) are at Bhaja, Kondane, Pitalkhora, and Ajanta (cave 10); the largest, finest, and latest (1st century A.D.) at Karli. Jain caves in the Udayagiri hills of Orissa are of similar date.

Scythian **Sakas** who, dislodged by the Yueh-chih from the Jaxartes, had overwhelmed the Greeks in Bactria (c. 135 B.C.), only to be expelled thence also by the Yueh-chih (shortly after 128), invaded the Punjab from Baluchistan and Sind (Greek Indo-Scythia).

(*Cont. p. 141.*)

8. CHINA, TO 221 B.C.

Present information indicates that the Chinese parent people, their language, and their civilization are alike native to North China. It seems probable that, at a primitive stage, they diverged from the Miao-tzu, who now find refuge in the southern mountains, the various T'ai peoples (Dioi, Laotians, Siamese) of Kwangsi and Indo-China, and the Tibeto-Burman peoples (Lolo, Mosso, Shan, and Tibetans) of southwestern China. **Peking Man,** who had some Chinese characteristics, lived in the Tertiary Pleistocene epoch. Paleolithic culture deposits (without skeletal material as yet) are known. Three independent Neolithic cultures are found, characterized by: (1) crude gray pottery with pointed foot; (2) red and black painted pottery similar to that found near Odessa and at Susa; (3) thin black pottery tentatively attributed to a Pacific civilization. The latter is linked with historic China through use of tripod vessels with hollow legs, and bone divination.

During the Shang dynasty the first systematic **astronomical observations** were made (Chinese astronomy represents the longest history of observational science). Use of the gnomon dates from this time, as do the first observations of eclipses and nova (14th century B.C.). By 240 B.C. **Halley's comet** was regularly observed. Mathematics developed to the point that by the 4th century B.C. a fully developed decimal, place-value system was in use. Within the next century Pythagoras' theorem was known and a symbol for zero used. In practical mechanics the balance, steelyard, and scaling ladder were understood. In optics the principles of refraction and reflection from plane and curved surfaces were also understood.

Two literary sources contain genealogies of **the early dynasties,** with chronologies which diverge prior to 841 B.C. Neither earlier chronology has any authority whatever. Nor can historical value be attached to legends which describe a predynastic golden age of fabulous culture-heroes and model rulers. Of the **Hsia Dynasty** we have only the calendar, honorific use of the name, and the putative genealogy of seventeen kings. It was followed by the **Shang** or **Yin Dynasty** of thirty kings, who practiced fraternal succession and who were masters of the Yellow River plain from the mountains of Shansi and the Mongolian plateau to the Shantung massif. Probably the last twelve ruled at An-yang from about the 12th century. The names of twenty-eight kings are found in oracular inscriptions from this site. Advanced pictographic and ideographic script; conventional decoration and perfect casting of bronze vessels; reliance upon ancestral guidance through divination.

c. 1000–950 B.C. The **WESTERN CHOU DYNASTY** established its capital at Hao in the Wei Valley. It exercised actual control over its feudatories only until the murder of King Yu in 771. The king was responsible for sacrifices to his ancestors and to gods of the soil, and for the agricultural calendar, as well as for administration. Tenure of land and office was restricted to a pedigreed aristocracy, whose clan names suggest a possible early matriarchate. The peasantry lived a communal life in the summer fields and winter villages, tilled common land for their prince, and practiced exogamic group betrothals and marriages. The Chinese communities were still surrounded and interspersed with "barbarian," i.e. less cultured, tribes.

770–256. The **EASTERN CHOU DYNASTY** reigned powerless at Loyang with diminishing moral authority over the frequently warring princes of surrounding (nominally) feudal states.

722–481. **"Annals" period** of loose confederation. The chief states were Ch'i and Lu, which divided modern Shantung; Sung, west of Lu; Yen, on the northeast; Chin, in modern Shansi; Ch'in, in the former Chou lands to the west; and Ch'u, in the middle Long River Valley.

458–424. **Partition of Chin** among three vassal houses: Han, Chao, and Wei.

412. Institution of **ever-normal granary** by Marquis Wen of Wei.

403–221. **Epoch of the Warring States,** opened by royal recognition of the partition of Chin.

391. **Change of dynasty in Ch'i,** which, with Chin, had been a chief bulwark of the "middle kingdoms" against the largely non-Chinese states of Ch'u and Ch'in.

334. **Ch'u** expanded eastward, annexing the coastal state of Yueh.

333. **"Vertical"** (i.e. north and south) **alliance of six states,** arranged by Su Ch'in, failed to restrain Ch'in, which conquered Shu (in modern Szechwan) in 316.

307. **Prince Wu-ling** of Chao gained military advantage for his state by adoption of Tatar dress (Iranian trousers, belt, and boots, which now gradually displaced the loose Chinese costume) and enlistment of cavalry archers, but the continual wars of the eastern states weakened them all, paving the way for

230–221. **CONQUEST BY CH'IN OF ALL ITS RIVALS.** Golden age of philosophy in China, as in Greece. Four major **schools of ethics,** which absorbed the practical Chinese to the exclusion of abstract speculation: (1) Coherent teaching embodied in *The Canon of the Way and of Virtue* (5th century or later?), attributed to **Lao-tzu,** of whom nothing is known: Man is part of an harmonious universe governed by transcendent law, and finds his best ethical guide in his own nature. **Yang Chu,** an individualist, sought self-expression in harmless hedonism. **Chuang Chou** (fl. 339–329), the most brilliantly imaginative and sub-

tle of all literary stylists, through parables taught *laissez faire,* mysticism, and relativity of truth. (2) **Mo Ti** (5th–4th century?) taught universal love, pacifism, economy, and the duty of the wise to set up standards. New dialectic method borrowed by all later writers. From him stem the schools of pacifists and sophists. (3) **K'ung Ch'iu** or **Confucius** (551–479 or later?) taught that clear thinking and self-discipline lead the superior man to correct action in all his relationships. Through moral influence and education he should lead the common herd with kindliness and justice; paternalism; golden rule. Having failed as minister of justice in Lu (500–496) to secure co-operation of his prince, he edited the *Annals* of that state (722–481) to illustrate his monarchical doctrine of political morality. (A much richer chronicle of the feudal states, composed c. 300, is now appended to these *Annals* as part of the *Tso Commentary.*) His precepts were gathered a century later. **Meng K'o** or **Mencius** (fl. 324–314) urged the now independent princes to win the world, i.e. North China, by exemplary conduct, declaring popular welfare to be the objective and condition of royal authority. A humanitarian, he elaborated the moral code to assure proper development of man's beneficent nature. **Hsun K'uang** or **Hsun-tzu** (c. 300–235) taught that man requires education and formation of correct habit to realize his capacity to order nature. He suggested forced conformity to standards. He synthesized earlier doctrines, and, although a muddy writer, so impressed his students that even mutually opposed thinkers for a century claimed succession from him. (4) **Shang Yang,** minister of Ch'in, 359–338, organized strong centralized government, created an official hierarchy, and encouraged agriculture in that state under a severe legal code. His reforms paved the way for the triumph of Ch'in. **Han-fei-tzu** (d. 233) and **Li Ssu** (d. 208), disciples of Hsün-tzu, developed further the legalist doctrine of compulsion to justify Ch'in's use of military force to unify the warring states.

Greek influence, probably traceable to Alexander's invasion of Sogdiana (c. 327), is seen in correct statement of the intervals of the Pythagorean musical scale by **Lu Pu-wei,** prime minister of Ch'in (c. 250), and in diagrammatic illustration of the Pythagorean theorem. (*Cont. p. 144.*)

B. GREECE

1. THE EARLY PERIOD, TO c. 500 B.C.

a. GEOGRAPHY AND CLIMATE

Mainland Greece is the southern extension and end of the Balkan Peninsula and marks the termination of various mountain ranges running north to south. The coastline is therefore much broken and the neighboring Aegean Islands are actually submerged mountains. The climate is dry and stimulating. Rainfall, which exceeds forty inches per annum in the Adriatic, is only about sixteen in Attica, making drought a constant menace. The weather, though chilly enough in winter, is rarely freezing, while in summer the mid-day heat is hard to bear in the valleys, though sundown invariably brings relief. Thus, the climate and the terrain demand vitality, and reward effort with enough wealth to encourage a robust civilization.

Most of Greece is divided into small compartments by the mountain ranges. This made natural the development of numerous small city states, characteristic of classical Greece. The towns, however, were essentially the dwelling places of an agrarian population, and the city states more or less unions of towns or villages. Boeotia, never really united, had 22 towns according to Homer; classical Athens (i.e. the union of all Attica) was exceptional, being a union of no fewer than about 120 towns and villages.

Over large areas of the country the soil was thin and rocky, making the cultivation of grain difficult, though olives and grapes ripened well in the rainless summers. Since much of the required grain had to be imported, sea-borne commerce developed at an early stage, the grain being paid for in terms of manufactured goods such as Greek vases, which are found in number throughout the Mediterranean world. But the civilization of ancient Greece at no time depended largely on manufacture or trade; it was basically agrarian.

Greece is almost split in two by the Gulf of Corinth, which runs in from the west, the narrow Isthmus of Corinth being the only link between the southern part, the Peloponnesus ("Island of Pelops"), and the northern. But this geographical division was less important than the difference in the degree of contact with lands of earlier civilization, notably Crete. Crete is the largest and southernmost of the Aegean Islands and its influence spread in mainland Greece through those valleys that faced south and east, such as Messenia and Laconia, the Argolid, Attica, and even Boeotia.

Thessaly, more distant, remained somewhat backward, while northern and western Greece, having fewer harbors and being constantly exposed to barbarian invasion from the north, remained savage until, late in Greek history, Alexander and the vigorous Macedonians were able to take over leadership of the Greeks and the government of most of the known world.

Greece's out-of-door climate and town life enabled the inhabitants to engage freely in social activity—gymnastics, politics, litigation, discussion in the agora (forum or market-place), festivals, athletic contests, dancing, drama, and banquets, to say nothing of war. Polis-dwelling became an essential characteristic of every Greek; the Greeks created **politics** and **political theory.**

b. THE MINOAN CIVILIZATION, c. 3000–c. 1100 B.C.

Long before the Greeks arrived in Greece, one of the world's distinctive civilizations had come into being on the largest of the Aegean Islands, Crete. This island (156 miles long) has, in its central and eastern sections, enough small plains and arable valleys, with enough rain in most winters, to enable its inhabitants, when they were reinforced from Asia Minor (not later than c. 2700 B.C.) to emerge into the Bronze Age earlier than any other people of Europe.

The Cretan civilization is called "Minoan" from the name of the legendary King Minos of Knossos, which was always the principal city. The language of the early Minoans remains unknown. Throughout a millennium and a half they were not invaded nor even much affected by outsiders. Their script, when they came to write (c. 1700 B.C.), was almost wholly their own, as was their art. It was a culture marked by color and gaiety. Their art, inspired by direct observation of nature, was freer than any in Europe prior to the 19th century. Their grandest palaces, built of stone, were aggregations of buildings around a large open court, with no insistence on symmetry. The Minoans were devoted to sports, including hazardous bull-jumping, rather than to war; their towns were at all times unwalled.

The form of government was probably monarchical, but for a long time was not highly organized. The king was evidently the chief figure in religious worship and his palace was the seat of religious cults. There were also other gods and goddesses, nature-derived and very human, worshiped in caves or at open-air shrines rather than in formal temples. Literature was doubtless oral, and was probably sung. The Minoans seem to have had little love for written records, but crafts such as pottery and painting were highly developed. The palaces reflect comfortable, varied, and refined living. They contained grand suites, commodious storerooms for goods and products paid as taxes (there was no coinage), light-wells with many-storied staircases, and sanitary arrangements superior to any in Europe before recent times.

Minoan civilization went through three main phases of development, each with three subdivisions, making nine successive periods in all. We thus have E(arly) M(inoan) I, II, III; M(iddle) M(inoan), I, II, III; L(ate) M(inoan) I, II, III. The evidence that distinguishes them is derived mostly from changes in pottery. Indeed, practically all that is known of Minoan Crete is based on the findings of archaeology. The various periods are dated (mostly approximately) from the quite infrequent contacts of Crete with Egypt and the evidence provided by Egyptian records. It suffices to mention

c. 2700–c. 1900 B.C. **Early Minoan**
c. 1900–c. 1600 B.C. **Middle Minoan**
c. 1600–c. 1100 B.C. **Late Minoan,** subdivided into
    c. 1600–c. 1450 Late Minoan I
    c. 1450–c. 1400 Late Minoan II (at Knossos only)
    c. 1400–c. 1100 Late Minoan III (the Mycenaean period)

EARLY MINOAN. This was a period of rapid development compared to the Stone Age, but slow compared to later periods. Stone and bone tools were still in use; bronze was only slowly introduced and, though of crucial importance, was never really abundant. Pottery was still shaped by hand, not on a wheel. People emerged from their cave dwellings and Neolithic hovels and began to live in towns. Some sort of community organization, the first government, must have come into being. Writing of a primitive kind began to appear on seals and as isolated markings.

MIDDLE MINOAN. During this period pottery was thrown on the wheel and was perfected to the point where it could be made as thin as eggshell. Free but well-judged design and profuse color suggest the vitality which led to the founding (in MMI) of the great palaces at Knossos, Phaistos, and Mallia. The process was one of uniting separate buildings. Government evidently was now more centralized: the palace became the royal court and the administrative center, with storerooms for taxes in kind and arsenals for whatever armed forces were maintained. It was also the center for religious observances, an arena for sports and theatrical exhibitions, and the home of the arts and literature.

Minoan Linear A is the name given to the writing of this period, to distinguish it from the earlier signs on images and seals (hieroglyphics) and to distinguish it also from the later **Linear B** script. Linear A took the form of fairly complex signs, most of them representing a consonant plus a vowel, so that it constituted a syllabary rather than an alphabet. Other signs were single symbols, such as for man, woman, sheep, goat, olive, etc., standing for whole words like the modern dollar or pound sterling sign. Counting was by simple signs for units—tens, hundreds, etc. on a decimal system. The numbers can be easily read, as can most of the symbols. But for the syllable signs even the vowels are not positively known in most instances, nor are the meanings of more than a very few words, since even the identity of the language has not yet been determined. Linear A was at first used for short inscriptions signifying ownership and the like. Later it was used for writing accounts on clay tablets. Not much of it survives, for there are fewer than two hundred even of the tablets extant and these are brief and careless. Paucity of the material adds to the difficulty of decipherment.

THE THALASSOCRACY OF MINOS. By MM III the Minoans, who had always carried on some trade with Egypt, the Levant, and more recently with some Aegean Islands (e.g. Melos), began a more aggressive foreign policy. Their legendary king, Minos, was said to have founded a sea empire (thalassocracy). The proofs that some such empire existed are: (1) the Athenian **Theseus legend,** which, for the purposes of the story, admits that Athens was then tributary to the **Minotaur** (the Minos Bull), i.e. to the ruler of the palace where the bull-sports were held; (2) the fact that no fewer than eleven different places, all seaports, later are known as bearing the name **Minoa.** They were probably trading, raiding, and tribute-collecting posts. The first European empire was doubtless primitive, loosely organized, semi-piratical. Archaeology has as yet discovered only a few actual overseas Minoan settlements, which, like others, were probably not very populous, since Crete hardly had the manpower needed to garrison many foreign establishments. But the tribute and booty collected abroad may well have financed the new palaces, and the thalassocracy, begun perhaps in MM III, continued into the next period, Late Minoan I.

c. THE GREEK MAINLAND IN THE BRONZE AGE

Mainland Greece had had Neolithic settlements, at least in Macedonia, for thousands of years. At the beginning of the Bronze Age, Greece like Crete was invaded by people from Asia Minor who used names ending in –ssos, such as Knossos, Parnassos, and in –inth, such as Labyrinth, Corinth. Certain names have survived. Narcissus comes to us from their language and Olympos probably meant "high mountain." Neither they nor their Neolithic predecessors spoke the Greek language.

Greek-speakers arrived in Greece at the beginning of the period that corresponds approximately to Early Minoan III in Crete, i.e. about 2200 B.C. They came from the north, wore heavier clothing, and designed their houses for protection against cold. Their pottery, which appeared also in Troy, was smooth-surfaced. But most of their civilization they acquired only in the course of centuries and from the Minoans.

The **Minoan influence** was naturally felt most strongly in the valleys that faced south toward Crete: Messenia, Laconia, the Argolid, Attica, but also Boeotia and certain localities in Thessaly. In time strong towns grew up, the richest and most powerful being **Mycenae**, at the head of the Argolid. The graves discovered by **Heinrich Schliemann** at Mycenae contained hundreds of objects of gold, wrought in a style that shows extensive Minoan cultural domination. But the Minoan thalassocracy never actually ruled Mycenae and even in culture differences remained. Thus each Greek king was buried with a small arsenal of swords; the Greeks were stern and warlike. In time, having greater resources, they would turn against their teachers.

THE GREEKS IN CRETE: LINEAR B. In A.D. 1900 **Sir Arthur Evans** discovered at Knossos large numbers (eventually some thousands) of clay tablets in a script obviously derived from Linear A and hence known as **Linear B.** Numerals, but little else, could be read, yet it was clear that the tablets were all accounts, that the language itself was different from that of Linear A, and that they had been preserved by being burned in a great fire that destroyed Knossos, apparently c. 1400 B.C. When, in 1939, **Carl Blegen** found similar tablets in the palace at **Pylos** (Messenia), scholars still refrained from believing that the language could be Greek, until in 1952 **Sir Michael Ventris** achieved the decipherment and it became evident that the language was undeniably Greek and that it antedated by half a millennium the Homeric epics, hitherto the earliest Greek known.

c. 1450 B.C. The Greeks must have captured Knossos sometime in the 15th century B.C.,

for their swords, chariots, and pottery as well as their tablets can be recognized at Knossos. They used writing for administrative purposes, the tablets giving us accounts of thousands of sheep and of other riches, likewise of great stores of weapons and also of cults with the names of gods familiar later—most of the Greek pantheon. A highly bureaucratic state was centered in the palace of Knossos and on the mainland at Pylos, at Mycenae, and at other places familiar to us from Homer.

d. THE MYCENAEAN AGE

Late Minoan III was dominated by Mycenae. Pottery shows that her trade extended from the Levant to Sicily. Hittite documents reveal the Greeks as a strong Aegean power and even Egypt felt her influence. This was a period of expansion abroad as well as grandeur at home. At Mycenae huge beehive tombs—their contents long since rifled—attest the manpower and engineering ability of the ancestors of Agamemnon. But wealth brought dangers: the palaces had to be fortified. Mycenae, Tiryns, Athens, Thebes still preserve great walls dating from this period.

Secure for the time at home, the Greeks united in a great joint **attack on Troy** which, once rich, was now poorer and weaker. The Trojans, threatened by siege, stocked their houses and held out for a long time before the city was taken and destroyed by the Greek host under Agamemnon. This was the city called Troy VIIa in the sequence of settlements.

e. THE DARK AGE

The Trojan War was the last effort of Greek expansion before a great invasion of peoples coming down through Asia Minor and going all the way to Egypt, where they fell back. Some among them, the Philistines, settled the country that was later named after them. As for the Greeks, Mycenaean trade was cut off and then Greece itself was invaded. **Pylos** which was never walled, was sacked and burned (c. 1200 B.C.). Unprotected buildings near Mycenae were also destroyed and eventually by about 1100 B.C. Mycenae itself had fallen, as had the other cities, including the half-ruined, half-inhabited palace at Knossos.

The **Dorians** were the new Greek invaders. They came in the age of iron and may have brought iron with them. In any case, the consequences of their invasion were terrific. Overnight the elaborate palace bureaucracies disappeared. Records in Linear B also vanished. The Greeks became illiterate and were reduced to small local communities. Their states had been beheaded and the old title of king (*wanax*) had no bearer. Even Athens, though itself uninvaded, suffered like the rest of the country.

Pottery had long since, in the imperial days of Mycenae, lost its easy naturalism. Forms had hardened; they were now stiff and the pottery style developed in the Dark Age was geometric. Once again pottery was the one continuing element. Archaeology is the method of knowing such details as can be discovered about the Dark Age. There is, however, some additional information available to us. In this period the Greeks, faced by distress and displacement at home, sailed to found cities at promising sites in Asia Minor, on the coast of which the Aeolians established settlements in the north, the Ionians in the center, and even the Dorians in the very south. This was the first massive Greek colonial movement.

f. THE GREEK POLIS

Split up and forced back on local resources, the Greeks now developed the unit that was to be central in the classical period: the **polis,** the roots of which were Mycenaean. Outwardly the poleis of the Dark Age, as earlier, were houses clustered around a palace, which usually stood on some strong hill, called the **Akropolis.** The king (now *basileus*) was the chief of the priests and also the highest judge and the commander of the forces. But there was no longer a bureaucracy nor any great concentration of wealth. There was not even any writing.

Yet Greek society had some organization. In Ionian cities the people were grouped into four tribes, each with its own head and cult. In Dorian cities there were only three tribes. Within the tribes "brotherhoods" (*phratriai*) appeared, composed of members sufficiently related to each other to certify proper birth, which was the qualification of membership. Hence the phratriai became guardians of citizenship, for which membership in some brotherhood was required. Families of tradition and substance formed smaller units (*gene*), virtually noble. These gene furnished the higher officials and the most eminent of them provided the king. Lesser citizens could attend an assembly, but until heavy-armed infantry learned to stand against cavalry, the horse-owning nobles were superior. Thus the royal powers were far more dependent on community goodwill than were the tight palace bureaucracies of the Mycenaean period. In the new poleis the way was open for royal powers eventually to be divided and shared by the nobles and for the other citizens also to participate in the city's management, as they already did in its defense and in its festivals. Nobles had no special titles or dress, nor any sort of a fenced-off status.

g. EPIC POETRY

Ruinous though the destruction had been, so that even quarrying was a lost art and large statues and stone buildings could not be constructed, memories of the grandeur of the past were still vivid in the impoverished present. Bards sang songs of the ancient heroes and songs preserved what the people loved: not the bureaucracy, but the wealth and might of Mycenae and the other great places, the prowess of the men of old, the names and ancestries of the leaders, the tales of mighty doings. Of all these heroic songs, there are preserved to us two, the *Iliad* and *Odyssey,* products (a) of the traditions handed down about the Bronze Age heroes; (b) of the illiterate Dark Age looking back with yearning and expressing itself in an oral art requiring life practice for mastery; (c) of a new acquisition of literacy in the Greek Renascence that followed the Dark Age.

h. THE GREEK RENASCENCE

The Greek revival was slow in coming, at least 300 years (c. 1100–c. 800 B.C.). Then, quickened by inspiration from the old civilizations of the East and by the accumulation of resources, the Greeks developed rapidly. Pottery shows the change: in **Proto-Corinthian** and **Proto-Attic** the stiffness of geometric design gives way to a new feeling for living, curved forms of men and animals; color reappears; ornament, often symmetrical, is vigorous. A whole new set of vase shapes is invented. Spread by the growing trade with distant places, then by colonies, Proto-Corinthian becomes the luxury pottery of the Mediterranean world.

Coinage, invented in Asia Minor, facilitated trade. Arts and crafts began to flourish as major activities in quarrying were resumed. Progress was made in ship construction, and exploration went beyond trade. The **oracle at Delphi** served as a gathering place for information and helped to guide new ventures.

Contact with the Phoenicians was inevitable, and from them the Greeks learned an alphabet of excellent simplicity and usefulness. A little adaptation made it fully adequate for the Greek language. Its virtue is clear from the fact that the Romans too found it good and passed it on to us. The Greek adaptation was made not earlier than 750 B.C. By the end of the 8th century some scribe, seeing the possibilities, persuaded the (oral) poet **Homer** to dictate his best songs about the heroes of the Trojan War.

Homer perceived that, relieved of the urgency of oral composition, he could form his expression at his leisure, and could bring to bear all his incomparable talent. And so we have the *Iliad* and *Odyssey*. "Homeric" hymns and the whole body of **Hesiodic verse** were set down before the oral narrative art vanished.

i. ARISTOCRACY AND TYRANNY. COLONIZATION

c. 900–600. Monarchies were replaced throughout Greece by aristocracies, and the kings vanished or were reduced to a titular office (the *archon basileus* at Athens), save in Sparta, which always continued to have two kings simultaneously, and in Macedonia, where ancient monarchy persisted unbroken. Elsewhere the nobles retained the dominant power in the state through the possession of good iron arms and the acquisition of property at the expense of the poor farmers.

c. 760–550. Love of exploration and adventure, distress and food shortage due to large holdings of land by the nobles led to **colonization,** encouraged first by the aristocrats to get rid of discontent and then by the tyrants for political and commercial advantage. The traditional dates of the more important colonies in east and west, which were entered almost simultaneously, follow: Miletus colonized Cyzicus (757) and Abydos (756) on the Euxine. Through friendship with Psammetichus I of Egypt, Miletus also joined other cities in founding the important trading post of Naucratis, in the Nile Delta (640). Phocaea settled Marssalia (Marseilles) in Gaul (600). Rhodes settled Gela (688) and Gela founded Acragas (580), both in Sicily. Thera colonized Cyrene in North Africa (630). Chalcis and Eretria in Euboea sent colonies to the Chalcidice (northern Aegean) and to Sicily, notably Catana and Leontini (728), Rhegium (730), also Cumae (Bay of Naples, 760). Megara colonized the Hellespont with Chalcedon (660) and Byzantium, as well as settling the Sicilian Megara Hyblaea (728). Corinth occupied the strategic Potidaea (northern Aegean, 609), Corcyra (735), and Syracuse in Sicily (735). In southern Italy (Magna Graecia) Achaea settled Sybaris (721) and Croton (710); while Sparta, occupied with the conquest of Messenia, founded only Taras (Tarentum, 705). Athens sent out no colonies until later. In the end, Greek colonies occupied most of the Mediterranean coasts all the way to Gibraltar, wherever the Etruscans, Carthaginians, Egyptians, and Levantines did not exclude them.

Trade had preceded colonization and in turn colonization encouraged trade, since not only the settlers but the peoples among whom they settled desired luxury products (oil, wine, and manufactures) from Greece, which they repaid with raw materials. But the colonies were formally and actually in the main independent. Greater skill in technical processes like metallurgy and pottery allowed the Greeks to compete favorably with the Phoenicians and encouraged the growth of an industrial population, as well as a trading one, in the cities. New farm land was, however, a strong motive. Slavery increased and coined money was introduced from Lydia into Ionia and thence into Greece, traditionally by King Pheidon of Argos (c. 680). The two prominent standards of currency were the Euboean and the Aeginetan.

c. 650–500. **Tyrannies** arose in Greece, for a variety of causes. The aristocracies refused political equality to the landless traders and manufactures, the peasants were oppressed by the rich and fell into debt and then were reduced to slavery or exile; slaves began to compete with free labor. Ambitious individuals capitalized this discontent to overthrow the constituted governments and establish themselves as tyrants in almost all the Greek cities, with the notable exception of Sparta, whose balanced constitution, organized to dominate the numerous serfs (*helots*), enabled it to preserve its aristocratic form. The tyrants were on the whole popular and successful; they kept the people happy with festivals and public works, they diminished the power of the nobles, and they reduced class and ethnic distinctions. They fostered, especially, the artistic and intellectual life. **Lyric poetry** flourished; **Archilochus** the father of satire (c. 700); the individual lyric of the Aeolians, **Alcaeus** and **Sappho** of Lesbos (c. 600); the choral lyric of the Dorians, **Stesichorus** (c. 650) and **Arion** (c. 600). Contact with the east led to the eclipse of the geometric style in art by the **oriental** (animal) **style.** Philosophy began with the Milesian school of **Thales** (predicted the eclipse of 585), **Anaximenes,** and **Anaximander,** who began to seek knowledge for its own sake, to find a rational explanation for natural phenomena; they were the first to try to prove any statements that they made, within a logical system. Among the important tyrants were: **Thrasybulus** of Miletus (c. 620); **Polycrates** of Samos (c. 530), noted for his navy, with which he almost dominated the Aegean, his building, and his alliance with Amasis of Egypt; **Cleisthenes** of Sicyon (c. 600); **Theagenes** of Megara (c. 640); **Periander** of Corinth (c. 600), patron of poetry, who recovered control of Corcyra from the oligarchs; and the **Peisistratids** in Athens. The tyrannies generally were overthrown in the second generation, since they had served their purpose, and the tyrants' sons, born to power, tended to become oppressive. Moreover, Sparta consistently opposed them.

j. FORMATION OF THE GREEK STATES

(1) Asia Minor

c. 690. The **Kingdom of Phrygia** (traditional kings Midas and Gordius), which had considerably influenced the Asiatic Greeks, was destroyed by the **Cimmerians**, invaders from southern Russia. Its place was taken by the **Kingdom of Lydia**, in which Gyges founded the active Mermnad Dynasty (c. 685). He and his successors raided the Greek cities, but were prevented from conquest by further incursions of the Cimmerians, who sacked Sardis and slew Gyges (c. 652).

585, May 28. **Alyattes**, third king of Lydia, and **Cyaxares**, king of Media, ended their war by a treaty defining their boundary at the river Halys. Thales is said to have predicted the eclipse which induced them to treat and which, therefore, determines the date. **Croesus** acceded to the Lydian throne (c. 560) and began to reduce the Ionian cities to a tributary condition, save for Miletus. His mild rule, however, did not check their political growth (tyrannies).

547. **CYRUS**, who had united his Persian kingdom with the Median by his defeat of Astyages (550), now defeated Croesus, crossed the Halys, sacked Sardis, and captured Croesus himself. His general, Harpagus, subdued the Ionian cities, save Miletus, which retained its favorable status, and put in pro-Persian tyrants. With the loss of freedom intellectual activity diminished.

(2) The Peloponnese

c. 800. **Sparta** had become mistress of Laconia and had colonized the coast of Messenia. She warred with **Tegea**, chief city of the backward and disunited Arcadians, who maintained a loose religious union centering about the primitive worship on Mt. Lycaeum. Politically, kingship survived in Arcadia into the 5th century. **Corinth**, under the close oligarchical rule of the Bacchiadae, had become commercially important and, until c. 720, dominated its smaller neighbor **Megara**. **Argos**, though claiming the hegemony of Greece as heir of Mycenae, remained a weak state.

c. 736–716. In the **FIRST MESSENIAN WAR**, Sparta, led by **King Theopompus**, conquered Messenia and divided the rich plain into lots, which the Messenians, as helots, worked for their Spartiate masters. Besides helots and Spartiates, there was a third class of Laconians, the *perioeci* (dwellers-around), who were free but not possessed of citizen rights. Sparta still, however, had an artistic and intellectual life equal to any in Greece, especially in respect to choral poetry.

c. 680. **King Pheidon** made Argos for a brief space powerful. He defeated Sparta allied with Tegea in the **battle of Hysiae** (669), and, in support of revolting Aegina, crushed Epidaurus and her ally Athens. Pheidon is said to have introduced coinage into Greece, perhaps with a mint on Aegina. After his death, the powers of the rulers were curtailed and Argos declined.

c. 650–630. In the **Second Messenian War**, Sparta with difficulty crushed her revolting subjects, who were led by Aristomenes, master of Arcadia, and who took refuge on Mt. Eira.

c. 610. By the so-called *Eunomia*, the Spartans, fearing further revolts, completely reorganized the state to make it more severely military. Citizen youth from the age of seven were taken for continual military training. Men of military age lived in barracks and ate at common messes (*syssitia, phiditia*). Five local tribes replaced the three Dorian hereditary ones and the army was correspondingly divided, creating the *Dorian phalanx*. The *gerousia*, comprising 28 elders and the two kings, had the initiative in legislation, though the *apella* of all citizens had the final decision. The chief magistrates, *ephors*, were increased to five, with wider powers especially after the ephorate of **Cheilon** (556). Later ages attributed the reforms to the hero **Lycurgus** in the 9th century, perhaps because the new laws were put under his protection.

c. 560. Sparta finally reduced the Tegeates to the status of subject allies, not helots. She then (c. 546, **battle of the 300 Champions**), took the plain of Thyreatis from Argos. The kings Anaxandridas and Ariston extended the policy of alliances to all the Peloponnesian states save Achaea and Argos to form the **Peloponnesian League**, in which the allies had equal votes on foreign policies, contributed two-thirds of their forces in war, and paid no tax except for war. Sparta's policy was hereafter anti-tyrant; she expelled the tyrants of Sicyon, Naxos, and, later, Athens (510), and sought to do so in Samos (c. 524, Polycrates).

c. 520. The young king **Cleomenes I** tried to reassert the royal power against the ephors. When the expulsion of the tyrants from Athens led not to a pro-Spartan oligarchy but to the democratic reforms of Cleisthenes, he led an expedition into Attica, which, however, failed because of the opposition of the other king,

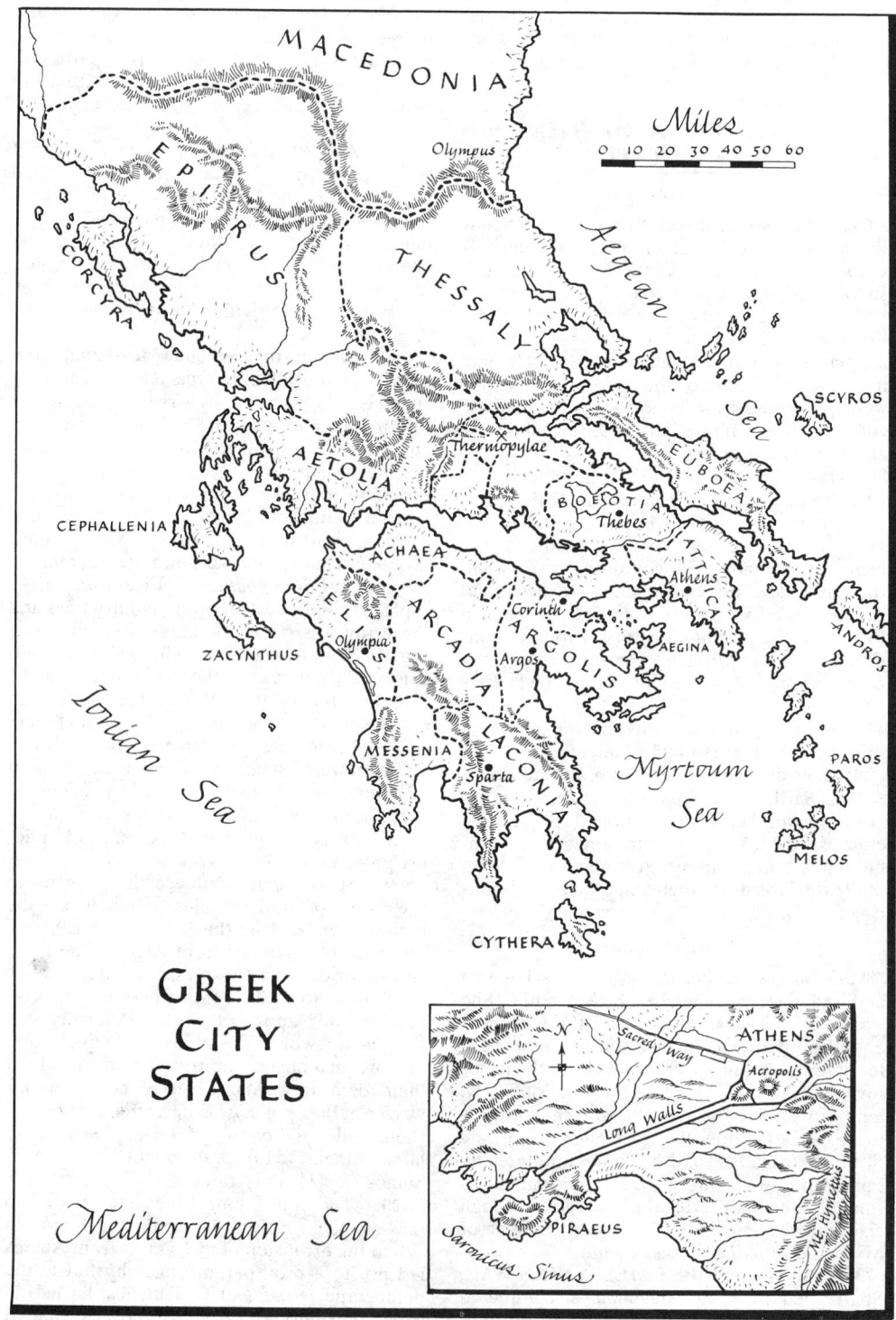

MACEDONIA

EPIRUS

Olympus

CORCYRA

THESSALY

Aegean

Sea

SCYROS

AETOLIA

Thermopylae

EUBOEA

CEPHALLENIA

BOEOTIA
Thebes

ATTICA

ACHAEA

Athens

ELIS

ARCADIA

Corinth

ARGOLIS

ANDROS

ZACYNTHUS

Olympia

Argos

AEGINA

Ionian

Sea

MESSENIA

LACONIA

Sparta

Myrtoum

Sea

PAROS

MELOS

CYTHERA

GREEK
CITY
STATES

Mediterranean Sea

N

Sacred Way

ATHENS

Acropolis

Long Walls

Saronicus Sinus

PIRAEUS

Mt. Hymettus

Damaratus, and the defection of Corinth through jealousy of Sparta's power. Nevertheless, by his defeat of Argos in the **battle of Sepeia** (494) he so increased the power of Sparta and of himself that he was emboldened to depose Damaratus, despite the opposition of the ephors, on a charge of illegitimacy. Public opinion then turned against him and he fled to Arcadia, whence he forced his return by arms. Traditionally, he soon after (c. 489) went mad, was imprisoned, and committed suicide, but this tale may conceal a real arrest and execution by the ephors. He was succeeded by **Leonidas.** Under Cleomenes the **Spartan League,** most enduring of all Greek leagues, was at its height.

(3) Athens

Attica was gradually unified or reunified by the device of *synoecism,* through which the numerous small independent cities surrendered their local citizenship for that of Athens. This process had by 700 taken in all Attica except Eleusis, which was soon added. Traditionally the whole process was accomplished by King Theseus.

In the **Ancient Constitution of Athens** the people were divided into four hereditary tribes (*phylai*), each made up of a number of brotherhoods (*phratriai*), which had common religious ceremonies and gave assistance to members in legal strife and blood feuds. The nobles (*eupatridai*) formed smaller associations of clans (*gene*); the *phratriai* contained eventually both members of these clans (*gennetai*) and common people (*orgeones*), although at first perhaps only the former. Each tribe was divided for administrative purposes into 12 *naucrariai*, which handled the revenue and cared for the navy. The people were grouped, chiefly for military purposes, into three classes: *hippeis* (knights), *zeugitai* (those with a yoke of oxen), and *thetes* (laborers). The nobles gradually restricted the power of the king by giving first his military functions to a *polemarch* and then his civil functions to an *archon.*

683. The hereditary kingship was abolished and made into an annual office (*archon basileus*) like the archon and polemarch. Six *thesmothetai* were created to determine the customary law. These, with the *archon eponymous* (civil archon), the archon basileus, and the polemarch, were known as the **nine archons.** They were chosen from the nobles by the **areopagus,** a council of nobles which was the greatest power in the state. The **ecclesia** (assembly of all the citizens) seems not to have had important powers.

632. Cylon, a noble related to Theagenes, tyrant of Megara, attempted to establish a tyranny, but was foiled. Many of his followers were tricked into surrendering and then slaughtered by Megacles of the Alcmaeonid clan ("Curse of the Alcmaeonids").

620. Publication of the law on homicide by **Draco,** the unfairness of the nobles in administering the traditional law having led to a demand for its publication.

c. 600. Athens seized Sigeum from Mytilene; the resulting war was arbitrated (c. 590) in favor of Athens by Periander of Corinth.

594. SOLON was made sole archon to remedy the distress caused by the introduction of coined money and high rates of interest; all parties agreed to give this man of the middle class complete powers of reform. He regulated the festivals, basis of the calendar, and made humane laws affecting private life. By the **Seisachtheia** (shaking-off-of-burdens) all debts on land were canceled; all debt slaves in Attica were freed; those sold abroad were redeemed at state expense; securing of debts by the person was forbidden. By his **judicial reforms** a new and milder code of laws replaced all of Draco's except the laws on homicide; a court of all the citizens, the *heliaea,* was created and a right of appeal to it from decisions of the magistrates was granted. By his constitutional reforms election of magistrates was given to the ecclesia of all freemen; a council (*boulé*) of 400 (100 from each tribe) was created as a deliberative body which had the initiative in all legislation: the assembly could only accept or reject its proposals. The areopagus, hereafter composed of ex-archons, continued as guardian of the laws to have large supervisory powers over the magistrates. Four classes of citizens were defined: *pentacosiomedimnoi* (who had revenues of 500 *medimni* of corn and/or *metretai* of wine or oil); the *hippeis* (300); the *zeugitai* (200); and the *thetes* (all the rest). Some time later these classes were redefined in terms of money, and based on property rather than income. Only the first two classes were eligible to the archonship; the first three to the lower offices; the fourth could participate only in the heliaea and the ecclesia. By his economic reforms, Solon devalued the drachma by about a quarter; weights and measures were increased in size; the exportation of all agricultural produce except oil was forbidden; and immigration of artisans was encouraged.

Solon's reforms were inadequate, perhaps because no provision was made to supply the freed slaves with land or to relieve the *hectemoroi* (sharecroppers), who received only one-sixth of the produce of the land for themselves. Sectional party strife continued immediately after Solon's archonship. The rich nobles of the plain (*pediakoi*) were led by **Lycurgus,** the middle class (*paralioi*) by **Megacles** the Alcmaeonid.

c. 565. Peisistratus acquired fame as the successful general in the **conquest of Salamis** from Megara. He organized a new party, the *diakrioi,* of the small farmers, artisans, shepherds, and other poor folk.

561–527. PEISISTRATUS made himself tyrant, but was almost immediately driven out by Megacles and Lycurgus. In 560–559 he won Megacles over and was restored. About 556 he was again expelled after a break with Megacles. After he had spent some years in gaining wealth from his mines in Thrace, he was restored with aid from Thessaly and Lygdamis of Naxos, whom he had made tyrant (c. 546). Peisistratus's opponents were now exiled and their confiscated lands used to provide for the poor. The *hectemoroi* were made landowners. Peisistratus encouraged industry and trade, and introduced the popular **cult of Dionysius,** in order to break down the power held by the nobles through their hereditary priesthoods. Miltiades and a few Athenians, with Peisistratus's encouragement, set up a tyranny over the Thracians of the Chersonese. Delos was purified. Abroad, Peisistratus pursued a policy of friendship with all near neighbors; at home, he ruled without abolishing existing forms.

527. On the death of Peisistratus his sons **Hippias and Hipparchus** succeeded to the tyranny. Athens protected Plataea against Thebes (519), which was trying to force her into the Boeotian League.

514. An attempt was made by **Harmodius** and **Aristogeiton** to overthrow the tyranny, but only Hipparchus was killed. Hippias was finally expelled by the exiled Alcmaeonids with Spartan aid (510). Party strife followed between the nobles led by Isagoras and the commons led by the Alcmaeonid **Cleisthenes,** who was finally victorious and inaugurated a

508. Structural reform of the Constitution. In order to combat sectionalism, *demes* (townships) were created to a number of over 140, and citizenship was made dependent on membership in one of these rather than as before in a phratria. A new system of 10 local tribes (*phylai*) was created: Attica was divided into three sections: Athens and its vicinity, the coast, and the interior. The demes in each section were associated in ten *trittyes,* and each tribe was composed of one trittys from each section, ordinarily not contiguous. A new council (*boulé*) of 500 replaced the Solonian 400; its members were chosen by lot, 50 from each tribe and from each deme in proportion to its population. The army was reorganized

into ten tribal regiments, each of which in 501 was put under an elective general (*strategos*).

507. At the appeal of Isagoras, **Cleomenes** of Sparta invaded Attica, expelled Cleisthenes, and tried to restore the aristocracy. The Athenians rose, expelled the Spartans, and recalled Cleisthenes.

506. A second expedition of Cleomenes was prevented by King Damaratus and by Corinth. The Athenians crushed the Boeotians and Euboeans and annexed part of Chalcis' territory. They disregarded an ultimatum from Darius of Persia that they restore Hippias, whom Darius had made tyrant of Sigeum.

498. The Athenians sent 20 ships to the aid of the revolting Ionians, but after one campaign withdrew and tried to conciliate Persia by electing Hipparchus, a Peisistratid, to the archonship (496).

493/2. **Themistocles** was elected archon by the anti-Persian party and commenced the fortification of the Piraeus, but his naval policy was opposed by Miltiades, also anti-Persian, who had fled the Chersonese after the failure of the Ionian revolt.

(4) Central and Northern Greece

Some time before 700 the cities of Thessaly had been grouped in four *tetrads,* each under a *tetrarch.* Now they were organized into a loose **Thessalian League,** which elected, when common action was necessary, a general (*tagos*). There was a federal assembly which levied taxes and troops on the members. Until the 6th century this league possessed the strongest army in Greece; Thessalian cavalry was always unsurpassed. The looseness of the organization, however, prevented Thessaly from playing a leading rôle in Greece. Thessaly dominated the **Amphictyony of Anthela,** a religious league that by 600 included all the states of central Greece.

c. 590. In the **FIRST SACRED WAR,** under the leadership of Thessaly, and with help from Sicyon and Athens, the Amphictyony of Anthela defeated and demolished Crisa (Cirrha), in whose territory the shrine of Delphi lay. The pretext was the tolls levied by Crisa on pilgrims to Delphi. Delphi was put under the administration of the Amphictyones and their headquarters were transferred thither; Athens and the Dorians of the Peloponnese were admitted to membership.

c. 570. In **Euboea** the two states of importance, Chalcis and Eretria, had been very active in colonization and industry (c. 750–650). The Euboean coinage and weights and measures spread through the Greek world.

c. 570. Chalcis, supported by Corinth, Samos, and Thessaly, now became engaged in the **Lelantine War** with Eretria, aided by Aegina,

Miletus, and Megara, over the possession of the rich Lelantine plain. Chalcis was victorious.

c. 600–550. Thebes formed a **Boeotian League** by bringing pressure on the other states of Boeotia. After a long struggle the powerful Orchomenos was reduced.

519–506. Plataea refused to join the league and entered into alliance with Athens. In the ensuing conflict, the Boeotians and Euboeans were defeated by the Athenians.

(5) Sicily and Magna Graecia

The original people of Sicily were Sicans; these were displaced by the Sicels from southern Italy. Before 800 the Elymians entered, probably from Spain, and occupied the western corner of Sicily. The Phoenician trading posts in Sicily (p. 47), which had covered the coast, were gradually driven out after 735 (foundation of Naxos) by the Greek colonization, except for Motya, Panormus, and Solus, in the west. Meanwhile **Carthage** (p. 48) had grown into an imperial power by founding colonies of her own and by protecting the older settlements after Tyre and Sidon were weakened by foreign domination after 669.

c. 580. An attempt of the Spartan **Pentathlus** to colonize western Sicily was defeated by the Elymians.

c. 570–554. **Phalaris**, tyrant of Acragas, pursued a policy of energetic and ruthless expansion, with extreme cruelty at home.

c. 550. The Carthaginian **Malchus** campaigned successfully in Sicily.

535. In the naval **battle of Alalia,** off Corsica, the Carthaginians and Etruscans defeated the Phocaean settlers and forced the abandonment of their colony. Shortly after this Massilia defeated Carthage and imposed a treaty limiting Carthaginian influence in the north and west.

510. **Sybaris** was destroyed by Croton, which was at this time ruled by the sect of the **Pythagoreans.** An attempt of the Spartan Dorieus to colonize western Sicily was prevented by the Carthaginians.

The conquest of Ionia by Persia led to a shift of intellectual and artistic effort to Greece proper and, thanks to their wealth, to the western colonies. **Tragedy** began at Athens with **Thespis** (539); the poets **Pindar, Simonides,** and **Anacreon** flourished c. 500. Attic black-figured vases gave way to red-figured (c. 525). **Sculpture** became more common, in the archaic style (Athens, Delphi). **Heraclitus of Ephesus,** last of the Ionian physicists, advocated "change" against the "one" of **Parmenides of Elea** (*Eleatic School*) in southern Italy. **Pythagoras** founded his sect of mystic philosophers in Croton.

2. THE PERSIAN WARS, 499–478 B.C.

499–494. The Ionians revolted under the leadership of **Aristagoras** of Miletus, against the Persians and the pro-Persian tyrants. Aristagoras made a trip to Greece to solicit aid; Sparta refused, but Athens responded with 20 ships (498) and Eretria with five. The rebels made a dash on Sardis, burned it, and retired to Ephesus. Greek disunion and the desertion of the Samians and Lesbians led to the defeat of the Greek fleet in a battle off the island of **Lade** (494). Darius's control of the sea now enabled him to take and sack Miletus. This practically ended the revolt. Darius subdued all the Greek cities, but did not again force tyrants upon them.

492. **First Persian expedition** under **Mardonius,** sent to punish Athens and Eretria for their aid to the rebel cities. Mardonius subdued Thrace and accepted the submission of Macedonia, but the Persian fleet was dashed to pieces while rounding the rocky promontory of Mt. Athos in a storm. Mardonius thereupon retreated.

490. **Second expedition** of the Persians, across the Aegean, under Artaphernes and Datis. Artaphernes besieged Eretria on Euboea while Datis landed at Marathon, the center of Peisistratid strength. When Eretria fell through treachery, Miltiades, one of the ten generals, persuaded the Athenians to attack. The Athenians won a complete victory in the **BATTLE OF MARATHON** (Sept. 12) and reached Athens in time to prevent its betrayal to Artaphernes by the now pro-Peisistratid Alcmaeonids. The Persians returned to Asia.

Miltiades failed to capture Paros and was condemned to a heavy fine. He died soon after.

489. Athens waged an indecisive **war with Aegina** until c. 483.

488–482. By a **reform of the Athenian constitution** (488/7), the nine archons were hereafter chosen by lot from 500 candidates elected by the demes; at some later time this was changed to ten preliminary candidates elected from each tribe, and still later the preliminary candidates also were chosen by lot. This change naturally reduced the power of the polemarch in favor of the ten elected generals, of whom one might be selected by the people at large as general-in-chief (*strategos autocrator*). To guard against tyranny, the device of **ostracism** was devised. In a meeting in which not less than 6000 votes were cast (*ostraka* were potsherds used for voting), the man with the greatest number was obliged to leave Athens for ten years; he remained a citizen, however, and his property was not confiscated. Hipparchus was ostracized in 487/6; Megacles the Alcmaeonid in 486/5; Xanthippus of the same party in 484/3. The anti-Persian party, of which the noble faction was led by **Aristides** and the commons by **Themistocles,** regained power. Themistocles prevailed upon the people to use a rich new vein of silver found in the state mine at Laurium for the building of 200 **triremes,** a newly invented type of warship. Aristides was ostracized due to his opposition to this measure, and from now on ostracism was used as a measure of party government. By 480 Themistocles headed the state as *strategos autocrator.*

480. CAMPAIGN OF THERMOPYLAE. Xerxes, who had succeeded Darius in 486, demanded earth and water (submission) from all the Greek states, most of which refused. Xerxes thereupon led a carefully prepared expedition of about 180,000 men (not the traditional 900,000) into Greece through Thrace and Macedonia. A Greek force sent to hold the pass of Tempe retired when it was found untenable; the Greek army then occupied the **pass of Thermopylae,** and the fleet the Gulf of Artemisium: the plan was for the army to hold the Persians while the fleet won a victory and thus compelled retreat. The naval fighting, however, was indecisive. Under the guidance of the Greek Ephialtes, a Persian company traversed a side path, routed a small Phocian outpost, and turned the Greek position at Thermopylae. Most of the Greeks withdrew, but **Leonidas,** with 300 Spartans and 700 Thespians, refused to retire and they were annihilated. The Boeotians, Phocians, and Locrians immediately "medized"; the Greek army retreated behind a wall built across the Isthmus of Corinth, and the fleet moved to the Saronic Gulf between Athens and Salamis. The Persians occupied Attica and destroyed Athens, whence the citizens had fled to Salamis and the Peloponnese.

BATTLE OF SALAMIS. The Greek fleet was bottled up in the Saronic Gulf by the superior Persian forces. Themistocles craftily warned Xerxes that the Greeks were about to escape by night, and the Persians thereupon rushed into the narrows, became entangled, and were thoroughly defeated. Since it was impossible to force the isthmus merely by assault, this meant the end of the year's campaign. Xerxes returned to Sardis with a third of the army, Artabazus to Thrace with another third, and Mardonius wintered in Boeotia with the rest.

479. BATTLE OF PLATAEA. After unsuccessfully trying to detach the Athenians from the Greek cause, Mardonius again invaded Attica. The Peloponnesians, urged by the Athenians, advanced to Plataea under the Spartan **Pausanias.** Mardonius attacked them as they were confusedly shifting their position, but the day was won by the superiority of the heavy-armed Greek *hoplites* and the discipline and bravery of the Spartans. Mardonius was killed, his camp plundered, and the Persian army routed. The Greeks then took Thebes by siege, and abolished the oligarchy in favor of a democracy. In the meantime, the Spartan **Leotychidas** had sailed with a small fleet to guard the Cyclades against Persia. The Samians and Chians prevailed upon him to attack the Persians, who were at Samos. The Persians, fearing to meet him on the open sea, drew up their ships on land at **Mycale** near Samos. Leotychidas stormed their position, but the Persians succeeded in burning their ships before the Greeks could seize them. The Ionians and several of the island cities (Samos, Lesbos, Chios) now revolted from Persia and joined the Greek fleet, which laid siege to Sestos in the Thracian Chersonese. The Spartans returned home in the fall, but the Athenians and Ionians succeeded during the winter in reducing Sestos (478).

3. THE 5TH CENTURY

a. THE PELOPONNESE, 479–461 B.C.

479.   Pausanias, in command of the allied fleet, reduced Cyprus and Byzantium. By his domineering he alienated the Ionians and caused the ephors to fear lest his power become excessive; they recalled him and after a first acquittal he was later (c. 471) starved to death in the temple of Athena of the Brazen House. The Ionians refused to recognize his successor Dorcis and went over to Athenian leadership. Thus Sparta's prestige in the Peloponnese fell very low. In 471 Elis united herself under a democratic government by *synoecism* and Tegea deserted Sparta to form an alliance with Argos, probably fostered by Themistocles.

470. After a drawn **battle at Tegea** all of Arcadia except Mantinea joined the anti-Spartan alliance. While Argos was occupied in reducing Tiryns and Mycenae (c. 469), however, Sparta crushed the allies at Dipaea and restored her hegemony.

464. An earthquake in Sparta gave the helots of Messenia a chance to revolt **(Third Messenian War);** after a defeat they retired to Mt. Ithome, where the Spartans besieged them. Unable to take the place, the Spartans called on the aid of their allies, including Athens. Athens sent a force under Cimon which was shortly dismissed (462), probably because many of its members were really hostile to Sparta; this marked the end of the Spartan-Athenian alliance. The fall of Ithome ended the revolt (461), and the Messenians were given safe-conduct to Naupactus, which Athens had just acquired from the Ozolian Locrians.

462. **Megara,** involved in a border war with Corinth, appealed unsuccessfully to Sparta and then made an alliance with Athens.

b. ATHENS AND THE DELIAN LEAGUE, 479–461 B.C.

479. Athens and the Piraeus were fortified by Themistocles, despite the opposition of Sparta.

478–477. The **Ionians,** disgusted with Spartan leadership, made an alliance with Athens for the expulsion of the Persians from all Greek territory. Each ally was to contribute either a quota of ships, or money in lieu of this: the smaller states chose the latter. **Aristides** ("The Just") assessed the tribute, using the old Persian tribute as a guide: the total was probably about two hundred talents at first. The league had a general assembly (*synedrion*) on Delos, which at first controlled league policy, although it was soon dominated by Athens.

476. **Cimon** made an expedition to Thrace and captured the Persian forts along the coast except Doriscus; the siege of Eion occupied the winter. Some time later Carystus in Euboea was compelled to join the league. These successes enabled Cimon to procure the ostracism of Themistocles (471), probably because the latter wished to follow an anti-Spartan policy. Themistocles went to Argos, where he conspired against Sparta; he was later (471) outlawed by Athens and fled to Persia, where Artaxerxes gave him a refuge (464).

467. When **Naxos** attempted to withdraw from the Delian League, though the treaty of alliance made no provision for withdrawal, Athens forced the city to raze its walls, surrender its fleet, and henceforth pay tribute. Athens after this often interfered in the internal affairs of the tributary states, which were soon considered subjects and not equal allies. Commercial disputes between citizens of two subject states or between those of a subject state and Athens, as well as capital criminal cases, were tried in the Athenian courts. Part of the rebels' lands was often taken, especially during Pericles's supremacy, to establish an Athenian *cleruchy* (colony), serving a military purpose as well as relieving unemployment in Athens. Garrisons were left under military captains (*phrourarchoi*) if necessary; sometimes only civil commissioners (*episkopoi*) were sent. Athenian surveyors (*taktai*) reassessed the tribute, and the Athenian people controlled its use, as well as the use of the contingents of the autonomous allies.

466. Cimon defeated the Persians in a great naval victory at the **Eurymedon River** on the south coast of Asia Minor. He then crushed a revolt of Thasos (465–463). Under the leadership of **Ephialtes,** a man of great probity and ability, a popular party was rising against the domination of Cimon. He was charged with having accepted a bribe from Alexander of Macedon, but was acquitted and prevailed over Ephialtes in having a force sent to Sparta against the helots (462). When the Spartans dismissed Cimon, the strong anti-Spartan feeling in Athens caused him to be ostracized (461). Ephialtes then succeeded in depriving the areopagus of all its powers except the jurisdiction in homicide cases; the other powers were distributed among the ecclesia, the council of 500, and the popular courts, which by this time, owing to the press of imperial business, had been changed from one panel of 6000 to several panels of from 201 up. Ephialtes was murdered shortly afterwards, and **Pericles** (born not long after 500, died 429), on his mother's side an Alcmaeonid, took his place in the leadership of the popular party.

c. THE FIRST PELOPONNESIAN WAR

460. **Inaros,** who had previously raised a revolt in Egypt and defeated a Persian force, appealed to Athens for aid and was sent a fleet (probably not of 200 sail), which took Memphis. Simultaneously war broke out between the Athenians and the Peloponnesians, caused in part by the Megarian alliance of 462, which the Athenians had followed with alliances with Argos and Thessaly.

459. The Athenians were defeated at **Halieis** by the Corinthians and Epidaurians, but their fleet won a victory at **Cecryphaleia.** The Aeginetans joined the Peloponnesians (458), but their combined fleet was defeated by the Athenians in a **battle off Aegina** and the island was invested by a force of Athenians under Leosthenes. The Corinthians raided the Megarid to create a diversion but were defeated by the Athenian old men and boys under Myronides.

457. The **Aeginetans** were forced to surrender, join the Delian League as tributaries, and surrender their fleet.

Sparta then entered the war, sent an army across the Corinthian Gulf, and restored the Boeotian League under the hegemony of Thebes. Athens was defeated at **Tanagra,** but the Spartans returned home, leaving the Athenians to defeat the Boeotians at **Oenophyta** and enroll all the cities except Thebes in her league; Phocis and Opuntian Locris also entered. The Athenians connected the Piraeus with Athens by two long walls.

456. A Persian force under **Megabyzus** defeated the Athenians, who were besieging Leukon Teichos, the citadel of Memphis. The Athenians were in turn besieged on the Nile island Prosopitis.

455. The Athenian **Tolmides** sailed around the Peloponnese, raiding the coast, burning the Spartan shipyard at Gytheum, and gaining Achaea for the Athenian League.

454. **Pericles** crossed the isthmus and made an unsuccessful campaign in the Corinthian Gulf. But meanwhile the Athenians in Egypt were defeated and slaughtered, and a relief squadron met the same fate. As a result the treasury of the Delian League was moved to Athens.

451. After three years of inactivity **Cimon** returned from exile and negotiated a five years' truce with Sparta. Thus, being unprotected, Argos had to make a thirty years' peace with Sparta. Cimon then took a large force to Cyprus (450) but a plague (famine?) caused his death and necessitated the return of the force to Athens. As it was departing, the fleet won a great **victory off Salamis,** a town of Cyprus. An understanding was then reached with Persia (the so-called **Peace of Callias**).

449–448. The **SECOND SACRED WAR** was begun when Sparta took Delphi from Phocis and made it independent; Athens immediately restored it to the Phocians.

447. **Boeotia** revolted and an inadequate Athenian force under Tolmides was crushed at Coronea. Moderate oligarchies were set up in all the Boeotian cities. The Boeotian League was re-established on a federal principle: a total of 11 Boeotarchs was sent by the cities in proportion to their sizes; for each Boeotarch a city was entitled to 60 seats on the federal council. Both local and federal councils were divided into four sections, of which each in turn served as council, while the four together constituted a plenary assembly. There was a federal treasury and coinage. Troops were

levied in proportion to population. Phocis and Locris followed Boeotia in quitting the Athenian League.

446. **Euboea revolted** and Pericles crossed over with an army. Simultaneously the Peloponnesians invaded the Megarid and drove out the Athenian garrison. Pericles returned, but not daring a battle retired to Athens and when the Peloponnesians reached Eleusis came to terms satisfactory to the enemy, who withdrew. Pericles then crushed the revolt in Euboea, and established a cleruchy on the territory of Histiaea. Negotiations with the Spartans continued, and during the winter

446/5. The **THIRTY YEARS' PEACE** was concluded: Megara returned to the Peloponnesian League; Troezen and Achaea became independent; Aegina was to be tributary but autonomous; disputes were to be settled by arbitration. Disgust among the Athenian conservatives at the failure of the anti-Spartan policy led to an attempt to ostracize Pericles, but it resulted in the ostracism (445) of their leader Thucydides, son of Melesias (not the historian). Pericles enjoyed undisputed control until 430.

d. ATHENS, 460–431 B.C.

457. **Pericles** made the zeugitai eligible to the archonship; the thetes were never legally eligible, but in fact were soon permitted to hold the office. Athenian imperialism was extended to the far west by an alliance with Segesta and Halicyae in Sicily (453). An extremely important measure for the development of the democracy was the institution (451) of pay for the *dicasts* (jurors) of the popular courts, which made it possible for the poorest citizens to serve. At the same time Pericles carried a bill restricting Athenian citizenship to those both of whose parents were Athenians (repealed 429, re-enacted 403), and when Athens received a gift of free corn from Egypt in 446/5 the lists were revised and 5000 citizens removed. The western policy was continued with the foundation of Thurii (443) and the alliances made with several Ionic cities of Sicily.

441. Miletus, involved in a war with Samos, appealed to Athens, which replaced the oligarchy in Samos with a democracy.

440. **Samos** revolted and threw out the democracy, but the Athenians after a long siege took the city (439) which lost its fleet, its walls, and its autonomy, being made tributary. Chios and Lesbos were now the only autonomous allies in the league.

437. A policy of expansion in the north was begun with the foundation of **Amphipolis** in

Thrace, controlling the mines of Pangaeus; it also relieved unemployment and served as a garrison against disaffected allies. Perhaps in the same year Pericles made an expedition into the Euxine and established good relations with the princes of Panticapaeum, who exported the grain badly needed by Athens. Athenian settlers were sent to various Pontic cities. In the Corinthian Gulf about this time Phormio made an alliance with some of the Acarnanians.

e. SICILY, 499–409 B.C.

The first decades of the 5th century witnessed the rise of tyrants in the Sicilian cities, of whom the most important were **Theron of Acragas** (488–472) and **Gelon of Gela,** later of Syracuse (485–478). Gelon made Syracuse the first city of Sicily, largely by transporting thither populations from conquered neighbors. He differed from the usual tyrant in favoring the landed nobles (*gamoroi*) at the expense of the commons.

480. **Terillus,** tyrant of Himera until Theron conquered that city, appealed for Carthaginian help. Carthage, fearing the alliance of Gelon and Theron, responded with a force under Hamilcar, which was utterly defeated at Himera by the allies. Hamilcar was killed and Carthage forced to pay an indemnity.

478–466. **Hieron I,** brother of Gelon, marks the height of the first Syracusan tyranny. He moved the citizens of Catana to Leontini and resettled Catana with his mercenaries under the name Aetna. In alliance with Aristodemus of Cumae he defeated the Etruscans in a naval **battle off Cumae** (474).

472. **Thrasydaeus,** a cruel and hated ruler, succeeded his father Theron at Acragas. He immediately became involved in a war with Hieron and was decisively defeated. The people of Acragas and Himera expelled him and set up a democracy.

467/6. **Rhegium and Taras** were defeated with heavy losses by the native Italian Iapyges. A democracy was established in Taras and the Pythagoreans were expelled from the Italian cities generally.

466. **Thrasybulus** succeeded his brother Hieron at Syracuse, but was expelled directly; a democracy was established. The attempted tyranny of **Tyndaridas** (Tyndarion) led to the introduction of *petalism,* like Athenian ostracism.

463–460. After a series of conflicts the mercenaries of the deposed Sicilian tyrants were left in possession of **Messana** (formerly Zancle).

459/8. The Sicels united under **Ducetius** and founded a capital at Palice.

453. The Elymian towns of Segesta and Halicyae became involved in a war with Selinus and made an alliance with the aid of Athens.

450. Syracuse and Acragas finally succeeded in defeating Ducetius at Noae; he was exiled to Corinth and the Sicel federation fell apart. As a result of this victory Syracuse and Acragas fell out over the division of territory (c. 445). Syracuse was finally victorious and became the recognized leader of Sicily. In fear of her, Rhegium, Leontini, Catana (?), and Naxos (?) made alliances with Athens (443). Athens at the same time refounded the site of Sybaris as Thurii, calling in colonists from all of Greece.

440/39. **Ducetius,** who had returned in 446, restored the Sicel federation, and after founding Cale Acte, died; his federation was completely ended; Syracuse destroyed Palice.

427–424. A **general war** broke out in Sicily. Naxos, Catana, Leontini, Rhegium, Camarina, and most of the Sicels opposed Syracuse, which was supported by Gela, Messana, Himera, Lipara, and Locri. Gorgias of Leontini went to Athens and made an appeal for aid, which was granted. After indecisive fighting the aristocrat Hermocrates of Syracuse persuaded the warring cities, which had assembled in the **Conference of Gela,** to make peace and cease to call in the Athenians.

416. **Segesta,** at war with Selinus, again obtained Athenian aid under the treaty of 453.

415–413. The **Athenian expedition** against Syracuse, during the Peloponnesian War. The Athenians were finally defeated at the Assinarus. A democratic reform was instituted in Syracuse by Diocles (412); privileges of the lower classes were extended and many offices were made elective by lot. Hermocrates, who had commanded a naval squadron in aid of Sparta, was banished after the **battle of Cyzicus** (410).

f. THE GREAT PELOPONNESIAN WAR

Thucydides considered the war of 431–421 (the **Archidamian War**) and that of 414–404 (the **Decelean** or **Ionian War**) to be in reality one, and together they are called the **Peloponnesian War.** Thucydides' incomplete history covers the period to 410. The basic cause of the war was the fact that there existed in Greece two great rival systems of alliances, comprising practically all of continental and Anatolian Greece, each of which was deemed essential by its leader. Thus neither leader could afford to tolerate any action threatening the solidity of its league, nor could it afford to allow the other to attain power appreciably superior to its own. Hence any minor conflict was bound to involve all Greece, and such a conflict was sure to arise.

435. Corcyra, quarreling with Corinth over the latter's interference in their joint colony Epidamnus, defeated the Corinthian fleet in the **battle of Leucimne.** Corinth began preparation of a great expedition, and the Corcyreans in fear appealed (433) to Athens for an alliance, which was granted, since Athens desired a station on the route to the west (to a small degree for commercial reasons), and especially since she feared Corinth's prospective naval power should the latter acquire the Corcyrean fleet. Ten ships were dispatched to Corcyra. The Corinthians attacked at Sybota, but when it was clear they were winning, the Athenians entered the battle, and the arrival of 20 more ships caused the Corinthians to return home. Athens then demanded that her subject Potidaea, a Corinthian colony, cease to receive her annual magistrate from Corinth, and raze her seaward walls.

432. Assured of Peloponnesian aid, the **Potidaeans** revolted in the spring. An Athenian force won a battle before Potidaea in the fall. Pericles passed a bill barring the Megarians from all the harbors of the Athenian Empire, ruining them economically; the Peloponnesians alleged that this was contrary to the Thirty Years' Peace, but the truth is uncertain. The Corinthians, Megarians, and Aeginetans forced the Spartans to take action and, although opposed by King Archidamus, the ephor Sthenelaïdas persuaded the Spartan assembly to declare the peace broken. The **Peloponnesian League** was then assembled and declared war. The winter was taken up by fruitless negotiations.

431. The war began when a band of Thebans by treachery entered Athens' ally Plataea; the Thebans were induced to surrender and were then killed.

The strategy of the Athenians, devised by Pericles, was to refuse a land battle, in which they would almost certainly be defeated, remain within their walls, and let their country be ravaged; they could support themselves through their control of the sea, and hoped to wear down the Peloponnesians by coastal raids and destruction of their commerce. They also ravaged the Megarid twice annually, when the Peloponnesian army was not assembled. The strategy of the Peloponnesians was to ravage the land of Attica annually and, if possible, lure the Athenians into battle; they also gave encouragement and support to revolting allies of Athens.

431. The Athenians expelled the inhabitants of Aegina and replaced them with Athenian cleruchs. Thucydides put in Pericles's mouth the famous *Funeral Oration* for the war dead of this year.

430. A **great plague** broke out at Athens. When an Athenian expedition against Epidaurus failed, it was sent to Potidaea, but returned after infecting the troops there with the plague. Disgusted, the Athenians deposed Pericles. During the winter Potidaea surrendered.

429. The plague continued. Pericles was reelected *strategos* in the spring, but died soon after. Instead of invading Attica, the Peloponnesians laid siege to Plataea. The Athenians sent Phormio to block the Corinthian Gulf. Off **Naupactus** he won two battles against superior forces.

428. **Cleon** succeeded to the leadership of the radical party in Athens, which favored war; the conservatives, opposed to war, were led by **Nicias.** All Lesbos except Methymna revolted on the promise of Spartan aid. To meet this emergency the Athenians levied the first direct property tax (*eisphora*) since 510 and sent out a large fleet under Paches.

427. **Mytilene** fell before the dilatory Spartan admiral, Alcidas, arrived. The leaders were executed and Athenian cleruchs were sent to the island. Plataea was finally taken by the Spartans; half the garrison had previously escaped; those who remained were executed. The oligarchs in Corcyra, wishing to end the alliance with Athens, opened civil war on the democrats, but the latter, with Athenian help, put down the rebellion; many oligarchs fled to the mainland opposite.

426. The Spartans offered peace to Athens, but it was refused.

425. The Athenian general, **Demosthenes,** in co-operation with the Acarnanians, took Anactorium. He was then sent to reinforce a fleet in Sicily but on the way seized **Pylos,** on the west coast of the Peloponnesus. Demosthenes was left with five ships to use this station to stir up the Messenian helots against Sparta. But the Spartans besieged this force on Pylos by landing a force on Sphacteria, an island in the bay. The Athenian fleet returned, defeated the Peloponnesians, and blockaded Pylos. Cleon, in Athens, accused Demosthenes of dilatoriness and, on the motion of Nicias, was sent himself to do better. To everyone's surprise, Cleon and Demosthenes captured the 120 Spartiates on Sphacteria. These were held as hostages to prevent another invasion of Attica.

424. Nicias seized **Cythera.** Cleon almost tripled the tribute assessment; pay for the dicasts was raised from two to three obols a day. Demosthenes and Hippocrates seized Nisaea but were prevented by Brasidas, on his way to Thrace, from taking Megara. **Brasidas,** with 700 helot hoplites and 1000 Argive mercenaries, continued to Thrace, Athens' only vulnerable point, and raised rebellion in several cities. Demosthenes and Hippocrates planned a synchronized invasion of Boeotia from the west and east respectively, to be aided by Boeotian democrats. The Thebans prevented Demosthenes from invading Boeotia from Acarnania and inflicted a heavy defeat on his colleague Hippocrates at Delium. Brasidas took Amphipolis. Thucydides, the historian, commanded a fleet nearby and was exiled at Cleon's instance on a charge of negligence. The fleet in Sicily returned after the **Conference of Gela.**

423. The Athenians made a year's truce with Sparta. Brasidas, however, continued to raise rebellions in the Thracian cities, so the Athenians broke off negotiations.

422. Cleon took a force to Thrace, but was routed and killed before **Amphipolis;** Brasidas was also killed: thus the leaders of the war parties on both sides were eliminated and negotiations reopened. Sparta's position in the Peloponnese was being shaken by trouble with Mantinea and Elis, the imminent expiration of the peace with Argos, and the Athenian possession of Pylos, Cythera, and the 120 captives. Athens had exhausted its reserves, which had amounted to 6000 talents in 431.

421. The **PEACE OF NICIAS** was negotiated, to last for 50 years. The Athenians were to keep Nisaea until the Boeotians restored Plataea; the Chalcidian cities were to be autonomous but tributary; Amphipolis was to be restored; the captives on both sides were to be freed. The Spartans restored the Athenian prisoners, but Brasidas' successor, Clearidas, refused to give over Amphipolis. The Corinthians, Megarians, Eleans, and Boeotians refused to sign the treaty: the former two because they received no benefits from the whole struggle, the Eleans because of a private quarrel over Lepreum, and the Boeotians because they did not wish to restore Plataea. To protect herself, Sparta made an alliance with Athens for 50 years. Thereupon, Elis, Mantinea, Corinth, and the Chalcidian cities made an alliance with Argos, whose treaty with Sparta had expired. Megara and Boeotia delayed action.

420. Sparta broke the terms of the Athenian alliance by making a separate treaty with Boeotia, whereby Boeotia was to restore Panactum to Athens. The Boeotians, however, first razed Panactum, and the Athenians continued to hold Pylos. The action of Boeotia caused Corinth to quit the Argive League. Athens formed the **Quadruple Alliance** with Argos, Mantinea, and Elis, for 100 years. The two latter states at this time were already at war with Sparta.

418. The Spartans under **Agis** invaded Argos and, after considerable delay, the Athenians sent troops to Argos' support. Agis decisively defeated the Athenians, Argives, and Mantineans (the Eleans dropped out) in the **battle of Mantinea** and restored Sparta's hegemony in the Peloponnese. The Spartans then sent an ultimatum to Argos, which proceeded to repudiate the Quadruple Alliance and make a 50 years' alliance with Sparta. In the spring of 417, the Spartans put an oligarchic government into Argos, but it fell immediately and the democrats renewed the treaty with Athens for 50 years. During the next two years various Spartan armies raided Argos; the Athenians each time sent troops which arrived too late to encounter the Spartans.

416. Athens took by siege the island of Melos, which had refused to join the empire. The men were killed, the women and children enslaved; a cleruchy was established.

Selinus attacked Segesta, which appealed to Athens. Athens had by now a reserve of 3000 talents; the industrial and trading elements desired westward expansion. Against Nicias' opposition an expedition to Sicily was voted, to be commanded by Nicias, Alcibiades (the prime mover), and Lamachus.

415–413. The **Sicilian expedition** set out with a fleet of 134 triremes, carrying 4000 hoplites. Nicias refused Lamachus' proposal to attack Syracuse immediately. Alcibiades was recalled on charges of sacrilege, mutilating the *Hermae,* and profaning the Eleusinian Mysteries. He fled to Sparta. The Athenians won over Naxos and Catana, but accomplished nothing more.

414. Hermocrates was elected to command the defense of Syracuse. The Athenians almost succeeded in enclosing the city by a wall, but were prevented by the arrival of the Spartan Gylippus with a small force; his seizure of the heights called *Epipolae* permanently prevented circumvallation.

413. Reinforcements were sent under Demosthenes. His night attack on Epipolae failed and he advocated immediate return, but was prevented by Nicias' superstitious fear of an eclipse (Aug. 27). When the Athenians finally attempted to leave, the Syracusans, who had strengthened their fleet, defeated them in two naval battles. The Athenians withdrew by land; the rear under Demosthenes lagged behind and was defeated; the van under Nicias was crushed at the **Assinarus.** The generals were executed; the prisoners were kept for a time in the stone quarries and then sold into slavery.

414. The Athenians sent a fleet against the coasts of Sparta. The Spartans declared the peace broken.

413. The Spartans seized **Decelea** in Attica. This post was fortified and a garrison kept there continually; the Athenians were thus absolutely prevented from using their own land. The radical party in Athens, led by Peisander and Androcles, fell after the Sicilian defeat and a conservative reform took place. A college of 10 "deliberators" (*probouloi*) received many of the functions of the old council. The imperial tribute was replaced by a 5 per cent import and export levy in all harbors of the empire.

412. A small Spartan squadron stirred up revolts along the coast of Ionia. The Athenians voted to use their last 1000 talents, laid away for extreme emergency, and built rapidly a large fleet, which recovered Lesbos and Clazomenae. The **treaty of Miletus** was negotiated by Alcibiades between Sparta and Tissaphernes, satrap of Sardis. Sparta recognized the Persian king's rights to all lands ever belonging to any of his ancestors, while Persia was to furnish the money to maintain the Peloponnesian fleet.

The Athenians laid siege to **Miletus,** but were forced to withdraw by the arrival of the Peloponnesian fleet. The Athenian fleet at Samos received reinforcements and sent a detachment to blockade Chios. During the winter the Peloponnesian fleet was united at Caunus, but had difficulty in paying its crews, since Tissaphernes' policy, suggested by Alcibiades, was to wear out both sides and let neither win a real victory. The Peloponnesians took Rhodes, where they obtained supplies and money.

411. Sparta made a new treaty with Persia, signed by both Tissaphernes and Pharnabazus, satrap of Phrygia. The king's claims were limited to Ionia.

Alcibiades claimed that he could win Tissaphernes to the Athenians if the democracy were abolished. The oligarchic clubs in Athens (*hetairai*) by terrorism carried a motion to restrict citizenship to about 5000 of the wealthiest Athenians. Pay for public offices was abolished; all citizens except the 5000 were to be completely without political rights. A provisional committee of 400 was to rule until the 5000 had been chosen. The 400, however, continued to rule without choosing the 5000. The crews at Samos, who refused to recognize the new government and constituted themselves as the Athenian people, elected new generals, notably Thrasybulus and Thrasyllus. They forcibly prevented an attempt by Athenian and Samian oligarchs to restore the oligarchy in Samos which had been put down the year before. Alcibiades was recalled and made commander-in-chief; he demanded the abolition of the 400 in Athens, although he ap-

proved of the 5000. When the extremists among the 400 seemed ready to surrender to Sparta after four months of rule, the moderates, led by Theramenes, secured their deposition. Nine thousand citizens were enrolled as councilors, to serve in four sections as in Boeotia (so-called **Government of the 5000**). Pay for civic offices was not restored. This government fell before the beginning of the civil year 410/9, and the democracy was restored, with pay for the dicasts.

Meanwhile the Spartans raised revolts in many Hellespontine and Thracian cities and especially in Euboea. The Athenians under Alcibiades defeated the Spartans at Cynossema and Abydos.

410. In the **battle of Cyzicus,** Alcibiades annihilated the Peloponnesian fleet. Sparta offered peace on the *status quo,* but the radical party in Athens, which had risen again under the leadership of **Cleophon,** rejected the offer. Pharnabazus paid for the building of a new Peloponnesian fleet.

409. An Athenian expedition under Thrasyllus failed to take Ephesus. Sparta recovered Pylos; Megara had already recovered Nicaea.

408. The Athenians made a truce with Pharnabazus and sent ambassadors to the king, but before they arrived the king had received a Spartan embassy and decided to help Sparta energetically. He sent his son **Cyrus** to replace Tissaphernes. Alcibiades recovered Byzantium.

407. **Thrasybulus** recovered Abdera and Thasos. Alcibiades was elected general and commander-in-chief at Athens and returned to the city in triumph. Cyrus arrived in Asia Minor and formed cordial relations with Lysander, the able Spartan admiral (*nauarchos*).

406. When **Alcibiades** went off to collect money, his guard squadron at Ephesus was **defeated off Notium** by Lysander. Alcibiades lost all influence and fled to the Hellespont. Callicratidas replaced Lysander, but could not get along with Cyrus. The Athenian Conon was defeated at **Mytilene.** The Athenians with a great effort built another fleet.

406. In the **battle of Arginusae,** Conon won a decisive victory over the Spartan fleet. Eight of the Athenian generals, however, were later tried and, despite Socrates' opposition, sentenced to death for not rescuing the shipwrecked sailors; two fled. The Spartans again offered peace on the *status quo,* but Cleophon again had the offer rejected. On Cyrus' demand, Lysander was sent with the Peloponnesian fleet, nominally as secretary, in reality to command.

405. The Athenians followed Lysander to the Hellespont and, through the gross carelessness of the commanders, the fleet was annihilated while drawn up on the shore at **Aegospotami.** Oligarchies of Ten (*decarchiai*) under Spartan harmosts were set up in all the Athenian subject states.

404.   **Theramenes** negotiated peace after Cleophon, who held out against surrender to the last, was finally tried and executed. Athens was to raze her long walls and the fortifications of the Piraeus, surrender her navy, and make an alliance with Sparta.

404.   The Athenian oligarchs, supported by Lysander and led by Theramenes, set up a **Commission of Thirty** which was to make a few immediate reforms and devise a new constitution. Instead of this, the Thirty with Critias at their head seized power and ruled as the **Thirty Tyrants.** They executed Theramenes when he advocated a more moderate course. Finally 3000 of the richest citizens were nominally enfranchised, but never exercised any real power. Many citizens were exiled or fled, and these were supported by Argos and by Thebes, who feared the excessive power of Sparta. In the autumn of 404 Thrasybulus led back some exiles, who occupied Phyle and then the Piraeus. In the beginning of 403, the Athenians deposed the Thirty, who fled to Eleusis, and elected a **Government of Ten.** These, instead of bringing in the democrats from the Piraeus, asked help from Sparta, which sent Lysander. Then the anti-Lysander party in Sparta replaced Lysander with King Pausanias, who brought about a settlement by which the democracy was restored, and a general amnesty with few exceptions decreed. The decarchies in the former Athenian dependencies were soon abolished.

g. ECONOMIC AND SOCIAL CONDITIONS

The decline of Ionia and the growing prosperity of the western Greeks led, after the Persian Wars, to a shift of trade and industry to Greece proper, toward which converged the routes from both west and east, where the Greeks now sought an outlet for manufactures and a source of raw materials. Corinth and Aegina were the leading commercial states in Greece at the beginning of the 5th century, but they were soon outstripped by Athens. This growth of industry caused a rapid rise in the number of slaves, and many **metics** (*metoikoia,* resident aliens) migrated to the commercial states of Greece, where they were well treated: Athens especially was liberal in granting citizenship from Solon's time until 451. The industrial states were all dependent on the **importation of food.** In Greece itself, only Thessaly, Macedonia, and Sicily exported grains; Sparta, Boeotia,

and the backward states of the west and north were self-sufficing. Athens exported wine and oil. The economy of almost all Greek states was now on a **money basis** (e.g. at Athens the Solonian classes had been converted into a money assessment of all property). The Athenian coinage became the predominant medium of exchange. **Prices** had risen tremendously since the 6th century. **Wages** were on a bare subsistence level, and the large number of slaves prevented any increase.

By 500 B.C. the mines at Mt. Laurion were important, economically, to Athens as a rich source of lead, silver, zinc, and iron. Mining was extensive, although laborious, the rock being hand cut or the veins being reduced by fire. The mines provided much of the revenue for the wars and financed the building of the Long Wall from Athens to Piraeus, its harbor. The main communications system of Greece was by sea, the terrain being too rugged to build roads; hence the building of harbors became important (e.g., Piraeus, Samos). Water supply was also a problem; towns were usually served by aqueducts, although the remains of pressure lines have been found. Building techniques included the use of timber frames, hoists, pulleys, and hydraulic cement.

Shipping and agriculture remained very primitive. In Sparta and Thessaly great estates existed, but elsewhere ownership of land was much divided, and even in an industrial state like Athens the large majority of the citizens remained landowners. Foreigners were usually prohibited by law from owning land.

Public finance was simple, with no public debt and few surpluses. The chief source of revenue was indirect taxation; Athens profited greatly from her state-owned mines and depended on semi-compulsory contributions by wealthy citizens (*liturgiae*) for such expenses as the equipment of triremes or production of plays. Direct property taxes were used only in case of extreme need. Expenses in most states were correspondingly low; Athens used the revenues from the empire for extensive public works, and also had a large number of citizens on the public payroll. The Peloponnesian War, however, not only exhausted the public finances throughout Greece, but also created economic dislocation, and impoverishment among individuals. These losses must, nevertheless, have been made good rapidly, as the 4th century witnessed a high level of prosperity.

During the 5th century **art and poetry** attained their finest expression in Greece, especially in Athens, whose prosperity favored an artistic life. This was fostered by **Pericles,** who herein, as in other policies, resembled the 6th-century tyrants. In the choral ode, **Pindar** of Thebes (518–

442) and **Bacchylides** (c. 480), in the epigram, **Simonides** (556–468), distinguished the early part of the century. At Athens the three great dramatists, **Aeschylus** (525–456), **Sophocles** (?496–405), and **Euripides** (480–406) developed tragedy from a crude choral performance to unsurpassed perfection. **Aristophanes** (c. 448–385), who overlapped into the 4th century, was the acknowledged master of the **Old Comedy.** Prose lagged behind verse, but the Ionian **Herodotus**, writing at Athens (484–425), made the Persian Wars the motif of a delightfully discursive history. **Thucydides** (471–c. 400) perfected history in his account of the Peloponnesian War. In philosophy the conflict of unity against multiplicity was solved by the atomic theories advanced by **Empedocles** in Sicily (c. 444), by **Anaxagoras**, an Ionian at Athens (500–425? mind or *nous*), and by **Leucippus** (c. 450?). But philosophy turned from physics to ethics and the **Sophists** became the teachers of Greece and advocates of the subjectivity of standards (*nomos*, convention, against *phusis*, nature). The leading Sophists were **Protagoras**, **Prodicus**, **Hippias**, and **Gorgias**, the last of whom came from Leontini in Sicily to Athens in 427.

In medicine **Hippocrates of Cos** (b. c. 460 B.C.) of the cult of Asclepius presented a common sense, natural medicine combined with personal hygiene. A school of medicine developed from his teaching, but the Hippocratic corpus is encyclopaedic, not a canon of medicine; it separated medicine from speculative philosophy, making it an empirical science.

In **architecture**, the heavy and luxurious temples of the early part of the century in Sicily, especially at Acragas (Agrigentum), were succeeded by the perfection of Pericles' Doric and Ionic buildings on the **Acropolis** at Athens, the **Parthenon**, or temple of Athens (447–432), the **Propylaea**, or entrance gate (437–432), and the **Erechtheum** (420–408), or temple of the hero Erectheus. **Sculpture** reached its height in the works of **Myron** (c. 450) and **Polycleitus** (c. 430) of the Argive School and **Pheidias** (500–431) the Athenian. Attic painters of red-figured vases developed line drawing in a series of exquisite styles (to 415), and **Polygnotus** (c. 480) mastered the technique of large-scale painting.

4. THE RISE OF MACEDON, TO 330 B.C.

a. SPARTAN HEGEMONY

401–400. **Darius II** of Persia had been succeeded in 404 by his eldest son, **Artaxerxes II.** A younger son, **Cyrus**, collected 10,000 Greek mercenaries in Asia Minor and marched against his brothers (the *anabasis* or "going up") in 401; he was killed in the **battle of Cunaxa**, and with great difficulty the Greeks, one of whose leaders was the Athenian **Xenophon**, made their way back to the Euxine by 400.

400–394. When **Tissaphernes** besieged Cyme in 400, Sparta sent Thibron to hire a mercenary army and to liberate the Ionians from Persia. Dercyllidas took over the command in 399 and ravaged some Persian territory. A truce was maintained (398–397) while Artaxerxes prepared his fleet and put the Athenian Conon in command. In 396/5 King Agesilaus, succeeding Dercyllidas, ravaged Persian territory. In 394 Agesilaus returned to Greece with most of the troops.

395–387. **The Corinthian War.** In the winter of 396/5 Persia sent Timocrates of Rhodes to bribe the leaders of Athens, Thebes, Corinth, and Argos to attack Sparta. Athens made a defensive alliance with Boeotia which Corinth, Argos, Megara, Euboea, and other states joined. In 394 the Spartans won battles at Nemea and at **Coronea**, but their fleet, under Peisander, was annihilated by the Persian fleet, under Conon, at **Cnidus**. Persia granted autonomy to the Asiatic Greek cities and withdrew her garrisons. The Ionians revolted from Sparta and established democracies; the Cyclades followed in 393. Conon returned to Greece, and rebuilt the Athenian long walls. Athens recovered Lemnos, Imbros, Scyrus, and Delos; and made alliances with Chios, Mitylene, Rhodes, Cos, and Cnidus. In 392 an attempt at a general settlement was rejected by the Athenian imperialists, who had just come to power. The Persians deposed Conon, who soon died. In 390 Evagoras of Cyprus revolted from Persia. In 389 the Athenian navy under Thrasybulus recovered Thasos, Samothrace, Tenos, the Chersonese, Byzantium, Chalcedon, *et al.*; garrisons were placed in the more important towns, and 5 per cent harbor tolls levied, which really constituted a **revival of the Athenian naval league.** Thrasybulus was killed in action (388).

387–386. **THE KING'S PEACE.** In 387 the Spartan Antalcidas negotiated with Persia a general Greek settlement. All Greek cities were to be autonomous except those in Asia, which were to belong to Persia. In 386 the Spartan navy forced Athens to accept by blockading the Hellespont; Thebes was frightened into acceptance. Thus the Boeotian and the new Athenian leagues were dissolved.

385–379. Sparta broke Mantinea up into villages (385), seized the citadel, or Cadmeia, of Thebes (382), and captured Olynthus and dissolved its Chalcidian League (379).

379–378. The Theban democratic exiles led by Pelopidas recovered the Cadmeia by a *coup* and established a democracy in Thebes. The raid of the Spartan Sphodrias on the Piraeus caused an Athenian alliance with Thebes (378). Sparta raided Boeotia in 378 and 377.

377. SECOND ATHENIAN LEAGUE AGAINST SPARTA. Shortly after 386 Athens had renewed her alliances with several naval powers. In 377 these, Thebes, and many others united in the "second" (really third) league against Sparta. All decisions were to be made jointly by a council (*synedrion*) of the allies, excluding Athens, and the Athenian ecclesia; funds were to be derived from contributions levied by the synedrion and handled by Athens; Athens was to command in war; Athens gave up all claims to its former cleruchies. A fleet was quickly built up. In 376 Chabrias crushed the Spartan fleet off **Naxos**, and gave Athens control of the sea. Meanwhile, Thebes restored the Boeotian League on a democratic basis.

372. Jason, who succeeded his father Lycophron in the tyranny of Pherae, unified Thessaly by having himself made perpetual commander (*tagos*) until his murder in 370.

371. A **general peace settlement** was reached with Sparta in the summer of 371; but when he was not permitted to sign for all Boeotia, the Theban **Epaminondas** withdrew. Sparta immediately sent King Cleombrotus to chastise Thebes, but he was decisively defeated at **Leuctra** by Epaminondas. This shattered Spartan prestige and ended her chance of hegemony over Greece. Thebes withdrew from the Athenian League, and with her Acarnania, Euboea, and the Chalcidian cities.

b. THEBAN HEGEMONY

370. An **Arcadian League** was formed under Theban protection as counterweight to Sparta. Mantinea was restored as a city. The government of the league comprised a general assembly **(the Ten Thousand)** of all free-born citizens, with sovereignty in matters of war, peace, etc.; a council of *damiurgoi*, which gave proportional representation to the member cities; a college of generals (*strategoi*) as civil and military executive; a standing mercenary army (*eparitoi*). The Theban army, under **Epaminondas**, liberated Messenia from Sparta

and the city **Messene** was built. In 369 Athens and Sparta made an alliance on equal terms. The Arcadians founded **Megalopolis** as a federal capital. In the following years, Thebes secured the union of all of Thessaly save Pherae under a single ruler (*archon*). The pro-Spartan party of Callistratus in Athens was replaced in power by the party of Timotheus, and peace was made with Thebes on the basis of the *status quo* (365). Pelopidas was killed in battle against Alexander of Pherae (364), whom Epaminondas then defeated (363).

362. Because of financial difficulties, the federal army of Arcadia was disbanded. The oligarchs, who could serve at their own expense, came into control of many cities, which then made peace with Elis. The radicals appealed to Epaminondas, and the league broke up: Tegea and Megalopolis remained pro-Theban, while the others made an alliance with Elis and Achaea; all these jointly made an alliance with Athens; Mantinea was allied with Sparta. Epaminondas faced this coalition at Mantinea, but was killed in battle. A general peace was made on the basis of the *status quo,* but it was not accepted by Sparta, which refused to recognize the independence of Messenia.

359 **Philip II** became regent and, in 356, by the deposition of his ward, **king of Macedon.** Since he was troubled by his unruly barbarian subjects and Athens was involved in war with the Thracian Odrysae, both were glad in 358 to make a treaty by which Philip gave up his claim to Amphipolis and Athens promised to surrender Pydna. Philip now thoroughly reorganized his army, placing more importance on the **phalanx** of infantry, and with it subdued the rebellious barbarians. By agreement with Athens, he conquered Amphipolis (357) to exchange it for Pydna, since Athens was occupied in recovering Euboea from Thebes and the Chersonese from the Thracians.

357–355. The Athenian allies were angry at Athenian policy, e.g. the sending of cleruchies to Samos (365) and Potidaea (361), the subjection of Ceos and Naxos to Athenian jurisdiction (363/2), and especially the arbitrary financial exactions of Athenian generals; further, the decline of Spartan power had removed the league's *raison d'être*. Under encouragement from **Mausolus** (Mausollos, 377–353), who had succeeded Hecatomnus (395–377) as ruler of Caria, the states of Chios, Rhodes, Cos, and Byzantium joined in revolt, known as the **Social War,** i.e. "War of the Allies." After the defeat and death of Chabrias at Chios, the Athenians, under the incompetent Chares, finally withdrew from Ionia and recognized the independence of many of their allies (355). Mausolus in 353 annexed Rhodes and Cos.

c. MACEDON UNDER PHILIP
AND ALEXANDER THE GREAT

359-336. PHILIP II

355-346. The **THIRD SACRED WAR** began when the Phocians refused to pay a fine levied on certain of their people by the Amphictyonic Council at the instigation of Thebes (355). The Phocians seized Delphi and made alliances with Athens and Sparta. When the Amphictyons declared war, the Phocians used the sacred money of Delphi to recruit a very large mercenary army. Though they were defeated by the Boeotians at **Neon** (354), they seized Thermopylae and Orchomenos (353). When Philip attempted to oppose them in Thessaly, their general Onomarchus twice defeated him, but in 352 Philip defeated and killed Onomarchus. Philip then united Thessaly, which continued loyal to him. His march south was stopped by Athenians, Achaeans, and Spartans at Thermopylae. The war continued indecisively in Phocis until Athens made the **Peace of Philocrates** with Philip (346). Philip then conquered Phocis, prohibited the carrying of arms, and spread the Amphictyonic fine in installments.

356-346. When Athens refused to surrender Pydna to Philip in return for Amphipolis, he conquered the former, kept the latter, made a treaty against Athens with Olynthus, and took Crenides, renamed **Philippi,** from the Odrysae. After the end of the **War of the Allies** (355), Athens was financially exhausted and the imperialist party of Chares and Aristophon was replaced by the pacifists under Eubulus. All financial surpluses were put into a **theoric fund** and used for the entertainment of the citizens. Athens allowed Philip to expand eastward almost unchecked. But in 351 Olynthus, suspicious of Philip, appealed to her for aid. **Demosthenes** appeared as the leader of the anti-Macedonian party, urging action in his three *Olynthiac Orations.* An alliance was made with Olynthus (349), but an attempt to divert the surplus from the theoric to the military fund failed. Philip induced Euboea to revolt from Athens and the latter, against Demosthenes' advice, divided its efforts by sending a force there as well as to Olynthus (348). Phocion was successful in Euboea, but his successor, Molossus, lost the country. Philip took Olynthus, which he razed, and enslaved the citizens (348). Athens could secure no help from the Greeks, and even Demosthenes was in favor of peace.

346. PEACE OF PHILOCRATES. On the motion of Philocrates, ten ambassadors, including himself, Aeschines, and Demosthenes, were sent at Philip's invitation to negotiate a peace: the terms restored the Chersonese, except Cardia, to Athens, canceled Athens' claim to Amphipolis, and left other possessions as they should be when the peace was sworn. Athens could not secure the inclusion of her ally Phocis in the terms. On the return of the ambassadors, the assembly accepted the terms and sent them back to swear the oaths; they delayed on the way and Philip profited by this to conquer more of Thrace. After the conclusion of the peace, Philip conquered the Phocians, took their seat in the Amphictyonic League, and, as its chairman, presided over the Pythian games; Athens refused to send a delegation until Philip's threats forced her to recognize his membership in the league.

344-339. Despite the friendly attitude of Philip, Demosthenes persuaded the Athenians to make alliances against him in Euboea (341) and the Peloponnese (340), and to help Byzantium repel him (339). Demosthenes, now in control in Athens, urged opposition to Philip in his *Philippic Orations.* He reformed the system of paying for the navy by replacing the individual liturgy (*trierarchia*) with more equitable and efficient groups of contributors (*symmoriae*). He devoted surplus income to the war fund instead of to the theoric. Philip tried to get the Amphictyons to fine Athens for insulting Thebes, but Aeschines cleverly diverted them against Amphissa.

339-338. When this caused the **Fourth Sacred War,** the Amphictyons called in Philip. Athens, terrified at this, made an alliance with Thebes on terms very favorable to the latter. The allies won some minor successes. But Philip annihilated their mercenaries near Amphissa.

338. In the **BATTLE OF CHAERONEA,** Philip crushed the allied citizen armies. He garrisoned Thebes, but let Athens go free. Philip called a **congress at Corinth,** and all states, except Sparta, entered a **Hellenic League.** There was proportional representation in the league council, which was presided over by the king in wartime, otherwise by a chairman; autonomy of the members was guaranteed; existing constitutions were not to be altered and no private property confiscated; no tribute was required and no garrisons left, except in a few places; the king had the military command; the Amphictyonic Council served as a supreme court. Philip announced plans for an Asiatic campaign.

337. A **second congress at Corinth** declared war on Persia, and Philip sent an army under his general, Parmenio, to Asia Minor (336).

336. Philip was assassinated, allegedly at the instigation of his recently divorced wife, Olympias.

336–323. ALEXANDER III, THE GREAT (b. 356), succeeded.

On the rumor that Alexander had died, Thebes revolted with Athens, Arcadia, Elis, and Aetolia, but Alexander swiftly took Thebes, destroyed it, and enslaved the inhabitants. The others submitted (335).

334–331. Alexander, leaving Antipater behind as his governor in Greece, crossed the Hellespont in the spring of 334 with an army of 32,000 infantry and 5000 cavalry, supported by a navy of 160 ships, mostly allied. Memnon of Rhodes, commander of Darius' Greek mercenaries, wished to retreat, laying waste the country, but the satraps, hoping to protect their provinces, forced him to take a stand at the river **Granicus,** where he was completely defeated by Alexander (334).

Most of the Greek cities revolted from Persia. Alexander subdued Caria and (spring, 333) Cilicia. Meanwhile, Memnon died and Darius summoned the mercenaries to Syria. Alexander went on to Myriandrus, where he faced Darius, who had raised a large but motley army. Since Alexander feared to come on to the open plain, Darius went behind him to the plain of Issus.

333. BATTLE OF ISSUS. Alexander attacked and completely defeated Darius III. Darius offered to give up all Asia west of the Euphrates and pay 10,000 talents, but Alexander demanded unconditional surrender. All Phoenicia, except Tyre, submitted after Issus, and, by a difficult siege of seven months, Tyre was reduced (332).

332–331. Alexander's **expedition to Egypt** was unopposed; while in Egypt, he founded **Alexandria** and visited the oracle of Ammon.

331. Leaving Egypt in the spring, Alexander met and defeated the Persian army at **Gaugamela** (Oct. 1) and went on to Arbela, where he seized much Persian treasure. Babylonia and Susa surrendered, but at Persepolis resistance was offered, so that the place was looted and burned and immense treasure was taken.

331. Sparta under King Agis III, aided by Persian money and in alliance with Elis, Achaea, and part of Arcadia, defeated a Macedonian force and besieged Megalopolis, but was crushed when Antipater arrived with a greatly superior force.

330. In the spring of 330, Alexander pursued Darius through Media, where Darius was murdered by the satrap Bessus. Alexander subdued the Caspain region and marched southward. When Parmenio's son Philotas had been executed for complicity in a plot, Alexander sent messengers who murdered Parmenio in Media: Alexander feared a revolt and Parmenio was too powerful to be discharged.

329. Alexander went on into Bactria and overcame the Iranians under Spitamenes only with a great deal of trouble (328). Alexander now commenced the **adoption of Persian dress** and court etiquette. In a drunken fury, he murdered his friend Cleitus who had reproached him. He had 30,000 natives trained in Macedonian fashion for the army. He married the Persian **Roxana.** He began to foster a **belief in his divinity** as the best means of dealing with the Greeks as an absolute ruler and yet without offending their sentiments of liberty. Though the Greeks had deified living men before this, Alexander's move met so much opposition that he dropped it temporarily.

327–324. Alexander was invited into **India** by Taxiles against Porus. In the **battle of the Hydaspes** (326), he defeated Porus and advanced as far as the Hyphasis. Here the army refused to go farther. Alexander, therefore, returned via the Hydaspes and Indus to the Indian Ocean (325). Thence **Nearchus** went back with the fleet to explore the Indian Ocean and Alexander returned through the desert of Gedrosia. They met in Caramania and, after a rest, went on to Susa (324).

324–323. In his policy of fusion of the Greek and Asiatic peoples, Alexander had left in office many of the native governors (satraps); most of these, and many of the Macedonian satraps, were now found to have ruled badly; some had enlisted private mercenary armies. These satraps were replaced, usually with Macedonians; the private armies were ordered disbanded. Pursuing the policy of fusion, Alexander, 80 officers, and 10,000 men married native women. Alexander paid all debts of his men. He ordered all exiles recalled by the Greek cities; to give himself a basis for this interference, contrary to the constitution of the Hellenic League, he ordered the Greek states to recognize him as **son of Zeus Ammon.** At Ecbatana Alexander's closest friend, Hephaestion, died.

323, June 13. Alexander died at Babylon. His exploration had fostered commerce; over 25 cities which he had founded served to Hellenize the east, although his policy of direct fusion failed. The organization of his complex empire he left much as he found it, differing in each area. The officers wished to make the unborn son of Alexander and Roxana king, but the privates preferred a Macedonian, the imbecile **Philip III Arrhidaeus,** son of Philip II. When a son, **Alexander IV,** was born to Roxana, a joint rule was established under the regents Craterus and Perdiccas.

330–322. Athens had recouped her strength under the financier **Lycurgus,** who, among other reforms, established compulsory military training for all young men (*epheboi*). In 330, Demosthenes had been acquitted in the trial brought by Aeschines on the justness of the award to Demosthenes of a civic crown. In 326 Lycurgus fell from power, and in 324 Demosthenes was exiled for embezzling some of the money which Alexander's treasurer, Harpalus, brought to Athens. On the report of Alexander's death, Athens, led by the radical orator **Hypereides,** organized a new Hellenic League in central Greece and the Peloponnese. The allies under Leosthenes besieged Antipater in Lamia (winter, 323), and eventually forced his retirement to Macedonia. There Craterus joined him from Asia (322).

322. The Athenian fleet was wiped out forever at **Amorgos.** When the allied army was indecisively defeated at **Crannon** the league broke up. Athens received a Macedonian garrison, took back her exiles, and accepted an oligarchic constitution by which only those possessing 2000 drachmas had the franchise, perhaps 9000 out of 21,000 free citizens. Demosthenes, who had been recalled, fled but was caught and committed suicide.

d. THE WEST DURING THE 4TH CENTURY

413-405. After the defeat of the Athenian expedition, **Syracuse** made democratic reforms. In 410 many oligarchs, including Hermocrates, were banished. Then Segesta, warring with Selinus (409), called in the **Carthaginians,** who, despite Syracusan opposition, sacked Selinus and Himera (408) and, in a second expedition, Acragas (406).

405-367. Dionysius I secured his election as one of the ten generals in Syracuse and then made himself tyrant. He made peace with the Carthaginian forces, who were suffering from a plague. He distributed the confiscated land of the oligarchs to the poor and enfranchised the serfs. He conquered Catana (403), Naxos, and Leontini (400). In a **first war with Carthage** (398-392), he attempted to drive the Carthaginians out, but failed. However, he reduced the Sicels, and then began the conquest of southern Italy (390-379), where he crushed the Italiote League at the **battle of the Elleporus** (389). But he suffered a severe defeat in a **second war with Carthage** (383-381?), which he failed to retrieve in a third (368).

366-344. On the death of Dionysius, his weak son, **Dionysius II,** succeeded under the regency of his uncle **Dion.** Dion brought in Plato to educate Dionysius, but both were forced out (366). Dion regained Syracuse in 357 and ruled tyrannically until his murder in 354. After two more sons of Dionysius I had seized

the power and fallen, Dionysius II returned (347), but the Syracusans called in first **Hicetas,** tyrant of Leontini (345), and then **Timoleon** of Corinth.

344-337. Timoleon defeated the Carthaginians at the **Crimissus** (341) and made peace, with the Halycus River as the boundary (339). The tyrants were expelled from the Greek cities, which formed a military league against Carthage. Timoleon established a moderate oligarchy in Syracuse, with the priest (*amphipolos*) of Zeus as chief magistrate and a council of 600 composed of rich citizens. He then retired (337).

338-330. The **Greeks in Italy** (Italiotes), hard pressed by the natives, called in first **Archidamus of Sparta** (338), who was killed, and then **Alexander of Epirus** (334). The latter defeated the natives and made an alliance with Rome, but was finally assassinated during a battle (330).

e. GREEK CULTURE IN THE 4TH CENTURY

The death of Alexander the Great marked the end of the great age of Greece in literature, philosophy, and art. **Xenophon** (431-354), though a writer far inferior to Thucydides, wrote an able continuation of his history from 410 to 362, as well as other historical works. The lesser writers of **Middle Comedy** were followed by **Menander** (343-c. 280), the most outstanding of the writers of **New Comedy,** or comedy of manners. But it was in **oratory** and **philosophy** that the 4th century was most distinguished. Of the ten Attic orators the best known were **Lysias** (445-c. 380), **Demosthenes** (384-322), and the advocate of pan-Hellenism, **Isocrates** (436-338). **Philosophy** was dominated by the figure of **Socrates** (469-399), executed by the Athenians for atheism. His greatest pupil, **Plato** (427-347), founded the **Academy** in the grove of the hero Academus, and **Aristotle** (384-322), the pupil of Plato and tutor of Alexander, founded the **Peripatetic** (walking about) **School** or **Lyceum,** in the grove of the hero Lycus. Plato, under the influence of the number mysticism of the Pythagoreans, established an idealistic ontology with mathematics as the prototype of reality, while Aristotle, who was primarily a botanist, developed an epistemology using biological models as a prototype for explaining change.

In **sculpture** a refined and less vigorous style was preferred by **Praxiteles** (385-c. 320), **Scopas** (400-c. 340), and **Lysippus** (c. 380-c. 318). The center of activity began to shift to Ionia, as seen in the tomb of Mausolus of Caria (the **Mausoleum**), completed c. 350, and the new **temple of Artemis at Ephesus** (the old one was burned by Herostratus in 356).

Engineering by this time had reached the stage where extensive tunneling could be undertaken by manual excavation. Lake Copias was drained to prevent flooding c. 325 B.C., and the tunnel at Samos was constructed using survey- ing techniques. The **lighthouse at Alexandria** (Pharos) was built c. 300 B.C. and remained an important navigational aid for 1600 years (one of the seven wonders of the Ancient World).

(*Cont. p. 87.*)

C. ROME, TO 287 B.C.

1. THE EARLY PERIOD, TO 509 B.C.

a. GEOGRAPHICAL FACTORS

ITALY IS A LONG, narrow peninsula of which the central portion comprises the mountains and isolated valleys of the Apennines. At the northern end, the Apennines swing west and enclose between themselves and the Alps a wide and fertile valley, Cisalpine Gaul, traversed by the Po, which flows east into the head of the Adriatic. The eastern (Adriatic) coast of Italy is infertile and lacks good harbors, while the Adriatic itself, because of prevailing northerly winds, hindered the penetration of the Greeks. Moreover, the rugged opposing shore of Illyria was occupied by wild and piratic tribes, whose forays constituted a continuous threat to commerce. The eastern Italian peoples, therefore, remained backward compared to the western. The western part, though mountainous at the northern end, contains fertile plains in its central portion (Etruria, Latium, and Campania), with good harbors, especially around the Bay of Naples. Its rivers, however (the Arno and the Tiber), are too swift to be readily navigable, so that early civilization sprang up along the coast, while the inland peoples remained rude and simple. The western (Tyrrhenian) sea is enclosed by the islands of Sardinia and Corsica, the former fertile and rich in metals, the latter a wild seat of pirates. Southern Italy, where the mountains begin to fall away, was a land of pastures where later herds moved seasonally from sea to hills under the charge of slave bands of shepherds, whose brigandage formed a constant threat to travelers. Around the Bay of Tarentum, however, the Greek settlers early found a hospitable welcome, and the western toe of Italy afforded ready access, across the narrow Straits of Messana, to the prosperous island of Sicily, whose rich Greek colonies and lavish crops played an important part in Roman history. The western apex of Sicily in turn led towards Africa and the Phoenician colony of Carthage, which became Rome's chief rival for the control of the western Mediterranean.

b. EARLY POPULATIONS OF ITALY

Early Cultures of Italy (p. 21).

c. 900 B.C. The **ETRUSCANS** first appeared in Italy, probably by sea from Asia Minor (Lydia?), in consequence of the break-up of the Hittite Empire. They established themselves north of the Tiber in Etruria, probably as a conquering minority among enserfed Villanovan (?) natives. The power was apparently held by an aristocracy of princes (*lucumones*), whose fortified cities (traditionally twelve, though the precise constituents varied from time to time) formed a loose league, and whose elaborate tombs were at first furnished with bronze utensils and armor, then painted and supplied with imported luxuries, notably Greek vases. They extended into the Po Valley and into Latium and Campania until the end of the 6th century, when the pressure of **Celtic invaders** into the Po Valley cut off their northern settlements and the Cumaeans and Hiero of Syracuse broke their control of the sea and Latium revolted. Thereafter they declined until their absorption by Rome during the 4th century. Their culture preserved its identity until the Sullan land distributions in the 1st century so disorganized it that within a century thereafter it had become dead. The Etruscans made no original contribution to Rome save for certain forms (lictors, curule chair, purple-striped toga of office) and a gloomy religion (perhaps the three divinities Latinized as Jupiter, Juno, and Minerva, and certainly the practice of prophesying by consulting the entrails, *haruspicium*), but they first introduced to Rome Greek culture, though in a debased shape, mythology, the heavy Tuscan temple (from the Doric), and perhaps the alphabet.

c. 760. **GREEK COLONIZATION** began in the Bay of Naples in southern Italy, and in Sicily. The Greeks were prevented from further expansion to the west and north, save for Marseilles (Marssalia), by the Phoenicians and the Etruscans. Despite victories over both peoples by the tyrants of Syracuse in the early 5th century, the Greeks never succeeded in dominating all of Sicily or southern Italy. From the 4th century their fortunes declined until their eventual absorption by Rome during the 3rd. Nevertheless they not only impregnated these areas with a Greek culture which lasted throughout the Roman period, but, by their contact with Rome during the formative period of her national culture, first through the Etruscans and then directly, so Hellenized the Romans that when the latter conquered the Mediterranean world they respected and extended the Hellenistic civilization and, by absorbing it, preserved for later ages the Greek heritage.

c. THE ROMAN MONARCHY

753. FOUNDATION OF ROME, according to Cicero's contemporary, the antiquarian Varro. Traditionally the founder, **Romulus,** was son of a princess of Alba Longa, Rhea Silvia, and the god Mars. The kings of Alba Longa, in turn, were descended from **Aeneas,** a fugitive of the Trojan War and son of the goddess Venus (Aphrodite). This tradition dates, however, from the period when Rome was assimilating Greek culture. Actually during the 8th and following centuries small settlements on the Palatine, Esquiline, Quirinal, and Capitoline Hills united into one, with a common meeting place in the valley between, the **Forum.** These peoples may have been of different racial stocks, chiefly Latin but partly Sabine, Etruscan, and perhaps pre-Italic. The importance of Rome is less likely to have been economic (trade up the Tiber or across the ford at this point is not attested by archaeology) than military, an outpost of the Latins against the encroaching Etruscans. This would account for the inculcation in the Romans from an early date of habits of obedience, organization, and military drill. The traditions of the four early kings (**Romulus,** 753–715, **Numa Pompilius,** 715–673, **Tullius Hostilius,** 673–641, and **Ancus Marcius,** 641–616) are historically unreliable.

Early government. Rome emerged into history with a **king** (elective, not hereditary), limited by the existence of a **senate** of 100 elders (*patres*) which was advisory, not compulsory, and by a popular assembly of the clans (*curiae*), the **comitia curiata,** which conferred upon the newly elected king his *imperium* and may have had slight legislative power. There were two classes in the state: **patricians,** who alone could belong to the senate, and **plebeians.** Most probably the patricians were simply the more prosperous farmers, who for their own advantage organized themselves in *curiae,* set themselves up as a superior class, and usurped certain privileges. (Another theory is that the plebeians were the conquered native people.) As a result of the plebeians' lack of power to defend themselves, many attached themselves as clients to patrician patrons, who protected them in return for attendance and service.

The **early religion** was simple, chiefly the worship of Mars (an agricultural divinity who only later became god of war) and of animistic forces. Religious ceremonies were simple to the point of being magical; by their proper performance the divine power (*numen*) inherent in gods or objects was compelled to act, and failure to get results indicated some fault in the ceremony.

c. 616. Tarquinius Priscus (616–578) and his successors, **Servius Tullius** (578–534) and **Tarquinius Superbus** (the Proud, 534–510), may represent the Etruscan domination in Rome and emerge more clearly than their predecessors. Tarquin the First was a great builder (*Cloaca Maxima, Temple of Jupiter Capitolinus, Circus Maximus*). To weaken the patrician influence, he is said to have increased the senate to 300. He fought successfully against Sabines, Latins, and Etruscans. **Servius Tullius,** traditionally of slave and Latin descent, fought against Veii and brought Rome into the **Latin League.** His chief achievement, traditionally, was to substitute for the hereditary clans a new military division into **classes** and **centuries,** based on wealth and arms (cf. reforms of Solon in Athens). It may be, however, that this reform should really be dated about 450 and, in any case, the surviving (and conflicting) descriptions of his arrangements probably portray them in the state which they reached after the 3rd century B.C. Upon this arrangement depended a new assembly, the **comitia centuriata.** Since group voting was taken over from the comitia curiata, the wealthy, who though few in numbers constituted the majority of the centuries, controlled this assembly as, presumably, the patricians had the former. The last, **Tarquin the Proud,** was expelled in a revolt which according to tradition was led by **L. Junius Brutus** and was due to the rape of Lucretia by Sextus Tarquinius, son of the king.

2. THE EARLY REPUBLIC, TO 287 B.C.

The **early constitution:** two annual **consuls,** originally called *praetors* (generals), held equally the undivided *imperium* of the king; either could prevent the other from acting, but could not force him to act. They had absolute command of the army in the field, including power over life and death; in the city they were provided with *coercitio,* a sort of summary police power, but with slight civil and no criminal jurisdiction. They were elected by the comitia centuriata, but their *imperium* was conferred by the comitia curiata (*lex curiata*), later represented by 30 lictors.

The **judicial system:** cases of high treason were handled by the *duouiri perduellionis;* all other criminal cases of which the state took cognizance were handled by the *quaestores parricidii* (investigators of murder), later known simply as *quaestors.* From their collecting of fines, the quaestors became the main financial officers of the state, and in this capacity they became attached to the consuls as comptrollers; later they lost their judicial functions. Civil cases were usually handled by arbitration, but gradually the consuls came to take a larger part, until in 367 there was created a special officer (*praetor*).

In time of crisis the senate could restore unity of command by instructing the consuls to appoint a **dictator** (*magister populi*), who appointed as his assistant a master of the horse (*magister equitum*); the dictator had absolute power in all fields, but had to resign when his task was completed, and in no case could remain in office for more than six months.

The **plebs** seem already to have had an organization of their own, the *concilium plebis,* with its own officers (?*tribunes* originally commanders of the tribal regiments) and *aediles* (custodians of the temple of Ceres on the Aventine, where were kept the plebeian treasury and archives). When the first 17 rustic tribes were organized shortly after the foundation of the republic (the four urban tribes are ascribed by tradition to Servius Tullius, but may be later), the concilium plebis was reorganized on the basis of these; some time later a *comitia tributa* of the whole people was organized on the same basis, perhaps to break up the power of the hereditary clans (cf. Cleisthenes, at Athens). It is uncertain how long the concilium plebis remained distinct from the comitia tributa; in the later republic the difference was merely technical. A resolution of the plebs alone was called a *plebiscitum,* and was originally binding only on the plebeians, as opposed to a *lex* of the entire *populus,* adopted in a *comitia.*

At the beginning of the republican period, Rome was probably the dominant power in the Latin League, but apparently lost this position because of the continued Etruscan pressure; the next two centuries (to c. 280) were characterized externally by Rome's conquest of the primacy in Italy and internally by the struggle of the oppressed plebs, of which the richer members desired social and political equality with the patricians, while the poorer wanted simply protection from unjust treatment at the hands of the patrician magistrates.

509. TRADITIONAL DATE OF THE FOUNDING OF THE REPUBLIC. L. Junius Brutus and **L. Tarquinius Collatinus** (husband of Lucretia) became consuls. Almost all of the history of the first century of the republic, including the names of the first two or three decades of consuls, is unreliable, but it is not yet possible to establish the truth. The dates given here are those of Cicero's contemporary, Varro, adopted by Livy. They are subject to errors of up to ten years in the first century of the republic, gradually decreasing to become practically certain from c. 300.

A **lex Valeria de prouocatione** is said to have been passed by the *consul suffectus* (filling another's unexpired term), P. Valerius Poplicola, guaranteeing citizens in Rome (not on military service) the right of appeal to the comitia centuriata from a consul who proposed to execute or flog them; probably a retrojection of later legislation, but such a right was recognized by the **Twelve Tables.**

508. A **treaty with the Carthaginians** recognized Carthage's exclusive interests in Africa and Rome's in Latium. Doubt has been cast on the genuineness of this treaty, but probably unjustly.

Lars Porsena of the Etruscan Clusium attacked Rome and probably restored the Etruscan domination for a short time, although Roman tradition claimed he had been turned back by the exploits of **Horatius Cocles** (defense of the *pons sublicius,* or wooden Tiber bridge), Cloelia, and Q. Mucius Scaevola.

496. The dictator A. Postumius, in the **battle of Lake Regillus,** defeated the Latins, who, with the help of Aristodemus of Cumae, had some time before freed themselves from Etruscan rule by the **battle of Aricia.**

494. The **plebeians,** oppressed by debt, **seceded to the Sacred Mount** (probably the Aventine). The patricians were forced to make some concessions before the plebs would return. The latter further protected themselves by swearing to the *leges sacrae,* by which they bound themselves to avenge any injury done to their officials, the tribunes, the aediles, and the *decemuiri stlitibus iudicandis*. These officials were therefore called *sacrosanct*. They were not officials of the state, but officers of a corporate group within the state. But because of the unanimous support of the plebes they had *de facto* great powers, which were never legalized but became gradually respected by custom. The basis of the tribunes' powers was the *ius auxilii*, by which they could intervene to save anyone threatened by the action of a magistrate. This *intercessio* against a specific act of a magistrate developed later (when the tribunes secured admission to the senate) into the right of interposing a veto against any proposed law or decree. They presided over the concilium plebis. The original number of the tribunes was two or four; it eventually became ten. The aediles handled the fines imposed by the tribunes or the concilium, and through the use of this money came to have control of the free distributions of corn to the poor and over the repair of public buildings, etc., which was later extended into a general police power. The *decemuiri stlitibus iudicandis* conducted trials in which the status of persons as slaves or freedmen was in question.

493. A treaty of **Sp. Cassius** with the Latin League provided that booty was to be equally divided; new territory to be colonized in common; the rights of *connubium* and *commercium* (to contract valid marriages between members of different states and to carry on commerce with full legal protection) were restored as they had been before Rome's break with the league (c. 508). The reason for this peace was certainly the increasing pressure of the attacks of the neighboring Volsci and Aequi. The Hernici were later admitted to the alliance on equal terms with the other two members (486).

491. Gn. Marcius Coriolanus traditionally tried to bribe the plebeians with free grain into giving up the tribunate; when he failed and was summoned to trial, he fled to the Volsci and led them against Rome, but was turned back by the prayers of his mother and wife.

486. The consul Sp. Cassius attempted to make himself tyrant but was executed. This much may be true, but the story that his method was a proposed division of the public land, which was of insignificant extent for a long time, is probably a retrojection from the Gracchan era.

477. Battle of the Cremera. War had broken out with the Etruscan Veii (483), which was supported by Fidenae, a town controlling the upper Tiber and thus essential to Rome. A large number of Fabii took up a position on the Cremera to prevent the two cities from joining their forces, but were annihilated by the Veientines. Traditionally, only one of 300 escaped. A peace was made in 474.

458. L. Quinctius Cincinnatus, called from his field to assume the dictatorship, rescued a Roman army and defeated the Aequi, who had pressed into the valley of the Algidus.

451. Agitation of the plebs for codification of the law to curb the arbitrariness of the patrician magistrates led to the creation of **ten patrician decemvirs** in place of consuls. According to legend, an embassy had been sent to Athens in 454 to procure the laws of Solon for study. The first decemvirs published ten tables, but since these proved insufficient new decemvirs were created in 450 and drew up two additional tables. Thenceforth the *Twelve Tables* constituted the fundamental law of Rome until the 2nd century. Tradition alleges that this decemviral board continued illegally in office in 449 under the extreme patrician **Appius Claudius.** When he attempted to get for himself by false legal process the maiden Virginia, her father Virginius stabbed her and the plebeians seceded to the Aventine and Sacred Mounts. The decemvirs had to abdicate and Appius committed suicide.

448. The moderate patrician consuls Valerius and Horatius passed a series of **Valerio-Horatian** laws weakening the patrician power. Traditionally, these (1) made the *plebiscita* as valid as *leges;* (2) compelled all magistrates, including the dictator, to allow appeals from their decisions; and (3) affirmed the inviolability of the tribunes and also the aediles. All these changes are probably mere retrojections of later reforms. Two more quaestors were added specially for the military treasury, making a total of four. Though patricians, they were elected in the comitia tributa, and in 421 the quaestorship was opened to the plebeians. The tribunes acquired the right of taking auspices (necessary before any public business and later convenient as a means of blocking action) and the privilege of sitting on a bench inside the senate, though near the door.

445. A law (plebiscite?) of the tribune Canuleius allowed marriage between patricians and plebeians, the children to inherit the father's rank.

444. As a compromise in the face of agitation that the consulate be opened to plebeians, **six (?three) military tribunes with consular power,** who might be plebeians, were substituted for the consuls. Two patrician *censors* were also created to hold office for five (?four) years, later reduced to eighteen months every fifth year. They had no *imperium,* but only a *potestas,* but because usually older and distinguished ex-consuls, they came to outrank even consuls. Their tasks gave them importance, since they made up the citizen lists for tax and military purposes (the *census*), enrolled senators (*lectio senatus*) and knights (*recognitio equitum*), and examined into public morals (*regimen morum*), so that at the end of their term they could perform the ceremony of purification for the state, the *lustrum,* a word which came to be applied to their five-year cycle. They also made up the state budget, handled its property, and let out contracts for public works.

439. Traditionally, Sp. Maelius was put to death by Servius Ahala, master of the horse for the dictator Cincinnatus, because his free distribution of grain to the people seemed an attempt at a tyranny.

431. The dictator A. Postumius Tubertus decisively defeated the Aequi at the Algidus and drove them out of the valley. The Volsci were then continually driven back and are said to have made peace in 396.

426. Fidenae, which, with Veii, had declared war in 438, was destroyed by the dictator Mamercus Aemilius and the master of the horse A. Cornelius Cossus; thus Veii was forced to make peace for 20 years (425).

405-396. In the **siege of Veii,** tradition alleged that, because the army had to be kept in the field all winter, pay for the troops was introduced. The dictator M. Furius Camillus finally took the town; it was destroyed, and, since the Latins had not contributed to the siege, the territory was annexed directly to Rome and organized in four new tribes. From this time on Rome really outweighed its ally, the Latin League; the Hernici had long been inferior to the other two.

390. Rome was sacked by the Gauls under Brennus, who defeated the defending army at the **Allia** on July 18. According to tradition the Gauls held all of Rome except the Capitol. Their withdrawal after seven months is attributed to Camillus, but they were probably bought off. The Latins and Hernici broke off their alliance with Rome.

384. The patrician M. Manlius Capitolinus was, according to tradition, convicted of aspiring to a tyranny by releasing plebeian debtors at his own expense, and was executed by being thrown from the Tarpeian Rock.

367. Licinio-Sextian Laws. After ten years of agitation the tribunes C. Licinius and L. Sextius secured the passage of reform measures: (1) some sort of relief was granted to debtors; (2) the amount of public land that one person could hold was limited to 500 iugera (one iugum = ⅝ acre). This provision is almost certainly a retrojection from the Gracchan era; (3) The practice of giving a consular *imperium* to military tribunes was abolished, and one consulship was opened to the plebs. Tradition in-

correctly states that both consulships were opened to the plebs, and that one of them had to be filled by a plebeian. At the same time a third praetor was created, to handle the judicial functions of the other two chief magistrates, who thenceforth were usually known as consuls. Two patrician *curule aediles* were created, with functions much like the plebeian aediles. The plebeians were soon admitted to all offices, the last being the religious colleges of *pontifices* and *augures,* by the **lex Ogulnia** of 300. As a result of these changes, a new nobility of office-holding families, both patrician and plebeian, grew up, and the patriciate lost all significance. This nobility soon became quite exclusive, so that a *novus homo* (a man without office-holding ancestors) had great difficulty in obtaining an office.

367-349. Four wars were waged against the Gauls, who made incursions from Cisalpine Gaul into central Italy. In them are supposed to have been fought the single combats against Gallic champions of T. Manlius Torquatus (361) and M. Valerius Corvus (349). Peace was finally concluded c. 334.

362-345. Wars with the peoples immediately around Rome. The Hernici and the revolting Latin cities were forced to rejoin the Latin League on severer terms; southern Etruria was brought under Roman supremacy; and the Volsci and Aurunci were reduced, thus putting Rome in contact with the Samnites.

348. Second treaty between Rome and Carthage; some sources and some modern authorities call this the first treaty.

343-341. The **FIRST SAMNITE WAR** was started by a request for aid from the Samnite tribes in the Campanian plain against the hill tribes. After minor Roman victories the war ended in a draw.

340-338. The **LATIN WAR** began with the revolt of the Latin cities from the league and their demand for complete equality. In the course of the war, P. Decius Mus sacrificed himself for the victory of his army. The consul T. Manlius brought the war to a close in the **victory of Trifanum.** The Latin League was dissolved and its members made dependent on Rome without even *commercium* and *connubium* among themselves. In Rome their inhabitants received private rights but not the vote (*ciuitas sine suffragio,* later called *latinitas*). Some cities ceded land for settlement of Romans, some were made into Roman colonies, others were made dependent states.

339. Leges Publiliae, passed by the plebeian dictator Q. Publilius Philo, gave *plebiscita* the force of law provided they obtained the subsequent consent of the senate (*auctoritas patrum*); for regular *leges* it was provided that this consent should now be given in advance, as a pure formality.

326-304. The **SECOND SAMNITE WAR** began when Rome made Fregellae a colony and the first pro-consul (an ex-consul whose *imperium* was extended for carrying on a military command), Q. Publilius Philo, captured Naples (327). The Romans had the support of the Apulians and Lucanians, and later of certain Sabellian cities. After initial successes the consuls Sp. Postumius and T. Veturius were surrounded in the **Caudine Forks** and forced to surrender with their whole army. The Romans only slowly recovered Campania, but in 312 the censor Ap. Claudius began the great military road, the **Via Appia,** from Rome to Capua to secure Campania. The northern Etruscans joined Rome's enemies but were defeated at **Lake Vadimo** in 310. In 308 the peoples of central Italy, Umbrians, Picentini, Marsians, etc., attacked Rome. The Romans countered by using their first war-fleet in the Adriatic. The Samnites were defeated by M. Fulvius and L. Postumius in 305. In 304 peace was made, slightly to Rome's advantage in that she got sole hegemony of Campania.

313. A law of the consul Poetilius (*lex Poetilia*) secured insolvent debtors against personal imprisonment if they surrendered their property entirely to their creditors.

312. **Appius Claudius** (later Caecus, "the blind"), as censor, is said to have distributed freedmen not holding land among all the tribes, but in 304 they, and freedmen of small landed property, were confined to the four urban tribes. This may reflect later debates as to the disposition of freedmen. In 304 a freedman of Appius, Gnaeus Flavius, is said to have made public the rules of legal procedure (*legis actiones*), to which he had access as clerk to the magistrates. This completed the work begun by the decemvirs in protecting the poor from manipulation of the law by the rich.

At about this time (or perhaps earlier, after the Gallic sack), the Roman army was reorganized so that in place of a solid phalanx with the long thrusting spear (*hasta*) the legion consisted of small groups, maniples of 120 men in two centuries (now purely titular), arranged in echelon in three lines (*hastati* and *principes* with the throwing javelin, *pilum,* and only the rearmost *triarii* with the spear) for greater mobility in mountainous areas.

During the ensuing years, Rome secured the Apennines by colonies, Sora, Alba Fucens, Carsioli, and Narnia, and built the **Via Flaminia** north to Narnia and the **Via Valeria** to Alba Fucens.

298-290. The **THIRD SAMNITE WAR** was a final effort of the Samnites, aided by the Luca-nians, Gauls, and Etruscans, to break the power of Rome. Their capital, Bovianum, was taken in 298, but their army managed to combine with the Gauls, only to be defeated in 295 at **Sentinum,** where a second Decius Mus secured a Roman victory by self-sacrifice, perhaps in fact the only instance. The Gauls scattered, the Etruscans sued for peace in 294, and the Samnites finally made peace as autonomous allies, though the colony of Venusia was planted in the south to watch them, as well as Minturnae, Sinuessa, and Haria farther north. The Sabines, northeast of Rome, were annexed and given Latin rights.

285-282. The Romans, despite defeats, annihilated the Gallic Senones, crushed the Etruscans at Lake Vadimo and Populonia, and occupied the Greek cities in Lucania: Locri, Croton, and Thurii. This advance brought on the war with Tarentum and Pyrrhus.

287. The **lex Hortensia,** passed by the dictator Q. Hortensius, fully equated *plebiscita* with *leges* by requiring the *auctoritas patrum* for the former to be given in advance as well as for the latter; its passage was brought about by another secession of the plebs, this time to the Janiculum. The plebs had thus achieved complete legal equality with the patricians, but the old problem remained in the oppression of the poor by the rich patricio-plebeian nobility, which was in full control of the concilium plebis and the comitia tributa because, since the voting was by tribes, only the rich members of the more distant tribes could afford to come to the meetings in Rome. Further, in the assemblies all initiative was in the hands of the presiding magistrates, and these were now almost always from the nobility and under the control of the senate. As the problems of government became more complex with the expansion of Rome, the control of the senate became still more effective.

Rome had now established her supremacy throughout central Italy. Her relations with the other communities may be summarized as follows:

(1) *Municipia* retained their own municipal administration and enjoyed only the private rights (*connubium* and *commercium*) of Roman citizenship, not the franchise or right of holding office (*ciuitas sine suffragio*).

(2) *Coloniae* were settlements established by Rome for military purposes, usually on land taken from the conquered peoples. Smaller ones, Roman, were real garrisons and their settlers retained full citizenship. At first they may have been administered directly from Rome. Larger ones reflected real attempts to relieve surplus population and included both Latins and Romans, the latter accepting only

Latin citizenship, or *ciutias sine suffragio.* They may have had some local government from the beginning. Ultimately, colonies came to have administrations closely modeled on the Roman, with two executive magistrates (*duumuiri*) and a senate or curia whose members were called *decuriones.*

Whatever the original form of government of the various *municipia* may have been, it tended to approximate the oligarchical model of Rome and the *coloniae,* with a small executive, often four (*quattuoruiri*), and a curia. Moreover, recent study suggests that this general pattern of municipality may not be at all early, may, in fact, date only from Caesar's municipal reforms, and that before that both *municipia* and *coloniae* were governed by officials sent out from Rome, as was certainly the

case with *municipia* which, by revolt, were deprived of self-government (e.g. Capua later).

(3) *Ciuitates foederatae* were independent allies (*socii*) of Rome, whose obligations were regulated by treaty. They enjoyed freedom from direct interference in their affairs and from taxation (*libertas et immunitas*) and usually provided auxiliary troops or ships rather than legionaries. But their foreign relations were determined by Rome, and, in fact, they suffered considerable control.

(4) There were, in addition, groups or communities which did not have a civic organization and which, consequently, were administered under various names (*fora, conciliabula, uici, pagi*) either directly from Rome, by *praefecti,* or by neighboring cities to which they were attached as *attributi.* (*Cont.* p. 97.)

D. THE HELLENISTIC WORLD, TO 30 B.C.

(*From p. 81*)

1. CULTURAL DEVELOPMENT

The **Hellenistic Age** was characterized politically by the **atrophy of the city state.** The cities of Greece were dominated increasingly by their richer or better educated members and the mass of the population lost power. In their external relations the cities either passed under the control of the various monarchs or joined together in leagues, whose attempts at representative federal government marked an advance in government which unfortunately bore no further fruit during the Roman period. Athens was a university town, respected for its past grandeur but of little political weight after 262. Sparta, however, played a lone and considerable hand in the Peloponnese. To offset the decay of Greece itself, the Hellenistic Age witnessed the **spread of Greek culture** by the conquests of Alexander and his successors as far as the Indus Valley, the creation of Greek cities throughout Asia, and the development of monarchical governments. In the new Greek cities, municipal administration and public building reached a high level, as at Priene (Asia Minor) or Alexandria (Egypt). **Social experiments** ranged from state control of the grain supply (Athens) or distribution of grain to citizens (Samos) to extreme agrarian reforms at Sparta. Private or royal munificence benefited the cities on a grand scale, and the cities themselves substituted for political rivalry that of the splendor of games, buildings, and honors. The administration of

the three chief kingdoms was conditioned by their background. In **Macedon** the army, representing the Macedonian people, retained considerable influence, and the king was never so absolute as his Asiatic *confrères.* The **Seleucids** developed a system of provincial administration and of communications based on the Persian satrapies; but their capital, Antioch, never attained the excellence of Egypt's Alexandria and its Hellenism was strongly affected by Syrian emotionalism. The **Ptolemies** administered Egypt as had the Pharaohs, as a state monopoly. They granted a privileged position, however, to Macedonian settlers and to the city of Alexandria, which was kept apart from the rest of Egypt as a Greek city, though it contained also a large Jewish population, for whom, during the 3rd century, a Greek translation was made of the Hebrew *Bible,* called the *Septuagint* from the 70 elders traditionally responsible for it. Alexandria was distinguished by its excellent administration and its splendid buildings, among which were a lighthouse (*pharos*) and an academy of scholars (*museum,* temple of the Muses) with a magnificent library.

The economic life of the eastern Mediterranean was much stimulated by unification in Greek hands, by the opening of new areas, and by improved navigation and communications. The cities became very rich. In particular, the opening of the treasures of the Near East vastly increased the amount of gold and silver in circulation. Two countries were, however, adversely affected. Greece, naturally poor, could no longer compete with the more fertile areas now opened for exploitation. Egypt's resources, though ample for her self-contained economy, were exhausted by the expenditures of the Ptolemies in their attempt to create an Aegean empire. Nevertheless, in general, the period was one of complacent prosperity throughout the eastern Mediterranean.

Under the great librarians of Alexandria, **Zenodotus** (c. 280), **Aristophanes** of Byzantium (257–180), and **Aristarchus** (217–145), philology, textual criticism, and kindred subjects replaced creative writing. Alexandria became the intellectual center of the world, whose museum not only contained a library said to have numbered 700,000 volumes (partially destroyed in 47 B.C.), but also botanical and zoological gardens, lecture rooms, and dissecting halls. The Hellenistics combined the mathematical emphasis of Plato with the epistemology of Aristotle to produce a physics that is recognizably modern. Astronomical measurements were made by **Aristarchus,** and the circumference of the earth computed by **Eratosthenes.** Mathematics advanced through the work of **Euclid** (c. 300) and physics through the work of **Archimedes** (287–212, in Syracuse), who must be acknowledged as one of the scientific geniuses of all time. **Herophilos** and **Erasistratos,** physiologists, conducted human as well as animal dissections in their investigations on the function of the brain and the nervous system. Beginning of the building of mechanical contrivances, Ctesibius (fl. c. 283–247 B.C.), Hero of Alexandria (1st century A.D.), and Archimedes, who designed siege instruments.

Literature became imitative, artificial, and overburdened with learning, as in the poetry of **Callimachus** (c. 260), or the epic *Argonautica* of **Apollonius Rhodius** (295–214). Only the pastoral achieved a delicate and spontaneous freshness in the poems of **Theocritus** (c. 270, from Syracuse). The Attalids, notably Eumenes II, tried to make Pergamum into an intellectual rival of Alexandria, but their capital became famous chiefly for its **Pergamene school of art,** whose exaggerated style is best seen in the friezes of the Altar of Pergamum. Another school flourished in the prosperous island of Rhodes. Much of Hellenistic art dealt with simple subjects of daily life in a realistic fashion, as in the charming pottery figurines from Tanagra, in Greece.

In **philosophy,** the Academy continued the Platonic tradition but with increasing skepticism about the possibility of attaining truth. The **Peripatetics** devoted themselves almost wholly to scientific and historical studies. Two new schools, however, answered the spiritual needs of the time. **Stoicism** was founded by **Zeno** (336–264), a half-Phoenician from Cyprus, who taught in the Painted Porch (*stoa poikile*) at Athens, and **Epicureanism** by **Epicurus** (342–270), who withdrew from the world into his garden. Both sought the same end, a mind which would be so self-sufficient through inner discipline and its own resources that it would not be disturbed by external accidents. The Stoics sought this undisturbed state of mind (*ataraxia*) by modifying the Cynic asceticism to a doctrine of neglect of outward honors and wealth and devotion to duty. A belief that the world was ruled by a universal reason in which all shared led them to a humanitarian view of the brotherhood of men which transcended national, racial, or social differences. This internationalism and the doctrine that the ruler should embody divine reason allowed them to support monarchical government. The Epicureans sought the same end by following the Cyrenaics in advocating an inactive life (*apraxia*) and a moderate, not an excessive, self-indulgence. To free the mind from wrong, they attacked religion and superstition and adopted the atomic metaphysics as a mechanical explanation of the universe.

In **religion,** the Hellenistic Age witnessed a loss of belief in the simple Greek pantheon and a turning to more emotional oriental worships, like those of **Cybele,** the Great Mother of Asia Minor, the Persian **Mithra,** or the Egyptian **Isis.** A fatalistic view of external events led to the personification of Fortune (*tyche*) as a goddess. And a combination of flattery, legalism (since a god could always rule a city without changes in the constitution), skepticism (since many considered that the gods were originally famous men), and real gratitude for the benefits of government introduced the worship of rulers, both dead and living, which the Macedonian monarchs alone refused.

2. THE WARS OF THE DIADOCHI, 322–275 B.C.

322–315. When **Perdiccas** became regent for Philip III Arrhidaeus, the other generals, Antipater, Antigonus, Craterus, and Ptolemy, refused obedience. Perdiccas was murdered when he attempted to dislodge Ptolemy from Egypt, but his general **Eumenes** defeated and slew Craterus in Asia Minor (321). Antipater and Ptolemy at Triparadeisus in Syria agreed

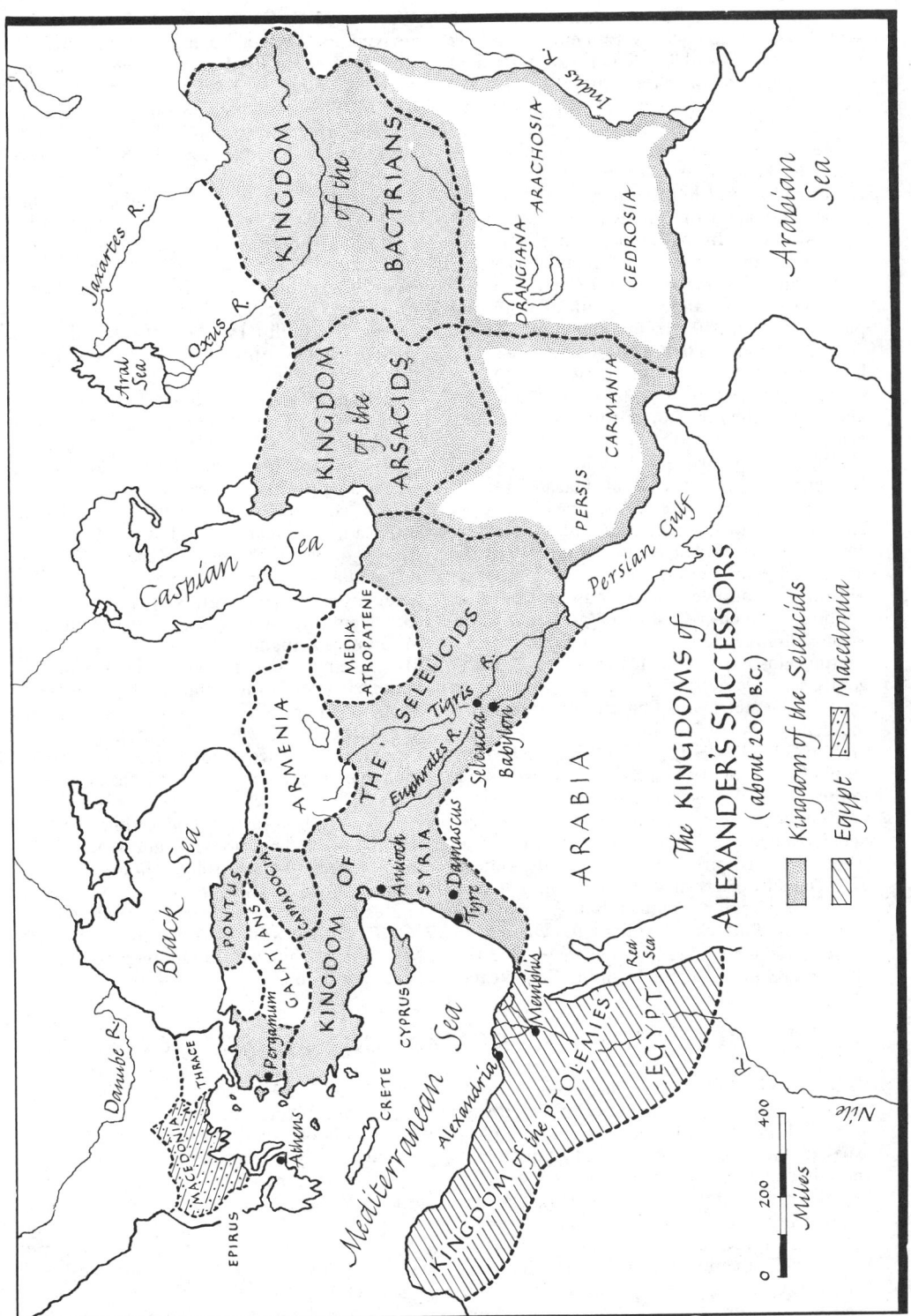

The KINGDOMS of
ALEXANDER'S SUCCESSORS
(about 200 B.C.)

Kingdom of the Seleucids
Egypt
Macedonia

that Antipater should be regent. Antipater sent Antigonus to dislodge Eumenes, who took refuge in the hills (320). When Antipater died (319), he left **Polyperchon** as regent, but Ptolemy defied him and annexed Syria. Antigonus seized Phrygia and Lydia. Polyperchon gave Eumenes command of the troops in Cilicia. Antipater's son, **Cassander,** seized the Piraeus, garrisoned it, and left Demetrius of Phalerum as virtual dictator of Athens (317). Cassander took Macedon from Polyperchon (317), executed Olympias and Philip Arrhidaeus when they attacked him, and imprisoned Roxana with her son Alexander IV, both of whom he put to death in 310. In the meantime, Antigonus, after a drawn **battle at Paraetacene** (317), had defeated Eumenes in Gabiene (316) and executed him. Ptolemy in Egypt, Cassander, and Lysimachus in Thrace formed a coalition against Antigonus (315).

315–307. Antigonus seized Syria, but his son, Demetrius, was defeated at Gaza (312) by Ptolemy, who had already occupied the Cyclades (314) and the Peloponnese (313). Ptolemy then sent **Seleucus** to capture Babylon from Antigonus. An attempted settlement in 311 merely allowed Antigonus to continue fighting Seleucus, Cassander to secure the throne of Macedon (above), and Ptolemy to continue his expansion in the Aegean. Antigonus sent Demetrius to Athens, whence he expelled Demetrius of Phalerum and restored the democracy (307).

307. ANTIGONUS I, MONOPHTHALMOS ("one-eyed") or Cyclops, and **Demetrius I Poliorcetes** ("besieger") took the title of king, whereupon Ptolemy and Seleucus, Cassander, and Lysimachus did the same. The unity of Alexander's empire was thus openly ended.

306. Demetrius crushed Ptolemy in a naval battle off Cyprian Salamis but Ptolemy repelled a land attack by Antigonus. Demetrius failed to reduce Rhodes by a year's siege (305–304), but relieved Athens from the **Four Years'** War waged by Cassander (307–304). He then revived the **Hellenic League** of Philip (302).

301. BATTLE OF IPSUS (in Phrygia). The allies, Cassander, Lysimachus, and Seleucus, but not Ptolemy, finally crushed and slew Antigonus. Demetrius, who had been recalled by Antigonus, escaped to Corinth. By the division of spoils, Seleucus was given Syria, Lysimachus western and central Asia Minor, Cassander kept Macedon, but his brother Pleistarchus received southern Asia Minor. Ptolemy, however, seized Coele-Syria.

299. Pleistarchus was driven out by Demetrius, and Cassander himself died in 298. His eldest son, Philip IV, died also, so that two younger sons, Antipater and Alexander V, divided his realm.

295. Demetrius, after a bitter siege, recovered Athens, where one Lachares had made himself tyrant. He then murdered Alexander V (294) and took Macedon. He mastered northern and central Greece save for Aetolia.

288. A coalition was formed against Demetrius, and Lysimachus and King Pyrrhus of Epirus drove him out of Macedon. He attempted a campaign in Asia Minor, but finally Seleucus captured him in Cilicia (285).

283. Demetrius died in captivity, leaving a son in Greece, Antigonus.

281. Seleucus defeated and slew Lysimachus at the **battle of Corupedium** and became master of Asia Minor. When he tried to seize Macedon, however, he was assassinated by Ptolemy Ceraunus, who acquired control of Macedon. Ptolemy, in turn, was slain in an invasion of Celts (279).

279. The **Celts** ravaged Macedon, defeated the Greeks at Thermopylae, and reached Delphi. A second band ruled Thrace until 210, while a third crossed to central Asia Minor and established the **kingdom of Galatia.**

276–275. Meanwhile, Antigonus recovered Macedon for himself, founding a dynasty that lasted until 168.

3. SICILY TO THE ROMAN CONQUEST, 216 B.C.

317–289. AGATHOCLES made himself tyrant of Syracuse in consequence of a civil war (c. 323–317) in which he, as democratic leader, expelled the oligarchs with Carthaginian aid and divided their property among the poor. He successfully defended himself against the neighboring cities and the exiled oligarchs until these appealed to Carthage.

311. The Carthaginian general **Hamilcar** defeated Agathocles at the Himera River and besieged Syracuse. In 310, Agathocles slipped across to Africa, where he maintained himself until 307. But his army, under his son, was annihilated during his absence.

305. Agathocles came to terms with Carthage and the oligarchs, and took the title of king. In the meantime the Tarentines had made peace with the Samnites (c. 320) and Rome (304), but were hard pressed by the Lucanians.

302. When a Spartan commander, Cleonymus, failed to relieve them, the Tarentines called in Agathocles. He also failed to accomplish much and died at Syracuse in 289, bequeathing their freedom to the Syracusans, who restored the democracy. Certain of the Campanian mercenaries of Agathocles, calling themselves **Mamertines** ("sons of Mars"), seized Messana.

282-275. The **Tarentines**, angered by Roman occupation of towns in southern Italy, destroyed a Roman fleet which, in violation of the treaty of 304, had passed the Lacinian promontory. They then drove the Romans from Thurii. When Rome declared war, they called in Pyrrhus. Upon his departure in 275, the Greeks of southern Italy remained under Rome, while those in Sicily passed under Carthaginian power, save for Syracuse.

269-216. **Hiero II** made himself tyrant of Syracuse and defeated the Mamertines at Mylae. He took the title of king (265), and joined the Carthaginians in besieging the Roman force which occupied Messana in 264. But when he was defeated and besieged in Syracuse, he made peace with Rome (263). At the end of the First Punic War all Sicily save Syracuse and a few other pro-Roman cities passed into Rome's possession. Syracuse was reduced in 211 during the Second Punic War.

4. MACEDON AND GREECE
TO THE ROMAN CONQUEST, 146 B.C.

290. Emergence of the **Aetolian League**, a military federation in western Greece. It had a council with proportional representation and a semi-annual assembly. Affairs were handled by a committee of 100 *apokletoi* and a single general (*strategos*) in wartime. The league expanded into Phocis (254) and Boeotia (245) and dominated Greece from sea to sea. It also included Elis and part of Arcadia (245) and made an alliance with Messene, thus separating Sparta from the Achaean League.

280. Formation of the **Achaean League**, consisting of twelve towns in the northern Peloponnese. It had a general (two until 255), a board of ten *demiourgoi*, a federal council with proportional representation of members. There was also an annual assembly of all free citizens. After 251, Aratus of Sicyon dominated its policy and was *strategos* in alternate years. He extended it to include many non-Achaean cities, especially Corinth (243).

276-239. ANTIGONUS II GONATAS ("knock-kneed"?) had to repel an invasion by **Pyrrhus of Epirus** (274-273). Pyrrhus was then called into Greece by the pretender Cleonymus, who sought to oust King Areus (309-265) from Sparta. Pyrrhus was slain at Argos by the Argives and Antigonus (272). Antigonus established tyrants in several cities of the Peloponnese and made peace with the Aetolian League.

266-262. **Ptolemy II of Egypt** stirred up Athens and Sparta to wage the **Chremonidean War** (from Chremonides, an Athenian leader) against Antigonus. Areus of Sparta was defeated and killed at the isthmus (265) and, when Ptolemy failed to give energetic aid, Athens was obliged to surrender after a two-year siege (262). Antigonus garrisoned several strong points of Attica and imposed a moderate oligarchy on Athens.

258 (?256). Antigonus defeated Ptolemy in a naval **battle off Cos** and took the Cyclades, though he had to reconquer them later in the **battle of Andros** (245).

c. 252. Antigonus' governor of the Peloponnese, Alexander, revolted and held the peninsula until his death (c. 246).

251. **Aratus of Sicyon** recovered that city from Antigonus' tyrant, and then joined the Achaean League, which he soon dominated.

245-235. **Sparta** had fallen into a serious economic crisis because of the excessive concentration of land and wealth in the hands of a few. Coined money had been introduced by King Areus. The number of full citizens who could contribute to their mess-tables (*syssitia*) had fallen to 700. When **King Agis IV** (244-240) tried to redistribute the land into 4500 equal lots, the great landowners executed him. **Cleomenes III**, who married Agis' widow, became king (235).

241. Antigonus sent the Aetolian League to ravage the isthmus.

239-229. **Demetrius II** succeeded his father, Antigonus. He protected Epirus against Aetolia, so that the latter broke with Macedon and made an alliance with Achaea. Demetrius attacked it in the **War of Demetrius** (238-229), but was recalled by invasions from the north (233). Argos expelled the pro-Macedonian tyrant Aristomachus and joined the Achaean League (229), while Athens asserted her independence.

229-221. **Antigonus III Doson** ("going to give," i.e. always promising) succeeded his cousin Demetrius as guardian of the latter's nine-year-old son, Philip, whom he deposed in 227 to become king himself. He made peace with Aetolia and drove the barbarians out of Macedon.

228-227. **Cleomenes** defeated the Achaeans under Aratus. He then seized the power in Sparta, redivided the land, and enfranchised

4000 *perioikoi* and abolished the *ephorate*. With an increased citizen army, he reduced Aratus to appeal to Antigonus (225).

222. Antigonus formed a new Hellenic League and crushed Cleomenes at the **battle of Sellasia** (222). Cleomenes fled to Egypt. Antigonus abolished the Spartan kingship, restored the ephors, and forced Sparta into his league.

221-178. Philip V, son of Demetrius II, succeeded Antigonus III. At his instigation the Hellenic League assembled at Corinth to declare

219-217. The **War of the Allies,** or Social War, against the Aetolians because of the latter's piracy. The Aetolians allied with Elis and Sparta, where an anti-Macedonian faction tried to recall Cleomenes. When he was slain in Egypt, the Spartans nevertheless restored the dual kingship. Philip ravaged Elis (219-218), molested the Aetolian sanctuary of Thermum, and laid waste Laconia.

217. Rhodes and Egypt negotiated the **Peace of Naupactus** between the discouraged Aetolians and Philip, who wanted freedom to act against Rome.

215-205. In the **FIRST MACEDONIAN WAR** Philip V of Macedon attempted to help Hannibal and the Carthaginians against Rome, but a Roman fleet in the Adriatic prevented him from crossing to Italy and the Romans secured the support of the Aetolian League and Pergamum (212), as well as of Elis, Mantinea, and Sparta (210). Sparta in particular, after a period of attempted social reform under King Cheilon (219), had risen to power under Machanidas, regent for the young King Pelops. When the Achaean League under Philopoemen (since the murder of Aratus in 213) slew Machanidas at Mantinea (207), Nabis became regent and soon, by deposing Pelops, king. The Greeks came to terms with Philip in 206 and Rome accepted the settlement by the **Peace of Phoenice** (205).

203-200. Philip, allied with Antiochus III against Egypt (203), began operations in the Aegean, but was defeated by Rhodes and Attalus of Pergamum in the **battle of Chios** (201).

200-196. The **SECOND MACEDONIAN WAR** arose from an appeal by Attalus and Rhodes to Rome (201). When Philip refused to keep the peace, all the Greeks joined Rome (200-198), and Flamininus defeated Philip at **Cynoscephalae** (197), and proclaimed the freedom of Greece at the Isthmian Games (196). Flamininus was forced to check Nabis of

Sparta (above), who had carried through agrarian reforms (207-204) and expanded his power in the Peloponnese, especially by acquiring Argos (198). He now lost Argos and much of Laconia, and gave control of his foreign policy to Rome (195). Upon the murder of Nabis (192), Sparta was forced into the Achaean League by Rome, and Messene and Elis soon joined, so that the league controlled all the Peloponnese.

192-189. The **Aetolians declared war on Rome** and secured the support of Antiochus III with a small force. The Achaeans and Philip supported Rome. The Romans drove Antiochus back to Asia in the **battle of Thermopylae** (191), and the Aetolians were finally made subject allies of Rome by M. Fulvius Nobilior (189).

189-181. Philopoemen humbled Sparta but lost his life in suppressing a revolt in Messenia (183). His successor in the Achaean League, Callicrates, was subservient to Rome and allowed Sparta to revive.

179-167. Perseus became king of Macedon on the death of his father Philip V. He had already persuaded Philip to execute his pro-Roman brother Demetrius, and now Eumenes II of Pergamum laid charges against him at Rome.

171-167. In the **THIRD MACEDONIAN WAR** Perseus was crushed by Aemilius Paullus at **Pydna** (168). He later died in captivity in Italy and the Antigonids came to an end. Rome made Macedon into four unrelated republics, paying a moderate yearly tribute (167). In Aetolia, 500 anti-Romans were slain. One thousand hostages, including the historian Polybius, were taken from Achaea to Italy.

149-148. The **FOURTH MACEDONIAN WAR** was begun by Andriscus, who pretended to be a son of Perseus. On his defeat, Macedon became a Roman province (148).

146. When the Achaean hostages had returned (151) and Callicrates had died (149), the Achaean League attacked Sparta, but was crushed by the Roman general Mummius (146). The Roman Senate ordered Mummius to abolish the leagues, substitute oligarchies for all democracies, sack Corinth, and place Greece under the supervision of the governor of Macedon. This marked the end of Greek and Macedonian independence, though some Greek states retained autonomy for a long time.

5. THE SELEUCID EMPIRE AND PERGAMUM, 305-64 B.C.

Under the Seleucids there developed, in Mesopotamia, a complex computational method of exact astronomical prediction, although apparently no physical model was used. The zodiac and the constellations against which the planets were seen became important for computational purposes.

305-280. SELEUCUS I NICATOR ("conqueror"), after securing his position against Antigonus (310-306) and assuming the royal title (305), ceded India to **Sandracottus** (Chandragupta) for 500 elephants (304-303). Though Ptolemy took Coele-Syria (301), Seleucus secured Cilicia from Demetrius (296-295). Seleucus failed to reduce **Mithridates I of Pontus,** but got control of western Asia Minor on the defeat of Lysimachus (281).

280-261. Antiochus I Soter ("saviour") succeeded upon the murder of Seleucus. He fought and finally defeated the Galatians (279-275) by terrifying them with his elephants. In the **Damascene War** (280-279) and **First Syrian War** (276-272) **War** he lost to Ptolemy II, Miletus, Phoenicia, and western Cilicia.

263-241. Eumenes I made himself virtually independent of Antiochus as ruler of Pergamum, where his uncle, Philetarus, had ruled as governor first for Lysimachus and then for the Seleucids.

261-246. Antiochus II Theos ("god"), son of Antiochus I, secured the support of Antigonus II and Rhodes against Egypt in the **Second Syrian War** (260-255). The succeeding peace restored to Antiochus: Ionia (including Miletus), Coele-Syria, and western Cilicia (255).

250-230. Diodotus I declared himself independent king of Bactria. In 248-247, Arsaces I of the nomad Parni established himself in the province of Parthia and founded the **Parthian Kingdom.**

246-226. SELEUCUS II CALLINICUS ("gloriously victorious"), son of Antiochus II by his divorced wife, Laodice I, succeeded. **Berenice II,** daughter of Ptolemy II, whom Antiochus married in 252, provoked the

246-241. Third Syrian War ("Laodicean War" or "War of Berenice") in favor of her infant son. Though she and her son were murdered in Antioch, her brother, Ptolemy III, invaded Asia and ultimately forced Seleucus to surrender the coasts of Syria and southern Asia Minor (241).

241-197. Attalus I Soter ("savior"), who succeeded his father's cousin Eumenes I, as ruler of Pergamum, took advantage of Seleucus' difficulties to secure for himself western Asia

Minor by crushing the Galatians near **Pergamum** (230), after which he took the title king and received the surname *Soter.*

237. Seleucus attacked **Antiochus Hierax** ("falcon"), a younger son of Laodice, whom Seleucus in 241 had recognized as ruler of Asia Minor. Hierax secured the aid of Mithridates II of Pontus and the Galatians. The Galatians crushed Seleucus at Ancyra (236).

229-226. Attalus I of Pergamum drove Hierax out of Asia Minor (229-228), after which Seleucus drove him out of Syria (227) to Thrace, where he died (226).

226-223. Seleucus III Soter or Ceraunus ("thunderbolt"), son of Seleucus II, was murdered during a war with Attalus I (224-221).

223-187. ANTIOCHUS III, THE GREAT, brother of Seleucus III, regained from Attalus most of the territory lost since 241. He recovered the Mesopotamian provinces from the revolting governor, Molon (221). But in the

221-217. Fourth Syrian War, despite initial successes, he finally retained on the Syrian coast only Seleucia, the port of Antioch.

209-204. In a number of campaigns, Antiochus reduced the Parthian Arsaces III Priapatius to vassalship, made an alliance with Euthydemus, who had usurped the Bactrian throne of Diodotus II, and even secured the submission of the Indian rajah Sophagasenus. Thus he restored the Seleucid kingdom to its former extent.

201-195. The **Fifth Syrian War** resulted from the treaty which Antiochus III had made with Philip V of Macedon in 203. The war was decided in 200 by Antiochus' **victory of Panium.** After several campaigns in Anatolia, Antiochus secured from Egypt most of Coele-Syria and southern Asia Minor (save Cyprus). Although Eumenes II Soter of Pergamum (197-159), son of Attalus I, induced Flamininus to order Antiochus out of Asia Minor, Antiochus did not heed, but confirmed his conquests by a peace with Egypt (195).

192-189. WAR WITH ROME, Antiochus' continued disregard of the senate led to a war in which he was driven from Greece (191) and his fleet was defeated at **Myonnesus** (190). The Roman army entered Asia Minor and defeated Antiochus himself at **Magnesia** (190). In the peace (189), Antiochus paid a large indemnity, lost his fleet, and surrendered Asia Minor, which was divided between Rhodes and Pergamum. This defeat led to the complete breaking away of Armenia (under Artaxias) and of Bactria, where a succession of Greek rulers preserved Hellenism until the invasions of the

The Maccabean Family

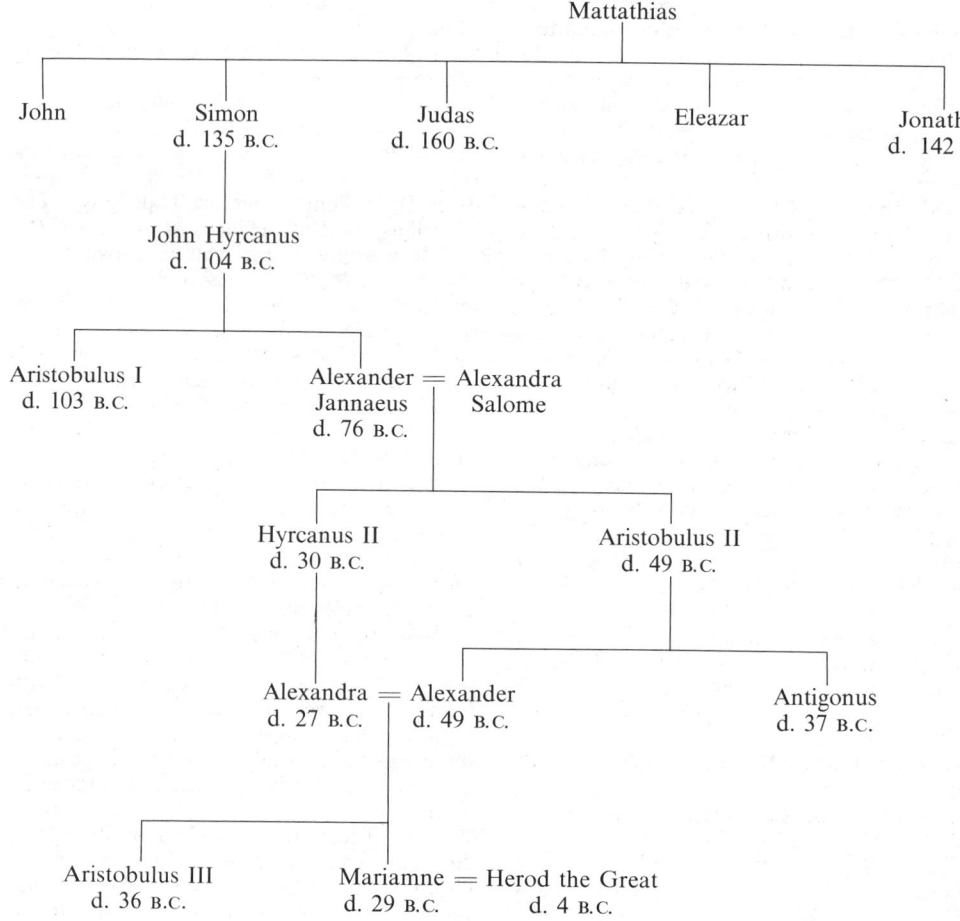

Mattathias

John   Simon
d. 135 B.C.   Judas
d. 160 B.C.   Eleazar   Jonathan
d. 142 B.C.

John Hyrcanus
d. 104 B.C.

Aristobulus I
d. 103 B.C.   Alexander = Alexandra
Jannaeus   Salome
d. 76 B.C.

Hyrcanus II
d. 30 B.C.   Aristobulus II
d. 49 B.C.

Alexandra = Alexander
d. 27 B.C.   d. 49 B.C.   Antigonus
d. 37 B.C.

Aristobulus III
d. 36 B.C.   Mariamne = Herod the Great
d. 29 B.C.   d. 4 B.C.

Sacae (c. 150–125). An offshoot of the Bactrian kingdom flourished in the Punjab (c. 175–c. 40), and though its rulers adopted Buddhism (c. 150) it introduced Hellenistic art and ideas into India.

187–175. Seleucus IV Philopater ("loving his father") succeeded his father, Antiochus III, and during his reign the empire gradually recovered strength. Meanwhile Eumenes II of Pergamum fought against Prusias I of Bithynia (186) and Pharnaces I of Pontus (183–179).

175–163. Antiochus IV Epiphanes ("god manifest") succeeded upon the murder of his brother Seleucus. Though friendly to Rome, he was prevented by the Romans from concluding successfully his war against Egypt (171–168). The Romans also weakened Rhodes by making Delos a free port (167).

168–165. Revolt of the Jews, under **Judas Maccabeus** (d. 160) and his brothers, Jonathan (d. 142) and Simon (d. 135). The Jews achieved religious freedom in 164 and eventually (141) succeeded in liberating Jerusalem. **Simon** established the **Hasmonean dynasty** and a theocratic state which, under his successors, **John Hyrcanus** (134–104) and **Alexander Jannaeus** (102–76), took advantage of the weakness of the Seleucid rulers to extend its power over neighboring territories. Eventually the rivalry between Aristobulus II (67–63) and his brother, Hyrcanus II, gave Pompey an excuse for annexing Judaea to the Roman Empire (63). Hyrcanus II remained as high priest and later as ethnarch (63–40). He was supplanted by his nephew, Antigonus (40–37), who, allying himself with the Parthians, incurred the wrath of the Romans. In 37 the Hasmonean dynasty came to an end and **Herod** (the Great, 37–4) was appointed king of Judaea by the Roman senate (p. 115).

163–162. Antiochus V Eupater, young son of Antiochus IV, king, with Lysias as regent.

162–150. Demetrius I Soter ("savior"), son of Seleucus IV, returned from Rome to eject Antiochus V, but was slain in 150 by a pretender, **Alexander Balas** (150–145), who claimed to be the son of Antiochus IV and was supported by Attalus II Philadelphus ("loving his brother") of Pergamum (159–138) (who had succeeded his brother Eumenes II), by Ptolemy VI of Egypt, and by Rome. Ptolemy, however, soon invaded Syria in favor of Demetrius II, the son of Demetrius I, who slew Balas in 145.

145–139. Demetrius II Nicator ("conqueror") won several victories (140) over Mithridates I of Parthia, who had seized Media (c. 150) and Babylon (c. 141). Mithridates, however, captured Demetrius by treachery in 139. In the meantime, a son of Alexander Balas, Antiochus VI Epiphanes Dionysus ("god manifest"), had held Antioch from 145 to 142, when he was expelled by the mercenary leader Diodotus, who took the title of King Tryphon (142–139). He was expelled in 139.

139–127. Antiochus VII Euergetes Eusebes Soter Sidetes ("benefactor, pious, savior") did much to restore the Seleucid power. However, after several victories over Phraates II of Parthia, he was finally defeated and killed at Ecbatana (127).

138–133. Attalus III Philomater ("loving his mother") **of Pergamum,** a son of Eumenes II, succeeded his uncle, Attalus II. In his will, he bequeathed his kingdom to Rome, apparently in order to protect his subjects from absorption by their neighbors. Rome had to suppress the pretender Aristonicus before it could make the kingdom of Pergamum into the province of Asia (129).

129–125. Demetrius II was sent back to Syria by Phraates II in 129 and was slain in 125 by a pretender with Egyptian support, Alexander Zabinas. Demetrius' son, **Seleucus V,** assumed the diadem but was put to death at once by his mother, Cleopatra Thea.

125–96. Antiochus VIII Epiphanes Philomater Callinicus "Grypus" ("god manifest, loving his mother, gloriously victorious, hook-nosed"), a younger son of Demetrius II, reigned with Cleopatra until her death (c. 120). The pretender, Alexander Zabinas, was killed in 123. In 117 Antiochus was forced into retirement by a half-brother, **Antiochus IX Philopater, "Cyzicenus"** ("loving his father, of Cyzicus"), son of Cleopatra and Antiochus VII. After an indecisive series of battles (113–112), they divided the realm in 111 and both reigned until Antiochus VIII was murdered in 96 by his favorite, Heracleon.

95–64. Seleucus VI, son of Antiochus VIII, defeated and killed Antiochus IX (95). The son of the latter, **Antiochus X,** defeated and killed Seleucus VI, but the latter's brother, Demetrius III, seized Damascus. Another son of Antiochus VIII, **Antiochus XI,** was defeated and killed, but his brother, Philip I, continued the war with Antiochus X. The latter was killed in 93 fighting the Parthians in Commagene. Demetrius III and Philip I engaged in civil war until Demetrius was captured by the Parthians in 88. **Antiochus XII,** another son of Antiochus VIII, seized Damascus, which he held until he was killed on an expedition against the Nabataeans in 84. An insurrection expelled Philip I from Antioch, and Tigranes of Armenia seized Syria and held it until he was defeated by Lucullus in 69. **Antiochus XIII,** son of Antiochus X, was installed at Antioch (68) and soon had to fight with Philip II, son of Philip I. The Arabian prince of Emesa slew Antiochus XIII by treachery in 67; Philip was unable to secure his rule. In 64 Pompey made Syria a Roman province.

6. PARTHIA, 312 B.C.–77 A.D.

331–323. Rule of Alexander the Great.

305–280. Seleucus I founded the dynasty of the Seleucids, ruling over Babylonia and Syria; he built the city of Seleucia near Ctesiphon on the Tigris.

248–212. Arsaces I founded the **kingdom of Parthia,** including at first only Parthia and Hyrcania, between the Seleucid kingdom in the west and the Bactrian kingdom in the east. In 238 Arsaces was expelled by Seleucus II, but returned when the latter withdrew to deal with a revolt in Syria.

212–c. 190. Arsaces II withstood the attacks of Antiochus III, the Great, in 209; he was followed by Arsaces III (Priapatius, 190–175) and Arsaces IV (Phraates I, 175–171).

171–138. Mithridates I conquered Babylonia and Media from the Seleucids; later he added to his kingdom Elam, Persia, and parts of Bactria, thus founding the Parthian Empire. Ctesiphon-Seleucia became the capital.

138–124. Phraates II (138–127) defeated Antiochus VII in Media (129), and as a result the Seleucids were permanently excluded from the lands east of the Euphrates; but he died in battle fighting the Tochari (the Scythians or *Sacae* of the Greeks), a tribe driven forth from Central Asia by the Yue-chi. The kingdom was devastated and Artabanus I (127–124) fell likewise fighting against the Tochari.

124–88. MITHRIDATES II, THE GREAT, defeated the Scythians and also Artavasdes, king of Armenia Major. In 92 he made a treaty with Rome.

88–70. Parthia suffered a collapse and was greatly reduced in territory by Tigranes I of Armenia.

70–57. Phraates III restored order, but was not strong enough to resist the Roman advance, led by Lucullus and Pompey.

57–37. Orodes I defeated Crassus at **Carrhae** (53) and regained Mesopotamia.

37–32. Phraates IV defeated Antony in 36, but could not prevent him from conquering Armenia in 34. After a period of dynastic disturbances

A.D. 51–77. Vologesus I, after a war with Rome, obtained recognition of his brother Tiridates as king of Armenia (63), thus establishing an Arsacid dynasty in that country. In Parthia itself the utmost confusion prevailed after 77, with two or more kings (all of them little known) ruling at the same time and constantly challenged by other claimants.

(*Cont. p. 124.*)

7. BACTRIA, 328–40 B.C.

328–323 B.C. Bactria under the rule of Alexander. A mutiny of Greek auxiliaries after Alexander's death was crushed at once by Perdiccas.

323–302. Bactria under Perdiccas (d. 321), Antipater (d. 319), Eumenes (d. 316), Antigonus (d. 301). In his wars against Antigonus, Seleucus I conquered the eastern provinces (311–302).

302–c. 250. Bactria under the Seleucids.

c. 250–c. 139. Diodotus, the satrap of Bactria, made himself an independent ruler and con-

quered Sogdiana. He founded a dynasty that withstood the attacks of the Seleucids.

After the defeat of Antiochus III at Magnesia (190), Euthydemus and his son Demetrius began the **conquest of the Indus Valley.** But Eucratides made himself king of Bactria (c. 170) while Demetrius was founding a kingdom in the Punjab. About 150 the Tochari (Scythians) occupied Sogdiana, and about 139 Bactria. The line of Eucratides maintained itself in Kabul until about 40 B.C., but most of the region was ruled by Scythian dynasties.

8. PTOLEMAIC EGYPT TO THE ROMAN CONQUEST, 305–30 B.C.

(*From p. 40*)

305–283. PTOLEMY I SOTER ("savior"), the son of Lagus (hence the "Lagid" house), had been governor of Egypt since 323 and king since 305. He had seized Coele-Syria in 301, and acquired from Demetrius, Pamphylia and Lycia (296–295), and Caria and the island of Cos (286).

285–246. PTOLEMY II PHILADELPHUS ("lover of his sister") adopted a Pharaonic practice by marrying his sister Arsinoe II (276), founder of the museum at Alexandria. He explored the upper Nile and extended his power along the Red Sea and into northern Arabia (278) for commercial purposes.

280–272. In the **Damascene War** (280–279) and **First Syrian War** (276–272), he suffered initial defeat from Antiochus I and the revolt of his half-brother Magas in Cyrene. But he finally defeated both and secured Miletus, Phoenicia, and western Cilicia. He subsidized

Pyrrhus against Antigonus (274), aided Athens and Sparta in the Chremonidean War (266–262), and incited Alexander II of Epirus to attack Macedon (264). He likewise incited Eumenes of Pergamum to revolt from Antiochus (262) and supported the seizure of Ephesus (262–259) by his own son, Ptolemy "the Son." These activities brought Antiochus II, Antigonus II, and Rhodes together to wage

260–255. The **Second Syrian War** (260–255), in which Antigonus defeated Ptolemy in the **battle of Cos** (258 or 256). Though by the resulting peace he lost Cilicia and western Pamphylia (255), he later recovered the Cyclades (250) and also Cyrene (c. 248), which had become independent in 258.

246–221. Ptolemy III Euergetes ("benefactor") supported his sister Berenice II in the **Third Syrian War** (246–241) and acquired the coasts of Syria and southern Asia Minor, as well as some Aegean ports, including Ephesus. But he lost the Cyclades to Antigonus through the **battle of Andros** (245). Height of the Ptolemaic power.

221-203. Ptolemy IV Philopater ("loving his father") was a weak monarch, dominated by his minister, Sosibius. In the **Fourth Syrian War** (221-217) he at first lost much of the Syrian coast to Antiochus III, but the victory of **Raphia** (217) brought the recovery of all save the port of Seleucia.

203-181. Ptolemy V Epiphanes ("god manifest"), a young boy, succeeded his father. While the Egyptian natives revolted in the Delta (201-200) Antiochus III attacked him in

201-195. The **Fifth Syrian War**, as a result of which Ptolemy retained only Cyprus of his Asiatic possessions. When he came of age (195), he succeeded in suppressing the native revolts.

181-145. Ptolemy VI Philomater ("loving his mother") followed Ptolemy V under the regency of his mother, Cleopatra I. In consequence of Ptolemy's cowardice during the war with Antiochus (171-168), the people of Alexandria forced him to associate his brother, **Ptolemy VII**, in the rule. Rome prevented Antiochus from capturing Alexandria (168). When Ptolemy VI was expelled by his brother (164), the Roman Senate restored him and gave Cyrene and Cyprus to Ptolemy VII, who, however, secured only Cyrene (163). Ptolemy VI expelled Demetrius I from Syria (152-151) and supported Demetrius II against Alexander Balas (147-145), but was slain in the war.

145-116. Ptolemy VII Euergetes II ("benefactor") or Physcon ("fat-bellied") reunited the empire after his brother's death and restored order. At his death, he left Cyrene separately to his son Apion, who willed it to Rome in 96, though it was not actually annexed until 75. Another son, Ptolemy IX, received Cyprus, which was ultimately bequeathed to Rome and annexed in 58.

116-47. Ptolemy VIII Soter II ("savior") or Lathyrus, son of Ptolemy VII, was eventually expelled by his brother **Ptolemy IX Alexander I** (108-88). The people of Alexandria, however, slew Ptolemy IX and restored Ptolemy VIII (88-80). **Ptolemy X Alexander II,** son of Ptolemy IX, succeeded but was at once slain by the people of Alexandria (80), who set up an illegitimate son of Ptolemy VIII, **Ptolemy XI Auletes** ("flute-player") or **Neos** ("new") **Dionysos.** Though expelled in 58, he bribed the "first triumvirate" to send Gabinus to restore him (55). On his death in 51, he left his throne jointly to his children, **Cleopatra VII** and **Ptolemy XII** (51-47). When Ptolemy expelled his sister, Caesar forced her restoration (48) and, since Ptolemy died during the fighting about Alexandria (48-47), Caesar joined with Cleopatra a younger brother, **Ptolemy XIII** (47-44), whom Cleopatra murdered on Caesar's death (44).

47-30. Cleopatra VII sought to restore the Ptolemaic Empire by winning to her support Caesar and later Antony (41), with whom she sought to establish a Hellenistic monarchy (36). Upon Antony's suicide after Actium (31), she sought to fascinate the young Octavian, but failed and committed suicide rather than adorn his triumph (30). This brought to an end the last of the Hellenistic monarchies.

E. ROME, THE REPUBLIC, TO 31 B.C.

(*From p. 87*)

1. THE PUNIC AND MACEDONIAN WARS, 282-132 B.C.

DURING the 3rd and 2nd centuries B.C. Rome's internal history was marked by the consolidation of the rule of the patricio-plebeian aristocracy. The extension of Rome's external relations and the consequent complexity of her internal problems raised questions impossible of settlement in the unwieldy and uninformed *comitia*, which came more and more to surrender the initiative in government to the senate, composed as it was of ex-magistrates, urban, military, and provincial, who had the necessary background and experience. They, in their turn, had come to regard government and office as a prerogative of themselves and their children. This distinction was furthered by the increased opportunities for wealth opened to the ruling group through conquest and provincial government. Since custom, confirmed by a *lex Claudia* of 218, forced senators to invest chiefly in land, they built up large estates, partly by renting public land, which through long tenure they came to regard as their own, and partly by acquiring the holdings of poorer farmers. The poorer farmers, in turn, subjected to the devastations of the Hannibalic Wars, and to the demands of long-term military service abroad, found it difficult to exist, and tended either to emigrate, remain in the army, or congregate as an idle mob in Rome. The political, social, and economic problems thus raised finally caused the ruin of the senatorial republic by the Gracchan troubles.

The republic saw notable achievements in **engineering.** These were based on abundant materials, superb organization, and cheap labor (freemen and legionaires as well as slaves were used). In road building no attention was paid to topography; the straight Roman roads, contrary to legend, were paved only through and along the approaches to cities. Aqueducts, which, from the 4th century B.C., supplied Rome with water, were continually enlarged and improved (e.g., the high-level aqueduct Marcia was added, 144 B.C.). Other techniques developed include the use of the arch (in vaulting and aqueducts), improvements in mine drainage and extraction of metals from ores, and the use of timber piles and hydraulic cement (*pozzulano*) for building foundations.

Rome's position in Italy became increasingly strong during these centuries. In consequence, the senatorial class began to act with increasing arbitrariness toward Rome's Italian allies and to impose on them the burdens of conquest while reserving the rewards for themselves or using them as sops to the Roman citizens. The citizens, who found that citizenship paid in privilege, in some share in the public land, in free entertainment at Rome, eventually in a government-controlled food supply, and probably in the indirect benefits of bribery and corruption, became unwilling to extend the franchise. The discontent of the Italians found ultimate expression in the Social War, which won for them Roman citizenship.

In the Mediterranean, Rome, without really so desiring, was forced to extend her sway, *imperium,* more and more widely. The senate, like such landed aristocracies as Sparta, was not imperialistic. Nor, on the whole, was the *populus.* But the fear of attack from strong powers led Rome to attack such as might threaten her, and experiments in allowing her rivals a feeble and divided independence (*diuide et impera,* divide and rule) proved unsatisfactory. Either her creations quarreled among themselves and forced her to intervene, or they became the willing or unwilling prey of stronger powers. Hence Rome was forced into annexation. But conquest led ultimately to the corruption of both senate and people, to the creation of a financial group, the *equites,* interested in imperialism, and to opportunities for self-aggrandizement on the part of generals and governors. In consequence, the discontented peoples of Asia supported Mithridates, the equestrian class became a possible rival to the senate, and the way was opened for the domination of the state by military commanders.

282-272. WAR WITH PYRRHUS arose from an attack by the Tarentines on Thurii and their destruction of a Roman fleet which entered the harbor in violation of a treaty forbidding Roman warships from sailing east of the western promontory of the Gulf of Tarentum. Tarentum called in **Pyrrhus of Epirus** (p. 91). In 280, with an army of 25,000 men and 20 elephants, he won a hard-fought victory over the Romans at **Heraclea.** Though the Bruttians, Lucanians, and Samnites then joined Pyrrhus, the senate, instigated by Ap. Claudius, the blind ex-censor, rejected the peace offers of Pyrrhus' ambassador Cineas. In 279 Pyrrhus won his second victory at **Ausculum,** but with losses so great that he exclaimed, "Another such victory and we are lost" (a "Pyrrhic victory"). Pyrrhus then crossed to Sicily. Rome rejected peace with Pyrrhus and made one with his enemy, Carthage. Pyrrhus returned to Italy after two years but was defeated at Beneventum in 275 and returned to Greece. His general, Milo, then surrendered Tarentum to the Romans (272), who destroyed its military resources, but left it its own municipal administration. Rome rounded out her subjugation of Italy by the recapture in 270 of Rhegium from the Mamertines and the reduction of the Bruttians, Lucanians, Calabrians, and Samnites.

264-241. The **FIRST PUNIC WAR** arose from the fact that certain of the Campanian mercenaries, or Mamertines, who were holding Messana against Hiero II of Syracuse appealed to Rome while others appealed to Carthage. The Roman assembly, though the senate hesitated, sent a fleet and army which found the Carthaginians already in possession. The Romans drove them out and were in turn besieged by the Carthaginians. In 264 the consul Ap. Claudius Pulcher relieved them, but failed to take Syracuse. During the following year two Roman armies invaded Sicily and Hiero shifted to a Roman alliance.

262. The Romans defeated the Carthaginian general Hanno and took Agrigentum (Acragas).

260. After losing the consul Cn. Cornelius Scipio with 17 ships off the Lipara Islands, the Romans under C. Duilius won the **naval victory of Mylae,** west of Messana.

257. The Romans sent 330 ships under the consuls M. Atilius Regulus and L. Manlius Vulso to carry troops from Sicily and effect a landing in Africa. This fleet defeated the Carthaginians off the south coast of Sicily at **Ecnomus** (256) and landed just east of Carthage. Regulus, left with half the troops, offered such stringent terms that Carthage continued her resistance under the leadership of the Spartan mercenary Xanthippus.

255. Xanthippus captured Regulus and part of his army. The Romans sent a fleet which took off the remainder, but was lost in a storm, as happened again two years later.

254. Rome seized Panormus and, in 251, defeated the new Carthaginian general, **Hasdrubal,** son of Hanno. On the advice, traditionally, of Regulus, who had been sent to negotiate an exchange of prisoners with the Carthaginians, they refused to do so and Regulus returned to die in Carthage.

249. The consul Claudius Pulcher, after throwing the sacred chickens overboard because they refused to give a good omen by eating grain, lost his fleet at **Drepana**. The Romans were unable to dislodge the Carthaginian **Hamilcar Barcas** ("lightning") from the strong promontory of Eryx, whence his ships harried their coasts.

241. At the **Aegates Islands,** off Lilybaeum, the Romans annihilated the Carthaginian fleet. Carthage received peace on condition of the surrender of Sicily and the payment of 3200 talents in ten years. Rome left eastern Sicily to Hiero of Syracuse but undertook to govern the remainder herself as her **first province,** regularly constituted in 227.

241–217. Some time during this period the comitia centuriata suffered a radical reform, probably because the centuries had lost their military significance. The centuries of *equites* lost the right of first vote, which was hereafter determined by lot among the centuries of the first class. The number of centuries was increased to harmonize in some way with the tribal divisions and divided into seniors and juniors. Perhaps there was one century each of seniors (over 46) and juniors from each of the five classes in each of the 35 tribes, i.e. $2 \times 5 \times 35 = 350$, $+18$ of knights and 5 of propertyless persons = 373. Though the reform passed for democratic, its basis remained one of property and age, since the first class (wealthy) probably had a proportion of centuries (almost one-fifth) in excess of its proportion of population and since the elders, naturally fewer than the younger, had nearly half of the centuries. At the same time (241) the final two tribes were added, making a total of 35. Thereafter new citizens were enrolled in the existing tribes, so that these lost their geographical significance.

238. Rome seized Sardinia, rich in minerals, during a revolt of the mercenaries in Carthage. It later (227) formed a province with Corsica.

235. The first recorded closing of the temple of Janus since its foundation by Numa indicated that Rome was at peace with all nations.

229–228. The first Illyrian War. Rome sent a fleet of 200 vessels to suppress the pirates of Queen Teuta. The grateful Hellenes admitted the Romans to the Isthmian Games and the Eleusinian Mysteries and thus recognized her as a civilized power. In a second war (219), Rome defeated Teuta's successor, Scerdilaidas.

225–222. Large hordes of **Celts** moved from the Po Valley to Etruria. The Romans surrounded and slew a considerable body at **Telamon** (225) and gradually reduced the Insubres, around Milan. In the **battle of Clastidium** (222) M. Claudius Marcellus slew a Gallic chief in single combat. The Romans founded the fortress colonies of Placentia, Cremona, and Mutina, and extended the Via Flaminia from Spoletum to Ariminum.

218. A *lex Claudia* forbade senators to own a ship of more than 300 *amphorae* (225 bushels), only enough to care for their farm produce; they were thus forced to invest in land rather than in industry or commerce.

218–201. The **SECOND PUNIC WAR** arose from Rome's jealousy of Carthaginian expansion in Spain, where Hamilcar Barcas (236–228) and, after his death, his son-in-law Hasdrubal (228–221) had established themselves. Rome made Carthage promise not to attack Saguntum or Emporiae, Greek foundations south of the Ebro, or to cross that river. After the assassination of Hasdrubal, his 25-year-old successor **Hannibal** destroyed Saguntum in 219, perhaps without the full support of his home government, the conservative element in which was jealous of the power and independence of the Barcids. Carthage, however, refused to disown him.

218. Hannibal executed a daring land march through southern France and by an undetermined Alpine pass advanced into the Po Valley. The Roman consul **Publius Cornelius Scipio** reached Marseilles with his fleet too late to stop Hannibal. He therefore sent his brother Cnaeus with most of the fleet to Spain and returned himself to meet Hannibal, who had perhaps 26,000 men and a few elephants, at the **Ticinus,** a branch of the Po. He was defeated, as was his colleague soon after at the **battle of the Trebbia,** another branch of the Po. As the Romans took refuge in Placentia and Cremona, the Gauls rallied to Hannibal.

217. Hannibal crossed the Apennines west of two new Roman armies posted at Ariminum and Arretium. The consul C. Flaminius followed him from the latter place and was led into an ambush and annihilated at **Lake Trasimene.** The Romans, terrified, appointed **Quintus Fabius Maximus** dictator. Hannibal moved east again to the Adriatic and then south, in hopes of a general Italian rising. The cities, however, refused to receive him, and Fabius, without joining battle (hence his title *Cunctator*), harried his army. The Romans were dissatisfied with this policy.

216. The consuls L. Aemilius Paullus (conservative) and C. Terentius Varro (popular) led an army of 86,000 Romans and Italians against Hannibal. Consuls, when together, now commanded on alternate days, and Varro, on his day, unwisely attacked Hannibal at **Cannae,** in Apulia. The Romans, including Paullus, were practically annihilated, though Varro escaped. When, during the same year, a legion was destroyed in Cisalpine Gaul, a rift appeared in the allegiance of Italy to Rome. Capua deserted, along with the Samnites, Lucanians, and other peoples of southern Italy. The Romans checked all public grief, refused Hannibal's terms, and sent out an army under M. Claudius Marcellus. Carthage made alliances with Philip V of Macedon, and Hieronymus, grandson of Hiero of Syracuse, who died in 217. Hannibal wintered at Capua.

215. **Marcellus,** now pro-consul, defeated Hannibal at **Nola** and forced him into Apulia. The government at Carthage gave Hannibal almost no support and he was unable to receive aid from his brother Hasdrubal in Spain.

218-211. **Publius Scipio** had rejoined his brother Cnaeus in Spain and between them, with varying fortune, they kept Hasdrubal busy and stirred up Syphax, king of western Numidia, against Carthage.

215-205. By using a few troops for the **First Macedonian War,** the Romans prevented the irresolute Philip from helping Hannibal. In 211 they organized a Greek alliance, under the lead of the Aetolians (**treaty of Naupactus**) including even Thracians, Illyrians, and Pergamum, against him. After her Greek allies quit in 206, Rome was forced to make the disadvantageous **peace of Phoenice.**

214-210. Marcellus carried the war into Sicily, where he defeated a Carthaginian army and sacked Leontini. Though Hieronymus had been murdered, the Syracusans renewed their alliance with Carthage (213), but, despite the ingenious defensive machinery devised by Archimedes, **Marcellus reduced Syracuse** in 211. The rest of Sicily quickly fell again under Roman control.

212. **Hannibal seized Tarentum,** save for the citadel. He compelled the Romans to raise the siege of Capua, defeated two armies, but retired again to Tarentum. Both Scipios were slain in Spain by the Carthaginians, who drove the Romans to the Ebro.

211. Hannibal returned to relieve Capua. The Romans this time refused to abandon the siege, so he marched to within a mile of Rome, but as they did not falter, he again had to retire. **Capua surrendered to Rome** and was deprived of all self-government. As Hannibal seemed unable to weaken Rome or reduce the citadel of Tarentum, his prestige sank and his Italian allies went back to Rome.

210. **P. Cornelius Scipio,** son of the late general, was sent to Spain with proconsular powers, though only 25 and a mere ex-aedile. In Sicily, the Romans reduced Agrigentum.

209. Scipio captured New Carthage in Spain. Marcellus defeated Hannibal and Fabius reduced Tarentum. In the following year, Hasdrubal evaded Scipio and reached the Po Valley.

207. In the **battle of the Metaurus River** (Sena Gallica), the consul M. Livius Salinator, supported by his colleague G. Claudius Nero, who had made forced marches from the south, where he was holding Hannibal in check, defeated and slew Hasdrubal. Hannibal withdrew to Bruttium.

206. **Scipio drove the Carthaginians out of Spain** and made a secret treaty with their ally Massinissa, king (in 208) of eastern Numidia. He returned to Italy and was elected consul under age, for 205.

205-178. **Spain was divided into two provinces** (197), Hither Spain (*Hispania Citerior*) in the Ebro Valley, and Farther Spain (*Hispania Ulterior*) in the south around Gibraltar and the Guadalquivir River. Constant warfare, however, was necessary to subdue the Lusitanians.

204. Scipio took a force to Africa and, with Massinissa's help, defeated the Carthaginians and Syphax (203). Carthage was forced to recall Hannibal, who attempted in vain to negotiate.

202. In the **battle of Zama,** Scipio annihilated the Carthaginian army, though Hannibal escaped.

201. Carthage accepted **Rome's terms:** surrender of Spain and all other Mediterranean islands; transfer of the kingdom of Syphax to Massinissa; payment of 200 talents a year for 50 years; destruction of all except 10 warships; promise not to make war without Rome's permission. Scipio, now entitled *Africanus,* celebrated a splendid triumph. The unfaithful Italian allies were in part forced to cede land, in part deprived of independence. Rome founded many colonies in southern Italy.

200-191. The resubjugation of the Po Valley

required considerable effort. Rome founded colonies and built the Via Aemilia as a continuation of the Via Flaminia from Ariminum to Placentia.

The newly acquired **overseas territories** could not be governed either from Rome or, as had been just possible in Sicily, by creating new praetors. This last method was tried in Spain, but it became more economical to retain the governors there for two years so that their *imperia* were "prorogued" for another year. The device of extending an *imperium* without renewing the corresponding magistracy was apparently first employed to keep the experienced commander Philo in command against Naples. As the number of provinces grew, this custom was regularly applied to the consuls and praetors, who came to expect a profitable year (for governorships were reduced to this) in a province to recoup themselves for the heavy expenses entailed in securing election (bribery) or incident to the tenure of office (games, etc.). A further effect of the transmarine provinces was that it became necessary to maintain a **standing army.** In the 2nd and 1st centuries B.C. the soldier not only could not return to his farm for harvest or the winter—that had long been impossible—but he could not look for a discharge at the end of a year of service, for the government could not afford to send new armies each year across the sea. Though the fiction of annual re-enlistment and the requirement of a property qualification were maintained, the soldiers became in fact professional and served for 20 years or more. They could not then return to farms which would have passed into other hands or fallen into decay, and so they had either to be settled in colonies or allowed to congregate in Rome. As they looked to their commander for rewards in war and protection of their interests at home, they shifted their loyalty, and oath (*sacramentum*), from the state to him. It is therefore extraordinary that for nearly a century the corporate class consciousness of the *nobiles* was sufficient to prevent disloyalty to the senatorial government.

200–197. Rome was drawn into the **SECOND MACEDONIAN WAR** by an appeal from Pergamum, Rhodes, and Athens, which were harried by Philip and Antiochus III of Syria. The senate, fearful of Philip's growing power, frightened an unwilling comitia centuriata into declaring war by visions of a renewed invasion of Italy. **T. Quinctius Flamininus,** supported by both the Aetolian and Achaean Leagues, finally (197) defeated Philip at **Cynoscephalae** in Thessaly and forced him to make peace (196) on the following terms: surrender of Greece; payment of 1000 talents in 10 years;

reduction of his forces to 5000 men and 5 ships; promise not to declare war without permission of Rome. At the ensuing Isthmian Games, Flamininus proclaimed the **independence of the Greek cities.** Rome sought to balance the Achaean League by curtailing but not destroying the power of King Nabis of Sparta.

192–189. THE SYRIAN WAR. Antiochus III, invited by the Aetolians, invaded Greece, but the consul, M. Acilius Glabrio, landed in Epirus, moved into Thessaly and, with M. Porcius Cato, repeated the maneuver of Xerxes at Thermopylae to rout Antiochus (191).

190. The Roman fleet, helped by the Rhodians, won two victories. The Roman army, under **L. Cornelius Scipio** (later *Asiaticus*) and his brother Scipio Africanus, crossed the Hellespont and defeated Antiochus in the **battle of Magnesia,** near Smyrna. Antiochus was obliged to make peace on the following terms: surrender of all European and Asiatic possessions as far as the Taurus Mountains; payment of 15,000 talents in 12 years; surrender of Hannibal, who had fled from his enemies at Carthage (195). Though Hannibal escaped, he finally poisoned himself (183) at the court of Prusias I of Bithynia, who was about to betray him. Rome divided the Anatolian territory of Antiochus between Pergamum and Rhodes and aided Eumenes II of Pergamum against the Galatians (189). In Greece, Rome subjected the Aetolians, but left the other cities free. Philip was not rewarded as he had hoped.

171–167. The **THIRD MACEDONIAN WAR** was waged against Rome by Perseus, the successor of Philip V. After several unsuccessful campaigns, the Romans sent L. Aemilius Paullus.

168. Battle of Pydna. Paullus utterly defeated Perseus and brought him back in his triumphal procession. So much booty accrued from his victory that Roman citizens were thereafter relieved of direct taxation, the *tributum*. Macedonia was broken up into four wholly distinct confederacies. Illyria was reduced to three tributary confederacies, and Epirus was devastated. From the Achaean cities 1000 of the chief citizens were taken as hostages and kept in Italy for 16 years. Rome likewise dictated to Eumenes of Pergamum, to Rhodes, and to Antiochus IV, who was prevented by the ambassador C. Popilius Laenas from making war on the Ptolemies of Egypt.

153. On account of an uprising in Spain, the consuls entered office on Jan. 1 instead of Mar. 15. Thus Jan. 1 became established as the beginning of the civil year.

151. A law forbidding re-election to the consulship superseded an earlier one of 342 which had imposed a 10-year interval between two tenures. It lasted, with some exceptions, until Sulla revived the older law. Possibly the same law raised the minimum ages for the tenure of all magistracies from those established by a *lex annalis* of the tribune Villius (180) to those of Cicero's time: quaestorship after the 30th year, aedileship after the 36th, praetorship after the 39th, and consulship after the 42nd.

149. The tribune L. Calpurnius Piso enacted a *lex Calpurnia* which set up a permanent commission to hear the suits of provincials to recover from governors money unjustly collected (*quaestio de rebus repetundis*). This commission differed from previous specially created boards of investigation (*quaestiones*) or panels of special judges (*reciperatores* or *iudices*) in being made always available (*perpetua*) without special legislation. Like its predecessors, the membership for different cases was drawn by lot from a panel of senators and the board met under the presidency of a praetor. The new court soon became an instrument whereby the senate could discipline governors. Decisions were motivated not by justice but by class selfishness. It is probable that further courts of this type were established before the revision of the system of Sulla.

149-146. The **THIRD PUNIC WAR** arose from alarm among conservative Romans over Carthage's revival, typified in the phrase with which Cato expressed his opinion on any question which was discussed in the senate: *ceterum censeo Carthaginem esse delendam* ("but I declare that Carthage must be destroyed"). The occasion was an attack by Carthage (150) on Rome's ally, the now aged Massinissa. When a Roman army landed in Africa, the Carthaginians offered submission, but refused to vacate the city. With almost no resources they withstood a siege until **Scipio Aemilianus** captured and **destroyed Carthage** (146). The Romans organized a small area around Carthage as the province of Africa, but left the rest to the sons of Massinissa (d. 149).

149-148. **THE FOURTH MACEDONIAN WAR.** A pretended son of Perseus, Andriscus, who called himself Philip, provoked the war, but was defeated by Q. Caecilius Metellus. In 148 Macedonia became a Roman province.

146. When the 300 surviving hostages returned to Achaea, the **Achaeans made war on Sparta.** Their leaders, Critolaus and Diaeus, were defeated by Metellus and L. Mummius. The latter took Corinth, sent its art treasures to Rome, sold its inhabitants into slavery, and burned the city (at the order of the Roman senate). The territory of Corinth passed in part to Sicyon, in part became Roman public land. The remaining Greek cities retained a certain measure of autonomy under the governor of Macedonia, though they paid tribute. Not until later (127) did they become organized as the Province of Achaea.

143-133. Continuous unrest in Spain grew into a **war in Lusitania**, led by Viriathus (assassinated 139, thanks to Roman bribery), and in northern Spain, where the city of Numantia took the lead. Numantia fell in 133 and all Spain, except the northwestern part, passed under Roman domination.

135-132. The **First Servile War** broke out when the ill-treated slaves of the large Sicilian estates revolted under the Syrian Eunus, who called himself King Antiochus. Eunus held Henna and Tauromenium against Roman armies, but was finally captured and his supporters brutally executed.

Rome now possessed **eight provinces:** Sicilia (241), Sardinia (238) with Corsica (c. 230?), Hispania Citerior (205), Hispania Ulterior (205), Gallia Cisalpina (191?), Illyricum (168), Africa (146), Macedonia and Achaea (146). The first four were initially governed by praetors and then, as these became useful at Rome for the new standing courts and as the system of proroguing *imperia* became regular, they were governed by pro-praetors (in the less important or "praetorian" provinces) or pro-consuls (in the more important or "consular"). After the middle of the 2nd century, consuls and praetors less frequently took command of a province or army while in office, though this was probably never forbidden by law. Wars were conducted either by the governors or by commanders specially endowed with an *imperium* and ranking usually as pro-consuls, even though they had not held the consulship.

Provinces were generally organized by their conqueror with the aid of a commission of ten senators sent out by Rome. The charter of organization was called a *lex data,* as it was authorized in advance by the comitia but not brought before it (*rogata*). Usually the senate rather than the comitia confirmed such arrangements. The Romans tended to leave undisturbed existing arrangements where they could; e.g. the charter of Sicily incorporated the usages of Hiero of Syracuse, the *lex Hieronica.* Moreover, organized cities were left to themselves for purposes of local government. The Roman governor was chiefly concerned with warfare and general police duties, with settlement of disputes between cities, of important native trials, of all cases involving Roman citizens, and with the public land and tax-collections. Since, however, Rome had no elaborate administrative organization, the actual management of such lands (when not distributed to Roman citizens) and the collection of taxes were auctioned off at Rome (but not the taxes of Sicily), as were contracts for public works, every fifth year by the censors to companies of private capitalists (*publicani*), whose members came to be called *equites* because they had the census requisite for membership in the centuries of knights. (The actual cavalry, composed usually of sons of senators and distinguished by the grant from the state of a horse, the *equus publicus*, had been abolished by Scipio Aemilianus at the siege of Numantia). The evils of the publican system lay not so much in extortionate collections, since the rates were laid down in the contract, as in the fact that on the one hand, a bad year might endanger the revenues, except in Sicily, and lead to undue hardship in the collection, and that on the other the municipalities, who were responsible to the publicani for the payments, might fall into arrears and have to borrow, which they did from the same publicani (acting as bankers, *negotiatores*) at very high rates. Once behindhand, they found it hard to get out of debt. The rates on such loans were in time laid down by law, but the governor, who was often a silent partner in the company (a senator could openly invest only in land), would connive at illegal practices, especially since for a time after the Gracchi, and again after 70 B.C. he would be likely to be called to account for his own administration before a court composed of equites.

Roman literature began with the production in 241 of a translation of a Greek play by **Livius Andronicus,** who had been captured at Tarentum in 272. The most important early writers, all strongly under Greek influence, were: for verse, **Naevius** (269–199), who wrote plays and an epic on the First Punic War (*Bellum Punicum*); **Plautus** (254–184), writer of comedies; **Ennius,** who dabbled in many fields and produced in quantitative (Greek) dactylic hexameters (instead of the old, native, accentual "Saturnians") an epic on all Roman history, the *Annales;* **Pacuvius** (220–130), a tragedian; **Caecilius** (d. 166) and **Terence** (190–159), authors of comedy; and **Lucilius** (180–103), the "inventor" of satire; for prose, a number of historians who wrote in Greek, like **Fabius Pictor** (c. 200), on the Second Punic War, and **Polybius; Cato** (234–149), "founder" of Latin prose with his *Origines* (Italian history) and his work on agriculture. Despite the conservative opposition, Greek rhetoric and philosophy were studied by the liberals who gathered about Scipio Aemilianus, whose "Scipionic circle" included Polybius, Terence, Laelius, and the Stoic Panaetius of Rhodes.

2. DOMESTIC STRIFE AND EASTERN CONQUEST, 133–31 B.C.

133. Ti. Sempronius Gracchus, a noble, was elected tribune on a platform of social reform. Traditionally his motive was to stop the spread of great estates (*latifundia*) at the expense of the small peasants, but since this tendency was restricted to Etruria and Campania, he was more probably motivated by the problem of the proletariat in Rome. He proposed an **agrarian law** (perhaps only a re-enactment of a law of 367) limiting holdings of public land to 500 iugera (312 acres) per person, with an additional 250 for each of two sons. This measure hurt both the great nobles and certain Italian cities. The senate persuaded a tribune, M. Octavius, to veto the measure, but Gracchus violated custom and had the assembly depose Octavius; the bill was then passed. A commission of three (Tiberius Gracchus, his brother Gaius, and his father-in-law Ap. Claudius) was appointed to recover land held in violation of this law and distribute it in inalienable lots of 30 iugera. To obtain funds for the new settlers Gracchus again violated custom, which left provincial affairs to the senate, and proposed that the people accept Attalus' legacy of the kingdom of Pergamum; probably this measure was not passed. Again contrary to custom, Tiberius stood for a second tribunate, on an even more radical program. The *optimates* (reactionary party of the nobles, contrasted with the democratic *populares*), led by **P. Cornelius Scipio Nasica,** murdered him and 300 of his followers during the election, and afterwards the senate had more of his partisans executed as public enemies.

133–129. Apparently the commission carried out in part the redistribution of the public land. In 129, Scipio Aemilianus, who had married a sister to Tiberius and, espousing a middle course, perhaps favored some concession to the increasing bitterness of the Italians, was found dead with suspicions of murder.

129. After the defeat of the pretender Aristonicus, Pergamum became the **province of Asia.**

125. The senate balked the attempt of the democratic consul **M. Fulvius Flaccus** to extend the franchise to all Italians and sent him to Liguria, where, by helping Marseilles against the Gauls, he began the conquest of southern

Gaul. The **revolt of Fregellae,** a town which despaired of peaceful means, was ruthlessly suppressed. In 123 the **Balearic Islands** were conquered and in 121 southern Gaul became the province of **Gallia Narbonensis,** so-called from the newly established colony of Narbo Martius (Narbonne).

123. Gaius Gracchus, the more forceful brother of Tiberius, became tribune. To the motive of social reform was added that of revenge, and in this and the following year, when he secured a second tribunate, he put through a far more extreme program than Tiberius had envisaged. The precise order and interrelation of his measures is uncertain, but the most important were the following: by a *lex iudiciaria* (probably the surviving *lex Acilia repetundarum*) he transferred membership in the court on extortion (*quaestio de rebus repetundis,* and any others that existed) from senators to equestrians. He also passed a law reorganizing the province of Asia, and particularly changing the tax rate into a tithe on produce, as in Sicily. The collection was to be auctioned off to the publicani, as heretofore. The two measures were probably intended to relieve the provincials, but they only served to separate the equestrians from the senate; the former were now able to avenge themselves on a governor who sought to check their rapacity or divert the profits to his own account.

In behalf of the proletariat Gaius passed three measures: (1) a revival of his brother's **land law;** (2) the foundation of **three commercial colonies** (Capua, Tarentum, and Carthage) to take care of veterans and Oriental freedmen, who comprised the majority of the Roman proletariat and who, it was recognized, would not make good farmers; (3) a **law obliging the government to provide grain at a fair price** (probably not below the average market level) to protect the poor against famine and speculation. The transmarine colonies failed because the proletarians preferred the pleasures of Rome to life in remote provinces. The **state control of the grain supply** became a means whereby demagogues could win popular support (by reducing the price and by increasing the number of eligible beneficiaries). Less important bills mitigated the conditions of military service and reaffirmed the laws against execution without appeal to the people. Finally, Gracchus planned to extend the full franchise to Latin cities and to grant Latin rights to all other Italians. This measure was naturally unwelcome to the Roman *populus,* now fully conscious of the advantages of citizenship. The senate took advantage of Gracchus' absence in Africa to undermine his influence, and he was defeated in the election

for his third tribunate. When a riot ensued over the repeal of his colonization bill, the senate invoked a right based on recent custom and of dubious validity, to declare a state of emergency and to call upon the consuls and other magistrates to see to it, even by use of force, that the state suffered no harm (*senatus consultum ultimum: ut consules . . . opera dent ne quid res publica detrimenti capiat*). This was a substitute for the dictatorship, the last effective use of which had been made in 216. In the ensuing struggles, Gaius Gracchus and many of his supporters were slain.

121–111. A series of measures, ending with the *lex agraria* of 111, recognized the failure of the land distributions by discontinuing them, by relieving the lots of rent, and by making them alienable. After various experiments, the courts also were completely restored to the control of the senate.

111–105. The **Jugurthine War** resulted from the usurpation of the African kingdom of Massinissa's descendants by King Micipsa's nephew, **Jugurtha.** The latter murdered one rival, bribed a senatorial commission to support his claim, and captured Cirta (Constantine), capital of the surviving son of the king. The death of some Italians at Cirta led Rome to declare war, but Jugurtha again bought peace. A second murder led to hostilities, waged with varying success by Q. Caecilius Metellus.

107. Gaius Marius, a self-made man and legionary commander (*legatus*) of Metellus, appealed to the Roman people over the head of a hostile senate and secured the consulship, with command in the war. Since the senate refused to grant him an army, he called for volunteers and took men without the requisite property qualification. There resulted a thorough **reform of the military system,** carried through by P. Rutilius Rufus in 105. For the manipular system with its three ranks was substituted a division of the legion (6000 men, gradually sinking to about 4500 during the 1st century) into 10 cohorts, each composed of three maniples; the old military tribunes lost their importance and the command was held by a delegate of the general (*legatus*); the backbone of the legion became the centurions (commanders of the maniples); to each legion was attached an equal number of auxiliary troops, levied from the subject peoples and usually organized in their own fashion; about 300 professional cavalry replaced the old noble *equites,* abolished by Scipio Aemilianus; from the time of Scipio the general had also a special bodyguard (called from his headquarters *praetorium*), the *cohors praetoriana* or praetorian guard.

107-105. Marius' aristocratic quaestor, **L. Cornelius Sulla,** secured the surrender of Jugurtha by the latter's ally and father-in-law, Bocchus, king of Mauretania. Marius triumphed in 105, Jugurtha died in prison, and his kingdom was divided between Bocchus and a grandson of Massinissa.

105. The **CIMBRI,** a German (or Celtic) people originally located east of the Rhine, who in 113 had moved into the Alpine regions and across the Rhone, ravaged Gaul and defeated two Roman armies at Arausio, on the Rhone.

Marius was elected consul for the second time, and then continuously for four more annual terms (contrary to the law of 151).

The Cimbri, defeated in Spain and again in northern France by native tribes, joined with the Germanic Teutons and other peoples. Most of the Cimbri then moved on Italy, while the Teutons, some Cimbri, and others advanced into southern Gaul to approach Italy from the west.

104. By a *lex Domitia* the pontiffs and augurs were made elective, but by a minority (17) of the 35 tribes, chosen by lot so that the gods might exercise their influence. This law was repealed by Sulla but revived by Caesar in 63 to secure his election as chief priest (*pontifex maximus*).

103-99. A **Second Servile War** in Sicily, under Tryphon and Athenion, was suppressed with difficulty by the consul, M. Aquillius.

102. **Marius,** having deflected the invading barbarians from the Little St. Bernhard Pass and having followed them to Aquae Sextae (Aix in Provence), annihilated them there. He then returned to the support of Catulus in northern Italy, which had been invaded by the main body of Cimbri coming over the Brenner Pass.

101. **Marius and Catulus** defeated the Cimbri at **Vercellae** (Campi Raudii). Marius became the national hero.

100. Marius, consul for the sixth time, but despised by the senate, turned to the demagogues C. Servilius Glaucia (a praetor) and L. Appuleius Saturninus (a tribune) to secure land with which to reward his veterans. A number of extreme bills were passed, including one which defined treason no longer as internal revolt (*perduellio*) but as impairing the "majesty" of the Roman people (*lex Appuleia de maiestate imminuta*—later *laesa*). When Glaucia secured the murder of his rival for the consulship, the senate passed the *senatus consultum ultimum* and Marius was obliged to besiege and kill his former supporters on the Capitoline. Marius then left for a tour of the east.

91. The tribune, **M. Livius Drusus,** son of an opponent of the Gracchi, brought forward several liberal bills: to compromise the problem of the courts by adding 300 equites to the senate; to distribute land; to cheapen the price of grain; and to extend the citizenship to all Italians. The first three measures were passed as one bill, whereupon the senate, in virtue of a recent law against such omnibus bills (*lex Caecilia Didia* of 98), declared them void.

91-88. The **Social War** (i.e. War of the Allies). The disappointed Italians, save for Latins, Etruscans, Umbrians, and some southern cities, flared into open revolt. They formed a republic, **Italia,** with a capital at Corfinium. Though Marius and Gn. Pompeius Strabo succeeded in suppressing it in the north, the consul **L. Julius Caesar** suffered reverses in the south.

90. The danger of the secession of the Etruscans and Umbrians led to the passage by Caesar of a *lex Iulia* by which citizenship was granted to all Italians who had remained faithful.

89. The war in the north was concluded and L. Cornelius Sulla won successes in the south. The two new consuls moved a *lex Plautia Papiria* which extended **citizenship to all Italians** who applied for it within 60 days, but enrolled them in only eight designated tribes, to prevent them from dominating the assemblies. Cities in Cisalpine Gaul received Latin rights by a *lex Pompeia,* though the precise status of the region between the Po and the Alps, the Transpadanes, remained a matter of dispute until 49. This concession brought the war to a close in 88 and showed that the Italians preferred to remain with Rome rather than to be independent. It also frankly recognized that citizenship was no longer a right, since personal participation in the assemblies at Rome was impossible for most Italians and no system of representation was devised, but a privilege which ensured to its possessors the special protection of Rome, favored treatment in the provinces, and a share in the profits of conquest.

88-84. **FIRST MITHRIDATIC WAR.** Contemporaneously with the Social War, **Mithridates IV Eupator,** ambitious king of Pontus since 120, made war on Rome. He had absorbed Colchis at the east end of the Pontus (Euxine, Black Sea), the kingdom of the Bosporus in the Tauric Chersonese (Crimea), Paphlagonia, and Cappadocia. He then came into conflict with Nicomedes of Bithynia, in northwestern Asia Minor, who was supported by the Romans. Mithridates routed both Nicomedes and the Romans, overran the province of Asia, and is said to have commanded the natives to put to death 80,000 "Romans" (Italian traders?) on a single day. Sulla, consul for 88, joined his army at Nola to start for Asia.

88–82. But **civil war** broke out in Rome. The demagogue **P. Sulpicius Rufus** carried several measures by violence, notably one distributing the new Italian citizens among all the tribes, and another conferring the eastern command on Marius. Sulla marched his troops to Rome, stormed the city, and slew Sulpicius and others. Marius fled to Africa. Sulla put through conservative reforms, which did not last, and went as pro-consul to Asia in 87.

87–84. The demagogic consul **L. Cornelius Cinna** turned to violence against the optimates under the other consul, Gn. Octavius. He was driven from the city, raised an army, and secured the support of Marius, who returned from Africa. They seized Rome, instituted a reign of terror, a **"proscription" of the optimates,** who were either slain or, if they escaped, lost their property. Cinna and Marius became consuls for 86 (Marius' seventh consulship). Marius soon died and his successor, **L. Valerius Flaccus,** went out to command in the east. Cinna tyrannized at Rome until his death in a mutiny in 84.

87–84. In the meantime, Sulla, in Greece, drove the generals of Mithridates, Archelaus and Aristion, back into the Piraeus and Athens respectively. When, in 86, Athens fell, Archelaus retired from the Piraeus by sea to Boeotia, where he was defeated by Sulla at **Chaeronea** and, in 85, at **Orchomenos.**

84. Sulla, supported by a fleet collected in Asia and Syria by **L. Licinius Lucullus,** moved around the Aegean into Asia, where Mithridates made peace on the following terms: evacuation of all his conquests, surrender of 80 warships, and an indemnity of 3000 talents. Sulla then won over the troops of the democratic general G. Fimbria, who had secured command by murdering Flaccus and now committed suicide. Sulla left these two legions to police Asia and to help Lucullus collect an immense fine of 20,000 talents from the Asiatic cities, while he himself returned to Italy.

83–79. Sulla made a cautious advance from Brundisium against the successors of Cinna, in the course of which the army of the consul Lucius Scipio deserted him after the defeat of the other consul, C. Norbanus. After wintering at Capua, Sulla conducted a brilliant campaign against the various opposing forces which culminated in the **battle of the Colline Gate** (Nov., 82), when he repulsed from Rome a large force of Samnites, who had taken advantage of the civil war to revolt. Sulla punished severely the cities that had sided with his opponents, and then had himself appointed

dictator for the purpose of restoring the state (*rei publicae constituendae*).

Sulla's dictatorship was only in name a revival of the old institution. It was not an "emergency" office and was not limited in time, so that actually it was a tyranny. Sulla's objective was to restore the old senatorial system. To this end he sought, by a series of laws (*leges Corneliae*), to subordinate to the senate all those powers that had been set up against it: magistrates, governors, knights, and people. The size of the senate was increased from 300 to 600 by the addition of new members, probably equestrians; admission became automatic for those who held the quaestorship, whose numbers had increased to 20. Thus the censors lost the control they had hitherto had over admissions to the senate, though probably Sulla only confirmed what had already become a general practice. But he also deprived the censors of the right to remove unworthy members. The *lex annalis* was revived, with permission for re-election to the consulship after ten years. The number of praetors was increased to eight. Governors were forbidden to take troops outside their province by a law that made such action treason. The number of **standing courts** (*quaestiones perpetuae*) was increased to at least seven: *de rebus repetundis, de maiestate, de ui* (violence), *de peculatu* (embezzlement), *de ambitu* (corrupt electioneering), *de falsis* (fraud), and *inter sicarios* (assassination). Membership was definitely restricted to senators, thus depriving both magistrates and people of judicial power. The **tribunes' veto** was confined to the protection of individuals (*auxilium*) and they were probably forbidden to bring any measure before the people without previous approval of the senate. Moreover, election to the tribunate disqualified a man for further political office, so that men of ambition would avoid it. The public distribution of grain, an instrument of demagoguery, was perhaps abolished.

Of these reforms, the only one of enduring importance was that of the **judicial system.** Though sentimentally the Laws of the Twelve Tables continued to be regarded as the fountainhead of the Roman law, in actual fact the *leges Corneliae* laid the foundations of Roman criminal law by defining the types of crime (which had naturally increased as Rome grew) and by providing a more expeditious system of court trial than the hearings before the *populus.* The importance of the praetors, who (except the *urbanus* and *peregrinus*) normally presided over the courts, was thus vastly increased. During this same period, by the *lex Aebutia* (probably c. 150), the civil law was liberated from the restraints of the old, ritualistic, narrow "actions at law" (*legis actiones*) by the recognition of the praetor's *formulae*. The formulae, borrowed by the urban praetor from the peregrine (i.e. praetor for foreigners), were general definitions of civil wrongs not covered by specific laws, for which remedies would be granted. Such formulas were published by the praetor either on special occasions (*edicta repentina*) or in the edict with which he assumed office (*edictum perpetuum*). A large body of such material was naturally passed on from praetor to praetor and became "tralatician" (*edictum tralaticium*). Thus the praetors, until the time of Hadrian, could widen the scope of civil law to meet new needs, and the praetor's edict became the chief authority for civil law.

As soon as his reforms were completed, Sulla voluntarily retired from public life (79). He died in the following year.

83-81. The **SECOND MITHRIDATIC WAR** resulted from a Roman invasion of Cappadocia and Pontus. After victory, peace was renewed on the terms of 84.

80-72. **Q. Sertorius,** the democratic governor of Hither Spain (83), was expelled by Sullan troops. When the Lusitanians invited him back in 80, he established an independent state modeled on Rome. He soon extended his sway over much of Spain and held the Romans at bay until he was murdered in 72 by a jealous subordinate, M. Perperna. Pompey, who had been sent to Spain in 77, quickly defeated and executed Perperna.

78-77. The democratic consul **M. Aemilius Lepidus** sought to undo Sulla's work. When he was blocked, he raised in Etruria an army of the discontented. He was defeated before Rome by his colleague Q. Lutatius Catulus and the remnant of his army was wiped out in northern Italy in 77 by the brilliant young Roman commander **Gnaeus Pompeius** (Pompey), son of a general in the Social War and a protégé of Sulla.

74. **Cyrene,** which had been tentatively bequeathed to Rome in 154 and again in 96, finally became a province.

73-71. **Third Servile War.** The Thracian gladiator **Spartacus** and other gladiators started a war by seizing Mt. Vesuvius, to which rallied many fugitive slaves. The praetor **M. Licinius Crassus** (b. 112), a favorite of Sulla who had enriched himself by buying the property of the proscribed, defeated Spartacus twice, and Pompey, returning from Spain, finished off the stragglers. For his achievements during this period, Pompey became known as "the Great" (*Magnus*).

70. **Crassus and Pompey** openly deserted the optimate cause and used their troops to win for themselves the consulship for 70, though both were under the age set in 151. As consuls, they secured the restoration to the tribunate of the privileges of which Sulla had deprived it. Already, in 75, the disqualification of tribunes for higher office had been abolished and, in 72, the censors had recovered the privilege of removing unworthy senators. Thus Sulla's restoration of the senate was largely undone. The prosecution of the corrupt pro-praetor of Sicily, Verres, by Cicero in 70 brought to a head discontent with the senatorial courts and the praetor L. Aurelius Cotta introduced a *lex Aurelia* under which the senators retained only one-third membership on the juries and the other two-thirds were filled from the equites and a group of slightly lower property census, the *tribuni aerarii,* whose origin is uncertain but whose sympathies were equestrian.

68-67. **Defeat of the Mediterranean pirates** by Q. Caecilius Metellus Pius. There had been a rapid increase of piracy (especially kidnapping for the slave market at Delos) in the eastern Mediterranean after the defeat of Carthage, Rhodes, and Syria and during the civil wars in Italy. The centers were Crete and Cilicia and the situation began to interfere seriously with Rome's grain supply. Efforts to suppress the pirates met with little success until Metellus took Crete (68). It was made a province (67) and later joined to Cyrene.

67. The tribune A. Gabinius secured the passage of the *lex Gabinia,* which conferred upon Pompey for three years the command of the Mediterranean and its coasts for 50 miles inland, equal to that of the governors in each province (*imperium aequum*). Thus enabled to mobilize all available resources, Pompey in three months cleared the sea of pirates and pacified Cilicia.

74-64. The **THIRD MITHRIDATIC WAR.** Mithridates, encouraged by Rome's troubles at home, supported his son-in-law, **Tigranes I of Armenia,** in the annexation of Cappadocia and Syria.

74. **Nicomedes III** of Bithynia bequeathed his kingdom to Rome, presumably to protect it against Mithridates, who nevertheless occupied it. The consul for 74, **L. Licinius Lucullus,** gradually drove Mithridates back and occupied Pontus (73). Mithridates fled to the court of Tigranes.

69. Lucullus defeated Tigranes at **Tigranocerta** and started to push on into the mountains of Armenia. His troops, many of them brought out twenty years before by Flaccus, mutinied and forced him to retire to Asia (68). This failure and his efforts to relieve Asia by wholesale reduction of the indebtedness of the publicani, to say nothing of his optimate sympathies, made him unpopular at Rome.

66.   The tribune C. Manilius moved a bill (*lex Manilia*), which was supported by the rising orator, **M. Tullius Cicero** (b. 106), that gave Pompey a command over all Asia equal to that of the governors and valid until the conclusion of the war (*imperium aequum infinitum,* i.e. without time limit).

Pompey quickly drove Mithridates to the east end of the Black Sea, after which he captured Tigranes at Artaxata and deprived him of all territories save Armenia, besides imposing a fine of 6000 talents.

65.   Pompey pursued Mithridates until the latter fled to the Crimea, where he committed suicide on hearing of the revolt of his son (63).

65-62.   Reorganization of Asia and Syria by Pompey.   He formed four provinces: Bithynia-Pontus (excluding eastern Pontus), which became a client kingdom; Asia, the old province, which was again heavily taxed; Cilicia, including Pamphylia and Isauria; and Syria, the region about Antioch.   As client kingdoms he left eastern Pontus, Cappadocia, Galatia (under King Deiotarus), Lycia, and Judaea.

64.   Pompey took **Jerusalem,** in order to pacify Judaea. He left in charge the Maccabean high-priest Hyrcanus and a civil adviser, Antipater, from the non-Jewish district of Idumaea.

Pompey's reorganization of Asia had enduring significance. He followed the Roman practice of making cities the responsible agencies of local government and founding new ones wherever advisable. In order to keep the support of the equestrian class, he extended the pernicious publican system throughout the east.   The senate was loath to confirm his arrangements or look after his veterans, but he did not turn against the government. Instead, he dismissed his army at Brundisium (61) and entered Rome as a private citizen.

64-63.   Conspiracy of Catiline.   The discontented classes at Rome (debtors, veterans, ruined nobles, those proscribed by Sulla, etc.) found a leader in **L. Sergius Catilina.** He may at first have had the support of Crassus and of Crassus' demagogic agent, **G. Julius Caesar** (b. 102 or 101). Caesar belonged to a poor branch of the patrician *gens Iulia,* but his aunt had been the wife of Marius and his (Caesar's) wife was a daughter of Cinna. Catiline tried to run for the consulship on a radical program in 66, but could not get his name presented to the comitia centuriata, as he was threatened with prosecution for extortion while pro-praetor in Africa. After a plot to murder the consuls failed (65), he ran again in 64, but was defeated by Cicero. Catiline turned to even more extreme methods (sedition in Rome and

levying a force in Etruria). Then, if not before, Crassus and Caesar abandoned him. The plot was detected, and Cicero, in virtue of a *senatus consultum ultimum,* arrested the conspirators. With the senate's approval he had them put to death as *hostes* without appeal, despite the law of Tiberius Gracchus. The forces in Etruria were dispersed. Cicero's famous *Orations against Catiline.*

60. THE FIRST TRIUMVIRATE. Caesar returned from a pro-praetorship in Spain and brought his master Crassus into alliance with Pompey, who had fallen out with the senate because of the unwillingness of the latter to confirm his eastern arrangements. This informal union became known as the first triumvirate.

59.   Caesar, as consul, put through the program of the trio: distribution of the Campanian land to Pompey's veterans; confirmation of Pompey's eastern settlement; grant to himself (*lex Vatinia*) for the unprecedented period of five years of the province of Cisalpine Gaul, with Illyria.   To this was added later Gallia Narbonensis, with the possibility of action throughout Transalpine Gaul.   The political union was cemented by the marriage of Caesar's daughter Julia to Pompey.

58-51.   CONQUEST OF GAUL by Caesar, both to enrich himself and to forge for himself an army and a military reputation to rival Pompey's. He used as an excuse the attempt of the Helvetii to move from Switzerland into Gaul.   His plan of campaign was to move down the Rhine, separate the Gauls from the Germans, and then turn back on the Gauls. In 58 he defeated the **Helvetii** at **Bibracte** (Autun) and the German Ariovistus near Vesontio (Besançon). He then reduced the Belgae (57), including the stubborn Nervii, in northwestern Gaul.   He defeated the **Veneti** on the southern coast of Brittany and the **Aquitani** in southwestern Gaul (56). After he had repulsed the Germanic Usipetes and Tencteri, Caesar built a wooden bridge over the Rhine near Coblenz to make a two weeks' demonstration in Germany (55).   He also tried with little success to invade Britain.

58.   To remove opposition at Rome, the triumvirs secured the mission of the irreconcilable **M. Porcius Cato** (the younger) to investigate the affairs of Cyprus, and allowed the violent demagogue and tribune **P. Clodius** to move a bill against Cicero for the execution of Roman citizens without appeal. Cicero voluntarily withdrew to Epirus, the bill was passed, and his property was confiscated. Clodius also made the distribution of grain free to a large number of poor, perhaps 300,000.

57.   An optimate tribune, **T. Annius Milo,** secured the recall of Cicero, and organized a following to oppose that of Clodius. The optimates summoned up enough courage to attack Caesar's land bill.

In consequence of the shortage of grain, the senate conferred on Pompey the supervision of the grain supply (*cura annonae*) and an *imperium aequum* over the areas concerned, but without what he really wanted, viz. military force.

56.   Worried by the revival of opposition, Caesar, Pompey, and Crassus met at Luca, on the southern boundary of Caesar's province, and laid plans for the future.

55.   In pursuance of these plans, Pompey and Crassus became consuls. By a consular *lex Pompeia Licinia,* Caesar's command in Gaul was prolonged for five years. By a tribunician law (*lex Trebonia*), Crassus was given Syria and Pompey both Spains for the same period. Crassus hurried east, but Pompey, contrary to custom, remained near Rome and governed Spain through his *legati.*

54.   INVASION OF BRITAIN.   Caesar was more successful than in 55 and defeated King Cassivellaunus somewhere north of the Thames, perhaps at Wheathampstead near Verulamium (St. Albans). Nevertheless, he withdrew to Gaul without any permanent result save to open Britain somewhat to the penetration of trade and Roman influence. In 53 he made a second demonstration across the Rhine.

54-51.   Breakup of the Triumvirate.   This began with the death of Julia in 54.

53.   **Crassus** was utterly defeated and slain by the Parthians at Carrhae in Mesopotamia.

52.   All Gaul flared into revolt under **Vercingetorix.** Caesar failed to take Gergovia (Clermont in Auvergne) and was himself surrounded while besieging Vercingetorix in Alesia (Alise near Dijon), but finally won a complete victory and captured Vercingetorix. He spent the year 51 ruthlessly suppressing the remaining insurgents.

52.   Milo's ruffians killed Clodius in a street fight at Bovillae.

As it had not yet been possible to elect magistrates for this year, the senate passed a *senatus consultum ultimum* and illegally appointed **Pompey sole consul,** i.e. in fact dictator. Milo, tried in a special court under Pompey's presidency, was condemned despite Cicero's faltering defense. Pompey then made the optimate Metellus Scipio, father of his new wife, Crassus' widow, his colleague, thus openly returning to the side of the senate. Afraid, however, of a decisive break with Caesar, he tried, by a series of indirect moves, to jockey him out of office long enough to leave him open for prosecution in the courts. Since

prosecutions could not be brought against one in office, Caesar had so arranged his tenure of Gaul (the details are uncertain) that, by being allowed to canvass in absence during 49, he could proceed direct to the consulship in 48.

49.   The senate finally passed a *senatus consultum ultimum* which declared Caesar a public enemy unless he should disband his army (Jan. 7). The tribunes favorable to him fled to Ravenna, where he was waiting. During the night of Jan. 10–11, Caesar with one legion crossed the **Rubicon** (*alea iacta est,* "the die is cast"), the brook south of Ravenna on the Adriatic which marked the limit of his province. He thus broke not only Sulla's law on treason, but also an old custom by which a general could bring armed forces into Italy only for a triumph. He justified his action as aimed to protect the sacrosanct tribunes.

49-46.   Pompey, fearful of the legions in Gaul, left Italy for Greece, where he might have the resources of the east behind him. Most of the senate went with him. Caesar, after failing to trap Pompey at Brundisium, turned to Spain, where he defeated the latter's commanders at **Ilerda** (Lerida) north of the Ebro. Marseilles surrendered to him on his way back to Italy.

48.   Caesar landed in Epirus and defeated Pompey at **Pharsalus.** Pompey fled to Egypt, where he was treacherously slain by order of the minister of the young king, Ptolemy XII.

48-47.   When Caesar reached Alexandria in pursuit of Pompey, he was besieged by Ptolemy and the natives during the winter, until he was rescued by an army from Asia. Since Ptolemy perished, Caesar made his sister **Cleopatra** and a younger brother, Ptolemy XIII, joint rulers of Egypt. Cleopatra soon disposed of her brother and set herself to restore the power of the Ptolemies with Roman aid. She charmed Caesar into remaining three months with her and perhaps siring her son Caesarion.

47.   Caesar advanced into Syria to meet a son of the great Mithridates, Pharnaces, who had invaded Pontus. On Aug. 2 Caesar defeated him at **Zela** (*ueni, uidi, uici*).

46.   On his return to Rome Caesar subdued a mutiny of his devoted Tenth Legion. He then crossed to Africa and defeated the Pompeians, led by Pompey the Great's son Sextus, at **Thapsus** (Apr.). Cato committed suicide at Utica (hence called *Uticensis*). A part of Numidia, whose Pompeian king, Juba, had committed suicide, was added to the province of Africa; the rest was left to the king of eastern Mauretania. After four simultaneous triumphs in Rome (July) Caesar went to Spain, where Sex. Pompey had joined his brother Gnaeus.

45.   Caesar utterly routed them at **Munda**

(Mar.). He then returned to Rome (Sept.).

Caesar's position was that of an absolute monarch. In 49 he had been dictator for 11 days to hold elections. In 48 he was consul for the second time. After Pharsalus he was given the consulship for a five-year term and was given the dictatorship annually; perhaps also some of the tribunician powers (*tribunicia potestas*), since being a patrician he could not be tribune. In 46 he was consul for the third time with Lepidus. After Thapsus he was made dictator for ten years and *praefectus morum* (supervisor of morals). In 45 he was sole consul. After Munda he was made consul for ten years; in 44, dictator and *praefectus morum* for life; his tribunician power was extended to include *sacrosanctitas*. Thus his position was essentially a revival of the Sullan dictatorship. His plans for the future are not definitely known, but while he certainly planned to continue as monarch, it is doubtful that he planned to take the crown or move the capital to Ilium.

The **senate was increased to 900** by enrolling ex-centurions and provincials, as much to weaken it as to make it representative of the empire. To provide for its maintenance at this size Caesar doubled the number of quaestors and praetors (to 40 and 16 respectively); the quaestors were later reduced. His agrarian and colonization program was like that of all reformers since the Gracchi. The citizenship was considerably extended, beginning in 49 with the confirmation of the Transpadanes' long disputed claim. The *lex Iulia municipalis* may perhaps have been a measure to give to the cities in the west something of the autonomy enjoyed by those in the east. The **calendar was reformed** in the light of Egyptian knowledge on the nearly correct basis of $365\frac{1}{4}$ days per year; this system continued in use in some countries into the 20th century. The number of those receiving free grain was reduced from 320,000 to 150,000. The publican system was somewhat restricted, since Caesar had considerable concern for the provinces and none for the *equites*.

44. ASSASSINATION OF CAESAR. Caesar's greatest weakness was an inability to choose trustworthy subordinates. A conspiracy of such people, together with the high-minded patriots and disgruntled optimates, led by M. Junius Brutus, Decimus Brutus, and G. Cassius Longinus, assassinated him in the senate on the Ides (15th) of March. The famous *Et tu Brute* ("Thou too, Brutus") may have been addressed to Decimus, not Marcus.

The conspirators had no organization ready to take charge. **M. Antonius** (Mark Antony), formerly Caesar's master of horse, got control,

in part by appealing to the sympathies of the proletariat by his funeral oration and in part by seizing Caesar's papers and treasure. The conspirators fled, Decimus Brutus to Cisalpine Gaul, Marcus Brutus to Macedonia, and Cassius to Syria, provinces already assigned to them, and over which the senate now gave them commands superior (not equal) to those of other governors (*imperia maiora*), so that they could raise armies against Antony. Antony secured from the people the transfer of Cisalpine Gaul and Macedonia to himself and Syria to his colleague, P. Cornelius Dolabella. In the meantime, Caesar's eighteen-year-old great-nephew, **Gaius Octavius,** whose mother, Atia, was daughter of Caesar's sister, Julia, and who had been named as heir and adopted in the will of Caesar, came to Rome to claim his inheritance. Antony refused to give him the money and prevented the passing of the *lex curiata* necessary to ratify his adoption. Octavius nevertheless called himself **Gaius Julius Caesar Octavianus.** He borrowed money and, illegally, as a private citizen, levied a force among Caesar's veterans in Campania.

43. **Antony** marched north to dislodge Decimus Brutus from Mutina (Modena). The senate sent the new consuls Hirtius and Pansa to relieve Decimus and joined to them Octavian with the command (*imperium*) of a pro-praetor. In two battles, **Forum Gallorum** and **Mutina,** Antony was forced to retire westward toward Gaul. But the consuls were killed. Octavian, marching to Rome (July), forced the senate to hold special elections in which he and Pedius were elected to replace the dead consuls. He had his adoption duly confirmed. By a *lex Pedia* vengeance was declared on the conspirators who had assassinated Caesar. In the meantime, **Marcus Lepidus,** governor of Transalpine Gaul, had allied with Antony, and Decimus had been slain. Octavian thereupon changed his support from the senate to Antony in a meeting at Bononia (Bologna).

43, Nov. SECOND TRIUMVIRATE. A tribunician *lex Titia* confirmed their arrangements: Antony, Lepidus, and Octavian were appointed a comission of three to establish the state (*triumuiri rei publicae constituendae*), which amounted to a Sullan dictatorship in commission and differentiated this second triumvirate from the first by recognizing it legally. The triumvirs proceeded with a widespread proscription inspired both by political hatred and by the need for money and lands with which to reward their troops. Octavian acquiesced in the **execution of Cicero** by Antony's agents (Dec. 7).

42. The triumvirs secured the erection of a temple to Caesar in the Forum, where he had been burnt, and his deification. The magistrates were forced to take an oath to support all Caesar's arrangements (*acta*). Antony and Octavian then crossed to Thrace, where they met the combined forces of Cassius and Brutus at **Philippi.** Cassius, defeated by Antony and misled by a false report of Brutus' defeat, committed suicide. Brutus, though actually victorious over Octavian, was finally defeated 20 days later and also killed himself. Antony betook himself to the eastern provinces, where he met Cleopatra at Tarsus in the summer of 41. Either fascinated by her charms or desiring to get control of her resources, he remained with her in Egypt for a year.

41–40. **Octavian,** who shared the western provinces with Lepidus, had a difficult war against Antony's wife Fulvia and brother Lucius Antonius before finally reducing them at **Perusia** (Perugia) in 40.

40. **By a pact made at Brundisium,** Antony married Octavian's sister Octavia (since Fulvia had recently died). Octavian took Gaul from Lepidus, who was left only Africa.

39. **Sextus Pompey,** who had conducted a piratical career since Munda, was now a power to be reckoned with, as he controlled Sicily and his fleet could interrupt Rome's grain supply. His possession of Sicily, Sardinia, Corsica, and the Peloponnese was recognized by the triumvirs in the **pact of Misenum.** Octavian divorced his second wife, Scribonia, and married **Livia,** previously wife of Tib. Claudius Nero.

37. Octavia engineered a **second pact at Tarentum.** Octavian gave troops to Antony for his Parthian War and Antony supplied ships for use against Pompey. The triumvirate was renewed for five years more, though the precise date set for its termination is uncertain.

36. Octavian's fleet, under his general **M. Vipsanius Agrippa,** defeated Pompey, who fled to Miletus, where he died. Lepidus, after landing in Sicily ostensibly to help Octavian, tried to secure the island. When, however, his troops deserted to Octavian, the latter annexed his rival's territory but, because Lepidus himself had become chief pontiff (*pontifex maximus*) on the death of Caesar, kept him in honorable captivity at Circeii until his death in 13. Octavian spent the following years consolidating Roman power in the Alps and Illyria.

36. Antony suffered a severe defeat from the Parthians in 36, but managed to retreat to Armenia. He openly married Cleopatra (though already married to Octavia).

34. At Alexandria he established her as a Hellenistic monarch and distributed Roman provinces to her children as subordinate rulers.

How far he intended to be her consort cannot be determined, but Octavian made the most of such a probability.

32. When Antony prepared to attack Octavian, the latter had the support of the west, which was both terrified by fear of an oriental domination under Cleopatra and angry at Antony's high-handed disposition of Roman territory. After the consuls, friends of Antony, fled to him, Octavian had the *imperium* of Antony under the triumvirate annulled by the *comitia.* He published a will purporting to be Antony's in which the Roman possessions in the east were bequeathed to Cleopatra. Italy, and perhaps all the western provinces, took a military oath (*coniuratio Italiae*) to support Octavian. In virtue of this, since he no longer had any legal *imperium* himself if the triumvirate was at an end, he levied troops, outwardly to meet Cleopatra. Antony formally divorced Octavia.

31, Sept. 2. **BATTLE OF ACTIUM.** The rival fleets met outside the bay. The course of the battle is uncertain, but Cleopatra fled to Egypt, followed by Antony, whose army then surrendered to Octavian. In the following year,

30. Antony, on hearing a false report of Cleopatra's suicide, killed himself. Upon Octavian's arrival at Alexandria, Cleopatra tried to win him as she had his predecessors. When she failed, she committed suicide (the story of the asp is perhaps false) lest she have to grace his triumph. Egypt passed finally into Rome's possession.

29. Octavian celebrated three triumphs and by closing the temple of Janus, something recorded only twice before (by Numa and in 235), signalized the restoration of peace throughout the Roman world.

If the crossing of the Rubicon marked the final fall of the republic, the battle of Actium signalized the final triumph of the empire. The last century of the republic was characterized by the collapse of popular government because of the wide extension of citizenship, the considerable adulteration of the citizen body at Rome by the introduction of un-Romanized Orientals, chiefly through the manumission of slaves, the growth in Rome of an unemployed proletariat, the rise of demagogues, and the complexity of the problems of government. The increasingly corrupt senate had lost control of the assemblies, the armies, and the generals. The financiers, as well as the governors, saw in the provinces only a field for exploitation. Italy had been exhausted by civil war, proscriptions (which especially reduced the upper classes), recruitment, and land confiscations.

The last century of the republic witnessed a vigorous **literary activity** at Rome. Hellenism, thoroughly absorbed into Roman education, formed a constituent element in thought rather than something imposed from without. At the same time the native talent of the Romans adapted Hellenism to their own particular needs. **Lyric poetry** found expression in **Catullus** (87–54) from Verona, who, besides his imitations of the Alexandrine poets, produced strongly personal and intense lyrics on his hates and loves. The Epicurean **Lucretius** (99–55), wrote his epic "On the Nature of Things" (*de Rerum Natura*) to expound a materialistic atomism. **Caesar's** (102–44) *Commentaries* on the Gallic Wars, continued by his officers for the other campaigns, are, despite their apologetic purpose, admirably clear and impartial. Minor writings which have survived are the historical monographs on Catiline and the Jugurthine War by **Sallust** (86–35) and the *Lives* by **Nepos** (100–29). Outstanding among antiquarians was **Varro** (116–27), while the **Scaevolae,** father and son, in the Sullan pe-

riod, were outstanding students of jurisprudence. But the figure who gave his name to the age was **Cicero** (106–43). In spite of his active public life, he not only published his forensic and judicial speeches but wrote extensively on philosophy, rhetoric, and politics. He passed on to the Middle Ages much of value from Greek thought, especially from Plato, the Stoics, and the New (Skeptic) Academy. But he added thereto a Roman color and much of his own thought and experience. Finally, his correspondence, published after his death, gives a deep insight into both the writer and his times.

Roman art began during this century to emerge with a definite character. Though buildings still preserved the heavy lines and ornament of the Etruscans, they acquired majesty and splendor under direct Greek influence. Portrait sculpture, though executed by Greeks, portrayed the individual to a degree unknown in idealizing Hellenic art.

F. THE ROMAN EMPIRE, TO 527 A.D.

1. THE EARLY EMPIRE, 31 B.C.–192 A.D.

[For a complete list of the Roman emperors see Appendix I.]

27 B.C.–14 A.D. IMPERATOR CAESAR OCTAVIANUS (b. Sept. 23, 63), later called **Augustus,** established his government in 27 (Jan. 23), with some modifications later, especially after a serious illness in 23. He proclaimed that he would "restore the republic," i.e. resign his extraordinary powers and put the senate and Roman people again at the head of the state. He held the consulship annually until 23, but only twice thereafter for a short part of the year. He also received, and retained after 23, a proconsular command superior to those of other senatorial pro-consuls and unlimited in time, though actually renewed at intervals (*imperium proconsulare maius infinitum*). Although he received a special dispensation to retain his *imperium* within the *pomoerium,* it is uncertain to what extent he could actually exercise it over Rome or even Italy, the sphere of the consuls. However, in virtue of the *imperium,* he controlled all the armed forces of the state and appointed as legionary commanders his own senatorial delegates (*legati*). He also divided the provinces between the emperor and the senate. Augustus himself took charge of all provinces in which the presence of troops was required and appointed to govern them other

senatorial delegates, called in this case *legati pro praetore.* The senate sent pro-consuls to the pacified provinces where troops were no longer needed. Thus Augustus hoped to prevent that rivalry of independent commanders that had brought about the downfall of the republic. He also sought to assure better government in the provinces by the payment of salaries to all governors, senatorial and imperial. Two major districts received special treatment. The command of the legions on the Rhine was given to a special legate, independent of the imperial government of the Gallic provinces, and only later did this command develop into two territorial provinces. Egypt was administered by Augustus as a private estate under an equestrian praefect (*praefectus Aegypti*) appointed by himself, who directed the elaborate machinery inherited from the Pharaohs and Ptolemies for the benefit of the new imperial treasury (*fiscus*), which was distinct from the old senatorial treasury (*aerarium Saturni*). Smaller districts were governed, not by senatorial *legati,* but by equestrian procurators or praefects. Imperial governors of all sorts tended to have longer terms than the senatorial and thus to perform their task better. Since, however, the imperial *legati,* in both

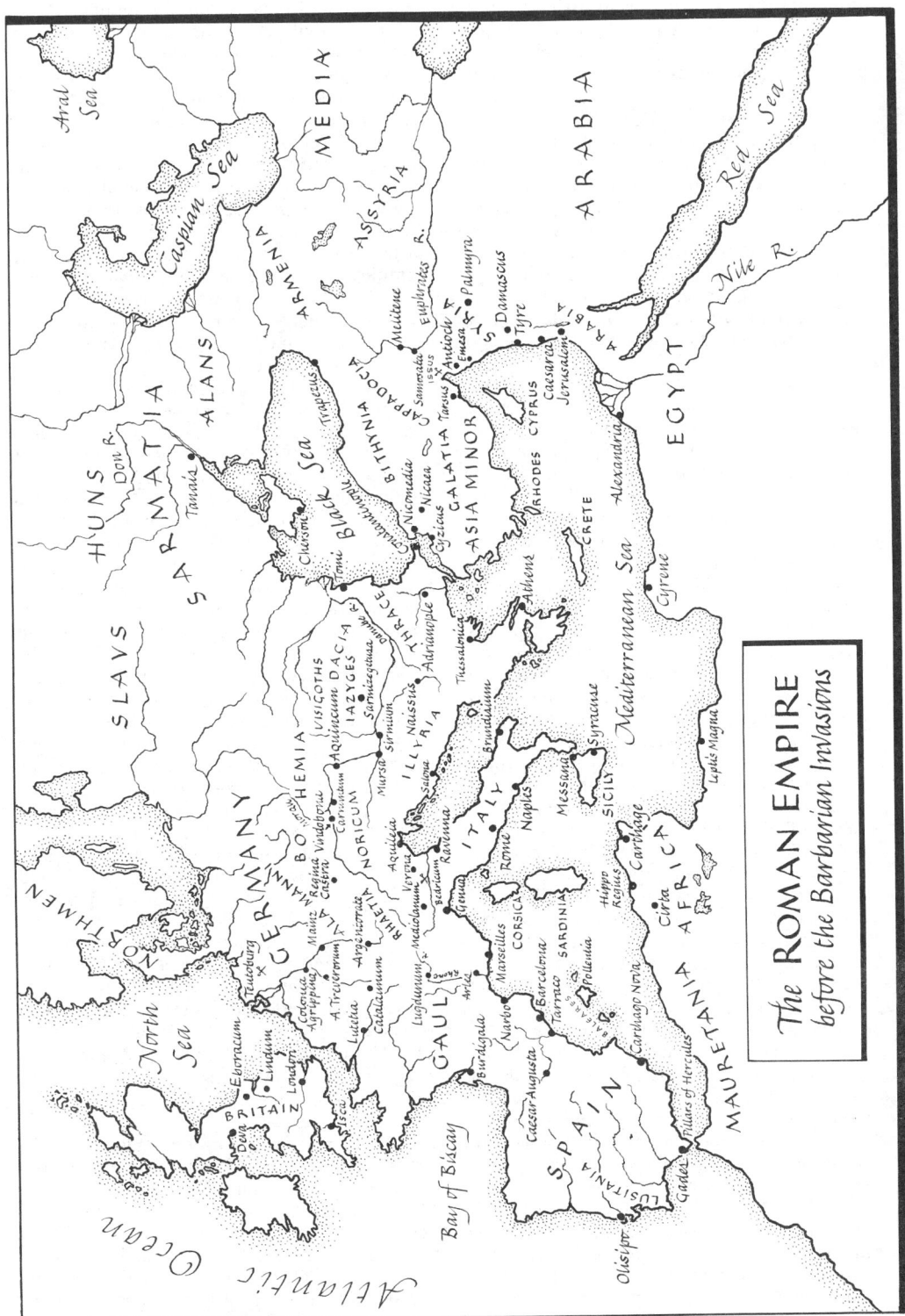

The ROMAN EMPIRE
before the Barbarian Invasions

provinces and the army, were drawn from the senate and usually held pro-consulships later, no sharp distinction was drawn between the republican and imperial administration in the upper ranks.

A distinct **imperial civil service** did, however, grow up among the equestrians, partly in the provinces where, besides the minor governorships above mentioned, they held financial posts as stewards (*procuratores*) of the emperor or of his treasury (*fiscus*) and partly in various administrative posts in Rome and Italy, of which the chief were those with which Augustus supplemented the inadequate republican administration of the city of Rome. The most important officer was a consular senator, the *praefectus urbi,* who had general supervision of the city with three "urban cohorts" of soldiers for police. This office, however, may have become permanent only under Tiberius. The other three major officials were equestrian. A *praefectus annonae* had charge of the grain supply for Rome. A *praefectus uigilum* had seven cohorts of freedmen as firemen, one for every two of the 14 regions into which Augustus divided the city. And a *praefectus praetorio* had charge of the nine cohorts of the imperial or "praetorian" guard (praetor-general), which Augustus kept scattered through Italy, but which Sejanus later concentrated in a camp at Rome. Because of the importance of this post, later emperors frequently divided it between two incumbents.

In 23 B.C. Augustus secured the consolidation and extension of certain tribunician privileges which had been granted to him because, as a patrician, he could not be a tribune. The value of this tribunician power (*tribunicia potestas*) was in part its traditionally popular appeal and in part the privileges of sacrosanctity, *auxulium,* veto, direct jurisdiction in Rome, consultation of the senate, and, most important, the initiation of legislation. Augustus, during his reign, initiated a series of far-reaching laws (*leges Iuliae*) in an attempt to reform the criminal law, regulate social classes, and revive morality and family life. With respect to the social order, he purified the senate of Caesarian intruders by a series of "selections" (*lectiones*); he restricted severely the freeing of slaves and the attainment of full citizenship by freedmen; and he bestowed the citizenship on provincials very grudgingly. However, he did increase the recipients of free grain from Caesar's 150,000 to 200,000. The final law in his effort to restore morality was the consular *lex Papia Poppaea* of 9 A.D., which supplemented his own *lex Iulia de maritandis ordinibus* of 18 B.C. These laws encouraged marriage in the senatorial and equestrian orders by penalizing the unmarried and offering privileges to the fathers of children, especially of three (*ius trium liberorum*).

Augustus likewise held a number of minor offices or titles. Though he did not become chief priest (*pontifex maximus*) until after the death of Lepidus in 13, he undertook to revivify the old Roman religion in the face of an influx of exotic eastern cults. He also allowed the worship of his genius, allied often with the goddess Roma, in Italy and the provinces. After his death he, like Caesar, was deified and temples were erected to him as *diuus Augustus;* but the official worship of living emperors during the early empire is questionable. Besides revising the rolls of senate, knights, and people either as censor or with censorial powers, he controlled admission to the senate by various methods. He alone could grant the wide stripe (*latus clauus*), the sign of a senatorial career, to those who did not inherit it as sons of senators. He appointed to the minor military posts which were a necessary qualification for the republican magistracies. And the privilege of either recommending (*nominatio*) or requiring (*commendatio*) the election of certain candidates for office allowed him to advance those whom he thought most fit. The republican magistracies continued with only minor changes save that the term of the consulship suffered progressive diminution until it averaged two months. When the opening pair of consuls (*consules ordinarii*) left office, there followed a succession of *consules suffecti.* Finally, in virtue either of specific enactments or of his general authority (*auctoritas*), Augustus undertook many improvements throughout the empire: roads, buildings, colonies, etc.

The title by which he is best known, **Augustus,** was bestowed on him by the senate in 27 (Jan. 16) and expressed a semi-religious feeling of gratitude for his achievements. He did not, however, set himself up outwardly as a monarch, and the term which he himself used informally, though not as an official title, to describe himself was **princeps,** chief among equals.

29. The **closing of the temple of Janus** for the first time since 235 signified the achievement of longed-for peace throughout the empire (cf. year 9, below).

20. By a **treaty with Parthia,** Augustus recovered the standards lost by Crassus and Antony and thereby vindicated Roman honor.

17. A celebration of the *ludi saeculares,* religious ceremonies, concluded the fifth era (*saeculum*) since the founding of Rome.

16–15. The **defeat of Lollius** by the Germans necessitated the presence of Augustus in Gaul and Tiberius in Germany. Rhaetia, Noricum, and Vindelicia were annexed so that the frontier reached the upper Danube.

12–9. **Tiberius** was summoned to Pannonia by a severe revolt. Drusus fought against the Germans until his death in 9.

9. The **altar of Peace** (*ara pacis*), voted by the senate four years before, was dedicated (cf. year 29, above).

9–7. Tiberius carried on the conquest of Germany, but was sent to Armenia in 6. For some reason now unknown, he retired to Rhodes until the death of the sons of Agrippa and Augustus' daughter, Julia, made him the only possible successor to Augustus. He returned to Rome in 2 A.D., on the death of Lucius Caesar at Marseilles, and was adopted in 4 A.D., after the death of Gaius Caesar in Asia.

4. B.C. Probable date of the **birth of Jesus,** following shortly the death of **Herod the Great** (37–4 B.C.), king of Judaea. Herod, who had rebuilt the temple in Jerusalem, was strongly disliked by the principal factions among the Jews: Saducees, Pharisees, Zealots, Essenes. He was succeeded by his sons **Archelaus** as ethnarch of Samaria (4 B.C.–6 A.D.); **Antipas** as tetrarch of Galilee (4 B.C.–39 A.D.); and **Philip** as tetrarch of Batanaea (4 B.C.–34 A.D.). Judaea itself was put under an imperial procurator. After the brief reign of **Herod Agrippa** (41–44 A.D.) and his son **Herod Agrippa II** (50–100), all Palestine was under direct Roman rule. The revolts of the Jews in 66–70 and 132–135 led only to the destruction of Jerusalem and the dispersal of the Jewish people.

The **DEAD SEA SCROLLS.** Much light has been cast recently on the religious and political life of the Jews in the centuries before and after Christ by the discovery of large numbers of scrolls and manuscripts in several localities to the west and north of the Dead Sea. These finds are without precedent in the history of modern archaeology and are of supreme importance for the understanding of primitive Christianity.

1. The **Qumran manuscripts,** the first of which were found in 1947 by a goatherd near **Khirbet Qumran,** site of the communal center of the **Essene sect.** In the sequel (1947–1956) further manuscripts and fragments, some 600 in number, were discovered by bedouin and archaeologists in eleven caves in the same general area, Cave IV containing the largest number. The finds include early texts, in Hebrew or Aramaic, of practically all books of the Old Testament, Apocrypha, commentaries, rules, laws, prayers, hymns, and psalms, dating from the late 3rd century B.C. to 68 A.D., when the community was destroyed by the Romans.

2. The **finds in the Wadi Murabba-at,** 18 km. south of Qumran, first made by bedouin in 1951. These records were left behind by fugitives of the army of **Bar Cocheba** (Bar Kokhba), who led the revolt of the Jews against Roman rule in 132–135. They consist of fragmentary biblical writings and legal documents in Hebrew, Aramaic, and Greek, but contain also a Hebrew papyrus of the 7th century B.C., the earliest yet known.

3. The **finds of Nahal Hever and Se-elim,** near En Geddi, in Israeli territory. The documents found here since 1952, like those of the Murabba-at caves, belong largely to the period of Bar Cocheba and the Jewish revolt.

4. Finds of the Wadi Daliyeh, 14 km. north of ancient Jericho, 1962–1964, consisting largely of papyri fragments dated 375–335 B.C. left in the cave by Samarians fleeing before the army of Alexander the Great in 331 B.C. They constitute the earliest extensive group of papyri to have been found in Palestine.

5. Finds at Masada, in the Judaean wilderness, in 1963–1964. This ancient fort was the site of the last stand of the Zealots against Rome (73 A.D.). The finds include valuable fragments of biblical writings.

After years of scholarly controversy paleologists and archaeologists are now generally agreed that the Qumran documents stem from the Essene sect that centered on that site. Secular records show this desert community to have been founded around 130 B.C. and to have existed until 68 A.D. It derived from the Pious (**Hasidim**) and seceded from the main Jewish community in protest against the policies and practices of Jonathan and Simon Maccabee, as did the Pharisees and Saducees. Persecuted by Simon, the Essenes, under their leader "The Righteous Teacher," fled into the wilderness, turned to apocalyptic visions, and looked forward to the establishment of their community as the true Israel, the Elect of God, in the dawning Messianic Age. Apparently many Essenes, like the more militant Zealots, took up arms against the Romans in 66–70 A.D. and were annihilated almost without leaving a trace.

In the light of the documents from the wilderness of Judah, early Judaism now appears far richer and more varied than scholars had previously suspected. The Essenes appear to have been the bearers, and in no small part the creators, of the late **Apocalyptic tradition.** Furthermore, the primitive Christian community is now shown to have stood in the same tradition of Jewish sectarianism. Its institutions, including its early practice of religious communism, its church organization, and even the sacraments of baptism and communion owe much to earlier Jewish institutions and

The House of Herod the Great

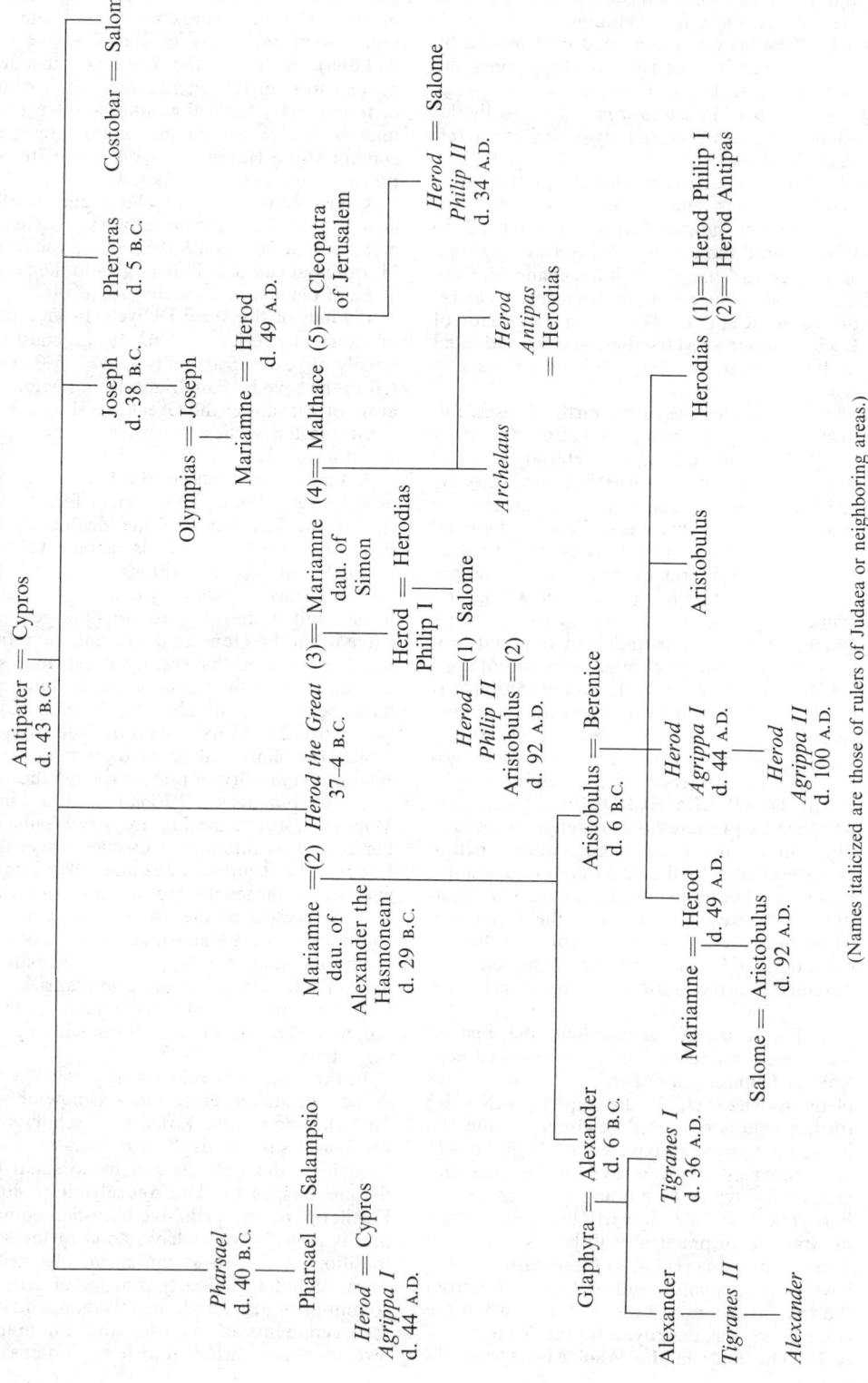

(Names italicized are those of rulers of Judaea or neighboring areas.)

liturgical practices of the Essene type. On the other hand, the early Christian community stood far closer to the Pharisaic societies than to the Essene sectaries in its freedom from priestly domination and in its participation in the ordinary life of the world. Again there is no real parallel between the place of the inspired Righteous Teacher in Essene doctrine and the central role of Jesus as Messiah in Christian teaching.

The **Christian Era** begins with the year 1 A.D., which follows directly on the year 1 B.C., since no year is numbered 0. Hereafter dates A.D. (*anno Domini,* "year of our Lord") will appear without designation and dates B.C. (before Christ) will be indicated as such.

4-6. Upon his adoption, Tiberius was sent again to Germany. From there he was recalled to suppress revolts in Pannonia and Dalmatia until 9. He finally established the frontier on the middle Danube. At the same time (6) the creation of the province of Moesia and the reduction of Thrace to a client state advanced the frontier to the lower Danube.

6. Augustus set up a special treasury, the *aerarium militare,* to pay bonuses to retiring legionary veterans. Though land grants to veterans occurred thereafter, this bonus system finally solved the problem of caring for veterans. Augustus reduced the number of legions from 70 or more to 27 or 28 at his death. These, with about an equal number of auxiliary troops, gave a total army of some 300,000 men.

9. The legate, **P. Quinctilius Varus,** with three legions, was annihilated by the German Arminius in the **battle of the Teutoburg Forest,** perhaps near Paderborn. This defeat put an end to Augustus' plans for the conquest of Germany to the Elbe and established the Rhine as the future border between Latin and German territory. Augustus discontinued his conquest because of the financial difficulties involved in replacing the lost legions and levying enough additional forces to subdue Germany permanently.

14. **AUGUSTUS DIED** at Nola on Aug. 19. Legally, his position could not be inherited, since the various powers and offices composing it ceased with his death and could be received by another only from the senate and Roman people. In fact, however, Augustus had throughout his life sought so to indicate a successor as to insure the perpetuation of the principate. In this attempt he tried to combine inheritance, by either blood, marriage, or adoption, with selection of the best available man, through the bestowal of a secondary proconsular *imperium* and the tribunician power. After several possible successors had pre-

deceased him, he selected **Tiberius,** son of his wife Livia by her first husband. Though, at the death of Augustus, Tiberius held the tribunician power and an unusually extensive *imperium,* he perhaps sincerely laid before the senate the option of restoring the republic. The senate, however, realized the impossibility of such a step or, according to ancient authorities, found its freedom of action impeded by the hypocrisy of Tiberius. Revolts of the legions in Pannonia and Germany showed the need of a single strong commander to prevent a recurrence of the civil wars of the later republic. Tiberius already occupied too strong a position for anyone else to be chosen. The senate therefore conferred on him the powers and titles of Augustus.

14-37. **TIBERIUS** Claudius Nero (b. 42 B.C.), emperor. He transferred the elections from the assemblies to the senate. Already the passage of laws in the assemblies had become a formality and though continued until the time of Nerva, the assemblies hereafter had no official share in the government save to confirm the grant of the *imperium* and *tribunicia potestas* to a new emperor. The Roman mob, however, continued by its frequent riots to exert a pressure upon the government out of proportion to its importance.

14-16. The **revolt of the Pannonian legions** was suppressed by Tiberius' son, the younger Drusus. The son of Tiberius' brother Drusus, who is known by his father's title, **Germanicus,** and whom Augustus had forced Tiberius to adopt as a possible successor, suppressed the German mutiny and campaigned in Germany with some successes. He defeated Arminius, whose kingdom then broke up, and recovered the eagles of Varus' legions. He was, however, recalled, probably not because Tiberius begrudged his victories, but because he found them too costly.

17. On the death of their kings, Cappadocia and Commagene became a province.

17-19. **Germanicus,** sent to install a king in Armenia, conducted himself in a high-handed manner both in Syria and in Egypt. When, however, he died in Syria the enemies of Tiberius rallied about his wife Agrippina, and charged the legate of Syria, Piso, before the senate with having poisoned him. Piso's consequent suicide gave color to the probably unjust suspicion that Tiberius, or even Livia, had encouraged the supposed poisoning.

19. **Maroboduus,** who had built up a strong kingdom in Bohemia, was forced by internal dissensions to take refuge with the Romans. Thereafter, the Romans were not seriously threatened on the Rhine or upper Danube until the time of Marcus Aurelius.

The Julian-Claudian House

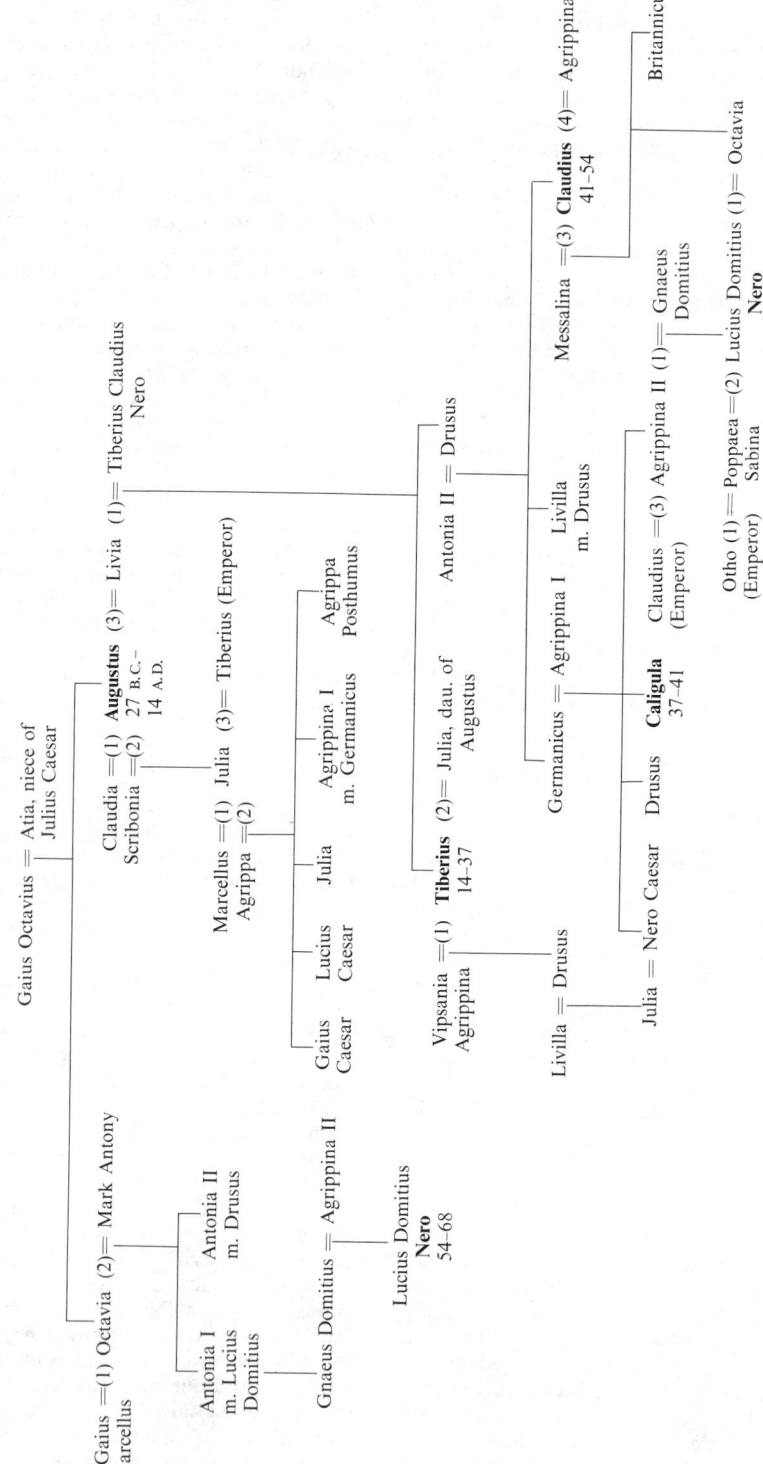

21. A **revolt broke out in Gaul** among the Treveri, led by Julius Florus, and the Aedui, led by Julius Sacrovir. Though soon suppressed by the commander in upper Germany, Gaius Silius, it showed that anti-Roman feeling was still strong in Gaul, even among the chiefs who had received Roman citizenship, as these Julii from Caesar or Augustus.

23–31. Tiberius fell increasingly under the influence of the ambitious and treacherous equestrian praefect of the guard, **Sejanus,** who quartered the praetorian cohorts in one camp outside Rome. He encouraged the gathering of information against those hostile to Tiberius by unscrupulous informers (*delatores,* many of whom were of the nobility) and the prosecution of the accused under the law of treason (*lex de maiestate imminuta*), since actions against the person of the emperor were regarded as harmful to the majesty of the state. When such trials involved senators or important equestrians, they were heard by the senate, which came increasingly to act as a court under the presidency of the emperor or the consuls. Ancient writers have, however, much exaggerated the abuse of this law under Tiberius. In 23, Sejanus probably poisoned Tiberius' son Drusus, in order to intrigue for his own succession.

26. Sejanus persuaded Tiberius to retire from the annoyances of an increasingly hostile Rome. Tiberius eventually settled on **Capreae** (Capri), an island in the Bay of Naples, where the popular imagination, probably wrongly, pictured him as giving way to the most abominable vices. Actually, Tiberius was of rigid morality and of the utmost conscientiousness in governing the empire and in carrying out the policies of Augustus.

29. **Livia,** accused of attempting to dominate the empire after Augustus' death, died. Sejanus secured the exile of **Agrippina,** wife of Germanicus (she died in 33), and the arrest of his two eldest sons, Nero (d. 31) and a third Drusus (d. 33).

(30). **PONTIUS PILATE,** procurator of Judaea (26–36), ordered the **crucifixion of Jesus** of Nazareth, called the Christ (the Greek *Christos* is a translation of Messiah, "anointed" in Aramaic), accused of sedition.

31. The plots of Sejanus finally came to the notice of Tiberius, who engineered his arrest and execution. Tiberius remained in rigid seclusion in Capreae.

36. Artabanus, **king of Parthia,** made peace with Rome. Rome was saved from a serious Parthian threat throughout this period by dynastic quarrels within Parthia and by disputes over the possession of Armenia.

37. **Tiberius,** dying at Misenum (Mar. 16), indicated as his successors his young grandson, **Tiberius Gemellus,** and the surviving son of Germanicus, **Gaius Caesar** nicknamed *Caligula* ("Little Boot"). Gaius at first favored Tiberius Gemellus, but soon put him to death.

37–41. **Gaius CALIGULA** (b. 12), emperor. If not insane at his accession, Caligula was at least a megalomaniac and soon became unbalanced. Though the follies ascribed to him may be exaggerated, his conduct was extremely irrational. Behind it may have lain the desire for an absolute monarchy after the pattern of his great-grandfather, Antony. He established many client kings, including Julius Agrippa I, wrongly called Herod Agrippa, a grandson of Herod the Great. He had himself worshiped as a god, though his attempt to erect a statue of himself in the temple of Jerusalem was blocked by the legate of Syria, Petronius.

39. Caligula's **campaign into Germany** was stopped by a conspiracy led by Gaetulicus.

40. A campaign against Britain was also a fiasco.

41, Jan. 24. **Caligula was assassinated** by conspirators led by Cassius Chaerea.

An attempt by the senate to revive the republic was frustrated when the praetorian guard found in the palace a scholarly, neglected younger brother of Germanicus, Claudius. Being loyal to the family, the guard imposed him upon the senate as emperor.

41–54. Tiberius CLAUDIUS Drusus (b. 10 B.C.), emperor.

He was regarded at Rome as a driveling imbecile, subject to the whims of his wives and freedmen. Of the former he had four. The third, **Messalina** (a great-granddaughter of Antony) used her power to gratify her lusts until her enemies, the freedmen, secured her execution in 48. The last wife was Claudius' niece, Agrippina the Younger. She used her power to insure the succession to Lucius Domitius Ahenobarbus, her son by a former husband. The most prominent of Claudius' freedmen were **Narcissus,** secretary for the imperial correspondence (*ab epistulis*), and **Pallas,** financial secretary (*a rationibus*). Henceforth these secretaryships and others like them, on petitions (*a libellis*), on legal precedents (*a studiis*), etc., which had hitherto been simply posts in the imperial household inherited from the establishments of the republican nobility, became real offices of state, heads of a great bureaucracy. Though they never again conferred such power as they had under Claudius, their administrative importance grew and they were later filled by equestrians. In fact, for all his domestic weaknesses, Claudius took a real and intelligent interest in the administration of the empire. Without departing widely from Augustan precedents, he extended the citizenship and opened the senate to noble Gauls (48). He incorporated the client provinces of Mauretania Tingitana and Mauretania Caesariensis (42), Lycia with Pamphylia (43), and Thrace (46). Though he made Agrippa king of all Judaea in 41, he resumed it as a procuratorial province on Agrippa's death in 44. He restored Macedon and Achaea to the senate in 44.

43. Aulus Plautius invaded Britain. The precise motives for the Roman conquest are unknown. Claudius himself visited the island to receive the surrender of Camulodunum (Colchester in Essex) in the same year. Thereafter the conquest proceeded slowly north to Lindum (Lincoln) and west to Deva (Chester) and Isca Silurum (Caerlon, i.e. *Castra Legionum*) on the Welsh border. The British leader **Caractacus** was finally captured in 51.

47. Claudius revived the censorship and celebrated secular games (*ludi saeculares*).

48. On the execution of Messalina, Claudius was permitted by a special senatorial enactment to marry his niece Agrippina. In 50 he adopted her son, Lucius Domitius Ahenobarbus, who took the name **Nero** and ousted from the succession Claudius' son by Messalina, Britannicus (b. 41 or 42 and inheriting his name from his father's British triumph). In 53 Nero married Claudius' daughter by Messalina, Octavia.

53. Claudius secured a decree of the senate by which jurisdiction was granted to imperial procurators in financial cases. This marked an important stage in the increase of the importance of imperial officials at the expense of senatorial.

54. Claudius died (Oct. 13), reputedly from poison administered in a dish of mushrooms by Agrippina. When Agrippina secured the recognition by the praetorian guard of **Claudius Nero Caesar** as successor, the senate had to confer on him the imperial powers.

54–68. NERO (b. 37), emperor. He began his rule well under the guidance of the philosopher **Seneca** and the praefect of the guard Burrus. But in spirit he was an actor and wished to play the monarch in the grand manner. He discharged the freedman financial secretary (*a rationibus*) Pallas and poisoned Britannicus in 55. He deserted Octavia, first for the freedwoman Acte and then for Poppaea Sabina, the wife of his friend Otho. Finally he murdered his mother Agrippina in 59. After the death of Burrus in 62, he divorced, exiled, and murdered Octavia, and married Poppaea.

55–63. The general **Corbulo,** who had been successful under Claudius in Germany, was sent to settle the Parthian problem. After spending three years building up the morale of his troops, Corbulo successfully invaded Armenia and took Artaxata (58) and Tigranocerta (59). In 61, however, Nero replaced him with Paetus, who was thoroughly defeated at **Rhandeia** (62). In 63, therefore, Corbulo's solution, peace without conquest, was accepted by Nero, whose vanity was satisfied when the Parthian Tiridates came to Rome in 66 to receive his crown.

56. By a decree of the senate, the tribunes were forbidden to usurp the judicial functions of higher magistrates and the power to fine of the tribunes and aediles was limited. At the same time the senatorial treasury (*aerarium Saturni*) was put under special praetorian praefects chosen by the emperor. The senatorial treasury constantly required subventions from the emperor. In 61 there is evidence that the city praefect (*praefectus urbi*), originally a military or police official, had acquired a jurisdiction which was competing with that of the city praetor (*praetor urbanus*). These instances show how even in Rome the imperial officials were gaining power at the expense of the republican.

60. St. Paul, before his conversion to Christianity a Jew of Tarsus named Saul belonging to the rigid sect of the Pharisees, was brought to trial before the procurator of Judaea, Felix, and appealed to the emperor.

61. While Suetonius Paulinus, governor of Britain since 59, was engaged in the subjugation of the Druidical center, Mona (Anglesey, an island off northwest Wales), the queen of the Iceni (Norfolk), **Boudicca** (not *Boadicea,* as usually spelled) led a determined revolt and sacked Camulodunum (Colchester), Verulamium (St. Albans), and Londinium (London). Paulinus succeeded in defeating and killing Boudicca.

64. A great fire destroyed most of Rome. Nero's "fiddling," if genuine, was singing to the lyre a poem on the burning of Troy. When suspected of having set the fire himself, Nero found convenient culprits in the new and despised sect of the **Christians,** already a considerable group in Rome, with their prophecies of an imminent second advent of Christ and a world-wide conflagration. They were put to death with refined tortures.

65. A widespread conspiracy was organized to put **Gaius Calpurnius Piso** into the principate. Its noble leaders conducted it with such pusillanimity that it was discovered and many senators including Seneca, his nephew Lucan the poet, Faenius Rufus (successor to Burrus as praetorian prefect), and Petronius (the writer and friend of Nero), were executed or forced to commit suicide.

66–70. REVOLT IN JUDAEA, resulting from misgovernment by a succession of Roman procurators. When the governor of Syria failed to suppress it, **Vespasian** was sent as special legate with three legions (67). He slowly reduced the country, took prisoner the pro-Roman Jewish historian, **Josephus,** and laid siege to Jerusalem (69). After his proclamation as emperor, Vespasian left his son **Titus** to continue the siege against the Zealot leader, John of Giscala, who had removed his rival Eleazar. Jerusalem fell (7 Sept. 70). Titus celebrated a triumph in 71, which is commemorated on the surviving Arch of Titus at Rome. Some of Judaea was given to Marcus Julius ("Herod") Agrippa II, son of Agrippa I, but most of it became imperial domain. The temple was destroyed, the sanhedrin (Jewish national council) and high-priesthood abolished, the two-drachma tax paid by Jews to the temple was diverted to a special account in the imperial treasury (*fiscus Iudaicus*), and a legion under a senatorial legate superior to the procurator, was quartered in Jerusalem.

67. Nero undertook an artistic tour in Greece, in the course of which he executed Corbulo, and two ex-legates of Germany.

68. On Nero's return to Italy, he heard that **G. Julius Vindex,** legate of Gallia Lugdunensis, had revolted. Though the revolt was put down by the legate of upper Germany, L. Verginius Rufus, who refused to be saluted as emperor (*imperator*) by his troops, the two legions in Hispania Tarraconensis, on the suggestion of Vindex, had already (Mar.) saluted as emperor their elderly legate, **Servius Sulpicius Galba.** When the praetorian guard, under the praefect Nymphidius Sabinus, recognized Galba, the senate declared Nero a public enemy (*hostis*). He committed suicide in a villa outside Rome ("*what an artist I perish*") and the Julio-Claudian line came to an end.

68–69. Servius Sulpicius GALBA (b. 5 or 3 B.C.), emperor. By the recognition of Galba, the helpless senate admitted that, in the words of Tacitus, "emperors could be made elsewhere than at Rome." The success of Augustus' compromise depended on the loyalty of the troops to the person to whom the senate might grant the powers of the principate. It had already been made clear that the senate could not resist accepting a candidate of the praetorian guard; now the provincial legions, disabused of their loyalty to the Julio-Claudian house by the unwarlike conduct of Nero, and jealous of the privileges of the praetorians, asserted themselves during this year of the four emperors (Galba, Otho, Vitellius, and Vespasian).

69, Jan. 1. The eight legions on the Rhine refused allegiance to Galba, and on Jan. 3 the four in lower Germany saluted as emperor their legate **Aulus Vitellius** (b. 15). He was also accepted by the four legions of upper Germany under Hordeonius Flaccus. Galba, whom Tacitus called "in the judgment of all, capable of ruling if he had not ruled" (*capax imperii nisi imperasset*), had reached Rome, where he adopted as his successor the aristocrat Piso Licinianus.

Thereupon, **Marcus Salvius Otho** (b. 32), the dissolute friend of Nero, who had been made legate of Lusitania so that Nero could marry his wife Poppaea and had returned with Galba, secured the support of the praetorians and had Galba and Piso murdered (Jan. 15). The helpless senate then recognized him.

Meanwhile, the troops of Vitellius approached Italy in two divisions under Valens and Caecina. They met in the plain of the Po and defeated the forces of Otho (Apr. 19) in the **first battle of Bedriacum** (near Cremona), whereupon **Otho** committed suicide. The senate immediately recognized Vitellius, who presently reached Rome himself.

In the meantime (July 1) the praefect of Egypt, Tiberius Julius Alexander, proclaimed as emperor, **Vespasian,** legate in Judaea. Mucianus, legate of Syria, lent his support. Antonius Primus, commander of the seventh legion in Pannonia, rallied all the Danubian legions to Vespasian and moved rapidly into northern Italy. There he defeated the forces of Vitellius in the **second battle of Bedriacum** and sacked Cremona (late Oct.). When Antonius approached Rome, Vespasian's brother seized the Capitol, which was burnt in the ensuing struggle. The Vitellians fought bitterly in the city streets, but Vitellius was finally slain (Dec. 20). The senate immediately recognized Vespasian. When Mucianus reached Rome in Jan. (70), he ruled it until Vespasian arrived during the summer.

69–79. Titus Flavius VESPASIANUS (b. 9), emperor and founder of the Flavian dynasty. He was the son of a humble tax collector from the Italian municipality of Reate. Vespasian was confronted with the task not only of restoring the principate but of equating himself with his aristocratic Roman predecessors. He himself, with his son Titus, held the opening consulship of every year of his reign save 73 and 78. A surviving law (*lex de imperio Vespasiani*) may be part of an inclusive measure whereby all the powers accumulated by preceding emperors were conferred specifically and together on Vespasian. Such events as the restoration of the Capitol (70, dedicated by Domitian in 82), the triumph of Titus (71), the erection of a temple of peace (71–75), the closing of the temple of Janus (71), the destruction of Nero's extensive "Golden House" and parks, on the site of which a vast public amphitheater, the Coliseum (or Colosseum, *amphitheatrum Flavianum*), was begun, served to surround the new dynasty with material glamor. To reorganize the senate, Vespasian felt compelled to revive the censorship with Titus in 73, instead of tacitly assuming the right of enrollment (*adlectio*) exercised by his predecessors. In 74 he granted Latin rights to all of Spain. He reorganized and rigidly controlled the finances.

69–71. The revolt of some Batavian auxiliaries under their native commander, Julius Civilis, won the support of some of the legions of Germany. This inflamed the Gallic Treveri under Julius Classicus and Julius Tutor and the Lingones under Julius Sabinus. Hordeonius Flaccus was slain at Novaesium (Neuss) on the lower Rhine. Petillius Cerealis, with six legions, took advantage of disagreements between Gauls and Batavians to crush the revolt piecemeal. The movement, though ostensibly begun in the interests of Vespasian, had in reality aimed at the establishment of an independent Gallic empire, the last instance of dangerous national separatism during the early empire. Thereafter auxiliaries were not employed in the country of their origin and the corps soon came to be composed of recruits of different nationalities. By this time the praetorian guards were alone recruited in Italy; the legions drew from Roman settlers in the provinces or Romanized provincials, to whom citizenship was often granted to secure their enlistment. Thus the army had become less Italian, more provincial in its sympathies. After the revolt, Vespasian disbanded at least four disloyal legions.

70. By putting Cappadocia in charge of the imperial governor of Galatia, by moving the eastern legions from Syria to forts on the upper Euphrates (Satala, Melitene, and Samosata), and by absorbing a number of small native principalities in Asia and Syria, Vespasian consolidated the eastern frontier against Armenia and Parthia and prepared the way for Trajan's expansion.

71. Titus, though a senator, was made praetorian praefect, a post hitherto equestrian. He also received both the proconsular command (*imperium*) and the tribunician power (*tribunicia potestas*), whereby Vespasian made it clear that he would follow the hereditary principle of succession.

73–74. Vespasian began the conquest of the territory east of the upper Rhine and south of the Main, the later *agri decumates* (or *decu-*

mathes; the meaning is uncertain). He furthermore reorganized the defenses of the upper and lower Danube.

73. At about this time Vespasian banished Helvidius Priscus, son-in-law of Thrasea and his successor as leader of the Stoic opposition to the empire. He also banished the professors of philosophy, perhaps because their doctrines encouraged disloyalty.

77–84. Conquest of Britain. Cn. Julius Agricola (40–93) as imperial governor continued the conquest carried on by his predecessors Cerialis (72–74) over the Brigantes around Eboracum (York) and Frontinus (74–77) over the Silures in Wales. In 83 he fought a successful engagement against the Caledonians at **Mt. Graupius** (not *Grampius*), possibly near Aberdeen in Scotland, the farthest point reached by Roman arms. But Domitian recalled him in the following year, due to the fact that troops were needed for the German war. Despite later revolts Romanization progressed rapidly thereafter in Britain.

79–81. TITUS Flavius Vespasianus (b. 39) emperor, succeeding on the death of his father, Vespasian (June 24). Though popular, Titus was more concerned with playing the prince charming than with the economical administration of the empire. Public opinion forced him to put away the Jewish princess Berenice, already thrice married sister of Agrippa II.

79. An **eruption of Mt. Vesuvius,** on the Bay of Naples, buried the cities **Pompeii** and **Herculaneum.** In 80 a severe fire occurred in Rome. During this year, however, Titus dedicated magnificently the Coliseum and some elaborate public baths (*thermae Titianae*).

81–96. Titus Flavius DOMITIANUS (b. 51) succeeded upon the death of his older brother, Titus (Sept. 13).

Naturally of a suspicious, perhaps cruel, temperament, Domitian had apparently borne with ill grace the favor and preference shown to his brother and came to the throne determined to rule without respect for others, especially the senate. Nevertheless, despite the hatred which his reign aroused, he appears to have been an able administrator and general. He legislated against immorality and strictly controlled the governors.

83. Domitian crossed the Rhine at Mainz to **campaign against the Chatti.** His victory allowed him to begin the construction of a series of forts connected by a road and later by an earth rampart surmounted by a wooden palisade which served to prevent the infiltration of barbarians into Roman territory and as a base for offensive or defensive operations, though it would not have withstood a full-fledged invasion. This system, which later extended along the central Rhine, then from Mainz outside the *agri decumates* to the upper Danube so as to straighten the dangerous reentrant angle of the frontier at that point, and along the upper Danube north of Rhaetia, was known as the *limes*.

84. Through his election as consul for ten years and censor for life, Domitian openly subordinated the republican aspect of the state (senate and magistrates) to the monarchical. By increasing the pay of the troops by one-third (probably in itself a needed reform), he secured their loyalty. And with lavish shows and buildings, he ingratiated himself with the Roman mob. He revived the excessive use of the law of treason with its attendant encouragement of informers. After the abortive **revolt of Saturninus**, legate of upper Germany, in 88, he proceeded bitterly against the opposition; expulsion of the philosophers in 89 was followed in 93 by the execution of Herennius Senecio, Junius Arulenus Rusticus, and Helvidius Priscus. Flavius Clemens, a first cousin of Domitian, was executed in 95 on a charge of atheism (Christianity?), though perhaps the real ground was fear of him as a possible rival. Domitian, besides widening the cult of his deceased father and brother, had himself addressed as "lord and god" (*dominus et deus*), in the tradition of Gaius and perhaps Antony.

85–89. An **invasion of the Dacians** across the Danube into Moesia in 85 was repulsed by Domitian in person. In 89, however, the complete reduction of Dacia was prevented by his defeat at the hands of the Marcomanni and Quadi, who had occupied Bohemia, west of Dacia. Domitian made a somewhat humiliating peace with the Dacian king, **Decebalus**, who retained his independence and defeated, but did not crush, the Marcomanni, Quadi, and Iazyges (a Sarmatian people) in 92. Thus the situation on the middle and lower Danube remained dangerous.

88. In consequence of the revolt of Saturninus, Domitian ceased the quartering of more than one legion in one camp to prevent any commander from gaining excessive power. The individual legions became permanently fixed in separate camps and no longer highly mobile, as they had been meant to be by Augustus.

96. **Assassination of Domitian** (Sept. 18) in a palace plot. The senate decreed the removal of his name from all public inscriptions (*damnatio memoriae*) and cancellation of his arrangements (*rescisio actorum*). Thus ended the Flavian house.

Since the conspirators, wisely, had a candidate ready to receive the senate's grant of powers, the armies remained quiet and **Nerva,** an elderly and distinguished senator, acceded

without difficulty. This marked the last attempt at self-assertion on the part of the old republican element in the principate. Already the old aristocratic families had become exhausted by persecution and race suicide. Their places had been taken by a new nobility of families elevated from the cities of Italy or the provinces through the imperial (equestrian) organization to senatorial rank. Despite a sentimental attachment to the traditions and forms of the Republic, the new generation admitted that the emperor was master, not, as Augustus had pretended, servant of the senate.

96–98. **Marcus Cocceius NERVA** (b. 35), emperor. He was forced to recognize that the wishes of the army should be consulted by adopting in the autumn of 97 as his successor the victorious general **Trajan.** Since Nerva and his three successors had no sons of their own, the principle of adoption, triumphing over heredity, secured a succession of capable rulers known as **the five good emperors** (Nerva, Trajan, Hadrian, Antoninus Pius, Marcus Aurelius). Nerva's two important contributions were to shift from the cities to the imperial treasury the cost of the postal service maintained for government dispatches (*cursus*) and to supplement existing private charity by a system of state aid for orphans (*alimenta*) supported by government grants or, under Trajan, by the interest of permanent loans to small farmers. Both reforms are symptomatic of the gradual breakdown of local economy and the municipal system. The last reference to legislation in the assemblies is to an agrarian law (*lex agraria*) in his reign. Nerva died Jan. 25, 98.

98–117. **Marcus Ulpius TRAIANUS** (b. 53), emperor. At the time he was in command in lower Germany, but was accepted at Rome without difficulty, though he was the first provincial emperor (born near Seville) and though he did not visit Rome until 99. On one Rhine frontier, Trajan continued the boundary palisade (*limes*) begun under Domitian.

101–107. In two **Dacian Wars** (101–102, 105–107), whose precise chronology is uncertain, Trajan first seriously exceeded the limits set to the empire by Augustus. Upon the death of Decebalus, Dacia, north of the Danube, became a Roman province. The war was commemorated by a column, covered with a spiral band of continuous reliefs in the magnificent Forum of Trajan in Rome. Trajan had many fine structures erected throughout the empire.

111–112. **Pliny the Younger** was sent by Trajan as special legate with proconsular power to reorganize the senatorial province of Bithynia. The appointment of Pliny is symptomatic of a spreading bankruptcy of municipalities, particularly in the Greek east, which necessitated imperial interference. The emperor not only sent special legates to senatorial provinces but appointed special supervisors for cities (*curatores rei publicae*). Extravagance and increased cost of administration, both municipal and imperial, thus started locally the crisis which disrupted the whole empire during the third century. Further indications of financial stringency appear in the enlargement of the alimentary system and in the burning of records of unpaid taxes in the forum. During his governorship, Pliny corresponded with Trajan on many problems, including the treatment of Christians, toward whom Trajan instructed him to be lenient.

113–117. Parthian War. When the Parthian monarch **Chosroes** set up his puppet in Armenia, thus violating the compromise reached under Nero, Trajan declared war on Parthia. In 114, on the death of the Parthian puppet, he annexed Armenia. As he advanced, he formed the provinces of Mesopotamia (115) and Assyria (116) and made the Tigris the eastern boundary of the empire. He was, however, recalled from the Persian Gulf by a widespread **revolt of the Jews** and of the newly conquered areas. Both were suppressed with great severity. In 117 Trajan was repulsed from the desert town of Hatra. He died at Selinus in Cilicia (June 22 or July 9) after having adopted on his deathbed (some suspected his wife Plotina of having invented the adoption) his ward and cousin, **Hadrian,** at the time legate of Syria. Trajan's conquests, though spectacular, were of no permanent value and probably hastened the financial collapse by increasing the military expenses.

117–138. Publius Aelius HADRIANUS (b. 75), emperor. He was recognized as emperor by the senate on Aug. 11. Almost immediately he abandoned the new provinces across the Euphrates. His lack of military ambition may have been responsible for the serious conspiracy, in 118, of four generals of consular rank, whom the senate put to death. Hadrian then took an oath, which had become a test of constitutionalism, not to execute senators without trial by their peers. Under him the appointment of equestrians rather than freedmen to the important posts in the imperial secretariat became regular. He spent most of his reign (121–126, 129–134) traveling through the provinces, where he erected many buildings. He especially favored the Greek cities, notably Athens. In Britain he built (122–127) the elaborate combination of road, ditches, and stone wall from the Tyne to the Solway which constituted a boundary (*limes*) between the Roman province and the unconquered Caledonians.

In Numidia he completed the extensive permanent camp of the Third Augustan Legion at Lambaesis.

In the collection of taxes, the companies of *publicani* had given way to individual collectors (*conductores*) under municipal supervision. Like his predecessors, Hadrian lightened or remitted certain taxes. Yet the economic difficulties continued. He had to deal with the problem of deserted farm lands (*agri deserti*), an indication that peasants were finding agriculture unprofitable, and with complaints from tenants (*coloni*) on the imperial estates in Africa. The replacement of slaves by tenants on large estates had begun when the cessation under Augustus of wars of conquest put an end to large supplies of cheap slaves. The oppression of tenants on both private and imperial estates by rising rents, heavier taxation, and forced labor rendered their lot ever more wretched.

131. The **Praetor's Edict** was definitively codified by the jurist Salvius Julianus under Hadrian's orders. Since no praetor could thereafter alter it, the extension of legal procedure by praetorian *formulae* ended. Senatorial decrees became only a confirmation of the imperial speech (*oratio principis*) that initiated them. The tribunician privilege of introducing business had been extended to the first five motions in any meeting so that the emperor presented all important matters. The only source of law was now the **edicts of the emperor.** The emperor hereafter summoned to his advisory council (*concilium*) distinguished jurists, who profoundly influenced the development of law.

132–135. The **Jews of Judaea revolted** upon the founding of a Roman colony (Aelia Capitolina) in Jerusalem and the dedication of a temple to Jupiter Capitolinus on the site of their temple. Their leaders were the rabbi **Akiba** and the fanatic **Simon Bar Cocheba.** The suppression of the revolt all but depopulated Judaea and thereafter Jews could enter Jerusalem but once a year. This completed the denationalization of the Jews begun by Vespasian. Until 1919 the Jews of the Dispersion (*Diaspora*), scattered among other peoples and generally despised, possessed only a racial and religious unity. The great edition of the *Talmud* was prepared in Babylon in the late 5th century.

138. Upon the death (Jan. 1) of his first choice for successor, **Lucius Ceionius Commodus,** Hadrian adopted (Feb. 25) the competent Titus Aurelius Fulvius Boionius Arrius **Antoninus,** who received the imperial powers and took the name Imperator Titus Aelius Antoninus. He, in his turn, had to adopt the young son of

Commodus, Aelius Aurelius Commodus (later Lucius Aurelius Verus) and his own nephew, Marcus Annius Verus, henceforth called Marcus Aurelius Antoninus. Hadrian died on July 10.

138–161. Titus Aurelius ANTONINUS PIUS (b. 86), emperor. Warned by Hadrian's unpopularity with the senate, he spent his reign in Rome. For his filial piety in securing the deification of Hadrian from a hostile senate, he received the title *Pius.* His uneventful reign marked the culmination of the happy age of the Antonines.

142–143. Quintus Lollius Urbicus, legate of Britain, suppressed a revolt of the Brigantes in Yorkshire and, along the temporary line of forts built by Agricola from the Forth to the Clyde, constructed a turf wall north of Hadrian's. This, however, was soon abandoned.

146. Marcus Aurelius, who had married Faustina, daughter of Antoninus, received the imperial powers. Antoninus apparently passed over the younger and incompetent Verus.

155. A brief **war with Vologesus of Parthia** ended in an inconclusive peace.

161–180. MARCUS AURELIUS Antoninus (b. 121) became emperor on the death of Antoninus (Mar. 7). Loyal to the wishes of Hadrian, he shared the imperial powers in full equality with **Lucius Aurelius Verus** (b. 130). This constitutes the first sure instance of complete collegiality in the imperial position, save for the office of chief pontiff (*pontifex maximus*), which remained unshared until Pupienus and Balbinus.

The reign of Marcus represents the **triumph of Stoicism.** Politically, the emperor was regarded as the human counterpart of the guiding reason of the universe and as obliged to rule for the good of his subjects. In law, the doctrine of the universal brotherhood of man, transcending limits of city or station, emphasized the humanizing trend which had long been operative, especially in legislation on slaves and women. Socially, the municipal and provincial aristocracy, which had appeared in the senate through the imperial service, had wholly replaced the old Roman nobility and worked in complete loyalty with the emperor. Economically, the empire most nearly approximated unification. Italy had yielded her economic supremacy to the increased prosperity of the provinces and was losing its favored political position. It received from the emperor four special judges (created by Hadrian, abolished by Antoninus, revived by Marcus).

162–165. Verus was sent by Marcus to command in the east against Parthia, adumbrating the later territorial division of the empire.

Though Verus dissipated at Antioch, his generals sacked Artaxata, Seleucia, and Ctesiphon, put a Roman puppet on the throne of Armenia, and made part of Mesopotamia a province.

166–167. The troops of Verus brought from the east a terrible plague, which seriously depopulated the empire.

166–175. The upper Danube was crossed by hordes of **Marcomanni** from Bohemia, with kindred tribes. Marcus created his young sons, Lucius Aelius Aurelius Commodus and Marcus Annius Verus, Caesars. He himself, with his colleague Verus, set out at once for the north. Verus died in 169. Just when Marcus had settled with the Marcomanni and had set an extremely important precedent by importing (172?) considerable numbers of them to occupy areas in the empire which had been depopulated by the plague, the **Sarmatians** attacked the lower Danube frontier.

175. Avidius Cassius, a distinguished general and legate of Syria, revolted, perhaps misled by a false report of Marcus' death. Though his revolt was crushed before Marcus could reach the east, it prevented a final settlement of the Sarmatian war.

177. Marcus' eldest son, **Commodus,** became Imperator, then Augustus, coequal with his father. The younger son had died in 169. Marcus is said to have issued a severe **rescript against the Christians.** In any case, they were subjected to increasingly bitter and far-reaching persecution, probably as fomenters of trouble by their prophecies of evil, and as disloyal to the state because they would not swear oaths to the emperor or offer incense to his statues or serve in the army.

178–180. The Marcomanni again opened war so that Marcus and Commodus had to go to the Danube. The wars of Marcus were commemorated on a column in Rome. Marcus died at Vindobona (Vienna) Mar. 17, 180.

180–192. Marcus Aurelius COMMODUS Antoninus (b. 161), as Marcus' son was now called, was the first emperor since Domitian to succeed by birth rather than by adoption. He made a peace with the Marcomanni which, though temporarily satisfactory, lost him favor with the troops. He returned to Rome, where he gave himself up to pleasure. The government was at first managed by the capable praetorian praefect **Perennis,** but on his unwarranted execution in 185, at the request of a deputation of mutinous soldiers from Britain, it fell to the mercenary freedman **Cleander,** who, in turn, was sacrificed in 189 to the Roman mob, which blamed him for a grain shortage. Commodus, already hostile to the senate in consequence of an abortive conspiracy in 182, became extravagantly despotic. He identified himself with Hercules and lavished wealth acquired from the treasury or by confiscation on his favorites, the praetorians, whose pay he increased by a quarter, and on hunts of beasts, in which he participated. On Dec. 31, 192, his concubine Marcia, his chamberlain Eclectus, and the praetorian praefect Laetus had him strangled by a wrestler named Narcissus. Thus ended the Antonine line.

The **important trends in the early empire** were: **politically,** the transformation of the *princeps,* agent of the republican senate and Roman people, into a Stoic king, head of a state in which all good men co-operated for the common weal; **administratively,** the subordination of the republican magistracies and organs to the will of the emperor and the growth of the imperial secretariat and equestrian civil service; **socially,** the substitution for the irreconcilable republican nobility of a new aristocracy drawn from the better classes throughout the empire, which, though sentimentally republican, accepted the empire if the emperor was good; **economically,** the financial breakdown of the municipal system, which was accompanied by a loss of local pride, and the increased burdens of the imperial government; and **militarily,** greater and more constant pressure on both frontiers, north and east, at the same time.

The **literature of the early empire** falls into two periods; the **Augustan Age,** which, with the preceding Ciceronian Age, forms the **Golden Age;** and (after 14) the **Silver Age** of the Julio-Claudians, Flavians, and Antonines. Under Augustus, the chief figures gathered around his friend, their patron **Maecenas: Publius Vergilius Maro** or Virgil (70–19 B.C.) author of the *Bucolica, Georgica,* and the *Aeneid,* and **Quintus Horatius Flaccus** or Horace (65–8 B.C.), author of *Odes, Epodes, Sermones* (satires), and *Epistolae.* Besides these, **Albius Tibullus** (54–19 B.C.) and **Sextus Propertius** (50–15 B.C.) wrote erotic elegies and **Publius Ovidius Naso** or Ovid (43 B.C.–17 A.D.) composed the erotic *Amores, Heroides, Ars Amatoria,* etc., and the longer *Metamorphoses, Fasti, Tristia, Epistolae ex Ponto,* etc. **Titus Livius,** or Livy (59 B.C.–17 A.D.) composed his *History of Rome* (*Libri ab urbe condita*), a prose glorification comparable to the *Aeneid.* The writers of the Silver Age are numerous and less outstanding: **Aulus Persius Flaccus** (34–62 A.D.) and **Decimus Iunius Juvenalis** (55–138) wrote satire, and **Marcus Valerius Martialis** (40–104) composed satirical epigrams. **Lucius Annaeus Seneca** the Philosopher (4 B.C.–65 A.D.), son of Seneca the Rhetorician (55 B.C.–40 A.D.), and his nephew,

Marcus Annaeus Lucanus (39–65), author of the epic *Pharsalis,* belong, like Martial, to the Spanish group of authors prominent in the 1st century, as does also **Marcus Fabius Quintilianus** (35–100), teacher of rhetoric and author of an *Institutio Oratoria.* **Gaius Petronius Arbiter** (d. 66), the Epicurean friend of Nero, probably composed the *Satyricon,* a picaresque novel. **Publius Cornelius Tacitus** (55–118?), author of the *Dialogus de oratoribus,* the life of his father-in-law *Agricola,* the *Germania,* the *Annales,* and the *Historiae,* **Gaius Plinius Caecilius Secundus** (61–113?), whose *Letters* are preserved, and nephew of the erudite Gaius Plinius Secundus (23–79), the author of the *Historia naturalis,* who died in the eruption of Vesuvius, and the biographer **Gaius Suetonius Tranquillus** (70–121?), whose *De vita Caesorum* extend from Caesar through Domitian, belonged to the literary circle that flourished under Trajan. Under Hadrian began a revival of interest in pre-Ciceronian Latin language and literature, while under the Antonines a school of African writers introduced a florid and exaggerated style. Its chief exponent was **Lucius Apuleius** (124–?), whose *Metamorphoses* and other writings cast light on the mystery religions and neo-Pythagoreanism. The surviving writings of emperors, apart from administrative edicts, etc., are the succinct account of his life by Augustus, preserved on inscriptions at Ancyra (Ankara, *Monumentum Ancyranum*) and, in fragments, elsewhere; some speeches and letters of Claudius in inscriptions or papyri; and the *Meditations,* in Greek, of Marcus Aurelius.

In **philosophy,** Stoicism remained dominant throughout the period and claimed among its chief exponents the statesman **Seneca** (1–65), the slave **Epictetus** (60–140), and the emperor **Marcus Aurelius.** But it had to compete with mystical tendencies which found expression in astrology, in such **oriental religions** as those of the Egyptian **Isis,** the Persian **Mithras,** and the Jewish **Jesus Christ,** and in a revival of the early Greek mystical philosophy of Pythagoras. **Christianity,** which had begun as a Jewish sect but was universalized and widely spread by the ardent convert **Paul,** soon developed both an organization and a literature. The organization consisted of independent churches governed by boards of elders (*presbyters*) among whom one frequently secured preeminence as bishop (*episcopos,* overseer). Those churches that traced their foundation to the immediate associates of Christ, the **Apostles,** or which arose in big cities, tended to overshadow the less important ones and their bishops, especially, in the west, the bishop of Rome, became authorities in ecclesiastical quarrels.

Heresies appeared from the beginning, like **Gnosticism** and, about 150, **Montanism.** Christian literature commenced with the *Gospels* and *apostolic* (or pseudo-apostolic) *writings.* The early martyrs, **Ignatius of Antioch** (d. 117?) and **Polycarp of Smyrna** (d. 155?), as well as the Greek bishop, **Irenaeus of Lyons** (c. 130–200), who attacked the heretical transcendentalism of the Gnostics, wrote largely for Christians. But the increasing hostility of the public and government occasioned apologetic writings addressed to non-Christians, like those of **Justin Martyr** (153?) and others.

Augustan art, like Augustan literature, achieved a happy blend of native Roman realism and Greek idealism, as best appears in the sculpture of the *Ara pacis* or the famous "Prima Porta" statue of Augustus. Julio-Claudian art aped the manner without attaining the excellence of Augustan. Under the Flavians, a certain heaviness and materialism, characteristic of the period, appeared. But two relief techniques were perfected, that of illusionism, the attempt to represent space, as on the panels of the Arch of Titus, and the continuous style, by which a series of events was represented in an unbroken sequence, as on the Column of Trajan. Hadrian's reign witnessed a revived interest in and copying of Greek archaic art. Under the Antonines, a crudeness appears on the Column of Marcus, though not in the reliefs from his arch. Mention should be made of the **wall-paintings** of all periods from the 2nd century B.C. to 79 A.D. preserved at Pompeii and of the common red pottery with appliqué reliefs known as **Arretine ware** (modeled on the Greek Samian ware) made first in Italy, at Arretium (Arezzo),

and then progressively at various places in Gaul and even in Britain.

In **science,** in outlying districts of the empire, the Greek scientific tradition was strong. **Galen** of Pergamon (c. 130–200) was a brilliant anatomist and physiologist who wrote prolifically on medicine and developed an all-embracing theory of medicine. **Ptolemy** (c. 85–165) collected the writings on astronomy into the *Almagest,* which also contained writings on optics and geography. Indigenous Roman science was little more than popular handbook science depending heavily on Greek sources, epitomized but not understood. The best of these was the *Historia naturalis* of **Pliny** (23–79), an uncritical compendium of good and bad information from a variety of sources, on technology as well as science.

In **architecture,** the grandeur of the Augustan Age, as in the porch of the Pantheon or the Maison Carrée at Nîmes, gave way to massiveness, as in the temple of Venus at Rome and the Coliseum. But the Roman engineers produced at all periods substantial and useful structures: aqueducts, theaters, circuses, baths, harbors, roads, etc. From the Augustan Age dates a treatise on architecture by Marcus Pallio **Vitruvius** (fl. in the Augustan Age), who described the instruments and techniques of surveying, hydraulic works, and bridge-building. Also included in the treatise are descriptions of war machines. Roman technology was empirical. Her engineers carried out vast and important projects; one such was **Agrippa** (c. 63–12 B.C.), who was director of Augustus' massive construction program. **Frontius** (fl. 35–103) wrote on the aqueduct system of Rome.

2. THE 3RD CENTURY, 192–284 A.D.

The 3rd century is characterized by the complete collapse of government and economics throughout the Mediterranean. Upon the death of Commodus, the armies asserted themselves against the senate as they had in 68. The ultimate victor, **Septimius,** finally and frankly unmasked the military basis of the imperial power. After an attempted revival of "constitutional" government under Alexander, the imperial position became the reward of successful generals of increasingly provincial and uncultured origins. The one ideal that still dominated the armies was the preservation of the frontiers against the Germans and Persians. Even the separatist movements were aimed, not at independence, but at the preservation of the *imperium Romanum.* To secure this end and their own support, the troops made and unmade

emperors and drained the scanty resources of the civilians by taxation, depreciation of coinage, and exactions of food, quarters, etc. The military wholly absorbed the civil administration. Intellectual life ceased, inscriptions became rare, and archaeological finds show a rapid decline in skill and taste.

193.   Publius Helvius PERTINAX, emperor. He was chosen by the senate, but his strict and economical rule led to his murder (Mar. 28) by the praetorian guard, which then auctioned off the empire to him who promised them the highest gift of money, **M. Didius Severus Julianus** (b. 133?). The British legions proclaimed as emperor the legate, **D. Clodius Septimius Albinus;** the Pannonian, the legate of Upper Pannonia **L. Septimius Severus** (April or May); and the Syrian, the legate **C. Pescen-**

nius **Niger Justus.** Severus at once seized Rome, where the senate deposed and executed Julianus (June 1).

193-211. L. SEPTIMIUS SEVERUS (b. 146, at Leptis in Africa), emperor. He dissolved the existing praetorian cohorts, composed of recruits from Italy, and enrolled new ones from deserving legionary veterans. He kept Albinus quiet by recognizing him as Caesar (i.e. heir). He then defeated Niger in **battles at Cyzicus** and **Nicaea** and at **Issus** (the Cilician Gates), and put him to death near Antioch (194). Byzantium held out until 196, when it was sacked and reduced to the status of a village. Albinus, who now claimed full equality, was defeated and slain (197, Feb. 19) at Lugdunum (Lyons), which was also sacked and never recovered its prosperity.

Severus created three new legions, one of which was quartered on the Alban Lake in Italy, hitherto free from the presence of legionary troops. He appointed equestrians to command these legions contrary to the Augustan rule and also put the new province of Mesopotamia under an equestrian. He thus initiated the replacement of senators by equestrians in military posts which culminated under Gallienus. Military marriages were recognized, since the immobilization of the legions had made these usual. Auxiliaries were settled on public land in return for military service and the legionary pay was raised. Severus humiliated the senate, which had supported Albinus, and put equestrian deputies to watch senatorial governors. When he closed down the now almost defunct courts (*quaestiones*), he transferred the jurisdiction over Rome and the area within 100 miles to the praefect of the city and over the rest of Italy to the praetorian praefect, who also exercised jurisdiction on appeal from the provinces. After the fall of the single and powerful praetorian praefect Palutianus (205), Severus returned to the practice of having two, one of whom was the distinguished jurist Papinian. In the criminal law, a distinction was drawn between the privileged classes (*honestiores*), who were treated favorably, and the ordinary people (*humiliores*). The emperor began the subdivision of provinces into smaller units, which culminated under Diocletian, and extended the organization of municipalities as the basis of tax-collecting even to Egypt, which shows how valueless municipal status had become. He created a new treasury in addition to the *fiscus* (the original imperial treasury) and the *patrimonium Caesaris* (originally the ruler's private property, then crown property), namely the *res privata,* his personal funds. He depreciated the silver content of the *denarius* to 60 per cent.

Despite all of these difficulties, his administration was good.

197-198. In a successful **Parthian war** Severus advanced as far as Ctesiphon and reconstituted the province of Mesopotamia under an equestrian governor with two legions.

205-211. A recurrence of **troubles in Britain,** which had suffered from invasion in 155 and revolt in 180, required the presence of Septimius himself to fight the Caledonians. He definitely withdrew from the wall of Antoninus to that of Hadrian, which he rebuilt He died at Eboracum (York) on Feb. 4, 211

211-217. CARACALLA (properly Caracallus), so named from a Gallic cloak which he wore He was the oldest son of Septimius and had been associated with him as Augustus (198) To strengthen the bond between the Severi and the Antonines he had changed his name from Septimius Bassianus to Marcus Aurelius (Severus) Antoninus (197). Upon his accession, he murdered his colleague (since 209 and younger brother, P. (originally L.) Septimius (Antoninus) Geta (b. 189), along with the jurist Papinian and many others. He increased the pay of the troops to a ruinous degree and called them all *Antoniniani.* To meet the consequent deficit he issued a new coin, the *antoninianus,* with a face value of two *denarii* but a weight of only one and two-thirds. He erected at Rome the vast **Baths of Caracalla** (*thermae Antoninianae*).

212. The **EDICT OF CARACALLA** (*constitutio Antoniniana*) extended Roman citizenship to all free inhabitants of the empire save a limited group, perhaps including the Egyptians. His motive has been much disputed; citizenship now meant so little that this step was a natural culmination of the leveling down of distinctions that had been continuous throughout the empire. Moreover, he may have hoped to extend to all inhabitants the inheritance tax paid by Roman citizens.

213-217. Caracalla successfully defended the northern frontier against the Alamanni in southern Germany and the Goths on the lower Danube (214), and in the east he annexed Armenia (216). But as he was preparing an invasion of Parthia, he was murdered by a group of his officers (217, Apr. 8).

217-218. M. Opellius (Severus) MACRINUS (b. 164?), emperor. He was a Mauretanian who had risen from the ranks to be praetorian praefect, and was the first equestrian emperor He surrendered Caracalla's eastern gains and sought to reduce the pay of the troops, who set up as a rival (218, May 16) at Emesa in Syria a grandnephew of Julia Domna, the Syrian wife of Septimius. Macrinus fell on June 8 218.

18-222. ELAGABALUS (Heliogabalus, b. c. 205), emperor. He derived his cognomen from the Emesa god, whose priest he was. To legitimize his rule, he changed his name from (Varius) Avitus to Marcus Aurelius Antoninus and claimed to be a son of Caracalla. While Elagabalus surrendered himself to license and introduced the worship of his god to Rome, the empire was really ruled by his forceful mother, **Julia Maesa.** She obliged him to adopt his cousin (Gessius) Bassianus (Alexianus?), son of her sister, Julia Mamaea. The praetorians murdered Elagabalus (222, Mar. 11).

22-235. Marcus Aurelius SEVERUS ALEX-ANDER (b. c. 208), emperor. He was the adopted son of Elagabalus and was dominated by his mother, Mamaea. She established a regency committee of senators and used the advice of the jurists Paulus and Ulpian. The new rule was an attempt to revive the Antonine monarchy. It was marked, however, by an extension of governmental control over the trade guilds (*collegia*) and further depreciation of the coinage.

27. The **New Persian (Sassanid) Empire** was founded by **Ardashir** (Artashatr, Artaxerxes), a Persian who overthrew the Parthian Arsacids, Artabanus V and Vologesus V. The strength of the new empire lay in a revival of **Zoroastrianism.**

34-235. Alexander was forced to buy peace from the Alamanni on the Rhine. The disgruntled troops murdered him (235, Mar.). With his death the last attempt to preserve a civil or "constitutional" government came to an end and military anarchy began.

35-238. G. Julius Verus MAXIMINUS "Thrax" (b. c. 172), a Thracian peasant of huge size and no culture, was elevated by the Rhine legions, but was not recognized by the senate, which put forward the senators **M. Clodius Pupienus Maximus** and **D. Caelius Calvinus Balbinus.** In the meantime (238), the African legions proclaimed the 80-year-old pro-consul **Marcus Antonius Gordianus I** and his son **Gordianus II.** The former committed suicide after his son was defeated and slain by the praefect of Mauretania. However, the populace of Rome forced the senate to join the grandson, **Gordianus III,** with Pupienus and Balbinus. Maximin was slain by his troops while besieging Aquileia (238, June) and the praetorians murdered Pupienus and Balbinus (238, June?).

38-244. Marcus Antonius GORDIANUS III (b. 225) was dominated by the wise praetorian praefect **C. Furius Timesitheus** (Misitheus?), whose daughter he married (241). Timesitheus drove the son of Ardashir, Shapur (Sapor), out of Antioch (241-243) but died of disease. The new praetorian praefect, and Arabian, made himself co-Augustus, then murdered Gordian (early in 244).

244-249. M. Julius PHILIPPUS "ARABS" bought peace with the Persians and, at Rome, celebrated the *ludi saeculares* for Rome's thousandth birthday (248). He was killed at Verona (249) in battle against his commander in Dacia, Decius.

249-251. G. Messius Quintus Traianus DECIUS (b. 200?), instituted the first general **persecution of the Christians,** and perhaps of all who would not sacrifice to the emperor. Emperor-worship seems now to have become a requirement of all loyal subjects, which indicates a growing belief in the actual divinity of the emperor. Decius was slain by the Goths in Dacia (251) because of the disloyalty of the legate of Moesia, Gallus.

251-253. G. Vibius Trebonianus GALLUS (b. c. 207) put to death his co-Augustus, **Hostilianus,** son of Decius. In his reign began a 15-year plague. When he marched against his successor in Moesia, the Moor M. Aemilius Aemilianus, his own troops slew him (before Oct., 253).

253. M. Aemilius Aemiliamus, emperor.

253-259. P. Licinius VALERIANUS (b. c. 193), commander in Germany, became emperor, with his son Gallienus as co-Augustus. He fought unsuccessfully against the Franks, who crossed the Rhine in 256, the Alamanni, who reached Milan, and the Goths. As the frontiers ceased to hold, cities within the empire began to build walls. Valerian recovered Antioch again from Shapur (256-258) but was treacherously seized at a parley (259?) and died a captive at an uncertain date.

259-268. P. Licinius Egnatius GALLIENUS (b. 218) continued to reign alone, though pretenders appeared throughout the empire and the period has been called that of the **"thirty tyrants."** He completed the substitution of equestrians for senators as legionary commanders and as governors.

The **Goths,** who had broken through to the Black Sea, harried Asia and the Aegean area from ships.

258-267. Odenathus, ruler of Palmyra in the Syrian Desert, kept the Persians out of Asia (260), but his queen and successor, **Zenobia,** declared her independence (267).

259-268. Postumus set himself up as emperor in Gaul. **Gallienus** was finally murdered by his own troops before Mediolanum (Milan), where he was besieging the pretender **Aureolus** (before Sept., 268). Aureolus in his turn was slain by Claudius II.

268-270. M. Aurelius CLAUDIUS II "Goth-

icus" (b.?) was the first of a series of capable Illyrian emperors who prepared the way for Diocletian. He repelled a Gothic invasion of the Balkans (269, whence his title) at **Naissus** (Nisch) and settled numbers of Goths in the vacant lands of the Danubian provinces. Upon his death from plague, his brother Quintillus was proclaimed as

270.   Marcus Aurelius Claudius QUINTILLUS, Deserted by his troops, he committed suicide, and was succeeded by an associate of Claudius II.

270–275.   L. Domitius AURELIANUS (b. c. 214?) was rightly entitled "restorer of the world" (*restitutor orbis*). He abandoned trans-Danubian Dacia and settled its Roman inhabitants in a new Dacia carved out of Moesia. He repulsed the Alamanni from Italy (271) and built the existing walls of Rome (271–276).

271–272.   Probus, and then Aurelian himself, defeated and captured Zenobia and, upon a second revolt, sacked Palmyra (273).

273 or 274. Aurelian recovered Gaul from the successor of Postumus, Tetricus, in a **battle at Châlons.** Both Zenobia and Tetricus adorned his magnificent triumph in Rome (274). He was murdered by some officers while preparing to invade Persia (275).

275–276.   M. Claudius TACITUS, an elderly senator, was appointed emperor against his will by the senate. Though he defeated the Goths and Alans, who had invaded Asia Minor, the troops slew him.

276.   Marcus Annius FLORIANUS, brother of Tacitus, was slain soon after assuming the purple.

276–282.   M. Aurelius PROBUS, an Illyrian, was saluted by the eastern armies (276). He repelled from Gaul the Franks and Alamanni and other peoples, who had inflicted great devastation. He also strengthened the Danube frontier, quieted Asia Minor, and suppressed pretenders in Gaul. When he tried to use the troops in works of peace, e.g. clearing the canals in Egypt, they murdered him (282, autumn?).

282–283.   M. Aurelius CARUS, an Illyrian (?) and praetorian praefect to Aurelian, succeeded and campaigned successfully against the Persian monarch Varahran. He perished in 283, and his son Marcus Aurelius Numerius **Numerianus,** co-Augustus with him, was murdered (284, autumn). A second son, M. Aurelius **Carinus** (emperor, 283–285), tried to hold the west against **Diocletian,** an officer whom the eastern army had elected emperor, but he was slain by his own troops during the battle at the river Margus in Moravia (285, summer?).

The **troubles of the 3rd century** had two main causes: the increased pressure on the frontiers from the new Germanic tribes and from the vigorous Persian Empire, and the economic collapse within, the causes of which cannot be wholly established. In part, at least the economic crisis was due to the heavy burdens of government and defense and to the oppressive and erratic system of taxation; in part, perhaps, to a "fatigue of spirit." Literature ceased almost entirely. Of art and building notable examples survive, like the Arch of Septimius, the Baths of Caracalla, and the Walls of Aurelian at Rome, but these are imitative and uninspired. **Roman law,** however, reached its heights under the Antonines and Severi. Though the two great schools of jurisprudence, the **Sabinians** and the **Proculian,** originated under Augustus or Tiberius, the great jurists were **Salvius Julianus** under Hadrian, who dealt with the **Praetor's Edict.** **Gaius** under the Antonines, whose *Institutes* became a standard textbook, and the triumvirate of **Papinian, Paulus, and Ulpian** under the Severi, whose various works provided most of the material for Justinian's *Institutes.* In philosophy, neo-Pythagoreanism gave way to neo-Platonism, whose chief exponents were **Plotinus** (204–270), **Porphyrius** (233–306), and, later **Iamblichus** (d. 333?).

Despite the persecutions under the Antonines, Severus, Maximin, and Decius, the **Christian Church** grew in numbers and power. Its chief competitor was the cult of the Persian **Mithras,** a god popular with the troops. The major internal problems of the church in the 3rd century were the heresy called Montanism (an extreme asceticism) and the acute question of the treatment of those who lapsed from their faith during persecutions (*lapsi*) or betrayed the sacred books (*traditores*). Those who had confessed their faith in the face of persecution (*confessores*) opposed the readmission of back-sliders to full communion, while the church as a whole, led in the west by the bishop of Carthage, **Cyprian,** and the bishop of Rome **Stephen,** advocated a milder policy. The extremists were called **Novatians** in the 3rd century and **Donatists** in the 4th, after a certain Donatus, whose riotous bands of schismatics (*circumcelliones*) terrorized the province of Africa. Christian apologetics gave way to homiletic and theological writings in the hands of the African **Tertullian** (150–225) and **Cyprian** (200–258) and the Alexandrians **Clement** (d. 215) and **Origen** (182–251), the last two of whom combined Platonism with Christianity in the manner of contemporary neo-Platonism.

3. THE LATER EMPIRE, 284–527 A.D.

**284–305. G. Aurelius Valerius DIOCLETI-
ANUS** (b. 245, saluted as emperor 284, Nov.
17?), was of humble Illyrian stock. Faced with
the task of bringing order out of chaos, he
desired to emulate Augustus, to revive the
happy days of the early empire, but he succeeded only in creating an oriental despotism.

Since it is difficult to distinguish how far
the reorganization of the empire was due to
Diocletian and how far to Constantine, a brief
outline will be given here. In general, all these
reforms were merely a regularization and crys-
tallization of practices developed in the 3rd
century. Although the senate continued to
meet and the higher republican magistrates
survived to varying dates, e.g. the consulship
in the east until its abolition by Justinian, and
although two provinces, Asia and Africa, still
received senatorial pro-consuls, nevertheless
the whole administration was organized in a
pyramid of interlocking bureaus emanating
from the emperor.

According to Diocletian's system, which
operated only sporadically, there were to be
two coequal emperors (*Augusti*), as in the case
of Marcus and Verus. Now, however, **the
empire was divided** for practical administrative
purposes into two spheres, eastern and western, the line between which ran from the Danube to the Adriatic south of Dalmatia. Each
part was administered by one of the Augusti.
But the edicts of the emperors were issued
conjointly and they might on occasion command in one another's spheres.

The emperors ruled absolutely, in virtue of
selection by the troops and without the consent
of the senate (since 282). Each surrounded
himself with the pomp of an oriental court.
No longer was he the first citizen among equals
(*princeps*), but since Aurelian, "lord" (*dominus*). All connected with him was "sacred"
(the "sacred court," *sacra aula*, appeared under
the Severi). Each emperor chose an assistant
and successor (*Caesar*).

Under these four rulers, praetorian praefects, now wholly civilian magistrates, administered the four praefectures, Gaul, Italy, Illy-
rium, and the east. Each praefecture was
divided into several dioceses under vicars
(*uicarii*) independent of the prefects and directly responsible to the emperor. The dioceses
were subdivided into provinces under presidents (*praesides* or *rectores*). These provinces
were subdivisions of those of the early empire
and their number increased from 60 to 116.

The military power, which during the 3rd
century had absorbed all the functions of government, was now wholly separated from the
civilian. Each province had a duke (*dux*) or
count (*comes*) in charge of its permanent garrison, which was not, as in the early empire,
concentrated in large camps, but scattered in
smaller posts along the frontier, often in the
guise of soldier-peasants (*limitanei, ripariensis,*
border or riverbank men). In each praefecture,
under masters of the infantry and of the horse
(*magistri peditum, equitum*), were mobile forces
that could be rushed to strengthen threatened
points (*comitatenses*, companions of the emperor). The emperors, moreover, had large
bodies of special guards (*protectores* or *domestici*). The old legions were split into smaller,
more mobile but less highly trained units of
about 2000 men. Heavy armed cavalry (*cata-
phractarii*) played a large part in warfare. The
auxiliary troops were mostly mercenary bands
of barbarians, whose chiefs became extremely
influential. The total forces now numbered
about 500,000 men, an increase over the Augustan 300,000, which accounts in part for the
financial problems of the later empire.

Besides the separate and elaborate administration for each territorial unit, the emperors
had an extensive central bureaucracy, the various "offices" (*officia*) under such officials like
the quaestor of the sacred palace (*quaestor sacri
palatii*, the chief judicial officer), the chancellor
(*magister memoriae*, master of records), and the
personnel manager (*magister officiorum*, master
of the offices, very powerful because he had a
finger in every department). These men automatically belonged to the senate, and other
high officials had the titles of honor formerly
reserved for equestrians, who vanished as a
class. The senators also now formed a class
of dominant and very wealthy landowners
throughout the empire, who might seldom actually attend the senate, but who enjoyed privilege and exemption. The rest of the population
were crushed by heavy taxes, which were
largely collected in kind (*annona*) after the collapse of the currency, and which were reassessed every 15th year by an "indiction"
(*indictio*). Both labor and property were evaluated in terms of a unit of wheat-producing
land (*iugum*). The taxation bore especially
heavily on the members of the municipal sen-
ates (*curiales, decuriones*), who continued to be
held responsible for the collection of taxes and
the payment of arrears, and on the small landowners, who had to provide recruits for the
army and see that waste lands (*agri deserti*)
were kept under cultivation. Thus freemen
found it wisest to flee the country, enter mon-

asteries, or become serfs (*coloni*) on large estates. Craftsmen and tradesmen were rigorously confined to their professions. The whole
caste system was arranged to insure the maintenance of the administration and the army.
Since, therefore, it benefited no one but the
great landlords or imperial officials, the vast
majority of the population lost interest and
either accepted the barbarian invasions su-
pinely or even welcomed relief from oppression. Whether, however, this lethargy, which
pervaded not only the political and economic
life but also the intellectual, save in the Christian Church, resulted from the system or
whether the unwieldy and inflexible system
indicated the poor mental caliber of the rulers,
so many of whom were of peasant or barbarian
origin, and the effeteness of the hereditary
upper class, cannot be determined.

285. Upon the defeat of Carinus, Diocletian
chose as his colleague (Caesar in 285, Augustus
in 286) the Illyrian **M. Aurelius Valerius Maximianus** (b. c. 240?), who was a harsh, unedu-
cated man but a competent general. They
assumed the titles respectively of *Jovius* and
Herculius. Diocletian took up his residence in
the east, at Nicomedia in Bithynia, from which
the main road to the upper Euphrates frontier
began, while **Maximian,** in the west, lived
mostly at Mediolanum (Milan) in northern
Italy, which was a better center for the defense
of the northern frontier than Rome. Despite
its sentimental pre-eminence, Rome thereafter
declined in practical importance. But the departure of the imperial court gave the bishop
of Rome increased scope.

293, Mar. 1. Diocletian chose as Caesar **G. Galerius Valerius Maximianus** (b. c. 250), who
became his son-in-law and received the government of Illyricum; Maximian chose **Flavius
Valerius Constantius** (misnamed **Chlorus**)
(b. ?) who divorced his wife Helena to marry
Maximian's daughter Theodora; he received
the praefecture of Gaul. He at once drove out
the rebel Carausius from Boulogne and subdued the Franks.

294. A revolt was raised in Egypt by Achilleus,
whom Diocletian besieged in Alexandria (295)
and captured.

296. Narses, king of Persia, invaded Roman
Mesopotamia and defeated Galerius, but the
latter gathered reinforcements in the winter
and returned to defeat Narses (297) and recover Mesopotamia; Roman influence was
restored in Armenia, whose king became
Christian.

297. Constantius crossed to Britain and his
lieutenant defeated and killed Allectus, who
had murdered and replaced Carausius.

298. Constantius returned to Gaul and defeated the Alamanni.

301. An edict limiting prices of goods and
labor was passed by Diocletian in an attempt
to end the economic distress caused by the
collapse of the currency; no attempt was made
to enforce it in the west, and in the east it
soon proved impracticable.

303, Feb. 23. Galerius persuaded Diocletian to
declare a **general persecution of the Christians,**
which, however, Constantius did not enforce in
his praefecture. The persecution was stopped
in the entire west in 306 but raged in the east
until 313.

**305, May 1. Diocletian and Maximian abdi-
cated; Galerius and Constantius became Augusti;** Diocletian and Galerius selected as
Caesars **Flavius Valerius Severus** under Constantius, receiving the praefecture of Italy, and
for Galerius his own nephew **Galerius Valerius
Maximinus Daia,** who received Syria and
Egypt. The hereditary claims of Maximian's
son Maxentius and Constantius' son Constantine were neglected.

**306–337. Flavius Valerius CONSTANTINUS I
THE GREAT** (b. 288? of Constantius and
Helena) fled from Galerius to his father in
Britain. On the death of the latter (July) Constantine was saluted as emperor by the troops,
but made an agreement with Galerius by
which he became Caesar and Severus became
Augustus. In Rome the praetorians and the
people proclaimed **Maxentius Augustus** (Oct.
28); he called his father Maximian to be Augustus and temporarily took the title of Caesar.
When the Emperor Severus came with an
army, it deserted and he surrendered to Maximian and was later executed by Maxentius.
In fear of Galerius, Maximian went to Constantine in Gaul; Constantine recognized him
as senior Augustus and married his daughter,
Fausta. Galerius attempted an invasion of
Italy (307), but disloyalty in his army forced
its abandonment. Maxentius took the title of
Augustus (308) and Maximian fled to Constantine; for four years Maxentius ruled in Italy
very oppressively. Galerius induced Diocletian
to preside over a conference at Carnuntum,
where it was decided that Maximian should
abdicate, **Valerius Licinianus Licinius** was to
be Augustus in the west, and Constantine was
to return to the rank of Caesar. Constantine
refused and Galerius gave him and Daia the
rank of *filius Augusti;* both were still unsatisfied, and were finally given the rank of Augustus (310). Maximian attempted to revolt, but
Constantine killed him. When Galerius died
of disease (311, May), Daia seized Asia Minor,
leaving the Balkans to Licinius.

312. Constantine suddenly invaded Italy and after winning a battle over Maxentius' general at Verona defeated and killed Maxentius himself near Rome at the **Milvian Bridge** (Saxa Rubra) (Oct. 28). Before the battle he is said to have seen in the sky a cross and the device *in hoc signo vinces.* Sometime later he became a Christian. He dissolved the praetorian guard. At a meeting with Licinius in Milan (early 313?) equal rights were proclaimed for all religions and the property confiscated from the Christians was restored by the **Edict of Milan.**

313. Daia crossed to Europe, but was defeated by Licinius at **Tzirallum** and fled to Tarsus, where he died soon after. Licinius now held the entire east and Constantine the west.

314. After a brief war, in which Licinius was defeated at **Cibalae** (Oct. 8), a peace was made giving Constantine all of the Balkans except Thrace.

323. Relations between the two were strained by Licinius' anti-Christian policy, and war finally broke out. Licinius was defeated at **Adrianople** (July 3), his fleet was defeated by Constantine's son Crispus, and Licinius was again defeated at Chrysopolis in Anatolia (Sept. 18). He surrendered and was executed in the next year.

324-337. CONSTANTINE REUNITED THE EMPIRE under his sole rule. He had already interfered in the affairs of the Church (at its invitation) when in 316 he tried to settle the Donatist schism.

325. He now summoned the **first ecumenical** (world-wide) **council of the Church,** to meet at **Nicaea** in Asia Minor. It was to settle a controversy that had arisen in Alexandria between the priest **Arius,** who maintained that Christ was of different substance from God (*heterousios*), and the Bishop Alexander (succeeded in 328 by **Athanasius,** who supported the doctrine that they were of the same substance (consubstantiality, *homo-ousios*). The council agreed on a creed favorable to Alexander (not the present "Nicene" creed); in addition it adopted certain canons giving privileges to the bishops (patriarchs) of Alexandria, Antioch, and Rome. Constantinople later acquired similar rights. The **primacy of Rome,** although in a very restricted sense, had been generally recognized in the west since the **Council of Arles** in 314. The prominent part taken by Constantine in this council laid the basis for the later supremacy of the emperor in the eastern Church. Though Arius died a horrible death in 336, Constantine and his successors swung the Church increasingly toward Arianism, and strife in the Church on this subject was not ended until the reign of Theodosius I. The west remained firmly Athanasian.

330, May 11. Constantine dedicated as his capital **CONSTANTINOPLE,** which he had spent four years in building on the site of Byzantium, commanding the strategic center of the east, the Bosporus.

337, May 22. Constantine died at Nicomedia. He had been induced (326) by his wife Fausta to execute Crispus, his son by his first wife. His heirs were three sons and two nephews. Of the sons, all Augusti, Constantinus II (b. 317) received the praefectures of Italy and Gaul; Constantius II (b. 317) took the east; and Constans (b. 323?) got Illyricum and part of Africa. The nephews, Dalmatius and Annibalianus, were at once executed by Constantius.

337-361. RULE OF CONSTANTINE'S SONS. While Constantius carried on an indecisive war against Persia, Constantinus attacked Constans, but was slain at Aquileia (340). Constans was killed by the pretender **Magnus Magnentius** (350, Jan.).

351, Sept. 28. Constantius defeated Magnentius at **Mursa,** near the confluence of the Danube and Drave. The latter slew himself at Lugdunum (353) and the empire was once more united.

351, Mar. 15. Constantius chose his cousin Gallus as Caesar, but had him executed in 354.

355, Nov. 6. Constantius chose as Caesar the half-brother of Gallus, **Julian,** who was given command against the Alamanni and Franks.

360. Julian marched against Constantius, who died before Julian reached the east (361).

361-363. JULIANUS, "the Apostate," (b. 332). He is known chiefly for his attempt to substitute paganism for Christianity and to organize a pagan church. After continuing his successes against the Franks, he campaigned against the Persians, but died on his way back from an attack on Ctesiphon (363, July 36). With him ended the line of Constantine.

363-364. JOVIANUS (b. c. 331), was elected by the troops. He surrendered Mesopotamia to the Persians and died soon after (364, Feb. 17).

364-375. FLAVIUS VALENTINIANUS I (b. 321) was the next choice of the troops. He ably defended the west against the barbarians and made his brother **Valens** co-Augustus in the east (364, Mar. 28).

367. Valentinian made his son **Gratian** co-emperor in the west. Valentinian died on an expedition against the Quadi and Sarmatians (375, Nov. 17).

375-383. GRATIANUS (b. 359) named his half-brother **Valentinian II** (b. 371) co-Augustus in the west.

376. The **Visigoths** (West Goths) crossed the Danube. Valens fell in battle against them at **Adrianople** (378, Aug. 9). The Goths continued to ravage the Balkan region.

379, Jan. 19. Gratian appointed as co-Augustus for the east, **Theodosius,** son of a successful general in Britain.

382. Gratian, at the request of Bishop Ambrose, removed from the senate-house the pagan altar of victory and gave up the title of *pontifex maximus.*

379–395. FLAVIUS THEODOSIUS "THE GREAT" (b. 346). He supported orthodoxy (i.e. Athanasianism) in the east, and came to terms with the Goths by settling them as military allies (*foederati*) in the Balkans.

383. The British legions proclaimed **Magnus Maximus,** who seized Gaul. Gratian was slain at Lugdunum (Aug. 25). Theodosius recognized Maximus.

387. When Maximus drove Valentinian II from Italy, Theodosius captured and executed him at Aquileia (388, July 28).

390. Theodosius cruelly massacred 7000 people at Thessalonica in revenge for an insurrection. Bishop Ambrose of Milan forced him to do penance for this act and emphasized thereby the independence of the western church from imperial domination.

392, May 15. The Frankish count (*comes*), **Arbogast,** murdered Valentinian II at Vienne and set up as emperor the pagan rhetorician **Eugenius.**

394, Sept. 5. Theodosius defeated and slew Eugenius and Arbogast at the Frigidus, just east of Aquileia. The empire was reunited for a brief space.

395, Jan. 17. Theodosius died at Milan. The empire was divided between his elder son **Arcadius** (made Augustus in the east in 383) and the younger son **Honorius** (made Augustus in the west in 393). The division proved to be permanent, though at the time the unity of the empire was fully accepted in theory and was always envisaged as a practical possibility. One consul regularly held office in Rome (until 472) and one in Constantinople (until 541).

395–408. ARCADIUS (b. 377), emperor of the east. He married Eudoxia, daughter of the Frank, Bauto (395). The praetorian praefect, Rufinus, managed to check the inroads of the Visigoths in the Balkans until his murder by the troops, but thereafter the eunuch Eutropius failed to prevent the invasions of the Visigoths or of the Huns, who overran Asia.

395–423. HONORIUS (b. 384), emperor of the west. He fell wholly under the influence of the Vandal **Stilicho** who, as master of the troops (*magister militum*), commanded all the forces and married his daughter Maria to Honorius (398).

396–397. Stilicho drove the Visigoths, led by Alaric, out of Greece.

402, Apr. 6. He frustrated their efforts to invade Italy (victory of the Romans at **Pollentia**).

406, Aug. 23. Stilicho at Florence broke up a miscellaneous force of barbarians which Radagaisus had led into Italy.

At about this time Gaul was overrun by Vandals, Alans, Suevi, and Burgundians.

407. EVACUATION OF BRITAIN by the Romans. Constantine, whom the troops in Britain had proclaimed emperor, crossed to Gaul with his forces and it is probable that Roman troops were never sent back. The Romanized natives were left to deal as best they could with the inroads of Caledonians (Picts) from the north and of various German tribes coming by sea. The Saxons seem to have secured a permanent footing at the mouth of the Thames about 441.

408, Aug. 22. Murder of Stilicho, at Honorius' order.

408–450. THEODOSIUS II (b. 401), emperor of the east. He was the son of Arcadius and was a weak ruler dominated by his sister Pulcheria. With Valentinian III, Theodosius issued the earliest collection of existing laws, the **Theodosian Code** (438).

The Huns, under Attila, continued to ravage the empire and extort tribute.

409. Alaric again invaded Italy and set up a usurper, **Attalus** (praefect of Rome, the last pagan "emperor"). Alaric soon deposed him again.

410, Aug. 14 or 24.   ALARIC SACKED ROME. He died soon after in southern Italy. His brother-in-law Ataulf led the Visigoths into Gaul (412) and thence began the conquest of Spain from the Vandals (415). There **Wallia** (416–419), successor of Athaulf, established the first recognized barbarian kingdom (419).

411. Constantine was defeated by Honorius' commander Constantius, near Arles.

423–425. Johannes usurped the purple on the death of Honorius at Ravenna (which he had made the capital in place of Milan).

425. Forces sent from the east by Theodosius II captured Johannes and put him to death.

425–455. VALENTINIAN III (b. 419), emperor of the west. He was the son of Honorius' half-sister Galla Placidia and the general Constantius, who had been made Augustus in 421, but had died almost at once. Valentinian was recognized by Theodosius II and married his daughter Eudoxia (437).

429. The general **Bonifatius** tried to set himself up as independent in Africa, with the aid of the Vandals, who crossed from Spain under Gaiseric (Genseric). But the Vandals seized Africa for themselves after a two-year siege of Hippo Regius (430-431) during which the bishop, **St. Augustine,** died (430, Aug. 28).

430. Aëtius, master of the troops, disposed of his rivals, Felix and Bonifatius (recalled from Africa in 432). He then devoted himself to clearing Gaul of barbarians, which he did by a resounding victory over the Visigoths (436) and by suppressing an uprising of the peasants and slaves (*Bagaudae,* 437).

435. The **Vandal kingdom in Africa** was recognized. The Vandals took Carthage in 439.

450-457. MARCIAN, emperor of the east. Pulcheria, sister of Theodosius II (d. 450), had married Marcian, an able general. He allowed the Ostrogoths (east Goths) to settle as military allies (*foederati*) in Pannonia.

450. Attila, leader of the Huns, decided to bring his people from the east into Gaul.

451, June. Aëtius, aided by the Visigothic king, Theodoric I (*Theoderich, Theoderid*), defeated the Huns in the **battle of Châlons** (actually the *campi Catalauni* or Mauriac plain, near Troyes).

452. Attila invaded Italy, but turned back, traditionally because warned by Pope Leo I, but probably because well paid. Attila died in 453 and his hordes broke up.

454, Sept. 21. Valentinian rewarded Aëtius by murdering him with his own hand.

455, Mar. 16. Valentinian was murdered by two of Aëtius' guards. End of the house of Theodosius.

455-472. A succession of puppet rulers in the west. In 455 Eudoxia, widow of Valentinian, set up **Petronius Maximus** at Rome. On his murder, in the same year, she called the Vandals from Africa.

455, June 2-16. Gaiseric and the Vandals sacked Rome. By the thoroughness of their destruction they attached a permanent stigma to their name.

456. Avitus advanced from southern Gaul to Rome, but was deposed by his able general, the Suevian **Ricimer.** Ricimer retained power by securing the consent of the eastern emperors to his nominees, who were **Majorianus** (457-461), **Severus** (461-465), and after a two-year interregnum, **Anthemius** (467-472), and **Olybrius** (472). When in 472 both Ricimer and Olybrius died, the eastern emperor, Leo I, appointed **Glycerius** (473), and **Julius Nepos** (473-475).

457-474. LEO I (b. ?), a Thracian (?), succeeded Marcian as emperor of the east. To offset his master of the troops, the Alan Aspar, he married his daughter Ariadne to Zeno, an Isaurian from the mountains of southern Asia Minor (467) and made Zeno's son, Leo, his colleague (473).

474. Leo II, who succeeded on the death of Leo I. His father, Zeno, made himself his colleague. Leo died the same year.

474-491. ZENO (b. 426), disposed of the pretender Basiliscus, brother-in-law of Leo I (475). He then tried to control the Goths by setting the rival chiefs, Theodoric, son of Strabo, and Theodoric the Amal, against each other.

475. The master of the troops, **Orestes,** removed Nepos in favor of his own son, whose name combined those of the founder of Rome and of the empire,

475-476. ROMULUS AUGUSTUS (nicknamed *Augustulus*).

476, Sept. 4. After defeating and killing Orestes at Pavia, the Herulian **Odovacar** (*Odoacer*) deposed Romulus Augustulus, the last emperor of the west, at Ravenna. **Traditional end of the Roman Empire.**

The eastern emperor, **Zeno,** apparently recognized Odovacar as "patrician" (*patricius* had become the title of honor for barbarian commanders). Nepos retained titular claim as emperor until his death in 480 and after that date the empire was theoretically reunited under the eastern emperors, but actually Odovacar ruled as an independent king in Italy.

481. On the death of Theodoric, the son of Strabo, Zeno recognized his rival as patrician and master of the troops. His people were established in Moesia as foederati.

488. Theodoric, ostensibly as **Zeno's** agent, invaded Italy.

493, Feb. 27. After a three-year siege of Ravenna, Odovacar surrendered. He was soon after murdered by Theodoric. Italy was united under Theodoric the Great (b. c. 455) as the kingdom of the Ostrogoths.

491-518. ANASTASIUS I (b. 431), emperor of the east. He married Zeno's widow and removed the Isaurians from power, thus causing a serious revolt in Isauria (suppressed only in 497).

The inroads of the Slavic Getae forced him to protect Constantinople by a wall.

502-506. The emperor waged a long war with the Persians.

514-518. Conflict with the pretender Vitalian, commander of the Bulgarian foederati. Anastasius died in 518 (July 1).

518-527. JUSTINUS I (b. 450?), a humble Illyrian who had risen to be commander of the imperial bodyguard. He took as his colleague his able nephew Justinian (527) and died the same year.

527-565. JUSTINIAN. (For his reign see Byzantine Empire, p. 186).

Diocletian and his successors managed to delay, but not to stop, the decay that had attacked the empire during the 3rd century. The administrative reforms added to the burdens of taxation without stopping the military domination and rivalry for the purple. The army became increasingly barbarized and immobilized by settlement on the land as peasant militia or barbarian foederati. The active defense was entrusted to barbarian mercenaries under their powerful chiefs, who came to dominate the state. Thus, the empire in the west did not fall: it petered out; and the establishment of the barbarian kingdoms simply recognized the end of a gradual process. In the east the empire, in Greek garb, maintained itself, at times as a very great and splendid power, until the conquest of Constantinople by the crusaders in 1204 and the definitive fall of the city into the hands of the Turks (1453).

In **architecture**, the later empire continued the able engineering of earlier days, as in the Baths of Diocletian at Rome, his palace at Spalato, or the Basilica of Maxentius and Constantine at Rome. But **art** showed a rapid decline, e.g. in the frieze of the Arch of Constantine at Rome.

The second half of the 4th century witnessed a revival of pagan **Latin literature** in **Symmachus,** the praefect of the city who vainly urged Valentinian II to restore the altar of victory (384), the Gallic poet **Ausonius,** consul in 379, and the Alexandrian **Claudius,** court poet of Honorius and Stilicho. **Boethius,** the last classical philosopher, compiled an elementary treatise on mathematics and translated the logic of Aristotle into Latin; whether he was pagan or Christian, he wrote the *De consolatione philosophiae* in prison before his execution by Theodoric the Ostrogoth, 524. **John Philopponus** (fl. first half of the 6th century) wrote critical commentaries on Aristotle widely quoted through the late Middle Ages.

Active intellectual life, however, appeared chiefly in the Church. The great Latin fathers were: **Lactantius** (d. c. 325), **Ambrose** (340–397), bishop of Milan (374), **Jerome** (340–420), who retired from Rome to Bethlehem, where he translated the Bible into Latin (the *Vulgate*), and **Augustine** (354–430), bishop of Hippo Regius in Africa (395), who founded Christian theology on Platonism. The important Greek fathers were: **Basil** of Caesarea (330–379), his

brother **Gregory** of Nyssa (d. c. 394), and **Gregory** of Nazianzus (329–389), all three Cappadocians, and **John Chrysostom** (329–389), patriarch of Constantinople (381). **Eusebius** (264–340), orthodox bishop of Caesarea (315), who should be distinguished from the contemporary Arian, Eusebius of Nicomedia, is noted for his *Historia ecclesiastica* and other historical works.

During the 5th and 6th centuries the eastern Church was torn by the **monophysite heresy,** whose doctrine was that Christ had a single nature. The orthodox doctrine, that Christ combined divine and human, had the support of Pope Leo of Rome and was approved at the **Council of Chalcedon** (451), but the eastern emperors on the whole were monophysite. In the west, as imperial authority weakened, and as rival bishoprics passed into barbarian hands, the bishop of Rome—or **pope** (*papa*) as he came to be known—became supreme, and such great popes as **Damasus** (pope, 366–383) and **Leo I, "the Great"** (pope, 440–461) became temporal as well as spiritual leaders of their people. A claim of territorial sovereignty began to be based on a fictitious **"Donation of Constantine"** to Pope Sylvester of the lands around Rome. A significant missionary effort of the Church was the sending of **Ulfilas to the Goths** (c. 340–348), who converted them to Arianism. But the chief feature of the Church during this period was the introduction of **monasticism.** In the east, the single solitary had long been common and **St. Antony** first gathered some of them together for a common life (*coenobite*) in Egypt in about 285. **Basil of Caesarea** established a monastic rule popular in the east. Monasticism spread to the west under the efforts of **Martin of Tours** (362) and **Jerome. Cassian of Marseilles** (c. 400) wrote *Institutes* for his monastery, but the rule that became dominant was that of **St. Benedict** (*regula Sancti Benedicti*), who founded his monastery at Monte Cassino, near Naples, in 529. His rule was adopted by Cassiodorus (480–575), secretary to Theodoric the Ostrogoth, who founded a monastery at Beneventum in 540. The closing of the schools at Athens by Justinian, the execution of Boethius, and the founding of Benedict's monastery mark the transition from classical to medieval intellectual life. (*Cont. p. 155.*)

G. THE EMPIRES OF ASIA

1. THE NEO-PERSIAN EMPIRE OF THE SASSANIANS, 226–651 A.D.

From p. 129)

226–240. Ardashir I (*Artaxerxes, Artashatr*), son of Papak, a vassal-king of the Parthian Empire ruling in Fars (Persia proper), revolted against Artabanus, last king of the Arsacid dynasty of Parthia, and defeated him finally at **Hormuz** (226–27), where Artabanus was slain.

Merv, Balkh, and Khiva conquered by Ardashir; submission of the kings of Kushan, Turan, and Makran received; India invaded and tribute levied on the Punjab.

229–232. War with Rome. Rome summoned to evacuate Syria and the rest of Asia. Armenia, the real objective of Ardashir's campaign, subjugated after the murder of its Arsacid king, Chosroes.

Under Ardashir a strongly centralized nation supported by the priesthood created; Zoroastrianism revived and the privileges of the Magi restored; collection of the text of the *Zend Avesta* under Arda-Viraf. He was succeeded by

240–271. Shapur I (*Sapor, Shahpuhri*). Revolts in Armenia and Hatra crushed (240).

241–244. FIRST WAR WITH ROME. Shapur invaded Mesopotamia and Syria, took Nisibis and Antioch, but was finally driven back across the Euphrates and defeated at Resaina by the Emperor Gordian. Gordian was murdered and peace was concluded by his successor, Philip. In the east, Balkh apparently independent.

258–260. SECOND WAR WITH ROME. Shapur again invaded Mesopotamia and Syria, taking Nisibis, Edessa, and Antioch, and defeating and capturing near Edessa the Emperor Valerian, who remained a captive until his death (265–66). Asia Minor also invaded, Caesarea Mazaca in Cappadocia taken, but no attempt made to consolidate and hold the conquered territory.

260–263. Palmyra. In a brilliant campaign **Odenathus,** the Arab prince of Palmyra, drove the Persians back across the Euphrates, defeated Shapur and besieged Ctesiphon, seized and occupied Mesopotamia, Syria, and other provinces west of the Euphrates, and was recognized by Gallienus as co-regent for the east. Palmyra had, by the mid-century, supplanted **Petra** as the chief junction of the caravan routes. Striking ruins of Petra, first described by Burckhardt in 1812: buildings and tombs hewn from rose-colored rock, some dating back to 5th century B.C.

Shapur's later years were devoted to public works, of which the greatest was the dam at Shuster. He also founded many cities, among them Nishapur. In his reign appeared Mani (215–273), founder of **Manichaeism,** whom Shapur at first favored, then banished.

271–293. Shapur was succeeded by his son, **Hormisdas I** (271–272), who was followed by his brother, **Varahran I** (272–275). Mani executed. Insufficient support given to **Zenobia of Palmyra,** the widow of Odenathus, against Aurelian, whose Persian expedition came to an end with his murder (275). Varahran succeeded by his son, **Varahran II** (275–293). An eastern campaign, in which the Sakae of Sistan were subdued, was brought to a close by a Roman invasion of Persia under the Emperor Carus, who conquered Mesopotamia and took Ctesiphon (283). The mysterious death of Carus ended the war (284). Armenia seized by Tiridates, the son of the murdered Chosroes, with the help of the Emperor Diocletian (286). **Varahran III,** son of Varahran II, reigned four months, and was succeeded by his brother.

293–301. Narses, who finally worsted his brother and rival, Hormisdas, and drove Tiridates from Armenia (296).

296–297. WAR WITH ROME. The Roman army under Galerius routed near **Carrhea** (296). The Persian army surprised by Galerius in the following year and almost annihilated. Peace concluded (297). Terms: (1) cession to Rome of the five provinces west of the Tigris; (2) the Tigris to be the boundary instead of the Euphrates; (3) cession to Armenia of Median territory up to the fort of Zentha; (4) Iberia (*Georgia*) to be a Roman protectorate.

Abdication of Narses and accession of his son, **Hormisdas II** (301–309), noted for his activity in building and for setting up a court of justice at which the poor were encouraged to make complaint against the oppression of the rich. Upon his death his natural heir, Hormisdas, was set aside by the nobles, who elected his posthumous son, the famous

309–379. SHAPUR II.

309–337. His minority and early campaigns. Persia invaded by the Arabs of Bahrain and Mesopotamia; Ctesiphon sacked. At the age of 17 Shapur grasped the reins of state, adopted an active policy, invaded Arabia, and exacted a terrible revenge upon the Arabs.

337-350. FIRST WAR WITH ROME. The Romans were defeated in the field, but Shapur was unable to capture the Roman strongholds. Nisibis invested three times in vain (338, 346, 350). Constantius routed at Singara (348). Persecution of the Persian Christians (from 339 on). **Treaty with Armenia** (341), but in 351 Armenia went over to Rome. Successful campaigns in the east against the Huns, Euseni, and Gilani (350–357).

359-361. SECOND WAR WITH ROME. Syria invaded, Amida taken after a heroic defense (359). Singara and Bezabde captured (360). Constantius attempted in vain to recapture the latter place, and died in the following year. His successor, Julian, invaded Persia, forced the passage of the Tigris, defeated the Persians north of Ctesiphon, but retreated before investing that city and was mortally wounded in a battle near Samarra (363). His successor, Jovian, concluded peace with Shapur for 30 years. Terms: (1) restoration of the five provinces ceded by Narses; (2) surrender of Nisibis, Singara, and a third fortress in eastern Mesopotamia to Persia; (3) Armenia declared to be outside the Roman sphere of influence. Conquest of Armenia by Shapur and invasion of Iberia.

371-376. THIRD WAR WITH ROME. No decisive results and an obscure peace. Persian power at its zenith at the death of Shapur II. His immediate successors weak and unenterprising. **Ardashir II** (379–383) and **Shapur III** (383–388). Shapur concluded a peace with Rome (384) by the terms of which Armenia was partitioned between Rome and Persia. **Varahran IV** (388–399). Khusru (*Chosroes*), the satrap of Persian Armenia, who had revolted, was deposed and succeeded by Varahran's brother. Varahran was killed in a mutiny and succeeded by his son,

399-420. Yezdigird the Wicked. A peaceful reign. A firman issued permitting Christians to worship openly and rebuild their churches (409), a decree as important to the eastern church as the **Edict of Milan** to the church of the west. The **Council of Seleucia** adopted the decrees and the creed of the **Council of Nicaea.** Yezdigird possibly contemplated baptism and persecuted the Magians, but returning to his old faith he authorized the destruction of the Christian sect. A terrible persecution for four years. Yezdigird succeeded by his son,

420-440. Varahran V. Brought up among the desert Arabs who supported him against his cousin, Khusru, the choice of the nobles, who finally accepted him peacefully. He continued

persecution of the Christians and declared war on Rome (420), when the Christians crossed the border seeking Rome's protection. Varahran was defeated and peace concluded (422), Christians to be allowed to take refuge in the Roman Empire, persecution of the Christians to cease. Declaration of the independence of the eastern church at the **Council of Dad-Ishu** (424). Persian Armenia reduced to a satrapy (428). Campaign of Varahran against the White Huns or Ephthalites (*Haytal*), of Turkish stock probably, in Transoxania. They invaded Persia, but were surprised and defeated by Varahran, who crossed the Oxus and forced them to sue for peace. Varahran succeeded by his son,

440-457. Yezdigird II. War declared upon Rome and peace concluded the same year (440). Successful campaigns against the Ephthalites of Transoxania (443–451). Armenia forcibly converted to Zoroastrianism (455–456), after the defeat of the Christian party at the hands of the Persians and their Armenian supporters. Persecution of Christians spread to Mesopotamia. Khorasan again invaded by the Ephthalites, who inflicted a severe defeat upon Yezdigird, after he had driven them across the Oxus. At his death his younger son Hormisdas, seized the throne, but the elder son,

459-483. Firuz (*Perozes*), defeated and captured Hormisdas with the aid of the Ephthalites. A famine of several years; wise measures adopted by Firuz. Unsuccessful campaigns adopted against the Ephthalites ending in a humiliating peace (464–480?). A further defeat at the hands of the Kushans of the maritime provinces of the Caspian Sea (481) led to the revolt of Iberia and of Armenia under Vahan (481–483). This was still smoldering when Firuz, breaking his troth, attacked the Ephthalites, was defeated and slain. Succeeded by

483-485. Balas (Vologesus), his brother. Tribute paid by Persia to Khush-Newaz, the Ephthalite Khan, for about two years. Conciliation of Armenia. **Edict of toleration** granted Christians, after **Vahan** aided Volagases in a civil war. Thereupon Armenia and Iberia contented provinces of the empire. Nestorian Christological doctrine of the two natures in Christ established by **Bar-Soma** in the Persian Church with royal authority; the college of Edessa driven out by Zeno and set up at Nisibis by Bar-Soma (489). Repudiation by Armenia of the **Council of Chalcedon** (491). Volagases succeeded by his son,

485-498. Kobad (first reign), who had taken refuge with the Ephthalites after an abortive attempt to seize the throne. Successful cam paign against the Khazars, dwelling between the Volga and the Don. Many converts gained for his communistic and ascetic doctrines by **Mazdak,** a high priest of Zoroastrianism, among them the king. Unrest in Armenia and Persia owing to the intolerant proselytism of the Mazdakites, leading to a conspiracy of the Chief Mobed, nobles, and army against Kobad, who was deposed and succeeded by his brother **Zamasp,** who reigned from 498 to 501. Kobad escaped to the Ephthalites, who espoused his cause with vigor. Zamasp resigned the crown voluntarily.

501-531. Kobad (second reign). Official support withdrawn from Mazdak.

503-505. FIRST WAR WITH ROME. Cause: non-fulfillment of the Eastern Empire's agreement to pay a share of the expenses of the defense of the pass of Derbend, the usual route taken by nomadic tribes in their invasions of Persia and the Eastern Empire. Roman Armenia invaded; Theodosiopolis taken; sack of Amida in northern Mesopotamia (502). An Ephthalite raid forced Kobad to conclude peace on the basis of the *status quo ante.*

503-523. Successful and final campaign against the Ephthalites (503-513). Massacre of the Mazdakites (523). Rebellion in Iberia.

524-531. SECOND WAR WITH ROME. Cause: Erection of the fortress of Daras within a day's march of Nisibis by the Emperor Anastasius. The first campaign ended in the defeat of the Romans (526), who were again defeated in 528, but were finally victorious in the **battle of Daras** (528) under Belisarius. An indecisive battle near Callinicum brought the war to a close. Kobad was succeeded by

531-579. ANUSHIRWAN THE JUST (*Chosroes*), his son. The most illustrious member of the Sassanian dynasty. Succession disputed. Execution of all his brothers and their male offspring with one exception. Massacre of Mazdak and his followers. Conclusion of the **Endless Peace with Rome** (533). Terms: (1) Rome to pay 11,000 pounds of gold toward the upkeep of the Caucasian defenses; (2) Rome to keep Daras as a fortress, but not as its headquarters in Mesopotamia; (3) restoration on both sides of captured strongholds in Lazica; (4) eternal friendship and alliance. Within seven years, however, Anushirwan, alarmed at Justinian's successes in Africa and Italy (533-539) and prompted by the Ostrogoths and Armenians, began a defensive war.

540-562. WAR WITH ROME. Syria invaded. Antioch sacked. Terms of peace agreed upon and ratification of the treaty received by Anushirwan at Edessa. He nevertheless extracted ransoms from the cities along the route of his return march, whereupon Jus-

tinian denounced the treaty.

540-557. Campaigns in Lazica. Lazica (ancient *Colchis*), a Roman protectorate since 527, appealed to Anushirwan for help to throw off the Roman yoke. Petra taken by the Persians (540). Lazica a Persian province. Petra retaken by the Romans (550), and the Persians driven out of the country (555). A truce agreed upon (557). **Definitive peace with Rome** (562). The terms included: (1) cession of Lazica to Rome; (2) payment by Rome of 30,000 pieces of gold annually; (3) free exercise of their religion guaranteed to the Christians of Persia; (4) commercial intercourse restricted to certain roads and marts; (5) Daras to remain a fortified town; (6) arbitration of all disputes and free diplomatic intercourse; (7) inclusion in the treaty of the allies of either party; (8) the defense of the Caspian gate to be undertaken by Persia alone; (9) the peace to hold for 50 years.

554. Subjugation of the Ephthalites with the aid of the Turks and the division of their territory with the Oxus as boundary. Successful campaign against the Khazars.

572. Declaration of war on Persia by Justin. Syria ravaged by Anushirwan and Daras taken (573). Abdication of Justin. A peace purchased by Tiberius.

576? Arabian campaign. The Abyssinians driven out of southern Arabia, which became a Persian province.

576-578. Alliance of the Turks with the Eastern Empire. Ill-success of their invasion of Persia. Armenian campaigns. An Indian campaign also reported.

Under Anushirwan the administration was reorganized. The empire was divided into four great satrapies: the east comprising Khorasan and Kerman; the west including Iraq and Mesopotamia; the north comprehending Armenia and Azerbaijan; and the south containing Fars and Khuzistan. A fixed land tax was also substituted for the former variable tax on produce, and its collection placed under the supervision of the priests. Irrigation and communications were improved, the army reformed, foreigners protected, agriculture encouraged, laws revised, the Christians granted toleration, learning subsidized, Indian tales and chess introduced. Anushirwan was succeeded by his son,

579-589. Hormisdas IV (*Hormazd*). War with Rome continued. The Persians were defeated at Constantia (581) and again at Arzanene near Martyropolis (588). In 589 the Persians took Martyropolis and defeated the Romans, who, however, gained a signal victory near Nisibis soon thereafter.

589. Invasion of Persia by Arabs, Khazars, and

Turks. The advance of the Turks constituted a real danger, but they were defeated by the great Persian general, Varahran (*Bahram*). **Bahram** was then ordered to invade Lazica, but was met and defeated by the Romans on the Araxes. Superseded and insulted by the king, he rebelled. Hormisdas was deposed and murdered, and succeeded by his son,

589–628. KHUSRU PARVIZ (*Chosroes II*), the last famous king of the Sassanian dynasty. Under him the Neo-Persian Empire reached its greatest extent and suffered also a sudden downfall. Defied by Bahram, Khusru was forced to flee to Constantinople, whereupon Bahram seized the throne and reigned as Bahram (*Varahran*) VI (590–591). Restoration of Khusru with the aid of the Emperor Maurice. Flight of Bahram to the Turks, by whom he was assassinated.

603–610. A victorious **war against Phocas,** the murderer of Maurice. Capture of Daras, Amida, Harran, Edessa, Hieropolis, Berhoea (Aleppo), etc. Armenia, Cappadocia, Phrygia, Galatia, and Bithynia ravaged.

610. A Persian force defeated by the Arabs at Dhu-Qar, a famous day in the annals of the tribes.

610–620. Accession of Heraclius as Roman emperor. War with Rome continued. Sack of Antioch and Apamea (611) by the Persians. Invasion of Cappadocia (612). Capture of Damascus (614). Sack of Jerusalem and capture of the "True Cross" (615). Capture of Pelusium and Alexandria by Shahr-Baraz. Subjugation of Egypt (616). Chalcedon taken. The Persians within a mile of Constantinople (617). Ancyra and Rhodes captured (620). Khusru had now restored the empire of Darius I, and the condition of the Roman Empire was desperate. Thrace was overrun by the Avars. Heraclius decided to flee to Carthage, but was prevented by the citizens of Constantinople. He determined as a forlorn hope to make use of his one great advantage, the possession of sea power, and carry the war to enemy territory.

622–627. The famous **campaigns of Heraclius.** Disembarkment at Issus and defeat of Shahr-Baraz (622). Expedition to Lazica and invasion of Armenia (623). Retreat of Khusru and wintering of Heraclius in Albania. The second invasion of Armenia. Surprise and defeat of Shahr-Baraz (624). Invasion of Arzanene and the recovery of Amida and Martyropolis.

Campaign in Cilicia. Indecisive **battle of the Sarus.** Retreat of Shahr-Baraz (625).

626. THE SIEGE OF CONSTANTINOPLE. Alliance between Khusru and the Avars. Two Persian armies placed in the field, one against Heraclius in Asia Minor, the other to co-operate with the Avars in the siege of Constantinople. The first under Shahen, the captor of Chalcedon, was defeated by the emperor's brother, Theodore. The second was prevented by the Roman command of the sea from assisting the Avar assault on Constantinople, which failed.

627. Invasion of Assyria and Mesopotamia by Heraclius. Defeat of the Persians near Nineveh. Flight of Khusru. Heraclius marched on Ctesiphon, but did not besiege it. His retreat to Canzaca. Mutiny of the Persian troops in Ctesiphon under Gurdanaspa, their commander. Imprisonment and murder of Khusru, he was succeeded by

628–629. Kobad II (*Siroes*), who made peace with Heraclius on the basis of an exchange of conquests and prisoners and the surrender of the "True Cross." The massacre of his brothers and his death by plague (629). The usurpation of Shahr-Baraz and his murder by his own troops (629). The reign of **Purandukht** and that of **Azarmidukht,** daughters of Khusru Parviz, followed by a period of anarchy, in which pretender after pretender aspired to the throne and perished almost immediately (629–634).

634–642. Yezdigird III, grandson of Khusru Parviz, and last Sassanian king of Persia, whose story is that of the expansion of the Muslim caliphate eastwards.

633–651. Arab invasion of Iraq under Khalid ibn al-Walid. Hira and Obolla taken. The Arab advance checked temporarily at the **Battle of the Bridge.** The Persians under Rustam were decisively defeated by the Arabs under Sa'd ibn-abi-Waqqas at **Qadisiya** (637). Mesopotamia invaded by Sa'd and Ctesiphon (*Madain*) captured. Defeat of the Persians at Jalula (637). Invasion of Susiana and Fars (639). Defeat of the Persians at Ram Hormuz; Shuster taken; conquest of Khuzistan (640). Final defeat of the Persians under Firuzan at **Nehawand** (642). Conquest of the Persian provinces and their incorporation into the caliphate. Flight of Yezdigird to Balkh; his appeal for help to the Emperor of China; his murder in a miller's hut near Merv (651).

2. INDIA, 72 B.C.–500 A.D.

(*From p. 56*)

a. NORTHERN INDIA

1st century B.C. Dating of the known Saka rulers, the **"Great King Moga"** or Maues, Azes, and Azilises, raises a complex chronological problem affecting the whole epoch from 100 B.C. to 200 A.D. It springs from multiplicity of eras, which are hardly ever explicitly identified.

The **Pahlavas** (Parthians closely related to the Scythians) under Vonones and his brother Spalirises became independent in eastern Iran with the title of "King of Kings" sometime (c. 30? B.C.) after the death of Mithridates II (88 B.C., supposed by L. de la Vallée Poussin to begin a Pahlava era). **Azes II**, son of Spalirises, succeeded the Sakas in the Punjab. Pacores was the last to rule as suzerain, although others probably continued as satraps.

The Kushana **Kujula Kadphises** forcibly united the five tribes of Yüeh-chih in Bactria (end 1st century B.C.) and seized from the Pahlavas the Kabul Valley and adjacent regions. His son **Vima Kadphises** conquered northwestern India and ruled it by deputy till his death at 80. An inscription near Panjtar speaks of a "Gushana Great King" under date "122" which is 64 or 34 A.D. by the Azes or Pahlava systems. The inscriptions of "136" similarly belongs to 78 or 48 A.D.

c. 78–176+ A.D. A second Kushana dynasty was founded by

c. 78–96+ A.D. KANISHKA, who extended his rule from Benares and Kabul to the Vindhyas, and established his capital at Peshawar. Whether or not the era he founded is the "Saka" era of 78 A.D., he probably came to the throne near that date. The Chinese *Later Han History* says:

84. A Yüeh-chih king was allied to Sogdiana by marriage, and by presents to him Pan Ch'ao secured the help of the latter against Kashgar.

88. The king presented precious stones and lions with a request for a Chinese princess, peremptorily refused by Pan Ch'ao.

90. A punitive army of 70,000 sent across the Pamirs under the Yüeh-chih viceroy Hsieh was starved into surrender by Pan, the ablest strategist of his time, who exacted payment of annual tribute. Although the king is not named, only a powerful ruler could have played so strong a hand across the mountains. Some scholars identify Kanishka rather with King Chien of Khotan, who was killed in error by a Chinese envoy in 152 A.D. The

Chinese source does not, however, suggest any connection of this king with the Yüeh-chih or with India.

Kanishka appears to have been tolerant in religion, and built a great stupa at Peshawar over relics of the Buddha. A fourth church council, unknown to the Pali sources, was apparently convoked at Jalandhara in the Punjab by the powerful Sarvastivadin, a realist sect of the conservative Theravacla. It probably supervised translation into Sanskrit of the canon which had been fixed in Prakrit in Mathura, the Punjab, and Kashmir in the last centuries B.C. The earliest and most vigorous classical Sanskrit is found in Asvaghosha's *Saundarananda* ("Conversion of Nanda") and the *Buddhacharita,* an artistic versified life of the Buddha, together with a work long supposed to be his *Sutralamkara,* which is now identified as the *Kalpanamanditika* of Kumaralata, a junior contemporary.

2nd century A.D. Kanishka's successors with their inscriptions (dated in terms of his reign) are: his son Vasishka (24, 28, 29); the latter's son Kanishka II (41); his younger brother Huvishka (29 or 33–60); Vasushka, son of Kanishka II (68, 74); and Vasudeva (76–98).

Asoka's inscriptions name three **Tamil states** in the Carnatic: Pandya (extreme south), Chola (southeast), and Chera or Kerala (southwest coast, chief port Muziris). These competed with Maesolia at the mouth of the Kistna and especially with the rich western port of Barygaza (Broach) in thriving trade with the Roman Empire. An embassy to Augustus (c. 22 B.C.) was sent by a king "Pandion" who may have been a Pandya. Strabo (d. 21 A.D.) speaks of fleets of 120 ships from Egypt to India, and Pliny (23–79) values annual imports from India at 50 million sesterces.

The **DECCAN** was dominated (from c. 100 B.C. to c. 225 A.D.) by a dynasty called **Andhra** by the late *Puranas* but **Satavahana** or **Satakani** in their own Prakrit inscriptions. Founded by Simuka on the ruins of the Sunga-Kanva power, with capital at Pratishthana (Paithan) on the upper Godavari, its early conquests to north and northwest were appropriated by the Saka satraps. A Saka satrap **Bhumaka** established Scythian power on the northwest coast (c. 70 A.D.). Nahapana, junior to him, ruled many years over Surashtra (Kathiawar) and the adjacent coast with capital probably at Junnar, east of Bombay. Named Mambanos in the *Periplus* (c. 89), his inscriptions are dated "41–46" (?119–124 A.D.), probably with reference to the Saka era of 78.

c. 109–132+. Gotamiputa Siri Satakani conquered Surashtra from Nahapana, and in an inscription at Nasik (18th year of his reign, c. 126) claimed not only the Deccan from the Vindhyas to Banavasi, but less probably Malwa as well. Very likely by this epoch the Satakani had extended control over the properly Andhra Telugu (Dravidian) lands of the Godavari and Kistna deltas. The Prakrit poems of the *Sattasai* in part date from this time. Liberal toward all religions, the Satakani especially exalted the Brahmans.

Sculptures about the great Buddhist stupa of Amaravati on the lower Kistna reveal union of Hindu traditional style with its crowding and naturalism, already more refined than at Bharhut and Sanchi, with Greco-Buddhist motifs which were borrowed from Gandhara and in turn transmitted to Malaya, Sumatra-Java, Cambodia, and Champa.

c. 120–c. 395. A DYNASTY OF WESTERN SATRAPS of Ujjain in Malwa was founded by Bhumaka's son Chashtana (Tiastanes of Ptolemy, c. 150).

c. 170. Rudradaman, Chashtana's grandson, in a Sanskrit inscription at Girnar in Kathiawar, records repair of a dam which broke in 150 A.D., defeat of northern tribesmen, and repeated rout of the southern Satakani.

Ujjayini (Ujjain) became a center of Sanskrit learning, and was taken as meridian by Indian astronomers. At Mathura, where sculpture early resembled that of Bharhut and Sanchi, and later imitated the forms of Gandhara, the heavy drapery of the Hellenistic school was rendered transparent, and schematized in decorative ridges, creating the so-called *Udayana Buddha,* carried to China and Japan.

The Buddhist community was now divided between two means to salvation: the **Hinayana** or Lesser Vehicle, which retained much of the primitive simplicity of the *Dharma,* "Law" by which Buddhism was then named; and the **Mahayana** or Great Vehicle, which emphasized personal devotion to Sakyamuni and exalted Bodhisattva (future Buddhas) as saviors. Although practically deified in the *Lalitavistara* (2nd century ?, Chinese trans. 308) and *Saddharma-pundarika-sutra,* "Lotus of the Good Law" (Chinese trans., 265–316), Buddha is regarded as but the human representative (*manushi-buddha*), for the current epoch, of an infinite series of buddhas. Popular bodhisattvas are Avalokitesvara (*Lotus Sutra,* ch. 24), Manjusri (*Avatamsaka-sutra,* 2nd–3rd centuries, Chinese trans. 317–420), Samantabhadra, and Kshitigarbha, all of whom have deferred their own illumination to succor struggling

mankind. The goal of effort is no longer sainthood or final absorption in nirvana, but direct attainment of buddhahood or rebirth to indefinite residence in a celestial paradise. Nagarjuna (2nd century), founder of the *Madhyamika Sutra* teaches that all sensory and mental experience is illusion, and comments on the *Prajñaparamita,* "*Perfect Wisdom*" (Chinese trans. 160) which consists in recognition of the Buddhist law as sole reality.

Already before our era Indian writers recognized and wrote treatises about three phases of human existence: *dharma,* religious and moral duty; *artha,* politics and practical life; and *kama,* love. The *Artha-sastra* (compounded from earlier materials c. 300–330) aims to teach a prince the whole science of successful rule according to accepted principles. It assumes autocratic monarchy, justification of all means by the end (personal aggrandizement), and chronic war. It advocates use of spies in all quarters; deception, intimidation, false witness, and confiscation to obtain money; cunning, and assassination. Virtuous rule is described because desirable to win affection of a conquered people. The *Kama-sutra* ("Laws of Love") by Vatsyayana Mallanaga (c. 4th century or later) imitates the *Artha-sastra* in both form and morals.

320–c. 535. The **GUPTA DYNASTY** united northern India after five centuries' division.

320–c. 330. Chandragupta I ruled from Pataliputra (Patna), having strengthened his position by marriage into the ancient Lichchavi tribe. His son

c. 330–c 375. Samudragupta completed the conquest of the north (Aryavarta) and won glory by traversing Telugu lands to force homage of the Pallava. Claiming to receive tribute from southeastern Bengal, Assam, and Nepal, with presents from the Kushan "son of Heaven and king of kings" (now actually vassal of the Sassanids) in Kabul-Kapisa-Gandhara, the satrap of Ujjain, the King Meghavanna (352–379) of Ceylon (who founded a monastery at Gaya for his subjects), he revived the Vedic horse-sacrifice which sanctified claim to the title of "universal monarch." He was a patron of poetry and music.

c. 375–c. 415. Chandragupta II Vikramaditya (on throne in 379) ended the satrapy of Ujjain by conquest of Malwa, Gujerat, and Surashtra (between 388 and 401). He moved his capital to Ayodhya (in Oudh) and then to Kausambi on the Jumna.

c. 415–455. Kumaragupta I probably founded the monastic community at Nalanda which was the principal Buddhist seminary till it burned c. 988.

455–c. 467. Skandagupta repulsed the White

Huns, as heir apparent and as emperor (455). 77-495+. **Budhagupta,** one of the last emperors of the dynasty, ruled from northern Bengal to eastern Malwa, perhaps to Surashtra. After c. 500 the chief branch of his house ruled as kings of Magadha till the 8th century.

The **Brahman legal writers** defined the social structure and ritual obligations. The *Dharma Sastra* of **Manu** (1st century B.C.?) was respected and freely utilized by later writers. The *Dharma Sutra* of **Vishnu** (3rd century A.D.), like the epics, recognized *suttee,* widow-burning, though it is not yet recommended. The days of the week were named from Greek sources. **Yanjavalkya** (4th century) admitted documentary evidence, and recommended use of ordeals of ploughshare, scales, and poison in addition to Manu's fire and water. **Narada** (5th century) first omitted religious and moral precepts from legal discussion. **Brihaspati** (c. 600 or 700) cited nine ordeals. Punishments: impalement, hanging, burning, mutilation, fines, and outcasting were adjusted to caste. A plaintiff might enforce justice by fasting to death on a debtor's premises. Fa-hsien, pioneer Chinese Buddhist pilgrim at the height of Gupta power, stated that fines were usually imposed, and that mutilation was reserved for brigands and rebels. He was enthusiastic about the peace and happiness of northern India (401-409) and Ceylon (410-411).

Six **schools of Hindu philosophy** (or rationalized religion) developed during the first centuries before and after Christ. They enjoy orthodox status in that all recognize the primordial and eternal character of the *Veda,* although in fact they do not derive from it. None is concerned primarily with ethics, but all seek freedom from bondage through deeds to rebirth. Escape for the soul is found in knowledge and cessation of thought. The *Purvamimamsa* is a systematization of rules for sacrifice. The *Vaiseshika-sutras* are variously dated from the 2nd century (Masson-Oursel) or 4th-5th centuries (Stcherbatsky). They elaborate an analysis of matter as composed of atoms combined in molecules under influence of time and direction. Souls are bound through linkage to such matter. The Nyaya is a system of logic calculated to attain that knowledge necessary to freedom. The *Yoga-sutras* (5th century?) teach rigid concentration of mind and body, a method open to all and regarded as valuable by many diverse religious groups. The *Samkhya-karika* is attributed to Isvarakrishna (3rd or 4th century? Chinese trans. c. 560). It sets forth a dualistic system teaching that the eternal soul can be freed by realization that it is not material like the world about it. The *Brahma Sutra* (c. 350-400) gives

the first clear expression of the Vedanta *darsana,* or "point of view," developed continuously from the older *Upanishads:* God is everything, the soul is God, and it is the task of the high-caste Brahman to realize in contemplation this identity.

Vasubandhu (c. 300-350), leading philosopher of Hinayana Buddhism, in his *Abhidharmakosa sastra* gave a classic summary of the Vibhasha and of the Vaibhashika school based upon it, with illuminating comments on the competing Sautrantika school founded by Kumaralabdha (c. 150-200) and developed by Harivarman. Vasubandhu was converted to the Mahayana by his brother Asanga, founder of the Vijñanavadin (Idealist) or Yogachara (Mystic) school, which explains phenomena as mere reflections of ideas and exalts the bodhisattvas, in particular Maitreya. The active translator to Chinese, **Kumarajiva** (c. 344-413), and the logician **Dignaga** (c. 5th century) were both adherents of this school, which developed important branches at Valabhi and Nalanda (6th-7th centuries). Fa-hsien first reported Mahayanist monasteries separate from those of the Hinayana.

Literary studies at Ujjain blossomed under the Guptas into the **golden age of classical Sanskrit. Arya Sura** in the *Jatakamala* (Chinese trans. 428) put into elegant *kavya* verse tales of former births of the Buddha which had been best known through the *Divyavadana* (Chinese trans. in part, 265). Secular fables gathered into the *Panchatantra* passed through Pehlvi (531-570), Syriac (570), and Arabic (750) into the languages of Europe. The *Sakuntala* and *Vikramorvasi* of **Kalidasa** (c. 400-455) rank first among Indian dramas (Greek influence), his *Meghaduta* equally high as a lyric poem, while his *Kumarasambhava,* and *Raghuvamsa* mark the apogee of *Kavya,* scholarly epic poetry. Literary taste survived the Gupta Empire: witness **Sudraka's** drama, *Mrichchakatika* ("Little Clay Cart"), and **Dandin's** romance *Dasakumaracharita* (both 6th century) and **Santideva's** brilliant poem of Mahayanist altruism, *Bodhicharyavatara* (late 7th century).

As in literature, so in **art** the Gupta period is one of dignity, restraint, and refinement: classicism in a land given to exaggeration.

Indian medicine largely parallels the Greek, but was limited, and surgery atrophied, by objection to dissection. An ethical code like the Hippocratic oath appears in works of Charaka and Susruta (prior to 4th century, though present texts date from 8th and 11th). Greek origin is clear for many astronomical ideas in the (4th century?) treatises summarized in **Varahamihira's** *Panchasiddhantika* (c. 550).

Zodiacal division of the ecliptic replaces the (Babylonian?) Nakshatras; planetary motion is explained by epicycles; parallax and eclipses are calculated, etc. But many Indian inconsistencies suggest that Greek astronomy was known imperfectly, perhaps through rule-of-thumb manuals. **Aryabhata** (499) taught rotation of the earth and the value of π as 3.1416 (epic value 3.5). **Brahmagupta** (b. 598) systematized the rules of astronomy, arithmetic, algebra, and geometry. His integral solution of an indeterminate equation, with another method given by **Bhaskara** in his *Siddhantasiromani* (1150) is called by Hankel the finest thing in numerical theory before Lagrange (1736–1813). The abacus was described in the *Abhidharmakosa* from 1st-century sources long before its use in China (1303–1383). More important, the zero (actually a superscribed dot) is attested in Indian literature (600), and the decimal position in a Sanskrit inscription in Cambodia (604) before they passed to the Arabs of Syria (662), and thence to the Europeans.

b. SOUTHERN INDIA

The whole Indian peninsula south of the Vindhyas, save for a part of Maharashtra (Nasik and Pratishthana) easily accessible from Malwa and already Aryanized before our era, was occupied by **Dravidians:** Canarese on the northwest, Telugu on the east, and Tamil in the Carnatic. Jainism, brought to Sravana Belgola in Mysore under Chandragupta (end 4th century B.C.), flourished in the Digambara, "naked clergy," form which the north rejected. Buddhism with its stupas and sculpture was brought to Amaravati and Mysore under Asoka. Sanskrit and Hindu culture were carried from the south to Cambodia about the opening of our era. Sanskrit influence is clear in the early Tamil grammar *Tolkappiyam*, and the *Kural* of Tiruvalluvar, lofty songs of a priest of pariahs (2nd–3rd centuries A.D.). Brahman colonies with Hinduism and the caste system were at various periods imported from the Ganges Valley and endowed by local rulers, as was done also in Bengal.

The south, however, placed its own impress on what it received, and developed linga-worship, *bhakti* devotion to Vishnu and Siva organization of Saiva monasteries and laymer occasional violent religious intolerance, an municipal and corporate life with a sacrificia spirit of personal loyalty.

c. 225. Breakup of the Satakani Empire led t establishment, in Maharashtra near Nasik, of

c. 250–c. 500. Traikutaka dynasty, probabl founded by chiefs of the pastoral Abhira tribe

c. 300–c. 500. The Vakatakas, extended thei power from the fortress of Gawilgarh in north ern Berar to Nagpur, Bundelkhand, and Kur tala, probably limiting Gupta expansion to th south.

Farther south the **Chutu branch of the Sa takani,** called Andhrabhrityas in the Purana: ruled at Banavasi (c. 200–c. 250) where the were succeeded by

c. 350–c. 500. The **Kadamba dynasty,** founde by a Brahman rebel from the Pallava. H great-grandson **Kakutsthavarman** (c. 435–47! married his daughters to a Gupta, a Vakatak (445), and a Ganga of Mysore.

In the Telugu lands, the Andhras were suc ceeded by the **Ikshvaku dynasty** (3rd century notable for donations to a Buddhist stupa o the Nagarjunikonda (hill), on the Kistna abov Amaravati; by the

c. 300–450. Salankayana of Vengi; and by th
c. 400–611. Vishnukundins, a dynasty of least ten kings at the same place.

c. CEYLON

Ceylon traditionally received Buddhism fro Asoka under

?247–?207 B.C. Devanampiya Tissa, wh founded the Mahavihara or Great Monaster at his capital Anuradhapura. The Pali *Trip taka,* which reflects Theravadin tradition, w; written under

89–40 or 29–?17 A.D. Vattagamani, wh founded the rival Abhayagiri Monastery. H epoch is supported by the geography (c. 9(200 A.D.) of the *Mahaniddesa,* a commentai admitted late to the Canon. Under

412–434. Mahanaman, Buddhaghosha of M. gadha, author of the *Visuddhimagga* or "W; of Purity," recorded in Pali Singhalese trad tions.   (*Cont. p. 355*

3. CHINA, 221 B.C.–618 A.D.

(*From p. 57*)

221–207 B.C. The **CH'IN DYNASTY** established by the self-styled "First Emperor" (**Shih Huang Ti,** b. 259; acceded 247; d. 210), ad-

vised by **Li Ssu.** Territorial reorganization in 36 *chün,* each under civil, military, ar supervisory officials. Disarmament by melti down weapons. Standardization of law, weights and measures, and axle length to facilitate interstate commerce.

14. Earlier ramparts linked by convict labor to form the **Great Wall** against the Turkish Hsiung-nu or Huns. Strategic roads. Wholesale transportation of families, especially criminals, to strengthen defenses and weaken particularism. Central South China conquered, from T'ai and Miao tribes, as far as the Southern Mountains and Canton, with the help of a new canal at Hsing-an, from present-day Hunan into Kwangsi.

13. **Proscription of books** that had been employed by enemies of the new order. Exception made for all scientific works and for those in the hands of 70 official scholars. Introduction of roll silk as writing material led to improvement of hair brush (attributed to Gen. Meng T'ien, d. 209) and to standardization and simplification of script (attributed to Li Ssu). Old complex characters were quickly forgotten.

6. **Epic struggle of Hsiang Yü against Liu Pang** (posthumous temple name [Han] Kao Tsu), who founded

2 B.C.–9 A.D. The **FORMER OR WESTERN HAN DYNASTY,** with capital at Ch'ang-an. Classic illustration of the typical Chinese dynastic pattern: foundation by rude warrior and administrator; gradual weakening of ruling line; renascence under a strong successor whose reign reveals cultural progress; further degeneration of dynasty, weakening of control over officials, oppression, revolts, dissolution. In general the Han continued the Ch'in system of administration, gradually increasing the *hün* from 36 to 108.

The study of number theory continued (concepts of negative numbers, fractions, and rules for measurement contained in a treatise that dates from 120 B.C.). In astronomy the sundial was introduced during the Han dynasty and first observations on sunspots were made (28 B.C.). The first maps also date from this period.

0. The emperor was surrounded for seven days by the Hsiung-nu, who had formed the first Turkish Empire in Mongolia during the preceding decade. The gift of an imperial princess as consort (repeated in 173), with other presents, secured peace till 166.

6. **Chao T'o** was recognized as king of southern Yüeh (the modern Kwang provinces), which he had conquered for the Ch'in in 218–14. An expedition against him in 181 ended in disaster.

1. Withdrawal of proscription of conservative literature permitted private scholars in the cultured East to begin its restoration and (equally vital) to transcribe it into modern characters.

155–130. **Liu Teh,** prince of Ho-chien, collected a library of archaic texts. His cousin, Liu An, prince of Huai-nan (d. 122), directed an inclusive compilation of early (especially Taoist) philosophy.

140–87. The **reign of Wu Ti,** "The Martial Emperor," was notable alike for foreign conquests and for the establishment of Confucian scholarship in control of civil administration.

140. **Tung Chung-shu** advocated Confucian training for a civil service, and urged limitation of private holding of land and slaves to remedy undue concentration of wealth resulting from commerce and mining on a national scale. As result of his efforts the emperor appointed in

136. **Doctors of the Five Classics.** These were the *I* or Changes (an early divination manual); the *Shih* or Odes; the *Shu* or History (documents compiled in the 6th century); the *Ch'un Ch'iu* or Annals of Confucius; and the *Shih-li* (now *I-li*) or Rituals. All were studied in terms of moralistic and ritual commentaries. The Han had followed the bad precedent of the Chou by granting fiefs to relatives and assistants, and found that direct efforts to weaken them resulted in revolt of seven princes (154).

127. **Chu-fu Yen** solved the problem by suggesting that younger sons should share by inheritance one-half of their father's fief. He thus also demonstrated the utility of the scholars.

126. **Chang Ch'ien** returned empty-handed, but with new knowledge of Central Asia and India, from a mission (138) to secure help against the Hsiung-nu from the **Yüeh-chih,** an Indo-European people who had been driven by the Hsiung-nu west from the Chinese border into Ili, and had thence invaded Hellenistic Bactria.

124. **Creation of a Grand College** to train officials for civil service through study of what was now fast becoming Confucian orthodoxy.

121–119. The Hsiung-nu were driven north of the Gobi by **Ho Ch'ü-ping** (d. 117, aged 22). They then split into northern and southern divisions (54).

111–110. **Subjugation of eastern Yüeh** and southern Yüeh (along the coast from modern Chekiang to Tonkin), and of the southwest. These conquests rounded out the frontiers of modern "China proper," and gave the Chinese all the best lands in their known world. During the next century Chinese officials traveled on the coasting vessels of local southern merchants at least as far as the Indian Ocean, exchanging gold and silk for glass and pearls.

110. Wu Ti inaugurated the sacrifice to Heaven which has since been the primary prerogative and obligation of imperial office.

108. Conquest of Ch'ao Hsien, a border kingdom of Korea.

102. Conquest of the petty states of the Tarim Basin and **Ferghana** (Ta Yüan) by Li Kuang-li and a large army. Indo-European languages were spoken throughout this region: Tokharian and Kuchean in the northern oases, Eastern Iranian or Shaka in those of the south, while Sogdian served as *lingua franca.*

Imperial finances, drained by war, were replenished by sale of military titles (123), monopolies of salt and iron (119), forced contributions by the nobility (112), and commutation by fines of judicial sentences (97). They were inflated by debasement of currency (119). The government, guided by Sang Hung-yang, entered the grain business (110), buying cheap and selling dear until exactions of greedy officials led to repeal under Chao Ti (86–73).

The *Shih Chi* or Historical Memoirs, first general history of China and a model for later dynastic histories, was compiled by **Ssu-ma Ch'ien** (d. c. 87). **Tai Teh** and **Tai Sheng** compiled standard repertories of early ritual texts, the *Ta Tai Li-chi* and *Li-chi.* **Liu Hsiang** (79–8) prepared a series of reports on the contents of the imperial library. His son **Liu Hsin** (d. 23. A.D.) digested these to form the first classified inventory of extant literature, and rescued from archaic script several important texts, notably the *Tso-chuan* (cf. supra) and the *Chou-li* or Chou Ritual.

1–8. A.D. **Wang Mang** served as regent for child-emperors.

6. All candidates for office were required to take **civil service examinations.** Tribute of a live rhinoceros was presented on request by the distant but unidentified southern state of Huang-chih.

9–23. WANG MANG reigned as emperor of the **Hsin Dynasty,** and undertook radical reforms: nationalization of land with division of large estates and manumission of slaves had to be repealed (12); a tax on slaveholding was substituted in 17. To monopolies of salt, iron, and coinage was added one on wine, and other mining profits were taxed. Seven regional commissions were directed to establish annual high, low, and mean price levels for staple products; to buy surplus goods at cost; and to peg the market by sales above the seasonal index. To curb usury, loans were offered free up to 90 days for funerals, and at 3 per cent a month or 10 per cent a year for productive purposes. Merchants and capitalists employed as administrators provoked revolts, in one of which Wang was killed.

25–220. LATER OR EASTERN HAN DYNASTY, founded by a collateral imperial scion, (Hou Han) Kuang Wu Ti (25–57) reigned at Loyang. **Buddhism** was introduced by missionaries from Central Asia and later from India, probably about the time of Christ. In 65 A.D. the presence of monks and lay believers at his brother's court was favorably mentioned in a decree by Emperor Ming (58–75). The story of official introduction following a dream of this emperor has been shown by Maspero to be a pious legend, complete in its main outlines by the end of the 2nd century.

43. Ma Yüan conquered Tonkin and Annam, much of which remained (except for brief revolts) under Chinese control until 939. A few natives adopted the Chinese classics, Confucianism, and Buddhism; but the masses retained their own language and customs. Commercial relations through the southern sea were gradually extended. "Java" (perhaps then Sumatra) sent tribute early in 132, and traders from the Roman Empire reached Cattigara or Chiao-chih (now Tonkin) in 166 and 226. A newly organized Malay people, the Chams, occupied Quangnam, the region of Tourane, c. 192; but when they came farther north they were repelled (270, 360, and 446).

74–94. Pan Ch'ao, by personal diplomacy and strategy, brought into submission all the petty states of Turkestan, opening the way for extensive silk trade with the Roman Orient (Ta Ch'in). His lieutenant Kan Ying penetrated the Persian Gulf (97). Even the Yüeh-chi, who had recently founded the Kushana Kingdom in the Indian Punjab, sent tribute in 90. The northern Hsiung-nu, as a result of successive defeats by the southern Hsiung-nu (85), by the Mongol Sien-pi (87), and by the Chinese general Tou Hsien (89), in part submitted, in part migrated westward, leaving their land to the Sien-pi, who in 101 in turn began raiding the frontier. To the west the Ch'iang Tibetans disturbed the peace of modern Kansu for several decades until repulsed by Chang Chung, 141–144.

After only two vigorous reigns the court was dominated by women, by their relatives, and by eunuchs by whom they were surrounded.

82. Empress Tou altered the succession, and with her family, ruled as dowager (88–97).

105–121. Empress Teng ruled as dowager for her infant son and his boy successor till his death, when her most prominent relative chose suicide.

124. A change in succession made by Empress Yen was violently reversed in the same year.

132. Empress Liang secured honors for her father, and ruled for three youthful emperors.

from 144 until her death in 150. A younger empress of the same family survived until 159.

159. Emperor Huan finally compassed the death of Liang Chi, brother of the elder empress.

184. Rebellion of the Yellow Turbans, provoked by the rapacity of the eunuchs, against whose influence and ruthless murder of scholars opposed to them there had been vigorous protests in 135–136.

189. Massacre of the eunuchs by Yüan Shao.

190–220. Emperor Hsien, last of the Later Han dynasty, never really governed, the actual power having passed to competing military dictators.

Insecurity of life and property contributed to the popularity of **religious Taoism,** a cult of mysticism and occultism which promised longevity or even immortality as a reward for support, faith, and monastic austerity. Its founders, **Chang Ling** (according to tradition he ascended into heaven in 156 at the age of 123) and his son **Chang Heng,** claimed authority from Lao-tzu and philosophic Taoism, but followed the practices of alchemy, breath-control, and magic inherited from charlatans who had infested the courts of Ch'in Shih Huang Ti and Han Wu Ti. Their successors slavishly imitated Buddhism by creation of a divine hierarchy, a voluminous textual canon, and a monastic community.

Cultural tradition was maintained by **Pan Ku** (32–92), who compiled the dynastic *History of the Former Han,* his sister **Pan Chao,** whose *Lessons for Women* codified the standard of feminine morality, and **Hsü Shen,** who completed in 100 the first lexicon of archaic script, *Shuo wen chieh tzu.* The rhymed and rhythmic prose-form *fu* was developed at this time. In 105 the eunuch **Ts'ai Lun** presented to court **paper** made of vegetable fibers: bark, hemp, fish nets, and rags. Paper rolls now rapidly supplanted bamboo or wooden slips strung with cords, and the costly roll silk and silk floss paper. The first mathematical text *Chou Pei Suan Ching* dates from the 3rd century and counting rods from the 5th century (rod numerals in evidence from the 1st century). The applications of mathematics are illustrated through the practical examples used in the texts. The first accurate figure for π is that of **Tsu Ch'ung-chih** and was computed between 430–501 A.D. In the 3rd century the first charts of the heavens appear and the astrolabe is used as an astronomical instrument. During the 5th century the foot stirrup was invented either in China, or Korea. **Ma Jung** invented the device of double-column commentary (138–140). Six classics were first engraved on stone (175–183) to perpetuate the academic victory of the conservative school of commentators, who accepted only the earliest renderings into modern script. Figure painting (portraits of 28 generals) and calligraphy (text for stone classics written by Ts'ai Yung) emerged as fine arts. Mortuary chapel of Wu Liang decorated with stone flat reliefs (151).

220–264. THREE KINGDOMS divided the empire, each claiming imperial status.

220–264. Wei dynasty formally founded by Ts'ao P'ei, son of Ts'ao Ts'ao, who had dominated the court since 196. Loyang remained the capital. Eunuchs excluded from government. Families of empresses excluded from future exercise of regency (222). Three classics cut in stone (240–248) to establish versions sponsored by the Archaic Text School, founded by Liu Hsin.

221–264. Shu or Shu-Han dynasty founded in the west by Liu Pei (d. 223), antagonist of Ts'ao Ts'ao since 194. Capital at Ch'eng-tu. Chuko Liang chief minister 221–234. Rapid development of Szechwan.

222–280. Wu dynasty founded by Sun Ch'üan in the lower Long River Valley with capital at Chien-K'ang (modern Nanking).

c. 245–250. K'ang T'ai mission to Fu-nan, Khmer state in southern Cambodia (first tribute 243), learned details of southern Asia from the envoy of the Indian king.

265–317. Nominal reunion under weak **Western Chin dynasty,** established by rebellion of Ssu-ma Yen against the Wei. Institution of the censorate.

317–589. Southern and Northern dynasties divided the empire. Six dynasties (counting the eastern Wu) ruled at Chien-K'ang. The later five are considered legitimate:

317–420. Eastern Chin dynasty.

420–479. Former (or **Liu**) **Sung dynasty,** so called from the eight emperors of the Liu family.

479–502. Southern Ch'i dynasty.

502–557. Southern Liang dynasty.

557–589. Southern Ch'en dynasty. Meantime a series of barbarian dynasties was established in the north by invasion and infiltration of diverse peoples who avidly sought Chinese culture, followed Chinese precedents, and were rapidly absorbed.

304–439. Sixteen kingdoms established along the northern marches by three Chinese and leaders of five northern peoples: three Turkish Hsiung-nu, five Mongol Sien-pi, three Ti, one Chieh, and one Tibetan Ch'iang.

386–534. Northern Wei dynasty, founded at Ta-t'ung by the Toba Tatars, who spoke a Mongol dialect strongly palatalized by contact with the Tungus. In 495 the capital was transferred to Loyang.

534–550. The **Eastern Wei dynasty** ruled at

Ye (present An-yang) as did their successors, **550–557. The Northern Ch'i.** Meanwhile at Ch'ang-an

535–556. The **Western Wei** were succeeded by **557–581.** The **Northern Chou,** who overthrew the Northern Ch'i in 577.

This long epoch of political division retarded cultural progress. Pseudo-reconstruction of texts which had been added to the *Canon of History* by K'ung An-kuo in the 2nd century B.C., but lost in the 1st century A.D., was probably carried out c. 250, and was presented to the throne in 317–322. Thirteen texts, including the *Bamboo Annals,* were recovered (281) from a tomb which was closed in 299 B.C. Gen. **Wang Hsi-chih** (321–379) provided the classic models (cut in stone) for formal and cursive calligraphy. **Ku K'ai-chih** (c. 344–c. 406) perfected the technical refinement of episodic figure-painting.

Buddhism flourished in China already by the close of the Han. The splendor of the Buddhist pantheon and ritual, with its novel conceptions which embraced 10 heavens, 10 hells, rebirth, and salvation of individual souls of common men, proved irresistible. Sutras were translated in terms borrowed from philosophic Taoism chiefly by Indian and Central Asiatic missionaries, among whom the most prolific was **Kumarajiva** (c. 344–413, to China 383), son of an Indian and of a princess of Kucha. Indian sectarian divergencies became reflected especially in versions of the monastic law (*vinaya*). Desire for direct intelligence of authoritative texts led at least 82 Chinese pilgrims to visit India during the period 200–600 (61 in the 5th century alone). Fa-hsien blazed the desert trail across Central Asia and returned by sea (399–414), and Sung-yun followed the land route to and from Udyana and Gandhara (518–522). Most popular text of the 6th century was the *Parinirvana-sutra,* which recounts the birth, illumination, first teaching, and death of the Buddha. Unfavorable Confucian appraisal of Indian asceticism, parasitic practices (celibacy, monasticism, mendicancy), and unrestrained imaginative metaphysical literature, together with hostility of the competing Taoist priesthood, led to brief persecution by the Northern Wei (446) and by the Northern Chou (574).

The Northern Wei cut **cave temples** in the Yün-kang cliffs near Ta-t'ung and decorated them with Buddhist sculpture in imitation of the "Caves of a Thousand Buddhas" at Tunhuang, then the point of bifurcation of trade routes north and south of the Tarim basin. After 495 new caves were cut at Lung-men near Loyang. The various Buddhas, bodhisattvas, Lohan (Skt. Arhat or Saints), and militant

guardians of the law reflect Indian iconography given form by Greek artisans in Gandhara, as well as Iranian influence.

In Central Asia the Juan-juan or Avars founded the **first Mongol Empire** throughout Mongolia (407–553). Revolt by the T'u-chüeh in the Altai (551) led to establishment in imitation of it of a Turkish Empire which shortly (572) split into eastern and western divisions. The Western Turks assailed Sassanian Persia from the east, and by weakening it contributed to the triumph of Islam a few decades later.

581–618. The **Sui dynasty** was founded at Ch'ang-an by Yang Chien (Wen Ti), chief minister (580) of the Chou.

585 and 607–608. Reconstruction of the Great Wall (as in 543 by the Eastern Wei and in 556 by the Northern Ch'i), against the Eastern Turks of the Orkhon.

589. REUNION OF THE EMPIRE by conquest of the southern Ch'en dynasty.

Active patronage of Buddhism, the common religion of north and south, multiplied shrines and images. Chinese Buddhists increasingly neglected the intangible goal of Indian theology, the eventual ending of the perpetual chain of sentient existences by nihilistic absorption into nirvana; and stressed more pratical objectives: immediate response to prayer by the protective Bodhisattva Kuan-yin (Avalokitesvara), direct rebirth into the Western Happy Heaven (Sukhavati) of O-mi-t'o (Amitabha), and salvation by the coming Buddha Mi-lo-fo (Maitreya). Early Chinese philosophic divergencies reappeared within Buddhist sectarian doctrine. Taoist thought was reflected in the increasingly influential **Ch'an sect,** which taught that the Buddha-nature is in every man, and that illumination is to be sought solely through meditation, to the exclusion of prayer, asceticism, and good works. Confucian reaction was evident in the emphasis by the **T'ien-t'ai school,** founded (575) in the mountains of Chekiang by Chih-i (531–597), upon education as necessary to realization of the Buddha-nature. Strongly synthetic, approval was given to ecstasy, ceremonial, discipline, and to a variety of texts that were interpreted as corresponding to stages in the Buddha's teaching. Perfection was reached in the Lotus (*Saddharmapundarika*) Sutra, which thenceforth surpassed all others in popular favor.

602–605. Liu Fang suppressed rebellion in Annam, repelled the Chams, and sacked their capital Indrapura (near Tourane). The Chams now paid tribute for a century and a half. They controlled (until the 10th century) the trade in spices for China, and in silk and porcelain for the Abbasids, which was largely in the hands of Persian merchants. Probably before this time the Cambodian kingdom of Chen-la overthrew its suzerain Fu-nan, and now resumed tribute missions to China (616 or 617).

605–618. Yang Ti, a parricide (604), was ruined by extravagance at home and fruitless foreign wars.

605. The **Grand Canal** was formed by linking existing waterways from the sumptuous new capital at Loyang (604) to the Long River. It was extended to Cho-chün (near modern Peking) by a million laborers in 608, and to Hangchow in 610.

606. The **National College** was enlarged and the doctoral *chin-shih* degree first awarded. The first Japanese embassy was received from the Empress Suiko.

607. Appointment of P'ei Chü to command in the west led to defeat (608) of the Mongol T'u-yü-hun, who had entered the Koko-nor region in the early 4th century, and submission of minor kingdoms (609), but provoked the Eastern T'u-chüeh, who invested the emperor in Yenmen (615).

610. The king of the Liu-ch'iu Islands (or Formosa?) was killed by Ch'en Leng.

611–614. Disastrous wars with Kao-li in the Liao Basin and Korea completed exhaustion of the empire and provoked

613–618. Domestic revolts which led to murder of Yang Ti.

618–907. The **T'ang dynasty** was founded.

(*Cont. p. 363.*)

4. KOREA, 300 B.C.–562 A.D.

Korea is a mountainous peninsula 100 to 150 miles wide and about 400 miles long, extending southward from Manchuria toward the western tip of Japan. High mountains and the cold Japan Sea have retarded the development of the east coast, but the milder climate and more suitable terrain of the west coast facing China and the south coast opposite Japan have made these regions the natural centers of Korean history.

The people since prehistoric times seem to have been closely related racially, linguistically, and culturally to the ancient peoples of Manchuria and Siberia as well as to the Japanese, but their post-Neolithic civilization came largely from China.

c. 300–200 B.C. A semi-Sinicized state called **Chosŏn** (Japanese: Chōsen) developed in the northwest, and other less civilized states appeared in the south and east.

108 B.C. Emperor Wu Ti of the Han dynasty of China conquered Chosŏn and established four prefectures covering central and western Korea and centering around Lo-lang near the modern P'yŏng-yang (Chinese Ping-yang, Japanese Heijo), where an extensive Chinese colony grew up.

c. 150 A.D. Koguryŏ, founded over 100 years earlier in Manchuria and northern Korea, and other states in the south and east asserted their independence of the Chinese colony.

c. 210. The **Kung-sun family** of southern Manchuria obtained control of Lo-lang and established Tai-fang to the south of it.

c. 238. The **Wei dynasty** of China captured Lo-lang and Tai-fang by sea.

c. 250. Northern invaders established the state of **Paekche** in the southwest.

313. The last remnants of the Chinese colonies were extinguished by native states, and Chinese civilization was diffused throughout the peninsula by the dispersed Chinese colonists. This marked the beginning of

313–668. THE THREE KINGDOMS PERIOD. After the elimination of China, Korea remained for several centuries divided between Koguryŏ in the north, Paekche in the southwest, and Silla, established probably in the 2nd or 3rd century, in the southeast.

c. 360–390. Period of greatest **Japanese influence** and activity in Korea through their foothold on the coast between Silla and Paekche.

372. Koguryŏ received Buddhism from China.

413–490. King Changsu brought Koguryŏ to the height of its power and moved the capital from the banks of the Yalu River to P'yŏngyang (427).

528. Silla adopted Buddhism. The last of the Korean states to do so and culturally the most backward, Silla at this time began to make rapid progress and to expand at the expense of the Japanese sphere.

554. Silla won an outlet on the East China Sea in central Korea, giving her easy sea communications with China.

562. Silla destroyed Japan's sphere in Korea.

(*Cont. p. 372.*)

5. JAPAN, 230–645 A.D.

GEOGRAPHY. Japan proper consists of a group of islands running eastward from the southern tip of the Korean peninsula for some 700 miles and then turning abruptly northward for about the same distance, approaching the Asiatic mainland once more off the coast of the Maritime Province of Siberia. The cold Japan Sea enclosed by this island arc gives the inner side of the archipelago a cold, damp climate, but because of the Japan Current the Pacific coast of southwestern Japan enjoys a warm, temperate climate. Consequently, here the main centers of civilization have developed. Four main islands account for most of the land area of Japan. Hondō, the largest, extends for the greater part of the arc. The next largest, Hokkaidō or Ezo, lies to the north of Hondō. Kyūshū at the southwestern extremity and Shikoku east of it, together with the westernmost portion of Hondō, almost surround a long narrow strip of water known as the Inland Sea. Among the many lesser islands Tsushima and Iki are of most significance, for they lie in the straits between Korea and Japan.

The two most important areas of Japan are the group of small plains lying in Hondō at the eastern end of the Inland Sea and the great Kantō Plain around Tōkyō Bay in eastern Hondō. The Inland Sea, as an artery of communications, and northern and western Kyūshū, which face the Asiatic mainland, are also important regions.

The rivers are all short and shallow and are consequently of little significance. Mountains cover almost the entire area and are particularly high in central Hondō. Many of them are volcanic, and eruptions and earthquakes are frequent. The climate is temperate throughout the land, and rain is abundant. Since antiquity rice has been the principal crop.

ETHNOLOGY. The origin of the Japanese people is still in question. Archaeology and physical anthropology indicate a close connection with the Koreans and the Tungusic peoples of northeastern Asia. Linguistic evidence, though more hotly disputed, tends to support this. However, ethnographical evidence and mythology suggest South Chinese, Malaysian, or even Polynesian origin. Furthermore, the Ainu (also called Ezo and Emishi), possibly a proto-Caucasian people, originally inhabited the northeastern half of Japan and undoubtedly contributed to the racial composition of the Japanese. One may conclude, therefore, that, though the early Japanese seem to have been primarily a Mongolian people, there was probably some admixture of blood from southeast-ern Asia and from the Ainu.

RELIGION. The primitive religion of Japan was a simple worship of the manifold manifestations of the powers of nature combined with a system of ritualistic observances, notable among which was an insistence on physical and ritual purity. The deities tended to become anthropomorphic and to merge with memories of past heroes. They were also affected by attempts to explain the origins of man and society in mythological terms. This eventually resulted in an organized mythology centering around the sun-goddess (Amaterasu) and her descendants, the imperial family. After the introduction of Buddhism this combination of nature-worship, ritualistic observances, and ancestor-honoring mythology was given the name of **Shintō** to distinguish it from the Indian religion.

CIVILIZATION. Japan's earliest known civilization was a Neolithic shell-mound culture, which before the Christian era gave way to a culture featured by sepulchral mounds over dolmens containing pottery and iron and bronze objects which show a predominantly north Asiatic influence. Prehistoric Japanese civilization seems to have come from what is known linguistically as the Altaic region and seems early to have been influenced strongly by the much higher Chinese civilization.

HISTORY. The first authentic historical accounts of Japan occur in Chinese histories of the 3rd century A.D., and picture western Japan, if not all of Japan, as divided among a great number of small political units, among which feminine rule was not uncommon. Some of these petty states had direct relations with the Chinese colonies in Korea, and embassies from Japanese states to the Chinese capital are recorded from 57 to 266.

Japanese historical mythology commences with the accession of the first emperor, **Jimmu,** in 660 B.C., a date arbitrarily chosen, probably over thirteen centuries later. The mythology hints at the migration of the future imperial clan from Kyūshū up the Inland Sea to the plain of Yamato or Nara, and a successful contest for supremacy with another clan in Izumo on the Japan Sea. The Izumo clan seems to have had a rather distinctive culture and to have had close relations with Korea. During the first four centuries of the Christian era the imperial clan in Yamato seems gradually to have established its suzerainty over most of central and western Japan in a long series of wars with neighboring clans and with the Ainu in the east and the Kumaso in the west, a peo-

le apparently of alien and quite possibly of
outhern origin.

, 230 A.D. With the accession of the tenth
emperor, **Sujin,** Japanese records begin to contain some material of probable historical accuracy. The victories of the half-legendary
Prince Yamatodake over the Kumaso and the
Ainu seem to reflect a period of rapid expansion in the early decades of the 4th century.

360. The story of the **conquest of Korea** by
the Empress Jingō, ruling in the name of her
deceased husband and later in the name of her
son, probably refers to Japanese campaigns in
the peninsula. Korean records mention Japanese inroads during this century, and a Korean
inscription of 391 proves that their armies were
widely active in the peninsula at that time.
From this period probably dates the establishment of a Japanese protectorate over a group
of miniature states in southern Korea known
as Kara or Imna (Japanese, Mimana), which
had for long constituted a Japanese sphere of
influence, and at the same time a semi-protec-
torate over Paekche, a larger state in southwestern Korea. Japan in the 5th century claimed
suzerainty over all of Korea, but in reality her
power was on the wane even in the south, as
Silla, a vigorous kingdom in the southeast,
gradually rose to supremacy. The chief significance of the Korean contacts was that Japan
through them was able to imbibe deeply of
Chinese civilization and was able to open the
way once more for direct relations with China,
which was accomplished in 413.

About the end of the 4th century or early
in the 5th, scribes able to read and write Chinese are said to have come from Korea. This
implies the official **adoption of Chinese writing,**
but not the first knowledge of it in Japan.
Writing spread slowly, but was early used for
historical records, for by the first half of the
6th century the traditional Japanese chronology becomes reasonably accurate.

Japan's **social organization** as it emerged at
that time was that of a large group of clans
(*uji*) under clan chiefs (*uji-no-kami*). The
members of a single clan all claimed descent
from a common ancestor, often the clan god
(*ujigami*). The clan chief acted as high priest
to the clan god, and his political rule was
tinged throughout with a sacerdotal flavor.
The chief and his immediate family often had
one of several hereditary titles (*kabane*), which
in time came to be grouped hierarchically.
Below the clans were hereditary occupational
groups (*be* or *tomo*), often called guilds or
corporations. They were the economic foundation of the clan system. Below them in turn
was an inconsiderable number of slaves.

The **imperial clan** at first was little more

than hegemon among the various clans. Its
chief was the emperor, and its clan god was
made the national deity. Its rule over the
country was extremely loose and feeble. The
clans with the two most important hereditary
titles, *Omi* and *Muraji,* were controlled through
a chief *Omi* (*Oomi*) and a chief *Muraji* (*Omu-
raji*). *Tomo-no-miyatsuko* were placed over
the imperial clan's hereditary occupational
groups and *Kunino-miyatsuko* over its rice
lands. Chieftains of the Kume, Otomo, and
Mononobe clans served as imperial generals
and those of the Nakatomi and Imube (also
pronounced Imibe and Imbe) clans were in
charge of the court religious ceremonies.

The **importation of Chinese civilization** and
an influx of Korean immigrants seriously
shook the clan system. In imitation of China
there developed a greater centralization of
power in the hands of the imperial clan and
its ministers, who at times even aspired to the
throne themselves. Imperial lands were
gradually extended, and imperial authority
grew, eventually leading to a complete political
and economic reorganization of Japan on the
Chinese model.

? 527. A serious **revolt in Kyūshū** prevented
the crossing of an army to Korea to aid Imna.
Dissension among the Japanese and the treason of some of their officers in Korea seriously
reduced their prestige in the peninsula and
opened the way for the conquest of Imna by
Silla.

? 552. The official introduction of **Buddhism**
from Paekche, which itself had received it in
384, marked the beginning of a new epoch in
Japan. There probably were Buddhist converts
in Japan prior to 552, but at this time Buddhism first began to play a significant rôle in
Japanese history and to stimulate the influx of
Chinese civilization by way of Paekche. Supported by the powerful Soga clan and strengthened by the arrival of clerics from Korea, Buddhism made headway at court, but soon a
temporary proscription of it was brought about
by the Nakatomi and Mononobe clans, the
political rivals of the Soga. It was presently
restored, and the Emperor Yōmei (585-587?)
embraced the faith shortly before his death.

? 562. Silla drove the Japanese out of Imna,
ending their long direct control of a portion
of Korea.

? 587. The Soga crushed their rivals in a short
civil war, thereby establishing their political
supremacy and the right of Buddhism to an
unhampered development in Japan.

592. **Soga Umako** (d. 626) had his nephew, the
Emperor Sushun (587-592), murdered.

593-628. **Suiko,** the first officially recognized
empress, ruled over the land at the crucial pe-

riod when Buddhism was taking root and the importation of Chinese civilization was strongly influencing the basic forms of Japanese government and society. The leading spirit during her reign was the crown prince, **Shōtoku** (d. 621 or 622), who was the real establisher of Buddhism in Japan, the pioneer in laying the foundations for the Sinicized form of government of the next several centuries, and the founder of such great monasteries as the Shitennōji (593), the Hōkōji (588–596), and the Hōryūji (607?).

604. Prince Shōtoku issued the so-called **Seventeen Article "Constitution,"** a moral code consisting of somewhat vague injunctions imbued with Confucian ethics and the Chinese political theory of a centralized imperial government. Thus it served as an ideological basis for political centralization. The constitution was also strongly influenced by Buddhism and shows that the prince was aware of its moral and philosophical import and not merely of its supposed magical powers, which chiefly attracted the contemporary Japanese. In this same year, in imitation of China, official grades known as "cap ranks" (*kan'i*), an official calendar, and regulations for court etiquette were adopted.

607. Ono Imoko, the first official envoy from the central government, was dispatched to the Sui court in China. This and a second embassy to the Sui in 608 were followed in the course of the next two and a half centuries by twelve embassies to the T'ang. Since Japanese students, scholars, and monks accompanied the envoys to China and sometimes remained there for prolonged periods of study, these embassies were a very important factor in the importation of Chinese civilization to Japan.

630. First embassy to the T'ang.

643. Prince Yamashiro no Oe, the heir of Prince Shōtoku, was forced to commit suicide by Soga Iruka (d. 645), the son of Emishi (d. 645), the kingmaker of the period. The prince had twice been overlooked in the imperial succession by the Soga, whose obvious imperial aspirations brought about

645. The **DOWNFALL OF THE SOGA** in a *coup d'état* led by the future Emperor Tenchi (661–672) and by Nakatomi Kamatari (d. 669), the founder of a new clan, the Fujiwara. The incident gave the progressive element at court a chance to begin a series of sweeping reforms along Chinese lines, which mark the beginning of a new era in Japan. (*Cont. p. 373*)

III. THE MIDDLE AGES

III. THE MIDDLE AGES

A. THE EARLY MIDDLE AGES

1. WESTERN EUROPE

(*From p. 136*)

a. CONDITIONS OF LIFE

SCIENCE AND TECHNOLOGY were separate from one another during this period. The science was based on the work of the early Latin Encyclopaedists, Pliny, Boethius, Cassiodorius, Isidore of Seville. Thought was profoundly influenced by Neo-Platonism; and observational science was abandoned since nature was seen as vivid symbols of moral realities. Technological developments were slow and came in small steps, which however added up to the increased pulse of life of the 11th century. Communication was difficult; roads and harbors were unused and in disrepair until about the 8th century, when commerce began again on a more than local basis. Building was stagnant; the art of bricklaying appears to have been lost; scarcely any stone buildings were erected in northern Europe. Metal working was still important, although stamping was unskilled and hence coins were crude. Precious metals were worked with enamel decorations, while silver and bronze could be cast. Unlike the light Mediterranean soils, those of northern Europe could not be pulverised for farming purposes; these heavy soils had to be "sliced, moved to one side and turned over." This was impossible until the introduction of the iron, wheeled plowshare, with moldboard. The basic farm tools evolved during this period: rake, spade, fork, pick, balanced sickle, scythe. Development of the horse collar was very important, for an efficient draft animal relieved the small, work force. With an effective harness and stirrup (the latter depicted in a drawing c. 900) and tandem rather than fan-hitched teams of horses or oxen, men were freed of even more work. Another important source of power was water: the Roman water mill (in use 536) spread throughout Europe.

b. THE EARLY PAPACY, TO 461

[*For a complete list of the Roman Popes see Appendix IV.*]

The Church before the emergence of the bishops of Rome. The center of gravity was in the east. Possession of the Holy Places and the presence of the emperor gave the east political and ecclesiastical supremacy.

Rise of the episcopate. The bishops, originally overseers (*episcopus*), thanks to their consecration, the tradition of apostolic succession, and their control of the sacraments, were distinguished among the clergy. Each church was originally independent, but the evolution of an ecclesiastical counterpart to the centralized civil state gave the bishop a clearly monarchical quality in the 3rd century. The lay and ecclesiastical states met in the person of the emperor, and the original loose autonomy of the independent churches began to be lost in a centralized system. The precedence of **metropolitans** (i.e. the bishops of the great sees) was recognized (341), without reducing the accepted superiority of the **patriarchs.** The five patriarchates (ecclesiastical equivalents of exarchates) were (save for Rome) in the east—Jerusalem, Antioch, Alexandria, Constantinople. The west (including Rome) was either poorly represented or not represented at all at the ecumenical councils in the east. Vague precedence in honor was conceded to Rome, but no more.

Ecumenical councils settled general problems of dogma and discipline. These councils were called by the emperor and presided over by him in person or by legate. Local problems were dealt with in synods.

EMERGENCE OF THE BISHOPS OF ROME. *Papa* was a title applied to all bishops until c. 425, and did not take on its present meaning until the 7th century. **Bishop Victor** of Rome (c. 190) exercised a kind of spiritual sovereignty which was continued in the 3rd century. Gradually the recession of the Church of the east, the loss of Africa, and the rise of powerful churches in the east, left Rome isolated in the west. As the sole western apostolic see, the scene of the martyrdom of Peter, and guardian of the tombs of Peter and Paul, Rome enjoyed a unique spiritual prestige, and until the reign of Diocletian (284–305) it was the administrative center of the empire. After that the capital was at Milan, and this see at times was almost equal to Rome in influence. With the removal of the imperial capital to Constantinople (330), Rome lost prestige, especially in the east. On the other hand, between 330 and 395, since there was no emperor permanently resident in the west, the bishop of Rome had no political rival.

(1) The emperors supported the Roman campaign against paganism and against heresy (e.g. Arians and Donatists) with civil penalties, and confirmed and deprived bishops.

(2) The Roman See, as early as the days of Diocletian, was rich, and was further enriched by the emperors until it was the wealthiest in the Church; the bishop of Rome enjoyed the "presidency in charity" throughout Christendom.

(3) Sporadic intervention (usually on appeal) was made outside his direct jurisdiction by the bishop of Rome, but until after 1000 he rarely pronounced on doctrinal points on his own authority, nor did he interfere between a bishop and his flock in ordinary diocesan affairs or collect money except within his own immediate episcopal jurisdiction.

(4) The **Petrine theory,** on the basis of Matthew 16: 18, 19, asserts that Peter was designated by Christ as the founder of the Church, and that Christ conferred the "power of the keys," i.e. "the power to bind and loose," upon Peter, who transmitted it to his successor, the bishop of Rome, through whom it passed to all bishops. This theory was given currency by **Pope Celestine I** (422–432). In effect this abandoned the original concept of the bishop of Rome as *episcopus inter episcopos* for the more radical monarchical concept of the Roman bishop as *episcopus episcoporum.* Early writers give no indication of such interpretations, and Cyprian (d. 258) in a famous passage avers that the bishop of Rome is no more than a bishop among other bishops.

340. The introduction of **eremitical monasticism** into the west by Athanasius marked the beginning of a strong ascetic reaction against the corruption of western life. Supported by Jerome, Ambrose, and Augustine, this development led to a great growth of monasticism. Bishop Eusebius of Vercelli (d. 371), by insisting that his clergy lead a monastic life, began a practice that led to the general ordination of monks. Martin of Tours founded (c. 362) a cenobitic community of monks near Poitiers.

343. The **Council of Sardika** apparently recognized the right of appeal from a provincial synod to the bishop of Rome.

The oldest extant decretal dates from the episcopacy of **Siricius** (c. 384–399).

THE LATIN FATHERS OF THE CHURCH. Jerome (c. 340–420), a Dalmatian, devoted to pagan learning despite his keen ascetic convictions. The first great western exponent of monasticism. One of the greatest scholars of the Latin Church, his translation of the *Bible* into Latin (the *Vulgate*) is still authoritative in the Roman Church today. This excellent version exerted stylistic and theological influence throughout the Middle Ages. **Ambrose** (c. 340–397) of Trier, a Roman provincial governor, elected (374) archbishop of Milan before he was baptized. His *Duties of the Clergy* (based largely on Cicero, *de Officiis*) was for centuries the standard work on ethics, and is probably the chief single source of the Stoic tradition in early western thought. He made Milan almost the equal of Rome in prestige, and forced the Emperor Theodosius to do penance, maintaining that in ecclesiastical matters a bishop was superior to an emperor. **Augustine** (354–430) of Hippo, greatest of the western fathers. Converted to Christianity after ventures in Neo-Platonism and Manichaeism, he was founder of western theology, the link between the classical tradition and the mediaeval schoolmen. Through him a great stream of Platonic and Neo-Platonic thought came into the Church. For a thousand years all thought was influenced by Augustine, and theology betrays his influence to this day. He gave wide currency to the doctrines of original sin, predestination, salvation through divine grace, and his influence was felt by Calvin and Luther. His *City of God* presents a dualism of the heavenly city (identified with the Christian Church) and the earthly city (Rome), and is written to prove that the misfortunes of Rome (e.g. the sack of 410) were not due to Christianity. The *Confessions* set the fashion in spiritual autobiography.

All knowledge was used as symbolic allegory. A model of this is seen in the *Physiologos,* where animals, real and imaginary, form the keys to moral teachings; in medicine the doctrine of signatures was popular; the external appearance of the plant held the key to its use.

401–417. INNOCENT I asserted that the pope was custodian of apostolic tradition and claimed universal jurisdiction for the Roman Church.

440–461. LEO THE GREAT, the first great pope, a highly cultivated Roman, vigorous foe of the Manichaean heresy. He procured an edict from Emperor Valentinian III (445) declaring that papal decisions have the force of law. Leo was probably the first pope to enunciate the theory of the mystical unity of Peter and his successors, and to attribute all their doings and sayings to Peter. Leo, repudiating the decrees of the Robber Council of Ephesus (449) at the Council of Chalcedon (451), dictated without discussion, and with imperial support, his solution of the greatest doctrinal controversy since 325. His *Tome* promulgated the doctrine of the union of the two natures. He refused to accept the decree of the council that the patriarch of Constantinople was supreme in the Church. The tradition of his miraculous arrest of Attila's advance and his efforts to stop Gaiseric's attack (455) won the papacy tremendous prestige in later days.

(*Cont. pp. 160, 164.*)

c. INVADERS OF THE WEST, TO 532

ORIGINS OF THE INVADERS. The Germanic race was established in Scandinavia (Denmark) and between the Elbe and Oder as early as the 2nd millennium B.C. Eastward lay the Balts (Letts) and to the west of the Elbe were the Celts.

EXPANSION. (1) The West Germans (Teutons) displaced (c. 1000 B.C.) the Celts, moving up the Elbe and Rhine (the Main reached c. 200 B.C.). South Germany was occupied (c. 100 B.C.); Gaul threatened (cf. Caesar's *Commentaries*). These invaders were a pastoral, agricultural folk, tending to settle down. By the time of Tacitus' (c. 55–c. 117 A.D.) *Germania* they were wholly agricultural. Later new tribal names and a new kind of federated organization appeared. (2) The East Germans (Scandinavians) crossed the Baltic (c. 600–300 B.C.) and pushed up the Vistula to the Carpathians. (3) The North Germans remained in Scandinavia.

NEW GROUPINGS AMONG THE WEST GERMANS. Alamanni (of Suevian stock) on the upper Rhine; **Franks** (i.e. "free" of the Romans) and **Saxons** between the Weser and the Elbe, inland to the Harz; **Thuringians,** south of the Saxons.

GOVERNMENT. All were tribal democracies, some under kings, others under *grafs.* In each case the head of the state was elected by the assembly of free men, the kings chosen from a royal house, e.g. Amals (Ostrogoths), Balthas (Visigoths), Mervings (Franks), the *grafs* without such restriction.

PROGRESS OF MIGRATIONS. The East Germans (Bastarnae, Burgundians, Gepids, Goths, Heruls, Rugians, Sciri) moved toward the Black Sea where they had arrived by 214 A.D. The division of Visigoth (West Goth) and Ostrogoth (East Goth) probably arose after their arrival at the Black Sea.

(1) The Huns

The **Huns,** nomadic Mongols of the Ural-Altaic race group, probably under pressure from the Zhu-Zhu Empire in Asia, swept into Europe in the 4th century and halted for some fifty years in the valley of the Danube and Theiss.

372. They defeated the Alans and Heruls, destroyed the Ostrogothic empire of Hermanric, absorbed the Ostrogoths for a time in their own empire, routed the Visigoths under Athanaric on the Dniester River, and then began a new thrust to the west.

445–453. Height of the Hun power under Attila. Honoria, sister of Valentinian III, to escape an unwelcome marriage, sent her ring to Attila and asked for aid. Attila claimed this to be an offer of marriage. About the same time Gaiseric the Vandal was intriguing to induce Attila to attack the Visigoths. By a clever pretense of friendliness to both sides, Attila kept the Romans and Goths apart, and set out westward with a great force (451) which included Gepids, Ostrogoths, Rugians, Scirians, Heruls, Thuringians, Alans, Burgundians, and Ripuarian Franks. Metz was taken and the Belgic provinces ravaged. To meet Attila the Roman Aëtius mustered a force of Salian Franks, Ripuarians, Burgundians, Celts, and Visigoths under Theodoric I, as well as his own Gallo-Romans. Attila apparently declined battle near Orleans and turned back.

451. Aëtius overtook him at an unknown spot near Troyes, the so-called *Lacus Mauriacus* **(Châlons),** and a drawn battle was fought. Attila continued his withdrawal. Still claiming Honoria, Attila turned into Italy, razed Aquileia, ravaged the countryside (foundation of Venice) and opened the road to Rome. Pope Leo, one of a commission of three sent by the emperor, appeared before Attila. Attila retreated after plague had broken out in his force, food supply had run low, and reinforcements arrived from the east for the Roman army. Attila's death (453) was followed by a revolt of his German vassals led by the Gepids, and (454) the defeat of the Huns on the Nedao (in Pannonia). The remnant of the Huns settled on the lower Danube, the Gepids set up a kingdom in Dacia, the Ostrogoths settled in Pannonia.

(2) The Visigoths

After their defeat by the Huns, the Visigoths (perhaps 80,000 in number) sought refuge in the Roman Empire.

376. The Emperor **Valens** ordered them disarmed and allowed to cross the Danube in order to settle in Lower Moesia. Faced with the unprecedented problem of these refugees, the Roman government bungled the administration, failed really to disarm the Goths, and ultimately had to fight a two-year war with them.

378. The Visigoths, under **Fritigern,** defeated

and killed **Valens** near Adrianople, thereby making the first decisive break in the Rhine-Danube frontier. This defeat of the Roman infantry by mounted warriors forecast the revolution in the art of war which determined the military, social, and political development of Europe throughout the Middle Ages.

Fritigern, hoping to carve a Visigothic empire out of the Roman provinces, ravaged Thrace for two years, but could not take Adrianople. After his death (379), the Emperor **Theodosius** arranged a pacification of the Visigoths as part of a general policy of assimilation. He won over some of the chieftains, including **Alaric** of the royal house of Balthas, who hoped for a career in the Roman service. Alaric, disappointed in his hopes at the death of Theodosius, was elected king by the Visigoths, and ravaged Thrace to the gates of Constantinople. Arcadius, emperor of the east (395–408), was helpless until the arrival of Stilicho, *magister utriusque militiae* (field marshal of both services) in the east.

Stilicho, a Vandal by blood, married to Theodosius' sister, was guardian of Theodosius' sons, Arcadius and Honorius. He faced Alaric in Thessaly and the Peloponnesus, avoiding battle, apparently on orders from Honorius. Alaric was made *magister militum* in Illyricum, and Stilicho, out of favor in Constantinople, was declared a public enemy.

401.   Alaric began a thrust into Italy, probably because of the triumph of an anti-German faction in Constantinople, and ravaged Venetia. Simultaneously Radagaisus (an Ostrogoth) began an invasion of Raetia and Italy. Stilicho, firmly against any Germanic invasion of the west, repulsed Radagaisus.

402.   Pollentia, a drawn battle between Stilicho and Alaric, was a strategic defeat for Alaric. Alaric's next advance was stopped, probably through an understanding with Stilicho. Halted again (403) at Verona, the Visigoths withdrew to Epirus.

406 The **Rhine frontier,** denuded of troops for the defense of Italy, was crossed by a great wave of migrants, chiefly East Germans: Vandals, Sueves, and Alans (non-German). The usurper **Constantine** having crossed from Britain to Gaul, Alaric in Noricum was paid a huge sum of gold by the senate, as a sort of retainer for his services against Constantine. Stilicho, his popularity undermined by these events and by the hostility of Constantinople, was beheaded (408). There is no evidence of treason by Stilicho. His execution was followed by a general massacre of the families of the barbarian auxiliaries in Italy, and some 30,000 of them went over to Alaric in Noricum.

410. ALARIC TOOK ROME after alternate sieges and negotiations. He sacked it for three days, and then moved south toward Africa, the granary of Italy. Turned back by the loss of his fleet, Alaric died and was buried in the bed of the Busento. His brother-in-law Ataulf was elected to succeed him. Ataulf, originally bent on the destruction of the very name of Rome, now bent his energies to the fusion of Visigothic vigor and Roman tradition.

412.   Ataulf led the Visigoths north, ravaged Etruria, crossed the Alps, ravaged Gaul, and married (against her brother Honorius' will) Galla Placidia (414) after the Roman ritual. He was forced into Spain (415), where he was murdered. **Wallia** (415–c. 418), after the brief reign of Sigeric, succeeded him.

Ulfilas (311–381), a Gothic bishop of Arian convictions, invented the Gothic alphabet for his translation of the *Bible.* This translation, the first literary monument of the German invaders, had enormous influence, and recalls the wide extent of the **Arian heresy,** which won every important Germanic invader except the Franks, a development with the greatest political consequences, since the lands where the Germans settled were peopled by orthodox Roman Catholics.

Spain had already been overrun by a horde of Vandals, Sueves, and Alans (409), and the Roman blockade made food hard to get. Wallia planned to cross to the African granary, but lost his ships, was forced to make terms with Honorius and restore Galla Placidia to her brother. He agreed to clear Spain of other barbarians. Succeeding in this he received the grant of *Aquitania Secunda* (i.e. the land between the Loire and the Garonne) with Toulouse as a capital. Thus began the

419–507.   KINGDOM OF TOULOUSE. The Visigoths received two-thirds of the land, the remainder being left to the Roman proprietors. A Gothic state was created within the Roman state. Honorius, hoping to counteract alien influences, revived a Roman custom of holding provincial councils, decreeing an annual meeting of the leading officials and the chief landowners for discussion of common problems. The most important rulers of Toulouse were

419–451.   Theodoric I, who fell in the **battle of Châlons,** and

466–484.   Euric, whose reign marked the apogee of the kingdom. He continued the pressure of the Visigoths upon Gaul and Spain, and by 481 extended his domain from the Pyrenees to the Loire and eastward to the Rhone, securing Provence from Odovacar (481). Euric first codified Visigothic law, but the *Breviary of Alaric* (506), a codification of Roman law for Visigothic use, had tremendous influence among the Visigoths and among many other barbarian peoples. Under Visigothic rule the administration in general remained Roman and the language of government continued to be a Latin vernacular. The Gallo-Roman population and clergy were hostile to the Visigoths as Arians, and this hostility opened the way for the **Frankish conquest** (507), which reduced the Visigothic power to its Spanish domains.

507-711. The **Visigothic Kingdom of Spain** dragged out a miserable existence under more than a score of rulers, some mere phantoms, until the arrival of the Moslems (p. 177).

554. **Belisarius' invasion of Spain**, part of Justinian's reconstruction of the Roman Empire (p. 160), was a brilliant campaign, but reduced only the southeast corner of Spain, later regained by the Visigoths, who also reduced the Sueves in the north.

(3) The Vandals

406. The **Vandals** (Asding and Siling), allied with the Sciri and Alani, crossed the Rhine near the Main, followed the Moselle and Aisne (sacking Reims, Amiens, Arras, Tournai), then turned southward into Aquitaine, and crossed the Pyrenees into Spain (409).

429-534. THE VANDAL KINGDOM IN AFRICA. The Vandals and Alani had been established in southern Spain under Gunderic. His brother **Gaiseric** received an appeal from Bonifatius, the revolted Roman governor of Africa, following which the Vandals (perhaps 80,000 in number) crossed into Africa (429).

430. The **first siege of Hippo** failed, but Bonifatius, now reconciled to the regency of Galla Placidia, was annihilated, and the city fell (431). **St. Augustine,** Bishop of Hippo, died during the siege. The creation of a great Vandal power in Africa, supported as it soon was by a powerful navy, distracted the attention of the Roman government from the new barbarian kingdoms of the west and had a decisive effect of a negative kind.

In Africa the Vandals spared nobody and nothing and the treaty made with the Romans was no restraint. After the arrival of a fleet from Constantinople, a second treaty was made. Eudocia, daughter of Valentinian, was betrothed to Gaiseric's son, Huneric, and the Vandals received most of the Roman territory except the region about Carthage.

439. **Gaiseric took Carthage** from the Romans, and made it his capital and naval base.

455. **Gaiseric attacked Rome,** on the invitation (according to tradition) of Valentinian's widow Eudoxia. He took it easily, and for two weeks pillaged the city, scientifically and ruthlessly, but without wanton destruction.

In Africa the Vandals were hated as Arians,

and they had to deal with serious **Berber revolts,** but their power was not broken until the

533-548. Vandalic Wars of Justinian. Belisarius quickly defeated the Carthaginian power of the Vandals; the ensuing Berber revolt was not put down until 548.

(4) The Burgundians

411-532. The **Burgundians,** arriving from the Oder-Vistula region, moved along the Main athwart the Rhine, entered Gaul under King Gundicar, and finally settled as federates of the Roman Empire in upper Burgundy (i.e. the lands including Lyons, Vienne, Besançon, Geneva, Autun, Macon). King **Gundibald** (d. 516) codified Burgundian law in the *Lex Gundobada.* The Burgundians were finally conquered by the sons of Clovis (c. 532), but the Burgundian state remained separate under Frankish control with Merovingian princes until 613. After 613 it was a province of the Frankish Empire.

d. THE OSTROGOTHS IN ITALY, 489-554

On the breakup of the Hunnic Empire (after Nedao, 454), the Ostrogoths settled in Pannonia (their first settlement inside the Roman frontier) as federates of the empire. Under the Huns the emergence of a single ruler had been impossible. Thiudareiks (ruler of the people), corrupted into Theodoric, educated as a hostage at Constantinople, was elected (471) merely a *gau* king, but soon became leader of his people on a march into the Balkan Peninsula where he forced the Emperor Leo to grant them lands in Macedonia. His ambition for imperial appointment was realized (483) when he was made *magister militum praesentalis* and (484) *consul.* He quarreled with the emperor and marched on Constantinople. To get rid of him the emperor commissioned him (informally) to expel Odovacar from Italy. Arriving in Italy (489) the Ostrogoths triumphed over Odovacar, but did not reduce Ravenna until 493. Theodoric killed Odovacar with his own hands and had his troops massacred.

489-526. THEODORIC THE GREAT. In general Theodoric continued Odovacar's policy, substituting Ostrogoths for Odovacar's Germans, and assigning one-third of the Roman estates (as Odovacar had probably done) to his people. Theodoric's rule was officially recognized (497) by Constantinople. Together with the emperors he named the consuls in the west, but never named an Ostrogoth. Theodoric was the only member of his people who was a Roman citizen; constitutionally the others were alien soldiers in the service of the empire. No Roman was in military command, no Ostrogoth in the civil service. Imperial legislation and coinage continued. The so-called *Edictum Theodorici* is a codification of Theodoric's administrative decrees rather than a body of legislation, as none of Theodoric's "laws" were anything more than clarifications of imperial legislation. Theodoric's secretary of state was the learned Italian, **Cassiodorus,** and the dual state was paralleled by a dual religious system. Theodoric was tolerant of the orthodox Catholics and a protector of the Jews. His chief aim was to civilize his people under the Roman environment and to keep peace.

Theodoric's co-operation with the other Germanic peoples was close, and he cemented his associations by marriage alliances (one daughter married Alaric II, the Visigoth, another Sigismund the Burgundian, and he himself married Clovis' sister). He intervened to protect the Alamanni from Clovis and tried to save the Visigoths. Provence was acquired from Burgundy and annexed to Italy. He was regent and protector of his grandson Amalaric after Alaric II's death, and virtually ruled the Visigothic Kingdom until his death (526):

To the Italians Ostrogothic rule was alien and heretical and they resented it. The end of Theodoric's reign was marked by a growing ill-feeling and suspicion that may have been due to this. **Boethius,** the Roman philosopher and commentator on Aristotle, author of the *De consolatione philosophiae,* an official of Theodoric's government, and his father-in-law, the brilliant and polished Roman **Symmachus,** were both executed (c. 524) on a charge of treasonable conspiracy.

535–554. RECONQUEST OF ITALY BY THE EMPEROR. Justinian, as part of his grandiose reconstitution of the Roman Empire, dispatched **Belisarius** and later **Narses,** who reduced the stubborn Ostrogoths and drove them over the Alps to an unknown end.

After the expulsion of the Ostrogoths the **Exarchate of Ravenna** was established under the Emperor Maurice (582–602). The exarch had military and civil powers and received full imperial honors. He exercised imperial control over the church, including the bishopric of Rome. War and pestilence had completely ruined northern Italy; Rome, in ruins, had sunk from her imperial position to be a provincial town; the way was open for the Lombard invaders.

Ravenna had been the capital of the west (c. 402–476) and was the home of Theodoric's brilliant court. The architecture of the city offers a unique series of examples of Roman and Romano-Byzantine buildings begun under the emperors and continued by Theodoric. The name and glory of Theodoric have survived in German tradition in Dietrich von Bern (i.e. of Verona, where he had a palace).

PROGRESS OF THE PAPACY. Gelasius (492–496) was the first pope to proclaim the independence of the Papacy from both emperor and church council in matters of faith. He asserted that two powers rule the world, the *sacerdotium* and the *imperium.* The *sacerdotium,* since it is the instrument of human salvation, is superior to the *imperium.*

As soon as Italy ceased to be a ruling state, there began a long effort to create national unity and to establish national independence. The barbarian invasions had isolated Italy, accentuated the break with the empire, and left the pope as the sole native representative of ancient unity and Italian hegemony. At the same time the Ostrogoths (half romanized as they were) did not destroy Italian culture, but allowed the Church to transmit the Greco-Roman tradition (linguistic, social, cultural, administrative, and religious) in the west.

529. Western monasticism, representing a wide ascetic reaction against current corruption in life and supported by Jerome, Ambrose, and Augustine, had expanded rapidly in the 6th century and reached a chaotic condition ranging from extremes of eremitical asceticism to the laxest kind of cenobitic worldliness. **Benedict** of Nursia, scandalized at conditions, withdrew to Monte Cassino where he founded a colony and gave it (traditionally in 529) the famous *Benedictine Rule.* This rule, which dominated western monasticism for centuries, was a remarkable and characteristic Roman compromise adapted to the average man. It placed the monks under the control of an abbot, made each house autonomous in a loose federation (not strictly an order at all), and provided for careful recruiting and probation. Discipline was efficient but not extreme, and great stress was laid on labor, especially in the open air (*laborare est orare*). The individual was merged in an ascetic, self-contained, self-sufficient corporation. The spread of the Benedictines was rapid, and soon the only important survival of eremitical monasticism was in the Irish monks of St. Columban. The order became the chief instrument for the reform of the Frankish (Gallic) Church, and for the conversion and civilization of England and Germany. In the course of history it gave the Church 24 popes, 200 cardinals, 5000 saints, 15,000 writers and scholars.

Ruined by invasion, its aqueducts cut, **Rome** was reduced in population from a half million to perhaps 50,000. Its aristocracy had fled, and mediaeval decay had replaced pagan grandeur. The city was not revived until the Renaissance.

554. Justinian's Pragmatic Sanction restored the Italian lands taken by the Ostrogoths and made a *pro forma* restoration of government, but agricultural lands were depopulated and grown into wilderness, the rural proprietors were sinking into serfdom. Town decline was similar. The Roman senate ceased to function after 603 and the local curiae disappeared at about the same time.

Duces were appointed, probably over each *civitas*, as part of the imperial administration, but they gradually became great landowners and their military functions dominated their civil duties. A fusion of the ducal title and landownership ensued and a new class of hereditary military proprietors emerged beside the clergy and the old nobles. The details of this process are, of course, hard to determine, the more so as evidence is scant.

e. THE FRANKISH KINGDOM, 481–752

The **Franks** first appear as settlers on the lower Rhine in two divisions, the **Salians** (dwellers by the sea, *sal*) and the **Ripuarians** (dwellers by the riverbank, *ripa*). By the end of the 4th century the Salians were established in the area between the Meuse and the Scheldt as federates of the Roman Empire; the Ripuarians in the tract between the Rhine and Meuse. They formed no permanent confederations, and, unlike the other Germanic peoples, did not migrate as a nation, but expanded.

431–751. THE SALIAN FRANKS UNDER THE MEROVINGIANS.

451. Chlodio (son of Merowech) invaded Artois, and was defeated by Aëtius. Salian Franks were in the Roman forces at the battle of Châlons. **King Childeric** (d. 481) fought as a federate of the empire at Orleans when Aëtius defeated the Visigoths, and he later defeated the Saxons on the Loire. His tomb was found (1653) at Tournai, the "capital" of the Salians.

481–511. CLOVIS (Chlodovech), son of Childeric, in the service of Julius Nepos and Zeno. He defeated the Gallo-Roman general Syagrius at Soissons (486), expanding Salian power to the Loire. The story of the **Soissons vase** is significant of the friendly relations between Clovis and Bishop Remigius. Sigebert, the Ripuarian, defeated an Alamannic invasion at Tolbiac (496) with Salian support. Clovis in the same year defeated the Alamanni (Strasburg?) and later, after election as king of the Ripuarians, emerged as master of the Franks on both sides of the Rhine.

496. The traditional date of the **conversion of Clovis** to Roman Catholicism is 496. He had previously married a Burgundian, Clotilda, who was of the Roman communion. The Burgundians in general were Arians, and Clovis' choice may have been deliberate. In any case his conversion won him powerful papal and episcopal support and opened the way to wide conquests from the heretic (i.e. Arian) German peoples. Burgundy was conquered (after 500), the Visigoths defeated at Vouillé (507), and their whole kingdom north of the Pyrenees (except Septimania and Provence) was soon subjugated. These conquests were warmly supported by the Gallo-Roman clergy as a religious war. Clovis founded the Church of the Holy Apostles (Ste. Geneviève) at Paris, and shortly moved his "capital" from Soissons to Paris. He was made an honorary consul by the Emperor Anastasius, a proceeding that brought the Franks technically into the empire.

511–628. Divisions of the Frankish lands after the death of Clovis: (1) His four sons established four capitals—Metz, Orleans, Paris, Soissons. Expansion eastward continued along the upper Elbe; Burgundy was added, and the territory of the Ostrogoths north of the Alps. After a period of ruthless conflict, only **Lothair** (Chlothar) survived, and for a brief time (558–561) the Frankish lands were under one head again. (2) Lothair's division of his lands among his four sons led to a great feud from which three kingdoms emerged: **Austrasia** (capital Metz) lying to the east (Auster) and mostly Teutonic; **Neustria** (the "new land" as the name implies) (capital Soissons), Gallo-Roman in blood; **Burgundy,** which had no king of its own but joined Neustria under a common ruler. The prince of Neustria exterminated the rival house in Austrasia, but the local baronage preserved the kingdom's identity. Under **Lothair II** all three kingdoms were united again (613) under one ruler.

629–639. Dagobert (Lothair's son), the last strong ruler of the Merovingian house, made wide dynastic alliances and found wise advisers in **Bishop Arnulf** and **Pepin of Landen.** His firm rule led to a revolt. Under the *rois fainéants* following Dagobert the **mayors of the palace** emerged from a menial position to a dominant rôle in the government both in Austrasia and Neustria.

Merovingian government retained the Roman civitas as a unit of administration and set a count (*comes* or *graf*) over it. The source of law was not the king, but local custom administered by the graf with the aid of local landowners. Military leaders of large districts were the duces who were over several counts. Land

The Merovingian Kings

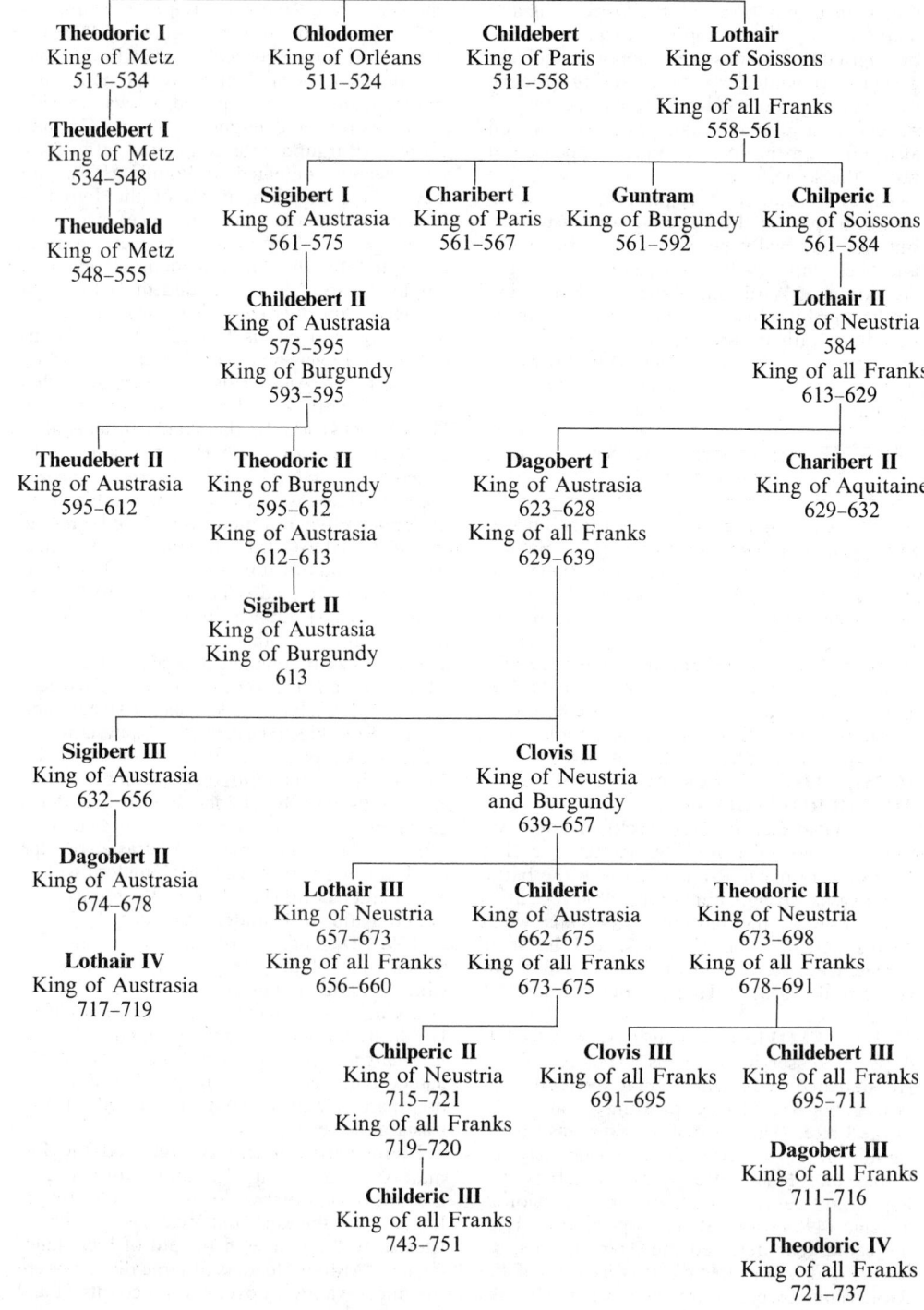

Clovis I
481–511

Theodoric I
King of Metz
511–534

Theudebert I
King of Metz
534–548

Theudebald
King of Metz
548–555

Chlodomer
King of Orléans
511–524

Childebert
King of Paris
511–558

Lothair
King of Soissons
511
King of all Franks
558–561

Sigibert I
King of Austrasia
561–575

Charibert I
King of Paris
561–567

Guntram
King of Burgundy
561–592

Chilperic I
King of Soissons
561–584

Childebert II
King of Austrasia
575–595
King of Burgundy
593–595

Lothair II
King of Neustria
584
King of all Franks
613–629

Theudebert II
King of Austrasia
595–612

Theodoric II
King of Burgundy
595–612
King of Austrasia
612–613

Dagobert I
King of Austrasia
623–628
King of all Franks
629–639

Charibert II
King of Aquitaine
629–632

Sigibert II
King of Austrasia
King of Burgundy
613

Sigibert III
King of Austrasia
632–656

Clovis II
King of Neustria
and Burgundy
639–657

Dagobert II
King of Austrasia
674–678

Lothair IV
King of Austrasia
717–719

Lothair III
King of Neustria
657–673
King of all Franks
656–660

Childeric
King of Austrasia
662–675
King of all Franks
673–675

Theodoric III
King of Neustria
673–698
King of all Franks
678–691

Chilperic II
King of Neustria
715–721
King of all Franks
719–720

Clovis III
King of all Franks
691–695

Childebert III
King of all Franks
695–711

Dagobert III
King of all Franks
711–716

Childeric III
King of all Franks
743–751

Theodoric IV
King of all Franks
721–737

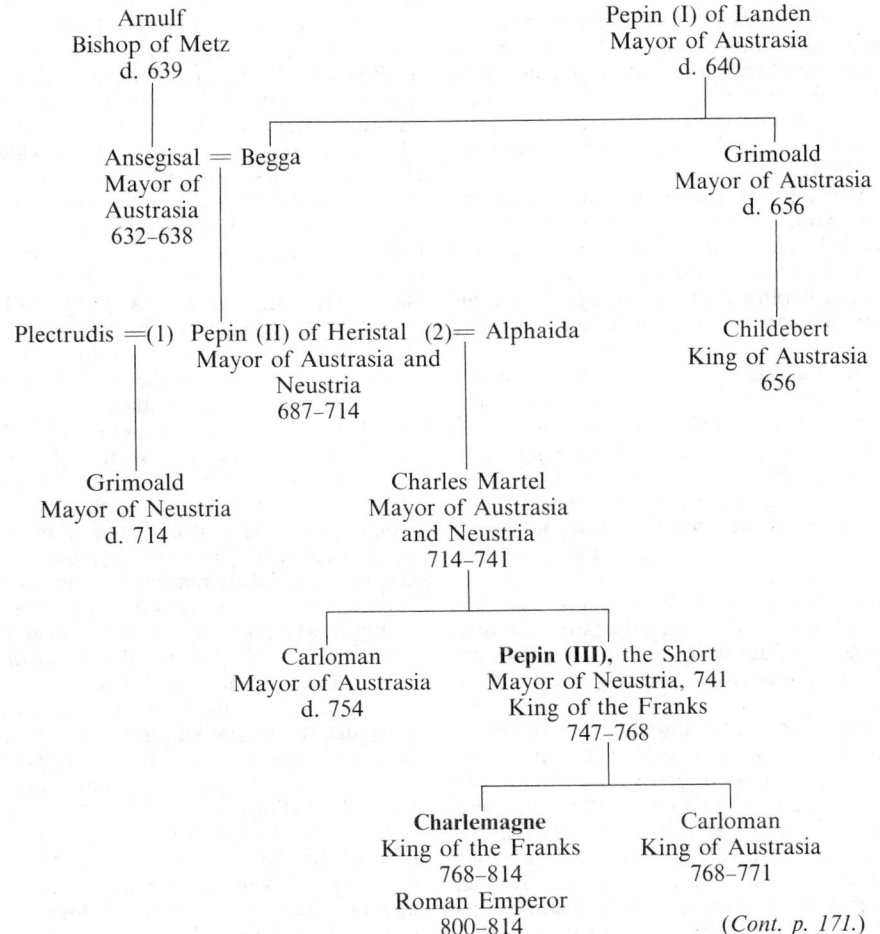

Arnulf
Bishop of Metz
d. 639

Pepin (I) of Landen
Mayor of Austrasia
d. 640

Ansegisal = Begga
Mayor of
Austrasia
632–638

Grimoald
Mayor of Austrasia
d. 656

Plectrudis =(1) Pepin (II) of Heristal (2)= Alphaida
Mayor of Austrasia and
Neustria
687–714

Childebert
King of Austrasia
656

Grimoald
Mayor of Neustria
d. 714

Charles Martel
Mayor of Austrasia
and Neustria
714–741

Carloman
Mayor of Austrasia
d. 754

Pepin (III), the Short
Mayor of Neustria, 741
King of the Franks
747–768

Charlemagne
King of the Franks
768–814
Roman Emperor
800–814

Carloman
King of Austrasia
768–771

(*Cont. p. 171.*)

grants were made in lieu of pay to officials.

Gregory, bishop of Tours (c. 540–594), a Frank, wrote in Latin the *Historia Francorum,* the best single source on the history of the Merovingian period.

Decline of the royal power under the last of the Merovingians, and beginning of **feudal decentralization.** (1) Concentration of land-ownership in the hands of a few (i.e. a landed aristocracy of which the mayors of the palace were representative). (2) The breakdown of the old clan and tribal organization without an effective state to replace it, leading to personal and economic dependence on private individuals rather than on the state (e.g. commendation, *beneficium,* immunity). (3) Military service on horseback became attached to the benefice as early as the 8th century; for example, Martel's cavalry (see *infra*) for service against the Saracens. Since these grants involved church lands to a considerable degree, Martel in effect compelled the Church to help support national defense. (4) The royal domain was exempt from visitation except by the king's personal administrators. This immunity was extended to royal lands granted to others, and then to lands never in the royal domain. The upshot of the system was complete decentralization by the delegation of the royal powers to local officials who tended to become entirely independent.

Emergence of the Carolingians in Austrasia. The son of Arnulf married the daughter of **Count Pepin I** (of Landen, d. 640), mayor of the palace, founding the line later called Carolingian.

656. Pepin's son, Grimoald, made a premature effort to usurp the crown, which cost him and his son their lives, and led to a reaction in favor of the Merovingians.

678–681. Ebroin, mayor in Neustria, united the mayoralties under one house; he was murdered (681).

687. Pepin II (of Heristal), grandson of Pepin I, gained supremacy in Austrasia and Neustria by his victory at Tertry. The kingdom was on the verge of dissolution (ducal separatism), and Pepin began an effort to reduce the landed aristocracy from which he himself had sprung.

714–741. Charles Martel (i.e. the Hammer), Pepin's son, an ally of the Lombards, supported Boniface's mission in Germany (Boniface testified that his achievements would have been impossible without Martel's aid).

732. Martel's great **victory at Tours** arrested the advance of the Moslems in the west, and was followed by their final retreat over the Pyrenees (759).

Pepin's **conquest of the Frisians** was continued, five wars were waged against the Saxons, and powerful decentralizing forces (notably in Burgundy and Alamannia) were broken down.

739. Pope Gregory III, threatened by the Lombards, sent an embassy to Martel, and offered the title of *consul* in return for protection. Charles, an ally of the Lombard king, ignored the appeal. At the end of his life Martel, like a true sovereign, divided the Merovingian lands between his sons, Austrasia and the German duchies going to Carloman, Neustria and Burgundy to Pepin. Carloman and Pepin ruled together, 741–747; Pepin ruled alone, 747–768.
(*Cont. p. 167.*)

f. THE LOMBARDS AND THE POPES, 568–774

(*From p. 161*)

[*For a complete list of the Roman popes see Appendix IV.*]

Under the Emperor Augustus the Lombards were still established on the lower Elbe (Bardengau) and were defeated (5 A.D.) by the Romans. Their history for the next 400 years is confused and often blank. They were members of the Hunnic Empire and were subdued by the Heruls (505), whom they then destroyed (508). They were probably Arians by this time. Resistance to the Gepids began (c. 546). They were given land by Justinian in Noricum and Pan-

nonia and aided (553) the imperial attacks on the Ostrogoths. The Avars arrived (c. 560) from the Volga, entered Thuringia (562), were defeated by the Franks, and allied themselves (c. 565) with the Lombards against the Gepids, who were annihilated. The Lombards moved on toward Italy and the Avars occupied Dacia. Alboin (d. 573), the Lombard king, killed the Gepid king, Cunimund, with his own hand and married his daughter Rosamund (story of Cunimund's skull as a drinking-cup). The Lombards took part in Belisarius' conquest, and soon they began to move south toward Italy.

568. THE LOMBARD CONQUEST OF ITALY. Italy, worn out by the Gothic wars, famine, and pestilence, offered little resistance. Constantinople was indifferent, and the conquest was easy. The Lombards, always few in numbers, had associated other peoples (including 20,000 Saxons, who soon departed, and some Slavs) in their invasion, but even then they were not numerous enough to occupy the whole peninsula. Rome and Naples were never held, and Ravenna only briefly. The coast was not really mastered. The Lombards (unlike even the Vandals) did not enter into a compact with the empire, and Italian feeling against them was bitter. Pavia became the capital (Italy, until 774, had always two and usually three capitals: Rome, the papal capital; Ravenna, the Byzantine capital; and Pavia, the Lombard capital after 573) and the peninsula was a mosaic of Byzantine, papal, and Lombard jurisdictions.

Lombard occupation (virtually military rule at first) covered inland Liguria, inland Tuscany, inland Venetia, the duchy of Spoleto and the duchy of Benevento. **Imperial Italy** comprised Venice and the land from north of Ravenna to the south of Ancona, and included the duchy of Rome and the duchy of Naples, as well as the toe and heel of Italy. *Hospitalitas* was revived and one-third the produce of the land (not one-third the land) was given to the Lombards. Lombards also took the lands of the dead and the exiled. At first lands were assigned with a full title, but Liutprand introduced (713, 735) leases, and the grant of estates without permanent tenure.

The Lombards took Roman titles and names, and in the end accepted Roman Catholicism. By the time of **Liutprand** (712–744) their speech was clearly Italian, but the natives were loyal to their past, and remained sharply divided from the Lombards. Legally there was a dual system of private law, and in Lombard territories there was a dual episcopal system (i.e. Arian and Roman).

573–584. Alboin's murder was followed by the

rule of Cleph (d. 575) and then by ten years of anarchy and private war under a loose federation of dukes (some 36 in number). Roman Catholic opposition and papal negotiations with the Franks alarmed the Lombards, and led to the election of

584-590. Authari, a grandson of Alboin, who was endowed with half the baronial lands as royal domain. The dukedoms were gradually absorbed (the marches like Fruili, Trent, Turin, survived longest).

Authari's widow Theodolinda, a devoted Roman Catholic, bidden to choose a husband who should also be king, selected a Thuringian.

590-615. Duke Agilulf, of Turin, who was friendly to the Roman Church and the true founder of the Lombard state. Gregory the Great blocked an Italian conspiracy against the Lombards. **Rothari** (636-652) became a Roman Catholic. He collected Lombard customary law in Latin and began the consolidation of Lombard power. Eventually Roman law triumphed and Lombard law survived only in the schools (e.g. Pavia).

The Italian bishops since 476 had been the leaders of the peaceful civilians in the cities, the protectors of the oppressed, and the dispensers of charity. Under the Lombards a system of **episcopal immunities** emerged which made the bishops virtually local temporal sovereigns and enabled them to preserve the local spirit of municipal independence and organization (e.g. consuls, guilds). The urban population was free of feudal bonds, and the town walls (often built by the bishops) were refuges. Milan resumed her greatness and almost equaled Rome. These developments prepared the way for the great assertion of Italian town independence against Roman clerical and German feudal encroachments. **Paul the Deacon** (c. 720–c. 800), the first important medieval historian, wrote the *Historia gentis Langobardorum.* **Martianus Capella** (fl. c. 600), encyclopaedist, formulated the seven arts (grammar, logic, rhetoric, geometry, astronomy, arithmetic, music) which were to guide education down to the Renaissance.

590-604. GREGORY THE GREAT. His family was a rich senatorial house and Gregory was prefect of Rome (573). He founded (c. 574) six monasteries in Sicily and one at Rome (St. Andrews) into which he immediately retired as a monk. Embassy to Constantinople (c. 579–586). As abbot of St. Andrews (586) his rule was severe. Elected pope (590) against his will, he began a vigorous administration. Discipline within his patriarchate was rigorous (stress on celibacy, close watch on elections,

insistence on exclusive clerical jurisdiction over clerical offenders). Church revenue was divided into four shares for the bishop, the clergy, the poor, and church buildings. His administration of the wide estates of the Church was honest and brilliant, and the revenue was expanded to meet the tremendous demands on Rome for charity. The pope continued the old imperial corn doles in Rome and elsewhere, aqueducts were repaired, urban administration, especially in Rome, reformed.

Outside his immediate patriarchal jurisdiction Gregory expanded the influence and prestige of the pope, maintaining that the pope was by divine designation head of all churches. Appeals to Rome were heard even against the patriarch of Constantinople, whose claim to the title of universal bishop was denied. Gregory boldly assumed the rôle of the emperor in the west, and the powers of a temporal prince, counterbalancing the prestige of Constantinople. From his administration date the foundations of later **claims to papal absolutism.** Gregory was the real leader against the Lombards, appointing governors of cities, directing the generals in war, and receiving from Constantinople pay for the army.

As the first monk to become pope, Gregory made a close alliance between the Benedictines and the papacy (at the expense of the bishops). The monks were given charters and protected from the bishops, the Benedictine Rule was imposed, and a great missionary campaign was begun with monkish aid: (1) the mission to Britain (596) under **Augustine of Canterbury** and the conversion of England provided a base from which the Frankish (Gallic) Church was later reformed and the German people converted; (2) campaigns against paganism in Gaul, Italy, and Sicily, and against heresy in Africa and Sicily.

Gregory was the last of the four great Latin Fathers, and first of the medieval prelates, a link between the classical Greco-Roman tradition and the medieval Romano-German. Not a great scholar, he was a great popularizer, and spread the doctrines of Augustine of Hippo throughout the west. At the same time he gave wide currency through his *Dialogorum libri* to the popular (often originally pagan) ideas of angels, demons, devils, relic worship, miracles, the doctrine of purgatory, and the use of allegory. Gregory reveals the clerical contempt for classical Latin which profoundly influenced the Latin of the Middle Ages. His *Regulae pastoralis liber* remained for centuries an essential in the education of the clergy. There was a school of music at Rome, but how much Gregory had to do with it, and how much with the introduction of the Gregorian chant, is doubtful.

Gregory introduced the papal style, *Servus Servorum Dei.*

CONTINUED ALIENATION OF ITALY FROM THE EAST. (1) The **Monothelite controversy:** condemnation by the **Lateran Synod** (649) of Emperor Heraclius' *Ecthesis* (of 638) and Emperor Constans II's *Typos* of 648. Arrest (653) by the exarch of Pope Martin I (649–655), who died in exile in the east. The **Council of Constantinople** (680–681) compromised on the controversy, taking a position in favor of Rome. The Council of Constantinople (692) reasserted the equality of the patriarchates of Constantinople and Rome. (2) **Emperor Leo the Isaurian's** (717–740) attempt to bring Italy back to obedience: heavy taxation to reduce the great landowners angered Pope Gregory II (the largest landowner in Italy) and Leo's iconoclastic decree (726) aroused all Italy. Gregory III excommunicated all Iconoclasts (731). Gregory's defeat and final humiliation weakened the pope and opened the way for the final Lombard advance.

712–744. DESTRUCTION OF THE LOMBARD KINGDOM. Liutprand, fearing Frankish, Slavic, Hungarian, Byzantine, and papal hostility, began to consolidate his kingdom, reducing the duchies of Benevento and Spoleto. Ravenna was taken temporarily. During the Iconoclastic controversy Liutprand's sincere efforts at rapprochement with the papacy met a brief success.

749–756. Aistulf continued Liutprand's policy of consolidation. The pope, alarmed at Lombard progress, had already (741) made overtures to Charles Martel. Martel, busy with the Moslems, remained faithful to his alliance with the Lombards, but Aistulf's continued advance brought a visit (753) from Pope Stephen II. Stephen had already begun negotiations with Pepin, and the mutual needs of the rising papacy and the upstart Carolingian dynasty drew them into alliance.

754, 756. Pepin in two expeditions forced Aistulf to abandon the Pentapolis and Ravenna (bringing the Lombards virtually to their holdings of 681). Legally the lands involved in the **Donation of Pepin** (756) belonged to the Eastern Empire. The Donation was a tacit recognition of implicit claims of the popes to be the heirs of the empire in Italy. Most important from the papal point of view was the fact that the Church had won a powerful military ally outside Italy. Henceforth the Carolingians maintained a protectorate over the papacy in Italy.

774. Charlemagne, heir to the traditions of Pepin, having repudiated the daughter of the Lombard king, Desiderius, appeared in Italy to protect the pope. After a nine-month siege Pavia was taken, Spoleto and Benevento were conquered, Charles absorbed the Lombard Kingdom into the rising Frankish Empire, and assumed the crown of the Lombards. On a visit (774) to Rome (the first of any Frankish monarch), Charlemagne confirmed the Donation of Pepin, but made it plain that he was sovereign even in the papal lands. At no time did Charlemagne allow the pope any but a primacy in honor (in this respect following the strict Byzantine tradition). The Donation of Pepin was the **foundation of the Papal States** and the true beginning of the temporal power of the papacy. Henceforth there was neither the Lombard menace nor the overlordship of the exarch to interfere with the rising papal monarchy. In this sense the fall of the Lombard Kingdom was decisive in papal history. It was equally decisive in Italian history, for the papal victory over the Lombards terminated the last effective effort to establish national unity and a national government until the end of the 19th century. For the Carolingian monarchy the episode was equally significant.

Under the successors of Charlemagne the emperors continued to participate in the papal elections and did what they could to protect Italy against the attacks of the Moslems from Africa.

827–831. The Moslems conquered Sicily.

837. They attacked Naples, pillaged Ancona (839) and captured Bari (840).

846. In the **battle of Licosa,** Duke Sergius of Naples defeated the Moslems at sea.

847–848. Construction of the **Leonine Wall** by Pope Leo IV (847–855) to defend St. Peter's from the Moslems.

POPE NICHOLAS I (858–867), one of the few great popes between Gregory I and Gregory VII, was the arbiter of western Christendom. Elected by the favor of Louis II. Three great controversies: **(1) Support of Ignatius,** patriarch of Constantinople, resulting in the excommunication (863) of Ignatius' rival, Photius. Photius' futile deposition (867) of Nicholas. This controversy brought the eastern and western churches closer to the final rupture (1054). **(2) Discipline of King Lothair** of Lorraine because of the divorce of his wife Theutberga. Lothair had been allowed (Synod of Aix) by his pliant bishops to remarry, and Nicholas reopened the case at the Synod of Metz (863), which found for Lothair. Nicholas (supported by Charles the Bald) quashed the entire proceeding, disciplined the bishops, and, despite the invasion (864) of the Leonine City by Louis II, compelled Lothair to submit.

(3) **Vindication of the right of appeal to Rome** by a bishop against his metropolitan—humiliation of the powerful Archbishop Hincmar of Reims. First papal citation (865) of the *Forged Decretals* (brought to Rome, 864). Emergence of the theory that no bishop may be deposed or elected without papal approval.

867- **Decline of the papacy,** after the pontificate of Nicholas and the death of Louis II. As the popes had no powerful protectors outside Italy until 961, they fell increasingly under the dominance of the Roman and Italian feudal aristocracy. The lapse of the imperial power left room for the insinuation of a new **doctrine of papal autonomy,** well formulated in the *Forged Decretals.* Outside Italy the relaxation of papal control and the decline of papal prestige, accompanied by the rise of dominant local feudal lords, accentuated the power of the bishops and made the unity of the western Church a mere shadow until the papacy, having learned to cope with feudalism in the second half of the 11th century, once again made its supremacy felt in the Church.

875-877. The Emperor **Charles the Bald** continued to support the papacy against the invader and came to Rome (875) to be crowned, having forced Charles the Fat to retreat and having induced his brother Carloman to sign a truce and withdraw. He was then elected king of Italy by the local magnates.

888. **Berengar of Friuli** was crowned king of Italy at Pavia.

894. **Guido of Spoleto** was consecrated emperor with his son Lambert as co-emperor and co-king.

893. Zwentibold (illegitimate son of Arnulf) was sent to Italy in response to an appeal from Pope Formosus (891–896), but he accomplished nothing. Arnulf then came in person (894) and received an oath of fealty from the Italian magnates, but Guido continued as emperor and was succeeded by

892-898. **Lambert.** Arnulf embarked upon a second expedition, took Rome, and was formally crowned (896). (*Cont. p. 230.*)

g. THE EMPIRE OF CHARLEMAGNE AND ITS DISINTEGRATION, 747-886

747-768. PEPIN THE SHORT, who attempted to conciliate the Church by granting and restoring lands to it.

752. **Pepin was elected king** by the Frankish magnates. Both the house of Pepin and the papacy (in the act of usurping political control from the emperor at Constantinople) needed each other's support. The immediate need of the popes was protection against the expanding Lombard monarchy. **Aistulf,** king of the Lombards, had taken Ravenna (751), the seat of the exarch, besieged Rome, and exacted tribute.

754. **Pope Stephen II** arrived in Gaul, anointed Pepin, and by conferring the title *Patricius* (which could legally come only from Constantinople) designated him in a sense regent and protector of Italy. The net result was to give some shadow of authority to Pepin's new title as king of the Franks.

754. Pepin marched into Italy, defeated the Lombards, and required them to hand over the exarchate and Pentapolis to the pope. The Lombards failed to do so.

756. Pepin returned and, after defeating the Lombards again, made his famous Donation. The **Donation of Pepin** (which Pepin had no legal right to make) established the Papal States (*Patrimonium Petri*) and began the temporal power of the papacy. It also established the Franks, a distant, non-Italian power, as the allies and defenders of the papacy.

759. Pepin conquered Septimania, disciplined Aquitaine, and so brought effective Frankish rule to the Pyrenees. On his death his lands were given to his sons: Charles receiving Austrasia, Neustria, and northern Aquitaine; Carloman, southern Aquitaine, Burgundy, Provence, Septimania. The brothers ruled together, 768–771; Charles alone, 771–814.

771-814. CHARLES THE GREAT (Charlemagne), a reign of the first magnitude in European history. Charles was a typical German, well over six feet tall, a superb swimmer, of athletic frame, with large, expressive eyes and merry disposition. He understood Greek, spoke Latin, but could not learn to write. He preferred the Frankish dress. In general he continued the Frankish policy: (1) expansion of Frankish rule to include all the Germans was completed (omitting only Scandinavia and Britain); (2) close understanding with the papacy; (3) support of church reform (which settled the foundations of medieval Christian unity.)

Italian conquest and reduction of German tribes: Already overlord of the Lombards, Charles married King Desiderius' daughter, soon repudiated her, conquered

773-774. Lombard Italy, and became king of the Lombards, whose kingdom was absorbed into the Frankish Empire. Charlemagne also established his rule in Venetia, Istria, Dalmatia, and Corsica.

787-788. Bavaria was incorporated, its duke, Tassilo, first made a vassal and then deposed.

785. Saxony, after a costly and bitter struggle of 30 years, involving 18 campaigns, was conquered, and Christianity forcibly introduced

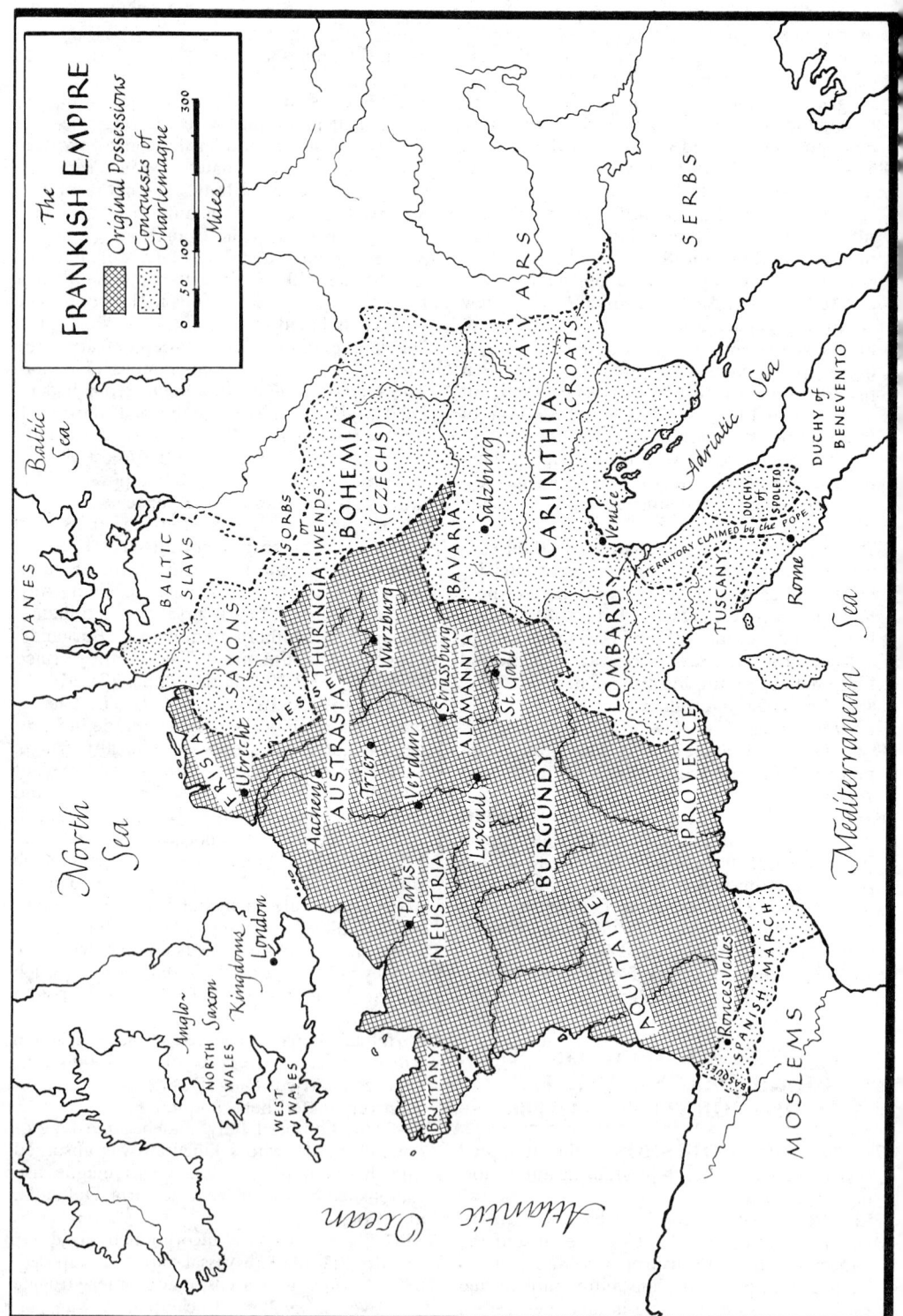

The FRANKISH EMPIRE

Original Possessions
Conquests of Charlemagne

Miles
0   50   100   300

despite stubborn pagan resistance. Foundation of the bishopric of Bremen (781).

795-796. The Avars (on the lower Danube) were reduced.

801. After the Frankish defeat at **Roncesvalles** (778), the Moslems in northeastern Spain were gradually reduced (Barcelona taken, 801), and the Spanish March created.

Establishment of marks (after c. 782) to hold the conquests: Dane Mark, the Altmark (against the Wends), Thuringian Mark, Bohemian Mark, Ostmark (against the Avars), Friulian Mark (on the Italian border), and the Spanish March. These marks were also centers of colonization and germanization.

Relation to the Church. Charlemagne held it to be his duty to defend the Church and the pope, and to maintain the faith. He treated the pope like any Frankish bishop, but recognized his unique spiritual prestige. His visit (774) to Rome was the first of a Frankish sovereign: the Donation of Pepin was confirmed, but the terms are not clear. The pope crowned Charles' son, Pepin, king of Italy (781), his son Louis, king of Aquitaine.

REVIVAL OF THE ROMAN EMPIRE IN THE WEST. Pope Leo III, a submissive pontiff, notified Charlemagne of his election to the Holy See, and dated his pontificate by Charlemagne's regnal years. Driven from Rome (799) by a conspiracy and riot, he sought refuge at Charlemagne's court and was restored by Frankish troops.

800. Charlemagne arrived in Rome, allowed Leo to clear himself of a series of charges by oath (avoiding the trial of a pope), and was crowned emperor in St. Peter's on Christmas Day. According to Einhard, Charlemagne avowed his regret at the coronation. He cannot have been unaware of the general plan, and his feeling may have been due to modesty or concern at Byzantine reactions or hostility to papal pretensions. Charlemagne disregarded the imperial title in a partition of the empire (806), and arranged to have his son Louis crown himself (813). Theoretically the coronation of 800 marked a return to the dualism of Theodosius I (i.e. two emperors over an undivided empire). In fact the Frankish Empire was more German than Roman in population and institutions. Byzantium regarded Charlemagne as a usurper; Charlemagne seems to have meditated a marriage with the Empress Irene as one solution of the difficulty. The papal coronation, an act of rebellion in Byzantine eyes, marked a definite **break between Rome and Constantinople.** The Emperor Michael I recognized (812) Charlemagne's title in the west in return for sovereignty in Venice, Istria, Dalmatia.

GOVERNMENT. (1) **In the Church:** Charlemagne's rule was a theocracy, and he insisted on supremacy over the Frankish Church, legislating on all subjects, settling dogmatic questions, deciding appointments, presiding at synods. (2) **In the Frankish state:** centralization continued; taxation in the Roman sense (which survived only under local and private auspices) was replaced by services in return for land grants (the economic basis of Carolingian society). Such services included forced labor on public works among the lower ranks, the provision of food for the court and public officials on duty, and judicial and military obligations (primarily among the upper ranks). Charlemagne's continuous campaigns reduced the small farmers, accentuating the tendency to serfdom. Charlemagne tried to offset this tendency by allowing groups of poorer farmers to cooperate in sending a single soldier, and by excusing the poorest from ordinary field service. Systematization of the army and of military service was also begun. Commendation and immunity continued, and the basis of later feudal development was firmly established.

Administration: The tribal dukes were largely eliminated and government was carried on by counts, appointed for life, but frequently removed. This system was extended to Italy, Bavaria, and Saxony. To prevent the counts establishing an hereditary tenure, and to limit local abuses, the *missi dominici* (usually a bishop and count) were introduced (802) as officers on circuit in a given district. The missi held their own courts, had power to remove a count for cause, and were charged with the supervision of financial, judicial, and clerical administration. They formed an essential link between the local and central government. Under the counts were viscounts and vicars (*centenarii*). Margraves (*Mark Grafen*) were set over the marks with extended powers to meet the needs of their position. Local administration of justice was reformed by the introduction of *scabini,* local landowners appointed by the counts to sit as permanent judiciary officers.

The Carolingian **revival of learning:** Charlemagne, perhaps out of concern for the improvement of ecclesiastical education, set up the Palace School under **Alcuin** from the School of York, later abbot of Tours. Various clerics were also given liberal grants that they might establish local schools, though no general system of education was introduced in the Frankish Empire. In general, the source of inspiration was Latin rather than Greek. **Einhard,** for example, who came to the Palace School from Fulda, wrote his biography of Charlemagne in the manner of Suetonius. At Charlemagne's court were gathered scholars and literary men of almost every nationality, including **Peter of Pisa,** the grammarian, the Visigothic poet **Theodulf,** the Lombard historian, **Paul the Deacon** (*Historia gentis Langobardorum*). Great care was given to the copying of texts, and the refined Carolingian minuscule was evolved.

814-887. THE DISINTEGRATION OF THE CAROLINGIAN EMPIRE.

Such efficiency as the Carolingian government possessed under Charlemagne derived rather from his personality than from permanent institutions. Local administration was carried on by unpaid officials whose compensation was a share of the revenue. Local offices tended to become hereditary. The tentative partitions of the empire in Charlemagne's lifetime followed Frankish tradition, and had no relation to any racial or national elements. One son, Louis the Pious, survived, and the empire was passed on to him (quite by accident) undivided. The decisive stage in the partition of the empire came under Louis and his heirs.

814-840. LOUIS the Pious (emperor), educated at the Palace School, crowned in his father's lifetime. Sincerely religious, a reformer of his court, the Frankish Church, and the monasteries, he allowed himself to be crowned again by the pope (816). Ineffectual as a soldier and ruler. Louis and his heirs concentrated on a long struggle (leading to civil war) over territorial questions, to the neglect of government, foreign policy, and defense, a program which hastened the breakup of the empire.

817-838. A significant series of **partitions** involving Louis' sons: Lothair (d. 855), Louis the German (d. 876), Pepin (d. 838), and their half-brother, Charles the Bald (d. 877).

The **division of 817:** Aquitaine and parts of Septimania and Burgundy went to Pepin as sub-king; Bavaria and the marches to the east were assigned to Louis the German as sub-king undivided; Francia, German and Gallic, and most of Burgundy were retained by Louis and his eldest son Lothair. Italy went to a third sub-king.

The **division of 838:** Charles the Bald was assigned Neustria and to this was added Aquitaine on the death of Pepin. Charles' holding, which had no name, approximated (accidentally) medieval France and was mainly Romance in speech.

840-855. LOTHAIR I (emperor). On the death of Louis the Pious the three heirs continued their struggle, and after the indecisive **battle of Fontenay** (841) Carolingian prestige sank to a new depth. Charles the Bald and Louis the German formed an alliance against Lothair (who was supported by the clergy in the interests of unity) in the bilingual (Teutonic and Romance) **Oaths of Strassburg** (842), sworn by the rulers and their armies, each in their own vernacular. They then forced a family compact upon Lothair at Verdun.

843. The **TREATY OF VERDUN** divided the administration and control of the Carolingian Empire as follows: (1) **Lothair** kept the (empty) title of emperor, and was king of Italy and of an amorphous territory (the "middle kingdom") which was bounded roughly by the Scheldt, the upper Meuse, Saône, and Rhone on the west, and by the Rhine and Frisia on the east (i.e. the territory of Provence, Burgundy, and what was later called *Lotharingia*); (2) **Louis the German,** as king of the (East) Franks, ruled a realm essentially Teutonic in blood, speech, and geography, extending from the Rhine (except Frisia) to the eastern frontier of the empire; (3) **Charles the Bald,** as king of the (West) Franks, received a realm (loosely called Carolingia for a time) made up of West Francia and Aquitaine, Gascony, Septimania, etc., mainly Romance in speech, approximating medieval France in general outline.

855-875. LOUIS II (emperor). At Lothair I's death his lands were divided as follows among his sons: Louis II received Italy, Charles (d. 863), the newly formed kingdom of Provence (centered around the city of Arles), and Lothair II the inchoate aggregate (from Frisia to the Alps and from the Rhine to Scheldt) which began to be called *Lotharii regnum* or *Lotharingia* (modern Lorraine).

870. **Treaty of Mersen,** following the death (869) of Lothair II, king of Lorraine. Louis the German forced Charles the Bald (crowned king of Lorraine, 869) to divide equally and solely on the basis of revenue the lands of Lothair outside of Italy. Thus Louis gained a strip of land which brought his frontier west of the Rhine.

875-877. CHARLES THE BALD, emperor.

877-881. Anarchy and interregnum in the empire.

879. The **kingdom of Burgundy** (Cisjuran Burgundy) was established by Boso of Provence.

888. The **kingdom of Juran Burgundy** (i.e. Besançon, Basel, Lausanne, Geneva, etc.) was erected by Rudolf I. It passed to the empire by bequest in the time of Conrad II.

c. 787-925. THE 9TH-CENTURY INVASIONS:

(1) **In the north.** Bands of Northmen (Scandinavians, p. 185), under pressure of population and resentful at the rise of local kings, pushed outward from Scandinavia. The Swedes penetrated into Russia, the Norwegians and Danes moved into the northern islands (including the

The Carolingian Dynasty (768-987)

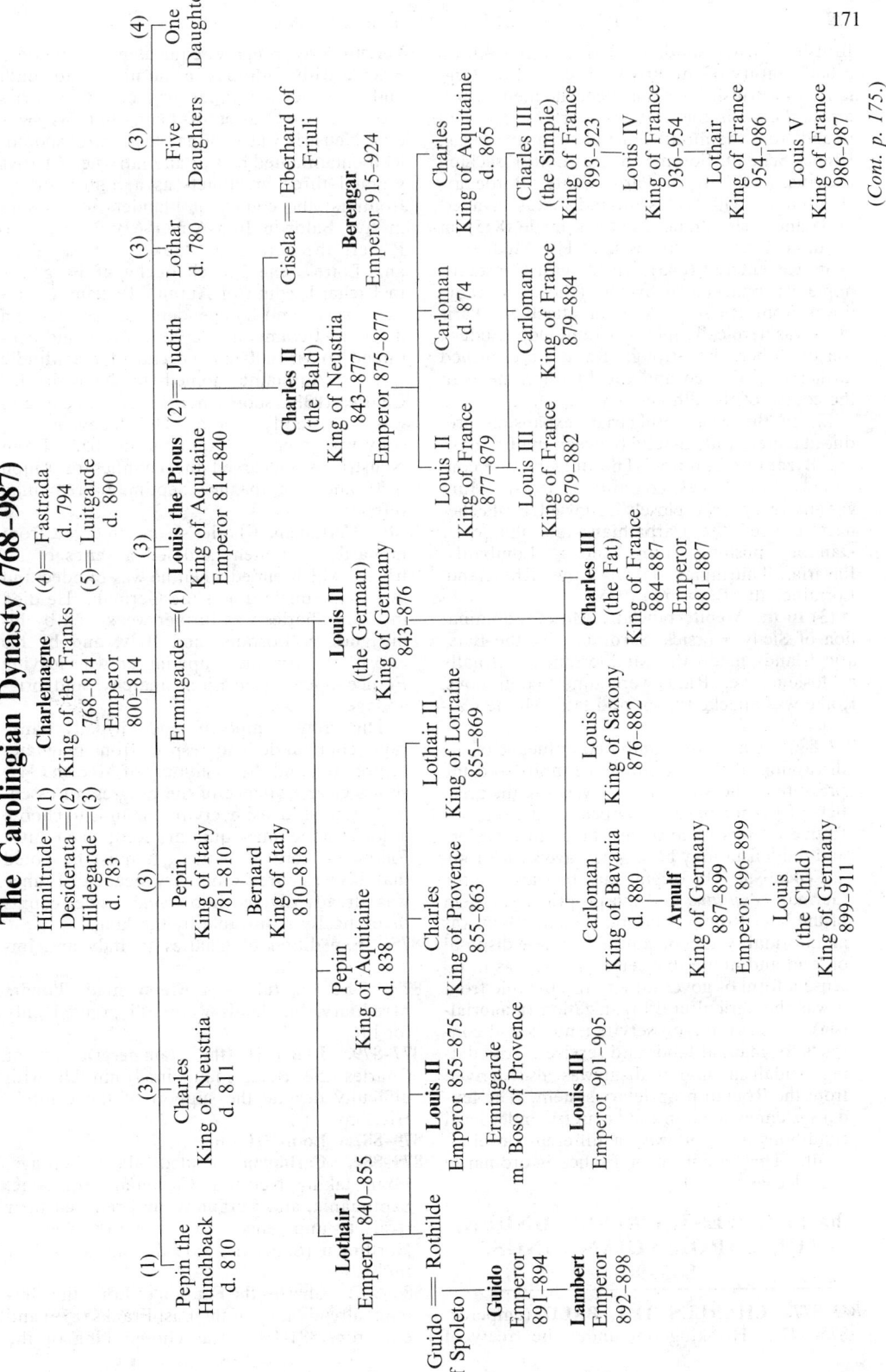

(Cont. p. 175.)

British Isles) and south to the Continent. Within a half century of the first raid (c. 787) on England, the British Isles had been flooded. Masters of the sea in the west, the Northmen pushed inland from the mouths of the great rivers (e.g. Rhine, Scheldt, Somme, Seine, Loire), sacking the cities (e.g. Utrecht, Paris, Nantes, Bordeaux, Hamburg, Seville). "Normandy" was invaded (841) and a simultaneous attack made (845) on all three Frankish kingdoms. The Mediterranean was entered (843). In the east Constantinople was attacked by Swedes (*Rus*), who came down from Russia. A great attack on Paris (885) was heroically met by Count Odo (Eudes), son of Robert the Strong. Raids were pushed farther into France and the Mediterranean in the course of the 9th century.

(2) **In the east.** Bulgarian expansion produced a great Bulgar state between the Frankish and Byzantine Empires. The Bulgars were converted to the Greek communion (870). Hungarians (Magyars), closely followed by Pechenegs, crossed the Carpathians and the lower Danube, pushing into Venetia, Lombardy, Bavaria, Thuringia, Saxony, the Rhineland, Lorraine, and Burgundy (925).

(3) **In the Mediterranean.** Moslem domination of Sicily, Corsica, Sardinia, and the Balearic Islands made the Mediterranean virtually a Moslem lake. Raids were almost continuous, Rome was attacked (846) and later Monte Cassino.

852-886. Under the combined influence of the disruption of the Carolingian Empire and the pressure of the 9th-century invasions, the **great fiefs** of France began to appear as the only effective centers of local resistance to invasion, and feudalism may be said to have struck root.

Feudalism. Its origins may be traced to the German *comitatus* and the proprietary system of the later Roman Empire. Essentially it was an informal system of contracts for the disposal of land and honorable services, and was in no sense a form of government. Inseparable from it was the agricultural organization (**manorialism**), which rested on servile tenures and contracts for manual labor and services. Antedating feudalism, manorialism was also derived from the Roman proprietary system. The feudal system evolved in each country under local conditions and followed a different development. The feudalism of France is ordinarily regarded as typical.

h. THE WEST FRANKS UNDER THE CAROLINGIAN KINGS, 843-987

843-877. CHARLES THE BALD (emperor, 875-877). His kingdom under the **treaty of** Verdun was roughly equivalent to modern France with additions in the north and south and a restricted frontier on the east. Charles was effective master of Laon, but his sway over Neustria was nominal, his control sporadically maintained by war and intrigue. Charles granted three great fiefs as a buffer for his frontiers: the county of Flanders to his son-in-law, Baldwin Iron-Arm (862); Neustria to Robert the Strong as "duke between Seine and Loire"; the French duchy of Burgundy to Richard, count of Autun. Brittany (Amorica) was semi-independent under its own dukes and counts in the 9th century and continued so virtually to the end of the Middle Ages. Aquitaine, joined to Neustria for Charles (838), soon emerged as a duchy and was consistently hostile. The duchy of Gascony was joined to Aquitaine in 1052. From Neustria were carved the counties of Anjou (870) and Champagne. Septimania remained refractory.

870. Carloman, Charles's son, emerged from monastic retirement and led a series of intrigues which ended when he was blinded and fled to his uncle, Louis the German. He died in 874. Charles was further weakened by his intrigues in Lorraine and Italy, and by his efforts to win the imperial crown, leaving France open to invasion, anarchy, and brigandage.

The crown, impotent and virtually bankrupt, commanded no respect from magnates or prelates, and the **Capitulary of Mersen** (847) shows clear evidence of the progress of essentially feudal ideas; every free man is to choose a lord; none may quit his lord; each must follow his lord in battle. It must be noted that this was purely a military measure. France was already divided into *comtés* under counts theoretically removable by the king.

875. Expedition of Charles to Italy and imperial coronation.

877. The **Capitulary of Kiersy** made honors hereditary, but lands were still granted only for life.

877-879. Louis II (the stammerer), son of Charles the Bald, maintained himself with difficulty despite the support of the Church. His sons

879-882. Louis III and

879-884. Carloman divided their heritage, Louis taking Neustria, Carloman Aquitaine, Septimania, and Burgundy, and reduced their rivals to impotence. Louis' victory over the Northmen (Saucourt, 881) did not stop their raids.

884-887. Charles the Fat, son of Louis the German, already king of the East Franks (879) and emperor (881-887), was chosen king of the

West Franks instead of Charles the Simple, the five-year-old brother of Louis and Carloman. Charles the Fat, having failed (886) to aid the gallant Odo (Eudes) against the Northmen, was deposed (887).

888-898. Odo (Eudes), count of Paris, marquis of Neustria (son of Count Robert the Strong, whence the name *Robertians* for the line before Hugh Capet) was elected king of the West Franks by one faction of magnates to avoid a minority on the deposition (887) of Charles the Fat. Another faction chose Charles III, the Simple, son of Louis II (Carolingian). Despite five years of civil war

893-923. Charles III ruled from Laon, the last Carolingian with any real authority in France. Charles, unable to expel the Northmen from the mouth of the Seine, granted (911) **Rollo** (Hrolf the Ganger, d. 931), a large part of what was later Normandy, for which Rollo did homage.

Formation of Normandy. Rollo was baptized (912) under the name **Robert,** acquired middle Normandy (the Bessin, 924) and the western part of the duchy (Cotentin and Avranche, 933). The colony was recruited with fresh settlers from Scandinavia for the best part of a century, and was able to retain a strong local individuality. Yet soon after 1000 the duchy was French in both speech and law. Between this period and the accession of Duke William I (the Conqueror) Norman history is fragmentary.

923-987. The French kingship. Robert, count of Paris, duke between the Seine and Loire, won the West Frankish crown with the aid of his sons-in-law, Herbert, count of Vermandois, and Rudolf, duke of Burgundy, but was killed (923), leaving a son (later Hugh the Great) too young to rule.

929-936. Rudolf followed Robert as the foe of Charles the Simple, and ruled with no opposition after Charles' death. **Hugh the Great,** master of Burgundy and Neustria, declined the crown, preferring to rule through the young Carolingian heir,

936-954. Louis IV, a son of Charles the Simple. Hugh's title, Duke of the French, seems to have implied governmental functions as much as territorial sovereignty, and he held most of the northern barons under his suzerainty.

954-986. Lothair succeeded his father Louis IV. On the death of Hugh the Great, his son Hugh, known as *Capet*, succeeded him (956).

978. Lothair's effort to gain Lorraine led to an invasion by Emperor Otto II to the walls of Paris. Hugh Capet, in alliance with Emperor Otto III, and aided by Gerbert of Reims, reduced Lothair's rule at Laon to a nullity. Lothair's son

986-987. Louis V was the last Carolingian ruler of France.

987. ELECTION OF HUGH CAPET, engineered by Adalbero, bishop of Reims, and by Gerbert. Hugh was crowned at Noyon with the support of the duke of Normandy and the count of Anjou. His title was recognized by the Emperor Otto III in exchange for Hugh's claims to Lorraine. The emergence of the new house of Capet was not the victory of a race, a nationality, or a principle, but the triumph of a family, already distinguished, over a decadent rival. (*Cont. p. 240.*)

i. GERMANY UNDER THE CAROLINGIAN AND SAXON EMPERORS, 843-1024

[*For a complete list of the Holy Roman emperors see Appendix V.*]

843-876. LOUIS THE GERMAN. Increasing Slavic and Norse pressure (general Norse attack, 845, on Carolingian lands). Louis had three sons: Carloman (d. 880), Louis (d. 882), and Charles the Fat. Carloman was assigned Bavaria and the East Mark; Louis, Saxony and Franconia; Charles, Alamannia. Contest with Charles the Bald for Lorraine. By the **Treaty of Mersen** (870) Louis added a strip of land west of the Rhine.

876-887. CHARLES THE FAT. He blocked Charles the Bald's advance toward the Rhine. Emergence of the kingdom of Cisjuran Burgundy (i.e. Dauphiné, Provence, part of Languedoc) under Boso (879). Expedition to Italy and coronation by John VIII (881). Negotiations (882) with the Northmen, now permanently established in Flanders. While Charles was in Italy settling a papal election, a great Norse invasion burst on France (Odo's defense of Paris, 886). **Deposition of Charles** by the Franconian, Saxon, Bavarian, Thuringian, and Swabian magnates at Tribur (887).

887 (896)-899. Arnulf (illegitimate son of Carloman, grandson of Louis the German). A certain supremacy was conceded to Arnulf by the various rulers of Germany and Italy who rendered a kind of homage to him. Victory over the Norse on the Dyle (Löwen, 891); resistance to the Slavic (Moravian) advance (893), with Magyar aid. Magyar raids after 900. Arnulf dared not leave Germany to answer the appeal of Pope Stephen V (885-891) for aid. His illegitimate son Zwentibold was sent on the call of Pope Formosus (891-896), but accomplished nothing (893). Arnulf went to Italy in person (894), was crowned king and received an oath from most of the magnates. On another appeal from Formosus (895) he took Rome and was crowned emperor (896).

899-911. Louis the Child (born 893), last of the Carolingians, elected king by the magnates at Forchheim (900). Increasing Norse, Slavic, and Magyar pressure and devastation.

The **weakening of the royal power** as the East Frankish kingdom of the Carolingians declined, and the survival of tribal consciousness left the way open for the emergence of the stem (German *Stamm,* a tribe) duchies. These duchies preserved the traditions of ancient tribal culture, and their independent development under semi-royal dukes (beginning in the 9th century) ensured the disruption of German unity for a thousand years. These stem duchies were: **Franconia** (the Conradiners ultimately drove the Babenbergers into the East Mark, later Austria); **Lorraine** (not strictly a stem duchy but with a tradition of unity); **Swabia** (the early ducal history is obscure); **Bavaria** (under the Arnulfings; repulse of the Magyars, acquisition of the mark of Carinthia); **Saxony** (under the Liudolfingers; repulse of the Danes and Wends, addition of Thuringia); **Frisia** (no tribal duke appeared).

911. End of the East Frankish line of the Carolingians, with the death of Louis the Child (911); the German magnates, to avoid accepting a ruler of the West Frankish (French) line, elected Conrad, duke of Franconia.

911-918. Conrad I. Magyar raids and ducal rebellions in Saxony, Bavaria, and Swabia met vigorous but futile resistance from Conrad. Lorraine passed (911) temporarily under the suzerainty of the West Frankish ruler, Charles the Simple. Conrad nominated his strongest foe, Henry, duke of Saxony, as his successor, and he was elected.

919-1024. THE SAXON (OR OTTONIAN) HOUSE.

919-936. KING HENRY I (called *the Fowler,* supposedly because the messengers announcing his election found him hawking). Tolerant of the dukes, he forced recognition of his authority; cool to the Church, he avoided ecclesiastical coronation.

920-921. Reduction of the duke of Bavaria; alliance with Charles the Simple.

923-925. Lorraine restored to the German Kingdom and unified into the **duchy of Lorraine,** a center of spiritual and intellectual ferment. Henry's daughter married the duke of Lorraine (928).

924-933. Truce (and tribute) **with the Magyars,** fortification of the Elbe and Weser Valleys (Saxony and Thuringia), palisading of towns, villas, monasteries, etc., establishment of *Burgwarde,* i.e. garrisons (which later often became towns like Naumburg, Quedlinburg), where one-ninth of the Saxon effectives were

on duty and trained as horsemen each year.

928. Saxon expedition across the frozen Havel River **against the Wends:** Branibor (Brandenburg) stormed; the Wends driven up the Elbe; creation of the marks of Branibor, Meissen, and (later) Lusatia as guardians of the middle Elbe.

933. Henry ended the Magyar truce with his **victory at Riade** on the Unstrut River, the first great defeat of the Magyars. Occupation of the land between the Schlei and the Eider (Charlemagne's Dane Mark), and erection of the mark of Schleswig, guardian of the Elbe mouth; the Danish king was made tributary and forced to receive Christian missionaries. Henry had prepared the way for his son, whose election was a formality, the succession becoming virtually hereditary.

936-973. KING OTTO I (the Great). Otto revived the policy of Arnulf, was crowned and anointed at Aachen, Charlemagne's capital; his coronation banquet revived the Carolingian coronation banquet (of Roman origin) at which the duke of Franconia served ceremonially as steward, the duke of Swabia as cup-bearer, the duke of Lorraine as chamberlain, and the duke of Bavaria as marshal.

Otto's vigorous **assertion of royal authority** (a three-year war reduced the dukes of Bavaria, Franconia, Lorraine, and Saxony). He followed the policy of keeping the great duchies (except Saxony) in his own hands or those of his family. Taking Conrad, the boy king of Arles (Provence and Burgundy), under his protection (937), Otto forced the recognition of his overlordship (forestalling Hugh of Provence); Conrad's sister, Adelheid, married Lothair, one of the claimants to the crown of Italy, and later Otto himself. The Bavarians defeated Otto (944) at Wels, but Otto conquered (950) Duke Boleslav of Bohemia and put the duchy under the suzerainty of Bavaria.

951-952. Otto's first expedition to Italy to keep the passes through the mountains open. Marriage to Adelheid and assumption of the crown of Italy; the pope refused him imperial coronation; Berengar of Ivrea, forced into vassalage, ceded the marks of Verona, Friuli, Istria (the keys to the passes), to Otto's brother Henry, duke of Bavaria.

953. Revolt of Otto's son (Ludolf, duke of Swabia), his son-in-law Conrad (duke of Lorraine), and others (suppressed, 955).

955. BATTLE OF THE LECHFELD. Otto, with an army recruited from all the duchies, ended the Magyar menace by a great victory. Defeat of the Wends on the river Recknitz. Re-establishment and colonization with Bavarians of Charlemagne's East Mark (Austria).

968. The bishoprics established among the

(*From p. 171*)

The Saxon and Salian Emperors (919–1125)

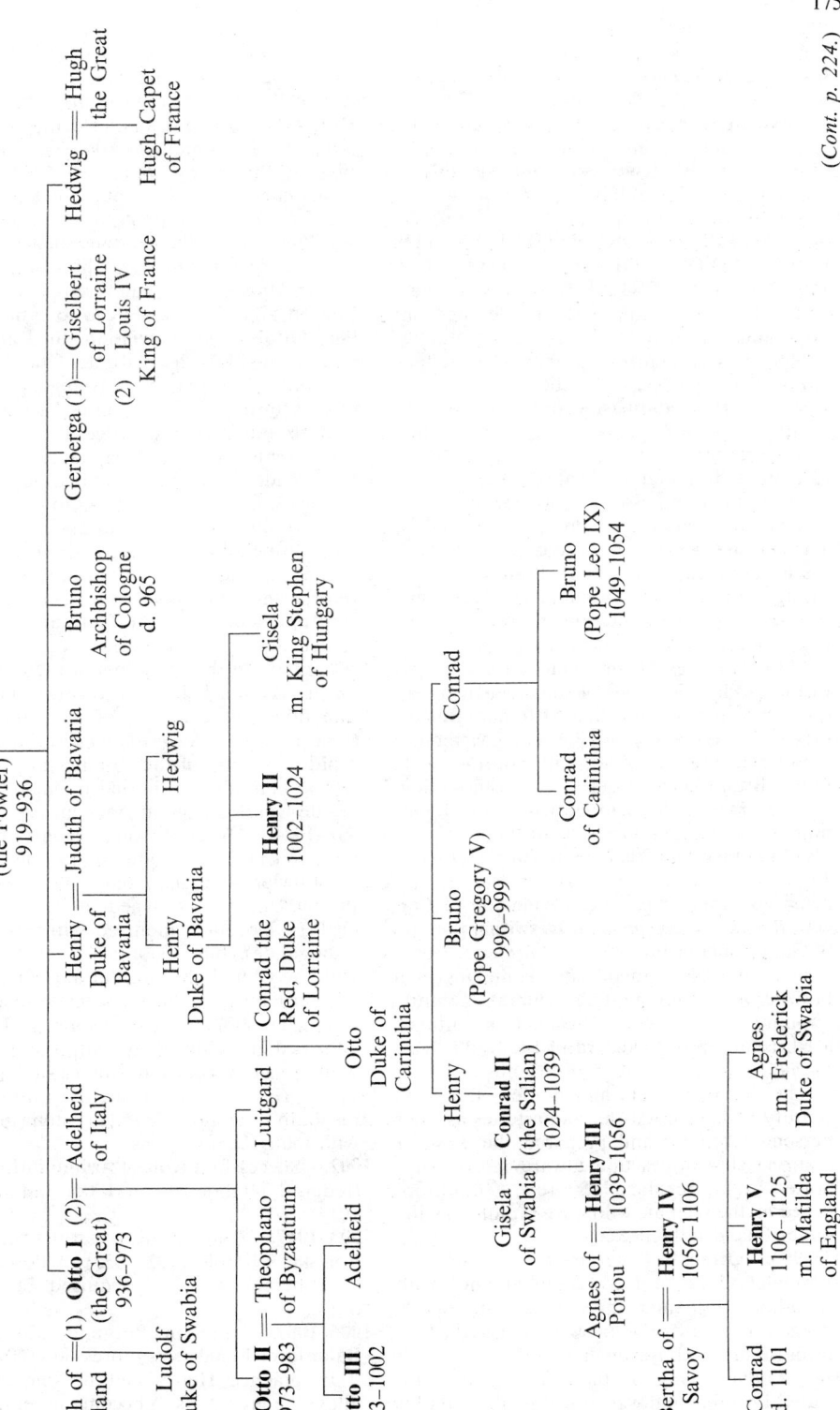

(*Cont. p. 224.*)

Slavs (e.g. Brandenburg, Merseburg, Meissen, Zeitz) were consolidated under the new **archbishopric of Magdeburg.** German bishoprics were everywhere filled with bishops loyal to the monarchy, marking the alliance of the king and the Church against feudal opposition.

961–964. Otto's second expedition to Italy on the appeal of Pope John XII for protection. Assumption of the crown of Italy at Pavia.

962. IMPERIAL CORONATION BY THE POPE: REVIVAL OF THE ROMAN EMPIRE IN THE WEST. Otto put a temporary end to feudal anarchy in Rome, deposed one pope and nominated another, and compelled the pope to recognize the emperor's right to approve or reject papal elections.

966–972. Otto's third expedition to Italy: deposition of one pope, restoration of another; nomination of a new pope; punishment of the Romans. Imperial coronation (967) of the future Otto II and assertion of suzerainty over Capua and Benevento (967). Betrothal of **Theophano** (probably a niece or grandniece of the Byzantine Emperor, John Tzimisces) to the future Otto II (969); coronation of Theophano (972) and marriage to Otto (supposedly bringing Greek Italy as her portion).

Otto, with the able assistance of his brother Bruno, archbishop of Cologne, began a cultural revival (the so-called **Ottonian Renaissance**) in the manner of Charlemagne; late in life, he learned to read, but not to speak, Latin; Bruno knew Greek. The cosmopolitan court literary circle included Irish and English monks, and learned Greeks and Italians, notably **Liutprand of Cremona** (*Historia Ottonis; Legatio Constantinopolitana*). Great literary activity of the monasteries: **Widukind of Corvey** (*Res Gestae Saxonicae*); **Roswitha,** the nun of Gandersheim, author of the *Carmen de Gestis Ottonis* and of learned Latin comedies in a bowdlerized Terentine style, celebrating saintly virginity; the vernacular *Heliand* (9th century), a Christian epic; **Ekkekard of St. Gall's** *Waltherius,* inspired by German legends.

The German rulers and nobles of the 9th century had regarded the monasteries as their personal property and prepared the way for a strong clerical reaction toward reform supported by the regular clergy (e.g. Cluny), opposed by the seculars who were rapidly passing under feudal influences.

973–983. Otto II. The revolt of Henry the Wrangler, duke of Bavaria, in alliance with Boleslav of Bohemia, and others, required five years to put down; Henry was banished (978). Repulse of a Danish incursion.

978. Lothair, king of the West Franks, invaded Lorraine and was forced to abandon his claims by Otto's invasion of France (980).

981–982. Otto's campaign in southern Italy, to expel the Saracens and reduce the Byzantine power, ended in defeat.

983–1002. Otto III (an infant of three years). Rule of his brilliant mother Theophano (983–991), his grandmother Adelheid, and Archbishop Willigis of Mainz (991–996). Under Theophano's influence his education was in the Byzantine tradition; his tutor **Gerbert of Aurillac,** one of the most learned men of his day, whose brilliance won him the nickname *Stupor Mundi.* Henry the Wrangler proclaimed himself king, but was forced to submit.

996. Otto's first expedition to Italy ended Crescentius II's sway in Rome; Otto designated his cousin Bruno as pope (Gregory V).

998. Returning to Rome on his **second expedition to Italy,** Otto deposed the Crescentine pope, John XVI, and decapitated Crescentius. Otto made Gerbert of Aurillac pope, as Sylvester II. Sylvester shared Otto's devotion to the Carolingian tradition of an intimate union and co-operation of pope and emperor. Otto's romantic antiquarianism led him to a plan of reform through universal imperial overlordship independent of the German crown. He settled down at Rome and began a theatrical restoration of the splendors of the city: palace on the Aventine, Byzantine court and Byzantine titles, futile revival of ancient formulae (seals inscribed *Renovatio imperii romani,* etc.); rapid alienation of the Roman populace. He left no heir and was buried by his own orders beside Charlemagne at Aachen.

1002–1024. Henry II (son of Henry the Wrangler, cousin of Otto, great-grandson of Henry the Fowler) emerged from the contest for the throne, and was crowned emperor at Rome (1014). Devout (canonized with his wife, St. Kunigunde), but a political realist and firm with the Church, he concentrated his attention on Germany. Against episcopal objections he founded (1007) the great bishopric of Bamberg, endowed it richly as an outpost of German culture against Slavdom; the cathedral, one of the glories of German architecture, contains his tomb. Vigorous (Gorzian) monastic reform with many confiscations.

1002. Successful **revolt of Ardoin** in Lombardy (reduced temporarily in 1004, and finally in 1014).

1003–1017. A long, unsuccessful struggle with Boleslav Chrobry (992–1025) of Poland, duke of Bohemia, who had acquired Lusatia and Silesia.

1006–1007. Unrest in Burgundy and **revolt of Baldwin of Flanders** (suppressed, 1007).

In practice Henry had no choice but to allow the great fiefs to become hereditary. He relied heavily on the clergy to supply advisers and administrators, and looked to the Church also for military and financial support, but he dominated the Church in Germany through his control of the episcopal appointments. Extensive secularization and reform of the monasteries of the Church resulted.

(*Cont. p. 220.*)

j. SPAIN

(1) The Visigothic Kingdom, 466-711

[*For a complete list of the Caliphs see Appendix III.*]

In the time of **Euric** (466-484) the Visigothic rule extended from the Loire to Gibraltar and from the Bay of Biscay to the Rhone. The capital was Toulouse.

507. Clovis' victory in the **battle of Vouillé** obliged the Visigoths to withdraw over the Pyrenees, retaining only Septimania north of the mountains. The new capital was Toledo.

The Visigoths in Spain were a small minority (about one in five) and were rapidly romanized (e.g. the *Breviary of Alaric*). The conversion of King Reccared (587) from Arianism to Roman orthodoxy brought an end to their religious separateness, accelerated the process of romanization and initiated the domination of the clergy over the monarchy. The **Synod of Toledo** (633) assumed the right to confirm elections to the crown. After 600 the Jews were forced to accept baptism, for which reason they later on welcomed the Moslem invasion. Visigothic speech gradually disappeared and the current vernacular was of Latin origin. Roman organization and tradition survived to a marked degree. **Isidore of Seville** (c. 560-636), a bishop, theologian, historian, man of letters, and scientist, produced in his *Etymologiae* a general reference work that remained a standard manual for 500 years and was a medium for transmitting much ancient knowledge to the medieval world.

(2) Moslem Spain, 711-1031

711-715. THE MOSLEM CONQUEST. In 711 a mixed force of Arabs and Berbers, led by the Berber **Tariq** (whence Gibraltar—*Gebel al-Tariq*) crossed from Africa. Roderick, the last Visigothic king, was completely defeated in the **battle on the Guadalete** (Rio Barbate), whereupon his kingdom collapsed. The Moslems took Córdoba and the capital, Toledo. Tariq was followed (712) by his master, **Musa,** who took Medina Sidonia, Seville, Merida, and Saragossa. The Moslems soon reached the Pyrenees (719), having driven the remnants of the Christians into the mountains of the north and west.

732. In the **battle of Tours** the Moslems, having crossed into France, were decisively defeated by Charles Martel and the Franks. By 759 they had been entirely expelled from France.

756-1031. THE OMAYYAD DYNASTY OF CÓRDOBA.

756-788. Abd ar-Rahman I, emir. He was the grandson of the Omayyad caliph of Damascus, and was the founder of the Moorish state in Spain. Christians were given toleration in return for payment of a poll tax. The Jews were very well treated. But Abd ar-Rahman met with vigorous opposition from the Arab nobility, which was supported from abroad by Pepin and Charlemagne.

777. Invasion of Spain by Charlemagne, checked by the heroic defense of Saragossa. Annihilation of his rear-guard by Basques at Roncesvalles (778—*Song of Roland*). Wars with the Franks continued throughout the rest of the century, Charlemagne ultimately conquering northeastern Spain as far as the Ebro River (capture of Barcelona, 801).

788-796. Hisham I, son of Abd ar-Rahman, emir, during whose reign Malikite doctrines were introduced in Spain.

796-822. Al-Hakam I, son of Hisham, emir. Revolts in Córdoba (805, 817) and Toledo (814). The Córdoban rebels, expelled from Spain, went to Alexandria and thence to Crete, which they reconquered.

822-852. Abd ar-Rahman II, son of Al-Hakam. During his reign Alfonso II of Leon invaded Aragon. He was defeated and his kingdom destroyed. The Franks too were driven back in Catalonia. The Normans first appeared on the coasts. In 837 a revolt of Christians and Jews in Toledo was suppressed, but Christian fanatics continued to be active, especially in Córdoba.

852-886. Muhammad I. He put down another Christian uprising in Córdoba, and carried on extensive operations against the Christian states of Leon, Galicia, and Navarre (Pampeluna taken 861).

886-888. Al Mundhir.

888-912. Abdallah, brother of Al Mundhir.

912-961. Abd ar-Rahman III. The ablest and most gifted of the Omayyads of Spain, who assumed the titles of *Caliph* and *Amir al-Mu'minin* in 929, thus asserting supremacy in Islam as against the Abbasid caliphs of Bagdad. Abd ar-Rahman's reign was marked by the pacification of the country, by completion of governmental organization (centralization), by naval activity, by agricultural advance, and by industrial progress. Development of huge paper mills by the 12th century. **Córdoba** (population c. 500,000) became the greatest intellectual center of Europe, with a huge paper trade, great libraries, and pre-eminent schools (medicine, mathematics, philosophy, poetry, music; much translation from Greek and Latin).

The height of **Moslem learning** was reached by **Averroës** (ibn Rushd, c. 1126–1198), philosopher, physician, and commentator on Plato and Aristotle, master of the Christian schoolmen.

The aristocracy, by this time almost extinguished, was replaced by a rich middle class and feudal soldiery. The Christians and Jews continued to enjoy wide toleration.

Abd ar-Rahman continued the wars with Leon and Navarre, which extended over most of his long reign. By the **Peace of 955** with Ordono III of Leon, the independence of Leon and Navarre was recognized and the Moslem frontier withdrawn to the Ebro; on the other hand, Leon and Navarre recognized the suzerainty of the caliph and paid tribute. This peace was soon broken by Ordono's brother Sancho (957) who, after his defeat, was expelled by his subjects but restored by the caliph (959).

961–976. Al-Hakam al Mustansír. He continued the wars against Castile, Leon, and Navarre and forced their rulers to sue for peace (962–970). At the same time he waged successful war against the Fatimid dynasty in Morocco, which was brought to an end (973) and replaced by the Omayyad power.

976–1009. Hisham II al Muayyad, whose reign marked the decline of the Omayyad dynasty. Power was seized by Muhammad ibn Abi'-Amir, with the title of *Hajib al-Mansur* (European: *Alamansor* = the Victorious Chamberlain), a brilliant reforming minister (army and administration). He carried on successful campaigns against Leon, Navarre, Catalonia, and Mauretania, and temporarily checked the religious and racial separatism which later on brought about the collapse of the Omayyad Caliphate. On his death in 1002 he was succeeded by his son, Abdulmalik al-Muzaffar (the Victorious), who several times defeated the Christians, and was followed by his brother, Abd ar-Rahman, named Sanchol. The latter obliged Hisham to proclaim him his heir, whereupon a revolt took place in Córdoba under the leadership of Muhammad, a member of the royal family. Hisham was compelled to abdicate in favor of Muhammad II al-Mahdi 1009–1010, and Sanchol was executed. In the meanwhile the Berbers nominated Sulaiman al-Mustain as caliph 1009–1010, 1013–1016. Civil war ensued, reducing Spain to more than a score of petty kingships (*taifas*) and making easier the Christian reconquest.

1027–1031. Hisham III, the last Omayyad caliph.

(3) Christian Spain, Castile and Leon, 718–1065

718–737. Pelayo, successor to Roderick the Visigoth, created the **kingdom of the Asturias,** a theocratic elective monarchy in the Visigothic tradition. Beginning of the reciprocal alliance of kings and clergy under

739–757. Alfonso I, who assigned to the Church a generous share of the lands conquered from the Moslems and used the clergy as a counterweight to the aristocracy.

899. Miraculous discovery of the bones of **St. James the Greater** and erection of the first church of Santiago de Campostella, which became the center of the Spanish national cult and one of the most influential shrines in Europe.

910–914. García, king of Leon, began a rapid expansion of his domain to the east (construction of numerous castles, hence the name *Castile*).

c. 930–970. Count Fernán González, count of Burgos (later Castile), marked the rise of the counts of Burgos. By intrigue and alliance with the Moslems he expanded his domains at the expense of Leon, and made the country of Castile autonomous and hereditary. His progress was arrested by Sancho the Fat of Leon (d. 966), who was in alliance with Abd ar-Rahman III.

1001–1035. Sancho the Great of Navarre effected a close union of Castile and Navarre and began the conquest of Leon.

1035–1065. Ferdinand (Fernando) I, of Castile, completed the work by conquering Leon (1037) and assuming the title of king of Leon.

(*Cont. p. 249.*)

k. THE BRITISH ISLES

(1) England, to 1066

Prehistoric Britain. The prehistoric inhabitants of Britain (called *Celts* on the basis of language) were apparently a fusion of Mediterranean, Alpine, and Nordic strains which included a dark Iberian and a light-haired stock. Archaeological evidence points to contacts with the Iberian Peninsula (2500 B.C.) and Egypt (1300 B.C.).

1200–600 B.C. The true **Celts** are represented by two stocks: Goidels (*Gaels*), surviving in northern Ireland and high Scotland, and Cymri and Brythons (*Britons*), still represented in Wales. The Brythons were close kin to the Gauls, particularly the Belgi. Their religion was dominated by a powerful, organized, priestly caste, the druids of Gaul and Britain, who monopolized religion, education, and justice.

55 B.C.-c. 450 A.D. ROMAN OCCUPATION began with Julius Caesar's conquests in Gaul and Britain (57–50 B.C.); Emperor Claudius' personal expedition and conquest (43 A.D.) were decisive in the romanization of Britain. Reduction of the "empire" (5–40 A.D.) of Cymbeline and suppression (61) of the national revolt of Boudicca (*Boadicea*). Conquest of Wales (48–79). Construction of the great network of Roman roads began (eventually five systems, four centering on London). Bath emerged as a center of Romano-British fashion.

78–142. Roman conquests in the north began under Agricola; results north of the Clyde-Forth line were not decisive. The Emperor Hadrian completed the conquest of Britain in person: construction of **Hadrian's Wall** (123) from Solway Firth to Tyne mouth. Firth-Clyde rampart (c. 142).

208. Emperor Septimius Severus arrived (208), invaded Caledonia (Scotland), restored Roman military supremacy in the north, and fixed Hadrian's Wall as the final frontier of Roman conquest.

300–350. Height of villa construction in the plain of Britain. Chief towns: Verulamium (St. Albans), Colchester, Lincoln, Gloucester, York. The skill of the artisans and clothworkers of Britain was already famous on the Continent in the 4th century. The island south of the wall was completely romanized.

c. 350. Piratic raids of Irish (*Scoti*) and **Picts** were common, and the Teutonic conquest of Gaul cut Britain off from Rome in the 5th century, leaving the Romano-British to defend themselves against Saxon attacks on the south and east which soon penetrated the lowlands.

410–442. Withdrawal of the Roman legions and the end of the Roman administration coincided with an intensification of Nordic pressure and the influx of **Jutes, Angles, and Saxons,** which permanently altered the racial base of the island. By c. 615 the Angles and Jutes had reached the Irish Channel and were masters of what is virtually modern England. A Celtic recrudescence appeared in the highlands of the west and northwest. The history of Britain for two centuries (c. 350–597) is obscure. Christianity had not made much progress under the Romans.

Seven Anglo-Saxon kingdoms, the *Heptarchy,* emerged after the Teutonic conquest: Essex, Wessex, Sussex (probably prevailingly Saxon as the names suggest); Kent (Jutes); East Anglia, Mercia, Northumbria (Angles).

560–616. The supremacy of **Ethelbert of Kent** in the Heptarchy coincided with the

597. Arrival of **Augustine the Monk** and the conversion of Kent to the Roman Church. The hegemony in the .eptarchy passed eventually to **Edwin of Northumbria** (which had also been converted).

633. The defeat and death of Ethelbert's brother-in-law Edwin at the hands of the heathen Mercians ended the Northumbrian primacy and temporarily overwhelmed the Roman Church. A period of anarchy ensued.

633. Oswald of Northumbria called Aidan from Iona, whose mission began the great influence of Celtic Christianity, which for a time threatened to replace the Roman Church.

664. The **Synod of Whitby** turned Britain back into the orbit of the Roman Church and the Continent, and prepared the way for the decisive rôle of

669–690. Theodore of Tarsus, archbishop of Canterbury. Theodore introduced a strictly Roman parochial system and a centralized episcopal system which became the model for the secular state and created a new concept of kingship. National synods brought the rival kingdoms together for the first time, and began the long evolution destined to create English nationality and national institutions, and to spread them through the civilized world.

Theodore's episcopate was marked by the reintroduction of Greco-Roman culture and the permanent establishment of a new cultural tradition which produced **Bede** (673–735), the father of English literature, and culminated in the wide influence of the great school at York, which extended to the Continent (e.g. **Alcuin** at the court of Charlemagne). The archbishopric of York was founded, 735. Romance ecclesiastical architecture and church music flourished.

757–796. Under Offa II the kingdom of Mercia, supreme south of the Humber, reached its maximum power, after which it broke up.

787. The first recorded **raid of the Danes** in England was followed by the Danish inundation of Ireland. In the pause before the great wave of Viking advance, Wessex under

802–839. Egbert, who had been in Charlemagne's service, emerged supreme (conquering Mercia), exercised a vague suzerainty over Northumbria, and received the homage of all the English kinglets.

856–875. Full tide of the **first Viking assault.** Wessex was the spearhead of resistance.

871–899. ALFRED THE GREAT purchased peace until he could organize his forces and build up a navy. Almost overwhelmed by the winter invasion of 878, he finally defeated the Danes and forced the **peace of Wedmore,** whereby Guthrun the Dane became a Chris-

ENGLAND
in
ALFRED'S DAY

Danish Boroughs
underlined - Lincoln

Chief Districts of
Danish Settlement

0   50   100
Scale of Miles

tian and divided England with Alfred. The *Danelaw,* north of the Thames-Lea line, went to Guthrun; the south, together with London, went to Alfred.

878-900. The Danes were masters of the northeast, and under Danish pressure **Scotland** began to take on shape and unity.

Alfred proceeded to organize the defense of his kingdom. London was walled and garri-

soned with burghers charged with its defense. Earth forts (*burhs*) of the Viking type were thrown up and garrisoned. The *fyrd* and the fleet were reorganized, the army increased, the *thegns* began to be used as a mounted infantry. All citizens of the requisite wealth were forced to thegnhood, i.e. to join the military class attached to the royal household. A Danish reaction (892–896) was firmly suppressed.

The Anglo-Saxon Kings of England (802–1066)

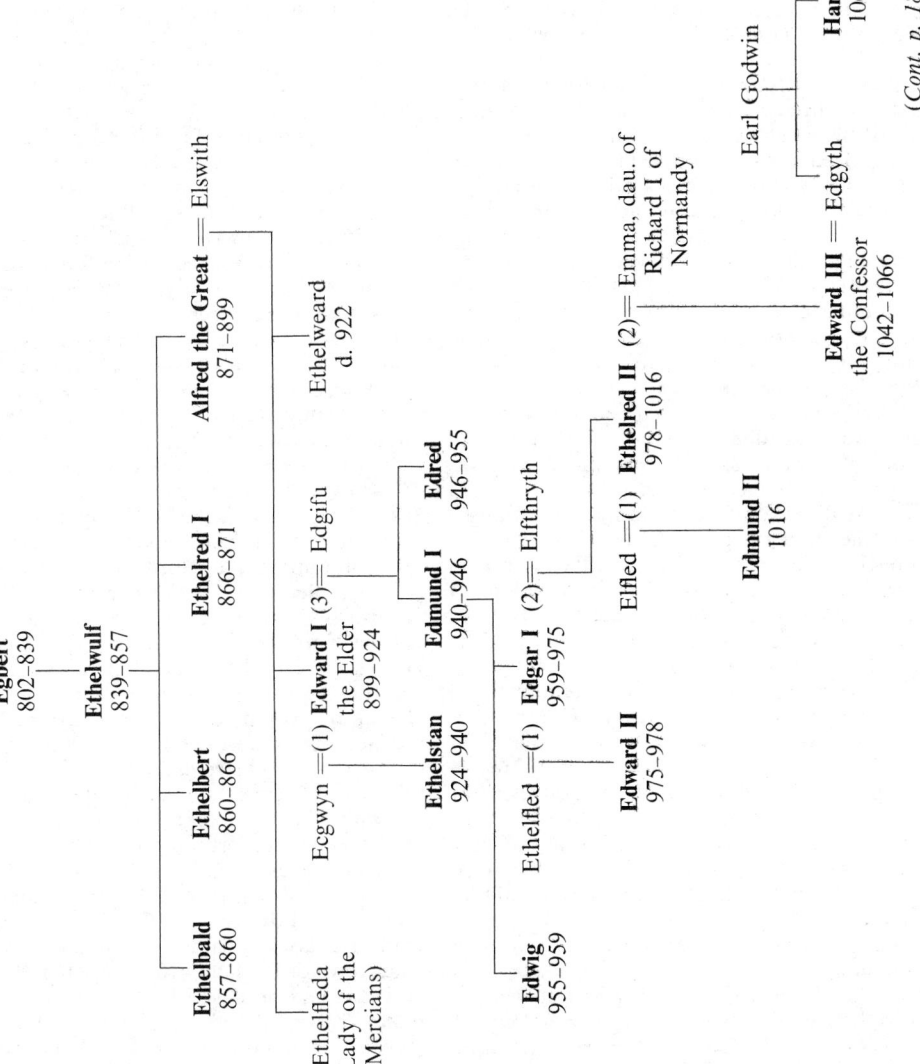

(Cont. p. 183.)

Alfred's **patronage of learning.** Foreign scholars and learned refugees were welcomed at court. Alfred translated Bede's *Historia,* Orosius, and Boethius' *Consolatio* into the vernacular. To provide trained administrators, Alfred established schools for the sons of thegns and nobles. The *Anglo-Saxon Chronicle* was started.

899-924. **Edward,** Alfred's son, succeeded him, and with his sister, Ethelfleda of Mercia, began the conquest of the Danelaw, which was completed under

924-940. **Ethelstan,** Edward's son. The descendants of Alfred were the first true kings of England; his great-grandson **Edgar** (959-975) was recognized as such. Archbishop Dunstan, Edgar's chief counselor, was a great ecclesiastical reformer (simony and morals) of the Church and the people. He followed a policy of fusion and conciliation toward the Danes, and Oda, a full-blooded Dane, became (942) archbishop of Canterbury. The absorption of the Danelaw by Wessex left the Celtic fringe in Scotland and Wales independent under a vague kind of vassalage to the king.

As the Danelaw was absorbed, the shire system was extended to it with the old Danish boroughs as a nucleus. The administration was often in the hands of men of Danish blood. The Anglo-Saxon farmers had no love for war, and the thegns began to emerge as a professional soldier class. The old tribal and clan organization was superseded by a system of quasi-feudal form whereby each man had a lord who was responsible for him at law. The great earldoms were beginning to emerge.

No common law existed; shire and hundred courts administered local custom with the freeman suitors under the king's representative-ealdorman, shire-reeve, or hundred-reeve. From the days of Edgar, the feudal element tended to encroach on royal authority, especially in the hundred courts. The old monasticism had been destroyed by the invasions, and the Church in England fell into corruption and decadence, only reformed by the influence of Cluny and Fleury and the Norman conquest.

991. An ebb in Viking raids was followed by a fresh onset during the reign of **Ethelred the Redeless** (978-1016), led by Sven I (Forked Beard), king of Denmark. *Danegeld* had been sporadically collected under Alfred; now it was regularly levied and used as tribute to buy off the invaders. This tax, and the invasions, led to a rapid decline of the freeholders to a servile status. Under Canute, the Danegeld was transformed into a regular tax for defense. Collection of the Danegeld, originally in the hands of the towns, fell increasingly to the lord

of the manor, and it was only a step from holding him for the tax to making him lord of the land from which the tax came.

1013-1014. **Sven I** (d. 1014) was acknowledged by the English, and Ethelred fled to Normandy, the home of his second wife, Emma.

1016-1035. **King Canute** (Cnut), one of the two sons of Sven, elected by the witan. The witan was a heterogeneous body of prelates, magnates, and officials without any precise constitutional status. Canute was "emperor," on the model of Charlemagne, over a northern empire which included Denmark, Norway, and England, and, but for his early death, might have played a more important rôle. His reign was marked by conciliation and fusion. The Church was under Anglo-Saxon clergy. Canute maintained a good navy, and his standing army included the famous *housecarls,* which soon had an Anglo-Saxon contingent. The four great earldoms, Wessex, East Anglia, Mercia, Northumbria, and seven lesser earldoms can be distinguished in this period. The greatest of the earls was **Godwin of Wessex.** Canute's sons were incompetent, and his line ended, 1042.

Godwin was chiefly responsible for the election of the successor to Canute's line, Edward, son of Emma and Ethelred, who married (1045) Godwin's daughter.

1042-1066. **Edward the Confessor,** of the line of Alfred, was under Godwin's domination. Brought up at the Norman court, speaking French, he tried to Normanize the English court. Godwin's influence led to the deposition of the Norman archbishop of Canterbury and the selection of the Saxon Stigand by the witan. As Stigand had supported an anti-pope, Alexander II favored the Normans, as did Hildebrand, the power behind the papal throne. Godwin's son, **Harold,** succeeded (1053) him as earl of Wessex, and dominated Edward as his father had. Another son of Godwin, Tostig, became earl of Northumbria. Harold (c. 1064) was driven ashore on the Channel, fell into the hands of William, duke of Normandy, a cousin of Edward the Confessor, and was forced to take an oath to aid William to attain the crown of England, which William declared Edward had promised him.

1066. **Tostig,** exiled after the Northumbrian revolt (1065), returned with **Harald Haardraade** to attack Northumbria. The Confessor died in January (1066) and William at once began vigorous preparations for the conquest of England.

1066. On Edward's death **Harold was chosen king** by the witan and was guarding the coasts of England against William when Tostig and Haardraade appeared in the north. After a brilliant dash northward, Harold defeated them at **Stamford Bridge** in September, at the very

183

The Danish Kings of England (1013–1066)

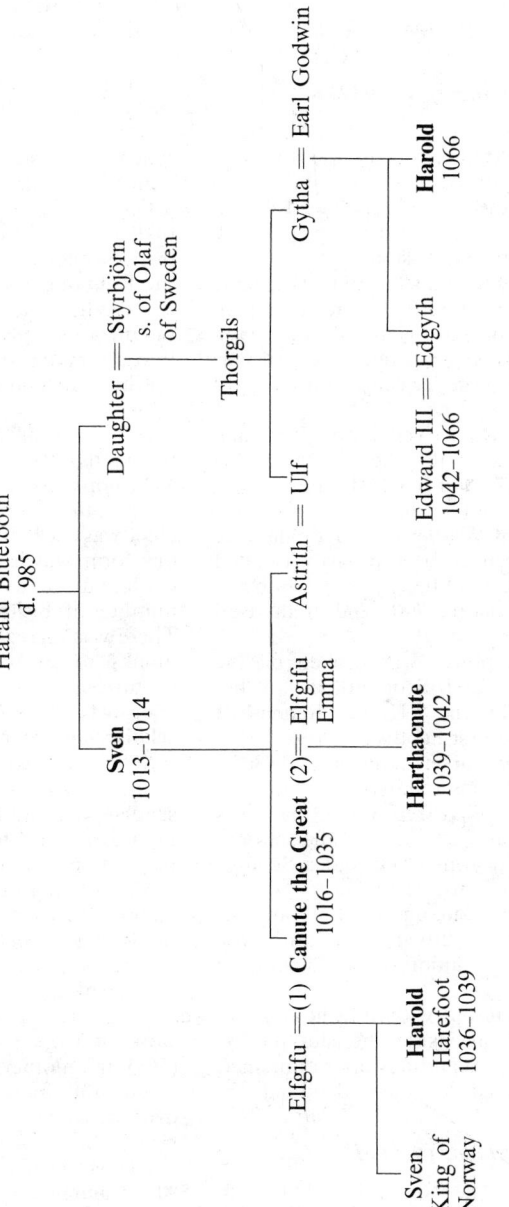

(*Cont. p. 211.*)

moment that the Norman invaders arrived in the Channel. Rushing southward after his victory, Harold confronted the Normans, who had already landed, with a reduced, wearied, and shaken force, and was beaten and killed in the

OCT. 14.   BATTLE OF HASTINGS, or Senlac. (*Cont. p. 206.*)

(2) Scotland, to 1034

Racial origins obscure. A wave of Neolithic peoples from the Mediterranean was followed by Celts, Goidels, Brythons, Saxons in the 6th century B.C., and then by Picts. The Romans arrived at the end of the 1st century, A.D., but made no permanent impression.

450-600. Four **political nuclei: Picts** (Pentland Firth to the central plain); **Dalriada** (Argyllshire and the islands of Jura and Islay); **"Welsh" refugees** in Strathclyde; **Ida of Bernicia's realm** (from the Tweed to the Firth of Forth).

c. 565.   COLUMBA arrived from Iona and converted the king of the Picts to the Celtic Church, giving Scotland her first cultural contact with the civilized world.

664. The **Synod of Whitby** turned England to the Roman Church and temporarily isolated Scotland. The Picts ultimately went into the Roman communion (c. 700) and Iona itself followed (716).

685. The English power was broken on the southern frontier, and Scotland began her independent evolution. Under **Kenneth I** (d. 858) began the first Scottish union.

794.   Arrival of the Norse. Iona burned (802); a series of devastations followed.

921.   Edward, son of Alfred the Great, was acknowledged lord of Scotland. Ethelstan enforced the bond in arms (934) and a Scottish effort to revolt was crushed (937).

1005-1034. Under **Malcolm II,** Lothian was added to the Scottish crown and Strathclyde completed (1034) the union of the four nuclei under

1034-1040.   Duncan, but without a homogeneous racial or political basis. The isles and the north were under Scandinavian dominance, and England aimed to make Scotland her vassal.   (*Cont. p. 217.*)

(3) Ireland, to 1171

Racial origins. The Neolithic inhabitants, followed by Celts and Goidels (c. 600-500 B.C.). The "fifths" (i.e. Ulster, Leinster, Connaught, East and West Munster) may date from the Goidel arrival. Belgic and other Brythonic migrations (300-150 B.C.) probably in the southeast. Supremacy of the Brythonic **kingdom of Tara** in the 4th century of the Christian Era.

The **Picts** pushed into Antrim and Down. There is an enormous body of legend dealing with the early origins.

431. Traditional date for the arrival of **Bishop Palladius** and his mission.

432.   PATRICK, a pupil of Germanus of Auxerre, especially trained for this mission, arrived to continue Palladius' work. He founded churches in Meath, Ulster, Connaught, and probably established the bishopric of Armagh. Chieftains were converted, but much paganism survived. Patrick began the education of the priesthood. Patrick's ecclesiastical organization was probably close to that of Britain and Gaul, but with the withdrawal of the Roman legions from the latter countries the Roman connection was cut, and there was a recrudescence of paganism. The diocesan organization of Patrick apparently slipped back into the native system.

Chieftains, on their conversion, made donations of land to the Church, and at first the ecclesiastical offices seem to have remained in the hands of the sept, with the *coarb* (inheritor) as bishop or abbot. The cenobitic organization of the 5th century was that of a sept, whose chief was a Christian. Later there was a rigorous form which separated the sexes. As the earlier diocesan organization declined, the number of bishops rose to fantastic figures. There was a great exodus of Irish scholars and monks to Europe during the 8th and 9th centuries.

c. 500-800. The **Golden Age of Irish monastic scholarship** occurred in the 6th to the 9th centuries. A great school founded by **Eudo,** prince of Oriel (c. 450-540), at Aranmore drew scholars from all Europe. Establishment of the monastery of **Clonard** (c. 520) under Welsh inspiration. Here there were said to be 3000 students living in separate, wattled huts under open-air instruction. From Clonard went forth the so-called **Twelve Apostles of Ireland,** founding schools all over Ireland and later the Continent.

c. 533.   True monasticism began with the work of Columba. Columba founded Iona (563), the mother Church of Scotland, whence Aidan, the apostle of England, founded Lindisfarne (635) for the conversion of Northumbria. The *Book of Kells* and the flowering of Gaelic vernacular poetry date from this period.

590.   Columban of Leinster, from Bangor, began his mission to Europe, founding Luxeuil and a great series of other foundations (e.g. Gall, Würzburg, Salzburg, Tarantum, Bobbio). The 8th century saw a great wave of missions from the Rhine-Meuse area inland to the Rhone-Alps line. This powerful advance of Celtic Christianity at one time seemed destined to win northern Europe from Rome. The chief formal differences from Rome were in tonsure, the date of Easter, the consecration of bishops. In the 7th century the Irish Church conformed to Roman usage, but the bond with Rome was not close.

723. Boniface (Winfred) the Anglo-Saxon arrived on the Continent to begin the organization on Roman lines of the Celtic establishments among the Franks, Thuringians, Alamanni, and Bavarians.

Before the coming of the Norse there were no cities, no stone bridges in Ireland, and no foreign trade of importance.

795. The first Norse attack. Dublin (840), Waterford, and Limerick founded as centers of Norse trade with the Continent. Soon a mixed race, the Gallgoidels (whence Galloway) arose, and a Christian decline set in. The Scandinavians remained chiefly in the ports.

1002-1014. Brian of Munster established his supremacy. A period of road- and fort-building. At Clontarf (1014) Brian defeated the Norse, ending the domination of Dublin, though the Norse remained in their cities. Brian fell in the battle and anarchy followed—the struggle of the O'Brians of Munster, the O'Neils of Ulster, the O'Connors of Connaught—which ended in an appeal to King Henry II of England by Dermond (or Dermot) MacMurrough.

1152. The **Synod of Kells** established the present diocesan system of Ireland, recognized the primacy of Armagh, and the archbishoprics of Cashel, Tuam, Dublin. Tithes were voted.

1167-1171. The Norman Conquest. Henry II, on his accession, had the idea of conquering Ireland. John of Salisbury records that on his request as Henry's envoy (1155), Pope Adrian IV sent Henry a letter granting him lordship of Ireland, and a ring as the symbol of his investiture. Henry seems never to have availed himself of the papal grant.

1167. On the appeal of Dermond MacMurrough, Henry issued a letter allowing Dermond to raise troops in England for his cause. Dermond came to terms with Richard of Clare, a Norman, earl of Pembroke, and with other Normans, most of whom were related to one another. A series of expeditions to Ireland brought into the island a group of Norman families (e.g. Fitzmaurices, Carews, Gerards, Davids, Barries, *et al.*), who began to establish a powerful colony. This greatly alarmed Henry.

1171. HENRY II, with papal sanction, landed in Ireland to assert his supremacy and to reconcile the natives. The **Synod of Cashel,** at which Henry was not present, acknowledged his sovereignty. (*Cont. p. 217.*)

I. SCANDINAVIA, TO 981

Origins. References in Pytheas, Pomponius Mela, Pliny the Elder, Tacitus, Ptolemy, Procopius, Jordanes. Archaeological remains indicate Roman connections in the 3rd century after Christ, but there is no evidence for close continental relations until the Viking period.

VIKING PERIOD. Scandinavia developed in isolation during the barbarian migrations until the 2nd century after Christ. The Viking expansion from Scandinavia itself prolonged the period of migrations in Europe for four hundred years. The traditional participation of Scandinavia was as follows: (1) **Norwegians** (outer passage): raids in Scotland, Ireland, France (Hrolf the Ganger, i.e. "Rollo"); (2) **Danes** (the middle passage): British Isles, France, the Low Countries; (3) **Swedes** (eastward passage): across Slavdom to Byzantium (foundation of Novgorod 862, Kiev, c. 900). There never was a mass migration, and probably all stocks shared in the various movements to some degree. **Causes:** (1) pagan reaction, including renegade Christians; (2) pressure of population; (3) tribal warfare and vassalage of the defeated, especially after 872 (this is the traditional explanation for Rollo's migration, 911); (4) love of gain; (5) fashion and love of adventure.

NORWEGIAN COLONIZATION. (1) **Ireland:** the Norwegian conquest began c. 823 and centers were established at Dublin (the kingdom endured until 1014), Waterford, and Limerick. Exodus of learned monks to Europe **(Scotus Erigena?).** Attacks by the Picts and Danes. The subsequent colonization of the Scottish Islands drew Norwegians from Ireland and accelerated the celtization of the colonists who remained there. (2) **The Islands:** Hebrides, Man, Faroes, Orkneys, Shetlands. (3) **Iceland:** reached by Irish monks c. 790; discovered by the Norsemen in 874 and colonized almost at once; establishment of a New Norway, with a high culture. (4) **Greenland:** visited by Eric the Red of Iceland (981) and colonized at once; expeditions from Greenland to the North American continent (p. 365). The Norse settlements in Greenland continued until the 15th century.

CIVILIZATION. Large coin hoards indicate the profits of raids and trade with the British Isles, Mediterranean, Byzantium, and Moslem Asia. Export of furs, arms (to eastern Europe), and mercenary services to rulers (e.g. bodyguards of Ethelred, Cnut, Slavic princes, Byzantine emperors). Trade eastward was cut off by the Huns and Avars (5th and 6th century), but resumed after Rurik's expedition (862) reopened Russia.

Runes (from a Scandinavian root, meaning

to inscribe) were already ancient in the Viking period, and probably are modified Roman letters. The *Eddas,* dramatic lays (prose and verse) of the Norwegian aristocracy (especially in Iceland) dealing with gods and heroes (many in the German tradition, e.g. Sigurd and the Nibelungs), are the highest literary production of heathen Scandinavia.

Scandinavian society rested on wealth from raids and commerce and consisted of a landed aristocracy with farmer tenants with the right and obligation to attend local courts; there were few slaves. The only general assembly was the *Allthing* of Iceland (established 930), the oldest continuous parliamentary body in existence.

Mythology and religion. The Norwegians had a more complicated mythology than any other Teutonic people: giants, elves, dwarfs, serpents, succeeded by the triumph of **Odin,** his wife **Friga,** and his son **Thor.**

Conversion to Christianity. The first Christians (probably captives) appeared in the 6th century. The first Christian missionary was the Anglo-Saxon, **Willibord** (c. 700), who accomplished but little. A Carolingian mission (c. 820) was welcomed by King Bjorn of Sweden. A few years later (c. 831) the archbishopric of Hamburg was established and became at once the center for missionary work in the north.

(Cont. p. 217.)

2. EASTERN EUROPE

a. THE BYZANTINE EMPIRE, 527–1025

[*For a complete list of the Byzantine emperors see Appendix II.*]

527–565. JUSTINIAN. A Macedonian by birth and the chief adviser of his uncle, Justin, since 518. Justinian was a man of serious and even somber temperament, but of strong, even autocratic character, sober judgment, grandiose conceptions. He was strongly influenced by his wife **Theodora** (d. 548), a woman of humble origin, probably unduly maligned by the historian Procopius. Theodora was cruel, deceitful, and avid of power, but a woman of iron will and unusual political judgment. Justinian's whole policy was directed toward the establishment of the absolute power of the emperor and toward the revival of a universal Christian Roman Empire. The entire reign was filled with wars in the east and in the west, punctuated by constant incursions of the barbarians from the north.

527–532. The **first Persian War** of Justinian. His commander, **Belisarius,** won a victory at Dara (530), but was then defeated at **Callinicum.** The conflict ended with the **Perpetual Peace** of 532, designed to free the imperial armies for operations in the west.

532. The **Nika Insurrection** (so called from the cry of the popular parties, *nika = victory*). This was the last great uprising of the circus parties and led to great violence and incendiarism. Much of Constantinople was destroyed by fire. Justinian was deterred from flight only through the arguments of Theodora. Ultimately Belisarius and the forces put down the insurrection with much cruelty (30,000 slain). Therewith the period of popular domination ended and the epoch of absolutism began.

533–534. CONQUEST OF NORTH AFRICA. Belisarius, with a relatively small force, transported by sea, defeated the Vandal usurper, Gelimer, and recovered the whole of North Africa for the empire.

535–554. THE RECONQUEST OF ITALY. Belisarius landed in Sicily, overran the island, conquered southern Italy from the Ostrogoths, and took Rome (Dec. 9, 536). The Ostrogoth king, **Witiges,** besieged the city for a whole year (537–538), but failed to take it. In the following year Belisarius advanced to the north, took Ravenna, and captured Witiges, but, after the recall of Belisarius, the new Ostrogoth leader, **Totila,** reconquered Italy as far as Naples (541–543). He took Rome (546) and sacked it. Belisarius returned, captured the city, but then abandoned it to the Goths (549). He was later replaced by **Narses,** who invaded Italy by land from the north with a large army composed chiefly of barbarian mercenaries. He defeated the Ostrogoths decisively in the **battle of Tagina** (552) and brought all of Italy under imperial rule.

540. The **Huns, Bulgars,** and other barbarian tribes crossed the Danube and raided the Balkan area as far south as the Isthmus of Corinth.

540–562. The great **Persian War against Khusru I** (Chosroes). The Persians invaded Syria and took Antioch, after which they attacked Lazistan and Armenia and raided Mesopotamia. In 544 they besieged Edessa, but in vain. A truce was concluded in 545, but hostilities were soon resumed in the Transcaucasus region. The Persians took Petra (549), but lost it again (551). By the fifty-year **Peace of 562,** Justinian agreed to pay tribute, but Lazistan was retained for the empire.

542–546. Constantinople and the empire were

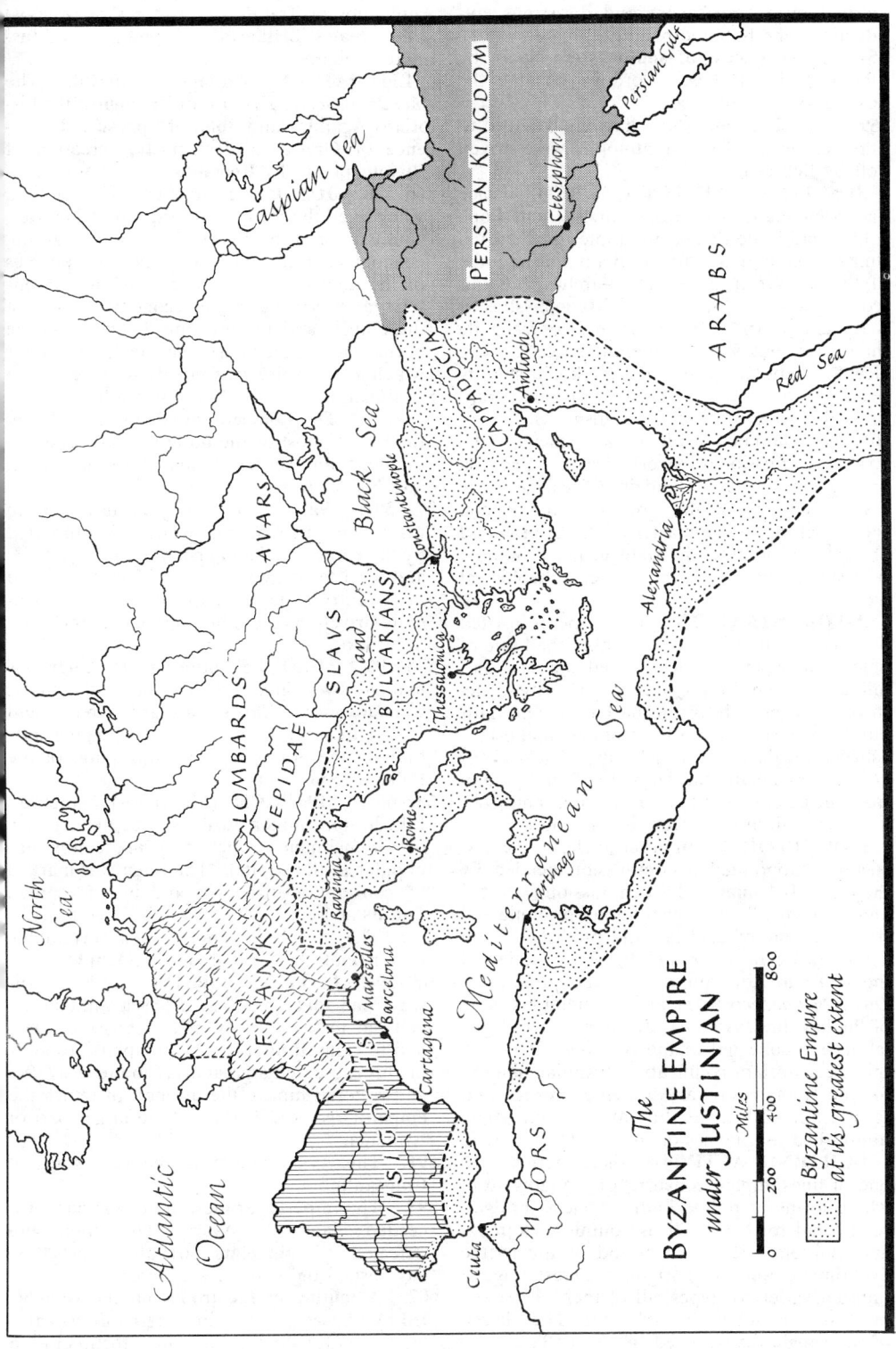

The
BYZANTINE EMPIRE
under JUSTINIAN

Miles

0   200   400   800

Byzantine Empire
at its greatest extent

visited by a very severe and disastrous epidemic of the bubonic plague.

554. The **conquest of southeastern Spain** by the imperial armies. Cordova became the capital of the province.

559. The **Huns and Slavs,** having advanced to the very gates of Constantinople, were driven off by Belisarius.

JUSTINIAN AND THE CHURCH. Peace had been made with Rome in 519 and Pope John I had visited Constantinople in 525. Justinian made a great effort to maintain the unity of the western and eastern churches, but this led him into trouble with the **Monophysites** of Syria and Egypt. He attempted to reconcile them also, but with indifferent success. The cleavage between Latin and Greek Christianity became ever more marked. Justinian suppressed all heresies and paganism (closing of the Neo-Platonic Academy at Athens, 529). Extensive missionary work was carried on among the barbarians and in Africa. For the rest, the emperor, with a great taste for dogma, set himself up as the master of the Church and arrogated to himself the right to make binding pronouncements in even purely theological matters.

ADMINISTRATION. The emperor insisted on honesty and efficiency. He abolished sale of offices, improved salaries, united the civil and military powers of provinicial authorities, etc. In order to hold back the barbarians, he built hundreds of forts along the frontiers and established a regular system of frontier forces (*limitanei*). Financially the empire suffered greatly from the extensive military operations and from the great building activities of the court.

LAW REFORM. In order to clarify the law, Justinian appointed a commission headed by the jurist, **Tribonian.** This commission collected and ordered all the constitutions promulgated since the time of Hadrian and published them as the *Codex Justinianus* (529). There followed the collection of opinions of the jurists, the *Digest* or *Pandects* (533), and a general textbook of the law, the *Institutes.* Justinian's own legislation was collected in the *Novellae* (565). By this great work of codification Justinian assured for the Roman Law an immense prestige and far-reaching influence, but at the same time diminished its chances of further development.

BUILDING ACTIVITY. The period was one of unexampled construction, ranging from whole towns to public baths, palaces, bridges, roads, and forts, as well as countless churches and cloisters. It was a period of much free experimentation and originality, resulting in unusual variety of types, all of them, however, marked by grandeur and splendor. The **Church of St. Sophia** (constructed between 532–537 by Anthemios of Tralles and Isidoros of Miletus) is the greatest of the many monuments of Justinian's reign.

LITERATURE. An age of revival. The *Anekdota* (*Secret History*) of **Procopius;** the historians **Agathias** and **John of Ephesus.** Renascence of Greek classical poetry; creation of religious poetry by **Romanos.**

565–578. JUSTIN II, nephew of Justinian, who seized the throne with the aid of Tiberius, commander of the guard. Justin was a careful, economical ruler, who continued the policies of his predecessor, but attempted to concentrate attention upon the economic plight of the empire and the growing danger from the barbarians. In 574 he became insane, after which the empire was ruled by Tiberius, in conjunction with the Empress Sophia.

568–571. The **Lombard invasion of Italy** led to the loss of most of the imperial possessions in the north and center, though Ravenna, Rome, and Naples were retained.

572–591. War with Persia, growing out of an insurrection in Armenia, which was supported by the emperor. The Persians took Dara (573) and devastated Syria. In 575, Khusru ravaged the country as far as Cappadocia, but was finally driven back by the imperial commander, Maurikios.

578–582. TIBERIUS, emperor. His reign was marked by a great inundation of the Slavs, who advanced into Thrace and Greece and settled in large numbers, thus changing profoundly the ethnographic composition of the Balkan populations.

582–602. MAURICE (Maurikios), emperor. Like his forerunner, Justin, he pursued a policy of retrenchment, which only made him unpopular in the capital. The reign was marked by constant disturbances and by widespread dissatisfaction.

583. The **Avars,** grown to be a formidable power, took the forts along the Danube.

589–591. Last phase of the Persian War. Khusru I had died in 579. In 589 a military revolt led to the deposition of Khusru II, who fled to Constantinople. The emperor, espousing his cause, led a great army to the east (591) and restored him to the throne. In return the emperor received Dara and the larger part of Armenia.

591. The Avars raided to the very gates of Constantinople.

593. The imperial armies, under **Priscus,** proceeded against the Avars. The latter were defeated at **Viminacium** (601) after which Priscus pushed on to the Tisza River.

602. A **mutiny of the troops on the Danube,** led by Phocas, resulted in a march to the capital, the outbreak of popular insurrection in the city, and the flight of the emperor.

602–610. PHOCAS, emperor. He was an untutored soldier, cruel and utterly incompetent. Maurice was captured and executed with his sons. All his supporters met with a like fate.

606–608. Resumption of the Persian War. The Persians again captured Dara and overran Syria and Mesopotamia (608) advancing through Anatolia as far as Chalcedon.

610. Conspiracy against Phocas, led by Priscus and supported by the exarch of Africa. The latter sent an army by land which conquered Egypt, while a fleet from Carthage arrived at Constantinople. The mob thereupon rose, slew Phocas, and proclaimed Heraclius, the son of the exarch, as emperor.

610–641. HERACLIUS I, founder of a new dynasty, in whose reign the empire became definitely a Greek (Byzantine) monarchy. Heraclius found the empire in a perilous state, threatened from the north by the Avars and from the east by the Persians. But he showed himself an able organizer, general, and statesman, and found in the Patriarch Sergius a courageous supporter.

611–622. The Persian advance. They took Antioch, Apameia, Emesa, and Kaisareia; Damascus (613); Jerusalem (614), which was sacked, the inhabitants and the Holy Cross being transferred to Ctesiphon. In 615 the Persians were at Chalcedon. In 619 they conquered Egypt.

616. The imperial possessions in Spain were lost to the Visigoths.

619. The **Avars appeared at Constantinople,** which was threatened on the Asiatic side by the Persians. Heraclius was deterred from flight to Africa only by the influence of the patriarch.

622–630. DEFEAT OF THE PERSIANS. Heraclius, with a newly organized army and supported by a tremendous outburst of religious enthusiasm (the *Byzantine Crusade*), took the offensive against the Persians and carried on three brilliant campaigns in the Transcaucasian region, refusing to allow himself to be distracted by the constant attacks of the Avars in the Balkans. In the **battle of Nineveh** (Dec. 12, 627) he won a decisive victory, which enabled him to advance to Ctesiphon (628). The death of Khusru (628) and dynastic disorders in Persia made possible the conclusion of a victorious peace. All the Persian conquests were returned and the Holy Cross restored to Jerusalem.

626. The Avars and Slavs attacked Constantinople by land and sea, but were unable to storm the walls. This marked the height of the Avar power.

634–641. The Arab conquests (p. 199). They took Bostra (634); Damascus (635); by the **battle of Yarmuk** (636) gained all Syria; forced the surrender of Jerusalem (637); overran Mesopotamia (639) and conquered Egypt (640–642).

635. Alliance between the emperor and Kuvrat, king of the Bulgars, intended to break the power of the Avars.

638. The *Ecthesis,* a formula elaborated by the Patriarch Sergius and other churchmen in the hope of reconciling the Monophysites, who were welcoming rather than opposing the Islamic advance. The formula recognized one will in the two natures of Christ (*monothelitism*), but failed to win acceptance in Syria and Egypt. On the contrary, it called forth much opposition in the strictly orthodox Italian and African possessions.

641. HERACLIUS CONSTANTINUS III, son of Heraclius, became emperor, but died in a few months under suspicious circumstances.

641. HERACLEONAS, younger son of Heraclius, emperor, under his mother's tutelage. He was almost at once overthrown by the army.

641–668. CONSTANS II (Constantinus), grandson of Heraclius, emperor. He was an energetic and able ruler, who did his utmost to check the Arab advance. With this object in view he reorganized the provincial administration by establishing **themes** (*themata*) under military governors with wide powers (*strategio*) and authority over the civil officials. This system greatly strengthened administrative control and was the basis of the imperial organization for centuries.

643. The Arabs took Alexandria, last outpost of the Greeks in Egypt.

647–648. Arab invasion of North Africa.

648. The Arabs, having assembled a fleet, took Cyprus.

649. Pope Martin condemned the teaching of the *Ecthesis,* but was soon arrested by the exarch of Ravenna (653) and sent to Constantinople.

653. The Arab advance continued. Armenia was conquered (653) and Rhodes plundered (654). In 655 the Arab fleet defeated an imperial armada under the emperor's own command off the Lycian coast. But in 659 a truce was concluded with the Arab commander in Syria.

663–668. Transfer of the court to Italy. Constans was intent on blocking the Arab conquest of Sicily and Italy and had dreams of restoring Rome as the basis of the imperial power. But he failed to make any conquests in Italy at the expense of the Lombards and in his absence the Arabs annually invaded and devastated Anatolia.

668. Constans was murdered in the course of a mutiny at Syracuse.

668-685. CONSTANTINE IV (Pogonatus), the son of Constans, a harsh character, but an able soldier. He had been in charge of affairs and had come to Sicily to put down the revolt that had resulted in his father's death. On his return to Constantinople, the troops obliged him to accept his brothers Heraclius and Tiberius as co-rulers, but after 680 Constantine was sole emperor. His reign witnessed the high point of the Arab attack, accompanied, as usual, by repeated incursions of the Slavs in the Balkans.

673-678. The **Arab attacks on Constantinople.** After a siege by land and sea (Apr.–Sept. 673), the assailants blockaded the city and attacked it every year for five years. The city was saved by the strength of its walls and by the newly invented **Greek fire,** which raised havoc with the Arab fleet. In 677 the Greeks destroyed the Arab fleet at **Syllaeum** and secured a favorable thirty-year peace (678). Never again did the Arab menace become so pressing. The empire had proved itself a formidable bulwark of Europe.

675-681. Repeated assaults of the Slavs on Thessalonica. The city held out, but the settlement of Thrace and Macedonia and northern Greece by Slavic tribes continued uninterruptedly.

679. Appearance of the **Bulgar menace.** The Bulgars, a people of Turkish race, had pressed westward through southern Russia and settled in Bessarabia. The emperor failed in his efforts to defeat them there. They crossed the Danube, settled in the region between the river and the Balkan Mountains, gradually fused with the Slavs and became largely Slavicized, and founded the first coherent Slavic power in the Balkans.

680-681. The **sixth ecumenical council** at Constantinople condemned the monothelite heresy and returned to pure orthodoxy. Since the loss of Syria and Egypt, there was no longer any need for favoring the monophysite view. The return to orthodoxy was a victory for the papal stand and was probably intended to strengthen the Byzantine hold on Italy. In actual fact the patriarch of Constantinople (now that the patriarchs of Antioch, Jerusalem, and Alexandria were under Moslem power) became more and more influential in the east and the primacy of the Roman pope was hardly more than nominal.

685-695. JUSTINIAN II, the son of Constantine and the last of the Heraclian dynasty. He ascended the throne when only sixteen and soon showed himself to be harsh and cruel, though energetic and ambitious like most members of his family.

689. The emperor defeated the Slavs in Thrace and transferred a considerable number of them to Anatolia.

692. The Byzantine forces were severely defeated by the Arabs in the **battle of Sevastopol.**

695. A revolt against the emperor, led by Leontius and supported by the clergy and people, initiated a period of twenty years of anarchy. Justinian was deposed and exiled to the Crimea (Cherson).

695-698. LEONTIUS, emperor. His reign was marked by the domination of the army.

697-698. The Arabs finally took **Carthage** and brought to an end the Byzantine rule in North Africa.

698-705. TIBERIUS II, made emperor by another revolt in the army. The reign was distinguished by an insurrection against Byzantine rule in Armenia and by constant Arab raids in eastern Anatolia.

705-711. JUSTINIAN II, who returned to the throne with the aid of the Bulgar king. He took an insane revenge on all his enemies and instituted a veritable reign of terror.

711. The emperor failed to suppress a serious **revolt in the Crimea,** supported by the Khazars. The insurgent troops, under Philippicus, marched on Constantinople and finally defeated and killed Justinian in an engagement in northern Anatolia.

711-713. PHILIPPICUS, emperor. He proved himself quite incompetent and was unable to check the raids of the Bulgars (reached Constantinople in 712) or the ravages of the Arabs in Cilicia (they took Amasia, 712).

713-715. ANASTASIUS II, emperor, the creature of the mutinous Thracian army corps. He attempted to reorganize the army, but this led to new outbreaks.

715-717. THEODOSIUS III, an obscure official put on the throne by the army. He was helpless in the face of the Arabs, who in 716 advanced as far as Pergamon. The invaders were finally repulsed by the strategos of the Anatolian theme, Leo, who forced the abdication of the emperor and was enthusiastically proclaimed by the clergy and populace of the capital.

717-741. LEO III (the Isaurian), founder of the **Isaurian dynasty,** an eminent general and a great organizer. Leo used drastic measures to suppress revolts in the army and re-established discipline by issuing new regulations. The finances were restored by heavy, systematic taxation, but steps were taken, by an **agrarian code,** to protect freemen and small holders. By the *Ecloga* (739) the empire was given a simplified law code, distinguished by the Christian charity of its provisions. In the administrative sphere Leo completed the **theme organization,** dividing the original units and making seven themes in Asia and four in Europe.

717-718. Second great siege of Constantinople by the Arabs. The siege, conducted by land and sea, lasted just a year and ended in failure, due to the energetic conduct of the defense.

726. Beginning of the great **iconoclastic controversy.** Leo found the empire generally demoralized and a prey to superstition and miracle-mongering. Like many devout persons (especially in the Anatolian regions), he disapproved of the widespread image-worship, which he proceeded to forbid. Behind these measures there undoubtedly lay the desire to check the alarming **spread of monasticism,** which withdrew thousands of men from active economic life and concentrated great wealth in the cloisters, which were free from taxation. The first measures led at once to a revolt in Greece (727), whence a fleet set out for Constantinople with an anti-emperor. This was destroyed by the Greek fire of the imperial fleet. The pope at Rome (Gregory II) likewise declared against the emperor's iconoclasm and the population of the exarchate of Ravenna rose in revolt and made an alliance with the Lombards. Only with the aid of Venice were a few crucial stations held by the imperial forces. A fleet from the east failed to restore Byzantine authority (731). In revenge the emperor in 733 withdrew Calabria, Sicily, and Illyria from the jurisdiction of the pope and placed them under the Constantinople patriarch.

739. The Byzantine forces won an important victory over the Arab invaders of Anatolia in the **battle of Akroinon.**

741-775. CONSTANTINE V (Kopronymos), the son of Leo and for years associated with him in the government. Constantine was autocratic, uncompromising, and violent, but withal able and energetic as well as sincere. A revolt of his brother-in-law, Artavasdos, was supported by the idolaters and by part of the army. It took fully two years to suppress it.

745. The emperor, taking the offensive against the Arabs, carried the war into Syria.

746. The Greek destroyed a great Arab armada and reconquered Cyprus.

746. The empire suffered from the greatest **plague epidemic** since the time of Justinian.

751-752. The emperor led a successful campaign against the Arabs in Armenia. The Arabs were weakened by the fall of the Omayyad Caliphate and the removal of the capital from Damascus to Baghdad (p. 204).

751. The Lombards conquered the exarchate of Ravenna. The pope thereupon called in the Franks and was given the former Byzantine territory by Pepin (**Donation of Pepin,** 756) (p. 166).

753. The **Church Council of Hieria** approved of the emperor's iconoclastic policy. Therewith began the violent phase of the controversy. The monks offered vigorous resistance, but the emperor was unbending. The monks were imprisoned, exiled, and some even executed; monasteries were closed and their properties confiscated; images were destroyed or whitewashed.

755-764. Nine successive **campaigns against the Bulgars.** The emperor won important victories at Marcellae (759) and Anchialus (763), and, despite some reverses, forced the Bulgars to conclude peace (764).

758. The Slavs were defeated in Thrace and a large number of them settled in Asia.

772. Renewal of the **war with the Bulgars,** marked by further victories of the emperor.

775-780. LEO IV, the son of Constantine. In religious matters he simply continued his predecessor's policy.

778-779. Victory over the Arabs at **Germanikeia** (778) and their expulsion from Anatolia.

780-797. CONSTANTINE VI ascended the throne as a child, wholly under the influence of his ambitious, unscrupulous, and scheming mother, **Irene,** and her favorites. Irene, anxious to secure support for her personal power, devoted herself almost exclusively to the religious question. The Arabs, who again advanced to the Bosporus (782), were bought off with heavy tribute (783). On the other hand, the general, Staurakios, carried on a successful campaign against the Slavs in Macedonia and Greece (783).

787. The **Council of Nicaea** abandoned iconoclasm and ordered the worship of images. Tremendous victory for the monkish party, which soon advanced far-reaching claims to complete freedom for the Church in religious matters.

790. The army, opposed to the monks, mutinied and put Constantine in power. Irene was forced into retirement. The emperor set out on campaigns against the Arabs and Bulgars, but met with indifferent success.

792. Constantine recalled his mother and made her co-ruler. She took a vile advantage of him and, after his divorce and a remarriage arranged by her (795), put herself at the head of a party of the monks in opposing the step. A rising of the army put her in control and she had her son taken and blinded (797).

797-802. IRENE, the first empress. Though supported by able generals (Staurakios and Aëtios), she preferred to buy peace with the

Arabs (798) and devote herself to domestic intrigue.

800.   Resurrection of the empire in the west, through the coronation of Charlemagne. The Eastern Empire refused to recognize the claim.

802-811.   NICEPHORUS, who was put on the throne by a group of conspiring officials of the government.   Irene, deposed, died in 803. Nicephorus was a firm ruler, who carried through a number of much-needed financial reforms.

803.   The emperor made **peace with Charlemagne,** the Eastern Empire retaining southern Italy, Venice, and Dalmatia.

804-806.   The Arabs resumed their raids in Anatolia and ravaged Cyprus and Rhodes, ultimately forcing the conclusion of a humiliating peace.

809.   Banishment of the monks of Studion, who, under **Theodoros of Studion,** took the lead in advancing claims to church freedom. They went so far as to appeal to the Roman pope and offer to recognize his primacy.

809-813.   War with Krum, the powerful king of the Bulgars. The emperor was defeated and killed in a great battle (811).

811.   STAURAKIOS, son of Nicephorus, was emperor for a few months.

811-813.   MICHAEL I (Rhangabé), brother-in-law of Staurakios, emperor. He proved himself quite incompetent, being unable to check the advance of Krum to Constantinople, or the success of the party of monks in domestic affairs.

813-820.   LEO V (the Armenian), called to the throne by the army.   Though personally not much moved by the religious controversy, he could not avoid taking up the challenge of the monks.

815.   The **COUNCIL OF ST. SOPHIA** marked the return to iconoclasm and the beginning of the second period of active and violent persecution of the monks.

817.   The emperor won a great victory over the Bulgars at **Mesembria,** Krum having died (814). The Bulgars were obliged to accept a thirty-year peace.

820-829.   MICHAEL II (Phrygian dynasty), succeeded to the throne after the murder of Leo by conspirators.

822-824.   Insurrection of the general, **Thomas,** in Anatolia. This was supported by the lower classes and encouraged by the Arabs. Thomas attempted twice to take Constantinople, but was ultimately defeated and executed in Thrace.

826.   Crete was seized by Moslem freebooters from Spain and until 961 remained the headquarters of pirates who ravaged the eastern Mediterranean.

827-878.   Conquest of Sicily by Moslems from North Africa.

829-842.   THEOPHILUS, emperor.   He was an arrogant, theologizing fanatic who promulgated a new edict against idolaters (832) and pushed persecution to the limit.

837-838.   War against the Arabs. The Byzantine armies, after invading the caliphate, were repulsed. After a long siege, Amorion, one of the key positions on the frontier, was taken by the Moslems (838).

842-867.   MICHAEL III, for whom his mother Theodora was regent.   Advised by her brother, **Bardas,** she decided to end the religious controversy.

843.   Image-worship was restored. This was a great victory for the opposition party, but only in the matter of doctrine. Politically the power of the emperor over the Church remained unimpaired, if not strengthened.

849.   Reduction of the Slavic populations of the Peloponnesus, followed by their conversion.

856.   Theodora was obliged to retire, but her brother Bardas, an able but unprincipled politician, remained the real ruler of the empire by exploiting to the full the weaknesses of the emperor.

860.   First appearance of the Russians (Varangians) at Constantinople.

863-885.   Missionary activity of **Cyril** and **Methodius** of Thessalonica among the Slavs of Moravia and Bohemia. They invented the **Glagolitic** (i.e. Slavic) **alphabet** and by the use of Slavic in the church service paved the way for the connection of Slavic Christianity with Constantinople.

865.   Tsar Boris of Bulgaria (852-889) allowed himself to be baptized. Although Michael III acted as godfather, the Bulgarian ruler was for a time undecided between the claims of Rome and Constantinople to religious jurisdiction in Bulgaria.

866.   Bardas was murdered by Michael's favorite, Basil.

867.   Michael himself was deposed and done away with at Basil's order.

867.   Schism with Rome. The great patriarch, **Photius,** had replaced **Ignatius** in 858, whereupon the latter had appealed to the pope for an inquiry.   Photius came to represent the Greek national feeling in opposition to Rome. He took a strong stand towards the papal claims and the **Council of Constantinople** (867) anathematized the pope, accused the papacy of doctrinal aberrations, rejected the idea of Rome's primacy, etc.

867-886.   BASIL I, founder of the Macedonian dynasty (he was really of Armenian extraction, though born in Macedonia).   His reign initiated what was probably the most glorious period of Byzantine history. The empire had by this time become a purely Greek monarchy, under an absolute ruler. Settlement of the iconoclastic controversy released the national energies and there followed a period of brilliant military success, material prosperity, and cultural development. An important departure was the recognition of the idea of legitimacy and of an imperial family. This was paralleled by the gradual emergence of a feudal system.

Basil I was himself an intelligent, firm, and orderly ruler, a good administrator and general, whose ambition was to restore the empire both internally and externally. He rebuilt the army and especially the navy, and did much to revise the legal system: the *Procheiros Nomos* (879), a compilation of the most important parts of the Justinian code; the *Epanagoge* (886), a manual of customary law.

869. The eighth ecumenical synod. Photius had been banished (867) and Ignatius recalled. The latter made peace with Rome on papal terms, but conflict and friction continued.

871–879. Campaigns in the east. Border warfare with the Arabs was chronic, but the campaign against the Paulicians (Christian purists hostile to the empire) was a new departure. The imperial armies advanced to the upper Euphrates and took Samosata (873). In 878–879 victorious campaigns were carried through in Cappadocia and Cilicia. By land the Byzantine forces were gradually taking the offensive against the Moslems, wracked by internal dissensions.

875. The Byzantine forces seized **Bari** in southern Italy. Some years later (880) they took Tarentum and then (885) Calabria, establishing two new themes in southern Italy, which became a refuge for Greeks driven from Sicily by the completion of the Saracen conquest (Syracuse taken, 878; Taormina taken, 902).

877. Photius was restored as patriarch.

880–881. A number of naval **victories over the Moslem pirates** of the eastern Mediterranean marked the beginning of a long campaign against this scourge.

886–912. LEO VI (the Wise), a somewhat pedantic philosopher, but nevertheless a determined ruler with a high sense of his office and obligations. He deposed Photius at once and put the Ignatians back in power. The result was a renewal of the **union with Rome** (900), which, however, could hardly be more than external. The reign of Leo was marked also by further legislative work. The *Basilika* (887–893) provided a series of 60 new law books, consisting largely of a compilation of decrees since the time of Justinian.

889– War with the Bulgarians, who now entered the period of greatness under **Tsar Symeon** (893–927). The emperor encouraged the Hungarians to attack by way of diversion and most of Symeon's reign was taken up with continued campaigns against this enemy. Symeon was educated at Constantinople and was deeply impressed by Greek culture, which he introduced in Bulgaria.

904. The Saracen corsair, **Leo of Tripoli,** stormed Thessalonica, plundered it, and carried off some 20,000 of the inhabitants.

907. The **Russians,** under their prince, Oleg, appeared again at Constantinople and secured rights of trade.

912–913. ALEXANDER II, the brother of Leo, emperor for less than a year.

912–959. CONSTANTINE VII (Porphyrogenetos) ascended the throne as a child, with a regency composed of his mother Zoë, the Patriarch Nikolas, and John Eladas. Constantine was a learned man of artistic tastes. He never really governed, leaving the actual conduct of affairs to strong men who were associated with him.

913–917. The Bulgarian threat. Tsar Symeon, who had established a brilliant capital at Preslav (seat also of the Bulgarian patriarchate), styled himself Emperor of the Romans, and undoubtedly hoped to possess himself of the imperial crown. In 913 he appeared at Constantinople; in 914 he took Adrianople, only to lose it again. But in 917 he defeated a Byzantine army at Anchialus. The war continued, indecisively, for years. In 924 Symeon again appeared at Constantinople.

915. A Byzantine victory over the Arabs at **Garigliano** assured the empire of its possessions in south Italy.

920–944. ROMANUS LECAPENUS, co-emperor with Constantine. He was the emperor's father-in-law, an able but ruthless Armenian, whose whole policy was designed to strengthen his own control and establish that of his family.

920–942. Brilliant campaigns of the Byzantine general, **John Kurkuas,** in the east. He took the modern Erzerum (928) and Melitene (934), and extended the imperial power to the Euphrates and Tigris.

920. Official reunion with Rome.

924. The piratical fleets of **Leo of Tripoli** were completely defeated off **Lemnos.** Nevertheless, the Moslem pirates continued to be the scourge of the Mediterranean.

927. The empire suffered from a **great famine,** which probably explains the stringent legislation of the government to prevent the purchase of small holdings by the great landed magnates.

The Macedonian Emperors (867–1054)

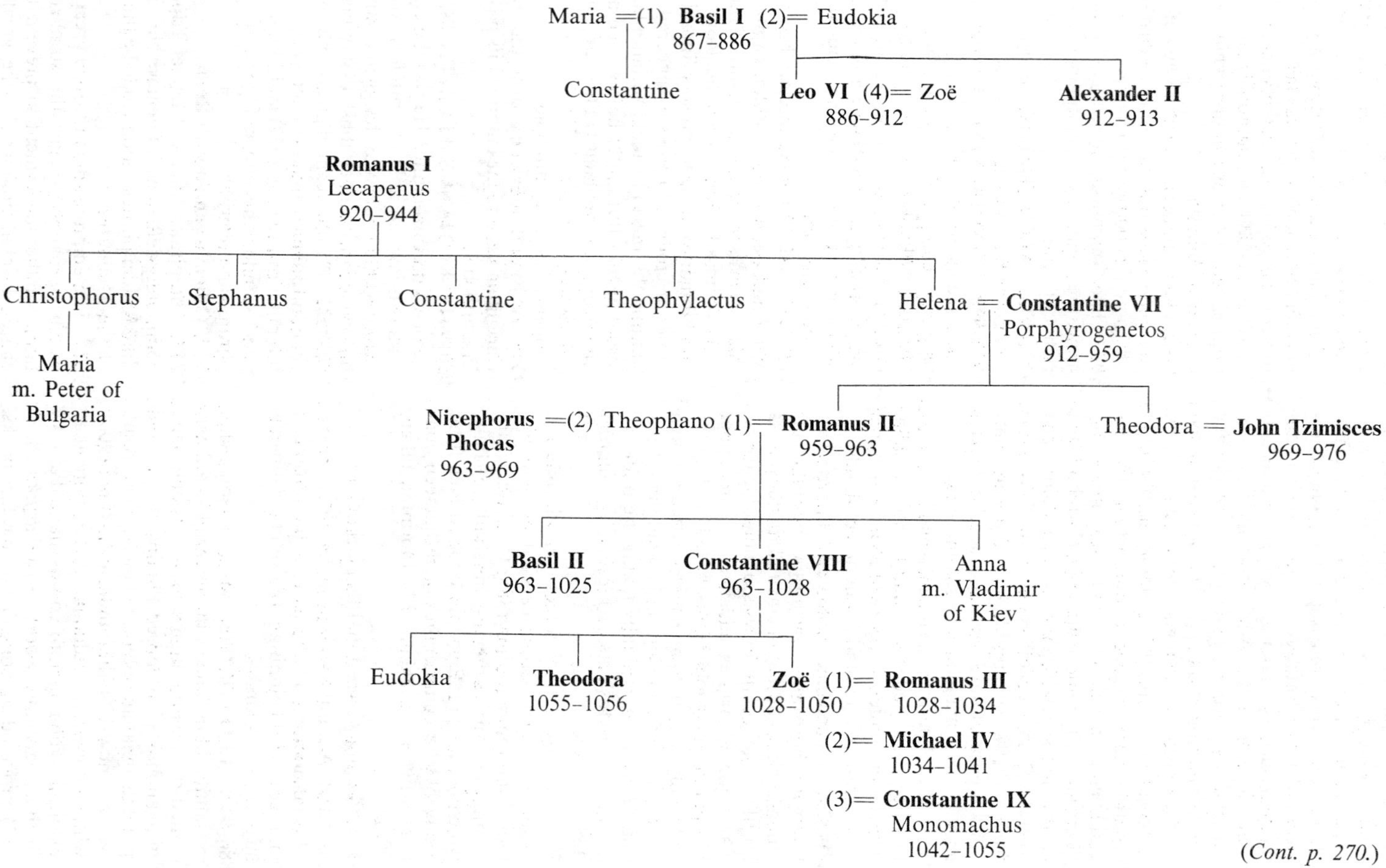

Maria =(1) **Basil I** (2)= Eudokia
867–886

Constantine   **Leo VI** (4)= Zoë   **Alexander II**
886–912   912–913

Helena = **Constantine VII**
Porphyrogenetos
912–959

Theodora = **John Tzimisces**
969–976

Romanus I
Lecapenus
920–944

Christophorus   Stephanus   Constantine   Theophylactus

Maria
m. Peter of
Bulgaria

Nicephorus =(2) Theophano (1)= **Romanus II**
Phocas   959–963
963–969

Basil II
963–1025

Constantine VIII
963–1028

Anna
m. Vladimir
of Kiev

Eudokia

Theodora
1055–1056

Zoë (1)= **Romanus III**
1028–1050   1028–1034

(2)= **Michael IV**
1034–1041

(3)= **Constantine IX**
Monomachus
1042–1055

(Cont. p. 270.)

941. A great armada of Russians, under **Prince Igor,** was signally defeated by the Greeks.

944. The **Emperor Romanus** was seized and imprisoned (d. 948) by the very sons whose interests he had attempted to serve. The Emperor Constantine became officially the sole ruler, but governed with the aid of the great general, **Bardas Phocas,** and under the influence of the Empress Helena and her favorite, Basil.

955. Visit to Constantinople and baptism of **Princess Olga** of Russia.

959-963. ROMANUS II, the young and dissipated son of Constantine.

961. Reconquest of Crete from the Saracen pirates. A great armada was sent out under Nicephorus Phocas. Candia was stormed, the Moslems expelled from the island or converted to Christianity.

962. Otto I, Roman emperor in the west, claimed suzerainty over the Lombards in southern Italy, initiating a period of friction with Constantinople, which was only temporarily broken by the marriage of Otto II and the Byzantine princess, Theophano (972).

963-1025. BASIL II, an infant at the death of his father. The principle of legitimacy was carefully respected, but before Basil II really assumed power, the empire was governed by two great generals associated with him.

963-969. NICEPHORUS II PHOCAS, who had carried on a successful campaign in the east. He seized control and married the widowed Empress Theophano. Never popular, especially with the clergy, Nicephorus, by his victories in the field, helped to raise the empire to its greatest glory.

964-968. Victorious campaign in the east. Adana was taken (964) and then Tarsus (965). Cyprus was reconquered and in 968 northern Syria was invaded. **Aleppo** and even **Antioch** fell into the hands of the Greeks.

966-969. The **Bulgarian campaign,** carried through with the aid of Sviatoslav and the Russians. The latter, with their fleets, were so successful on the Danube that the Greeks made peace with the Bulgars.

969. Nicephorus Phocas was overthrown by a conspiracy of officers led by his own nephew

969-976. JOHN I TZIMISCES, an Armenian by birth and one of the greatest of Byzantine generals.

969. Sviatoslav, the Russian, crossed the Balkan Mountains and took Philippopolis. John Tzimisces marched against him, defeated him near Adrianople, and, with the aid of the Byzantine fleet on the Danube, forced him to evacuate Bulgaria (972). John thereupon annexed eastern Bulgaria as far as the Danube

to the empire. The patriarchate of Preslav was abolished.

971. A great feudal insurrection, led by Bardas Phocas, was put down only with difficulty.

972-976. Continuation of the campaigns in the east. John took Edessa and Nezib (974), Damascus and Beirut (976), and advanced to the very gates of Jerusalem, where he was halted by the Moslem forces from Egypt.

976. Sudden **death of John Tzimisces,** at the early age of 51.

976. BASIL II (Bulgaroktonos = Slayer of the Bulgarians) now became sole emperor. He was only 20 years old, but serious and energetic, cynical and cruel. Until 989 he was much influenced by Basil the Eunuch, the illegitimate son of Romanus Lecapenus. The reign of Basil began with another great feudal upheaval, led by **Bardas Skleros,** who marched his armies from the east through Anatolia and to Constantinople. Basil appealed to Bardas Phocas, defeated leader of the earlier rising, to save the situation, which he did by defeating Skleros at Pankalia (979).

976-1014. Tsar Samuel of Bulgaria. He built up another great Bulgarian empire, with its capital at Ochrid, extending from the Adriatic to the Black Sea and from the Danube to the Peloponnesus. In 981 he defeated Basil near Sofia.

987. Rising of Bardas Phocas and Bardas Skleros against Basil and the imperial authority. The great feudal barons overran Anatolia. In 988 they threatened Constantinople, but the movement collapsed with the defeat of Phocas at Abydos (989) and his subsequent death. Skleros then submitted.

989. Conversion of Prince Vladimir of Russia, at Cherson. This initiated the general conversion of the Russians to eastern Christianity and the close connection between Kiev and Constantinople.

992. Extensive trade privileges in the empire were granted to **Venice,** by this time quite independent of imperial control, but in close co-operation with Constantinople in the Adriatic.

995. Victorious campaigns of the emperor in the east. Aleppo and Homs were taken and Syria incorporated with the empire.

996. Land legislation of Basil II. Many of the great estates were confiscated and divided among the peasants, and provision made to prevent the further development of feudalism.

996-1014. THE GREAT BULGARIAN CAMPAIGNS. In 996 Basil defeated Samuel on the Spercheios River and reconquered Greece. In 1002 he overran Macedonia. Samuel recovered, however, reconquered Macedonia, and sacked Adrianople (1003). In 1007 Basil subdued Macedonia again and after years of indecisive conflict annihilated the Bulgarian army at **Balathista** (1014). He sent several thousand blinded soldiers back to Samuel, who died of the shock. The Bulgarians finally submitted (1018), but were left their autonomy and an autocephalous church at Ochrid. Many of the Bulgarian noble families settled in Constantinople and merged with the Greek and Armenian aristocracy.

1018. The Byzantine forces won a great victory over the combined Lombards and Normans at **Cannae,** thus assuring continuance of the Greek domination in southern Italy.

1020. The **king of Armenia,** long in alliance with the Greeks against the Arabs, turned over his kingdom to Basil to escape the new threat from the Seljuk Turks. Thereby the empire became firmly established in Transcaucasia and along the Euphrates.

BYZANTINE CULTURE reached its apogee in the late 10th and early 11th centuries. The empire extended from Italy to Mesopotamia and its influence radiated much farther. Constantinople, indeed, was the economic and artistic center of the Mediterranean world.

Government. The emperor was an absolute ruler, regarded almost as sacred. Under the Macedonian emperors the idea of legitimacy became firmly established. The imperial court reflected the emperor's power and splendor. There was an extensive and elaborate ceremonial (cf. the *Book of Ceremonies* of Constantine Porphyrogenetos); the administration was highly centralized in Constantinople and was unique for its efficiency; the treasury was full and continued to draw a large income from taxes, customs, and monopolies; the army and navy were both at the peak of their development, with excellent organization and leadership; the provinces were governed by the strategoi; there were by this time 30 themes (18 in Asia and 12 in Europe), but throughout this period there was a steady growth in the number and power of the provincial magnates (*dunatoi*), feudal barons who acquired more and more of the small holdings and exercised an ever greater influence, even challenging the emperor himself. All the legislation of the Macedonian emperors failed to check this development.

The **Church** was closely connected with the throne, but during this period it too became more and more wealthy and gradually produced a clerical aristocracy. The union with Rome, when it existed, was a purely formal thing. The Greek patriarchate in practice resented the Roman claim to primacy and the popular dislike of the Latins made any real co-operation impossible.

Economic life. This was closely controlled by the state, which derived much of its income from the customs and monopolies. Yet it was a period of great commercial development, Constantinople serving as the entrepôt between east and west. It was also a great center of the industry in luxuries (organization of trades in rigid guilds, etc.).

Learning. The university of Constantinople (opened c. 850) had quickly become a center of philosophical and humanistic study, in which the emperors took a direct interest. In the 11th century there appeared the greatest of the Byzantine scholars, **Psellus,** reviver of the Platonic philosophy and universal genius. In the field of literature there was a conscious return to the great Greek models of the early Byzantine period; historians, **Constantine Porphyrogenetos, Leo the Deacon,** etc. The great popular epic, *Digenis Akritas,* describing the heroic life of the frontier soldiers (*Akritai*), dates from the 10th century.

Art. The period was one of extensive construction, especially in Constantinople; full exploitation of the St. Sophia type in church architecture; mosaics; ikons; gold and silver work. Byzantine influence in this period permeated the entire Mediterranean world, Moslem as well as Christian. (*Cont. p. 267.*)

b. THE FIRST BULGARIAN EMPIRE, TO 1018

The Bulgarians, first mentioned by name in 482 as a people living to the northeast of the Danube, were members of the Finno-Tatar race, probably related to the Huns and at first ruled by princes of Attila's family. They were organized on the clan system, worshiped the sun and moon, practiced human sacrifice, etc.

584-642. Kurt, or **Kubrat,** of the Dulo family, the first authenticated ruler. His dominions lay in the eastern steppes, from the Don to the Caucasus. In 619 he visited Constantinople to secure aid against the Avars, at which time he became converted to Christianity, though this step seems to have had no consequences for his people.

643-701. Isperikh (Asperuch), the son or grandson of Kurt. The old Great Bulgaria was disrupted by the attacks of Avars and Khazars, and various tribes of Bulgars moved westward into Pannonia and even into Italy. Those under Isperikh crossed the Danube (650-670) and established a capital at Pliska. In 680 they defeated a Byzantine army and occupied the territory between the Danube and the Balkan Mountains. At the same time they still held Wallachia, Moldavia, and Bessarabia. The amalgamation with the Slavic inhabitants was probably very gradual, the upper, military classes remaining strictly Bulgar for a long time.

701-718.   Tervel, to whom the Emperor Justinian II paid a subsidy or tribute, but only after the imperial forces had been defeated at Anchialus (708) and after Tervel had advanced to the very gates of Constantinople (712).

718-724.   Ruler unknown.

724-739.   Sevar, during whose reign the peace with the empire was maintained. The Dulo dynasty came to an end with Sevar, whose death was followed by an obscure struggle of noble factions.

739-756.   Kormisosh, of the Ukil family. Until the very end of his reign he maintained peace with the empire, until further domestic disorders gave the signal for Byzantine attacks (755 ff.).

756-761.   Vinekh, who was killed in the course of an uprising.

761-764.   Telets, of the Ugain family. He was defeated at Anchialus by the Byzantines (763) and put to death by the Bulgarians.

764.   Sabin, of the family of Kormisosh. He was deposed and fled to Constantinople.

? 764.   Pagan, who finally concluded peace with the emperor.

766.   Umor, who was deposed by

766.   Tokt, who was captured and killed by the Greeks. This entire period is one of deep obscurity, the years 766-773 being a complete blank.

? 773-777.   Telerig, whose family is unknown. The Greeks renewed their attacks, which were on the whole successful and resulted in the subjugation of Bulgaria.

777-791.   Ruler unknown.

? 791-797.   Kardam, whose reign marked the turning of the tide. He took advantage of the confusion in the empire to defeat the Greeks at **Marcellae** (792) and to rebuild the foundations of the state. What happened after his death is unknown.

808-814.   KRUM, one of the greatest Bulgarian rulers. He appears to have been a Pannonian Bulgar, who rose to power as a result of his victories over the Avars. During his short reign he organized the state and encouraged the Slav elements at the expense of the Bulgar aristocracy. His objective seems to have been the establishment of the absolute power of the khan. For four years (809-813) he carried on war with the Byzantine Empire. The Greeks sacked Pliska (809; 811), but Krum defeated and killed the emperor in a battle in the mountains (811). In 812 he took the important fortress of Mesembria and in 813 won another victory at Versinicia. In the same year he appeared at Constantinople. The city was too strong for him, but he retired, devastating Thrace and taking Adrianople.

814-831.   Omortag, the son of Krum. After a defeat by the Greeks (815), he concluded a thirty-year peace with them (817), returning Mesembria and Adrianople. Construction of the earthwork barrier (the Great Fence) on the Thracian frontier. Founding of the new capital, **Great Preslav** (821). During the peace in the east, the Bulgars began systematic raids into Croatia and Pannonia (827-829).

831-852.   Malamir, the son of Omortag, the period of whose reign is vague, excepting for gradual expansion into upper Macedonia and Serbia (839).

852-889.   BORIS I. He continued the campaigns in the west, but suffered severe defeats by the Germans (853) and a setback from the Serbs (860). Boris' reign was important chiefly for his

865.   Conversion to Christianity. The way had undoubtedly been prepared by numerous prisoners of war, but Boris was induced to take the step under pressure from Constantinople, where the government was eager to frustrate a possible German-Roman advance. Boris had all his subjects baptized, which led to a revolt and the execution of a number of noble leaders. For some time Boris was undecided whether to lean toward Rome or toward Constantinople. To counteract the aggressive Greek influence he accepted the primacy of Rome (866), but then turned to Constantinople (870) when the pope refused to appoint an archbishop for Bulgaria. In 885 the Slavonic liturgy was introduced among the Slavs of Bulgaria by the successors of Cyril and Methodius. In 889 Boris voluntarily retired to a monastery.

889-893.   Vladimir, the son of Boris, who was soon exposed to a violent aristocratic, heathen reaction.

893.   Boris re-emerged from retirement, put down the revolt, deposed and blinded his son, completed the organization of the church, and made the Slavonic liturgy general in its application. The capital was definitely moved to Preslav. Boris then returned to his monastery, where he died (907).

893-927.   SYMEON I, another son of Boris, the first Bulgarian ruler to assume the title *Tsar*. Symeon had been educated at Constantinople, as a monk. He was deeply imbued with Greek culture and did much to encourage translations from the Greek. Splendor of Great Preslav and Symeon's court; development of a second cultural center at Ochrid, under St. Clement and St. Nahum.

894-897.   Symeon's reign was filled with wars against the Byzantine Empire, which grew originally out of disputes regarding trade rights and ultimately developed into a contest for possession of the imperial throne. The war began in 894, with the defeat of a Greek army. The emperor thereupon induced the Magyars, located on the Pruth River, to attack the Bulgarians in Bessarabia (895). Symeon induced the Greeks by trickery to withdraw and then defeated the Magyars, after which he returned and fell on the Greeks at Bulgarophygon. Peace was made in 897, the emperor paying tribute.

In the meanwhile the **Magyars,** driven westward by the Patzinaks (Pechenegs), advanced into Transylvania and Pannonia, which were lost to the Bulgars.

913. Symeon, taking advantage of the dynastic troubles in the empire, advanced to Constantinople, but withdrew with many presents and the promise that the young emperor, Constantine Porphyrogenitus, should marry one of his daughters. Symeon evidently hoped to attain the crown for himself, but was frustrated by the seizure of power by Zoë. He thereupon made war (914), raiding into Macedonia, Thessaly, and Albania. But the Patzinaks, instigated by the Greeks, invaded and occupied Wallachia (917), while Symeon defeated the Greeks near **Anchialus** (917). In 918 Symeon defeated the Serbs, who had also been aroused by the empress.

919-924. Symeon four times advanced to the Hellespont and Constantinople, but was unable to take the city because of his lack of a fleet. In 924 he had an interview with the Emperor Romanus Lecapenus and finally made peace.

925. Symeon proclaimed himself **Emperor of the Romans and the Bulgars.** The Greek emperor protested, but the pope recognized the title.

926. Symeon set up Leontius of Preslav as a patriarch.

926. Conquest and devastation of Serbia.

927-969. Peter, the son of Symeon, a pious, well-intentioned but weak ruler, who married the granddaughter of Romanus Lecapenus. Peace with Constantinople was maintained, the Greek emperor recognizing the Bulgar ruler as emperor and acknowledging the Bulgarian patriarchate. Bulgaria was, during this period, occupied by the constant threat from the Magyars (raids, 934, 943, 958, 962) and the Patzinaks (great raid of 944). Internally the period seems to have been one of unrest and religious ferment (founding of monasteries;

St. John of Rila; beginning of the **Bogomil heresy,** c. 950, a dualistic creed possibly inspired by the Paulicians settled in the Thracian region by the Byzantine emperors).

967. Invasion of Bulgaria by Sviatoslav and the Russians. Tsar Peter roused the Patzinaks who attacked Kiev in 968 and forced Sviatoslav to withdraw.

969-972. Boris II. The reign was filled with the second invasion of Sviatoslav, who took Preslav and captured Boris and his family (969). The Greeks, in alarm, sent an army against him and defeated him at **Arcadiopolis** (970). In 972 the Emperor John Tzimisces attacked the Russians by land and sea. He took Preslav and destroyed it, besieged Sviatoslav at Dristra on the Danube, and finally forced him to evacuate Bulgaria. Boris was obliged to abdicate, the patriarchate was abolished, and Bulgaria came to an end as a separate state.

976-1014. SAMUEL, son of a governor of one of the western districts, which had been unaffected by the Russian invasion, set himself up as ruler. He soon expanded his domain to Sofia, and re-established the patriarchate (ultimately fixed at Ochrid, which was the center of the new state).

986-989. Samuel took Larissa after several annual raids into Thessaly and c. 989 took also Dyrrhacium on the Adriatic coast. In the east he extended his power to the Black Sea.

996-1014. The **campaigns of Basil II** (Bulgaroktonos = Slayer of the Bulgarians) against Samuel. Basil proceeded to reduce one stronghold after another. Samuel avoided open battle as much as possible, but throughout suffered from defection of his leaders, who were bribed by attractive offers by the emperor. The crowning defeat of the Bulgarians at Balathista (1014) and the sight of his 15,000 blinded warriors brought on Samuel's death.

1014-1016. Gabriel Radomir (or Romanus), the son of Samuel. He tried to make peace but was murdered by his cousin

1016-1018. John Vladislav, who continued the war, but was killed in a battle near Dyrrhacium. He left only young sons. The Bulgar leaders thereupon decided to submit. Bulgaria was incorporated into the Byzantine Empire (themes of Bulgaria and Paristrium), the patriarchate was abolished, but the Archbishop of Ochrid retained practical autonomy. The Bulgarian aristocracy settled in Constantinople and merged with the leading Greek families. (*Cont. p. 265.*

3. THE MOSLEM WORLD

a. MUHAMMAD AND ISLAM, 622–661

[For a complete list of the caliphs see Appendix III.]

Arabia before the time of Muhammad was inhabited by tribes of Semitic race, those in the desert areas (Bedouins) of nomadic, pastoral habits, those in the coastal valleys along the Red Sea (Hijaz, Yemen) much more settled, engaged in agriculture and trade. The towns of Mecca and Medina were centers of considerable commercial and cultural development, in which Greek and Jewish influence was probably quite marked.

570–632. MUHAMMAD. He was the posthumous son of Abdallah of the Hashimite sept of Mecca. Having lost his mother when about six, he was brought up by his grandfather, Abd al Muttalib, and his uncle, Abu Talib. Muhammad became a merchant in the caravan trade, serving Kadijah, a widow of means whom he married when he was about 25, thus achieving for himself a modest independence. Given to religious meditation and affected by Christian and Jewish ideas and practices, he began his prophetic career about 612, preaching the One God, the Last Judgment, alms, prayers, and surrender to the will of God (Islam). Gaining a few adherents, but rejected and persecuted by his townsmen, he and his followers fled to Medina, on July 2, 622.

622, July 16. The traditional (though erroneous) date of **Muhammad's flight** (*Hijrah, Hegira*). This date has been adopted as the beginning of the Moslem era.

622–632. In Medina, Muhammad organized the **commonwealth of Islam** by welding together the Meccan fugitives and the Medinan tribes in and around the town (the Aus and the Khazraj)—expelling or devoting the Jewish tribes—into a community based on the will of God as revealed to his prophet, and on the common law of the tribesmen. At the same time he carried on war against the Meccans.

624–630. The Moslems defeated the Meccans at **Badr** (624), but were themselves defeated at Ohod (625). The Meccans thereupon besieged Medina (627) but were repulsed. By the **treaty of Hudaybiya** (628), Muhammad and his followers were granted permission to make the pilgrimage to Mecca. When the treaty was broken by the allies of the Meccans, the war was resumed and Muhammad took Mecca (630). Many of the Arab tribes

were subdued before Muhammad's death (632).

The **essential articles of the Moslem faith** are: Belief in the One God, **Allah,** in his angels, and in his prophet, **Muhammad,** the last of the prophets; belief in his revealed books, of which the *Koran* is the last and the only one necessary; belief in the Day of Resurrection, and in God's predestination, which determines the fate and the actions of men.

The **six fundamental duties** are: the recitation of the profession of faith; attesting the unity of God and the mission of Muhammad; the five daily prayers; the fast in the month of Ramadhan; the pilgrimage to Mecca; and the Holy War.

632–661. The **Orthodox Caliphate,** including the first four caliphs.

632–634. Abu Bakr, the first caliph or vicegerent of the prophet, chosen by acclamation. Defeat of the so-called false prophets, Tulayha and Musaylima; reduction of the rebellious tribes (632).

632–738. EXPANSION BEYOND ARABIA. First incursion into Iraq under **Khalid ibn al-Walid** (633). Hira, the ancient Lakhmid capital, and Obolla taken and put to ransom. The main advance, however, was against Syria. Defeat of Theodore, brother of the Emperor Heraclius, at Ajnadayn (Jannabatayn) between Gaza and Jerusalem (634). Death of Abu Bakr, who appointed as his successor

634–644. Omar, who first assumed the title of *Amir al-Mu'minin* (Prince of the Faithful) and established the primacy of the Arabs over their taxpaying subjects.

Conquest of Syria. Defeat of the Byzantines under Baanes at Marj al-Saffar, near Damascus, by Khalid (635). Damascus and Emessa taken, only to be given up, however, under the pressure of superior forces. Decisive defeat of the Byzantines at **Yarmuk,** south of the Lake of Tiberias (636). Damascus and Emessa retaken. Subjugation of northern Syria, Aleppo and Antioch taken. Capitulation of Jerusalem (638). Caesarea captured (640). The seacoast occupied. Northern boundary of the caliphate the Amanus Mountains. Subjugation of Mesopotamia (639–641).

Conquest of Persia. After a disastrous defeat at the **battle of the Bridge,** the Moslems resumed their attack on Persia. Invasion and occupation of Iraq (635–637). Defeat of the Persians under Mihran at Buwayb by Muthanna (635). The Persian chancellor, Rustam, defeated by Sa'd ibn-abi-Waqqas at **Qadisiya** (637). Al-Madain (Ctesiphon) taken (637).

Persians defeated again at Jalula, fifty miles north of Madain (637). Invasion and occupation of central Persia (638–650). Final defeat of the Persians at Nehawand (642).

Conquest of Egypt. Invasion of Egypt by the Arabs under Amr ibn al-'As (639). Pelusium taken (640). Byzantine defeated at Heliopolis (640). Death of the Emperor Heraclius (641). Capture of Babylon (642). Capitulation of Egypt arranged by Cyrus, patriarch of Alexandria (642). Terms: security of person and property guaranteed to the inhabitants on payment of a tribute and free exercise of their religion. Omar assassinated (644). His successor was chosen by a body of electors.

644–656. Othman, a member of the Omayyad family of Mecca, notorious for his nepotism. The official redaction of the *Koran* made by Zayd ibn Thabit in this reign.

Occupation of Barqa and the Pentapolis (642–643). Revolt of Alexandria, inspired by the appearance of the Byzantine fleet (645). The city retaken by assault (645). Creation of an Arab fleet by Abdallah ibn Sa'd, governor of Egypt. Capture of Cyprus (649) and Aradus (650). Expedition against Constantinople, annihilation of the Byzantine fleet at Dhat al-Sawari on the Lycian coast (655). Disaffection of Arab troops in Iraq and Egypt owing to Othman's nepotism, led to the assassination of Othman in Medina. He was succeeded by

656–661. Ali, the prophet's cousin and son-in-law, whose succession was disputed.

First civil war. Revolt of Talha and Zobayr, two old companions of the prophet, and Aishah, the prophet's favorite wife, in Iraq. They seized Basra, but were defeated by Ali in the **battle of the Camel,** near that town.

Revolt of Muawiya, Omayyad governor of Syria, who demanded revenge for the murder of his kinsman, Othman. Indecisive battle of **Siffin** (657). Hostilities suspended by an agreement to arbitrate the dispute. Arbitration of Adhroh (658). Rejection of the decision by Ali, who was deserted and opposed by a party of his followers, the Kharijites, whom he decimated at Nahrawan. Egypt taken for Muawiya by its first conqueror, Amr (658). Murder of Ali by a Kharijite.

b. THE OMAYYAD CALIPHATE, 661–750

[*For a complete list of the caliphs see Appendix III.*]

661–680. Muawiya, founder of the Omayyad dynasty.

Ḥasan, Ali's eldest son, was proclaimed caliph, but abdicated in the face of Muawiya's advance on Iraq. Muawiya, who had been proclaimed caliph in Jerusalem in 660, moved the seat of government to Damascus. Expedition against Constantinople, Chalcedon taken, Constantinople besieged (669). Ifriqiya (North Africa from the eastern limits of Algeria to the frontiers of Egypt) invaded and the conquest consolidated by the founding of Qairawan by 'Oqba ibn Nafi' (670). In the east under Muawiya's brilliant viceregent, Ziyad ibn Abihi, Sind and the lower valley of the Indus were overrun by Muhallib. Eastern Afghanistan invaded. Kabul taken (664). The Oxus was crossed and Bokhara captured (674). Samarkand taken (676). Moslem advance to the Jaxartes.

Blockade of Constantinople by the Moslem fleet (673–678). Failure of the Moslem attack. Peace concluded for thirty years (678). Death of Muawiya, who had proclaimed as his successor in 676

680–682. Yazid I.

The second civil war. Husayn, the second son of Ali, was invited by the Kufans in Iraq to assume the caliphate. Advancing from Mecca he was basely deserted by the Kufans, defeated, and slain at the famous **battle of Kerbela** (680), whence the Shi'ite celebration of the martyrdom of Husayn each year in the month of Muharram.

Revolt of Abdallah ibn Zubayr, the candidate for the caliphate supported by the Meccans and Medinans. Defeat of the Medinans on the Harra near the town. Siege of Mecca; the Ka'ba burned. Death of Yazid.

The son and successor of Yazid, **Muawiya II,** died some months after his father. **Ibn Zubayr's** caliphate accepted in Arabia, Iraq, Egypt, and by the adherents of the Qais tribe in Syria. The Omayyad party with its adherents of the Kalb tribe chose **Marwan ibn al-Hakam,** a distant cousin of Muawiya I. The Qais were defeated with great slaughter at Marj Rahit (684), north of Damascus, which began the disastrous feud between the so-called northern and southern Arabs, which was largely responsible for the fall of the Arab kingdom of the Omayyads.

684–750. THE MARWANIDS.

684–685. Marwan I. Proclaimed caliph in Syria. Egypt was recovered from **Ibn Zubayr.** Death of Marwan. He was succeeded by his son,

685–705. Abdalmalik, creator of the Arab administration of the empire.

Inroads of the Mardaites of the Amanus, encouraged by the Byzantines, occupied Abdalmalik's first years. His rival, Ibn Zubayr, was occupied by Shi'ite and Kharijite revolts

The Quraysh (Koreish) Tribe

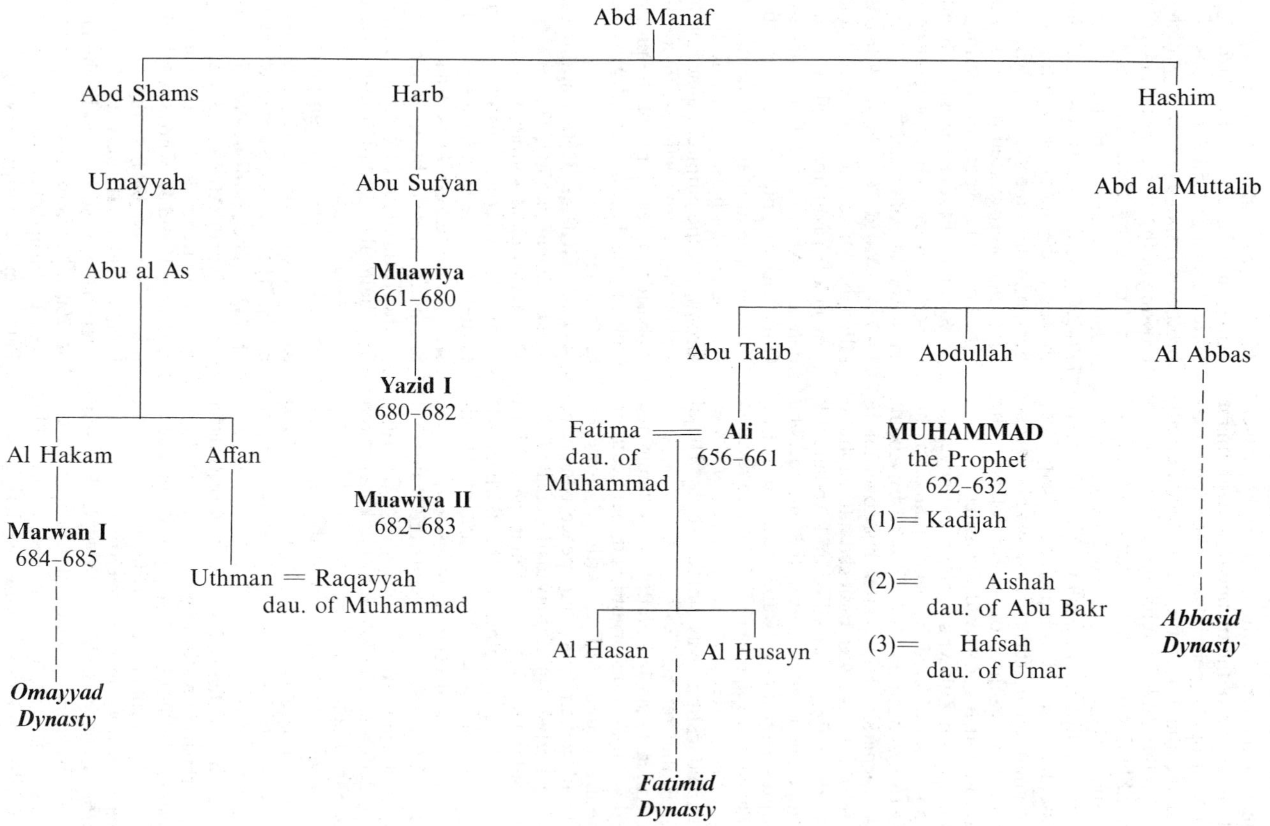

Abd Manaf

Hashim

Abd al Muttalib

Al Abbas — — — — — *Abbasid Dynasty*

Abdullah

MUHAMMAD
the Prophet
622–632

(1)= Kadijah

(2)= Aishah
dau. of Abu Bakr

(3)= Hafsah
dau. of Umar

Abu Talib

Ali
656–661

Fatima = dau. of Muhammad

Al Hasan

Al Husayn — — — — *Fatimid Dynasty*

Abd Shams

Umayyah

Abu al As

Harb

Abu Sufyan

Muawiya
661–680

Yazid I
680–682

Muawiya II
682–683

Affan

Uthman = Raqayyah
dau. of Muhammad

Al Hakam

Marwan I
684–685 — — — — *Omayyad Dynasty*

in Kufa and Basra, Arabia and Persia.

The **Shi'ite sect** were supporters of the claims of the "House of the Prophet," the descendants of the Caliph **Ali,** and of the prophet's daughter, Fatima. Later they developed the dogma of the **Imamate,** that the Imam (the leader of the people) was the representative or incarnation of the deity and the only seat of authority both religious and civil.

The **Kharijites** held that any Moslem in good standing could be elected by the community as caliph. They held that works were an essential part of religion and that those who committed mortal sins were unbelievers. Both sects were bitter opponents of both the Omayyad and the Abbasid dynasties.

Mus'ab, Ibn Zubayr's brother and governor in Iraq, was defeated by Abdalmalik on the Tigris (690). Medina was captured by Abdalmalik's general, Hajjaj, later his governor in Iraq (691). Mecca was besieged and captured (692). Ibn Zubayr was killed and Abdalmalik became undisputed master of the empire. The Kharijites (Azraqites) were crushed in Iraq and Persia by Muhallib (693-698). A rebellion in the east under Ibn al-Ash'ath, who was proclaimed caliph, was put down by Hajjaj (699). Kabul retaken.

In Africa **Oqba ibn Nafi,** now a saint, had raided as far as Tangier, but had met death on his return march (683). Carthage, however, was finally taken (698), and peace concluded with the Berbers, after they had defeated the Arabs under Hassan ibn No'man near Mons Aurasius (703). Thereupon the Berbers became allies of the Arabs. Death of Abdalmalik. He was succeeded by his son,

705-715. Walid I, who built the cathedral mosque at Damascus. Conquest of Transoxania under Qutayba (705-715). Bokhara taken (709), Samarkand (712), Ferghana (714). It is reported that Qutayba invaded China and reached Kashgar (c. 713). Conquest of Sind and part of the Punjab by Mohammed ibn Qasim (708-715).

Invasion of Cilicia (710-711) **and of Galatia** (714). Preparations for a grand attack on Constantinople by land and sea. Subjugation of the western Berbers and pacification of North Africa by Musa ibn Nusayr (708-711).

711-715. CONQUEST OF SPAIN. Invasion of Spain by a mixed force of Arabs and Berbers under Tariq, a freed slave of Musa (711). The Goths under their king, Roderick, were totally defeated in Wadi Bekka, near Rio Barbate (not at Xeres de la Frontera) (July, 711). Fall of Ecija, Córdoba, and the capital, Toledo. Tariq master of half of Spain. The advance of Musa himself (712). Capture of Medina Sidonia, Carmona, Seville (712), Merida (713),

and Saragossa. Resistance to Arab arms continued only in the mountains of Asturias. Death of Walid. He was succeeded by his brother,

715-717. Sulaiman. Conquest of Jurjan (Hyrcania) and Tabaristan by Yazid ibn Muhallib (716). Siege of Constantinople by the caliph's brother, Maslama (717-718), which failed. The crossing of the Pyrenees and invasion of southern France by Hurr, the successor of Musa. Sulaiman succeeded by his cousin,

717-720. Omar ibn Abdul-Aziz, who attempted to reorganize the finances of the empire. Members of the subject races, who had become Moslems, were placed on the same footing as the Arabs in respect to taxation. Narbonne in southern France taken by Samh, the successor of Hurr. Omar was succeeded by the third son of Abdalmalik,

720-724. Yazid II. Samh was defeated and killed by Duke Eudo before Toulouse (721). Revolt of Yazid ibn Muhallib in Iraq. His defeat at Akra on the Euphrates by Maslama. Outbreak of internecine strife between the Yemenites (Kalb) and Modharites (Qais) (the so-called southern and northern Arabs) throughout the empire, especially in Khorasan and Transoxania, where propaganda for the Abbasids (descendants of the prophet's uncle, Abbas) also began. Yazid was succeeded by his brother.

724-743. Hisham. Defeat of the Khazars, conquest of Georgia (727-733).
732. Invasion of southern France by Abd ar-Rahman, governor of Spain; his defeat at Poitiers (Tours) by Charles Martel.
738. Kharijite revolts in Iraq, insurrection of Sogdians and Arabs in Khorasan supported by the Turkomans of Transoxania, was quelled by Khalid ibn Abdallah al-Kasri, governor of Khorasan.
740. Shi'ite revolt in Iraq under Zayd, grandson of the martyred Husayn; his defeat and death. Hisham was succeeded by his nephew.
741-742. The revolt of the Kharijites and Berbers in North Africa was put down by Hanzala, the viceroy in North Africa.
743-744. Walid II, who was killed in a Yemenite revolt led by his cousin, who succeeded him as **Yazid III,** only to die a few months later. He was succeeded by the last Omayyad,
744-750. Marwan II, the grandson of Marwan I. Insurrections in Syria at Homs and in Palestine. Kharijite revolt in Mesopotamia (745), and in Arabia (745-746). Mecca and Medina seized by the rebels. Shi'ite insurrection in Iraq and Persia under Abdallah, grandson of Ali's brother, Ja'far, which was joined by Kharijites and Abbasids (745-747). The black standard of the Abbasids was raised by

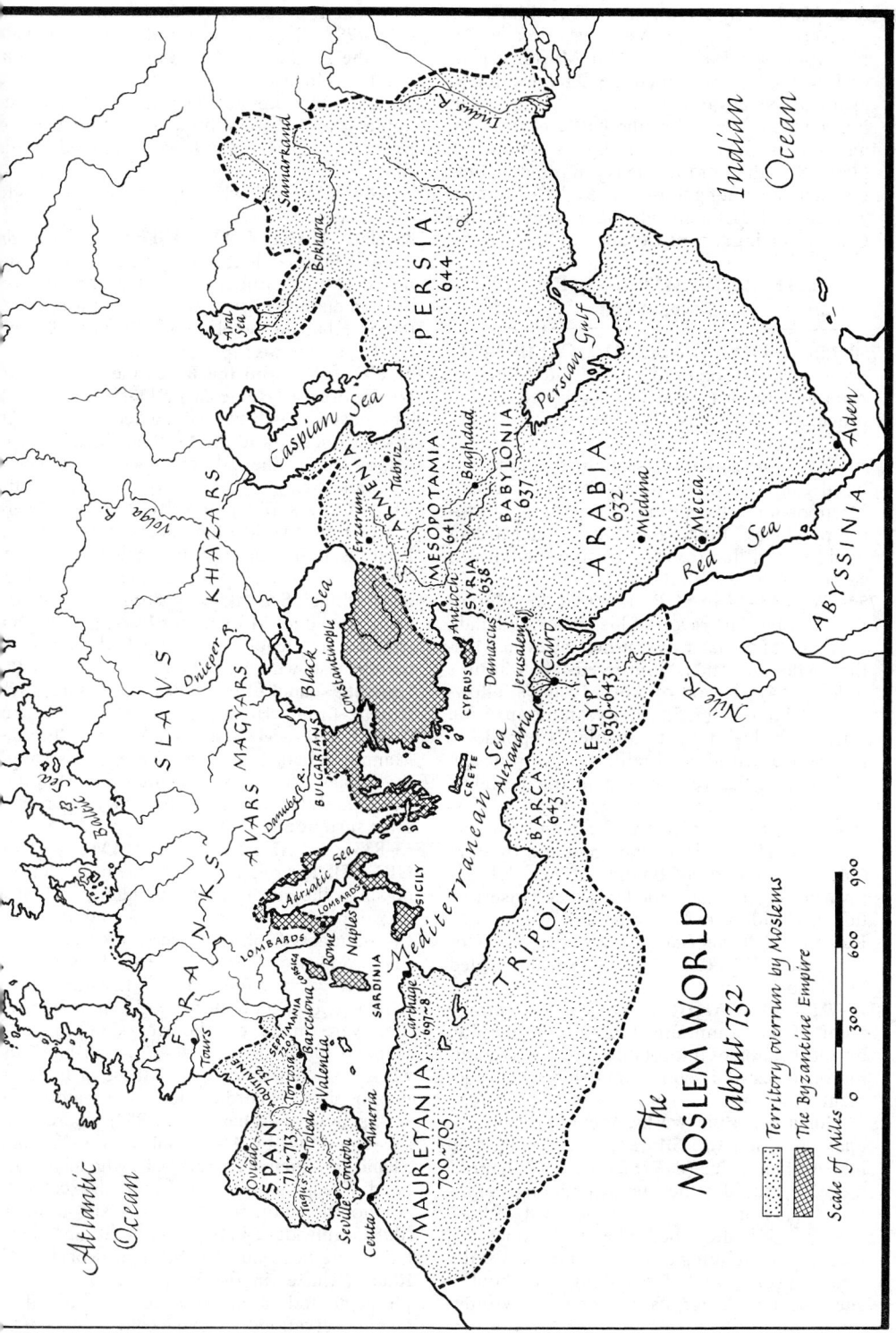

Atlantic
Ocean

Indian
Ocean

The
MOSLEM WORLD
about 732

Territory overrun by Moslems

The Byzantine Empire

Scale of Miles

0   300   600   900

SLAVS

KHAZARS

Aral
Sea

Samarkand

Bokhara

PERSIA
644

AVARS

MAGYARS

Caspian Sea

Volga R.

Dnieper R.

FRANKS

Baltic
Sea

Black Sea

BULGARIAN

ARMENIA

Erzerum

Tabriz

Baghdad

MESOPOTAMIA
641

Antioch

SYRIA
638

Damascus

Jerusalem

BABYLONIA
637

Persian Gulf

ARABIA
632

Medina

Mecca

Red Sea

Aden

ABYSSINIA

Constantinople

Tours

SPAIN
711-713

Oviedo

Tagus R.

Toledo

Seville

Cordova

Almeria

Valencia

Barcelona

Tortosa

SEPTIMANIA

CATALONIA

Ceuta

MAURETANIA
700-705

Carthage
697-8

SARDINIA

CORSICA

Rome

Naples

LOMBARDS

SICILY

Adriatic Sea

CRETE

CYPRUS

Alexandria

Cairo

EGYPT
639-643

BARCA
643

TRIPOLI

Mediterranean Sea

Nile R.

Danube R.

Tigris R.

Abu Muslim in Khorasan (747). Marwan's governor of Khorasan, Nasr, was defeated at Nishapur and Jurjan by Abu Muslim's general, Kahtaba, who routed the Omayyad forces again at Nehawand and Kerbela. Marwan himself was defeated at the **battle of the Zab,** and was pursued to Busir, Egypt, and killed (750). Slaughter of the Omayyad princes. Few escaped, but among those was Abd ar-Rahman, grandson of Hisham, who later founded the Omayyad Kingdom of Córdoba in Spain (755).

c. THE ABBASID CALIPHATE, 750–c. 1100

750–1258. THE ABBASID CALIPHATE. Spain never recognized it, nor did Morocco. Abbasid authority was re-established in the province of Africa as far as Algiers in 761, but only for a short period.

750–754. Abu-l-Abbas al-Saffah, the first Abbasid caliph. Omayyad revolts in Syria and Mesopotamia. Byzantine raids into the northern provinces. First paper mill of the Moslem world established (c. 751). Abu al-Saffah was succeeded by his brother,

754–775. AL-MANSUR, the real founder of the dynasty. The revolt of his uncle, Abdallah, governor of Syria, was crushed by Abu Muslim, who was then murdered at Mansur's orders (754). Revolt of Abu Muslim's followers in Khorasan (755). A Byzantine invasion was repulsed with great slaughter. Cappadocia reoccupied; Malitia (Melitene), Mopsuestia, and other cities rebuilt and fortified against Byzantine raids (758). Annexation of Tabaristan (759); Shi'ite revolt in Iraq and Medina under the Hasanids, Muhammad and Ibrahim (762). Foundation of Baghdad (762). Khazar invasion of Georgia repelled (762). Insurrection of Ustad Sis in Khorasan and Sistan (767). Rise of the **Barmecides** to power as vizirs of the realm (752–803). Mansur was succeeded by his son,

775–785. AL-MAHDI, noted for his improvement of the communications of the empire, his fortification of important centers, his founding of towns and schools, and his encouragement of the arts.

Hindu scientific works, including the *Siddhautas, Charaka, Sustrata,* were translated into Arabic. Jabir (fl. 776) known as Gebir to the West, recorded the chemical methods of his time, many of which were concerned with alchemy. He described chemical apparatus, techniques—refining of metals and the distillation of alcohol, and glassmaking. A school of chemists and a corpus of chemical writings arose.

Persecution of the Manichaeans. Revolt of the veiled prophet, **Mokanna,** in Khorasan (775–778). Rise of a communistic, nihilistic sect, the Zindiqs, in Khorasan, western Persia and Iraq. Invasion of the Byzantines, who were routed. Moslem advance against Constantinople; the Empress Irene forced to sue for peace (783–785). Mahdi was succeded by his son,

785–786. Al-Hadi, who reigned only a year and was succeeded by

786–809. HARUN AL-RASHID (of *Arabian Nights'* fame). Kabul and Sanhar were annexed to the empire (787). Khazar invasion of Armenia (799). Fall of the Barmecides (803). Kharijite revolts. A collection of original Greek manuscripts ordered.

791–809. War with the Byzantines. Defeat of Nicephorus at Heraclea or Dorylaeum (798). The peace, which was concluded, was broken by Nicephorus, and the Moslems invaded Asia Minor led by the caliph in person. Capture of Tyana (806). Advance to Ancyra. Meanwhile Cyprus (805) and Rhodes (807) were ravaged by the Moslem fleet. Iconium and Ephesus in Lydia captured, Sideropolis, Andrasus, and Nicaea reduced. Heraclea Pontica on the Black Sea taken by storm. Nicephorus again invaded Moslem territory in 808, but troubles in Khorasan compelled Harun to march east, where he died. In his reign the **Hanafite school of law** began to assume a systematic form. He was succeeded by his son,

809–813. AL-AMIN, against whom his brother Mamun rebelled and was accepted as caliph in Persia. Siege of Baghdad by Mamun's general, Tahir (813). Amin was murdered after surrendering on terms.

813–833. AL-MAMUN (MAMUN THE GREAT). His reign probably the most glorious epoch in the history of the caliphate. A **House of Knowledge** was set up in Baghdad, where translations of philosophical, literary, scientific works from Greek, Syriac, Persian, and Sanskrit were made. The translations were scholarly, especially those, with commentaries that were made on the works of Aristotle. **Hunayn Ibn-Ishaq** (c. 809–877) translated the works of Galen and some of those of Ptolemy, Hippocrates. Astronomical observatory was set up by **Al-Farghani** (d. c. 850) whose work was continued by **Al-Battani** (c. 858–929) and **Thabit Ibn-Quarra** (c. 826–901), who also translated Greek mathematical and physical texts Apollonius, Ptolemy, Euclid). **Al-Khwarizm** (d. 835) introduced Hindu numerals and calculation methods to the Moslem world. **Al Rhazi** (Rhazes in the West d. c. 924), was a physician and an encyclopaedist; he added his own observations in gynaecology, obstetrics ophthalmic surgery. **Ibn-Sina** (Avicenna wrote a comprehensive canon of medicine. Many of the above men became important to the West, as indicated by their Latinized names, since they preserved the knowledge of the Greeks, transmitted to the West by the Arab world. A liberal religious attitude adopted. **Mu'tazilitism** became the established faith. The Mu'tazilites maintained, like the Qadarites of the later Omayyad period, man's free will, also that justice and reason must control God's action toward men, both of which doctrines were repudiated by the later orthodox school of the Ash'arites.

Transference of the capital by Mamun from Merv to Baghdad, owing to Omayyad and Shi'ite revolts in Arabia, Iraq, and Mesopotamia. To meet this crisis he had proclaimed as his heir-apparent, Ali al-Ridha, a descendant of the caliph Ali (817).

Conquest of Crete (from Egypt) by Arabs who had been expelled from Spain by the Omayyads (825); of Sicily by the Aghlabites of North Africa (827). Palermo taken (831). Only Syracuse and Taormina left in Byzantine hands.

Terrorization of the northern provinces by the Magian, **Babek,** leader of the communistic Khurramites, from his stronghold in Azerbaijan (816–833). Byzantine invasions in his support were repulsed by Mamun in person (829–833). In his reign the Tahirids of Khorasan became practically independent (820–872). Mamun was succeeded by his brother,

33–842. Al-Mu'tasim. Transference of the capital to Samarra (836). Formation of a standing military corps composed of Turkish slaves and mercenaries, of whom the later caliphs were the mere puppets.

Revolt of the Jats or **Gypsies** on the lower Tigris (834). Babek was defeated by Afshin and put to death (837–838). **War with Byzantium** (837–842). Defeat of the Byzantines at Anzen on the Halys, Ancyra destroyed; Amorium, the place of origin of the Byzantine dynasty, captured (838). Preparations for the siege of Constantinople. Arab fleet destroyed by a tempest. Death of Al-Mu'tasim (842) and his succession by his son,

42–847. Al-Wathiq, who continued his father's policy of aggrandizing the Turks at the expense of the Arabs and Persians. Interchange of prisoners between the Byzantines and Moslems. Al-Wathiq's reign marks the beginning of the decline of the caliphate. He was succeeded by his brother,

47–861. Al-Mutawakkil, who sought to reestablish the traditional Moslem faith. Mu'tazilite doctrines were abjured, their professors persecuted. Shi'ites, Jews, and Christians also persecuted. The mausoleum of Husayn, the

martyr of Kerbela, was razed to the ground. Damietta in Egypt was taken and Cilicia ravaged by the Byzantines. Al-Mutawakkil was murdered by his Turkish guard and was succeeded by his son,

861–862. Al-Muntasir, who reigned only six months, when he was deposed by the Turkoman chiefs of his guard, who raised to the throne another grandson of Al-Mu'tasim, **Al-Musta'in** (862–866), who escaped from the Turks to Baghdad, but was forced by them to abdicate and was later murdered by an emissary of his successor, **Al-Mu'tazz** (866–869), in whose reign Egypt became virtually independent under **Ahmad ibn Tulun,** founder of the Tulunid dynasty. Al-Mu'tazz was murdered by his mutinous troops and succeeded by **Al-Muqtadi** (869–870), a son of Al-Wathiq, who was compelled to abdicate by the Turks, who chose as his successor the eldest surviving son of Al-Mutawakkil,

870–892. Al-Mu'tamid, who transferred the court to Baghdad; and for this and the next two reigns the power of the Turkish guard was successfully checked.

The **Zenj rebellion** in Chaldaea (869–883), which devastated this region for fifteen years, was put down finally by the caliph's brother, Al-Muwaffiq. A Byzantine invasion of Syria was repelled by the Tulunid governor of Tarsus.

In this reign the caliphate lost its eastern provinces. The **Saffarid dynasty** was founded by Ya'qub ibn Layth, who established himself in Sistan, drove out the Tahirids of Khorasan, and became master of the whole of modern Persia. The dynasty lasted from 870 to 903, when it was extinguished by the Samanids of Transoxania, who had succeeded the Tahirids there (872), and who, after the overthrow of the Saffarids, ruled from the borders of India to Baghdad and from the Great Desert to the Persian Gulf. Their power was finally broken by the Ilak Khans of Turkestan (999), who then ruled over Transoxania, Kashgar, and eastern Tatary from Bokhara (932–1165). Under the Samanids, Bokhara was the intellectual center of Islam.

Al-Mu'tamid was succeeded as caliph by his nephew,

892–902. Al-Mu'tadid, who restored Egypt to the caliphate and reformed the law of inheritance. His successor, Al-Muqtafi (902–908), brought Egypt under his direct control and repulsed the Byzantines, storming Adalia.

891–906. The Carmathian revolt. These communistic rebels overran and devastated Arabia, Syria, and Iraq, took Mecca, and carried away the sacred **Black Stone.** Al-Muqtafi was succeeded by

908–932. Al-Muqtadir, his brother, during

whose reign occurred the **conquest of North Africa** by the Fatimid, Obaydullah al-Mahdi, who also drove out the last Aghlabite, Ziyadatullah, from Egypt. Establishment of the Ziyarids in Tabaristan, Jurjan, Isfahan, and Hamadan ,as independent sovereigns (928–1024). **Rise of the Buwayhids** (932–1055) under the patronage of the Ziyarids. Conquest and division of Persia and Iraq by the three Buwayhid brothers, Imad al-Dawla, Rukn al-Dawla, and Mu'izz al-Dawla. Mu'izz granted the title of Amir al-Umara (Prince of the Princes) by the caliph Al-Mustaqfi (945). The caliphs became puppets of the Amir al-Umara. The Buwayhid dominions fell piecemeal to the Ghaznavids, the Kakwayhids of Kurdistan (1007–1057), and the Seljuks, owing to divisions among the Buwayhid rulers.

During the first half of the 10th century the **Brotherhood of Purity** was organized. A secret organization, it sponsored educational projects and artisans' guilds, and was influential in publicizing the work of the alchemists.

962–1186. THE GHAZNAVIDS. Founder of the dynasty was **Subaktagin,** a Turkish slave of Alptagin, himself slave and commander-in-chief of the Samanids in Khorasan and independent prince of the petty fief of Ghazni in the Sulayman mountains. Subaktagin defeated the Rajputs and received Khorasan from the Samanids (994). His successor, **MAHMUD** (the Idol-Breaker), one of the greatest figures in the history of Central Asia, became master of Khorasan (1000) and invaded India several times. His court was the resort of famous scholars and poets, such as Beiruni and Firdausi. The Ghaznavids were overthrown by the Seljuks.

929–1096. In Syria and Mesopotamia four Arab dynasties and one Kurdish held sway.

929–1003. The **Hamdanids of Mosul and Aleppo,** the most famous of whom, **Sayf al Dawla,** took Aleppo from the Ikhshidids of Egypt (944) and warred successfully against the Byzantines. His court was one of the brilliant centers of Islam in the 10th century. The great Arab poet, **Mutannabi,** was its chief ornament. The Hamdanids were descendant of the Arab tribe of Taghlib. Their dominions were absorbed by the Fatimids and the Buwayhids.

1023–1079. The **Mirdasids of Aleppo,** of the Arab tribe of the Banu Kilab, engaged in continual warfare with the Fatimids and the Buwayhids, and were finally driven out by the

996–1096. **'Uqaylids of Mosul,** a division of the Banu Ka'b tribe, who succeeded the Hamdanids in Mosul, and whose dominions under **Muslim ibn Quraysh** extended from the neighborhood of Baghdad to Aleppo. Their domain was ultimately merged in the Seljuk Empire.

990–1096. The **Marwanids of Diyar-Bakr,** established by the Kurd, Abu-l Ali ibn Marwan, ruled over Amid, Mayyarfariqun, and Aleppo. They too fell before the Seljuks.

995. Under the Fatimid caliphate a House of Science was established in Cairo. Among the scholars there were Al-Hazen (c. 965–1038) who worked on optics; Al-Mushudi (d. 957) who wrote an encyclopaedia of natural history, containing the first description of a wind mill; Ibn al-Nafis (1210–1288), who described the lesser circulation of the blood. The first block-printing in the West occurred in Egypt between 900 and 1350.

1012–1050. **Mazyadids of Hilla,** a tribe of the Banu Asad. The fourth ruler of this dynasty the Sadaqa, was one of the great heroes of Arab history. The state was ultimately absorbed by the Zangids. (*Cont. p. 272.*)

B. THE AGE OF THE CRUSADES

1. WESTERN EUROPE

a. THE BRITISH ISLES

(*From p. 184*)

(1) England, 1066–1307

[*For a complete list of the kings of England see Appendix VI.*]

1066–1087. WILLIAM I (the Conqueror), of medium height, corpulent, but majestic in person, choleric, mendacious, greedy, a great soldier, governor, centralizer, legislator, innovator.

1066–1072. Rapid collapse, speedy submission or reduction of the south and east. The Confessor's bequest, acceptance by the witan and coronation "legalized" William's title. Reduction of the southwest (1068). Reduction of the rest of England (1067–1070): a series of local risings leniently dealt with; construction by forced native labor of garrison castles (Norman mounds). Great **rising of the north** (Edwin and Morca's second) with Danish aid (1069) put down by William in person. The "harrying of the north" (1069-1070), a devastation (often depopulation) of a strip from York to Durham (the consequences survived to modern times) ended Scandinavian opposition in England. **Reduction of Hereward's last stand** (the "last of the English") in the Isle of Ely (1070-1071); raid into Scotland (1072).

Norman fusion, conciliation, innovation: (1) Feudalization on centralized Norman lines (on the ruins of the nascent Saxon feudalism) followed military reduction and confiscation of the rebel lands (1066-1070). Theoretically every bit of land in England belonged to the crown; in practice only the great estates changed hands and were assigned to William's followers on Norman tenures. The king retained about one-sixth of the land; less than a half of the land went to Normans on feudal tenures. Except on the border few compact holdings survived; the earldoms, reduced in size, became chiefly honorific. Some 170 great tenants-in-chief, and numerous lesser tenants emerged. A direct oath (the *Oath of Salisbury*) of primary vassalage to the crown was exacted from all vassals, making them directly responsible to the crown (1086). Construction of castles (except on the borders) subject to royal license; coinage a royal monopoly; private war prohibited. (2) The **Anglo-Saxon shires** (34) and hundreds continued for local administration and for local justice (bishops no longer sat in the shire courts and the earls were reduced) under the sheriffs (usually of baronial rank), retained from Anglo-Saxon days, but subject to removal by the king. The sheriffs were an essential link between the (native) local machinery and the central (Norman) government. Communities were held responsible for local good order; sporadic visitations of royal commissioners. Anglo-Saxon laws little altered. (3) Early grant of a charter to London guaranteeing local customs. (4) **Innovations of the centralizing monarch:** a royal council, the **great council** (*curia regis*), meeting infrequently (three stated meetings annually) replaced the Anglo-Saxon witan and was of almost the same personnel: tenants-in-chief, the chancellor (introduced from Normandy by Edward the Confessor), a new official, the justiciar (in charge of justice and finance, and William's viceroy during his absences), the heads of the royal household staff. This same body, meeting frequently, and including only such tenants-in-chief as happened to be on hand, constituted the **small council**, a body which tended to absorb more and more of the actual administration.

The **church** retained its lands (perhaps a fourth of the land in England). Pope Alexander II had blessed William's conquest, and

William introduced the (much-needed) Cluniac reforms. Archbishop Stigand and most of the bishops and great abbots were deprived or died, and were replaced by zealous Norman reformers; **Lanfranc** (an Italian lawyer, a former prior of Bec), as archbishop of Canterbury, carried through a wide reform: celibacy enforced, chapters reorganized, new discipline in the schools, numerous new monastic foundations. By royal decree episcopal jurisdiction was separated from lay jurisdiction and the bishops given their own courts, a decisive step in the evolution of the common law as an independent force. William refused an oath of fealty to Pope Gregory VII for his English conquests, and (despite the papal decree of 1075) retained control of the appointment of bishops and important abbots, from whom he drew his chief administrators (thereby making the church, in effect, pay for the administration of the state). No papal bull or brief, no papal legate might be received without royal approval and no tenant-in-chief or royal officer could be excommunicated without royal permission. The king retained a right of veto on all decrees of local synods. The great prelates were required to attend the great council, even to do military service.

1086. The great **Domesday survey:** royal commissions on circuit collected on oath (sworn inquest) from citizens of the counties and vills full information as to size, resources, and present and past ownership of every hide of land. The results, arranged by counties in *Domesday Book,* gave a unique record as a basis for taxation and administration.

Royal finance: (1) non-feudal revenues: Danegeld, shire farms, judicial fines; (2) the usual feudal revenues.

Military resources of the crown: (1) (non-feudal) the old Anglo-Saxon *fyrd* (including *ship fyrd*) was retained (i.e. a national non-feudal militia, loyal to the crown, was used, e.g. against the Norman rebellion of 1075); (2) (feudal) about five thousand knights' fees owing service on the usual feudal terms. The prosperity of England under Norman rule was great and an era of extensive building (largely churches, cathedrals, and monasteries) began under the Conqueror and continued even through the anarchy of Stephen and Matilda.

1087-1100. WILLIAM II (Rufus), a passionate, greedy ruffian, second son of the Conqueror, designated by his father on his death-bed (Robert, the eldest, received Normandy; Henry, cash). A Norman revolt (1088) was put down, largely with English aid, and William firmly settled on the throne. Justice was venal and expensive, the administration cruel and unpopular, taxation heavy, the Church exploited. On Lanfranc's death (1089), William kept the revenues of the see of Canterbury without appointing a successor until he thought himself dying, when he named (1093) Anselm (an Italian, abbot of Bec, a most learned man, and a devoted churchman), who clashed with William over the recognition of rival popes; Anselm maintained church law to be above civil law and went into voluntary exile (1097). William, deeply hated, was assassinated (?) in the New Forest.

1100–1135. HENRY I (Beauclerc, Lion of Justice), an educated, stubborn, prudent ruler, a good judge of men, won the crown by a dash to the royal treasury at Winchester and a quick appeal to the nation by his so-called *Coronation Charter,* a promise of reform by a return to the good ways of the Conqueror (a promise often broken). Henry married Edith (of the line of Alfred), whose name became Matilda out of deference to the Norman's difficulties with Saxon names. Anarchy in Normandy under Robert's slack rule, an invitation from the revolting Norman barons, and the victory of **Tinchebray** (1106), gave Henry Normandy (Robert remained a prisoner until his death), and made a later struggle between the new English kingdom and the rising Capetian power in France inevitable. **Anselm,** faithful to the reforming program of the revived papacy, on his recall from exile refused homage for the archiepiscopal estates (i.e. he refused to recognize lay investiture) and refused to consecrate the bishops who had rendered such homage. Henry temporized until firmly on the throne, then seized the fiefs and exiled Anselm. Adela, Henry's sister, suggested the **Compromise of 1107,** which terminated the struggle by establishing clerical homage for fiefs held of the king, while the king allowed clerical investiture with the spiritual symbols. The crown continued to designate candidates for the great prelacies.

This reign was marked by a notable expansion, specialization, and differentiation of function in the royal administration (e.g. the exchequer, influenced by accounting methods from Lorraine or Laon). Extension of the jurisdiction of royal courts: growing use of royal writs, detailing of members of the small council as judges on circuit (hitherto a sporadic, now a regular practice), who not merely did justice but took over increasingly the business formerly done by the sheriffs (e.g. assessment and negotiation of aids and other levies), and brought the curia regis into closer contact with shire and hundred courts.

Prosperity was general and trade in London attracted Norman immigrants. The **Cistercians** arrived (1128) and began an extensive program of swamp reclamation, mill and road building, agricultural improvement, and stock-breeding. Henry began the sale of charters to towns on royal domain.

Influence of the Conquest on English culture: (1) architecture: wide introduction of the Norman (Romanesque) style (e.g. St. John's Chapel in the Tower of London, end of the 11th century; Durham Cathedral, c. 1096–1133); (2) **literary:** Anglo-Saxon, the speech of the conquered, almost ceased to have a literary history, rapidly lost its formality of inflections and terminations, and became flexible and simple if inelegant. Norman French, the tongue of the court, the aristocracy, the schools, the lawyers and judges, drew its inspiration from the Continent until the loss of Normandy (1204). The Normans then began to learn English, and the Anglo-Saxon was enriched with a second vocabulary of Norman words, ideas, and refinements.

Anglo-Norman culture: (1) historical writing: Geoffrey of Monmouth, *History of the Kings of Britain* (written in Latin, before 1147), created the tale of Arthur for Europe; **Walter Map** (c. 1140–c. 1200), author of Goliardic verse, welded the Grail story into the Arthurian cycle, giving it a moral and religious slant; **Wace** (c. 1124–c. 1174) *Roman de Brut* and *Roman de Rou;* **Marie de France;** all three were at the court of Henry II. (2) **Science: Walcher of Malvern** observed the eclipse of 1092 and attempted to calculate the difference in time between England and Italy; Walcher began to reckon in degrees, minutes, and seconds (1120); **Adelard of Bath,** a student of Arabic science, in the service of Henry II, observed and experimented (e.g. the comparative speed of sound and light), translated Al-Khwarizmi's astronomical tables into Latin (1126) and introduced Al-Khwarizmi's trigonometric tables to the West; **Robert of Chester** translated Al-Khwarizmi's algebra into Latin (1145); **Alexander Neckham** (1157–1217), encyclopedist, wrote on botany and on the magnet. (3) **Philosophy: John of Salisbury** (d. 1180), pupil of Abelard, the best classical, humanistic scholar of his day, attached to the court of Henry II, and later bishop of Chartres, wrote the *Policraticus,* etc. **Beginnings of Oxford University** (c. 1167) on the model of Paris, a center of national culture.

1135–1154. STEPHEN. Henry's son drowned on the White Ship (1120), and Henry had had his daughter **Matilda** (widow of the Emperor Henry V) accepted as his heir and married to Geoffrey of Anjou, as protector. Stephen of Blois (son of Henry's sister Adela) asserted and maintained his claim to the throne at the price of a dynastic war (till 1153) with Matilda,

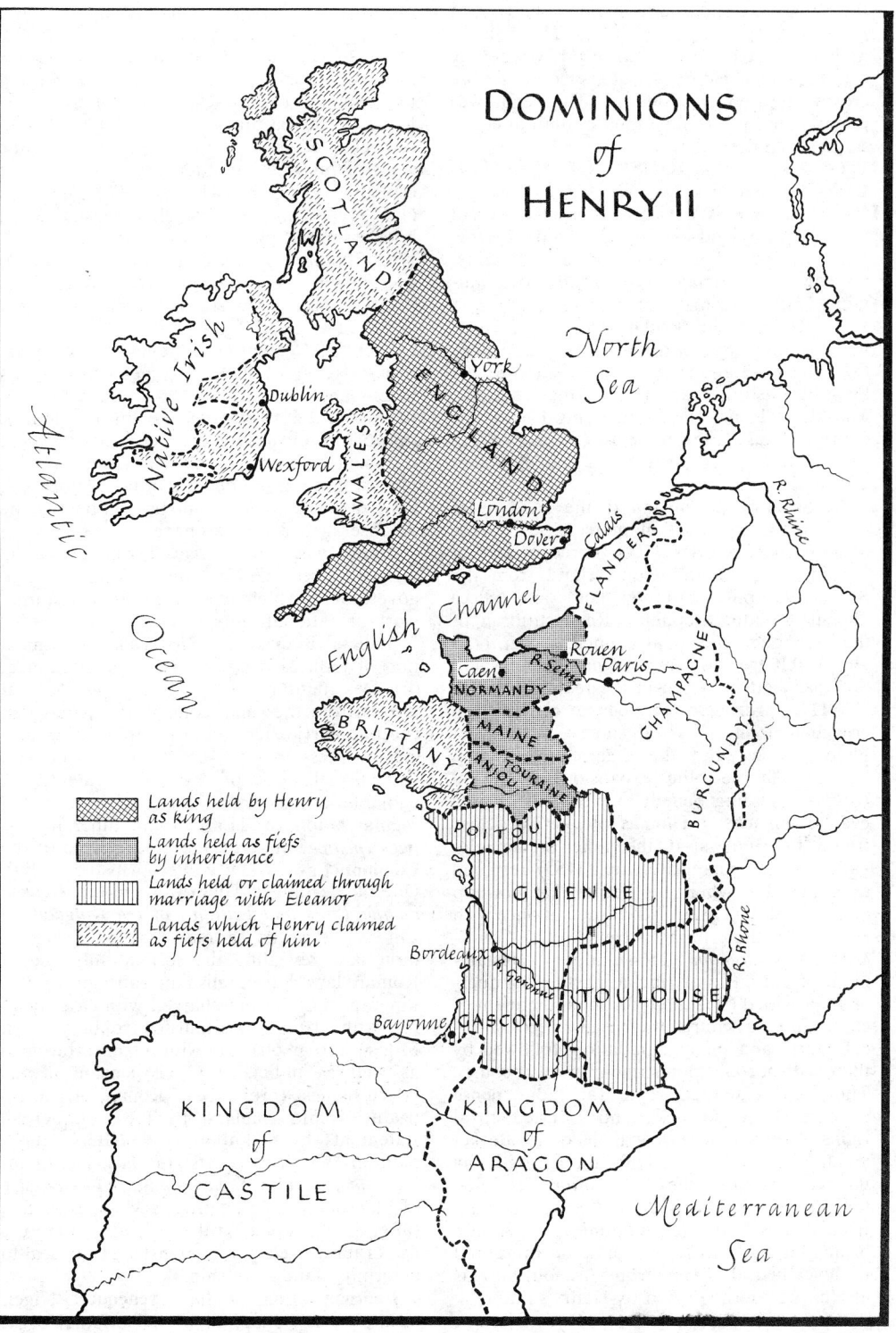

DOMINIONS
of
HENRY II

Lands held by Henry
as king

Lands held as fiefs
by inheritance

Lands held or claimed through
marriage with Eleanor

Lands which Henry claimed
as fiefs held of him

the climax of feudal anarchy, and the ruin of English prosperity. Archbishop Theobald finally negotiated a compromise (1153) whereby Matilda's son Henry should succeed to the crown on Stephen's death. The reign was remarkable for a tremendous amount of ecclesiastical building.

1154-1399. THE HOUSE OF PLANTAGENET (Angevin).

1154-1189. HENRY II. Master of a hybrid "empire" (England, Normandy, Anjou, Maine, Touraine, by inheritance; Poitou, Aquitaine, Gascony, by marriage with Eleanor of Aquitaine [1152]; Brittany [acquired, 1169], and Wales, Ireland, and Scotland [on a loose bond] without unity save in the person of the ruler). **Dynastic marriages:** daughter Eleanor to the king of Castile, Joan to the king of Sicily, Matilda to Henry the Lion. King Henry was a man of education, exhaustless energy, experience as an administrator, a realist, violent of temper.

Restoration of England to the good order of Henry I: dismissal of mercenaries, razing of unlicensed castles (1000?), reconquest of Northumberland and Cumberland from the Scots, resumption of crown lands and offices alienated under Stephen. Reconstitution of the exchequer and great council. After 1155 Henry felt free to leave England, and spent less than half his reign in the realm.

1155-1172. Struggle to reduce clerical encroachment on the royal courts: Under Stephen anarchy and the theories of Roman law had favored the expansion of clerical courts, extending benefit of clergy to include even homicides. **Thomas Becket** (a close friend of Henry's at the time of his elevation to the chancellorship, 1155) resigned as chancellor when he became archbishop of Canterbury (1162), and clashed at once with Henry over the criminous clerks. The *Constitutions of Clarendon* (1164), largely a restatement of old customs (including the Conqueror's), provided (*inter alia*) for the indictment of clerics in royal courts, their trial in ecclesiastical courts, and their degradation, followed by their sentence and punishment in royal courts. They also extended royal (at the expense of clerical) jurisdiction, and asserted royal rights of control in episcopal elections. Becket yielded, was dispensed from his oath by the pope, violated the *Constitutions,* and fled to France. Reconciled (1170) with Henry, Becket returned, excommunicated certain bishops friendly to Henry, and was murdered in the cathedral of Canterbury by four knights of Henry's court, spurred by Henry's outbreak of fury against Becket, but not by Henry's orders. Henry escaped excommunication by

promising to abide by the papal judgment, and was reconciled with the papacy (1172) after an oath denying all share in the crime. After this incident Henry had no choice but to tolerate benefit of clergy, which continued to be an increasing scandal in England until the reign of Henry VII. Henry retained the right of presentation and virtual control over espicopal elections. The *Assize of Clarendon* (1166) contains the first civil legislation on heresy since Roman days.

1170. Extensive replacement of the (baronial) sheriffs with men of lower rank, trained in the royal service. Henceforth the barons ceased to hold the shrievalty.

1173-1174. Reduction of the last purely feudal revolt; Henry's only use of mercenary troops in England.

1181. The Assize of Arms. By this reorganization of the old *fyrd* every freeman was made responsible, according to his income, for his proper share in the defense of the realm. The king thus ensured a national militia for the defense against the baronage.

Henry was not a great legislator, but he initiated a remarkable series of innovations in government which fixed the political framework of national unity.

Judicial Reforms: (1) Increasing concentration of judicial business in the small council. (2) Designation (1178) of five professional judges from the small council as a **permanent central court;** extension of the transfer of judicial business to royal courts by the increase and specialization of royal writs (the fees a valuable source of revenue); formalization and regularization (c. 1166) of the itinerant justices (*justices in eyre*), the great source of the **Common Law** (a law universal in the realm). One of the judges, **Glanvil,** wrote the *Treatise on the Laws and Customs of the Kingdom of England,* the first serious book on the common law, revealing the formal influence of Roman law, but English in substance. The itinerant judges were charged with cases dealing with crimes like murder, robbery (soon forgery and arson), and with financial business as well as judicial. (3) **Expansion of the sworn inquest** (probably of Roman origin, introduced into England by the Conqueror): statements by neighbors (freeholders) under oath in the shire courts: (a) *jury* (12 members) *of presentment in criminal cases* (Assize of Clarendon, 1166), a process which expanded (after 1219), replacing the ordeal; and (b) the use of juries (recognitions) instead of ordeal to determine landownership.

Reorganization of the exchequer: Nigel, bishop of Ely (nephew of the original organizer, Roger of Salisbury), restored the ex-

(From p. 183)

England: The Norman and Plantagenet Kings (1066–1377)

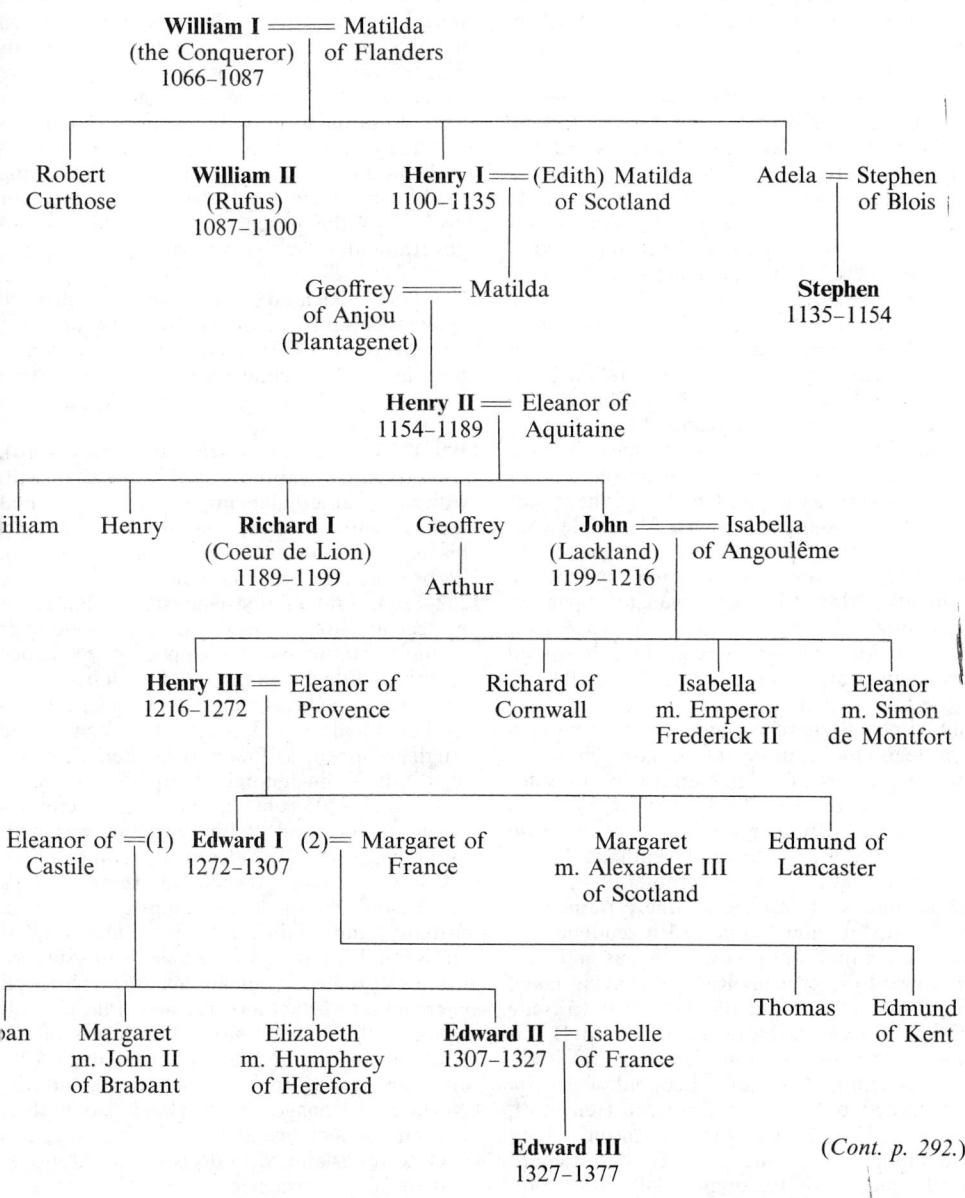

(*Cont. p. 292.*)

:hequer to the general form of Henry I. **Inno-ations in the raising of revenue:** (1) *tallage,* evied by local negotiations (i.e. by the itiner-nt justices) with boroughs and tenants: (2) *idage (carucage)* replaced the Danegeld; (3) *cutage,* levied by Henry I on the clergy, now xtended to knights' fees in lieu of military ervice (due to Henry's need of non-feudal evies across the Channel); (4) *personal prop-erty taxes* (the first, 1166), Saladin tithe (1188), assessed by neighborhood juries. *The Dia-logue of the Exchequer* written by one of the officials of the exchequer.

Extension of trade: German merchants were well established in London by 1157; there was a large Italian business in wool; and there was extensive development of domestic trade.

Foreign affairs: (1) **Norman penetration of Wales** since the Conquest bred a sporadic national resistance; Henry by three expeditions reduced Wales to nominal homage to the English crown; (2) **Ireland,** despite a brilliant native culture, was in political chaos under rival tribal kinglets and economically exhausted. Pope Adrian IV, hoping that Henry would reform the church in Ireland, "gave" Ireland (1154) to Henry. Richard of Clare's (Strongbow) expedition (1169–1170) established a harsh rule; Henry landed (1171), temporarily reduced the rigors of the baronial administration, and reformed the Irish Church (Synod of Cashel, 1172). **John Lackland** (Henry's son) was appointed lord of Ireland (1177), arrived (1185), but was soon recalled for incompetence.

Intrigues and revolts (beginning 1173) of Henry's sons, supported by their mother Eleanor, King Louis VII, and later Philip II of France, as well as by disgruntled local barons.

The ruling class continued to speak French during this reign, but the establishment of primogeniture as applied to land inheritance insured that younger sons would mingle with the non-aristocratic sections of society and accelerate the fusion of Norman and native elements. Manor houses began to appear in increasing numbers as domestic peace continued. Numerous Cistercian houses spread new agricultural methods and especially improved wool-raising.

1189–1199. Richard I (Coeur de Lion). Neither legislator, administrator, nor statesman, but the greatest of knights errant, an absentee ruler who spent less than a year of his reign in England, visiting his realm only twice, to raise money for continental ventures. Taxation was heavy. The government remained in the hands of ministers largely trained by Henry II, but there appeared a tendency toward a common antipathy of barons and people toward the crown. Richard (having taken the Cross, 1188) went on the Third Crusade with Frederick Barbarossa and Philip II, his most dangerous foe. On his return trip Richard was captured by Duke Leopold of Austria and turned over to the Emperor Henry VI, who held him for a staggering ransom. John and Philip bid for the prisoner, but Richard finally bought his freedom (1194) with a ransom raised partly by taxation in England. The crusade gave Englishmen their first taste of eastern adventure, but drew few except the adventurous portion of the baronage. The domestic reflection was a series of anti-Semitic outbreaks. John Lackland (despite his known character) was given charge of several counties; his plot against Richard was put down by **Hubert Walter** with the support of London.

Hubert Walter, archbishop of Canterbury and Justiciar (1194–1198), ruled England well, maintained the king's peace, and began a clear reliance on the support of the middle class in town and shire. Charters were granted towns (London received the right to elect its mayor)—and the knights of the shire were called on to assume a share of county business as a balance to the sheriffs. Knights (elected by the local gentry) served as coroners and chose the local juries, a departure looking to the day when local election and amateur justices of the peace would be the basis of government. The first known merchant guild, 1193.

1194–1199. Richard's continental struggle against Philip II, in which Richard more than held his own. Château Gaillard, a new departure in castle architecture based on eastern lessons, built by Richard on the Seine, as an outpost against Philip.

1199–1216. JOHN (Lackland, Softsword), cruel, mean, licentious, faithless, weak of will, without counterbalancing virtues. Crowned with the support of the Norman barons against his nephew Arthur's claims (by primogeniture), he became Arthur's guardian.

1202–1204. John's first contest with Philip (to protect his French possessions): struggle over Brittany, Maine, Anjou (temporary acceptance of John's title by Philip, 1200). John's marriage to Isabella of Angoulême (already betrothed to his vassal Hugh of Lusignan) led Hugh to appeal to Philip II as their common overlord. John ignored Philip's summons to judgment (1202); his French fiefs were declared forfeit, and Philip began a war with rapid successes. The death of Arthur (1203), possibly by John's own hand, ruined John's cause, and Philip, already master of Anjou, Brittany, and Maine, took Normandy (1204) and soon Touraine. John's vassals in southern France (preferring an absent Angevin to an encroaching Capetian) resisted Philip's advance south of the Loire. John's loss of the lands north of the Loire reduced the power and prestige of the English crown, cut the Norman baronage in England from their French connections, and turned their interests back to the island, with decisive constitutional and social consequences.

1205–1213. John's struggle with Pope Innocent III: after a double election to the see of Canterbury, Innocent rejected both elections (including John's nominee) and named (1207) **Stephen Langton,** a noted scholar and theologian. John refused to accept Langton, confiscated the estates of the see, expelled the monks of Canterbury; Innocent laid an interdict on England (1208). John confiscated the property of the English clergy who obeyed Innocent's ban without arousing serious public opposition. Innocent excommunicated John (1209), but John, holding as hostages the children of some of the barons, weathered the storm. Innocent deposed John (1213) and authorized Philip II to execute the sentence. John, aware of treason and mounting hostility, promised indemnity to the clergy, did homage to the pope for England and Ireland, agreed to an annual tribute, and was freed of the ban.

1213-1214. Final contest with Philip II (to regain the lands north of the Lorie): John's great coalition (including his nephew, Emperor Otto IV, and the Count of Flanders) against Philip; most of the English baronage held aloof. Crushing defeat of the coalition at **Bouvines** (1214) ended all hope of regaining the lands north of the Loire (formal renunciation of English claims, 1259).

1215. MAGNA CARTA. The first politico-constitutional struggle in English history: in origin this struggle resulted from an effort of the feudal barons, supported by Archbishop Langton (notwithstanding papal support of John) and public opinion, to enforce their rights under their feudal contract with the king; it did not aim to destory the monarchy or the royal administration. Preliminary demands of the barons (1213); John's concessions to the Church and negotiations with Pope Innocent; civil war. London opposed John (despite his liberal charter to the city). John's acceptance of the **great charter** at Runnymede. Magna Carta was essentially a feudal document, exacted by feudal barons from their lord but with national implications in its reforms: (1) concessions to the barons: reform in the exaction of scutage, aid, and reliefs, in the administration of wardship and in the demands for feudal service; writ of summons to the great council to be sent individually to the great magnates, collectively proclaimed by the sheriffs to the lesser nobles (i.e. knights); (2) concessions to the agricultural and commercial classes: Mesne tenants granted the privileges of tenants-in-chief; uniform weights and measures; affirmation of the ancient liberties of London and other towns; limitation on royal seizure of private property; reform of the forest law; reform of the courts; (3) concessions to the Church (in addition to John's charter of 1214): promise of freedom and free elections.

The **most significant provisions of the great charter:** (1) chapter 12: no scutage or aid (except for the traditional feudal three) to be levied without the consent of the great council; (2) chapter 14: definition of the great council and its powers; (3) chapter 39: *"No freeman shall be arrested and imprisoned, or*

dispossessed, or outlawed, or banished, or in any way molested; nor will we set forth against him, nor send against him, unless by the lawful judgment of his peers and by the law of the land." Even these clauses were feudal and specific in background, but centuries of experience transformed them into a generalized formula of constitutional procedure, making them the basis of the modern English constitution. At the time their chief significance lay in the assertion of the supremacy of law over the king. Careful provisions were made for the enforcement of the charter by the barons, even by force of arms, but in practice such enforcement was impossible. The charter was repeatedly reissued by succeeding rulers. The pope, as John's feudal suzerain, declared the great charter void. Civil war followed; a Francophile section of the barons called Louis, son of Philip II, to the throne (1216). John opportunely died; his young son Henry, with the support of the Anglophile barons, succeeded him, and Louis abandoned his pursuit of the crown (1217).

1216-1272. Henry III (a boy of nine). Guardianship (1216-1219) of **William Marshal, Earl of Pembroke;** an able, patriotic regime: two reissues (1216, 1217) of the (modified) great charter; elimination of French influence and interference, opposition to papal encroachments, reduction of feudal castles. William Marshal had designated the pope as Henry's guardian, and the government passed on his death (1219) to the papal legate Pandulph, the justiciar Hubert de Burgh, and Peter des Roches, tutor to Henry. Arrival of the **Dominicans** (1220) and the **Franciscans** (1224). Henry's personal rule (1227-1258) was marked by a major constitutional crisis.

Growth of national consciousness. After a futile but expensive effort (1229) to recover Aquitaine, Henry, always devoted to the papacy, gave free reign to papal exactions. At the same time the increase of papal provisions filled the English Church with alien (usually absentee Italian) appointees, to the exclusion of natives. A bitter anti-papal outbreak (perhaps supported by de Burgh) drove de Burgh from office; des Roches succeeded him (1232-1234), filling the civil offices with fellow Poitevins. Henry's French marriage increased the alien influx and public opinion grew bitter. The papal collector was driven out (1244), and the great council refused (1242) a grant for Henry's effort to recover Poitou, which failed. Henry's acceptance of the crown of Sicily from the pope for his second son Edmund (1254), and his permission to his brother, Richard of Cornwall, to seek election as emperor (1257), both costly ventures, added to public ill-feeling. Finally, in a period of great economic distress, Richard asked the great council for one-third of the revenue of England for the pope. This grant was refused and the barons set out to reform the government with public approval (1258). A committee of twenty-four, representing king and barons equally, brought in a proposal.

1258. The **PROVISIONS OF OXFORD,** a baronial effort to restore the charter, with strong clerical and middle-class support; creation of a council of fifteen (containing a baronial majority) with a veto over the king's decisions; the great council to be superseded by a committee of twelve, meeting thrice a year with the permanent council of fifteen; the chancellor, justiciar, and treasurer were to be chosen annually by the council. All officials, including the king and his son, took an oath of loyalty to the Provisions.

1260–1264. The **knights,** alienated by the baronial oligarchy, appealed to Edward (Henry's eldest son). Gradually there emerged a group of progressive reformers (younger barons, many of the clergy and knights, townsmen, notably of London and Oxford); the more conservative barons turned to the king. Henry obtained papal release from his oaths (1261) and replaced the council of fifteen with his own appointees; chaos was followed by civil war (1263). Papal exactions continued. Louis IX (asked to arbitrate the Provisions of Oxford), in the *Mise of Amiens* (1264), decided in favor of the king. This decision was rejected by London and the commercial towns, and civil war soon broke out.

1264. **Simon de Montfort** (son of Simon of the Albigensian crusade), Henry's brother-in-law, of French blood and education, a friend of Grosseteste, bishop of Lincoln (a lifelong champion of ecclesiastical and governmental reform), emerged as leader of the reforming group. This group, ahead of its time, manifested strong religious fervor, and even traces of democratic ideas. Simon's victory at **Lewes** (1265), capture of Henry, and exaction of the *Mise of Lewes* (a return to the reforms of 1258).

In the course of this reign the great council came to be called **Parliament** (c. 1240) and at various times knights of the shire were summoned to share in its deliberations. Parliament was still as much concerned with administration and justice as with "legislation"; its membership, control of finance, and specific functions were by no means precisely defined. The summoning of the knights in effect merely transformed the negotiation of shire business into a collective negotiation by the same men who managed it locally.

1265. **De Montfort's Parliament:** two knight from each shire, and two burgesses from eacl borough were summoned, probably the firs summons to townsmen in parliamentary his tory.

1265. **Edward,** now leader of the baronial, con servative opposition, defeated de Montfort a **Evesham** (death of de Montfort).

Henry's return to power was formal, a Edward was the real ruler, and Edward an(the barons were aware of the need of reform Edward, on a crusade with Louis IX whei Henry died, was proclaimed king while stil absent, spent a year in Gascony on the wa· back, and was not crowned until 1274.

1272–1307. **EDWARD I** (Longshanks; the Eng lish Justinian), an able ruler and a great legis lator, fit to rank with Frederick II, Louis IX and Alfonso the Wise. He observed his mottc *Pactum serva* (Keep troth), but tempered i with realism. The first truly English king, h surrounded himself with able ministers an(lawyers. The reign was marked by a frequen consultation of the knights and townsmen, nc always in parliament. The institutions of th English state began to take shape.

EXTERNAL AFFAIRS

1276–1284. **Reduction of Wales.** Wales dur ing the reign of Henry III had gotten out c hand, and a national revival had set in (bardi poetry and tribal union under the Llewelyn around Snowdon in the north). **Llewelyr** prince of Wales, joined de Montfort's opposi tion, refused homage (1276), and, with hi brother David, renewed war with the Englisl (1282). Edward marched into Wales, killec Llewelyn, and executed David (1283), assertin the full dominion of the English crown. Il these wars Edward became aware of the effi ciency of the Welsh longbow. Edward's fourtl son, Edward (later Edward II), was born a Carnarvon (1284), and with him began th customary title, **Prince of Wales,** bestowed o· the heir to the English throne. Local govern ment was organized in Wales, and the *Statut of Wales* settled the legal status of the newl disciplined Welsh.

1285–1307. **Scotland.** William the Lion ha(purchased freedom from homage to the Eng lish king from Richard I in 1189, but hi successors continued to do homage for thei English lands. The Scottish nobility wer largely Normanized. Margaret, the *Maid c Norway* (daughter of Erik of Norway), wa granddaughter and heir of King Alexander II of Scotland. After Alexander's death (1286 Edward arranged a marriage for her with th Prince of Wales (1290), but she died on he way to England and Edward's hope of a personal union of the two crowns vanished. There were three collateral claimants to the Scottish crown: **John Baliol, Robert Bruce, John Hastings.** Edward, asked to arbitrate, demanded (1291) homage and acknowledgment of paramountcy from the Scots, which was given (the commons protested). He awarded the crown to Baliol (1292), who did homage for Scotland. Edward's insistence on appellate jurisdiction alienated the Scots and disposed them toward France, and an alliance began (1295) which endured intermittently for 300 years. Edward invaded Scotland, defeated Baliol at **Dunbar** (1296), declared himself king of Scotland, received the homage of the nobles, took away the coronation stone of Scone. Oppressive administration by Edward's officials led to the rising of **William Wallace** (1297), who was supported by the gentry and commonalty, but got little aid at first from the nobles. Wallace won a victory at Stirling. Edward, using the longbow to open the way for a cavalry charge, defeated Wallace at **Falkirk** (1298), drove him into exile, and completed his second conquest of Scotland (1304). Wallace was taken (1305) and executed and Scotland incorporated under the English crown. Scottish law was retained, Scottish representatives sat in parliament, but the nobles had to yield their fortresses, and an English lieutenant was sent to rule Scotland with a council and with power to amend the laws. Scottish nationalism found a leader in **Robert Bruce** (grandson of the claimant to the crown), who was crowned at Scone. Edward died (1307) on an expedition against Bruce.

1293-1303. France. Ill-feeling between sailors from the Cinque Ports (Sandwich, Dover, Rommey, Hythe, Hastings, and [later] Rye and Winchelsea) and the French, culminated in a victory for the Anglo-Gascon fleet (1293) and Edward's summons to the court of his French overlord, King Philip IV. Under a *pro forma* compromise (1294), Edward turned over his Gascon fortresses to Philip, who refused to return them, and declared Gascony forfeited. Futile expeditions of Edward (1294, 1296, and 1297, in alliance with the count of Flanders) against Philip. Philip, busy with his contest against Boniface VIII and other matters, returned Gascony to Edward (1303).

DOMESTIC AFFAIRS

1290. Expulsion of the Jews: Hitherto the Jews had been protected by the kings, as they were important sources of loans. By this time public opinion was hostile to the Jews, and the Italian houses, like the Bardi and Peruzzi, were ready to finance royal loans. Foreign trade, like

banking, was in the hands of foreigners, and there were few native merchants, except for wool export, where Englishmen did about 35 per cent of the business, Italians 24 per cent. The English wool staple was established in Antwerp under Edward.

1296. The clash with Pope Boniface VIII: Winchelsea, archbishop of Canterbury, in accordance with the bull *Clericis laicos,* led the clergy in refusing a grant to the crown. Edward, with the general support of public opinion, withdrew the protection of the royal courts, and thus promptly brought the clergy to an evasion of the bull through "presents" to the crown; the lands of recalcitrant clergy were confiscated, the pope soon modified his stand, and the victory of Edward was complete.

Institutional and "legislative" developments: (1) The parliament of 1275 granted (hitherto permission had not been asked) an increase of the export duty on wool and leather to the king, to meet the rising cost of government. (2) **Distraint of knighthood:** various enactments (beginning in 1278) to insure that all men with a given income (e.g. £20 a year from land) should assume the duties of knighthood. Probably primarily an effort to raise money, the acts also ensured a militia under royal control. (3) *Statute of Gloucester* (1278), providing for *quo warranto* inquests into the right of feudal magnates to hold public (i.e. not manorial) courts. (4) *Statute de religiosis* (statute of mortmain, 1279), forbade gifts of land to the clergy without consent of the overlord (a usual policy elsewhere in Europe). Such consent was often given; the statute frequently evaded. (5) Second *Statute of Westminster* (*De donis conditionalibus,* 1285) perpetuated feudal entail (i.e. conditional grants of lands), and led to the later law of trusts. It also reorganized the militia and provided for care of the roads. (6) Third *Statute of Westminister* (*Quia emptores,* 1290) forbade new sub-infeudations of land. Land could be freely transferred, but the new vassal must hold direct of the king or from a tenant-in-chief.

1295. The Model Parliament. The writs of summons included (probably by accident) the famous phrase, *quod omnes tangit ab omnibus approbetur* (let that which toucheth all be approved by all). Bishops, abbots, earls, barons, knights, burgesses, and representatives of the chapters and parishes were summoned. The clergy did not long continue to attend parliament, preferring their own assembly (*Convocation*) and left only the great prelates, who sat rather as feudal than ecclesiastical persons.

1297. The Confirmation of Charters (*Confirmatio cartarum*), a document almost as important as Magna Carta, extorted by a coalition of the barons (angered by taxation and the Gascon expedition) and the middle classes (irritated by mounting taxes) under the leadership of Archbishop Winchelsea. In effect the Confirmation included Magna Carta (and other charters) with the added provision that no non-feudal levy could be laid by the crown without a parliamentary grant. Edward left the actual granting of this concession to his son Edward as regent, and Pope Clement V later dispensed Edward from the promise in exchange for the right to collect (for the first time) annates in England. Edward did not surrender tallage, despite the so-called statute *de tallagio non concedendo.*

1303. The *carta mercatoria* granted the merchants full freedom of trade and safe conduct, in return for a new schedule of customs dues.

1305. The petition from the barons and commonalty of the parliament of Carlisle to end papal encroachments, notably in provisions and annates. Edward enforced the petition except in the matter of annates.

The reign is remarkable for frequent consultation of the middle class (in parliament and out), for the encouragement of petition to parliament (now one of its chief functions), and for frequent meetings of parliament, which educated the nation not merely in the elements of self-government but in ideas, and kept the crown in close contact with public opinion. The word *statute* as used of this reign means any formal royal regulation intended to be permanent, and does not imply formal parliamentary enactment.

Judicial developments. Under Edward the differentiation of the great common law courts is clear: (1) **Court of King's Bench** (concerned with criminal and crown cases); (2) **Court of Exchequer** (dealing with royal finance); (3) **Court of Common Pleas** (handling cases between subjects). The **King's Council** (small council) still remained supreme as a court by virtue of its residual and appellate jurisdiction, and the councilors were expected to take the councilor's oath to the king. Edward began the practice of referring residual cases which did not readily come within the jurisdiction of the common law courts to the chancellor with a committee of assessors from the council. This chancellor's court tended to absorb the judicial business of the council and finally emerged as a court of equity. The **Year Books,** unofficial, verbatim reports in French (the language of the courts) of legal proceedings, a record unique for completeness in the period, began in this reign. Coherence and continuity of tradition among the lawyers was greatly facilitated by the establishment of the **Inns of Court** under the three Edwards. Here the lawyers assembled their libraries, lodged, and studied, transmitting with increasing strength the living force of the common law, to the virtual exclusion of Roman law.

PROGRESS OF ENGLISH CULTURE

Architecture. Early English Gothic (under French influence): Canterbury, begun 1175; Lincoln, 1185–1200; Salisbury, 1220–1258. Decorated Gothic: Choir of Lincoln, 1255–1280; York, west front, 1261–1324.

Painting and minor arts. St. Albans at the opening of the 13th century was the greatest artistic center in Europe (manuscript painting by Matthew Paris). The court of Henry III was a mecca for European craftsmen, especially Frenchmen.

Literature. Orm's *Ormulum* (early 13th century), a translation into English of portions of the Gospels; the *Ancren Rewle,* rules for the ascetic life tinged with the cult of the Virgin (c. 1200); **Layamon's** *Brut,* an English verse translation of Wace's *Brut.* Political songs and satires of the Barons' War, etc. (e.g. *Song of the Battle of Lewes;* the *Husbandman's Complaint*). **Matthew Paris** (c. 1200–1259), a friend of Henry III, monk of St. Albans, in his compilation, the *Historia Maior,* covered the history of the world, but in the portion dealing with the years 1235–1259 produced a work of original research in which he glorified England and things English.

Foundation of Cambridge University (1209). Foundation of University College (1249); Balliol (1261); Merton (1264) began the collegiate system of Oxford.

Science and learning. Bartholomew Anglicus (c. 1230), *On the Properties of Things,* a popular encyclopedia influenced by Pliny and Isidore, combining accurate observation (e.g. the domestic cat) with discussion of the fantastic (e.g. the griffin).

The English Franciscans at Oxford. Robert Grosseteste (d. 1253), bishop of Lincoln: insistence on the study of the sources (the Fathers and the Bible); knew Greek and Hebrew, a precursor of the Christian humanists; student of philosophy, mathematics, astronomy, physics, teacher of Roger Bacon. **Roger Bacon** (d. 1292), greatest mediaeval exponent of observation and experiment. Foresaw the application of mediaeval power to transport, including flying; "formula" for gunpowder; author of the *Opus Maius* and *Opus Minus.*

Opponents of the Thomist rationalists. Duns Scotus (c. 1270–1308) and **William of Occam** (c. 1300–1349).   (*Cont. p. 287.*)

(2) Scotland, 1034-1304

1034-1286. Racial and political turmoil. Duncan I was followed by his murderer, the usurper
1040-1057. Macbeth, and his son and avenger
1057-1093. MALCOLM CANMORE. Malcolm was forced to do some kind of homage by William the Conqueror (1072) and by William Rufus (1091), and Anglo-Norman penetration began. Malcolm's wife (Saint) Margaret (sister of Edgar Aetheling, grandniece of Edward the Confessor) was a masterful and remarkable woman whose Anglicizing influence on Scottish culture, on the national life, and the native Church was profound. Her three sons, especially
1124-1153. DAVID I, continued the so-called "bloodless Norman conquest," and the new Anglo-Norman aristocracy (e.g. Baliols, Bruces, Lindsays, Fitz Alans, i.e. Stewarts) became the bulwark of the crown.
1153-1286. The new four reigns were notable for the consolidation of Scotland, and for signs of impending collision with the English monarchy. William the Lion, captured in a raid by the English, accepted (1174) the feudal lordship of the English crown and did ceremonial allegiance at York (1175). Richard I weakened England's position, John tried to restore it.
1249-1286. ALEXANDER III did homage (1278) to the English king for his English lands, "reserving" his Scottish fealty. All of Alexander's issue were dead by 1284, leaving only his granddaughter Margaret, the *Maid of Norway.* Margaret's death (1290) made impossible the personal union of England and Scotland (by Margaret's marriage to Edward I's heir). Thirteen claimants to the Scottish crown were narrowed down to the candidacy of **Robert Bruce** and **John Baliol.** Edward I of England, called upon to arbitrate, awarded the crown to Baliol (1292), but when Baliol ignored a summons to attend Edward and instead embarked upon an alliance with France (1295), the English invaded the country and, after some years of warfare, reduced it in 1304 (p. 215). *(Cont. p. 294.)*

(3) Ireland, 1171-1307

(From p. 185)

The period following the **expedition of Henry II** (1171) was marked by a steadily developing conflict between the feudal system of the incoming Normans and the old tribal organization of the Irish. In its later phases this struggle bred centuries of discord and bloodshed. Henry's authority was precariously maintained by a viceroy who had orders to be fair to the natives, a policy which estranged the Norman elements.
1185. Henry's son, John Lackland, returned to England after a short and inglorious rule as lord of Ireland, but his authority was maintained by his representative, **William Marshal,** earl of Pembroke, who married the daughter of Richard of Clare.
1213. John abandoned Ireland, along with England, to Pope Innocent III.
1216-1272. Under Henry III the power and possessions of the Anglo-Norman colony expanded rapidly: bridges and castles were built, towns prospered and guilds were formed.
1272-1307. Edward I's revolutionary legislation in England was extended to Ireland, which continued to prosper, at least in the Anglo-Norman sections. But the cleavage between the two races had become very marked and the native clans remained restive.
(Cont. p. 296.)

b. SCANDINAVIA

(From p. 186)

(1) Denmark, 950-1320

c. 950-985. Harald II (Bluetooth), whose reign saw a steady advance of Christianity and expansion of Danish power over Schleswig, the Oder mouth, and Norway. But the kingship was of little importance until the reign of
985-1014. SVEN I (Forked-beard). He defeated the Norwegians, Swedes, and Wends and conquered England (1013).
1014-1035. CANUTE II, THE GREAT (Knut), Sven's son, was king of Denmark, Norway (1028), and England (1016-1035), the first "northern empire." Canute's conversion completed the conversion of his people. He imported priests, architects, and artisans from his English realm, and new influences spread from Denmark to Norway and Sweden. On his death Norway broke away, England passed to Edward the Confessor.
1157-1182. Under **WALDEMAR I, THE GREAT,** the founder of the **Waldemarian dynasty,** a great expansion eastward took place at the expense of the Wends; Copenhagen was established as the capital.
1182-1202. CANUTE VI made conquests in (Slavonic) Mecklenburg and Pomerania.
1202-1241. WALDEMAR II (the Conqueror) led crusading expeditions into Livonia, Estonia (Reval founded), and penetrated the Gulf of Finland, making the southern Baltic a Danish lake (the second "northern empire"). This empire collapsed in 1223, and the advance was in fact more in the nature of a crusade than of permanent imperial expansion. The mon-

218

Kings of Scotland (1040-1390)

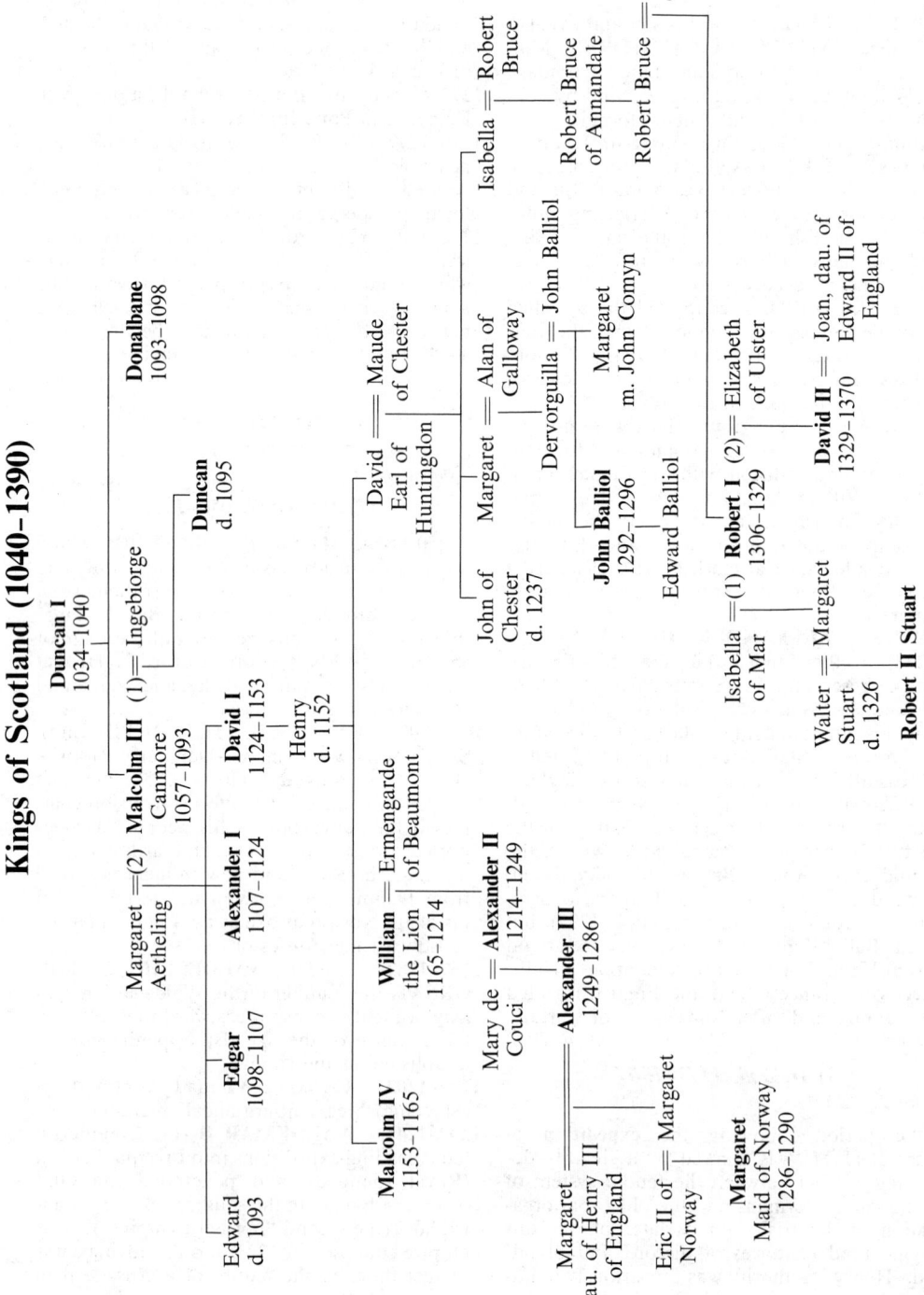

(*Cont. p. 295.*)

archy was now dominant, the nobles largely feudalized, the clergy (with royal grants) powerful, the bourgeoisie vigorous (fisheries and cattle-raising), the yeoman class strong and independent.

1241-1250. ERIC IV (Plowpenny), whose reign was taken up with civil war against his brothers Christopher and

1250-1252. ABEL, who was supported by his brother-in-law, the count of Holstein, and also by the Swedes and by the city of Lübeck.

1252-1259. CHRISTOPHER I. His effort to tax the Church opened a struggle that lasted nearly a century.

1259-1286. ERIC V (Glipping). He was forced by the nobility to sign a charter, the **Danish Magna Carta** (1282), recognizing the national assembly and initiating the subordination of the king to the law. He continued the contest with the clergy, fought against dynastic rivals, planned expansion in Mecklenburg and Pomerania, and lost Scania and North Halland to Sweden.

1286-1319. ERIC VI (Menved), during whose reign the conflict between the crown and the Church came to a head. By a compromise (1303) the rights of the Church were guaranteed, but the king's right to levy military service on church lands was upheld.

(*Cont. p. 334.*)

(2) *Sweden, 993-1319*

The origins of the Swedish kingship are obscure, but the kingdom may be dated back to the **union of Gothia and Svealand** (prior to 836). The conversion of the country to Christianity took place in the 9th century and

993-1024. OLAF SKUTKONUNG was the first Christian ruler. He was the son of Eric the Conqueror, the founder of the Northern Kingdom, and brought to Sweden many Anglo-Saxon workers. His wars with St. Olaf of Norway led to some conquests, which were soon lost. The century following his death was marked by wars between the Goths and the Swedes and by what appear to have been religious conflicts.

1134-1150. SVERKER. Amalgamation of the Swedes and Goths with alternation of rulers from the two peoples (an arrangement which continued for a century). The monarchy gradually became established on a firm basis and the progress of Christianity was marked by the foundation of many bishoprics (including Uppsala, 1163). The first monasteries also belong to this period.

1150-1160. ERIC IX (the Saint), whose reign was a short golden age. He led a crusade into Finland, the first real expansion of Sweden. The line of St. Eric ended with

1223-1250. ERIC XI (Laespe), whose reign was dominated by his brother-in-law, Jarl i.e. Earl) **Birger Magnusson,** the greatest statesman of mediaeval Sweden. He controlled the government from 1248-1266 and had his son elected king in 1250, thus founding the **Folkung line.**

1250-1275. WALDEMAR. As regent, Jarl Birger abolished judicial ordeal by fire, ended serfdom by choice, encouraged commerce, favored the settlement of German artisans, checked the power of the baronage. He attempted to introduce typical European feudalism, setting up his other sons in quasi-independent duchies.

1279-1290. MAGNUS LADULOS, who had dethroned and imprisoned his brother Waldemar. Magnus continued his father's feudal innovations, extended the powers of the clergy, and set up an hereditary nobility. Town charters became numerous as the burghers became prosperous through trade and mining.

1290-1319. BIRGER (son of Magnus). His rule was chaotic, due to civil war with his brothers, whom Birger ultimately captured and executed. This led to a popular uprising and the expulsion of Birger, who was followed by his three-year-old nephew. (*Cont. p. 334.*)

(3) *Norway, 872-1319*

Norway was a region with little natural unity, which in the earlier mediaeval period was ruled by numerous petty kings.

872-930. HAROLD I (Haarfager) began the unification of the country by deposing many of the chieftains (traditionally including Hrolf of Rollo). It was in this period that the Norsemen supposedly made their conquests in Iceland, the Faroes, Shetlands, Orkneys, Hebrides, Scotland, and Ireland.

935-961. HAAKON I (the Good), who attempted, prematurely, to convert the country to Christianity.

995-1000. OLAF I, TRYGVESSON, who with the aid of English clergy, converted Norway, Iceland, and Greenland. He was defeated by the kings of Denmark and Sweden, who supported the Norwegian nobility. There followed a period of feudal disruption.

1016-1028. OLAF II (St. Olaf) reunited the country and established Christianity on a firm footing.

1046-1066. HARALD III, HAARDRAADE, who was defeated by King Harold of England in the **battle of Stamford Bridge** (p. 182). There followed another period of confusion, marked by constant wars of succession, and by a struggle against the growing power of the clergy. Nevertheless the expansion of trade brought increasing prosperity.

1184-1202. SVERRE. He was able to maintain a strong monarchy in the face of aristocratic and clerical opposition, thanks to support from the small landowners. Nevertheless Norway continued to be troubled with dynastic conflict.

1223-1263. HAAKON IV, a strong king, who temporarily restored order, conquered Iceland, but was defeated in a war with Scotland.

1280-1299. ERIK II (the Priest-Hater), whose reign was marked by a war with the Hansa towns, in which he suffered a reverse. As a result he was obliged to grant the towns full privileges in Norway and to join the Hanseatic League.

1299-1319. HAAKON V, marking the culmination of decline of the royal power.

The crown in Scandinavia depended on its vassals for soldiers and for administration. The introduction of cavalry (first recorded in Denmark, 1134) accentuated this feudal tendency, and a new nobility emerged. This nobility was a professional military class always ready for war, exempt from taxes; it quickly became a governing class receiving local offices and lands as a reward for military services. From Denmark this new society spread to Norway and Sweden. Henceforth the nobles added a further complication to dynastic wars, causing a series of crises, and restricting the normal evolution of royal power.

German capital and German merchants began to penetrate Scandinavia, achieving by the second half of the 13th century a dominating position. The growth of the Hanseatic League delayed the progress of the native bourgeoisie, but commerce led to the active growth of towns and town life. Population was increasing rapidly, lands were cleared, the arts were advancing in distinction and perfection under the patronage of wealthy kings and prosperous prelates.

The **heroic age of the Icelandic** *skalds* (court poets) in the 10th and 11th centuries brought the art to an involved perfection and a concentration on war that ultimately killed it. Meantime the kings, interested in politics as well as war (notably Sverre of Norway, 1185) began to patronize the Norwegian story-tellers, particularly the Icelanders, and the **Sagas** emerged. The greatest master of the new form was an Icelander, **Snorri Sturleson** (1179-1241), an active political figure in both Iceland and Norway. Snorri's *Younger Edda* (*Edda Snorra Sturlusonar*) in prose and verse, containing the rules of versification, the old myths, and a collection of ancient Icelandic poems, is unique. History was written by **Saxo Grammaticus** (c. 1208), whose *Historia Danica* is the chief source for the Hamlet story. Both Snorri and Saxo were preoccupied with the ideals of national unity, strong royal power, and resistance to baronial particularism.

(*Cont. p. 336.*)

c. GERMANY UNDER THE SALIAN AND HOHENSTAUFEN EMPERORS, 1024-1268

(*From p. 177*)

[*For a complete list of the Holy Roman emperors see Appendix V.*]

1024-1125. THE FRANCONIAN (or Salian) **HOUSE.** Dawn of the great imperial age.

1024-1039. CONRAD II (the Salian). He continued the general policy of Henry: personally interested only in the churches of Limburg and Speyer, he was firm in his dealings with the Church in general and relied on the lesser nobles to balance the clergy and magnates. The *ministeriales,* laymen of humble or even servile origin, were used to replace the clergy in many administrative posts; regalian rights were retained and exploited. Dukedoms were not regranted as they fell vacant, but were assigned to Conrad's son Henry, who on his accession to the crown held all but the duchies of Lorraine and Saxony. By encouraging the making of fiefs heritable Conrad weakened the dukes and got the support of the lesser nobles, but insured the ultimate feudalization of Germany. Conrad's imperial coronation (1027), one of the most brilliant in mediaeval Rome, was witnessed by two kings, Canute the Great and Rudolf III of Burgundy. Burgundy, willed to Conrad by Rudolf III, guardian of one road to Italy, was reincorporated (1033) in the empire on the death of Rudolf. Failure of an expedition (1030) against Stephen of Hungary; successful disciplinary expedition (1031) against the Poles; recovery of Lusatia; payment of homage by the Poles.

1039-1056. HENRY III (the Black). Imperial authority at its height. A period of great town prosperity, due to development of trade. His wife, Agnes of Poitou, was an ardent devotee of Cluny; Henry, an honest reformer, abandoned simony, purified the court along Cluniac lines, but retained a firm hold on the Church. Strongest of the German emperors, he asserted his mastery in Poland, Bohemia, and Hungary; Saxony was the only duchy to keep a trace of its original independence; resumption of the dangerous practice of granting duchies outside the royal house made Germany a feudal volcano; use of the *ministeriales* in administration, but retention of the bishops as principal advisers and administrators.

Henry's reforms alienated the bishops, the magnates, and the nobles.

1043. Henry proclaimed the **"Day of Indulgence,"** forgiving all his foes and exhorting his subjects to do likewise; Brĕtislav of Bohemia forced (1041) to do homage; pagan reaction in Hungary put down (1044); final peace in Hungary (1052), which became a fief of the German crown. Homage of Denmark, repudiated soon after.

1046. Synods of Sutri and Rome. Deposition at Henry's instigation of three rival popes and election of his nominee, Clement II, the first of a series (Clement, Leo IX, and Nicholas II) of reforming German popes; reaffirmation of the imperial right of nomination to the papacy.

1047. Godfrey the Bearded, duke of Upper Lorraine, disappointed at Henry's refusal to award him Lower Lorraine, stirred up serious disaffection, and finally joined Baldwin of Flanders in a revolt at first supported by Henry of France (1047); he married (1054) Beatrice, widow of Boniface, marquis of Tuscany, one of the most powerful Italian supporters of the popes.

1056–1106. HENRY IV. (Aged six at his accession; nine-year regency of his pious, colorless mother, Agnes.) During the regency lay and clerical magnates appropriated royal resources and sovereign rights with impunity, and dealt a fatal blow to the German monarchy.

1062. **Anno,** archbishop of Cologne, kidnaped the young king and with **Adalbert,** archbishop of Hamburg-Bremen, governed in his name, dividing the monasteries (one of the chief resources of the crown) between themselves.

1066. The **Diet of Tribur,** thanks to the reaction of the clergy and nobles against Adalbert, freed Henry from Adalbert and his personal government began.

Henry was a remarkable but undisciplined man, intelligent, resolute, ill-balanced, and headlong, with the odds against him from the start; under papal pressure he was reconciled (1069) with his wife Bertha, reformed his personal life, and began a vigorous rule. His policy was a return to the Ottonian habit of using the Church as a major source of revenue; simony was open, and the reforming party appealed to Rome against Henry. Henry began the recapture, reorganization, and consolidation of royal lands and revenues, especially in Saxony, and probably planned to consolidate the monarchy in the Capetian manner around a compact core of royal domain in the Harz-Goslar region.

1073. A great **conspiracy of the leading princes** led to a rising of virtually all Saxony. Henry came to terms with the pope, played one faction off against the other, won the South German baronage, and finally defeated the rebels (1075).

1074. Charter of Worms, the first imperial charter issued direct to citizens without episcopal intervention.

Theophilus the Presbyter (fl. second half of the 11th century) described the techniques of building a cathedral, including the making of stained glass.

1075–1122. THE STRUGGLE OVER LAY INVESTITURE. The German bishops, alarmed at Hildebrand's reform policy (p. 232), opposed his confirmation as pope, but Henry, in the midst of the Saxon revolt, sanctioned it, and apparently promised reforms in Germany. The sudden abolition of lay investiture would have reduced the emperor's power in Germany and would have made government impossible. With the end of the Saxon revolt Henry's interest in reform vanished.

1075. Pope Gregory, at the Lenten Synod, issued a rigorous reform program and later sent a stern warning to the emperor and the German episcopate. Henry, under pressure from his bishops, called

1076. The Synod of Worms. The bishops repudiated their allegiance to Pope Gregory, addressed a list of (ridiculous) charges to him, and declared him deposed. Henry's letter to the pope associated him with the charges and demanded Gregory's abdication in the most insolent and violent terms. Public opinion was shocked at the letter, but the North Italian bishops at Piacenza supported Henry. Gregory at the Lenten Synod (1076) in Rome, suspended and excommunicated the German and Lombard prelates involved, and deposed and excommunicated Henry, absolving his subjects from allegiance and producing political and ecclesiastical chaos in Germany. Henry was isolated, the Saxon rebellion broke out again, and a powerful coalition of German magnates eager to regain power was formed against him. The **Diet of Tribur** (October) compelled Henry to humble himself and agree to stand trial and clear himself of Gregory's charges before Feb. 22, 1077, on pain of the withdrawal of their allegiance. The princes called a synod to meet at Augsburg, inviting Gregory to preside; Gregory accepted and started for Germany.

1077. Henry, after a midwinter dash across the Alps with his wife, was welcomed by the North Italians and avoided the humiliation of a public trial in Germany by presenting himself as a penitent at Canossa (Jan. 21). Gregory, outmaneuvered, hesitated three days, and finally, on the appeals of the Countess Matilda and Abbot Hugh of Cluny (Henry's godfather), accepted Henry's promises and solemn oaths of contrition, and absolved him. The **penance at Canossa** is hardly mentioned by contemporaries, and made much less impression in Germany than the excommunication; the chief source on the episode is Gregory's letter of justification to the disappointed German nobles; Gregory, after some months of waiting for a safe conduct into Germany, turned back.

1077. A faction of the nobles elected an anti-king, **Rudolf of Swabia,** with the approval of Gregory's legates, but without papal confirmation.

1077–1080. Civil war ensued, but Henry, loyally supported by the towns, gained strength steadily; Rudolf of Swabia was defeated and killed (1080); Gregory again excommunicated and deposed Henry, but a synod of German and North Italian prelates then deposed Gregory, naming as his successor Guibert of Ravenna, a reforming bishop and former friend of Gregory (1080).

1083. Henry, at the end of a series of expeditions to Italy (1081–1082), besieged Rome; after futile efforts at reconciliation he gained entrance to the city and Gregory called in his Norman allies. Henry, crowned at Rome by his anti-pope, invaded Apulia; **Robert Guiscard** expelled him from Rome and sacked the city. (1084). The horrors of the Norman sack made it impossible for Gregory to remain in Rome and he departed with his allies, dying as their "guest" in Salerno (1085). The papal position was justified by **Manegold of Lautenbach's** theory that an evil ruler violates a contract with his subjects and may therefore be deposed by the pope, who is responsible for the salvation of mankind. Henry's advocate, **Peter Crassus,** based his denial of this right on historical precedent backed by citations of Justinian (one of the earliest examples of such quotations).

1093–1106. Gregory's successors, unbending champions of reform, supported the revolts of Henry's sons in Germany and Italy: **Conrad** (1093), and the future **Henry V** (1104). Henry was elected king, but his father retained the loyalty of the towns to the end. Henry V shamefully entrapped and imprisoned his father, who abdicated, escaped, and was regaining ground when he died.

1106–1125. HENRY V (married to Matilda, daughter of Henry I of England in 1114). A brutal, resourceful, treacherous ruler, Henry continued his father's policies. Skillfully pretending to be dependent on the princes, he continued lay investiture, opposed papal interference in Germany, and retained the support of the lay and clerical princes; meantime, relying on the towns and *ministeriales,* he built up the nucleus of a strong power. Wars against Hungary, Poland, and Bohemia (1108–1110).

1110–1111. Imposing **expedition to Italy** to secure the imperial crown, universally supported in Germany. In Italy the Lombard towns (except Milan) and even the Countess Matilda yielded to Henry. Pope Paschal II (1099–1118) offered to renounce all feudal and secular holdings of the Church (except those of the see of Rome) in return for the concession of free elections and the abandonment of lay investiture, a papal humiliation more than equal to the imperial mortification at Canossa. At Henry's coronation the clergy repudiated Paschal's renunciation, there was a scuffle, Henry took the pope and cardinals prisoners, and forced the pope to acknowledge the imperial powers. The net result was nil, but papal prestige was badly damaged.

1114–1115. A series of revolts (Lorraine, along the lower Rhine, in Westphalia, and soon in East Saxony and Thuringia). Henry was saved by the loyalty of the South Germans.

1115. Matilda, countess of Tuscany, who had made over all her vast holdings to the papacy, retaining them as fiefs with free right of disposition, willed these lands to Henry on her death, and Henry arrived in Italy to claim them (1116–1118).

Both pope and emperor were weary of the investiture controversy, Europe was preoccupied with the Crusades (p. 274), and the time was ripe for compromise. The first important compromise negotiated by the pope was with Henry I of England (1107) and provided that the king should not invest with the spiritual symbols (the ring and the staff), but that he was to be present or represented at all elections. After due homage the king should then invest with the symbols of temporal authority. In France a similar compromise was reached in practice with Philip I (c. 1108). Pope Calixtus II convinced Henry that neither Henry of England nor Philip of France had suffered by their compromise.

1122. At the Synod of Worms, under the presidency of a papal legate, the **Concordat of Worms** was drawn up in two documents of three brief sentences each which provided that: (1) elections in Germany were to be in the presence of the emperor or his representative, without simony or violence; in the event of disagreement the emperor was to decide; the emperor was to invest with the temporalities before the spiritual investiture; (2) in Italy and Burgundy consecration was to follow within six months of election; the emperor to invest with the regalia after homage. This concordat ended the investiture struggle, but not the bitter rivalry of pope and emperor, for the papacy, now clearly the independent spiritual leader of Europe, could not long tolerate an imperial rival.

1125. Henry left no direct heir, and at the bitterly fought election of 1125 the archbishops of Mainz and Cologne, foes of the anticlerical Salian line, cleverly prevented, with papal aid, the election of the nearest heir, Frederick of Swabia, of the house of Hohenstaufen, on the ground that the hereditary principle was dangerous, and Lothair of Supplinburg, duke of Saxony, was chosen, opening the great struggle of Welf and Waiblinger (Hohenstaufen) in Germany (**Guelf** and **Ghibelline** in Italy).

1125-1137. LOTHAIR II. Elected with the support of the clergy, he remained loyal to the Church, was the first German king to ask papal approval of his election, and did not exercise his rights under the Concordat of Worms for some years. Bitter civil war against the Hohenstaufens (1125-1135); vigorous policy of German expansion among the Wends and Scandinavians; renewal of Wendish conversions (1127).

1133. Influenced by Bernard of Clairvaux, Lothair decided in favor of Pope Innocent II (against Anacletus II) and went to Italy to settle the papal schism; he was crowned, had the Concordat of Worms confirmed, and received the lands of Matilda as fiefs.

1135. The **"year of pacification"** in Germany—general peace proclaimed. Lothair apparently planned to create a vast dynastic holding for his son-in-law, the Welf Henry the Proud, to include Bavaria, Swabia, Saxony, the allodial lands and fiefs of Matilda of Tuscany, and to secure him the imperial crown. Lothair died suddenly on his return from an expedition against King Roger II of Sicily, and in the election (1138) the clergy, led by Adalbert of Trier, had the Waiblinger, Conrad of Hohenstaufen, chosen. Conrad almost at once put Henry the Proud under the ban, gave Saxony to Albert the Bear, Bavaria to Leopold of Austria, his half-brother, and reopened the civil war.

1138-1268. THE HOUSE OF HOHENSTAUFEN (from Staufen, their Swabian castle). The first German dynasty to be conscious of the full historical implications of the imperial tradition and the significance of Roman law for imperial pretensions. Their consequent devotion to a policy of centralization and to the aggrandizement of the lay imperial power in the face of the new spiritual supremacy and political aspirations of the Papacy precipitated a second great struggle between the popes and the emperors, centering in Italy but turning upon a sharp conflict between rival spiritual and political concepts.

1138-1152. CONRAD III, a gallant, knightly, attractive, popular hero, but no statesman. The Welf, **Henry the Lion** (son and successor of Henry the Proud), acknowledged Conrad's title, but regained Saxony by force and was granted it by the peace (1142); the struggle of Welf and Waiblinger reduced Germany to chaos and Conrad left on the Second Crusade. On his return Conrad found Germany in worse confusion.

The most significant development of the reign was the renewal of **expansion against the Slavs and Scandinavians** (chiefly on the initiative of Albert the Bear and Henry the Lion): a regularly authorized German crusade against the Slavs (1147); colonization of eastern Holstein; foundation of Lübeck (1143); conversion of Brandenburg and Pomerania; Albert the Bear began to style himself margrave of Brandenburg; Henry the Lion began the creation of a principality east of the Elbe. Conrad took no share in these developments; was the only king since Henry the Fowler not to attain the imperial title. Alienated from the Church toward the end of his life, Conrad was preparing a more vigorous assertion of the imperial position, and supported the strong imperialist Frederick of Swabia, his nephew, as candidate for the throne. On Conrad's death anarchy was so prevalent in Germany that even the magnates favored a strong ruler, and Conrad's candidate, Frederick, duke of Swabia, was unanimously elected.

1152-1190. FREDERICK I (Barbarossa, i.e. Red Beard), a handsome man with flowing golden hair, who could both frighten and charm, the embodiment of the ideal medieval German king. A close student of history and surrounded with Roman legists, he regarded himself as heir to the tradition of Constantine, Justinian, and Charlemagne (whom he had canonized by his anti-pope), and aimed at restoring the glories of the Roman Empire. He began the style *Holy Roman Empire.*

Policy of consolidation and expansion of royal lands. Burgundian lands regained by marriage (1156) with Beatrice, heiress of the county of Burgundy; purchase of lands from the Welfs in Swabia and Italy; exploitation of regalian rights.

Conciliation of the magnates. (1) **Henry the Lion,** recognized as virtually independent beyond the Elbe; confirmed in Saxony; regranted Bavaria (1156). (2) **Austria made an independent duchy** (1156), granted to Henry of Austria in return for Bavaria. (3) **Alliance with the episcopate.** Free exercise of rights under the Concordat of Worms; reforming

224

(From p. 175)

The Welf and Hohenstaufen Families

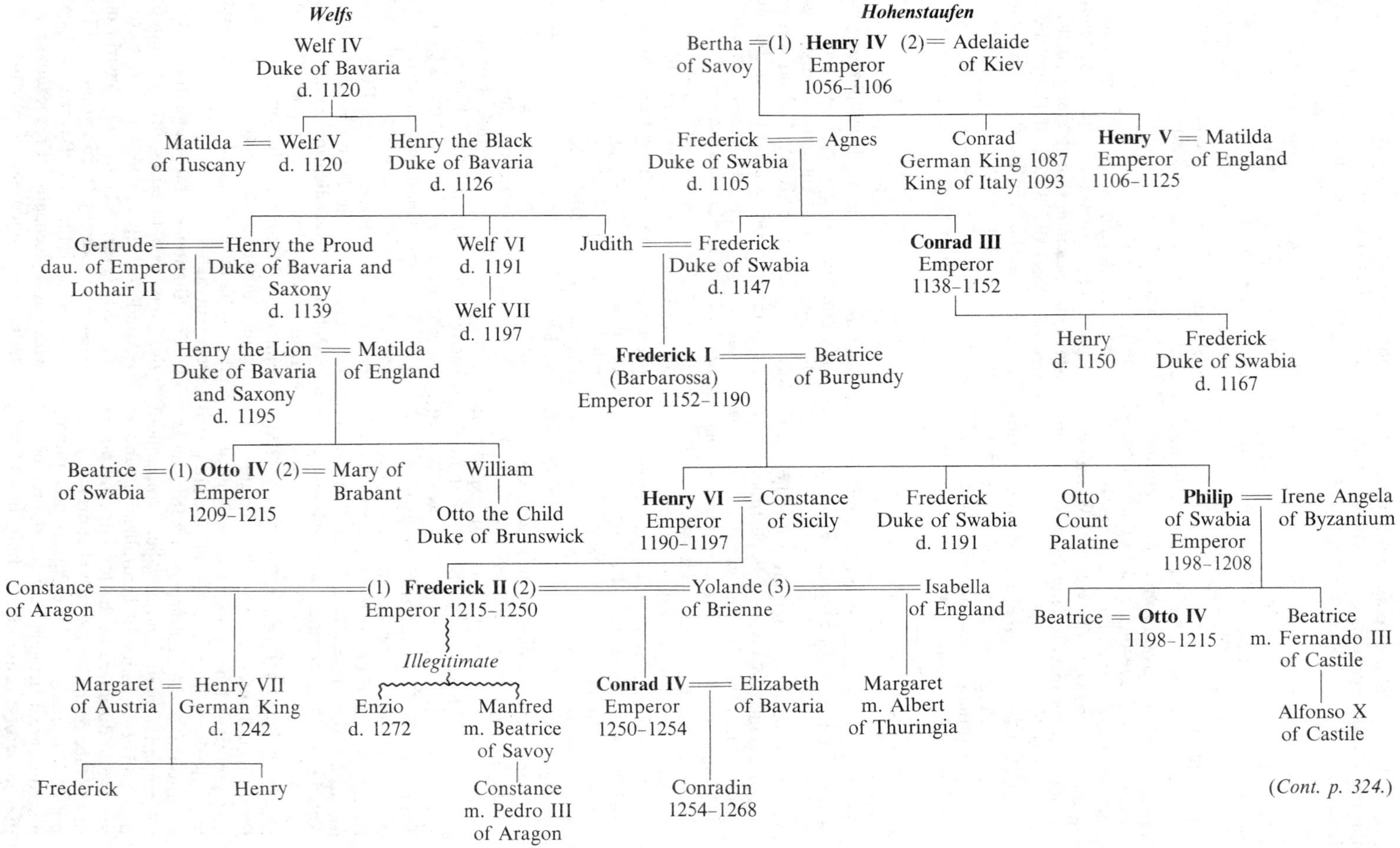

Welfs

Hohenstaufen

Bertha =(1) **Henry IV** (2)= Adelaide
of Savoy   Emperor   of Kiev
      1056–1106

Frederick == Agnes   Conrad   **Henry V** = Matilda
Duke of Swabia   German King 1087   Emperor   of England
d. 1105   King of Italy 1093   1106–1125

Frederick == Beatrice   **Conrad III**
Duke of Swabia   of Burgundy   Emperor
d. 1147   1138–1152

Welf IV
Duke of Bavaria
d. 1120

Henry the Black
Duke of Bavaria
d. 1126

Frederick
Duke of Swabia
d. 1167

Henry
d. 1150

Matilda == Welf V
of Tuscany   d. 1120

Judith === Frederick
Duke of Swabia
d. 1147

Frederick I
(Barbarossa)
Emperor 1152–1190

Welf VI
d. 1191

Welf VII
d. 1197

Henry VI === Constance
Emperor   of Sicily
1190–1197

Frederick
Duke of Swabia
d. 1191

Philip = Irene Angela
of Swabia   of Byzantium
Emperor
1198–1208

Otto
Count
Palatine

Beatrice = **Otto IV**
1198–1215

Beatrice
m. Fernando III
of Castile

Alfonso X
of Castile

Gertrude === Henry the Proud
dau. of Emperor   Duke of Bavaria and
Lothair II   Saxony
             d. 1139

Henry the Lion === Matilda
Duke of Bavaria   of England
and Saxony
d. 1195

William

Otto the Child
Duke of Brunswick

Beatrice =(1) **Otto IV** (2)= Mary of
of Swabia   Emperor   Brabant
      1209–1215

Isabella
of England

Yolande (3)

Margaret
m. Albert
of Thuringia

Conrad IV === Elizabeth
Emperor   of Bavaria
1250–1254

Conradin
1254–1268

(1) **Frederick II** (2)
Emperor 1215–1250

Illegitimate

Enzio
d. 1272

Manfred
m. Beatrice
of Savoy

Constance
m. Pedro III
of Aragon

Constance
of Aragon

Margaret === Henry VII
of Austria   German King
d. 1242

Henry

Frederick

(Cont. p. 324.)

bishops replaced with hard-headed appointees of the old school, loyal to the crown. Administration delegated to the *ministeriales*. Successful maintenance of public order; Frederick won the title *pacificus*.

Expeditions to Italy (p. 235, *seq.*). (1) 1154–1155; (2) 1158–1162; (3) 1163–1164; (4) 1166–1168; (5) 1174–1177; (6) 1184–1186.

1156–1180. Henry the Lion's "principality" beyond the Elbe: military progress against the Slavs and colonization (Hollanders, Danes, Flemings); Bremen taken from the archbishop (1156), Lübeck from Adolf of Holstein (1158); commercial relations with Denmark, Sweden, Norway; alliance with Waldemar II of Denmark; reduction of Slavic pirates; colonization of Mecklenburg, extension of Christianity; war with Albert the Bear; refusal of aid to Frederick in Italy (1176); confiscation of Henry's holdings and exile (1180); dismemberment of Saxony.

1156. Diet of Regensburg. Emergence of the **prince electors** as a substantive body in the German state.

1157. Diet of Besançon. Emissaries from Rome, France, England, the Spanish princes, Apulia, Tuscany, Venice, and the Lombard towns did honor to Frederick. Frederick saved the life of the papal legate, Cardinal Roland, whose statement of papal claims enraged the German nobles (translation of *beneficia* as "fiefs"). Boleslav, duke of Bohemia, granted the style of "king" (1158).

1174–1177. Frederick's fifth expedition to Italy. Vain siege of Alessandria, futile efforts at reconciliation with the pope.

1176. LEGNANO. Decisive defeat of Frederick by the Lombard League, the first major defeat of feudal cavalry by infantry, herald of the new rôle of the bourgeoisie.

1183. Final peace of Constance between Frederick, the pope, and the Lombard towns: restoration of all imperial confiscations during the papal schism confirmed, recognition of general imperial suzerainty in Italy; the Lombard towns virtually autonomous city states under a loose administration by imperial legates and vicars. Frederick retained the Matildan lands without a specific definition of their status. Henceforth there was no shadow of unity in the empire, as Germany and Italy followed a divergent development.

1184. Great Diet of Mainz. A tremendous medieval pageant for the knighting of Frederick's two sons in the presence of a great concourse, 70 (?) princes, 70,000 (?) knights.

1186. Marriage of the future Henry VI to Constance (daughter of Roger II of Sicily), heiress of King William II; possibly arranged in the hope of permanent peace with the empire. The net result of the marriage was the transfer of the center of gravity in the struggle between the popes and the emperors to Sicily, the final destruction of German unity, and the ruin of the house of Hohenstaufen. The pope refused imperial coronation to Henry.

1186. Triple coronation at Milan. Frederick as king of Burgundy; Henry as *Caesar* (a deliberate revival of the title), and Constance as queen of the Germans.

1186. Frederick took the Cross, and until his death led the Third Crusade (p. 275) in the traditional rôle of the emperor as the knightly champion of Christendom.

1190–1197. HENRY VI (already Caesar and regent, crowned emperor, 1191). The medieval empire at its maximum, ideally and territorially. Henry was not robust, and lacked the usual Hohenstaufen good nature. A good soldier, learned, practical, a shrewd diplomat, stern, cruel, but of heroic and original mind.

1190–1195. Intermittent struggles with the Welfs in Germany under Henry the Lion.

1191–1194. Restoration of order in Sicily. Struggle with the Norman anti-king, Tancred of Lecce (d. 1194); coronation of Henry as king of Sicily (1194); birth of Frederick (later Frederick II) at Jesi (1194).

1192–1194. Henry used the captivity of King Richard I of England to make the crown of England a fief of the empire, and to extort an enormous ransom.

Henry's plans to unite the German and Sicilian crowns, and to crown Frederick without election, thereby establishing the heredity of the German crown, were blocked by powerful German and papal opposition. Frederick was elected king of the Romans (1196). Plans (traditional with the Norman kings of Sicily) for the foundations of a Mediterranean empire on the ruins of the Byzantine Empire as the basis for a universal dominion; dynastic marriage with the Greek imperial house; active preparations for a crusade; advance in central Italy and conciliation of northern Italy. Sicilian outbreak against the German administration brutally crushed. Henry's sudden death was followed by a bitter anti-imperial reaction in Italy, by fourteen years of civil war in Germany.

1197–1212. Civil war in Germany, chaos in the empire. Rival kings; Henry's brother, the Waiblinger **Philip of Swabia** (supported by King Philip II of France) and the Welf **Otto of Brunswick,** son of Henry the Lion (supported by King Richard I of England). The German nobles played one side off against the other. Chaos in Sicily, where Pope Innocent III acted as guardian of Frederick (after 1198). Otto's title validated by Innocent (1201); assassination of Philip (1208); imperial coronation of Otto (1209); papal break with Otto (1210) and support of Frederick (with Philip II); Frederick's second election (1211) and dash to Germany.

1212-1250. FREDERICK II (Stupor Mundi), a valetudinarian of middle height, courteous, amiable, charming, pitiless, arrogant; the most brilliant ruler and one of the most learned men of his day; a legislator of the first order, able soldier, diplomat, skeptic, one of the leading scientific investigators of his time; an astrologer with the mind of a Renaissance rationalist; Sicilian by taste and training, half Norman by blood, with little of the German about him. Crowned: king of the Romans, 1212; king of the Germans, at Aachen, 1215; emperor, at Rome, 1220.

1212. Alliance with King Philip II of France.

1213. The **Golden Bull of Eger:** Frederick, who had already sworn an oath to keep his two crowns separate and to support the pope, abandoned the German church to Innocent (conceding the free election of bishops, the right of appeal to Rome) and undertook to support the pope against heretics.

1214. The **battle of Bouvines** (p. 246): Frederick and Philip II completed the defeat of Otto and the Welfs. On the death of Innocent III (1216) Frederick's personal rule may be said to have begun.

1216-1227. Frederick on tolerable terms with Pope Honorius III, his old tutor: election (1220) of Frederick's son Henry as king of the Romans (a violation of Frederick's promise); Frederick allowed to retain Sicily during his lifetime; renewal of his crusading oath; grant of generous privileges (1220) to the clergy: exemption of the Church from taxation and of clerics from lay jurisdiction, making clerical princes virtually independent territorial princes; support of the bishops against the towns; promises to suppress heresy. Crusade postponed until 1225.

1223. **First appearance of the Mongols in Europe** (p. 284); capture of Cracow (1241); defeat of the Hungarians and Silesians.

1226. The **conversion of Prussia** undertaken by the Teutonic Order (p. 229).

1226-1232. Renewal of the ancient imperial claims in Lombardy, formation of the **Second Lombard League,** and appearance of the **First League of the Rhineland;** town leagues in central Italy; Pope Gregory alienated.

1227-1229. **Frederick's crusade** (p. 277): return of Frederick due to illness; first excommunication (1227); resumption of crusade (1228); violent papal and imperial propaganda and recrimination; the Teutonic Knights under Hermann of Salza remained faithful to Fred-

erick. Aware of the commercial value of Moslem friendship Frederick negotiated a ten-year truce (1229) with El-Kamil, sultan of Egypt, which restored Jerusalem, Nazareth, and Bethlehem to Christian hands. Frederick crowned himself king of Jerusalem. Papal war (1228-1229) of devastation in Apulia (first known papal mercenaries, the *soldiers of the keys*); Frederick on his return expelled the papal forces and threatened the *Patrimonium Petri* with invasion.

1230. Hollow **peace of San Germano** with Pope Gregory IX: Frederick promised to protect the papal domains, confirmed papal rights over Sicily, and was absolved. In preparation for the next struggle Frederick concentrated on Italy, especially Sicily. Frederick's son Henry on his majority (1228) devoted himself to Germany, and favored the towns. Frederick, like Barbarossa, had leaned heavily on the German episcopate, especially Engelbert of Cologne, and had increased the independence of the lay princes and ministeriales; administrative offices tended to become hereditary, and after Engelbert's death (1225) the administration had become less efficient. Settlement of the Teutonic Knights in Prussia: union (1237) with the Livonian Brothers of the Sword and eastward expansion: foundation of Thorn (1231), Kulm (1232), and Marienwerder (1233).

1231. Privilege of Worms. Hoping for German support for his Italian policy, Frederick extended to the lay princes his generous grants of 1220 to the clergy, giving them control over local justice, minting rights, roads, and streams, etc. From this grant dates a clear emergence in Germany of the territorial sovereignty of both lay and clerical princes. The **Decree of Ravenna** (1232) allowed expansion of the power of the princes at the expense of the towns. Henry objected, revolted (1234), and tried to win the German and Italian towns to his side.

1231. Completion of the **reorganization of Sicily:** clean sweep of private titles and royal privileges in the Norman manner; resumption of royal domain; destruction of private garrisons and feudal castles; ban on private war; criminal jurisdiction transferred from feudal to royal courts; towns deprived of magistrates and put under royal officers; clergy taxed and excluded from civil office. Sicily reduced to order (1221-1225): feudal revolts put down, towns brought to heel; large Saracen garrison-colonies (loyal to Frederick and indifferent to papal threats) established at Lucera and Nocera. Recognizing in Sicily the true source of his strength in money and men, Frederick aimed to unify Sicily and Italy into a kingdom of the empire. Local risings (1228-1230 and 1232) in Apulia and Sicily; unrest (1234) in southern Italy.

1231. The **Constitutions of Melfi,** the most conspicuous and constructive single piece of "legislation" in the Middle Ages, completed the Sicilian reorganization: an efficient divine right absolutism (much of it a return to the policy of Roger II) profoundly influenced by Roman law; centralization under an expert departmentalized bureaucracy; clerical jurisdiction limited to ecclesiastical matters; heresy a civil crime; simony in civil office a capital offense; gift or sale of Church land forbidden. Feudal, clerical, and municipal administration replaced by royal officials; supreme court at Capua; justices on annual circuits; careful financial organization. The University of Naples (the first European university on a royal charter) founded (1224) to train state officials, and given a monopoly of higher education; Salerno revived as a school of medicine.

Advanced economic policy in Sicily based on Arab practice: abolition of internal tolls; mercantilistic regulation, state monopolies. Replacement of feudal dues by fixed payments; direct taxation in crises, efficient customs collection and internal prosperity.

1235-1237. **Frederick's last visit to Germany.** Deposition, arrest, and imprisonment of Henry, who committed suicide in prison (1242) and was succeeded by his brother Conrad (1237); conciliation and peace with the Welfs strengthened Frederick in Germany. Great reform **Diet of Mainz** (the German Melfi, 1235); issue of the model *Landfrieden.* Frederick was unable to stem the steady progress of towns (resting on expanding commerce) in Germany or Italy.

1237. Frederick at **Cortenuova** smashed the Second Lombard League and humiliated Milan.

1239. Pope Gregory's **second excommunication of Frederick,** followed by a tremendous battle of pamphlets and preaching: Frederick painted as a heretic, rake, anti-Christ. He retorted with a demand for reform of the Church and an appeal to the princes of Europe, proposing a league of monarchs against the papacy.

Beginning of the amalgamation of northern and central Italy with the imperial administration on Sicilian lines: a system of general vicariates under imperial vicars, each city with an imperial *podestà* (generally Apulians, and often relatives of Frederick).

1241. Gregory's call for a **synod at Rome** to depose Frederick. Frederick ravaged papal territory, almost took Rome, and his fleet captured a large delegation of prelates off Genoa on their way to the synod; annexation of papal

Tuscany to the empire. Gregory's death (1241). Celestine IV (1241). During the two-year interregnum in the Papacy Frederick intrigued for a friendly pope, and welcomed

1243. The **election of Sinibaldo de'Fieschi** (Innocent IV), who turned out to be the architect of his ruin.

1244. **Frederick's invasion of the Campagna** and vain efforts at reconciliation with the pope; Innocent's flight to Lyons, and call for a synod.

1245. **The Synod of Lyons.** Appeal to the Germans to revolt and elect a new king; deposition of Frederick; Louis IX's efforts at conciliation and Frederick's offers rebuffed by the pope: Innocent unleashed the Franciscans and Dominicans in a war of propaganda and proclaimed a crusade against Frederick. Henry Raspe, duke of Thuringia (d. 1247), was set up (1246) as an anti-king in Germany, followed by

1247-1256. **William of Holland,** who was supported by a newly formed **league of Rhenish towns.** Innocent's ruthless but vain campaign against Frederick's episcopal allies in Germany; bitter warfare in northern Italy with extreme cruelty on both sides; Italian conspiracy to assassinate Frederick (probably with Innocent's knowledge) put down in cold blood; Piero della Vigne, Frederick's most trusted official, supposedly implicated. He was arrested, blinded, and died a suicide (1249); capture of Frederick's son Enzio (1249), who died in prison (1272).

1248. The **defeat of Frederick** after a long siege of Parma did not destroy his hold on northern Italy.

1250. Sudden **death of Frederick;** burial in the cathedral at Palermo, where his sarcophagus still remains.

1250-1268. **Relentless persecution of the Hohenstaufens by the popes:**

1250-1254. **CONRAD IV,** king of Germany, and king of Sicily by the will of his father, Frederick; Manfred, his illegitimate half-brother, regent of Sicily; Pope Innocent IV's offer (1253) of the Sicilian crown under papal suzerainty to Edmund (son of Henry III of England); renewal of Conrad's excommunication and proclamation of a crusade against him; papal invasion of the kingdom (i.e., southern Italy and Sicily).

1254-1273. **THE GREAT INTERREGNUM.** An epilogue to the medieval struggle of the popes and the emperors, marks the end of the medieval Holy Roman Empire and the failure of imperial efforts to establish German unity; it was a prologue to the complete triumph of particularism which dominated German life until well into the 19th century.

1255-1261. **Manfred** regained southern Italy

(1255) and Sicily (1256), was crowned king of Sicily (1258), and after the Sienese (Ghibelline) victory over Florence at Montaperto (1260) almost dominated Italy; Alexander IV's peace offers were rejected by Manfred (1261).

1257. Double election in Germany of two foreigners: **Richard of Cornwall** (brother of Henry III of England, brother-in-law of Frederick II), and **Alfonso X** of Castile.

1266. Charles of Anjou (brother of Louis IX of France), accepting Urban IV's offer (1262) of the Sicilian crown under papal suzerainty, invaded southern Italy in accordance with papal plans and with his own ambitions to create a Mediterranean empire. He defeated Manfred, who fell in the battle (**Benevento,** 1266), ending any hope of a native ruler for Italy.

1268. Conradin (Conrad IV's son, aged 15), called from Germany by the Italian Ghibellines, was defeated at **Tagliacozzo,** betrayed to Charles of Anjou, and beheaded at Naples with at least the tacit approval of Pope Clement IV. European public opinion was shocked, and Henry III of England and Louis IX of France were aroused. The heir of the house of Hohenstaufen was Constance, daughter of Manfred, whose husband, Pedro III of Aragon, was destined to become the first Aragonese king of Sicily (1282–1285) (p. 306).

The imperial title remained (1268–1806) an appendage of the German monarchy, but as the Germans were little interested in the title the way to the imperial throne was opened to ambitious foreigners. The bitter struggle of the Hohenstaufens and the popes, followed by removal of the Papacy to French soil, alienated the German people from the Roman popes and bred a lasting suspicion of the Latin Church that bore fruit in the nationalism of the Reformation.

The princes of Germany, busy consolidating their own power, were not eager to elect a king, and there was no election until Pope Gregory X, alarmed at the progress of Charles of Anjou and the degeneration of Germany, which reduced papal revenue and indirectly strengthened France, and needing an imperial leader for the crusades, threatened to name an emperor.

SIGNIFICANT ELEMENTS IN 13TH-CENTURY GERMANY

I. **Great tenants-in-chief:** (1) Four ancient princely houses: the **Ascanians** (Brandenburg and eastern Saxony with the ducal title); the **Welfs** (Brunswick); the **Wittelsbachs** (Upper Bavaria, the County Palatine of the Rhine, Lower Bavaria); the **Wettins** (Saxony after the 15th century); (2) **Ottokar,** king of the Slavic kingdom of Bohemia (1253–1278), with claims to Austria, Styria, Carinthia, Carniola.

II. **Great ecclesiastical tenants-in-chief:** especially in the Rhineland (notably the archbishops of **Mainz, Trier,** and **Köln**).

III. **Three minor houses** about to emerge into importance: (1) **Luxemburgs,** (2) **Hapsburgs,** (3) **Hohenzollerns.**

IV. **Lesser tenants-in-chief** (the so-called *Ritterschaft*), who regarded the central power as their defense against the great princes.

V. **Imperial cities** (*Reichsstädte*), growing richer and more powerful and disposed to support the crown against the princes. Tendency of the cities to organize as leagues.

The informal (until the 14th century) constitution of the German monarchy: (1) Election of the king (originally by tribal chieftains) devolved upon the tenants-in-chief, then upon a group of them; election to be followed by ratification by the others. In the 13th century the group election became final election and was confined to a body of **seven electors** (of varying personnel).

(2) The ancient feudal *Reichstag* (*curia regis*) became (in the 13th century) the German Diet (equivalent to parliament or the estates-general) divided into two houses: princes and electors. Its functions remained vague and amorphous. Towns were admitted in 1489.

The great ecclesiastical states of the Rhineland and their feudal satellites reached the zenith of their power in the 13th century, and strove to maintain their position in the face of the rising lay states to the east (Saxony, Brandenburg, Austria, and Bohemia) by electing to the monarchy feeble princes who could pay well for election and would remain amenable. The lay states became dynastic principalities primarily concerned with their own fortunes and anti-clerical in policy.

Epic poetry flourished in the Middle High German period, in national epics such as the *Nibelungenlied* (c. 1160) and *Gudrun* (c. 1210–1220); court epics, the romance of chivalry, as sung by **Hartmann von Aue, Wolfram von Eschenbach** (c. 1200), **Gottfried von Strassburg** (*Tristan*), and **Conrad von Würzburg** (1220–1287). The art of the *Minnesang* reached its peak with **Walther von der Vogelweide** (c. 1165–1230) and **Neidhart von Reuenthal** (c. 1215–1240).

(1) The Teutonic Knights, 1190–1382

1190–1191. Crusading origin. Merchants of Lübeck and Bremen founded a hospital at Acre which soon became attached to the German church of Mary the Virgin in Jerusalem.

1198. The brethren of this hospital were raised

to a military order of knighthood (as the *Order of the Knights of the Hospital of St. Mary of the Teutons in Jerusalem*) by the Germans gathered for Henry VI's crusade. Henceforth membership in the order was open only to Germans, and knighthood only to nobles. Pope Innocent III gave them the rule of the Templars. Headquarters were successively at Acre (1191–1291), Venice, and (after 1309) Marienburg, clear evidence of the new orientation of the Knights. Intense rivalry existed between the order and the Templars and Hospitalers in the Holy Land until the failure of the crusades turned them to other fields of action. The robes of the Teutonic Knights were white with a black cross.

Reconstitution of the order and **transfer to the eastern frontier** of Germany. The eastward advance (*Drang nach Osten*) of the Germans, begun under Charlemagne, had never wholly ceased, and colonization with Netherlandish farmers and German merchants, coupled with Cistercian efforts during the days of Adolf of Holstein, Albert the Bear (self-styled margrave of Brandenburg), and Henry the Lion of Saxony, established the Germans firmly in Mecklenburg and Brandenburg. Lübeck (founded 1143) early became an important commercial center. The foundation of Riga (1201), as a crusading and missionary center, the establishment of the Livonian *Brothers of the Sword,* and an influx of Westphalian nobles and peasant immigrants insured the continued advance of Germanization and the progress of Christianity (largely under Cistercian auspices) in Livonia. The defeat of the Danes at Bornhöved (1227) by the combined princes of North Germany, cost them Holstein, Lübeck, Mecklenburg, and Pomerania, leaving only Estonia to Denmark. The Poles had already begun the conversion of the Prussians and East Pomeranians.

1210–1239. Under **HERMANN VON SALZA,** the first great grand master, the order, at the invitation of Andrew of Hungary, was established (1211–1224) in Transylvania as a bulwark against the Comans (Cumani) until their progress alarmed the Hungarian monarch.

Hermann was an intimate friend of Emperor Frederick II, and was the real founder of the greatness and prosperity of the (still relatively poor and insignificant) order.

1226. By the **Golden Bull of Rimini,** Frederick laid down the organization of the order (on Sicilian lines) and prepared the Knights for a new career as pioneers of Germanization and as Christian missionaries on the eastern frontier. Frederick repeatedly made them generous gifts, used them for his own crusade, and employed individual knights on important missions. The grand master was given the status of a prince of the empire.

Organization of the order. Districts, each under a commander; a general chapter, acting as advisers to the grand master; five chief officers; the grand master elected for life by the Knights. The order was nominally under the pope and the emperor, but in the days of its might only strong popes exerted any influence.

1229. The call of Prussia. (The name *Prussia* is probably derived from a native word *Prusiaskai* and not from *Bo-Russia*.) An appeal (1225–1226) from Conrad of Masovia, duke of Poland, for aid, coinciding with Frederick's reorganization, was accepted by Hermann von Salza, and the Knights embarked on a unique crusade comparable only with that in the Iberian Peninsula, as champions of Christianity and Germanism. Conrad gave (1230) them Kulmerland, and promised them whatever they conquered from the Prussians. Frederick confirmed their rights.

1234. The Knights transferred all their holdings to the pope, receiving them back as fiefs of the church and thus had no other lord than the distant Papacy.

1237. Union with the Livonian Brothers was followed by notable progress in Livonia and plans for the conversion of the Russians from the Greek Church to the Roman, which led to a serious defeat for the order. Courland was also gained and Memel founded (1252) to hold the conquests. Eventually the southern Baltic coast from the Elbe to Finland was opened by the order to the missions of the Church and the trade and colonies of the Germans.

A **great era of town foundations** (some 80 in all) opened under the order: Thorn (castle, 1231), Kulm (castle, 1232), Marienwerder (1233), Elbing (castle, 1237), Memel (1252), Königsberg (1254), *et al.*

1242–1253. A **Prussian revolt** was put down, and the conquest of Prussia continued with aid from Ottokar of Bohemia, Rudolf of Hapsburg, Otto of Brandenburg.

1260. The **battle of Durben,** a disastrous defeat of the order by the Lithuanians, was followed by another Prussian revolt which had national aspects and was put down with Polish aid. The suppression was marked by deliberate extermination and the virtually complete Germanization of Prussia ensued. Castle Brandenburg was built (1266) and the reduction of Prussia completed (1285).

The order allowed great freedom to the towns (especially after 1233); no tolls were collected, only customs dues. The large commercial towns joined the Hanseatic League (p. 330). The Knights were also generous (after 1236) in charters to German (and Polish) nobles, the peasants were well treated, and mass migrations into territories of the Knights became common.

1263. The pope granted the order permission to trade, not for profit, a concession later expanded (by devious means) into full commercial freedom. As a result the order, founded as a semi-monastic crusading society, eventually became a military and commercial corporation of great wealth and selfish aims, and a serious competitor of the very towns it had founded. The Knights escaped the fate of the Templars, though temporarily on the defensive.

Great state was kept at the headquarters in Marienburg, and under Grand Master Winrich (1351–1382) the order was the school of northern chivalry, just as later it became a great cultural influence through the foundation of schools everywhere in its domains and the maintenance of its houses as centers of learning.   (*Cont. p. 333.*)

d. ITALY AND THE PAPACY, 888–1314

(*From p. 167*)

[*For a complete list of the Roman popes see Appendix IV.*]

The Papacy was a local and secular institution until 1048; Italy was without effective native rule.

888–924. Berengar I, last of the phantom "emperors" (vacancy in the empire, 924–962), was the grandson of Louis the Pious. Surviving rival "emperors" were Guido of Spoleto, Lambert his son, and Louis of Provence (901–905). **Raids of Saracens** (c. 889) and **Magyars** (c. 898) into Lombardy; a Saracen stronghold at Freinet controlled the Alpine passes; Saracen settlements in southern Italy, and the **Moslem conquest** (827) **of Sicily** began the isolation of that area; Italian urban life had become almost extinct; the invasions were checked, not by the shadowy monarchs, but by the rise of feudal defenders.

914–963. The **nadir of the Papacy** (the *pornocracy*): the landed aristocracy of Rome, under the leadership of the senator Theophylact, his wife Theodora, and his daughter Marozia (mistress of Pope Sergius III, and mother of Sergius' son John, later Pope John XI) dominated the curia.

928. Marozia, having imprisoned Pope John XI, took control of Rome until her son

932–954. Alberic II assumed power; the *Patrimonium Petri* was a plaything of the **Crescentii** (Marozia's family), who maintained an intermittent supremacy in Rome during the 10th century. The Papacy was without political power or spiritual prestige and the western Church for all practical purposes became a loose organism under its bishops, who gave "national churches" such coherence as they had, and acknowledged a vague kind of allegiance to Rome.

924. Rudolf of (Juran) Burgundy elected king, followed by

926–945. Hugh of Provence.

945. Lothair II (d. 950), Hugh's son and coregent, was declared sole king, Lothair's rival,

950–961. Berengar II, imprisoned his widow, Adelheid, who appealed (according to tradition) to Otto the Great.

951–952. Otto the Great's first expedition to Italy.

961–964. Otto's second expedition to Italy, in answer to the appeal of the profligate pope, John XII, for protection against Berengar. Otto's coronation at Pavia as king of Italy and his coronation by the pope as Roman emperor, marked the

962. REVIVAL OF THE ROMAN EMPIRE. Otto confirmed his predecessors' grants in the *Patrimonium Petri* (probably with additions), but made careful reservation of the imperial right to sanction papal elections, and treated the pope like a German bishop (i.e. subject to the state). Otto also exacted a promise from the Romans not to elect a pope without imperial consent. He established a precedent by calling a synod at Rome which deposed (963) Pope John XII for murder and other crimes, and selected a (lay) successor, Leo VIII (963–964). This synod opened a period of about a hundred years when the papacy was dominated by the German emperors and by the counts of Tusculum, vassals of the emperors, with the title of *patricius* in Rome. In the same period the bishops in the west lost the position they had won in the 9th century, and became increasingly dependent on the kings and feudal nobility, and increasingly secular in outlook. The homage of Pandolf I for Capua and Benevento (967) and his investiture with the duchy of Spoleto mark the beginning of the long imperial effort to include southern Italy in the empire.

964. Leo VIII was expelled by the Romans shortly after his election, and **Benedict V** was (964) elected by the Romans without imperial consent.

966–972. Otto's third expedition to Italy. Otto held a synod which deposed Benedict. **Pope John XIII** (elected with imperial co-operation) was soon expelled by the Romans, and Otto, after a terrible vengeance on Rome, restored him. Imperial coronation of the future Otto II (967) by John XIII, coronation of Theophano and her marriage to Otto in Rome (972).

980-983. Otto II's expedition to Italy. Otto crushed Crescentius I, duke of the Romans, restored Pope Benedict VII (981), and was utterly defeated in his effort to expel the Saracens from southern Italy by a Greco-Moslem alliance (982). Otto nominated **Pope John XIV** (983-984).

983. Great Diet of Verona. Remarkable unity of the Italian and German magnates; resolve on a holy war against the Moslems; election of the future Otto III as successor to his father. Venice, already profiting by her Moslem trade, refused ships and defied the emperor.

996. Otto III, on his first expedition to Italy deposed the *Patricius,* Crescentius II, and (at the request of the Roman people) nominated as pope his cousin Bruno, **Gregory V** (996-999), the first German pope, an ardent Cluniac. Gregory and Otto compelled Gerbert to yield the archbishopric of Reims to the German Arnulf, and forced the French episcopate to acquiesce. Gregory censured King Robert of France. As the successor of Pope Gregory, Otto named **Gerbert of Aurillac.**

999-1003. SYLVESTER II (Gerbert of Aurillac), the first French pope, a man of humble origin, one of the most learned men of his day (Arabic, mathematics, and science). An intriguer and diplomat who co-operated with Otto in his mystic renewal of the empire; he was a moderate reformer, asserting that simony was the worst evil of the Church.

1012-1046. The **Tusculan popes** were either the relatives or the creatures of the counts of Tusculum: **Benedict VIII** (1012-1024), something of a reformer; **John XIX** (1024-1033), his brother, and **Benedict IX** (1033-1045), a debauchee who sold the Papacy for cash (i.e. the Peter's Pence from England) to his godfather, a priest, **Gregory VI** (1045-1046), who bought the See of Peter in order to reform it. The emperors, preoccupied with German affairs, made only rare visits to Italy.

Notable local efforts were made by the Church to reform itself and society:

(1) Local synods decreed clerical celibacy (e.g. Augsburg, 952; Poitiers, 1000; Seligenstadt, 1023; Bourges, 1031), attacked simony.

(2) Foundation (910) of the **Abbey of Cluny** by William the Pious, duke of Aquitaine, as a reformed Benedictine house, wholly free of feudal control, directly under the Holy See. Centralization of all daughter and affiliated houses (priories) under a single abbot of Cluny; rapid spread of Cluniac organization (France, Lorraine, Germany) and ideas of reform into western Europe: celibacy of the clergy; abolition of lay investiture and of simony.

(3) Gerard, lord of Brogne, founded (923) a monastery on his own estate which became a center of ecclesiastical reforms among existing foundations in Flanders and Lorraine.

(4) **Synods in Aquitaine and Burgundy** (where monarchical opposition to feudal anarchy was weak) pronounced (c. 989) anathema on ravagers of the Church and despoilers of the poor, initiating a long series of clerical efforts throughout Europe to force feudal self-regulation, which go by the name of the **Peace of God.** These decrees, repeatedly renewed and extended, were supplemented (after c. 1040) by the **Truce of God,** an effort to limit fighting to certain days and seasons of the year.

(5) An effort to restore the central authority of the Church by reference to past decrees, of which the most notable were the so-called *Isidorean* (or Forged) *Decretals,* attributed to Isidorus Mercator, and produced (c. 850) by a Frankish cleric. A combination of authentic and forged papal decrees, they aimed to establish the authority and power of the bishops and the position of the pope as supreme lawgiver and judge, and to make him supreme over councils.

(6) Notable increase in new ascetic orders in Italy and monastic schools north and south of the Alps; outstanding individual reformers (e.g. **Peter Damian,** d. 1072; **Lanfranc,** d. 1089; **Anselm,** d. 1109).

ITALY AT THE OPENING OF THE 11TH CENTURY. Sicily was in the hands of the Saracens; Apulia and Calabria under the feeble rule of Constantinople; Gaeta, Naples, Amalfi, were city republics; Benevento, Capua, and Salerno the capitals of Lombard principalities. Norman pilgrims arriving (1016) at the shrine of St. Michael on Monte Gargano began the penetration of the south by Norman soldiers of fortune in the service of rival states: the first permanent Norman establishment was at Aversa (c. 1029); the sons of the Norman Tancred of Hauteville (including Robert Guiscard) appeared (after c. 1035), and their steady advance at the expense of the Greeks led Benevento to appeal for papal protection (1051). Feudal anarchy prevailed in the north.

1027. Conrad II, in Italy for his coronation, restored order in the north, reducing the Lombard nobles.

1037. On a second expedition he disciplined Archbishop Aribert of Milan, restored order in the south; his *constitutio de feudis* made Italian fiefs hereditary.

1045-1046. GREGORY VI purchased the papal throne to reform the Papacy, but the end of his reign saw three rival popes (Gregory, Sylvester III, and Benedict IX). All three were deposed by the **Synods of Sutri and of Rome** (1046) under pressure from the reforming emperor, Henry III, who made Suitgar, bishop of Bamberg, pope as **Clement II** (1046–1047), the first of a series of German pontiffs: Damasus II (1048), Leo IX (1049–1054), Victor II (1055–1057), representing strong Cluniac influences. Henry pacified southern Italy, reaffirmed the imperial right of nomination to the Papacy, and left Italy in sound order.

1049–1085. Restoration of the independence of the Papacy, resumption of papal leadership in the Church and of spiritual supremacy in the west.

1049–1054. LEO IX (Bruno of Toul, a kinsman of Henry III) began the identification of the Papacy with Cluniac reforms, and the restoration of the spiritual primacy of the Holy See. He insisted on his own canonical election to the papal throne, reorganized the chancery on the imperial model, reformed the Church by personal or legatine visitation, giving reform reality in the west. The **Synod of Rome** (1047) had issued stern decrees against simony and clerical marriage.

1052. Henry III granted the duchy of Benevento to the Papacy.

1053. Leo, in his personal effort to enforce papal rights in the south, was utterly defeated by the Normans at Civitate.

1054. The long doctrinal **controversy with the Greek Orthodox Church,** which really hinged on fundamental divergences between east and west, ended with the final schism between the eastern (Orthodox) and western (Roman) Church (p. 267).

1055–1057. VICTOR II. Elected at the urging of Hildebrand (later Gregory VII), who dominated this pontificate and the following one and who made the Papacy the leader in reform. Beatrice, mother of Matilda, and widow of Count Boniface of Tuscany, married (1054) Godfrey the Bearded, duke of Upper Lorraine, Henry's most dangerous foe in Germany, as Boniface had been in Italy. Henry arrested Beatrice and her daughter Matilda, Boniface's heiress; Godfrey fled; Matilda remained all her life a powerful ally of the Papacy, and kept middle Italy loyal to the popes.

1057–1058. STEPHEN IX (brother of Godfrey the Bearded), a zealous Cluniac. The **Pataria** (c. 1056), a popular movement (the result of a preaching campaign), gained wide currency in the Milan region for its demands of clerical celibacy, the end of simony, and for apostolic simplicity among the clergy. It came into sharp conflict with the bishop and clergy. Peter Damian, sent by the pope, maintained the papal position (1059), and brought

the archbishop to terms; there was a later outbreak of the Pataria.

1058–1061. NICHOLAS II.

1059. The **Synod of the Lateran,** by its electoral decree, replaced the vague traditional rights of the Roman clergy in papal elections by an electoral **college of cardinals:** the prerogative voice in the election went to the seven cardinal bishops; the cardinal clergy represented the clergy and people at large; a Roman prelate (if worthy) was to be preferred; the election to be at Rome if possible. Henry's rights were provided for, but the provision seems to have been personal rather than general.

1059. Under Hildebrand's influence an alliance was made with the Norman, Richard of Aversa, and Nicholas after exacting an oath later invested Robert Guiscard with the duchy of Apulia and Calabria, and promised him Sicily if he could conquer it, thereby establishing papal suzerainty over southern Italy, the first great expansion of temporal suzerainty by the popes. The **Synod of Melfi** condemned (1059) the marriage of clergy.

1061–1073. ALEXANDER II. His election without consultation of Henry IV created serious tension; the **Synod of Basel** declared the election invalid, and chose an anti-pope. Alexander, on friendly terms with William the Conqueror, blessed the Norman conquest of England.

1071. Robert Guiscard (d. 1085) captured Bari, ending the Greek power in Italy; his capture of Palermo (1072) began the

1072–1091. Norman conquest of Sicily. Roger I (d. 1101) succeeded Guiscard as lord of southern Italy (except Capua, Amalfi, and papal Benevento).

1073–1085. GREGORY VII (Hildebrand). Short, corpulent, with glittering eyes, the son of an Italian peasant educated at Rome under strong Cluniac influence. Inspired by Gregory the Great, Gregory VI, and the study of the Decretals, he was neither an original thinker nor a scholar, but was intensely practical and of lofty moral stature. After a brilliant career in the Curia he was acclaimed pope by the Romans before his election. German bishops protested the election, and Gregory postponed his consecration, awaiting Henry's decision in a sincere effort to live up to his ideal of perfect co-operation between pope and emperor in the interest of peace, reform, and the universal monarchy of the Papacy. His program was summed up by his *Dictatus,* an informal memorandum which asserted: (1) the Roman Church has never erred, can never err; (2) the pope is supreme judge, may be judged by none, and there is no appeal from

233

The House of Tancred (1057-1287)

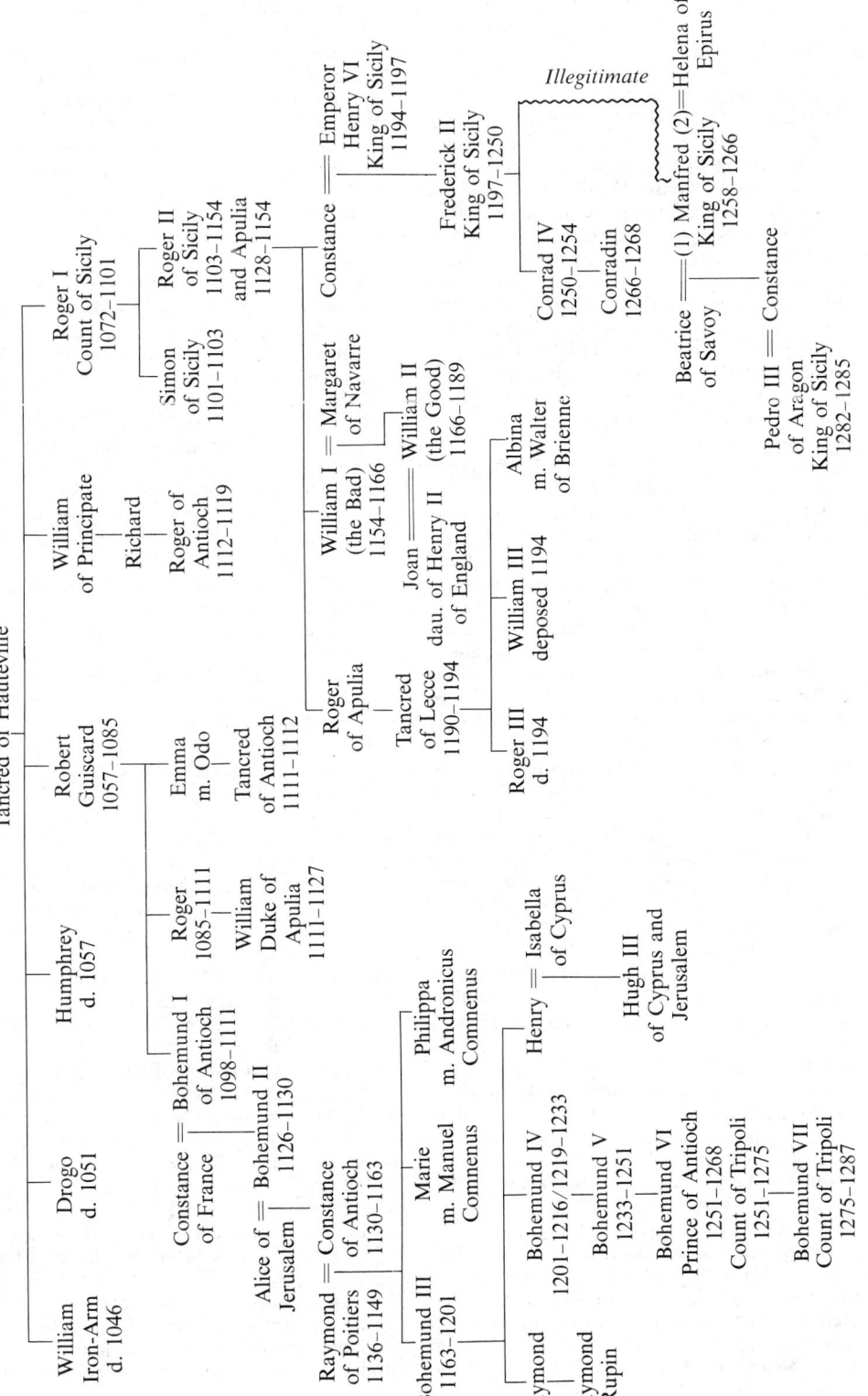

him; (3) no synod may be called a general one without his order; (4) he may depose, transfer, reinstate bishops; (5) he alone is entitled to the homage of all princes; (6) he alone may depose an emperor.

1075-1122. THE INVESTITURE STRUGGLE. Vindication of the spiritual supremacy and leadership of the Papacy (p. 221).

The Emperor Henry IV after his Saxon victory forgot his promises of reform in Germany. The **Synod of Rome** (1075) passed severe decrees against simony, clerical marriage, and (for the first time) against lay investiture, providing deposition for clerical offenders, excommunication for laymen. Gregory's letter of remonstrance and rebuke to Henry was ignored, and Henry, on the urging of the German bishops, called a **Synod at Worms** (1076). This synod deposed Gregory. Henry's first excommunication and the so-called humiliation at Canossa (1077) profited neither party; Henry's second deposition (1080) was without serious effect. After a series of invasions (1081-1084), Henry entered Rome and was crowned by his anti-pope, only to be expelled by Gregory's Norman ally, Robert Guiscard, with a motley army which included Saracens; the atrocity of the Norman sack made it impossible for Gregory to remain and he died a virtual exile, almost a prisoner of his allies at Salerno, leaving Henry and his anti-pope master of Rome for the time.

Gregory was on excellent terms with William the Conqueror and responsible for Alexander's blessing of the Conquest (1066), but William, true to the Norman conception of strong monarchy, ignored Gregory's pressure to make England a fief of the Papacy, and forbade the circulation of papal bulls in England without his permission. Gregory asserted papal suzerainty over Hungary, Spain, Sardinia, and Corsica. After a vacancy of a year, a close friend of Gregory was elected pope, **Victor III** (1086-1087), an aged, unwilling pontiff, soon driven from Rome by Henry's partisans.

1088-1099. URBAN II. A Frenchman of noble blood, long intimate with Gregory; handsome, eloquent, learned, he continued Gregory's policy of maintaining the complete independence of the Papacy and vigorous opposition to the emperors. Urban arranged the marriage of Countess Matilda and the son of the (Welf) duke of Bavaria (1089).

Henry invaded northern Italy successfully, but Matilda held out in the hills; Urban, profiting by the anarchy in Germany, urged Henry's son Conrad to a revolt (1093) which was taken up by half of Lombardy. Urban at the **Synod of Piacenza** (1095) renewed the decrees against simony and clerical marriage, added a ban on clerical homage to laymen, and received the appeal of the Byzantine emperor for help against the Turks at the **Synod of Clermont** (1095). Urban excommunicated King Philip I of France for adultery, and proclaimed the **First Crusade,** directing his appeal to the nobles and peoples rather than the monarchs, most of whom were hostile to the Papacy. On a visit to southern Italy Urban made Roger of Sicily his legate (1098), thus exempting him from the visits of an ordinary legate. At the **Synod of Bari,** Urban was as much interested in keeping the papal leadership in the crusade as he was in the debates on the procession of the Holy Ghost. The First Crusade was the first great victory for the reformed Papacy; the papal dominance of the military effort to defend Christendom is significant of the new prestige of the Papacy and the decline of the emperors.

1099-1118. PASCHAL II renewed the excommunication of Henry IV; intrigued with Henry, his son; Anselm waged the investiture battle in England (1103-1107), ending in a compromise (1107), followed almost at once by the lapse of lay investiture in France (formerly one of the worst offenders). Paschal's humiliating renunciation (1111) of papal fiefs and secular revenues, his repudiation by his clergy, and his arrest by Henry V made a much more profound impression in Europe than Canossa. Paschal recalled (1112) his concessions.

1115. The **Countess Matilda,** having made a donation (1086 and 1102) of her allodial lands (the second great addition to papal holdings) to the Papacy (subject to free testamentary disposition), willed them at her death (1115) to Henry V, who came and occupied the Matildine lands (1117), destined to be a bone of contention between the popes and emperors for a century.

1118-1119. GELASIUS II was forced to flee Rome; Henry V appointed his own pope; Gelasius, having excommunicated (1118) Henry, was finally driven to France.

1119-1124. CALIXTUS II, a Burgundian, related to half the rulers of Europe and a skilled diplomat, arranged the **Concordat of Worms** (1122), which closed the investiture controversy with a compromise. The **Synod of Reims** (1119) renewed the decrees against simony, clerical marriage, and lay investiture, as well as the excommunication of Henry V.

1130-1138. Papal schism. Precipitated by the corrupt election of the (Cluniac) Cardinal Pierleone (son of a rich converted Jewish banker of Rome), as **Anacletus II** (1130-1138), and the hostility of the rival houses of Corsi and Frangipani. The rival pope, **Innocent II**

(1130-1143), supported by Bernard of Clairvaux and most of Europe, was given military support by Lothair in return for confirmation of his rights under the concordat of 1122, imperial coronation, and investiture with the Matildine lands. Anacletus confirmed Roger II's title as king in return for his support.

1139. The **Second Lateran Council** (the tenth general council in the west) was attended by a thousand bishops. It marked the end of the schism.

1143. The **Commune of Rome** established in opposition to the non-Roman pope, it defied three feeble popes (Celestine II, Lucius II, Eugene III). **Arnold of Brescia,** pupil of Abelard, emerged as the eloquent leader with bitter denunciations of clerical wealth and papal bloodshed and burning appeals for a return to apostolic poverty and simplicity. Temporary restoration of the ancient Roman state, appeal to the emperor's protection. **Bernard of Clairvaux** agreed with Arnold's indictment (cf. *De Consideratione,* addressed to Pope Eugenius), but saw salvation for the Church in purification from within, not in diminution of its great powers, and opposed Arnold as he had Abelard.

1147-1149. **The Second Crusade** (p. 275).

1154-1159. **Adrian IV** (Nicholas Breakspear, the only English pope). Son of a poor man, learned, kindly, of high character, he had risen by his own merits; Roman anarchy ended by a stern interdict. Arnold expelled; alliance with **Frederick Barbarossa** against William, king of Sicily; altercation with Frederick over his haughty refusal of ceremonial service to the pope (stirrup episode). The bitter hostility of the Romans to pope and emperor forced a surreptitious coronation and hurried departure from Rome.

1155. Frederick executed Arnold as a heretic, but abandoned Adrian to the Normans and forced him to an independent Italian policy (i.e. alliance with an anti-Norman league of southern barons and with Constantinople) which brought William of Sicily to his knees as the pope's vassal. Adrian accepted the Roman Commune and returned to Rome.

1158-1162. Frederick's second expedition to Italy: the **League of Pavia** (Brescia, Cremona, Parma, Piacenza) supported Frederick; Milan and its league were reduced to submission. The great **Diet of Roncaglia:** Frederick, using Roman law to justify an extreme assertion of imperial rights and a brusque resumption of imperial regalia, substituted an imperial *podestà* for the consuls in the Lombard cities, drove Milan into open revolt (1159-1162), and turned the towns to alliance with the pope.

Renewal of the papal alliance with Byzantium; formation of an alliance of Lombard towns under papal auspices.

1159-1181. **ALEXANDER III** (imperialist anti-popes: Victor IV, Paschal III, Calixtus III). Frederick, citing precedents from Constantine, Charlemagne, and Otto the Great, held a synod at Pavia to adjudicate the claims of Alexander III and Victor IV. Alexander ignored the synod, Victor was recognized. Alexander, after an exile in France, returned and excommunicated Frederick (1165). Renewal of the town leagues (1164); Milan rebuilt, expulsion of imperial *podestàs.*

1167-1168. Frederick's **fourth expedition to Italy:** Alexander's flight to the Normans; Frederick's capture of Rome; renewal of the Lombard League (1168): promises of mutual aid; organization for federal administration; erection of Alessandria, a great fortress city (named for the pope), to guard the passes (1168); Italy virtually independent.

1174. Frederick's **fifth expedition to Italy:** vain siege of Alessandria, complete **defeat at Legnano** (1176); preliminary peace of Venice (1177, the centenary of Canossa).

1179. The **Third Lateran Council** decreed a two-thirds vote of the conclave to be necessary for a valid papal election.

1181-1198. A series of unimportant popes, often exiled from Rome by local anarchy until 1188, when papal recognition of the Commune of Rome made peaceful residence again possible.

1183. **Peace of Constance:** imperial suzerainty in Italy recognized; resumption by the Lombard towns of all regalia they had ever enjoyed, including the right to maintain an army, to fortify, to keep the league or expand it, full judicial jurisdiction, control of their own coinage, abolition of the imperial *podestàs.* The only relic of imperial control was the reservation of the emperor's right to confirm elected consuls, the right of appeal to the imperial court, and the retention of the *fodrum* as a contribution to military needs. The Lombard towns were autonomous for all practical purposes under a very loose system of imperial legates and vicars.

1184. Frederick's **sixth expedition to Italy:** utilizing the split in the Lombard League (after 1181) and local feuds in Tuscany and Bologna, Frederick created a strong imperial party in middle Italy and by a liberal charter (1185) even won over Milan.

1189-1192. **The Third Crusade** (p. 275).

1198-1216. **INNOCENT III.** A tough-minded Italian patrician of German blood (whose family provided the Church with eight popes), chosen by the cardinals to restore the political power of the Papacy. Animated by an historical mysticism, he looked on Christendom as a single community in which he aimed to combine moral unity with a world-state under papal guidance. He deduced the papal powers from the *Petrine Theory,* the *Old Testament,* the *Donation of Constantine,* and from the duty of the pope to insure justice, maintain peace, prevent and punish sin, and aid the unfortunate. With a clear grasp of essentials, he never lost sight of this concept, but his frequent opportunism destroyed his moral grandeur. Insistence, not on moral or theological, but on historical grounds (i.e. the Translation of the Empire) on the right (claimed by Gregory VII) to pass on imperial elections. A brilliant administrator, he first brought the papal chancery into systematic organization (division into four sections under experts, careful systematized treatment of documents) and made a great collection of canons and decretals. This pontificate was the zenith of the medieval Papacy.

Restoration of the Papal States (Spoleto, Ancona, Romagna regained); many towns succeeded in escaping and keeping their local autonomy. Tuscany: an anti-imperial league under papal auspices; towns like Florence, Lucca, and Siena retained their appropriations of the Matildine lands (a partial foundation of their later power); the rest of the Matildine lands were regained by the Church. Innocent used his position first as protector, then as guardian of Frederick II, in an attempt to alienate Sicily from the Hohenstaufens.

Steady **insistence on a crusade.** The Fourth Crusade (p. 275) combined opportunity to attack the infidel with a chance to reunite the Roman and Orthodox Churches; Innocent reconciled himself to the sack of Constantinople by the organization of the new Latin church of Constantinople. The **Albigensian Crusade** (p. 245), directed against the spreading heresy of southern France, drenched that region with blood and exterminated one of the most advanced local cultures in Europe, under revolting circumstances of feudal cynicism and clerical intolerance. Simon de Montfort nullified Innocent's efforts to divert the crusaders' ardor to Spain against the Moslems.

Vindication of the political claims of the Papacy. (1) Asserting his right to pass on imperial elections, Innocent rejected the Hohenstaufen claimant (Philip of Swabia) to the imperial crown, ignored the undoubted rights of Frederick, crowned and supported Otto (in return for large promises of obedience to papal authority), and then procured (in alliance with King Philip II) the election of Frederick II. (2) By excommunicating Philip II

(1198) he forced him to a formal recognition of his wife Ingeborg, but was coldly rebuffed when he intervened in Philip's struggle with the Angevins. (3) Maintaining the rights of his nominee to the See of Canterbury (Langton), Innocent forced King John of England (interdict, 1208) to cede England to the Holy See and receive it back as a fief (1213). (4) Innocent received the homage as papal vassals of the following states: Aragon, Bulgaria, Denmark, Hungary, Poland, Portugal, Serbia, and brought the Roman Church to its closest approximation to an ideal Christian, universal commonwealth.

The struggle against urban heresy. The Church, long organized to deal with a predominantly rural society, was increasingly out of touch with the rising bourgeoisie and urban proletariat as town life revived and expanded; the anti-clericalism of the cities had become a major problem. The Italian, **Francis of Assisi,** and the Spaniard, **Dominic,** organized the spontaneous response within the Church to this crisis: Francis (d. 1226), a converted gilded youth, as the joyous "troubadour of religion" began preaching the beauties of humbleness, poverty, simplicity, and devotion, of the brotherhood of man, of man and the animals, of man and nature. His cheerful vernacular hymns won tremendous success in the towns of Italy. Founded as a brotherhood, whence the name **Friars Minor** (Minorites, Grey Friars, also Cordeliers), the **Franciscans** won cautious support from Innocent, but not formal ratification as a corporation until 1223.

The second of the mendicant orders, the **Dominican,** born of Dominic's campaign against the Albigensian heresy, was sanctioned by Innocent (1215). Organized as a preaching order, the Dominicans (Friars Preachers, Black Friars, or Jacobins in Paris) patterned their constitution on the Franciscan. These two mendicant orders were not monastic, rural monks, but town-dwellers devoted to preaching and charity. The conduct of the Inquisition was entrusted to them (1233) and their direct influence on education (especially that of the Dominicans) was enormous.

1215. The **Fourth Lateran Council** was the climax of Innocent's pontificate (attended by 400 bishops, 800 abbots and priors, and the representatives of the monarchs of Christendom) and its decrees were of tremendous significance: (1) the Church was pronounced one and universal; (2) the sacraments were decreed the channel of grace, and the chief sacrament, the Eucharist; (3) the dogma of transubstantiation was proclaimed; (4) annual confession, penance, and communion were enjoined; (5) careful rules were made as to episcopal elections and the qualifications of the clergy, and (6) injunctions for the maintenance of education in each cathedral and for theological instruction were formulated; (7) the Albigensian and Catharist heresies were condemned; (8) trial by ordeal and by battle forbidden; (9) relic worship regulated, and (10) rules of monastic life were made more rigorous. Finally, another crusade was proclaimed.

1216-1227. HONORIUS III, a high-minded noble of conciliatory disposition who managed to keep on relatively good terms with Frederick II.

1227-1241. GREGORY IX, a relative of Innocent III, aged and fiery, he never relaxed his relentless pressure on Frederick. **Canonization of Francis of Assisi** (1228) and **Dominic** (1234).

Leonardo of Pisa (Fibonacci) (c. 1170-1240), the mathematician, who wrote the first rigorous, systematic demonstration of Hindu mathematics. He also wrote treatises on geometry and algebra, including quadratic and cubic equations.

1243-1254. INNOCENT IV, a canon lawyer. Supposedly friendly to Frederick, he continued the uncompromising attack on the emperor, and encompassed the final ruin of the Hohenstaufen.

1271-1276. GREGORY X (Visconti), a high-minded pope with three aims: to pacify Italy, to check Charles of Anjou and the rising power of France, and to pacify Germany. At the **Synod of Lyons** (1274) he provided for the seclusion of conclaves to avoid corruption. His successors were occupied with Italian affairs (the war of Naples and Sicily, baronial anarchy in Rome, etc.), and the advancement of their own houses: **Nicholas III** (Orsini) (1277-1280), a foe of Charles of Anjou; **Martin IV** (1281-1285), a puppet of Charles of Anjou; **Honorius IV** (Savelli) (1285-1287); **Nicholas IV** (1288-1292). The rivalries of the great houses were so close that two years were required to elect Nicholas' successor, a hermit dragged unwilling (as a result of Cardinal Malabranca's dream) to the Holy See, **Celestine V** (1294), who never saw Rome, a puppet of Charles of Anjou and Cardinal Gaetani. Induced (probably) by Gaetani (the midnight voice, a megaphone over the papal couch) he resigned (*The Great Refusal*, Dante, *Inf.* III, 60) and was kept a prisoner by his successor, Boniface VIII (Gaetani).

1294-1534. THE SECULARIZED PAPACY. Absorption in secular politics to the exclusion of spiritual leadership.

1294-1303. BONIFACE VIII (Gaetani). Surpassed all his colleagues in the Sacred College as lawyer, diplomat, and man of affairs. A skeptic in religion, but a believer in amulets and magic, well-read in the pagan classics, he was the last pope to claim the universal authority of the papacy as asserted by Gregory VII and maintained by Innocent III. Addicted to low company, he was not as vicious as contemporary propaganda painted him. Handsome and vain, he substituted on occasion imperial dress and regalia for papal vestments (*I am pope, I am Caesar*). Rude beyond belief, domineering and well-hated, his chief aim was the aggrandizement of the Gaetani family. An intelligent patron of architecture and art: Giotto in Rome.

1295. Bent on regaining Sicily for the papacy, Boniface continued the support of the Angevin claimant, Charles II of Naples, arranged the **Peace of 1295,** by which James of Aragon exchanged Sicily for the investiture of Sardinia and Corsica, and the extinction of French claims in Aragon.

1296. The **Bull *Clericis laicos*,** designed to bring the kings of France and England to accept papal intervention, forbade the payment of taxes by the clergy to lay rulers without papal consent (a vain attempt to maintain a medieval custom in the face of rising national states). Philip IV of France answered with an embargo on the export of bullion; Edward I of England with outlawry of the clergy; both were supported by public opinion expressed in their national assemblies (pp. 215, 247-248).

1297. Angered by the Colonna, their insistence on the validity of Celestine V's election, their appeal to a general council, and their support of the Aragonese in Sicily, the pope began a veritable crusade which exiled the Colonna (Palestrina, the family stronghold, razed).

Recognition of the rights of Robert (second son of Charles II) in Naples. Beginning of the formation of a Gaetani state as a threat to the barons.

1300. The **GREAT JUBILEE,** zenith of the pontificate, one of the magnificent pageants of the medieval Papacy, managed with tremendous pomp by Boniface; huge donations (raked over public tables by papal "croupiers"); the proceeds intended by Boniface for the second Gaetani state to be formed in Tuscany and for the subjection of Sicily.

1302. Charles of Valois' failure to dislodge Frederick, the Aragonese claimant in Sicily, forced Boniface to the **Peace of 1302** which ended the War of the Sicilian Vespers, left Frederick king, and provided for the ultimate reunion of Naples and Sicily under the Aragonese.

1302-1303. Boniface's defeat and humiliation by the national states.

The **Bull *Unam sanctam*** (1302) marked the climax of papal claims to superiority over national states and lay rulers. Philip IV (his appeal for a compromise rejected) dispatched Nogaret to bring the pope to French soil for trial by a general council called by Philip.

1303, Sept. 8. The **"Terrible Day at Anagni."** Nogaret and Sciarra Colonna penetrated to the papal apartment, found Boniface in bed, threatened him with death, tried to force his resignation, took him prisoner. Faced with a public reaction against them as foreigners, Nogaret and Colonna fled, and Boniface died shortly of humiliation. The papacy, so lately triumphant over the empire, found itself defeated by a new force, national feeling supporting national monarchy, and the defeat vindicated the claim of the new states to tax clerics and to maintain criminal jurisdiction over them.

1303-1304. **BENEDICT XI.** Exiled to Perugia by the anarchy in Rome, he promulgated a bull condemning the principals in the affair at Anagni, and died almost immediately (reputedly by poison). The cardinals, almost evenly divided for and against Boniface, after a conclave of ten months, chose a compromise candidate, the French archbishop of Bordeaux, Bertrand de Got (supposed to be a bitter foe of Philip IV), who assumed the name

1305-1314. **CLEMENT V.** Clement never entered Italy and became friendly (bribed?) to Philip. The **Synod of Vienne** (1311-1312) exonerated Boniface's memory despite Philip's pressure, but Philip had his way with the Templars (1307). Italy was in anarchy, but Clement was bent on returning there as soon as he had made peace between England and France and launched a crusade. To escape Philip, Clement established the papal **court at Avignon**. (Avignon was an enclave in the Venaissin, which was papal territory). (*Cont. p. 308.*)

(1) The Norman Kingdom in South Italy and Sicily, 1103-1194

1103-1154. The Norman count **Roger II of Sicily** (1103-1154) succeeded the Norman duke William of Apulia (1111-1127) and assumed the title of king of Sicily, Apulia, and Capua with the approval of anti-Pope Anacletus II. Excommunicated by Pope Innocent II (1139) for his alliance with Anacletus, he defeated Innocent (1140), took him prisoner, and forced recognition of his title. By skillful diplomacy he prevented a joint invasion of Sicily by the Greek and Roman emperors. Planning a Mediterranean commerical empire, Roger established an extensive North African holding (at its maximum, 1153).

1154-1166. **William I,** continuing Roger's policy, defeated (1156) the Byzantine allies of Pope Adrian IV and compelled Adrian to recognize his title in Sicily, Apulia, Naples, Amalfi, and Salerno. He supported Pope Alexander III against Frederick I.

1166-1189. **WILLIAM II** continued this policy, but as he planned a Mediterranean empire and wished a free hand, he welcomed the marriage (1186) of Constance (Roger II's daughter), his heiress, to the future emperor Henry VI. He himself married Joan, sister of King Richard I of England, and intended to lead the Third Crusade as part of his imperial plans. On his death,

1190-1194. **Tancred of Lecce** (son of Roger, duke of Apulia, the brother of Constance) led a vigorous native resistance to the emperor Henry VI (king, 1194-1197) with the support of the pope and Richard I. Henry reduced Sicily, southern Italy, and part of Tuscany, with the aid of Pisa and Genoa, retained the Matildine lands in central Italy, organized an imperial administration of his holdings, and planned a great empire with Italy as its base. Purely Norman rule ended with Tancred.

The Norman kingship in southern Italy and Sicily was theocratic, on Byzantine lines; the administration was an efficient, departmentalized bureaucracy. Tremendous prosperity and efficient taxation made the Sicilian monarchs perhaps the richest in Europe. Dealing with a cosmopolitan kingdom containing Italian, Greek, and Saracen elements, and needing settlers, the Norman rulers practiced a tolerant eclecticism which provided for wide racial divergences in law, religion, and culture.

Roger II's cosmopolitan court and generous patronage of the learned produced a brilliant circle including the Arab geographer **Edrisi, Eugenius,** the translator of Ptolemy's *Optics,* and **Henry Aristippus,** translator of Plato's *Phaedo* and Book IV of Aristotle's *Meteorologica.*

(2) The Development of Italian Towns

No continuous tradition of medieval and classical town government in Italy can be traced. The post-Carolingian anarchy left defense in local hands and rural refuges and town walls were the work of local co-operation. The bishops in Lombardy, traditional guardians of their flocks, with large episcopal and comital powers delegated from the monarchs, played a decisive rôle in communal organization for defense (e.g. Bergamo, 904). The first cases of true urban autonomy were in Amalfi, Benevento, and Naples (1000-1034), a development cut short by the advent of the Normans.

The great urban evolution took place in the

north, and particularly in Lombardy, where sworn municipal leagues and urban associations appeared (probably) in the 10th century. In these cities the nobles (since ancient times town-dwellers for at least part of each year) played an important part, though they were always balanced by the bishops. The emperors, busy in Germany or preoccupied with the popes, made wide grants of regalian rights over local coinage, tolls, customs dues, police powers, and justice (diplomas of Henry I, Lothair II, and Conrad II); there were also considerable delegations of local episcopal powers. Full-fledged communes appeared in the 11th and 12th centuries (e.g. Asti, 1093; Pavia, 1105; Florence, 1138; and Rome itself, by papal charter, 1188). Expansion in the great maritime and commercial republics was rapid (e.g. Pisa's new walls, 1081; Florence's second wall, 1172-1174; Venetian expansion in the Adriatic after the capture of Bari from the Saracens, 1002).

As a result of revolt and negotiation the towns of Lombardy were largely self-governing communes by the opening of the 12th century, and the consulate or its equivalent was in full activity by the end of the century. Typical town organization: an assembly (legislation, declaration of war and peace, etc.); the consuls, core of the magistracy, usually four to twenty in number, serving a one-year term, and chosen from the leading families; the town council and minor magistrates.

The development of the merchant and craft guilds led to a vigorous class warfare as the rising bourgeoisie asserted itself, and brought in the podestate (the *podestà*), a kind of local dictator, during the last quarter of the 12th century.

In Tuscany the towns treated the counts as the Lombards had treated their bishops. Venice, thanks to her peculiar circumstances, evolved a unique commercial oligarchy.

(3) The Rise of Venice, to 1310

Fugitives from the Huns found refuge among the fishing villages of the lagoons; the permanent establishment of Venice seems to date from the Lombard invasion (568). Venetian aid to Belisarius began the formal connection between Venice and Constantinople and a (largely) theoretical connection with the Eastern Roman Empire. The *tribuni maiores* (a central governing committee of the islands) dated from c. 568.

687. Election of the first doge. A salt monopoly and salt-fish trade were the sources of the first prosperity of Venice. Two great parties: (1) pro-Byzantine aristocrats favoring an hereditary doge; (2) democrats friendly to the Roman church and (later) the Franks. Venice offered asylum to the exarch of Ravenna flee-ing from Liutprand, and gained trading rights with Ravenna. When Charlemagne ordered the pope to expel the Venetians from the Pentapolis and threatened the settlement in the lagoons, Venice turned again to Constantinople, and in a treaty

810. Charlemagne and Nicephorus recognized Venice as Byzantine territory and accepted her mainland trading rights.

1000. After a 200-year expansion in the Adriatic, Venice completely reduced the Dalmatian pirates, and the doge took the title of duke of Dalmatia. Venice was mistress of the sea route to the Holy Land (commemorated in the wedding of the doge and the sea).

1032. The aristocratic effort to establish an hereditary doge was defeated. Establishment of a council and senate.

1043. The construction of the **church of St. Mark** begun; one of the most notable and influential examples of Byzantine architecture in the west.

1063. The first three crusades established Venetian trading rights in a number of Levantine ports (e.g. Sidon, 1102, Tyre, 1123) and founded the power of a wealthy ruling class. A war with the Eastern Empire (financed by the first known government bonds) was unsuccessful, and led to the institution of a deliberative assembly of 480 members (the germ of the **great council**).

1171. Appointment of the doge was transferred to this council, a complete triumph for the commercial aristocracy.

1198. A coronation oath (in varying terms) began to be exacted of the doge.

1204. In the **FOURTH CRUSADE** (p. 275) Venice gained the Cyclades, Sporades, Propontis, the Black Sea coasts, Thessalian littoral, and control of the Morea. She administered this vast empire on a kind of feudal tenure, portioning it out to families charged with defense of the seaways. Venice had also gained a further foothold in Syrian ports.

From this period dates a great epoch of building and increasing oligarchic pressure as the government began to become a closed corporation of leading families.

1253-1299. The STRUGGLE WITH GENOA for the Black Sea and Levantine trade. The feud of Genoa and Venice was ancient, and trouble began at Acre (1253). The first war with Genoa ended in the complete defeat (1258) of the Genoese.

1261. The Greeks seized Constantinople during the absence of the Venetian fleet; they favored Genoa, turning over Galata to her.

1264. The Venetians destroyed the Genoese fleet at **Trepani**, and soon returned to their old status in Constantinople.

1289-1299. The **advance of the Turks** (capture of Tripoli, 1289, of Acre, 1291) led Venice to a treaty with the new masters of Asia Minor. Genoa met this by an effort to close the Dardanelles, and won a victory (1294) at Alexandretta; Venice forced the Dardanelles and sacked Galata. The Genoese defeated the Venetians at **Curzola** (1299), but Matteo Visconti negotiated an honorable peace (1299) for them.

1284. The **first ducat** was coined.

1290-1300. The perfection of the great galleys. Establishment of the **Flanders galleys** (1317).

1297. The **great council** was restricted in membership to those who had been members within the preceding four years. A commission added other names and then the council was closed to new members (except by heredity). In effect this excluded a large section of the citizens from any share of the government in favor of a narrow, hereditary, commercial oligarchy. Popular reaction led to a revolt (1300), the leaders of which were hanged.

1310. **Tiepolo's rebellion,** the only serious uprising in Venetian history, was crushed. This seems to have been a patrician protest against the extreme oligarchy, and led to the creation of an emergency committee of public safety, the **council of ten,** which soon became permanent (1335).

The **Venetian government** thus consisted of: the great council (i.e. the patrician caste); the senate (a deliberative and legislative body dealing with foreign affairs, peace, war, finances, trade); the council of ten, a secret, rapidly acting body concerned with morals, conspiracy, European affairs, finance, the war department, which could override the senate; the *collegio* or cabinet (the administrative branch); the doge and his council, which, sitting with the ten, made the council of seventeen.   (*Cont. p. 322.*)

e. FRANCE, 987-1314

(*From p. 173*)

[*For a complete list of the kings of France see Appendix VII.*]

987-1328. DIRECT LINE OF THE CAPETIAN HOUSE (the dynasty continued until 1792).

987-996. HUGH (called *Capet,* from the cloak he wore as abbot of St. Martin de Tours). At Hugh's accession the kingship was at its nadir; such power as Hugh had was feudal; the royal title meant little more than an hegemony over a feudal patchwork, an ill-defined area called France, and the prestige of ancient monarchical tradition sanctified by ecclesiastical consecration. Hugh's own feudal domain consisted of the Île de France (extending from Laon to Orleans, with its center at Paris) and a few scattered holdings. The great barons of the so-called royal fiefs recognized Hugh as their suzerain, but never did homage nor rendered service. Hugh's special interest was to maintain his control over his chief resources, the archbishopric of Reims and the great bishoprics (Sens, Tours, Bourges) and abbeys of the Île de France, and to wean northeastern France away from the Carolingian and imperial interest. Despite clerical pressure, he avoided submission to imperial suzerainty, a policy that facilitated the demarcation between France and Germany. In defiance of pope and emperor he forced his own candidate into the archbishopric of Reims. Hugh crowned his son shortly after his own coronation and began a practice (*co-optation*) which the early Capetians continued (until Philip II no longer felt it necessary), thus insuring the succession, and weakening the principle (dear to the feudality) of elective kingship.

996-1031. ROBERT II (the Pious), an active, well-educated, polished, amiable ruler, a good soldier, supported by the duke of Normandy in constant wars against his neighbors, and by the religious houses of Burgundy in attacks on the dukes of Burgundy. The duchy of Burgundy escheated to the crown, and was given to Robert, a younger son. Robert the Pious, like his father, supported the Cluniac reformers. Minor territorial additions signify the revival of royal power.

1031-1060. HENRY I, an active, brave, indefatigable ruler, whose reign nevertheless marked the lowest ebb of the Capetian fortunes. The rebellion of his brother Robert, supported by Eudes, count of Chartres and Troyes, was put down with the aid of the duke of Normandy, and Robert was pacified by the grant of the duchy of Burgundy (which continued in his family until 1361). Henry supported the duke of Normandy (1047), but led a coalition against him two years later, and was defeated. He boycotted the pope and his synod at Reims, and, like his son and successor, opposed the reform movement in the church. The *prévôts* were introduced to administer justice and taxation in the royal lands. The kingdom of Burgundy passed (1032) to the empire.

1035-1066. RISE AND EXPANSION OF NORMANDY. William I became duke (1035) and until 1047 faced a series of baronial revolts. With the aid of his feudal suzerain, King Henry of France, William defeated his revolting barons (1047) and razed their castles. The union of Normandy and Maine was completed (1063) against powerful opposition from the counts of Anjou. William's alliance with Henry was broken (1053), and Henry ravaged the heart of Normandy (1058). Normandy was now a fully developed feudal state under firm ducal control. Military service, assessed in knights' fees, was attached to specific pieces of land, no castles could be built or maintained without ducal license. Private warfare and blood feud were strictly limited. Coinage was a ducal monopoly. The legal jurisdiction of the duke was wide, local government was under the duke's representatives (the *vicomtes*), who commanded the local forces, guarded the castles, did justice, collected the revenue (a large part of which was cash). The Church had been revivified, but here too the duke was supreme, naming bishops, most of the abbots, and sitting in provincial synods.

Norman **relations with England** had grown closer, and this tendency culminated (1002) in the marriage of Duke Robert's sister Emma with King Ethelred. The son of this marriage, Edward the Confessor, educated largely at the Norman court, came to the throne of England (1042), and died without heirs (1066). The witan at once elected Harold, Earl Godwin's son. **William I** of Normandy with a volunteer force (perhaps 5000-6000) collected from Normandy and the Continent, defeated Harold in the **Battle of Hastings** (Oct. 14) and was crowned king of England on Christmas Day (p. 184). The *Bayeux Tapestry* forms a unique and probably contemporary record of this expedition.

1060-1108. PHILIP I, enormously fat, but active and vigorous; excommunicated and unpopular with the clergy as the result of an adulterous marriage (1092) and because of his hostility to clerical reform. He defeated (1079) Duke William of Normandy (the Conqueror) and steadily supported **Robert Curthose,** William's son, against Anglo-Norman pressure. Systematic expansion of the resources of his house, and regular annexations to its domains in the face of stubborn feudal resistance. The *Chanson de Roland,* the national epic of France, was probably composed during this reign.

The growth of feudalism tended to diminish anarchy and to improve the general security of life, and ultimately led to decisive economic recovery in western Europe, a trend toward urban economy, and the emergence of a bourgeoisie who were beginning to accumulate capital. This development was a determining factor in the economic, social, and monarchical evolution of the 13th century. The **Peace of God** in the 10th century, and the **Truce of God** (first mentioned, 1027), promoted by the Church with Capetian support, were significant rather than effective attempts to reduce warfare.

1108-1328. A period in which the Capetians reduced the great feudatories north of the Loire and began the transformation of the vague ecclesiastical, judicial, and military rights derived from Carolingian tradition into royal powers over the French people as a whole.

1108-1137. LOUIS VI (the Fat). A brave soldier, of tremendous physique, intelligent, affable, avaricious, but liked by the peasantry, commercial class, and clergy, the first popular Capetian. Consolidation of his Norman frontier (wars with Henry I of England: 1109-1112; 1116-1120), and steady reduction of his lesser vassals as far as the Loire. His charters to colonizers (*hôtes*) of waste lands, and frequent if inconsistent support of the communes, especially on the lands of the Church and the baronage, began the long alliance of the Capetians with bourgeois interests; Louis's *charter of Lorris,* widely copied in town charters, was a significant sign of the great **urban development** setting in all over Europe in this period. As protector of the Church, Louis gained a foothold in the lands of his vassals. Careers at court were opened to talented clergy and bourgeois: great influence of **Suger** (see below). Louis's compromise with the Church over feudal patronage and investiture initiated the king of France's effective rôle as *eldest son of the Church.* He was the first Capetian to intervene effectively outside his own feudal lands. He defeated the alliance of Henry I of England with the Emperor Henry V, and stopped (1124) a German invasion. The marriage (1137) of his son Louis to Eleanor, heiress of William X of Aquitaine (i.e. Guienne [*Aquitania Secunda*] and Gascony), marked the Capetian effort to balance the Anglo-Norman menace in the north by additions of territory south of the Loire. The Anglo-Norman danger had appeared in aggravated form when in 1129 Geoffrey became count of Anjou, Maine, and Touraine. He had in 1128 married Matilda (daughter of Henry I of England), and proceeded (1135) to conquer Normandy.

DEVELOPMENT OF ROYAL ADMINISTRATION under the early Capetians. The court of the king, usually known as the *curia regis,* consisting as it did of magnates, royal vassals, and court officials (mainly chosen from the baronage), was essentially feudal in spirit and tradition. Meeting at royal summons and relatively frequently, its early duties were undifferentiated, its functions judicial, advisory, legislative. The royal administration was in control of the great officers of the crown whose aim was to concentrate power in their own

France: The Capetian Kings (987–1328)

(From p. 171)

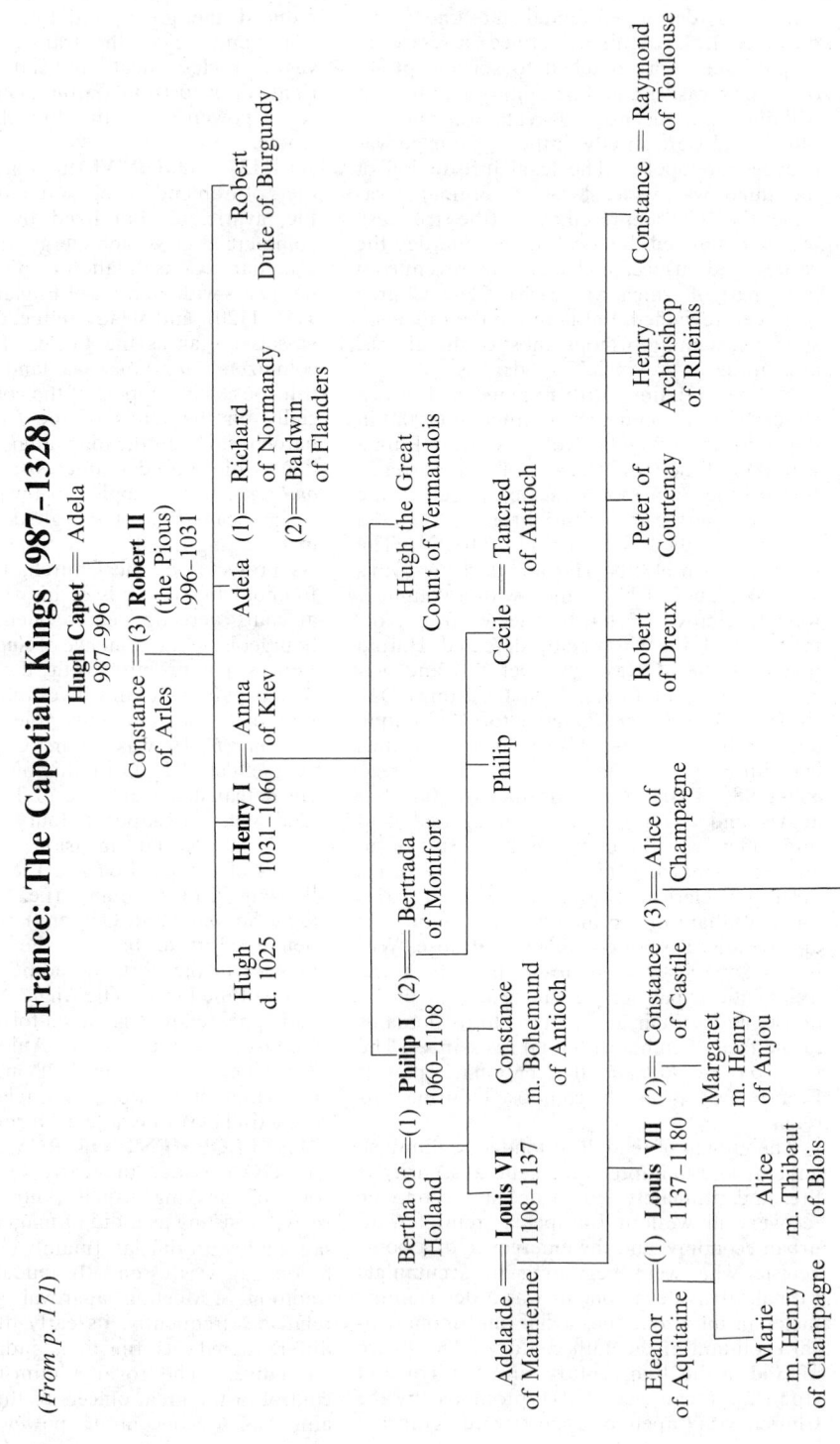

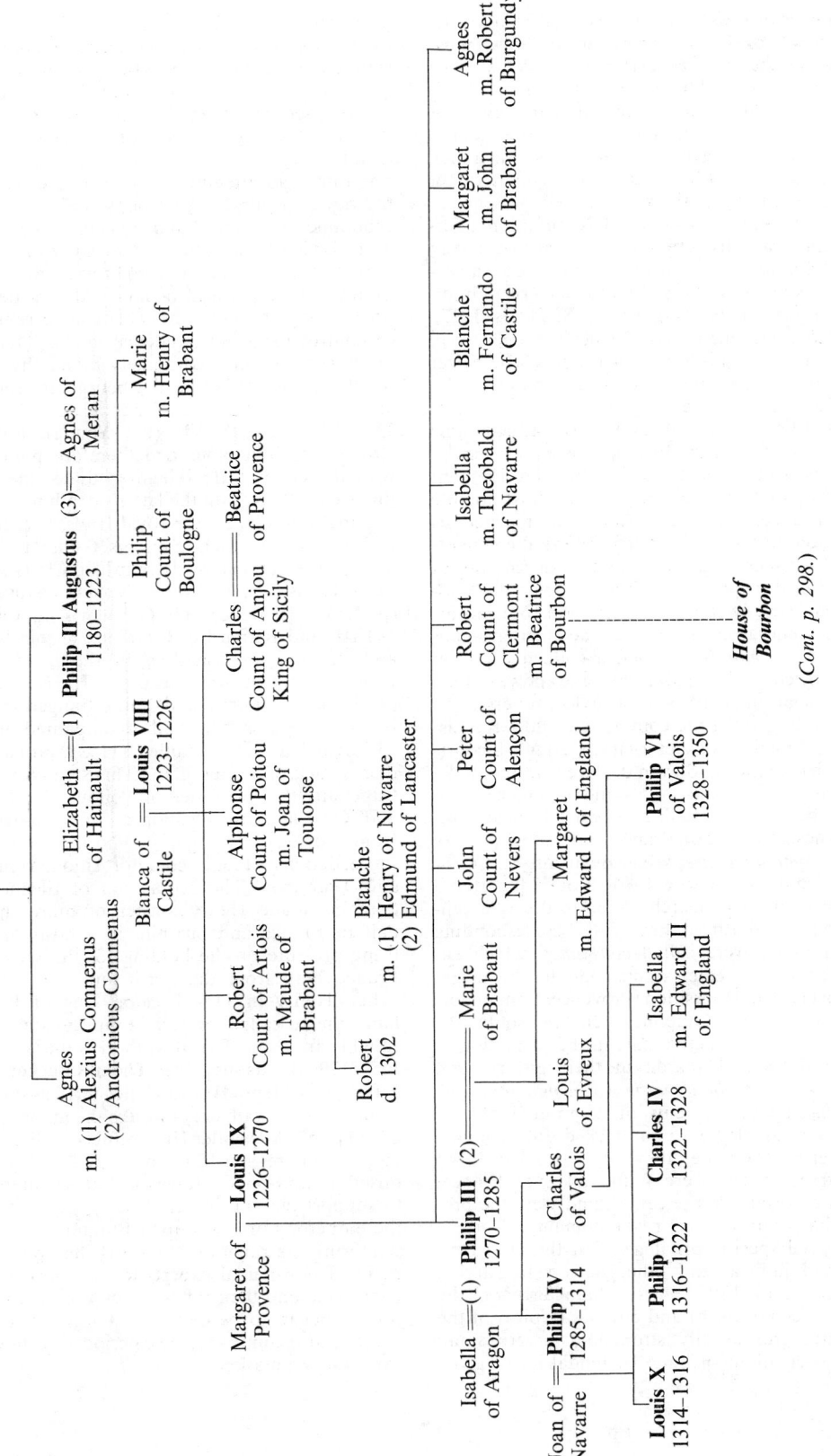

(Cont. p. 298.)

hands, a process which culminated in a virtual monopoly of such power by the **Garlande family** early in the 12th century. Louis VI, after a struggle (1128–1130), terminated their dominance, and thenceforth the Capetians relied increasingly on lesser and more docile nobles, clerics, and bourgeois men of affairs. Such men were career men devoted to the crown rather than to feudal ambitions, and their presence in the *curia regis* began the differentiation of its functions and its subjection to royal rather than feudal influences. Most notable of these career-ists was **Suger**, Louis's old tutor, a cleric of humble origin, who became abbot of St. Denis (1122). An able statesman, his influence was decisive in the reign of Louis and his son Louis VII. Suger began (c. 1136) the new abbey church of St. Denis, the first edifice wholly Gothic in design.

1100–1400.   RISE OF TOWNS. The economic revival of western Europe was paralleled by a resumption of town life and development throughout the west, which was most notable in France, where the movement reached its apogee in the 12th century, before the consistent advance of the Capetian monarchy began to retard its progress. Types of town development were by no means uniform, but important general categories can be distinguished: (1) The *commune* proper, a collective person endowed with legal rights and powers (e.g. financial, judicial), able to hold property. As a feudal person the commune could have vassals, render and exact homage, establish courts for its tenants, and even declare war and make treaties. Symbols of its independence were the belfry, town hall, and seal. Typical communes of northern France and Flanders were the *communes jurées* (e.g. Beauvais, St. Quentin [chartered before 1080], Rouen [chartered 1145], and Amiens [chartered in the 12th century]); in southern France the corresponding communes were called *consulates*, which enjoyed even greater rights than in the north, especially in Roussillon, Provence, Languedoc, Gascony, and Guienne. In the south the nobles took an active part in the formation of consulates and shared in their government. (2) *Villes de bourgeoisie* (or *communes surveillées*) had elements of communal powers in varying degrees, but lacked full political independence (i.e. they were privileged but unfree). They were found all over France, but especially in the center, and were the prevailing type on the royal domain. Citizens enjoyed specific privileges, but the crown retained judicial and other powers in varying degrees. (3) *Villes neuves* (characteristic of the commercial north) and *bastides* (typical of the south, and usually strongholds) were small rural creations of kings or feudal lords, given

a charter from the first, establishing their status. (4) *Peasant associations* and village federations (influential in the north) which sought to define and guarantee the rights of their citizens. Governmentally town development seems to have been hardly the result of conscious effort to introduce a new political dispensation. It was rather an attempt to establish and define the rights of non-feudal groups, and aimed at economic prosperity and personal security. The movement constantly enjoyed royal support, but royal policy toward it was governed by immediate political or financial considerations, and the crown always strove to reduce or control town independence in the interest of its own power. Ultimately monarchy triumphed, but not before the bourgeois groups and the serfs had gained substantial advantages.

1137–1180.   LOUIS VII (the Young), not a strong king, but pious and therefore popular with the clergy. He remained under the influence of Suger until the latter's death in 1151. A papal interdict on the royal lands, resulting from Louis's insistence on his feudal rights, led to intervention by Bernard of Clairvaux.

1147. Louis inspired the **Second Crusade** (p. 275). He induced the German king, Conrad III, and Bernard of Clairvaux to join him and, leaving the kingdom in the hands of Suger, he set out for the east. He returned (1149) beaten, humiliated, and estranged from his wife Eleanor, who had accompanied him. The marriage was annulled (1152), probably due to lack of a male heir. This step cost the Capetians the territories of Poitou, Guienne, and Gascony, for Eleanor at once married Henry, duke of Normandy, who in 1151 had succeeded his father as count of Anjou, Maine, and Touraine. The acquisition of Eleanor's domains made Henry master of more than half of France and put him in a position to bring pressure on the holdings of the king of France both from the north and the south. When Henry in 1154 became king of England, the so-called Angevin Empire extended roughly from the Tweed to the Pyrenees.

1165–1170. Louis supported **Thomas Becket** (p. 210) against Henry II of England, and was saved from Henry's wrath only through the mediation of the pope, Alexander III, a refugee in France against whom the Emperor Frederick had raised an anti-pope. It was in Louis's interest to support the anti-imperial party, because of the emperor's pressure upon Burgundy.

During the reign of Louis VII the appointment of non-feudal experts to the *curia regis* continued, and their influence on the administration began to be decisive. Grant of town charters also continued. The period was, moreover, one of marked

Cultural progress: The guild of masters (germ of the University of Paris) was recognized (c. 1170) and a number of eminent scholars appeared on the scene: **St. Bernard of Clairvaux** (1091-1153), member of the Cistercian Order, a great preacher, fervent reformer, and dominant spiritual figure of the west; **Roscellinus** (died c. 1121), champion of nominalism; **Anselm** (d. 1109), abbot of Bec, later archbishop of Canterbury, champion of realism; **Peter Abélard** (d. 1142), eminent master at Paris (after about 1115), supporter of conceptualism, a middle ground in the great controversy over universals. Abélard's *sic et non* presented without solution the conflicting theological arguments on 158 important problems. **John of Salisbury** (d. 1180), bishop of Chartres, favored the humanistic rather than the dialectical approach to knowledge. Before the rise of the University of Paris, Chartres was the cultural center where Ptolemaic astronomy and Aristotelian logic were taught. **Thierry of Chartres** put forward a rational explanation of the creation, within the Mosaic framework, as well as a cosmology based on the Aristotelian pattern. **Peter Lombard,** bishop of Paris (1159), in his *Sententiae* offered a cautious solution of theological and philosophical problems that became a standard text of the Paris schools. In literature the period produced the *chansons de geste* such as *Chanson de Roland,* the epics of poets like Chrétien de Troyes, and the troubadour lyrics.

1180-1223. PHILIP II (Augustus). He began his rule at fifteen and had no time for education (he knew no Latin). A calculating realist, perhaps the outstanding figure of his time, he was the consolidator of the monarchy and the founder of the organized state. As the "maker of Paris" he paved the streets, walled the city, and began the building of the Louvre.

1180. A six-year alliance with King Henry II of England enabled Philip to defeat Philip of Artois and the counts of Champagne, to crush a baronial league against him, and to gain recognition for his title to Artois and Vermandois. Philip intrigued with the sons of Henry, welcomed the rebellious Richard (1187), and, joining him, defeated Henry (1189), who died the same year.

1191. Philip, under pressure of public opinion, joined King Richard on the **Third Crusade;** eclipsed by Richard, he quarreled with him, returned to France, and intrigued against him with John during his (Richard's) captivity (1192-1194).

1194-1199. Richard, in a pitiless war of vengeance, built Château Gaillard on the Seine and restored the Angevin power in northern France.

1198. Excommunicated by Pope Innocent III for his divorce of Ingeborg of Denmark, Philip was forced by public opinion to a reconciliation, but sharply refused Innocent's offer of mediation with John, who succeeded Richard (1199).

1202-1204. The final duel with John for, and conquest of, the Angevin lands north of the Loire. On King John's refusal to stand trial as Philip's vassal on charges by Philip's vassal, Hugh of Lusignan, Philip declared John's French fiefs forfeited (1203), and supported John's nephew, Arthur of Brittany. The murder of Arthur (1203) cost John his French support, Château Gaillard was lost (1204), Normandy and Poitou followed, and Philip emerged master of the Angevin lands north of the Loire.

New royal officials, the *baillis* (*sénéchaux* in the south), paid professionals (often Roman lawyers), superseded the now feudalized *prévôts* as the chief local administrators (financial, judicial, military) on the Capetian lands (c. 1190). In the course of the 13th century baillis began to be assigned to regular districts (*baillages*), but they continued responsible to and removable by the king. As the royal domain expanded, royal administration was extended to it, and the foundation laid for a national, specialized, professional system.

Philip, henceforth master in the north, left the conquest of the south to his successors and devoted himself to statecraft rather than war. He played the barons off against each other, used his position as protector of the Church to weaken them further, and sought the support of the towns and rich bourgeoisie as a balance to the feudality. Part of this process involved the systematization of the royal finance, the regular exaction of feudal aids and obligations due to the crown as well as the systematic collection of customs, tolls, fines, and fees, though as yet there was no such thing as taxation in the modern sense. The levy of the Saladin tithe (1188) was, however, a forerunner of true taxation. Philip's reign also saw the formation of a semi-permanent royal army.

1208-1213. The Albigensian-Waldensian Crusade. The Albigensians (Catharists of Albi) and the Waldensians (followers of Peter Waldo) represented originally a reaction of the lower classes against clerical corruption, but the movement was soon espoused by the nobles, who saw in it a chance to appropriate church lands. Innocent III, after a vain appeal to Philip, proclaimed a crusade against these heretics. Philip took no direct part in the action, but allowed his northern vassals to begin the penetration of the south and thus prepare the way for the advance of the Capetian power.

Simon de Montfort (the elder), a baron of the Île de France, emerged as the leader of the crusaders. His **victory at Muret** (1213) sealed the fate of the brilliant Provençal culture, of the leading southern barons, and of the heretics. After a long chapter of horrors the conquest was finally completed in a campaign by Louis VIII (1226). In the reign of Louis IX the county of Toulouse passed under Capetian administration and the royal domain was extended to the Mediterranean.

1213–1214. The great **anti-Capetian Alliance** (John of England, Emperor Otto IV, the counts of Boulogne and Flanders, and most of the feudality of Flanders, Belgium, and Lorraine).

1214, July 27. BATTLE OF BOUVINES. Philip, in alliance with Emperor Frederick II, defeated the coalition near Tournai and thereby established the French monarchy in the first rank of the European powers, at the same time ruining John of England, assuring Frederick II of the imperial crown, and bringing Flanders under French influence. Militarily speaking the battle was a triumph of Philip's professional cavalry and bourgeois militia over the older infantry.

1223–1226. LOUIS VIII, a pallid reflection of his father. The first Capetian king not crowned in his father's lifetime.

1224. Temporary conquest of the lands between the Loire and the Garonne; the English soon regained all but Poitou, the Limousin, and Perigord (1225).

1226. Renewal of the Albigensian Crusade and Louis's **conquest of the south.** Louis began the dangerous practice of bestowing great fiefs as appanages on the princes of the blood, a practice which later had almost fatal consequences to the monarchy (the case of Burgundy).

1226–1270. LOUIS IX (St. Louis, canonized 1297). The most chivalrous man of his age and the ideal medieval king. Handsome and lofty in character, Louis's careful education prepared him for a unique reign, in which ethics dominated policy. His justice won him national support and made him the arbiter of Europe. His reign was the golden age of medieval France.

1226–1234. Minority of Louis IX and regency of his able and devout mother, Blanche of Castile. With the support of the Church, the royal officials, and the people, Blanche was able to suppress a number of feudal rebellions (1226–1231). By the **treaty of Paris** (1129) Raymond of Toulouse surrendered, and his heiress was betrothed to Louis's brother, Alphonse. Louis himself was married to Margaret of Provence and thus began the severance of that province from the empire.

1233. As part of the campaign against heresy, Pope Gregory IX granted independent authority to investigate heresy to the **Dominicans,** requiring the bishops to co-operate with them. Louis later supported the **Inquisition,** despite episcopal objections.

1241. Louis induced the Emperor Frederick II to release the prelates and delegates captured off Genoa while en route to a synod at Rome but, without directly attacking the Church, he associated himself with Frederick's grievances against the pope and refused to intervene against the emperor (1247).

1242. Invasion of France by Henry III of England, in coalition with the rebellious feudal lords of southern France. The whole movement collapsed and was followed by the final submission of Aquitaine and Toulouse (1243).

1244. Louis took the Cross, against his mother's advice, and sailed on his first crusade (1248). His aim was to free Palestine by the capture of Egypt, but the expedition was poorly managed, Louis was captured (1250), and most of his army was put to the sword. Louis himself was ransomed and returned to France.

1258. The **treaty of Corbeil,** representing a peaceful adjustment of conflicting claims between France and Aragon, to the advantage of France. Louis's son, Philip, was betrothed to Isabella of Aragon.

1259. Treaty of Paris. Louis, in the interest of amity, yielded Perigord and the Limousin to the king of England, despite protests from both provinces. In return he received the renunciation of English claims to Normandy, Maine, Poitou. Henceforth Guienne became distinct from Aquitaine. This pacific gesture displeased opinion in both countries and weakened the French position in the south as the Hundred Years' War approached.

1265. Louis permitted his brother, Charles of Anjou, to accept the crown of Sicily, a step which later involved France in Italian problems, with decisive consequences.

1270. Louis's second crusade. Probably influenced by Charles of Anjou, who cherished far-reaching Mediterranean ambitions, Louis set out for Tunis. He died of pestilence without accomplishing anything.

Louis's reign was marked by rigorous insistence on inherent royal rights even at the expense of the Church, and despite episcopal protests. Royal justice was notably efficient and was constantly expanded. The right of appeal from feudal to royal courts was clearly established. The old *curia regis* had already become somewhat differentiated: a *chambre des comptes* and a *parlement* (i.e. high court) were already recognizable. Louis introduced the *enquêteurs,* itinerant investigators, to supervise the baillis and sénéchaux, but he made few other administrative innovations. Many of his diplomats, baillis, and other officials were chosen from the royal household, notably from the so-called *chevaliers du roi,* and from the clergy. Assemblies of royal vassals, irregularly held, gave such "national" sanction as there was to royal policy. Louis was the first king to issue *ordonnances* (i.e. legislation) for the whole realm on his sole authority. By ordonnance he outlawed private warfare, the carrying of arms, and trial by battle as part of the royal judicial process, and extended the royal coinage to the whole realm. By 1270 the communal movement was already in decline and the crown profited by enforcing a more rigorous control over the towns. Only one new charter (to the port of Aigues Mortes) was granted during the reign. The bourgeois oligarchy of the towns got on increasingly bad terms with the lower orders, often reducing the town finances to chaos. Louis took advantage of this state of affairs to introduce a town audit (1262). The country at large was prosperous in this period, but the financing of the two crusades and of the grandiose schemes of Charles of Anjou led to complaints that royal taxation was leading to bankruptcy and formed a bad precedent for Philip IV.

A brilliant **cultural advance** accompanied the general material and political progress of the time of Philip II and Louis IX; perfection of the **French Gothic:** Cathedral of Chartres (c. 1194, Romanesque and Gothic); Amiens (c. 1200); Reims (1210); Louis IX's *Sainte Chapelle;* progress of naturalism in Gothic sculpture. **University of Paris:** foundation charter (1200); regulations of Innocent III (1215); endowment of Robert de Sorbon (hence Sorbonne) in 1257. Advance of **vernacular literature:** Villehardouin's (d. c. 1218) *Conquête de Constantinople* (the first vernacular historical writing); **Chrétien de Troyes** and the Arthurian romances; Goliardic verse (with pagan touch); *fabliaux* (risqué, semi-realistic bourgeois tales); *Aucassin et Nicolette* (a *chante fable* marked by irony and realism); **Jean de Meun's** (d. 1305) completion of William of Lorris's *Roman de la Rose* (a satire on the follies of all classes, especially women and clergy); **Jean de Joinville's** *Histoire du roi Saint Louis* (1309), the first vernacular classic of lay biography. Paris the center of **13th century philosophy:** harmonization of the Greek philosophy, especially Aristotle (newly recovered during the Renaissance of the 12th century in Latin translations, with Christian orthodoxy: **Vincent of Beauvais's** (d. 1264) *Speculum Maius* (a compendium of

contemporary knowledge); **Albertus Magnus** (a German, d. 1280), chief of the great Dominican teachers in Paris; **Thomas Aquinas** (an Italian, d. 1274), the pupil of Albertus Magnus. Thomas Aquinas' *Summa Theologiae* reconciled reason and religion, completed the integration of the classical learning and the Christian theology, and remains to this day the basis of all Catholic theological teaching. Also at Paris was **Jordanus Nemorarius** (d. 1237), a German, who wrote arithmetical and geometrical treatises as well as working in physics.

1270-1285. PHILIP III (the Bold), a hasty, ill-balanced king, victim of his favorites. The death of Philip's uncle, Alphonse of Poitiers, brought Languedoc under royal sway and established the royal power firmly in southern France (1272). The walls of Carcassonne and Aigues Mortes were built, the latter place giving access to the Mediterranean. Unsuccessful candidacy (1273) of Charles of Anjou for the imperial crown. Crusade (1282) against the king of Aragon, Philip acting as papal champion against the successful rival of the house of Anjou in Sicily.

1281-1285. The pontificate of Martin IV brought to an end an anti-French period of papal policy; papal support of Charles of Anjou's ambitious dreams of Byzantine conquest until the **Sicilian Vespers** (p. 313). There followed another period of papal opposition to French ambitions.

1285-1314. PHILIP IV (the Fair). His reign had a distinctly modern flavor and was marked by ruthless expansion of the royal power and notable consolidation of the monarchy: royal finance superseded the feudal; Roman lawyers (trained at Bologna and Montpellier) rather than clerics dominated the government; papal pretensions were reduced and the national Church made virtually autonomous under royal domination.

1286. Edward I of England did homage for Guienne.

1293. Philip treacherously confiscated Gascony, which had been temporarily surrendered by Edward as a pledge, after a Gascon-Norman sea-fight.

1294-1298. War with Edward I over Guienne. Philip announced a war levy on the clergy and followed a protest with a violent antipapal pamphlet campaign. To finance the war Philip debased the coinage. He first made an **alliance with the Scots** (1295) and excluded English ships from all ports. In 1297 Edward invaded northern France, in alliance with the count of Flanders, but the war was brought to a close by a truce negotiated by Pope Boniface VIII.

1296-1303. Philip's **conflict with Pope Boni-**

face VIII, who put forward extreme claims to papal supremacy. The bull *Clericis laicos* (1296) forbade secular rulers to levy taxes on the clergy without papal consent. Philip retorted by forbidding the export of precious metals (a serious threat to the papal finances) and by a vigorous propaganda campaign. Boniface, engaged in a feud with the Colonna in Rome and absorbed in Sicilian affairs, gave way and practically annulled the bull (1297). But the great papal jubilee of 1300 was followed by a resumption of the quarrel, culminating in 1302 in the bull *Unam sanctam,* the most extreme assertion of the doctrine of papal theocracy in the Middle Ages. On the "Terrible Day" of Anagni (1303, p. 238), Nogaret and Sciarra Colonna attacked the papal palace, demanded the resignation of the pope, and had a violent scene with Boniface. The death of the aged pontiff followed shortly.

1302. The first well-authenticated convocation of the **estates-general,** including representatives of the towns in their feudal capacity. The meeting was called mainly to insure national support for the king's struggle with the pope.

1302, July 11. Battle of the Spurs (at Courtrai), brought about by the troubles in Flanders. Philip had antagonized the count of Flanders by his efforts to penetrate his territory, and the count had turned to Edward I of England for support. The Flemish nobility betrayed him (1300) and he lost both his liberty and his county. But French rule soon alienated the independent burghers and led to the massacre of the French (*Matin de Bruges*), followed by the **battle of Courtrai,** in which the burghers defeated the flower of the French chivalry.

1305. Election of Clement V (a Frenchman) as pope. Clement reluctantly accepted French royal domination, lingered in France after his election, and finally took up his residence at Avignon, thus beginning the **Babylonian** or **Avignonese Captivity** of the Papacy (p. 308). During the captivity (1305–1376) the French monarchy exercised an important influence on the Papacy. Clement was obliged to quash the bulls of Boniface, to absolve the assailants of Anagni, and to support Philip's suppression of the Knights Templar (see below). Philip may properly be called the founder of **Gallicanism** (i.e. of the autonomy of the French Church).

1306. The Jews were arrested, despoiled, and expelled from France.

1307. The **Order of the Knights Templar,** a rich, decadent organization which acted as banker to the popes and was a creditor of Philip, had become almost a state within the state. Philip now launched an attack upon it. He had its lands occupied by royal officers and its property sequestrated. The country was stirred up against the Order by a vigorous propaganda campaign and by an appeal to the estates-general (1308). Clement was obliged to co-operate and the Inquisition was made use of in the trial, the entire affair being conducted with unparalleled ruthlessness and horror (torture freely used to extort confessions).

1312. The Order of the Templars was abolished by the **Synod of Vienne.** Its property was transferred to the Hospitalers (except in Spain and in France, where it passed to the crown). Philip made the Temple treasury a section of the royal finance administration.

New economic and social alignments. The rapid expansion of France, and especially the wars of Philip III and Philip IV against England and Flanders, raised an acute financial problem. Philip IV tried every device to raise money (feudal *aides,* war levies to replace military service, tallage of towns, special levies on clergy and nobles, "loans" and "gifts," the *maltôte* or sales tax, debasement of the coinage, attacks upon the Jews and Templars), but without finding an adequate solution. It was this situation primarily that explains the emergence of the

Estates-General. Levies on the nobles and clergy had long been arranged in meetings of representatives of these two orders; by negotiations between the towns and the royal agents the burghers had been brought to contribute. Provincial estates had been called frequently during the 13th century. The convocation of the estates-general simply meant the substitution of national for provincial or local negotiation, and implied no principle of consent or control over royal taxation. The royal revenue was increased perhaps tenfold between the time of Louis IX and the time of Philip IV, but this meant overtaxation of all classes, harmful effects upon economic life, and estrangement of public opinion. Anti-tax leagues were organized and local assemblies drew up lists of grievances. Philip was obliged to call the estates-general again in 1314, but as the bourgeoisie and the nobility distrusted each other, no effective measures were taken and no permanent constitutional development took place. Characteristic of the period was

Pierre Dubois's *De Recuperatione Sanctae Terrae* (c. 1306), ostensibly an appeal to Philip to undertake a crusade to recover the Holy Land from the Saracens, in reality an extensive program of reform in the interests of stronger national monarchy. Dubois envisaged the formation of a European league to enforce peace through common military action and economic boycott, disputes between parties to be settled by judicial methods. He called also for a system of universal education and for the secularization of Church property.

(*Cont. p. 296.*)

f. THE IBERIAN PENINSULA, 1037-1284

(*From p. 178*)

(1) Moslem Spain

1037-1086. THE MULUK AL-TAWA'IF (i.e. *Party Kings*). These were petty dynasties founded on the ruins of the Omayyad caliphate: the Hammudids of Malaga (from 1016 onward) and of Algeciras (1039-); the Abbadids of Sevilla (1031-); the Zayrids of Granada (1012-); the Jahwarids of Córdoba (1031-); the Dhul-Nunids of Toledo (1035-); the Amirids of Valencia (1021-); the Tojibids and Hudids of Saragossa (1019- and 1031-). Most of these dynasties were absorbed by the most distinguished of them, the **Abbadids,** who summoned the Almoravids from Africa to aid them against Alfonso VI of Castile.

1056-1147. The **ALMORAVIDS,** a Berber dynasty, founded by the Berber prophet **Abdullah ibn Tashfin.** They conquered Morocco and part of Algeria and were called into Spain by the Abbadids to help in the defense against the Christians. They defeated Alfonso of Castile at **Zallaka** (1086) and proceeded to annex Moorish Spain, with the exception of Toledo and Saragossa.

1130-1269. The **ALMOHADES,** a dynasty founded by the Berber prophet **Mohammed ibn Tumart.** His successor, Abdul-Mu'min, annihilated the Almoravid army (1144), after which Morocco was conquered (1146).

1145-1150. The Almohades invaded and conquered Moorish Spain, after which they conquered Algeria (1152) and Tunis (1158). They were finally defeated by the Christian kings of Spain in

1212, July 16. The **battle of Las Navas de Tolosa,** which was followed by their expulsion from Spain. Thereafter only local Moslem dynasties remained, of which the **Nasrids of Granada** (1232-1492) alone offered much resistance to the Christians until union of the Christian states brought about their defeat.

(2) Castile

1072-1109. ALFONSO VI, of Castile. He captured Toledo from the Moors (1085) and created his son-in-law, Henry of Burgundy, count of Portugal (1093).

1086. The Moslems, alarmed by Alfonso's progress, called from Africa the great **Yusuf ibn Tashfin** (d. 1106), leader of the newly dominant sect of Berber fanatics, the Almoravids. Ibn Yusuf landed at Algeciras (1086), and with the support of Sevilla began a successful counter-thrust against the Christians (defeat of Alfonso at **Zallaka,** 1086). Yusuf, recalled by the African situation, did not at once exploit his advantage, but on his return to Spain his energetic, puritanic reforms strengthened the Moslems and brought them into an integral relation (c. 1091) with his great African empire which was centered in Morocco. This empire quickly disintegrated on Yusuf's death.

Alfonso resumed the Christian reconquest with the aid of **Rodrigo (Ruy) Diaz** of Bivar, the **Cid** (*Cid* as applied by the Moslems means *lord* or *master*). Alfonso's style of "emperor" represented personal prestige and a vague hegemony rather than political reality.

The **Cid,** a Castilian originally in the service of Sancho II of Castile, later passed to that of Alfonso VI; was exiled (1081); returned to Castilian service (1087-1088); went over to the Moslem king of Saragossa after his second exile. Eventually he became ruler of Valencia. The Cid served both sides, was cruel, selfish, and proud. Despite these characteristics the legendary figure of the man became the great national hero of Spain. On his death (1099) Valencia was soon abandoned to the Almoravids.

In the course of the 11th century French influence began to penetrate the peninsula. The Cluniacs, already (1033) strong in Catalonia, Castile, and Aragon, reinforced French influence, and stimulated clerical reform and the reconquest. A literary reflection of this is to be found in the *Cantar de mio Cid* (c. 1140), which already shows French elements in the cycle of the Cid (a cycle which continued into the 15th century).

1126-1157. ALFONSO VII, crowned "emperor" (1135) on the basis of military ascendancy and an intense feeling of equality with rival monarchs, especially the Holy Roman emperors. The weakening of the Almoravids by luxury, and the rise of rivals (the Almohades) in Africa (c. 1125), made possible a resumption of the reconquest (1144-1147) with wide raids into Andalusia. The Almohades, summoned from Africa (1146), completed (1172) the second **restoration of Moslem unity,** and made Moslem Spain a province of their African empire, reducing the Arab influence in Spain to nothing in favor of Berber fanatics. Alfonso's death was followed by a minority and an eight-year dynastic crisis from which his son Alfonso VIII finally emerged as master.

1158-1214. ALFONSO VIII. After a series of

250

Spanish Rulers (970-1285)

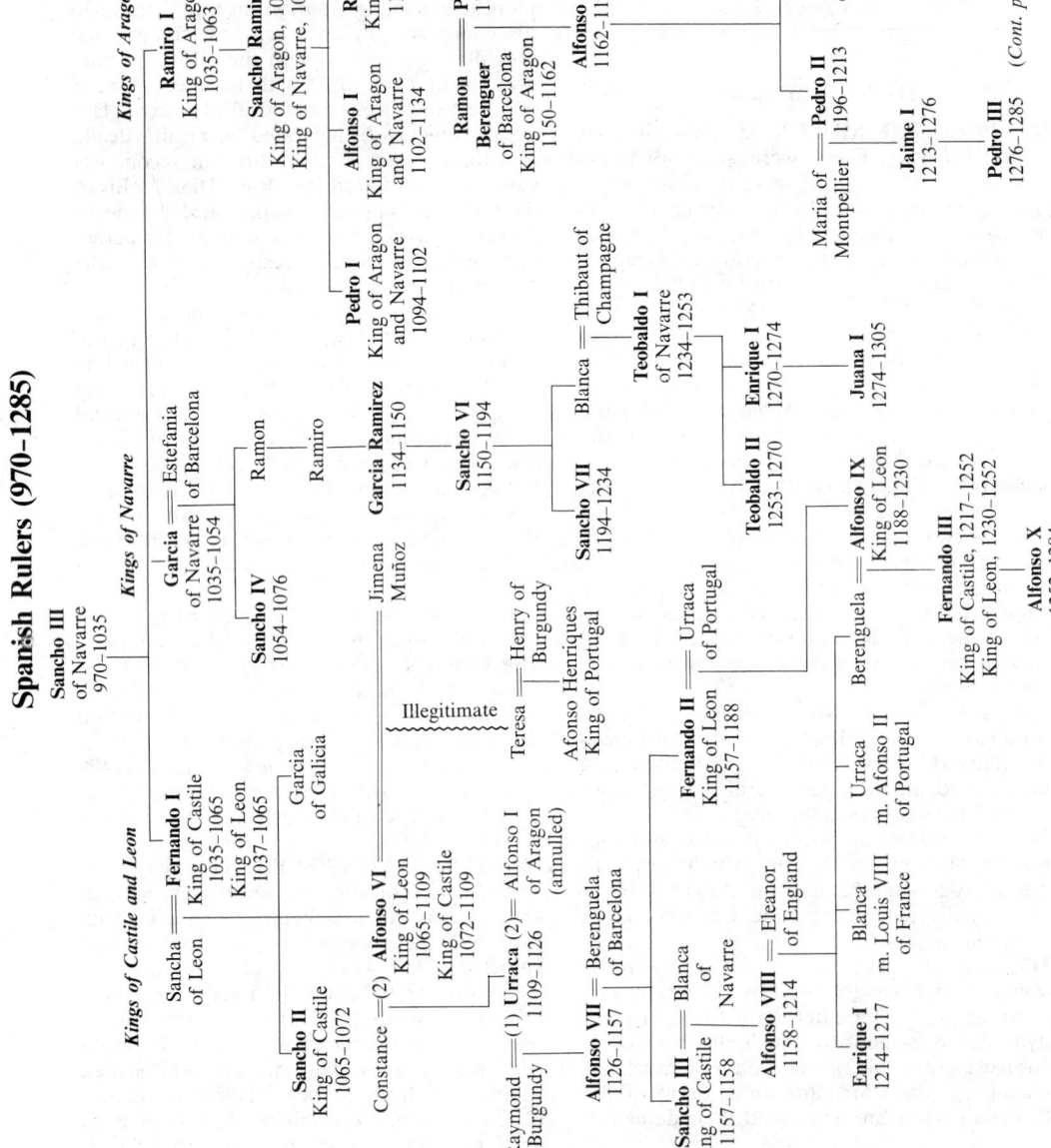

(Cont. pp. 305, 307.)

successful attacks on the Moslems, Alfonso was overwhelmingly defeated (**Alarcos,** 1195) by the Almohades, then at the zenith of their power. Leon and Navarre promptly invaded Castile, but Alfonso triumphed over them, and, with the aid of Pope Innocent III and the clergy, began the preparation of a unified general assault on the Moslems which led to the greatest victory of the reconquest, **Las Navas de Tolosa** (1212), soon followed by the decline of the Almohade power in Spain and Africa and by Christian dissension.

179. Portugal's independence and royal title were recognized by Pope Alexander III.

217-1252. FERDINAND III ended the dynastic war in Castile and attacked the Moors in the Guadalquivir Valley, taking Córdoba (1236) and Sevilla (1248). On the appeal of the Almohade emperor he sent aid to him, gaining in return a line of African fortresses, and permission to establish a Christian church at Marrakah. His plans for an invasion of Africa were cut short by death. After the capture of Jaen (1246), the emir was allowed to establish himself at Granada, the last Moorish stronghold, as Ferdinand's vassal.

The long history of guerrilla warfare in Castile disorganized tillage, made the people averse to agriculture, led to a concentration of population in the towns, and accounts for the poverty of Castilian agriculture, the tremendous influence of municipalities in medieval Castile, the development of a race of soldiers, and the isolation of Spanish thought from general European currents. In general the Moors were not disliked, and intermarriages were not unusual until the 13th century. Then the preaching of crusades as part of the reconquest and papal propaganda prepared the Spanish mind for the burst of intolerance and fanaticism which began in the second half of the 15th century.

The war of Christian reconquest gave birth to three great native military orders, modeled partly on Moorish societies for border defense, partly on the international crusading orders, notably the Templars, already established in the Peninsula. Some members took the regular monkish vows, others did not. Two Cistercian monks assumed (1158) the defense of Calatrava (when the Templars gave it up), and the **Order of Calatrava** which grew up was confirmed by the pope (1164). The **Order of Santiago** (established 1171) was the largest and richest, the **Order of Alcántara** (founded c. 1156), an offshoot of Calatrava, was the most clerical in type. By 1493 these orders had grown to stupendous size (the largest, Santiago, having 700,000 members and vassals, and a vast annual income.

In the period following 1252 fear of the infidel was no longer a dominant force in Iberian politics and the nobles turned from assaults on the Moors to attacks upon the monarchy. The struggle between crown and baronage (which found a parallel all through Europe) was notable in Spain for the depth of governmental degradation which it produced. The new elements in the situation were clearly indicated in the reign of

1252-1284. ALFONSO X (the Learned), a versatile savant, distinguished as an astronomer (*Alfonsine Tables*), poet, historian, patron of learning, a pre-eminent lawyer and codifier (*las Siete Partidas*), devoted to the Roman ideal of centralized absolute monarchy, but a futile, vacillating monarch. Lavish concessions to the nobles (1271) to avoid civil war established the aristocracy in a position from which it was not dislodged until the reign of Ferdinand and Isabella. Debasement of the coinage to relieve poverty produced economic crises; alternate alliance and war with the vassal king of Granada, and hostilities with Aragon, accomplished nothing. The kingdom of Murcia was regained (1266) with the aid of James I of Aragon, and was then incorporated with Castile.

In foreign affairs Alfonso abandoned the long peninsularity of Spanish sovereigns, made a series of dynastic alliances, and attempted to give Castile an important European position. **1263-1267.** Efforts to rectify the Portuguese boundary with advantage to Castile ultimately produced an actual loss of territory (in Algarve); Alfonso began the long effort to regain Portugal, which finally succeeded under Philip II (1580). Claims to (English) Gascony were revived (1253) and abandoned (1254); desultory wars fought with France. A twenty-year effort to win the crown of the Holy Roman Empire (despite papal opposition and public opinion) met with two defeats (1257 and 1273). The death of Alfonso's eldest son Ferdinand (1275) led at once to a bitter struggle over the succession organized by Alfonso's son Sancho.

(3) Barcelona and Catalonia

The **Spanish Mark** was established as a result of the conquest of Catalonia by Charlemagne (785-811). The county of Barcelona (erected 817) under the Frankish crown became independent, perhaps as early as the 9th century. By the beginning of the 12th century the counts of Barcelona had large holdings north of the Pyrenees (notably in Provence), to which they added for a brief period (1114-1115) Majorca and Iviza, and permanently Tarragona.

1137. The **union of Catalonia and Aragon,**

begun by Ramon Berenguer IV of Catalonia, was epochal, for it created a powerful state with access to the sea. Catalonian territories included Cerdagne, a large part of Provence, etc., with the later addition of Roussillon (1172), Montpellier (1204, under French suzerainty), Foix, Nîmes, Béziers (1162–1196). **1213.** The **battle of Muret** (see below) definitely turned Catalonia back into the Spanish orbit.

In the 13th century **Barcelona,** utilizing the skill of her native sailors and the local (mostly Jewish) accumulations of capital, and profiting by Italian commercial pioneering, began an extensive slave trade in Moorish prisoners. Aragonese imperial expansion in the Mediterranean (Sicily and the Greek Archipelago), gave Barcelona further commercial advantages and made it one of the most active Mediterranean ports.

Ramon Lull (1232–1315) was the greatest Catalonian intellectual figure of the Middle Ages, a vernacular poet, novelist, missionary, mystic, educator, reformer, logician, scientist, and traveler.

(4) Navarre

Navarre gained its independence from Carolingian rule in the 9th century and fell heir to the Carolingian rights in Aragon, which was absorbed by Navarre in the 10th century. **Sancho the Great** (970–1035) secured the succession of Castile, conquered most of Leon and temporarily united the Iberian kingdoms. By his will Aragon passed to his son Ramiro (d. 1063) and the union came to an end. On the death of **Alfonso the Warrior** (1104–1134), Navarre returned to its old ruling house until it passed under French control (1234) for two centuries.

(5) Aragon

Aragon, beginning as a county on the river Arago under Carolingian control, emerged from Carolingian domination in the middle of the 9th century, passed under the control of Navarre, and then became independent under Ramiro (d. 1063). The period from 1063 to 1134 is marked by confusion, intrigue, some progress against the Moors, and the annexation of Navarre (1076).
1102–1134. **ALFONSO I** (the Warrior) advanced to the Ebro, captured Saragossa (1118), and made raids to the Mediterranean. On Alfonso's death, Aragon chose his brother, **Ramiro,** a monk who emerged from retirement long enough to marry and produce a daughter, Petronilla, whom he betrothed to Ramon Berenguer IV (1131–1162), count of Barcelona. He then returned (1137) to his monastery, leaving Petronilla under the guardianship of Ramon. On his marriage to Petronilla in 1150, Ramon became king of Aragon. The resulting **union of Catalonia and Aragon** was a decisive event in Spanish history.

After the union the Aragonese kings, preoccupied with Spanish affairs, let Provence drift, and on the death of Alfonso II (1162–1196) it passed to his son Alfonso, nominally under the suzerainty of his brother Peter **(Pedro) II** (1196–1213), but, in fact, lost for good. Alfonso tried to keep his Provençal holdings clear of the Albigensian heresy, but Raymond, count of Toulouse, a supporter of the heresy, sought to win Peter II to his views. Peter went to Rome (1204) for a papal coronation, declared himself a vassal of the Holy See, and bore an honorable part at Las Navas de Tolosa, but was forced by the horrors of the Albigensian Crusade and the legitimate appeals of his vassals to oppose Simon de Montfort at Muret, where he fell.
1213. The **battle of Muret** marked the real end of Aragonese interests north of the Pyrenees.
1258. By the **Treaty of Corbeil** the king of France renounced his claims to Barcelona, Urgel, etc., Cerdagne, Roussillon, etc. Aragon ceded: Carcassonne, Foix, Béziers, Nîmes, Narbonne, Toulouse, etc. All rights in Provence passed to Margaret, wife of Louis IX; a marriage was arranged between Louis's son Philip and Isabella, daughter of James I of Aragon.
1213–1276. **JAMES (Jaime) I** (the Conqueror). After the weakness and anarchy of his minority, James, one of the greatest soldiers of the Middle Ages, conquered Valencia in an intermittent campaign (1233–1245), took the kingdom of Murcia for Castile (1266), and freed the Aragonese frontier of the Moslem menace. James also attempted to establish his overlordship over Tlemcen and Bugia in North Africa, and to secure a hold in Tunis. Against the will of his Aragonese nobles, but with the support of his Catalonian and French vassals, James conquered the Balearic Islands (1229–1235), thus beginning the creation of an Aragonese Mediterranean empire.

SPANISH CULTURE in the Middle Ages was very largely conditioned by external influences. The Moslem tradition of scholarship continued and the translations from the Arabic to the Latin made Spain the avenue by which the knowledge of antiquity came to the West. **Gerard of Cremona** translated the works of Ptolemy, Euclid, Galen, and the Hippocratic corpus. Toledo, which had been a center of learning of the Arabic world, became a center for the translation of Arabic and Greek works into Latin. **John of Sevilla** (fl. 1135–1153), also at Toledo, translated Arabic texts on mathematics, astronomy, and philosophy into Latin and the vernacular. Abraham bar-Hiyya (d. 1136) (**Sarasorda**) was one of the earliest to introduce Moslem mathematics to the West. Moses ben Maimon (**Maimonides**) (1135–1204), born in Córdoba, who became one of the most influential thinkers of the West, also translated medical and astronomical texts from Arabic. **Ibn-Rushd** (1126–1198), born in Córdoba, was known as "the commentator," through whom the West relearned the works of Aristotle.

Architecture: (1) **Pre-romanesque** architecture revealed traces of Visigothic, Carolingian, Persian, Byzantine, and Moslem traditions. (2) **Romanesque** architecture showed particularly the influence of Auvergne and Languedoc (e.g. second church of Santiago de Compostella). (3) The **Gothic** was marked by strong elements of the Burgundian style, brought by the Clunics. The full tide of the Gothic was probably introduced by the Cistercians (e.g. cathedrals of Toledo, c. 1230; Burgos 1126; Leon, c. 1230). Catalan Gothic shows German influences (cathedrals of Barcelona, 1298; Gerona, 1312). The later Spanish Gothic revealed French, German, and Flemish currents (e.g. cathedral of Sevilla, begun 1401; west towers of Burgos cathedral, 1442). (4) **Moorish** architecture had a development of its own: the great mosque of Córdoba (completed 1118), the Alcazar, Sevilla (c. 1181), and the Alhambra (mostly 14th century).

Foundation of the first universities: Valencia (1209); Salamanca (1242).   (*Cont. p. 303.*)

(6) Portugal

1055– Reconquest from the Moors of much of present-day Portugal by **Ferdinand the Great** of Leon and Castile. Ferdinand organized the territory as a county, with Coimbra as the capital.

1093–1112. Henry of Burgundy, a descendant of King Robert of France, came to Spain with other knights-adventurers, to fight against the Moors. In return the king of Castile granted him the county of Portugal and gave him the hand of his (illegitimate) daughter, Teresa. Henry himself was a typical crusader, restless and enterprising, whose main hope appears to have been to establish a dynasty in Castile.

1112–1185.   AFONSO HENRIQUES, the founder of the Portuguese monarchy and of the Burgundian dynasty. Afonso was only three years old at the death of his father. His mother Teresa ruled as regent, but soon became involved in a struggle with Galicia and Castile. Being defeated, she agreed to accept Castilian domination, but

1128. Afonso assumed authority, repudiated the agreement, and, after defeating the Span-iards, drove his mother into exile.

1139. Afonso, one of the most famous knights of his age, began a long series of struggles against the Moors by defeating them in the **battle of Ourique.**

1143. Afonso was proclaimed king by the cortes. The pope arranged the **Treaty of Zamora** between Portugal and Castile, the latter recognizing Portuguese independence, while Portugal accepted the suzerainty of the pope.

1147. The Portuguese took Lisbon and established a frontier on the Tagus.

1169. Further conflicts with Castile led to Afonso's attack on Badajoz. He was defeated and captured, but soon released.

1185–1211. SANCHO I, the son of Afonso Henriques. His reign was noteworthy for the development of towns and for the establishment of military orders of knighthood. Sancho did much to settle colonists on the lands that were won back in the prolonged wars against the Moors.

1211–1223. AFONSO II. Beginning of the king's conflict with the clergy, which led to interference by the pope and to restlessness among the nobility.

1223–1245. SANCHO II. His trouble with the clergy and nobility led ultimately to his deposition by the pope, who offered the crown to

1245–1279. AFONSO III, the brother of Sancho II and count of Boulogne. His title being weak, Afonso was much dependent on the cortes, in which the commons were for the first time represented. **War with Castile** was ended by a peace in 1253.   (*Cont. p. 306.*)

g. DEVELOPMENTS IN EUROPEAN TECHNOLOGY

The increased pulse of life in the later Middle Ages was felt throughout society as well as in literature, science, and technology. The technological developments are known, but sparsely and not chronologically recorded. The water mill was used for fulling, stone cutting, and wood cutting after the introduction of the geared wheel. The windmill (documented from the 12th century), was more complex than that used in the East, due to the more variable winds of Europe. As a fuel, coal was being used as the forests were depleted (coal was mined in Liège during the 13th century). Communications improved partly because bridge and road building was considered a Christian duty and partly because of the more effective use of animal power. Communication by sea was improved by the Lateen sail, in use in Italy in the 11th century, and by the sternpost rudder and compass (the latter was introduced in the 13th century).

Portugal: The Burgundian House (1112–1325)

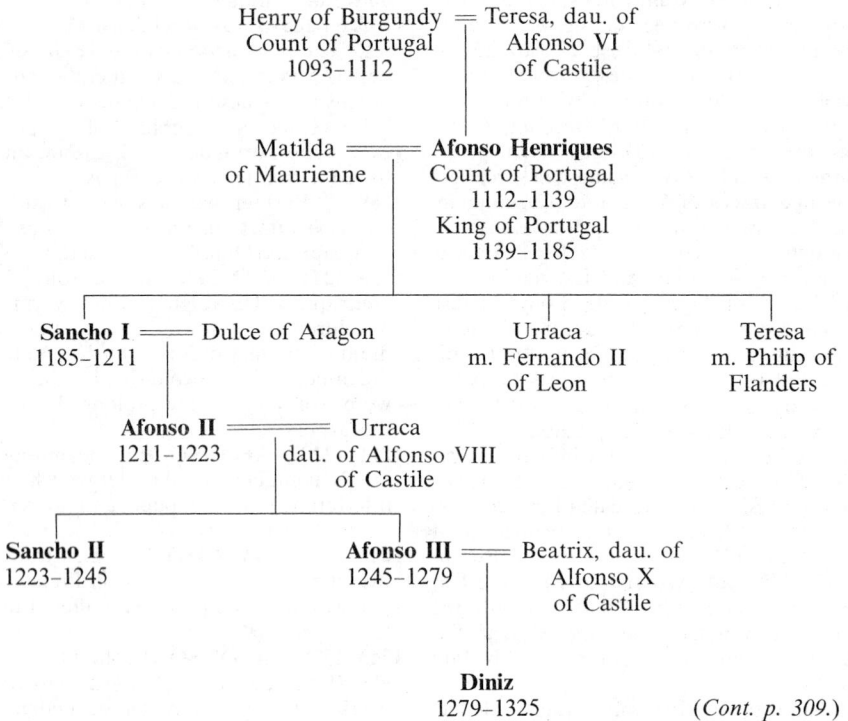

Henry of Burgundy ══ Teresa, dau. of
Count of Portugal | Alfonso VI
1093–1112 | of Castile

Matilda ════ **Afonso Henriques**
of Maurienne | Count of Portugal
1112–1139
King of Portugal
1139–1185

Sancho I ══ Dulce of Aragon | Urraca | Teresa
1185–1211 | m. Fernando II | m. Philip of
| of Leon | Flanders

Afonso II ════ Urraca
1211–1223 | dau. of Alfonso VIII
of Castile

Sancho II | **Afonso III** ══ Beatrix, dau. of
1223–1245 | 1245–1279 | Alfonso X
of Castile

Diniz
1279–1325 (*Cont. p. 309.*)

Along with the increase in the building of stone bridges came an increase in the number of stone buildings and greater empirical knowledge of building techniques (e.g., improvements in the arch and the knowledge of the distribution of roof weight). The textile industry developed, employing wool, linen, cotton, and silk. The spinning wheel dates from the 13th century and is the first example of belt power transmission. Soap was also invented and produced on a large scale by the 12th century. Mining had declined from the end of the Roman Empire to the 10t century after which it increased rapidly bot with the discovery of new sources and by th conquest of the Spanish mines from the Mo lems. The most important development was i the discovery of iron-casting techniques; too and weapons could be more efficiently pro duced. Gunpowder, although known in Europ in the 13th century, did not become revolution ary until the 14th century, when it was fir used to propel missiles. (*Cont. p. 458*

2. EASTERN EUROPE

a. THE SLAVS

The Slavs, an eastern branch of the Indo-European family, were known to the Roman and Greek writers of the 1st and 2nd centuries A.D. under the name of *Venedi* as inhabiting the region beyond the Vistula. The majority of modern scholars agree that the "original home" of the Slavs was the territory to the southeast of the Vistula and to the northeast of the Carpa- thian Mountains, in the upper basins of th Western Bug, the Pripet, and the Dniester. I the course of the early centuries of our era th Slavs expanded in all directions, and by th 6th century, when they were known to Gothi and Byzantine writers as *Sclaveni,* they wer apparently already separated into three mai divisions: (1) the western Slavs (the present-da Poles, Czechs, Slovaks, and Moravians); (2) th southern Slavs (the Bulgarians, Serbs, Croat and Slovenes); (3) the eastern Slavs (the Russians, subsequently subdivided into the Great Russians, the Little Russians or the Ukrainians, and the White Russians).

Closely related to the Slavs were the Lithuanians who, together with the Letts and the ancient Prussians, formed the Baltic branch of the Indo-European family. They inhabited the southeastern coast of the Baltic Sea, between the present location of Memel and Estonia.

b. BOHEMIA AND MORAVIA, TO 1306

The earliest recorded attempt at the construction of a Slavic state was that made by

c. 623-658. Samo, who appears to have been a Frankish tradesman traveling in central Europe. Probably taking advantage of the defeat of the Avars by the Greeks in 626, he managed to unite the Czechs and some of the Wends, and succeeded in repulsing not only the Avars, but also the Franks under King Dagobert (631). But on the death of Samo the union of the tribes disintegrated.

833-836. Mojmir, founder of the Moravian state, maintained himself against pressure from the East Franks.

846-869. Rastislav, prince of Moravia, made an alliance (862) with **Michael III,** the Byzantine emperor, to counteract the close relationship between the East Franks and the Bulgarians.

863. Conversion of the Moravians by Cyril (Constantine, 826–869) and **Methodius** (815–885), two monks from Saloniki sent at Rastislav's request. Beginning of Slavic church language and liturgy. **Cyrillic alphabet.**

869. Rastislav captured and blinded by Carloman.

870-894. Sviatopluk, a Moravian prince, succeeded in uniting under his authority Moravia, Bohemia, and present-day Slovakia, and managed to maintain his position as against the Germans. During his reign the western Slavs were converted to Christianity by Cyril and Methodius but in the last years of the century the German clergy redoubled its efforts and won Bohemia and Moravia for the Latin Church, thus establishing the ecclesiastical dependence of the western Slavs on Rome.

906. The **kingdom of Moravia** was dissolved as the result of a great defeat by the Hungarians.

920-929. St. Wenceslas, duke of the Premysl house. He was murdered in 929 at the instigation of his brother Boleslav, leader of the heathen reaction, who ascended the throne as

929-967. BOLESLAV I. He seems to have carried on constant warfare against the encroaching Germans, until forced (950) to accept German suzerainty. To the eastward he made many conquests and included Moravia, part of Slovakia, part of Silesia, and even Cracow in his kingdom. Furthermore, he appears to have established a fairly strong royal power over the old tribal chiefs.

967-999. BOLESLAV II, son of the preceding. He apparently continued the policies of his father and saw to the final victory of the Christian faith (foundation of the bishopric of Prague, 973). Missionaries from Bohemia took an active part in the conversion of Hungary and Poland.

The entire 11th and 12th centuries were filled with chronic dynastic conflicts between members of the Premysl family and the various claimants appealing to Poland and more particularly to the German emperors for support. The result was an ever-increasing German influence and the gradual integration of Bohemia with the empire.

999-1000. Boleslav the Brave of Poland took advantage of the anarchy in Bohemia to conquer Silesia, Moravia, and Cracow. In 1003 he became duke of Bohemia, but was driven out in the next year by a German army. There followed another period of disorder, marked only by

1031. The reacquisition of Moravia, which thenceforth remained connected with Bohemia.

1034-1055. BŘETISLAV I (the Restorer), who overran Silesia, took Cracow (1039) and for a time ruled Poland, which had now entered upon a period of disruption.

1041. Emperor **Henry III,** alarmed by the expansion of the Bohemian power, invaded the country and advanced to Prague. Bratislav agreed to give up his Polish conquests and pay tribute to the emperor.

1055-1061. Spytihnev, son of Břetislav, whose reign was uneventful.

1061-1092. VRATISLAV II, who, throughout his reign, loyally supported the German emperor, Henry IV, in his struggle with the Papacy and took part in the Italian campaigns. He was rewarded by Henry with a crown (1086), but only for his own person.

1092-1110. Břetislav II.

1111-1125. Vladislav I.

1125-1140. Sobeslav I.

1140-1173. VLADISLAV II. Like his predecessors, he supported the German emperors in the main, and was rewarded (1156) by Frederick Barbarossa with an hereditary crown for his aid against the Italian cities.

1173-1197. Another period of dynastic conflict, during which there were some ten rulers.

Bohemia: The Premyslid Kings (1198–1378)

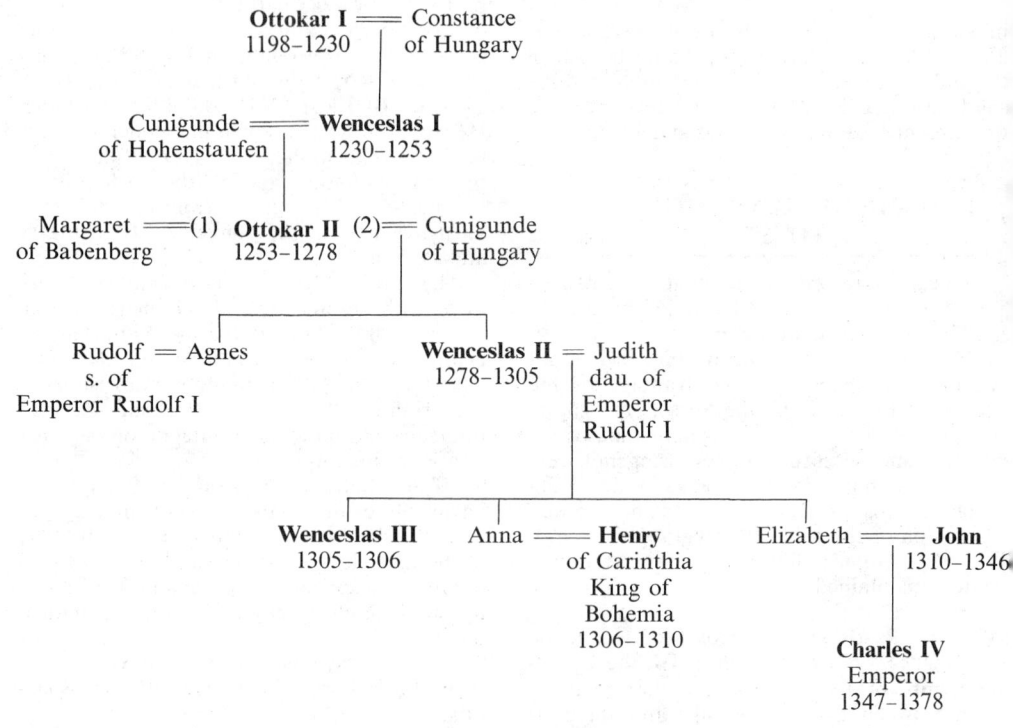

1198–1230. OTTOKAR I. He took full advantage of the struggles for the succession which now began to wrack the German Empire. Siding now with one party, now with another, he made the Bohemian king (an imperial elector since the early 12th century) one of the decisive powers in German affairs. On the other hand, a long-drawn conflict with the clergy (1214–1221) led to the almost complete independence of the Church.

1212. The **Golden Bull** of Frederick II recognized the right of the Bohemian nobility to elect its own ruler.

1230–1253. WENCESLAS (VACLAV) I. His reign was marked by large-scale immigration of Germans, encouraged by the ruler, possibly to counteract the growing power of the nobility. Germans had been coming in for a long time (chiefly clergy and nobility), but they now began to open up large forested tracts and to build cities, which were given practical autonomy under German (Magdeburg) law.

1247–1250. Rising of the nobility against the king, possibly in protest against the favor shown the Germans.

1251. The Austrian estates, after the death of the last Babenberg duke, elected Ottokar, son of Wenceslas, as duke.

1253–1278. OTTOKAR II (the Great) whose reign marked the widest expansion of Bohemian power and was characterized by great prosperity (opening of the famous silver mines, which made Bohemia one of the wealthiest countries in the later Middle Ages).

1255. Ottokar carried on a successful campaign in support of the Teutonic Knights against the heathen Prussians.

1260. After defeating the Hungarians, Ottokar took from them the province of Styria.

1267. A second northern campaign, against the Lithuanians, achieved little.

1269. Ottokar, taking advantage of the interregnum in the German Empire, extended his power over Carinthia, Carniola, and Istria.

1273. Election of **Rudolf of Hapsburg** as king of Germany. Ottokar refused to recognize him. The Diet of Regensburg (1274) therefore declared all Ottokar's acquisitions void. The king, supported by the Hungarians and by some of the Bohemian nobility, attacked

Ottokar, who agreed to give up all but Bohemia and Moravia, and to recognize Rudolf's suzerainty even over these.

278. New war between Rudolf and Ottokar. Ottokar was decisively defeated on the **Marchfeld** (Aug. 26) and killed.

278-1305. **Wenceslas II**, a boy of seven, for whom Otto of Brandenburg at first acted as regent.

290. Wenceslas was elected and crowned king of Poland.

301. His son, Wenceslas, was elected king of Hungary (ruled to 1304).

305-1306. **Wenceslas III.** He gave up the claim to Hungary and was murdered while en route to Poland to suppress a revolt of the nobles. **End of the Premyslid line.**

(*Cont. p. 327.*)

c. POLAND, TO 1305

The Polish state emerged in the 10th century, ɪe result of the unification of some six tribes nder the **Polani,** who were ruled by the membɪs of the semi-mythical **family of Piast.** From ɪe outset the Poles were obliged to fight against ɪe encroachment of the Germans from the ɪest, the Prussians from the north, the Bohe-ɪians from the south, and the Hungarians, ɪlso in the south.

960-992. **MIESZKO I,** of the house of Piast, the first historical ruler. He conquered the territory between the Oder and the Warthe Rivers, but was defeated by Markgraf Gero and obliged to recognize German suzerainty ᴄ973).

66. Mieszko was converted to Christianity by Bohemian missionaries, probably for political ɪeasons, to deprive the Germans of any further excuse for aggression. The acceptance of Latin Christianity meant the connection of Poland, like Bohemia and Hungary, with west-ɪrn European culture.

�)2-1025. **BOLESLAV I** (Chrobry = the Brave). He ascended the throne at 25 and ɪvas the real organizer of the Polish state. An ɪnergetic, but at times treacherous and cruel ɪuler, he built up an efficient military machine, ɪaid the basis for an administrative system (*comites = castellani = Burggrafen,* with civil ɪnd military powers), organized the Church (establishment of Benedictine monasteries, ɪtc.). Politically his aim appears to have been ɪhe union of all western Slavs under his rule. ɪie conquered eastern Pomerania and gained ɪccess to the Baltic (992-994), added Silesia, Moravia, and Cracow to his domain (999), and ɪnduced Otto III to erect an independent arch-ɪishopric of Gnesen (1000). On the death of ɪtto he took advantage of the confusion in

Germany to occupy Lusatia and Meissen, and in 1003 made himself duke of Bohemia. The new emperor, Henry II, carried on long wars against Boleslav to break his power (1004-) and ultimately forced the abandonment of Bohemia and Lusatia (1005). But by the **treaty of Bautzen** (1018) Boleslav was given Lusatia as an imperial fief, and just before his death he was able to make himself king of Poland (1025).

1025-1034. **MIESZKO II,** a much weaker ruler. The Poles, like the other Slavs, divided the domain among the various sons of a deceased king, thus creating endless dynastic conflict and ample opportunity for intervention by neighboring rulers. During Mieszko's reign most of the territorial gains of Boleslav were lost: St. Stephen of Hungary conquered Slovakia (1027); Bretislav of Bohemia took Moravia (1031); Yaroslav of Russia acquired Ruthenia (1031); Canute of Denmark took Pomerania (1031). In 1032 the Emperor Conrad actually divided Poland between Mieszko and two of his relatives.

1034-1040. A period of violent dynastic struggle and general insurrection, including a heathen reaction (burning of monasteries, massacre of the clergy) and a peasant uprising against the landlords. Meanwhile Brětislav of Bohemia seized Silesia (1038).

1038-1058. **CASIMIR I** (the Restorer), who succeeded, with the aid of the Emperor Henry III, in reconquering his domain, re-establishing Christianity, and restoring order. Silesia was recovered (1054). In return Casimir was obliged to give up the royal title (becoming merely a *grand duke*) and to make numerous concessions to the nobility and clergy, thus initiating a baneful practice.

1058-1079. **BOLESLAV II** (the Bold), one of the great medieval rulers. In the great struggle between the emperor and the pope he consistently supported the latter, as a counterweight to German influence. At the same time he did his utmost to throw off the pressure of the nobility. In his countless campaigns he reconquered upper Slovakia (1061-1063) and marched as far as Kiev to put his relative upon the Russian throne (1069). In 1076 he reassumed the royal crown, with the pope's approval. But his entire policy estranged the nobility, which ultimately drove him from his throne.

1079-1102. **Vladislav I** (Ladislas), **Hermann,** an indolent and unwarlike ruler, brother of Boleslav. He resigned the royal title and attempted to secure peace by supporting the Emperor Henry IV, as well as by courting the nobility and clergy.

1102-1138. **BOLESLAV III** (Wry-mouth), who

acquired the throne only after a violent struggle with his brother Zbigniew. He was one of the greatest Polish kings, who defeated the Pomeranians (**battle of Naklo,** 1109) and, by the incorporation of Pomerania (1119–1123), re-established the access to the sea. At the same time he defeated the Emperor Henry V (1109, **battle of Hundsfeld,** near Breslau) and checked the German advance. On the other hand, his campaigns in Hungary (1132–1135) had no permanent results.

Boleslav completed the organization of the state, in which the great landlords (*nobiles* = magnates), gentry (*milites* = knights = *szlachta*) had become well-defined social classes, the peasantry having steadily lost in the periods of confusion. The Church was reorganized under the archbishop of Gnesen, by the papal legate Walo. In order to avoid dispute, Boleslav fixed the royal succession by senority. Poland was divided into **five principalities** (Silesia, Great Poland, Masovia, Sandomir, Cracow) for his sons; Cracow was established as the capital, and was to go, with the title of *grand duke,* to the eldest member of the house of Piast. In actual fact this arrangement by no means eliminated the dynastic competition, but introduced a long period of disruption, during which the nobility and clergy waxed ever more powerful and the ducal or royal power became insignificant. Only the weakness of the neighboring states saved Poland from destruction.

1138–1146. Vladislav II (Ladislas).

1146–1173. Boleslav IV, an ineffectual ruler, during whose reign the Germans, under Albert the Bear and Henry the Lion, supported by Waldemar of Denmark, drove back the Poles from the entire territory along the Baltic and west of the Vistula (1147). The Emperor Frederick Barbarossa intervened and forced the humble submission of Boleslav (1157).

1173–1177. Mieszko III, a brutal and despotic prince who antagonized the nobility and was soon driven out by them.

1177–1194. CASIMIR II (the Just) was practically elected by the magnates, who extorted privileges from him. In the **Assembly of Lenczyca** (1180) the clergy was also given far-reaching concessions. Casimir attempted to preclude further strife by making the principality of Cracow hereditary in his own line.

1194–1227. Leszek I (the White), whose reign was punctuated by constant wars against Mieszko III, who attempted to regain the throne (d. 1202), and against the latter's son Vladislav Laskonogi (1202–1206). The period was one of complete feudal anarchy, with the nobility and clergy controlling the situation.

1227–1279. Boleslav V, whose unhappy reign was marked by complete disruption and by constant aggression by neighboring states.

1228. Arrival of the **Teutonic Knights,** called to Prussia by Duke Conrad of Masovia (p. 229). Within the next 50 years they conquered Prussia and erected a most formidable barrier to Polish access to the sea.

1241. Beginning of the great **Mongol invasions** (p. 261), of which there were constant renewals throughout the rest of the century. The Poles managed to stave off Mongol domination, but the country was devastated. One result was the calling in of large numbers of German settlers, some of whom cleared forest land and colonized new areas in Silesia and Posen, others of whom settled in the towns. In all cases large concessions in the direction of autonomy were made (Magdeburg law). The German influence meant greater and more efficient exploitation of the soil, development of trade, cultural advance.

1279–1288. Leszek II (the Black).

1288–1290. Further dynastic and feudal warfare, with the brief reign of Henry Probus.

1290–1296. Przemyslav II. He was crowned king with the consent of the pope (1295), but was murdered soon afterward.

1300–1305. Wenceslas I, son of the king of Bohemia, elected by the nobility but challenged by claimants of the Piast family. He soon resigned the position and returned home.
(*Cont. p. 337.*)

d. RUSSIA, TO 1263

The **eastern Slavs** settled on the territory of present-day European Russia in the period from the 5th to the 8th century A.D. Little is known of their political history during these centuries, but undoubtedly there were attempts at political organization in the shape of both tribal principalities and city states formed around important commercial centers. In the 8th century some of the eastern Slavs were under the protectorate of the **Khazars,** a Turkish tribe which established a strong and prosperous state along the lower Volga. After the end of the 8th century the northern part of Russia began to be penetrated by the Scandinavian Vikings called in the old Russian chronicles **Varangians** or *Rus* (hence the name of *Russia*). In the course of the 9th century the Varangians constantly moved southward along the main waterway leading from the Baltic to the Black Sea, gradually establishing their political domination over the Slav communities. According to tradition, the Scandinavian chieftain **Rurik** ruled in Novgorod in the 860's. Later he was recognized as the founder of the Russian princely dynasty.

860. The first recorded appearance of the Rus

sians (Varangians) at Constantinople. This
was a raid not unlike those of the Norsemen
on Britain and France in the same period.

880–912. PRINCE OLEG, who succeeded
in uniting under his control both Novgorod
and Kiev (on the Dnieper River). Kiev subsequently became the political center of a
loose federation of Russian states.

1. The Russians again appeared at Constantinople and extracted trade privileges from
the Byzantine emperor. Trade became a leading occupation of the Russian princes, who,
with their followers (*druzhina*) protected the
merchant ships. Russians also began to take
service with the Greek emperors in considerable number and came to play an important
rôle in the mercenary corps.

45. Further trade agreements with the Greek
Empire testify to the ever closer economic
connections and no doubt to an increasing
cultural contact.

57. The Russian princess, **Olga,** visited Constantinople and was converted to the Christian
faith. This was, however, a personal conversion, and may in fact have been Olga's second.

4–972. SVIATOSLAV, the son of Olga. He
was the first of the great conquering princes.
In 965 he defeated the Khazars on the lower
Volga and proceeded to establish a Russian
state in place of the Khazar Empire. Called
to the Balkans to aid the Greek emperor
against the powerful Bulgars, he carried on a
successful campaign (967) and decided to establish himself on the lower Danube. At this
time his power extended from Novgorod in the
north to the Danube in the southwest and to
the lower Volga in the southeast. He was
forced to abandon Bulgaria in order to resist
the **Patzinaks** (Pechenegs), who had entered
southern Russia from the east and were threatening Kiev. Having repulsed them (968), Sviatoslav returned to Bulgaria, but he was no
more welcome to the Greeks than were the
Bulgars. In 971 he was defeated and driven
out by the Emperor John Tzimisces (p. 198).
Sviatoslav was defeated and killed by the Patzinaks on his way back to Kiev (972).

2–980. A dynastic struggle between the sons
of Sviatoslav ended in the victory of

0–1015. VLADIMIR THE SAINT, in whose
reign (c. 990) the Russians were converted in
mass to Christianity in the eastern (Byzantine)
form. The Russian church was organized on
the Greek pattern and was considered to be
under the canonical authority of the patriarch
of Constantinople. From this time on the cultural relation between Constantinople and
Kiev was very close.

15–1019. Further dynastic conflict between
the sons of Vladimir.

1019–1054. YAROSLAV (the Wise), the greatest ruler of Russia in the Kievan period. He
was finally successful in the struggle with his
brother Sviatopolk, but was obliged to leave
to another brother, Mstislav, that part of the
principality east of the Dnieper River until
Mstislav's death in 1036. Yaroslav was then
supreme ruler of all Russia. Extensive building activity at Kiev (Cathedral of St. Sophia).
Religious activity (Metropolitan Hilarion and
the Monastery of the Caves). Promotion of
education. Revision of the *Russian Law* (the
earliest known Russian law code), under Byzantine influence. Dynastic alliances with western states (Yaroslav's daughter, Anna, married
Henry I of France).

The period following the death of Yaroslav
the Great was one of disintegration and decline. Technically the primacy of Kiev continued and the power remained concentrated
in the family of Yaroslav. Actually Kiev continued to lose in importance, and authority became divided between members of the
princely family on a system of seniority and
rotation, leading of necessity to much dynastic
rivalry and countless combinations, sometimes
with Poles and Hungarians.

At the same time the Kievan state was subjected to ever greater pressure from the nomads (Patzinaks and Cumans) moving into
southern Russia from the east. The period
witnessed also a shifting of the older trade
routes, due to the decline of the Baghdad
Caliphate and the conquest of Constantinople
(1204) by the Latin crusaders.

Emergence of new political centers: Galicia
and Volynia in the southwest, principalities
characterized by a strongly aristocratic form
of government; Novgorod the Great, in the
north, controlling territory to the east to the
Urals. In Novgorod the assembly of freemen (*Vieche*) reached its fullest development;
Suzdal-Vladimir in central Russia, the precursor of the grand duchy of Moscow. In
this region the princely power was dominant.

1113–1125. VLADIMIR MONOMAKH,
prince of Kiev. He carried on numerous campaigns against the Cumans of the steppes and
his reign marked the last period of brilliance
at Kiev, which soon thereafter became a bone
of contention between the princes of Volynia
and Suzdal.

1147. First mention of **Moscow** in one of the
chronicles.

1157–1174. ANDREI BOGOLIUBSKI, prince
of Suzdal. He repressed the rising power of
the nobles (*boyars*), united a large block of territory, and established his capital at Vladimir.

1169. Andrei conquered Kiev, which became
part of the Vladimir principality. But the new

Russia: Grand Princes of Kiev (862–1212)

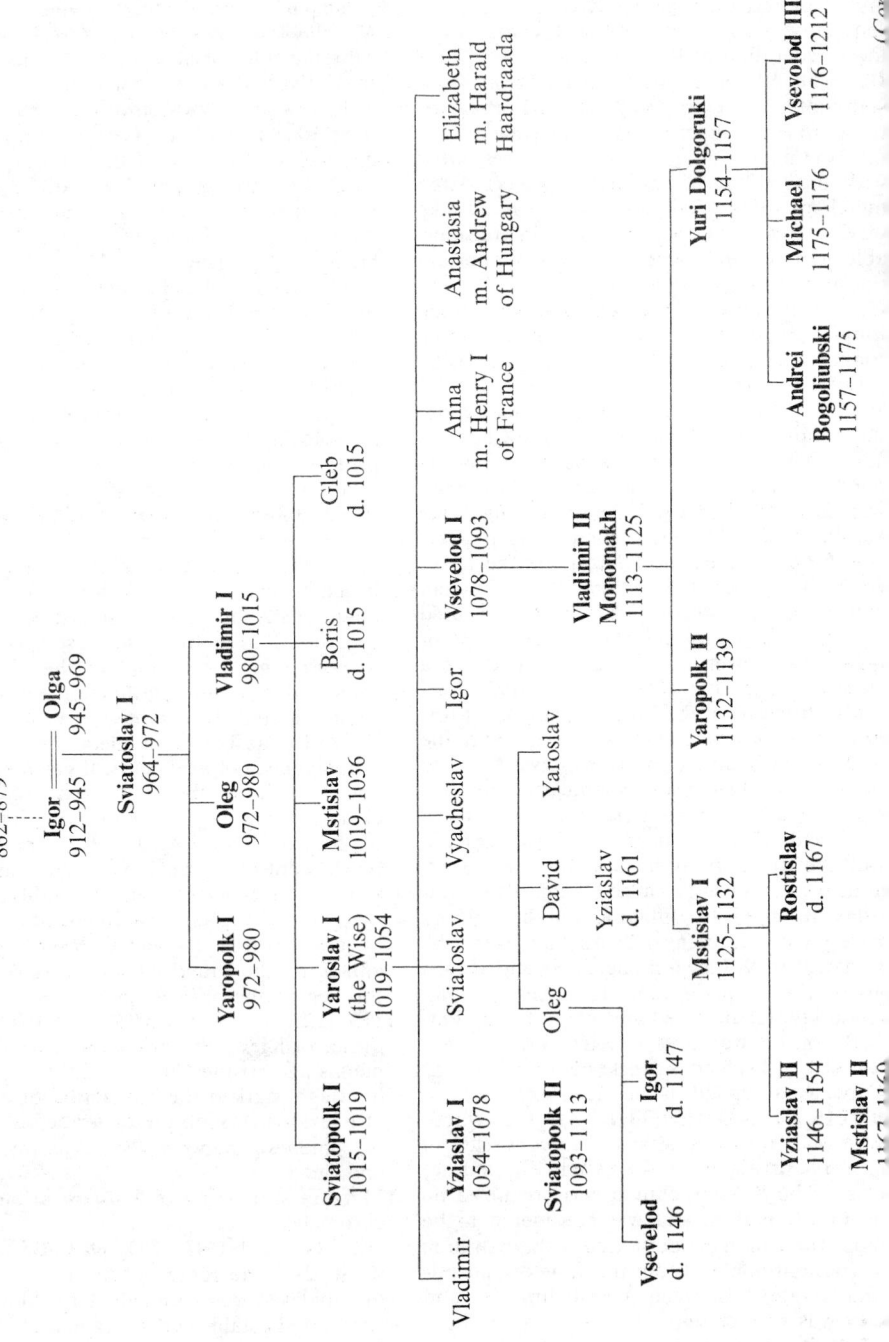

(Cont. p. 341)

state underwent a marked decline on the death of the ruler.

199-1205. Zenith of the Galician principality under Prince Roman.

201. Foundation of Riga, which became the center of German missionary enterprise and commercial expansion.

202. Foundation of the German Order of Swordbearers by Bishop Albert of Livonia (Latvia).

219. Conquest of Estonia by Waldemar II of Denmark.

223. BATTLE OF THE KALKA RIVER, near the Sea of Azov. The Mongols (Tatars, see p. 284), under Subutai, invaded southern Russia from the Transcaucasus region and completely defeated a coalition of Russian princes and Cuman leaders. They retired, however, without pressing their conquests.

226. The **Teutonic Knights** (p. 228) were commissioned to conquer and convert Prussia. They united with the Swordbearers in 1237.

236-1263. ALEXANDER NEVSKI, prince first of Novgorod and after 1252 of Vladimir.

237-1240. The **MONGOL CONQUEST,** under the leadership of Batu. The great armies of the invaders swept over southern and central Russia and into Europe, coming within 50 miles of Novgorod. They took Kiev (1240) and ultimately established themselves (1242) at Sarai on the lower Volga. The **Khanate of the Golden Horde** for two centuries thereafter acted as suzerian of all Russia, levying tribute and taking military contingents, but for the rest leaving the princes in control, respecting the Russian church and interfering little.

240. Alexander Nevski defeated the Swedes under Birger Jarl on the Neva River and thus broke the force of the Swedish advance.

242. Alexander defeated the Teutonic Knights in a **battle on Lake Peipus.**

252. As prince of Vladimir, Alexander Nevski did his utmost to prevent insurrections against Tatar rule and built up a system of protection based upon submission and conciliation.

253. Daniel of Volynia attempted to organize a crusade against the Tatars. In order to secure papal aid he accepted the union of the Russian church with Rome, but his efforts came to nothing.

263. Death of Alexander Nevski on his way back from the Golden Horde.

RUSSIAN CULTURE in this period was all primarily religious and largely Byzantine character. Noteworthy churches were built Kiev, Novgorod, and Cernigov in the 11th and 12th centuries, decorated with fine frescoes. Church literature was voluminous and there appeared further the first chronicles and epics fights against the nomads. (*Cont. p. 340.*)

e. HUNGARY, TO 1301

896. The Hungarians, organized in a number of tribes, of which the **Magyar** was the leading one, occupied the valley of the middle Danube and Theiss (Tisza). Under **Arpad** (d. 907) they had come from southern Russia by way of Moldavia, driven on by the Patzinaks (Pechenegs) and other Asiatic peoples. The Hungarians were themselves nomads of the Finno-Ugrian family. For more than half a century after their occupation of Hungary they continued their raids, both toward the east and toward the west.

906. The Hungarians destroyed the rising Slavic kingdom of Moravia.

955. Battle of Augsburg, in which Emperor Otto 1 decisively defeated the raiding Hungarians. From this time on the Hungarians began to settle down and establish a frontier.

972-997. Geza, duke of the Magyar tribe, and the organizer of the princely power. He began to reduce the tribal leaders and invited Christian missionaries from Germany (Pilgrin of Passau, 974; **St. Adalbert of Prague,** 993). Christianization had already begun from the east, and was furthered by large numbers of war prisoners.

997-1038. ST. STEPHEN (I), greatest ruler of the Arpad dynasty. He suppressed eastern Christianity by force and crusaded against paganism, which was still favored by the tribal chiefs. Stephen took his stand definitely by the west, married a Bavarian princess, called in Roman churchmen and monks (Benedictines), and endowed them with huge tracts of land. With the help of the clergy he broke the power of the tribal chieftains, took over their land as royal domain, administered through counts (*Ispan*), placed over counties (*Comitat*). The counts and high churchmen formed a royal council. Every encouragement was given to agriculture and trade and a methodical system of frontier defense was built up (large belt of swamps and forests, wholly uninhabited and protected by regular frontier guards; as time went on this frontier was gradually extended).

1001. Stephen was crowned with a crown sent by the pope. He was canonized in 1083.

1002. Stephen defeated an anti-Christian insurrection in Transylvania.

1030. Attacks of the Germans under Conrad II, who tried to enforce German suzerainty over Hungary, were repulsed.

1038-1077. A period of dynastic struggles over the succession, every member of the Arpad family claiming a share of the power, and sometimes calling in the Germans for support.

1038-1046. Peter Urseolo, son of Stephen's

The Arpad Dynasty (907–1301)

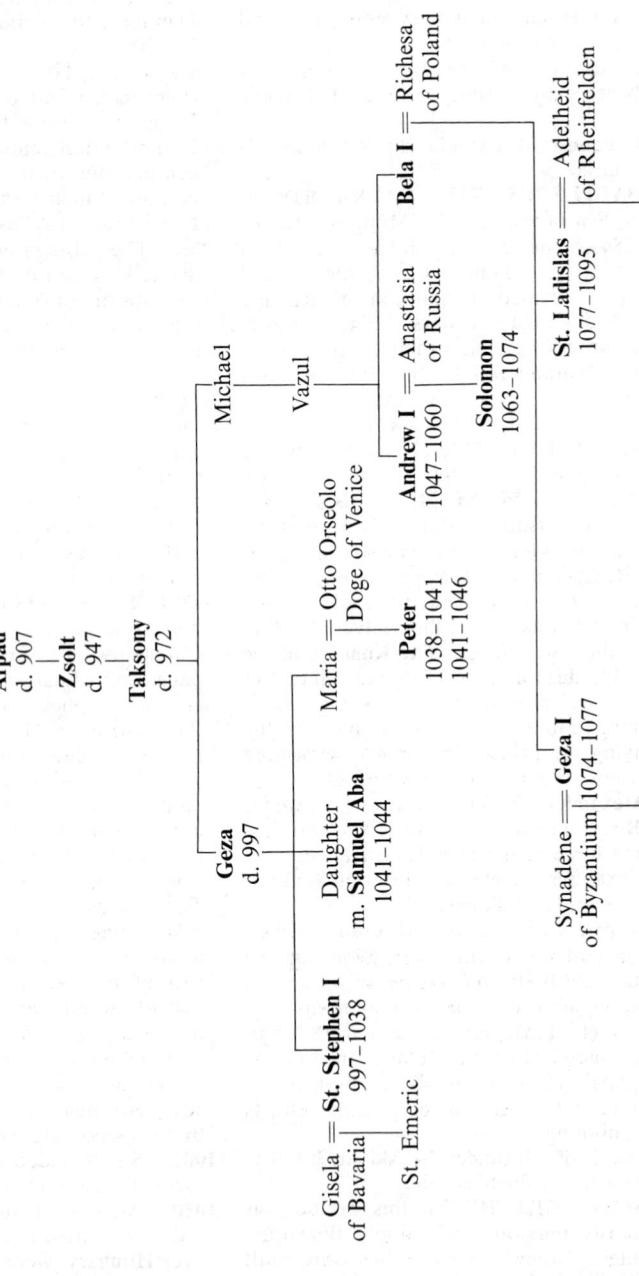

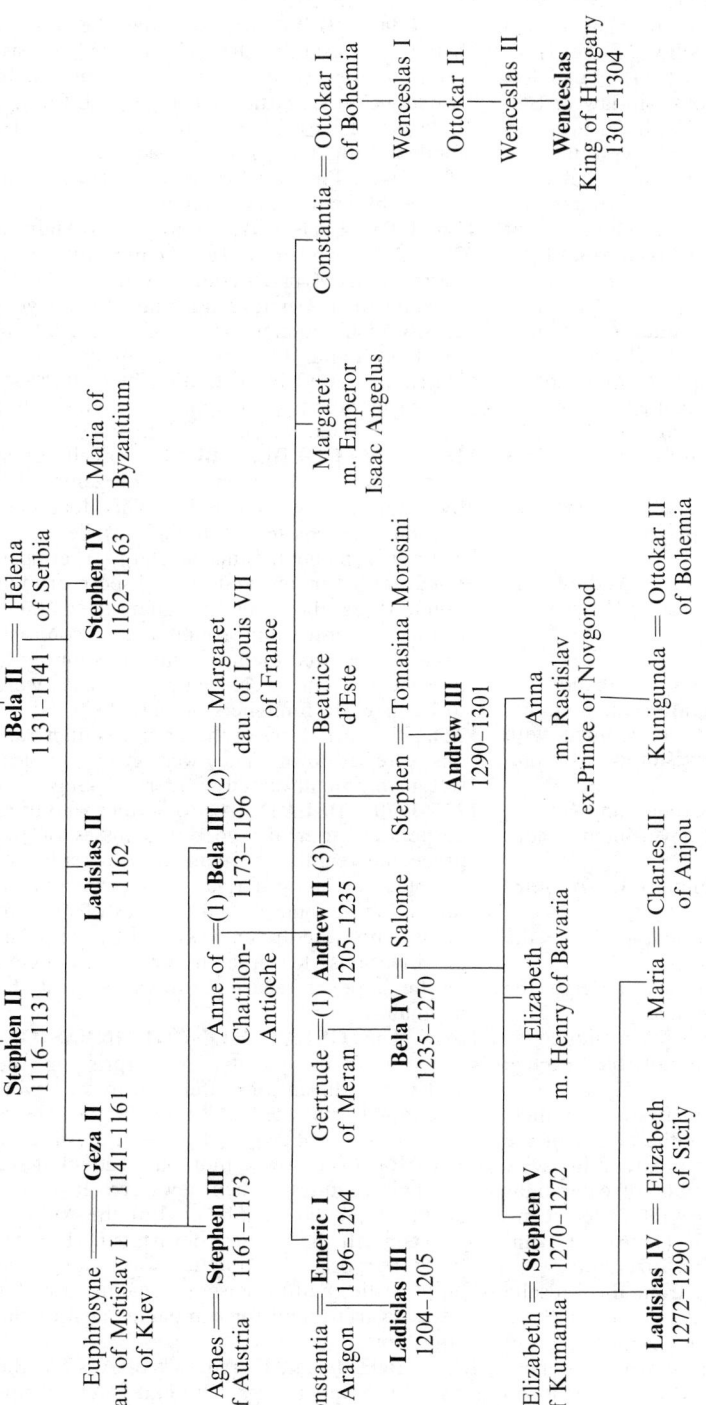

sister and the doge of Venice, succeeded to the throne. He called in German and Italian favorites, aroused the hostility of the Hungarians, and was driven out (1041). For a few years Samuel Aba, the brother-in-law of Stephen, occupied the throne, but he in turn was expelled by Peter, who returned with the Emperor Henry III, to whom he swore fealty.

1046. Peter was overthrown in the course of a great **pagan rising** of the tribal chiefs under Vatha, who massacred the Christians and destroyed the churches. This was the last serious revolt of the kind.

1047-1060. Andrew I, who managed to restore the royal power.

1049-1052. The three campaigns of Emperor Henry III against the Hungarians. Andrew managed to hold his own, and in 1058 the emperor recognized Hungary's independence of the empire.

1061-1063. Bela I, brother of Andrew and popular hero of the campaigns against the Germans.

1063-1074. Solomon, the son of Andrew, the candidate of the German party. He was defeated by his cousin

1074-1077. Geza I.

1077-1095. ST. LADISLAS I (canonized 1192), the first great king after St. Stephen. He supported the pope in his conflicts with the emperor, and at home restored order and prosperity.

1091. Ladislas conquered Croatia and Bosnia, but left these regions self-government under a *ban.*

1095-1116. Coloman (Kalman) **I.** Another strong ruler, who, in

1097-1102. Conquered Dalmatia from the Venetian Republic.

1116-1131. Stephen II, in whose reign the dynastic struggles were resumed.

1131-1141. Bela II. He had been blinded by Coloman, and now took a horrible revenge on his opponents.

1141-1161. Geza II. The intestine conflicts were greatly complicated by the efforts of the Greek emperor, Manuel I, to extend his sway over Hungary. But a number of campaigns carried out to this end (1097-1102) led to no success, though at one time (1156) the Hungarians recognized Byzantine suzerainty.

1150. Saxon (i.e. Germans from the Moselle region) **settlement** in the Zips and southern Transylvania regions. They were called in to help defend the frontiers against Poland and against the Greeks, and had much to do with developing agriculture, trade, and town-building. In this period many Pechenegs and Szeklers were also established for frontier protection.

1161-1173. Stephen III.

1173-1196. BELA III, who had been educated at Constantinople. He married the sister of Philip Augustus of France and established a close dynastic connection with France. Bela was a strong ruler who successfully defended Dalmatia against Venice.

1196-1204. Emeric I, whose position was challenged by his brother Andrew.

1204-1205. Ladislas III, dethroned by Andrew.

1205-1235. ANDREW II. The most disastrous reign in the Arpad period. Andrew was renowned for his extravagance and for his generosity to his foreign favorites. A crusade to the Holy Land (1217) cost him much money, which he raised by alienating huge tracts of the royal domain, facilitating the emergence of large landed magnates or oligarchs.

1222. The **GOLDEN BULL,** forced upon Andrew by the lesser nobility or gentry, led by Andrew's own son, Bela. This document became the charter of feudal privilege. It exempted the gentry and the clergy from taxation, granted them freedom to dispose of their domains as they saw fit, guaranteed them against arbitrary imprisonment and confiscation, and assured them an annual assembly to present grievances. No lands or offices were to be given to foreigners or Jews.

1224. The privileges of the Transylvanian Saxons were set down. They were given practical self-government, directly under the king.

1235-1270. BELA IV. A strong ruler who tried desperately to make good the losses of the preceding reign. The magnates, in reply, attempted to set up a rival ruler, and Bela in turn allowed some 40,000 families of the Cumans, who were driven westward by the Mongol invasions, to settle in the Theiss region in the hope of securing support against the magnates.

1241. The **GREAT MONGOL INVASION,** which took the country by surprise in the midst of its dissensions. Bela's army was overwhelmingly defeated at Muhi on the Theiss and he was obliged to flee to the Adriatic. The Mongols followed him, but suddenly gave up their conquests when news arrived of the death of the Great Khan. But the Mongol invasion left the country devastated. For defense purposes the nobility was allowed to build castles and these soon became bases for feudal warfare and for campaigns against the king himself.

1246. Bela defeated Frederick of Austria, the last of the Babenbergs, who had taken advantage of the Mongol invasion to appropriate some of the western provinces.

1265-1270. Wars of Bela against Ottokar II of Bohemia.

1270–1272. Stephen V, a weak ruler.

1272–1290. Ladislas IV. His efforts to curb the feudal aristocracy were of little avail, but in alliance with Rudolf of Hapsburg he succeeded in breaking the power of Ottokar in the **battle of Dürnkrut** (1278).

1290–1301. Andrew III, last of the native dynasty. He continued the struggle against the domination of the feudal aristocracy, but with little success. (*Cont. p. 342.*)

f. SERBIA, TO 1276

650. Approximate date of the completion of the Slav occupation of the Balkan area. Part of the Slav people extended as far west as Carniola and Carinthia, but these (the Slovenes) were conquered by the Franks in the early 9th century and were thenceforth part of the German Empire.

818. The **Croats,** who had also been conquered by the Franks, revolted, but were again subdued.

924. Tomislav became king of Croatia, accepting his crown from the pope. He ruled over later-day Croatia and over the territory as far south as Montenegro, though the coastal towns were mostly under Byzantine control.

960. Death of Chaslav, who had made the first effort to unite the Serbs. The Serbs, inhabiting a mountainous area, were divided into tribes and clans, under headmen or *zupans.* The grand zupan held an honorary pre-eminence. Technically the territory was under Byzantine suzerainty, which, when the Eastern Empire was strong, was effectively exercised. By the end of the 10th century the inhabitants of present-day Serbia and eastern Bosnia had for the most part accepted eastern Christianity, while western Bosnia and Croatia leaned toward Roman Catholicism. But the conflict of the churches drew the southern Slavs this way and that, becoming frequently an important political as well as religious issue.

1077. Mikhail of Serbia was crowned by a papal legate.

1081–1101. Bodin established a Serbian state in Zeta (i.e. Montenegro).

1102. Croatia was joined with Hungary in a dynastic union, after the defeat of the last ruler, Petar, by King Ladislas. This involved the definitive victory of the western orientation in Croatia and the separation from the other southern Slavs.

1168–1196. STEPHEN NEMANYA, founder of the Nemanyid dynasty in the Raska (i.e. *Rascia* or Serbia proper). Though only grand zupan, Stephen appears to have made considerable progress in uniting the various clans. He definitely adopted the Greek Orthodox faith and persecuted the **Bogomils,** who were forced across the frontier into Bosnia, which at that time was ruled by a strong prince, Kulin (d. 1204). The death of Manuel I Comnenus (1180) and the subsequent decline of the Eastern Empire gave Stephen an opportunity to establish his independence of Constantinople and to conquer extensive territories to the south. In 1196 he retired to a monastery on Mt. Athos which had been founded by his son, **St. Sava.** Stephen died in 1200.

1196–1223. STEPHEN NEMANYA II, the son of the preceding. The beginning of his reign was marked by a struggle with his elder brother, Vukan, to whom Montenegro had been assigned. The Hungarians, who became an ever greater meance to Serbia, supported Vukan, and Stephen was forced to flee to the Bulgarian court. He returned with an army of Cumans supplied by Kaloyan (see below), who appropriated for himself most of eastern Serbia, including Belgrade and Nish. Stephen's brother, St. Sava, finally mediated between the two contestants and Stephen became ruler of Serbia proper.

1217. Stephen was crowned king by a papal legate (hence Stephen the First-Crowned).

1219. St. Sava, fearful of the Roman influence, visited Nicaea and induced the Greek patriarch to recognize him as archbishop of all Serbia and as head of an autocephalous church.

1222. Stephen was recrowned by St. Sava with a crown from Nicaea, thus re-establishing the eastern orientation.

1223–1234. Radoslav, the son of Stephen, a weak ruler, who was deposed by his brother

1234–1242. Vladislav. He married a daughter of Tsar John Asen II of Bulgaria and during this period much of eastern Serbia was under Bulgarian domination.

1242–1276. Urosh I, brother of the preceding two rulers. He married a daughter of the deposed Latin emperor, Baldwin II, and established an alliance with Charles of Anjou, heir of the Latin claims to Constantinople.

1254. The Hungarians, who already held part of northern Serbia, established their suzerainty over Bosnia and Herzegovina. (*Cont. p. 343.*)

g. THE SECOND BULGARIAN EMPIRE, TO 1258

(*From p. 198*)

Following the collapse of the First Bulgarian Empire in 1018, Bulgaria was, for 168 years, an integral part of the Byzantine Empire. The more stringent taxation and other grievances led to a serious revolt in 1040, led by **Peter Delyan,** a son of Gabriel Radomir, and confined to the northwest and western parts of the former empire. Delyan had himself proclaimed *tsar,* but the movement suffered from his rivalry with Tikhomir of Durazzo. In 1041 Delyan was defeated and captured by the imperial troops. Another uprising, led by **George Voitech,** in 1072–1073, never assumed the same proportions and was suppressed without much difficulty. During the Byzantine period the country was constantly exposed to marauding raids by the Patzinaks (1048–1054), many of whom settled in northeastern Bulgaria, and by invasions of the Cumans (1064). The **Bogomil heresy** continued to spread, despite persecution by the government (1110 ff.). Under the leadership of the monks it became to a certain extent a reaction to the Greek influence exerted by the higher clergy.

1185. RISING OF JOHN AND PETER ASEN, two Bulgarian lords from the vicinity of Tirnovo. Defeated by the Emperor Isaac II Angelus (1186) they fled to the Cumans and returned with an army of the latter. After raiding into Thrace, they accepted a truce which left them in possession of Bulgaria north of the Balkan Mountains.

1189. The Asens attempted to effect an alliance with Frederick Barbarossa and the leaders of the Third Crusade, against the Greeks. This came to nothing, but the Bulgarians resumed their raids into Thrace and Macedonia. An imperial army under Isaac Angelus was completely defeated in **a battle near Berrhoe.**

1196. Peter Asen succeeded to leadership of the movement after the murder of John by boyar (i.e. noble) conspirators.

1197. Peter himself fell a victim to his boyar rivals.

1197–1207. KALOYAN (Joannitsa), the younger brother of John and Peter. He made peace with the Greeks (1201) and then engaged (1202) in campaigns against the Serbs (taking of Nish) and the Hungarians, whom he drove back over the Danube.

1204. The **collapse of the Byzantine Empire** (p. 272) gave Kaloyan an excellent opportunity to reaffirm his dominion. By recognizing the primacy of the pope, he succeeded in securing the appointment of a primate for Bulgaria and in getting himself crowned king by the papal legate. At the same time he took over the whole of western Macedonia.

1205. Supported by the Cumans and the local Greeks, Kaloyan completely defeated the Frankish crusaders near Adrianople and captured the Emperor Baldwin I.

1206. Kaloyan put down a revolt of the Greeks and besieged Adrianople and Thessalonica. He was murdered in 1207.

1207–1218. Boril, the nephew of Kaloyan, whose position was not recognized by all other leaders, some of whom attempted to set up independent principalities.

1208. Boril was completely defeated by the Franks under Henry I in the **battle of Philippopolis,** and ultimately (1213) was obliged to make peace.

1217. Ivan (*John*) **Asen,** son of Kaloyan, supported by the Russians, began a revolt in northern Bulgaria. He besieged and took Tirnovo, and captured and blinded Boril (1218).

1218–1241. JOHN ASEN II, whose reign marked the apogee of the Second Bulgarian Empire. John was a mild and generous ruler, much beloved even by the Greek population.

1228–1230. Owing to the youth of the Emperor Baldwin II, a number of Frank nobles at Constantinople projected making John Asen emperor and thereby securing themselves against the aggression of Theodore of Epirus (p. 282). The scheme was opposed by the Latin clergy and ultimately came to nothing.

1230. John Asen defeated Theodore of Epirus at **Klokotnitsa** on the Maritza River and captured him. He then occupied all of western Thrace, Macedonia, and even northern Albania, leaving Thessalonica and Epirus to Theodore's brother Manuel, who became his vassal.

1232. John broke with Rome and the Bulgarian church became independent.

1235. Alliance of John with the Greek emperor of Nicaea against the Franks. The Greeks recognized the patriarch of Tirnovo. Together the allies besieged Constantinople, which was relieved by a fleet and forces from Achaia.

1236. The Hungarians, instigated by the pope, began to threaten the Bulgarians and forced John to withdraw from operations against the Latin Empire.

1241–1246. Kaliman I, the son of John Asen II. His reign was distinguished chiefly by the great incursion of the Mongols, returning from the expedition into central Europe (1241).

1246–1257. Michael Asen, the youngest son of John, and a mere child. The Nicaean emperor, John Vatatzes, took advantage of the situation to conquer all southern Thrace and Macedonia, while Michael of Epirus appropriated western Macedonia.

1254. On the death of John Vatatzes, Michael Asen attempted to recover the lost territories, but was badly defeated by Theodore II Lascaris at **Adrianople** and later (1256) in Macedonia.

1257–1258. Kaliman II, who, with support of the boyars, drove out Michael Asen, only to be deposed and expelled in his turn. He was the last ruler of the Asen dynasty.

(*Cont. p. 345.*)

3. THE NEAR EAST

a. THE BYZANTINE EMPIRE, 1025-1204

rom p. 196)

'or a complete list of the Byzantine emperors
see Appendix II.]

The period of the later Macedonian emper-
s (to 1050) and the succeeding thirty years
as a period of decline, marked by the rule
women, barbarian invasions in the Balkans,
e advance of the Normans in Italy, and the
pansion of the Seljuk Turks (p. 272) in Ana-
lia. Within the empire there was a steady
velopment of the clerical and bureaucratic
bility in the capital and of the feudal baron-
e in the provinces, leading ultimately to sharp
nflict between the two interests.

25-1028. CONSTANTINE VIII, the younger
rother of Basil II, a man suspicious of the
military commanders, who granted many high
offices to court favorites.

27. The Patzinaks, who had invaded the
alkans, were finally driven back over the Dan-
be by the general, Constantine Diogenes.

28-1050. ZOË, empress. She was the third
daughter of Constantine and, though 48 years
ld at her accession, married three times, asso-
iating her husbands in the imperial office.

28-1034. ROMANUS III (Argyropolus), an
official 60 years old, first husband of Zoë. He
made great efforts to gain popularity by cater-
ng to the populace, the nobility, and espe-
ially the church. The patriarchate was permitted to persecute the Monophysites of Syria,
housands of whom fled to Moslem territory.
The hatred engendered by this policy helps
o explain the Seljuk advance in subsequent
ears.

30. Romanus suffered a severe defeat in a
campaign against the Moslem emirs who at-
acked Syria.

31. The situation was saved by the victories
of Georgios Maniakes, greatest imperial gen-
ral of the period.

32. A combined Byzantine-Ragusan fleet
completely defeated the Saracen pirates in the
Adriatic.

34-1041. MICHAEL IV (the Paphlagonian),
econd husband of Zoë. He was a man of
owly origin, who promptly established his
rothers (mostly men of energy and ability) in
igh office.

34-1035. The Byzantine fleets, manned by
he Norseman Harald Haardraade and Scandi-
avian mercenaries, repeatedly defeated the
Saracen pirates off the Anatolian coast and
avaged the coasts of North Africa.

1038. Maniakes and Haardraade with Scandinavian and Italian mercenaries and with the
support of the Byzantine fleets, stormed Messina and defeated the Sicilian Saracens, first at
Rametta (1038), then at **Dragina** (1040).

1040. **Revolt of the Bulgarians** under Peter
Delyan, a descendant of Tsar Samuel. The
revolt was directed against the harsh fiscal
policy of the government. The Bulgars attacked Thessalonica, but the city held out.
Ultimately the movement collapsed, as the
result of dissension among the leaders. Bulgaria was then incorporated in the empire and
the autocephalous church of Ochrid became a
prey of the patriarchal hierarchy.

1041-1042. MICHAEL V (Kalaphates), one of
Zoë's favorites. He attempted to secure sole
power by shutting the empress in a cloister,
but this led to a rising of the Constantinople
nobility and to the incarceration of Michael
in a monastery.

1042-1055. CONSTANTINE IX (Monomachus), the third husband of Zoë, a scholarly
person, wholly out of sympathy with the army
and with the military aristocracy. He systematically neglected the frontier defenses and
the forces.

1042. Maniakes totally defeated the Normans,
who had begun the attack on southern Italy,
in the **battle of Monopoli** (near Naples).

1043. Revolt of Maniakes, representing the
disaffection of the military classes. Maniakes
landed at Durazzo and prepared to march on
the capital, but he was accidentally shot and
killed on the way.

1046. The Byzantine forces occupied Ani and
took over the government of Armenia, which
became another field for clerical exploitation.

1047. Another military uprising, led by Leo
Tornikios, failed.

1048. The imperial generals defeated the advancing Seljuk armies at **Stragna.**

1050. **Death of Zoë.** Her husband Constantine
continued to reign alone.

1051. Expulsion of the Patzinaks from Bulgaria, after years of ravaging and unsuccessful
Byzantine campaigns.

1042-1056. THEODORA, empress. She was
the elder sister of Zoë, an intelligent, vigorous,
and popular ruler, but already advanced in
age.

1054. **Final schism between Rome and Constantinople.** The long-standing friction between the Papacy and the eastern patriarch
had come to a head with the conquest of parts
of southern Italy by the Normans, who were
supported by the Papacy. The Patriarch Michael Kerularios disputed the claim of Pope

Leo IX to jurisdiction in southern Italy. Negotiations were opened, but each side assumed an uncompromising attitude and the rift became unbridgeable. The enmity it left behind was of the utmost importance for the development of the following years.

1056-1057. MICHAEL VI (Stratioticus), who was overthrown almost at once by a revolt of the Anatolian feudal barons.

1057-1059. ISAAC I COMNENUS, proclaimed by the insurgents. He was an able and energetic army man, who promptly abolished a host of sinecures, undertook the reform of the finances, etc. Isaac, already advanced in years, soon found his work too arduous and abdicated in favor of

1059-1067. CONSTANTINE X (Dukas), a high official of the finance department. Constantine introduced a period of domination by the civil officials, church, and scholars, during which the army was viewed with suspicion, neglected, and driven into hostility.

1060. The Normans took Rheggio, completing the conquest of Calabria.

1064. The Seljuks, under Alp Arslan, took Ani and ravaged Armenia.

1065. The Cumans, having crossed the Danube, flooded the Balkan area as far as Thessalonica. They were finally driven back by local forces.

1068-1071. ROMANUS IV DIOGENES, who, on Constantine's death, married the widowed empress, Eudoxia. Romanus was an ambitious soldier, who did his best to check the advance of the enemy in the east and the west.

1068. The Normans took Otranto, and then Bari (1071), the last Byzantine outpost. This marked the **end of the Byzantine rule in Italy.**

1068-1069. Romanus succeeded in repulsing the Seljuks, though they repeatedly raided through the whole of eastern Anatolia.

1071. BATTLE OF MANZIKERT (north of Lake Van). Romanus had concentrated huge forces for a decisive battle, and he rejected all offers of a settlement. In the course of a hard-fought battle he was deserted by Andronicus Dukas and other Byzantine magnates. Romanus was defeated and captured, but then released by the Seljuks. He attempted to regain the Byzantine throne, but was defeated by his opponents and blinded. He died soon afterward.

1071-1078. MICHAEL VII (Parapinakes), a son of Constantine X. His elevation meant another victory for the bureaucratic group. Michael made the great scholar **Michael Psellus** his chief adviser and devoted himself to the pursuit of learning. The military system was again allowed to fall into neglect.

1074. The emperor concluded a **treaty with the Seljuks** in order to secure their aid against h[is] uncle, who had set himself up as a pretende[r]. The Seljuks defeated the pretender, but too[k] advantage of the situation to spread them selves over a large part of Anatolia.

1078. Revolt of Nicephorus Briennius in Alba[...]nia. Another military revolt broke out i[n] Anatolia, led by Nicephorus Botaniates, wh[o] was supported by the Seljuks.

1078-1081. NICEPHORUS III (Botaniates[)] emperor after Michael's abdication. His acce[s]sion was met by a number of insurrections i[n] various parts of the army, but these were su[p]pressed by the able general Alexius Comnenu[s]

1081. Revolt of Alexius Comnenus himsel[f] He seized Constantinople with a force of me[r]cenaries, who thereupon plundered the capita[l] The victory of Comnenus meant the final su[c]cess of the military aristocracy and the begi[n]ning of a new period of military achievemen[t]

1081-1118. ALEXIUS I COMNENUS, an abl[e] general, vigorous administrator, conscientiou[s] ruler, and shrewd diplomat. Having to rel[y] upon the great feudal families, he attempte[d] to win their support by lavish grants of hono[rs] and ranks. At the same time he tried to us[e] the high clergy to counterbalance the influenc[e] of the nobility. He reformed the judicial an[d] financial systems and systematically used hi[s] resources in money to buy off the enemies h[e] could not conquer.

1081-1085. The war against the Norman[s] under **Robert Guiscard.** The latter landed i[n] Epirus with a large force and besieged Durazz[o] (Dyracchium). Alexius bought the support [of] the Venetians with extensive trade privilege[s] (1082), but Guiscard defeated the emperor i[n] the **battle of Pharsalus,** after which he too[k] Durazzo. The war was continued by Robert['s] son, Bohemund, who again defeated Alexiu[s] and in 1083 conquered all Macedonia as far a[s] the Vardar. But the advance was broken b[y] the resistance of Larissa, by the guerrilla tac[-]tics of the natives (who hated the heretic[al] Latins), and by the Seljuk cavalry employe[d] by the emperor. In 1085 the combined Byzan[-]tine and Venetian fleets defeated the Norman[s] near Corfu. The death of Robert Guiscard [in] the same time led to dissension among his son[s] and the abandonment of the Balkan projec[t].

1086-1091. Revolt of the Bogomils in Thrac[e] and Bulgaria. The heretics were supported b[y] the Patzinaks and Cumans and were able t[o] defeat Alexius and a large army (**battle [of] Drystra** or Dorostolon, 1087). The Cuman[s] then ravaged the entire eastern Balkan regio[n] as far as Constantinople until Alexius bough[t] them off, took them into imperial service, an[d] used them (1091) to annihilate the Patzinak[s] (**battle of Leburnion**).

1092. Death of Malik Shah, ruler of the Seljuk empire of Iconium, which controlled almost all of Anatolia. The death of Malik led to disputes as to the succession and paved the way for the partial reconquest of Anatolia.

1094. Constantine Diogenes, a pretender to the throne, crossed the Danube with an army of Cumans and besieged Adrianople, but was then defeated in the battle of **Taurocomon.**

1096–1097. THE FIRST CRUSADE (p. 274). The crusaders, of whom Bohemund was one of the leaders, were looked upon with great suspicion in the east, where there was little interest in a movement organized by the heretical Latin pope. But Alexius was unable to stop the crusaders, and therefore devoted himself to managing the movement. He induced them to promise to do homage to the empire for all territory reconquered from the infidel. The crusading **victories at Nicaea** and **Dorylaeum** (1097) enabled Alexius to recover the entire western coast of Anatolia.

1098–1108. Second war with the Normans. The crusaders, having regained Antioch (lost to the Turks only in 1085), turned it over to Bohemund, who refused to recognize Alexius' suzerainty. War broke out. Bohemund returned to Italy and raised a huge army, with which he appeared in Epirus (1104). He failed in his siege of Durazzo, and Alexius wisely avoided open battle. Ultimately (1108) Bohemund agreed to make peace, recognizing Byzantine suzerainty over Antioch.

1110–1117. War against the Seljuks, who again advanced to the Bosporus. In 1116 Alexius won a resounding victory at **Philomelion,** which induced the Turks to make peace at **Akroinon** (1117); they abandoned the entire coastal area of Anatolia (north, west, and south) and all of Anatolia west of a line from Sinope through Ancyra (Ankara) and Philomelion.

1111. Trade privileges granted to the Pisans. This was part of the emperor's effort to draw the Pisans away from the Normans and at the same time to counterbalance the extensive trade position of the Venetians in the empire.

1118–1143. JOHN II COMNENUS, a ruler of high moral integrity, mild, brave, and sincere. He devoted his attention chiefly to the east, with the object of recovering the old frontier of the Euphrates and of subjecting the Latin states of Syria to the empire.

1120–1121. In a successful campaign against the Seljuks, John recovered southwestern Anatolia. He was diverted from further conquests by continued incursions of the Patzinaks in the Balkans.

1122. The Patzinaks were completely defeated and thenceforth did not threaten the empire.

1122–1126. War with Venice, resulting from John's refusal to renew the extensive trading privileges, which the Venetians had been exploiting to the full. The Venetian fleets ravaged the islands of the Aegean, occupied Corfu and Cephalonia, and ultimately (1126) forced John to renew the privileges.

1124. Intervention of the emperor in behalf of Bela II in Hungary, initiating a policy which continued throughout the century. The objective of the Comneni was to prevent the Hungarians from establishing control over the Slavic regions of Dalmatia, Croatia, and Serbia. By the **Peace of 1126** the emperor secured Branicova, a vital bridgehead on the Danube.

1134–1137. Conquest of Cilician (Little) Armenia, which was allied with the Latin kingdom of Antioch. John forced Raymond of Antioch to do homage for his domain.

1143. John died from a wound incurred while hunting. He was just about to renew his campaigns in Syria.

1143–1180. MANUEL I COMNENUS, the son of John, a noble, intelligent, chivalrous idealist, and yet an adroit statesman and ambitious soldier. He was the greatest of the Comneni and the most splendid. In his reign Constantinople came to be accepted as the capital of the world and the center of culture. Its brilliant art was imitated in the east as in the west. Manuel married a Latin princess (Maria of Antioch) and throughout his career cherished the hope of resurrecting a universal empire. Hence his association with and employment of Latin nobles, who intermarried with the Greek aristocracy, his constant toying with the idea of reunion with Rome, his designs on Italian territory, and his antagonism to the Hohenstaufen emperors. All this tended to arouse much hostility among the Greeks (accentuated by the high-handed activities of the Italian traders), cost the empire inordinate sums of money, and involved repeated conflict with the Normans. The emperor's preoccupation in the west at the same time forced him to neglect the east, where the Seljuk sultanate of Iconium (Rum) was able to effect a marked recovery.

1147–1158. War with Roger of Sicily. The Norman fleets ravaged Euboea and Attica, took and plundered Thebes and Corinth, carried away large numbers of the silk-workers, who were established at Palermo. The emperor, having neglected the Byzantine fleet, was obliged to buy the aid of Venice with extensive trading rights (1148). The Venetians helped to reconquer Corfu (1149) and paved the way for the Byzantine conquest of Ancona (1151). But efforts to extend the Greek power in Italy met with failure (1154) and Manuel in

270

(*From p. 194*)

The Comneni and Angeli (1057–1204)

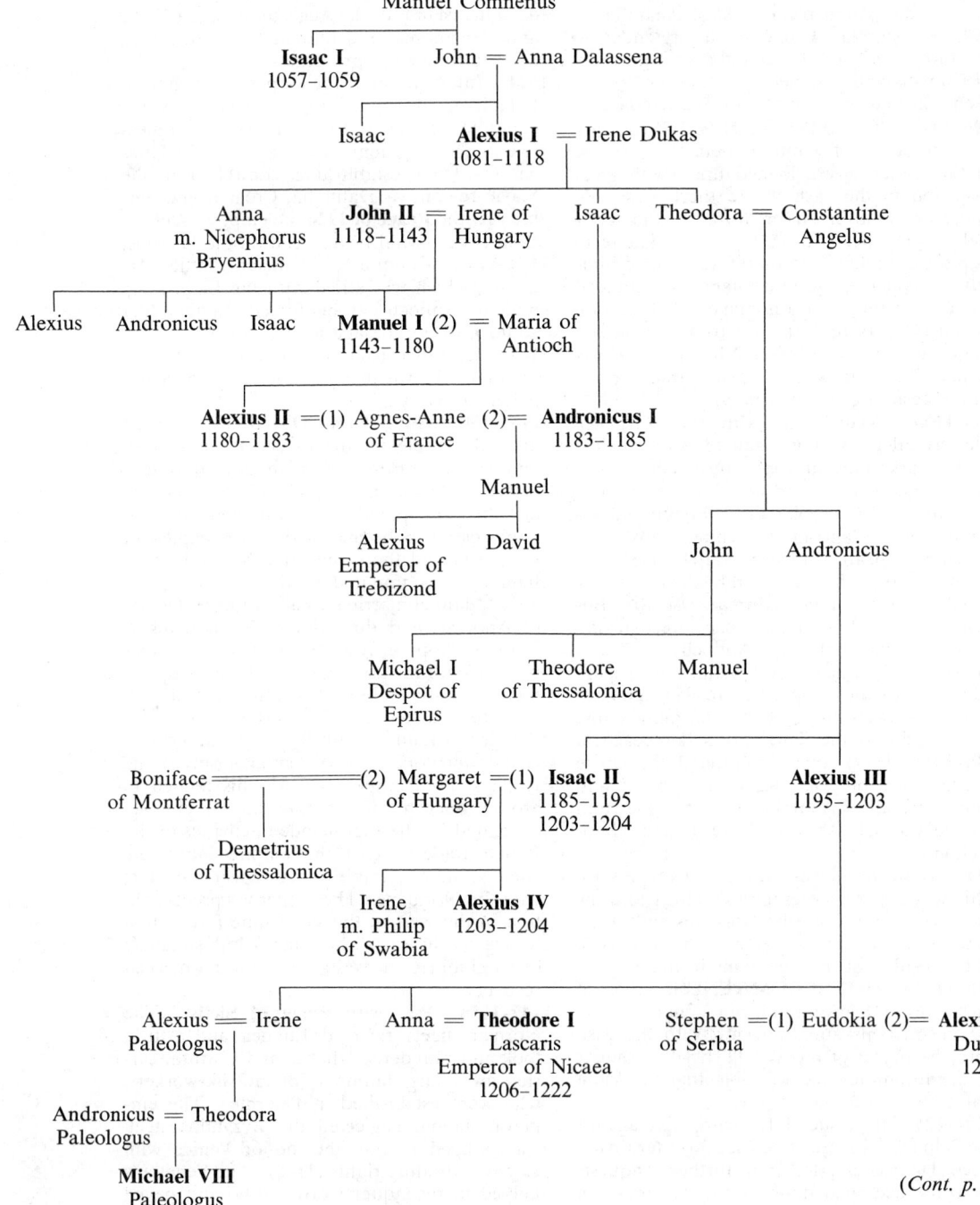

(*Cont. p. ...*)

the end had to agree to an inconclusive peace (1158).

1147-1149. THE SECOND CRUSADE (p. 275). The crusaders, having plundered the Balkan region, almost came to blows with the Greeks at Constantinople, but Manuel by diplomacy prevented a clash. The Greeks did nothing to prevent the defeat of the crusaders in Anatolia.

1152-1154. Successful war against the Hungarians, who attempted to make good their claims to Serbia and Bosnia. Peace was made in 1156, the Hungarians recognizing the emperor's suzerainty.

1155. Trade privileges granted to Genoa, the emperor hoping thereby to counteract the domination of the Venetians.

1158-1159. An expedition against Raymond of Antioch forced the latter to renew his homage.

1161. Kilidj Arslan IV, sultan of Rum, made peace with the empire, recognizing the emperor's primacy.

1165-1168. War with the Hungarians. The imperial forces took Dalmatia and in the final peace (1168) received also part of Croatia. The following years Manuel interfered actively in Hungarian dynastic affairs. Bela III was practically his vassal.

1170-1177. War with Venice, the natural result of the Byzantine acquisitions in Dalmatia and in Italy. The emperor arrested all Venetian traders in Constantinople and confiscated their goods, but with a neglected fleet he was able to do little. The Venetians conquered Ragusa (1171) and Chios (1171), though they failed in an attack on Ancona (1173). In 1175 the Venetians made an alliance with the Normans against the empire and thereby forced Manuel to yield. By the **Peace of 1176** the trade privileges were renewed and the emperor paid a heavy indemnity.

1176-1177. War against the Seljuks. The Byzantines were defeated at **Myriocephalon** (1176), but in the next year Manuel defeated the enemy in Bithynia, while John Vatatzes drove them out of the Meander Valley.

1180-1183. ALEXIUS II COMNENUS, the son of Manuel, who ruled under the regency of his mother, Maria of Antioch. The regent relied almost entirely upon Latins in her service.

1182. Revolt of the populace of Constantinople against the Latins, officials, and traders, who were brutally cut down in a great massacre. The mob forced the proclamation of

1183-1185. ANDRONICUS I COMNENUS, an uncle of the boy-emperor, who ruled first as co-emperor, but in 1183 had Alexius strangled and became sole ruler. Andronicus had intrigued innumerable times against Manuel and was renowned for his lack of principle. But

he was a man of great personal charm, intelligent, vigorous, unscrupulous, and cruel. Through persecution, confiscations, and executions he cleaned the court circle, got rid of the hated Latins, abolished sale of offices, sinecures, etc.; reformed the judiciary, lightened the taxes. All this was a policy directed against the powerful official and landed aristocracy and might, had it been carried through, have led to a thoroughgoing reform of the empire.

1185. The Norman attack. The Normans took Durazzo, sent an army and a navy against Thessalonica, which they stormed, and massacred the Greeks. This attack led to a revolt of the Greek nobility against Andronicus, who was deposed, tortured, and executed.

1185-1195. ISAAC ANGELUS, leader of the insurgents. His accession meant a return of the old negligence and corruption. Within a brief space the entire empire began to disintegrate. In the provinces the powerful feudal families (i.e. Sguros in Greece; Gabras at Trebizond) began to set up as independent potentates.

1185. Victory of the Byzantine general, Alexius Branas, over the Normans at Demetritsa. By 1191 the Normans were driven out of the Balkans and even out of Durazzo and Corfu.

1185-1188. The **great insurrection in Bulgaria,** led by Peter and John Asen. This was due primarily to the extortion of the imperial fiscal agents. The revolt was supported by the Cumans and resulted in the devastation of much of the Balkan region, with the annihilation of much of the Greek population. Though at times successful, the Greek commanders were unable to suppress the movement, which resulted in the formation of a new Bulgarian state north of the Balkan Mountains (1188).

1187. Fall of Jerusalem. Isaac, in fear of another crusade, allied himself with Saladin.

1189. THE THIRD CRUSADE (p. 275). Frederick Barbarossa was welcomed in Bulgaria by John Asen, who offered him an army for use against the empire. But Frederick avoided friction as well as might be, and Isaac did not oppose the crossing of the crusaders into Anatolia. The death of Saladin (1193) relieved the danger from the east.

1190-1194. Continuation of the war in Bulgaria. The Byzantine forces were defeated at Berrhoe (1190) and at Arcadiopolis (1194).

1195-1203. ALEXIUS III, the brother of Isaac, whom he deposed and blinded.

1196. The western emperor, Henry VI, heir to the Norman domains, demanded Durazzo and Thessalonica. Alexius settled for a huge money payment, and Henry's death (1197) removed the immediate threat from that quarter.

1201. Peace with the Bulgars, who were allowed to retain most of the eastern Balkan area, under the younger brother of the Asens, John (Joannitsa, Kaloyan, 1197–1207).

1202–1204. THE FOURTH CRUSADE (p. 275). The leaders were the Venetian doge, **Enrico Dandolo,** and **Boniface of Montferrat.** Alexius, the son of Isaac, appealed for aid against his uncle and promised great concessions. Dandolo succeeded in diverting the expedition against Constantinople. The crusaders took Durazzo (1203) and arrived at Constantinople (June, 1203). The emperor thereupon fled to Adrianople (July). His deposed brother, Isaac, was set upon the throne with his son, the accomplice of the crusaders.

1203–1204. ALEXIUS IV. He was wholly under the control of the crusaders and was forced to pay a heavy tribute. Popular discontent led to

1204, Jan. 25. A revolution and the proclamation of

1204. Alexius V (Dukas). Alexius IV was killed. The new ruler refused payments to the crusaders and demanded their withdrawal.

Apr. 12. The crusaders stormed the city, which was given over to a merciless sack. The emperor succeeded in escaping. (*Cont. p. 280.*)

b. THE SELJUK TURKS, 1037–1109

(*From p. 206*)

1037. The **Seljuks,** a sept of the Ghuzz Turks, under the brothers Tughril Beg and Chagar Beg, invaded Khorasan and defeated the Ghaznavid armies. They then conquered Balkh, Jurjan, Tabaristan, and Khwarezm.

1055. Entry of Tughril Beg into Baghdad, where he was proclaimed sultan, with the title *King of the East and the West.* Invasion of Byzantine Cappadocia and Phrygia by Tughril Beg.

1063–1072. Alp Arslan, brilliant nephew of Tughril, succeeded the latter. He conquered Georgia and Armenia.

1071. BATTLE OF MANZIKERT (Malaz Kard). Alp Arslan defeated the Byzantine emperor, Romanus IV Diogenes, and virtually destroyed the Byzantine power in Asia Minor.

1073–1092. Malik Shah, son of Alp Arslan. His vizir, **Nizam al-Mulk,** was one of the ablest administrators of Oriental history. At the same time he was a patron of learning, founder of colleges in Baghdad (the Nizamiya) and other principal cities. Under him the calendar was reformed by the last of the intellectuals of the Baghdad school, **Omar Khayyam** (d. 1123), poet and mathematician (worked on cubic equations).

1084. The Seljuks took Antioch.

1090. Rise of the Ismailian fraternity of the **Assassins,** founded by Hasan Sabbah, a schoolfellow of Nizam al-Mulk, and a Fatimid propagandist. He captured the mountain stronghold of Alamut in the Elburz range in Mazandêran. The Assassins later became masters of many mountain fortresses in northern Persia, Iraq, and Syria. The crusaders came into contact with the Syrian branch.

1091. Nizam al-Mulk was murdered by one of Hasan's emissaries, after two expeditions against the Assassins had failed.

1094–1104. Barkyaruk (Rukn al-Din), son of Malik Shah, sultan. Civil war broke out between the new ruler and his brother, Mohammed, over Iran and Khorasan, and separate branches of the Seljuk family attained virtual independence in different parts of the empire, although the main line still preserved the nominal sovereignty down to 1157. The **Seljuk Empire of the East** ultimately fell before the attack of the Khwarezm shah (1157). The Seljuks of Kirman (1041–1187) were overthrown by the Ghuzz Turcomans; the Seljuks of Syria (1094–1117) by the Burids and Ortuqids; the Seljuks of Iraq and Kurdistan (1117–1194) by the shahs of Khwarezm. The Seljuks of Rum (Iconium, Koniah), who ruled most of Anatolia, absorbed the Danishmandid princedom in Cappadocia, but were ousted by the Mongols and the Othmanli (Ottoman) Turks (p. 350).

1100–1200. During the 12th century the whole of the Seljuk Empire, excepting Rum, fell into the hands of captains of the Seljuk armies, the so-called *Atabegs* (regents). The **Burid dynasty** of Damascus (1103–1154) was founded by Tughtugin. The **Zangid dynasty** of Mesopotamia and Syria (1127–1250) by Imad al-Din Zangi, whose son, Nur al-Din, was famous as an opponent of the crusaders. The Zangids absorbed the Burids (1154). The **Ortuqid dynasty** of Diyar-Bakr (Diarbekr) was founded by Ortuq ibn Akrab (1101), whose sons, Sukman and Il-Ghazi, both won renown in the wars against the Latin princes of Palestine. The dynasty lasted until 1312. Sukman Qutbi was the first of the shahs of Armenia (1100–1207). The Atabeg house of Azerbaijan (1136–1225) was founded by Ildigiz, whose son, Mohammed, was the actual ruler of the Seljuk kingdom of Iraq. The Salgharids held Fars (1148–1287), the Hazaraspids Luristan (1148–1339); and Anushtigin, a Turkish slave of Balkatigin of Ghazni, was the grandfather of the first independent shah of Khwarezm, Atsiz. At one time the rule of the Khwarezm shah was almost co-terminous with the Seljuk Empire.

273

Seljuk Sultans (1055–1194)

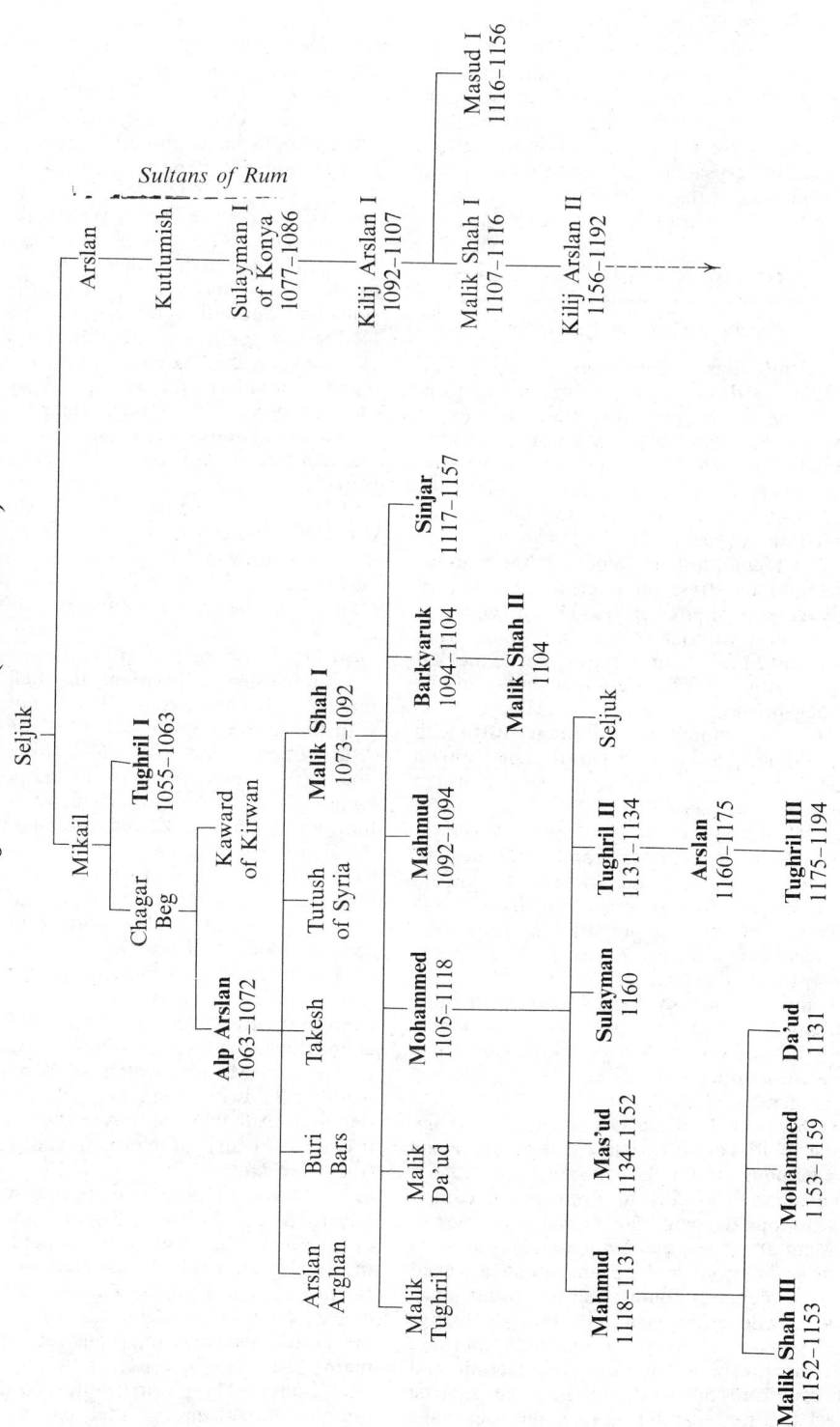

Seljuk

Mikail

Arslan

Sultans of Rum

Kutulmish

Sulayman I
of Konya
1077–1086

Kilij Arslan I
1092–1107

Malik Shah I
1107–1116

Masud I
1116–1156

Kilij Arslan II
1156–1192

Chagar
Beg

Kaward
of Kirwan

Tughril I
1055–1063

Alp Arslan
1063–1072

Takesh

Tutush
of Syria

Malik Shah I
1073–1092

Barkyaruk
1094–1104

Malik Shah II
1104

Sinjar
1117–1157

Arslan
Arghan

Buri
Bars

Malik
Da'ud

Mohammed
1105–1118

Mahmud
1092–1094

Malik
Tughril

Mahmud
1118–1131

Mas'ud
1134–1152

Sulayman
1160

Tughril II
1131–1134

Seljuk

Da'ud
1131

Mohammed
1153–1159

Malik Shah III
1152–1153

Arslan
1160–1175

Tughril III
1175–1194

1095. The crusaders, having invaded the dominions of the sultan of Rum, took Antioch, with frightful slaughter. They stormed Jerusalem (1099) and founded the Latin kingdom of Jerusalem. By 1109 Caesarea, Tripoli, Tyre, and Sidon were captured. Constant warfare between the crusaders and the Moslems (Fatimids, Burids, Zangids, Ortuqids, and finally Saladin, the sultan of Egypt). (*Cont. p. 348.*)

c. THE CRUSADES, 1096–1291

Precursors of the Crusades

(1) **Penitentiary pilgrimages** probably dating from the days of Helena, mother of Constantine the Great; after the Arab conquest of Jerusalem (638) the Holy City was a joint shrine of Christian and Moslem; protectorate of Charlemagne over the Holy Places (recognized by Harun al-Rashid, 807); abrogated by the mad Caliph Hakim (1010); (2) **Charlemagne's war** of Christian reconquest in Spain; (3) the **Cluniac revival** and its stress on pilgrimages led to a steady increase of pilgrimages (117 known in the 11th century) without serious opposition from the tolerant Moslems until the advent of the Seljuks; (4) **wars of Christian reconquest** in the west began European reaction to Moslem pressure; Pisan reconquest of Sardinia (c. 1016) with papal support; alliance of Castile and Aragon in the reconquest of Spain (c. 1050); Norman reconquest of Sicily (1060–1090).

1087. Genoa and Pisa, by capture of Mahdiyah in Africa, gained command of the western Mediterranean from the Moslems. Appeal of the Greek emperor after Manzikert (1071) to Pope Gregory VII; preparation of an army (alliance with Roger Guiscard) by Gregory (1074) to aid the Greeks.

Transformation by Pope Urban II of military assistance to Constantinople into a new kind of holy war (a sort of ecclesiastical imperialism) under the auspices of the revived and regenerated Papacy.

1095. Appeal from the Greek emperor at the **synod of Piacenza;** Urban's call at the **synod of Clermont** (1095): Urban, a Cluniac and a Frenchman, speaking to Frenchmen, recited the glorious deeds of the French and tales of Moslem atrocities, made open allusions to the chances of profit and advancement, attacked feudal violence at home, and brought the audience to wild enthusiasms; he himself distributed crosses. Urban's propaganda journeys and the preaching of **Peter the Hermit** and others stirred the west, but had the greatest effect in France and Lorraine, the area most under Cluniac influence. The great rulers were all at odds with the Papacy or busy at home; the rest of Europe indifferent, and the Crusades began as they continued, largely under French auspices.

1096–1099. THE FIRST CRUSADE. Five popular, aimless mass migrations (1096), emptying whole villages and often accompanied by pillage and anti-Semitic outbreaks, of which two (perhaps 7000 under Peter the Hermit and perhaps 5000 under Walter the Penniless) reached Asia Minor and were annihilated. The Norman-French baronage flocked to the Cross and converged in three divisions on Constantinople: the Lorrainers under **Godfrey of Bouillon** and his brother Baldwin via Hungary; the Provençals under **Count Raymond of Toulouse** and the papal legate, Adhemar of Puy, via Illyria; the Normans under **Bohemund of Otranto** (the most effective leader) via Durazzo by sea and land. Perhaps they were 30,000 in all.

The Greek emperor, Alexius I Comnenus, expecting mercenaries and unprepared for crusaders, provided food and escort and punished the plunderers. He exacted an oath of fealty from the leaders (Raymond refused) in an effort to insure his title to any recovered "lost provinces" of the Greek Empire.

The **Moslem opposition:** the Seljuks had merely garrisoned Syria and were not popular with the native population. Moslem unity in Asia Minor ended with the death of Malik Shah (1092), and Syria was divided politically, racially, and theologically (Sunnite *vs.* Shi'ite; the Fatimite capture of Jerusalem (1098) from the Sunnites).

1097. Nicaea, the Seljuk capital in Asia Minor, taken by the combined Greek and crusading force; defeat of the Moslem field army at Dorylaeum; excursion of Baldwin and Tancred, and rivalry in Cilicia; Bohemund established himself in the Antioch area. Siege and capture (by treachery) of Antioch (1097–1098); countersiege of the Christians in Antioch by the emir of Mosul; election of Bohemund as leader. Baldwin's conquest of Edessa (1097); death of Adhemar of Puy (1098); Christian divisions: rivalry of Norman and Provençal (the *Holy Lance*).

1099. March to Jerusalem (Genoese convoy and food supply); siege, capture, and horror of the sack. The death of the papal legate left the organization of the government of Jerusalem to feudal laymen. **Godfrey of Bouillon,** elected king, assumed the title of *Defender of the Holy Sepulcher* (for pious reasons). The main body of the crusaders soon streamed back home. The Norman effort to dominate the government through their patriarch Dagobert led to his deposition by the anti-Norman party and Jerusalem became a feudal kingdom rather than theocracy under papal domination. The government (as revealed by the *Assizes of Jerusalem,* the most complete feudal code extant) was narrowly feudal, the king a feudal suzerain, not a sovereign, the tenants-in-chief dominant. Besides the feudal organization there were burgher and ecclesiastical organizations, with their own courts.

Continued divisions among the Moslems and the weakness of the Greeks favored the progress of the Latin states: the **kingdom of Jerusalem,** in close commercial alliance with the Italian towns (Genoa, Pisa, and later Venice), profited by the commerce through its ports and extended south to tap the Red Sea trade. The other states: the **county of Edessa** (established by Baldwin), the **principality of Antioch** (established by Bohemund), and the **county of Tripoli** (set up by Raymond of Toulouse), were fiefs of Jerusalem (divided into four great baronies and into lesser fiefs). The departure of the main body of the crusaders left the Franks without enough forces to prevent their orientalization and decline. After the capture of Jerusalem (1187) the kingdom of Jerusalem ceased to be an organized state.

Moslem unification in Syria was completed by the Atabegs of Mosul and signalized by the capture of Edessa (1144). Mosul soon mastered Egypt; Saladin emerged supreme in Egypt (1171), quickly reduced Damascus and Aleppo, and brought Syria and Egypt under a single efficient rule.

1147-1149. THE SECOND CRUSADE. Bernard of Clairvaux, persuaded by Pope Eugenius III, somewhat against his will, preached (1145) the Second Crusade. Conrad III and King Louis VII of France took the Cross. To avoid conflicts the two monarchs went by separate routes; there never was coherent direction or unity of command. The Norman Roger of Sicily profited by the Second Crusade to seize the Greek islands and to attack Athens, Thebes, and Corinth. Nothing of importance was achieved by the Second Crusade and the movement was discredited throughout Europe.

1184. Saladin's steady advance led to a great appeal to the west; King Philip II of France and Henry II of England declined the crown of Jerusalem, but levied a **Saladin tithe** (1188) to finance a crusade. Christian attack on a caravan (said to be escorting Saladin's sister) provoked Saladin's holy war (1187-1189): **capture of Jerusalem** (1187) without a sack (Saladin's humanitarianism) and reduction of the Latin states to the cities of Antioch, Tyre, Tripoli, and a small area about each.

1189-1192. THE THIRD CRUSADE. Precipitated by the fall of Jerusalem, a completely lay and royal affair despite the efforts of the Papacy to regain control. It was supported partly by the Saladin tithe, and was led by the three greatest monarchs of the day: (1) **Frederick Barbarossa** (a veteran of the Second Crusade) as emperor, the traditional and theoretical military leader of Christendom, headed a well-organized and disciplined German contingent starting from Regensburg (1189), which marched via Hungary, entered Asia Minor, and disintegrated after Frederick was drowned (1190); (2) **King Richard I of England** and (3) **King Philip II of France,** who went by sea. Already political rivals, they quarreled in winter quarters in Sicily (1190-1191); Richard turned aside in the spring and took Cyprus which he sold to Guy de Lusignan. The quarrels of Philip and Richard continued in the Holy Land, and Philip returned to France after the capture of Acre (1191). Richard's negotiations with Saladin (Richard proposed a marriage of his sister Joan to Saladin's brother, who was to be invested with Jerusalem) resulted (1192) in a three-year truce allowing the Christians a coastal strip between Jaffa and Acre and access to Jerusalem. Captivity of Richard (1192-1194) and heavy ransom to the Emperor Henry VI. The Third Crusade ended the golden age of the crusades.

1202-1204. THE FOURTH CRUSADE. Emperor Henry VI, king of Sicily (by virtue of his marriage to the Norman Constance) and heir of the traditional Norman plan of creating an empire on the ruins of the Greek Empire, was determined to continue his father Frederick's crusade, and began to encroach on the Greek lands: homage of Cyprus and Lesser Armenia (1195); the marriage of Henry's brother Philip to Irene, daughter of the deposed Emperor Isaac II Angelus, established a Hohenstaufen claim to the Greek throne. Henry died 1197.

Pope Innocent III, determined to regain control of the crusading movement, and hoping to unite the Greek and Latin churches, issued a call to the monarchs; it was ignored (Philip II and King John of England were at odds, Germany in chaos, the Spanish rulers busy with the Moors), and the brunt fell again on the French baronage. Egypt, the objective, could only be reached by water; negotiations with Venice (1201): terms, 85,000 marks and half the booty. **Meeting of Hagenau** (1201) between Philip (brother of Henry VI), Boniface of Montferrat, and (?) Alexius; decision to divert the crusade to Constantinople (a return to the plans of Henry VI); Venice may have shared in the decision. As it was impossible to raise 85,000 marks, Venice agreed to fulfill her bargain if the Christian city of Zara

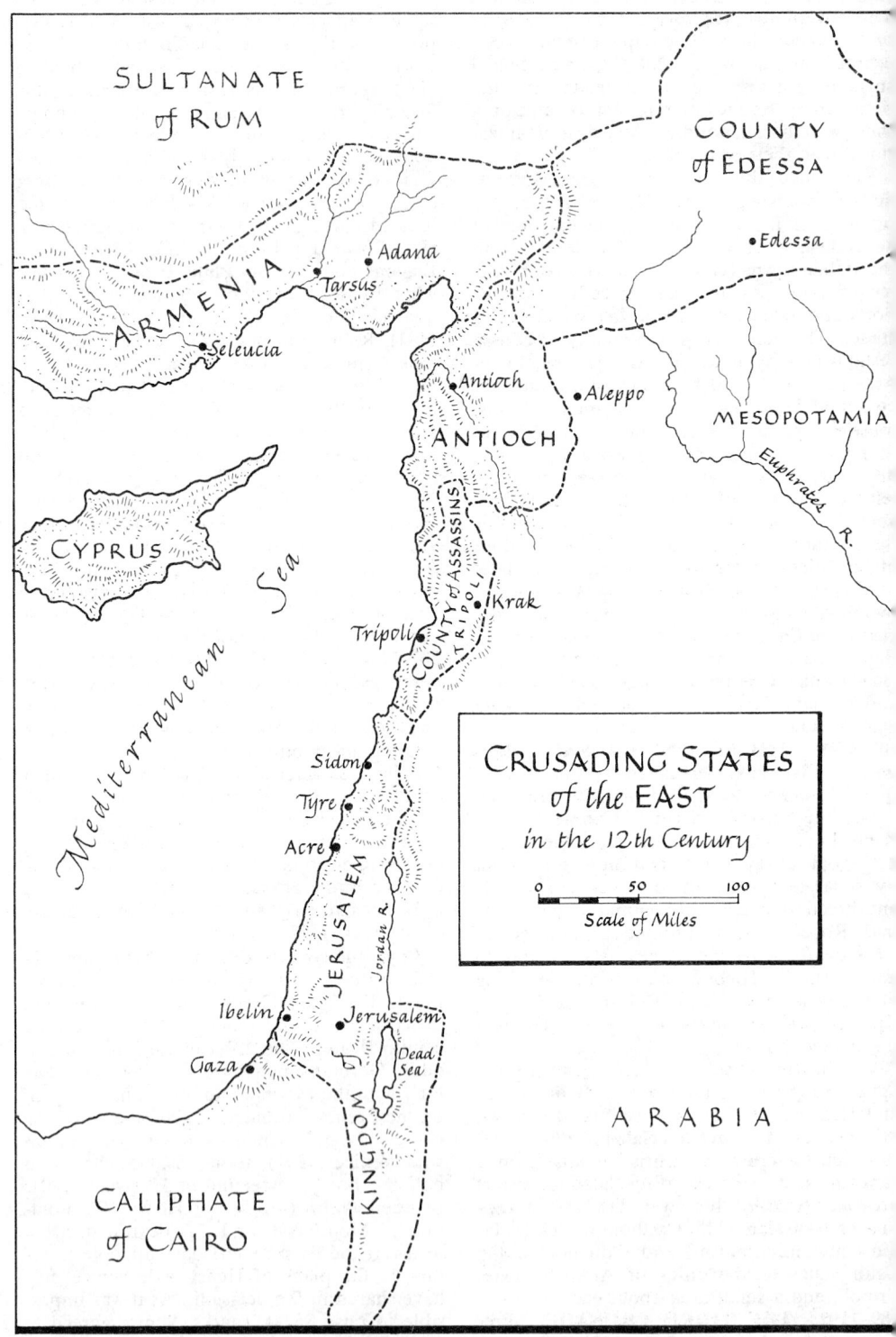

SULTANATE of RUM

COUNTY of EDESSA

• Edessa

ARMENIA

• Adana

• Tarsus

• Seleucia

• Antioch

• Aleppo

MESOPOTAMIA

ANTIOCH

Euphrates R.

CYPRUS

Mediterranean Sea

COUNTY of ASSASSINS

TRIPOLI

• Krak

Tripoli •

Sidon •

Tyre •

Acre •

JERUSALEM

Jordan R.

CRUSADING STATES
of the EAST
in the 12th Century

0   50   100

Scale of Miles

Ibelin •

• Jerusalem

Dead Sea

Gaza •

KINGDOM of

ARABIA

CALIPHATE
of CAIRO

were taken by the crusade. Despite Innocent's furious opposition, Zara was taken and sacked (1202); Innocent excommunicated the crusade. Constantinople was entered (1203); Isaac II Angelus and his son Alexius IV were restored; Greek opinion was furious at the new exactions to pay the clamorous crusaders, and Alexius V soon succeeded Isaac. The crusaders stormed and took Constantinople (1204), the first **capture of Constantinople** in history, and sacked it with unparalleled horrors. The Latin Empire of the East (*Romania*) replaced the Greek Empire at Constantinople from 1204 to 1261; the first emperor, Baldwin of Flanders; a Latin patriarch, a Venetian (Morosini), replaced the Greek patriarch, and technically the schism was ended; actually the Greeks refused all union. Venice acquired three-eighths of the city, plus Adrianople, Gallipoli, Naxos, Andros, Euboea, Crete, and the Ionian islands. Innocent III was horrified and helpless. The government of the Latin Empire was completely feudal under the *Assizes of Romania* (copied from the *Assizes of Jerusalem*). The Greek emperors ruled at Nicaea (1204–1261) until Michael VIII surprised and took Constantinople, 1261. The Fourth Crusade shocked Europe, discredited the Papacy and the whole crusading movement, and facilitated the advance of the Turks.

08.   The **ALBIGENSIAN CRUSADE,** a European crusade against the Albigensian heretics in southern France, proclaimed by Innocent III (1208) (see p. 245).

12.   The so-called **Children's Crusade,** preached by the lad Stephen of Vendôme and by Nicholas of Cologne in Germany. Stephen's contingent reached Marseilles and was sold into slavery. Nicholas' company was turned back. The whole episode is supposed to have been the origin of the story of the Pied Piper.

18–1221. THE FIFTH CRUSADE. Innocent III, unwilling to let the crusading idea lapse, preached the Fifth Crusade at the Fourth Lateran Council. Egypt was to be the objective; the date 1217; John of Brienne, king of Jerusalem, was replaced by the papal legate Pelagius as leader (1218). Capture of Damietta (1219); rejection (in the expectation of Frederick II's arrival) of the offers of the sultan (1219) to exchange Jerusalem for Damietta; failure of the march on Cairo; **treaty 1221:** eight-year truce, Damietta lost; retreat.

8–1229. The **SIXTH CRUSADE,** of the Emperor Frederick II. Essentially lay, the crusade continued the policy of Frederick's father, Henry VI. Frederick, king of Jerusalem by his marriage (1225) to Yolande of Brienne, sailed (1227) after careful preparation, returned ill with fever, and was excommunicated. He sailed again (1228); the pope proclaimed a crusade against Frederick's Sicilian lands and renewed the excommunication; Hermann von Salza, master of the Teutonic Order, remained loyal to Frederick. Frederick, the first crusader to understand the Moslems, negotiated a treaty (1229) with Malik al-Kamil, nephew of Saladin, sultan of Egypt; peace for ten years, grant of Nazareth, Bethlehem, Jerusalem, etc., and a corridor from Jerusalem to the coast for the Christians. The patriarch of Jerusalem opposed Frederick at every turn, and Frederick had to crown himself king (1229) in the Church of the Holy Sepulcher. He returned home at once to repel the papal crusade in his lands. The capture of Jerusalem by a rush of Moslem mercenaries (1244) led to the crusades of King Louis IX of France, but Jerusalem was not again in Christian hands until General Allenby arrived [1917].

The **crusades of Theobald of Navarre** (1239) and **Richard of Cornwall** (1240–1241) were forbidden by the pope and were fruitless.

1248–1254. The **SEVENTH CRUSADE,** the first of King Louis IX of France. Poorly organized; Damietta taken without a blow; march to Cairo (1249); rout of the army; capture of Louis; massacre of the army; loss of Damietta. Louis, ransomed, spent four years on a pilgrimage to Jerusalem (1251–1254).

1267.   Charles of Anjou, aiming at the conquest of Constantinople, became heir (by treaty) to the Latin Empire. He planned to unite Sicily and Jerusalem, but was balked by the Sicilian Vespers (1282).

1269.   James the Conqueror, of Aragon, under papal pressure, made a futile crusading expedition to Asia Minor.

1270. The **EIGHTH CRUSADE,** the second of King Louis IX and Edward of England (the last of the western crusaders who arrived [1271] and did nothing permanent). Attack on Tunis, possibly at the insistence of Charles of Anjou; death of Louis; the expedition continued by Charles; nothing accomplished.

1274. Preaching of a crusade at Lyons by Pope Gregory X; every ruler took the Cross; Gregory's death ended the project. Acre fell, 1291.

Local and specific crusading expeditions were subsequently undertaken under various circumstances at different times; there was a revival of crusading zeal with the fall of Constantinople (1453) under papal urging, but the true crusades were over.

The crusades gave rise to great orders of knighthood which combined chivalry and monasticism.

The **KNIGHTS OF ST. JOHN** or the Hospitalers (black mantle with a white cross), orig-

278

Kings of Jerusalem (1099-1489)

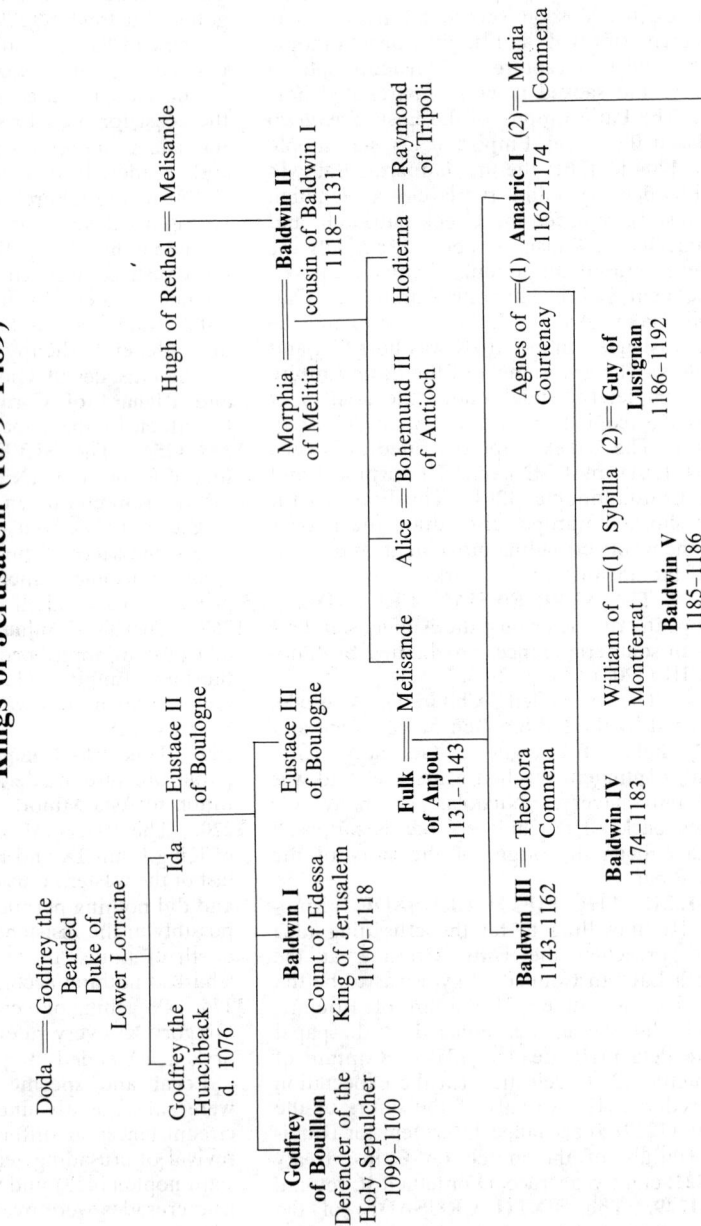

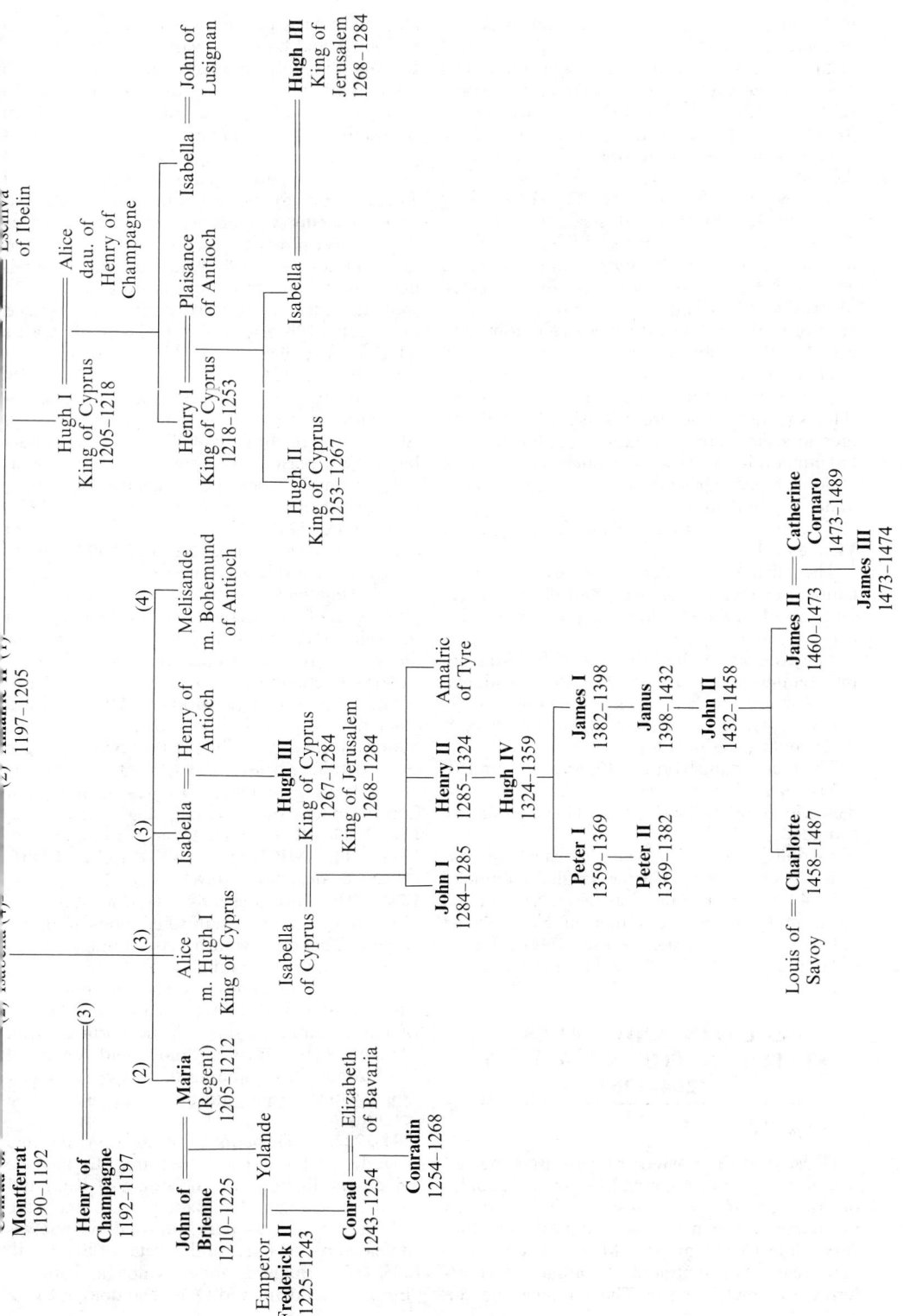

inally an order founded at Jerusalem by Amalfitan merchants (c. 1070) to care for the Hospital of St. John; militarized (c. 1130) on the model of the Knights Templar; transferred to Cyprus (1291); to Rhodes (1310–1522) (the **Knights of Rhodes**) and then to Malta **(Knights of Malta)**. Noble blood was a requisite to knighthood in the order.

The **KNIGHTS OF THE TEMPLE** (their house in Jerusalem stood near the Temple) or Templars (white mantle with a red cross) founded (c. 1120) by Hugh of Pajens to guide and protect pilgrims; confirmed by the **synod of Troyes** (1128) and Pope Honorius II. Bernard of Clairvaux drew up their rule, a modification of the Cistercian; they took the threefold monastic vows of poverty, chastity, and obedience, and their rule in general was that of the canons regular. The Order consisted of knights, men-at-arms, and chaplains. Admission to knighthood in the order was open only to those of noble blood. Organization: by commanderies under a grand master. Transferred to Cyprus (1291), the order was dissolved by the **synod of Vienne** (1312).

The other great orders were associated with national or racial influences, and do not represent the older international aspects of knighthood:

The **Knights of the Hospital of St. Mary of the Teutons** in Jerusalem (Teutonic Knights) (white mantle with a black cross) founded (c. 1190); headquarters at Acre. (For their history in Germany, see p. 228.)

The great Spanish orders: **Calatrava** (founded, 1164); **Avis** (Portuguese, founded 1166); **St. James of Compostella** (founded 1175); **Alcántara** (founded, 1183).

Famous orders of chivalry of royal foundation: the **Order of the Garter** (English), founded c. 1344; the **Order of the Star** (French), founded 1351, replaced by the **Order of St. Michael** (1469–1830); the **Order of the Golden Fleece** (Burgundian), founded 1429, became Hapsburg 1477.

d. LATIN AND GREEK STATES IN THE NEAR EAST, 1204–1261

(*From p. 272*)

Division of the Eastern Empire after the fall of Constantinople: A council, composed equally of crusaders and Venetians, decided to award the imperial crown to **Count Baldwin of Flanders**, while a Venetian (Pier Morosini) was made patriarch of Constantinople. **Boniface of Montferrat** was made king of Thessalonica and the remaining parts of the empire were assigned to various feudal barons as vassals of the emperor. In Anatolia the crusaders were never able to establish themselves excepting in a part of Bithynia near the Bosporus. In Europe they were constantly exposed to the attacks of the Bulgarians. The kingdom of Thessalonica at first extended over part of Thrace, Macedonia, and Thessaly, but to the westward the Greek, **Michael Angelus Comnenus,** set himself up as despot of Epirus and soon began to expand his dominion eastward. Attica and the Peloponnesus were conquered by crusading barons in a short time, and these territories were organized on a feudal basis as the **lordship of Athens** (Otto de la Roche, 1205–1225; Guy I, 1125–1263; John I, 1263–1280), and the **principality of Achaea** (conquered by Guillaume de Champlitte and Geoffroy de Villehardouin in 1205). Achaea was in turn divided into twelve feudal baronies, a perfect example of the French feudal system. Under the Villehardouin family (Geoffroy I, 1209–1218; Geoffroy II, 1218–1246; Guillaume, 1246–1278) it was well-governed and popular with the Greco-Slavic population, which was considerately treated.

The **Venetians** took as their share of the empire most of the islands and other important strategic or commercial posts. They kept for themselves part of Constantinople, Gallipoli, Euboea, Crete, the southwestern tip of the Peloponnesus (Coron and Modon), Durazzo, and other posts on the Epiran coast, as well as the islands of the Ionian and Aegean Seas. For the most part these possessions were granted as fiefs to the leading Venetian families (triarchies of Euboea, duchy of the Archipelago, etc.).

1204–1205. BALDWIN I, Latin emperor.

1204–1214. MICHAEL ANGELUS COMNENUS, despot of Epirus.

1204. Theodore Lascaris, with most of the Byzantine leaders, established himself in Bithynia; Theodore Mancaphas set himself up at Philadelphia; Leo Gabalas took over Rhodes; Manuel Maurozomes established himself in the Meander Valley; Alexius and David Comnenus organized a state on the north coast of Anatolia, with David at Sinope and Alexius at Trebizond, thus founding the **empire of Trebizond,** which lasted until the Ottoman conquest of 1461.

1204–1222. Theodore I (Lascaris) became founder of the Nicaean Empire. In 1204 he made an alliance with the sultan of Rum and with Mancaphas of Philadelphia to resist the advance of the crusaders into Anatolia, but was defeated by the latter under Peter of Bracheuil.

1205. The **Bulgars,** under Kaloyan, defeated Emperor Baldwin and Doge Dandolo in **battle**

The Lascarid Dynasty (1206-1261)

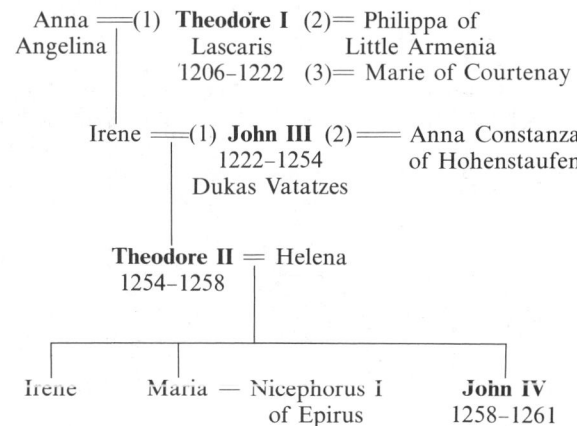

Anna =(1) **Theodore I** (2)= Philippa of
Angelina | Lascaris Little Armenia
| 1206-1222 (3)= Marie of Courtenay

Irene =(1) **John III** (2) = Anna Constanza
1222-1254 of Hohenstaufen
Dukas Vatatzes

Theodore II = Helena
1254-1258

Irene Maria — Nicephorus i **John IV**
of Epirus 1258-1261

---

near Adrianople. Baldwin was captured and died in captivity. The Bulgars then overran much of Thrace and Macedonia, exterminating a large part of the Greek population.
1205-1216. HENRY I, Latin emperor. He was the brother of Baldwin, and the ablest of the Latin emperors.
1207. Kaloyan and the Bulgarians besieged Thessalonica, but in vain. Kaloyan died suddenly, probably murdered.
1207. Theodore Lascaris, allied with the Seljuks of Rum, defeated David Comnenus and drove him back to Sinope. Theodore then concluded a truce with the Emperor Henry, in order to oppose the advance of Alexius of Trebizond, who was now allied with the Seljuks.
1209. Theodore repulsed a second attempt by Peter of Bracheuil and the crusaders to conquer Bithynia.
1210. The **Parliament of Ravennika,** at which the feudal lords of Greece finally recognized the suzerainty of the emperor at Constantinople. In practice this meant little, and the emperor was left to shift for himself, with such support as the Venetians saw fit to give him.
1211. Theodore Lascaris defeated Alexius of Trebizond and the sultan of Rum, both of whom were captured. As a result a large part of the Anatolian coast was added to the empire of Nicaea.
1212. Henry I defeated Theodore at Luparcos and began the invasion of Anatolia. Theodore made peace, abandoning to the Latin Empire part of Mysia and Bithynia.
1214-1230. Theodore Dukas Angelus, nephew of Michael, became despot of Epirus. He

began the work of expansion at the expense of the Latins and Bulgars, taking Durazzo and Corfu from the Venetians (1214).
1216-1217. PETER OF COURTENAY, Latin emperor. He was the brother-in-law of Baldwin and Henry and was in Europe when Henry died. On the way from Durazzo to Thessalonica he was captured by Theodore Dukas of Epirus. He died in 1218.
1217-1219. Regency of Yolande, the wife of Peter of Courtenay.
1219-1228. ROBERT OF COURTENAY, Latin emperor. His domain was reduced to Constantinople and he spent most of his time soliciting aid in the west.
1222. Theodore Dukas of Epirus captured Thessalonica and extinguished the kingdom. He then had himself proclaimed Emperor of the West, and before long had extended his conquests to the vicinity of Philippopolis and Adrianople.
1222-1254. JOHN III (Dukas Vatatzes), emperor at Nicaea. He proved himself a great ruler as well as an able general. During his reign agriculture was encouraged, trade and industry developed, the finances reformed. The Nicaean Empire enjoyed a period of real prosperity and power.
1224. John Vatatzes defeated the Franks at Poimanenon. In succession he took the islands near the Anatolian coast (Samos, Chios, Lemnos) and subjected Rhodes. An army was even sent across the Straits to capture Adrianople.
1224. Theodore of Epirus defeated an army of the Latin emperor at Serres and then drove the invading Nicaean army away from Adrianople.

(*From p. 270*) **Latin Emperors of Constantinople (1204–1373)**

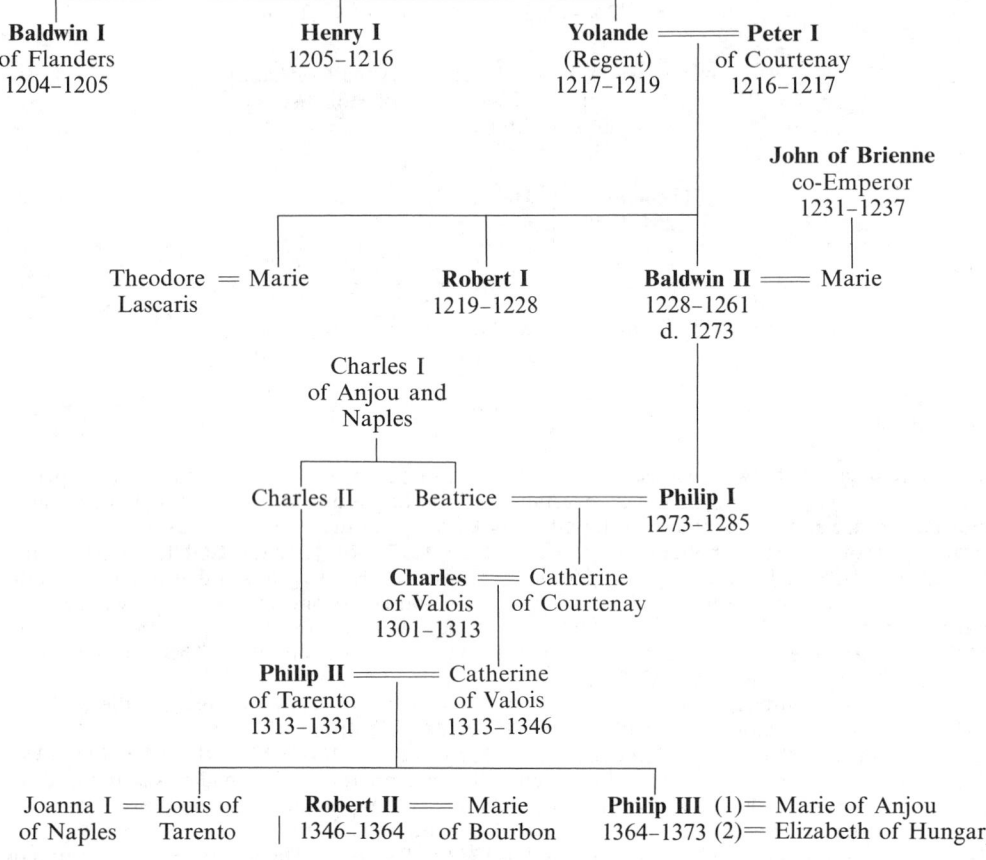

Baldwin I of Flanders 1204–1205

Henry I 1205–1216

Yolande (Regent) 1217–1219 ══ **Peter I** of Courtenay 1216–1217

John of Brienne co-Emperor 1231–1237

Theodore ═ Marie Lascaris

Robert I 1219–1228

Baldwin II 1228–1261 d. 1273 ══ Marie

Charles I of Anjou and Naples

Charles II   Beatrice ══════════ **Philip I** 1273–1285

Charles ══ Catherine of Valois │ of Courtenay 1301–1313

Philip II ══════ Catherine of Tarento │ of Valois 1313–1331   1313–1346

Joanna I ═ Louis of of Naples   Tarento

Robert II ══ Marie 1346–1364   of Bourbon

Philip III (1)═ Marie of Anjou 1364–1373 (2)═ Elizabeth of Hungary

(*Cont. p. 346.*)

1228. On the death of Robert of Courtenay, it was proposed that a regency be established under the Bulgarian ruler, John Asen II (1218–1241), but this suggestion was frustrated by the Latin clergy.

1228–1261. BALDWIN II, Latin emperor. He was the eleven-year-old son of Peter of Courtenay. The reign was a helpless one, during which the emperor was reduced to the point of peddling the Constantinople relics through Europe.

1229–1237. Regency of John of Brienne, former king of Jerusalem, for the boy-emperor. John became co-emperor in 1231.

1230. Theodore of Epirus was defeated and captured by John Asen in the **battle of Klokotnitsa.** The Bulgarian ruler thereupon ap-

propriated most of the eastern sections of the Empire of the West. Thessalonica and Thessaly passed to

1230–1236. MANUEL, the brother of Theodore.

1235. An expedition sent by John Vatatzes against the Venetians in Crete failed to achieve anything.

1236. An attack of the Nicaean Greeks, allied with John Asen of Bulgaria, on Constantinople. The city was saved by the Venetians and by a force sent by the duke of Achaia.

1236–1244. JOHN, the son of Theodore Dukas of Epirus, became despot of Thessaly and Emperor of the West.

1236–1271. MICHAEL II, despot of Epirus.

1242. John Vatatzes, in company with Theo-

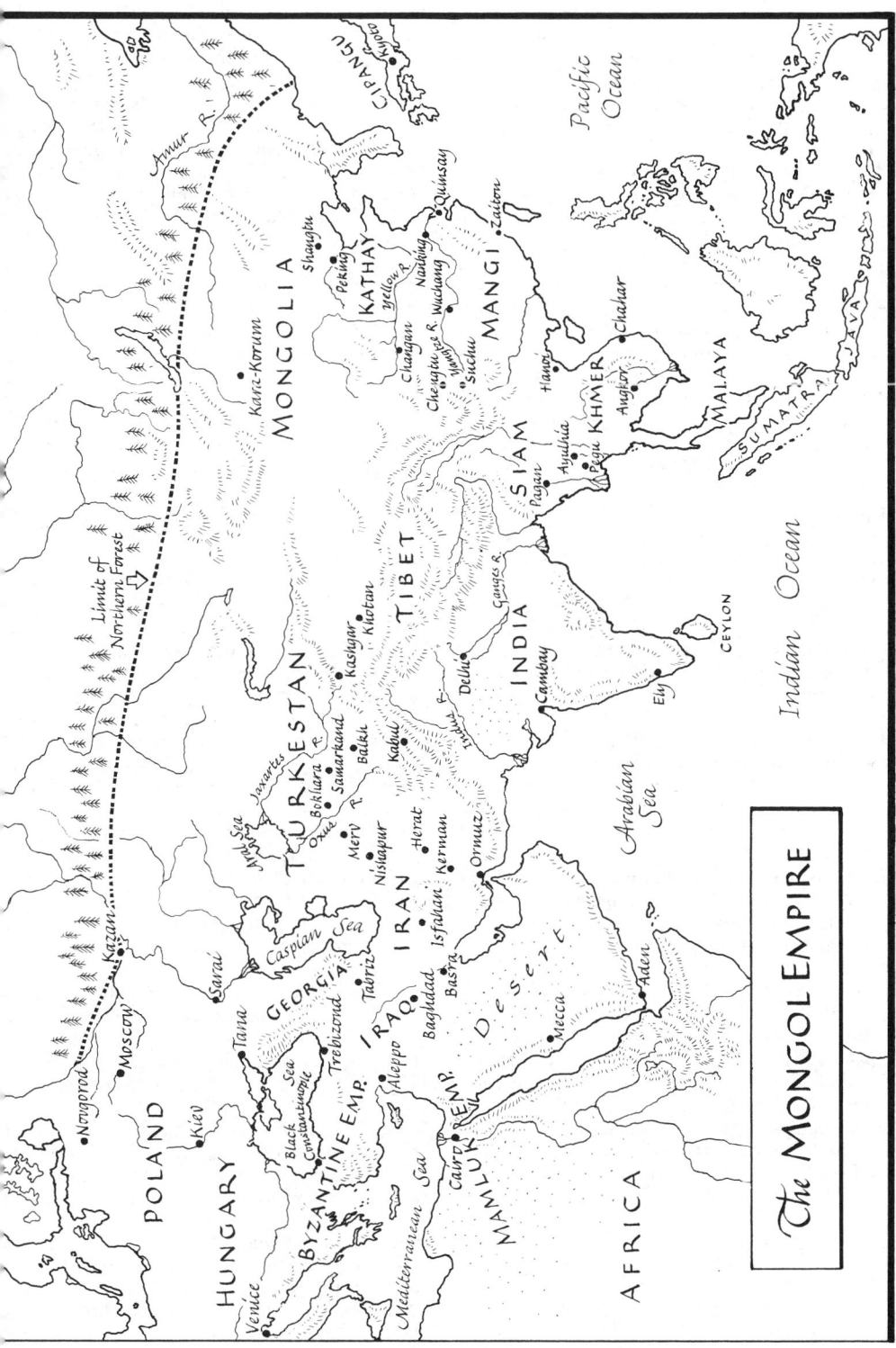

The Mongol Empire

dore, who had been liberated by the Bulgarians, set out with an army and besieged Thessalonica. He failed to take the city, owing to his lack of seapower, but John, the despot of Thessaly, was obliged to give up the title Emperor of the West and to recognize the suzerainty of the Nicaean emperor.

1244. The **Mongol invasion** of Anatolia, after the defeat of the Seljuks in the **battle of Erzinjan.** The Mongols reached Ancyra (Ankara). John Vatatzes established friendly relations with them and succeeded to much of the Seljuk territory in central Anatolia.

1246. Second expedition of John Vatatzes to the Balkans. He conquered northern Macedonia and finally took Thessalonica, deposing Demetrius Angelus, despot since 1244.

1254. Michael II, of Epirus, recognized Nicaean suzerainty, after a defeat by the forces of John Vatatzes.

1254-1258. THEODORE II (Lascaris), Greek emperor at Nicaea.

1255. Theodore defeated the Bulgarian armies of Michael Asen in northern Macedonia.

1257. Revolt of Michael II of Epirus, who managed to defeat the Nicaean forces sent against him.

1258-1261. JOHN IV (Lascaris), emperor. He was a mere child and his accession led to a military uprising, led by Michael Paleologus, who became regent and then (1259) co-emperor.

1259-1282. MICHAEL VIII (Paleologus), who was first co-emperor with the boy John, whom in 1261 he had imprisoned and blinded. Michael was an able and energetic general, whose great objective was to re-establish the Greek power at Constantinople.

1259. Michael II of Epirus, allied with the king of Sicily and with the prince of Achaea, attacked Thessalonica, but was defeated and driven back by the Nicaeans **(battle of Pelagonia).**

1261. RECONQUEST OF CONSTANTINOPLE. Michael made an alliance with the Bulgarians and concluded the **treaty of Nymphaion** with Genoa, promising the Genoese all the privileges hitherto enjoyed by the Venetians. On July 25 a Greek army under **Alexius Stragopulos,** taking advantage of the absence of the Venetian fleet, crossed the Bosporus and retook Constantinople without much difficulty. Baldwin II fled (d. 1273). End of the Latin Empire. *(Cont. p. 345.)*

e. THE MONGOLS, 1206-1349

Under the last caliphs, the Caliphate had regained its temporal power in Mesopotamia and Fars, and its spiritual authority was greater than at any time since the death of Wathiq (847), bu the Caliphate was soon threatened by the Mongols, who, in the late 12th century, had advance from Mongolia.

1206. The Mongol chief, **Temujin** (1162-1227), was proclaimed supreme ruler, *Jenghi Khan* (Very Mighty King), of all the Mongols Under his leadership the Mongol armies swep over northern China and over Azerbaijan Georgia, and northern Persia. Transoxani was invaded and Bokhara taken (1219); Samarkand captured (1220) and Khorasan devastated Destruction of Merv and Nishapur. Capture o Herat.

1223. Battle of the Kalka River, in souther Russia. The Mongols defeated a strong forc of Russians and Cumans, but after their victor returned to Asia.

1237-1240. Mongol armies under **Batu** (ac tually commanded by Subutai) overran an conquered southern and central Russia an then invaded Poland and Hungary.

1241. The Mongols defeated the Poles an Germans in the **battle of Liegnitz** (Wahlstatt in Silesia, while another army defeated th Hungarians. But because of political compli cations arising from the death of the Grea Khan, Batu withdrew from western Europe subjugating, on the way back, Bulgaria, Walla chia, and Moldavia. Subsequently he settle on the lower Volga, where a Mongol (Tatar state was organized under the name of **Golde Horde,** with Sarai as the capital. The Golder Horde, like other Mongol khanates, recog nized the supreme authority of the Grea Khan, whose capital was first at Kara-Korun in Mongolia, then at Khanbalyk (present-da Peip'ing) in China. But after the death o Kublai Khan (1294) the unity of the empir was purely nominal.

1245-1253. Continued ravages of the Mongol in Mesopotamia, Azerbaijan, Armenia, an Georgia.

1256-1349. THE ILKHANS OF PERSIA Hulagu, the grandson of Jenghiz Khan, wa sent by his brother, Mangu, to crush the Assas sins and extirpate the Caliphate.

1256. Suppression and **extinction of the Assas sins.**

1258. CAPTURE AND SACK OF BAGH DAD. Hulagu executed the caliph, Musta'sim He then invaded Syria and took Aleppo.

1260. Great victory of the Mamluks of Egypt under Baybars, at **Ain Jalut.** This victor checked the Mongol advance and saved Egypt the last refuge of Moslem culture. **Baybar** revived the Caliphate by inviting to Cair Ahmad Abu-l-Qasim, a scion of the Abbasi house, who was acknowledged as caliph unde the title of *Mustansir l' Jllah.*

The Successors of Jenghiz Khan (1227-1336)

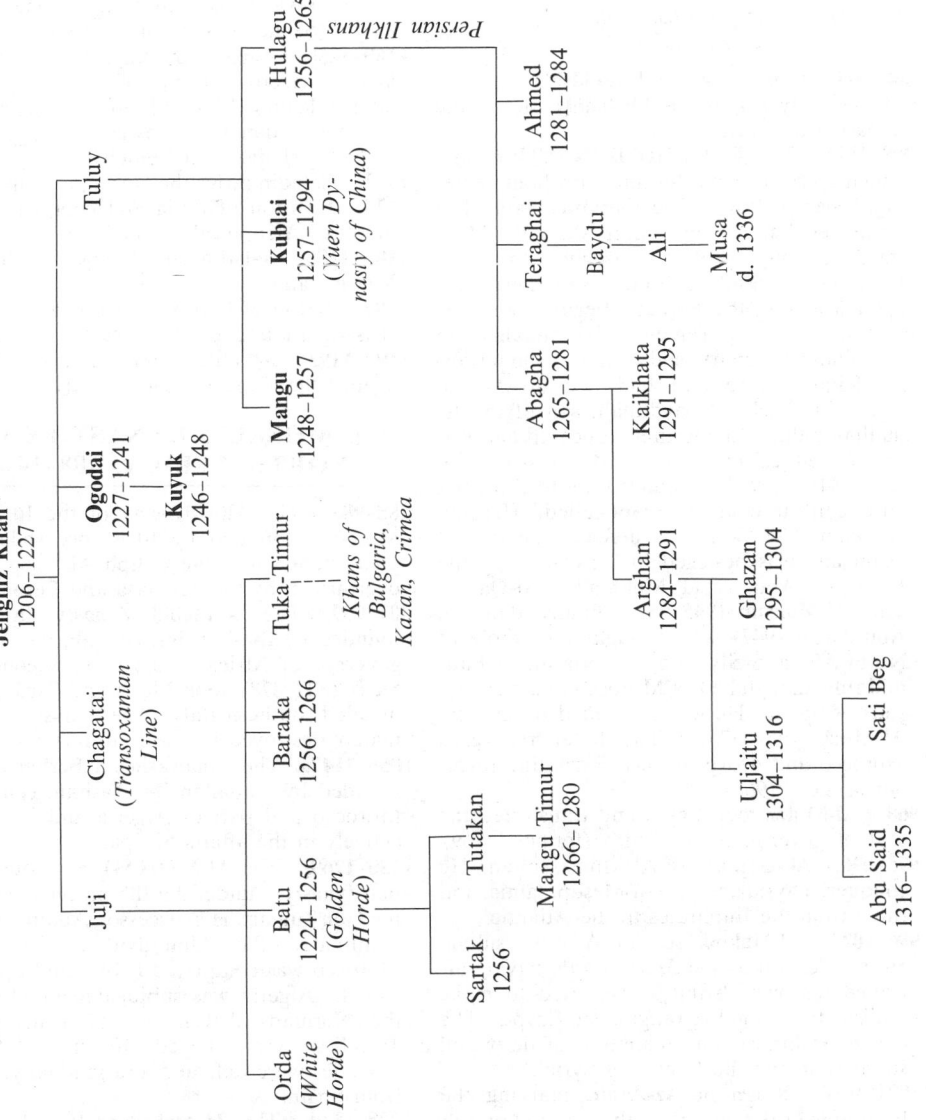

1344-1349. Reign of Nushirwan, last of the Ilkhans of Persia. The dynasty was succeeded by a number of lesser families. (*Cont. p. 354.*)

f. MOSLEM EGYPT, 868-1193

(*From p. 206*)

[*For a complete list of the caliphs see Appendix III.*]

868-905. Dynasty of the Tulunids.
934-969. Dynasty of the Ikhshidids. Both these dynasties also ruled Syria.
968-1171. The **FATIMID DYNASTY,** under which Egypt became the most brilliant center of Moslem culture. The Fatimids claimed to be descendants of the Caliph Ali, and of Fatima, the daughter of the Prophet. They rose to power as a result of Shi'ite (Ismailian) propaganda among the Berbers, begun about 894 and directed from Yemen. Abu Abdallah, an Ismailian missionary, had won over the powerful Kitama tribe and had overthrown the Aghlabids (909). Obaydullah, son of the Ismailian hidden Imam, then appeared and was proclaimed caliph and mahdi in Qairowan (909-934). In 922 he reduced the Idrisids, but an attempt to conquer Egypt failed. His son, Al-Qaim (934-945), was defeated again and again and was besieged in his capital by the Kharijite, Abu Yazid Makhlad. Al-Qaim's son, **Al-Mansur** (945-952), finally defeated Abu Yazid (947), and brought the whole of North Africa, Sicily, and Calabria under Fatimid rule, though he lost Morocco to the Omayyads of Spain. He was succeeded by his son, Al-Muizz (952-975). The latter recovered Morocco and drove the last Byzantine forces out of Sicily (966).
968. Al-Muizz took Egypt and transferred the seat of government to Cairo (founded 969).
975-996. Al-Aziz, son of Al-Muizz, sultan. He conquered Syria and part of Mesopotamia, and ruled from the Euphrates to the Atlantic.
996-1021. Al-Hakim, son of Al-Aziz, sultan. He was known as the *Mad Caliph*, having affirmed his own divinity. He tried to make Shi'ism the orthodox religion of Egypt. The cult of Hakim as an emanation of deity still survives among the Druses of Syria.
1021-1036. Reign of **Az-Zahir,** marking the beginning of the decline of the Fatimid power. Most of Syria was lost.
1036-1094. Reign of **Al-Mustansir.** The holy cities of Mecca and Medina disclaimed their allegiance (1047) and North Africa threw off the Fatimid yoke. On Al-Mustansir's death civil war broke out among his sons, Nizar and Ahmad. Nizar was defeated and killed, and Ahmad reigned as

1094-1101. Al-Mustadi. He lost Jerusalem to the crusaders (1099). The Fatimid power continued to decline.
1167. Shirkuh, general of the Zangid Nur al-Din of Damascus, entered Egypt to assist the second-last Fatimid caliph, Al-Adid (1160-1171). Shirkuh was appointed vizir, in which office he was succeeded by his nephew, **Salah al-Din** (Saladin), who founded the
1169-1250. Ayyubid dynasty. Saladin ruled at first as viceroy of Nur al-Din, but on the latter's death (1173) asserted his independence and consolidated his power over Egypt, part of Nubia, Hijaz, and Yemen.
1172. Saladin drove the Normans from Tripoli.
1174. Invasion of Syria and conquest of Damascus. Aleppo taken (1183).
1185-1186. Saladin seized Mosul and reduced Mesopotamia.
1187. Battle of Hittin. Saladin destroyed the crusading kingdom of Jerusalem.
1190-1193. Saladin defended his conquests against the Third Crusade. (*Cont. p. 450.*)

g. MOSLEM DYNASTIES OF NORTH AFRICA, 788-1470

788-985. The **Alid dynasty** of the Idrisids in Morocco, founded by Idris ibn Abdallah, a great-grandson of the Caliph Ali's son Hasan, overthrown by the Miknasa and Berbers.
801-909. The **Aghlabid dynasty** in Tunis, founded by Ibrahim ibn Aghlab, the Abbasid governor of Africa. This dynasty conquered Sicily (827-878), took Malta and Sardinia and invaded southern Italy. The dynasty was ultimately destroyed by the Fatimids.
1056-1147. The **Almoravids,** a Berber dynasty founded by Abdallah ibn Tashfin, conquered Morocco and part of Algeria and intervened actively in the affairs of Spain.
1130-1269. The **ALMOHADES,** another Berber dynasty founded by the prophet, Mohammed ibn Tumart. His successor, Abdul-Mu'min, annihilated the Almoravid armies (1144). Morocco was conquered (1146) and Spain invaded. Algeria was subjugated in 1152, and the Normans driven out of Tunis (1158). Tripoli too was annexed. But in 1235 the Almohades were defeated and gradually ejected from Spain.
1228-1534. The **Hafsid dynasty,** which succeeded the Almohades in Tunis.
1235-1339. The **Ziyanids,** successors of the Almohades in Algeria. They were ultimately absorbed by the
1296-1470. Marinids of Morocco, a dynasty founded in 1195 which took the Moroccan capital from the Almohades in 1296.

(*Cont. p. 450.*)

C. THE LATER MIDDLE AGES

1. WESTERN EUROPE

a. THE BRITISH ISLES

(*From p. 216*)

(1) England, 1307–1485

[*For a complete list of the kings of England see Appendix VI.*]

1307–1327. EDWARD II. Married to Isabelle, daughter of Philip IV of France. Ignorant of his task and bored with the business of kingship, Edward was dominated by his favorite, **Piers Gaveston,** a Gascon. The Scottish war was continued in desultory fashion. The baronage, angered by Gaveston, followed the leadership of Edward's nephew, Thomas, duke of Lancaster, an ambitious, incompetent person. They forced Edward to accept a committee of reform, the twenty-one **Lords Ordainers** (1310), whose reform ordinances, suggestive of the Provisions of Oxford, were confirmed by parliament (1311). The ordinances required a baronial consent to royal appointments, to a declaration of war, and to the departure of the king from the realm, this consent to be given through parliament. Gaveston was captured and slain (1312).

1313–1314. The Scottish War. By 1313 only the castle of Stirling remained in the hands of the English. Edward set out (1314) to relieve the castle; Lancaster and the baronial party refused to support the expedition. At **Bannockburn** (1314) Edward was overwhelmingly defeated, and Scottish independence won.

In Gascony the French kings began a policy of egging Edward's vassals on to resistance, a process which culminated in the French conquest of Gascony and its retention by the French with the consent (1327) of the regents who ruled after Edward's abdication.

1314–1322. Supremacy of Lancaster. Lancaster offered no opposition to Scottish raids; private wars broke out in England; Edward was under a new favorite, Hugh le Despenser. Parliament exiled Despenser (1321). Edward defeated Lancaster at **Boroughbridge** (1322) and beheaded him. The parliament of York repealed the ordinances.

1322–1326. Rule of the Despensers, father and son: Scottish truce (1323); decline of the popularity of the Despensers; alienation of Queen Isabelle. Isabelle went to France (1325), arranged the marriage of her son, the future Edward III, to Philippa of Hainault, and returned (1326) with Mortimer and foreign troops. Supported by the barons, Isabelle

gained London, the Despensers were hanged, and the **parliament of Westminster** (1327), dominated by Isabelle and by Edward's enemies, forced an abdication that was tantamount to deposition. Edward was brutally murdered in prison eight months later.

Baronial reform was cynical and selfish in aim, but made no effort to destroy the monarchy. Burgesses and knights sat in the parliaments of 1311, 1322, and 1327, and retained a share in the grant of taxes.

1327–1377. EDWARD III (aged fifteen at his accession). Council of regency and rule (1327–1330) under Mortimer, Isabelle's paramour; Bruce's invasion of England forced the acknowledgment of Scottish independence (1328). Edward led the baronial opposition to Mortimer (hanged, 1330) and opened his personal rule (1330).

1338. Outbreak of the **HUNDRED YEARS' WAR.** Edward did homage (1329) for his French lands and renewed it (1331). French support of Scottish aggression continued and Edward, profiting by civil war in Scotland, supported Baliol; after a series of expeditions he avenged Bannockburn at **Halidon Hill** (1333). French intrigues sought to alienate Aquitaine continued; Edward sought allies in the emperor, the German princes, and his wife's relatives in Hainault and Holland, but could not win the count of Flanders, the vassal of Philip VI. The economic interdependence, due to the wool trade, of England and the Flemish cities made an English alliance with them inevitable. Philip continued his advance into the English lands south of the Loire (1337) and open hostilities broke out (1338). Edward ravaged northern and eastern France without a decisive battle. Urged on by the Flemings, Edward proclaimed himself king of France (in right of his mother Isabelle), and enabled the Flanders towns under Jan van Arteveldt to support him without violating their oaths.

1340. The **naval victory of Sluys** transferred the mastery of the Channel from France to England (until 1372). Intermittent truces (1340–1345) were followed by Edward's invasion of France, and

1346, Aug. 26. Great victory at **CRÉCY** where English longbowmen, supported by dismounted horsemen, routed the undisciplined chivalry and mercenary crossbowmen of France. This tactical innovation, the result of English experiences in Wales and Scotland, began the joint participation of the yeomanry and the aristocracy in war, and gave the English a unique military power and new social orientation.

1346. The invasion of Philip's Scottish allies was halted at **Neville's Cross,** and the king of Scotland captured.

1347. Calais was taken after a long siege in which artillery was used. (Philippa's intervention in behalf of the burghers of Calais.) Calais remained an English military and commercial outpost in France until 1558.

1347-1355. A **series of truces** with France was ended by the expedition of Edward's son, **the Black Prince,** to Bordeaux, followed by ruthless plundering raids from there as a base, which enriched the English and alienated the populace.

1356, Sept. 19. BATTLE OF POITIERS. The Black Prince, using the tactics of Crécy, defeated King John, capturing him, his son, and the king of Bohemia, as well as the flower of French chivalry.

1359-1360. Edward's last expedition to France penetrated to the walls of Paris; the south had been so devastated that the English could hardly find food.

1360. PEACE OF BRETIGNY, ending the first period of the war. (1) France, utterly exhausted and in chaos, surrendered the full sovereignty of Aquitaine, Calais, Ponthieu; and (2) fixed John's ransom; (3) Edward waived his claims to the crown of France.

THE BLACK PRINCE IN THE SOUTH. The Black Prince, ruling as duke of Aquitaine, supported Pedro the Cruel of Castile against Henry of Trastamara (allied with Charles V and aided by Du Guesclin). Having defeated Du Guesclin and Henry (**Navarrete,** 1367), the Black Prince, disgusted at Pedro's character, his army dissipated by illness, and seriously ill himself, withdrew. Taxation in Aquitaine to pay for the expedition led the southern baronage to appeal to Charles V, who summoned the Black Prince to answer to him as his feudal lord (alleging a technical defect in the **peace of Bretigny**). The prince defied Charles, and parliament advised Edward to resume his claims to the French crown. Du Guesclin avoided open battle, pursuing a warfare of attrition which wore out the Black Prince and alienated the Aquitanians from the English. After the hideous **sack of Limoges** (1370) the Black Prince returned to England (1371) and was replaced (1372-1374) by his brother, **John of Gaunt,** duke of Lancaster, an incompetent soldier, who lost town after town until only Calais, Cherbourg, Brest, Bayonne, and Bordeaux remained in English hands (1375).

Edward's personal rule and domestic developments in England. Edward, a majestic, affable man, opened his reign with generous concessions to the baronage, and a courteous welcome to the complaints of the middle class. He grew steadily in popularity. He was fond of war and the war was popular; the nation backed him.

Progress of parliament. The necessities of war finance played into the hands of parliament, and (after 1325) the knights and burgesses began to establish a privileged position for their common petitions. Without immediate redress when the king broke promises of reform, they were able to apply financial pressure in crises. The king could still legislate outside parliament by ordinances in council, but parliament was gaining the initiative: non-feudal levies and changes in levies require parliamentary sanction (1340); a money grant made conditional on redress, and auditors of expenditure appointed (1340-1341); all ministers of the king declared (1341) to be subject to parliamentary approval (soon repealed); demand that a grant be spent as directed (1344); a specific grant voted for defense against the Scots (1348); appointment of parliamentary treasurers and collectors (1377). Parliament continued to sit as a single body, but deliberated in sections: the magnates and prelates sitting in the parliament chamber with the king's council (thus forming the **Great Council**); the knights and burgesses met separately until 1339-1349, when they began joint sessions (i.e. emergence of the **Commons**) and designated (before 1377) a representative, the speaker, to voice their views in debate. Royal officials ceased to attend the council-in-parliament, leaving the council to the prelates and magnates (now sitting virtually by hereditary right). The outline of the **house of lords** began to appear.

Development of **justices of the peace.** The conservators of the peace established under Henry III to keep the peace had no judicial powers; the statute of 1327 allowed them to receive indictments for trial before the itinerant judges. In 1332 their jurisdiction was made to include felonies and trespass. Established as police judges in each county (1360), they were also charged with price and labor regulation. By 1485 they had absorbed most of the functions of the sheriffs. Chosen from the local gentry, under royal commission, they constituted an amateur body of administrators who carried on local government in England until well into the 19th century.

1348-1349. The ravages of the **Black Death** probably reduced the population one-third; coupled with tremendous war prosperity, this dislocated the wage and price structure, producing a major economic and social crisis. Wages and prices were regulated by a royal ordinance (1349) followed by the **Statute of Laborers** (1351), fixing wages and prices, and attempting to compel able-bodied unemployed to accept work when offered. The labor shortage accelerated the transition (already begun) from servile to free tenures and fluid labor; the statute in practice destroyed English social unity without markedly arresting servile emancipation or diminishing the crisis.

War prosperity affected everybody and led to a general surge of luxury (e.g. the new and generous proportions of contemporary Perpendicular Gothic). Landowners, confronted with a labor shortage, began to enclose for sheep-raising, and the accumulation of capital and landholdings founded great fortunes, which soon altered the political and social position of the baronage. The yeomanry, exhilarated by their joint military achievement with the aristocracy, and their share of war plunder, lost their traditional passivity, and a new ferment began among the lower sections of society.

Growth of national and anti-clerical (anti-papal) **feeling.** Hostility to the francophile Papacy at Avignon: **statute of Provisors** (1351), an effort to stem the influx of alien clergy under papal provisions (renewed several times); **statute of Praemunire** (1353), forbidding appeals to courts (i.e. Avignon) outside England (renewed several times); rejection (1366) by parliament of the papal request that John's tribute (intermitted by Edward, 1333) be renewed, and declaration that no king could make England a papal fief without parliament's consent; parliament declared bishops unfit for state offices (1371). **Progress of the vernacular.** English became, by statute (1362), the language of pleading and judgment in the courts (law French retained in documents). English began to be taught in the schools (1375). Parliament was opened (1399) with a speech in English.

c. 1362. Growth of social tension. Langland's *Piers Plowman,* a vernacular indictment of governmental and ecclesiastical corruption, and an appeal (unique in Europe) in behalf of the poor peasant. Langland, a poor country parson, typical of the section of the church directly in contact with public opinion, was the voice of the old-fashioned godly England bewildered and angered by a new epoch. Preaching of scriptural equalitarianism by various itinerant preachers (e.g. John Ball); growing bitterness against landlords and lawyers.

c. 1376. JOHN WICLIF, an Oxford don and chaplain of Edward, already employed (1374) by the government in negotiations with the Papacy over provisions, published his *Civil Dominion,* asserting in curious feudal terms that, as Christians hold all things of God under a contract to be virtuous, sin violates this contract and destroys title to goods and offices. Wiclif made it plain that his doctrine was a philosophical and theological theory, not a political concept, but extremists ignored this point. A remarkable precursor of the Reformation, Wiclif advocated a propertyless Church, emphasizing the purely spiritual function, attacked the Caesarian clergy, and insisted on the direct access of the individual to God (e.g. abolition of auricular confession, reduction of the importance of the sacraments, notably penance) and the right of individual judgment. He also was responsible (with Purvey and Nicholas of Hereford) for the first complete, vernacular **English Bible.** He wrote pamphlets, both in Latin and English, and carried on a wide agitation through his poor priests for his doctrines (**Lollardy**) until it was said every fourth man was a Lollard.

1369–1377. Edward, in his dotage, was under the domination of Alice Perrers; the Black Prince (after his return, 1371) was ill and lethargic; government in church and state was sunk in the depths of corruption, society in an orgy of luxury.

1374. John of Gaunt, returning from France, struck a bargain with Alice Perrers, became the leader of the state, set out to use the strong anti-clerical feeling and social unrest for his own ends, and probably aimed at the succession.

1376. The Black Prince, awakened from his lethargy, led the **Good Parliament** in a series of reforms: the commons refused supply until an audit of accounts; two notorious aristocratic war profiteers (Lyons and Latimer) were impeached before the king's council (i.e. the future Lords), the first impeachment of officials by parliament in English history.

1377. After the death of the Black Prince (1376) John of Gaunt's packed parliament undid the reforms and passed a general poll tax (4*d.*).

1377. Gaunt, aiming at the confiscation of clerical estates, supported Wiclif, but the bishops, unable to touch Gaunt, had Wiclif called to account. A violent scene between Gaunt and Bishop Courtenay ended with public opinion on the bishop's side and Gaunt in flight. Attempts to discipline Wiclif failed because of public opinion, but his denial of transubstantiation (1380) alienated Gaunt and his aristocratic supporters.

ART, LITERATURE, AND SCIENCE

Perpendicular Gothic: Gloucester, transepts and choir (1331–1335); cloisters (1351–1412). Minor arts: *Louterell Psalter* (opening of the 14th century), illuminations. English influence on craftsmen of the Rhineland, Paris, Lorraine.

Popular songs: Anti-French songs in celebration of victories at Halidon Hill, Sluys, the capture of Calais, etc., c. 1377 first mention of Robin Hood. Popular performances of miracle and mystery plays.

Historical writing: Higden's *Polychronicon* (before 1363), a brilliant universal history in Latin; Walsingham of St. Albans' (end of the 14th century) *Chronicle,* in Latin, rivaling Froissart in brilliance of description. English translation (1377) of the fictional account of the *Travels of Sir John Mandeville* by Jean de Bourgogne.

The Pearl, a mystical poem of lament for a dead daughter, influenced by the *Roman de la Rose,* and suggestive of Dante's mystical visions.

Geoffrey Chaucer (c. 1340–1400), son of a London burgher, a layman, attached to the circle of John of Gaunt, a diplomat, active at court, later member of parliament, combined observation with learning. Translator of Boethius' *Consolatio,* etc. Representative of the new cosmopolitanism of English society, he was under Italian and French influences; probably knew Petrarch. Creator of English versification; recaster of the English vocabulary by adding continental grace to the ruder Anglo-Saxon word-treasury. The influence of Wiclif, Oxford, Cambridge, the court, and above all, Chaucer, fixed Midland English as the language of the English people. The *Canterbury Tales* are a witty, sympathetic, sophisticated, realistic picture of contemporary society (omitting the aristocracy). John Gower (d. 1408), last of the Anglo-Norman poets, wrote in both Latin and French, and later (perhaps due to Chaucer) in English: *Confessio Amantis; Vox Clamantis* (expressing the alarm of a landowner at the Peasants' Revolt).

Foundation of Winchester College (St. Mary's College) by William of Wykeham (1393). **Merton College,** Oxford, became a center for scientific investigations, especially in mechanics. **Robert Grosseteste, Roger Bacon, Richard Swineshead, Thomas of Bradwardine** began a tradition of logical analysis and experiment which remained influential until the Renaissance.

1377–1399. RICHARD II (son of the Black Prince, aged ten at his accession).

1377–1389. Minority. Marriage to Anne of Bohemia (1382); rule by the council under the domination of John of Gaunt; activity of parliament: insistence by the commons on the nomination of twelve new councillors. Renewal of war in France (1383): loss of the Flanders trade, complaints at the cost by parliament. Poll taxes (1370 and 1380); sporadic violence, growing tension in the lower orders of society.

1381. PEASANTS' REVOLT. Efforts by the landlords to revert to the old servile tenures culminated in a peasant rising, the burning of manors, destruction of records of tenures, game parks, etc., assassination of landlords and lawyers, and a march (100,000[?] men) from the south and east of England on London led by **Jack Straw, Wat Tyler,** and others (release of John Ball from prison). London admitted the marchers; lawyers and officials were murdered, their houses sacked, the Savoy (John of Gaunt's palace) burned. Significant **demands:** commutation of servile dues, disendowment of the Church, abolition of game laws. The Tower was seized, Archbishop Sudbury (mover, as chancellor, of the poll taxes) was murdered. Richard met the rebels (Mile End), rapidly issued charters of manumission, and started most of them home. After the murder of Wat Tyler, Richard cleverly took command of the remnant (possibly 30,000), deluded them with false promises, and dispersed them. Cruel reaction ensued: Richard and parliament annulled the charters; terrible repression followed, and a deliberate effort was made to restore villeinage. This proved impossible and serfdom continued to disappear.

1381. Passage of the first **Navigation Act,** followed by clear signs of growing national monopoly of commerce.

1382. Wiclif, who had alienated his upperclass supporters by a denial of transubstantiation, was discredited by the Peasants' Revolt, and condemned by the Church, and withdrew to Lutterworth (1382–1384), where he continued to foster Lollardy until he died (1384). His body, by order of the council of Constance, was dug up and burned (1428).

1382. Archbishop Courtenay purged Oxford of Lollardy, thus separating the movement from the cultured classes and destroying academic freedom, with serious results alike for reform and education in England. Parliament refused to allow persecution of the Lollards. The position of the English church was not wholly due to its own corruption nor to the paralysis of the Avignonese Captivity, but was partly a result of the fact that secular learning, secular society, and the secular state had overtaken the position of the Church.

1385. Futile **expedition of Richard to Scotland;** threatened French invasion (1386); general demands for reform in government. Parliament blocked Richard's effort (1385) to set up a personal government, and appointed a commission of reform. The lords appellant (led by Richard's uncle, the duke of Gloucester) secured the impeachment and condemnation (1388) of five of Richard's party (in the *Wonderful,* or *Merciless Parliament*).

1389-1397. Richard's personal and constitutional rule. Truce with France (1389), peace negotiations, marriage to Isabelle, infant daughter of Charles VI (1396). Richard was on good terms with parliament, England prosperous and quiet. Livery and maintenance forbidden by statute (1390); re-enactment of the statutes of: provisors (1390); mortmain (1391); praemunire (1393).

1397-1399. Richard's attempt at absolutism. Richard, furious at a parliamentary demand for financial accounting, had the mover (Haxey) condemned for treason (not executed). In the next parliament (commons, packed for Richard; lords friendly) three of the lords appellant were convicted and executed for treason, Richard was voted an income for life (1398) and the powers of parliament delegated to a committee friendly to Richard. Heavy taxation, ruthless exactions, and a reign of terror opened the way for the **conspiracy of Henry of Bolingbroke** (exiled son of John of Gaunt).

1399. Bolingbroke landed while Richard was in Ireland, got him into his power on his return, and forced him to abdicate. Richard thrown into the Tower and later died (murdered?) in prison (1400). Parliament accepted the abdication and, returning to the ancient custom of election, made Henry king. Henry's title by heredity was faulty; his claim was based on usurpation, legalized by parliament, and backed by public opinion.

1399-1461. THE HOUSE OF LANCASTER.

1399-1413. HENRY IV. The reign, in view of the nature of Henry's title to the throne, was inevitably a parliamentary one. Henry, an epileptic, was not a great king, but a national monarch was now a necessity to England. To retain the support of the Church, Henry opposed the demand (1404) of the commons (perhaps a reflection of Lollardy) that church property be confiscated, and applied to poor relief. The request was renewed (1410). The statute, *de Heretico Comburendo* (1401), increased the power of the Church over heresy (primarily, of course, against Lollardy) and was the first law of its kind in England.

1400-1406. Rebellions and invasions: (1) revolt in behalf of Richard (1400); (2) Scottish invasion (1402) stopped by the Percies, the leading barons of Northumberland, at **Homildon Hill**; (3) Owen Glendower's revolt in Wales (1402-1409) joined by (4) the revolt of the Percies (1403-1404); (5) French landing in Wales (1405); (6) archbishop (of York) Scrope's rebellion (1405); (7) attack by the duke of Orléans in Guienne (1406).

1413-1422. HENRY V, a careful king, whose military achievements brought England to the

first rank in Europe. Bent on the revival of the Church, he led a strong attack on Lollardy: **Sir John Oldcastle** (Lord Cobham), the leading Lollard, was excommunicated by Archbishop Arundel, but escaped; a Lollard plot against the king's life was discovered; Henry attacked (1414) and captured a Lollard group, most of whom were hanged; anti-Lollard legislation allowing seizure of their books; Oldcastle, the last influential Lollard, executed (1417). Henceforth Lollardy was a lower-class movement driven undergound until the Reformation.

1415. Henry, in alliance with Burgundy, reasserted his claims (such as they were) to the throne of France. Relying on the anarchy in France and hoping by military successes to unite the English behind the house of Lancaster, he advanced into France.

1415, Oct. 25. BATTLE OF AGINCOURT. Henry's great victory over vastly superior forces opened the way to

1417-1419. The **reconquest of Normandy** and an advance to the walls of Paris (1419). The temporary union of the Armagnac and Burgundian factions in France was broken by the assassination (1419) of the duke of Burgundy, followed by the renewal of Anglo-Burgundian alliance and

1420. The treaty of Troyes. The dauphin (later Charles VII) was disinherited; Henry V was designated regent of France and successor to the mad Charles VI, was given control of northern France, and was married to Charles's daughter Catherine. Henry, busy in the reconquest of France, died suddenly, followed shortly by Charles VI (1422).

1422-1461. Henry VI (aged nine months on his accession), acclaimed king of France; his uncle, the duke of Gloucester, regent (under the council) in England; another uncle, the duke of Bedford, regent in France.

1424. Bedford defeated the French at **Verneuil**, but his ally, the duke of Burgundy, was angered by Gloucester's foolish invasion of Hainault. Bitter feud of Gloucester and Beaufort, bishop of Winchester and chancellor.

1428-1429. English failure at Orléans; coronation of Charles VII at Reims (1429).

1431. The English burned **Joan of Arc** (p. 301) at Rouen and crowned Henry VI king of France in Paris. Steady advance of Charles VII; unpopularity of the war in England; parliamentary resistance to grants; loss of the Burgundian alliance (1435) and of Paris (1436).

1436-1437. Richard, duke of York (heir to throne), regent in France. He was replaced, after a few successes, by the earl of Warwick (1437-1439), but later returned to France (1440-1443). Continued rivalry of Beaufort

292

(From p. 211)

The Houses of Lancaster and York (1377–1485)

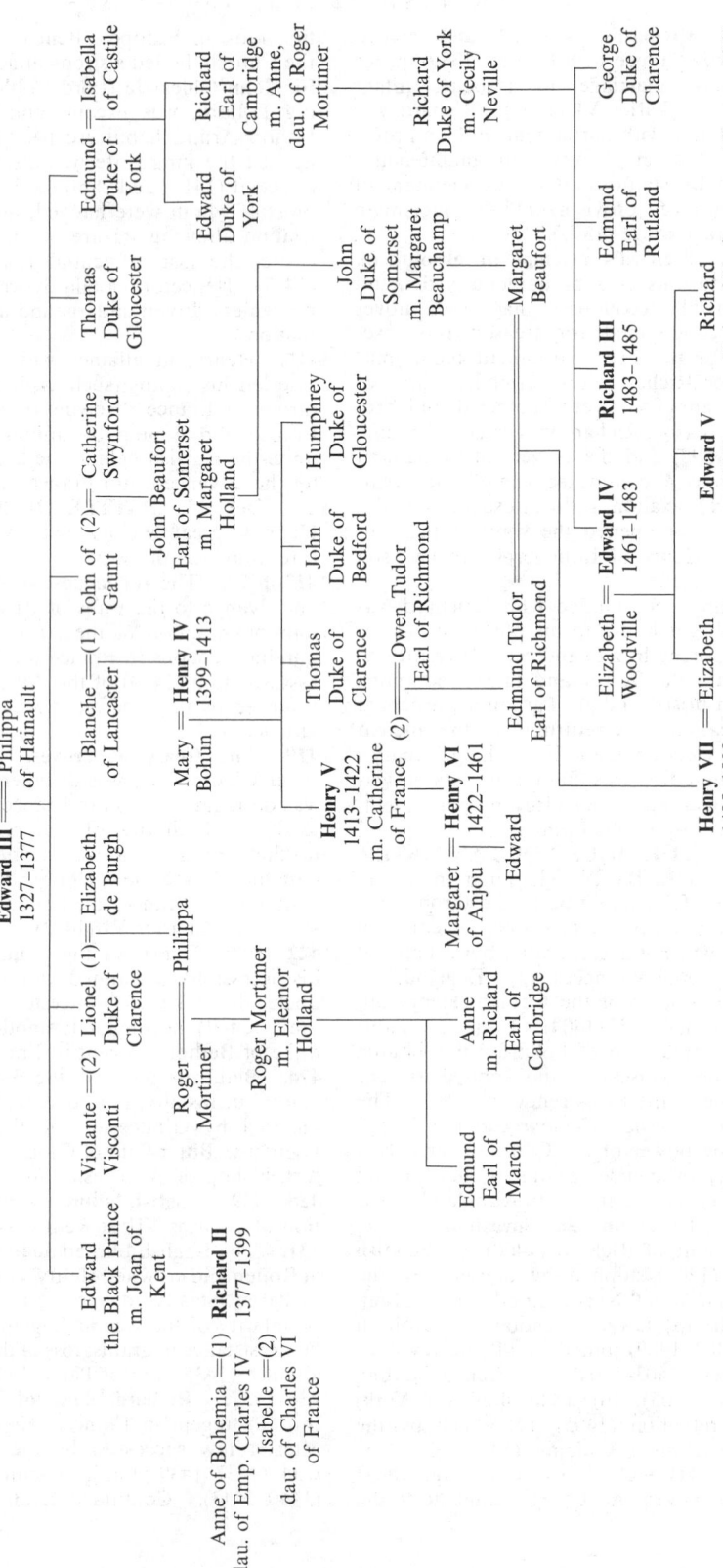

(Cont. p. 396.)

and Gloucester. Beaufort, supported by the king, who liked his peace policy, attended the conference of Calais (1439).

1442. French conquest of Gascony except Bordeaux and Bayonne.

1444. The king's new favorite, the duke of Suffolk, arranged the marriage of Henry and Margaret of Anjou, concluded a truce of two years, and promised to surrender Maine to Charles VII. Margaret was unpopular in England and Maine was not turned over.

1448. Charles VII, in a vigorous renewal of the war, took Maine, completed the conquest of Normandy (1450), and regained Bordeaux and Bayonne (1451). The English effort to reconquer Gascony failed (1453), leaving only Calais in English hands at the end of the Hundred Years' War.

 Domestic disorders. Henry, declared of age (1437), was unfit to rule; the council continued in power, factions and favorites encouraged the rise of disorder. The nobles, enriched by the war and the new sheep-farming and progress of enclosures, maintained increasing numbers of private armed retainers (livery and maintenance) with which they fought one another, terrorized their neighbors, paralyzed the courts, and dominated the government. The government lost prestige; Gloucester, arrested (1447) for treason, died in prison, Suffolk (impeached 1450) was killed as he sailed into exile.

1450. Cade's rebellion: a revolt of perhaps 30,000 men of Kent and Sussex, including many respectable small landowners, who marched on London to demand reform in government and the restoration of the duke of York to power. Admitted to London, the marchers were finally crushed after they resorted to violence. **Richard of York** returned from Ireland and forced his admission to the council (1450). York was regent during Henry's periods of insanity (1453–1454; 1455–1456), but on his recovery (1454) Somerset returned to power.

1455-1485. THE WARS OF THE ROSES. A dreary civil war between the houses of Lancaster and York (the Yorkists wearing a white rose, the Lancastrians [later] a red rose). The nation as such took little part. **Battle of St. Albans** (1455): Somerset defeated and killed. **Battle of Northampton** (1460): the Yorkists defeated the royal army and took Henry prisoner. York asserted his hereditary claim to the throne, and the lords decided that he should succeed Henry on his death (excluding Henry's son, Edward).

1460. Queen Margaret raised an army in the north, defeated Richard of York, who fell on the field (Wakefield, 1460). Southern England rallied to Richard's son Edward (aged nineteen) who defeated the Lancastrians at **Mortimer's Cross** (1461), but was defeated at the **second battle of St. Albans** (1461), and lost possession of King Henry. London stood firm against Margaret, admitted Edward to the town, and after his victory at Towton acclaimed him king (1461).

 Growth of the powers of parliament under the Lancastrians: Profiting by the cloud on the royal title and by the pressing needs for war supply, parliament reached the zenith of its influence: (1) Grant of supply delayed until the end of the session after redress of grievances; agreement by the king not to alter petitions when drafted into statutes. Petitions began to take the form of bills, which when approved by the king became statutes in the modern sense. (2) Beginnings of the commons' control over the initiation of financial legislation. (3) Enforcement of reform (1404) in the royal administration; members of the council named in parliament; appointment of the new council enforced (1405). (4) Parliament forced a reversal of the Haxey judgment (1399), establishing its right to freedom of speech in debate. (5) Opposition to packing began to develop and a statute was passed defining the franchise for elections (1430); this statute was in force until the great reform bill of 1832.

 The king could still legislate by ordinances in council. Under Henry VI the autocratic council ruled, and in the end dominated parliament; finally the chaos of the Wars of the Roses saw the temporary eclipse of parliament as well as of ordered government.

1461-1485. THE HOUSE OF YORK.

1461-1483. EDWARD IV. Parliament declared the three Lancastrian kings usurpers and Henry VI, his wife, son, and chief adherents, traitors. Edward closed the session with a speech of thanks to the commons, the first time an English king had addressed that body. The mass of Englishmen now wanted a monarch to keep order in the state, and allow them to attend to trade, industry, and agriculture. Civil war continued intermittently, and Henry VI was finally captured (1465) and put in the Tower. Edward's marriage to the commoner, Elizabeth Woodville, and the beginnings of the creation of a new nobility, angered the older nobles, especially the earl of Warwick. Edward's sister Margaret was married to Charles the Bold, duke of Burgundy, and master of the Netherlands (1468). Warwick abandoned the king for his brother, the duke of Clarence, and began to foment trouble for Edward, now increasingly unpopular (1469–1470). Edward's victory (partly due to artillery) at **Stamford** (1470) was followed by the flight of Warwick and Clarence.

1471. Warwick next turned to the Lancastrians (under the astute guidance of King Louis XI of France), returned to England with Lancastrian support. Edward's victory at Barnet (1471), where Warwick was killed. Edward then turned on Queen Margaret at Tewksbury, and defeated her. Henry VI died (in all probability murdered) in the Tower. The only surviving claimant to the crown was Henry, earl of Richmond, an exile aged 14, descended from John of Gaunt and his mistress, Catherine Swynford.

Edward's vigorous plans for war against Louis XI: parliamentary grants were too small, so he began a new practice—benevolences (supposedly free, but in fact forced gifts).

1475. Landing in France, Edward got no support from Charles the Bold, and was bought off by Louis XI. Charles the Bold was killed (1477) and Edward was left without an ally.

1483. EDWARD V, aged twelve. **Richard, duke of Gloucester,** Edward's uncle, an able man, good soldier, cruel and cynical, skilled at winning popular support, had been appointed guardian by Edward's will. Fearing the Woodvilles (family of Edward's mother), Richard struck at them, taking Earl Rivers and Sir Richard Grey prisoners; the queen mother took sanctuary at Westminster; assassination of Lord Hastings (a supporter of the queen); execution of Grey and Rivers; attacks on the legitimacy of Edward; parliament declared Gloucester the heir and he was crowned Richard III. Edward was sent to the Tower.

1483–1485. RICHARD III. The duke of Buckingham, a former supporter of Richard, led (under the skilled direction of Morton, bishop of Ely) a rebellion in behalf of Henry, earl of Richmond. The rebellion failed, Buckingham was beheaded, Edward and his brother were murdered in the Tower (1483), and universal indignation was aroused. Richard and the earl of Richmond were both candidates for the hand of Elizabeth of York, daughter of Edward IV, now heiress to the throne. As she was Richard's niece, even his own followers were shocked.

1485. Henry, earl of Richmond, landed at Milford Haven, there were open defections from Richard by the nobles, and Henry defeated Richard on **Bosworth Field** (Aug. 22), where Richard fell. The crown of England was found on a bush and passed to the first ruler of the great **house of Tudor,** by virtue of his victory in arms and a later act of parliament.

Cultural movements. The Italian humanist, Poggio Bracciolini's visit (1418–1423) to England. *The Paston Letters* (1422–1509), a remarkable collection of the correspondence (in the vernacular) of a middle-class English family. *The Libel of English Policie* (c. 1436), a militant nationalistic exposition of the economic value of sea power. **Eton founded** by Henry VI.

Humphrey, duke of Gloucester (d. 1447), influential patron of classical learning and Italian humanism, was the donor of 279 classical manuscripts to Oxford, the nucleus of the university library. **Sir John Fortescue** (d. c. 1476), chief justice of the king's bench, a Lancastrian exile during the anarchy of the Wars of the Roses, wrote *On the Governance of the Kingdom of England,* and *De Laudibus Legum Angliae,* contrasting the "political" (i.e. constitutional) spirit of the English common law with the absolutism of the Roman law, and comparing the French monarchy unfavorably with the English. Many of his ideas foreshadowed the policies of Henry VII, in form if not in spirit.

Trade guilds and other lay groups gradually took over production of miracle plays and later morality plays.

Caxton's printing press set up at Westminster (1476) under the patronage of Edward IV. Malory's *Morte Arthure* printed (1484), the first book in poetic prose in the English language. (*Cont. p. 395.*)

(2) Scotland, 1305–1488

(From p. 217)

1305. The conquest of Scotland by Edward I of England saved the country from civil war. Edward's plan of union seemed possible for a brief period until the emergence of Bruce's great-grandson, Robert, who turned against the English and maintained himself until the incompetence of Edward II gave him a chance to extend the opposition to the English.

1311–1313. Bruce began a great advance into England and besieged Stirling (1314).

1314, June 24. BATTLE OF BANNOCKBURN. Bruce completely defeated the English and established himself on the throne, thus postponing for centuries the union with England. Bruce's daughter, Margaret, married Walter "the Steward" and became the founder of the house of Stuart.

1315–1318. Edward Bruce, brother of the king, led an unsuccessful invasion of Ireland.

1323. A truce of five years with England was followed by the **treaty of Northampton,** which recognized Robert Bruce's title and provided for the marriage of his son David to Joan, daughter of Edward II.

1329–1370. DAVID II, son of Robert, king.

(From p. 218)

The House of Stuart (1370–1625)

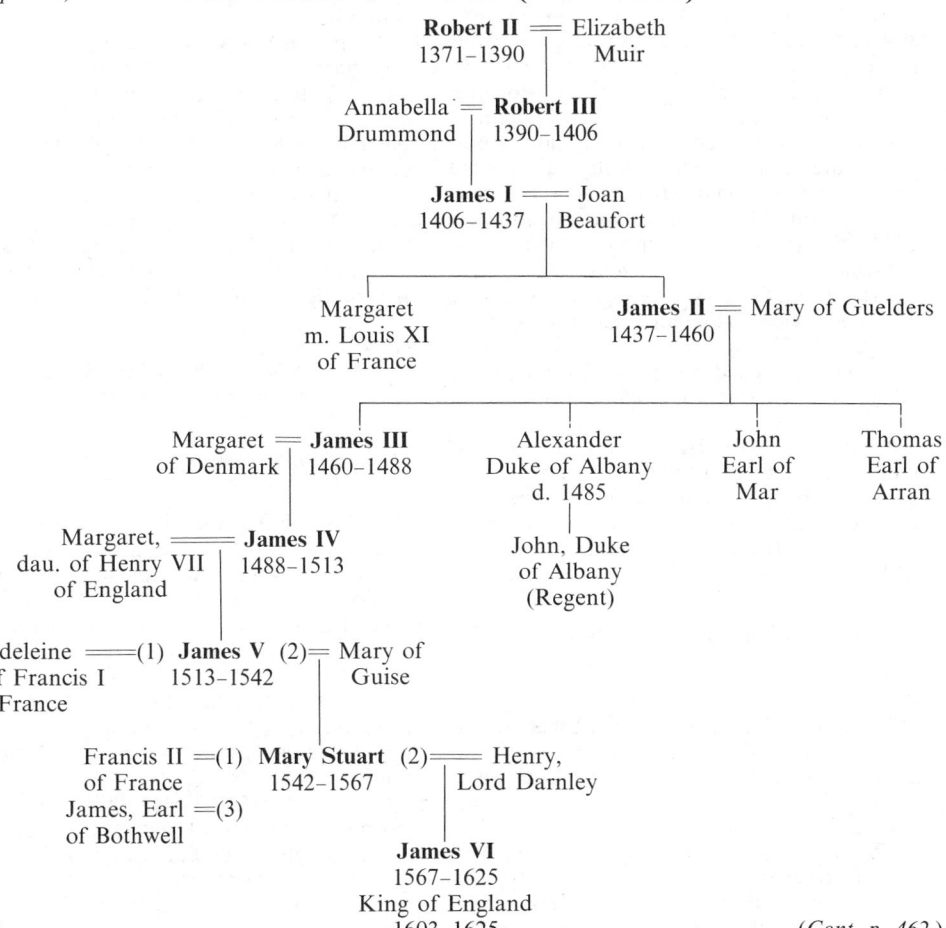

Robert II = Elizabeth
1371–1390   Muir

Annabella = **Robert III**
Drummond   1390–1406

James I == Joan
1406–1437   Beaufort

Margaret   **James II** = Mary of Guelders
m. Louis XI   1437–1460
of France

Margaret = **James III**   Alexander   John   Thomas
of Denmark | 1460–1488   Duke of Albany   Earl of   Earl of
               d. 1485   Mar   Arran

Margaret, === **James IV**   John, Duke
dau. of Henry VII | 1488–1513   of Albany
of England   (Regent)

Madeleine ===(1) **James V** (2)= Mary of
dau. of Francis I   1513–1542 | Guise
of France

Francis II =(1) **Mary Stuart** (2)=== Henry,
of France   1542–1567 | Lord Darnley
James, Earl =(3)
of Bothwell

James VI
1567–1625
King of England
1603–1625

(Cont. p. 462.)

His minority was followed by an incompetent rule.

1332. Edward Baliol, with English support, was crowned, and Bruce fled to France. After Baliol's recall to England, Bruce returned and was defeated and captured at

1346. The **battle of Neville's Cross,** in an effort to aid France by invading England. He was not ransomed until 1357.

This futile reign gave the Scottish parliament its chance; the burghs had sent representatives to the parliament of 1326, but the practice was not a regular one until 1424. On at least two occasions the parliamentary majority went home (1367, 1369), leaving the session to commissions, thus establishing the **Lords of Articles,** who assumed deliberative functions and soon became tools of the crown. Never-

theless, parliament managed to establish a considerable control over royal acts, and kept its hand on the declaration of war and peace and the coinage. The lower clergy began sending representatives to parliament (e.g. 1367, 1369, 1370).

1356. Edward Baliol handed over his crown to Edward III.

1363. David Bruce's scheme for a union with England if he died childless was blocked by parliament's refusal to approve it (1364).

1371. The **STUART LINE** was established on the Scottish throne by the accession of

1371–1390. ROBERT II, grandson of Robert Bruce. The family maintained itself for three centuries despite a succession of futilities and minorities. The rival **house of Douglas** was finally extinguished (1488).

1390-1406. ROBERT III. Due to physical infirmity he rarely exercised royal power.

1406-1437. JAMES I. After a long imprisonment (since 1405) in England began a vigorous, if premature, reform, reduction of violence, restoration of the judicial process, and new legislation which ended anarchy and disciplined the church. The country lairds were given representation in parliament as a support to the crown (1428). James was assassinated, 1437. St. Andrew's University founded.

1437-1460. JAMES II. From James I to Charles I (1625) every sovereign was a minor on his accession. The reduction of the earls of Douglas (1452), followed by confiscation of their lands, enriched the crown. Rosburgh was taken from the English, leaving only Berwick in alien hands.

1460-1488. JAMES III, a feeble figure, was kidnaped (1466) by Lord Boyd, who ruled as governor (by vote of parliament). The Orkneys and Shetlands were acquired from Norway (1472). France kept Scotland in contact with the Continent. *(Cont. p. 395.)*

(3) Ireland, 1315-1485

(From p. 217)

1315. Edward Bruce, brother of Robert Bruce of Scotland, landed in Ireland and, with the aid of native chieftains, had himself crowned (1316). But he was able to maintain himself only until 1318.

The Anglo-Norman colony began to weaken from internal quarrels while Edward III was preoccupied with the Hundred Years' War. The chieftains thereupon seized their opportunity to encroach still further upon the position of the outsiders. From this period dates the gradual ebb of English influence. The Black Death (1348-1349) made matters even worse.

1366. The **statute of Kilkenny** (passed during the viceroyalty of Lionel, duke of Clarence) had two aims: (1) to maintain the allegiance of the English colony and keep it to the English tradition, and (2) to reduce the grounds of racial conflict. Marriages with the Irish were forbidden, though this was not an entirely new measure. English was enjoined as the speech of the colonists, and English law was insisted on. Nevertheless, the viceroys and governors were unable to maintain order.

1398. Expedition of Richard II to reduce Ireland. This was without permanent results. Under Henry V misery in Ireland reached a new peak and perhaps half of the English colony returned home. The danger in this situation is mentioned in the *Libel of English*

Policie (c. 1436). Fear that Ireland might pass into other hands was widespread.

1449. Richard of York arrived as viceroy and ingratiated himself equally with colonists and natives. He departed to England in 1450, but on his return made Ireland virtually independent, with the approval of the Irish parliament. English rule was repudiated and a separate coinage established. Richard continued this policy until his death, but Edward IV resumed a harsh and anarchic policy. Under Richard III the strongest figure in Ireland was **Kildare,** leader of the Yorkists. *(Cont. p. 395.)*

b. FRANCE, 1314-1483

(From p. 249)

[For a complete list of the kings of France see Appendix VII.]

1314-1316. LOUIS X (the Quarrelsome). The real ruler was Louis's uncle, Charles of Valois. A reaction against the monarchy forced concessions from the king.

1316. Louis was succeeded by his posthumous son, John I, who lived only a few days. Louis's daughter by his first wife, Jeanne, was also an infant. A great national council therefore decreed that there could be no queen regnant in France (so-called) and awarded the crown to Louis's brother.

1316-1322. PHILIP V (the Tall). There were frequent meetings of assemblies which included burghers. Philip, in an enormous number of royal ordinances, gave definitive form to the Capetian government. He left no male heir.

1322-1328. CHARLES IV (the Fair), the last Capetian of the direct line, succeeded his brother Philip, to the exclusion of Edward III of England, grandson of Philip IV. This established the principle, later called the **Salic Law,** that the throne could pass only through males. On Charles's death, an assembly of barons declared that "no woman nor her son could succeed to the monarchy."

1328-1498. In this period the **Capetian house of Valois** freed the soil of France from the alien occupation of the English; completed the creation of French national unity and the establishment of a strong national monarchy; prepared France for its brilliant political and cultural rôle in the Renaissance, and began French expansion south of the Alps.

1328-1350. PHILIP VI (nephew of Philip IV, son of Charles of Valois), the nearest male heir. Jeanne, daughter of Louis X, became queen of Navarre. Edward III did homage for his French fiefs (1329 and 1331). Brittany,

Flanders, Guienne, and Burgundy remained outside the royal sway. The Papacy was located in France under powerful French influence; rulers of the Capetian house of Anjou were seated on the thrones of Naples, Provence, and Hungary; French interests were firmly established in the Near East; French culture was dominant in England and northern Spain, and was making headway on the fringes of the empire; Dauphiné, the first important imperial fief added to French territory, was purchased (1336). The king had become less accessible; the kingdom, regarded as a possession rather than an obligation, was left to the administration of the royal bureaucracy.

1338–1453.   THE HUNDRED YEARS' WAR. English commercial dominance in Flanders precipitated a political crisis. The communes made the count of Flanders, Louis of Nevers, prisoner (1325–1326); Philip marched to his relief, massacred the burghers on the field of Cassel (1328), and established French administration in Flanders. Edward III retorted with an embargo on wool export from England (1336); the weavers of Ghent, under the wealthy Jan van Arteveldt, became virtual masters of the country and made a commercial treaty with England (1338). On van Arteveldt's insistence, Edward declared himself king of France; the Flemings recognized him as their sovereign, and made a political alliance with him (1340).

1338.   Philip declared Edward's French fiefs forfeited and invested Guienne. Edward was made vicar of the empire and his title as king of France was recognized by the emperor. Thus began the **Hundred Years' War,** really a series of wars with continuous common objectives: the retention of their French "empire" by the English, the liberation of their soil by the French.

1340.   Philip, by dismissing two squadrons of Levantine mercenary ships, lost his mastery of the Channel until 1372 and was overwhelmingly defeated by Edward at the **naval battle of Sluys** (June 24). This opened the Channel to the English and gave them free access to northern France.

1341–1364.   A dynastic contest in Brittany, in which both Edward and Philip intervened.

1341.   First collection of the *gabelle* (salt tax) in France; increasing war levies and mounting dissatisfaction.

1346.   Edward's invasion of Normandy and overwhelming **VICTORY AT CRÉCY,** Aug. 26 (10,000 English defeated some 20,000 French). The French military system was outmoded, the people unaccustomed to arms, and the chivalry inefficient. Blind King John of Bohemia was slain. Artillery came into use (1335–1345).

Continued war levies led to open refusal (1346) of a grant by the estates-general of Langue d'Oïl, and a demand for reforms. The king attempted some reforms.

1347.   Edward's siege and **capture of Calais** gave the English an economic and military base in France that was held until 1558.

1348–1350.   The **Black Death** penetrated northern Europe, reducing the population by about a third, and contributing to the crisis of 1357–1358 in France.

1350–1364.   JOHN II (the Good Fellow), a "good knight and a mediocre king," a spendthrift who repeatedly debased the currency.

1355.   English **renewal of the war** in a triple advance: into Brittany; from the Channel; and from Bordeaux by the Black Prince. Virtual collapse of French finance. The estates-general of Languedoc and Langue d'Oïl (the latter under the leadership of **Etienne Marcel,** the richest man in Paris, provost of the merchants), forced the king (ordinance of 1355) to agree to consult the estates before making new levies of money, a policy already in practice, and to accept supervision of the collection and expenditure of these levies by a commission from the estates. John cleverly induced the estates to adjourn, debased the coinage in the interest of his treasury, and organized his opposition to the estates.

1356.   The **Black Prince** (the English "model of chivalry") defeated John, the last "chivalrous" king of France, at **Poitiers** (Sept. 19). King John, his son Philip, and two brothers were taken prisoner with a multitude of the French aristocracy. The royal authority in France was reduced to a shadow; civil chaos reigned. Charles, the eighteen-year-old son of John, became regent.

1357.   Climax of the power of the **estates-general:** The estates-general again had to be called and passed the **Great Ordinance** which provided for supervision of the levy and expenditure of taxes by a standing committee of the estates, regular and frequent meetings of the estates, poor relief, and many other reforms, but did not attempt to reduce the traditional powers of the monarchy. The estates had met too frequently, were divided, and had no real coherence or skill in government. They were discredited by Marcel's alliance with Charles the Bad of Navarre (a son of Jeanne, daughter of Louis X), who had a better claim to the throne than Edward III. The regent Charles fled from Paris and created a powerful coalition against the estates and Charles the Bad.

1358.   The *Jacquerie* (a violent peasant reaction against war taxes, the weight of the ransoms of the captives at Poitiers, and the pillage of

The French Succession (1328)

298

(From p. 243)

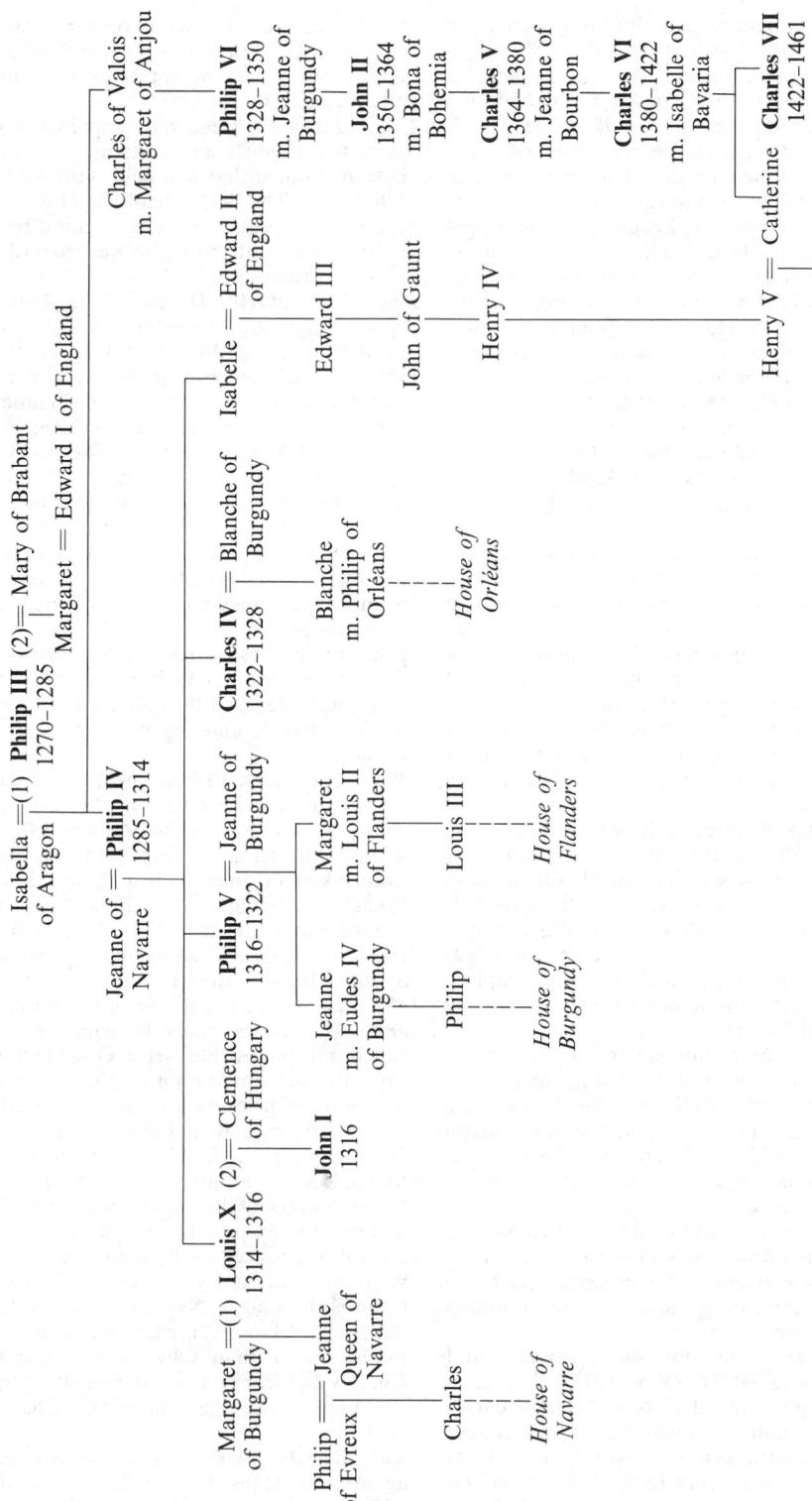

Charles of Valois
m. Margaret of Anjou

Philip VI
1328–1350
m. Jeanne of Burgundy

John II
1350–1364
m. Bona of Bohemia

Charles V
1364–1380
m. Jeanne of Bourbon

Charles VI
1380–1422
m. Isabelle of Bavaria

Charles VII
1422–1461
m. Marie of Anjou

(Cont. p. 300.)

Isabella =(1) Philip III (2)= Mary of Brabant
of Aragon   1270–1285
              Margaret = Edward I of England

Jeanne of = Philip IV
Navarre   1285–1314

Isabelle = Edward II
of England

Edward III

John of Gaunt

Henry IV

Henry V = Catherine

Henry VI
King of England
and France

Charles IV = Blanche of Burgundy
1322–1328

Blanche
m. Philip of Orléans

House of Orléans

Philip V = Jeanne of Burgundy
1316–1322

Margaret
m. Louis II of Flanders

Louis III

House of Flanders

Jeanne
m. Eudes IV of Burgundy

Philip

House of Burgundy

Margaret =(1) Louis X (2)= Clemence of Hungary
of Burgundy   1314–1316

John I
1316

Philip = Jeanne Queen of Navarre
of Evreux

Charles

House of Navarre

the free companies) led to a merciless reaction by the nobles. Marcel, already distrusted, was further discredited by intrigues with the revolted peasantry and with the English. Charles, after the murder of Marcel (1358), returned to the capital, repressed disorder with a firm hand, and refused to approve John's preliminary peace (1359), which virtually restored the old Angevin lands in France to Edward.

1360. The **PEACE OF BRETIGNY** (Calais) (virtually a truce of mutual exhaustion): Edward practically abandoned his claims to the French crown; Charles yielded southwestern France (Guienne), Calais, Ponthieu, and the territory immediately about them, and promised an enormous ransom for John. King John was released on partial payment of the ransom, but returned after the flight of a hostage to die in his luxurious and welcome captivity in England. The southern provinces protested their return to English rule, and there were clear signs of national sentiment born of adversity.

1361. The **duchy of Burgundy** escheated to the crown, and John handed it to his son Philip as an appanage (1363). Charles negotiated (1369) the marriage of Duke Philip to Margaret, daughter and heiress of Louis de Male, last count of Flanders, in order to keep Flanders out of English hands. As Margaret brought Flanders, the county of Burgundy, Artois, Nevers, and Rethel under control of the dukes of Burgundy, this marriage added a new danger on the east and north to the Plantagenet threat in the west. Philip further strengthened his house by marriage alliances with the children of the Wittelsbach, Albert of Bavaria, which added holdings in Hainault, Holland, and Zealand.

1364-1380. **CHARLES V** (the Wise), neither strong of body, handsome, nor chivalrous; a pious, refined, realistic statesman of modern cast. He saved France and made it plain to the nation that national well-being depended on the monarchy rather than on the estates-general.

The reign opened with a bad harvest, plague, and pillage by the free companies (discharged soldiers). The Breton, **Bertrand Du Guesclin,** the first great soldier on the French side in the Hundred Years' War, was sent with some 30,000 of these men to support Henry of Trastamara against Pedro the Cruel of Castile, who had become an ally of the Black Prince.

Charles managed to dominate the new financial machinery set up by the estates-general, continued the war levies (e.g. hearth-tax, *gabelle,* sales taxes) and utilized the peace for general reform and reconstruction: castles were rebuilt, and royal control of them strengthened; permanent companies of professional cavalry and infantry were established; artillery was organized and supported by pioneers and sappers; a military staff and hierarchy of command established in the army (1374); the navy was reorganized, and French sea power restored. New walls were built around Paris.

The government and finance were reorganized and the general frame of the financial structure fixed until 1789. The grant of the estates-general of Langue d'Oïl (1360) for John's ransom had been for a term of six years; their grant of a hearth-tax (1363) was without a time limit. Following these precedents, Charles was able (1369) to induce the estates to agree to the general principle that old grants of funds need not be renewed by the estates unless their terms were to be changed. This freed the king from control by the estates unless new taxes were needed and meant that the estates no longer had a vital function. The financial control established by the estates (1357) was transferred to the royal *chambre de comptes* in Paris.

1369. The appeal of the count of Armagnac to Charles against the Black Prince and the Black Prince's refusal to appear at Charles's court served as an excuse for the **resumption of the war.** Du Guesclin became (1370) constable of France (a title usually reserved for great nobles), abandoned chivalrous tactics, and allowed the English to parade through France. Avoiding pitched battle, he harassed the invaders with a picked force. The reconquest of Poitou and Brittany (1370-1372) was followed by the death of the Black Prince (1376); the French fleet, supported by the Castilian, regained control (La Rochelle, 1372) of the Channel, and blocked English transport in the north. By 1380 the English held only Bordeaux, Bayonne, Brest, Calais, Cherbourg, Valais, and their immediately surrounding territory. France was cleared of the enemy, but was in ruins.

1378. With the end of the Avignonese Captivity (1376) the **Great Schism** in the Church began; Charles and his successors supported the French line of popes. On his deathbed Charles forbade the hearth-tax.

1380-1422. CHARLES VI. A minority reign accompanied by the disruptive rivalry of the king's uncles (the dukes of Anjou, Berri, and Burgundy, the "Princes of the Lilies"), who exploited France for their own ends. This was followed by the intermittent insanity of the king, and paralysis in the government.

General economic distress, popular unrest, and general revolts, usually against taxes (vigorously repressed): the *Tuchins* (1381) in Languedoc; the *Maillotins* (1382) in Paris, and elsewhere; and the outbreak in Flanders (1382)

The House of Valois (1328–1515)

(From p. 298)

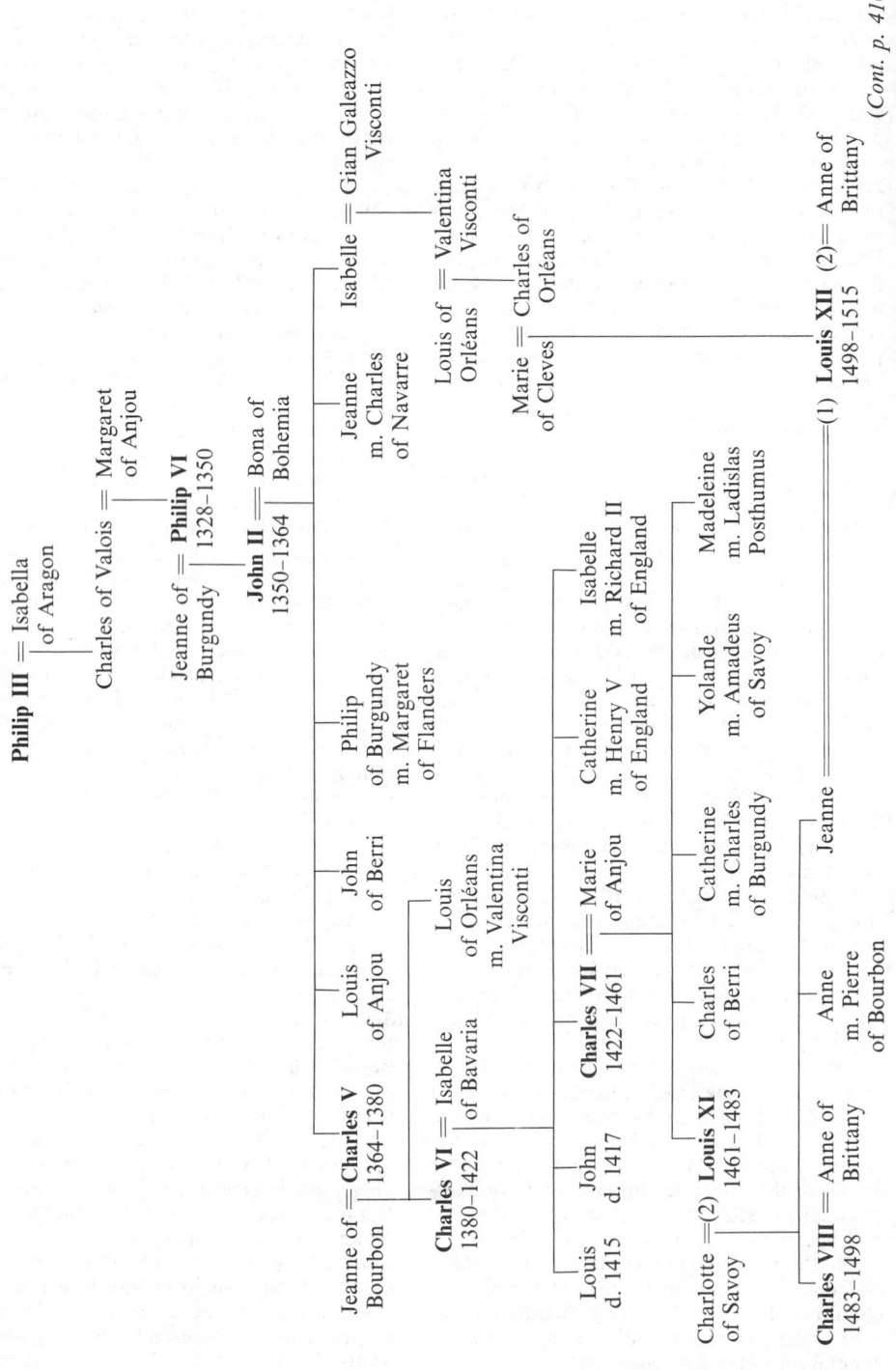

(Cont. p. 410.)

under Philip (son of Jan) van Arteveldt. The French feudality, under leadership of the duke of Burgundy, ended this revolt by the victory of **Roosebeke** (1382), following it up with atrocious repression. Flanders on the death of the count (1384) passed to Burgundy; its pacification was completed in 1385. The hearth-tax was renewed and taxation remained heavy.

1388. The death (1384) of the duke of Anjou had left the duke of Burgundy in a position of great power, and Charles, angered at Philip of Burgundy's policies, began his personal rule by replacing the duke by his own brother, Louis, duke of Orléans, and by restoring (1389) his father's old advisers, men of humble birth (whence their nickname, the *Marmousets*). Louis of Orléans was a refined, talented spendthrift, unpopular in Paris, and Philip of Burgundy (supported by Queen Isabelle) was able to pose as a reformer and lead the opposition, bringing the rivalry of Burgundy and Orléans into the open.

1392. **Charles's first** (brief) **attack of insanity** was soon followed by longer seizures; Philip of Burgundy (as regent) replaced Louis of Orléans in power and the situation returned to what it was before 1389.

1396. **Twenty-year truce with England;** annihilation of the French knights on a crusade to free Hungary from the Turk (Nicopolis, p. 350).

1404. **John** (the Fearless), an able, ambitious man, became **duke of Burgundy.** After the sudden transfer of Isabelle's support to Louis of Orléans, John's orders led to the assassination of Louis, duke of Orléans (1407). John became the hero of Paris, but caused the emergence of two great factions in France and began the civil war of the **Armagnacs** against the Burgundians. The Armagnacs, named for their head, the count of Armagnac (father-in-law of Charles, the new duke of Orléans), were strong among the great nobles, drew their power from the south and southeast, were a reactionary, anti-English, war party. The Burgundians, supported by the people, the University of Paris, and the Wittelsbachs, were strong in the north and northeast, favored peace, were pro-English, and supported Pope Clement VII and his papal successors.

1413. The **Cabochian revolt** (named for the skinner, Simon Caboche) in Paris forced attention to reform, and led to the **Cabochian Ordinance** (1413), inspired by the University of Paris and aimed at efficiency in government rather than democracy. It provided for three councils to conduct public business, and a general detailed program of reform. The Armagnacs returned to control in Paris and led a feudal reaction, which destroyed all hope of reform and opened the way for the English.

The duke of Armagnac (Constable, 1415) repeated the traditional military errors of the feudal class, which understood tournaments but not war.

1415, Oct. 25. THE BATTLE OF AGINCOURT. Henry V, with 10,000 men, defeated three times that number of French; the duke of Orléans was taken prisoner; **Normandy was reconquered** by the English, undoing for the time the work of Philip Augustus; the dauphin (later Charles VII) fled to the south of France (1418); the Burgundians returned to power and there was a massacre of Armagnacs in Paris (1418).

1419. Rouen fell; the Burgundians, alarmed at the English advance, began negotiating with the Armagnacs; John of Burgundy was assassinated at a conference with the dauphin at the bridge of Montereau, and the Burgundians returned to the English alliance.

1420. Charles, under Burgundian influence, and supported by his wife Isabelle, accepted the **treaty of Troyes** (which repudiated the dauphin as illegitimate), adopted Henry V of England as his heir and immediate regent (with the approval of the University of Paris and the estates-general, 1421). Charles's daughter, Catherine, was married to Henry V and, also under the treaty, the English were allowed to retain all their conquests as far as the Loire. King Henry V drove the forces of the dauphin across the Loire and began the steady conquest of France which continued uninterrupted until his death (1422). The dauphin remained at Bourges (whence his nickname, *the Roi de Bourges*).

1422–1461. CHARLES VII (the Roi de Bourges, not crowned until 1429). Physically weak, bowed and lethargic from misfortune, the puppet of unscrupulous advisers until the advent of a better group (including Dunois, Richemont, brother-in-law of the duke of Burgundy, La Hire, *et al.*), after 1433, when he became known as "Charles the Well-Served." **Regency of the duke of Bedford** (1422–1428) for the infant Henry VI of England, who was recognized as king of France in the north, supported by the Burgundians, and crowned in Paris (1436).

1424. Bedford's decisive **victory at Cravant** was followed by the defeat of the Armagnacs and the Scots at Verneuil.

1428. The English began the **siege of Orléans. Jeanne d'Arc** (Joan of Arc, The Maid of Orléans), born in 1412 at Domrémy, was of comfortable village family, illiterate, but a good seamstress. A devout mystic, she began to have visions at the age of thirteen.

1429. Jeanne presented herself to the king at Chinon, and was allowed to lead an army (with the empty title of *Chef de Guerre*) to the relief of Orléans. The relief of the city, followed by **Charles's coronation** (1429) at Reims, was the turning point of the war and marked a decisive change in the spirit of the king and the nation. Jealous ministers (*e.g.* La Trémoille) of Charles soon undermined Jeanne's position, despite the progress of the royal cause.

1430. Jeanne was captured at Compiègne by the Burgundians, ransomed by the English. Without intervention by Charles on her behalf, she was tried for witchcraft. The process was probably a typical ecclesiastical trial. After her confession and its repudiation she was burned (1431) by the English at Rouen ("We have burned a saint"), and Charles returned to his old ways.

1432. Charles favored the **council of Basel,** which was pro-French and anti-papal.

1435. Separate **peace of Arras,** reconciliation with Burgundy: Charles agreed to punish the murderers of Duke John of Burgundy and recognized Philip as a sovereign prince for life. Burgundy was to recognize Charles's title; the Somme towns were to pass to Burgundy (subject to redemption). The English refused to make peace on acceptable terms. **Charles recovered Paris** (1436).

1436–1449. Period of military inaction, utilized by Charles for reforms of the army paid for from the *taille.* The estates-general agreed to permanent taxation for support of the army. Charles entered Paris and was welcomed (1437).

1437–1439. Famine, pestilence, the anarchy of the *écorcheurs,* but steady progress against the English.

1438. THE PRAGMATIC SANCTION OF BOURGES. Assertion that a church council is superior to a pope; suppression of the annates; provision for decennial councils; maintenance of the autonomy of the French national church (*Gallicanism*) and its isolation from Rome.

1440. The **Praguerie,** part of a series of coalitions of great nobles against the king, with support from the dauphin (later Louis XI), was put down; the dauphin was ordered to the Dauphiné, where he continued his intrigues.

1445–1446. **Army reforms:** establishment of the first permanent royal army by the creation of 20 companies of élite cavalry (200 *lances* to a company, six men to a *lance*) under captains chosen by the king; a paid force, the backbone of the army, assigned to garrison towns; regularization of the auxiliary free archers (*francs-archers*), a spontaneous body dating from the reign of Charles V (opposed by the nobles), under royal inspection (1448) and under territorial captains (1451). Establishment of artillery (the Bureau brothers).

1444. Louis the dauphin made a treaty of **alliance with the Swiss cantons.** The alliance was strengthened (1452) and an alliance made with the towns of Trier, Köln, *et. al.* (1452), and with Saxony, as part of a developing anti-Burgundian policy. Intermittent support for the house of Anjou in Naples and the house of Orléans in Milan. Under **Jacques Coeur,** the merchant prince of Montpellier, royal finances were reformed, control of the public revenue by the king established, and French commercial penetration of the Near East furthered (c. 1447).

1449–1461. Expulsion of the English: Normandy and Guienne regained; Talbot slain (1453).

1456. Retrial and **rehabilitation of Jeanne d'Arc,** to clear Charles's royal title.

1461–1483. LOUIS XI (the Spider), of simple, bourgeois habits, superficial piety, and feeble, ungainly body, the architect of French reconstruction and royal absolutism. He was well-educated, a brilliant diplomat, a relentless statesman, an endless traveler throughout his kingdom. He perfected the governmental system begun under Charles V (revived by Charles VII), and established the frame of the constitution until 1789. The recognized right of the king to the taille, the aides, and the gabelle made a good revenue available for defense and diplomacy. Louis improved and perfected the standing army with added emphasis on the artillery, but seldom waged war. Feudal anarchy and brigandage were stopped; a wise economic policy restored national prosperity despite grinding taxes.

1461. Louis's first step in the reconstruction of the kingdom was a rapprochement with the Papacy by the formal **revocation of the Pragmatic Sanction of Bourges.** Little of the royal power was sacrificed, and the national church remained under the firm control of the crown. Louis steadily reduced urban liberties and began the extinction of local and provincial administrative independence in the interests of royal centralization.

1462. Acquisition of Cerdagne and Roussillon; redemption of the Somme towns (1463) revealing the resumption of national expansion.

1465. League of the Public Weal, a conspiracy against Louis by the dukes of Alençon, Burgundy, Berri, Bourbon, Lorraine.

1465. Louis's defeat by the league at Montl'héry. The **treaty of Conflans** restored the Somme towns to Burgundy, and Normandy to the duke of Berry. Louis began to evade the treaty at once, and split the league by diplomacy.

Louis's greatest rival was **Duke Philip the**

Good of Burgundy. Philip was head of the first union of the Low Countries since the days of Charlemagne, a curious approximation of the ancient Lotharingia, which included: the duchy and county of Burgundy, Flanders, Artois, Brabant, Luxemburg, Holland, Zealand, Friesland, Hainault. The dukes lacked only Alsace and Lorraine and the royal title.

1467. The accession of **Charles the Bold** as duke of Burgundy opened the final duel with Burgundy.

1468. Anglo-Burgundian alliance; marriage of Charles the Bold to Margaret of York.

1468. The **affair at Péronne:** Charles, assuming Louis's treachery in the revolt of Ghent, arrested him at a conference at Péronne.

1469. The Duke Sigismund ceded Charles's rights in Alsace; Charles occupied Alsace and Lorraine (1473). Louis formed an alliance with the Swiss (1470) and seized the Somme towns (1471).

1474. Louis formed the **Union of Constance** (a coalition of the foes of Burgundy, under French subsidies) which opened the war on Charles.

1475. **Edward IV,** an ally of Charles, invaded France; Louis met him at Piquigny and bought him off.

1476. Charles's conquest of Lorraine and war on the Swiss cantons: defeat of Charles at **Grandson** and **Morat.**

1477, Jan. 5. DEFEAT AND DEATH OF CHARLES AT NANCY (triumph of the Swiss pikeman over cavalry); end of the Burgundian menace. Louis united the duchy of Burgundy to the crown and occupied the county of Burgundy (Franche Comté). Flanders stood by the daughter of Charles, Mary of Burgundy, and was lost to France forever. Mary hurriedly married the Hapsburg Archduke Maximilian, the "heir" to the empire.

1480. On the **extinction of the house of Anjou,** Anjou, Bar, Maine, and Provence fell to the French crown. Bar completed Louis's mastery on the eastern frontier.

The most significant internal fact of the reign was the development of a clear basis for royal absolutism. Only one meeting of the estates-general was held (1469), and on that occasion the estates asked the king to rule without them in future. Legislation was henceforth by royal decree, a situation which facilitated Louis's thoroughgoing reform of the government and administration.

CULTURAL DEVELOPMENTS

Jean Froissart (1337-1410) wrote his *Chroniques,* a colorful history of his times.

Philippe de Commines, (1447-1511), a Flem-

ing who left the service of Charles the Bold for that of Louis, produced in his *Mémoires* the finest piece of critical history since the days of the great historians of antiquity, and was a precursor of Machiavelli.

François Villon (1430-1470), a lyric poet of the first rank.

Jan (d. 1441) **and Hubert van Eyck** (d. 1426), Flemish painters in the service of the court of Burgundy, perfected oil technique; religious painting; portraiture, raising the painter's art to the highest stage of proficiency and perfection.

The Burgundian school of music flourished under the patronage of Charles the Bold: **Gilles Binchois** (d. 1470); **Guillaume Dufay** (d. 1474).
(Cont. p. 408.)

The only professional engineering document of the Middle Ages is the notebook of **Villard de Honnecourt** (fl. late 14th century), a French architect who worked in Cambrai, Laon, Reims, Meaux, Chartres, as well as in Hungary. His notebook contains architectural plans, practical geometry, descriptions of machines. In France around the University of Paris arose a school of mechanists who developed the ideas of the group at Merton College. **Jean Buridan** (d. 1358) used the concept of impetus as an explanation for motion and acceleration. **Nicole Oresme,** College of Navarre, used geometrical diagrams to display the variation of physical quantities under various conditions.

c. THE IBERIAN PENINSULA

(From p. 253)

(1) Castile, 1312-1492

The successors of Alfonso X were not conspicuous for capacity. Frequent minorities and constant dynastic contests still further weakened the authority of the crown. Most outstanding of the Castilian rulers in this period was

1312-1350. ALFONSO XI, who decisively defeated the joint attack of the Spanish and Moroccan Moslems. His **victory at Rio Salado** (Oct. 30, 1340) ended the African menace forever and was the chief battle in the whole history of the reconquest.

Throughout the **Hundred Years' War** Castile supported France, but attempted to avoid hostility with England as much as possible.

1350-1369. PETER (Pedro, the Cruel). His reign was in fact little more than a nineteen-year dynastic conflict with his half-brother, the bastard **Henry of Trastamara.** The French, alienated by Peter's outrageous treatment of his wife, Blanche of Bourbon, supported Henry and sent Du Guesclin to Spain. The English (the Black Prince) supported Peter. Henry was defeated at **Navarrete** (1367), but the English were soon estranged by Peter's vicious character. Ultimately Henry defeated and killed Peter (1369).

1369-1379. HENRY (ENRIQUE) II (Trastamara), who renewed the alliance with France. The Castilian fleet, by its victory over the English in the **battle of La Rochelle** (1372), restored command of the Channel to the French. Peace between Castile on the one side and Portugal and Aragon on the other concluded at **Almazan** (1374).

1375. Rapprochement of Castile and Aragon, through the marriage of Henry's son, John, to Eleanor, daughter of Peter IV of Aragon.

Castilian leadership in the reconquest of Moslem Spain led to a maximum of local and municipal self-government between the middle of the 12th and the middle of the 14th centuries. The cortes apparently originated from councils of nobles dating from Visigothic days. The Castilian rulers freely granted *fueros* (charters of self-government) to towns in the early stages of the reconquest, and definite elements of democracy appeared in municipal government in this period. By calling the burghers to the córtes, the kings found allies against the baronage, and this process began in Castile and Leon at least as early as 1188 (in Aragon probably not before 1250). The córtes reached its zenith in the 14th and 15th centuries, but petitions to the crown were received and embodied in legislation as early as the 13th century.

Urban groups, the *hermandades* (brotherhoods), sworn to defend the laws of the realm and the lives and property of their members, were clearly developed in the 13th century (e.g. Sancho's, 1282, directed against his father, Alfonso X) and usually supported the kings in periods of crisis (minorities, succession struggles, baronial assaults). The decline of the hermandades is associated with the municipal decline and the appearance of the royal *corregidores* (mayors) in the towns (14th century), but it is not clear whether the crown hastened the decay of the towns and the brotherhoods or sought to stave it off.

Despite all this support, the battle of the kings with the aristocracy, firmly entrenched during the early stages of the reconquest, was a losing one. The nobles were exempt from taxes and from many laws; in general the same was true of the clergy, and some of the great bishops were virtual sovereigns.

The status of the lower classes of Castile was, however, far from desperate: Jew and Moslem were protected for their economic value, though the tendency toward jealousy and toward the segregation of the Jews was already appearing and the Jewish population was declining. The status of rural workers and serfs tended to improve by the definition and limitation of the landlord's rights. Slavery had probably disappeared by the 15th century.

1454-1474. HENRY (ENRIQUE) IV, during whose reign the feudal anarchy reached its apogee. The monarchical power was saved primarily through the support of the towns.

1469. Marriage of Isabella, half-sister and heiress of Henry IV, to **Ferdinand,** heir of the king of Aragon.

1474. ISABELLA succeeded to the Castilian throne. Isabella's succession was challenged by the daughter of Henry IV, supported by Afonso V of Portugal. But the córtes of Segovia (1475) recognized Isabella and Ferdinand and the latter defeated the Portuguese in 1476 **(battle of Toro).**

1479. FERDINAND (FERNANDO) succeeded to the rule of Aragon, Catalonia, Valencia. A form of dyarchical government was set up for the united Castilian and Aragonese crowns. Rule of the **Catholic kings** (Ferdinand and Isabella). Restoration of the royal power in Castile: by revising the town charters, the towns were made centers of resistance to feudal aggression; formation of the *Santa Hermandad,* a union of Castilian towns in the interest of royal authority and order. The great feudal magnates were deprived of many of their possessions and rights and a royal administration was gradually established. The *Libro de Montalvo* (1485), an early codification of Spanish law. **Concordat of 1482** with the pope, carefully restricting the power of Rome over the Spanish church: the king became grand master of the powerful religious orders of knighthood. The **Inquisition** (established in 1478) wholly under royal control, used primarily for the persecution of the Marranos (converted Jews secretly practicing their old faith). Confiscations of property did much to increase the financial power of the rulers and to strengthen them in the work of subduing the feudal opposition.

1492. Fall of Granada, marking the end of the reconquest of Spain from the Moors. This was speedily followed by a spiritual reconquest, the work of the Inquisition. The **expulsion of the Jews** (possibly as many as 200,000) in 1492 was followed by that of the Moors in Castile (1502).

Art and literature. Castilian painting showed the influence of the school of Giotto (after c. 1380), and in the 15th century came under Flemish inspiration (visit of Jan van Eyck, 1428-1429). In general literature and learning followed the same foreign tendencies as architecture and painting: French influence came

The House of Castile (1252-1504)

(From p. 250)

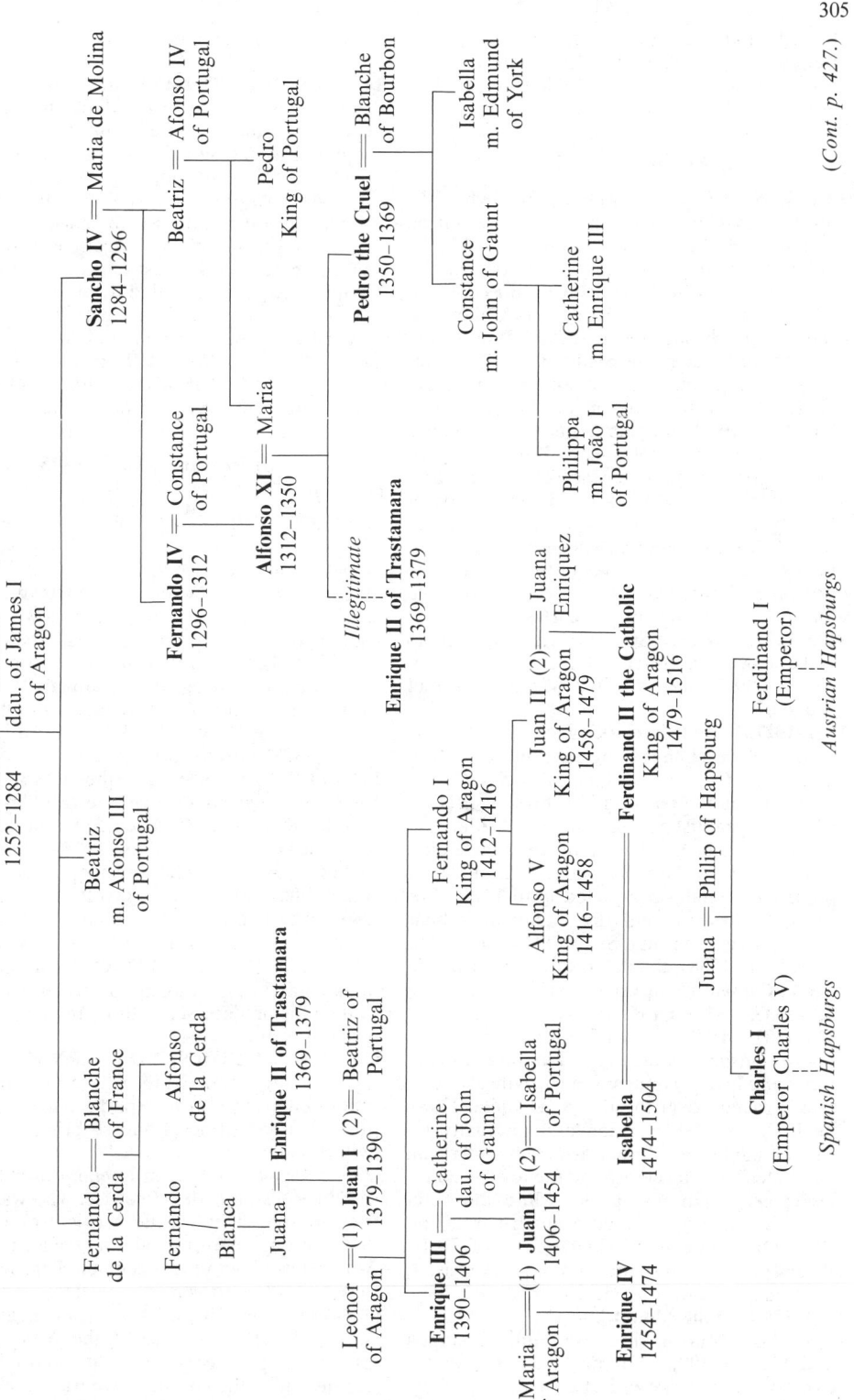

(Cont. p. 427.)

in early, followed later by Italian and English (notably Dante, Petrarch, Boccaccio, Gower). Introduction of printing at Valencia (c. 1474) and in Castile (c. 1475).

(2) Aragon, 1276–1479

1276–1285. PETER (PEDRO) III, who was married to Constance, daughter of Manfred and heir of the Hohenstaufen. In 1282 he sailed on a long-planned expedition for the **conquest of Sicily** (which he disguised as an African crusade). He landed at Collo, was called to the throne, defeated Charles of Anjou, and became Peter I of Sicily (1282–1285), refusing to do homage to the pope for his island kingdom. This expansion of the Aragonese kingdom gave Aragon for a time predominance in the western Mediterranean. But it estranged the Aragonese aristocracy, as well as the towns. The nobility therefore formed the **Union for Liberty** and, in the cortes of 1283, extorted from Peter a **General Privilege** which defined the rights and duties of the nobles, affirmed the principle of due process of law, and provided for annual meetings of the córtes.

1285–1291. ALFONSO III was obliged to make a sweeping re-grant of the Privileges of Union (1287), the so-called **Magna Carta of Aragon.**

1291–1327. JAMES II (king of Sicily, 1285–1295). He exchanged the investiture of Sardinia and Corsica for that of Sicily (1295), which thereupon passed to his brother Frederick, who established the separate Sicilian dynasty. James began the expulsion of the Genoese and Pisans from Sardinia (1323–1324), a process not finally completed until 1421. For a period Aragon held the duchy of Athens (first indirectly through Sicily, 1311–1377, then directly, to 1388), thanks to the activity of the **Grand Catalan Company** (p. 347).

1327–1336. ALFONSO IV.

1336–1387. PETER (PEDRO) IV. He was virtually a prisoner of the revived union of the nobility and had to confirm their privileges. But, after a victory over the union (at **Epila,** 1348), he broke up the coalition and gradually restricted the power of the aristocracy in Aragon and Valencia. The clergy and the towns had far less power than in Castile, while the rural workers and serfs suffered a much harder lot.

1377. On the death of Frederick II of Sicily, Peter IV, as the husband of Frederick's sister, sent his son Martin as viceroy to Sicily.

1387–1395. John (Juan) king.

1395–1410. Martin, king. He reunited Aragon and Sicily (1409). On his death the native dynasty came to an end after a period of dynastic struggle.

1412–1416. Ferdinand (Fernando) I, of Castile, a grandson of Peter IV, succeeded to the throne.

1416–1458. ALFONSO V (the Magnanimous). His attention was engrossed by the desire to conquer Naples. After long diplomatic intrigues and occasional combats, he succeeded (1435) in being recognized as king by the pope in 1442. Alfonso, a lover of Italy and passionate devotee of the Renaissance, shifted the center of gravity of the Aragonese empire and subordinated the interest of Aragon to that of Naples. Aragon was ruled by his brother John, as viceroy. On the death of Alfonso, Naples passed to his son Ferrante (1458–1494).

1458–1479. John (Juan) II, king.

1479–1516. FERDINAND (FERNANDO) II, king. **Union of Aragon with Castile.**

(*Cont. p. 415.*)

(3) Portugal, 1279–1495

(*From p. 253*)

1279–1325. DINIZ (the Worker), the best-known and best-loved king of medieval Portugal. An ardent poet, he did much to raise the cultural level of the court. His interest in agriculture and constant effort toward economic development (commercial treaty with England, 1294) resulted in greater prosperity. Beginning of **Portuguese naval activity** (under Venetian and Genoese guidance). Foundation (1290) of the University of Lisbon, which was soon (1308) moved to Coimbra.

1325–1357. AFONSO IV (the Brave), whose reign was scarred by dynastic troubles. The **murder of Inez de Castro** (1355), the mistress and later the wife of Afonso's son Peter, at the behest of Afonso. This episode, the subject of much literature, led to a revolt of Peter.

1340. The Portuguese, in alliance with Castile, defeated the Moors in the **battle of Salado.**

1357–1367. PETER (PEDRO) I (the Severe), a harsh and hasty, though just, ruler, who continued his predecessor's efforts in behalf of the general welfare.

1367–1383. FERDINAND (FERNÃO) I (the Handsome), a weak ruler whose love for Leonora Telles led him to repudiate his betrothal to a Castilian princess and so bring on a war with Castile.

1383. Regency of Queen Leonora in behalf of Ferdinand's daughter, Beatrice, who was married to John I of Castile. This arrangement led to strong opposition among the Portuguese, who detested both the regent and her lover and resented all control from outside.

1385–1433. JOHN (JOÃO) I, an illegitimate son of Peter I, established the **Avis dynasty** after leading a successful revolt and driving the regent out of the country. He was proclaimed king by the cortes of Coimbra, but his position

The House of Aragon (1276–1516)

(*Cont. p. 427.*)

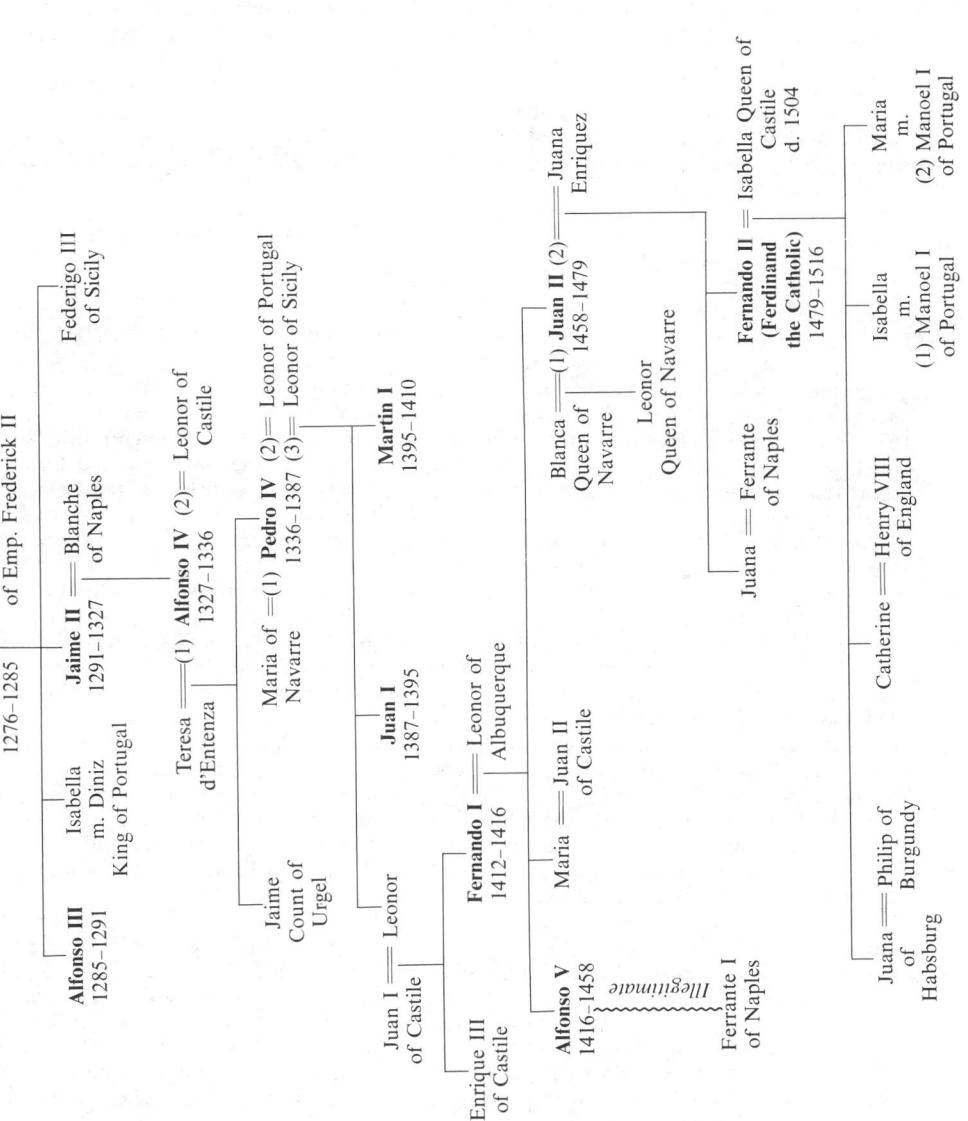

was at once challenged by the Castilians, who twice invaded Portugal and besieged Lisbon.

1385, Aug. 14. The **BATTLE OF ALJUBAR-ROTA,** in which the Portuguese defeated the Castilians. A decisive date in the history of the country, this battle established the **independence of Portugal** beyond all possibility of challenge. With the Avis dynasty Portugal entered upon the greatest period of her history. The king himself was an able and enlightened ruler, who enjoyed the aid of five outstanding sons, of whom **Henry the Navigator** (1394–1460) became the greatest figure in the history of the epoch-making discoveries of the 15th century (p. 384).

1386, May 9. The **treaty of Windsor,** by which England and Portugal became permanently allied. King John married Philippa, the daughter of John of Gaunt. The dynasty thereby became part English.

1411. Peace was finally concluded with Castile.

1415, Aug. 24. The Portuguese took **Ceuta** from the Moors, thus initiating a policy of expansion on the African mainland.

1433–1438. Edward (Duarte) I, a learned and intelligent prince, eldest son of John. His short reign was marked by a terrific epidemic of the plague and by

1437. The **disaster at Tangier,** where the Portuguese were overwhelmingly defeated. They were obliged to promise to return Ceuta, and to leave in Moorish hands the youngest brother of the king, **Ferdinand** (the Constant Prince), who died in captivity after five years of suffering. Ceuta was not returned.

1438–1481. AFONSO V (the African), an attractive and chivalrous ruler, but lacking the hard-headed realism of his predecessors. The reign began with the regency of the king's mother, Eleonora, a Spanish princess, who again was confronted with Portuguese opposition to a Spanish connection. The nobility revolted, the regent fled, and the king's uncle, Peter, was made regent. His able and enlightened rule came to an end when the king, having reached his majority, allowed himself to be persuaded by favorites to make war on Peter. The latter and his son were defeated and killed in the **battle of Alfarrobeira** (1449).

1446. The *Ordenaçoes Affonsinas,* the first great law code of the Portuguese, representing an amalgam of Roman, Visigothic, and customary law.

1463. Campaigns against the kingdom of Fez. The Portuguese captured Casablanca and

1471. Tangiers.

1476. Battle of Toro. Defeat of the Portuguese by the Castilians, after Afonso, who had married a sister of Isabella, attempted to dispute the latter's succession to the throne.

1481–1495. JOHN (JOÃO) II, an energetic prince who at once undertook to restrict the property and power of the nobility, which had become very great during the preceding reign. This led to a revolt of the nobles, led by **Ferdinand of Braganza** and supported by the Catholic kings of Castile and Aragon. The revolt was suppressed in 1483; Braganza and many of his followers were executed. The royal power thenceforth was more firmly established than ever before. (*Cont. p. 418.*)

d. ITALY AND THE PAPACY

(*From p. 238*)

(1) The Papacy, 1305–1492

[*For a complete list of the Roman popes see Appendix IV.*]

1305–1378. THE AVIGNONESE PAPACY (Babylonian Captivity): during seven pontificates the popes, exiled from the spiritual capital of the West, preferred to contend against the pressure of the French crown rather than face the disorder of Rome and Italy.

1310–1313. Expedition of the Emperor Henry VII to Italy (p. 323). Henry asserted his independence of the spiritual power and claimed control of Italy. Clement V and Philip IV (opposed to him as a rival of the Angevins) combined against him.

1316–1334. JOHN XXII, who supported the Angevins in Naples. His attempt to decide the validity of Emperor Louis IV's title led to a long struggle (1323–1347). Louis was supported by the German people, who resented the Avignonese Papacy, and by the Franciscans. John was unable to return to Italy because of the continued anarchy.

1334–1342. Benedict XII, and

1342–1352. CLEMENT VI, whose pontificate was marked by the

1347. REVOLUTION OF COLA DI RIENZI at Rome. With the support of the populace, Cola overthrew the rule of the patricians, set himself up as tribune of the people, and summoned an Italian national parliament. Expelled by his opponents (1348), he returned in 1352 and was appointed senator by the pope (1354), but was in the same year slain by his baronial opponents. The lords of the Papal States resumed control and were, to all intents and purposes, independent of papal authority.

1352–1362. INNOCENT VI. He sent the Spanish cardinal, Albornoz, to Italy and the latter succeeded in reducing the powerful barons to obedience, thus making possible an eventual return of the pope.

REFORM OF THE CURIA during the Avi-

Kings of Portugal (1248–1521)

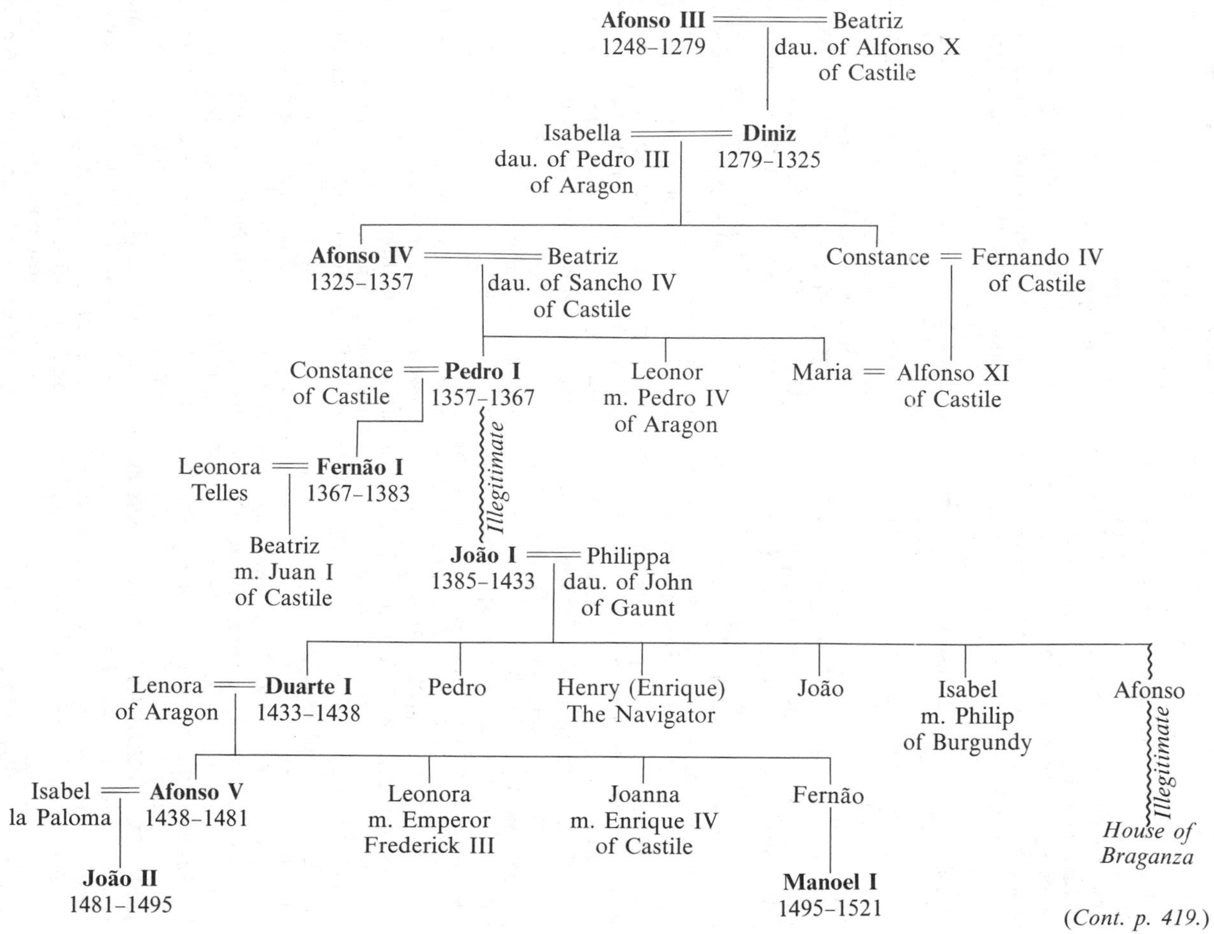

(From p. 254)

Afonso III — Beatriz
1248–1279 — dau. of Alfonso X
of Castile

Isabella ══ Diniz
dau. of Pedro III 1279–1325
of Aragon

Constance ══ Fernando IV
of Castile

Afonso IV ══ Beatriz
1325–1357 — dau. of Sancho IV
of Castile

Maria ══ Alfonso XI
of Castile

Leonor
m. Pedro IV
of Aragon

Constance ══ Pedro I ~~Illegitimate~~
of Castile 1357–1367

Leonora ══ Fernão I
Telles 1367–1383

Beatriz
m. Juan I
of Castile

João I ══ Philippa
1385–1433 dau. of John
of Gaunt

Pedro

Henry (Enrique)
The Navigator

João

Isabel
m. Philip
of Burgundy

Afonso
~~Illegitimate~~
House of
Braganza

Duarte I
1433–1438

Leonora
m. Emperor
Frederick III

Joanna
m. Enrique IV
of Castile

Fernão

Manoel I
1495–1521

Lenora ══ Duarte I
of Aragon 1433–1438

Isabel ══ Afonso V
la Paloma 1438–1481

João II
1481–1495

(Cont. p. 419.)

gnon period. General work of centralization and departmentalization: (1) the *camera apostolica;* (2) the chancery; (3) justice; (4) the penitentiary (punishments and dispensations). Centralization put important clerical appointments throughout Europe under direct papal control through an extraordinary extension of the papal rights of reservation and provision; made a virtual end of local elections, filled ecclesiastical offices with aliens and strangers, and outraged public opinion everywhere. A parallel reorganization and departmentalization of the papal financial administration led to a new efficiency in the levy and collection of papal taxes, fees, etc., which bore hard on the clergy, and drained large sums from the national states, stirring public opinion still further, especially in England. Significant items of the budget of John XXII: war, 63.7 per cent; upkeep and entertainment, 12.7 per cent; alms, 7.16 per cent; stables, 0.4 per cent; art, 0.33 per cent; library, 0.17 per cent.

Vying with the growing magnificence of the monarchies of Europe, the Avignonese popes and cardinals became proverbial for their pomp and luxury, and these tendencies spread to the episcopate despite the thunders of the Franciscans and the decrees of local synods. The insubordination of outraged reformers like the **Fraticelli,** the Bohemian preachers, and **Wiclif** soon penetrated to the masses.

Virtually every pope (notably Clement V and John XXII) made serious and honest efforts to combat these alarming developments, but the general anarchy in Europe made success impossible. There was a notable **expansion of missions to the Far East:** China (an archbishop and ten suffragans, 1312; fifty Franciscan houses, 1314; missions to Persia). Rome, the ancient spiritual center of the West, was reduced to an anarchic, poverty-stricken, provincial city, and clamored for the return of the popes. Petrarch's extreme denunciations of the Avignonese popes had little justification.

1362–1370. URBAN V. Return to Rome with the co-operation of Emperor Charles IV; the city a dismal ruin; return to Avignon on the entreaties of the cardinals (a majority of whom were French).

1370–1378. GREGORY XI visited Rome and died before he could leave. The conclave, under threat of personal violence from the Roman mob, yielded to demands for an Italian pope, electing

1378–1389. URBAN VI, a blunt, avaricious man, who alienated the cardinals by announcing that his reform of the Church would begin with the sacred college.

1378–1417. The GREAT SCHISM: the papacy divided and dishonored. Thirteen cardinals, meeting at Anagni, elected

1378–1394. CLEMENT VII, thus dividing western Christendom into obediences:

The Roman Line	The Avignonese Line
Urban VI	Clement VII
(1378–1389)	(1378–1394)
Boniface IX	Benedict XIII
(1389–1404)	(1394–1423)
Innocent VII	
(1404–1406)	
Gregory XII	
(1406–1415)	

Allegiance to the rivals was determined partly by practical considerations, but often was settled after careful study of the claims of each and consultation with the clergy (e.g. King Charles V of France, John of Castile); England's decision was based largely on hostility to France; Scotland's on its hostility to England; in Naples and Sicily the rulers and their subjects took opposite positions.

EMERGENCE OF THE CONCILIAR MOVEMENT. The basic ideas were inherent in such writers as **Marsiglio of Padua;** specific arguments that a general council is superior to a pope, can be called by a king, and is competent to judge a pope or call a new conclave, were advanced in 1379 (**Henry of Langenstein**) and from then on grew in importance. King Charles VI of France (influenced by the University of Paris) called a **national synod** (1395), which voted overwhelmingly to urge the resignation of both popes. The Avignonese cardinals approved with only one negative; the popes refused to resign. The French clergy voted (1398) to withhold papal taxes and dues, and were endorsed by the king. Benedict's cardinals deserted him in panic and he fled, producing a reaction of public opinion against the king of France. Two Roman popes were elected with the understanding that they would resign if Benedict XIII would do so. The two colleges of cardinals joined in a call for a general council to meet at Pisa, 1409.

1409. The COUNCIL OF PISA, attended by 500 prelates and delegates from the states of Europe. Two parties: (1) a moderate majority with the sole aim of ending the schism; (2) radical reformers (including d'Ailly and Gerson from Paris), who were compelled to accept postponement of reform to a council supposed to meet in 1412. After hearing specific charges against both popes, the council deposed both. The conclave chose **Alexander V** (d. 1410) and then the ecclesiastical *condottiere,* Cardinal Baldassare Cossa, a man without spiritual qualities. Neither the Roman nor the Avignonese pope resigned, and the schism became a triple one.

1410–1415. JOHN XXIII, expelled from Rome

ITALY *in the* 15th CENTURY

by Ladislas of Naples, was forced by the Emperor Sigismund to issue a call for the **Council of Constance** (1414) in return for protection. This marked the passing of the initiative in reform from the king of France to the Roman emperor, a return in theory to the days of the Ottos.

1414–1417. The **COUNCIL OF CONSTANCE:** one of the greatest assemblies of medieval history; three aims: (1) **restoration of unity to the Church;** (2) **reform in head and members;** (3) **extirpation of heresy,** particularly the Hussite heresy (p. 327). Following university practice, voting was by nations and the numbers of the Italian prelates did no good to Pope John. John, seeing a chance to divide the council and the emperor, allowed the imprisonment of Hus (in violation of the imperial safe-conduct).

Hus, heard three times by the whole council (and cleverly induced to expand his doctrine that sin vitiates a clerical office to include civil office as well), lost Sigismund's support, was condemned and executed (1415) as was his companion, Jerome of Prague (1416).

John XXIII, having agreed to resign if his rivals did so, fled the council, was brought back, tried, and deposed (1415); **Gregory XII** resigned (1415); Sigismund, unable to induce Benedict XIII to resign, won away his supporters, and isolated him. Reform was again postponed, but two decrees are significant: *Sacrosancta* (1415), asserting that a council is superior to a pope; and *Frequens* (1417) providing for stated meetings of general councils.

The conclave elected Cardinal Colonna as Martin V. Christendom ignored the obstinate Benedict, and the schism was over.

1417–1431. MARTIN V (Colonna), a Roman of Romans, declared it impious to appeal to a general council against a pope and dissolved the council of Constance. Evasion of general reform and the threat of general councils supported by powerful monarchs, through the negotiation of concordats with the heads of states (i.e., by dealing with the bishops through lay rulers, a complete negation of the theory of a universal papal absolutism, and a virtual recognition of national churches). **Recovery of the Papal States:** most of the cities were under their own lords who bore *pro forma* titles as papal vicars but were in fact independent. Concentration on Italian political problems at the expense of the universal spiritual interests of Christendom.

1431–1447. EUGENE IV, an obstinate Venetian who favored summoning the **council of Basel.**

1431–1449. The **COUNCIL OF BASEL,** dominated by strong anti-papal feeling. Dissolved

by Eugene because of negotiations with the Hussites, the council ignored the order and decreed (with the support of the princes) that no general council can be dissolved without its consent, continued in session, and summoned Eugene and the cardinals to attend. Eugene ignored the summons, but was forced (1433) to accept the council. Temporary compromise with the Hussites registered in the *Compactata.* **Reforms voted:** abolition of commendations, reservations, appeals to Rome, annates, etc.; provision for regular provincial and diocesan synods; confirmation of the right of chapter elections; appeal from a general council to a pope pronounced heresy. Already divided over these reforms, the council split over reunion with the Greek church. Eugene and his cardinals ignored a second summons, were pronounced contumacious; Eugene dissolved the council and called another to meet at Ferrara; the papalists left Basel. The rump council continued to meet, deposed Eugene (1439), elected Amadeus of Savoy,

1439–1449. FELIX V, because he could pay his own way. Moved to Lausanne, the council continued with dwindling numbers and prestige.

1438–1445. The **COUNCIL OF FERRARA-FLORENCE** (under the presidency of Eugene). After months of futile discussion (over the *filioque* question, unleavened bread at the sacrament, purgatory, and papal supremacy), the Greeks were forced to accept the Roman formula for union (1439) and the schism between East and West, dating from 1054, was technically healed. As the Greeks at home repudiated the union, it was of no effect. Isidore of Kiev and Bessarion remained as cardinals of the Roman church.

1438. A **French national synod** and King Charles VII accepted the *Pragmatic Sanction of Bourges* embodying most of the anti-papal decrees of the council of Basel (basis for the Gallican liberties). It checked the drain of money from France to the Papacy.

1439. The **diet of Mainz** accepted the *Pragmatic Sanction of Mainz,* abolishing annates, papal reservations, provisions, and providing for diocesan and provincial synods.

Enea Silvio de'Piccolomini, sent to win Germany back for the Papacy, came to an agreement with Emperor Frederick III on such cynical terms that the German princes flocked to Felix V, but a provisional concordat, embodying the Pragmatic of 1439 enabled Enea Silvio to detach the princes one by one.

1448. Concordat of Vienna, Eugene's greatest triumph, accepted the supremacy of a general council, but restored the annates and abandoned most of the restrictions on papal patronage.

1449. Dissolution of the Council of Basel: abdication of Felix V (who became a cardinal). Papal celebration of the triumph over the conciliar movement in the **Jubilee of 1450.** Postponement of moderate reform made the radical Reformation of the 16th century inevitable.

1447-1455. NICHOLAS V, former librarian of Cosimo de' Medici, scholar, humanist, collector of manuscripts, founder of the **Vatican Library.** Rome temporarily a center of humanism: Nicholas' circle included: **Poggio Bracciolini, Alberti,** and **Lorenzo Valla** (a scientific humanist and critic who had just demolished the *Donation of Constantine* as a forgery). Plans for a new St. Peter's.

1453. The **Turkish capture of Constantinopie** (p. 352) ended the Greek Empire of the East and removed all serious rivalry by the patriarch to the position of the Roman pope.

1455-1458. CALIXTUS III (an Aragonese), an aged invalid, anti-humanist, energetic supporter of war against the Turk, an ardent nepotist (three Borgia nephews, one of them later Pope Alexander VI).

1458-1464. PIUS II (Aeneas Sylvius Piccolomini). In his youth a gay dog; in later life austere; most brilliant and versatile of the literary popes, a humanist, lover of nature, eloquent essayist, orator, and Latin stylist. A short, bent man with smiling eyes, a fringe of white hair, seldom free of pain, a tireless worker, always accessible. Advocate of papal supremacy, obstinate foe of conciliar reform. His appeals for a crusade ignored by a preoccupied Europe, he gallantly took the Cross himself to shame the princes of Christendom, and died at Ancona. His family was large and poor and he was a nepotist.

1464-1471. PAUL II, a Venetian, rich, kindly, handsome, a collector of jewels and carvings, founder of the Corso horse-races. A strong centralizer, supporter of the Hungarian crusade. The Turkish victory at **Negroponte** (1470) gave the Turks mastery of Levantine waters.

1471-1484. SIXTUS IV (della Rovere) aimed to consolidate the Papal States and reduce the power of the cardinals; methodical nepotist (three nephews, the Riarios, one of them later Pope Julius II).

1475. Rapprochement with Ferrante of Naples; alienation of the Medici who were replaced as papal bankers by the Pazzi. The Riarios organized with Sixtus' knowledge, if not approval, the **Pazzi Conspiracy** (assassination of Giuliano de' Medici, 1478). This destroyed the alliance of Florence, Naples, Milan, to maintain the Italian balance of power

and led to a war involving most of Italy; the war was terminated by the capture of Otranto (1480) and by the diplomacy of Lorenzo de' Medici. Sixtus' coalition with Venice led to the Ferrarese War (1482-1484). Sixtus and Julius II were the great beautifiers of Rome: **Sistine Chapel** (c. 1473), paving and widening of streets and squares; patronage of **Ghirlandaio, Botticelli, Perugino, Pinturicchio,** *et al.*

1484-1492. INNOCENT VIII, a kindly, handsome Genoese, a compromise cipher, the first pope to recognize his children and to dine publicly with ladies. A baronial revolt (1485-1487) in Naples (supported by Innocent and, secretly, by Venice) led to a revival of the Angevin claims to Naples. Florence and Milan, fearing French intervention in Italy, opposed the war, and peace and amnesty were arranged. Ferrante's cynical violation of the amnesty led the exiles (on Ludovico Sforza's advice) to call in King Charles VIII of France. Sforza struck an alliance with Charles to protect Milan and opened the road into Italy to this alien invader (1494). Italy was not again to know full independence from foreign domination until the end of the 19th century.

Girolamo Savonarola (1452-1498), a Dominican, prior of San Marco in Florence (1491), eloquent reforming preacher and precursor of the Reformation, was already denouncing the new paganism of the Renaissance, the corruption of the state and the Papacy, and foretelling the ruin of Italy.

(*Cont. p. 422.*)

(2) Sicily and Naples, 1268-1494

(*From p. 237*)

1268-1285. CHARLES I (Angevin) king of Naples and of Sicily (1268-1282). His grandiose scheme for the creation of a Mediterranean empire in succession to the Byzantine (a revival of the Latin Empire under French auspices) was frustrated by the **Sicilian Vespers** (1282) and the war in Sicily which continued until 1302. Sicily maintained its independence and offered the crown to **Peter III of Aragon** (husband of Constance, heiress of the Hohenstaufen), an ally of Constantinople against Charles. Peter accepted the offer (1282), ejected the Angevins, and established the house of Aragon on the throne.

1282- SICILY UNDER ARAGONESE RULE: Peter (1282-1285); **James** (1285-1295). James exchanged the investiture of Sardinia and Corsica for that of Sicily, and Sicily passed to his brother, **Frederick** (1295-1337). Frederick brought to a close the war with Naples (**Peace of Caltabelotta,** 1302), marrying the daughter of Charles I and accepting the stipulation that the Sicilian crown should pass to the Angevins

on his death. This agreement was not fulfilled, with the result that the struggle continued until, in 1373, Joanna of Naples abandoned Sicily to the Aragonese in return for
tribute. Sicily was ruled as a viceroyalty until
the reunion with Aragon in 1409.

1285–1309. Charles II (Angevin) of Naples.

1309–1343. Robert (Angevin) of Naples. He
was the leader of the Italian Guelfs and, having been appointed imperial vicar on the death
of Emperor Henry VII, planned to create an
Italian kingdom.

1343–1382. Joanna (Giovanna) I, queen of Naples.

1382–1386. Charles III, a grandnephew of
Robert.

1386–1414. Ladislas, son of Charles III, finally succeeded in establishing some measure
of order in the kingdom and began a vigorous campaign of expansion in central Italy.
In 1409 he bought the States of the Church
from Pope Gregory XII, but his designs were
blocked by Florence and Siena.

1414–1435. JOANNA (GIOVANNA) II, sister
of Ladislas. The amazing intrigues of this
amorous widow with her favorites, successors
designate, and rival claimants to the throne
kept Italian diplomacy in a turmoil, and
culminated in a struggle between **René,** the
Angevin claimant (supported by the pope),
and **Alfonso V of Aragon** (supported by Filippo
Maria Visconti). This conflict ended in the
triumph of Alfonso, who secured Naples in
1435 and was recognized as king by the pope
in 1442.

1435–1458. ALFONSO (the Magnanimous)
reunited the crowns of Naples and Sicily and
made Naples the center of his Aragonese Mediterranean empire (p. 306). He supported
Filippo Maria Visconti of Milan, who apparently willed his duchy to him on his death.
Alfonso avoided arousing Italy by claiming the
duchy, but Ferdinand of Aragon later revived
the claim. Alfonso's pressure drove Genoa
into the arms of France. Loyal to the pope,
Alfonso supported Eugene IV against Francesco Sforza. He centralized the administration, reformed taxation, and arranged a series
of dynastic marriages in Italy. But he failed to
subdue his barons entirely. He preferred Italy
to Aragon, was a passionate devotee of Italian
culture and acted as a Renaissance Maecenas,
the patron of Lorenzo Valla. The **Academy of
Naples** was composed mostly of poets. Alfonso
divided his domain, Aragon and Sicily passing
to his brother, John, and Naples (correctly
called the kingdom of Sicily) going to his illegitimate son

1458–1494. FERRANTE (FERDINAND I),
one of the most notoriously unscrupulous Ren-

aissance princes. He triumphed in his struggle for the succession with the aid of Francesco
Sforza and Cosimo de' Medici (who was
alarmed at the presence of the French in
Genoa). Ferrante generally supported the
triple Italian alliance except for the period
1478–1480. Pope Innocent V, angered at Ferrante's suspension of tribute, supported the
Angevin pretender, and Ferrante made a hollow peace until he could crush a baronial
revolt. Then, supported by the Colonna and
Orsini in Rome, he turned on Innocent, who
was saved only by Lorenzo de' Medici. Innocent (1492) guaranteed the succession in Naples. Alexander VI stood by the bargain, and
opposed Charles VIII's demand for investiture.

The **CLAIMS OF THE VALOIS KINGS**
to Naples. Based on (1) the marriage of
Margaret (daughter of Charles II of Naples) and
Charles of Valois, the parents of King Philip VI;
and on (2) the claims of the so-called "second"
house of Anjou founded by Duke Louis I (d.
1384) of Anjou, count of Provence. Louis was
grandson of Philip VI, and grandfather of (1)
Maria, wife of Charles VII of France, mother of
Louis XI; and of (2) Duke Louis III (d. 1434)
and his brother René of Lorraine (d. 1468).

(Cont. p. 426.)

(3) Florence, to 1492

EARLY HISTORY. The **margraviate of
Tuscany,** set up by the Carolingians, extended
from the Po to the Roman state under the Margrave Boniface (d. 1052), whose daughter, the
great **Countess Matilda** (1052–1115), was probably the strongest papal supporter in Italy. Associated with her in the government was a council
of *boni homines,* whose administration during her
frequent absences, and after her death, laid the
foundation for the emergence of the commune.
Florence, already a great commercial center,
opposed the Ghibelline hill barons, who preyed
on her commerce. The burghers continued
Guelf in sympathy; trade and financial connections with France made them Francophile and
friendly to Charles of Anjou. Under Matilda
the **guild organization** emerged, which came to
form the basis of the city government. Control
of the government was concentrated in the
hands of the great guilds (one of which included the bankers). Consuls appeared after
1138. The populace was divided into two great
groups, the *grandi* (nobles) and the *arti* (guilds).
Consuls were chosen by the grandi.

On the breakup of the margraviate following
Matilda's death, Florence began her advance,
and by 1176 was master of the dioceses of Florence and Fiesole. The institution of the *podestate* (magistrates) after 1202 was favored by the
feudal elements and the lesser guilds. Intermit-

315

The House of Anjou (1266–1435)

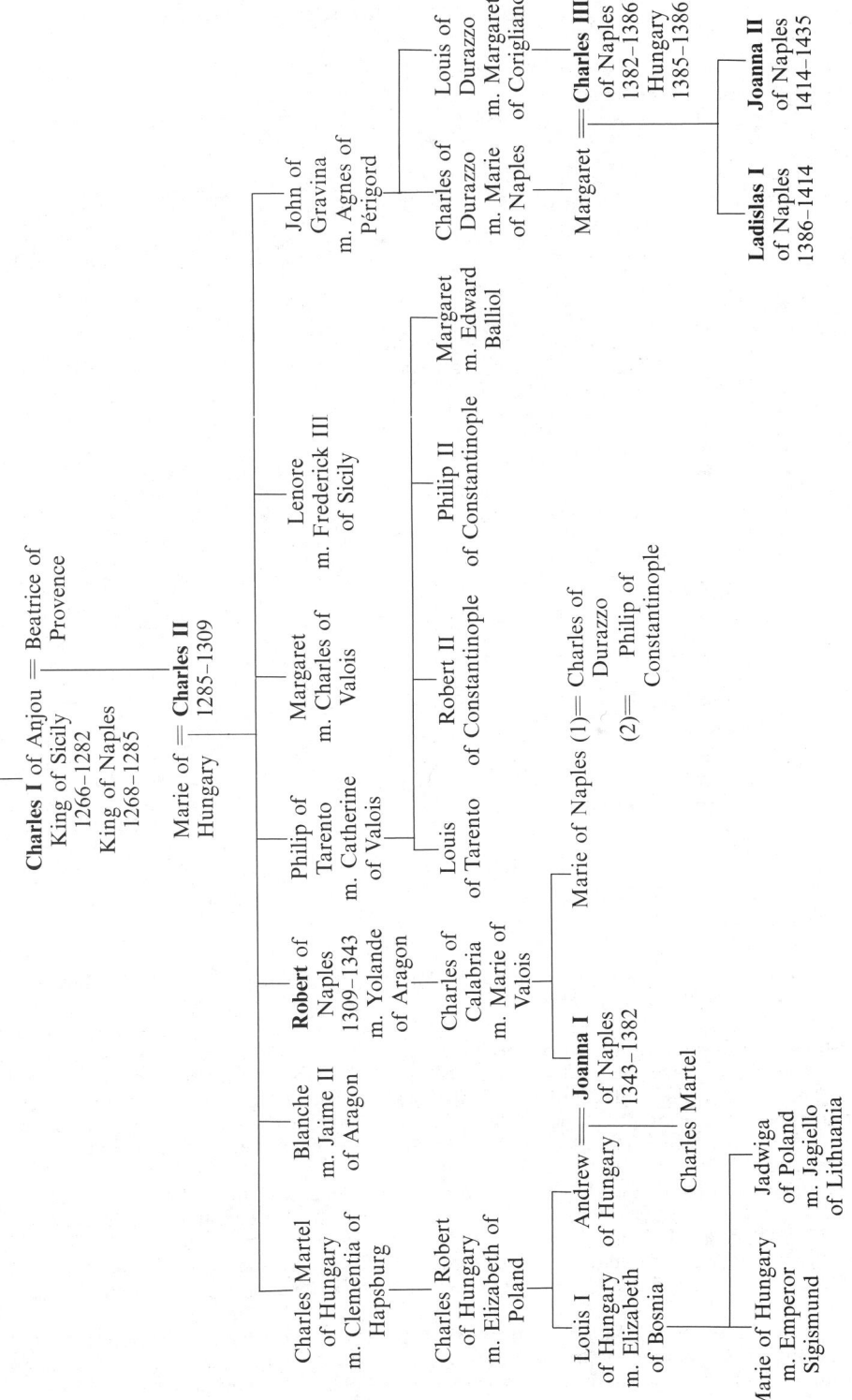

(From p. 243)

Louis VIII of France

Charles I of Anjou = Beatrice of Provence
King of Sicily
1266–1282
King of Naples
1268–1285

Marie of = **Charles II**
Hungary   1285–1309

Blanche
m. Jaime II
of Aragon

Charles Martel
of Hungary
m. Clementia of
Hapsburg

Charles Robert
of Hungary
m. Elizabeth of
Poland

Louis I   Andrew = **Joanna I**
of Hungary   of Hungary   of Naples
m. Elizabeth   1343–1382
of Bosnia

Charles Martel

Marie of Hungary
m. Emperor
Sigismund

Jadwiga
of Poland
m. Jagiello
of Lithuania

Robert of
Naples
1309–1343
m. Yolande
of Aragon

Charles of Calabria
m. Marie of Valois

Marie of Naples (1) = Charles of Durazzo
                   (2) = Philip of Constantinople

Philip of
Tarento
m. Catherine
of Valois

Louis
of Tarento

Margaret
m. Charles of
Valois

Robert II
of Constantinople

Lenore
m. Frederick III
of Sicily

Philip II
of Constantinople

Margaret
m. Edward
Balliol

John of
Gravina
m. Agnes of
Périgord

Charles of
Durazzo
m. Marie
of Naples

Louis of
Durazzo
m. Margaret
of Corigliano

Margaret = **Charles III**
of Naples
1382–1386
Hungary
1385–1386

Ladislas I
of Naples
1386–1414

Joanna II
of Naples
1414–1435

The Neapolitan Anjous (1350–1481)

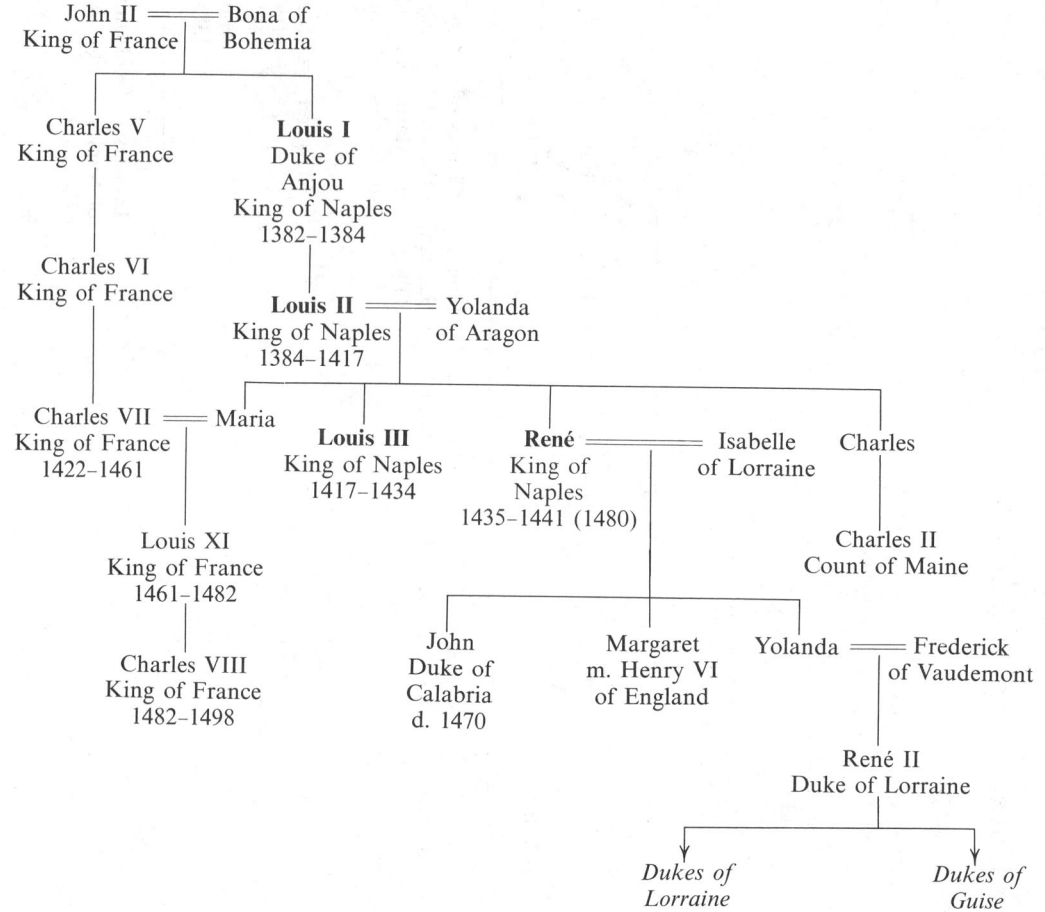

John II King of France === Bona of Bohemia

- Charles V, King of France
  - Charles VI, King of France
    - Charles VII, King of France 1422–1461 === Maria
      - Louis XI, King of France 1461–1482
        - Charles VIII, King of France 1482–1498
- Louis I, Duke of Anjou, King of Naples 1382–1384
  - Louis II, King of Naples 1384–1417 === Yolanda of Aragon
    - Louis III, King of Naples 1417–1434
    - René, King of Naples 1435–1441 (1480) === Isabelle of Lorraine
      - John, Duke of Calabria d. 1470
      - Margaret m. Henry VI of England
      - Yolanda === Frederick of Vaudemont
        - René II, Duke of Lorraine
          - *Dukes of Lorraine*
          - *Dukes of Guise*
    - Charles
      - Charles II, Count of Maine

tent rivalry of the noble houses continued. Wars were fought with Pisa, Lucca, Pistoia, Siena. Under the *podestà* the commune developed a strong organization paralleled by the growth of the *popolo* (populace) under its *capitano* (chief).

The great struggle of **Guelf and Ghibelline** was reflected in Florentine civil strife. After a Guelf régime, Frederick of Antioch (son of Frederick II) as imperial vicar instituted the first mass expulsion in Florentine history by driving out the Guelfs (1249).

1252. The first **gold florin** was coined, and soon became the standard gold coin in Europe.

1260. Siena, with the aid of Manfred and the Florentine Ghibellines, inflicted a great defeat on the Florentine Guelfs **(Montaperti),** beginning a Ghibelline dominance that lasted until Manfred's death (1266). This was followed by a reaction, and the expulsion of the Ghibellines. Under the Ghibelline régime the popolo lost all share in the government.

In the reaction following the Ghibelline régime, Ghibelline property was confiscated to support persecution of the Ghibellines. Under Charles of Anjou the formulae of the old constitution were restored; the party struggle continued. The Sicilian Vespers (1282) weakened Charles, strengthened the commune, and the Florentine "republic" became in effect a commercial oligarchy in the hands of the greater guilds.

1282. By the **Law of 1282** nobles could participate in the government only by joining a guild. The last traces of serfdom were abolished (1289) and the number of guilds increased to 21 (seven greater, 14 lesser).

1293. The **ordinance of 1293** excluded from the guilds anyone not actively practicing his profession, and thus in effect removed the nobles from all share in the government.

Two factions arose: the **Blacks** (*Neri*), extreme Guelfs led by Corso Donati; the **Whites** (*Bianchi*), moderate Guelfs (and later Ghibellines) under Vieri Cerchi. The Neri favored repeal of the ordinance of 1293.

Emperor Henry VII was unable to capture Florence, but

1320–1323.   Castruccio Castracani, lord of Lucca, humiliated the city in the field. Growing financial troubles, partly the result of Edward III's repudiation of his debts to the Florentine bankers, culminated in the failures of the Peruzzi (1343) and Bardi (1344), and damaged Florentine banking prestige. The government was discredited and civil war ensued. **Walter of Brienne** (duke of Athens) was called in, reformed the government, began a usurpation, and was expelled (1343). The restored commune was under the domination of the business men who had three objectives: access to the sea (hence hostility to Pisa), expansion in Tuscany (to dominate the trade roads), and support of the popes (to retain papal banking business). Social conflict continued and grew as the oligarchy gained power and the Guelfs opposed the increasing industrial proletariat. The lesser guilds were pushed into the background, the unguilded were worse off. The first social revolt came in 1345.

1347–1348. Famine followed by the **Black Death** reduced the population seriously.

1351. The commutation of military service for cash marked the decline of citizen militia and the golden age of the *condottieri* (mercenary captains). War with Milan resulted (1351) from Giovanni Visconti's attempt to reduce Florence and master Tuscany.

1375–1378. Papal efforts to annex Tuscany led Florence into a temporary alliance with Milan.

1378. Continued pressure by Guelf extremists to exclude the lesser guilds led to a series of violent explosions. **Salvestro de' Medici,** gonfalonier, ended the *admonitions,* which were the basis of the Guelf terrorism, and a violent **revolt of the ciompi** (the poorest workmen) broke out. The ciompi made temporary gains, but Salvestro was exiled, and by 1382 the oligarchy was back in the saddle and even the admonitions were revived.

FLORENTINE CULTURE: Precursors of the Renaissance. (1) **Dante** (1265–1321): *Vita Nuova,* in the Tuscan vernacular; the *Divina Commedia,* a brilliant poetic synthesis of medieval ideas and culture which established Tuscan as the literary vernacular of Italy; *De Vulgari Eloquentia,* a defense of the vernacular, written in Latin. **Petrarch** (1304–1374), of Florentine origin, greatest of Italian lyrists, brilliant Latin-

ist, the first great humanist; interested in every aspect of humanity; a lover of nature; a universal mind. **Boccaccio** (1313–1375), friend of Petrarch, knew both Greek and Latin, the first modern student of Tacitus, collector of classical manuscripts, first lecturer on Dante (1373). His *Decameron,* an epitome of bourgeois sophistication. Founder of Italian prose. **Giotto** (1276–1337), architect (employed on the cathedral), sculptor, painter, revealing Renaissance tendencies. **Villani** (d. 1348), *Chronicon Universale* with clear bourgeois elements. **Chrysoloras** (called from Constantinople), the first public lecturer on Greek in the West (1396–1400); he had many famous humanists as pupils.

1382–1432. A half-century of oligarchic domination in Florentine politics, in many ways the **zenith of Florentine power.** Constitutional reform (1382) broadened popular participation in government, but nothing much was done for the ciompi, and sporadic revolts continued as the Guelfs slowly regained power.

1393.   Maso degli Albizzi's long control of the government began with the exile or disenfranchisement of the Alberti and their supporters. Capitalism had destroyed the guild organization as a vital political force, and Albizzi ruled for the advantage of his own house and the *Arte della Lana* (wool) with which he was associated. Democratic elements in the state had vanished.

1397–1398. Florence resisted the Visconti advance into Tuscany.

1405.   Pisa was bought and reduced to obedience (1406), giving Florence direct access to the sea. Livorno (Leghorn) was purchased (1421) and the *Consuls of the Sea* established. Filippo Maria Visconti's drive into Tuscany led Florence to declare war. The peace party was led by **Giovanni de' Medici,** a wool dealer and international banker, probably Italy's richest man. Several defeats of Florence were accompanied by a decline of Florentine credit and a number of serious bankruptcies. Alliance with Venice and defeat of the Visconti, who accepted peace on onerous terms (1429); Venice monopolized the gains of the war.

1427.   Taxation reform, the *catàsto,* an income tax intended to be of general and democratic incidence, supported (?) by the Medici.

1433. The fiasco of the war on Lucca (1429–1433) led to Cosimo (son of Giovanni) de' Medici's imprisonment as a scapegoat, and his sentence to ten-year exile. The next election to the signory (governing body) favored the Medici, and Cosimo was recalled (1434). Rinaldo degli Albizzi, Rodolfo Peruzzi, *et al.,* were in turn exiled, and the Medici dominance in Florence began, opening three centuries of close identity between the fortunes of the

The Medici Family (1434–1737)

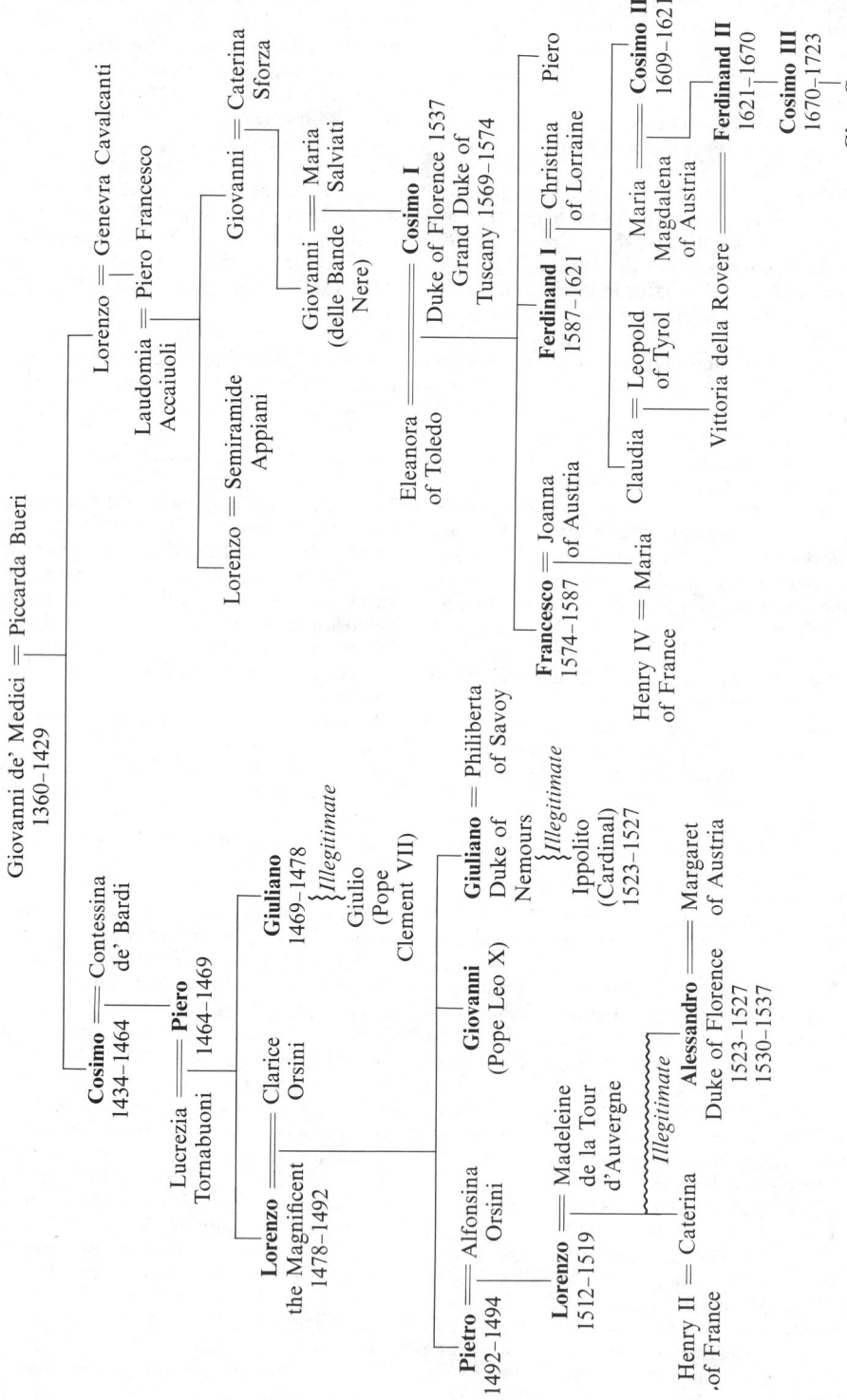

family and those of Florence. Cosimo, without holding office, dominated the government, determining who should hold office.

1434-1494. DOMINATION OF THE MEDICI.

1434-1464. COSIMO (Pater Patriae).

1440. Florence and Venice in alliance defeated Filippo Maria Visconti at **Anghiari.** The catàsto was replaced by a progressive income tax designed to lighten the burdens of the poor (i.e. the Medici adherents). Cosimo supported Francesco Sforza's contest for the duchy of Milan and aided him in his war with Venice. For commercial reasons he favored France, but backed Ferrante of Naples against the Angevin claims. He was thus the real creator of the **triple alliance** of Florence, Milan, and Naples in the interest of the Italian equilibrium and security.

1464-1469. Piero the Gouty, son of Cosimo, a semi-invalid who was opposed by Luca Pitti.

1469-1478. Lorenzo and Giuliano de' Medici, and

1478-1492. LORENZO DE' MEDICI (the Magnificent) alone. Lorenzo continued the general policy of Cosimo. He enjoyed the power and prestige of a prince, though he had neither the title nor the office. His marriage to Clarice Orsini was the first princely marriage of the Medici.

1471. Lorenzo's effort to conciliate Pope Sixtus IV netted him a confirmation of the Medici banking privileges and the appointment as receiver of the papal revenues.

1474. Pope Sixtus and Ferrante of Naples were asked to join the alliance of Florence, Venice, and Milan (concluded in 1474), but Ferrante, feeling isolated, and Sixtus, angered at Lorenzo's opposition to his nephews, the Riarios, drew together. Italy became divided into two camps. The Pazzi family, rivals of the Medici, were given the lucrative position as receivers of the papal revenues.

1478. The Pazzi Plot. The Riarios (apparently not without Sixtus' knowledge), plotted to have Lorenzo and Giuliano assassinated in the cathedral at Easter Mass. Giuliano was killed, Lorenzo wounded. The Medici almost exterminated the Pazzi and hounded the fugitives all over Italy. Sixtus laid an interdict on Florence, excommunicated Lorenzo; Alfonso of Calabria invaded Tuscany. Venice and Milan stood by Florence, Louis XI sent Commines as his representative. Ferrante engineered a Milanese revolt, the Turks diverted Venice at Scutari, plague broke out. Desperate, Lorenzo visited Ferrante (the cruelest and most cynical despot in Italy), and by his charm and the threat of a revival of Angevin claims, arranged (1480) a peace. Florence suffered considerable losses, but Lorenzo was a popular hero and succeeded in establishing the council of seventy, a completely Medici organ, the instrument of *de facto* despotism, but a source of real stability in government.

Lorenzo's brilliant **foreign policy** was costly; he had neglected the family business and apparently used some of the state money for Medici purposes; he also debased the coinage. Florentine prosperity, under the pressure of rivals, heavy taxation, and business depression, was declining. Nonetheless, Lorenzo, the leading statesman of his day, brought a twelve-year calm before the storm to Italy, resuming the Medici alliance with Naples and Milan to balance the Papacy and Venice, and to keep a united front against alien invasion. Florence, on good terms with Charles VIII, regained most of her Tuscan losses. **Savonarola,** prior of San Marco (1491), had already begun his denunciations of Florentine corruption and his attacks on Lorenzo (p. 313).

1492. PIERO succeeded Lorenzo on his death. Son of an Orsini mother, married to an Orsini, he supported Naples, angered Milan, and threw Ludovico Sforza into alliance with the Neapolitan exiles who summoned Charles VIII.

1494. Charles's invasion began the age-long subjugation of Italy to alien invaders who dominated the national evolution until 1870. Piero, alarmed at public opinion, fled the city.

Florence, center of the Italian Renaissance. For over a century the Medici were the greatest patrons of the Renaissance, and led the rich bourgeoisie of Florence in fostering the most brilliant development of culture since the days of Pericles. **Cosimo** was an enthusiastic patron of manuscript collectors, copyists, and humanists, established the **library of San Marco** and the **Medici library.** The council of Ferrara-Florence sat in Florence (1439) and brought a number of learned Greeks who stimulated Platonic studies. Under Cosimo's auspices **Ficino** was trained to make his great translation of Plato (still ranked high) and the **Platonic Academy** was founded. **Lorenzo,** a graceful poet (carnival songs, etc.), ardent champion of the vernacular, and lover of the countryside, a generous patron, drew about him a brilliant circle. He continued the support of Ficino. Florentine leadership in Renaissance: (1) **painting: Masaccio** (1401-1429?), **Botticelli** (1444-1510), **Leonardo da Vinci** (1452-1519) (sculptor and polymath); (2) **architecture: Brunelleschi** (1377-1446); **Alberti** (1405-1471); (3) **sculpture: Donatello** (c. 1386-1466), **Ghiberti** (1378-1455); **Verrocchio** (1435-1488); **Michelangelo** (1475-1564) (also painter, poet, architect); (4) **history and**

political theory: **Machiavelli** (1469–1527); **Guicciardini** (1485–1540); (5) **romantic poetry: Pulci** (1432–c. 1487). (*Cont. p. 426.*)

(4) Milan, to 1500

EARLY HISTORY. Milan, ancient center of the agriculture of the Lombard plain, self-sufficient in food, master of important passes (Brenner, Splügen, St. Gothard) of the Alps, was for a long time surpassed in wealth only by Venice.

Establishment of Pavia as the Lombard capital (569). Emergence of Milan as the center of Italian opposition in the Lombard plain to alien and heretical domination. Rise of the archbishop as defender of native liberty and orthodoxy laid the basis for the evolution of archiepiscopal temporal power (military, administrative, judicial) exercised through his viscounts. The end of Lombard domination (774), followed by Carolingian destruction of the great Lombard fiefs, strengthened the episcopal power still further.

The spirit of municipal independence emerged from intense rivalries for the archiepiscopal see and the necessities of defense; Milan became an island of safety and justice in the Lombard plain, a populous, self-sufficient, city-state. Under **Archbishop Heribert** (1018–1045) the *carroccio* (arc of municipal patriotism) was set up; expansion in the Lombard plain began (reduction of Lodi, Como, Pavia). The moat was dug after Emperor Frederick I's destruction (1162); the city was rebuilt by its allies, Bergamo, Brescia, Mantua, and Verona. (For the Lombard League and the wars with Frederick, see p. 235.) Rapid growth, extension of the walls (after 1183). Chief industry: armor manufacturing and the wool trade, later silk manufacture; irrigation made the plain productive.

Government: (1) *parlamento* (*consiglio grande*) (membership successively reduced to 2000, 1500, 800); (2) *credenza,* a committee of twelve for urgent and secret business; (3) *consuls* (the executive) elected for a year, responsible to the assembly.

Bitter warfare between populace and nobles led to the rise of two great families, the Della Torre (lords of the tower, i.e. castle) and the Visconti (i.e. the viscounts).

1237–1277. Rule of the (Guelf) **DELLA TORRE.** Martino established the catàsto, a tax of democratic and uniform incidence. The title *signore,* i.e. lord of Milan, established (1259); defeat and capture of the (Ghibelline) Visconti and their adherents. Milan established her power over Bergamo, Lodi, Como, and Vercelli.

1277–1447. Rule of the **VISCONTI.** Established by Archbishop Otto Visconti. Brief restoration of the Della Torre (1302) in a Guelf reaction with outside support. Establishment (1312) of the Visconti supremacy (Matteo designated *imperial vicar*). Ruthless Visconti rule and expansion over northern Italy (including Genoa). Stefano's sons, Bernabò, Galeazzo, Matteo, divided the domains but ruled jointly until Matteo was assassinated (1355) by his brothers. Intolerably harsh joint rule of Bernabò (1354–1385) at Milan and Galeazzo (1354–1378) at Pavia; ostentatious patronage of learning and art.

1378–1402. GIAN GALEAZZO succeeded his father Galeazzo and did away with Bernabò (1385), thereafter ruling alone (1385–1402). Gian Galeazzo married Isabelle, daughter of King John of France; one of his daughters, Valentina, married Louis of Orléans (the source of Louis XII's claims to Milan). Gian Galeazzo began the creation of a northern Italian kingdom: mastery of Verona, Vicenza, Padua (1386–1388); Tuscan advance blocked by Florence (1390–1392) and by the rebellion of Padua. Created hereditary duke (1395) by Emperor Wenceslas, he added Pisa and Siena (1399), Assisi and Perugia (1400) to his domains, and routed (1401) Elector Rupert III (in Florentine pay). The *Certósa* (Charterhouse) and *Duomo* (Cathedral) were begun. Gian Galeazzo's death (1402) saved Florence and opened a period of anarchy in Milan under his sons Gian Maria, (1402–1412) and Filippo Maria (1402–1447), which undid much of their father's work.

1402–1447. FILIPPO MARIA, after the assassination (1412) of Gian Maria, regained Gian Galeazzo's lands (even Genoa). Venice joined Florence against Filippo and took Bergamo, Brescia (1425). Filippo, last of the Visconti, was followed by

1447–1450. The **Republic** and the supremacy of Francesco Sforza, son-in-law of Filippo, who fought his way to mastery, defeating Venice and conquering the Lombard plain.

1450. Francesco Sforza was invested with the ducal title by popular acclaim.

1450–1500. Rule of the **SFORZA.** Francesco, eager for peace, came to terms with Cosimo de' Medici and Naples (the so-called triple alliance for the Italian balance of power). Louis XI was on intimate terms with Francesco and made him his political model. Francesco completed the Certósa and the Duomo with Florentine architects under Renaissance influence and began the *Castello* (Castle). Patron of the humanist **Filelfo,** Francesco gave his son Galeazzo and his daughter Ippolita a humanist education; Ippolita was famous for her Latin style. His court was full of humanists and learned Greeks.

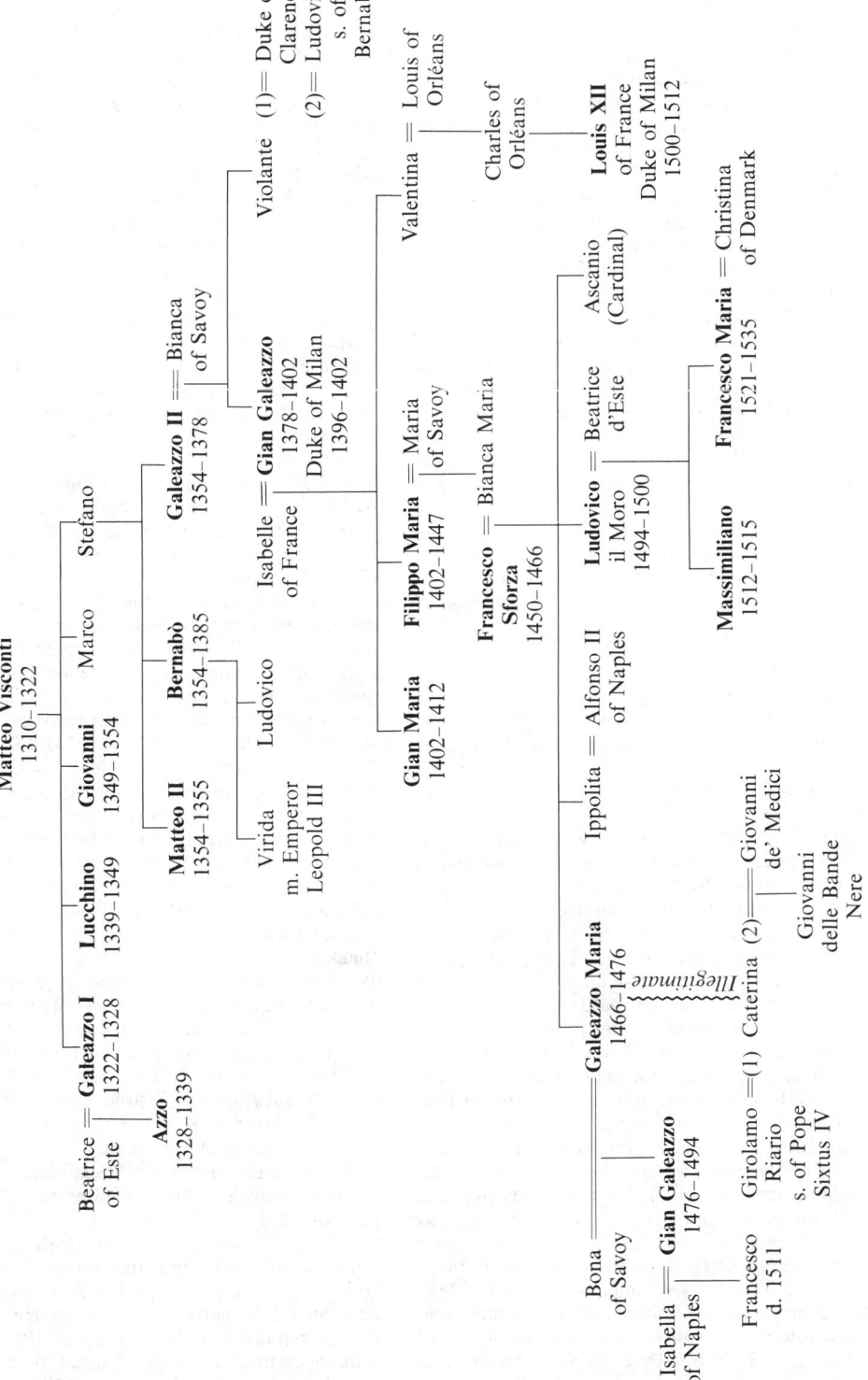

The Visconti and Sforza Families (1310–1535)

Matteo Visconti
1310–1322

Beatrice = **Galeazzo I**
of Este   1322–1328

Azzo
1328–1339

Lucchino
1339–1349

Giovanni
1349–1354

Marco

Stefano

Matteo II
1354–1355

Bernabò
1354–1385

Galeazzo II = Bianca
1354–1378   of Savoy

Virida
m. Emperor
Leopold III

Ludovico

Violante   (1)= Duke of
                    Clarence
           (2)= Ludovico
                  s. of
                  Bernabò

Isabelle = **Gian Galeazzo**
of France   1378–1402
            Duke of Milan
            1396–1402

Valentina = Louis of
             Orléans

Charles of
Orléans

Louis XII
of France
Duke of Milan
1500–1512

Gian Maria
1402–1412

Filippo Maria = Maria
1402–1447   of Savoy

Francesco = Bianca Maria
Sforza
1450–1466

Ludovico = Beatrice
il Moro   d'Este
1494–1500

Ascanio
(Cardinal)

Francesco Maria = Christina
1521–1535   of Denmark

Massimiliano
1512–1515

Ippolita = Alfonso II
of Naples

Giovanni
de' Medici (2)= Caterina =(1) Girolamo
                              Riario
                              s. of Pope
                              Sixtus IV

Giovanni
delle Bande
Nere

Illegittimate

Galeazzo Maria
1466–1476

Bona
of Savoy

Isabella = **Gian Galeazzo**
of Naples   1476–1494

Francesco
d. 1511

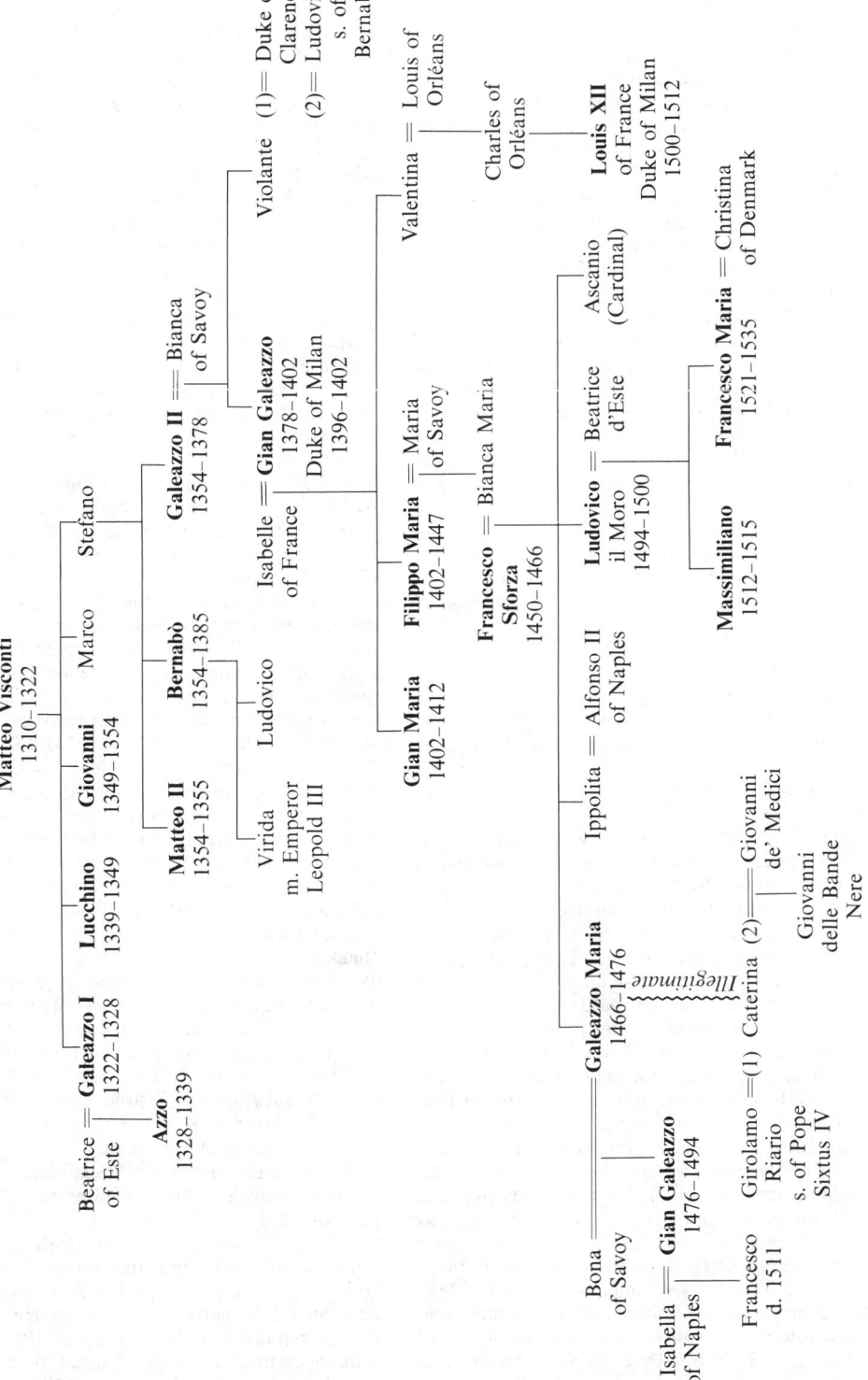

321

1466-1476. GALEAZZO MARIA SFORZA was assassinated after a cruel but able rule. His son

1476-1479. GIAN GALEAZZO, husband of Isabella of Naples, under the regency of his mother, supported Florence against Naples after the Pazzi conspiracy (1478). Gian Galeazzo's uncle Ludovico usurped the duchy (1479).

1479-1500. LUDOVICO (il Moro), alarmed at his isolation after the death (1492) of Lorenzo de' Medici, supported the appeals of Neapolitan refugees to Charles VIII of France, whose expedition (1494) began the destruction of Italian independence. In Charles's train came Louis of Orléans, who, as Louis XII (1498-1515), added claims to Milan to his other Italian claims, took Milan (1499) and captured Ludovico (1500), who ended his days (1508) as prisoner of Louis.

Ludovico's generous patronage marked the **golden age of the Renaissance in Milan.** Ludovico, an artist, man of letters, economist, and experimenter, beautified the city, improved irrigation, bettered agriculture. He was the patron of Bramante and Leonardo.

(*Cont. p. 425.*)

(5) Venice, 1310-1489

(*From p. 240*)

In the early 14th century Venice already dominated the trade of the Adriatic and possessed many colonies throughout the Near East. Her position in the eastern trade was challenged primarily by Genoa, at that time at the height of her power.

1353-1355. War between Venice and Genoa. The Venetians were defeated at **Sapienza** (1354) and suffered the loss of their fleet. Peace was mediated by Milan.

1378-1381. The **WAR OF CHIOGGIA** between Venice and Genoa. This grew out of the grant, by John V Paleologus, of the island of Tenedos, key to the Dardanelles. Luciano Doria, the Genoese admiral, defeated the Venetians at **Pola,** seized Chioggia and blockaded Venice. The Venetians, under **Vittorio Pisano,** blocked the channel and starved out the fleet of Pietro Doria, forcing its surrender. From this blow Genoa never recovered. Henceforth Venice was mistress of the Levantine trade, which made an outlet for her goods over the Alpine passes more urgent than ever. The war with Genoa had demonstrated the importance of a mainland food supply and thereby inaugurated an inland advance which had a decisive influence on Italian politics. Venice had already taken Padua from the Scaligers of Verona (1339), but by agreement had turned it over to the Carrara family. Treviso and

Belluna, however, were retained.

1388. Treaty of the Venetians with the Ottoman Turks, the first effort to assure trade privileges despite the rise of the Turkish power.

1405. Venice seized Padua, Bassano, Vicenza, and Verona after the breakup of the Visconti domains (1402) and the defeat of the Carrara family.

1416. First war of Venice against the Ottoman Turks, the result of Turkish activity in the Aegean. The **Doge Loredano** won a resounding victory at the Dardanelles and forced the sultan to conclude peace.

1423. The Venetians took over Thessalonica as part of a plan of co-operation with the Greek emperor against the Turks.

1425-1430. Second war against the Turks. The Turkish fleets ravaged the Aegean stations of the Venetians and took Thessalonica (1430). The Venetians were obliged to make peace in view of

1426-1429. The **war with Filippo Maria of Milan,** by which the Venetians established a permanent hold over Verona and Vicenza, and gained in addition Brescia (1426), Bergamo (1428), and Crema (1429).

1453. Participation of the Venetians in the **defense of Constantinople** against Mohammed II (p. 352). After the capture of Constantinople, Mohammed proceeded to the conquest of Greece and Albania, thus isolating and endangering the Venetian stations.

1463-1479. The great **WAR AGAINST THE TURKS.** Negroponte was lost (1470). The Turks throughout maintained the upper hand and at times raided to the very outskirts of Venice. By the **treaty of Constantinople** (1479) the Venetians gave up Scutari and other Albanian stations, as well as Negroponte and Lemnos. Thenceforth the Venetians paid an annual tribute for permission to trade in the Black Sea.

1482-1484. War with Ferrara, as a result of which Venice acquired Rovigo. This marked the limit of Venetian expansion on the mainland. The frontiers remained substantially unaltered until the days of Napoleon.

1489. Acquisition of Cyprus (partly by gift, partly by extortion), from Catherine Cornaro, widow of James of Lusignan.

Venetian culture in the Renaissance. Preoccupied with her commercial empire, her expansion on the mainland, and the advance of the Turk, Venice, despite her wealth, unique domestic security, and the sophistication of wide travel, long stood aside from the main currents of the early Renaissance. Her architecture remained under Gothic and Byzantine influences until the end of the 15th century, and the Palazzo Vendramini (1481) is perhaps the first important example of the new style. The **Bellinis** (Jacopo, 1395–1470, and his two sons) were the most notable early Venetian painters, but there was little promise of the brilliant if late achievement of the 16th century. The printing press apparently appealed to the practical Venetian nature and the senate decreed (1469) that the art should be fostered. Much of the finest early printing issued from the Venetian presses of the 15th and 16th centuries.   (*Cont. p. 425.*)

e. THE HOLY ROMAN EMPIRE, 1273–1486

[*For a complete list of the Holy Roman emperors see Appendix V.*]

(*From p. 230*)

1273. The election fell to **Rudolf of Hapsburg** (b. 1218), who ranked as a prince, wished to restore and retain in his family the duchy of Swabia, and had three daughters to marry off. The Hapsburgs or Habsburgs (from *Habichts-Burg,* Hawk-Castle) originally (10th century) of the district of Brugg (junction of the Aar and Reuss) had steadily expanded their lands in the Breisgau, Alsace, and Switzerland, emerging as one of the leading families of Swabia.

1273–1291. RUDOLF I. Indifferent to the Roman tradition, he concentrated on the advancement of his own dynasty, and founded the greatness of the Hapsburgs on territorial expansion of the family holdings and dynastic marriages. Edicts for the abolition of private war and support of local peace compacts (*Landfrieden*).

1276–1278. Struggle with Ottokar, king of Bohemia, over the usurped imperial fiefs of Austria, Styria, Carinthia, Carniola. Rudolf expelled Ottokar from Austria by force (1276), but allowed him to retain Bohemia and Moravia (after homage) as a buffer against Slavdom; dynastic alliance with the Hapsburgs. Ottokar was ultimately defeated and killed (1278, Aug. 26, **battle of the Marchfeld**); investiture of Rudolf's sons with the imperial fiefs of Austria, Styria, Carniola (1282) established the Hapsburgs on the Danube until 1918.

Rudolf threw away the last remnants of Frederick II's great imperial fabric: confirmation of papal rights in Italy and Angevin rights in southern Italy (1275); renunciation of all imperial claims to the Papal States and Sicily (1279).

1291. Alarmed at the rapid rise of the Hapsburgs to first rank, the electors passed over Rudolf's son, choosing instead **Adolf of Nassau** in return for substantial considerations.

1291. Revolt of the three Forest Cantons, Uri, Schwyz, and Unterwalden, and formation of a (Swiss) confederacy (p. 329).

1292–1298. ADOLF, a strong imperialist, and able. He supported the towns and lesser nobles and entered into alliance with Edward I of England against Philip IV of France to protect the imperial fiefs of Franche Comté, Savoy, Dauphiné, Lyonnais, and Provence, long under French pressure; the alliance came to nothing, as the German princes were indifferent. The princes, alarmed at Adolf's advance in Meissen and Thuringia, deposed him (1298), electing Rudolf's rejected son Albert.

1298–1308. ALBERT (ALBRECHT) I. Firm reduction of the ecclesiastical electoral princes (aid of the French and the towns); double dynastic marriage with the Capetians; acquisition of the crown of Bohemia (on the extinction of the Premyslids, 1306); Albert supported the Angevin Carobert's acquisition of Hungary; the Rhineland was filled with Francophile clerical appointees of the pope, and the election of 1308 was dominated by French influence. Charles of Valois procured the election of Henry of Luxemburg, brother of the archbishop of Trier.

1308–1313. HENRY VII (Luxemburg), Francophile, devoted to Italian culture, and bent on restoring the empire. The marriage of his son John to the sister of King Wenceslas of Bohemia brought the throne of Bohemia to the house of Luxemburg (1311–1489).

1310–1313. Expedition to Italy at the urging of Pope Clement V and the Ghibellines; order restored, Milan, Cremona, Rome reduced; imperial coronation (1312); alliance of the pope and King Philip IV of France to save Naples from Henry.

1314–1347. LOUIS IV (Wittelsbach). A Hapsburg anti-king, **Frederick the Handsome,** and civil war (until 1325). Bitter papal opposition (1323–1347, refusal of confirmation of Louis's title to the empire); Louis, backed by the German people, against the Avignonese pope. Violent war of propaganda: **Marsiglio of Padua** (*Defensor Pacis,* 1324) and **William of Occam,** defending the imperial position, gave wide currency to pre-Reformation ideas; **Dante's** *De Monarchia;* papal supporters, **Augustino Trionfans** and **Pelagius.**

1327–1330. Louis's futile expedition to Italy and "lay" coronation (1328); his demand for a general council welcomed by the Italian Ghibellines.

Effort to give the German monarchy a formal constitution.

1338. The Day at Rense: formation of a strong electoral union (*Kurverein*); declaration by the electors that election by a majority of the electors without papal confirmation is valid.

The House of Hapsburg (1273–1519)

(From p. 224)

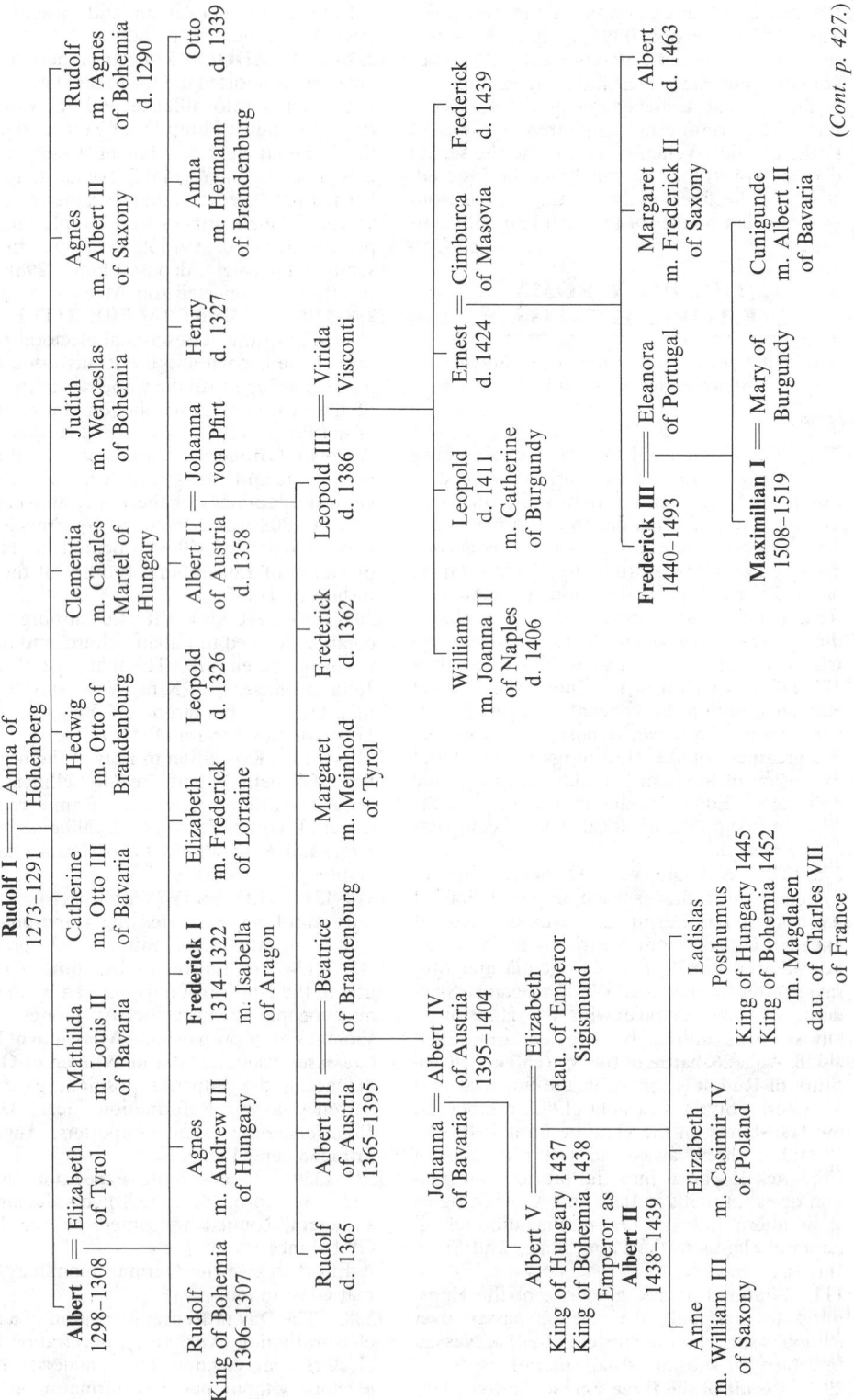

(Cont. p. 427.)

The **diet of Frankfurt:** declaration (the *Licet juris*) that the electors are competent to choose an emperor (i.e. papal intervention is not necessary); in effect the Holy Roman Empire was divorced entirely from the Papacy.

1346. Louis was deposed, but fought against his successor, Charles (son of King John of Bohemia, who had been elected after an open alliance with the pope).

1347-1378. CHARLES IV (Luxemburg). Concentration on the advancement of his dynasty (in Silesia, the Palatinate, Lusatia, Brandenburg) and on the progress of Bohemia. Prague became one of the chief cities of the empire (the university founded, 1348). The **Black Death** (1348-1349); the Flagellants; anti-Semitic massacres. Promulgation of the Swabian League and numerous *Landfrieden* reduced private warfare. Dauphiné and Arles continued to drift into the French orbit.

Further elaboration of a formal constitution of the empire.

1356. The **GOLDEN BULL** (in force until 1806) transformed the empire from a monarchy into an aristocratic federation, to avoid the evils of disputed elections. Seven **electors,** each a virtual sovereign: the archbishops of Mainz, Trier, and Köln, the count palatine of the Rhine, the duke of Saxony, the margrave of Brandenburg, the king of Bohemia. Secular electorates to be indivisible and pass by primogeniture. Elections to be by majority vote and without delays; urban leagues forbidden without specific license; other restrictions on the towns. No mention of papal rights or claims. The electors to exercise supervision over the empire, a new function. The crown to remain in the house of Luxemburg.

Charles openly regarded the empire as an anachronism, but valued the emperor's right to nominate to vacant fiefs.

1364. **Treaty of Brünn** with the Hapsburgs, whereby either house (Luxemburg or Hapsburg) was to succeed to the lands of the other upon its extinction.

Little improvement in internal anarchy; climax of localism and the *Faustrecht;* the only islands of order and prosperity were the walled towns; the only basis of order were the town leagues (e.g. revival of the **Rhine League** [1354]; the **Swabian League**); bitter warfare of classes, and princely opposition to the towns. Charles's vain appeal to the princes of Europe to resist France and end the Avignonese Captivity.

Apogee of the **Hanseatic League** (p. 330).

1378-1400. WENCESLAS (Wenzel, son of Charles IV, king of Bohemia, 1378-1419). Formation of the **Knights' League** (*League of the Lion*) followed by a series of political quarrels between the knights and lords on one side and the towns on the other, ending in the town war (1387-1389) and the defeat of the towns, but not their ruin. Rising Bohemian nationalism: revolts, 1387-1396.

1400. Deposition of Wenceslas for drunkenness and incompetence. He refused to accept the decision, and the result was that at the end of the confused period (1400-1410) there were **three rival rulers** (Sigismund, Jobst, and Wenceslas) to correspond to the three rival popes.

1410-1437. SIGISMUND (Luxemburg; king of Bohemia, 1419-1437; king of Hungary by marriage). His main concern was to end the Great Schism, and he succeeded the king of France as protagonist of conciliar reform by forcing Pope John XXIII to call the **council of Constance** (p. 312). Establishment of the **house of Wettin** in Saxony (1423); the **Hohenzollerns (Frederick)** in Brandenburg (1415). Sigismund's failure at Constance not merely alienated Bohemia, but also ended any hope of German unification.

1410. Utter **defeat of the Teutonic Knights** by the Polish-Lithuanian army at **Tannenberg;** beginning of the decline of the Teutonic Knights.

1411. Peace of Thorn, halting of the Slavic advance.

1420-1431. Emergence of **Bohemian Nationalism** and the **Hussite Wars** (p. 327).

1433. Called to the **council of Basel** (p. 312), the Hussites finally accepted the *Compactata* (which embodied the *Four Articles*), but the Church by its devious dealings alienated them, and they began a final break. Bohemian nationality asserted itself increasingly in the 15th century, and Bohemia never returned to the German orbit.

Sigismund struggled against the Turkish advance (1426-1427) and was crowned at Rome (1433). In the election of 1438, Frederick of Brandenburg (candidate of the political reformers in Germany) withdrew, making the choice of Albert of Hapsburg (Sigismund's son-in-law) unanimous. Albert also succeeded Sigismund on the thrones of Hungary and Bohemia. Henceforth the imperial crown in practice became hereditary in

1438-(1740) 1806. THE HOUSE OF HAPSBURG.

1438-1439. ALBERT II.

1439. The **Pragmatic Sanction of Mainz** (abolition of annates, papal reservations, and provisions), a preliminary agreement between the Papacy and the emperor, left the German church under imperial and princely control and postponed reform until the days of Martin Luther.

1440-1493. FREDERICK III. The last em-

(*From p. 224*)

Luxemburg Rulers (1308–1437)

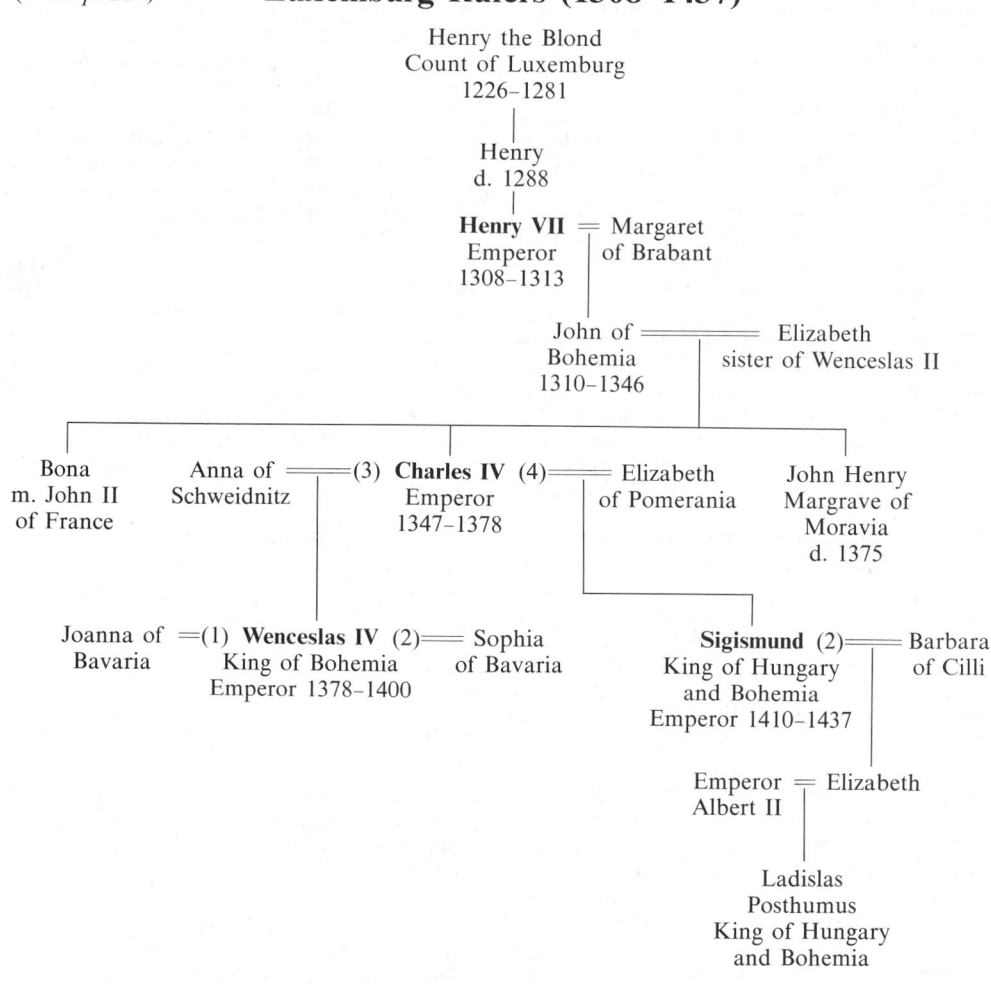

Henry the Blond
Count of Luxemburg
1226–1281

Henry
d. 1288

Henry VII = Margaret
Emperor   of Brabant
1308–1313

John of ═══════════ Elizabeth
Bohemia   sister of Wenceslas II
1310–1346

Bona .... Anna of ═(3) **Charles IV** (4)═ Elizabeth .... John Henry
m. John II ...... Schweidnitz .... Emperor .... of Pomerania .... Margrave of
of France .... 1347–1378 .... Moravia
.... d. 1375

Joanna of =(1) **Wenceslas IV** (2)═ Sophia .... **Sigismund** (2)═ Barbara
Bavaria ...... King of Bohemia .... of Bavaria .... King of Hungary .. of Cilli
.... Emperor 1378–1400 .... and Bohemia
.... Emperor 1410–1437

Emperor = Elizabeth
Albert II

Ladislas
Posthumus
King of Hungary
and Bohemia

(*Cont. p. 339.*)

peror crowned (1452) at Rome by the pope; a handsome, placid *fainéant*, amateur astrologer, botanist, mineralogist, he ignored the existence of diets, debates, and appeals for crusades.

Ladislas Posthumus (d. 1457), ward of Frederick, became duke of Austria (1440), was acknowledged king of Hungary (1445) and elected king of Bohemia (1452) with a council of regency. **George Podiebrad** (champion of the *Compactata*) emerged (1452) from the Bohemian civil war (Catholics vs. Utraquists) as regent of Bohemia, and later king (1458–1471) (p. 329).

1448. The **Concordat of Vienna:** a compromise on cynical terms between the pope and the emperor on the reform issue: the Papacy triumphed over the conciliar movement for reform, by dividing profits with the princes and emperor; external episcopal jurisdiction was excluded, the princes retained rights of presentation, obtained a share in episcopal taxation, and established an authority over the German church which survived even the Reformation.

1453. The **capture of Constantinople** (p. 352) and end of the Eastern Empire left the Holy Roman Empire without a rival and brought the Turkish menace to the frontier of Germany.

1454. Traditional date for the **invention of printing** from movable metal type. This invention is usually attributed to **Johann Guten-**

berg (?1400-1468) of Mainz, printer of the so-called **Mazarin Bible** (1456). Printing had been in process of development for many years and was probably perfected not only by Gutenberg, but by others like Lourens Coster at Haarlem (1440), Albrecht Pfister of Bamberg, Peter Schoeffer and Johann Fust of Mainz.

Schools sprang up, especially in South Germany, to teach the art of *Meistergesang* in accordance with very strict and complicated rules.

1456. **John Hunyadi** (without imperial support) repulsed the Turk from Belgrade.

1458. Election of Hunyadi's son **Matthias Corvinus,** king of Hungary (to 1490) and **George Podiebrad,** king of Bohemia (to 1471), the climax of national spirit in Bohemia and Hungary.

1462. Pius II's **annulment of the Compactata** and the excommunication and deposition (1466) of Podiebrad reopened the Bohemian religious wars. **Ladislas** (elected 1468) succeeded on Podiebrad's death as king of Bohemia (1471-1516), becoming king of Hungary in 1490 (see below).

1473. **Frederick,** faced with the threat of (French) Burgundian expansion in the empire, avoided giving Charles the Bold, duke of Burgundy, the royal title (p. 303), and married his son Maximilian to Charles's daughter Mary (1477), bringing the Hapsburg fortunes to their zenith, and giving reality to his own monogram: **A.E.I.O.U.** (*Austriae est imperare orbi universo,* or, *Alles Erdreich ist Oesterreich unterthan.*)

1485. Expelled from Vienna by Mathias Corvinus, Frederick became a cheery imperial mendicant.

1486. **Maximilian,** elected king of the Romans, became the real ruler of Germany and began the creation of the Hapsburg dynastic empire. (*Cont. p. 426.*)

(1) Bohemia, 1306-1471

(*From p. 257*)

1306. The **Premyslid dynasty** came to an end with the death of Wenceslas (Vaclav) III. There followed an interregnum, during which the Bohemians were driven out of Poland. The interregnum ended with the election of

1310-1346. **JOHN OF LUXEMBURG,** son of the Emperor Henry VII. The circumstances of his accession forced John to issue a charter guaranteeing the rights and privileges of the nobility and clergy. Thus limitations of the royal power were fixed by written law. At the same time the national diet, theretofore called only on special occasions, became a regular institution. During this reign Bohe-

mian overlordship over Upper Lusatia and Silesia was established.

John supported the Teutonic Knights against the Lithuanians and participated in three campaigns (1328, 1337, 1346). For a time (1331-1333) he ruled western Lombardy, as well as the Tyrol (1336-1341). John was killed in the **battle of Crécy,** where he fought on the side of the French. While he had shown little concern for Bohemian domestic affairs, he had made Bohemia a power in international politics.

1346-1378. **CHARLES I** (Charles IV as German Emperor), the son of John of Luxemburg. His reign is regarded as the "golden age" of Bohemian history. A series of charters issued in 1348 established an order of dynastic succession and determined Bohemia's place in the Holy Roman Empire. Moravia, Silesia, and Upper Lusatia were to be indissolubly connected with the Bohemian crown. By the **Golden Bull** (1356, see p. 325) the king of Bohemia was given first place among the empire's secular electors. At the same time Bohemia's internal independence was guaranteed. Acquisition of Lower Lusatia (1370) and Brandenburg (1373). Charles ruled as a constitutional king and spared no effort to promote material well-being and cultural progress. A new code of laws, the *Maiestas Carolina,* was published. Prague was rebuilt and beautified. The **University of Prague** founded (1348), the first university in central Europe.

1378-1419. **WENCESLAS** (Vaclav) IV, son of Charles. Gradual weakening of the connection with the German Empire. Loss of Brandenburg (1411). Continued conflicts with the barons. This was hastened by the development (since the end of the 14th century) of a national-religious movement which culminated in **Hussitism. JOHN HUS** (1369-1415), a professor at the University of Prague and a popular preacher in the vernacular, was deeply influenced by the teaching of Wiclif and the Lollards in England. He attacked sale of indulgences, demanded reforms in the Church, challenged the primacy of the pope, and emphasized the supreme authority of the Scriptures. He also supported the native element in the university in the struggle which ended in the exodus of the alien Germans (1409), becoming rector of the university. Excommunicated by the pope and eager for vindication, he went to the **council of Constance** (1415) under a safe-conduct from the emperor. His arrest in violation of this guaranty, his trial and burning (July 6), identified religious reform with Bohemian nationalism and split the empire in the

The House of Wittelsbach, Main Line (1180–1508)

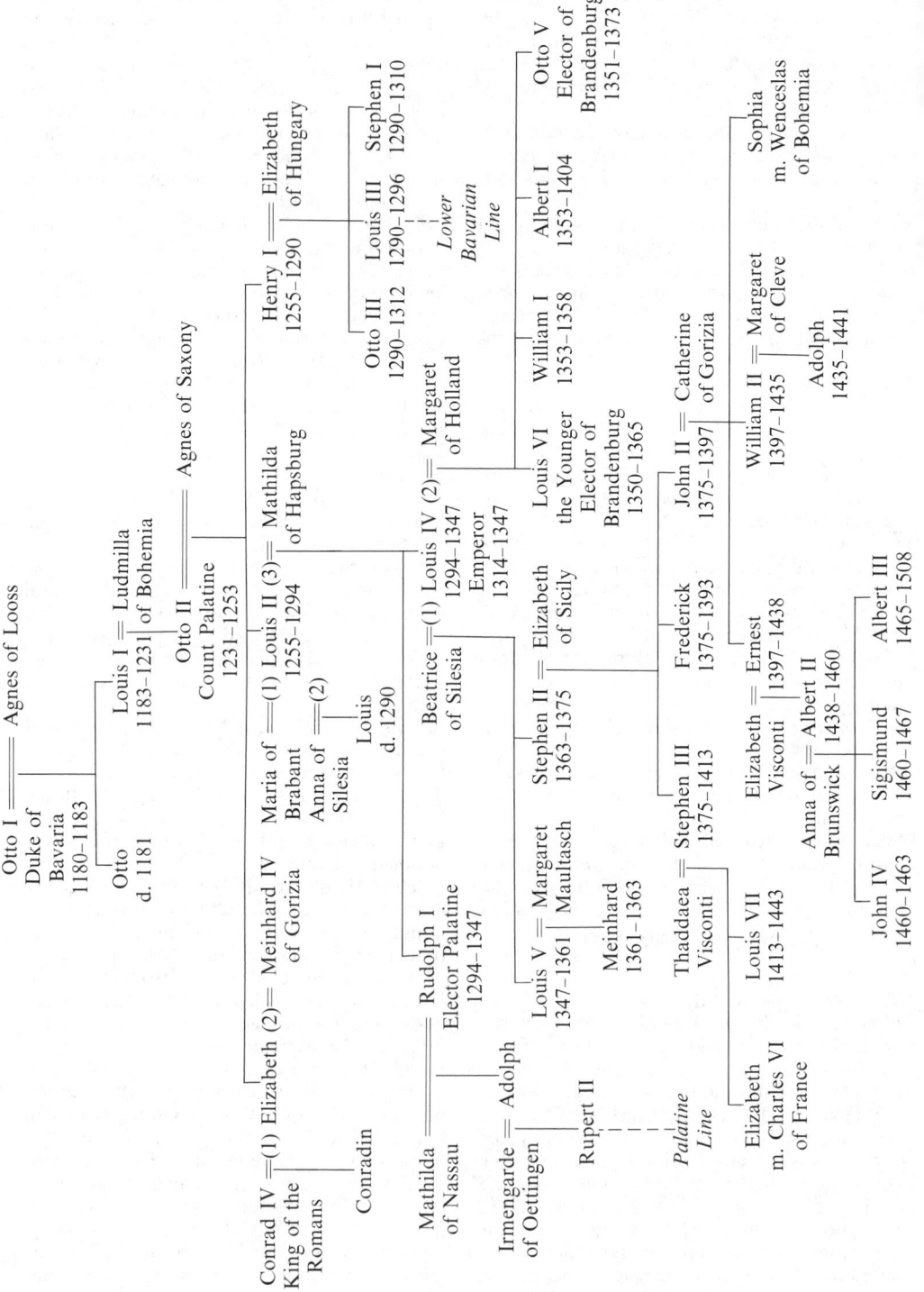

1420-1433. HUSSITE WARS. Refusal to recognize Sigismund as king. The reformers divided into two groups: (1) The moderate **Calixtines,** with the university as a center, favored separation of religious and political reform and formulated their program in the **Four Articles of Prague** (1420): full liberty of preaching, the cup to the laity (*Utraquism*), exclusion of the clergy from temporal activity and their subjection to civil penalties for crime. (2) The radical **Taborites,** under extreme Waldensian, Catharist, and Wiclifite influences, with a program of democracy and apostolic communism. The papal proclamation of a **Bohemian Crusade** (not opposed by the Emperor Sigismund) united the nation behind **John Ziska,** a brilliant soldier, who led the Hussites in a series of victories (1420-1422). Ziska's "modernization" of tactics: improved, mobile artillery, use of baggage wagons for mobile cover. Ziska's death (1424) did not affect the movement. Under a priest, **Procop the Great,** the Hussites defeated one crusade after another (1426, 1427, 1431) and carried the war into neighboring regions of Germany, on one occasion (1432) advancing as far as the Baltic. Then civil war broke out between the Calixtines and the Taborites (led by Procop the Great), the latter suffering defeat (1434).

1431-1436. The council of Basel. The Hussites finally accepted a compromise, the *Compactata* (1436), recognizing them as true sons of the Church and conceding them the cup in the communion.

1436. Sigismund was finally accepted as king by all parties. He attempted a Catholic reaction, which was cut short by his death in the following year. Disputes continued between the Catholics and the Hussites, complicated by factional struggles between Hussite moderates and radicals and by social tension between nobility, townsmen, and peasantry.

1437-1439. ALBERT OF AUSTRIA (son-in-law of Sigismund), elected king. An opposition group chose Ladislas, king of Poland. Albert died in the course of a civil war.

1439-1457. LADISLAS POSTHUMUS, the son of Albert. The Emperor Frederick III acted as his guardian, and for many years kept him from Bohemia. In the midst of continued factional conflict, a young nobleman, **George Podiebrad,** rose to power.

1448. George seized Prague and became head of the Hussites. He was recognized as administrator of the kingdom (1452) and devoted himself to the task of reconciling Catholics and Hussites. The radical wing of the latter was completely suppressed by the **capture of Tabor** (1452). George ultimately succeeded in

bringing the young king to Prague, but Ladislas died before he could accomplish much in behalf of the Catholics.

1458-1471. GEORGE PODIEBRAD elected king. Policy of conciliation: vigorous persecution of the **Bohemian Brotherhood,** a puritanical sect with outspokenly democratic leanings, dating from the teaching of **Peter of Chelchich** (d. 1460), and, like the Taborites, rejecting all subordination to Rome. George, an avowed Hussite of the moderate school, was technically a heretic and soon found himself in conflict with the pope.

1462. The pope denounced the agreements of Basel, and deposed George (1465). Thereupon the Catholic nobility of Bohemia elected **Matthias of Hungary** as king. George defeated him in a series of engagements, but the issue was undecided when George died.

(Cont. p. 448.)

(2) The Swiss Confederation, to 1499

Lake Lucerne and the original **Forest Cantons** belonged to the duchy of Swabia, and the expansion of powerful Swabian families during the Great Interregnum led the Forest Cantons to a determined effort to replace feudal allegiances to various nobles with a single direct allegiance to the emperor. Most powerful of the Swabian families was the rising **house of Hapsburg** (whose original lands expanded in the 13th century into the Aargau, Breisgau, and Alsace). **Rudolf I** (b. 1218) of Hapsburg sought to restore the duchy of Swabia under his house.

The **Forest Cantons of Uri** (already acknowledged independent of any but a loose imperial allegiance in 1231), **Schwyz,** and **Unterwalden,** emerged as champions of local independence and masters of the St. Gothard Pass into Italy. Rudolf during the Interregnum expanded his suzerainty, but as emperor was too busy to assert it.

1291. First (known) **League of the Three Forest Cantons,** an undertaking for mutual defense, a kind of constitution, but not an independent federal league, as the cantons did not claim independence. Emperor Adolf confirmed the status of Uri and Schwyz, Henry VII that of Unterwalden, and henceforth the three Forest Cantons were thought of as a unit. The Swiss sent Henry VII three hundred soldiers for his Italian expedition, the first recorded use of Swiss troops outside their own borders.

1315, Nov. 15. Battle of Morgarten. Leopold of Austria, in an effort to crush the Swiss and punish them for support of Louis IV against the Hapsburg Frederick the Handsome, was thoroughly beaten at Morgarten, a battle which began the brilliant career of the Swiss infantry in Europe. Renewal and strengthening of the league and its confirmation by Louis IV.

1332–1353. Additions to the three Forest Cantons: canton of Lucerne (1332); canton of Zürich (1351); canton of Glarus (1352); canton of Bern (1353), bringing the number to seven, half of which were peasant cantons, the other half urban.

1386, July 9. BATTLE OF SEMPACH. The confederation, supported by the Swabian League, defeated the Hapsburg Leopold III of Swabia. In 1388 another victory was won at **Näfels.**

1394. Twenty-year truce between the confederation and the duke of Austria. Austria abandoned claims on Zug and Glarus. The confederation became solely dependent on the empire, which amounted to practical independence.

The confederation was controlled by a **federal diet** (1393), but the cantons retained the widest possible autonomy. Throughout the succeeding period there was but little evidence of union. The various cantons followed their own interests (Lucerne and Schwyz looked to the north; Bern to the west; Uri to the south) and wrangled among themselves. Only the threat from Austria invariably united them against the common enemy. Meanwhile the 15th century was marked by continual struggles and conflicts with neighbors, as a result of which further territories were brought into the confederation and some approach was made to natural frontiers.

1403. The canton of Uri began expansion southward, to get control of the passes to the Milanese. In 1410 the whole Val Antigorio was conquered, with Domodossola. The Swiss were driven out by the duke of Savoy in 1413, but in 1416 regained mastery of the country.

1415. Conquest in the north of the Aargau, from Frederick of Austria, at the behest of his rival, the Emperor Sigismund.

1419. Purchase of Bellinzona, which, however, was seized by the Visconti of Milan (1422).

1436–1450. Civil war between Zürich and some of the neighboring cantons over the succession to the domains of the count of Toggenburg. Zürich allied itself with Emperor Frederick III (1442), but was defeated by Schwyz (1443); Zürich besieged (1444). Frederick called in the French, but after a defeat near Basel, the French withdrew. The emperor made **peace at Constance** (June 12, 1446) and in 1450 peace was made within the confederation. The general effect of the war was to strengthen the confederacy.

1460. Conquest of the Thurgau from Austria

gave the confederation a frontier on Lake Constance.

1474–1477. The great war against **Charles the Bold of Burgundy,** whose designs on Alsace were regarded as a menace to the confederation. The Swiss allied themselves with the South German cities. This combination was joined by the emperor (perpetual peace, Mar. 30, 1474: Austria again renounced claims to Swiss territory). Louis XI of France also joined, but in 1475 both the emperor and the king withdrew again. Great victories of the Swiss at **Grandson** (Mar. 2, 1476), **Morat** or Murten (June 22, 1476), and at **Nancy** (Jan. 5, 1477) sealed the fate of Charles's plans and established the great military reputation of the Swiss, who were thenceforth sought far and wide as mercenaries.

1478. War with Milan. Victory of the Swiss at **Giornico** (Dec. 28). Alliance with the pope, who was allowed to engage Swiss forces.

1481. Solothurn and Fribourg were admitted to the confederation after a long dispute among the members. The **diet of Stans** drew up a covenant by which federal relations were regulated until 1798. Henceforth the urban cantons were in a majority.

1499. War with the emperor over disputed territories in the east. The emperor was supported by the South German cities, while the Swiss enjoyed the support, especially financial, of the French. The Swiss won a series of victories (especially **Dornach,** July 22) and forced the emperor to conclude the **treaty of Basel** (Sept. 22) which granted the confederation independence of the empire in fact, if not formally (this came only in 1648). By the inclusion of **Basel** and **Schaffhausen** (1501) and later **Appenzell** (1513), the confederation rounded out its northern frontier.

The Swiss at the end of the 15th century enjoyed immense military prestige, but within the confederation there was much social unrest, especially among the peasants, and a good deal of demoralization in the towns. **Hans Waldmann,** bürgermeister of Zürich (1483–1489), was only the most outstanding of the typical ruthless, mercenary, cynical figures which dominated the scene and remind one of the contemporaneous Italian despots.

(*Cont. p. 437.*)

(3) The Hanseatic League, 1000–1669

Hansa (Old French *Hanse;* Med. Latin *Hansa*), meaning a group, company, or association.

Associations (*Hansas*) and partial unions of North German towns date from the 13th century and were an important aspect of the great town development of Germany in that period.

c. 1000. German traders were established on the island of Gothland and in London.

c. 1150–c. 1250. Revival of the German river trade, notably along the Rhine, centering in the towns of Köln, Dortmund, Soest, and Münster. At the same time the German expansion toward the Slavic east extended the sphere of German trade along the Baltic coasts. In the later 12th century the German settlement on Gothland **(Wisby)** became autonomous and established an offshoot at **Novgorod** (*St. Peter's Yard*) which became the focus of the important Russian trade.

1226. Lübeck (founded 1143) secured an imperial charter from Frederick II. Hamburg followed in 1266–1267.

1237. Wisby secured trading rights in England, and soon afterward in Flanders.

1241. Lübeck and Hamburg formed an alliance to protect the Baltic trade routes.

1256. The **Wendish towns** (Lübeck, Stralsund, Wismar, Rostock, Greifswald, and later Lüneburg), held their first recorded meeting. Lübeck began to emerge as the dominant North German town, a position it retained throughout the history of the Hanseatic League. Most of the commercial towns followed the *Code of Lübeck,* which was an early source of unity between them. By the end of the century the Wendish towns had taken the leadership from the Gothland merchants.

1282. The **Germans in London** formed a corporation and established their own guildhall and steelyard. Other German yards were opened at York, Bristol, Yarmouth, Lynn, and Boston. The London trade was dominated by Köln, but the yards at Lynn and Boston were under the control of Lübeck and Hamburg.

THE HANSEATIC LEAGUE. No date can be fixed for its organization, which was evidently the result of the lack of a powerful German national government able to guarantee security for trade. Its formation was no doubt facilitated by the medieval affinity for co-operative action and for monopoly. The term *Hanseatic League* was first used in a document in 1344. The exclusion of Germans abroad (1366) from the privileges of the Hansa indicates a growing sense of unity, but league members spoke of the association merely as a *firma confederatio* for trade, and throughout its history it remained a loose aggregation. This looseness of organization allowed a maximum of independence to its members and was not modified until the league was put on the defensive in the 15th century. The league never had a true treasury or officials in a strict sense; its only common seal was that of Lübeck; it had no common flag. Assemblies of the members (*Hansetage*) were summoned by Lübeck at irregular intervals and were sparsely attended, except in time of crisis. The objectives of the league were mutual security, extortion of trading privileges, and maintenance of trade monopoly wherever possible. The chief weapon against foreigners or recalcitrant members was the economic boycott and (rarely) war. Primarily concerned with the North European trade, the Hansa towns dealt chiefly in raw materials (timber, pitch, tar, turpentine, iron, copper), livestock (horses, hawks, etc.), salt fish (cod and especially herring), leather, hides, wool, grain, beer, amber, drugs, and some textiles. The four chief *kontors* were Wisby, Bergen, London, and Bruges.

1340–1375. WALDEMAR IV of Denmark, who freed his country of the German domination and took up the struggle against the powerful Hansa towns. He threatened the Hanseatic monopoly of the herring trade by his seizure of Scania, and in 1361 cut the Russian-Baltic trade route by his capture of Wisby. In 1362 he defeated the German fleets at **Helsingborg.** By the **peace of Wordingborg** (1365) the Hansa was deprived of many of its privileges in Denmark.

1367. The **CONFEDERATION OF KÖLN (COLOGNE),** effected by a meeting of representatives of 77 towns, organized common finance and naval preparations for the struggle. Reconstruction of Scandinavian alliances to meet the threat from Waldemar. After a series of victories, the German towns extorted from the Danish *Reichsrat*

1370. The **PEACE OF STRALSUND,** which gave the league four castles in Scania (dominating the Sound), control of two-thirds of the Scanian revenues for 15 years, and the right to veto the succession to the Danish throne unless their monopoly was renewed by the candidate. The treaty marked the **apogee of Hanseatic power** and virtually established control over the Baltic trade and over Scandinavian politics. The Baltic monopoly was not finally broken until 1441, after a war with the Dutch. Wisby itself never recovered from Waldemar's sack, and was long a nest of pirates (e.g. the famous **Victual Brothers**).

FLANDERS. The Germans in Bruges received a special grant of privileges in 1252, which allowed them their own ordinances and officials. They later (1309) established exemption from the usual brokerage charges levied on foreigners and eventually won an influential voice in the affairs of the city, notably in foreign policy. The revised statutes of the Bruges kontor (1347) recognized the division of the Hanseatic League into thirds: the Wendish-Saxon, the Prusso-Westphalian, and the Goth-

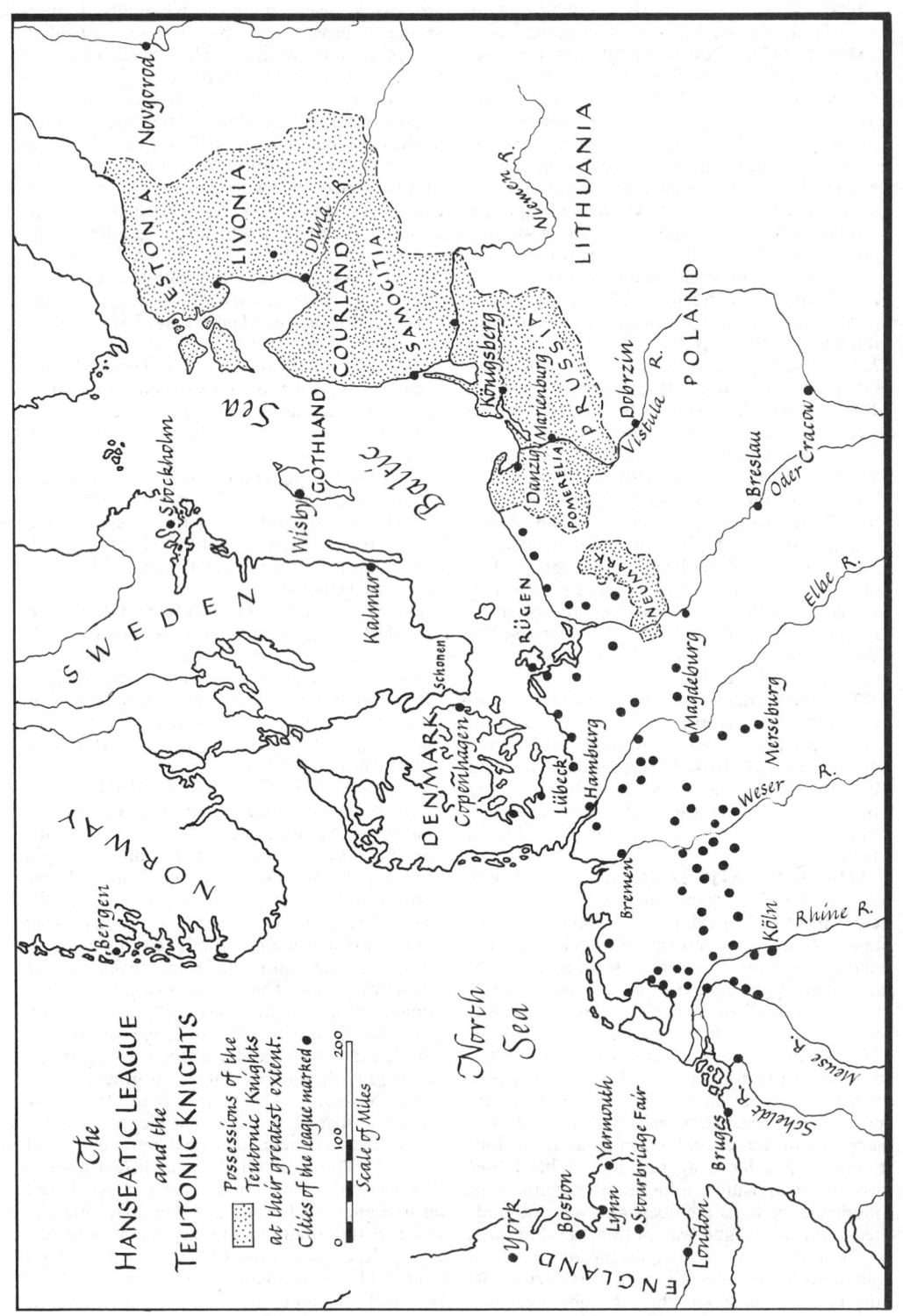

The
HANSEATIC LEAGUE
and the
TEUTONIC KNIGHTS

Possessions of the
Teutonic Knights
at their greatest extent.
Cities of the league marked ●

Scale of Miles
0   100   200

ENGLAND

North
Sea

York
Boston
Lynn
Yarmouth
Sturbridge Fair
London
Bruges

Scheldt R.
Meuse R.
Rhine R.
Köln
Bremen
Weser R.
Merseburg
Magdeburg
Hamburg
Lübeck
Copenhagen
Schonen
DENMARK
RÜGEN
NEUMARK

NORWAY
Bergen

SWEDEN
Stockholm
Wisby
GOTHLAND
Kalmar

Baltic Sea

ESTONIA
LIVONIA
Düna R.
COURLAND
SAMOGITIA
PRUSSIA
Königsberg
Marienburg
Danzig
POMERELIA
Dobrzin
Vistula R.
Niemen R.
LITHUANIA
POLAND
Breslau
Oder
Cracow
Elbe R.

Novgorod

land-Livland thirds. Bruges was the most ardent champion of Hanseatic unity, and, with Lübeck, was the chief source of such cohesion as the League attained. A boycott in 1360 brought the town into complete submission to the League.

ENGLAND. The Hansa towns, by maintaining friendly relations with the crown, were able to ignore the growing national hostility to alien traders (directed at first mainly against the Italians) and to avoid granting reciprocal privileges to the English in return for their own exclusive rights (notably those claimed under Edward I's *Carta Mercatoria* of 1303). One source of Hanseatic influence derived from loans to the crown, especially during the Hundred Years' War. The English themselves began to penetrate into the Baltic (c. 1360) and growing public resentment against the League led to increased customs dues, but Richard II in 1377 renewed the privileges of the League, thus firmly establishing the Hanseatic power in England. The Sound was opened to the English in 1451, and the League, profiting by the Wars of the Roses, secured full title to the steelyard in London (1474) and the renewal of rights in Boston and Lynn. Not until the days of Elizabeth were the Hanseatic privileges finally reduced.

DECLINE OF THE LEAGUE. **Externally** the league was weakened by the disorders of the Hundred Years' War; by the rise of Burgundy and the new orientation thereby given to Dutch trade (e.g. Brill wrested the monopoly of the herring trade from the League); and by the great discoveries and the opening of new trade routes. But above all, the monopolistic policies of the League aroused ever sharper opposition in the countries where the League operated (notably in England, Holland, Scandinavia, and Russia; Ivan III destroyed the Novgorod kontor in 1494). **Internally** the League continued to suffer from lack of organization. The inland towns held aloof from the Baltic policy and Köln sent no representatives to the assembly until 1383. The assembly itself was summoned only at irregular intervals. The delegates were strictly bound by their mandates and their votes were subject to review by their home towns. Decisions were not binding on all members until 1418. In the 15th century the League was further weakened by the struggle within the member towns between the democratic guildsmen and the patrician oligarchy. The League threatened the expulsion of "democratic" towns. The German princes (notably the Hohenzollerns of Brandenburg) gradually reduced the freedom of various powerful members of the League and rivalries broke out within the League itself (Köln and the Westphalian towns stood together, as did Danzig and the Prussian towns,

especially after 1467). The South German towns opened direct trade relations of their own with Flanders, Breslau, Prague, and other centers, and began to establish their own fairs. Leipzig, for example, replaced Lübeck as the center of the fur trade.

1629. The assembly entrusted the guardianship of the common welfare to Lübeck, Hamburg, and Bremen.

1669. The last assembly (attended by six towns) was held. The League by this time was the merest shadow of its former self, but its kontors survived in Bergen until 1775, in London until 1852, and in Augsburg until 1863.

(4) The Teutonic Knights, 1382–1561
(*From p. 230*)

The 14th century marked the apogee of the power of the **Teutonic Order** in eastern Europe. The knights began the penetration of Poland, where Germans settled some 650 districts and where the middle class of the towns became German in speech and law, much to the alarm of the rulers and nobles. At the same period the knights advanced into Lithuania, a huge region extending from the Baltic to the Black Sea, the last heathen area in Europe. German colonization and town-building first opened and civilized this region.

1326–1333. The **FIRST POLISH WAR,** marking a sharp reaction to German penetration and putting the Order for the first time on the defensive. With the aid of John of Bohemia, Louis of Hungary, Albert of Austria, Louis of Brandenburg, and others, the Order emerged triumphant and the Poles were obliged to conclude a truce.

1343. PEACE OF KALISCH. The Poles, despite papal support of their claims to Pomerelia, were obliged to recognize the Order's possession of the territory, in return for a promise of aid against the Lithuanians. Poland was thus cut off from the Baltic.

1343–1345. The **Estonian Revolt,** one of the worst *jacqueries* of the Middle Ages. Estonia was taken by the Order from the Danes in 1346.

1386. Union of Poland and Lithuania under Jagiello and Jadwiga, thus creating a strong barrier to the further advance of the Germans and, indeed, sealing the ultimate fate of the Order.

1410, July 15. Defeat of the Knights in the **battle of Tannenberg** by a huge army of Poles and Lithuanians. Poland, unable to exploit the victory, concluded

1411. The **FIRST PEACE OF THORN,** which cost the Knights only Samogitia and an indemnity.

1454. The **Prussian Revolt,** a great uprising against the oppressive rule of the Order in which the Prussian nobility and towns took part. The movement was supported by the Poles, and Casimir of Poland declared war on the Order.

1466. SECOND PEACE OF THORN: Prussia was divided: (1) **West Prussia** (including Danzig, Kulm, Marienwerder, Thorn, and Ermeland) went to Poland, thus cutting East Prussia off from the rest of Germany and securing for Poland access to the sea. (2) **East Prussia** was retained by the Order, with Königsberg as capital. East Prussia, Brandenburg, and Memel were all to be held as Polish fiefs. The Order was opened to Polish members. This peace marked the definitive end of the German advance until the partitions of Poland.

The **decline of the Order** continued (growing commercialization, exclusiveness, lack of new blood, loss of discipline, Slavic pressure) despite efforts at reform by various grand masters.

1525. East Prussia was finally secularized by the grand master, Albrecht (Hohenzollern) of Brandenburg, and became a fief of the Hohenzollerns under the Polish crown.

1561. The Livonian holdings were similarly transformed and became the duchy of Courland.

The Order itself survived in Germany until 1809 and was later revived in 1840 under Hapsburg auspices with its original functions (e.g. ambulance service in war).

f. SCANDINAVIA

(1) Denmark, 1320–1387

(*From p. 219*)

The active and on the whole successful reign of **Eric Menved** (1286–1319) was followed in Denmark by a period of weakness and decline, marked by the ascendancy of the nobility and the constant advance of German influence.

1320–1332. CHRISTOPHER II, elected king after a capitulation, the first in Danish history, limiting the royal power in the interest of the nobility and clergy. The Hansa towns, having acquired a monopoly of trade in Denmark, soon became dominant in Danish politics.

1332–1340. A period of complete anarchy. Christopher was driven from the throne by Gerhard, count of Holstein, who parceled out the territories of the crown, established German nobles in all the important fortresses, and gave the German traders full rein. Gerhard was murdered in 1340.

1340–1375. WALDEMAR IV, the youngest son of Christopher and one of the greatest Danish

kings. At home he did his utmost to break the German influence and to restrict the power of the nobility and the clergy. The Church was subordinated to the royal power and the nobles and towns obliged to perform their military obligations. Abroad Waldemar devoted himself to the reconquest of the territories lost by his father. In wars with Sweden, Holstein, and Schleswig he regained Zeeland (1346), most of Fünen and Jutland (1348), and Scania (1360). His seizure of Gothland (1361) brought him into direct conflict with the powerful Hansa towns, which were supported by Sweden.

1361–1363. First War against the Hansa. Copenhagen was sacked, but Waldemar defeated the Hansa fleets at **Helsingborg** (1362) and forced the Hansa to accept peace (1363) which greatly curtailed their privileges.

1368. A revolt against heavy taxation led to Waldemar's flight. His return (1370) was purchased by tremendous concessions. Meanwhile

1368–1370. The **SECOND WAR WITH THE HANSA** had broken out. The German towns were supported by Sweden, Norway, Holstein, Mecklenburg, and even by some of the Danish nobles. Waldemar, badly defeated, was obliged to accept

1370. The **PEACE OF STRALSUND,** renewing the privileges of the German Hansa, turning over the larger part of the revenues of four places, and accepting interference in the royal succession. This treaty marked the **ascendency of the Hansa** in the Baltic.

1376–1387. Olaf, grandson of Waldemar, who, until his death, ruled with his mother Margaret as regent.

1387–1412. MARGARET, mother of Olaf, was queen, ruling at the same time Norway and Sweden and thus uniting Scandinavia.

(*Cont. p. 438.*)

(2) Sweden, 1319–1387

(*From p. 219*)

1319–1365. MAGNUS II (Smek), aged three at his accession and, until 1333, ruler under the regency of his mother. He was a weak and ineffectual ruler, but through his mother succeeded (1319) to the Norwegian crown and, during the troubled period in Denmark, managed to acquire, temporarily, Scania, Halland, and Bleking (given up again in 1360, to Waldemar IV). His long minority and his reliance on unworthy favorites led to a striking weakening of the royal power and an equally striking rise of the aristocratic party (first *Riksdag*, including burghers 1359). Magnus was ultimately deposed and was succeeded by

1363–1388. Albert of Mecklenburg, who from

Scandinavian Rulers (1263-1533)

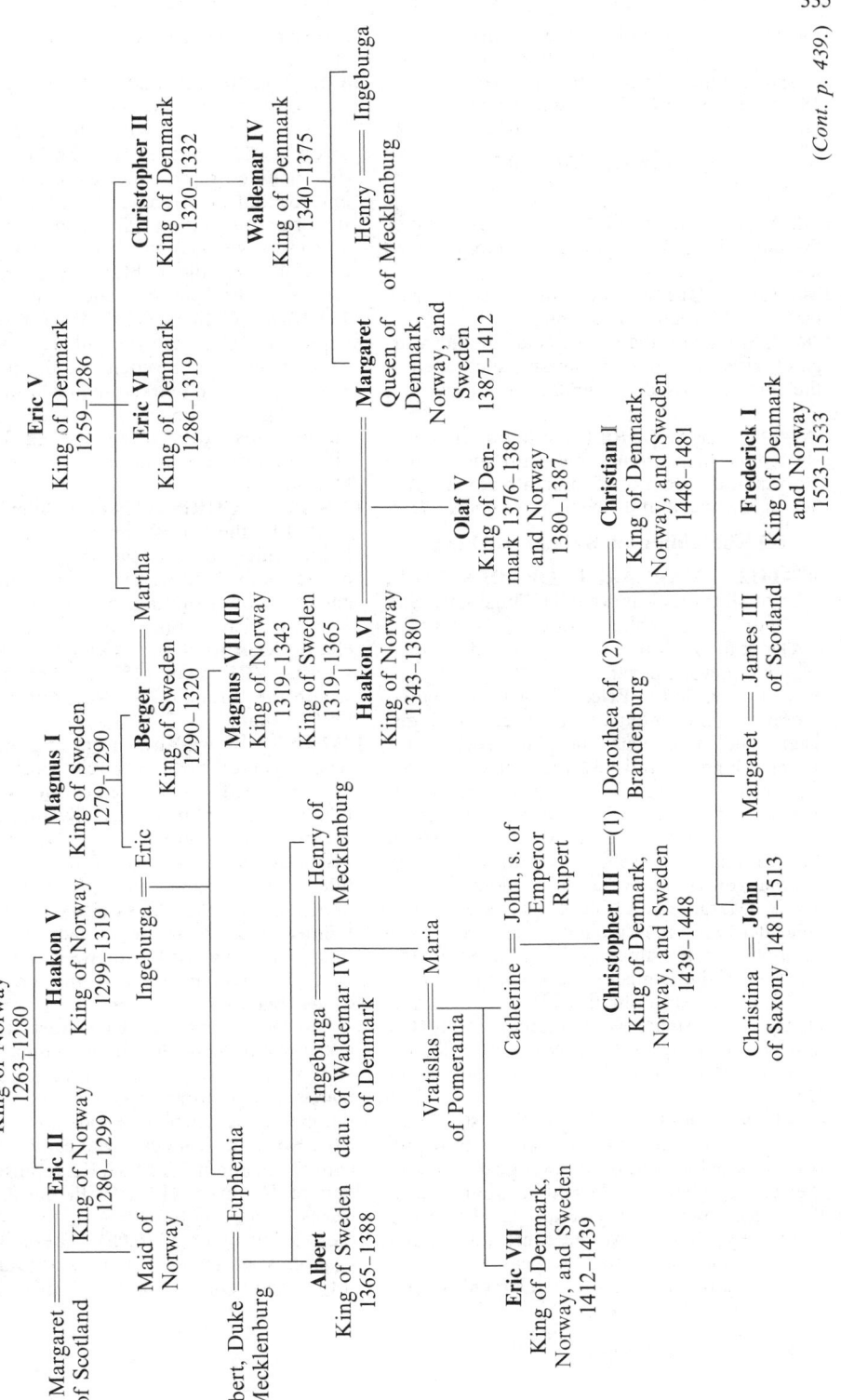

(*Cont. p. 439.*)

the outset was merely a tool of the nobility. The magnates eventually deposed him and defeated him, calling to the throne

1387-1412. MARGARET, the regent of Denmark. *(Cont. p. 439.)*

(3) Norway, 1320-1387

(From p. 220)

1319-1343. Magnus VII, who was also king of Sweden. In 1343 he turned over Norway to his son

1343-1380. Haakon VI, who was married (1363) to Margaret of Denmark.

1380-1387. Olaf, the son of Haakon and Margaret, already king of Denmark, succeeded to the throne. His death ended the Norwegian line.

1387-1412. MARGARET, mother of Olaf, was elected to the throne, thus introducing into Norway the system of election already in practice in Denmark and Sweden. *(Cont. p. 438.)*

(4) The Union of Kalmar, to 1483

1387-1412. MARGARET OF DENMARK, ruler of all three Scandinavian kingdoms. She had her grand-nephew, Eric of Pomerania, elected king of all three countries, but retained effective power herself.

1397. Coronation of Eric. Margaret presented a draft for the union of the three kingdoms. Vague and incomplete, the plan provided for a single king, established rules of succession, and set up a system of common defense. It was never ratified by the councils of the three kingdoms, but as long as Margaret lived, it worked relatively well. The union left the internal government of each kingdom much as it was. Margaret, an able despot (the Lübeck delegates called her "the lady king"), repressed the nobles, maintained order, and began the recovery of the Danish royal domain. In general the Danes profited by the union, and Danes and Germans were gradually insinuated into power in Sweden and Norway. Effective government of Scandinavia was centered in Denmark.

1412-1439. ERIC, Margaret's successor, proved himself less able. His efforts to regain control in Schleswig led to a long contest with the dukes of Holstein, who, in alliance with the Hansa towns, finally conquered Schleswig completely (1432). At the same time much unrest developed among the peasantry (especially in Sweden, where **Engelbrecht Engel-** brechtson emerged as a leader of the lower classes).

1434. Engelbrecht marched through eastern and southern Sweden, seizing castles and driving out bailiffs, until the **diet of 1435** recognized his demands, electing him regent. This diet included representatives of all four orders and for four hundred years continued to be an important institution. The movement of revolt spread to Norway, where it was taken up and controlled by the nobles. Eric finally took flight and the Danish council called in

1439-1448. CHRISTOPHER (of Bavaria), nephew of Eric, who again ruled all three countries (elected in Sweden, 1440; in Norway, 1442). His reign marked the **nadir of the monarchy,** for Christopher was entirely dependent on the Hansa towns and was obliged to renew all their privileges, despite protests from the Danish burghers.

1448-1481. CHRISTIAN I (of Oldenburg) was elected by the Danish council under a capitulation which left all real power in the hands of that body. He had to accept a similar engagement on assuming the crown of Norway. The Swedish nobility, on the other hand, elected **Knut Knutsson** as king with the title of **Charles VIII** (1449-1457). Charles tried to secure the throne of Norway, but was ousted by Christian.

1457. Charles was driven out of Sweden by a revolt inspired by the Church. Christian I was then crowned, but the real power was in the hands of the **Stures** (Sten, Svante, and Sten the Younger). Christian kept a great state, but his court, like that of Christopher and Eric, was filled with Germans, and he was financially dependent on the Hansa cities. The **union of Schleswig and Holstein,** each autonomous under the crown of Denmark, was arranged in 1460. Christian founded the **university of Copenhagen** (1479).

Sweden in the later 15th century: The crown was a plaything of the nobles, while the clergy supported the king of Denmark. A rising commerce and industry was, however, creating a burgher class which was soon to assert itself. **Sten Sture the Younger,** who came into power with the death of Charles VIII, repulsed Christian of Denmark (1471) with the aid of the towns (especially Stockholm) and returned to the reforms of Engelbrecht. The **university of Uppsala** was founded (1477) and **printing** was introduced soon afterward. *(Cont. p. 438.)*

2. EASTERN EUROPE

a. POLAND, 1305-1492

(From p. 258)

The history of Poland in this period was concerned chiefly with the efforts of the kings to reunite the various duchies and to establish the royal power. This policy was opposed, with success, by the nobility, which, as elsewhere in Europe, managed to extract countless privileges and to erect a type of oligarchical government. Externally the Poles were involved in a long struggle with the Teutonic Knights, designed to secure an outlet to the Baltic. This conflict alternated with a policy of expansion to the southeast toward the Black Sea.

1305-1333. VLADISLAV IV (Lokietek), under whom Poland regained its independence after a brief period of Bohemian domination. Vladislav was obliged to continue the struggle against Bohemia, and was not crowned until 1320. For protection he concluded dynastic alliances with Hungary (his daughter married Charles Robert of Anjou) and Lithuania (his son Casimir married the daughter of Gedymin). He did much to reunite the various duchies and established a new capital at Cracow. But he failed to secure Pomerania, which in 1309 passed from Brandenburg to the Teutonic Order. A papal decision in 1321 awarded the region to Poland, but the Knights ignored the order to turn it over, and continued their raids into Polish territory (1326-1333).

1333-1370. CASIMIR III (the Great), an astute and cautious statesman. He introduced an improved administration, reduced the influence of the German town law (a new law code published), developed national defense, and promoted trade and industry (extensive privileges to the Jews, 1334). In 1364 he founded a school at Cracow, which became a university in 1400 and the chief intellectual center of eastern Europe. Here **Johannes Dlugosz** (1415-1480) wrote the first critical history of the country. There was a printing press in Cracow as early as 1474.

In **foreign affairs** Casimir abandoned claims to Silesia and Pomerania, turning his attention toward the southeast, where dynastic problems in the Ukraine called forth dangerous rivalry between Poles, Lithuanians, and Hungarians. By an agreement with Hungary (1339), Casimir, who had no direct heir, promised that on his death the Polish crown should pass to Louis, the son of Charles Robert of Hungary. Louis was to reconquer the lost territories and to respect the privileges of the Polish nobility. This marks the beginning of the disastrous elective system, which gave the magnates an unequaled opportunity for extracting further rights (first real diet—*colloquia*—in 1367). In 1340 Casimir seized Halicz, Lemberg, and Volhynia. War ensued with Lithuania over Volhynia, and ultimately the Poles retained only the western part (1366).

1370-1382. LOUIS (of Anjou). He paid but little attention to Poland, which he governed through regents. To secure the succession to his daughter Maria (married to Sigismund, son of Emperor Charles IV) he granted to the nobility the *Charter of Koszyce* (Kaschau), the basis of far-reaching privileges.

1382-1384. Opposition to Sigismund led to the formation of the **confederation of Radom** and civil war between the factions of the nobility.

1384-1399. JADWIGA (Hedwig), a daughter of Louis, was elected queen.

1386. Marriage of Jadwiga to Jagiello, grand duke of Lithuania, who promised to become a Christian and to unite his duchy (three times the size of Poland) with the Polish crown. As a matter of fact, though the marriage prepared the way for union, Jagiello was obliged to recognize his cousin, **Witold,** as grand duke of Lithuania, and the connection continued to be tenuous.

1386-1434. JAGIELLO (title **Vladislav V**). He had great difficulty in keeping his fractious nobility in order and in 1433 was obliged to grant the *Charter of Cracow,* reaffirming and extending their privileges.

1410, July 15. BATTLE OF TANNENBERG (Grünwald), a great victory of the Poles, using Bohemian mercenaries under John Ziska and supported by the Russians and even the Tatars, against the Teutonic Knights. The Poles thereupon devastated Prussia, but Jagiello, unable to keep his vassals in order, concluded the

1411, Feb. 1. FIRST PEACE OF THORN, which left matters much as they were and failed to secure for the Poles an access to the Baltic.

1434-1444. VLADISLAV VI, son of Jagiello, succeeded to the throne. Since he was only ten years old, the country was ruled by a regency. Vladislav's brother, Casimir, was offered the Bohemian throne by the Hussites (1438); Vladislav himself became **king of Hungary** (1440). Thenceforth he devoted himself to Hungarian affairs, leaving Poland in the hands of the magnates. Vladislav lost his life in 1444 at the **battle of Varna** (p. 351) against the Turks.

1444-1447. An interregnum, followed by the reign of

1447-1492. CASIMIR IV, brother of Vladislav. He was able to make use of a rift be-

POLAND, LITHUANIA
and RUSSIA
in the 15th Century

0   100   200   300   400   500

Scale of Miles

Rulers of Hungary, Poland, and Lithuania (1205–1492)

(*From p. 326*)

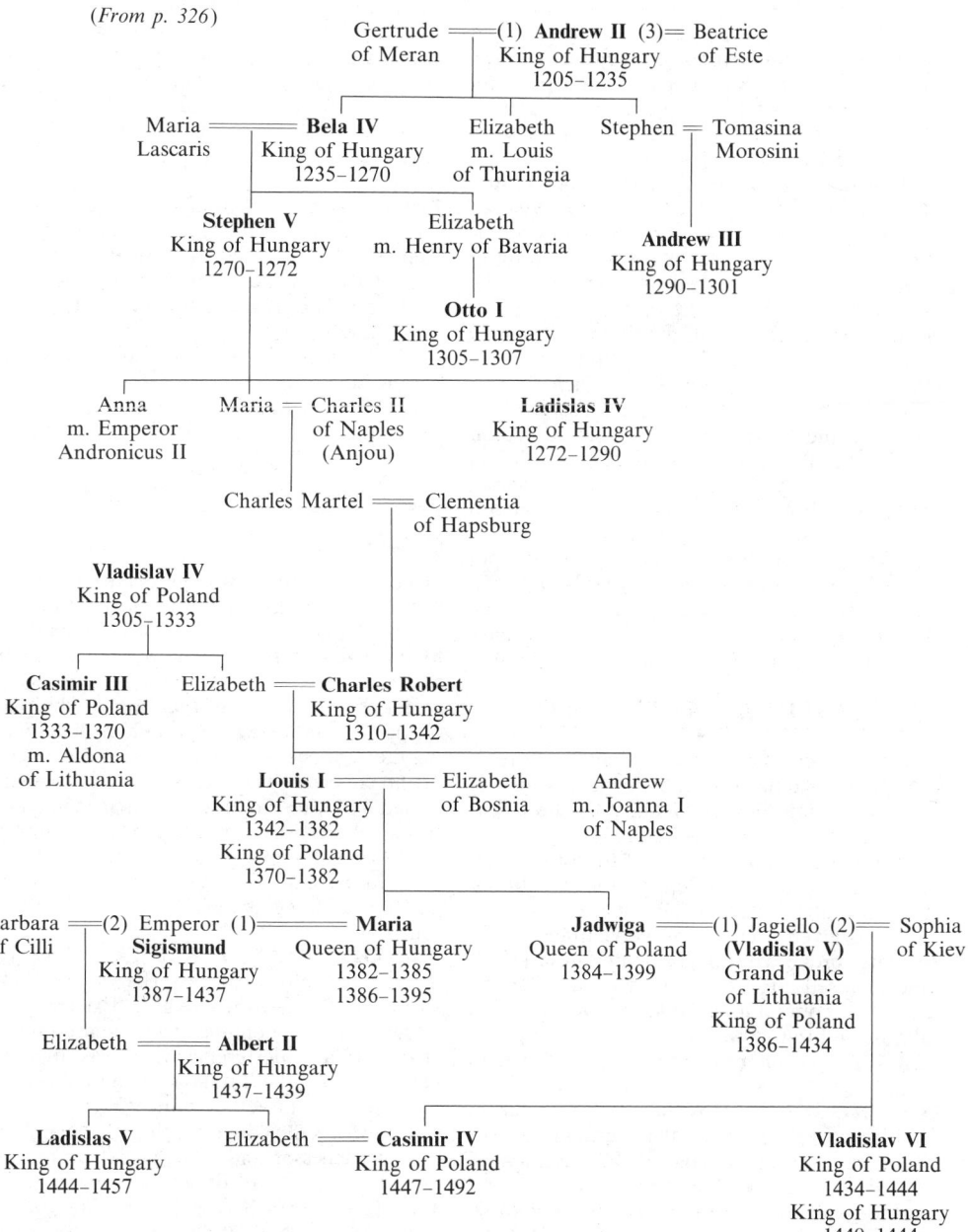

(*Cont. p. 443.*)

tween the great nobles (magnates) and the gentry (*szlachta*). The *statute of Nieszawa* greatly limited the power of the former and granted substantial rights to the latter (no laws to be passed, no war to be declared without their consent). At the same time the independence of the Church was curtailed (bishops to be appointed by the king).

1454-1466. War against the Teutonic Order. The Poles took advantage of the Prussian Union (Prussian nobles and towns in opposition to the Order). The war was carried on in desultory fashion, marked by constant shifting of the feudal forces and of the mercenaries from side to side, but the Poles ultimately gained the upper hand and secured

1466, Oct. 19. The **SECOND PEACE OF THORN,** by which Poland finally secured an outlet to the Baltic. Poland acquired Kulm, Michelau, Pomerania, Marienburg, Elbing, and Christburg. The Order became a vassal of the Polish crown, and half its membership became Polish.

1471-1516. Vladislav, the son of Casimir, became king of Bohemia, which involved a long and indecisive war with Hungary (1471-1478). Eventually Vladislav became king of Hungary as Ladislas II (1490). (*Cont. p. 442.*)

b. LITHUANIA, 1240-1447

Of the early history of Lithuania little is known. The numerous heathen tribes were first brought to some degree of unity by the threat of the German Knights (after 1230).

c. 1240-1263. Mindovg, one of the Lithuanian chieftains, in order to deprive the Knights of their crusading purpose, accepted Christianity and was given a crown by Pope Innocent IV. He later broke with the Teutonic Order (1260) and relapsed into paganism. He was killed by one of his competitors. Of the following period almost nothing is known.

1293-1316. Viten re-established a Lithuanian state.

1316-1341. GEDYMIN, the real founder of Lithuania. Blocked by the Germans on the Baltic, he took advantage of the weakness of the Russian principalities to extend his control to the east and south (acquisition of Polotsk, Minsk, and the middle-Dnieper region). **Vilna** became the capital of the new state.

1341-1377. OLGERD, the son of Gedymin, was the ablest of the dynasty. Defeated by the Knights (1360), he too turned eastward. Siding with Tver in the dynastic conflicts of Russia, he advanced several times to the very outskirts of Moscow. During his reign the domain of Lithuania was extended as far as the Black Sea, where Olgerd defeated the Tatars (1368).

1377-1434. JAGIELLO, the son of Olgerd, married Jadwiga of Poland (1386) and established the **personal union with Poland.** Through him Lithuania became converted to Roman Catholicism and the Polish and Lithuanian nobility gradually became assimilated. In 1387 and 1389 Moldavia and Wallachia, and in 1396 Bessarabia, accepted Lithuanian suzerainty.

1398. Jagiello was obliged to recognize his cousin, **Vitovt** (Witold) as grand duke of Lithuania. Vitovt hoped to re-establish the independence of the country from Poland, but his failure in a crusade against the Tatars greatly weakened him.

1447. Casimir IV of Poland, having been grand duke of Lithuania before his accession, once again united the grand duchy and the Polish kingdom. (*Cont. p. 442.*)

c. RUSSIA, 1263-1505

(*From p. 261*)

The period following the death of **Alexander Nevski** (1263) was marked by the continued and repeated disruption of the Russian lands, due to the complicated and unfortunate system of succession in the princely family. Russia was under the **suzerainty of the Tatars,** who played off one candidate against another, thus increasing the confusion and perpetuating the weakness of the country. The **rise of Moscow** (first mentioned 1147) to prominence among the Russian principalities was perhaps the most important development looking toward the future. Centrally located, Moscow was in the most favorable position to serve as nucleus for a revived Russian state.

1328-1340. IVAN I KALITA (Moneybag), grand prince of Moscow. His was the first of a series of noteworthy reigns. Extremely cautious and parsimonious, Ivan bought immunity from Tatar interference and was ultimately entrusted by the Tatars with the collection of tribute from the other princes.

1340-1353. Simeon I continued the policy of his predecessor and was placed, by the Tatar overlord, above all the other princes.

1353-1359. Ivan II Krasnyi (the Red).

1359-1389. DMITRI DONSKOI (of the Don), who ascended the princely throne at the age of nine. His reign was filled with a struggle against **Michael of Tver,** his chief rival, who was supported by Olgerd of Lithuania. At the same time he began the conflict with the Tatars, whose power was fading, but who also enjoyed the support of Lithuania.

1380, Sept. 8. THE BATTLE OF KULIKOVO. Dmitri completely defeated the Tatar armies

rom p. 260)

Grand Princes of Moscow (1176-1505)

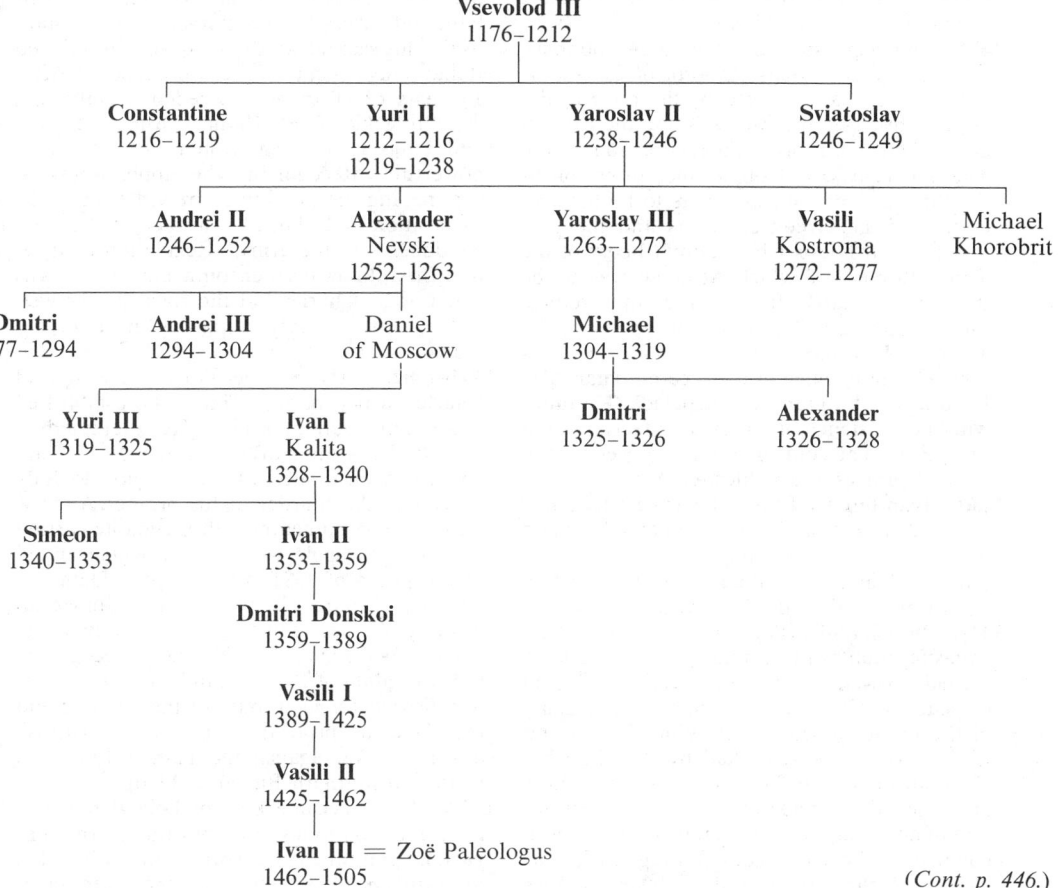

Vsevolod III
1176-1212

Constantine
1216-1219

Yuri II
1212-1216
1219-1238

Yaroslav II
1238-1246

Sviatoslav
1246-1249

Andrei II
1246-1252

Alexander
Nevski
1252-1263

Yaroslav III
1263-1272

Vasili
Kostroma
1272-1277

Michael
Khorobrit

Dmitri
77-1294

Andrei III
1294-1304

Daniel
of Moscow

Michael
1304-1319

Yuri III
1319-1325

Ivan I
Kalita
1328-1340

Dmitri
1325-1326

Alexander
1326-1328

Simeon
1340-1353

Ivan II
1353-1359

Dmitri Donskoi
1359-1389

Vasili I
1389-1425

Vasili II
1425-1462

Ivan III = Zoë Paleologus
1462-1505

(Cont. p. 446.)

before the Lithuanians arrived. The victory was in no sense decisive, for the Tatars on several occasions thereafter advanced to the very gates of Moscow. But Kulikovo broke the prestige of the Tatar arms and marked the turning point.

1389-1425. Basil I (Vasili). He annexed Nishni-Novgorod and continued the struggle with the Tatars and the Lithuanians, without forcing a decision.

1425-1462. Basil II, whose reign was distinguished by a relapse into anarchy. A long civil war with his rivals, Yuri and Shemyaka, was followed by Tatar invasion (1451, the Tatars beaten back from Moscow). Nevertheless the Moscow principality managed to maintain itself. In 1439 Basil refused to accept the union of the eastern and western churches, arranged for at the council of Flor-

ence. Thenceforth the Russian metropolitan, who had moved to Moscow in the time of Ivan Kalita, became more and more the head of an independent Russian church.

1462-1505. IVAN III (the Great), who may be regarded as the first national sovereign of Russia. By a cautious but persistent policy he annexed most of the rival principalities and, after a series of wars, subjected Novgorod, where the patrician elements tended to side with Lithuania. In 1471 Novgorod was obliged to renounce the alliance of Lithuania and to pay tribute. After a second war, in 1478, **Novgorod's independence was ended** and the troublesome upper classes were deported to central Russia. In 1494 Ivan drove out the German merchants and closed the Hanseatic kontor. Thus he acquired the huge territory of Novgorod, extending eastward to the Urals. Indirectly he greatly reduced the danger of Lithuanian interference. The **annexation of Tver** (1485) put an end to the most formidable rival of Moscow.

1472. Marriage of Ivan with Zoë (Sophia), niece of the last Greek emperor of Constantinople. This was arranged by the pope in the hope of bringing the Russians into the Roman church, but all efforts in that direction failed. The marriage was of importance in establishing the claim of Russian rulers to be the successors of the Greek emperors and the protectors of Orthodox Christianity (theory of the Three Romes, of which Moscow was to be the third and last). It also served to introduce into Moscow the Byzantine conception of the autocrat (Ivan took the title of *Tsar,* i.e. Caesar) and the practice of court ceremonial. Rebuilding of the grand ducal palace (Kremlin) with the assistance of Italian architects brought in by Zoë. The court hierarchy (precedence in rank of princes and nobles, etc.).

1480. Ivan threw off the Tatar yoke after a last Tatar advance on Moscow. Ivan avoided open warfare, but took advantage of the Tatars' disunion. Mengli Girai, the khan of the Crimea, joined him against the Lithuanians.

1492. Invasion of Lithuania, made possible by dynastic troubles in Lithuania and Poland. A **second invasion** (1501) led to the conclusion of peace in 1503, which brought Russia many of the border territories of White Russia and Little Russia. Moscow had by this time become an important factor in European affairs and enjoyed a considerable prestige. Resumption of active diplomatic relations with western countries. The art of icon-painting reached its apogee in the 15th century: Master **Andrew Rublyor** (1370–1430)   (*Cont. p. 444.*)

d. HUNGARY, 1301–1490

(*From p. 265*)

At the beginning of the 14th century Hungary was already an essentially feudal country, in which the great magnates and the bishops, richly endowed with land, ruled as virtually independent potentates ("little kings"), while the lower nobility, organized in the *Comitats* (provincial governments), had, to a large degree, control of the administration. The nobility, freed of taxation, was responsible for defense, but acted only as it saw fit.

1301–1308. The **extinction of the Arpad dynasty** led to a period of conflict, during which Czech, German, and Italian parties each attempted to put their candidates on the throne. **Wencelas,** son of the king of Bohemia, thirteen years old, was first elevated, but could not maintain himself, nor could **Otto of Bavaria.**

1310–1342. CHARLES I (Charles Robert of Anjou), a grandson of Maria, the daughter of Stephen V, was elected and founded the brilliant and successful **Anjou line.** Charles established his capital at Visegrad and introduced Italian chivalry and western influences. After 15 years of effort he succeeded in subduing the "little kings" of whom **Matthias of Csak** and **Ladislas of Transylvania** were the most powerful. Recognizing the hopelessness of suppressing the nobility entirely, he regulated its position and obliged it to furnish specified contingents to the army. Regulation of taxation (first direct tax); encouragement of towns and trade. Charles left the royal power well entrenched, but only as part of an avowedly feudal order.

1342–1382. LOUIS (the Great), the son of Charles, a patron of learning who established a brilliant court at Buda. He attempted to solidify the position of his house in Naples and embarked on a successful expedition to Italy to avenge the murder of his brother Andrew (1347). In conjunction with Genoa he carried on a long struggle with Venice, which ended in the **peace of 1381:** Venice ceded Dalmatia and paid tribute. In the east the Hungarian power made itself felt throughout the Balkans: Serbia, Wallachia, and Moldavia recognized the suzerainty of Louis; foundation of the border districts (*banats*) south of the Danube and the Save, as protection against the Turkish advance. **War against the Turks:** Hungarian victory in northern Bulgaria (1366).

1370. Louis became king of Poland but paid little attention to his new obligations. In Hungary he continued the work of his father: the *jus aviticum* (1351) restricted the freedom of the great magnates to dispose of their property.

1382–1385. Maria of Anjou, queen. She was married to Sigismund of Luxemburg, who became guardian of the kingdom. His position was challenged by Charles of Durazzo and Naples, who had many adherents, especially in southern Hungary and Croatia.

1385–1386. Charles II (of Naples). He was assassinated after a very brief reign, which led to a new revolt in Croatia.

1387–1437. SIGISMUND (of Luxemburg), who became German emperor in 1410 and king of Bohemia in 1436. His reign marked a great decline in the royal power, due in large measure to Sigismund's constant absence from the country and his practice of selling royal domains in order to get money for his far-reaching schemes elsewhere. In general Sigismund relied on the towns and lesser nobility against the great magnates (who imprisoned him for four months in 1401). Hence the grant of ever greater rights to the comitats.

1396. The disastrous **crusade of Nicopolis** against the Turks (p. 000). Loss of Dalmatia to the Venetians. Hussite invasions of Hungary, resulting from Sigismund's attempts to gain the Bohemian throne.

1437-1439. Albert (Albrecht) of Hapsburg, son-in-law of Sigismund, also German emperor and king of Bohemia. He was obliged to sign far-reaching capitulations (nobles not obliged to fight beyond the frontiers).

1437. First victory of John Hunyadi over the Turks. Hunyadi was a powerful frontier lord of uncertain origin.

1440-1444. Vladislav I (Vladislav VI of Poland), a weak ruler, whose reign was distinguished chiefly by the continued victories of Hunyadi (1443). Crusade against the Turks.

1444, Nov. 10. Disaster at Varna and death of Vladislav.

1444-1457. Ladislas V, the son of Albert of Hapsburg, also king of Bohemia. He was only four years old at his accession and Hunyadi was therefore appointed governor of the kingdom until 1552.

1456. Crusade against the Turks, preached by John of Capistrano and led by Hunyadi. The Turks were turned back from the siege of Belgrade, but Hunyadi died in the same year.

1458-1490. MATTHIAS CORVINUS (the Just), the son of John Hunyadi and one of the greatest of the Hungarian kings. He was fifteen at his election, but soon distinguished himself as a soldier, statesman, and patron of art and learning. Intelligent, firm, crafty, yet just and noble, he re-established the power of the crown and made Hungary the dominant power in central Europe, if only for the brief space of his reign. He once again broke the power of the oligarchs and drew on the support of the lesser nobility. Development of a central administration; regulation and increase of the taxes. Great wealth and luxury of the court. The *Bibliotheca Corvina,* consisting of more than 10,000 manuscripts and books, many beautifully illuminated by Italian artists. Matthias the patron of Renaissance learning. Famous law code (1486). University of Buda (c. 1475) re-founded 1635. Development of Magyar literature. Creation of a standing army (Black Troop), composed first of Bohemian, Moravian, and Silesian mercenaries. This gave Matthias one of the most effective fighting forces in the Europe of his day. **Matthias' aims:** to secure the Bohemian throne and ultimately the empire and then to direct a united central Europe against the Turks. Long struggles against **George Podiebrad** of Bohemia ended with George's death in 1471, after Matthias had been proclaimed king of Bohemia (1470). Equally prolonged struggle

against Emperor Frederick III, who had been elected king of Hungary by a faction of nobles in 1439. Frederick was finally bought off (1462), but trouble continued. Matthias, disposing of much greater funds and forces than Frederick, conquered not only Silesia and Moravia, but also lower Austria. His capital established at Vienna (1485). Matthias died at 47, leaving Hungary the dominant state in central Europe and a decisive factor in European diplomacy. *(Cont. p. 448.)*

e. THE SERBIAN STATES, 1276-1499

(From p. 265)

By the end of the 13th century the Serbian states, like others of eastern Europe, had evolved a strong secular and clerical aristocracy which, to a large extent, controlled even the more outstanding rulers. In view of the general unsettlement of the law regarding succession and inheritance, the tendency toward dynastic conflict and territorial disruption was very pronounced. In the western Balkans the situation was further complicated by the rivalry of the western and eastern forms of Christianity, to say nothing of the persistence of the heretical Bogomil teaching, especially in Bosnia.

1276-1281. Dragutin, with the aid of the Hungarians, seized the Serbian throne from his father, **Urosh I.** Having been defeated in battle by the Greeks, he abdicated after a short rule.

1281-1321. Milyutin (Stephen Urosh II), the brother of Dragutin. He was a pious and yet dissolute ruler, but above all a political and religious opportunist. Taking full advantage of the growing weakness of the Byzantine Empire, he gradually extended his possessions in Macedonia, along the Adriatic, and, in the north, toward the Danube and the Save.

1321-1331. Stephen Dechanski (Stephen Urosh III), the illegitimate son of the preceding. His reign was marked chiefly by the great victory of the Serbs over the Greeks and Bulgarians near **Küstendil** (Velbuzhde) in 1330. The Serbs now held most of the Vardar Valley.

1331-1355. STEPHEN DUSHAN (Stephen Urosh IV), the greatest of the Serbian rulers in the Middle Ages. Dushan began his career by deposing his father, who was strangled soon afterward. For most of his reign he attempted to maintain friendly relations with Hungary and Ragusa, in order to have a free hand to exploit the dynastic war in the Byzantine Empire between the Palaeologi and John Cantacuzene. By 1344 he had subjected all of Macedonia, Albania, Thessaly, and Epirus. His daughter was married to the Bulgarian tsar and Bulgaria was under Serbian supremacy.

1346. Dushan set up his capital at Skoplye (üsküb) and proclaimed himself *Emperor of the Serbs, Greeks, Bulgars, and Albanians.* At the same time he set up a Serbian patriarchate at Peč (Ipek), for which he was anathematized by the Greek patriarch. Dushan established a court wholly Byzantine in character, with elaborate titles and ceremonial. In the years 1349–1354 he drew up his famous law code (*Zabonnik*), which gives an invaluable picture of Serbian conditions and culture at the time.

1349. Attack upon Dushan by the ruler of Bosnia. This led to the invasion of Bosnia by the Serbs, who found much support among the Bogomils, resentful of the Catholic proclivities of their rulers. The conquest of Bosnia was not completed because of Dushan's diversion elsewhere.

1353. Dushan defeated Louis of Hungary, who had been instigated by the pope to lead a Catholic crusade. The Serbs now acquired Belgrade.

1355. Dushan died at the age of 46 as he was en route to Constantinople. Thus perished his hope of succeeding to the imperial throne and consolidating the Balkans in the face of the growing power of the Ottoman Turks (p. 350).

1355–1371. Stephen Urosh V, a weak ruler who was faced from the outset by the disruptive ambitions of his uncle Simeon and other powerful magnates. He was the last of the Nemanyid house.

1358. Hungary obtained most of Dalmatia, after defeating Venice. Ragusa became a Hungarian protectorate.

1371. Battle of the Maritza River, in which the Turks, having settled in Thrace, defeated a combination of Serbian lords.

1371. Zeta (Montenegro) became a separate principality under the Balsha family (until 1421).

1371–1389. Lazar I, of the Hrebelyanovich family, became prince of Serbia.

1375. The Greek patriarch finally recognized the patriarchate of Peč.

1376. TVRTKO I, lord of Bosnia from 1353–1391, proclaimed himself *King of Serbia and Bosnia,* taking over parts of western Serbia and controlling most of the Adriatic coast, excepting Zara and Ragusa. Tvrtko was the greatest of the Bosnian rulers and made his state for a time the strongest Slavic state in the Balkans.

1389 (traditional June 15). **BATTLE OF KOSSOVO,** a decisive date in all Balkan history. **Prince Lazar,** at the head of a coalition of Serbs, Bosnians, Albanians, and Wallachians, attempted to stop the advance of the Turks under **Murad I.** Murad was killed by a Serb who posed as a traitor, but his son Bayazid won a victory. Lazar was captured and killed, due to the reputed desertion of Vuk Brankovich. Henceforth Serbia was a vassal state of the Turks.

1389–1427. STEPHEN LAZAREVICH, the son of Lazar I. He was a literary person, but withal an able statesman. During the early years of his reign he loyally supported the Turks, being present with his forces at the **battles of Nicopolis** (1396) and **Angora** (1402). In return the Turks recognized him as *despot of Serbia,* and supported him against Hungary and other enemies.

1391. Death of Tvrtko I of Bosnia; gradual disintegration of the Bosnian Kingdom.

1392. Venice acquired Durazzo, beginning the process of establishment on the Dalmatian and Albanian coasts. Scutari was acquired in 1396, and when, in 1420, Venice secured **Cattaro,** she possessed practically all the fortified coast towns.

1393. Hungary recovered Croatia and Dalmatia from the Bosnian Kingdom. Hungarian campaigns against Bosnia itself continued for years, until the native elements in 1416 called in the Turks.

1427–1456. GEORGE BRANKOVICH, the nephew of Stephen Lazarevich, despot of Serbia. He built himself a new capital at Semendria (Smederovo) on the Danube and attempted, with Hungarian support, to hold his own against the Turks. This policy led to a Turk invasion (1439) and conquest of the country, the Hungarians, however, saving Belgrade. But in 1444 Brankovich, with the aid of **John Hunyadi** (p. 351), recovered his possessions and the Serbian state was recognized in the **treaty of Szegedin.** Thereafter Brankovich deserted Hunyadi and tried to maintain himself through close relations with the Turks.

1456–1458. Lazar III, the son of George Brankovich. On his death he left his kingdom to

1458–1459. Stephen Tomashevich, the heir to the Bosnian throne. Stephen, as a Roman Catholic, was much disliked by the Serbs, who consequently offered less resistance to the Turks.

1459. The Turks definitively conquered and incorporated Serbia with the empire.

1463. The Turks overran and conquered Bosnia.

1483. Turkish conquest of Herzegovina (Hun).

1499. Conquest of Zeta (Montenegro) by the Turks.

f. THE BYZANTINE EMPIRE, 1261-1453

(*From p. 284*)

After the recapture of Constantinople by the Greeks in 1261, the **empire of the Paleologi** was still a relatively small domain, consisting of the former Nicaean Empire, the city of Constantinople and its immediate surroundings, the coastal part of Thrace, southern Macedonia with Thessalonica, the islands of Imbros, Samothrace, Lesbos, and Rhodes. In Anatolia the northeastern part was still held by the Greek **empire of Trebizond,** which in the course of the 13th century had managed to hold a balance between the Seljuk Turks and the Mongols and had become the great entrepôt of the eastern trade coming to the Black Sea by way of Persia and Armenia. The city and the court reached their highest prosperity and brilliance under the Emperor **Alexius II** (1297-1330), whose reign was followed by a period of dynastic and factional struggle, marked by unbelievable degeneracy and cruelty. The reign of **John Alexius III** (1350-1390) marked a second period of splendor, but the 15th century was one of decline. The empire of Trebizond ended with the Ottoman conquest in 1461 (last ruler, **David,** 1458-1461).

The European territories of the earlier empire were divided between the Greek despotate of Epirus and the Greek duchy of Neopatras (Thessaly, Locris), the Latin duchy of Athens, the Latin principality of Achaea, and the Venetian duchy of the Archipelago.

1259-1282. MICHAEL VIII (Paleologus). He was the ablest of the Paleologi, a man who devoted himself to the restoration of Byzantine authority throughout the Balkan area, persisting despite many setbacks.

1261. Michael established a foothold in the southeastern part of the Peloponnese (Morea). **Mistra** (Misithra) became the capital of a flourishing principality and one of the great centers of late-Byzantine culture.

1262. Michael II of Epirus was forced to recognize the suzerainty of the Constantinople emperor. In a series of campaigns much of the despotate was regained for the empire (Janina taken, 1265).

1264-1265. Constant raids of the Bulgars into Thrace led to a formidable campaign against them and the reconquest of part of Macedonia.

1266. Charles of Anjou became king of Sicily. He made an alliance with Baldwin II, the last Latin emperor, and, through the marriage of his son with the heiress of the Villehardouins, extended his authority over Achaea. He soon became the most formidable opponent of the Greeks, for by the **treaty of Viterbo** (1267) he took over the claims of Baldwin II.

1267. Michael permitted the Genoese to establish themselves at Galata, across from Constantinople. This was part of his policy of encouraging the Genoese at the expense of the Venetians, to whom, however, he had to grant privileges also (1268).

1269. Defeat of the Greeks by the Turks at Baphaeon.

1271. Death of Michael II of Epirus. Charles of Anjou had already taken Corfu (1267) and now undertook the conquest of the Epiran coast, the essential base for any advance on Thessalonica and Constantinople. Durazzo was taken in 1272. **John Angelus,** driven out of Epirus, set up as lord of Neopatras (to 1295). **Nicephorus I** was the titular ruler of a much-reduced Epiran state (to 1296). Charles of Anjou proclaimed himself *king of Albania* and entered into alliance with the Serbs, who had begun the construction of a large state by advancing down the Vardar Valley.

1274. THE COUNCIL OF LYON. Michael, in order to escape from the Angevin danger, accepted the Roman creed and the primacy of the pope, thus effecting the **reunion with Rome.** This move, purely political in intent, met with vigorous resistance on the part of the Orthodox Greek.

1274. Campaigns of Michael against the Angevins in Epirus. These campaigns were carried on year after year, with varying success.

1278. The death of William of Villehardouin, prince of Achaea, gave the Greeks an opportunity to expand their holding in the southeastern part.

1281. Michael VIII won a great victory over the Angevins at **Berat.** Thereupon Charles made an alliance with the papacy and with Venice, with which the Serbs and Bulgars were associated. Michael in reply effected a rapprochement with Peter of Aragon.

1282. The Sicilian Vespers (p. 313). This blow at the Angevin power in Sicily served to relieve the pressure on the Greek Empire.

1282-1328. ANDRONICUS II, the son of Michael, a learned, pious, but weak ruler, whose first move was to give up the hated union with Rome and conciliate the Orthodox clergy.

1285. Venice deserted the Angevin alliance and made a ten-year peace with the Greeks.

1295-1320. MICHAEL IX, son of Andronicus, co-emperor with his father.

1296. The Serbs, continuing their advance, conquered western Macedonia and northern Albania. Andronicus was obliged to recognize these losses (1298).

1302. Peace between the Angevins and the

346

The Paleologus Family (1260–1453)

(From p. 270)

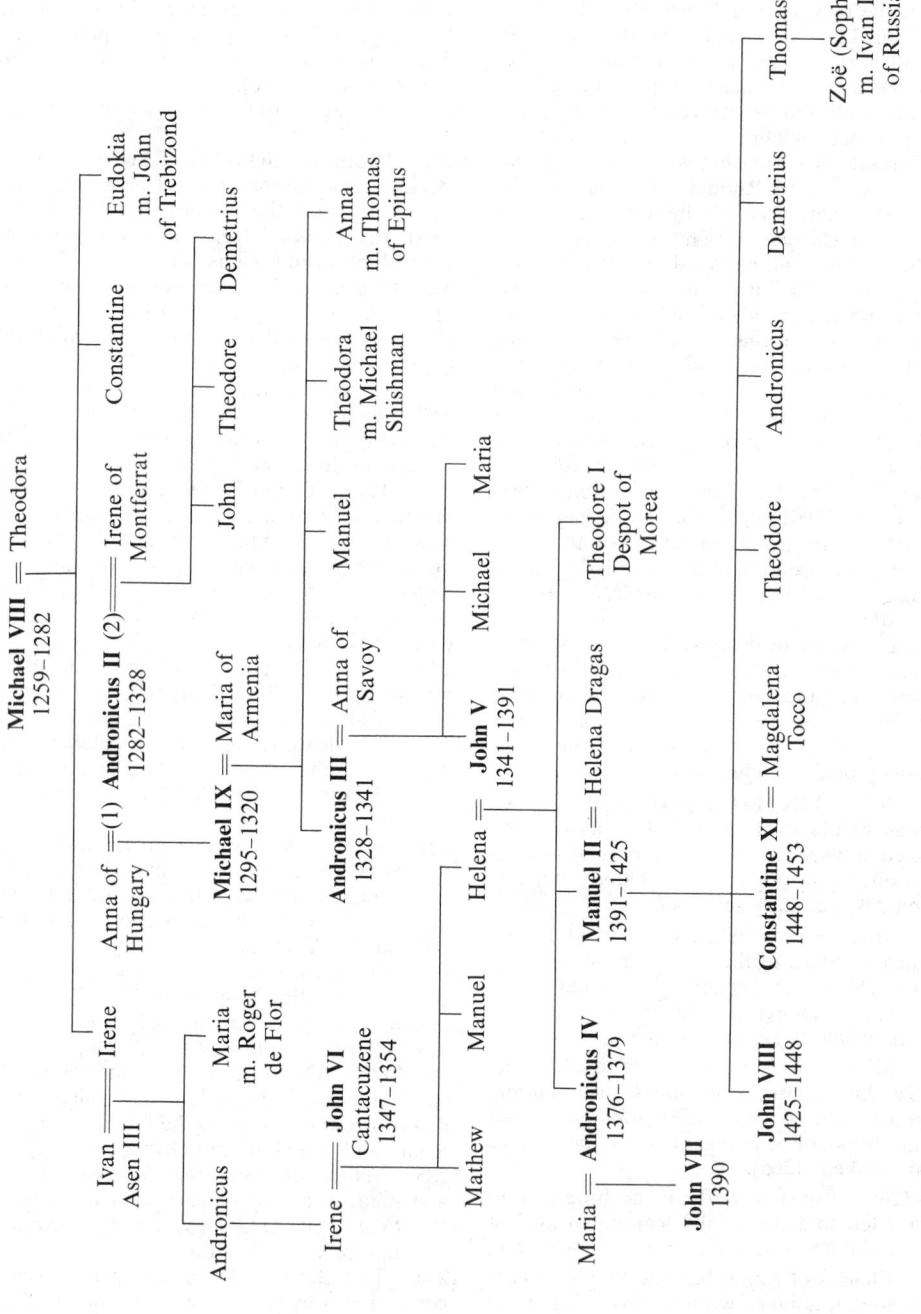

(Cont. p. 451.)

Aragonese. Andronicus, once again exposed to Angevin ambition, engaged **Roger de Flor** and 6000 Catalan mercenaries (the Catalan Company) to fight against the Italians. They raised havoc at Constantinople, where 3000 Italians are said to have been killed in the disorders.

1304. The Catalans repulsed an attack of the Turks on Philadelphia, but they then turned and attacked Constantinople (1305–1307), without being able to take it.

1305. Murder of Roger de Flor. The Catalan Company became a veritable scourge, roaming through Thrace and Macedonia and laying the country waste.

1311. The Catalans, having advanced into Greece, took the duchy of Athens, where they set up a dynasty of their own.

1321–1328. Civil war between the emperor and his grandson Andronicus. In the course of the struggle much of the empire was devastated.

1325. Andronicus was obliged to accept his grandson as co-emperor.

1326. RISE OF THE OTTOMAN TURKS in northwestern Anatolia. In 1326 they took Brusa (Bursa) from the Greeks, and in 1337 Nicomedia (p. 350).

1328–1341. ANDRONICUS III, the grandson of Andronicus II, who finally forced the emperor's abdication (d. 1332). Andronicus III was a frivolous and irresponsible ruler, wholly unequal to the great problems presented by the rise of the Turkish and Serb powers (Sultan Orkhan, 1326–1359; Tsar Stephen Dushan, 1331–1355).

1329. The Greeks managed to take the important island of Chios from the Genoese.

1330. The Serbs defeated the Bulgars in a decisive battle and put an end to the Bulgar power.

1334–1335. Andronicus conquered Thessaly and part of Epirus from the despot, John II Orsini.

1336. The Greeks reconquered Lesbos.

1340. Stephen Dushan, having conquered the Albanian coastal territory (as far as Valona) from the Angevins, drove the Greeks out of the interior and took Janina.

1341–1376. JOHN V, the son of Andronicus III, ascended the throne as a child, under the regency of his mother, Anna of Savoy.

1341–1347. CIVIL WAR IN THE EMPIRE. John Cantacuzene, supported by the aristocratic elements, set himself up as a rival emperor. John V was supported by the popular elements. In the ensuing war much of Thrace and Macedonia was ravaged. The war was the undoing of the empire, since both sides freely called in Serbs or Turks to support them.

1341–1351. The **HESYCHAST CONTROVERSY** in the Greek church, which added to the confusion. The controversy was really a conflict between the mystic teachings emanating from the monasteries of Mt. Athos (founded 962 ff.) and the rationalism of the clergy. The Hesychasts (Zealots) supported Cantacuzene and were victorious with him. In the interval the dispute led to a great popular, almost socialistic **rising in Thessalonica,** where the extremists set up an almost independent state (1342–1347).

1343. The Venetians, taking advantage of the civil war, seized Smyrna.

1346. Stephen Dushan was crowned emperor of the Serbs and the Greeks and made preparations to seize Constantinople and replace the Greek dynasty.

1347. Cantacuzene managed to take Constantinople, through treachery.

1347–1354. JOHN VI (Cantacuzene), sole emperor. He made his son Manuel despot of the Morea (1348). The Serbs held all of Macedonia.

1351. Stephen Dushan besieged Thessalonica.

1353. The **Ottoman Turks,** called in by Cantacuzene, defeated the Serbs.

1354. The Turks established themselves in Europe, at Gallipoli, thus beginning their phenomenal career of expansion (p. 350).

1354. John V took Constantinople and forced the abdication of Cantacuzene (d. 1383). At the same time Dushan, having taken Adrianople, was advancing on the capital. His sudden death (1355) led to the disintegration of the Serb Empire and to the removal of a great threat to the Greeks. On the other hand, it left the Christians an easier prey to the advancing Turks.

1365. The Turks, having overrun Thrace, took Adrianople, which became their capital.

1366. John V, who had been captured by Tsar Shishman of Bulgaria, was liberated by his cousin, Amadeus of Savoy.

1369. John V appeared before the pope at Avignon and agreed to union of the churches, in order to secure the aid of the west against the Turks.

1376–1379. ANDRONICUS IV, the son of John V, who dethroned his father with the aid of the Genoese.

1379–1391. John V, supported by the Turks, managed to recover his throne.

1386. The Venetians recovered Corfu, which they held until 1797.

1388. The Venetians purchased Argos and Nauplia.

1389. Battle of Kossovo (p. 344). End of the great Serb Empire.

1390. John VII, a grandson of John V, deposed the latter, but after a few months the old emperor was restored by his second son, Manuel.

1391–1425. MANUEL II, an able ruler in a hopeless position. By this time the empire had been reduced to the city of Constantinople, the city of Thessalonica, and the province of Morea. The Turks held Thrace and Macedonia.

1391–1395. The Turks, under Bayazid I, blockaded Constantinople, and only the Christian crusade that ended in the disastrous **battle of Nicopolis** (1396) gave the Greeks some respite.

1397. Bayazid attacked Constantinople, which was valiantly defended by Marshal Boucicaut. This time the advance of the Tatars under Timur distracted the Turks. The defeat and capture of Bayazid in the **battle of Angora** (1402), led to a period of confusion and dynastic war among the Turks (p. 351).

1422. The Turks again attacked Constantinople, because of Manuel's support of the Turkish pretender Mustapha, against Murad II.

1423. The Venetians bought the city of Thessalonica.

1425–1448. JOHN VIII, the son of Manuel, whose position was, from the outset, desperate.

1428. Constantine and Thomas Paleologus, brothers of the emperor, conquered Frankish Morea, with the exception of the Venetian ports.

1430. The Turks took Thessalonica from the Venetians.

1439. THE COUNCIL OF FLORENCE. John VIII, having traveled to Italy, once again accepted the union with Rome and the papal primacy. As on earlier occasions this step raised a storm of opposition among the Greeks and to some extent facilitated the Turk conquests.

1444. A second crusade from the west ended in disaster when the Turks won a decisive victory at **Varna.**

1446. The Turks frustrated an attempt of the Greeks to expand from the Morea into central Greece. Corinth fell into Turkish hands.

1448–1453. CONSTANTINE XI, the last Byzantine emperor.

1453. The siege and **capture of Constantinople** by **Mohammed the Conqueror** (p. 352). **End of the Byzantine Empire** after a thousand years of existence.

1460. Conquest of the Morea by the Turks. End of the rule of the Paleologi in Greece.

1461. Conquest of the empire of Trebizond, the last Greek state, by the Turks.

BYZANTINE CULTURE in the time of the Paleologi. The territorial and political decline of the empire was accompanied by an extraordinary cultural revival, analogous to the Renaissance in Italy. The schools of Constantinople flourished and produced a group of outstanding scholars (philosophy: **Planudes, Plethon, Bessarion**). In theology the dominant current was one of mysticism (**Gregory Palamas** and the Hesychasts; **George Scholarius**). Historical writing reached a high plane in the work of **John Cantacuzene, Nicephorus Gregoras,** and, in the last years of the empire, of **Phrantzes, Ducas, and Chalcocondylas.** Art, especially painting, was distinctly humanized and three different schools (Constantinople, Macedonia, and Crete) cast a flood of splendor over the closing years of the empire. **Mistra,** the capital of the Morean province, became in the early 15th century the center of a revived Greek national feeling and a home of scholars and artists.

g. THE OTTOMAN EMPIRE, 1300–1481

(From p. 274)

The presence of the Turks in central Asia can be traced back to at least the 6th century (**Orchon inscriptions,** in Turkish, dealing with the period 630–680). These Turks, of the Oghuz family, were conquered by the Uighur Turks in 745 and continued under their rule until 840, when the Uighurs in turn were conquered by the Kirghiz Turks coming from the west. In the 9th and 10th centuries the Turks were converted to Islam, and in the 11th century, having pushed their advance into southeastern Russia and Iran, they began to attack the Byzantine Empire. The **Seljuks,** a branch of the Oghuz Turks, took **Baghdad** in 1055, and in the following two centuries built up an imposing empire in Anatolia and the Middle East (p. 272).

1243. The **Mongols** defeated the Seljuks at **Kösedagh.** Anatolia under Mongol suzerainty; disintegration of the Seljuk Empire in Anatolia.

1261–1310. Foundation of new **Turkish principalities** on the Aegean coast, which was conquered from the Byzantines by Turkish chiefs or lords of the border. The influx of Turkish population, the revival of the Holy War, as well as the withdrawal of the Byzantine frontier guards to the Balkans were the main reasons for this development.

1290 (?)–1326. OSMAN, son of one of the border chiefs, was the founder of the principality called Osmanli (Ottoman) in Bithynia. The immigration into these frontier states consisted not only of semi-nomadic tribesmen, but also of civilized townsmen from central Anatolia. Osman allied himself with the **Akhis,**

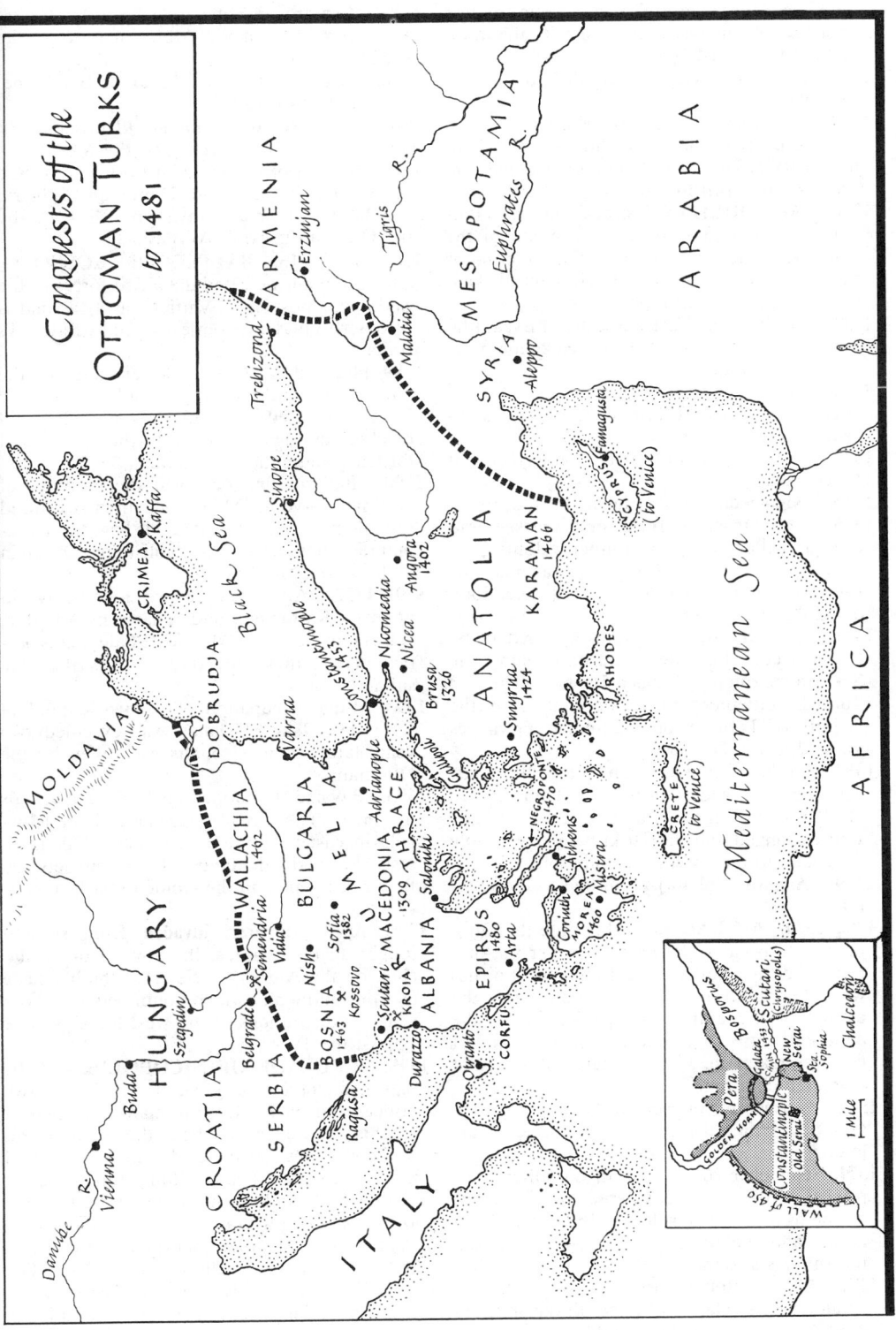

Conquests of the
OTTOMAN TURKS
to 1481

members of a fraternity, who became the first organizers of the Ottoman state, with the traditional Islamic institutions.

1301. Turkish victory over the Greeks at **Baphaeon.**

1304. The Turks conquered **Ephesus.**

1317–1326. Siege of Brusa (Bursa) by the Ottoman Turks. The town was finally starved into submission (April 6).

1326–1362. ORKHAN I struck the first Ottoman coin and took the title of sultan of the **Ghazis** (warriors of the faith). His dominions came to extend from Ankara in central Anatolia to Thrace in Europe.

1329, June 10. The Turks defeated a Byzantine force under Andronicus III at **Pelekanon,** near the present Maltepe.

1331, March 2. Nicaea (Iznik) taken by the Turks. The first Turkish college was established there.

1333. Orkhan's victory over the Greeks at **Pelekanon.**

1335. Nicomedia (Ismid) taken by the Turks.

1345. The **Ottoman Turks first crossed into Europe,** called in by the Emperor John Cantacuzene to support his claims against the Empress Anna. Orkhan married Theodora, daughter of Cantacuzene.

1352. The Ottoman Turks again called in by Cantacuzene, this time to aid him against the Serbian conqueror, **Stephen Dushan.** The first Turkish settlement in Europe made in the vicinity of Tzympe, on Gallipoli. Privileges granted to the Genoese.

1354, March. Gallipoli taken by the Ottomans. They then spread rapidly over Thrace. On Orkhan's death the Ottoman state was already well organized and the Turkish ruler was able to dictate to the Byzantine emperors.

1359. Angora (Ankara) submitted to the Ottomans.

1362–1389. MURAD I. In his time the Ottoman state became the leading power in Anatolia and the Balkans. **Adrianople** (Edirne) was taken in 1361, and after 1402 became the capital of the empire. Organization of the **Janissary corps** (date uncertain), composed of captives taken in war, and later of levies of Christian children.

1366. Crusade of Amadeus of Savoy. He took Gallipoli, which the Turks recovered ten years later.

1371, September 26. Defeat of the allied Serb princes of Macedonia at **Chermanon** (Chirmen) on the Maritza. The rulers of Bulgaria, Macedonia, and the Byzantine Empire recognized the sultan's suzerainty.

1377–1386. Ottoman expansion in central Anatolia; first clash with the **Karamanids of Koniah** (siege of Koniah in 1387).

1385. Capture of Sofia by the Turks; defeat and submission of the Albanian lords at the **battle of Voissa.**

1386. Capture of Nish. Lazar of Serbia became a Turkish vassal.

1387. Capture of Saloniki (Thessalonica); Turkish raids into Greece and the Morea.

1388. Defeat of the Turks in Bosnia; coalition of Serbia, Bosnia, and Danubian Bulgaria against the Ottomans. Invasion of Bulgaria by the Ottoman general, Ali Pasha.

1389, June 15. BATTLE OF KOSSOVO. The Ottomans defeated the allied forces of the Serbs and Bosnians. Murad was assassinated by a Serb, and Lazar was executed by Bayazid's order.

1389–1402. BAYAZID I. Chosen sultan on the battlefield of Kossovo, he had his brother Yakub strangled. Saloniki was lost. Bayazid reached an agreement with the Serbs and turned his attention to Anatolia.

1390. Bayazid first occupied the emirates of Saruhan, Aydin, Mentezhe, then captured Philadelphia. He defeated Ali beg, the Karamanid ruler, thus re-establishing Ottoman authority in Anatolia.

1391–1392. After two expeditions, Bayazid annexed **Kastamonu** and **Amasia** in Anatolia. Raids into Albania. Manuel II Paleologus participated in these operations as vassal of the sultan.

1393. Final occupation of **Trnovo,** capital of Bulgaria. **Tsar Shishman** was executed two years later when **Nicopolis** was taken by the Ottomans.

1393. Bayazid summoned his European vassals to Serez. The threat of **Timur and the Mongols** in eastern Anatolia encouraged them to resist Bayazid's demands. Coalition between Bayazid, Egypt, and the Golden Horde against Timur.

1395, April. Bayazid invaded Hungary and fought against **Mircea,** the voyvod of Wallachia, on the Argesh. He started the **blockade of Constantinople,** which continued for seven years. Preparations in the west for a crusade against the Turks.

1395. CRUSADE OF NICOPOLIS, led by **Sigismund of Hungary,** supported by Balkan princes and by French, German, and English knights, as well as by both the Roman and Avignon popes. Venice and Genoa negotiated with both sides. The crusading forces assembled at Buda and advanced along the Danube to Nicopolis, pillaging and slaying as they went. On September 25 they met the Turks about four miles south of Nicopolis. The knights ignored all advice and pressed forward; after an initial success they were completely overwhelmed and many were captured. The

pressed forward; after an initial success they were completely overwhelmed and many were captured. The forces numbered about 20,000 on each side.

1397. The **siege of Constantinople** pressed more vigorously by the sultan, while Evrenuz made further conquests in Greece. Bayazid again defeated the Karamanids and occupied Konia.

1398–1399. The sultan took **Sivas** and annexed the entire area west of the Euphrates, thus incurring the enmity of the sultan of Egypt. At the same time depossessed Turkish emirs called Timur into Anatolia.

1400. Timur took and sacked Sivas. War between him and Bayazid became inevitable when the latter retaliated by taking **Erzinjan.**

1402, July 28 (not 20). **BATTLE OF ANGORA** (Ankara). Bayazid, deserted by most of his Turkish vassals, was completely defeated and captured. Timur restored many of the Turkish emirs and himself advanced as far as Smyrna and Bursa. The Ottoman Empire on the verge of dissolution. Dispute of Bayazid's sons for the succession.

1403–1413. Civil War. Bayazid died in captivity (1403) and his three sons, **Isa** in Bursa, **Suleiman** in Edirne, **Mehmed** in Amasia, began to fight each other for control of Bursa and Edirne and for the acquisition of supreme power.

1404. Mehmed defeated Isa and took Bursa, whereupon Suleiman intervened.

1405. Suleiman crossed to Anatolia and drove Mehmed into the mountains. Most of the emirs restored by Timur were reduced to obedience.

1409. Mehmed sent his brother **Musa** to Wallachia to threaten Suleiman's European possessions.

1410. Suleiman returned to Europe and defeated Musa near Constantinople. Meanwhile Mehmed reoccupied Bursa.

1411, June 5. Suleiman was attacked by Musa, who was joined by the warlike frontier elements and by the Serbs. Suleiman was defeated and killed at Edirne, but Musa's radical policy soon alienated his supporters.

1413. Musa threatened Constantinople and the Serbs who had allied themselves with Mehmed. The latter finally defeated and killed Musa and thereupon was able to reunite the Ottoman possessions.

1413–1421. Mehmed I (the Restorer *or Kirishdji*). He conciliated the Serbs and the Byzantine emperor, who held as a hostage **Mustafa,** Mehmed's elder brother and a pretender to the throne.

1414. Mehmed defeated the Karamanids and restored the Ottoman overlordship over the emirs of Anatolia. Nonetheless, the Karamanids remained restless for some years to come.

1415. Mustafa attempted to overthrow Mehmed. A great social-religious rising led by **Sheikh Bedreddin** was put down with difficulty in 1416.

1416. First war with Venice, due chiefly to Turkish activity in the Aegean. The Venetian admiral, **Giovanni Loredano** (later doge), destroyed a Turkish fleet off Gallipoli, whereupon the sultan made peace.

1417. Mehmed invaded Wallachia to punish Mircea, who had supported both Mustafa and Bedreddin.

1421–1451. MURAD II proclaimed sultan in Bursa.

1421. Mustafa, released by the Byzantine emperor, was proclaimed sultan in Adrianople. In 1422 he attempted to take Bursa, but was taken prisoner and executed. Murad, to revenge himself on the Greek emperor, undertook a serious **siege of Constantinople,** but when his brother Mustafa rose against him in Anatolia he had to abandon the siege (June–August). A treaty of peace with the Greek emperor was signed in February 1424.

1439. Murad annexed the whole of Serbia, whose prince (despot), **George Brankovich,** fled to Hungary.

1440. Murad's vain **siege of Belgrade,** which had been in Hungarian possession since 1427.

1441–1442. Two Ottoman armies were defeated in Transylvania by its governor, **John Hunyadi,** who became famous as the Christian champion in defense against the Turks.

1443. Battle of Zlatica (Izladi). An army under **Vladislav,** king of both Hungary and Poland, supported by Hunyadi and by George Brankovich, took Nish and Sofia and was stopped in its advance only at Zlatica (a Balkan pass) by Murad. This daring campaign evoked great enthusiasm and agitation for a crusade in the west.

1444, June 12. Truce of Adrianople (Edirne), which was ratified in Szegedin (Hungary) in August. Under its terms Brankovich was restored to his despotate. Murad also made **peace with Karaman** and then voluntarily abdicated in favor of his twelve-year-old son, Mehmed (August). **THE VARNA CRUSADE.** The Hungarians, encouraged by the papal representative, thereupon broke the truce and renewed the crusade (September). They advanced through Bulgaria to the coast at Varna. Murad was called from his retirement to take command of the army. The Venetian fleet, cruising in the Dardanelles, tried to prevent the Ottoman forces from crossing from Asia to Europe, but was foiled when Murad crossed and defeated the crusaders (only the Hungarians and the Wallachians took part) at **Varna** on November 10. Vladislav was killed and a great many knights taken prisoner.

1444–1446. Mohammed (Mehmed) II, whose first short reign was unsuccessful.

1446–1451. Second reign of Murad II. An insurrection in Adrianople, instigated by grand vizir **Khalil,** brought Murad back to the throne.

1448. Turkish expedition against **Scanderbeg** (George Castriota), an Albanian chieftain, followed by the **second battle of Kossovo,** where Murad defeated Hunyadi.

1450. Second Turkish expedition against Scanderbeg, again without decisive result.

1451–1481. MOHAMMED II (the Conqueror). He can be considered as the real founder of the Ottoman Empire with its centralist administration and its firm territorial basis in Rumelia and Anatolia. In this huge area he put an end to all local dynasties, and drove out the Hungarians and the Venetians. Mohammed was at once an inexorable conqueror and a broad-minded ruler, who assembled at his court Muslim, Greek, and Italian scholars.

1451. Mohammed campaigned in Anatolia to reassert Ottoman authority over the rebellious Turkish emirs.

1452. Mohammed completed the **Castle of Europe** (*Rumili Hisar*) at the narrowest point of the Bosporus, opposite the older **Castle of Asia** (*Anadoli Hisar*). This assured him freedom of passage between Anatolia and Rumelia and at the same time enabled him to control the supply of Constantinople. Its construction led at once to war between Mohammed and the last Greek emperor, Constantine (June).

1453, Apr. 6–May 29. SIEGE AND FALL OF CONSTANTINOPLE, at that time largely depopulated and very poor. Constantine had only some 10,000 men at his command and was unpopular because of his efforts to reunite the eastern and western churches. He received some aid from the Venetians and Genoese, but his chief asset was the tremendous system of fortifications which had defended the city for a thousand years. The Turks concentrated between 100,000 and 150,000 men outside the city. Though the sultan had a substantial fleet, this was shut out from the Golden Horn by a great iron chain. The most important role was played by the Turkish artillery, especially by the huge guns built by a Hungarian renegade, **Urban.** The walls were continuously bombarded, but for a long time the defenders managed to close the breaches. Finally Mohammed had some 70 small ships dragged overland from the Bosporus to the Golden Horn, thereby forcing the defenders to divide their attention. On May 29, the

Turks delivered a great attack on the Romanos Gate and forced an entry. **Constantine was killed** in the ensuing melée and many of the defenders took refuge on the Venetian and Genoese ships. The city was given up to pillage for three days. Mohammed tried at first to populate it with Turks but then began to settle Greeks and other Christians, chiefly artisans. He gave the patriarch, **Gennadios,** considerable civil as well as religious authority over the Orthodox inhabitants of the entire empire. Somewhat later similar authority over the Armenian and Jewish communities was conferred upon the Armenian patriarch and the Grand Rabbi (*millet system*). Constantinople (Istanbul) soon became the Ottoman capital, with a population of some 70,000 at the end of the reign. Churches were transformed into mosques (notably *Santa Sophia*) and palaces built (*Old Serai,* completed 1458; *New Serai,* completed 1467). The seat of government now became firmly fixed and the Ottoman administrative system was developed, with an elaborate system of training (palace school; slave household). Some of the court ceremonial could be traced to the Greeks, but most institutions were fundamentally Turkish and Islamic.

1455. Mohammed annexed southern Serbia; treaty with the despot. Genoese colonies in the Black Sea made tributaries.

1456. The sultan besieged **Belgrade,** which was relieved by Hunyadi shortly before his death (Aug.).

1458–1459. The Turks annexed the rest of Serbia, with Smederovo.

1458–1460. Conquest of the Morea.

1461. Conquest of the Black Sea coast, with the principality of **Kastamonu** and the **empire of Trebizond.**

1463–1464. Mohammed invaded Bosnia and Herzegovina, while the Hungarians recaptured Yaiche, the Bosnian capital.

1463–1479. GREAT WAR BETWEEN THE TURKS AND THE VENETIANS, resulting from Turkish interference with Venetian privileges in the Levant trade, and from Venetian apprehension about the future of the outposts on the Greek and Albanian coasts. The humanist pope, **Pius II,** attempted to organize a crusade and Hungary did in fact join Venice. But only a small, miscellaneous force of crusaders was assembled at Ancona. In 1470 a huge Turkish fleet and landing force took Euboea (Negroponte) from the Venetians, but in 1472, a Venetian-Papal fleet burned Smyrna (Izmir) and Adalia and tried to supply firearms to Venice's ally, **Uzun Hasan** of the Akkoyunlu. On August 11, 1473, in the critical **battle of Ot-**

luk-beli (on the upper Euphrates) Mohammed defeated Hasan and not only assured his
own rule over Anatolia, but deprived Venice of
its most formidable ally. In 1477 Turkish raiders reached the very outskirts of Venice, and in
1478 Mohammed took **Kroia, Alessio** and **Dri-
vasto** from the Venetians. Scutari held out.
On January 25, 1479, peace was concluded:
the Venetians gave up Scutari and the other
Albanian stations, but kept Dulcigno, Antivari,
and Durazzo; they accepted the loss of Negro-

ponte and Lemnos and thenceforth paid an
annual tribute of 10,000 ducats for trade privileges in the Ottoman Empire.

1480, Aug. 11. A Turkish force occupied
Otranto in southern Italy. On the other hand,
Mohammed failed to take **Rhodes**, which was
besieged from May until August and valiantly
defended by the Knights of St. John.

1481, May 3. Mohammed died as he was about
to begin another campaign in Anatolia.

(*Cont. p. 450.*)

D. AFRICA DURING THE MIDDLE AGES

AFRICA

(*For the history of Mediterranean Africa see p. 286.*)

THE EARLIEST HISTORY of Africa is shrouded in
obscurity. In the north the original inhabitants
appear to have been of some white stock (the
ancestors of the Berbers), while south of the
Sahara the country was populated by Negrillos,
a small race of Negroes of whom the Pygmies,
Bushmen, and Hottentots are probably the descendants. The Negrillos were evidently pushed
to the northwest and south by a great invasion
(possibly c. 30,000 B.C.) of a larger Negro race
arriving from the other side of the Indian Ocean
and landing on the central part of the eastern
coast. From the newcomers the Bantu derive.
A second great invasion from overseas followed
and pushed the Negrillos even farther to the
west, though there seems to have been much
intermixture in the region north of the equator,
forming the various Sudanese tribes. In all
likelihood there was also a good deal of infiltration of Semitic stocks into the northern part of
the continent, both west (Carthage) and east
(Syria). The earlier inhabitants were chiefly
hunters, but the Negro invaders brought pastoral
and agricultural pursuits and introduced polished stone and iron. Very few monuments of
the earlier ages have survived. The great stone
ruins **(Zimbabwe)** of Rhodesia have been variously dated from the 10th century B.C. to the
15th century A.D. They may have been built by
the Bantu, though the weight of expert opinion
seems to favor the Sabaeans from the Yemen
(10th century A.D.) or Dravidians from India.
c. 1st to 6th centuries A.D. The **kingdom of
Axum** in northern Ethiopia and southwestern
Arabia (obelisks of Axum); direct contact with
the Greek world; conversion of the country to
Christianity by **Frumentius** (early 4th century).
The connection with the Christian east was
broken by the Arab conquests (640–).

**640–710. CONQUEST OF NORTH AFRICA
BY THE ARABS,** beginning with Egypt and
spreading westward (p. 200 et seq.).

c. 980. Settlement of Arabs from Muscat and
Persians from Shiraz and Bushire along the
eastern coast, south as far as Cape Corrientes.
They founded Mogdishu, Melinde, Mombasa,
Kilwa (Quiloa), and Sofala and traded with
the interior natives in slaves, ivory, and gold
that was shipped to India and Arabia.

10th century. Apogee of the kingdom of Ghana
(capital Kumbi), which had been founded in
the 4th century, supposedly by people of Semitic extraction. It extended from near the
Atlantic coast almost to Timbuktu and was an
essentially Negro state consisting of a group of
federated tribes with a surprisingly developed
culture (visits of the Arabs Ibn Haukal and
Masudi in the late 10th century). There appears to have been an active trade with Morocco by way of the Sahara.

1054. Beginning of the **Islamic conquest** of
West Africa by the Almoravids under Abdallah
ben Yassin. Several of the native dynasties
were converted, though the masses appear to
have retained their original beliefs.

1076. The Almoravids pillaged Kumbi, the
capital of Ghana, which never entirely recovered. Its decline was evidently hastened by
the growing barrenness of the region. The
breakup of the Ghana Empire led to the formation (11th century) of succession states
(Diara, which existed till 1754, Soso, the two
Mossi states south of the bend of the Niger,
and Manding). Both the rulers of Manding
and Songhoy were converted to Islam, Songhoy
being a great empire which rose (c. 690) on
the middle Niger ·and came to divide West
Africa with Manding.

1203. Sumanguru, greatest of the rulers of Soso, plundered Kumbi.

1224. Sumanguru conquered and annexed Manding.

1235. Sun Diata, powerful king of the Mandingos, defeated the ruler of Soso and re-established his independence. In 1240 he destroyed Kumbi.

1307-1332. Apogee of the Mandingo Empire under **Gongo Musa,** who extended his dominions until they covered most of West Africa, after defeating and subjecting the Songhoy Empire (1325). Brilliant culture of Timbuktu (founded 12th century).

1352-1353. The great Arab traveler, **Ibn Batuta,** having crossed the Sahara, visited the Mandingo Empire, of which he wrote a description.

1433. The Tuaregs from the Sahara took and sacked Timbuktu.

1433. The **Portuguese explorers** first rounded Cape Bojador, beginning a long series of expeditions along the coast (p. 385).

1468. The Songhoy ruler recaptured Timbuktu from the Tuaregs.

1471. The Portuguese founded the post of San Jorge d'el Mina on the Guinea coast.

1490. The Portuguese ascended the Congo for about 200 miles and converted the king of the Congo Empire (14th century-). They established a post at **São Salvador** and exercised a wide influence in the region until the end of the 16th century.

1493-1529. Greatness of the Songhoy Empire under **Askia Mohammed,** who conquered the larger part of the Mandingo Empire and pushed his conquests to the east beyond the Niger. Visit of Leo Africanus (1507).

1505-1507. The Portuguese took Sofala and Kilwa from the Arabs and founded Mozambique. In 1513 they ascended the Zambezi, establishing posts at Sena and Tete. Missionaries probably penetrated much of the hinterland, but details are not known.

(*Cont. p. 563.*)

E. ASIA DURING THE MIDDLE AGES

1. PERSIA, 1349-1497

(*From p. 286*)

1349. The end of the troubled reign of **Nushirwan** was also the end of the dynasty of the Il-Khans of Persia. They were succeeded by

1336-1411. The Jalayrs, in Iraq and Azerbaijan;

1313-1393. The Muzaffarids in Fars, Kirman, and Kurdistan;

1337-1381. The Sarbadarids in Khorasan. The Muzaffarids and Sarbadarids were overthrown by Timur, and the Jalayrs by

1378-1469. The **Turkomans of the Black Sheep,** who ruled Azerbaijan and Armenia until they were succeeded by

1387-1502. The **Turkomans of the White Sheep.**

1369-1405. TIMUR (Tamerlane), the vizir of the Mongol Chagatay Khan Suyurghatmish, usurped the power of his master. Between the years 1380 and 1387 he overran Khorasan, Jurjan, Mazandaran, Sijistan, Afghanistan, Fars, Azerbaijan, and Kurdistan. In 1391 he completely defeated Toqtamish, the khan of the Golden Horde.

1393. Timur took Baghdad and reduced Mesopotamia. After an invasion of India (1397) he marched against Anatolia and routed the Ottoman Turks at **Angora** (p. 351). The empire of the Timurids (until 1500) was soon restricted to Transoxania and eastern Persia.

1404-1447. SHAH RUKH, fourth son of Timur, whose reign was noted for its splendor. He carried on successful campaigns against Kara Yusuf, head of the Turkoman dynasty of the Black Sheep (1390-1420), who ruled Azerbaijan, Shirvan, and other regions of the northwest. Kara Yusuf was obliged to recognize the suzerainty of the Timurids, though Kara Yusuf and his successor, Kara Iskender (1420-1438), and Jehan Shah (1435-1467) were effective rulers of all northwestern Persia. Jehan Shah for a brief period (1458) held even Herat.

1452-1469. Abu Said, last of the Timurid dynasty. This period was marked by the great expansion of the Turkoman power under

1453-1478. UZUN HASAN, of the dynasty of the White Sheep. This dynasty had established itself under Hasan's grandfather, Osman Beg Kara Iluk (d. 1435) and ruled the territory about Diabekr. Hasan rapidly extended his authority over Armenia and Kurdistan. His defeat by the Ottoman Turks (1461) turned his attention eastward, and led to five large-scale raids into Georgia.

1467. Uzun Hasan defeated and killed Jehan Shah of the Black Sheep and took over his territories.

1469. Uzun defeated, captured, and killed Abu Said, the Timurid sultan, who had marched against him. Thereupon Hasan became effective ruler of Armenia, Kurdistan, Azerbaijan, and Iran. He entered with Venice into a treaty directed against the Ottoman Turks, but the artillery that was sent him never reached him, and he was defeated by Mohammed II in

1473.   The battle of Erzinjan (Otluk-beli). On his death he was succeeded by his son

1478-1490.   JAQUB, who continued his father's policies and gave the country firm and enlightened rule.

1492-1497.   RUSTAM SHAH, who succeeded to the throne after a severe dynastic conflict. His death was followed by confusion and by the emergence of the new Safavid dynasty, under Shah Ismail   *(Cont. p. 565.)*

2.   INDIA

(From p. 144)

a. NORTHERN INDIA, 500-1199

The **White Huns** or Hephthalites, a branch of the Mongol Juan-juan who dominated Central Asia (407–553), had occupied Bactria (425) and, after defeat by Sassanid Bahram Gor (428), Gandhara. Victory over Sassanid Peroz (484) freed them for raids from the Punjab into Hindustan.

c. 500-502.   Toramana ruled as far as Eran.

502-c. 528.   Mihirakula from Sialkot controlled Gwalior and Kashmir. Bhanugupta probably expelled him from Eran (510). Yasodharman of Mandasor (?) boasts (533) of victory over him. Although the Huns in Central Asia were crushed by Turks and Sassanians (553–567), their chiefs kept rank in the Punjab and Rajputana till the 11th century.

606-647.   HARSHA, fourth king of Thanesar, north of Delhi (new era Oct. 606), succeeded his brother-in-law as king of Kanauj (royal title 612), and quickly conquered an empire across northern India, to which he left no heir. He received an embassy (643) from the Emperor T'ang T'ai-tsung. A poet and dramatist, he patronized men of letters. He is well known through **Bana's** poetic romance *Harshacharita,* and by the *Hsi yü chi (Record of Western Lands)* of his guest, the pilgrim **Hsüan-tsang,** whose exact observations in India (630–643) have given priceless guidance to modern archaeology.

   Tantrism meanwhile sought to secure for its adepts in magic arts, through esoteric texts (*tantra*) and charms, rapid attainment of Buddhahood or at least supernatural powers. Partial syncretism with Sivaism led to a cult of Vairochana and various new divinities, largely terrible or erotic. Spells (*dharanis*) appear early (Chinese trans. 4th century), but the *Panchakrama* is in part the work of Sakyamitra

(c. 850). Tantrism seems to have flourished chiefly along the northern borderland. Buddhism, however, progressively disappeared from India from the 9th century, lingering in Bengal and Bihar until the Moslem conquest (1202). It was largely absorbed by Hinduism.

647.   A second Chinese embassy, under Wang Hsüan-tse, having been attacked by a usurper on a local throne (Tirhut, north of Patna ?), secured 7000 troops from Amsuvarman, king of Nepal, and 1200 from his son-in-law, Srong-tsan-sgampo, king of Tibet; captured the malefactor, and haled him to Ch'ang-an (648).

c. 730-c. 740.   YASOVARMAN, king of Kanauj, an author, patronized the Prakrit poet **Vakpatiraja** and **Bhavabhuti,** a Sanskrit dramatist ranked by Indian criticism next to **Kalidasa.**

c. 725-1197. The Pala Buddhist kings ruled Bengal (till c. 1125) and Magadha. Leading rulers: Dharmapala (c. 770–c. 883), and Devapala (c. 881–c. 883), who endowed a monastery founded at Nalanda by Balaputradeva, king of Sumatra.

c. 1125-c. 1225? Senas from the Carnatic gradually advanced from North Orissa into Bengal.

c. 1169-c. 1199. Lakshmanasena patronized Jayadeva, whose *Gitagovinda,* mystic call to love of Krishna, is considered a Sanskrit masterpiece. Tightening of caste restrictions was accompanied by origin of **kulinism:** prohibition of marriage of any girl below her own caste, which led to infanticide; and rise in caste by marriage to man of higher caste, which led to polygamy of high-caste husbands to collect dowries.

b. WESTERN INDIA, 490-1490

Western India, thanks to many impregnable fortresses in Rajputana, was usually divided among local dynasties from the time of the Gupta power to the advent of the Moslems.

c. 490–766. A dynasty of **Maitrakas,** foreigners of the Rajput type, usually independent at Valabhi in Surashtra, created a Buddhist scholastic center which rivaled Nalanda. Their gifts reveal that Buddhist images were honored with *puja* of the kind devoted to Hindu gods.

c. 550–861. The **GURJARA** horde of central Asiatic nomads established a dynasty of twelve kings at Mandor in central Rajputana. Two retired to Jain contemplation, and a third to self-starvation.

712– **Arab raids** from Sind devastated Gujarat and Broach (724–743) and finally shattered the Maitraka dynasty (766).

c. 740–1036. The **GURJARA-PRATHIHARA DYNASTY,** by uniting much of northern India, excluded the Moslems till the end of the 10th century. Prominent early rulers were Nagabhata I (c. 740–c. 760), who defeated the Arabs; Vatsaraja (c. 775–c. 800); and Nagabhata II (c. 800–836), conqueror of Kanauj.

746–c. 974. The Chapas (or Chapotkatas), a Gurjara clan, founded Anahillapura (or Anandapura, 746), the principal city of western India until the 15th century.

831–1310. A **Dravidian dynasty of Chandellas** (in present Bundelkhand) built numerous Vaishnava temples, notably at Khajuraho, under Yasovarman (c. 930–954) and Dhanga (954–1002).

c. 840–c. 890. **Mihira,** or Bhoja, devoted to Vishnu and the Sun, ruled from the Sutlej to the Narmada, but failed to subdue Kashmir.

c. 950–c. 1200. The **Paramaras of Dhara,** near Indore, were known for two rulers: Munja (974–c. 994) who invaded the Deccan, and Bhoja (c. 1018–1060), author of books on astronomy, poetics, and architecture, and founder of a Sanskrit college.

c. 974–c. 1240. The **Chalukya** or Solanki Rajput clan, led by Mularaja (known dates 974–995) ruled from Anahillapura over Surashtra and Mt. Abu.

977–1186. The **Ghaznavid** (Yamini) **dynasty** ruled at Ghazni and Lahore. It was founded by **Subaktagin** (977–997), a Turkish slave converted to Islam, who extended his rule from the Oxus to the Indus and broke the power of a Hindu confederacy which included King Jaipal of Bhatinda, the Gurjara-Prathihara king of Kanauj, and the Chandella King Dhanga.

998–1030. **MAHMUD OF GHAZNI** made 17 plundering raids into the Punjab (defeat of Jaipal, 1001) to Kangra (1009), Mathura and Kanauj (1018–1019), Gwalior (1022), and Somnath (1024–1026). Vast destruction, pillage of immensely rich Hindu temples, and wholesale massacre resulted only in enrichment of Ghazni and annexation of the Punjab. Ghazni,

heir to the rich artistic heritage of the Samanids of northeastern Persia, was now one of the most brilliant capitals of the Islamic world. **Alberuni** (973–1048) of Khiva, the leading scientist of his time, followed Mahmud to the Punjab, learned Sanskrit, and wrote the invaluable *Tahkik-i Hind* (*Inquiry into India*).

1093–1143. The Chalukya ruler, **Jayasimha Siddharaja,** a patron of letters, although himself a Saiva, organized disputations on philosophy and religion, and favored a Jain monk, **Hemachandra,** who converted and dominated

1143–1172. Kumarapala. As a good Jain, he decreed respect for life (*ahimsa*), prohibited alcohol, dice, and animal fights, and rescinded a law for confiscation of property of widows without sons. He also built (c. 1169) a new edifice about the Saiva temple of Somanatha, which had been reconstructed by **Bhimadeva I** (1022–1062) after destruction by the Moslems.

1151–1206. The Shansabani Persian princes of Ghur (Ghor) having burned Ghazni (1151), drove the Yamini to the Punjab and deposed them there (1186).

1172–1176. Ajayapala, a Saiva reactionary, ordered the massacre of Jains and sack of their temples until he was assassinated, when Jain rule was restored under a mayor of the palace whose descendants displaced the dynasty (c. 1240).

Two Jain temples at Mt. Abu are the work of a governor, **Vimala Saha** (1031), and a minister, **Tejpala** (1230). Built of white marble with a profusion of ornamented colonnades, brackets, and elaborately carved ceilings, they are the most elegant version of the northern or Indo-Aryan architectural style.

Kashmir, already (c. 100 A.D.) an important home of the Sarvastivadin Buddhist sect, remained a center for Buddhist studies (till the 10th century; degenerate before the Moslem conquest, 1340) and of Sanskrit literature (until today). Its history from c. 700 is rather fully known through the *Rajatarangini*, the only extant document by **Kalhana** (c. 1100), the sole early Indian historian, who consulted literary sources and inscriptions but accepted even absurd tradition without criticism.

1175–1206. Mohammed of Ghur, Mu'izz-ud-Din, undertook conquest of Hindustan by capture of Multan and Uch. He ruled from Ghazni as governor for his elder brother, **Ghiyas-ud-Din Mohammed,** whom he succeeded as ruler of Ghur (1203).

1192. A **battle at Tararori** (14 miles from Thanesar) decisively crushed a new Hindu confederacy led by the Chauhan king of Ajmer and Delhi. Cumbersome traditional tactics, disunited command, and caste restrictions handicapped the Hindu armies in conflict with

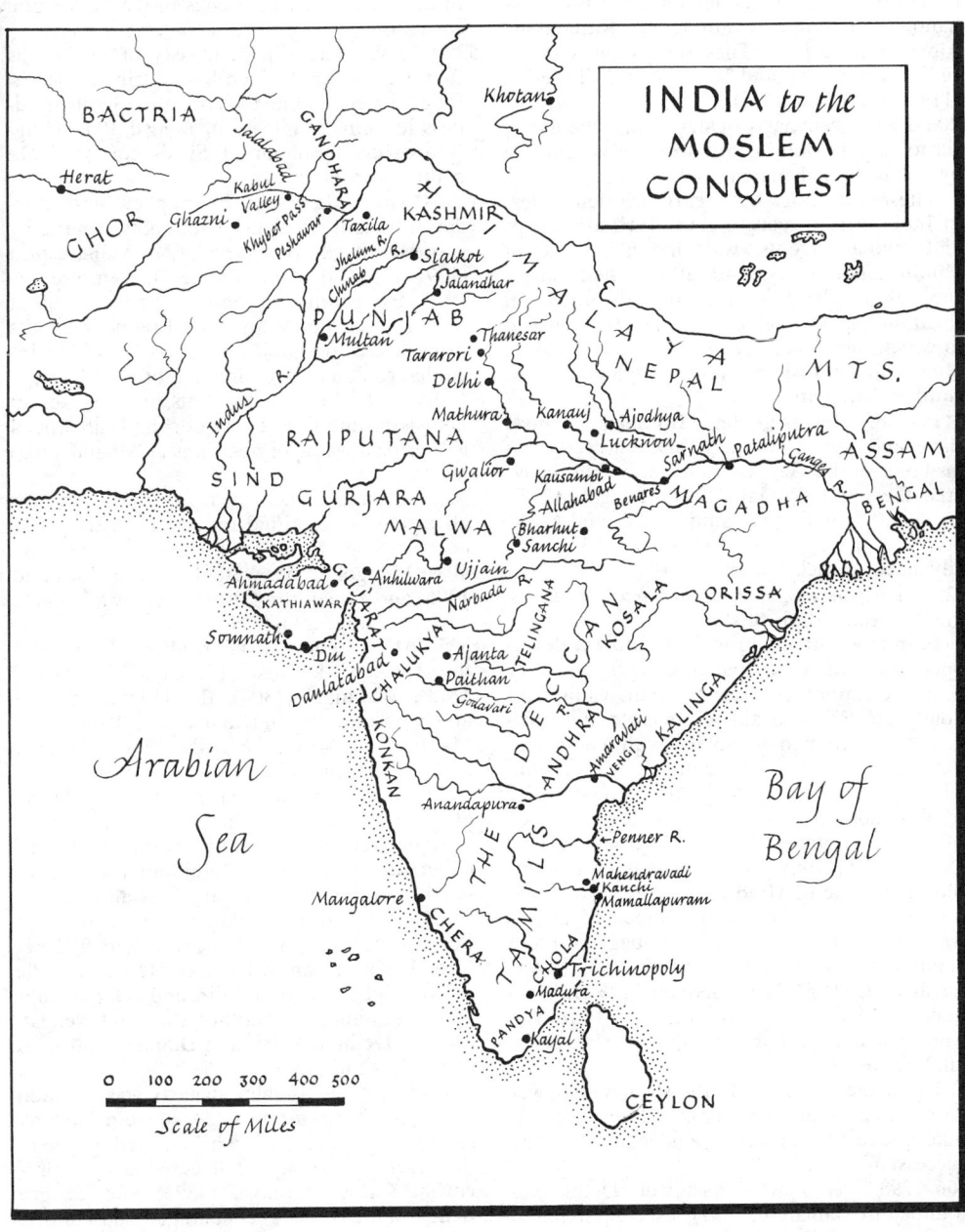

INDIA *to the* MOSLEM CONQUEST

the mounted archers from the northwest. Victory led to occupation of Delhi (1193), to conquest of Bihar, where the organized Buddhist community was extinguished (c. 1197), Bengal (c. 1199), and the Chandella state in Bundelkhand.   Mohammed appointed **Kutb-ud-din Aibak,** a slave from Turkestan, viceroy of his Indian conquests, and left him full discretion (1192, confirmed 1195).

1206–1266. A dynasty of slave kings, the first of six to rule at Delhi (until 1526), was founded by Aibak (killed playing polo, 1210).

The numerically weak early Moslem rulers in India were forced to employ Hindu troops and civilian agents, welcome allegiance of Hindu landholders, and afford their native subjects much the same limited protection (including tacit religious toleration) and justice to which they were accustomed. Rebels, both Hindu and Moslem, were slaughtered with ruthless barbarity.

1211–1236. Shams-ud-din Iltutmish, ablest slave and son-in-law of Aibak, succeeded to his lands in the Ganges Valley only, but recovered the upper Punjab (1217), Bengal (1225), the lower Punjab with Sind (1228), and Gwalior after a long siege (Feb.–Dec. 1232). He advanced to sack Ujjain (1234).

1229. He was invested as sultan of India by the Abbasid caliph of Baghdad.

Islamic architects brought to India a developed tradition of a spacious, light, and airy prayer chamber covered by arch, vault, and dome, erected with aid of concrete and mortar, and ornamented solely with color and flat linear, usually conventional, decoration. This formula was applied with recognition of local structural styles and of the excellence of Hindu ornamental design. Aibak built at Delhi (1193–1196) with the spoils of 27 temples a mosque of Hindu appearance to which he added (1198) an Islamic screen of arches framed with Indian carving. He began (before 1206) a tower for call to prayer, which was finished (1231–1232) and named *Kutb Minar* to honor a Moslem saint (d. 1235) by Iltutmish, who also enlarged the mosque in strictly Islamic style.

Upon the death of Iltutmish actual power passed to a group of 40 Turks who divided all offices save that of sultan, and controlled the succession.

1266–1290. A new dynasty at Delhi was founded by **Balban** (d. 1287), a slave purchased by Iltutmish (1233); made chamberlain (1242), father-in-law and lieutenant (1249–1252 and 1255–1266) of King Mahmud (1246–1266). Balban as king, aided by an effective army and corps of royal news-writers, repressed the 40 nobles, ended highway robbery in south and

east, and rebellion in Bengal. His son repelled the Mongols established in Ghazni (since 1221), but was killed by them (1285).

The **tomb of Balban** is the first structure in India built with true arches instead of Hindu corbelling.

1290–1320. The **Khalji dynasty of Delhi** was founded by **Firuz** of the Khalji tribe of Turks, long resident among the Afghans. Senile mildness led him to release in Bengal 1000 Thugs (murderers in honor of Siva's consort Kali) captured in Delhi.

1296–1316. Ala-ud-din, his nephew and murderer, bought allegiance with booty secured by surprise attack upon Devagiri in Maharashtra (1294–1295).   He consolidated the empire.

1297. He conquered and despoiled Gujarat with its rich port Cambay. Frequent revolts prompted a program of repression which included espionage; confiscation of wealth (especially of Hindus), endowments, and tax-exempt lands; prohibition of liquor and all social gatherings. Mongol invasions (1299 and 1303) led to

1303. Decrees which by fixing low prices for all products permitted reduction of army pay and increase of strength to nearly 500,000 cavalry. Mongol armies were destroyed (1304 and 1306) and expeditions, usually led by a eunuch, Kafur, entitled Malik Naib, effected

1305–1313. Conquest of Malwa (1305) and the Deccan: Devagiri (1306–1307, annexed 1313), Warangal (1308), the Hoysala capital at Dvarasamudra and that of the Pandyas at Madura (1310–1311), and the central Deccan (1313), with enormous treasure.

The *Alai Darwaza* (1311), southern gateway of a proposed vast enlargement of Aibak's mosque, represents the finest ornamental architecture of the early Delhi sultanate, fortunately continued in Gujarat. **Amir Khusrav** (1253–1325), greatest Indian poet to write in Persian, was son of a Turk who had fled before Jenghiz Khan to Patiala. He was prolific as court poet to Ala-ud-din and later in religious retirement. Another excellent Persian poet of Delhi was **Hasan-i-Dihlavi,** who died at Daulatabad (1338).

1320–1413. The **Tughluk dynasty** was founded by the old but vigorous **Ghiyas-ud-din Tughluk** (d. 1325), a pure Turk who boasted 29 victories over the Mongols. He reduced to provincial status Warangal (1323) and eastern Bengal (1324). He encouraged agriculture, corrected abuses in tax collection, and perfected a postal system by which runners covered 200 miles a day. At Multan he erected a splendid octagonal tomb of Persian character for the saint, Rukn-i-Alam. Increasing austerity marked the architecture of his house.

1325-1351. Mohammed Tughluk hastened to the throne by deliberate parricide. A military genius, his administrative measures were warped and defeated by his own unwisdom, inordinate pride, inflexibility, and ferocious cruelty. Revolt of a cousin in the Deccan (1326) led to

1327. Transfer of the capital to Devagiri, renamed Daulatabad, handsomely rebuilt with European feudal fortifications about an impregnable rock citadel. As a punitive measure

1329. All remaining citizens of Delhi were forced to move thither. He raised taxes so high in the Doab as to force rebellion and then destroyed both fields and cultivators.

1330. Emission of copper fiat money equivalent to the silver *tanga* of 140 grains failed because of easy counterfeiting.

1334. Ibn Batuta, a Moorish traveler, was welcomed with fantastic gifts like other foreigners who might help in world conquest. He left on a mission to China (1342).

1334-1378. Madura revolted under a Moslem dynasty, ended by Vijayanagar.

1337-1338. An army of 100,000 horse, sent through Kangra into the Himalaya to conquer Tibet and China, was destroyed by rains, disease, and hill-men; and with it resources needed to avert

1338. Loss of Bengal to the house of Balban, independent until 1539. Moslem architects used at Gaur, its capital, local brick and terra cotta to build, e.g., the bold *Dakhil Gateway* (1459-1474?).

1340. Mohammed sought recognition (received 1344) from the caliph in Egypt. He vainly tried to restore prosperity by redistricting, and appointing undertakers to supervise fixed (unscientific) crop rotation, and to maintain a mounted militia. Increased penal severity culminated when he began

1344-1345. Wholesale extermination of his centurions, revenue collectors who usually failed to meet his quotas. Rebellion begun by them in Gujarat led to permanent loss of the whole south.

1346-1589. Shah Mirza (1346-1349) founded a Moslem dynasty in Kashmir. He substituted the usual land tax of one-sixth for the extortionate rates of the Hindu kings.

1347-1527. The **Bahmani dynasty,** founded by rebels against Mohammed Tughluk, who elected **Bahman Shah** (1347-1348), at first ruled four provinces: Gulbarga, Daulatabad, Berar, and Bidar. The capital at Gulbarga and many other fortresses were built or strengthened with European science to serve against Gujarat, Malwa, and Khandesh in the northwest, the Gonds, Orissa, and Telingana in the northeast, and Vijayanagar in the south.

1351-1388. Firuz Tughluk (b. 1305) restored rational administration. He exacted tribute from Orissa (1360), Kangra (1361), and Sind (1363). He refused to disturb the Bahmani kingdom of the Deccan, its tributary Warangal, or the rebels from it, the khans of Khandesh between the Tapti and Narbada (independent 1382). He built several towns, notably Jaunpur north of Benares (1359), many mosques, palaces, hospitals, baths, tanks, canals, and bridges; but with cheap materials and little artistic quality. His successors were too weak to prevent further dissolution of the empire.

1358-1375. The Bahmani **Mohammed I** gave lasting organization to the government of the new dynasty.

1363-1364. Warangal was forced to cede Golconda, with much treasure.

1367. Victory of the Bahmani over immense but ineffectual armies of Vijayanagar. It was the first of several successes and was won with artillery served by Europeans and Ottoman Turks. The subsequent massacre of 400,000 Hindus led to agreement to spare noncombatants. The **Great Mosque at Gulbarga** was completely roofed with domes.

1392-1531. Malwa (formally independent in 1401) was ruled by the Ghuris and the Khaljis (1436). **Hushang Shah** (1405-1435) fortified the capital at Mandu above the Narbada, and erected there the durbar hall *Hindola Mahall,* together with a great mosque. These buildings are impressive through structural design rather than surface ornament.

1394-1479. Jaunpur, with Oudh, became independent under the Sharki (eastern) dynasty, founded by the eunuch, Malik Sarvar, and his adopted sons, probably of African Negroid descent. The second ruler, **Ibrahim Shah** (1402-1436), was a cultured and liberal patron of learning.

1396-1572. Gujarat prospered under a Moslem Rajput dynasty.

1398-1399. INVASION OF TIMUR (Tamerlane) of Samarkand, who had already conquered Persia, Mesopotamia, and Afghanistan (p. 354). He desolated the whole kingdom of Delhi. Crossing the Indus (Sept. 24), he marched 80 miles a day for two days (Nov. 6-7) to overtake fugitives at Bhatnair, massacred 100,000 Hindu prisoners before Delhi (Dec. 12), sacked the city (Dec. 17), stormed Meerut (Jan. 9), and fought his way back along the Himalaya to the Indus (Mar. 19).

1411-1442. Ahmad Shah built Ahmadabad as a capital and beautified it with the *Tin Darwaza* (Triple Gateway) and *Great Mosque,* one of the most imposing structures in the world.

1414-1526. The **KINGDOM OF DELHI,** reduced to the Jumna Valley, with tenuous control over the Punjab, was ruled by the Sayyids, who laid nebulous claim to Arab descent from the Prophet, but could collect their revenues only by force. Later the Afghan **Buhlul Lodi** (1451-1489) founded the Lodi dynasty.

1420-1470. Zain-ul-Abidin, learned and tolerant, recalled the exiles, permitted Brahman rites, employed convicts on public works, and exacted communal responsibility for order.

1422-1436. Ahmad Shah enrolled 3000 foreign mounted archers, who, like the Turks, Arabs, Mongols, and Persians, when employed as ministers, earned by superior qualities and disdain the envy and hostility (massacre 1446) of the native-born Deccanis, Africans, and Muwallads, half-breed offspring of the latter.

1429. Bidar, rebuilt under Persian decorative influence, became capital.

1458-1511. Mahmud I, called Begarha (Two Forts) because of his conquest of Girnar (with Kathiawar, 1469-1470) and Champanir (near Baroda, 1483-1484), when 700 Hindu Rajputs preferred ritual death (*jauhar*) to Islam. He built magnificently and in exquisite taste: the great mosque at Champanir; the palace at Sarkhej; the step-well at Adalaj; and the pierced stone window-screens of Sidi Sayyid's mosque. The tiny Rani Sipari mosque at Ahmadabad (1514) displays harmonious perfection of the ornamental style.

1463-1482. Mohammed III conquered the Konkan and Telingana to both coasts. He died at 28 of drink, the curse of nearly all his house, and of remorse at having slain (while drunk) his best minister, Mahmud Gavan, the builder of the large quadrangular college at Bidar.

1490. Ahmadnagar (1490-1633), Bijapur (1490-1686), and Berar (1490-1574) became in fact independent of Mahmud (1482-1518), the incompetent prisoner of his minister, Kasim Barid, whose dynasty mounted the throne of Bidar in 1527 (till 1619).

c. SOUTHERN INDIA, 100-1565

100-200. King Karikalan of early Tamil poems is credited with construction of a great irrigation dam on the Kaveri River, east of Trichinopoly.

c. 300-888. The **Pallava warrior dynasty** of foreign (Pahlava?) origin, using Prakrit and later Sanskrit, held from Kanchi (near Madras) hegemony of the Deccan, which it disputed with the Chalukyas of Vatapi (550-753), the Rashtrakutas of Malkhed (753-973) and the Chalukyas of Vengi (611-1078).

c. 500-753. The **first Chalukya dynasty** in Maharashtra advanced from Aihole on the upper Kistna to near-by Vatapi (or Badami, c. 550)

and to Banavasi (566-597) at the expense of the Kadambas. Construction of the earliest temples at Aihole was followed by that of Mahakutesvara (c. 525) and completion of the cave-temple to Vishnu at Vatapi (578).

c. 575. The Pallava **Simhavishnu** seized the Chola basin of the Kaveri, which his family held until after 812.

c. 600-625. The Pallava **Mahendravarman I,** converted from Jainism to Sivaism, destroyed a Jain temple, but dug the first (Saiva) cave-temples in the south (at Trichinopoly, Chingleput, etc.). From his reign date **Buddhist monasteries** (in part excavated) and *stupas* on the Samkaram Hills (near Vizagapatam).

609-642. The Chalukya **Pulakesin II** placed his brother on the throne of Vengi, where he ruled as viceroy (611-632), repulsed an attack by Harsha of Kanauj (c. 620), sent an embassy to Khosroes II of Persia (625), and enthroned a son, who headed a branch dynasty in Gujarat and Surat (c. 640-740). Hsüan-tsang (641) describes the prosperity of the country just before the Pallavas pillaged the capital (642), a disaster that was avenged by pillage of the Pallava capital, Kanchi, by Vikramaditya (c. 674).

611-c. 1078. The **Eastern Chalukyas** of Vengi (independent after 629-632), were continually at war with Kalinga on the north, the Rashtrakutas on the west, and the Pandyas on the south.

c. 625-c. 645. The Pallava **Narasimhavarman** defeated Chalukya Pulakesin II (c. 642) and took Vatapi. He defeated also his southern neighbors and enthroned Manavalla in Ceylon (?). He improved the port of Mamallapuram, near Kanchi, and cut there the first of five *raths,* monolithic sanctuaries in the form of cars, the earliest monuments of the Dravidian style; also the cliff-relief depicting the descent of the River Ganges from Heaven.

c. 675-c. 705. The Pallava **Narasimhavarman II** built in stone and brick the Shore temple at Mamalla, and the central shrine of the Kailasa temple at Kanchi, completed by his son.

c. 700. Conversion of King Srimaravarman to Sivaism by Tirujnana Sambandhar, the first of 63 *nayanmars* or Tamil saints, led the king to impale 8000 Jains at Madura in a single day, since celebrated by the Saivas. Another saint, Manikka Vasagar (9th century), wrote poems of his own religious experience which correspond to our *Psalms.* The Tamil Vaishnavas, too, had their saints, twelve *alvars,* who also expressed emotional religion and whose works were collected c. 1000-1050.

733-746. The Chalukya **Vikramaditya II** thrice took Kanchi, and distributed presents to the temples. He imported Tamil artists and his

queen commissioned Gunda, "the best southern architect," to build the temple of Viru-
paksha. The **frescoes of Ajanta caves** 1 and 2
are believed to date from this period. So too
the Saiva and Vaishnava sculptures of the Das
Avatara cave-temple at Ellora.

c. 735–c. 800. Nandivarman II, a collateral
kinsman twelve years of age, accepted the
Pallava throne offered him by the ministers
and elders, who defended him against rival
claimants.

753–973. The **Rashtrakuta dynasty** of Canarese
kings, already enthroned in North Berar (631)
and in Gujarat (c. 700) was elevated to empire by Dantidurga, who soon overthrew the
Chalukyas.

758–772. Rashtrakuta **Krishnaraja I** cut from
the cliff and decorated with Saiva sculpture the
Kailasa (natha) temple at Ellora to rival that
of Kanchi. To the same Canarese dynasty if
not to the same reign belong the equally classic Saiva sculptures of the **cave-temples at
Elephanta** (an island in Bombay harbor). The
successors of Krishnaraja were Govinda II
(779) and Dhruva (783), who defeated the
Pallava Nandivarman II and the Gurjara Vatsaraja.

774–13th century. The **Eastern Gangas** ruled
Kalinga, waging constant war with the Chalukyas of Vengi and the princes of Orissa.

c. 788–c. 850. Samkara of Malabar revitalized
the Vedanta, creating an unobtrusively new
but consistent synthesis of tradition, which he
speciously traced to the *Upanishads* and to
Badarayana, author of the *Brahma sutra.* His
doctrine became accepted as orthodox Brahmanism. He taught a rigorous monism (*ad-
vaita*) which admits release for the soul only in
union with *brahman* through the higher knowledge that the phenomenal world (and individual personality) do not exist save for those
who think objectively. For these latter, however, engrossed in worldly phenomena (*maya*),
he recognized that a simpler kind of knowledge was necessary; and for them he was a
practical apostle of Sivaism. Although he
denounced Buddhism he imitated its moral
teaching by opposition to sectarian extravagance, its ecclesiastical strength by organization of an ascetic order for zealous youth
(hitherto debarred till later life from religious
activity). He founded four scholastic monasteries (*maths*) which still survive at Sringeri
(Mysore), Puri (Orissa), Badrinath (the Himalaya), and Dwaraka (western Kathiawar).
Ramanuja (c. 1055–1137) of Kanchi (Con-
jeeveran, near Madras) also interpreted the
Vedanta. For him souls are distinct from
brahman, whose representatives they are, and
from the material world with which they are

entangled. It is through piety toward Vishnu
and his saving grace that they may recover
their divine nature.

c. 790. The Chalukya **Vikramaditya II** was defeated by the Rashtrakuta Dhruva (779–794).

794–813. Rashtrakuta **Govinda II** seized Malwa
with Chitor from the Gurjaras, and enthroned
his brother as head of a second Rashtrakuta
dynasty in Gujarat (till c. 900). He took from
the Pallava (c. 800) tribute and territory as far
as the Tungabhadra.

c. 812–844. Pallava **Nandivarman III** helped
Govinda III to crown Sivamara II as Ganga
king of Mysore. At the same time

c. 812– Pandya **Varaguna I** imposed suzerainty on the Pallavas.

817–877. Rashtrakuta **Amoghavarsha I** moved
the capital from Nasik to Malkhed, the better
to carry on war against the Vengi. He abdicated and died in saintly Jain fashion. The
last of his line found death in Jain starvation (982).

c. 825–1312. The **Yadavas,** early suzerains of a
score of petty vassal kings, occupied in turn
three capitals: (modern) Chandor and Sinnar
(1069), both near Nasik, and the fortress of
Devagiri (c. 1111) renamed Daulatabad (1327).
They fell heir to the northern possessions of
the Chalukyas of Kalyani.

843–1249. The **Silaharas,** another petty dynasty, under Chalukya or Rashtrakuta suzerainty, provided 45 kings in three different
areas along the west coast north of Goa. The
Parsis (Parsees), refugees in Kathiawar, had
probably already reached Thana near Bombay
during the 8th century.

844–888. Gunaga **Vijayaditya III** fought successfully against western and northern enemies
and by the defeat of the Pallava Aparajita and
the Pandya Varaguna II helped the rising
Chola to supersede both. His association of
two brothers as kings-consort led ultimately to
succession struggles which placed eight kings
on the throne in ten years (918–927).

c. 844–870. Pallava **Nripatungavarman** recovered Tanjore and obtained the submission of
Varaguna II (862–) and of Ganga Prithivipati I.

c. 870–888. Pallava **Aparajitavarman,** with
Ganga Prithivipati, crushed Varaguna II, but
was himself defeated and killed by the Chola
Aditya I. Numerous Pallava chiefs continued
to rule locally. Perungina, in the Tamil South,
claimed imperial titles for at least 31 years.

888–1267. The **Chola dynasty of Tamil kings**
from Tanjore, under **Aditya I** (870–c. 906),
with the aid of the Chalukyas of Vengi, replaced the Pallavas at Kanchi. The Chola
territory extended along the east coast from
Telugu to the Pandya lands.

927–934. A royal inscription is the earliest

extant specimen of Telugu literature. It records the erection of a Saiva temple and sectarian hostel.

973–c. 1190. The Chalukyas of Kalyani (near Bombay) were restored to power by Taila II (or Tailapa), who spent his reign fighting the Cholas and Paramaras.

985–1014. Chola **Rajaraja I** acquired hegemony over the Deccan.

994. Conquest of the Cheras and Pandyas justified the title *Thrice-crowned Chola,* marking the first historical union of the southern peninsula.

999. The conquest of Vengi drove a usurper from the East Chalukyan throne and was extended (1000) to Kalinga.

1001–1004. A successful **invasion of Ceylon** permitted assignment of Singhalese revenues to the Saiva great pagoda of Rajarajesvara, which Rajaraja I built at Tanjore, the masterpiece of baroque Dravidian architecture. He also endowed a Buddhist monastery built at Negapatam by a king of Srivijaya (Sumatra).

1014–1042. Rajendra Choladeva, who had helped his father since 1002.

1014–1017. A second invasion of Ceylon secured the regalia and treasure of the Pandya kings, so that a son of the Chola could be consecrated king of Pandya.

1024. An **invasion of Bengal** enabled the Chola to assume a new title and establish a new capital near Trichinopoly.

c. 1030. By use of sea power, the Chola exacted tribute from Pegu, Malaiyur (Malay Peninsula), and the empire of Srivijaya.

1040–1068. (Chalukya) **Somesvara I** founded Kalyani, the capital until c. 1156. He drowned himself with Jain rites in the Tungabhadra, a sacred river of the south.

1042–1052. Chola **Rajadhiraja I,** who had aided his father since 1018. He was killed in battle at Koppam against Somesvara I of Kalyani.

1062–1070. Chola **Virarajendra** defeated the Chalukyas and gave his daughter to Vikramaditya VI. He founded a vedic college and a hospital. His two sons fell into conflict and extinguished their line by assassination (1074).

1073–1327. The **Hoysalas,** at first a petty dynasty, ruled at Dvarasamudra (Halebid) in Mysore.

1074–1267. The **Chalukya-Chola dynasty,** founded by Rajendra, son and grandson of Chola princesses, king of Vengi (1070–), who took the vacant throne of Kanchi (1074) and thenceforth ruled Vengi through a viceroy. His authority was recognized by the Ganga king of Kalinga.

1075–1125. Vikramaditya VI of Kalyani began a new era in place of the Saka era, but with small success. One of his many inscriptions is

at Nagpur in the northern Deccan, while in the south one of his generals repelled the Hoysalas. His people enjoyed unwonted security. He built temples to Vishnu, but made gifts also to two Buddhist monasteries which must have been among the last in the south to withstand Hindu reaction and absorption. **Bilhana of Kashmir,** in return for hospitality, a blue parasol, and an elephant, wrote the *Vikramankácharita* in praise of his host.

1076–1147. Anantavarman Codaganga extended his authority from the Ganges to the Godavari, and built at Puri (south of Cuttack) the temple of Jagannath (Vishnu) which, at first open to all Hindu castes, is now barred to fifteen. The great Sun temple, in form of a solar car, known as the *Black Pagoda,* at Konarak, may be earlier than its attribution to Ganga Narasimha (1238–1264).

1111–1141. Bittideva, independent, fought successfully against Chola, Pandya, and Chera. As viceroy before accession he was converted from Jainism to Vishnu by Ramanuja, at that time a refugee from Saiva persecution by the Cholas. He began construction at Belur and Halebid of temples in a distinctively ornate Hoysala style, featured especially by a high, richly carved plinth of stellate plan.

c. 1150–1323. The **Kakatiyas** reigned in the east at Kakati or Warangal between the Godavari and the Kistna. They held an important kingdom under **Ganapati** (1197–1259) and his daughter (1259–1288), whom Marco Polo knew.

c. 1156–1183. A revolt against the Chalukya ruler **Taila III** (known dates 1150–1155) led to usurpation by a general who was soon assassinated by Basava, who was in turn compelled to commit suicide. Basava created and organized the Lingayat sect of fanatic, anti-Brahman worshipers of Siva under a phallic emblem. The movement at the outset appeared in the form of a religious and social (equalitarian) war.

1183. Taila's son **Somesvara IV** regained Kalyani, but was unable to resist the Hoysalas (last date 1189).

1292–1342. The Hoysala ruler **Viraballala III** inherited an empire comprising most of southern India.

1327. After sack of Halebid by **Mohammed Tughluk,** Viraballala moved his capital to Tiruvannamalai (South Arcot).

c. 1335–1565. Vijayanagar (present Hampi), founded by two brothers from the region of Warangal, fought steadily against the Moslem sultans north of Kistna and Tungabhadra. It became an important center for Brahman studies and for Dravidian nationalism and art. **Madhava** wrote at Sringeri (c. 1380) the *Sarva* *darsana samgraha,* which remains the classic summary of the various Brahman philosophical points of view.

1520. Division of the Moslems into five rival sultanates (late 15th century) gave Krishnadeva (c. 1509-1529) a chance to win a victory over the sultan of Bijapur.

1542-1565. Ramaraja sought to profit by further division of the Moslems but provoked a coalition which crushed him and razed Vijayanagar.

d. CEYLON, 846-1284

846. The capital was moved south to Polonnaruva to escape Tamil invasions, which later culminated in

1001-1017. The **two great invasions** (1001-1004 and 1014-1017) by Chola Rajaraja and his son Rajendra.

1065-1120. **Vijayabahu** ruled prosperously despite further incursions (1046, 1055).

1164-1197. **Parakramabahu I** repelled the Tamils (1168), invaded Madura, and united the two rival monasteries.

1225-1260. **Parakramabahu II** repelled two attacks (c. 1236 and c. 1256) by a king of Tambralinga (Ligor on the Straits of Malacca), with Pandya help.

1284. The king sent a relic of the Buddha to Kublai Khan. (*Cont. p. 569.*)

3. CHINA, 618-1471

(*From p. 149*)

618-907. The **T'ANG DYNASTY,** founded by
618-626. LI YÜAN (T'ai Tsu) and his son Li Shih-min. The T'ang used Loyang and Ch'ang-an as eastern and western capitals. Sui institutions were in general retained. The central administrative organization remained essentially unchanged from this time until 1912. The emperor ruled through daily audience with a grand council composed of (1) heads of a secretariat and chancery, which for safety divided transaction of business (a feature later discarded); (2) representatives of the six ministries of civil office, finance, ceremonial, war, justice, and public works; and (3) specially appointed dignitaries. The censorate and nine independent offices, notably a clan court and a criminal high court, together with three technical services including the national college and flood-prevention bureau, reported to him directly. Although the empire was divided into ten (627), later fifteen (733), districts for supervisory purposes, the prefectures (*chou*) depended directly from the central administration, the prefect being responsible for duties corresponding to those of the six ministries. Each prefecture sent an annual quota of candidates to join graduates of two state universities in civil service examinations. These led to the eighth or ninth (bottom) ranks in the official hierarchy. Appointment to a corresponding office depended on a further searching examination before each term until the sixth rank was reached. Promotion was based on performance.

627-649. The reign of **T'AI TSUNG** (Li Shih-min) is illustrious not alone because of the military conquests which established stimulating contacts with Iranian and Indian civilizations, but still more for the liberal, tolerant spirit of the emperor and his patronage of art and letters.

630. The eastern Turks, who had attacked Ch'ang-an in 624 and 626, were crushed.

631-648. Chinese suzerainty was acknowledged by the petty states of western and eastern Turkestan. The western Turks were divided and defeated (641).

635. A Nestorian missionary, A-lo-pen, was officially welcomed to Ch'ang-an; and given (638) both freedom of the empire and an imperial church at the capital.

641. A Chinese princess was married to the first king of Tibet, Srong-tsan-sgam-po, and helped convert Tibet to Buddhism, later (after 749) modified by Padmasambhava toward Tantrism.

645. Hsüan-tsang, returned from a pilgrimage to India, recorded his precise observations, and headed a commission which translated 75 books in 1335 volumes, creating for the purpose a consistent system for transcription of Sanskrit. He introduced the scholastic doctrine of **Vasubandhu** (which still survives), that the visual universe is only a mental image. The **Pure Land** or **Lotus School** of Buddhism for the next seventy years enjoyed far more popular favor. Based on texts translated in the 2nd and 5th centuries, it is called the *Short-Cut School* because it teaches direct salvation by faith in Amitabha and invocation of his name. Religious **Taoism,** fully organized on the Buddhist model, now also received imperial patronage on the ground that Lao-tzu, whose surname legend gives as Li, was the ancestor of the ruling house. A 4th century apocryphal text, *Hua Hu Ching*, which claims Lao-tzu to be a prior avatar of Buddha, was actively debated. It was proscribed (668) but again tolerated (696). Imperial commissions completed or newly compiled eight standard histories to bring the series down to date from the Three Kingdoms. Another prepared the first literary encyclopedia, *I Wen Lei Chü*.

657–659. Dispersal of the western Turks (T'u-chüeh), some of whom eventually migrated across southern Russia to Hungary while others followed Mahmud of Ghazni to India.

671–695. I-ching made the pilgrimage to India by sea, stopping to learn Sanskrit in Srivijaya (southeastern Sumatra), a state which became tributary (670–673), and remained powerful until the close of the 14th century.

684–704. Empress Wu temporarily altered the dynastic title to *Chou* (690–704), and decreed use of capriciously deformed written characters.

712–756. HSÜAN TSUNG, popularly known as Ming Huang, ruled over a court of brilliant High Renaissance literary and artistic attainment. He founded the **Academy of Letters** (725) and established schools in every prefecture and district in the empire (738). **Li Po** (705–762) and **Tu Fu** (712–770) created and excelled in lyric verse. In painting, continuous composition was substituted for episodic treatment. **Wu Tao-hsuan** (c. 700–760) ranks foremost among figure-painters. **Li Ssu-hsün** (651–c. 720) and **Wang Wei** (698–759) created two of the first and most influential landscape styles. Slackening of genuine religious enthusiasm is conspicuous alike in the tone of Buddhist votive inscriptions and in the monumental realism of the sculpture which becomes increasingly secular, then perfunctory. T'ang potters freely borrowed forms of Iranian flask and ewer, Indian ritual drinking vessel, and Greek amphora. They made these resplendent with new colors in soft lead glaze applied over slip with new technical versatility. From about this time dates probably also the first true porcelain with high-fired felspathic glaze. **I-hsing** (c. 725), a Buddhist astronomer, invented the first known clock-escapement. The Buddhists, too, now enlarged the seal and produced wood blocks for **printing on paper** (earliest extant printed book dated 868).

732. Manichaeism was condemned as perverse doctrine, but was permitted to Persians and Tokharians who had introduced it (694 and 719) and who were favored for their competence in astronomy and astrology.

738. The title *King* was conferred on a T'ai ruler who (730) united six principalities as **Nan-chao** with capital at Ta-li (741). After two disastrous efforts at conquest (750 and 754), the T'ang made peace (789–794), leaving the kings of Nan-chao full autonomy. They still had to be repelled, twice from Cheng-tu (829 and 874), once from Hanoi (863).

745. Uighur Turks overthrew the eastern Turks and set up their own empire on the Orkhon, ruling from Ili to Tibet and the Yellow River. Their *kaghan* was given a title and a Chinese princess (758).

747. Kao Hsien-chih led an army across the Pamirs and Hindukush, but

751. Defeat by the Arabs at Talas lost Turkestan to China.

751–790. Wu-k'ung made the pilgrimage to India through Central Asia on the eve of displacement of Buddhism by Islam.

755. Revolt of An Lu-shan, a Turkish adventurer who had been adopted by the emperor's favorite concubine, Yang Kuei-fei, and had united three military commands, plunged the empire into particularly sanguinary and destructive civil war.

756–757. The emperor fled to I-chou (renamed Cheng-tu) which was developed rapidly as a cultural center. He there abdicated in favor of his son. Despite gradual suppression of the rebellion by Kuo Tzu-i and Li Kuang-pi, power remained in hands of territorial military leaders.

762–763. The Uighur kaghan sacked the eastern capital at Loyang, then in rebel hands, but was himself there converted to Manichaeism, which became the Uighur state religion.

763. The Tibetans, by a surprise attack, sacked Ch'ang-an. Through fear of the Uighur, who tried to convert the T'ang, Manichaeans were allowed to build temples in the capitals (768) and seven other cities (771 and 807). The kaghans were given rich gifts of silk, and a princess (821).

840–846. Overthrow of the Uighur Empire by the Turkish Kirghiz and Karluk led to migration of many tribes from the Orkhon to the Tarim basin, where they carved out a second Uighur Empire in which the Turkish language extinguished the Indo-European dialects.

841–846. The reign **of Wu Tsung,** under Taoist influence, was filled with persecution of Manichaeans (843), Buddhists, Nestorians, and Mazdeans (845). Buddhism alone was now naturalized and able to survive. The most prominent place in an epoch of increasing anarchy was taken by the **Ch'an** (Sanskrit, *Dhyana,* Japanese, *Zen*) **sect** which offered refuge in introspective contemplation. **Bodhidharma,** an aged Persian who had come to Loyang from India prior to 534, was now hailed as fabulous founder of the school, although in fact he was still obscure as late as 728.

CULTURAL PROGRESS continued despite military alarms. **Wei Pao** was commanded (744) to prepare an authentic version of the *Canon of History* by collation of variant manuscripts. It was included, together with all three competing rituals and all three commentaries on the *Annals,* among twelve classics which were cut in stone at Ch'ang-an (836-841). **Han Yü** (768-824) not only wrote excellent poetry, as did **Po Chü-i** (772-846), but created and set the classic model for the essay style. The first historical encyclopedia, the *T'ung Tien,* was compiled (766-801) by **Tu Yu;** and the practice of writing monographs on individual prefectures and districts was begun.

907-959. FIVE DYNASTIES of short duration asserted imperial authority but seldom exercised it outside the Yellow River Basin: Later Liang (907-923), Later T'ang (923-936), Later Tsin (Chin) (936-947), Later Han (947-950), and Later Chou (951-960). Among ten competing secession states the most considerable were southern Han at Canton (904-971), and southern T'ang, which from Nanking ruled much of the east and south (937-975).

932-953. Nine classics were first printed from wood blocks, as cheap substitute for stone engraving, at the Later T'ang capital at Loyang by **Feng Tao,** who had seen the process in Shu (Szechwan). The text was that of the stone inscriptions of 836-841.

907-1123. KHITAN MONGOLS under their dynastic founder Ye-lü A-pao-chi (907-926) conquered all Inner Mongolia, the kingdom of Po Hai in the Liao Valley, and 16 northern districts of China. His suzerainty was recognized even by the Uighurs. His son Ye-lü Te-kuang (927-947) first helped set up the Later Tsin dynasty at Ta-liang (modern Kaifeng) and then destroyed it. He took Yen-ching (Peking) as his own southern capital (938), and adopted the Chinese dynastic name *Liao* with periodic reign-titles (947-1125).

960-1279. The **SUNG DYNASTY** marks the advent of modernity, not only in governmental and social organization, but in thought, belief, literature, and art; not least in the diffusion of learning through print. It was an age of humanism, of scholar statesmen who were at once poets, artists, and philosophers. The first half of the dynasty is often distinguished as the Northern Sung (960-1127) when the capital was at Kaifeng, then variously called Ta Liang, more properly Pien-liang, or Pien-ching.

960-976. Chao K'uang-yin or (Sung) T'ai Tsu gradually restored unity and order under accustomed forms with the help of a paid army.

965. The Annamese secured independence before South China could be subdued and shortly (c. 982) sacked the Cham capital Indrapura before Chinese pressure forced them to peace. Although the Chams (c. 1000) moved their capital south to Vijaya (Cha-ban, near Binh-dinh), the Annamese resumed the war (1043) and sacked it also.

967. The emperor deliberately refused to invade the territory of the native kings of Nanchao in Yünnan, a policy observed by his successors. He permitted temporary autonomy to the king of Wu Yüeh (modern Chekiang) who had retained his throne (897-978) by pledging loyalty to each Chinese dynasty.

972 ff. The **Buddhist canon** was printed in Szechuan by imperial order from 130,000 blocks. It was reprinted with additions in Fukien (1080-1104), and elsewhere thereafter.

976-997. T'ai Tsung completed reunion of the empire (979), but was twice repulsed from Peking by the Liao (979 and 986).

997. Division of the empire into 15 provinces (*lu*), later extended to 18 (1023-1031) and 23 (1078-1085).

990-1227. The **western Hsia** (Hsi Hsia) kingdom of Tangut on the northwest frontier with capital at Ning-hsia appealed often to arms (996, 1001-1003, 1039-1042) despite grant of the imperial surname *Chao* and office (991, 997, 1006) and royal investiture (1044).

1004. An invasion by the Liao reached the Yellow River near Pien-liang. They were granted annual tribute. These payments, increased in 1042, and the hire of a large standing army bade fair to bankrupt the treasury.

1006. Granaries for emergency relief were established in every prefecture. In 1069 grain so stored was valued at 15 million strings of cash.

1069-1074. WANG AN-SHIH (1021-1086) carried out a program of radical reform with the full confidence of Shen Tsung (1068-1085), and in face of bitter opposition of conservative statesmen.

Through a new **financial bureau** (1069) he cut the budget 40 per cent and raised salaries to make honesty possible for ordinary officials. To avoid excessive transport costs and to control prices he empowered the chief transport officer to accept taxes in cash or kind, to sell from the granaries, and to buy in the cheapest market, using capital of 5 million strings of cash. Further to protect poor farmers against usurers and monopolists, loans of cash or grain were offered in spring against crop estimates to be repaid in autumn with interest of 2 per cent a month (moderate in China). Ambitious officials forced these loans upon merchants and others who did not want them. Objection to both principle and administration of these measures, which were accompanied by alarming centralization of power and disregard for precedent, led to wholesale resignations and transfers of the best officials, whose help alone might have made them successful. **Conscript militia** were organized (1070) and trained for police purposes and national defense. The standing army of over a million inefficient men was gradually cut in half. By 1076 the militia, volunteer guards, and border bowmen numbered over 7 million men. **Cash assessments** graded in proportion to property were substituted (1071) for compulsory public services which had borne too heavily upon thrifty rural families. The exemption of officials, clergy, and small families was reduced by half. Necessary local services were now performed by paid volunteer agents. **State banking** and barter offices were opened (1072) first at the capital and later in every prefecture, with the object of controlling prices for the popular benefit.

1074–1085. The reform program was continued, despite complaints of excessive cash levies and other malpractices, until the emperor's death, for a time (1075–1076) by Wang himself.

1085–1093. Regency of the hostile grand dowager empress (under the reign title Yüan Yu) and recall of Ssu-ma Kuang, Su Shih, and the conservative faction to rescind the whole of the reform scheme (1085–1086). Extreme reaction in turn provoked reaction. On the death of his grandmother,

1093–1100. Che Tsung again favored reform, as did his younger brother

1101–1125. Hui Tsung, who permitted Ts'ai Ching to proscribe (1102) 98 of the Yüan-Yu partisans, finally (1104) 309 conservatives, living and dead, headed by Ssu-ma Kuang. Eventually much that was good in the measures of 1070 and 1071 was retained. Hui Tsung, himself an able painter, was an active patron of the arts and letters. He founded the **Imperial Academy of Painting,** and sponsored catalogues of his collections of painting and of archaic bronzes, some of which were obtained by excavation.

The Northern Sung period was the golden age of **landscape painting,** when compositions of majestic breadth and exquisite detail were rendered in monochrome and color on long rolls or broad panels of silk. **Tung Yüan** (late 10th century) and **Kuo Hsi** (c. 1020–1090) combined mastery of continuous composition and linear technique with that of suggestion of atmosphere through gradations of ink-tone. **Li Kung-lin** (c. 1040–1106) excelled in vigorous contrasts of light and shade, of broad and delicate line, and in airy architectural renderings in ruled and measured style. **Mi Fei** (1051–1107) used hardly any lines, building mountains and forests from graded accumulations of blobs of ink.

Scholarship flourished no less. Two great encyclopedias were compiled by imperial order, the *T'ai Ping Yü Lan* (977–983) and the *Ts'e Fu Yüan Kuei* (1005–1013). **Ou-yang Hsiu** (1007–1072), a prominent statesman, prepared the *New History of the T'ang,* the first repertory of early inscriptions, and a monograph on the peony. **Ssu-ma Kuang's** greatest work was an integrated history of China, 403 B.C.– 959 A.D., compiled 1066–1084. **Su Shih** (1036–1101), better known as **Su Tung-p'o,** was distinguished as an independent statesman, and one of China's greatest essayists, poets, and calligraphers. **Wang An-shih** held his own with these as a brilliant writer of state papers and classical expositor.

Use of tea, first mentioned as substitute for wine under the Wu dynasty (222–280), spread through North China.

It is not known when or by whom the **principle of magnetic polarity,** known to the Chinese at least since the 1st century A.D., was applied in the mariner's compass with floating needle. The Malays in the 16th century employed, like the Chinese, a compass rose with 24 points, in contrast to the Arab rose of 32 points; which suggests, but does not prove, that the Malays received both compass and rose from the north. The compass is plainly mentioned by Chinese writers of the early 12th century. The volume of **maritime commerce** swelled greatly as Arabs in the 9th and 10th centuries entered into competition with Persians at Canton and Ch'üan-chou (Zayton), later at Lin-an. It was trade in cotton goods that brought 70 families of Jews from Persia and India to settle at the capital Pien-liang, where they remained unmolested until gradually absorbed.

1114–1234. Jürchen Tungus tribes overthrew their Khitan rulers in Manchuria (1114–1116) and, with short-sighted Chinese aid, seized all the Liao lands in China (1122–1123). Ye-lü Ta-shih of the Khitan led the remnant of his people to found a new state, Kara-Khitai, in eastern Turkestan (1130) and Turkestan proper (1141–1211). Meantime

1122. The Jürchen prince declared himself emperor of the **Chin** (or Kin) **dynasty.** He attacked the Sung so vigorously that although

1125. Hui Tsung abdicated in favor of his son,

1126. Ch'in Tsung and his father were both captured with the entire court in the capital. Hui Tsung died in captivity (1135).

1127–1279. THE SOUTHERN SUNG. A

junior prince fled southeastward across the Long River from city to city, even by sea to Wen-chou; but, when the Chin retired north of the Long River (1130) and set up the puppet buffer state of Ch'i (1130-1137), the capital was established (1135) at Lin-an (modern Hangchow). The gallant general Yüeh Fei won several successes until put to death by Ch'in Kuei who made

1141. A peace dictated by economic exhaustion, accepting as frontier the line of the Huai and upper Han Rivers.

1161. Explosives were used by **Yü Yün-wen** in defeating the Chin at Ts'ai-shih (in Anhuei near Nanking). The Chin, like the Liao before them, avidly absorbed and adopted Chinese culture.

Early **Chinese philosophers** devoted nearly all their effort to the practical study of ethics. Buddhism, however, insistently raised the problems of ontology and epistemology. It is the merit of the Sung philosophers to have achieved a synthesis of ancient ethics with a new rationalized metaphysics. **Chou Tun-i** (1017-1073) revived a diagram of the ancient diviners to illustrate his conception of causation: emergence of paired forces from primal unity and differentiation of natural phenomena by their interaction. **Ch'eng Hao** (1032-1085), the leading member of a commission which initiated the valuable public services act of 1071, was in philosophy a mystic synthesist who found benevolence in all things. His brother **Ch'eng I** (1033-1107) was an analyst who discovered in the *Li Chi* the *Ta Hsüeh* or "Great Learning," a short work on method which stresses knowledge as essential to self-improvement on which all human welfare depends. Ideas of the school were systematized and crystallized by **Chu Hsi** (1130-1200), who equated as universals primary unity, an impersonal but just and benevolent heaven, and righteousness, which correspond to the physical, metaphysical, and ethical spheres. From these proceed as co-ordinates the dual modes of production, the decrees of heaven, and the processes of self-improvement. The final products are, respectively, the diversity of natural phenomena, conscience, and character. All these activities of parallel evolution are expressions of a universal divine law. Acceptance of knowledge as an element in self-improvement, and consequent emphasis on objective study, pointed the way toward scientific research; but this tendency was promptly combated by **Lu Chiu-yüan** (1139-1192), who stressed the teaching of Mencius that goodness springs from within.

Painters under the Southern Sung reproduced most often the mild misty landscapes of the Hang-chow region rather than the beetling crags found south of Ch'ang-an that had often inspired northern artists. **Ma Yüan** (1190-1224), **Hsia Kuei** (c. 1180-1230), and their school placed special emphasis on economy of line and representation of mists and clouds. Secular painters came increasingly under domination of conventions which grew up in the academy founded by Hui Tsung, and elegance, charm, and impeccable taste tended to replace more virile virtues; but religious painters, both Buddhist and Taoist, continued to produce vigorous work until the close of the dynasty. **Ch'en Jung** (c. 1235-1255) ranks as China's greatest painter of dragons.

Sung **ceramists** applied to pottery and porcelain in forms of subtle and sophisticated elegance both incised and molded decoration, together with a wide variety of high-fired glazes, some of which have never since been equaled. Although most wares were ostensibly monochrome, the potters learned to control color-transmutation of their pigments. The potters of Tz'u-chou for the first time employed penciled decoration both under and over glaze.

Science developed so that in mathematics the complete properties of the circle were known. Astronomical instruments became very large, to increase the accuracy of the measurements. The calendar month had been computed to be 29.53 solar days. By 1200 the first windmills appeared in China, spreading there from Afghanistan.

c. 1190-1294. THE MONGOLS. In central Asia, **Temujin** (c. 1162-1227) created a new Mongol empire which was rapidly expanded by strategy and a military machine employing discipline, extreme mobility, espionage, terrorism, and superior siege equipment.

1194. The **Yellow River**, after repeated alterations of its bed, flowed south of the Shantung massif until 1853.

1206. **Temujin was proclaimed** *Jenghiz Khan* ("Emperor within the Seas") at Karakorum. He employed as chancellor a Uighur scholar Tatatonga, who applied to Mongol the Uighur script that was derived from Phoenician through Aramaic, Old and New Sogdian. Enforcement of peace and order within the empire promoted both commerce and cultural exchanges.

1211-1222. The Chin were driven south to the Yellow River (from Yen-ching, 1215).

1227. After several campaigns (1205, 1207, 1209) the Hsi Hsia Kingdom was destroyed, with massacre at Ning-hsia. Temujin bequeathed the empire to a grandson and three sons: to **Batu,** son of his eldest, Juchi, Kipchak in Russia; to **Chagatai,** the former Kara-Khitai empire; to **Ogadei,** Outer Mongolia; and to

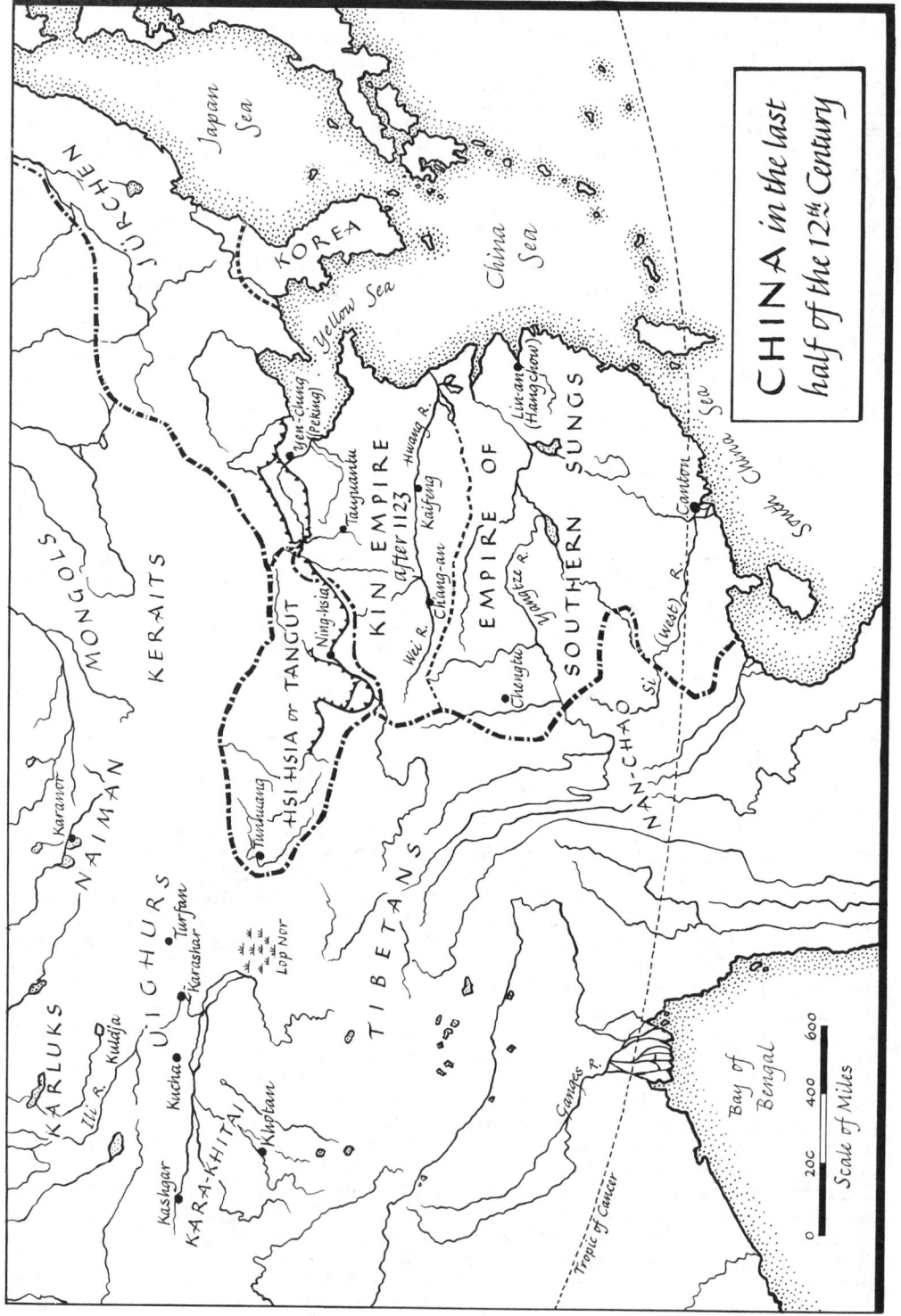

CHINA in the last half of the 12th Century

Tului (regent 1227–1229), eastern Mongolia and North China.

1229–1241. Ogadei was elected khan by plenary kuriltai on the Kerulen.

1231. Ye-lü Ch'u-ts'ai (1190–1244), a sinicized scion of the Khitan royal house and adviser to Temujin since 1215, proved his ability to collect taxes in China by traditional methods, and was appointed chancellor. Korye (Korea) conquered and placed under 72 Mongol residents.

1233. Pien-liang fell after a flanking campaign by Tului through Hanchung and Szechwan (1231–1232), and a long siege by Subutai in which the Chin defenders used explosive bombs.

1234. The Chin Empire was annexed. Belated Chinese attack provoked Mongol seizure of Szechwan (1236–1238).

1237. Ye-lü Ch'u-ts'ai secured 4030 scholars one-quarter of whom were freed from slavery through civil service literary examinations, and restored full civilian administration.

1237–1241. Subutai subjugated Russia and led an invasion through Hungary to Cattaro which was recalled only by death of Ogadei (p. 264).

1246–1248 or 1249. Guyuk, son of Ogadei and his widow Turakina (regent 1242–1246), was elected khan in presence of Plano Carpini, envoy of Innocent IV.

1251–1259. Mongka, son of Tului, was elected over the son of Guyuk's widow (regent 1249–1251).

1252–1253. Mongka's brother Kublai crushed Nan-chao. The king was named *maharaja* and hereditary administrator under the eyes of a Mongol garrison commander and Chinese resident. More autonomy and an imperial princess were conferred in 1284.

1254. Mongka, the son of a Nestorian woman and employer of a Nestorian chancellor, told William of Rubruck, envoy of Louis IX of France, that religions are like the fingers of one hand. He yet favored Buddhism, and after public disputation (1255) proscribed Taoist books for forgery. Kublai shortly followed this example (1258).

1257. The capital was transferred to Shang-tu, north of present Peking.

1258. The Mongols pillaged Hanoi, while, at the other end of the empire, Hulagu with a Nestorian wife and general destroyed the Abbasid caliphate of Baghdad.

1260–1368. The **YÜAN DYNASTY** (as distinguished from the Mongol Empire) was effectively founded when **Kublai** (1214–1294) had himself elected khan by his own army at Shang-tu (1260), although he adopted the dynastic title only in 1271. He ruled in China according to Chinese precedents. His dynastic name is Shih tsu.

1264. The **Mongol Empire** was reunited by capture of Kublai's brother Arikboga, who had been proclaimed khan at Karakorum (1260). Twice (1277 and 1287–1288) its unity was defended against Khaidu, head of the house of Ogadei. Kublai's authority was respected by his brother Hulagu and the succeeding ilkhans of Persia, and in theory by the Golden Horde on the Volga. He transferred (1264) the winter capital to Yen-ching where he constructed Khanbalig, modern Peking (1267). He erected an astronomical observatory on the city wall, wherein were installed bronze instruments cast by Kuo Shou-ching (1279).

1268–1273. A siege of Hsiang-yang and Fanch'eng on the Han was ended after four years five months only by engineers and machines from Mesopotamia. Thereafter the Mongols were free to descend toward the sea.

1276. Capitulation of the empress-regent and boy-emperor at Lin-an (Hangchow) was followed by capture of Canton (twice, 1277) and destruction of a fleet carrying the last youthful Sung pretender (1279).

1281. Disastrous **attack upon Japan.** An assault in 1274 having failed, a Mongol army of 45,000 from Korea joined (June) a tardy armada with 120,000 men from the southern Chinese coast in landing at Hakozaki Bay. The invaders were repulsed by the well-prepared Japanese until (Aug. 15) a typhoon destroyed their fleets, leaving them to death or slavery.

1282–1283. An army sent by sea from Canton to subdue Champa took the capital Vijaya, but was forced by epidemics to withdraw.

1285 and **1287–1288.** Abortive expeditions against Annam and Champa by land and sea were massacred and repulsed, but secured admission of vassalage.

1287. The Mongols pillaged Pagan, capital of Burma, received homage (1297), and returned (1300) to pacify competing Shan chiefs.

1292–1293. A naval **expedition to Java,** after temporary success, was forced to re-embark.

1294. Tribute was received from the Siamese kingdoms of Xieng-mai and Sukhotai.

1295–1307. Temur Oljaitu, grandson of Kublai, was the second and last effective ruler of the Yüan dynasty.

1296. A Mongol embassy accompanied by Chou Ta-kuan found Chen-la (Cambodia) much weakened by the attacks of Sukhotai, which had now become a powerful state under its second ruler Rama Kamhing.

ECONOMIC DEVELOPMENTS. Kublai devoted special attention to economic matters: the grand canal was restored (1289–1292) from the former Sung capital, Lin-an at Hangchow (the Kinsay of Marco Polo), now a great and rich city, to the Huai River, and carried north to the outskirts of Peking. Imperial roads were improved, and postal relays of 200,000 horses established. Charitable relief was organized (1260) for aged scholars, orphans, and the sick, for whom hospitals were provided (1271). Imperial inspectors every year examined crops and the food supply with a view to purchase when stocks were ample for storage against famine.

The T'ang first employed paper money orders, to which the Sung and Chin added various bills of exchange. When issue of paper currency was suggested to Ogadei (1236), Ye-lü Ch'u-ts'ai secured limitation to value of 100,000 ounces of silver. Under Kublai, a Mohammedan financier, Saiyid-i Edjill Chams al-Din Omar (1210–1279), kept annual issues at an average of 511,400 ounces (1260–1269). His successor Ahmed Fenaketi increased emissions (1276–1282) to 10,000,000 ounces annually. After Ahmed's murder, inflation increased until a Uighur, Sanga, reduced the rate of printing to 5,000,000 ounces (1290–1291). Circuit stabilization treasuries (1264 and 1287) were given reserves inadequate to redeem the flood of bills at $2\frac{1}{2}$ per cent discount, the official rate of 1287. The issue of 1260 depreciated until replaced 1 for 5 by that of 1287, which again was replaced 1 for 5 in 1309. All printing was discontinued in 1311; but the credit, financial and moral, of the dynasty was already on the wane. The southern provinces of the empire rapidly fell from its control.

Marco Polo, in the service of the khan (1275–1292), traveled widely in Cathay (from Khitai, hence North China), and Manzi (South China), and to Burma (p. 383). Through his "Division of the World" he first brought detailed and accurate knowledge of eastern Asia to Europe. In his time, and even in that of the Arab, Ibn Batuta (c. 1345), Zayton (Ch'üan-chou) was the busiest deep-sea port in the world, leading Kinsay (Lin-an), Foochow (Fu-chou), and Canton in shipping silks and porcelains to Java, Malaya, Ceylon, India, and Persia in exchange for spices, gems, and pearls. The itineraries given by Chao Ju-kua (1225) imply in the precision of their bearings the use of a compass needle mounted on a dry pivot.

The **MOSLEM COMMUNITIES** of Persian and Arab traders at these ports were small compared to those which now grew up in North China and in Yünnan. Saiyid-i Edjill as governor of Yünnan (1274–1279) built the first two mosques in what became a stronghold of Islam. Most popular religion with all the Mongols was Buddhism. Kublai welcomed a gift of relics of the Buddha from the raja of Ceylon. He conferred the title *Teacher of the State* upon a Tibetan lama Phags-pa, whom he employed to convert the Mongols and to whom he entrusted government of the three provinces of Tibet.

NESTORIAN CHRISTIANS enjoyed full protection. The patriarch of Baghdad created an archbishopric at Peking (1275); churches were built in Chen-kiang (1281), Yang-chou, and Hangchow; and a special bureau was created (1289) to care for Christianity. **Mar Yabalaha,** pilgrim from Peking to Jerusalem, was elected patriarch (1281), and his companion Rabban Sauma was sent by him and Argun, ilkhan of Persia, to Rome and France. He negotiated with Pope Nicholas IV an entente between the Nestorian and Roman churches. **John of Montecorvino** was the first of several Roman missionaries to China (1294–1328). He baptized 5000 converts and was named by the pope (1307) archbishop of Peking. He received a three-year visit from **Oderic of Pordenone** who reported to Europe the custom of foot-binding, which had spread through South China under the Southern Sung, but which was unknown to the Chin and early Yüan.

SCIENCE AND TECHNOLOGY. Meteorology developed to the extent that by the 14th century the correlation between the climate changes and the sunspot cycle was known. By 1500 a rotary disc-cutter was being used to cut jade, highly valued in China since the 13th century B.C. By 1593 a modern form of the abacus was in use.

LITERATURE. The Mongol period introduced the novel and the drama, the latter accompanied by raucous percussion music. Although neither was at once admitted as a form of polite letters, both are now recognized to possess artistic merit.

PAINTING. One group of artists continued traditions of the Southern Sung while another boldly swept away the mists which had shrouded landscape. **Ch'ien Hsüan** (1235–c. 1290) is perhaps the greatest painter of flowers and insects. **Chao Meng-fu** (1254–1322) was particularly adept at depicting the horses and other livestock that were prominent in Mongol economy. Yüan porcelain reveals in arabesques no less than in the technique of penciling in cobalt blue directly on clear white paste the debt of Chinese potters to Persian models. From these also is derived the Byzantine form of cloisonné enamel.

1368–1644. The **MING DYNASTY** was founded by **Chu Yüan-chang** (Ming T'ai Tsu, 1328–1398), a monk turned insurgent amidst anarchy, who seized Chiang-ning (Nanking) in 1356, set up there an orderly government, and proceeded to annex the holdings of surrounding southern war-lords until in 1368 he was strong enough to drive the Mongols from Peking with Shensi, Kansu (1369), and Szechwan (1371). Like all the emperors of this and the following dynasty he ruled under a single reign-title, *Hung-wu* (1368–1398), which is accordingly often used instead of his personal name.

1382. Yünnan was completely conquered, and its prince executed at Nanking. The whole territory of China was now under direct government.

1388. The Mongols were driven from Karakorum and defeated on the Kerulen.

1392-1910. The **Li dynasty** was founded in Korea upon the ruins of that of Wang, which had reigned since 918 (p. 373).

1403-1424. The **Yung Lo reign** of Ch'eng Tsu was established by violence against his nephew, who disappeared in a palace fire (1402).

1403-1433. A series of **naval expeditions** through the southern seas was motivated by desire for commerce and military prestige, but also by uneasiness lest the deposed nephew emerge thence to claim his throne. Secret inquiry by Hu Jung within the empire also was protracted (1407–1416, 1419–1423). A claimant actually appeared in Honan in 1440.

1405-1407. **Cheng Ho,** the chief eunuch (a Moslem whose real surname was Ma), brought back in chains the prince of Palembang (Sumatra), who had been defeated in battle, as he did

1408-1411. The **king of Ceylon** and his family, who had attacked the mission. As a result of

1412-1415. A third cruise as far as Hormuz, sixteen southern states sent tribute. Cheng Ho was appointed to lead three more embassies during this reign: 1416–1419 (as far as Aden), 1421–1422, and 1424. Other eunuchs led additional missions.

1410, 1414, 1422-1424. **Campaigns into Outer Mongolia** were directed at destruction of whatever chieftain or group momentarily possessed sufficient prestige to threaten recreation of the Mongol power.

1421. **Transfer of the capital to Peking** was mooted in 1409, decreed in 1420. Wisdom of the move is reflected by the fact that the northern frontier was never successfully violated during the five centuries Peking remained capital, save when the Manchus were invited in.

1428-1788. The **later Le dynasty in Annam,** after a quarter century of fighting, secured recognition of independence (1431) from Hsüan Tsung in the Hsüan Te reign (1426–1435). The royal title was conferred in 1436.

1431-1433. **Cheng Ho** led a seventh and final embassy to twenty states. As result tribute was sent by Mecca and ten others.

1449. **Emperor Ying Tsung** (1436–1449 and 1457–1464) was captured in battle by the chief of a new Mongol confederation (Oirat) of four tribes. Although released next year, he recovered his throne from his brother Ching Ti only in 1457.

c. 1470-1543. **Dayan,** a descendant of Jenghiz, restored unity to Mongolia, but then divided it among his own descendants.

1471. Annam finally annexed its southern neighbor, Champa. (*Cont. p. 575.*)

a. BURMA, 1044-1365

From early times Burma was under Indian influence. By the 3rd century A.D. expanding Hindu peoples had established commercial settlements on the Tenasserim coast and at the principal river mouths which developed into small kingdoms in contact with the Tibeto-Burman tribes of the Irrawaddy Valley. Commercial relations with China were less influential, although an embassy from a Burmese state reached Ch'ang An in 802.

1044. **Anawrata** seized royal power at Pagan and by his patronage of Hinayana Buddhism and conquests, both north and south, made it the political, religious, and cultural center of Burma; the Burmese written language was developed and Buddhist scriptures translated; architectural monuments followed the inspiration of Ceylon and southern India; able rulers succeeded Anawrata.

1106. A Burmese embassy at the Sung capital in China was received as from a fully sovereign state.

1287. Following the rejection of Mongol demands for tribute (1271 and later), Burmese raids into Yünnan, and the death of Narathihapate (who ruled 1254–1287), **Mongol forces looted Pagan** and destroyed its power. The invasion of Shan tribes, forced southward by the Mongols, led to the division of Burma into a number of petty states, chief among them being Toungoo (established 1280), Pegu in southern Burma, and Ava in the middle and lower Irrawaddy Valley (established as capital 1365). (*Cont. p. 579.*)

b. SIAM, to 1557

During the early centuries of the Christian Era, the **Khmer** peoples of the Menam Valley came under the influence of Hindu civilization, and about the 6th century there was organized, in the region of Lopburi, the **kingdom of Dvaravati,** which was Buddhist rather than Brahman in religion, and from which during the 8th century migrants to the upper Menam Valley established the independent and predominantly Buddhist **kingdom of Haripunjaya,** with its capital near the present Chiengmai. Early in the 11th century Dvaravati was annexed to Cambodia; but Haripunjaya retained its independence.

Splendor of Khmer architecture; vast funerary temples for the god-kings (**Angkor Wat,** early 12th century). In the 13th century Haripunjaya was overrun by a migration of Tai, or Shan, peoples from the north. This migration, accelerated by the Mongol conquest of the Tai state of Nan-chao (in modern Yünnan and southern Szechwan) in 1253, led eventually to the suppression of the Khmer kingdoms and the setting up of the Tai Kingdom of Siam with its capital at Ayuthia, founded by Rama Tiboti in 1350. The early Siamese state was from the first under the influence both of Hinayana Buddhism and of Chinese political institutions. Toward the end of the 13th century a form of writing had been invented for the Siamese language.

1350-1460. Siamese **invasion of Cambodia** finally led to the abandonment of Angkor (1431) and collapse of the Khmer Empire.

1371. A Siamese embassy at Nanking inaugurated tributary relations with the newly founded Ming dynasty.

1376-1557. Intermittent friction between Siam and the Tai state of Chiengmai in the northern Menam Valley ended only with the destruction of Chiengmai by the Burmese.

During the 14th and 15th centuries strong Siamese influence was exerted over the disunited states of Burma and the northern part of the Malay Peninsula. (*Cont. p. 580.*)

c. MALAYSIA, to 1407

Early Indian commercial settlements in Sumatra and Java, at first Brahman in religion and later influenced by Buddhism, became the centers of organized states. Toward the end of the 7th century A.D., **Srivishaya** became the dominant state of Sumatra and built up a commercial empire which at its height (c. 1180) controlled the Straits of Malacca and of Sunda, all of Sumatra and the Malay Peninsula, and the western half of Java; its authority was recognized as far away as Ceylon and Formosa, and in many colonies throughout the East Indies. The **Sailendra dynasty,** rulers of Srivishaya, were ardent patrons of Buddhism, as is shown in the great Borobudur victory monument in central Java. The consolidation of petty Javanese states, begun after the middle of the 9th century, led to the rise of **Singosari** in eastern Java, which under Kartanagara (who ruled 1268-1292) challenged and finally destroyed the power of Srivishaya.

1293. A Mongol expedition, sent to avenge insult offered by Kartanagara, was forced out of Java by a new kingdom, **Madjapahit,** which during the 14th century built up a commercial empire with authority extending over Borneo, Sumatra, and parts of the Philippines and of the Malay Peninsula, and profited by an extensive trade with China, Indo-China, and India. After the

1389. Death of Hayam Wuruk, the power of Madjapahit disintegrated.

1405-1407. The first Chinese expedition under Cheng Ho established tributary relations between many Malay states and the Ming Empire; and the authority of Madjapahit rapidly gave way to that of the Moslem Arabs. During the 15th century Moslem commercial operations, based chiefly on Malacca, were extended to the whole archipelago, and some twenty states accepted Islam as the state religion. (*Cont. p. 580.*)

4. KOREA, 612-1451

(*From p. 149*)

612. Emperor Yang-ti of the Sui dynasty of China invaded Koguryŏ but was repulsed.

645-647. Two T'ang expeditions against Koguryŏ failed.

663. The T'ang destroyed Paekche.

668. The T'ang and Silla together destroyed Koguryŏ.

670. Silla robbed the T'ang of Paekche and southern Koguryo, but did not break its allegiance to China.

670-935. SILLA PERIOD.

670-780. Height of Silla power and culture, when Buddhism and art flourished, particularly at the capital near the modern Kyŏngju (Japanese Keishū).

780-935. Period of political decline, but of closer relations with and increasing imitation of China.

c. 880. Serious rebellions broke out.

918. The state of **Koryŏ** was founded in west central Korea.

935. Silla peacefully submitted to Koryŏ.

935-1392. KORYŎ PERIOD.

935-1170. Height of Koryŏ power and culture centering around the capital, Kaesong (modern Sŏngdo; Japanese, Kaijō), in west central Korea and P'yŏngyang, the secondary capital.

936. Koryŏ destroyed Later Paekche, thus uniting Korea once more.

996. The **Khitan** (Liao dynasty) forced Koryŏ

to recognize them, and not the Sung dynasty of China, as overlords of Korea.

1044. A great wall was completed across northern Korea as a defense against the Manchurian peoples.

1123. The **Jürchen** (Chin dynasty) forced Koryŏ to recognize their suzerainty.

1170. Military officers seized the government and proscribed Buddhism.

1196. The **Ch'oe family** established its control over the government with the title of *Kongnyŏng*.

1223. Beginning of over 200 years of attacks on coastal regions by Japanese pirates.

1231. The **Mongols** invaded Korea, and the Ch'oe removed the government to the island of Kanghwa off the west coast.

1258. The Im (Lim; Japanese, Rin) family supplanted the Ch'oe as *Kongnyŏng*.

1259. Koryŏ submitted to the Mongols, and the Koryŏ kings through intermarriage became merely a branch of the Mongol imperial family and their representatives in Korea. This situation and the rise of Confucianism at this time led gradually to the unquestioning acceptance of Chinese suzerainty and leadership in political and cultural matters.

1356. Koryŏ revolted successfuly against the Mongols.

1356-1392. Period of great disorder. The Koryŏ kings, who had depended on Mongol prestige for their authority, were unable to suppress their unruly vassals, and the Japanese pirates were at their worst.

1369. Koryo submitted to the Ming dynasty of China.

1392. **I** (Li; Japanese, Ri) **Sŏnggye** declared himself king after a series of *coups d'état* and assassinations, thus founding the

1392-1910. **I** (Li; Japanese, Ri) **DYNASTY** with its capital at Kyŏnsŏng (modern Sŏul [Seoul]; Japanese, Keijō). This new dynasty based its claims to legitimacy on its championing of the Ming cause as opposed to the Mongols, considered by them not to be the legitimate rulers of China. Like their predecessors they remained unswervingly loyal and subservient to China.

1392-1494. Period of greatest prosperity and cultural development.

1419-1451. **King Sejong** was a patron of learning, and in his time the native phonetic script called *ŏnmun* was introduced. During this reign the Japanese pirates ceased to ravage the Korean coast, and the northeastern corner of present-day Korea was brought under Korean rule. (*Cont. p. 581.*)

5. JAPAN, 645-1543

(*From p.* 152)

645-784. PERIOD OF THE IMITATION OF CHINA. An edict outlining the general principles of national reorganization was promulgated as early as 646 (the *Taika Reform*), but it was only in the course of several decades that the principles were put into practice and even then the reforms often remained on paper. The major features of the new system were: (1) the nationalization of the land, in theory; (2) the adoption of the T'ang system of land distribution and taxation; (3) the reorganization of local government and other measures intended to increase the authority of the central government in the provinces and its income from them, and (4) the reorganization of the central government. The principles and many of the details of the reforms were borrowed directly from China, but in Japan, dominated as it was by an hereditary aristocracy, it was well-nigh impossible to carry them out in full, and from the start they were basically modified in practice. (1) Although the land was nationalized in theory, in actuality the large hereditary estates of the clan chiefs were

returned to them as lands held as salary for their official positions and ranks. (2) The land was to be periodically divided among the agriculturalists in accordance with the membership of each family as determined by census, and uniform taxes were to be levied on all alike. These were (a) the land tax (*so*), paid in rice; (b) the corvée (*yōeki*), often commuted at a fixed rate into a textile tax; and (c) the excise (*chō*), levied on produce other than rice. The system was too closely patterned after the Chinese and functioned badly in Japan from the beginning. Powerful families and institutions, hungry for land, were always ready to deprive the public domain of taxpaying lands, and the peasants, impoverished by taxes, were often anxious to transfer themselves and their lands from the taxpaying public domain to the care of privately owned manors (*shōen*). As a result the history of economic development during the next several centuries is primarily the story of the return of the land into private hands and the emergence of large tax-free estates owned by the court nobility and great religious institutions. (3) The improvement of means of communication helped in the centralization of government and in the collection of taxes, but, although the officials of the provincial governments were to have been appointees of the central government, in practice local leaders retained their supremacy by occupying the lower posts, and it soon became the accepted custom for the high provincial officials to remain at the capital and to delegate their powers to underlings in the provinces. (4) An essential and permanent feature of the reforms was the complete reorganization and great elaboration of the central government. A department of religion (*jingikan*) and a great council of state (*dajōkan*) were established as two parallel organs controlling the spiritual and political aspects of the state. Below the great council were eight ministries, and below them in turn many smaller bureaus. The organization was too ponderous for the Japan of that day. Moreover, with the collapse of the economic supports of the central government through the growth of tax-free estates, this elaborate organism was literally starved to death. Although in theory it continued little changed until the 19th century, actually during most of that period it was merely a skeleton devoid of most of its former substance. In adopting the Chinese form of government the Japanese made one significant change: the official hierarchy of Japan remained a hereditary aristocracy and, with rare exceptions, there was little opportunity for the able or learned of low rank to rise far in this hierarchy.

This period was the **classic era of Japanese culture.** Poetry and prose in pure Chinese were composed, and native Japanese poetry reached an early flowering. Japan in the preceding century had already been imitating continental artistic styles, and now the art of T'ang China found fertile soil in Japan and produced there many of the greatest extant examples of Far Eastern art of that day in the fields of architecture, sculpture, painting, and the applied arts.

663. The **Japanese withdrew from Korea,** after the defeat of a Japanese army and fleet, sent to the aid of Paekche, by a combined force from China and Silla (662). Thus ended the first period of Japanese continental expansion. The fall of Paekche in 663 and of Koguryŏ (a North Korean kingdom) in 668 left Silla supreme in the peninsula and resulted in a great immigration of Korean refugees into Japan.

697. The **Empress Jitō** (686–697) abdicated in favor of her grandson, **Mommu** (697–707). This was the first case of the accession of a minor and the second of the abdication of a ruler, but both were soon to become the rule.

702. New **civil and penal codes** known as the *Taihō Laws* were promulgated. This may have been the first complete codification of the laws embodied in the reforms commenced in 646, although there is mention of an earlier code. These laws, together with a revision of 718 (*Yōrō Laws,* not enforced until 757), have come down to us only through later commentaries, the *Ryō no Gige* of 833 and the *Ryō no Shūge* of 920. A supplementary code, the *Engishiki,* was completed in 928.

710. **Heijō** (or Nara) was laid out on the model of Ch'ang-an, the T'ang capital, as the first permanent capital of Japan. The period during which it was the capital is known as **710–784. THE NARA PERIOD.**

712. The *Kojiki,* which records the history of the imperial line since its mythical origins, was written in Chinese characters (used to a large extent phonetically) to represent Japanese words. This is Japan's oldest extant book.

720. The *Nihonshoki* (or *Nihongi*), a more detailed history of Japan written in Chinese, was compiled. It was continued to 887 by five other official histories written in Chinese, which together with it constitute the **Six National Histories** (*Rikkokushi*).

724–749. **Shōmu's reign,** which included the brilliant Tempyō year period (729–748). This and the period during which Shōmu dominated the court as the retired emperor (749–756) marked the apogee of the Nara Period and its classic semi-Chinese culture.

737. The death of the four grandsons of Kamatari delayed for several decades the complete domination of the imperial court by the Fujiwara clan.

741. Government monasteries and convents (*Kokubunji*) were ordered erected in each province.

752. The dedication of the **Great Buddha** (*Daibutsu*) at Nara marked the completion of the devout Shōmu's most cherished project. The 53-foot bronze figure of the Buddha Rushana (Sanskrit, *Vairocana*) and the huge hall built over it was a tremendous undertaking for the Japanese court and gave witness to the great Buddhist fervor of the time. Many of the objects used in the dedication service together with the personal belongings of Shōmu form the basis of the unique collection of 8th century furniture and art preserved at the imperial treasury in Nara (the *Shōsōin,* commenced in 756).

Shortly before the erection of the Great Buddha the famous monk, **Gyōgi** (670–749), is said to have propagated the concept that Buddhism and Shintō were two aspects of the same faith. Such beliefs served as a justification for the growing amalgamation of the two religions, which was to lead by the 12th century to the development of **Dual Shintō** (*Ryōbu Shintō*), in which Shintō gods were considered to be manifestations of Buddhist deities. Faced with a highly developed foreign religion backed by all the prestige of the more advanced Chinese civilization, the simple native cult became for a period of almost 1000 years the handmaiden of Buddhism in an unequal union.

754. The Chinese monk **Ganjin** (also pronounced Kanshin, etc.; Chinese, *Chien-chên*, d. 763), after five unsuccessful attempts to reach Japan, finally arrived at Nara, where he set up the first ordination platform (*kaidan*) and firmly established the **Ritsu** (Sanskrit, *Vinaya*) **Sect,** which stressed discipline rather than doctrine. The Ritsu Sect together with five other sects formed the so-called **Nara Sects,** the oldest sectarian division of Japanese Buddhism. These others were the **Sanron** (Sanskrit, *Madhyamika*) **Sect,** said to have been introduced in 625; the **Hossō** (Sanskrit, *Dharmalaksana*) **Sect,** brought from China by Dōshō (d. 700), who had gone there to study in 653; the **Kegon** (Sanskrit, *Avatamsaka*) **Sect,** which was largely responsible for the cult of Rushana, the universal and omnipresent Buddha; the **Kusha** (Sanskrit, *Abhidharmakosa*) **Sect;** and the **Jōjitsu** (Sanskrit, *Satyasiddhi*) **Sect;** which last two may never have existed as independent religious bodies in Japan.

759. The *Man'yōshū*, a collection of over 4000 poems in pure Japanese, composed largely by the court nobility between 687 and 759, was compiled shortly after the latter date. It was followed in later centuries by similar anthologies. In 751 the *Kaifusō,* a small collection of poems in Chinese, had been compiled; it likewise was continued by similar works.

764. A clash for power between **Fujiwara Nakamaro** (also known as Emi Oshikatsu), the leading statesman during Junnin's reign (758–764), and Dōkyō, the monk favorite of the retired nun empress, Kōken (749–758), led to the death of Nakamaro, the exile of Junnin, his subsequent assassination and the reascension to the throne of Kōken as the Empress Shōtoku.

764–770. Dōkyō was all-powerful during Shōtoku's reign and may even have aspired to the throne. Strong opposition and Shōtoku's death led to his ultimate downfall. Perhaps because of the memory of Dōkyō's influence over Shōtoku, for almost nine centuries thereafter no woman occupied the throne.

781–806. The reign of the energetic **Kammu** witnessed the conquest of much of northern Hondō in a prolonged but successful border struggle with the Ainu. After several initial failures the natives of this region, both Ainu and intractable Japanese frontiersmen, were definitely brought under the imperial sway by **Sakanoue Tamuramaro** (d. 811). His campaigns concluded centuries of slow advance into Ainu territory. After a final outbreak in 812 the Ainu menace in the north never again assumed major proportions.

794. Kammu moved the capital from Nagaoka, where it had been since 784, to Heian, the modern Kyōto, where it remained until 1868. The reasons for his abandoning of Nara are not definitely known but were probably: (1) a desire to make a new departure politically and economically; (2) a desire to escape the oppressive influence of the powerful Nara monasteries; (3) the superior location of Nagaoka and Kyōto, which had better water communications with the sea; and (4) the influence of the Hata family (?), which had lands in that region. The reasons for the sudden removal of the capital from Nagaoka to Kyōto, a few miles farther inland, are still more obscure, but may have been connected with Kammu's fear that the first site had incurred the curse of certain spirits. The establishing of the capital at Kyōto marked the beginning of

794–1185. The **HEIAN PERIOD,** a long era marked by few violent upheavals but one in which the transition from the period of the imitation of China to the feudal and more strictly Japanese Kamakura period was slowly made. These centuries were characterized by a somewhat effete dilettantist court society, becoming increasingly divorced from political and economic realities; the gradual decline and collapse of the economic and political system borrowed from China; the growth of tax-free manors; the slow emergence of a new military class in the provinces; the full glory and subsequent decline of the Fujiwara family; the appearance and development of the Buddhist sects and cults that dominated much of Japan's religious history; a sounder understanding of the borrowed Chinese civilization and a greater ability to synthesize it with what was natively Japanese, or to modify it to fit the peculiar needs of Japan; a resultant growing cultural independence of China, and the reappearance of more purely Japanese art and literature.

800–816. New offices in the central government, which were to affect profoundly the whole administration, appeared at this time. These were: (1) the *kageushi* (audit office) (c. 800), which in time usurped the prerogatives of the original audit and revenue offices; (2) the *kurōdo-dokoro* (bureau of archivists) (810), which gradually attained control of palace affairs and became the organ for issuing imperial decrees; (3) the *kebiishichō* (police commission) (c. 816), which in time became the primary law enforcement organ of the state and eventually created outside of the official codes its own code of customary law.

804. **Tendai** and **Shingon,** the two leading sects of the Heian period, were founded by **Saichō** (Dengyō Daishi 767–822) and **Kūkai** (Kōbō Daishi 774–835) respectively. Both monks accompanied the eleventh embassy to the T'ang in 804. Saichō returned to Japan the next year to found the Tendai Sect, named after Mt. T'ien-t'ai in China. The syncretistic inclusive nature of the philosophy of the sect appealed to the Japanese, and its central monastery, the Enryakuji, which Saichō founded on Mt. Hiei overlooking Kyōto (788), became the center from which sprang most of the later significant movements in Japanese Buddhism. Kūkai returned from China in 806 bringing with him the Shingon or Tantric Sect, a late esoteric and mystic form of Indian Buddhism. Because of his tremendous personality and the natural appeal of Shingon to the superstitious propensities of the people, the new sect won considerable popular support, and the Kongōbuji monastery on Mt. Kōya, which Kūkai founded (816), became one of the great centers of Buddhism. Tendai and Shingon were more genuinely Japanese in spirit than were the Nara sects, and the Shingon Sect in particular furthered the union of Shintō and Buddhism.

838. The twelfth and **last embassy to the T'ang** was dispatched. When in 894 Sugawara Michizane (845–903) was appointed to be the next envoy, he persuaded the court to discontinue the practice on the grounds that China was disturbed and no longer able to teach Japan. Although some unofficial intercourse continued between the two countries, this brought to an end the three centuries of the greatest cultural borrowing from China and marked the beginning of a period in which peculiarly Japanese traits asserted themselves increasingly in all phases of Japanese life.

858. The complete **domination of the Fujiwara clan** over the imperial family was achieved by Yoshifusa (804–872) when he became the *de facto* regent of the child-emperor, Seiwa (858–876). In 866, after Seiwa had attained his majority, Yoshifusa assumed the title of regent (*sesshō*), becoming the first non-imperial regent. Seiwa was the first male adult emperor to have a regent. The typical inner family control which the Fujiwara exercised over the emperors can be seen in the relationship that existed between Seiwa and Yoshifusa, for the latter was both the grandfather and the father-in-law of the young ruler. It was the definite policy of the Fujiwara to have a young imperial grandson of the head of the clan occupy

the throne and to have him abdicate early in favor of another child. The period of the domination of the Fujiwara family is often called

866–1160. THE FUJIWARA PERIOD.

880. **Fujiwara Mototsune** (836–891) became the first civil dictator (*kampaku*), a post thereafter customarily held by the head of the clan when an adult emperor was on the throne, while the post of regent came to be reserved for the clan head in the time of a minor emperor.

889. The branch of the warrior **Taira clan** which was to rule Japan for part of the 12th century was founded when a great-grandson of Kammu was given this surname. The clan was established in 825 by another imperial prince. In 814 the rival military **clan of Minamoto** was founded by other members of the imperial clan, and in 961 the princely progenitor of the later Minamoto rulers received this surname. The descendants of such imperial princes, reduced to the rank of commoners, often went to the provinces to seek their fortunes, and there some of them merged with the rising class of warriors, who were soon to dominate the land.

891. The **Emperor Uda** (887–897), who was not the son of a Fujiwara mother, made a determined effort to rule independently without Fujiwara influence and refused to appoint a new civil dictator after Mototsune's death. To further this end he used the brilliant scholar, **Sugawara Michizane** (845–903), as his confidential minister, but after Uda's abdication (d. 931), Fujiwara Tokihira (871–909) managed to obtain the removal of Michizane to a provincial post, where he soon died. He was posthumously loaded with honors and deified because it was believed that his vengeful spirit had caused certain calamities. Tokihira throughout his official career strove valiantly but in vain to stem the tide of governmental corruption and disintegration.

905. The *Kokinshū,* an anthology of over a thousand poems in Japanese, was compiled by imperial order in a revival of interest in Japanese poetry. For over a century almost all literary effort and scholarship had been devoted to prose and poetry in the Chinese language, but **Ki Tsurayuki** (d. 946) wrote the preface to the *Kokinshū* in Japanese and followed it in 935 by a travel diary (*Tosa Nikki*) also in Japanese. Within the short compass of a century Japanese prose was to rise to great heights of literary achievement. An important contributing factor to the revival of Japanese literature at this time was the fact that in the preceding century a simple syllabary for writing Japanese phonetically had been evolved from the complicated Chinese characters.

930. The offices of regent and civil dictator were revived after a lapse of four decades when **Fujiwara Tadahira** (880–949) became regent in 930 and civil dictator in 941.

935–941. Civil strife in the provinces broke out on an unprecedented scale, giving witness to the rise of the provincial military class. From 936 until his death in 941 Sumitomo, a member of the Fujiwara clan and a former provincial official, controlled the Inland Sea as a pirate captain, while in eastern Japan an imperial scion, Taira Masakado, after waging war on his relatives and neighbors, declared himself emperor (940), but was presently killed.

949. The **Emperor Murakami** (947–967) did not appoint a successor to Tadahira, but after the former's demise

967–1068. The successive heads of the Fujiwara clan occupied the posts of regent and civil dictator almost uninterruptedly for a full century. This was the heyday of the Fujiwara clan and the core of the so-called Fujiwara period. Court life was ostentatious and extravagant and was characterized by amatorial dilettantism and moral laxity. At the same time petty jealousies and intrigues disrupted the Fujiwara clan, members of the provincial warrior class began to appear on the capital stage as petty military officers and came to be used by the court nobles in their disputes, manors continued to grow apace, further limiting government resources, and the general collapse of the central government continued unabated.

985. The *Ojōyōshū* by the monk **Genshin** (942–1017) gave literate expression to new religious currents that were stirring the nation. A belief had sprung up that the age of *mappō* ("the latter end of the law"), a period of degeneracy to come 2000 years after the Buddha's death, had already commenced. There was a growing belief in the **Pure Land** (*Jōdo*), Paradise of Amida (Sanskrit, *Amitabha*) and salvation through his benign intervention in favor of the believer and not only through one's own efforts, as earlier Buddhism had taught. Emphasis was increasingly placed on *nembutsu*, the repetition of Amida's name or a simple Amidist formula. **Kūya** (903–972), an itinerant preaching monk, was the first articulate voice to express this new religious movement, and Genshin gave it sound literary formulation. It continued to develop, and in the 12th and 13th centuries produced important new Buddhist sects.

995–1028. FUJIWARA MICHINAGA'S (966–1028) rule over clan and state saw the zenith of clan power and some of the most brilliant decades of artistic and literary achievement of the epoch. Although he was never officially civil dictator and was regent for only a short period prior to his official retirement in 1017, he was perhaps the most powerful leader the Fujiwara produced. At this time the classic prose literature of Japan reached its height in the *Genji Monogatari* (c. 1008–1020), a long novel by **Murasaki Shikibu**, a court lady, and in the *Makura no Sōshi* (Pillow Book) (c. 1002), a shorter miscellany by another court lady, **Sei Shōnagon**. The refined and somewhat feminine art of the epoch also was at its height. **Jōchō** (d. 1057), a famous Buddhist sculptor, was already active, and Michinaga's successor, **Yorimichi** (992–1074, regent 1017–1020; civil dictator 1020–1068), built the *Byōdōin*, the outstanding architectural work remaining from the age.

1039. Armed Enryakuji monks invaded Kyōto to force their will upon the government, but were driven off by Taira troops at Yorimichi's command. Such descents upon the capital, known as "forceful appeals" (*gōso*), were common during the 11th and later centuries and sometimes led to actual fighting. The turbulence of the monks, who fought fiercely among themselves as well as with the court, made it necessary for the court to appeal to the Taira and Minamoto for military aid, and the warrior clans consequently became more influential at court.

1051–1062. In the **Earlier Nine Years' War** Minamoto Yoriyoshi, on imperial command, destroyed the **Abe**, a powerful military clan of northern Japan. Thereby he firmly established the prestige of his branch of the Minamoto clan in eastern and northern Japan. Yoriyoshi's ancestors had already started the military renown of the house, and its status at court as "the claws and teeth of the Fujiwara" greatly increased its power.

1068–1073. The **Emperor Sanjō II,** who was not the son of a Fujiwara mother, ruled directly without the interference of the Fujiwara. Although the latter continued to occupy the posts of regent and civil dictator, they never again gained full control of the government. Sanjō II established a records office (*kirokujo*) to examine title deeds of manors in an effort to check their growth, but in this attempt he was blocked by the opposition of the Fujiwara.

1083–1087. In the **Latter Three Years' War** Minamoto Yoshiie (1041–1108) destroyed the Kiyowara family of northern Japan, thereby increasing Minamoto prestige in that region.

1086–1129. The **Emperor Shirakawa** (1073–1086) continued to rule after his abdication as a retired emperor (*jōkō*) and after 1096 as a priestly retired emperor (*hōō*). He built up a complete governmental organization of his own (*insei*, camera government) which was continued during much of the next two and a half centuries by other retired emperors and priestly retired emperors, but after 1156 they lost control of the government to the warrior clans.

1129-1156. The **Emperor Toba** (1107-1123) ruled after Shirakawa's death as a priestly retired emperor.

1156. **Civil war** (the *Hōgen no Ran*) broke out between the reigning emperor **Shirakawa II** (1155-1158), and the retired emperor, Sutoku (1123-1142). Both were supported by prominent members of the Fujiwara, Minamoto, and Taira clans. Shirakawa II's partisans, among whom were numbered Minamoto Yoshitomo (1123-1160) and Taira Kiyomori (1118-1181), were victorious. Sutoku was exiled, and many of his supporters were executed. This war brought no lasting peace and was soon followed by

1160. A **second civil war** (*Heiji no Ran*), in which Minamoto Yoshitomo and an adventurous young Fujiwara noble, Nobuyori (1133-1160), gained temporary control of the capital by a successful *coup d'état*, but were soon crushed by the Taira. This war left

1160-1181. **Taira Kiyomori** in control of the nation. The two wars of 1156 and 1160 had not been a struggle for power between the court and the military clans, but the result had been to make a single victorious warrior, backed by personal troops, the dominating figure in Japanese politics. Shirakawa II as retired emperor (1158-1192) had some influence in the government, but in 1167 Kiyomori had himself appointed prime minister (*dajō-daijin*), and gave important posts in the central and provincial governments to his clansmen. Kiyomori married his daughters into both the imperial and the Fujiwara families. In 1180 his infant grandson, Antoku, was placed on the throne. Thus he attained the same hold over the imperial family that the Fujiwara had once had.

1175. The **Pure Land** (*Jōdo*) **Sect** was founded by Genkū (Hōnen Shōnin) (1133-1212). It was the first of the Amidist Sects, and this event marked the beginning of a great new sectarian movement.

1179. The **death of Shigemori** (1138-1179), Kiyomori's eldest son and perhaps the wisest of the Taira, removed a stabilizing check on Kiyomori, whose desire for more power was leading him to excesses which were alienating the sympathies of the imperial family, the court nobility, and the Buddhist monasteries. The rapid adoption on the part of Kiyomori and his family of the customs and mentality of the court nobles also estranged many of the provincial supporters of the clan.

1180. An abortive uprising against the Taira led by an imperial prince and by Minamoto Yorimasa (1106-1180), together with certain monasteries, started a general uprising of the remnants of the Minamoto clan under the leadership of Yoshitomo's son, Yoritomo (1147-1199), backed by Taira and other clansmen of eastern Japan.

1183. The Taira were driven out of Kyōto by Yoshinaka (1154-1184), a cousin of Yoritomo. A long campaign in the Inland Sea region followed and culminated in

1185. The **battle of Dan no Ura,** at the western outlet of the Inland Sea, where Yoritomo's younger brother, Yoshitsune (1159-1189), annihilated the Taira. The child-emperor, Antoku, whom the fleeing Taira had taken with them, died in the battle. The elimination of the Taira left Yoritomo, as head of the Minamoto clan, the virtual ruler of the nation and marked the beginning of the first period of feudal rule in Japan known as

1185-1333. THE KAMAKURA PERIOD. The outstanding feature of the era was the clear division between the now powerless civil and religious government of the imperial court at Kyōto and the military government (*Bakufu*) of the Minamoto established at Kamakura, near the clan estates in eastern Japan and away from the enervating influence of the court nobility. The transition from civil to feudal military rule had begun with the Taira and was not completed until centuries later, but it was in the Kamakura period that the most drastic changes occurred and the political and economic institutions of the next several centuries began to take shape.

Feudalism. The usurpation of the powers of the imperial court was largely unconscious and developed naturally out of the economic and political conditions of the late Heian period. Primary factors in this evolution were: (1) The wars of the 11th century had hastened the transfer of the prerogatives of ownership of the great manors of the nobles to the military men who resided on these manors as bailiffs or wardens and who often had feudal ties with the warrior clans. The actual ownership of the estates usually remained unchanged, but ownership was robbed of most of its meaning by a complicated series of feudal rights (*shiki*) which ranged from rights to cultivate the land up through an ascending scale of rights to the income from it. (2) Because of the breakdown of the old centralized government and the need for self-defense feudal military groups had grown up in the provinces with their own "house laws," governing the conduct and the relations of the members of a single group. Moreover, a feudal code of ethics had been developed which emphasized personal loyalty to a feudal chief rather than to a political ideal. (3) Minamoto prestige had for long induced landed warriors to commend themselves and their lands to the Minamoto for the sake of protection. The victory over the Taira greatly increased Minamoto feudal authority both through new additions of this sort and through the confiscation of vast Taira lands. The single Minamoto feudal union consequently had grown so large that it now controlled the nation, and its military government, not the impotent Kyōto administration, was the real government of the land.

Foreign Relations. For four and a half centuries only a few Japanese monks had gone abroad, and foreign trade had been in the hands of the Koreans and Chinese, but in the Kamakura period the Japanese once more began to take part in foreign commerce. At the same time they began to raid and plunder the coasts of both Korea and China, and in time they became a serious nuisance and occasionally even a national menace to both countries.

Art. Kyōto, though remaining the scene of a colorful court life, was forced to share honors with Kamakura as a center of art and culture. Many Kyōto scholars moved to Kamakura to aid in the civil administration of the military government, and the warrior class brought a new creative energy to art and literature, which were approaching sterility in the late Heian period. Significant artistic trends were: (1) a final great flowering of sculpture before its gradual extinction in following centuries; (2) the introduction from China of two new architectural styles known as the Chinese (*Karayō*) and the Indian (*Tenjukuyō*) styles, which came to blend with the traditional style (*Wayō*), and (3) the perfection of the narrative picture scroll (*emakimono*). Significant literary trends were: (1) the increasing use of Japanese in preference to Chinese; (2) the revival of native poetry in the *Shinkokinshū*, an imperial anthology of 1205, and (3) the popularity of historical military tales written in rhythmical prose.

Religion. The Kamakura period was one of great religious and intellectual ferment. It witnessed the birth and development of new sects growing out of the popular movements of the late Heian period. It saw the introduction of the **Zen Sect** from China and the growth of a military cult glorifying the sword, Spartan endurance, and loyalty. From these two elements was born the combination of the aesthetic and mystical penchants of the Zen monk with the qualities of the Kamakura warrior—a combination which remains one of the chief characteristics of the Japanese people.

1185-1199. Yoritomo, as the feudal military dictator, organized the new military government with the aid of Kyōto scholars like Ōe Hiromoto (1148-1225). Already in 1180 he had created a *Saburaidokoro* to perform police duties and to control affairs of the warrior class. In 1184 he had established an administrative board, renamed the *Mandokoro* in 1191. In 1184 the *Monchūjo* had also been established as a final court of appeal. Impartial administration of justice characterized the rule of the Kamakura military government and was one of the chief reasons for its long duration.

In 1185 Yoritomo appointed constables (*shugo*) in some of the provinces and placed stewards (*jitō*) in many of the large manors. A few such appointments had been made in preceding years, but now this system was expanded in order to strengthen his influence in regions over which he had hitherto had no direct control. The constables were special military governors in charge of the direct vassals of the Minamoto. The stewards, who represented Yoritomo on estates not otherwise under his control, levied taxes on the estates for military purposes. Thus the fiscal immunity of the manors was violated, and Kamakura retainers were scattered in key positions all over the country. The constables and stewards gradually grew in importance in the economic and political life of the provinces and in time developed into the feudal lords of later centuries.

1189. Yoshitsune was killed at the orders of Yoritomo, who apparently was jealous of the fame the latter had won as the brilliant general responsible for the greatest victories over the Taira. Yoritomo similarly disposed of other prominent members of the family, including his cousin Yoshinaka (1184), who as a warrior ranked next only to Yoshitsune, his uncle Yukiie (1186), who was one of the prime movers in the Minamoto uprising, and his brother Noriyori (1193), who also was one of the clan's great generals. His cruel treatment of his own relatives contributed to the early extinction of the family.

1189. Yoritomo crushed the powerful Fujiwara family of northern Japan on the grounds that they had killed Yoshitsune, albeit at his own command. The northern Fujiwara in the course of the previous century had become a great military power and had made their capital, Hiraizumi, a brilliant center of culture. Their elimination removed a serious menace to Minamoto supremacy.

1191. Eisai (1141-1215) propagated the Rinzai branch of the Zen (Sanskrit, *Dhyana*) Sect after his return from a second study trip to China. The Zen Sect enjoyed the official patronage of Kamakura and the special favor of the warrior class in general.

1192. Yoritomo was appointed *Seiidaishōgun* ("barbarian-subduing great general"), or *shōgun* for short. He was not the first to bear this title, but he was the first of the long line of military dictators called *shōgun*.

1199-1219. Transition period from Minamoto to Hōjō rule. Yoritomo was succeeded as head of the Minamoto by his eldest son, Yoriie (1182-1204), who was not appointed *shōgun* until 1202, but his mother, Masako (1157-1225), actually ruled with the aid of a council headed by her father, **Hōjō Tokimasa** (1138-1215). The latter, though a member of the Taira clan, from the start had cast his lot with Yoritomo and had exercised great influence in the Kamakura councils before Yoritomo's death. The Hōjō, though loyal to the military government, unscrupulously did away with Yoritomo's descendants and crushed their rivals among the other Minamoto vassals.

1203. Yoriie was exiled and his younger brother, Sanetomo (1192-1219) was made *shōgun* by Tokimasa. The following year Yoriie was murdered.

1205. Tokimasa was eliminated from the government by Masako. His son, Yoshitoki (1163-1224), then became regent (*shikken*) of the *shōgun*, a post held by successive Hōjō leaders, who were the real rulers.

1219. The Minamoto line came to an end when Sanetomo was assassinated, probably with Hōjō connivance, by his nephew, who in turn was executed.

1219-1333. The **PERIOD OF HŌJŌ RULE** as regents for weakling *shōgun* of Fujiwara and imperial stock was characterized by administrative efficiency and by justice.

1221. An uprising under the leadership of the retired emperor, **Toba II** (1183-1198), was the gravest menace the Hōjō had to face, but was quickly crushed. Two prominent Hōjō leaders were left in Kyōtō as joint civil and military governors of the capital region (*Rokuhara Tandai*). The estates confiscated from the defeated partisans of Toba II gave Kamakura much needed land with which to reward its followers, and the abortive uprising gave the Hōjō a chance to extend the system of constables, stewards, and military taxes to regions hitherto unaffected by it.

1224. Shinran Shōnin (1173-1262), a disciple of Genkū, founded the **True Pure Land** (*Jōdo Shin*) **Sect** as an offshoot from the Pure Land Sect of his master. The True Pure Land Sect introduced innovations such as marriage for the clergy. It was destined to become the most popular of all Japanese Buddhist sects with Zen its only close rival.

1226-1252. Fujiwara nobles as figurehead *shōgun*.

1229. Dōgen (1200-1253) introduced the Sōtō branch of the Zen Sect after his return from study in China.

1232. The *Jōei-skikimoku*, a law code based primarily on custom rather than on earlier sinicized law codes, was adopted for all those directly under the feudal rule of Kamakura. It remained the basis of law codes until modern times.

1252-1333. Imperial princes as figurehead *shōgun*.

1253. Nichiren (1222-1282) founded the **Lotus** (*Hokke*) **Sect,** popularly known as the Nichiren Sect. In it the Lotus Sutra was venerated much as the Amidist Sects venerated Amida. A fiery religious and political reformer, Nichiren was an ardent nationalist, and his writings illustrate the gradual emergence of a definite national consciousness at this time. Imbued with the turbulent nature of its founder, the sect had a stormy career.

1274. FIRST MONGOL INVASION. The Mongols, already masters of Korea and most of China, repeatedly sent embassies (1268-1273), enjoining the Japanese to submit, but the Kamakura government under the bold leadership of the regent, Hōjō Tokimune (1251-1284), refused. Finally in 1274 the Mongols dispatched an expedition aboard a Korean fleet. The islands of Tsushima and Iki were reduced, a landing was made in Hakata (Hakozaki) Bay in northern Kyūshū, and an inconclusive encounter, in which superior weapons and military organization gave the Mongols the advantage, was fought with the local warriors. But the same night, because of their insecure position and the threat of a storm, the invaders set sail for Korea.

1281. SECOND MONGOL INVASION. Mongol envoys sent to Japan in 1275 and again in 1280 were summarily executed, and the military government hastily prepared defense works in western Japan. In 1281 the Mongols embarked a huge force on two large fleets, one Korean and one Chinese, and again, after capturing Tsushima and Iki, landed in northern Kyūshū. Although the invaders numbered some 150,000, the Japanese checked their advance on land with walls they had prepared for this emergency and worsted them on the sea because of the greater mobility of their smaller craft in close quarters. After almost two months of fighting a terrific storm destroyed a large portion of the invading armada, and the remainder departed with serious losses. The Mongols continued plans for another invasion of Japan until the death of their emperor, Kublai (1294), and the Japanese continued their defense preparations still longer.

The Mongol invasions no doubt spurred on Japan's nascent national consciousness, but it also contributed greatly to the final collapse of the Kamakura government. Military preparations against the Mongols had seriously taxed the nation's resources, and at the end of the two invasions the military government, lacking land confiscated from the enemy, was without the usual means of rewarding its vassals for their valiant efforts. This state of affairs helped undermine the loyalty of the warrior retainers of Kamakura. At the same time the monasteries were becoming increasingly unruly, the court nobility was beginning again to intrigue with disaffected warriors against the Hōjō, and the latter themselves had lost the virtues of frugality and justice that had once characterized the family.

The Hōjō during the final decades of their rule began to resort to **Acts of Grace** (*Tokusei*) cancelling certain indebtedness in an effort to save the lands of their vassals from mortgages, but such obviously unfair measures antagonized certain powerful interests and failed adequately to protect the Kamakura vassals.

1331–1333. The **IMPERIAL RESTORATION** of **Daigo II** and the fall of the Hōjō. The energetic and able emperor, Daigo II (1318–1339), after bringing to an end in 1322 the domination of the court by retired emperors, organized an abortive plot to overthrow the Hōjō as early as 1324. In 1331 open warfare broke out between Daigo II, supported by his able sons, some of the large monasteries in the capital region, and various local nobles and warriors like **Kitabatake Chikafusa** (1292–1354) and **Kusunoki Masashige** (1294–1336), the two outstanding patriot heroes of medieval Japan. The following year the emperor was captured and exiled to Oki, but in 1333 he escaped. Most of western Japan declared for the imperial cause. Ashikaga Takauji (1305–1358), one of the two chief generals dispatched by the Hōjō from eastern Japan, deserted to Daigo II's standards, and the sudden capture of Kamakura by another prominent Hōjō vassal, Nitta Yoshisada (1301–1338), brought the military government of Kamakura to an end.

1333–1336. **Daigo II** in a short period of personal rule, failing to face economic and political realities, attempted to revive the civil imperial rule of the 8th century. However, he did make his able son, Morinaga (1308–1335), *shōgun* and appointed his leading generals

military governors of large sections of the land. Because of his dissatisfaction with his share of the spoils in northeastern Japan,

1335. **Takauji** revolted against the throne. Defeating the Nitta, Kitabatake, and other loyal families,

1336. Takauji drove Daigo II out of Kyōto and set up a new emperor from a branch of the imperial family which had been jealously contending the throne with Daigo II's branch for several decades. He thereby became the virtual dictator of the central government, and, although he was not appointed *shōgun* until 1338, with his capture of Kyōto commenced

1336–1568. **THE ASHIKAGA** (or Muromachi) **PERIOD.** The Ashikaga *shōgun* continued the outward forms of the military rule of the Minamoto and Hōjō, but during most of the first and last centuries of the period open warfare disrupted the nation, and at best the Ashikaga exercised only a shadowy control over the great feudatories who made their appearance at this time. The age was characterized by quickly shifting allegiances and by political instability, which at times amounted to anarchy. There was a general redistribution of feudal and economic rights, and the Kyōto nobility, which now lost most of its few remaining lands and provincial sources of income, was reduced to penury. The complicated feudal relations of the Kamakura period broke down into simpler, more compact divisions with practically independent lords, often the former provincial constables, ruling large territories, which were in turn subdivided into smaller units administered by their direct vassals. The collapse of clan unity and an organized feudal system necessitated stronger solidarity within the smaller family and feudal units. The division of patrimonies among heirs was abandoned, and women were reduced to a subordinate status. Lords exercised a closer paternalistic supervision over their vassals, and the latter in turn served their lords with greater personal loyalty.

The **overseas trade** and pirate enterprises of the Japanese increased in the Ashikaga period; the central government once more established official relations with China; and another important period of borrowing from abroad commenced. Foreign trade stimulated the growth of towns and provincial ports, such as Sakai (part of the modern Ōsaka), Hyōgo (the modern Kōbe), and Hakata (part of the modern Fukuoka). Despite political disruption and incessant warfare, a phenomenal economic development took place. Nascent industries grew and expanded, and trade guilds (*za*), usually operating under the patronage of some religious institution, appeared and flourished.

However, the unrestricted multiplication of various levies and of customs barriers proved a serious curb to the development of trade.

Kyōto was once more the undisputed political and cultural capital, and there the warrior class and the court nobility tended to fuse. Constant warfare made the period in some respects the intellectual dark ages of Japan, but political disunity helped to diffuse learning throughout the land. Zen monks dominated the intellectual and artistic life of the nation and through their intimate contacts with China, where many had lived and studied, expanded Japan's intellectual and artistic horizons. Although this was a great age of Zen, the other sects, particularly the Amidist sects, flourished and sometimes developed powerful military organizations. It was still a thoroughly Buddhist age, but intellectual life began to free itself from the bonds of Buddhism, Sung Confucian philosophy was introduced from China, and stirrings of new life appeared in Shintō, where for the first time systematic syncretic philosophies were developed.

Despite the violent internecine strife of the early and late Ashikaga period, in the middle decades literature and art, ruled by Zen standards of restraint and refinement, flourished. The *Literature of the Five Monasteries*, as the Zen school at Kyōto was called, revived poetic composition in Chinese, and a great lyric drama called *Nō* appeared. The Sung style of painting, often in monochrome and usually of landscapes, reached its height in Japan with such great masters as **Shūbun** (c. 1415) and **Sesshū** (1420–1506), and the two greatest Japanese schools of painting, the **Tosa** and **Kano,** flourished. The independent architectural styles of the Kamakura period were blended to form a composite style. Minor arts like landscape gardening and flower arrangement grew up, and the tea ceremony was popular among the upper classes. Under Zen tutelage there developed a refined simplicity of taste and a harmony with nature that has had a lasting influence on Japanese art and psychology.

1336–1392. CIVIL WARS OF THE YOSHINO PERIOD. When Takauji drove Daigo II out of Kyōto and set up a rival emperor, Daigo II and his partisans, the Kitabatake, Kusunoki, and others, withdrew to the mountainous Yoshino region south of Nara, where Daigo II and three imperial successors maintained for almost six decades a rival court, called the *Southern Court* because of its location. During this period, known as the *Yoshino period* or the *Period of the Northern and Southern Dynasties,* civil war convulsed Japan. In support of the legitimacy of the southern court

1339. Kitabatake Chikafusa wrote the *Jinnōshōtōki,* a history of Japan imbued with extreme nationalistic and patriotic sentiments. It is an important landmark in the growth of a national consciousness and the imperial cult.

1392. The reunion of the two courts. Although at times the Yoshino warriors even captured Kyōto, the hopes of the southern court gradually waned. Eventually in 1392 peace was made, and Kameyama II (1383–1392) of the southern line abdicated in favor of **Komatsu II** (1382–1412) of the northern line, with the understanding that the throne should henceforth alternate between members of the two branches of the imperial family, as it had done for several reigns preceding that of Daigo II. However, the northern line never yielded the throne to its rivals despite futile uprisings in their behalf. Official history regards the southern line as the legitimate rulers during the Yoshino period.

1395–1408. Rule of Yoshimitsu as retired *shōgun.* Yoshimitsu, the third Ashikaga *shōgun* (1369–1395), after crushing his principal opponents, uniting the two imperial courts, and bringing the Ashikaga power to its apogee, passed on the title of *shōgun* to his son and retired as a monk to his Kitayama estate on the outskirts of Kyōto. The **Golden Pavilion** (*Kinkaku*) he erected there is the outstanding remaining architectural work of the day, and his coterie of artists was the center of the artistic movements of the most creative epoch of the Ashikaga period. There **Kan-ami** (1333–1384) and his son **Se-ami** (1363–1444) perfected the highly refined *Nō* drama from earlier dramatic and terpsichorean performances. The luxurious but artistically creative life of the Kitayama estate was continued for several decades after Yoshimitsu's death by his successors.

1449–1490. Rule of Yoshimasa as *shōgun* (1449–1474) and retired *shōgun.* This was the second great creative period of Ashikaga art. In his Higashiyama estate on the edge of Kyōto, Yoshimasa built the **Silver Pavilion** (*Ginkaku*), which as an architectural work ranks second only to the Golden Pavilion of Yoshimitsu, and here he and a brilliant group of artists and aesthetes, presided over by Nō-ami (1397–1476), enjoyed a life of luxury and artistic elegance.

At the same time the complete collapse of what little authority the Ashikaga exercised over the nation became apparent, and there was great social unrest, resulting in numerous popular uprisings. Under the pressure of popular demands, Yoshimasa, like other Ashikaga *shōgun,* repeatedly issued Acts of Grace (*Tokusei*), which, unlike those of the Kamakura period, were sweeping debt cancellations for the benefit of the whole debtor class.

1465. The monks of the Enryakuji destroyed the Honganji, the central monastery of the True Pure Land Sect in Kyōto. Such affrays between the great monasteries were common at this time. Rennyō (1415–1499), the eighth hereditary head of the sect, fled to the region north of Kyōto, where his teachings met with great success and his numerous followers built up a military organization to defend their interests.

1467–1477. The **Ōnin War,** ostensibly a contest over the succession in the Ashikaga and other great military families, was actually a reshuffling of domains and power among the feudal lords, who divided into two camps under the leadership of two great war lords of western Japan, **Yamana Mochitoyo** (Sōzen) (1404–1473) and his son-in-law, **Hosokawa Katsumoto** (1430 [1425?]–1473), long the chief minister (*kanryō*) of the military government (1453–1464, 1468–1473). Kyōto was soon laid waste, but both leaders died in 1473, and exhaustion eventually brought peace in 1477. However local struggles went on unabated. In fact, the Ōnin War was merely the prelude to over a century of almost uninterrupted warfare. This period, which is aptly called the *Epoch of a Warring Country,* witnessed a continual shifting of fiefs and power, the elimination of many of the old feudal families, and the emergence of a new group of territorial lords, now known as *daimyō.*

1488. The **True Pure Land Sect** believers north of Kyōto defeated and killed a local lord. This is considered the first of the *Ikkōikki,* or Uprisings of the Ikkō Sect, another name for the True Pure Land Sect. Such uprisings became increasingly common and acted as a medium for popular manifestations of discontent.

1493. **Hosokawa Masamoto** (1466–1507) drove the *shōgun,* Yoshitane (1490–1494, 1508–1521) out of Kyōto and set up a puppet *shōgun* (1494), acts which were repeated by his adopted son, Takakuni (1484–1531), in 1521. Yoshitane's successors suffered similar indignities as the prestige of the Ashikaga dwindled further.

(*Cont. p. 581.*)

F. THE GREAT DISCOVERIES

1. ASIA

THE CRUSADES left Europe with a greatly expanded horizon, with much more extensive trade interests and connections, and with an accentuated hostility toward Islam. The great conquests of the Mongols in the 13th century (**Jenghiz Khan,** 1206–1227; period of greatness under **Kublai Khan,** 1259–1294), in uniting most of Asia, the Near East, and eastern Europe under one sway opened direct communication between Europe and the Orient and raised the prospect of an alliance against the Moslems.

1160–1173. Rabbi **Benjamin of Tudela** (in Navarre) traveled through Persia, central Asia, and to the very confines of China, but for religious reasons his records had little influence on Christian Europe. The same was true of the researches of the great Arab geographer **Yaqut,** who lived in the late 12th and early 13th centuries and wrote a great geographical dictionary.

1245–1247. Travels of **John of Pian de Carpine,** an Umbrian sent to the court of the Great Khan to propose an alliance against Islam and if possible to convert the Mongols. Traveling by way of southern Russia and the Volga, Carpine crossed central Asia and reached the Mongol court at Karakorum. Though well received his mission proved abortive.

1253–1255. Mission of **William of Rubruck,** a Fleming sent by St. Louis to the court of the Great Khan. Rubruck followed much the same route as Carpine and left one of the finest travel accounts of the Middle Ages.

1255–1266. **First journey of the Polo brothers,** Nicolo and Maffeo, Venetian traders in the Black Sea, who traveled to central Asia, spent three years in Bokhara and proceeded thence to China. They returned to Acre in 1269, bearing letters to the pope from the Mongol ruler.

1271–1295. **Second journey of the Polos,** accompanied this time by Nicolo's seventeen-year-old son, **Marco,** greatest of all medieval travelers. They took the route Mosul-Baghdad-Ormuz-Kerman-Khorasan-Pamir-Kashgar and thence across the Gobi Desert to the court of the Great Khan. The Mongol ruler was so favorably impressed that he took them into his service. During the next fifteen years Marco became acquainted with much of China, Cochin-China, Burma, and India. The Polos returned by sea by way of Sumatra, India, and Persia. Marco's famous *Book of Various Experiences* was dictated, probably in 1297, while he was a prisoner in Genoa. It was almost immediately popular and colored the whole geographic outlook of the succeeding period. Marco died in 1324.

1290-1340. During this period lively trade relations sprang up between Europe and Asia. Specific records are few, but such as they are they indicate the existence of commercial colonies and missionary groups in Persia (Tabriz), in India (Gujerat and Malabar coast), and in China (Peking and other cities). The great trade routes from Central Asia through southeastern Russia and the Black Sea, and from Trebizond through Persia were wide open. Embassies were constantly passing between western rulers and the ilkhans of Persia, whose emissaries on various occasions came as far as England (1287, 1289, 1290, 1307).

1289. The pope sent out Friar **John of Montecorvino** to take charge of the newly established archbishopric of Peking. John re-

mained at his post until his death in 1328 and seems to have built a flourishing Christian community.

1324-1328. Friar **Oderic of Pordenone** traveled to China, leaving one of the best accounts of the country.

1328. The pope established a bishopric of Quilon and sent out **Jordanus of Severac** to take charge.

1338-1346. **John Marignolli** was sent out to Peking as legate of the pope.

1340. **Francesco Pegolotti,** a Florentine trader at the Genoese station at Kaffa (Black Sea, founded 1266), wrote his *Merchants' Handbook* (*Della Pratica della Mercatura*), most valuable business manual of the time, which gives an unrivaled account of the commercial communications with Asia.

1368. Overthrow of the Mongol domination in China. Under the succeeding Ming dynasty foreigners were again excluded. The conquests of Timur the Great, shortly after, served to block the Near Eastern trade channels once more.

2. AFRICA

During the Middle Ages much of Africa was familiar to the Arabs. **Ibn Batuta,** greatest of Arab travelers, between the years 1325 and 1349 journeyed from his home in Morocco across northern Africa, through Egypt, the Near East, Arabia, eastern Africa, and thence to India. Later he traveled northward to the Crimea and thence through central Asia to India. After spending eight years at Delhi, he went on to Ceylon and China. On his return to Morocco in 1349, he set out across the Sahara and visited Timbuktu and the Niger region. His remarkable journeys serve to record not only the Arab trade from Egypt down the east coast of Africa and to India and beyond, but also the regular caravan trade from southern Morocco across the desert to the **kingdom of Ghana** (i.e. Guinea) in Nigeria.

1225. Under the tolerant rule of the Almohades and Marinides in Morocco, the Franciscans and Dominicans were allowed to establish their missionary centers in the country. By the end of the 13th century Christian, and more particularly Jewish, European merchants were engaged in the trans-Saharan trade, dealing chiefly in gold and ivory. In 1447 the Genoese Antonio Malfante penetrated far to the south.

1316. Having heard of a Christian king in East Africa (legend of **Prester John,** widespread in Europe after the spurious letter of

1165), the pope sent eight Dominicans to Ethiopia. Others seem to have been sent in the course of the century.

1402. An **Ethiopian embassy** reached Venice. There were others in 1408 and 1427. In 1452 Ethiopian emissaries arrived at Lisbon and in 1481 at Rome. The object of these embassies, and of those sent in return (especially by the pope in 1453) was to establish a Christian alliance against the Moslem Mamluks in Egypt and later against the Ottoman Turks. Nothing came of this project, but the exchange of missions served to acquaint Europe with that part of Africa.

1270. Beginning of **Portuguese exploration** of the west coast of Africa. The Portuguese Malocello visited the Canary Islands (1340-1341). These were assigned by the pope to the crown of Castile (1344).

1291. The two Genoese, Doria and Vivaldo, set out to find a route to India by sea; they never returned and nothing is known of their explorations.

1394-1460. PRINCE HENRY THE NAVIGATOR, the greatest patron of cosmography and discovery. Prince Henry, as general of the *Order of Christ,* was able to turn the crusading enthusiasm as well as the funds of the order into the fields of science and discovery. From 1418 onward he sent out, almost annually, expeditions carefully prepared and ably conducted. There can be little doubt that the religious factor dominated the work of the prince, though the scientific and commercial factors were hardly less important. That Prince Henry hoped to open up direct communications with Guinea by sea is clear. That he hoped ultimately to find a sea route to Ethiopia and thence to India has been questioned by some, but is reasonably certain.

1418-1419. Exploration of the **Madeira Islands,** some of which had been known before. The **Azores,** some of which appear on the *Medicean Portolano* of 1351, but probably as imaginary islands, were discovered by Diogo de Sevilla in 1427-1431.

1425. Expedition sent by Prince Henry to conquer the **Canaries** from Castile. Thereafter the prince tried hard to secure the islands by negotiation and so exclude Castile from any share in the West African trade. Further attacks were made upon them in 1450-1453, but by the **treaty of Alcaçovas** (1480, Mar. 6) they were definitely assigned to Castile, while West Africa, Guinea, and the islands of the ocean were assigned to Portugal.

1433. After more than ten years of repeated efforts, the Portuguese (under Gil Eannes) succeeded in doubling **Cape Bojador.** The advance then became rapid. Gold and natives were brought back and slave-raiding (later forbidden by Prince Henry) began.

1444. **Nuño Tristam** reached the Senegal River.

1445. **Dinis Dias** rounded Cape Verde. By this time the most barren part of the coast was passed and a lively trade with West Africa (c. 25 caravels a year) developed.

1455-1457. **Alvise da Cadamosto** (Ca da Mosto), a Venetian in the service of Prince Henry, explored the Senegal and Gambia Rivers and discovered the Cape Verde Islands.

1469. After the death of Prince Henry there was a slackening of activity and the king, Afonso V, for financial reasons leased the Guinea trade for five years to **Fernão Gomes,** with the stipulation that exploration be carried forward at least 100 leagues annually.

1470-1471. Under Gomes' auspices, **João de Santarem** and Pedro de Escolar reached Mina on the Gold Coast, where the Portuguese established a factory (fort, 1482) and did a rich trade in gold.

1472. **Fernando Po** discovered the island which bears his name. Lopo Gonçalves crossed the equator and Ruy de Sequeira reached latitude 2° south.

1481. With the accession of **John (João) II** (1481-1495) the crown once more took in hand the work of exploration, and with greater energy than ever.

1482-1484. **Diogo Cão** reached the mouth of the Congo River and Cape St. Augustine. In 1485-1486 he advanced to Cape Cross and Cape Negro.

1487. King John organized expeditions by land and by sea in the hope of reaching Ethiopia and India. **Pedro de Covilhã** and Afonso de Paiva were sent out by way of Cairo and Aden. Covilhã reached India and on his return followed the east coast of Africa as far south as the mouth of the Zambezi.

1487, Aug.-1488, Dec. VOYAGE OF BARTOLOMEU DIAS. Having followed the African coast, Dias was driven by a great storm (Dec.-Feb.) south of the tip of Africa. He turned east and soon discovered hills running to the northeast, showing him that he had rounded the **Cape of Good Hope.** He followed the east coast of Africa as far as Mossel Bay and the Great Fish River and then was obliged by his crew to return.

1497, July 8-1499, Aug. 29 or Sept. 9. VOYAGE OF VASCO DA GAMA. This would have been undertaken sooner, excepting for internal troubles in Portugal and disputes with Castile arising from the discoveries of Columbus. Da Gama left with four ships to find the way to India, the feasibility of the route being perfectly clear after the discoveries of Covilhã and Dias. He rounded the Cape in Nov. 1497, reached Quilimane (Jan. 1498), Mozambique (Mar.), and then Mombasa. Despite trouble with the jealous Arab traders, he was finally able to get a pilot from Melindi. He reached Calicut on the Malabar coast (May 22). He started for home in August 1498, touched Melindi (Jan. 1499) and rounded the Cape (Mar.). The exact date of his arrival at Lisbon is disputed.

1500, Mar. 9.-1501, June 23. VOYAGE OF PEDRO CABRAL, who set out with 13 ships to establish Portuguese trade in the east. After touching Brazil he went on to India, which he reached in September. The fleet loaded pepper and other spices and arrived safely in Lisbon. From this time on Portuguese trading fleets went regularly to India, and Lisbon soon became the chief entrepôt in Europe for oriental products.

1501. Vasco da Gama was sent out with 20 ships to punish the Arabs and to close the Red Sea, in order to cut the trade route through Egypt to Alexandria.

1505. **Francisco de Almeida** sent out as first governor of the Indies. He took Quiloa and Mombasa on the African coast and established forts at Calicut, Cananor, and Cochin on the Malabar coast.

1509, Feb. 2. Almeida destroyed the Moslem fleet in the **battle of Diu,** definitely establishing Portuguese control in Indian waters.

1509-1515. Governorship of **Afonso de Albuquerque,** who in 1507 had conquered Ormuz on the Persian Gulf. He made Goa the capital of the Portuguese possessions (1510), and in 1511 took Malacca. He opened communication with Siam, the Moluccas, and China.

1513. **Jorge Alvarez** first landed near Canton.

1517. **Fernão Peres de Andrade** appeared with a squadron at Canton.

1542. **Antonio da Mota** and two companions, driven by a storm, first reached Japan.

1557. The Portuguese established themselves at Macão (near Canton) and initiated regular trade with China.

The opening of the direct route to India at once began the revolution in the conditions of trade between Europe and Asia. The Mamelukes in Egypt had controlled the main routes, from the Persian Gulf to Syrian ports and from the Red Sea to Alexandria, and from these ports the Venetians shipped to western Europe. The Egyptian sultan kept the consignments small (210 tons of pepper per year) and the prices were therefore high. By 150 the price of pepper in Lisbon was only one fifth what it was in Venice. When the Portuguese succeeded in blocking the Red Sea route the Egyptian-Venetian trade was more or less ruined. The conquest of Syria and Egypt by the Turks (1516–1517), though frequently described as a stimulus to the discovery of new routes, had almost nothing to do with the situation. On the contrary the Turkish sultans (notably Suleiman, 1520–1566) did what they could to reopen the Near Eastern routes.

(*Cont. p. 563.*

3. AMERICA

a. PRE-COLUMBIAN AMERICA

The aborigines of America, varying among themselves in certain racial characteristics, migrated from Asia to North America in successive waves by way of the Bering Strait. These migrations began at a very early date, and apparently continued until relatively recent times. The migrants, when they arrived, were in a very primitive state. Becoming isolated from other peoples, they slowly expanded throughout both continents and developed autochthonous cultures which ranged from savagery to a relatively high degree of civilization. Many groups at a comparatively early date attained the agricultural stage, and the Inca of Peru achieved the use of bronze. The use of iron and the principle of the wheel were unknown. The dog universally, the turkey, the duck, and, in the Peruvian highlands, the llama, alpaca, and guanaco were the only existing domestic animals, the llama being the sole beast of burden.

At the time of the discovery the peoples of highest culture, most complex society, and greatest political importance were the **Aztec,** with their center in the Valley of Anáhuac; the **Maya** of Yucatan and portions of Mexico and Central America; the **Chibcha** of the Colombian plateau; and the **Inca,** whose empire centered in the highlands of Peru. Between the higher civilizations of Mexico, Yucatan, and Central America and between those of the Andean region there was extensive interchange of culture over a lengthy period, and it is possible that there was cultural interchange between the peoples of Central America and those of the Andean region. The civilizations of the Aztec and the Inca were built upon preceding cultures of a high order.

The **AZTECS** were originally a minor tribe of the great Nahua group. This group evolved the high **Toltec civilization** which, receiving through cultural transmission mathematical and astronomical knowledge and a calendar from a lowland people, possibly the Maya, reached its height in the 13th century and declined thereafter, being followed by the transitional Chichimec culture. Reaching the shores of Lake Tezcuco in 1325, the Aztecs erected an impregnable capital, **Tenochtitlán,** in the marshes of the lake and, through superior political and military capacity and alliance, extended their control over central and southern Mexico from the Gulf to the Pacific and established colonies in Central America. In 1519 Tenochtitlán was a city of some 60,000 house-holders and the Aztec Empire included perhaps 5,000,000 inhabitants. The government was relatively centralized, with an elective monarch, provincial governors appointed by the central authority, a well-organized judicial system, and a large and efficient army. The Aztecs attained a high degree of development in engineering, architecture, art, mathematics, and astronomy. Principal buildings were of mortar and rubble faced with stucco. There existed a body of traditional history, philosophy, and poetry that was orally transmitted. Picture writing which was rapidly approaching phonetic was evolved. Music was rudimentarily developed. Agriculture was far advanced and commerce and simple industry flourished. The working of gold and silver and the production of pottery and textiles were highly developed. The religion of the Aztec was polytheistic, and although it included many lofty concepts the deity of war, Huitzilopochtli, was the principal god and his worship led to the development of one of the most extensive systems of human sacrifice that has ever existed. The priesthood constituted a powerful group, political as well as religious. Certain of the peoples subjected by the Aztecs were restive under their domination and were prepared to rebel at the first opportunity. In the mountains to the east of Lake Tezcuco there existed the powerful republic of **Tlaxcala,** which, maintaining its independence, regarded the Aztec as hereditary enemies. These conditions created a situation favorable to the Spaniards during the conquest.

The **MAYAS,** before the Christian Era, established themselves in the peninsula of Yucatan, Tabasco, Chiapas, northern, central, and eastern Guatemala, and western Honduras. They developed a civilization which, reaching its apogee well before 1000 A.D., was in certain cultural aspects the highest in the New World. The Maya culture in the earlier period extended with considerable uniformity throughout the greater part of their general area, but after about 1000 A.D., tended to center in the northern part of the peninsula of Yucatan. During the period of highest development the Mayas did not evolve a unified empire, the area being divided into city states governed by politico-religious rulers or ruling groups. Art, architecture, mathematics, engineering, and astronomy were far advanced, and the Mayas had evolved the conception of zero, a vigesimal numerical system, and a calendar more accurate than the Julian. Temples and other major buildings were constructed of stone and mortar and were faced with carved stone. A system of causeways existed. Codices were formed for religious and astronomical purposes, but writing did not exist. A body of traditions, history, and religious prophecies were orally preserved. Religion was polytheistic and relatively humane, and the priestly class, exercising political authority as well as religious, possessed, with the ruling groups, a monopoly of learning. Widespread commerce existed, and weaving and pottery-making were well developed. Agriculture was on an exceedingly high level. Civil war occurred during the 13th century and certain Mexican groups conquered the Mayas of northern Yucatan. Mexican cultural influences were consequently introduced, especially in art and religion. In the same century a greater degree of political cohesion appears to have been established in the northern part of the peninsula, and this resulted in a period of peace which endured until the 15th century, when internecine strife led to the destruction of Mayapan in 1451 and the abandonment of the great cities Chichen Itzá and Uxmal. The Mayan civilization was decadent culturally and politically when the Spaniards arrived, although certain of the independent provinces were relatively powerful militarily. The Mayas of Yucatan numbered perhaps 400,000 to 500,000 on the eve of the Spanish conquest.

The **CHIBCHAS.** The political organization of the Chibchas, who numbered some 1,000,000, was comparatively cohesive. The Zipa at Bacatá and the Zaque at Tunja were the political rulers, and supreme religious authority was held by the high-priest known as the *Iraca.* The Chibchas possessed a well-developed calendar and numerical system and employed pictographs. Extensive commerce and simple industry existed, ceramics and textiles being highly developed. In gold-working the Chibchas were in certain respects unequaled. They employed wood and thatch in the construction of buildings.

The **INCAS,** with their capital at Cuzco, successors to the high coastal and upland cultures of Chimú, Nasca, Pachacamac, and Tiahuanaco, which flourished during the early centuries of the Christian Era, extended their control over the area from Ecuador to central Chile along the coast and inland to the eastern slopes of the Andes including the Bolivian plateau. Expansion was particularly rapid from the 14th century onward and one of the greatest of the conquerors, **Huayna Capac,** lived until the eve of the Spanish conquest. The empire, with a population of perhaps 6,000,000 to 8,000,000, was a thoroughly organized, absolute, paternal, socialistic, and theocratic despotism. All power emanated from the Inca as the ruler and representative of the Sun Deity, whose worship constituted the religion of the Incas. There existed a close-knit and graduated system of provincial and local administration. Each individual had a fixed place in society, and the state benignly provided for the welfare of all. The army was large and well organized, and a system of post and military roads extended to all portions of the empire. In mathematics and astronomy the Incas were not as accomplished as the Mayas and Aztecs, but in engineering, architecture, and the production of textiles and ceramics they were far advanced. The Incas did not evolve writing, but possessed a device to aid memory in the form of the *quipu,* through which governmental records were kept, tradition was preserved, and messages were sent. In gold-working a high degree of skill was attained. Commerce, entailing extensive navigation along the coast, was well developed. A great body of oral tradition and poetry existed, and music was comparatively well developed. Principal buildings were of stone. Politically the Incas were the most advanced of the peoples of the New World. At his death Huayna Capac, contrary to practice, divided the empire between Huáscar, his son by a lawful wife, and Atahualpa, his son by a concubine. A civil war followed, in which Atahualpa, shortly before the arrival of the Spaniards, triumphed and imprisoned his half-brother.

b. PRE-COLUMBIAN DISCOVERIES

790. **Irish monks,** searching for religious retreats and for new fields of missionary enterprise, reached **Iceland,** after discovering the Faroe Islands in the 7th century.

874. The **Norsemen** (Normans, Vikings) arrived in Iceland and settled.

981. The Norsemen, under **Erik the Red,** discovered **Greenland** and settled on the southwest coast (985–986).

1000. **LEIF ERICSSON,** returning from Norway to Greenland, was driven onto the American coast. In 1963 a Norwegian expedition under **Dr. Helge Ingstad** discovered and excavated nine buildings near L'Anse aux Meadows, at the northern tip of Newfoundland. The settlement dated from c. 1000 A.D. and was incontrovertibly Norse. It was therefore in all probability the *Wineland* (*Vinland*) mentioned by Leif Ericsson.

1003-1006. **THORFINN KARLSEFNI** set out from Greenland with three ships to settle Wineland. He and his party spent three winters on the American continent. There is no general agreement regarding the localities visited by him, which have been placed by different authorities as far apart as Labrador and Florida. One writer puts the *Helluland* (Flatstone Land) of the Greenlandic-Icelandic sagas in northeastern Labrador; *Markland* (Wood Land) in southern Labrador; *Furdustrand* (Wonder Strand) on the north side of the Gulf of St. Lawrence; *Straumfjord* (Stream Fjord), where the first and third winters were spent, on Chaleur Bay (New Brunswick); and *Hop* (Lagoon) on the New England coast, either north or south of Cape Cod. Another writer is convinced that Karlsefni visited only the Labrador coast and both sides of the northern peninsula of Newfoundland, Straumfjord being, perhaps, in the vicinity of Hare Bay. Wineland was first mentioned in the *Hamburg Church History* of **Adam of Bremen** (1074 ff.), but most of our knowledge derives from the Norse sagas written down in the 14th century. Supposed Norse remains on the American continent (Dighton Rock, Old Stone Mill at Newport) have all been rejected by

scholars as spurious, as has also the Kensington Stone, found near Kensington, Minnesota, in 1898, under the roots of a tree. The stone contains a long runic inscription purporting to record the presence there of a group of Norsemen in 1362. Though long the subject of heated disputation, the stone is now generally held to be a forgery.

How long the Norsemen continued to visit America is an open question. The last definite mention is for 1189 A.D., but there is some reason to believe that they came at least as far as southern Labrador for ship's timber as late as 1347. After that date the Greenland colonies declined, though the West Colony (in southeast Greenland) continued to exist until at least the mid-15th century and ships appear to have gone there periodically, probably trading in walrus hides and tusks.

1470-1474. Between these years two Germans in the Danish service, **Didrick Pining** and **Hans Pothorst,** undertook a voyage to Iceland and the west, supposedly at the request of the king of Portugal. Pining was a great seaman and the terror of the English; from 1478 to 1490 he was governor of Iceland. There is no reason why he should not have been able to reach America, but the evidence does not show that he and Pothorst went beyond Greenland. On a map of 1537 it is stated that a famous pilot, **Johannes Scolvus** (claimed by some to have been a Pole—Jan Szkolny), reached Labrador at this time. It has been held by some scholars that he must have accompanied Pining and Pothorst, but, since Labrador at this time was a name generally used for Greenland, it seems unlikely that Scolvus went beyond the old Norse settlements. From the Portuguese connection with the expedition it has been concluded by some that **João Vaz Corte Real** went along. There is no satisfactory evidence of this. The markings on early maps make it likely that he too failed to get beyond Greenland. It is not unlikely, though there is no real evidence, that Breton, Gascon, or Basque fishermen regularly visited the Grand Banks in this period. In any event there is no conclusive proof of any pre-Columbian discovery, or of any influence on later attempts.

A great many theories have been advanced in recent years, notably by the Portuguese, but also by others, to show that the Portuguese knew of the existence of America before Columbus sailed. Most of the theories rest upon conjecture and clever deductions. All that can be said is that, after the translation of Ptolemy's *Geography* into Latin (1410), the idea of the sphericity of the earth (never entirely lost during the Middle Ages, cf. Roger

Bacon's *Opus Maius* of the late 13th century) spread rapidly in scientific circles and revived the idea of reaching Asia by sailing westward. Prince Henry the Navigator, for all his interest in the African route, sent expeditions to the west. In 1427–1431 Diogo de Sevilla discovered seven of the Azores, which may have been known to the Italians as early as 1351. Flores and Colvo were discovered in 1451–1452. The map of Andrea Bianco (1448) shows land of the proper conformation where Brazil lies. It is clear that after 1450 many Portuguese expeditions set out in search of legendary islands (St. Brandan's, Brazil, Antillia, Island of the Seven Cities, etc.) and, according to some scholars, the Lisbon government enforced a policy of rigorous secrecy with regard to new findings. Nevertheless, no present evidence of Portuguese knowledge of America before 1492 can be regarded as conclusive.

c. THE VOYAGES OF COLUMBUS

1451, bet. Aug. 26 and Oct. 31. CRISTOFORO COLOMBO (Spanish Cristóbal Colón) born near Genoa, the son of Domenico Colombo, a weaver. Almost nothing definite is known of his youth (general unreliability of the biography by his son Fernando). He was probably himself a weaver and probably went to sea only in 1472, when he made a trip to Scio. He seems to have come to Portugal in 1476 and to have made a voyage to England in 1477 (the story of his visit to Iceland is rejected by almost all authorities). In 1478 he appears to have made a voyage to the Madeiras and in 1482 possibly to the Guinea coast. In 1480 he married the daughter of Bartholomew Perestrello, hereditary captain of Porto Santo, near Madeira. By this time Columbus must have learned much about Portuguese discoveries and certainly about the ideas current in Lisbon. His appeal to the great Florentine geographer, **Paolo Toscanelli**, and the latter's reply (1474) urging a voyage to the west, have been called in question by some writers and may be spurious. In any event the idea of seeking India or China in the west was not novel.

1483 or 1484. Columbus appealed to King João II of Portugal to finance a voyage to the west, but whether to seek new islands or a route to Asia is not clear. At this very time the king was authorizing self-financed expeditions to the west of the Azores (1486, Ferman Dulmo) and he might have licensed Columbus had the latter been willing to finance himself. Others maintain that the Portuguese already knew that Asia could not be reached in this way. Apparently Columbus, whose geographical knowledge appears to have been very incomplete, was regarded as a vain boaster. His project was rejected.

1486. Columbus, through the mediation of some Franciscan monks, was able to submit his project to **Ferdinand and Isabella** of Spain. His religious fervor and personal magnetism impressed the queen, but the project was again rejected by experts. In the following years Columbus met the three Pinzón brothers, wealthy traders and expert navigators, from whom he doubtless learned much.

1492. After being recalled to court, Columbus finally induced the queen to finance his expedition. His objective was to find a route to the Indies, rather than to discover a new world. He was made admiral and governor of the territories to be discovered, but also carried letters to the great khan.

1492, Aug. 3–1493, Mar. 15. THE FIRST VOYAGE. Columbus left Palos with three ships, of which Martin Pinzón commanded one, and the famous pilot Juan de la Cosa another. He left the Canaries (Sept. 6) and reached land in the Bahamas (probably Watling Island) (Oct. 12), naming it *San Salvador*. He then discovered Cuba, which he thought was the territory of the great khan, and Santo Domingo (Española). A post, Navidad, was established on Santo Domingo, after which Columbus returned (1493, Jan. 4), touching at the Azores (Feb. 15), landing at Lisbon (Mar. 4) and finally reaching Palos (Mar. 15). He announced that he had discovered the Indies, news of which spread over Europe with great rapidity and caused much excitement.

1493, May 4. The Line of Demarcation. At the instance of the Spanish rulers, who feared counterclaims by Portugal, Pope Alexander VI granted to the Catholic kings exclusive right to and possession of all lands to the south and west toward India not held by a Christian prince on Christmas Day, 1492, beyond a line drawn one hundred leagues west of the Azores and Cape Verde Islands.

1493, Sept. 25–1496, June 11. SECOND VOYAGE OF COLUMBUS. He left with 17 caravels and 1500 men to establish Spanish power. On this voyage he discovered Dominica, Puerto Rico, and other of the Antilles and Jamaica, explored the southern coast of Cuba, and circumnavigated Española, where he founded the town of Isabella. He left his brother Bartholomew in charge, who in 1496 transferred the settlement to the southern coast (Santo Domingo).

1494, June 7. TREATY OF TORDESILLAS, between Portugal and Spain. The line of demarcation was moved 270 leagues further west, Portugal to have exclusive rights to all lands to the east of it, and Spain of all lands to the west. The making of this treaty is not entirely clear, and it has often been used as an argument to prove that Portugal already knew of Brazil, which, by the treaty, was brought into the Portuguese sphere.

1498, May 30–1500, Nov. 25. THIRD VOYAGE OF COLUMBUS. Discovery of Trinidad Island (1498, July 31) and South America (Aug. 1) near the mouth of the Orinoco. He explored the coast westward as far as Margarita Island. He then went to Española, where a revolt broke out against him. He requested the crown to send out a judge. The government sent out to the Indies **Francisco de Bobadilla** (1499), who sent Columbus and his brother to Spain as prisoners. Columbus was released and treated with distinction, but, despite the earlier rights granted him, was never restored to his former authority or monopolistic grants. With Bobadilla direct royal control was established.

1502, May 11–1504, Nov. 7. FOURTH VOYAGE OF COLUMBUS. He reached the coast of Honduras and passed south to Panama, returning after having suffered shipwreck at Jamaica.

1506, May. 21. Columbus died in relative obscurity at Valladolid. It is reasonably clear that he believed to the end of his days that he had discovered outlying parts of Asia, despite the fact that ever since 1493 the conviction had spread among experts (e.g. **Peter Martyr**) that a New World had been discovered.

d. POST-COLUMBIAN DISCOVERIES

1497, May 2–Aug. 6. VOYAGE OF JOHN CABOT. Cabot was a wealthy Italian merchant (born in Genoa, resident in Venice) who had traveled in the east (Black Sea, Alexandria, Mecca) and who settled in England about 1495. For several years British merchants had sent out expeditions to seek the island of Brazil. Columbus' supposed discovery of Asia in the west spurred Cabot on. His expedition reached land (June 24) evidently on Northern Newfoundland, whence it then cruised along the eastern and part of the southern coast of Newfoundland. Cabot was convinced that he had discovered the country of the great khan and intended to return, passing south along the coast to the region of Brazil.

1498, May. John Cabot sailed with five ships on a second voyage. One of them put back to Ireland after a few days. The other four were lost with all hands.

1498. King João of Portugal sent out the famous captain, explorer, and scientist, **Duarte Pacheco Pereira,** to investigate the lands in the west. Duarte's account (written in 1505 but published only in 1892) indicates that he may have reached the South American coast. He speaks of a vast continent extending from 70° N.L. to 28° S.L.

1499, May–1500, June. Voyage of **Alonso de Ojeda** and **Amerigo Vespucci** in the service of Spain. They landed in French Guiana, discovered the mouth of the Amazon, and proceeded as far as Cape St. Roque, after which they returned north and west along the coast as far as the Magdalena River and reached home by way of Española. An earlier voyage (1497–1498) by Vespucci, of which he himself tells in the confused and probably spurious sources, has been generally rejected by scholars. Vespucci (1451–1512) was a Florentine resident in Sevilla, probably an agent of the Medici banking firm.

1499, Sept.–1500, Dec. Voyage of **Vicente Yañez Pinzón.** Pinzón made a landfall near Cape St. Roque (1500, Jan.) and thence followed the coast northwestward. At about the same time the Spaniard **Diego de Lepe** explored the Brazilian coast from Cape St. Roque to about 10° S.L.

1500, Apr. 21. The Portuguese commander **Pedro Cabral,** sailing to India with 13 caravels, and accompanied by such distinguished captains as Dias and Duarte Pacheco, landed in Brazil, coming from the Cape Verde Islands. The party stayed only about ten days, but took official possession of the country which Cabral named *Tierra de Vera Cruz.* The idea of Cabral having been the first to discover Brazil, like the idea that his landing there was accidental, has now been given up by some scholars, but the question remains open.

1500. The Portuguese **Gaspar de Corte Real,** son of João Vaz, voyaged to the east coast of Greenland and to Labrador. In 1501 he set out on a second expedition, exploring Labrador and thence turning south. He himself was lost on this expedition, but his brother Michael carried out yet another voyage in 1502 to the Newfoundland coast. He too was lost at sea.

1501, May–1502, Sept. SECOND VOYAGE OF AMERIGO VESPUCCI, this time in the service of Portugal. The voyage took him south along the Brazilian coast to about 32° S.L. if not farther. It was from the published account of this voyage and from Vespucci's conviction that what had been found was a *New World* that the geographer **Martin**

Waldseemüller was led to propose that this New World be called *America* (1507). The name was at first applied only to South America and the use of it spread slowly until its general adoption toward the end of the 16th century.

Further explorations need not be listed in detail. **Rodrigo de Bastidas** traced the coast from Panama to Port Manzanilla (1500–1502); **Vicente Pinzón** followed the mainland from the Bay of Honduras to beyond the easternmost point of Brazil (1508); **Florián de Ocampo** circumnavigated Cuba (1508), which was conquered by **Diego Velázquez** (1511); **Juan Ponce de León,** the governor of Puerto Rico, discovered Florida (1512).

1513, Sept. 25. VASCO NUÑEZ DE BALBOA crossed the Isthmus of Panama and discovered the **Pacific Ocean.**

1515–1516. Juan Diaz de Solis, chief pilot of Spain, searching for a strait to the Pacific, explored the coast of South America from near Rio de Janeiro to the Rio de la Plata, where he was slain.

1517. Francisco Hernández de Córdoba discovered Yucatan, finding traces of large cities and great wealth.

1518. Juan de Grijalva followed the coast north from Yucatan to the Panuco River.

1519. Alvárez Pineda completed exploration of the Gulf of Mexico by coasting from Florida to Vera Cruz and back. **Francisco de Gordillo** advanced up the Atlantic coast to South Carolina (1521), and **Pedro de Quexos** as far as 40° N.L. (1525). At the same time (1524–1525) **Esteban Gómez,** sailing from Spain, followed the coast from Nova Scotia in the north to Florida in the south.

1519–1522. CIRCUMNAVIGATION OF THE GLOBE BY FERDINAND MAGELLAN (Fernão de Magalhães, 1480–1521). Magellan was sent out by the Spanish crown to find a strait to the Moluccas. He sailed on September 20, 1519 and reached the Brazilian coast near Pernambuco, explored the estuary of the Rio de la Plata and, after wintering at Port St. Julian, passed through the strait which bears his name and entered the South Sea, to which the name *Mare Pacificum* was given. After following the coast to about 40° S.L. he turned northwest and then west, and eventually after sighting only two tiny atolls reached Guam (March 6) and the Philippines (March 15, 1521). At Macton, near Celon, he was killed by Filipinos (April 27). His ship *Victoria* under **Juan Sebastian del Cano,** continued westward and reached Spain (September 6, 1522), thus completing the circumnavigation of the globe.

(*Cont. p. 923.*)

IV. THE EARLY MODERN PERIOD

IV. THE EARLY MODERN PERIOD

A. EUROPE AND THE NEAR EAST, 1500–1648

1. ENGLAND, SCOTLAND, AND IRELAND, 1485–1649

[For a complete list of the kings of England see Appendix VI.]

(*From p. 294*)

1485–1603. HOUSE OF TUDOR.
1485–1509. HENRY VII. Henry's first act was to imprison the **earl of Warwick,** son of the duke of Clarence. His first parliament (1485) confirmed the crown to him and his heirs. Though the traditional medieval checks on the power of the crown were maintained in theory, in practice Henry went a long way toward developing royal absolutism—establishment of the administrative court later called the **Star Chamber** (1487), suppression of private feudal armies, development of an efficient, if arbitrary, royal financial system (Empson, Dudley, "Morton's Fork").
1487. The pretended earl of Warwick (Simnel) landed in England, but was defeated at **Stoke** (June 16, 1487), and became one of the king's scullions.
1488–1499. Attempts of **Perkin Warbeck,** a Fleming who personated the duke of York, to overthrow Henry. Disavowed by Charles VIII in the **peace of Étaples** (Nov. 9, 1492), which ended the war in which Henry had engaged on account of the annexation of Brittany by Charles VIII (1491), Warbeck found a warm reception in Flanders from the duchess of Burgundy, sister of Edward IV. Expelled from Flanders, he fled to Scotland, where his claim was recognized. Warbeck and James IV of Scotland invaded England in 1496. In 1497 a formidable insurrection broke out in Cornwall on occasion of an imposition of a tax by parliament. It was suppressed by the defeat at **Blackheath** (June 22, 1497), and the leaders executed (Flammock). **Peace with Scotland** (Sept. 1497). Warbeck was soon taken and imprisoned in the Tower, whence he escaped, but was recaptured. Plotting another escape with the earl of Warwick, both Perkin and Warwick were executed (1499).
1494. STATUTE OF DROGHEDA (*Poyning's law*): (1) No Irish parliament should be held without the consent of the king of England. (2) No bill could be brought forward in an Irish parliament without his consent.

(3) All recent laws enacted in the English parliament should hold in Ireland.
1496. *Intercursus magnus,* commercial treaty with Netherlands, granted mutual privileges to English and Flemings and provided fixed duties.
1502. Marriage of Henry's eldest daughter, Margaret, with James IV, king of Scotland.
1509–1547. HENRY VIII. He was six times married: (1) **Catherine of Aragon,** widow of his brother Arthur, mother of Mary the Catholic (married June 3, 1509, divorced March 30, 1533). (2) **Anne Boleyn,** mother of Elizabeth I (married Jan. 25, 1533, beheaded May 19, 1536). (3) **Jane Seymour** (married May 20, 1536, died after the birth of her son Edward VI, Oct. 24, 1537). (4) **Anne of Cleves** (married Jan. 6, 1540, divorced June 24, 1540). (5) **Catherine Howard** (married Aug. 8, 1540, beheaded Feb. 12, 1542). (6) **Catherine Parr** (married July 10, 1543, outlived the king). Henry united in his person the claims of both Lancaster and York.
1511. Henry a member of the **Holy League** (pp. 409, 415). Having laid claim to the French crown, he sent troops to Spain, which were unsuccessful (1512). In 1513 the king went to France in person and with Emperor Maximilian won the bloodless victory of
1513, Aug. 17. Guinegate, the battle of the Spurs.
1513, Sept. 9. Battle of Flodden Field. Defeat and death of James IV of Scotland, who was allied with France.
1514, Aug. Peace with France (Tournay ceded to England, afterward [1518] bought by France for 600,000 crowns) and with Scotland.
1515. Thomas Wolsey (1475?–1530), the king's favorite, cardinal and chancellor, papal legate.
1520, June 7. Meeting of Henry VIII and Francis I of France near Calais (Field of the Cloth of Gold).
1521. Execution of the **duke of Buckingham** on a charge of high treason. Buckingham was descended from Edward III.

The House of Tudor (1485–1603)

(From p. 292)

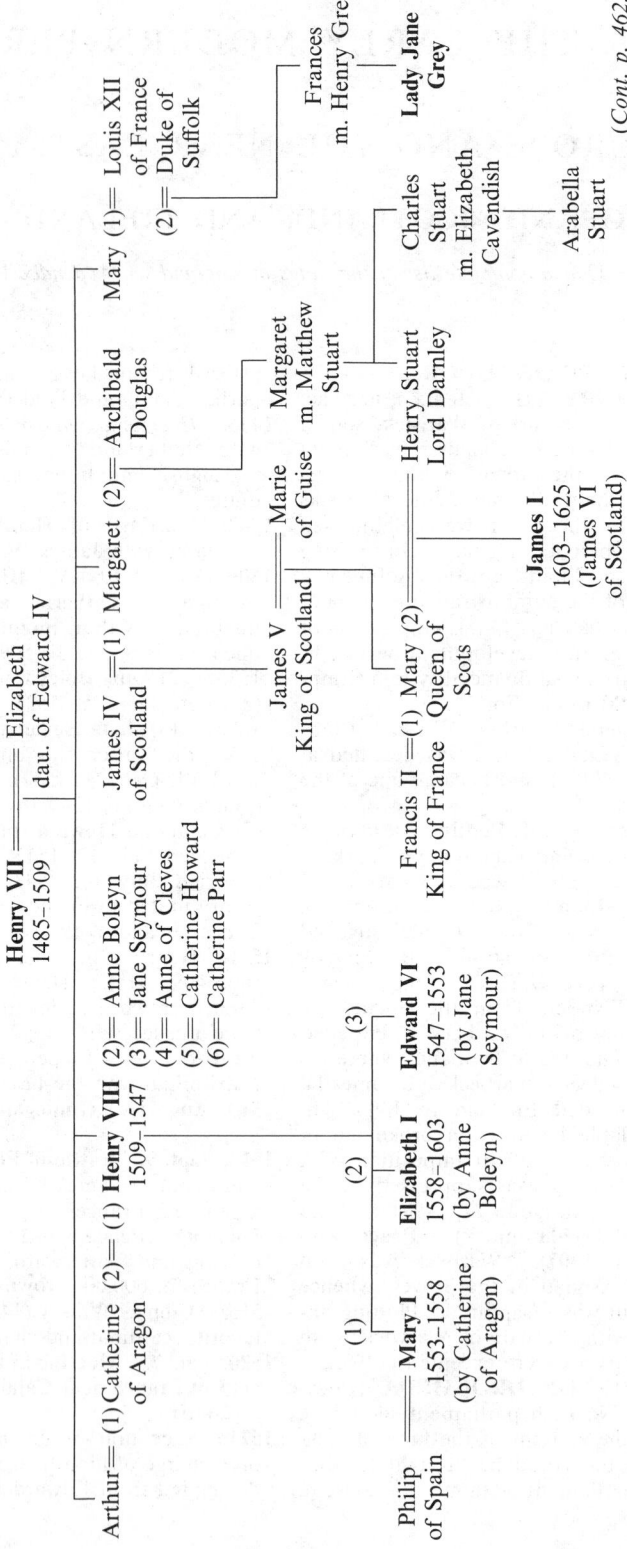

(Cont. p. 462.)

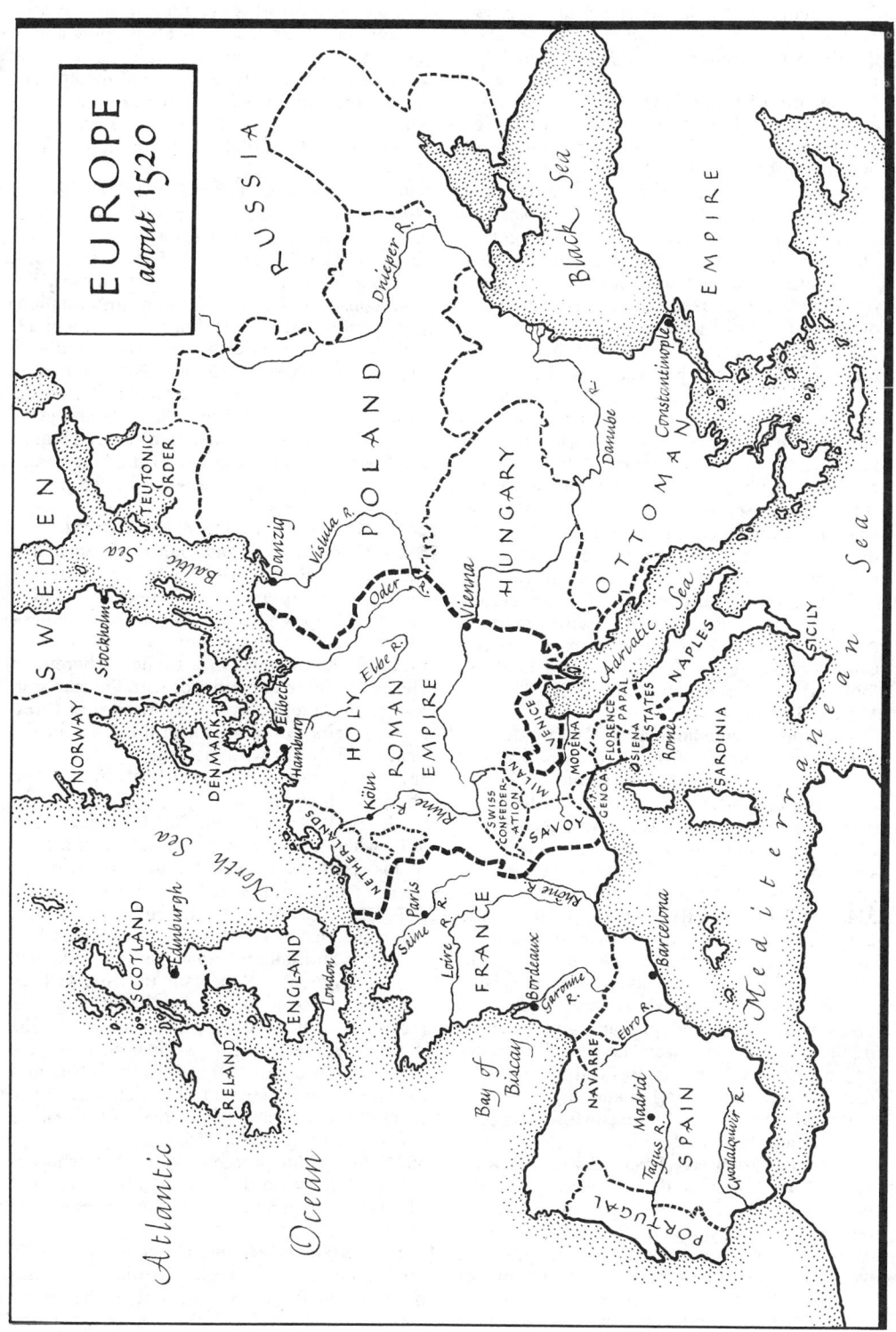

EUROPE about 1520

RUSSIA

SWEDEN

NORWAY

Stockholm

Baltic Sea

TEUTONIC ORDER

Danzig

Vistula R.

POLAND

Dnieper R.

Black Sea

OTTOMAN EMPIRE

Constantinople

Danube R.

HUNGARY

Vienna

Oder R.

DENMARK

Lübeck

Hamburg

Elbe R.

HOLY ROMAN EMPIRE

Köln

Rhine R.

SWISS CONFEDER- ATION

MILAN

SAVOY

GENOA

MODENA

VENICE

Adriatic Sea

FLORENCE

PAPAL STATES

SIENA

Rome

NAPLES

SARDINIA

SICILY

Mediterranean Sea

NETHERLANDS

Paris

Seine R.

Loire R.

FRANCE

Rhône R.

Bordeaux

Garonne R.

Bay of Biscay

NAVARRE

Ebro R.

Barcelona

SPAIN

Madrid

Tagus R.

Guadalquivir R.

PORTUGAL

North Sea

SCOTLAND

Edinburgh

ENGLAND

London

IRELAND

Atlantic

Ocean

1521. Henry wrote the *Assertion of the Seven Sacraments* in reply to Luther, and received the title of *Defender of the Faith* from Pope Leo X.

After the **battle of Pavia** (p. 415), the relations between Henry and the emperor, which had been weakened by the double failure of the emperor to secure the promised election of Wolsey as pope, became so strained that war seemed inevitable, and a forced loan was assessed on the kingdom, which brought in but little. In 1523 an attempt to force a grant from parliament met with no success, but a rebellion was provoked which was suppressed only by abandoning the demand.

1527. Henry, desiring to divorce his wife in order to marry **Anne Boleyn,** alleged the invalidity of marriage with a deceased brother's wife, and appealed to Rome. The delays of the pope and the scruples of Wolsey enraged the king, who in 1529 deprived the latter of the great seal and gave it to **Sir Thomas More** (1478-1535). Sentence and pardon of Wolsey, who, however, died in disgrace (1530). At the suggestion of **Thomas Cranmer** (1489-1556) the question was referred to the universities of England and Europe, and, a number deciding in the king's favor, Henry married Anne Boleyn. Henry also broke with the Church of Rome. Confiscation of the annates, followed by the resignation of Sir Thomas More (1532).

The **pope excommunicated Henry** and annulled his divorce from Catherine, which Cranmer, now archbishop of Canterbury, had pronounced. After the birth of **Elizabeth,** parliament confirmed the divorce, recognized Elizabeth as heir to the throne (1534), and secured the succession to other children of Anne in case of the death of the princess.

1534. ACT OF SUPREMACY, appointing the king and his successors *Protector and only Supreme Head of the Church and Clergy of England.* This may be taken as the decisive beginning of the **English Reformation.** The break with Rome had political and personal origins; at first there were no real differences in dogma and liturgy. Refusal to take the oath of supremacy was made high treason, under which vote Sir Thomas More was condemned and beheaded (1535).

Thomas Cromwell (1485?-1540), a former servant of Wolsey and his successor in the favor of the king, now vicegerent in matters relating to the Church in England, issued a commission for the inspection of monasteries which resulted in the suppression of the smaller ones in 1536 and the larger ones in 1539, and the confiscation of their property. Abbots now ceased to sit in parliament.

1536. Execution of Anne Boleyn on a charge of adultery. Princess Elizabeth proclaimed illegitimate by parliament. The crown was secured to any subsequent issue of the king, or should that fail, was left to his disposal.

1536. Publication of **Tyndale's translation of the Bible,** by Coverdale, under authority from the king.

1536. Suppression of the Catholic rebellion of **Robert Aske,** aided by **Reginald Pole,** son of Margaret, countess of Salisbury.

1539. STATUTE OF THE SIX ARTICLES, defining heresy; denial of any of these positions constituted heresy: (1) transubstantiation; (2) communion in one kind for laymen; (3) celibacy of the priesthood; (4) inviolability of vows of chastity; (5) necessity of private masses; (6) necessity of auricular confession.

1540. Execution of Cromwell, on a charge of treason. Cromwell had fallen under Henry's displeasure by his advocacy of the king's marriage with **Anne of Cleves,** with whom the king was ill-pleased.

1542. IRELAND MADE A KINGDOM.

1542. War with Scotland. James V defeated at the **battle of Solway Moss** (Nov. 25). James V died shortly afterward. Henry proposed a marriage between his son, Edward, and James's infant daughter, Mary, but the Scottish court preferred an alliance with France, whereupon Henry concluded an alliance with the emperor.

1544. Parliament recognized **Mary** and **Elizabeth** as heirs to the crown in the event of the death of Edward without issue.

1547. Execution of the **earl of Surrey,** on charge of high treason.

Henry VIII died Jan. 28, 1547, leaving a will, wherein the crown was left to the heirs of his sister, **Mary, duchess of Suffolk,** in the event of failure of issue by all of his children.

1547-1553. EDWARD VI, ten years of age; his uncle, earl of Hertford, was appointed lord protector and **duke of Somerset,** and assumed the government. **Repeal of the Six Articles** (1547). Introduction of Protestant doctrines (1549). Execution of Seymour, brother of the duke of Somerset, who wished to marry the Princess Elizabeth. Establishment of uniformity of service by act of parliament; introduction of Edward VI's *Book of Common Prayer* (1549) (second, 1552).

1550. Fall of the protector, Somerset, who was superseded by Lord Warwick, afterward **duke of Northumberland.** Execution of Somerset (1552).

1551. Forty-two articles of religion published by Cranmer. These were essentially the basis of Anglican Protestantism, though their form was not final until the thirty-nine articles of Elizabeth's reign.

1553. Edward assigned the crown to **Lady Jane Grey,** daughter of his cousin, Frances Grey, eldest daughter of Mary, daughter of Henry VII, to the exclusion of Mary and Elizabeth, daughters of Henry VIII. Lady Jane was married to the son of the duke of Northumberland. **Death of Edward VI** (July 6).

1553-1558. MARY, who had been brought up a Catholic.

The proclamation of **Lady Jane Grey** as queen by Northumberland meeting with no response, Northumberland, Lady Jane, and others were arrested. **Execution of Northumberland** (Aug. 22, 1553). Restoration of Catholic bishops. **Stephen Gardiner,** bishop of Winchester, author of the Six Articles, lord chancellor.

1553. Marriage treaty between Mary and **Philip of Spain,** son of Charles V, afterward Philip II. Philip was to have the title of *King of England,* but no hand in the government, and in case of Mary's death could not succeed her. This transaction being unpopular, an insurrection broke out, headed by Sir Thomas Carew, the duke of Suffolk, and Sir Thomas Wyatt. The suppression of the rebellion was followed by the **execution of Lady Jane Grey** (Feb. 12, 1554) and her husband. Lady Jane was an accomplished scholar (pupil of **Roger Ascham**) and had no desire for the crown. Imprisonment of Elizabeth, who was soon released on the intercession of the emperor.

1554, July 25. Marriage of Mary and Philip.

1555. Return to Catholicism and persecution of the Protestants (**Bonner,** bishop of London). Oct. 16, **Ridley** and **Latimer;** March 21, 1556, **Cranmer** burnt at the stake. About 300 are said to have been burnt during this persecution. **Cardinal Pole,** archbishop of Canterbury and papal legate (1556).

1557. England drawn into the Spanish war with France. Defeat of the French at the **battle of St. Quentin** (Aug. 10, 1557).

1558, Jan. 7. Loss of Calais, which was captured by the duke of Guise.

1558-1603. ELIZABETH I, brought up a Protestant. **Sir William Cecil** (Baron Burleigh, 1571), secretary of state. **Sir Nicholas Bacon,** lord privy seal. Repeal of the Catholic legislation of Mary; re-enactment of the laws of Henry VIII relating to the Church; **act of Supremacy, act of Uniformity.** Revision of the prayer-book.

1559, Apr. 3. Treaty of Cateau-Cambrésis with France. Calais to be ceded to England in eight years.

On the accession of Francis II, king of France, Mary Stuart, his wife, assumed the title of *Queen of England and Scotland.* Conformity exacted in Scotland. **Treaty of Berwick** (Jan. 1560), between Elizabeth and the Scottish reformers. French troops besieged at Leith. **Treaty of Edinburgh** between England, France, and Scotland (1560, July 6). French interference in Scotland withdrawn. Adoption of a **Confession of Faith** by the Scotch estates. Mary returned to Scotland (1561) after Francis II died and was at once involved in conflict with the Calvinists **(John Knox).**

1563. Adoption of the **Thirty-Nine Articles,** in place of the forty-two published by Cranmer. Completion of the **establishment of the Anglican church** (Church of England, Episcopal Church). A compromise Church, largely Protestant in dogma (though many of the thirty-nine articles are ambiguous), but with a hierarchical organization similar to the Catholic, and a liturgy reminiscent of the Roman Catholic. Numerous **dissenters** or **nonconformists: Puritans**—even then a broad, inexact term, covering various groups which wished to "purify" the Church; to substitute a simple early-Christian ritual for the existing ritual, to make the Church more "Protestant"; **Separatists,** Puritans who left the Anglican church entirely to organize their own churches; **Presbyterians,** Puritans who sought to substitute organization by presbyters and synods for organization by bishops within the Anglican church: **Brownists,** extreme leftist Puritans religiously, the nucleus of the later **Independents** or **Congregationalists;** Brownists and Catholics alone of the Elizabethan religious groups could not be brought under the queen's policy of toleration within the Anglican church. Elizabeth therefore did not "tolerate" and did "persecute" Catholics, Brownists, and, of course, Unitarians (who denied the doctrine of the Trinity).

1564. Peace of Troyes with France. English claims to Calais renounced for 222,000 crowns.

In Scotland Mary married her cousin Henry Stuart, **Lord Darnley,** who caused her favorite, David Rizzio, to be murdered (1566) and was himself murdered (Feb. 10, 1567) by Earl Bothwell. The exact part played by Mary in these intrigues is still debated by historians. **Marriage of Mary and Bothwell** (May 15, 1567). The nobles under Earl Moray, Mary's natural brother, revolted, defeated Mary at **Carbury Hill,** near Edinburgh, and imprisoned her at Lochleven Castle. **Abdication of Mary** in favor of her son, by Darnley, **James VI** (July 24, 1567). **Moray** (Murray), regent. In May 1568 Mary escaped from captivity; defeated at **Langside,** May 13, she took refuge in England, where, after some delay, she was placed in confinement (1568).

1577. Alliance of Elizabeth and the Netherlands.

1583-1584. Plots against the queen (Arden, Parry); Spanish plot of Throgmorton; execution of the **earl of Arundel** for corresponding with Mary. **Bond of Association.**

1585. Troops sent to the aid of the Dutch Republic under the **earl of Leicester. Victory of Zutphen** (Sept. 22, 1586), death of **Sir Philip Sidney.**

1586. Expedition of **Sir Francis Drake** to the West Indies, sack of Santo Domingo and Carthagena; rescue of the Virginia colony.

1586. Conspiracy of **Savage, Ballard, Babington,** etc., discovered by the secretary of state, **Sir Francis Walsingham;** execution of the conspirators. The government involved Mary, queen of Scots, in the plot. She was tried at Fotheringay Castle (Oct.), and convicted on the presentation of letters which she alleged to be forged. She was convicted Oct. 25 and executed Feb. 8, 1587.

1587. WAR WITH SPAIN. Construction of an English fleet of war. The Spanish fleet, called the *Invincible Armada* (132 vessels, 3165 cannon), was defeated in the Channel by the English fleet **(Howard, Drake, Hawkins),** July 31–August 8, 1588, and destroyed by a storm off the Hebrides.

1597. Rebellion of the Irish under **Hugh O'Neill, earl of Tyrone;** the failure of the earl of Essex to cope with the insurrection led to his recall, and his successor Lord Mountjoy quickly subjugated the country (1601). Capture of Tyrone, flight of the **earl of Desmond.** A rebellion of **Essex** in London was followed by his execution (1601).

1600. Charter of the **East India Company.**

1601. Elizabethan Poor Law, preceded by various measures regulating apprenticeship (1563), vagrancy, etc. This famous law charged the parishes with providing for the needy.

1603-1649 (1714). THE HOUSE OF STUART. Personal Union of England and Scotland.

1603-1625. JAMES I (as king of Scotland **James VI**), son of Mary Stuart. The Scots had brought him up in the Protestant faith. He was rather pedantic, and not popular with a people used to the hearty Tudors. Divine right of kingship, divine right of the bishops (*no bishop, no king*). In this century the after-effects of the Reformation made themselves felt in England as on the Continent, and in both places resulted in war. In England, however, owing to the peculiar circumstances of the Reformation, these effects were peculiarly conditioned; the religious questions were confused and overshadowed by political and constitutional questions. Under stress of their quarrel, both the first two Stuarts and the parliamentarians sought to bend the medieval

English constitution, the Stuarts toward royal absolutism, the parliamentarians toward government by an oligarchy of great nobles and city merchants. Only at the end of the struggle, in the 1640's, did advanced democratic ideas, coupled usually with extreme religious doctrines, appear in minority groups **(Levelers, Fifth Monarchy Men).**

1603, Mar. 24. James I was proclaimed king; he entered London on the 7th of May, and was crowned July 25. Presentation of the **millenary petition** immediately after James's arrival in London, signed by 1000 (800) ministers, asking for the reform of abuses.

The Main and the Bye. The Main was a plot to dethrone James in favor of **Arabella Stuart** (see genealogical table), concocted by Lords Cobham, Grey, and others. **Sir Walter Raleigh** was also implicated and was imprisoned till 1616 (*History of the World* written in prison). The Bye or the *surprising treason* was a plot to imprison the king. **Alliance with France,** negotiated by Sully.

1604, Jan. Hampton Court Conference, between the bishops and the Puritans, James presiding. The Puritans failed to secure any relaxation of the rules of the Church. James issued a proclamation enforcing the **act of Uniformity,** and another banishing Jesuits and seminary priests. Friction between the king and parliament over a disputed election in Bucks **(Goodwin** and **Fortescue).**

1604, Mar. 19-1611, Feb. 9. First parliament of James I. The king's scheme of a real union of England and Scotland unfavorably received. Appointment of a commission to investigate the matter.

Convocation (ecclesiastical court and legislature, at first established [Edward I] as an instrument for ecclesiastical taxation; afterward convened by archbishops for the settlement of church questions; since Henry VIII, convened only by writ from the king, and sitting and enacting [canons] only be permission of the king) adopted some new canons which bore so hard upon the Puritans that 300 clergymen left their livings rather than conform.

1604. Peace with Spain. James proclaimed *King of Great Britain, France, and Ireland* (Oct. 24). Punishment of many recusants (under the recusancy laws of Elizabeth, whereby refusing to go to church, saying Mass, or assisting at Mass was severely punished).

1605, Nov. 5. GUNPOWDER PLOT, originating in 1604 with **Robert Catesby,** after the edict banishing the priests. Preparations for blowing up the houses of parliament with thirty-six barrels of gunpowder. Disclosure of the plot through an anonymous letter. Arrest of **Guy Fawkes** in the vaults on Nov. 4, the day before the meeting of parliament. Trial and execution of the conspirators.

1606. Penal laws against papists. Plague in London. **Episcopacy restored in Scotland.** James urged the union anew, but in vain.

Impositions. The grant of customs duties made at the beginning of every reign (*tonnage* and *poundage,* established by Edward III) proving insufficient to meet James's expenditure, he had recourse to impositions without parliamentary grant, which Mary and Elizabeth had used to only a small extent. Trial of Bates for refusing to pay an imposition on currants. The court of exchequer decided in favor of the king.

1610. The **Great Contract;** in return for the surrender of some feudal privileges, the king was to receive a yearly income of £200,000. The agreement was frustrated by a dispute over the impositions. Dissolution of parliament (Feb. 9, 1611).

1611. Plantation of Ulster, which was forfeited to the crown by the rebellion of Tyrone.

1611. Completion of the **translation of the Bible,** which was authorized by the king and had occupied 47 ministers since 1604.

1613. Robert Carr, the king's favorite (Viscount Rochester in 1611), created duke of Somerset and lord treasurer, on the death of the earl of Salisbury (Robert Cecil). Death of Henry, prince of Wales (Nov. 1612).

1614, Apr. 5–June 7. Second parliament of James I. Three hundred new members, among whom were **John Pym** (Somersetshire), **Thomas Wentworth** (Yorkshire), **John Eliot** (St. Germains). The whole session was spent in quarreling with the king over the impositions, and parliament was dissolved without making an enactment, whence it is called the *Addled Parliament.*

1615. Renewal of the negotiation for the marriage of James's son to a Spanish princess (opened in 1611). Imposition of a benevolence, which was resisted by Oliver St. John and condemned by the chief justice, **Sir Edward Coke,** who was afterward dismissed from office. **Rise of George Villiers** in the king's favor; Viscount Villiers, earl, marquis, **duke of Buckingham.**

1617. Sir Walter Raleigh, released from the Tower, allowed to sail for the Orinoco, where he hoped to discover a gold mine. Failing in this he attacked the Spanish towns on the Orinoco. On his return to England in the following year, he was executed under the old sentence, as reparation to Spain.

1621, Jan. 30–1622, Feb. 8. Third parliament of James I. The parliament granted a supply for the prosecution of the war in the Palatinate

(p. 431), in which James was half-hearted, and then took up the subject of grievances. Impeachment of Mompesson and Mitchell, who had bought monopolies of inn-licensing and the manufacture of gold and silver thread; they were degraded, fined, and banished. **Impeachment of Francis Bacon** (1561–1626), famous essayist and writer on scientific method, lord chancellor since 1618. Bacon admitted that he had received presents from parties in suits, but denied that they had affected his judgment. He was fined £40,000 (which was remitted) and declared incapable of holding office in the future. Petition of the commons against popery and the Spanish marriage. The angry rebuke of the king for meddling in affairs of state (*"bring stools for the ambassadors"*) drew from the parliament

1621, Dec. 18. The **GREAT PROTESTATION:** "That the liberties, franchises, privileges, and jurisdictions of parliament are the ancient and undoubted birthright and inheritance of the subjects of England, and that the arduous and urgent affairs concerning the king, state, and defense of the realm . . . are proper subjects and matter of council and debate in parliament." The king tore the page containing the protestation from the journal of the commons, dissolved parliament (Feb. 8, 1622), and imprisoned **Southampton, Coke, Pym,** and **Selden.**

1623. Charles, prince of Wales, and the **duke of Buckingham** went to Spain and negotiated a marriage treaty, the provisions of which were so favorable to the Catholics as to excite great dissatisfaction in England; finally, being unable to secure any help from Spain in regard to the Palatinate, Charles and Buckingham returned in anger.

1624, Feb. 12–1625, Mar. 27. Fourth parliament of James I. The Spanish marriage was broken off, but even the anger of Buckingham could not drive the parliament into a declaration of war with Spain. Supplies voted for defense. Mansfeld raised 1200 men in England who reached Holland, but nearly all perished there from lack of proper provisions. This was, in fact, a breach with Spain. Marriage treaty with France for the marriage of Prince Charles with **Henriette Marie,** sister of Louis XIII.

1625–1649. CHARLES I.

1625, May 11. Marriage of Charles I and Henriette Marie. Ships sent to Louis XIII secretly engaged not to fight against the Huguenots.

1625. First parliament of Charles I. (Assembled June 18; adjourned to Oxford July 11; dissolved August 12). Grant of tonnage and poundage for one year only, and of £140,000 for the war with Spain. Proceedings against

Montague. Unsuccessful expedition of Wimbledon against Cadiz.

1626, Feb. 6–June 15. Second parliament of Charles I. Charles had hoped for a more pliable parliament, as he had appointed several of the leaders of the first parliament sheriffs, and so kept them out of the second. But this parliament, under the lead of **Sir John Eliot,** was more intractable than the last. Lord Bristol, to whom no writ had been sent by order of the king, received one on the interference of the lords, but was requested not to appear. He took his seat and brought **charges against Buckingham,** on which that lord was impeached (May). Imprisonment of Sir John Eliot and Sir Dudley Digges, who were set at liberty only upon the refusal of parliament to proceed to business without them.

1626–1630. War against France. Inglorious expedition of Buckingham to the relief of Rochelle (1627).

Exaction of a **forced loan** to raise money for the French war, and for the subsidy which Charles had agreed to supply to Christian IV of Denmark.

1628, Mar. 17–1629, Mar. 10. Third parliament of Charles I. (May): Passage of the **PETITION OF RIGHT:** (1) Prohibition of benevolences, and all forms of taxation, without consent of parliament. (2) Soldiers should not be billeted in private houses. (3) No commission should be given to military officers to execute martial law in time of peace. (4) No one should be imprisoned unless upon a specified charge. Assent of the king (June 7). Grant of five subsidies.

Charles having, after the first year of his reign, continued to levy tonnage and poundage, the commons drew up a remonstrance against that practice. **Prorogation of parliament** (June 26). Seizure of goods of merchants who refused to pay tonnage and poundage.

Assassination of Buckingham (Aug. 23), by Felton.

1629, Jan. New session of parliament. The Commons at once took up the question of **tonnage and poundage;** claim of privilege in the case of Rolle, one of the merchants, whose goods had been seized, and who was a member of parliament. Turbulent scene in the house of commons; the speaker held in the chair while the **resolutions of Eliot** were read: Whoever introduced innovations in religion, or opinions disagreeing with those of the true Church; whoever advised the levy of tonnage and poundage without grant of parliament; whoever voluntarily paid such duties, was an enemy of the kingdom.

1629. Eliot and eight other members were arrested (Mar. 5); Eliot died in the Tower in Nov. 1632 and the others made submission. **Parliament dissolved** (Mar. 10). For eleven years (1629–1640) Charles governed without a parliament, raising money by hand-to-mouth expedients, reviving old taxes, old feudal privileges of the crown, selling monopolies. These were rarely wholly illegal, but seemed to parliamentarians contrary to recent constitutional developments. **Charles's advisers: William Laud** (1573–1645), bishop of London, 1628, archbishop of Canterbury, 1633; **Thomas Wentworth** (1593–1641), earl of Strafford and lord lieutenant of Ireland, 1639. Both were extremists. Strafford's policy of *thorough* further embittered Ireland. **Peace was made with France** (Apr. 1630) **and with Spain** (Nov. 1630). Conformity was enforced, and the communion table inrailed.

1634. The tax which focused hatred on Charles was **ship-money,** by which a writ issued in 1635 extended to the whole country a tax hitherto levied only on seaboard towns. **John Hampden,** a Buckinghamshire country gentleman, defying the tax, was tried, 1637–1638, and lost his case in court but won it with the public.

1637. An attempt to read the English liturgy in Edinburgh, ordered by Charles, produced a **riot at St. Giles'** (June 23). This was followed by the organization of the Scottish Presbyterians to resist episcopacy. On February 28, 1638 was signed the **Solemn League and Covenant** (whence *Covenanters*) for the defense of the reformed religion. In November a general assembly at Glasgow abolished episcopacy, settled liturgy and canons, and gave final form to the **Scottish Kirk.**

1639. The First Bishops' War. The Scots seized Edinburgh Castle and raised an army. Charles marched to meet them near Berwick, but concluded with them, without battle, the **pacification of Dunse** (June 18). After the armies had been disbanded, the questions were to be referred to a new general assembly and a new (Scottish) parliament. At the Edinburgh assembly the work of the Glasgow assembly was confirmed, and parliament proved intractable.

1640. Charles, in trouble in Scotland and financially distressed in England, now called his **fourth parliament,** the *Short Parliament* at Westminster (Apr. 13–May 5). This parliament, refusing to vote money until grievances were settled, was immediately dissolved. Riots, attacks on Laud's palace. The Scottish trouble broke out in the **Second Bishops' War,** and the royalists were beaten in a skirmish at **Newburn on the Tyne** (Aug. 28). By the **treaty of Ripon** (Oct. 26) Charles agreed to pay the Scottish army £850 a day until a permanent settlement could be made. These obligations made the calling of a parliament inevitable.

1640. The **LONG PARLIAMENT, the fifth parliament of Charles I** (Nov. 3, 1640–Mar. 16, 1660). First session until September 8, 1641.

The fact that the Scottish army was not to be disbanded until paid gave the commons an unusual hold over Charles. On November 11, **Strafford was impeached,** followed by **Laud,** and both were sent to the Tower. At the trial of Strafford in the following March, the result of impeachment being uncertain, it was dropped, and a bill of attainder introduced, which passed both commons and lords in April. Strafford was executed on May 12. Meanwhile, parliament passed the revolutionary **Triennial Act,** requiring the summoning of parliament every three years even without the initiative of the crown (May 15, 1641). This was followed in May by a bill to prevent the dissolution or proroguing of the present parliament without its own consent, which Charles reluctantly signed, along with Strafford's attainder. The culmination of radicalism was the introduction of a bill for the abolition of bishops. This was the **Root and Branch Bill,** on which the moderate Puritans split with the more radical Presbyterians.

1641, July. Abolition of the courts of Star Chamber and **High Commission.** These courts were a part of the constitution of England, and their abolition shows that parliament was determined to effect a revolution. In August a **treaty of pacification with Scotland** was made, and Scottish and English armies were paid with the proceedings of a special poll-tax granted by parliament. Charles took refuge with the Scots. On the proroguing of parliament in September, each house appointed a committee to sit in the vacation (**Pym,** chairman of the commons' committee). Charles attempted to conciliate the moderate parliamentarians by giving office to their leader, Lucius Cary, Lord Falkland.

In Scotland, the **marquis of Montrose** plotted the seizure of the **earl of Argyll,** Presbyterian leader. The discovery of the plot seemed to involve Charles himself, who was thus thrown into the hands of Argyll. Charles practically surrendered all control over Scotland to Argyll and the Presbyterians, receiving from the latter only a promise not to interfere in English religious affairs (Oct. 1641).

1641, Oct. 21. Parliament assembled and heard the news of the **massacre of Protestants in Ulster** (30,000 killed). Still unwilling to entrust Charles with an army, it presented him with the **Grand Remonstrance** (Dec. 1) passed in the Commons in November by eleven votes, a summary of all the grievances of his reign. It was ordered printed by parliament on December 14.

1642, Jan. 3. Charles ordered the impeachment of Lord Kimbolton, and of **Pym, Hampden, Haselrig, Holles, Strode,** of the commons, for treasonable correspondence with the Scots in the recent troubles. The commons refusing to order the arrest, Charles with a few hundred soldiers went to the house and attempted to seize the five members (Jan. 4). Failing to find them, he withdrew. The five members had taken refuge in London, where the commons followed them, and formed a committee at the Guildhall under the protection of the citizens of London. Charles left London on January 10 and the five members returned. The victorious commons, emboldened, put before the king bills excluding bishops from the lords and giving command of the militia to parliament. From York he refused to sign the latter (March) and there he was joined by 32 peers and 65 members of the commons. He also had the great seal. The parliament at Westminster now was obliged to pass ordinances which were not submitted to the king and did not appear under the great seal.

June 2. Parliament made a final approach to Charles, submitting the **nineteen propositions:** that the king should give his assent to the militia bill; that all fortified places should be entrusted to officers appointed by parliament; that the liturgy and church government should be reformed in accordance with the wishes of parliament; that parliament should appoint and dismiss all royal ministers, appoint guardians for the king's children, and have the power of excluding from the upper house at will all peers created after that date. The propositions were rejected.

July. Parliament appointed a **committee of public safety,** and put Essex in charge of an army of 20,000 foot and 4000 cavalry. When on August 22 Charles raised the royal standard at Nottingham, the military phase of the **Great Rebellion** began.

1642–1646. THE CIVIL WAR. Roughly, northern and west-central England stood by the king; East Anglia, London, and the south with parliament. Socially, the gentry, the Anglican clergy, and the peasantry were royalist; the middle classes, the great merchants, and many great nobles were parliamentarians. But neither *Roundhead* (parliamentarian, Puritan) nor *Cavalier* (royalist) describes completely an economic or social class. Armies were small. Until Cromwell's *Ironsides* the royalist cavalry was superior. The war was relatively free from excesses.

1642. After the drawn **battle of Edgehill** (Oct. 23), where **Prince Rupert** (royalist cavalry leader, son of the Elector Palatine and Elizabeth of England) distinguished himself, the king marched on London, but turned back at Brentford when confronted by Essex (Nov. 12).

The associated counties of Norfolk, Suffolk, Essex, Cambridge, Hertford, and Huntingdon raised a force entrusted to **Oliver Cromwell** (1599–1658), which as the *Ironsides* finally became the best troops in the war. Meantime, the war was a series of raids and indecisive battles. **Capture of Reading** by Essex (Apr. 27, 1643); skirmish at **Chalgrove Field** in which Hampden was mortally wounded (June 18). **Capture of Bristol** by Rupert (July 25), counterbalanced by Essex's **relief of Gloucester** (Sept.), gallantly defended by Massey. **First battle of Newbury** (Sept. 20).

1643, July 1. Through all this the **Westminster Assembly,** which sat until 1649, debated religious and theological problems.

Sept. 25. The **SOLEMN LEAGUE AND COVENANT,** signed by 25 peers and 288 members of the commons, agreeing to make the religions of England, Ireland, and Scotland as nearly uniform as possible and to reform religion *"according to the word of God, and the examples of the best reformed churches."* All civil and military officials were required to sign the covenant (nearly 2000 clergymen refused and lost their livings). The Scots now consented to help the English parliamentarians; a Scottish army crossed the Tweed (Jan. 1644). Charles rashly enlisted Irish Catholic insurgents with whom he concluded peace, thus alienating many Englishmen.

1644, Jan. Charles convened a **royalist parliament at Oxford.** His opponents established (Feb. 15) a joint committee of the two kingdoms of Scotland and England. At the **battle of Nantwich** (Jan. 25) the royalist Irish were beaten by **Sir Thomas Fairfax,** who, in junction with the Scots, besieged York while Essex and Waller besieged Oxford.

July 2. BATTLE OF MARSTON MOOR. Prince Rupert, after defeating the Scots, was decisively beaten by Cromwell and his Ironsides. This was the crucial battle of the war, and gave the north to parliament. York surrendered (July 16); Newcastle (Oct. 16). In the south Waller was beaten at **Cropredy Bridge** (June 29) and Essex's infantry surrendered to Charles in Cornwall. The indecisive **second battle of Newbury** (Oct. 27), in which Charles was pitted against Essex, Waller, and Manchester, prefaced the so-called **treaty of Uxbridge,** a truce in January and February 1645, during which parliament's proposals were rejected by Charles, who had hitherto had the best of the war in south and southwest.

In Scotland, **Montrose,** after slipping into the country in disguise (Aug. 1644), raised highland clans for Charles and gained several victories over the Covenanters (**Tippamuir,** Sept. 1; **Inverlochy,** Feb. 2, 1645; **Auldcarn,** May 1; **Alford,** July 2). At one time he held most of Scotland, but his armies melted away when the parliament sent General Leslie into Scotland after Naseby, and at **Philiphaugh** (Sept. 13, 1645) the Stuart partisans were decisively beaten. Montrose fled to the Continent.

1645, Jan. Laud, tried in March 1644, was attainted and executed. England was fast moving toward extreme Protestantism. With Cromwell, the **Independents** rose to leadership. **Presbyterianism,** with some reservations for the Independents, became the established Church. The **Self-Denying Ordinance** (April 3) having excluded members of either house from military command, Fairfax superseded Essex as captain-general, and Cromwell, with the ordinance suspended in his case, became lieutenant-general. The army was reformed into the *New Model* on the lines of the Ironsides.

1645, June 14. BATTLE OF NASEBY, decisive defeat of the king, ruin of his cause. Royalist towns and houses surrendered rapidly: Leicester (June 18), Bridgewater (July 23), Bristol (Sept. 11), Carlisle, Winchester, Basing House (Oct.), Latham House (Dec.). At **Stowe-on-the-Wold** (Mar. 26, 1646) Lord Ashley was beaten and captured in the final battle of the war. Charles surrendered himself to the Scots (May 5).

1646, July. Parliament submitted to the captive Charles the **Newcastle proposals:** that parliament control the militia for twenty years; that Charles take the Covenant; that he support the Presbyterian establishment. Hoping to profit by the obviously impending breach between the Presbyterians in parliament and the Independents in the army, Charles rejected the propositions.

1647, Jan. 30. The **Scots surrendered Charles to parliament** in return for their back pay (£400,000). He was brought to Holmby House in Northamptonshire. **Army and parliament in open conflict.** Parliament reappointed Fairfax commander-in-chief, re-enacted the self-denying ordinance, and voted the disbandment of all soldiers not needed for garrisons or for service in Ireland. This the army refused to accept, claiming full payment for arrears in salary. A detachment headed by Cornet Joyce seized Charles at Holmby House (June 4), and carried him prisoner to the army, thus forestalling an agreement between king and Presbyterians.

June 4. On the same day Cromwell fled from parliament to the army at **Triptow Heath,**

where it had taken an oath not to disband until freedom of conscience was secured, and had erected a council of adjudicators. From St. Albans the army addressed to parliament a *humble representation* (June 10) and demanded the exclusion of eleven members, among them Holles, obnoxious to it. The two speakers, fourteen lords, and about one hundred of the commons fled to the army (July). Proposals were presented to the king by the army: that worship be free for all; that parliament control army and navy for ten years and appoint officers of state; that parliament serve for three years **(triennial parliaments)**. The king rejected them, and moved to take refuge with the Presbyterian members of parliament; but the army entered London (Aug. 6) and forced parliament to take back the members who had fled to the army. Charles removed to Hampton Court, where he rejected a modified form of the previous proposals and fled to the Isle of Wight, where he was detained by the governor of Carisbrooke Castle (Nov. 11).

Dec. 24. The **Four Bills** presented to the king by parliament: (1) parliament to command the army for twenty years; (2) all declarations and proclamations against the parliament to be recalled; (3) all peers created since the great seal was sent to Charles to be incapable of sitting in the house; (4) the two houses should adjourn at pleasure. Charles, who was only playing with the parliament in the hope of securing aid from Scotland, rejected the four bills (Dec. 28), after he had already signed a **secret treaty with the Scots** (Dec. 26). Charles agreed to abolish Episcopacy and restore Presbyterianism; the Scots, who looked with horror on the rising tide of toleration in England, agreed to restore him by force of arms.

1648, Jan. 15. Parliament renounced allegiance to the king, and voted to have no more communication with him.

1648. SECOND CIVIL WAR. At once a war between Scotland and England, a war between the royalists and the Roundheads, and a war between the Presbyterians and the Independents.

Mar. At a meeting of army officers at Windsor it was decided to bring the king to trial. Parliament having reassembled with 306 members and the Presbyterians again in control, repealed the non-communication resolution and attempted to reopen negotiations with the king (July).

Aug. 17-20. Battle of Preston. Under the duke of Hamilton, a Scottish army invaded England, but was beaten by Cromwell. This ended the second civil war. The so-called **treaty of Newport,** between king and parliament, had no result, as Charles was seized by the army (Dec. 1) and, parliament having again attempted to treat with the king, **Colonel Thomas Pride,** by order of the council of affairs, forcibly excluded 96 Presbyterian members from the parliament (*Pride's Purge,* Dec. 6, 7), which is henceforth known as the *Rump Parliament* (some 60 members).

Dec. 13. The **Rump** repealed the vote to continue negotiations with Charles, and voted that Charles be brought to trial. Appointment of a high court of justice of 135 members to try the king was rejected by the lords (1649, Jan. 2) whereupon the commons resolved that the legislative power resided solely with the commons (Jan. 4; passed Jan. 6 without concurrence of the lords).

1649, Jan. 20. The army council drew up a temporary *Instrument of Government.* Charles was tried before the high court (67 members present, Bradshaw presiding) whose jurisdiction he simply denied (Jan. 20-27). **The king was sentenced to death and beheaded at Whitehall** (Jan. 30). (*Cont. p. 459.*)

BRITISH CULTURE

(1) Architecture

Inigo Jones (1573-1652) built Lincoln's Inn Chapel, the Banqueting-Hall at Whitehall, the Queen's House at Greenwich.

(2) Education

University of Glasgow (1452); University of Aberdeen (1494); St. Paul's School, London (1510); Rugby (1567); Harrow (1571); Trinity College, Dublin (1591).

(3) Literature

Prose: **Archbishop Cranmer,** *Book of Common Prayer;* **Thomas More** (1478-1535), *Utopia,* 1516; **Roger Ascham** (1515-1568), *The Schoolmaster;* **Raphael Holinshed** (d. 1580), *Chronicles of England, Scotland, and Ireland;* **Richard Hakluyt** (1553-1616) *Principall Navigations, Voyages and Discoveries of the English Nation,* 1589; **Richard Hooker** (1554-1600), *Laws of Ecclesiastical Polity;* **Sir Philip Sidney** (1554-1586), poet and critic, *Defense of Poesie;* **Sir Walter Raleigh** (1552-1618), *The History of the World;* **John Lyly** (1554-1606), *Euphues; The Anatomy of Wit;* the essayist **Francis Bacon** (1561-1626), *Essays, New Atlantis,* 1621; the dramatists **Thomas Nashe** (1567-1601); **Thomas Dekker** (1570-1641); **Robert Burton** (1577-1640), *Anatomy of Melancholy;* the political philosophers **Thomas Hobbes** (1588-1679), *Leviathan,* 1651; and **James Harrington** (1611-1677), *Oceana,* 1656; **Izaak Walton** (1593-1683), *The Compleat*

Angler, 1653; **Sir Thomas Browne** (1605–1682), *Religio Medici.*

Poets: John Skelton (1460–1529); **Sir Thomas Wyatt** (c. 1503–1542); **Edmund Spenser** (c. 1552–1599), *Faerie Queene;* **Sir Walter Raleigh; Sir Philip Sidney; Michael Drayton** (1563–1631); **Ben Jonson** (1573–1637); **John Donne** (1573–1631); **Sir John Suckling** (1609–1642); **Thomas Carew** (1605–1639); **Richard Lovelace** (1618–1658). **Thomas Campion** (1567–1620) was composer and poet. Other composers: **Thomas Tallis** (c. 1505–1585); **William Byrd** (1540–1623); **Orlando Gibbons** (1583–1625).

Dramatists: Miracle plays ceased after the Reformation, but dramas in a popular vein were written by **John Lyly** (see above) and **Thomas Kyd** (*The Spanish Tragedy*, 1585). **Christopher Marlowe's** use of blank verse in his morality plays (*Dr. Faustus*, 1588; *The Jew of Malta*, 1589) established its use in the English theater.

William Shakespeare (1564–1616) was the greatest dramatist of the Elizabethan or any other age. The force of his dramas is dependent on his careful development of individual characters, his forceful and precise vocabulary, the universal and enduring appeal of his plots to other ages and other cultures. Many of his plays, especially the tragedies, relied on actual history for their stories (*Julius Caesar, King Lear, Henry IV, Henry V, Henry VI*); among the comedies are *A Midsummer Night's Dream* (1595–1596), *As You Like It, Twelfth Night.* Shakespeare also wrote some of the best sonnets in the English language, using a rhyme scheme of his own devising; also lyrics, often incorporated in the plays and the narrative poems *Venus and Adonis* and *The Rape of Lucrece.*

Shakespeare established the drama as a respected literary medium. The comedies of his contemporary, the poet **Ben Jonson,** dared to criticize the foibles of the age (*Volpone,* 1605). The collaborators **Francis Beaumont** (1579–1625) and **John Fletcher** (1584–1616) dared to poke fun at their society (*The Knight of the Burning Pestle,* 1607).

John Milton (1608–1674), the blind poet of the Puritan Revolution, composed sonnets and lyric poems (*L'Allegro, Il Penseroso, Lycidas*) in his youth; published his three major poems after the Restoration (*Paradise Lost,* 1667; *Paradise Regained,* 1671; *Samson Agonistes,* 1671), and a *History of Britain to the Conquest* (1670). During the twenty years of political unrest he wrote prose tracts in support of liberty—in religion, education, and in the press (*Areopagitica,* 1644).

2. THE NETHERLANDS, TO 1648

The provinces of the **Low Countries,** originally inhabited by Batavians and other Germanic tribes, had formed a part of the empire of Charlemagne and, after the **treaty of Mersen** (870), belonged in large part to Germany, forming a dependency of the kingdom of Lotharingia. The decline of the ducal power favored the growth of powerful counties and duchies, such as Brabant, Flanders, Gelders, Holland, Zeeland, Hainault, and the bishopric of Utrecht. After 1384 the provinces were brought under the control of the dukes of Burgundy in the following manner: **Philip II** (the Bold), fourth son of **John II** of France, became the duke of Burgundy in 1363. He acquired Flanders and Artois (1384) through marriage with Margaret, heiress of Count Louis II. Their son was **John the Fearless,** duke of Burgundy (1404–1419), who was succeeded by his son, **Philip the Good** (1419–1467). Philip acquired Namur by purchase (1425). Brabant and Limburg came to him by bequest (Joanna, daughter of John III, duke of Brabant, left them to her great-nephew, Antoine, brother of John the Fearless). In 1433 he acquired Holland, Hainault, and Zeeland by cession from Jacqueline, countess of Holland; and in 1443, Luxemburg, by cession from Elizabeth of Luxemburg. He also added Antwerp and Mechlin. His son, **Charles the Bold** (duke of Burgundy 1467–1477), acquired Gelderland and Zutphen by bequest from Duke Arnold (1472).

Mary, the daughter and heiress of Charles the Bold, married **Maximilian,** archduke of Austria and later emperor (p. 327). Their son, **Philip the Handsome** (duke of Burgundy), married **Joanna,** the daughter of Ferdinand of Aragon and Isabella of Castile, and thus the Netherland provinces passed ultimately into the hands of Philip's son, **Charles I** (Charles V as emperor).

1548. Charles annexed the seventeen provinces (Brabant, Limburg, Luxemburg, Gelderland, Flanders, Artois, Hainault, Holland, Zeeland, Namur, Zutphen, East Friesland, West Friesland. Mechlin, Utrecht, Overyssel,. Groningen) to the Burgundian circle of the empire.

1556. Abdication of Charles. The Netherlands, like Spain, passed to his son,

1556–1598. PHILIP II.

1568–1648. REVOLT OF THE NETHER-

The House of Burgundy (1312–1477)

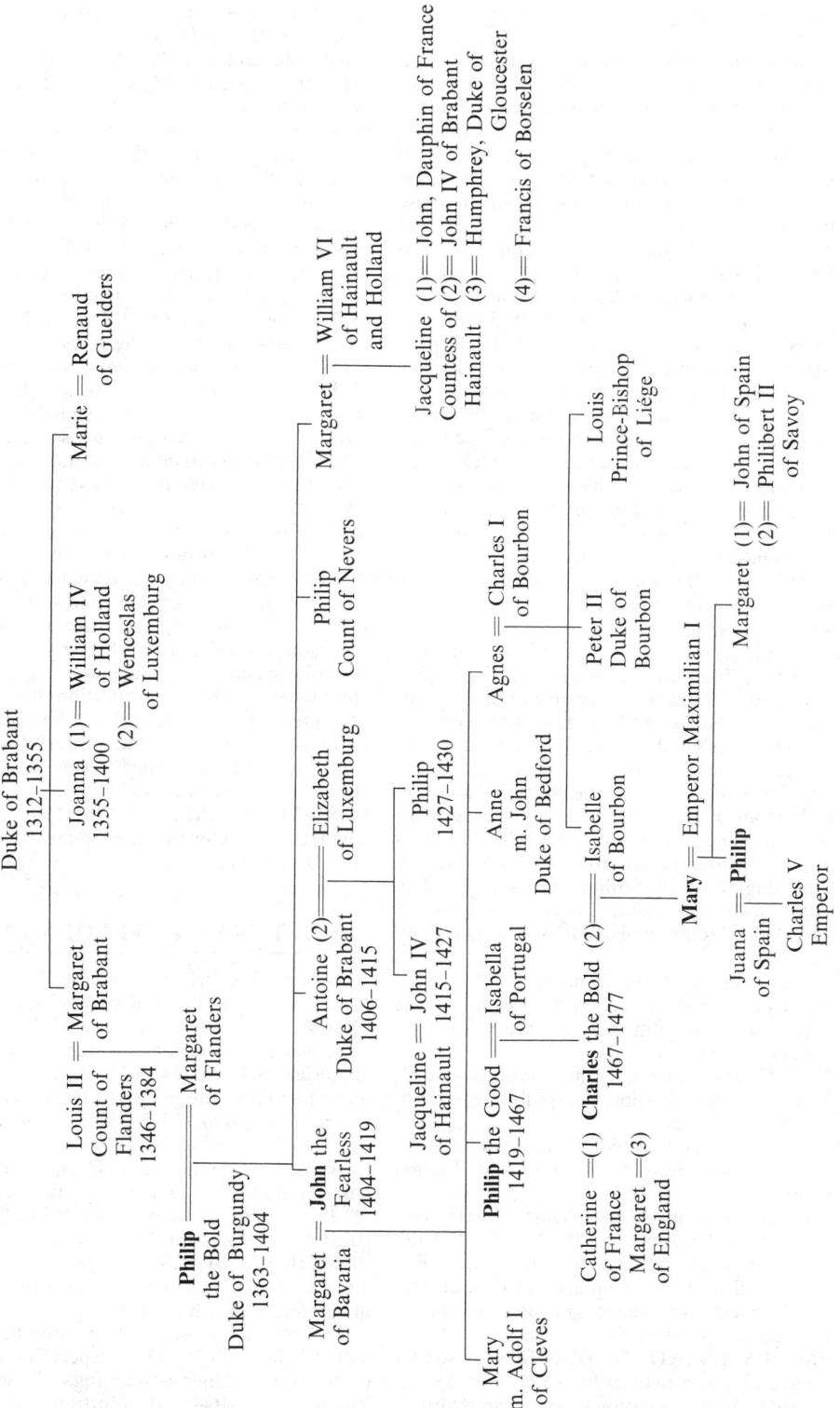

John III
Duke of Brabant
1312–1355

Louis II = Margaret
Count of   of Brabant
Flanders
1346–1384

Joanna (1)= William IV
1355–1400   of Holland
        (2)= Wenceslas
              of Luxemburg

Marie = Renaud
          of Guelders

Philip ===== Margaret
the Bold   of Flanders
Duke of Burgundy
1363–1404

Margaret = Elizabeth
Antoine (2)===== of Luxemburg
Duke of Brabant
1406–1415

Philip
Count of Nevers

Margaret = William VI
               of Hainault
               and Holland

Jacqueline (1)= John, Dauphin of France
Countess of (2)= John IV of Brabant
Hainault   (3)= Humphrey, Duke of
                        Gloucester
         (4)= Francis of Borselen

Margaret = John the
of Bavaria   Fearless
               1404–1419

Jacqueline = John IV
of Hainault   1415–1427

Philip
1427–1430

Anne
m. John
Duke of Bedford

Agnes = Charles I
            of Bourbon

Louis
Prince-Bishop
of Liége

Mary
m. Adolf I
of Cleves

Philip the Good ==== Isabella
1419–1467   of Portugal

Catherine =(1) Charles the Bold (2)= Isabelle
of France   1467–1477   of Bourbon
Margaret =(3)
of England

Peter II
Duke of
Bourbon

Mary = Emperor Maximilian I

Margaret (1)= John of Spain
        (2)= Philibert II
              of Savoy

Juana = Philip
of Spain

Charles V
Emperor

LANDS. The provinces had long enjoyed ancient and important privileges. The estates (*staaten, états*) granted taxes and troops. **Calvinism** had taken firm root in the northern provinces (commonly called Holland), but the southern provinces (now Belgium) remained Catholic. The Spanish garrison, the penal edicts against heretics, the dread of the introduction of the Spanish Inquisition, all these factors led (during the rule [1559-1567] of **Margaret of Parma,** the natural sister of Philip II, and her adviser, **Cardinal Granvelle**) to the formation of a **league of nobles** (*Compromise of Breda*), headed by Philip Marnix of St. Aldegonde. Presentation of a petition by 300 nobles (*Gueux = Beggars,* a party name, originating in the contemptuous remark of the count of Barlaimont: *"Ce n'est qu'un tas de gueux"*). Insurrection of the lower classes. Destruction of images and sack of the churches. These disturbances were opposed by **Lamoral, count Egmont** (1522-1568) and **William of Nassau,** prince of Orange (**William the Silent,** 1533-1584), the leaders of the higher nobility, who, however, soon lost control of the movement. Protestant and Catholic parties soon emerged.

1567. Philip sent to the Netherlands the **duke of Alva** (1508-1582) with an army of 20,000 Spaniards. William of Orange and many thousands of Netherlanders fled the country. Margaret resigned her regency and also departed. Creation of the Council of Blood. Ruthless suppression of opposition. **Execution of Egmont, Hoorn,** and many other prominent figures. The estates of those who failed to appear before the tribunal were confiscated, including those of William of Orange. The latter, with his brother Louis, thereupon invaded the Netherlands, but was repulsed by Alva.

The arbitrary taxes imposed by Alva (the tenth pfennig from the price of every article sold, the hundredth part of every income) produced a new revolt.

1572. Capture of Brill, by the "Water Beggars." The insurrection spread rapidly, especially throughout the north.

1573. Alva was recalled at his own request. His successor, **Luis de Requesens y Zuñiga,** gained a

1574. Victory at Mookerheide, where two brothers of the prince of Orange fell. But the Spaniards could not suppress the revolt. Requesens died (1576). **Capture and sack of Antwerp, Maestricht, Ghent,** and other towns by the Spaniards led to the

1576. PACIFICATION OF GHENT, a treaty among all the provinces by which they united, without regard to national or religious differ-

ences, to drive out the Spaniards. The new governor, **Don John of Austria,** was unable to quiet the country, despite disputes between the various parties. He died in 1578, and was succeeded by

1578-1592. Alexander Farnese (duke of Parma), a shrewd statesman and an excellent general. Parma ultimately subdued the southern provinces, on the promise that their old political freedom should be restored. The seven northern provinces (Holland, Zeeland, Utrecht, Gelderland, Groningen, Friesland, Overyssel), thereupon concluded

1579. The **UNION OF UTRECHT,** followed by a proclamation of **independence from Spain** (1581). The *stadholdership* was settled on **William of Orange.** After his murder at Delft (July 10, 1584), he was succeeded by his son.

1584. Maurice of Nassau, only seventeen years old. Parma continued his victorious campaigns and managed to capture Antwerp. Thereupon the English came to the aid of the insurgents.

1588. Philip II, hoping to put an end to the Anglo-Dutch combination, organized the **Great Armada,** which was defeated by the English and destroyed in a terrible storm (p. 400).

1609. The **Twelve Years' Truce** put an end to sporadic and inconclusive fighting and virtually established the independence of the northern provinces. After its expiration the war was resumed by the Spaniards. The Hollanders, who had grown rich and powerful at sea in the course of the struggle, were well able to hold their own, and finally

1648. The **TREATY OF WESTPHALIA** recognized the independence of the Republic of the United Provinces. (*Cont. p. 474.*)

CULTURAL DEVELOPMENTS

Josquin Des Près (c. 1445-1521) composed sacred songs in the polyphonic style of the Flemish school which dominated 16th-century Renaissance music: for example, the madrigals of **Adrian Willaert** (1480-1563), the sacred and secular songs of the greatest Flemish composer, **Orlando di Lasso** (1532-1594). The religious tradition in painting carried over from the **Van Eycks, Hans Memling** (c. 1433-1495), and **Hieronymus Bosch** (1460-1516), to the engravings of **Lucas Van Leyden** (1494-1533), and the paintings of **Quentin Massays** (c. 1466-1530). **Pieter Breughel** (1525-1569) painted both religious and everyday subjects, with the addition of humorous, earthy touches.

The golden age of painting came in the first half of the 17th century, especially with the portraits and religious paintings of **Peter Paul Rubens** (1577-1640); the portraits of **Anthony**

Van Dyck (1599–1641), court painter to Charles I of England, and **Franz Hals** (1580–1666); the landscapes of **Meyndaert Hobbema** (1638–1709) and **Jacob Ruysdael** (1628–1682); the genre works of **Jan Vermeer** (1632–1675); and culminating in the work of **Rembrandt van Rijn** (1606–1669): his numerous paintings of himself and of Saskia (1633–1641), *The Anatomy Lesson* (1632), *The Night Watch* (1642), his etchings, and his religious paintings.

Hugo Grotius (1583–1645) laid the bases of international law in his *Mare liberum* (1609) and *De jure belli ac pacis* (1625).   (*Cont. p. 474.*)

3. FRANCE, 1483–1641

(*From p. 303*)

[For a complete list of the kings of France see Appendix VII.]

1483–1498. CHARLES VIII.   Death of the duke of Brittany (1488) called forth a coalition of the empire, Spain and England to preserve the independence of the duchy, but this proved futile.   Charles married Anne, the heiress, in 1491, and concluded the **treaties of Senlis** (with the emperor) and **Étaples** (with England). Spain was bought off by the cession of Roussillon and Cerdagne.

1495–1496.   Charles's expedition to Italy to claim the inheritance of Naples (through his father from Charles, duke of Maine and Provence; see genealogical table). Charles marched victoriously through Italy and conquered Naples, but was soon obliged to withdraw in the face of the **Holy League** (Emperor Maximilian, Pope Alexander VI, Spain, Venice, Milan, and ultimately England), formed to protect Italy from foreign domination. Importance of the expedition in furthering the introduction of the Renaissance into France.

1498–1589.   HOUSES OF ORLÉANS AND ANGOULÊME.   Branch lines of the house of Valois (since 1328) whose relation to the main line is shown on page 410.

1498–1515.   LOUIS XII obtained a divorce from Jeanne, daughter of Louis XI, and married **Anne of Brittany,** widow of Charles VIII, in order to keep this duchy for the crown; as grandson of Valentina Visconti he laid claim to Milan, drove out Ludovico Moro, who was imprisoned when he tried to return (1500).

1501.   Louis, in alliance with Ferdinand the Catholic, king of Aragon, conquered the kingdom of Naples.   The Spaniards and French soon falling out, the latter were defeated by the Spanish general Gonzalvo de Córdoba on the Garigliano (1503).   Louis XII gave up his claims to Naples.

1508.   Louis a party to the **league of Cambrai** (p. 426).   In 1511 the pope, Ferdinand the Catholic, and Venice renewed the **Holy League,** with the object of driving the French out of Italy.   The latter, under the young **Gaston de Foix,** duke of Nemours, nephew of Louis XII, were at first successful in the war, taking Brescia (1512) by storm (**Seigneur de Bayard,** *sans peur et sans reproche,* 1476–1524), and defeating the united Spanish and papal armies at **Ravenna,** with the aid of 5000 German mercenaries, in the same year; they were, however, compelled by the Swiss to evacuate Milan. In 1513 the French formed a new alliance with Venice, but were defeated by the Swiss at **Novara** and withdrew from Italy. **Henry VIII of England,** who had joined the Holy League in 1512, and the **Emperor Maximilian,** who had joined in 1513, invaded France, and defeated the French at

1513, Aug. 17.   Guinegate, called the *battle of the Spurs* from the hasty flight of the French.

France concluded peace with the pope, with Spain (1511), with the emperor, and with Henry VIII (1514).   Anne of Brittany having died, Louis took as his third wife Mary, the sister of Henry VIII.   He died soon after the marriage (1515) and was succeeded by his cousin and son-in-law, the count of Angoulême, who had married Claude, heiress of Brittany, which, however, was not actually incorporated with France until later.

1515–1547.   FRANCIS I.
1515, Sept. 13–14.   Francis reconquered Milan by the brilliant **victory of Marignano** over the Swiss.   Peace and alliance between France and Switzerland.   **Treaty of Geneva** (Nov. 7, 1515); **treaty of Fribourg** (Nov. 29, 1516). The latter (*la paix perpétuelle*) endured till the French Revolution.

1516.   Increase of the royal power by the **concordat of Bologna** with the pope, which rescinded the Pragmatic Sanction of 1438 and placed the choice of bishops and abbots in the hands of the king; the pope on the other hand received the annates, or the first year's revenue of every ecclesiastical domain where the king's right of presentation was exercised.   Francis also abandoned the principle of the council of Basel, that the pope was subordinate to an ecumenical council.

410

The Last Valois Kings (1498–1589)

(From p. 300)

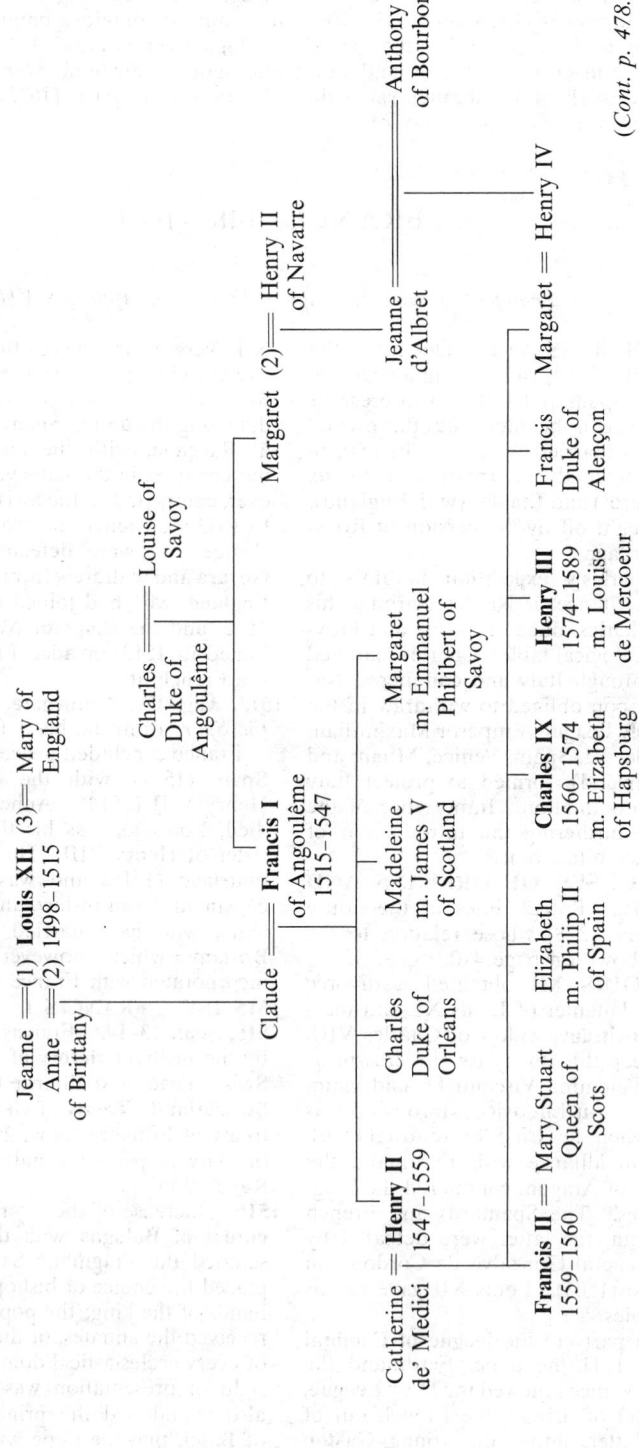

Jeanne ═(1) **Louis XII** (3)═ Mary of
Anne   ═(2) 1498–1515   England
of Brittany

Charles ═ Louise of
Duke of   Savoy
Angoulême

Margaret (2)═ Henry II
of Navarre

Jeanne ═ Anthony
d'Albret   of Bourbon

Claude ═ **Francis I**
of Angoulême
1515–1547

Margaret
m. Emmanuel
Philibert of
Savoy

Margaret ═ Henry IV

Charles
Duke of
Orléans

Madeleine
m. James V
of Scotland

Elizabeth
m. Philip II
of Spain

Charles IX
1560–1574
m. Elizabeth
of Hapsburg

Henry III
1574–1589
m. Louise
de Mercoeur

Francis
Duke of
Alençon

Catherine ═ **Henry II**
de' Medici   1547–1559

Francis II
1559–1560

Mary Stuart
Queen of
Scots

(Cont. p. 478.)

1520. Meeting of Francis and Henry VIII of England in the neighborhood of Calais (*Field of the Cloth of Gold*). The wars of Francis with Charles V (pp. 415 ff.) occupied the rest of the reign. Restrictions upon the political rights of the *parlements*. Beginnings of French Protestantism. Reformers of Meaux, **Lefebvre d'Étaples** (1455–1537). King and *parlements* condemned the movement.

1547–1559. HENRY II, son of Francis. Growing power of the **house of Guise (Francis,** duke of Guise, and **Charles,** cardinal of Lorraine).

Henry's mistress, **Diane of Poitiers,** duchess of Valentinois, ruled him almost absolutely. **Montmorency,** constable. Persecution of the Protestants in France; assistance to German Protestants.

1547. Final union of Brittany with the French crown.

1552. War with Charles V. Seizure of the three bishoprics (Toul, Metz, and Verdun) by the French.

1556–1559. War with Spain. The French were defeated by the Spaniards, supported by the English, in the **battle of St. Quentin** (1557), and by Egmont at **Gravelines** (1558).

1558. Calais, the last English possession in France, was captured by the duke of Guise.

1559, Apr. 3. PEACE OF CATEAU-CAMBRÉSIS, which ended the Hapsburg-Valois wars. The French restored all their conquests except Calais and the three bishoprics. Henry II, who died of a wound received in a tournament, was succeeded by his son

1559–1560. FRANCIS II, the first husband of Mary Stuart of Scotland, who was a niece of the Guises. Measures against the Protestants (*chambres ardentes*). The king's mother, **Catherine de' Medici** (1519–1589), struggled for power and influence against the Bourbon princes: **Anthony** (king of Navarre); and **Louis de Condé,** who were descended from Louis IX. The **Guises,** at first rivals of the queen-mother and then in alliance with her, conducted all the affairs of state and surpassed in influence their opponents, the Catholic constable, **Montmorency,** and his nephews, the three Châtillon brothers: **Gaspard, Admiral de Coligny; François d'Andelot,** and **Cardinal Châtillon,** later leaders of the Huguenots. **Conspiracy of Amboise** against the Guises. This was defeated (1560). Death of Francis II.

1560–1574. CHARLES IX (ten years old), the brother of Francis. He was wholly under the influence of his mother.

1562–1598. THE RELIGIOUS WARS. Persecution compelled the **Huguenots** (as the French Protestants were called—derivation uncertain) to take up arms. At the same time they formed a political party. The ensuing struggles, therefore, did not constitute a purely religious war, but also a political, civil war, in which the leaders of both parties endeavored to exploit the weakness of the crown and get control of the government. The Huguenots were recruited primarily from the nobility (between two-fifths and one-half of the French nobility were at one time Protestant) and from the new capitalist-artisan class. Save in the southwest very few peasants became Protestants. Paris and the northeast in general remained Catholic throughout.

The **first three wars** form properly one war, interrupted by truces called peaces (**Amboise,** 1563; **Longjumeau,** 1568; **St. Germain,** 1570), which bore no fruit. Battles, in which the Huguenots were worsted, were fought at **Dreux** (1562); **Jarnac** (1569); and **Moncontour** (1569). Huguenot cavalry, recruited from the nobility, was excellent; the infantry was generally weak.

The issue of the first period was that the Huguenots, despite defeat, were given conditional freedom of worship, which was guaranteed them, for two years, of four strongholds (La Rochelle, Cognac, Montauban, La Charité).

1572, Aug. 23-24. MASSACRE OF ST. BARTHOLOMEW. Murder of Coligny and general massacre of Protestants in Paris and in the provinces, on the occasion of the marriage of **Henry of Bourbon,** king of Navarre, with the sister of Charles IX, **Margaret of Valois.** Henry of Navarre saved his life by a pretended conversion to Catholicism. The massacre led to the

1572–1573. Fourth War. La Rochelle, besieged by Henry, brother of Charles IX, made a brave defense. The election of the duke of Anjou to the crown of Poland brought about a compromise. **Edict of Boulogne** (July 8, 1573) ended the war favorably to the Huguenots.

Charles IX died May 30, 1574. His brother, who fled from Poland, became king.

1574–1589. HENRY III.

1574–1576. The **Fifth War,** during which **Henry of Navarre** reassumed the Protestant faith, was concluded by conditions more favorable to the Huguenots than those of any previous peace. **Peace of Chastenoy** (*Paix de Monsieur,* after the duke of Alençon) May 6, 1576. Hence dissatisfaction among the Catholics. Origin of the **Holy League** (1576), which, in alliance with Philip II of Spain, purposed the annihilation of the reformed party, and the elevation of the Guises to the throne. The king, out of fear of the league, proclaimed himself its head and forbade the exercise of the Protestant religion throughout France. The Protestants and moderate Catholics had joined forces in 1575 by

The Houses of Lorraine and Guise (1480–1625)

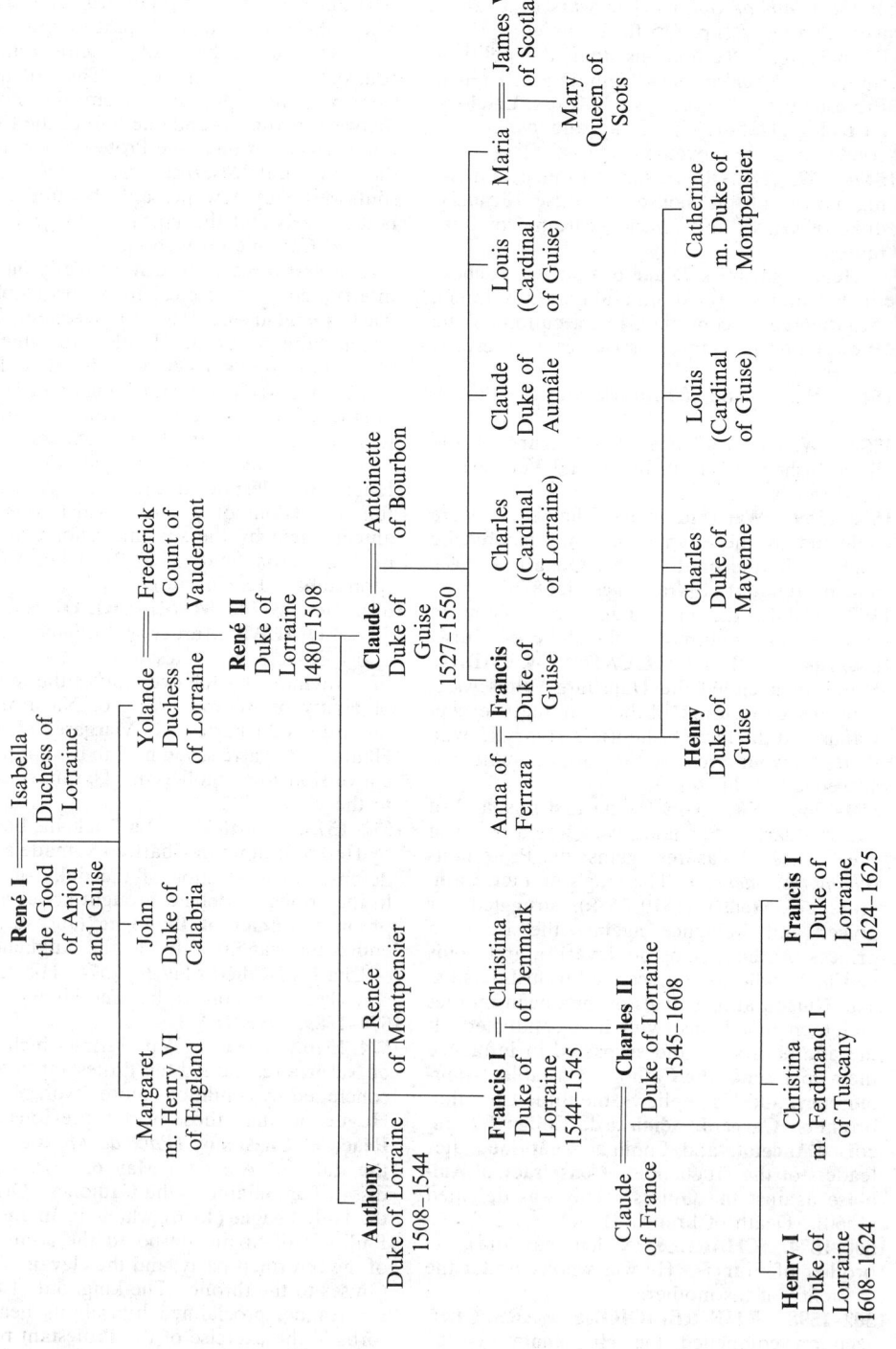

the **confederation of Milhaud.**

1577. Sixth War, wherein the Huguenots were defeated, but obtained favorable terms at the **peace of Bergerac** or **Poitiers** (Sept. 17), as the king was unwilling to let the league become too powerful. In spite of the renewal of the treaty of peace, not one of its articles was executed. This caused the

1580. Seventh War, which was ended in the same year by the **treaty of Fleix** (Nov. 26), in which the conditions granted the Huguenots in former treaties were confirmed.

1584. The death of Francis, duke of Alençon (since the accession of Henry III, duke of Anjou), the younger brother of the king, rendered the extinction of the house of Valois certain. As it was the intention of the league to exclude from the throne Henry of Navarre, who belonged to the reformed religion, and to give the crown to the latter's uncle, the **cardinal of Bourbon,** and as the league meantime had induced the king to revoke the concessions granted to the Huguenots, there broke out the

1585-1589. Eighth War, called the *War of the Three Henrys* (Henry III of Valois, Henry of Navarre, Henry of Guise). The Catholic party triumphed in spite of the **victory of Coutras** (Oct. 20, 1587), gained by Henry of Navarre. Formation of the **league of Sixteen** at Paris, which purposed the deposition of the weak king. Guise entered Paris, was received with acclamation (*King of Paris*); the timid resistance of the king was broken by a popular insurrection (*Day of the Barricades,* May 12, 1588). Henry III fled to Blois, where he summoned the estates-general of the kingdom. Finding no support among them against the league, he caused Henry, duke of Guise, and his brother, Louis the Cardinal, to be murdered (Dec. 23, 1588). At this news, a revolt of the Catholic party broke out, headed by the brother of the murdered men, the **duke of Mayenne.** Henry III fled to Henry of Navarre in the Huguenot camp, where he was murdered before Paris, at St. Cloud, by the monk **Jacques Clément** (July 31).

1589-1792. HOUSE OF BOURBON, descended from Louis IX's younger son Robert, count of Clermont, husband of Beatrice of Bourbon.

1589-1610. HENRY IV. The Catholic party refused to recognize Henry and made the old cardinal of Bourbon king under the name of **Charles X** (1590). Some wished the duke of Mayenne to be his successor, while others joined themselves to Philip II of Spain, who laid claim to the throne of France on behalf of his daughter by his third marriage with Elizabeth of Valois, sister of Henry III. Victory of Henry IV over the duke of Mayenne

at **Arques** (1589) and at the

1590, Mar. 14. Battle of Ivry, crucial battle of these wars. Henry besieged Paris, which was relieved by Mayenne and the Spanish duke of Parma. Henry's ultimate success was made possible by the *politiques,* usually moderate Catholics, but above all French patriots who wished a strong national monarchy. **Michel de L'Hôpital** (1505-1573) their precursor and founder. Henry abjured the reformed religion at St. Denis (1593) and was crowned at Chartres (1594). Brissac having thereupon surrendered Paris to him, the power of the league was broken. Not, however, until Henry, after public penance by his ambassadors at Rome, had been freed from the papal ban, was he generally recognized (by Mayenne too). The civil wars of religion were ended by the

1598, Apr. 13. EDICT OF NANTES, which gave the Huguenots equal political rights with the Catholics, but by no means secured them entire freedom of religious worship. The edict granted the exercise of the reformed religion to nobles having the right of criminal jurisdiction (*seigneurs hauts justiciers*), and to the citizens of a certain number of cities and towns, but prohibited it in all episcopal and archiepiscopal cities, at the court of the king, and in Paris, as well as within a circle of twenty miles around the capital. Public offices were opened to the Huguenots and **mixed chambers** were established in four *parlements* (Paris, Toulouse, Grenoble, Bordeaux). The Huguenots obtained some fortified towns, and were recognized, to a certain extent, as an armed political party. The edict of Nantes was registered by the *parlement* only after a long delay. Though it established nothing like a "free church in a free state," it did give legal status to a kind of toleration not yet formally recognized elsewhere. **Treaty of Vervins** (May 2, 1598) with Spain; restoration of all conquests to France.

Adoption of measures looking to the improvement of the finances and the general prosperity, which had gone to decay, especially by Rosny, afterward **duke of Sully** (1560-1641). *Grand Design,* attributed to Henry IV by Sully in his *Mémoires,* for the ensurance of perpetual peace through organization of a Christian Republic with the Holy Roman Emperor as first magistrate and a general council of Europe to discuss affairs of common interest and if possible settle disputes. Intended primarily to limit the Hapsburg power, this plan is nevertheless interesting as the first of many projects for organizing Europe and ending war. Question of Cleves-Jülich succession. Henry IV supported the claims of Brandenburg. In the midst of great preparations for war, **Henry was assassinated** at Paris, 1610 (May 14) by the fanatic **François Ravaillac.**

1610-1643. LOUIS XIII, his son, nine years old. Regency of his mother, **Marie de' Medici** (1573-1642). Sully removed from office; the Italian **Concini** was placed in control of affairs. Louis XIII, declared of age in 1614, was in fact all his life under the guidance of others. **Summons of the estates-general,** 1614, being the last before the Revolution of 1789. Arrest and murder of Concini; the queen-mother banished to Blois (1617). The king under the influence of his favorite, the duke of Luynes. By the mediation of Armand-Jean du Plessis (1585-1642), **cardinal-duke of Richelieu,** a treaty was concluded between Luynes and the queen-mother (1619). New **civil war.** Contest of the crown with the nobility and the Huguenots. After the death of Luynes (1621) Marie de' Medici and her favorite, Richelieu, obtained control of affairs. The influence of the latter soon became supreme, and the queen-dowager quarreled with him.

1624-1642. Administration of Richelieu, whose influence over the king was henceforward unbroken. Numerous conspiracies against him instigated by Gaston of Orléans, the king's brother.

1625. Revolt of the Huguenots under the dukes of Rohan and Soubise.

1627-1628. Siege of La Rochelle, under the personal supervision of Richelieu. In spite of the dispatch of three fleets from England to the aid of the Huguenots, the city surrendered October 28, 1628, after an heroic resistance of fourteen months. Defeat of the duke of Rohan, and complete subjugation of the Huguenots, who thereafter were no longer an armed political party, but only a tolerated sect.

War in Italy with Spain; subjugation of Savoy, Richelieu at the head of the army.

1631. Treaty of Cherasco. France renounced all conquests in Italy, but by a secret treaty with Victor Amadeus, duke of Savoy, Pignerol was surrendered to France (negotiators of these treaties, Richelieu's confidant, **Father Joseph,** and the pope's agent, **Mazarin**).

A final attempt of Marie de' Medici to overthrow the cardinal failed ignominiously (Nov. 11, 1630, the *Day of Dupes*).

1632, Oct. 30. Defeat of the conspiracy of Gaston and the duke of Montmorency. Execution of Montmorency.

1631-1648. FRENCH PARTICIPATION IN THE THIRTY YEARS' WAR (pp. 435-437).

1641. Conspiracy of Henry d'Effiat, marquis of Cinq-Mars (*Monsieur le Grand*). His secret treaty with Spain. The plot was discovered by Richelieu.

Richelieu, though not a good financial administrator, helped somewhat to further the power of the royal bureaucracy (*intendants*) at the expense of the nobles, the Huguenots, and the *parlements*. His true greatness, however, lay in the field of foreign affairs. He restored French influence in Italy, in the Netherlands and in Germany, and established it also in Sweden. It was his work that laid the foundation for the power of Louis XIV, and became the traditional basis of French foreign policy (*Cont. p. 477.*)

CULTURAL DEVELOPMENTS

The literature of the French Renaissance bore the stamp of Italy. **François Rabelais** (1494-1553), a former monk, satirized the foibles of his society in *Pantagruel* (1532) and *Gargantua* (1534). His books also bear testimony to the importance the Renaissance placed on humanistic education. The reformer **John Calvin** (1509-1564) was his contemporary and complete antithesis. The poets **Pierre de Ronsard** (1524-1585) and **Joachim du Bellay** (1522-1560) were the leaders of **La Pléiade,** a group of young poets who urged the use of the French language in literature, at the same time reverting to a classical style. **Michel Eyquem de Montaigne** (1533-1592) introduced a question-and-answer technique in his *Essais* (1580-1595); his influence on the philosophy, style, and form of later writers such as Rousseau and the essayist Charles Lamb was marked.

In the 16th century several of the chateaux in the Loire valley were built. The sculptors **Michel Colombe** (1430-1512), **Jean Goujon** (1515-1560), and **Germain Pillon** (1535-1590) were active; and **François Clouet** (1516-1572) painted royal portraits.

In the field of political theory **Jean Bodin's** (1530-1596) *Six livres de la République* (1576) was outstanding.

4. THE IBERIAN PENINSULA

(*From p. 306*)

a. SPAIN, 1479-1659

1479-1516. REIGN OF FERDINAND of Aragon and his wife, **ISABELLA,** queen of Castile (1474-1504). During this period much progress was made, notably in Castile, toward the suppression of the fractious aristocracy and the regulation of the Church. Aragon, on the other hand, retained most of its privileges. The **conquest of Granada** (1492) ended Moorish power in the peninsula, while the **discovery of America** in the same year opened up endless possibilities of overseas empire. In matters of foreign policy, Ferdinand devoted his efforts to the conclusion of profitable marriage alliances and to the furtherance of his designs in Italy, which brought him into conflict with France and other Italian powers.

1493, Jan. 19. Treaty of Narbonne with Charles VIII of France. The latter, about to invade Italy, ceded to Ferdinand Roussillon and Cerdagne, in the hope of securing support. Ferdinand, with his usual duplicity, joined the pope, the Emperor Maximilian, Milan, and Venice, and helped to frustrate Charles's plans.

1494. Foundation of the *Consulado* for foreign trade at Burgos. This chamber, and the *Casa de Contratación* at Seville (1503) undertook to regulate Spanish trade and had much to do with the commercial expansion of the 16th century.

1500. By the **treaty of Granada,** France and Spain again engaged to co-operate in Italian affairs, but friction over Naples soon led to hostilities. Victories of the great Spanish commander, **Gonzalvo de Córdoba** (especially at **Garigliano,** 1503). Aragon retained Naples. By the **treaty of Blois** (1505), Louis XII of France ceded his rights to Naples to his niece, Germaine de Foix, whom Ferdinand, a widower since 1504, married.

1504. The **death of Isabella** made **Joanna** (wife of Philip, archduke of Austria) legal heiress to Castile. Ferdinand, who had long planned the union of Castile and Aragon, in Joanna's absence secured from the cortes authority to carry on the government in his daughter's behalf. In 1506 Philip and Joanna came to claim their inheritance. **Treaty of Villafavila** between Philip and Ferdinand, the former securing the regency. Philip's death in the same year and the **insanity of Joanna** (kept in confinement for 49 years, d. 1555) allowed Ferdinand to resume control.

1509-1511. African campaigns, organized, financed, and led by **Cardinal Jiménez de Cis-** neros (1436-1517), aided by **Pedro Navarro.** Cisneros was one of the ablest statesmen of his time who, having reformed the Spanish church, now devoted himself to the crusade. The Spanish forces took Oran, Bougie, and Tripoli and forced the Moslem rulers to pay tribute.

1511. The **Holy League** (the pope, Ferdinand, and Venice) against France and the Empire. **Victory of the League at Novara** (1513). At the same time (1512) the Spaniards conquered **Navarre,** which was annexed to the Castilian crown, though it retained its own government (1515).

1516. Death of Ferdinand. **Regency of Cardinal Cisneros,** who vigorously repressed incipient disturbances by the nobles. The crowns now passed to the son of Philip and Joanna, Charles of Ghent, who became

1516-1556. CHARLES I of Spain, founder of the **Hapsburg dynasty.** Charles, who had been educated in Flanders, arrived (1517) with a large Flemish following, which regarded the Spaniards with disdain. Dissatisfaction of the Spaniards with Charles's election to the imperial throne (1519) led to widespread opposition to his leaving the country and using Spanish money and men for his imperial purposes.

1520-1521. UPRISING OF THE *COMUNEROS*. A group of cities (led by Toledo and by the Toledan **Juan de Padilla**) took issue with the government and organized a **Holy League** (*Santa Junta*) at Avila (July 1520). Though this was originally as much an aristocratic as a bourgeois movement, radical tendencies soon appeared and the upper elements withdrew. After the **defeat of the *comuneros* at Villalar** (Apr. 23, 1521) the leaders were executed and government authority re-established. But in future Charles avoided as much as possible any infringement of traditional rights.

1521-1529. War between France and Spain, the result of French support of the *comuneros* and French designs on Navarre. The French took Pampeluna and Fontarabia, but Charles, supported by the pope, Florence, and Mantua, expelled the French from Milan (1522). In 1524 the Spanish commanders, the **Constable de Bourbon** and the **Marqués de Pescara,** invaded Provence and advanced to Marseilles. Francis I was decisively defeated and captured at the **battle of Pavia** (Feb. 24, 1525) and in captivity at Madrid was obliged to sign the **treaty of Madrid,** by which he abandoned his Italian claims and ceded Burgundy. On his release he violated his promises and the war was resumed. By the **treaty of Cambrai** (1529), Charles was obliged to renounce Burgundy, while Francis once more abandoned his claims to Naples.

1535. The expedition of Charles to Tunis (p. 452), part of a great duel between Spain and the formidable Turkish power.

1535–1538. Another war with France, arising from the succession to Milan (p. 425), led to another invasion of Provence (1536) and to the inconclusive **treaty of Nice** (1538).

1541. Reverse of the Spaniards at Algiers.

1542–1544. Further hostilities with France.

1551–1559. The last war between Charles and the French kings, ending in the **treaty of Cateau-Cambrésis** (Apr. 3, 1559). (See below.)

Charles I (Charles V as emperor) gave Spain efficient government, continuing the work of Ferdinand and Isabella. On the other hand, his imperial position resulted in the involvement of Spain in all general European problems and in the expenditure of much blood and money, a drain not so noticeable at the time because of the great influx of gold from the New World. Culturally speaking, the whole 16th century and the first half of the 17th century was Spain's golden age, a period of humanism: **Luis Vives** (1492–1540), for a time professor at Oxford; **Elio Antonio de Nebrija** (or Lebrija), the leading humanist (1444–1532); **Juan del Encina** (c. 1469–1529), popular dramatist; poets **Garcilaso de la Vega** (1503–1536) and **Juan Boscán Almogáver** (d. 1542); and Spain's great mystical poet **Juan de la Cruz** (1542–1591); **Luis Ponce de León** (b. 1528), theologian, poet, and one of those who made Castillian a great literary language. To this period belong the first printings of the chivalrous romance *Amadis de Gaul* (1508), the first realistic novel *Celestina* (c. 1499), and the first important picaresque novel *Lazarillo de Tormes* (anon., 1554). It was also a time of **religious leadership** in the cause of Roman Catholicism: **Arias Montano** (1527–1598) was one of the outstanding scholars at the **council of Trent**; **Luis de Granada** (1504–1588) was one of the greatest preachers of the century and a religious writer whose books were translated into all leading languages; **Francisco Suarez** (1548–1617), a Jesuit, was a neo-scholastic and an outstanding jurist (*De Legibus ac Deo Legislatore,* 1612); while **Francisco de Vitoria** (1486–1546) wrote extensively on the government of the colonies and became a pioneer of international law (*De Indis et de iure belli relectiones,* 1532). In political theory **Juan Marquez** (1564–1621), *El Gobernador cristiano* (1612) and **Diego Saavedra Fajardo** (1584–1648), *Idea de un Principe político cris-*

tiano (1640). At the same time the Spaniards took the lead in the work of the Catholic Reformation. **Ignatius de Loyola** (1491–1556), after receiving a serious wound in war, made a pilgrimage to Jerusalem (1523–1524) and then studied at Paris (1528–1535). In 1534 he founded the **Society of Jesus** at Rome, the Jesuit organization from the beginning being placed on a military basis, and engaging in widespread missionary and teaching activity. At the same time **Sta. Teresa de Jesús** (1515–1582) undertook the reorganization of the Carmelite nunneries and, in her autobiography and her *Castillo interior,* made outstanding contributions to mystical literature. **San Juan de la Cruz** (1542–1591), her disciple, effected similar reforms of the monasteries.

The period was one of equal greatness in the realm of literature and art. **Juan de Mariana** (1536–1624) wrote a popular history of Spain, and an important work on political theory, *De Rege et Regis Institutione* (1599), while **Bartolomé de Las Casas** (1474–1566), **Fernandez de Oviedo,** and **Lopez de Gómara** distinguished themselves in treatment of the New World. **Felix Lope de Vega** (1562–1635), who produced over 2000 plays, poems, and stories, was one of the great literary figures of all time and a founder of the modern drama; **Tirso de Molina** (c. 1571–1648) and **Pedro Calderón** (1600–1681) continued the drama on a high plane; **Miguel de Cervantes Saavedra** (1547–1616) in his *Don Quijote* (1605) produced an incomparable picture of the Spain of his day and at the same time one of the world's most popular masterpieces. In the same year, **Mateo Alemán** (1547–1610) published the second part of *Guzmán de Alfarache,* a picaresque novel with a moral for each adventure.

In the field of **art** the Italian influence was very strong, though the **Escorial** (begun in 1563 and built by **Juan de Herrera**) had a severe style of its own. Prominent sculptors of the age were **Gregorio Fernández** (d. 1636); **Alonso Cano;** and **Martínez Montañés** (d. 1649), but the achievements of painting overshadowed those of the other arts. **El Greco** (1541–1614; really a Greek [Kyriakos Theotokopoulos] from Crete, trained in Italy) came to Spain in 1575 and lived at Toledo until his death in 1614. One of the greatest painters of the Renaissance, he was the first of a number of world-famous artists: **José Ribera,** called Spagnaletto (1588–1652); **Francisco de Zurbarán** (1598–1664); **Bartolomé Murillo** (1617–1682); **Juan de Valdés Leal** (1630–1691) and above all the incomparable **Diego Rodríguez de Silva y Velásquez** (1599–1660). In music **Tomás Luis de Vittoria** was a worthy contemporary of Palestrina.

On the abdication of Charles I, Spain and the colonies, as well as the Netherlands, Franche-Comté, Naples, and Milan passed to his son

1556-1598. PHILIP II (b. at Valladolid in ·1527), the most Spanish of the Hapsburg rulers and a monarch who spent most of his reign in Spain. Affable, yet dignified and serious, Philip was a very hard-working bureaucrat as well as an autocrat, and at the same time a hard-hearted and vindictive religious fanatic. His entire policy centered about his determination to defend the faith and to stamp out Protestantism, and further to stand by the Hapsburg interests, outside as well as inside Spain. This involved constant intervention in general European affairs and many costly wars that drained the country. During this period the Spanish infantry (largely volunteer and with a considerable noble element) reached the pinnacle of its prestige.

Philip married four times: (1) **Mary of Portugal,** mother of Don Carlos; (2) **Mary the Catholic,** queen of England; (3) **Elizabeth of Valois;** (4) **Anne of Austria,** daughter of Maximilian II.

1556-1559. Continuance of the **war with France.** Victories of the Spaniards under the **duke of Alva,** at **St. Quentin** (Aug. 10, 1557) and at **Gravelines** (July 13, 1558), led to

1559, Apr. 3. The **treaty of Cateau-Cambrésis,** which reaffirmed the Spanish possession of Franche-Comté and the Italian states. Philip married Elizabeth, the daughter of Henry II.

1560. The capital was definitively established at **Madrid.** In 1563 the construction of the Escorial Palace was begun.

1567. Beginning of the prolonged **struggle for independence in the Netherlands** (p. 408).

1568. Death of Don Carlos, the son of the king, whom Philip is sometimes accused of having put away. Don Carlos appears to have been deranged and unmanageable, for which reason he was kept in confinement. There is no evidence of unnatural death.

1569-1571. Revolt of the Moriscos (converted Moslems suspected of secretly retaining their original faith). The rising was put down with great severity and ultimately (1609) the Moriscos were expelled from Spain.

1571, Oct. 7. Battle of Lepanto, the outstanding event in the long naval duel between the Spaniards and the Turks. **Don John of Austria** (natural brother of Philip), with the aid of a papal and a Venetian fleet, inflicted a tremendous defeat on the Turks (p. 453).

1574. The Spaniards lost Tunis.

1580. Philip succeeded to the **Portuguese throne** (p. 418).

1587. Sir Francis Drake destroyed the Spanish fleet at Cadiz. England had for some time been incurring the displeasure of Philip, partly because of the succession of Elizabeth and the progress of Protestantism, partly because of the aid given the Dutch rebels, and partly because of the piratical raids on the Spanish treasure ships. The **execution of Mary Stuart** (1587) brought matters to a crisis, and Philip sent against England

1588. The **GREAT ARMADA,** which met with complete disaster (p. 400). The war with England continued in a desultory way until 1603.

1589-1598. War with France, arising from Philip's intervention against Henry IV. The Spaniards played an important rôle in this last phase of the religious wars in France, but failed to attain their objectives. The war ended with the **treaty of Vervins** (p. 413).

1598-1621. PHILIP III, the son of Philip II by his last marriage. A melancholy, retiring, and deeply religious man, the king devoted himself to the interests of the Church (9000 monasteries in this period, and one-third of the population in the church service). Philip left the government to his favorite (*privado*), the **duke of Lerma,** who initiated the system of court intrigue and corruption. Formation of a court nobility; growth of huge estates; marked decline in agriculture (depopulation through wars and emigration to the colonies). Spain became to a large extent a wool-raising country. Industry and trade, so flourishing in the 16th century, suffered a marked decline.

1609. Expulsion of the Moriscos (see above).

1618. Beginning of the Thirty Years' War (p. 431), into which Spain was drawn by Hapsburg interests and by religious considerations.

1621-1665. PHILIP IV, an amiable prince, not interested in politics and therefore quite content to leave the conduct of affairs to his *privado,* the **Count-Duke Olivares** (1587-1645; count of Olivares, duke of Sanlúcar), an able and patriotic administrator who, until his fall in 1643, made valiant efforts to modernize the governmental system by means of greater centralization and increase of the royal power.

1622. The occupation of the **Valtelline Pass** (between Milan and the Austrian lands) by the Spanish led to war with France, which, in a sense, was merely one aspect of the Thirty Years' War. France, under the able leadership of Richelieu, gradually established her ascendancy over Spain.

1640-1659. The great **REVOLT IN CATALONIA,** a direct result of the policy of Olivares. The king's failure to summon the Catalan cortes, the imposition of new taxes, the demands for aid for the foreign wars, the quartering of troops in the country, and in general the centralizing tendencies of the count-duke precipitated the conflict. The movement was supported by France, which even recognized a **Catalan republic.** After the struggle had gone on for twelve years, Barcelona was finally obliged to submit (1652, Oct.). In the final settlement (1659) the Catalans retained most of their former rights and privileges.

1642. The French occupied Roussillon.

1643, May 19. The battle of Rocroi. Defeat of the Spaniards. This battle is generally taken as marking the end of the supremacy of the Spanish forces.

1647. Revolt of Naples, under **Masaniello** (p. 426).

1648. The peace of Westphalia (p. 436). This did not apply to the war between France and Spain, which continued for another eleven years.

1658, June 14. Battle of the Dunes; decisive defeat of the Spaniards.

1659, Nov. 7. TREATY OF THE PYRENEES (signed on the Isle of Pheasants, in the Bidassoa River). Spain was obliged to cede to France the frontier fortresses in Flanders and Artois, and also Roussillon and Cerdagne. Louis XIV married Maria Teresa, daughter of Philip IV.   (*Cont. p. 486.*)

b. PORTUGAL, 1495-1640

(*From p. 308*)

1495-1521. MANOEL I (the Great, the Fortunate), brother-in-law of John II. His reign and that of his successor mark the apogee of Portuguese power and empire, following the great discoveries (**Vasco de Gama's** voyage to India, 1497-1498; **Pedro Alvares Cabral's** discovery of Brazil, 1500; **Magellan's** circumnavigation of the globe, 1519-1522, p. 391). The new empire was at first ruled by men of exceptional ability and courage (**Francisco de Almeida,** first viceroy of the Indies, 1505; **Afonso de Albuquerque,** viceroy, 1507-1511) and brought in large returns. Lisbon very soon displaced Venice as the entrepôt for Asiatic goods, and became a center of wealth and luxury. Colonial trade was a royal monopoly, and the court became a mecca for concession-seekers. The old agrarian system became undermined by the introduction of black slavery, while the aristocracy to a certain extent abandoned itself to imperial war, to corruption at home, and to exploitation abroad. In short, the 16th century, outwardly brilliant, was already the beginning of decadence.

1497. Expulsion of the Jews from Portugal. This step was taken chiefly to please Ferdinand and Isabella of Spain, whose daughter, Isabella, Manoel married (1497; she died in the next year). Persecution and massacre followed the expulsion order, which deprived Portugal of many of its most educated and wealthiest inhabitants.

1521-1557. JOHN (João) III (the Pious), during whose reign

1536. The **Inquisition** was established in Portugal and the **Jesuit Order** invited in. The consequences were much like those in Spain.

1557-1578. SEBASTIAN I, the grandson of John, succeeded. Regency of his mother, Joanna of Austria, a daughter of Charles V, until 1562, followed by the regency of **Cardinal Henry** (Enrique), brother of John III and grand inquisitor. Sebastian himself was educated by the Jesuits and was consumed with the idea of a crusade against the infidel, which he undertook despite the contrary advice of Philip II of Spain and of the pope.

1578, Aug. 4. The **BATTLE OF AL KASR AL-KABIR** (Alcazar-Qivir), in which the Portuguese and their mercenary troops were completely defeated by the Moors. Sebastian, the king of Fez, and the Moorish pretender all lost their lives (*battle of the three kings*).

1578-1580. CARDINAL HENRY, king.

1580. Death of **Luis de Camões,** (b. 1524), greatest of Portuguese poets (*The Lusiads,* published 1572), whose work not only brought to culmination the literary flowering of the 16th century (dramas of **Gil Vicente**), but served as a profound commentary on Portuguese national life and imperial enterprise.

1580. A **regency of five** was established to govern the country on the death of Cardinal Henry. There were no less than seven claimants to the throne, of whom the most powerful was **Philip II of Spain** (son of Isabella, the daughter of Manoel I) and the most popular was **Antonio,** the prior of Crato (illegitimate son of Luis, the brother of John III). Philip's candidacy was supported by the high clergy and by part of the nobility. Antonio enjoyed the support of the townsmen and of the peasants, and was backed by France.

Aug. 25. The Spaniards, under the duke of Alva, invaded Portugal and defeated their opponents in the **battle of Alcántara,** near Lisbon.

1580-1598. PHILIP I (Philip II of Spain), who was accepted by the cortes. Philip promised to respect the rights of the country and to rule only through Portuguese. He himself generally observed this obligation, but under his successors it was more and more ignored. First Portugal itself, then the Portuguese Empire, was turned over to Spanish officials. The result was growing discontent in Portugal and

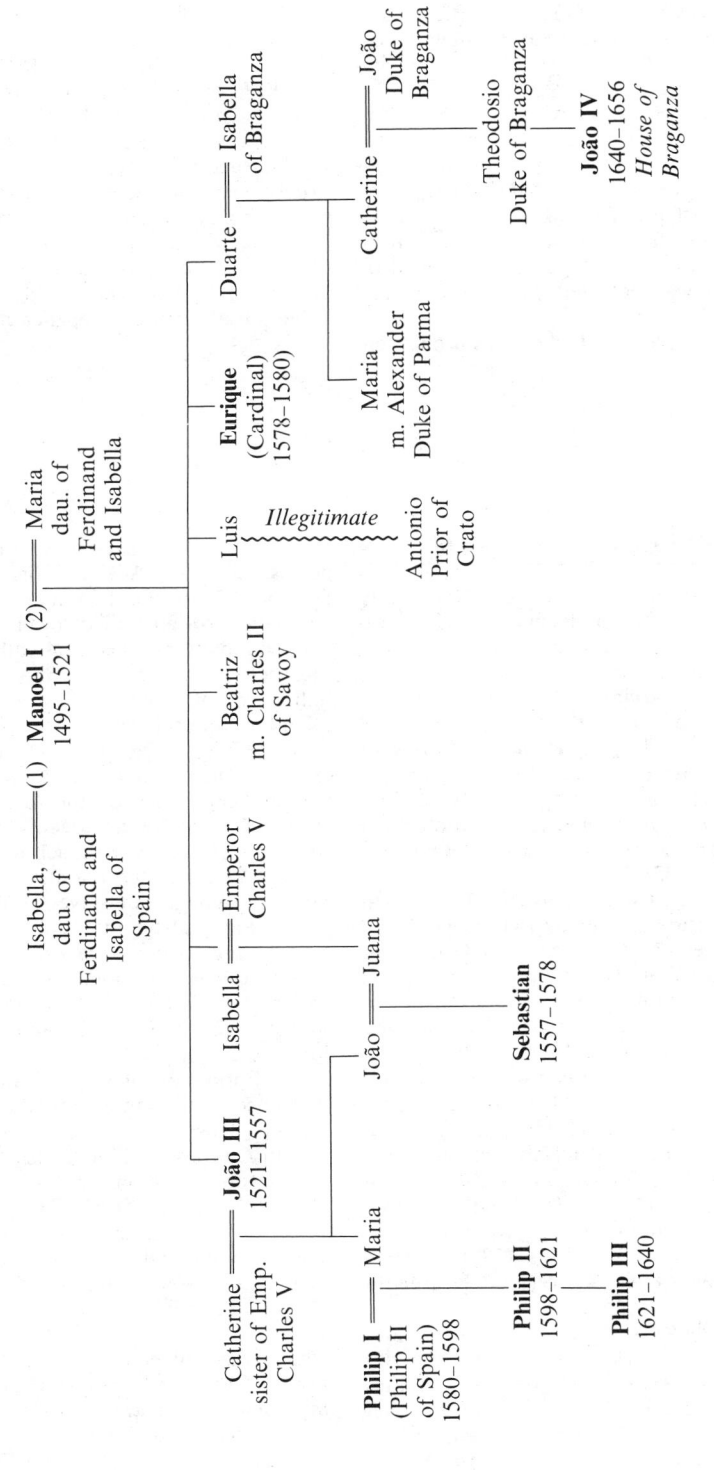

Kings of Portugal (1495–1640)

(From p. 309)

(Cont. p. 491.)

increasing weakness abroad. After the defeat of the Spanish armada (1588), the British and the Dutch began to attack the Portuguese possessions, many of which were conquered before 1640.

1583. Antonio of Crato, with a French fleet, established himself in the Azores and prepared to reconquer the throne, but the French-Portuguese fleet was defeated by a Spanish fleet off the island of St. Miguel.

1589. Antonio, now supported by the British, made a landing in Portugal and marched on Lisbon, but was defeated by the Spaniards. He died at Paris in 1595.

1598. Dutch trade with Lisbon was prohibited.

This marked the beginning of Dutch enterprise in the east and of the gradual conquest of Portuguese possessions.

1640, Dec. 1. REVOLT OF THE PORTUGUESE, inspired and organized by **João Ribeiro,** a professor at the University of Coimbra, and supported by the nobility and clergy. The insurgents, all disillusioned about Spanish rule, took advantage of the revolt in Catalonia. Like the Catalonians they were supported by France, which was at war with Spain. The Spanish government, unable to devote much attention to Portugal, could not prevent the **election of John of Braganza** to the throne.

(*Cont. p. 490.*)

5. ITALY

(*From p. 323*)

a. THE ITALIAN WARS, 1494–1559

The period from about 1450 to 1550 not only marked the apogee of the Renaissance, but also the intellectual and artistic primacy of Italy. In the field of history and political science, **Francesco Guicciardini** (1483–1540; *Istoria d' Italia* published only in 1561) and **Niccolò Machiavelli** (1469–1527; *Il Principe*, 1513) were outstanding. **Pietro Aretino** (1492–1552) was a famous publicist of the time, while **Baldassare Castiglione** (*Il Cortegiano*, 1528) produced a famous handbook of the courtier. **Ludovico Ariosto** (1474–1533; *Orlando Furioso*, 1516) was one of the greatest epic poets of all time. In the field of music **Giovanni da Palestrina** (1525–1594; at St. Peter's after 1551) and **Orlando di Lasso** were men of the first rank. Architects and painters of eminence were too numerous to be listed, and it will suffice to recall names like **Leonardo da Vinci** (1452–1519); **Raffael Santi** (1483–1520; *Sistine Madonna*, 1516); **Michelangelo Buonarroti** (1475–1564; Sistine Chapel paintings, 1508–1512, 1534–1541; dome of St. Peter's, 1547); **Andrea del Sarto** (1486–1530); **Giorgione da Castelfranco** (1477–1510); **Titian** (Tiziano Vecelli, 1477–1576); **Gentile Bellini** (1429–1507); **Tintoretto** (Jacopo Robusti, 1512–1594); **Paolo Veronese** (1528–1588); **Andrea Mantegna, Allegri da Correggio, Benvenuto Cellini,** etc.

Politically, however, Italy was divided and soon became the "cockpit" of Europe, the victim of the rivalries of the strong monarchies which were arising in the west and all of which coveted the wealth of the peninsula. There were, at the time, five major states: **Venice,** the strongest of all, deriving her wealth and influence from the extensive eastern trade, from her possessions in the Adriatic, Ionian, and Aegean Seas, and from domination of the neighboring mainland; **Milan,** ruled by Ludovico Sforza and commanding the rich valley of the Po; **Florence,** long one of the most progressive of Italian communities, having attained to great splendor under Lorenzo the Magnificent; the **Papal States,** carved from the central part of the peninsula and in process of expansion under the political popes of the late 15th century; the **kingdom of Naples,** deeply involved in the Near East, ruled by a branch of the Aragonese house. These states maintained a precarious balance among themselves, but were almost all so imperialistic that they were constantly endeavoring to victimize each other and ultimately reached the point of calling in the foreigner, with the result that Italy became the prey of French, German, and Spanish ambitions.

1492. Formation of a secret alliance between Florence and Naples for the spoliation of Milan. This led to Ludovico Sforza's appealing to Charles VIII of France to make good the Anjou claims on Naples.

1494–1495. THE FRENCH INVASION OF ITALY. Charles arrived in September and met with no real resistance. Florence submitted, but then drove out **Piero de' Medici** (Nov.) and abandoned the French connection. Thereupon Charles attacked and took Florence, which was obliged to give up Pisa and other towns. Charles advanced on Rome (Jan. 1495) and thence into Naples. Alfonso fled to Sicily, leaving Naples to his son Ferrante, who was driven out by a revolt. The French entered Naples (Feb. 22, 1495), but their very success led to the formation of a coalition directed against them: Milan, Venice, Emperor Maximilian, Pope Alexander VI, and Ferdinand of Aragon leagued together against Charles, forcing his retreat to the north. Ferrante and the Spaniards (Gonzalvo de Córdoba) soon reconquered Naples. This first French invasion of Italy was poorly planned and carelessly executed, but had much importance in opening up the international side of the Italian problem as well as in disseminating the learning and art of Italy throughout western Europe.

1499, Feb. Venice agreed to support the claims of Louis XII of France to Milan, in return for a promise of Cremona. The French thereupon invaded Italy a second time (Aug.) and forced **Ludovico Sforza** to flee from Milan to Germany. Milan surrendered (Sept. 14). The next year Sforza returned with an army of German mercenaries and obliged the French to evacuate. Before long the German forces began to disintegrate and the French returned to Milan. Ludovico was captured and died (1508) in a French prison. Milan thus became French.

1500, Nov. 11. By the **treaty of Granada,** Ferdinand of Aragon agreed to support Louis's claim to Naples, which was to be divided between France and Spain. In 1501 (June) the French army, marching south, entered Rome, whereupon the pope declared Federigo of Naples deposed and invested Louis and Ferdinand with the kingdom. The French took Capua (July), while the Spanish fleet seized Taranto (Mar. 1502). So much having been gained, the two allies fell to quarreling over the division of the spoils, and war resulted (July). The Spaniards at first suffered reverses, but in 1503 defeated a French fleet and won a decisive victory at **Cerignola** (Apr. 28). They took Naples (May 13), and, after another victory at **Garigliano** (Dec. 28), forced the French to surrender at **Gaeta** (Jan. 1, 1504). This completed the Spanish conquest of Naples, which, with Sicily, gave them control of southern Italy, as the French had control of Milan in the north.

1508, Dec. 10. The **LEAGUE OF CAMBRAI,** organized to despoil Venice of her possessions on the mainland and in Apulia. Emperor Maximilian promised Louis XII the investiture of Milan in return for support. Ferdinand of Aragon and Pope Julius II joined the coalition. The French attacked and defeated the Venetians at **Agnadello** (May 14, 1509). Surrender of Verona, Vicenza, and Padua, which were handed over to Maximilian, while the pope occupied Ravenna, Rimini, Faenza, and other Venetian possessions in the Romagna. The Apulian towns, Brindisi, Otranto, etc., fell to Ferdinand. But the Venetians soon rallied and retook Padua (July 17), which was besieged in vain by Maximilian. Vicenza too rose against the emperor and recalled the Venetians. In 1510 the pope, fearful of the power of the Germans, deserted the league and joined Venice, while Ferdinand, having secured his share of the spoils, turned neutral. The papal forces took Modena and Mirandola (Jan. 1511), but the French conquered Bologna (May 13). In October Ferdinand completed a *volte face* and joined Venice and the pope, while Henry VIII of England also adhered. After a French victory at **Ravenna** (Easter, 1512), even the emperor and the Swiss cantons joined the coalition against the French, who were driven out of Milan (May). In a **congress of the league at Mantua** (Aug.) the Spaniards forced the Florentines to take back the Medici and join the league. Milan was given to Maximilian Sforza (son of Ludovico). The war continued until the French were badly defeated at **Novara** (June 6, 1513), after which the pope, Ferdinand, and Henry of England all made peace.

1515. The new French king, **Francis I,** as deeply interested in Italy as his two predecessors, and quite as adventurous, concluded an alliance with Henry VIII and Venice against the Emperor Maximilian, the pope, Ferdinand, Milan, Florence, and the Swiss. The French won a great victory at **Marignano** (Sept. 13) by which they recovered Milan. Thereupon the pope came to terms, surrendered Parma and Piacenza, and in return secured the **concordat of Bologna** (p. 409). After the death of Ferdinand (Jan. 1516), his successor, Charles I (later Emperor Charles V), confronted with serious problems in Spain and Germany and eager to secure European co-operation against the advance of the Turks, concluded with Francis the **treaty of Noyon** (Aug. 13, 1516), by which the French retained Milan, but gave up their claims to Naples. Maximilian returned Brescia and Verona to Venice in consideration of a money payment.

1522–1523. First of the **Hapsburg-Valois wars,** for many of which Italy became a battlefield. The pope and England supported Charles V against Francis. Having been driven out of Milan, Parma, and Piacenza, the French were defeated at **Bicocca** (Apr. 27, 1522) and retained only the citadel of Milan. In May they were even driven from Genoa, their all-important sea-base. But in October 1524 the French invaded Italy with a large army. They retook Milan (Oct. 29). The pope changed sides and joined the French.

1525, Feb. 24. The **BATTLE OF PAVIA,** the most important engagement of the long Italian wars. The Spanish commanders, **Constable de Bourbon** (prominent French noble and opponent of Francis), and **Marquís de Pescara,** completely defeated the French. Francis himself was captured and sent to Madrid. There he concluded the **treaty of Madrid** (Jan. 14, 1526), by which he promised to surrender his Italian claims, give up Burgundy, and abandon his suzerainty over Artois and Flanders. These engagements he never meant to observe, and they were repudiated by him as soon as he was liberated.

1526, May 22. The **LEAGUE OF COGNAC,** a coalition of Francis I, the pope, Sforza, Venice, and Florence against Charles and the Spaniards. The league was the natural result of the too great success of the Spaniards in Italy and the objective was to restore the *status quo* of 1522. But the Spaniards forced Sforza out of Milan (July 24) and before long attacked Rome (Sept. 21). The pope was helpless and could not prevent

1527, May 6. The **SACK OF ROME** by the Spanish and German mercenaries of Charles. The sack was horrible even when judged by the customs of the day, and ended Rome's pre-eminence in the Renaissance. The pope himself was captured.

May 17. Florence rose against the Medici, who were again driven out and replaced by a republic (under **Niccolò Capponi**). **Genoa also revolted,** under **Andrea Doria** (formerly in French service). The French were expelled and a republican constitution established. The French, however, having overrun Lombardy (Oct.), began to march south. Meanwhile the pope, who had fled to Orvieto (Dec.), made his peace with Charles (**treaty of Barcelona,** June 29, 1529—the Papal States to be restored and the Medici returned to Florence). The war was ended by

1529, Aug. 3. The **treaty of Cambrai** (*Paix des dames,* because negotiated by Charles's aunt, Margaret, and by Francis' mother, Louise of Savoy). Francis once more renounced his Italian claims and the overlordship of Artois and Flanders. Venice was obliged to disgorge her conquests (Apulian towns, Ravenna, etc.). The duchy of Milan was given to Francesco Maria Sforza, Charles V retaining the citadel. Florence was forced, after an eight months' siege, to take back Alessandro de' Medici as duke. On Feb. 23, 1530, Charles was crowned by the pope as emperor and king of Italy.

1535. The **death of Francesco Sforza** opened the question of the Milanese succession. Charles V claimed it as suzerain, but the French invaded Italy and took Turin (Apr. 1536). After an invasion of Provence by the imperialists, the **truce of Nice** was concluded

for ten years (June 18, 1538). It reaffirmed the treaty of Cambrai, but the French remained in occupation of two-thirds of Piedmont and the emperor retained the rest.

1542-1544. The **war between Francis I and Charles V,** though fought out in the Netherlands and in Roussillon, had repercussions in Italy. The **treaty of Crespy** (Sept. 18, 1544) involved abandonment of French claims to Naples, but provided that the duke of Orléans should marry either Charles's daughter, with the Netherlands and Franche-Comté as a dowry, or else Charles's niece, who would bring Milan. The plan failed through the death of Orléans (1545). Piedmont and Savoy were to be restored to the legitimate ruler.

1556. Alliance of Pope Paul IV and Henry II of France to get Naples. The French, under the **duke of Guise,** invaded Italy, but were obliged to withdraw after their defeat at **St. Quentin** (1557). This practically ended the French struggle for Italy. The **treaty of Cateau-Cambrésis** (Apr. 3, 1559) involved the abandonment of French possessions, except Turin, Saluzzo, and Pignerol. Margaret, sister of Henry II, was to marry Emmanuel Philibert of Savoy.

b. THE PAPACY, 1484-1644

[For a complete list of the Roman popes see Appendix IV.]

(*From p. 313*)

The earlier part of this period marked the nadir of the Papacy viewed from the moral standpoint. Most of the popes were typical products of the Renaissance, patronizing the arts, living in splendor and luxury, using their position either to aggrandize their families or to strengthen the temporal position of the Church. Of religious leadership there was almost none, yet politically speaking the period was one of the utmost importance.

1484-1492. INNOCENT VIII (Giovanni Cibo), an indolent and altogether corrupt pontiff, who was entirely under the influence of Cardinal Giuliano della Rovere. A long-drawn conflict with Naples ended in marriage alliances of the pope's family with the Aragonese house and with the Medici.

1492-1503. ALEXANDER VI (Rodrigo Lanzol y Borgia), a stately, energetic, ruthless, and thoroughly immoral pope, whose life was a scandal even in the Italy of his time. The main objective of his policy was to establish the rule of his family in central Italy. He broke the power of the great Roman families (Orsini, Colonna), and, through his son, **Caesar Borgia** (1475-1507), a former cardinal and the hero

The Borgia Family (1455–1600)

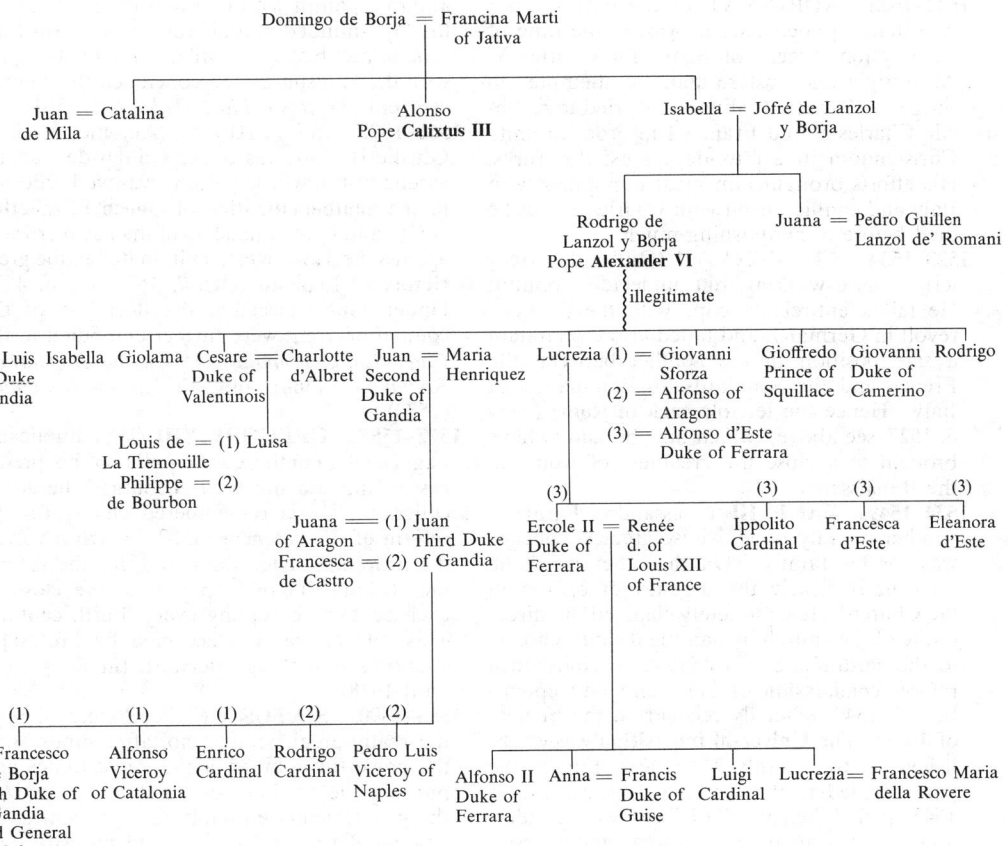

Domingo de Borja = Francina Marti of Jativa

Juan = Catalina de Mila   Alonso Pope **Calixtus III**   Isabella = Jofré de Lanzol y Borja

Rodrigo de Lanzol y Borja Pope **Alexander VI**   Juana = Pedro Guillen Lanzol de' Romani

illegitimate

...ro Luis ..t Duke ...andia   Isabella   Giolama   Cesare = Charlotte Duke of d'Albret Valentinois   Juan = Maria Second Henriquez Duke of Gandia   Lucrezia (1) = Giovanni Sforza (2) = Alfonso of Aragon (3) = Alfonso d'Este Duke of Ferrara   Gioffredo Prince of Squillace   Giovanni Duke of Camerino   Rodrigo

Louis de = (1) Luisa La Tremouille Philippe = (2) de Bourbon

Juana == (1) Juan of Aragon Third Duke Francesca = (2) of Gandia de Castro

(3) Ercole II = Renée Duke of d. of Ferrara Louis XII of France   (3) Ippolito Cardinal   (3) Francesca d'Este   (3) Eleanora d'Este

(1) ..t. Francesco de Borja ..rth Duke of Gandia ..ird General of the ..esuit Order   (1) Alfonso Viceroy of Catalonia   (1) Enrico Cardinal   (2) Rodrigo Cardinal   (2) Pedro Luis Viceroy of Naples

Alfonso II Duke of Ferrara   Anna = Francis Duke of Guise   Luigi Cardinal   Lucrezia = Francesco Maria della Rovere

---

of Machiavelli's *Prince,* undertook the conquest of the Romagna. Caesar reduced most of the principalities (1499–1501) and became duke of the Romagna. In 1501 the Borgias joined France in the attack on Naples, and the French aided Caesar in putting down a revolt of his captains at Sinigaglia (Dec. 1502). But the death of the pope and the hostility of the new pontiff, Julius II, frustrated Caesar's schemes. Forced to disgorge his conquests, he turned to Spain for aid. In 1506 he was arrested at Naples and sent to Spain, where he died (1507).

1503. PIUS III (Francesco Piccolomini, a nephew of Pius II), died within 26 days of his election.

1503–1513. JULIUS II (Giuliano della Rovere), one of the greatest of the popes and the real founder of the Papal States, a man of great intelligence and boundless energy, more a statesman than a priest. He not only regained the Romagna, but took the lead in the effort to expel the foreigner from Italy. In 1508 he was in the forefront of the **league of Cambrai,** through which he hoped to acquire the Venetian possessions in the Romagna. Having humbled Venice, he turned on the French. In reply Louis XII summoned a church council at Pisa (1511), which obliged the pope to convoke a rival **council at the Lateran** (1512). This remained in session for several years, and first undertook reform of abuses in the Church.

1513–1521. LEO X (Giovanni de' Medici, son of Lorenzo the Magnificent), a noteworthy patron of art, but an easy-going churchman, whose pontificate was noted chiefly for the **beginning of the Reformation** in Germany (1517, see p. 428). There is no evidence that the pope realized the gravity of the situation and the only solution he could offer was to ban Luther (1521).

1522-1523. ADRIAN VI (of Utrecht), the last non-Italian pope. Adrian was, at the time of his election, regent of Spain for Charles V. An upright and austere man, he attempted to purge the Papacy of abuses and tried to reconcile Charles V and Francis I in order to unite Christendom in a crusade against the Turks. His efforts brought him great unpopularity in Italy and conflict, even with Charles V, but he died before accomplishing much.

1523-1534. CLEMENT VII (Giulio de' Medici), a hard-working but undecided pontiff. He failed entirely to cope with the religious revolt in Germany, and failed also to maintain a safe position in the conflict between the French and the Spaniards for domination of Italy. Hence the terrible **sack of Rome** (May 6, 1527, see above), which may be said to have brought to a close the greatness of Rome in the Renaissance.

1534-1549. PAUL III (Alessandro Farnese), another worldly pope, whose greatest concern was for his family. On the other hand, he recognized clearly the urgency of reform in the Church. He completely changed the directorate of the church by naming devout scholars to the cardinalate. In 1536 he established a **reform commission** of nine, and on September 27, 1540, officially recognized the **Society of Jesus.** The **Universal Inquisition** was established at Rome (July 21, 1542). Finally the pope yielded to the demand of years, and in 1545 opened the **council of Trent,** which undertook the reform of the Church, under Jesuit guidance. The work of the council was several times interrupted and therefore divides into three periods: 1545-1547; 1551-1552; 1562-1563. The first period was perhaps the most important, both for organizational and doctrinal reform.

1550-1555. JULIUS III (Giovanni Maria del Monte), an elegant pope whose reign marked a short return to the Papacy of the Renaissance.

1555. Marcellus II (Marcello Cervini), whose election marked the victory of the strict reform party. The pope died within 22 days, and was succeeded by

1555-1559. PAUL IV (Gian Pietro Caraffa), a sincere and vigorous reformer and one of the chief inspirers of the **Counter-Reformation.** The powers and activities of the Inquisition were extended and the **first index of forbidden books** was drawn up (1559). As a Neapolitan the pope detested the Spanish rule and was soon in conflict with the Hapsburgs. He allied himself with France, but was defeated by the duke of Alba.

1559-1565. PIUS IV (Giovanni Medici, not related to the famous Florentine family), an amiable pontiff who followed the guidance of his high-minded and able nephew, **Carlo Borromeo,** archbishop of Milan. He made peace with the Hapsburgs and concluded the council of Trent (*Professio Fidei Tridentina,* 1564).

1566-1572. ST. PIUS V (Antonio Michele Ghislieri). Pius was an exceedingly devout and ascetic priest, whose attitude was well reflected in the **anathematization of Queen Elizabeth I** (1570) and in the financing of the naval crusade against the Turks which culminated in the great **victory of Lepanto** (Oct. 7, 1571, see p. 453). Under Pius's direction the decisions of the council of Trent were further embodied in the *Catechismus Romanus* (1566), the *Breviarium Romanum* (1568), and the *Missale Romanum* (1570).

1572-1585. GREGORY XIII (Ugo Buoncampagni), who continued the policy of his predecessor and did much to encourage the Jesuit colleges. He is remembered chiefly for his **reform of the calendar** (1582), which involved the dropping of ten days, and, for the future, the striking out of leap year at the close of each century, excepting every fourth century. This reform was not accepted by Protestant countries until long afterward (in Russia not until 1918).

1585-1590. SIXTUS V (Felice Peretti), one of the really great popes, who, after suppressing the powerful nobility of the Papal States and purging the territory of bandits, reorganized the government, re-established the finances on a sound basis, and encouraged industry (silk culture). In the same way he remade the papal curia (college of cardinals fixed at 70; establishment of 15 congregations or commissions of cardinals to deal with particular aspects of church affairs). New edition of the Vulgate Bible. Beautification of Rome, which now took on its characteristic baroque appearance (construction of the Vatican Palace and Library, the Lateran Palace, the Santa Scala; completion of the dome of St. Peter's according to Michelangelo's plans). There followed three brief pontificates of

1590. Urban VII, who died in 14 days,

1590-1591. Gregory XIV, and

1591. Innocent IX, who died in two months.

1592-1605. CLEMENT VIII (Ippolito Aldobrandini), a pious, serious pope, who supported the Catholic cause in France and ultimately mediated the peace between France and Spain (1598). His reign was distinguished by the great cardinals, **Robert Bellarmine** (1542-1621), eminent theologian and defender of the papal right to interfere in temporal affairs (*De potestate summi pontificis in rebus* *temporalibus,* 1610; *De officio principis christiani,* 1619), and **Caesar Baronius** (1538–1607), the great historian of the Catholic Church (*Annales ecclesiastici,* 1588–1607). During this pontificate Ferrara was added to the Papal States by reversion (1597).

1605. **Leo XI** lived only 25 days, and was succeeded by

1605–1621. **PAUL V** (Camillo Borghese), whose high idea of the papal power brought him into conflict with Venice and led to a compromise. On the outbreak of the Thirty Years' War the pope gave financial support to the Hapsburgs.

1621–1623. **GREGORY XV** (Alessandro Ludovisi), a weak old man who was guided by his able nephew, **Ludoviso Ludovisi.** He regulated the papal elections and organized the *Congregatio de propaganda fide* (1622), which united all missionary activity of the Church.

1623–1644. **URBAN VIII** (Maffeo Barberini). He secured Urbino by reversion (1631), thus completing the dominions of the Papal States. In the Thirty Years' War he attempted to maintain a neutrality which brought him much criticism from the imperialist side. His main concern appears to have been for the States of the Church, which he carefully fortified.

(*Cont. p. 493.*)

c. VENICE, 1500–1573

(*From p. 323*)

The discovery of the new route to the Indies struck at the old traditional trade through the Levant and at once began to undermine the prosperity of Venice. At the same time the steady advance of the Turks left the Venetians the choice between active opposition or accommodation. In general the latter policy was followed (much to the disgust of other European states), but nevertheless Venice became involved in a number of disastrous conflicts, which cost her most of her outposts in the east. The assault upon the possessions of Venice in Italy (**league of Cambrai,** see p. 426) proved less successful than the powers had expected, but thenceforth Venice was obliged to remain on the defensive and to observe, as well as might be, a neutral attitude as between France and Spain and later between France and Austria.

1570. The **Turks attacked Cyprus,** the largest and most important base of Venetian power in the east. In the course of the ensuing war, the allied Spaniards and Venetians, supported by the papal fleet, won the great

1571, Oct. 7. Battle of Lepanto, which, however, was not effectively followed up. The Venetians took the earliest opportunity to make peace, and

1573. Venice abandoned Cyprus and agreed to pay a heavy indemnity. Thenceforth only Candia (Crete), Paros, and the Ionian Islands remained in Venetian hands. (*Cont. p. 496.*)

d. OTHER ITALIAN STATES, 1525–1675

(*From p. 322*)

After the treaty of Cateau-Cambrésis (1559, see p. 411) all the Italian states, with the possible exception of Venice, were more or less directly under Spanish influence. The Counter-Reformation was soon in full swing, and by the end of the 16th century Italy was already losing the intellectual and cultural primacy which she held during the Renaissance.

MILAN declined rapidly in economic and political importance after 1525. The death of the last Sforza (**Francesco II**) in 1535 brought Milan under direct Spanish rule. In 1556 the duchy of Milan became an appanage of the Spanish crown, though held as a fief of the empire.

GENOA had been, in the later 15th century, a bone of contention between France and Milan. Torn by internal struggles of rival families (**Adorno** and **Fregoso**), it had lost its great commercial power and was important chiefly as a base of operations for France. In 1528 (Sept. 9), however, the great Genoese admiral, **Andrea Doria,** having left the French service, seized the town and re-established the republic, with a pronouncedly aristocratic constitution. Efforts of the French to recapture it failed. **Gian Luigi Fieschi** (Fiesco) in 1547 staged a spectacular conspiracy that was supported by France. Gianettino Doria, nephew of Andrea, was murdered and Andrea himself forced to flee. The conspirators secured most of the town, but then Fieschi was accidentally drowned and the movement collapsed. **Andrea Doria** returned as doge and the constitution was restored. On Andrea's death (1560) he was succeeded by **Gian Andrea Doria.** The **loss of Chios** to the Turks (1566) marked the end of Genoese power in the east.

SAVOY was an independent state, the rulers of which governed also Piedmont. Lying astride the Alps and commanding the passes from France into Italy, the state was one of considerable importance, but the feudal organization resulted in such weakness that for long the dukes were unable to pursue an independent policy. In the early 16th century Savoy was decidedly under French influence, and when, in 1536, the duke departed from the traditional policy, his dominions were overrun and for the larger part occupied by the French. **Emmanuel Philibert** (1553–1580) was the first really outstanding ruler. By following the Spanish lead he secured his dominions again in 1559, and in the course of his reign acquired Asti and other territories by negotiation. He made much progress in breaking the power of the nobility and in organizing a central government and an effective army. His successor, **Charles Emmanuel I** (1580–1630), squandered much of his father's achievement, waging war and neglecting the economic development of the country. **Victor Amadeus I** (1630–1637) was a wise and just ruler, but his short reign was followed by a civil war, and when finally **Charles Emmanuel II** (1638–1675) ascended the throne, his mother **Christina** (daughter of Henry IV of France) dominated the situation as regent.

MANTUA played a fleeting rôle on the international stage in the years 1627–1631, when the death of **Vincenzo II** (Gonzaga) without heirs provoked the **war of the Mantuan succession.** The best claim was that of **Charles of Nevers,** of the French branch of the Gonzaga line, but the emperor, at Spain's suggestion, sequestered the territory in order to keep the French out. The Spaniards overran the duchy, but the pope and Venice championed Nevers, appealing to France for aid. During 1629 the French fought the Spaniards in the duchy, but both sides were diverted by the larger obligations of the Thirty Years' War. The invasion of Germany by Gustavus Adolphus finally turned the scales in France's favor and by the **treaty of Cherasco** (Apr. 26, 1631), Nevers was invested with the duchy.

FLORENCE, like Milan, sank rapidly in importance during the 16th century. The Medici, restored in 1512, were expelled for a second time in 1527, when the republic was re-established. But in 1530 Charles V appointed **Alessandro de' Medici** hereditary ruler. **Cosimo de' Medici** became duke in 1537 and ruled until 1574. During this period Siena was incorporated with Florence (1555) and Florence became the **grand duchy of Tuscany** (1569).

NAPLES, conquered by the Spaniards in 1504, became an appanage of the Spanish crown and was, throughout this period, the headquarters of Spanish power in Italy. Though unpopular, the Spaniards were not threatened in their position excepting by the **revolt of Masaniello** (Tommaso Aniello, a fisherman), in July 1647. The insurrection, at first completely successful, led to extremism and confusion, in the midst of which Masaniello was murdered.

(*Cont. p. 496.*)

6.   GERMANY, 1493-1648

[For a complete list of the Holy Roman emperors see Appendix V.]

(*From p. 327*)

a. GERMANY, 1493-1618

1493–1519. MAXIMILIAN I, who first took the title of *Roman Emperor elect.*
1495. The diet of Worms. Constitutional reform. Attempted "modernization" of the medieval empire. Perpetual public peace. Imperial chamber (*Reichskammergericht*), first at Frankfurt, then at Speier, and finally at Wetzlar (1689). At the **diet of Köln** (1512) the reorganization of the empire was carried further: establishment of ten circles for the better maintenance of public peace (*Landfriedenskreise*): (1) Austria; (2) Bavaria; (3) Swabia; (4) Franconia; (5) Upper Rhine; (6) Lower Rhine; (7) Burgundy (ceded to the Spanish line of the Hapsburgs, 1556); (8) Westphalia; (9) Lower Saxony; (10) Upper Saxony. In all there were 240 states in the empire, exclusive of the imperial knights. Bohemia and the neighboring states (Moravia, Silesia, Lusatia) with Prussia and Switzerland (which was already completely independent in fact) were not included in the circles. Establishment of the **Aulic Council,** a court more under the control of the emperor than the imperial chamber, and to which a large part of the work of the latter was gradually diverted.
1508. The **league of Cambrai,** between Maximilian, Louis XII, Pope Julius II, and Ferdinand the Catholic. The purpose of the league was to break the power of Venice. Maximilian took possession of a part of the republic's territory, but he besieged Padua in vain (1509). The pope withdrew from the league, and concluded with Venice and Ferdinand the
1511. Holy League, directed against France. Maximilian finally (1513) joined in this.

The genealogical table shows the **claim of the Hapsburgs to Spain,** and division of the house into Spanish and German lines. Through these marriages the central European lands of the Hapsburgs, the Burgundian lands in what are now France and Belgium, and the united lands of the crowns of Castile and Aragon (Spain, Naples, and the Americas)

The House of Hapsburg (1493–1780)

(From pp. 305, 307, 324)

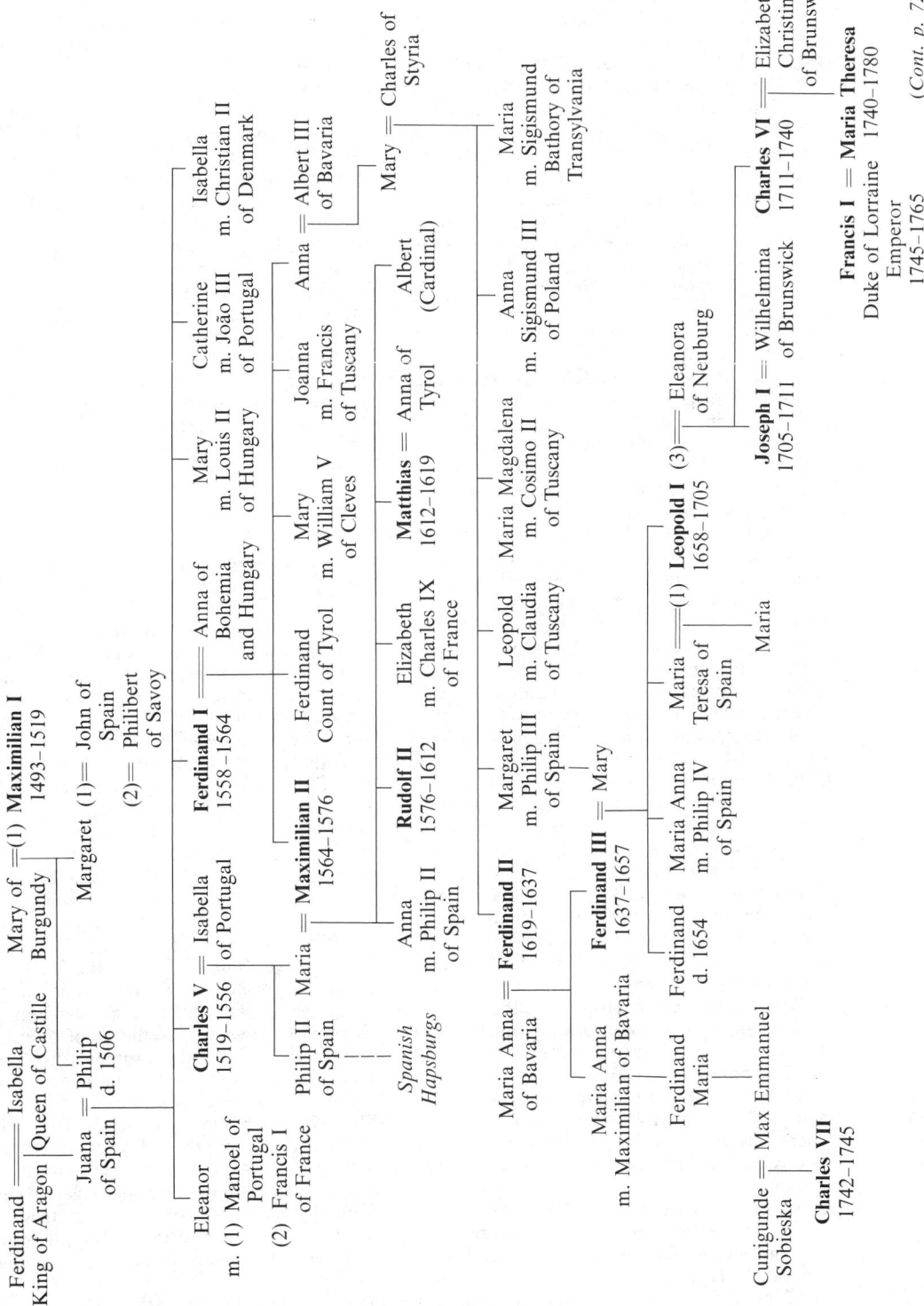

(Cont. p. 721.)

all came by birth to **Charles I of Spain** (eldest son of Philip and Joanna). He acquired the empire and his better known title of **Charles V** by election in 1519.

1517. BEGINNING OF THE REFORMATION. Background: Wiclifite (Lollard), Hussite, and other preceding rebellions against the Roman Church; the Babylonian Captivity and the Great Schism, which weakened the prestige of Rome; corruption and worldliness of the Church during the Renaissance; the development of critical scholarship, as represented by **Desiderius Erasmus** of Rotterdam, whose editions of the Church Fathers and whose Greek text of the New Testament (1516) revealed the shortcomings of basic ecclesiastical writings; rise of national feeling and dislike of foreigners, especially in Germany and England; growth of a middle class and a capitalist economy, which felt Roman Catholicism as a restraint (economic interpretation of the Reformation in modern writings of Max Weber and R. H. Tawney); great landed wealth of the Church available for confiscation by ambitious and unscrupulous princes.

Martin Luther (1483–1546), born at Eisleben, the son of a miner; monk in the Augustine monastery at Erfurt; priest (1507); professor at Wittenberg (1508); visit to Rome (1511).

1517, Oct. 31. Luther nailed on the door of the court church at Wittenberg his **95 theses** against the misuse of absolution or indulgences (especially by the Dominican monk **Johann Tetzel**). In the following year another reformatory movement was begun in Switzerland by **Ulrich Zwingli** (1484–1531).

1518. Summoned to Augsburg by Cardinal de Vio of Gaëta (Cajetanus), Luther refused to abjure, but appealed to the pope. Mediation of the papal chamberlain, Karl von Miltitz.

1519. Discussion at Leipzig between **Andreas Bodenstein** (called Karlstadt) and **Johann Eck.** The latter secured a papal bull against 41 articles in Luther's writings. Luther burned the papal bull and the canon law (1520). Thereupon he was excommunicated.

Basic Lutheran doctrine: justification by faith alone, which makes priestly offices of the Catholics an unnecessary intermediary between the individual and God.

In the meantime the German electors, despite the claims of Francis I of France, had chosen as emperor the grandson of Maximilian, King Charles I of Spain, who as emperor became

1519–1556. CHARLES V. He came to Germany for the first time in 1520, to preside at a grand **diet at Worms** (1521). There Luther defended his doctrines, coming under a safe-conduct. The ban of the empire having been pronounced against him, he was taken to the Wartburg by Frederick the Wise of Saxony, and there enjoyed protection. The **edict of Worms** prohibited all new doctrines. Luther's translation of the Bible.

1521–1526. First war of Charles V against Francis I of France. Charles advanced claims to Milan and the duchy of Burgundy. Francis claimed Spanish Navarre and Naples. The French, under Lautrec, were driven from Milan, which was turned over to **Francesco Sforza** (1522). The French constable, **Charles de Bourbon,** transferred his allegiance to Charles V. Unfortunate invasion of Italy by the French, under Bonnivert (1523–1524). Imperial forces thereupon invaded southern France. Francis I crossed the Mt. Cenis Pass and recaptured Milan.

1522. Progress of the Reformation. Luther, hearing of Karlstadt's misdoings, returned to Wittenberg and introduced public worship, with the liturgy in German and communion in both kinds in Electoral Saxony and in Hesse. The spread of the Reformation was favored by the fact that the emperor was deeply engrossed in the war with France.

1522. The Knights' War. Franz von Sickingen and **Ulrich von Hutten** advocated the Reformation. Sickingen stood at the head of a league of nobles directed against the spiritual principalities. He laid siege to Trier (1522), but in vain. He was then himself besieged in Landstuhl and fell in battle. Hutten fled the country and died on the island of Ufnau in the Lake of Zurich (1523).

1524–1525. The PEASANTS' WAR, in Swabia and Franconia. The peasants took the occasion of the disorders attendant on Luther's revolt (inspiration of his passionate attacks on the constituted authorities) to rise against the social and economic inequalities of German feudalism. They incorporated their demands in the revolutionary **Twelve Articles.** Luther himself repudiated the peasants. They were defeated at **Königshofen** on the Tauber and cruelly punished. Another religious-social revolt was that of the **Anabaptists** in Thuringia, who denied the efficacy of infant baptism and put forward a program strongly colored with communism. Their leader, **Thomas Münzer,** was captured and executed.

1524. Ferdinand of Austria, younger brother of Charles V, to whom the emperor had entrusted the government of Germany in 1522, at the instigation of the papal legate, **Lorenzo Campeggio,** formed an alliance with the two dukes of Bavaria and the bishop of southern Germany, in the hope of checking the religious changes.

1525. The **BATTLE OF PAVIA** (p. 421).

Francis was completely defeated and captured by the imperial forces. In the **peace of Madrid** (1526) he renounced all claim to Milan, Genoa, and Naples, as well as the overlordship of Flanders and Artois; he also assented to the cession of the duchy of Burgundy, and gave his sons as hostages.

1526. The **league of Torgau** formed by the Protestant princes (John of Saxony, Philip of Hesse, Lüneberg, Madeburg, Prussia, etc.) to oppose Ferdinand and his Bavarian allies. The league procured the enactment of the **diet of Speier,** favorable to the new doctrine.

1526–1532. War with the Turks (p. 451).

1527–1529. Second war between Charles V and Francis I, who had declared that the conditions of the peace of Madrid were extorted by force, and hence void. **Alliance of Cognac** between Francis, the pope, Venice, and Francesco Sforza against the emperor. The imperial army, unpaid and mutinous, took Rome by storm under the Constable de Bourbon, who fell in the assault; the pope besieged in the Castle of St. Angelo (1527). The French general, **Lautrec,** invaded Naples, but the revolt of Genoa (Doria), whose independence Charles V promised to recognize, and the epidemic of plague, of which Lautrec himself died, compelled the French to raise the siege of the capital and to retire to France.

1529, Aug. 3. Treaty of Cambrai (*Paix des dames*), negotiated by Margaret of Austria, Charles's aunt, and Louise of Savoy, duchess of Angoulême, mother of Francis. Francis paid two million crowns and renounced his claims upon Italy, Flanders, and Artois; Charles promised not to press his claims upon Burgundy *for the present,* and released the French princes.

1529. Second diet at Speier, where Ferdinand and the Catholic party took a more decided position. The strict execution of the decree of Worms was resolved upon. The evangelical states protested against this resolution, whence they were called **Protestants.**

1530. Charles crowned emperor at Bologna by the pope. This was the last coronation of a German emperor by the pope.

1530. Brilliant **diet at Augsburg,** the emperor presiding in person. Presentation of the **confession of Augsburg** drafted by **Melanchthon** (Philipp Schwarzert) but read at the diet by Chancellor Brüch. The enactment of the diet commanded the abolition of all innovations.

1531, Feb. 6. Schmalkaldic League, agreed upon in 1530, between the majority of Protestant princes and imperial cities.

Charles caused his brother, Ferdinand, to be elected king of Rome, and crowned at Aachen. The elector of Saxony protested against this proceeding in the name of the evangelicals. In consequence of the new danger which threatened from the Turks, Ferdinand concluded the

1532. Religious peace of Nürnberg. The Augsburg edict was revoked, and free exercise of their religion permitted the Protestants until the meeting of a new council to be called within a year.

1534–1535. The Anabaptists in Münster (**Johann Bockelsohn** of Leyden). Extreme anarchistic (*Antinomian*) consequences of Luther's doctrine of justification by faith alone.

1534. Philip, landgrave of Hesse, restored the Lutheran duke, Ulrich of Württemberg, who had been driven out (1519) by the Swabian league of cities. The emperor had invested his brother Ferdinand with the duchy, but the latter was obliged to agree to a compact, whereby he was to renounce Württemberg and in turn be recognized as king of Rome by the Evangelical party.

1534. FOUNDATION OF THE JESUIT ORDER. Ignatius de Loyola (Iñigo Lopez de Recalde, 1491–1556) with five associates founded the *Society of Jesus,* commonly known as the Jesuit Order. It was approved by Pope Paul III, in 1540. The Jesuits, organized with military strictness, under direct papal control, were the chief agents in spreading the Catholic (or Counter) Reformation.

1535. Charles's successful expedition against Tunis (p. 452).

1536–1538. Third war of Charles against Francis I of France. The latter, having renewed his claims to Milan after the death of Francesco Sforza II, without issue, Charles invaded Provence anew, but fruitlessly. Francis made an inroad into Savoy and Piedmont, and besought the alliance of **Suleiman,** who thereupon pressed his advance on Hungary and sent his fleets to ravage the coasts of Italy. The war was ended by

1538, June 18. The **truce of Nice,** which was concluded on the basis of possession, and for ten years.

1541. JOHN CALVIN (1509–1564) introduced the Reformation into Geneva. Calvin was born at Noyon, France, and published the *Christianae Religionis Institutio* in 1536. He was head of the state in Geneva, save for a short exile to Strassburg (1538–1541), until the time of his death. He systematized Luther's rather emotional revolt, adapting from St. Augustine the rigorous **doctrine of predestination.** Calvinist churches had a strict moral code, and, unlike Lutheran, maintained independence of the Church from the lay authority. In Geneva, in Scotland (**John Knox,**

1505–1572), and briefly in England and even in the New World (at Boston), the Calvinists erected theocratic states. In France and Hungary they became an important minority. In Holland and parts of Germany they were soon the dominant Protestant group.

1541. Charles's unsuccessful expedition against Algiers.

1542–1544. Fourth war between Charles and Francis, occasioned by the investiture of Charles's son, Philip, with Milan. The fact that two secret agents whom Francis had sent to Suleiman were captured in Milan and put to death served Francis as a pretext. Francis in **alliance with Suleiman** and the duke of Cleve. The allied Turkish and French fleets bombarded and plundered Nice. Charles, in alliance with Henry VIII of England, defeated the duke of Cleve, and advanced as far as Soissons. Suleiman invaded Hungary and Austria.

1544, Sept. 18. Treaty of Crespy. Francis' second son, the duke of Orléans, was to marry a princess of the imperial family and receive Milan. He died in 1545, however; Milan continued in the possession of the emperor. Francis gave up his claims to Naples, and the overlordship of Flanders and Artois; Charles renounced his claims to Burgundy.

1545–1563. COUNCIL OF TRENT (not attended by the Protestants). The **Tridentine Decrees** effected a genuine internal reform in the Roman Catholic Church, and reaffirmed the supremacy of the pope as against conciliar claims. Under Jesuit guidance the doctrine of the church was rigidly formulated in direct opposition to Protestant teaching.

1546–1547. SCHMALKALDIC WAR. Charles V sought to crush the independence of the states of the empire in Germany, and to restore the unity of the Church, to which he was urged by the pope, who concluded an alliance with him, and promised money and troops. The leaders of the league of Schmalkalden, John Frederick, elector of Saxony, and Philip, landgrave of Hesse, placed under the ban. Duke Maurice of Saxony concluded a secret alliance with the emperor. Irresolute conduct of the war by the allies in upper Germany. They could not be induced to make a decisive attack, and finally retired, each to his own land. John Frederick reconquered his electorate, which Maurice had occupied. Charles V first reduced the members of the league in southern Germany, then went to Saxony, forced the passage of the Elbe, and defeated in the

1547, April 24. Battle of Mühlberg, the elector of Saxony, captured him, and besieged his capital, Wittenberg. Treaty mediated by

Joachim II of Brandenburg. The electoral dignity and lands given to the **Albertine line** (Duke Maurice). The **Ernestine line** retained Weimar, Jena, Eisenach, Gotha, etc. The elector was kept in captivity. Philip of Hesse surrendered, and was detained in captivity. **Interim of Augsburg** (1548), not generally accepted by the Protestants. The city of Magdeburg, the center of the opposition, placed under the ban. **Maurice of Saxony,** entrusted with the execution of the decree, armed himself in secret against Charles V and

1552. Surprised the emperor, after the conclusion of the **treaty of Friedewalde** (1551) with Henry II of France, and forced him to liberate his father-in-law, Philip of Hesse, and to conclude the **convention of Passau:** Free exercise of religion for the adherents of the confession of Augsburg until the next Diet.

1552–1556. War between **Charles V** and **Henry II,** who, as the ally of Maurice, had seized Metz, Toul, and Verdun. Charles besieged Metz, which was successfully defended by Francis of Guise. The **truce of Vaucelles** left France, provisionally, in possession of the cities which had been occupied.

1553. Maurice defeated Albert, margrave of Brandenburg-Culmbach, at **Sievershausen,** but was mortally wounded.

1555, Sept. 25. RELIGIOUS PEACE OF AUGSBURG. The territorial princes and the free cities, who, at this date, acknowledged the confession of Augsburg, received freedom of worship, the right to introduce the Reformation within their territories (*jus reformandi*), and equal rights with the Catholic states. No agreement reached as regarded the **ecclesiastical reservation** that bishops and abbots who became Protestant should lose their offices and incomes; but this provision was inserted by imperial decree. This peace secured no privileges for the reformed (Calvinist) religion.

1556. ABDICATION OF CHARLES V at Brussels (effective 1558).

The crown of Spain with the colonies, Naples, Milan, Franche-Comté, and the Netherlands, went to his son **Philip;** the imperial office and the Hapsburg lands to his brother **Ferdinand I.** Charles lived in the monastery of Yuste as a private individual, but not as a monk, and died there in 1558.

1558–1564. FERDINAND I, husband of Anna, sister of Louis II, king of Bohemia and Hungary, after whose death he was elected king of these countries by their estates. Constant warfare over the latter country, which he was obliged to abandon, in great part, to the Turks (p. 452).

1564–1576. MAXIMILIAN II, son of Ferdinand, was of a mild disposition and favorably inclined to the Protestants, whom he left undisturbed in the free exercise of their religion. War with John Zápolya, prince of Transylvania, and the Turks. Sultan **Suleiman I** died in camp before Szigeth, which was defended by the heroic Nicholas Zrinyi. By the **truce with Selim II** (1566) each party retained its possessions (p. 452).

REACTION AGAINST PROTESTANT-ISM: Catholic, or Counter, Reformation.

1576-1612. RUDOLF II, son of the Emperor Maximilian II, a learned man, an astrologer and astronomer, but incapable of governing. New quarrels over the ecclesiastical reservation. The imperial city of Donauwörth, placed under the ban by the emperor because a mob had disturbed a Catholic procession, was, in spite of the prohibition of the emperor, retained by Maximilian of Bavaria, who had executed the ban (1607). These troubles led to the formation of a

1608. Protestant Union (leader, **Frederick IV,** Elector Palatine), which was opposed by the

1609. Catholic League (leader, **Maximilian,** duke of Bavaria). Both princes were of the house of Wittelsbach.

Rudolf, from whom his brother, Matthias, had forced the cession of Hungary, Moravia, and Austria, hoping to conciliate the Bohemians gave them the

1609. Royal Charter (*Majestätsbrief*), which permitted a free exercise of religion to the three estates of lords, knights, and royal cities.

1609. Beginning of the quarrel about the **succession of Cleves-Jülich** on the death of John William, duke of Cleve. The elector of Brandenburg and the prince of Neuburg were the principal claimants.

Rudolf, toward the close of his life, was forced by Matthias to abdicate the government of Bohemia.

1612-1619. MATTHIAS, being childless, and having obtained the renunciation of his brothers, secured for his cousin Ferdinand, duke of Styria, Carinthia, and Carniola, who had been educated by the Jesuits in strict Catholicism, the succession in Bohemia and Hungary, in spite of the objections of the Protestant states.

LITERATURE AND ART

The greatest of the *Meistersinger* was **Hans Sachs** (1494-1576), composer also of numerous *Fastnachtspiele,* the popular plays which emerged as drama became more secular. Satire appeared in prose and poetry, in fable

and in *Schwank,* or comic anecdote (**Sebastian Brant,** *Narrenschiff,* 1494); in the writings of **Thomas Murner** (1475-1537) and **Johann Fischart** (c. 1550-c. 1591); most particularly in the writings of the humanist scholar, the great Reformation author **Desiderius Erasmus** (b. Rotterdam c. 1466, d. 1536). His *Encomium Moriae* (*Praise of Folly,* 1509) satirized the foibles of individuals and of institutions, especially the Church; his *Colloquia* likewise contain criticisms of contemporary usage. The *Volkslied* remained a popular vehicle for lyric poetry, gradually having expanded to a polyphonic *Lied* in style.

The drama was further popularized by touring English players late in the 16th century. *Dr. Faustus,* first published anonymously in 1587 as a "chap-book," was immediately popular and translated into English.

Pre-Reformation artists continued to be concerned with church decoration: the sculptors **Tilman Riemenschneider** (1468-1531) and the two **Peter Vischers;** the artist **Matthias Grünewald** (1460-1527; *Isenheimer Altar*). The influence of the Reformation and a trend toward secularism are evident in the works of **Albrecht Dürer** (1471-1528), whose careful studies and theoretical treatises exerted tremendous influence on the development of techniques in the graphic arts. The paintings of **Lucas Cranach** (1472-1553) and **Hans Holbein the Younger** (1497-1543), court painter to Henry VIII of England, reflect the growing secularism in art.

b. THE THIRTY YEARS' WAR

1618-1648. The **Thirty Years' War** is generally divided into four periods, which were properly as many different wars. The first two, the Bohemian and the Danish, had a predominantly religious character; they developed from a revolt in Bohemia into a general conflict of Catholic Europe with Protestant Europe. The two latter, the Swedish and the French-Swedish, were primarily political struggles, wars directed against the power of the Hapsburg house and wars of conquest by Sweden and France, fought upon German soil.

(1) The Bohemian Period, 1618-1625

Origin of the war: closing of a (Protestant) Utraquist church in the territory of the abbot of Braunau, and destruction of another in a city of the archbishop of Prague. The irritation of the Bohemian Protestants was increased by the transference of the administration to ten governors, seven of whom were Catholics. Meeting

The Cleves–Jülich Succession (1609)

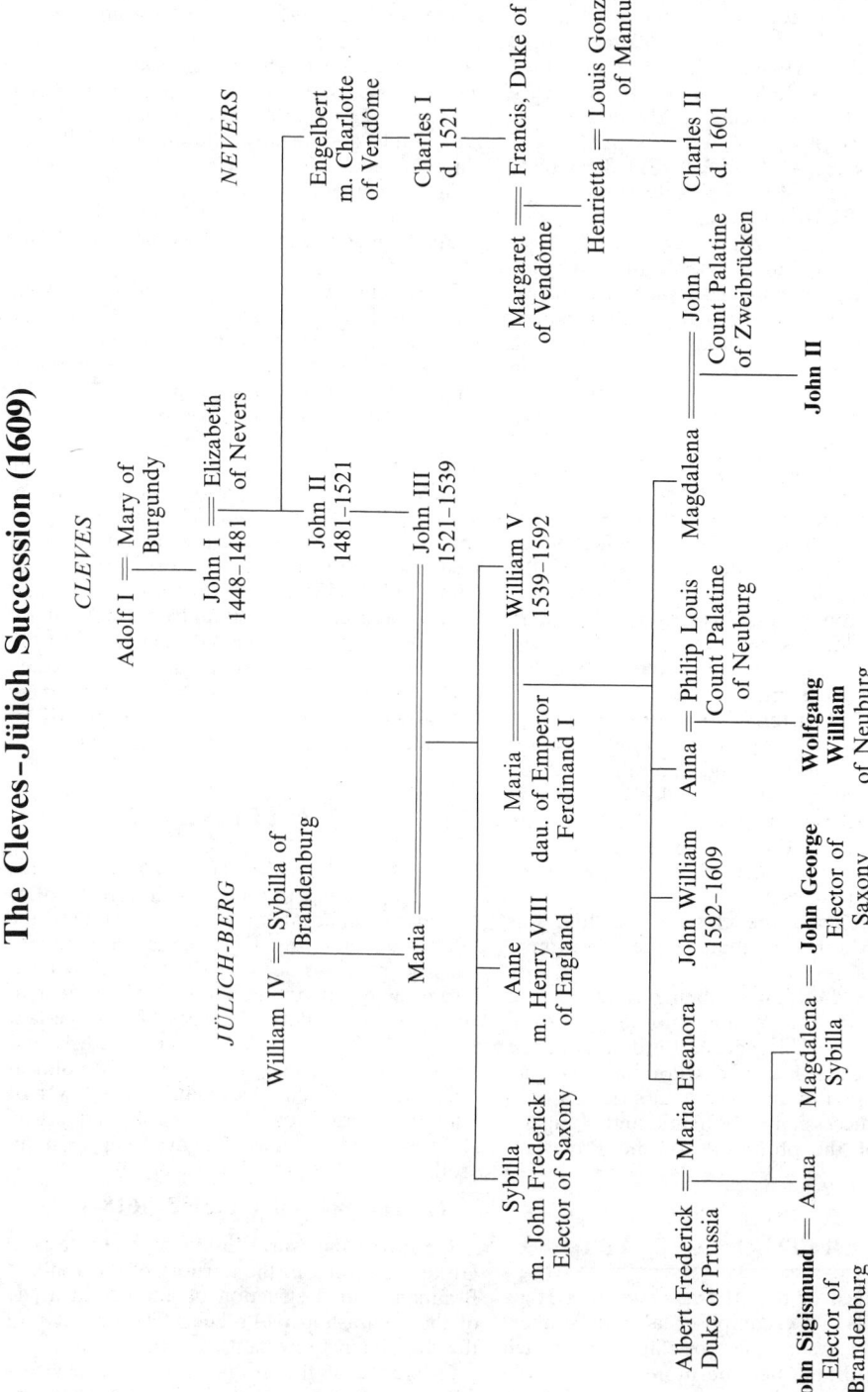

Names in **boldface** are those of claimants in 1609.

of the defensors, and revolt in Prague, headed by **Count Matthias von Thurn.**

1618, May 23. Defenestration of Prague. The governors, Martinitz and Slawata, were thrown from a window in the palace of Prague. They fell fifty feet into a ditch, but escaped with their lives. The rebels then appointed thirty directors. The Protestant Union sent Count Peter Ernst Mansfeld to their aid, and from Silesia and Lusatia came troops under Margrave John George of Jägerndorf. The imperial forces were defeated by Mansfeld and Thurn.

1619-1637. FERDINAND II. Thurn marched upon Vienna. The Austrian estates, for the most part Protestant, threatened to join the Bohemians, and made rough demands upon Ferdinand, who, by his courage and the arrival of a few troops, was rescued from a dangerous situation. Thurn, who arrived before Vienna shortly afterward, was soon obliged to retire by an unfavorable turn of the war in Bohemia. Ferdinand went to Frankfurt, where he was elected emperor by the other six electors.

Meantime the Bohemians had deposed him from the throne of Bohemia and elected the young **Frederick V** (*The Winter King*) elector palatine, the head of the Union and of the German Calvinists, son-in-law of James I, king of England.

Thurn, for the second time before Vienna, allied with **Bethlen Gabor** (i.e. Gabriel Bethlen), prince of Transylvania (Nov. 1619). Cold, want, and the inroad of an imperial partisan in Hungary, caused a retreat.

Ferdinand leagued himself with (1) **Maximilian,** duke of Bavaria, head of the Catholic League, the friend of his youth, who helped him subdue the Austrian estates; with (2) Spain (Spinola invaded the County Palatine; **treaty of Ulm,** July 3, 1620; neutrality of the Protestant Union secured); and with (3) the Lutheran elector of Saxony, who resubjugated Lusatia and Silesia. Maximilian of Bavaria, with the army of the league commanded by **Tilly** (Jan Tserkales, baron von Tilly, in Brabant, 1559-1632), marched to Bohemia and joined the imperial general Buquoy. They were victorious in the

1620, Nov. 8. BATTLE OF THE WHITE MOUNTAIN, over the troops of Frederick V, under the command of **Christian of Anhalt.** Frederick was put under the ban, and his lands confiscated; he himself fled to Holland. Christian of Anhalt and John George of Brandenburg-Jägerndorf also put under the ban. Subjugation of the Bohemians, destruction of the royal charter, execution of the leading rebels, extirpation of Protestantism in Bohemia. Afterward, violent counter-reformation in Austria, and, with less violence, in Silesia.

Dissolution of the Protestant Union and transfer of the seat of war to the Palatinate, which was conquered in execution of the imperial ban by Maximilian's general, Tilly, aided by Spanish troops under Spinola.

1622, Apr. Battle of Wiesloch; defeat of Tilly by Mansfeld.

May. Battle of Wimpfen; victory of Tilly over the margrave of Baden-Durlach.

June. Battle of Höchst; victory of Tilly over Christian of Brunswick, brother of the reigning duke and administrator of the bishopric of Halberstadt.

1623. Maximilian received the electoral vote belonging to Frederick V and the Upper Palatinate; Saxony obtained Lusatia in pledge for the time being.

(2) The Danish Period, 1625-1629

Christian IV, king of Denmark and duke of Holstein, was the head of the Lower Saxon circle of the empire, and leader of the Protestants.

Albert (Albrecht) von Wallenstein (1583-1634), born in Bohemia of an Utraquist family, but educated in the Catholic faith, made duke of Friedland in 1624, became the commander of an imperial army recruited by himself and provisioned by a system of robbery.

1626. Wallenstein defeated Mansfeld at the **Bridge of Dessau,** and pursued him through Silesia to Hungary, where Mansfeld joined Bethlen Gabor. Death of Mansfeld and of Christian of Brunswick (1626).

Aug. Tilly defeated Christian IV at **Lutter am Barenberge,** in Brunswick.

1627. Tilly and Wallenstein conquered Holstein. Wallenstein alone subdued Schleswig and Jutland, drove the dukes of Mecklenburg from their country, and forced the duke of Pomerania into submission.

1628. Wallenstein besieged **Stralsund.** Heroic defense of the citizens for ten weeks obliged Wallenstein to raise the siege.

1629, Mar. 29. EDICT OF RESTITUTION: (1) Agreeably to the ecclesiastical reservation, all ecclesiastical estates that had been confiscated since the convention of Passau (1552) should be restored. This affected two archbishoprics: Magdeburg and Bremen; twelve bishoprics: Minden, Verden, Halberstadt, Lübeck, Ratzeburg, Meissen, Merseburg, Naumburg (the latter three were, however, left in the possession of the elector of Saxony), Brandenburg, Havelberg, Lebus, and Camin, besides very many (about 120) monasteries and foundations. (2) Only the adherents of the Augsburg Confession were to have free exercise of religion; all other "sects" were to be broken up. Beginning of a merciless execution of the edict by Wallenstein's troops and those of the League.

1629, May 22. TREATY OF LÜBECK, between the emperor and Christian IV. The latter received his lands back, but promised not to interfere in German affairs, and abandoned his allies. The dukes of Mecklenburg put under the ban. Wallenstein invested with their lands.

1630. Electoral Assembly at Regensburg. The party of Bavaria and the League was hostile to Wallenstein and took up a position of determined opposition to the too powerful general. An excuse was found in the well-grounded complaints of all states of the empire, particularly the Catholics, of the terrible extortion and cruelty practiced by Wallenstein's army. The emperor consented to decree the dismissal of the general and a large part of the army.

(3) The Swedish Period, 1630–1635

1630, July.   GUSTAVUS II ADOLPHUS (1594–1632), king of Sweden, landed on the coast of Pomerania.

Object and grounds of his interference: protection of the oppressed Protestants; restoration of the dukes of Mecklenburg, his relatives; rejection of his mediation at the **treaty of Lübeck;** anxiety in regard to the maritime plans of the emperor.

Political position of Sweden: Finland, Ingermannland, Estonia, Livonia, belonged to the kingdom of Gustavus; Courland was under Swedish influence; the acquisition of Prussia and Pomerania would have made the Baltic almost a Swedish sea. Gustavus concluded a subsidy treaty with France **(Richelieu);** drove the imperial forces from Pomerania and captured Frankfurt-on-the-Oder. Negotiations with his brother-in-law, George William, elector of Brandenburg (1619–1640), who was under the influence of Schwarzenberg. Spandau was at last surrendered to him. Negotiations in regard to the surrender of Wittenberg. Saxony, which endeavored to maintain the position of a third, mediatory party in the empire, a sort of armed neutrality **(diet of princes of Leipzig,** 1631), was with difficulty brought to form an alliance with an enemy of the empire. Meanwhile

1631, May 20. Capture of Magdeburg by Tilly. The storm was conducted by Count Gottfried Pappenheim. Terrible massacre and sack of the city by the unbridled soldiery of Tilly, who did what he could to check the outrages. Fire broke out suddenly in many places far removed from one another, and the whole city with the exception of the cathedral was consumed (*not* by Tilly's command).

Tilly took possession of Halle, Eisleben, Merseburg, and other cities, and burned them. John George, elector of Saxony, formed an alliance with Gustavus Adolphus, who crossed the Elbe at Wittenberg. Leipzig occupied by Tilly. The imperial army and that of the Swedes and Saxons, each about 40,000 strong, were face to face.

1631, Sept. 17. BATTLE OF LEIPZIG or BREITENFELD. The Saxons were at first put to rout by Tilly, but after a bloody fight Gustavus Adolphus won a brilliant victory.

The Saxons entered Bohemia. Gustavus crossed Thuringia and Franconia to the Rhine, and occupied Mainz.

Meantime Prague was captured by the Saxons under Arnim (Boytzenburg), a former subordinate of Wallenstein. The emperor held fruitless negotiations with the Saxons.

At the urgent request of Ferdinand, Wallenstein collected an army, over which he received unrestricted command. He recaptured Prague, and drove the Saxons from Bohemia. Their eagerness for the war and the Swedish alliance was already chilled.

1632. Gustavus advanced to the Danube by way of Nürnberg to meet Tilly. Conflict at **Rain,** near the confluence of the Lenz and the Danube. Tilly, mortally wounded, died at Ingolstadt.

Gustavus went to Augsburg, vainly besieged Maximilian in Ingolstadt, but forced Munich to surrender. Wallenstein summoned to the assistance of Maximilian.

1632, July–Sept. Fortified camp near Nürnberg. Gustavus and Wallenstein face to face for eleven weeks. Wallenstein declined battle. Reinforced by Bernhard of Saxe-Weimar, the Swedes attacked Wallenstein's entrenchments, but were repulsed with heavy loss. Gustavus advanced to the Danube. Wallenstein turned upon Saxony, now defenseless, Arnim having marched through Lusatia to Silesia with the Saxon and Brandenburg troops. Terrible ravages committed by the bands of Wallenstein. At the call of the elector of Saxony, Gustavus hastened back by way of Kitzingen and Schweinfurt, joined Bernhard of Saxe-Weimar at Arnstadt, marched upon Naumburg and, hearing that Wallenstein had dispatched Pappenheim from Leipzig to the Rhine, attacked the imperial forces (18,000 against 20,000 Swedes) in the

1632, Nov. 16. BATTLE OF LÜTZEN. Death of Gustavus Adolphus. Pappenheim, recalled in haste, took part in the battle with his cavalry, after three o'clock; he was mortally wounded. The victory of the Swedes was completed by **Bernhard von Saxe-Weimar.**

Bernhard, Gustavus Horn, and Johann Baner took command of the Swedish forces. The conduct of foreign affairs was assumed by the Swedish chancellor, **Axel Oxenstierna** (1583-1654). **League of Heilbronn** between the circles of Swabia, Franconia, Upper and Lower Rhine, on the one part, and Sweden on the other.

1633. Expedition of Bernhard to Franconia. He took Bamberg and Hochstädt, drove back the Bavarians under Aldringer, and joined Horn. Bernhard received from the chancellor the investiture, with the bishoprics of Würzburg and Bamberg, under the name of the duchy of Franconia, and occupied the upper Palatinate.

Feb. After Wallenstein had tried and punished with death many of his officers in Prague, and had filled their places with new recruits, he marched to Silesia, fought with the Saxon, Brandenburg, and Swedish troops, and negotiated frequently with Arnim. Negotiations with Oxenstierna.

Nov. Regensburg captured by Bernhard von Saxe-Weimar. Wallenstein found himself unable to go to the assistance of the elector of Bavaria, as the emperor urged, and went into winter quarters in Bohemia.

Growing **estrangement between Wallenstein and the imperial court.** The Spanish party and the League wished him removed from his command. Wallenstein conducted secret negotiations with the Saxons, the Swedes, the French. He intended to create, with the help of the army, an independent position for himself, whence he could, with the aid of the two North German electors, liberate the emperor from the control of the Spanish party, and, if necessary, *compel* him to make peace and reorganize the internal affairs of the empire. He had resolved upon open revolt if the hostile party continued in power. Whether he harbored a wish for the crown of Bohemia, along with other fantastic plans, it is hard to decide. The court of Vienna succeeded in detaching the principal generals (Piccolomini, Gallas, Aldringer, Marradas, Colloredo) from his cause. Ilow, Trzka, Kinski, remained faithful.

1634, Jan. 24. Imperial proclamation: *"Friedland was concerned in a conspiracy to rob the emperor of his crown."* The chief officers of the army commanded to obey him no longer.

Feb. 18. Second proclamation, formally deposing Wallenstein. On the 24th Wallenstein went to Eger, where he was to be met by Bernhard von Saxe-Weimar and Arnim. There occurred the

Feb. 25. Assassination of Wallenstein by Captain Devereux, at the instigation of the Irish general, Butler, after his intimate friends had been treacherously massacred. The emperor had not commanded the murder, nor had he definitely desired it; but he had given rein to the party which he knew wished "to bring in Wallenstein, alive or dead," and, after the deed was done, he rewarded the murderers with honor and riches.

1634. Victory of the imperialists under Ferdinand, the emperor's son, and Gallas and the Bavarians (Johann von Werth), over the Swedes at **Nördlingen.**

1635, May 30. TREATY OF PRAGUE, between the emperor and the elector of Saxony. (1) The elector received Lusatia permanently, and the archbishopric of Magdeburg for his second son, August, for life. (2) Those ecclesiastical lands, not held immediately of the emperor, which had been confiscated before the convention of Passau, should remain to the possessor forever; all others should remain for forty years (from 1627), and in case no further understanding was reached before the expiration of that period, forever, in the condition in which they were on November 12, 1627. (3) Amnesty, except for participants in the disturbances in Bohemia and the Palatinate; common cause to be made against Sweden. The Lutherans alone to be allowed freedom of worship. Brandenburg and most of the other Protestant states accepted the peace.

(4) The Swedish-French Period, 1635–1648

The policy of Sweden was determined by **Oxenstierna,** that of France by **Richelieu,** and afterward by **Mazarin.** France fought at first in the person of Bernhard of Saxe-Weimar only, with whom subsidy treaties had been concluded, and who was trying to conquer for himself a new state in Alsace, in place of the duchy of Franconia, which he had lost by the **battle of Nördlingen. Capture of Breisach** (1638). After his death (1639) France took control of his army.

1636. Victory of the Swedes under Baner at **Wittstock** over the imperialists and the Saxons. Death of Ferdinand II (1637).

1637–1657. FERDINAND III, his son, was desirous of peace. After the death of Baner (1641) **Count Lennart Torstenson** became commander-in-chief of the Swedes.

1640. Death of George William. Frederick William, elector of Brandenburg (the **Great Elector,** 1640–1688).

1641. Discussion of the preliminaries of peace in Hamburg. A congress agreed upon.

1642. Second battle of Leipzig (Breitenfeld). Torstenson defeated the imperialists under Piccolomini. He then threatened the hereditary states of the emperor. These Swedish successes aroused the envy of Christian IV of Denmark. Hence

1643-1645. War between Denmark and Sweden.
1643, Sept. Torstenson hastened by forced marches to the north, conquered Holstein and Schleswig, and invaded Jutland.

Meanwhile the French in South Germany, under Marshal Guébriant, had penetrated to Rottweil. Guébriant fell in battle. Shortly afterward the French, under Josias von Rantzau, were surprised at **Tuttlingen** by an Austro-Bavarian army under Franz von Mercy and Johann von Werth, and totally defeated.

1643. Opening of the negotiations for peace in Osnabrück with the Swedes; 1644 in Münster with the French.

Marshal Turenne and the twenty-one-year-old prince of Bourbon, duke of Enghien, afterward **prince of Condé,** appointed commanders-in-chief of the French troops.

1644. The French forced the Bavarians under Mercy to retreat. Condé captured Mannheim, Speier, and Philippsburg. Turenne took Worms, Oppenheim, Mainz, and Landau.

Meanwhile an imperial army, under Count Matthias Gallas, had been sent to the aid of the Danes, who were hard pressed, both by land and by sea, by the Swedish admiral, Gustavus Wrangel.

1645, Jan. The imperial force was repulsed by Torstenson and Königsmark, pursued into Germany, and almost annihilated at Magdeburg.

Mar. Brilliant victory of Torstenson over the imperialists at **Jankau** in Bohemia, whereupon, in union with the prince of Transylvania, George Rákóczi, he conquered the whole of Moravia, and advanced hard upon Vienna.

May. Turenne defeated by Werth at **Mergentheim** in Franconia.

Aug. Turenne, at the head of the French and Hessians, defeated the Bavarians at **Allersheim.**

Peace between Sweden and Denmark at **Brömsebro.**

After a futile siege of Brünn, the plague having broken out in his army, Torstenson returned to Bohemia. He resigned his command on account of illness, and was succeeded by Wrangel.

1646. Wrangel left Bohemia, united to his own force the Swedish troops under Königsmark in Westphalia, and joined Turenne at Giessen. Swedes and French invaded Bavaria and forced the Elector Maximilian to conclude the

1647. Truce of Ulm, and to renounce his alliance with the emperor. After Turenne had been recalled, from envy at the Swedish successes, and Wrangel had gone to Bohemia, Maximilian broke the truce and joined the imperialists again.

1648. Second invasion of Bavaria by the French

and Swedes; terrible ravages. A flood on the Inn prevented the further advance of the allies, who returned to the Upper Palatinate.

Terrible condition of Germany. Irreparable losses of men and wealth. Destruction of towns and trade. Reduction of population; increase of poverty; retrogradation in all ranks.

1648, Oct. 24. TREATIES OF WESTPHALIA. Negotiations from 1643 to 1648. Imperial ambassadors, Count Maximilian Trautmannsdorf and Dr. Volmar. French, Count d'Avaux and Count Servien. Swedish, Count Oxenstierna, son of the chancellor, and Baron Salvius. France and Sweden, against the will of the emperor, secured the participation of the states of the empire in the negotiations.

Terms of the treaties: (A) **Indemnifications:** (1) **Sweden** received as fief of the empire the whole of Hither Pomerania and Rügen, with a part of Farther Pomerania, the city of Wismar (formerly a possession of Mecklenburg), and the bishoprics of Bremen (not the city) and Verden as secular duchies. Indemnity of five million rix dollars. Sweden became a member of the German diet with three votes. (2) **France** received absolute sovereignty over the bishoprics and cities of Metz, Toul, and Verdun (in French hands since 1552); also Pignerol, the city of Breisach, the landgravate of Upper and Lower Alsace (which belonged to a branch of the Austrian Hapsburgs), and the government of ten imperial cities in Alsace. These cities and the other imperial states of Alsace (particularly Strassburg) retained their membership in the empire. France received also the right to garrison Philippsburg. (3) **Hesse-Cassel** received the abbey of Hersfeld and part of the county of Schaumburg. (4) **Brandenburg** received, as indemnification for Pomerania (all of which had belonged to Brandenburg by right of inheritance, though only the larger part of Farther Pomerania had been taken over), the bishoprics of Halberstadt, Minden, and Kammin as secular principalities; the archbishopric of Magdeburg as a duchy, with the reservation that it should remain in possession of the administrator, August of Saxony, during his life (d. 1680). (5) **Mecklenburg** received the bishoprics of Schwerin and Ratzeburg, as principalities. (6) **Brunswick** was given the alternate presentation to the bishopric of Osnabrück, where a Catholic and an Evangelical bishop alternated until 1803.

(B) **Secular affairs of the empire:** (1) General amnesty and return to the condition of things in 1618. (2) The electoral dignity and the possession of Upper Palatinate were left to the Wilhelmian (Bavarian) line of the house of Wittelsbach, while a new electorate (the eighth) was created for the Rudolfian (Palatinate) line. (3) The territorial sovereignty (*Landeshoheit*) of all the states of the empire, as regarded their relation to the emperor, was recognized. This involved the right of concluding alliances with one another and with foreign powers, provided they were not directed against the empire or the emperor. (4) The republics of the United Netherlands and of Switzerland were recognized as independent of the empire.

(C) **Ecclesiastical affairs:** (1) The convention of Passau and the peace of Augsburg were approved and extended to include the Calvinists. (2) Catholic and Protestant states were to be on complete equality in all affairs of the empire. (3) January 1, 1624, was adopted as the norm (*annus normalis*) by which questions of ownership of ecclesiastical states and the exercise of religion should be determined. As things were on that date, so they were to remain forever, i.e. the ecclesiastical reservation was acknowledged to be binding for the future. The subjugated Protestants of Austria and Bohemia obtained no rights by the treaties, but those Evangelical states which had been won to the Counter-Reformation during the war (i.e. the Lower Palatinate, Württemberg, Baden, etc.) were allowed to resume the exercise of that religion which had been theirs in 1618. The *jus reformandi*, the privilege of deciding by fiat the religion of those subjects to whom the year 1628 did not secure free exercise of religion, was retained for the future by the territorial lords. The right of emigration was, however, reserved to the subjects in such cases. The imperial court (*Reichskammergericht*) was restored and its members were equally divided between Protestants and Catholics.

The treaties of Westphalia were guaranteed by France and Sweden.   (*Cont. p. 498.*)

Literary output during the Thirty Years' War was sparse: hymns of **Paul Gerhardt** (1607-1676); mystical poems of **Angelus Silesius** (1624-1677), who was indebted to **Jakob Böhme** (1575-1624); poems and plays of another Silesian, **Andreas Gryphius** (1616-1664), especially his satiric comedy *Horribilicribrifax* (c. 1650); the acknowledged "prose classic of the century," *Simplicissimus* (1669), a vivid picture of contemporary life and manners by **Hans Jakob von Grimmelshausen** (c. 1625-1676). Another Silesian, **Martin Opitz** (1597-1639), won recognition as purifier of the language by his insistence on proper form in *Das Buch von der deutschen Poeterey* (1624).

Music in the period was chiefly for church use: **Heinrich Schütz** (1585-1672) composed vocal and instrumental music in various forms;

his influence was apparent on Buxtehude and J. S. Bach.

c. THE SWISS CONFEDERATION, 1503-1648

(*From p. 330*)

The confederation, at the beginning of the 16th century, was still a loose union of practically independent cantons, each sending two representatives to a federal diet. There were, after 1513, thirteen cantons, of which six (Schwyz, Uri, Zug, Unterwalden, Glarus, and Appenzell) were rural, and seven (Lucerne, Zürich, Bern, Solothurn, Fribourg, Basel, and Schaffhausen) were urban. The Aargau, Thurgau, Ticino, and parts of Vaud were governed by the confederation or one or more of its members. Franche-Comté was under Swiss protectorate. In addition there was a number of states allied with the confederation (St. Gall, Upper Valais, Neuchâtel, Rothweil, Mülhausen, Geneva, etc).

Swiss military prestige had reached its zenith in the latter part of the 15th century. Swiss mercenaries took an important part in the Italian expedition of Charles VIII and continued to form a crucial part of the French and Italian armies.

1503. The Forest Cantons seized Bellinzona after the French conquest of Milan.

1510. The Swiss joined in the **Holy League** against France. In partnership with the Venetians they restored the Sforza to the Milanese duchy (1512), taking for themselves Locarno, Lugano, and Ossola. Great victory of the Swiss over the French in the **battle of Novara** (June 6, 1513).

1515, Sept. 13-14. In the **battle of Marignano** (p. 409) the French won a decisive victory over the Swiss and Venetians. This led to the conclusion of peace (Nov. 12, 1515): the Swiss retained most of the Alpine passes and received a French subsidy in return for the right for the French to enlist mercenaries.

1519, Jan. 1. Beginning of the **REFORMATION IN SWITZERLAND**, under the leadership of **Ulrich Zwingli** (b. 1484; educated at Basel and Bern; priest at Glarus, 1506; after taking part in the Italian campaigns, became priest at Einsiedeln, 1516; preacher at Zürich, 1518). Zwingli denounced indulgences and other abuses in the Church and made a great impression in Zürich. In 1521 he denounced the hiring of mercenaries, and in 1522 condemned fasts and celibacy (he himself married in 1524). The town, following his teaching, abolished confession (1524) and closed the monasteries. Zwingli acted independently of Luther, from whom he was separated chiefly by difference of opinion on transubstantiation.

1524. Five cantons (Lucerne, Uri, Schwyz, Unterwalden, and Zug) banded together against Zürich and the Reformation movement.

1528. Bern and Basel accepted the Reformation, and were followed by three others. Fribourg and Solothurn remained Catholic and sided with the original five (rural) cantons.

1531. War of the Catholic cantons against Zürich. The Zürichers were defeated in the battle of Kappel (Oct. 11) and Zwingli was killed. Thus the division of the confederation was complete; the weakness resulting therefrom made impossible all effective action in the ensuing century.

1536. Geneva (allied with Bern) adopted the Reformation, largely through the efforts of William Farel. In the same year John Calvin (1509–1564) arrived in the city. His teaching made a deep impression, but also aroused much opposition. In 1538 he was banished and retired to Strassburg.

1536. Bern subdued Vaud, Chablais, Lausanne, and other territories of the duke of Savoy, thus laying the basis for a long-drawn duel between the two powers.

1541–1564. CALVIN, recalled to Geneva, organized the town as a theocratic state (*City of God*). A consistory of twelve laymen and six clericals controlled the council and the government. Drastic suppression of all godlessness (i.e. everything at variance with Calvinist doctrine).

1553. Execution of Servetus for denying the Trinity.

1555. Ruthless suppression of an anti-Calvinist uprising. Geneva a center for Protestant refugees from England and France and a radiating point for Calvinist doctrine. But the Protestant cantons of Switzerland remained predominantly Zwinglian.

1564. Bern was obliged, under pressure from the Spanish power in Italy, to retrocede Gex and Chablais to Savoy. The Savoyards, supported by Spain and also by the Catholic cantons, began a prolonged offensive against Geneva and Bern, which drove the Protestant cantons into the French fold.

1577. Opening of a Jesuit seminary at Lucerne, marking the most active phase of the Counter-Reformation, directed chiefly by Cardinal Carlo Borromeo of Milan.

1584. Alliance of Bern, Geneva, and Zürich against Savoy and the Catholic cantons, followed by an alliance of the latter with Spain (1587).

1602. Savoyard attack on Geneva. This was frustrated, but one important result was the renewal of the alliance between the whole confederation and France (the Catholic cantons, however, retained also their alliance with Spain).

1620–1639. Struggle for control of the Valtelline Pass, the most important link in the communications between Hapsburg Austria and the Spanish Hapsburg possessions in Italy. The pass was controlled by the Grisons League, but in 1620 was seized by the Spaniards, who enjoyed the support of the Catholic faction (under Rudolf Planta). Thereupon Bern and Zürich sent aid to the Protestant faction, led by the pastor George Jenatsch (1596–1639). The Protestants were at first successful, but in 1621 were expelled by the Austrians, Spain taking over control of the pass. In 1625 it was seized by a Swiss force in French pay. Governorship of the duke de Rohan. But in 1637 Jenatsch, having turned Catholic in the interest of patriotism, secured Austrian aid and once more drove out the foreigner. By treaty with Spain (Sept. 3, 1639) the passes were left open to the use of Spanish troops. The war had been conducted by both sides with the utmost cruelty, typical of the Thirty Years' War. In that great struggle the Swiss Confederation remained officially neutral, being paralyzed by the division between Catholic and Protestant cantons. Nevertheless, by

1648. The treaties of Westphalia, the confederation, owing to the efforts and diplomacy of John Rudolf Wettstein, burgomaster of Basel, was able to secure a European recognition of its independence of the German Empire.   (*Cont. p. 497.*)

7. SCANDINAVIA

(*From pp. 334, 336*)

a. DENMARK AND NORWAY, 1513–1645

During this period the union of the three Scandinavian kingdoms became dissolved. The attempt of the Danish king,

1513–1523. CHRISTIAN II, to assert Danish supremacy in Sweden by invading the latter and executing the leaders of the national Swedish party (the massacre of Stockholm, 1520) led to a

1520. National revolt headed by Gustavus

Kings of Denmark and Norway (1448-1730)

(From p. 335)

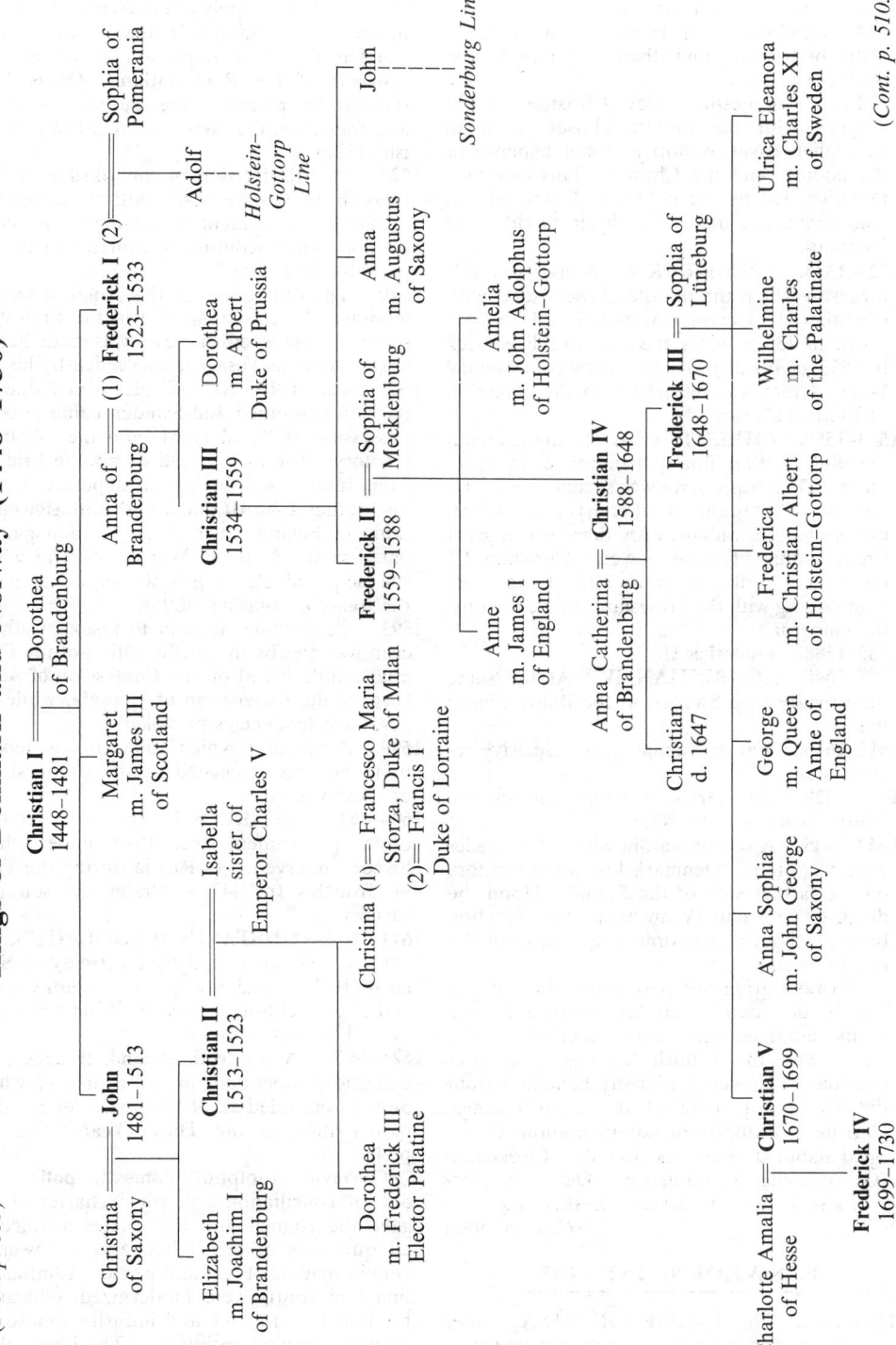

(Cont. p. 510.)

Ericksson Vasa, a young Swedish nobleman. The Danes were defeated, and

1523. Gustavus Vasa became first administrator of the kingdom, then king (see below, Sweden).

In his domestici policy Christian II, in alliance with the middle classes, tried to strengthen royal authority at the expense of the nobility and the Church. This caused a rebellion, led by the nobles and the bishops, who invited the duke of Holstein to rule over Denmark as

1523-1533. FREDERICK I. A civil war followed in which the middle classes sided with Christian II. Christian was defeated and deposed in 1532. After the death of Frederick in 1533, civil war broke out anew (the **Counts' War**). Order was restored with the accession of Frederick's son

1534-1559. CHRISTIAN III. During his reign the **Reformation** finally triumphed in Denmark. Church property was secularized and a national Protestant (Lutheran) church was established. Simultaneously there was a great strengthening of royal power. Christian III intervened in the religious struggle in Germany siding with the Protestant princes against the emperor.

1559-1588. Frederick II.

1588-1648. CHRISTIAN IV. At the same time rivalry with Sweden in the Baltic caused the

1611-1613. War of Kalmar with indecisive results, and

1625-1629. Denmark's participation in the **Thirty Years' War** (P. 433).

1643-1645. A second war, in which the Swedes were victorious. Denmark lost some territory on the farther side of the Sound. Upon the death of Christian IV an aristocratic reaction brought about a temporary weakening of the royal power.

Norway during this period remained under Danish domination: all the important posts in the administration were occupied by the Danes and the Danish language was predominant. However, Norway benefited from the activity of some of the Danish kings. Christian IV improved administration, developed national resources, founded **Christiania** (Oslo). Under the influence of Denmark, Norway also became Protestant (Lutheran).

(*Cont. p. 509.*)

b. SWEDEN, 1523-1654

1523-1654. The **HOUSE OF VASA,** under whom Sweden became the strongest power in the Baltic.

1523-1560. GUSTAVUS I. War with Lübeck, concluded by the **treaty of 1537,** put an end to the trade monopoly of the Hanseatic League in the Baltic region. In the internal life of Sweden the most important event was the progress of the **Reformation. Olaus Petri** successfully preached the Lutheran doctrine and translated the New Testament into Swedish (1526).

1527. By the decision of the **riksdag of Västeras,** bishops were made entirely dependent on the king, payment of the Peter's pence to the pope was discontinued, church estates were partially secularized.

1529. The ordinances of the **synod of Örebro** modified the church service in the Protestant sense. As the Swedish crown was made hereditary, Gustavus Vasa was succeeded by his son

1560-1568. ERIC XIV. Under him Baltic expansion continued and Sweden came into the possession of Reval (1561) and the adjoining territory. Toward the end of his life Eric became insane, and finally was deposed. Under his brother **John III** and John's son **Sigismund** (king of Poland since 1587), Sweden participated in the **Livonian War** (p. 442) in which she acquired all of Estonia with Narva, by the **treaty of Teusina** (1595).

1593. Sigismund's attempt to restore Catholicism was met by the reaffirmation of the Protestant faith, based on the **Confession of Augsburg,** at the **Convention of Uppsala,** while his absolutist tendencies provoked

1599. A rebellion which ended in his deposition. He was succeeded by the youngest son of Gustavus Vasa,

1604-1611. CHARLES IX (in virtual control of the government since 1599) under whom Sweden intervened in Russia during the **Time of Troubles** (p. 447). Under his son and successor,

1611-1632. GUSTAVUS II ADOLPHUS, war with Russia was ended by the **treaty of Stolbovo** (1617): Sweden acquired eastern Carelia and Ingria, cutting Russia off from the Baltic Sea. This was followed by

1621-1629. A war with Poland, the result of dynastic competition, in the course of which Sweden occupied all of Livonia. For Swedish participation in the **Thirty Years' War** see p. 434).

Gustavus Adolphus' **domestic policy** was one of conciliation. A royal charter (1611) gave the council and the estates a voice in all questions of legislation, and a power of veto in matters of war and peace. Administration and courts were modernized, education promoted, commerce and industry sponsored, foreign immigration invited. The king's chief collaborator was his chancellor, **Axel Oxenstierna** (1583-1654), who became the actual

The House of Vasa (1523-1818)

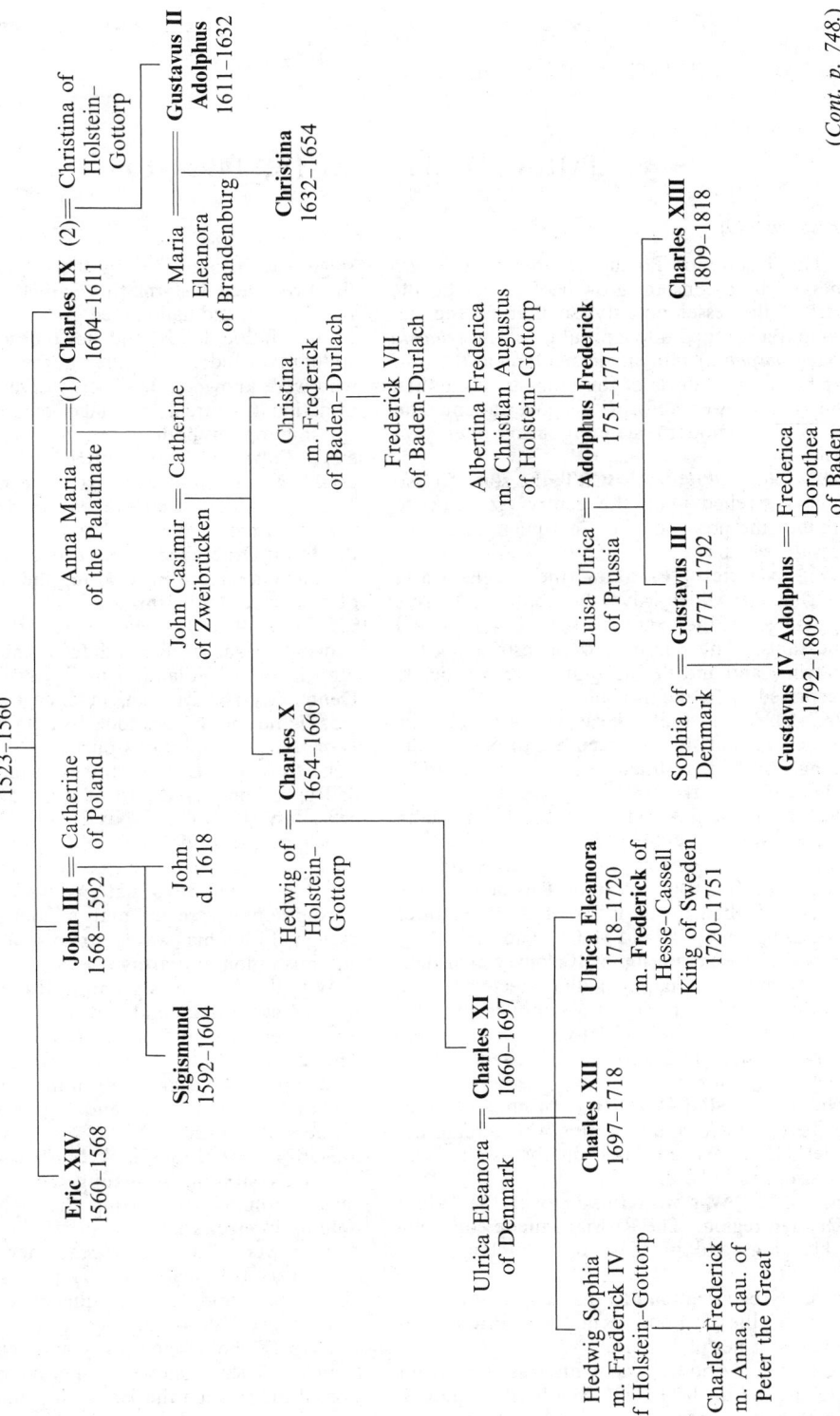

(Cont. p. 748.)

ruler of Sweden under Gustavus Adolphus' daughter,

1632-1654. CHRISTINA. For Swedish acqui-

sitions under the **treaties of Westphalia** see p. 436. (*Cont. p. 506.*)

8. POLAND-LITHUANIA, 1492-1648

(*From p. 340*)

The history of Poland in this period was marked by a constant growth of power on the part of the lesser nobility, so that Poland became transformed into a republic of the *szlachta* (*Rzeczpospolita*) with an elected king as the titular head. All efforts of the kings to strengthen the royal power, reform the government, and establish a modern standing army met with failure.

1492-1501. JOHN ALBERT, the son of Casimir IV, relied upon the gentry (szlachta) to reduce the power of the great magnates. The result was the

1496. Statute of Piotrkow (the Magna Carta of Poland) which gave the gentry extensive privileges at the expense of the burghers and peasants. The burghers were restricted from buying land and the peasants were practically deprived of freedom of movement.

1497-1498. A futile **invasion of Moldavia,** which was intended to secure a throne for the king's brother, resulted in a devastating invasion by the Turks.

1501-1506. ALEXANDER I, brother of John Albert and, since 1492, grand duke of Lithuania. His reign was important only for the **war with Ivan the Great** of Russia (p. 342), which resulted in the loss of the left bank of the Dnieper by Poland (1503), and for

1505. The **Constitution of Radom,** which definitely made the national diet, elected by the nobles at their provincial assemblies (the *dietines*), the supreme legislative organ. Henceforth no new laws were to be passed without the diet's consent.

1506-1548. SIGISMUND I, brother of John Albert and Alexander, during whose reign the diet (1511) passed laws finally establishing serfdom in Poland.

1512-1522. War with Russia over the White Russian region. The Russians made considerable gains and in 1514 took Smolensk, the key city.

1525. Secularization of Prussia and end of the rule of the Teutonic Knights. Prussia remained a fief of Poland.

1534-1536. Another war with Russia brought no success to the Poles. Smolensk remained in Russian hands.

1548-1572. SIGISMUND II (August). His reign was distinguished by the wide spread of the **Protestant Reformation,** which had taken root in 1518 and had gained ground, especially in the Baltic lands and in the towns, despite many edicts penalizing the adherents, who were known as **Dissidents.** Demands for a national church, marriage of the clergy, communion in both kinds, Slavonic liturgy, etc. **Calvinism** and **Antitrinitarianism** also established themselves. After the **council of Trent** (p. 424) the crown, backed by the recently formed Polish-Lithuanian chapter of the Jesuit Order (1565), succeeded in checking the movement and in restoring the supremacy of Roman Catholicism.

1557-1571. The **Livonian War,** arising from a disputed succession and from the conflicting claims of Poland, Russia, Sweden, and Denmark. The Russians invaded the country (1557) and the Swedes took Estonia, while the Danes acquired part of Courland. In 1561 the Poles took over Livonia, but Ivan the Terrible of Russia conquered part of it in 1563.

1569, July 1. The **UNION OF LUBLIN,** which, despite opposition on the part of Lithuania, merged that country with the Polish kingdom. The two nations were to have a common sovereign, and a common diet, though Lithuania was to retain a separate administration and army.

With the death of Sigismund II the **Jagellon dynasty** came to an end and the Polish crown, already elective in theory, became so in fact. The result was a tremendous weakening of the royal power, constant embroilment in the rivalries of other nations, and a growing hopelessness of reform.

1573-1574. HENRY OF VALOIS was elected king on condition of signing the *Pacta Conventa,* formally recognizing the right of the nobility to elect kings and strictly limiting the royal power. The diet was to meet at least once every two years. Henry paid richly for his election and for the alliance of Poland with France, but, on the death of his brother, Charles IX, he slipped away and returned to France. There followed a period of confusion, during which the Hapsburgs made great efforts to secure the crown. The Poles ultimately elected

Rulers of Poland and Hungary (1447–1668)

(From p. 339)

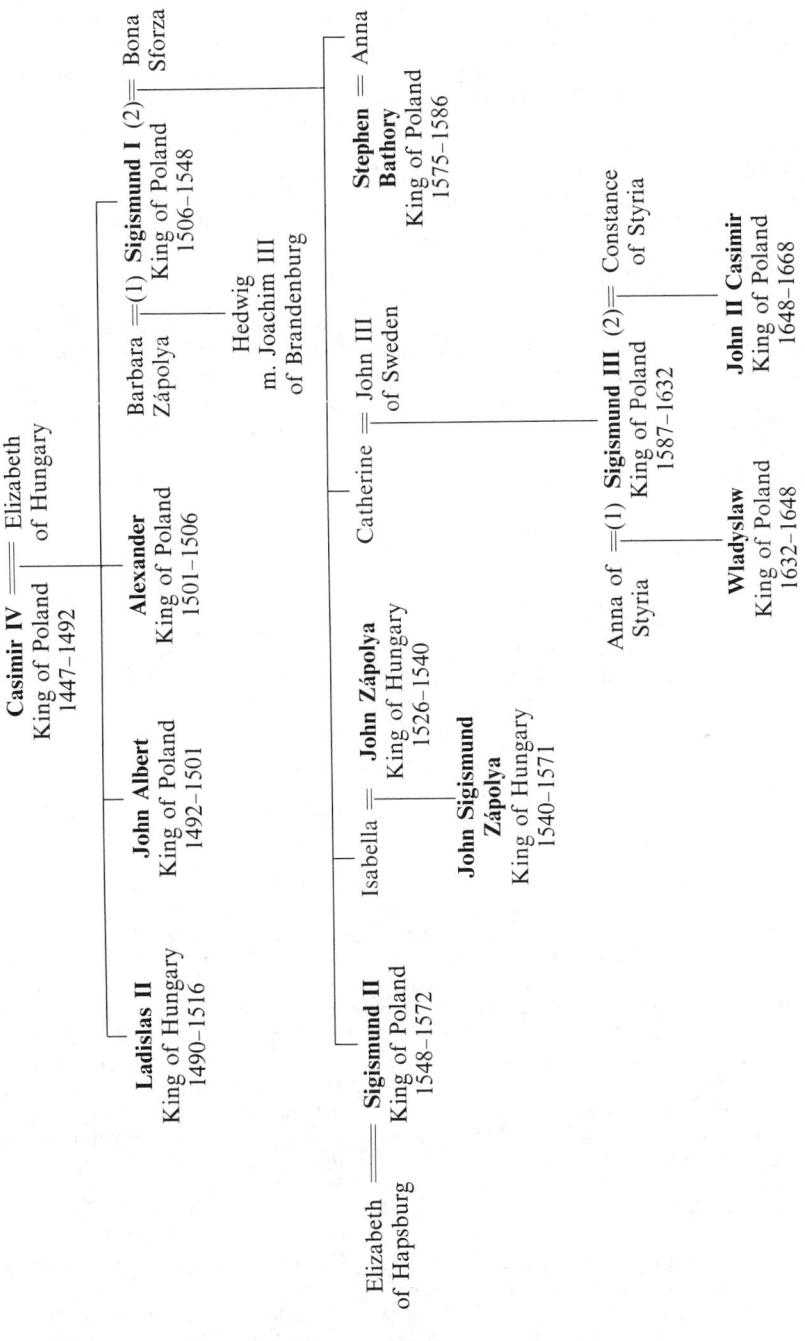

Casimir IV ═══ Elizabeth
King of Poland   of Hungary
1447–1492

Ladislas II
King of Hungary
1490–1516

John Albert
King of Poland
1492–1501

Alexander
King of Poland
1501–1506

Barbara ══(1) **Sigismund I** (2)══ Bona
Zápolya   King of Poland   Sforza
1506–1548

Hedwig
m. Joachim III
of Brandenburg

Stephen ═══ Anna
Bathory
King of Poland
1575–1586

Elizabeth ═══ **Sigismund II**
of Hapsburg   King of Poland
1548–1572

Isabella ═══ **John Zápolya**
King of Hungary
1526–1540

**John Sigismund
Zápolya**
King of Hungary
1540–1571

Catherine ═══ John III
of Sweden

Anna of ══(1) **Sigismund III** (2)══ Constance
Styria   King of Poland   of Styria
1587–1632

Wladyslaw
King of Poland
1632–1648

John II Casimir
King of Poland
1648–1668

1575-1586. STEPHEN BATHORY, husband of Anna, the last Jagellon. Stephen was a strong ruler, but was unable to make much progress against the powerful nobility. His great success was in the field of foreign affairs and war. Plan for a union of eastern Europe under his leadership, preparatory to a united attack upon the Turk. This came to nothing, but Stephen, with a new army of peasant infantry, raised on the royal estates, was able, in the last phase of the Livonian War (1579–1582) to retake Polotsk and to put an end to the steady encroachment of Russia upon the White Russian regions.

1587-1632. SIGISMUND III (Vasa), son of King John of Sweden. He had been educated by the Jesuits and threw his entire influence on the side of the Counter-Reformation. For the rest he demonstrated little statesmanship and involved Poland in endless wars with Sweden because of his claims to the Swedish throne.

1595-1596. Attempts to reunite the Greek Orthodox Church in Poland with Rome foundered on the obstinacy of the Jesuits. However, part of the Orthodox formed the so-called **Uniate Church,** retaining Eastern rites but recognizing papal authority. The result was the **confederation of Vilna** (1599), an alliance between the Orthodox and the Dissidents against the power of the Roman church.

1609-1618. Polish intervention in Russia during the **Time of Troubles** (p. 447). An attempt to put Sigismund's son, Wladyslaw, on the Russian throne ended in the expulsion of the Poles from Moscow.

1629. The **treaty of Altmark,** a truce in the long conflict with Sweden, signalized the defeat of the Poles and confirmed the loss of Livonia.

1632-1648. WLADYSLAW, the son of Sigismund. He was elected without opposition and pursued a policy diametrically opposed to that of his father. But his efforts to restrict the powers of the Jesuits were in vain.

1632-1634. War with Russia, which was ended by the **treaty of Polianov** (1634): Wladyslaw renounced his claims to the Russian throne, but regained the Smolensk region for Poland.

(*Cont. p. 509.*)

Literature: *Aesop's Fables* were paraphrased and a life written by **Bernard of Lublin** (c. 1515). The spread of Renaissance culture and of the Reformation culminated in a "golden age" of prose and poetry: poets **Nicholas Rej of Naglowice** (1505–1569) and **Jan Kochanowski** (1530–1584). Prose writers **Lucas Gornicki** and **Peter Skarga** (1536–1612). Foremost poet of the 17th century: **Waclaw Potocki** (1625–1696).

9. RUSSIA, 1505-1645

(*From p. 342*)

In Russia, as in many other countries, the period was one of conflict between the crown and the powerful landed nobility, accompanied by a decline in the influence of the townsmen and a gradual relapsing of the peasantry into serfdom. In Russia the latter problem was closely connected with defense and territorial expansion. Since 1454 the grand dukes of Moscow granted non-hereditary military fiefs (*pomestye*) to secure a supply of fighting men for use in the struggle against the Tatars. The corollary was a steady debasement in the position of the peasants, who consequently tended to run off to newly conquered territories in the southeast. Depopulation in the center resulted in ever more drastic measures to hold the cultivator on the land. At the same time there grew up on the borders the Cossack colonies, wild, free communities which were to play a great rôle in this period.

1505-1533. BASIL III, the son of Ivan the Great and Sophia. The reign was a fairly quiet one, during which the work of consolidation was continued by the reduction of Pskov (1510), Smolensk (1514), and Riazan (1517).

1533-1584. IVAN IV (the Terrible), the son of Basil. He ascended the throne at the age of three. The regency was in the hands of his mother, **Helen Glinski** (of Lithuanian family), until 1538, and thereupon fell into the hands of powerful noble (*boyar*) families, notably the **Shuiskys** and **Belskys,** whose oligarchic policy presented the young ruler with an almost insuperable problem.

1547. Ivan assumed power and had himself crowned *tsar,* the first Russian ruler to assume the title formally. At the same time he established a *chosen council,* composed of personally selected advisers, which he hoped to make a counterweight to the power of the **council of boyars** (*duma*). This was followed in 1549 with the convocation of the first national assembly or *zemski sobor,* also meant to broaden the support of the crown. In these early years Ivan made considerable progress in breaking down the power of the provincial

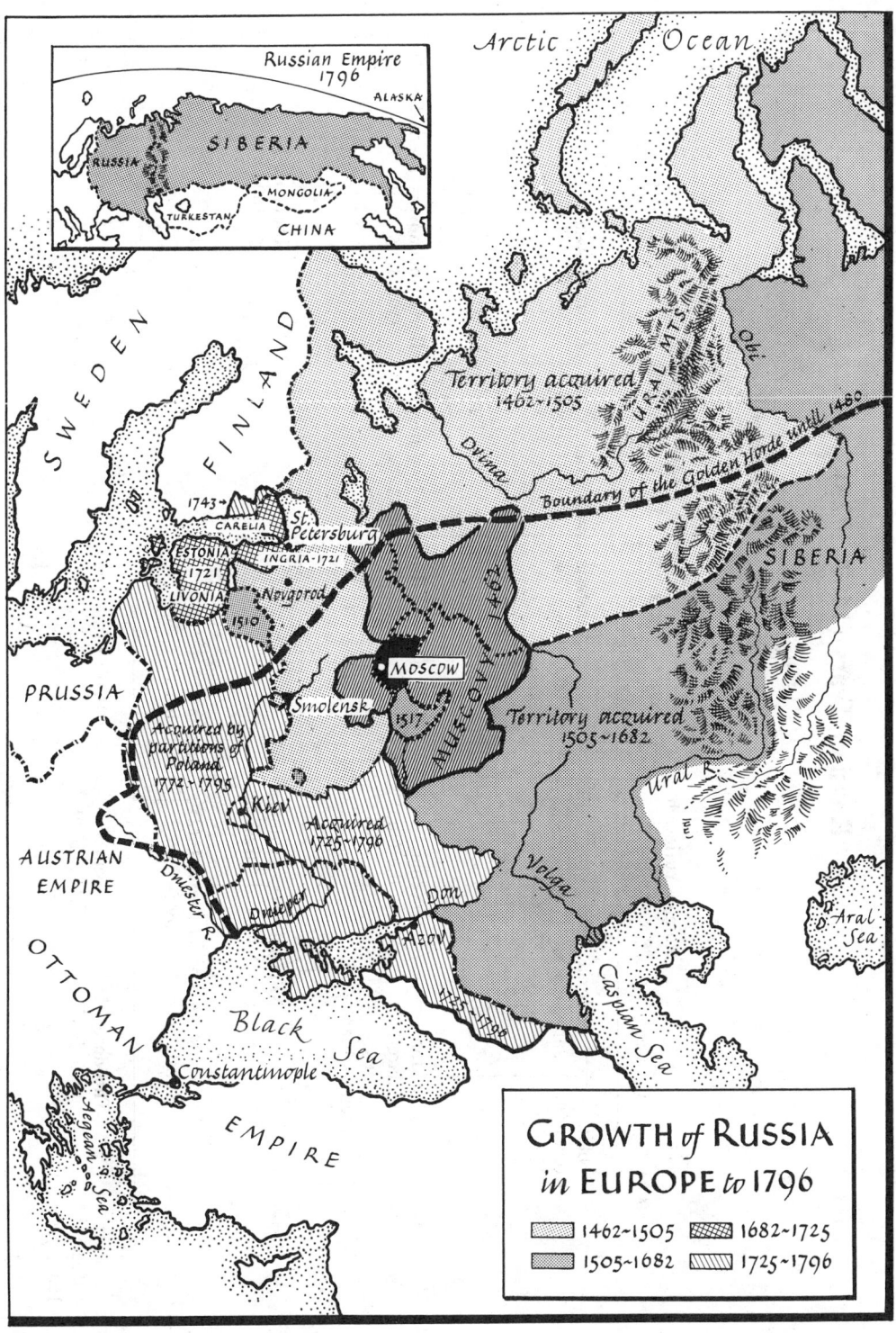

Russian Empire 1796

ALASKA

SIBERIA

RUSSIA

MONGOLIA

TURKESTAN

CHINA

Arctic Ocean

SWEDEN

FINLAND

Territory acquired 1462-1505

URAL MTS.

Obi

Dvina

Boundary of the Golden Horde until 1480

SIBERIA

1743

CARELIA

St. Petersburg

ESTONIA 1721

INGRIA-1721

LIVONIA

Novgorod

1510

MOSCOW

PRUSSIA

Smolensk

1517

Territory acquired 1505~1682

MUSCOVY 1462

Acquired by partitions of Poland 1772-1795

Ural R.

Kiev

Acquired 1725~1796

AUSTRIAN EMPIRE

Dniester R.

Dnieper

Don

Volga

D. Aral Sea

1620

OTTOMAN

Black Sea

Constantinople

Caspian Sea

EMPIRE

Aegean Sea

GROWTH of RUSSIA
in EUROPE to 1796

| | 1462~1505 | | 1682~1725 |
| 1505~1682 | | 1725~1796 | |

446

Russian Tsars (1462–1725)

(*From p. 341*)

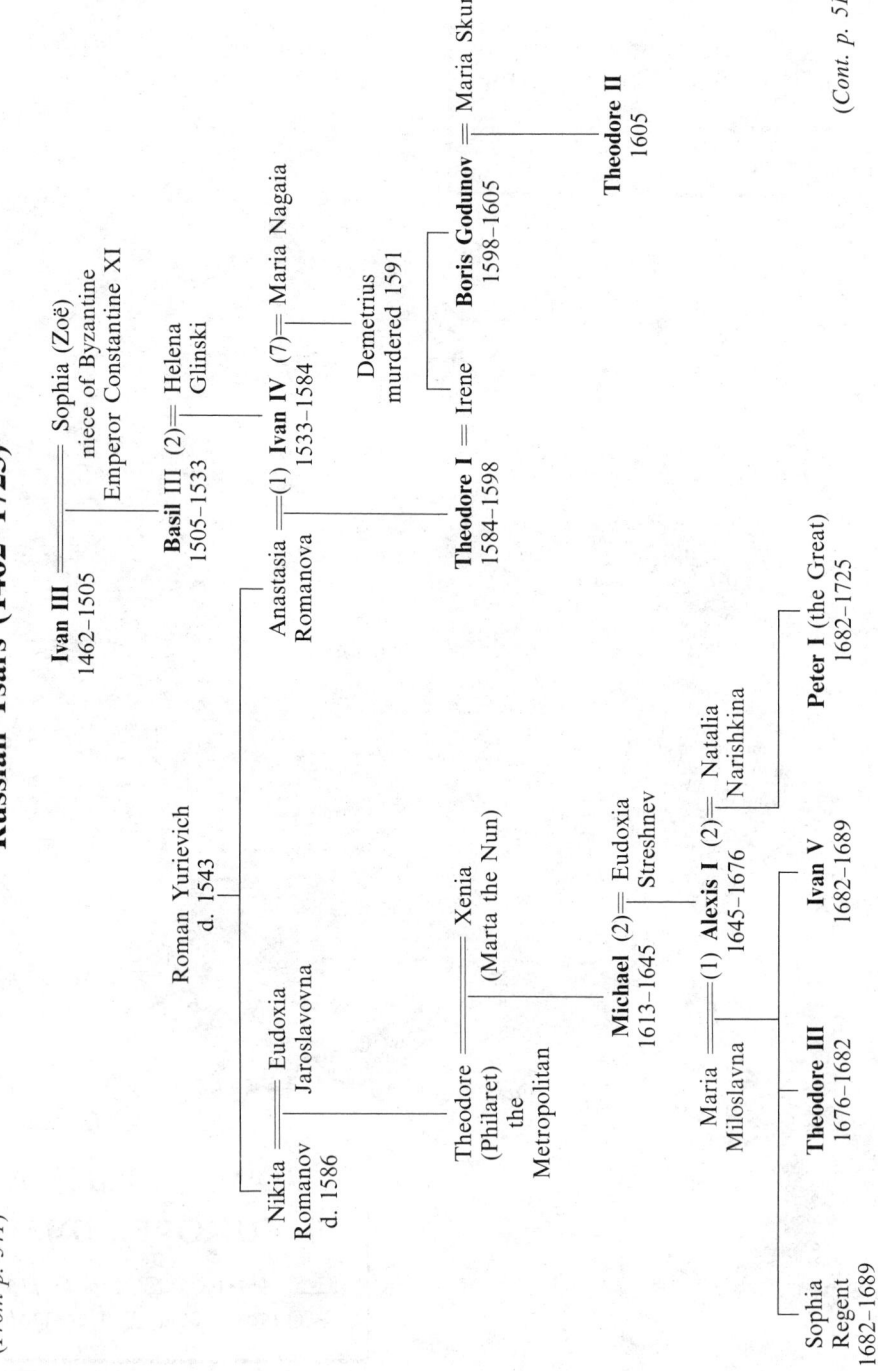

(*Cont. p. 515.*)

governors and in establishing a measure of local government.

1552-1556. The **conquest of Kazan and Astrakhan** from the Tatars gave Russia control of the entire course of the Volga and opened the way for expansion to the east and southeast. Already in the last years of Ivan's reign (1581–1583) Russian traders (the Stroganov family) established themselves east of the Urals and Cossack pioneers, under **Yermak,** began the conquest of Siberia.

1553. The British, under Richard Chancellor, reached Moscow by way of the White Sea and Archangel. They were given trade rights in 1555 and formed an important link in Russian communications with the west, which were otherwise cut off by Poland-Lithuania and Sweden.

1557-1582. The **LIVONIAN WAR,** arising from the disputed succession to the Baltic territories ruled by the Teutonic Knights. Ivan appreciated to the full the importance of an outlet to the Baltic, and seized Narva and Dorpat. In 1563 he conquered part of Livonia, which had been taken over by the Poles.

1564. Conflict of Ivan with the powerful boyars, led by **Prince Andrei Kurbski.** Ivan eventually withdrew from Moscow and issued an appeal to the people, who, through the metropolitan, urged him to return. He took a terrible revenge on his opponents and began a reign of terror marked by incredible excesses and fantastic self-debasement. At the same time Ivan set aside about half of the realm as his personal domain (*oprichnina*), in which he established a new administration and a separate royal army.

1570. **Ivan ravaged Novgorod** and massacred many of the inhabitants, whom he suspected of sympathy for the Poles.

1571. The **Crimean Tatars** attacked and sacked Moscow.

1578. **Defeat of the Russians by the Swedes** at Wenden, in the course of the struggle for the Baltic lands. Polotsk was lost in the following year.

1581. **Stephen Bathory,** king of Poland, invaded Russia and advanced victoriously to Pskov.

1582. Peace between Russia on the one hand and Poland and Sweden on the other, mediated by the Jesuit **Antonio Possevino,** who had been sent by the pope in the hope of effecting a union of the Orthodox and Roman churches. Ivan was obliged to accept most of his recent losses.

1584-1598. **THEODORE (FEDOR) I,** the son of Ivan, a feeble and utterly weak ruler. The actual government fell again into the hands of the boyars, notably Nikita Romanov (related to

Ivan IV's first wife) and Boris Godunov, brother-in-law of Theodore.

1589. **Establishment of the Russian patriarchate** as separate from that of Constantinople. The Russian church thus became entirely independent. Theodore dying without issue, a national assembly elected to the throne

1598-1605. **BORIS GODUNOV,** an intelligent but none too courageous ruler, faced with the jealousy of other boyar families. Against these he acted by intrigue and persecution.

1604-1613. The **TIME OF TROUBLES,** which began with the appearance of a **false Dmitri,** i.e. a pretender who claimed to be the supposedly murdered son of Ivan IV. Dmitri was an able and forceful person who soon found extensive support among the Poles and the Cossacks. Boris' death at this crucial time initiated a period of utmost confusion during which boyar families struggled for supremacy while their position was challenged by the lower classes (led by the Cossacks), and while foreigners (Poles and Swedes) took full advantage of the situation to further their own interests.

1605. **Theodore II,** the son of Boris, succeeded to the throne. He was soon deposed and murdered by the boyars, many of whom accepted Dmitri. The latter advanced to Moscow and established himself on the throne.

1606. **Basil Shuisky** and a faction of the boyars succeeded in driving out the pretender and murdering him. Shuisky thereupon became tsar. But new pretenders soon appeared, and the situation became desperate when the Cossacks and peasants in the south and east rose in revolt.

1608. The new Dmitri defeated Basil and advanced to Tushino, outside Moscow. In urgent need, Basil ceded Carelia to the Swedes in return for aid.

1609. **Sigismund of Poland** advanced to Smolensk and made extensive promises to the Russian boyars in the hope of acquiring the crown.

1610. **Skopin-Shuisky,** nephew of Basil, with a Swedish force under De La Gardie, relieved Moscow, but the Poles continued their advance. The Russians then deposed Basil and a boyar faction offered the throne to Wladyslaw son of Sigismund. The latter, jealous of his son and anxious to secure the throne himself, evaded the offer and advanced to Moscow.

1611. The turn of the tide was marked by the death of the pretender and by a powerful reaction against the Poles, especially in the northern and eastern provinces. A national militia was formed under **Pozharsky** and this in

1612. Relieved Moscow and drove out the Poles.

1613, Feb. 21. A **national assembly** (*zemski sobor*) elected to the throne

1613-1645. MICHAEL ROMANOV, grandnephew of Ivan IV and son of the patriotic leader, **Philaret.** Michael was crowned on July 11 and therewith began the **Romanov dynasty,** which ruled until 1917. Michael himself was a man of no ability, who was guided by his father and later fell under the influence of favorites. The reign saw the gradual restoration of order, but also the firmer establishment of serfdom and the gradual disappearance of local self-government. The national assembly, which was frequently summoned, failed to establish a regular organization or to develop beyond the status of a consultative body.

1617. Treaty of Stolbovo, with Sweden. The Swedes restored Novgorod, which they had occupied, but Russia was obliged to abandon the few towns that had still been held on the Gulf of Finland.

1634. Treaty of Polianov, with Poland, bringing to a temporary end a long period of conflict. In return for recognition of his title, Michael was obliged to give up many of the frontier towns (including Smolensk) which had been taken by the Poles.

1637. Russian pioneers reached the coast of the Pacific, after a phenomenally rapid advance over the whole of Siberia.

1637. The **Cossacks** managed to take the important fortress of **Azov** from the Crimean Tatars. They offered it to Michael, who refused it (1642) in order to avoid conflict with the Turks. The fortress was thereupon returned. (*Cont. p. 512.*)

10. BOHEMIA, 1471-1627

(*From p. 329*)

1471-1516. LADISLAS II, son of the king of Poland, first ruler of the **Jagiello family,** a boy of sixteen at his accession. Ladislas proved himself a gentle but weak and undecided ruler, wholly unsuited to the position. He continued the persecution of the Bohemian Brotherhood, but made no progress toward unifying the country. As king of Hungary also, he spent most of his time at Pressburg, leaving open the way for the domination of Bohemia by powerful nobles. During the entire later 15th century the aristocracy extended its possessions and power at the expense of the crown and Church. The towns declined in power and the peasantry sank back into serfdom or a status close to it. Great influx of German peasants in the west and north, and also in the towns.

1516-1526. LOUIS, son of Ladislas, who ascended the throne of Bohemia and Hungary at the age of ten. Conditions continued as under Ladislas, further complicated by the spread and persecution of Lutheranism.

1526. Louis was defeated and killed by the Turks at the **battle of Mohács. Ferdinand,** brother of Emperor Charles V and brother-in-law of Louis, was elected king, opening a long period of Hapsburg rule.

1547. The Bohemian crown was proclaimed hereditary in the house of Hapsburg. Constant growth of the royal prerogative at the expense of the diet and of town government.

1618. Defenestration of Prague and beginning of the Thirty Years' War (p. 433). Ferdinand II was declared deposed and the Protestant Frederick of the Palatinate was elected king (*the Winter King*).

1620, Nov. 8. BATTLE OF THE WHITE MOUNTAIN; defeat of Frederick and the Bohemians. Bohemia was virtually deprived of independence and a wholesale confiscation of the lands of the native nobility took place.

1627. A **new constitution** confirmed the hereditary rule of the Hapsburgs and strengthened royal power. The incorporation of Bohemia with the Hapsburg Empire was completed in the 18th century with the extension of the imperial administration under Joseph I (1705-1711) and with the **Pragmatic Sanction of 1720** (p. 501).

11. HUNGARY, 1490-1648

(*From p. 343*)

1490-1516. LADISLAS II, king of Bohemia, was elected king of Hungary by the nobles. A weak and ineffectual ruler, he allowed the work of Matthias Corvinus to be undone within a few years. In order to secure recognition from the Hapsburgs, he gave up Matthias' conquests and arranged dynastic marriages with the Hapsburgs (his infant son Louis was married to Mary, granddaughter of Maximilian; his own daughter, Anne, was married to Maximilian's grandson Ferdinand). This policy led to the formation of a national party among the Hungarian nobility, which was led by Stephen Zápolya (Szapolyai), the vaivode (prince) of Transylvania. The nobles refused Ladislas all effective financial support, so that he was unable to maintain an army and was soon at the mercy of the feudal elements.

1514. A great **revolt of the peasants,** led by George Dózsa, was directed against the ruthless exploitation by the aristocrats. It was suppressed in a sea of blood by John Zápolya, leader of the nobility.

1514. The *Tripartitum,* a constitution worked out by Stephen Verböczy, was passed by the diet. It established the equality of all nobles and at the same time fixed the system of serfdom on the peasantry.

1516-1526. **LOUIS II,** the son of Ladislas, succeeded his father at the age of ten. A dissolute youngster, devoted to pleasure, he did nothing to stop the disintegration of the royal power. His reign was marked chiefly by the spread of the **Protestant Reformation.** The movement first took root in the German areas and in the towns, and was vigorously opposed by the nobles. In 1523 it was declared punishable by death and confiscation of property, but despite all edicts it took firm hold of the country.

1521. The Turks took Belgrade, beginning their victorious advance into Hungary.

1526, Aug. 29-30. BATTLE OF MOHÁCS. Defeat and death of Louis when the Turks completely overwhelmed his disorganized feudal army of 20,000.

1526-1528. Louis's death was followed by a hot contest over the succession. Part of the nobility, hoping for German aid against the Turks, elected **Ferdinand of Hapsburg,** brother of Emperor Charles V. The national party, on the other hand, elected **John Zápolya** as king. After a civil war lasting two years, Zápolya was defeated. He appealed to the Turks, who supported him vigorously. By the **peace of Nagyvarad** the two kings recognized each other, each ruling part of the territory. Zápolya became a vassal of the Turks, but Ferdinand continued the war against them which was interrupted only by occasional truces (p. 450).

1540. Death of John Zápolya. The Turks recognized his infant son, **John II** (Sigismund) **Zápolya** (1540-1571). This led to a new clash with Ferdinand, who began the invasion of eastern Hungary. The Turks again invaded and took Buda. They now took over the entire central part of Hungary (the great plain), which was organized in four *pashaliks.* There was no settlement by the Turks, but the territory was granted in military fiefs and subjected to heavy taxation. Religious tolerance of the Turks. Transylvania, under Zápolya, was a vassal state of the Turks, but was left almost entirely free. Under **Cardinal Martinuzzi** it was organized as a state (three nations: Magyars, Szeklers, and Germans, meeting in a *Landtag,* elected the king and passed laws). The Transylvanians (even the nobility) soon accepted **Calvinism,** so that during the later 16th century the larger part of Hungary was either Lutheran or Calvinist. In 1560 religious toleration was established in Transylvania. The **Hapsburgs,** on the other hand, held only a narrow strip of western and northern Hungary, and even for this they long paid tribute to the Turks. Warfare was incessant on this frontier (blockhouses and constant raids). The Hapsburgs employed Italian and Spanish mercenaries to defend their possessions, and these ravaged the country as much as the Turkish territory. Ferdinand and his successors governed from Vienna or Prague and with little reference to the traditional rights of the Hungarian nobility. This led to growing friction and later to serious conflict.

1581-1602. Sigismund Bathory, prince of Transylvania. His efforts to unite with the Hapsburgs for a grand assault on the declining Turk power met with vigorous opposition on the part of the Transylvanian nobility.

1604. Beginning of the Counter-Reformation, under Hapsburg auspices. This resulted in a revolt of the Hungarians, who were supported by the Transylvanians.

1604-1606. STEPHEN BOCSKAY became prince of Transylvania and, after defeating the Hapsburgs, secured the **treaty of Vienna,** by which Protestantism was given equal status with Catholicism. Nevertheless, the Counter-Reformation made great strides, especially among the nobility, due to the efforts of Cardinal Pazmany and the Jesuits.

1613-1629. BETHLEN GABOR (Gabriel Bethlen), prince of Transylvania. He was one of the greatest rulers of the country and made his state the center of Hungarian culture and national feeling. On the outbreak of the **Thirty Years' War,** he openly sided with the enemies of the Hapsburgs and made Transylvania a vital factor in European politics.

1630-1648. GEORGE RÁKÓCZI I, another eminent prince of Transylvania. He continued the policy of his predecessor and managed to guide the country through the storms of the European crisis. At the same time he took full advantage of the growing weakness of the Turks, making Transylvania virtually an independent state, which played a part of some importance in international affairs.

Literary efforts of the 16th and early 17th centuries centered on Scripture translations, along with the poetry of **Valentine Balassa, John Rimay,** and **Nicholas Zrinyi** (1620-1664).

12.   THE OTTOMAN EMPIRE, 1481-1656

(From p. 353)

1481-1512.   BAYAZID II, a man of intellectual tastes, but the least significant of the first ten sultans. He was raised to the throne with the support of the Janissaries, but his position was challenged by his younger brother, Jem **(Djem),** who had himself proclaimed sultan at Bursa, and then proposed a division of the empire. Jem was defeated by Bayazid's forces at Yeni-Shehr and fled, first to Egypt, then to Rhodes. The Knights of St. John sent him to France and extracted from Bayazid a treaty of peace. As a valuable hostage many of the European powers tried to get control of Jem, but he was finally (1489) turned over to the pope, who tried to use him to extract money and support from Bayazid against Charles VIII of France. During the latter's invasion of Italy, Jem fell into his hands. He died under suspicious circumstances at Naples (1495).

1481.   Surrender of the Turks at Otranto.

1484-1491.   War with Egypt for control of Cilicia. Six inconclusive campaigns.

1489.   The Venetians acquired Cyprus from the Christian ruler by bequest, and tried to take advantage of Bayazid's weakness to strengthen their position in the Aegean.

1499-1503.   Venetian-Turkish War, joined by Hungary in 1500. The Turkish fleet, under **Kemal Re'is** (possibly a Greek) defeated the Venetians and took Modon, Koron, and Lepanto. Turk cavalry raided as far as Vicenza. The peace deprived Venice of the lost stations, but left it Nauplion and some of the Ionian islands.

1511.   **Ismail,** shah of Persia, incited an uprising of the Turkish nomads of the Taurus Mountains.

1512-1520.   SELIM I (the Grim). He forced his father to abdicate after a civil war between Bayazid's three sons, Ahmed, Corcud, and Selim. Death of Bayazid.

1513.   Selim defeated his brother Ahmed in Anatolia and had him executed.

1514.   War against Shah Ismail of Persia, who had supported Ahmed. The struggle was accentuated by religious differences, the Kizilbashes in Anatolia being Shi'ites and wholly in sympathy with the Persians. Selim, a fanatic Sunnite, is said to have slaughtered 40,000 of his own heretic subjects before proceeding against the Persians.

1514, Aug. 23.   Selim completely defeated the Persians at **Chaldiran,** east of the Euphrates. He took and plundered Tabriz, but was obliged to fall back because of the objections of the Janissaries to further advance.

1515.   Conquest of eastern Anatolia and Kurdistan by the Turks.

1516.   Selim embarked on a second campaign against Persia, but was diverted by the Mameluke sultan of Egypt, Kansu al-Gauri, who was allied with Persia and appeared at Aleppo with an army.

1516, Aug. 24.   BATTLE OF MARJ DABIK, north of Aleppo. Selim, with the use of artillery, completely defeated Kansu, who was killed. Aleppo and Damascus at once surrendered to the Turks. Selim, anxious to proceed against Persia, offered peace to the new sultan, Tuman Bey, on condition that he accept Turkish suzerainty. This was refused.

1517, Jan. 22.   The Turks took Cairo, and sacked it. The **sherif of Mecca** surrendered voluntarily. The caliph **Mutawakkil** was sent to Constantinople, but after Selim's death returned to Egypt (legend of his having transferred his authority as caliph to Selim). The important thing was that Selim secured control of the Holy Places in Arabia. Tuman Bey was executed, but Egypt left under the rule of the Mameluke beys, under a Turkish governor-general. Legend of the Turks cutting the routes of oriental trade: these had really been cut by the Portuguese, operating at the entrance of the Red Sea.

1520-1566.   SULEIMAN I (the Magnificent), only son of Selim, a highly cultivated but proud and ambitious ruler, generally rated as the greatest of the sultans. In reality he left affairs largely to his famous viziers. **Ibrahim Pasha,** son of a Greek of Parga, practically ruled the empire from 1523 to 1536. In 1524, after an attempt of the Turkish governor of Egypt to set himself up as sultan, Ibrahim completely reorganized the government of the country with more effective control by the Turks.

1521.   Capture of Belgrade, after several assaults. In the succeeding years the Turks raided regularly in Hungary and Austria, creating a panic throughout central Europe.

(*From p. 346*)

Ottoman Sultans (1451–1648)

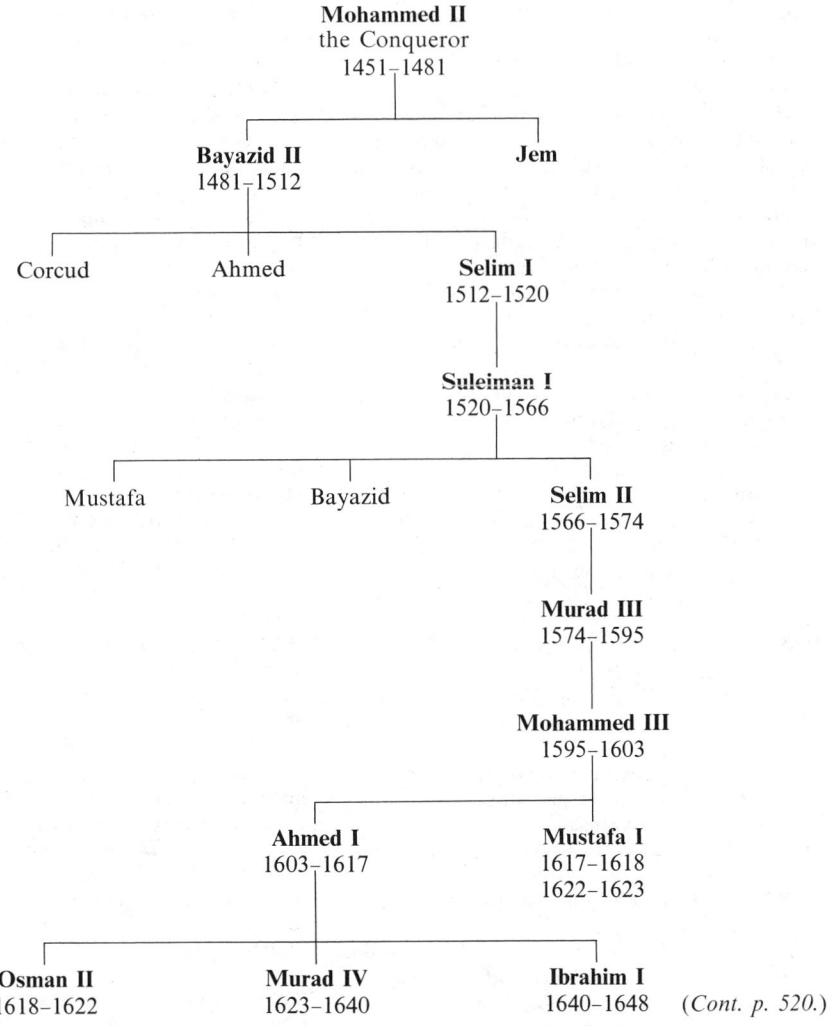

Mohammed II
the Conqueror
1451–1481

Bayazid II
1481–1512

Jem

Corcud   Ahmed

Selim I
1512–1520

Suleiman I
1520–1566

Mustafa   Bayazid

Selim II
1566–1574

Murad III
1574–1595

Mohammed III
1595–1603

Ahmed I
1603–1617

Mustafa I
1617–1618
1622–1623

Osman II
1618–1622

Murad IV
1623–1640

Ibrahim I
1640–1648   (*Cont. p. 520.*)

1522. Capture of Rhodes, which had become the headquarters for Catalan and Maltese pirates who threatened Turkish communications with Egypt. The Knights of St. John put up a valiant defense, but the help expected from the West did not materialize. They thereupon capitulated. In 1530 they were established at Malta by Charles V.

1526, Aug. 29-30. BATTLE OF MOHÁCS. Defeat of King Louis of Hungary and his 20,000 ill-disciplined knights and peasants. Louis was killed and the Turks advanced and took Ofen. Disputed succession in Hungary: John Zápolya elected in Transylvania, Ferdinand of Hapsburg at Pressburg. After two

years of civil war Zápolya was defeated. He appealed to Suleiman.

1528. Second campaign in Hungary. Ofen retaken by the Turks.

1529, Sept. 26. FIRST SIEGE OF VIENNA. After several assaults the Turks withdrew (Oct. 16), partly because of valiant resistance of the garrison, partly because of wretched weather and inability to bring up the heavy artillery. But Suleiman rejected repeated offers of Ferdinand to pay tribute for Hungary in return for recognition.

1529. Khaireddin Pasha, famous Turkish admiral and corsair (originally a Greek of Mytilene in the service of the bey of Tunis, 1512;

entered Turkish service in 1516), took the Peñon of Algiers.

1532.   Turkish campaign in Hungary. The Turks took Güns, after a valiant resistance. Suleiman then retired, because of the threat from Persia.

1533.   Peace between Suleiman and Ferdinand. The latter retained that part of Hungary that he still held; Zápolya remained king of the rest; both paid tribute to the Turks. No peace made with Charles V, so that the naval war in the Mediterranean (Khaireddin and Andrea Doria) continued. Khaireddin evacuated thousands of Moors expelled from Spain.

1533.   Khaireddin drove out the bey of Tunis and ravaged the coasts of Sicily and southern Italy.

1534.   War against Shah Tahmasp of Persia, who had been negotiating with Charles V. The Turks marched to Tabriz, and conquered Baghdad and Mesopotamia.

1535, June–July.   Great **expedition of Charles V to Tunis,** the fleet commanded by Andrea Doria. The town was taken after Khaireddin had been defeated off the coast. Horrible sack of three days. The bey, Mulai Hassan, was reinstated.

1536, Mar.   Formal **alliance between Suleiman and Francis I** of France, against the Habsburgs. This had been under discussion since 1525 and had led to some measure of co-operation.

1537–1540.   War with Venice, forced by the Turkish threat to close the Straits of Otranto. The sultan and Khaireddin raided Apulia and besieged Corfu, with French aid, but were obliged to give up the project.

1538.   Holy League against the Turks (Charles V, the pope, and Venice). Abortive efforts of Charles V to buy off Khaireddin. After a defeat at sea **(battle of Prevesa)** the Venetians made peace (1540), losing Nauplion, their last station in the Morea, and paying a large indemnity.

1538.   Turkish naval expedition through the Red Sea to the northwest coast of India. The entire east coast of the Red Sea (Yemen, Aden) was taken over.

1540.   Death of John Zápolya, leaving an infant son as his successor, whom Suleiman recognized. Invasion of Hungary by Ferdinand, who tried to make good his claim to the whole country.

1541.   Suleiman's campaign in Hungary. He marched to Buda and took over control during the minority of John Sigismund Zápolya. Direct Turkish administrative control established.

1543.   A combined French and Turkish fleet took **Nice.**

1547.   Five years' truce between Suleiman and Ferdinand; the Turks retained the larger part of Hungary and Ferdinand paid tribute for the small strip remaining to him.

1548.   Second expedition against Persia. Tabriz again occupied.

1551–1562.   Renewal of war with Ferdinand. This was carried on in desultory fashion and consisted chiefly of sieges. After Ferdinand's succession to the imperial throne peace was made, Zápolya receiving Transylvania, the Turks retaining Hungary proper, and Ferdinand paying tribute for the western section.

1552.   The Persians took the offensive and captured Erzerum.

1553.   Suleiman proceeded against the Persians and ravaged the western part of the country. Peace was made in 1555, Suleiman retaining his conquests in Mesopotamia.

1554.   Dragut, successor of Khaireddin (d. 1546), took Mehedia, a stong base on the Tunisian coast, from the Spaniards. The **conquest of the North African coast** was completed in the following two years.

1565.   Turkish siege of Malta, the headquarters of the Spanish corsairs. After taking one of the three main forts the Turks were obliged to withdraw.

1566, Sept. 5.   Death of Suleiman, at the siege of Szigeth. His last years had been embittered by family troubles. His wife, **Roxelana** (probably a Russian captive), and her son-in-law, the grand vizir **Rustem Pasha,** so poisoned his mind against his eldest son, Mustafa, that he had him strangled in 1553. There ensued a conflict between the sons of Roxelana, Selim and Bayazid. The latter took up arms in 1559, but was defeated at Konia. He fled to Persia, where he and his sons were executed in return for a high money payment by Suleiman. But Suleiman left the empire the greatest in Europe and the best organized, an easy match for the European powers, rent by dynastic and religious antagonisms.

1566–1574.   SELIM II (the Sot), an intelligent but indolent ruler, much given to drink. Divided counsels of **Mehmed Sökullu** (grand vizir, 1560–1579), who favored close relations with Venice and continuance of the war against Spain (peace made with Maximilian in 1568), and the friend of Selim, **Don Joseph Nasi,** most prominent of the thousands of Spanish Jews who settled in Constantinople, Saloniki, Adrianople, and other towns of the empire after the expulsions from Spain and Italy. Nasi had come to Constantinople in 1553 and had financed Selim in the struggle with Bayazid. In return Selim had induced Suleiman to grant Nasi the region about Lake Tiberias, where Nasi undertook to settle Jewish refugees from Italy. In 1566 Selim made him duke of

Naxos and other Aegean islands. Nasi was hostile to France and Venice, for personal reasons.

1569. Ottoman expedition against the Russians. Siege of Astrakhan followed by conclusion of peace (1570).

1570. Nasi persuaded the sultan to declare **war on Venice,** after the latter had refused to cede Cyprus, which Nasi may have intended to make a refuge for Jews. Spain joined Venice in the war, but the two allies were unable to co-operate successfully and their fleets delayed the relief of Cyprus until too late.

1571, May 20. **Pope Pius V** finally succeeded in organizing a **Holy League** against the Turks. A great armada, under **Don John of Austria,** assembled at Messina.

Aug. 3. The Turks took Famagusta, after a siege of eleven months and six assaults.

Oct. 7. **BATTLE OF LEPANTO,** between the allied fleets (208 galleys, including 6 immense galleasses) and the Turks (230 galleys) under supreme command of **Ali Pasha.** After a ferocious fight of three hours, 80 Turkish galleys were sunk and 130 captured; 40 escaped from the wing. Greatest naval battle since Actium. Tremendous joy throughout Europe. But the advantages of the victory were lost through continued dissension between the Spaniards and the Venetians, the former insisting on the reconquest of North Africa, the latter desiring to reconquer Cyprus. The Turks rebuilt their fleet with astounding rapidity, and Don John refused to attack it in the Adriatic in 1572.

1572. **Don John took Tunis,** which had been captured by the Turks in 1569.

1573. Mar. The Venetians deserted the Spaniards and made peace, abandoning Cyprus and paying an indemnity of 300,000 ducats.

1574. The Turks drove the Spaniards out of Tunis again. Despite the Lepanto disaster, the Turks continued to ravage the coasts of the western Mediterranean during the rest of the century.

1574–1595. MURAD III.

1581. **Peace between Spain and the Turks** (definitive 1585) based on the *status quo.*

1585. Beginning of the phenomenal **decline of the empire,** due to the degeneracy of the sultans, the abandonment of the government to vizirs (mostly favorites), the growth of corruption and harem influence, the emergence of governing cliques (Jews, Greeks, etc.) and the inevitable decline of the military organization, especially the Janissary corps, to which Turks were gradually admitted. As the empire had advanced to the frontier of strong European states, conquests became more difficult and military grants fewer. The soldiers had to be kept quiet with presents and favors. Before long the Janissaries became a veritable praetorian guard, making and unmaking sultans. The period was marked by rising taxation and general decline in the treasury. On the other hand, the Dutch, English, and French began to develop an extensive trade in the Levant.

1590. **Peace between the Turks and Persia,** after a long and desultory war that had begun in 1577. The Turks acquired Georgia, Azerbaijan, and Shirwan, thus extending their frontiers to the Caucasus and Caspian.

1593–1606. War between Austria and the Turks, in which **Sigismund Bathory,** prince of Transylvania, took the side of the emperor.

1595–1603. MOHAMMED III.

1596. **Turkish victory at Keresztes** (near Erlau in northern Hungary). The campaigning, however, remained desultory, due to the preoccupation of the emperor with Transylvania, which he took successively from Bathory and from Michael the Brave of Moldavia. The Turks thereupon supported **Stephen Bocskay** and helped him drive out the Austrians (1605).

1602–1618. War with the Persians **(Abbas the Great),** who had completely reorganized their forces (with the help of **Sir Anthony** and **Sir Robert Shirley;** mission of Sir Anthony to Europe to secure co-operation).

1603. **Abbas retook Tabriz,** and then Erivan, Shirwan, and Kars. After a great victory at Lake Urmia, **Abbas took Baghdad,** Mosul, and Diarbekr. Peace was made in 1612, but the war was renewed in 1616. By the **treaty of 1618** the Turks abandoned Azerbaijan and Georgia.

1603–1623. AHMED I.

1606. **Treaty of Zsitva-Török** (first peace treaty signed by the Turks outside Constantinople) between the Turks and Austrians. The Austrians abandoned Transylvania to Bocskay, but were recognized by the Turks as equals and ceased paying tribute for their part of Hungary.

1623–1640. MURAD IV, a boy of fourteen, who found the empire wracked by revolts and at the mercy of insubordinate Janissaries. By savage ruthlessness Murad asserted his authority.

1625. Murad's efforts to retake Baghdad were foiled by new uprisings, which he again suppressed with great ferocity.

1630. Murad took Hamadan from the Persians.

1635. The Turks reconquered Erivan and Tabriz.

1638. Murad retook Baghdad. By the **treaty of Kasr-i Shīrīm** (1639) a permanent border was finally established, the Persians keeping Erivan, the Turks Baghdad.

1638. Murad abolished the tribute in Christian children, reorganized the system of military fiefs, reduced the Janissary corps, and began the organization of a new military system. This first effort at reform was ended with his death in 1640.

1645-1664. Long **WAR WITH VENICE,** occasioned by Turkish designs on Candia (Crete). The Venetians showed themselves far stronger than the Turks and sent their fleets into the Straits. The Janissaries thereupon revolted, deposed **Ibrahim I** (1640–1648) and put on the throne

1648-1687.   MOHAMMED IV, a boy of ten. There followed another period of anarchy, brought to an end in 1656 by a great Venetian victory off the Dardanelles.

1656.   Mohammed Kiuprili, made grand vizir. He was a simple Albanian pasha, noted for his energy and firmness.   (*Cont. p. 518.*)

B. SCIENCE AND LEARNING, 1450–1700

1. SCIENCE

1469. Publication of Pliny's *Historia naturalis,* the first scientific book to be printed.

1500.   Hieronymus Brunschwig (1450–c. 1512) published *Das Buch der rechten kunst zu distillieren;* its bold woodcuts were the first illustrations to depict chemical apparatus and operations.

1527-1541.   Philippus Paracelsus [Theophrastus von Hohenheim] (1493–1541) crusaded for the use of chemicals in the treatment of disease. He introduced the system of salt, sulphur, and mercury as the three prime "elements," from which all things are made.

1537.   Niccolò Tartaglia (?1500–1557), in *Nova scientia,* discussed the motion of heavy bodies and the shape of the trajectory of projectiles.

1540. Posthumous publication of *De la pirotechnica,* a handbook of metallurgy containing information about smelting and ore reduction compiled by **Vannoccio Biringuccio** (1480–1539).

1542.   Leonhart Fuchs (1501–1566) used the botanical work of his contemporaries, **Otto Brunsfels** (1488–1534), **Jerome Bock** (1498–1554), and **Conrad Gesner** (1516–1565) to prepare a great herbal, describing some four hundred plants, illustrated by realistic woodcuts.

1543.   NICOLAUS COPERNICUS [Niklas Kopernik] (1473–1543) published *De revolutionibus orbium coelestium,* which asserted that the planets, including the earth, circle around a stationary sun. He believed this theory represented the true structure of the world.

1543.   ANDREAS VESALIUS (1514–1564) produced *De fabrica corporis humani,* an illustrated, systematic study of the human body. This work is a union of Renaissance artistic endeavor and of a revived interest in the empirical study of **human anatomy.**

1545.   Jerome Cardan (1501–1576) published the solution of the **cubic equation** in *Ars Magna.* This solution, the first major advance in mathematics in the European Renaissance, was due to **Niccolò Tartaglia** (?1500–1557), and was used without his permission.

1545-1573.   Ambroise Paré (1510–1590) encouraged a **pragmatic approach to surgery.** He promoted the dressing of gunshot wounds rather than the traditional practice of cauterizing them with boiling oil.

1546.   Georgius Agricola [Georg Bauer] (1494–1555) applied observation rather than mere speculation to the study of rocks, publishing *De natura fossilium,* an early handbook of mineralogy, and *De re metallica* (1556), which dealt with mining and metallurgy.

1546.   Girolamo Fracastoro (?1483–1553) developed the theory that **contagion** (infectious disease) is caused by a living agent transmitted from person to person.

1551.   Erasmus Reinhold (1511–1553) issued the *Prutenic Tables* (*Tabulae Prudenticae*), astronomical tables based on numerical values provided by Copernicus. These were an improvement on the *Alfonsine Tables* then widely in use.

1551-1555.   Pierre Belon (1517–1564) and **Guillaume Rondolet** (1507–1566) initiated the study of **comparative anatomy** with their studies of fishes.

1551-1587.   Conrad Gesner (1516–1565) amassed in the first great Renaissance encyclopedia, *Historia animalium,* ancient and contemporary knowledge of the animal kingdom.

1554.   Jean Fernel (1497–1558) codified the practical and theoretical medicine of the Renaissance, rejecting magic and astrology but emphasizing the functions of organs.

1572.   TYCHO BRAHE (1546–1601) observed a bright new star, a *super nova,* and determined that it was beyond the moon, thereby destroying the prevailing Aristotelian notion that no change occurred in celestial regions. Through systematic observation, using instruments designed by himself, Tycho accumulated very accurate data on planetary and lunar positions and produced the **first modern star catalog.**

1572. Volcher Coiter (1543–1576) revived interest in **descriptive embryology.**

1582. Pope Gregory XIII (1502–1585) introduced, into the Catholic nations, the **Gregorian** or **New Style calendar.** This reformed calendar utilized astronomical data compiled during the 16th century.

1583. Andrea Cesalpino (1519–1603) compiled the first modern **classification of plants** based on a comparative study of forms.

1585. Simon Stevin (1548–1620) published *La disme,* introducing decimal fractions into arithmetic. A year later he published treatises on **statics and hydrostatics.** The work on statics gave a mathematical proof of the law of the lever, elegantly proved the law of the inclined plane, and showed that two unequal weights fell through the same distance in the same time.

1591. François Viète [Vieta] (1540–1603) introduced **literal notation** in algebra, i.e., the systematic use of letters to represent both coefficients and unknown quantities in algebraic equations.

c. 1600. Dutch lens-grinders in Middleburg are thought to have constructed the **first refracting telescope** and the **compound microscope.**

1600. William Gilbert (1540–1603) provided in *De magnete* a methodical experimental study of the **electric and magnetic properties of bodies,** and established that the earth itself is a magnet.

1603. Johann Bayer (1572–1625) produced a **celestial atlas** which introduced the use of Greek letters to indicate the brightest stars in every constellation.

1603. Foundation of the **Accademia dei Lincei,** one of the earliest learned societies, at Rome.

1609. JOHANNES KEPLER (1571–1630) announced in *Astronomia nova* his first two **laws of planetary motion:** planets move in ellipses with the sun in one focus; the radius vector from the sun to a planet sweeps out equal areas in equal times. In *Harmonices mundi* (1619) he added his third law: the squares of the periods of revolution of all planets are proportional to the cubes of their mean distances from the sun.

1610. GALILEO GALILEI (1564–1642), in *Sidereus nuncius,* revealed the results of the first telescopic observations of celestial phenomena. He used these observations to destroy the Aristotelian-Ptolemaic cosmology and to argue for the plausibility of the Copernican system.

1614. John Napier (1550–1617) introduced **logarithms** as a computational tool.

1627. Kepler, on the basis of Tycho Brahe's observations and his own theories, compiled the *Rudolphine Tables* (*Tabulae Rudolfinae*) which made possible the calculation of future planetary positions and other astronomical events; they were standard for over a century.

1628. WILLIAM HARVEY (1578–1657) in his classic *Exercitatio anatomica de motu cordis et sanguinis in animalibus* blended reason, comparative observation, and experimentation to demonstrate the **circulation of the blood.**

1632. Galileo fashioned in *Dialogo sopra i due massimi sistemi del mondo Tolemaico e Copernicano* a brilliant polemical masterpiece, which clearly showed the superiority of the Copernican system over the Ptolemaic system of the world. This work led to **Galileo's trial and recantation** before the Roman Inquisition of the Catholic Church.

1637. RENÉ DESCARTES (1596–1650) published *Discours de la méthode,* an introduction to his philosophy, which served as a preface to his works on dioptrics, meteorology, and geometry. In the same year he published *La géometrie,* setting forth an **analytic geometry,** i.e., representation of geometric figures by algebraic equations and algebraic equations by geometric figures. **Pierre de Fermat** (?1608–1665) simultaneously and independently developed an analytic geometry. Both Descartes and Fermat applied analytic geometry to the finding of tangents to curves; Fermat also devised a general method for finding maxima and minima.

1638. Galileo in *Discorsi e demonstrazione matematiche intorno a due nuove scienze* established the basic principles of a mathematical description of falling bodies and projectile motion.

1642–1671. Blaise Pascal (1623–1662) constructed the first **adding machine** that could perform the operation of carrying. Some thirty years later, **Gottfried Wilhelm Leibniz** (1646–1716) invented a more complex calculating machine which would multiply rapidly by repeated additions.

1644. Descartes in his *Principia philosophiae* provided mechanistic explanations in terms of matter and motion of a wide variety of physical, chemical, and biological phenomena, and presented his **vortex theory of planetary motion.**

1648. Jan Baptista van Helmont (1577–1644), in his posthumously published collected works,

Ortus medicinae, assigned the name "gas" to the "wild spirits" which were produced in various chemical processes and argued that acid fermentation, not "innate heat," was the operative agent of digestion.

1654. Correspondence between Pascal and Fermat on mathematical treatment of games of chance resulted in the beginning of **probability theory.**

1655. John Wallis (1616-1703) published *Arithmetica infinitorum,* which studied infinite series, infinite products, solved problems of quadratures, and found tangents by use of infinitesimals.

1657. The foundation of the **Accademia del Cimento** of Florence, the first organized scientific academy and a center for the new experimental science which stemmed from the work of Galileo.

1659. Christiaan Huygens (1629-1695) revealed, in *Systema Saturnium,* that Saturn is surrounded by a thin, flat ring.

1660-1674. ROBERT BOYLE (1627-1691) described his first **pneumatic pump,** an improvement on that invented by **Otto von Guericke** (1602-1686), in *New Experiments Physicomechanical, Touching the Spring of the Air.* In the second edition (1662) Boyle noted the relation between pressure and volume now called **Boyle's Law.** With this pump Boyle showed that animals die from a lack of air, not from the accumulation of noxious vapors. So began an era in respiration studies that included the elucidation of lung structure (1661) by **Marcello Malpighi** (1628-1694), the proof that fresh air is necessary for respiration (1667) by **Robert Hooke** (1635-1703), the observation that blood changes color when in contact with air (1667-1669) by **Richard Lower** (1631-1691), and the demonstration that the volume of air is reduced in respiration (1674) by **John Mayow** (1640-1679).

1661. Boyle published his *Sceptical Chymist,* which contained a vigorous criticism of the Aristotelian theory of elements and the Paracelsian theory of principles.

1662. Charles II of England chartered **The Royal Society of London,** an independent organization that became the major center of English scientific activity during the 17th and 18th centuries.

1662. Jeremiah Horrocks (1619-1641) predicted and was the first man to observe (1639) a **transit of Venus** across the disk of the sun. His work was posthumously published in *Venus in sole visa* (1662).

1664. Publication of Descartes' posthumous work *L'homme,* expounding a mechanistic interpretation of the animal body. **Giovanni Borelli** (1608-1679), in *De motu animalium*

(1680), linked Galilean mechanics to Cartesian mechanistic biology.

1663. Pascal reported his principles and experiments on hydrostatics and pneumatics.

1664-1668. Isaac Barrow (1630-1677), the teacher of **Isaac Newton,** showed, in his mathematical lectures at Cambridge University, that the method of finding tangents and the method of finding areas were inverse processes.

1665. The Royal Society of London published the first issue of its *Philosophical Transactions* (March 1665), the first scientific journal in the English-speaking world.

1665. Robert Hooke published *Micrographia,* containing descriptions of his microscopic observations. He first used the word *cells* to describe the lacework of rigid walls seen in cork. The observations of Hooke and other classical microscopists—**Marcello Malpighi, Nehemiah Grew** (1641-1712), **Jan Swammerdam** (1637-1680), **Antony van Leeuwenhoek** (1632-1723)—revealed the complex minute structure of living matter and the existence of micro-organisms.

1666. Louis XIV of France founded the **Académie Royale des Sciences,** a government-controlled and financed organization dedicated to experimental science. The activity of the Académie was regularly recorded in the *Journal des Savants,* one of the earliest scientific periodicals. In 1667 the king founded the **Observatoire de Paris** and named the Italian astronomer **Giovanni Domenico Cassini** (1625-1712) as its first director (1669).

1669. Erasmus Bartholin (1625-1698) published his observations on double refraction in crystals of Iceland spar.

1669. ISAAC NEWTON (1642-1727) announced his **calculus,** in *De analysi per aequationes numero terminorum infinitas,* which circulated in manuscript but was first published in 1711. He further developed the calculus in *Methodus fluxionum et serierum infinitarum* (1671, published 1736), using as fundamental notions "fluxions" (time derivatives) and "fluents" (inverse of fluxions), fluents being interpreted as areas.

1669. Nicolaus Steno [Niels Stensen] (?1631-1687?) established the fundamental concept of the superposition of strata settling from water, and also observed the constancy of interfacial angles in quartz crystals, basic to mineralogy.

1669. Jan Swammerdam, by his study of insect metamorphosis, provided the apparent proof which entrenched for the next century the **doctrine of preformation.** Preformation held that the foetus exists before fertilization as a complete miniature in either the egg or the sperm.

1669. Johann Joachim Becher (1635-1682) asserted that all bodies are composed of air, water, and three earths: *terra lapida, terra mercurialis,* and *terra pinguis.* In combustion the "fatty earth" (*terra pinguis*) burns away, and in calcination it is driven off by the action of fire. This was a forerunner of the phlogiston theory (1723).

1671–1684. Cassini discovered four new **satellites of Saturn** and observed a dark marking in Saturn's ring.

1671–1673. Jean Richer (1630–1696), on a scientific expedition to Cayenne (latitude 5°N), found the **intensity of gravity** was less near the equator than in higher latitudes.

1672. Newton presented to the Royal Society a **reflecting telescope** which he constructed on principles learned in his optical studies. Newton also published his "New Theory about Light and Colors" showing notably that white light is composed of the various spectral colors, each of which has a different index of refraction.

1673. Christiaan Huygens announced in *Horologium oscillatorium* the invention and theory of the **pendulum clock.** This work included theorems on centrifugal force in circular motion.

1674. John Mayow asserted in his *Tractatus quinque medico-physici* that the air contains "nitro-aërial particles," which he thought necessary to support combustion and respiration.

1675. Olaus Roemer (1644–1710), by studying the eclipses of Jupiter's moons, determined that light is transmitted with a finite, though very great, speed.

1675. Charles II of England established the **Royal Observatory, Greenwich** and designated **John Flamsteed** (1646–1719) as the first Astronomer Royal.

1676. Thomas Sydenham (1624–1689) rejected the view that the diseased state was an exception to natural law. He emphasized the importance of clinical observation, experience, and common sense in therapy.

1678. Robert Hooke provided an account of the law of elastic force, *ut tensio, sic vis* (stress is proportional to strain), which is now known by his name.

1679. Edmé Mariotte (?1620–1684) announced his discovery of the constant **relation between the pressure and volume** of an enclosed quantity of air (discovered independently of Robert Boyle).

1681. Thomas Burnet (1635–1715) published *Telluris theoria sacra,* the most popular of several religiously orthodox cosmogonical treatises of the late 17th century, focusing on Noah's flood as the central fact of earth history.

1684. LEIBNIZ first published his **differential calculus,** based on work done independently of Newton during the period 1673–1676. Leibniz based his calculus on the finding of differentials, which he understood as infinitesimal differences, and defined the integral as an infinite sum of infinitesimals; the operations of summing and of finding the differences were mutually inverse. His vision of a universal symbolic language led him to devise notation of great heuristic power, such as *d* for differential and ∫ for integral.

1686–1704. John Ray (1627–1705) in the three volumes of *Historia generalis plantarum* provided an able account of the structure, physiology, and distribution of plants and laid the foundations of modern **systematic classification.**

1687. NEWTON in his *Philosophiae naturalis principia mathematica* founded mechanics, both celestial and terrestrial, on his three axioms or **laws of motion.** He demonstrated that the sun attracts the planets and the earth attracts the moon with a force inversely proportional to the square of the distance between them. In his **principle of universal gravitation** he states that any two bodies attract each other with a force proportional to the product of their masses and inversely proportional to the square of the distance between them.

1688. Francesco Redi (1621–1697) challenged the ancient belief in spontaneous generation and began a two-century-long debate on the subject by his controlled experimentation on the production of maggots.

1690. Christiaan Huygens developed in his *Traité de la lumière* a mechanistic theory which presents light as a propagation of impulses in a subtle aether. He used this theory to explain reflection, refraction, and double refraction.

1696. Guillaume de L'Hôpital (1661–1704) published the first textbook of the **infinitesimal calculus,** *Analyse des infiniment petits,* based on the lectures of his teacher, **Johann Bernoulli** (1667–1748).

1697. Bernoulli showed that the curve of quickest descent was the cycloid, thereby solving the first problem of the **calculus of variations.**

(*Cont. p. 522.*)

2. MECHANICAL INVENTIONS AND TECHNOLOGICAL ACHIEVEMENTS

c. 1450. **Printing** with moveable type introduced into Europe by **JOHANNES GUTENBURG** (?1400–1468). **Laurens Coster** (fl. 1440), cheapened and widened the diffusion of knowledge. This development accompanied an increased use of wood-block illustrations.

1485. Publication of **Leon Battista Alberti's** (1404–1472) *De re aedificora* exemplifies the extended interests of Renaissance architects and artists in the realm of applied science. A more famous example is **Leonardo da Vinci** (1452–1519), who was a military engineer and speculated on various types of machines. Structural theory did not advance until the work of **Galileo Galilei** (*Dialogues concerning Two New Sciences,* 1638), **Christopher Wren,** and **Robert Hooke.** The revival of interest in classical architecture, sparked by the rediscovery of the works of Vitruvius, led architects to develop new techniques, flat ceiling, and the dome. Some architects of the period were **Filippo Brunelleschi** (?1377–1446), **François Mansard** (1598–1666), **Claude Perrault** (1613–1688), **François Blondel** (1617–1686), **Inigo Jones** (1573–1652), and **Christopher Wren** (1632–1723).

1500. The expansion of trade brought a **development in ship construction.** Galleys were in use until the 17th century but the fully rigged ship with stern-post rudder developed during the 15th century, and by 1700 the four-masted galleon had evolved.

c. 1510. First of the handbooks on metallurgy appeared, *Probierbergbüchlein* on assaying, *Bergbüchlein* on mining. In 1540 **Vannocio Biringuccio's** (1480–1539) *Pyrotechnica* published, the first practical, comprehensive metallurgy text by a professional metallurgist. Included were descriptions of alloying and cannon-molding processes. In 1556 *De re metallica* of Agricola (Georg Bauer), a physician in the mining area of Saxony, appeared. It covered all aspects of mining from the survey of the site through the equipment and methods of mining to assaying, blast and glass furnace descriptions as well as the treatment of iron, copper, and glass. Agricola was concerned with miners' health, and described the diseases to which they are prone.

1520. **Wheel lock** invented, probably in Italy, one of the steps to a single-handed pistol. **Rifling** of the gun barrel was a known technique, 1525, and by 1697 **iron cannon** were cast directly from the blast furnace.

1533. The principle of **triangulation** in surveying discovered by **Gemma Frisius,** a German. More technical maps began to appear to replace the earlier Portalan maps (first **road map of Europe** appeared in Germany, 1511). **Maritime charts** were improved; in 1536 **Pedro Nuñez** (1492–1577) wrote on the errors in the plain charts used at sea. In 1569 **Gerhard Mercator** [Kremer] (1512–1594) devised the mercator chart; in 1600 the first seaman's calendar appeared. The **telescope,** invented c. 1590, and the back-staff (1595) of **John Davis** (?1550–1605), superseded the older navigational instruments, the astrolabe and cross-staff.

c. 1589. **William Lee** (d. 1610) invented the first frame **knitting machine,** slowly accepted during the 17th century.

1560–1660. Increased **use of coal,** especially in England, as a power source. The output of coal in Newcastle rose from 32,951 tons in 1563–1564 to 529,032 tons in 1658–1659. The use of coal was dictated by serious deforestation both in England and on the Continent. By 1615 wood-fired glass furnaces were illegal in England; thus technology was stimulated by the necessity of using coal.

1575–1680. The evolution of the **glass-maker's "chair."** Many new techniques were introduced into glass-making, including those of producing ruby glass (before 1620), lead and white glass (1679).

1603. **Cannon** were bored in Spain. By 1650 lead shot was molded by means of a split mold.

1698. **Thomas Savery's** (?1650–1715) steam engine. The steam mill of **Giovanni Branca,** 1629, was ill conceived, and the engine of **Denis Papin,** 1688, was not developed and had no effect on the Industrial Revolution.

1700. By this date many **foods and crops** were exchanged between Europe, Asia, and the Americas. From the New World came the **potato** (in Spain c. 1570), maize, tea, chocolate, **tobacco. Coffee** grew wild in Ethiopia (known c. 1450) and was introduced into Europe (in England by 1650). By this date **sugar** was a common, cheap commodity in England; cane was shipped to America to form the basis of the industry in the Caribbean in the 18th century. **Cotton** was exported to America where it became an important crop.

(*Cont. p. 526.*)

C. EUROPE AND THE NEAR EAST, 1648–1812

1. ENGLAND, SCOTLAND, AND IRELAND, 1648–1812

[For a complete list of the kings of England see Appendix VI.]

(From p. 405)

1649–1660. The **COMMONWEALTH**, a republican form of government. Power in the army and its leader **Oliver Cromwell.** Theoretically legislative power still in the Rump (some 50 Independent members of the Long Parliament), executive power in a council of state of 41 (three judges, three officers of the army, five peers, 30 members of the commons). Title and office of king abolished, as was the house of lords.

1649, Feb. 5. The Scots proclaimed **Charles II** in Edinburgh and the Irish rose in his favor under Ormonde. Cromwell went to Ireland himself and quickly suppressed the rebellion at the **storming of Drogheda** (Sept. 12) and **Wexford.** Massacres of both garrisons. Cromwell returned to London (May) leaving Ireton to complete his work. By 1652 the Cromwellian settlement had been achieved. Catholic landholders were dispossessed in favor of Protestants; many Catholics killed. The Irish question took on a new bitterness.

1650. **Montrose** came again to Scotland, was beaten at **Corbiesdale** (April 27), captured and executed at Edinburgh (May 21).

June 24. **Charles II** landed in Scotland, took the covenant, and was proclaimed king. At the **battle of Dunbar** (Sept. 3) the Scots under Leslie were totally defeated by Cromwell. Charles II, however, was crowned at Scone and marched on into England while Cromwell took Perth (Aug. 2, 1651). Cromwell then turned and pursued the king, completely defeated the royal army at the **battle of Worcester** (Sept. 3). Charles in disguise escaped to France, after romantic adventures.

1651, Oct. 9. **First Navigation Act** passed forbidding the importation of goods into England except in English vessels or in vessels of the country producing the goods. This typical measure of mercantile economy helped the British merchant marine to gain supremacy over the Dutch.

1652, July 8. **War with the Dutch** broke out because of this act. It was almost wholly naval. English commanders, Blake, Monk; Dutch, Tromp, Ruyter. The English won off the **Downs** (May, before the declaration of war); defeated Tromp off **Portland** (Feb. 18, 1653) and off the **North Foreland** (June 2–3).

Monk won an important victory of the **Texel** (July 31) where Tromp died. **Peace with the Dutch** (April 5, 1654).

Trouble had long been brewing between the Rump and the army. Negotiations for the return of confiscated royalist estates led to charges of bribery of members. After an **Act of Indemnity and Oblivion** (Feb. 1652) and an **Act of Settlement for Ireland** (Aug.) had been passed,

1653, Apr. 20. Cromwell turned out the Rump and dissolved the council of state. He set up a new council and a nominated parliament of 140 members, called **Barebones'** or the **Little Parliament** (July 4). The Cromwellians in parliament resigned their powers to Cromwell (Dec. 12), who set up the **Protectorate** (Dec. 16).

1653, Dec. 16–1658, Sept. 3. CROMWELL, LORD PROTECTOR OF THE COMMONWEALTH OF ENGLAND, SCOTLAND, AND IRELAND. The *Instrument of Government,* a written constitution. The executive (lord protector) had a co-operative council of 21; there was a standing army of 30,000; parliament was to be triennial, and composed of 460 members; once summoned, it could not be dissolved within five months. The protector and council could issue ordinances between sessions, but parliament alone could grant supplies and levy taxes.

1654, Sept. 3. The **new parliament** quarreled with the protector, who ordered an exclusion of members (Sept. 12). After voting that the office of protector should be elective instead of hereditary, the parliament was dissolved (Jan. 22, 1655).

1655, Mar.–May. The **rising of Penruddock** at Salisbury was suppressed and Penruddock executed. England was divided into 12 military districts, each with a force supported by a tax of 10 per cent on royalist estates. Anglican clergy were forbidden to teach or preach. Catholic priests ordered out of the kingdom. Censorship of the press. Rigid "puritanical" rule in arts and morals.

Oct. **Pacification of Pinerolo,** with France: the duke of Savoy stopped the persecution of the Vaudois and Charles II was to be expelled from France.

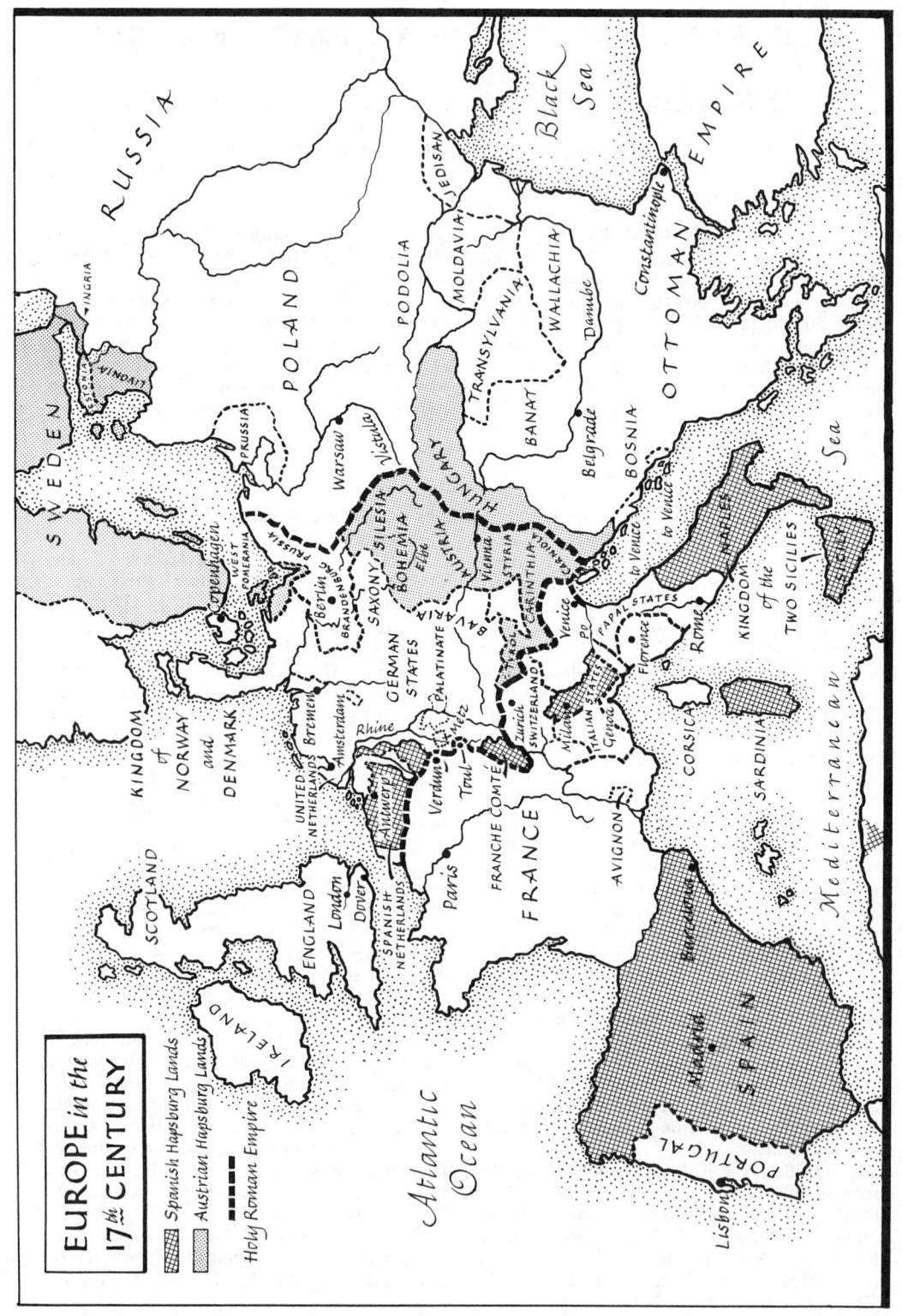

EUROPE in the 17th CENTURY

Spanish Hapsburg Lands
Austrian Hapsburg Lands
Holy Roman Empire

1656–1659. War with Spain. An English raid under Penn and Venables which had captured Jamaica in the West Indies (May) brought on the war. Capture of Spanish treasure ships off **Cadiz** (Sept. 9, 1656). Victory of Blake off **Santa Cruz** (April 20, 1657).

1656, Sept. 17–1658, Feb. 4. Cromwell's third parliament witnessed another exclusion of members, and the **Humble Petition and Advice** (March–May, 1657) altering the constitution. Establishment of a second house; reduction of the power of the council of the state; the protector deprived of the power of excluding members; fixed supply for army and navy; toleration for all trinitarian Christians except Episcopalians and Catholics. Cromwell rejected the title of king (May 8).

1658. Dunkirk besieged by the English and French. A Spanish relieving force was beaten in the **battle of Dunes** (June 4). Dunkirk surrendered to the English, who retained it at the **peace of the Pyrenees** (p. 477).

1658, Sept. 3. Death of Oliver Cromwell.

1658, Sept. 3–1659, May 25. Richard Cromwell, Oliver's son, lord protector. A new parliament met (Jan. 27, 1659) and was soon involved in a dispute with the army, which induced Richard to dissolve parliament (Apr. 22). The Rump Parliament came together under Lenthall as speaker (May 7) and Richard was induced to resign as lord protector. After the futile insurrection of Booth (Aug.) the army, under Lambert, expelled the Rump and appointed a military committee of safety (Oct.). There was a reaction against military *coups d'état,* and the Rump was restored (Dec. 26).

1660, Feb. 3. General George Monk led his army from Scotland to London, assumed control as captain-general, and re-established the Long Parliament with the still living members excluded by Pride's Purge restored (Feb. 21). Final dissolution (Mar. 16).

1660, Apr. 14. Charles issued his **declaration of Breda,** proclaiming amnesty to all not especially excepted by parliament, promising liberty of conscience and the confirmation of confiscated estates in the hands of the actual holders. A **Convention Parliament,** 556 members chosen without restrictions (Apr.), returned a favorable answer to Charles (May 1) and proclaimed him king (May 8); on May 29 he entered London.

1660–1685. CHARLES II. The king's brother, James, duke of York, appointed lord high admiral and warden of the Cinque Ports; Monk (later duke of Albemarle), captain-general; Sir Edward Hyde (later earl of Clarendon), chancellor and prime minister. Abolition of the rights of knight service, worship, and purveyance in consideration of a yearly income for the king of £1,200,000. Restoration of the bishops to their sees and to the house of lords. Acts of indemnity for all political offenses committed between January 1, 1637, and June 24, 1660 (the regicide judges were excepted from this act). All acts of the Long Parliament to which Charles I had assented were declared in force. This meant that the Restoration was by no means a restoration of "divine right" monarchy, but rather a restoration of the moderate parliamentarian régime aimed at by Pym and Hampden. The army was disbanded (Oct. 2) except some 5000 men. The Cromwellian settlement of Ireland was reaffirmed.

1660, Dec. 29. Dissolution of the Convention Parliament. Rising of Fifth Monarchy men in London put down (Jan. 1661). Bodies of Cromwell, Ireton, Bradshaw disinterred and scattered. Royalist parliament in Scotland abolished the covenant and repealed all preceding parliamentary enactments for the last twenty-eight years.

1661, May 8–1679, Jan. 24. First parliament of Charles II. The **Cavalier Parliament,** overwhelmingly royalist. Social reaction against puritanism; revival of games, dancing, the theater. Parliament enacted a series of repressive measures since known as the **Clarendon Code** (Clarendon himself was opposed to many of these measures). They were: (1) The **Corporation Act** (Nov. 20, 1661), by which all magistrates were obliged to take the sacrament according to the Church of England, to abjure the covenant, and to take an oath declaring it illegal to bear arms against the king. (2) The **Act of Uniformity** (Aug. 24, 1662), which required clergymen, college fellows, and schoolmasters to accept everything in the Book of Common Prayer (those who refused were the *Nonconformists*). (3) The **Conventicle Act** (May 1664), which forbade nonconformist (dissenting) religious meetings of more than five persons, except in a private household. (4) The **Five-Mile Act** (Oct. 1665), which required all who had not subscribed to the Act of Uniformity to take an oath of non-resistance, swearing never to attempt any change in church or state; and which prohibited all who refused to do this from coming within five miles of any incorporated town, or of any place where they had been ministers. The code, and especially this last act, was impossible of strict enforcement.

1662, May 20. Charles married Catherine of Braganza, daughter of John IV of Portugal. Dunkirk was sold to France for £400,000.

1665–1667. War with Holland, marked by the defeat of the Dutch by the English fleet off

462

(From pp. 295, 396)

The House of Stuart (1603–1714)

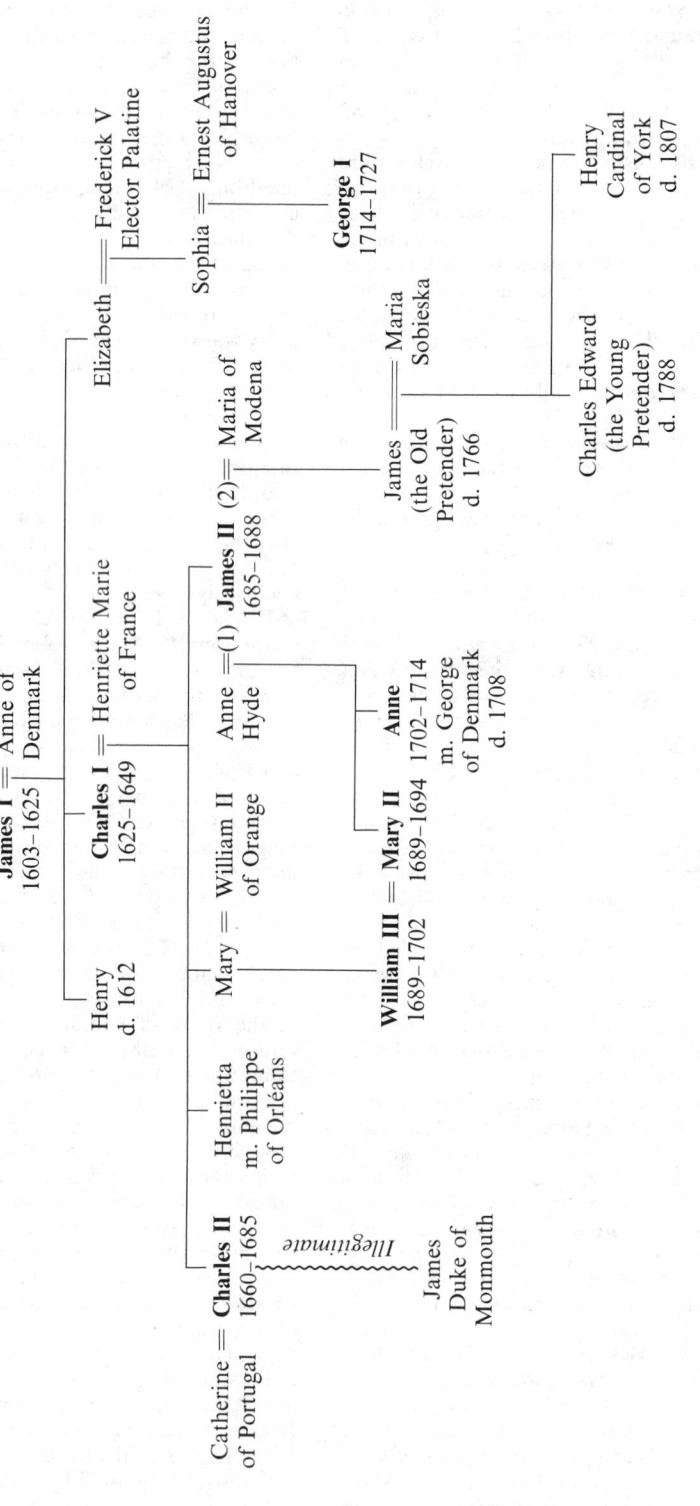

(Cont. p. 469.)

Lowestoft (June 3, 1665). France entered the war against England (Jan. 1666). Albemarle beaten by de Ruyter and De Witt off the North Foreland. Defeat of the Dutch in another naval fight (July 25). The Dutch rallied, burnt Sheerness, entered the Medway (June 1667); low point of English naval power.

1665-1666. Two great domestic disasters: the **great plague** in London (April 1665); the **great London fire** (Sept. 2-9, 1666), burning 450 acres. St. Paul's Cathedral rebuilt by Wren.

1666. The **Scottish Covenanters revolted** against restrictions laid on them by the triumphant Episcopalians, and were crushed by Dalziel in the **battle of Pentland Hills** (Nov. 28).

1667, July 21. **Treaties of Breda** between England, Holland, France, Denmark. England received from France Antigua, Montserrat, St. Kitts; France received Acadia; England and Holland adopted the *status quo* of May 21, 1667, England retaining New Amsterdam and Holland, Surinam. The navigation acts were modified to permit the bringing to England in Dutch vessels of goods brought down the Rhine.

1667. **Clarendon,** who had had to bear the burden of unpopularity for much of the work of the Cavalier Parliament, was forced to resign, and was impeached and exiled. The chief officers of state now began to be looked on as a distinct (if perhaps unconstitutional) council, the nucleus of the future cabinet system. This was emphasized by the accession to power of the so-called **Cabal** (Clifford, Arlington, Buckingham, Ashley, Lauderdale). There was no cabinet solidarity, and no clear party system. The court and the country factions did, however, foreshadow the later **Tories** and **Whigs.** The court (Tory) party were supporters of the royal prerogative, and in a sense heirs of the Cavaliers; the country (Whig) party, supporters of the power of parliament and heirs of the majority group in the Long Parliament, but *not* democrats or radicals. Both *Whig* and *Tory* were originally terms of reproach, the first Scottish, the second Irish in origin.

1668, Jan. 23. The **Triple Alliance** between England, Holland, and Sweden negotiated by Sir William Temple and John De Witt as a check on Louis XIV. Charles II went behind parliament and signed with Louis the **treaty of Dover** (May, 1670) in secret provisions of which he agreed that he and his brother James would openly join the Church of Rome as soon as expedient, and that he would support Louis in his wars with Spain and Holland. Louis promised Charles £200,000 a year while the war lasted and the assistance of 6000 men

in case of an insurrection. James, duke of York, at once professed his belief in Roman Catholicism.

1672, Mar. Charles issued a **Declaration of Indulgence,** which aimed to free both nonconformist Protestants and Catholics from restrictions. Parliament, insisting that the royal power of dispensing from statutory obligations could be applied only to particular, never to generalized, cases, forced him to withdraw the indulgence (1673).

1672, Mar. 17-1674, Feb. 9. **WAR WITH HOLLAND,** pursuant to the policy of the treaty of Dover. English naval victory at **Southwold Bay** (May 28, 1672). **William of Orange,** Dutch stadholder. Marriage of the duke of York with the Catholic Maria d'Este of Modena (Nov. 21, 1673). The war was concluded by the **treaty of Westminster** (Feb. 9, 1674).

1673. The **Test Act,** an attempt to salvage something from the Clarendon Code, and to attack the duke of York and his supporters. All persons holding office were compelled to take oaths of allegiance and of supremacy, to adjure transubstantiation, and to take the sacrament of the Church of England. This act was not repealed until 1828, but it was nullified after 1689 by the typically English practice of passing bills of indemnity to legalize the acts of magistrates who had not conformed—i.e. taken communion in the Established Church—while in office. Such officials were commonly dissenters rather than Roman Catholics.

1673. Shift in the ministry; the duke of York, Shaftesbury, Clifford resigned, being superseded by Prince Rupert, Sir Thomas Osborne (later earl of Danby), Sir Heneage Finch (later earl of Nottingham). Buckingham out of office.

1677, Nov. 4. **Marriage of Mary,** daughter of the duke of York, with **William of Orange** (later William III).

1678, Sept. **The Popish plot.** **Titus Oates** began the scare by alleging that Don John of Austria and Père La Chaise had plotted to murder Charles and establish Roman Catholicism in England. In the ensuing wave of frenzy against the "papists," five Catholic lords (Powys, Bellassis, Stafford, Petre, Arundel) were sent to the Tower. Coleman, confessor of the duchess of York, convicted and executed. Passage of the **Papists' Disabling Act,** excluding Roman Catholics from parliament (repealed 1829).

1679, Jan. 24. **Dissolution of the Cavalier parliament.** Danby, who had been impeached (Dec. 1678) on a charge of criminal correspondence with France, was dismissed from the office of lord high treasurer. The duke of York left the kingdom.

1679, Mar. 6-1680, May 27.   Third parliament of Charles II. Danby's impeachment resumed, but not carried; he remained in the Tower until 1685. A new cabinet council composed of Sir William Temple, Viscount Halifax, the earl of Essex, the earl of Sunderland, and Shaftesbury (afterward in opposition). Introduction of a bill to prevent the duke of York, as a Catholic, succeeding to the throne. Charles fought various exclusion bills, which were backed by Shaftesbury, until he had secured his brother's succession.

1679, May.   The Habeas Corpus Act. Judges were obliged on application to issue to any prisoner a writ of *habeas corpus,* directing the jailer to produce the body of the prisoner, and show cause for his imprisonment; prisoners should be indicted in the first term of their commitment, and tried not later than the second; no person once set free by order of the court could be again imprisoned for the same offense.

1679. The **Covenanters** again rose in Scotland against the repressive measures of Lauderdale. Murder of Archbishop Sharpe (May 3). Defeat of Claverhouse by the Covenanters under Balfour at **Drumclog** (June 1). Defeat of the Covenanters by the duke of Monmouth at **Bothwell Brigg** (June 22). Covenanters, Conventiclers, Cameronians—all shades of Presbyterians repressed, but not successfully. Passage of a **Test Act** against the Presbyterians (1681) caused some eighty Episcopalian bishops to resign. Trial and condemnation of Argyle (Dec. 1681), who fled the kingdom.

1679, Oct. 7. **Charles,** without advice of the cabinet, prorogued his third parliament before it had done any business. Temple, Essex, and Halifax resigned, and were succeeded by the earl of Godolphin and Laurence Hyde, earl of Rochester. Another alleged papist conspiracy **(meal-tub plot)** disclosed by Dangerfield. Petition that parliament be called; whence **petitioners** (country party, Whigs) and those who expressed their abhorrence at this interference with the prerogative, **abhorrers** (court party, Tories).

1680, Oct. 21-1681, Jan. 18.   Fourth parliament of Charles II. The exclusion bill passed the commons, but lost in the lords (Halifax).

1681, Mar. 21-28.   Fifth parliament called at Oxford, and immediately dissolved when the exclusion bill was introduced.

1683, June. Judgment given against the city of London on a *quo warranto;* forfeiture of the charter, which was ransomed. The process repeated for other corporations. Confederacy of leaders of the country party against the policy of Charles, which seemed to them a repetition of earlier Stuart attempts to extend the power of the crown (Essex, Russell, Grey, Howard, Sidney, Hampden, Monmouth). This was supplemented by, and at the same time confused with, the **Rye House plot,** a plan concerted by quite different persons to assassinate the king. Both plots were revealed. Essex committed suicide; Russell and Sidney were executed, becoming republican martyrs for later generations; Monmouth (natural son of Charles and Lucy Walters) was pardoned, and retired to Holland. The duke of York was reinstated in office (Sept.) and Oates, now known to be a liar, was fined.

1685, Feb. 6.   Charles died knowing that his brother would succeed and that the Whigs were at the moment worsted.

1685-1688.   JAMES II, a Roman Catholic, whose tactless attempt to secure freedom of worship for his co-religionists united against him Whigs and Tories in defense of the Anglican Church (*not,* as far as the Tories were concerned, in defense of parliamentary supremacy).

1685, May 19-1687, July 2.   Parliament of James II. Halifax, president of the council; Sunderland, secretary of state; Godolphin, chamberlain; Clarendon, lord privy seal; Rochester, treasurer. Trial and condemnation of Baxter, a dissenting clergyman. Danby and the five Catholic lords were liberated. Oates and Dangerfield were tried, condemned, and sentenced to whipping, from which Dangerfield died (May 1685).

1685.   Rebellion of Monmouth and Argyll. Argyll landed in Scotland, but could not arouse the Covenanters. He was captured and executed (June 30). Monmouth landed in Dorsetshire and proclaimed himself king, but his motley followers were easily beaten at the **battle of Sedgemoor** (July 6)—the last formal warfare in England until German naval attacks and Zeppelin raids in 1914-1918. **Monmouth was executed,** and **Jeffreys** sent on a circuit in the west to try the rebels (*the Bloody Assizes*). Jeffreys became lord chancellor; Halifax was dismissed; Sunderland, converted to Catholicism, took his place.

1686. James set out to test the **anti-papal laws.** By dispensation, he appointed a Catholic, Sir Edward Hales, to office. In a test suit, decision was rendered in favor of the king by judges he had appointed. Compton, bishop of London, refused to remove the rector of St. Giles', who had disobeyed a royal order against violent doctrinal sermons. He was tried before a new court of ecclesiastical commission (July) and suspended. The fellows of Magdalen College, Oxford, having refused to accept Farmer, a Catholic, whom James had appointed their president, were expelled from the college (1687). These and other specific cases were rapidly rousing opinion against the king.

1687. James generalized his action; he issued the first **Declaration of Liberty of Conscience,** granted liberty to all denominations in England and Scotland (Apr.).

1688, Apr. A second **Declaration of Liberty of Conscience** was ordered to be read in all churches. Sancroft, archbishop of Canterbury, and six other bishops were committed to the Tower for having petitioned the king not to insist on their reading what they held to be an illegal order.

June 10. **Birth of a son to James,** said by Whigs at the time to have been introduced in a warming-pan. The knowledge that James's policies might be continued by a son to be brought up as Catholic turned against him many Tories hitherto loyal.

June 29, 30. **Trial of the bishops for seditious libel.** The bishops were acquitted. Great popular enthusiasm. An invitation was dispatched to William of Orange to save England from Catholic tyranny: it was signed by the *seven eminent persons* (Devonshire, Shrewsbury, Danby, Compton, Henry Sidney, Lord Lumley, Admiral Russell).

Sept. 30. **Declaration of William** accepting the invitation. William's real purpose in accepting was to bring England into the struggle against Louis XIV, begun by the **League of Augsburg.** His success reversed the policy of Charles II and James II, which had been broadly pro-French, and re-established English foreign policy along lines which were later considered "traditional"—opposition to any overwhelmingly powerful continental state, especially if that power threatened the Low Countries.

James, frightened by the declaration, dismissed Sunderland and tried to retrace his steps. William left Helvoetsluys with 14,000 men (Oct. 19), but was driven back by a gale.

Nov. 5. **William succeeded in landing** at Torbay. Risings in various sections of England. **Grafton** and **Churchill** (later **duke of Marlborough**) went over to William (Nov. 22). James issued writs for a new parliament and endeavored to treat with William. The queen and the baby prince were sent to France (Dec. 10) and James, throwing the great seal into the Thames, fled on Dec. 11. **Interregnum,** rioting in London, seizure of Jeffreys.

Dec. 12. The peers set up a **provisional government** in London. James, stopped at Sheerness, was brought back to London, but succeeded in escaping to France (Dec. 22),

after William had entered London (Dec. 19). Louis XIV set up the exiled Stuarts at the Court of St. Germain.

1689, Jan. 22–1690, Jan. 27. Convention Parliament, summoned by advice of the peers. On Jan. 28 the commons declared: "That King James II, having endeavored to subvert the constitution of the kingdom by breaking the original contract between king and people, and by the advice of Jesuits and other wicked persons having violated the fundamental laws, and having withdrawn himself out of the kingdom, has abdicated the government, and that the throne is vacant." Also: "That it hath been found by experience to be inconsistent with the safety and welfare of this Protestant kingdom to be governed by a popish prince." The lords objected to the use of the word "abdicated," and to the declaration of the "vacancy" of the throne, but an agreement being reached in a conference of the two houses, the crown was offered to Mary and the regency to William; this being refused, parliament offered the crown to William and Mary jointly.

1689, Feb. 13. The offer was accompanied by the **Declaration of Rights,** asserting the "true, ancient, and indubitable rights of the people of this realm": (1) that the making or suspending law without consent of parliament is illegal; (2) that the exercise of the dispensing power is illegal; (3) that the ecclesiastical commission court and other such like courts are illegal; (4) that levying money without consent of parliament is illegal; (5) that it is lawful to petition the sovereign; (6) that the maintenance of a standing army without the consent of parliament is illegal; (7) that it is lawful to keep arms; (8) that elections of members of parliament must be free; (9) that there must be freedom of debate in parliament; (10) that excessive bail should never be demanded; (11) that juries should be empaneled and returned in every trial; (12) that grants of estates as forfeited before conviction of the offender are illegal; (13) that parliament should be held frequently. William and Mary were declared king and queen of England for life, the chief administration resting with William; the crown was next settled on William's children by Mary; in default of such issue, on the Princess Anne of Denmark and her children; and in default of these, on the children of William by any other wife. The crown was accepted by William and Mary, who were on the same day proclaimed king and queen of Great Britain, Ireland, and France.

1689–1702.   WILLIAM III AND MARY II (until 1694). Privy councillors: earl of Danby (marquis of Carmarthen), president; Nottingham, Shrewsbury, secretaries of state; marquis of Halifax, privy seal; Schomberg (duke of Schomberg), master-general of ordnance; Bentinck (earl of Portland), privy purse.

1689, Feb. 22. The **Convention Parliament** was transformed by its own act into a regular parliament. **Oaths of allegiance and supremacy** were taken by the houses, the clergy, etc. Six bishops and about 400 clergymen refused them, and were deprived of their benefices (1691). These **non-jurors** ordained their own bishops, and maintained their own private Church of England until the 19th century.

Mar. 14. James landed in Ireland with a few followers, was joined by **Tyrconnel,** and entered Dublin (Mar. 24) amid popular enthusiasm. Irish parliament (May 7). James besieged the Protestant town of Londonderry (April 20–July 30), which was finally relieved by Kirke.

The first **Mutiny Act,** to punish defection in the army, made necessary by the **Declaration of Rights** (Mar.), passed henceforth annually. The Protestant dissenters who had disdained James's gift of freedom were rewarded by the **Toleration Act** (May 24) which exempted dissenters who had taken the oaths of allegiance and supremacy from penalties for non-attendance at the services of the Church of England.

1689, May 7. WAR BROKE OUT WITH FRANCE. In Scotland Claverhouse (Viscount Dundee) raised his standard for James among the Highlanders, after episcopacy had been abolished by law. At the **battle of Killiecrankie** (July 17) he defeated the Whig general, Mackay, but fell on the field. The revolt gradually petered out.

1689–1690. A series of measures made the constitutional adjustments necessitated by the **Glorious Revolution.** The system of requiring estimate and accounts for supplies, and of specific appropriations—i.e. the nucleus of modern budgetary systems—now became fixed. The **Bill of Rights** (Dec. 16, 1689) was a parliamentary enactment of the **Declaration of Rights,** repeating the provisions of that paper, settling the succession, and enacting that no Roman Catholic could wear the crown. William's **second parliament** (Mar. 20, 1690–May 3, 1695) by an act of recognition further legalized the already legal acts of the Convention Parliament, settled William's civil list (at a smaller figure than James's or Charles's) and by the **Act of Grace** (May 20, 1690) gave indemnity to all supporters of James II except those in treasonable correspondence with him. Shrewsbury and Halifax resigned.

1690. William went to Ireland, and defeated James at the crucial **battle of the Boyne** (July

1). James fled to France. Dublin and Waterford fell quickly. Limerick resisted successfully under Sarsfield (Aug). In the open field Ginkel defeated Sarsfield and the French St. Ruth at the **battle of Aughrim** (July 12, 1691). Limerick, besieged a second time, surrendered (Oct. 3) under the conditions known as the **pacification of Limerick:** free transportation to France of all Irish officers and soldiers so desiring. (The Irish Brigade in the French armies had a long and distinguished history.) All Irish Catholics to have the religious liberty they had had under Charles II, carry arms, exercise their professions, and receive full amnesty. The English parliament confirmed the treaty, but the Irish parliament, consisting wholly of Protestants, refused to ratify it (1695) and enacted severe anti-Catholic legislation contrary to the pacification terms.

1690, June 30. Defeat of the English fleet by the French at the **battle of Beachy Head.** Lord Torrington, the English admiral, was tried by court martial and acquitted, but dismissed from the service. This defeat was redeemed by the **English naval victory** under Russell over the French under Tourville at **Cap de La Hogue** (May 19, 1692).

1692, Feb. 13. Massacre of Glencoe. The Highlanders, incompletely pacified after Dundee's rising, had been given until December 31, 1691 to take oath to William. This had been done by all the chieftains save MacIan of the MacDonalds of Glencoe. He took the oath on January 6, 1692, but this fact was suppressed by William's agent, the Master of Stair. A company of soldiers commanded by a Campbell (hereditary foes of the MacDonalds), quartered peacefully at Glencoe, turned suddenly on the Highlanders, killed MacIan and some forty others. The incident was of great political use to William's enemies.

William's land campaigns were unsuccessful; he was defeated by the French at **Steinkirk** (July 24, 1692) and at **Neerwinden** (July 29, 1693) (p. 480). At home he was obliged to turn for support to the **Whig Junto**—Somers, lord keeper; Russell, Shrewsbury, Thomas Wharton, secretaries of state; Montague, chancellor of the exchequer. **Marlborough** had been detected in correspondence with James (Jan. 1692) and disgraced. Sunderland returned to parliament.

1693, Jan. Beginning of the national debt. £1,000,000 borrowed on annuities at 10 per cent.

1694, July, 27. Charter of the Governor and Company of the **Bank of England,** a company of merchants who, in return for certain privileges, lent the government £1,200,000. Bill for preventing officers of the crown from sitting in the house of commons **(Place Bill).** Unsuccessful **attack on Brest.**

1694, Dec. 22. The **Triennial Bill** became law; **Queen Mary died** (Dec. 28); the **Licensing Act** ran out, and was not renewed for the next year, thus abolishing censorship of the press.

1695, Nov. 22-1698, July 5. Third parliament of William III (first triennial parliament). Whigs in majority. **Recoinage Act.** Isaac Newton, master of the mint. **Trials for Treason Act** (1696); two witnesses required to prove an act of treason. Plot to assassinate William discovered, and conspirators executed; one of them, Fenwick, was the last person to be condemned by a bill of attainder and executed (1696). Formation of a loyal association. Suspension of the Habeas Corpus Act.

1697, Sept. 20. TREATY OF RYSWICK (p. 480).

1698, Dec. 6-1700, Apr. 11. Fourth parliament of William III. London Stock Exchange, the first true stock exchange, formed (1698). **Disbanding Act,** reducing the army to 7000 men (Feb. 1699). Act for the resumption of forfeited estates, aimed at William's Dutch favorites. Further anti-papal measures: Catholic teachers and priests liable to life imprisonment (repealed 1778).

1701, Feb. 6-June 24. Fifth parliament of William III. Tories in a majority. Harley (later earl of Oxford) speaker. Portland, Somers, Orford (Russell). Halifax impeached (Apr.-June).

June 12. ACT OF SETTLEMENT. The crown was settled on **Sophia,** princess of Hanover, granddaughter of James I, and her issue. The sovereigns of Great Britain were to be Protestant and not leave the kingdom without consent of parliament; the country should not be involved in war for the defense of the foreign possessions of the sovereigns; no foreigner should receive a grant from the crown, or hold office, civil or military; ministers should be responsible for the acts of their sovereigns; judges should hold office for life unless guilty of misconduct.

Sept. 16. Death of James II. His son **James Edward** (the **Old Pretender**) proclaimed king of Great Britain and Ireland by Louis XIV.

1701, Dec. 30-1702, July 2. Sixth parliament of William III. Attainder of James Edward, "pretended" prince of Wales. Oath of abjuration reimposed.

1702, Mar. 8. Death of William III.

1702-1714. ANNE, second daughter of James II, wife of Prince George of Denmark. In the first part of her reign Anne was under the influence of her favorite, **Sarah, duchess of Marlborough,** and her husband, the duke.

1702, May 4. War declared upon France by the Grand Alliance; for this **War of the Spanish Succession,** see p. 481. **Marlborough** was captain-general of the land forces. Godolphin, lord high treasurer; Nottingham, secretary of state. Halifax and Somers not in the privy council.

1702. The campaign: **capture of Venloo and Liège** by the allies, loss of the lower Rhine to France. Sir George Rooke failed to take Cadiz, but seized part of the Spanish treasure fleet at Vigo Bay (Oct.).

1702, Oct. 20-1705, Mar. 14. First parliament of Anne. Harley, speaker.

1703, Nov. Establishment of **Queen Anne's Bounty,** a grant of the first fruits and tithes that Henry VIII had confiscated for the crown, in trust for increasing the incomes of small benefices.

Dec. 27. Treaty between England and Portugal, known from its English negotiator as the **Methuen Treaty.** England admitted Portuguese wines at duties one-third less than those paid by French wines, while Portugal agreed to import all her woolens from England.

1703-1706. Progress of the war: Marlborough took Bonn, Huy, Limburg, and Guelders (1703). Rooke took **Gibraltar** (July 24, 1704). Marlborough's great victory at **Blenheim** (Aug. 13, 1704). Capture of Barcelona by Lord Peterborough (Oct. 4, 1705). **Battle of Ramillies** (May 23, 1706) won by Marlborough.

1707, May 1. UNION OF ENGLAND AND SCOTLAND under the name of **Great Britain.** This measure, which was made necessary by the omission of Scotland from the Act of Settlement, provided that: (1) Sophia, princess of Hanover, and her Protestant heirs should succeed to the crown of the united kingdom; (2) there should be one parliament, to which Scotland should send sixteen elective peers and forty-five members of the commons. No more peers of Scotland to be created. Scottish law and legal administration to be unchanged; the Episcopal Church in England and Presbyterian in Scotland to be unchanged. **Adoption of the Union Jack** (Crosses of St. George and St. Andrew) as the national flag of Great Britain.

Oct. 23. Second parliament of Anne. First parliament of Great Britain. The influence of Marlborough and his wife had been gradually weakened by Harley and by the influence of the queen's new favorite, Abigail Hill, now Mrs. Masham. Marlborough, however, was still so strong that a hint at resignation secured the dismissal of Harley and St. John from the cabinet, and the substitution of Boyle and Robert Walpole (secretary-at-war). Last royal veto.

1708, Mar. James Edward landed in Scotland; the French fleet sent to help him was beaten by

Admiral Byng. The pretender soon returned to France.

1708, Nov. 16–1710, Apr. 5. Third parliament of Anne. Whig majority. Somers, president of the council. Leaders of the Whigs (*Junto*): Somers, Halifax, Wharton, Orford, Sunderland.

1708–1709. The progress of the war: Marlborough won at **Oudenarde** (July 17, 1708) and again after a bloody battle, at **Malplaquet** (Sept. 11, 1709). Marlborough called by his Tory enemies "the butcher."

1710, Feb.–Mar. Trial of Dr. Henry Sacheverell for preaching sermons of an ultra-Tory cast. His conviction further endeared him to the people, and helped the Tory cause.

1710, Nov. 25–1713, July 16. Fourth parliament of Anne. Tory majority clear in the commons. In the lords it was made certain in 1712 by the creation of twelve Tory peers for the purpose. Complete change in ministry. This election was the first clean-cut peaceful transfer of power under the modern party system in England. Harley (earl of Oxford in 1711), lord high treasurer. St. John (Viscount Bolingbroke in 1712), secretary of state. Godolphin dismissed. Mrs. Masham had a large part in this transfer of power. The duke of Marlborough was accused of peculation (Nov. 1711), dismissed from his offices, and supplanted as commander-in-chief by the duke of Ormonde. British participation in the war reduced by Tory policy to a negligible point. Complicated peace negotiations begun with France.

1711. South Sea Company incorporated by vote of parliament in a bill dated 1710. Passage of the **Occasional Conformity Bill**, directed against dissenters who technically satisfied the Test Act by one communion in an Anglican Church, and then attended a nonconformist "chapel" regularly. **Landed Property Qualification Act**, an attempt by landed proprietors to exclude merchants, financiers, and industrialists from parliament (repealed 1866). Neither of these Tory measures were long successfully enforced.

1713, Apr. 11. TREATY OF UTRECHT. Articles affecting **Great Britain:** renunciation of the pretender by Louis XIV, who recognized the Protestant succession in Great Britain; crowns of France and Spain *not* to be united under one head; fortifications of Dunkirk to be razed and its harbor filled up; cession by France of Hudson's Bay and Acadia, Newfoundland and St. Kitts to Great Britain. **Great Britain and Spain:** cession of Gibraltar and Minorca to Britain; grant of the Asiento (*el pacto del asiento de negros*), or contract for supplying slaves to Spanish America, to the subjects of Great Britain for thirty years (Royal African Company).

1714, Feb. 16–Aug. 25. Fifth parliament of Anne. Death of Sophia of Hanover (May 28). **Schism Act.** Oxford dismissed (July 27) and succeeded as lord high treasurer by the earl of Shrewsbury. Many leading Tories, who foresaw that the Hanoverian succession would mean a Whig monopoly of power, attempted negotiations with the pretender.

Aug. 1. Death of Anne.

1714. HOUSE OF HANOVER or **BRUNSWICK,** changed (1917) to house of Windsor. None of Anne's seventeen children having survived her, the crown, according to the Act of Settlement, descended to the Protestant house of Hanover, the Catholic line of the Stuarts being excluded.

1714–1727. GEORGE I.

1714, Sept. 18. The king landed in England. George I favored the Whigs in the formation of the first government; Lord Townshend, secretary of state; Shrewsbury resigned, and Halifax was made first lord of the treasury (Shrewsbury was the last lord high treasurer); Sunderland, lord lieutenant of Ireland; Lord Cowper, chancellor; earl of Nottingham, president of the council; Marlborough, commander-in-chief.

1715, Mar. 17–1722, Mar. 7. First parliament of George I. Impeachment of Bolingbroke, Ormonde, Oxford. Flight of Bolingbroke and Ormonde. Oxford in the Tower. Jacobite riots in England.

1715–1716, Sept. "The Fifteen," Jacobite rising in Scotland under the earl of Mar. **Battles of Sheriffmuir** and **Preston.** Arrival of the pretender ("James III") from France (Dec. 1715). The duke of Argyll (John Campbell) dispersed the Jacobite troops without a battle, and the pretender fled (Feb. 5, 1716). Impeachment of Jacobite leaders, execution of Derwentwater and Kenmure (Feb. 24).

1716. Partly because of this Jacobite scare, parliament passed the **Septennial Act,** prolonging its own life to seven years, and making that the full legal term for future parliaments.

1717, Jan. 4. Triple alliance between Britain, France, and Holland because of the intrigues of the pretender, Charles XII, and Alberoni; Empire joined these in the **quadruple alliance** (Aug. 2, 1718). War between Great Britain and Spain (see p. 487).

1718, Jan. Repeal of the Occasional Conformity Act and the Schism Act.

1719. Abortive Spanish expedition to Scotland to help the pretender. **Treaty of Stockholm** (Nov. 20, 1719): Sweden ceded Bremen and Verden to George I (as elector of Hanover) for 1,000,000 rix dollars.

The House of Hanover (1714–1837)

(From p. 462)

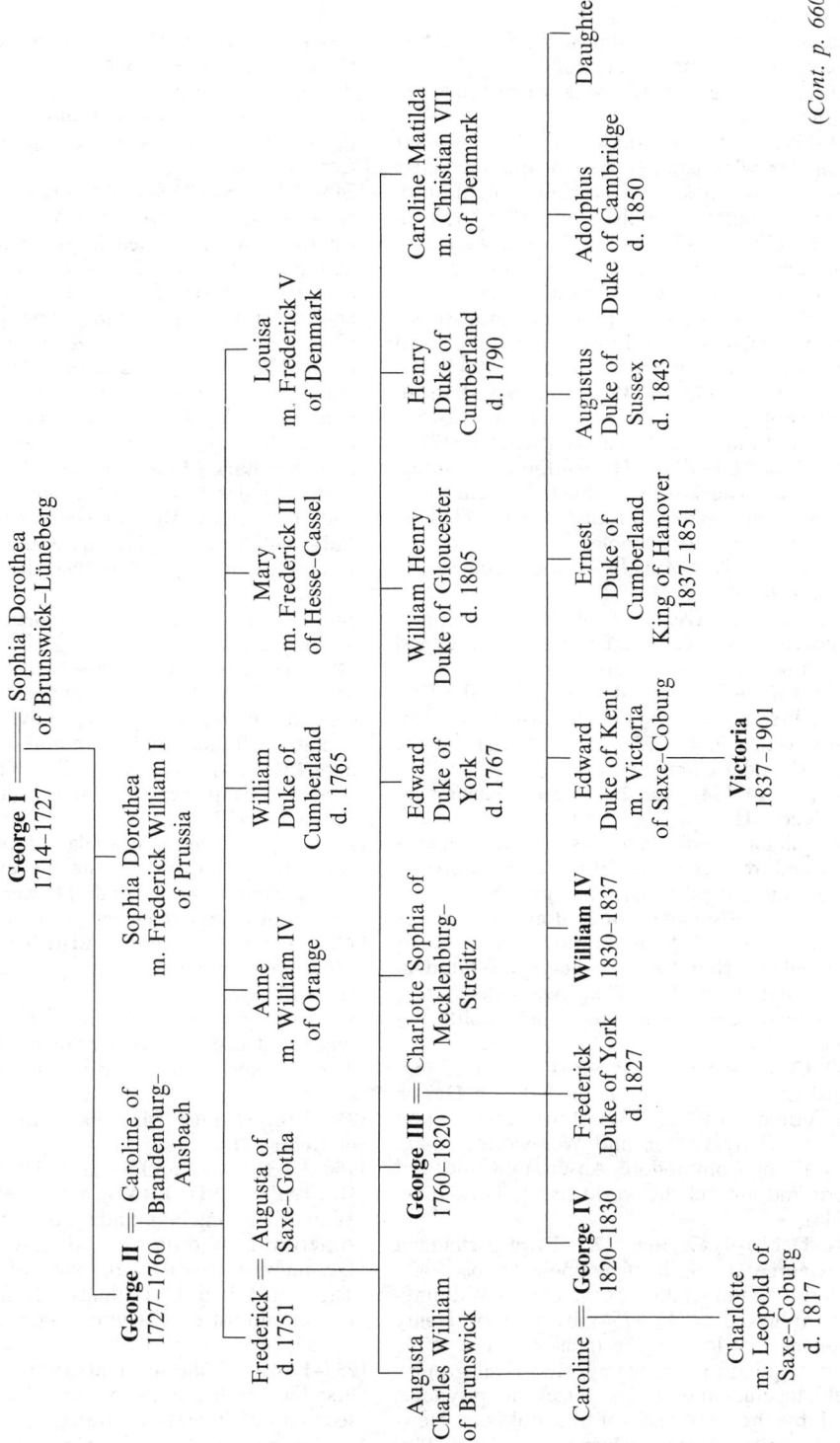

(Cont. p. 660.)

1720, Jan. Spain joined the quadruple alliance, making peace with Great Britain.

1720, Jan. Bursting of the **South Sea Bubble:** disastrous financial panic influenced by the earlier bursting of Law's **Mississippi Bubble** in France (p. 484).

1721-1742. Administration of Sir Robert Walpole. The cabinet system and the party system now took the form they held until 1832. Parallel administration of Fleury in France (1726-1742). Both ministers were cautious and peace-loving, anxious to restore prosperity after the ravages of the "first World War." Period of stability, of common sense, the **Augustan Age** of European letters, great advances in commerce and industry.

1722, Oct. 9-1727, July 17. Second parliament of George I. **Treaty of Hanover** between Britain, France, and Prussia (Sept. 3, 1725).

1727-1760. GEORGE II. Walpole continued in office. The king was much influenced by his wife, the capable Caroline of Ansbach, who remained loyal to Walpole.

1728, Jan. 23-1734, Apr. 16. First parliament of George II.

1729, Nov. 9. Treaty of Seville with Spain: restoration of conquests; Britain retained Gibraltar; the *asiento* confirmed.

1731, Mar. 16. Treaty of Vienna with the Empire; dissolution of the Ostend East India Company, which had been formed as rival to the English India Company, by the emperor.

1735, Jan. 14-1741, Apr. 25. Second parliament of George II.

1736. **John Wesley** and his brother **Charles** returned from Georgia, set up the little groups of evangelical Christians out of which came the **Wesleyan societies,** and, after the death of John Wesley (1791), the various independent **Methodist churches.** **George Whitefield** was ordained in 1736. The Methodists were emotional and revivalistic, but politically conservative.

1739-1748. WAR WITH SPAIN (War of Jenkins' Ear). Capture of Porto Bello in Darien by Vernon (Nov. 22, 1739). Futile attack upon Cartagena by Vernon and Wentworth (1740). Voyage of Commodore Anson to Chile and Peru and around the world (Sept. 1740-June, 1744).

1741, Dec. 1-1747, June 17. Third parliament of George II. Fall of Walpole (Feb. 1742). Interim administration of the earl of Wilmington, followed (1743-1754) by that of **Henry Pelham,** first lord of the treasury. The Whig party tended to disintegrate into rival groups, held together loosely by place and privilege, and by the "interest" of the duke of Newcastle. **Broadbottom ministry.** Pelham, Pitt,

Newcastle, Harrington (later Earl Stanhope), Bedford.

1740-1748. WAR OF THE AUSTRIAN SUCCESSION. Britain took part on the side of Austria. For further details see p. 501.

1745, May 11. Battle of Fontenoy, victory of the French under Saxe over the allies under Cumberland.

1745-1746. SECOND JACOBITE REBELLION (The Forty-five). The Young Pretender, **Charles Edward,** landed in Scotland (July 25) and proclaimed his father as **James VIII** of Scotland and III of England. The Jacobites entered Edinburgh with some 2000 men (Sept. 11), won the **battle of Prestonpans** (Sept. 21), and under Charles Edward himself marched down into England, where they reached Derby, his farthest point, on December 4. Jacobite victories at **Penrith** (Dec. 18) and at **Falkirk Moor** (Jan. 17, 1746). But only in the Highlands was the Jacobite cause strong, and here they were beaten decisively at **Culloden** (Apr. 16). The pretender escaped to France (Sept. 20). This was the last Stuart effort.

1747, Nov. 10-1754, Apr. 6. Fourth parliament of George II.

1748. Treaty of Aix-la-Chapelle, p. 503. Britain emerged from this war a defeated nation, except in North America. The divisions of the Whigs continued, and their ablest man, **William Pitt** (earl of Chatham in 1766), was not trusted with power save at the crisis of the **Seven Years' War** (1757).

1752. The **Gregorian calendar** adopted in Britain and the colonies. The eleven days between September 2 and 14 were omitted. ("Give us back our eleven days!")

1753. Foundation of the **British Museum** by government purchase of the collection of Sir Hans Sloane.

1754. On the death of Pelham (Mar.) he was succeeded as prime minister by his brother, the duke of Newcastle. Henry Fox, secretary of state.

1754, May 31-1761, Mar. 19. Fifth parliament of George II.

1756-1763. Land and Naval **WAR BETWEEN BRITAIN AND FRANCE.** (Seven Years' War) originating in boundary disputes in North America, carried on by land in America (and Germany), by sea in all parts of the world. The British had the ultimate advantage of the French almost everywhere. (War in America, p. 556; in India, p. 573).

1757-1761. Coalition ministry of Newcastle, first lord of the treasury, and the elder **Pitt,** secretary of state, to centralize war policy and administration. Pitt was the real leader, and helped make possible Britain's victory in the duel with France.

1759, Sept. 13. Battle of Quebec, death of **Wolfe** and **Montcalm.** Naval **battle of Quiberon Bay** (Nov. 20); defeat of the French by Sir Edward Hawke.

1760-1820. GEORGE III.

1761, Aug. 15. Bourbon family compact between France and Spain, with the assumption of the accession of Naples and Parma, for reciprocal guarantee of all possessions and an offensive and defensive alliance.

Oct. 5. **Pitt,** insisting that war be declared against Spain, resigned. **Lord Bute,** adviser to the king. George attempted to exercise influence and authority, but in a way thoroughly consonant with the organization of politics in 18th century England. He built up in parliament, with Tory aid and by the usual means of patronage and bribery, a party of **king's friends,** and thus brought the Tories into power for the first time since 1714. Newcastle continued prime minister in the new cabinet (Oct. 5, 1761). Egremont and Bute, secretaries of state, George Grenville, leader of the commons.

1761, Nov. 3-1768, Mar. 10. First parliament of George III. War declared against Spain (Jan. 1762). Bute became prime minister (May 29, 1762), Grenville, secretary of state.

1763, Feb. 10. TREATY OF PARIS between Great Britain, France, and Spain. (1) France ceded to Britain: in North America, Canada, and Cape Breton Island; the Mississippi was recognized as the boundary between Louisiana and the British colonies; in the West Indies, Grenada; in Africa, the French possessions on the Senegal. Britain restored to France Goree in Africa, and Pondichéry and Chandernagor in India. (2) Spain ceded to Britain Florida, as indemnification for which France had already ceded Louisiana to Spain; Spain received from Britain all conquests in Cuba including Havana. In consequence of this peace and her acquisitions in India, Great Britain approached the apogee of her extent and power; the North American colonies had gradually developed into virtually self-governing states.

1763, Apr. 1-1765, July; Ministry of George Grenville; Halifax and Egremont, secretaries of state; Fox created Lord Holland.

1763-1764. No. 45 of the *North Briton* (Apr. 23, 1763), containing insulting remarks concerning the king by **John Wilkes;** general warrants for the apprehension of the authors, printers, and publishers, were issued. Wilkes was arrested and expelled from the commons (Jan. 19, 1764). General warrants declared illegal by the chief justice. Wilkes outlawed.

1765, July-1766, July. Ministry of the marquis of Rockingham; Conway, leader of the commons. This was succeeded by a ministry headed by **Chatham** (Aug. 1766-Dec. 1767) and then by the ministry of the **duke of Grafton** (Dec. 1767-Jan. 1770); Townshend, chancellor of the exchequer; Conway, Shelburne, secretaries of state; the earl of Chatham, lord privy seal. Lord Hillsborough the first colonial secretary.

1768, May 10-1774, June 22. Second parliament of George III. Wilkes returned and was elected to the commons from Middlesex. He was expelled from the house by votes of the "king's friends," but was thrice elected and thrice rejected; at the last election his opponent, Colonel Luttrell, who received a small minority of votes, was declared elected. This was a Pyrrhic victory for George. The affair of the **Middlesex election** stirred up animosities against him, and resulted finally in establishing freedom of election of the house of commons.

1769-1772. *Letters of Junius,* containing bitter attacks on the duke of Grafton, Lord Mansfield, and other members of the government, appeared in the *Daily Advertiser.* The author is still unknown, but the weight of evidence favors **Sir Philip Francis.**

1770, Jan.-1782, Mar. Ministry of Lord North, first lord of the treasury and chancellor of the exchequer, and George's favorite. Full Tory government. Under North, third parliament of George III (Nov. 29, 1774-July 8, 1780) and fourth parliament (Oct. 31, 1780-Mar. 24, 1784).

Constitutional developments: Establishment of publication of speeches in the commons, in spite of their protests (1771). Wilkes made lord mayor of London and member for Middlesex. The sixth motion to expunge the resolution rejecting him, as "subversive of the rights of electors," carried (May 3, 1782). Repeal of some of the penal laws against Roman Catholics (1778) helped bring on the **Lord George Gordon riots** in London (June 1780), originating as a protest against further Catholic emancipation, but degenerating into drunken orgies and brawls. London in the hands of the mob for three days.

The failure of North to subdue the American colonies resulted in a series of motions hostile to him, culminating in that of Sir J. Rous (Mar. 15, 1782) "that the House could no longer repose confidence in the present ministers" (lost by only nine votes). On threat of renewal of the motion, **North resigned,** thus setting a further precedent in parliamentary government.

1775-1783. WAR OF AMERICAN INDE-PENDENCE (see p. 557). The war widened in 1778 with the entrance of France against Great Britain, in 1779 with the entrance of Spain against her. Gibraltar, defended by Elliott, besieged by French and Spanish in vain (1779-1782). Holland entered the war against Great Britain (Dec. 30, 1780). In 1781 the British lost Pensacola, Tobago, St. Eustace, Demerara, St. Kitts, Nevis, Monserrat; Cornwallis surrendered at **Yorktown** (Oct. 19, 1781). Minorca lost (1782). In the **battle of the Saints** (Apr. 12, 1782) the British under Rodney defeated a French fleet and convoy under De Grasse in the strait between Guadeloupe and Dominica. By forestalling a French junction with the Spanish and an assault on Jamaica, Rodney restored British command in the Caribbean. But England was sick of the war, and the new government had, without a formal election, a mandate to make peace.

1782, Mar. 20-July 1. Ministry of Rockingham: Shelburne and **Charles James Fox** (1749-1806), secretaries of state; Thurlow, lord chancellor; **Edmund Burke** (1729-1797), paymaster of the forces; **Richard Sheridan** (1751-1816), undersecretary of state. The golden age of English oratory. On Rockingham's death (July 1), Lord Shelburne became prime minister in a cabinet (July 1, 1782-Feb. 24, 1783) from which Fox, Burke, and Sheridan were excluded, and **William Pitt** (1759-1806) included as chancellor of the exchequer.

1782, Nov. 30. PRELIMINARY TREATY OF PARIS with the United States (p. 562) followed by the general **treaty of Paris** (Jan. 20, 1783-Sept. 3) between the United States, Great Britain, France, Spain, and Holland. (1) Recognition of the independence of the thirteen United States. (2) Britain surrendered Tobago and Senegal to France. (3) Spain retained Minorca and Florida. (4) Holland, badly worsted (separate peace, May 20, 1784), gave Negapatam and the right of free navigation in the Moluccas to Britain.

1783, Apr. 2-Dec. 13. Coalition ministry of North and Fox, nominally headed by the duke of Portland. The alliance of two such bitter opponents as North and Fox shocked public opinion and paved the way for the ministry of the younger Pitt.

1783, Dec. 26-1801, Mar. 17. First ministry of William Pitt the Younger, formed after Fox's bill to reform the government of India was lost in the lords. Pitt's bill was also rejected, whereupon parliament was dissolved (1784, Mar. 25) and new elections held.

1784, May 18-1795. Fifth parliament of George III.

Aug. 13. **Pitt's India bill** became law (p. 574).

1788. Temporary insanity of George III. In the course of discussion regarding the regency, the king recovered.

1793, Feb. 1. The **French Republic declared war on Great Britain** (p. 631). The government at once took measures against revolutionary agitation (Traitorous Correspondence Bill; suspension of the Habeas Corpus Act, [1794] renewed annually until 1801).

1794, May. Trial of Hardy, Horne Tooke, and Thelwall, on charge of high treason, all of whom were eventually acquitted (Dec.).

Nov. **Jay's treaty** between the United States and Great Britain (p. 806).

1796, Sept. 17. The sixth parliament of George III convened.

1797, Apr. 15. The mutiny at Spithead. The sailors' demands for better treatment were reasonable and were met by the government (May 17), but immediately afterward a more serious outbreak occurred at the **Nore,** which had to be suppressed by force (June 30).

1799. Supression of the **insurrection of the United Irishmen.** This organization had been formed in 1791 to secure the complete separation of Ireland from England. The French had sent several expeditions to aid them (notably that of Hoche, which was scattered by a storm, Dec. 1796), but the United Irishmen were defeated at **Vinegar Hill** (June 21, 1798) and the insurrection stamped out. As a result

1801, Jan. 1. The **LEGISLATIVE UNION OF GREAT BRITAIN AND IRELAND,** under the name of the *United Kingdom,* was brought about. The Act of Union provided that there should be one parliament, to which Ireland should send four spiritual lords, sitting by rotation of sessions; 28 temporal peers, elected for life by the Irish peerage; and 100 members of the commons. The churches of the two countries were to be united into one Protestant Episcopal church. Pitt proposed to make some concessions to the Roman Catholics, but the king was persuaded that this would involve a breach of his coronation oath. Thereupon

Feb. 3. Pitt resigned.

Mar. 14. His friend **Henry Addington** then headed the cabinet, with Pitt advising, and concluded peace with France, embodied (Mar. 27, 1802) in the **treaty of Amiens.**

The passage of the **Health and Morals of Apprentices Act** in this year marks a step toward government supervision of labor conditions. The act forbade the hiring out of pauper children for work in the cotton mills until they were nine years of age, restricted their working day to 12 hours, and prohibited their employment at night work.

1803, May 16. The war between Britain and France was renewed. (See p. 640.)

1804, May 10. Pitt returned to office and helped to organize the **Third Coalition** against France. He was stricken by the news of Napoleon's victory at Austerlitz and died on Jan. 23, 1806.

1806. Pitt's place was taken by **Lord William Grenville,** with **Charles James Fox** as foreign secretary until the latter's death, Sept. 13.

1807. Abolition of slavery decreed in the British dominions. The **duke of Portland** formed his second ministry (March) and held office until May 1809, when **Spencer Perceval** replaced him, to be followed (June 1812) by the **earl of Liverpool,** whose unusually long ministry lasted until April 1827.   (*Cont. p. 653.*)

BRITISH ART AND LITERATURE, 17th AND 18th CENTURIES

(1) Architecture

Christopher Wren (1632–1723): chief architect of the Greenwich Observatory (1676) and Royal Hospital (1696–1705), St. Paul's Cathedral (1710). **James Gibbs** (1682–1752): churches in London, buildings at Oxford and Cambridge Universities. The brothers **Adam** (James, John, Robert, William) designed many buildings in the West End of London; Robert (1728–1792) set the fashion in his design of furniture and interiors.

(2) Literature, Late 17th Century

Prose: John Dryden (1631–1700) was the foremost prose writer of the latter part of the 17th century and his style established a pattern for later writers (*Essay of Dramatic Poesy,* 1668, rev. 1684; preface to *Fables,* 1700); he also wrote poetry and plays (*Conquest of Granada,* 1672).

Diaries: Samuel Pepys (1633–1703); **John Evelyn** (1620–1706).

Philosophy: John Locke (1632–1704) founded the empirical school (*Essays Concerning the Human Understanding,* 1690) and laid the basis for political liberalism.

History and biography: Anthony à Wood, with John Aubrey, *Athenae Oxoniensis* (1691–1692); William Dugdale, with Roger Dodsworth, *Monasticon Anglicanum* (1655–1673); Edward Hyde, first **earl of Clarendon** (1609–1674), *History of the Rebellion* (1702–1704).

A dictionary was compiled by Edward Phillips: *A New World in Words* (1658).

John Bunyan (1628–1688), an itinerant preacher jailed after the restoration of Charles II, wrote *The Pilgrim's Progress* (1678) during his imprisonment; written in everyday language and hence immensely popular among the poor classes; an allegory full of simple but colorful prose.

Drama: In addition to Dryden (see above), **William Congreve** (1670–1729; *Love for Love,* 1695; *Way of the World,* 1700) created outstanding dialogue; comedies of manners also written by **William Wycherley** (*The Country Wife,* 1675) and **Sir George Etherege** (*The Man of Mode,* 1676).

Poets: John Dryden (*Absalom and Achitophel,* 1681) and **Samuel Butler** (*Hudibras,* 1663–1664); also **Robert Herrick** (1591–1674), **George Wither** (1588–1667), **Abraham Cowley** (1618–1667), **Andrew Marvell** (1621–1678), **Henry Vaughan** (1622–1695).

Music: John Blow (1647–1708), composer of the first English opera (*Venus and Adonis,* c. 1685); **Henry Purcell** (c. 1658–1695), composer of opera (*Dido and Aeneas,* c. 1689), songs, church and chamber music.

(3) Literature and Art, 18th Century

In general, literature showed a reaction to the puritanism of the Commonwealth and the laxity of the Restoration; discussion of mores and ideas became more generally accepted; new impetus was given the newspapers by the failure to renew the Licensing Act with its censorship provisions. The essay was a popular literary vehicle; *The Tatler* (1709–1711) and the *Spectator Papers* (1711–1712), under the editorship of **Joseph Addison** (1672–1719) and **Richard Steele** (1672–1729), offered all kinds of social criticism.

The prose novel, often a satire, was a popular form: **Daniel Defoe** (1660–1731; *Robinson Crusoe,* 1719; *Moll Flanders,* 1722); **Jonathan Swift** (1667–1745; *Gulliver's Travels,* 1726); **Samuel Richardson** (1689–1761; *Pamela,* 1740; *Clarissa,* 1747–1748); **Henry Fielding** (1707–1754; *Joseph Andrews,* 1742; *Tom Jones,* 1749); **Tobias Smollett** (1721–1771; *Roderick Random,* 1748, suggested by *Gil Blas*); **Laurence Sterne** (1713–1768; *Tristram Shandy,* 1759–1767). The Gothic horror novels began to appear with **Horace Walpole,** *Castle of Otranto* (1764).

Biography and literary criticism: Samuel Johnson (1709–1784), in his *Lives of the English Poets* (1779–1781), gave sound reasons for his critical observations; his *Dictionary of the English Language* (1755) established the pattern for later models. **Anthony Ashley Cooper** earl of Shaftesbury (1671–1713), *Characteristics of Men, Manners, Opinions, Times* (1711); **James Boswell** (1740–1795), *Life of Samuel Johnson* (1791).

Poetry: Alexander Pope (1688–1744) translated the *Iliad* and portions of the *Odyssey;* wrote *The Rape of the Lock* (1712). Lyric poetry of **William Blake** (1757–1827), mystic, who created engraved illustrations for many of his poems; the Scot **Robert Burns** (1759–1796).

Also: **James Thomson** (1700-1748), **Thomas Gray** (1716-1771), **William Cowper** (1731-1800), **William Collins** (1721-1759).

Drama: Richard Brinsley Sheridan (1751-1816) satirized his age in *The Rivals* (1775) and *The School for Scandal* (1777).

Music: George Frederick Handel (1685-1759), German-born composer of oratorio and orchestral works, spent much of his life in England, becoming a naturalized British subject in 1726. **John Gay** (1685-1732) and **John Christopher Pepusch** (1667-1752) collaborated on the comic *Beggar's Opera* (1728).

Painting: William Hogarth (1697-1764) was the artist-critic of his society (*A Rake's Progress,* 1735; *Marriage à la Mode,* 1744). The favorite technique of the 18th century was the portrait: **Sir Joshua Reynolds** (1723-1792); **Thomas Gainsborough** (1727-1788); **George Romney** (1734-1802); **Sir Henry Raeburn** (1756-1823); **John Hoppner** (1758-1810). Also landscapes by **Gainsborough** and by **Richard Wilson** (1714-1782). The **Royal Academy of Art** in London was founded in 1768.

2. THE DUTCH REPUBLIC, 1602-1810

(*From p. 408*)

The first half of the 17th century, during which the Dutch provinces were still at war with Spain to secure their independence, was nevertheless the golden age of the Netherlands, a period of unexampled flowering in art (p. 408). This was probably due primarily to the unprecedented expansion of Dutch commerce, which resulted from the closing of Lisbon to Dutch trade after the annexation of Portugal to Spain. The Dutch were obliged to find their own way to the east and within a remarkably short time they were disputing the command of the Indies with the Portuguese, whom they soon displaced. The **Dutch East India Company** (founded 1602), was given extensive political and military authority and became one of the chief organs of Dutch imperialism. In the east, Batavia was founded in 1619. The Portuguese were expelled from Ceylon (1638-1658), and Malacca taken from them (1641). In 1652 the Dutch established themselves at the Cape of Good Hope and in 1667 they took Sumatra. The **Dutch West India Company** (founded 1621) had the same extensive control over the American and African coast trade. In 1623 the Dutch seized Pernambuco and began extensive conquests in Brazil (till 1661). They took the islands of St. Eustace and Curaçao (1634-1635), Saba (1640), and St. Martin (1648). With this far-flung colonial empire, the Dutch provinces became the commercial center of Europe, Amsterdam easily holding the lead as a financial center.

The provinces, however, were politically connected only in the loosest fashion. Despite the stadholdership of the house of Orange, there continued to be (especially in Holland, the chief province) strong suspicion of all centralizing tendencies and an almost fanatical attachment to state rights.

1647-1650. **WILLIAM II,** a young man of 23, succeeded his father, Frederick Henry, in the stadholdership. Able, ambitious, and restless, William disapproved of the **treaty of Münster** (1648), which recognized the independence of the provinces, and would have preferred to continue the war. He soon became involved in conflict with the states-general and, by arresting some of the leaders of Holland and attacking Amsterdam itself (1650), he forced the submission of the state-rights group.

1650, Nov. 6. **William's early death** gave the decentralizing party a golden opportunity, for William's son was born posthumously and there was no one to dispute the taking over of control by the states-general. In 1653 **John De Witt** became pensionary of Holland, and thereby controlled general policy. An able statesman and adroit diplomat, he easily maintained Dutch prestige and greatness.

1652-1654. The **FIRST ANGLO-DUTCH WAR,** the direct outgrowth of the **English Navigation Act** (1651) and the steadily growing competition of English and Dutch, especially in the east. The English and the Dutch, led by outstanding commanders like Blake, Monk, Tromp, de Ruyter, and De Witt, fought no less than twelve naval engagements, most of them indecisive. By the **treaty of Westminster** (Apr. 5, 1654) the Dutch agreed to enter a defensive league with England and to pay indemnity. The province of Holland secretly agreed to exclude all members of the house of Orange from the stadholdership (this was due to Cromwell's uneasiness about the relationship of the Stuarts and Oranges—William II having married the daughter of Charles I).

1657-1660. The Dutch interfered successfully in the Swedish-Danish War in order to prevent the entrance of the Baltic from falling into exclusively Swedish control.

1657-1661. **War with Portugal,** over conflicting interests in Brazil.

The House of Orange-Nassau (1558–   )

William I   (1)= Anna of Egmont
(the Silent) (2)= Anna of Saxony
Stadholder (3)= Charlotte of Bourbon
1558–1584 (4)= Louise de Coligny

(1)   **(2)**   **(3)**   **(3)**   **(4)**

Philip William   **Maurice**   Louisa Juliana   Amalia   **Frederick Henry** = Amalia
d. 1618   1584–1625   m. Frederick IV   m. Frederick   1625–1647   of Solms
   of the Palatinate   Casimir of
Charles I   Zweibrücken
of England

James II   Mary = **William II**   Louisa   Henrietta   Albertina = William
of England   1647–1650   Henrietta   Catherine   Agnes   Frederick
Mary ===== **William III**   m. Frederick William   m. John George   of Nassau–
   1672–1702   of Brandenburg   of Anhalt–   Dietz
   Dessau

Henry Casimir

John William Friso

Anne of England = **William IV**
Regent   1748–1751
1751–1766

Wilhelmina = **William V**
of Prussia   1766–1795

William I = Frederica Wilhelmina
King of the   of Prussia
Netherlands
1813–1840

Anna of = **William II**   Marianne   Frederick = Louisa of
Russia   1840–1849   m. Albert of   Prussia
   Prussia

Sophia of ==(1) **William III** (2)= Emma of   Louisa   Marie
Württemberg   1849–1890   Waldeck   m. Charles XV   m. William
   of Sweden   of Wied

   Wilhelmina ===== Henry of
   1890–1948   Mecklenburg–Schwerin

William Nicholas   Alexander
d. 1879   d. 1884

Juliana === Bernhard of
1948–   Lippe–Biesterfeld

Beatrix Wilhelmina   Irene Emma   Margriet   Maria Christina
b. 1938   b. 1939   Francisca   b. 1947
m. Claus Gerd   m. Carlos Hugo   b. 1943
von Amsberg   of Bourbon–Parma   m. Pieter
   von Vollenhoven

Willem   Johan   Constantijn
Alexander   Friso   b. 1969
b. 1967   b. 1968

1660. On the restoration of the Stuarts in England, the Dutch states-general at once rescinded the exclusion of the house of Orange from the stadholdership.

1662. The Dutch allied themselves to the French to provide against the danger of attack by the British.

1664. The **British seized New Amsterdam** (New York) and appropriated various Dutch stations on the African coast.

1665–1667. SECOND ANGLO-DUTCH WAR. France and Denmark supported the Dutch, who, on the whole, maintained the upper hand at sea (attack on the English fleet in the Medway, etc., but by the **treaty of Breda** (July 21, 1667) they abandoned claims to New Amsterdam in return for Surinam.

1668, Jan. 23. Triple Alliance of England, Holland, and Sweden to check the aggression of Louis XIV in the Spanish Netherlands. Louis soon managed to buy off the English and the Swedes and thereafter concentrated his hatred upon the Dutch.

1672–1678. WAR WITH FRANCE AND ENGLAND (p. 479). The Dutch were quite unprepared for a land war and consequently the French were able to overrun much of the country. The result was much agitation against **John De Witt,** who, with his brother Cornelius, was brutally murdered by a mob (Aug. 27, 1672).

1672–1702. WILLIAM III (son of William II), stadholder. With the aid of the emperor and of Brandenburg he was able to hold his own against the French and indeed to force their retirement. The British abandoned the war (1674) and by the **treaty of Nijmwegen** (Nimwegen, Nimeguen) of 1678, the Dutch came off without losses.

1688, Nov. 5. William III (married in 1677 to **Mary,** the daughter of James II of England) landed in England in response to an appeal from the opponents of James II. In 1689 he was proclaimed king and joint ruler with Mary (p. 465).

1688–1697. WAR OF THE LEAGUE OF AUGSBURG against Louis XIV (p. 480). William was very decidedly the leader in the coalition and threw the whole weight of England as well as of the Netherlands into the struggle. Though rarely successful in the field, William's perseverance and able management saved him from disaster. By the **treaty of Ryswick** (1697), France and the Netherlands returned to the *status quo ante.*

1702, Mar. 8. The **death of William III,** without children, brought to an end the direct line of the house of Orange, which, however, was continued by the related house of Nassau. For the time being, however, the states-general, conducted by **Antonius Heinsius,** since 1688 close collaborator of William III, dominated the provincial estates, especially of Holland. Heinsius remained in power until his death in 1720.

1702–1713. The **WAR OF THE SPANISH SUCCESSION** (p. 481), in which the Dutch again played their part in conjunction with England. These wars, costly in men and money, reacted most unfavorably on the Dutch position. After 1715 there was a marked and steady economic decline. The republic was soon overshadowed by Britain and became more and more an adjunct of the British system.

1715, Nov. 15. By the **Barrier Treaty,** the Empire ceded to the Dutch a number of strong places on the French frontier of the (since 1713) Austrian Netherlands, as protection against attack by France.

1731. The Dutch signed the **Pragmatic Sanction** of Emperor Charles VI in return for abolition of the Ostend Company, which had been set up as a rival to the Dutch East India Company.

1734. The prince of Orange-Nassau married Anne, the daughter of George II.

1743. The Dutch Republic joined Britain in the alliance with Maria Theresa against Prussia and France. The French conquests in the Austrian Netherlands constituted a direct danger to the republic.

1748–1751. WILLIAM IV of Orange-Nassau (grandson of William III's cousin) proclaimed stadholder, a dignity which now became hereditary in the family.

1751. On the death of William IV, his widow, Anne, acted as regent for the three-year-old heir.

1766–1795. WILLIAM V assumed the position of stadholder. He proved himself a weak and ineffectual ruler.

1780–1784. The Dutch went to war with Britain over the question of the right to search ships at sea. As a result the Dutch lost some of their possessions in both the East and the West Indies.

1785. Beginning of serious conflict between William and the states-general, due to the emergence of the **Patriot Party** (representing the French influence). William ultimately had to call in Prussian troops (1787) to restore his authority.

1793. **France declared war on the Dutch Republic** as well as on Britain (friction over the opening of the Scheldt by the French in 1792).

1794–1795. The French general, Pichegru, overran the country, capturing the Dutch fleet while it was frozen in the ice in the Texel. William V fled to England.

1795-1806. The **BATAVIAN REPUBLIC,** modeled on France and governed by the Patriots under more or less direct French influence. In the interval the British, still at war with France, seized the Dutch colonies.

1806-1810. **LOUIS,** the brother of Napoleon, king of Holland. His policy, aimed at the good of his adopted kingdom, brought him into conflict with his brother.

1810. The **KINGDOM OF HOLLAND** was incorporated with France as an integral part of the empire. (*Cont. p. 672.*)

3. FRANCE, 1643-1788

[For a complete list of the kings of France see Appendix VII.]

(*From p. 414*)

1643-1715. **LOUIS XIV,** who ascended the throne at the age of five. His mother, **Anne of Austria** (daughter of Philip III of Spain) acted as guardian. The government, even after Louis's arrival at majority, was conducted by **Cardinal Mazarin.**

1648-1653. Disturbances of the **Fronde (Cardinal Retz; Prince of Condé;** resistance of the *parlement* of Paris), the last attempt of the French nobility to oppose the court by armed resistance. The parlementary, as contrasted with the noble, Fronde, was, however, an attempt to substitute government by law for government by royal or any other irresponsible will. Condé, at first loyal, afterward engaged against the court, fought a battle with the royal troops under Henri de la Tour d'Auvergne, Vicomte de **Turenne,** in the Faubourg Saint Antoine, and took refuge in the city. The first conspiracy, the old Fronde, ended in 1649, with the second **treaty of Rueil;** the second conspiracy, the new Fronde, which involved treasonable correspondence with Spain, failed in 1650. A union of the two was crushed in 1653. (Gaston of Orléans, and his daughter "Mademoiselle.")

1648. Acquisitions of France in the **treaties of Westphalia,** p. 436.

The war with Spain, which sprang up during the Thirty Years' War (victory of Condé at **Rocroi,** May 19, 1643; alliance with England, 1657; Cromwell sent 8000 men of his army to the assistance of Turenne) was continued till the

1659. **TREATY OF THE PYRENEES:** (1) France received a part of Roussillon, Conflans, Cerdagne, and several towns in Artois and Flanders, Hainault and Luxemburg; (2) the duke of Lorraine, the ally of Spain, was partially reinstated (France received Bar, Clermont, etc., and right of passage for troops; the prince of Condé entirely reinstated; (3) marriage between Louis XIV and the infanta **Maria Teresa,** eldest daughter of Philip IV of Spain, who, however, renounced her claims upon her inheritance for herself and her issue by Louis forever, in consideration of the payment of a dowry of 500,000 crowns by Spain.

1661. **Death of Mazarin.** Personal government of Louis XIV (1661-1715), absolute, at least in the theory of certain royalist pamphleteers, and perhaps of Louis himself, without estates-general, without regard to the remonstrances of the parlement of Paris (*L'état, c'est moi*). Louis was in practice, however, limited by his inability to do everything himself. The French bureaucracy was a privileged group, often owning their offices (*vénalité des offices; Paulette,* a tax to the crown paid by office owners). Three constitutional limitations on the crown: king must be a Catholic; no woman may occupy the throne (**Salic law**); king may not alienate his lands by *appanage* system. **Jean Baptiste Colbert,** controller general of the finances from 1662-1683. **Reform of the finances;** mercantile system. Construction of a fleet of war. François Michel Le Tellier (**Marquis de Louvois**), minister of war, 1666-1691. Quarrel for precedence in rank with Spain. Negotiations with the pope concerning the privileges of French ambassadors at Rome. The ambition of Louis for fame and his desire for increase of territory were some of the causes of the following wars, in which these generals took part: Turenne, Condé, Luxembourg, Catinat, Villars, Vendôme, Vauban (inventor of the modern system of military fortification).

1667-1668. **FIRST WAR** (War of Devolution) on account of the Spanish Netherlands.

Cause: After the death of his father-in-law, Philip IV of Spain, Louis laid claim to the Spanish possessions in the Belgian provinces (Brabant, Flanders, etc.), on the ground that, being the personal estates of the royal family of Spain, their descent ought to be regulated by the local *droit de dévolution,* a principle in private law, whereby in the event of a dissolution of a marriage by death, the survivor enjoyed the usufruct only of the property,

The French Bourbons (1589–1883)

(From p. 410)

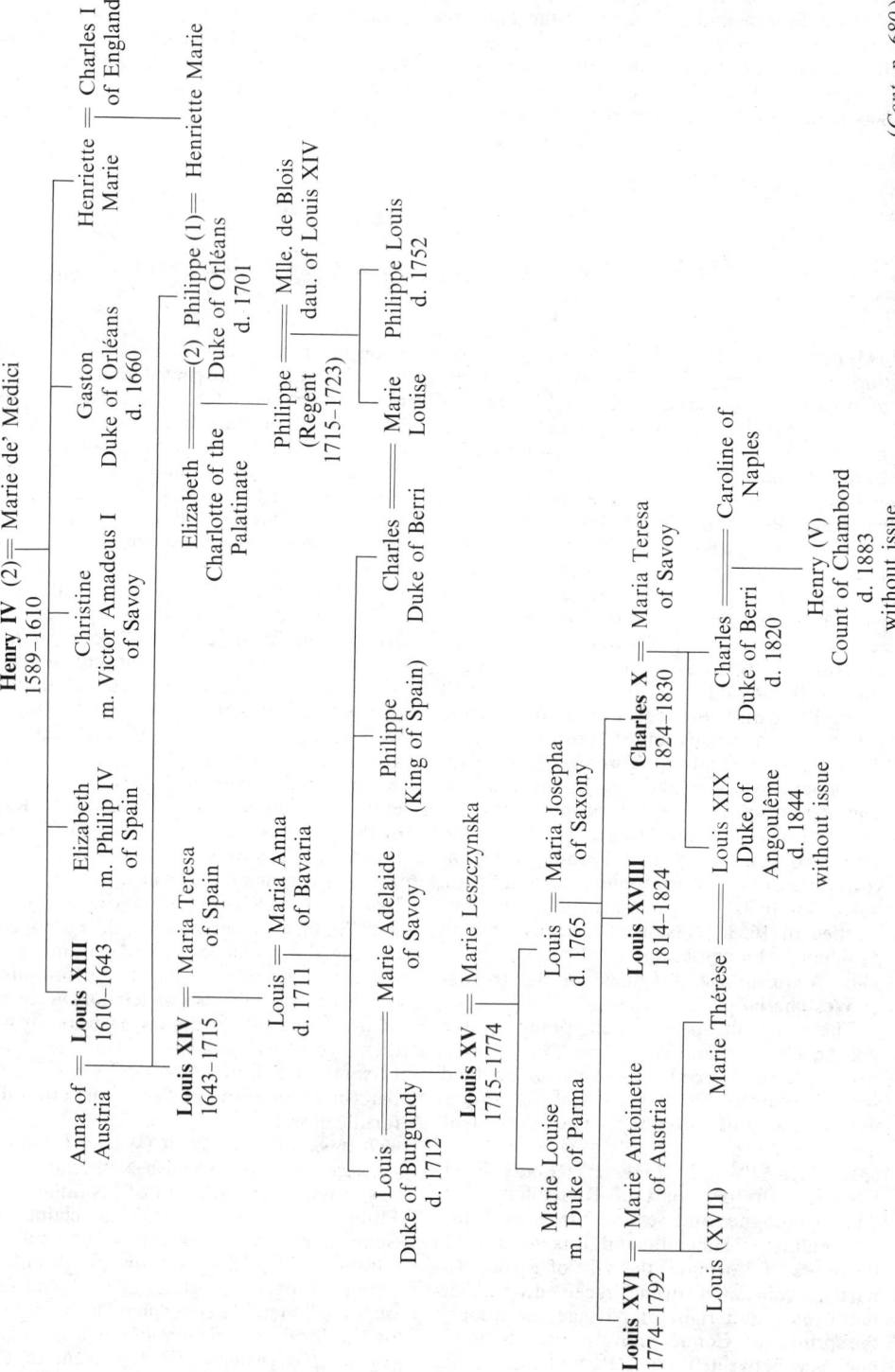

(Cont. p. 680)

the ownership being vested in the children, whence it followed that daughters of a first marriage inherited before sons of a second marriage. The renunciation of her heritage which his wife had made was, Louis claimed, invalid, since the stipulated dowry had never been paid.

1667. **Turenne** conquered a part of Flanders and Hainault. By the exertions of John De Witt, pensionary of Holland, and Sir William Temple, England, Holland, and Sweden concluded the **Triple Alliance** (1668, Jan. 23) which induced Louis, after Condé had occupied the defenseless free county of Burgundy (Franche-Comté), to sign the

1668, May 2. **Treaty of Aix-la-Chapelle:** Louis restored Franche-Comté (the fortresses having been dismantled) to Spain, in return for twelve fortified towns on the border of the Spanish Netherlands, among others Lille, Tournay, and Oudenarde. The question of the succession was deferred.

1672–1678. **SECOND WAR** (against Holland). The course of Holland in these transactions had inflamed the hatred of Louis against her, a hatred made still stronger by the refuge given by the provinces to political writers who annoyed him with their abusive publications. In revenge, Louis secured the disruption of the Triple Alliance by a private treaty with Charles II of England (the **treaty of Dover,** 1670, p. 463), and between France and Sweden (1672). Subsidy treaties with Köln and Münster; 20,000 Germans fought for Louis in the following war.

1672. **Passage of the Rhine.** Rapid and easy conquest of southern Holland by Turenne, Condé, and the king, at the head of 100,000 men. The brothers De Witt, the leaders of the aristocratic republican party in Holland, were killed during a popular outbreak (Aug. 20), **William III of Orange,** who had been made captain-general in February and stadholder in July, now became the head of the state. The opening of the sluices saved the province of Holland, and the city of Amsterdam. Alliance of Holland with Frederick William, elector of Brandenburg (1640–1688), afterward joined by the emperor and by Spain.

1673. Frederick William concluded the separate **peace of Vossem,** in which he retained his possessions in Cleves, except Wesel and Rees.

1674. Declaration of war by the Empire. Peace between England and Holland. Louis conquered Franche-Comté in person; Condé fought against Orange (drawn **battle at Senef**) in the Netherlands. Brilliant campaign of **Turenne** on the upper Rhine (first ravaging of the Palatinate) against Montecucculi, the im-

perial general, and the elector of Brandenburg. The latter, recalled by the inroad of the Swedish allies of Louis XIV into his lands, defeated the Swedes in the

1675, June 28. **Battle of Fehrbellin.** Turenne fell at Sasbach, in Baden (July 27). The French retreated across the Rhine.

1676. Naval successes in the Mediterranean against the Dutch and Spanish. Death of de Ruyter.

1678. Surprise and capture of Ghent and Ypres by the French. Negotiations with each combatant, which had been for some time in progress, resulted in the

1678–1679. **TREATIES OF NIJMEGEN** (Nijmwegen, Nimeguen). **Holland** and **France** (Aug. 10, 1678); **Spain** and **France** (Sept. 17, 1678); the **emperor,** with **France** and **Sweden** (Feb. 6, 1679); **Holland** with **Sweden** (Oct. 12, 1679). At Fontainebleau, **France** and **Denmark** (Sept. 2, 1679). At Lund, **Denmark** and **Sweden** (Sept. 26, 1679).

(1) Holland received its whole territory back, upon condition of preserving neutrality. (2) Spain ceded to France: Franche-Comté, and on the northwest frontier, Valenciennes, Cambray, and the Cambrésis, Aire, Poperingen, St. Omer, Ypres, Condé, Bouchain, Maubeuge, and other towns; France ceded to Spain: Charleroi, Binche, Oudenarde, Ath, Courtray, Limburg, Ghent, Waes, etc.; and in Catalonia, Puycerda. (3) The emperor ceded to France: Freiburg in the Breisgau; France gave up the right of garrison in Philippsburg; the duke of Lorraine was to be restored to his duchy, but on such conditions that he refused to accept them.

Louis XIV forced the elector of Brandenburg to conclude the

1679, June 29. **Peace of St. Germain-en-Laye,** whereby the elector surrendered to Sweden nearly all of his conquests in Pomerania, in return for which he received only the reversion of the principality of East Friesland, which became Prussian in 1744, and a small indemnification.

Louis was now at the height of his power. Stimulated by the weakness of the Empire, he established the

1680–1683. **Chambers of Reunion** at Metz, Breisach, Besançon, and Tournay. These were French courts of claims with power to investigate and decide what dependencies had at any time belonged to the territories and towns which had been ceded to France by the last four treaties of peace. The king executed with his troops the decisions of his tribunals. Saarbrücken, Luxemburg, Zweibrücken, Strassburg (1681), and many other towns were thus annexed to France.

1683. Invasions of the Spanish Netherlands, occupation of Luxemburg, and seizure of Trier (1684). Lorraine permanently occupied by France. To the weakness of the Empire, the wars with the Turks, and the general confusion of European relations since the peace of Nimwegen, is to be attributed the fact that these aggressions were met by nothing more than empty protests, and that

1684. A truce for twenty years was concluded at Regensburg between Louis and the emperor and the Empire, whereby he retained everything he had obtained by reunion up to August 1, 1681, including Strassburg.

Louis's mistresses: Louise de la Vallière; Madame de Montespan; Madame de Maintenon, a devout Catholic whose influence over the king was boundless. Maria Teresa died 1683. Louis privately married to Madame de Maintenon. **War upon heresy.** The dragonnades in Languedoc. Wholesale conversions of Calvinists.

1685, Oct. 18.   REVOCATION OF THE EDICT OF NANTES. The exercise of the reformed religion in France was forbidden, children were to be educated in the Catholic faith, emigration was prohibited. In spite of this more than 50,000 families, including military leaders (Schomberg), men of letters, and a large part of the artisans of France, made their way to foreign countries. Their loss was a blow to the industry of the country that perhaps hastened the approach of the revolution. The exiles found welcome in Holland, England (Spitalfields), Brandenburg, English North America, and South Africa. The Protestants of Alsace retained the freedom of worship that had been secured to them.

1688–1697. THIRD WAR. (War of the League of Augsburg).

Cause: After the extinction of the male line of the electors palatine in the person of the **Elector Charles** (d. 1685), whose sister was the wife of Louis XIV's brother, the duke of Orléans, the king laid claim to the allodial lands of the family, a claim he soon extended to the greater portion of the country. Another ground for war was found in the quarrel over the election of the archbishop of Köln, which Louis was resolved to secure for Von Fürstenberg, bishop of Strassburg, in place of Prince Clement of Bavaria (1688).

Meantime the unfavorable impression produced throughout Protestant Europe by the revocation of the edict of Nantes had contributed to the success of the plans of William of Orange, and on July 9, 1686, the **League of Augsburg,** directed against France, was signed by the emperor, the kings of Sweden and Spain, the electors of Bavaria, of Saxony,

and the Palatinate. In 1688 occurred the revolution in England that placed William of Orange on the throne of that country, and added a powerful kingdom to the new foes of Louis. The exiled James II took refuge with the French monarch (court at St. Germain).

1688, Oct. Invasion and devastation of the Palatinate, by order of Louvois. The military successes of the French on the Rhine were unimportant, especially after 1693, when **Prince Louis of Bavaria** assumed the chief command against them.

1689, May 12. The **Grand Alliance,** between the powers who had joined the League of Augsburg and England and Holland (Savoy had joined the league in 1687). The principal scene of war was in the Netherlands.

1690, June 30. Battle of Fleurus, defeat of the prince of Waldeck by Louis's general, Marshal **Luxembourg.** The French expedition to Ireland in aid of James had but a temporary success, and ended in defeat, 1690. French successes in Piedmont; Catinat reduced Savoy; defeat of Victor Amadeus at Staffarda.

1692, May. Defeat of the French fleet under Tourville by the English and Dutch at **Cap La Hogue.** The mastery of the sea passed from the French to the English. Death of Louvois.

July 24. Battle of Steinkirk (Steenkerken). Victory of Luxembourg over William III.

1693, June 30. Battle of Lagos; defeat of the British fleet by the French under Tourville.

July 29. Battle of Neerwinden. Victory of Luxembourg over William III, who in spite of his many defeats still kept the field.

In Italy Marshal Catinat defeated the duke of Savoy at **Marsaglia.** Rise of **Prince Eugene of Savoy** (1663–1736).

1695. Death of Luxembourg, who was succeeded by the incapable Villeroy.

1695, Sept. Recapture of **Namur** by William III.

1696, May 30. Separate peace with Savoy at Turin. All conquests were restored to the duke (Pignerol and Casale), and his daughter married Louis's grandson, the duke of Burgundy. Savoy promised to remain neutral.

1697, Sept. 30.   TREATY OF RYSWICK between France, England, Spain, and Holland. (1) Confirmation of the separate peace with Savoy. (2) Restoration of conquests between France and England and Holland; William III acknowledged as king of England, and Anne as his successor, Louis promising not to help his enemies. (3) It was agreed that the chief fortresses in the Spanish Netherlands should be garrisoned with Dutch troops as a barrier between France and Holland. (4) France restored to Spain all places which had been "reunited" since the treaty of Nimwegen, with the exception of 82 places, and all conquests. (5) Holland restored Pondichéry in India to the French East India Company and received commercial privileges in return.

Oct. 30. Treaty between France and the emperor (and Empire). (1) France ceded all the "reunions" except Alsace, which henceforward was lost to the Empire. (2) Strassburg was ceded to France. (3) France ceded Freiburg and Breisach to the emperor, and Phillipsburg to the Empire. (4) The duchy of Zweibrücken was restored to the king of Sweden, as count palatine of the Rhine. (5) Lorraine was restored to Duke Leopold (excepting Saarlouis). (6) The claims of Cardinal Fürstenberg to the archbishopric of Köln were disavowed. (7) The Rhine was made free.

1701–1714. WAR OF THE SPANISH SUCCESSION. The family relations that led to the war will be made clear by the genealogical table.

Leopold I had, besides his daughter **Maria Antonia,** two sons by his third marriage, **Joseph I,** emperor from 1705 to 1711 and **Charles VI,** emperor from 1711 to 1740.

Charles II, king of Spain, was childless; the extinction of the Spanish house of Hapsburg in the near future was certain; hence the question of the Spanish succession formed the chief occupation of all the European cabinets after the **treaty of Ryswick.** The question had two aspects: (a) The *legal,* according to which there were three claimants: (1) **Louis XIV,** at once as son of the elder daughter of Philip III and husband of the elder daughter of Philip IV. The solemn renunciations of both princesses were declared null and void by the parlement of Paris. (2) **Leopold I,** the representative of the German line of Hapsburg, as son of the younger daughter of Philip III, and husband of the younger daughter of Philip IV. Both princesses had expressly reserved their right of inheritance. (3) The **electoral prince of Bavaria,** as great-grandson of Philip IV, and grandson of the younger sister of the present possessor, Charles II. (b) The *political* aspect with regard to the balance of power in Europe, in consideration of which the naval powers, England and Holland, would not permit the crown of the great Spanish monarchy to be united with the French, or to be worn by the ruler of the Austrian lands. On this account Leopold I claimed the Spanish inheritance for his second son Charles only, while Louis XIV's claim was urged in the name of his second grandson, Philip of Anjou.

1698, Oct. 11. First Treaty of Partition. Spain, Indies, and the Netherlands to the electoral prince of Bavaria; Naples and Sicily, seaports in Tuscany, and the province of Guipuzcoa, to the dauphin; the duchy of Milan, to Archduke Charles. The negotiations of the powers in regard to the succession, and the conclusion of a treaty of partition without the participation of Charles II, provoked that monarch. In order to preserve the unity of the monarchy, he made the prince elector of Bavaria, then seven years old, sole heir of the whole inheritance; a settlement to which the naval powers agreed.

1699, Feb. 6. Sudden death of the prince elector. New intrigues of France (Harcourt ambassador, Cardinal Portocarrero) and Austria at Madrid, while both parties were negotiating a new treaty of partition with the naval powers.

1700, Mar. 13. Second Treaty of Partition. Spain and the Indies to Archduke Charles; Naples and Sicily and the duchy of Lorraine to the dauphin; Milan to the duke of Lorraine in exchange. Finally Charles II, although originally more inclined to the Austrian succession, signed a new will, making Louis's grandson, Philip of Anjou, heir. Immediately afterward

1700, Nov. 1. Charles II died. Louis XIV soon decided to follow the will rather than the treaty with England. The duke of Anjou was proclaimed as **Philip V,** and started for his new kingdom. (*Il n'y a plus de Pyrénées.*)

1701, Sept. 7. Grand Alliance of the naval powers with the Emperor Leopold I, for the purpose, at first, of securing the Spanish possessions in the Netherlands and in Italy for the Austrian house, while France allied herself with the dukes of Savoy and Mantua, the electors of Bavaria and Köln. The other states of the Empire, especially Prussia, joined the emperor. Portugal afterward joined the Grand Alliance, and in 1703 Savoy did likewise, deserting France. Three men were at the head of the Grand Alliance against France: **Eugene, prince of Savoy,** imperial general; **Marlborough,** English general, formerly John Churchill; **Antonius Heinsius,** after the death of William III, 1702, pensionary of Holland. Spain, the real object of the war, had but little importance in the campaigns, the chief seats of war being Italy, the Netherlands, and Germany. Philip of Anjou was recognized in Spain as **King Philip V.** His strongest support was in Castile.

1701. Commencement of the war by Eugene's **invasion of Italy.** Victory over Catinat at Carpi, over Villeroy at **Chiara;** the latter was captured at Cremona (1702).

1702. Eugene and Vendôme fought a drawn **battle at Luzzara,** after which the French had the advantage in Italy until 1706.

1703. The **Bavarians invaded Tyrol,** but were

The Spanish Succession (1700)

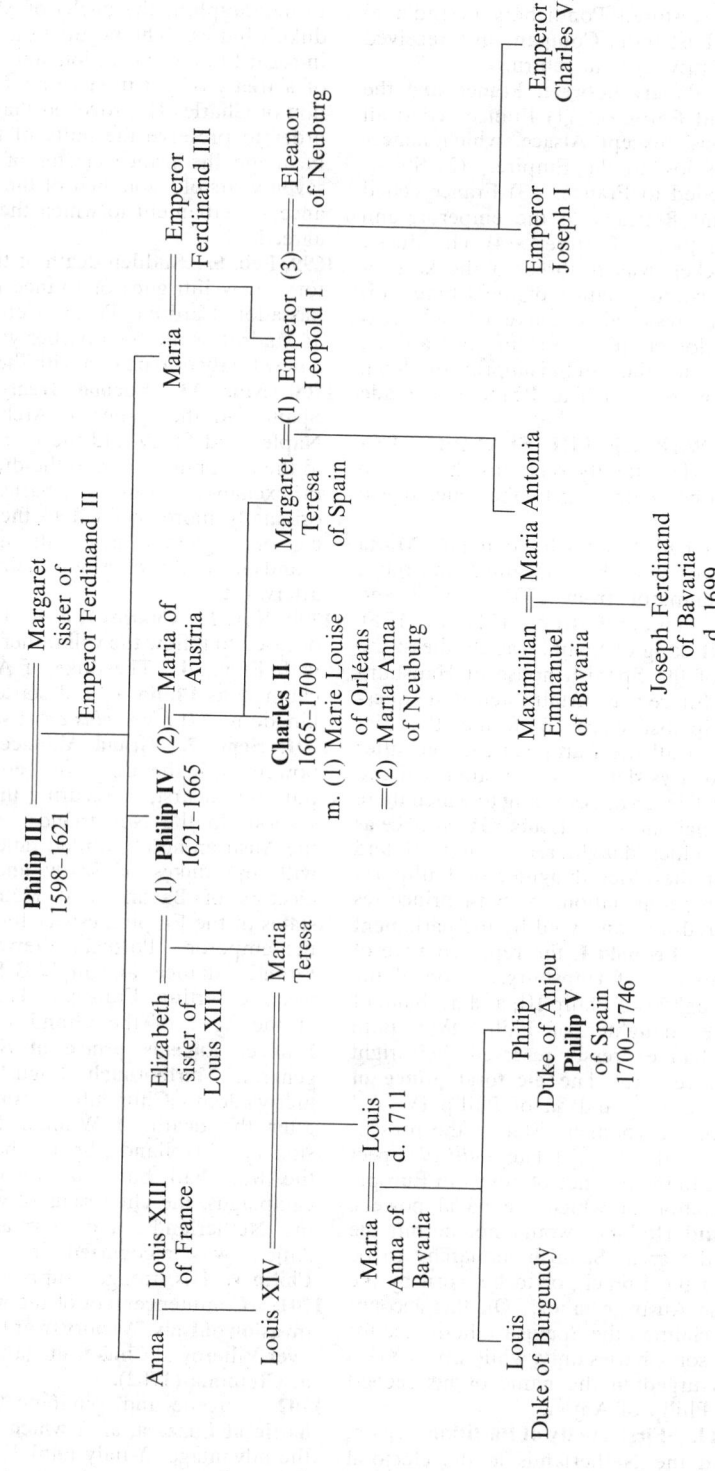

repulsed. Eugene went to Germany along the Rhine. Marlborough invaded the Spanish Netherlands. The Archduke Charles landed in Spain, and invaded Catalonia, where he established himself as Charles III. **The English captured Gibraltar** (1704).

1704, Aug. 13. BATTLE OF HÖCHSTÄDT AND BLENHEIM (BLINDHEIM), (between Ulm and Donauwörth), Bavarians and French (Tallard) defeated by Eugene and Marlborough.

1706. Charles conquered Madrid but held it for a short time only.

May 23. VICTORY OF MARLBOROUGH AT RAMILLIES over Villeroy. Submission of Brussels, Antwerp, Ghent, Ostend, etc.

Sept. 7. VICTORY OF EUGENE AT TURIN, over Marsin and the duke of Orléans with the help of the Prussians under Leopold of Dessau. Submission of all Lombardy. Charles III proclaimed at Milan. **The French excluded from Italy.**

1708, July 11. VICTORY OF MARLBOROUGH AND EUGENE AT OUDENARDE over Vendôme and the duke of Burgundy. Siege and surrender of Lille.

Negotiations for peace. Demands of the allies: surrender of the Spanish monarchy to Charles of Austria, and of the border fortresses of the Netherlands to the Hollanders; restoration of all matters relating to the Empire and the emperor to the state prescribed in the peace of Westphalia, i.e. the cession of Strassburg, Breisach, etc. Britain insisted on the recognition of Anne and the Protestant succession and the banishment of the Pretender. These terms Louis was willing to accept, but when the demand was added that he should drive his grandson from Spain with French weapons, it was too much. The negotiations were broken off, Louis made a successful appeal to the people of France, and the war was continued.

1709, Sept. 11. BATTLE OF MALPLAQUET. The French were again beaten by Eugene and Marlborough, but, by no means broken, retired in good order. The bloodiest battle of the war. The argument of "butchery" helped overthrow the Whigs in England. The allies lost 20,000 men. New approaches on the part of Louis. Capture of Douai, Mons, etc. (1710). In Spain Philip, by the aid of Vendôme, had the advantage of Charles. The Spanish people favored Philip. Renewal of the negotiations at Gertruydenburg. Louis offered to pay subsidized troops against his grandson. The allies demanded that he should send his armies against Philip. Renewal of the war. Victories of Vendôme over the British (**Brihuega**, 1710)

and the imperialists (**Villaviciosa**, in Spain).

1710, Aug. Fall of the Whig ministry in England, and accession of the enemies of Marlborough.

1711. Death of the Emperor Joseph, whereby Charles became heir of all the Austrian possessions, so that the monarchy of Charles V would have been restored had the Spanish inheritance also devolved upon him. These events completely altered all political relations, in favor of Louis XIV. **Marlborough** removed from command, the Grand Alliance dissolved, preliminaries of peace between Britain and France. Death of the dauphin, of Adelaide of Savoy, her husband, and their son, the duke of Brittany.

1712. Victory of the French commander Villars at **Denain** over Lord Albemarle. Recapture of Douai, Le Quesnoy, and Bouchain. Opening of the **congress at Utrecht.** Each of the allies presented his demands separately. Dissensions between the allies caused the conclusion of separate treaties of peace, which are comprehended under the name of the

1713, Apr. 11. TREATY OF UTRECHT.

(1) **Britain:** Recognition of the Protestant succession in England; confirmation of the permanent separation of the crowns of France and Spain. France ceded to Britain Newfoundland, Nova Scotia (Acadia), and Hudson Bay territory, but retained New France (Quebec); Spain ceded to Britain Gibraltar, the island of Minorca, and the *asiento,* or contract for supplying the Spanish colonies with African slaves.

(2) **Holland:** Surrender of the Spanish Netherlands to the Republic of Holland, in order that they should be delivered to the Austrians, after the conclusion of a barrier treaty, in regard to the fortresses along the French border from Furnes to Namur, which were to be garrisoned by the Dutch. Lille restored to France. Demolition of the fortifications of Dunkirk.

(3) **Savoy** received the island of Sicily as a kingdom, and an advantageous change of boundary in upper Italy, renounced its claims upon Spain, reserving, however, its right of inheritance in case the house of Bourbon should become extinct.

(4) **Prussia** received recognition of the royal title, and possession of Neuchâtel and the upper quarter of Guelders. Prussia's claim upon the principality of Orange, on the Rhône, was transferred to France.

(5) **Portugal** obtained a correction of boundaries in South America.

Philip V (founder of the Spanish branch of the Bourbons) was recognized as king of Spain and the colonies.

Reservations in the peace: (1) for the emperor, the possession of the appanages of the Spanish monarchy, the Netherlands, Milan, Naples, Sardinia, but *not* Sicily; (2) for the Empire the *status quo* of the treaty of Ryswick, only.

1713. The emperor and the Empire continued the war. Unsuccessful campaign of Eugene, who was wretchedly supported. Landau and Freiburg taken by Villars. After these losses the emperor concluded peace with France, in his own name at Rastatt, in that of the Empire at Baden (in Switzerland).

1714, Mar.-Sept. TREATY OF RASTATT AND BADEN. Austria took possession of the Spanish Netherlands, after the barrier for Holland had been agreed upon, and retained Naples, Sardinia, and Milan, which she had already occupied. For the Empire: ratification of the treaty of Ryswick; the electors of Bavaria and Köln, who had been placed under the ban of the Empire, were reinstated in their lands and dignities. Landau was left in the hands of France. No peace between Spain and the emperor, who did not recognize the Bourbons in Spain.

FRENCH LITERATURE AND ART, 17TH CENTURY

The 17th century was the **golden age of French literature,** with the baroque giving way to classicism, new status given to intellectual matters, the establishment of the *Académie française* (1635). The poet **François de Malherbe** (1555–1628) was critical of his baroque predecessors; the philosopher **Blaise Pascal** (1623–1662) wrote his *Pensées sur la religion* (1669) under the influence of Cornelius Jansen (1585–1638). The drama was the most important literary medium of the period. **Pierre Corneille** (1606–1684) violated the classical dramatic unities of time, place, and action in *Le Cid* (1636), thereby creating a great controversy as to their observance; the classical tradition, upheld by the Royal Academy, eventually won, and Corneille conformed to its dictates as did the other great tragedian, **Jean Racine** (1639–1699; *Phèdre,* 1677; *Bérénice,* 1670). **Molière** (Jean Baptiste Poquelin, 1622–1673) raised the standards of French comedy to a new level with his comedies of manners (*Les précieuses ridicules,* 1659; *Le misanthrope,* 1666; *Tartuffe,* 1669). This was also an age of fable, with the verse *Fables* of **Jean de La Fontaine** (1621–1695) and the *Contes de ma mère l'oye* of **Charles Perrault** (1628–1703); and an age of essays and letters (**Nicolas Boileau-Déspreaux,** 1636–1711; **Madame de Sévigné,** 1626–1696). In the field of history **Jean Mabillon** (1632–1707) *De re diplomatica*

(1681); **Jacques Bossuet** (1627–1704) *Discours sur l'histoire universelle* (1681); **Pierre Bayle** (1647–1706) *Dictionnaire historique et critique* (1695–1697), a criticism of existing beliefs and institutions, commonly regarded as the first important work of the Enlightenment.

The classical style prevailed in the paintings of **Nicolas Poussin** (1594–1665), **Claude Lorrain** (1600–1682), and **Charles LeBrun** (1619–1690). The tradition carried over too into the music of **Robert Cambert,** whose *Pastorale,* performed at the **Académie royal de musique** in Paris (1659), was the first opera in French, and to the operas of **Jean-Baptiste Lully** (1632–1687), who introduced ballets into his operas and collaborated with Molière to write *Le bourgeois gentilhomme* (1670).

The second half of the 17th century also marked the beginning of construction of many outstanding royal buildings in and about Paris (Versailles, Louvre, Hôtel des Invalides).

1715–1774. LOUIS XV, five years old, greatgrandson of Louis XIV. **Philip, duke of Orléans,** became regent during the minority of Louis XV (1715–1723), thus setting aside the will of Louis XIV. An attempt was made to use the higher nobility in government by means of councils, but this failed. Under the regent's favorite, **Cardinal Dubois,** a man of low birth who had risen through political skill, the foreign policy of Louis XIV was reversed. **Alliance with Britain and Holland.**

1718–1720. War with Spain (p. 487). By the **treaty of The Hague** (Feb. 17, 1720) the emperor received Sicily, and Savoy received Sardinia in exchange. In domestic policy, increased religious toleration of Protestants and Jansenists.

1718–1720. Law's Mississippi scheme. In his financial distress the regent grasped at the dazzling plans of the Scotsman **John Law.** Royal bank, Company of the West, grant of Louisiana. Characteristic boom phenomena—rise in value of stock of the Mississippi Company, inflation (made worse by paper). Sudden collapse of the company bringing widespread disaster (1720). Law's boom, like most such speculative manias, left behind it some definite achievements—increased shipping, some colonization in Louisiana, private fortunes for those who had sold out in time. With the contemporary English **South Sea Bubble,** Law's scheme forms an introduction to modern speculative finance.

1723–1726. Administration of the duke of Bourbon. Louis XV married (1725) the daughter of the deposed king of Poland, **Stanislas Leszczynski,** having broken off a projected marriage with the infanta of Spain and sent her back, to the great indignation of Philip V. Louis was under the influence of his tutor, **Cardinal Fleury,** who replaced Bourbon and his favorite Prie, and banished them from court.

1726–1743. Administration of Fleury, generally peaceful, and marked by economic growth. Quarrels over the papal bull *Unigenitus,* marked by the government's abandonment of the Jansenists and their defense by the courts (*parlements*). Wave of religious revivalism, similar to Methodism in England (*convulsionnaires,* Archdeacon Pâris). Growth of deism among the literate classes.

1773–1738. France, with Spain and Sardinia, took part in the **War of the Polish Succession** (p. 501) and occupied Lorraine (1733).

1740–1748. War of the Austrian Succession (p. 501). France supported the claims of the Bavarian elector and allied with Frederick the Great against Maria Theresa (1741). This involved France in conflict with Britain, especially in North America and India (pp. 554, 573).

1756–1763. The **Seven Years' War** (p. 503) in which France played a leading rôle, but this time on the Austrian side, against Prussia. The war overseas led to the loss of most of the French colonial empire.

After the **death of Fleury,** a series of administrations influenced by the royal mistresses, especially the **marquise de Pompadour** (1745–1764), who helped make possible the Austrian alliance of 1756 (*The Diplomatic Revolution,* p. 503). Heavy expenditures, growth of luxury. The king, once *Louis le bien-aimé,* now hated. **Damiens,** who attempted to assassinate the king (Jan. 5, 1757), was tortured and killed. In spite of general failure in war, France added in this reign Lorraine (1766) and Corsica (1768). In his old age, Louis came under the influence of the politically least able of his mistresses, the plebeian Jeanne Vaubernier, by marriage with a superannuated courtier, **Comtesse du Barry.**

Throughout the reign, quarrels with the parlements, especially that of Paris, which asserted a claim to something like a power of judicial review over the royal decrees. The parlements were abolished in 1771 by the chancellor, Maupéou, and a more simple and efficient system of courts set up, but the reform was very unpopular, and Louis XVI restored the parlements as one of the first acts of his reign. The crown was made still more unpopular by the affair of the *pacte de famine,* an attempted corner in the grain trade in which the king himself was implicated. Steady growth of a literature of attack on the government.

1774–1792. LOUIS XVI, grandson of Louis XV. The new king's personal morality and good will were neutralized by a lack of energy and understanding. As dauphin he had (1770) married **Marie Antoinette,** daughter of the Empress Maria Theresa. The queen, always unpopular with the anti-Austrians at court, was a proud and tactless woman, fond of dances, theaters, parties, and was easily made unpopular with the masses by the propaganda of the *philosophes* and their friends. (*"Let 'em eat cake."*) The scandal of the **diamond necklace** (1785) was especially disastrous to her reputation. She did much, by purely personal choices of favorites, to prevent any consistent or thoroughgoing reforms in French administration.

Yet the early years of the reign were marked by an effort, in keeping with the spirit of "Enlightened Despotism," to achieve reforms. **Robert Turgot,** minister of marine and finance (1774–1776), by the **Six Edicts** made reforms in taxation, dissolved the old trade guilds, and tried to carry out the *laissez-faire* economics of the **physiocrats,** of whom he was one of the leading thinkers. He was dismissed, partly by court intrigue, partly by the opposition of the guilds, and his work largely undone. **Jacques Necker,** a Swiss banker, was minister of finances (1777–1781) and effected piecemeal reforms. The greatest achievements of Louis's reforming ministers were those of the **comte de St. Germain** at the war office. The standing army was improved, especially in the artillery. St. Germain and his aids, **Guibert** and **Gribeauval,** did much to make the victories of the armies of 1792–1794 possible. **Maurepas** was the head of the ministry, 1774–1781, and on his death was succeeded by the **comte de Vergennes** (1781).

1778–1783. France intervened in the **War of American Independence** on the side of the colonists (p. 561). Her expenses in this war added disastrously to her financial deficit.

1781. Necker, dismissed from office, published a somewhat disingenuous *compte rendu* of the finances, the effect of which was to bring the deficit dramatically before the public. The next seven years were filled with the desperate expedients of a series of ministers to solve the financial problem. A solution was probably impossible without taxing heavily the *privilégiés* (nobles, state officials, clergy, and even certain commoners). These resisted the efforts of the government, no matter how well intentioned.

1783–1787. Calonne (minister of finances), a facile courtier, contracted an immense debt, but came in the end to the sensible decision to reform the land-tax thoroughly. He encountered resistance, and was forced out in

favor of **Loménie de Brienne.** Meanwhile
1787, Feb. 22. An **assembly of notables,** a
purely consultative body, with not very clear
constitutional precedents, called to Versailles, was dissolved (May 25) without having
achieved any real reform. Loménie de Brienne
attempted to issue reform edicts on lines Calonne had worked out, but the parlements,
headed by the parlement of Paris, refused to
register them. The parlement of Paris was
banished to Troyes (Aug. 14). Public opinion
was in favor of the parlement, and its president,
d'Espréménil, became a hero, largely because
he had defied the government. The parlement
was recalled (Sept. 24), but continued its resistance when Brienne proposed new loans. In
January 1788 it presented a list of grievances,
and was abolished in favor of a *cour plénière*
(May 8). Louis and his advisers now decided
to give in to many pressures, and summon the
old medieval legislative body of the realm,
the **estates-general,** which had last met in
1614. In August 1788 Brienne resigned and
amid popular rejoicing **Necker was recalled** to
arrange for the estates.   (*Cont. p. 627.*)

FRENCH LITERATURE AND ART, 18TH CENTURY

The 18th century was the **"Age of Enlightenment"** and its best authors wrote mostly prose.
Charles-Louis de Secondat, **Baron de Montesquieu** (1689–1755) wrote letters and essays (*Lettres persanes,* 1721) and *L'Esprit des lois* (1748)
which played a considerable part in establish-

ing the ideas that culminated in the French
Revolution. **Denis Diderot** (1713–1784) edited
a 34-volume *Encyclopédie, ou dictionnaire raisonné des sciences, des arts et des métiers* to
which the great contemporary writers contributed, using it as the medium for airing their
views on individual liberty. The novel flourished: **Alain Lesage** (1668–1747), *Gil Blas* (1715)
a picaresque novel; **L'Abbé Prévost** (1696–1763),
Manon Lescaut (1731); and finally **Jean-Jacques
Rousseau** (1712–1778; *Julie ou la nouvelle Héloïse,* 1761; *Émile,* 1762). It was in his essays
(*Discourses,* 1750, 1755; *Le contrat social,* 1762)
that Rousseau expounded his views of the
"noble savage," of the "inalienable right" of
the individual to equality before the law.

The political writings of **Voltaire** (Francois-Marie Arouet, le jeune, 1694–1778) were so
critical of French institutions that he was forced
to flee from France. He also wrote drama,
poetry, histories (*Siècle de Louis XIV,* 1751;
Essai sur les moeurs, 1756), literary criticism,
letters, and message novels (*Candide,* 1759).

The paintings of the period were characteristically rococo in spirit: **Antoine Watteau**
(1684–1721), **François Boucher** (1703–1770),
Jean-Honoré Fragonard (1732–1806). Most
prominent sculptor was **Jean-Antoine Houdon**
(1741–1828), whose subjects were the leading
literary and political figures of the day.

The composers **François Couperin** (1668–
1733) and **Jean-Philippe Rameau** (1683–1764)
carried on the operatic tradition of Lully. **Jean
Marie Leclair** (1697–1764) founded a French
school of violin playing.

4. THE IBERIAN PENINSULA

(*From p. 418*)

a. SPAIN, 1659–1807

The **peace of the Pyrenees** (1659) marked the
end of the Spanish ascendancy in Europe,
which now passed to France. Thenceforth
Spain came to be looked upon increasingly as
suitable spoil for the stronger states.
1665–1700. CHARLES II, the four-year-old
son of Philip IV and the last of the Spanish
Hapsburgs. Until 1676 his mother, **Maria
Anna of Austria,** headed the council of regency. She, in turn, was wholly under the
influence of her Jesuit advisers (**Everard Nitard,**
et al.). The general laxity and incompetence
of the government, as well as the queen-mother's preference for foreigners, aroused
much opposition, led by **John Joseph of Austria** and some of the nobles. These ultimately
effected the downfall of Nitard and even the

departure of the queen-mother. Thereafter
John Joseph controlled the king until the
former's death in 1679.
1667–1668. The **War of Devolution** (p. 477),
representing an attack by Louis XIV on the
Spanish possessions in the Netherlands. He
was forced, by the combined action of England, Holland, and Sweden, to restore most of
his conquests, but by the **treaty of Aix-la-Chapelle** (May 2, 1668) Louis retained twelve
fortified places in Flanders.
1674. Spain joined the coalition against France
occasioned by Louis's attack on Holland. By
the **treaty of Nimwegen** (Sept. 17, 1678) Spain,
as the ally of Holland, lost to France Franche-Comté, Artois, and sixteen fortified places in
Flanders (p. 479).
1680. Charles II married Marie Louise of Orléans. On her death he

1689. Married Maria Anna, daughter of the elector palatine.

1690. Spain joined the League of Augsburg (p. 480) against Louis XIV. By the **treaty of Ryswick** (1697), which concluded the war, Spain was obliged to cede Haiti to France.

1698, Oct. 11. First partition treaty between England, Holland, and France, regarding the succession to Spain and the Spanish Empire. Charles, naturally irritated by this cavalier treatment,

1700, Oct. 3. Named **Philip of Anjou**, grandson of Louis XIV, heir to his dominions. The king, long ill, died on November 1.

1700-1746. PHILIP V, the first Bourbon king, 17-years-old at the time of his accession: a mediocre, irresolute, but pious ruler.

1701-1714. WAR OF THE SPANISH SUCCESSION (p. 481).

1703. The powers of the Grand Alliance against France proclaimed Archduke **Charles of Austria** as king of Spain.

1704, Aug. 4. The **English took Gibraltar,** which they have held ever since.

1705. Charles landed in Catalonia and took Barcelona (Oct. 14). Catalonia and Valencia, ever strongholds of anti-French sentiment, accepted Charles and supported him.

1706, June. The **Portuguese**, acting with the Grand Alliance, invaded Spain and occupied Madrid, but were driven out by Philip in October.

1707, Apr. The forces of the allies were defeated at **Almanza** by the duke of Berwick, in Spanish service.

1709. The British seized **Minorca.** Philip was defeated by the Austrians at **Almenara** and **Saragossa,** and

1710, Sept. 28. Charles took Madrid. Before long, however, Philip and the French won victories at **Brihuega** and **Villaviciosa** (Dec. 10) and Charles was obliged to abandon Madrid again.

1713, Apr. 11. The **treaty of Utrecht** (p. 483). Philip was recognized as king of Spain by Britain and Holland, on condition that the French and Spanish crowns should never be united. At the same time he ceded to his father-in-law, Victor Amadeus of Savoy, the island of Sicily. The British retained Gibraltar and Minorca and secured the *asiento,* a contract allowing them to import into the Spanish colonies 4,000 Negroes a year and to keep one ship stationed at Porto Bello.

1713, May. The **Salic law** was introduced in Spain to govern the succession to the throne.

1714, Mar. 6. Treaty of Rastatt, ending the war with Austria. Spain gave up her possessions in Flanders (henceforth the Austrian Netherlands), Luxemburg, and Italy.

Sept. 11. Barcelona finally capitulated to Berwick. The privileges of Catalonia and Valencia had already been declared abolished (1707). The provinces were now put under Castilian law and the use of the Catalan language was forbidden in the courts.

With the end of the War of Succession the **Bourbon rule in Spain** may be said to have begun, properly speaking. The rulers of the line soon proved themselves to be no more efficient than the later Hapsburgs and the court continued to be a hotbed of intrigue, dynastic and personal. On the other hand, the Bourbon kings regarded themselves as absolute rulers and did their utmost to reduce the old feudal privileges. They reorganized the administration (central secretariats in the place of the old commissions) and established a bureaucracy (intendants, corregidores). An impressive number of **reforming ministers** succeeded each other through the century, of whom may be mentioned Patiño, Ensenada, Aranda, Floridablanca, Campomanes, Jovellaños, and Godoy. They succeeded in putting the finances on a sounder basis, in rebuilding the army and navy (introduction of conscription—every fifth man), and above all devoted themselves to economic development—road- and bridge-building, encouragement of industry and trade, establishment of technical schools, agricultural improvements, etc.

1714. Philip married Elizabeth Farnese of Parma, on the death of his first wife, Maria Louisa of Savoy. Elizabeth was a handsome, alert, and very ambitious woman, who soon had the king wholly under her influence. With the aid of her adviser, Abbé (later Cardinal) **Giulio Alberoni,** an Italian of humble extraction, she devoted herself to the problem of supplanting the Austrian power in Italy and providing Italian thrones for her children. Philip, on the other hand, appears to have hoped for many years to succeed to the French throne and did his utmost to undermine the position of the French regent, the duke of Orléans. Thus Spain antagonized both France and Austria at the same time.

1717. Philip secretly sent an expeditionary force which seized Sardinia, and, later (July 1718), Sicily also.

1718, Aug. 2. Conclusion of the **Quadruple Alliance** (Britain, France, Holland, and Austria) to counteract the attempts of Philip to overturn the peace settlements. The British fleet landed an Austrian force in Sicily, while the French invaded the Basque country and Catalonia. The war was concluded by

1720, Feb. 17. The **treaty of The Hague,** by which Philip abandoned his Italian claims in return for an Austrian promise of the succes-

488

(From p. 482)

The Spanish Bourbons (1700–1833)

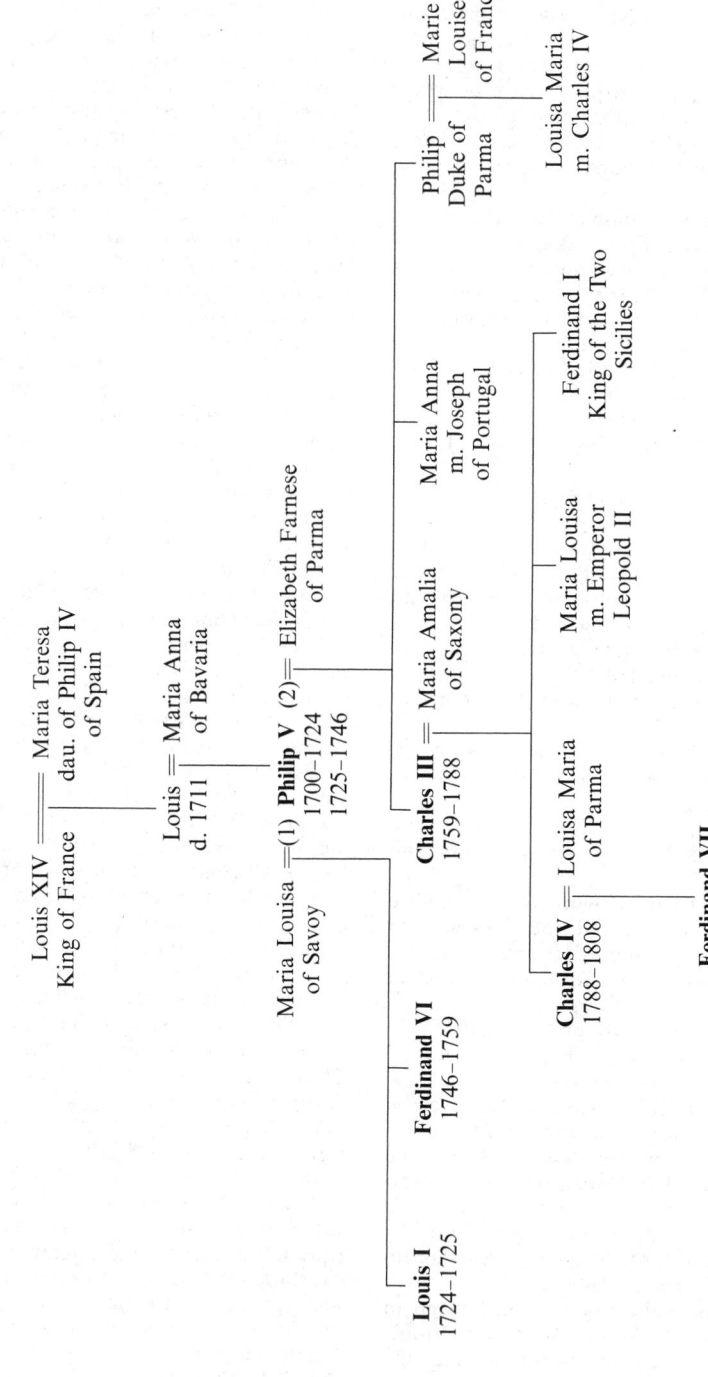

Louis XIV === Maria Teresa
King of France   dau. of Philip IV
   of Spain

Louis === Maria Anna
d. 1711   of Bavaria

Maria Louisa ===(1) **Philip V** (2)=== Elizabeth Farnese
of Savoy   1700–1724   of Parma
   1725–1746

Louis I
1724–1725

Ferdinand VI
1746–1759

Charles III === Maria Amalia
1759–1788   of Saxony

Maria Anna
m. Joseph
of Portugal

Philip === Marie
Duke of   Louise
Parma   of France

Louisa Maria
m. Charles IV

Charles IV === Louisa Maria
1788–1808   of Parma

Maria Louisa
m. Emperor
Leopold II

Ferdinand I
King of the Two
Sicilies

Ferdinand VII
1814–1833

(Cont. p. 695.)

sion to Parma, Piacenza, and Tuscany for Charles, the eldest son of Philip and Elizabeth Farnese. At the same time the emperor gave up his claims to Spain. Savoy was given Sardinia in place of Sicily, which was turned over to Austria.

1721, June. Spain joined the alliance of Britain and France. Louis, son of Philip by his first wife, married Louise Elizabeth of Orléans (1722), while Louis XV of France was betrothed to a daughter of Philip and Elizabeth, who was then only five years old.

1724. Abdication of Philip, for reasons not clear. He was succeeded by his son

1724. LOUIS I, who, however, died in the same year. Philip then resumed the crown.

1725. The **duke of Bourbon,** chief minister of Louis XV of France, eager for an heir to the throne, cancelled the engagement of the king to the girl-princess of Spain. In reply Philip allied himself with Austria (work of the adventurer, Baron de Ripperdá) by the **treaty of Vienna** (Apr. 30, 1725). This alliance, in turn, provoked the **treaty of Hanover** (Sept. 3) between Britain, France, Prussia, and Holland.

1727-1729. War with Britain and France. By the **treaty of Seville** (Nov. 1729), Britain and France agreed to the Spanish succession in the Italian duchies.

1731. Charles, the son of Philip and Elizabeth, on the extinction of the Farnese family, succeeded to the Italian duchies. At the same time Spain recognized the **Pragmatic Sanction** of Charles VI (p. 501).

1733. First *pacte de famille* between France and Spain. Spain thereupon joined France in

1733-1735. The **War of the Polish Succession** (p. 501) against Austria. A Spanish force was sent to invade Lombardy, while another seized Naples and Sicily (1734). By the **treaty of Vienna** (Nov. 13, 1738) Austria gave up Naples and Sicily (p. 501) and received Parma and Piacenza.

1739-1741. War of Jenkins' Ear, with Great Britain (p. 470).

1740-1748. War of the Austrian Succession (p. 501). Spain took part in the war as the ally of France against Austria. By the **treaty of Aix-la-Chapelle** (1748), Philip, the second son of Philip V and Elizabeth, was given the duchies of Parma, Piacenza, and Guastalla, while his brother Charles retained Naples and Sicily. Thus the dynastic aspirations of their mother were realized.

1746-1759. FERDINAND VI, the second son of Philip V by his first wife. Ferdinand was a good but timid ruler, who did but little to impress his age or his people.

1754. Concordat with the Vatican. Thereby the Spanish church became practically independent of Rome and was placed under the control of the government.

1756-1763. The **Seven Years' War** (p. 503). Spain at first remained neutral, though Spanish troops recovered **Minorca** (1756).

1759-1788. CHARLES III, son of Elizabeth Farnese and thitherto king of the Two Sicilies, which he now passed on to his son Ferdinand. Charles has been classified as one of the enlightened despots and he did, in fact, give considerable impetus to administrative and economic reform.

1761, Aug. 15. Second *pacte de famille* with France, against Britain. In this generally defensive arrangement the Bourbon states of Italy were included.

1762. Spain joined in the war against Britain. The British seized Cuba and the Philippines. By the **treaty of Paris** (Feb. 10, 1763) Spain recovered these possessions, but lost Minorca and Florida. In return for the loss of Florida, France ceded Louisiana to Spain.

1767, Mar. 1. Without warning or trial the king secretly expelled the **Jesuits** from Spain. Some 10,000 of them were deported to the Papal States.

1779, June. Spain joined France in the **War of American Independence** against Britain. The Spaniards seized Florida and Honduras and Minorca (1782), but failed to retake Gibraltar (1779-1783). By the **treaty of Versailles** (Sept. 3, 1783), Spain retained both Minorca and Florida.

1788-1808. CHARLES IV, the son of Charles III, a well-intentioned but weak and undecided ruler. A portrait of his family was painted (1800) by the great Spanish artist **Francisco Goya** (1746-1828). His ministers, **Conde de Floridablanca** and **Conde de Aranda,** made great efforts to shut out the teaching and influence of the French Revolution, and the Spanish court did its utmost to save the life of Louis XVI, but the queen effected the overthrow of Aranda and brought into power her favorite, **Manuel Godoy.**

1793, Mar. 7. FRANCE DECLARED WAR ON SPAIN. Spain made an alliance with Great Britain (Mar. 13) and the Spaniards invaded Roussillon and Navarre. But in 1794-1795 the French took the offensive, invading Catalonia and Guipúzcoa. By the **treaty of Basel** (June 22, 1795), the French returned their conquests and secured in return Santo Domingo. Godoy was given the title *Prince of the Peace.*

1796, Aug. 19. Treaty of San Ildefonso. Spain joined France in the war against Britain. Defeat of the Franco-Spanish fleet at **Cape St. Vincent** (Feb. 14, 1797). The British seized Trinidad.

1800, Oct. 1.   Second treaty of San Ildefonso. France secured Louisiana in return for a promise to enlarge Parma. By agreement of January 20, 1801, Spain promised to detach Portugal from Britain, by force if necessary. This latter provision resulted in the **War of the Oranges,** between Spain and Portugal.

1802, Mar.   Treaty of Amiens, between Great Britain, France, and Spain. The Spaniards secured Minorca but abandoned Trinidad.

1805, Jan. 4.   Spain entered the **War of the Third Coalition** on the side of France. Defeat of the Franco-Spanish fleet at **Trafalgar** (Oct. 21, 1805). Growing opposition of the Spanish people to the disastrous Francophile policy of Godoy. Ferdinand, the heir to the throne, soon emerged as the leader of the opposition.

1807, Oct. 27.   Treaty of Fontainebleau, between Napoleon and Spain. Portugal was to be divided between Charles IV and Godoy (who was to become prince of the Algarves, under Spanish suzerainty). The French were to aid in the conquest, and a French army, under **Junot,** soon arrived in Spain. Invasion of Portugal and capture of Lisbon (Nov. 30, 1807).

1807, Mar. 17.   Popular uprising against Godoy at Aranjuez.   Charles thereupon abdicated (Mar. 19), but **Murat,** who arrived soon afterward at Madrid, induced the king to retract his abdication and persuaded both Charles and Ferdinand to meet Napoleon.

Apr. 30.   The Bayonne Conference. Napoleon told Ferdinand to abdicate the throne he had just assumed. Then Charles was forced to abdicate in Napoleon's favor (May 10). Both princes were given estates in France and handsome pensions.

June 6.   JOSEPH, Napoleon's brother, became king of Spain.

In the early 18th century encouragement was afforded Spanish culture with the founding of the National Library (1712), the Royal Spanish Academy (1714), and the Academy of History (1735); but there was little significant literary production in the period (a novel, *Fray Gerundio* [1758], by **José Francisco de Isla y Rojo,** 1703–1781).   (*Cont. pp. 643, 694.*)

b. PORTUGAL, 1640–1807

(*From p. 420*)

The story of Portugal in this period parallels that of Spain. The period was one of growing weakness, economically and socially, accompanied by a growth of the royal power. The last cortes was called in 1697. The nobility became more and more a court group, dependent on royal favor. The Church, too, was subjected to the state, though within the country the Church possessed great wealth and exercised immense influence.

1640–1656.   JOHN (João) IV, first king of the house of Braganza. He was recognized almost at once by France and Holland, but Spain fostered a plot of Portuguese nobles against him. This was discovered and the leaders executed. Hostilities with Spain continued in desultory fashion. In 1644 the Portuguese, supported by England and France, took the offensive and invaded Spain **(victory of Montijo).** This brought a suspension of operations for some years.

1654.   The **Dutch** were finally driven from Brazil, where they had established themselves during the Spanish period.

1656–1667.   AFONSO VI, a frivolous, profligate, and vicious young man, during the first period of whose reign his mother, **Luisa María de Guzmán,** served as regent. In these years hostilities with Spain were reopened. The Spaniards were defeated at **Elvas** (Jan. 14, 1659), and, when they attempted to invade Portugal (1662) were again overwhelmed (**battle of Ameixal,** June 8, 1663) in a series of Portuguese victories in 1664–1665.

1662.   Charles II of England married Catherine, the daughter of John IV, thus preparing the way for ever closer relations between England and Portugal.

1667.   Peter (Pedro), the brother of Afonso, led the opposition to the outrageous conduct of the king. He set himself up as regent and exiled Afonso to the Azores (d. 1683). Peter's rule was more respectable and enjoyed wide popular support.

1668, Feb. 13.   Conclusion of **peace with Spain,** through the mediation of Charles II of England.   Spain at last recognized Portuguese independence.

1683–1706.   PETER II ruled as king after the death of Afonso. His reign was memorable for the conclusion of the

1703, Dec. 27.   Methuen-Alegrete agreement, by which British wool and woolens were to be admitted into Portugal duty-free, and Portuguese wine to be admitted into England at a greatly reduced rate. The agreement resulted in great gains in the Portuguese trade for the British, at French and Spanish expense.

1704.   Invasion of Portugal by a French-Spanish force, as a result of Portuguese participation in the War of the Spanish Succession. The British landed a force at Lisbon and joined the Portuguese in driving out the enemy.

1706.   Anglo-Portuguese invasion of Spain and brief **occupation of Madrid** (June).

1706–1750.   JOHN V, the son of Peter II, a

Portugal: The House of Braganza (1640-1853)

om p. 419)

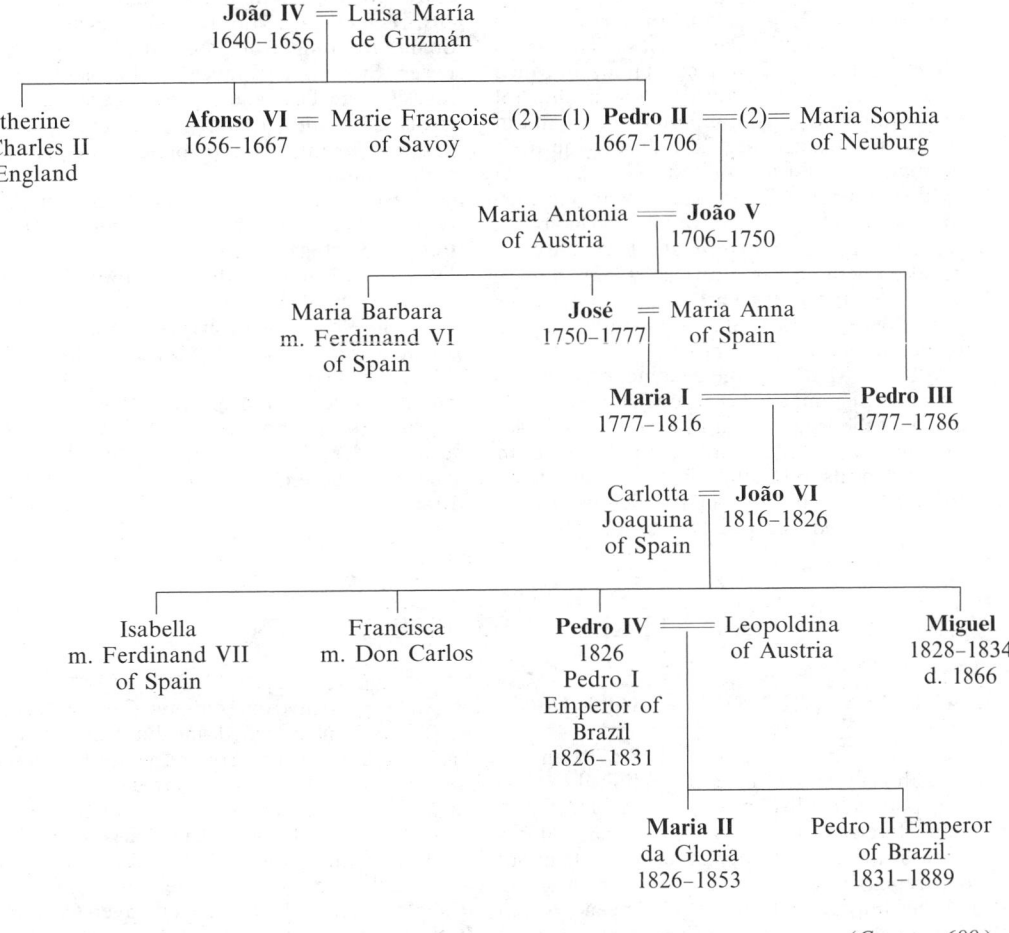

Joāo IV = Luisa María
1640–1656 | de Guzmán

Catherine
. Charles II
of England

Afonso VI = Marie Françoise (2)=(1) Pedro II ==(2)= Maria Sophia
1656–1667 of Savoy 1667–1706 of Neuburg

Maria Antonia ==== Joāo V
of Austria 1706–1750

Maria Barbara   José = Maria Anna
m. Ferdinand VI   1750–1777 of Spain
of Spain

Maria I =========================== Pedro III
1777–1816 1777–1786

Carlotta = Joāo VI
Joaquina | 1816–1826
of Spain

Isabella   Francisca   Pedro IV ==== Leopoldina   Miguel
m. Ferdinand VII m. Don Carlos 1826   of Austria   1828–1834
of Spain   Pedro I   d. 1866
                                Emperor of
                                Brazil
                                1826–1831

Maria II   Pedro II Emperor
da Gloria   of Brazil
1826–1853   1831–1889

(Cont. p. 699.)

profligate, extravagant, and bigoted ruler, during whose reign the court became another Versailles (construction of the **Mafra palace**), filled with mistresses and favorites.

1707, Apr. 25. Battle of Almanza. Defeat of the Anglo-Portuguese army by the French forces under Marshal Berwick. Thereafter Portugal played no further part in the war.

1750–1777. JOSEPH I, during whose entire reign the government of the country was in the hands of the **marquis de Pombal** (Sebastião José de Carvalho e Mello, who became marquis de Pombal only in 1770), the most remarkable statesman of modern Portuguese history. Pombal was a ruthless and heartless dictator, but at the same time a man affected by the French philosophy of the enlighten-

ment. He devoted himself to breaking the power of the privileged nobility and even more of the Church. On the other hand, he reformed the finances and the army, encouraged industry and trade (establishment of trade companies with monopolistic powers), tried to revive agriculture (silk-raising), and did much to develop primary and technical education.

1755, Nov. 1. The **GREAT EARTHQUAKE AT LISBON,** which was accompanied by fire and by flood of the Tagus. Tens of thousands lost their lives in the disaster. Lisbon was destroyed, with many of its treasures. The city was rebuilt under Pombal's energetic direction.

1758, Sept. Conspiracy of the Tavoras, a plot

by a group of nobles against the king and more especially against Pombal. The leaders, among them members of the highest aristocracy, were tortured and executed.

1759, Sept. 3. Expulsion of the Jesuits, who were deported to the Papal States. This was a direct result of the Tavora conspiracy, in which some Jesuits were involved. Pombal thus set the example for Spain and other states and in fact took a leading part in inducing the pope to abolish the Society of Jesus (1773).

1761. During the Seven Years' War, the Portuguese stood by Great Britain. The result was an invasion by Spanish and French forces, repulsed with British aid (Dec. 1762).

1774. Insanity of Joseph I, and regency of his wife, **Maria Anna.** She began gradually to reduce the power of Pombal.

1777-1816. MARIA I, the daughter of Joseph I, queen. She married her uncle, Peter, who assumed the title of king as **Peter III,** but who died in 1786. Under Maria the nobility began to recover its position. Pombal was exiled (d. 1782), but his reform policies were continued at a reduced pace.

1792. Insanity of Maria and regency of her son John. John, ardently supported by the clergy, undertook a drastic repression of all revolutionary agitation and thought.

1801, Feb.-Sept. War of the Oranges, with Spain, resulting from the bargain made between Spain and France. After a Spanish invasion the Portuguese made peace. By the **treaty of Madrid** (Sept. 29) Portugal paid a heavy indemnity and renounced the treaties with Britain.

1807, Oct. 27. Treaty of Fontainebleau between France and Spain, envisaging the **partition of Portugal.** The provinces of Entre-Douro and Minho (with Oporto) were to go to Louis, king of Etruria, who was to become king of Northern Lusitania. Alentejo and Algarve were to go to Godoy as prince of the Algarves; Beira, Tras-ós-Montes, and Estramadura were to be disposed of later.

Nov. 30. Lisbon was taken by a French army under Junot, assisted by the Spanish. The Portuguese royal family thereupon fled to Brazil.   (*Cont. pp. 643, 698.*)

5. ITALY AND THE PAPACY

(*From p. 426*)

a. ITALY (GENERAL), 1600-1800

Italy remained, during the late 17th and in the 18th centuries, a mere geographical expression, politically divded and for the most part under foreign rule. But the cultural decadence of the 17th century gave way in the 18th to a remarkable flowering which again made Italy an important factor in European art and thought and contributed much to the general European enlightenment. In music Italy was outstanding. **Niccolò Amati** (1596-1684) and **Antonio Stradivari** (1644-1737) built the finest stringed instruments; the **opera** (dating from 1600) was brought to a high stage of development by **Claudio Monteverdi** (1567-1643), **Giovanni Pergolesi** (1710-1736), **Domenico Cimarosa** (1749-1801), and **Giovanni Paisiello** (1741-1816). **Girolamo Frescobaldi** (1583-1643), composer of organ music; **Arcangelo Corelli** (1653-1713), eminent violinist and composer of sonatas and concerti grossi; **Alessandro Scarlatti** (1659-1725), of operas; and **Antonio Vivaldi** (c. 1678-1741), of chamber music. Two great schools of music at Venice and Naples.

Giovanni Lorenzo Bernini (1598-1680), architect and sculptor, was one of the leading artists of the baroque period, which preceded the rococco of the 18th century and the classical

revival represented by **Antonio Canova** (1757-1822). **Bernini** designed and built the Vatican Palace and St. Peter's Square, while **Francesco Borromini** (1599-1667) reconstructed St. John Lateran and built other Roman churches.

In painting, **Giambattista Tiepolo** (1696-1770) for a time brought Venice a final burst of glory. Other artists: the painter Antonio Canale (**Canaletto,** 1697-1768); the engraver **Giovanni Battista Piranesi** (1720-1778), whose etchings of Rome appeared in *Le antichità romane;* the sculptor **Antonio Canova.**

The **Academy of Arcadia** (1692) started a widespread vogue of the conventional and artificial in literature, which, however, was counterbalanced by the comedies of **Carlo Goldoni** (1707-1793) and the serious patriotic dramas of **Vittorio Alfieri** (1749-1803). A return to classicism was apparent in the dramas of Goldoni as well as in the work of Alfieri and the poetry of **Giacomo Leopardi** (1798-1837). **Alessandro Manzoni** (1785-1873), lyric poet and dramatist, wrote the one great historical novel of Italy, *I promessi sposi* (*The Betrothed,* 1826).

But Italy was pre-eminent also in the fields of social and physical science. **Pietro Giannone** (1676-1748) created a profound stir with his anti-clerical *Istoria civile del regno di Napoli* (1723); **Antonio Genovesi** (1712-1769) was an outstanding physiocrat; another distinguished economist was **Pietro Verri** (1728–1797); **Giambattista Vico** (1668–1744), with his *Scienza nuova* (1725), laid the basis of the modern philosophy of history; while **Cesare Beccaria** (1738–1794) in his *Dei delitti e delle pene* (1764) founded the modern science of penology. In the natural sciences **Lazzaro Spallanzani** (1729–1799) made fundamental contributions to the study of digestion, while **Luigi Galvani** (1737–1798) and **Alessandro Volta** (1745–1827) were in the front rank among the pioneers of electricity.

b. THE PAPACY, 1644–1799

[For a complete list of the Roman popes see Appendix IV.]

(*From p. 425*)

Most of the popes of the later 17th and 18th centuries were altogether worthy men, but the currents of the time were against the Papacy. By attempting to remain neutral in the great conflicts between the Bourbons and the Hapsburgs, the popes sacrificed the support of both. Furthermore, the Church before long became divided on the question of **Jansenism** (from **Cornelius Jansenius,** bishop of Ypres, who died in 1638, leaving a famous book, *Augustinus,* published in 1640. In this he emphasized inner regeneration rather than external reorganization of the Church, as represented by the Jesuits). Jansenism and Jesuitism soon came into conflict and the Papacy was sapped in the process. The enlightenment of the 18th century completed the development and by the time of the French Revolution the Papacy appeared as an ineffectual and outworn, as well as superfluous institution.

1644–1655. INNOCENT X (Giambattista Pamfili), a pope who was entirely under the control of his sister-in-law, **Olympia Maidalchini,** whose machinations brought about almost complete financial collapse. The pope denounced the **treaty of Westphalia** because of the abolition of bishoprics, etc., but the protest was of no effect. By the bull *Cum occasione impressionis libri* (May 31, 1653) the pope condemned five propositions in the work of Jansenius, thus initiating the **Jansenist controversy.**

1655–1667. ALEXANDER VII (Fabio Chigi), an honest and cultured, but apathetic pontiff, who left the conduct of affairs to his nephew, **Flavio Chigi.** Beginning of friction with Louis XIV over the prerogatives of the Church.

1667–1669. CLEMENT IX (Giulio Rospigliosi), elected by French influence. He attempted to mediate between Jesuits and Jansenists, but died before much could be achieved.

1670–1676. CLEMENT X (Cardinal Altieri), regarded as pro-Spanish. He disapproved of the French alliance with the Turks and did what he could to support the war of the Hapsburgs against the enemy.

1676–1689. INNOCENT XI (Benedetto Odescalchi), one of the outstanding popes of the period. He undertook a much-needed financial reorganization of the Papacy, refused to practice nepotism, enforced regulations to improve the morality of the clergy. At the same time he financed the Austrians in their campaigns against the Turks. The **conflict with Louis XIV** came to a head when the French ruler called a church assembly at St. Germain (1682) which adopted the **four articles:** (1) sovereigns are not subject to the pope in temporal matters; (2) a general council is superior to a pope; (3) the power of the pope is subject to the regulations of a council and a pope cannot decide contrary to the rules of the Gallican Church; (4) decisions of the Papacy are not irrevocable. In reply to these articles the pope refused to invest as bishops any French clerics who had taken part in the assembly. Ultimately 35 French bishoprics were vacant. Further friction developed. The pope protested against the suppression and expulsion of the Huguenots and actually approved the expedition of William III to England, as part of an anti-French policy.

1689–1691. Alexander VIII (Pietro Ottoboni).

1691–1700. INNOCENT XII (Antonio Pignatelli), another able pope. By the bull *Romanum decet pontificem* (1692) he definitely limited the number of offices that could be held by relatives of the pope, thus putting an end to nepotism in its worst form. He also checked the sale of offices. In 1697 he made peace with France, winning a substantial victory. **Louis XIV abrogated the four articles** of 1682, probably in order to win support in the matter of the Spanish succession.

1700–1721. CLEMENT XI (Gian Francesco Albani), an upright priest, who, though he inclined toward France, attempted to maintain neutrality in the Bourbon-Hapsburg struggle. The Austrians therefore ignored papal claims. In the course of the war they occupied Parma and Piacenza, marched through the Papal States and conquered Naples. In 1709 the pope was obliged to recognize Charles as king of Spain. But Clement's pontificate was noteworthy chiefly for the renewed **condemnation of Jansenism,** which had made extraordinary progress in France. The bull *Unigenitus* (Sept. 8, 1713) was a landmark in the controversy.

1721–1724. Innocent XIII (Michelangelo dei Conti), a kind but ineffectual pope, who was followed by two other unimportant pontiffs,

1724-1730. Benedict XIII (Pietro Francesco Orsini), and

1730-1740. Clement XII (Lorenzo Corsini).

1740-1758. BENEDICT XIV (Prospero Lambertini), a charming, learned, and serious-minded pope. He was much influenced by the enlightenment in Europe, was a friend of Voltaire and Montesquieu, did much to encourage agriculture and trade. His policy was to seek a compromise with the absolute rulers, whose efforts to establish national churches had so much weakened the Papacy. Conclusion of **concordats with Naples** (1741) and **Spain** (1753) were important steps in this direction, though they cost the Papacy far-reaching concessions.

1758-1769. CLEMENT XIII (Carlo Rezzonico), a pope elected through the efforts of the Jesuits (*Zelanti*), but who proved too weak and mild to save them. The Jesuits had become unpopular as a result of Jansenist attacks, and because of their interference in politics, their engagement in commercial and industrial enterprise, etc. Their expulsion from Portugal (1759) and France (1762) set the ball rolling, and the next pope,

1769-1774. CLEMENT XIV (Lorenzo Ganganelli), was unable to resist the pressure of the Bourbon governments. By the breve *Dominus ac redemptor noster* (July 21, 1773) the **Society of Jesus was ordered dissolved.**

1775-1799. PIUS VI, during whose pontificate the Papacy felt the full force of the revolutionary doctrine. The pope tried to deter Emperor Joseph II from his anti-clerical policy, but was soon confronted with the radical anti-clericalism of the French Revolution. As a result the French armies invaded papal territory (1796) and, after a short truce, intervened in Rome to set up the revolutionary **Roman Republic** (1798). The pope was taken off to southern France (Valence), where he died in the next year. (*Cont. pp. 638, 645, 711.*)

c. SAVOY (SARDINIA), 1638-1796

(*From p. 425*)

The beginning of the period was one of almost complete eclipse for Savoy, where the **regency of Duchess Christine** for her son, Charles Emmanuel II, formed a long interlude of conflict between the French and Spanish factions and brought on a decisive weakening of the ducal power. In the 18th century, however, Savoy re-emerged as a strong military state (the Prussia of Italy).

1638-1675. CHARLES EMMANUEL II, who came of age in 1648, submitted to the domination of his mother until her death in 1663.

His reign was scarred by the horrible **massacres of the Waldenses** (1655) which stirred the indignation of Europe.

1675-1730. VICTOR AMADEUS II. His mother, **Jeanne de Nemours,** acted as regent not only until the young duke attained his majority, but until 1684. She continued the Francophile orientation of Savoyard policy. In 1681 Louis XIV appropriated Casale as part of his reunion plan.

1685. Further persecution of the heretics, at the behest of Louis XIV.

1690. The duke at last made a break in the pro-French policy and joined the League of Augsburg against the French. But in 1696, hoping to make better terms with Louis, he reversed himself and received Pinerolo in return. The French and Savoyard forces obliged the powers of the league to evacuate Italy and agree to its neutralization for the duration of the war.

1701, Apr. War of the Spanish Succession (p. 481). Victor Amadeus stuck by the French connection and allowed the French to occupy Milan and Mantua. But once again the duke changed sides, joining the Grand Alliance in 1703. As a result the French, under Vendôme, overran Savoy in 1704, but the Austrians, under **Prince Eugene of Savoy,** relieved the situation in 1705. During the following year the French again invaded and besieged Turin until, in September, they were again driven out by Prince Eugene. Occupation of Milan by the Austrians and Savoyards (Sept. 24). This practically ended the war in Italy.

1713. By the **treaty of Utrecht,** Victor Amadeus was awarded Sicily as his share of the Spanish spoils. At the same time he assumed the royal title.

1717. A Spanish raid on Sicily resulted in war (p. 487) and a new peace settlement, by which

1720. Victor Amadeus gave up Sicily to Austria and received in exchange the island of Sardinia. Henceforth he was king of Sardinia.

1730-1773. CHARLES EMMANUEL III, king. He joined France and Spain in the War of the Polish Succession, in the hope of driving the Austrians out of Italy. By the **treaty of Vienna** (Oct. 3, 1735), however, his possessions remained unchanged.

1742-1747. Savoy sided with Austria in the War of the Austrian Succession, and by the **treaty of Aix-la-Chapelle** (1748) was rewarded with that part of the duchy of Milan which lay west of the Ticino.

Savoy-Piedmont had relatively little share in the intellectual and artistic life of Italy, being essentially a military state. The army, however, was not nearly strong enough to resist the storms of the French Revolution.

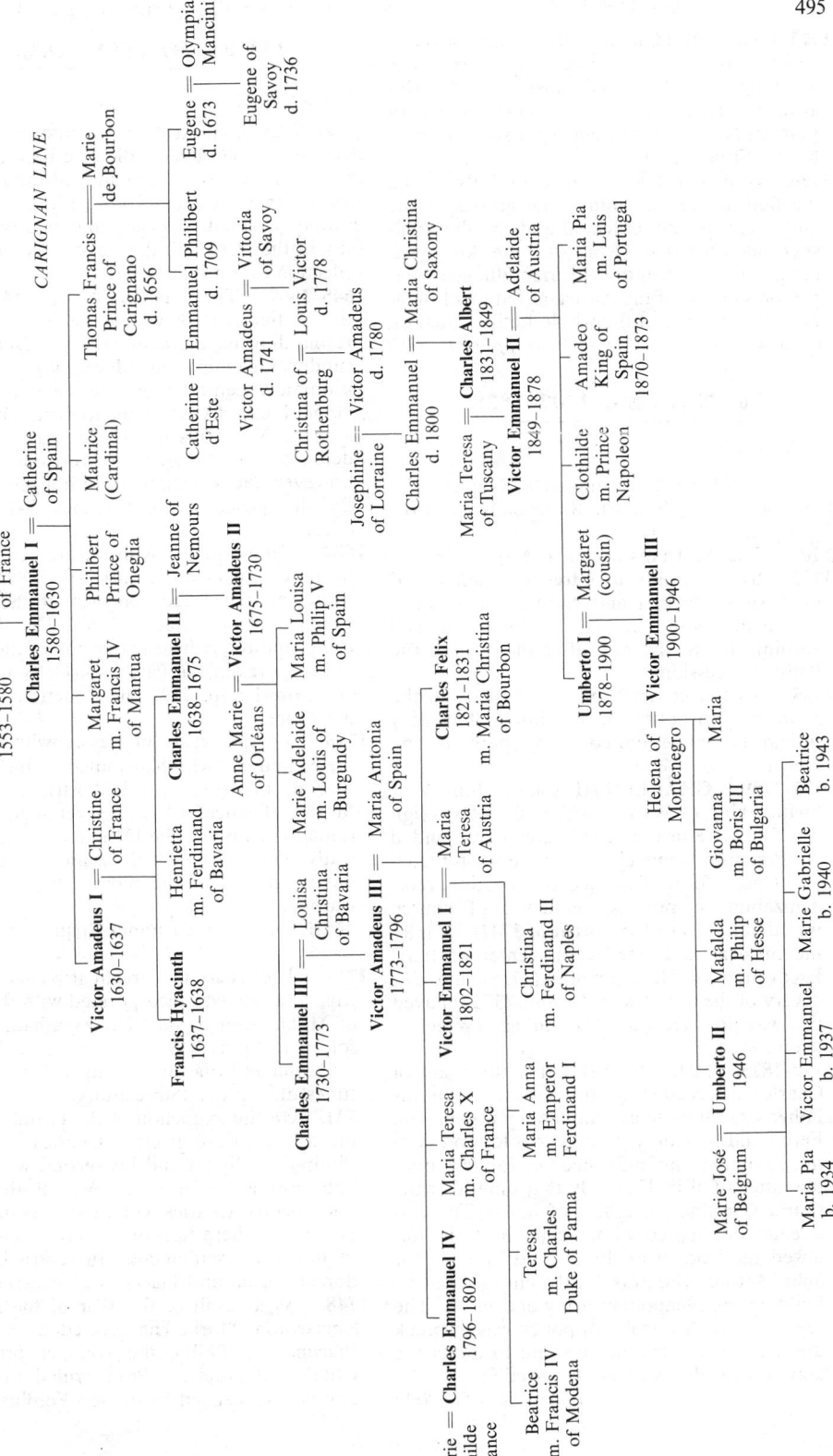

The House of Savoy (1553-1946)

1773-1796. VICTOR AMADEUS III. Strongly anti-revolutionary by temperament and policy, the king in 1792 joined Austria in the war against France, rejecting French offers of Lombardy. His territories were soon overrun by the French and

1796. Napoleon's appearance in Italy sealed the fate of the kingdom. The armies of the king were quickly defeated and, by the **armistice of Cherasco** (Apr. 28) the king was obliged to abandon the Austrian alliance. Napoleon's defeat of the Austrians led to a fundamental remaking of the whole Italian situation (p. 634). *(Cont. pp. 634, 700.)*

d. NAPLES, 1707-1825

(From p. 426)

The Spanish rule continued in Naples until the War of the Spanish Succession (p. 481). During this conflict

1707. The Austrians occupied Naples, and

1713. By the **treaty of Utrecht,** Spain ceded to Austria Sardinia and Naples, while Sicily passed to Savoy. In 1720 Austria exchanged Sardinia for Sicily, but, after the War of the Polish Succession

1735. Austria ceded Naples and Sicily to the Spanish Bourbons, on condition that they should never be united with Spain as one crown.

1735-1759. CHARLES III (son of Philip V of Spain), king of Naples and Sicily. His reign was one of reform and enlightenment, guided by **Bernardo Tanucci.** Restriction of feudal privilege, reform of finance and taxation, reorganization of prisons, reduction of church wealth and power **(concordat of 1741).** Naples the musical and intellectual center of Italy. Excavation of Herculaneum (1738) and discovery of the temples at Paestum (1752) paved the way for neo-classicism in art (Winckelmann, etc.).

1759-1825. FERDINAND I, the third son of Charles, succeeded to the throne when his father was called to assume the Spanish crown. Ferdinand was only nine years old, and continued under the influence of Tanucci until the latter's fall in 1771. By that time his wife, **Maria Carolina** (daughter of Maria Theresa) already dominated him. She, in turn, followed the lead of an English adventurer, **Sir John Acton,** who was busily engaged in rebuilding the Neapolitan army and navy. The result of Maria Carolina's policy was to break down the Spanish influence and to direct the king toward the Austrian connection.

(Cont. pp. 651, 700.)

e. OTHER STATES, 1645-1790

(From p. 426)

VENICE continued to fall into ever deeper decline, the old aristocratic rule becoming ever more unsuited to the demands of the European world. In international affairs Venice became entirely devoted to peace and neutrality, and only in the wars with the Turks was there some reflection of earlier glory.

1645-1669. The **Candian War** (p. 454), during the earlier part of which the Venetians won resounding naval victories at the Dardanelles (under Grimani and Mocenigo). The war ultimately centered on the siege of Candia (1658-1669). France came to the aid of Venice and the Venetians themselves put up a stout defense, under **Francesco Morosini.** Finally, however, the Venetians were obliged to yield. By the peace settlement they lost Candia (Crete).

1684. Venice joined with Austria and Poland in the war against the Turks (p. 518). In 1685 Morosini began the **conquest of the Morea,** which was completed in 1687. The Venetians even captured Athens (explosion of the ammunition stores in the Parthenon). By the **treaty of Karlowitz** (p. 519), the Venetians retained the Morea.

1718. By the **treaty of Passarowitz** (p. 519), the Venetians, who had joined in the Turkish War at the side of the Austrians, lost Morea. Thenceforth Venice retained only the Ionian Islands and the Dalmatian coast. Politically Venice stagnated, while artistically it remained one of the most active centers in Europe.

MILAN remained under Spanish rule until, by

1713. The **treaty of Utrecht** it passed to Austria. Mantua was incorporated with the duchy of Milan, after the last Gonzaga had, in 1701, sold it to Louis XIV.

Parma and Piacenza changed hands several times during the 18th century.

1731. On the extinction of the Farnese family, the duchies were given to Charles, the son of Philip V of Spain and his second wife, Elizabeth Farnese. In 1733 (War of the Polish Succession) Charles conquered Naples and Sicily, and these territories were awarded him in the peace settlement. In return he abandoned Parma and Piacenza to Austria.

1748. As a result of the **War of the Austrian Succession,** Maria Theresa ceded Parma and Piacenza to **Philip,** the younger brother of Charles of Naples. Philip ruled until 1765 and was succeeded by his son **Ferdinand,** who married a daughter of Maria Theresa and generally followed the lead of the Vienna government.

The **GENOESE REPUBLIC,** like the Venetian, remained independent, though constantly exposed to encroachment by Savoy, France, and Austria.

1730. Revolt of Corsica against Genoese rule. After a long and variable struggle, during which a German adventurer, Baron Neuhof of Westphalia, appeared for a time as **King Theodore I** (1736), the Genoese called upon the French for assistance. After many engagements (especially against **Pasquale Paoli,** the Corsican leader), the French subjugated the island, which the Genoese ceded to them (1768).

TUSCANY (Florence) continued under the decadent and unedifying rule of the Medici (**Cosimo III,** 1670-1723; **Gian Gastone,** 1723-1737) until the extinction of the line in 1737.

1737-1745. Francis of Lorraine, grand duke of Tuscany. He became the husband of Maria Theresa and, after his election as German emperor (Francis II, 1745), turned over Tuscany to a regency, and eventually to his son,

1747-1790. Leopold I, who devoted himself to the thoroughgoing reform of his dominion. The administration was remade, serfdom abolished, trade and industry encouraged. Tuscany became perhaps the best ruled and most progressive region of Italy. In 1790 Leopold was elected Roman Emperor as Leopold II.

(*Cont. p. 700.*)

6. THE SWISS CONFEDERATION, 1650-1798

(*From p. 438*)

The century from 1650 to 1750 was one of stagnation and decline in Switzerland. The confederation continued to be the loosest kind of union, the cantons divided against each other by religious issues. Within the cantons patrician oligarchies became dominant and ruled in a reactionary fashion. The main occupation of the Swiss continued to be fighting, and mercenaries were engaged by foreign states (especially France) by the tens of thousands. Only after 1750 was there a renaissance, which brought Switzerland to the threshold of the French Revolution.

1653. A peasant revolt, led by Nicholas Leuenberg, brought the insurgents to the very gates of Bern, but was suppressed with the aid of other cantons.

1655. Proposals for the establishment of a more centralized state, put forward by Zürich, were defeated by the Catholic cantons.

1656. The **FIRST VILLMERGEN WAR,** in which Bern and Zürich were pitted against the Catholic cantons. The Protestants were defeated at Villmergen (Jan. 24) and complete control of religious affairs had to be left to the individual members of the confederation.

1663. Renewal of the **alliance with France,** enabling Louis XIV to draw as many mercenaries as he chose from the cantons. The alliance was opposed by Zürich and some of the Protestant cantons, and in the ensuing period there was much friction between France and Switzerland over the question of service with France against Protestant states, over the reception of Huguenots expelled from France, etc.

1663-1776. During more than a century there was no meeting of the federal diet, indicating the almost complete collapse of the federal connection.

1678. Franche-Comté, hitherto under federal protection, was annexed to France.

1693. The Protestant cantons, incensed by French use of mercenaries against the Dutch, agreed to supply soldiers to the Dutch, and later to the English. Thereupon the Catholic cantons made an agreement to supply men to the Spaniards. In the War of the Spanish Succession the Swiss fought by the thousands on both sides.

1707. A popular insurrection at Geneva, led by **Peter Fatio,** was suppressed with the aid of the Bern and Zürich oligarchies.

1708. The **house of Hohenzollern** succeeded to the principality of Neuchâtel. Louis XIV was prevented by the war from pressing the claims of the prince of Conti.

1712. The **SECOND VILLMERGEN WAR,** another conflict between Catholics and Protestants. This time the Bernese won a decisive victory, again at Villmergen (July 25), after which the dominance of the Protestant cantons was firmly established.

1723. Revolt of Abraham Davel in the Vaud, against the oppressive rule of Bern. The whole affair was a harebrained undertaking, inspired by noble motives. After taking Lausanne, Davel was easily outmaneuvered, captured, and executed.

1725. Renewal of the treaty with France, but this time with the abstention of the Protestant cantons.

1734, 1737. Further uprisings in Geneva led to some constitutional revision in the popular direction.

With the middle of the century there came a distinct economic improvement in Switzerland, marked by the expansion of industry. This brought with it a falling-off of the mercenary system, but also a rise of the middle class and an intellectual renaissance: Zürich (with **Johannes J. Bodmer,** 1698-1783, **Albrecht von Haller,** 1708-1777, and **Johannes C. Lavater,** 1741-1801) became an important center of German literature and thought; Geneva (with **Rousseau,** 1712-1778, **Voltaire,** resident in the vicinity after 1755, etc.) became a refuge for advanced thinkers of the French school. The **Helvetic Society** (founded 1762) was an exuberant organization devoted to the new ideas. The educational reformer **Johann Heinrich Pestalozzi** (1746-1827) was strongly influenced by Lavater. After publication of *How Gertrude Teaches her Children* (1801) his influence became international.

1776. The whole confederation once more allied itself with France, but Swiss mercenaries in French service fell to less than 10,000.

1789-1792. In the first years of the **French Revolution** the Swiss oligarchies were strongly hostile and seriously considered intervention by the side of Austria and Prussia. In the end they determined on neutrality, though pursuing at home a repressive policy (crushing of unrest in the Vaud by the Bern government).

1792, Dec. 5. A revolutionary **coup at Geneva** put the government in the hands of the popular party. Thenceforth the developments in France were faithfully mirrored in Geneva.

1793. The French Republic annexed the bishopric (not the town) of Basel.

1797, Oct. Napoleon, following his successes in Italy, annexed the Valtelline and Chiavenna to the Cisalpine Republic.

Dec. Revolutionists seized the town of Basel.

1798, Jan. 23. The French declared the Vaud free from Bernese rule and organized it as the **Lemanic Republic.**

Feb. 9. France decreed the establishment of a **Helvetic Republic.** The move was inspired by the Helvetic Committee in Paris, a revolutionary group headed by **Frédéric-César de La Harpe,** 1754-1838, a Vaudois whose great aim was the liberation of his homeland from the hated Bernese aristocracy, and by **Peter Ochs,** a less high-minded radical. The new republic was to be organized along French lines; excepting for territory annexed to France, all the cantons, together with the subject territories, were to be made into 23 cantons, bound together by a centralized government consisting of an elected chamber of deputies (eight members from each canton), and a senate (four from each canton). At the head was to be a directory of five.

The French move finally convinced the Swiss oligarchies of the danger. Bern declared war and the Bernese defeated the French army under Brune at **Laupen** (Mar. 5). But another Bernese force was vanquished on the same day by Schauenberg. Bern surrendered and was sacked. Indemnity of 17 million francs.

Apr. Five Forest (Catholic) **Cantons** revolted against the French under Aloys von Reding. They won some successes, but then made peace, accepting the Helvetic constitution on condition that the French should not interfere or occupy territory of the five cantons.

Apr. 26. Geneva was annexed to France.

(*Cont. pp. 635, 714.*)

7. GERMANY, 1658-1792

[For a complete list of the Holy Roman emperors see Appendix V.]

(*From p. 437*)

1658-1705. LEOPOLD I, the son of Ferdinand III. After 1663 a permanent **diet at Regensburg,** consisting of representatives of the 8 electors, the 69 secular princes, and the imperial cities; an ineffectual legislature, often degenerating into a squabble for precedence ("a bladeless knife without a handle"). *Corpus Catholicorum* and *Corpus Evangelicorum,* the corporate organizations of the Catholic and Protestant states, the latter being the most important. This organization of the Protestant states had existed, in fact, since the latter half of the 16th century, but it was legally recognized in the treaty of Westphalia, which decreed that in the diet matters relating to religion and the Church should not be decided by a majority, but should be settled by conference and agreement between the Catholic and Protestant states, as organized corporations.

1661-1664. War against the Turks (p. 518).

1666. Settlement of the contested **succession in Cleve-Jülich:** Cleve, Mark, and Ravenstein,

The House of Hohenzollern (1417–1713)

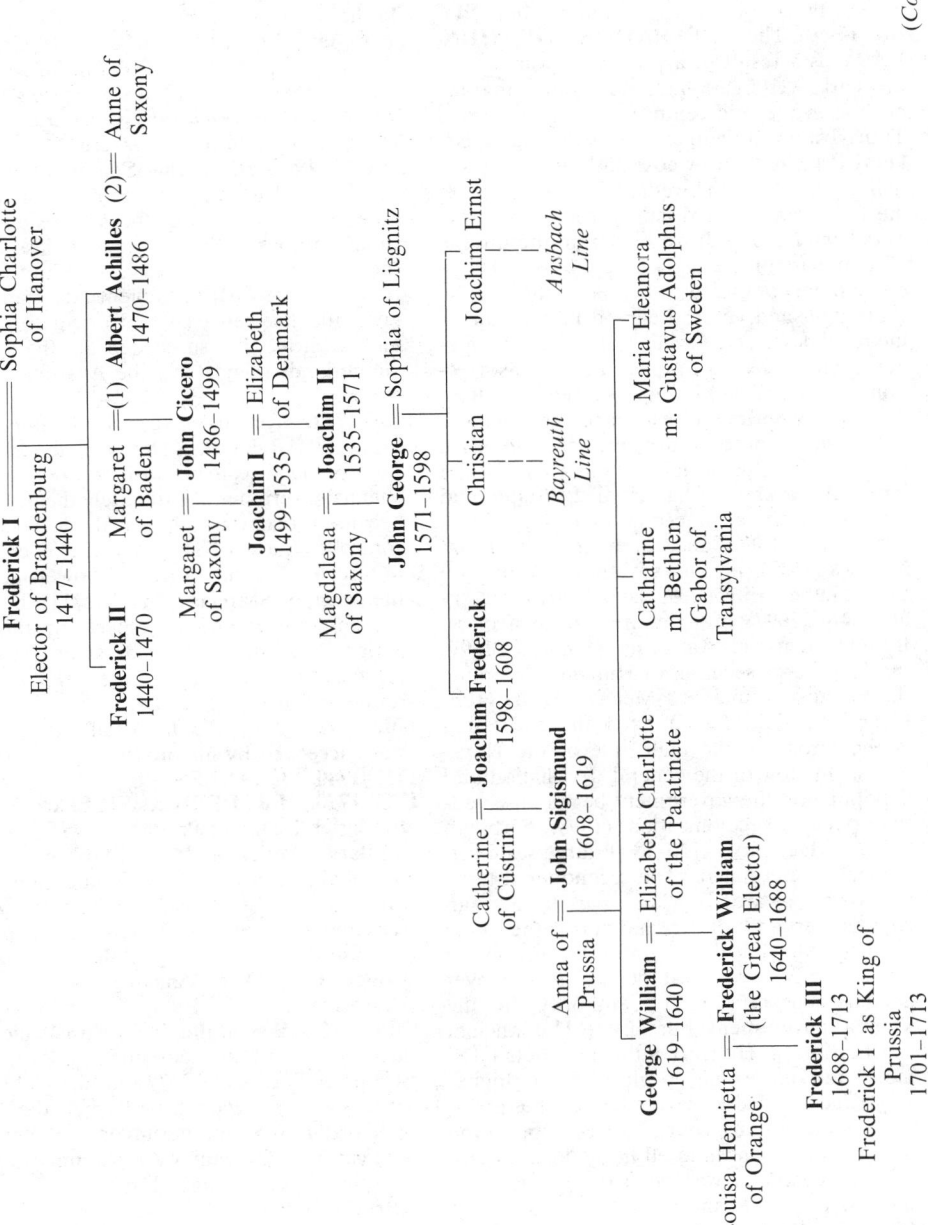

(Cont. p. 727.)

as well as half of Ravensberg, were given to Brandenburg; afterward the whole of Ravensberg in place of Ravenstein.

1668. The Empire joined in the **War of Devolution,** against Louis XIV of France (p. 477), and likewise in

1674. The **Dutch War,** siding with the Dutch against the ambitious aggression of Louis XIV.

1682-1699. The **LIBERATION OF HUNGARY** as a result of a prolonged war against the Turks. Hungary had undergone a marked decline in the mid-century. The greatness of Transylvania came to an end with **George Rákóczi II** (1648-1660) whose ambitious dynastic policy (alliance with Sweden; attempt to secure the Polish crown) had led to trouble with the Turks, who finally drove him from the throne. In that part of Hungary ruled by the Hapsburgs there continued to be persecution of the Protestants and, under Leopold I, extension of the royal power, confiscation of estates of opponents, etc. This led to much unrest (insurrection of **Imre Tökölli**), but the reconquest of the country entirely transformed the situation.

For details of the **war against the Turks** see p. 518. After the siege of Vienna (1683), the imperial generals, Charles of Lorraine and Louis of Baden, advanced into Hungary. Buda was taken (1686) and, after the **victory at Mohács** (1687) the Turks were driven beyond the Danube. Eugene of Savoy's great **victory at Zenta** (1697) brought the war to a close. By the **treaty of Karlowitz** (Jan. 26, 1699) the Hapsburgs secured all Hungary excepting the Banat of Temesvar. Meanwhile the Hungarian diet had (1687) fixed the succession to the throne in the male line of the Hapsburgs. In view of the general devastation and depopulation the government began an extensive policy of colonization (1690: Serbs in southern Hungary; 1720-1800: large-scale settlement of Germans). The reconquered territories were awarded in large part to German commanders and soldiers and during the whole century following the reconquest there was a steady increase of royal power and an ever greater concentration of authority in the Vienna government bureaus. The ancient constitution of Hungary subsisted, but it fell more and more into neglect. The higher aristocracy tended to devote itself to the pleasures of the Vienna court, and the opposition of the gentry (concentrated in the local assemblies or comitats) was not sufficient to stem the tide of absolutism.

1688-1697. **War of the League of Augsburg,** against Louis XIV (p. 480). This war distracted the empire to such an extent that the reconquest of Hungary was delayed for a decade.

During this period several of the German princes were elevated in rank:

1692. **Hanover became an electorate** (the ninth).

1697. **Augustus II,** elector of Saxony, was elected king of Poland on the death of John Sobieski. He thereupon adopted the Catholic faith.

1701, Jan. 18. **FREDERICK III,** elector of Brandenburg (1688-1713), with the consent of the emperor, assumed the title of *king in Prussia* (*König in Preussen*) (Frederick I) and crowned himself at Königsberg.

1701-1714. **War of the Spanish Succession** (p. 481). The emperor, though he and his allies failed to prevent the succession of the Bourbon house in Spain, nevertheless effected the breakup of the Spanish dominions in Europe. By the final settlement Austrian power and influence replaced that of Spain in Italy, and Austria also succeeded to the Spanish Netherlands (henceforth the Austrian Netherlands).

1703-1711. Revolt of the Hungarians under **Francis II Rákóczi.** This was the result of widespread discontent with the policy of the Vienna government. Ultimately the movement became a real social upheaval. Rákóczi soon controlled most of Hungary and even began to threaten Vienna. But his followers accepted the **peace of Szatmar** (May 1, 1711), by which the emperor promised respect for the Hungarian constitution and redress of grievances. Rákóczi himself refused these terms and took refuge in Turkey (d. 1735).

1705-1711. **JOSEPH I,** son of Leopold. He was succeeded by his brother,

1711-1740. **CHARLES VI.**

1713-1740. **FREDERICK WILLIAM I,** son of Frederick I, king of Prussia, by wise economy, military severity, and the establishment of a formidable army, laid the foundation of the future power of Prussia. Maintenance of a standing army of 83,000 men, with a population of two and a half million inhabitants. **Prince Leopold of Anhalt-Dessau** (*der alte Dessauer*).

1714-1718. **War of the Turks with Venice,** and after 1716 with the emperor (p. 519). The seizure of Sardinia (1717) and Sicily (1718) by Spain, where Elizabeth of Parma, the second wife of Philip V, and her favorite, the minister and cardinal **Alberoni,** were planning to regain the Spanish appanages lost by the **treaty of Utrecht,** brought about the

1718, Aug. 2. **Quadruple Alliance** for the maintenance of the **treaty of Utrecht,** between France, Britain, the emperor, and (1719) the Republic of Holland. After a short war and the fall of Alberoni, who went to Rome (d.

1752), the agreements of the Quadruple Alliance were executed in 1720: (1) **Spain** evacuated Sicily and Sardinia, and made a renunciation of the appanages forever, in return for which the emperor recognized the Spanish Bourbons; (2) **Savoy** was obliged to exchange Sicily for Sardinia. After this time the **dukes of Savoy** called themselves **kings of Sardinia.**

The Emperor Charles VI was without male offspring. His principal endeavor throughout his reign was to secure the various lands which were united under the scepter of Austria against division after his death. Hence he established an order of succession under the name of the **Pragmatic Sanction,** which decreed that: (1) the lands belonging to the Austrian Empire should be indivisible; (2) that in case male heirs should fail, they should devolve upon Charles' daughters, the eldest of whom was **Maria Theresa,** and their heirs according to the law of primogeniture; (3) in case of the extinction of this line the daughters of Joseph I and their descendants were to inherit.

To secure the assent of the various powers to the Pragmatic Sanction was the object of numerous diplomatic negotiations. The Hungarian diet accepted it in 1723. A special agreement between Austria and Spain (1725), in regard to this measure, produced the **alliance of Herrenhausen,** in the same year, between Britain, France, and Prussia in opposition. Prussia soon withdrew from the alliance and joined Austria by the **treaty of Wusterhausen.** The alliance between Austria and Spain was also of short duration.

1733–1735. WAR OF THE POLISH SUCCESSION, after the death of Augustus II.

Cause: The majority of the Polish nobles, under the influence of France, elected **Stanislas Leszczynski,** who had become the father-in-law of Louis XV, king, a second time. Russia and Austria induced a minority to choose **Augustus III,** elector of Saxony (son of Augustus II), and supported the election by the presence of troops in Poland. France, Spain, and Sardinia took up arms for Stanislas.

The seat of war was at first in Italy, where Milan, Naples, and Sicily were conquered, and the Austrians lost everything except Milan; and afterward on the upper Rhine, where the old **Prince Eugene** fought unsuccessfully, and Francis Stephen, duke of Lorraine, the future husband of **Maria Theresa,** alone upheld the honor of the imperial arms. Lorraine occupied by the French. Kehl captured. Preliminaries of peace (1735), and, after long negotiations,

1738, Nov. 18. TREATY OF VIENNA: (1) **Stanislas Leszczynski** made a renunciation of the Polish throne, receiving as compensation the duchies of Lorraine and Bar, which at his death were to devolve upon France. Stanislas died 1766. (2) The duke of Lorraine, **Francis Stephen,** received an indemnification in Tuscany, whose ducal throne had become vacant by the extinction of the family of Medici, 1737. (3) **Austria** ceded Naples and Sicily, the island of Elba and the Stati degli Presidi to Spain as a *secundogeniture* for Don Carlos, so that these lands could never be united with the crown of Spain, receiving in exchange Parma and Piacenza, which Don Carlos had inherited in 1731 upon the death of the last Farnese, his great-uncle. (4) **France** guaranteed the Pragmatic Sanction.

1736–1739. Unsuccessful war with the **Turks** (p. 519).

1740, May.   Death of Frederick William I of Prussia.

1740–1786.   FREDERICK II, THE GREAT of Prussia.

1740, Oct. With the **death of Charles VI,** the male line of the Hapsburgs was extinct.

1740–1780. MARIA THERESA, queen of Bohemia and Hungary, archduchess of Austria, etc., married **Francis Stephen** of the house of Lorraine, grand duke of Tuscany (co-regent).

1740–1748. WAR OF THE AUSTRIAN SUCCESSION:

Cause: The following claimants for the Austrian inheritance appeared: (1) **Charles Albert,** elector of Bavaria, who had never recognized the Pragmatic Sanction, a descendant of Anna, the eldest daughter of Ferdinand I. He based his claim upon the marriage contract of Anna, and upon the will of Ferdinand I, whereby the Austrian inheritance was (he claimed) secured to the descendants of Anna, in case the *male* descendants of her brother should become extinct. (The *original* will, however, will read, in case the *legitimate* descendants of her brother became extinct.) (2) **Philip V,** king of Spain, relying on a treaty between Charles V and his brother Ferdinand, on occasion of the cession of the German lands, and upon a reservation made by Philip III in his renunciation of the German lands. (3) **Augustus III** of Saxony, the husband of the *eldest* daughter of Joseph I.

The claims advanced by **Frederick II** to a part of Silesia, and his desire to annex the whole of Silesia to his kingdom, the rejection of the offer which he made at Vienna to take the field in favor of Austria if his claims were recognized, brought about, before the commencement of hostilities by the other claimants, the

1740–1742. FIRST SILESIAN WAR. Legal claims of Prussia to a portion of Silesia: (1) The principality of Jägerndorf was purchased in 1523 by a younger branch of the electoral line of Hohenzollern, and the future acquisition of Ratibor and Oppeln secured at the same time, by an hereditary alliance. In 1623 Duke John George was placed under the ban by the Emperor Ferdinand II, as an adherent of Frederick V, the elector palatine, and in spite of the peace of Westphalia, neither he nor his heirs had been reinstated. (2) The elector Joachim II had made an hereditary alliance in 1537 with the duke of Liegnitz, Brieg, and Wohlau, which Ferdinand I had forbidden as king of Bohemia and feudal superior of the duke. After the extinction of the ducal house (1675) Austria took possession of the inheritance.

In 1686, Frederick William, the great elector, of Brandenburg, renounced his claims to the Silesian duchies in return for the cession of one of them, viz. Schwiebus. His son Frederick, however, in an agreement concealed from his father, undertook to retrocede to Austria the Schwiebus district. This was done (1695) after Frederick had succeeded to the electorate.

1740. Occupation of Silesia by Frederick's troops. Capture of Glogau.

1741, Apr. 10. Prussian victory at **Mollwitz.**

May. Secret **alliance of Nymphenburg** against Austria concluded by France, Bavaria, and Spain, afterward joined by Saxony, and lastly by Prussia. The allied French (Belle-Isle) and Bavarian army invaded Austria and Bohemia. Prague taken in alliance with the Saxons. Charles Albert caused himself to be proclaimed archduke in Linz, while Frederick II received homage in Silesia. Charles Albert was elected emperor in Frankfurt as

1742–1745. CHARLES VII. Meantime **Maria Theresa** had gone to Hungary. **Diet at Pressburg** (1741); enthusiasm of the Hungarian nobility which was guaranteed immunity from taxation; two armies raised; alliance concluded with Britain. An Austrian army conquered Bavaria, where Maria Theresa received the homage of Munich; a second besieged the French in Prague.

1742, May 17. The victory of Frederick at **Czaslau** and **Chotusitz,** and Maria Theresa's desire to rid herself of a dangerous enemy led to the separate

June and July. Treaty of Breslau and Berlin between Austria and Prussia: (1) **Frederick** withdrew from the alliance against Maria Theresa. (2) **Austria** ceded to Prussia upper and lower Silesia and the county of Glatz, retaining only the principality of Teschen, and the southwestern part of the principalities of Neisse, Troppau, and Jägerndorf, the Oppa forming the boundary. (3) **Prussia** assumed the debt upon Silesia held by English and

Dutch creditors, to the amount of 1,700,000 rix dollars.

Austria prosecuted the war against the allies with success, driving them entirely out of Bohemia (1742) and Bavaria (1743); the Pragmatic army (British, Hanoverians, Hessians), under King George II, defeated the French in the

1743, June 27. Battle of Dettingen. The Emperor Charles VII was a refugee in Frankfurt.

These Austrian successes and the treaties with Sardinia and Saxony (1743) made the king of Prussia anxious about his new acquisitions. He concluded a second alliance with Charles VII and France, and began the

1744–1745. SECOND SILESIAN WAR, by forcing his way through Saxony with 80,000 men and invading Bohemia. He took Prague, but, deserted by the French, was soon driven back into Saxony (1744).

1744. East Friesland, upon the extinction of the reigning house, fell to Prussia.

1745, Jan. Alliance between Austria, Saxony, Britain, and Holland against Prussia. The French and Bavarians took Munich. Charles VII died (1745, Jan.). His son **Maximilian Joseph** concluded the

Apr. Separate **treaty of Füssen,** with Austria. (1) **Austria** restored all conquests to Bavaria. (2) The **elector of Bavaria** surrendered his pretensions to Austria and promised Francis Stephen, the husband of Maria Theresa, his vote at the imperial election.

The French under Marshall **Maurice of Saxony** (*Maréchal de Saxe,* son of Augustus II and the Countess Aurora of Königsmark) defeated the Pragmatic army in the

May 11. BATTLE OF FONTENOY (Irish Brigade), and began the conquest of the Austrian Netherlands.

Frederick the Great defeated the Austrians and Saxons under Charles of Lorraine in the

June 4. Battle of Hohenfriedberg, in Silesia, and the Austrians alone in the

Sept. 30. Battle of Soor, in northeastern Bohemia.

By the election of the husband of Maria Theresa as emperor, the

1745–1806. HOUSE OF LORRAINE-TUSCANY acceded to the imperial throne in the person of the emperor,

1745–1765. FRANCIS I.

After a victory of the Prussian general, Leopold von Dessau, over the Saxons at **Kesseldorf,** December 15, the

1745, Dec. 25 TREATY OF DRESDEN was concluded between Prussia and Austria (Saxony). (1) Ratification of the **treaty of Breslau and Berlin** in regard to the possession of Silesia. (2) **Frederick II** recognized Francis I as emperor. (3) **Saxony** paid Prussia one million rix dollars.

After the flower of the British army had been recalled to England, where it was needed in the contest with the "young pretender" (p. 470), **Marshal Saxe** obtained at **Raucoux** (1746) a second victory over the allies of Austria and completed the conquest of the Austrian Netherlands.

At the same time, the naval war between France and Great Britain, and the war in Italy between Spain, France, and Austria, were carried on with varying fortune. Sardinia had concluded peace with Austria as early as 1743. At last the empress of Russia, **Elizabeth** (p. 516), joined the combatants as the ally of Austria and sent an army to the Rhine. Congress, and finally,

1748, Oct. TREATY OF AIX-LA-CHAPELLE. (1) Reciprocal restoration of all conquests. (2) Cessions of Parma, Piacenza, and Guastalla to the Spanish infant, Don Philip, making the second *secundogeniture* of the Spanish Bourbons in Italy. The following guaranties were given: that Silesia should belong to Prussia; that the Pragmatic Sanction should be sustained in Austria; that the house of Hanover should retain the succession in its German states and in Great Britain.

Change in the relations of European states induced by the rise of Prussia to the rank of a great power. Envy between Prussia and Austria; the latter seeing a disgrace in the loss of Silesia to a smaller power, and intriguing for the recovery of the lost province. Thus began the

1756–1763. THIRD SILESIAN, or **SEVEN YEARS' WAR.**

Cause: Before the treaty of Aix-la-Chapelle Maria Theresa had concluded a **defensive alliance** with Frederick's personal enemy, Elizabeth, empress of Russia (May 1746). Secret articles of this treaty provided for the reunion of Silesia with Austria under certain specified conditions. In September 1750, George II of Great Britain, moved by anxiety for his principality of Hanover, signed the main treaty, the secret articles being excepted. Saxony (minister, Count Brühl) signed the treaty unconditionally. **Count** (Prince in 1764) **Wenzel von Kaunitz** (until 1753 Austrian ambassador in France, then chancellor of the Empire in Vienna) succeeded in promoting a reconciliation between the cabinets of Versailles and Vienna, and securing the marquise de Pompadour in favor of an Austrian alliance. Formation of a party inimical to the Prussian alliance at the French court.

Maria Theresa and Kaunitz induced Britain to conclude a new subsidy treaty with Russia in 1755. In June of the same year, however, hostilities broke out between Britain and France in North America without any declaration of war. Dreading a French attack upon Hanover, George II concluded, in January 1756, a treaty of neutrality with Frederick at Westminster, which caused a rupture between Britain and Russia. Kaunitz made skillful use of the indignation at Versailles over the **treaty of Westminster.** In May 1756 conclusion of a defensive alliance between France and Austria. In June 1756 war broke out between France and Britain in Europe.

Frederick, well informed concerning the alliances of the powers, and knowing that Russia and France were not in condition to take the offensive against him in 1756, decided to take his enemies by surprise.

1756, Aug. He invaded Saxony with 67,000 men and took Dresden (Sept. 2). On October 1 he defeated the Austrians at **Lobositz,** and on October 15 the Saxons (18,000) surrendered at **Pirna.**

1757, Jan. 10. War was declared on Frederick in the name of the Empire. Hanover, Hesse, Brunswick, and Gotha, however, continued in alliance with Prussia. Conclusion of an agreement between Austria and Russia (Jan.) concerning the partition of the Prussian monarchy. Offensive treaty between Austria and France (May 1).

Frederick invaded Bohemia in four columns, and won a

May 6. Victory over the Austrians at **Prague.** Death of Schwerin. Frederick besieged Prague and attacked the army of Count Daun, who attempted to relieve the city. But Frederick was defeated in the

June 18. Battle of Kolin, as a result of which he had to evacuate Bohemia.

July 26. Victory of the French over the British at **Hastenbeck,** which led to the capitulation of the British army (duke of Cumberland) at **Kloster-Zeven** (Sept. 8). The French occupied Hanover, though the treaty was rejected by the British government.

July 30. Battle of Grossjägerndorf, in which the Russians, under Apraxin, after invading East Prussia with a large force, defeated the Prussians under Lehwald. Nevertheless the Russians withdrew from East Prussia and did not exploit their success. But the Swedes in the meanwhile began to occupy Pomerania, promised them in return for participation in the war.

Nov. 5. BATTLE OF ROSSBACH, one of the most spectacular victories of Frederick. The French, under Soubise, had joined the imperial army, under Duke Frederick William, for the purpose of liberating Saxony. But

Frederick surprised them on the march and completely overwhelmed them. He then led his victorious army into Silesia, where the Austrians had just won a victory over the duke of Brunswick-Bevern at Breslau (Nov. 22).

Dec. 5. Battle of Leuthen. Frederick completely defeated the Austrians under Charles of Lorraine and Daun.

1758. Frederick campaigned in Moravia, but failed to take Olmütz. In the west, Ferdinand of Brunswick drove the French back over the Rhine and defeated them in the

June 23. Battle of Crefeld. But the greatest Prussian victory of the year was Frederick's defeat of another invading Russian army in the

Aug. 25. Battle of Zorndorf. But this was counterbalanced by the

Oct. 14. Battle of Hochkirch. The Austrians had invaded Lusatia and Frederick had hurried to the relief of his brother Henry. Daun defeated the Prussians at Hochkirch, but was not able to drive Frederick out of Saxony and Silesia.

1759. The French resumed the offensive in the west and, under the duke of Broglie, defeated Ferdinand of Brunswick at **Bergen,** near Frankfurt (Apr. 13). Later in the year Ferdinand made good this defeat by his victory over the French in the

Aug. 1. Battle of Minden. The Russians once again advanced into Germany and defeated the Prussian general, Wedell, at **Kay** (July 23). Frederick was unable to prevent their union with the Austrians under Laudon and suffered a major reverse in the

Aug. 12. BATTLE OF KUNERSDORF. The Austrians thereupon captured Dresden. On November 20 Daun surrounded and captured 13,000 Prussians under Finck at **Maxen.**

1760, June 23. The Prussians, under Fouqué, were defeated and captured by the Austrians in the battle of **Landshut,** but

Aug. 15. Frederick's victory over Laudon in the battle of **Liegnitz** (Pfaffendorf) enabled him to prevent the union of the Austrians and Russians. The latter, under Tottleben, nevertheless

Oct. 9-12. Surprised and burned **Berlin,** retreating only as Frederick hurried to the relief.

Nov. 3. Victory of Frederick over Daun at **Torgau.**

1761. Frederick established a defensive position opposite the united Austrians and Russians near Bunzelwitz. But on October 1 the Austrians took Schweidnitz and the Russians occupied Kolberg before the year was out (Dec. 16). By this time Frederick, deprived of the British subsidies by the accession of

George III (1760), was in great distress. His position was saved by the

1762, Jan. 5. The **death of Elizabeth** of Russia. Her successor, **Peter III,** was an admirer of Frederick and very soon concluded the

Mar. 16. Truce of Stargard, which was followed by the

May 5. Treaty of St. Petersburg. Russia restored all conquests and both parties renounced all hostile alliances. The defection of Russia brought with it also the

May 22. Treaty of Hamburg between Sweden and Prussia, which restored the *status quo ante bellum.* The alliance between Prussia and Russia was soon broken off by the deposition of Peter III (July 9). His successor, **Catherine II,** recalled her troops from Frederick's army; nevertheless their inactivity upon the field contributed to the

July 21. Victory of Frederick at Burkersdorf (Reichenbach) over the Austrians (Daun). After Prince Henry in the

Oct. 29. Battle of Freiburg had defeated the Austrians and the imperial forces, and the preliminaries of the **treaty of Fontainebleau** between England and France had made it certain that the French armies would be withdrawn from Germany, Austria and Prussia concluded the

1763, Feb. 15. TREATY OF HUBERT(U)S-BURG: (1) Ratification of the treaties of Breslau and Berlin, and of Dresden, i.e. Prussia retained Silesia. (2) Prussia promised her vote for the Archduke Joseph at the election of the king of Rome. Saxony (restoration to the *status quo*) and the Empire were included in the peace.

Frederick's endeavors to heal the wounds inflicted by the war upon his kingdom; distribution of the magazine stores; remission of taxes for several provinces; establishment of district banks, of the Bank (1765) and the Maritime Company (1772) at Berlin. Afterward, however, introduction of an oppressive financial administration; tobacco and coffee were made government monopolies. Drainage of the marshes along the Oder, Werthe, and Netze. Canal of Plauen, Finow, and Bromberg. Reform of the jurisdiction. Codification of the common law by grand chancellor von Carmer, a part of which was published in 1782.

1765-1790. JOSEPH II, emperor, for the Austrian lands co-regent only with his mother, **Maria Theresa,** until 1780, and without much influence.

1778-1779. WAR OF THE BAVARIAN SUCCESSION. Cause: Extinction of the electoral house of Bavaria with Maximilian Joseph (1777). **Charles Theodore,** elector palatine, the legal heir of the Bavarian lands, as head of the house of Wittelsbach, and in consequence of various treaties, was persuaded by Joseph II to recognize certain old claims of Austria to Lower Bavaria, and a part of the Upper Palatinate. **Treaty of Vienna** (1778, Jan.): occupation of Lower Bavaria by Austrian troops. Charles Theodore was childless; his heir presumptive was Charles Augustus Christian, duke of the palatinate of Zweibrücken (Deux-Ponts). **Frederick II** opened secret negotiations with this wavering and irresolute prince through Count Eustachius von Görz and encouraged him, under promise of assistance, to make a formal declaration of his rights against the Austrian claims. Saxony and Mecklenburg, also incited by Frederick, protested as heirs presumptive of a part of the Bavarian inheritance. As direct negotiations between Austria and Prussia were without result, Joseph and Frederick joined their armies, which were already drawn up face to face on the boundary of Bohemia and Silesia.

Saxony allied with Prussia. No battle in this short war. Frederick and Prince Henry invaded Bohemia (July 1778). Impossibility of forcing Joseph from his strong position along the upper Elbe, or of getting around it. The armies maintained their positions of observation so long that want began to make itself felt. In the autumn Prince Henry retired to Saxony, Frederick to Silesia. Unimportant skirmishes along the frontier. A personal correspondence between **Maria Theresa** and **Frederick,** commenced by the former, led in the following spring, with the help of Russian and French mediation, to a truce and a congress, and soon after to the

1779, May 13. TREATY OF TESCHEN. (1) The treaty of Vienna with Charles Theodore was abrogated. Austria retained only the district of the Inn, in Bavaria, i.e. the part of Lower Bavaria between the Inn, Salzach, and Danube. (2) Austria agreed to the future union of the margravates of Ansbach and Baireuth with the Prussian monarchy. (3) Saxony obtained some hitherto disputed rights of sovereignty and nine million rix dollars; Mecklenburg the *privilegium de non appellando.*

1780–1790. JOSEPH II. Period of his reign alone and of his attempts at reform. The prudent government of Maria Theresa (d. 1780), with its carefully matured scheme of reform, was succeeded by the essentially revolutionary reign of Joseph II, whereby the ancient forms were shaken to their foundations, and their substance, reluctant and stiff from lack of change, forcibly subjected to experiments made in sympathy with the enlightenment of

the century. Joseph II is the best representative of the contradictions of the 18th century, and of its philanthropy and its devotion to right, and again of its severity and lack of consideration, where there was question of executing some favorite theory. Filled with dislike of the clergy and the nobility, and entertaining the ideal of a strong, centralized, united state, Joseph pursued his reforms with the purpose of breaking the power of the privileged classes mentioned above, of destroying all provincial independence, and of establishing unity in the administration (centralization). Despite all his failures, despite the fact that, with few exceptions his reforms did not outlive him, Joseph's reign regenerated the Austrian monarchy, lending it mobility and vitality.

1781, Oct. 13.   Edict of tolerance. Within eight years 700 monasteries were closed and 36,000 members of orders released. There still remained, however, 1324 monasteries with 27,000 monks and nuns. For those which remained a new organization was prescribed. The connection of the ecclesiastical order with Rome was weakened, schools were established with the property of the churches, innovations in the form of worship were introduced, nor did the interior organization of the Church escape alteration. Futile journey of Pope **Pius VI** to Vienna (1782), undertaken to prevent these changes. Reform of jurisdiction. The feudal burdens were reduced to fixed norms, and attempts were made to abolish completely personal servitude among the peasants.

1781. Disputes between Joseph and the Dutch; the emperor arbitrarily annulled the **Barrier Treaties** (p. 476). He demanded that the Scheldt, which had been closed by the treaty of Westphalia to the Spanish Netherlands, in favor of the Dutch, should be opened. Finally, after four years of quarreling, French mediation brought about the **treaty of Versailles** (1785). Joseph withdrew his demands in consideration of ten million florins.

Joseph attempted to improve the legal system of the Empire. His encroachments in the Empire. Violent proceedings in the case of the **bishop of Passau** (1783).

1783. The endeavors of Frederick the Great to conclude a union of German princes (1783), which should resist the encroachments of the emperor, and to strengthen Prussia in her political isolation by a "combination within the Empire," were at first but coldly supported by his own ministers and the German princes. Frederick's plan was not taken into favor until news was received of

1785.   Joseph II's plan of an exchange of territory, according to which Charles Theodore was to cede the whole of Bavaria to Austria, and accept in exchange the Austrian Netherlands (Belgium), excepting Luxemburg and Namur, as the kingdom of Burgundy. France maintained an attitude of indifference. Russia supported the project and endeavored by persuasion and threats to induce the heir of Bavaria, the count palatine of Zweibrücken, to consent to the scheme. The latter sought help from Frederick the Great, who, a year before his death (d. 1786, Aug. 17), succeeded in forming the

1785, July. League of the German Princes between Prussia, Electoral Saxony, and Hanover, which was afterward joined by Brunswick, Mainz, Hesse-Cassel, Baden, Mecklenburg, Anhalt, and the Thuringian lands, directed against Joseph's scheme.

Opposition to Joseph's reforms in the Austrian Netherlands and in Hungary. The removal of the crown of Hungary to Vienna produced so great a disturbance that the emperor yielded and permitted its return. The revocation of the constitution of Brabant caused a revolt in the Belgian provinces (1789). War with the Turks (p. 521). **Death of Joseph II** (1790). His brother became

1790–1792. LEOPOLD II, emperor. He suppressed the Belgian insurrection, but restored the old constitution and the old privileges. A **conference at Reichenbach** prevented a war with Prussia, which (Jan. 31, 1790) had concluded a treaty with the Turks, in order to procure more favorable conditions for the latter from Austria and Russia (p. 521).

(*Cont. pp. 631, 715.*)

CULTURAL DEVELOPMENTS

German literature began to revive after the appearance of **Johann Christoph Gottsched's** *Kritische Dichtkunst* (1730), which was answered by the Swiss **Johann J. Breitinger's** treatise (1739) of the same name, pleading for greater freedom of inspiration and imagination in literature. The first poet of this modern period was **Friedrich Gottlieb Klopstock** (1724–1803), whose epic *Messias* appeared in twenty cantos. **Gotthold Ephraim Lessing** (1729–1781)

was the first great German critic of literature and of art (*Laokoon,* 1766) and a classical dramatist whose plays gave new stature to German drama (*Minna von Barnhelm,* 1767; *Nathan der Weise,* 1779). The later German novel owed much to **Christoph Martin Wieland's** *Agathon* (1766–1767), a pyschological study.

The **Sturm und Drang** movement, reflecting much of Rousseau's emphasis on the return to naturalism and individual liberties, was in part founded by **Johann Gottfried Herder** (1744–1803); he stressed the national quality in the folk-songs he collected; stated in four volumes his *Ideen zu einer Philosophie der Geschichte der Menschheit* (1784–1791); had considerable influence on the young **Johann Wolfgang von Goethe** (1749–1832), the foremost poet of the Sturm und Drang period, author of the first important drama of the movement (*Götz von Berlichingen,* 1773) and of the first novel (*Werthers Leiden,* 1774).

Goethe soon came under the influence of **Johann J. Winckelmann** (1717–1768), the great historian of classical art; his plays (*Iphigenie auf Tauris,* 1787; *Torquato Tasso,* 1790) conformed to the classical ideal. *Faust,* the first part of which was begun in the Sturm and Drang period, is highly classical in its second part.

Goethe's contemporary and great friend, **Friedrich von Schiller** (1759–1805), also bridges the gap from the excessive demands of the Sturm und Drang period (*Die Räuber,* 1781) to purely classical dramas (the trilogy *Wallenstein,* 1798–1799; *Die Jungfrau von Orleans,* 1801). These were the two great authors of Germany's classical period of literature.

Music: Influence of sacred music of **Dietrich Buxtehude** (1637–1707) on **Johann Sebastian Bach** (1685–1750). Baroque music of **George Frederick Handel** (1685–1759) followed by operas of **Christoph Willibald Gluck** (1714–1787), symphonies and chamber music of **Joseph Haydn** (1732–1809) and of **Wolfgang Amadeus Mozart** (1756–1791), who also composed several operas in the rococco style (*Marriage of Figaro,* 1786; *Don Giovanni,* 1787; *Così fan tutte,* 1790). Greatest composer of classical symphonies was **Ludwig van Beethoven** (1770–1827); also chamber music, oratorio, opera, and piano music.

8. SCANDINAVIA

a. SWEDEN, 1654–1792

(*From p. 442*)

Gustavus Adolphus and his able lieutenants and successors took advantage of the Thirty Years' War to raise Sweden to the rank of a

first-class power, with dominance over the whole Baltic area. But the greatness of Sweden was to be short-lived. During the later 17th century the royal power was greatly strengthened, but nevertheless Sweden lacked the resources to compete with the neighboring powers, like Prussia and Russia. The attempts of the Swedish kings to establish control in Poland and the extravagant schemes of Charles XII soon reduced Sweden to the position of a second-class power.

1654. Queen Christina, the daughter of Gustavus Adolphus, abdicated the throne and spent the rest of her life as a converted Catholic, devoted to religion and art. She left the throne to her cousin, Charles Gustavus of Pfalz-Zweibrücken, son of a sister of Gustavus Adolphus, who became

1654–1660. CHARLES X GUSTAVUS. His reign was pre-eminently one of military activity, devoted to

1655–1660. The First Northern War. Charles declared war on Poland on the pretext that John Casimir (of the house of Vasa) refused to acknowledge him. Actually Charles' purpose was to extend the Swedish possessions on the southern Baltic coast.

1656. The Swedes, allied with the elector of Brandenburg **(treaties of Königsberg and Marienburg)** invaded Poland and won a great **battle at Warsaw.** Thereupon Russia, Denmark, and the Empire declared war on the Swedes, and Brandenburg soon deserted the Swedish cause to join the coalition (Poland recognized the elector's sovereignty over East Prussia).

1657. The Swedes were driven out of Poland, but

1658. Charles twice invaded Denmark. The valiant defense of Copenhagen saved the Danish monarchy from annihilation and the death of Charles facilitated the

1660, May 3. Treaty of Oliva: John Casimir of Poland abandoned his claims to the Swedish throne and ceded Livonia to Sweden. By the **treaty of Copenhagen** Denmark surrendered to Sweden the southern part of the Scandinavian Peninsula, but retained Bornholm and Trondheim. The **treaty of Kardis** (1661) between Sweden and Russia re-established the *status quo ante bellum.*

1660–1697. CHARLES XI.

1672–1679. Sweden took part in the Dutch War as an ally of France, but the Swedes achieved little. The invasion of Brandenburg resulted in the

1675, June 28. Battle of Fehrbellin, in which the Swedes were defeated by the forces of the Great Elector. A severe blow to Swedish military prestige. The elector then invaded Swedish Pomerania, took Stettin, Stralsund, and Greifswald; but, by the **treaty of St. Germain-en-Laye** (1679), Sweden, through her French ally, was able to recover all that had been lost.

In the internal history of Sweden this reign was marked by the establishment of an **absolutist government.** The council was reduced to impotence, and the estates were kept in submission.

1680. Under the pressure of the king the estates passed a law by the terms of which all earldoms, baronies, and other large fiefs should revert to the crown. This wholesale confiscation of properties dealt a severe blow to Swedish aristocracy.

1697–1718. CHARLES XII. He ascended the throne at the age of 15, but was soon to prove himself one of the military geniuses of modern times. His reign was taken up almost entirely by the

1700–1721. GREAT NORTHERN WAR, which, in a sense, was one aspect of the general war in Europe during the first fifteen years of the century.

The **Northern War** was caused by the common opposition of Russia, Poland, and Denmark to the Swedish supremacy in the Baltic region. **Peter of Russia** was firmly determined to make his country a naval power, and to get possession of harbors on the Baltic; **Augustus II,** elector of Saxony and king of Poland, had a scheme for the reunion of Livonia with Poland; the **king of Denmark,** besides desiring the general weakening of Sweden, resented Swedish support of the duke of Holstein-Gottorp in his struggle with Denmark. A secret alliance between the three sovereigns was concluded in the fall of 1699, and next year the war opened with an invasion of Schleswig by the Danes, and of Livonia by Augustus' Saxon troops. Unexpected landing of Charles XII of Sweden in Zeeland; he threatened Copenhagen and extorted from the Danes the

1700, Aug. 18. Treaty of Travendal: (1) Indemnification of the duke of Holstein. (2) Denmark promised to abstain from hostilities against Sweden for the future.

Meantime the Saxons were besieging Riga (in Livonia), and the Russians Narva (in Ingermanland).

Nov. 30. Landing of Charles XII with 8000 men and decisive **victory of Narva** over the Russians. Instead of pursuing the Russians, Charles turned west, relieved Riga (1701, June 17) and then invaded Poland.

The following six years were spent by Charles in an effort to defeat Augustus II. After a series of victories over the Poles and Saxons, Charles invaded Saxony and compelled Augustus to sign the

1706, Sept. 24. Treaty of Altranstädt: (1) Augustus abdicated the Polish crown and recognized the previously elected **Stanislas Leszczynski** (the candidate of the pro-Swedish party) as king of Poland. (2) Augustus broke his alliance with the Russian tsar.

1707, Sept. After this, Charles took the field against Peter, who had employed the interval in making conquests and establishing his power in the Baltic (St. Petersburg founded at the mouth of the Neva in 1703, Narva captured in 1704), and in forming a trained and well-supplied army.

1708. Charles advanced in the general direction of Moscow, and then suddenly turned south into the Ukraine where his secret ally, the Cossack hetman, **Mazeppa,** had promised him a general anti-Russian uprising. The uprising failed to materialize, and the Swedish army found itself in a difficult situation. Meanwhile the Russians had intercepted and defeated an auxiliary Swedish corps, under Loewenhaupt, which was moving south from Livonia with supplies for Charles' army. In an attempt to seize the city of Voronezh, Charles besieged the fortress of Poltava which lay on his way there, and Peter led his main army to the rescue of the stronghold.

1709, July 8. BATTLE OF POLTAVA. The Russian army, superior in numbers and equipment, completely defeated the Swedes, who were exhausted by long marches and lack of food. The Swedish army was broken up, and a large part of it captured. Charles, accompanied by Mazeppa, found refuge in Turkey. Two years later he induced the Porte to declare war against Peter.

1711. Peter, allied with the rulers of Moldavia and Wallachia, moved to the river Pruth, but was surrounded by a much larger Turkish army and was obliged to conclude the **treaty of the Pruth:** (1) Azov given back to the Porte. (2) Charles allowed to return to Sweden.

Charles XII, indignant at this treaty, refused to depart, and remained in Turkey for three more years. Meanwhile (1709) Augustus II drove King Stanislas from Poland. Peter occupied all of Livonia, Estonia, Ingermanland, Karelia, Finland. The Danes took Schleswig from the duke of Holstein-Gottorp, conquered the Swedish duchies of Bremen and Verden, which they afterward sold to Hanover upon condition that that state should take part in the war against Sweden, and jointly with the Poles invaded Pomerania. The Prussians occupied Stettin.

1714. Charles XII at last returned to his kingdom through Hungary and Germany. After this the war dragged on for several years with Russia, Saxony, Poland, Denmark, Prussia, Hanover allied against Sweden.

1718, Dec. 11. Charles XII was shot near Fredrikshald during a military expedition to Norway. He was succeeded by his sister

1718-1720. ULRICA ELEANORA, who was accepted on condition that the riksdag should be allowed to draw up a constitution. The **new constitution** provided for joint rule of the monarch and the council when the riksdag was not in session. While the riksdag was sitting, the principal decisions were to be made by a secret committee composed of members of the three higher estates (nobility, clergy, and burghers). The peasants were, however, to be heard in matters of taxation. This new system involved the re-establishment of the political power of the nobility and clergy and continued until 1771. But the ruling class was divided in the 18th century, between the party of the *Caps,* who favored a prudent foreign policy, and that of the *Hats,* who were eager to regain Sweden's supremacy in the Baltic.

1720-1751. FREDERICK I (of Hesse-Cassel), the husband of Ulrica Eleanora, to whom she turned over the government. Cautious policy of the minister, **Count Arvid Horn,** a Swedish Fleury, who allowed the dangerous connection with France to lapse, and sought better relations with Great Britain and Russia. In 1738 he was overthrown by **Count Gyllenborg,** leader of the Hats and wholly under the French influence (alliance of 1738). This brought Sweden before long into conflict with Russia. The Hats remained in power until 1766.

1720-1721. Conclusion of the Northern War. By the **treaties of Stockholm:** (1) The *status quo ante bellum* was restored as between Sweden, Saxony, and Poland. (2) Hanover was allowed to retain Verden, but paid Sweden 1,000,000 thalers. (3) Prussia received Stettin, western Pomerania as far as the Peene, the islands of Wollin and Usedom, but paid Sweden 2,000,000 thalers. (4) Denmark restored all conquests, in return for which Sweden paid 600,000 rix dollars, gave up its freedom from customs duties in the Sound, and abandoned the duke of Holstein-Gottorp, whom Denmark deprived of his share of Schleswig.

1721, Aug. 30. Treaty of Nystadt, between Sweden and Russia: Sweden ceded to Russia: Livonia, Estonia, Ingermanland, part of Karelia, and a number of islands, among others Oesel and Dagö. Russia restored Finland and paid 2,000,000 rix dollars.

The main results of the great war were the destruction of Sweden's preponderance in the Baltic and the emergence of Russia as a great European power.

1741-1743. War against Russia, provoked by the Hats, who were under French influence and were thirsting for revenge. By the **treaty of Åbo** (Aug. 7, 1743), Sweden ceded to Russia more territory in Finland.

1751-1771.   ADOLPHUS FREDERICK of Oldenburg-Holstein-Gottorp, king, introducing a collateral line.

1771-1792.   GUSTAVUS III, the son of Adolphus Frederick. Gustavus, fearful lest Sweden should be victimized by Russia and Prussia, restored absolute government by means of a military *coup d'état* (Aug. 19, 1772). The power of the council was ended and the king again acquired full authority over the administration. The riksdag lost its initiative in legislation. Gustavus tried to be an "enlightened despot." He abolished torture, improved the poor laws, proclaimed religious toleration and liberty of the press, and encouraged trade. But with the outbreak of the French Revolution his policies became more reactionary.

1788-1790.   War with Russia. Gustavus invaded Russian Finland and achieved several victories, but was attacked by the Danes and in the end was obliged to conclude the **treaty of Wereloe,** which left Finland and Karelia in Russian hands.

1789, Feb.   By the Act of Unity and Security, Gustavus, taking advantage of his victory over the Danes, effected another *coup* and established his despotic power in Sweden.

1792, Mar.   Gustavus III was murdered by Jacob Johan Ankarström, a Swedish aristocrat.

(*Cont. pp. 644, 747.*)

b. DENMARK AND NORWAY, 1648-1788

(*From p. 440*)

1648-1670.   FREDERICK III. A few months after the conclusion of peace with Sweden (1660), a monarchical *coup d'état,* supported by the clergy and the burghers, transformed the king into an hereditary and virtually absolute ruler, with the council relegated to the position of a mere advisory body. A treatise expressing absolutist ideas was composed for the king by **Peter Schumacher** (afterwards **Count Griffenfeld**). Published under the title of *Kongelov* (*King's Law*), it guided Griffenfeld's administration during the early years of

1670-1699.   CHRISTIAN V's reign.

1699-1730. Under **FREDERICK IV,** Denmark took part in the **Northern War** (p. 507). As a result of the war a certain balance between Denmark and Sweden was established in the Baltic region: Denmark was no longer afraid of a Swedish invasion, and on her part gave up ideas of reconquering her lost possessions in the south of the Scandinavian Peninsula. In his domestic policies, Frederick IV perfected the machinery of royal absolutism.

These gains, however, were partially lost during the reigns of his feeble successors (**Christian VI,** 1730-1746; **Frederick V,** 1746-1766) characterized by the rule of royal favorites mostly of German origin. Under the mentally unbalanced

1766-1808.   CHRISTIAN VII an attempt at radical internal reform was made during the administration (1770-1771) of the German, **John Frederick Struensee,** an exponent of "enlightened despotism": Struensee tried to make the royal power independent of the nobility by suppressing the council, attacked aristocratic privileges, reorganized the administration, abolished torture and censorship of the press.

1772.   Struensee was overthrown by a palace revolution and subsequently executed. This was followed by the rule of a reactionary aristocratic group, headed by **Guldberg,** and after his fall (1784) by the

1784-1788. Administration of an able and enlightened statesman, **Count Andreas Peter Bernstorff,** who began by regulating relations between the landlords and their peasant tenants, and then passed a series of measures (1787-1788) virtually abolishing serfdom in Denmark.

In **NORWAY,** which remained under Danish domination, this period saw the vigorous growth of a national cultural movement: literary activity of **Ludwig Holberg** (1684-1754), formation of the **Norwegian Society** among the university students in Copenhagen (1772).

(*Cont. pp. 642, 746.*)

9. POLAND, 1648-1795

(*From p. 444*)

1648-1668.   JOHN II CASIMIR. His reign was marked by grave internal disturbances and unsuccessful foreign wars against the Swedes, Russians, and Turks. Frequent uprisings of the serfs and of the Ukrainian Cossacks.

1654. The hetman of the Cossacks, **Bogdan Khmelnitsky,** placed himself under the protection of Russia, thus precipitating a prolonged conflict between Russia and Poland for possession of the Ukraine.

1655-1660.   War between Sweden and Poland (p. 507). Invasion of the Swedes. By the

(From p. 439)

The Danish Royal House (1699–   )

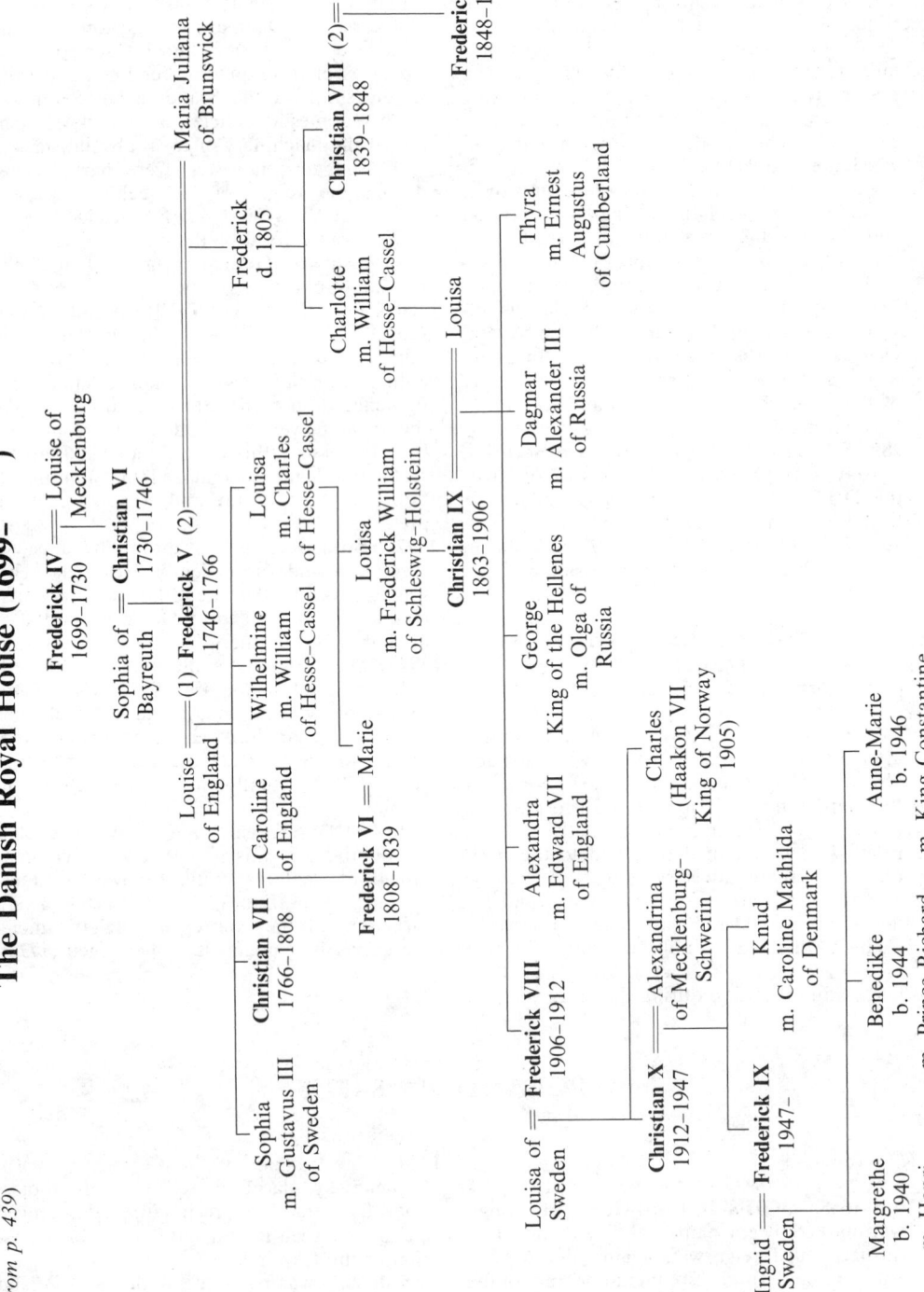

treaty of Oliva (May 3, 1660), Poland lost to Sweden her last Baltic territories.

1667, Jan. 20. Treaty of Andrussovo, ending the conflict with Russia. Poland ceded to Russia the eastern Ukraine and Smolensk.

1668. John Casimir abdicated and there followed a period of ardent struggle for the throne. The Poles finally elected a national candidate,

1669-1673. MICHAEL WISNIOWIECKI, during whose short reign the Cossacks again rose in revolt and appealed to the Turks for aid.

1672-1676. War with Turkey. The Turks, having taken Kameniec, secured from the disheartened Polish king the **treaty of Buczacz** (1772), by which Poland lost Podolia and recognized the western Ukraine as independent under Turkish protectorate. The Polish diet refused to ratify the treaty and the Poles resumed the struggle under the lead of **John Sobieski,** an able commander who gradually drove the Turks back.

1674-1696. JOHN III SOBIESKI, king after the death of Michael. After a victory over the Turks at Lemberg (1675), he concluded with them the

1676, Oct. Treaty of Zuravno, by which the Turks retained only part of the Ukraine.

1683, Mar. 31. John Sobieski made an **alliance with Austria** in order to present a united front to the Turkish advance on Vienna. The Poles then played an important rôle in the relief of Vienna from the famous second siege (p. 518). Sobieski continued to participate in the reconquest of Hungary until 1685.

These military successes, however, were not enough to arrest the process of decline which resulted from the basic defects of the Polish political organization, viz. the absence of real unity, the lack of strong central authority, the impotence of the national diet (repeatedly paralyzed by the use of the *liberum veto* or right of each individual member of the diet to defeat a resolution by his protest, and thus to break up the session).

1697-1733. AUGUSTUS II (elector of Saxony), king of Poland. He attempted to strengthen the royal power, but without much success.

1699, Jan. 26. Treaty of Karlowitz, ending the long war against Turkey (p. 519). By this settlement the Poles regained Podolia and the Turkish part of the Ukraine.

1700-1721. The **Great Northern War** (p. 507), which was fought largely on Polish soil. The Poles had made an agreement with Russia to despoil Charles XII of Sweden. They invaded Livonia (1700), but in 1701-1702 Charles invaded Poland, taking Warsaw and Cracow

(1702). The Polish magnates then dethroned Augustus, and elected

1704-1709. STANISLAS LESZCZYNSKI as king. By the **treaty of Altranstädt,** with Sweden (1706), Augustus gave up his claims. The Empire, Brandenburg, England, and Holland all recognized Stanislas. But after the defeat of Charles at Poltava (1709), Augustus returned and drove out his rival. Poland suffered tremendously from the Swedish invasion and the civil war, yet gained nothing whatever from the defeat of Charles.

1715-1717. Further disorders, resulting from a rising of the nobles against the absolutist policies of Augustus. This offered an opportunity for Russian intervention and initiated the gradual subordination of Poland to Russia.

1733-1735. WAR OF THE POLISH SUCCESSION. The Poles, supported by France, elected Stanislas Leszczynski, who had become the father-in-law of Louis XV. The Russians and Austrians insisted on the election of Augustus of Saxony, son of Augustus II. A huge Russian army invaded the country and drove out Stanislas, who withdrew to Danzig. France, supported by Spain and Sardinia, declared war on the Empire. French expedition to the Baltic to relieve Danzig (besieged by the Russians from October 1733 onward).

1734, June 2. Capitulation of Danzig; Stanislas fled to Prussia. Meanwhile the main fighting was done in Italy (French and Spanish victories, p. 501) and on the Rhine (indecisive). The war was finally ended by the **treaty of Vienna** (Oct. 5, 1735, ratified 1738), which wrought profound changes in Italy and assured the victory of the Russian-Austrian policy in Poland.

1734-1763. AUGUSTUS III, king. He spent but little time in Poland, and did little to prevent Russian encroachment, especially during the Seven Years' War. Growing agitation for reform in Poland after 1740: two parties, led by the **Potocki** and **Czartoryski** families. The former looked to France for support and aimed at the establishment of an aristocratic constitution; the latter, relying on Russian support, envisaged strengthening of the royal power, abolition of the *liberum veto,* etc.

1764-1795. STANISLAS PONIATOWSKI, king. He was a nephew of Prince Czartoryski and was the favorite of Catherine II of Russia. By agreement of April 11, 1764, Russia and Prussia had arranged for co-operation in Polish affairs. Poniatowski and the reformers attempted to introduce changes, but Russia soon showed herself lukewarm on the subject.

1766-1768. Question of the Dissidents (Greek Orthodox Catholics and Protestants), who were granted equal rights with Roman Catholics, at the insistence of Russia and Prussia. This raised a storm of protest in Poland and led (1768) to the formation of the **Confederation of Bar,** an anti-Russian association which soon enjoyed the active support of France. Civil war of the most violent type broke out in Poland; invasion and campaigns of the Russians against the Confederates. Ultimately the Turks, encouraged by the French, declared war on Russia, in support of Polish "liberties."

1772, Aug. 5. THE FIRST PARTITION OF POLAND. This resulted directly from the Russian victories against the Turks, which so alarmed the Austrians that they came to the point of making war on Russia. Frederick the Great, fearing involvement in a general European conflict, engineered the partition of Poland, by which Russia might make gains unobjectionable to Austria, while Prussia and Austria might participate in the spoils. By the first partition **Russia** acquired White Russia and all territory to the Dvina and Dnieper, about 1,800,000 inhabitants (mostly Greek Orthodox); **Austria** took Red Russia, Galicia, and western Podolia, with Lemberg and part of Cracow (2,700,000 inhabitants); **Prussia** took Polish Prussia, except Danzig and Thorn (416,000 inhabitants). In all Poland lost about one-third of its territory and about one-half of its inhabitants.

1773. The **Polish diet,** forced to accept the partition, began to effect reforms (council of state, divided into five ministries, to govern when the diet was not in session). Intellectual awakening under the influence of French ideas, educational reforms, etc.

1788-1792. The **Four Years' Diet,** dominated by the progressive patriotic party, while Prussia, Austria and Russia were at war with the Turks. The Prussian minister **Hertzberg** hoped to secure Danzig and Thorn by agreement with a reformed Poland. Developments in France led to an agreement between Prussia and Austria and to postponement of the scheme.

1791, May 3. The Polish patriots put through a **new constitution** which (1) converted the elective monarchy into an hereditary monarchy (the elector of Saxony to succeed Poniatowski and to establish a Saxon dynasty); (2) conferred the executive power upon the king and council of state; (3) vested the legislative power in a diet of two chambers; (4) abolished the *liberum veto.* Prussia and Austria accepted this change, but the Russians organized

1792, May 14. The **Confederation of Targowicz,** in defense of the old constitution. Russian invasion was followed by similar action on the part of the Prussians, and finally led to a bargain between the two powers in the

1793, Jan. 23. SECOND PARTITION OF POLAND. Russia took most of Lithuania and most of the western Ukraine, including Podolia (3,000,000 inhabitants); **Prussia** took Danzig and Thorn, as well as Great Poland (1,100,000 inhabitants). In addition, Russia forced Poland to accept a **treaty of alliance,** whereby Russia was given free entry for her troops in Poland and the right to control Poland's relations with other powers.

1794, Mar. 24. NATIONAL UPRISING in Poland, led by **Thaddeus Kosciuszko.** After an unequal struggle against the forces of Russia and Prussia, the Poles were defeated (capture of Kosciuszko, surrender of Warsaw to Suvorov), and Austria joined Russia and Prussia in the

1795, Oct. 24. THIRD PARTITION OF POLAND. Russia took what remained of Lithuania and the Ukraine (1,200,000 inhabitants); **Prussia** secured Mazovia with Warsaw (1,000,000 inhabitants), while **Austria** obtained the remainder of the Cracow region (1,000,000 inhabitants). Courland, long under the suzerainty of Poland, but since 1737 practically under Russian influence (Biron, duke of Courland), was incorporated with Russia.

The "Age of Enlightenment" produced much satirical writing: **Ignatius Krasicki** (1735-1801), poet, novelist, author of satires and fables. With the establishing of the first public theater in 1765 in Warsaw, new dramatists emerged: **Francis Zoblocki** (1754-1821) and **Julian Ursyn Niemcewicz** (1757-1841), also translator of English poems, author of novels, memoirs, *Collection of Historical Songs (Spiewy historyczne).*

10. RUSSIA, 1645-1801

(From p. 448)

1645-1676. ALEXIS, the son of Michael Romanov, who ascended the throne at the age of sixteen. His reign was marked by much internal unrest (serious revolt in Moscow, 1647) and by the adoption by a national assembly (1649) of a new code of law (in force until 1832) designed to improve the administration and to eliminate various abuses. In some of its provisions, however, it involved the final establishment of peasant serfdom in Russia.

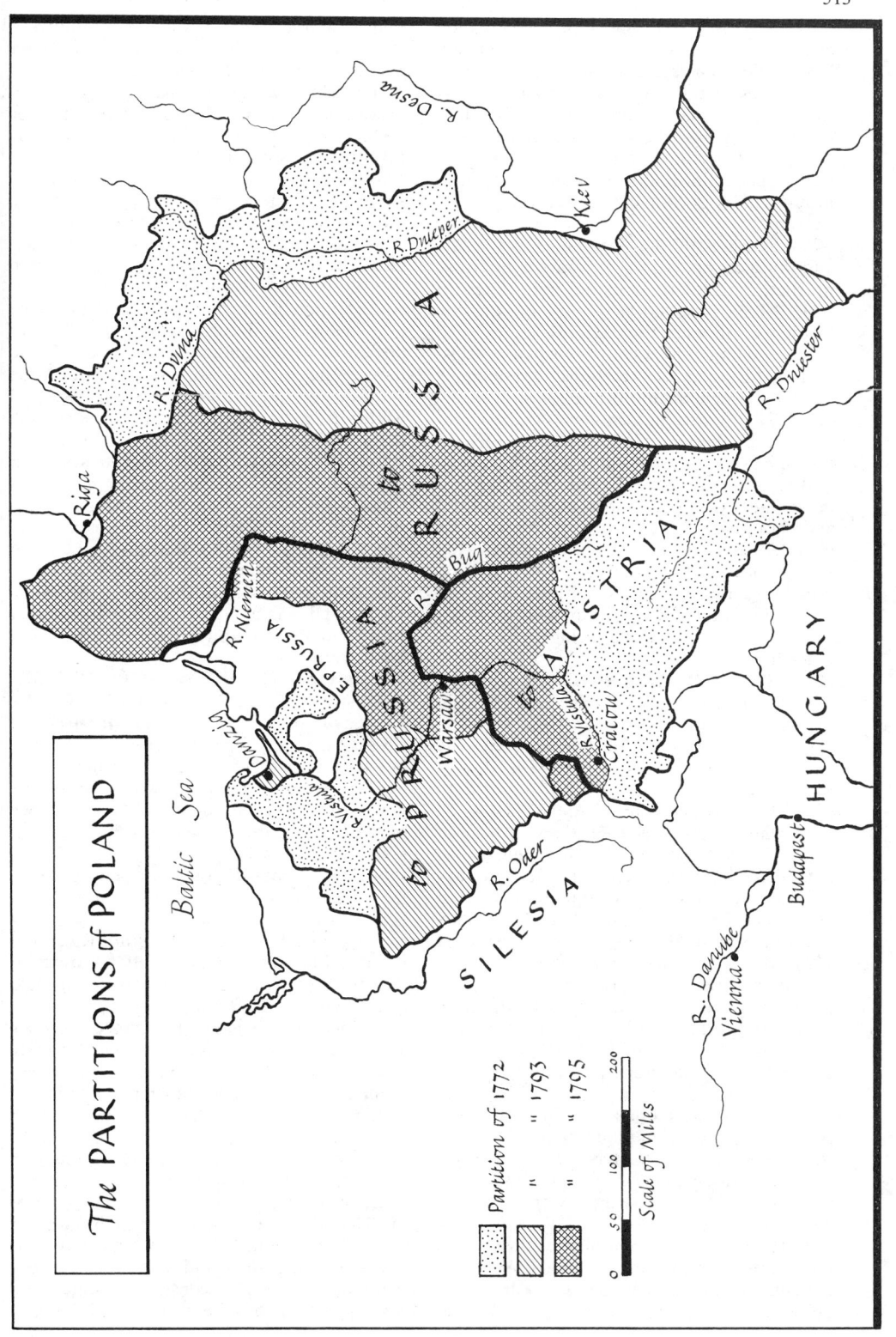

The PARTITIONS of POLAND

Baltic Sea

Riga

Danzig

R. Niemen

E. PRUSSIA

to PRUSSIA

Warsaw

R. Vistula

R. Oder

SILESIA

R. Duna

R. Dnieper

to RUSSIA

Kiev

R. Desna

R. Bug

to AUSTRIA

R. Vistula

Cracow

R. Dniester

HUNGARY

Budapest

Vienna

R. Danube

Partition of 1772
" " 1793
" " 1795

Scale of Miles

0   50   100   200

1654-1667. War with Poland for the possession of the Ukraine, after the Cossack hetman, **Bogdan Khmelnitsky,** had placed himself under Russian protection. By the **treaty of Andrussovo** (Jan. 20, 1667) Russia obtained the Smolensk region and the eastern Ukraine, with Kiev. The outcome of the war was of great importance, since the Russian gains first brought them in contact with the Turks in the Balkans.

1667. Revision of the Russian church ritual and liturgical books in accordance with Greek practice. This reform, undertaken by the patriarch, **Nikon,** resulted in secession from the Church of the so-called **Old Believers,** who were condemned by a church council as schismatics. Epistles of **Archpriest Avvakum** (c. 1620-1681) denouncing the reforms.

1670-1671. A great **peasant revolt** in the southeast, led by the Don Cossacks, under **Stephen Razin,** was suppressed with great difficulty.

By the end of the reign of Alexis the government had established more effective control and the crisis of the early 17th century was definitely overcome. The tsar, indeed, felt strong enough to discontinue calling the national assembly. At the same time there was a rapid infiltration of western influences, which foreshadowed the westernizing reforms of Peter the Great.

1676-1682. THEODORE III, the son of Alexis, during whose short reign Russia fought the first of many wars against the Ottoman Turks. By the **treaty of Radzin** (1681) the Turks abandoned most of the Turkish Ukraine to Russia.

1682-1689. IVAN V (son of Alexis' first wife), with whom was associated **Peter I** (son of Alexis' second wife) as co-tsar. **Sophia,** the daughter of Alexis, acted as regent. In 1689 the partisans of Peter overthrew Sophia and

1689-1725. PETER I (the Great) was effectively the sole ruler, though Ivan V lived until 1696. Peter, an intelligent but ruthless and headstrong ruler (b. 1672), spent the first years of his reign in a process of self-education (chiefly technical and military). He established close relations with members of foreign colonies in Moscow and prepared for his later campaigns through his military and naval "games."

1689. Conflict with China, resulting from the penetration of Russian pioneers into the Amur region. By the **treaty of Nerchinsk** (1689)—the first Russian treaty with China—the Russians were obliged to withdraw from the occupied territory.

1695-1696. Peter's **expeditions against Azov,** the fortress commanding the Sea of Azov and the entrance to the Black Sea. The first expedition, by land, was unsuccessful, but the second, supported by a naval force, resulted in the capture of the stronghold (July 28, 1696).

1697-1698. Peter's **European journey,** which he undertook *incognito* as part of a grand embassy sent to secure allies in western Europe for a crusade against the Turks. Peter was the first Russian sovereign to go abroad and his travels in France, England, and Holland strengthened him in the determination to "westernize" Russia. He returned to Moscow to suppress a **revolt of the streltsy** (soldiers of the Moscow garrison, among whom there were many Old Believers), and then embarked upon his first reforms. At the same time he prepared for war with Sweden for possession of the Baltic coast, having failed to induce the western powers to continue the Turkish war beyond the year 1699 (**treaty of Karlowitz,** p. 519). Peace was concluded with the Turks in 1700, Russia retaining Azov.

1700-1721. The GREAT NORTHERN WAR (p. 507). Peter was at first no match for Charles XII, who defeated him at **Narva** (Nov. 30, 1700). But Charles spent the next years campaigning in Poland, thus giving Peter an opportunity to reorganize his army on European lines and to construct a fleet in the Baltic. The capital was moved to the newly founded city of **St. Petersburg** (modern Petrograd and Leningrad) in 1703.

1709, July 8. The BATTLE OF POLTAVA, a decisive battle in Russian history. Charles XII, having allied himself with **Mazeppa,** the Cossack hetman, began to march on Moscow, but then turned off south. At Poltava Peter won a resounding victory which broke the power of Charles and marked the emergence of Russia in place of Sweden as the dominant power in the north.

1710-1711. War with Turkey, due to pressure from Charles XII (a refugee in Turkey) and France (p. 519). The Russians were surrounded by the Turks on the Pruth River and Peter had to buy himself off. By the **treaty of the Pruth** (July 21, 1711), he was obliged to return Azov to the Turks.

1721, Aug. 30. Treaty of Nystadt, between Russia and Sweden, concluding the Northern War. Russia acquired Livonia, Estonia, Ingermanland, part of Karelia and a number of Baltic islands. Thus Peter had achieved his great purpose of acquiring a "window" on the Baltic which would open up connections with the west. Russia now definitely took her place as a European power.

INTERNAL REFORMS: centralization of the administration. The old council of the boyars was abolished and was replaced by a governing *senate* (1711), consisting of nine members appointed by the tsar. New govern-

(From p. 446)

Russian Tsars (1645-1917)

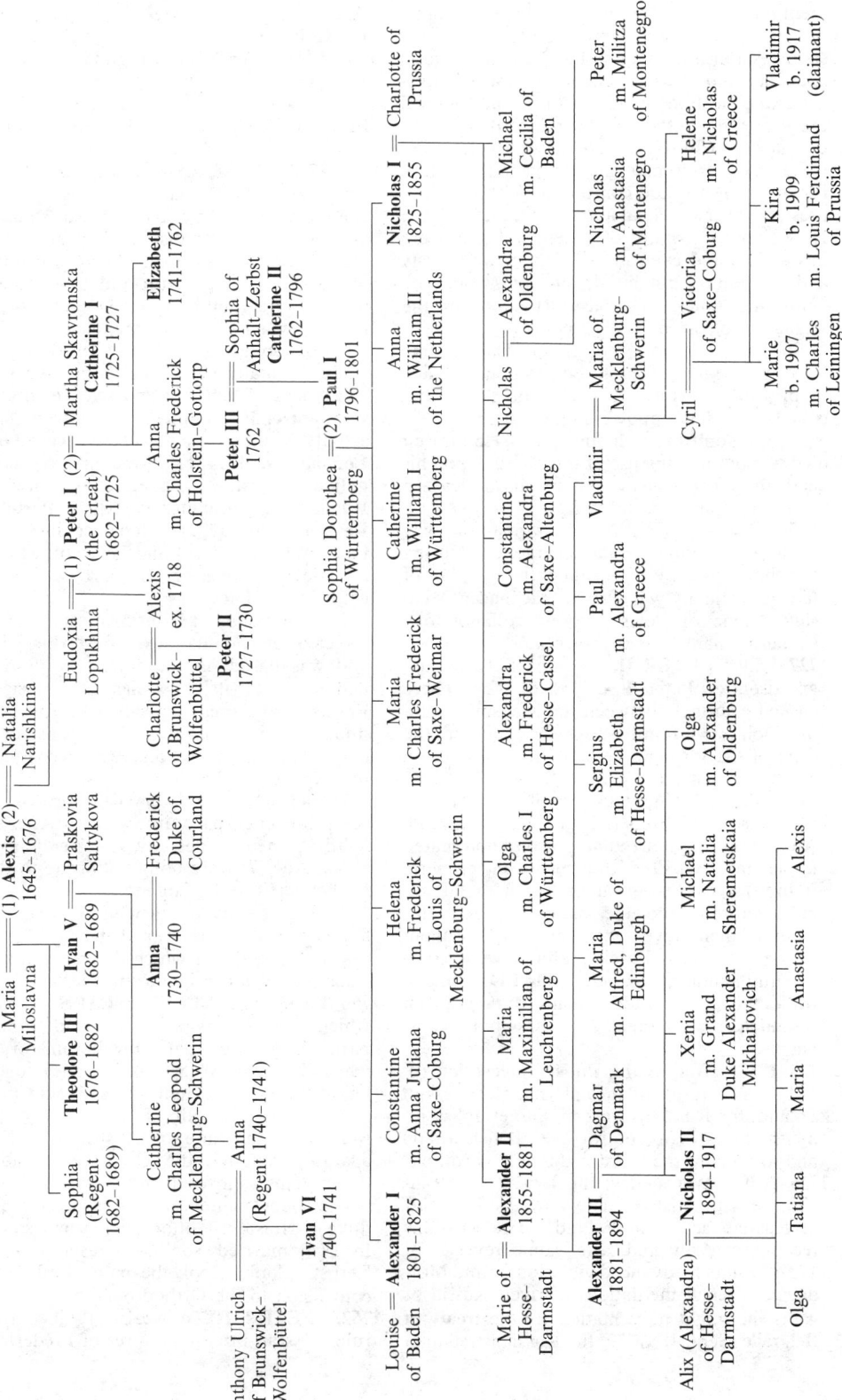

ment bureaus were set up (1718) under the name of *colleges.* The nobility was made to serve the state (establishment of a hierarchy of offices) and Peter did much to encourage trade, industry, and education (Academy of Science opened the year after Peter's death). In order to subordinate the Church to state control, Peter abolished the patriarchate and in its place established (1721) a synod composed of bishops, but presided over by a layman (procurator of the Holy Synod). Many of Peter's reforms were incomplete and even more of them were hasty and premature, but his drastic innovations no doubt did much to arouse Russia from the stagnation of the preceding period.

Alexis, the son of Peter I, who had become the center of opposition to Peter's policies, died in prison of torture in 1718. In 1722 Peter issued a law that empowered the reigning sovereign to appoint his own successor. He himself died without making use of this right. Upon his death the officers of the palace guard elevated to the throne his second wife,

1725–1727. CATHERINE I, a woman of lowly birth, but intelligent and energetic. During her short reign the most influential member of the government was **Prince Alexander Menshikov,** one of Peter's closest collaborators. Catherine named as her successor

1727–1730. PETER II, the son of Alexis and grandson of Peter I, a boy of 12. There ensued a struggle between the Menshikov and the Dolgoruki families, which ended in the exile of the former. Peter II died young and was succeeded by

1730–1740. ANNA, daughter of Ivan V, who was married to Frederick, duke of Courland. Anna was an ineffectual person, dominated by her favorite, **Ernst Johann Biron** (properly Bühren). The government began to fall almost entirely into the hands of Germans, many of them adventurers, but many of them extremely able. Foreign affairs were competently handled by **Count Andrei Ostermann,** while the army, under **Count Burkhard von Münnich,** scored great successes in its campaigns.

1733–1735. War of the Polish Succession (p. 501). As a result of the internal weakness of Poland, the Russians were able to establish on a firm basis their control over Polish affairs and to prepare the way for the final partitions.

1736–1739. War against the Turks (p. 519), in alliance with Austria. The war was the result of Russian action in Poland. The Russians recaptured Azov and, after some reverses in 1737, Münnich advanced victoriously into Moldavia. French mediation deprived Russia of gains she might have made. By the **treaty of Belgrade** (Sept. 18, 1739) the Russians retained

Azov, but agreed to raze the fortifications and not to build a fleet on the Black Sea.

1740–1741. IVAN VI, the grandson of Anna's sister Catherine. Ivan's mother conducted the government for a short time after the fall of Biron (effected by Münnich), but a military revolt soon placed on the throne

1741–1762. ELIZABETH, the youngest daughter of Peter the Great, a thoroughly Russian character, politically keen, but dissolute and easy-going. Nationalist reaction against German favorites. Elizabeth set up a brilliant if somewhat uncouth court and gave wide rein to the court nobility. **Golden age of the aristocracy,** which began to emancipate itself from onerous obligations of service to the state, while gradually increasing its privileges. Development of learning and science: **first Russian university** founded at Moscow (1755); activity of the Academy of Sciences (**Mikhail Lomonosov,** 1711–1765, the first outstanding native scientist. Also poet, founder of modern Russian literature, literary stylist). **Bartolomeo Restrelli** (1700–1771) built palaces in St. Petersburg (Winter Palace) and Peterhof, as well as a castle and monastery in Zarskoye Selo and a cathedral in Kiev.

Foreign policy was, during most of the reign, directed by **Count Alexis Bestuzhev-Riumin,** and was based on the alliance with Austria and Great Britain as against Prussia and France. The great objectives of Russia continued to be expansion at the expense of Sweden, domination of Poland, and conquest at the expense of the Turk.

1741–1743. War with Sweden, provoked by the pro-French party in Sweden. After some fighting, the Swedes, by the **treaty of Abö** (1743, Aug. 7) were obliged to cede to Russia further territory in Finland.

1746, June 2. By treaty with Austria, Russia finally joined in the **War of the Austrian Succession** (p. 501), in which, however, the Russians played an insignificant rôle.

1756–1763. The **SEVEN YEARS' WAR,** in which Russia took an active and important part. The "diplomatic revolution" of 1756, which brought Austria and France together, led to the estrangement of Russia and Britain, and to the downfall of Bestuzhev. Russia fought on the side of Austria and France against Frederick the Great, but made no direct gains as a result of the war.

Elizabeth named as her successor **Peter,** duke of Holstein-Gottorp, her sister's son, who in 1744 married Sophia-Augusta of Anhalt-Zerbst. Sophia took the name Catherine on conversion to the Orthodox faith.

1762. PETER III, a weak and incompetent ruler. As an intense admirer of Frederick the

Great, he effected Russia's withdrawal from the war, thereby causing much resentment among the officers and the aristocracy (despite the fact that he proclaimed the freedom of the nobility from obligatory state service). After a six months' reign, Peter was deposed (July) by a military revolution led by the **Orlov brothers.** A few days later he was killed while in captivity. Peter was succeeded by his wife

1762–1796. CATHERINE II (the Great), an exceptionally astute and energetic ruler, who completed the work initiated by Peter the Great. In domestic affairs Catherine was guided by the teachings of the French Enlightenment (especially Voltaire) and tried to establish a benevolent despotism. On the other hand, she was obliged to cultivate the good will of the nobility, to which she owed her power. In order to codify the Russian law and also in order to learn the needs of the country, she convoked at Moscow a **legislative commission** (1767–1768), consisting of representatives of all classes excepting the serfs. Although no law code was produced, Catherine made good use of the commission's findings in planning her later legislation.

1766–1768. Drastic interference of Catherine in the **affairs of Poland,** where one of her favorites, Stanislas Poniatowski, had been placed on the throne (p. 511). The Russian advance in Poland led to

1768–1772. WAR WITH THE TURKS (p. 519), in which the Russians won unprecedented victories. The prospective gains of Russia so excited the Austrians (thitherto the partners of the Russians in the advance against the Turks) that the two powers came to the very verge of war. In order to prevent a general conflagration, Frederick the Great engineered the

1772, Aug. 5. FIRST PARTITION OF POLAND (p. 512). The Russian operations against Turkey were hampered further by

1773–1775. Pugachev's revolt, a formidable insurrection of the peasants and Cossacks of southeastern Russia, which was suppressed only with great difficulty.

1774, July 21. The **treaty of Kuchuk Kainarji** ended the war against Turkey. Russia acquired Kinburn, Yenikale, and Kertch in the Crimea and secured the right of free navigation for commercial ships in Turkish waters. The Tatars of the Crimea were recognized as "independent" and Russia was given important rights of intervention in Moldavia and Wallachia and in behalf of Christians in the Ottoman Empire (for details see p. 519).

1775. The statute of **provincial administration** was a direct result of Pugachev's revolt, which convinced Catherine of the need for reform.

It completely reorganized local government (small administrative units, better division of functions among the branches of government, some measure of self-government, more particularly for the nobility). Catherine did not dare, however, to touch the evil of serfdom. On the contrary, this institution reached its fullest development in her reign. Catherine's encouragement of education, art, and letters contributed to the growth of a liberal public opinion on the social problem. After the outbreak of the French Revolution, Catherine became decidedly hostile to this movement. **Alexander Radishchev** (1749–1802) was arrested and exiled to Siberia (1790) for having published his *Journey from St. Petersburg to Moscow,* which contained a vigorous protest against serfdom.

1780. Armed neutrality at sea, an idea advanced by Russia during the War of American Independence, as a method of protecting commerce. The idea was supported by Denmark and Sweden (1780) and later by Prussia, Austria (1782), and Portugal (1783); France and Spain recognized the principle, but Britain prevented Holland from joining the league by declaring war on the Dutch. The demands of the **League of Armed Neutrality** were: (1) free passage of neutral ships from port to port and along the coasts to combatants; (2) freedom of enemy goods in neutral ships (*le pavillon couvre la marchandise*), excepting for contraband; (3) definition of blockade (nominal, "paper" blockade not sufficient; a blockade, to be legal, must be effective).

1780. Visit of the Emperor Joseph II to Catherine and conclusion (1781) of an **Austro-Russian treaty.** Catherine's **Greek Scheme** for the disruption of the Ottoman Empire and division of the Balkans between Russia and Austria (p. 519). In keeping with her Near-Eastern plans, Catherine carried through

1783. The **annexation of the Crimea,** on the plea of restoring order. The Turks were with difficulty dissuaded by Britain and Austria from declaring war on Russia.

1785. Charter to the nobility, recognizing their corporate rights. A similar charter was issued for the towns, but not for the peasantry.

1787–1792. Second war of Catherine against the Turks (p. 521). Austria joined in the war. The Russians advanced to the Danube, but were badly distracted by

1788–1790. War with Sweden, and the Swedish invasion of Finland (p. 509). Under Prussian pressure, the Austrians finally backed out of the Turkish war, and Russia concluded the **treaty of Jassy** (1792, Jan. 9), by which she secured Oczakov and the boundary of the Dniester River.

1793, Jan. 23. The **second partition of Poland,** between Russia and Prussia (p. 512). Catherine, though very hostile to the French Revolution, took care not to become involved. Instead, she furthered her own designs in Poland, and, by

1795, Oct. 24. The **third partition of Poland** (p. 512) helped to extinguish the kingdom. By her immense gains in Poland, Russia advanced far into central Europe and became an ever more important factor in European affairs. Catherine was succeeded by her son

1796-1801. PAUL I, a tyrannical and mentally unbalanced ruler. Nevertheless, he was the first Russian ruler who tried to put certain limits to the spread of serfdom (1797, manifesto limiting the peasants' work for the landlord to three days a week).

1797. Paul repealed the law of succession of Peter the Great and decreed that succession should be by genealogical seniority.

1799-1801. Russia participated in the **War of the Second Coalition** against France (p. 636).

1801, Mar. 24. Paul was assassinated in the course of a palace revolution, and was succeeded by his son

1801-1825. ALEXANDER I.

(Cont. pp. 636, 749.)

11. THE OTTOMAN EMPIRE, 1656-1792

(From p. 454)

1656-1661. Mohammed Kiuprili, grand vizir. Through unlimited ruthlessness he tamed the restless Janissaries, executed incapable commanders, purged the court, raised the finances (taxes and confiscations). The war with Venice was vigorously pressed and Lemnos and Tenedos retaken (1657). **George II Rákóczi** of Transylvania was defeated and deposed.

1661-1678. Ahmed Kiuprili (son of Mohammed), grand vizir. Order having been restored, he ruled with a lenient hand, humoring the sultan and outwitting his enemies. The war with Venice he tried, in vain, to bring to an end by compromise.

1663-1664. War with Austria. After the treaty of Westphalia, Austria was able to devote attention to the Near East once more.

1664, Aug. 1. Battle of St. Gotthard, a victory of the imperial general, Montecuccoli, over the Turks. A 20-year truce concluded at Vasvar, the Turks losing no territory, but recognizing the election of the prince of Transylvania by the local estates.

1669. Fall of Candia, after a long siege. In the peace with Venice (1670) the latter retained only three fortified posts on the island.

1672-1676. War with Poland, the result of countless border raids (Tatars and Cossacks) and rivalry for control of the Ukraine. The Turks raided as far as Lemberg, but were twice defeated by King John Sobieski. In the **treaty of Zuravno** (Oct. 16, 1676) the Turks acquired most of Podolia and the Polish Ukraine, thus coming in contact with Russia.

1677-1681. First war with Russia, following Cossack raids. By the **treaty of Radzin** (1681) the Turks were obliged to give up most of the Ukraine and accord the Cossacks trading rights on the Black Sea.

1678. Kara Mustafa (brother-in-law of Ahmed Kiuprili), grand vizir. He was an incompetent but ambitious man, who at once supported Imre Tökölli as king of Hungary against the Emperor Leopold I.

1682-1699. War with Austria, which was allied to Poland.

1683, July 17-Sept. 12. SIEGE OF VIENNA by Kara Mustafa. Violent assaults on the walls; extensive mining operations; valiant defense by the garrison under **Rüdiger von Stahremberg.** Successful relief of the city by a united German and Polish army under **Charles of Lorraine** and **John Sobieski.**

1684. Venice joined Austria and Poland in a **Holy League,** sponsored by the pope. The Poles, however, soon withdrew, influenced thereto by Louis XIV of France. The Austrians advanced rapidly to Budapest (1686), while the Venetians took most of the fortresses in the Morea and the Russians laid siege to Azov (1687, 1689).

1687, Aug. 12. Second battle of Mohács. Charles of Lorraine defeated the Turks and the diet of Pressburg conferred hereditary succession to the Hungarian throne upon the male line of Austria. Panic in Constantinople; **deposition of Mohammed IV,** who was succeeded by **Suleiman III** (1687-1691).

1688. The Austrians took Belgrade and then (1689) Vidin.

1689. Mustafa Kiuprili (brother of Ahmed), grand vizir.

1690. The Turks drove the Austrians out of Bulgaria, Serbia, and Transylvania and retook Belgrade (flight of the Serbs into southern Hungary).

1691, Aug. 19. The Turks defeated by Louis of Baden in the **battle of Slankamen;** Mustafa killed. The war continued, but was not pressed by Austria, which had become involved in war with France (**War of the League of Augsburg,** 1688–1697).

1696, July 28. Peter the Great finally took Azov from the Turks.

1697, Sept. 11. Battle of Zenta, a great victory of **Eugene of Savoy** over the Turks.

1699, Jan. 26. TREATY OF KARLOWITZ, concluded for 25 years: **Austria** received all of Hungary (except the Banat of Temesvar), Transylvania, Croatia and Slavonia; **Venice** received the Morea and most of Dalmatia; Poland obtained Podolia. **Russia** continued the war until 1700, when the peace treaty recognized the Russian conquest of Azov. Peter was obliged to postpone his far-reaching plans to liberate his coreligionists in the Balkans.

1710–1711. War with Russia, instigated by France and by Charles XII of Sweden, who had fled to Turkey after his defeat by the Russians at Poltava (1709). Peter posed as the champion of the Balkan Christians and made efforts to stir up revolts. But in 1711 he was surrounded on the Pruth River by a vastly superior Turkish army and had to buy himself off. By the **treaty of the Pruth** (1711, July 21) Russia was obliged to give up Azov again.

1714–1718. War with Venice. Corinth and the Venetian stations in Candia were taken, but Austria entered the war and pressed the campaign in Hungary.

1716, Aug. 5. Eugene of Savoy won a victory at **Peterwardein** and captured Belgrade (1717).

1718, July 21. TREATY OF PASSAROWITZ: The Turks lost the Banat of Temesvar, northern Serbia, and Little Wallachia, but they retained the Morea.

1725–1727. The Turks, by agreement with Russia, secured the western part of Transcaucasia. This led to war with Persia (**Nadir Shah**), who drove the Turks out (1730).

1736–1739. War with Austria and Russia, partly the result of Turkish protests against Russian action in Poland, partly of French pressure. The Russians retook Azov and raided the Crimea, but in the campaigns of 1737 the Turks were successful against both Russians and Austrians.

1739. Spectacular advance of the Russian general, Münnich, to Jassy. Austria, alarmed by the successes of Russia, accepted French mediation.

1739, Sept. 18. TREATY OF BELGRADE. Austria gave up northern Serbia and Belgrade. The Russians, deserted by Austria, joined in the peace, agreeing to raze the fortifications of Azov and not to build a fleet on the Black Sea.

1743–1746. An indecisive **war with Persia,** marking, in a general way, the end of a long

duel. The mid-century was, on the whole, a period of peace (European powers involved in the War of the Austrian Succession and the Seven Years' War) and cultural progress (**Raghib Pasha,** grand vizir, 1757–1763). But the unaggressiveness of the central government soon led to the rise of the **Derebeys** (lords of the valley), who established themselves in many parts of Anatolia and set themselves up as semi-independent potentates.

1768–1774. First war of Catherine the Great against the Turks. This arose from the Russian policy in Poland, the rising of the Poles, and their subsequent flight into Turkey, whither they were pursued by Russian troops. The Turks, instigated by France, declared war. Catherine, though she did not want the war, threw herself into it energetically. Her generals overran Moldavia and Wallachia and sent agents to Greece to raise a revolt, which was officered by Russians.

1770, July 6. Battle of Chesmé, in which a Russian fleet, officered by British, having come from the Baltic to the Anatolian coast, defeated the Turkish fleet.

1771. The Russians conquered the Crimea. Frederick the Great, alarmed by the Russian successes, offered mediation and arranged the first partition of Poland (p. 512), but the war went on until the Russians were diverted by the great revolt of Pugachev (1773).

1774, July 21. TREATY OF KUCHUK KAINARJI (a village near Silistria on the Danube); Russia received Kinburn, Yenikale, and Kertch in the Crimea and obtained the right of free navigation for trading vessels in Turkish waters; the Tatars of the Crimea were recognized as "independent" on condition that they accept the sultan as caliph (first move of the sultan to exploit his claim to religious leadership of Islam); Moldavia and Wallachia were returned to Turkey on condition that they be leniently ruled (Russia reserved the right to intervene on their behalf); Russia was given the right to build a Greek church in Galata (foreign quarter of Constantinople); the Turks promised protection to the Christian churches and recognized the right of Russia to make representations in behalf of the church to be built in Galata. These provisions were to become the basis of much Russian interference later.

1781. Austro-Russian Treaty, following a famous meeting of Catherine and Joseph II (1780). Catherine's **Greek Scheme** to drive the Turks out of Europe and restore the Greek Empire, with her grandson Constantine (born 1779) as emperor. The Austrians were to receive the whole western half of the Balkans.

1783. The Russians incorporated the Crimea,

Ottoman Sultans (1640–1922)

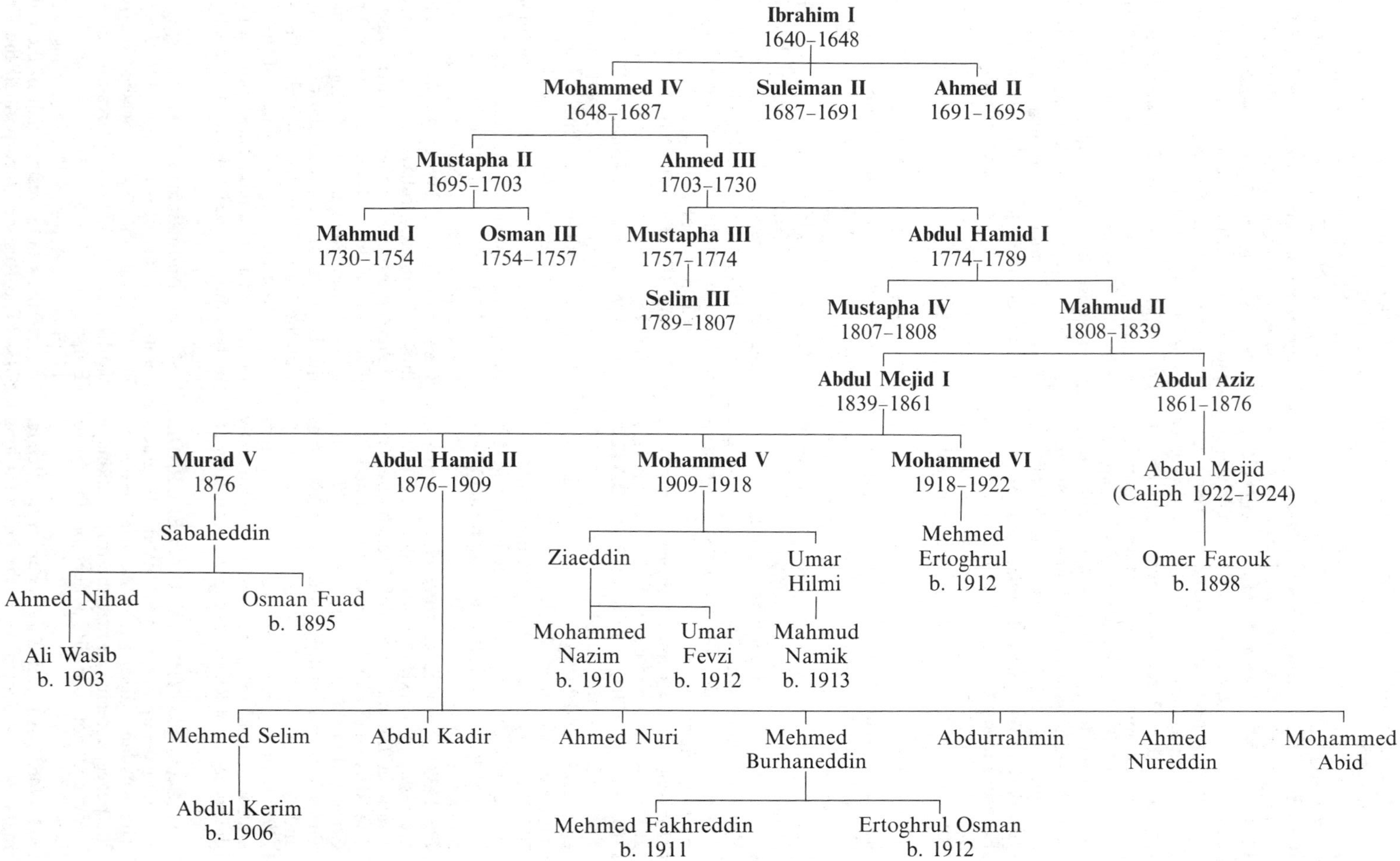

(From p. 451)

Ibrahim I
1640–1648

Mohammed IV
1648–1687

Suleiman II
1687–1691

Ahmed II
1691–1695

Mustapha II
1695–1703

Ahmed III
1703–1730

Mahmud I
1730–1754

Osman III
1754–1757

Mustapha III
1757–1774

Abdul Hamid I
1774–1789

Selim III
1789–1807

Mustapha IV
1807–1808

Mahmud II
1808–1839

Abdul Mejid I
1839–1861

Abdul Aziz
1861–1876

Abdul Mejid
(Caliph 1922–1924)

Omer Farouk
b. 1898

Murad V
1876

Abdul Hamid II
1876–1909

Mohammed V
1909–1918

Mohammed VI
1918–1922

Mehmed
Ertoghrul
b. 1912

Sabaheddin

Osman Fuad
b. 1895

Ahmed Nihad

Ali Wasib
b. 1903

Ziaeddin

Mohammed
Nazim
b. 1910

Umar
Fevzi
b. 1912

Umar
Hilmi

Mahmud
Namik
b. 1913

Mehmed Selim

Abdul Kerim
b. 1906

Abdul Kadir

Ahmed Nuri

Mehmed Fakhreddin
b. 1911

Mehmed
Burhaneddin

Ertoghrul Osman
b. 1912

Abdurrahmin

Ahmed
Nureddin

Mohammed
Abid

on the plea of restoring order. Britain and Austria persuaded the outraged Turks to accept the inevitable.

1787-1792. Second War of Catherine against the Turks, resulting from Turkish intrigues with the Crimean Tatars and from Russian designs on Georgia. Austria joined Russia (1788) under the terms of the alliance treaty of 1781.

1788. The campaign was indecisive, the Russians being unprepared and the Turks having difficulty in getting troop contingents from the derebeys.

1789-1807. SELIM III, an intelligent ruler, bent on victory and reform of the empire.

1789. The Austrians took Belgrade and the Russians, under Prince Gregory Potemkin and Count Alexander Suvorov, advanced to the Danube.

1791, Aug. 4. The Austrians, under Prussian pressure, made the separate **treaty of Sistova,** giving back Belgrade in return for a strip of northern Bosnia.

1792, Jan. 9. TREATY OF JASSY, between Turkey and Russia, which, worried by Prussian activity in Poland and deserted by Austria, decided to end the war: Russia obtained Oczakov and a boundary along the Dniester River, but returned Moldavia and Bessarabia.

(*Cont. pp. 635, 767*)

D. SCIENCE AND SOCIETY, 1700-1800

1. PHILOSOPHICAL, RELIGIOUS, AND SOCIAL THOUGHT

THE 18TH CENTURY is commonly referred to as the **Age of Enlightenment,** during which European thinkers, strongly influenced by the advances in scientific knowledge, reviewed the institutions of human society in the light of pure reason. As a result almost all accepted ideas were called in question. It was an age of destructive criticism, but also one of healthy skepticism and broad humanitarianism.

1697. Pierre Bayle (1647-1706) brought out his *Dictionnaire historique et critique,* which set the tone for 18th-century thought.

1710. Bishop George Berkeley (1685-1753), in his *Treatise concerning the Principles of Human Knowledge,* inaugurated the empiricist school of philosophy.

1721. Louis, Baron de Montesquieu (1689-1755), in his *Lettres persanes,* viewed European society through the eyes of two imaginary Persians.

1725. Giambattista Vico's (1668-1744) *Principi di una scienza nuova intorno alla commune natura delle nazione* combated the intellectualism prevalent in his day and attempted to set up a philosophy of history based on the notion of cyclical change.

1734. The *Lettres anglaises ou philosophiques* of **Voltaire** (Francois-Marie Arouet, 1694-1778) glorified the English constitution, with particular reference to representative government.

1739. David Hume (1711-1776), in his *Treatise on Human Nature* and later in his *Philosophical Essays* (1748), developed the empiricist philosophy and advanced a doctrine of extreme

skepticism with respect to the possibilities of human knowledge.

1748. Montesquieu's *L'Esprit des lois,* one of the greatest and most influential of all works on political theory.

1751. In his *Le siècle de Louis XIV,* followed by his *Essai sur les moeurs* (1756), **Voltaire** established the new genre of cultural history.

1751-1772. Publication of the *Encyclopédie, ou dictionnaire raisonné des sciences, des arts et des métiers,* in 28 volumes, followed by a six-volume supplement (1776-1777). Edited by **Denis Diderot** (1713-1784) and **Jean d'Alembert** (?1717-1783), it numbered among its contributors Rousseau, Voltaire, Buffon, Holbach, Turgot, Quesnay, Mirabeau, and Montesquieu. Building on the critical analysis of Bayle, the *Encyclopédie* stands as a monumental digest of 18th-century rationalism.

1755. Posthumous publication of **Richard Cantillon's** (d. 1734) *Essai sur la nature du commerce en général,* the earliest systematic analysis of wealth and economic process. Cantillon's book influenced the **Physiocratic School,** a group of economists who stressed agriculture as the source of wealth and attempted to establish the working of natural law in economic life. Pre-eminent in this group were **François Quesnay** (1694-1774), author of *Tableau économique* (1758); **Pierre Dupont de Nemours** (1739-1817: *La physiocratie,* 1768); **A. R. J. Turgot** (1727-1781: *Réflexions sur la formation . . . des richesses,* 1766).

1758. Emanuel Swedenborg (1688-1772), eminent Swedish naturalist and scientist, published *De nova Hierosolyma,* one of his many religious treatises and revelations which served as the foundation of the **Church of the New Jerusalem.**

1761. Johann P. Süssmilch (1707–1767) pioneered the study of statistics and demography in his fundamental work *Die göttliche Ordnung in den Veränderungen des menschlichen Geschlechts aus der Geburt, dem Tode, und der Fortpflanzung desselben erwiesen.*

1762. Jean-Jacques **Rousseau's** (1712–1778) *Le contrat social* and his *Émile, ou traité de l'éducation,* setting forth the political theory of democracy and the doctrine of rational elementary education.

1764. Cesare **Beccaria** (1738–1794) established the science of modern penology in his classic *Tratto dei delitti e delle pene.*

1765-1769. The *Commentaries on the Laws of England* by William **Blackstone** (1723–1780), a landmark in the history of the common law.

1776. *An Inquiry into the Nature and Causes of the Wealth of Nations* by Adam **Smith** (1723–1790), an epoch-making treatise on economics, formulating the doctrine of economic liberalism and inaugurating the classical school of political economy.

1776-1788. Edward **Gibbon's** (1737–1794) *The History of the Decline and Fall of the Roman Empire,* an immortal masterpiece of rationalist historiography, based on wide as well as intensive study of the sources.

1781. Immanuel **Kant** published his *Die Kritik der reinen Vernunft,* to be followed by his *Kritik der praktischen Vernunft* (1788) and his *Kritik der Urteilskraft* (1790). These basic works of the greatest of modern philosophers examined the limitations of the human understanding and established the rationalism of pure experience.

1784-1791. Johann Gottfried **Herder** (1744–1803) published his four-volume *Ideen zur Philosophie der Geschichte der Menschheit* in which, drawing on his earlier researches in primitive literatures, he argued that institutions reflect the soul of a people (*Volksgeist*), in constant process of development. The book provided the foundation for the doctrine of cultural nationalism.

1789. The *Introduction to the Principles of Morals and Legislation,* by Jeremy **Bentham** (1748–1832) set forth a comprehensive system of rational legislation and expounded the philosophy of utilitarianism.

1790. Edmund **Burke** (1729–1797), in his *Reflections on the Revolution in France,* criticized vigorously the political theories of liberalism and inaugurated modern traditionalist doctrine.

1791-1792. *The Rights of Man,* by Thomas **Paine** (1737–1809), an eloquent defense of the French Revolution, its aims and achievements.

1792. Mary **Wollstonecraft's** (1759–1797) *Vindication of the Rights of Women,* the basic text of the modern feminist movement.

1793. William **Godwin's** (1756–1836) *Enquiry concerning Political Justice,* a restatement of the political tenets of the Enlightenment, eventuating in a system of philosophical anarchism.

1794. Elaborating the Kantian philosophy, Johann Gottlieb **Fichte** (1762–1814) expounded a philosophy of transcendental idealism: *Grundlage der gesamten Wissenschaftslehre* (1794); *Grundlage des Naturrechts* (1796–1797); *System der Sittenlehre* (1798); *Ueber die Bestimmung des Menschen* (1800).

1795. Marie-Jean **Condorcet** (1743–1794) in his *Tableau historique des progrès de l'esprit humain* provided a classic exposition of the idea of human progress and of the ultimate perfectibility of mankind.

1797. Friedrich von **Schelling** (1775–1854), deriving from the teaching of Kant, developed a pantheistic philosophy of nature which was highly influential in the Romantic Age: *Ideen zu einer Philosophie der Natur* (1797); *Von der Weltseele* (1798); *System des transcendentalen Idealismus* (1800).

1798. First edition of Thomas **Malthus'** (1766–1834) *Essay on the Principle of Population,* the most influential of all treatises on demography. The second, greatly enlarged edition, appeared in 1803.

1799. Friedrich **Schleiermacher** (1768–1834), in his *Reden über die Religion,* initiated the attempt to reconcile religion with modern science and learning.   *(Cont. p. 591.)*

2. SCIENTIFIC THOUGHT

(From p. 457)

1700. Gottfried Wilhelm **Leibniz** (1646–1716) was instrumental in the foundation of the **Berlin Academy,** Germany's first stable scientific organization.

1701-1713. Jakob (Jacques) **Bernoulli** (1654–1705) worked on problems (1701) which later became the calculus of variations. His *Ars conjectandi,* posthumously published in 1713, on probability theory, permutations and combinations, and binomial distribution.

1704. Isaac Newton (1642–1727), reporting on the optical researches he had undertaken since the 1660's, published his *Opticks*. He treated experimentally of the reflection, refraction, diffraction, and spectra of light.

He investigated the dispersion and composition of white light, showing that it is not homogeneous, as was traditionally thought, but decomposable into simple colors. The *Opticks* concluded with a group of "Queries," which in later editions developed Newton's speculations and conjectures concerning heat, chemical affinity, pneumatics, physiology, atomism, the nature of gravitation and the aether, the relation of the world of nature to God, and the proper manner of scientific inquiry. These speculations determined much of the experimental science of the 18th century.

1705. Edmund Halley (1656–1742) noted the resemblance in the paths of the comets of 1531, 1607, and 1682, and conjectured that these were different appearances of the same comet, now called *Halley's Comet*. He correctly predicted the return of this comet in 1758.

1708. Hermann Boerhaave (1668–1738) systematized physiology in the mechanistic terms of chemistry. As teacher of theoretical medicine at Leyden he influenced a whole generation of physicians.

1713. Publication of the second edition of Newton's *Principia*, to which was added the famous *General Scholium* containing the phrase "Hypotheses non fingo" (I feign no hypotheses).

1715. Brook Taylor (1685–1731) published *Methodus incrementorum directa et inversa*, the first treatise on finite differences and the source of *Taylor's series*. The series took on great importance in the work of **Leonhard Euler** (1707–1783) and **Joseph-Louis Lagrange** (1736–1813).

1717. Gabriel D. Fahrenheit (1686–1736) proposed the *Fahrenheit System* and a mode of calibrating thermometers.

1718. Etienne F. Geoffroy (1672–1731) published the first table of *chemical affinities*, a chart designed to indicate the reactivity of individual chemicals toward each other.

1723. Georg E. Stahl (1660–1734) popularized the views of **Johann Becher** (1669). Stahl renamed *terra pinguis, phlogiston,* which he thought to be an inflammable principle given off into the air by combustible bodies in burning.

1725. Peter the Great founded the **Academy of Sciences** at St. Petersburg. The original resident membership of sixteen included thirteen Germans, two Swiss, and one Frenchman.

1725. John Flamsteed's (1646–1719) *Historia coelestis britannica,* a catalog of the positions of nearly 3,000 stars published posthumously. This replaced the catalog of **Tycho Brahe** as the standard reference source.

1727–1733. Stephen Hales (1677–1761) in *Vegetable Staticks* (1727) and *Haemastaticks* (1733) recorded a series of experiments in plant and animal physiology and demonstrated that biological phenomena, such as blood pressure, could be investigated on a quantitative basis. He also invented a pneumatic trough, an indispensible apparatus for collecting gases.

1728. James Bradley (1693–1762) explained an anomalous motion of the fixed stars by his discovery of the aberration of light.

1732. Boerhaave published *Elementa chemiae,* a standard chemistry textbook influential until the end of the 18th century.

1733. Abraham de Moivre (1667–1754) published the discovery of the normal curve of error.

1734–1742. Berkeley, in *The Analyst* (1734), attacked the calculus as based on unclear and fallacious premises. This attack stimulated **Colin Maclaurin** (1698–1746) to write *A Treatise on Fluxions* (1742) in which he tried to provide a rigorous foundation for the calculus on the basis of Greek geometry and first applied the calculus to dynamics.

1736. Leonhard Euler published *Mechanica sive motus analytice exposita,* generally considered to be the first systematic textbook of mechanics. During his life, Euler made fundamental contributions in many areas of analytical mechanics, e.g., the theory of the motion of rigid bodies, hydrodynamics, the application of variational principles in mechanics, and celestial mechanics.

1738. Pierre de Maupertuis (1698–1759) published *Sur la figure de la terre,* a report of a scientific expedition to Lapland which confirmed Newton's view that the earth is a spheroid flattened near the poles with a bulge near the equator.

1738. Daniel Bernoulli (1700–1782), in *Hydrodynamica,* presented investigations of the forces exerted by fluids, and presented an early version of the **kinetic theory of gases.**

1743. Jean d'Alembert (1717–1783) published *Traité de dynamique,* which formulated *d'Alembert's principle,* and successfully applied it to the solution of many difficult problems in mechanics.

1743. Alexis Clairaut (1713–1765) presented his *Théorie de la figure de la terre,* a mathematical investigation on hydrostatic principles of the shape of the earth.

1743–1744. Benjamin Franklin (1706–1790) was instrumental in the establishment of the **American Philosophical Society** at Philadelphia, America's first scientific society, devoted to "the promotion of useful knowledge."

1744. César Cassini (1714-1784) directed the triangulation of France, the first national survey, which was completed during the French Revolution.

1748.   James Bradley reported his discovery, made earlier, of the **mutation of the earth's axis.**

1748. Euler published *Introductio in analysin infinitorum,* systematizing the calculus and emphasizing the study of functions, classifying differential equations, and treating trigonometric functions and equations of curves without reference to diagrams. He gave an elegant and highly influential exposition of the Leibnizian calculus, together with many new results of his own, in his *Institutiones calculi differentialis* (1755) and *Institutiones calculi integralis* (1768-1770).

1748. John Tuberville Needham (1713-1781), in *Observations upon the Generation, Composition, and Decomposition of Animal and Vegetable Substances,* reported that boiled, sealed flasks of broth teemed with "little animals" when opened. His rival **Lazzaro Spallanzani** (1729-1799) devised controlled experiments to test such factors as the amount of heating necessary to kill micro-organisms.

1749.   George Leclerc, Comte de Buffon (1707-1788), in the fifty-four volumes of his celebrated treatise *Histoire naturelle,* posed a majority of the problems dominating evolutionary biology for the next 150 years: geographical distribution, progressive development, isolation, transmutation, correlation, and variation.

1750.   Thomas Wright (1711-1786) suggested that the appearance of the Milky Way from the earth is due to the distribution of the visible stars in a disc.

1751.   Robert Whytt (1714-1764) explicitly distinguished voluntary from involuntary motions, recognized that only a segment of the spinal cord is necessary for reflex action, and established the **study of reflexes** as a distinct branch of physiology.

1751-1754. Franklin published *Experiments and Observations on Electricity,* in which he explained his theory that electricity is a single fluid and used it to account for the properties of the Leyden jar and other known electrical phenomena. He deduced the principle of the **conservation of electric charge** from his theory, and established that lightning is identical with electricity produced by friction.

1752.   Jean Guittard (1715-1786) noted the existence of extinct volcanoes in the Auvergne region, thereby beginning an extended controversy over the origin of certain kinds of rocks.

1755.   Mikhail Lomonosov (1711-1765) played a leading role in the founding of **Moscow University.** Known for his work in chemistry, electricity, mechanics, and history, his major contribution was the establishment of the scientific tradition in Russia.

1756-1762.   Joseph Black (1728-1799), in *Experiments upon Magnesia Alba* (1756), announced the isolation of a new gas, "fixed air" (carbon dioxide). In researches conducted between 1759 and 1762, but published posthumously (1803) in his *Lectures on the Elements of Chemistry,* he distinguished between temperature and quantity of heat, and introduced the terms and concepts *latent heat, heat of fusion, thermal capacity,* and *caloric.*

1756.   Johann Lehmann (d. 1767) contributed to knowledge of geological succession by classifying orders of strata. Similar work was carried on by **Giovanni Arduino** (1713-1795), who gave the names *primitive, secondary,* and *tertiary* to lithologically distinct sequences of strata; and earlier by **John Strachey** (1671-1743), whose "Observations on the Strata in the Somersetshire Coal Fields" (1719) established stratigraphical divisions and offered an early attempt at a structure section.

1758.   Carl Linnaeus (1707-1778) in the tenth edition of his *Systema naturae* catalogued all known flora and fauna, (including man), and laid the basis for modern taxonomy by his consistent use of a **binomial nomenclature.**

1759-1766.   Albrecht von Haller (1708-1777) delineated the phenomena of "irritability" and "sensibility" in animal tissues and searched for the problems and laws peculiar to physiology.

1760-1761.   Joseph-Louis Lagrange presented a complete *calculus of variations,* incorporating both old and new results in an elegant and systematic treatment.

1761.   Giovanni Morgagni (1682-1771) presented in *De sedibus et causis morborum* a correlation of clinical symptoms and anatomic lesions challenging the notion of disease as an imbalance of humors.

1761-1769.   Transits of Venus across the face of the sun were observed by astronomical expeditions sent out by France, Britain, Germany, Russia, and the American colonies: an early example of international scientific cooperation.

1765-1780.   The creation of provincial English scientific societies—Lunar Society of Birmingham; Manchester Literary and Philosophical Society—marked the decline of the **Royal Society of London** and a new alliance between science and industry.

1768-1779.   Captain James Cook (1728-1779), an English naval officer, led three expeditions opening the Pacific to scientific explorers and collectors (p. 621).

1770–1771. Lagrange published *Réflexions sur la résolution algébrique des équations,* considering the question of why the methods which solve equations of degrees less than 5 do not work for the quintic. He considered the rational functions of the roots and their behavior on permutation of the roots, leading **Evariste Galois** (1811–1832) and **Niels Henrik Abel** (1802–1829) to their results on solvability.

1771. Charles Messier (1730–1817) published the first installment of a star catalog which eventually recorded 103 nebulae and clusters.

1771–1794. John Hunter (1728–1793) raised surgery from a technical trade to the ranks of a science by connecting morphology with physiology and emphasizing the natural healing powers of the body.

1773–1784. Pierre Laplace (1749–1827) and **Lagrange** in a long series of papers finally solved the "long-term inequality" of Jupiter and Saturn, thus giving important evidence for the stability of the solar system.

1774–1817. Abraham Werner (1749/50–1817) propagated his view that features of the earth's crust are of aqueous origin (neptunism). Werner's methodical systematization of rocks and their formations helped found mineralogy as a science.

1774. Nicholas Desmarest (1725–1815) established the igneous origin of basalt in a study of the Auvergne volcanoes, thereby challenging neptunism.

1774–1786. Joseph Priestley (1733–1804) in his *Experiments and Observations on Different Kinds of Air* reported his studies on gases and announced the discovery of a number of water soluble gases, including ammonia, sulfur dioxide, and hydrogen chloride. In 1774 Priestley isolated **oxygen,** which he called "dephlogisticated air," in experiments with red calx of mercury.

1777. Carl Scheele (1742–1786) published his *Chemische Abhandlung von der Luft und dem Feuer.* He reported on his production of hydrogen in 1770 ("inflammable air"), his isolation of oxygen in 1773 ("fire air"), and his discoveries of many new and important substances, both organic and inorganic.

1778. Buffon argued in *Epoques de la nature* that the earth is far older than the 6000 years allowed by contemporary theological doctrine.

1779. Jan Ingenhousz (1730–1799) showed that plants make the atmosphere fit for breathing by producing oxygen during the day, that green leaves and stalks are the functional parts in this process, and that plants carry out respiration concomitantly with photosynthesis.

1780–1781. Claude Berthollet (1748–1822) and **Antoine Lavoisier** (1743–1794), using the new chemical techniques of pneumatic and combustion analysis, isolated carbon, oxygen, and hydrogen as the elements of organic substances. Their work opened a new era in elementary organic analysis and physiological chemistry.

1781. William Herschel (1738–1822) discovered by telescopic observation the planet **Uranus,** the first planet to be discovered in recorded history.

1783. John Goodricke (1764–1786) observed regular variations in the brightness of the star Algol and demonstrated that Algol was an eclipsing binary.

1784. René-Just Haüy (1743–1821/22) gave an exposition of the laws of crystal form in *Essai d'une théorie sur la structure des cristaux.*

1784. Henry Cavendish (1731–1810) published *Experiments on Air,* in which he showed from experimental results obtained in 1781 that the explosion of a mixture of two volumes of "inflammable air" (hydrogen) with one volume of "dephlogisticated air" (oxygen) produced water.

1784. Lavoisier and **Laplace** measured the amount of oxygen consumed and of carbon dioxide and heat produced in respiration and combustion.

1785–1789. Charles Augustin de Coulomb (1736–1806) published *Mémoires sur l'électricité et le magnétisme,* in which, by using a torsion balance, he measured the force of electric and magnetic attraction and repulsion and found it inversely proportional to the square of the distance between point charges or magnetic poles.

1788. Lagrange published *Méchanique analitique,* a strictly analytical treatment of mechanics. Here statics is founded on the principle of virtual velocities and dynamics on d'Alembert's principle.

1788. Tobern Bergman (1735–1784) published his *Traité des affinités chymiques, ou attractions electives,* which included lengthy affinity tables summarizing the results of extensive investigations of displacement reactions.

1789. Lavoisier published his *Traité élementaire de chimie* rejecting the phlogiston theory. He championed his new **theory of combustion** which maintained that oxygen supports combustion and respiration, and combines with metals to form a calx. He also presented a new and empirically determined list of chemical elements. Two years earlier, in collaboration with **Guyton de Morveau** (1737–1816), **Claude-Louis Berthollet** (1748–1822), and **Antoine Fourcroy** (1757–1809), he published a treatise outlining a new method of chemical nomenclature, essentially the one used today.

1790-1801. The revolutionary government of France decreed the adoption of a **decimal system** of weights, measures, and coinage (the **metric system**).

1791. *The Ordnance Survey of Great Britain* was instituted; during the next several decades the entire island was mapped.

1791. Luigi Galvani (1737-1798) in a series of experiments reported in *De viribus electricitatis in motu musculari animalium,* postulated the existence of "animal electricity."

1793. The **Académie Royale des Sciences** was first suppressed by the revolutionary government and then reopened as a section of the **Institut de France.** Motivated by a new concern for applied science, the government established the **École Polytechnique** (1794), providing training and posts for eminent French scientists.

1795. James Hutton (1726-1797) published his *Theory of the Earth,* setting forth the uniformitarian principle that geological change is produced by continuous natural forces.

1797. Lagrange published his *Théorie des fonctions analytiques,* studying real valued functions by means of their Taylor series expansions, and giving the first form for the remainder term as an estimate of error in the Taylor series.

1798. Edward Jenner (1749-1823) described his success at using the scrapings from cowpox as a "vaccination" against smallpox.

1798. Benjamin Thompson (Count Rumford) (1753-1814), in "Inquiry Concerning the Heat which is Caused by Friction," explained, on the basis of experiments in the boring of a cannon's barrel, that the caloric or fluid substance theory of heat was untenable, and suggested that heat of a body was identical with the motions of a body's particles.

1799. Carl Friedrich Gauss (1777-1855) gave the first rigorous proof of the fundamental theorem of algebra, that an nth degree algebraic equation with real coefficients has n roots.

1799. Joseph Louis Proust (1754-1826) announced the **law of definite proportions,** according to which the same chemical compound, however it is prepared, always contains the same elements combined in the same proportions by weight.

1800. Alessandro Volta (1745-1827), in his essay "On the Electricity Excited by the mere Contact of Conducting Substances of Different Kinds," disagreeing with **Luigi Galvani** (1791), showed that the electrically produced effects in muscular contraction arise not from innate animal electricity, but from the moist contact of different metals. This observation led him to construct the **voltaic pile,** the forerunner of the modern battery and the first source of a continuous electric current.

(*Cont. p. 594.*)

3. TECHNOLOGICAL ACHIEVEMENTS

(*From p. 458*)

Technical achievements of this century in agriculture, mining, metallurgy, and machinery (prime movers, textiles, and machine tools) laid the groundwork for the Industrial Revolution, commencing about the mid-century, which was markedly to change the nature of society and civilization. Industrialization, commencing first in England and first in the textile industry, was to urbanize society, transform the international power structure, and put its mark upon every aspect of modern life.

c. 1700. Christopher Polhem (1661-1751), the "Father of Swedish Technology," developed an improved **rolling mill** and utilized water power for primitive mass production.

1709-1717. Abraham Darby (1677-1717) produced iron from a **coke-fired blast furnace** at Coalbrookdale; despite shortage of charcoal, it took 50 years and improvements made in the method by his son Abraham Darby II before coke was regularly used for this purpose.

1712. Low pressure **steam pump** ("atmospheric engine") of **Thomas Newcomen** (1663-1729) used to pump water from mines. Newcomen utilized some features of **Denis Papin's** (1647-1714) atmospheric engine of 1695, but his invention was quite independent of **Thomas Savery's** (?1650-1715) first useful "fire-engine" of 1698. **John Smeaton** (1724-1792) made many empirical improvements of the Newcomen engine; he also designed bridges, harbors, canals, and the Eddystone Lighthouse (1759), and lowered the price of iron by his water-powered bellows (1761).

1716. Corps des Ponts et Chaussées established in France for civil engineering works; clear distinction made between civil engineer and architect. First improvements in **road-making** since Roman times with work of **P. M. J. Trésaguet** (1716-1794) in France, and **John L. McAdam** (1756-1836) ("metalled" or "macadamized" roads) and **Thomas Telford** (1757-1834) in England. Trésaguet and Telford emphasized a road foundation of large stones, with smaller stones for top layer; McAdam stressed a roadtop impervious to water.

1722. First technical treatise on iron, *L'Art de convertir le fer forgé en acier et l'art d'adoucir le fer fondu*, by **René A. F. de Réaumur** (1683–1757). **Metallurgical techniques** developed during this century included **Benjamin Huntsman's** (1704–1776) crucible process for casting steel (1751), utilized for cutlery and instruments but not commercially successful until 1770; **Henry Cort's** (1740–1800) puddling process to produce wrought (bar) iron from cast iron in a reverberatory furnace (1784); and Cort's perfected rolling mill with grooved rollers (1784).

1732. Publication of **Jethro Tull's** (1674–1741) *New Horse Hoeing Husbandry* in which he described his innovations in **scientific cultivation**: seed drill (1701) to plant seed in rows rather than the older, casual method of tossing seeds; the horse-hoe (introduced by Tull from France in 1714); and the technique of soil pulverization. **Robert Bakewell** (1725–1795) introduced selective breeding of livestock, and **Charles Townshend** (1674–1738) introduced useful new crops, turnips and clover, for winter fodder. The work of these pioneers in scientific cultivation, publicized by **Arthur Young** (1741–1820), helped to produce the **Agricultural Revolution,** which effected radical transformations in agricultural crops and techniques and a large increase in the production of foodstuffs and animal materials (wool, hides).

1733. **John Kay** (d. 1764?) patented the **flying shuttle,** the first of a series of inventions which were to transform the manufacture of textiles, substitute the factory system for the older method of domestic production, introduce power-driven machinery into manufacuring processes, and mark the first steps in the Industrial Revolution. Other landmarks in the industrialization of textile production were the **spinning jenny** invented (1764) by **James Hargreaves** (d. 1778); the spinning machine **(waterframe)** developed (1769) by **Richard Arkwright** (1732–1792), perhaps based on earlier machines for roller spinning (especially that devised by Lewis Paul in 1733 with some assistance from John Wyatt), and which made Arkwright Lancashire's largest cotton-manufacturer and one of England's richest men; the **spinning "mule"** (1784) of **Samuel Crompton** (1753–1827); the power-loom (1785) of **Edmund Cartwright** (1743–1823), and the cotton gin (1793) of **Eli Whitney** (1765–1825).

1753. Publication by **Johann Heinrich Pott** of the *Lithogeoginoise pyrotechnique* on the **ceramic arts,** which developed during this period as Europeans sought to reproduce the much admired Chinese porcelain introduced to Europe in the later 17th century. First to produce quality china were the **Meissen** works in Saxony (Dresden China), followed by the French state manufactory at **Sèvres** (1768). The English developed bone-china (utilizing bone-ash as an ingredient). **Josiah Wedgwood** (1730–1795) was appointed royal potter (1762) and established his **Etruria** works in 1769. By the 1750's The Potteries, a series of towns in Staffordshire, had become the center of world production of inexpensive earthenware.

1754. Society for the Encouragement of Arts, Manufactures and Commerce (later, **The Royal Society of Arts**) established, inspiring the organization of similar societies in France, Netherlands, and Russia. The first exhibition of the industrial arts was held in Paris (1763). The French *Encyclopédie* (1751–1772) provided a comprehensive treatise, with illustrations, of contemporary technology.

1770. Completion of the English **Grand Trunk Canal** linking the Trent and the Mersey Rivers, giving the industrial towns of the Midlands a direct water route for exports and initiating a **canal-building** fever in England, which reached America and France in the early 19th century. Principal English canal engineers were **James Brindley** (1716–1772), **John Rennie** (1761–1821), and **Thomas Telford** (1757–1834).

1774. **John Wilkinson** (1728–1808) invented the **boring-mill.** Originally designed to bore cannon, this machine was to find its most important use in the boring of cylinders for

1776. The **steam engine** of **James Watt** (1736–1819). Based upon the older Newcomen engine, the first working model (1768, patented 1769) contained the separate steam condenser. Put into practical use in 1776, Watt's engine was not a commercial success until 1785, when Watt went into partnership with the entrepreneur **Matthew Boulton** (1728–1809) and only after further improvements had been made: the epicyclic (sun-and-planet) gear (1781) producing rotary motion by the reciprocal piston action, and the double-acting expansive engine (1782). (The "steam engine," actually a two-cylinder atmospheric pressure engine, of the Russian **Polzunov** [1729–1766] operated only for a short time [1767] and had no influence on subsequent engine development.)

1783. **First balloon ascent** by **Montgolfier brothers** in France, using a paper balloon lifted by hot air. (Balloons a Chinese invention.) Later ascents (1784) by the **Roberts brothers** utilized hydrogen for lifting power. First military use for observation at battle of Fleurus (1794).

1785. Introduction of **chemical bleaching** with chlorine (*eau de Javel*) by the French chemist **C. L. Berthollet** (1748–1822).

1789. The **Leblanc process** for obtaining soda

from common salt invented by **Nicolas Leblanc** (1742–1806) in France, but first exploited in England.

1793. Claude Chappe (1763–1805) developed the **semaphore** (visual telegraph); rapid spread after success of first line from Paris-Lille.

1794. Establishment of **École Polytechnique**, premier institution of higher technological education in France; emphasis upon mathematics and applied science.

1797. Henry Maudslay (1771–1831) designed a **screw-cutting lathe,** made entirely of metal and utilizing a slide-rest. This tool was the culmination of much previous precision tool development, including the drill and lathe

(1768–1780) of **Jacques de Vaucanson** (1709–1782), the screw-cutting lathe (1770) of **Jesse Ramsden** (1735–1800); the marine chronometer (1759) of **John Harrison** (1693–1776); the spring-winding machine of **Joseph Bramah** (1748–1814), who also invented the modern water closet (1778) and a hydraulic press (1796).

1798. P. L. Guinand (1748–1824), a Swiss, patented a stirring process for making optical glass which became the foundation of the great German **optical industry** of the 19th century.

1798. Aloys Senefelder (1771–1834) of Prague invented **lithography.**   (*Cont. p. 603.*)

E. LATIN AMERICA, 1500–1803

1. NATURE OF THE CONQUEST

IN THE BROADER SENSE the conquest and colonization of Spanish America progressed logically outward from the earliest colony in Santo Domingo until by 1600 the territory from New Mexico and Florida on the north to Chile and the Río de la Plata on the south was, with the exception of Brazil, effectively under the rule of the crown of Castile.

The motives which inspired the Castilian sovereigns to create a vast empire in the Americas were the desire to achieve more extensive realms, propagate Christianity, and obtain increased revenues. The early *conquistadores* were impelled by several motives which varied in intensity with regard to individuals, time, and place: desire to gain wealth and position, desire to add to the glory of the Castilian crown, zeal to propagate Christianity, and love of adventure. The most important of the early conquests were achieved at no direct cost to the crown. Individual leaders by their own initiative, in the name of the sovereign or by virtue of royal patents, conquered territory at their own expense, hoping to receive or to be assigned authority and revenues in the lands subjugated. In this manner Cortés conquered Mexico, Alvarado Guatemala, Pizarro Peru, Jiménez de Quesada New Granada, and Montejo Yucatan. The crown of Castile soon established direct and absolute control and evolved complex machinery of government to rule its vast colonial empire. The Church, over which the crown exercised patronage, achieved complete organization and exercised vast influence. The military triumphs of the Spaniards over incredible numerical odds were the triumph of indomitable representatives of a more highly developed society over those of a lesser. The conquest was accompanied by great cruelty, but it was no greater than that of contemporary conquest elsewhere. Ruthless exploitation of the natives followed colonization, but such was the common lot of subject peoples during the period. The intent of the Castilian crown toward the Indian masses, if not the actual practice, was beneficent. While the production of gold and silver was the chief source of crown revenues in the Indies and became the basis of much private wealth, agriculture, grazing, and commerce were soon highly developed and local industries of various types came into existence. Certain colonies like Chile, Yucatan, and the Río de la Plata were almost exclusively agricultural and pastoral. A relatively large measure of intellectual activity came into being in the larger cities and within the Church. The existence of a large Indian population, many groups of which possessed high cultures of long standing and the impact of European culture and Christianity on the New World civilizations led to fundamentally important social, cultural, and racial developments.

2. THE WEST INDIES AND THE ISTHMUS, 1501-1531

Santo Domingo became the first seat of Spanish government in the Indies. Immigration to Española, although not heavy, increased and mining and agriculture were developed.

1501. **Negro slavery** was introduced. The Indian population rapidly diminished as a result of warfare, enslavement, and disease.

1508-1511. **Puerto Rico** was conquered, San Juan being founded, and **Jamaica** was settled.

1511-1515. **Diego Velázquez,** as lieutenant of the viceroy, Diego Columbus, conquered Cuba and founded Santiago and San Cristóbal de la Habana.

1509-1513. Under royal patents **Alonso de Ojeda** founded a colony on the coast of South America east of the Isthmus of Panama and **Diego de Nicuesa** founded Nombre de Dios on the Isthmus. The settlement founded by Ojeda was transferred to the Isthmus at the suggestion of Vasco Nuñez de Balboa (1474–1519). There the colonists united with those of Nicuesa.

1513. **Balboa** became governor of the colony and as such he discovered the South Sea (Pacific Ocean) and took possession for the crown of Castile.

1513-1514. A jurisdiction independent of Española, **Castilla del Oro** (Darien); was created in the region of the Isthmus and **Pedro Arias de Ávila** (1442-1531) was appointed royal governor, bringing some 1500 colonists from Spain.

1514-1519. Ávila dispatched expeditions by land and sea to adjacent areas, including the Gulf of Nicoya, Zenú, and the Gulf of San Miguel, founded **Panama** as the seat of government, refounded Nombre de Dios, and established a route across the Isthmus. Balboa, as *adelantado* of the South Sea and subordinate to Ávila, continued explorations on the Pacific coast, but as a result of quarrels with the governor, was executed by him (1519).

1522-1523. Under authority independent of Ávila, **Gil González Dávila** and Alonso Niño led a combined land and sea expedition westward from the Isthmus. Dávila conquered the area about the Gulf of Nicoya and Lake Nicaragua and Niño sailed to Fonseca Bay. Ávila then dispatched **Francisco Hernández de Córdoba** to conquer Nicaragua for himself.

1523-1531. Dávila, returning to Española, secured license to continue exploration and conquest, and returned to Central America by way of Honduras. Hernández de Córdoba, after establishing a short-lived colony on the Gulf of Nicoya, entered Nicaragua and founded León and Granada. Forces sent northward by him were defeated by Dávila, who in turn was overcome by Cristóbal de Olid. Hernández de Córdoba rebelled against Ávila and was executed, after which Ávila became governor of Nicaragua. In this capacity he dispatched an expedition along the San Juan River to the sea, exploration which was continued after his death (1531). (*Cont. p. 536.*)

3. VENEZUELA AND NEW GRANADA, 1521-1549

Early efforts to colonize the eastern portion of the north coast of South America failed.

1521. An attempt made by **Bartolomé de Las Casas** (1474-1566) to found a colony at Cumaná in accord with his theories of peaceful reduction failed.

1530. **Antonio de Sedeño** achieved but little success in an effort to occupy Trinidad Island.

1531-1535. The efforts of **Diego de Ordaz** to explore the region of the Orinoco led to no result. Ordaz lost his life. In the western areas permanent colonization was established at an early date.

1527. **Juan de Ampués,** commissioned by the *audiencia* of Santo Domingo, founded Santa Ana de Coro. This territory was granted by the Emperor Charles V to the **Welsers,** the great Augsburg banking firm to which he was heavily indebted.

1529. The Welsers at once sent out colonists and established an administration. Exploration was carried on through the valley of the Orinoco and into the Andes. The government of the Welsers was marked by ruthless enslavement and maltreatment of the Indians. On that account and because of protests in Spain against grant of lands in the New World to foreigners, their concession was ultimately revoked (1546-1556). The conquest and colonization of Venezuela was then undertaken by the Spaniards. Caracas was founded by Diego de Losada in 1567.

1525. **Rodrigo de Bastidas** founded Santa Marta, the first permanent settlement in what was to become New Granada. **Cartagena** was founded in 1533 by Pedro de Heredia, acting directly under royal authority.

1536-1538. **Gonzalo Jiménez de Quesada**

Colonial LATIN AMERICA

TEXAS

Zacatecas
Guadalajara
Tlaxcala
Vera Cruz
Mexico
Oaxaca
Tehuantepec
Havana
Campeche
YUCATAN
Santiago
CUBA
ESPAÑOLA
PUERTO RICO
GUATEMALA
Guatemala
HONDURAS
COSTA RICA
Porto Bello
Nombre de Dios
Cartagena
Sta Marta
Caracas 1567
Cumaná
Trinidad
Darien
VENEZUELA
GUIANAS
Panama 1519
Cali
Bogotá 1558
Popayán
Orinoco R.

Viceroyalty of NEW SPAIN

Equator

Quito 1587
Guayaquil
Túmbez
Cajamarca

Viceroyalty of NEW GRANADA

Amazon River
Belém (Para)
Saō Luiz de Maranhão
Natal
Paraiba
Recife (Pernambuco) 1536

Lima 1535
Cuzco
L. Titicaca
Potosí
Charcas 1558

BRAZIL

São Francisco

Salvador 1549 (Baia)
MINAS GERAIS
Porto Seguro, 1537

Viceroyalty of PERU

LA PLATA

Paraná R.
São Paulo
Asunción
Córdoba
Valparaiso
Santiago
Mendoza
BANDA ORIENTAL
Rio Grande do Sul, 1736
Montevideo 1723
Buenos Aires 1580
Rio de la Plata

Rio de Janeiro
Santos 1532

Viceroyalty of LA PLATA

Cg. of Chile

Pacific Ocean

Atlantic Ocean

Str. of Magellan

Cape Horn

(1495–1576), under commission from the governor of Santa Marta, moved up the Magdalena River, reached the plateau of Bogotá, reduced the Chibchas (p. 387), and founded **Santa Fé de Bogotá.**

1539. Nikolaus Federmann, an agent of the Welsers, arrived at Bogotá after three years of wandering in the lowlands. Very soon afterward there appeared from the west coast **Sebastian de Belalcázar,** one of Pizarro's lieutenants. A dispute arose regarding jurisdiction. Finally the three captains went to Spain to lay the controversy before the crown. Federmann died. Belalcázar was confirmed in the governorship of Popayán, but Quesada's claims were rejected in favor of those of the son of the deceased governor of Santa Marta.

1549. The *audiencia* of **New Granada** was created. It included Santa Marta, Cartagena, Popayán, and Santa Fé (Bogotá), the latter town being the seat of government over this large area. (*Cont. p. 536.*)

4. PERU AND THE WEST COAST, 1522–1581

1522. Continuing exploration southward from Panama, **Pascual de Andagoya** (c. 1495–1548) reached a point south of the Gulf of San Miguel and advanced into **Biru (Peru),** where he learned of the rich and powerful **Inca Empire** (p. 387). Andagoya planned the conquest of the lands reported, but was forced to relinquish the project by ill health.

1524–1528. Francisco Pizarro (1470–1541), under authority of Ávila, in association with Diego de Almagro (1475–1538) and Hernando de Luque, a priest, determined upon the conquest of Peru. An initial expedition reached the San Juan River and a second the Gulf of Guayaquil and Túmbez, where evidence of the high civilization and great wealth of the Inca was encountered.

1528–1529. Pizarro went to Spain and concluded a capitulation with the crown by which he was granted the right of discovery and conquest in Peru for a distance of 200 leagues south of the Gulf of Guayaquil with the offices of *adelantado,* governor, and captain general. Almagro was assigned command of the fortress of Túmbez, and Luque was named bishop of Túmbez.

1531. Returning to Panama, accompanied by his brothers, Gonzalo (c. 1505–1548) and Hernando, and a small group of recruits, Pizarro organized an expedition of 180 men, with 27 horses and two pieces of artillery, and sailed for the conquest. Pizarro consolidated his position at Túmbez and founded San Miguel. After having been joined by further recruits, Pizarro moved into the interior with 62 horse and 102 foot, invited by the Inca **Atahualpa,** and reached Cajamarca on the central plateau, near which the Indian monarch was encamped with a large army.

1532, Nov. 16. When Atahualpa visited the Spanish camp, Pizarro seized him. This bold stroke produced great moral effect among the Inca and paralyzed the machinery of government. While a prisoner, Atahualpa caused his rival, his half-brother Huascar, to be murdered.

1533. The Inca paid an enormous ransom in gold and silver, but for political reasons was executed by the Spaniards. Having been joined by Almagro, Pizarro occupied **Cuzco,** the Inca capital, and set up **Manco,** brother of Huascar, as Inca.

1535. Pizarro, having left Cuzco, founded **Lima,** which became the capital of the later viceroyalty of Peru. In Pizarro's absence the natives revolted under Manco and conducted a lengthy but unsuccessful **siege of Cuzco.** This was the only serious attempt of the Incas to expel the Spaniards (1535–1536).

In the following years the area of Spanish dominion was greatly extended. In the south the region about Lake Titicaca was reduced and Chuquisaca founded (1536–1539). The rich silver mines of **Potosí** were opened in 1545. To the north the region of Quito, where lieutenants of Atahualpa had established control after his seizure, was reduced in 1534 by Pizarro's subordinate, Belalcázar (1495–1550). **Pedro de Alvarado,** governor of Guatemala, having heard of rich lands in Peru, led an expedition of some 500 men from Central America and sought to secure control of Quito in 1534–1535. Alvarado was ultimately induced to relinquish his claims in return for monetary compensation. Belalcázar founded Cali and Popayán (1535–1536) and advanced to the Bogotá plateau, where in 1539 he encountered Quesada. In the same year Gonzalo Pizarro, governor of Quito, led an expedition across the Andes and reached the upper Amazon. One of his lieutenants, **Francisco de Orellana,** seeking to gain territory for himself, continued down the Amazon and reached the sea (1541). He went to Spain and secured authority to conquer the Amazonian area, but died on the return to the New World. His followers accomplished nothing.

1537. After a dispute with Pizarro regarding jurisdiction over the city of Cuzco, Almagro occupied the city, thus beginning a series of civil wars between the Spaniards. Almagro was defeated and executed (1538).

1541. Dissension continued. Partisans of Almagro assassinated Pizarro and set up Almagro's son as governor, but the younger Almagro was, in turn, overthrown by the royal governor Vaca de Castro (1542).

Meanwhile the Spaniards had begun **expansion into Chile.**

1535-1537. Almagro the elder had advanced as far as the Maule River.

1540-1553. **Pedro de Valdivia** (c. 1498-1553) penetrated the fertile valley and founded **Santiago** (1541). A series of wars ensued with the **Araucanian Indians,** most warlike of the tribes.

Valdivia having lost his life in the wars (1553), the conquest was continued by **García Hurtado de Mendoza** (1557-1561) whose forces advanced to the Straits of Magellan. The conquest was extended into Cuyo and the town of Mendoza founded.

With the creation of the viceroyalty and *audiencia* of Peru (1542), **Blasco Núñez Vela,** the first viceroy, proclaimed the **New Laws,** with provision for eventual abolition of *encomiendas* (1544). This aroused much opposition, culminating in open revolt under the leadership of **Gonzalo Pizarro.** Vela was deposed and Pizarro assumed the position of governor (1544). The viceroy sought to quell the revolt, but was defeated and killed (1546).

1546-1550. The emperor, fearing a separatist movement, appointed **Pedro de la Gasca,** a churchman with high qualities of statesmanship, his representative and endowed him with virtually unlimited powers. Gasca, adopting a conciliatory policy and promising remedy of the causes of complaint, won over many of the opposing party, defeated Pizarro in the **battle of Xaquixaguana** (1548), and restored direct royal authority. Gonzalo Pizarro was executed.

1550-1551. **Antonio de Mendoza** was named viceroy of Peru, but died after a short period in office. The *audiencia* exercised interim authority, crushing a revolt of yet dissatisfied elements led by Francisco Girón, until the arrival of Andrés Hurtado de Mendoza (1557).

1569-1581. **Francisco Alvarez de Toledo,** a proved soldier and diplomat, and one of the greatest of the magistrates of the colonial period, as viceroy of Peru systematized the administration. Codes were promulgated, mining was stimulated and regulated, *corregimientos* on the Castilian model were erected for both Spanish and Indian districts, the tribute of the natives was regularized, the *mita,* or system of enforced labor of the Indians in the mines, on the *haciendas,* and for public works was established, the natives were concentrated in towns to facilitate administration and indoctrination, and public works were constructed. **Francis Drake** raided the coast of Peru during the incumbency of Toledo.

(*Cont. p. 536.*)

5. THE RÍO DE LA PLATA, 1526-1580

1526-1532. **Sebastian Cabot,** in the service of a group of merchants of Seville, set out with an expedition to reach the Moluccas, but diverted it to the **Río de la Plata** in search for a passage to the east. The expedition passed up the Paraná and Paraguay Rivers and founded a short-lived settlement on the lower Paraná.

1535. Permanent colonization of the La Plata was undertaken by the expedition of **Pedro de Mendoza,** to whom the conquest of the area was assigned.

1536. Mendoza founded **Buenos Aires** (Santa María de Buenos Aires) on the estuary of the La Plata. Expeditions were sent to explore the Paraná and Paraguay and search for a route to Peru. A fort was established at Asunción (1537) to which the colony at Buenos Aires was soon transferred. Mendoza died (1537) on a voyage to Spain, and Domingo Martínez de Irala was elected governor.

1542-1544. **Alvar Núñez Cabeza de Vaca,** named by the crown to replace Mendoza, reached Asunción with more colonists, having traveled overland from southern Brazil. He was opposed by Irala, who again became governor and was at length confirmed by the crown.

1573. **Juan de Garay,** with colonists from Asunción, founded Santa Fé and a few years later refounded Buenos Aires (1580).

(*Cont. p. 536.*)

6. NEW SPAIN, 1518–1574

a. THE CONQUEST OF MEXICO, 1518–1522

1518–1519. To continue the discoveries of Hernández de Córdoba and Grijalva (p. 391), Diego Velázquez and **Hernándo Cortés** (1485–1547) organized an expedition of some 600 men, with 17 horses and 10 cannon. Cortés was put in command. Sailing from Cuba despite Velázquez's orders, he followed the coast of Yucatan, subjugated Tabasco and reached San Juan de Ulloa. There he renounced the authority of Velázquez and, acting as a direct agent of the crown, founded **Villa Rica de la Vera Cruz.** Cortés was elected chief magistrate by the soldiers and sent representatives to Spain to secure confirmation.

After negotiations with **Moctezuma** (Montezuma), ruler of the Aztecs (p. 386), and after winning the support of the **Totonac,** a people subject to the Aztec, Cortés moved into the interior, overcame Tlaxcala, and formed an alliance with the republic. Moving on the Aztec capital, Cortés thwarted a treacherous attempt to destroy his force at Cholula and entered **Tenochtitlán** (1519, Nov. 8), where he was amicably received by Moctezuma. To safeguard his position, Cortés soon made the native ruler a prisoner, and the latter and his chiefs swore fealty to the Castilian sovereign. **1520.** Meanwhile Velázquez, named royal *adelantado* of the lands discovered by Hernández de Córdoba and Grijalva, sent an expedition under **Pánfilo de Narváez** to reduce Cortés to obedience. Cortés, placing Pedro de Alvarado (1485–1541) in command at Tenochtitlán, went to the coast and by combined subterfuge and vigorous action won over the majority of the force of Narváez, thereupon returning to the Aztec capital. Harsh rule by Alvarado aroused the Aztecs to revolt against the Spaniards and Moctezuma, and Cortés was forced to evacuate Tenochtitlán with heavy losses (1520, June 30). Moctezuma, who had been injured by his own subjects, died or was killed by the Spaniards at the time of the evacuation. Cortés retreated around the northern end of Lake Tezcuco, overcame an overwhelming Aztec army at **Otumba** (1520, July 7), and reached Tlaxcala, which remained loyal. At Tlaxcala Cortés reorganized his forces. He then conquered the province of Tepeaca, founding Segura de la Frontera. An expedition was sent into southern Vera Cruz, and two outposts were established. Having received reinforcements, among them the members of the Garay expedition to Pánuco, Cortés established his base at Tezcuco and undertook the investment of Tenochtitlán by land and water.

1521, May 26–Aug. 13. After a prolonged and desperate siege the Spaniards, aided by a horde of native allies, captured the Aztec capital, making prisoner **Cuauhtémoc,** who had become emperor and had organized resistance. Spanish control was firmly established over the immediate vicinity and the conquest was rapidly extended. Tenochtitlán was razed and **Mexico City,** which became the seat of government of the later viceroyalty of New Spain, was erected. A bitter suit between Cortés and Velázquez, carried on before the crown during the period of the conquest, terminated in favor of Cortés and the emperor named him *governor* and *captain-general of New Spain* (1522, Oct. 15).

b. EXPANSION TO THE SOUTH, 1522–1546

1522–1524. Cristóbal de Olid subdued Colima and part of Jalisco. Another settlement was made in Michoacan, the territory of the independent and civilized Tarascans, whose ruler had given allegiance to Cortés. Farther south Oaxaca and Tehuántepec were reduced, the latter by Alvarado.

1523–1525. Embassies from certain towns of Guatemala having made submission, Cortés sent Alvarado to that region. Alvarado conquered the civilized Quiché and Cakchiquel and founded the city of Guatemala. The conquest was then extended into **Salvador,** and Alvarado became governor of the general district of Guatemala. Chiapas was reduced by expeditions from New Spain (1523–1528).

1524–1526. Cortés then sent Olid to conquer and settle **Honduras.** Olid sought to free himself from the authority of Cortés and overcame Gil González Dávila, but was defeated and later killed by a lieutenant of Cortés. Trujillo was founded during this period (1523–1526). Cortés led an expedition overland to Honduras by way of Tabasco and Petén, and established his authority, thereupon returning to Mexico (1524–1526).

1526–1536. Almost complete anarchy continued in Honduras, despite appointment of royal governors. The acting governor, **Andrés de Cerezeda,** established the majority of the colonists in the area of the Río de Ulúa (Higueras), and soon summoned Alvarado to preserve the colony (1534–1536). Alvarado as governor founded **San Pedro** and dispatched an expedition to found Gracias a Dios, but departed for Spain without definitely reducing the area (1536).

1527–1535. The **conquest of Yucatan** was assigned to **Francisco de Montejo** (c. 1473–1553) as *adelantado*. The first attempt of Montejo to conquer the Maya failed after eight years of effort, and he was diverted to Honduras upon appointment as governor. The final conquest and colonization of Yucatan were achieved by the son and nephew of Montejo under his general direction. Campeche, Mérida, Valladolid, and Salamanca (Bacalar) were founded (1539–1545).

1537–1539. **Francisco de Montejo,** as royal governor, conclusively subjugated Higueras, founding Comayagua. Alvarado, upon returning, again became governor, but after his death (1541) governmental affairs fell into confusion. Stability was created with the establishment of the *audiencia* of Confines (1542–1544).

1546. A serious **revolt of the Maya** was crushed.

Tabasco, which had been colonized at an early date but was in danger of abandonment, was assigned to the jurisdiction of Montejo and was pacified by him and his son (1529–1540). The area of Petén was not conquered until the close of the 17th century.

c. EXPANSION TO THE NORTH, 1522–1795

1522–1527. The initial efforts of Garay to colonize Amichel having failed, Cortés subdued the region of the Panuco River and founded a town. Further efforts by Garay were forestalled, and a revolt of the natives was put down by one of Cortés' lieutenants (1523). The Panuco district became a special jurisdiction under the crown, with Nuño de Guzmán as governor (1527).

1531–1550. In the interior Spanish expansion was slower. **Querétaro** was reduced and the town of that name was founded. The Zacatecas and Guanajuato **silver mines** were opened, the former proving to be the richest in New Spain. **San Luis Potosí,** in which mining was soon developed, was conquered by Francisco de Urdiñola, whose son continued the work of colonization.

1539. Reports brought by Cabeza de Vaca and the legend of the *Seven Cities of Cíbola* caused the viceroy, Mendoza, to send the Franciscan **Fray Marcos de Niza** northward. Having reached the Zuñi pueblos of New Mexico, the friar returned with exaggerated accounts.

1540–1542. **Francisco Vásquez de Coronado,** governor of New Galicia, with the authority of the viceroy, led an expedition overland to the new lands, while **Hernando de Alarcón** proceeded by sea along the west coast. Coronado reached the Zuñis and his lieutenants reached the Moqui pueblos and the **Grand Cañon** of the Colorado. In search of Gran Quivira, Coronado traversed northern Texas, Oklahoma, and eastern Kansas before his return.

1562–1570. **Francisco de Ibarra,** governor and captain-general, conquered New Vizcaya and founded **Durango.**

1598–1608. Under royal patent, **Juan de Oñate** secured the submission of New Mexico and sent out expeditions which explored the region from Kansas to the Gulf of California. **Santa Fé** was founded soon after the resignation of Oñate.

Meanwhile the Spaniards had extended their conquests far up the Pacific Coast.

1529–1531. **Nuño de Guzmán,** president of the first *audiencia* of New Spain, subjugated a considerable area to the north and west of Mexico City, including Jalisco and Sinaloa. This region was called *New Galicia,* of which Campostela became the capital.

1532–1533. In search of a strait and of new lands, Cortés dispatched expeditions which reached northern Sinaloa and Lower California.

1535. Cortés himself attempted, though without success, to found a colony in Lower California, but **Francisco de Ulloa,** in command of an expedition organized by Cortés, reached the head of the **Gulf of California** (1539). Alarcón, co-operating by sea with Coronado's expedition to New Mexico, reached the same district and passed up the **Colorado River** (1540).

1541. In the absence of Coronado, the natives of New Galicia rose in revolt, but were finally subdued by the viceroy, Antonio de Mendoza.

1542–1543. As part of his project for South Sea discovery, Mendoza sent **Juan Rodríguez de Cabrillo** to search for a northern strait. Cabrillo, and, after his death, the pilot Bartolomé Ferrelo, explored the Pacific coast as far as **Oregon,** but failed to discover the Bays of Monterey and San Francisco.

1548. An *audiencia* was created to govern New Galicia, **Guadalajara** becoming the political and ecclesiastical capital.

1602. The occupation of the Philippines (p. 580), the development of trade, and the need for protection against English, French, and Dutch aroused renewed interest in the California coast and the possibility of a northern strait. The Madrid government having ordered the exploration of the coast, **Sebastian Vizcaino** proceeded to a point above San Francisco Bay, which, however, he did not discover. Plans to colonize the Monterey Bay region did not materialize.

1680. The Spaniards, driven from New Mexico by a revolt of the natives, reconquered the area somewhat later (1696).

1720-1722. Fearing loss of territory to France, the Spaniards permanently occupied **Texas,** mainly through the efforts of the marquis of Aguayo, governor of Coahuila.

1769-1786. Under Gálvez's direction Upper California was occupied. San Diego (1769), Monterey (1770), Los Angeles (1781), and San Francisco (1776), were founded and a system of *presidios* and missions, the latter under the Franciscan order, was established.

1774-1776. Juan Pérez, Bruno de Heçeta, Bodega y Quadra, and other Spanish explorers were sent north along the coast to counter British and Russian activity. They discovered the mouth of the **Columbia River** and advanced as far as 60° N.L.

1776. **José de Gálvez,** minister of the Indies, erected New Vizcaya, Sinaloa, Sonora, the Californias, Coahuila, New Mexico, and Texas into the *Provincias Internas* under the governorship of a commandant-general responsible directly to the crown.

1789-1795. Attempts were made to colonize the region north of California. Settlements were made on Vancouver Island and at Cape Flattery, but without permanent results.

d. THE GULF COAST, FLORIDA, AND THE CAROLINAS, 1521-1574

1521. **Juan Ponce de León,** under royal patent, tried unsuccessfully to colonize Florida.

1526-1528. A colony, **San Miguel de Gualdape,** was established in the Carolinas by **Lucas Vásquez de Ayllón,** but was abandoned on his death.

1528. **Pánfilo de Narváez,** having secured authority to colonize the territory assigned to Garay on the Gulf coast and to Ponce de León in Florida, landed in Florida with colonists from Spain. After exploration he tried to reach the area of the Pánuco River. The expedition was wrecked on the coast of Texas and most of the colonists died of hunger and disease, or at the hands of the Indians.

1536. **Alvar Núñez Cabeza de Vaca** and three companions, after six years of captivity, escaped and traversed Texas and northern Mexico, reaching Culiacán.

1539-1543. **Hernando De Soto** (1499-1542), granted a patent for the colonization of the Gulf coast (Florida), headed an expedition from Spain, landed in Florida, explored the southeastern portion of the United States, **discovered the Mississippi River** (1541), traversed Arkansas and Oklahoma to the Arkansas River, and followed the latter river to the Mississippi. While moving down the Mississippi, De Soto died (1542) and the expedition, under Luis de Moscoso, continued on to the area of the Pánuco (1543). Luis De Cancer, a Dominican, and certain companions sought to bring the nations of Florida to obedience by peaceful means, in accord with theories of Las Casas, but De Cancer was killed, and the attempt was abandoned (1549).

1559-1561. Under directions from the crown, the viceroy, Velasco, dispatched a large expedition under **Tristán de Luna** to colonize the region of the Carolinas (Santa Elena). Luna established a garrison at Pensacola, moved inland, and founded a settlement. The colonists were soon transferred to Pensacola. Villafañe replaced Luna as governor and sought without success to colonize the Carolinas. The garrison left at Pensacola was soon withdrawn. In view of constant failure, Philip II ordered that no further attempt be made to colonize Florida (1561), but need for protection of the Bahama Channel (the route for the return to Spain of plate and merchant fleets) and French attempts to occupy the region led to a reversal of this policy.

1562. **Jean Ribaut** failed in an attempt to establish a French Huguenot settlement at Port Royal (in South Carolina), but shortly afterward **Laudonnière** founded Fort Caroline, on the St. John's River (1564). Ribaut arrived with a third expedition, with instructions to establish a fortified place to command the route of the Spanish plate fleets. As a result of these activities Philip II determined upon the expulsion of the French and the permanent colonization of Florida.

1565. As *adelantado* of Florida **Pedro Menéndez de Avilés founded St. Augustine,** captured Fort Caroline, and slew the garrison. Thus danger of French occupation was removed.

1565-1574. Menéndez de Avilés established *presidios* and posts throughout a wide area and explored and sought to colonize the area north of the peninsula. **Jesuits,** and later **Franciscans,** supported by the *adelantado*, established missions as far north as Virginia. The peninsula of Florida was secured for Spain by Menéndez de Avilés, but the attempts to achieve permanent possession of the territory to the north failed. (*Cont. p. 536.*)

7. FOREIGN ENCROACHMENTS AND TERRITORIAL CHANGES, 1580–1800

The commercial and territorial monopoly of Spain in the Indies, international war, and religious conflict caused England, France, and the Netherlands to attack Spanish shipping and coastal towns in the colonies and to colonize within areas controlled by Spain.

16th cent. French corsairs early attacked Spanish vessels off the coasts of Europe and at the Azores and Canaries and soon extended their activities into the Caribbean, where they attacked towns as well as commerce. In the latter half of the 16th century English freebooters, with the tacit approval of the crown, became active in the Atlantic, Caribbean, and Pacific. The raiding of the Pacific coast by **Drake** during his voyage around the world (1577–1580) is the most outstanding example of English activity in the Pacific during this period. The activities of English freebooters became official after the outbreak of war between Spain and England. Spanish commerce suffered greatly, and many towns were held for ransom or sacked, among them Nombre de Dios, Cartagena, Santo Domingo, and Valparaiso. **Drake, Hawkins, Oxenham,** and **Cavendish** were the most important of the English mariners, and two of the expeditions commanded by Drake constituted formidable armaments. Coincident with the struggle for independence in the Netherlands, Dutch mariners became active.

17th cent. With the decline of Spanish power, official **colonization of the Lesser Antilles,** neglected by Spain, was undertaken by England, France, and Holland. Settlements were established by these powers in the Guianas. England colonized Bermuda and the Bahamas, the Netherlands unsuccessfully sought to colonize the Pacific coast of South America, and France and Holland sought to gain possession of portions of Brazil. Powerful Dutch armaments were dispatched to American waters, one of which, under Piet Heyn, captured a plate fleet from New Spain (1628). An expedition sent against Spanish possessions by Cromwell captured Jamaica (1655), of which England remained in permanent possession. Western Española, in which French buccaneers had secured a foothold and official colonization had later been undertaken, was ceded to France by the **treaty of Ryswick** (1697). The activity of English, French, and Dutch freebooters in the Caribbean reached its height during the 17th century, and played an important part in the decline of Spanish commerce. The Englishman **Henry Morgan** was the most important of these freebooters, who during his career captured numerous cities and towns, including Porto Bello and Panama (1655–1671).

18th cent. The European wars in which Spain was involved in the 18th century and the early part of the 19th had important consequences in the Americas. Control of the seas by Great Britain rendered protection of the colonies increasingly difficult. The Spanish commercial monopoly was, moreover, incapable of enforcement, and extensive illicit commerce participated in by British, French, and Dutch merchants developed.

1701–1713. During the **War of the Spanish Succession** there was considerable fighting between the allied Spaniards and French in the West Indies and Florida. By the **treaty of Utrecht** (1713) Great Britain was granted the *asiento,* or monopoly of the slave trade with the Spanish possessions and the right to send one ship each year to trade with Atlantic ports of the Spanish colonies.

1718–1720. Incident to war between France and Spain, military operations took place in Florida and Texas, as a result of which Spanish possession of Texas was assured, although the boundary remained disputed.

1739–1748. In the "War of Jenkins' Ear," which merged into the **War of the Austrian Succession,** Spain, as a result of reforms introduced by the Bourbons, maintained a successful defense of her possessions. Inconclusive operations took place in Florida and on the frontier of Georgia, and a powerful British expedition under Admiral Vernon was repulsed at Cartagena, which had been heavily fortified as a principal bulwark of colonial defense (1741). The **treaty of Aix-la-Chapelle** (1748) provided for no important territorial changes.

1762. When Spain entered the **Seven Years' War** as an ally of France, British expeditions captured Havana and Manila (1762). By the **treaty of Paris** (1763) Spain ceded Florida to Great Britain and received Havana, Manila being restored later. France ceded Louisiana to Spain, although Spanish authority was not established in the latter without opposition from the French colonists.

With the temporary elimination of France by the Seven Years' War, Great Britain and Spain became the great colonial powers, and **Charles III** (1759–1788), convinced that Great Britain would seek to possess itself of the Spanish colonies, believed a decisive conflict inevitable. Internal and colonial reforms introduced by Charles III raised Spain to the highest position of power and influence enjoyed since the 16th century, and she was comparatively well prepared for an eventual conflict.

1771. A dispute between Spain and Great Britain concerning possession of the **Falkland Islands** brought the two nations to the verge of war, but France refused to afford the support anticipated under the **Family Compact** (p. 489) and Spain was obliged to accept an accommodation.

1775–1783. The **American War of Independence,** becoming a European war after the alliance between France and the colonies, afforded Spain a desired opportunity to check British expansion, and she entered the conflict (1779). Spanish forces captured Mobile and Pensacola, overran the Bahamas, and blocked British attempts to gain control of the Mississippi (1779–1783). By the **treaty of Versailles** (1783) Spain regained Florida, but relinquished the Bahamas.

1789. Controversy between Great Britain and Spain arose over the seizure of British ships at Nootka. Considering sovereignty involved, Spain invoked the **Family Compact** and prepared for war. The French revolutionary government failed fully to support Spain and she yielded. Great Britain and Spain adjusted the incident by treaty (1790–1794).

1795. By the **treaty of Basel** Spain relinquished the eastern two-thirds of Española to France. This territory was returned to Spain by the **treaty of Paris** (1814). Trinidad was forced to capitulate (1797) and was ceded to the British by the treaty of Amiens (1802). Great Britain during the 18th century gained permanent control of Belize and established a protectorate over the Mosquito Indians of Honduras and Nicaragua.

Controversy arose with the **United States** concerning the navigation of the Mississippi, the mouth of which Spain controlled through the acquisition of Louisiana.

1800. France under the consulate forced Spain to return **Louisiana,** guaranteeing that the territory would not be transferred to any power other than Spain.

1803. France, notwithstanding, soon sold Louisiana to the United States. As a result of increasing pressure from the United States, Spain sold **Florida** to that nation (1819–1821).

The establishment of territorial jurisdiction in South America in accord with the **Line of Demarcation** (p. 389) created much friction between Spain and Portugal. **Colonia** was established on the left bank of the estuary of the Río de la Plata by the Portuguese (1680–1683) and Montevideo was founded some years later by the Spaniards to prevent Portuguese expansion (1723). Colonia soon became a base for illicit British and Portuguese trade with the province of the Río de la Plata. The **treaty of Madrid** (1750), an attempted settlement, provided that Colonia should be given to Spain in return for seven Jesuit *reductions* on the east bank of the Uruguay; that Portuguese claims to the basins of the Amazon and Paraná and Spanish claims to the Philippines be recognized, and that boundaries be surveyed. The Guaraní of the seven *reductions,* incited by the Jesuits, rebelled against transfer, and it became necessary for the Portuguese to subdue them by force, the **War of the Seven *Reductions*** (1752–1756). Portugal, notwithstanding, retained Colonia, and Charles III annulled the treaty of Madrid (1761). Spanish forces captured Colonia (1762) and invaded Río Grande do Sul (1762), but these territories were returned by the **treaty of Paris** (1763). Pombal (p. 491) desired to expand Portuguese territory, and, relying on British support, encroached upon Spanish territory. Rivalry between Spain and Portugal continued, and when Great Britain, because of developments in Europe and North America, failed effectively to support Portugal, Charles III dispatched a strong force which captured Colonia and moved against other Portuguese territories (1776–1777). With the dismissal of Pombal (1777) hostilities were suspended and the **treaty of San Ildefonso** was concluded (1777), by which Colonia and disputed Paraguayan territory were assigned to Spain, and Portuguese claims to the interior were recognized. Meanwhile the **Viceroyalty of La Plata** had been created as a defensive as well as an administrative measure (1776). The Portuguese later occupied the disputed missions territory incidental to European hostilities (1801), but by posterior settlements Spain received Colonia and Uruguay while Portugal secured Río Grande do Sul. Attempts of Great Britain to secure territory in the region of the Río de la Plata failed completely (1806–1807).   (*Cont. p. 838.*)

8. THE SPANISH COLONIAL SYSTEM

a. POPULATION

Emigration to the Indies was rigidly controlled by the crown and the *Casa de Contratación*. Heretics, Moors, Jews, and their descendants were excluded. The vast majority of immigrants were from the realms of the crown of Castile. In the early 16th century the crown adopted active measures to encourage immigration. Negro slavery, introduced at the opening of the century, was extensive only in the West Indies and northern South America. Intermixture between male Spaniards and native women produced a large mixed group (*mestizos*). In 1574 the Spanish population was estimated at some 160,000, and at the close of the colonial period the estimated population was 3,276,000 whites, 5,328,000 *mestizos*, 7,530,000 Indians, and 776,000 Negroes (New Spain, 1,230,000 whites. 1,860,000 *mestizos*, 3,700,000 Indians; Guatemala, 280,000 whites, 420,000 *mestizos*, 880,000 Indians; Peru and Chile, 465,000 whites, 853,000 *mestizos*, 1,030,000 Indians; Colombia and Venezuela, 642,000 whites, 1,256,000 *mestizos*, 720,000 Indians; Río de la Plata, 320,000 whites, 742,000 *mestizos*, 1,200,000 Indians; Cuba and Puerto Rico, 339,000 whites, 197,000 mixed, 389,000 Negroes). Negroes in all colonies except Cuba and Puerto Rico numbered 387,000.

Social composition. There existed six relatively distinct groups in the population of the colonies: Spanish colonial officials; upper grade creoles (those of Spanish blood born in the Indies) and socially superior Spanish immigrants; lower grade creoles and Spanish immigrants, high rank *mestizos* and Indian nobility; *mestizos* (mixed white and Indian), mulattoes, *zambos* (mixed Negro and Indian), and certain Indians; Indians, who constituted the largest group numerically; Negro slaves. The two upper classes possessed virtually all the wealth of the colonies.

b. ADMINISTRATION

The discovery of America was accomplished under commission of the sovereign of Castile and the new lands consequently became realms of the Castilian crown, from which all authority emanated. In accord with the theory of royal absolutism the crown abrogated governmental authority granted Columbus and the early conquistadores and established direct royal control. The machinery of royal government was fully formed by the third quarter of the 16th century.

After appointment to supervise preparations for the second voyage of Columbus (1493) **Juan Rodríguez de Fonseca** became virtual minister of the Indies, and as such laid the foundation for the expansion of the machinery of royal government. With the development of trade the *Casa de Contratación* was established at Seville to control colonial commerce and maritime enterprise (1503). The nucleus of a council to administer the Indies was evolved and this body, under the presidency of Rodríguez de Fonseca, rapidly developed into a formal **Council of the Indies** (*Consejo de Indias*). Upon the death of Rodríguez de Fonseca the *Consejo de Indias* was reorganized (1524) and by the close of the reign of Charles V its organization and functions were fully developed. The *Consejo de Indias* exercised supreme administrative, judicial, and ecclesiastical authority over the Indies and possessed supervisory authority over the *Casa de Contratación*. The legislation for the Indies promulgated by the crown and *Consejo de Indias* was codified in the *Recopilación de Leyes . . . de las Indias,* one of the greatest of colonial codes (1680). At the opening of the 17th century a *Junta de Guerra y Armadas de Indias,* to administer the armed forces and the dispatch of fleets to the Indies, and a *Cámara de Indias,* to control ecclesiastical affairs and appointments, were created as adjuncts to the *Consejo de Indias.* Early in the Bourbon period the office of *Minister of the Indies* was created with the establishment of a *Secretaría de Guerra, Marina e Indias* (1714). This secretariat underwent numerous changes and before the close of the century a separate **secretariat of the Indies** was formed. With the creation of these institutions the *Consejo de Indias* declined in importance.

Direct royal government in the Indies was instituted with the appointment of **Francisco de Bobadilla** as judge and governor of Española and the removal of Columbus (1499–1500). Bobadilla was succeeded by Nicolás de Ovando (1502), and he by Diego Columbus, son of the admiral, named governor at the will of the crown (1509). A tribunal of three royal judges was created in Santo Domingo as a check on the governor (1511), and this body was later established in a fully developed form as the *audiencia of Santo Domingo* and given governmental authority over the West Indies (1526).

On the mainland government was at first permitted to rest with those who had conquered the several areas under royal patent or with crown recognition and who governed with the titles of *adelantado,* governor, or captain-general. The threat to royal absolutism inherent in government by powerful vassals with privileged positions caused early extension of direct government to the mainland.

The institution of the *adelantado* was of great importance during the period of conquest. By capitulation with the crown the *adelantado* undertook the conquest of a specified area at his own cost and in return was assigned governmental authority and hereditary privileges. The institution was of value in bringing new lands under Spanish dominion, but its character threatened royal authority and the powers granted were revoked after achievement of the royal purpose.

An *audiencia* was created to govern New Spain (1527), but proved weak in its executive aspects and shortly after a viceroy, Antonio de Mendoza, was appointed (1529), although he did not take office for some years (1535). The **viceroyalty of Peru** was created by the New Laws (1542), which also established an *audiencia* at Lima. The **viceroyalty** (or *Reino*) **of New Spain,** with its capital Mexico City, came to include all Spanish territory north of Panama, the West Indies, Venezuela, and the Philippine Islands. That of Peru, with its capital Lima, included Panama and all Spanish territory in South America except Venezuela.

Audiencias, each with its definite area, were created for Guatemala (1542), New Galicia (1548), New Granada (1549), Charcas, or Upper Peru (1556), Quito (1563), and the Philippine Islands (1583–1593).

The viceroys, as direct representatives of the sovereign, possessed wide civil and military authority, and certain ecclesiastical powers. They were presidents of the *audiencias* of their capitals. The *audiencias,* composed of a president, *oidores,* a *fiscal* (crown prosecutor), and lesser officials, exercised supreme judicial authority within their districts, and the *audiencias* not directly under viceroys exercised governmental authority. The viceregal *audiencia* acted as an advisory council to the viceroy and in this function evolved legislative power. The *audiencias* were co-ordinate in judicial affairs, appeals going directly before the *Consejo de Indias,* and they were empowered to correspond directly with the crown. The *audiencias* varied in status according to the rank of the presiding officer, i.e., viceroy, president and captain-general, or president. The presidents of the *audiencias* of Santo Domingo, Guatemala, and New Granada were early accorded military authority and became presidents and captains-general. As such they became practically independent of the viceroys. Guadalajara, Quito, and Charcas remained presidencies. In the absence of the viceroy or president and captain-general the *audiencia* assumed the government. During the Bourbon period New

Granada, Panama, Venezuela, and Quito were erected into the **viceroyalty of New Granada** (1717–1739), the **viceroyalty of La Plata** was established (1776), the captaincies-general of Venezuela (1773), Cuba (1777), and Chile (1778) were created, and *audiencias* were established in Buenos Aires (1783), Caracas (1786), and Cuzco (1789).

Major administrative areas were divided into *gobiernos, corregimientos,* and *alcaldías mayores,* of which the *gobiernos* were, in general, the more important and frequently consisted of more than one province. This organization persisted until the reign of Charles III, when a system of intendants was established throughout the Indies (1769–1790). The intendants possessed administrative, judicial, financial, and military authority, and in fiscal and economic matters were directly responsible to the crown.

In accord with medieval Castilian traditions the **municipalities** at first enjoyed a large measure of self-government under their *cabildos,* composed of *regidores* (councilmen) and *alcades* (mayors), the former elected by the householders and the latter by the *regidores.* Before the close of the 16th century the election of *regidores* gave way to royal appointment, hereditary tenure, and venality of office. *Cabildos abiertos* of all citizens were at times held to discuss important matters. The municipal government exercised executive, legislative, and judicial authority within its district, although frequently under control of royal officials.

Fiscal administration was from the first directly under the crown through the *Casa de Contratación* and *contadores, factors, tesoreros,* and *veedores* in the New World jurisdictional areas. With the establishment of the intendants those officials assumed administration of fiscal affairs.

The Castilian institutions of the *residencia, visita,* and *pesquisa* were early instituted in the New World.

The principal sources of **crown revenues** were the *quinto,* or one-fifth of the products of the subsoil (gold, silver, precious stones) under the theory of crown ownership of the subsoil; the *almojarifzgo* (customs imposts); the *alcabala* (sales tax); the tributes of the natives; the *media anata* of civil and ecclesiastical offices, and the sale of the *Crusada.* Although revenues from the Americas were great, they at no time during the period of Spanish greatness exceeded 25 per cent of the total income of the crown.

The presence of a great **Indian population** created extraordinary administrative problems. Municipal governments on the Castilian model were established in the Indian towns. Local Spanish officials had jurisdiction over the native towns in their districts. Protectors of the Indians were created for general and local districts to guard their interests. The *repartimiento-encomienda,* which early developed, was an institution of great political, social, and economic importance. In the earlier period this institution involved the assignment of specified towns to *conquistadores* and colonists, the Indians of which gave tribute, labor, and service to the *encomendero,* who was obligated to afford protection, indoctrination in Christianity, and instruction. Abuses caused the crown to regulate the system. Fixed quotas of tribute were established and labor and service were eliminated about the middle of the 16th century. Before the close of the century the *encomienda* was virtually reduced to the right to enjoy the revenues from specified towns. The crown after the publication of the **New Laws** (1542-1543) assumed control of many towns, and grants of *encomiendas* were brought under control of higher authorities. Attempts were made to abolish the system, notably in the New Laws, but it was not until the first part of the 18th century that abolition was definitely decreed. In certain areas the institution persisted almost until the close of the colonial period. The *mita,* forced labor of the natives in the mines, on the *haciendas,* and for public works, was established late in the 16th century. Indians not within the *encomienda* system were required to pay an annual tribute and after the abolition of the *encomienda* this was required of all.

Extensive **enslavement of Indians** took place during the period of conquest under the law of just war, but this was prohibited by the New Laws. The natives were regarded as wards of the crown and throughout the colonial period legislation was promulgated for their welfare and protection, notable examples of such legislation being the Laws of Burgos (1512), and the New Laws. A section of the Laws of the Indies was devoted to Indian legislation (1680). The beneficent intent of the crown was to a large degree rendered nugatory by the difficulties of administration and the conflict of theory and practice. Many Spaniards acted as advocates of the Indians, the greatest of whom was **Bartolomé de Las Casas** (1474-1566).

c. THE CHURCH AND THE MISSIONS

The union of State and Church in the Spanish Americas was exceedingly close. The crown early secured almost complete control of ecclesiastical affairs through the patronage of the Indies (*real patronato de Indias*) granted by Alexander VI in the bulls *Inter caetera* (1493, May 4) which assigned dominion over the Indies and exclusive authority to convert the natives,

and *Eximiae devotionis* (1501, Nov. 16), which granted the titles and first fruits of the Church in the Indies, and by Julius II in the bull *Universalis ecclesiae* (1508, July 28), which conceded universal patronage. The extent and nature of the patronage was further defined by bulls issued at intervals throughout the colonial period. The crown exercised ecclesiastical control through the *Consejo de Indias* and later through that body and the *Cámara de Indias.* Papal bulls were not permitted to be placed in effect without the approval of the crown.

The full **organization of the Church** in the Indies followed closely upon the conquest and colonization, and at the close of the colonial period there existed seven archbishoprics and some 35 dioceses. The Church possessed its own courts, with jurisdiction over all cases touching the clergy and spiritual affairs. The **Spanish Inquisition** was introduced (1569), and tribunals were established in Mexico City and Lima (1570-1571). This institution rapidly achieved great religious and political influence. Indians, considered incapable of rational judgment, were exempt from the Inquisition.

The Church played an important part in the Indies through conversion of the natives, aid in the maintenance of Spanish political authority, transmission of culture, and education. It achieved vast wealth and a privileged position, and at the close of the colonial period is estimated to have controlled half of the productive real estate in the Indies.

The **religious orders,** Franciscan, Dominican, Jesuit, Augustinian, Capuchin, and others, early achieved complete organization and carried on an exceedingly important work in converting the natives and instructing them in the rudiments of European civilization. The task of preserving and extending Spanish control in outlying areas was assigned to the religious orders, especially the Franciscan, Dominican, Capuchin, and Jesuit, as official agencies of the crown. Missionaries, accompanied by small groups of soldiers, and frequently by colonists, established missions and instructed the natives in Christianity. They developed agriculture, grazing, and simple industry. *Presidios* were established to protect the missions. Civilian colonists occupied the territory and secularization followed. Carrying forward on the northern frontier of New Spain, toward the close of the 17th century, Jesuits under the leadership of **Eusebio Kino** began the establishment of missions in Pimería Alta (Arizona) and under **Juan María Salvatierra** in Lower California, over which the order was granted complete authority. A wide area was eventually brought under Spanish control. Early in the 18th century a system of missions and *presidios* was established in Texas and late in the century in California. Dominicans and Franciscans were active in Guatemala, Capuchins in the area of the lower Orinoco—to check French, English, and Dutch encroachments— and Jesuits in the territory of the Araucanians and Paraguay. The mission system in Paraguay was one of the most important in the New World. Granted complete authority to convert and organize the Guaraní east of Asunción, the Jesuits established missions (reductions) along the upper Paraná. The natives were later transferred farther south because of Portuguese slave raids. A complete governmental organization was established, controlled by a father superior at Candelaria, the natives were instructed in Christianity, and the rudiments of European civilization, and agriculture and industry were extensively developed. By the **treaty of Madrid** (1750) seven reductions were transferred to Portugal. The Guaraní, incited by the Jesuits, rose in revolt to resist transfer, but were defeated. By later adjustments the territory remained in Spanish possession. With the expulsion of the Jesuits (1767) the Paraguayan reductions were given to Franciscans, but failed to prosper.

d. ECONOMIC CONDITIONS AND POLICIES

Mining of gold and silver, fostered by the crown, rapidly became the most important industry in the Spanish colonies. Rich silver deposits were early discovered throughout central Mexico, especially in the districts of Zacatecas, Guanajuato, Pachuca, Taxco, and San Luis Potosí, and at Potosí in Upper Peru (1530–1600). Gold deposits were worked throughout the Indies. Silver production came to surpass that of gold, and after the third quarter of the 16th century Peru produced about two-thirds of the total output of precious metals.

Agricultural and pastoral pursuits were highly developed. All plants and animals of Spain were introduced into the Indies and native plants, especially maize, potatoes, cotton, tobacco, and cacao were cultivated.

Local textile, iron, pottery, shipbuilding, gold and silver working, and sugar (West Indies) industries developed.

The **principal imports** into the colonies were manufactured goods, and **exports** consisted almost exclusively of precious metals, raw materials and agricultural products.

The **economic policy of Spain** was based upon mercantilist theory. Trade was a monopoly of the metropolis under direct crown control and economic activity in the colonies which competed with that of Spain was prohibited or restricted.

The economic privileges of Columbus were almost immediately rendered inoperative and the crown assumed direct control over all phases of economic activity. In the earliest period Juan Rodríguez de Fonseca as de facto minister of the Indies controlled commerce (1493–1503), and trade under license was authorized by the crown (1495–1501). The Casa de Contratación, "a board of trade, a commercial court, and a clearing-house for the American traffic," was established at Seville (1503). This body came under the supervisory authority of the Consejo de Indias. Seville was accorded a monopoly of the American trade. In the New World, Vera Cruz, Cartagena, and Porto Bello alone were permitted direct trade with Spain. General intercolonial commerce was early prohibited, and before the close of the 16th century commerce with the Philippines was restricted to Acapulco. Trade between Manila and China was confined to Chinese.

Naval warfare, attacks by corsairs, and the necessity of protection for gold and silver shipments caused the establishment of a system of **convoyed fleets,** one each year for New Spain (the flota) and one for Peru (the galeones) (1543–1561). On the return the fleets united at Havana and sailed for Spain together. Fairs for the exchange of goods were held annually at Porto Bello and Jalapa (Mexico). Trade between Acapulco and the Philippines (Manila) was restricted to one vessel a year each way. With the period of Spanish decadence trade declined greatly.

Under the Bourbons many reforms were introduced. By the treaty of Utrecht (1713) Great Britain was conceded the monopoly of the slave trade with the colonies (asiento) and the privilege of sending one vessel each year to Porto Bello to trade. With the establishment of the office of the minister of the Indies early in the 18th century (1714) the Casa de Contratación tended to decline in importance. The Casa de Contratación and trade monopoly were transferred to Cadiz (1717–1718). To develop trade the monopolistic **chartered companies** of Honduras (1714), Guipúzcoa, or Caracas (1728), Havana (1740), and Santo Domingo (1757) were formed. With the decline in trade the sailings of the fleets became irregular. Supplies were increasingly carried to the Indies in registered vessels and by the chartered companies and in the middle of the 18th century the fleet system was abolished (1748). Charles III promulgated a series of reform measures authorizing trade between more than twenty Spanish ports besides Seville and Cadiz and a large number of ports throughout the Indies, and permitting direct intercolonial trade between New Spain and Peru and Guatemala and New Granada (1764–1782). A great increase in trade resulted. Royal secretaries having increasingly assumed its functions, the *Casa de Contratación* was abolished (1790). During the wars of the French Revolution neutral vessels were permitted to engage in the carrying trade with the colonies (1797).

e. EDUCATION, LEARNING, AND FINE ARTS

Education in Spanish America, with the exception of the rudimentary instruction afforded the Indians by the Church, was largely confined to the upper classes. The earliest universities were those of **Mexico** (1551), **San Marcos de Lima** (1551), and **St. Thomas Aquinas** of Santo Domingo (1558), founded by royal decree. They were modeled after the University of Salamanca. A school of mines was established in Mexico by Charles III (1783).

A vast body of **historical writing,** much of it of high quality, was produced during the colonial period, and important anthropological and linguistic studies were made. In the sciences the most important figures were **Carlos Sigüenza y Góngora** (1645–1700) and **Pedro de Peralta Barnuevo Rocha y Benavides** (1663–1743).

Juan Rúz de Alarcón (d. 1639), a Mexican creole, achieved a high place in the Spanish drama and **Sor Juana Inés de la Cruz** (b. 1651), also a Mexican creole, attained recognition for her poetry.

The first **printing press** was introduced into Mexico by the Viceroy Mendoza (1535). At the close of the colonial period there were a number of presses in operation in the larger cities. Newssheets and scientific and literary publications appeared in Lima and Mexico City toward the close of the 18th century.

Intellectual activity was, in general, seriously hampered by the Inquisition.

In **art and architecture** Spanish models were followed. Local schools of painting developed in Mexico and Quito. Charles III founded the **San Cárlos Academy of Fine Arts** in the former city (1778). An outstanding architectural achievement was the **Cathedral of Mexico,** begun late in the 16th century and completed in the first part of the 19th. (*Cont. p. 838.*)

9. PORTUGUESE AMERICA, 1500–1821

1500–1521. Absorbed by interests in the Orient, **Manuel the Fortunate** (1495–1521) made no effective effort to colonize the territory claimed by Portugal in South America, although certain royal expeditions were dispatched and trading posts were established through private enterprise.

1521–1530. French activities having menaced Portuguese possession, **John III** (1521–1557) undertook systematic colonization.

1530–1532. **Martin Afonso de Souza,** as captain-major and leader of a colonizing and exploratory expedition, founded São Vicente and actively furthered colonization, introducing cattle and European grains and fruits and laying the foundations of a sugar industry.

1532–1536. A system of feudal **hereditary captaincies** under *donatarios* with virtually sovereign authority was established by the crown, but proved unsuccessful and a more centralized administration with a directly responsible governor-general at its head was created.

1549. **Thomé de Souza,** the first governor-general, founded **São Salvador** (Bahia), which was made the seat of government. Souza firmly established the administration and effectively furthered colonization. This task was ably continued by **Mem de Sá** (1558–1572). **São Paulo** was founded shortly after the middle of the century.

1549. **Jesuits,** headed by Manuel de Nobrega and José de Anchieta, undertook the conversion of the natives and established missions, playing an important part in colonization.

1551. The fundamental relationship between Church and State was established by a bull of Julius III which conceded to the crown complete spiritual jurisdiction over conquests and the right to nominate bishops, collect tithes, dispense church revenues, and receive appeals from ecclesiastical tribunals. The bishopric of Bahia, suffragan to the archbishop of Lisbon, was erected (1551).

France, Holland, and England did not permit Portugal to remain in possession of Brazil unchallenged. French efforts to establish an empire in South America passed through two distinct phases.

1555. With the intention of creating an "Antarctic France," a colony was founded on the Bay of Rio de Janeiro under **Nicolas Durand de Villegagnon.**

1565–1567. The Portuguese under leadership of Mem de Sá destroyed the colony and founded the city of **Rio de Janeiro,** ending French attempts in that area. Henry IV projected the establishment of an "Equinoctial France."

1612. After his death, although without direct royal aid, a town was founded on the island of **Maranhão** and exploration was conducted on the mainland with the purpose of occupying the area of the mouths of the Amazon. The state of Maranhão was created (1621), directly subordinate to the home government. The Jesuits established missions along the Amazon and gave France control of the vast river basin. Maranhão was independent of Brazil until 1777.

1615. The Portuguese forced the surrender of the colony, and shortly thereafter founded Belem, ending French efforts to establish an extensive empire in South America.

The personal union of the crowns of Spain and Portugal (p. 418) carried important consequences for Brazil. **English attacks** on coastal towns occurred in the final decades of the 16th century, Santos being sacked.

1624-1625. Dutch activities were far more serious. Shortly after the organization of the **Dutch West India Company** (p. 474), the Dutch captured Bahia (1624), but were forced to capitulate to a Spanish fleet (1625).

1630. Continuing the effort, a powerful Dutch armament captured Recife and Olinda. The conquest was extended over a wide area.

1637. The West India Company named **Prince Maurice of Nassau-Siegen** governor, and under his able administration Dutch control was established over an area extending from the São Francisco River to Maranhão.

1644. As the West India Company displayed greater interest in profit than in colonization, Prince Maurice returned to Holland.

1645. Immediately thereafter, in a truly popular movement, the Portuguese rebelled and within a decade forced the Dutch to capitulate (1654). These events ended Dutch occupation of Brazilian territory, a situation later recognized by treaty (1661, Aug. 6).

Slave-raiding parties began to penetrate into the interior from São Paulo (1629) and by the middle of the century these Paulistas had explored an extensive area of southern Brazil. They attacked the Spanish Jesuit *reductions* on the upper Paraná, forced their transfer to a more southern area, and made possible Portuguese possession of the region. Simultaneously Portuguese Jesuits established missions in the south, coming into conflict with the Paulistas in their efforts to protect the Indians, in which they received royal support.

1680-1683. Seeking to gain possession of the left bank of the Río de la Plata (*Banda Oriental*), the Portuguese founded **Colonia.** Spain and Portugal immediately came into conflict over this area; **Montevideo** being founded by the Spaniards (1726). The territory changed hands frequently during the remainder of the colonial period.

1693. Decreasing profits from slaving operations and increasingly effective protection afforded the Indians by the Jesuits caused the Paulistas to direct their efforts to a search for gold, and toward the end of the 17th century extensive deposits were discovered in **Minas Gerães.** An influx of gold-seekers ensued, among them many newly arrived Portuguese.

1701-1713. The alliance of Portugal with England during the War of the Spanish Succession led to French attacks on Brazilian ports, **Rio de Janeiro** being sacked and held for ransom by Duguay-Trouin (1711).

1708-1709. Efforts of the Portuguese to displace the Paulistas resulted in open warfare, the **War of the Emboabas,** in which the former were successful. Through the efforts of the Paulistas, Matto Grosso and Goyaz, far to the west of the Line of Demarcation, were gained for Portugal.

1709. With the colonization of the interior the crown created the captaincy of **São Paulo and Minas Gerães,** with a captain-general directly responsible to the sovereign, erected Minas Gerães into a separate jurisdiction (1720), and established the captaincies of Matto Grosso (1744) and Goyaz (1748).

1710-1711. The War of the Mascates. Rivalry between the native Brazilians of Olinda, the political capital of Pernambuco, and the Portuguese of the commercial town of Recife, concerning the elevation of the latter to *villa* status, led to armed conflict. Recife, notwithstanding, was accorded municipal privileges and eventually superseded Olinda as the seat of government.

The **Line of Demarcation** never having been surveyed, as Portuguese expansion progressed, efforts were made to establish limits.

1750. In the **treaty of Madrid** Spain recognized Portuguese claims to extensive areas in the basins of the Amazon and Paraná, and although this treaty was abrogated, the bases of settlement were reaffirmed by the **treaty of San Ildefonso** (1777). While the limits were not definitely surveyed, Portuguese claims to territory vastly greater than that assigned under the **treaty of Tordesillas** (p. 390) were permanently established.

1750-1777. Pombal as minister of Joseph I (p. 491) introduced far-reaching colonial reforms. Administration was unified, the capital being transferred from Bahia to Rio de Janeiro and Maranhão being incorporated with Brazil (1777). Commerce between Portugal and Brazil was encouraged, certain restrictions and taxes were removed, and trading companies were organized. Native Brazilians were appointed to important governmental posts, racial equality was advocated, and defenses were improved. Pombal strongly pressed Portuguese territorial claims. The **Jesuits were expelled** from Portugal and its possessions during his ministry (1759).

1789. The Conspiracy of Minas. Maladministration, heavy taxes, and reactionary government led to an abortive attempt at revolution in Minas Gerães, led by **Joaquim José de Silva Xavier** (*Tiradentes*).

1807. The determination of Napoleon to force Portuguese adherence to the Continental System and his plan to partition Portugal exercised a decisive influence on Portuguese and Brazilian history.

1807–1808. Apprised of the designs of the emperor, upon the approach of a French army, **Prince John,** regent after 1792 because of the insanity of Maria I, created a regency in Portugal, fled to Brazil, and established his government at Rio de Janeiro.

1808–1816. The regent adopted many reforms advantageous to Brazil. Decrees were issued establishing free trade, removing restrictions on industry, promoting agriculture and communications, establishing a royal press, founding the Bank of Brazil, and encouraging the arts and sciences. Brazil was erected into a coordinate member of the **United Kingdom of Portugal, Brazil, and Algarves** (1815, Dec. 16).

The regent became **John VI** upon the death of Maria I (1816, Mar. 1).

1808. Prince John declared war on France and dispatched an expedition which occupied **French Guiana.** This territory was returned by the **treaty of Paris** (1814). The regent sought also to annex the *Banda Oriental* and supported the designs of his wife, Carlotta Joaquina, sister of Ferdinand VII of Spain, to establish her rule over the provinces of the **Río de la Plata.**

1812. The opposition of the viceroy and the revolutionary *junta* of Buenos Aires and British influence caused the regent temporarily to renounce intervention in the area of the Río de la Plata.

1816–1821. After becoming king, John took advantage of the situation arising from the struggle for independence in the *Banda Oriental* and the violation of Brazilian territory by the leader of the movement, **José Artigas** (p. 840). He then intervened again in the *Banda Oriental.* Portuguese troops occupied Montevideo and defeated Artigas, and the territory was incorporated into Brazil as the **Cisplatine Province** (1821). Projects against other provinces of the Río de la Plata were renounced under threat from Ferdinand VII and in face of a potentially united Argentina.

10. THE PORTUGUESE COLONIAL SYSTEM

Population and Race. A complex racial situation developed in Brazil. Intermixture between Portuguese males and Indian women gave rise to a large group of *mestizos.* From the middle of the 16th century onward Negro slaves were introduced in large numbers to meet labor requirements and extensive intermixture of Negro and white blood occurred. There was also intermixture between Negroes and natives. In 1583 the population was estimated at 25,000 whites, 18,000 civilized Indians, and 14,000 Negro slaves. In the mid-17th century, considerable immigration having taken place, the population was estimated at 150,000 to 200,000, three-fourths of whom were Indians, Negroes, and mixed. At the close of the 18th century at 3,000,000, a population already greater than that of Portugal. In 1818 the population was estimated at 843,000 whites, 1,887,500 Negroes, 628,000 mixed, and 259,400 civilized Indians. The bulk of the population was concentrated in São Paulo, Minas Gerães, Pernambuco, and Bahia. Originally the crown permitted any person of Catholic faith to enter Brazil, but after 1591 aliens were excluded.

Portuguese **colonial administration** was not clearly differentiated from that of the metropolis prior to the union of the crowns of Portugal and Spain. For general purposes there existed an inspector of finances and a *Casa da India.* The *Mesa da Consiencia e Ordems,* with ecclesiastical and financial powers, was created in 1532. Upon the establishment of a more centralized government in Brazil, a commissioner of finances and a chief justice were appointed for the colony (1548). For local administration there were *corregedores,* with judicial and military functions. Municipal organization was patterned on that of Portugal. The fundamental code was the *Ordenanças Manuelinas* (1521).

During the period of the union of the thrones of Spain and Portugal (1580/1581–1640) Spanish administrative forms were introduced. The inspector of finance was replaced by a council, the *Consejo da Fazenda.* A Council of the Indies (*Conselho da India*) was created (1604), a supreme court was established in Bahia (1609), and the title of *viceroy* was introduced (1640). Under Philip III (1598–1621), the *Ordenanças Philippinas,* which permitted greater local autonomy, superseded the *Ordenanças Manuelinas.* Most of these innovations were permanent.

By the close of the 18th century the structure of royal government was fully formed. The **Transmarine Council** (*Conselho do Ultramar*), formerly the Council of the Indies, exercised general religious and military authority over Brazil. Pará, Maranhão, Pernambuco, Bahia, São Paulo, Minas Gerães, Goyaz, Matto Grosso, and Rio de Janeiro were captaincies-general, provinces of the first rank, under captains-general usually appointed by the crown. The viceroy, who was also captain-general of Rio de Janeiro, possessed legal authority over the captains-general in certain matters, but the latter frequently received instructions from the crown, with which they could correspond directly. A tendency toward local autonomy existed. There were a number of districts of inferior status, captaincies, subordinate to the captaincies-general. Two superior judicial districts existed, with high tribunals at Bahia and Rio de Janeiro (founded 1757) respectively. Appeals from these courts went directly to Lisbon. The municipalities, with their councils (*senados da camera*), enjoyed a certain degree of self-government.

Portuguese **economic policy** was founded upon mercantilist theory. Commerce was a monopoly of Portugal until 1808 and trade was restricted to Lisbon and Oporto. In 1649 a monopolistic **Commercial Company of Brazil** was organized and greatly developed commerce. The **Maranhão Company,** also monopolistic, was formed in 1682. Both companies aroused opposition and were abolished in the first part of the 18th century. To foster commerce two chartered companies, one with a monopoly of the trade of Pará and Maranhão and the other with a monopoly of that of Pernambuco and Parahyba, were formed during the period of Pombal, but were abolished after his fall. Between 1548 and the formation of the Commercial Company of Brazil commerce was carried on through convoyed fleets. Discontinued during the existence of the company, the system was re-established upon its abolition and continued until finally abolished by Pombal.

Restrictions were placed upon **industry and agriculture** which competed with that of Portugal, and a government monopoly, which produced important crown revenues, existed for the exploitation of Brazil wood, mining of diamonds, and other activities. Customs duties were levied, and a royal fifth (*quinto*) of the product of mining activity was required. Agriculture and pastoral pursuits were highly developed. Cotton and sugar cane were the principal agricultural products. The cultivation of coffee was introduced. The mining of gold and diamonds (rich deposits of the latter were discovered in 1721), the gathering of Brazil wood, and the production of sugar and hides were the chief industries. Brazilian sugar production became the greatest in the world and was the basis of the wealth of the colony.

The Church and education. In 1676 Innocent XI created the **archbishopric of Brazil,** with Bahia as the metropolitan see, at the same time erecting the suffragan bishoprics of Rio de Janeiro and Pernambuco. At the close of the 18th century there were nine bishoprics, two of which were suffragan to the archbishop of Lisbon. The **Inquisition** was not introduced into Brazil. The **Jesuits,** until their expulsion, (1759) played an important rôle through conversion of the natives, extension of Portuguese influence, and establishment of schools and colleges, the earliest being that of São Paulo (1554). No institution of university status was created in Brazil during the colonial period, but seminaries and academies were established, among them the seminaries of São Pedro and São José at Rio de Janeiro (founded 1736).

(*Cont. p. 838.*)

F. NORTH AMERICA, 1500-1788

1. EXPLORATION AND SETTLEMENT

a. THE FRENCH IN NORTH AMERICA, 1500-1719

Norman and Breton fishermen visited Newfoundland coasts perhaps as early as 1500. There are unconfirmed reports of attempts to explore the Gulf of St. Lawrence in 1506 and 1508, and of an unsuccessful colony on Sable Island in 1518.

1524. **Giovanni de Verrazzano,** sent out by Francis I, probably explored the coast from Cape Fear to Newfoundland.

1534-1541. Voyages of **Jacques Cartier.** On the first voyage he sighted the Labrador coast, passed through the Straits of Belle Isle and explored the Gulf of St. Lawrence. On the second (1535-1536) he sailed up the St. Lawrence, stopped at the site of Quebec, proceeded to the La Chine Rapids and to the site of Montreal. On the third (1541) he was accompanied by M. de Roberval, a Picard nobleman, whom Francis I had made viceroy of Canada, Newfoundland, and Labrador. Unsuccessful attempts were made to establish a settlement at Quebec, and therewith the French efforts to colonize the St. Lawrence Valley came to an end until the 17th century.

In the south the activities of the French necessarily led to conflict with the Spaniards.

1562. Admiral Coligny, as part of his plan to attack Spain, sent **Jean Ribaut** to establish a colony in Florida. A colony on Port Royal Sound failed, but in 1564 Ribaut and **René de Laudonnière** established **Fort Caroline** on St. John's River. In the very next year the Spaniards, led by Menéndez de Avilés, massacred the French colonists and took the fort. Commanded by the Chevalier de Gourgues, the French (1567) avenged themselves by attacking the Spanish fort on the St. John's and putting the garrison to death.

1598. **Marquis de La Roche** attempted to found a colony on Sable Island. The survivors were rescued five years later.

1600. **Pontgravé, Chauvin,** and **De Monts,** with a grant of the fur-trade monopoly, made another unsuccessful attempt to colonize, this time at **Tadoussac** on the lower St. Lawrence.

1603. Pontgravé, accompanied by **Samuel de Champlain,** explored the St. Lawrence as far as La Chine Rapids. Champlain also explored the Acadian coast. In the next three years De Monts and Champlain organized a settlement on St. Croix Island, but moved later to **Port Royal.** Champlain followed the New England coast as far as Cape Cod, and returned to France in 1607.

1608, July 3. Champlain, acting as lieutenant for De Monts, founded the settlement of **Quebec.** In the following year, accompanied by a party of Algonquin and Huron Indians, he ascended the Richelieu River to the lake that now bears his name.

1610. Poutrincourt re-established Port Royal.

1613. Champlain explored the Ottawa River to about 100 miles above the present city of Ottawa. In 1615 he went up the river to Lake Nipissing and thence to Georgian Bay, being the first white man to blaze the fur-trader's route into the interior.

1615. Four **Recollet friars** arrived at Quebec, marking the beginning of French missionary activity. In 1625 five **Jesuits** arrived, beginning the work of that order.

1625-1664. French settlements in the West Indies. The first was St. Christopher (1625). The **Company of St. Christopher** was formed in 1626, to extend the settlement. This was superseded in 1635 by the **Company of Isles of America.** Guadeloupe, Martinique, and Tor-

tuga were occupied, and between 1648 and 1656 settlements were made on St. Martin, St. Bartholomew, St. Croix, The Saints, Maria Galante, St. Lucia, and Grenada.

1627. Richelieu organized the **Company of the Hundred Associates** to colonize New France. The company was given all lands between Florida and the Arctic Circle, with a monopoly of trade, except in cod and whale fisheries.

1628. Acadia and Quebec captured by the English, but restored in 1632.

1634. Champlain, hearing of a great waterway in the west and believing it might be a passage to China, sent **Jean Nicolet** on an exploring expedition. Nicolet reached Sault Ste. Marie, explored the south shore of the upper peninsula of Michigan, and reached the southern extremity of Green Bay.

1642. Paul de Maisonneuve founded Montreal.

1658-1659. Radisson and Groseillers traded and explored in the country at the western end of Lake Superior.

1665. Father Allouez established the La Pointe Mission near the west end of Lake Superior.

1673. Father **JACQUES MARQUETTE** and **LOUIS JOLIET,** a trader, followed the Fox and Wisconsin Rivers to the Mississippi, which they descended to the confluence of the Arkansas. In the same year **Count Louis de Frontenac,** governor of New France, founded Fort Frontenac on Lake Ontario.

1679-1683. Explorations of Robert de La Salle, along the shores of Lake Michigan and in the Illinois country. He erected **Fort Crèvecoeur** near present Peoria (1679) and sent Hennepin to explore the upper Mississippi while he himself returned to Fort Frontenac. In 1682 La Salle reached the mouth of the Mississippi and took possession of the whole valley in the name of the king of France.

1683-1689. Attempts of La Salle to establish a French colony at the mouth of the Mississippi, in order to control the fur trade and to provide a base for attack upon Spain in America. He left France with some 400 men in 1684 and reached the West Indies. Continuing his voyage he missed the mouth of the Mississippi and landed at Matagorda Bay, on the coast of Texas. In the meanwhile, **Tonty** had descended the Mississippi, but had failed to find La Salle (1686). La Salle conducted four expeditions to the northeast in the hope of finding the Mississippi. On the fourth of these (1687) he was murdered by his companions. His colony was completely wiped out by an Indian attack (1689).

1699-1702. To check the Spanish advance, to control the Gulf coast and to forestall possible English occupation of the lower Mississippi, French forces under **Pierre d'Iberville** estab-

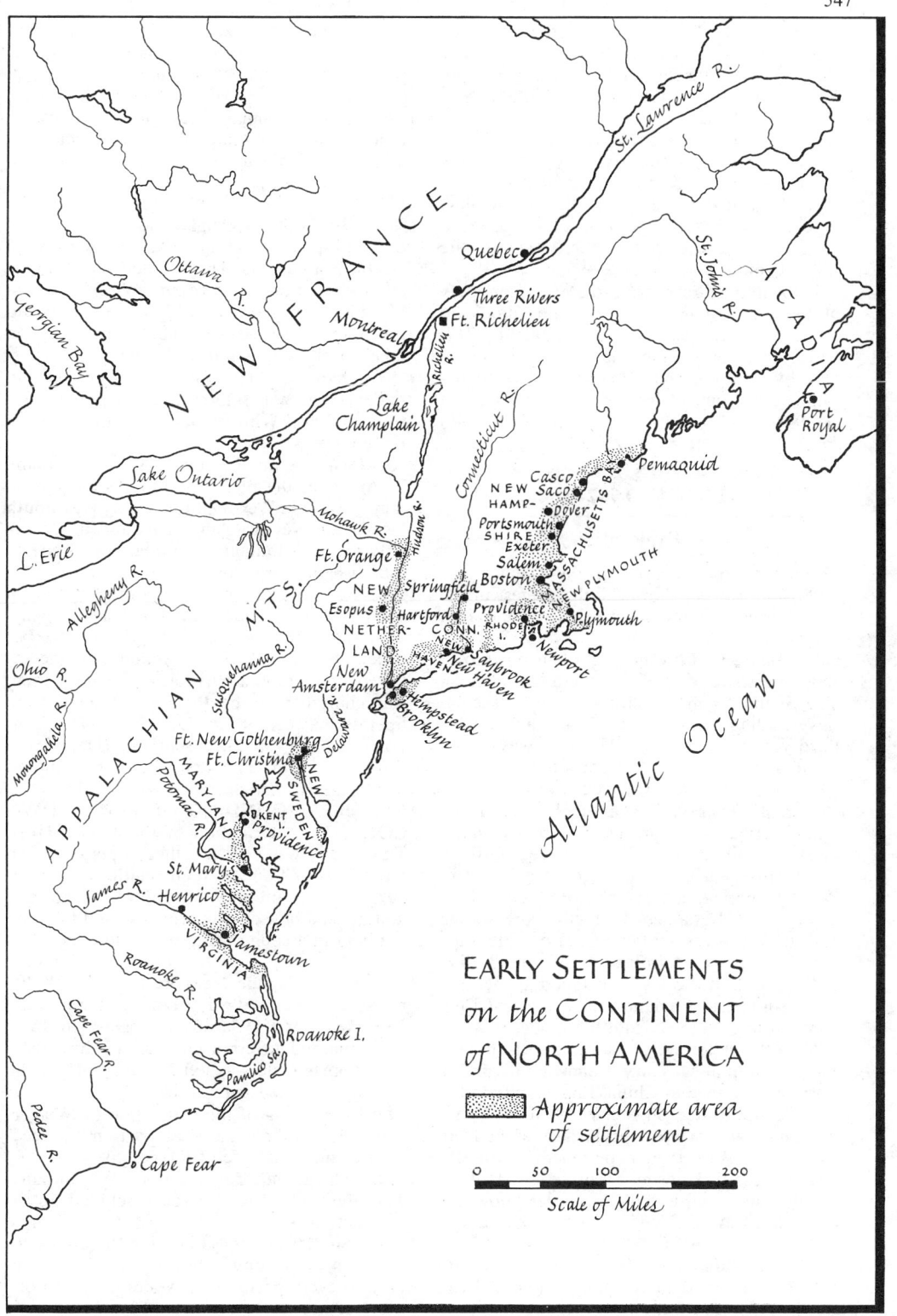

EARLY SETTLEMENTS
on the CONTINENT
of NORTH AMERICA

Approximate area
of settlement

0   50   100   200

Scale of Miles

lished posts at Biloxi and started the French colony in **Louisiana** (1699). The post was moved to Mobile Bay in 1702 and named St. Louis. **Mobile** was founded in 1710 and **New Orleans** in 1718.

1699. A Sulpician mission was set up at Cahokia in the Illinois country. In 1700 Jesuits moved down the Illinois River to Kaskaskia.

1701. **Detroit founded by Antoine de Cadillac,** to control the entrance from Lake Erie to Lake Huron and to control the trade with the Illinois country.

1712. **Antoine Crozat** was granted a monopoly of the trade in the territory from Illinois to the coast. Crozat surrendered his patent (1717) and Louisiana was in the same year taken over by the **Compagnie d'Occident,** which became the **Compagnie des Indes Orientales** (1719).   (*Cont. p. 554.*)

b. THE ENGLISH IN NORTH AMERICA, 1562–1640

(1) Exploration

Following the voyages of the **Cabots** (see p..390) the English showed little interest in the New World until the second half of the 16th century.

1562. **John Hawkins,** having taken a cargo of slaves in Africa, disposed of them in Española. The Spaniards made efforts to stop a second slave-trading voyage (1564–1565), and on his third voyage (1567–1568) Hawkins was driven by a storm into the harbor of Vera Cruz, where his fleet was largely destroyed.

1572–1580. **Francis Drake,** nephew of Hawkins, carried out reprisals on Spanish commerce. Sailing in 1577 he passed through the Straits of Magellan, up the west coast of South America, and north to Drake's Bay, California. He named the region **New Albion** and took possession for England. He then sailed to the East Indies, across the Indian Ocean, around the Cape of Good Hope, and thence home to England, being the first Englishman to circumnavigate the globe.

1576–1578. After unsuccessful efforts by explorers of the **Muscovy Company** to find a northeast passage to China, English efforts became concentrated on the search for a northwest passage. **Martin Frobisher** sailed from England in June 1576, explored the Labrador coast, crossed Hudson Strait, coasted along Baffin Land, and entered the inlet known as **Frobisher Bay.** In 1577–1578 he made a second voyage (p. 612).

1583. **Sir Humphrey Gilbert** took possession of Newfoundland in the name of Elizabeth, but lost his life on the return voyage.

1585. **John Davis** explored Davis Strait, but failed to find a northwest passage. A second attempt (1586) was equally unsuccessful (p. 612).

1586–1588. **Thomas Cavendish,** following Drake's course, plundered Spanish commerce and circumnavigated the globe.

(2) Virginia

1584. **Sir Walter Raleigh,** under patent, sent out Philip Amadas and Arthur Barlow to establish a colony. They landed on Roanoke Island and named the country **Virginia.** Supply ships were sent out in 1586, but they found the colony deserted, the colonists having been taken back to England by Drake.

1587. Another party of colonists was sent out, under Governor **John White.** Upon his return in 1591, White found only the ruins of the colony.

1602–1606. A number of voyages were made to America, the most important having been that of **George Weymouth** in 1604. Weymouth visited the New England coast and his favorable report did much to stimulate the desire to establish further colonies.

1606, Apr. A group of London men was given a charter to organize the **London Company,** with the object of colonizing the region between 34° and 41° N.L. Another group, composed of Plymouth, Bristol, and Exeter men, was chartered as the **Plymouth Company,** to operate between 38° and 45° N.L. The London Company at once sent out (Dec. 1606) three ships with 120 colonists, under command of Captain **Christopher Newport.**

1607, May. **FOUNDING OF JAMESTOWN COLONY** at the mouth of the James River. The colony was held together largely through the efforts of Captain **John Smith.**

1609. The London Company was enlarged and given a new charter which vested the government in a council with power to appoint its own officers.

1610, May. **Captain Newport** arrived with 400 more colonists and with **Lord Delaware,** the new governor. Delaware left again in 1611, but remained governor until his death in 1618. **Sir Thomas Dale** was left in command of the colony and ruled with an iron hand.

1612. Beginning of the **cultivation of tobacco,** which was to play a vital part in the economic and social life of the colony.

1612. Third charter of the London Company. The Bermuda Islands were included in its jurisdiction.

1618. **Sir Edwin Sandys** became the dominant figure in the colony. He assigned 50 acres of land to every person who would transport one more settler to the colony.

1619. Arrival of the first **Negro slaves** in the colony.

1619. Sir Thomas Yeardley arrived as governor, bringing instructions for each plantation to elect two burgesses to a general assembly. The assembly met at Jamestown on July 30 and was the **first representative assembly** in America.

1621. Sir Francis Wyatt, the governor, brought over new regulations providing for government through a governor, council of state, and assembly, the latter consisting of two burgesses each elected from every plantation and town.

1624. Revocation of the charter. This step was taken as a result of dissension within the company and because of the king's disapproval of popular government and of the raising of tobacco, as well as because of his desire to please the Spanish, who had protested against the founding of the colony. Virginia became a royal colony, with a governor and council appointed by the crown.

(3) New England

(a) Massachusetts

1606. Granting of the charter to the **Plymouth Company.** In this very year two unsuccessful attempts were made to found colonies. In 1607 settlers were landed at the mouth of the **Kennebec River,** but the enterprise was abandoned the next spring.

1614. Captain John Smith, of the Virginia settlement, explored the coast of New England and mapped it. He was made *Admiral of New England* by the Plymouth Company (1615) and made an abortive effort to start a colony. Several fishing and trading voyages were made to the New England coast between 1615 and 1620 under the direction of **Sir Ferdinando Gorges,** a member of the Plymouth Company.

1620, Nov. 13. The Council for New England. The Plymouth Company having failed to found a colony, Gorges and others secured the incorporation of the council, which was given jurisdiction between 40° and 48° N.L.

1620, Nov. ARRIVAL OF THE PILGRIMS at Cape Cod. The Pilgrims were a group of separatists who had migrated from Scrooby to Amsterdam and thence to Leyden in Holland. In 1617 they decided to seek a new home in order to preserve their English identity. They obtained a patent from the London Company and **John Carver** was made their governor. They left England in the *Mayflower* and reached Cape Cod, which they found to be outside the jurisdiction of the London Company. They therefore drew up the **May-**flower Compact,** by which they formed themselves into a body politic and agreed to enact laws for the welfare of the colony. The basis of government, then, was the will of the colonists rather than that of the crown. **Plymouth** was selected as the site of the settlement.

1621. William Bradford became governor on the death of Carver.

1623. Settlements at Portsmouth and Dover (New Hampshire) and at **Casco Bay** and **Saco Bay** (Maine) were made under the auspices of the Council for New England. A group of Dorchester merchants settled on Cape Ann (1624).

1628, Sept. John Endicott and some 50 colonists arrived at Salem, acting under a patent obtained by Rev. **John White** of Dorchester from the Council for New England. This patent ran for lands between the parallel three miles north of the source of the Merrimac River and that three miles south of the Charles River.

1629, Mar. ROYAL CHARTER issued confirming the grant to Endicott and his associates, which members of the Gorges family had protested. The new corporation was known as the **Governor and Company of Massachusetts Bay** in New England.

    June 27. Five ships, with some 400 settlers, arrived at Salem. **John Winthrop** and other prominent men meeting at Cambridge (England) agreed to emigrate to Massachusetts Bay, provided the charter and government might be legally transferred to America. The company decided to make the transfer and Winthrop was named governor.

1630. Seventeen ships brought about 1000 persons to the colony. By the end of the year settlements had been made at Dorchester, Boston, Watertown, Roxbury, Mystic, and Lynn. The first **general court** of the colony was held at Boston (Oct. 19). From then on no person was to be admitted as a freeman of the corporation unless a member of some church within the colony. In 1634 a representative system was introduced into the general court, because the growth of the colony prevented attendance of all freemen.

1630-1642. The **Great Migration** to Massachusetts Bay Colony. During these years some 16,000 settlers arrived from England.

1635. The coast of New England was reapportioned. **Gorges** received the land in Maine between the Penobscot and Piscataqua Rivers; **John Mason** received New Hampshire and northern Massachusetts as far as Cape Ann; **Edward Gorges** from Cape Ann to Narragansett Bay. In this same year the Council for New England gave up its charter and the king demanded also the charter of the Massachusetts

Bay Colony, because of Archbishop Laud's dislike of the Puritan Commonwealth. The king was unsuccessful.

1636. The general court voted £400 toward the founding of a college. In 1638 **John Harvard** bequeathed to the college £780 and 260 books. The institution was named **Harvard College** in 1639.

(b) Connecticut and Rhode Island

1631. The **earl of Warwick,** to whom the Council for New England had granted much of the Connecticut River Valley, transferred his rights to William Fiennes, **Lord Saye and Sele.**

1633. The **Dutch,** who had explored the coast, erected a fort on the river near the present **Hartford.**

1635. Lord Saye, with his associates, sent out settlers under John Winthrop, Jr., who established **Fort Saybrook,** at the mouth of the river. In the same year settlers from Dorchester (Massachusetts), seeking better land, established themselves at Windsor. In 1636 Rev. **Thomas Hooker** led Cambridge settlers to Hartford, while other colonists from Watertown settled at **Wethersfield.**

1638. Rev. **John Davenport** and **Theophilus Eaton** founded a theocratic colony at **New Haven.**

1639. Hartford, Windsor, and Wethersfield drew up **Fundamental Orders,** which provided that the governor and assistants, with four representatives from each town, should constitute the general court. These three settlements were commonly referred to as **Connecticut.**

Meanwhile **Roger Williams** had arrived at Boston, from England (1631). After spending some time at Salem, he repaired to Plymouth, where he concluded that the land rightfully belonged to the Indians and that the king had no right to grant it. He returned to Salem, where he argued that the Church and the State should be separated. He denied the right of the magistrate to control the churches, and objected to enforced oaths, since they obliged wicked men to perform a religious act, thereby destroying the freedom of the soul. In October 1635 he was banished from Salem.

1636, June. ROGER WILLIAMS SETTLED AT PROVIDENCE, where he organized a government democratic in character, with separation of Church and State.

1638. Mrs. Anne Hutchinson, the center of a controversy which shook Massachusetts Bay Colony to its foundations, was banished and took refuge on the island of Aquidneck, later called **Rhode Island,** where she and a small group of associates founded the settlement of **Portsmouth.** The following year another settlement was made at **Newport.**

(4) Maryland

George Calvert (later Lord Baltimore) had bought the southeastern peninsula of Newfoundland from **Sir William Vaughan** (1620) and had secured a charter (1623) for a colony, which he called **Avalon.** He visited Newfoundland in 1627 and resolved to abandon the colony because of the unfavorable climate. He then asked for a grant in Virginia, which was made in 1632, despite opposition from the Virginians.

1632, Apr. The charter of the new colony was drawn up in the name of Cecilius Calvert, George Calvert having died. The province was named **Maryland,** and Calvert, as proprietor, was given the right to collect taxes, make grants of land, create manors, appoint ministers, and found churches according to the laws of England. As the charter did not forbid the establishment of other churches than the Protestant, Baltimore (Calvert) made use of it to help his co-religionists, the Catholics.

1633, Oct. Baltimore dispatched to Maryland two vessels with some 20 gentlemen, mostly Catholics, and about 200 laborers, chiefly Protestants. Arriving at the mouth of the Potomac (1634, Mar.), they founded the settlement of **St. Mary's.**

(5) Island Settlements

1609. A Virginia supply ship, under command of **Sir George Somers,** was wrecked on one of the Bermuda Islands. On his return to England Somers interested a number of persons, mostly members of the Virginia Company, in the islands, with the result that the **Somers Islands Company** was formed (1612) for the colonization of Bermuda. The island had 600 settlers in 1614 and between 2000 and 3000 in 1625. It became an important producer of tobacco.

1625. St. Christopher was settled, and **Sir William Courten** established the first colony on Barbados. Nevis was occupied by the British in 1628, and settlements were made on Antigua and Montserrat in 1632. By 1640 the island possessions of England had a population of 20,000, devoted chiefly to the cultivation of sugar, which soon supplanted tobacco as the leading crop. (*Cont. p. 551.*)

c. DUTCH AND SWEDISH SETTLEMENTS, 1602-1655

1602. The **United East India Company** was chartered by the states-general of Holland.

1609. The company employed **Henry Hudson,** an Englishman, to search for the northwest passage. He sighted land at Newfoundland, explored the New England coast, rounded Cape Cod, proceeded south to Virginia, probably entered Chesapeake Bay, entered Delaware Bay, and explored the **Hudson River** to Albany. Friendly relations with Iroquois Indians.

1612. Dutch merchants sent **Christianson and Block** to Manhattan Island to engage in fur trade. A post was established in 1613.

1614. Fort Nassau, later Fort Orange, built near present Albany. Exploration by Adrian Block of Long Island Sound, Connecticut coast, Narragansett Bay, and Cape Cod. As a result the **New Netherland Company** was formed and given monopoly of trade between the 40th and 45th parallels. Fur trade carried on and the coast explored.

1621. The **Dutch West India Company** was chartered and given a monopoly of trade in Africa and America.

1626. **Peter Minuit** became director-general of the company. He purchased **Manhattan Island** from the Indians for 24 dollars and founded the settlement of **New Amsterdam.** The company also made settlements in Con-

necticut, New Jersey, Delaware, and Pennsylvania. Men, known as *patroons,* were given large areas of land on condition that they bring over a stipulated number of settlers. The Dutch, under Governor Kieft of New Netherland, protested in vain against the founding of New Haven.

Meanwhile the attention of Gustavus Adolphus of Sweden was called to the Delaware country by **William Usselincx,** who had withdrawn from the Dutch West India Company. Usselincx received a charter for the **South Company** which came to naught. In 1633 the **New South Company** was organized, but it too failed to achieve anything. In 1637 the **New Sweden Company** was organized, chiefly as a result of the encouragement of two Dutchmen, Samuel Blommaert and Peter Minuit.

1638. Two Swedish vessels arrived on the Delaware and **Fort Christina** was established. This intrusion of the Swedes angered **Peter Stuyvesant** of New Netherland, who urged the West India Company to occupy New Sweden, which was done in 1655.

2. COLONIAL HISTORY

a. NEW ENGLAND, 1641–1728

1641. The **Body of Liberties,** a code of 100 laws, was established by the general court of the Massachusetts Bay Colony.

1643, May 19. The **New England Confederation** was formed by Connecticut (Hartford, Windsor, and Wethersfield), New Haven, Plymouth, and Massachusetts Bay for purposes of defense.

1644. Union of Providence and the Rhode Island towns (Newport and Portsmouth) under a charter obtained by Roger Williams. Union of Saybrook and Connecticut under the latter name.

1646. In Massachusetts, **John Eliot** began his missionary work among the Indians, translating the Bible into Massachusetts dialect, 1661–1663.

1649. Incorporation in England of the **Society for Propagating the Gospel in New England.**

1653. Settlements in southern Maine accepted the jurisdiction of Massachusetts.

1662. Charter of Connecticut granted by the king. Assembly composed of the governor, deputy-governor, 12 assistants, and two deputies from each town.

1663. Charter of Rhode Island and Providence Plantations, kept throughout the colonial period and the constitution of the state until 1842.

1664. Union of Connecticut and New Haven, because of the latter's fear of annexation to New York.

1665. Maine was restored to the heirs of Sir Ferdinando Gorges.

Royal commissioners, after an unsuccessful attempt to hear complaints in New England, left the provinces.

1668. Massachusetts reassumed the government of Maine.

1675–1676. KING PHILIP'S WAR in New England. Although primarily due to the advance of the frontier of settlement upon the Indian hunting grounds, there were numerous minor infractions of the law. Christianizing of Cape Cod Indians by John Eliot aroused the suspicions of the Wampanoags, who saw in it an attempt to weaken their power. **Philip,** son of **Massasoit,** chief of the Wampanoags, formed a league comprising most of the Indians from Maine to Connecticut. Border attacks were followed by the white attack upon the stronghold of the Narragansetts near Kingston, Rhode Island, in December 1675, with heavy losses to the Indians. Deerfield was attacked by Indians and most of the houses were burned. During the war 500 white men were captured or killed and nearly 40 towns damaged, 20 being destroyed or abandoned. Chief Canonchet of the Narragansetts was shot (Apr. 1676) and the war came to a close with the death of Philip (Aug. 1676).

1677. The dispute between Massachusetts and the heirs of Sir Ferdinando Gorges regarding Maine having been decided in favor of the latter by the English courts, Massachusetts bought all of the province except that granted to the duke of York.

1680. New Hampshire was separated from Massachusetts by royal charter.

1684. ANNULMENT OF THE MASSACHU-SETTS CHARTER. The independent course of Massachusetts had long irritated the crown. The heirs of Mason and Gorges charged that Massachusetts has usurped their rights. London merchants claimed the colony evaded the navigation acts by sending tobacco and sugar directly to Europe. Lack of respect for the king's authority and the exercise of powers not warranted by the charter were also charged. In 1679 **Edward Randolph** arrived in Boston as collector of the customs, bearing instructions for the colony to relinquish jurisdiction over New Hampshire and Maine, the latter of which was disregarded. Friction continued, as did Randolph's complaints against the colony, until legal action in 1684 resulted in the annulment of the charter.

1686. DOMINION OF NEW ENGLAND formed through consolidation of the New England colonies. **Sir Edmund Andros** was made governor. *Quo warranto* proceedings were instituted against Connecticut and Carolina. Andros arrived in Boston (Dec. 20) and assumed the government of Plymouth and Rhode Island. In 1687 he assumed the government of Connecticut and demanded the charter, which Captain William Wadsworth concealed in a hollow tree, the famous *Charter Oak.*

1689. Upon news of the flight of James II from England, the people of Boston rose in revolt, imprisoned Andros and restored charter government. Similar action was taken in Rhode Island and Connecticut.

1691. New charter for Massachusetts, which included Plymouth, Maine, Nova Scotia, and all land north to the St. Lawrence. A governor, to be appointed by the crown, was vested with the power of calling and dissolving the general court, appointing military and judicial officers, and vetoing acts of legislature. The electoral franchise was extended and religious liberty secured to all except Catholics. **Sir William Phips** was made governor.

1692. Salem witchcraft trials.

1701. Founding of Yale College, New Haven, Connecticut.

1728. William Burnet, governor of Massachusetts, became involved in a quarrel with the legislature over the question of a fixed salary

for the governor, which the court refused to grant "because it is the undoubted right of all Englishmen, by Magna Carta, to raise and dispose of money for the public service, of their own accord, without compulsion."

Death of **Cotton Mather,** (b. 1663), prolific author of Puritan tracts. More liberal were the writings of a later divine, **Jonathan Edwards** (1703–1758).

b. NEW YORK, NEW JERSEY, PENNSYLVANIA, 1664–1735

1664. Grant of New Netherland, from the Connecticut to the Delaware, to the king's brother, **James, duke of York.** The grant included the eastern part of Maine and islands south and west of Cape Cod. The region between the Hudson and the Delaware was granted by the duke of York to **Lord Berkeley** and **Sir George Carteret.**

1664, Aug. 27. SURRENDER OF NEW AMSTERDAM to the English. Name of the colony changed to **New York.** On September 24 surrender of Fort Orange, whose name was changed to **Albany.**

1673. In the war between England and Holland, the **Dutch captured New York** and established temporary control over Albany and New Jersey. These places were restored when peace was made in 1674.

1676. Line of demarcation between East and West New Jersey. **Settlement of Quakers** in West New Jersey (1677–1681).

1681, Mar. 4. CHARTER OF PENNSYLVANIA signed, granting to **William Penn** the region between 40° and 43°, extending 5° west from the Delaware River. These limits brought the colony into conflict with New York on the north and Maryland on the south. The dispute with Maryland was finally adjusted when in 1767 two surveyors, **Mason and Dixon,** ran the present boundary between the two states. The form of government of the colony was to be determined by the proprietor. The first body of colonists arrived in 1681 and a frame of government was provided for the government of the colony.

1682–1683. Penn arrived in the colony and **Philadelphia** was laid out (1682). Penn entered into a treaty with the Indians (1683) which had the effect of keeping the colony free from Indian wars.

1683. In response to persistent demands of the people, the duke of York conceded a legislative assembly to New York. In October, 17 representatives drew up a **Charter of Franchises and Liberties,** which the duke signed, only to reject it when he became king.

1688. The **Lords of Trade** determined to bring

New York and New Jersey under the government of Andros. In 1689 New York proclaimed William and Mary.

1702. New Jersey reunited as a royal province.

1715-1750. SETTLEMENT OF THE PIEDMONT, partly by newcomers and old settlers, who crossed the fall line into the areas, partly by Germans, Swiss, and Scotch-Irish entering at the port of Philadelphia and pushing southward through the valleys, especially the Shenandoah. **German immigration,** which began with the founding of Germantown, Pennsylvania (1683), increased greatly in volume after 1710. Occupation of the piedmont resulted in the formation of a restless, aggressive frontier society which was to become increasingly important.

1720-1726. William Burnet, governor of New York, began efforts to counteract French attempts to hem in the English colonies in the west. He prohibited trade between the Iroquois and the French. In 1722 he established a trading post at **Oswego** and carried on negotiations at Albany with the Six Nations. A treaty with the Senecas, Cayugas, and Onondagas (1726) added their lands to those of the Mohawks and Oneidas, which were already under English protection.

1732. Benjamin Franklin (1706–1790), journalist as well as statesman, published *Poor Richard's Almanac.*

1735. Trial in New York of **John Peter Zenger,** printer of a paper, for libel. The court contended that it should decide the libelous nature of the statements made, and that the jury should determine the fact of publication. Zenger's lawyer, Andrew Hamilton, argued that the jury must decide whether or not the publication was libelous. He won his suit, thereby materially safeguarding the freedom of the press.

c. VIRGINIA, DELAWARE, AND MARYLAND, 1652-1716

1652. Parliament assumed control of Maryland and suspended the governor.

1659. Virginia proclaimed Charles II king of England, Scotland, and Ireland, and restored the royal governor, **Sir William Berkeley.**

1662. Lord Baltimore was confirmed in the government of Maryland.

1676. Bacon's Rebellion in Virginia. Led by Nathaniel Bacon, this revolt was largely the result of the indifference of Governor Berkeley to the problem of frontier defense against the Indians. Jamestown was burned, but the rebellion collapsed with the death of Bacon.

1689. Virginia and Maryland proclaimed William and Mary.

1693. College of William and Mary founded in Virginia.

1716. Governor Alexander Spotswood of Virginia led an expedition to the Blue Ridge, and into the Shenandoah Valley. He recommended the securing of the mountain passes and the establishment of settlements on Lake Erie.

d. THE SOUTHERN COLONIES, 1663-1737

1663. Grant of Carolina by the king to eight proprietors, including the earl of Clarendon. The grant included land between 31° and 36° N.L. After Raleigh's unsuccessful effort, the region between Virginia and the Spanish settlements in Florida had received little attention until the grant of the region to Sir Robert Heath (1629), which also came to naught.

1667. Grant of the Bahamas to the Carolina proprietors.

1669. Adoption of the Fundamental Constitutions, drawn up for Carolina by John Locke, which provided for an archaic feudal régime totally unsuited to the needs of a frontier colony.

1711. Tuscarora War in North Carolina. The Tuscaroras massacred some 200 settlers. Virginia and South Carolina sent aid and the Indians were defeated (1712). Remnants of the Tuscaroras moved to New York and were incorporated in the Iroquois as a sixth nation.

1715. Defeat of the Yamassees and allied Indian tribes in Carolina. They were driven across the Spanish border into Florida.

1719-1729. REORGANIZATION OF THE CAROLINAS. Economic differences between the northern and southern portions of Carolina had resulted in governmental differentiation. The governor was located at Charleston with a deputy governor in the north. In 1713 the proprietors appointed **Charles Eden** governor of North Carolina and from this time the provinces were virtually separate. Popular discontent with the proprietors because of their indifference to defense against Indians and pirates. The situation was aggravated by refusal of the proprietors to allow the distribution of the Yamassee lands. Meanwhile the proprietors had incurred the ill-will of the British government. Their incompetence in the Yamassee War was the last straw which convinced the Board of Trade that a change was necessary. It upheld the people against the proprietors and in 1729 an act of parliament established royal governments in both North and South Carolina.

1733. FOUNDING OF GEORGIA, the last of the 13 English colonies on the continent. In the triangle between the Carolinas, Florida, and Louisiana, British, French, and Spanish claims conflicted. The international boundaries had never been defined. In 1716 the Carolinians had established a fort on the Savannah River and from 1721 to 1727 had maintained **Fort George** on the Altamaha. In 1730 **Sir Alexander Cuming** was sent on a mission to the Cherokees which resulted in their acknowledgement of British supremacy. The need of a buffer colony on the southern boundary had long been realized by the British. In 1717 **Sir Robert Montgomery** had secured from the Carolina proprietors a grant of the land between the Savannah and Altamaha Rivers, known as the **margravate of Azilia.** Plans for its settlement proving unsuccessful, **James**

Oglethorpe became interested in the settlement of the region. An advocate of a strong policy against the Spanish and a humanitarian interested in improving the condition of imprisoned debtors, he conceived the idea of a barrier colony. In 1732 he secured a charter, granting to him and his associates the region between the Savannah and the Altamaha from sea to sea. Proprietary government was to prevail for 21 years, when the colony was to become a royal province. Religious liberty was guaranteed to all except Catholics. Colonists left England in the autumn of 1732, arriving at Charleston in January 1733. The town of **Savannah** was immediately laid out; and in 1737 a fort was established at **Augusta.**

3. WARS OF ENGLAND WITH FRANCE AND SPAIN, 1651-1775

1651-1673. The British Navigation Laws. These applied mercantilist doctrine to colonial trade. The **Act of 1651,** designed to strike a blow at Dutch shipping, required that colonial products be shipped to England in ships of Great Britian or the Plantations. This law was re-enacted in 1660, with the additional provision that certain enumerated articles of colonial production could be shipped only to England. The **Staple Act** of 1663 required that articles of European production destined for the colonies must be shipped first to England. The **Act of 1673** imposed intercolonial duties on sugar, tobacco, and other products.

1667. Treaty of Breda between England and France. Antigua, Montserrat, and the French port of St. Christopher surrendered to England

1670. The Hudson's Bay Company incorporated and given a monopoly of the trade in Hudson's Bay Basin.

1689-1697. KING WILLIAM'S WAR, with France. This was the American phase of the general war against Louis XIV known as the **War of the League of Augsburg** (see p. 480). The French were aided by the Indians of Canada and Maine, while the Iroquois supported the English. In 1690 the French and Indians massacred colonists at Schenectady, Salmon Falls, and Casco Bay. An English force under **Sir William Phips** captured Port Royal (1690, May 11), but a Massachusetts expedition against Quebec, led by Phips, resulted in failure. The **treaty of Ryswick** restored all conquests (1697).

1696-1698. Renewed efforts of the English government to control colonial trade. A **Board of Commissioners for Trade and Plantations** was organized (1696) and a navigation act of the same year was designed to prevent further evasion of earlier regulations. Since the war with France had interrupted the usual trade, the New Englanders had taken up manufacturing. The **Woolens Act** (1698) forbade the colonists to ship wool or woolen products from one colony to another.

1702-1713. QUEEN ANNE'S WAR, the American phase of the **War of the Spanish Succession** (see p. 481). In 1702 the English plundered and burned St. Augustine in Florida, while in 1704 the French and Indians surprised Deerfield in the Connecticut Valley. Their attacks soon spread over much of the frontier and even to the outskirts of Boston. In 1707 the English organized an **expedition against Acadia.** Troops from New England laid siege to Port Royal, but failed to reduce it. The French province was, however, conquered in 1710, when 4000 colonists under **Francis Nicholson,** aided by British ships and a regiment of marines, attacked and captured Port Royal. Acadia then became the British province of **Nova Scotia** and the name of Port Royal was changed to **Annapolis Royal.** For the year 1711 a joint land and sea campaign against Canada was planned. Nicholson's colonials and Iroquois were to attack Montreal, while an expedition was to be led against Quebec by Admiral Sir Hovenden Walker and General Sir John Hill. Seven of Marlborough's best regiments were included. The force gathered at Boston, where it was reinforced by 1500 colonials. In August the fleet entered the St. Lawrence, but the destruction of ten ships compelled the abandonment of the attack. News of this reached Nicholson and induced him to give up the campaign against Montreal. By the **treaty of Utrecht** (1713) Great Britain secured recognition of its claims in the Hudson's Bay country and the possession of Newfoundland and Acadia. The claim of the British to the Iroquois country was also admitted, and St. Christopher was ceded to Britain. The French were excluded from fishing on the Acadian coast, but were allowed to retain Cape Breton Island. The *asiento* gave the English the exclusive right for 30 years of bringing Negroes into the Spanish possessions.

1733. The Molasses Act. The increased production of sugar in the French and Dutch West Indies after 1715, the disposition of the English colonists on the mainland (especially the New Englanders) to take advantage of the low prices of sugar, molasses, and rum in the foreign islands, and their desire to avail themselves of the market afforded for their own products in the islands contributed to bring about a severe depression among the sugar planters of the British island possessions. In response to pleas from the West Indian planters, parliament enacted the Molasses Act, which placed prohibitive duties on sugar and molasses imported into the colonies from other than British possessions. In 1732 parliament had stopped the importation of hats from the colonies and had restricted their manufacture. This was in accord with the mercantilist policy of encouraging the production of raw materials (including furs) and of discouraging manufactures that would conflict with those of the mother country.

1739. WAR BETWEEN SPAIN AND ENGLAND (War of Jenkins' Ear, see p. 470). Dissatisfied with the provisions of the treaty of Utrecht with respect to trade with Spanish possessions, British merchants had resorted to extensive smuggling, which, in turn, had led to the seizure of British ships and the rough treatment of British sailors by the Spaniards. The loss of Jenkins' ear was merely one of many similar episodes. In the course of the ensuing war the British captured Porto Bello and demolished its fortifications (1739). In 1740 they bombarded Cartagena and captured Chagres, while Oglethorpe led an expedition of Georgia, Carolina, and Virginia troops into Florida and made an unsuccessful attack on St. Augustine. The British were likewise unsuccessful in an attack on Santiago (Cuba) in 1741. In the next year they planned, but then abandoned, an attack on Panama. The Spanish attacked Georgia (1742), but soon withdrew again to Florida. In 1743 Oglethorpe once more invaded Florida, but failed to take St. Augustine.

1743-1748. KING GEORGE'S WAR, the American phase of the **War of the Austrian Succession** in Europe (see p. 501). The outstanding event in the war in America was the **capture of Louisburg** (1745). The French had made the fortress one of the strongest in the New World. After an invasion of Nova Scotia by the French, Governor William Shirley of Massachusetts assembled volunteers from Massachusetts, New Hampshire, and Connecticut and placed them under the command of **William Pepperell.** Transports were supplied by the colonies, while warships were provided by the British navy. The expedition appeared before Louisburg on April 30 and the fortress capitulated after a siege (June 16). An attempt of the French to recover Cape Breton and Nova Scotia was made in 1746, but was doomed to failure when a storm destroyed the fleet off the coast. In the interior an abortive attempt of the northern colonies to conquer Canada spurred the French and Indians to attack the frontier as far south as New York (1746-1748). The New York and Pennsylvania frontiers were protected by **Sir William Johnson,** British superintendent of the Six Nations, who kept the Mohawks friendly, and by **Conrad Weiser,** whose support of the Iroquois land claims as against the Delawares kept the Six Nations on the English side. At sea the British twice defeated the French in the West Indies (1745, 1747) and in 1748 the British admiral, Sir Charles Knowles, captured Port Louis on the southern coast of Haiti, bombarded Santiago, and attacked the Spanish fleet off Havana.

1748. The **treaty of Aix-la-Chapelle,** based upon European rather than colonial considerations, restored all the conquests of the war. In America the treaty was merely a truce, for Nova Scotia, the Ohio Valley, and the Cherokee country continued to be areas of conflict. In order to strengthen the British hold on Nova Scotia, Lord Halifax sent out 2500 settlers in 1749 and founded the town of **Halifax.** In the Ohio Valley traders from Virginia and Pennsylvania pushed westward as far as the Indian villages on the Mississippi. Virginia frontiersmen made a settlement at **Draper's Meadow** on the Greenbrier River in 1748.

1749. The **Ohio Company,** organized by a group of Virginians and a number of prominent Englishmen. The company obtained a grant of 500,000 acres on the upper Ohio and sent out **Christopher Gist** (1750) to explore the region as far as the falls of the Ohio. His favorable report led to the erection of a trading house at **Wills's Creek,** the present Cumberland (Maryland), and to the blazing of a trail to the junction of Redstone Creek and the Monongahela River. This activity roused the French to action. In an effort to detach the Iroquois from the British they founded the mission at present-day **Ogdensburg** (1748). To divert trade from Oswego they established **Fort Rouillé** on the site of present-day **Toronto** (1749). Another post was located at **Niagara** portage, **Detroit** was strengthened, and in 1749 the governor of Canada sent **Céloron de Blainville** to take possession of the Ohio Valley.

1753. **Marquis Duquesne** sent an expedition of 1500 men to occupy the Ohio country. **Fort Presqu'Isle** was erected and a road was cut to French Creek, where **Fort Le Boeuf** was built. It was planned to establish another fort at the forks of the Ohio. In the same year Governor Robert Dinwiddie of Virginia sent out **George Washington,** a young surveyor, to demand the withdrawal of the French. He proceeded to Fort Le Boeuf, but was told that Dinwiddie's letter would be forwarded to Duquesne. It was quite clear that the French would not leave the valley peacefully.

1754. Virginia troops dispatched to the Ohio, with Washington second in command. The French had, in the meanwhile, built **Fort Duquesne** at the forks of the Ohio. Washington pushed on to Great Meadows where he constructed **Fort Necessity.** He was attacked by the French and forced to surrender.

1754, June 19. The Albany Convention. The advance of the French had shown the need for a common plan of defense. Representatives of New York, Pennsylvania, Maryland, and the New England states met with the Six Nations. Upon the suggestion of **Benjamin Franklin,** the convention drew up a plan of union which was, however, rejected by the colonies. The plan called for union under a president appointed by the crown, with a grand council of delegates elected by the colonial assemblies, this body to have legislative power subject to approval by the president and the crown.

1755-1763. The **FRENCH AND INDIAN WAR,** the American phase of the **Seven Years' War** in Europe (see p. 503). In 1755 the governors of Virginia, North Carolina, Pennsylvania, Maryland, New York, and Massachusetts met in conference at Alexandria (Virginia) with **General Edward Braddock,** the British commander, recently arrived. They planned a fourfold attack on the French: upon Fort Duquesne, Niagara, Crown Point, and Fort Beauséjour. Braddock led the expedition into the Ohio country, but was surrounded and defeated near **Fort Duquesne** (July 9). In the

Crown Point campaign the French were defeated in the **battle of Lake George** (Sept. 8), but the British made no attempt to capture Crown Point itself. They built **Fort William Henry** at the southern end of Lake George, while the French fortified **Ticonderoga.** In 1756 war was formally declared between France and Great Britain. **Lord John Loudoun** was named commander-in-chief of the British forces in America. The French were commanded by **Marquis Louis de Montcalm,** who took and destroyed Forts Oswego and George (Aug.) and in 1757 took Fort William Henry (Aug. 9). The garrison, whose retreat to Fort Edward had been guaranteed by Montcalm, was massacred by his Indian allies.

The resistance of the British was weakened by the friction between Loudoun and the Massachusetts general court over quartering of troops, and between the governor and assembly of Virginia over various matters of taxation. In 1758 (July 8) General James Abercromby was defeated before Ticonderoga, but General Jeffrey Amherst and General James Wolfe took Louisburg (July 26), Bradstreet took Fort Frontenac (Aug. 27) and Forbes took Fort Duquesne (Nov. 25).

For the year 1759 the English planned four campaigns: against Niagara, against settlements on Lake Erie, against Ticonderoga and Crown Point, and against Quebec. The **battle of the Plains of Abraham** (Quebec) was fought on September 13, both Wolfe and Montcalm losing their lives. Quebec surrendered to the British on September 18. On September 8, 1760 Montreal surrendered and all Canada passed into the hands of the British. In 1762 **Admiral George Rodney** forced the surrender of Martinique, Grenada, St. Lucia, St. Vincent, and the other French West Indies.

1763, Feb. 10. The **TREATY OF PARIS,** between Great Britain, France, Spain, and Portugal. France ceded to Britain all claim to Acadia, Canada, Cape Breton, and all that part of Louisiana situated east of the Mississippi except the Island of Orleans. France retained certain fishing rights on the Newfoundland Banks and was given the islands of St. Pierre and Miquelon. Britain restored to France the islands of Guadeloupe, Martinique, Belle Isle, Maria Galante, and St. Lucia. Britain restored Havana to Spain, in return for which Spain ceded Florida to Britain. France, by a previous treaty (1762, Nov. 3) had ceded to Spain all French territory west of the Mississippi and the Island of Orleans, as compensation for the loss of Florida to Britain.

1763. The Conspiracy of Pontiac. This was an aftermath to the war. Indian tribes north of the Ohio, fearing eviction by the British, embittered by the arrogance and dishonesty of British traders, and disappointed by the economy of General Amherst in the matter of presents, were ready to revolt against British occupation of the posts recently held by the French. Pontiac, chief of the Ottawas, organized a rising of the Algonquins, of some of the Iroquois, and of tribes on the lower Mississippi. In a simultaneous attack all but three of the northwestern posts fell in May. By 1765, however, the British forces were in possession of the last of the French posts in the west.

1763, Oct. 7. Proclamation of 1763, issued by George III. It created four distinct provinces from the recent conquests: Quebec, East Florida, West Florida, and Grenada. It also temporarily closed to white settlement all lands west and north of the streams flowing into the Atlantic Ocean. Fur trade in this Indian reserve was opened to licensed subjects. In 1764 **Lord Hillsborough** drew up a plan for the management of the Indians and the fur trade. It continued the northern and southern departments for Indian affairs (created in 1755) and provided that in the north all trade must be conducted at regularly established posts and in the south at the Indian towns.

1763–1775. Expansion beyond the mountains. Numerous colonies had been planned by land companies before 1763. With these the Proclamation of 1763 interfered. In 1768, however, a plan for the gradual and controlled establishment of colonies in the west was worked out. In that year treaties with the Creeks, Cherokees, and Iroquois extinguished Indian rights to large areas. A group of Pennsylvanians, including Franklin, organized the **Vandalia Company** for the establishment of a colony in what is now West Virginia. Purchase of land was made in 1769 and by 1775 the proposed colony of Vandalia had been approved by the king and council. The outbreak of the Revolution rendered the plan abortive.

The **Watauga settlement** in eastern Tennessee was made in 1769 and was augmented by the arrival of Virginians and North Carolinians under **James Robertson** and **John Sevier** (1770–1771). Finding themselves beyond the pale of organized law, the settlers, proceeding on the compact theory, formed the **Watauga Association** (1772), organized as Washington County (North Carolina) in 1777.

Richard Henderson, of North Carolina, together with his associates, organized the **Transylvania Company,** purchased land from the Cherokees, and established the Transylvania settlement in Kentucky in 1775. **Daniel Boone** was Henderson's agent and cleared the wilderness road to Kentucky. The **settlement of Kentucky** (1775–1777) was facilitated by the peace forced on the Indians as a result of **Lord Dunmore's War** (1774).

4. THE AMERICAN REVOLUTION, 1763–1788

1763–1775. The Preliminaries of the American Revolution. By 1761 the British government was thoroughly aroused by the systematic evasion of the **Molasses Act** of 1733 through colonial smuggling, and by the illicit trade which the colonies had carried on with the enemy during the War of the Austrian Succession and the Seven Years' War. British officials felt that the trade prolonged French resistance. To prevent smuggling, the British resorted to **writs of assistance,** general search warrants, which made possible the search of all premises where smuggled goods might be found. This aroused the opposition of merchants who alleged the writs were illegal. In 1761, when Boston customs officers applied for the writs, the merchants contested their use. **James Otis** argued cogently against their legality before the Massachusetts supreme court. Although the court decided they were legal, the argument of Otis did much to shape public opinion.

1763. The **Parsons' Cause,** argued in Virginia by **Patrick Henry,** still further aroused and molded public opinion against British policy, in this instance the disallowance of a Virginia statute.

1763–1765. George Grenville in power in England. The acquisition of the vast territory from France in America necessitated increased revenues for defense and Indian administration. The ministry decided to enforce the navigation laws, tax the colonies directly, and use the revenue to maintain an army in America. Powers of the admiralty courts were enlarged, and colonial governors were instructed to enforce the trade laws.

1764. Enactment of the **Sugar Act,** with the avowed purpose of raising revenue in the colonies and reforming the old colonial system, both economically and administratively.

The **Colonial Currency Act** prevented colonies from paying their debts in England in depreciated currency and forbade issues of unsound money. This act created a shortage of money in the colonies at a time when the

Sugar Act injured the West Indian trade of the colonies, which had previously supplied the necessary specie.

1765. Disregarding colonial protests against the two previous acts, Grenville pushed through parliament the **Stamp Act,** providing for stamps on commercial and legal documents, pamphlets, newspapers, almanacs, playing cards, and dice.

The **Quartering Act** was passed, providing that, in the event of insufficiency of barracks in the colonies, British troops might be quartered in public hostelries.

May 29. Patrick Henry introduced into the Virginia house of burgesses a series of resolutions boldly challenging the position of the British government.

June. The Massachusetts general court sent an invitation to colonial assemblies to send delegates to meet in New York and consider the Stamp Act. Meanwhile the arrival of the stamp officers led to riots in various cities, including Boston, where the house of Lieut.-Gov. Thomas Hutchinson was sacked.

Oct. 7. Stamp Act Congress at New York. Twenty-eight delegates from nine colonies drew up memorials to the king and parliament and adopted a **Declaration of Rights and Liberties** (Oct. 19).

1766, Mar. Repeal of the Stamp Act, followed by the **Declaratory Act** (Mar. 18), declaring that the king, by and with consent of parliament, had authority to make laws to bind the colonies in all respects.

1767. Suspension of the New York Assembly because of its refusal fully to comply with the Quartering Act.

The **Townshend Acts** imposed duties on glass, lead, painters' colors, tea, and paper imported into the colonies. Out of these revenues fixed salaries were to be paid to royal officials in the colonies. A Boston town-meeting adopted a **non-importation agreement.**

1768. The Massachusetts general court drew up a petition to the king, sent letters to the ministry, and dispatched a circular letter to the other colonies.

June. The seizure of John Hancock's sloop *Liberty,* because of false entry, led to a riot.

Oct. British troops arrived in Boston and the town refused to provide quarters.

1769. Parliament advised the enforcement of a statute of Henry VIII, allowing the government to bring to England for trial those alleged to have committed treason outside the realm. Resolutions of protest adopted by the Virginia house of burgesses.

1770, Mar. 5. The Boston Massacre. Popular hatred of the British troops in the city led to a brawl in which several citizens were killed or wounded. Preston, the commanding officer, was acquitted, being defended by John Adams and Josiah Quincy.

An **act repealing duties** on paper, glass, and painters' colors, but retaining that on tea. This gesture produced a conservative reaction in the colonies, in which the merchants worked for conciliation. This truce was broken by the arbitrary acts of crown officials and by the announcement in

1772. That salaries of governors and judges in Massachusetts were to be paid by the crown, thus rendering them independent of the assembly's control of the purse, and by

June 10. The **Gaspée Affair,** in which a revenue boat, whose commander's conduct had enraged public opinion in Rhode Island, was burned by a mob in Narragansett Bay.

1772, Nov. 2-1773, Jan. Formation of 80 town **committees of correspondence** in Massachusetts under the leadership of **Samuel Adams.**

1773, Mar. 12. The Virginia house of burgesses appointed a **Provincial Committee of Correspondence** to keep in touch with sister colonies. By February 1774 all the colonies except Pennsylvania had appointed such committees.

To provide relief for the East India Company the government allowed it a drawback of the tea duty in England, but the full duty was to be paid in the colonies. There was a protest to the landing of the tea in Charleston, Philadelphia, and New York, while in Boston there occurred

Dec. 16. The **Boston Tea Party** in which citizens, disguised as Indians, boarded the ships and dumped the tea into the harbor.

1774. The resistance to the landing of the tea provoked the ministry to the adoption of a punitive policy. The so-called **Coercive Acts** were passed, including: The **Boston Port Act,** closing the port after June 1; the **Massachusetts Government Act,** depriving the people of most of their chartered rights, and greatly enlarging the governor's powers; the **Administration of Justice Act,** providing that persons accused of a capital crime in aiding the government should be tried in England or a colony other than that in which the crime was committed; the **Quartering Act;** and the **Quebec Act,** extending the boundary of that province to the Ohio River, cutting athwart the claims of Massachusetts, New York, Connecticut, and Virginia. Although not designed as a punitive measure the Quebec Act was so regarded by the colonies.

County conventions in Massachusetts protested against the acts (Aug.-Sept.). The **Suffolk Convention** resolved that they should be "rejected as the attempts of a wicked admin-

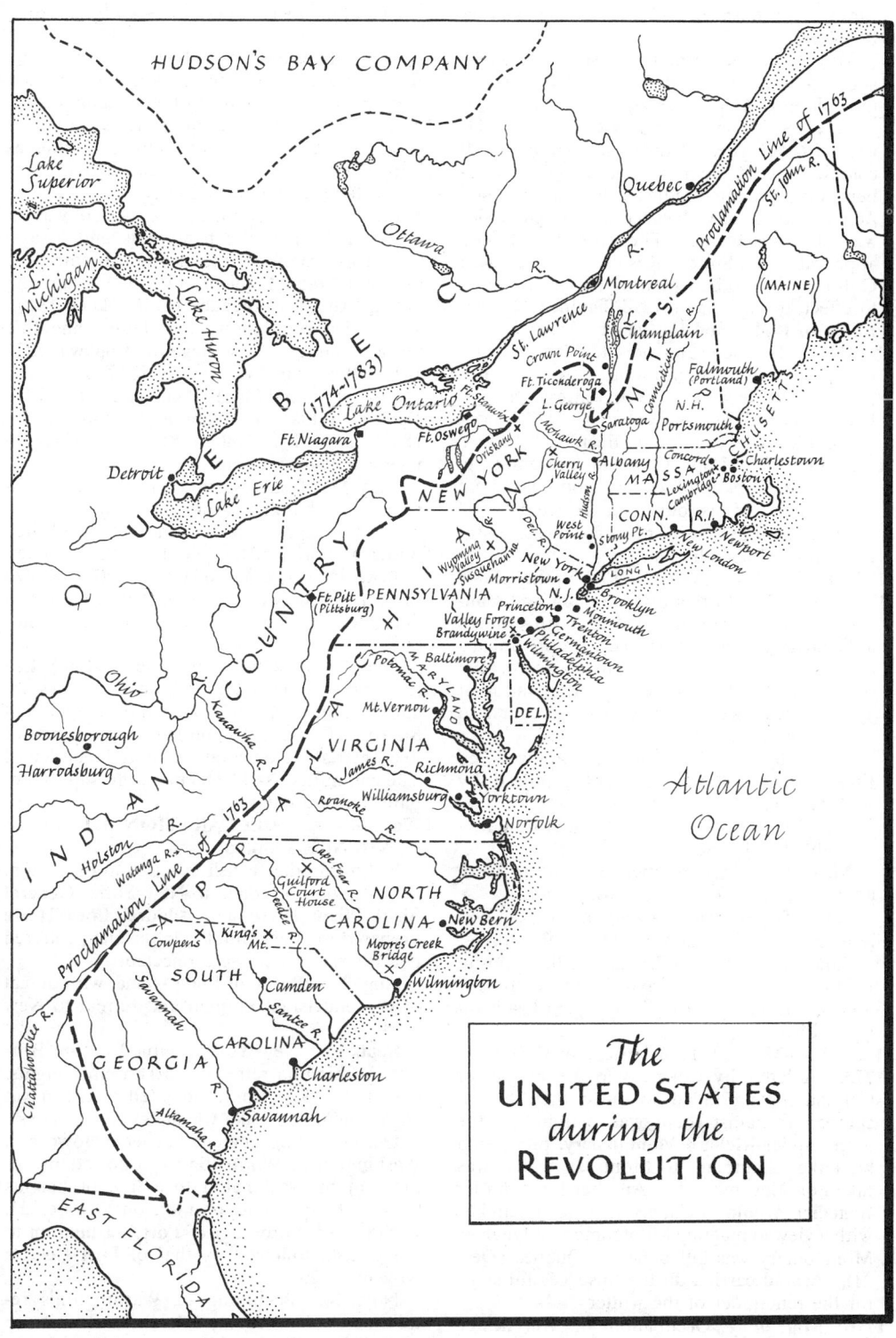

The
UNITED STATES
during the
REVOLUTION

istration to enslave America" **(The Suffolk Resolves).**

May 27.   The Virginia house of burgesses adopted resolutions calling for a congress of the colonies. Copies sent to other assemblies.

Sept. 5.   The **FIRST CONTINENTAL CONGRESS** assembled at Philadelphia. All colonies except Georgia represented. Members divided into radicals led by **Samuel Adams** and conservatives led by **Joseph Galloway** of Pennsylvania. The radicals obtained approval of the Suffolk Resolves and defeated Galloway's proposed plan of union, designed to effect an adjustment of difficulties. **Declaration of Rights and Grievances** drawn up.

Oct.   The delegates adopted the *Association* providing for non-importation of English goods after December 1. If redress had not been obtained by September 11, 1775, non-exportation was to go into effect.

1775, Feb. 1.   **Lord Chatham** presented to parliament a plan of conciliation, based on mutual concessions, but it was rejected.

Feb. 20.   **Lord North** made an unsuccessful effort toward conciliation.

1775–1783.   WAR FOR INDEPENDENCE.

1775, Apr. 19.   Battles of Lexington and Concord.   British troops detailed to destroy stores at Concord became embroiled with provincials at Lexington. Proceeding to Concord, the troops destroyed the stores, but after the fight at the bridge were forced to retreat, first to Lexington, then to Boston.

May 10–12.   **Ticonderoga** captured by **Ethan Allen** and **Crown Point** captured by **Seth Warner.**

May 10.   The **Second Continental Congress** assembled at Philadelphia.

May 31.   Troops before Boston were adopted as the **Continental Army** and on

June 15.   **George Washington** (1732–1799) appointed commander-in-chief of the forces.

June 17.   Battle of Bunker Hill, opposite Boston. Americans driven from entrenchments, but only after inflicting great losses on the British.

1775, July–Mar. 17, 1776.   Siege of Boston.

1775.   A letter by Congress to the people of Canada having failed to enlist their aid, a campaign against them was planned. One force, under **Richard Montgomery,** proceeded by Lake Champlain to Montreal, which was taken on November 12. Another force, under **Benedict Arnold,** advanced by the Kennebec with a view to meeting Montgomery at **Quebec.** Montgomery was killed before Quebec (Dec. 21). Arnold carried on the unsuccessful siege for the remainder of the winter.

1776, Mar. 4.   Occupation of **Dorchester Heights** by Washington.

Mar. 17.   Evacuation of Boston by the British forces.

Meanwhile the unyielding attitude of the British government, the hiring of German mercenaries, the events on the Canadian frontier, and the burning of Norfolk inflamed public opinion. The appearance of **Thomas Paine's** *Common Sense* crystallized that opinion in favor of independence.

Most of the writing of the period was in the form of patriotic pamphlets and essays. Only two prominent literary figures emerged: the poet **Philip Freneau** (1752–1832) and the novelist **Charles Brockden Brown** (1771–1810).

America could now also claim some fine portrait painters: **John Singleton Copley** (1737–1815), **Benjamin West** (1738–1820) in whose studio in England **Charles Willson Peale** (1741–1827) and his son **Rembrandt Peale** (1778–1860), as well as **Gilbert Stuart** (1755–1828) received some training.

May 15.   Congress announced that the authority of the British crown should be suppressed and power of government established under authority of the people of the colonies.

May 15.   The **Virginia Convention,** called to form a new government, instructed Virginia delegates in Congress to propose independence.

June 7.   Resolution of **Richard Henry Lee** in Congress, "That these United Colonies are and of right ought to be free and independent States." Congress appointed a committee of five to draft a declaration of independence. The committee asked **Thomas Jefferson** to prepare the document.

1776, July 4.   DECLARATION OF INDEPENDENCE adopted.

Following the British evacuation of Boston, Washington proceeded to New York. **General Sir William Howe** and **Admiral Lord Howe** prepared to attack, but the latter first proffered peace terms which were rejected.

Aug. 27.   Battle of Long Island, with defeat of General Israel Putnam and retreat to New York.

Sept. 15.   New York occupied by the British; Washington retreated to Harlem Heights.

Oct. 11–13.   Arnold defeated in two naval engagements on **Lake Champlain.**

Oct. 28.   Engagement between Howe and Washington at **White Plains,** followed by retirement of Washington to a line of heights back of his previous position on October 31.

Nov. 16.   Surrender of **Fort Washington** to the British, followed by that of **Fort Lee** on November 20.

Nov. 28.   Beginning of Washington's retreat across New Jersey into Pennsylvania.

Dec. 26.   Battle of Trenton. Crossing the

Delaware by night, Washington surprised and captured about a thousand Hessians at Trenton. This was followed by the defeat of the British at the

1777, Jan. 3. Battle of Princeton. The British plan of campaign for 1777 was to divide the states by the line of the Hudson. General John Burgoyne was to proceed from Canada by way of Lake Champlain, General Barry St. Leger was to co-operate with Burgoyne from Lake Ontario, while Howe was to ascend the Hudson and join Burgoyne.

Aug. 16. Battle of Bennington, in which General John Stark defeated Colonel Baum, sent by Burgoyne to seize stores.

Sept. 19. First battle of Bemis Heights, in which Burgoyne held the field, although suffering heavy losses.

Oct. 7. Second battle of Bemis Heights, or **Saratoga.** Burgoyne was defeated and, finding himself surrounded, called a council of war at which it was decided to negotiate terms.

Oct. 17. Burgoyne surrendered his entire force to General Horatio Gates.

Howe's campaign. Instead of advancing up the Hudson, Howe, on August 25, disclosed his purpose of attacking **Philadelphia.** Washington offered battle, but in the

Sept. 11. Battle of Brandywine, the Americans, under General Nathanael Greene, were defeated.

Sept. 27. Howe occupied Philadelphia.

Oct. 4. Attempting to surprise the camp at Germantown, Washington was defeated in the **battle of Germantown.** With the capture of Fort Mifflin and Fort Mercer on November 16 and 20, British control of the Delaware was complete.

1777–1778. Winter suffering of Washington's army at **Valley Forge.** Unsuccessful attempt of the **Conway Cabal** to remove Washington from command.

1777, Nov. 15. ARTICLES OF CONFEDERATION and perpetual union agreed upon in Congress. These provided for a confederacy to be known as *The United States of America,* and were sent to the states for ratification.

Burgoyne's defeat and surrender stirred France to action in support of the United States. To re-establish French prestige in Europe, so greatly weakened in the Seven Years' War, was the aim of **Count Charles de Vergennes,** the French minister of foreign affairs. After supplying secret aid in money and supplies to the Americans for two years, France signed

1778, Feb. 6. Treaties of Commerce and Alliance with the United States. **Marquis Marie Joseph de Lafayette** and **Baron Johann de Kalb**

had arrived the previous summer to offer their services. **Pierre de Beaumarchais,** French playwright, had drawn heavily on his personal resources to aid the Americans.

Feb. 17. Lord North presented to parliament his plan for conciliating the Americans, which included renunciation of the right of taxation. Commissioners sent to the United States with a peace offer, which was rejected by Congress (June 17). With the French alliance an assured fact, only independence would now satisfy the Americans.

June 18. Evacuation of Philadelphia by Sir Henry Clinton, who started to march across New Jersey, where on

June 28. Washington won the **battle of Monmouth.**

July 4. Wyoming massacre in Pennsylvania.

July 8. Arrival of **Count Jean Baptiste d'Estaing's** fleet off Delaware Capes. He and Washington planned a land and sea attack on the British in Newport. After a storm on August 9, which prevented a clash between the French and British fleets, d'Estaing sailed to Boston for repairs, leaving General John Sullivan unsupported, who on August 29 gave up the siege of Newport.

Nov. 11. Massacre of Cherry Valley in New York.

1779, Feb. George Rogers Clark, with a force of Virginians, completed the conquest of the Old Northwest, capturing Hamilton, the British commander, at **Vincennes.**

June. Spain entered the war against Britain, on the promise of France that she would assist Spain to recover Gibraltar and the Floridas.

Sept. 23. Naval victory of **John Paul Jones** of the *Bonhomme Richard* over the *Serapis* and the *Countess of Scarborough.*

Meanwhile the British had decided to try, with the aid of loyalists, to overrun the southern states. In 1778 **Savannah** was captured and in 1780 Sir Henry Clinton laid siege to Charleston.

1780, May. Charleston surrendered.

July. Count Jean Baptiste de Rochambeau arrived at Newport with 6000 French troops.

Despite brave resistance of Thomas Sumter and Francis Marion, South Carolina was overrun by the British, and in the

Aug. 16. Battle of Camden, Gates was defeated by General Charles Cornwallis.

Aug. 18. Sumter's force was defeated by Tarleton, and Marion retreated to North Carolina.

Sept. 23. A plot of **Benedict Arnold** to surrender West Point to Sir Henry Clinton was revealed through capture of the British agent,

Major John André. Arnold escaped, but on
  Oct. 2. André was hanged as a spy.
  Oct. 7. **Battle of King's Mountain,** in North
Carolina, in which the British, under Major
Ferguson, were defeated.
1781, Jan. 17. **Battle of the Cowpens,** in which
the British cavalry under Sir Banastre Tarleton
was defeated by General Daniel Morgan.
  Mar. 15. **Battle of Guilford;** British victory
and withdrawal.
  Sept. 8. **Battle of Eutaw;** defeat of Greene,
followed by retreat of British to Charleston.
  Meanwhile British forces under Cornwallis
were concentrating in Virginia, where they
fortified themselves at **Yorktown.** While Cornwallis remained inactive, Washington, Lafayette, and Rochambeau closed in on him at
Williamsburg, and Count François de Grasse,
with the French fleet, entered Chesapeake Bay.
  Sept. 30–Oct. 19. **Siege of Yorktown.** Finding himself bottled up,
  **Oct. 19. CORNWALLIS SURREN-
DERED** with 7000 men.
  In the peace negotiations, Vergennes was in
the difficult position of trying to please both
of his allies, Spain and the United States.
This led to delay which aroused the impatience
of the American commissioners, who, disregarding their instructions not to negotiate a
separate peace with Great Britain, proceeded to
do so. The British, eager to win American
friendship and trade, thereby defeating the
aspirations of the French, readily acceded to
the American demand for the Mississippi as
the western boundary and full rights in the
fisheries off the Canadian coast.
**1783, Sept. 3. DEFINITIVE TREATY OF
PEACE** between Great Britain and United
States, signed at **Paris.** It recognized the independence of the United States. Provisions
of the treaty with respect to the northeastern
and northwestern boundaries led to later difficulties with Britain, while the southern
boundary provision led to trouble with Spain.
  Full rights in the Newfoundland fisheries
were guaranteed to the United States. Creditors of neither country were to encounter legal
obstacles to collection of debts, while the Congress would recommend to the states the restoration of the confiscated estates of loyalists.
  Navigation of the Mississippi was to be open
to both Great Britain and the United States.
**1783-1787. THE CRITICAL PERIOD OF
AMERICAN HISTORY.** The Articles of Confederation had gone into effect in 1781, and
with the achievement of independence in 1783
the young nation found itself in a difficult
economic situation, not due primarily to the
particular forms of government then in operation. Treated as a foreign people by Britain

as well as by other European countries, and
denied participation of their ships in the trade
of the British West Indies, so important in
their economy before the Revolution, far-
reaching economic dislocations resulted, producing a deep depression in 1784–1785, from
which the country began to recover as early
as 1787. While not fundamentally responsible
for the unfortunate situation, the Articles of
Confederation received the blame and were
widely believed to be inadequate. The economic situation was aggravated by paper-
money experiments of the states and by the
inability of Congress to raise an adequate
revenue. The weakness of the central government was dramatized by **Shays's Rebellion**
(1786) in Massachusetts, in which the use of
state troops was necessary to protect the federal arsenal at Springfield.
1785. The **Land Ordinance** enacted. The cession by the landed states of their claims to
western lands, made necessary by Maryland's
refusal to ratify the Articles of Confederation
unless such cessions should be made, created
the public domain of the United States, for the
administration of which a land policy was
necessary. (*See map on page 807.*) This ordinance established the rectangular system of survey, provided for survey in advance of sale, and
laid down terms and conditions of sale.
1787. The **NORTHWEST ORDINANCE** enacted, providing for the government of the
northwest. The region was to be divided into
not less than three and not more than five
districts, which, after passing through territorial or colonial stage, should be admitted to
statehood. This **principle of co-ordinancy** or
ultimate statehood became the basic and dis-
tinguishing feature of the American colonial
system of the 19th century. Slavery and involuntary servitude were prohibited in the area.
1787, May. The **CONSTITUTIONAL CON-
VENTION** assembled at Philadelphia. The
inability of Congress to raise revenue, the outbreaks of disorder, and the obstructions to
commerce resulted in an increasing desire for
a more perfect government. Commissioners
from Virginia and Maryland met at **Mount
Vernon** in 1785 to consider the possibility of
a uniform commercial code. This conference
made clear the need for wider co-operation,
so Virginia invited all the states to send delegates to a convention at **Annapolis** (1786). This
convention was attended by delegates from
only five states, who proposed a convention to
meet at Philadelphia in May 1787. Congress
officially called such a convention to convene
on May 5. All states except Rhode Island
were represented. After four months of labor,
1787, Sept. 17. The **Constitution was signed**

by the delegates present. The document was sent to the states for ratification, with the provision that it should become operative upon the acceptance of nine states.

1788, June. Ratification by New Hampshire, the ninth state, placed the constitution in operation. In several states the anti-Federalists exacted promises of amendments in return for unconditional ratification. *(Cont. p. 805.)*

(Cont. p. 805.)

G. AFRICA, 1517–1800

(From pp. 354, 386)

1517. Conquest of Egypt by Selim I (p. 450). The country was put under a Turkish governor, but the Mamluk beys were left in effectual control, acting as a landholding oligarchy.

1517. Regular establishment of the **slave trade** through a concession granted by Charles I of Spain to a Flemish merchant.

1517. Defeat of the Songhoy ruler by the forces of the **Haussa Confederation,** which became the dominant power east of the Niger, under the leadership of Kebbi.

1520–1526. Mission of **Francisco Alvarez** to Ethiopia. He wrote the first detailed description of the country.

1527. Ethiopia was overrun by the Moslem Somali chief, Ahmed Gran, who used firearms. The negus thereupon called upon the Portuguese for aid.

1534. The Turks, under Khaireddin Barbarossa, took **Tunis** (p. 452).

1535. Spanish conquest of Tunis, completing the conquest of the North African coast begun in 1496 with the acquisition of Melilla.

1541. Abortive expedition of Charles V to Algiers (p. 452)

1541. Portuguese expedition to Ethiopia under **Christopher da Gama,** son of Vasco. The Portuguese succeeded in expelling Ahmed Gran.

1555–1633. THE PORTUGUESE (Jesuit) **MISSIONS IN ETHIOPIA.** Conversion of two successive rulers. Remarkable influence and work of **Pedro Paez.** The conversion led to repeated religious wars against the Portuguese faction. Ultimately the Portuguese were expelled and all Catholic missions prohibited.

1562–1568. John Hawkins initiated the British slave trade, making three voyages from West Africa to the New World with slave cargoes.

1571–1603. Apogee of the **EMPIRE OF KANEM** or **BORNU** (dating from the 13th century) under **Idris III.** It controlled most of the territory about Lake Chad.

1574. The Spaniards lost Goletta. End of the Spanish rule in Tunis, which became a Turkish regency, with an elected bey.

1574. The Portuguese began the settlement of Angola at **São Paulo de Loanda.**

1578. Sebastian of Portugal, called upon to intervene in the dynastic struggles in Morocco and determined to conquer the country for himself, was overwhelmingly defeated at **Kasr al-Kabir. Ahmed al Mansur** established the Sharifian dynasty.

1580. The Spaniards occupied **Ceuta,** which remained technically a possession of Portugal till 1688.

1581. The Moroccans took Tuat, beginning the penetration of the Sahara.

1591. A force of Spanish and Portuguese renegades in the service of the Moroccans crossed the desert and defeated the forces of **Songhoy** by use of firearms. Gao was destroyed and the Moroccans established themselves at **Timbuktu.** The entire Negro culture was destroyed and the country fell a prey to rival pashas. These made themselves independent of Morocco in 1612 and continued to rule at Timbuktu until 1780.

1595. First establishments of the **Dutch** on the **Guinea coast.**

1598. The Dutch took Mauritius (Isle de France).

1616. The Portuguese, **Gaspar Boccaro,** journeyed from the upper Zambezi to Kilwa on the coast, one of the first recorded explorations of the interior.

1618. Journey of the Frenchman, **Paul Imbert,** to Timbuktu.

1618–1619. G. Thompson ascended the Gambia River for about 400 miles.

1621. The Dutch took **Arguin and Goree** from the Portuguese.

1626. The French established themselves at St. Louis at the mouth of the Senegal.

1626. First French settlements on **Madagascar** (inhabited by various primitive tribes and by the **Hovas,** who had arrived from overseas about 1000 A.D.).

1637. The Dutch took Elmina from the Portuguese and built numerous forts on the Gold Coast.

1637. The French, under de Rochefort, explored the Senegal for about 100 miles and established posts.

1645. Capuchin monks ascended the Congo River, possibly as far as Stanley Falls.

1650. **Ali Bey** made himself hereditary bey of Tunis.

1652, Apr. 7. **CAPETOWN FOUNDED** by the Dutch under **Jan van Riebeeck.**

1660. Rise of the **BAMBARA KINGDOMS** (Segu and Kaarta) on the upper Niger. They defeated and replaced the **Manding Empire** (1670) which thenceforth became a minor state.

1662. Portugal ceded **Tangier** to England.

1662. The British built a fort at James Island at the mouth of the Gambia.

1668. A Dutch exploring party advanced as far as Mossel Bay, but the first farms were established in that area only in 1740 and a new frontier in 1750.

1672. Foundation of the **Royal African Company.**

1677. The French conquered the Dutch posts on the Senegal.

1683. The Prussians built the fort of **Grossfriedrichsburg** on the Guinea Coast (abandoned 1720).

1684. The British abandoned Tangier to the sultan of Morocco.

1684. French expeditions against the piratical deys of **Algiers.** Various coast towns were bombarded and the deys were obliged to surrender Christian slaves.

1686. Louis XIV proclaimed the annexation of **Madagascar.**

1688. The arrival of Huguenot refugees from France strengthened the Dutch settlement in South Africa.

1697. The French, under **André de Brue,** completed the conquest of the Senegal region and advanced up the river to Mambuk (1715).

1698. The Portuguese were expelled from their posts on the east coast by Arabs from Oman. Mombasa was abandoned in 1730, but the Portuguese retained Mozambique.

1699. **C. Poncet,** an emissary of Louis XIV, traveled overland from Cairo to Gondar in Ethiopia.

1705. Hussein ibn Ali founded the **Husseinite dynasty** in Tunis and threw off Turkish authority.

1708. The Spaniards were expelled from Oran.

1713. The *Asiento treaty* (p. 468) gave Britain the right to import African slaves into the Spanish colonies in the New World, thus initiating the most active period of the British slave trade.

1714. **Ahmed Bey** made himself ruler of Tripoli, founding the Karamanli dynasty which lasted until 1835.

1715. The French took the island of Mauritius.

1723. **Bartholomew Stibbs,** for the African Company, took over the Gambia region as far as the Barrakonda Falls.

1732. The Spaniards retook Oran.

1757–1789. Reign of **Sidi Mohammed** in Morocco. He established law and order and abolished Christian slavery (1777).

1758. The British captured the French possessions on the Senegal.

1760. The Dutch in South Africa crossed the Orange River and began penetration of Great Namaqualand. The Orange River became the official boundary in 1801.

1761. A Dutch hunter, Hendrik Hop, crossed the Orange River, but this became the official boundary only in 1801.

1766. **Ali Bey** established himself as ruler of Egypt and proclaimed independence of the Turks. His successor, Mohammed Bey, recognized Turkish suzerainty again (1773).

1768–1773. **James Bruce** explored Ethiopia, traveling from Massawa to Gondar and thence to the Blue Nile. He returned by way of Egypt and reported the Ethiopian Empire in decline, restricted to the area north of the Blue Nile and wracked by rebellion.

1770. The Dutch in South Africa first encountered the African tribes beyond Algoa Bay, thus beginning a century of frontier wars.

1776. Rise of the Tukulor power in West Africa.

1778. The French recovered their possessions on the Senegal.

1778. Explorations of **W. Paterson** in the Kafir country.

1783. By the treaty of Paris the British secured the Senegal again. They held it until 1790.

1787. The British acquired **Sierra Leone** from the natives. In 1791 it was devoted to the settlement of freed slaves.

1788. **Sir Joseph Banks** founded the *African Association* for the furtherance of exploration and the development of trade.

1791. The Spanish abandoned Oran, retaining only Melilla and Ceuta and a few minor stations on the North African coast.

1792. **Denmark prohibited the slave trade,** the first country to take this step.

1801. Conquest of the Haussa power by **Usman dan Fodio,** a Tukulor chief, who converted this area to Islam and founded the **kingdom of Sokoto.** (*Cont. p. 863.*)

H. ASIA, 1500–1800

1. PERSIA, 1500–1794

(From p. 355)

1502–1524. SHAH ISMAIL, founder of the **Safavid dynasty,** the first national dynasty in many centuries. Ismail traced his descent to **Safi al-Din** of Ardabil (1252–1334), a supposed descendant of Ali, the fourth caliph. Safi al-Din founded among the Turk tribes an order of dervishes devoted to mystic teachings and Shi'a doctrine. His influence and that of his successors spread over northwestern Persia and into eastern and southern Anatolia. Sheikh Joneid, head of the order from 1448–1460, attempted to extend his temporal power and ultimately secured the protection and alliance of **Uzun Hasan,** whose sister he married. His son, Haidar, married a daughter of Uzun Hasan and devoted himself to the reorganization of the order, which became a powerful military instrument (*Kizilbashes i.e.* red heads, from their headdress). Haidar was defeated and killed by Jaqub of the White Sheep, but left several sons, of whom Ismail was one. After years spent in hiding, Ismail was able to take advantage of the confusion following the death of Rustam Shah.

1501. Battle of Shurur, in which Ismail defeated Alwand of the White Sheep. He soon took Tabriz and had himself proclaimed shah. With his accession the Shi'a doctrine became officially established in Persia.

1507–1622. The Portuguese established themselves at Hormuz.

1510. Ismail defeated the Uzbeks and drove them out of Khorasan.

1514. BATTLE OF CHALDIRAN, following the invasion of Persia by the Turks under Selim I (p. 450). Ismail was defeated and Tabriz taken, though later evacuated by the Turks. Beginning of a long duel between Turks and Persians, resulting largely from religious conflict.

1524–1576. SHAH TAHMASP I, the son of Ismail, who ascended the throne at ten. His reign was marked by continuous raids and campaigns against the Uzbeks of Transoxiana and by repeated incursions of the Turks, who conquered Mesopotamia and on several occasions took Tabriz, Sultanieh, and Isfahan. **Peace with the Turks** was finally concluded in 1555.

1561–1563. Anthony Jenkinson, of the English Muscovy Company, reached Persia overland through Russia and opened commercial relations which continued until 1581.

1576–1578. ISMAIL II, fourth son of Tahmasp, who succeeded on the death by poison of his father. He killed off all his relatives and rivals, but himself died after a year of office.

1578–1587. MOHAMMED KHUDABANDA, the half-blind eldest son of Tahmasp, who had escaped his brother's vengeance. Renewal of the Turkish attack; which was less decisive than before.

1587–1629. SHAH ABBAS I (the Great), most highly esteemed of the Persian rulers. He was a man of broad outlook and strong will, though personally suspicious and cruel (he had one son murdered and two others blinded). In his early years Abbas was wholly under the domination of the Kizil-bash chiefs, but he later succeeded in counteracting their influence by organizing a new tribe of "friends of the shah," and by building up a new infantry and artillery force, modeled on the Turkish. In this he was greatly aided by **Anthony** and **Robert Shirley,** two brothers who came with 26 followers in 1598. Robert remained in Persian service during most of Abbas' reign.

1590. Abbas made peace with the Turks, abandoning Tabriz, Shirvan, Georgia, and Luristan. This he did in order to be free to deal with the Uzbeks, who, under Abdullah II, had taken Herat, Meshed, and other towns of Khorasan.

1597. The Persians defeated the Uzbeks, whose invasions of Khorasan were stopped for many years.

1602–1627. Further **wars with the Turks** (mission of Sir Anthony Shirley to Europe to enlist the co-operation of the emperor and king of Spain). In 1603 Abbas managed to retake Tabriz, and then Erivan, Shirvan, and Kars. A great victory was won over the Turks at **Lake Urmia.** Thereafter Abbas conquered Baghdad, Mosul, and Diarbekr. Peace was made in 1612, but war broke out again in 1616. Efforts of the Turks to retake Baghdad (1625) failed.

1616. The **English East India Company** began trading with Persia from Surat. The activity of the English was resented by the Portuguese, who attacked them, but were defeated in the **battle of Jask** (1620).

1622. The English merchants, co-operating with a Persian army, took **Hormuz** from the Portuguese, receiving special privileges there.

The Safavid Dynasty

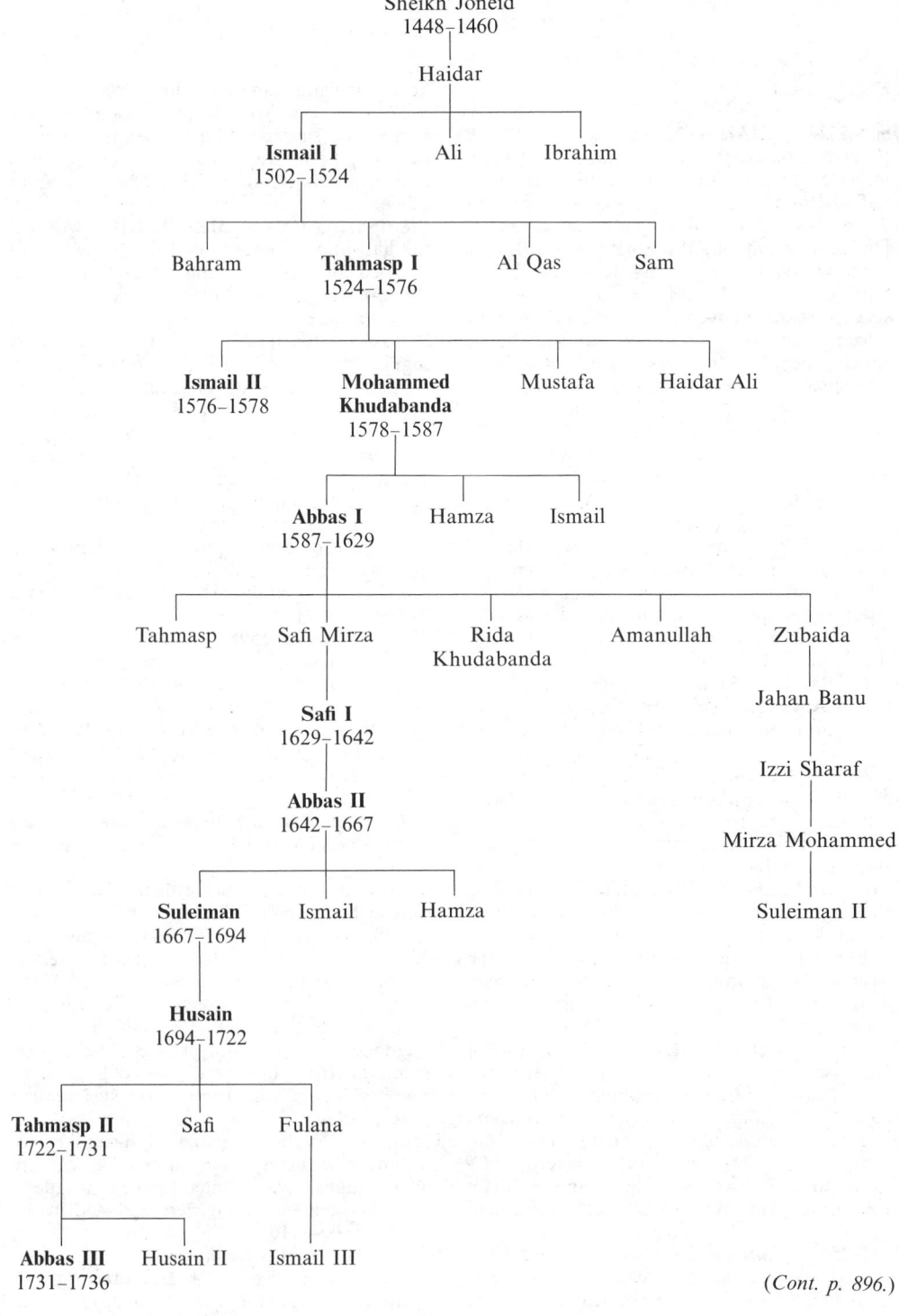

Sheikh Joneid
1448–1460

Haidar

Ismail I
1502–1524 — Ali — Ibrahim

Bahram — **Tahmasp I**
1524–1576 — Al Qas — Sam

Ismail II
1576–1578 — **Mohammed Khudabanda**
1578–1587 — Mustafa — Haidar Ali

Abbas I
1587–1629 — Hamza — Ismail

Tahmasp — Safi Mirza — Rida Khudabanda — Amanullah — Zubaida

Safi I
1629–1642

Jahan Banu

Abbas II
1642–1667

Izzi Sharaf

Suleiman
1667–1694 — Ismail — Hamza

Mirza Mohammed

Husain
1694–1722

Suleiman II

Tahmasp II
1722–1731 — Safi — Fulana

Abbas III
1731–1736 — Husain II — Ismail III

(*Cont. p. 896.*)

1629-1642. SHAH SAFI, the grandson of Abbas. Beginning of harem rule and rapid decline, as in the Ottoman Empire fifty years before. Like his contemporary, Murad IV (p. 453), Shah Safi distinguished himself by wholesale executions.

1630. Murad IV took and sacked Hamadan, the first move in the campaign to retake the conquests of Abbas the Great.

1635. The Turks took Erivan and Tabriz.

1638. The Turks took **Baghdad** and forced the shah to make peace. Erivan was left to the Persians, while the Turks retained Baghdad.

1642-1667. SHAH ABBAS II, the son of Safi. He was only ten when he reached the throne and at no time showed any particular ability.

1664. First Russian mission to Isfahan. Beginning of Cossack raids on the Caucasus front. In the same year the French secured permission to trade in Persia.

1667-1694. SHAH SULEIMAN, the son of Abbas II, another dissolute ruler who did nothing to check the decline.

1694-1722. SHAH HUSSEIN, a devout ruler whose renewed emphasis on Shi'a doctrine gave his Sunnite neighbors an excuse for making trouble.

1709. Rising of the Afghans at Kandahar, led by **Mir Vais,** a Ghilzai chieftain and a Sunnite. Mir Vais succeeded in defeating the Persian armies sent against him (1711) and established the independence of the Afghan state.

1715-1717. Mir Abdullah, ruler of Kandahar in succession to Mir Vais. He was overthrown when he attempted to make peace on the basis of Persian suzerainty over Kandahar.

1717-1725. Mir Mahmud, ruler of Kandahar. In 1717 the Abdalis of Herat also revolted and established another Afghan state.

1722. Invasion of Persia by Mir Mahmud and an army of Afghans. The Persian court and army were completely demoralized and offered little real resistance. They were defeated at **Gulnabad,** after which Mahmud took Isfahan. Husain abdicated and

1722-1725. Mahmud became shah. Husain's son, **Tahmasp,** however, escaped to Mazandaran and tried to organize national resistance.

1722. Peter the Great, taking advantage of the confusion, took Derbent on the plea of supporting Tahmasp. In 1723 he added Resht and Baku, and Tahmasp agreed to cede all of Shirvan, Daghestan, Gilan, Mazandaran, and Astrabad in return for effective aid.

1723. The Turks, hoping for a share of the spoil, took Tiflis.

1724. Russia and Turkey made an agreement for the dismemberment of Persia, the Turks reserving for themselves Tabriz, Hamadan, and Kermanshah. These places they occupied in 1724-1725.

1724-1725. Reign of terror in Isfahan, where Mahmud, gone mad, ordered the massacre of the Persian nobility and of all available Safavid princes, to say nothing of large numbers of soldiers and inhabitants.

1725-1730. ASHRAF SHAH, in succession to Mahmud. He was more conciliatory, but from the outset failed to get much sympathy from the Persians, or much support from Kandahar.

1726. Ashraf defeated the Turks, who were advancing on Isfahan. Peace was concluded in 1727, Ashraf securing recognition from the sultan in return for the cession of the conquered territories.

1726-1728. Tahmasp, supported by Nadir Kuli, a powerful chief of the Afshar tribe of Khorasan, conquered Meshed and Herat and, after defeating an Afghan army, retook Isfahan.

1730. Final defeat of the Afghans near Shiraz. Ashraf was murdered on his way to Kandahar and his followers fled from Persia as best they could.

1730-1731. SHAH TAHMASP II was hardly more than a figurehead, the real ruler being **Nadir Kuli,** who married Tahmasp's sister. Nadir, having defeated the Afghans, turned against the Turks, whom he forced to give up Hamadan, Kermanshah, and Tabriz. He then marched east to deal with the Abdalis, and Tahmasp, thinking to complete the victory over the Turks, met with disaster and lost all that Nadir had gained. He agreed to the terms submitted by the Turks, for which Nadir deposed him.

1731-1736. ABBAS III, the eight-months-old son of Tahmasp, was elevated to the throne as a mere puppet. He was the last of the Safavid dynasty.

1732. By the **treaty of Resht** the Russians gave up their claims to Mazandaran, Astrabad, and Gilan, which had never been effectively occupied.

1733. Nadir, having been seriously defeated by the Turks in the **battle of Kirkuk,** managed to retrieve his position and blockade Baghdad. But these operations were interrupted by the need for a further campaign in Transcaucasia (1734).

1735. Russia, by treaty, gave up the last Persian acquisitions of Peter the Great, Baku and Derbent, and joined in alliance with Nadir against the common enemy, the Turk. Nadir won a great victory over the Turks at **Baghavand,** and took Tiflis.

1736-1747. NADIR SHAH became ruler on the death of Abbas III. He accepted the throne on condition that the Persians renounce the Shi'a heresy. He himself, being a Turk by race, was also a Sunnite. But he never succeeded in making orthodoxy acceptable to the Persians.

1737. Nadir and his generals reduced Baluchistan and Balkh.

1738. Capture of Kandahar. Nadir thereupon proceeded to invade India. Kabul, Peshawar, and Lahore were taken and in 1739 a huge army of the Mogul emperor was defeated at **Karnal,** near Delhi. **Delhi** was taken and a tremendous massacre followed. Nadir left the Mogul emperor on the throne, but levied an indemnity of almost half a billion dollars and took all the territory north and west of the Indus.

1740. Nadir subjected **Bokhara and Khwarezm** (Khiva). This marked the greatest extent of his dominion and at the same time marked a turning-point in his career. Nadir was a great soldier, but he lacked real statesmanship and administrative ability. His efforts to stamp out Shi'ism resulted in growing unrest, and the need for suppressing discontent made the shah ever more ruthless and cruel. In the end he ruined the country by his huge exactions and despotic exploitation.

1743-1747. Resumption of **war with the Turks,** the sultan having refused the Persian terms. In 1745 Nadir won a resounding victory near **Kars** and in 1747 was able to secure peace: he gave up his demand for recognition of a fifth (Persian) orthodox sect, but secured recognition for the frontier as it had been in the time of Murad IV.

1747. Nadir Shah was assassinated by one of his own tribesmen.

1747-1750. A period of anarchy, during which the succession was hotly disputed. **Ahmad Khan Durani** established himself at Kandahar, took Meshed and Herat, and annexed Sind, Kashmir, and parts of the Punjab, founding a powerful Afghan state.

1747-1748. Adil Shah, the nephew of Nadir, became shah, but was soon dethroned and executed.

1748-1751. Shah Rukh, grandson of Nadir, was elevated to the throne. He was defeated and blinded by a Shi'a rival, but ultimately established his rule in Khorasan (to 1796). The rest of Persia continued to be hotly disputed between competing chieftains, until

1750-1779. KARIM KHAN, of the **Zand dynasty,** succeeded in maintaining himself against the powerful Kajar leader. Karim Khan, whose strength was in the south (Shiraz the capital), was a just and benevolent ruler, during whose reign the country was enabled to recover.

1763. The British established a factory at Bushire, and somewhat later (1770) at Basra.

1775-1776. Karim Khan sent an expedition against Basra. This important station was taken, but was voluntarily abandoned on the death of Karim.

1779-1782. Another period of anarchy, during which Karim's brothers disputed the succession and the Kajar chief, Aga Mohammed, again took the field.

1782-1785. Ali Murad Shah. He re-established the capital at Isfahan.

1785-1789. Jafar Shah. Continuation of the confusion, marked by cruelty and barbarity.

1789-1794. Lutf Ali Khan, last of the Zand dynasty; a brilliant and chivalrous, but arrogant ruler. Unable to get the better of his rivals, Lutf was finally defeated and killed.

1794. Aga Mohammed founded the Kajar dynasty. (*Cont. p. 894.*)

2. AFGHANISTAN, TO 1793

(*From p. 360*)

Prior to the 18th century, Afghanistan was in part ruled by Persia, in part by India and in part by the central Asian khanate of Bokhara. In 1706 **Kandahar** made itself independent and there followed the Afghan conquest of Persia (1722, see p. 567). This remained but an episode, for in 1737 Nadir Shah, having driven the Afghans out of Persia, carried the offensive eastward and subjected all of Afghanistan and western India.

1747-1773. AHMAD SHAH, one of the Afghan generals of Nadir Shah, on the murder of the latter assumed control of the Afghan provinces. He was a member of the Durani (Sauzai) clan of the Abdali tribe and established the **Durani dynasty** and empire. Most of his reign was filled by his nine **expeditions to India,** where he successfully asserted his claim to the Indian provinces of Nadir's empire. The dying Mogul Empire was unable to offer effective resistance. Ahmad took Lahore (1752) and then Delhi, which he plundered (1755). In 1761 he won a resounding victory over the Marathas at **Panipat,** and in 1762 over the Sikhs near Lahore. On his death the Afghan Empire extended from eastern Persia

(Meshed) over Afghanistan and Baluchistan and eastward over Kashmir, and the Punjab.

1773–1793. Timur Shah, the son of Ahmad, proved to be a weak and ineffectual ruler. He moved the capital from Kandahar to Kabul, but was unable to prevent the loss of some of the Indian territory or the gradual disintegration of his authority even in Afghanistan.

(*Cont. p. 898.*)

3. INDIA, 1498–1796

(From p. 363)

1498. VASCO DA GAMA, having rounded the Cape of Good Hope, reached Malabar. The Portuguese, after constructing forts at Cochin (1506) and Socotra (1507), soon diverted the spice trade from the Red Sea route.

1504. Yusuf Adil Shah of Bijapur, having annexed Gulbarga, established the Shi'a form of Islam, despite protest from many Sunnites.

1509. The Portuguese, under **Francisco de Almeida,** at Diu destroyed an Egyptian-Indian fleet which had, in the previous year, defeated a Portuguese squadron at Chaul.

1510. The **Portuguese acquired Goa** as headquarters, in place of Cochin.

1512. Golconda became independent (till 1687).

1526–1537. Bahadur, the last active sultan, with the aid of Khandesh, captured Mandu and annexed Malwa (1531), after which he captured Chitor (1534).

1526–1761 (1857). The **MOGUL EMPIRE** in India was founded by **Babar** (1483–1530), descendant of Timur in the fifth generation, who had seized Kabul (1504) and Lahore (1524) as compensation for loss of Ferghana and Samarkand. Decisive victory at **Panipat** over Ibrahim Shah Lodi gave him Delhi and Agra, which he defended in the

1527. Battle of Khanua against Rana Sanga of Chitor, chief of a Rajput confederacy.

1529. Victory on the Gogra, where it meets the Ganges, completed conquest of the kingdom of Delhi to the frontier of Bengal.

Babar's acts, problems, and personality appear in his Turki *Memoirs.*

1530–1556. Humayun drove Bahadur Shah of Gujarat to flight before Chitor and captured Mandu and Champanir (1535), but lost both through a year of inaction. The same fault and treachery of his brothers lost the empire to the

1539–1555. Sur dynasty of the Afghan **Sher Shah** (1539–1545) who had consolidated his power in Bihar and drove Humayun to seek refuge in Persia, whence he returned precariously to Delhi and Agra (1555).

1535. The Portuguese secured by treaty Bassein, and were allowed to fortify Diu, which they defended against an Ottoman fleet and a Gujarati army (1538).

1546. Efforts to expel the Portuguese failed miserably.

1556–1605. AKBAR (b. 1542, personal rule 1562) restored and consolidated the empire throughout northern India.

1556. Guided by **Bairam Khan,** his guardian (till 1560), he crushed the Afghans at Panipat.

1559. Constantine de Braganza seized Daman.

1561. Conquest of Malwa was effected by the harem party (dominant 1560–1562).

1562. Akbar's marriage to a Rajput princess of Amber (mother of Jahangir) and abolition of the *jizya* tax on non-Moslems (1564) marked a new policy of impartiality and conciliation of subjects.

1564. The Gond Chandels (capital Chauragarh) were conquered. (Construction of the stone fort at Agra was begun.)

1565. A coalition of Ahmadnagar, Bijapur, Bidar, and Golconda decisively defeated Vijayanagar at **Talikota,** and led to the execution of the rajah. In 1574 Ahmadnagar annexed Berar, which had hindered the allied campaign.

1568. Chitor was taken by Akbar and about 30,000 Rajputs massacred.

1571. A new city at Fathpur Sikri, near Agra, was founded and magnificently built, but abandoned on Akbar's death.

1572–1573. Conquest of Gujarat gave Akbar access to the sea, new ideas, and revenues. To defend his conquest he rode with 3000 horsemen 450 miles in 11 days.

Reorganization of administration was begun by (1) resumption to the crown of all lands, hitherto held by officials as temporary assignments, but now to be administered and revenue collected directly; (2) establishment of the **Mansabdari system,** a unified state service of officers arranged in a hierarchy of military (cavalry) rank, but performing civil (mainly financial) as well as military functions if required; (3) substitution of a single tax of one-third produce of the land for the traditional

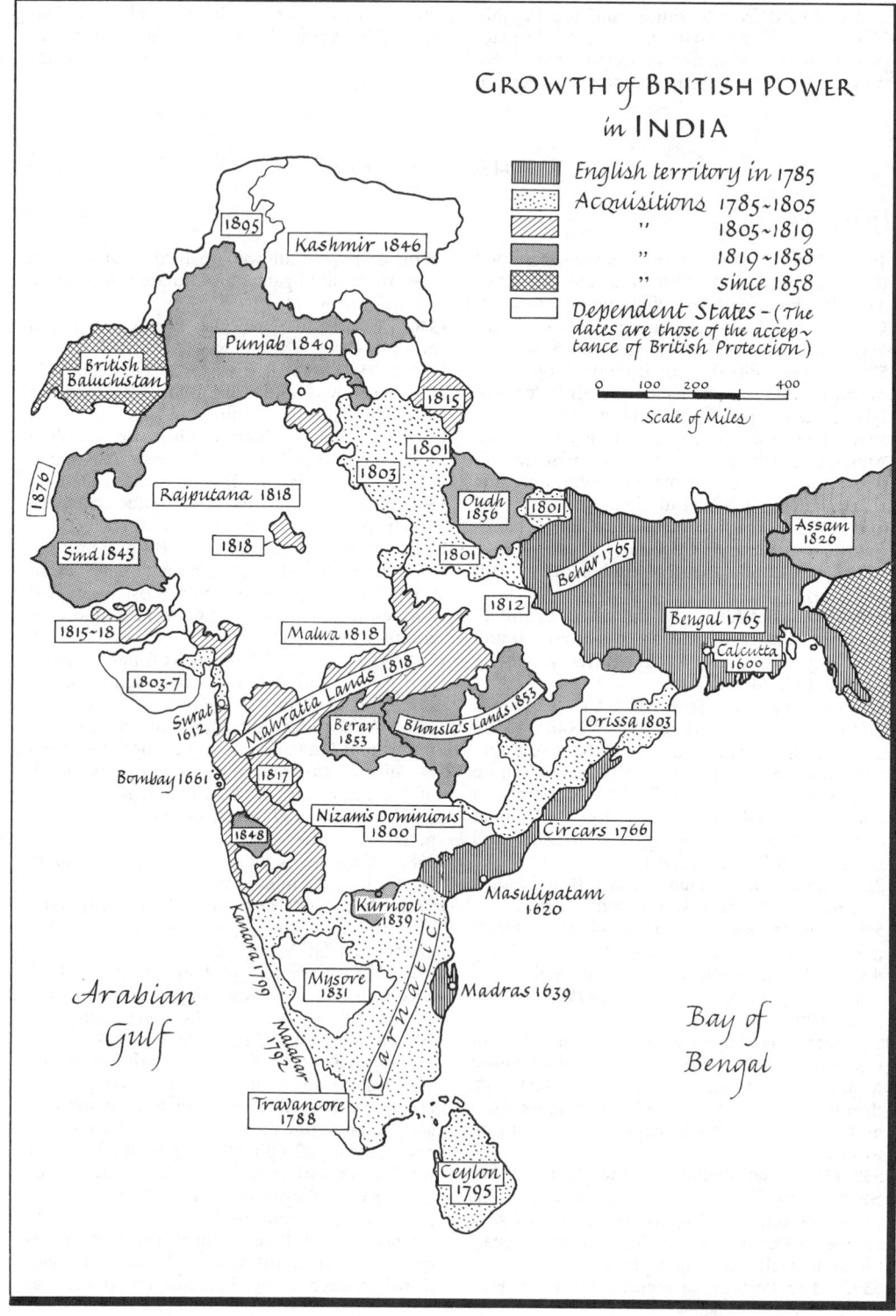

GROWTH of BRITISH POWER
in INDIA

English territory in 1785
Acquisitions 1785~1805
" 1805~1819
" 1819~1858
" since 1858
Dependent States ~ (The dates are those of the acceptance of British Protection)

0   100 200   400
Scale of Miles

1895
Kashmir 1846
Punjab 1849
British Baluchistan
1876
1815
1801
1803
Rajputana 1818
1818
Sind 1843
Oudh 1856
1801
Assam 1826
1801
Behar 1765
Bengal 1765
Calcutta 1600
Malwa 1818
1812
Mahratta Lands 1818
Surat 1612
Berar 1853
Bhonsla's Lands 1853
Orissa 1803
Bombay 1661
1817
Nizam's Dominions 1800
Circars 1766
1848
Masulipatam 1620
Kurnool 1839
Kanara 1799
Mysore 1831
Madras 1639
Arabian Gulf
Malabar 1792
Carnatic
Travancore 1788
Bay of Bengal
Ceylon 1795

The Mughal (Mogul) Emperors (1526–1858)

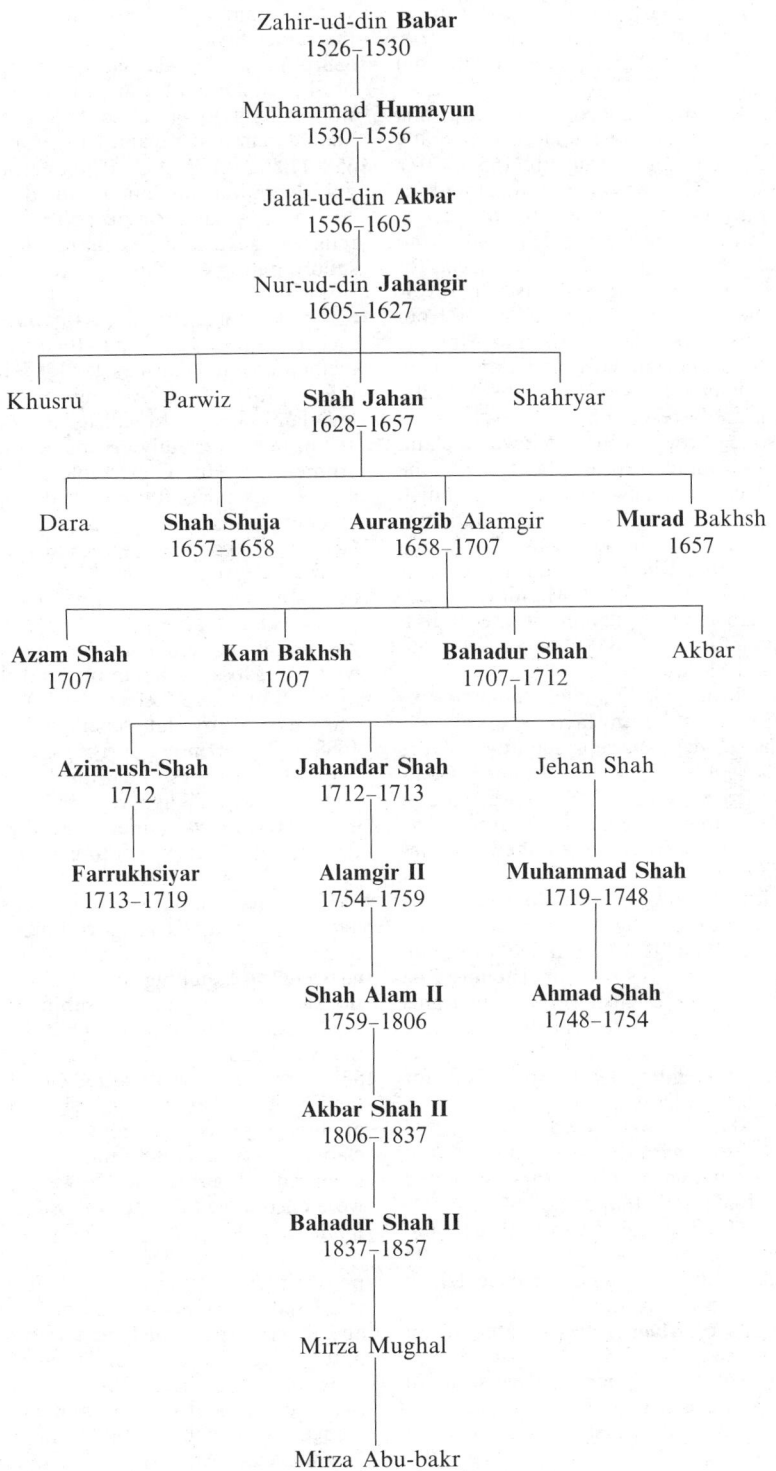

Zahir-ud-din **Babar**
1526–1530

Muhammad **Humayun**
1530–1556

Jalal-ud-din **Akbar**
1556–1605

Nur-ud-din **Jahangir**
1605–1627

Khusru Parwiz **Shah Jahan**
1628–1657 Shahryar

Dara **Shah Shuja**
1657–1658 **Aurangzib** Alamgir
1658–1707 **Murad** Bakhsh
1657

Azam Shah
1707 **Kam Bakhsh**
1707 **Bahadur Shah**
1707–1712 Akbar

Azim-ush-Shah
1712 **Jahandar Shah**
1712–1713 Jehan Shah

Farrukhsiyar
1713–1719 **Alamgir II**
1754–1759 **Muhammad Shah**
1719–1748

Shah Alam II
1759–1806 **Ahmad Shah**
1748–1754

Akbar Shah II
1806–1837

Bahadur Shah II
1837–1857

Mirza Mughal

Mirza Abu-bakr

levy of one-sixth plus numerous cesses which were now declared abolished; (4) the branding of all horses maintained for government service, to prevent usual fraud.

1576. **Bengal** was definitely conquered from the Afghans.

1577. **Khandesh** was induced to submit as first step toward reconquest of the Deccan, actually accomplished only by Aurangzib (1659–1707).

1578. Public debates on religion, instituted for Moslems only in 1575, were thrown open to Hindus, Jains, Zoroastrians, Sabaeans, and Christians. Akbar showed new respect for animal life (Jain *ahimsa*), Zoroastrian reverence for the sun, and invited to court from Goa the Portuguese Jesuits Antonio Monserrate and Rodolfo Acquaviva (1579; arr. 1580). These, like later missions (1590, 1595), failed despite a friendly reception.

1582. In spite of revolt which followed a claim to infallibility under Moslem law (1579), the emperor decreed a new *Divine Faith* much influenced by Sufi practice. The limited support he won for it collapsed at his death.

1589–1591. **Jamal Khan,** minister of Ahmadnagar, an adherent of the Mahdavi heresy which anticipated the advent of the Mahdi (world savior) in A. H. 1000, persecuted both Sunnites and Shi'ites.

1601–1604. Prince Salim, later Jahangir, rebelled but was restored to favor.

1603. **John Mildenhall,** representative of the English East India Company (London Company, founded December 31, 1600) arrived at Agra, but secured no concession until 1608.

1605–1627. **JAHANGIR** maintained his father's empire in northern India but, himself given to drink, allowed power to pass to his wife Nur Jahan (1611).

1609–1611. **William Hawkins** failed to secure a treaty for James I, as did **Sir Thomas Roe** (1615–1619), but the English won trading rights at Surat after defeating a Portuguese fleet (1612).

1616. **Bubonic plague,** clearly identified for the first time, became epidemic.

1628–1657. **SHAH JAHAN** (d. 1666) ruled with even less regard for his subjects, but destroyed Ahmadnagar (1632) and defeated Golconda (1635) and Bijapur (1636).

1632–1653. The **Taj Mahal** was built as tomb for his wife, Mumtaz Mahal, for whom he had already built the splendid palace Khass Mahal on the fort at Agra.

1639. The site of **Madras** was granted to an Englishman.

1647. **Aurangzib** campaigned unsuccessfully in Badakhshan and Balkh, and

1649–1653. Failed to wrest Kandahar from the Persians.

1653–1657. Again governing the Deccan, he campaigned ambitiously and arrested the revival of Bijapur; but failed to check the Maratha raider Sivaji.

1658. **Aurangzib rebelled,** following the illness of Shah Jahan and competition for the succession among his four sons. He imprisoned Shah Jahan and became emperor.

1658–1707. **AURANGZIB** emperor. The Mogul dominion was undermined, in part by Aurangzib's sacrifice of political stability to religious zeal, and his failure to control his subordinates, of whom he was inordinately suspicious.

1659–1680. Sivaji reduced Bijapur (1659) and sacked Surat (1664 and 1670); the English factory escaped harm. In 1667 he won the title of *rajah* from Aurangzib and began to levy land taxes in Mogul territory (Khandesh, 1670); he successfully organized Maratha government on Hindu principles with the guidance of the poets Ramdas and Tukaram, and was enthroned as an independent ruler (1674).

1666. Chittagong was annexed for Aurangzib by the Bengal governor.

1669. In the first purely religious persecution since Akbar's accession, the **Hindu religion was prohibited** and Hindu temples destroyed, with great loss to Indian art, and the *jizya* reimposed on non-Moslems (1679). The period was marked by Jat rebellions (1669, 1681, 1688–1707), Hindu uprisings, and troubles with Afghan tribes and with the now militant and theocratic Sikhs (1675–1678).

1679. **Marwar** was annexed in war against the Rajputs; hostilities continued nearly thirty years.

1681. Prince Akbar revolted unsuccessfully against his father's misgovernment, and died in exile.

1681–1707. Assuming personal command in the Deccan, Aurangzib subjugated Bijapur (1686) and Golconda (1687) but failed to check the Marathas.

1685–1688. **Aurangzib seized Surat** (1685), intending to expel the English, whose unwise attempt to seize Chittagong lost them all their claims in Bengal (1688); their naval superiority menaced Mogul trade, however, and they were encouraged to return to Bengal (**Calcutta founded,** 1690).

Following the decline of the Portuguese power in India, that of the English had been increased by the acquisition of **Bombay** (1661) and the absorption of Dutch ambitions chiefly in the Spice Islands. Foundation of the French *Compagnie des Indes Orientales* (1664) under strict government control, and numerous settlements (Pondichéry, 1674), now opened the way for acute Anglo-French rivalry.

1689. Capture of Sivaji's successor, **Sambhaji,** failed to crush the Marathas and indecisive warfare continued until 1707.

The intellectual curiosity and luxurious tastes of the Mogul rulers, except Aurangzib, fostered brilliant cultural progress. Histories, annals, and memoirs, chiefly in Persian, a dictionary supported by Jahangir, and the unsurpassed poems of **Tulsi Das** (1532–1623), formed important literary contributions. Slavish imitation of Persian painting was modified by Hindu and even European influences; a height of keen observation and delicate rendering was attained under Shah Jahan. Under him also the building of palaces, mausoleums, and mosques in Indo-Persian style attained an exquisite elegance.

1707– Following Aurangzib's death the empire rapidly disintegrated; various provincial governors became virtually independent (1722 ff.), and wars of succession and foreign invasions culminated in anarchy.

c. 1708. The **Sikhs,** who had been founded in the 15th century as a strictly religious order, proclaiming Moslem and Hindu fellowship and monotheism, and opposing caste restrictions and priestcraft (except for the secular and religious authority vested in the Guru Hargovind, 1606), became a thoroughly militant order under the last Guru, **Govind Singh** (1666–1708); they menaced Mogul rights in the Deccan but their strength was broken by Bahadur Shah (1707–1712).

1717. The **English East India Company,** through gifts and medical service, secured from the Mogul emperor exemption from customs duties and other concessions.

The reorganized Maratha government gradually became pre-eminent in India, exacting taxes from the whole Deccan excepting Hyderabad, which became virtually independent of Delhi (1724) under its governor, the **Nizam-ul-Mulk** (d. 1748). The governors of Avadh (Oudh) (1724) and Bengal (1740) also became independent, but maintained the fiction of allegiance to the Mogul emperor.

1739. A pillaging invasion of Persians under **Nadir Shah** checked the Maratha expansion northward, defeated imperial troops, and withdrew, retaining possession of Afghanistan and the wealth of Delhi.

1746–1748. Following the outbreak of the **War of the Austrian Succession** in Europe, the French, strengthened by their participation in Indian intrigue under the guidance of **Joseph Dupleix,** captured Madras (1746) and defeated the protesting nawab of the Carnatic. The **treaty of Aix-la-Chapelle** (1748) restored Madras to Britain.

1748–1754. **Anglo-French rivalry** continued, each side supporting candidates for the positions of nizam of the Deccan and nawab of the Carnatic. French domination, at its height in 1751 when **Bussy** virtually ruled the Deccan and Dupleix the Carnatic, was checked by **Robert Clive's** (1727–1774) brilliant seizure of Arcot (Sept. 12, 1751). The recall of Dupleix (1754) left English prestige firmly established.

1756. The nawab **(Siraj-ud-Daulah)** of the Bengal region captured Calcutta (June 20) and imprisoned unescaped residents in a small storeroom in the fort (later called the "Black Hole"), where over a hundred perished from suffocation, wounds, and the heat.

1757. British forces under **Watson** and Clive retook Calcutta and, being again at war with France, seized Chandernagor (Mar. 23). Clive formed a conspiracy with Hindu bankers and the nawab's general, **Mir Jafar,** which enabled his forces to rout those remaining loyal to the nawab at **Plassey** (June 23). Mir Jafar, having executed Siraj-ud-Daulah, was installed as nawab under a virtual English protectorate of Bengal.

1758–1760. Maratha occupation of the Punjab (1758) and renewed northern activity (1760) excited allied opposition of the Rohilla Afghans and **Ahmad Shah Abdali** (the Durani Afghan chief, who had invaded the Punjab almost annually between 1748 and 1759). The Marathas were crushingly defeated by this coalition in

1761. Jan. 14. The battle of Panipat. Subsequent mutiny caused Ahmad Shah's withdrawal, leaving India in dissension.

British supremacy in India's foreign relations was assured by their defeat of the Dutch (1759) and capture of **Pondichéry** from the French, who by the **treaty of Paris** (1763) retained only Pondichéry, Chandernagor, and other scattered stations, with limited numbers of troops. The *Compagnie des Indes Orientales* was dissolved in 1769.

1764, Oct. 22. Victory at Baksar over forces of the deposed nawab of Bengal, the nawab of Avadh, and the titular Mogul emperor gave the British uncontested control in Bengal and Bihar.

1765–1767. Clive administered Bengal affairs for the company: the powerless Mogul emperor was induced to grant it *diwani* (revenue control) in Bengal, Bihar, and part of Orissa, the company taking over the actual collection of revenue in 1771. Official perquisites were reduced among the company's servants, whose rapacity since 1757 Clive had encouraged by his own example.

The militarism of the Moguls and the predatory policy of the Marathas led to an emphasis on warfare and piracy as sources of prestige and wealth, and a gradual decline of industry, education, and cultural progress except as maintained by some Moslem and Hindu poets and scholars, notably the Delhi reformer **Shah Wali-Ullah** (1703–1760) and the Bengali poet **Bharatchandra** (1717–1760). General economic chaos ensued, with Europeans profiting greatly from gifts, forced sales, and usury. One exception was Indore (1765–1795) under the rule of the pious **Ahalya Bai.**

During dissension in the Maratha confederacy, **Haidar Ali** (1721–1782) gained power, usurped the throne of Mysore (1761), and

1769. Compelled the British at Madras, who became involved in war against him (1767), to sign a treaty of mutual assistance.

1769–1770. Disastrous famine in Bengal wiped out an estimated one-third of the population.

1772–1785. As governor of Bengal, **Warren Hastings** (1732–1818) initiated reforms, including simplification of the revenue system, improved coinage, government control of salt and opium manufacture, reduction of dacoity, and study of Moslem and Hindu law (Calcutta Madrasa, 1781). He was styled governor-general, with certain supervisory powers over the other two company presidencies (Bombay and Madras) under the

1773. REGULATING ACT, by which parliament also established a supreme court for British subjects in the company's territories, limited the rights of the company's directors, and prohibited officers' private trade and receipt of presents. Hastings' high-handed measures kept the company solvent and relatively secure in a turbulent period, but incurred the censure of jealous colleagues, notably Philip Francis, and led to his impeachment (after his retirement in 1785) with a trial (1788–1795) resulting in acquittal.

1775–1782. First Anglo-Maratha War, the result of the Bombay government's alliance with the would-be Maratha peshwa, **Raghoba.** Hastings sent an expedition across the peninsula from Calcutta to Surat (1778, arrived 1779), and broke the coalition between the Marathas, Haidar Ali, and the nizam. The **treaty of Salbai** (1782) obtained for Bombay twenty years' peace with the Marathas and the cession of Salsette and Elephanta.

1778. France and Britain being again at war, Hastings took Pondichéry and Mahé. Provoked by this action,

1780–1784. Haidar Ali, with French help, attacked the British in the Carnatic, but was defeated at **Porto Novo** (1781) and died (1782); the **Second Anglo-Mysore War,** continued by his son, **Tipu Sultan,** was terminated when French aid was withdrawn.

1784. PITT'S INDIA ACT, in an endeavor to check territorial expansion, forbade interference in native affairs or declaration of war except in case of aggression, and made the company's directors answerable to a board of control appointed by the crown.

1786–1793. Lord Cornwallis (after a 20-month interregnum of Sir John MacPherson) became governor-general and commander-in-chief, with power to overrule his council. Under injunctions to preserve peace, he made administrative reforms: company officers given adequate fixed salaries and their private trade eliminated; separation of administrative from commercial branches of service.

1790–1792. Tipu attacked Travancore, opening the **Third Anglo-Mysore War;** Cornwallis allied himself with the peshwa and the nizam, and Tipu was defeated and ceded half his territory, paying a large indemnity (Mar. 19, 1792).

1791. The Sanskrit College was established at Benares by Jonathan Duncan.

1793. Cornwallis' Code inaugurated substantial reforms. The *Permanent Settlement* stabilized the revenue system by fixing the assessment in Bengal, Bihar, and Orissa (and Benares Province, 1795) with collection through *zamindars,* but failed to check the latter's exploitation of the peasantry; it also effected ruthless sale of *zamindar* rights in case of default, and closed the way to later reassessments, thereby eventually causing great financial loss to the government. The **judicial system** was reshaped on the British model, but with a paucity of courts. **Indians were excluded from all higher posts.** *Zamindars* were left only revenue duties, their magisterial and police functions being transferred to European district judges and Indian police (*darogas*).

In the Madras presidency a careful survey along the lines of local practice led to a system of direct levy (periodically reassessed) from the *ryot* (peasant), later extended to Bombay presidency; in the Northwest and Central Provinces, somewhat later, the *mahalwari* system was introduced, collecting revenue through villages or estates.

Meanwhile the principal Maratha leader, **Mahadaji Sindhia** (d. 1794) assumed protection of the emperor, reclaimed Delhi, and extended his power in northern India.

1793. Sir John Shore, governor-general.

1796. Ceylon conquered from the Dutch, and administered jointly by the East India Company and the crown until 1802, the latter assuming full responsibility thereafter.

(Cont. p. 900.)

4. CHINA, 1520–1798

(*From p. 371*)

1520–1521. The **Portuguese,** who under Albuquerque had seized Malacca (1511), sent Thomé Pires to Peking. Piratical conduct of Simao d'Andrade and others led to their expulsion from China in 1522.

1522–1566. The **CHIA CHING REIGN** of Shih Tsung was filled with the effort to repel attacks (especially 1542 and 1550) of Altan Khan, prince of the Ordos; and of Japanese pirates (1523 and 1552), who even besieged Nanking (1555).

1557. A Portuguese settlement was permanently established at **Macao.**

1577. So-nam gya-tso, third successor of Tsong-kha-pa (1357–1419), who reformed **Tibetan Buddhism** by foundation of the yellow-capped "Virtuous" church, and himself an incarnation of Avalokitesvara, presided over a Mongol assembly beside Koko-nor. Altan Khan entitled him *Dalai Lama* (Lama of all within the seas), and formally accepted his spiritual authority for his people. The hold of the Tibetan church over Mongolia was cemented by recognition of two new divine incarnations: **Manjusri** in the Dongkur Hutuktu of the Ordos (1579) and **Maitreya** in the Jebdzun-damba Hutuktu of Urga (c. 1602).

1573–1620. The **WAN LI REIGN** of Shen Tsung is famous for cultural achievements.

1592–1593, 1597–1598. Japanese invasions of tributary Korea sent by Hideyoshi were repelled, the first from P'yŏng-yang (1593), the second from southern Korea.

1615. Nurhachi gave military organizations as eight banners to a group of Tungus tribes in eastern Manchuria.

1616. He adopted the title *Chin Khan* and the surname *Aisin Gioro,* "Golden Tribe," to identify his people as heirs of the Chin (1116–1234). They later (1652) called themselves *Manchus* (Man-chou, probably from the Bodhisattva of learning, Manjusri).

1621. He expelled the Ming from the Liao Basin and moved his capital to Liaoyang.

1636. The **MANCHUS** proclaimed an imperial Ta Ch'ing dynasty at Mukden, and set up a civilian administration copied closely from the Chinese.

1644. The **last Ming emperor** hanged himself when a bandit, Li Tzu-ch'eng, seized Peking.

MING THOUGHT was at first almost wholly dominated by authority of **Chu Hsi** and his school. The *Hsing Li Ta Ch'üan,* a digest of moral philosophy from the works of 120 of these scholars, was published under imperial

authority in 1416. Opposition to the positive and authoritarian aspects of such teaching was most vigorously expressed by **Wang Shou-jen** (pen-name *Wang Yang-ming*) (1472–1528 or 1529), who insisted that moral judgments spring from the intuitive faculties within all men. Sages differ from common men in quantity, not quality, of true perceptions. Experience is for him the test of truth. Chu Hsi, through emphasis on objective study, had opened the door to scientific research. Wang, by insistence on subjectivity, did much to prevent it.

The early part of the dynasty saw a vigorous national reaction led by the **Academy of Letters** (*Han Lin Yüan*) against all things foreign. Buddhism was now almost completely naturalized as Chinese, and Islam was too strongly entrenched in the north and southwest to be eradicated; but both Nestorian and Roman Christianity were suppressed. So too were various secret fraternities with obscure social and authoritarian objectives, like the **White Cloud** and the **White Lotus,** which had enjoyed official status under the Mongols.

Matteo Ricci (1552–1610, Macao, 1582) won toleration for the Jesuits and a salary at court (1601) by presenting clocks, etc., to the throne and preparing a huge map of the world. News in Peking (1606) of the arrival in Kansu of **Benedict de Goez,** who had come overland from India (1603–1605), first established for modern Europe identity of Marco Polo's **Cathay** with maritime China (*Thinai* in the *Periplus,* A.D. 80–89, from Sanskrit *Cina*). Rapid conversions and private church services at Nanking brought suspicion of secret aims like those of the White Lotus, and consequent deportation (1616) of the missionaries to Macao, whence they gradually returned. **Johann Schall von Bell** (1591–1666, Peking, 1622) was charged (1630) to reform the dynastic calendar (already begun by Jesuits, 1611 and 1629). He cast astronomical instruments; and (1636–1637) twenty 40-pound cannon, with camel-guns for use against the Manchus.

The **Academy of Letters** supervised an imposing series of official compilations. The *Yung Lo Ta Tien,* an encyclopedia into which numerous whole works were transcribed, was compiled in 10,000 manuscript volumes of folio size (1403–1409). The precedents of the T'ang, Sung, and Yüan were followed by issue, in numerous editions, of the dynastic legal and administrative codes and a territorial survey of the empire. The practice was begun of gathering many small choice works by various authors into uniform collections. **Mao Chin** published from his private library the *Chi Ku Ko*, fine critical editions of the *Thirteen Classics with Commentaries,* the *Seventeen Standard Histories,* and many other works.

Ming painters, besides much imitation of Sung ink landscape, which was now reduced to conventional formulae, revived a coloristic tradition of vivid blues and greens. **Tai Chin** (fl. c. 1446) especially developed a new style of free rapid composition in ink which was better adapted to representation of life and movement than the exquisite but somewhat static Sung technique. The potters of the Hung Wu and Yung Lo reigns achieved bold effects by application of "three-color" glazes (aubergine, turquoise, and yellow) with dark blue to monumental potiches. In the Hsüan Te period they learned to control copper oxide red for decoration of white paste under clear glaze, in addition to the cobalt "Mohammedan blue" of which the purest supply came intermittently from Turkestan. Decoration in overglaze enamels, often in combination with underglaze blue, was used brilliantly on rather bombastic vases in the Chia Ching and Wan Li periods. The imperial kilns at Ching-te-chen in Kiangsi were developed to supply immense quantities of porcelain to the palace.

1644–1912. The **CH'ING DYNASTY** entered Peking by surprise when the Manchu regent **Dorgun** (1643–1650) had helped the Ming general Wu San-kuei to drive off the bandit Li Tzu-ch'eng.

1644–1661. The **SHUN CHIH REIGN** of Shih Tsu was filled with military effort to destroy Ming resistance, which centered about Prince Fu at Nanking (1644–1645), Prince T'ang in Fukien (1645–1646), Prince Lu at Shaohsing, Amoy, Chusan (1645–1651), and Prince Kuei from Canton to Yünnan (1646–1659). Conquest was accompanied by imposition of the Manchu shaven head with queue. Foot-binding, at first forbidden (1638, 1645, 1662), was at length permitted to Chinese only (1668). Manchus were appointed as colleagues of Chinese in all principal posts of central administration, and garrisons from the eight Manchu banners were distributed among strategic provincial cities; but Chinese were appointed in the provinces both to civil posts and to command of Chinese auxiliary troops. Four Chinese were sent as viceroys to hold the south and southwest.

1645–1683. A pirate dynasty upheld the Ming. Chen Chih-lung (1645–1646, executed at Peking 1661) was succeeded by **Cheng Ch'eng-kung,** known to the Portuguese as *Koxinga* (1646–1662). Koxinga seized Amoy (1653), Ch'ung-ming Island (1656), attacked Nanking (1657), and by a long siege of Fort Zelandia (1661–1662) wrested Formosa from the Dutch. So formidable was his naval power that the Manchus decreed (1661) evacuation of the whole coastal population to a depth of ten miles from the sea.

1662–1722. The **K'ANG HSI REIGN** of Sheng Tsu (b. 1654, personal rule in form 1667, in fact 1669) opened a period of cultural achievement which surpassed the greatest of earlier dynasties. The fifteen provinces of the Ming were increased to eighteen by separate recognition of Anhuei (1662), Hunan (1664), and Kansu (1705).

The **Dutch** had founded Batavia (1619), a Formosan station (1624–1625), and captured Malacca (1641) from the Portuguese, who lost their commercial empire, but retained Macao. A mission of Pieter van Goyer and Jacob van Keyser (1656) secured nothing better than tributary status, only slightly improved (1667) by the mission of Pieter van Hoorn. Disgruntled by loss of Zelandia,

1663–1664. Balthasar Bort with a Dutch fleet helped a Chinese army drive Koxinga's son and successor, Cheng Chin (1662–1681), from the Fukien coast to Formosa.

1670. A Portuguese embassy under **Manoel de Saldanha,** like that of Bento Pereyra de Faria (1678–1679), won only confirmation of the status of Macao. The much later missions of A. M. de Souza y Menezas (1726) and F.-X. Assis Pacheco y Sampayo (1742) achieved no more.

1674–1681. Revolt of three viceroys followed imperial orders providing for their withdrawal (1673).

1674. Viceroy Wu San-kuei from Yünnan held Szechuan, Kueichou, Hunan, and Kwangsi for five years (1674–1679). Keng Ching-chung, grandson and heir of the Fukien viceroy, joined him and invaded Kiangsi.

1675. A revolt by Burni in Chahar was quickly suppressed. Cheng Chin's pirates resumed depredations in Chekiang and Fukien.

1676. Shang Chih-hsin forced his aged father, viceroy of Kwangtung, to surrender Canton to the rebels.

1681. Re-entrance of imperial armies to Yünnan City marked complete military triumph, supplemented by

1683. Surrender of Formosa by Cheng Chin's son Cheng K'o-shuang (1681–1683). Formosa was for the first time given imperial administration, as appendage of Fukien.

The Russian **Poyarkhov** explored the Amur (1643–1646) and Khabarov built a fort at Albazin (1651). A mission under Baikov (1656) proved futile, but Spatar Milescu (1676) performed the kotow (*k'ou t'ou*) with dignity on a

The Manchu (Ta Ch'ing) Dynasty (1644–1795)

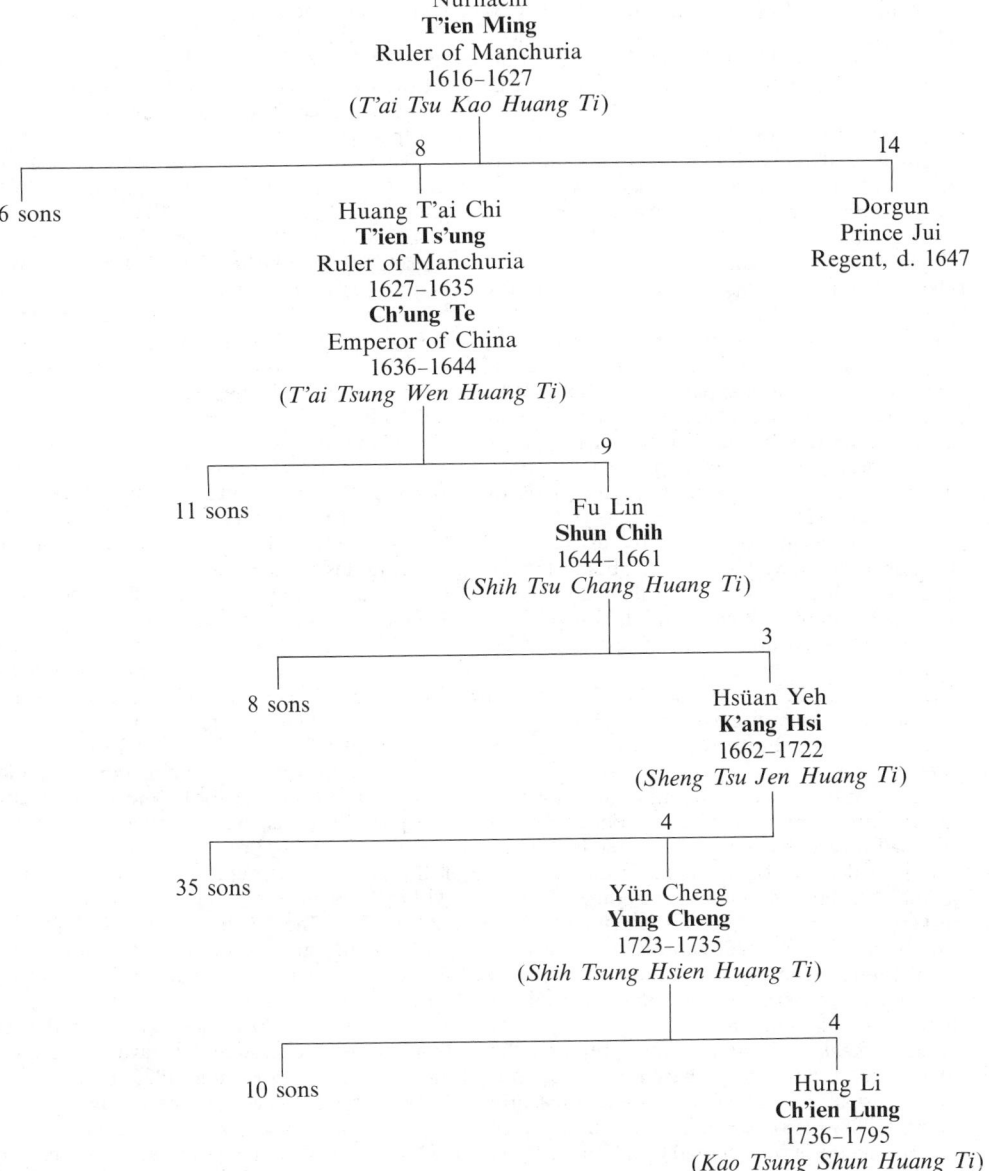

Nurhachi
T'ien Ming
Ruler of Manchuria
1616–1627
(*T'ai Tsu Kao Huang Ti*)

8   14

16 sons

Huang T'ai Chi
T'ien Ts'ung
Ruler of Manchuria
1627–1635
Ch'ung Te
Emperor of China
1636–1644
(*T'ai Tsung Wen Huang Ti*)

Dorgun
Prince Jui
Regent, d. 1647

9

11 sons

Fu Lin
Shun Chih
1644–1661
(*Shih Tsu Chang Huang Ti*)

3

8 sons

Hsüan Yeh
K'ang Hsi
1662–1722
(*Sheng Tsu Jen Huang Ti*)

4

35 sons

Yün Cheng
Yung Cheng
1723–1735
(*Shih Tsung Hsien Huang Ti*)

4

10 sons

Hung Li
Ch'ien Lung
1736–1795
(*Kao Tsung Shun Huang Ti*)

NOTE: Names in plain type are personal names, taboo after a ruler ascended the throne.
Names in boldface type are reign titles, or year names, adopted for reckoning time, but often applied by Westerners to the emperor himself.
Names in italic type are dynastic titles, or temple names, conferred posthumously to refer to the ruler. *Huang Ti* means simply "emperor." (*Cont. p. 910.*)

reciprocal basis, and mapped Siberia.

1689. By the **treaty of Nerchinsk** the Russians adopted advice of the Jesuit negotiator Jean-François Gerbillon to abandon Albazin and military pressure for commercial penetration. L. V. Izmailov (1720-1721) established a trading agent and an Eastern Orthodox church in Peking.

1691. The emperor, at a great assembly of Mongols at Dolon Nor, reorganized the four Khalkha states of central Mongolia which he had just defended (1690) against the provoked attack (1688) of Galdan, chief of the Olöt (West Mongol) Jungars.

1696. Galdan was crushed near Urga and took poison (1697).

1705. Forcible enthronement as dalai lama at Lhasa of an imperial candidate aroused Tibetan opposition and appeal to the Olöt (1714).

1712. Domestic peace since 1681 and vigilant administration with frugality not only paid for foreign wars, but led to a permanent settlement of land and poll-taxes on the basis of returns for 1711.

1717. Olöt **seizure of Lhasa** by direction of Galdan's nephew, Tsewang Rabdan (1697-1727), was learned in Peking too late to save a relief column from annihilation (1718). Well-prepared armies from Kansu and Szechwan.

1720. Enthroned a popular dalai lama and established imperial garrisons in Tibet.

1721. Revolt in Formosa led by Chu I-kuei was suppressed.

The **Jesuits** enjoyed toleration and favor in return for scientific services. **Johann Schall von Bell** prepared the dynastic calendar (1630-1664) until imprisoned on representations of jealous Moslem astronomers. **Ferdinand Verbiest** (1623-1688, arr. 1659) was reinstated in control of the almanac (1669), installed a new set of instruments on the observatory (1674), and promulgated a perpetual calendar (1678). **Fontaney** cured the emperor of fever with quinine (1693). **Régis** and eight others prepared the first maps of China to be based on astronomical observation, triangulation, and measurement (1708-1718). Benefits of an edict of toleration (1692) were ruined by a bitter quarrel over Jesuit acceptance of Chinese rites toward Heaven, Confucius, and ancestors. These rites were condemned (1693) by Mgr. Maigrot. Appeal to the emperor (1700) accentuated conflict of imperial and papal authority, which neither of two patriarchs, De Tournon (1705) and Mezzabarba (1720), sent by Clement XI, could reconcile. Dabbling in intrigue for succession among the twenty adult sons of the emperor won only (1722) permanent hostility of the victor, the end of the active mission.

From his accession **Sheng Tsu** labored to win support of the scholar class by daily classical study, honors to Confucius and the Sung Neo-Confucianists (*Ju*), and patronage of scholarship. He founded (1677) the **College of Inscriptions** (*Nan San So*) affiliated to the Academy of Letters. Most important among many books compiled by his order, in addition to the several administrative and archival works prescribed by precedent, were the standard *Ming History* (53 scholars appointed, 1679), *Complete T'ang Poetry* (1707), the *P'ei Wen Chai Shu Hua P'u* repertory of works on painting (1708), the *Yüan Chien Lei Han* encyclopedia (1710), *P'ei Wen Yün Fu* thesaurus of literary phrases (1711), *K'ang Hsi* dictionary (1716), and the *T'u Shu Chi Ch'eng* encyclopedia (5020 volumes 1726). Private scholars were also active: **Huang Tsung-hsi** (1610-1695), the philosopher and critical historian of Sung, Yüan, and Ming philosophy; **Ku Yen-wu** (1613-1681), historical geographer and critic; **Chu I-tsun** (1629-1709), author of the critical bibliography of the classics *Ching I K'ao;* **Hsü Ch'ien-hsüeh** (1631-1694), who brought together 480 volumes of choice classical comment, *T'ung Chih T'ang Ching Chieh;* **Mei Wen-ting** (1633-1721), the mathematician; and many others.

The most brilliant epoch in the history of the imperial kilns at Ching-te-chen followed appointment of **Ts'ang Ying-hsüan** as supervisor (1682). The techniques of enameling on the biscuit, of composite monochrome glazing over colored glaze, of application of underglaze blue in powder form, and of decoration overglaze in transparent *famille verte* enamels were perfected. Progress of the minor arts followed establishment of 28 kinds of artisans within the palace precincts (1680).

1723-1735. The **YUNG CHENG REIGN** of Shih Tsung, although peaceful at home, was filled with inconclusive war against Mongols and western tribesmen.

1727. The **Kiakhta treaty** fixing the Russian frontier was concluded by Sava Vladislavich after a mission to Peking (1726-1727).

1729. Large-scale operations against the Jungars led to

1732. Establishment of an advisory military council (*Chün Chi Ch'u*) which gradually usurped the executive functions of the grand secretariat (*Nei Ko*).

1736-1795. The **CH'IEN LUNG REIGN** of Kao Tsung marks a new advance in population and wealth, which supported imposition of imperial control throughout Central Asia. Cultural activity continued to enjoy imperial patronage and leadership. Corruption of the civil service led by the venal Ho Shen (1750-1799) during the last twenty years of the reign provoked revolts which continued until the end of the dynasty.

1747-1749, 1755-1779. Campaigns of exceptional difficulty were waged to pacify the native tribes of the Tibetan border.

1750. Violence by and against the imperial residents at Lhasa led to the

1751. INVASION OF TIBET and establishment of control over the succession and the temporal acts of the dalai lama.

1755. Amursana, grandson of Tsewang Rabdan, after ten years' succession struggle, was enthroned by imperial troops as prince of the Jungars, but revolted. Suppression of the revolt, following a smallpox epidemic, depopulated the Ili Valley. The Jungars were annihilated or dispersed.

1757-1842. Restriction of foreign maritime trade to Canton was maintained despite efforts of the British interpreter Flint at Tientsin (1759), Capt. Skottowe at Canton (1761), and the earl of Macartney at Jehol and Peking (1793).

1758-1759. Kashgaria was conquered by Chaohui from the Turkish Khoja dynasty.

1765-1769. Invasion of Burma failed to reach Ava, but secured recognition of suzerainty.

1771. The Torgud, who had fled beyond the Volga to escape the Jungars, now dared accept an invitation by T'u-li-ch'en (1712), and migrated back to Ili.

1774. The first Chinese rebellion in nearly a century broke out in Shantung and was traced to the White Lotus Society.

1781, 1784. Revolts in Kansu by Moslems, including the Wahabis, were suppressed.

1784. The **United States** entered the profitable Canton trade.

1786-1787. Revolt in Formosa was suppressed.

1792. Invasion of Nepal under Fu-k'ang-an, provoked by attack on Tashilunpo, the seat of the panchan lama, resulted in defeat of the Gurkhas and their recognition of imperial suzerainty.

1795-1797. Revolt by the Miao tribes of Hunan and Kueichou was suppressed.

The best critical edition of the 24 *Standard Histories* was issued by imperial authority (1739-1746). Chief among many later imperial literary enterprises was the assemblage (1772-1781), by manuscript transcription, of a select library, *Ssu K'u Ch'üan Shu* or *Complete Work of the Four Treasuries,* embracing 3462 works in 36,300 volumes. Seven copies were eventually distributed. The printed critical *General Catalogue* in 92 volumes (1789) contains additional notices of 6734 works not included in the library. The emperor exploited the occasion of compilation to expurgate from Chinese literature all derogatory references to the Manchus

and their northern predecessors. More than 2000 works were condemned to total destruction (1774-1782), most of them minor writings of the period 1616-1681. Contrary to precedent, two propagandist histories were compiled fraudulently to identify the Manchus as descendants of the Jürchen Chin. The technique of textual criticism was perfected and applied by numerous able scholars to the classics, especially by **Lu Wen-ch'ao** (1717-1795), **Chiang Sheng** (1721-1799), and **Tuan Yüts'ai** (1735-1815). **Wang Ming-sheng** (1722-1797) and **Ch'ien Ta-hsin** (1728-1804) distinguished themselves as commentators on the standard histories. **Pi Yüan** (1730-1797) compiled a supplement to the general history of Ssu-ma Kuang. The practice of gathering choice literature of diverse kinds into uniform collections was spurred by issue from the imperial Wu Ying Tien of a series of 138 works printed from movable wooden type in 800 volumes (1773-1783). **Pao T'ing-po** (1728-1814) published his *Chih Pu Tsu Chai Ts'ung Shu* in 240 volumes.

Under direction of **T'ang-Ying** (1736-1749) the imperial kilns at Ching-te-chen developed the elaborate *famille rose* palette of opaque overglaze enamels, which is distinguished by mixed colors and replacement of ferric oxide red by carmine derived from gold.

1795. Kao Tsung abdicated, but continued to direct affairs until death (1798).

(*Cont. p. 909.*)

a. BURMA, 1519-1767

(*From p. 371*)

Following the arrival during the 15th century of a few European travelers (Nicolo di Conti, c. 1435), in

1519. The Portuguese by treaty secured trading privileges at Martaban, and an increasing portion of the foreign trade was conducted by Europeans.

1539. Tabin Shwehti, ruler of Toungoo (1531-1550), captured Pegu, was crowned king of Lower Burma (1542), and after extending his power northward to Pagan (1546) assumed the title of *King of all Burma.* With Portuguese mercenaries he attacked unsuccessfully both Arakan to the west and Siam to the east.

1555. His successor, **Bayin Naung** (ruled 1551-1581), took Ava, destroyed the Tai kingdom of Chiengmai (1557) in northern Siam, and subdued Ayuthia (1563) temporarily. Exhausted by these wars, the central power declined; in

1600. Pegu was destroyed and Burma broke up into a number of petty states.

1619. The Dutch and English East India Companies opened factories. They did not flourish and were closed later in the century.

1753. Alaungpaya reunited Burma, with assistance from the English East India Company and in opposition to the French. His second successor destroyed Ayuthia (1767) and subdued Siam for a time, retaining the Tenasserim coast in Burmese possession. (*Cont. p. 904.*)

b. SIAM, 1602–1782

(*From p. 372*)

Portuguese trading stations were established in the 16th century and about the beginning of the 17th century large numbers of Japanese were active in Siam, in war and trade.

1602. A Dutch trading post was established at Patani, where the English soon followed, until their withdrawal from Siam in 1623.

1664. By a commercial treaty, the Dutch gained a monopoly of Siamese foreign trade, which was, however, thwarted by French intrigue; a French embassy and military expedition (1685) in turn failed to secure the acceptance of Christianity and French influence, and led to

1688. A popular revolt which began a period of prolonged civil war.

1767. A **Burmese invasion** destroyed Ayuthia and compelled temporary acceptance of Burmese rule until

1782. Rama I founded a new Siamese dynasty, with its capital at Bangkok. (*Cont. p. 906.*)

c. MALAYSIA, 1511–1790

(*From p. 372*)

1511. The Portuguese, under **Albuquerque, captured Malacca,** center of the spice trade. They then sent envoys to open trade relations with native states and set up fortified posts to protect the trade.

1594. The Lisbon spice market was closed to Dutch and English traders, thus providing an incentive to direct trade with the Far East. The English and Dutch **East India Companies** (1600, 1602) presently destroyed the Portuguese forts in Malaysia.

1596. The Dutch set up a factory at **Palembang** (Sumatra).

1602. The English established themselves at **Bantam** (northwest Java).

1605. The Dutch seized Amboina, then settled in western Timor (1613) and in

1619. Built Batavia. It became the headquarters of the Dutch East India Company, which worked trade to the limit.

1623. Massacre of the English by the Dutch at **Amboina.** The English forced to abandon trade in Siam, Japan, and the East Indies.

1639. Expulsion of the Portuguese from Japan.

1641. Capture of Malacca by the Dutch, who thenceforth dominated the East Indies.

1666. The Dutch took Celebes from the Portuguese.

1685. The British set up a **factory at Bengkulen** (Sumatra).

During the 18th century the Dutch continued to hold the upper hand. Growing ruthlessness and corruption of the company. In order to control the trade, the company had to widen its control over northern Java.

1769. The **British East India Company** opened stations in northern Borneo, but the settlements (especially **Balambangan,** 1773) had to be given up under pressure from the natives (1775).

1781. The British conquered all the Dutch settlements on the west coast of **Sumatra,** Holland having joined the armed neutrality against Britain.

1783. By the **treaty of Paris** the British returned the Dutch colonies, but secured the right to trade throughout the Dutch island possessions.

1786. The British East India Company secured a grant of Penang (permanent cession 1790), which made a fourth Indian presidency (1805), but proved useless as a naval and commercial base. (*Cont. p. 908.*)

5. THE PHILIPPINES, 1521–1764

1521, Mar. 15. The islands were discovered by **Magellan,** who was killed there (Apr. 25) in a fight with the natives.

1525–1527. In order to strengthen Castilian claims against Portugal, Charles V sent out an expedition under **García Jofre de Loyasa,** who died en route. The expedition visited Mindanao, but Portuguese opposition was encountered and no results were obtained.

1527. Under orders from home, **Cortés** (in Mexico) sent out **Alvaro Saavedra Ceron,** whose fleet was dispersed without accomplishing anything.

1529. Lack of success in these efforts induced Charles V to conclude with Portugal the **treaty of Saragossa,** by which the line of demarcation in the Far East was fixed 297.5 leagues east of the Moluccas, which remained Portuguese. The Philippines, though within Portuguese jurisdiction, were not occupied by Portugal.

1532. Charles V granted **Pedro de Alvarado** authority to conduct discovery and colonization in the Pacific. Alvarado abandoned the project in order to attempt the conquest of Quito.

1541. The viceroy of New Spain, **Antonio de Mendoza,** was given authority for the same purpose but was to share the results with Alvarado.

1542–1543. Mendoza sent out **Ruy Lopez de Villalobos,** who landed and named the islands, though he was then driven off by the natives and later captured by the Portuguese.

1565–1571. Under instructions from Philip II, the viceroy **Luis de Velasco** sent out an expedition under **Miguel Lopez de Legazpi,** who made the first settlement (San Miguel), subjugated the natives, and founded **Manila** (May 19, 1571). An *audiencia* was established at Manila (1583) and the islands were subordinated to the government of New Spain.

1762, Sept. 22. A British fleet bombarded Manila and took the city (Oct. 5).

1764, Mar. 31. The British evacuated Manila on the conclusion of peace.   (*Cont. p. 937.*)

6. KOREA, 1506–1800

(*From p. 373*)

1506. A revolt against the cruel ruler, Yonsangun, brought to the throne

1507–1544. Chungjong, whose attempt to curb the great families by means of the Confucian scholars led to the defeat of the latter.

c. 1570. The Confucian scholars gradually established their control over the court, but, although only the orthodox Chu Hsi school of philosophy was tolerated, they broke up into bitterly antagonistic factions. Meanwhile the decline of the Ming brought a similar political and cultural decline in Korea.

1592–1598. Japanese invasions laid waste the land (p. 583).

1623. Injo was put on the throne by the so-called western faction of Confucianists, which had triumphed over the big northern faction (one branch of the northern faction), which previously had superseded the western faction.

1627. The Manchus overran Korea.

1637. Korea became a vassal state of the Manchus (Ch'ing dynasty) after an invasion led by T'ai-tsung, but the court and people remained loyal to the Ming.

1675–1720. Under Sukchong the western faction of Confucianists returned to power and divided into the old and young factions, which fought bitterly with each other.

1725–1800. A period of great intellectual activity, for the most part limited to moral philosophy and to genealogical research or fabrication.

(*Cont. p. 916.*)

7. JAPAN, 1542–1793

(*From p. 383*)

1542 or 1543. Portuguese landed from a Chinese ship on the island of Tanegashima, off the southern coast of Kyūshū. These were the first Europeans to visit Japan. They introduced the musket, which soon modified Japanese warfare. Other Portuguese ships followed and entered into trade relations with the lords of western Japan.

1549–1551. ST. FRANCIS XAVIER (1506–1552), the famous Jesuit missionary, introduced Christianity into Japan, proselytizing in the feudal domains of the west and also at Kyōto, but with no great success. On the whole he was well received and in some cases the feudal lords even encouraged conversions in the hope of attracting Portuguese trade. But the dogmatic intolerance of the missionaries soon earned them the bitter enmity of the usually tolerant Buddhist clergy and led to proscriptions of the new religion in certain fiefs. Xavier left behind two Jesuits and the Japanese converts, who formed the nucleus of the new church.

1568. Oda Nobunaga (1534–1582) seized Kyōto and set up a puppet *shōgun,* Yoshiaki (1568–1573, d. 1597). Lord of the provinces of Owari, Mino, and Mikawa east of Kyōto, Nobunaga had acted in response to a secret appeal from the emperor. By this daring blow he became the virtual dictator of central Japan, and with this date commenced

1568–1600. The **PERIOD OF NATIONAL**

UNIFICATION (usually called the *Azuchi-Momoyama Period*). The process of political disintegration of the nation had already run its course, and in these few decades, through the efforts of three great leaders, the nation was again united as the periphery was gradually subjugated by the military hegemons of the capital region. This was unquestionably one of the most dynamic epochs of Japanese history. The Japanese pirate traders were at their height and were active even in Siamese and Philippine waters. Excess national energy also expressed itself in a great **invasion of Korea.** Closer contacts with the Asiatic mainland and with Europeans resulted in an influx of new intellectual and artistic currents. Buddhism was in decline, and its monasteries were being deprived of their military power, but militant Christianity was at its height in Japan, and there was a revival of lay learning after the years of warfare. New skills and new products from the Occident profoundly affected the economy of the land, and in these years of relative peace the wealth and productivity of the nation expanded rapidly. The private customs barriers which had hampered trade were abolished, and the old monopolistic guilds (*za*) for the most part came to an end.

The artistic and intellectual spirit of the period was almost the antithesis of what it had been in Ashikaga times. It was an exuberant, expansive age. Refined simplicity had given way to ostentatious pomp and faddism. Architecture, which perhaps most clearly expressed the spirit of the age, showed a love of gorgeous decoration and majestic size. Castles and palaces rather than monasteries were the typical structures of the day.

1570. Nagasaki was opened to foreign trade by the local lord, Ōmura (sometimes dated 1567 or 1568). A hitherto unimportant fishing village, it soon became Japan's greatest port for foreign commerce.

1571. Nobunaga destroyed the Enryakuji on Mt. Hiei, thus eliminating this, the most powerful of all the monasteries, as a military force. In these same years he also waged usually successful wars against other Buddhist groups, especially the militant groups of the True Pure Land sect (Ikkō sect), as in the siege of their central monastery, the Ishiyama-honganji in Ōsaka (1570-1580). Nobunaga's violent opposition to Buddhism as an organized political force finally broke the temporal power of the monasteries.

1576. Nobunaga commenced work on the **Azuchi castle** on the shores of Lake Biwa. This was the first great castle of Japan and heralded the beginning of several decades of widespread castle-building. Azuchi was de-stroyed at the time of Nobunaga's death.

1577-1582. Toyotomi (at this time Hashiba) **Hideyoshi** (1537-1598), the brilliant but basely born chief general of Nobunaga, conquered much of western Japan from the Mōri family in the name of Nobunaga.

1578. The death of **Uesugi Kenshin** (1530-1578), together with the earlier demise of his great enemy, **Takeda Shingen** (1521-1573), removed Nobunaga's two most formidable rivals in eastern Japan.

1578. The conversion of **Ōtomo Yoshishige** (Sōrin) (1530-1587), one of the greatest lords of Kyūshū, to Christianity gave the foreign religion a greater foothold in the island, where it had already become quite strong since the conversion of some lesser lords of the western littoral, such as Ōmura (1562) and Arima (1576). The Christians, who were for the most part confined to the fiefs with Christian lords, were estimated at 150,000 in 1582.

1582. Nobunaga was killed by a discontented general, Akechi Mitsuhide (1526-1582). Hideyoshi returned from his western campaigns and destroyed Mitsuhide. A contest for power with the remaining members of the Oda family, supported by **Tokugawa Ieyasu** (1543-1616), one of Nobunaga's vassal lords in eastern Japan, brought about the elimination of the Oda and an understanding with Ieyasu, resulting in

1584. The hegemony of Hideyoshi over central Japan. The preceding year he had already commenced the construction of the great Ōsaka castle as his home base.

1585. Hideyoshi was appointed civil dictator (*Kampaku*), and two years later he became prime minister (*Dajodaijin*) as well.

1585-1587. A greater stratification of the classes (1, gentlemen-warriors; 2, farmers; 3, artisans; 4, merchants) was brought about by legislation (1585, 1586) and by the disarming of the peasantry (1587).

1587. The subjugation of the Shimazu family of southern Kyūshū completed Hideyoshi's conquest of western Japan.

1587. Hideyoshi issued a decree banishing the Portuguese missionaries from Japan, but failed to enforce it for ten years. His motive for this sudden opposition to Christianity was probably fear of the growing political and military strength of the Christians.

1590. The capture of the stronghold of the Hōjō family at Odawara induced all eastern and northern Japan to accept Hideyoshi's rule and completed the political unification of the land. At this time Hideyoshi's prominent vassal, Tokugawa Ieyasu, moved his administrative and military base to Edo (the modern Tōkyō), a strategic spot for the domination of the great plain of eastern Japan.

1592. The INVASION OF KOREA. Possibly motivated by the fear of the excess of experienced warriors in Japan, the ambitious Hideyoshi planned the conquest of China. When Korea refused to grant the Japanese transit, he invaded the peninsula. Under the leadership of **Katō Kiyomasa** (1562–1611) and **Konishi Yukinaga** (d. 1600) the expeditionary force of some 200,000 overran almost the whole of Korea, but was forced by a large Chinese army to withdraw to the southern coast in 1593.

1597. The Korean campaign was resumed, but with no great success. After Hideyoshi's death (1598) all the Japanese soldiers returned to Japan. The lasting political results of the Korean venture were negligible, but a rapid development and expansion of the ceramic industry in Japan was brought about by many Korean potters who were taken back to Japan by the retreating captains.

1597. Hideyoshi, irritated by the bickerings between the Portuguese Jesuits and the Spanish Franciscans (who had come to Japan in 1593), and suspecting that Christian proselytizing was merely an opening wedge for the subsequent conquest of Japan by the Europeans, executed three Jesuits, six Franciscans, and seventeen Japanese Christians. The remaining missionaries were ordered to leave, but only a small number did so. Hideyoshi did not press the persecution further, because he did not wish to drive away the Portuguese traders, who were then especially welcome, since direct commercial intercourse with China had been stopped.

1598. Hideyoshi's death was soon followed by a contest for power among his former vassals, culminating in

1600. The **battle of Sekigahara**, where Ieyasu defeated a coalition of his rivals. This victory made Ieyasu the virtual ruler of the whole land, and although he was not appointed *shōgun* until 1603, from this time is usually dated

1600–1868. The TOKUGAWA (or Edo) PERIOD. Ieyasu established the military capital at Edo (Tōkyō), which grew phenomenally to become the economic and cultural as well as political capital of the nation. Because of the fate of the Oda and Toyotomi families, Ieyasu made the perpetuation of the rule in his family his major objective, and this colored the whole spirit as well as the political organization of the epoch, giving them strong conservative and even reactionary tendencies. The feudal lords were divided into the *Fudai* and *Tozama Daimyō*. The former, who were the vassals and allies of Ieyasu before Sekigahara, now occupied the central provinces. The latter, who had only submitted after Sekigahara, were located in more remote regions and were usually excluded from the central government. Both groups were compelled to leave hostages in Edo and to spend alternate periods there and in their fiefs. Important cities were ruled directly by Edo. The building and repairing of castles were strictly limited. The conduct of the warriors was closely regulated, and the emperor and his court, though financially generously treated, were strictly controlled.

The **administrative hierarchy,** which grew out of the Tokugawa family organization, consisted in order of rank of a *shōgun;* at times, and especially between 1638 and 1684, one or more prime ministers (*tairō*); four or five elders (*toshiyori* or *rōju*) as a council of state; a group of junior elders (*wakadoshiyori*), who controlled the direct petty vassals of Edo; a class of officials known as *metsuke,* who served as censors or intelligence officers; and a large group of civil administrators called *bugyō.* The laws lacked coherent organization, but were based on certain fundamental moral precepts, primarily that of loyalty. Criminal codes were severe and cruel. There was a stringent stratification of the classes. *Daimyō* were to a large extent autonomous rulers in their own domains, but Edo kept a watchful eye on them, and there was a strong tendency for the feudatories to adopt the laws and organization of Edo.

The peace and prosperity of the early Tokugawa period brought a gradual rise in the standard of living and an increase in population as well as in the national wealth. With the **growth of industry and commerce,** a powerful merchant class grew up in the larger cities, and a gradual transition from a rice economy to a money economy commenced. This transition, together with the rise in living standards and the increase in population, tended to make production inadequate and brought about great economic ills during much of the period.

Political conservatism and **isolation** from the rest of the world made the Tokugawa period outwardly stagnant, but it was inwardly a time of great intellectual development. Buddhism was in decline, and Christianity was early stamped out, but there was a great **revival of lay learning,** the old feudal code of conduct received definite formulation under the name of *bushidō,* Confucian philosophy enjoyed a protracted period of unparalleled growth and popularity, philosophers and teachers of ethics abounded, there was a revival of interest in Japanese antiquity, Shintō developed new life both as a nationalistic philosophy and as a

The Tokugawa Shoguns (1603–1867)

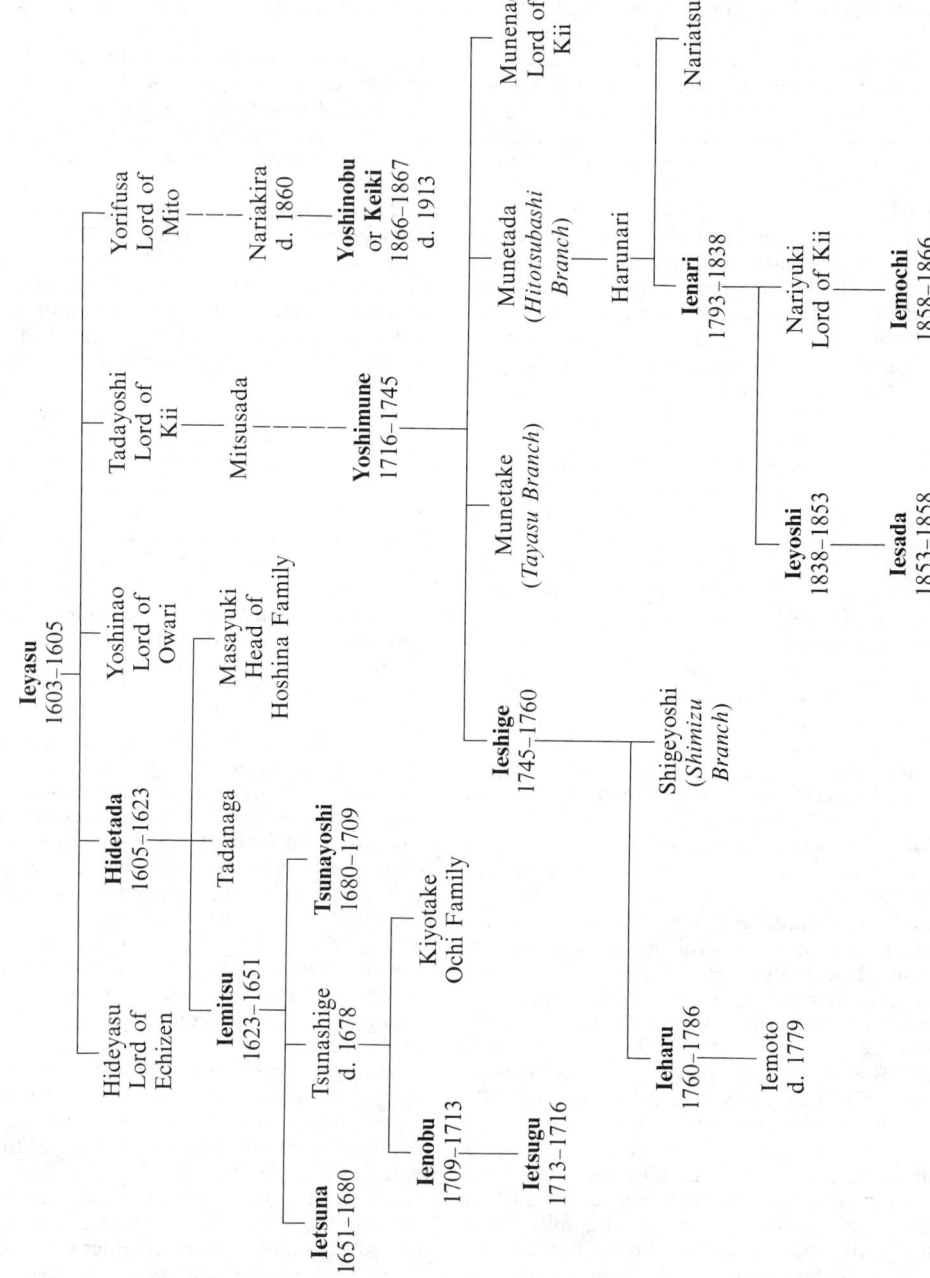

popular religion, and the newly arisen merchant class contributed greatly to the intellectual and cultural growth of the land.

Literature and art in the Tokugawa period were comparatively free from Chinese influences and were less aristocratic and more popular than in earlier periods because of the influence of the merchant class. A new poetic form, the *haiku,* which consists of only 17 syllables as opposed to the classic form of 31 syllables, was popularized at this time. The novel enjoyed a second great period of flowering. The refined *Nō* drama slowly gave way to more realistic, more exciting, and decidedly less restrained forms, the *Kabuki* and puppet plays, which both developed from long poetic recitations called *Jōruri.* Applied arts reached great heights of technical excellence, but architecture was an uninspired and often debased imitation of 16th-century styles. Painting was largely traditional, but there were able masters of design and an important new school of realism. The most interesting development in painting was the so-called *ukiyo-e* school, a school of popular artists who chose for their subject matter not Chinese scenes, and historical events but the people, street scenes, and landscapes of contemporaneous Japan. The style was introduced in the 17th century and found its most popular expression in the prints of the great wood-block masters of the 18th and first half of the 19th centuries.

c. 1602. The arrival of **Spanish traders** in eastern Japan. Ieyasu befriended Spanish missionaries, hoping thereby to persuade Spanish traders to trade directly with eastern Japan, but, although a formal treaty was negotiated with the Spanish acting governor of the Philippines in 1610, few traders ever came.

1605–1623. HIDETADA as *shōgun* (d. 1632). This was the formative period of the Edo government, first under the direction of the retired *shōgun,* Ieyasu (d. 1616), and then under that of his uninspired but dependable son, Hidetada.

1608. Hayashi Razan (1583–1657), a Confucian scholar, was appointed attendant scholar (*jidoku*) to Ieyasu. This marked the beginning of a Tokugawa policy of using **Confucianism** as a stabilizing force in politics and society. Razan, who founded the Edo Confucian temple in 1623, represented the orthodox Sung Confucian school of Chu Hsi (Japanese *Shushi*), which was the orthodox school in Japan throughout the period. Other schools of Confucian philosophy were those of **Wang Yang-ming** (Japanese *Ōyomei*); of Ming China (represented by Nakae Tōju [1608–1648] and Kumazawa Banzan [1619–1691]); and the **Ancient School** (*Kogakuha*), a reformed school

which returned to pre-Sung Confucian commentators (represented by Itō Jinsai [1627–1705] and Ogyū Sorai [1666?–1728]). The Japanese Confucianists made many contributions in various fields of learning and some attacked the pressing economic problems of the time.

1609. The **Dutch** established a trading post at Hirado in western Japan after an invitation from Ieyasu in 1605. This invitation had been obtained by Will Adams (d. 1620), the English pilot of a Dutch vessel wrecked in Japan in 1600. Adams was forced to remain in Japan by Ieyasu, who made of him an honored adviser.

1612. A definite **persecution of Christianity** commenced after a series of anti-Christian edicts beginning in 1606. Ieyasu's mounting fears of the political menace from Christianity and his realization that trade with Europe could be maintained without the presence of Catholic missionaries as decoys had made him gradually abandon his at first friendly attitude toward the missionaries.

1613. Cocks established an English factory at Hirado.

1613. Date Masamune (1565–1636), a prominent lord of northern Japan, dispatched an embassy to Spain and to the pope.

1614–1615. The Siege of Ōsaka Castle. Hideyori (1593–1615), the son and heir of Hideyoshi, and the former's mother, **Yodogimi** (1577–1615), had remained in the Ōsaka Castle after the battle of Sekigahara, constituting a dangerous rallying-point for disaffected elements. Their ultimate destruction was deemed necessary by Ieyasu. In 1614 on a trumped-up charge he laid siege to the castle, and after a short truce captured and destroyed it and its inmates in 1615.

1615. The **Bukeshohatto,** a collection of general maxims for the warrior class, was issued.

1616. Death of Ieyasu.

1617. Hidetada, aroused by the mutual recriminations of the various European nationalities and religious associations in Japan, intensified the persecution of the Christians (estimated then at 300,000), and for the first time since 1597 European missionaries were executed. Jesuits, Franciscans, and native believers were executed in increasing numbers in the following years (particularly 1622–1624). This marked the height of the Christian persecution. Catholic missionaries still continued to arrive, but eventually all were killed or forced to leave or to apostatize.

1623–1651. IEMITSU as *shōgun.* This was the period of consolidation of Tokugawa rule. As means of achieving this goal the **suppression of Christianity** was carried to a successful end and the policy of national isolation was adopted.

1623. The English voluntarily left Hirado because their trade with Japan had not proved profitable.

1624. All Spaniards were driven from Japan and all intercourse with the Philippines was stopped.

1636. Japanese were forbidden to go abroad, and those abroad were not allowed to return. Two years later the building of large ships was also proscribed.

1637-1638. The Shimabara uprising. The peasants of the peninsula of Shimabara and the island of Amakusa near Nagasaki, which had been a thoroughly Christianized region for decades, rose in desperation over economic and religious oppression. Some 37,000 of them defended themselves in the dilapidated Hara Castle on the coast of Shimabara for almost three months against vastly superior forces, aided by a Dutch vessel, until food and musket ammunition, on which they depended, failed them. They were killed almost to a man in the fall of the castle, and with this slaughter Christianity was virtually stamped out.

1638. The Portuguese traders were expelled because of suspicions as to their complicity in the Shimabara uprising. When they sent an embassy in 1640 to reopen trade, almost the whole party was summarily executed. This left the Dutch at Hirado and some Chinese traders at Nagasaki as Japan's sole means of contact with the outside world.

1641. The Dutch traders were moved from Hirado to the islet of Deshima in Nagasaki Harbor, where they were in virtual imprisonment and were subjected to many inconveniences and indignities.

1651-1680. IETSUNA as *shōgun.*

1651-1652. Two successive abortive *coups d'état* at Edo were the last revolutions the Tokugawa had to face until the 19th century.

1657. Tokugawa Mitsukuni (1628-1701), lord of Mito, commenced the compilation of a *History of Japan* (*Dainihonshi*) on the model of Chinese dynastic histories. Among the many scholars who aided him were Chinese *émigrés.* The original task was not officially completed until 1720, and supplementary work was continued until 1906. The school of Japanese historians that grew up around this enterprise was one of the important factors in the imperial revival movement.

1657. A great fire destroyed most of Edo and the Edo castle buildings.

1680-1709. TSUNAYOSHI as *shōgun.* Sakai Tadakiyo (1624-1681), prime minister at the time of Ietsuna's death, proposed to have an

imperial prince succeed the heirless Ietsuna, but on the insistence of Hotta Masatoshi (1634?-1684) Ietsuna's brother, Tsunayoshi, was made *shōgun,* and presently Masatoshi succeeded Tadakiyo as prime minister. The early years of this period were characterized by vigorous administrative measures until

1684. The **assassination of Hotta Masatoshi** left Tsunayoshi with inferior counsellors who allowed him to ruin the Edo finances and to bring great hardships on the people by edicts inspired by Buddhism prohibiting the killing of any living creature and extending special protection and privileges to dogs.

1688-1704. The **Genroku year period** is regarded as the apogee of the vigorous culture of the merchant class of the Tokugawa period. Already by this time the warrior class was becoming mired in debt to the merchants, into whose hands the wealth of the nation was beginning to pass. Consequently, this was a time of ebullient and unsuppressed self-expression on the part of the merchant class. The gay and extravagant life of the cities centered in the puppet and *Kabuki* theaters and the licensed quarters, the famous Yoshiwara in the case of Edo. Among the great spirits of the age were **Matsuo Bashō** (1644-1694), who made of the *haiku* a great poetic medium; **Ibara Saikaku** (1642-1693), the author of *risqué* novels about courtesans; **Chikamatsu Monzaemon** (1653-1725), Japan's greatest playwright; and **Hishikawa Moronobu** (1638-1714), an early *ukiyo-e* master. Repressive measures and a gradual amalgamation of the merchant and warrior classes in time tempered the Genroku spirit.

1703. The **Chūshingura** (called the "Forty-Seven *Rōnin*") **Incident.** Kira Yoshinaka was killed by a group of former retainers of Asano Naganori, lord of Akō, whose execution in 1701 they felt to be Yoshinaka's fault. The deed thrilled the nation, for, although they had broken the laws of the land, they were but following Confucian ethics in avenging their lord's death. They were eventually ordered to commit suicide.

1703. A great earthquake and fire at Edo was followed in the next five years by several other catastrophes, including the last eruption of Mt. Fuji (1707).

1709-1713. IENOBU, as *shōgun.* With the aid of the orthodox Confucian scholar, **Arai Hakuseki** (1657-1725), this able and vigorous ruler carried out a series of much-needed financial reforms.

1713-1716. The infant **Ietsugu** as *shōgun.*

1715. The quantity of copper allowed exported by the Dutch was greatly reduced. Copper was the mainstay of the Dutch trade, but its export by them and by the Chinese was a drain on the metal resources of the land. This reduction was followed later by even greater reductions and resulted in the limitation of the number of Dutch vessels calling at Japan to two a year.

1716–1745. YOSHIMUNE as *shōgun* (d. 1751). Since Hidetada's line had come to an end the new *shōgun* was chosen from the Tokugawa house of Kii, which, with the houses of Owari and Mito, were made by Ieyasu the three Tokugawa cadet branches (*Gosanke*) from which *shōgun* were to be selected when needed. Perhaps next to Ieyasu the ablest and wisest of the Tokugawa rulers, Yoshimune attempted to revive the feudal regimentation and military virtues of Ieyasu's day and to carry through economic reforms. He also encouraged scholarship in all fields, and the Confucian scholar, **Muro Kyūsō** (1658–1734), was one of his chief advisers. Despite this able leadership, economic and social ills began to become acute in Yoshimune's time. The peasants were losing the ownership of their land, and the farm population began to decline because of infanticide and movements to the towns. The military class was badly indebted to the merchants, and to save them from ruin a long series of petty laws in favor of the debtor class was commenced at this time. These economic conditions led to a mingling of the classes, which began to efface the old rigid class barriers.

1720. Yoshimune removed the ban on the study of Europe and on the importation of European books, exclusive of those on religion. This broadminded move made possible the development of a small but vigorous group of students of Dutch and through this medium of occidental sciences, particularly medicine. A manuscript Dutch-Japanese dictionary was produced in 1745, and in 1774 **Sugita Gem-**

paku translated a text on anatomy. This early start in the occidental scientific method produced achievements in cartography and military science and proved of great value in Restoration days.

1732–1733. A great famine in western Japan was met with positive measures of relief by Yoshimune.

1742. The criminal law of the land was codified for the benefit of judges and administrators. This codification remained the basis of criminal law during the rest of the Tokugawa period.

1745–1760. IESHIGE as *shōgun* (d. 1761). An incompetent sensualist, Ieshige made no attempt to stem the rapid administrative and economic decline which set in after Yoshimune's death in 1751.

1758. **Takenouchi Shikibu** (1714?–1768), a scholar favoring an imperial restoration, and his noble disciples in Kyōto were punished by Edo.

1760–1786. IEHARU as *shōgun.* Though an able man, Ieharu was dominated by the tyrannical and avaricious **Tanuma Okitsugu** (often called Mototsugu) (1719–1788), and Tokugawa rule continued its downward course. During this period peasant uprisings became frequent and serious, and they continued to be so until the fall of the Tokugawa.

1783. A great **eruption of Mt. Asama** and a famine in the north came as a double climax to a series of disasters resulting in

1787. Rice riots in Edo.

1787–1793. Matsudaira Sadanobu (1759–1829) as head of the government for the child *shōgun,* **Ienari,** carried through a series of reforms. At this same time imperialist opposition to Edo became apparent in Kyōto and the military government became aware of the menace of the rapidly expanding European powers.

(*Cont. p. 918.*)

V. THE MODERN PERIOD

V. THE MODERN PERIOD

A. SCIENCE AND SOCIETY, 1800–1960

1. PHILOSOPHICAL, RELIGIOUS, AND SOCIAL THOUGHT

(*From p. 522*)

1802. The French author, **François René de Chateaubriand** (1768–1848), initiated the Catholic revival with his *Génie du christianisme,* stressing the aesthetic rather than the theological aspect of the faith.

1803. The *Traité d'économie politique* of **Jean-Baptiste Say** (1767–1832) was one of the most lucid and influential expositions of economic liberalism. Say followed it in 1828–1830 with a much more extensive *Cours complet d'économie politique pratique.*

1806. **Johann F. Herbart's** (1776–1841) *Allgemeine Pädogogik,* a landmark in the development of modern education based on psychology and ethics.

1807. The Hegelian philosophy of the absolute, the dominant philosophy of the early 19th century, was introduced by **Georg W. F. Hegel** (1770–1831) in his *Phänomenologie des Geistes,* followed by *Wissenschaft der Logik* (1812–1816) and *Grundlinien der Philosophie des Rechts* (1821).

1810. The political philosophy of conservatism was further elaborated in the brilliant writings of **Joseph de Maistre** (1754–1821), the *Essai sur le principe générateur des constitutions politiques* (1810) and especially *Du pape* (1819), with its emphasis on the importance of papal authority.

1813. **Robert Owen** (1771–1858), British industrialist and philanthropist, is generally regarded as the first of the **Utopian Socialists.** In his *New View of Society* (1813) he argued for co-operation in production and advocated the organization of new social units, many of which (notably **New Harmony,** Indiana, 1825–1828) were established in Europe and the United States. Subsequently the French reformer, **Charles Fourier** (1772–1837), proposed the setting up of *phalanstères* or co-operative communities in a rural setting; and **Étienne Cabet** (1788–1856) in his *Voyage en Icarie* (1840) pictured an imaginative, highly planned, and regulated community. **Louis Blanc** (1811–1882) in his *Organisation du travail* (1839) urged the foundation of state-financed producers' associations, while **Pierre-**

Joseph Proudhon (1809–1865), the great French polemicist, demanded justice, equality, and anarchy as the only remedies for the corruption of society. In exile in Paris, the self-educated German tailor, **Wilhelm Weitling** (1808–1871), came under the influence of French socialist ideas. In his *Garantien der Harmonie und Freiheit* (1842) he presented a system not unlike those of Fourier and Cabet. **Johann Karl Rodbertus** (1805–1875) was also instrumental in introducing French ideas into Germany.

1815–1831. **Friedrich Karl von Savigny** (1779–1861) in his six-volume *Geschichte des römischen Rechts im Mittelalter* contributed greatly to the development of the historical school of jurisprudence.

1816–1826. **Karl Ludwig von Haller** (1768–1854) published his six-volume *Restauration der Staatswissenschaften,* one of the most comprehensive as it was one of the last refutations of 18th-century political theory and restatements of the principles of absolutism and paternalism.

1817. The *Principles of Political Economy and Taxation* by the British banker **David Ricardo** (1772–1823) provided a classical formulation of economic doctrine. Ricardo set forth the law of "differential rent" and explained wages as tending to seek the minimum subsistence level. He also analyzed the conflicting interests of social classes, thereby foreshadowing the doctrine of the class struggle. His teaching was enthusiastically adopted by the rising manufacturing class and was further elaborated in England by the utilitarian **James Mill** (1773–1836), **John Ramsay McCulloch** (1789–1864), and **Nassau William Senior** (1790–1864), and in France by **Pellegrino Rossi** (1787–1848), **Charles Dunoyer** (1786–1863), **Michel Chevalier** (1806–1879), and **Frédéric Bastiat** (1801–1850).

1817–1818. **Count Henri de Saint-Simon** (1760–1825), eccentric scion of the high French aristocracy, published his four-volume study of industry (*L'industrie, ou discussions politiques, morales et philosophiques*) followed by *Du système industriel* (1821) and *Le catéchisme des industriels* (1823). In these writings he called for a reorganization of society to accord with modern methods of production and to assure the greatest good of the greatest number. He dreamed of integrating the sciences in a new sociology and forecast modern technocracy. His disciples, **Prosper Enfantin** (1796-1864) and **Saint-Amand Bazard** (1791-1832) not only systematized and expounded his thought but, on the basis of his late book *Le nouveau christianisme* (1825), organized a Saint-Simonian sect on communist principles. This was soon suppressed by the authorities. Meanwhile Saint-Simon's secretary, **Auguste Comte** (1798-1857), developed his scientific thought and founded the philosophy known as positivism (*Cours de philosophie positive*, six volumes, 1830-1842; *Système de politique positive*, four volumes, 1851-1854).

1817-1821. The Abbé **Felicité de Lamennais** (1782-1854) wrote an eloquent defense of papal and royal authority in his *Essai sur l'indifférence en matière de religion*, but after 1830 became converted to liberalism. With **Count Charles de Montalembert** (1810-1870) he launched the liberal Catholic movement, which was condemned by the papacy. Eventually Lamennais became identified with the socialist movement. His fervent booklet *Paroles d'un croyant* (1833) was at once translated into many languages and aroused much sympathy for the lower classes.

1819. **Arthur Schopenhauer's** (1788-1860) *Die Welt als Wille und Vorstellung* formulated a philosophy of pessimism which, though generally ignored for a generation, became highly influential in the later 19th century.

1819-1837. **Jakob Grimm's** (1785-1863) *Deutsche Grammatik* was a landmark in the development of modern philogy. Jakob and his brother Wilhelm (1786-1859) collaborated in collecting folktales, myths, and laws, and in publishing a great dictionary of the German language (Vol. I, 1854).

1819. The Swiss historian **Simonde de Sismondi** (1773-1842) in his *Nouveaux principes d'économie politique* attacked the *laissez-faire* doctrines of the liberal school and was one of the first to call for state action in behalf of the helpless working classes.

1821-1822. *Der christliche Glaube nach den Grundsätzen der evangelischen Kirche*, one of the great theological treatises of the century, by **Friederich Schleiermacher** (1768-1834). The book emphasized the individual and emotional side of the Protestant religion and contended against dogmatism and rigidity.

1825. **Augustin Thierry's** (1795-1856) *Histoire de la conquête de l'Angleterre par les Normands* provided a highly colored, romantic narrative history and at the same time pictured the rul-

ing aristocracies as brutal conquerors and exploiters of "the people." The French statesman, **François Guizot** (1787-1874), in his brilliant lectures *Histoire de la civilisation en Europe* (1828), likewise stressed the importance of the middle class and the rise of representative institutions.

1825. **James Mill's** (1773-1836) *Analysis of the Phenomena of the Human Mind* was a basic work of modern psychology.

1826. Beginning of the publication of the *Monumenta Germaniae Historica*, the first of many scholarly collections of historical sources and a landmark in the development of national history.

1833. Establishment of a historical seminar by **Leopold von Ranke** (1795-1886) as a center for advanced training in historical writing. Ranke's emphasis on criticism of sources and the utmost objectivity in presentation marked the beginning of modern professional history. His *Die römischen Päpste* (1834-1839) was only the first of various historical studies of the 16th and 17th centuries.

1834-1840. *La Démocratie en Amérique* by **Alexis de Tocqueville** (1805-1859), a most discerning analytical study of democracy, based largely on personal observation and study.

1835-1836. **David Friedrich Strauss** (1808-1874) published *Das Leben Jesu* (two volumes), a critical examination of the sources that led him to question the historicity of Jesus. Strauss's book marked the appearance of the **Young Hegelians,** a group that interpreted the Hegelian philosophy in a radical and destructive sense: **Bruno Bauer** (1809-1882): *Kritik der evangelischen Synoptiker* (1841); **Ludwig Feuerbach** (1804-1872): *Das Wesen des Christentums* (1841); **Max Stirner** (1806-1856): *Der einzige und sein Eigentum* (1845).

1841. **Friedrich List** (1789-1846) in his *Nationales System der politischen Ökonomie* stressed national welfare rather than individual gain and propounded a theory of relativity in economic policy: countries in the early stages of industrialization should protect their industries until free trade should become feasible.

1843-1845. In a series of brilliant writings (*Euten-Eller*, 1843; *Begrebet Angst*, 1844; *Stadier paa Livetsvej*, 1845) the Danish philosopher **Sören Kierkegaard** repudiated the Hegelian philosophy and preached a religion of acceptance and suffering on the part of the individual. His teaching presaged the philosophy of existentialism.

1848. **John Stuart Mill's** (1806-1873) *Principles of Political Economy* was the most logical and persuasive exposition of classical economics, with some concessions to state intervention where private initiative could not work.

1848.   Karl Marx (1818–1883) and **Friedrich Engels** (1820–1895) issued the *Communist Manifesto,* a fiery appeal to the workers of all countries to unite in the struggle against capitalist exploitation, and at the same time a succinct presentation of "scientific" as contrasted with "utopian" socialism.

1851.   Herbert Spencer's (1820–1903) *Social Statics,* the first work of the author of *Synthetic Philosophy* (*First Principles,* 1862), an attempt to organize the corpus of human knowledge and to establish the laws of social evolution.

1851.   The *Ensayo sobre el Catolicismo, el Liberalismo y el Socialismo,* by **Juan Donoso Cortés** (1809–1853), the Spanish statesman who clearly reflected the fears inspired by the revolutions of 1848 and the ensuing disillusionment with liberalism and radicalism.

1853–1855.   Count Joseph de Gobineau's (1816–1882) *Essai sur l'inégalité des races humaines,* the basis for much later writing on racial superiority.

1855.   *Kraft und Stoff,* by **Ludwig Büchner** (1824–1899), a classic of modern materialism.

1857.   Publication of the first volume of **Henry T. Buckle's** (1821–1862) *History of Civilisation in England,* a valiant attempt to approach history scientifically.

1860.   *Die Cultur der Renaissance in Italien,* by the Swiss historian **Jakob Burckhardt** (1818–1897), was a masterpiece of cultural history and a brilliant essay in interpretation. Likewise Burckhardt's posthumous *Weltgeschichtliche Betrachtungen* (1898) was a highly provocative critique of the materialistic, democratic culture in which he lived.

1861.   Johann J. Bachofen's (1815–1887) study *Das Mutterrecht* explored the matriarchal institutions of primitive man and greatly stimulated anthropological investigations.

1863.   Ernest Renan's (1823–1892) *Vie de Jésus* was the first of a series of studies of the origins of Christianity. Translated into all European languages, it was a classic of urbane skepticism and rationalism. In his *Réforme intellectuelle et morale* (1871) he called in question the democratic system and envisaged government by an intellectual elite.

1864.   The foundation of the **First International Workingmen's Association** by Karl Marx, with headquarters first in London, then in New York. Designed to unite the workers of all countries in support of Marxian socialism, it was eventually wrecked (1876) by the conflict between Marx and Bakunin, who advocated "direct action" to hasten the advent of anarchy. After Bakunin's death anarchist doctrine was further elaborated by **Prince Peter Kropotkin** (1842–1921) and in the later 19th century

gained many adherents, especially in the Latin countries, where a series of assassinations and other outrages were committed in the 1880's and 1890's.

1867, 1885, 1895.   *Das Kapital* (three volumes) by Karl Marx, an elaborate analysis of economic and social history and at the same time the basic exposition of "scientific" socialism.

1879.   Wilhelm Wundt (1832–1920) established the first psychological laboratory. **Ivan Petrovich Pavlov** (1849–1936) discovered the "conditioned reflex" and induced "experimental neurosis" in dogs.

1883–1888.   The provocative and highly original works of cultural criticism of **Friedrich von Nietzsche** (1844–1900): *Also sprach Zarathustra* (1883); *Jenseits von Gut und Böse* (1886); *Zur Genealogie der Moral* (1887); *Der Wille zur Macht* (1888). Nietzsche denounced the morality of slaves and called for the utmost development of the individual, even at the cost of much suffering and sacrifice. Tremendous influence of his doctrine of the "superman" in the early 20th century.

1886–1890.   The *Lehrbuch der Dogmengeschichte* of **Adolf von Harnack** (1851–1930) was only the most outstanding of that scholar's many studies of Christian dogma and of the influence of Greek thought and religion on the development of Christianity.

1889–1914.   The **Second International Workingmen's Association,** which held periodic meetings of representatives of the various national Social Democratic parties. It never had any central authority and at all times suffered from divergence of interest among its constituents. It was finally discredited by the patriotic participation of the Socialist parties in the First World War.

1890.   Gabriel Tarde (1843–1904) published his *Les lois de l'imitation* a pioneer work in the field of social psychology. At the same time **Pierre Janet** (1859–1949) carried on studies of hypnosis and hysteria. In 1895 **Gustave Le Bon** (1841–1931) published his *Psychologie des foules.*

1890.   William James (1842–1910), the American psychologist, published his *Principles of Psychology,* to be followed by *The Will to Believe* (1897), *The Varieties of Religious Experience* (1902), and *Pragmatism* (1907). James' "pragmatism" viewed thinking and knowledge as aspects of the struggle to live. This school of thought went back to the American logician **Charles Sanders Peirce** (1839–1914) and was espoused also by **John Dewey** (1859–1952): *How We Think* (1909); *Democracy and Education* (1916). In Europe the related "logical empiricists" included **Pierre Duhem** (1861–1916). **Ernst Mach** (1838–1916), and **Henri Poincaré** (1854–1912).

1893. *Appearance and Reality,* by **Francis H. Bradley** (1846–1924), rejected utilitarianism and attempted a return to absolute idealism.

1897–1922. The philosophical writings of **Henri Bergson** (1859–1941) stressing intuition and irrational forces: *Matière et mémoire* (1897); *Évolution créatrice* (1906); *Durée et simultanéité* (1922).

1899. The revisionist or reformist current in social democracy was established by **Eduard Bernstein** (1850–1932) in his *Die Voraussetzungen des Sozialismus und die Aufgaben der Sozialdemokratie,* in which he queried Marx's predictions and advocated evolutionary as distinguished from revolutionary socialism.

1900. *Traumdeutung,* by **Sigmund Freud** (1856–1939), may be taken to mark the beginning of **psychoanalysis.** Other important works: *Über Psychoanalyse* (1910); *Vorlesungen zur Einführung in die Psychoanalyse* (1917); *Das Ich und das Es* (1923); *Die Zukunft einer Illusion* (1927); *Das Unbehagen in der Kultur* (1930); *Neue Folge der Vorlesungen* (1932). Among Freud's earlier adherents were **Alfred Adler** (1870–1937) and **Carl G. Jung** (1875–1964), both of whom broke away and established schools of their own.

1902. **John A. Hobson** (1858–1940) published *Imperialism: A Study,* undoubtedly the most comprehensive critique of economic imperialism. Through the German theorists **Rosa Luxemburg** and **Rudolf Hilferding** his arguments found their way into Lenin's famous pamphlet: *Imperialism, the Highest Stage of Capitalism* (1916), which constitutes the official Communist view.

1904–1905. **Max Weber** (1864–1920), the eminent German economist-sociologist, published *Die protestantische Ethik und der Geist des Kapitalismus,* in which he concluded that the teachings of Luther and Calvin were among the main springs of the capitalist spirit. This thesis was further developed by **Richard H. Tawney** (1880–1962): *Religion and the Rise of Capitalism* (1926).

1908. **Georges Sorel's** (1847–1922) *Réflexions sur la violence* supplied a theoretical background for the syndicalist movement, an outgrowth of anarchism which aimed at destruction of the state through a general strike engineered by trade unions.

1910–1913. *Principia Mathematica,* by **Bertrand Russell** (1872–1970) and **Alfred North Whitehead** (1861–1947), setting forth the principles of mathematical logic which were to be applied to sociology, education, and politics.

1912. **Gestalt psychology** expounded by **Max Wertheimer** (1880–1943) and developed further by **Kurt Koffka** (1886–1941) and **Wolfgang Köhler** (1887–1967).

1916. **Vilfredo Pareto** (1848–1923), in his *Trattato di Sociologia Generale,* provided a comprehensive mathematical analysis of economic and sociological problems, based on the distinction between the fundamental motivations of human nature (*residues*) and their outward appearance or rationalization (*derivations*).

1918–1922. **Oswald Spengler** (1880–1936), in a learned and brilliantly written study, *Der Untergang des Abendlandes,* produced a cyclical interpretation of history and forecast the eclipse of western civilization as inevitable.

1934–1954. *A Study of History* (ten volumes) by **Arnold J. Toynbee** (1889–   ) constituted an exhaustive re-examination of human development in the light of an idealist philosophy of history.

1936. **John Maynard Keynes** (1883–1946), in his *General Theory of Employment, Interest and Money,* explained how and why an economy might fail to maintain a level of activity required for full employment. Though dealing primarily with short-run phenomena, the "Keynesian economics" became crucial in the development of theories of economic growth.

2. SCIENCE AND LEARNING

(*From p. 526*)

a. MATHEMATICS, PHYSICS, ASTRONOMY

1799–1825. **Pierre Laplace** (1749–1827) published his *Traité de mécanique céleste,* in which he aimed at presenting analytically all of the developments in gravitational astronomy since the time of Newton.

1800. The **Royal Institution of Great Britain,** center for the diffusion of technical and scientific knowledge, was founded by the American **Benjamin Thompson (Count Rumford)** (1753–1814).

1801. **Giuseppi Piazzi** (1746–1826) discovered the first asteroid *Ceres;* its orbit was computed by Gauss.

1801. **Carl Friedrich Gauss** (1777–1855) published *Disquisitiones arithmeticae,* developing the theory of congruences, quadratic forms, and quadratic residues, using methods and concepts basic to the subsequent progress of number theory and algebra.

1802. Thomas Young (1773–1829) demonstrated in his paper "On the Theory of Light and Colours" that the properties of light, including interference phenomena, are satisfactorily explained by considering it as a periodic wave motion in an aether.

1803–1804. William Herschel (1738–1822) reported observations on six cases of double stars, and concluded that each was a binary or connected pair of stars in which each member influenced the motion of the other. This was the first observation of changes taking place under gravity beyond the solar system.

1809. Gauss expounded his new "least-squares" method of computing planetary orbits in *Theoria motus corporum coelestium.*

1815–1821. Augustin Fresnel (1788–1827), through a series of mathematical and experimental researches on interference, diffraction, polarization, and double refraction, was able to establish the **transverse wave theory of light.**

1817. Joseph von Fraunhofer (1787–1826), following the 1802 observations by **William Wollaston** (1766–1828) that the solar spectrum contains black lines, and using an improved spectroscope, charted these lines, naming the principal ones.

1820. Hans Oersted (1777–1851) showed that a magnetic needle placed near a current-carrying wire deviated from its position, and that the direction of deviation depended on the direction of current flow.

1820. André-Marie Ampère (1775–1836) repeated Oersted's experiments (1820), and reported his discovery that two current-carrying wires exercise a reciprocal action upon one another. He later established a mathematical theory of known electrical phenomena, and experimentally demonstrated the principles of the electrodynamics of adjacent current-carrying conductors.

1821–1859. Michael Faraday (1791–1867) demonstrated electromagnetic rotation (1821) and discovered electromagnetic induction (1831). He independently discovered self-induced currents (1834), found two years earlier by **Joseph Henry** (1797–1878). He found the laws of electrochemical decomposition and conduction, and established a general theory of electrolysis. He also introduced the concept of *field* into physics. These and other investigations were collected in his *Experimental Researches in Electricity* (1839–1855) and in his *Experimental Researches in Chemistry and Physics* (1859).

1821–1823. Augustin-Louis Cauchy (1789–1857), who successfully sought rigor in analysis, gave the first essentially correct definition of limit in *Cours d'analyse* (1821). This work also contained the first systematic study of convergence of series and general tests for it, and the first theory of functions of a complex variable. He defined the derivative and integral in terms of limit, and obtained the fundamental theorem of calculus (1823).

1822. Joseph Fourier (1768–1830) published *Théorie analytique de la chaleur,* giving a mathematical theory of heat conduction. He introduced trigonometric series, *Fourier series* of arbitrary, piecewise, continuous functions, thus extending the notion of function.

1824. Niels Abel (1802–1829) proved that the general quintic cannot be solved by radicals.

1824. Nicolas Sadi Carnot (1796–1832) published *Réflexions sur la puissance motrice du feu.* Here he showed that the transformation of heat into motive power depends on the quantity of heat ("caloric"), and the temperature difference between the source and sink of heat. He also introduced the reversible cycle of a heat engine—now called the *Carnot cycle.*

1827–1829. Niels Abel and **Karl Jacobi** (1804–1851) independently founded the theory of elliptic (doubly periodic) functions.

1827. Georg S. Ohm (1789–1854) found that the ratio of electromotive force to the current, in an electric circuit, is a constant (*Ohm's Law*) and called this constant the resistance of the circuit.

1829–1832. Nikolai Lobachevskii (1793–1856) and **János Bólyai** (1802–1860) independently developed the first **non-Euclidean geometries.**

1831. The foundation of the **British Association for the Advancement of Science,** dedicated to the promotion and professionalization of British science. The B.A.A.S. was based on a German model, **Gesellschaft deutscher Naturforscher,** and served as an example for the **American Association for the Advancement of Science** (1848).

1832. Evariste Galois (1811–1832) left posthumous papers using group theory to give necessary and sufficient conditions for the solution of equations by radicals. He emphasized the importance of the invariant or normal subgroup.

1833. Charles Babbage (1792–1871) conceived an "analytical engine" (a large-scale digital calculator). In 1822, he had made a working model of a smaller, "difference engine" to calculate tables of functions by finite difference methods.

1833. Gauss, in his *Intensitas vis magnetica terrestris,* presented a rigorous mathematical analysis of the earth's magnetic field, and proposed a system of absolute units for the measurement of terrestrial magnetism.

1834. Adolphe Quetelet (1796–1874) initiated the **London Statistical Society,** and later helped found several other such groups. He applied the theory of probability to the statistics of society, especially in *Sur l'homme* (1835).

1835. Cauchy published the first existence proof for the solution of a differential equation.

1838-1839. Friedrich Bessel (1784–1846), **Friedrich Struve** (1793–1864), and **Thomas Henderson** (1798–1844) measured *stellar parallax* for the first time.

1842. Julius von Mayer (1814–1878) stated that the total amount of energy in the universe is constant (a form of the **first law of thermodynamics**), and that in natural processes energy is never lost, but only transformed from one kind to another.

1843-1846. John Adams (1819–1892) and **Urbain LeVerrier** (1811–1877) independently predicted the existence of a new planet and constructed its orbit from a consideration of irregularities in the motion of Uranus. This planet, later named *Neptune*, was sighted in 1846 by **Johann Galle** (1812–1910)—a great triumph for gravitational astronomy.

1843. James Joule (1818–1889) sought the connection between electricity, heat, and mechanical energy in "The Calorific Effects of Magneto-Electricity, and the Mechanical Value of Heat," and determined by four different procedures the mechanical equivalent of heat. In 1847 he enunciated the principle of the **conservation of energy.**

1846. The **Smithsonian Institution** for the increase and diffusion of knowledge was established by the United States Congress, utilizing the funds bequeathed by England's **James Smithson** (1765–1829).

1847. Hermann Helmholtz (1821–1894) announced the principle of the conservation of energy in *Über die Erhaltung der Kraft.* He discussed the principle in great theoretical detail and elucidated its meaning.

1848. William Thomson (Lord Kelvin) (1824–1907) established the absolute thermodynamic scale of temperature, which is named after him.

1849. Armand Fizeau (1819–1896) for the first time successfully measured the **speed of light** by observations which do not involve astronomical constants.

1849. Jean Bernard Foucault (1819–1868) measured the speed of light accurately in media other than air, and thereby determined that the speed of light in air is greater than in water. Later, in a famous pendulum experiment, he demonstrated that the earth rotates (1851).

1850. William Cranch Bond (1789–1859), using the Harvard College Observatory's 15-inch refractor, took the first photograph of a star.

1850. Rudolph Clausius (1822–1888) announced the **second law of thermodynamics:** heat cannot of itself pass from a colder to a warmer body. In *Über die bewegende Kraft der Wärme* (1865) he introduced the term *entropy,* stating that the entropy of the universe tends to increase.

1851. Bernhard Riemann (1826–1866) introduced topological considerations into analysis.

1853. The first **International Statistical Congress** was held at Brussels, organized and inspired by **Adolphe Quetelet.**

1854. Riemann established the mathematical importance of non-Euclidean geometries, discussing them in his general theory of manifolds. In the same year he gave the most comprehensive and general definition of the classical definite integral, since called the *Riemann integral.*

1854. George Boole (1815–1864) published *The Laws of Thought,* an expansion of his 1847 work, *The Mathematical Analysis of Logic,* which marks the beginning of **symbolic logic,** i.e., the attempt to express the laws of thought in algebraic symbols.

1856. Karl Weierstrass (1815–1897) began to lecture at the University of Berlin. In these lectures, which spanned over thirty years, he gave the modern (delta-epsilon) definition of a limit, eliminated the remaining vagueness in the concepts of the calculus, introduced the notion of uniform convergence, and founded the theory of functions of a complex variable on power series.

1860-1877. James Clerk Maxwell (1831–1879) and **Ludwig Boltzmann** (1844–1906) developed statistical mechanics, a theory of the behavior of a gas considered as a collection of large numbers of molecules obeying the laws of classical mechanics.

1863. The United States Congress approved creation of the **National Academy of Sciences** as a scientific adviser to the federal government and promoter of scientific research.

1868. William Huggins (1824–1910), noting a slight shift toward the red in the spectrum of Sirius, calculated the radial velocity of a star for the first time.

1870-1883. Georg Cantor (1845–1918) published his major works, founding the **theory of sets** (1870) and the **theory of transfinite numbers** (1883).

1872-1882. Richard Dedekind (1831–1916) gave arithmetic definitions of irrational numbers (the *Dedekind cut*), constituting the first rigorous theory of irrationals.

1873. Johannes van der Waals (1837–1923) found an equation of state for imperfect gases.

1873. Maxwell published his *Treatise on Electricity and Magnetism* where he described the properties of the electromagnetic field in a series of equations (*Maxwell equations*) which entailed the electromagnetic theory of light.

1877. **Giovanni Schiaparelli** (1835–1910) observed long, narrow, straight, intersecting, dark lines on Mars, which he called *canali.*

1877–1893. **Francis Galton** (1822–1911) and **Karl Pearson** (1857–1936) developed the major statistical tools of present-day social science, e.g. regression (Galton, 1877), correlation coefficients (Galton, 1888), moments and standard deviation (Pearson, 1893).

1878. **William Crookes** (1832–1919) showed that cathode rays proceed in straight lines, are capable of turning a small wheel, can be deflected by a magnet, excite fluorescence in certain substances, and heat and sometimes even melt some metals.

1884. **Gottlob Frege** (1848–1925) published *Grundlagen der Arithmetik,* in which arithmetical concepts were defined in logical terms.

1887. **Heinrich Hertz** (1857–1894) demonstrated the existence of electromagnetic waves in the space about a discharging Leyden jar, and found that electromagnetic waves were propagated with the velocity of light as Maxwell had predicted (1873). Hertz's work led to modern radio communications.

1887. **Albert Michelson** (1852–1931) and **Edward Morley** (1838–1923) announced that they were unable to detect any effect of the earth's motion through the aether in experiments with an extremely sensitive interferometer.

1895. **Wilhelm K. Röntgen** (1845–1923) announced the discovery of x-rays in *Eine neue Art von Strahlen.*

1895. **John W. Strutt (Lord Rayleigh)** (1842–1919) and **William Ramsay** (1852–1916) discovered the "inert" or "noble" gas *argon.* Ramsay later discovered the other noble gases: helium, krypton, neon, xenon, and radon.

1895. **Henri Poincaré** (1854–1912) founded **algebraic topology.** He first applied topology to celestial mechanics (1892–1899).

1896. **Alfred B. Nobel** (1833–1896) endowed prizes for outstanding achievements in physics, chemistry, medicine, and physiology. The first prizes were awarded in 1901, to **Wilhelm K. Röntgen** in physics, **Jacobus H. van't Hoff** (1852–1911) in chemistry, and **Emil A. von Behring** (1854–1917) in medicine and physiology.

1896. **Antoine H. Becquerel** (1852–1908) discovered radioactivity in uranium compounds.

1897. **Joseph John Thomson** (1856–1940) announced the discovery of the **electron,** the first sub-atomic particle, and determined experimentally the ratio of its mass to its charge.

1900. **Max Planck** (1858–1947) stated that energy is not emitted continuously from radiating bodies, but in discrete parcels, or **quanta.**

1902–1904. **Henri Lebesgue** (1875–1941) gave a theory of measure and the Lebesgue integral, extending the notions of integration and area to more general sets.

1904. **Marie Sklodowska Curie** (1867–1934) showed that pitchblende (uranium ore) contained two new radioactive elements: **radium** and **polonium.**

1904. **Ernst Zermelo** (1871–1953) published a proof that every set can be well ordered, which made possible the use of transfinite methods in mathematics.

1905. **Albert Einstein** (1879–1955) announced his **special theory of relativity,** which required a fundamental revision in the traditionally held Newtonian views of space and time, and introduced the celebrated equation $E = mc^2$.

1905. **Einstein** attributed to radiation itself a particle structure, and by supposing each particle of light **(photon)** to carry a quantum of energy, explained the photoelectric effect.

1910–1913. **Bertrand Russell** (1872–1970) and **Alfred North Whitehead** (1861–1947) published *Principia Mathematica,* carrying out the reduction of arithmetic to symbolic logic. This work is the foundation of the calculus of propositions and modern symbolic logic.

1911. **Robert A. Millikan** (1868–1953) established that electric charge always consists of an integral multiple of a unit charge, which he determined with great accuracy, in his oil-drop experiment.

1911. **Ernest Rutherford** (1871–1937) introduced the nuclear **model of the atom,** i.e., a small positively charged nucleus, containing most of the mass of the atom, surrounded by electrons.

1911–1913. **Ejnar Hertzsprung** (1873–1967) studied double stars and their colors, especially in the Pléiades, and with **Henry Norris Russell** (1877–1957) devised the Hertzsprung-Russell Diagram, a graphic way of grouping stars by the relation between their absolute magnitudes and spectral types.

1912. **Max von Laue** (1879–1960) discovered **X-ray diffraction,** a powerful technique for directly observing the atomic structure of crystals.

1913. **Niels Bohr** (1885–1962) devised a new model of the atom by applying quantum theory to Rutherford's nuclear atom. Although this model violated classical electromagnetic theory it successfully accounted for the spectrum of hydrogen.

1915. **Einstein** announced his **general theory of relativity,** which explained the advance of Mercury's perihelion, and predicted the subsequently observed bending of light rays near the sun.

1918. **Harlow Shapley** (1885–   ), from an extensive study of the distribution of globular clusters and cepheid variable stars, increased the estimated size of our galaxy about ten times. He envisioned the galaxy as a flattened lens-shaped system of stars in which the solar system occupied a position far from the center.

1919. Rutherford found that the collision of alpha particles with nitrogen atoms resulted in the disintegration of the nitrogen and the production of hydrogen nuclei (protons) and an isotope of oxygen. He was the first person to achieve artificial transmutation of an element.

1919. Arthur S. Eddington (1882–1944) and others, by studying data obtained during a total solar eclipse, verified Einstein's prediction of the bending of light rays by the gravitational field of large masses.

1919-1929. Edwin P. Hubble (1889–1953) detected cepheid variable stars in the Andromeda Nebula, a discovery that allowed him to determine the distances between galaxies.

1924. Louis-Victor de Broglie (1892–) determined from theoretical considerations that the electron, which had been considered a particle, should behave as a wave under certain circumstances. Experimental confirmation was obtained in 1927 by **Clinton Davisson** (1881–1958) and **Lester H. Germer** (1896–).

1925. Wolfgang Pauli (1900–1958) announced the **exclusion principle** (in any atom no two electrons have identical sets of quantum numbers). This principle was an important aid in determining the electron structure of the heavier elements.

1925-1926. Werner Karl Heisenberg (1901–) and **Erwin Schrödinger** (1887–1960) independently, and in different ways, laid the theoretical foundations of the new **quantum mechanics** which, though violating classical notions of causality, successfully predicts the behavior of atomic particles.

1927. George Lemaître (1894–), in order to explain the red shift in the spectra from distant galaxies, introduced the concept of the **expanding universe. Eddington** pursued research in this subject from 1930.

1928. Paul A. Dirac (1902–), by combining quantum mechanics and relativity theory, devised a relativistic **theory of the electron.**

1930. Vannevar Bush (1890–) and his associates placed into operation a "differential analyzer," the first modern analog computer.

1931. Ernest O. Lawrence (1901–1958) invented the **cyclotron,** a device for accelerating atomic particles, which has become the fundamental research tool in high-energy physics and has made possible the creation of transuranium elements.

1931. Kurt Gödel (1906–) published *Uber*

formal unentscheidbare Sätze der Principia Mathematica und verwandter Systeme, showing that in any formal mathematical system in which elementary arithmetic can be done, there are theorems whose truth or falsity cannot be proved.

1932. Karl Jansky reported the reception of radio waves from cosmic sources, making **radio astronomy** possible.

1938-1939. Otto Hahn (1879–1968) and **Otto Strassmann** bombarded uranium with neutrons and found an isotope of barium in the product (1938). **Lise Meitner** (1878–1968) and **Otto Frisch** (1904–) explained this result by assuming the fission of the uranium nucleus (**nuclear fission**).

1939. Nicolas Bourbaki (pseudonym assumed by a group of mathematicians) published the first of a long series of expository works on modern mathematics.

1939. Hans A. Bethe (1906–) and **Carl von Weizsäcker** (1912–) independently proposed two sets of nuclear reactions to account for stellar energies: the carbon-nitrogen cycle and the proton-proton chain.

1939-1945. World War II research needs stimulated the formation of large groups or teams of research workers to concentrate effort on a single problem, e.g., radar and atomic bomb. Such group research has become a common feature of post-war science.

1940. Gödel in *The Consistency of the Axiom of Choice and of the Generalized Continuum Hypothesis with the Axioms of Set Theory,* proved that transfinite methods could not introduce inconsistencies into mathematics.

1942. Enrico Fermi (1901–1954) and associates built the first controlled self-sustaining **nuclear reactor.** Fermi was one of the chief architects of the theory of the atomic nucleus.

1944. Mark I, the Harvard-IBM Automatic Sequence Controlled Calculator was put into operation at Harvard University. This was the first large-scale digital calculating machine.

1945. Vannevar Bush issued the report *Science: The Endless Frontier,* recommending the creation of a United States foundation for the support and encouragement of basic research and education in science. In 1950 the United States Congress established the **National Science Foundation** to implement this recommendation.

1946. The foundation of the **United States Atomic Energy Commission** assured civilian control of United States developments in atomic energy.

1946. ENIAC (Electronic Numerical Integrator and Calculator) was put into operation at the University of Pennsylvania, the first electronic high speed digital calculating machine.

1951. **Harold I. Ewen** and **Edward M. Purcell** (1912–) detected the 21-centimeter hydrogen spectral line in galactic radiation, which had been predicted in 1944 by **Hendrik van de Hulst** (1918–). This discovery has enabled astronomers to map the structure of the Milky Way.

1956. **Tsung Dao Lee** (1926–) and **Chen Ning Yang** (1922–) showed theoretically that a basic symmetry principle, previously thought to hold in all atomic interactions (conservation of parity), is invalid for weak interactions. **Chien-Shiung Wu** (1915–) in the same year experimentally demonstrated the violation of conservation of parity.

1962. **Neil Bartlett** announced that he had combined xenon with platinum and fluorine to form xenon-platinum hexafluoride; other compounds of xenon and radon were found, thus destroying the notion that the noble gases are all nonreacting.

b. CHEMISTRY, BIOLOGY, GEOLOGY

1799–1805. **Georges Cuvier** (1769–1832) founded **comparative anatomy** on functional grounds maintaining that the parts of the organism are correlated to the functioning whole.

1800–1802. **Marie-François Bichat** (1771–1802) stimulated the separate and systematic study of each anatomical structure and physiological function by his classification of the body into textures or *tissus* each with its particular vital property.

1801. **Claude Berthollet** (1748–1822) opposed the prevailing doctrine of elective affinities with his **law of mass action.**

1802. **John Playfair** (1748–1819), friend and disciple of **James Hutton** (1726–1797), produced *Illustrations of the Huttonian Theory of the Earth,* bringing a clear exposition of uniformitarianism to a wide audience and establishing this philosophy as the basis of modern geology.

1802–1804. **Jean d'Aubuisson de Voisins** (1769–1819) and **Leopold von Buch** (1774–1853), two of the most illustrious students of **Abraham Werner** (1749/50–1817), accepted the volcanic origin of basalt, signalling the defeat of Wernerian neptunism.

1804. **Nicholas de Saussure** (1767–1845) explained the process of photosynthesis in terms of the new chemistry of **Antoine Lavoisier** (1743–1794).

1807. **Humphry Davy** (1778–1829), using the new voltaic battery, isolated the metals potassium and sodium.

1807. Establishment of **United States Coast Survey,** the first United States scientific agency.

1807. Foundation of the **Geological Society of London,** which served as a center for research and discussion and as a model for similar societies in other countries.

1808. **John Dalton** (1766–1844) published his *New System of Chemical Philosophy,* which established the **quantitative atomic theory** in chemistry.

1808. **Joseph Gay-Lussac** (1778–1850) announced his discovery of the law of combining volumes for gases, i.e., the ratios of the volumes of reacting gases are small whole numbers.

1809. **Jean-Baptiste Lamarck** (1744–1829), in *Philosophie zoologique,* gave the most complete explanation of his **theory of evolution.** He argued that through a combination of unconscious striving, the physiological effects of use and disuse, and the influence of the environment, anatomical parts became modified. Furthermore, he believed that by the "inheritance of acquired characteristics" living forms evolved in an ever-ascending scale of perfection.

1809. **Lorenz Oken** (1779–1815), one of the leaders of the German **Naturphilosophie** movement, published an anti-mechanist treatise which taught the superiority of intuitively derived concepts, expressed a belief in the archetypal polarities of nature, and championed a search for ideal types and a teleological unity in nature.

1809. **Ephraim McDowell** (1771–1830) performed a successful ovariotomy, thus showing that surgery of the abdominal cavity was not necessarily fatal.

1811. **Amedeo Avogadro** (1776–1856) concluded that equal volumes of all gases at the same temperature and pressure contain equal numbers of molecules; in effect he distinguished between atoms and molecules, but his ideas were neglected until 1858.

1811. **Georges Cuvier** (1769–1832), the founder of modern vertebrate paleontology, and **Alexandre Brongnïart** (1770–1847) brought out their *Essai sur la géographie minéralogique des environs de Paris* with a map, ordering important tertiary strata.

1812. **Jöns Berzelius** (1779–1848) developed a dualistic electrochemical theory to account for electrolysis and chemical combination.

1815. **William Prout** (1785–1850) published an anonymous paper in which he advanced the hypothesis that the atoms of all other elements were really aggregates of hydrogen atoms.

1815. **William Smith** (1769–1839) published his famous **geological map of England and Wales,** and established that specific strata can be identified by their fossil content, the principle upon which historical geology is founded.

He also worked out the main divisions of the **Secondary** or **Mesozoic** strata.

1819. Pierre Dulong (1785–1838) and **Alexis Petit** (1791–1820) formulated the rule that the product of the relative atomic weight and the specific heat of an element is a constant. This made possible the experimental determination of relative atomic weights.

1819. René Laënnec (1781–1826) invented the **stethoscope.**

1822. François Magendie (1783–1855) showed that the sensory and motor functions arise from different spinal roots. He was anticipated in 1811 by the more discursive work of **Charles Bell** (1774–1842).

1824. Justus von Liebig (1803–1873) obtained the chair of chemistry at Giessen, where he established the first truly effective laboratory for the teaching of chemistry. He greatly improved methods of organic analysis and, with his students, accurately analyzed a great number of organic compounds.

1826-1840. Johannes Müller (1801–1858) developed his doctrine of specific nerve energies. He taught some of the most productive men in German physiology.

1828. Friedrich Wöhler (1800–1882) announced the **synthesis of urea,** a typical product of animal metabolism. Urea synthesis and subsequent advances in organic synthesis crippled the vitalistic notion that a special force controls life processes.

1828. Karl von Baer (1792–1876) founded modern comparative embryology with the publication of *Über Entwickelungsgeschichte der Thiere.* Here he proclaimed that embryonic development is the history of increasing specificity.

1830-1833. Charles Lyell (1797–1875) published his *Principles of Geology,* a powerful synthesis expounding and extending Hutton's uniformitarian theory.

1831-1836. Charles Darwin (1809–1882), as naturalist aboard *H. M. S. Beagle,* studied South American flora and fauna, and gathered information he was later to use in his theory of evolution.

c. 1831-1852. Roderick Murchison (1792–1871) and **Adam Sedgwick** (1785–1873) described the succession of Paleozoic strata in Wales, Murchison defining the *Silurian* system (1839) and Sedgwick defining the *Cambrian* system.

1838-1842. The **United States Exploring Expedition,** under the command of Lieut. **Charles Wilkes** (1798–1877), explored the Pacific Ocean, the first example of a United States government-sponsored scientific maritime venture.

1839. Theodor Schwann (1810–1882) extended the 1838 observations on plants cells of **Matthias Schleiden** (1804–1881) into the generalization that cells are the common structural and functional unit of all living organisms.

1840. Louis Agassiz (1807–1873) elucidated the role of glaciers in geological change and enunciated his **ice age theory.**

1841. Carlo Matteucci (1811–1868) demonstrated that a difference of electropotential exists between an excised nerve and damaged muscle. This stimulated **Emil du Bois-Reymond** (1818–1896) to work in electrophysiology and to champion the German school of physiologists who wished to reduce physiological phenomena to physical and chemical processes.

1842. Liebig published *Die Thierchemie,* which promoted the analysis of organic compounds and described all physical and mental actions of animals as the result of chemical reactions.

1846. William T. G. Morton (1819–1868) gave the first public demonstration of the use of **ether as an anaesthetic** in surgery.

1847. Carl Ludwig (1816–1895) perfected the **kymograph,** which became an invaluable measuring instrument for physiology.

1848. Louis Pasteur (1822–1895), in a series of brilliantly conceived and executed experiments, demonstrated the connection between the optical activity of organic molecules and crystaline structure, thus founding **stereochemistry.**

1848. Claude Bernard (1813–1878) demonstrated the ability of the liver to store sugar in the form of glycogen. His widely read *Introduction à l'étude de la médecine expérimentale* (1865) influenced literary men as well as scientists.

1852. Edward Frankland (1825–1899) announced his **theory of valency,** i.e., each atom has a certain "valency," or capacity for combining with a definite number of other atoms.

1856-1864. Bernard evolved the concept of the *milieu interieur,* envisioning that cells were autonomous physiological units, yet were dependent upon and protected by the internal environment of the whole organism.

1856-1866. Hermann Helmholtz (1821–1894) extended the doctrine of specific nerve energies developed by **Johannes Müller** to vision and hearing, indicating the penetration of physics and physiology into psychology.

1857-1860. Louis Pasteur demonstrated that fermentation was a product of yeast cell activity. This challenged the view of Liebig that the ferment was merely an unstable chemical substance.

1858. Rudolph Virchow (1821–1902) in *Die*

Cellularpathologie declared that disease reflects an impairment of cellular organization. Here, too, he stated his famous generalization *"omnis cellula e cellula"* (all cells arise from cells) and described the cell as the basic element of the life process.

1858. Friedrich A. Kekulé (1829–1896) published *Über die Konstitution und die Metamorphosen der chemischen Verbindungen und über die chemische Natur des Kohlenstoffs,* in which he recognized that carbon is quadrivalent, and that carbon atoms link together to form long chains that serve as skeletons for organic molecules.

1858. Stanislao Cannizzaro (1826–1910) showed that one could unambiguously determine atomic weights. He was thus able to provide a table giving the correct molecular formulas of many compounds.

1859. Gustav R. Kirchhoff (1824–1887) and **Robert W. Bunsen** (1811–1899) began researches that made **spectrum analysis** a powerful method for the investigation of matter. They showed that a chemical element was clearly characterized by its spectrum, and by spectrum analysis they were able to discover previously unknown elements.

1859. Darwin amassed twenty-five years of careful research in *The Origin of Species.* Inspired by the evidence in geology, paleontology, zoogeography, and domestic animal breeding, he declared that species evolved through variation and the natural selection of those individuals best suited to survive in given environmental conditions. A similar theory was developed independently by **Alfred R. Wallace** (1823–1913).

1860. Marcelin Berthelot (1827–1907) published *Chimie organique fondée sur la synthèse,* which showed that total synthesis of all classes of organic compounds from the elements carbon, hydrogen, oxygen, and nitrogen was possible.

1861. Alexander M. Butlerov (1828–1886) introduced the term "chemical structure" at a chemical meeting in Germany. Butlerov shares credit with **Kekulé** for the development of the theory of the structure of organic compounds.

1861. Pasteur, in a classic paper "Mémoire sur les corpuscles organisés qui existent dans l'atmosphère," described a series of experiments which confuted the doctrine of the spontaneous generation of micro-organisms.

1862–1877. Pasteur investigated several types of micro-organisms to advance the **germ theory of disease.** His evidence encouraged **Joseph Lister** (1827–1912) to initiate the practice of **antiseptic surgery** (1865).

1863. Ivan M. Sechenov (1829–1905) published *Reflexes of the Brain,* one of the earliest attempts to establish the physiological basis of psychic processes. His teaching and research was a decisive influence on the development of physiology in Russia.

1865. Gregor Mendel (1822–1884), an Augustinian monk, described cross-breeding experiments with peas which demonstrated the particulate nature of inheritance. He concluded that many traits segregated into dominant and recessive alternatives and that combined traits assorted independently. Little attention was paid to his results until 1900 when cytological work suggested such unit characters existed.

1869. Dmitri I. Mendeleev (1834–1907), in *Principles of Chemistry,* devised his periodic table of the chemical elements, which arranged the elements in the order of increasing atomic weight, noted the periodic recurrence of similar properties in groups of elements, and successfully predicted the properties of elements yet to be discovered.

1872–1876. H. M. S. *Challenger* made an extended voyage of scientific investigation, led by **Wyville Thomson** (1830–1882). The information gathered and reported largely by **John Murray** (1841–1914) gave much impetus to the science of **oceanography.**

1874. Jacobus van't Hoff (1852–1911) and **Achille LeBel** (1847–1930) independently interpreted the 1848 results of **Pasteur** and developed the stereochemistry of carbon.

1878. Josiah W. Gibbs (1839–1903), in his rigorously mathematical thermodynamic study on the *Equilibrium of Heterogeneous Substances,* used the concept of chemical potential and introduced the phase rule.

1879. Ivan P. Pavlov (1849–1936) showed the production of gastric juices could be achieved without the introduction of food into the stomach. His work in the physiology of digestion led him to develop the concept of the acquired or *conditioned reflex.*

1879. The **United States Geological Survey** was founded, consolidating under one office the several surveys which had been gaining valuable information in western North America for over a decade. Under the directorship of **John W. Powell** (1834–1902) after 1881, the survey grew into a powerful agency for the progress of science in the United States.

1880. John Milne (1850–1913) developed the first accurate **seismograph,** permitting the careful study of earthquakes and opening the way to new knowledge of the earth's interior.

1882. Robert Koch (1843–1910) described the etiology of the **tubercle bacillus.** This discovery led him (1884) to state *Koch's postulates,* a method for isolating micro-organisms and proving that they are specific causes, not merely concomitants, of disease.

1883.   Ilia I. Mechnikov (1845–1916) described the action of phagocytic cells in transparent starfish larvae. His discovery led to a general explanation of local inflammation.

1883.   Edouard van Beneden (1845–1901) described how the chromosomes are derived in equal numbers from the conjugating germ cells. This led to the discovery of reduction division in the formation of the gametes.

1887.   Svante A. Arrhenius (1859–1927) announced his theory of electrolytic dissociation, according to which most of the molecules of an electrolyte are immediately dissociated into two ions when dissolved.

1888–1891.   Wilhelm Roux (1850–1924) destroyed half of the two-cell stage of a frog's embryo (1888). The remaining cell developed into half an embryo. In 1891 **Hans Driesch** (1867–1941) working with sea urchin embryos got results contradictory to Roux's. This drew attention to the relative rôles of the internal and external environment on the development of cells.

1890.   Emil von Behring (1854–1917) and **Shibasaburo Kitasato** (1856–1931) demonstrated that the serum of immunized rabbits neutralized the toxin of tetanus. This discovery opened the possibility that disease could be prevented through the stimulation of specific antibody production.

1892.   August Weismann (1834–1914) described in *Das Keimplasma* his theory of the continuity of the germ plasm and a scheme for the unfolding of a particulate hereditary pattern in embryogenesis.

1893.   Theobald Smith (1859–1934), in "Investigations into the Nature, Causation and Prevention of Southern Cattle Fever," demonstrated that parasites could act as vectors of disease.

1895.   Wilhelm K. Röntgen (1845–1923) discovered x-rays and immediately realized that his discovery had a practical application in medicine.

1897.   Eduard Buchner (1860–1917) discovered that *zymase,* a cell-free yeast extract, caused fermentation, thus resolving a longstanding controversy over "vital" and "inorganic" ferments.

1900.   Hugo de Vries (1848–1935), **Carl Correns** (1864–1933), and **Erich Tschermak** (1871–1962) independently rediscovered the 1865 work of **Gregor Mendel** while searching the literature to confirm their own experimental results.

1903.   Walter S. Sutton (1876–1916) pointed out that the Mendelian ratios could be explained by the cytological behavior of the chromosomes.

1906.   Charles Sherrington (1861–1952) described in *The Integrative Action of the Nervous System* the properties of the synapse and the complex integration of reflexes in behavior.

1907.   Ross G. Harrison (1870–1959) announced a technique for culturing tissue cells outside of the body.

1909.   Paul Ehrlich (1854–1915) showed that the synthetic compound, *Salvarsan,* was an effective treatment for syphilis. This discovery was a tremendous stimulus to the field of chemotherapy.   In 1935 **Gerhard Domagk** (1895–1964) made the fundamental discovery which led to the introduction and widespread use of **sulfa drugs.**

1911.   Thomas H. Morgan (1866–1945) claimed that certain traits were genetically linked on the chromosome, thus visualizing a linear arrangement of genes and stimulating the construction of genetic maps.

1915.   Alfred Wegener (1880–1930) gave the classic expression of the controversial theory of continental drift in *Die Entstehung der Kontinente und Ozeane.*

1921.   Hans Spemann (1869–1941) postulated an organizer principle which was responsible for the formative interaction between neighboring embryonic regions. He stimulated contemporary embryologists to search for the inductive chemical molecule.

1927.   Hermann J. Muller (1890–1967) announced that he had successfully induced mutations in fruit flies with x-rays. This provided a useful experimental tool, yet in retrospect gave warning to the generations of the 1940's and 1950's of a danger in the release of atomic energy.

1929.   Alexander Fleming (1881–1955) announced that the common mold *Penicillium* had an inhibitory effect on certain pathogenic bacteria. It was not until 1943 under the pressures of World War II, however, that the first antibiotic, penicillin, was successfully developed.

1930.   Ronald A. Fisher (1890–1962) established in *The Genetical Theory of Natural Selection* that superior genes have a significant selective advantage, thus testifying that Darwinian evolution was compatible with genetics.

1941.   George W. Beadle (1903–   ) and **Edward L. Tatum** (1909–   ) described an experimental assay which evaluated the exact relationships between specific mutant genes in mold and particular stages in the metabolic process.

1944.   Ostwald T. Avery (1877–1955) and collaborators announced they had transmuted one type of pneumococcus bacteria into a second type by the transfer of DNA molecules.

1946.   Willard F. Libby (1908–   ), and associates, developed *radiocarbon dating,* a method for ascertaining the absolute age of materials containing carbon.

1953. Francis H. C. Crick (1916–   ) and **James D. Watson** (1928–   ) offered a model for the structure of DNA which accounted for gene replication and conceived a biochemical code that could transmit a great variety of genetic information.

3. TECHNOLOGICAL ACHIEVEMENTS

(From p. 528)

The Industrial Revolution, begun in the latter half of the 18th century, expanded into new geographical areas, revolutionized older technologies, created new ones, and continued to transform society and human life during the 19th and 20th centuries. Although historians might debate as to whether several industrial revolutions occurred during this two-century span, whether there were different phases of the same revolution, or whether industrialization had reached the point of a "continuing revolution," there was no doubt that technological advances from the mid-18th century to the present had given man greatly increased mastery over his environment, while at the same time posing problems and even threats to man's continued existence.

The culmination of Britain's leadership in the Industrial Revolution was reached at the **Great Exhibition of 1851** in London; after that Britain's position declined relatively while new industrial giants, America and Germany near the close of the 19th century, and Russia in the 20th century, gained in technological strength and capabilities. More recently, the "underdeveloped nations" (so-called because they are not so advanced technologically as some of the Western nations) have sought their own industrial development.

a. ENERGY AND POWER SOURCES

1800. The **galvanic cell,** or Voltaic pile, of **Alessandro Volta** (1745–1827) was the first electric battery (converting chemical energy into electrical energy).

1802. Richard Trevithick (1771–1833) built the first **high-pressure steam engine,** although the American **Oliver Evans** (1755–1819) had patented one in the United States in 1797. Other advances in steam-engine technology included the compound engine (adding a high pressure cylinder to the original Watt engine) by **William McNaught** (1813–1881) in 1845.

1806. First gas-lighting of cotton mills. Improvements made in production and distribution of gas as heat source (**Bunsen burner,** 1855) and for illumination (**Welsbach gas-mantle,** 1885).

1827. Benoit Fourneyron (1802–1867) developed the **water-turbine.**

1832. The first mechanical generation of electricity by **Hippolyte Pixii.** Major improvements in **electric generators** followed: the improved armature (1856) designed by **Werner von Siemens** (1816–1892); and the ring-armature (1870) of **Zénobe T. Gramme** (1826–1901), which represented the first practical dynamo.

1854. Abraham Gesner (1797–1864) manufactured kerosene.

1859. William M. J. Rankine (1820–1872) published the first comprehensive manual of the steam engine. The steam engine stimulated theoretical studies in thermodynamics by Clapeyron, Clausius, Joule, Lord Kelvin, and Gibbs.

1859. Edwin L. Drake (1819–1880) drilled the **first oil well** in Titusville, Pennsylvania, opening up the Pennsylvania oil field and starting the large-scale commercial exploitation of petroleum. **First oil pipeline** (two-inch diameter, six miles long) constructed 1865 in Pennsylvania.

1876. Nicholas August Otto (1832–1891) built the first practical gas engine, working upon the so-called **Otto cycle,** which is now almost universally employed for all internal combustion engines. Otto's work was based upon previous engines of **Étienne Lenoir** (1822–1900) and **Alphonse Beau de Rochas** (1815–1891). The Otto cycle was employed in the gasoline engine patented (1885) by **Gottlieb Daimler** (1834–1900).

1882. The Pearl Street (New York City) electric generating station, a pioneer central power station designed by **Thomas A. Edison** (1847–1931), commenced operations a few months after Edison dynamos had been installed at Holborn Viaduct Station in England.

1884. Charles A. Parsons (1854–1931) patented the **steam turbine.** The steam turbine (1887) of the Swede **Gustav de Laval** (1845–1913) proved successful for engines of smaller power.

1886. Beginning of the first great **hydro-electric installation** at Niagara Falls.

1888. Nikola Tesla (1856–1943) invented the

alternating current electric motor: he also made possible the polyphase transmission of power over long distances and pioneered the invention of radio.

1892.   Rudolf Diesel (1858–1913) patented his heavy oil engine, first manufactured successfully in 1897.

1921.   Tetraethyl lead, gasoline anti-knock additive, produced by **Thomas Midgley** (1889–1944).

1930–1937.   Development of gas turbine unit for jet propulsion in aircraft by **Frank Whittle.**

1930–1935.   Development of first commercially practicable **catalytic cracking system** for petroleum by **Eugene J. Houdry** (1892–1962).

1942.   DAWN OF THE NUCLEAR AGE. The first self-sustaining **nuclear chain reaction** achieved at Stagg Field, Chicago, by **Enrico Fermi** (1901–1954). The first full-scale use of nuclear fuel to produce electricity occurred at Calder Hall (England) in 1956.

1954.   The **solar battery** developed by Bell Telephone Laboratories, making it possible to convert sunlight directly to electric power.

b. MATERIALS AND CONSTRUCTION

1800.   Pioneer **suspension bridge,** hung by iron chains, built by **James Finley** (c. 1762–1828) in Pennsylvania; wire suspension employed by **Marc Seguin** (1786–1875) in bridge near Lyons (1825). The American, **Ithiel Town** (1784–1844), patented his truss bridge (1820).

1817–1825.   Building of the **Erie Canal,** the first great American civil engineering work.

1818.   The **Institute of Civil Engineers** (London), the first professional engineering society, founded.

Marc Isambard Brunel (1769–1849) patented the cast-iron **tunnel shield; Thomas Cochrane** (1830) used this shield to construct foundations on marshy ground.

1824.   Joseph Aspdin (1779–1855) patented **Portland cement,** a hydraulic cement (impervious to water) as durable as that employed by the Romans.

1827.   Gay-Lussac tower introduced in manufacture of sulphuric acid, largely replacing John Roebuck's lead-chamber process (1746). **Herman Frasch** (1851–1914) developed process (1891) for mining sulphur (by superheated water and pumping to the surface).

1836.   Galvanized iron introduced by Sorel in France. Galvanized fencing and barbed wire (c. 1880) helped to fence off large tracts of cattle land in American west during latter part of 19th century.

1839.   Charles Goodyear (1800–1860) **vulcan-**

ized rubber. Although introduced into Europe in 1615, rubber had not been commercially successful until a solvent for the latex was found (1765); bonding of rubber to cloth to produce raincoats (macintoshes) had been developed (1824) by **Charles Macintosh** (1766–1843).

1855.   John A. Roebling (1806–1869) completed **wire cable bridge** at Niagara; Roebling utilized this same method for the **Brooklyn Bridge** (completed by his son, W. A. Roebling, in 1883), and it became standard construction technique for all great suspension bridges.

1856.   Henry Bessemer (1813–1898) perfected the technique (*Bessemer process*) for converting pig iron into steel by directing an air blast upon the molten metal.

1856.   *Mauve,* first of the **aniline** (coal-tar) **dyes,** discovered by **William H. Perkin** (1838–1907). Beginning of the synthetic dye industry, which was to develop greatly in Germany.

1861.   Ernest Solvay (1838–1922) patented the Solvay ammonia process for the manufacture of soda.

1863.   The **open-hearth process** for the manufacture of steel developed by the Martin brothers in France using the regenerative furnace devised (1856) by **Frederick Siemens** (1826–1904) (also known as the Siemens-Martin process).

1867.   Alfred Nobel (1833–1896) manufactured **dynamite.** Guncotton and nitroglycerine both discovered in 1846, had previously been used for blasting purposes. In 1875 Nobel discovered blasting gelatine, from which arose the gelignite industry. Cordite, another explosive, patented 1889 by Frederick Abel and James Dewar.

1863.   Henry Clifton Sorby (1826–1908) of Sheffield discovered the microstructure of steel, marking the beginning of **modern metallurgical science.**

1868.   Robert F. Mushet (1811–1891) began the manufacture of **tungsten steel.** Other steel alloys also developed: chromium steel (France, 1877); manganese steel (Robert Hadfield, England, 1882); nickel steel (France, 1888); stainless steel (many inventors, 1911–1920).

1872.   John W. Hyatt (1837–1920) began commercial production of celluloid, discovered by Alexander Parkes (1855).

1877.   Joseph Monier (1823–1906) patented a **reinforced concrete** beam. In the 1890's two other Frenchmen, Edmond Coignet and Francois Hennibique, utilized reinforced concrete for pipes, aqueducts, bridges, tunnels; E. L. Ransome employed it extensively in building construction.

1879.   Percy Gilchrist (1851–1935) and **Sidney G. Thomas** (1850–1885) developed a method for making steel from phosphoric iron ores, thereby doubling in effect the world's potential steel production.

1886. Charles M. Hall (1863-1914) developed the electrolytic method of obtaining aluminum from its oxide (bauxite).

1889. Completion of the **Eiffel Tower;** wrought-iron superstructure on reinforced concrete base. Cast iron used for building construction earlier in the century by James Bogardus (1800-1874) for office buildings in New York and by Joseph Paxton (1801-1865) for Crystal Palace at Great Exhibition of 1851 (also employing wrought iron and glass, and prefabricated units). The first complete steel-frame structure was built in Chicago in 1890; steel made possible skyscrapers, as did the earlier invention (1854) of the elevator by **Elisha G. Otis** (1811-1861).

1902. Arthur D. Little (1863-1935) patented rayon, the **first cellulose fiber,** and also artificial silk. Earlier (1884) Louis, Count of Chardonnet (1839-1924), had produced an artificial thread which was woven into a silk-like material. Cellophane developed by J. E. Brandenberger (1912); further developed by W. H. Church and K. E. Prindle (1926).

1909. The first polymer, **Bakelite,** discovered by **Leo H. Baekeland** (1863-1944). Subsequent development of polymers include neoprene, arising from work of Father Julius A. Nieuwland beginning in 1906; nylon, developed by Wallace H. Carothers and first manufactured in 1938; acrilan; orlon; dynel; and dacron (called terylene by its British inventors, J. R. Whinfield and J. T. Dickson, 1941). Synthetic polymers include elastomers, fibers, plastics. Silicon polymers developed c. 1945.

1928. The first steel-frame, glass-curtain-wall building completed. By 1960 this technique was practically universal for high buildings; developed particularly by **L. Mies van der Rohe** (1886-1969).

1941. Shell molding, a revolutionary process producing more accurate castings cheaply, invented by **Johannes Croning.** Powder metallurgy, although known since Wollaston's work at the beginning of the 19th century, achieved extensive application in mid-20th century.

1945. Industrial development of silicones proceeded apace for a wide variety of applications, including lubricants for exceedingly high and low temperatures; binding of fiberglass; water-repellent agents; etc.

1947. Frank Lloyd Wright (1869-1959) extended pure cantilever technique (earlier employed with iron and steel construction in bridges) by using concrete slab cantilevers for S. C. Johnson Research Building (Racine, Wisconsin).

1950 ff. Basic-oxygen process for manufacture of steel developed in Austria.

c. MACHINES AND INDUSTRIAL TECHNIQUES

1800. Eli Whitney (1765-1825) credited with introduction of **interchangeable parts** for manufacturing muskets. Although it had European precedents, the system of interchangeable parts became known as "the American system" because it was most fully exploited in the United States and became the foundation of the mass production characteristic of American industry at a later date.

1801. Joseph M. Jacquard (1752-1834) invented a loom for figured silk fabrics, later introduced into the making of worsteds. **William Horrocks** (1776-1849) developed the power loom (1813), improved (1822) by **Richard Roberts** (1789-1864). Machine combing of wool developed (1845); ring spinning frame (1830); the Brussels power loom invented by Erastus B. Bigelow (1814-1879) of Massachusetts for the weaving of carpets (1845); and the loom of J. H. Northrop of Massachusetts (1892), which was almost completely automatic.

1810. Friedrich Koenig's (1774-1833) **power-driven press** in use, followed by the flat bed press (1811). Other developments leading to mass production of printed matter, especially newspapers, were the rotary press of Robert Hoe (1846) and the web printing press, allowing for printing on a continuous roll (web) of paper by a rotary press, invented (1865) by William A. Bullock. In 1885 the linotype of **Ottmar Mergenthaler** (1854-1899) replaced monotype.

1823-1843. Charles Babbage (1792-1871) attempted to build calculating machines (following the lead of Thomas de Colmar, who built the first practical calculating machine in 1820); Babbage's machines were never completed, being too advanced for the technology of the time, but his theories formed a basis for later work in this field.

1830. Joseph Whitworth (1803-1887) developed the **standard screw gauge** and a machine to measure one-millionth of an inch, for standards. Made possible more precise machine tools for planing, gear-cutting, and milling.

1837 ff. Rapid **development of armament,** keeping pace with improvements in metallurgy, machines, and explosives: **Henri J. Paixhans'** (1783-1854) shell-gun, adopted by France, 1837; rifled, breech-loading artillery used by Piedmont, 1845; the French '75, the first quick-firing artillery piece, firing both shrapnel and high explosive, 1898; the cast steel breech-loading Prussian artillery manufactured by the Krupps from 1849 on. In small arms, there was the Colt revolver (1835), the Dreyse needle-gun (1841), the Minié bullet (1849), Winchester repeating rifle (1860), Gatling machine gun (1861), French chassepot (1866), and the Maxim gun (1884). The self-propelled torpedo was invented by Robert Whitehead (1823–1905) in 1864; smokeless powder appeared in 1884.

1839. **Steam hammer** invented by **James Nasmyth** (1808–1890). Also developments in drop-forging and die-stamping at this time.

1846. **Elias Howe** (1819–1867) invented the lock-stitch **sewing machine;** in 1851 **Isaac M. Singer** (1811–1875) invented the first practical domestic sewing machine. This became the first major consumer appliance, soon followed by the **carpet sweeper** of M. R. Bissell (1876), and the **vacuum cleaner** (I. W. McGaffey, 1869; J. Thurman, 1899).

1849–1854. Exploiting the increasing accuracy of machine tools, **Samuel Colt** (1814–1862) and **Elisha Root** (1808–1865) developed a practical system for manufacturing interchangeable parts, especially in connection with Colt's revolver.

1855. Development of **turret lathe** by American machine-tool makers. First true **universal milling machine** designed (1862) by **Joseph R. Brown** (1810–1876). Other machine-tool improvements included Mushet's tool steel, increasing the cutting speed (high speed tool steel, 1898, by Taylor and White), gear-box mechanisms for better control, multiple-spindle lathes (1890), and tungsten carbide tools (1926).

1873. First **use of electricity to drive machinery,** Vienna. Quickly adopted, usually with the motor incorporated into the machine rather than separate.

1877. **Elihu Thomson** invented a **resistance welder.** N. V. Bernardos of Russia patented carbon-arc welding, although arc welding (most popularly employed process today) did not come into its own until invention of the coated electrode in the 1920's. Oxyacetylene torch (invented in 1900 by Edmund Fouche) and gas welding was the dominant process until recently. Development of inert-gas-shielded arc welding after 1942.

1882 ff. Invention and use of electric appliances for consumer market: electric fan (S. S. Wheeler); flatiron (H. W. Seely, 1882); stove (W. S. Hadaway, 1896); separate attachable plug (H. Hubbell, 1904); sewing machine (Singer Co., 1889); washing machine (Hurling Co., 1907).

1884. **Dorr E. Felt** (1862–1930) made first accurate **comptometer.** **William S. Burroughs**

(1857–1898) developed first successful recording **adding machine** (1888); Brunsviga calculating machine (1892).

1895. **Carl Linde** established **liquid air** plant. He had previously (1876) introduced the ammonia compressor machine (the first vapor compression machine invented by Jacob Perkins, 1834). Other refrigerating machines were: ammonia absorption machine (Carré, 1860), air refrigerator (Gorrie, 1845; improved by Kirk, 1862), open-cycle air machine (Giffard, 1873, and later by Bell and Coleman).

1895. **King C. Gillette** (1855–1932) invented **safety razor** with throwaway blades. **J. Schick** invented **electric razor** (1928). Stainless steel throwaway blades invented in Sweden (1962).

1898. **M. J. Owens** (1859–1923) invented automatic **bottle-making machine.**

1905–1910. Electric precipitation equipment, for prevention of atmospheric pollution by industry, developed by Frederick G. Cottrell (1877–1948).

1913. **G. Sundback** invented a slide fastener **(zipper);** earlier version patented by W. L. Judson (1891).

1914. **Conveyer-belt mass production** employed in the United States most dramatically in Henry Ford's assembly line for Model T Ford automobile, which became the symbol for American industrial technique.

1915. Development of **tank in warfare** by British (Sir Ernest Swinton).

1920 ff. **Managerial techniques** improved through development of "Scientific Management," whose principles were first enunciated by **Frederick W. Taylor** (1856–1915) in the first decade of the century. Taylor concentrated on time-motion studies. Other proponents of "rationalized" production were Frank Gilbreth and Charles Bedaux. Quality control developed 1926 ff.

1920. **J. C. Shaw** developed a **sensing device,** controlled by a servomechanism, for a milling machine. Hydraulic trace of J. W. Anderson (1927) allowed the reproduction of complex shapes. Machine tools further supplemented by electrolytic and ultrasonic machines, and cutting machines guided by an electron beam. **Development of laser** (light amplification by simulated emission of radiation) by Theodore N. Maiman (1960), also used for precision cutting.

1923. First mill for hot continuous wide strip rolling of steel, based on work of John B. Tytus.

1938. Ladislao J. and George Biro patented the **ball-point pen.**

1941–1945. Development of **rockets and missiles** during World War II.

1944. Harvard IBM Automatic Sequence Controlled Calculator, the first automatic general-purpose **digital computer,** completed. ENIAC (electronic numerical integrator and calculator), the first electronic digital computer, built in 1946. Development of special purpose computers and data processors (1950 ff.), including programmed **teaching machines.**

1947. Word *Automation* coined by John Diebold and D. S. Harder, to define "self-powered, self-guiding and correcting mechanism," and later extended to include all elements of "automated factory" and extension to office and clerical procedures.

1953. **Electronic computers** with feedback mechanism (servomechanisms), made possible new field of **Cybernetics,** defined by **Norbert Wiener** (1953) as "the study of control and communication in the animal and the machine."

d. AGRICULTURAL PRODUCTION AND FOOD TECHNOLOGY

1801. **Franz K. Achard** (1753–1821) built the first **sugar-beet factory** (Silesia). Sugar-beet cultivation and beet-sugar industry developed primarily in France and Germany.

1810. **Nicolas Appert** (c. 1750–1840) described system for food preservation by canning, using glass jars. Tin cans introduced 1811.

1834. **Cyrus H. McCormick** (1809–1884) patented his **reaper,** and began commercial manufacture c. 1840. Obed Hussey (1792–1860) invented a similar reaper simultaneously and independently.

1837. **John Deere** (1804–1886) introduced the **steel plow.** In 1819 Jethro Wood (1774–1834) had developed a cast-iron plow; and John Lane had introduced a steel-blade plowshare in 1833. James Oliver's (1823–1908) chilled plow of 1855 was improved by the Marsh brothers (1857). Mechanical power applied to plowing with the introduction of **cable plowing** (1850); by 1858 John Fowler had introduced the **steam plow.**

1850–1880. **Improvements in farm implements** included the revolving disc harrow (1847), binder (1850), corn planter (1853), two-horse straddle-row cultivator (1856), combine harvester (1860), combine seed drill (1867), and sheaf-binding harvester (1878).

1860. **Gail Borden** (1801–1874) opened the first factory for the production of **evaporated milk.**

1861. After Louis Pasteur's work on microorganisms, **pasteurization** was introduced as a preservative for beer, wine, and milk.

1865 ff. Development of **mechanical refrigeration** for preservation of food products, especially Thaddeus Lowe's (1832–1913) compres-

sion ice machine (1865) and Linde's ammonia compression refrigerator (1873).

1869 ff. Transcontinental railway aided development of **meat-packing industry** in Chicago.

1877. **Gustav de Laval** (1845–1913) invented the centrifugal **cream separator.**

1880 ff. Application of **chemical fertilizers** increased food production. J. B. Lawes manufactured superphosphates (1842); Chilean sodium nitrate beds exploited from c. 1870 until methods of fixing atmospheric nitrogen were developed after 1900 by Fritz Haber (1868–1934); use of potash as an inorganic fertilizer from Strassfurt deposits.

1889. **Angus Campbell** tested the first spindle type **cotton picker;** this type of machine was not fully developed and marketed successfully until the 1940's, competing with the machine devised by John and Mack Rust in 1924 and also commercially produced in the 1940's.

1892. **Gasoline tractor** came into use for farming. **Caterpillar tractor** developed 1931.

1902. W. Normann patented a process for hardening liquid fats by hydrogenation, making available an ample supply of solid fats for soap and food.

1917. **Clarence Birdseye** (1886–1956) began development of method for quick **freezing of foods** in small containers; placed on market in 1929.

1939. Paul Muller synthesized DDT for use as an insecticide. Othmar Zeidler had prepared DDT in 1874, but its insecticidal qualities had not been suspected.

1940 ff. Development of **artificial insemination** to improve livestock breeding.

1945 ff. Unit **packaging of foodstuffs** improved by development of plastic packaging films. Trend toward prepared "convenience" foods for household use.

1950 ff. Mass-production, battery-raising of poultry increased production, lowered prices, and converted chicken and turkey from a holiday and Sunday luxury to an everyday food item.

e. TRANSPORTATION AND COMMUNICATION

1802. **Richard Trevithick** (1771–1833) patented a **steam carriage;** earlier attempts to use steam power for transport purposes had been made by Nicolas Cugnot in France (1769), William Murdock in England (1785), and Oliver Evans in the United States. In 1804 Trevithick designed and built a locomotive to run on rails.

1807. **Robert Fulton** (1765–1815) sailed the *Clermont* from New York to Albany. This was by no means the first steamboat: the Marquis Claude de Jouffroy d'Abbans (1751–1832) had built a paddle-wheel steamer in France (1783); John Fitch (1743-1798) had launched a steamboat on the Delaware (1787); James Rumsey (1743-1792) on the Potomac (1787); and John Stevens (1749-1838) had designed a successful screw-propeller steamboat (1802). However, Fulton's boat was the first steamboat to represent a commercial success. By 1819 steam augmented sail on the first transatlantic steamship crossing of the *Savannah*.

1814. George Stephenson (1781-1848) built his **first locomotive,** and in 1829 his *Rocket*, designed with the aid of his son Robert (1803-1859), won out in a competition with locomotives of other design and thereby set the pattern for future locomotive developments.

1825. Opening of the **Stockton-Darlington Railway,** the first successful railroad system, using a steam engine built by Stephenson. In 1829 the first railroads were opened in the United States (Pennsylvania) and France (Lyon-St. Étienne), both employing English-built locomotives. The first American locomotive was built (1830) by Peter Cooper (1791-1883).

1837. Charles Wheatstone (1802-1875) and **William F. Cooke** (1806-1879) patented the **telegraph,** which was also independently invented by the American **Samuel F. B. Morse** (1791-1872), whose **telegraphic code** was universally adopted. By 1866, **Cyrus W. Field** (1819-1892) succeeded in laying a **transatlantic cable,** after two previous failures and after overcoming tremendous financial and technical difficulties.

1839. Louis J. M. Daguerre (1787-1851) evolved the **daguerreotype photographic process,** based on the work of Joseph Nicéphore Niepce (1765-1833). Although **William H. F. Talbot** (1800-1877) produced paper positives (1841), the first fully practical medium for photography was the wet collodion plate process (1851) of Frederick S. Archer (1813-1857).

1860. Construction began on the **London underground railway** system, which was electrified in 1905. Construction began on the Paris *metro* in 1898, on New York City subway in 1900.

1864. George M. Pullman (1831-1897) built the first **sleeping car** specially constructed for that purpose.

1867. Ernest Michaux invented the **velocipede,** the first bicycle to put cranks and pedals directly on the front wheel; the "safety" bicycle with the geared chain-drive to rear wheel was introduced in 1885.

1869. Union Pacific and Central Pacific Railroads met to complete the **first transcontinental line** in America. The **Trans-Siberian Railway** was begun in 1891.

1869. Opening of the Suez Canal, the work of the French engineer, **Ferdinand de Lesseps** (1805-1894).

1873. The Remington Company began manufacture of the **typewriter** patented by **Christopher L. Sholes** (1819-1890); shift-key system, with capital and small letters on same type bar, introduced in 1878.

1874. Stephen D. Field's (1846-1913) electrically powered **streetcar** began operation in New York City, replacing the horsecars introduced in 1832. The cable streetcar, invented by Andrew S. Hallidie (1836-1900), was put into use in San Francisco (1873). The first streetcars with overhead trolley lines were in use in Germany by 1884 and first installed in the United States at Richmond, Virginia in 1888.

1876. Alexander Graham Bell (1847-1922) patented the **telephone.** The first telephone exchange installed in New Haven (1877) and an automatic switching system introduced in 1879. Much previous experimentation had been done on telephones, including that of Philip Reis of Germany (1861), Antonio Meucci of Italy (1857), and Elisha Gray (simultaneously with Bell). The periodic insertion of loading coils (inductors), originated by M. I. Pupin (1899), made possible long distance transmission of telephone calls.

1878-1879. Joseph W. Swan (1828-1914) of England made the first successful carbon filament **electric lamp** in 1878; working independently Thomas A. Edison patented his **incandescent bulb** in 1879. Improved vacuum in the lamp bulb made possible by the high vacuum mercury pump developed by Hermann Sprengel (1865). At the same time successful experiments in public lighting were carried on with the use of arc lamps, the most successful systems being those of P. Jablochkoff (Paris, 1876) and Charles F. Brush (Cleveland, 1879). Tungsten filament lamp introduced in 1913.

1885 ff. Karl Benz (1844-1929) produced the prototype of the **automobile** using an internal combustion motor operating on the Otto four-stroke cycle principle; the same year **Gottlieb Daimler** (1834-1900) also patented his **gasoline engine,** trying it first on a motorcycle, then on a four-wheeled vehicle. These may be said to have been the first automobiles, although there had been experiments with battery-powered electric automobiles from 1851 on and some previous internal combustion vehicles had been attempted by the Frenchman Étienne Lenoir (1859) and the Austrian Siegfried Marcus (1864). Other automobile pioneers included the Frenchmen Peugeot and Panhard. The first automobile patent in the United States was taken out by George B.

Selden (1879), but the Duryea (1895) was the first auto made for sale in the United States. **Henry Ford** (1863–1947) made his first car in 1896 and founded the Ford Motor Co. in 1903. Important in the development of the automobile was the invention (1888) of the **pneumatic tire** by **John B. Dunlop** (1840–1921).

1889–1890. **Thomas Edison** improved his first **phonograph** (patented 1878) by substituting wax for the tinfoil-coated cylinders and by adding a loudspeaker to amplify the sounds produced by the diaphragm. Emile Berliner (1851–1929) improved the quality of sound reproduction (1890) by utilizing disk-records and better cutting technique.

1888. **George Eastman** (1854–1932) perfected the **hand camera** (*Kodak*); he had previously invented the first successful roll film (1880). Leo Baekeland perfected (1893) a photographic paper (*Velox*) sufficiently sensitive to be printed by artificial light. Work of Rudolph Fischer and Siegrist in dye-coupler color processes (1910–1914) provided the basis for the development of a commercially practicable color film (*Kodachrome*) by Leopold Godowsky, Jr., and Leopold Mannes (1935).

1895. The first public **motion picture** showing in Paris, by **Louis** (1864–1948) and **Auguste** (1862–1954) **Lumière,** inventors of the **cinématographe.** This followed by a year the opening of Edison's Kinetoscope Parlor (New York City) where the motion picture (peepshow) could be viewed by but one person at a time. Both these successful attempts at motion pictures had been preceded by earlier devices: the "thaumatrope" of J. A. Paris (1826); the magic lantern, devised by A. Kircher (1645) and improved by Pieter van Musschenbroek (1736); the multi-camera apparatus of Edward Muybridge (1872); the "photographic gun" of E. J. Marey (1882); the celluloid motion-picture film of William Friese-Green (1889). Prototype of the modern **film projector** was the Vitascope (1896), devised by **Charles Francis Jenkins** (1867–1934) and Thomas Armat on the basis of Edison's kinetoscope.

1895. **Guglielmo Marconi** (1874–1937) invented the **wireless telegraph,** based on the discovery (1887) of radio waves by Heinrich Hertz (1857–1894) (existence of these waves had been deduced by James Clerk Maxwell in 1873). Other contributors to wireless development were E. Branly, Thomas Edison, Alexander Popov (who contributed the aerial), Reginald E. Fessenden (improved transmitter, 1901). In 1901 Marconi succeeded in sending a wireless signal across the Atlantic.

1898. **Valdemar Poulsen** of Denmark invented the **magnetic recording of sound** (1898). F. Pfleumer of Germany replaced steel wire by plastic tape coated with magnetic material (1930's), and Marvin Camras of the United States made further developments in magnetic recording (1940's).

1900. Count **Ferdinand von Zeppelin** launched the first of the **rigid airships** which were to be called by his name.

1903. Orville (1871–1948) and **Wilbur** (1867–1912) **Wright** made the first flight in a **heavier-than-air plane** on December 17 at Kitty Hawk, North Carolina. This flight was the culmination of a long series of developments: George Cayley's glider (1804) and studies in aerodynamic theory; the glider flights (1895) of Otto Lilienthal and Octave Chanute; Samuel P. Langley's (1834–1906) steam-powered model plane (1896); Alberto Santos-Dumont's (1873–1932) model airplane with an internal combustion engine (1898); and others.

1904. **John Ambrose Fleming** (1849–1945) devised the diode thermionic valve **(radio tube); Lee de Forest** (1873–1961) invented the Audion (1906), a three-electrode vacuum tube (triode amplifier), thereby providing the basis for the development of **electronics.**

1909–1927. The "heroic age" of **aviation,** commencing with **Louis Bleriot's** (1872–1936) flight (1909) across the English Channel, and including the exploits of the aerial "aces" of World War I, the flight (1919) of John W. Alcock (1892–1919) and Arthur W. Brown (1886–1958) across the Atlantic (Newfoundland to Galway), Richard E. Byrd's (1888–1957) flight (1926) across the North Pole, and culminating in **Charles A. Lindbergh's** (1902–   ) solo non-stop flight New York to Paris in *The Spirit of St. Louis* (1927). Many technical improvements made, including the first engine specifically intended for aircraft by Glenn Curtiss (1904), and the **gyroscope stabilizer** of Elmer A. Sperry (1913).

1911. **Charles F. Kettering** (1876–1958), who had previously invented lighting and ignition systems for the automobile, perfected the **electric self-starter.** The first fully **automatic transmission,** perfected by Earl A. Thompson, was introduced commercially in 1939. Harry Vickers and Francis W. Davis began work on hydraulic **power-assisted steering** systems in 1925 and 1926 respectively, and in 1951 power steering was introduced for passenger cars.

1913. **Diesel-electric railway engines** first used in Sweden. Coming into use in the United States during the later 1930's, they have largely replaced steam-locomotives.

1920. **Frank Conrad** (1874–1941) of the Westinghouse Co. began broadcasting radio programs in Pittsburgh, marking the **beginning of radio** as a mass communication medium.

1922. **Herbert T. Kalmus** developed **Techni-**

color, first commercially successful color process for motion pictures.

1926. Sound Motion Pictures. Although Edison had attempted to put together his phonograph and motion picture inventions for sound movies as early as 1904, it was 1923 before de Forest successfully demonstrated his phonofilm system for recording sound on the motion picture film. The first motion picture with sound accompaniment was publicly shown in 1926, the first talking picture in 1927.

1926 ff. John L. Baird (1888-1946) successfully demonstrated **television** in England. His mechanical system of television, similar to that of C. F. Jenkins in the United States, was based on Paul von Nipkov's rotating disk (1886), but had technical limitations; modern electronic television developed from the cathode-ray tube (1897) of Ferdinand Braun and A. A. Campbell-Swinton's proposals (1911) for use of a cathode ray to scan an image. The crucial invention was the Iconoscope of the Russian-American **Vladimir Zworykin** (1889-   ), the device which transmits television images quickly and effectively. Philo Farnsworth of the United States contributed the image dissector tube (1927). General broadcasting of television began in England in 1936, in the United States in 1941, but languished until after World War II. Peter C. Goldmark of Columbia Broadcasting System demonstrated (1940) sequential method of color television which gave way to compatible electronic system developed by R. C. A. in the 1950's.

1932. Edwin H. Land (1909-   ) invented the first practical synthetic light-polarizing material **(polaroid glass),** found useful in sunglasses, cameras, and scientific optical instruments. In 1947 he invented the **Polaroid Land camera,** which developed the film inside the camera and produced a photograph print within one minute; in 1962 he introduced color film for his camera.

1933. Fluorescent lamps introduced for floodlighting and advertising. Developments leading up to this included experiments by George Stokes (1852) and Alexandre Becquerel (1859) to excite fluorescent materials by ultraviolet rays or in a discharge tube; Peter Cooper-Hewitt's invention of the mercury vapor lamp (1901); the introduction of the **Neon lamp** by Georges Claude and the work on cathodes by D. M. Moore and Wehnelt in the 1900's; and J. Risler's application of powder to the outside of tubular discharge lamps (1923). Subsequent developments have included increased cathode life and improved fluorescent powders.

1933. Edwin H. Armstrong (1890-1954), pioneer radio inventor (regenerative, i.e., feedback, circuit, 1912, and superheterodyne circuit, 1918), perfected **frequency modulation (FM)** providing static-free radio reception.

1937. Chester Carlson patented a new dry photographic process (*Xerography*) based upon principles of photoconductivity and electrostatics.

1939. Igor Sikorsky (1889-   ) flew the first **helicopter** of his design. The first helicopter capable of flight was the work of Ellehammer of Denmark (1912), based on C. Renard's articulated rotor blade (1904) and G. A. Crocco's cyclic pitch control (1906). Juan de la Cierva invented the autogiro (1922), differing from the helicopter in that its rotor autorotated and the engine drove a normal propeller. Further development work was done (1934-1936) by Louis Breguet and Heinrich Focke.

1939. First test flight of a **turbo-jet airplane** (Heinkel) with an engine designed by Hans von Ohain. Simultaneous and parallel work on jet airplanes in Britian, based on turbo-jet engine designed by Frank Whittle (1930). In 1958 **jet-powered transatlantic airline** service was inaugurated by BOAC and Pan-American Airways. In 1962 the British and French governments announced plans to co-operate on the production of a jet-propelled supersonic transport plane (the Concorde), and the U.S. government proposed American production of a supersonic commercial plane the following year. The first plane to exceed the speed of sound in level flight was the American rocket-propelled Bell X-1, which reached Mach 1.06 (approximately 750 m.p.h.) on October 14, 1947.

1940-1945. Development of radar ("radio-detection-and-ranging") stimulated by World War II, for detection of aircraft, blind-bombing techniques, and naval search equipment. Based on Heinrich Hertz's demonstration (1887) that radio waves are reflected similarly to light rays, the technique was first applied by Edward Appleton in Britain (1924) and G. Breit and M. A. Tuve in the United States (1925) for investigating ionization in the upper atmosphere. Robert A. Watson-Watt showed the possibilities of employing radio waves to detect aircraft (1935); J. T. Randall and H. A. H. Boot developed the cavity magnetron for high-power microwave transmission. Simultaneously, radar development had been going on in Germany and the United States, including the development of equipment by Robert H. Page of the Naval Laboratory. After 1940 Britain and the United States co-operated in radar development, much of the work being done at the Radiation Laboratory in Cambridge, Mass.

1941-1945. Construction of 2500 miles of large

diameter (20-inch–24-inch) **pipelines** to deliver petroleum from oil-producing regions in Southwest United States to East Coast depots. Development of welding of steelpipe sections (1913–1914) cut leakage and made possible large-scale pipeline construction.

1948. Long-playing phonograph record introduced, based on Peter Goldmark's development of the narrow-groove vinyl plastic record, a light-weight pickup, and a slow-speed (33⅓ r.p.m.), silent turntable.

1948. Basic research in semi-conductors at the Bell Telephone Laboratories resulted in the invention of the **transistor** by a group which included William Shockley, John Bardeen, and Walter H. Brattain. This tiny, rugged, amplifying device was increasingly used to replace vacuum tubes in electronic instruments. In 1954 the silicon transistor was developed.

1950 ff. Development of **nuclear propulsion** for submarines and surface ships. The United States submarine *Nautilus* (1955), built under the stimulus exerted by Admiral Hyman Rickover, was the first submarine to pass under the North Polar ice cap. The Soviet icebreaker *Lenin* was the first nuclear-powered surface vessel.

1953 ff. "Cinerama" system (invented and developed by Fred Waller) to produce three-dimensional films, released for commercial exhibition. At about the same time Cinemascope, employing a single large concave screen, and stereophonic sound were introduced for motion picture exhibition.

1954. Charles H. Townes (1915–) invented the **maser** (microwave amplification by the simulated emission of radiation), making it possible to transmit signals over great distances.

1957. Launching of first **man-made satellite,** *Sputnik I,* by Russia (Oct. 4) marked the beginning of the **Space Age.** This was the product of millennia of human dreams but, more materially, of the rocket researches of **Robert H. Goddard** (1882–1945) of the United States (first liquid-fuel rocket launched, 1926), the theoretical studies of the Russian **Konstantin Tsiolkovsky** (1903), and the German **Herman Oberth** (1923). Practical rocket development, for military purposes, took place in Germany during World War II, largely under Oberth, Walter Dornberger, and Wernher von Braun, who produced the V-2. Rocket development after the war was largely concentrated on missiles (in the United States: the *Redstone, Thor, Jupiter, Titan, Polaris*), but rocket launching of satellites was an outgrowth of the **International Geophysical Year** (IGY), a coordinated study of the earth's atmosphere, shape, magnetic field, etc. by the world's scientists.

1961. First controlled, individual free flight by Harold Graham (April 20), using rocket-belt designed by Wendell Moore of Bell Aerosystems.

4. ARCTIC EXPLORATION, 870–1940

a. EARLIEST EXPLORATIONS

The first known civilization within the Arctic regions appears to have been that of the **Norsemen,** who, before the birth of Christ, seem to have superseded the Finns in Scandinavia. For a thousand years the Norsemen developed a rude form of political democracy and, from their own rocky coasts, ranged the coasts of western Europe.

c. 870. The Norseman, **Ottar** (Othere), claimed to have sailed around northern Norway, along the Murman Coast, and into the White Sea as far as the Kola Peninsula, in search of the walrus. Thereupon King Harald of Norway declared annexed all territory as far as the White Sea. His successors made various expeditions to that region, both for trade and conquest.

875–900. COLONIZATION OF ICELAND (previously discovered by Irish anchorites, see p. 388)

877. Günnbjorn Ulfsson, driven westward from Iceland, sighted Greenland.

982–985. Eric the Red, outlawed from Iceland, founded a colony in **western Greenland** (c.

61° N.L.). The Norsemen seem to have carried on sealing and whaling expeditions as far north as Disco Bay. The settlement lasted until the 14th or 15th century.

1000–1006. LEIF ERICSSON and THORFINN KARLSEFNI, from Greenland, explored and tried to settle the **North American coast** (p. 388).

1194. Iceland annals record the discovery of modern **Spitsbergen** (*Svalbard*). In the course of hunting, the Norsemen reached Novaya Zemlya. But after 1300 Norse enterprise seems to have fallen off (loss of Norwegian independence [1349] and domination of the Hanseatic League).

b. THE 16th CENTURY

During this period the initiative in Arctic discoveries was taken by England. **Bristol** had long carried on trade with Iceland and the Bristolers were therefore well acquainted with the northern routes. After the Portuguese discovery of the route to India, the English hoped to find an alternative passage to Cathay either by the northwest, around North America (rediscovered by the Cabots, 1497, see p. 390), or to the northeast, around Siberia. The Cabots, intent on finding a **northwest passage,** having failed in their quest, attention became focused on the Siberian route.

1553–1554. Expedition of **SIR HUGH WILLOUGHBY and RICHARD CHANCELLOR.** Two of their three ships reached the Russian coast near the mouth of the Pechora River and some new land which may have been Novaya Zemlya or Kolguev Island. They turned back to winter on the Kola Peninsula, where Willoughby and all his men died. The third ship, under Chancellor, reached the site of modern Archangel, whence Chancellor made a trip to Moscow. In 1554 he reached England with a letter from the tsar. One result of the expedition was the

1555. Foundation of the **Association of Merchant Adventurers** (the *Muscovy Company*), to trade with Russia. The company at once took the lead in northern exploration. Chancellor left on a mission to Moscow in 1555, but was lost on the return voyage (1556).

1565. The **Dutch,** under Olivier Brunel and Philip Winterkönig (a Norwegian) made a trade settlement on the Kola Peninsula, followed by another (1578) near present-day Archangel. Brunel traveled overland as far as the Ob and visited Novaya Zemlya.

1576. Expedition of **SIR MARTIN FROBISHER** to find a northwest passage. Frobisher had the support of Queen Elizabeth I as well as the London merchants. He dis-covered Frobisher Bay in southern **Baffin Land,** which he was sure was the desired passage. Rumors of gold in some earth that he took back led to further expeditions in the succeeding years. On the last of these Frobisher penetrated **Hudson Strait,** but was deterred from "sailing through to China" by orders to bring back loads of "gold ore."

1585–1587. Voyages of **JOHN DAVIS,** sent out to follow up the work of Frobisher. Davis landed on the west coast of Greenland at Gilbert's Sound and thence crossed the strait named for him. He cruised along the Baffin coast south to Cumberland Sound, convinced that he had found the passage. In 1587 he explored the Greenland side of **Davis Strait** as far as 72° 41'. On his return voyage he followed up Cumberland Sound and passed Hudson Strait without realizing its importance.

1594–1597. The three voyages of **WILLEM BARENTS and CORNELIS NAY.** Barents and his Dutchmen explored much of the western coast of Novaya Zemlya, while Nay sailed into the Kara Sea and reached the west coast of the **Yalmal Peninsula.** Finding the sea open beyond, he was convinced that he had found the northeast passage. In 1595 he and Barents tried to get through, but in vain. In 1596 Barents struck north through the sea that bears his name, discovered **Bear Island** and sighted and named **Spitsbergen,** which he supposed to be part of Greenland. He rounded the north end of Novaya Zemlya and wintered at Ice Haven (the first expedition to weather an Arctic winter successfully). Barents died on the return voyage (1597), having laid the foundation for the lucrative Dutch whale and seal fisheries of the 17th and 18th centuries.

c. THE 17th AND 18th CENTURIES

During the 17th century the English and the Dutch continued their efforts to find a passage to China not under Spanish or Portuguese control. The Muscovy Company and individual members of it promoted most of the British expeditions (notably **William Sanderson,** who supported Davis, and **Sir Thomas Smith,** first governor of the East India Company). **Richard Hakluyt's** *Voyages* (1582) and *Principal Navigations* (1598–1600) as well as the collections of his successor, **Samuel Purchas,** were intended to preserve the records of English achievement and actually provided a great stimulus to exploration and colonization.

1607–1611. Voyages of **HENRY HUDSON,** commissioned by the Muscovy Company. In 1607 he set out in the *Hopewell* for China by way of the North Pole. He discovered the East Greenland coast at 73°, passed thence to

The ARCTIC REGIONS

0   200   400   600   800   1000
Scale of Miles

ARCTIC CIRCLE

SIBERIA

Lena R.

120

90

60 E. Long.

70

75

80

85

150

30

180

0

150

30

120 W. Long.

Taimyr Peninsula

KARA SEA

Yamal Pen.

Vaigach I.

Kolguev I.

Nordenskiold Sea

Lonely I.

Novaya Zemlya

Kola Pen.

FINLAND

Nicholas II Land

BARENTS SEA

North Cape

NORWAY

C. Chelyuskin

Franz Joseph Land

Liakhov Is.

Bear I.

New Siberian Is.

Bennett I.

Northeast Land

SPITSBERGEN

Jeannette I.

Henrietta I.

E. Siberian Sea

ARCTIC OCEAN

North Pole

ARCTIC OCEAN

Greenland Sea

Jan Mayen

Wrangel I.

Herald I.

ICELAND

Pt. Barrow

PEARY LAND

GREENLAND

Axel Heiberg I.

Borden I.

GRANT LD.

Kane Basin

Etah

ELLESMERE LD.

Prince Patrick I.

BEAUFORT SEA

McClure Str.

Melville I.

Bathurst

Jones Sd.

Devon I.

Upernivik

ALASKA

Banks

Melville Sound

Pr. of Wales I.

Somerset

Lancaster Str.

BAFFIN BAY

Victoria Land

G. of Boothia

Boothia Pen.

BAFFIN LAND

Davis Str.

King William Land

Melville Pen.

Foxe Basin

ARCTIC CIRCLE

CANADA

HUDSON BAY

LABRADOR PENINSULA

Spitsbergen. On the return he discovered **Jan Mayen Island.** In 1608 he examined the edge of the ice pack between Spitsbergen and Novaya Zemlya in the vain search for a through passage. In 1609 he made yet another attempt, this time in behalf of the Dutch East India Company. Finding his way barred in the Barents Sea, he turned west to North America, where he discovered the Hudson River. In 1610, with English support, he sailed through Hudson Strait and explored the eastern coast of Hudson Bay. On the return voyage the crew mutinied and set out Hudson and the sick to perish in a small boat. Hudson's Spitsbergen explorations had much to do with the development of the Spitsbergen fisheries. In 1612 the Muscovy Company was given a monopoly over fishing in those waters. In 1613 it fitted out a large fleet under Benjamin Joseph. But the English were never able to exclude the Dutch and the Danes, who finally secured the best fishing grounds on the northern shore of Spitsbergen.

1610–1648. The **Russian Cossacks,** in the course of the conquest of Siberia, reached the Siberian north coast at the mouths of the great rivers (Yenisei, 1610; Lena and Yana, 1636; Kolyma, 1644). In 1648 a Cossack named **Simon Dezhnev** led an expedition from the Kolyma through Bering Strait into the Gulf of Anadyr.

1612–1613. **Sir Thomas Button** reached the western coast of Hudson Bay and spent the winter at the mouth of the Nelson River. In the following summer he explored the shore of Southampton Island.

1615–1616. **Robert Bylot** (a former member of Hudson's crew) and **William Baffin** explored the coasts of Hudson Strait. On their second voyage they penetrated Baffin Bay and explored the coast far beyond the point reached by Davis. Baffin's fine scientific observations enabled Prof. Hansteen of Christiania to draw up his **first magnetic chart.**

1664. **Willem de Vlamingh,** in search of new whaling grounds, rounded the northern end of Novaya Zemlya and sailed east as far as 82° 10′.

1670. Royal charter granted to **Hudson's Bay Company,** under the auspices of Prince Rupert, for the purpose of trading with the Indians. The company sent out a reconnoitering expedition under **Zachariah Gillan** (Gillam), who wintered on Rupert's River and established a station at Fort Charles. Trading stations multiplied rapidly, but exploration was badly neglected for nearly a century, the only fruitful expeditions being those sent out by the admiralty to look for a northwest passage.

1721. **Hans Egede,** a Norwegian pastor, began the modern colonization of Greenland. He founded Gotthaab and began to convert the Eskimos. Other colonists, including missionaries, spread along the west coast. Trade (skins of seal, reindeer, fox, and bear, eiderdown, whale-bone, walrus tusks, and dried cod) was organized as a monopoly in private hands from 1750 to 1774, and, after it became less profitable, passed into government hands.

1725. **Vitus Bering,** a Dane in Russian service, was dispatched by Peter the Great to explore the waters off northeastern Siberia. In a series of voyages (1728–1741) he discovered **Bering Strait,** explored the Aleutian Islands, and discovered and named Mt. St. Elias on the American side.

1732–1743. **Great survey of the whole Siberian coast,** sponsored by the Russian government. Two Russian officers in 1738 made the voyage from Archangel to the mouths of the Ob and the Yenisei. In an effort to effect a passage from the Yenisei to the Lena, a journey was made (1738–1739) eastward past Taimyr Bay to Cape Sterlegov, and repeated attempts were made to round the northernmost point of Siberia by boat. These efforts were blocked by the ice. But in 1743 **S. Chelyuskin** succeeded in making the trip by sledge. **Dmitri Laptiev** in a series of voyages (1737, 1742) completed the delineation of the coast east from the mouth of the Lena to Cape Baranov.

1750–1820. Height of the British whaling industry in the Spitsbergen and Greenland Seas. Outstanding among the whaling captains for exploration and scientific work were the **William Scoresbys,** father and son.

1770–1773. **Liakhov,** a Russian fur merchant, discovered three of the New Siberian Islands.

1778. **Capt. James Cook,** sent by the admiralty to Bering Strait to find a passage northeast or northwest from the Pacific to the Atlantic, sailed north from Kamchatka in the *Resolution* and the *Discovery.* He rounded Cape Prince of Wales, cleared Bering Strait and penetrated eastward to Icy Cape before turning west again to discover and name Cape North on the Asiatic side.

d. THE 19th CENTURY

1806. **William Scoresby** reached a record north in the Spitsbergen region (81° 30′). In 1820 William Scoresby, Jr., published his *Account of the Arctic Regions,* which at once became the standard work.

1818. The British government, at the instigation of **Sir John Barrow,** renewed the offer of £20,000 for making the northwest passage and £5000 for reaching 89° N.L.

1818. **Capt. John Ross** and **Lieut. Edward Parry**

set out on a twin expedition to Baffin Bay and pointed the way to the subsequent lucrative whale fishery in that region.

1819-1820. Parry penetrated Lancaster Sound and Barrow Strait, discovered Wellington Channel, Prince Regent Inlet, and the island of North Somerset, and finally advanced westward to **Melville Sound** and Melville Island, where the expedition wintered.

1819-1826. **Exploration by land,** carried on by the Hudson's Bay Company to fill in the "missing" coastline of northern Canada. The work was entrusted to Lieut. (later Sir) **John Franklin.** In 1820-1821, with Dr. John Richardson, George Back, and Robert Hood, he made a trip from Great Slave Lake to the Coppermine River and down the river to the polar sea. They explored 550 miles of coast east to Cape Turnagain.

1820-1823. **Baron Wrangel** explored the Siberian coast from Cape Chelagskoi to the mouth of the Kolyma.

1821-1823. **Parry's second expedition,** in quest of a passage at a lower latitude. During the summer of 1821 he verified the dead end of Repulse Bay. In 1822 he turned north to Fox Channel and discovered the ice-choked Fury and Hecla Strait.

1822. **William Scoresby, Jr.,** in the specially constructed *Baffin,* forced his way through the ice and reached the east coast of Greenland, which he surveyed for 400 miles (75° to 69°).

1823. **Capt.** **Douglas Clavering** continued Scoresby's work and charted the East Greenland coast from 72° to 76°, while his associate, **Capt. Edward Sabine,** established for the admiralty a magnetic observatory on Pendulum Island.

1824. **Parry's third expedition,** on which he hoped to follow the Fury and Hecla Strait west to Prince Regent Inlet. He had to abandon the attempt when one of his ships was badly damaged.

1825-1826. **Franklin's second expedition** by land. He descended the Mackenzie River to the sea and advanced westward to Cape Beechey. A party under Dr. Richardson reached the shore between the Mackenzie and Coppermine Rivers, discovered and named Union and Dolphin Strait and Wollaston Land.

1826. **Capt. F. W. Beechey** led an expedition to the Arctic by way of Bering Strait, to connect with Franklin's explorations. He traced the coastline as far east as Point Barrow, and narrowly missed connection with Franklin's party.

1827. **Parry tried to reach the North Pole** from northern Spitsbergen, using sledge-boats, but the party did not get beyond 82° 45′ N.L. This remained the record north for fifty years.

1829-1833. **Capt. John Ross** and his nephew, **James Clark Ross,** embarked on a private quest for the northwest passage through Prince Regent Inlet. They found their way into the Gulf of Boothia, where they wintered. In 1830 James Ross crossed the Isthmus of Boothia by sledge, discovering to the west King William Land. In

1831, June 1. **JAMES ROSS** located and planted the British flag on the **north magnetic pole.** The expedition remained in the Arctic until 1833 and was rescued in Lancaster Sound by a whaler.

1833. **Sir George Back** and **Dr. Richard King** made an effort to reach the Rosses overland from Great Slave Lake and Great Fish River, which they descended to the mouth. Failure of supplies forced them to turn back.

1837. **Thomas Simpson** and **P. W. Dease,** of the Hudson's Bay Company, descended the Mackenzie and explored the remainder of the coast westward from Cape Beechey to Point Barrow. In 1839 Simpson explored east from the mouth of the Coppermine to Simpson Strait and the mouth of the Great Fish River. From there he went on to Montreal Island and as far as Castor and Pollux River. On the return trip he explored the southern coasts of King William Land and of Victoria Land.

1845-1848. The **EXPEDITION OF SIR JOHN FRANKLIN,** in the *Erebus* and *Terror,* to seek a northwest passage by way of Lancaster Sound. In 1846 he sailed south down Peel Sound and Franklin Strait and in the winter 1846-1847 was beset by heavy polar ice drifting on the northwest coast of King William Land. In the spring a party went south as far as Cape Herschel, thus completing the **discovery of the northwest passage,** although unable to navigate its full length. Sir John died in June, as did twenty-three others in the course of the following winter. The rest abandoned ship (Apr. 22, 1848) and started for Great Fish River. According to later reports by Eskimos "they fell down and died as they walked." Not one member of the expedition survived.

1847. **Dr. John Rae** closed the gap remaining in the Canadian coastline between Boothia and Fury and Hecla Strait. He and his men of the Hudson's Bay Company explored 655 miles of new coast, on foot, and established the fact that Boothia is the northernmost extremity of the American continent.

1848-1859. **THE FRANKLIN RELIEF EXPEDITIONS:**

1848-1849. **Sir James Ross** followed Franklin's route by way of Lancaster Sound and explored the northern and western coasts of North Somerset, never realizing, when he turned back, how near he had come to solution of the Franklin mystery.

1848-1851.   Dr. Rae and **Sir John Richardson** searched the American coast between the mouth of the Mackenzie and the mouth of the Coppermine.

1850-1851. A great relief expedition was organized in various sections and dispatched by the admiralty: **Capt. Horatio Austin** led a renewal of the search from Barrow Strait. He found Franklin's Beechey Island camp but found no further trace of Franklin.

1850-1854.   Capt. Richard Collinson and **Capt. Robert M'Clure** were sent out by the admiralty to attack the problem from Bering Strait. M'Clure wintered in Prince of Wales Strait, whence he could see Banks Strait, blocked by ice. Once again the northwest passage was found, but could not be navigated. Collinson traced the shore of Prince Albert Land and reached Melville Island, thus connecting with previous explorations from the east.

1852.   Capt. Edward A. Inglefield advanced north in Baffin Bay to Smith Sound, which he correctly surmised to be a channel to the Arctic Ocean. He named Ellesmere Land and explored 600 miles of new coast.

1852-1854.   Sir Edward Belcher was sent out by the admiralty on a last effort to solve the Franklin mystery from the east. He and Sherard Osborn completed the exploration of Melville Island and Prince Patrick Island.

1853-1855. An American relief expedition under **Dr. E. K. Kane** advanced up Smith Sound and in 1854 discovered the great Humboldt Glacier.

1854.   Dr. Rae, exploring in the region of King William Land, secured from the Eskimos the first information and relics of the Franklin expedition, thus winning the £10,000 admiralty award.

1857. Lady Franklin sent out **Capt. Leopold M'Clintock,** to complete the search. His party went over the Boothia and King William Land regions, and at Point Victory and Point Felix found the records and many relics of Franklin's party. In the last analysis the Franklin catastrophe resulted in the exploration of more than 7000 miles of coastline.

1860-1871. Expeditions of **Charles Hall,** an American. He explored Countess of Warwick Land and came across the ruins of a house built by Frobisher in 1578.

1863.   Capt. E. Carlsen first circumnavigated Spitsbergen.

1869-1870. The Germans, inspired by Dr. A. Petermann, organized a great Greenland expedition under **Capt. Karl Koldewey.** He and his lieutenant, **Julius Payer** (an Austrian), explored the east coast of Greenland by sledge

to Cape Bismarck in Germania Land. One of the ships, the *Hansa,* was crushed by the ice and for nearly a year her crew drifted 1100 miles south on a floe, eventually landing near Cape Farewell.

1870. Prof. A. E. Nordenskiöld and Dr. Berggren explored the interior of Greenland, advancing 35 miles from Auleitsivikfjord on the west coast and reaching an altitude of 2200 feet.

1871-1874.   DISCOVERY OF FRANZ JOSEPH LAND by the Austrians Julius Payer and Carl Weyprecht. In 1872 they sought a northeast passage around Novaya Zemlya.

1875-1876. The British, under **Sir George S. Nares,** resumed the effort to penetrate the northwest passage. In 1876 **Albert H. Markham,** of the expedition, reached a new record north (83° 20′ on May 11). Another member, Lieut. Aldrich, explored the north coast of Ellesmere Land to Cape Columbia, while Lieut. Beaumont followed the north coast of Greenland to Cape Britannia.

1876. Foundation of the Danish committee for the geographical and geological investigation of Greenland. This committee stimulated popular interest and sent out many expeditions.

1878. The **Dutch,** under **Koolemans Beynen,** began sending out annual expeditions in the specially constructed *Willem Barents* to make scientific observations in the Spitsbergen area.

1878-1879.   NORDENSKIÖLD for the first time made the **northeast passage** in the *Vega.* Rounding the northernmost point of Siberia (Cape Chelyuskin) on August 19, 1878, he was frozen in and obliged to winter on shore. The voyage was completed in the next year, Bering Strait being reached on July 20, 1879.

1879-1881. The American expedition of **Lieut. G. W. de Long** in the *Jeannette.* The purpose was to explore the northern coast of Siberia from Bering Strait. The ship was crushed in the ice and sank (June 13, 1881). De Long and most of the party perished, but a few reached the coast by way of the New Siberian Islands.

1880.   Leigh Smith, an Englishman, reached Franz Joseph Land from Spitsbergen and explored the southern coast, naming it Alexandra Land.

1882. Establishment of **international polar stations,** an idea put forward in 1875 by Weyprecht and promoted at the polar conferences of 1879-1880. Norwegians, Swedes, Danes, Russians, Dutch, British, Germans, Austrians, and Americans agreed to co-operate. The Dutch were unsuccessful in establishing a station at the mouth of the Yenisei, but the other expeditions carried out their assignments. An American mission, under **Lieut. Adolphus**

W. Greely, carried on observations in Lady Franklin Bay for two years (1881–1883). Greely explored the north coast of Greenland and reached a **new record north** (83° 24′) at Lockwood Island. In 1882 Greely penetrated Grinnell Land. In 1883 **Lieut. James Lockwood** crossed Grinnell Land to Greely Fjord. Relief ships having failed to arrive, the party had to winter in Smith Sound. All but six of the party of 24 were dead of starvation when the relief ships arrived in June 1884.

1883. Nordenskiöld penetrated 84 miles into the interior of Greenland, reaching an altitude of 5000 feet.

1886. Lieut. Robert E. Peary advanced 50 miles inland from Disco Bay and reached an altitude of 7500 feet.

1888. FIRST CROSSING OF GREENLAND, by **Dr. Fridtjof Nansen, Otto Sverdrup,** and five others. From near Kjoge Bay on the east coast they covered 260 miles of glacier on skis, reaching an altitude of nearly 9000 feet and striking the west coast near Gotthaab.

1892. Peary made a 1200-mile dog-sledge journey from Inglefield Gulf in northwest Greenland, north and east over the inland ice to Independence Fjord and back again.

1893-1896. EXPEDITION OF NANSEN in the *Fram.* Surmising that there was a drift across the polar basin, Nansen decided to be frozen in and travel with it. With Sverdrup he entered the pack off the New Siberian Islands in September 1893, drifted northwest until November 15, 1895. Thence the ship moved southward until it broke free off northern Spitsbergen (Aug. 1896). The ship reached 85° 55′ N.L. in the summer of 1895, but Nansen and Hjalmar Johansen in March left the ship and traveled north with skis and dog-sledges, reaching a **record north** of 86° 14′ on April 7. They wintered on Frederick Jackson Island and in the spring started for Spitsbergen, and were picked up by the relief ship *Windward.*

1894-1897. The **Jackson-Harmsworth expedition** to Franz Joseph Land reached 81° 19′ N.L. and surveyed a number of islands. Jackson covered about 600 miles of new coastline and demonstrated the complexity of the archipelago.

1897. S. A. Andrée, a Swedish flyer, undertook a balloon flight northeastward from Spitsbergen. His decapitated body was found on White Island in Barents Sea in 1930, with a diary which revealed that the balloon had come down on the ice pack after 65 hours and that the party had reached White Island, where all had perished.

1898-1902. Capt. Otto Sverdrup in the *Fram,* blocked by ice in his effort to circumnavigate Greenland, made several journeys over Ellesmere Land, discovering its western coast.

1899. The Russian admiral, **Makarov,** arranged a trial trip into the ice off Spitsbergen, using the great icebreaker *Yermak.* Though unsuccessful, he paved the way for later development of the icebreaker.

1899-1900. Expedition of the **DUKE OF THE ABRUZZI** to Franz Joseph Land. From Rudolf Land his lieutenant, **Capt. Umberto Cagni,** led a dog-sledge party on a 753-mile trip and reached a **new northern record** of 86° 34′ N.L. (200 miles from the pole).

1900. Peary, from his base in Lady Franklin Bay, made a journey along the northern coast of Greenland, rounding the northernmost point and reaching Cape Wyckoff, where he built a cairn (82° 57′ N.L.).

e. THE 20th CENTURY

(1) Conquest of the North Pole

1905-1906. Peary, with **Capt. Robert Bartlett,** went by ship to northern Grant Land and thence westward by sledge to Cape Hecla. From there he claimed to have reached 87° 6′ early in 1906. The claim is questioned by some geographers, since Peary was the only white man in the final party and because the record is unsatisfactory in certain respects.

1907-1908. Expedition of Dr. F. A. Cook. He followed a route discovered by Sverdrup (from Cape Sabine across Ellesmere Land and north along the coast to the northern tip of Axel Heiberg Island).

1908, Apr. 20. Cook claimed that he reached the pole on this date. Experts regard the claim as improbable, though not impossible. His observations were fuller than Peary's, but not very good. His chronological table of distances was entirely reasonable. The claim has not yet been accepted by authoritative opinion.

1909. Apr. 6. Peary claimed to have reached the pole on this date, from Cape Columbia, the northernmost extremity of Grant Land. Though generally accepted, the claim is questioned by some experts because of the inadequacy of the observations and the incredible time-table submitted. Possibly neither Cook nor Peary actually reached the pole.

No further progress in polar exploration was made until the airplane began to open up new possibilities.

1925, May. Roald Amundsen (Lieut. Riiser-Larsen as pilot) and **Lincoln Ellsworth,** in two flying-boats, flew from King Bay, West Spitsbergen, to 87° 43′ N.L., where they landed.

They finally got one of their craft into the air again and managed to return.

1926, May. COMM. RICHARD BYRD and **FLOYD BENNETT** flew from King Bay and **reached the pole** (May 9). Using the Fokker monoplane *Josephine Ford,* they covered the 750 miles and return in 15 hours.

1926, May. ROALD AMUNDSEN, GEN. UMBERTO NOBILE, and **LINCOLN ELLS-WORTH,** forestalled by Byrd in their effort to reach the pole first, took off in the dirigible *Norge* to fly from King Bay across the pole to Alaska. They landed safely near Nome, having sighted no land in the Beaufort Sea area.

1928, May. Nobile, in the dirigible *Italia,* made a number of flights from King Bay, one of which covered almost 20,000 square miles of unexplored regions. No new land was seen. The last flight was made (May 24) over northeastern Greenland to the pole. On the return flight the ship encountered a storm and crashed on the ice. Among many relief expeditions, Amundsen's ended disastrously in Barents Sea. Amundsen was lost. The *Italia* survivors were rescued by other planes and by the Russian icebreaker *Krassin.*

1937. May 26-1938, February 19. A **SOVIET POLAR STATION** organized by Prof. Schmidt, and consisting of four members, led by Ivan Papanin, was transported by plane to a floe near the pole (89° 26′ N.). Oceanographical and meteorological observations were taken over a period of nine months. The drift ultimately carried the party to the east coast of Greenland.

1937, June. Three Russian aviators (V. P. Chkalov, G. P. Baidukov, and A. V. Beliakov) flew non-stop from Moscow over the North Pole to Vancouver.

1937, July 14. Mikhail Gromov and two companions, all Russians, flew non-stop over the pole from Moscow to Riverside, California (6262 miles in 62 hours 17 minutes, a non-stop distance record).

(2) The Canadian Arctic

1903-1906. Capt. Roald Amundsen navigated the northwest passage by way of the east coast of King William Land, spending two winters at Petersen Bay and charting the coast of Victoria Land. In August 1906, he finally reached Bering Strait. This was the **first time a ship passed from sea to sea.**

1908-1910. The **CANADIAN GOVERNMENT** took formal possession of all islands to the north of the continent. **Capt. J. E. Bernier,** sent out by the government, formally annexed Banks and Victoria Islands.

1913-1917. Donald B. MacMillan led the Borup Memorial Expedition to Ellesmere Land. From a base at Etah observations were made over a period of four years and a permanent meteorological station was established.

1913-1918. Stefansson led the **Canadian Arctic Expedition,** one section of which made observations for three years in the Coronation Gulf district, while the other, in command of Stefansson, was beset off northern Alaska. Stefansson himself remained in the field for four years and continued his investigations in a series of remarkable sledge journeys in the vicinity of Banks Island and Melville Island.

1921-1924. Knud Rasmussen, with two companions, carried out a 20,000-mile expedition across Arctic America by way of Fox Channel, Hudson Bay, King William Land, Coronation Gulf, and the Mackenzie Delta to Alaska.

1922- The Canadian government established an **annual police patrol** of the islands and opened a large number of government stations designed for observation, exploration, and the development of the Eskimos.

1934-1935. The **Oxford University Ellesmere Land Expedition** organized by **Edward Shackleton,** son of the famous antarctic explorer, and led by **Noel Humphreys,** made a sledge journey from Etah to northern Grant Land where the British Empire Mountains were discovered.

1936- The **British-Canadian Arctic Expedition,** under **T. H. Manning,** carried out scientific surveys around Southampton Island, Repulse Bay, and Melville Peninsula.

During and after the Second World War the Arctic became increasingly important as providing the most direct air-route from the United States to Europe and thereby acquired great strategic as well as commercial significance. Northern Canada was equipped with a great system of radar stations for early warning of attack by way of the Arctic and the Canadian Arctic has been intensively explored for raw materials such as coal and iron. In

1954. Scandinavian Airlines System initiated commercial flights from Copenhagen to Los Angeles by way of the Arctic.

1958, Aug. Commander W. R. Anderson (American) navigated the nuclear-powered submarine *Nautilus* under the North Pole, covering 1830 miles in 96 hours, from Point Barrow to a point between Greenland and Spitsbergen.

1959, Mar. The United States nuclear submarine *Skate* surfaced at the North Pole.

(3) Greenland

1905. The **duke of Orléans** in the *Belgica* traced the northeastern coast from Cape Bismarck to a new northern point (78° 30′, Duc d'Orléans Land).

1906-1908. L. Mylius-Erichsen led a Danish

expedition from near Cape Bismarck to North-east Foreland. A party under **Lieut. J. P. Koch** advanced to the northwest and connected with Peary's earlier explorations, thus completing the discovery of the entire Greenland coast.

1909–1912. Einar Mikkelsen led an American expedition to settle the question whether Peary Channel was really a channel or a fjord.

1912. Knud Rasmussen made two crossings of interior Greenland, the first eastward from Inglefield Gulf to Danmark Fjord, whence he explored Peary Land and Independence Fjord. Finding that Peary Channel did not exist, he was obliged to make a second crossing from Navy Cliff to Inglefield Gulf.

1912. Dr. de Quervain, a Swiss scientist, crossed Greenland from Disco Bay to Angmagssalik, discovering the lofty mountain chain that contains Mt. Forel.

1912–1913. J. P. Koch and **Dr. Alfred Wegener,** a German, led a party on the long 700-mile crossing over the unknown middle part of Greenland.

1917. Denmark strengthened her claim on Greenland by treaty with the United States, ceding the Virgin Islands in settlement of American claims to areas discovered by Peary.

1919. Foundation of the **Danish East Greenland Company.** This led to the establishment of trapping stations at Danmark Harbor and Germania Harbor and later at other places.

1920–1923. Lauge Koch led a Danish expedition to northern Greenland to complete the survey of Peary Land.

1921. Denmark proclaimed sole sovereignty over the whole country and closed the coasts to foreigners. The Norwegians, however, continued to press a long-standing claim based on original discovery and settlement by the Norsemen.

1924. Greenland Agreement between Denmark and Norway, providing that, until 1944, Norwegian hunters and landing parties should suffer no restrictions on the east coast between 60° 27' and 81°, except at Angmagssalik and the new Eskimo colonies around Scoresby Sound. Similar concessions made to the British. **Greenland became a crown colony of Denmark,** which exercises a trade monopoly and has undertaken a paternalistic program to preserve Eskimo culture.

1926, 1929. J. M. Wordie led two Cambridge University expeditions to East Greenland, mapping in detail a large area of mountains and glaciers around Clavering Island. On the second expedition Petermann Peak (9600 feet) was ascended.

1926–1927, and 1931–1934. Lauge Koch continued the Danish government surveys from Scoresby Sound northward. Four winter stations were established with radios, and various air surveys were carried out.

1930. Capt. Ahrenberg made an airplane flight from Sweden to Angmagssalik. In the same year **Wolfgang von Gronau** flew over the southern end of Greenland and landed at Ivigtut on his way from Iceland to the United States.

1930–1931. The **German Inland Ice expedition** under Dr. Alfred Wegener established parties at Scoresby Sound and at Kamarujuk Bay (West Greenland) and set up meteorological stations for winter observation.

1930–1932. The **British Arctic Air-Route Expedition,** led by twenty-three-year-old **H. G. Watkins,** established a base west of Angmagssalik and set up a weather station at an altitude of 8000 feet. Much of the coast was photographed from the air, and the lofty Watkins Mountains were discovered. In 1931 a party climbed Mt. Forel (11,100 feet). Another party crossed the icecap to Ivigtut, while yet another section crossed by a more northern route to Holsteinsborg.

1931, July 10. Norway formally annexed the coastal region north of Scoresby Sound, calling it *Eric the Red's Land.* After protests by Denmark the matter was referred to the Hague Court which decided in favor of Danish sovereignty (Apr. 5, 1933).

1932–1933. The **Danish Scoresby Sound Committee** undertook large-scale aerial photography.

1934. Martin Lindsay led the **British Trans-Greenland Expedition** from Disco Bay to the west slope of the Watkins Mountains, following the range southward for 350 miles. The expedition traversed one of the largest "blank spots" and reached an icecap altitude of 10,400 feet.

1935–1936. The **Oxford University Greenland Expedition,** under **H. Hayward,** continued extensive investigations in West Greenland.

1935. A. Courtauld, a former companion of Watkins, scaled the highest known peak in the Arctic (about 12,200 feet) in the Watkins Range.

During the Second World War Greenland became important for the staging of aircraft flying from the United States to Britain. Various bases were built on the southwest coast and eventually, in 1951, a great radar-protected base was constructed at **Thule** in northwest Greenland. During the entire post-war period there have been many expeditions, mostly air-supported, studying weather conditions and exploring the Greenland ice-sheet. Among the most important were

1948–1957. The French **Expéditions polaires,** led by **Paul-Émile Victor.**

1952-1954. The British North Greenland Expedition, led by **C. J. W. Simpson,** and

1959-1961. The **International Expedition** to Greenland, led by Victor.

(4) The Spitsbergen Area

1907-1920. **Dr. W. S. Bruce** in a series of six expeditions made a complete cartographical, geological, and zoological survey of Prince Charles Foreland. In addition he staked a mining claim on which the Scotch Spitsbergen Syndicate was founded (1909), and took an active part in developing the mineral resources of the country.

1911. **Count Zeppelin** in the *Mainz* set up a German meteorological station at Ice Fjord.

1921-1924. A series of three **Oxford University expeditions,** largely promoted by **George Binney,** initiated the University School of Explorers, composed largely of undergraduates and professional scientists. In Spitsbergen these expeditions carried out extensive scientific investigations, as they did in Greenland.

1923. **Lieut. Mittelholzer,** a Swiss aviator, made a successful 500-mile flight over Spitsbergen and Northeast Land.

1925. **Norway acquired sovereignty** over the Spitsbergen Archipelago and Bear Island, the whole area becoming officially known by the old Norse name *Svalbard.* Since 1906 the government has supported annual surveying cruises, mostly under the leadership of **Prof. Adolf Hoel.** Since 1911 meteorological and other stations have been established and in 1936 aerial mapping was begun.

1925. **Beginning of the polar flights** of Amundsen, Byrd, Nobile, etc., which all started from King Bay (p. 617).

1931. The **Norwegian-Swedish expedition** to Northeast Land, under **Prof. H. Ahlmann,** carried out a sledge tour over the inland ice and made many valuable scientific contributions.

1933-1936. **Two Oxford University expeditions,** led by **A. R. Glen,** concentrated on the little known New Friesland icecap in West Spitsbergen, explored and mapped the greater part of the interior, and carried on extensive biological researches. The second expedition (1935-1936) went to Northeast Land and carried out the most comprehensive scientific program of any British Arctic expedition.

(5) The Russian Arctic

The development of Siberia and the need for better communications with the Far East served as an important stimulus to Arctic work.

1910. The government inaugurated annual hydrographic cruises along the Siberian coast by the icebreakers *Taimyr* and *Vaigach,* and

between 1912 and 1914 established five meteorological stations in the Arctic.

1913. **Capt. B. Vilkitski,** in an attempt to navigate the northeast passage from east to west, discovered the new and extensive Severnaya Zemlya (North Land), about 50 miles north of Cape Chelyuskin.

1914-1915. **Capt. Otto Sverdrup** first used radio successfully in the Arctic, communicating with the icebreakers off Cape Chelyuskin.

1915. Vilkitski arrived at Archangel, having completed the east-west passage.

1916. The **Russian government annexed Franz Joseph Land** (claimed by Austria after the discovery in 1873). At the same time the government claimed Wrangel Island, Henrietta Island, and Herald Island, all discovered by Americans in the late 19th century.

1918-1925. **Capt. Roald Amundsen,** with **Dr. H. Sverdrup,** in the specially built *Maud,* navigated the northeast passage and spent two winters (1918-1920) in the ice preparatory to his projected drift over the pole. The drift was carried out in 1922-1925, nearly duplicating that of the *Fram,* but without important geographical results.

1921. **Stefansson** attempted to plant a British colony on Wrangel Island, which he regarded as a possible future air base. Most of the colonists died before they could be relieved in 1923.

1921. **Prof. R. Samoilovich,** of the new Institute for the Exploration of the North (founded 1921), initiated the annual exploration cruises into the Barents Sea, Kara Sea, and Russian Arctic.

1924. The **Soviet government** founded a colony on Wrangel Island, which has been maintained ever since.

1924. The government created the **Islands Administration of the U.S.S.R.** and placed Novaya Zemlya, Kolguev, and Vaigach under its jurisdiction.

1925-1928. Prof. S. V. Obruchev explored the practically unknown territory between the Kolima and Indigirka Rivers, discovering some very high mountain ranges.

1926. The **Soviet government** hoisted the flag over Herald Island, and, after Amundsen's flight in the *Norge,* claimed all lands and islands that might be discovered north of Russia and Siberia by flight across the Arctic.

1927. The Soviet established a permanent station on the New Siberian Islands. **First Russian hydroplane flight** from Cape North to Wrangel Island.

1931. The German dirigible, *Graf Zeppelin,* commanded by **Dr. Hugo Eckener,** cruised over the Franz Joseph Archipelago, Severnaya Zemlya, the Taimyr Peninsula, and unexplored parts of northern Novaya Zemlya.

1932. The **Soviet government** claimed Victoria Island, though this is generally regarded as part of the Spitsbergen group.

1932. Prof. Schmidt, in the icebreaker *Sibiriakov,* made a record passage by the northeast route from Archangel (July 28) to Yokohama (Nov. 5), that is, 3000 miles in nine weeks. It was the first time the passage had been made in one season. Since then at least one ship has gotten through each year. In 1936 fourteen ships made the passage.

1932. The government established a **polar radio station** on Prince Rudolf Land, in the Franz Joseph group.

1932. **Prof. N. N. Zubow** first circumnavigated the Franz Joseph Archipelago.

1935. Foundation of the **CENTRAL ADMINISTRATION OF THE NORTHERN SEA ROUTE** by the Soviet government. This was a chartered company entrusted with the exploration and development of all Soviet territory north of 62°. Under Prof. Schmidt it employed about 40,000 people. The extensive new program included: navigation of the great Siberian rivers and building of ports at their mouths (to be kept open by icebreakers); establishment on the coast of permanent stations (there were 57 in 1936) with radio and other scientific equipment; maintenance of planes for reconnaissance of ice conditions, etc.; charting of coasts and currents (warm currents discovered along the edge of the continental shelf in 1935); construction of a railway from the Yenisei to the Dudinka and Norilsk mining regions (coal, nickel, platinum, and copper); agricultural stations to develop a food supply for colonists (work on rapidly maturing wheat, etc.); education and development of the natives, and protection of reindeer herds, etc.

The Second World War saw the development of the Northern Sea Route as a regular part of the Soviet communications system. The Soviet government has supported intensive exploration of its entire Arctic coast and has, in the post-war period, organized several expeditions to study the Arctic drift.

1948. A Russian expedition discovered the **Lomonosov Ridge,** a great chain of submerged mountains running from Ellesmere Land to the New Siberian Islands and thus dividing the great polar basin.

5. ANTARCTIC EXPLORATION, 1738-1940

A legend dating from Greek antiquity and supported by Ptolemy related to the existence of an enormous continent in the southern hemisphere. This land-mass was shown by medieval cartographers, and even on maps as late as the end of the 16th century, on many of which it is extended to tropical latitudes in each of the three oceans. A series of voyages in southern latitudes during the 15th, 16th, and 17th centuries (Da Gama, 1497; Magellan, 1520; Drake, 1579; Tasman, 1642; and others, who were blown southward from their courses) progressively reduced the possible area of this legendary continent by pushing its limits farther and farther southward.

1738-1739. **Pierre Bouvet,** a French naval officer, deliberately set out to prove or disprove the existence of the southern continent, and 1400 miles south of Capetown he sighted land (Bouvet Island, 54° S.L.).

1756. The Spanish ship *Leon* discovered South Georgia (54°–55° S.) in the Atlantic.

1768. **Capt. James Cook,** on his first voyage, circumnavigated New Zealand, hitherto supposedly part of the Antarctic continent.

1771-1772. **Capt. Yves Kerguélen** sent out by France to look for "a very large continent." He discovered Kerguelen Island in the Indian Ocean (50° S.), which he named *New France.*

1772-1775. **SECOND VOYAGE OF CAPT. COOK.** He was the first to cross the Antarctic Circle (Jan. 17, 1773). He circumnavigated Antarctica, and made extensive exploratory cruises in the surrounding waters, pushing to 71° 10′ S. on January 30, 1774 (1130 miles from the pole and the **record south** for the 18th century). He discovered the South Sandwich Islands, annexed South Georgia, and reported the presence there of enormous herds of seals.

1778-1839. **Explorations by the sealers.** The discoveries made in this period were in the main incidental to the operations of British and American whalers and sealers drawn south by Cook's reports.

1819. **Capt. William Smith** discovered and took possession of the South Shetland Islands for the British.

1820. **Edward Bransfield** charted 500 miles of the southern coast of the South Shetlands, discovered his strait, and sighted Graham Land.

1820-1821. **Capt. Fabian Gottlieb von Bellingshausen,** sent out by Alexander I of Russia, circumnavigated Antarctica, and discovered Alexander I Land and Peter Island (68° S.), the first land sighted within the Antarctic Circle.

1821. **George Powell,** a British sealer, and

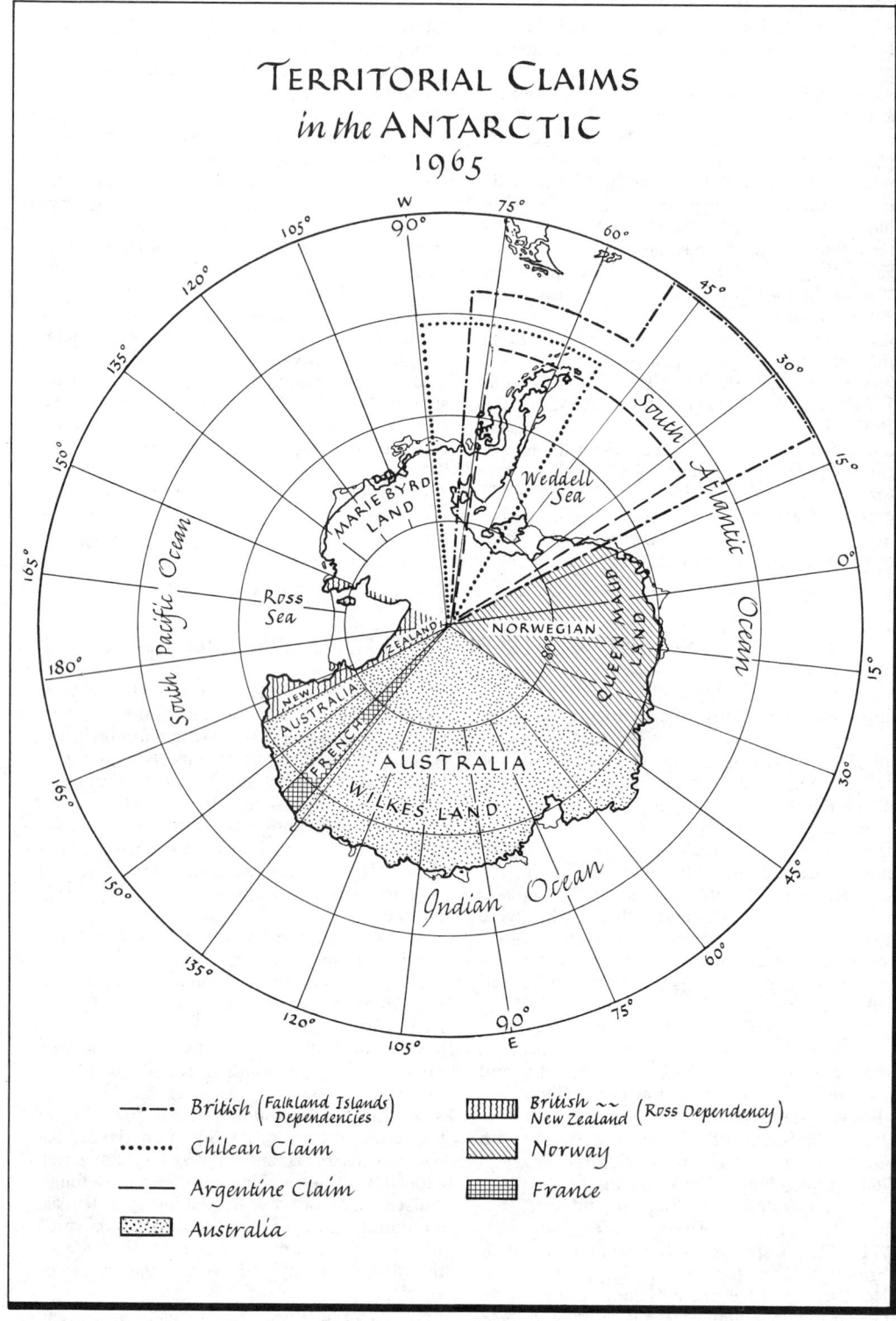

TERRITORIAL CLAIMS
in the ANTARCTIC
1965

British (Falkland Islands Dependencies)

Chilean Claim

Argentine Claim

Australia

British ~ New Zealand (Ross Dependency)

Norway

France

Nathaniel B. Palmer, an American sealer, discovered the South Orkney Islands, and Powell annexed them for the British. Palmer and other American sealers further explored Palmer Archipelago, which skirts Graham Land.

1823. Capt. James Weddell, an Englishman, discovered and penetrated Weddell Sea, establishing on February 20, 1823, the **record south** of his day (74° 15', 945 miles from the pole).

1831-1832. John Biscoe, an English sealer, circumnavigated Antarctica, named and annexed Graham Land, discovered the Biscoe Islands, Queen Adelaide Island, and sighted Enderby Land.

1837-1840. Capt. J. S. C. Dumont d'Urville of the French navy, in the *Astrolabe* and *Zelée,* sighted Joinville Island, Louis Philippe Land (in Graham Land), and Adélie Land on the mainland due south of Tasmania.

1839-1840. Capt. Charles Wilkes of the U.S. Navy cruised westward along the coast of Antarctica from 148° E. to 108° E., where he found his way blocked by Termination Barrier (Shackleton Ice Shelf).

1841-1843. CAPT. JAMES CLARK ROSS (sent out by the British admiralty) in the *Erebus* and the *Terror* hoping to plant the Union Jack on the south magnetic pole and reach as high a latitude as possible. He got through the ice pack, but, finding his way barred by the lofty Admiralty Range, cruised southward for 430 miles into Ross Sea, along the scarped eastern coast of South Victoria Land. There he sighted and named, besides the Admiralty Range, the Prince Albert Range, and the volcanic mountains Erebus and Terror on Ross Island. Finding further passage southward barred at the latter point by the **Great** (Ross) **Ice Barrier,** he cruised eastward along it for 350 miles, before returning to Hobart, Tasmania (Apr. 1, 1841). The following summer he returned to the head of Ross Sea near King Edward VII Land and made a **record south** (78° 9', 710 miles from the pole) which held for 60 years. Altogether Ross charted about 1000 miles of coastline. He also took possession for Great Britain of all the continental land and islands that he discovered in 1841.

After the voyages of Ross there was a lull of 30 years in systematic exploration of the Antarctic, attention having shifted to the North Pole.

1872-1874. H.M.S. *Challenger* (Capt. George S. Nares), the first steam-propelled vessel to cross the Antarctic Circle, renewed the study of oceanography in the Antarctic.

1873-1875. Capt. Eduard Dallmann (German) established that Palmer Land was an archipelago by sailing behind it, and, beyond, discovered Bismarck Strait and the Kaiser Wilhelm Archipelago to the south off Graham Land.

1893. Capt. C. A. Larsen (Norwegian) explored Weddell seacoast, discovering and naming Foyn Coast in Graham Land, King Oscar Land, Mt. Jason, and Robertson Island.

1894-1895. Capt. Leonard Kristensen (Norwegian) discovered Ridley Beach at Cape Adare, where the **first landing on the continent** was made in January by Carsten Borchgrevink. He found the first vegetation—a lichen at Possession Island.

1895. The Sixth International Geographical Congress in London described Antarctic exploration as the most pressing geographical requirement of the time.

1897-1899. Lieut. Adrien de Gerlache (Belgian) with **Roald Amundsen** as mate, coasted Graham Land, discovered and made several landings in Belgica Strait (subsequently Gerlache Channel), discovered and named Danco Land to the east, and passed south of Peter Island. Here on March 3, 1898, they were beset and remained, the first prisoners through an Antarctic night, drifting with the pack ice until February 14, 1899.

1898-1900. Carsten Borchgrevink led the first party (British and Scandinavian) to winter on the continent, at Cape Adare, where meteorological observations were taken, penguin life studied, and geological collections made. Picked up by their ship in January 1900, they made several landings on the eastern shore of Victoria Land, discovered the Emperor Penguin rookery at Cape Crozier, and cruised along the Ross Barrier. February 19 they made a sledge journey on its surface to 78° 45', a new **record south.**

1901-1903. The **German National Expedition,** led by **Prof. Erich von Drygalski,** discovered and named the Gaussberg and Kaiser Wilhelm II Land, where they sent out the first sledge parties on the Antarctic ice coast.

1901-1903. The **Swedish Expedition,** led by **Dr. Otto Nordenskiöld** and Capt. Larsen in the *Antarctic,* made exploratory cruises around Graham Land and in Weddell Sea, and discovered and charted the Crown Prince Gustav Channel and James Ross Island as well as the northern archipelago lying around it. The *Antarctic* was crushed and sunk by the pack ice and the expedition was obliged to spend two winters at Snow Hill Island, where it was finally rescued by an Argentine ship.

1902-1904. CAPT. ROBERT F. SCOTT (British), commanding a large expedition, including **Lieut. Ernest H. Shackleton** and **Dr. E. A. Wilson,** in the *Discovery,* reached Cape Adare,

January 1902. Cruising southward along Ross's course in 1842, he discovered and named the Drygalski and Nordenskiöld ice tongues, Granite Harbor, and the Royal Society Mountains. He succeeded in surpassing his predecessor's record, reached the eastern end of Ross Barrier, sighted and named King Edward VII Land. Upon the return to winter at Ross Island in McMurdo Sound, Mt. Erebus was found to be an active volcano.

1903, Nov.-1904, Feb. Scott, Wilson, and Shackleton made a southern trip of 930 miles over the Ross Barrier in an effort to ascertain its limits. They discovered that its western boundary was formed by 350 miles of scarped coastline, backed by the lofty Britannia and Queen Alexandra Ranges, the latter containing 15,000-foot Mt. Markham. Their **record south** was 82° 17′ (500 miles from the pole), near Shackleton Inlet, where they were obliged to turn back. At the same time a reconnaissance party under **Lieut. Albert Armitage** made a western trip on to the continental ice-sheet of South Victoria Land's 9000-foot inland plateau, discovering and naming the Ferrar, Taylor, and Blue Glaciers. The following season (1903–1904) a party under Scott pushed 200 miles farther over the plateau and on the return trip discovered and explored Dry Valley.

1903-1905. The **Scottish National Expedition,** led by **Dr. W. S. Bruce,** carried on oceanographical explorations in Weddell Sea, and wintered on Laurie Island.

1903-1905. Jean B. Charcot (French) operated off the west coast of Graham Land, charted the western side of Palmer Archipelago, sighted Alexander I Land, and discovered Loubet Land.

1907-1909. SIR ERNEST SHACKLETON (British), privately financed in the *Nimrod,* led an expedition including Douglas Mawson and Prof. T. W. E. David to the Ross Sea sector. **First ascent of Mt. Erebus** and discovery of the live crater (Mar. 5–10, 1908). From a base at Cape Royds on Ross Island, Shackleton and three others started on a journey to the pole (Oct. 29, 1908). Surpassing Scott's record, they discovered and passed the southern end of Ross Barrier, and struggled (Dec. 7–27) more than a hundred miles up to the head of Beardmore Glacier, where they discovered a seam of low-grade coal. At its head (9820 feet) they emerged upon the South Polar Plateau, across which they traveled to 88° 23′ S., on January 9, 1909, where a desperate food shortage obliged them to turn back, only 97 miles short of their goal.

1908, Oct. 5-1909, Feb. 4. David, Mawson, and Mackay on a 1260-mile sledge trip, explored 200 miles northward along the coast of Victoria Land, crossed Drygalski Glacier, and turning inland climbed up the 7000-foot Northern Plateau to plant the British flag on the **south magnetic pole** (1200 miles from the true South Pole) on January 16, 1909. Altogether Shackleton's expedition discovered about 1000 miles, and explored 300 miles more of territory previously discovered. All the new land explored was formally declared to be British.

1908. Great Britain issued letters patent constituting the *Falkland Dependency* (South Georgia, the South Shetlands, the Sandwich Group, and Graham Land) under the jurisdiction of the governor of the Falkland Islands. The Dependency established a sector between 80° and 20° W. Long. running from 50° S. Lat. to the pole.

1908-1910. Second expedition of Jean Charcot. Advancing southward Charcot first reached Alexander I Land, but could not determine whether it was an island or mainland. In 1910 he discovered Charcot Land, farther to the southwest, and verified Bellingshausen's discovery of Peter Island.

1910-1912. DISCOVERY OF THE SOUTH POLE BY CAPT. ROALD AMUNDSEN. Beaten by Peary at the North Pole, Amundsen hoped to anticipate Scott at the South Pole. He chose a base on the Bay of Whales and with four others made the trip with dog-sledges (1911, Oct. 19–Dec. 14). The Norwegian flag was hoisted at the pole on December 16, 1911. On the trip Amundsen discovered the 15,000-foot Queen Maud Range which bounds Ross Barrier. He ascended this range to the Polar Plateau by way of Axel Heiberg Glacier, and discovered the Devil's Glacier beyond.

1910-1913. SCOTT'S LAST EXPEDITION. He aimed for the pole, but was interested mainly in scientific research. From a base at Cape Evans in McMurdo Sound, he and four others started (Nov. 3, 1911) and followed Shackleton's route up Beardmore Glacier. Failure of transport and insufficient food resulted in ever slower progress. **The pole was reached January 16, 1912,** but the party was so exhausted that before getting back it was overtaken by bad weather. Halfway across Ross Barrier they all died in a blizzard (about March 29).

1911-1912. Dr. Wilhelm Filchner (German) discovered Leopold Land, delimited the southern boundary of Weddell Sea, and discovered the Wilhelm Ice Barrier, which fills its head.

1911-1913. Dr. Douglas Mawson (British) led a large-scale, well-equipped expedition to explore the 2000 miles of practically unknown coast between Cape Adare and the Gaussberg.

He was the first Antarctic explorer to use wireless. The larger section of the expedition broke through the pack ice and discovered Mertz Glacier. Here the party made its base on Commonwealth Bay and (Nov. 1911-Jan. 1912) Mawson, Mertz, and Ninnis sledged 280 miles over the great ice plateau into King George V Land, crossing the Mertz and the still larger Ninnis Glacier, but Mawson was the only one who got through alive. Another party explored the coast to the east for 275 miles, and a third contingent was taken 1200 miles westward in the *Aurora* past the great ice barrier which they named Shackleton Ice Shelf, discovered Davis Sea, and named the land on its shores Queen Mary Land. The party camped on Shackleton Ice Shelf, on which Denman and Scott Glaciers were discovered. From here also a party made a 215-mile trip to Gaussberg in Kaiser Wilhelm Land and back.

Mawson discovered that the greater part of Antarctica is bordered by ice coasts. Altogether his expedition discovered and explored 1320 miles of land, mapped 800 miles of coastline, and made more geographical and scientific discoveries than any previous expedition, although it worked under far worse weather conditions in the most desolate, blizzard-ridden part of the continent.

1914-1917. SIR ERNEST SHACKLETON, in the *Endurance,* proposed to cross Antarctica from Weddell to Ross Sea via the pole (1800 miles, half over unknown territory) to meet the complementary party under **Mackintosh** in the *Aurora.* This aim was defeated, Shackleton's way south to the destined landing-place being barred by heavy pack ice in Weddell Sea, but he discovered Caird Coast, which contains the Dawson Lampton Glacier—probably the world's largest. February 22, 1915, the *Endurance* was fast beset and drifted 570 miles northwest with the pack until November 21, 1915, when she was crushed and sunk by the pressure ice. The party drifted on the disintegrating floe until April 9, 1916, when they took to small boats. On April 14 they reached Elephant Island, where they were obliged to winter. Shackleton and five others made the 800-mile trip to South Georgia for help in a 20-foot open boat in 16 days, arriving May 10, 1916. A fourth relief expedition to Elephant Island was finally successful in removing the marooned party on August 30, 1916.

The Ross Sea party in the *Aurora* was left stranded with insufficient equipment at its base at Cape Evans when the ship was carried away by the pack in May 1915. Scantily-clad, half-starved, and suffering from scurvy, the land party nevertheless fulfilled its part of the plan, laying depots all the way to Beardmore Glacier for Shackleton to use on the last lap of his polar journey. This party was rescued by the *Aurora* in January 1917.

1921-1922. J. L. Cope and **G. H.** (now **Sir Hubert) Wilkins** (British), landed by Norwegian whalers on the west coast of Graham Land, were foiled in their plan to cross it to Weddell Sea, because the country was too rugged for sledging.

1923, July 30. A **British order in council** constituted the Ross Sea sector a British dependency, known as the *Ross Dependency,* under the governor-general of New Zealand, and fixed as its boundaries the meridians of 150° W., 160° E., and the 60th parallel S., a delimitation which included a large part of Amundsen's discoveries and excluded part of Scott's route to the pole across King Edward Plateau, part of Oates Land, and all of the extensive lands discovered by Mawson, including the south magnetic pole area, which had been claimed for the British by David in 1908.

1924. The **French government** put **Adélie Land** (between 136° 20′ and 142° 20′ E. Long.) under the governor of Madagascar.

1928-1930. FIRST ANTARCTIC FLIGHTS, BY SIR HUBERT WILKINS. The expedition was sponsored by the American Geographical Society and largely financed by W. R. Hearst. From Deception Bay, Wilkins, piloted by C. B. Eielson, made a 1200-mile flight (Dec. 20, 1928) southwest over Graham Land, discovering Crane Channel, the Lockheed Mountains, and Stefansson Strait, which separates Graham Land from the mainland (named Hearst Land). On December 31, 1929, Wilkins, piloted by A. Cheesman, flew over Charcot Land, discovered that it was an island and dropped a flag claiming it for Britain. Altogether Wilkins mapped about 80,000 square miles, discovered a new portion of the continent, and determined the insularity of Graham Land.

1928-1930. COMM. RICHARD E. BYRD (American) led a large, scientifically equipped expedition with three airplanes. In January 1929 they built the base *Little America* on Ross Barrier. A flight on January 27 revealed the new Rockefeller Mountains and neighboring Scott Land. Another on November 18 discovered the Charles V. Bob Mountain Range east of the Queen Maud Range.

1929, Nov. 28-29. Byrd, Balchen, June, and McKinley, in the plane *Floyd Bennett,* flew to the pole and back (1700 miles) by way of the 10,000-foot pass over Liv's Glacier. In a further flight on December 5 Byrd went beyond the Rockefeller Mountains and discovered the huge Edsel Ford Range in a new territory which he named *Marie Byrd Land* and claimed for the United States (between 150° and 120° W.).

1929-1931. SIR DOUGLAS MAWSON led the co-operative British, Australian, and New Zealand Antarctic Research Expedition, in the *Discovery* (Capt. Davis), to explore the 2500-mile uncharted coastline between King Wilhelm II Land and Coats Land, including Kemp and Enderby Lands. Planes were carried along, to be used where pack ice prevented approach to the mainland coasts. December 29, 1929: Discovery of MacRobertson Land near Kemp Land by flight from the *Discovery*. January 13, 1930: Landing in Enderby Land, of which formal possession was taken for the crown. January 14, 1930: The *Discovery* met the *Norvegia* (Capt. Riiser-Larsen), which was also exploring. It was decided that the British should keep to the east and the Norwegians to the west of 40° E. (later changed to 45° E. by the two governments). The following (1930-1931) season a landing was made on Commonwealth Bay and all land from there eastward to Oates Land was claimed for the British crown under the name *King George V Land*. The coast west of Cape Denison was explored by plane and additional surveys of Adélie Land were made. Further discoveries were: Banzare Land (west of 127° E.), Sabrina Land (between 115° and 116° E.), Princess Elizabeth Land (between the Gaussberg and MacRobertson Land), and Mackenzie Sea, a huge bay in MacRobertson Land. These two cruises resulted in the discovery of new coasts covering 29° of longitude, about 1000 miles of which was charted. Mawson's major achievement on his two expeditions (1911-1914 and 1929-1931) was the demonstration that the coastline is continuous from Cape Freshfield in King George V Land to Enderby Land—more than 2500 miles.

1933. The British government accepted the **Australian claim** to the huge sector between 45° and 160° E. Long., exclusive of French Adélie Land.

1929-1931. Capt. Hj. Riiser-Larsen (Norwegian) led an expedition in the *Norvegia* to look for new whaling grounds and new land. He carried two planes and on December 22, 1929 flew to the coast of Enderby Land. January 15, 1930, he discovered Queen Maud Land (southwest of Enderby Land) and (Feb. 18) Crown Princess Martha Land (by flight), to which 150 miles of coastline was added by a flight on February 20. The following (1930-1931) season he extended his explorations of Queen Maud Land 200 miles farther to the west, the new land (between 24° and 30° E.) being called *Princess Ragnhild Land*.

1934-1935. THE SECOND EXPEDITION OF COMMANDER BYRD. The equipment included four planes, four tractors, and an autogyro, and from January 17, 1934 to February 6, 1935 a comprehensive set of observations was taken in the fields of meteorology, biology, geophysics, botany, and cosmic rays. Byrd himself undertook to man single-handed a weather observation station 100 miles inland through the Antarctic winter, but fell ill and injured himself after three months, so that a relief expedition had to be sent in one of the tractors. Dr. Poulter's investigations of Ross Barrier bore out the Japanese contention that much of it was aground. One tractor party explored a new plateau discovered to the southeast of Little America, and another, aiming south, pushed up the glaciers bordering the Barrier, explored mountains only two hundred miles from the pole, where they found plant-fossils, coal, fossilized wood, and other indications that the climate had once been subtropical, and discovered a huge plateau to the east of Thorne Glacier.

Explorations were also carried on by flight, the main achievement being the demonstration that no strait connects Ross and Weddell Seas and that Antarctica is thus one continent. A new range called the *Horlick Mountains* was discovered east of Thorne Glacier.

1934-1937. The **British Graham Land Expedition,** under **John Rymill** (Australian). In 1935-1936 it operated from a base at the Argentine Islands, exploring the Graham Land coast to Cape Evensen and discovering that it consists of an 8000-foot plateau, rising abruptly from the sea. In July 1936 two parties surveyed the coastline north from a base at Barry Island (Fallières Coast). On August 15 a flight was made westward along the shore of Alexander I Land, which was photographed. A flight on September 15 revealed to the south a long, ice-covered strait (King George VI Channel), which the expedition attempted to penetrate with sledges. At 72° S.L. the channel appeared to open into a large bay, which proved that Alexander I Land is larger and extends farther south than previously supposed. Meanwhile another sledge party penetrated the interior of Graham Land, discovered and scaled a 7500-foot pass and reached a point overlooking the east coast, which was mapped for 140 miles, south to 70° 40'. The expedition revealed that what looked like straits to Wilkins were in reality glaciers several thousand feet high and that Stefansson Strait, Casey Channel, and probably Crane Channel are fjords. Graham Land may, after all, be part of the Antarctic continent.

1935-1936. LINCOLN ELLSWORTH (American) in the *Wyatt Earp,* commanded by Sir

Hubert Wilkins, succeeded in his third attempt at a **transcontinental Antarctic flight.** On November 23, 1935, with Herbert Hollick-Kenyon (Canadian), he took off in the *Polar Star* from Dundee Island in the northern part of the Antarctic Archipelago for the Bay of Whales, 2300 miles away. The trip was made in six stages, the last one by sledge after the exhaustion of their fuel. They reached Little America December 15 and were picked up January 15, 1936 by the *Discovery II,* an Antarctic research ship. The new territory between Hearst Land and Marie Byrd Land (80° to 120° W.) was named *James W. Ellsworth Land* and claimed for the United States, and a high mid-continental plateau was named after Hollick-Kenyon. Ellsworth also discovered the 12,000-foot Eternity Range in Hearst Land and the Sentinel Range in James W. Ellsworth Land.

1936. Australia proclaimed her control over all Antarctic territory south of the 60th parallel between 160° and 45° E. Long. (except Adélie Land), this being the territory explored by Mawson on his two expeditions. It constitutes an area almost as large as that of Australia.

1938-1939. Ellsworth, on another expedition, surveyed a large part of eastern Antarctica by air, claiming some 430,000 square miles for the United States. The Australian government at once protested against this claim.

1939, Jan. 14. The **Norwegian government** laid claim to Queen Maud Land, Princess Ragnhild Land, and Crown Princess Martha Land and the sector running inward to the Pole, about 1,000,000 square miles covering roughly one-fifth of the Antarctic continent.

In the Antarctic scientific and political considerations together led to ever increasing activity in exploration, charting, and settlement.

1939-1941. An American expedition under Admiral Byrd attempted to establish permanent bases in the sector of American interest, but failed for lack of financial support.

1940. Chile claimed a sector running from 53° to 90° W. L., thus overlapping the Argentine claim. Competing Argentine, Chilean, and British expeditions were sent to the area.

1943. The British government established more than a dozen meteorological stations throughout its Falkland Islands Dependencies.

1946-1947. The United States government announced that it would make no specific territorial claim but would not, at the same time, recognize the claims of other nations to Antarctic territory.

1946-1947. A huge American expedition under Byrd explored in the region of Ross Bay. In February 1947 Byrd made a **second flight to the South Pole.**

1949. A **Norwegian-Swedish-British expedition** (the first international one) initiated a series of annual expeditions in Queen Maud Land.

1954. The first permanent **Australian base** was established in MacRobertson Land.

1956-1957. The American **Amundsen-Scott station** was set up at the South Pole.

1957-1958. The **International Geophysical Year** devoted major attention to scientific work in the Antarctic.

1957, Nov. 24-1958, Mar. 2. First crossing of Antarctica by land by a party under leadership of **Sir Vivian Fuchs.** The hugh area between the Pole and Weddell Sea explored for the first time.

1959, Dec. 1. International **ANTARCTIC TREATY** signed in Washington. The signatories undertook, for a period of thirty years, to make use of the Antarctic continent for peaceful purposes only, and to ensure freedom for scientific research. Existing territorial claims remained unaffected, but new claims and the enlargement of existing claims were prohibited.

B. THE REVOLUTIONARY AND NAPOLEONIC PERIOD, 1789-1815

(*From p. 486*)

The period of the Revolution and Empire may be divided into these subperiods, distinguished by changes in the form of government:

(1) **Estates-General** and **Constituent Assembly** (*Constituante*) from May 5 (June 17), 1789, to September 30, 1791. Government a limited, constitutional monarchy. Dominance of the upper middle classes.

(2) The **Legislative Assembly** (*Législatif*), from October 1, 1791, to September 21, 1792. The monarchy continued as before, until suspended. Rising power of the lower classes.

(3) The **National Convention** (*Convention Nationale*), from September 21, 1792, to October 25, 1795. Height of the revolution. The convention, called to frame a new constitution, first abolished the monarchy and condemned the king to death; it supported the Reign of Terror, and then

overthrew it. It led the resistance to foreign foes.

[N.B. In modern party terms the *Left* of the Constituent was the *Right* of the Legislative (though the actual *personnel* was by law different), and the *Left* of the Legislative was (at first) the *Right* of the Convention.]

(4) The **Directory** (*Directoire*), from October 26, 1795, to November 9, 1799 (18 Brumaire, An. VIII). The middle classes recovered their influence. Party divisions. The army. General Bonaparte's *coup d'état*. Form republican.

(5) The **Consulate** (*Consulat*), at first provisional, then definitive, from December 25, 1799, to May 20, 1804; civil and military rule, virtually of one man; progress of French arms. Form still nominally republican.

(6) The (first) **Empire,** from May 20, 1804, to (April 1814) June 22, 1815. **Napoleon I** made France the controlling power on the Continent, but was finally overthrown.

1. BACKGROUND OF THE REVOLUTION

The spirit of the 18th century—a spirit devoted to the destruction or reformation of existing institutions. Attacks of French writers upon church and state.

Agrarian conditions. The peasantry was almost wholly free (300,000 out of some 20,000,000 still subject to certain servile restrictions), and in many regions owned land. Often its holdings were too small for adequate support. It was subject to certain surviving feudal dues, not in the aggregate large, but annoying, and in 1789 no longer paid for protection. There is evidence that in the last half of the 18th century nobles and other owners of these dues were attempting to collect them to the full, and revive those that had lapsed (the so-called *feudal reaction*). Taxation bore heavily on the peasantry, especially the *taille,* a land-tax from which nobles and clergy were exempt. Yet as a whole French peasants were certainly better off than most European peasants, and they took part in the revolution, not because they were hopelessly downtrodden, but because they were well enough off to wish to better themselves.

The **rise of a middle class,** generally excluded from politics, and particularly from local politics (access to the royal bureaucracy was open to able and ambitious bourgeois), but which had been growing richer with the expansion of French trade, and which read and listened to the *philosophes.*

An **unwieldy and inefficient machinery of government,** not so much tyrannical as irresponsible and unsuited to the needs of a large commercial and agricultural state. Taxation was inequitable, neither clergy nor nobility paying their full share (the clergy did pay a not inconsiderable *don gratuit,* and nobles paid the *vingtième* and *capitation*). Moreover, the indirect taxes were farmed out, and the *fermiers généraux* most unpopular. The *gabelle,* or salt-tax, was particularly irregular in its incidence. There was no true representative assembly, though the parlements, and especially the parlement of Paris, sometimes took upon themselves in the 18th century the rôle of such an assembly. Justice was by no means arbitrary, and the judges (*noblesse de robe*), though they owned their offices, were generally competent and conscientious. The famous *lettres de cachet,* royal orders imprisoning without benefit of *habeas corpus* or similar proceedings, were less important in fact than in anti-governmental propaganda. Sometimes used against political offenders, their chief use was to back up the family discipline of the upper classes by providing a means of shutting up wayward sons and otherwise keeping the power of the *pater familias* intact.

An **ever-growing deficit,** which proved impossible of reduction. The estates-general were called to remedy practical bankruptcy. Once called, they took upon themselves the wholesale reform of the state. France in 1789 was a fairly prosperous society with a bankrupt government.

2. THE NATIONAL ASSEMBLY

1789, May 5. MEETING OF THE ESTATES-GENERAL at Versailles, with a **double representation** of the middle classes as the third estate (*tiers état*): nobles 300, clergy 300, commons 600. Dispute about the manner of debating and voting (whether votes should be cast by the orders as such, or by each member individually) which broke out during the verification of the powers of the members. The nobles and the clergy demanded a separate verification, the third estate wished that it should take place in common. The true question was whether the legislative body should consist of a lower house of commons, and an upper house (or two houses) of nobles and clergy which would check the lower, or of **one house** in which the commons equaled in number the nobles and clergy together. Upon the motion of the **Abbé Siéyès** (author of the remarkable pamphlet asking, *What is the Third Estate?*) the representatives of the third estate assumed the title of the

1789, June 17–1791. NATIONAL ASSEMBLY (*Constituante*) and invited the other orders to join them.

June 20. Suspension of the meetings for three days; the hall closed to the members, who at last resorted to a neighboring **tennis court** (*jeu de paume*) and took an **oath** not to separate until they had given the realm a constitution. President Bailly. Many of the clergy and some nobles joined the assembly.

June 23. Fruitless royal sitting; the king ordered the assembly to meet in three houses. Principal orator of the assembly: **Count Honoré de Mirabeau** (1749–1791), a Provençal nobleman elected by the third estate. The representatives of the clergy and the nobility joined the third estate by request of the king. Concentration of troops near Paris. Rumors of the king's intention to dissolve the national assembly, and the **dismissal of Necker** (July 11) caused the

July 14. STORM AND DESTRUCTION OF THE BASTILLE in Paris (murder of its governor, Jordan de Launay). Paris in the hands of the mob scarcely controlled by the electors who had chosen the deputies from Paris and who now sat at the Hôtel de Ville as a provisional government. **Necker recalled. Lafayette** commander of the newly established **National Guard.** Bailly mayor of Paris. Adoption of the tricolor: blue, red (colors of Paris), white (color of France).

Beginning of the emigration of the nobles, headed by the **count of Artois**, second brother of the king, **prince of Condé, duke of Polignac.**

Rising of the peasants against the feudal lords in Dauphiné, Provence, Burgundy, and throughout France. This *grande peur* was not systematically spread from Paris but occurred sporadically as a series of mass movements with numerous centers. Riots, provisional governments, guards in the provincial cities.

Aug. 4. Voluntary surrender by the representatives of the nobles (Vicomte de Noailles) of all feudal rights and privileges, but only gradually over a period of years, and with compensation to the owners (this compensation was in most cases never paid; under the convention these provisions were repealed); abolition of titles, prohibition of the sale of offices, dissolution of the guilds, etc.

Aug. 27. Declaration of the rights of man, a bill of rights compounded from English and American precedents and from the political theories current with the *philosophes*. Discussion of the veto power.

Oct. 5, 6. Outbreak of the mob of Paris, caused by hunger and rumors of an intended reaction. March of a band, consisting principally of women, to Versailles. The royal family, rescued by Lafayette, was obliged to go to Paris, whither the national assembly followed them. Two hundred members resigned.

Liberal monarchical constitution: one chamber with legislative power and the sole right of initiation. The royal veto was suspensive only, delaying the adoption of a measure for two legislative terms. The king could not declare war and conclude peace without the consent of the chamber, ratification by which was necessary for the validity of all foreign treaties.

In order to relieve the financial distress the ecclesiastical estates were declared public property. *Assignats,* notes of the government, having for security the public lands, the value of which was not to be exceeded by the issue of notes (a check which was inoperative). The state assumed the support of the clergy.

1790, July 14. National federation in Paris; the constitution accepted by the king. Abolition of the old provinces and governments; France divided into 83 *départements,* named after rivers and mountains; these departments being subdivided into 374 *districts* and *cantons.* The *communes* were left unchanged (44,000); tax qualifications for the exercise of *active* suffrage in the primary assemblies, which chose electors, who then elected the representatives (745) for a legislature with a term of two years. The administrative officers of the departments and districts were selected from the electors; the municipal officers and the judges were taken from the great body of voters, the *active* citizens. Active citizens, who voted, paid direct taxes equal to three days' wages of common labor in their locality: *passive* citizens, who did not vote, paid no direct taxes, or less than the above minimum. Each department and each district had a local assembly. Abolition of the parlements and the old judicial constitution. Juries. Abolition of hereditary nobility, titles, and coats-of-arms. Dissolution of all ecclesiastical orders, excepting those having education and the care of the sick for their objects. Civil organization of the clergy; the priests to be chosen by the voters of the districts, the bishops by the voters of the departments. Somewhat less than half of the clerics submitted to the new constitution by taking the required oath, creating a distinction between the *prêtres asser-*

mentés and the *prêtres réfractaires.*

Growing power of the clubs, which had existed since 1789. The *Jacobins* (meeting in a monastery formerly occupied by Dominicans in the Rue St. Jacques), under the leadership of **Maximilien Robespierre** soon became the greatest power in the state, making use of a network of daughter societies in the provinces. The *Cordeliers,* who met in a Franciscan monastery (leaders **Georges Jacques Danton, Jean Paul Marat, Camille Desmoulins, Jacques Hébert**). The *Feuillants,* moderate monarchists who had separated from the Jacobins (**Lafayette, Bailly** belonged to this group).

Reorganization of the municipality (*commune*) **of Paris:** 48 sections, with 84,000 voters in a population of 800,000; general council; executive board (44). Each section had a primary assembly.

Sept.   Fall of Necker. Alliance between the court and Mirabeau, who endeavored to stem the revolution and prevent the overthrow of the throne.

1791, Apr. 2.   Death of Mirabeau.

June 20–25.   FLIGHT OF THE KING and his family to the northeast frontier, where loyal troops were to protect them. The party was recognized and stopped at Varennes, then brought back to Paris. At first suspended, then reinstated by the moderate party (Sept.), **Louis accepted the constitution** (Sept. 14) as revised and completed.

Sept. Annexation of Avignon and Venaissin to France.

Sept. 30.   Dissolution of the assembly, after it had voted that none of its members should be eligible for election to the next assembly.

3. THE LEGISLATIVE ASSEMBLY

1791, Oct. 1–1792, Sept. The **LEGISLATIVE ASSEMBLY,** composed of 745 members, elected by the active citizens, still represented primarily the middle class. **Parties:** The *Right* (constitutionalists, royalists, Feuillants, etc.) became weaker almost day by day. The *Left,* comprising the majority, was divided into (1) the *Plain,* an unorganized group of moderate republicans or timid monarchists, swayed in turn by the next two groups; (2) the *Girondists,* so called because the leading members came from Bordeaux (department of the Gironde), had in **Elie Guadet, Pierre Vergniaud,** and **Jacques Brissot** a group of brilliant orators, advocating the establishment of a form of federal republic; (3) the *Mountain* (la Montagne, Montagnards), so called from their seats, which were the highest on the left side of the hall, was composed of the radicals, champions of a united, indivisible republic. The Mountain drew its strength from the Jacobin and Cordelier clubs. The division between Girondists and the Mountain did not attain its clearest form until the meeting of the convention (below), but its beginnings were evident in the legislative assembly. **Jerome Pétion,** the mayor of Paris, was a Girondist.

Aug. 27. Meeting at Pillnitz of **Frederick William II** of Prussia (1786–1797) and **Leopold II** (1790–1792), the emperor. The two sovereigns and their ministers reached a preliminary understanding regarding Near Eastern affairs (p. 521) and above all regarding the French situation. The **declaration of Pillnitz** was a carefully worded statement that the two rulers would intervene in French affairs only with the unanimous consent of the powers, including Great Britain. But the French interpreted it as a bald threat of interference.

1792, Feb. 7.   Alliance of Austria and Prussia against France.

1792–1806.   FRANCIS II, emperor in succession to Leopold.

1792–1797.   WAR OF THE FIRST COALITION against France. A Girondist ministry (Roland, Dumouriez) took the place of the constitutionalist ministry, whose fall was caused by the Pillnitz declaration. The Girondists actually sought the war, while on the Austrian side Francis fell completely under the influence of the war party. The French *émigrés* had long been trying to provoke intervention, while certain German princes with feudal rights in Alsace (*princes possessionés*) were demanding compensation for losses under the decrees of August 4, 1789. Many Prussian and Austrian leaders thought that France, weakened by the revolutionary dissension, would be easily beaten. Exact responsibility for the war is hard to allocate. In April 1792 both sides wanted it.

Apr. 20. The **French declared war against Austria** and put three armies in the field: Rochambeau (48,000) between Dunkirk and Philippeville; Lafayette (52,000) between Philippeville and Lauterburg; Luckner (42,000) between Lauterburg and Basel. The French suffered reverses, which increased the revolutionary exictement in Paris.

June 13.   Fall of the Roland ministry.

June 20.   Attack of the mob on the Tuileries; calm behavior of the king.

July 11. The assembly pronounced the country in danger. Formation of a voluntary army throughout the country. Threatening **manifesto of the duke of Brunswick,** Prussian commander-in-chief. The Paris council was broken up and its place usurped by commissioners from the sections (new commune of 288 members).

Aug. 10. STORMING OF THE TUILERIES by the mob, in consequence of a command of the king ordering the Swiss guard to cease firing. Massacre of the Swiss guards. The king took refuge in the hall of the assembly, was suspended from his functions, and confined in the Temple (old house of the Knights Templar). Arrests of suspected persons. **Provisional government: Danton** (1759–1794), minister of justice; Lebrun, Roland, Servan, Monge, Clavière. The assembly virtually abdicated its powers, which passed to the Paris commune and the Jacobin clubs. Convocation of a national convention, to be elected by manhood suffrage, to draw up a new constitution.

Aug. 20. Lafayette, having been impeached and proscribed, fled from his army, was captured by the Austrians and imprisoned at Olmütz (till 1796). Verdun taken by the Prussians.

Sept. 2-7. The **SEPTEMBER MASSACRES** at Paris. Suspects were taken from the prisons and, after hasty trials by improvised tribunals, were summarily done away with by the mob. Blame seems to lie chiefly with Sergent, Panis, and other Paris ward politicians. **Danton,** if he cannot be proved to have instigated the massacres, certainly allowed them to run their course. Similar scenes were enacted at Versailles, Lyons, Rheims, Meaux, and Orléans.

Sept. 20. BATTLE OF VALMY. The French, under **Generals Charles Dumouriez** and **François Kellermann,** defeated the Prussians in an artillery duel fought in a heavy fog. The engagement, far from important in the military sense, was yet a crucial test. It gave heart to the revolutionary armies and was to prove a turning-point.

4. THE NATIONAL CONVENTION

1792, Sept. 21-1795, Oct. The **NATIONAL CONVENTION,** longest-lived of the revolutionary assemblies. It was elected by manhood suffrage and was composed entirely of republicans (749 members, of whom 486 were new men). **Parties:** The **Girondists** now formed the Right, while the **Mountain,** under Robespierre, the duke of Orléans (Philippe Egalité), Danton, Collot d'Herbois, etc., formed the Left. The **Plain** (scornfully called the *Marsh* and the *Belly*) appeared as in the preceding assembly. Numerically it had the majority, but it was dominated first by the Girondists, then by the Mountain.

1792, Sept. 21. ABOLITION OF THE MONARCHY. France declared a republic.

Sept. 22 was the **first day of the year one** of the French republic. *Citoyen et citoyenne;* decree of perpetual banishment against emigrants; *tu et toi.* Inglorious retreat of the Prussians through Champagne to Luxemburg and across the Rhine. The French general, **Adam de Custine,** took Speier, Mainz, and Frankfurt-on-the-Main. Occupation of Nice and Savoy (Sept.).

Nov. 6. Victory of the French general Dumouriez at **Jemappes.** He took Brussels and conquered the Austrian Netherlands. The Prussians retook Frankfurt.

Nov. 19. Proclamation of the convention offering French assistance to all peoples who wished to throw off their government.

Nov. 27. Savoy and Nice annexed; the Scheldt opened to commerce.

1792, Dec.-1793, Jan. Trial of **Louis XVI** before the convention. Barère prosecutor; Malesherbes, Desèze, Tronchet, for the defense. Proposed appeal to the nation rejected. January 15, 683 votes out of 721 declared the king guilty. January 16, 361 votes, exactly a majority (among them that of the duke of Orléans) were cast unconditionally for death, 360 being cast for imprisonment, banishment, or death with respite.

1793, Jan. 21. EXECUTION OF LOUIS XVI.

Feb. 1. War declared against Great Britain, Holland, Spain. Britain, Holland, Spain, and the Empire joined the alliance against France, Sardinia having been at war with the latter power since July 1792. **Annexation of Belgium.** The *émigrés,* under the prince of Condé, proclaimed the young son of the dead king as **Louis XVII,** who was a prisoner in the Temple.

Mar. Royalist revolt in the **Vendée,** upon occasion of a levy of recruits. (Charette, Stofflet, Cathelineau, La Rochejaquelein.)

Mar. 18. The Austrians under the duke of Coburg defeated Dumouriez at **Neerwinden,** and recaptured Brussels. Dumouriez went over to the Austrians with the duke of Chartres, **Louis Philippe,** son of Egalité.

At Paris, in the convention, struggle for life

and death, between the **Girondists** and the **Mountain.** After the failure of the plan of the Orléanists, belonging to the Mountain, to make the duke of Orléans protector, all power centered in the **Committee of General Security** and the

Apr. 6. Committee of Public Safety (*Comité du salut public*). Composed of nine (afterward 12) members, who exercised dictatorial power. Leaders: **Danton** (from the very start); **Robespierre, St. Just, Couthon** (these three in July); **Carnot,** who concerned himself exclusively with military matters; **Collot d'Herbois** (Sept.). The third power in the state was the **commune of Paris,** now reorganized on the basis of manhood suffrage and acting through its committee (reduced to 20) at the Hôtel de Ville. **Leaders: Chaumette** and **Hébert** (editor of *Le Père Duchesne*).

Financial difficulties: New issues of *assignats,* based on the lands of the emigrant nobles, the sale of which was ordered. Attempts to check depreciation of the *assignats* by severe penalties.

June 2. Arrest of 31 Girondist deputies, forced on the convention by an uprising engineered by the commune and the Jacobin "machine," with the national guard, commanded by Henriot. Brissot, Vergniaud, Pétion were among the victims. Complete domination of the Mountain, itself the organ of the Paris commune.

June 22. The **Constitution of 1793,** an out-and-out democratic system, was sent to the primary assemblies for ratification, but was never actually put into effect.

July 13. Assassination of Marat by **Charlotte Corday,** an ardently patriotic girl from the provinces.

1793–1794. THE REIGN OF TERROR. **Robespierre** gradually came to dominate the whole government. He was never "dictator" in the modern sense, being checked by his colleagues in the committee of public safety, by the opposing Hébertist faction in the commune and convention, and by the commissioners of the convention sent into the provinces (*représentants en mission*). These commissioners, sent out to suppress counterrevolutionary movements, were often responsible for extreme terrorism in their districts. They collaborated with the local Jacobin clubs and revolutionary committees (*comités de surveillance, comités révolutionnaires*). Horrors perpetrated by Tallien at Bordeaux, Lebon at Arras, Carrier at Nantes, Couthon, Fouché, Collot d'Herbois at Lyons. Some commissioners, however, were fairly clement and spared their regions (the younger Robespierre in the east and south, Lakanal in the southwest).

1793, July. Mainz recovered by the Prussians after a three-months' siege. The Allies also took Condé and Valenciennes. Custine executed by the French for negligence. British **siege of Toulon.** The troops of the republic were driven back on almost all fronts, with the result that revolts multiplied in the interior, frequently inspired by Girondists who had escaped the purge and had fled Paris. Energetic counter-measures of the committee of public safety.

Aug. 23. Levy of the entire male population capable of bearing arms. Fourteen armies hastily organized and put in the field. Caen, Bordeaux, Marseilles conquered by the republicans.

Sept. 29. Establishment of the maximum price for a large number of commodities; fixation of wages. The system was never fully worked out and the *maximum* was frequently violated. It did, however, prevent a catastrophic fall of the *assignats* and insured the provisioning of the armies. The whole experiment was less a socialistic measure than a way to ration goods during an emergency.

Oct. Lyons captured after a two-months' siege. The city was partially destroyed and large numbers of the inhabitants were massacred.

Oct. 16. Execution of Marie Antoinette.

Oct. 20. Defeat of the Vendéans at **Chollet,** and at **Le Mans** (Dec. 12). Revolutionary tribunal at Nantes (15,000 put to death in three months by Carrier: *noyades, fusillades, mariages républicains*).

Oct. 31. Execution of the Girondists (21). Reign of the revolutionary tribunals and the guillotine (Place de la Révolution, now Place de la Concorde). **Fouquier-Tinville,** public prosecutor. Neglect of legal forms; sixty executions a month (including Bailly, Philippe Egalité, Madame Roland, etc.).

Nov. 10. Abolition of the worship of God. Cult of Reason (Hébert, Chaumette, Cloots). Profanation of the royal sepulcher at St. Denis.

Revolutionary calendar, dating from the year one of the revolution (Sept. 22, 1792). The months: Vendémiaire, Brumaire, Frimaire; Nivose, Pluviose, Ventose; Germinal, Floréal, Prairial; Messidor, Thermidor, Fructidor. Each month had 30 days, leaving five intercalary days (*sans culottides*) in the year. Every tenth day a holiday.

Creation of the new army, really an amalgamation of recruits with loyal elements of the old army. Successes of the new forces throughout the autumn, under Jourdan, Hoche, and Pichegru.

Dec. Retreat of the Allies across the Rhine. The French captured Worms and Speier, and took Toulon from the British (first appearance of **Napoleon Bonaparte,** a young artillery officer, closely connected with Robespierre and Jacobins).

1794. Robespierre (representing the committee of public safety) finally succeeded in crushing the rival powers represented by Hébert and Danton. Playing off Danton against the Hébertists, he engineered

Mar. 24. The **execution of the leaders** (Hébert, Chaumette, Cloots, etc.). Thereupon he turned on the Dantonists, whose past gave ample opening for accusation.

Apr. 6. **Execution of Danton,** Desmoulins, Hérault de Sechelles, etc.

Apr. 19. **Treaty of The Hague** between Britain and Prussia, Britain paying subsidies for 60,000 men.

May 18. **Victory of Pichegru's army** at Turcoing.

June 8. **Festival of the Supreme Being,** a cult of which Robespierre was the high-priest, having abolished the cult of reason.

June 10. **Law of 22 Prairial,** bestowing great power on the revolutionary tribunal: juries to convict without hearing evidence or argument. Tremendous increase of executions (up to 354 a month).

June 25. **Capture of Charleroi** by the French.

June 26. **BATTLE OF FLEURUS,** a French victory which obliged the duke of Coburg to evacuate Belgium.

July. **Conspiracy against Robespierre,** by members of the Mountain and by the more moderate elements (Tallien, Fréron, Fouché, Collot d'Herbois, Billaud-Varenne). This was due to jealousy of Robespierre within the committee of public safety, and to rivalry between the two "great committees."

July 27 (9 Thermidor). **FALL OF ROBESPIERRE.** He and his brother, as well as **Couthon** and **St. Just,** were arrested. Being released by friends, they were outlawed, surprised at the Hôtel de Ville, and executed, with 18 others. On the following days over 80 of the party met the same fate. The Paris commune was nearly extinct. This *coup d'état* was carried through by disparate elements, personal enemies of Robespierre, who were opposed to his effort to make France a "republic of virtue." The objective was to remove Robespierre, not to end the Terror. Public opinion, however, forced his successors to adopt more moderate policies.

1794-1795. **End of the Terror.** The convention dominated by the moderates (*Thermidoreans*), who gradually broke the power not only of the commune, but of the Jacobin clubs (the Paris club closed November 12).

Dec. 8. The **Girondists** who had escaped with their lives were readmitted to the convention.

Dec. 24. **Repeal of the maximum.** New issues of *assignats;* increased depreciation.

1795, Apr. 1 (Germinal 12). **Bread riots in Paris;** attack on the convention suppressed; transportation of Billaud, Collot, Barère, Vadier, and other radicals. Growing reaction in the capital and throughout the country. *Jeunesse dorée;* revival of monarchist agitation; return of some of the *émigré* nobility; the **White Terror.**

May 20 (Prairial 1). Further riots and outbreaks. Fierce attack on the convention. Firmness of the president, Boissy d'Anglas. The movement was finally gotten in hand and resulted only in the extermination of the remnants of the Mountain.

Meanwhile the armies had been uniformly successful. Having overrun Belgium, Pichegru invaded Holland in the winter of 1794–1795, the prince of Orange-Nassau fleeing to England (p. 476).

1795-1806. The **BATAVIAN REPUBLIC** founded by the French. Flanders was surrendered to France.

1795, Mar. 5. **TREATY OF BASEL** between France and Prussia. Prussia, financially exhausted and at odds with Austria, withdrew from the war. Saxony, Hanover, and Hesse-Cassel followed suit. France was to retain the left bank of the Rhine until peace should be concluded with the Empire, but was to evacuate the right bank. Northern Germany was to be neutralized. Secret articles: Prussia consented to the absolute cession of the left bank to France and was given assurance of compensation through secularization of ecclesiastical territory on the right bank. On June 22 Spain and France concluded peace at Basel, Spain ceding St. Domingo but recovering other lost territories.

June 8. **Death of the dauphin** (Louis XVII, ten years old) in the Temple. Later numerous pretending dauphins appeared, even in the United States. The death of the dauphin is, however, as certain as such matters can ever be.

June 27. Landing of the British and *émigrés* at Quiberon (Brittany) to aid the royalists of the region (*Chouans*).

July 16–21. Victories of Hoche over the invaders. Over 700 *émigrés* executed. Retaliatory massacre of 1000 republican prisoners by Charette.

Aug. 22. The **Constitution of 1795** (third of the revolution): the executive power vested in a directory of five; legislature of two chambers (*Council of Elders,* or Ancients, 250;

Council of Five Hundred); for the first term, two-thirds of the members of both houses were to be taken from the rolls of the convention. This self-protective proviso led to opposition in Paris and the provinces. The Paris royalists instigated an outbreak of the sections. On the motion of Barras, the convention placed Gen. Bonaparte in charge of its troops.

Oct. 5. (Vendemiaire 13). **The Day of the Sections.** Bonaparte's "whiff of grape-shot." Cannonade from the Church of St. Roch. Complete victory of the convention.

Oct. 26.   The **convention dissolved,** after voting that relatives of *émigrés* should not be permitted to hold office.

5. THE DIRECTORY

1795–1799. THE DIRECTORY. The new government, much maligned by historians and frequently accused of dishonesty and corruption, was faced by an acute financial crisis, the *assignats* having fallen to a fraction of 1 per cent of their face value. Substitution of *mandats territoriaux,* convertible into a specified amount of land, for the *assignats.* The *mandats* in turn depreciated almost at once.

1796, Mar. 5.   Final suppression of the insurrection in the Vendée and in Brittany, by Hoche.

In the **war against the Empire,** the directory, on advice of Carnot, arranged for a triple attack: (1) the army of the Sambre and Meuse, under **Jourdan,** was to advance from the lower Rhine to Franconia; (2) the army of the Rhine and the Moselle, under **Moreau,** was to penetrate from the upper Rhine into Swabia and Bavaria; (3) the army of Italy, under **Bonaparte,** was to drive the Austrians out of Italy and unite with the other armies by way of the Tyrol.

1796. The campaign in Germany. Jourdan and Moreau invaded South Germany, and Baden, Württemberg, and Bavaria were obliged to conclude truces (Aug.), but suddenly the **Archduke Charles** (brother of Emperor Francis II) took the offensive against Jourdan and defeated him at **Amberg** (Aug.) and **Würzburg** (Sept. 3).   Jourdan resigned his command. The archduke then turned on Moreau, who retreated through the Black Forest to the upper Rhine.

Mar. 9.   Marriage of Bonaparte with Josephine de Beauharnais, former friend of Barras and one of the lights of Paris society.

1796–1797. BONAPARTE'S ITALIAN CAMPAIGN. Following the coast from Nice, he defeated the Austrians at **Millesimo** (Apr. 13) and the Piedmontese at **Mondovi** (Apr. 22), compelling Victor Amadeus to conclude a separate peace with France: Savoy and Nice ceded to the French Republic, and the French given the right to garrison Piedmontese fortresses. Napoleon then pursued the Austrians, whom he defeated in

1796, May 10.   The **battle of Lodi** (storming of the bridge over the Adda).

May 15.   Napoleon entered Milan, and then conquered all Lombardy as far as Mantua. The dukes of Parma and Modena, the pope, and the king of Naples purchased truces at the price of large payments in money and art treasures.

May 16.   Napoleon set up the **Lombard Republic.**

July–1797, Feb.   Siege of Mantua by the French.   Four attempts by the Austrians to relieve the fortress.   They were defeated in the **battles of Castiglione** (Aug. 15), **Roveredo, Bassano,** and in

Nov. 15–19.   The **battle of Arcola,** and

1797, Jan. 14.   The **battle of Rivoli.**

Feb. 2.   Mantua surrendered, and Napoleon started on an advance to Rome. The pope thereupon hastily concluded with him

Feb. 19.   The **treaty of Tolentino,** ceding the Romagna, Bologna, and Ferrara.

Mar.–Apr.   Bonaparte crossed the Alps to meet the Archduke Charles, advancing from Germany.   The inhabitants of Venetia rose against the French, and in the Tyrol too the population was called to arms.   In danger of being cut off, Bonaparte opened negotiations which led to

Apr. 18.   The **PRELIMINARY PEACE OF LEOBEN: Austria** ceded the Belgian provinces to France; a congress was to arrange peace between France and the Empire on the basis of the integrity of imperial territory; Austria ceded the region beyond the Oglio, receiving in return the Venetian territory between the Oglio, Po, and Adriatic (which she was to conquer for herself), Venetian Dalmatia and Istria, and the fortresses of Mantua, Peschiera, and Palma Nova. **Venice** was to be indemnified with the Romagna, Bologna, and Ferrara. Austria recognized the **Cisalpine Republic,** which was to be formed in northern Italy.

May.   The French declared **war upon Venice,** under pretext of an outbreak at Verona. Abolition of the aristocracy and establishment of popular government. Occupation of the republic by French troops; also of the Venetian islands of Greece (Ionian).

July 9. Proclamation of the **Cisalpine Republic** (Milan, Modena, Ferrara, Bologna, Romagna). Transformation of the Republic of Genoa into the **Ligurian Republic** under French control.

Sept. 4 (18th Fructidor). **COUP D'ÉTAT AT PARIS.** Victory of the republican party over the party of reaction, which was represented in the council of five hundred, in the council of ancients, and in the directory. The three republican directors, Barras, Rewbell, and La Révellière, defeated their colleagues, Barthélemy and Carnot. The latter escaped by flight; Barthélemy and many of his adherents, including Pichegru, were transported to Cayenne.

Oct. 17. TREATY OF CAMPO FORMIO. (1) Austria ceded the Belgian provinces to France.   (2) A congress was convened at **Rastatt** to discuss peace with the Empire. (3) Austria received the territory of Venice as far as the Adige, with the city of Venice, Istria, and Dalmatia. (4) France retained the **Ionian Islands.** (5) Austria recognized the Cisalpine Republic and indemnified the duke of Modena with the Breisgau.   Secret articles: (1) Austria agreed to the cession of the **left bank of the Rhine** from Basel to Andernach, including Mainz, to France; the navigation of the Rhine was left open to France and Germany in common; those princes who lost by the cession were to receive indemnification in Germany. (2) France was to use her influence to secure to Austria, **Salzburg,** and that portion of Bavaria which lay between Salzburg, the Tyrol, the Inn, and the Salza. (3) Reciprocal guaranty that Prussia should not receive any new acquisition of territory in return for her cession on the left bank of the Rhine.

1796–1801. PAUL I, emperor of Russia, succeeded his mother Catherine II (p. 518).

1797–1840. FREDERICK WILLIAM III, king of Prussia.

1797, Dec.–1799, Apr. Congress of Rastatt. No agreement.

1798, Feb.   The French occupied Rome. Proclamation of the **Roman Republic. Captivity of the pope, Pius VI** (p. 494).

Apr.   French invasion of Switzerland. Organization of the **Helvetic Republic** (p. 498). Geneva annexed to France.

1798–1799.   BONAPARTE'S EGYPTIAN EXPEDITION, prepared under the mask of an invasion of England (*Army of England* concentrated at Boulogne).   Napoleon, having convinced himself of the impracticability of crossing the Channel, persuaded the directory to deliver a blow at Britain's Indian empire, by way of Egypt, a country that had long attracted the interest of French political writers. Napoleon sailed from Toulon with 35,000 men and a corps of scientists (May 19, 1798), surprised and took **Malta** (June 12), and landed in Egypt (July 1).   **Capture of Alexandria** (July 2).

July 21.   BATTLE OF THE PYRAMIDS, outside Cairo. The French easily defeated the medieval Mamluk cavalry, and took Cairo (July 22).

Aug. 1.   BATTLE OF THE NILE. The British admiral, **Horatio Nelson,** having sought the French in vain throughout the eastern Mediterranean, finally located the French fleet in the harbor of **Abukir,** east of Alexandria. Without much difficulty he managed to destroy the fleet, which, being crowded in the anchorage, was unable to maneuver.   Thus Nelson cut Napoleon and his force off from France.

1799, Feb.   The Syrian campaign. The Ottoman government having declared war on France, Napoleon invaded Syria, stormed **Jaffa** (massacre of 1200 prisoners), but was frustrated in his efforts to take **Acre.** Outbreak of plague in the French army; hasty retreat to Egypt.

July 25.   Battle of Abukir. The Turks, supported by the British, had landed at Abukir, but were completely defeated by Napoleon and Murat.

Napoleon left Egypt (Aug. 24) to return to France. **Kléber** in command. After long negotiations, he concluded with the Turks the **convention of El Arish** (Jan. 24, 1800), providing for evacuation of the French forces. This was opposed by the British. Kléber was assassinated (June) and succeeded by Menou, whom the British defeated at Alexandria (Mar. 21, 1801). The French force was repatriated and, by the **treaty of Amiens** (p. 638), Egypt was restored to the sultan.

6. THE WAR OF THE SECOND COALITION

1798, Dec. 24. Alliance between Russia and Great Britain, to which Austria, Naples, Portugal, and the Ottoman Empire adhered. This **Second Coalition** against France was the work primarily of Paul I of Russia, whom the Knights of Malta had elected as grand master.

Plan of campaign: An Anglo-Russian army under the duke of York was to drive the French from the Netherlands; an Austrian army under Archduke Charles was to expel them from Germany and Switzerland; a Russo-Austrian army was to force the French out of Italy.

A Neapolitan army, commanded by the Austrian general, Mack, had attacked the Roman Republic and occupied the city of Rome (Nov. 29), thus beginning hostilities. The French, under Championnet, recaptured the city (Dec. 15) and then overran the entire kingdom of Naples; Ferdinand was obliged to flee to Sicily, while the French proclaimed

1799, Jan. 23. The **Parthenopean Republic,** a client state of France. Even before this (Nov.-Dec. 1798) Gen. Joubert had conquered Piedmont and forced the king to flee to Sardinia (Dec. 9). On March 25, 1799 the grand duke of Tuscany was driven from his dominions and the French occupied Florence.

Mar. 25. The Archduke Charles defeated Jourdan and the army of the upper Rhine, at **Stockach.** Jourdan retreated across the Rhine and laid down his command. His army and that of the middle Rhine (Bernadotte) were united under command of **Masséna.**

Apr. 5. Battle of Magnano, in which the French army of Italy, under Schérer, was defeated by the Austrians under Kray. **Moreau** succeeded to the command, but was in turn defeated in the

Apr. 27. Battle of Cassano, by the Austrian general Melas and the Russian army under Suvorov. The Allies entered Milan and extinguished the Cisalpine Republic. Meanwhile,

Apr. 8. The **congress of Rastatt** had been dissolved. Mysterious murder of the French delegates, Roberjot, and Bonnier, on their way home, by Austrian hussars (Apr. 28).

May 27. Suvorov occupied Turin, and shut up remnants of Moreau's army in Genoa.

June 4–7. BATTLE OF ZÜRICH. The Archduke Charles defeated Masséna.

June 17–19. BATTLE OF THE TREBBIA. Suvorov defeated the French army under MacDonald, which had hurried north from Naples. In the interval the king of Naples returned from Sicily and overthrew the Parthenopean Republic (ruthless vengeance, with massacres). The Roman Republic met with the same fate. The directory now sent to Italy Gen. Joubert with a new army.

Aug. 15. BATTLE OF NOVI. Suvorov and Melas completely defeated Joubert as he attempted to advance from Genoa. Joubert himself was killed.

Suvorov then crossed the Alps by the St. Gothard Pass in order to unite with the second Russian army under Korsakov, who had taken the place of the Archduke Charles in Switzerland.

Sept. 26. Korsakov was defeated and driven out of Zürich by Masséna. Suvorov was unable to recover the position in Switzerland and was obliged to fall back to the Grisons with an army decimated by starvation and want. Masséna took Constance and threatened the flank of the Archduke Charles, who was preparing the invasion of France from the Rhine.

Oct. 18. Convention of Alkmar, by which the British surrendered all prisoners taken in Holland, in return for unobstructed evacuation. The campaign in Holland had been an unqualified failure. The British and Russians had not co-operated effectively and the French, under Brune, had more than held their own in the fighting around Bergen (Sept. 19).

Oct. 22. The **Russians withdrew** from the coalition, disgusted with the conduct of their allies, especially the Austrians. In the interval (May 1799) a Russian-Turkish fleet had wrested the Ionian Isles from French control. The islands were organized as a republic **(Septinsular Republic)** under Turkish protection and under Russian guaranty. The Russians occupied them until 1807.

Nov. 9 (18 Brumaire). **THE COUP D'ÉTAT OF BRUMAIRE. Napoleon** had landed at Fréjus unannounced from Egypt (Oct. 8) and had effected an alliance with the directors Siéyès and Roger-Ducos. With the aid of his brother Lucien (president of the council of five hundred), he overthrew the directory and broke up the council on the following day.

7. THE CONSULATE

1799–1804. The **CONSULATE,** representing a new system worked out by Siéyès in conjunction with Napoleon. **Napoleon was first consul** (term ten years) and was assisted by two other consuls appointed by him (Cambacérès and Lebrun), who had only consultative powers. **1799, Dec. 24. Constitution of the Year VIII,** which was submitted to popular vote (3,011,107 in favor; 1567 opposed). It preserved the appearance of the republic, but in reality established the **dictatorship of Napoleon.** Below the consuls were the following institutions: the *senate* (80), appointed for life from lists of names sent in by the departments, legislative bodies, higher officials; the *tribunate* (100), which discussed measures submitted by the government, but without voting on them; the *legislative chamber* (300), which accepted or rejected these measures, but without debate; the *council of state,* appointed by the first consul, and his chief support in the work of legislation.

The people voted for notables of the communes, who then elected one-tenth of their own number as notables of the departments, of whom one-tenth again became notables of France. From this final sifting were chosen, by the senate, the members of the legislative bodies.

Establishment of prefectures (administration of the departments) and **subprefectures** (for the districts or *arrondissements*). The administration was gradually centralized. **New system of tax-collection:** a *receveur-général* for each department, and a *receveur particulier* for each *arrondissement.*

The new system, which proved to be highly efficient and which has, to a large extent, been retained to the present day, owed much to experiments and experience of the revolutionary assemblies and the directory. The civil service was recruited largely from former Jacobins. In his policy Napoleon, as first consul, followed closely the course marked out by his predecessors.

Napoleon's offers of peace. These were rejected by the Allies, though Russia had left the coalition. Defensive alliance between Russia and Sweden (1799); drawing together of Russia and Prussia. Friction between Russia and Britain over Malta. Renewal of the **armed neutrality** of 1780. Northern convention (1800). **1800. RENEWAL OF THE CAMPAIGN AGAINST AUSTRIA.** In Italy the Austrians, having defeated Masséna at **Voltri,** advanced to Nice (Apr.). Obstinate **defense of Genoa** by Masséna and Soult. Capitulation of the city (June 4) after a horrible famine.

May. Napoleon crossed the St. Bernard Pass with 40,000 men, to attack the flank of the Austrians.

June 2. The French took Milan and restored the Cisalpine Republic.

June 14. BATTLE OF MARENGO, a great victory won by Napoleon, but by an extremely narrow margin. Truce between Napoleon and Melas: all fortresses west of the Mincio and south of the Po were surrendered to the French.

In Germany, Moreau was in command. He had crossed the Rhine in April and had advanced into southern Germany.

July. Moreau took Munich, after which operations were suspended for some months, causing dissatisfaction on both sides.

Dec. 3. BATTLE OF HOHENLINDEN. Moreau completely defeated the Archduke John, who had been appointed to take the place of his brother Charles. The French then advanced to Linz. Another army, under MacDonald, advanced into Tyrol, and in January 1801 Brune, with the army of Italy, crossed the Adige and began the invasion of Austria from the south. This decided the emperor to make peace.

1801, Feb. 9. TREATY OF LUNÉVILLE, which practically involved the destruction of the Holy Roman Empire. **Conditions:** (1) Ratification of the cessions made by and to Austria in the treaty of Campo Formio (p. 635). (2) Cession of the grand duchy of Tuscany (Austrian *secundogeniture*) to Parma, to be indemnified in Germany. (3) The emperor and Empire consented to the cession of the left bank of the Rhine to France, the valley of the Rhine (i.e. the middle of the river) to be the boundary. The princes who lost by this operation received indemnification in Germany. (4) Recognition of the Batavian, Helvetian, Cisalpine, and Ligurian Republics. Germany lost by this peace, taking the Belgic territory into account, 25,180 square miles with almost 3,500,000 inhabitants. The German princes received an increase of territory. The negotiations over the indemnifications lasted more than two years (p. 638), during which time the ambassadors of German princes haunted the antechambers of the first consul to beg for better terms, and bribed French ambassadors, secretaries, and their mistresses.

Tuscany was transformed into the **kingdom of Etruria,** for the satisfaction of Parma. Besides losing Parma (a Spanish *secundogeniture*), Spain ceded **Louisiana** to France, which afterward sold it to the United States (1803). The treaty of Lunéville was succeeded, after conclusion of a truce, by the

Mar. 18. Treaty of Florence with Naples. **Conditions:** (1) Closure of the harbors to British and Turkish vessels. (2) Cession of the Neapolitan possessions in central Italy and the island of Elba. (3) Reception of French garrisons in several Italian towns.

Prussia joined the Northern convention against Britain. **Occupation of Hanover.**

1801-1825. ALEXANDER I, tsar of Russia. Reconciliation between Russia and Britain (in 1801 Britain had attacked Denmark, the ally of Russia, and forced her to withdraw from the Northern convention). The Northern convention was now dissolved.

1801. CONCORDAT BETWEEN FRANCE AND THE PAPACY, concluded after long and trying negotiations. This was part of Napoleon's policy of pacification. The concordat provided that French archbishops and bishops should be appointed by the government, but confirmed by the pope. Clergy paid by the government. The pope agreed to accept as valid the titles of those who had bought former church property confiscated by the revolutionary government. **Pius VII** (elected 1800) was given possession of the Papal States, but without Ferrara, Bologna, and the Romagna. The liberties of the Gallican Church were strongly asserted. By the new organization of the **Université,** an incorporated body of teachers who had passed a state examination, the entire system of higher education was made dependent upon the government. The **Institut National** was reorganized and divided into four (later five) academies: (1) *Académie Française* (1635); (2) *A. des Inscriptions et Belles-Lettres* (1663, 1701); (3) *A. des Sciences* (1666); (4) *A. des Beaux Arts* (1648); (5) *A. des Sciences Morales et Politiques* (1832).

After the withdrawal of the younger Pitt from the British cabinet, and after long negotiations, the

1802, Mar. 27. TREATY OF AMIENS was concluded between Great Britain and France, thus achieving a complete pacification of Europe. (1) Surrender of all conquests made by Britain to France and her allies, excepting Trinidad, which was ceded by Spain, and Ceylon, which was ceded by the Batavian Republic. (2) France recognized the Republic of the Seven Ionian Islands. Malta must be restored to the Order of the Knights of Malta. In consequence of this treaty, peace was concluded also between France and the Porte.

Creation of the **Order of the Legion of Honor** (May 19, 1802). Assumption of regal

state and authority. By a popular vote (plebiscite, $3\frac{1}{2}$ millions),

Aug. 2. Napoleon became consul for life, with the right of appointing his successor.

New (fifth) constitution. The powers of the senate, which was ruled by the first consul, were enlarged; the importance of the legislative bodies and the tribunate was very decidedly reduced.

Napoleon had already become president of the **Italian Republic,** as the Cisalpine Republic was henceforward called. Elba and Piedmont were annexed to France. Military interference of the French in Switzerland, which was torn with civil dissensions. The **act of mediation** restored the independence of the separate cantons, but the country remained still so far a single state that it was represented by a landamman and a diet.

As regards the internal relations of Germany, the treaty of Lunéville was executed according to a plan of indemnification established by France and Russia by the

1803, Feb. Enactment of the delegates of the Empire (*Reichsdeputationshauptschluss*): Of the ecclesiastical estates there were left only: (1) The former elector of Mainz, now electoral archchancellor, with a territory formed out of the remains of the archbishopric of Mainz on the right bank of the Rhine, the bishopric of Regensburg, and the cities of Regensburg and Wezlar. (2) The masters of the Order of St. John and the Teutonic Order. (3) Of the 48 free imperial cities which still existed, only six were left, (the three Hanseatic cities: Lübeck, Hamburg, Bremen, and Frankfurt, Augsburg, Nürnberg). All other ecclesiastical estates and imperial cities were devoted to indemnifications. The electoral bishoprics of Trier and Köln were abolished. Four new electorates: Hesse-Cassel, Baden, Württemberg, Salzburg.

Principal indemnifications: (1) To the **grand duke of Tuscany:** Salzburg, and Berchtesgaden. (2) To the **duke of Modena:** Breisgau (in exchange for which Austria received the ecclesiastical foundations of Trent and Brixen). (3) To **Bavaria:** bishoprics of Würzburg, Bamberg, Freising, Augsburg, the majority of the prelacies and imperial cities in Franconia and eastern Swabia, in return for which, (4) **Baden** received that portion of the Palatinate lying on the right bank of the Rhine (Heidelberg, Mannheim). Baden also received: the portion of the bishoprics of Constance, Basel, Strassburg, Speier, on the right bank of the Rhine, and many ecclesiastical foundations and imperial cities. (5) **Württemberg:** many abbeys, monasteries, and imperial cities, especially Reutlingen, Esslingen, Heilbronn, etc.

The House of Bonaparte

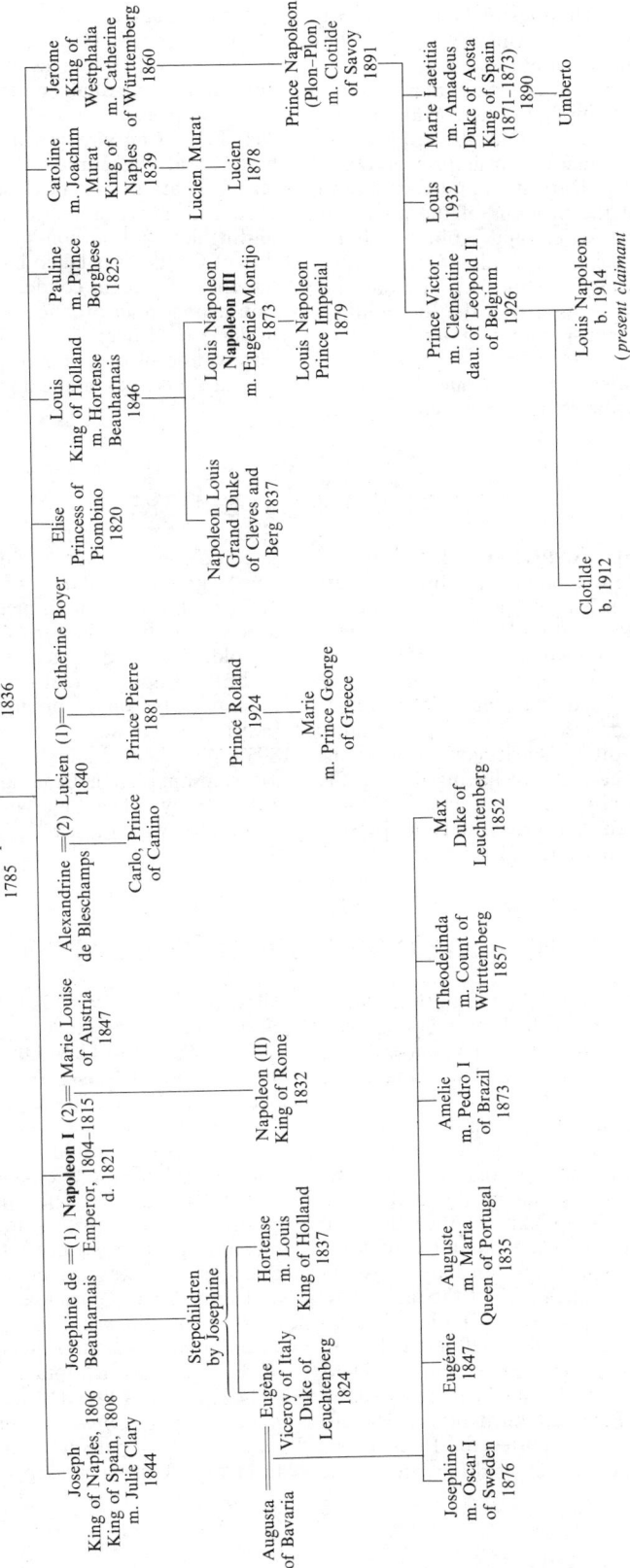

Single dates, unless otherwise indicated, are death dates.

(6) **Prussia:** the bishoprics of Paderborn, Hildesheim, the part of Thuringia which had belonged to Mainz (Eichfeld and Erfurt), a part of Münster, many abbeys, particularly Quedlinburg, and the imperial cities, Mühlhausen, Nordhausen, Goslar. (7) **Oldenburg:** bishopric of Lübeck. (8) **Hanover:** bishopric of Osnabrück. (9) **Hesse** (Darmstadt and Cassel) and **Nassau** divided the portions of the archbishoprics of Mainz, Trier, and Köln which remained upon the right bank of the Rhine. (10) **Nassau-Orange:** bishopric of Fulda, and abbey of Corvey. As a rule the indemnified princes gained considerably in territory and subjects.

New dissensions between France and England, caused by the refusal to surrender Malta and the quarrels of the journalists. The French occupied Hanover, where they nearly exhausted the resources of the state. The encampment at **Boulogne** threatened England with an invasion.

1804, Feb. Conspiracy against the life of the first consul discovered. Pichegru met a mysterious death in prison, **Georges Cadoudal** was executed. **Moreau** fled to America. The **duke of Enghien,** a Bourbon prince of the branch line of Condé, was taken by violence from the territory of Baden, condemned by a commission acting in accordance with the wishes and under the order of Napoleon, without the observation of the ordinary forms of law, and shot at Vincennes on the night of March 20–21.

8. THE FIRST EMPIRE

1804–1814 (1815). **NAPOLEON I,** emperor of the French. He was proclaimed by the senate and tribunate on May 18, and consecrated at Paris by Pope Pius VII on December 2. Napoleon placed the crown on his own head (in imitation of Pepin and Charlemagne). His elevation was ratified by a plebiscite (3,572,329 in favor, 2569 opposed). The imperial office was made hereditary, succession to be in the male line and the emperor having the right to adopt the children of his brothers; in default of such children, the crown was to pass to Napoleon's brothers, Joseph and Louis.

Napoleon at once established a brilliant court: grand dignitaries of the Empire; the eighteen marshals of France; development of a new nobility, with many of the privileges of the old, but based on achievement rather than on birth. Napoleon really revived the absolute monarchy, but on a more modern and efficient basis.

1805. Napoleon made himself king of Italy. His stepson, Eugène Beauharnais, became viceroy of Italy. The **Ligurian Republic** was incorporated with France.

9. THE WAR OF THE THIRD COALITION

1805. Formation of the Third Coalition against France. Great Britain had been at war with France since May 16, 1803, and was now joined by Austria, Russia, and Sweden. Spain was allied with France.

Napoleon hastily broke up the camp of Boulogne and shelved his plans (genuine or pretended) for an invasion of England. The French armies, under Davout, Soult, Lannes, and Ney, marched quickly to the Rhine to meet the Austrian armies under Archduke Ferdinand and Gen. Mack. In Italy, Masséna commanded the French against the main Austrian army under Archduke Charles. Napoleon then took over the chief command in Germany, crossed the Rhine, and marched toward Bavaria, which had been invaded by the Austrians. Bavaria, Württemberg, Baden, Hesse, and Nassau supported the French.

Oct. 17. Mack was obliged to surrender at Ulm, with an army of 30,000 men, whom the French had surrounded.

Oct. 21. BATTLE OF TRAFALGAR, a great victory of **Nelson** (who died of wounds) over the combined French and Spanish fleets. This victory broke the naval power of France and established Britain as the mistress of the seas throughout the 19th century.

The French, after Ulm, marched down the course of the Danube and took **Vienna** without meeting much resistance. In Italy the Archduke Charles was driven back by Masséna, and returned to Germany. Meanwhile, however, a Russian army under Kutuzov and a second under **Tsar Alexander I** came to the aid of the Austrians in Moravia.

Dec. 2. BATTLE OF AUSTERLITZ (*battle of the three emperors*), one of the greatest victories of Napoleon. The combined Austrian and Russian armies were defeated, the

Austrians hastily agreed to a truce, and the Russians retreated.

Dec. 15. Treaty between Prussia and France. The Prussians had been on the point of joining the coalition, but after Austerlitz agreed to cede to France the remaining part of Cleve on the left bank of the Rhine, and also Ansbach and Neuchâtel, in return for Hanover.

Dec. 26. TREATY OF PRESSBURG, between France and Austria. (1) **France** received Piedmont, Parma, and Piacenza. (2) **Austria** ceded to the kingdom of Italy all that she had received of Venetian territory by the treaty of Campo Formio, as well as Venetian Istria and Dalmatia; Austria also recognized Napoleon as king of Italy. (3) **Austria** ceded to Bavaria the Tyrol, Vorarlberg, the bishoprics of Brixen and Trent, Burgau, Eichstädt, Passau, Lindau; Bavaria also received the free city of Augsburg. (4) **Austria** ceded to Württemberg and Baden what remained of the western lands of the Hapsburgs. (5) **Württemberg** and **Baden** were recognized as kingdoms. (6) **Austria** was indemnified by being given Salzburg, Berchtesgaden, and the estates of the Teutonic Order, which were secularized. The elector of Salzburg received from Bavaria Würzburg as compensation.

Dec. The **Bourbons** in Naples were dethroned by a proclamation of Napoleon from Schönbrunn.

1806. Joseph Bonaparte, elder brother of Napoleon, became king of Naples. The Bourbons withdrew to Sicily, where they enjoyed the protection of the British fleet.

Joachim Murat, brother-in-law of Napoleon, was created grand duke of Berg; Marshal Bertheir became prince of Neuchâtel; **Louis,** third brother of Napoleon, became king of Holland (the former Batavian Republic).

July 12. The **CONFEDERATION OF THE RHINE,** organized under French auspices. Napoleon was protector. **Members:** the prince primate, formerly electoral archchancellor; the kings of Bavaria and Württemberg; the grand dukes of Baden, Hesse, Darmstadt, Berg; the duke of Nassau, etc. Afterward all German princes joined the confederation except Austria, Prussia, Brunswick, and the elector of Hesse. Thus a large part of Germany came under French domination. Territorial changes were constantly made: many princes who held immediately of the empire were mediatized; Bavaria was given the free city of Nürnberg; Frankfurt passed to the prince primate (grand duke of Frankfurt).

Aug. 6. END OF THE OLD HOLY ROMAN EMPIRE. The Austrian emperor, Francis II, had already assumed the title of *Francis I, Emperor of Austria* (1804). He now laid down the old imperial crown.

1806–1807. WAR AGAINST PRUSSIA AND RUSSIA. Reasons for Prussia's entry into the war: establishment of the Confederation of the Rhine; annexation of Wesel; seizure of Verden and Essen; garrisoning of French troops throughout half of Germany; Napoleon's offer to Britain to take Hanover away from Prussia (on whom he had forced it a short time before). The Prussians were also embittered by the high-handed execution of Johann Palm, a book-seller of Nürnberg, who had published some strictures on Napoleon.

Dangerous **position of Prussia** at the outbreak of the conflict: the complete separation of the military and civil administration had resulted in the safety of the state resting on a half-trained army composed in part of foreigners, on a superannuated general, and on subordinate commanders who, overconfident in the military fame of Prussia since the time of Frederick II, regarded the French with contempt. Prussia had no allies, excepting Saxony and far-off Russia. Relations with Britain were filled with dissension.

The Prussian army was commanded by the duke of Brunswick, and was concentrated in Thuringia. As it advanced, it was defeated by the French at **Saalfeld** (Oct. 10) and in the

Oct. 14. BATTLES OF JENA AND AUERSTÄDT. The main Prussian armies were completely routed and quickly fell to pieces. A reserve force under the prince of Württemberg was defeated and scattered at **Halle** (Oct. 17).

Oct. 27. Napoleon occupied Berlin. The prince of Hohenlohe and 12,000 men were forced to surrender at **Prenzlau** (Oct. 28). Blücher, after a valiant defense of Lübeck, was also obliged to surrender at Ratkau (Nov. 7). Hasty surrender of the fortresses of Erfurt, Spandau, Stettin, Küstrin, Magdeburg, Hameln; only Kolberg (Gneisenau, Schill, Nettelbeck) and Graudenz (Courbière) defended themselves resolutely.

Nov. 21. BERLIN DECREE: Napoleon proclaimed a (paper) **blockade of Great Britain** and closure of the Continent to British trade, thus inaugurating the *Continental System.*

The French, supported by the Bavarians and Württembergers, invaded Silesia and called on the Poles to revolt.

Dec. 11. Separate peace between France and Saxony. The elector became *king,* allied himself with France, and joined the Confederation of the Rhine.

The war also became extended to the Near East. The French emissary, **Gen. Horace Sebastiani,** induced the Turks to abandon the alliance with Britain and Russia. Deposition of the Russophile governors (*hospodars*) of Moldavia and Wallachia (Aug. 1806) resulted in

1806-1812. WAR BETWEEN RUSSIA AND TURKEY.

1807. The French captured most of the Hanseatic towns and took Breslau and most other fortresses of Silesia. Meanwhile the Russians advanced to the aid of the Prussians. The combined armies fought against the French in the

Feb. 7-8. Battle of Eylau, a bloody but indecisive engagement. The armies then went into winter quarters. King Frederick William withdrew to Memel.

Feb. 17. A British squadron, under Admiral Sir John Duckworth, forced the **passage of the Dardanelles** and appeared before Constantinople. Duckworth was, however, obliged to retire with a loss of two ships (Mar. 3), because of the threatening preparations of the Turks, inspired by Sebastiani.

Mar. 18. The **British occupied Alexandria,** but, meeting with vigorous opposition from the Turkish forces, evacuated again on September 25.

May 26. The **French captured Danzig** and, advancing eastward, fought

June 14. The **BATTLE OF FRIEDLAND** against the Russians. The French were victorious and the Russians fell back. Napoleon then occupied Königsberg and all the country as far as the Niemen River. After the conclusion of a truce, Napoleon met Alexander I and Frederick William III on a raft in the Niemen and concluded

July 7-9. The **TREATIES OF TILSIT,** between (A) France and Russia, and (B) France and Prussia.

A. (1) **Russia** recognized the grand duchy of Warsaw, which was formed from Polish territory acquired by Prussia through the partitions, under the king of Saxony. (2) Danzig restored to the condition of a free city. (3) A part of New East Prussia (Bialystock) ceded to Russia. (4) Russia recognized Joseph Bonaparte as king of Naples, Louis Bonaparte as king of Holland, Jerome Bonaparte as king of Westphalia, a new kingdom yet to be created; Russia, moreover, recognized the Confederation of the Rhine, and accepted the mediation of Napoleon in concluding peace with the Turks, while Napoleon accepted the like good offices from Alexander in regard to Britain. In a secret article, Alexander agreed to an alliance with France against

Britain, in case the latter refused to accept the proffered peace.

B. (1) **Prussia** ceded: (a) to Napoleon for free disposal, all lands between the Rhine and Elbe; (b) to Saxony, the circle of Cottbus; (c) all lands taken from Poland since 1772 for the creation of a duchy of Warsaw, also the city and territory of Danzig. (2) Prussia recognized the sovereignty of the three brothers of Napoleon. (3) All Prussian harbors and lands were closed to British ships and British trade until the conclusion of a peace with Great Britain. (4) Prussia was to maintain a standing army of not more than 42,000 men. In regard to the restoration and evacuation of the Prussian provinces and fortresses, it was settled by the **treaty of Königsberg** (July 12), that Prussia should first pay all arrears of war indemnities.

These indemnities, fixed at 19 million francs by the Prussian calculations, were set at 120 millions by the French, which sum was raised to 140 millions in 1808. After 120 millions had been paid the fortresses were evacuated, excepting Stettin, Küstrin, and Glogau. Until this occurred the Prussian state, reduced as it was from 89,120 to 46,032 square miles, was obliged to support 150,000 French troops.

Aug. Foundation of the **kingdom of Westphalia** (capital, Cassel) by a decree of Napoleon, who reserved for himself half of the domains.

Sept. High-handed proceeding of the British against Denmark, which had been summoned to join the Continental system. A British fleet bombarded Copenhagen, and carried off the Danish fleet. Alliance of Denmark with France. Russia declared war upon Britain. Stralsund and Rügen occupied by the French.

Nov. Portugal, which refused to join the Continental system, occupied by a French army under **Junot** (duke of Abrantes). The royal family fled to Brazil.

Dec. 17. Milan Decree, reiterating the blockade against British trade. On paper, Napoleon had closed the entire European coastline to the British.

1808, Mar. Spain invaded by 100,000 Frenchmen under the pretext of guarding the coasts against the British. Charles IV (p. 490) abdicated in favor of his son Ferdinand, in consequence of an outbreak which had occurred against his favorite, Godoy. Father and son, with Godoy, were enticed by Napoleon to Bayonne and compelled to renounce the throne (May). Napoleon's brother **Joseph** became king of Spain, Murat taking the throne of Naples instead of Joseph. General uprising of the Spaniards.

10. THE PENINSULAR WAR

1808–1814. War of the British against the French in Portugal and Spain. The British landed in Portugal, under command of **Sir Arthur Wellesley** (later the duke of Wellington) and defeated the French under Junot at **Vimeiro** (Aug. 21, 1808). Nevertheless, Wellesley's successor, Gen. Dalrymple, instead of continuing the campaign, agreed to

Aug. 30. The **convention of Cintra,** by which Junot agreed to evacuate Portugal.

The **popular insurrection in Spain** (May 1808) led to retirement of the French, under Murat, behind the Ebro. But on July 20 the French managed to recover Madrid. On the same day another French force, advancing toward Cadiz, was defeated by the insurgents and forced to capitulate at **Baylen.**

Sept. The **congress of Erfurt,** a conference between Napoleon and Alexander I of Russia, attended also by four kings and thirty-four princes, mostly obsequious German satellites. Ostensible reinforcement of the Franco-Russian alliance. Napoleon at the height of his power and splendor. But in secret the French statesman, **Charles de Talleyrand,** was negotiating with Alexander behind Napoleon's back, to frustrate further measures against Austria. Immediately after the Erfurt meeting Napoleon proceeded to Spain in person, with an army of 150,000. He advanced at once upon Madrid (which the French had again abandoned), while his marshals defeated the Spaniards at **Burgos** (Nov. 10) and **Espinosa** (Nov. 11).

Dec. 13. Madrid capitulated to Napoleon. To distract the French from invasion of the south, the British, under **Sir John Moore,** invaded northwestern Spain from Portugal. Napoleon turned against him, forcing his retreat.

1809, Jan. 16. Battle of Corunna. Marshal Soult, succeeding Napoleon in the command, defeated and killed Moore. The British were forced to evacuate Spain. But in Spain guerrilla warfare continued: heroic **defense of Saragossa** (Palafox), which, however, was obliged to capitulate (Feb. 21). The French, meanwhile, invaded Portugal and took **Oporto.** To protect Lisbon, the British sent out Wellesley with reinforcements. Soult was driven out of Oporto, and the British again invaded northwestern Spain.

July 28. Battle of Talavera, an indecisive engagement, which, however, protected Portugal against further invasion. Meanwhile the French pushed on with the conquest of the south.

Nov. 12. Battle of Ocaña, in which the Spaniards were defeated. The French thereupon overran all Andalusia, excepting Cadiz.

11. THE WAR AGAINST AUSTRIA

After the disasters of 1805–1806, both Prussia and Austria undertook far-reaching political and social reforms, designed to modernize the state and develop greater strength for the further contest with Napoleon. In Prussia the greatest reformer was **Karl, Freiherr vom Stein** (1757–1831), assisted by **Prince Karl von Hardenberg.** Reorganization of town government, liberation of industry from burdensome restrictions, abolition of hereditary serfdom, reform of taxation and the whole financial system. Reorganization of the army, on the basis of universal military service, by **Gneisenau, Grolmann, Boyen, Clausewitz, Scharnhorst.** Foundation of the **University of Berlin** (1810), by **Humboldt, Altenstein, Niebuhr,** and **Schleiermacher.** **Fichte's** famous *Addresses to the German Nation* (1807–1808), a tremendous stimulus to national feeling; foundation of the *Tugendbund,* a patriotic organization; development of gymnastics by **Friedrich Jahn;** patriotic poems of **E. M. Arndt,** etc.

Similar, though less extensive, reforms were introduced in Austria, where **Count Johann von Stadion** became the leading figure. Reorganization of the army by **Archduke Charles.** The Austrians, impressed by the difficulties Napoleon was meeting with in Spain, and encouraged by the British, who promised subsidies, decided to take advantage of the situation.

1809, Apr. The **Archduke Charles** appealed to the whole German people to embark on a war of liberation, and with an army of 170,000 began the invasion of Bavaria. Only Tyrol heeded the appeal, and rose in revolt, under **Andreas Hofer.** Napoleon, having hurried back from Spain, engaged the Austrians in Bavaria (using German troops), drove the archduke across the Danube into Bohemia **(battles of Abensberg, Landshut, Eckmühl, Regensburg,** Apr. 19–23) and

May 13. The French took Vienna. Napoleon then crossed the island of Lobau, in the Danube, and fought the

May 21–22. BATTLE OF ASPERN AND

ESSLING. Napoleon was defeated and forced to recross the Danube, where he united his forces with those of the Italian viceroy, **Eugene**, who had driven the Austrians, under Archduke John, from Italy into Hungary. With the combined forces Napoleon recrossed the river and defeated Archduke Charles in the

July 5-6. BATTLE OF WAGRAM. The Austrians, completely exhausted, agreed to the **Oct. 14. TREATY OF SCHÖNBRUNN:** Austria lost 32,000 square miles of territory, with 3,500,000 inhabitants, as follows: (1) to **Bavaria:** Salzburg and Berchtesgaden, the Innviertel and half of the Hausrückviertel; (2) to the **grand duchy of Warsaw:** West Galicia; (3) to **Russia:** the Tarnopol section of East Galicia; (4) to **France:** all the lands beyond the Save River (circle of Villach, Istria, Hungarian Dalmatia, and Ragusa). These territories were, together with the Ionian Islands (ceded to France by Russia in 1807), organized by Napoleon as a new state, the **Illyrian Provinces,** under **Auguste Marmont** as duke of Ragusa. Austria further joined the Continental system and agreed to break off all connections with Britain.

The **Tyrolese,** left to themselves, continued the war against the Bavarians and French with heroic courage, but in the end were subdued. In November 1809, **Hofer was captured and shot** by the French at Mantua. Southern Tyrol was annexed to the kingdom of Italy.

Similar **outbreaks in Germany** ended likewise in disaster: The bold attempt of Major Schill, a Prussian, to precipitate a war of liberation in April 1809 was frustrated by news of Napoleon's victories on the Danube. Schill fell while fighting at Stralsund (May 31). Eleven of his officers were court-martialed and shot at Wesel, while the captured soldiers were condemned by Napoleon to hard labor; after serving for six months in the French galleys, they were enrolled in the coast guard. Another effort was made in 1809 by the duke of Brunswick, who, with a force of volunteers from Bohemia and Silesia, made his way across Germany to Brunswick (July 31). Forced by superior numbers to withdraw, he managed to reach Bremen and transported his men to England.

12. EUROPE, 1810-1812

1810, Apr. MARRIAGE OF NAPOLEON WITH ARCHDUCHESS MARIE LOUISE, daughter of Emperor Francis I of Austria. Napoleon had divorced Josephine and was eager for an heir to his great empire. The marriage was arranged by **Count** (later Prince) **Klemens von Metternich,** the Austrian foreign minister after 1809, whose policy was that of alliance with France as the only protection for Austria during the period of recuperation. Birth of an heir to the throne, the king of Rome (Mar. 1811).

July 1. Abdication and flight of **Louis, king of Holland,** who had refused to ruin his country by joining the Continental system. Thereupon **Holland was annexed to France** (July 9), followed by the annexation also of the canton of Wallis, of Oldenburg, of a large part of the kingdom of Westphalia, of the grand duchy of Berg, of East Friesland, and of the Hanseatic cities. The French Empire thenceforth comprised 130 departments and extended along the entire Channel and North Sea coast. These annexations were provoked chiefly by the desire to stop smuggling of British goods, but as such they proved rather ineffectual.

THE REVOLUTION IN SWEDEN. By the **treaty of Tilsit,** Alexander of Russia had been given a free hand to conquer Finland, which he did in 1808, meeting with but feeble opposition from the Swedes. In the course of the war the Russians, under Gen. Barclay de Tolly, crossed the Gulf of Bothnia on the ice, captured the Aaland Islands, and threatened Stockholm. This situation, complicated by an unfortunate war between Sweden and Denmark, resulted in a military overturn. On March 13, 1809, **King Gustavus IV** was arrested by Generals Klingspor and Adlerkreutz, and forced to abdicate (Mar. 29). His uncle became king as **Charles XIII** (1809-1818) and a new constitution was promulgated, restoring the power of the aristocracy. The new king concluded with Russia the **treaty of Fredrikshamm** (Sept. 17) by which the Swedes abandoned Finland as far as the Tornea River, and also the Aaland Islands. Through the mediation of Russia, the Swedes secured also the **treaty of Paris,** with France. By this Sweden joined the Continental system, and received in return Swedish Pomerania. In January 1810, the Swedish estates elected as heir to the throne Prince Christian of Holstein-Augustenburg, and on his sudden death (May) they chose **Marshal Jean Baptiste Bernadotte** (prince of Ponte Corvo) as crown prince. Napoleon was unable to resist this compliment and Bernadotte accepted the position (Nov. 5).

Thenceforth he controlled the Swedish army and foreign affairs.

ROME AND THE PAPACY. Growing friction between Napoleon and Pius VII after 1805, when the pope returned to Rome. Difficulties about the working of the concordat of 1801, high-handed action of Napoleon in depriving the pope of some of his territories. Pius steadfastly refused to join in the Continental system, as directed, so that on February 2, 1808, the French, under Gen. Miollis, occupied Rome. On May 17, 1809, the **Papal States were declared incorporated with France.** To this act Pius replied by excommunicating Napoleon (June 10), whereupon the emperor had him arrested (July 6) and taken to Savona, near Genoa, where he was held prisoner. Pius continued his attitude of opposition and in 1812 was removed to Fontainebleau.

PORTUGAL AND SPAIN. The British force in Portugal, under Wellesley, was in 1810 threatened by a twofold attack by the French, under Masséna in the north, and under Soult in the south. The French took **Ciudad Rodrigo** (July 10) and the British fell back toward Lisbon, where they held the lines of **Torres Vedras** (Oct.). All through the winter the two armies confronted each other, until finally Masséna fell back into Spain. The British pursued and besieged **Almeida** and **Badajoz.** In the **battle of Fuentes de Onoro** (May 5) Masséna was defeated, while another British force, under Gen. William Beresford, defeated Soult in the south (**battle of Albuera,** May 16). In 1812 (Jan. 19) the British took **Ciudad Rodrigo,** and somewhat later (Apr. 6) captured **Badajoz.** On July 22 Wellesley (Wellington) completely defeated the French under Marshal Marmont at **Salamanca.** Joseph Bonaparte had to abandon Madrid (Aug. 12) and fall back to the Ebro River. Meanwhile, a national assembly (cortes) elected in 1810 in the only part of the country then free, viz. Cadiz and vicinity, promulgated a famous **constitution** (May 8, 1812) of an advanced, democratic type (one-chamber parliament, universal suffrage, popular sovereignty, etc.).

THE OTTOMAN EMPIRE. War against Great Britain and Russia (1806–1812). This was conducted in desultory fashion by both sides. 1807: **Revolutions in Constantinople** (p. 767). 1809, Jan. 5: The British concluded the **treaty of the Dardanelles** with the Turks and withdrew from the war. In the same year the Russians won a victory at **Silistria,** which was followed, in 1810, by the occupation of **Bessarabia, Moldavia,** and **Wallachia.** In 1811 the Russians crossed the Danube and began the advance through Bulgaria. These operations had to be broken off in view of the impending invasion of Russia by Napoleon. Despite French efforts to induce them to continue the war, the Turks were glad to accept the **treaty of Bucharest** (May 28, 1812), by which they gave up to Russia the province of Bessarabia.

13. THE FRENCH INVASION OF RUSSIA

Causes: Latent rivalry between Napoleon and Alexander, both eager for leadership in Europe. Dissatisfaction of Alexander, aroused by Napoleon's marriage and alliance with Austria. Unwillingness of the Russians to carry through fully the Continental system. Irritation of the tsar over Napoleon's unwillingness to grant him free hand in the matter of Constantinople. Addition of West Galicia to the grand duchy of Warsaw (by the **treaty of Schönbrunn,** 1809) aroused Alexander's fear that Napoleon was planning the restoration of Poland. Deposition of the duke of Oldenburg and annexation of his territory to France offended Alexander, who was a near relative of the duke.

Preparations: Alliance of Napoleon with Austria (which agreed to furnish 30,000 men) and **Prussia** (20,000). **Denmark,** however, maintained neutrality throughout the war. **Sweden,** which had been forced by Napoleon to declare war on Britain (1810), now, under Bernadotte's guidance, shook off the French yoke and secured compensation for the loss of Finland. The French having reoccupied Swedish Pomerania and Rügen (Jan. 1812), the Swedes concluded with Russia

1812, Apr. The **treaty of St. Petersburg:** Russia promised Sweden the annexation of Norway, which belonged to Denmark, the latter to be indemnified elsewhere; Sweden agreed to make a diversion against the French in northern Germany.

May 28. Russia made peace with the Turks at Bucharest (above).

June. Great Britain made peace with Russia and Sweden.

Military preparations: the Grand Army of Napoleon, originally about 420,000 men, ultimately, with reinforcements, about 600,000, probably the greatest army ever assembled up to that time. It was only in part French, for there were large contingents of Italians, Poles, Swiss, Dutch, and German (from the Confederation of the Rhine members, as well as

646

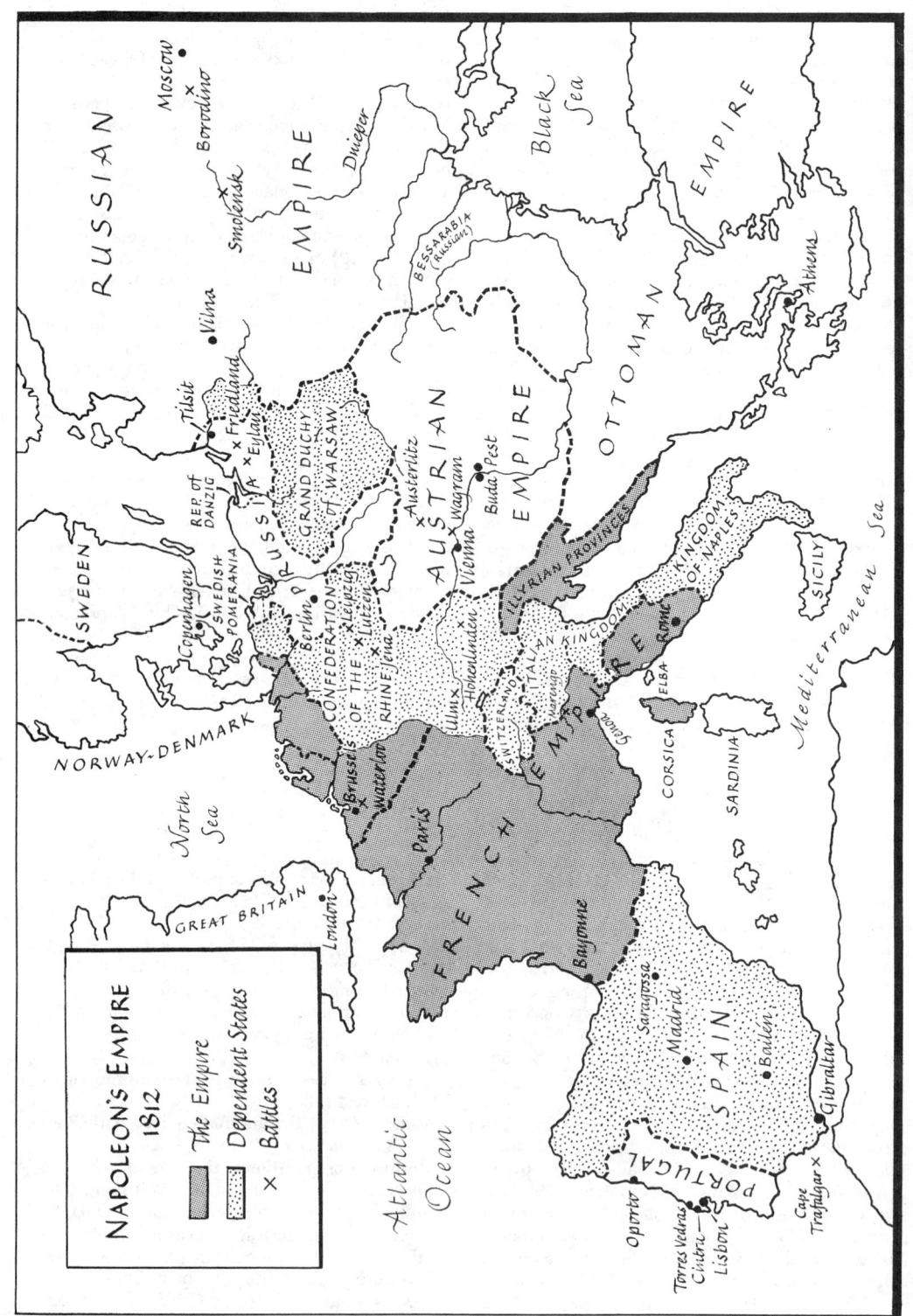

NAPOLEON'S EMPIRE
1812

The Empire

Dependent States

× Battles

Austria and Prussia). The **Austrians, under** Prince Karl von Schwarzenberg, formed a separate army on the right wing, the **Prussians,** under Count Hans York von Wartenburg, held the left wing.

1812, June. Passage of the Niemen River and **occupation of Vilna.** The Russians, under Barclay de Tolly, retreated, allowing the French main army to reach Smolensk without offering battle. The Prussians meanwhile besieged **Riga** and the Austrians penetrated into **Volhynia.**

Aug. 17-18. Destruction of Smolensk by the French. Barclay de Tolly, criticized for his failure to resist the invasion, was replaced by **General Michael Kutuzov,** who fought the French in the bloody

Sept. 7. BATTLE OF BORODINO, on the Moskova River (terrific losses on both sides). The Russians were obliged to retreat farther, and abandoned Moscow.

Sept. 14. The **French occupied Moscow,** which had been deserted by most of the inhabitants. Napoleon established himself in the Kremlin.

Sept. 15-19. BURNING OF MOSCOW, evidently a disaster planned and executed by the Russians **(Count Fedor Rostopchin)** to make the place untenable. Napoleon offered Alexander a truce, which Alexander rejected. After waiting for five weeks in Moscow, Napoleon, frustrated in his hope of bringing the Russians to terms and unable to maintain himself so far from his bases, began the

Oct. 19. RETREAT FROM MOSCOW toward Smolensk. Attacks on the invaders by Kutuzov's army and by swarms of Cossacks and irregulars. Separate corps of the Grand Army fought at **Jaroslavetz** (Oct. 24) and at **Viazma** (Nov. 3). By the beginning of November very severe weather began to set in. Suffering of the troops from hunger and frost, combined with constant attacks by the enemy (e.g. at **Krasnoi** and **Borissov**).

Nov. 26-28. CROSSING OF THE BERESINA, one of the most horrible episodes in the retreat. Ney and Oudinot, with 8500 men, forced the passage against 25,000 Russians. From this point on, the remaining fragments of the army became completely disorganized and the retreat became a wild flight. Napoleon left the army and hastened to Paris, where he arrived on December 18. At about the same time the remnants of the army (not more than 100,000 men) straggled across the Niemen.

14. THE WARS OF LIBERATION

Soon after the catastrophic invasion of Russia, the Prussians deserted the French and joined the tsar in a campaign in Germany. On December 30 General York concluded the **convention of Tauroggen** (an agreement of neutrality) with the Russian general, Count Ivan Diebitsch. Great pressure was brought to bear upon Frederick William III by his generals and advisers.

1813, Feb. 3. Appeal of Frederick William III, issued from Breslau and calling upon his people to form volunteer corps. Enthusiastic response, especially among the younger men and students.

Feb. 28. Treaty of Kalisch, between Prussia and Russia: (1) offensive and defensive alliance, enumeration of auxiliary armies to be furnished by either side; (2) in the event of victory Prussia to be given as much territory as she possessed in 1806; (3) invitation extended to Austria and Britain to join the alliance.

Mar. 3. Treaty between Great Britain and Sweden: Britain paid one million rix dollars in subsidies and promised not to oppose the union of Norway with Sweden. Sweden furnished the allies an army of 30,000 men under command of **Crown Prince Bernadotte.**

Mar. 17. Appeal of Frederick William III "to my people," and "to my army." Establishment of the **Landwehr** and the **Landsturm.** Iron Cross.

Mar. 18. Outbreak in Hamburg. A force of Russians occupied the city. The dukes of Mecklenburg withdrew from the Confederation of the Rhine.

Great preparations on both sides. The Elbe was the boundary between the combatants; Danzig, Stettin, Küstrin, Glogau, Modlin, and Zamosc, being, however, in the hands of the French.

Mar. 27. Occupation of Dresden by Russians and Prussians under Prince Ludwig Wittgenstein and General Gebhard von Blücher, after the withdrawal of Marshal Davout. Flight of the king of Saxony.

The French army and the contingents of the Confederation of the Rhine concentrated in Franconia, Thuringia, and on the Elbe. Napoleon, after the end of April, was at the head of 180,000 men in Germany. He was unexpectedly attacked by the armies of the allies, numbering 85,000 men.

May 2. Battle of Gross-Görschen or **Lüt-**

zen. Victory remained with the French, in spite of their losses. The Allies withdrew through Dresden to Lusatia. Napoleon in Dresden, in close alliance with the king of Saxony, who had returned from Prague.

May 20 and 21. Battles of Bautzen and Wurschen. Napoleon attacked the Allies at Bautzen, forced them to retreat across the Spree, and completed the victory at Wurschen, with great loss to himself. Duroc killed. The Allies retreated to Silesia.

May 30. Hamburg occupied by Davout, after the withdrawal of the Russians. The combatants, exhausted, waited for reinforcements and strove to secure the alliance of Austria.

June 4–July 26. Armistice of Poischwitz, afterward prolonged until August 10 (16).

June 15. Great Britain concluded a subsidy treaty with Prussia and Russia at Reichenbach.

July 5 (28)–Aug. 11. Congress at Prague. Austria played the part of mediator. After futile negotiations (Metternich, Caulaincourt, William von Humboldt), the congress was dissolved.

Aug. 12. AUSTRIA DECLARED WAR ON FRANCE.

The Allies, all supported by British subsidies, put three armies into the field: (1) **the Bohemian army,** under **Schwarzenberg** (with Kleist and Wittgenstein), was accompanied by the three monarchs; (2) **the Silesian army,** under **Blücher** (with York, Sacken, and Langeron); (3) **the Northern army,** under **Bernadotte** (with Bülow, Tauenzien, and Winzingerode).

Napoleon began operations by attacking Blücher, who retired behind the Katzbach. Meanwhile Schwarzenberg advanced from Bohemia upon Dresden. Napoleon left MacDonald to oppose Blücher and hurried to Saxony. Oudinot and Reynier were to march on Berlin, with the support of Davout, coming from Hamburg.

Aug. 23. Battle of Grossbeeren. Oudinot and Reynier were defeated by Bülow, the crown prince of Saxony having looked on inactive. Berlin was saved by this victory.

Aug. 26. Battle of the Katzbach. MacDonald's army was defeated by Blücher, who was made prince of Wahlstatt.

Aug. 26–27. BATTLE OF DRESDEN. Napoleon defeated the Allied army under Schwarzenberg. It was his last major victory on German soil.

Aug. 30. Battle of Kulm and Nollendorf. Vandamme, with a French force that tried to intercept the retreating Bohemian army, was defeated by Ostermann and Kleist.

Sept. 6. Battle of Dennewitz, in which Marshal Ney, attempting to take Berlin, was defeated by Bülow and Tauentzien.

Sept. 9. TREATY OF TEPLITZ, between Russia, Prussia, and Austria: (1) firm union and mutual guaranty for their respective territories; (2) each party to assist the others with at least 60,000 men; (3) no separate peace or armistice to be concluded with France. **Secret articles** provided for the restoration of the Austrian and Prussian monarchies to their territorial status of 1805.

Oct. 3. Battle of Wartenburg. York forced a passage across the Elbe for the army of Silesia. The Northern army also crossed the Elbe.

Oct. 8. Treaty of Ried, between Austria and Bavaria. Bavaria withdrew from the Confederation of the Rhine and joined the alliance against Napoleon. In return, the king was guaranteed his possessions as of the time of the treaty.

Oct. 16–19. BATTLE OF LEIPZIG (*Battle of the Nations*). Napoleon had left Dresden in order to avoid being cut off from France by the three allied armies, which were attempting to unite in his rear. The decisive battle was fought around Leipzig. **Oct. 16:** inconclusive engagement between Napoleon and the army of Bohemia at **Wachau** (south of Leipzig); victory of Blücher over Marmont at **Möckern,** north of Leipzig. **Oct. 17:** the main armies were not engaged; Napoleon sent peace offers to the emperor, who rejected them as too extravagant; toward evening the Allies united, being reinforced with a Russian reserve under Bennigsen (100,000); formed in a huge semicircle, they greatly outnumbered the forces of Napoleon. **Oct. 18:** general attack of the Allies, ending in complete victory after nine hours. The French army was driven back to the gates of Leipzig. The Saxon and Württemberg corps went over to the Allies. **Oct. 19: storming of Leipzig** by the Allies; capture of the king of Saxony. The army of Napoleon, having lost 30,000 men, began the retreat, harried by the Allied forces **(battle of the Unstrut,** and of **Hanau).**

As a result of the French defeat at Leipzig, King Jerome fled from Cassel and the **kingdom of Westphalia came to an end.** The same was true of the **grand duchies of Frankfurt and of Berg.** The old rulers were restored in Cassel, Brunswick, Hanover, and Oldenburg. The central administrative bureau, which had been created under Freiherr vom Stein at the beginning of the war to govern recovered territories, had only Saxony to concern itself with.

THE CAMPAIGN IN SPAIN. The British, unable to take Burgos, had been obliged to fall back again, and King Joseph was able to recover Madrid. But in February 1813, Soult and a large part of the French army had to be recalled to Germany. Once more Wellington advanced to the northeast, to cut off the communications of King Joseph with France.

June 21. Battle of Vittoria. Wellington completely defeated Marshal Jourdan. Joseph fled to France and the French abandoned most of the country. The British stormed **San Sebastian** (Aug. 21) and besieged **Pampeluna.** In the east, Marshal Suchet was driven out of Valencia into Barcelona. Pampeluna fell to the British and Spaniards (Oct. 31). **Wellington crossed the French frontier,** defeated Soult (Nov. 10), and invested **Bayonne** (Dec.).

Nov. Napoleon crossed the Rhine at Mainz. Württemberg, Hesse-Darmstadt, Baden, and the remaining members of the Confederation of the Rhine joined the alliance. One city after another surrendered to the Allied forces: Dresden (Nov. 11), Stettin (Nov. 21), Lübeck (Dec. 5), Zamosc, Modlin, Torgau (Dec. 26), Danzig (Dec. 30), Wittenberg (Jan. 12, 1814), Küstrin (Mar. 7). But Hamburg (Davout), Glogau, Magdeburg, Erfurt, Würzburg, Wesel, and Mainz remained in French hands until the conclusion of peace.

Nov. 8. The **Allies offered Napoleon peace,** leaving France the boundaries of the Alps and the Rhine. When Napoleon failed to accept, the Allies (Dec. 1) adopted a resolution to prosecute the war vigorously and to pass the Rhine and invade France.

Nov. 15. Revolt of the Dutch, who expelled the French officials. The allied army of Bülow entered Holland, while Bernadotte, with the northern army, invaded Holstein, and in a short winter campaign forced Denmark to accept the

1814, Jan. 14. TREATY OF KIEL: (1) **Denmark** ceded Norway to Sweden, with a guaranty to the Norwegians of the maintenance of their rights; (2) **Sweden** ceded to Denmark Western Pomerania and Rügen. At the same time peace was made between **Great Britain and Denmark,** Britain restoring all conquests except Heligoland.

Meanwhile the **Allied armies had crossed the Rhine** (Dec. 21–25). The army of Schwarzenberg crossed through Switzerland, whose treaty of neutrality was disregarded. On January 1, 1814, Blücher crossed the river at Mannheim and Coblenz. Altogether about 200,000 men invaded France. The main army proceeded through Burgundy, while Blücher advanced through Lorraine. Napoleon attempted to prevent their junction by attacking Blücher

at Brienne and driving him back (Jan. 29). But Blücher united with part of the main army and defeated the emperor in the

Feb. 1. Battle of La Rothière. Napoleon retired behind the Aube River. Difficulties of supply forced the Allied forces to divide again. The main army was to advance on Paris by the Seine River, while Blücher was to follow the course of the Marne. Hearing of the division, Napoleon suddenly hurled himself on the various corps of Blücher's army and defeated them in four battles: **Champaubert, Montmirail, Château-Thierry, Vauchamps** (Feb. 10–15). Then, turning on the main army, he defeated it in engagements at **Nangis** and **Montereau** (Feb. 17–18). Blücher was obliged to fall back to Etoges, and Schwarzenberg to Troyes. Meanwhile the Allies met with Napoleon's envoy, **Marquis Armand de Caulaincourt,** in the

Feb. 5–Mar. 19. Congress of Châtillon (sur-Seine). Napoleon was offered the French frontier of 1792, but, elated by his recent successes, he overplayed his hand and the negotiations failed.

Feb. 27. Battle of Bar-sur-Aube. Schwarzenberg defeated Oudinot and MacDonald. Blücher, forced to retire across the Marne and Oise, joined the army of the north under Bülow and Winzingerode.

Mar. 9. TREATIES OF CHAUMONT, between the Allies. These were arranged by **Lord Castlereagh,** the British foreign minister, who had hurried to the Continent to forestall any breakup of the coalition. The treaties provided for continuance of the struggle and guarded against a separate peace. The alliance to continue for twenty years.

Mar. 9–10. Battle of Laon. The allied armies, combined, defeated Napoleon.

Mar. 12. The British, under Wellington, captured **Bordeaux.** The campaign in the south came to an end with Soult's final defeat in the **battle of Toulouse** (Apr. 10).

Mar. 20–21. Battle of Arcis-sur-Aube. Napoleon suffered another reverse. He then formed the desperate plan of throwing himself on the rear of the Allies in Lorraine, summoning the garrisons of the fortresses to his aid, and calling the population to arms. The Allies, with equal boldness, advanced on Paris, and, in

Mar. 25. The **battle of La Fère-Champenoise** defeated Marshals Marmont and Mortier. The French generals threw themselves upon the capital, which was valiantly defended, but which, after

Mar. 30. The **storming of the Montmartre** by the Allies, was obliged to capitulate.

Mar. 31. VICTORIOUS ENTRY OF THE

ALLIES INTO PARIS. The senate, under Talleyrand's influence, declared that Napoleon and his family had forfeited the throne. The emperor, hastening to the defense of the capital, arrived a few hours too late. His marshals refused to join him in a foolhardy assault on the city, so in the end he was obliged to abdicate in favor of his son (Fontainebleau, Apr. 6). The Allies rejected this solution, and on

Apr. 11. Napoleon abdicated unconditionally. The Allies granted him the **island of Elba** as a sovereign principality, with an annual income of 2,000,000 francs, to be paid by France. His wife, **Marie Louise,** received the duchies of Parma, Piacenza, and Guastalla, with sovereign power. Both Napoleon and Marie Louise retained the imperial title. On May 4 the emperor arrived at Elba.

15. THE PEACE SETTLEMENTS

1814-1824. LOUIS XVIII, king of France. He was the elder of the two surviving brothers of Louis XVI. His restoration to the throne was due in part to the failure of other candidacies (notably that of Bernadotte), in part to the clever managing and maneuvering of Talleyrand. The British were sympathetic and Alexander I of Russia was easily persuaded. Louis was induced by Talleyrand and his other advisers to issue a **constitution,** modeled on that of the British, but with many limitations. This was the charter (*Charte constitutionelle*), for which see p. 677.

May 30. THE FIRST TREATY OF PARIS. Leniency of the Allies, due to their desire to strengthen the Bourbon régime: (1) **France** retained the boundaries of 1792, which included Avignon, Venaissin, parts of Savoy, and parts of the German Empire and Belgium, all of which had not belonged to France in 1789; (2) **France** recognized the independence of the Netherlands, of the German states, the Italian states, and of Switzerland; (3) **Britain** restored the French colonies, excepting Tobago, Ste. Lucia and Mauritius (Isle de France); Britain also retained Malta; (4) the Allies abandoned all claims for indemnity, etc.; (5) **France** promised to abolish the slave trade.

Discussion of the general settlement of the reconquered territories among the Allies at Paris, and during the visit of Alexander I and Frederick William to England (June). In view of the complexity of the problem, it was decided to hold a congress at Vienna.

1814, Sept.-1815, June. The **CONGRESS OF VIENNA,** one of the most brilliant international assemblies of modern times. Lavish entertainment offered by Emperor Francis. Most of the rulers of Europe attended the congress, to say nothing of the host of lesser potentates, ministers, claimants, etc. The chief negotiators were: for Austria, **Prince Metternich;** for Prussia, **Hardenberg** and **William von Humboldt;** for Great Britain, **Castlereagh** and **Wellington;** for Russia, the tsar himself and

his many advisers (**Czartoryski, Stein, Razumovsky, Capo d'Istrias, Nesselrode**); for France, **Talleyrand;** for the Papacy, **Cardinal Consalvi.**

The main decisions were made by the chief representatives of the four major Allied powers, the other members of the grand alliance (Spain, Portugal, Sweden) being allowed to participate only in the treatment of fairly obvious or unobjectionable subjects. The full congress never met officially. Talleyrand, in order to gain admission to the inner councils, tried to raise the **principle of legitimacy** to support his claim, but he was taken into the inner group only when the dispute between the Allies as to the fate of Poland and Saxony led them (Jan. 1815) to the verge of war and the deadlock between the two opposing groups (Russia and Prussia against Austria and Britain) had to be broken by enlisting the support of France on the anti-Russian side.

The work of the congress of Vienna was interrupted by the **return of Napoleon from Elba** and the reopening of the war (p. 651), but the various settlements were brought together and signed as

1815, June 8. THE ACT OF THE CONGRESS OF VIENNA. Chief provisions:

(1) **Restoration of the Austrian and Prussian monarchies:** (*a*) **Austria** received, besides her former domain, the Italian provinces of Lombardy and Venetia (to be called the *Lombardo-Venetian Kingdom*); the Illyrian provinces (French kingdoms of Illyria and Dalmatia); Salzburg and the Tyrol (from Bavaria); Galicia. (*b*) **Prussia** received part of the grand duchy of Warsaw (Posen) and Danzig; Swedish Pomerania and Rügen, in return for which Denmark was given Lauenburg; the former Prussian possessions in Westphalia, somewhat enlarged, as well as Neuchâtel; the greater part of Saxony, as compensation for the loss of former possessions, like Ansbach and Baireuth (ceded to Bavaria), East Friesland (to Hanover), and part of the Polish territory (to Russia).

(2) **Formation of the kingdom of the Netherlands,** comprising the former Republic of Holland and the Austrian Netherlands (Belgium), under the former hereditary stadholder as King William I. Britain returned the former Dutch colonies, but not Ceylon or the Cape of Good Hope.

(3) **Creation of the Germanic Confederation,** to take the place of the old Holy Roman Empire. Schemes for a unified German state, advanced by the so-called "patriots," were put aside, and the federal bond was hardly more than a mutual defensive alliance. The confederation comprised 39 states, including four free cities. All other princes remained mediatized. The **Act of Confederation** was signed on June 8, 1815 and was later supplemented by the **Final Act of Vienna** (May 15, 1820).

(4) **The kingdom of Poland:** Most of the former grand duchy of Warsaw was handed over to Russia, and became a Polish kingdom, with the Russian tsar as king. Poland received from Alexander a liberal constitution; Polish was the official language and Poland had her own institutions, including a separate army. **Cracow** became a free state under the protection of Russia, Austria, and Prussia.

(5) **Great Britain** retained Malta, Heligoland, some of the French and Dutch colonies (see above), and assumed a protectorate over the Ionian Islands **(treaty of November 5, 1815).**

(6) **Sweden** retained Norway, which had been acquired by the treaty of Kiel (p. 649). **Norway** was given a separate constitution. **Denmark** was indemnified with Lauenburg.

(7) **Switzerland** was re-established as an independent confederation of 22 cantons. Geneva, Wallis, and Neuchâtel (a principality belonging to the king of Prussia) were now included in the federation.

(8) **Restoration of the legitimate dynasties** in Spain, Sardinia (which received Genoa), Tuscany, Modena, and the Papal States. The Bourbons were not reinstated in Naples until 1815, since Murat had secured possession of Naples for the time being through his desertion of Napoleon.

16. THE HUNDRED DAYS

News of the discontent in France with the government of the Bourbons, and knowledge of the discord at the congress of Vienna, to say nothing of the encouragement of his adherents, induced Napoleon to make another effort to recover his throne.

1815, Mar. 1. Landing of Napoleon at Cannes, with 1500 men. He marched at once upon Paris. Troops sent to oppose him (even Ney's corps) espoused his cause.

Mar. 13. Ban against Napoleon, issued by the Allied monarchs from Vienna. **Flight of Louis XVIII** to Ghent.

Mar. 20. Napoleon entered Paris and began the short rule generally called the *Hundred Days* (Mar. 20–June 29).

Mar. 25. Austria, Britain, Prussia, and **Russia** concluded a new alliance against Napoleon: each engaged to supply 180,000 men. All European nations were invited to join the coalition, and most of them did, but not Sweden, which was engaged in the conquest of Norway. The contingents furnished against Napoleon amounted to over a million men. The **duke of Wellington** in command.

May 3. Murat, who had declared for Napoleon again, was defeated by an Austrian force at **Tolentino.** Naples was captured (May 22); Murat fled to France. The Bourbon king, **Ferdinand,** restored to the Neapolitan throne.

June 14. Napoleon, forced to fight, crossed the frontier into Belgium. Engagement at **Charleroi;** the advanced guard of the Prussians, under Ziethen, forced back.

June 16. Battle of Ligny. Napoleon obliged Blücher to fall back. The Prussians marched to Wavre. On the same day the prince of Orange defeated Marshal Ney in battle of **Quatre Bras.**

Meanwhile the army of Wellington had been concentrating. This consisted of British, Hanoverians, Dutch, and Germans from Brunswick and Nassau.

June 18. BATTLE OF WATERLOO (Belle Alliance). Napoleon hurled himself upon Wellington's army, believing that he had insured against the junction of Blücher and Wellington by ordering **Grouchy** to engage the Prussians. But Grouchy had allowed Blücher to get away. At Waterloo Wellington's army held its lines all day under terrific assaults from the French. The arrival of Blücher toward evening probably saved the day. The French were completely defeated, and the army, pursued by Gneisenau, was soon scattered.

June 22. SECOND ABDICATION OF NAPOLEON. The emperor was soon obliged to flee before the victorious Allies. He reached Rochefort where, after futile attempts to escape to America, he surrendered himself to the British admiral, **Hotham.** He was conveyed to England on the warship *Bellerophon.* By unanimous resolution of the Allies, he was taken, as a prisoner of war, to the island of **St. Helena,** in the South Atlantic Ocean. There he arrived in October. The remainder of his life he spent under close supervision. He died May 5, 1821.

July 7. Second capture of Paris by the Allies. Return of Louis XVIII ("in the baggage of the Allies"). Arrival of the Allied monarchs.

1815, Sept. 26. The **HOLY ALLIANCE,** a document drawn up by the Tsar Alexander I, signed by the Emperor Francis I and by Frederick William III and ultimately by all European rulers, excepting the prince regent of Britain, the pope, and the sultan of Turkey. It was an innocuous declaration of Christian principles, which were to guide the rulers in their relations with their subjects and with each other. These vague and unexceptionable principles were probably meant by the tsar merely as a preface to some form of international organization, along the lines recommended by the Abbé de St. Pierre a century earlier. The importance of the document lay not in its terms, but in its later confusion in the public mind with the **Quadruple Alliance** and more particularly with the reactionary policy of the three eastern powers, which were regarded as bound by a pact

directed against the liberties of the people, camouflaged by religion.

Oct. 13. Murat, who had made a reckless attempt to recover his kingdom by landing in Calabria, was captured, court-martialed, and shot.

Nov. 20. SECOND PEACE OF PARIS. Terms: (1) France was obliged to give up the fortresses of Philippeville and Marienburg to the Netherlands, and Saarlouis and Saarbrücken to Prussia; Landau became a fortress of the Germanic Confederation; the surrounding region, as far as the Lauter River, was ceded to Bavaria. To Sardinia, France was obliged to cede that part of Savoy which she had retained in the first treaty of Paris. In general she was restricted to the boundary of 1790. (2) Seventeen fortresses on the north and east frontiers were to be garrisoned for not more than five years by troops of the Allies (at French expense). (3) France was to pay 700,000,000 francs for the expense of the war. In addition, art treasures which the French had taken from all over Europe were now to be returned to their original owners.

Nov. 20. RENEWAL OF THE QUADRUPLE ALLIANCE, between Great Britain, Austria, Prussia, and Russia. The members promised to supply each 60,000 men in the event that a violation of the treaty of Paris should be attempted. (*Cont. p. 677.*)

C. WESTERN AND CENTRAL EUROPE, 1815-1914

1. THE CONGRESS SYSTEM, 1815-1822

DURING THE **congress of Vienna** there was general agreement between the powers that some measures should be taken to maintain the peace settlements and to guard against the recurrence of war. But efforts to establish a guaranty of the peace terms came to nothing.

1815, Sept. 26. THE SIGNING OF THE HOLY ALLIANCE (p. 652.)

Nov. 20. The **QUADRUPLE ALLIANCE,** signed by the four victorious powers after the battle of Waterloo and the **second treaty of Paris** (p. 652). It developed the principles laid down in the **treaties of Chaumont** (p. 649) and was concluded for 20 years. It aimed at preventing the return of Napoleon or his dynasty; at preservation of the territorial settlement with France; at the protection of Europe against French aggression through cooperative action by the signatories. It was further provided, at the urgent request of Lord

Castlereagh, that representatives of the signatory powers should meet periodically to discuss common interests and problems (**government by conference**).

1818, Sept. Congress of Aix-la-Chapelle, the first of the meetings. This settled the question of the French indemnity payments and arranged the withdrawal of Allied troops from France. France was admitted to the newly constituted **Quintuple Alliance** (the old Quadruple Alliance being retained, however). Questions of the slave trade, the status of Jews, etc., were also raised and there was indication that the congress system would develop into an effective international machine.

1820-1821. Congresses of Troppau and Laibach, called to consider the revolutions in Spain and Italy. Metternich induced the three eastern powers to accept the **Troppau protocol,** directed against revolutions which might disturb the peace. Castlereagh was prevented by English liberal opinion and by British tradition from accepting a policy of interference in the affairs of other states (cf. British state paper of May 5, 1820). This difference of view marked the first serious weakening of the congress system.

1822, Oct.   Congress of Verona, last of the congresses, summoned to consider the Spanish and Greek situations. Castlereagh had committed suicide on the eve of the meeting. His successor, **George Canning** (1770–1827), was unsympathetic to the "European Areopagus," tended to stress the divergence between the "liberal" and the "conservative" powers, and was, above all, determined to prevent intervention in Spain for fear that the effort might be made to extend it to Spanish colonies in the New World. He refused to co-operate with the other powers and, though unable to prevent intervention in Spain, succeeded in destroying the congress system.

2.   THE BRITISH ISLES

[For a complete list of the kings of England see Appendix VI.]

(From p. 473)

a. THE END OF THE TORY RÉGIME, 1815–1830

1815–1820. The cessation of the Napoleonic wars brought, not the anticipated prosperity, but widespread distress. A long and severe **economic depression** followed. Continental markets failed to absorb the overstocked supplies of British manufacturers; governmental demands for military supplies ceased; prices fell; thousands were thrown out of work. The ranks of the unemployed were swelled by more than 400,000 demobilized men. A complete dislocation of the country's war-time economic organization took place.

Remedial legislation took the form of: (1) further protection for agriculture (primarily in the interest of the landlords) by the **Corn Law of 1815,** which virtually excluded foreign grain from England until home-grown corn should reach the "famine price" of 80 shillings per quarter, after which it was to be admitted duty free (this measure was in part a blow at the working classes in the form of higher prices for bread); (2) **abolition of the 10 per cent income tax** (1816, Mar.), but with the concomitant enactment of duties on many articles (raising prices); (3) **deflation of the currency** (1821, May) by the resumption of specie payments by the Bank of England. But the meager and unsatisfactory character of these "remedies" gave rise to widespread dissatisfaction.

Radical agitation turned particularly to **demands for parliamentary reform,** viewed as a panacea for social and economic ills by such leaders as the journalist, **William Cobbett.** Clubs were formed, petitions presented to parliament. As distress became more general, the radical movement revealed more extreme elements, violence was resorted to, middle-class moderates were driven more and more into the arms of the reactionary Tory ministry.

1816, Dec. 2. Acts of violence by a crowd gathered in **Spa Fields,** London, to hear an address on parliamentary reform precipitated the

1817, Mar.   Coercion Acts: (1) temporarily suspending *habeas corpus;* (2) extending the act of 1798 against seditious meetings; (3) renewing the act for the prevention and punishment of attempts to seduce soldiers and sailors from their allegiance; (4) extending to the prince regent all the safeguards against treasonable attempts which secured the king himself. The government's repressive policy stimulated the activity of extremists in the radical movement, which reached a climax in the

1819, Aug. 16.   Peterloo Massacre: a crowd gathered at St. Peter's Fields, Manchester, to hear a speech on parliamentary reform and the repeal of the corn laws was charged by soldiers ordered to arrest the speaker; several were killed and hundreds injured. The result was the passage of the repressive code known as the

Dec.   Six Acts: (1) provided for the speedy trial of "cases of misdemeanor"; (2) increased the penalties for seditious libel; (3) imposed the newspaper stamp duty on all periodical publications containing news (a blow at the radical journalists); (4) once more greatly curtailed public meetings; (5) forbade the training of persons in the use of arms; (6) empowered magistrates to search for and seize arms dangerous to the public peace. The Six Acts rendered the cabinet unpopular, but its prestige was again momentarily revived when a band of twenty extremists plotted the assassination of the whole cabinet (they were to be blown up as they dined together), and the seizure of enough cannon to overawe the populace, occupy the Bank of England, and establish a provisional government. This was the famous

1820, Feb. 23. Cato Street conspiracy. The plot was discovered in time; the conspirators were arrested at their rendezvous. This conspiracy stimulated anew fears of radicalism, and the cause of moderate reform was dealt a serious blow.

Jan. 29. George III, declared insane and represented by the prince of Wales as regent since 1811, died. The regent became king as **1820-1830. GEORGE IV,** promptly had his cabinet institute **divorce proceedings** against the queen, Caroline of Brunswick, whom he had married (Apr. 8, 1795) in accordance with an arrangement of his father, but from whom he had separated shortly after the marriage. With the accession of George IV she returned from the Continent to claim her position as queen, was received with tumultuous demonstrations by the public, which viewed her as wronged by a prince whom it had learned to know as debauched and treacherous. The ministry brought in

July 5. A **Bill of Pains and Penalties,** depriving the queen of her royal title and dissolving the marriage. The bill passed the house of lords by a margin of nine votes, but was dropped by the government (Nov. 10) in face of certain defeat in the commons. The result of the fiasco was a serious decline in the cabinet's prestige.

1822-1830. Following the **death of Castlereagh** (1822, Aug. 12), the cabinet received a series of liberal accessions: **George Canning** as foreign minister; **Robert Peel** as secretary for home affairs—son of a self-made factory owner, Oxford-trained, independent, with a mind open to arguments for reform; **William Huskisson,** liberal financier of wide talent, as president of the board of trade. Between 1822 and 1830 the liberal wing of the Tory cabinet was responsible for a number of moderate but important reforms: (1) Peel secured passage of **legislation revising the antiquated criminal code** by which more than 200 offenses had become punishable by death. The reforms reduced the number of offenses so punishable by about 100, thus making conviction for many misdemeanors more certain, making the punishment more nearly approximate the offense (reflecting the growing humanitarian sentiment of the 19th century). (2) The **first breach in the protectionist mercantile system** was made by Huskisson in the budget of 1823-1825, which reduced duties on certain imports (silk, wool, iron, wines, coffee, sugar, cottons, woolens, etc.), and lifted the secular prohibition on the exportation of wool. Huskisson's reform was a foretaste of the sweeping movement

toward free trade which began in the mid-forties. (3) The **repeal of the Combination Acts** was largely the work of **Francis Place,** master tailor who had retained his interest in the worker's cause from less fortunate days. Place collected a mass of evidence on the hardships occasioned for labor by the Combination Acts, and interested **Joseph Hume,** radical member of parliament, in the cause. Hume secured appointment of a select committee to investigate conditions, and the evidence produced convinced Peel and Huskisson. The acts were repealed (1824, June 21). Phenomenal, though short-lived, **development of trade-unionism.** Many strikes followed, accompanied by violence. A new law (1825, July 6) allowed workers to combine to secure regulation of wages and hours of employment, but, in effect, forbade them to strike by prohibiting the use of violence or threats, and introducing summary methods of conviction.

The sharp divergences in the cabinet between liberal and right-wing Tories had been smoothed over by the conciliatory **Lord Liverpool,** continuously prime minister from 1812 till 1827, when a stroke of apoplexy obliged him to resign.

1827, Apr. 30. Canning succeeded as prime minister with a cabinet of liberal Tories and moderate Whigs, but died soon after (Aug. 8).

1827, Aug.-1828, Jan. Cabinet of the conciliatory but incapable **Lord Goderich.**

1828, Jan.-1830, Nov. Cabinet of the **duke of Wellington,** from whose great distinction and wide popularity much was hoped. But Wellington was sympathetic with the reactionary group in his cabinet and alienated the liberal Tories, who resigned. The complete failure of Wellington's policy in the Near Eastern crisis (p. 770) seriously discredited the cabinet.

1828, July 15. The corn law. The patent hardships (for consumers) of the corn law of 1815 obliged Wellington to introduce a measure permitting grain to be imported at any time and fixing duties on a sliding scale (high when the price of English corn was low and reducing the duty as the English price advanced). The act alienated the landlords, yet won Wellington no credit with the liberals, who remembered that the duke had earlier defeated the law when it was introduced by Canning.

1829. The Wellington cabinet again alienated its own supporters by its **Catholic emancipation policy.** When **Daniel O'Connell,** leader of the Catholic emancipation movement, was elected to parliament in 1828 from the county of Clare in Ireland, the Wellington cabinet was faced by a crisis. Under the provisions of the **Test Act** (p. 463), no Catholic (or Protestant Nonconformist) could hold public office. Welling-

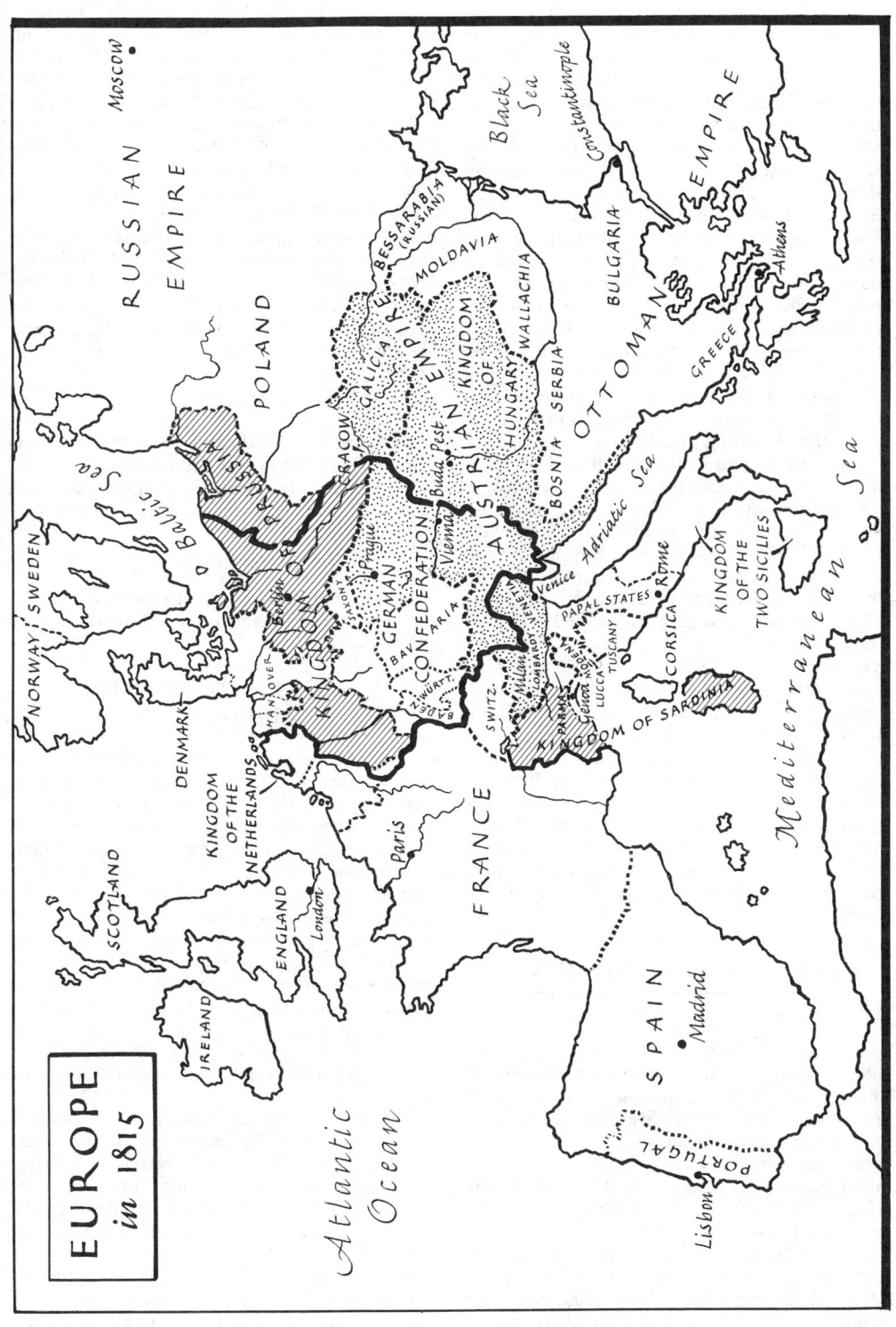

EUROPE
in 1815

Atlantic
Ocean

IRELAND

SCOTLAND

ENGLAND
London

NORWAY SWEDEN

DENMARK

KINGDOM
OF THE
NETHERLANDS

Paris

FRANCE

SPAIN
Madrid

PORTUGAL
Lisbon

RUSSIAN EMPIRE
Moscow

Baltic Sea

POLAND

HANOVER

SAXON

BAV.

W.URTT.

BADEN

SWITZ.

GERMAN CONFEDERATION

KINGDOM OF

Prague

Vienna
Buda Pest

BOHEMIA

CRACOW

GALICIA

BESSARABIA
(RUSSIAN)

MOLDAVIA

WALLACHIA

AUSTRIAN EMPIRE

KINGDOM OF HUNGARY

SERBIA

BOSNIA

BULGARIA

OTTOMAN EMPIRE

GREECE

Athens

Constantinople

Black Sea

Adriatic Sea

Venice
Milan

LOMBARDY

VENETIA

PARMA

MODENA

Genoa

LUCCA

TUSCANY

PAPAL STATES

Rome

CORSICA

KINGDOM OF SARDINIA

KINGDOM
OF THE
TWO SICILIES

Mediterranean Sea

ton and Peel were bitterly opposed to emancipation, but feared that failure to relieve the Catholics of their disabilities would precipitate civil war in Ireland (the Catholic movement had been gathering strength steadily since the turn of the century).

1828, May 9. The **Test Act was repealed,** and **1829, Mar.-Apr.** The **Catholic Emancipation Bill** was driven through parliament by Wellington in the face of vigorous opposition from the reactionary Tories. It granted the Catholics the right of suffrage and the right to sit in parliament, and declared their eligibility for any public office, save those of lord chancellor of England and lord lieutenant of Ireland—all this in return for an oath denying the pope any power to interfere in the domestic affairs of the realm, recognizing the Protestant succession, and repudiating every intention to upset the established church.

The radical and violent **agitation for parliamentary reform** which followed the Napoleonic wars yielded in the twenties to more moderate demands advocated by individual Whigs, notably **Lord John Russell.** The **July Revolution** in France, a triumph for the middle class (p. 678), stimulated the movement.

1830, June 26. **George IV died,** and was succeeded by his brother

1830-1837. WILLIAM IV. The accession necessitated a general election (a requirement abolished by the Reform Bill of 1867), and the reform of the house of commons became a campaign issue. There was a turnover of some 50 seats, almost all of them going to proponents of reform. In caucus the Whigs adopted reform as their program. Wellington maintained an intransigent attitude, but was forced to resign (Nov. 16), ending a continuous Tory rule (with one brief interval) of nearly half a century.

CULTURAL DEVELOPMENTS

(1) Literature

The early decades of the 19th century were characterized by the Romantic movement in England as on the Continent. Lyric poetry flourished. **William Wordsworth** (1770-1850) and **Samuel Taylor Coleridge** (1772-1834) together published *Lyrical Ballads* (1798). The major poets were George Gordon, **Lord Byron** (1788-1824); **Percy Bysshe Shelley** (1792-1822); and **John Keats** (1795-1821).

Essays: In this period, subjective criticism received recognition; the new reviews which began to appear monthly and quarterly gave opportunity for expression of individual opinion on a variety of subjects (*Edinburgh Review,* 1802;

William Cobbett's *Weekly Political Register,* 1802; *Quarterly Review,* 1809; *Blackwood's Magazine,* 1817; *London Magazine,* 1820; *Manchester Guardian,* 1821). **Charles Lamb** (*Essays of Elia,* 1823-1833) and **William Hazlitt** (*Table Talk,* 1821-1822) wrote outstanding critical essays; also **Walter Savage Landor** (1775-1864) and **Leigh Hunt** (*The Examiner,* 1808-1821).

Novels: The popular historical novels of the Scotsman **Sir Walter Scott** (1771-1832) overshadowed the earlier Gothic novels (*Waverly,* 1814; *Ivanhoe,* 1819; *Kenilworth,* 1821; *Talisman,* 1825). In England the domestic novel of **Jane Austen** (1775-1817) proved the local contemporary scene worthy of portrayal (*Sense and Sensibility,* 1811; *Pride and Prejudice,* 1813; *Emma,* 1816).

(2) Painting

Landscapes of **Joseph Mallord William Turner** (1775-1851) and **John Constable** (1776-1837); **Thomas Lawrence** (1769-1830) painted a series of official portraits at the congress of Vienna.

(3) Music

In music there was little of interest except for the church and organ music of **Samuel Wesley** (1766-1836).

b. AN ERA OF REFORM, 1830-1846

1830-1834. The Tory cabinet of Wellington was succeeded by the Whig cabinet of **Earl Grey** (1764-1845), including a membership of distinguished talents, widely representative of liberal opinion and determined on **parliamentary reform.** The existing system of representation reflected gross inequalities, the result of ancient provisions whose effect was greatly exaggerated by the growth and migration of population under the impact of the industrial revolution. In *pocket boroughs* the patron enjoyed the absolute right of returning candidates. In *rotten boroughs* the elections were controlled by bribery and influence. On the eve of the reform not more than one-third of the house of commons was freely chosen. Electoral inequalities constituted a second serious abuse: in various boroughs the right to vote rested on the possession of a forty-shilling freehold or some other financial basis, certain residence qualifications, membership in the governing body of the municipality (*close boroughs*). Even in boroughs of democratic electoral qualification the number of electors was usually small enough to be effectively bribed. Electoral conditions in the counties were better, but abuses were many.

Grey's ministry undertook to reform this situation by redistributing parliamentary seats and extending the franchise.

1831, Mar. 22. The **First Reform Bill,** the work of Lord John George Durham and Lord John Russell, was passed on second reading by a majority of one, but defeated by amendment in the committee stage.

Apr. 19. Grey secured a **dissolution of parliament,** followed by a bitterly fought election, with public opinion warmly supporting "The Bill, the whole Bill, and nothing but the Bill." The election was a Whig triumph.

Sept. 21. The **Second Reform Bill** passed the new house of commons with a majority of 109, but the house of lords threw the measure out on second reading (Oct. 8). The ministry prorogued parliament and prepared a new bill. Extraparliamentary agitation now became violent, riots broke out, the mob held Bristol for two days.

1832. The **THIRD REFORM BILL** was passed by the commons with a larger majority (Mar. 23). But the lords in committee demanded amendments unacceptable to the ministry. They were greeted by a new blast of popular agitation. With the country on the verge of civil war, Grey advised the king to create enough new peers to pass the measure. The king refused, the cabinet resigned, Wellington was unable to form a ministry. The king recalled Grey, promised to appoint the new peers, but instead induced the recalcitrant Tories to withdraw during the final vote in the lords (June 4).

The act disfranchised 56 *pocket* and *rotten* boroughs (returning 111 members); 32 small boroughs were deprived of one member each. The available 143 seats were redistributed: 22 large towns received two each, 21 towns a single member each; county membership was increased from 94 to 159; 13 remaining members went to Scotland and Ireland. Extension of the franchise took the form of eliminating antiquated forms in the boroughs and giving the vote to all householders paying £10 annual rental. In the counties the area of enfranchisement was enlarged by retaining the 40-shilling freehold qualification for those owning their own land; other cases were covered by a £10 qualification for freeholders, copyholders, leaseholders for 60 years; and a qualification of £50 was fixed for leaseholders of shorter terms and tenants-at-will.

July–Aug. Scotland and Ireland were subjects of separate bills, in which the franchise was remodeled upon lines similar to those adopted in England.

The Reform Bill shifted the balance of power to the industrial and commercial class,

revealed that the house of lords could not defy popular will, opened an era of reform. It failed to concede the secret ballot and left the bulk of the population still disfranchised.

1831. Tithe War in Ireland. The Irish, overwhelmingly Catholic, resented the enforced payment of **tithes** to support the established Episcopal Church and resorted to violence.

1833, Apr. A **Coercion Bill** gave the lord lieutenant unlimited powers of suppressing public meetings, of subjecting disturbed districts to martial law.

Aug. 2. The **Irish Church Temporalities Bill** introduced by the government as a counterpoise to coercion. The bill established a graduated tax on clerical incomes to relieve ratepayers from the burden of parish expenses, and provided for the reduction of the Irish episcopate. The bill failed to provide for the application to secular purposes of the savings effected and so outraged O'Connell and his following.

Aug. 23. Abolition of slavery in the colonies. Edward Stanley, secretary for Ireland, had incurred such unpopularity that he was transferred to the colonial secretaryship, where he carried the bill emancipating the slaves in the British colonies. The law was the crowning act in the long campaign of the abolitionists, led by **William Wilberforce,** agitation dating particularly from the abolition of the slave trade (p. 863). The act provided for the immediate emancipation of children under six, a period of apprenticeship for those over six (eliminated four years later), and compensation of £20,000,000 to slaveowners.

Aug. 29. Factory Act. Investigations had revealed the frightful working conditions to which children were often subjected and against which the factory acts of 1802 and 1816 gave quite inadequate protection. The result was the factory act of 1833, carried in the face of opposition from the Tories and many Whigs (imbued with *laissez-faire* doctrine). It forbade employment of children under nine years, restricted labor of those between nine and 13 to 48 hours a week or nine in a single day, and of those from 13 to 18 years to 69 hours a week or 12 in a day. Children under 13 were to have two hours' schooling per day. A system of paid inspectors was set up. The law applied only to factories in the textile industries and was in itself inadequate, but it was the forerunner of further remedial legislation.

1834. Growth of trade-unionism. The movement had taken a phenomenal but short-lived spurt after the repeal of the Combination Laws in 1825, and was given momentum by the general dissatisfaction of the workers with the Reform Act of 1832. The pioneer was **John Doherty,** at whose instigation the **National Association for the Protection of Labor** (a federation of about 150 unions) had been formed in 1830. As the movement spread after 1832, Doherty and **Robert Owen** decided to attempt to form a general union of skilled and unskilled laborers.

Jan. The **Grand National Consolidated Trades Union** was organized. Within a few weeks it had over 500,000 members. The avowed policy was to promote a **general strike** for an eight-hour day. But the organization suffered from the confusion of trade-union aims with the co-operative and socialist aspirations of Owen and his disciple, **William Thompson.** The Grand National made one or two small and futile experiments in co-operative production, but spent most of its energies in a series of aggressive and unsuccessful strikes. The government became seriously alarmed and resorted to drastic measures.

Mar. **Six Dorchester laborers,** who had formed a lodge of the Grand National, were sentenced to seven years' imprisonment. The Grand National dissolved in October, Owen quit the field, and a period of general apathy followed in the labor movement.

Apr. 22. **Quadruple Alliance** with France, Spain, and Portugal (p. 652).

July 9. **Grey resigned.**

July–Nov. First cabinet of **Lord Melbourne,** a right wing Liberal (the terms *Liberals* and *Conservatives* were beginning to replace the older *Whigs* and *Tories*). The king had hoped for a coalition government (with Peel), was disappointed at the reconstitution of the Whig ministry, and welcomed an early opportunity to accept the **resignation of Melbourne** (Nov. 15), who felt the strength of his party shaken by the loss of the leader in the house of commons, **Lord John Althrop,** who became Earl Spencer on the death of his father.

Aug. 14. **The new poor law.** Earlier relief legislation was fundamentally altered and given coherent form by the new law, which limited payment of charitable doles to sick and aged paupers and established workhouses where ablebodied paupers were put to work. The law ended the vicious system of giving the dole to laborers as a supplement to low wages. It supplanted the great poor law of 1601 and its amendments of 1722, 1782, and 1795.

Nov.–1835, Apr. The short-lived **first Peel ministry.** In the general election of January 1835 Peel set forth his conceptions of a new **liberal Conservatism** (*Tamworth Manifesto*): acceptance of the Reform Act of 1832, readiness to proceed further with "judicious reforms." He won wide support from the moderates of both parties, actively undertook the cause of reform, but was defeated shortly thereafter on the Irish question.

1835–1839. **Second Melbourne cabinet.** Melbourne promptly undertook the reform of the internal organization and administration of municipal government—untouched by the Reform Act, generally in the hands of self-elected, irresponsible, and corrupt councils.

1835, Sept. 9. The **Municipal Corporations Bill** provided a uniform plan of government for all boroughs and cities (London and 67 small towns excepted): a town council was to consist of mayor, aldermen, and councilors, the last-named elected for three years by the ratepayers, together with the freemen who had survived the Reform Act (the freemen were a limited number of privileged persons who had formerly chosen the corporations). The mayor was to be chosen annually, the aldermen every six years by the councilors from among their own number.

Further reforms followed in 1836, notably legislation permitting civil marriages, some equalizations of episcopal and clerical incomes, permission to prisoners charged with felony to have full benefit of counsel, etc.

William IV died (1837, June 20) and was succeeded by his youthful niece,

1837–1901. **VICTORIA** (1819–1901), then eighteen. Victoria was the daughter of the duke of Kent (d. 1820) and the duchess, a princess of Saxe-Coburg (for the Hanoverian dynasty see p. 469), who had brought up Victoria in England, but surrounded her by German influences, notably that of her brother Leopold (king of the Belgians, 1831, p. 673). Victoria's education had been solid and sensible, and she brought to her heavy duties graciousness and poise rarely associated with one of her age. She was self-willed on occasion, "rebuked" her ministers, but made no serious attempt to invade their rights under the parliamentary system despite the influence of her German adviser, **Baron Christian von Stockmar,** who urged her to take a stand of greater independence.

The Melbourne government favored a conciliatory Irish policy (opposed by the Conservatives); it was faced by three Irish problems—poor relief, municipal reform, and the settlement of tithes.

1838, July 31. The **poor law bill** extended provisions similar to those in the **new poor law** to Ireland. It was opposed by the Irish members of the house of commons on the ground that the poor were too numerous to be provided for in workhouses. A second bill **converted the tithes** into a fixed rent charge, 75 per cent of their nominal value and payable by the landlord. The municipal corporations in Ireland were controlled by self-appointed Protestant councils. A **new municipal act** (1840) conferred the right to vote on all persons paying £10 rent a year.

Weakened by attack on its policy in England, Ireland, and Canada (p. 833) the Melbourne government was in no position to survive the disaffection occasioned by the settlement of the

1839, Apr. 9.   Jamaica problem. Following emancipation of the slaves, economic conditions had grown rapidly worse for the planters, who were guilty of great brutality toward their former slaves. The upshot was the suspension for five years of the **Jamaica constitution,** a drastic measure carried by only five votes in the commons. Melbourne felt his position seriously shaken, resigned soon after (May 7).

May.   Cabinet crisis. The queen turned regretfully to Wellington, then to Peel. The latter refused to form a ministry unless certain that the queen's lady attendants (all members of Whig families) were changed (the **Bedchamber Question**). The queen was indignant and turned again to Melbourne, who formed

1839, May–1841, Aug.   The third Melbourne ministry.

1839.   CHARTIST AGITATION. The Chartist movement was a direct outcome of dissatisfaction with the reforms of the Whigs among the laboring classes and of the failure of the trade-union movement. It had its origin when (1836) a **Workingmen's Association** in London set forth its program in a petition or **charter** to parliament. This demanded: (1) manhood suffrage; (2) vote by ballot; (3) abolition of property qualification for members of parliament; (4) payment of members; (5) equal electoral districts; (6) annual parliaments. The working public was rapidly converted to this program by missionaries who toured the country, held huge meetings, and organized torchlight processions. Gradually more radical elements emerged, notably **Feargus O'Connor,** who headed a **party of physical force** opposed by **William Lovett's party of moral force,** both within the larger movement.

Feb. The first **National Convention of Chartists** met in London.

May 13. The **charter was presented to parliament,** which rejected it. The convention adjourned to Birmingham, issued a radical manifesto appealing to members to defend liberty by use of arms.

July.   Serious riots in Birmingham and elsewhere.

Nov. 4. In a **riot at Newport** (Wales) the crowd was fired on by the constables and 20

were killed. **John Frost,** the leader, and others were sentenced to death, but ultimately transported to the penal colonies. The movement then turned back to more moderate channels.

Nov. 3.   Outbreak of the Opium War with China (p. 910).

1840, Jan. 10. A pamphlet by **Rowland Hill** on postal reform led to the institution of **uniform penny postage** (for letters under half an ounce to any point in the United Kingdom), a substitute for the previous exorbitant rates and the cumbersome system of charges varying with size, weight, and shape of letters—a revolution in communication.

Feb. 10. The **queen married** her first cousin, **Albert of Saxe-Coburg-Gotha,** a sober and sensible prince, to whom she became profoundly devoted. The marriage was generally condemned by Conservative leaders, and Albert suffered from rumors that he was a "papist" (although all his family were Lutheran), from the demands of the queen that he be named *king consort* (he was made *prince consort* by royal letters patent only in 1857), and that he be voted a civil list of £50,000 (reduced to £30,000), etc. Albert succeeded Melbourne as royal private secretary, and in time became, with the queen, joint ruler of the nation, in fact if not in name.

In the spring of 1841 Melbourne's government was twice defeated on a tariff measure in the commons, appealed to the country, and was again defeated by the Conservatives.

1841, Aug. 28. Melbourne finally resigned following a vote of censure, and was succeeded by

1841, Sept.–1846, June. The **second Peel cabinet,** which included a number of men of distinction and young men of promise, notably **William Ewart Gladstone** as vice-president of the board of trade. Peel turned first to the deficit, the most pressing problem. He **modified the sliding scale of 1828 on corn imports** (1842, Apr. 29) to encourage importation; **removed prohibitory duties** and drastically reduced duties on a vast number of imports, especially raw materials and prime foodstuffs; **revived the income tax** to provide against possible losses from lower tariffs; **abolished import and export duties on wool.** Peel, a protectionist, was already moving in the direction of free trade.

1842, Apr. 12–May 12.   Second National Convention of Chartists in London. A second petition to parliament was again rejected (May 3) and a "turn-out" followed in August. In Lancashire the strike spread rapidly and the moderates were again outmaneuvered by the radicals. Nevertheless the movement gradually collapsed. It remained in eclipse until

The House of Saxe–Coburg–Windsor (1837–   )

(From p. 469)

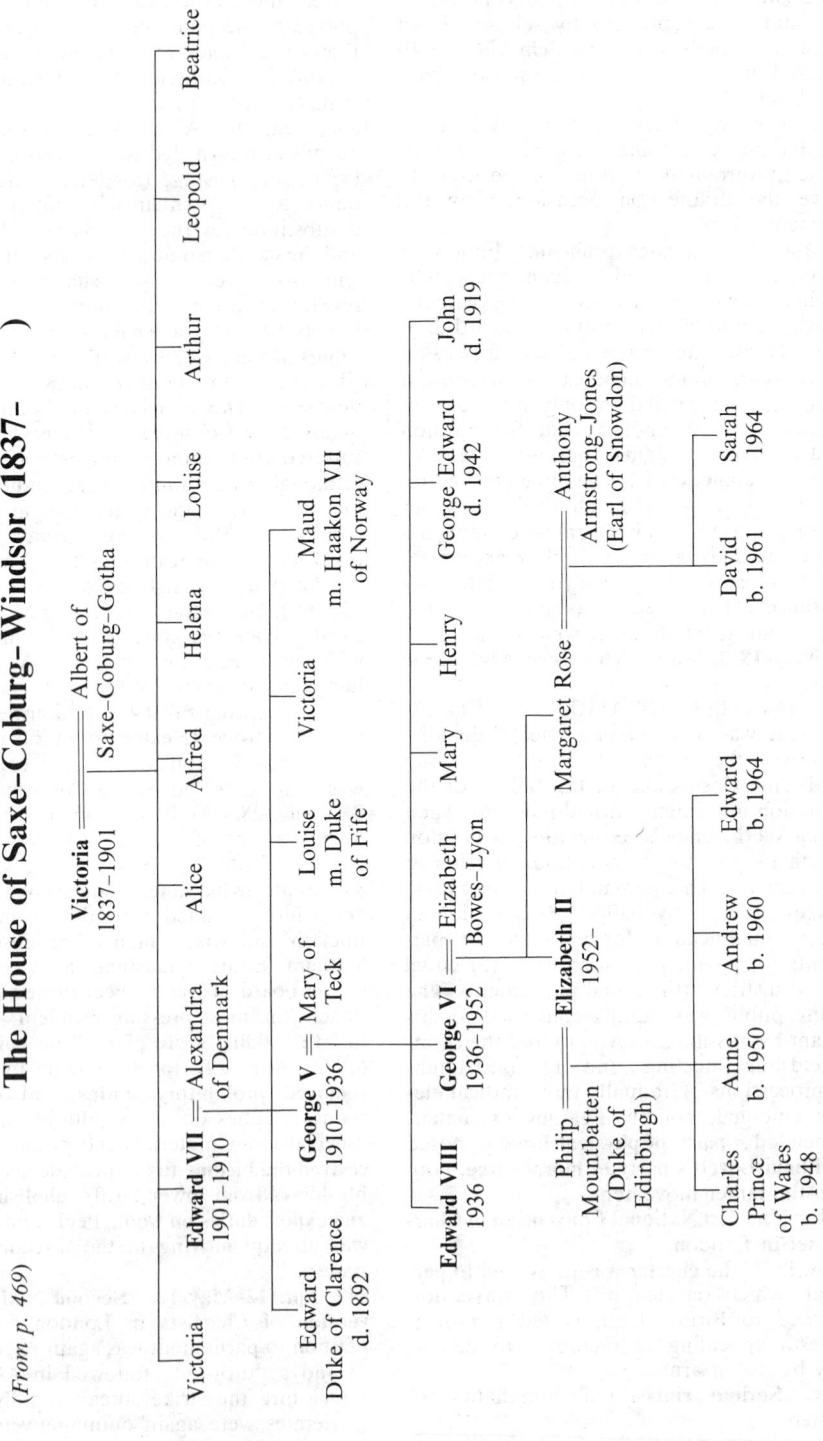

1848, when a last national convention was held, a huge demonstration arranged, and the charter once more presented to parliament.

Aug. 9. Webster-Ashburton treaty with the United States (p. 813).

1844. The **Bank Charter Act,** designed to meet the problem presented by the rapid growth of joint-stock banks. These issued great quantities of paper money at a time when British gold reserves were being depleted by shipments abroad, largely to the United States. The Bank Charter Act separated the banking department from the note-issuing department of the Bank of England; required that note issues of the bank should be covered by coin or bullion, except for £14,000,000 covered by government securities; prohibited new banks from issuing notes and limited old banks to the existing amount. The tendency of the act was to eliminate by degrees all notes except those of the Bank of England.

1845. Peel's second free-trade budget eliminated export duties entirely, and also duties on cotton, glass, etc.

1845. Formation of the **National Association of the United Traders for the Protection of Labor,** marking the revival of the trade-union movement. The new organization undertook to deal with disputes between master and men, and to look after the interests of labor in parliament. The program showed that the movement had discarded the aggressive policy and ambitious aims of the years 1830–1834. Strikes were deprecated and the idea of the general strike abandoned in favor of conciliation and arbitration.

1845–1846. Anti-corn law agitation. This gradually absorbed much of the interest of the working classes. It centered in Manchester and was fostered by the political leaders of the **Manchester School,** notably **Richard Cobden** and **John Bright,** both manufacturers of middle-class origin. Their interests extended not only to free corn (i.e. grain import), but to **free trade** in general, in which they saw a boon both for the workers (cheap food and higher wages) and factory owners (cheap raw materials and the expansion of markets). The **Manchester Anti-Corn Law Association** (1838) was launched in the midst of the economic depression which began in 1837. Similar organizations rapidly appeared elsewhere, and all joined to form the **Anti-Corn Law League** (1839). The widespread propaganda of the league was met by the bitter opposition of Conservative landlords, but was carried to the farmers as well as the workers. The farmers were attracted by the argument that free trade meant low prices for means of subsistence, and cheap food meant low wages, by which

Britain would be able to meet successfully foreign competition. The argument that appealed to the workers was as follows: the abolition of the corn duties would reduce the price of food, which would enable the people to spend more on manufactured goods and so increase the demand for them. This in turn would lead to more employment and higher wages in industry.

Peel's support for corn law reform finally came as a result of the ruin of the Irish potato crop and the consequent threat of famine in the island unless prompt relief measures were taken.

1845, Nov. 22. The Whig leader, **Lord John Russell,** announced his conversion to free trade. Unable to forestall a Whig success by the enactment of a repeal measure, **Peel resigned** (Dec. 5), but returned to office (Dec. 20) when Russell was unable to form a government.

1846, Jan. ff. New free-trade proposals met with stiff resistance from a block of Conservatives led by **Benjamin Disraeli,** who denounced Peel for betraying the protectionist principles of his party. A struggle of two months was followed by the

1846, June 6. REPEAL OF THE CORN LAWS. After passage of both the corn and customs bills by the commons (May 15), Wellington again induced the lords to yield. The **corn law** provided for the immediate repeal of earlier legislation and fixed the duty on corn at a shilling a quarter from 1849, preserving a small protective duty in the intervening years. The **customs law** abolished the duties on all live animals and nearly every kind of meat, and reduced the duties on cheese, butter, and other foods. Many duties on manufactured goods were abolished and others greatly reduced.

June 15. Oregon Boundary Treaty with the United States (p. 814).

June 29. Peel's government was overthrown by a revolt led by **Benjamin Disraeli,** who objected to a new coercion bill for Ireland.

c. PALMERSTON AND RUSSELL, 1846–1868

1846, July–1852, Feb. Cabinet of Lord John Russell.

1847–1848. Young Ireland. The Irish famine of the forties resulted in the growth of a revolutionary movement in the island. Even before the **death of Daniel O'Connell** (1847), the leadership of the Irish nationalists had passed to the **Young Ireland Party** (founded 1840), under **William Smith O'Brien.** This radical group rejected O'Connell's peaceful methods to secure repeal of the union. A series of agrarian crimes in the autumn of 1847 was followed by the suspension of the *Habeas Corpus* Act for Ireland. This measure, together with news of the revolutions on the Continent, precipitated an **insurrection in Tipperary** (1848, July 29), O'Brien hoping that the peasantry would support it. The rising proved abortive, as the rebels were unequal to the forces of the constabulary.

1850. The **Don Pacifico affair.** Don Pacifico was a Moorish Jew, but a British subject. He held large claims against the Greek government which he pressed with vigor until an anti-Semitic mob burned his house in Athens (1849, Dec.). Palmerston ordered a British squadron to the Piraeus to force a settlement of this and other claims on the Greek government. The Greeks proving obstinate, the British laid an **embargo on all Greek vessels** in the Piraeus and finally seized them (1850, Jan.). After abortive mediation by the French, the Greeks were eventually forced to comply (Apr. 26). Palmerston defended his action in his greatest parliamentary speech (June 29), in which he appealed to British pride and nationalism (*civis Romanus sum*).

1850–1851. Formation of the **Amalgamated Society of Engineers,** a new type of labor organization based on high contributions and provision of benefits as well as direct action and collective bargaining. A number of further "amalgamated societies" were organized and their leaders gradually assumed control of the trade-union movement.

The **Oxford Movement** centered at Oxford, and had as its chief **John H. (later Cardinal) Newman.** It endeavored to prove that the doctrines of the Anglican Church were identical with those of the Roman Catholic Church, therefore that every Catholic doctrine might be held by Anglicans. In 1845 Newman and many of his associates seceded to the Church of Rome, whereupon the English people, thoroughly Protestant, became alarmed, fearing that the real object of the *Tractarians* (so called from the tracts they published) was to reconcile England with Rome. Popular apprehension of "papal aggression" was stirred by a papal bull (1850, Sept. 30) setting up a hierarchy of bishops in England who were to derive their titles from English sees created by the bull. The sympathies of the Whig ministry, and especially of Lord John Russell, the prime minister, were with the people.

1851, Feb. The **Ecclesiastical Titles Bill,** which forbade the assumption by priests and bishops of the Roman Catholic Church of titles taken from any territory or place within the United Kingdom, and declared null and void all acts of possessors of such titles. The law remained a dead letter and was repealed in 1871.

May 1–Oct. 15. The **Great Exhibition of 1851** (Crystal Palace) in Hyde Park, for which Prince Albert was largely responsible, included exhibits from all nations, and was the first of its kind. *Prosperity* was the note it sounded, and it was confidently expected that the exhibition would inaugurate an era of international peace.

Dec. Conflict between the queen and Lord Palmerston. Victoria had long been dissatisfied by the foreign minister's indiscretions and boisterous nationalistic policy, to say nothing of his tendency to ignore royal suggestions and advice. After the Don Pacifico incident, the queen, assisted by Prince Albert and Baron Stockmar, drew up a memorandum demanding that the queen be kept informed and that, once she had approved a measure, it should not be arbitrarily altered. Palmerston promised to mend his ways, but in the following months a new crisis occurred. Palmerston at once approved of the *coup d'état* of Louis Napoleon in France (Dec. 2), but the cabinet, adopting the queen's attitude, on December 5 instructed the ambassador at Paris to carry on as though nothing had occurred, passing no judgment. The resulting embarrassment enabled the queen to force **Palmerston's dismissal** (Dec. 19).

1852, Feb. 20. Lord John Russell's cabinet was defeated on a militia bill.

Feb. 27–Dec. 17. Cabinet of Lord Derby (Conservative).

1852, Dec. 28–1855, Jan. 20. Lord Aberdeen's ministry, with a coalition of Whigs and Peelites.

1854, Mar. 28. Outbreak of the Crimean War (p. 773).

1855, Feb. 5–1858, Feb. 22. First Palmerston cabinet, resulting from popular dissatisfaction with Aberdeen's policy in the war.

1857. The Indian Mutiny (p. 902).

1857–1858. War with China (p. 911).

1858, Feb. 25–1859, June 11. Second Derby ministry, after Palmerston's government was defeated on a bill to increase the penalty for conspiracy to murder (following French representations after the **Orsini bomb affair,** p. 706).

1858, June. An act brought to an end the property qualifications for members of parliament.

July 23. Removal of disabilities on Jews.

Aug. 2. India Bill, by which the British East India Company's political powers were brought to an end and the government of India was assumed by the crown (p. 902).

1859, June 18–1865, Nov. 6. Second Palmerston ministry, after the defeat of Lord Derby's reform bill.

1860, Jan. 23. The important **commercial treaty signed with France** (Cobden-Chevalier Treaty) marking a great advance toward free trade on the part of France.

1861, Nov.–Dec. The *Trent* **affair.** Crisis in Anglo-American relations resulting from the Civil War (p. 817).

Dec. 14. Death of the Prince Consort. For a period of many years Queen Victoria withdrew from all public functions and thereby suffered a period of marked unpopularity.

1864, June 5. Great Britain abandoned the protectorate over the **Ionian Islands** (assumed in 1815) and made over the islands to Greece, in order to stabilize the new Danish dynasty (p. 756).

1865, Oct. 18. Death of Lord Palmerston.

1865, Nov. 6–1866, June. Second ministry of Lord John Russell. On the death of Palmerston, Russell succeeded as prime minister. He was faced by urgent demands for further electoral reform, which he had previously sponsored in a perfunctory way. Only one man in six possessed the vote, and workers were virtually excluded. Repeated measures for franchise extension had been defeated in the commons, while industrial growth had exaggerated electoral anomalies left by the act of 1832.

1866, Mar. Russell introduced an anodyne measure which was defeated as the result of the defection of a section of the Liberals. Russell resigned in June.

1866, July 6–1868, Feb. 25. The **third Derby ministry,** in which the dominant figure was to be **Benjamin Disraeli,** once more leader of the house of commons. Workers' demands for suffrage reform spread rapidly, and Disraeli was literally obliged to adopt the Liberal program of electoral reform, which in the end he had to extend radically, despite the opposition of many Conservatives.

1867, Aug. 15. The **SECOND REFORM BILL** extended the suffrage: in *boroughs* to all householders paying the poor rates and all lodgers of one year's residence paying an annual rent of £10; in the *counties,* to owners of land of £5 annual value, to occupying tenants paying £12 annual rental. All boroughs of fewer than 10,000 population lost the right of sending two members to the commons; Manchester, Birmingham, Liverpool, Leeds were given each a third member; two other large towns, Salford and Merthyr, received a second member; nine *new boroughs* were created; 25 additional members were allotted to the counties. The **Scottish Reform Bill** of 1868 (July 13) founded generally upon the same principles as the English bill, gave Scotland seven new seats. The **Irish Reform Bill** of 1868 (July 13) reduced the borough franchise requirement, left the county franchise unaltered, and left the Irish representation unchanged. A radically democratic step had been taken: the electorate was increased from roughly 1,000,000 to 2,000,000. Disraeli had "dished the Whigs," but had violated his party pledges and had taken a step bitterly opposed by many Conservatives and described even by Derby as a "leap in the dark."

1867–1868. Abyssinian expedition (p. 870).

d. DISRAELI AND GLADSTONE, 1868–1894

1868, Feb. 29–Dec. 2. First Disraeli ministry, which came to an end after the sweeping Liberal victory in the elections of November 1868.

1868, Dec. 9–1874, Feb. 17. First Gladstone ministry. Gladstone was the son of a Liverpool merchant, a product of the aristocratic influences of Eton and Christ Church, Oxford. He was learned, profoundly devout, possessed of typical Scottish industry. He had entered politics as a Tory, seceded with the Peelites, ended as a Liberal. He possessed a vast knowledge of internal problems, especially of financial questions. In the field of foreign relations he was hampered in an age of imperialist expansion by humanitarian principles and sympathies with minorities abroad.

1868–1869. The Irish Question. Prior to taking office Gladstone had declared: "My mission is to pacify Ireland." The **Fenian Brotherhood,** formed in 1858 in New York, collected funds among the American Irish, aimed to overthrow British rule in Ireland. **O'Donovan Rossa** and **James Stephens** were arrested (Sept., Nov. 1865) and supplies of arms were taken. A Fenian invasion of Canada (1866) failed (p. 835). A general rising in Ireland miscarried (1867, Mar.). Further "outrages" followed, notably the attempt to deliver two prisoners from Clerkenwell, London (Dec. 13), when a blast in the wall caused the death of 12, the injury of 120 more. Gladstone attacked what he considered the causes of the discontent—disestablishment and land tenure (neither of which had figured among Fenian aims).

1869, July 26. The **Disestablishment Act** provided that the Irish (Episcopal) Church should cease to exist as of January 1, 1871. The Church's endowments were to be taken away with compensation for interests affected; church buildings, etc., were to be reserved to a new voluntary organization; the tithe rent-charge on estates, the Church's chief source of revenue, was to be purchased by the landlords for some £8,212,500; provision was made for the care of Episcopal clergymen during their lifetime. Irish Catholics were no longer to be obliged to support a state church of which they were not communicants. Despite the opposition of the Episcopal clergy, the Conservatives in general and the house of lords in particular (again threatened with the creation of new peers), the bill passed.

1870, Aug. 1. Irish Land Act. The sufferings of the Irish were in considerable measure due to the prevalent system of **land tenure.** There was a vast difference between the rural landlord in England and his Irish counterpart—the former putting money into the land and making improvements for the tenants; the latter merely drawing rack-rent which he often spent in England, leaving the tenants to do everything for themselves, and often evicting them wholesale without compensation for improvements. In 1850 a **Tenant-Right League** was founded to obtain for the tenant the "three F's"—a **fair rent, fixity of tenure,** and **free sale.** The movement spread rapidly. In 1870 Gladstone introduced an Irish land bill. It contained no recognition of the "three F's," but gave the tenant the right to compensation for disturbance (that is, eviction) and for improvements (if, without fault on his side, he was evicted, but not where the ejection was for non-payment of rent). The **Bright clauses** of the bill facilitated the creation of a peasant proprietorship by allowing government loans to be granted to tenants who wished to buy their holdings from their landlords. The act did not extinguish the evils with which it was designed to deal. It interfered with the landlord's right of disposing of his land on the absolute basis of free contract, but it did not protect the tenant against increased rent, nor did it give him security of tenure. The act of 1870 was important chiefly as the first of a great series of Irish agrarian laws. It did not allay Irish agitation. Even while the bill was in progress, in the spring of 1870, agrarian outrages occurred in County Mayo. By the **Peace Preservation Act** (Apr. 4), the government increased its powers of repression.

1870, Aug. 9. An important **Education Bill** aimed to remedy the existing chaotic situation: nearly half of the 4,000,000 children of school age were unprovided for; about 1,000,000 attended schools attached to the Church of England, government inspected and supported by voluntary subscriptions supplemented by government grants; another million attended schools unsupported by the government and uninspected. On the whole English education was far inferior to that in Prussia, Switzerland, the United States. The Education Bill,

brought in by **W. E. Forster,** provided for two types of schools: (1) those voluntary schools doing good work were to be retained, government grants were to be increased, but they were to receive no aid from local rates; (2) elsewhere *board schools* (under the control of locally elected boards) were to be set up and maintained by government grants, parents' fees, local rates (the question of compulsory attendance was to be passed on by each local board). The question of religious education was crucial: the voluntary schools were permitted to continue religious instruction; all denominational religious instruction was prohibited in the board schools—a compromise satisfying neither of the extreme groups.

1870, June 4. Order in council reforming the civil service, by providing that candidates for ordinary posts should, in the discretion of department heads, be given competitive examinations. The new order was speedily adopted by almost all the chief departments, the foreign office remaining a notable exception.

1871, June. The **University Tests Act** conferred on Cambridge and Oxford students the right to obtain university degrees and to hold lay offices in colleges and universities without subscribing to any religious tests.

The **Army Regulation Bill** virtually reorganized the British army, a reform associated with the name of **Edward Cardwell,** the secretary of war. The system of purchasing commissions was abolished; short service was introduced, which made possible a well-trained reserve (six years with the colors and six in the reserves, instead of twelve years' service); etc.

1872. The **Ballot Act** made voting secret for the first time.

Sept. 14. Settlement of the *Alabama* claims (p. 822).

The prestige of the Gladstone ministry rapidly declined: the education act alienated nonconformists and high churchmen alike; reduction in the number of dockyard workers caused dissatisfaction; the elimination of the purchase of army commissions irritated the upper classes. When Gladstone introduced a bill to unite Irish colleges in a single university open to Catholics and Protestants alike, he was defeated and resigned (1873, Feb.). Disraeli was reluctant to take office as yet, Gladstone returned, sponsored a notable reform of the law courts in

1873. The **Judicature Act,** which, along with supplementary acts, consolidated the three common law courts, chancery, and various other tribunals into one **supreme court of judicature,** to consist of two principal divisons: (1) The *high court of justice*—(*a*) queen's bench, (*b*) chancery, (*c*) probate, divorce, and admiralty; (2) the *court of appeal,* from which appellate jurisdiction lay to the house of lords, strengthened in 1876 by the addition of three (later four) law lords of life tenure.

1874, Feb. Gladstone appealed to the country in a **general election,** was overwhelmed by the Conservatives, who succeeded to power with Disraeli as prime minister.

1874, Feb. 21–1880, Apr. 22. The **second Disraeli ministry** came to power with the expressed purpose of "giving the country a rest" at home and pursuing a foreign policy more in accord with the demands of British prestige and interests. Certain measures of a domestic character were passed, notably a

1875. Public Health Act, a codification of earlier legislation which remains even today the backbone of English sanitary law; an

1875. Artisans' Dwelling Act, the first serious attempt by the government to grapple with the problem of the housing of the poor;

1876. The **Merchant Shipping Act,** aimed to prevent overloading ships or permitting use of unseaworthy vessels (the act a result of persistent efforts of **Samuel Plimsoll,** the "sailors' friend").

But the country's attention was riveted on foreign and colonial affairs.

1875, Nov. 25. Purchase of the Suez Canal shares. The completion of the Suez Canal under the direction of a Frenchman, Ferdinand de Lesseps, and under the auspices of an international company, greatly shortened the distance to India and the east and heightened British interest in Egypt. **Khedive Ismail** of Egypt, who held 44 per cent of the shares, was in perennial financial difficulties, and finally considered mortgaging his shares in Paris. This information came to Disraeli's attention; he sprang a *coup* by negotiating purchase of the shares on his own responsibility. A grateful parliament subsequently ratified the act. This marked the beginning of British penetration and presently occupation of Egypt (p. 867).

1876, Apr. The **Royal Titles Bill** declared the queen *Empress of India,* deeply flattered Her Majesty, was the occasion of great enthusiasm in India, caused considerable opposition among educated Englishmen—the title was "un-English" and in disrepute through the fall of Emperor Napoleon III and the tragedy of Emperor Maximilian of Mexico (the opposition was allayed by the promise that she would not use it in England).

Aug. Disraeli was elevated to the peerage as the **earl of Beaconsfield.** During the remainder of its term of office the government was absorbed by the crisis of 1875–1876 in the Near East, culminating in the **Russo-Turkish War** and the **congress of Berlin**

(p. 780), by the **Afghan War** of 1878–1879 (p. 781), and by the war with the **Zulus** in South Africa (p. 887). Beaconsfield's popularity had reached its zenith when he returned from the congress of Berlin.

1879. A severe **agricultural depression** with the worst harvest of the century accompanied by a decline in trade, strikes, the unpopular Afghan and Zulu wars, obstruction by the new **Irish Home Rule Party** in the house of commons.

Nov. **Gladstone** roundly denounced the government, alike for its imperialism and its domestic policy, in a series of speeches to his **Midlothian** constituents.

1880, Mar. 8. Beaconsfield appealed to the country in a general election, his party was defeated, and he resigned (Apr. 18), to be succeeded by Gladstone.

1880, Apr. 28–1885, June 8. Second Gladstone ministry. Much of the session of 1880 was occupied by the case of **Charles Bradlaugh,** newly elected to the commons, who as an atheist refused to take the oath (including the words "So help me God") and insisted on an affirmation instead. An **Affirmation Bill** was twice defeated (1881, 1883); Bradlaugh changed his mind, offered to take the oath, was refused the right (as a freethinker). Subsequently he was involved in eight lawsuits, was unseated and re-elected repeatedly, was finally permitted to take the oath (1886, Jan.). Bradlaugh secured passage of a bill (1888) legalizing affirmation both in the commons and the courts, removing the last religious disability for membership in the house.

1880, Sept. 13. First Employers' Liability Act, granting compensation to workers for injuries not their own fault.

1881–1882. The Irish Question. Foundation (1871) of the parliamentary **Home Rule for Ireland Party** by **Isaac Butt,** who aimed at securing by peaceful means a separate legislature for Ireland. The dominant figure soon became **Charles Stewart Parnell,** descendant of English Protestant settlers in Ireland, but consumed by hatred for England; brilliant orator, elected to parliament in 1875. Parnell hoped to unite all elements of Irish opposition and to force the grant of home rule by the use of obstruction in parliament. The Peace Preservation Act of 1875 expired in 1880 and the government, unable to maintain order under ordinary law, was obliged to resort to new **coercive measures.**

1881, Aug. Gladstone then passed the **Land Act,** which aimed to correct the defects in his Act of 1870 and to meet the Irish demand for the three "F's." The act recognized a dual ownership of land and provided for the creation of a court to mediate between landlord and tenant and fix a "fair" rent for a period of 15 years; it gave increased fixity of tenure to tenants who paid those rents, with the right to sell their interest in the holdings to the highest bidder. While it established a land court, with authority to cut down excessive rents, the act made no provision for dealing with accumulated arrears. It pleased neither landlords nor tenants.

Oct. 13. Parnell and others were sent to Kilmainham Prison for inciting Irishmen to intimidate tenants taking advantage of the act. They were released (1882, May 2) when they agreed in the "Kilmainham treaty" to cease "boycotting" and co-operate with the Liberal party.

1882, May 6. **Lord Frederick Cavendish,** new chief secretary for Ireland, and **Thomas Burke,** permanent undersecretary, were murdered in broad daylight by Fenians in **Phoenix Park,** Dublin. Parnell repudiated all connection with the crime and offered to resign his leadership of the Home Rule party.

July. The government put through the draconian **Prevention of Crimes Bill** (limited to three years) suspending trial by jury and giving the police unlimited power to search and arrest on suspicion. Irish extremists, with whom Parnell denied all connection, resorted to a **campaign of terrorism,** punctuated by dynamiting of public buildings in England.

1883, Aug. The **Corrupt and Illegal Practices Act** in effect limited the total amounts that might be spent (all parties) in a general election to £800,000 (£2,500,000 had been spent in the general election of 1880); no candidate might spend more than a fixed sum for election purposes; penalties for corrupt practices were greatly increased.

1884. Gladstone's **Franchise Bill** aimed to extend the rights enjoyed by the borough voters to the rural classes and to unify substantially the franchise throughout the United Kingdom. The measure virtually provided manhood suffrage—only domestic servants, bachelors living with their families, and those of no fixed abode being excluded. Some 2,000,000 voters were to be added, nearly four times the number added in 1832, nearly twice that added in 1867. The bill passed the commons, was rejected by the lords, the Conservatives insisting on the importance of a concomitant redistribution of seats. Negotiations followed; Gladstone yielded in the matter of redistribution; the Franchise Bill itself passed easily (Dec.).

1885, June. A **Redistribution Bill** followed—London received 37 additional members, Liverpool six, Birmingham four, Glasgow four, Yorkshire 16, Lancashire 15; single-member constituencies became the rule, except in the city of London and in cities and boroughs with a population between 50,000 and 165,000; boroughs of fewer than 15,000 population were merged with their counties. By this legislation the historic counties and boroughs ceased to be, as such, the basis of the house of commons. The individual for the first time became the unit, and numerical equality ("one vote, one value") the master principle.

Despite his resistance to the imperialist policy of Disraeli, his withdrawal from Afghanistan (p. 899), his concessions to the Boers in South Africa (p. 887), Gladstone was fated to play an active rôle in the field of **colonial expansion.**

1882. **Britain was obliged to intervene in Egypt** (p. 868), and the prestige of the cabinet was seriously damaged when it failed to rescue General Charles G. Gordon, isolated in the Sudan (p. 869).

1884-1885. **Russian encroachments in Afghanistan** nearly led to war, and the pacific policy of the foreign minister, Lord Granville, led to Conservative accusations of truckling to the Russians (pp. 783, 899).

1885, June 9. A hostile amendment to his budget led to **Gladstone's resignation.**

1885, June 24-1886, Jan. 27. **First Salisbury ministry.** Salisbury had become head of the Conservative Party on the death of Beaconsfield (1881, Apr. 19).

1885, Aug. **Ashbourne Act.** The Conservatives had previously been the party of Irish coercion, but Salisbury reached an understanding with Parnell that this policy should be reversed in return for Irish Nationalist support. A fund of £5,000,000 was provided by the Ashbourne Act for loans with which Irish tenants could purchase their holdings on an easy-interest, long-term basis (extending a feature of the Liberal land act of 1881). **Further land purchase acts** were adopted in 1887, 1891, 1896, and 1903 (the last named providing an eventual sum of £100,000,000).

1886, Feb. 12-July 20. **Third Gladstone ministry.** Gladstone's support for home rule had been secured (1885, Dec.), and during his third ministry he introduced his

1886, Apr. 8. **First Home Rule Bill,** providing for a separate Irish legislature of two orders (one of 28 representative peers, with 75 other members elected by and from the propertied classes, the other of 204 elected members). The Irish legislature was to have important powers, but legislation relating to the crown, the army and navy, trade and navigation, etc., were still to be dealt with by the British parliament, in which Irish members were no longer to sit. The measure was bitterly attacked by the Conservatives, caused a secession from the Liberal party of the **"Liberal Unionists"** (Marquis of Hartington, Joseph Chamberlain), and was finally defeated (July). A general election was called and produced a new defeat for the Liberals.

1886, July 26–1892, Aug. 13. Second Salisbury ministry. Arthur J. Balfour, the prime minister's nephew, was made chief secretary for Ireland and carried a new **Crimes Bill** (1887) whose passage was facilitated by the publication of a notorious series of articles by the *Times* on "Parnellism and Crime," including an alleged letter of Parnell's declaring he had condemned the Phoenix Park murders only as a matter of policy. Parnell denied authorship of this and other letters, was cleared (1890) by a governmental commission (the author was Richard Piggott, broken-down Irish journalist and subsequent suicide). Soon thereafter Parnell's position was ruined when he was named co-respondent in a divorce suit brought by Captain O'Shea, one of his followers. Gladstone dropped him, a schism followed among the Nationalists, **Justin McCarthy** became leader of the majority. When Parnell died (1891, Oct. 6), **John E. Redmond** succeeded him as leader of the minority.

1889, May 31. Naval Defense Act, designed to meet growing sea power of France and Russia. It provided that the British fleet should always be as strong as the fleets of the two next strongest powers combined **(two-power standard).**

1889, Aug. 15–Sept. 16. Great **London dock strike,** in which almost all riverside workers joined. This great strike and the formation of the **Miners' Federation of Great Britain** (1888) marked the extension of trade-unionism from the skilled classes (represented in the Amalgamated Societies) to the less skilled.

1892. In the **general election** Gladstone made home rule the principal issue of the campaign, advocating also a series of additional reforms **(Newcastle program):** disestablishment of the Church of England in Wales, and of the Church of Scotland; local veto on liquor sales; abolition of plural voting; extension of the Employers' Liability Act; restriction of hours of labor. The election gave Gladstone sufficient votes, with the aid of 81 Irish Nationalists, to carry his home rule plank.

1892, Aug. 18–1894, Mar. 3. Fourth Gladstone cabinet.

1893, Feb. 13. Second Home Rule Bill. Its principal difference from the first bill was the provision that 80 Irish representatives should sit at Westminster. It passed the commons (Sept. 1), but was overwhelmed by the lords (Sept. 8). A period of comparative peace followed in Ireland and home rule sank in importance, to be revived only two decades later. **John Morley,** secretary for Ireland (1892–1895), ruled with sympathy and wisdom. The Conservative régime (1895–1905) continued its traditional tactics of killing home rule by kindness (new land purchase acts, 1896, 1903).

1893, Jan. Foundation of the Independent Labor party, a frankly socialist party. Socialism, which had declined in the forties, had revived in the eighties under the influence of the American Henry George's *Progress and Poverty* (1879). In 1884 **Henry M. Hyndman** founded the **Social Democratic Federation,** a Marxist organization. In 1883 was founded the **Fabian Society,** which became prominent with the publication (1889) of the *Fabian Essays.* Prominent among the Fabians were **Sidney** and **Beatrice Webb** and **George Bernard Shaw.** They preached practical possibilities—municipal socialism and state control of the conditions of labor—and expected socialism to come as a sequel to the full application of universal suffrage and representative government. In 1892 the first two avowed socialists were elected to parliament. One of them, **James Keir Hardie,** was mainly responsible for the foundation of the Labour party.

1894, Mar. Gladstone had lost his fight for home rule, had shattered the Liberal party. He resigned the premiership and was succeeded by the Liberal imperialist Lord Rosebery.

1894, Mar. 5–1895, June 21. Cabinet of Lord Rosebery. Sir William Harcourt, now leader of the house of commons, brought in a bill adding £4,000,000 to the budget by equalizing death duties on real and personal property and providing a graduated tax of 1 to 8 per cent—an attempt further to shift the burden of taxation to the wealthy. The cabinet was defeated on a matter of minor importance, and resigned.

e. A DECADE OF UNIONISM, 1895–1905

1895, June 25–1902, July 11. Third Salisbury ministry, with Salisbury himself as foreign minister, Balfour as first lord of the treasury and leader of the commons. The cabinet included some of the principal Liberal Unionists, notably Hartington (duke of Devonshire since 1891) and **Joseph Chamberlain.** The latter's political beginnings had been as a radical; as colonial secretary he now devoted his great energy and ability to the cause of enhancing British imperial prestige. The new government's attention was almost entirely absorbed by events abroad—the **Venezuela boundary dispute** with the United States (p. 828), the **Armenian massacres** and the **Greco-Turkish war** (pp. 788, 789), the struggle for power in the **Far East** (pp. 789, 790), the **Hague conference of 1899** (p. 791), the **South African problem** which culminated in the **Boer war** (p. 890).

1900, Feb. Formation of the **Labor Representation Committee,** with **J. Ramsay MacDonald** as secretary. The committee represented the Independent Labour party, Trade-Union congress, and various socialist organizations. Its aim was to establish a distinct labor group in parliament, but it had a hard struggle for existence. Only about 5 per cent of the unions affiliated themselves with it, the Social Democratic Federation soon withdrew, the attitude of the Fabians was cool, and the miners were hostile. At the general election of 1900 the committee ran 15 candidates, of whom only two were returned. But the decision of the lords in the **Taff Vale case** (1901, July), which declared unions legal entities capable of being sued, consolidated the ranks of labor and created the **Labour party,** which returned 29 members in the election of 1906.

1901. Jan 22. Death of Queen Victoria after one of the longest reigns in European history. She was widely mourned, reflecting the respect for her courage, strength of character, and the tact with which she had recognized the constitutional limitations of the crown and yielded to the steadily enlarging powers of her ministries. In the last decades Victoria had come to be regarded above all as the symbol of imperial unity, an aspect of the monarchy upon which attention had been brilliantly and effectively focused by the **Jubilee of 1887** (celebrating the fiftieth anniversary of the queen's accession) and by the **Diamond Jubilee of 1897.** The reign had witnessed a period of incredible industrial expansion and increasing material prosperity. The population of the United Kingdom had increased from 16,261,183 in 1831 to 37,518,052 in 1901.

1901-1910. EDWARD VII (b. 1841). Edward was nearly sixty, and Victoria had deprived him until recently of serious participation in matters political. He was possessed of great social charm and tact, read little, cared nothing for routine, gathered information largely from personal contact. He was gay and fond of pleasure, a yachting and racing enthusiast, supporter of philanthropic causes, widely popular with all classes before his accession.

1902, July 11-1905, Dec. 4. Cabinet of Arthur Balfour, following the retirement of Lord Salisbury.

1902, Dec. The **education act** was the most important legislative achievement of the Balfour government. For some time it had been felt that the school boards of the education act of 1870, although they had worked well in the towns, were on the whole too parochial in personnel and policy. The act of 1902 abolished the boards, placed elementary and secondary education in the hands of statutory committees of the borough and county councils. The denominational schools, hitherto belonging to and maintained by the Anglicans and Catholics, were brought into the reorganization *pari passu* with the undenominational board schools. For the first time in England the provision of secondary education was recognized as the duty of the state and was brought under public control. Educational progress under the act was rapid; in five years the number of secondary schools doubled.

1903, May. Joseph Chamberlain and the **Tariff Reform League** advocated a sweeping tariff reform, with moderate duties on corn, flour, meats, dairy produce, and foreign manufactures. The new system was to give Britain a basis for bargaining with the colonies, of preventing foreign dumping in Britain, of increasing the revenue. Balfour was unwilling to go so far, and Chamberlain resigned (Sept. 18).

1904. Committee of Imperial Defense. The South African war had revealed serious defects in the army. The report of the commission of inquiry was an "unsparing condemnation of war office methods." The upshot was the organization of the Defense Committee with the prime minister as its head; the commander-in-chief was replaced by an army council which included the war secretary, four military members, one civil and one finance member; a board of selection (duke of Connaught, president) was to control appointments.

Foreign relations bulked large in a period when Britain settled her differences with France in the **Entente cordiale** of 1904 (p. 794), European peace was threatened in the **Moroccan crisis of 1905** (p. 795), and the naval rivalry of Britain and Germany became increasingly embittered (p. 790 *ff.*).

Balfour's cabinet steadily lost prestige because of its dilatory tactics regarding the tariff question; opposition to its Education Act of 1902, which roused the ire of Nonconformists because it left in existence state-supported denominational schools largely controlled by Anglicans; etc. Balfour resigned, expecting to be recalled, but was succeeded by

Descendants of Queen Victoria

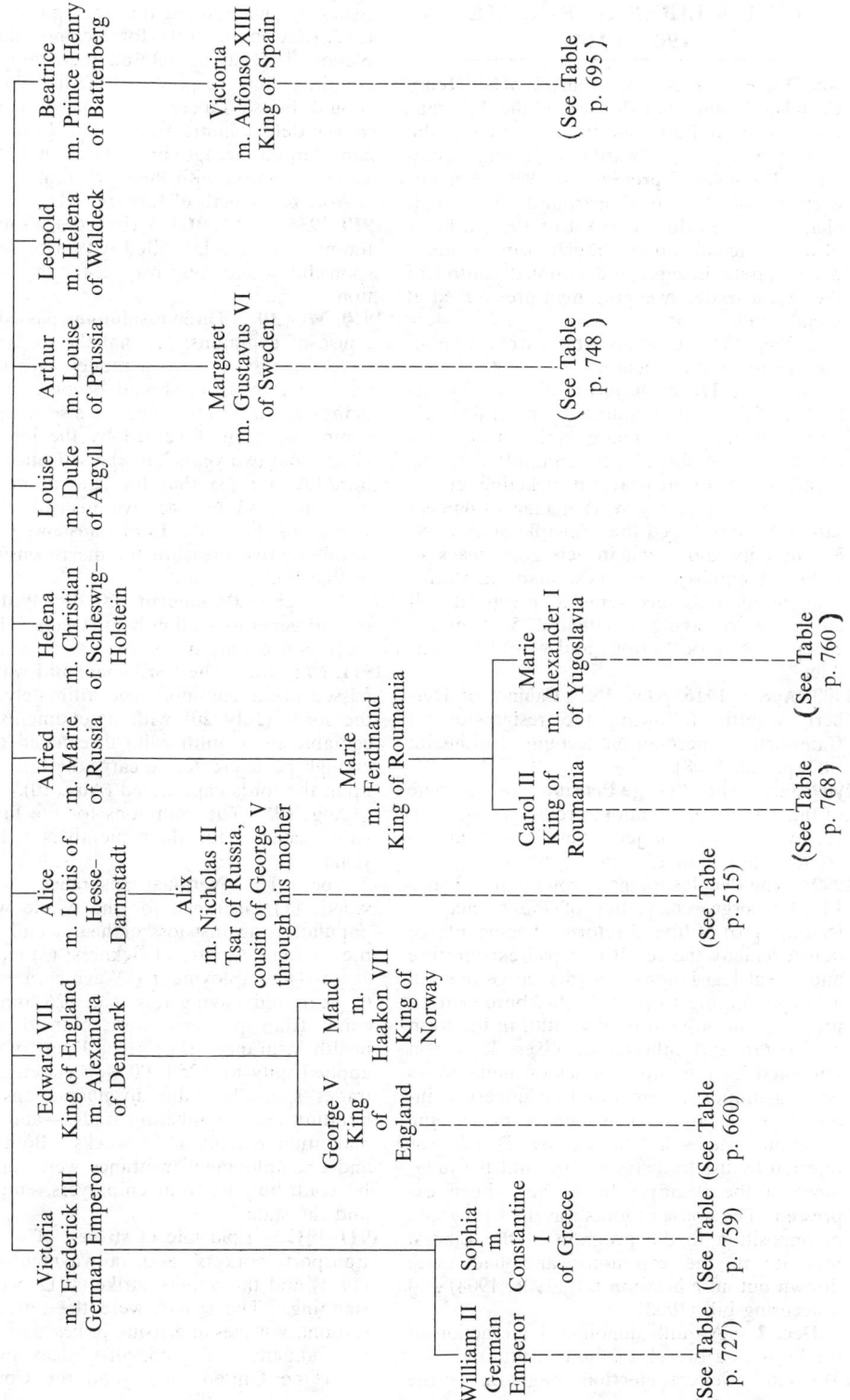

f. THE LIBERAL RÉGIME, 1905-1914

1905, Dec. 5-1908, Apr. 5.   Cabinet of Sir Henry Campbell-Bannerman, leader of the Liberals. It included **Herbert Asquith,** chancellor of the exchequer, and **Sir Edward Grey,** foreign secretary. The **Liberal program of 1906** included: exclusion of Chinese labor from the Transvaal; change of the Education Act of 1902 in favor of the Nonconformists; reduction in the number of liquor licenses and national control of the liquor trade; sweeping measures aimed at social amelioration.

1906, Jan.   The Liberals won an overwhelming victory in the elections.

Dec.   A Trade Disputes Bill met the demands of the trade-unionists by providing that a union could not be made liable for damages on account of illegal acts committed by its members; legalized peaceful picketing, etc.

At the same time a **Workingman's Compensation Act** developed the principle of employers' liability laid down in acts going back to 1880; the employer was now made liable for compensation for accidents to practically all employees receiving less than £250 annually except in case of "serious and willful misconduct."

1908, Apr. 5-1916, May 15.   Cabinet of Herbert Asquith, following the resignation of Campbell-Bannerman on account of ill health (d. Apr. 22, 1908).

1909, Jan.   The Old-Age Pension Law, outcome of thirty years of agitation, provided a pension for every British subject over 70 with an income of less than £31 10s.

1909.   The Peoples Budget, brought in by **David Lloyd George,** chancellor of the exchequer, leading spirit of liberal reform. Facing a large deficit (chiefly the result of naval expenditure and social legislation), Lloyd George devised a budget aiming to shift the tax burden from producers to possessors of wealth, in the form of income and inheritance taxes, levies on unearned income, heavy rates on monopolies (such as liquor licenses) and on unearned increments of land. The budget passed the commons after a hot fight (Nov. 5), but was rejected by the lords (Nov. 30) until the judgment of the country should have been expressed. The house of lords was the stronghold of opposition to the program of the Liberal majority in the commons, and had twice thrown out an education bill (1906, 1908) and a licensing bill (1908).

Dec. 2.   Asquith denounced the action of the lords as a breach of the constitution.

1910, Jan.   General election, fought out on the issues of the budget, the veto power of the lords, and home rule for Ireland (the Irish Nationalists having offered their support on condition that the power of the house of lords should be so far reduced that it could no longer defeat home rule). The Liberals lost considerable strength in the election, but determined to go on with their program.

May 6.   Death of Edward VII.

1910-1936.   GEORGE V (b. 1865), a sound but unimaginative ruler, filled with a sense of responsibility and rigid respect for the constitution.

1910, May 10.   Three resolutions passed in the house of commons: (1) that the lords should have no right to veto a money bill; (2) that any other measure should become law after being passed in three successive sessions of the commons, even if vetoed by the lords, providing that two years had elapsed since its first introduction; (3) that the maximum life of parliament should be five instead of seven years. In the lords, **Lord Lansdowne** offered an alternative measure for the reconstruction of that body.

Nov. 28.   Parliament was dissolved and a second general election held (Dec.). The Liberals gained only two seats.

1911, May 15.   The Parliament Bill was again passed in the commons and ultimately passed the lords (July 20) with amendments unacceptable to Asquith, who threatened to have enough peers created to carry the bill. Thereupon the lords capitulated (Aug. 10).

Aug. 10.   The commons for the first time voted salaries for their members (£400 per year).

Dec.   The National Insurance Act provided: (1) insurance for the whole working population against loss of health and for the prevention and cure of sickness; (2) insurance against unemployment. Wage-earners 16 to 65 years old having less than £26 annual income from property were obliged to take health insurance. The second part of the act applied only to 2,250,000 workers engaged in trades specially liable to fluctuations—large building and engineering trades—and gave a maximum benefit of 15 weeks. Both health and unemployment insurance were supported by contributions from employers, employees, and the state.

1911-1912.   Epidemic of strikes, of which the transport workers' and railwaymen's strikes (1911) and the miners' strike (1912) were outstanding. The strikes were the reflection of stationary wages and rising prices, and showed the influence of syndicalist ideas imported from the United States and the Continent.

The **coal strike** (1912), involving 1,500,000 men, brought government action and

1912, Mar. 29. A **Minimum Wage Law,** which, however, did little to relieve unrest.

Apr. 11. The government introduced a bill for **home rule in Ireland.** It provided for a bicameral parliament for Ireland, but with continued representation in the house of commons. The bill was attacked for its injustice to Protestant Ulster, which would be submerged in a united Catholic Ireland. Opposition brilliantly led by **Sir Edward Carson.**

1913. The **Home Rule Bill** was twice passed by the commons (Jan. 16, July 7) and twice rejected by the lords (Jan. 30, July 15). Meanwhile Ulster opposition grew steadily hotter. A **covenant** was signed at Belfast (1912, Sept. 28) pledging resistance to home rule and refusal to accept it if it were voted.

July 12. A resolution was adopted by a meeting of 150,000 Ulstermen at Craigavon to resist home rule by force of arms if necessary. By December 100,000 **Ulster volunteers** had been raised. Civil war appeared imminent if the government persisted·in its home rule program, which it had pledged to the Irish Nationalists.

1914, Feb. 10. When parliament met, Unionist opposition had reached its peak. Asquith offered a compromise (Mar. 9): electors in each of the nine Ulster counties might determine whether their county should be excluded from the new arrangement for six years. The Home Rule Bill was passed for a third time by the commons (May 26). Under the Parliament Act of 1911 no further action by the lords was necessary: Ireland had now been given a unitary parliamentary system, with no separate position for Ulster.

June 23. **Asquith introduced his compromise** of March 9 on Ulster into the house of lords, which changed the bill to exclude the whole of Ulster without time limit. A three-cornered struggle of lords, commons, and Irish Nationalist leaders was overtaken by the World War.

Sept. 18. The **Home Rule Bill** received the royal assent and became law; but by a simultaneous act it was not to come into force until after the war, and the government pledged that, before it was put into force, an amending bill dealing with the question of Ulster would be introduced. The third Home Rule Bill, which never came into operation, was subsequently replaced by the Home Rule Bill of December 1920 (p. 984).

Sept. 18. Welsh disestablishment. The parliamentary course of the Welsh Disestablishment Bill was almost exactly parallel with that of the Home Rule Bill. A bill for the disestablishment of the Anglican Church in Wales had failed in 1894-1895, again in 1909. Introduced in 1912 (Apr. 12), it passed the commons twice, but was rejected by the lords (1913, Feb. 13, July 22). The bill was finally passed by the commons in 1914 (May 19) and received the royal assent (Sept. 18); but along with it was passed a **Suspensory Bill,** postponing its action until the end of the war. The bill provided that the four Welsh dioceses should no longer form part of the province of Canterbury, that the Welsh bishops should no longer sit in the house of lords, that all ecclesiastical jurisdiction should be abolished, and the Welsh Anglicans should be free to set up their own church government.

(*Cont. p. 980.*)

CULTURAL DEVELOPMENTS

(1) Literature

In the Victorian era the novel was a favorite form, both as re-creation of history and as social commentary. In the former category: **Edward George Bulwer-Lytton** (1803-1873), *Last Days of Pompeii* (1834); **Charles Dickens** (1812-1870), *Tale of Two Cities.* The two foremost novelists of the period were **William Makepeace Thackeray** (1811-1863), who drew true pictures of a period in *Vanity Fair* (1847) and *Henry Esmond* (1852), and **Charles Dickens,** equally skilled in his portrayal of a lower stratum of society (*David Copperfield,* 1850; *Oliver Twist,* 1838). Also concerned with problems of their day; **Anthony Trollope** (1815-1882), **Charlotte Brontë** (1816-1855, *Jane Eyre,* 1847); George Eliot (1819-1880); George Meredith (1828-1909). The implications of *Alice in Wonderland* (1865) and *Through the Looking Glass* by Lewis Carroll (Charles L. Dodgson) continue to occupy students. The Scot Robert Louis Stevenson (1850-1894) is remembered chiefly for his adventure stories *Treasure Island* (1883), *Kidnapped* (1886), and his verses for children.

Thomas Carlyle (1795-1881) and **Thomas Babington Macaulay** (1800-1859) were essayists and historians: Carlyle's *French Revolution* (1837) and his lectures *On Heroes* (1841); Macaulay's *History of England* (1848-1861). Other critics and essayists: **John Ruskin** (1819-1900); **Matthew Arnold** (1822-1888); **Thomas Huxley,** the scientist (1825-1895); **Walter Pater** (1839-1894).

Poetry: Alfred Lord Tennyson (1809-1892; *Idylls of the King,* 1859-1885); **Robert** (1812-1889) and **Elizabeth Barrett Browning** (1806-1861; *Sonnets from the Portuguese,* 1850); the

Pre-Raphaelite Brotherhood of **Dante Gabriel Rossetti** (1828-1882), **Christina Rossetti** (1830-1894), **Algernon Charles Swinburne** (1837-1909), **Edward Fitzgerald** (1809-1883), the translator of the *Rubaiyat* of Omar Khayyam, and **William Morris** (1834-1896).

(2) Music

William Sterndale Bennett (1816-1875); **John Stainer** (1840-1901); **Sir Arthur Sullivan** (1842-1900), best known for his "operas" written in collaboration with W. S. Gilbert.

(3) Painting

A group of Pre-Raphaelite painters followed the philosophy of the Brotherhood of poets, stressing faithfulness to nature, which resulted in a mystical quality in their art: **Edward Burne-Jones** (1833-1898); **Sir John Millais** (1829-1896); the poet and journalist **Dante Gabriel Rossetti** (see above). **Aubrey Beardsley** (1872-1898) illustrated Malory's *Morte d'Arthur,* Oscar Wilde's *Salomé,* Pope's *Rape of the Lock.*

3. THE LOW COUNTRIES

(From p. 477)

a. THE KINGDOM OF THE NETHERLANDS, 1814-1830

1814, June 21.   Protocol of the Eight Articles, concluded between the prince of Orange and the representatives of the allied powers after the defeat of Napoleon. In order to create a bulwark against France, it was agreed to unite Belgium (the Austrian Netherlands) and Holland to form the **Kingdom of the Netherlands.** This arrangement was confirmed by the congress of Vienna (1815, June 9).

1815-1840.   WILLIAM I, the former prince of Orange, a well-meaning but rather arbitrary and obstinate ruler. He granted a moderately **liberal constitution** (1815, Aug. 24), but failed to make the union of Belgium and Holland work. Traditions, customs, religion, and interests were different and the Belgians felt throughout that they were put in an inferior position. The seat of the government was in Holland, the king a Dutchman and a Calvinist; despite her larger population, Belgium had only equal representation in the lower chamber of the states-general or assembly; the majority of officers and officials were Dutch; the public establishments (banks, schools) were predominantly Dutch; Dutch was made the official language in all except the Walloon districts of Belgium; the public debt was equally divided, though in 1814 that of Holland was many times greater than that of Belgium; the Catholic Church in Belgium resented the equality of religious denominations; the Belgians disliked the Dutch tariff system, which, being liberal, gave inadequate protection to Belgian industry.

1828, July. The two Belgian parties (Clericals and Liberals) united after the king had estranged the Clericals by concluding a **concordat with the pope** (1827) giving the king the right to veto the election of bishops, and had estranged the Liberals by a harsh press law. The program of the two parties called for freedom of press, instruction, and worship, and for ministerial responsibility. Increased agitation for the redress of grievances, accompanied by much economic distress.

1830, Aug. 25. The **BELGIAN REVOLUTION,** stimulated by the **July Revolution in Paris** and by unrest among the lower classes. The moderate liberal elements asked only an autonomous administration and were willing to accept the king's son as viceroy.

Sept. 23-26.   Violent fighting in Brussels between the workers and the troops, who were obliged to evacuate the city. A provisional government was set up with **Charles Rogier** as leader.

Oct. 4.   Proclamation of independence. A national congress was summoned to draw up a constitution.

Oct. 27.   Bombardment of Antwerp by the Dutch made the Belgians irreconcilable.

Nov. 4. At the suggestion of Great Britain, a **conference of the powers** met at London and ordered an armistice.

Nov. 10. The Belgian national congress declared the house of Orange deposed, but voted for constitutional hereditary monarchy.

Nov. 15. Advent of **Lord Palmerston** to the British foreign office, following the downfall of the Wellington ministry. Palmerston was not unsympathetic to the Belgian claims, but was above all eager to check the spread of French influence in Belgium and to prevent war. Louis Philippe, confronted with a serious domestic situation in France, followed Britain and the two powers induced Russia (paralyzed by the Polish insurrection, p. 750), Austria, and Prussia to abandon the principle of legitimacy.

Dec. 20. The conference practically recognized the independence of Belgium by declaring the **dissolution of the Kingdom of the Netherlands.**

1831, Jan. 20, Jan 27. Two protocols set forth the bases of separation. The Dutch accepted the terms, but the Belgians refused.

Feb. 3. The Belgian national congress elected as king the **duke of Nemours,** second son of Louis Philippe. Energetic warnings and threats of Palmerston induced Louis Philippe to reject the election.

Feb. 7. The Belgians set up a regency under **Surlet de Chokier,** and the congress drew up a constitution on the British pattern, one of the most liberal in Europe.

June 4. The Belgians elected as king **Prince Leopold of Saxe-Coburg,** widower of Princess Charlotte of England and uncle of the future Queen Victoria, a cultured and shrewd prince.

June 26. The London conference, having approved of Leopold, drew up the **Eighteen Articles,** regulating the separation and more favorable to the Belgians. It was accepted by the Belgians, but rejected by King William of Holland.

Aug. 2. Breaking off the armistice, William sent a large army over the frontier, which quickly defeated an improvised Belgian force. A French army thereupon invaded the country and forced the Dutch to retire.

Oct. 14. The **Twenty-Four Articles,** drawn up by the London conference and more favorable to Holland. Still King William refused to agree or to evacuate Antwerp.

1832, Nov.-Dec. A French army and a Franco-British and French to conclude an armistice

1833, May 21. The Dutch were obliged by the British and French to conclude an armistice of indefinite length on the basis of the *status quo.*

1839, Apr. 19. King William finally accepted a settlement much like that of the Twenty-Four Articles. He recognized Belgium and accepted substantially the frontier of 1790, except for Luxemburg and. Limburg. The Belgians had claimed the whole of **Luxemburg,** but only the western part was given them; the rest, including the capital, remained a grand duchy with the king of Holland as grand duke. **Limburg** was also divided, the Belgians receiving about one-half. The **Scheldt** was declared open to the commerce of both countries and the national debt was divided. Article VII recognized Belgium as an **"independent and perpetually neutral state"** under the collective guaranty of the powers.

b. THE KINGDOM OF BELGIUM, 1830-1914

1831-1865. LEOPOLD I. During the early part of his reign the Clerical-Liberal coalition continued to rule the country, devoting itself to the consolidation of the kingdom, ably guided by the king.

1847. The coalition gave way to a party system and ministerial responsibility. Until 1884 the Liberals were generally in control of the government, first under the leadership of **Charles Rogier,** then of **Walther Frère-Orban.**

1848. A **new electoral law** lowered the franchise and doubled the number of voters. The success of the régime was attested by the fact that Belgium was almost alone among the Continental powers in escaping revolution.

1850. The **national bank** was founded as part of a general policy devoted to economic development.

1861-1862. Commercial treaties with France and Britain ushered in a period of free-trade policy.

1863. The **navigation of the Scheldt** was made free.

1865-1909. LEOPOLD II, like his father an able, energetic, strong-willed ruler and a man of vision.

1867-1870. A period of international uncertainty, arising from the **designs of Napoleon III** upon Belgium (p. 685) and culminating in the effort (1869) to secure control of the Belgian railways.

1870, Aug. 9, 11. Under British auspices, treaties were concluded between Great Britain, Prussia, and France guaranteeing **Belgian neutrality** during the Franco-Prussian War.

1879, July 1. Education act secularizing primary education. The public or "neutral" schools were to be supported by the communes with subventions from the government; no public support was to be given to the "free" or Catholic schools. This measure, passed by the Liberals, estranged the Clericals.

1880, June. The **Clericals won a majority** in the elections. They now replaced the Liberals and remained in power until the time of the First World War.

1884, Sept. 10. A **new education law** reversed that of 1879 and gave public support for church schools in Catholic districts.

1885, May 2. Establishment of the Congo Free State, with Leopold II as ruler. This great African empire had been built up by Leopold as a personal enterprise. Its recognition by the powers was a most unusual achievement (pp. 783, 878).

1886-1894. Labor unrest, with a series of major strikes. Economic development had been very rapid, with the result that social problems emerged in an acute form. With extensive coal mines, Belgium was able to industrialize to the point where it was the fourth manufacturing power in Europe. Under the circumstances socialism made great strides. The **Labor Party**

was founded in 1885 and soon took the place of the declining Liberal Party as the chief organ of opposition to the Clericals The Socialists demanded universal manhood suffrage and organized strikes as a method of bringing pressure.

1893, Apr. A general strike was proclaimed.

Apr. 27. The government introduced **universal suffrage,** but with a system of **plural voting** which gave two or three votes to about two-fifths of the voters who fulfilled certain requirements as to age, income, education, and family.

1895, Aug. 30. Instruction in the Catholic religion made compulsory in all public schools.

1899, Dec. 24. Adoption of **proportional representation** for the protection of political minorities. An alliance was formed between the Liberals and Socialists to demand "one man, one vote."

1901–1905. Another period of **strike activity,** punctuated by anarchist outrages, especially dynamitings.

1903–1904. The **Congo scandal,** arising from the revelation in England of labor conditions under Leopold's rule. A commission of inquiry was sent out in 1905. The Congo was ceded by the king to the Belgian nation in 1908 and became the Belgian Congo.

1909–1934. ALBERT I (b. 1875) succeeded his uncle, Leopold II.

1913, Apr. 14–24. A **political general strike** ended on the assurance of the government that the electoral system would be revised. The reform was delayed by the World War, but was finally accomplished on May 6, 1919, when universal suffrage without plural voting was established and certain women were given the vote.

Aug. 30. **Army Law** enacted, with the introduction of universal military service in place of the earlier system by which one son was taken from each family.

1914, Aug. 2. **German ultimatum to Belgium** demanding free passage for German armies. Belgium rejected the ultimatum and appealed to Britain and France.

Aug. 4. Beginning of the **invasion of Belgium** and German declaration of war (p. 805). (*Cont. p. 985.*)

c. THE KINGDOM OF THE NETHERLANDS, 1830–1914

1840, Oct. 7. **Abdication of William I,** who had become very unpopular because of his obstinate opposition to reform. He died in 1844.

1840–1849. WILLIAM II (b. 1792).

1848, Oct. The king, moved by the European revolutions of 1848 and pressed by the Liberals, under the distinguished jurist and statesman **Johan Thorbecke,** conceded a **revision of the constitution:** the power of the king was reduced and that of parliament greatly increased. Ministerial responsibility was provided and the upper house (thus far appointed by the king) was to be elected by the provincial assemblies. The lower house was still elected by a restricted suffrage.

1849–1890. WILLIAM III (b. 1817), an enlightened and benevolent ruler. His reign was marked by great **commercial expansion** and much internal development (canals, etc.). The political life of the country centered on the struggle of parties over the questions of religious education and the extension of the suffrage. The Liberals, largely representative of the trading classes and the towns, demanded a system of free secular schools. They were opposed by the Protestant Conservatives, the Calvinist peasantry and the Catholics, all of whom favored religious control of the public schools.

1862. **Slavery abolished** in the Dutch West Indies.

1867, Mar. The king made a treaty with France for the **sale of Luxemburg.** This gave rise to an international crisis and the dropping of the project. (p. 735).

1887, June 17. Introduction of **suffrage reform,** after a long period of agitation. The electorate was about doubled. The first Socialist was elected to parliament.

1889, Dec. 6. A **Calvinist-Catholic coalition,** following on a period of Liberal rule (1871–1888), passed a law providing financial assistance for all private denominational schools. Non-sectarian public schools continued to be state-supported.

1890–1948. WILHELMINA (b. 1880). Until 1898 the queen-mother, **Emma,** acted as regent.

1894. A **serious revolt** broke out in the **Dutch East Indies.** Another rising, in 1896, was put down only with considerable difficulty.

1896, June 29. A **new electoral law,** carried by a Liberal cabinet, again doubled the electorate (from 300,000 to 700,000), but the system was still far removed from universal suffrage and drew fire from the working classes.

1897–1901. The **Borgesius ministry** (Liberal), which passed much **social legislation,** such as accident insurance, improvement of housing, compulsory education for children, etc.

1901, Feb. 7. The **queen married Duke Henry of Mecklenburg-Schwerin.**

1901–1905. **Ministry of Abraham Kuyper** (Clerical).

1903, Apr. Great **railway and dock strikes,** which the government broke up by the use of

Belgium: The House of Saxe–Coburg (1831–   )

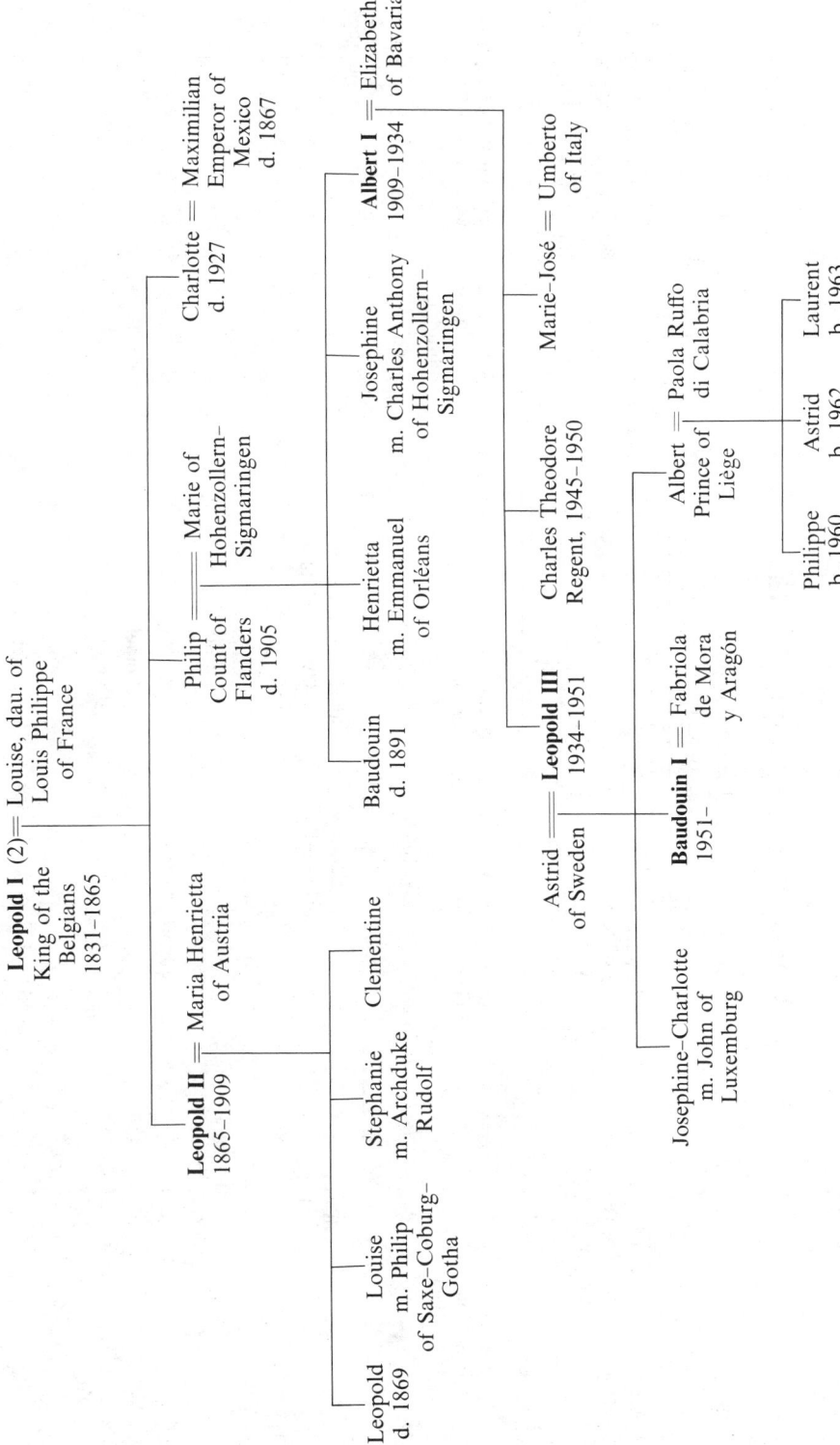

The House of Saxe–Coburg–Gotha (1800–   )

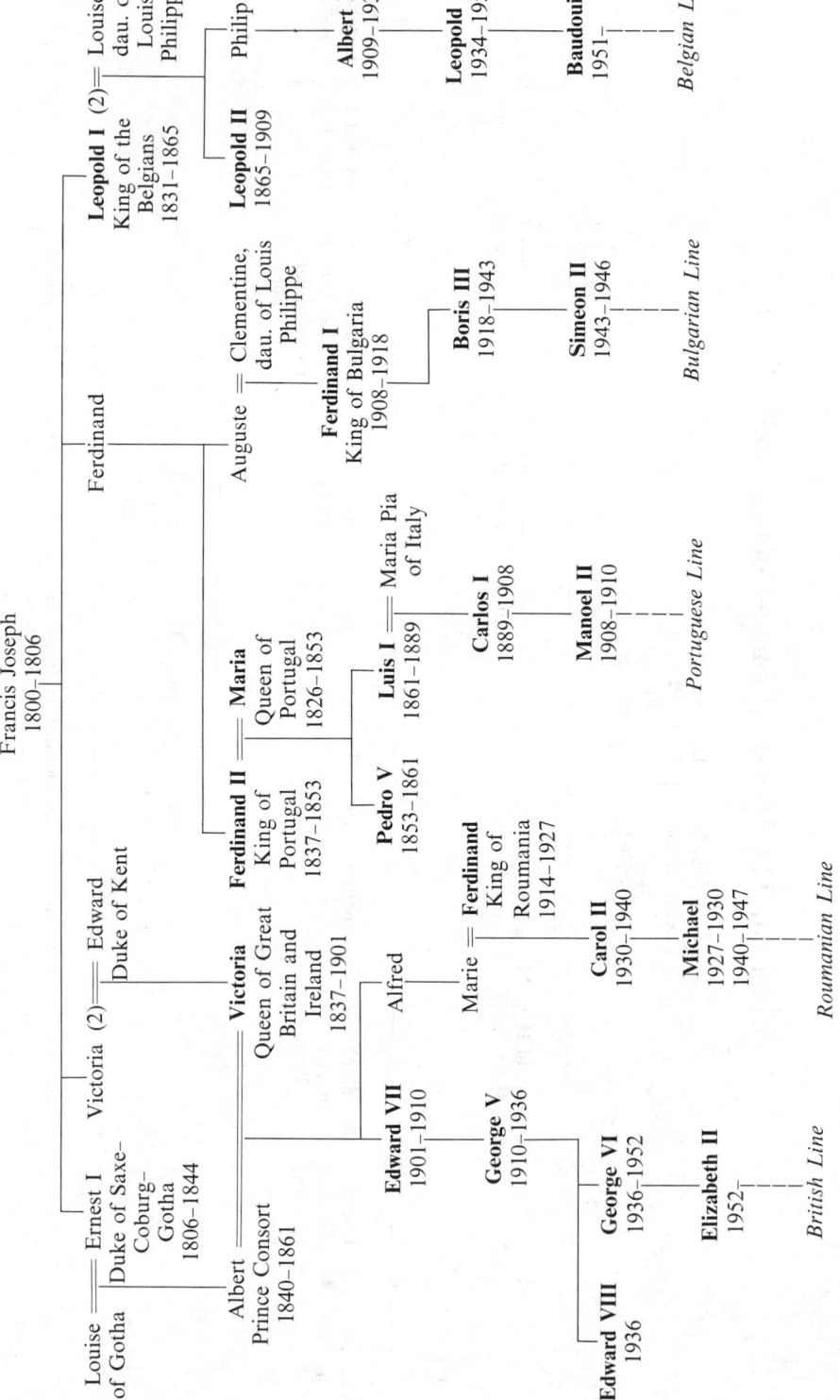

the military, thus arousing the forces of trade-unionism and socialism.

1905. The elections restored the Liberals to power, but the party, never very disciplined, continued to disintegrate.

1913, Aug. 25. An **extra-parliamentary cabinet** was formed by Cort van der Linden (Moderate Liberal) and set out to settle the suffrage and education questions. In 1917 (Nov.) **universal suffrage** and proportional representation were introduced. At the same time the Clericals were satisfied by the concession in full of the principle of absolute equality with regard to financial support for public nondenominational schools and private sectarian instruction.

(*Cont. p. 986.*)

4. FRANCE

[*For a complete list of the kings of France see Appendix VII.*]

(*From p. 652*)

a. THE RESTORATION MONARCHY, 1814–1830

1814–1824. LOUIS XVIII (b. 1755), brother of Louis XVI, easy-going, disillusioned, reasonable. He was permitted by the allies to return after the defeat of Napoleon, mainly through the influence of Tsar Alexander of Russia.

1814, June 14. The king granted the *charte constitutionnelle,* or **constitution,** a reflection of the tsar's liberalism and of Louis's desire to meet the demands of the middle classes. It created a system akin to that of the British, with an hereditary monarch, a chamber of peers nominated by the king, a chamber of deputies elected by a limited suffrage, and various guaranties of civil and religious liberty.

1815, Mar. 13. The sudden **return of Napoleon** from Elba obliged Louis to flee from Paris and remain in exile during the **Hundred Days** (p. 651). After Waterloo he made an undignified return to the capital "in the baggage of the allies" (July 7), whereupon the **second restoration** was accomplished. The king's influence was much reduced and he was unable to prevent a so-called **White Terror,** carried on by fanatical royalists, especially in the south, against revolutionaries and Bonapartists.

Aug. 22. The first parliamentary elections yielded a large majority for the **Ultra-royalist** group (*chambre introuvable*), whose reactionary policy was opposed by the ministry headed by the duke of Richelieu. The reaction went to such extremes that the king, under pressure from the allied representatives,

1816, Sept. Dissolved the chamber and called new elections. In the new chamber a majority of moderates supported the policy of Richelieu and that of his immediate successors, Dessolles (1818–1819), Decazes (1819–1820).

1816–1820. Moderate measures characterized the period of these ministries, among others laws freeing the press (1819, May 1).

1818. The **payment of the French indemnity** and the consequent evacuation of French soil by allied troops, the most notable achievement of Richelieu.

1820, Feb. 13. The **murder of the duke of Berri,** presumed to be the last of the Bourbon line, by an obscure fanatic, Louvel, was providential for the Ultras. The ministry of the duke of Decazes, favorite of the king, was overthrown and succeeded by a second Richelieu ministry (1820–1821).

1820. To preserve the country from the increasing danger from the Left, a **new electoral law** was passed (the *Law of the Double Vote*), which established a complicated system of election of two degrees, increased the electoral weight of voters in the upper tax brackets, and aimed to increase the influence of landed proprietors (source of Ultra support) at the expense of the middle class. This law, together with legislation on the press, personal liberty, etc., marked the beginning of the "reaction," which was to end only in the revolution of 1830.

1823, Apr. Invasion of Spain by French troops, in behalf of Ferdinand VII (p. 694).

1824–1830. CHARLES X (b. 1757).

1821–1827. Under the **Villèle ministry,** a resolute attempt was made to restore, in as large a measure as possible, the position which the monarchy had occupied under the old régime.

1825, Apr. A **Law of Indemnity** compensated the nobles for the losses of their lands during the revolution, at the expense of the holders of government bonds, largely the upper *bourgeoisie.* The Church was favored in various ways, notably by the adoption of the notorious

1826. Law of Sacrilege, imposing a death sentence for certain offenses of a "sacrilegious" character. The *bourgeoisie* was further alienated by the king's

1827, Apr. 30. Dissolution of the national guard, a preserve of the middle class. Secret societies sprang up, notably the Liberal electoral society, *Aide-toi, le ciel t'aidera.* Confident of his position, Charles X called a general election to strengthen his majority in the chamber.

1827, Nov. 17, 24. The election returned a Liberal majority, and the king was obliged to part with his Ultra minister, Villèle, and replace him with

1828, Jan. 3. Count Gay de Martignac, a moderate who, the king hoped, would please neither the Liberals nor the Ultras.

1829, Aug. 6. The **dismissal of Martignac** was followed by a revolutionary step, when the king appointed

Aug. 8. A ministry dominated by the **prince of Polignac,** "Ultra of the Ultras," which for the first time since 1816 did not possess the confidence of the chamber, a departure from the principle of ministerial responsibility, not stated in the constitution of 1814, but now generally accepted.

1830, Mar. 18. The king's act was censured in the answer to the address from the throne, signed by 221 Liberal deputies. Charles X dissolved the chamber.

May 16. New **elections** returned a majority unfavorable to the king, who, relying on the effect of the conquest of Algiers (June–July, p. 873), replied with the

July 26. FIVE "JULY" ORDINANCES, establishing a rigid governmental control of the press, dissolving the chamber, changing the electoral system in an attempt to insure an Ultra majority.

July 26. Adolphe Thiers, journalist and Liberal, drew up a protest against the ordinances on behalf of the Parisian journalists. The Liberal majority of the chamber also prepared a protest. But the dynamo of the **revolution of 1830** was radical Paris, in whose ranks a republican movement had been for some years forming.

July 28. The insurgents raised barricades, took the Hotel de Ville, and were masters of Paris (July 29.) The **marquis de Lafayette,** patriarch of the republican cause, headed the radical movement, which aimed to make him president of a French republic. The Liberal deputies hastily turned to **Louis Philippe,** duke of Orléans and representative of the younger Bourbon line, as the savior of the cause of constitutional monarchy.

July 30. Orléans was offered the lieutenant-generalship of the realm, was accepted by Lafayette on behalf of radical Paris, and was proclaimed *King of the French* by the Liberals sitting as a rump chamber (Aug. 7) under the charter of 1814, revised to insure the perpetuation of the new constitutional régime.

b. THE JULY MONARCHY, 1830–1848

1830–1848. REIGN OF LOUIS PHILIPPE (b. 1773).

1830–1836. Agitation of Republicans and other radicals, who had accepted Louis Philippe as a revolutionary monarch only to discover their mistake too late. The radicals were disillusioned by the cautious policy of the

1830, Nov. 2–1831, Mar. 13. Laffitte ministry with respect to the revolutions in Italy and Poland and by the government's opposition to the demands of the workers.

1831, Mar. 13–1832, May 16. Ministry of Auguste Casimir-Périer, a strong man who managed to restore order, but died in the great cholera epidemic of 1831–1832. Radical agitation and violence continued.

1831, Nov. A large-scale **insurrection of workers at Lyons** was put down with difficulty. Rapid spread of secret societies. Under a régime of press freedom the king was unsparingly attacked in the radical newspapers and mercilessly caricatured (notably by **Honoré Daumier).**

1832, Oct. 11–1834, July 15. Ministry of Marshal Soult, which included the duke of Broglie, Thiers, and Guizot, and represented the more conservative wing of liberalism.

1833, June 28. The **Primary Education Law,** brought in by Guizot. In the interests of safe doctrine it gave the Church (formerly attacked by the Liberals) extensive control of the primary schools.

1834, Apr. Climax of the radical movement in the **great revolts in Paris and Lyons,** repressed with great severity.

1835, Mar.–1836, Feb. Ministries of the duke of Broglie.

1835, July 28. Sanguinary attempt on the life of Louis Philippe by the Corsican radical, **Fieschi.**

1835, Sept. The **September Laws,** including a severe press law and other acts to accelerate the trials of insurgents and assure their conviction. These repressive laws brought the radical movement under control.

1836, Feb.–Sept. First Ministry of Adolphe Thiers.

1836–1839. Ministries of Count Louis Molé, the king's personal friend. Louis Philippe managed to establish something like personal rule by playing off the strong men in the Liberal movement and by appointing weak men to office. But the two groups of the opposition (Right Center: *party of resistance,* led by Guizot; Left Center: *party of movement,* led by Thiers) united and overthrew Molé, who was followed by a short-lived Soult ministry (1839, May–1840, Feb.).

1840, Mar.–Oct. Ministry of Thiers, who led France to the brink of war during the acute Near Eastern crisis (p. 772).

1840–1847. Ministry of Soult, in which **François Guizot** was the commanding figure. Guizot became premier in 1847 and remained in power until February 1848. He dominated the political scene through political and electoral manipulation and followed the direction of the king in a conservative policy.

1840–1848. Revival of radicalism and emergence of "utopian" socialism. The period was one of rapid industrial development (600 steam engines in France in 1830, 4853 in 1847; consumption of coal increased fivefold) and extension of communications (**Railway Act** of 1842: provided for government construction of roadbeds, bridges, tunnels, etc.). All this tended to raise a social question, which was treated by such eminent writers as **Henri de Saint-Simon, Charles Fourier, Étienne Cabet, Louis Blanc** (p. 591). The radical movement had been driven underground by the **September Laws,** but continued behind the façade of innocent **friendly societies** and in secret organizations of many kinds. Gradual merging of radical, republican, and socialist movements.

1846–1847. A severe **agricultural and industrial depression** caused widespread unemployment and suffering among the workers and predisposed them to revolutionary action when opportunity offered.

1847–1848. The **parliamentary opposition** to Guizot, led by Thiers and Odilon Barrot, demanding electoral reform (extension of suffrage) and an end of parliamentary corruption (office-holding by members, bribery, etc.), embarked upon an extra-parliamentary **campaign of banquets,** culminating in a great banquet in Paris, arranged for February 22, 1848, but prohibited by the government. The unrest engendered by this demonstration led to street disorders and to the revolution of February.

CULTURAL DEVELOPMENTS

The Romantic period of French literature flourished after the fall of Napoleon. Lyric poetry was revived by **Alphonse Louis-Marie de Lamartine** (1790–1869). The first novels of the Romantic period came from the pens of **Madame de Staël** (1766–1817), **François-René de Chateaubriand** (1768–1848), and **George Sand** (1804–1876); Alfred Victor, Comte **de Vigny** (1797–1863), wrote the first French historical novel (*Cinq-Mars,* 1826), in addition to poems

and plays. **Victor-Marie Hugo** (1802–1885) was poet, novelist (*Notre Dame de Paris,* 1831; *Les Miserables,* 1862), and dramatist (*Hernani,* 1830; *Ruy Blas,* 1838). The poet **Alfred de Musset** (1810–1857) also wrote some prose and a few plays. **Alexandre Dumas** the Elder (1802–1870) wrote plays and historical novels of action and suspense (*The Three Musketeers,* 1844; *The Count of Monte Cristo,* 1844–1845; *The Black Tulip,* 1845). **Théophile Gautier** (1811–1872) was the author of short tales as well as novels. Charles Augustin de **Saint-Beuve** (1804–1869) gave up romantic poetry in favor of a *History of Port-Royal* (1840–1860) and numerous critical writings. An interest in historical studies was evident following the Revolution in the work of **Augustin Thierry** (1795–1856), **François Guizot** (1787–1874), **Jules Michelet** (1798–1874).

The novels of **Honoré de Balzac** (1799–1850) provide detailed realistic descriptions of people and places; the novels of both **Prosper Mérimée** (1803–1870) and **Stendhal** (Henri Beyle, 1783–1842) remain partly in the Romantic tradition.

In the field of painting, **Eugène Delacroix** (1798–1863) and **Jean Auguste Ingres** (1780–1867) led the field; **Honoré Daumier** (1808–1879) was acclaimed for his lithographed caricatures. **François Rude** (1784–1855) was the creator of the powerful "Marseillaise" sculpture of the Arc de Triomphe, Paris.

Hector Berlioz (1803–1869) composed symphonic music and opera; **Frédéric Chopin** (1810–1849) composed for the piano.

c. THE SECOND REPUBLIC, 1848–1852

1848, Feb. 22. Workers, students, and others gathered to demonstrate in Paris. Barricades went up, and fighting began.

Feb. 23. The king replaced Guizot with Molé, satisfying the middle class but not the workers, who continued the struggle, and by the morning of February 24 had become masters of Paris.

Feb. 24. LOUIS PHILIPPE ABDICATED in favor of his grandson, the count of Paris, but the latter was ignored by a rump meeting of the chamber of deputies into which the Paris mob had filtered; the latter chose a provisional government, dominated by moderate republicans, which fused in turn at the Hôtel de Ville that evening with a more radical slate. The same evening the **republic was proclaimed** at the insistent demand of the mob (for the second time in France). The right wing of the government, dominated by the

(From p. 478)

The House of Bourbon-Orléans (1700-   )

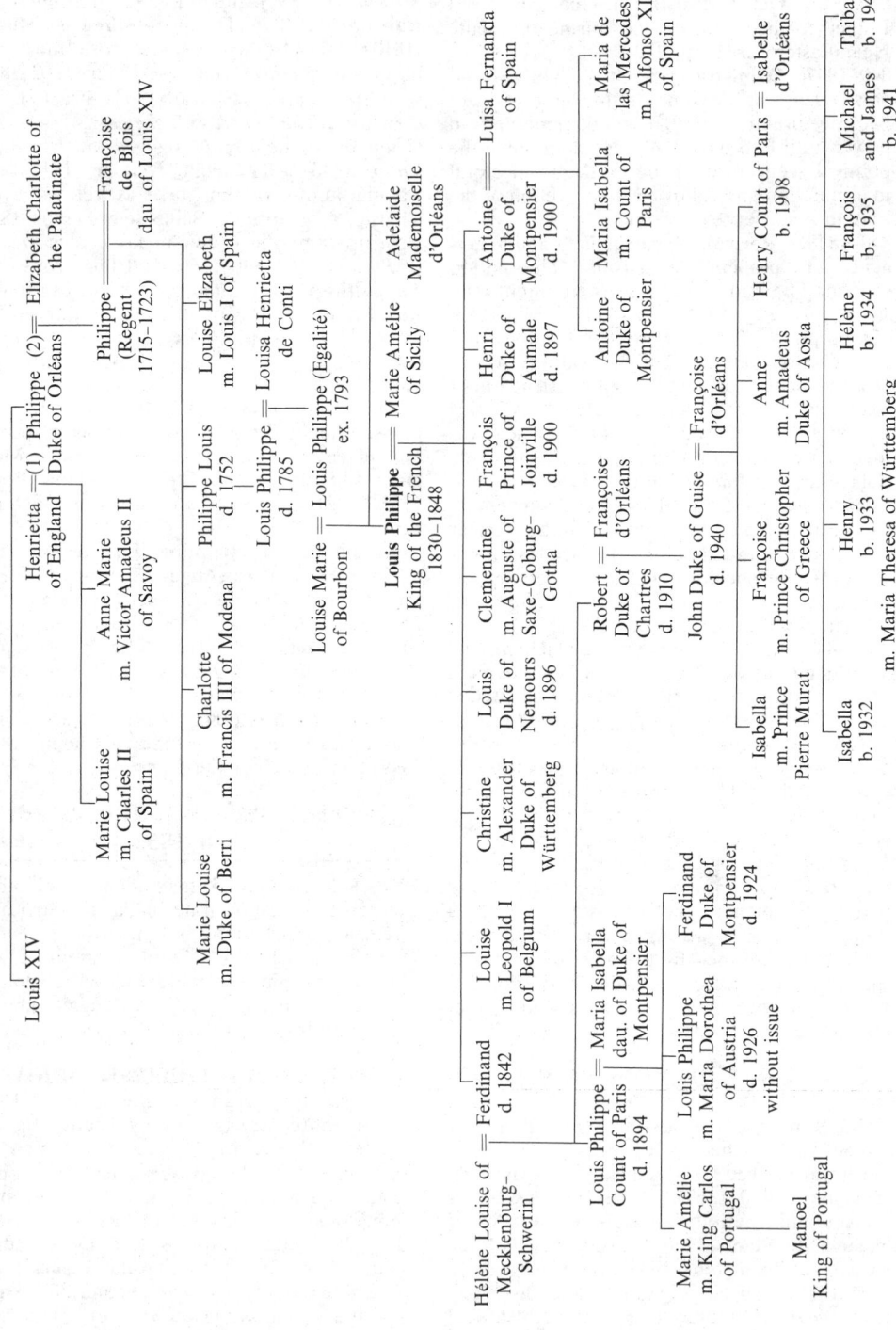

poet, **Alphonse de Lamartine,** was composed of members of the parliamentary opposition, willing to accept a republic and universal suffrage so long as the republic's program were moderate. The left wing, dominated by **Louis Blanc,** viewed the republic as the vestibule to far-reaching economic and social reforms, along the general lines sketched in Blanc's *Organisation du travail* (1839). The right wing had perforce to make concessions to the radicals, who had armed control of Paris during the days following the revolution.

Feb. 25. The government recognized the **right to work** (government guaranty of work relief) and implemented this promise with the

Feb. 26. Establishment of the national workshops, a large-scale but inefficient work-relief scheme in Paris. It also permitted Louis Blanc to set up

Feb. 28. The **Commission of the Luxembourg,** a kind of parliament of workers and employers to discuss questions of common interest, soon, however, deserted by the employers and accomplishing little. Meanwhile the right wing prepared to regain control of the situation by arranging for elections, by bringing troops to Paris, taking steps to render the national guard loyal to the "cause of order," etc. The workers became alarmed, organized

Mar. 17. A **monster radical demonstration** which might have overturned the government but for Louis Blanc, who guided it into moderate channels. Conservatives everywhere now became alarmed by the "specter of communism" which was raising its head.

Apr. 16. A **second demonstration** of workers in Paris completely miscarried.

Apr. 23. The **elections to the national or constituent assembly,** which was to give France a new constitution, were a victory for the moderate Republicans (**Lamartine**) with some 500 seats; the left wing (**Louis Blanc**) had fewer than a hundred; the Legitimists (seeking the return of the Bourbon line) had about a hundred; the Orléanists (supporters of the fallen dynasty of Louis Philippe), about 200.

May 15. In the face of the unfriendly national assembly, the workers prepared a new protest, organized a huge procession, which marched to the hall of the assembly, invaded it during a sitting, overturned the government, set up a new provisional government. The movement quickly collapsed. But the forces of order were by now terrified. They determined to dissolve the national workshops, whose membership had grown to more than a hundred thousand, denounced as "pretorians of revolt." The reply of the Parisian workers was

June 23–26. The **INSURRECTION OF JUNE,** which witnessed the bloodiest street-fighting Europe had seen. The executive commission, vacillating successor of the provisional government, was swept away; **General Louis Cavaignac** was made dictator *pro tempore* and suppressed the movement.

July–Aug. A **reaction** followed, punctuated by severe press legislation (aiming to eliminate radical newspapers), the suppression of secret societies, and laws for the rigid control of clubs and political associations.

Nov. 4. The assembly completed the **new constitution,** providing for a single chamber and a strong president (with a separation of powers and direct election under universal suffrage). The moderate Republicans' candidate, Cavaignac, was opposed by **Prince Louis Napoleon Bonaparte** (1808–1873), nephew of Napoleon I and pretender to the Napoleonic succession. Louis Napoleon had profited by the flowering of the "Napoleonic legend"; by the publicity attending two personal attempts at a *coup d'état* in France (Strasbourg, 1836; Boulogne, 1840); and by the demand after the June Days for a "strong man" to govern France.

Dec. 10. The **presidential elections** gave Louis Napoleon 5,327,345 votes; his opponents, 1,879,298.

Dec. 20. PRINCE LOUIS NAPOLEON took the oath as **president of the French Republic,** and promptly gave evidence of his "republicanism" by appointing a ministry dominated by Orléanists, headed by **Odilon Barrot,** despite the fact that the majority of the national assembly was Republican. The president had the support of five million electors, the constituent assembly was already obsolete.

1849, Jan. 29. Under the menace of troops quartered in Paris for that purpose, the assembly was obliged to vote its own dissolution, after the budget and certain organic laws completing the constitution should have been passed.

The conservative forces in society—such diverse elements as Legitimists, Orléanists, Bonapartists, some moderate Republicans—were united by means of a central committee (*Union électorale*) to win the elections to the new chamber on a program of "saving society" ("threatened" by the radical elements of 1848) through revival of the influence of the Catholic Church.

Apr.–June. The **French intervention against the Roman Republic** (p. 703) was part of this program, connived at by the president. After **Oudinot's** first defeat (Apr. 30), "the honor of the country and of the army" was turned to account as a slogan by the Conservatives, who won a large majority of the seats in the election. Actually the Radical Republicans (the "Mountain") fared much better in the elections than they had anticipated. Their leader, **Alexandre Ledru-Rollin,** was returned in five departments by two million votes.

June 13. He engineered an **abortive revolt in Paris,** which played into the hands of the Conservatives: severe measures were taken against the Radical Republicans—arrests were made in Paris and the provinces, banquets forbidden, mutual benefit societies dissolved. The severity of these measures overshot the mark, stimulated Republican propaganda in turn. The history of the new legislative assembly (*Corps législatif*) now became that of the struggle between the royalist Catholic majority and the Liberal and radical, Republican opposition groups. Louis Napoleon was determined to be captured by neither, to use the struggle for his own ends.

Oct. 31. Although French troops had restored Rome to Pius IX, Louis Napoleon opposed reintroduction of an absolutist régime. In this he was supported neither by his Catholic majority, nor by his own ministry. He accordingly dismissed Odilon Barrot and summoned **General d'Hautpoul** as premier, with a cabinet "devoted to his own person," in which the dominating figure was **Eugène Rouher,** minister of justice. With a ministry of his own men, the president had in fact established a thinly veiled dictatorship.

1850, Jan. 9. The president extended his control through a government bill, placing school teachers under the control of prefects.

Mar. 15. A **second education bill,** the so-called *Falloux Law* (prepared by the Catholic Legitimist, Vicomte Frédéric de Falloux), was grudgingly acquiesced in by the government, a concession to the Catholic majority. Its effect was to extend greatly Catholic influence in education, providing lower standards for Catholic than for state teachers, giving the clergy participation in school inspection, permitting the substitution of Catholic for lay schools by communes and departments (seeking to avoid the expense of maintaining state schools).

May 31. A further attack on radicalism was made in an **electoral law** requiring three years' residence in one place for all voters, to be attested by a tax receipt or employer's affidavit (affecting above all industrial workers, at once migratory and radical.)

June 9. Another act **forbade clubs and public meetings,** even for election purposes. Republican propaganda was paralyzed by various other means: newspapers overwhelmed

with lawsuits and fines, houses of Republicans searched, Republican civil servants dismissed on the slightest suspicion, etc.

By now, the empire was on the horizon. Was it to be accomplished legitimately or by force? Louis Napoleon turned first to legal methods, the **revision of Article 45 of the constitution,** which forbade two consecutive four-year terms for a president. The president had a clear majority in the assembly, but a vote of three-quarters was essential to revision.

1851, July 15. The proposal to revise was defeated by nearly 100 votes more than were needed. Not without considerable vacillation the president now decided to resort to force to accomplish his objects.

Dec. 2.   THE COUP D'ÉTAT. Plans were laid in great secrecy late in November. During the night of December 1–2 (December 2 was the anniversary of the victory of Napoleon I at Austerlitz) **Count Auguste de Morny,** the president's half-brother, had a proclamation printed, informing the people of the dissolution of the assembly, the restoration of universal suffrage (Louis Napoleon was here posing as the friend of the people tricked by an unfriendly legislature), convening the electors for a plebiscite concerning fundamental revision of the constitution. The people of Paris found themselves confronted by the army which occupied the Palais Bourbon, seat of the assembly. Leading deputies, Republican and Royalist (notably generals), prominent journalists, *et al.* were arrested in their beds. Two hundred deputies who met and proclaimed the fall of Louis Napoleon were arrested.

Dec. 3. A group of Republican deputies organized a **popular rising** (Faubourg St. Antoine); barricades went up.

Dec. 4. Troops were hurled against the workers by General **Jacques de Saint-Arnaud,** minister of war; the movement promptly collapsed, but not before many insurgents had been killed and unarmed crowds of pedestrians had been fired upon (Massacre of the Boulevards). Large numbers of arrests followed in Paris and the provinces, where numerous risings were summarily repressed.

Dec. 21. The **plebiscite,** feverishly "prepared" by Morny (now minister of the interior), gave to the president (7,500,000 votes to 640,000) the right to draw up a constitution: the great majority of Frenchmen was weary of parliamentary struggles, alarmed by popular risings, and ready to seek security beneath the authority of a second Napoleonic dictatorship. Repressive measures continued: nearly 20,000 persons were sentenced— 10,000 of them to transportation to Algeria.

1852, Jan. 14. The **new constitution** declared the chief of the state "responsible to the nation," but gave him "free and unfettered authority"; he commanded the forces on land and sea, could make war and peace, alone could initiate laws, promulgate laws, and issue decrees and regulations necessary to carry them into effect, etc. The constitution set up a **council of state,** chosen by the president, to formulate laws in secret sessions; a **senate,** with members appointed by the president, sitting in secret, empowered to reject laws judged unconstitutional, and to modify the constitution through its *consulta,* subject to the consent of the president; a **legislative assembly** (*Corps législatif*), which could accept or reject legislation, but which had no power to introduce or amend bills. Hence effective power rested in the hands of the president, who appointed the members of the council of state and the senate, and who exercised wide influence over the election of members of the legislative assembly through presentation of "official candidates," openly supported by the prefects. The constitution expressly stated: "The emperor governs *by means of* the ministers, the council of state, the senate, and the legislative assembly."

Sept. The president made a **provincial tour.** Under the influence of handpicked prefects, there were frequent cries of **Vive l'Empire!** The empire was the logical and obvious next step.

Nov. 2. The *senatus consultum* ratified by plebiscite (Nov. 21) and promulgated by decree (Dec. 2), declared the empire re-established.

d. THE SECOND EMPIRE: THE AUTHORITARIAN PERIOD, 1852–1860

1852–1870. NAPOLEON III, emperor.

1852, Feb. 17. Repressive measures. The **press** was kept under strict supervision by the police; newspapers could be established only with government permission and were obliged to deposit a large sum (50,000 francs in Paris) as guaranty of good behavior. The minister of the interior discharged and appointed editors, on nomination of the owners; he had power to suspend publication at any time.

Feb. 28. Promotion of material prosperity. The government authorized formation of joint-stock banks issuing long-term credit. The government-subsidized *Crédit foncier* (1852) was obliged to make loans at 5 per cent and later (1854) became a state institution. The *Crédit mobilier* (founded 1852 by the Pereire brothers) was a joint-stock bank whose func-

tion it was to initiate and support large companies, participate in public loans, etc. It played a large rôle in the development of railroads, shipping companies, public utilities. Napoleon embarked also upon an active **social policy:** improvement of workers' dwellings, donations to charitable institutions, formation of friendly societies. A huge program of **public works** was initiated, especially the rebuilding of Paris by **Baron Georges Haussmann,** made prefect of the Seine. Streets were widened and new boulevards opened. Paris soon became a new city, enlarged from 12 to 20 arrondissements by the annexation of the suburbs (1860). Its population grew from 1,297,064 in 1851 to 1,825,274 in 1866.

Dec. 25. The **powers of the emperor** were further extended by a *senatus consultum.* He was given authority to conclude treaties of commerce; the budget of every ministry was voted by the legislative assembly, but the subdivision of sums granted was to be settled by imperial decree.

1853, Jan. 30. Marriage of the emperor to Eugénie de Montijo, countess of Téba, daughter of a Spanish grandee. Beautiful and charming, the empress was simple and dignified in manner, but she was impulsive and ignorant, incapable of grasping affairs of state. Her rigorous religious training made her an enemy of liberalism and a leader of the Clerical party at the palace.

Napoleon III continued the policy of **concessions to the Church** initiated by the Falloux law: Catholic missions were developed, government grants were made to churches and religious bodies of a charitable or educational character, Catholic schools were favored and offered increased competition to state schools. Catholics as a whole welcomed and supported the empire as a "heaven-sent blessing," although the Liberal Catholic wing, notably **Count Charles de Montalembert,** urged the importance of a liberal political régime as the only type under which Catholicism could flourish.

1854, Mar. 28. FRANCE DECLARED WAR ON RUSSIA (Crimean War, p. 773). The war grew out of a dispute between France and Russia regarding the custody of holy places in Palestine (1850–1853). In part to please the Clericals, in part to assert French claims and maintain French prestige, Napoleon III, mindful of the poor impression made by Louis Philippe's cautious foreign policy, took a strong line and carried Britain with him.

1855, May–Nov. The **Paris International Exposition** bore witness to the technological and economic progress of France. Wages were rising rapidly, though costs of living rose even more. General prosperity. Height of Napoleon's popularity.

1856, Feb.–Apr.   Peace congress at Paris (p. 774). France once again the leading power in Europe, enjoying great military prestige.

Mar. 16.   Birth of the Prince Imperial, assuring the succession to the throne.

1857.   A railway law encouraged railway companies through an elaborate system of state guaranties of bonded interest. Railways developed rapidly from 3627 kilometers in 1851 to 16,207 in 1858.

1858, Jan. 14.   Attempt of Felice Orsini to assassinate Napoleon and the empress. Two persons were killed and a hundred wounded. This unfortunate episode initiated Napoleon's active participation in the problem of Italy, resting on his interest in oppressed nationalities and national self-determination, as well as the desire to acquire for France her "natural frontiers."

1859, May 12–July 12.   WAR OF FRANCE AND PIEDMONT against Austria (p. 706). The war, which took a turn not intended by Napoleon, estranged the Clerical elements in France, but brought France

1860, Mar. 24. The **annexation** of the Piedmontese provinces of **Savoy** and **Nice.**

1860, Jan. 23.   Commercial treaty with Great Britain, marking the initiation of a free-trade policy.

e. THE LIBERAL EMPIRE, 1860–1870

1860, Nov. 24.   Extension of the powers of the legislature. Napoleon, his popularity shaken by the Italian war and the commercial treaty with Britain, decided to revive parliamentary life, create parties, and exercise his power more indirectly by acting as mediator. The decrees of 1860 empowered the senate and legislative assembly to move and discuss freely a reply to the address from the throne; parliamentary debates were to be fully reported (thus saving governmental prestige in cases of failure by emphasizing the approval of a measure by a parliamentary majority). Both parties seized upon these concessions as an opening wedge to demand wider powers, the eventual revival of parliamentary institutions.

1861, Nov. 4. The **financial powers of the legislature** were next extended. A grandiose program of public works, an extravagant foreign policy had entailed rapidly mounting expenses. The annual deficit was about 100 million francs; by the end of 1861 the floating debt had reached nearly a billion francs. Financial policy was unsettled by the emper-

or's power to redistribute the estimates for the various departments after the budget had been voted *en bloc* and by his power to authorize supplementary loans on his own responsibility. To restore the confidence of the business world and to oblige the legislature to share imperial responsibility, Napoleon renounced the right to borrow money while the legislature was not in session and agreed that the budget should be voted by sections. But the emperor retained the right to alter the estimates, section by section. This defeated parliamentary control, gave rise to constant demands for an enlargement of the chamber's financial powers.

An opposition coalition rapidly grew up in the country, composed of such diverse elements as Catholics (outraged by the papal policy of Napoleon), Legitimists, Orléanists, Protectionists, and even Republicans—republican opposition had been reborn in the legislature when "the Five" (Emile Ollivier, Louis Darimon, Jacques Hénon, Louis Picard, Jules Favre) were returned in the elections of 1857 and by-elections of 1858.

Napoleon's position was rapidly undermined during the sixties by a series of failures in foreign policy.

1861–1867.   THE MEXICAN EXPEDITION (p. 859). Owing to the refusal of the revolutionary Juarez government to meet its obligations, France, Britain, and Spain decided (**convention of London,** Oct. 13, 1861) to force fulfillment of these obligations. They all landed troops at Vera Cruz (Dec. 1861), but the British and Spanish soon withdrew when they recognized Napoleon's more far-reaching plans, viz. to establish a Catholic Latin empire in Mexico while the United States was engaged in the Civil War. French troops took Mexico City (June 1863) and proclaimed Archduke Maximilian (brother of Francis Joseph I of Austria) as emperor. Maximilian was unable to maintain himself without French support. By 1866 the United States was vigorously demanding the withdrawal of the French and Napoleon was in dire need of his troops because of European complications. He therefore deserted Maximilian, who refused to abdicate (1866, Dec.). He was captured and executed by the Mexicans (June 19, 1867).

1862, Sept. 25. An attempt to conciliate the Papacy by warning the Italian government against a march on Rome succeeded only in estranging the Italian government.

1863. Napoleon's efforts to intervene against Russia in the **Polish Insurrection** (p. 750) broke down through the lukewarm attitude of the British and Austrians and through Prussia's support of Russia. The effect of the policy was to estrange Russia, with which power France had been on close terms of friendship since 1857.

1864. The September Convention. Reversing his attitude on the Roman question, Napoleon agreed to withdraw his troops from Rome within two years in return for a promise from the Italian government not to attack papal territory. This move outraged French Catholic opinion. The pope issued the encyclical *Quanta cura* and the *Syllabus of Errors* (p. 712) which were in part an attack on the French government (e.g. condemnation of the supremacy of the nation and of universal suffrage). Napoleon at once forbade publication of the *Syllabus* in France, and thereby further aroused the ire of the clergy.

These failures led to a more outspoken attitude on the part of the parliamentary opposition, which, in the elections of 1863, had polled a vote of almost two million and had returned 35 deputies to the chamber, of whom 17 were Republicans. Thiers denounced the extravagance in Mexico (Jan. 11, 1864) and demanded "the indispensable liberties" which became the slogan of his group.

1866, Mar. More than 40 members of the government majority in the chamber broke away and formed a **Third Party** which asked the emperor "to further the natural development of the great Act of 1860."

July 3. Prussian victory over Austria at Sadowa (p. 731). The French, who had expected a long war ending with French mediation and compensation, regarded the victory as a national humiliation. But the army was not ready and Napoleon's will was crippled by physical suffering occasioned by bladder stones. He failed to mobilize and acquiesced in the formation of the North German Confederation. His belated attempts to secure compensation from Prussia in the Rhineland, Luxemburg, or Belgium (1866–1867) failed completely and left him badly discredited.

1867, Jan. 19. The **right of interpellation** was granted the chamber, but every interpellation required the previous approval of four committees, so that the majority could forestall undesired questions.

Mar. 12. The senate demanded and was accorded the **right to examine the projected laws** in detail (instead of merely passing on their constitutionality) and to return them to the legislative assembly for further action. Thus the senate became a collaborator in legislation, though a reactionary one.

Nov. 3. Napoleon again alienated the Liberals and Republicans by sending troops to crush the Garibaldians before they could at-tack Rome (Mentana, p. 708).

1867–1870. ALLIANCE NEGOTIATIONS WITH AUSTRIA AND ITALY. These were part of the preparation for ultimate conflict with Prussia (regarded as inevitable after the Luxemburg affair of 1867, p. 735). **Napoleon met Francis Joseph at Salzburg** (1867, Aug. 18–21) and Francis Joseph paid a visit to Paris (Oct.). After the reorganization of the French army had begun (**army law of January 1868** adding 100,000 men and providing for complete rearmament), negotiations were initiated first with Austria, then with Italy, leading in 1869 to a draft treaty and to an exchange of letters between the sovereigns. The main obstacles to a firm agreement were the unwillingness of the Austrians to commit themselves to immediate action in a dispute between France and Prussia on a purely German issue, and the insistence of the Italians on the evacuation of Rome by the French. Nevertheless the French government mistakenly proceeded on the supposition that in case of war with Prussia, Austria and Italy could be relied upon to participate.

By 1868 there had been a marked **revival of republicanism** and **radicalism.** Strikes had been permitted by an act of May 1864 and trade unions, though still illegal, were connived at after an act of March 25, 1868. The result was a growing epidemic of strikes and a widespread of trade-unionism, with a corresponding strengthening of the republican sentiment. By 1868 the enemies of the imperial régime could be silenced only by candid concessions.

1868, May 11. A **liberal press law** made possible establishment of a newspaper by simple declaration; eliminated administrative interference in the form of warning, suspension, and suppression.

June 11. Limited right of public meeting was granted, each meeting to be held, however, in a closed building subject to supervision by a police officer empowered to dissolve it. Republican newspapers promptly multiplied; workers met to discuss economic problems, to end in attacking the political régime.

1869, May 23, 24. Parliamentary elections gave the government 4,438,000 votes to 3,355,000 for the opposition; the new chamber included 30 Republicans.

June 28. The Third Party interpellated the government, demanded the creation of a responsible ministry. With the co-operation of 40 deputies of the Left, the "116" of the Third Party had a majority. The emperor had to yield or embark on a struggle with at least one-half of his subjects.

July 12. He adopted the program of the 116. By decree of the senate (Sept. 6), the new régime was initiated: the legislative assembly was given the right to propose laws, criticize and vote the budget, choose its own officers; the senate became a deliberative body with public sessions, had the right to discuss laws voted by the assembly and send them back for consideration; ministers were declared responsible but were to "depend on the emperor alone"—an equivocal position casting doubt on how far the new régime could be considered "parliamentary."

Dec. 28. The Third Party pressed Napoleon for clarification of this situation, and he entrusted their chief, **Emile Ollivier,** with the formation of a "homogeneous cabinet, representative of the majority of the legislative assembly." Ollivier was faced by divisions within his own party, by growing revolutionary agitation in the country. **Leon Gambetta's** Republican **program of Belleville** demanded universal suffrage, freedom of the press, right of meeting, of combination, trial by jury for all political offenses, separation of Church and State, suppression of the standing army. Labor was rapidly organizing in trade unions, on one hand, and its more radical elements in the Marxist **First International.** This was twice dissolved in France by official action (Mar. 1868; June 1870). France was swept by an epidemic of strikes.

1870, Jan. 10. When the Republican journalist, **Victor Noir,** was shot by Prince Pierre Bonaparte, cousin of the emperor, his funeral was the occasion for a demonstration against the empire of some hundred thousand people. Ollivier's problem was no longer that of converting a liberal into a constitutional monarchy, but of saving the empire by concessions. Sweeping constitutional reforms followed:

Apr. 20. The senate was made an **upper house,** sharing legislative power with the assembly; constituent authority was taken from the senate and given to the people (no constitutional change was to be made without a plebiscite). The Bonapartists then sought a plebiscite (to strengthen the hand of the emperor): the nation was asked "whether it approved the liberal reforms effected in the constitution since 1860 . . . whether it ratified the *senatus consultum* of April 20, 1870." Battle was joined between empire and republic (Right Republicans, however, as the *Gauche ouverte,* supporting the government).

May 8. The **plebiscite** gave 7,358,786 "ayes," 1,571,939 "noes"; the Napoleonic empire seemed to have won new strength by this sweeping triumph. Within four months it was to be swept away by the war of 1870 (p. 736).

f. THE THIRD REPUBLIC, 1870-1914

1870, Sept. 2. The **capitulation of Napoleon III at Sedan** (p. 736) was a blow the empire was unable to survive.

Sept. 4. When the news became general in Paris, the mob invaded the Palais Bourbon and obliged the reluctant members of the rump of the legislative assembly to join in proclaiming the fall of the empire. In accordance with accepted revolutionary ritual, the **republic was proclaimed** at the Hôtel de Ville after a provisional **government of national defense** had been set up, of which **Gambetta** was the outstanding member, **General Louis Trochu** (who had recently sworn to die defending the Napoleonic dynasty) the president. The new government seemed faced by a hopeless task—winning a war already lost.

Sept. 19. After Sedan two German armies swept on and invested Paris. The government devoted itself to a desperate defense of the country, sent a delegation to Tours to organize resistance in the provinces, which was presently joined by Gambetta, who escaped from besieged Paris in a balloon and virtually governed France (beyond Paris) in the succeeding months.

The populace of Paris was disgusted by the inactivity of Trochu, who possessed a force superior in size to the investing army; was further outraged by the "treasonable"

Oct. 27. Surrender of General Achille Bazaine at Metz, with 173,000 men.

Oct. 31. This discontent crystallized in a Paris *putsch* of **socialists and radicals,** aiming to establish a commune in the tradition of 1792 and carry on the war to the finish. The movement collapsed. By January the Parisian populace was reduced to a miserable state. With only eight days' supply of food remaining,

1871, Jan. 28. Paris capitulated. The armistice agreement yielded the forts to the Germans, provided for an indemnity of five billion francs, and disarmed the troops of the line in the city. By the armistice Bismarck also agreed to permit election of a representative assembly to determine whether the war should be continued or on what terms peace should be made.

Feb. 8. Elections were held.

Feb. 13. The national assembly met at Bordeaux. From Tours Gambetta had organized armed resistance in the provinces, with the aid of a young mining engineer, **Charles de Freycinet;** the obstinate fighting of these hastily improvised forces amazed the German command. But by mid-January this resistance had been substantially crushed, the country was exhausted, the majority of Frenchmen wanted peace. Under these conditions only the **Radical Republicans** and **Socialists** wanted to continue the war "to the last ditch." Hence the country elected an assembly two-thirds of whom were conservatives.

Feb. 16. The assembly elected **Adolphe Thiers,** who had won a reputation as the Cassandra of imperial collapse, **chief of the executive power.**

Feb. 28. Thiers introduced the **terms of a peace treaty** negotiated with Bismarck by **Jules Favre** and himself providing for the **cession of Alsace and a part of Lorraine,** an indemnity of five billion francs, an army of occupation to remain until the indemnity should have been paid. The terms were hotly opposed by the representatives of Alsace and Lorraine, by Louis Blanc, Gambetta, Georges Clemenceau, and others; but accepted, 546 to 107 (Mar. 1).

May 10. The definitive **treaty of peace was signed at Frankfurt,** embodying the terms accepted March 1, but with certain territorial rectifications, etc. Thiers proclaimed his own neutrality in the face of party division within the assembly and urged the necessity of the co-operation of all in the task of national recovery (**pact of Bordeaux,** Feb. 19). The assembly adjourned (Mar. 11) to meet again at Versailles (Mar. 20).

Mar.–May. THE PARIS COMMUNE. Mar. 1–3. Radical Paris, which had undergone the fruitless suffering of four months' siege, felt itself further humiliated by the entry of German troops into the capital and by the peace terms accepted by the national assembly; it was alarmed by the composition of the assembly, whose majority was obviously unfriendly to the republic. Discontent spread rapidly. The national guard, which the Germans had failed to disarm by the armistice of January 28, appointed a central committee, seized cannon belonging to the regular army, prepared for the eventualities of conflict.

Mar. 18. Thiers sent troops of the line to seize the cannon; they fraternized with the crowd, refused to fire; the mob seized and executed Generals **Lecomte** and **Thomas;** the troops retired, leaving Paris in the hands of the radicals. Election of a municipal council (the **Commune of 1871**) was called by the central committee of the national guard for March 26. The **Commune** included Moderate Republicans, Radical Republicans (of the 1793 Jacobin tradition), followers of Proudhon, followers of Blanqui, members of the **First International.** A body of such diverse tendencies had no clear-cut program, "socialist" or otherwise. It sought to decentralize France by

enlarging the powers of municipalities; to substitute the national guard for the standing army; to separate Church and State **(law of April 2).** But opportunity for carrying through a legislative program was cut short by the armed struggle with the government of the national assembly at Versailles.

Apr. 2. The Versailles troops took the offensive, defeated the troops of the Commune repeatedly, entered Paris, reduced the city in the face of desperate but unorganized resistance behind barricades in the **Bloody Week** (May 21–28). Hostages taken by the Communards, including **Archbishop Darboy** of Paris, had been executed. The victors replied by visiting summary and sanguinary punishment through courts-martial on a large but indeterminate number of prisoners; others in large numbers were deported or imprisoned.

1871–1873. THE MONARCHIST OFFENSIVE. The Monarchist majority of the national assembly, summoned to answer the question of war or peace, was determined to settle the question of a new régime for France before separating. The Monarchists were divided: of those originally elected, some 200 were **Legitimists** (supporters of the "legitimate" Bourbon line and of its pretender, the **count of Chambord**), the same number **Orléanists** (supporters of the **count of Paris,** grandson of Louis Philippe), some thirty **Bonapartists.** Legitimists and Orléanists would hear nothing of a restoration of the "parvenu" Napoleonic dynasty.

1871, July 6. The **count of Chambord** alienated both the Orléanists and the country by declaring categorically that he must rule under the white flag of the Bourbons. Meanwhile Republicans gained ground in by-elections to the national assembly.

Aug. 31. Thiers's title became *President of the Republic* by the **Law Rivet-Vitet,** which, however, also declared that the assembly possessed constituent powers. Thiers, originally a staunch Orléanist, was rallying to the *conservative republic* as a *pis aller* ("the government which divides us least"). The Monarchist majority permitted him to accomplish the patriotic task of paying the German indemnity (through two government loans, June 21, 1871, July 15, 1872), bringing with it **evacuation of French territory** (the last German soldier crossed the frontier September 16, 1873). They then condemned the government of Thiers as insufficiently "conservative" (vote of 360 to 344).

1873, May 24. Thiers promptly resigned, and **Marshal Marie Edmé MacMahon** was elected president at the same session. MacMahon, soldier by profession, monarchist by predilection, neophyte in politics, was to prepare the way for the restoration.

Aug. 5. The count of Chambord and the count of Paris became reconciled, and it was agreed that the latter should succeed the former, who was childless.

Oct. 27. The plan foundered when the count of Chambord insisted once again on the white flag.

Nov. 20. To give itself time to reform its forces, the Monarchist majority conferred the powers of president on MacMahon for seven years **(Law of the Septennate).**

1875.   THE CONSTITUTION OF 1875. After prolonged discussion of various constitutional projects, a **Law on the Organization of the Public Powers** was introduced.

Jan. 21.   Henri Wallon proposed an amendment: "The president of the republic is elected by an absolute majority of the votes of the senate and the chamber of deputies sitting together as the national assembly. He is chosen for seven years. He is eligible for re-election." The term *republic* was crucial: acceptance of the amendment meant acceptance of the republic. The *impasse* caused by the failure of the Monarchists had resulted in some disintegration in their ranks.

Jan. 30. The **Wallon amendment was adopted** by one vote—353 to 352. The **Law on the Organization of the Public Powers** was accepted as a whole (Feb. 25); the **Law on the Organization of the Senate** had been accepted (Feb. 24). A **Law on the Relation of the Public Powers** (passed July 16) completed the so-called **Constitution of 1875.** The executive was a president (who was not to be a member of the legislative body) elected according to the Wallon amendment, possessed of the usual executive powers (command of the army and navy, right to choose civil officials and military officers, etc.), but requiring a counter-signature for each of his acts by the relevant minister. The ministers were declared responsible, each for his own acts, together for the general policy of the government. The senate was to have 300 members, 225 chosen for nine years, on the basis of a complicated and indirect system of election, 75 named by the national assembly (later by the senate) for life (senators for life were discontinued in 1884). The senate shared the right to initiate legislation (except finance laws) with the chamber of deputies, whose members were elected by universal, direct, manhood suffrage. The chamber could be dissolved only by the president, with the consent of the senate. The seat of the government was fixed at Versailles, reflecting fear of Republican Paris.

Apr.–May. The famous **war scare** during which the duke of Decazes, French foreign minister, secured the intervention of Britain and Russia at Berlin (p. 778).

1877, May 16.   CRISIS OF *SEIZE MAI.* The national assembly came to an end and the new senate and chamber met for the first time (1876, Mar. 8). The senate had a Conservative majority, the chamber was overwhelmingly Republican. In the next quarter-century the new republican institutions were to be repeatedly attacked by their enemies of the Right. The first test came in the affair of the *Seize Mai* when MacMahon, irritated by what he considered inadequate opposition of the premier, **Jules Simon,** to the anti-clerical attitude of the Left, forced Simon to resign. Had the power of dismissal of ministries been conceded to the president, the chamber's control of ministries would have disappeared, and the president would have been given the powers held by Louis Napoleon, 1848–1851 (p. 682).

June 19. A new cabinet, headed by the Orléanist **duke of Broglie,** was given a vote of "no confidence" by the chamber, 363 to 158; MacMahon dissolved the chamber with the consent of the senate (the only dissolution in the history of the Third Republic).

Oct. 14, 28. In the elections, despite vigorous governmental pressure, the Republicans lost only 36 seats.

Nov. 19. The Broglie ministry was forced to retire by an adverse majority (312 to 205); its successor, the presidential **Rochebouët ministry** (Nov. 24) fared the same.

Dec. 13. MacMahon was forced to retreat, named **Jules Dufaure** to head a ministry with the confidence of the chamber. The principle of ministerial responsibility had won over that of the personal power of the president.

1879, Jan. 5. In the **senatorial election** the Republicans gained 58 seats; faced by a hostile majority in the senate and chamber.

Jan. 30.   MacMahon resigned (although his term of office had more than a year to run), and was succeeded by a Conservative Republican, **Jules Grévy.**

1879–1887.   PRESIDENCY OF JULES GRÉVY. The Conservative Republicans **(Opportunists),** in power from 1879 to 1885, proceeded to a series of **anti-clerical laws:**

1880, Mar. 29, 30. Two decrees (1) enjoining all non-authorized **religious associations** to regularize their position within three months; (2) ordering dissolution and **dispersion of the Jesuits** within three months and dissolution of all religious teaching associations within six months (giving effect to the decree of 1762 and later legislation).

July 11. A law providing virtually **full amnesty to the Communards** of 1871.

1881, Mar.-May. French occupation of Tunis (**treaty of Bardo,** May 12), largely the work of Jules Ferry (1832–1893); important as marking the emergence of French imperialism and the expansion of the second French Empire (pp. 782, 873).

1882, Mar. 29. Primary education law, making education from six to thirteen free, obligatory, and "neutral" (i.e. public schools were to give no religious education).

1884, July 27. Law re-establishing divorce substantially as it had been permitted under the civil code (divorce had been abolished by the law of May 8, 1816).

Further important legislation included

1884, Mar. 21. The **Trade-Union Act** legalizing unions forbidden by the *Loi Chapelier* (of 1791) and subsequent legislation, but tolerated since 1868. By this time the **labor movement,** temporarily in eclipse after the Commune, had begun to revive and to veer in a Marxian direction. In 1876 **Jules Guesde** had returned from exile and had begun to propagate Marxian ideas. At the **third congress of French workers** (Marseilles) in October 1879 the Guesdists had won the day over the more idealistic cooperative socialists and steps were taken to organize a socialist political party, the *Fédération du Parti des Travailleurs Socialistes de France.* In the party the more moderate group (**Possibilists**) were at first dominant. In 1882 the Guesdists withdrew and formed the *Parti Ouvrier Français,* while the Possibilists reorganized the majority as the *Parti Ouvrier Socialiste Révolutionnaire Français.*

1884–1885. French advance in Tonkin, resulting in war with China (p. 912) and downfall of the second Ferry ministry (1883–1885).

1886–1889. THE BOULANGER CRISIS. This arose from widespread discontent with the Conservative Republican régime. The Radical Republicans wished to democratize further the constitution and to separate the Church and State; the workers were suffering from depression and demanding state action in their behalf; the Monarchists continued to hope for an eventual restoration. The **elections of 1885** were a victory for the Right (202 seats as against 80 in 1881), although the various Republican groups still had 372 seats.

1886, Jan. 4. General Georges Boulanger became minister of war in the Freycinet cabinet. He was the friend and protégé of **Georges Clemenceau,** dominant figure among the Radical Republicans, who had imposed Boulanger on Freycinet. Boulanger won popularity in the army through various reforms (improvement of soldiers' food and living conditions, etc.); among the people by frequent and impressive appearances in public, notably on July 14, 1886. He was celebrated in poem and song, became a national figure with the **Schnaebelé incident** (p. 785) and the attacks of the German press, and was greeted as the incarnation of the *révanche.*

1887, May 18. When **Boulanger** left office (fall of the Goblet cabinet), his popularity only increased. The government became alarmed, exiled Boulanger to Clermont-Ferrand as commandant of the 13th Army Corps. The **Wilson scandal** shook the prestige of the republic and offered Boulanger an opportunity to widen his contacts. Daniel Wilson, son-in-law of President Grévy, was discovered to have been trafficking in medals of the Legion of Honor: Grévy, although not guilty of complicity, was forced to resign the presidency (Dec. 2). He was succeeded by **Marie François Sadi-Carnot.**

1887–1894. Presidency of Sadi-Carnot, an honest but undistinguished politician, grandson of Lazare Carnot, "organizer of victory" in 1793.

During the Wilson crisis, Boulanger maintained relations with the Radical Republicans and made contact with the Orléanist leaders (*Nuits historiques,* Nov. 28–30, 1887)—apparently ready to satisfy his ambitions by whatever path offered. Boulanger, although ineligible for the chamber, permitted his candidacy to be posed repeatedly as a test of his popularity.

1888, Mar. 27. The government, alarmed, put him on the retired list; he was now eligible for the chamber, to which he was promptly elected (Apr. 15). He initiated a vigorous **campaign for revision of the constitution** (in what sense was not specified); demanded dissolution of the chamber as an essential preliminary; resigned from the chamber (July 12) and was returned in three constituencies simultaneously (Aug. 19).

1889, Jan. 27. Boulanger won a striking victory in Paris. It was believed he would march on the Elysée Palace that night and make himself master of France. But he failed to seize the opportunity to make himself dictator and his popularity rapidly declined. The government prepared to have him tried for treason by the senate; and he fled into exile (Apr. 8), where he eventually committed suicide on his mistress' grave in Brussels (1891, Sept. 30).

July 17. Meanwhile a law was adopted forbidding **multiple candidacies.** The general elections of 1889 were a triumph for the Republicans, a crushing defeat for the Boulangists.

1890 ff. The Ralliement. The Boulangist fiasco was a blow to the monarchists and their ally, the Church. **Pope Leo XIII,** discouraged by the failures of the monarchists, turned to a policy of conciliation of the republic.

1890, Nov. 12. **Charles Cardinal Lavigerie,** primate of Africa, in a famous toast at a banquet to French naval officers at Algiers **(Algiers Toast),** declared it the duty of all citizens to "rally" to the support of the existing form of government, once that form of government had been accepted by the people. This so-called *ralliement* to the republic was vigorously combated by Monarchists and Clericals on the one-hand, and by Radical Republicans and Socialists on the other. But the pope was influenced, notably by the international situation (p. 713), to espouse Lavigerie's policy.

1891, May 15. The encyclical *Rerum novarum* (on the condition of the workers) attempted to win the support of both Radical and Conservative Republicans through a more liberal (though by no means radical) statement of papal views on the social question; more specific support to the movement came in the encyclical *Inter innumeras* (Feb. 16, 1892), which declared that a government once established was legitimate. Despite opposition, the *ralliement* introduced a new spirit into the relations of Church and State in France: the period of the **Méline ministry** (1896–1898) has been termed "the Golden Age of Clericalism." Eventually the *ralliement* foundered in the struggle over Dreyfus (p. 691).

July. Visit of a French squadron to Cronstadt. Beginning of the **Franco-Russian Alliance** negotiations (p. 786).

1892–1893. **THE PANAMA SCANDAL.** Attracted by the name of **Ferdinand de Lesseps,** builder of the Suez Canal, and president of the Panama Company (*Compagnie du Canal Interocéanique*), French investors, from peasant to capitalist, had contributed to the Panama Canal project to the extent of 1,500,000,000 francs. The company collapsed (1889, Feb.) as a result of corruption and mismanagement, but despite the uproar, it was nearly four years before legal action was taken against Lesseps and his associates (1892, Nov. 19). In the course of a parliamentary investigation and two trials, it was revealed that the company had made lavish distributions to the press and to a certain number of deputies and senators (in the interest of securing their support for parliamentary authorization of a stock lottery). The company's intermediary was **Baron Jacques Reinach,** Jewish banker of German origin, who was found dead the day after he was summoned for trial. The revelations caused widespread consternation, increased by knowledge that the government had attempted to silence the whole affair.

1893, Feb. 9. Ferdinand de Lesseps and some of his associates were condemned by the court of appeal to pay large fines and serve prison sentences, but the decree of the court was set aside by the *cour de cassation* (June 15) on the grounds that the three years under the criminal statute of limitations had expired. Of the numerous senators, deputies, and others tried before the court of assizes, only three were found guilty, one (Baïhaut) on his own confession that he had received 375,000 francs.

Further development of **socialism** and the **labor movement.** In 1890 a further split in the ranks of the Possibilists had taken place, precipitated by **Jean Allemane,** who criticized the majority for accepting public office and co-operating with the bourgeoisie. The new faction took the name *Parti Ouvrier Socialiste Révolutionnaire*. With the progress of the industrial revolution and the consequent growth of the proletariat, the social question became ever more acute. Collisions between workers and the forces of "order" became more and more frequent. In the **Massacre of Fourmies** (1891, May 1) the troops fired on a crowd of demonstrating workers and killed women and children, causing a great sensation. The government of the Conservative Republicans continued lukewarm in the matter of social reform, with the result that extremist elements in the labor movement became more and more active. The **anarchists** (disciples of **Michael Bakunin** and **Prince Peter Kropotkin**) began a long series of outrages (dynamiting and assassination). In March 1892 a number of bombings were carried out by **Francois Ravachol,** an anarchist.

Oct. Visit of a Russian squadron to Toulon, followed by the conclusion (1893, Dec.–1894, Jan.) of the **Franco-Russian Alliance** (p. 786).

Dec. 9. **Auguste Vaillant,** another anarchist, exploded a bomb in the chamber of deputies.

1894, June 24. **President Carnot was stabbed** at Lyons by an Italian anarchist, **Santo Caserio.**

Meanwhile, the various socialist parties had begun to concert action. In 1893 they had elected some 50 deputies. The trade unions, which had developed rapidly after the law of 1884, organized nationally in the *Fédération des Syndicats* (by trades) and in the *Fédération des Bourses du Travail* (each representing the different trades in one locality). Under the influence of anarchism

1894. The **Trade-Union Congress at Nantes** adopted the principle of the **general strike.**

1894, June 27–1895, Jan. 17. **Presidency of Jean Casimir-Perier,** who resigned in disgust.

1895. The **Trade-Union Congress** at Limoges

organized the *Confédération Générale du Travail* (C.G.T.) with a program of direct action, seeking to destroy the capitalist régime and the state by means of the general strike and to prepare for this eventual cataclysm through local strikes, boycotts, and sabotage (a theory later given classic formulation by **Georges Sorel** in his *Reflections on Violence*, 1908). By the end of the century the workers' organizations—radical revolutionaries harking back to Auguste Blanqui; socialists of various stamps; anarchists; syndicalists—constituted a real power in the country, which was, however, dissipated by divergences of view and mutual antagonism.

1895–1899. Presidency of Félix Faure (1841–1899), prosperous and conservatively minded business man and politician. During his presidency the **ministry of Félix Méline** marked the last flowering of conservative, protectionist, clerical republicanism.

1894–1906. THE DREYFUS AFFAIR. Captain Alfred Dreyfus, probationer (*stagiaire*) of the general staff of the army, was arrested (1894, Oct. 15) charged with treason. He was tried by a court-martial *in camera*, condemned (Dec. 22), degraded, deported to Devil's Island in French Guiana. The evidence was a list of military documents (the *bordereau*), apparently submitted by a treasonable member of the general staff to the German military attaché, later purloined from the latter's mail by a French spy and submitted to the French intelligence service. The latter's handwriting experts disagreed as to whether the writing was that of Dreyfus; further "secret" evidence, subsequently shown to be irrelevant or forged, was also introduced and was said to have been considered conclusive. The presence of treason in the general staff had been aired in the press and had excited public opinion; the honor of the army seemed to be engaged; a victim was needed, and Dreyfus was the only one to whom the evidence pointed at all. Moreover, the real culprit was a friend of a member of the general staff, **Major Hubert Henry,** who sought to protect him. Dreyfus was a Jew, intensely disliked by most of his conservative colleagues of the general staff, who were Catholic, royalist, anti-Semitic. Dreyfus, wealthy and ambitious, son of an Alsatian patriot who had opted for France after the cession of 1871, apparently had no motive for treason.

1896, Mar. Colonel Georges Picquart, new chief of the intelligence service, had delivered to him a second document (the *petit bleu*), a card of the type used in the Paris pneumatic postal service. The card was addressed to a former member of the general staff, **Major**

Count Walsin-Esterhazy, then stationed at Rouen, French by birth, former officer in the Austrian army, in the papal zouaves, in the foreign legion; *débauché,* gambler, *arriviste.* Picquart compared a specimen of Esterhazy's writing with that of the *bordereau,* concluded they were identical, submitted his evidence to General Gonse (second in command of the general staff), was told to say nothing of the matter—that the affair could not be reopened. Picquart was transferred to a frontier post in Tunis.

1897, Nov. 15. Mathieu Dreyfus, brother of Alfred, discovered independently that the *bordereau* was in Esterhazy's writing, and demanded the latter's trial.

1898, Jan. 11. Esterhazy was tried by a military tribunal, and triumphantly acquitted.

Jan. 13. The novelist **Émile Zola** promptly published an open letter (*J'accuse*) to the president of the republic, denouncing by name the members of the general staff associated with the condemnation of Dreyfus.

Feb. 23. Zola was tried and condemned to one year imprisonment.

It was presently discovered that a decisive document in the secret Dreyfus *dossier* had been forged by **Colonel** (formerly Major) **Henry,** now chief of the intelligence service.

Aug. 30. When Henry admitted the forgery (only the first of a series to be discovered), **General de Boisdeffre,** chief of the general staff, resigned. Henry was imprisoned and committed suicide the next day. A rehearing for Dreyfus was promptly sought by his wife (Sept. 3).

Sept.–Nov. The **Fashoda crisis** (p. 791) brought France and England to the brink of war.

By this time France was divided into two camps, and the *Affair* had taken on a profound political complexion: **Dreyfusards** (those interested in preserving the republic) ranged themselves against **anti-Dreyfusards** (the army and a large body of Royalists and Catholics—forces interested in a restoration of the monarchy). A violent campaign in the press, both Nationalist and Republican followed. Street clashes were frequent. The various socialist parties, who had at first considered the *Affair* a mere "*bourgeois* quarrel," now saw the republic threatened.

Oct. 16. In a mass meeting in Paris the socialists concerted forces to defend the republic against its "attackers."

1899, Feb. 16. The sudden **death of President Faure,** opponent of a retrial for Dreyfus, was followed by the election of the colorless **Émile Loubet,** considered a friend of revision.

1899–1906. Presidency of Émile Loubet.

1899, June 3. The *cour de cassation* (highest court of appeal) set aside the condemnation of Dreyfus, and summoned a court-martial at Rennes.

Sept. 9. Dreyfus was again found guilty, this time with "extenuating circumstances"; he was condemned to ten years' imprisonment.

Sept. 19. By presidential decree, he was pardoned—first act of pacification of the **ministry of René Waldeck-Rousseau,** formed June 22, 1899, to bring internal peace to the country. The Dreyfusards painfully accumulated new evidence, and Dreyfus finally asked a rehearing. On July 12, 1906 the *cour de cassation* set aside the judgment of the court-martial at Rennes, declaring it "wrongful" and "erroneous." The government decorated Dreyfus (July 13) and raised him to the rank of major.

1901–1905. SEPARATION OF CHURCH AND STATE. The outcome of the Dreyfus affair was a victory for the republic, a defeat for its enemies (monarchists, the clergy, the army). In matters affecting the Church, Waldeck-Rousseau wished to remain faithful to the Napoleonic **concordat** (p. 638), but was a proponent of stringent regulation (not suppression) of religious associations, many of whose members had intervened on the side of the anti-Dreyfusards.

1901, July 1. The result was the **Associations Law,** whose terms relative to religious "congregations" were most important: (1) no congregation could be formed without a law defining its scope and activity; (2) all congregations lacking authorization, or which parliament failed subsequently to authorize, were to be dissolved. Since the treatment of congregations was to depend on the will of the legislature, the general elections were all-important. The elections were a victory for the Radical Republicans and Socialists.

The **Republican bloc** (formed in 1900 to defend the republic against its anti-Dreyfusard opponents) was determined to proceed with vigor against the Church, viewing the Associations Laws as a *pis aller.*

1902, June 2. Waldeck-Rousseau, unsympathetic with extreme measures, **resigned,** an unprecedented act for a premier who possessed the confidence of the majority of the chamber. His successor was **Émile Combes,** known for his probity and anti-clerical convictions. His ministry proceeded to enforce the Associations Law with vigor: closing some 3000 unauthorized schools until they should apply for, and receive, authorization; preparing 54 bills refusing the applications for authorization of as many male congregations (all 54 bills were passed by parliament, 1903, Mar.); etc.

1904, July 7. All teaching by congregations was forbidden by a further law, such congregations to be suppressed within ten years.

Relations of the French government with the Papacy were rapidly embittered.

1904, Mar. President Loubet's visit to the king of Italy, the pope's enemy, irritated the papal government, which sent to the Catholic powers an official protest against this offense to papal dignity.

May 21. The French ambassador to the Vatican was recalled.

Nov. Combes, who thus far had wished to preserve the concordat of 1801, introduced a bill for the **separation of Church and State.** It was not Combes's bill (his ministry came to an end, January 19, 1905), but that ably defended by **Aristide Briand,** reporter of the chamber's committee on the separation of Church and State, that was carried, the law being promulgated December 9, 1905: (1) it guaranteed complete liberty of conscience; (2) it suppressed all connection of the Church with the state—henceforth the state would have no connection with the appointment of Catholic ecclesiastics or with the payment of their salaries; (3) the property of the Church was to be taken over by private corporations formed for that specific purpose. Thus ended the relationship of the state to the Catholic Church as established by the concordat of 1801, as well as the separate régimes establishing the relation of the state to the Protestant and the Jewish faiths (the Protestant Church had been state-supported and controlled since 1802, under the Organic Articles of April 8; the Jews had been under state control since 1808 and had been given state support in 1831).

Apr. 8. Conclusion of the Entente Cordiale with Great Britain (p. 794).

1905. An acute **crisis in Franco-German relations,** arising from the Moroccan question (p. 795). Dramatic downfall of **Théophile Delcassé** (June 6), foreign minister since June 1898.

1906–1913. Presidency of Clément Armand Fallières.

1906–1911. Striking **revival of French nationalism and royalism.** This was an outcome of the conflict over Dreyfus and particularly of the international tension resulting from the Moroccan crisis. The new "integral nationalism" assumed a sophisticated form in the writing of **Charles Maurras** and **Léon Daudet** in the newspaper *Action Française* (founded 1899). They sought the restoration of the monarchy, the aggressive development of French power at home and of French prestige abroad. **Maurice Barrès,** the eminent novelist, though unsympathetic to the restoration of the monarchy, also sought the promotion of national unity in terms of French "traditional development," with decentralization and harmonizing of the forces of nationalism and socialism, an ideology in some respects foreshadowing National Socialism.

1906–1911. Epidemic of strikes and labor troubles. Decline in wine prices caused a crisis in that industry and the organization of vineyard workers in the *Confédération Générale des Vignerons* (1907). There were manifestations on a grand scale in the south, and considerable violence.

1909, Apr.–May. Strike of the Paris postal workers. Civil servants had demanded the right to unionize and affiliate with the *Confédération Générale du Travail.* The former demand had been granted, the latter refused. The government of **Georges Clemenceau** (1906–1909) met the strikers with severe measures: more than 200 employees were discharged and the right of civil servants to strike was denied. Labor agitation was accompanied by violent passages between radicals and socialists, notably between Clemenceau and **Jean Jaurès,** the outstanding figure of French socialism.

1909–1910. The first ministry of Aristide Briand.

1910, Oct. 10. A strike of railway workers on the Northeastern Railway was answered by Briand (long a socialist) by calling out the troops. The National Union of Railway Workers and Employees thereupon called a **general strike,** but when it became clear that the movement was collapsing, the strike committee ordered the resumption of work (Oct. 18). Briand defended the use of force to maintain the functioning of the railroads as essential to the life of the nation and its defense.

1911. New strikes of vineyard workers in Champagne, similar to those in the south in 1907.

1911, June–Nov. The second Moroccan (Agadir) **crisis** (p. 799). The ministries of **Joseph Caillaux** (1911, June 27–1912, Jan. 10) and **Raymond Poincaré** (1912, Jan. 14–1913, Jan. 18) were taken up largely with the Moroccan problem and other questions of international import, notably those arising from the Tripolitan War (p. 800) and from the Balkan Wars (pp. 801, 802).

1913, July–Aug. The government of **Louis Barthou** (1862–1934) carried a **law increasing the military service** from two to three years. This measure was vigorously opposed by the Radical Socialists and Socialists and its revoca-

tion was hotly debated until the very eve of the First World War.

1913–1920. Presidency of Raymond Poincaré, ardent patriot, one of the most eminent French statesmen in modern times.

(*Cont. pp. 943, 987.*)

CULTURAL DEVELOPMENTS

Realism was the means and the end for prose writers after mid-century. The greatest of these were **Gustave Flaubert** (1821–1880; *Madame Bovary,* 1857), **Alphonse Daudet** (1840–1897), **Émile Zola** (1840–1902), and **Guy de Maupassant** (1850–1893), master of the short story. **Anatole France** (1844–1924) appears as a satirist in his novels (*Penguin Island,* 1908). The Belgian-born dramatist **Maurice Maeterlinck** (1862–1949) is recognized for his contributions to French literature as one of the foremost of the symbolists (see under Low Countries). **Edmond Rostand** (1868–1918) was the poet-dramatist who created *Cyrano de Bergerac* (1897) from the 17th-century figure. The poet **Frédéric Mistral** (1830–1914) wrote in Provençal.

In painting a parallel movement is apparent: the romantic-realist qualities of paintings of **Jean-Baptiste Camille Corot** (1796–1875) and **Jean François Millet** (1814–1875); the realism of **Gustave Courbet** (1819–1877); the horror of **Gustave Doré's** illustrations (*Gargantua, Don Quixote, La Bible*); the impressionist influence in the works of **Edouard Manet** (1832–1883), **Henri de Toulouse-Lautrec** (1864–1901); the neo-impressionism of **Georges Seurat** (1859–1891) and **Paul Signac** (1863–1935); the post-impressionism of **Paul Cézanne** (1839–1906), from whom "modern art" is said to date; and the expressionism of **Paul Gauguin** (1848–1903), **Henri Rousseau** (1844–1910), and **Henri Matisse** (1869–1954).

Composers **Giacomo Meyerbeer** (1791–1864; *Les Huguenots,* 1836) and **Charles Gounod** (1818–1893; *Faust,* 1859) were best known for their operas; organ music was the medium of **César Franck** (1822–1890), while **Camille Saint-Saëns** (1835–1921), **Claude Debussy** (1862–1918), and **Maurice Ravel** (1875–1937) composed orchestral works; **Gabriel Fauré** (1845–1924) composed songs, piano music, and a *Requiem.*

For the **Paris Exposition of 1889,** Alexandre Gustave Eiffel designed the **Eiffel tower.**

Antoine Baryé (1796–1875) was the foremost sculptor of animals in his era, but the sculptor whose influence was greatest was **Auguste Rodin** (1840–1917).

5. THE IBERIAN PENINSULA

a. SPAIN, 1814-1914

(*From p. 643*)

1814-1833. FERDINAND VII, restored to the throne (1814, Mar.) after the conquest of Spain by Wellington in the Peninsula War (p. 643). The king had promised to maintain the liberal **constitution of 1812** (p. 645), but refused to keep his promise, knowing the absolutist temper of the country and relying on the support of the Church and the army. Ferocious persecution of the liberals and the king's capricious and incapable rule caused widespread dissatisfaction, notably in the army. The loss of the colonies in America (p. 838) deprived the government of one of the chief sources of income and determined Ferdinand (who was encouraged by Russia and France) to undertake their reconquest. Forces were concentrated at Cadiz, one of the chief centers of disaffection, where the troops became demoralized.

1820, Jan. Mutiny of the troops under Colonel Rafael Riego. They began to march to Madrid. Other revolutionary movements broke out in the north and ultimately the garrison in Madrid mutinied. Ferdinand yielded and restored the constitution. The revolutionaries held him practically a prisoner until 1823.

1822. The **congress of Verona** (p. 653), after much previous debate among the powers, gave France a mandate to suppress the movement. Great Britain, under Canning, did its utmost to prevent intervention, but in vain. A French army crossed the Pyrenees in the spring of 1823, marched to Madrid to the cheers of the unenlightened peasantry, and drove the revolutionaries south to Cadiz, taking the king with them.

1823, Aug. 31. The **battle of the Trocadero** brought the revolution to an end. Ferdinand was restored. He ignored the advice of the French to introduce a moderate constitutional régime and delivered the country over to an orgy of repression which lasted until his death.

Dec. 2. **Monroe's message to Congress (Monroe Doctrine,** p. 812). This warned European countries against intervention in South America, and was the outcome of Canning's approaches to the American minister, Richard Rush, for joint action to oppose reconquest of the colonies. The danger of such action was almost nil on account of the attitude and sea power of Britain.

1833, June 30. To assure the succession of his infant daughter **Isabella,** Ferdinand, under the influence of his energetic queen, **Maria Cristina,** set aside the Salic Law, thus depriving his brother, **Don Carlos,** of the throne. The king died September 29.

1833-1868. ISABELLA II. She was represented by her mother, Maria Cristina, as regent. Realizing that she must depend on the Liberals for support, the latter granted

1834. The **Estatuto Real** (royal constitution): Spain was divided into 49 administrative provinces, on the model of the French *départements;* a bicameral legislature (*cortes*) was given financial powers, but the government retained the right of dissolution and control of the ministry. The constitution was less advanced than that of 1812, and led to a split in the ranks of the Liberals: the *Moderados* accepted the statute; the *Progresistas* demanded restoration of the constitution of 1812.

1834-1839. THE CARLIST WAR. Don Carlos, claiming the throne, was supported by the conservative elements, the Church, and much of the north of the country (Basques, Navarre, Aragon, Catalonia) where regional and autonomous feeling revolted against the centralizing tendencies of the Liberals.

1834, Apr. 22. Quadruple Alliance between Great Britain, France, Spain, and Portugal, aimed at the support of the constitutionalists against the pretenders. The British government went so far as to suspend the Foreign Enlistment Act and allow the formation of a foreign legion, under **Sir De Lacy Evans.** In 1836-1837 the Carlists were defeated, and the war was concluded by the **convention of Vergara** (1839, Aug. 31). Don Carlos left the country for France.

1836, Aug. 10. Progressist insurrection in Andalusia, Aragon, Catalonia, and Madrid. Cristina, who had become very unpopular through her secret marriage to **Ferdinand Muñoz** (1833), was obliged to restore the constitution of 1812 and summon a Progressist ministry, which had the cortes adopt the **constitution of 1837,** a compromise between the constitution of 1812 and the statute of 1834.

1840, Oct. Revolt of General Baldomero Espartero, "Duke of the Victory," who had embraced the Progressist cause. Cristina was forced to leave the country and Espartero became practically dictator, acting as regent.

1841, Oct. Espartero defeated a Cristina insurrection at Pampeluna.

1842, Nov. Rising in Barcelona, accompanied with much bloodshed. A republic was proclaimed, but was suppressed by Espartero (Dec.).

The Spanish Bourbons (1814–1931)

(From p. 488)

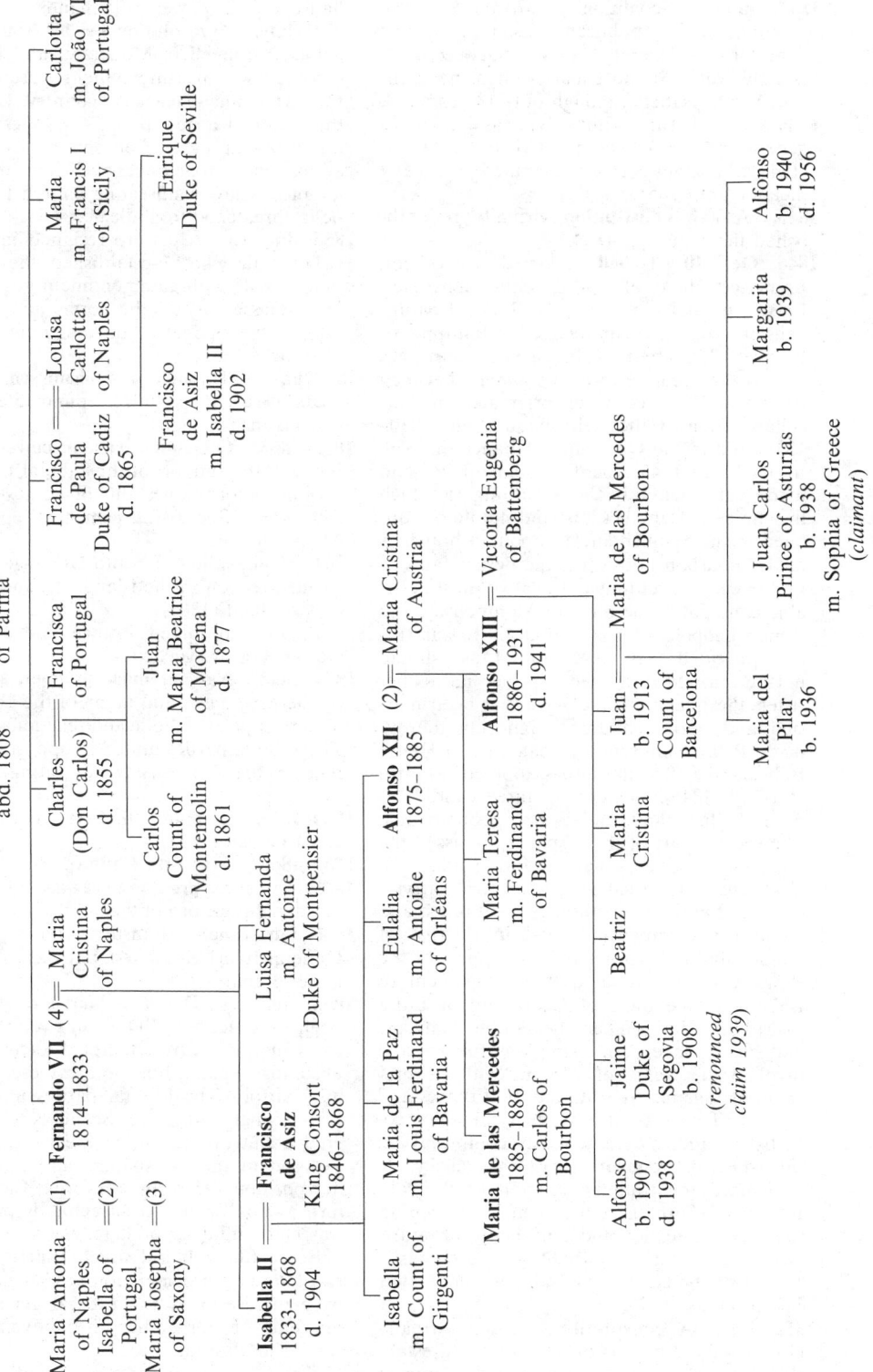

Carlos IV = Louisa Maria
abd. 1808   of Parma

Maria Antonia =(1) **Fernando VII** (4)= Maria
of Naples   1814–1833   Cristina
Isabella of   =(2)   of Naples
Portugal
Maria Josepha =(3)
of Saxony

Charles = Francisca
(Don Carlos)   of Portugal
d. 1855

Francisco = Louisa
de Paula   Carlotta
Duke of Cadiz of Naples
d. 1865

Maria
m. Francis I
of Sicily

Carlotta
m. João VI
of Portugal

Carlos
Count of
Montemolin
d. 1861

Juan
m. Maria Beatrice
of Modena
d. 1877

Francisco
de Asiz
m. Isabella II
d. 1902

Enrique
Duke of Seville

Isabella II = **Francisco**
1833–1868   **de Asiz**
d. 1904   King Consort
               1846–1868

Luisa Fernanda
m. Antoine
Duke of Montpensier

Isabella
m. Count of
Girgenti

Maria de la Paz
m. Louis Ferdinand
of Bavaria

Alfonso XII
1875–1885

Eulalia
m. Antoine
of Orléans

Maria Cristina
of Austria

Maria Teresa
m. Ferdinand
of Bavaria

Alfonso XIII = Victoria Eugenia
1886–1931   of Battenberg
d. 1941

Maria de las Mercedes
1885–1886
m. Carlos of
Bourbon

Beatriz

Maria
Cristina

Juan = Maria de las Mercedes
b. 1913   of Bourbon
Count of
Barcelona

Alfonso
b. 1907
d. 1938

Jaime
Duke of
Segovia
b. 1908
*(renounced
claim 1939)*

Maria del
Pilar
b. 1936

Juan Carlos
Prince of Asturias
b. 1938
m. Sophia of Greece
(claimant)

Margarita
b. 1939

Alfonso
b. 1940
d. 1956

1843, June. A coalition of *Moderados, Progresistas,* and republicans declared against Espartero. **General Ramón Narváez took Madrid** (July 15) and Espartero fled the country (Aug.). Isabella, though only 13 years old, was declared of age, with Narvaez as lieutenant-general of the kingdom. Cristina returned (1844, Mar.), but Narváez remained practically dictator until 1851.

1845. A **new constitution** virtually re-established the statute of 1834.

1846, Oct. 10. **Isabella** married her cousin, Francisco, duke of Cadiz, while her sister, **Luisa Fernanda,** married the duke of Montpensier, youngest son of Louis Philippe of France. The **affair of the Spanish marriages** caused the breakdown of the *entente* between Britain and France which originated in their collaboration in the Belgian question (1830-1831) and in the Quadruple Alliance of 1834. In 1843 and 1845 Aberdeen and Guizot had made **agreements at Eu,** according to which the choice of Isabella's husband should be confined to the Spanish and Neapolitan branches of the Bourbon house (i.e. the descendants of Philip V). This eliminated the two most desirable candidates, the duke of Montpensier and Prince Leopold of Saxe-Coburg. It was further provided that the Infanta Luisa should not be married to a French prince unless her sister, the queen, should have first been married and borne children. Ignoring the Eu pacts, Palmerston sent a dispatch to Sir Henry Bulwer, the British ambassador at Madrid (July 19, 1846), mentioning three candidates for Isabella's hand, and Prince Leopold first. The second part of the dispatch discussed the Spanish domestic situation and condemned the French-supported *Moderados* for their violence and arbitrary methods. The French and Spanish governments, united in distrust of Palmerston and fearing British support of the *Progresistas,* precipitated the engagement of Isabella to the duke of Cadiz and of Luisa to Montpensier. When the double marriage had taken place Palmerston was furious and invoked the treaty of Utrecht with its precautions against the union of France and Spain. This was of no effect, but Franco-British relations were seriously compromised.

1851, Mar. 16. Concordat with the Papacy. It recognized the Catholic religion as the sole authorized faith, gave the Church sweeping control of education and censorship; in return the Papacy recognized abolition of ecclesiastical jurisdictions and the sale of confiscated church lands.

1852, Dec. A **constitutional reform** virtually eliminated the powers of the cortes and established the dictatorship in law. A **camarilla** had complete power in its hands.

1854, July. A revolution led by General Leopoldo O'Donnell (a Moderate) and Espartero (Progressive) overthrew the government and forced Cristina to leave the country. O'Donnell then formed a new party, the **Liberal Union,** espousing a program between that of the moderates and progressives. When the cortes adopted a law confiscating church lands, Isabella threatened to abdicate.

1856, July 15. Espartero resigned in favor of O'Donnell, who re-established the constitution of 1845 with an amendment guaranteeing annual assembly of the cortes and presentation of the budget at the beginning of each session.

Oct. **O'Donnell was dismissed** and two years of reaction followed, punctuated by numerous insurrections.

1858-1863. O'Donnell back in power, governing with the support of the Liberal Union and avoiding thorny questions of domestic policy.

1859-1860. Successful **campaign against the Moors** in Morocco.

1861. Annexation of Santo Domingo followed by insurrection in the island. Relinquishment of the island (1865).

Spain also joined France and Britain in intervention in Mexico.

1864, Sept. Narváez made premier, supported by the *Moderados* and many of the absolutists. Reversion to a Catholic and reactionary policy. The Liberal parties united in opposition to the régime, the *Progresistas* boycotting the elections.

1864-1865. Dispute with Peru over the Chincha Islands (p. 851).

1865-1866. War with Chile (p. 847).

1865. A severe **press law** was accompanied by the dissolution of political clubs.

1866, Jan.-June. An insurrection organized by General Juan Prim failed, but was followed by many executions.

1868, Apr. 23. Death of Narváez, which had been preceded by O'Donnell's (d. 1867, Nov. 5). **Gonzalez Bravo** attempted to continue the absolutist régime, but the army escaped from his control. The Liberal parties united on a revolutionary program. Scandals which gathered about the queen's name were ruthlessly exposed in the newspapers and undermined her position. Her latest favorite, **Carlos Marfori,** a cook's son and an actor by profession, was made minister of state.

Sept. 18. Admiral Juan Topete issued a revolutionary proclamation at Cadiz, followed by a manifesto by the Liberal generals. By the end of September the movement had spread to all Spain.

Sept. 28. Royal forces defeated at **Alcolea**

by Marshal Francisco Serrano. The queen fled to France (Sept. 29) and was declared deposed.

Oct. 5. A **provisional government** was formed, with **Serrano** at the lead and with **Prim** as the moving spirit. Reactionary laws were annulled, the Jesuit and other religious orders abolished. The government established universal suffrage and a free press.

1869, Feb. A **constituent cortes** met.

May 21. The cortes voted for the continuance of monarchical government.

June 6. The new constitution promulgated.

June 15. Marshal Serrano made regent. Prim head of the ministry. The new régime was bothered by Carlist and republican uprisings and other disturbances, but its chief concern was to find a ruler. The duke of Montpensier was passed over out of consideration for Napoleon III; the duke of Aosta; Prince Ferdinand of Saxe-Coburg; the duke of Genoa; General Espartero, all these declined the throne when offered. Finally the offer was made to **Prince Leopold of Hohenzollern-Sigmaringen,** who accepted, but then withdrew. This candidacy became the occasion for the war between Germany and France (p. 735).

1870, Dec. 30. The **duke of Aosta,** son of Victor Emmanuel II of Piedmont, was prevailed upon to accept. Death of Prim, victim of an assassin.

1871–1873. AMADEO I, the duke of Aosta (b. 1845). Amadeo ruled for two years—isolated, opposed on every side, greeted as a "foreigner"—and then abdicated (1873, Feb. 12).

1873–1874. The **FIRST SPANISH REPUBLIC,** proclaimed (Feb. 12) by the radical majority in the cortes elected in August 1872 (the Carlists having abstained).

1873, May 10. A **constituent cortes,** now elected, was divided among partisans of different types of federal republic.

Sept. 8. In the midst of Carlist risings, **Emilio Castelar,** partisan of a centralized republic, was made head of the government, with the mission of restoring order.

1874, Jan. 2. Castelar retired. A military *coup* promptly followed, with Marshal Serrano as head of a provisional government. The Carlist war continued, marked by exceptional brutality.

Nov. 24. Alfonso, son of Isabella, came of age and declared for a constitutional monarchy. A party of Liberal Unionists and Moderates supported him.

Dec. 29–31. A **group of generals,** disgusted with the republic, **rallied to Alfonso,** who was proclaimed king.

1875–1885. ALFONSO XII. Continuation of the Carlist War, until February 1876, when Don Carlos again fled. The pope, who had recognized Carlos as **Carlos VII,** king of Spain, was won over to recognition of the new régime by a governmental increase of the ecclesiastical budget, closing of Protestant schools and churches, abolition of civil marriages, and other concessions.

1876, July. A **new constitution** accepted by the cortes elected in January was a compromise between the constitutions of 1845 and 1869 and established a system midway between Carlist "absolutism" and republican "anarchy." It provided for a bicameral legislature and a responsible ministry, but with a limited suffrage—a parliamentary régime in appearance only. The cortes, as before the revolution, was "ministerial" (i.e. elected under government auspices and obedient to the ministry). The ministry, in turn, was selected by the king, who thus remained the effective ruler of the state. Constitutional forms were, however, observed, and during the succeeding decades there was neither *camarilla* nor insurrection. The ministerial power alternated between two parties, both supporting the régime: the **Conservatives** (led by **Canovas del Castillo**) and the **Liberals** (under **Práxedes Sagasta**). The country prospered, but the king, though courageous and humane, was indulgent and lost much popularity through scandals at court. In foreign policy he followed the lead of the central powers. From 1887 to 1895 Spain was associated with Britain, Italy, and Austria in the **Mediterranean Agreements** (p. 784 *ff.*).

1885–1902. Regency of Maria Cristina, widow of Alfonso, who ruled for her son, born 1886, May 17, after the death of his father. The Conservatives and Liberals continued to alternate in power.

1890. Universal suffrage was again introduced. The economic development of the country led to increasing labor unrest, especially in centers like Barcelona. **Anarchist outrages** became frequent and resulted in many executions and in much repressive legislation.

1895. The **Cuban Revolution** (p. 827). It continued for three years and ended in the loss of both Cuba and the Philippines.

1898. THE SPANISH-AMERICAN WAR (p. 827). It left Spain weak and discredited, and resulted in further disintegration of the parliamentary régime. The **Conservatives** divided into an authoritarian wing (led by **Juan La Cierva,** allied to the clergy), and the **Liberal Conservatives** (followers of **Augustino Silvela**). The **Liberals** (Progressives) were led by **Sigismondo Moret** after the death of Sagasta. A small **Carlist Party** continued to exist in the mountains of the north. A **Republican Party** had headquarters in Madrid, Andalusia, and Catalonia. A **Socialist Party** was rapidly winning recruits among the laborers of Catalonia and the miners of the Basque region. Anarchists continued their activities and even made attempts upon the king's life. The centralized character of the government system gave rise to a **regionalist movement** in Catalonia, where the **United Catalans** (*Soldiarios*) demanded an autonomous administration and a separate budget. In its literary and linguistic aspects this movement took the form of a cultural revival.

1902-1931. ALFONSO XIII. Though declared of age, he at first allowed his mother to continue the government.

1904. Agreement between Spain and France regarding Morocco (p. 795). This marked the veering of Spanish policy to the side of France and Britain.

1906, May 31. Marriage of Alfonso to Princess Eugenia of Battenberg, granddaughter of Queen Victoria. The succeeding period was one of internal conflict. Army influence secured the passage of a law (1906) to try press offenses "against the fatherland and the army" by court-martial.

1909. When troops were embarked for Morocco, protests of extremists followed, directed against the inequality of the military service régime, under which obligatory service fell on the poorer classes. A **general strike** was proclaimed at Barcelona and extended to other Catalonian cities under the direction of a revolutionary committee.

July. At Barcelona the insurgents burned convents and massacred priests and monks. Vigorous repression followed, and **Francisco Ferrer,** propagandist of the anti-clerical opposition, was executed (Oct. 13), with resulting criticism throughout Europe and many repercussions in Spain.

Oct. 21. The king called a Liberal ministry. In the succeeding years he even consulted with the Republican leader, **Gumersindo Azcarate,** and declared himself accessible to all parties, even those of anti-dynastic complexion.

1910-1913. The **Liberals were in power,** supported by the king.

1912, Nov. 12. Assassination of the advanced Liberal premier, **José Canalejas,** pledged to an anti-clerical program. He had passed (1910, Dec. 23) the **Padlock Law,** forbidding the establishment of more religious houses without the consent of the government. The industrial enterprises of the religious orders were taxed, and public worship of non-Catholic bodies was expressly permitted.

Nov. 27. Treaty with France, defining their respective spheres in Morocco (p. 875).

1913, Oct. 27. The **Conservatives returned to power** after the king's unsuccessful attempts to reconcile the Liberals, who had split up after Canalejas' death.

1914, Aug. 7. Spain declared neutrality in the First World War, the king having given France assurances that she might denude her Pyrenees frontier of troops. (*Cont. p. 991.*)

Spanish literature in the 20th century was characterized first by romanticism, later by realism (**José de Espronceda y Delgado,** 1808-1842), a romantic poet; **Ramón de Campoamor** (1817-1901), writer of epigrams and narrative poems; **José María de Pereda** (1833-1906), realistic novelist. Turn-of-the-century composers in the romantic tradition were **Isaac Albéniz** (1860-1909) and **Enrique Granados** (1867-1916).

b. PORTUGAL, 1820-1912

(*From p. 643*)

1820, Aug. 29. Revolution at Oporto, stimulated by the revolution in Spain. The insurgents drove out the regency, established in November 1807 under British auspices to rule the country during the sojourn of **King John VI** (ruled 1792-1826) in Brazil.

1822. A constitution was adopted similar to the democratic Spanish constitution. Brazil declared independence. King John accepted the invitation to return as constitutional monarch and left the government of Brazil to his eldest son, **Dom Pedro.**

1823, June 5. John revised the constitution in the interest of absolutism. His second son, **Dom Miguel,** in the meantime started a civil war (1823-1824) supported by the reactionaries.

1826, Mar. 10. Death of King John. He left the throne to Dom Pedro of Brazil, who became **Peter IV.** Peter drew up a charter providing for moderate parliamentary government of the British type. But he refused to leave Brazil and eventually handed over the Portuguese throne to his infant daughter, **Maria da Gloria,** with Dom Miguel as regent.

1826-1853. MARIA II. Miguel united the reactionaries and clericals in a movement against constitutional government.

1827, Jan.-1828, Apr. 28. A British force landed at Lisbon to support the constitutionalists. They withdrew when Miguel promised to respect the constitution.

1828, May. *Coup d'état by Miguel,* who abolished the constitution and had himself proclaimed king (July 4). Maria da Gloria fled to England.

1828-1834. The Miguelite Wars.

(*From p. 491*) # Portugal: The House of Coburg–Braganza (1826–1910)

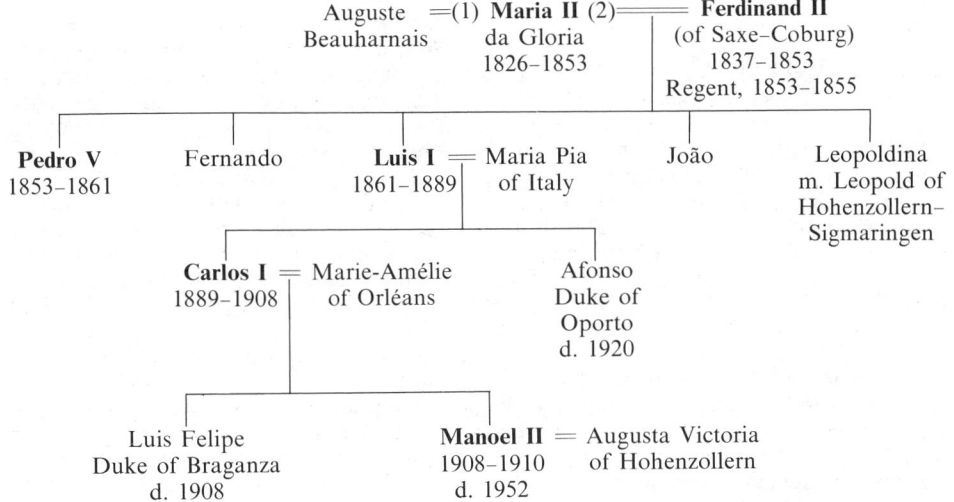

Auguste ═(1) **Maria II** (2)═════ **Ferdinand II**
Beauharnais   da Gloria   (of Saxe–Coburg)
         1826–1853   1837–1853
                       Regent, 1853–1855

Pedro V   Fernando   **Luis I** ═ Maria Pia   João   Leopoldina
1853–1861   1861–1889   of Italy   m. Leopold of
                                              Hohenzollern–
                                              Sigmaringen

Carlos I ═ Marie-Amélie   Afonso
1889–1908   of Orléans   Duke of
                            Oporto
                            d. 1920

Luis Felipe   **Manoel II** ═ Augusta Victoria
Duke of Braganza   1908–1910   of Hohenzollern
d. 1908   d. 1952

1831, Apr. 7. Dom Pedro abdicated the Brazilian throne and returned to Europe (England), to fight for the restoration of Maria.

1832, July 8. Pedro, with the connivance of Britain and France, organized an expedition and **took Oporto.** The Miguelists were defeated and

1833, Sept. Maria was restored.

1834, Apr. 22. Quadruple Alliance between Great Britain, France, Spain, and Portugal, aimed at the expulsion of Miguel.

May 26. Final defeat of Miguel, who left the country.

1834–1853. A period of ministerial instability and chronic insurrection, reflecting the conflict between those championing the radical constitution of 1822 and those supporting the charter of 1826.

1836, Apr. 9. The queen married Duke Ferdinand of Saxe-Coburg.

1853–1861. PETER (PEDRO) V.

1861–1889. LOUIS (LUIS) I. Under these two reigns Portugal had some respite from civil strife, and the country was ruled by two opposing factions of professional politicians, the **Regenerators** (or Conservatives) and the **Progressives** (or Liberals), who adopted the system of *rotavism:* skillful manipulation of the electorate, enabling the two parties to hold office in rotation. This sterile, pseudo-parliamentary system resulted in the formation of a **Republican Party** (1881).

1889–1908. CARLOS I, who gained notoriety by his extravagance and licentiousness. Discontent grew, especially in the cities, and there were sporadic revolts, strikes, and conspiracies.

1906, May 19. The king appointed **João Franco** as prime minister, with dictatorial powers. Parliamentary government was suppressed, the press gagged, and all opposition to the government sternly punished.

1908, Feb. 1. Assassination of King Carlos and the crown prince in the streets of Lisbon.

1908–1910. MANUEL (MANOEL) II. He put an end to Franco's régime and restored constitutional government, but, like his father, was scandalously extravagant.

1910, Oct. 3–5. Insurrection in Lisbon. The king was forced to flee to England.

Oct. 5. PROCLAMATION OF THE PORTUGUESE REPUBLIC. A provisional government was organized under **Dr. Theophilo Braga.** It proceeded to a frontal attack upon the Catholic Church, which was regarded as the backbone of royalism. Religious orders were expelled, their establishments closed and their property confiscated. Religious teaching in primary schools was forbidden.

1911, Apr. 20. Separation of Church and State, along the lines followed in France.

Aug. 20. A constituent assembly adopted a very **liberal constitution.**

Aug. 24. Dr. Manoel de Arriaga elected first president. He was confronted with royalist plots and with growing unrest among the workers, who were disappointed when the revolution failed to bring them relief.

1912, Jan. A serious **general strike** broke out in Lisbon. The city was put under military rule and hundreds of syndicalists were arrested. But radical outbreaks continued throughout the rest of the period. (*Cont. p. 995.*)

6. ITALY

(*From p. 497*)

a. THE ITALIAN STATES, 1815-1848

With the collapse of the Napoleonic Empire in 1814, the states of the Italian peninsula were reconstituted under the effective domination of Austria, which attempted a thoroughgoing restoration of the old régime. The new states were nine in number: kingdom of Sardinia (Piedmont), Modena, Parma, Lucca, Tuscany, Papal States, kingdom of Naples, the republic of San Marino, and Monaco. Lombardy and Venetia were annexed by Austria. The only important territorial changes, as compared with the pre-Napoleonic situation, were the annexation of the former Venetian Republic by Austria, of the former Genoese Republic by Piedmont.

In cultural matters the early part of the century was marked by the writings of **Alessandro Manzoni** and **Giacomo Leopardi** (p. 492) while Italy's traditionally dominant position in opera was maintained by **Gioacchino Rossini** (1792–1868, *Barber of Seville,* 1816), **Vincenzo Bellini** (1801–1835, *La Sonnambula,* 1813) and **Gaetano Donizetti** (1797–1848, *Lucia di Lammermoor,* 1835).

1815, May. The Bourbon **Ferdinand I** (1759–1825), restored to the throne of Naples by Austrian arms, despite his promises of political liberty and the maintenance of French reforms (**decrees from Messina,** May 20–24, 1815), quickly descended to a rule of almost unrelieved despotism. In the **Papal States, Pope Pius VII** returned from his long exile to re-establish the obscurantist and semi-feudal ecclesiastical rule of the 18th century and to restore the Company of Jesus (suppressed in 1773). In **Modena, Duke Francis IV** entered upon a policy of candid reaction, rigorously concentrating power in his own hands, turning the universities over to the Jesuits. In **Parma** and **Lucca** the return to the old régime was rapid but less violent than in Modena and the south. **Maria Louisa of Parma** (former empress of the French) and the infanta **Maria Louisa of Bourbon-Parma,** duchess of Lucca, owed their thrones to Austria and heeded the wishes of Metternich. In **Lombardy** and **Venetia,** with separate governments, Metternich organized a thoroughly Austrian administration. Despite the arbitrary features of the government, Lombardy was in most respects (education, communications, administrative efficiency) the most advanced part of Italy. **Victor Emmanuel I of Piedmont** returned in

1814 hoping to restore the old régime intact, even to the return of officials who were holding office in 1798. The Jesuits were cordially welcomed, religious toleration denied, the French code swept away, old and brutal punishments restored.

The Italian conquests of Napoleon and the reorganization of Italy (1) had revealed to Italians the advantages of enlightened laws and administration; (2) had awakened a desire to free themselves from foreign rule. The restorations of 1815 lost for the Italians in large measure the advantages of French rule and substituted the foreign domination of Austria. Hence revolutionary sentiment grew, aiming at first to overthrow existing governments and gradually embracing the idea of unity for all of "Italy." Secret societies multiplied, most famous being the **Carbonari** (*Charcoal-Burners*), inspired by Christian and humanitarian principles, organized on republican lines, borrowing Masonic ritual. The Carbonari prepared to combat "tyranny," to overthrow existing governments. They grew rapidly in numbers in the kingdom of Naples, and spread to other Italian states.

1820, July 2. The Neapolitan Revolution. Encouraged by news of the success of the revolution in Spain (p. 694), the Carbonari in the army, led by **General Guglielmo Pepe,** precipitated a revolt.

July 13. Ferdinand I granted a constitution similar to that introduced in Sicily under British auspices in 1812. The representatives of the powers, meeting in congress at Troppau and Laibach to consider the Spanish situation, were persuaded by Metternich (Britain dissenting because of British public opinion, but not opposing) to adopt the principle of intervention (**Troppau protocol**) against revolutions that might endanger the European peace. Austria was given a mandate to restore order in Italy. An army was marched to Naples, overthrew the revolutionary government (1821, Mar.) with little difficulty, and restored Ferdinand I to his former position.

1821, Mar. 10. Rising in Piedmont, engineered by the Carbonari, who hoped that **Charles Albert,** prince of Carignan, would place himself at the head of a constitutional government.

Mar. 12. Victor Emmanuel I abdicated in favor of his brother, Charles Felix, then absent from Turin. Charles Albert was made regent and granted a constitution like that of Spain.

Mar. 22. Charles Felix arrived, ordered Charles Albert to flee, which he did.

Apr. 8. The **Piedmontese revolution collapsed** with the defeat of the constitutionalists near **Novara** by a combined force of royalists and Austrians.

1831, Feb. Risings in Modena and Parma inspired by the July Revolution in Paris (p. 678) and connected with a general movement aiming to free all northern Italy; they were accompanied by widespread revolts in the Papal States.

Mar. With the aid of Austrian troops the insurrections were put down.

May 21. The ambassadors of the powers demanded certain reforms in the Papal States, but the pope contented himself with an amnesty and a few concessions in the administration and the judiciary. Fresh revolts broke out in the Papal States at the end of 1831. Order was again restored by Austria (Jan. 1832), which led to the **occupation of Ancona** by the French (Mar. 1832). It was not until 1838 that the foreign troops were withdrawn.

The failure of insurrections indicated the ineffectiveness of secret societies, notably of the Carbonari, and of small-scale, sporadic risings which they promoted. The importance of unified effort by Italians everywhere and of careful preparation through propaganda and organization was recognized by **Giuseppe Mazzini** (1805–1872), former Carbonaro, who launched a

Mar. New revolutionary society (*Young Italy*). From early youth Mazzini had dreamt of freeing Italy from her present rulers and giving her a republican constitution—as a prelude to a free confederation of all Europe dominated by a spirit of Christian brotherhood. Through the widely ramifying channels of Young Italy, Mazzini launched his propaganda from exile in Marseilles. Before a general rising in Italy (planned for June 1832) could take place,

1832, Mar. Piedmontese authorities discovered existence of the plans; arrests followed, the rising collapsed.

1834, Feb. Another Mazzinian **attack on Savoy** ended in ludicrous failure. Mazzini now extended the scope of his activity by organizing the **Young Europe movement,** composed of Young Italy, Young Germany, Young Poland, and kindred organizations. From London he carried on his work of direction and propaganda. Abortive risings followed with almost monotonous regularity, but accomplished nothing but the creation of martyrs to the cause.

1843. Publication of **Vincenzo Gioberti's** *On the Moral and Civil Primacy of the Italians,* and of **Count Cesare Balbo's** *The Hopes of Italy.* These two books represented the views of the Italian moderate Liberals, especially in northern Italy. They found Mazzini's republicanism offensive and his methods dangerous and impractical. The moderates distrusted universal suffrage and advocated constitutional reform and some type of unification for the peninsula. Some favored a federation of states under the presidency of the pope. These were the **Neo-Guelphs,** led by Gioberti. Balbo and his followers were intent chiefly on the extrusion of Austria (by peaceful means if possible) and the organization of Italy under Piedmontese leadership.

1846, June 15. ELECTION OF PIUS IX (Cardinal Mastai-Ferretti) as pope led to an outburst of liberal enthusiasm and to boundless hopes. In contrast to his predecessor, Gregory XVI, Pius was democratic in his attitude. He proclaimed an amnesty for political prisoners and refugees, relaxed the censorship laws, organized an advisory council composed of laymen, replaced the mercenary army by a civil guard, and established a municipal council for Rome. These reforms were opposed by the reactionaries (Gregorians) at every step, but the pope's popularity grew throughout Italy.

1847, July 17. Occupation of Ferrara by Austrian troops (actually exercising a right conferred by the treaty of Vienna). This step called forth a storm of indignation among Liberals in all Italy and did much to fan the anti-Austrian sentiment.

Oct. Charles Albert of Piedmont (succeeded Charles Felix in 1831), though conservatively inclined, dismissed his reactionary minister, **Solaro della Margarita,** and began to yield to the liberal agitation (*King Wobble, Re Tentenna*). He consented to the revision of the criminal code, mitigation of the censorship, amendment of the law on public meeting.

1848, Jan. 12. A **revolutionary movement** broke out in **Sicily** and stimulated the Neapolitan liberals to action.

Feb. 10. Ferdinand II (*Bomba,* 1830–1859), unable to secure Austrian aid in the face of the pope's opposition to the crossing of his territory, promulgated a liberal constitution modeled on the French charter of 1830.

Feb. 17. Grand Duke Leopold of Tuscany was obliged to grant a constitution.

Mar. 4. Charles Albert promulgated a constitution for Piedmont (the *Statuto,* the basis for the later constitution of the kingdom of Italy).

Mar. 14. The pope followed suit, introducing a constitution establishing an elective council of deputies, but reserving a veto power to the pope and college of cardinals.

The Neapolitan Bourbons (1735–1860)

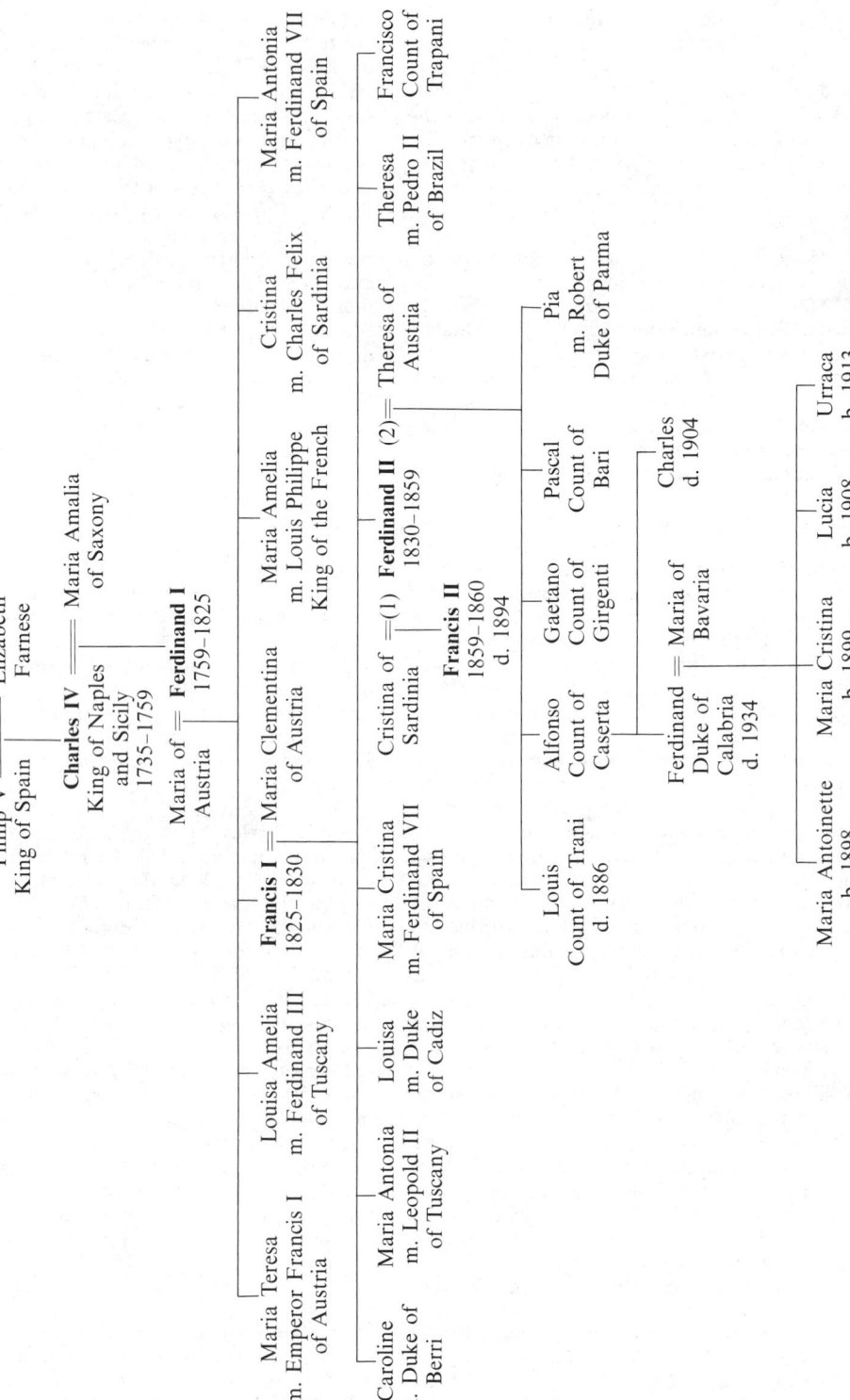

b. THE ITALIAN WAR OF INDEPENDENCE, 1848-1849

1848, Mar. 18-22. The **FIVE DAYS OF MI-LAN,** marking the culmination of dissatisfaction with Austrian rule and the influence of the news of the revolution in Vienna (Mar. 13). Barricades were thrown up in the narrow streets. The Austrian general, **Josef Radetzky,** held the entire circle of fortifications, preventing the insurgents from communicating with the outside world. The rebels, fighting without plan or organization, but greatly outnumbering the Austrian forces, gradually reduced the garrisons inside the town and, after repeated assaults, took **Porta Tosa** (Mar. 22). Radetzky was obliged to order a general retreat to the famous **Quadrilateral** (four fortresses: Mantua, Peschiera, Legnano, Verona, between Lombardy and Venetia).

Mar. 22. Proclamation of the Venetian Republic, following agitation and some violence after the arrival of the news from Vienna. A provisional government was established, with **Daniele Manin** as president.

Mar. 22. PIEDMONT DECLARED WAR ON AUSTRIA, in response to an appeal from the Milanese. Charles Albert was very hesitant about allying with the revolution and very suspicious of possible action by the radical French Republic, but finally yielded for fear of radicalism in his own territory.

Apr. 25. Papal forces under **General Giacomo Durando** joined the Piedmontese. Contingents also arrived from Naples and other parts of Italy. Wild enthusiasm, but little discipline.

Apr. 29. A **papal encyclical,** the result of Austrian protests, disclaimed all intention of making war on the Catholic Austrians. This paralyzed all action by the papal troops.

May 15. Collapse of the revolution in Naples, after a counter-offensive by the king's Swiss mercenaries. Neapolitan troops withdrawn from the north.

May 30. The Piedmontese won the **battle of Goito,** but failed to follow up their advantage. Acute danger of intervention by the French Republic, which had concentrated 30,000 troops on the Alps. Austrian efforts to secure British support **(Hummelauer mission).** Palmerston urged the abandonment of both Lombardy and Venetia.

June 15. The Austrian government ordered Radetzky to seek an armistice to permit an offer of independence to Lombardy. Radetzky sent **Prince Felix Schwarzenberg** to Vienna and induced the government to continue the war.

July 24. BATTLE OF CUSTOZZA. Radetzky overwhelmingly defeated the Piedmontese and (Aug. 4) drove them out of Lombardy. Charles Albert finally appealed to the French for mediation, but after the **June Days** (p. 681) the French government was too deeply engrossed in domestic affairs to be willing to embroil itself with Austria and Britain.

Aug. 9. Armistice of Salasco (the general who negotiated it). The Piedmontese gave up Lombardy. Charles Albert accepted joint Anglo-French mediation, on the understanding that he would get Lombardy later. The Austrians accepted mediation after much resistance (Sept. 3), but nothing came of it, especially after the formation of the Schwarzenberg ministry (Nov. 21), which refused to entertain the suggestion of territorial cessions.

Sept. 16. The pope appointed **Count Pellegrino Rossi** prime minister, after several ephemeral cabinets and a steady growth of radicalism at Rome. Rossi was a disciple of Guizot, a moderate, clear-headed administrator, whose aim was to restore order. His efforts at reform earned him the hatred of all factions.

Nov. 15. Rossi was murdered by a fanatical democrat.

Nov. 16. Popular insurrection in Rome. The pope was forced to appoint a democratic ministry under Monsignor **Carlo Muzzarelli.**

Nov. 25. Pius, alarmed by radical agitation (clubs), fled from Rome to Gaeta where he enjoyed Neapolitan protection. He attempted unsuccessfully to maintain his power in Rome through a commission of regency.

1849, Feb. 9. Proclamation of the Roman Republic, after the meeting of a constituent assembly (Feb. 5).

Mar. 12. Piedmont denounced the armistice with Austria, the king yielding to radical pressure.

Mar. 23. BATTLE OF NOVARA. Radetzky again decisively defeated the Piedmontese. Charles Albert abdicated in favor of his son, **Victor Emmanuel II.** Peace negotiations dragged on through the spring and summer, the size of the indemnity being the chief point in dispute. Peace was finally signed August 9, Piedmont agreeing to an indemnity of 65,000,000 francs.

Mar. 29. On news of the Piedmontese defeat at Novara, the leaders at **Rome set up a triumvirate** (Mazzini, Saffi, Armellini) which introduced a moderate, conciliatory régime and restored order. But since January there had been discussion of intervention by France or Austria, or both, to restore the pope.

Apr. 14. The French assembly voted funds for an expedition, being led by the government to suppose that the purpose was to forestall the Austrians. In reality the aim of Louis Napoleon was to win the approval of the Catholics.

Apr. 24. The **French expedition,** under General **Nicolas Oudinot,** landed at Città Vecchia.

Apr. 29-30. **Oudinot,** supposing that Mazzini's followers were a minority in Rome, attacked the city, but was repulsed by improvised forces led by **Giuseppe Garibaldi,** republican patriot and guerrilla leader.

May 29. **Ferdinand de Lesseps,** later builder of the Suez Canal, having been sent by the French government to negotiate, signed a treaty with the Roman Republic by which the city gates were to be opened to the French in return for a promise to respect the rights of the republic and to guarantee it against foreign aggression.

June 1. **Lesseps was abruptly recalled** and later disavowed. Oudinot was reinforced and ordered to take the city.

June 3. He attacked without warning, but Garibaldi and his men fought so valiantly that the French had to settle down to a siege.

June 30. **Garibaldi,** regarding the situation as hopeless, made terms with the French.

July 2. After reviewing his troops, Garibaldi marched forth with some 5000 men on his famous retreat. All were presently killed, captured, or dispersed, Garibaldi himself escaping after dramatic adventures.

July 20-Aug. 28. **Austrian siege and bombardment of Venice.** The city surrendered, ravaged by cholera and faced with starvation.

By this time the revolutionary movement had been everywhere suppressed. Neapolitan troops had reconquered Sicily and entered Palermo (May 15) and the Austrians had entered Florence to support the restored Grand Duke Leopold (May 25).

c. THE UNIFICATION OF ITALY, 1849-1870

The abysmal failure of the revolutionary movements of 1848-1849 revealed the military weakness of the Italian states (hence the need of foreign aid for the extrusion of Austria); demonstrated the unsuitability of the pope as a leader of the unity movement; undermined the prestige of the Mazzinians and republicanism in general; pointed to the steadfastness of Piedmont, only state to retain its liberal constitution. Piedmont was henceforth recognized as the hope of liberal Italy. In the parliamentary life of Piedmont there rapidly came to the fore a new man,

1851-1861. **Count Camillo Benso di Cavour,** a liberal who had drawn his ideas from French

and especially English sources; believer in the *juste milieu,* profound admirer of British parliamentarism, convinced of the importance of reforms (commercial, industrial, agricultural, political) if Piedmont were to take its place as the leader of the movement for Italian independence. Scientific farming on western lines he introduced on his father's estates, and then made it the subject of wider propaganda through the medium of the **Agrarian Society** (founded 1842). He was active in the promotion of banking, railroads; welcomed the repeal of the Corn Laws in England. He entered actively into the necessarily veiled political activity of the forties; founded the first **Whist Club** at Turin, innocuous façade for political discussions. When Charles Albert reformed the censorship (1847), Cavour promptly founded, with Cesare Balbo, *Il Risorgimento,* a newspaper urging the independence of Italy, a league of Italian princes, and moderate reforms. Cavour assumed a leading rôle in the demand for a constitution during January 1848. The king yielded (Feb. 8); published the new constitution (Mar. 4) providing for a system modeled principally after that of Great Britain, with a senate, whose life-members were to be appointed by the king; a chamber of deputies, with members elected on the basis of a limited suffrage (leaving electoral influence in the hands of the nobility and middle class); a ministry responsible to parliament. Parliament met for the first time, May 8, 1848. Despite vigorous opposition of democratic elements, suspicious of Cavour as an aristocrat, he played an increasingly important rôle in the period following the disasters of 1848-1849.

1850, Mar. On the advice of Cavour, **Giuseppe Siccardi** was made keeper of the seals by Premier Massimo d'Azeglio. Siccardi brought in a bill (of which Cavour was the author) seriously curbing the powers of the Catholic Church—abolishing ecclesiastical courts, and all their special jurisdictions; eliminating the right of asylum; limiting the number of holidays; restricting the right of religious bodies to acquire real property. Elsewhere these questions had been settled by concordat with the pope; in Piedmont they were settled by unilateral action (Oct. 10).

1850-1851. Cavour entered d'Azeglio's government as minister of agriculture and commerce, the portfolio of the navy being shortly added, and later that of finance.

1852, Nov. 4. After a short period out of office, **Cavour became premier,** a post he was to hold uninterruptedly for seven years. Cavour by now had deserted the Right and governed with the aid of a coalition of the Liberals of the Right Center and Left Center

FRANCE

AUSTRIA~HUNGARY

SWITZERLAND

TRENTINO

VENETIA

LOMBARDY
• Milan.

Venice •

Trieste •

ISTRIA

CROATIA

SAVOY
(To France
1860)

PIEDMONT

Turin •

PARMA

MODENA

ROMAGNA

MARCHES

BOSNIA

DALMATIA

NICE
(To France
1860)

LUCCA

Florence •

TUSCANY

UMBRIA

STATES of
the CHURCH

KINGDOM of SARDINIA

CORSICA
(FR.)

Rome

★

SARDINIA

Naples •

KINGDOM of the
TWO SICILIES

Palermo •

SICILY

The UNIFICATION
of ITALY

Kingdom of Sardinia (Piedmont)

Area added 1860

"   "   1866

"   "   1870

(the *connubio*). His government reorganized finances; negotiated commercial treaties and revised tariffs (first approach to free trade); fostered legislation on co-operative societies, agrarian credit, banks; accelerated railroad construction; reorganized the army.

1855, Jan. 26. Cavour managed to insinuate his country into the **Crimean War** on the side of France and Britain. The Piedmontese troops took part in the victory of the **Chernaia** (Aug. 16) and thereby regained morale and prestige. Though Piedmont received no reward as a result of its participation (unwillingness of Britain to estrange Austria), Cavour was given an opportunity at the **congress of Paris** (p. 774) to expound the grievances of Italy. His moderation made a most favorable impression on the British and French.

1856. Foundation of the National Society by Giuseppe Farina, Daniele Manin, and Giorgio Pallavicino. The organization, aiming at the unification of Italy under the king of Piedmont, enjoyed the secret encouragement of Cavour, and at the same time was backed by many Mazzinian republicans, like Garibaldi.

1858, Jan. 14. The attempt of **Felice Orsini** to assassinate Napoleon III and the empress. From prison Orsini appealed to Napoleon to help free Italy. The effect of the episode was to prick Napoleon (himself originally an Italian conspirator) into action.

July 20. SECRET MEETING OF NAPOLEON III AND CAVOUR AT PLOMBIÈRES. Agreement: Napoleon to join Piedmont in war on Austria provided it could be provoked in a manner to justify it in the eyes of French and European opinion; after expulsion of the Austrians, Italy to be organized as a federation of four states, under presidency of the pope—(*a*) an **upper Italian kingdom** of Piedmont, Lombardy, Venetia, Parma, Modena, and the Papal Legations; (*b*) a **kingdom of Central Italy,** Tuscany with Umbria and the Marches; (*c*) **Rome** and the surrounding territory, to which the temporal power of the pope was to be restricted; (*d*) the **kingdom of Naples;** France was to be compensated by Savoy and Nice; Princess Clotilde, 15-year-old daughter of Victor Emmanuel, was to marry Prince Joseph Charles Bonaparte, cousin of the emperor.

Dec. 10. The **formal treaty signed** by France and Piedmont, after Napoleon had assured himself of the good-will of Russia (mission of Prince Jerome to Warsaw, September).

1859, Jan. 1. Napoleon's warning remarks to the Austrian ambassador let the secret out. Strong protests of Napoleon's ministers and of some sections of French opinion. Desperate efforts (Jan.–Apr.) of the British to prevent a clash. These proved abortive, since there was no will to peace on the French and Italian side.

Mar. 9. Piedmontese reserves called to the colors including volunteers, chiefly fugitives eluding conscription in Lombardy (a direct provocation to Austria).

Apr. 7. Austria mobilized.

Apr. 23. Austrian ultimatum to Piedmont, directing her to demobilize in three days. This was a blunder, since it supplied Cavour with the provocation he needed. The ultimatum was rejected.

Apr. 29. The **Austrians,** under General Franz Gyulai, **invaded Piedmont,** but Gyulai delayed action so long that the French had ample opportunity to arrive on the scene.

May. Peaceful revolutions in Tuscany, Modena, and Parma, engineered by the National Society. The rulers fled the country.

May 30. Piedmontese victory at Palestro. The allies crossed the Ticino into Lombardy.

June 4. BATTLE OF MAGENTA, a disorganized fight ending in the retirement of the Austrians.

June 13-15. Insurrection in the Papal Legations (Ravenna, Ferrara, Bologna).

June 24. BATTLE OF SOLFERINO and San Martino, sanguinary but indecisive. The Austrians began to withdraw to the Quadrilateral.

Napoleon III had been depressed by the sight of bloodshed on the fields of Magenta and Solferino; was alarmed by the risings in Tuscany and the Papal States with the threat of rapid spread of the unification movement; was faced by the possibility of a Prussian attack on the Rhine and the reality of a prolonged siege of the Quadrilateral fortresses, into which the Austrian army had retired. Without preliminary understanding with Victor Emmanuel, Napoleon proposed an armistice to Emperor Francis Joseph, concluded July 8, followed by the

July 11. Meeting of the two emperors at **Villafranca,** with agreement that Lombardy (except Mantua and Peschiera) should be ceded to France and might then be ceded by France to Piedmont; Venetia was to remain Austrian; Italian princes should be restored to their thrones subject to amnesty of their revolting subjects. These terms were accepted as preliminaries of peace by Victor Emmanuel who reserved his liberty, however, respecting the risings in central Italy. **Cavour resigned** in a rage. The final **treaty of Zürich** (Nov. 10) embodied substantially the provisions of the preliminaries of Villafranca.

Aug.-Sept. In Parma, Modena, Tuscany, and Romagna, representative assemblies decreed the downfall of their late rulers and union with constitutional Piedmont. The Piedmontese government dared not accept without the consent of Napoleon.

1860, Jan. 20. Cavour returned to power as premier, negotiated the annexations with Napoleon, whose price was the cession of Nice and Savoy.

Mar. 13-15. Plebiscites in Parma, Modena, Romagna, and Tuscany resulted in vote for annexation to Piedmont.

Mar. 24. Treaty of Turin, by which Piedmont ceded Savoy and Nice to France, after plebiscite.

Apr. 4. Abortive rising in Sicily against the Bourbons.

May 5. Garibaldi and his Thousand Redshirts sailed from Genoa for Sicily. They had been preparing an expedition to Nice, Garibaldi's natal city, which he meant to hold against the French. He was diverted to Sicily by Cavour, who secretly supported this filibustering expedition.

May 11. Garibaldi and his force landed at **Marsala,** in western Sicily. He marched inland, gathering recruits as he went.

May 15. He defeated the Neapolitans at **Calatafimi** and marched on Palermo.

May 27. Garibaldi took Palermo and set up a provisional government.

July 20. He defeated the Neapolitans at **Milazzo,** whereupon they evacuated Sicily, except Messina.

Aug. 22. Garibaldi crossed the straits, with the connivance of the British government (Lord Palmerston).

Sept. 7. He took **Naples** after a triumphal march, during which the Neapolitan army faded before him. **Francis II** (succeeded Ferdinand II in May 1859) fled to Gaeta. He had made desperate attempts to ward off the danger by forming a Liberal ministry (June 28) and re-establishing the constitution of 1848 (July 2), but was faced by defection on all sides.

Garibaldi's plan was to defeat the remnants of the Neapolitan army, march on Rome, and then proceed to the conquest of Venetia. Despite Garibaldi's loyalty to Victor Emmanuel, Cavour became alarmed, fearing French intervention on behalf of the pope and possible action by the Austrians. He therefore decided to take a hand and march Piedmontese troops to the scene, a course favored by the British to thwart supposed French schemes for a Muratist restoration in Naples.

Sept. 8. An **uprising in the Papal States** gave Cavour an excuse to intervene. He called upon **Cardinal Antonelli,** papal secretary of state, to disband his "adventurers" (the *Zouaves,* an international force of ardent Catholics). The demand was rejected.

Sept. 10. The Piedmontese crossed the papal frontier.

Sept. 18. They virtually annihilated the papal forces at **Castelfidaro** and advanced into Neapolitan territory, joining forces with Garibaldi.

Oct. 21-22. Naples and Sicily voted by plebiscite for union with the north. Similar votes were taken in the **Marches** (Nov. 4) and in **Umbria** (Nov. 5).

Oct. 26. Garibaldi defeated the Neapolitans on the **Volturno.**

Nov. 3-1861, Feb. 13. Siege of Gaeta. The operations were much hampered by the French fleet, which made attack by sea impossible until it was withdrawn (Jan. 19).

1861, Mar. 17. The **KINGDOM OF ITALY** proclaimed by the first Italian parliament, with Victor Emmanuel as first king and a government based on the Piedmontese constitution of 1848.

June 6. Cavour died at the age of 51.

1861-1862. Ministry of Baron Bettino Ricasoli, ardent Tuscan patriot, who embarked upon a vast national **agitation for the annexation of Rome,** still garrisoned by French troops. Garibaldi left his place of retirement, the island of Caprera, and organized the

1862, Mar. 9. Society for the Emancipation of Italy. He organized an abortive conspiracy against Austria, then made a triumphant visit to the scenes of his victories in Sicily. Defying the government, he raised the cry *Rome or Death,* crossed to the mainland (Aug. 24) and advanced north.

Aug. 29. Battle of Aspromonte, a skirmish in which Garibaldi and his volunteers were defeated by government troops. Garibaldi wounded and captured. He and his men were amnestied soon after (Oct. 5).

1864, Sept. 15. The **September convention,** by which Napoleon finally agreed to evacuate Rome within two years (beginning February 5, 1865), in return for an Italian promise to move the capital from Turin to Florence. Napoleon regarded this as the renunciation of Rome. The agreement raised a storm of protest in Piedmont and was denounced by Garibaldi, but was approved by the parliament.

1866, May 12. Alliance of Italy and Prussia, encouraged by Napoleon (p. 729).

June 20. Italy declared war on Austria.

June 24. Italians defeated at **second battle of Custozza,** by Archduke Albert.

July 3. VENETIA CEDED TO ITALY after its cession to France by Austria.

July 20. Resounding **defeat of the Italian fleet** by the Austrians under Admiral Wilhelm von Tegetthoff, near **Lissa.**

Oct. 12. **Treaty of Vienna,** ending the war.

Dec. Last **French troops withdrawn from Rome.** Garibaldi again placed himself at the head of volunteers and began the invasion of the papal territory, despite disavowals of the government. He was twice captured, but escaped (1867, Sept.).

1867, Oct. 27. A plan for an insurrection in Rome failed, but Garibaldi defeated a papal force.

Oct. 28. A French force landed at Cività Vecchia and marched to Rome.

Nov. 3. **BATTLE OF MENTANA.** Garibaldi defeated by papal troops supported by French, who mowed down the enemy with the new breech-loading *chassepots.* Garibaldi was captured and sent to Caprera. Napoleon tried at first to summon an international congress to discuss the Roman question, but accomplished nothing. The Roman question continued to be an open sore in Franco-Italian relations, and did much to prevent the formation of an alliance (p. 685).

1870, Aug. 19. Final withdrawal of French troops from Rome, in view of the **Franco-German War** (p. 736).

Sept. 20. After a short bombardment the **Italians,** capitalizing the defeat of France at Sedan, **entered Rome** after making a breach at the Porta Pia.

Oct. 2. After a plebiscite, **Rome was annexed** to Italy and became the capital.

d. THE KINGDOM OF ITALY, 1870-1914

1871, May 13. The **LAW OF GUARANTIES,** defining the relations between the government and the Papacy: the person of the pope was to be inviolable; he was granted royal honors and prerogatives and full liberty in the exercise of his religious functions (free intercourse with Catholics throughout the world, liberty to hold conclaves, control of papal seminaries, etc.); representatives of foreign powers at the Vatican were conceded diplomatic rights and immunities; the pope was to have an annual income of 3,250,000 lire from the Italian treasury (the equivalent of his previous income from his territories); he was left in full enjoyment of the Vatican and other palaces, with rights of extraterritoriality. This law was not accepted by the pope, who henceforth posed as *the prisoner of the Vatican.* Relations between the Papacy and the Italian government were not regularized until the **Lateran treaty** of 1929 (p. 1002).

1873-1876, Ministry of Marco Minghetti following that of Giovanni Lanza. The outstanding statesman was **Quintino Sella,** minister of finance, whose great aim was to balance the budget and organize the economic life of the new kingdom. He exercised "economy to the bone" (cutting down the civil list, salaries of ministers, etc.) and imposed taxes on cereals, incomes, land, etc. The government **reorganized the army** (350,000 men in peacetime) and re-created the navy (Italy the third sea-power by 1885). **Railroads** were pushed to the south (mileage 1758 kilometers in 1860; 7438 in 1876) and the **merchant marine** developed (10,000 tons in 1862; 1,000,000 in 1877, next to Britain and France).

1876, Mar. 18. **FALL OF THE MINGHETTI CABINET** and of the party of the Right (the party of enlightened conservatism following the teaching of Cavour, which had ruled the country since 1849).

Mar. 28. **First ministry of the Left,** under **Agostino Depretis.** Depretis was an early disciple of Mazzini, but had been converted to monarchism. Cold, cynical, disillusioned, he relied for maintenance of his power upon adroit parliamentary tactics, upon corruption and upon political alliances (*trasformismo*). By generous use of government pressure the Right was overwhelmingly defeated in the elections and returned to parliament a mere rump. Depretis remained premier, with two short interruptions, until his death in 1887. The unpopular taxes, against which the Left had protested, were restored and free rein was given to agitation against Austria (*irredentism*), aiming to acquire the **Trentino** and **Trieste** (*Italia Irredenta*), Italian-speaking districts still under Austrian rule. Italian stock in international affairs reached a low point.

1878, Jan. 9. **Death of King Victor Emmanuel.**

1878-1900. **UMBERTO I,** king.

1878, Feb. 7. **Death of Pius IX.**

1878-1903. **LEO XIII** (Cardinal Pecci), pope. Various attempts were made to reach an agreement on the Roman question (notably in 1886) but they all foundered on the pope's demand for at least some part of Rome.

1881. **Extension of the franchise,** by reduction of the age limit from 25 to 21 and lowering the tax-paying requirement from 40 to 19 lire. The result was an increase of the electorate from about 600,000 to about 2,000,000.

1882, May 20. **Triple Alliance** of Italy, Austria, and Germany (p. 782).

1885. An act of parliament farmed out the **state railways** to three private companies for 60 years, with possible termination at the end of 20 or 40 years.

Another act introduced **employers' liability**

for accidents, but was so poorly administered as to be ineffective, like the act (1877) making elementary education compulsory for children from six to nine years.

1885. Italian occupation of Assab and Massowa on the Red Sea, after the French (1881) had frustrated Italian hopes for Tunis (pp. 782, 873).

1887, July 29. Death of Depretis.

1887–1891. First ministry of Francesco Crispi, minister of interior under Depretis, former republican and member of Garibaldi's "Thousand," a proud, self-centered, vigorous individual. After abortive negotiations with the Papacy he turned to a violently **anti-clerical policy:** abolition of ecclesiastical tithes and of compulsory religious instruction in elementary schools. The erection of the **statue of Giordano Bruno** confronting the Vatican (1889) brought relations to such a pitch of tension that the pope seriously considered leaving Rome.

In **foreign policy** Crispi took his stand unwaveringly by the alliance with Austria and Germany (p. 784). He suppressed radical and irredentist organizations. Relations with France became so strained that they almost resulted in a rupture.

1887–1889. The Ethiopian venture. Crispi was a convinced imperialist and was determined to expand the Italian footing on the Red Sea. This led to war with Ethiopia and to a serious setback at **Dogali** (Jan. 25, 1887). Nevertheless the Italians were able to strengthen their position by backing **Menelek,** king of Shoa, against the Ethiopian king of kings, Johannes.

1889, May 2. The **treaty of Uccialli** by which, according to the Italian version, Menelek accepted an Italian **protectorate over Ethiopia.** Menelek became king of kings (Nov.) on the death of Johannes.

1891, Jan. 31. Fall of Crispi, after a gratuitous outburst against the Right.

1891–1892. Ministry of Marquis Antonio di Rudini, member of the Right, who governed with a coalition cabinet and support from the Left. He attempted to balance the budget, notably by reducing the expenditures for army and navy.

1892–1893. First ministry of Giovanni Giolitti. In the midst of a banking crisis, Giolitti made the managing director of the *Banca Romana,* Signor Tanlongo, a senator. The senate refused to confirm the appointment; an interpellation resulted in the arrest of Tanlongo and other prominent persons. A parliamentary investigation revealed that he had issued large sums in duplicate bank notes, that two preceding cabinets had been aware of his irregularities, that loans had been made by him to deputies,

etc. Giolitti was overthrown and left the country for a time.

1893, Dec. 10–1896, Mar. 5. Second Crispi ministry. The cabinet was faced with serious peasant troubles in Sicily (*fasci*), which were ruthlessly put down by the military. In similar manner Crispi dealt with anarchist outrages. Laws of July 11 and October 22, 1894, suppressed anarchist and socialist organizations.

The desperate financial situation was attacked by **Baron Sidney Sonnino,** the minister of finance. The Bank of Italy had been established by a law of August 10, 1893, to liquidate the insolvent Banca Romana. The law forbade state banks to make loans on real estate, limited their powers of discount, and reduced the paper money maximum. Other measures sought to increase economy and produce larger income. By 1896 Sonnino had practically balanced the budget despite the added expenses of the war in Africa.

1895–1896. THE ETHIOPIAN WAR. Menelek had, in 1891, rejected the Italian interpretation of the **treaty of Uccialli** and all efforts at compromise had failed. By 1895, after Menelek had secured the necessary munitions, he was ready to take up the Italian challenge.

1895, Dec. 7. The Italians, having advanced into northern Ethiopia, were badly defeated at **Amba Alagi** by Ras Makonen, who then besieged the key fortress of **Makallé,** which fell January 20, 1896. Crispi now felt that Italian honor and his own position were at stake. He insisted that **General Oreste Baratieri** make an advance and secure a victory. The general, against his better judgment, obeyed orders.

1896, Mar. 1. BATTLE OF ADUA (Adowa). The Italians (25,000) were completely defeated by some 100,000 Ethiopians under Menelek. Those who were not killed were for the most part captured and held for ransom. One of the worst colonial disasters in modern history. The Italians were obliged to sue for peace and signed the **treaty of Addis Ababa** (Oct. 26), in which they recognized the independence of Ethiopia and restricted themselves to the colony of Eritrea.

Mar. 5. Downfall of Crispi, resulting from a storm of public indignation and unrest.

1896–1898. Second Rudini ministry, based on an understanding with **Felice Cavalotti,** the radical leader. There followed a period of acute unrest.

1896, Sept. 30. Agreement between France and Italy with respect to Tunis. The Italians gave up many of their claims. First step in the policy of assuaging French hostility.

1898, May 3–8. THE "FATTI DI MAGGIO."

Serious bread riots in various parts of the country culminated in open conflict with the troops in Milan. Martial law was proclaimed, but order was restored only after considerable loss of life. Heavy sentences by courts-martial, especially against socialists, ensued. Rudini was obliged to resign.

1898, June 28-1900, June 18. Ministry of General Luigi Pelloux. He presented to parliament a drastic **Public Safety Law,** which was violently opposed by all radical groups. An attempt was made to change the chamber's standing orders, but this was again opposed. Pelloux appealed to the country (1900), but the elections only strengthened the radical elements. Having already granted an amnesty (Dec. 30, 1899), Pelloux was forced to resign.

1898, Nov. 21. A **commercial treaty signed with France,** bringing to an end the tariff war that had been raging since 1886, much to the detriment of Italy.

1900, July 29. King Umberto assassinated by an anarchist at Monza.

1900-1946. VICTOR EMMANUEL III, king. He was regarded as more liberal than his father and the government's policy gradually turned more and more to the Left for support.

1900, Dec. 14. Franco-Italian agreement exchanging a free hand in Morocco (for France) for a free hand in Tripoli (for Italy). An important stage in the Franco-Italian rapprochement (p. 793).

1901. Development of a large-scale **strike epidemic,** reflecting the growth of socialism, the organization of labor, and the more active spread of radicalism.

1902, Jan.-Feb. Strike of the employees of the Mediterranean Railway, demanding, among other things, recognition of their union. In February there was real danger of a general strike, following a strike of gas employees in Turin. The government met the situation by calling up all railway workers who were reservists. By mediation a settlement was finally reached in June.

1903, Oct.-1905, Mar. 4. Giolitti prime minister. Strikes and disorders continued unabated.

1904, Sept. General strike proclaimed. Much violence in Milan and other large cities.

Oct. In the **general elections** the socialists and radicals lost considerably, evidently a popular protest against the excesses of the labor organizations, but probably influenced also by the attitude of the pope (Pius X since 1903), who gave permission to Catholics to take part in political struggles involving the safety of the social order.

1906, May 30-1909, Dec. 2. Ministry of Gio-

litti, following the short-lived cabinets of Fortis and Sonnino.

1908. Giolitti continued his policy of **concession to the Church** by sponsoring a measure of facilitate religious education, such education to be optional with the communal councils, which were, however, obliged to supply such education if parents desired it.

Dec. 28. An **earthquake** of appalling severity shook southern Calabria and eastern Sicily, completely destroyed **Reggio** and **Messina** and many villages, with loss of life estimated at 150,000. At Messina a "tidal wave" added to the destruction.

1909, Dec. 2. Giolitti's government was overturned and was followed by the **cabinets of Sonnino** (1909, Dec.-1910, Mar.) and **Luzzatti** (1910, Mar.-1911, Mar.).

1911, Mar. 29-1914, Mar. 10. Giolitti prime minister again.

1911, Sept. 29-1912, Oct. 15. The **TRIPOLITAN WAR,** with Turkey. By various agreements (with Germany and Austria, 1887; with Britain, 1890; with France, 1900; with Russia, 1909) Italy had secured approval for eventual action to acquire Tripoli. The second Moroccan crisis (p. 799) and the prospects of a French protectorate in Morocco induced the Italian government to act before it was too late. Its decision may have been influenced by the pressure exerted by the **revived nationalist movement** (writings of **Gabriele d'Annunzio, Enrico Corradini,** et al.) after 1908. The pretext used was Turkish obstruction of Italian peaceful penetration. An ultimatum was sent (Sept. 28), but was rejected by the Turks.

1911, Oct. 5. The **Italians landed a force at Tripoli** and occupied the town. The other coastal towns were taken in rapid succession.

Nov. 5. The Italian government proclaimed the **annexation of Tripoli,** though the country was far from being conquered (valiant opposition of a small Turkish force under **Enver Bey,** supported by the Arabs).

1912, Jan.-Feb. Naval operations in the Red Sea and on the Syrian coast. The Italians bombarded several coastal cities, but the general operations were much hampered by Austrian refusal to permit war on the Balkan or Aegean coasts (forbidden by the Triple Alliance and other agreements). All efforts at mediation by the powers were frustrated by the refusal of the Turks to abandon Tripoli.

Apr. 16-19. Italian naval demonstration at the Dardanelles. The Turks closed the Straits (till May 4) causing much loss to Russian commerce.

May 4-16. The **Italians occupied Rhodes** and the other Dodecanese Islands. Peace negotiations were finally opened in July, but neither side was ready to yield an iota of its claims and only the threatening Balkan War finally induced the Turks to give in. The preliminary **treaty of Ouchy** (definitive **treaty of Lausanne,** October 18) ended the war: the Turks abandoned sovereignty of Tripoli, but the Italians were to recognize a representative of the sultan as caliph (i.e. Turkish religious authority); the Italians were to restore the Dodecanese Islands as soon as the Turks evacuated Tripoli.

June 29. Extension of the franchise, increasing the number of voters from about three to about eight and a half million. This amounted to practically universal suffrage. The same bill provided for salaries for members of parliament.

1913, Oct. The **general election** gave the Liberals a majority, but showed a marked increase of various socialist groups (78 seats together in place of the previous 41) and the Catholics (35 instead of 14).

1914, Mar. 9. General strike proclaimed at Rome, largely the outcome of popular resistance to taxation made necessary by the war.

Mar. 10. Cabinet of Antonio Salandra, following the resignation of Giolitti. The revolutionary railway union demanded an increase in wages, but the question was finally compromised.

June 7. On the national holiday of the *Statuto,* **riots broke out in Ancona,** where an anti-militarist demonstration had been prohibited. A general strike followed in the town and spread to other parts of the Marches, Romagna, etc. The leader was **Enrico Malatesta.** **Benito Mussolini** (p. 997), then editor of the socialist newspaper *Avanti,* took a prominent part. Mobs held a number of towns for a week until nationalists and troops restored order.

Aug. 3. Italy proclaimed neutrality in the World War. (*Cont. pp. 951 ff., 997.*)

Giuseppe Verdi (1813–1901) was the greatest composer of Italian opera. He adapted Shakespearean plots (*Macbeth,* 1847; *Otello,* 1887; *Falstaff,* 1893) as well as episodes from his country's history and heritage (*Rigoletto* 1851; *Il Trovatore,* 1853; *La Traviata,* 1853; *Simon Boccanegra,* 1857; *La Forza del Destino,* 1862; *Aïda,* 1871). The operas of **Giacomo Puccini** (1858–1924) have remained popular (*La Bohème,* 1896; *Madama Butterfly; La Tosca,* 1900).

The poet **Giosuè Carducci** (1835–1907) was an outstanding exponent of neo-classicism.

7. THE PAPACY

[For a complete list of the Roman popes, see Appendix IV.]

(*From p. 494*)

In the period of the restoration the Papacy recaptured much of the ground lost during the chaos of the revolutionary era. Throughout Europe there was a revival of Catholicism, and even in Protestant states sympathy had grown for the Catholic Church as the mainstay of the throne and the most effective force for holding the revolutionary spirit in check. The governing classes regarded as axiomatic this "union of throne and altar" against the disruptive tendencies of liberalism and nationalism. The Papacy was also assisted by the Romantic movement, with its idealization of the past, and by the influential writings of men like **René de Chateaubriand, Felicité de Lamennais,** and **Joseph de Maistre** (*Du Pape,* 1819), which glorified the Catholic Church and the authority of the pope.

1814, May 24. Ultramontanism reigned in Rome upon the return of the gentle and courageous **Pius VII.** The **Jesuit Order** and the **Inquisition** were re-established in Rome (Aug. 7), and the **Index** was reconstituted.

1815. Through the efforts of his able secretary of state, **Cardinal Consalvi,** the pope obtained from the congress of Vienna the **restitution of the States of the Church.** The temporal administration was reorganized, a bureaucracy established on the French model. Considerable opposition developed against this highly centralized administration, which excluded laymen from all high offices. Discontent against the "rule of the priests" centered in the **Carbonari,** a Liberal secret society (p. 700).

1821, Sept. 13. After the **rising in Naples** (p. 700), Consalvi had their leaders prosecuted, and the pope condemned their principles.

The chief activity of the Papacy in the reign of Pius VII was concerned with efforts to recover its international influence in Europe. Toward the accomplishment of this program, Consalvi negotiated a series of valuable **concordats** with all the Roman Catholic powers save Austria.

1823–1829. LEO XII (Annibale della Genga)

continued the policy of Pius VII and secured further advantageous concordats, extending the policy to the South American republics. His extreme **reactionary policy** in domestic affairs strengthened the underlying current of liberalism. He persecuted the Jews, harshly supervised morals, condemned the Protestant Bible societies and all dissenters (1824, 1826), and made vigorous efforts to root out the Carbonari. On the constructive side, Leo promoted missions, encouraged scholars, improved the educational system in Rome, reduced taxes, made justice less costly, and found money for public improvements. Of noble character, Leo lacked insight into, and sympathy with, the temporal developments of his period.

1829-1830. PIUS VIII (Francesco Castiglione) —a short, reactionary reign noteworthy for the **Catholic Emancipation Act in England** (p. 656).

1831-1846. GREGORY XVI (Bartolomeo Alberto Cappellari). Apogee of the reaction. The new pope was greeted by revolts which had broken out under his predecessor and which were promptly suppressed (p. 701).

1832, Aug. 15. The encyclical *Mirari vos* condemned complete and unrestrained liberty of conscience, liberty of the press, and revolt for any reason against an established government. Though Gregory did much to promote **public welfare** (establishment of a decimal coinage and a bureau of statistics, and of a steamship service at Ostia; foundation of public baths, hospitals, and orphanages; lightening of various imposts), he would not concede the demand for separation of the ecclesiastical and the civil administration. The secretary of state, **Cardinal Lambruschini,** suppressed all aspirations for political liberty with extreme severity. The last three years were again occupied with rebellions in the Papal States. The embarrassing financial condition in which Gregory left his dominions was due to his lavish expenditure on architectural and engineering works, and to his liberal patronage of learning.

1846-1878. PIUS IX (Giovanni Mastai-Ferretti), wildly greeted in Italy as the "pope of progress" (p. 701).

1848, Apr. 29. Placing the universal significance of the Papacy above national aspirations, Pius proclaimed his neutrality in the national war against Austria. For this he was denounced as a traitor, and forced to flee (for details on Pius IX and the Revolution of 1848, see p. 703).

1850, Apr. 12. Pius returned to Rome, embittered, and henceforth stubbornly hostile to liberalism in all its forms. The constitution of 1848 was not restored, though half-hearted efforts were made to modernize the state through the grant of self-government, with participation of laymen. In the reactionary policy which prevailed, **Cardinal Antonelli,** secretary of state, with medieval views and Machiavellian temperament, exerted a paramount influence. In the achievement of Italian unity (1859-1860) the Papal States were lost, to be followed by the taking of Rome in 1870 (p. 708). Pius and his successors persistently refused the offer of the Italian government to accord the pope the rights and honors of a sovereign, and an annual endowment (p. 708). Faced by the loss of his temporal sovereignty, Pius sought compensation by strengthening the machinery of the Church and the spiritual influence of the Papacy. The political reaction following the stormy years 1848-1849 offered promising soil for the pope's efforts to conclude advantageous concordats, and in several countries, notably Spain (1851) and Austria (1855), he was able to regulate church-state relations to the advantage of the curia. Pius also re-established Roman Catholic hierarchies in England (1850) and Holland (1853). Seeking popularity, the pope, unaided by an ecumenical council, promulgated a new dogma, the first since the council of Trent.

1854, Dec. 8. Dogma of the Immaculate Conception of the Virgin, which made a belief long widely held in the Church an article of faith. The "infallibility" of the pope implied in this act was openly acknowledged in 1870 by the Vatican council.

1864, Dec. 8. When the temporal power of the Papacy was tottering to its fall, Pius flung down the gauntlet of defiance to the new social and political order in the encyclical *Quanta cura,* with the appended *Syllabus errorum.* The pope censured the "errors" of pantheism, naturalism, nationalism, indifferentism, socialism, communism, freemasonry, and various other 19th-century views. He claimed for the Church the control of all culture and science, and of the whole educational system; denounced the enjoyment of liberty of conscience and worship, and the idea of tolerance; claimed the complete independence of the Church from state control; upheld the necessity of a continuance of the temporal power of the Roman See, and declared that "It is an error to believe that the Roman Pontiff can and ought to reconcile himself to, and agree with, progress, liberalism, and contemporary civilization." The Ultramontane party was loud in its praise of the *Syllabus,* but the Liberals were amazed, and treated it as a declaration of war by the Church on modern civilization. It was also a blow aimed at the **Liberal Catholics,** who were reconciled to religious liberty and democratic government.

1869, Dec. 8–1870, Oct. 20. THE VATICAN COUNCIL. The zenith of Pius' pontificate was attained when the Vatican council (the first general council since that of Trent, three centuries earlier) proclaimed (1870, July 18) the **dogma of papal infallibility**—the dogma that the pope, when speaking *ex cathedra,* possesses infallibility in decisions regarding faith or morals, in virtue of his supreme apostolic power. The new dogma was attended by important results. It marked the final triumph of the Papacy over the episcopal and conciliar tendencies of the Church. It attempted to exalt the Papacy above all secular states and to extend "faith and morals" to the political domain.

1870, July 30. Austria immediately annulled the **concordat of 1855.** In Prussia the *Kulturkampf* broke out (p. 738), and in France the council so accentuated the power of ultramontanism that the state took steps to curb it. At his death in 1878, Pius left the Church shaken to its foundations and in feud with almost every secular government.

1878–1903. LEO XIII (Gioacchino Pecci), a gifted diplomat, marked a change. Leo possessed a more liberal and tolerant spirit than his predecessor. He narrowed the intellectual gulf between the Church and modern society: by encouraging a renewed study of St. Thomas Aquinas in all Catholic seminaries (the result of which was to spread the doctrine that between true science and true religion there was no conflict); by fostering the study of Church history (on the theory that it would augment the prestige of the Church by showing its contributions to the progress of civilization); by supporting experimental science among eminent Catholics.

1885. Leo was appointed arbitrator in a dispute between **Germany and Spain** over the possession of the Caroline Islands. He also acted as arbitrator in a number of other cases. As his reign wore on, Leo perceived that democracy might prove fully as useful as monarchy for preserving and strengthening Catholic principles. He therefore encouraged Catholic political parties, with distinctly liberal tendencies, in Germany and Belgium, and adopted a friendly attitude toward the government of the French Republic. Instructions were given to French Catholics to break with monarchical principles, and to support the republic.

1890. However, the policy of the *Ralliement* in France (p. 690) was also motivated by the pope's desire to secure French aid for the **solution of the Roman question,** the mainspring of his whole policy. Relations with the Italian government had grown steadily worse, and in an encyclical addressed to the Italian clergy (1898, Aug. 5) Leo insisted on the duty of Italian Catholics to abstain from political life while the pope remained in his "intolerable position."

1891, May 15. The encyclical on labor questions, *Rerum novarum,* aimed to apply Christian principles to the relations between capital and labor, and won for Leo the title of "the workingman's pope." It pointed out that the possessing classes, including the employers, have important moral duties to fulfill; that it is one of the first duties of society (state and church collaborating) to improve the position of the workers.

Of the political principles of Pius IX, Leo altered little. He expressed in his encyclicals the same condemnation of many phases of liberalism and nationalism, and reiterated the view that the Church should superintend and direct every form of secular life. But, unlike his predecessor, Leo never appeared as a violent partisan of any particular form of government. It was his object to bring about harmonious collaboration between church and state. In the *Kulturkampf* he adopted a moderate and conciliatory attitude, and succeeded in obtaining the repeal of the legislation against the Church.

1903–1914. PIUS X (Giuseppe Sarto), known as the "pope of the poor and the humble," applied himself with determination to the task of fortifying the inner life of the Church. He carried out (1908) an extensive reorganization of the curia in order to modernize its machinery. Another important reform, the codification of canon law (1904), was undertaken (completed under Benedict XV, promulgated June 28, 1917).

Encouraged by the liberal tendencies in Leo's reign, a group of Catholics known as **Modernists** (notably **Father George Tyrrell** in England, the **Abbé Loisy** in France, and **Antonio Fogazzaro** in Italy) had begun to agitate for a revision of the dogmas and policies of the Church to bring them in line with the findings of scientific scholarship and the modern spirit. Pius had only bitter scorn for the Modernists.

1907, Sept. 8. The encyclical *Pascendi gregis* expounded and condemned the Modernist system, and set up a new and effective censorship to combat it.

Pius was not greatly interested in political affairs. Relations with the Italian government improved, and the pope qualified the absolute prohibition imposed by his predecessors of the participation of Catholics in political elections (p. 710). But the pope experienced great bitterness in his relations with France, which adopted legislation for the separation of church and state (p. 692).

1914, Aug. 2. Pius' last circular was an appeal for peace addressed to the Catholics of the world on the eve of the World War.

1914-1922. BENEDICT XV (Giacomo della Chiesa), whose reign was taken up by efforts to maintain an even balance between the warring nations, many of them essentially Catholic. The pope twice (1915, July 30; 1917, Aug. 1) appealed to the belligerents to make peace, but these appeals earned him nothing but a reputation for pro-Germanism.

With the victory of the Allies and Italy, the pope began to give up opposition to the Italian government. He definitely revoked (1919) the decree forbidding Catholics to participate in politics, and authorized (1920) Catholic sovereigns to visit the king in Rome. Negotiations were opened which led ultimately to the Lateran treaty of 1929 (p. 1002).

(*Cont. p. 997.*)

8. SWITZERLAND

(*From p. 498*)

1815, Mar. 20, 29. Two acts of the **congress of Vienna** regulated the Swiss problem. They laid down the principle of the **perpetual neutrality** of Switzerland, restored the old frontiers, with two exceptions, and smoothed over the internal difficulties of the country. A constitutional convention drew up a new **federal pact** which restored the old institutions, and gave wide autonomy to the 22 cantons. The diet had very restricted powers, being little more than a congress of ambassadors representing the cantons. Racial and religious differences, and differences in political ideals, still existed among the cantons, which made for division and disunion.

1815-1828. The early part of the restoration period was characterized by a serious economic crisis, due to the war. Swiss industry, no longer protected by the Continental blockade, found itself unable to compete with English industry, especially in the textile trade. The cantons were unable to agree upon a common customs policy. In the political sphere most of the cantons followed reactionary policies. Under the pressure of the Holy Alliance, Switzerland was obliged to persecute the liberal refugees from neighboring countries, and in 1823 was compelled to restrict the freedom of the press.

1828-1848. The so-called **"Era of Regeneration,"** in which revision of the constitutions of several cantons was undertaken.

1828-1829. The cantonal governments were wise enough to grant the concessions demanded, such as universal suffrage, freedom of the press, and equality before the law. The movement was strengthened by the July Revolution in Paris. Between 1830 and 1833 some ten cantons liberalized their constitutions.

1832, Mar. 17. The Siebener Concordat. The liberal cantons joined together to guarantee their new liberal constitutions.

July 17. The question of revising the federal pact in the direction of a stronger central government was brought before the diet by a large majority of the cantons, whereupon the conservative cantons concluded an alliance **(league of Sarnen)** to maintain the pact of 1815.

1834, Jan. 20. The struggle for the revision of the constitution was transformed into a **religious quarrel** when the liberal cantons adopted the *Articles of Baden,* which contained a program of ecclesiastical reform. The Liberal party stood for freedom of worship, secular education, a lay state, and was especially irritated by the paramount position in the Catholic cantons of the **Jesuits,** who had returned after 1814. By increasing the power of the central government, the Liberals hoped to be able to impose their views upon the whole confederation. Religious and political passions gradually rose to fever pitch.

1845, Dec. 11. THE *SONDERBUND*. The seven Catholic cantons—Lucerne, Uri, Schwyz, Unterwalden, Zug, Freiburg, and Valais—replied to the organized armed bands of the Liberal cantons by concluding a league (the *Sonderbund*) for the purpose of protecting their interests.

1847, July 20. The Liberals were able to get a vote through the diet ordering the **dissolution of the *Sonderbund*** as being contrary to the constitution. The seven cantons refused, and war resulted.

Nov. 10-29. The federal general **Guillaume Dufour** quickly defeated the forces of the *Sonderbund.* Lord Palmerston's policy of masterly inactivity and Dufour's rapid victory averted an intervention being planned by Metternich and Guizot. The *Sonderbund* was dissolved, the Jesuits were expelled, and the victors proceeded to strengthen the federal government.

1848, Sept. 12. The **NEW CONSTITUTION,**

replacing the **pact of 1815.** It organized Switzerland as a federal union closely modeled on that of the United States. While preserving the historic local government of the cantons, it established a strong central government. Legislative authority resided in two chambers: The **council of state** (*Ständerat*) consisting of two members from each canton; the **national council** (*Nationalrat*), members of which were elected by universal suffrage in numbers proportional to the population of each canton. The executive was a **federal council** (*Bundesrat*) of seven members, elected by the two chambers. Its annual chairman was given the title *President of the Confederation,* but he enjoyed no wider powers than his colleagues.

1848-1857. The Neuchâtel problem. The canton of Neuchâtel (part of the confederation, but under the sovereignty of the king of Prussia) had proclaimed a republic (Mar. 1848), the constitution of which was guaranteed by the federal diet. In 1856 a conservative revolution aimed at the restoration of the king. War with Prussia was narrowly averted by the mediation of Napoleon III. In May 1857 the king renounced his rights, in return for a money payment, which he later renounced. He kept his title, but this was discontinued by William I.

Swiss internal history in the ensuing period was dominated by economic problems and by a general trend toward **government centralization.** The public services (telegraph and postal systems, customs, currency, weights and measures) had been brought under federal control, and were reorganized.

1874, Apr. 19. A revision of the constitution further enlarged the powers of the federal government, especially in military affairs. Free elementary schools under federal supervision were authorized and the principle of referendum was introduced for national legislation. Thereafter, by means of the initiative and referendum, federal authority was extended to many fields.

Oct. The **International Postal Congress** met at Berne. Switzerland became a favorite meeting-place for international conventions

and headquarters for many international organizations.

1882, May 20. Opening of the St. Gothard Railway; first of the great railroad tunnels through the Alps.

1887, May. The federal government was given a **monopoly of sale of spirits.**

1889. Acute tension in relations with Germany, resulting from the expulsion of a police officer on the trail of political offenders. Switzerland had long been a haven for political refugees and for radicals and conspirators of all hues. The asylum extended to them caused constant friction with neighboring powers.

1890, June. The federal government was empowered to enact measures of **social insurance.**

1898, Feb. The federal government was authorized to **purchase privately owned railways.**

Nov. The federal government was empowered to unify and enforce the **civil and penal codes.**

1907, Apr. 12. A **new army bill** reorganized the forces. Although Swiss neutrality was guaranteed by the powers in 1815, growing international tension necessitated precautions. A unique military system was built up (1847, revised 1907): the army was a type of standing militia, with short periods of required training biennially.

Switzerland made steady progress in the economic sphere, but despite growing prosperity and the expansion of federal power, democracy remained. In six of the smallest cantons the people continued to exercise their local powers through mass meetings (*Landesgemeinden*) without the intervention of any assembly. In the larger cantons representative systems were used, but they were based on universal suffrage and in most of them the initiative and referendum were employed. (*Cont. p. 1003.*)

German-Swiss literature in the 19th century: novels of **Jeremias Gotthelf** (1797-1854); stories and verses of **Gottfried Keller** (1819-1890) and **Conrad Ferdinand Meyer** (1825-1898); historical writings of **Jakob Burckhardt** (1818-1897); poetry of **Carl Spitteler** (1845-1924).

Artists: Arnold Boecklin (1827-1901) and **Ferdinand Hodler** (1853-1918).

9. CENTRAL EUROPE

a. GERMANY, 1815-1848

1815. THE "METTERNICH SYSTEM." After the Napoleonic wars central Europe (the German states and the Austrian Empire) was subjected to the "Metternich System." Through rigid censorship, elaborate espionage,

supervision of the universities, etc., Metternich opposed constitutional and nationalist aspirations awakened during the Napoleonic wars. In the German states he made his will felt through the **Germanic Confederation** (called into being by the congress of Vienna). It was composed of 38 sovereign powers; its object was to guarantee external and internal peace of Germany, and the independence of the member states (Austria brought only its German states into the confederation); its organ was a diet sitting at Frankfurt-on-the-Main, organized on a complicated basis into two "assemblies," over both of which the Austrian representative presided. The diet was a diplomatic congress, not a parliament: its members were instructed delegates of the various governments. In Metternich's view, it was a loose confederation (*Staatenbund*) to protect German monarchs against their foreign foes (Russia and France) and their domestic enemy (liberalism).

In 1815 **Prussia** had been the great hope of the Liberals, but with the decay of the influence of the king's principal minister, Karl August von Hardenberg, reactionary influences came to the fore, capitalizing the growing fear of radical activity and the fact of fundamental disunity (territorial and moral) in Prussia. The constitutional movement was a disappointment elsewhere, except in Bavaria, Baden, and Saxe-Weimar.

1815–1819. The *Burschenschaften.* Universities became the centers of the liberal movement; students were organized in Liberal societies (*Burschenschaften*). The center of the agitation was the University of Jena, where an extremist group followed the lead of **Karl Follen.**

1817, Oct. 18. The **Wartburg Festival** (organized by Jena students as a joint celebration of the Reformation and the battle of Leipzig), at which emblems of reaction were burned.

1819, Mar. 23. **August von Kotzebue,** poetaster, reactionary journalist, formerly in the tsar's service, was murdered at Mannheim by a Jena student, **Karl Sand,** as an enemy of liberalism. Metternich was alarmed by this Liberal activity, won King Frederick William of Prussia over to repressive measures, embodied in the

July. **CARLSBAD DECREES,** sanctioned by the diet of the Germanic Confederation (Sept. 20), binding sovereigns to control the universities through commissioners, providing a strict censorship of all publications, establishing at Mainz an inquisition into secret societies—an act held to have "fettered opinion and postponed constitutional liberty in Germany for a generation."

1819–1844. **THE GERMAN** *ZOLLVEREIN.* A more serious threat to Austrian hegemony in Germany now had its unostentatious beginnings in the movement for a *Zollverein* (customs union). The multiple tariff systems existing in Germany imposed irksome and hampering restrictions on a steadily growing commerce. Prussia took the lead in this situation by establishing a uniform tariff for all her

territories and signing an initial tariff treaty with Schwarzburg-Sondershausen (1819, Oct.). Prussia was feared for her power and hated for her reaction by the smaller states, which combated her leadership and attempted to set up rival customs unions.

1829, May. Prussia won over the league of Bavaria and Württemberg and gradually added other states. By 1844 the Zollverein included practically the whole of Germany, except German Austria, Hanover, Oldenburg, Mecklenburg, and the three Hanse cities. By forming a close economic union of the great majority of the states in the Germanic Confederation, Prussia had won a political victory over Austria.

1830. The **July Revolution in Paris** (p. 678) not unnaturally had repercussions in Germany, where the revolutionary movement had revived in the hands of the reorganized university movement (1827), in secret clubs, etc. The rulers were forced to abdicate in Brunswick, Saxony, and Hesse-Cassel (Sept.); in these states and in Hanover (1833) new constitutions were introduced. Prussia escaped revolution, due to respect for the king, and especially to administrative reforms which had removed the worst evils of misgovernment.

Metternich saw in the revolutions the working of international radicalism, seeking to undermine the bases of existing society.

1832, May. The new movement was typified for Metternich in the **Hambach Festival,** where a gathering of 25,000 toasted Lafayette, demanded a republic and German unity, resolved to adopt not only peaceful methods of press and platform, but of armed revolt.

June 28. Metternich's answer was the adoption by the Germanic Confederation of **six articles:** imposing on every German sovereign the duty of rejecting petitions of his estates impairing his sovereignty; repudiating the right of estates to refuse supplies or to use this method to secure constitutional changes; providing against legislation by the states prejudicial to the Germanic Confederation, etc.

July. Additional repressive measures included prohibition of all public meetings; surveillance of suspicious political characters; renewal of edicts against universities. The reply of the revolutionists was a crazy plot engineered by international conspirators (probably connected with Mazzinian secret societies), aiming to seize Frankfurt, dissolve the diet, unify the German states on liberal principles.

1833, Apr. 3. The **attempt on Frankfurt** was made and promptly collapsed. The diet's reply (June) was to appoint, at Metternich's instance, a central commission to co-ordinate preventive measures and supervise prosecutions in the various states.

1837. The Metternichian reactionist policy was next extended to **Hanover,** where, on the death of William IV of England, the kingdom passed (in accordance with the Salic Law) to **Ernest Augustus, duke of Cumberland,** eldest surviving son of George III. The latter set aside the Liberal constitution granted by William IV (1833). (Dismissal of seven eminent professors for refusal to take the oath.) A new constitution, cloak for the king's absolutism, was vigorously opposed in Hanover; the opposition was supported in the federal diet by Bavaria and other states; but Metternich secured the support of Prussia for the principles of monarchical absolutism, and the diet decided that the constitution of 1833 was invalid, the king justified in overthrowing it.

1840, Aug. Ernest Augustus then imposed a constitution of his own, reducing the legislature to a nullity and recognizing the state domains as the king's private property. Constitutionalists in Germany were outraged by this act, even Conservatives were stirred; Liberals declared the Germanic Confederation a national disgrace.

The long reign of Frederick William III of Prussia came to an end, June 7, 1840, and he was succeeded by his son,

1840–1861.   FREDERICK WILLIAM IV (b. 1795), a romanticist, deeply imbued with poetic and mystical conceptions, his ideas often far removed from reality. Like the Liberals, he aimed at greater political freedom and stronger national unity. But he sought to attain these ends, not through constitutionalism, but through the rule of the estates, reviving the position of the nobles and corporations, reflecting the "mystic glories of a divinely consecrated and patriarchal monarchy." In place of the Germanic Confederation, he dreamt of reviving the Holy Roman Empire, in which Prussia would play a glorious rôle, but secondary to that of the Hapsburgs.

1841–1842. The reign began auspiciously. The censorship was made less stringent, but abuses of the new system resulted in its prompt withdrawal, causing mutual recrimination between government and public opinion.

1841. Provincial diets, established in 1823, were given the right to elect committees to meet in Berlin and discuss legislation for all Prussia.

1842. At the first meeting of the committees, the king explained that they were not to regard themselves as a popular assembly, an irritating and ambiguous statement. They separated after accomplishing but little. The king was impelled to move forward also by financial difficulties which he hoped to ease by some sort of popular representation.

1847. The eventual result was the order summoning the **United** *Landtag* (combined provincial diets). The king, who affected to despise the formalism of "Liberal constitutions," now presented to the Landtag an incredibly complicated and unreal scheme which gave the Landtag no effective power over legislation or the budget, made no provision for regular meetings. Opposition developed at once, demanding above all periodicity of meetings. Two government bills were introduced at this session (dealing with financial matters); both were rejected. The session came to an end amid great discontent of the Liberals.

Having failed in the Landtag, the king sought to recover his prestige through a scheme for reform of the Germanic Confederation, giving the diet new powers and transforming the system in the direction of a federal state. The plan was presented at Vienna (end 1847) by **Joseph Maria von Radowitz,** but no decision had been reached when the scheme was overtaken by the stormy events of 1848.

CULTURAL DEVELOPMENTS

(1) Literature

Poetry was the chief form of expression of the Romantic movement: **Friedrich Hölderlin** (1770–1834), **Joseph von Eichendorff** (1788–1857), and **Heinrich Heine** (1797–1856); dramas of **Heinrich von Kleist** (1777–1811) and the Austrian **Franz Grillparzer** (1791–1872); dramas and tales of **Ludwig Tieck** (1773–1853), who with **August Wilhelm Schlegel** (1767–1845) translated Shakespeare's plays (1797–1810). **Friedrich Schlegel** (1772–1829) and his brother were the foremost literary critics. The **Grimm brothers** (Jakob and Wilhelm, 1785–1863 and 1786–1859 respectively) were the first to study and formulate the history of the German language.

(2) Music of the Romantic School

Operas of **Carl Maria von Weber** (1786–1826, *Der Freischütz,* 1820); choral music, oratorios, and symphonies of **Felix Mendelssohn** (1809–1847); songs of **Franz Schubert** (1797–1828) and **Robert Schumann** (1810–1856); symphonic music and songs of **Johannes Brahms** (1833–1897) and **Franz Liszt** (1811–1886).

b. THE HAPSBURG MONARCHY, 1815–1848

(1) Austria

The **Austrian Empire** was an anomalous congeries of territories and peoples, united by common obedience to the house of Hapsburg-

Lorraine, as provided by the Pragmatic Sanction (p. 501) and by such common institutions as the capital (Vienna), the Austrian court, the army, the bureaucracy, foreign service, the Austrian Church. Held together by the centripetal forces of these institutions, Austria was a monarchical machine. She was increasingly weakened by the centrifugal forces of nationalism and the discords of inharmonious peoples gathered within her heterogeneous territories. The empire embraced (1) the hereditary lands (principally Austria proper and the territories inhabited by the Slovenes to the south); (2) the lands of the Bohemian crown; (3) the province of Galicia, acquired in the partitions of Poland; (4) the kingdom of Italy—Venetia, and Lombardy; (5) the lands of the crown of St. Stephen —Hungary, Transylvania, Croatia.

Among these peoples **nationalist movements** took root and flourished, e.g.: (1) the **Illyrian renaissance,** beginning as a literary movement among the Croats and their neighbors and eventuating in resistance to the rule of the Magyars, dominant racial group in the lands of the crown of St. Stephen; (2) the **Czech renaissance,** beginning also as a literary movement and turning in the forties to demands for the restitution of constitutional rights for Bohemia; (3) most important of all, the rise of a nationalist movement among the **Magyars** (p. 720).

1806-1835. FRANCIS I (b. 1768). He was, until the dissolution of the Holy Roman Empire (1806), Holy Roman Emperor as Francis II. Until 1805 he had been assisted by a cabinet minister (in effect a prime minister) who was in direct control of the various elements in the government. Thereafter Francis acted as his own minister, permitting **Metternich** wide powers in foreign affairs, but holding the threads of domestic government in his own hands. The governmental machine was extremely complicated, the emperor alone representing any synthesis of the various administrative departments. "Austria was administered, but not ruled," remarked Metternich. The infrequent meetings of the various provincial estates were mere form. The police were supreme; spies were everywhere; letters were opened; censorship was extremely severe; instruction was made to conform with conservative principles. The emperor's alarm at popular movements increased.

1832. He combated Metternich's suggestion of a new constitution to reconcile the "opposition between the monarchist principle and the democratic." His will warned his successor to "displace none of the foundations of the edifice of state. Rule, and change nothing."

1835-1848. FERDINAND I, the weak-minded and incapable son of Francis I. He followed his father's advice in leaving Metternich in control of foreign affairs. But he permitted court circles to induce him to create, as supreme governmental organ,

1836. The **state conference** (*Staatskonferenz*), composed of Archdukes Ludwig and Francis Charles, **Count Franz Anton Kolowrat,** Metternich. In fact the state conference met less and less often, and the dominant influence in the state was exercised by individual ministers over their several departments, notably by Metternich over foreign affairs, Kolowrat over finance.

Publications within Austria were still subjected to a strict censorship, but Liberal pamphlets, newspapers, etc., were secretly introduced from abroad. University professors were (in fact) allowed considerable latitude. Western European Liberal ideas rapidly took root among the educated classes of Austria. In Austria proper these ideas found expression in agitation for constitutional changes. This agitation was least important in the Alpine districts, most significant in Lower Austria and especially Vienna. The assembly of estates in Lower Austria had during the past century lost its political significance, but now began to press for legislative and tax reforms, more effective parliamentary representation for the cities, etc. The movement for constitutional reform was stimulated by the industrial progress of Austria, giving Vienna and other cities an increasingly large middle class, cultivated, self-confident, eager to take its place in the political life of the country. Industry also brought a city proletariat with more radical views, destined to play an important rôle in the revolution of 1848. The masses were goaded by severe economic depression; riots of workers became more frequent. This was the setting for the events of March 1848.

(2) Hungary

1813-1825. In Hungary, whose constitution remained unchanged, the reactionary Emperor Francis I attempted to rule without summoning the diet, demanding troops and subsidies directly from the counties. When the latter refused compliance, he was obliged once again to summon the diet (1825), promise triennial meetings and the exclusive right to grant taxes and recruits. The Hungarian diet represented exclusively the still semifeudal nobility. The upper house (*table of magnates*) had as members the great nobles (some 130 in number) and certain ecclesiastical dignitaries and high office-holders. The lower house (*table of deputies*) was recruited from members of the gentry (about 700,000), with representatives elected by the county assemblies (two each); it included also two members representing all the cities, and delegates from the diet of the kingdom of Croatia.

A movement, at once liberal and national, made rapid progress in Hungary in the thirties and forties. Its moderate wing, inspired by **Count Stephen Széchenyi,** aimed primarily at a cultural renaissance and the economic development of the country along western European lines. The radicals, led by **Louis Kossuth,** sought complete autonomy and parliamentary government for Hungary. Between these two groups, but much nearer Széchenyi, **Francis Deák** urged a middle course to assure Hungary at once her rightful position of autonomy within the empire and a modern parliamentary régime. All groups were interested in extending the use of the Magyar language; all favored maintenance of the dominant position of Magyars over other peoples within Hungary.

1836-1844. The diet won its first victory when Magyar was substituted for Latin as the official language in Hungary. Agitation for reform gathered vigor in the forties. As editor of a newly founded (1841) organ of the radicals, the *Pesti Hirlap* (*Pest Journal*), Kossuth extended the influence of his revolutionary propaganda, attacking Austria violently, fostering Magyar chauvinism by denying the rights of Slavic minorities in Hungary.

1847. The **elections of 1847** returned a large majority of Liberals to the table of deputies. Deák now united the various Liberal groups on a compromise program of reform, the so-called **Ten Points,** afterward known as the *March Laws:* responsible government; popular representation; larger liberty for the press; incorporation of Transylvania; right of public assembly; complete religious liberty; universal equality before the law; universal taxation; abolition of serfdom with compensation to the landlords; abolition of the *aviticitas,* the rigid system of entail dating from 1351. Deák's program was accepted by the table of deputies, but was combated by the conservative table of magnates. The deputies negotiated with the imperial government and had reached a deadlock when news of the February Revolution in Paris reached Budapest and precipitated the revolutionary movement there.

CULTURAL DEVELOPMENTS

In **literature** the period was an exceptionally active one. Among poets of the classical and romantic schools may be mentioned **Benedict Virág,** who was also the author of *Magyar Szazadok* (*Pragmatic History of Hungary,* 1808),

Francis Kazinczy (1759-1831), **John Bacsányi** (1763-1845), **Alexander Kisfaludy** (1772-1844), whose brother **Charles** (1788-1830) was one of the first successful dramatists; **Francis Kölcsey** (1790-1838), **Michael Vörösmarty** (1800-1855), and especially **Alexander Petöfi** (1823-1849) and the great epic poet **John Arany** (1812-1882). **Nicholas Jósika** wrote historical romances and Baron **Josef Eötvös** (1813-1871) in his *Faln Jegyzöje* (*The Village Notary,* 1845) gave a vivid picture of Hungarian country life in the pre-1848 period.

c. THE REVOLUTION OF 1848-1849 IN THE HAPSBURG DOMINIONS

1848, Mar. 3. The news of the February Revolution in Paris (p. 679) aroused much excitement in Vienna and Budapest. In a daring speech **Kossuth** denounced the Vienna system and demanded responsible government for Hungary.

Mar. 12. Stimulated by the boldness of the Hungarians, the Viennese began to demonstrate and draw up petitions to the emperor. Through mismanagement the popular commotion led (Mar. 13) to clashes between the troops and the demonstrators (largely students).

Mar. 13. METTERNICH RESIGNED and left the country.

Mar. 15. An imperial manifesto abolished the censorship and promised the convocation of a constitutional assembly. On the same day the Hungarian table of deputies adopted the entire Ten Points of Deák, which thus became the **March Laws,** equivalent to a constitution. The table of magnates opposed the program vigorously, but the king-emperor accepted it (Mar. 31) as well as further demands (Apr.) which made **Hungary** all but independent, joined to the rest of the Hapsburg possessions only through a personal union. On the same day also the **Croats** organized a national committee which sought autonomous government, i.e. separation from Hungary.

Mar. 18-22. The **glorious Five Days in Milan,** initiating the revolution in Lombardy (p. 703).

Apr. 8. The **Czechs** obliged the Vienna government to promise a constituent assembly for the kingdom of Bohemia. Other revolutionary movements took place in Moravia, Galicia, Dalmatia, and Transylvania.

Apr. 25. The emperor promulgated a **constitution for Austria** instead of awaiting the work of the assembly promised in March. The constitution set up a constitutional régime with a responsible ministry.

May 15. Dissatisfaction with the constitu-

The House of Hapsburg-Lorraine (1740–1918)

(From p. 427)

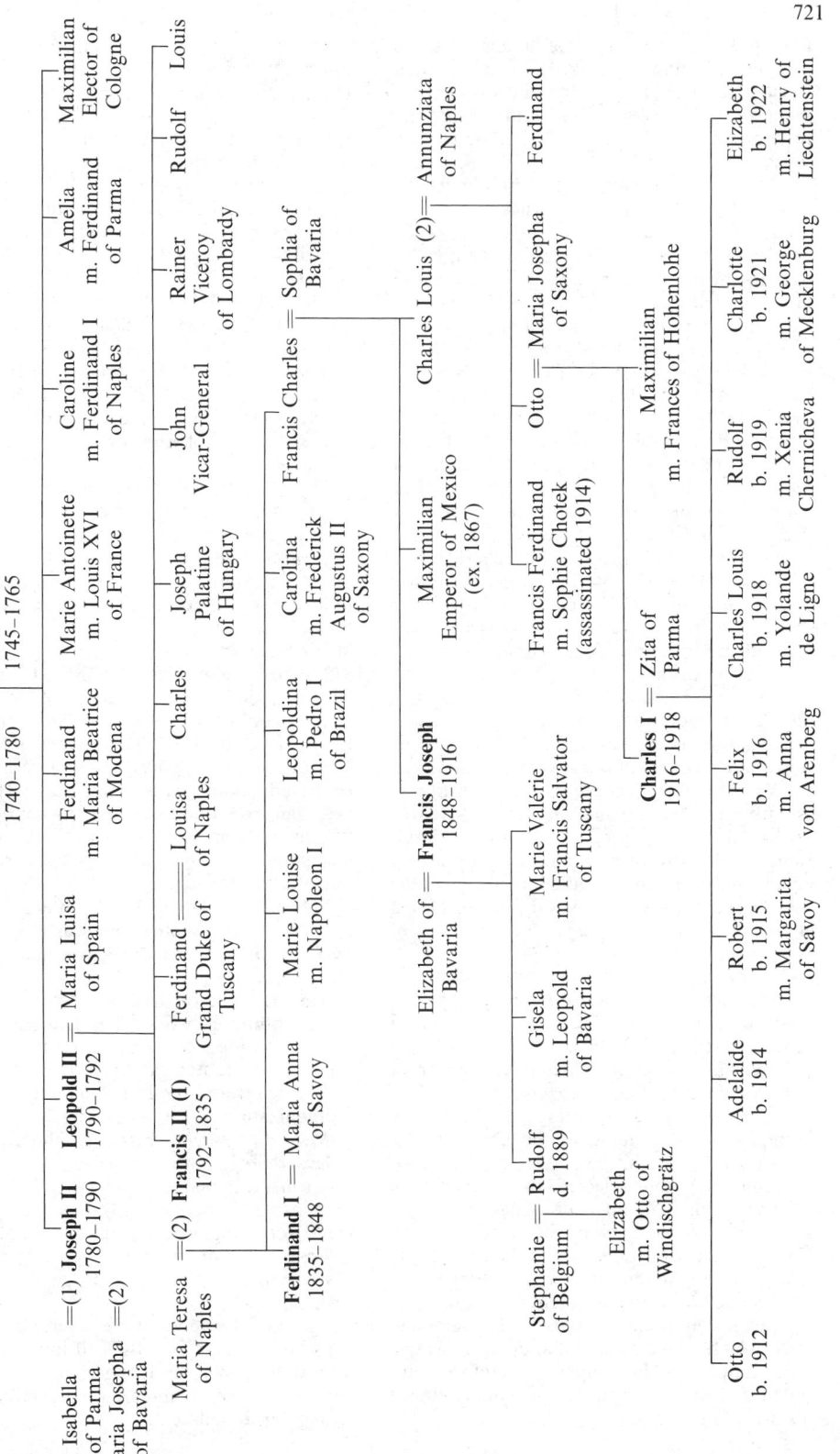

tion and the dissolution of a committee of students and national guard led to a popular demonstration. The government was forced to reconstitute the committee and to promise revision of the constitution in a democratic sense.

May 17. The **emperor and his family fled** from radical Vienna to Innsbruck.

May 26. An attempt to dissolve the academic legion resulted in another demonstration, the raising of barricades, and the creation of a **committee of safety,** which controlled Vienna during the following months.

June. The **first Pan-Slav congress** (composed, however, almost entirely of Czech delegates) met at Prague under the presidency of **Francis Palácky,** the eminent Bohemian historian and national leader. It proclaimed the solidarity of the Slavic peoples (as against the Germans), but stressed also the equality of all peoples, and proposed a European congress to deal with outstanding international problems.

June 12. The Princess Windischgrätz, wife of the commander of the forces at Prague, was accidentally shot and killed during a demonstration. **Prince Alfred Windischgrätz,** who favored strong repressive measures, seized this opportunity to bring up reinforcements.

June 17. He bombarded **Prague,** crushed the Czech revolutionary movement and established a military dictatorship in Bohemia. First step in the recovery of the governmental power.

July 22. The general diet or constituent assembly (*Reichstag*) met in Vienna. It discarded the constitution previously promulgated by the government and drew up a new document, pronouncedly democratic. Its only act of lasting importance was the **emancipation of the peasants** from feudal burdens (law of September 7).

July 24. General Radetzky overwhelmingly defeated the Piedmontese-Italian army in the **battle of Custozza** and re-established control of Lombardy (p. 703).

Sept. 17. Baron Josef Jellachich, governor (*ban*) of Croatia, began an invasion of Hungary. He had been appointed on March 23, in reply to the demand of the Croatians for autonomy. Under his leadership the Croatian-Slavonic diet had rejected the authority of Hungary (June 5), an action that led to the suspension of Jellachich by the emperor. After Custozza the court party urged the emperor to take vigorous action against the Hungarians, who made no secret of their sympathy with the revolutionary movements in Germany and Italy, which aimed at the breakup of the Hapsburg Empire. The emperor therefore reinstated Jellachich (Sept. 4) and countenanced his attack on Hungary.

Oct. 3. Jellachich was made commander-in-chief of the forces operating against the Hungarians, who drove him back, invaded Austria, and came within sight of Vienna.

Oct. 6. Barricades went up in Vienna when it was learned that the court was moving to suppress the Hungarian revolutionary movement. **Count Theodor Latour,** the minister of war, was murdered and a radical rump of the constituent assembly declared itself in permanent session.

Oct. 31. Windischgrätz, aided by Jellachich, bombarded **Vienna** into submission. The radical leaders (including **Robert Blum,** delegate from the Frankfurt parliament, p. 723) were ruthlessly executed. The assembly had already (Oct. 22) been adjourned to the little Moravian town of **Kremsier,** where it attracted less attention.

Dec. 2. Abdication of the Emperor Ferdinand. This was engineered by **Prince Felix Schwarzenberg,** diplomatic adjunct of Radetzky, iron-willed adherent of the restoration and even extension of the imperial power. He induced the heir to the throne, Archduke Francis Charles, to forego his rights in favor of his eighteen-year-old son,

1848–1916. FRANCIS JOSEPH I (b. 1830), who ascended the throne, according to Schwarzenberg unbound by any of the promises of his predecessor to the Hungarians and others. The efforts of the government were now concentrated on the campaign against Hungary.

1849, Jan. 5. Windischgrätz, in command of the invading armies, won an initial success by occupying **Budapest,** which surrendered without offering resistance.

Feb. 26–27. He defeated General Henry K. Dembinski at **Kapolna,** but was then obliged by General Arthur Görgei to evacuate nearly all of Hungary (Apr.).

Mar. 1. The Austrian Reichstag completed its constitutional work. The **Kremsier constitution** provided for a decentralized, federal form of government and is regarded by many as having offered the last chance for a healthy reorganization of the monarchy.

Mar. 4. Having dissolved the Reichstag, **Schwarzenberg** promulgated a constitution of his own, designed to apply to all the Hapsburg possessions, including Hungary. It provided for a highly centralized system, with a representative diet and a responsible ministry. "Provisionally" the emperor governed autocratically.

Apr. 13. Goaded into resistance by the new constitution and rapidly drifting into more radical channels, the Hungarian diet, meeting temporarily at Debreczen, proclaimed the **Hungarian Republic.**

Apr. 14. **Kossuth** was elected *"responsible governor-president"* by the Hungarian diet.

June. Francis Joseph accepted the offer of Tsar Nicholas of Russia to aid in the suppression of the Hungarian revolution.

June 17-18. The Russian general **Ivan Paskievich** invaded Hungary from the north while the Austrian general **Julius Haynau** led the invasion from the west. At the same time the Hungarians were faced with serious revolutionary movements among the Serbs in the south and the Roumanians in Transylvania. **Görgei** put up a vigorous resistance, but the Hungarians were unable to face such odds for long.

Aug. 9. The Hungarians were decisively defeated in the **battle of Temesvar.**

Aug. 11. **Kossuth** abandoned his position in favor of Görgei and fled (with many other leaders) across the frontier into Turkey.

Aug. 13. GÖRGEI SURRENDERED to the Russian commander **at Világos.** Despite promises of clemency, Haynau visited sanguine vengeance on the Hungarians at the **bloody assizes of Arad.** Nine generals were hanged and four shot.

d. THE REVOLUTION OF 1848-1849 IN GERMANY

The **February Revolution in Paris** (p. 678) acted as a catalytic agent to precipitate widespread discontent in Germany. First in the south and west, then in the central states and Prussia, there were popular demonstrations and demands for constitutional changes and reform. As in the Hapsburg Monarchy, the movement was both national and liberal. But whereas in Austria the revolution aimed at the dissolution of one sovereign state, in Germany its objective was the unification of numerous sovereign states into one new empire. In the excitement of the first days, the German rulers, taken off their guard, yielded everywhere. Ministries were refashioned along liberal lines and profuse promises of reform were made. Revolutionary changes were effected rapidly and almost without bloodshed.

1848, Mar. 15. Beginning of the **March Days** in Berlin. The raising of barricades led to efforts of the soldiers to clear the streets, and to some bloodshed (Mar. 16). King Frederick William, convinced that the whole trouble was due to the machinations of foreign agitators and unwilling to slaughter his beloved subjects, determined to make concessions.

Mar. 18. The censorship was abolished and a patent was issued summoning the **United Landtag.** The king announced his readiness to collaborate in giving Germany as a whole a constitution. The crowd, milling about the palace, was greeted by accidental shots from the troops. No one was hurt, but barricades went up again and the insurrection became general in Berlin.

Mar. 19. The king, extremely agitated, issued a proclamation "to his beloved Berliners" urging them to quit the barricades and promising them that the troops would then be withdrawn. Before the evacuation of the barricades was at all complete, the king ordered the withdrawal of the military. The palace was unprotected, the king was obliged to grant the popular demand for arms, and had to face the humiliation of saluting the corpses of insurgents as the mob carried them by.

Mar. 21. The king issued a second proclamation "to my people and the German nation," promising that he would assume the leadership of the German people and that Prussia would henceforth be "merged in Germany." On the same day the king suffered a second humiliation when he paraded through the streets wearing the tricolor of black, red, and gold (recently adopted by the diet as the flag of the new Germany) and making liberal addresses to the students.

Mar. 31. The **Frankfurt *Vorparlament*** met. On March 5 a self-constituted committee of 53 Liberals from various states had met at Heidelberg and had decided to arrange for a constituent body for all Germany. The *Vorparlament* (preliminary parliament) ordered the holding of elections by direct, manhood suffrage.

May 18. The **FRANKFURT NATIONAL ASSEMBLY** (*Nationalversammlung*) or parliament met for the first time in the Church of St. Paul at Frankfurt-on-the-Main. Its membership was about 830. Many of the conservatives who had been elected refused to take their seats in a revolutionary assembly, but the parliament nevertheless was weighted heavily in favor of rank, office, property, and education. It was preponderantly a middle-class body, composed of some 200 lawyers, about 100 professors, many physicians, judges, officials, plus about 140 businessmen. "The most distinguished constituent body in history." Its debates, though often of exasperating length and technicality, were of a surprisingly high order.

May 19. The parliament chose **Heinrich von Gagern** as president and devoted itself to the work of organization.

May 22. Meeting of the Prussian constituent assembly. It continued its debates throughout the summer, becoming gradually more and more radical.

June 28. The **Frankfurt parliament,** having

suspended the diet of the Germanic Confederation, appointed **Archduke John of Austria** (uncle of Emperor Ferdinand) imperial regent (*Reichsverweser*) as head of a provisional executive power. He was recognized by the various state governments and appointed a ministry in which Anton Schmerling (an Austrian) was minister for foreign affairs and the interior and General Eduard von Peucker (a Prussian) and Johann Heckscher (from Hamburg) ministers of war and justice respectively. The provisional government, lacking all material power (army), never established its authority firmly, and the attention of the parliament itself was riveted during the summer of 1848 on the **Schleswig-Holstein question,** a test case of the solidarity of German national feeling and of the power of the parliament over the state governments.

The two provinces of **Schleswig** and **Holstein** (the former half German, the latter almost wholly so) were possessions of the king of Denmark. Holstein was a member state of the Germanic Confederation. In January 1848 Frederick VII succeeded to the Danish throne. He was wholly under the influence of the Danish nationalists **(Eider Danes)** whose object was to integrate Schleswig with the rest of the monarchy. The duchies refused to recognize descent in the female line and supported the claim of the duke of Augustenburg to succession in the duchies. When Danish troops began to occupy Schleswig, the **duchies rose in revolt** and established a provisional government at Kiel (Mar. 24). The Frankfurt parliament thereupon decided to intervene and commissioned Prussia to send federal troops, which the Prussians did, despite warnings from both Britain and Russia, which powers were interested in keeping Prussia from the North Sea coast, and in maintaining Denmark at the entrance to the Baltic. Various British efforts at mediation (June, July) failed, but Frederick William, whose heart had never been in the intervention,

Aug. 28. Concluded the **armistice of Malmö** for seven months: Danes and Prussians both to evacuate the duchies, which were to be provisionally administered by a joint commission of Danes and representatives of the Germanic Confederation. This arrangement, so favorable to Denmark, raised a storm of protest in the duchies and in the Frankfurt parliament. The parliament rejected the armistice at first, but, after a change of ministry,

Sept. 16. The Frankfurt parliament yielded. Ultimately it accepted a proposal of Palmerston (Feb. 3, 1849) for a separate constitution for Schleswig, but soon afterward (Feb. 26) the Danes denounced the armistice. The war was resumed March 31, the Germans invading Jutland. On July 10 a new armistice was concluded and long-drawn negotiations were initiated. They finally led to the conclusion of **peace between Prussia and Denmark** (July 2, 1850), in which both sides reserved their rights. The **London protocol** (May 8, 1852), between Great Britain, Russia, France, Austria, Prussia, Sweden, and Denmark (not signed by the duchies or by the Germanic Confederation) fixed the succession, the duke of Augustenburg's claims being settled by a money payment.

By the time the parliament was ready to devote itself to the constitutional problem, loose parties had emerged from the ranks of deputies. The **Right** (Radowitz, Vincke, Prince Lichnowsky) held to the idea of an imperial constitution in harmony with the separate state governments; the **Left** (Vogt, Ruge, Blum) proclaimed the sovereignty of the people and endeavored to establish a republican, strongly centralized, federal government; the **Right Center** (Gagern, Dahlmann, Gervinus, Arndt, Bassermann, J. Grimm) hoped to persuade the governments to recognize a constitutional monarchy for all Germany; the **Left Center** (Römer, Fallmerayer) insisted on the subordination of the states to the central monarchy. As the various groups debated, the chief governments recovered their authority.

Oct. 31.   Windischgrätz took Vienna (p. 722).

Nov. 9.   King Frederick William of Prussia, encouraged by the success of the Austrian court and prodded by his generals, exiled the Prussian constituent assembly to Brandenburg-on-the-Havel, as a reply to its action in striking the phrase "by the grace of God" from the royal title, and other radical measures.

Dec. 5. The **Prussian constituent assembly was dissolved** and the government promulgated a constitution (based upon the work of the assembly, but maintaining the ultimate authority of the king). As elaborated in the succeeding years, the constitution came to provide for an upper house (*Herrenhaus*), bulwark of the privileged orders, and a lower house (Landtag), chosen by universal suffrage but under a three-class system of voting based on taxpaying ability, so that 83 per cent of the electorate controlled only one-third of the seats. Though the Landtag was given power to vote *new* laws and taxes, there was no ministerial responsibility, and when parliament was not in session, ordinances, with the force of law, could be issued by royal fiat. This constitution remained in force from 1850 to 1918.

The conservatives and the radicals in the Frankfurt parliament had become seriously divided on the question of what territory should be included in the projected German national state. The radicals were in favor of bringing in the German provinces of Austria (in which they included Bohemia), though this would have involved the disruption of the Hapsburg Monarchy. This group was known as the Big-German (*Grossdeutsch*) party, while the Little-German (*Kleindeutsch*) group thought it wiser to leave Austrian territory out of account. The question became more and more academic as the Austrian government recovered its position and made known its hostility to any infringement of its unity. The whole matter was finally compromised (Oct.) by a decision to include all German territory, but with the proviso that no part of the new state should be connected with non-German territory. In effect this meant the victory of the *Kleindeutsch* group, which looked to Prussia and Frederick William for aid in the constitution of a German national state.

1849, Mar. 27. THE FRANKFURT CONSTITUTION. This followed upon the Austrian constitution of March 4 which reasserted the unity of the Hapsburg dominions and ended all talk of including part of Austria. The Frankfurt constitution created a federal state under an hereditary "Emperor of the Germans," who was to have a suspensive veto over legislation passed by a national parliament. Ministers were to be responsible to the parliament, which was to consist of two houses: an upper house (*Staatenhaus*) the members of which were to be chosen, one-half by the state governments, one-half by the lower houses of the state legislatures. The members of the lower house (*Volkshaus*) were to be elected on the basis of universal, direct, secret, equal ballot, with single-member constituencies. Over the courts of the various states was set a supreme court for the *Reich*, with final jurisdiction. The federal government was to have complete control of foreign policy, the army, regulation of economic questions. The constitution was never put in force, but exercised important influence on the later constitution of the North German Confederation (p. 735) and the constitution of the German Republic (p. 1005).

Mar. 28. The Frankfurt parliament elected **Frederick William of Prussia as emperor.**

Apr. 3. The king told the parliament's deputation that he could agree only after the princes and free cities had accepted the constitution.

Apr. 21. When the small states had already accepted, the king torpedoed the movement through a declaration that Prussia could not accept the constitution as it stood—a king by

"divine right" could not receive a crown at the hands of a popularly elected assembly. The majority of the governments now withdrew their representatives from Frankfurt.

June 18. A "rump parliament" removed to **Stuttgart,** where government troops finally dispersed its members. The attempt to unite Germany under a parliamentary system had failed.

1849–1850. The Prussian Union Scheme. Though unwilling to accept the crown from an elected assembly, Frederick William still hoped to achieve German unity in accordance with his own ideas and with the consent of his fellow princes. His friend, **Radowitz,** produced a plan for a larger confederation to include the German states and the whole of the Austrian dominions, German and non-German, thus creating a great **Middle European bloc** with a population of 60,000,000, with immense economic possibilities. This great empire was to be divided for administration into two parts: (1) an **inner confederation** comprising non-Hapsburg Germany, under the leadership of Prussia; (2) the **Hapsburg Monarchy,** which would thus remain intact.

1849, May 26. A draft constitution for the inner confederation **(Prussian Union),** not substantially different from that of the later North German Confederation, was accepted by Prussia, Saxony, and Hanover, however, reserving the right to withdraw if it were not accepted by the other German governments, apart from Austria. Nearly all the petty governments, fearing Prussia, promptly joined the new union.

Oct. 19. A **national assembly** was summoned to meet at **Erfurt.** Saxony and Hanover now withdrew, leaving the union substantially a combination of Prussia and the smaller states (Württemberg and Bavaria refusing to join).

1850, Mar. 20. The **Erfurt parliament** met, the constitution as proposed by Prussia was accepted, and the parliament was soon afterward prorogued.

Apr. 29. Frederick William told the princes that he left them free to adhere to the union, but gave them the impression that it was in fact suspended until more auspicious times. With the Hungarian revolution crushed, **Schwarzenberg** was now prepared for an active policy in Germany.

May 16. At his invitation, representatives of a number of the petty states and Austria met at Frankfurt and reconstituted the old **diet of the Germanic Confederation.** If Prussia insisted on the perpetuation of the Erfurt Union, war with Austria appeared inevitable. When a dispute arose from an appeal of the elector of Hesse to the Frankfurt diet for support against his parliament, the Austrians sent federal troops into the district, while the Prussians, arguing a right to intervene in view of the fact that Hesse was a member of the Prussian Union, did likewise. Both powers mobilized and war seemed imminent. Tsar Nicholas of Russia, irritated by the pseudo-liberalism of the Prussian ruler, sided with Austria, and Frederick William, who had been averse to war from the very outset, decided to beat a retreat. He sent his new minister, **Otto von Manteuffel,** to negotiate with Schwarzenberg at Olmütz.

Nov. 29. THE PUNCTATION OF OLMÜTZ. The Prussians abandoned the Prussian Union and recognized the re-established Germanic diet at Frankfurt. It was decided that the future constitution of Germany should be discussed in "open conferences" of all the German states. This was merely a screen to conceal the Prussian retreat, and the whole affair is generally spoken of by Prussian historians as the *Humiliation of Olmütz.*

1850, Dec.-1851, Mar. Conference of the German states at Dresden. This proved fruitless and the old Germanic Confederation was re-established in the original form.

e. THE AUSTRIAN EMPIRE, 1849-1867

1849-1860. The Bach system. The constitution of March 4, 1849, having been suspended (1851), the empire was ruled from Vienna by bureaucratic methods and a concerted effort was made to undermine the national movements by a policy of vigorous **Germanization.** This policy was associated especially with the name of **Alexander Bach,** minister of the interior. Hungary lost its historic identity and was divided into five administrative "governments," ruled by German officials and by gendarmerie directed from Vienna. Croatia, Transylvania, and southern Hungary became separate provinces, and the Slavs and Roumanians in these territories (who had been loyal in 1848) suffered the same fate as the Hungarians.

1855. A concordat with the Catholic Church gave the Church extensive power, especially in matters of education, thus breaking with the tradition of Joseph II, in the interests of counteracting the revolutionary spirit.

1856-1859. The Austrian government felt acutely the results of the **Crimean War** (p. 773), which undermined Austria's international position and ruined the finances through prolonged mobilization.

1859. WAR WITH FRANCE AND PIEDMONT (p. 706), brought to an abrupt end in part because of financial stringency, in part because of the danger of revolt in Hungary. The government felt impelled to scrap the Bach system and come to an agreement with the national groups.

1860, Oct. 20. The **October Diploma,** issued by the emperor, set up a federal constitution which recognized wide autonomy for the various "Lands," with an imperial diet of limited powers, to be elected by the provincial Landtage. The Hungarians opposed this settlement and demanded the restoration of their own constitution.

1861, Feb. The **February Patent,** "interpreting" the October Diploma, but really a new constitution which set up a bicameral parliament with an electoral system designed to give the German bourgeoisie (the mainstay of the empire) an influence wholly disproportionate to their numbers. Negotiations with the Hungarians failed; Hungary was again ruled administratively and autocratically. The emperor resumed negotiations with the Hungarians in 1865. They were facilitated by the overwhelming defeat of Austrian arms at Königgrätz (p. 731) and by the loyal participation of the Hungarians in the war against the Germans. The result was the

1867, Oct. COMPROMISE OF 1867 (largely the work of **Francis Deák,** seconded by **Julius Andrássy**), which established a political organism *sui generis.* In **Hungary** (the ancient *lands of the crown of St. Stephen*) the Magyars were permitted to dominate the subject peoples through the constitutional system of 1848. In **Austria** (the remaining seventeen provinces of the empire) the Germans were to dominate the other peoples through a constitution, based on the February Patent, extended and made perpetual. The two states were joined in personal union in the monarch; in common ministries of foreign affairs, war, and finance (merely an administrator of the common treasury which received the funds contributed by both states for common purposes); in the annual *delegations,* composed of sixty members of each of the two parliaments, empowered to decide matters of common interest; in a decennial treaty regulating tariffs, currency, etc. The "autocrat of the fifties" now ruled through responsible ministries in both parts of the empire.

f. THE UNIFICATION OF GERMANY, 1850-1871

1850-1853. Despite the extent of the humiliation of Prussia by Austria at Olmütz (above), Prussia was able to thwart Austria's effort to

The House of Hohenzollern (1701–1918)

(From p. 499)

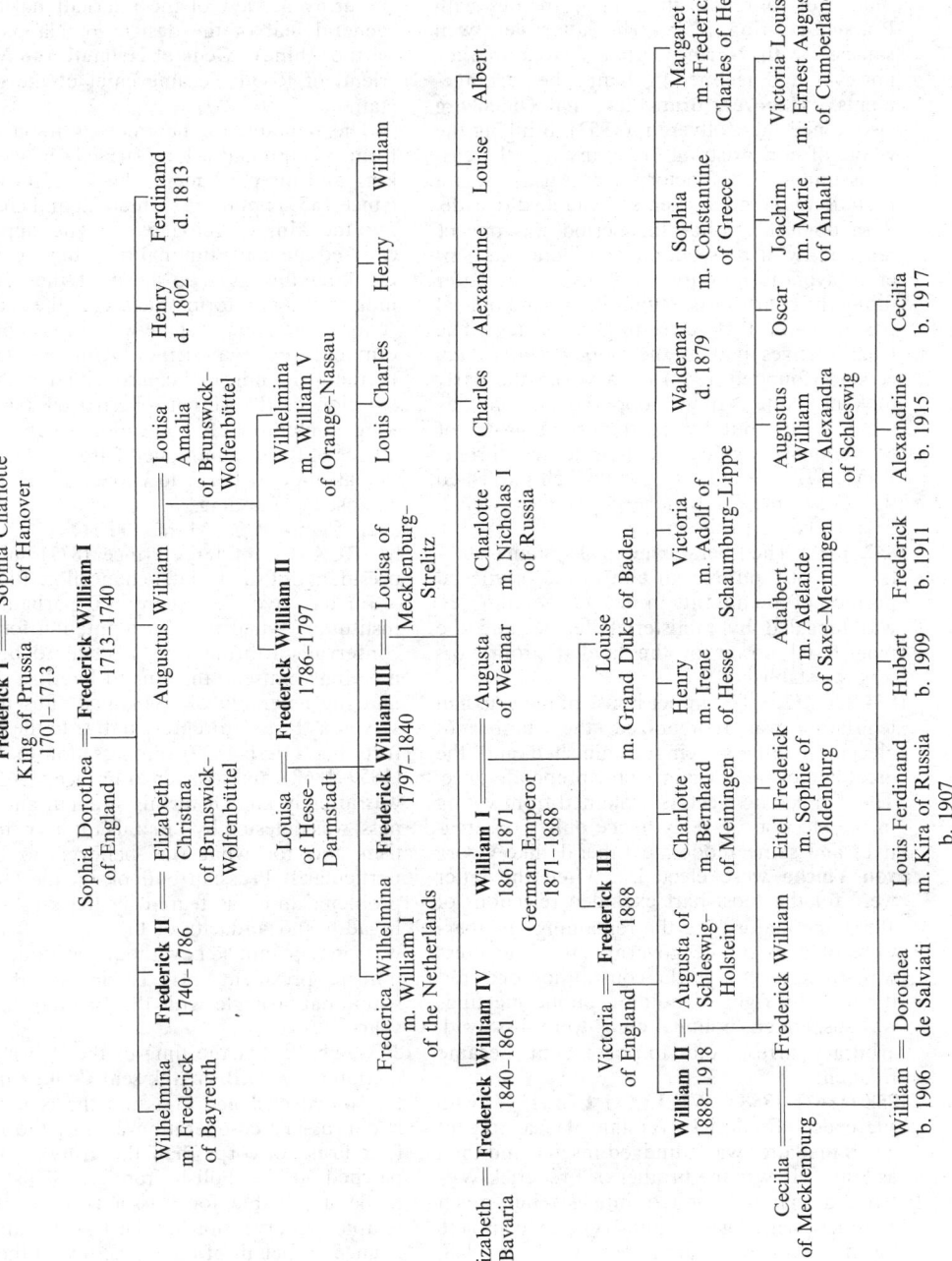

enter the Zollverein. Tariff duties were reduced to a point too low for Austrian industry to bear. Thwarted, Austria attempted to break up the Zollverein by inducing South German states not to renew their tariff treaties with Prussia, expiring 1852. The latter were well satisfied with North Germany as a market, however, and declined to change their arrangements. **Hanover, Brunswick, and Oldenburg** also joined the Zollverein (1853), bringing the whole of non-Austrian Germany into the customs union. This victory over Austria was a prelude to the great events of the next decade.

In domestic policy the period was one of reaction, with persecution of Liberals in general, favors to nobility and Junkers, the latter filling the court posts, high military and official positions—in fact, directing the state. The Conservatives had as their organ the *Kreuzzeitung* (founded 1848) from which the party took its name. It was opposed not only by the Liberals, but by an important group of Moderates to which the heir to the throne, Prince William, adhered and which published its views in the *Preussische Wochenblatt*, which gave its name to the group.

1852, Jan. The liberal **municipal system** (established 1850), putting an end to the privileged position of the nobility in village communities, was repealed by ministerial decree, and the magisterial power of the landed proprietors was re-established.

1854, Oct. 12. The upper house of the Prussian legislature was reorganized, the number of elected members being diminished and the great landowners regaining the preponderance. The democratic electors abstained from voting in the election of 1852, hence only Conservatives and some moderate Liberals like **Georg von Vincke** were elected. When the latter were for the most part excluded (elections of 1855), the majority of the remaining members were officials of the government. The press was stifled (although the constitution declared it free), the right of holding public meetings was suspended, political clubs were dissolved, arbitrary arrest and imprisonment became frequent.

1858 (1861)–1888. WILLIAM I (b. 1797) who succeeded Frederick William IV as regent when the latter was adjudged insane, and then as king. He was the brother of Frederick William, a man of limited intellect but much common sense, great industry, and complete loyalty. Though an arch-conservative in 1848, he had come to see the need for living up to the constitution as granted. Many restrictive measures were abrogated and a new era was introduced. The success of the Italians in 1859–1860 (p. 706) aroused a storm of liberal and nationalist sentiment in Prussia and all Germany.

1859, Dec. 5. The regent appointed **General Albert von Roon** minister of war to reform the army in view of the international tension (general fear of the designs of Napoleon III on the Rhine). **General Helmuth von Moltke,** friend of Roon, became chief of the general staff.

The demand for new credits for army reform precipitated a long struggle between the king and his parliament, the Liberal majority (since 1859) opposing militarism and challenging the king's prerogative. The opposition claimed the constitutional right to vote credits; the king the right, as head of the army, to make military reforms and secure the necessary funds. The issue at stake was responsible government versus autocracy, with the rights of neither side indicated clearly either in the constitution or the Hohenzollern tradition. The king contemplated abdication; then, on the advice of Roon, summoned Otto von Bismarck, ambassador to Paris, to carry on the struggle against the Landtag.

1862, Sept.–1890, Mar. OTTO VON BISMARCK (Count 1865, Prince 1871), minister-president of Prussia, later chancellor. Bismarck—Junker, avowed enemy of parliamentary institutions—had made a reputation for ultra-conservatism through his staunch advocacy of the king's cause in the United Landtag of 1847 and the assembly of 1848; had subsequently served as Prussian representative to the Frankfurt diet (1851–1859), ambassador to Russia (1859–1862), ambassador to France (1862). He was already known for his strength and boldness, was detested by Liberals for his conservatism and for what was believed to be his particularist Prussian outlook on the German problem, and was feared by the king for the breadth and audacity of his views. Bismarck was made minister without portfolio, then minister-president. He carried on the constitutional struggle with the Landtag for four years.

1863, Feb. 8. At the time of the Polish insurrection (p. 751) Bismarck sent **Count Constantin von Alvensleben** to assure the tsar that he had Prussia's co-operation against the rebels; four Prussian corps (half the army) were dispatched to the Polish frontier. This action made it possible for Russia to resist the attempted intervention by Austria, Britain, and France on behalf of the Poles; it won the tsar's trust and friendship during the three wars necessary to German unification.

Agitation for the unification of "Germany" had revived rapidly after 1859. Austria and the South German states favored reform of the Germanic Confederation. German Liberals generally favored a parliamentary *Kleindeutschland* after the Frankfurt tradition of 1848. Bismarck had learned at the Frankfurt diet to distrust Austria, was convinced she must be extruded from Germany, preliminary to German union under the leadership and domination of Prussia.

1863, Aug. A **congress of princes,** summoned by Emperor Francis Joseph to reform the Germanic Confederation, but really meant as a bait to German liberalism, miscarried when Bismarck induced King William to refuse to attend. Bismarck's next opportunity came in connection with the highly complicated **Schleswig-Holstein question.** A royal proclamation of King Frederick VII of Denmark (1863, Mar. 30) in substance announced the annexation to Denmark of the duchy of Schleswig. This act was a breach of the **London protocol** (1852) by which the powers had guaranteed at once the inseparability of the duchies and their personal union with Denmark under the king, and also of an engagement given by Denmark to Austria and Prussia (Dec. 1851) not to incorporate Schleswig or treat it separately. Frederick's act also thrust a new charter on the duchy of Holstein (which retained its autonomy), without consulting its representatives. This was to fly in the face of the Germanic Confederation, of which Holstein was a member. Expectation of British and Swedish support was an important factor in shaping Danish policy during 1863 and early 1864.

July. The diet of the Germanic Confederation demanded that the two duchies be taken forcibly from Denmark and submitted to the rule of the German duke of Augustenburg (son of one of the claimants to the succession).

Oct. 1. The diet voted federal execution (i.e. action against Denmark) and instructed Hanover and Saxony to furnish troops.

Nov. 15. Frederick VII died, and was succeeded by

Nov. 18. Christian IX, who promptly signed a newly drafted constitution (of November 13), not formally incorporating Schleswig, but clearly tending to that end.

Dec. 24. Federal troops entered Holstein. The diet was still supporting the duke of Augustenburg, whose claims had been discarded by the London protocol. Hence Bismarck could now separate Prussia from the action of the diet and declare Prussia the upholder of the protocol.

1864, Jan. 16. Austria joined Prussia in an alliance, and the two powers agreed to send an ultimatum to Denmark demanding repeal of the constitution (otherwise they would invade), to settle the future course of the duchies only "by mutual agreement."

Feb. 1. Austrian and Prussian troops invaded Schleswig, the new Prussian army of Roon and Moltke receiving its baptism of fire.

Feb. 5. The Danes quickly abandoned the defense of the *Dannewirke;* all Schleswig except Düppel and the island of Alsen were in the enemy's hands. The Düppel forts were not taken until April 18; the Germans were now invading Denmark.

Apr. 25–June. The **London conference,** engineered by the British to save the Danes, miscarried, due to the cleverness of Bismarck and the stubbornness of the Danes.

June 26. The war was renewed, resulted in a crushing defeat for the Danes, the **surrender of the duchies of Schleswig, Holstein, and Lauenburg** to Austria and Prussia (definitive **peace of Vienna,** Oct. 30).

What was to become of the duchies, now the joint possession of Austria and Prussia? After prolonged negotiations, Bismarck maneuvered Austria, seriously embarrassed at home by political demands of the Magyars (p. 726), into

1865, Aug. 14. The **convention of Gastein:** joint sovereignty was to be maintained, but Austria was to administer Holstein, Prussia to administer Schleswig (Lauenburg going to Prussia in return for a money payment to Austria). An impossible situation was created: Austrian Holstein became a virtual enclave in unfriendly Prussia. Under the skillful hand of Bismarck, Austro-Prussian relations rapidly worsened. Prussian relations with Russia were excellent.

Oct. At Biarritz **Bismarck met Napoleon III,** and appears to have dropped vague hints of compensation for France in the Rhineland, in return for which he won a promise of French neutrality from the emperor, convinced that Austria would be victor in the coming war.

1866, Apr. 8. Bismarck, aided by Napoleon, concluded an offensive and defensive **alliance with Italy:** Italy to join Prussia if war broke out between Austria and Prussia within three months, with Venetia as a reward.

Apr. 9. Bismarck introduced a motion for **federal reform** into the Frankfurt diet, evidently with the idea that Austria would reject it and precipitate a conflict. Both parties began to mobilize. Last-minute efforts to compromise **(Gablenz mission)** proved fruitless.

June 6. The Austrian governor of Holstein summoned the Holstein diet in order to discuss the future of the duchy. Bismarck denounced this as a violation of the Gastein convention and ordered Prussian troops into the duchy.

Kings of Hanover (1814–1866)

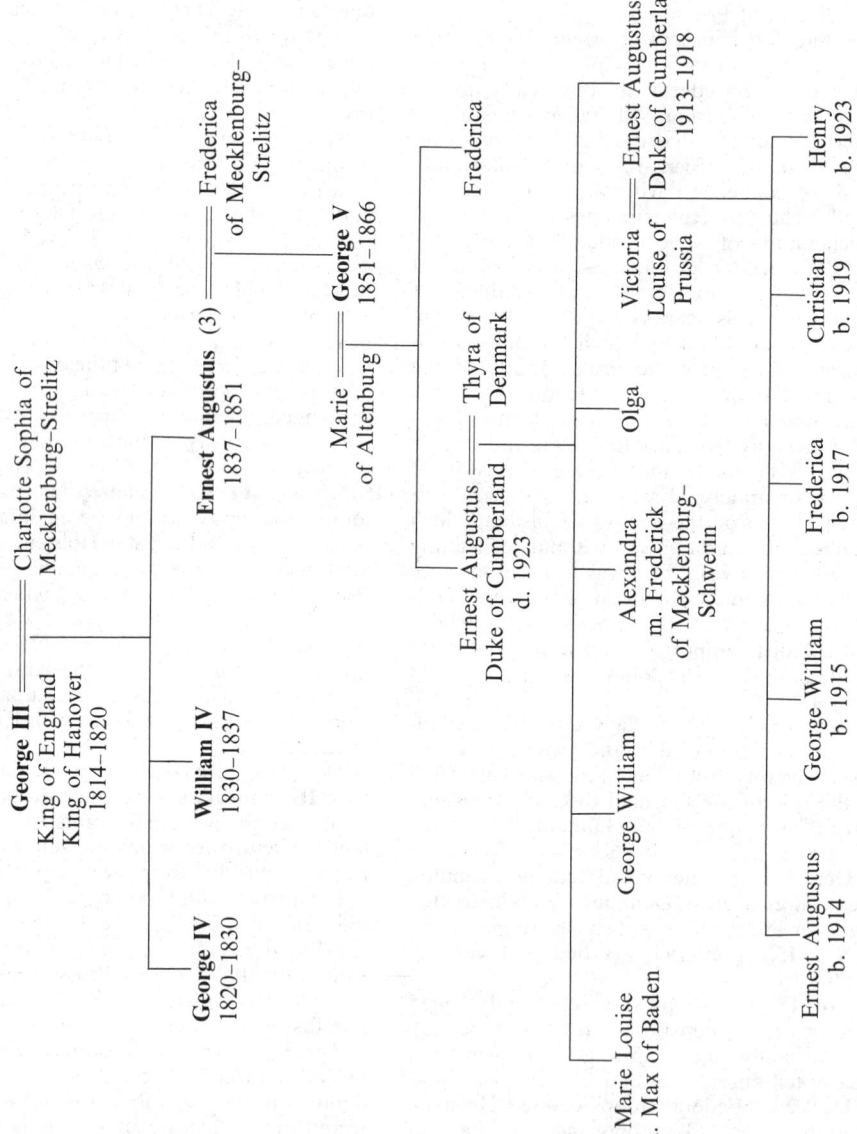

June 12. Austria, realizing that conflict was inevitable, signed a **secret treaty with Napoleon III.** In return for French neutrality, Austria promised to cede Venetia to Napoleon (who was to retrocede it to Italy), whether Austria won or lost the war. In the event of Austrian victory, Austria was to be free to make what changes it wished in Germany, but if these changes disturbed the European balance of power (as they were bound to do), Austria was to consult with Napoleon before making them. Verbally the Austrians agreed in this case not to oppose the erection of a **neutral buffer state** (client of France) **along the Rhine.**

June 14. On Austria's motion, the Frankfurt diet voted **federal execution against Prussia** for violating federal (Holstein) territory. Most of the German states, including the larger ones like Bavaria, Saxony, and Hanover, sided with Austria against Prussia. The Prussian government declared the federal constitution violated and the **confederation at an end.** The war began.

1866, June–Aug. The SEVEN WEEKS' WAR. The war was fought in three theaters:

(1) **Italy:** the Italians were defeated on both land and sea (pp. 707–708).

(2) **Germany:**

June 27–29. General Vogel von Falkenstein, with an army of some 50,000 men, defeated the Hanoverians at **Langensalza,** and forced them to capitulate. He turned to the South German allies of Austria, but before he could reach them the die had been cast in

(3) **Bohemia:** Moltke had learned golden lessons from the American Civil War on the uses of the telegraph and railroad. To acclerate concentration of his forces near Gitschin (Bohemia), he formed three armies, advanced them separately in order to make greatest use of existing railways, co-ordinating their movements from headquarters in Berlin by telegraph.

June 22–23. The First Army **(Prince Frederick Charles)** and the Army of the Elbe **(General Herwarth von Bittenfeld)** entered Bohemia through passes in the Erzgebirge and Riesengebirge. The Second Army **(Crown Prince Frederick)** moved south through Silesia. The experience of the Austrian commander-in-chief, **Field Marshal Ludwig von Benedek,** had been limited to Italy, and he had never been called upon to command large numbers of troops. He was summoned to Bohemia so that an Austrian archduke, Albert, might be assured a victory in Italy. Benedek was, as it turned out, a sacrifice to the prestige of the house of Hapsburg.

July 2. Benedek's army was discovered to be within striking distance of the Prussian First Army and Army of the Elbe. At this critical moment the telegraph broke down. Late at night Moltke took the fateful decision: instructed the First Army and Army of the Elbe to attack at dawn while he sent a courier twenty miles to fetch the crown prince's Second Army.

July 3. Battle of Königgrätz (Sadowa). The Austrians had the better of the battle until early afternoon, when the crown prince came up on the east and decided the issue in favor of the Prussians, who were much advantaged by the breech-loading "needle-gun," enabling the infantry to fire from prone positions at the standing Austrians (using muzzle-loaders).

The sudden and complete victory of the Prussians at Königgrätz was a stunning defeat for the policy of Napoleon, who had expected a long war, exhausting both belligerents.

July 5. Napoleon offered mediation, which Bismarck accepted only on condition that the terms of peace should be determined before an armistice was concluded. Napoleon—ill, his will crippled, unwilling to envisage the use of force—yielded; accepted Prussian terms imposed in the

July 26. Preliminary peace at Nikolsburg: Hanover, Electoral Hesse, Nassau, Frankfurt were to be incorporated in Prussia; Austria was to be excluded from Germany (the Germanic Confederation came to an end); German states north of the Main River were to form a North German Confederation under Prussian leadership; the South German states were to remain independent and to be permitted to form a separate confederation. King William insisted on taking Austrian Silesia, territory from the South German states, and Saxony. Bismarck had seen the importance of not provoking Napoleon for the moment, of not alienating Prussia's potential allies for the future. He resisted and won his point.

Aug. 5. Napoleon advanced his **claims for compensation:** the frontiers of 1814 (Saarbrücken, Landau) and possibly the Bavarian Palatinate or Rhenish Hesse (with Mainz), or Luxemburg. Bismarck brusquely rejected these claims as an offense to German national feeling.

Aug. 16. Napoleon instructed his ambassador, Count Vincent Benedetti, to ask for Luxemburg and for Prussian support for the **acquisition of Belgium** by France. Benedetti was induced by Bismarck to put these demands in writing, along with the French offer to sanction the union of North and South Germany in return (the **Benedetti treaty**). Bismarck then took advantage of illness (Sept.–Dec.) to evade a definite reply. The draft treaty was communicated to the British in 1870 and in-

Kings of Saxony (1806–1918)

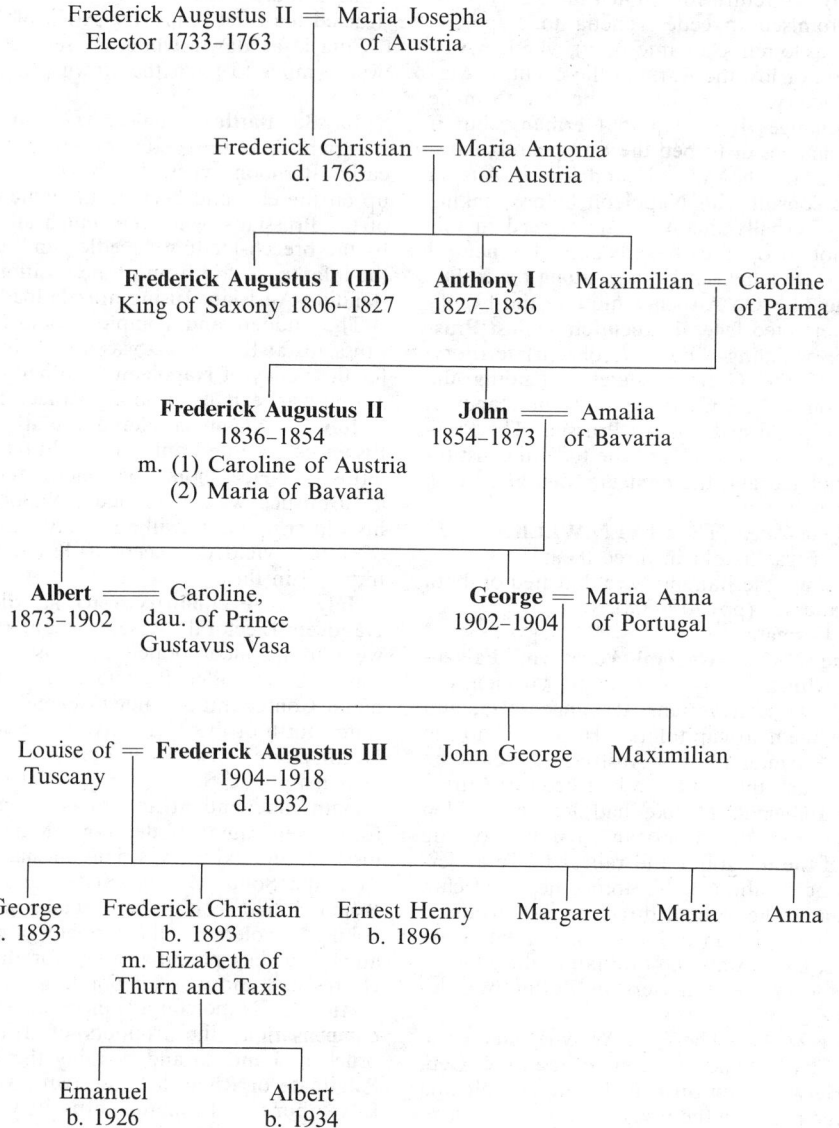

fluenced British opinion in favor of Prussia during the war with France.

Aug. 9–22. Bismarck took advantage of the French demands to push his peace negotiations with the **South German states** (Baden, Württemberg, Bavaria). They were let off on very generous terms, but were induced, in return, to conclude with Prussia **military alliances** in the event of French attack.

Aug. 23. The **definitive treaty of Prague**

brought the war to a close.

Sept. 8. Bill of indemnity, by which Bismarck concluded the struggle with the Prussian parliament. An election during the war had strengthened the Conservatives at the expense of the Liberals. Many of the latter had come over to Bismarck in view of the fact that he was accomplishing their program of national unification. The bill of indemnity gave retroactive assent to previous expenditures of the

Kings of Württemberg (1806–1918)

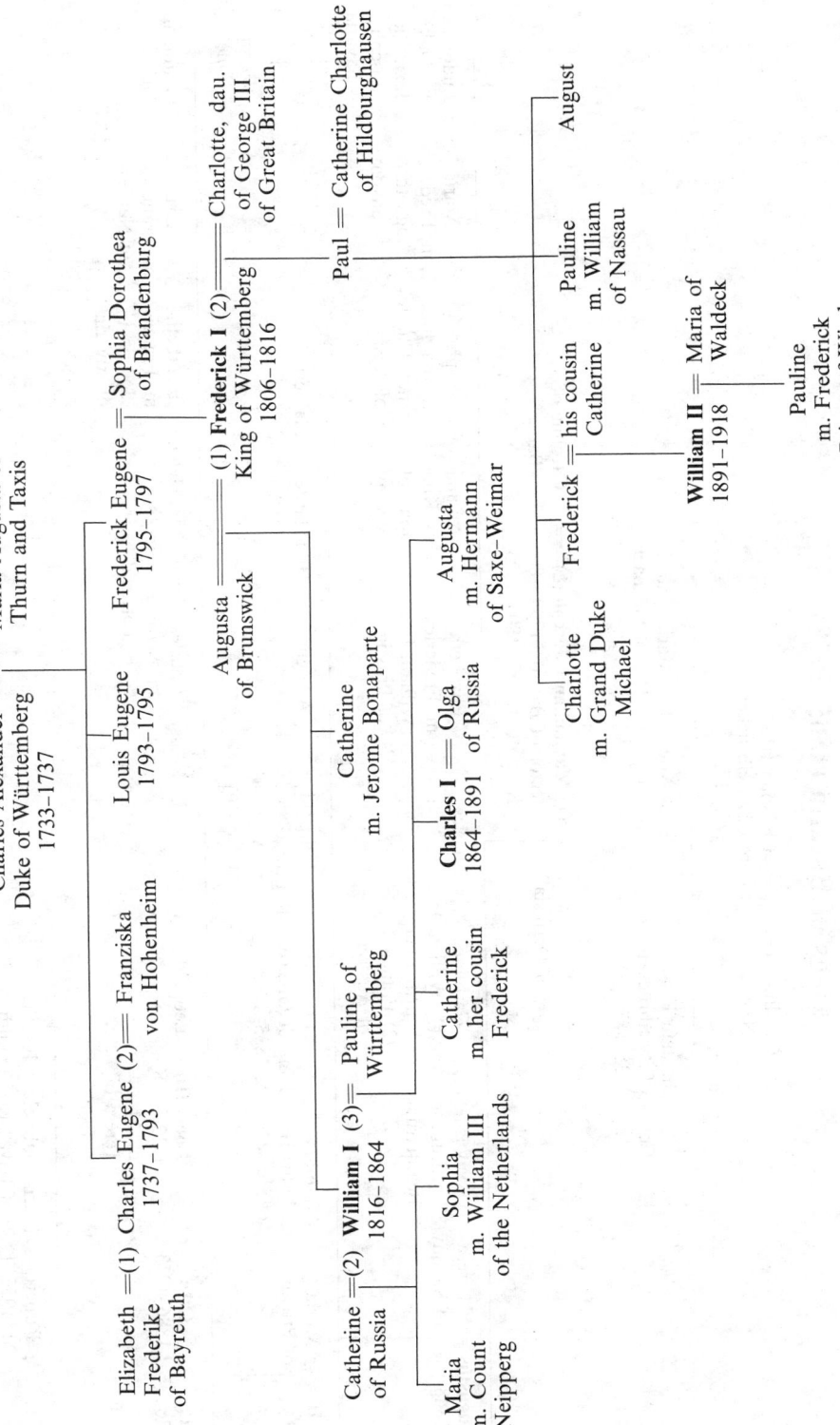

734

Kings of Bavaria (1805–1918)

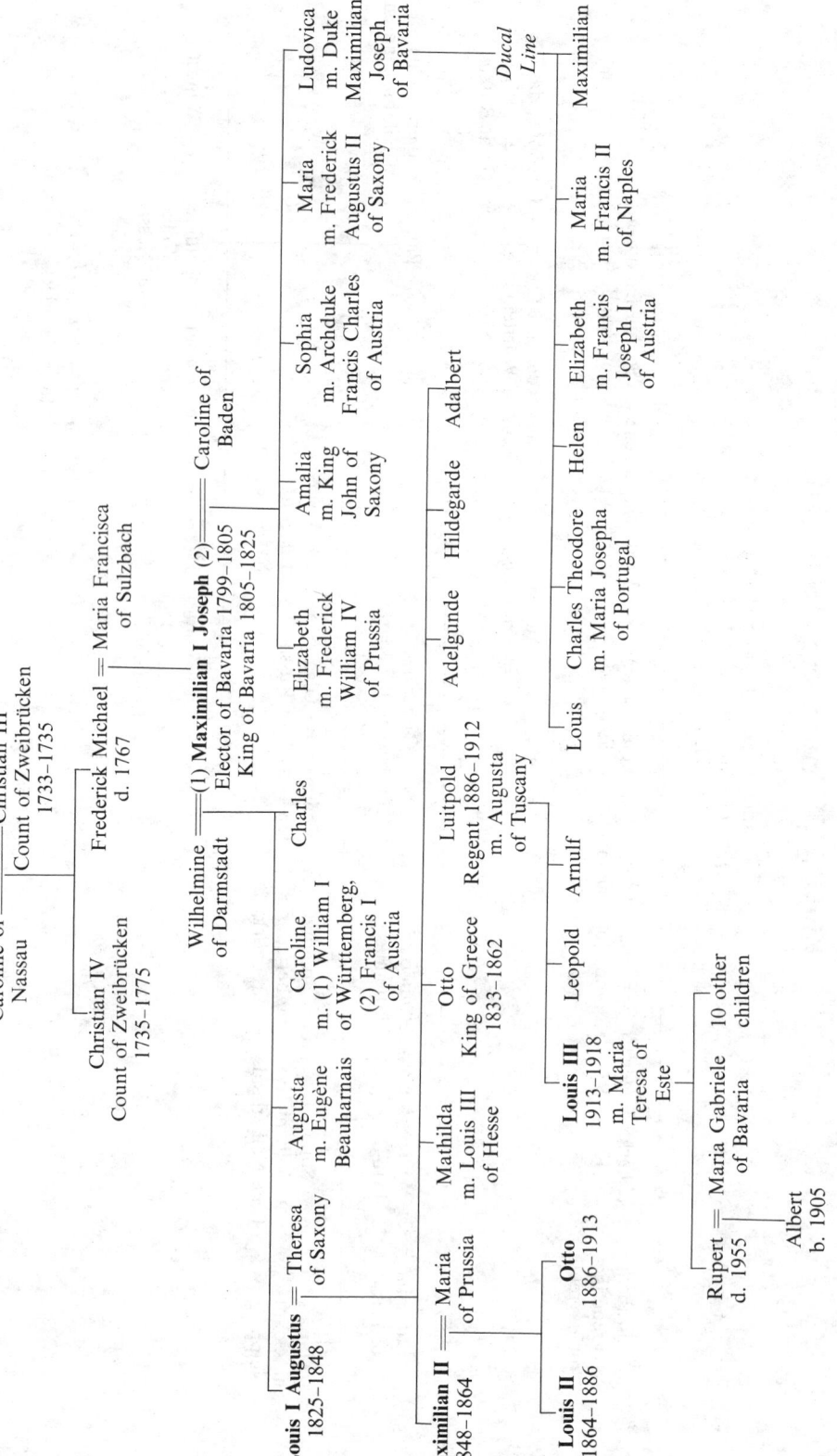

government without the consent of Landtag. It caused an important split in the ranks of liberalism, the majority of the Liberals rallying to Bismarck as the new **National Liberal Party** (leader, **Rudolf von Bennigsen**).

1867. The **NORTH GERMAN CONFEDERATION,** formed through treaties between Prussia and the other states north of the river Main. The constitution was primarily the work of Bismarck himself. The new confederation was one in which the component states retained their own governments, but in which the military forces were controlled by the federal government (the king of Prussia, commander-in-chief). The **presidency** (*praesidium*) was held by the king of Prussia, represented by a **chancellor** (Bismarck), responsible to him alone. The **federal council** (*Bundesrat*) was composed of instructed delegates of the various states, among whom 43 votes were divided, Prussia having 17 and unofficially controlling the votes of several small North German states. The Bundesrat had constituent powers, but a two-thirds vote was required for constitutional changes. The **lower house** (*Reichstag*) shared equally with the Bundesrat in legislation. It was composed of deputies elected from single-member constituencies on the basis of universal suffrage. Bismarck had thus achieved two objects: the predominancy of Prussia in the new state, and the maintenance of the royal power against Liberal demands for responsible government.

1867, Apr. The Luxemburg crisis. This grew out of Napoleon's efforts (winter 1866–1867) to acquire the duchy of Luxemburg from the king of the Netherlands, who was suzerain. Bismarck had promised not to oppose the deal, provided it were so engineered that German national feeling should not be aroused. The French mismanaged the affair, the news leaked out, Bismarck was interpellated in the new North German Reichstag, and the king of the Netherlands drew back from the arrangements he had made. There followed a period of acute crisis, which was closed by a compromise.

May 7–11. An **international conference at London,** which finally signed the **treaty of London** (Sept. 9): Prussia abandoned her previous right to garrison the fortress of the town of Luxemburg. The duchy ceased to be a member of the Germanic Confederation. Its neutrality and independence were guaranteed by the powers. This settlement was a profound humiliation for Napoleon, who henceforth looked upon a final reckoning with Prussia as inevitable, reorganized his army and initiated negotiations for an alliance with Austria and Italy (p. 685).

July 8. Bismarck brought the four South German states into the Zollverein and established a *Zollparlament* (customs parliament) consisting of the North German Reichstag plus representatives of the South German states. This was effectively a parliament for all Germany, though still empowered to deal only with customs questions. In South Germany there was still much opposition to union with Prussia, due to cultural and religious differences and general suspicion, as well as attachment to states' rights. It became increasingly evident to Bismarck that only war with France and the specter of French domination in the Rhineland would drive the South German states into the union. War he regarded as inevitable, convinced as he was that France would not peaceably permit the inclusion of the South German states in the confederation. The sudden appearance of the greatly strengthened neighbor alarmed the French and led to the demand of revenge for Sadowa and to much loose talk about the need of chastising overbearing Prussia.

1868–1870. The **Hohenzollern candidacy** for the Spanish throne. After the Spanish revolution (Sept. 1868) and the expulsion of Queen Isabella (p. 696), the provisional government of Marshal Serrano and General Prim made several attempts to secure one of the Portuguese Coburgs or one of the Italian princes as king. From the outset there had been talk of offering the throne to Prince Leopold of Hohenzollern-Sigmaringen, distant relative of both King William of Prussia and of Napoleon III. The part played by both French and Prussian diplomacy in the various candidacies is still obscure, but the Hohenzollern candidacy was taken up by Bismarck at least as early as March 15, 1870 (**mission of Eusebio Salazar** with letters from Prim, **Hohenzollern "family" council**). Prince Leopold refused to accept unless ordered by the king, but William, averse to the whole business, refused to take an active part. Bismarck, possibly seeking a reply to the French alliance project with Austria and Italy and desiring a connection with Spain that would oblige French troops to guard the frontier in the event of a Franco-Prussian war, sent special emissaries to Spain who returned (May) with glowing accounts.

1870, June 19. Leopold was induced to change his decision and accept the offer. King William gave a grudging consent, on condition that Leopold should be elected by a substantial vote of the Spanish cortes.

July 2. Through misunderstanding, the Spanish cortes was adjourned before a vote was taken. The secret leaked out and created a wave of consternation in France, fanned by the French foreign minister, duke of Gramont.

July 6. **Gramont** made a speech in the French chamber indicating war unless the Prussian government withdrew the candidacy. The Prussian government, however, disclaimed all knowledge of the affair, which it insisted on describing as a family matter.

July 9, 11. The French ambassador, **Count Vincent Benedetti,** having followed King William to Ems, where he was taking a cure, asked that he order Leopold to withdraw. The king refused, but sent a secret emissary to advise Leopold to that effect.

July 12. **Prince Charles Anthony,** father of Leopold, withdrew the candidacy in behalf of his son, who was absent in the Alps. Not content with this diplomatic victory, Gramont and the French government now proceeded to demand satisfaction and guaranties from King William (he was to write Napoleon a letter of apology, officially disavow the candidacy, and promise that it would never be renewed).

July 13. At a famous **interview at Ems,** the king rejected Benedetti's demands and repulsed all efforts of the ambassador to continue the discussion. On the same day Bismarck met with Roon and Moltke in Berlin. On receiving a report of the happening at Ems, he revised it for publication, giving it a brusque quality and conveying the impression that the negotiations at Ems had ended in what was tantamount to a rupture of relations. The importance of the **Ems telegram** has probably been exaggerated, for it is now clear that the French court (with the possible exception of Napoleon himself) was determined on a humiliation of Prussia, even at the cost of war.

July 15. The **French took the decision for war,** relying on the preparedness of the army and on the support of Austria and Italy.

July 19. **France declared war on Prussia.**
1870-1871. **THE FRANCO-GERMAN WAR.** Bismarck had at once the armed support of the South German states and the benevolent neutrality of Russia. The war party in Vienna was a threat that would become serious in case of Prussian defeats. In England Gladstone was interested only in the preservation of **Belgian neutrality,** reassured in new treaties with France and Prussia (Aug. 9).

Three German armies invaded France. **General Karl von Steinmetz** from the Moselle, **Prince Frederick Charles** from the Palatinate on Metz, **Crown Prince Frederick** from the upper Rhine on Strasbourg. A French army advanced into the Saar, won a minor victory at Saarbrücken. Then the German avalanche began.

Aug. 4, 6. The crown prince won victories over Marshal MacMahon at **Wörth** and **Weissenburg,** forced him to evacuate Alsace, invested Strasbourg, advanced on Nancy. **Marshal Achille Bazaine** was soon shut up in Metz by the other two German armies.

Aug. 16, 18. In bloody battles at **Mars-la-Tour** and **Gravelotte** Bazaine's attempts to break through the Prussian lines were repulsed. Metz was besieged, the advance on Châlons begun. When MacMahon attempted to relieve Bazaine at Metz, he found the road closed, and was decisively defeated in the

Sept. 1. **Battle of Sedan.** The army, with the Emperor Napoleon himself, capitulated the following day. (For the siege of Paris and remaining events of the war, see p. 686.)

1871, Jan. 18. **FOUNDATION OF THE GERMAN EMPIRE.** During the war German public opinion demanded the union of North and South Germany. Bismarck negotiated separately with each state, making essential concessions. By the end of November treaties had been signed with all. On December 2, King Ludwig II of Bavaria addressed a letter to King William (drafted by Bismarck at Ludwig's invitation) inviting him to assume the imperial title. The king was averse to having the Prussian title subordinated to that of the empire, but yielded to the general wish.

Jan. 18. **William I was proclaimed German Emperor** in the Hall of Mirrors at Versailles. The constitution of the North German Confederation was then remodeled in terms of the agreements reached with the various states and was adopted (Apr. 14) by a freshly elected Reichstag, representative of the new empire. The new Reich included 25 states—four kingdoms (Prussia, Bavaria, Saxony, Württemberg); five grand duchies; 13 duchies and principalities; three free cities (Hamburg, Bremen, Lübeck). **Alsace-Lorraine** (annexed as a result of the war) was designated *Reichsland,* given an imperial governor (*Statthalter*), and made the common property of all the German states.

CULTURAL DEVELOPMENTS

(1) Literature

Realism in the dramas of **Christian Friedrich Hebbel** (1813-1863; *Agnes Bernauer,* 1852) and **Otto Ludwig** (1813-1865; *Der Erbförster,* 1850); in the later stories of **Theodor Storm** (1817-1888; *Der Schimmelreiter,* 1888); in the stories and novels of the Swiss writers **Conrad Ferdinand Meyer** (1825-1898) and **Gottfried Keller** (1819-1890).

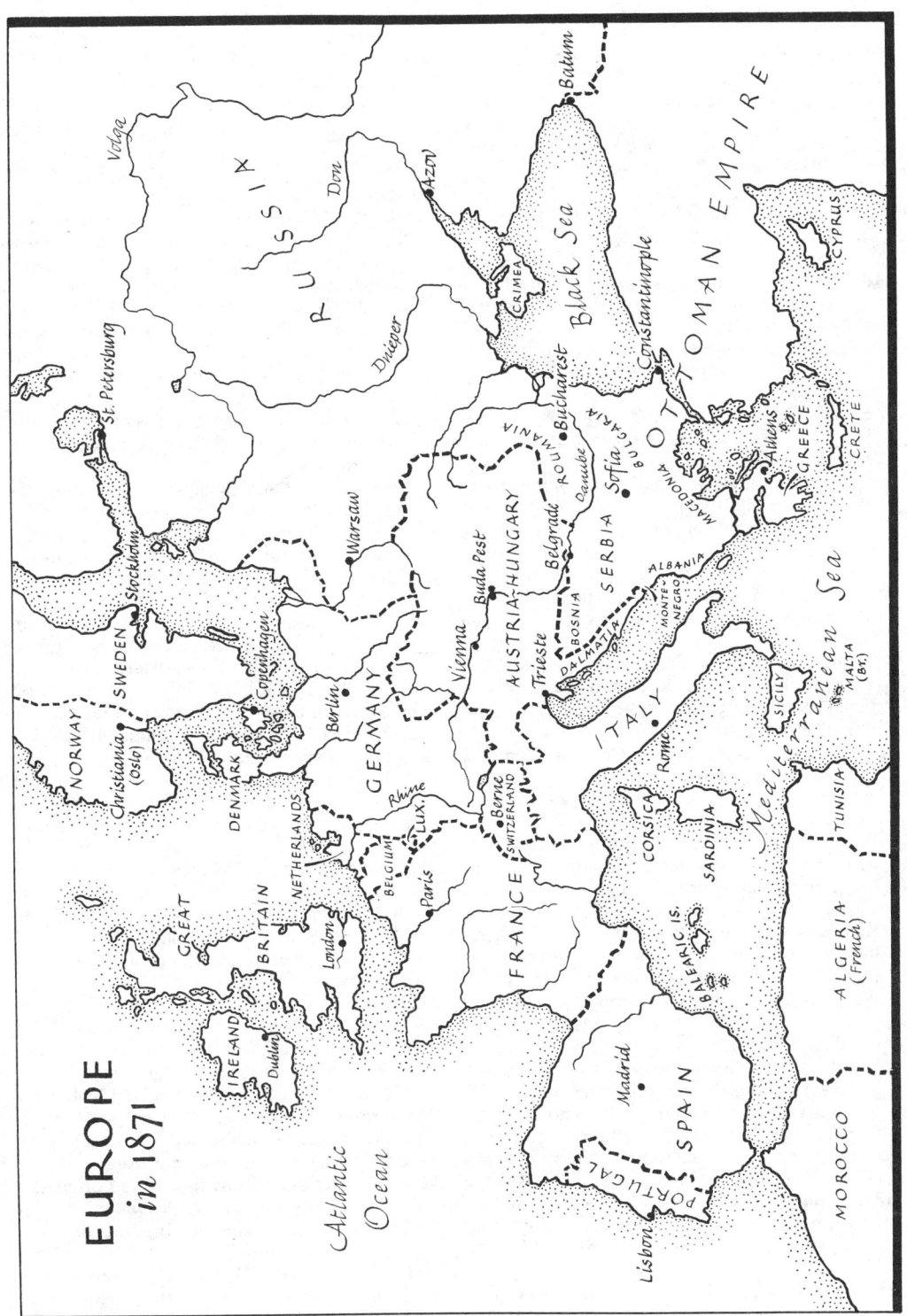

EUROPE
in 1871

Atlantic
Ocean

NORWAY

Christiania
(Oslo)

SWEDEN

Stockholm

St. Petersburg

RUSSIA

Volga

Don

Dnieper

Azov

Batum

Black Sea

Constantinople

OTTOMAN EMPIRE

CYPRUS

DENMARK

Copenhagen

Warsaw

GERMANY

Berlin

Vienna

Buda Pest

AUSTRIA-HUNGARY

ROU-
MANIA

Bucharest

Crimea

Sofia

BULGARIA

Danube

SERBIA

Belgrade

Athens

GREECE

CRETE

IRELAND

Dublin

GREAT
BRITAIN

London

NETHERLANDS

BELGIUM

LUX.

Rhine

Paris

FRANCE

Berne

SWITZERLAND

Trieste

BOSNIA

DALMATIA

MONTE-
NEGRO

ALBANIA

MACEDONIA

ITALY

Rome

CORSICA

SARDINIA

SICILY

MALTA
(Br.)

Mediterranean Sea

TUNISIA

ALGERIA
(French)

BALEARIC IS.

Madrid

SPAIN

PORTUGAL

Lisbon

MOROCCO

737

(2) Music

A wholly new concept of opera composition employed by **Richard Wagner** (1813–1883) in his "music dramas," attaching equal importance to music, libretto, and dramatic art (*Lohengrin*, 1845; *Der Ring des Nibelungen*, a tetralogy, 1852–1874; *Parsifal*, 1882).

g. THE GERMAN EMPIRE, 1871–1914

1871–1883. The *Kulturkampf.* As chancellor of the new German Empire, Bismarck's first struggle was with the Catholic Church in the so-called *Kulturkampf*, from the words used by Rudolf Virchow in the Prussian diet (1873, Jan. 17): "The contest has taken on the character of a great cultural struggle (*Kulturkampf*)." The conflict grew out of the coincident expansion of papal pretensions and German power: the promulgation of the **dogma of papal infallibility** (p. 713), implying the extension of papal pretensions to defend the Church against encroachments of the state, came just at the time of the creation of the German Empire, determined to subordinate all groups within the state to its sovereign power.

German bishops and the vast majority of lay Catholics promptly accepted the dogma of papal infallibility, despite the resistance of the liberal group (*Old Catholics*).

1871, Mar. Heterogeneous Catholic elements organized the **Center Party** during the first elections to the imperial Reichstag to defend Catholic interest—leader, **Ludwig Windthorst.** In general, the Center Party represented particularist Catholic interests in opposition to the pretensions of Protestant Prussia, hence it was anti-imperial. When, of all parties in the Reichstag, only the National Liberals supported the new state, the anti-imperial attitude of the Center irritated and alarmed Bismarck. Hence the Prussian government supported Catholic teachers in state schools who refused to accept the dogma of papal infallibility, and

July 8. Abolished the Roman Catholic **department for spiritual affairs** (recognized by the constitution of 1850). "Have no fear—to Canossa we shall not go, either in body or spirit," declared Bismarck to the Reichstag (1872, May 14).

1872, June 25. An imperial law permitted the **expulsion of the Jesuits;** the Jesuit organization was dissolved, the Jesuits expelled from Germany.

1873, May. The **May Laws or Falk Laws.** Dr. Adalbert Falk, Prussian minister of public worship, was responsible for four drastic measures: (1) making it a punishable offense for servants of the Church to impose penalties in matters not of a religious character; (2) placing education of the clergy under state supervision and giving the government a right of veto on all clerical appointments; (3) facilitating secession from the Church for those who wished to leave it; (4) subjecting ecclesiastical discipline of the Catholic clergy to state control. The struggle rapidly became embittered.

1875, Feb. 6. Civil marriage was made obligatory for the empire. A papal letter to Prussian bishops at the same time declared null and void all Prussian laws which denied and sought to undermine the divine sanction and authority of the Church. Publication of this letter was forbidden by the Prussian government.

Apr. 6. The Prussian diet passed the **Breadbasket Bill,** suspending all grants to the Church in sees whose clergy refused obedience to Prussian laws.

May 8. Catholic religious orders and congregations, with the exception of those engaged in nursing the sick, were dissolved.

May. The **war scare,** an acute crisis in the relations of Germany and France (p. 778).

May. SOCIALIST CONGRESS AT GOTHA. Adoption of the Gotha program and formation of the **Socialist Workingmen's Party.** The growth of socialism was the result of the rapid industrial development of Germany and the conversion of the working classes to political action. **Ferdinand Lassalle,** son of a prosperous merchant, was the founder of German social democracy. In lectures on the "Workers' Program" (1862) he insisted on the importance of universal suffrage as a means of obtaining state help for producers' cooperative societies. He opposed all violence. In May 1863 he organized the **Universal German Workingmen's Association,** of which he became president, with almost dictatorial power. It numbered fewer than 5000 members at the time of Lassalle's death in a duel (Aug. 31, 1864). Leadership soon passed to the **Marxian Socialists.** After the organization of the International Workingmen's Association (the **First International**) at London in 1864, Karl Marx (p. 593) sent **Wilhelm Liebknecht** to Germany to organize labor along Marxian lines. Expelled from Prussia, Liebknecht took refuge in Saxony, where he met **August Bebel,** a woodturner of Catholic family and originally of monarchist sympathies. Liebknecht won Bebel to the cause and he became the outstanding parliamentary leader of the movement. At the **Eisenach congress** of representatives of workingmen's associations (Aug. 1869) the Marxians had a majority and formed the **Social Democratic Workingmen's Party,** devoted to political action. Liebknecht and Bebel, the only two Socialist members of the North German Reichstag, withheld their votes when war credits were granted in July 1870 and joined the Lassalleans in voting (Sept. 1870) against the continuation of a war which they regarded as no longer defensive. Bismarck's attacks upon both groups drove them into union. At the **Gotha congress** (1875) they united on an essentially Lassallean program, which Marx bitterly criticized.

1876, Jan. Opening of the Imperial Bank (*Reichsbank*), an institution which was to play a major part in the economic development of the country.

1878, May 11. Attempt on the life of the emperor by **Emil Hödel,** a deranged radical. Bismarck's proposal for repressive legislation rejected by the Reichstag (May 24).

June 27. Another attempt on the emperor's life by **Dr. Karl Nobiling,** an educated radical. The emperor was badly wounded.

June 13–July 13. The congress of Berlin (p. 780).

July 30. In the elections for the Reichstag the Conservatives made substantial gains at the expense of the National Liberals.

Oct. 19. Passage of the **ANTI-SOCIALIST LAW,** renewed at intervals until 1890. The electoral campaign was waged largely on the question of repressing socialism, though neither of the would-be assassins of the emperor was a socialist. The law prohibited meetings, publications, and collections of money which by "means of social democratic, socialistic or communistic designs, aim at the overthrow of the existing order of state or society." Rigorous measures were provided for its execution, though the Reichstag steadfastly refused (Mar. 7, 1879) to gag debate in parliament or to interfere with the Socialist deputies. In the next twelve years socialism was driven underground.

1878–1879. Negotiations with the Papacy for the cessation of the *Kulturkampf*. By this time half the bishops in Germany had been displaced and many of them had fled abroad. Hundreds of clerics had been removed and many imprisoned, yet the fight continued as obstinately as ever. In 1878 Pius IX died and was succeeded by Leo XIII, a much more diplomatic pope, who at once opened negotiations with the German government. He demanded the abrogation of the May Laws, but Bismarck would agree to nothing more than administrative dilution of the laws, and only with the proviso that the pope would guarantee pre-notification of clerical appointments to the government, which could object. This proposal was rejected by Rome.

1879, June 30. Resignation of Falk, the minister officially connected with the policy. Bismarck, satisfied by this time that he had overrated the danger from organized Catholicism and requiring the support of the Center Party for his new tariff program, began to introduce ameliorative measures on his own initiative. Repressive laws were abrogated or neglected over a period of years until by 1883 the *Kulturkampf* may be said to have come to an end.

July 12. The new (protective) **TARIFF LAW.** Thus far Germany had been following a policy of free trade, which was supported by the National Liberals, though opposed by the landholding Conservative groups. But German industry was hard hit by the **financial crisis of 1873** and the ensuing depression, as well as by the **crisis in agriculture** produced by foreign competition. Both the industrialists and the landowners began to inveigh against free trade. The government itself was influenced to return to protection because, depending upon customs and excise duties for its income, it found itself in perennial need of funds. The new tariff gave protection to both industry and agriculture. It was supported by the Conservatives, who gave up their earlier opposition to the empire and became supporters of the government, by the Catholic Center, and by part of the National Liberals, representing industry. The Liberal Party split for a second time, the dissidents going over to the Progressive Party.

In the decades following the introduction of protection, German industry underwent a phenomenal development comparable to that of the United States. Possessed of vast supplies of coal and extensive iron deposits, German industry was able to meet competitors. Between 1860 and 1913 pig iron production grew from 529,000 metric tons to 19,309,000: Germany passed France and England as producers and was second only to the United States on the eve of the war. She occupied the same position as a producer of steel. Railway mileage grew from 18,887 kilometers (1870) to 61,749 (1914); the merchant marine from 980,000 tons (1870) to 5,450,000 (1914), placing the Germans third after Great Britain and the United States. Foreign trade grew with similar rapidity, doubled between 1902 and 1913; at the latter date Germany was close on the heels of Britain for first place. With the development of industry, the German social scene rapidly changed: from 1882 to 1907 the number of persons employed in and dependent upon industry rose from 16,058,080 to 26,386,537, while the total number dependent on agriculture decreased more than a million and a half. Urbanization was equally striking:

8,600,000 persons lived in cities of 20,000 or more (1885), representing 18.4 per cent of the population; by 1910 this number had increased to 22,400,000, 34.5 per cent of the population.

1879, Oct. 7. Signature of the alliance between **Germany and Austria,** the foundation of the **Bismarckian alliance system** (p. 781).

1881, June 18. Conclusion of the **Three Emperors' League** (Germany, Austria, and Russia, p. 782). Renewed, 1884, for three years.

1882, May 20. Conclusion of the **Triple Alliance** (Germany, Austria, Italy, p. 782).

1883, May. **Sickness Insurance Law,** the first of Bismarck's great measures of "state socialism" by which he hoped to wean the workers from socialism. The law insured workers during sickness; the costs to be paid two-thirds by the workers, one-third by employers. This measure was followed by the **Accident Insurance Law** (June 1884), paid for entirely by the employers and extended to practically all wage-earning groups; the **Old-Age and Invalidity Insurance Law** (May 1889), of which the costs were divided between the employers and workers, with state contributions to pensions.

1883-1885. **Foundation of the German colonial empire.** Friction with Britain (p. 783).

1886, Dec.-1887, Mar. Parliamentary conflict over an **army bill,** the Liberal parties making an effort to secure control over appropriations. After elections the government, through the intervention of the pope, secured the support of the Center Party and won its point.

1887, Apr. The **Schnaebelé affair,** marking the height of tension in Franco-German relations and in European affairs generally. Renewal of the Triple Alliance, conclusion of the **Reinsurance treaty** with Russia, formation of the **Mediterranean coalition** (p. 784).

1888, Mar. 9-June 15. **FREDERICK III** (b. 1831) who succeeded on the death of William I.

1888-1918. **WILLIAM II** (1859-1941), who followed on the death of his father, Frederick III, by cancer of the throat. The young emperor, intelligent, charming, idealistic, but impulsive and headstrong, soon evinced the desire to rule the state himself. He showed sympathy for the workers and was called the *Labor Emperor.*

1890, Jan. After two readings of a bill to prolong the anti-socialist law it was rumored that the emperor had changed his mind and favored a policy of mildness. The bill was lost, but it opened a rift between the chancellor and the emperor, which was widened when the latter proposed (Feb.) an international conference on labor questions, opposed by Bismarck as a further weak concession to the Socialists. The emperor wished to set aside the right of the chancellor to be present at interviews of the emperor and ministers. On Russo-German policy the two differed basically (p. 785). The fundamental question was who should rule the empire—the emperor or Bismarck? After further irritating incidents, Bismarck was ordered to "ask permission to resign," but refused.

Mar. 18. **RESIGNATION OF BISMARCK,** on imperial command. He was made duke of Lauenburg, but unceremoniously "ejected" from the chancery palace.

1890-1894. **Chancellorship of General Georg Leo von Caprivi,** able soldier, sober and capable administrator, but without political experience, chosen to carry out the emperor's wishes. The emperor hoped through social legislation to win the workers from socialism.

July 29. **Industrial courts** were set up to adjust wage disputes. Weekday employment of women and children was restricted, Sunday rest made obligatory for all workers.

1891, June 1. **Factory inspection** was made more efficient. Workers were given the right to form committees to negotiate with employers on conditions of employment.

1892, Mar. 26. A **labor department** was formed in the imperial statistical office, to bring the whole province of labor under more complete survey. But the emperor's hopes of winning the workers from socialism were disappointed. Socialism spread rapidly after the repeal of the anti-socialist legislation and attracted much non-socialist, liberal support. In the elections of 1890 the Socialists returned 35 deputies to the Reichstag. At the **Erfurt congress** (1891) the party adopted a more strictly Marxian program.

1892-1894. The Caprivi **commercial treaties,** with Austria, Italy, Switzerland, Spain, Serbia, Rumania, Belgium, and ultimately Russia (1894). They substantially reduced agricultural duties, thereby relieving the prices on foods (seriously high in 1891-1892) and laying the basis for the expansion of German trade in industrial products in the treaty countries. These treaties recognized the preponderance of German industry over agriculture and drew upon Caprivi's head the wrath of the landowners, who organized (1894) the **Agrarian League** (*Bund der Landwirte*), with which the older German **Peasants' League** (*Deutscher Bauernbund*) amalgamated. The Agrarian League wrung numerous concessions to agriculture from the government and came more and more to serve as a spearhead for conservatism in the political sense.

1894, Oct. 26. **Resignation of Caprivi,** who had estranged not only the agrarians, but the Center (through his failure to carry the **Prussian**

School Bill in 1890), the colonialists (through the **East Africa agreement** with England, 1890, p. 786), and the militarists (through the **reduction of the term of service in the infantry** from three to two years, 1893). Caprivi was also harassed by the independence and unexpected initiatives of the emperor, with whom he found it increasingly difficult to work.

1894–1900. Chancellorship of Prince Chlodwig zu Hohenlohe-Schillingsfürst, former Bavarian statesman, diplomat, governor of Alsace-Lorraine, *grand seigneur,* now in his old age and little inclined to oppose openly the will and vagaries of the emperor.

1895, June. Opening of the Kiel Canal from the North Sea to the Baltic.

1896, Jan. 3. The **Kruger telegram** episode, marking the first violent outbreak of popular hostility between Germany and Britain (p. 788).

July 1. The **Civil Code** (in process of elaboration since 1871) was enacted, to come into effect January 1, 1900.

1897, Nov. German occupation of Kiaochow, on the Chinese coast (pp. 789, 913).

1898, Mar. 28. Passage of the **first German Navy Law,** through the efforts of **Admiral Alfred von Tirpitz,** minister of marine since 1897. It marked the beginning of German naval expansion and the gradual emergence of friction with Britain on this score.

Nov. 27. Preliminary concession for the **Baghdad Railway** secured by the *Deutsche Bank,* marking active German expansion in the Near East and the development of friction with Britain and Russia (p. 792).

1899, Dec. 7. A law permitting the **federation of societies** of all kinds. This was Hohenlohe's reply to Liberal and Socialist agitation for broadening of the association laws.

1900, Oct. 16. Hohenlohe resigned.

1900–1909. Chancellorship of Count (later Prince) **Bernhard von Bülow,** diplomat, who had been foreign minister and intimate adviser of the emperor since June 1897. Bülow was a man of brilliant parts, an accomplished *causeur* and orator and a finished manipulator of men, but he lacked Bismarck's seriousness of purpose, strength of character, and breadth of view. His tenure of office was marked primarily by major issues in foreign and colonial policy (p. 793). In domestic policy the chief developments were the extension of social insurance.

1900. Accident insurance was extended to new occupations. The **Old-Age and Invalidity Law** had already been amended (June 1899) to increase old age and invalid pensions and extend compulsory insurance to various new groups.

June 11. Prussia enacted a law empowering local authorities to remove children from their homes if they were in danger of demoralization and place them in institutions—a law much criticized as invading parental rights.

June 12. The **second German Naval Law,** providing for a seventeen-year building program and the construction of a high-seas fleet which would be second only to that of Great Britain. Tirpitz' idea of risk—Germany to have a navy so strong that even the strongest naval power would hesitate before attacking it.

1902, Dec. 14. The **new Tariff Law,** enacted on the expiration of the Caprivi treaties. It restored the higher duty on agricultural products and was the reflection of the power of the Agrarian League. The Conservatives supported the naval policy (advocated especially by big business interests) in return for adequate protection in their own lines.

1903, Apr. 30. The **Sickness Insurance Law** amended to give longer and more generous help to workers in ill health (26 weeks instead of 13).

1905–1906. The first Moroccan crisis (p. 795).

1906, Dec. Parliamentary crisis. The Center Party, which had held the balance since 1890 and had extracted many favors from the government, turned against the administration, defeated a bill for the reorganization of the colonial office, and refused funds for military operations against the Hereros in Southwest Africa (in revolt since 1904). The Reichstag was dissolved and Bülow called on the Conservatives, National Liberals, and Progressives to subordinate party to national interests, to combat the Center and the Socialists. In the elections the Socialists suffered heavily and the government was able to form a coalition of parties in its support.

1906–1910. Bernhard Dernburg, minister for the colonies. He studied British methods of administration, revolutionized the German system and made sweeping changes in favor of the natives.

1908, Dec. 9. A law restricted **hours of factory work** by young people and women (no children under 13 to be employed, 6-hour day for children 13–14, 10-hour day for those 14–16, etc.).

Nov. The *Daily Telegraph* episode, resulting from the publication in an English paper of an interview with the emperor on Anglo-German relations. The emperor pictured the German people as hostile to Britain, while he was friendly. The affair created a furor in the Reichstag and a widespread demand for some check on the emperor's power. Bülow, who was responsible, directly or indirectly, for the publication of the interview, defended the emperor but weakly.

1909, July 14. Bülow resigned.
1909-1917. Chancellorship of Dr. Theobald von Bethmann-Hollweg. Bethmann had won a high reputation as minister of the interior. He was a typical bureaucrat of the best type, sound, industrious, honest, well-intentioned, but lacking in imagination and brilliance.
1910. Religious affairs. A violent controversy had developed from the papal encyclical *De pascendi dominici gregis* (1907, Sept. 18), directed against "modernist" heresies and requiring priests and teachers of the Church to take an oath against modernism. This seemed to threaten again an invasion of the state province of education. But the pope promised (in a letter to the German prelacy, 1910, Feb. 1) that the oath would be restricted to priest-professors and would not be required of professors engaged in purely lay functions. Protestant sentiment had also been aroused by the encyclical *Editio saepe* (1910, May 26) which referred in scathing terms to the Reformation and association of certain German princes with it. In reply to a tactful remonstrance from the Prussian government, the pope denied (June 11) any intention of wounding Protestant susceptibilities and decided that the encyclical should not be circulated in Germany.
1910, Nov.-1911, Aug. The **Potsdam agreement** between Germany and Russia concerning their interests in the Near East (p. 799).
1911, May 26. A law was passed organizing **Alsace and Lorraine as a state,** with a two-chamber legislature and a large measure of autonomy.
May 30. The **Imperial Insurance Code** consolidated all previous workers' insurance laws and amended and extended their provisions. Certain groups of white-collar workers were insured against sickness, old age, and death, by a separate and simultaneous law.
July 1. Mission of the gunboat *Panther* to Agadir, thereby precipitating the **second Moroccan crisis** (p. 799).
1912, Jan. Elections to the Reichstag. The Socialists polled 4,250,000 votes and, with 110 deputies, became the strongest party in the Reichstag. By this time the movement had become much modified through the "revisionist" tendency introduced by **Eduard Bernstein.** The revisionists sought to divert interest from the "ultimate goal" of socialism and to fasten attention on the importance of gradual advancement, through parliamentary reforms, toward a new social world. This theory was denounced as a heresy at the **Lübeck congress** (1901, especially by **Karl Kautsky** and **Rosa Luxemburg**), but it nevertheless colored the outlook of the party, which was further in-

fluenced by the rapid progress of the trade-union movement, dominated by moderate views. After the serious setback of the Socialists in the election of 1907, revisionism became more and more generally accepted. The party began to take an active part in work for social reform and collaborated with the Progressives in organizing the Reichstag in 1912. In 1914 the Social Democrats voted for the war credits, defending their action as necessary for the defense of the fatherland against autocratic Russia.
    Feb. Visit of Lord Haldane to Berlin. Abortive attempt to effect a naval agreement between Britain and Germany (p. 800).
1913, June 30. The Army and Finance Bills. In the midst of the tension which preceded the outbreak of the First World War, the government had little difficulty in securing the passage of its army bills. But all previous bills were eclipsed by the bill of 1913, providing for the addition of 4000 officers, 15,000 non-commissioned officers, 117,000 men, as part of a program to increase the peacetime strength of the army from 544,000 to 870,000 men. The Socialists, Poles, and Alsatians voted against it, but all other parties supported the government, and the bill passed. The cost of the measure was estimated at one billion marks, of which 435,000,000 was to fall due in 1913. In the **Finance Law** there was provision for a special national defense tax (*Wehrsteuer*), to be levied only once on real and personal property and income. The incidence was to be on the well-to-do classes, as a concession to the Socialists and other radicals: the Socialists therefore voted the funds, though they had voted against the military measures for which the funds were intended.
    Dec. The **Zabern affair,** resulting from the action of a German officer in striking and wounding a lame cobbler with his sword and insulting Alsatian recruits. The incident created much excitement and embittered Franco-German relations. *(Cont. pp. 943 ff., 1004.)*

CULTURAL DEVELOPMENTS

Literature: Plays treating serious social and psychological problems by **Hermann Sudermann** (*Die Ehre,* 1889) and **Gerhart Hauptmann** (*Vor Sonnenaufgang,* 1889; *Die Weber,* 1892), **Arthur Schnitzler** (1862-1931), and **Frank Wedekind** (1864-1918). Lyric poetry of **Richard Dehmel** (1863-1920), **Stefan George** (1868-1933), **Hugo von Hofmannsthal** (1874-1929), and **Rainer Maria Rilke** (1875-1926).
    Music: Symphonic works of **Anton Bruckner** (1824-1896), **Gustav Mahler** (1860-1911), and **Richard Strauss** (1864-1949).

Art: Painters **Käthe Kollwitz** (1867–1945); **Vassili Kandinski** (1866–1944). One of the early modern sculptors was **Wilhelm Lehmbruck** (1881–1919).

h. AUSTRIA-HUNGARY, 1867–1914

The task of the Emperor Francis Joseph was to make the dualist system work. In law he ruled through responsible ministries in both Austria and Hungary, but in fact little could be done in either state without affecting "common concerns" and in these the emperor-king was able to make his will felt. In foreign affairs and military questions he enjoyed far-reaching powers. The foreign minister was officially responsible to the delegations, but in practice it was almost impossible not to endorse his policy so long as he enjoyed the confidence of the emperor.

(1) Austria

1867, Dec. 21. Four **fundamental laws** of a liberal character reformed the February Patent (p. 726) and became the **constitution of 1867.** This was a concession aimed to win the approval of the German Liberals for the compromise with Hungary.

1867, Dec.–1870, Jan. **Ministry of Count Adolf Auersperg,** representing the German Liberals, who were a minority of all the Germans (these in turn constituting hardly more than a third of the total population). The Liberals were determined to maintain administrative centralization and oppose the federalist pretensions of the Slavs. Once in power they passed a number of anti-clerical measures:

1868, May 25. **Civil marriage was restored.**

1870, July 30. The **concordat with the Papacy** (of 1855) was suspended as a reply to the promulgation of the dogma of papal infallibility.

1871, Feb.–Oct. 25. **Ministry of Count Karl Hohenwart,** representing the federalist groups. The Czechs and other Slavs had protested vigorously against the compromise, had boycotted the parliament and had demanded local autonomy. When hopes of recovery of the Austrian position in Germany had disappeared, the emperor, who distrusted the anti-clericalism of the German Liberals, turned to these opposition groups. Hohenwart prepared a scheme to meet the demands of the Czechs, to whom far-reaching promises were made.

Sept. 12. The Bohemian diet went further, and demanded a position in Austria similar to that of Hungary in the Dual Monarchy. This was opposed by the Hungarians as endangering the "unity" of the empire, and was rejected by the emperor. Hohenwart was obliged to resign.

1871, Nov.–1878. **Second ministry of Count Auersperg** and the German Liberals. The position of the ministry was unstable after the financial crisis of 1873, when a number of leading Liberals and even ministers were discredited by speculation. The Liberal group rapidly dissolved into conflicting factions.

1875–1878. **Acute Near Eastern crisis,** arising from the insurrection in Bosnia-Herzegovina and the war of Russia against Turkey (p. 780).

1878, June–July. The Austrian government, by European mandate, was given the right to occupy **Bosnia** and **Herzegovina,** which were put under the administration of the ministry of common finance. The step aroused much opposition among both Germans and Magyars, who disliked the annexation of more Slavs. In the provinces a serious revolt broke out (1882), which was not suppressed until October.

1879, Aug.–1893, Oct. 29. **Ministry of Count Eduard Taaffe,** a boyhood friend of the emperor. Faced by the opposition of the German Liberals, Taaffe was obliged to rule with a coalition of Czechs, Poles, and German Conservatives and Clericals (the *Iron Ring*), which in turn extracted from him numerous concessions (language rights, etc.).

In the face of a rising **labor movement,** Taaffe adopted a policy much like that of Bismarck. Socialism was repressed with great severity, but the government passed legislation providing protection for workers, shortening of the working day, measures of insurance, etc.

1879, Oct. 7. Signature of the **Austrian alliance with Germany** (p. 781).

1881, June 18. Austria-Hungary joined Germany and Russia in the **Three Emperors' Alliance** (p. 782).

1882, May 20. Austria joined Germany and Italy in the **Triple Alliance** (p. 782).

1885–1888. Acute tension between Austria and Russia resulting from the development of the **Bulgarian problem.** Non-renewal of the Three Emperors' Alliance (1887), renewal of the Triple Alliance (1887), and conclusion of the Mediterranean agreements with Britain and Italy (Feb., Dec. 1887, see pp. 784–785).

1889, Jan. 30. **Suicide of Archduke Rudolf,** only son of Francis Joseph and heir to the throne, at Mayerling. The Archduke Francis Ferdinand (1863–1914), nephew of the emperor, became heir.

1893, Oct. 29. **Resignation of Count Taaffe,** due to the breakdown of his governing coalition. The opposition of the Germans, who had formed a nationalist group, and the rise of the **Young Czechs** (more radical than their predecessors) had rendered his policy of muddling along impossible. Taaffe had tried to solve the problem by introducing a bill providing for **universal manhood suffrage** (1893, Oct. 10), hoping thereby to counteract the nationalist agitation with the weight of socialism. The bill was rejected by Conservatives and Liberals of all stamps.

1895, Sept.-1897, Nov. Ministry of Count Casimir Badeni, a Polish landlord. He attempted to solve the nationality problem by conciliating the Czechs.

1897, Apr. 5. The **Badeni Language Ordinances,** establishing parity between German and the local language in a given district.

Apr. Austro-Russian agreement to maintain the *status quo* in the Balkans (p. 789).

Nov. 28. Badeni was forced to resign as a result of violent German agitation against his language ordinances and hot debate on the decennial renewal of the economic arrangements with Hungary. There followed a period of acute constitutional crisis, which brought the monarchy to the verge of dissolution and made parliamentary government utterly impossible.

1898, Mar. New laws divided Bohemia into a Czech, a German, and a mixed linguistic district, but this effort at compromise satisfied no one. On October 14, 1899, the original arrangements were restored, despite objection and obstruction from the Czechs, who engaged in widespread disorders.

Sept. 10. Assassination of the Empress Elizabeth at Geneva, by the Italian anarchist, Luigi Luccheni.

1900, Jan.-1904, Dec. Ministry of Ernst von Körber, an able bureaucrat, who governed with a ministry of officials, chiefly by decree. His efforts to effect a compromise on the language question proved as fruitless as those of his predecessors.

1907, Jan. 26. Law introducing **universal, equal, and direct suffrage** for parliamentary elections. This subject had been hotly debated for years and was vigorously demanded by the Socialists. The effect of it was to stress social stratification and interests, though the nationality problem remained an open sore.

The ministries from 1907 to 1914 were for the most part non-parliamentary (i.e. lacked a parliamentary majority), ruling by decree and making concessions to particular groups to secure support for particular measures.

1908, Oct. 6. Annexation of Bosnia and Herzegovina by decree. This ushered in the acute **Bosnian annexation crisis** and a period of tension in Austro-Russian relations that lasted until the World War (p. 798).

1912-1913. The Balkan Wars (p. 801 *f.*). The victories of Serbia and Austrian efforts to block Serbian expansion led to a marked growth of Yugoslav agitation and to a revival of Slavic activity within the monarchy.

1914, June 28. Assassination of the Archduke Francis Ferdinand at Sarajevo. He was known to be hostile to the Magyar pretensions and favorably disposed toward a reorganization of the monarchy along "trialistic" lines, i.e. giving the Slavic elements a position on a par with that of Germans and Magyars.

(*Cont. pp. 947 ff., 961.*)

(2) Hungary

1867, Feb. 17. The **constitution of 1848** was restored in Hungary. A ministry was formed under **Count Julius Andrássy,** remaining in power until November 1871.

June 8. Francis Joseph crowned king of Hungary at Budapest.

1868, May 4. In face of opposition from the Independence party, Andrássy's government agreed to the establishment of a common army for the Dual Monarchy, with German the language of command.

Sept. The king agreed to the **reunion of Croatia** with Hungary (separated since 1848). Despite opposition from military circles, the king also permitted **abolition of the military frontier province** (*Militärgrenze*), adjacent to the southern boundary of Hungary, which had been administered for two centuries by the Austrian war office as a safety zone against the Turks. It was now incorporated with Croatia.

1875, Feb. Formation of the Liberal Party by Kálmán Tisza (1830–1902). It was composed of the larger part of the Independence Party, which had fought the compromise of 1867, and the larger part of the Deák Party, which had disintegrated.

Aug. The elections gave the new party a great majority.

1875, Oct.-1890, Mar. 7. Ministry of Kálmán Tisza. Accepting the compromise, Tisza devoted his energies to strengthening the Magyar position in Hungary, notably by various school and language regulations designed to Magyarize the new generation among the subject nationalities.

1876, Jan. 28. Death of Francis Deák.

1894, Mar. 20. Death of Louis Kossuth, at Turin. In the previous decade there had been a marked revival of the Independence Party, the leadership of which was assumed by Kossuth's son, Francis. This party kept stressing the weaknesses of the compromise and demanding fuller independence for Hungary. Economic differences between industrial Austria and agrarian Hungary served to sharpen the tension, as demonstrated in the heated arguments over the renewal of the economic compromise in 1897.

1903. The dispute reached the acute phase in the **struggle over the army,** the Magyars resenting the unified system. An increase in the number of recruits was vigorously opposed by the Independence Party, which insisted on the use of Magyar insignia in the Hungarian regiments and the substitution of Magyar for German as the language of command. This the king flatly refused to consider.

Sept. 16. In a proclamation to the army, Francis Joseph declared that he would "never yield the rights and duties guaranteed to its supreme commander," and that he would maintain the army, common and unified, at all costs. This declaration raised a storm in Hungary.

Oct. 26-1905, Feb. 1. Ministry of Count Stephen Tisza (1861–1918), son of Kálmán Tisza.

1904, Mar. 11. Tisza secured the passage of the recruits bill after he had threatened drastic measures (*guillotine bill*) to deal with parliamentary obstruction.

1905, Jan. In the **elections** Tisza and the Liberal Party, having refused to make use of the customary corruption, were completely defeated. The Independents had 163 seats as against the Liberals' 152. Kossuth formed a coalition with several of the smaller parties and renewed the demand for the Magyar language of command, refusing to recognize the non-parliamentary government set up by Baron Géza Fejérváry. The crisis, which continued despite innumerable efforts to reach a compromise, dragged on until broken by the king's threat to introduce universal suffrage. This was designed to break the preponderance of the Magyars and was hotly resisted by all parties.

1906, July. The **Universal Suffrage Bill** was actually brought before the Hungarian parliament. This brought the Independence Party to its senses. The military demands were abandoned.

1906–1910. Parliamentary government of Dr. Alexander Wekerlé, governing with the support of the coalition parties.

1910–1913. Ministry of Count Károlyi Khuen-Héderváry, in which Tisza was the dominating figure. Tisza was convinced of the importance of ending the internecine struggles in Hungary and of strengthening the common army in face of European danger of war. By expending large sums of money he reorganized the old Liberal Party as the **National Party of Work,** and won an overwhelming victory in the elections of 1910. Nevertheless the Independents, again in opposition, continued obstructive tactics.

1912. **Tisza,** as president of the lower house, succeeded in modifying parliamentary procedure and forced through the army bill, after ejecting the opposition by force.

1913, June 15-1917, May 23. Tisza prime minister, exercising far-reaching authority not only in Hungary, but in the councils of the Dual Monarchy.

In Hungary, as in Austria, though to a less extent, the disintegrating forces of nationalism made themselves felt. There was constant friction with the **Croatians** (especially in 1903) which the government tried to meet by encouraging the Serb elements against the Croats. In Transylvania the **Roumanian irredentist agitation** developed rapidly. The government suppressed it to the best of its ability, but thereby created much ill-feeling in Roumania proper. Tisza was eager for an understanding, especially with the Roumanians, but like all Magyar statesmen, he rejected the idea of universal suffrage, which would have given the subject nationalities a voice in political affairs (they were 52 per cent of the total population) and would at the same time have enabled the lower classes (both agrarian and industrial proletarians) to challenge the domination of the upper classes. In 1914 Hungary was still essentially a feudal state, ruled by a Magyar aristocracy.

(Cont. pp. 947 ff., 1019.)

CULTURAL DEVELOPMENTS

Literature: One of the most prolific writers of plays was **Edward Szigligeti; Charles Obernyik** wrote one of the best historical tragedies, *George Brankovics.* Novels, especially with national flavor, were coming from the pens of such writers as **Baron Sigismund Kemény** (1816–1875), **Maurus Jókai** (1825–1904), **Koloman Mikszath** (1847–1910). The most controversial modern poet was **Andrew Ady** (1877–1919).

Art: Foremost Hungarian painters of the late 19th century were **Mihaly Munkacsy** (1844–1900) and **Ladislas Paal** (1846–1879).

Music: Béla Bartók (1881–1945) was one of the greatest modern composers; with the composer **Zoltán Kodaly** (1882–1967) he collected Magyar and Turkish folk songs. In Bohemia **Bedřich Smetana** (1824–1884) and **Antonin Dvořák** (1841–1904) were their precursors in composing with nationalistic feeling.

D. NORTHERN AND EASTERN EUROPE, 1801–1915

1. SCANDINAVIA

a. DENMARK, 1808–1915

(*From p. 509*)

During the Napoleonic period Denmark sided with France, thereby becoming involved in war with Great Britain and Sweden (p. 642). By the **treaties of Vienna** (1815) **Denmark** abandoned **Norway** to Sweden and **Pomerania** to Prussia, receiving as compensation the little duchy of **Lauenburg.**

1808–1839. FREDERICK VI, king. The reign was devoted primarily to the work of reconstruction and recovery, especially in finance. Marked growth of **liberal and nationalist feeling,** stimulated by the Paris revolution of 1830.

1831–1834. Institution of representative government: four provincial diets established for (1) the islands; (2) Jutland; (3) Schleswig; (4) Holstein. But these bodies had only deliberative and advisory powers.

1839–1848. CHRISTIAN VIII (grandson of Frederick V). Continuation of reform; improvement of the finances; development of communal self-government; prison reform; constitution granted to Iceland.

1848–1863. FREDERICK VII. His reign began with a **war with the German states** resulting from the efforts of the Danish nationalists to incorporate Schleswig with the monarchy (p. 724).

1849, June 5. Promulgation of a new constitution: Denmark proper became a limited monarchy in which the king shared legislative power with a bicameral national assembly; civil liberties guaranteed. Schleswig and Holstein continued to be governed in the old fashion, since an effort made in 1855 to include Schleswig in the Danish constitutional system resulted in further friction with the German powers.

1857. Abolition of the historic Sound dues, in return for compensation.

1863–1906. CHRISTIAN IX, of a collateral branch of the family.

1864. WAR AGAINST PRUSSIA AND AUSTRIA, over the two disputed duchies. The Danes had tried, by the constitution of November 13, 1863, to settle the Schleswig problem by violating promises given to Prussia and Austria in 1851. When these two powers demanded the abolition of the objectionable constitution, the Danes, relying on the support of Britain, Sweden, and possibly France, accepted the challenge. No aid from others having been offered, the Danes were bound to lose in so unequal a struggle. By the peace settlement they had to **cede Schleswig, Holstein,** and **Lauenburg** to the victors, thus losing some 200,000 Danes resident in northern Schleswig.

1866, July 28. Revision of the constitution of 1849. The upper chamber (*Landsthing*) was to consist in part of members named by the king, in part of members chosen by indirect vote. The upper chamber was given extensive power at the expense of the lower (*Folkething*): ministers could govern with support of the upper chamber even in defiance of the lower. This arrangement led to an acute struggle between the **Liberal Party,** aiming at parliamentary government, and the **Conservative Party,** defending the existing political order. After 1875 the Conservatives were in control for nearly two decades, under the leadership of **Jacob Estrup.**

The last decades of the 19th century were marked by unusual **economic and cultural development** in Denmark. *Society for the Cultivation of Heaths* (1866); improvement of agriculture; expansion of dairy-farming (English market); growth of co-operative enterprise; development of industry and commerce.

1891–1892. Social legislation: the **Old-Age Pension Law** and the **Health Insurance Law** passed. At the same time the peasants were aided in transforming their leasehold tenancies into freeholds (by 1905 about 94 per cent of the farms were freeholds). Continued vigorous growth of co-operatives, which greatly increased the economic well-being of the rural population.

Liberal agitation for a democratic constitution was supported (after 1880) by the new **Social Democratic Party.**

1901. Formation of a Liberal government, without, however, any constitutional change.

1906–1912. FREDERICK VIII, king.

1912–1947. CHRISTIAN X, king.

1914–1915. Constitutional amendments passed. The suffrage was extended to all men and most women, and the age limit reduced from 30 to 25 years. The appointive seats in the upper house were abolished, and its former predominance broken. **Establishment of regular parliamentary government.** (*Cont. p. 1043.*)

Denmark's greatest story-teller was **Hans Christian Andersen** (1805–1875). It was a Danish sculptor, **Bertel Thorwaldsen** (1770–1844), who carved the famed *Lion of Lucerne* (1820). **Nikolai Grundtvig** (1783–1872), poet, educator, hymnist, did much to stimulate national feeling (*Northern Mythology*, 1808; *Songs for the Danish Church*, 1837–1841).

b. SWEDEN AND NORWAY, 1809–1914

(From p. 509)

Sweden, by participating in the **War of the Third Coalition** against France (p. 640), for a time lost Pomerania, which, however, was restored in 1810. Following the deposition of Gustavus IV in 1809,

1809–1818. CHARLES XIII ascended the throne and was obliged to accept a **new constitution.** In 1810 the French marshal, **Jean-Baptiste Bernadotte,** was elected crown prince under the name of Charles John. Under his lead

1812. Sweden joined Russia in the coalition against France, as a result of which

1814. Sweden acquired Norway from Denmark but lost Finland to Russia. Under pressure from the Norwegians, the Danes had, since 1807, granted Norway some national institutions including a national university. On taking over the country, the Swedes had to agree to

May 17. A new constitution for Norway, providing for a single-chamber national assembly (*Storting*) and denying the king an absolute veto or the right of dissolving parliament. The Norwegians attempted to elect as their king the Danish prince, **Christian Frederick,** but after an invasion of the country by Bernadotte, they were obliged to accept Charles XIII.

Nov. 4. At a meeting at Christiania (Oslo) the Norwegian assembly declared **Norway** a free, independent, and indivisible kingdom, united with **Sweden** under one king.

1815. A special **act of union** was ratified by both Sweden and Norway.

1818–1844. CHARLES XIV JOHN (Bernadotte), king and founder of a new dynasty. He was a firm defender of the royal prerogative and tended to lean toward a reactionary policy. This led to a chronic **conflict between the king and the estates,** which tried to check royal absolutism.

1832. Opening of the Göta Canal, connecting the North Sea with the Baltic.

1842. An **Elementary-School Statute** provided for the maintenance of at least one school in every parish.

1844–1859. OSCAR I. Continued growth of Liberal opposition.

1845. The government was obliged to grant some liberal concessions (right to abrogate periodical publications abolished).

1859. Complete religious freedom established.

1859–1872. CHARLES XV. Insistence of the Liberals on electoral reform finally led to

1864, Dec. 8. Revision of the Constitution (promulgated Jan. 1866), framed by **Louis de Geer,** the Liberal prime minister. The traditional division of the *Riksdag* into four estates was given up and a modern **bicameral parliament** was established: the upper chamber to be elected by provincial assemblies and for a nine-year term; the lower chamber by direct popular vote, for a three-year term. The franchise was still subject to property qualifications, but was wide enough to include a large part of the peasantry.

GROWTH OF NORWEGIAN NATIONALISM in this period: formation of the **Young Norway Party** by Henrik Wergeland; cultural and intellectual activity: **Magnus Landstad** published his *Norwegian Folksongs* (1853), while **Peter Andreas Munch** brought out his *History of the Norwegian Nation* (1852–1863). **Ivar Aasen** wrote a Norwegian grammar and a dictionary of the folk language (1848, 1850). The great figures of the Norwegian **literary revival: Henrik Ibsen** (1828–1906), **Björnstjerne Björnson** (1832–1910), **Jonas Lie** (1833–1908), **Alexander Kielland** (1849–1906).

1872–1907. OSCAR II (brother of Charles XV). During his long reign Sweden underwent an **economic and social transformation.** The first twenty years of the new constitutional régime were a period of agrarian domination in politics, but after 1880 the commercial and industrial classes began to come to the fore. The conflict between free-traders and protectionists ended in

1888. The introduction of a **protective tariff.**

1889. Passage of the **first Factory Laws** (extended in 1900). Meanwhile the industrial workers organized the **Social Democratic Party** (under **Hjalmar Branting**). Development of trade-unionism and the co-operative movement. Extensive **emigration to America** (between 1870 and 1914 Sweden lost about 1,500,000 inhabitants).

1898. Universal manhood suffrage was introduced in Norway, where the democratic elements, led by **Johan Sverdrup,** dominated the *Storting* after 1884. Rapid growth of the movement for complete independence in Norway. This led to a conflict with Sweden about Norway's foreign representation. The Norwegians, a great trading people, demanded a national flag and a consular service of their own. These concessions the Swedish king refused to make.

1905, June 7. THE NORWEGIAN *STORTING* DECLARED THE UNION WITH

748

(From p. 441)

The House of Bernadotte (1818–   )

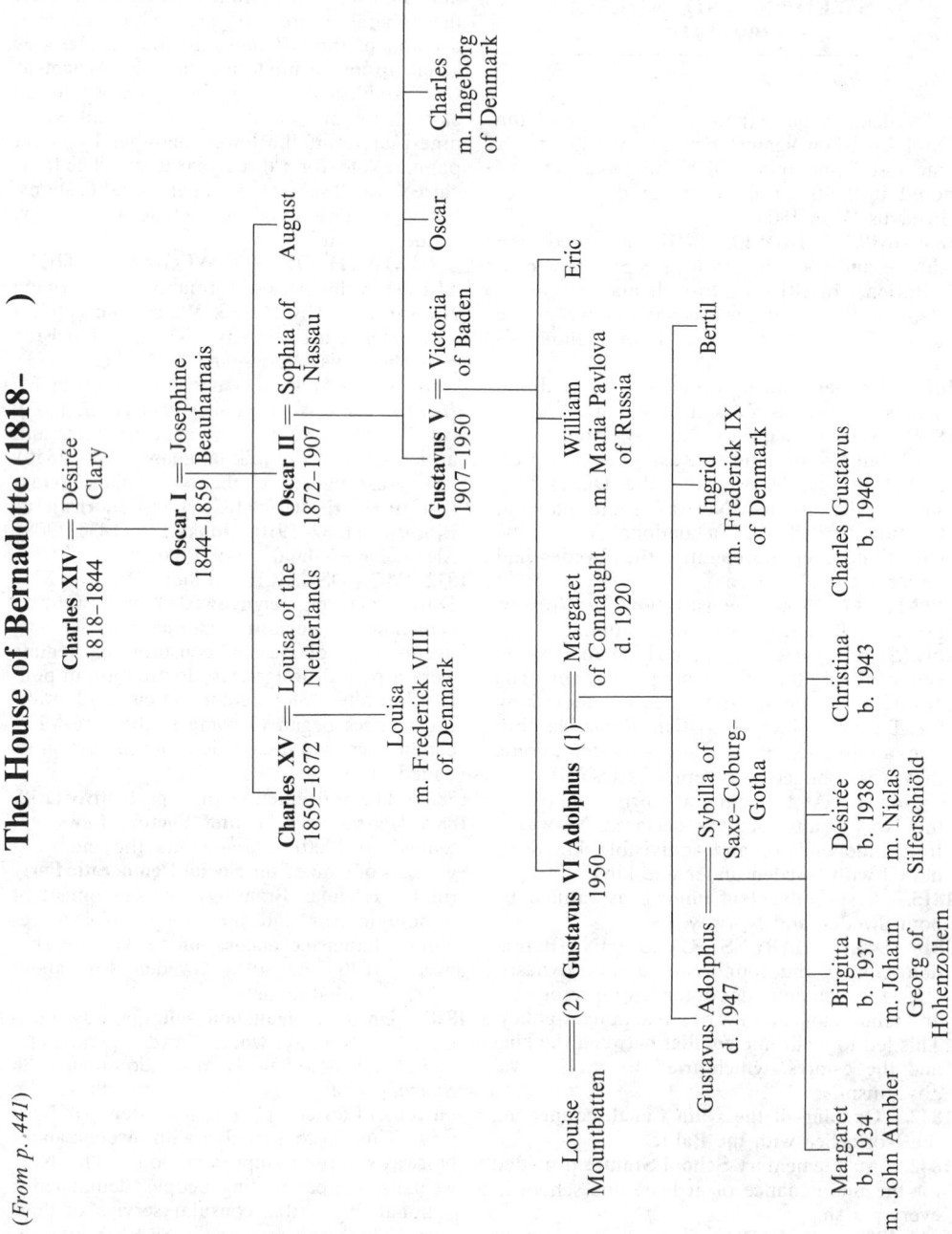

SWEDEN DISSOLVED. The decision was ratified by a popular plebiscite (Aug. 13).

Sept. 24. The **Swedish *Riksdag*** acquiesced.

Oct. 26. The **treaty of separation** was signed. Oscar II laid down the Norwegian crown and the Norwegians elected as their king Prince Charles of Denmark, who ascended the throne as

1905–1957. HAAKON VII, king of Norway. His reign was marked by further democratic reforms: suffrage extended to women (1907); royal veto (suspensive) abolished.

1907. Parliamentary government and almost universal suffrage were introduced in **Sweden.**

1907–1950. GUSTAVUS V, king of Sweden. Further constitutional amendments based the elections to the lower house upon real universal suffrage, combined with proportional representation. Property qualifications for election to the upper house were considerbly reduced. Conflict between the government and parliament over expenses for national defense led to the growth of radical opposition. In the elections of 1914 the Socialists won about one-third of the seats in the lower chamber.

(*Cont. p. 1044.*)

CULTURAL DEVELOPMENTS

Norway's national poet was **Henrik Wergeland** (1808–1845) and its foremost dramatist **Henrik Ibsen** (1828–1906), whose plots, full of symbolism and criticism, dealt with current social problems: *Peer Gynt* (1867), *A Doll's House* (1879), *Hedda Gabler* (1890). Likewise **Björnstjerne Björnson** (1832–1910) and, in Sweden, **August Strindberg** (1849–1912) wrote problem plays (*Miss Julie,* 1888).

A Norwegian counterpart of Denmark's Hans Christian Andersen was **Peter Christen Asbjörnsen** (1812–1885). The leading Norwegian musician was **Edvard Grieg** (1843–1907), whose songs and piano compositions are prevaded by a feeling of nationalism.

In Finland the great philologist and folklorist, **Elias Lönnrot** (1802–1884), collected and compiled the *Kalevala* (1835–1849), one of the great epics of European literature.

2. RUSSIA, 1801–1914

(*From p. 518*)

1801–1825. ALEXANDER I. He had been educated by the Swiss rationalist **Jean Francois de Laharpe,** and began his reign by granting an amnesty to political prisoners and exiles, abolishing torture, repealing the prohibition of foreign books, etc. With a group of intimate friends (the *Informal Committee:* **Czartoryski, Kochubei, Novosiltsov, Stroganov**) Alexander discussed various reforms and the project of a constitution for Russia. Though the constitution was not introduced, the central government was reorganized, **modern ministries** replacing the old "colleges."

1803. A law was passed regulating the **liberation of the peasant serfs** of owners who desired to make the change. This was important chiefly as the first move of the government toward abolition of serfdom. Further reforms were postponed because of the many wars in which Alexander became involved.

1804–1813. War with Persia, resulting from Russian annexation of the **kingdom of Georgia.** The Russians were victorious and Persia recognized the annexation, besides ceding to Russia **Daghestan** and **Shemakha.**

1805–1812. Russian expansion in North America. Forts were built in Alaska (occupied by Russian pioneers in the late 18th century) and even in northern California.

1805–1807. WAR OF THE THIRD COALITION against France (p. 640). This ended in Russia's defeat and the conclusion of the **treaty of Tilsit,** by which Alexander and Napoleon became allies.

1806–1812. War against Turkey (p. 642). This was hurriedly concluded in 1812 by the **treaty of Bucharest,** which gave Russia not only **Bessarabia,** but rather extensive rights in the Danubian Principalities.

1808–1809. War with Sweden, through which Russia conquered **Finland.** Finland was organized as an autonomous grand duchy, with the Russian tsar as grand duke. Constitutional government was guaranteed the Finns by a special act.

After these wars, Alexander resumed his reform schemes, with **Michael Speransky** as his chief counselor.

1810. A **council of state** was established to draft new laws and watch over the legality of administration. The ministries were also reorganized and a regular system of state budgets introduced. Speransky presented a **plan for a constitution,** but it too remained unrealized. Opposition of the conservatives and personal disagreement with the tsar led to Speransky's downfall and temporary exile (1812).

1812. INVASION OF RUSSIA by Napoleon (p. 645). Formation of the **Grand Alliance** and the campaigns in Germany and France led

Alexander to devote himself almost entirely to foreign affairs. For his participation in the **congress of Vienna** and his project of a **Holy Alliance,** see pp. 650, 652.

1815. By the treaty of Vienna, Russia acquired most of the **grand duchy of Warsaw,** which Alexander organized as an autonomous **kingdom of Poland,** in permanent union with the Russian Empire. The **constitution of Poland** provided for a diet, a separate administration and army, official use of the Polish language, etc. General Josef Zaionczek was made viceroy, and the Grand Duke Constantine became commander of the Polish army. After 1820 Alexander's relations with the Poles became ever more strained, partly because of his unwillingness to abide by the constitution (failure to summon the diet), partly because the Polish nationalists advanced claims to White Russia, Lithuania, and the western Ukraine.

In **domestic affairs,** Alexander continued to discuss constitutional projects, but in practice he became more and more reactionary, as was shown by his selection of **General Alexis Arakcheiev** as his chief adviser. This new departure led to the **growth of opposition,** more particularly among the younger army officers who had imbibed liberalism in the west. After 1817 **secret societies** were formed in the army. These finally took the shape of a **Northern Society** at St. Petersburg (favored constitutional monarchy, abolition of serfdom, etc.), and a **Southern Society** at Kiev (republican, advocating division of land among the peasants, etc.) under the leadership of **Paul Pestel.**

1825, Dec. 13. Death of Alexander I in the Crimea. As he had no children the succession would normally have passed to his brother **Constantine,** but the latter had, in 1822, renounced his claims in favor of the younger brother, **Nicholas.** This arrangement, however, had been kept secret and Nicholas refused to believe in it until he had secured a further renunciation from Constantine (at Warsaw). The interregnum and the general uncertainty gave an opportunity for

Dec. 26. The DECEMBRIST RISING, a military revolt started by the Northern Society. The whole affair was ill-planned and halfhearted. Nicholas suppressed it the same day. Of the leaders several were executed and the rest sent into exile. An attempted uprising in the south was also frustrated.

1825-1855. NICHOLAS I, a firm believer in autocracy and a determined enemy of liberalism both at home and abroad. In foreign policy he combined defense of legitimism with an attempt to secure Russia's commercial interests, especially in the east.

1826-1828. War with Persia, resulting from a Persian attack on Russian possessions in Transcaucasia. The war ended in a Russian victory and in the **treaty of Turkmanchai:** Russia secured part of **Armenia** with Erivan; Persia recognized Russia's exclusive right to have a navy on the Caspian Sea, and granted Russia important commercial concessions.

1828-1829. War against Turkey, growing out of the Greek Revolution and conflict between Russia and Turkey over the terms of the treaty of Bucharest. For the campaigns see p. 770. By the **treaty of Adrianople** (1829) Russia secured the mouth of the Danube and the eastern coast of the Black Sea.

1830-1831. The **POLISH REVOLUTION,** long prepared by the Polish nationalists, but provoked by the Paris revolution and the tsar's proposal to use the Polish army to suppress the new governments in Belgium and France. The Russian garrison was expelled from Poland, a revolutionary government proclaimed, the Romanov dynasty declared deposed, and the union with Lithuania celebrated. The Russian army, commanded first by General Hans Diebitsch and then by General Ivan Paskievich, defeated the Poles (divided by internal dissensions between moderates and radicals) at **Ostrolenka** (May 26, 1831) and finally took Warsaw (Sept. 8). The revolution collapsed and most of the Polish leaders escaped to the west, where they formed a powerful revolutionary faction, especially in Paris. The **Polish constitution was abrogated** and replaced by an **organic statute:** Poland lost its political rights and retained only a small measure of administrative autonomy. Beginning of the policy of Russification in Poland.

DOMESTIC POLICY. Nicholas, while recognizing the need for reform, was sternly opposed to all independent public activity. **Growth of bureaucracy** and of the tsar's personal government. Publication of a **new code of law** (1832), edited by Speransky. This, with some modification, remained in force until the revolution of 1917. Partial measures to alleviate the condition of the serfs and to limit the power of the landlords. Progress of technical education. **First Russian railroad** (St. Petersburg to Tsarskoe Selo, 1838). At the same time drastic **repression of all liberal manifestations** and tendencies; activity of the secret police (**third section** of "His Majesty's Own Chancery"); strict **censorship;** control of the universities; official championship of **orthodoxy, autocracy, and nationalism.** Despite all the repressive measures, public opinion nevertheless developed. Formation of two schools of thought: the *Westerners,* who held that Russia must follow the lead of western countries in political and social development; and the *Slavophiles,* who insisted on the peculiarities of Russian culture and historical evolution, and on the need for independent development. But both groups opposed bureaucratic rule and demanded freedom of thought, abolition of serfdom, etc. Beginnings of **Russian socialism** (under the influence of the Utopian socialists in France): **Alexander Herzen, Michael Bakunin.** The revolutions of 1848–1849 simply resulted in more thoroughgoing repression in Russia, but opposition broke through as soon as Russia began to meet with defeats in the Crimean War.

CULTURAL DEVELOPMENTS. Foreign influence, especially French, began to appear in literature: lyric poetry of **Gavriil Derzhavin** (1743–1816); Indian, Persian, and Greek epics translated by **Vasili Zhukovski** (1783–1852; *Odyssey,* 1847); elegies of **Constantine Batyushkov** (1787–1855); *Fables* of **Ivan Krylov** (1809). Influence of **Nikolai Karamzin** (1765–1826) in introducing ideas from French romanticism.

Alexander Pushkin (1799–1837), first poet to criticize the social order (*Ruslan i Lyudmila,* 1820; *Boris Godunov,* 1825; *Kapitanskaia Dochka,* 1832; *Yevgeni Onegin,* 1832). The one outstanding drama of the period: *Gare ot uma* (*Woe from Wit,* 1825), a comedy by **Alexander Griboyedov** (1795–1829).

1833. The **Near Eastern crisis,** resulting from Mohammed Ali's victory over the sultan. Interference of Russia and **treaty of Unkiar Skelessi** (p. 771).

1839–1840. Second Mohammed Ali crisis. Russian co-operation with Britain. **Straits convention,** etc. (p. 772).

1848–1849. Revolutions in central and western Europe. Intervention of Russia to suppress the Hungarian revolutionary movement (p. 723).

Advance in Asia. The Russians were pressing on steadily. During the reign of Nicholas they conquered the Khirghiz Steppe and prepared for the **advance into Turkestan.** In the Far East **Nicholas Muraviev** (1809–1881) became governor-general of Siberia in 1847.

1850. The Russians established a settlement at the mouth of the Amur River.

1853–1856. The **CRIMEAN WAR,** the outcome of the dispute between Russia and France over the holy places in Palestine and of Russian claims to a protectorate over the Christians in the Ottoman Empire. For details of the war see p. 773 *f.* By the **treaty of Paris** (1856) Russia lost control of the Danube mouth and ceded to Turkey the southern part of **Bessarabia.** Russia was obliged to accept **neutralization of the Black Sea** and to agree to build no fortifications and to keep no navy in that sea.

1855–1881. ALEXANDER II (the Tsar Liberator), whose reign was distinguished by a number of fundamental reforms, of which the most important was the liquidation of the serf problem.

1858–1860. Advance of Russia in the Far East. By the **treaty of Aigun** (1858) China ceded to Russia the left bank of the Amur River, and by the **treaty of Peking,** the Ussuri region. **Foundation of Vladivostok** (1860).

1861, Mar. 3. The **EMANCIPATION EDICT,** liberating the serfs. The subject had been discussed for years by a special committee, which collected huge masses of material from provincial bodies. Temporary freedom of discussion in the press had also produced much information and difference of viewpoint. The landowners were, on the whole, ready to give the serfs freedom, but not ready to give up much of their land. At the other extreme were the radicals and socialists, who insisted that the land belonged to those who worked it. The final solution was a compromise imposed by the tsar.

Terms: All serfs were given **personal freedom,** together with **allotments of land** for which the owners were paid by the state in treasury bonds. The peasants in turn were to refund the treasury by installments **(redemption payments)** spread over a period of 49 years. The land was not given to individuals, but to the **village communes** (*mir*), which distributed it among the village members according to the size of the peasant family. To assure equality of treatment the land was to be redistributed every 10 or 12 years. The members of the commune were held jointly responsible for the redemption payments.

1863–1864. THE SECOND POLISH REVOLUTION. Attempts of Alexander to win the support of the Poles by a mild and liberal policy: the arrangements of 1815–1830 substantially restored in 1862. This policy met with support from the Polish moderates (**Marquis Alexander Wielopolski**), but was not enough to satisfy the extreme nationalists (*Reds*), who aimed at complete independence. After considerable disorder the government decided to draft the malcontents (especially students) into the army. This provoked the insurrection of January 1863, which spread rapidly to Lithuania and White Russia. The Poles having no army, most of the fighting was done by guerrilla bands. **Diplomatic intervention by Great Britain, France, and Austria** (similar but not identical protests of April, June, and August) produced a strong **nationalist reaction in Russia,** led by the former radical journalist, **Michael Katkov.** The Russian government was able to ignore the protests of the western powers because of the support and co-operation of the Prussian government (**Alvensleben convention,** February 8, 1863). But the insurrection was not finally suppressed until May 1864, and then with great severity. Polish autonomy was again abolished and Russian administration re-established; Russian language made obligatory in Polish schools; proceedings of the government against the Roman Catholic clergy; rupture of relations with the Vatican.

1864. ZEMSTVO LAW, one of the most important features of the great reforms. By the law a system of local self-government was organized: local boards (*zemstvos*), on which the nobility, the townsmen, and the peasants were represented (no one class to have a majority of the seats), were empowered to levy taxes for local economic and cultural requirements (roads, bridges, schools, hospitals, etc.).

1864. Reform of the judiciary: the old system of class courts was abolished and a new hierarchy of courts, on the French model, was set up, with thoroughly modernized procedure and jury trial for criminal offenses. **Justices of the peace** were provided to deal with minor civil suits, and the old **peasant courts** were retained for those who wished to use them.

1867. Cession of Alaska to the United States (p. 837). The Russian settlements in California had been abandoned in 1844 and the Russian government now sold Alaska itself to the American government.

1865-1876. Russian advance in central Asia. Conquest of the khanates of **Kokand, Bokhara, and Khiva,** followed by the annexation of the entire Transcaspian region in 1881. This forward policy created much friction between Russia and Britain, which was fearful for India.

1870. Reform of municipal government, the last of the great reform measures. The old patrician system was abolished and the towns were given self-government, under councils elected by the propertied classes.

1871, Mar. 13. Abrogation of the Black Sea clauses of the treaty of Paris. The Russian government had taken advantage of the Franco-German War (p. 736) to denounce its obligations. British protests led to the convocation of a **conference at London,** which accepted the fact, but reaffirmed the principle that international obligations cannot be abrogated without consent of all signatory powers.

1874. Army reform, introducing the principle of **universal military liability** in place of the former system of taking recruits only from among the lower classes.

1875. Cession of the Kurile Islands to Japan, in exchange for the southern part of the island of **Sakhalin.**

1875-1878. The NEAR EASTERN CRISIS, the Russian-Turkish War, and the **treaties of San Stefano** and **Berlin** (p. 780 *f.*). As a result of the war the Russians received **Bessarabia** (which had been lost in 1856), **Kars,** and **Batum.**

Growth of opposition to the tsarist régime, due to the incompleteness of the government reforms. The liberal elements demanded a constitution, while the radicals and socialists aimed at the complete overturn of the social order and a resettlement of the land question. The radicals soon became avowedly revolutionary. Under the leadership of **Herzen, Bakunin, Peter Lavrov,** and **Nicholas Chernyshevsky** they organized

1876. A **secret society** under the name *Land and Liberty.* This became the spearhead of the so-called **Populist movement** (the *Going among the People*). The movement met with a qualified reception from the suspicious peasants and was soon persecuted by the police.

Meanwhile the unsatisfactory outcome of the war with Turkey broadened the base of popular discontent. The liberals were further estranged by the grant of a constitution to the Bulgarians, while the adherents of the new **Panslav movement** (foundation of the *Slavonic Welfare Society* at Moscow 1857; Panslav congress at Moscow, 1867) became extremely critical of the government for failure to complete the work of liberating the Balkan Slavs. After 1878, therefore, the revolutionary movement secured more popular support.

1879. Organization of the society *Will of the People,* composed of the most radical wing of the older Populist group. The new society was out-and-out terrorist and carefully planned attempts on the lives of prominent officials, finally of the tsar himself.

1880. Appointment of General Michael Loris-Melikov as minister of the interior. After two abortive attempts to assassinate him, the tsar had decided on a policy of concessions, accompanied, however, with ever more stringent police measures against the terrorists. Loris-Melikov propounded a scheme for summoning representatives of the zemstvos to co-operate with the council of state in the discussion of new laws. This compromise plan was approved by Alexander on

1881, Mar. 13. But on the very same day he fell a victim to the bombs of the terrorists.

1881-1894. ALEXANDER III. He was determined to suppress the revolutionary movement and throughout his reign followed the advice of his former teacher and close friend, **Constantine Pobiedonostsev,** who was made procurator of the Holy Synod. After some debate, Loris-Melikov's plan was dropped and the **autocratic system reaffirmed.** Drastic repression of revolutionary activity and silencing of all liberal opposition. Curtailment of the reforms of the preceding reign and restoration of the pre-eminence of the nobility. **Persecution of religious dissenters,** Roman Catholics, Protestants, and especially Jews (beginning of the pogroms in the Ukraine). **Discrimination against national minorities** and attempts at Russification in the border provinces.

1881, June 18. Conclusion of the **Alliance of the Three Emperors** between Germany, Russia, and Austria (p. 782). This was renewed in 1884, but in 1887 was replaced by a separate pact between Russia and Germany (the **Reinsurance treaty,** p. 785). For the rest, Russian policy was concerned primarily with Balkan affairs, and more particularly with the abortive effort to maintain a predominant position in Bulgarian affairs (p. 764).

1884-1887. Continued advance in central Asia (conquest of Merv, 1884) brought the Russians to the frontier of Afghanistan, where a clash of Russian and Afghan troops in 1885 brought Russia to the very verge of war with Great Britain (pp. 666, 783). The matter was finally disposed of by agreement on a Russian-Afghan frontier.

BEGINNING OF THE INDUSTRIALIZATION OF RUSSIA. The government inaugurated a high protective tariff and began to give extensive support to native industry. The rapid expansion of railroads and the opening of the coal and iron fields of southern Russia served as an important stimulus. The guiding spirit in the whole process was **Sergei Witte,** first minister of communications and later minister of finance. Heavy borrowing abroad, especially in France, in the hope that the increased productive power of Russia would make repayment easy. But the growth of industry involved also the emergence of an **industrial proletariat,** living in misery and most inadequately protected by the first factory laws (1882-1886). Unrest in the cities was accompanied by growing disorder in the country, where the plight of the peasants was such (**great famine** of 1891-1892) that the government was obliged to abolish the poll-tax and reduce the redemption payments.

1891-1894. Conclusion of the **Franco-Russian Alliance,** which was to become one of the main features of pre-war international relations (p. 786).

1894-1917. NICHOLAS II, an intelligent but weak-willed ruler, deeply devoted to the memory and to the system of his father. During the first decade of his reign the reaction continued unabated and at the same time the policy of economic development was maintained (**introduction of the gold standard** by

Witte in 1897). Liberal tendencies of the zemstvos were vigorously combated and the policy of Russification was extended to Finland, thitherto practically autonomous. But as time went on it became more and more difficult for the government to uphold the policy of Alexander III. Opposition revived in various forms:

1898. Formation of the **Social Democratic Party** among the industrial workers. Marxism had been introduced into Russia by **George Plekhanov,** whose fairly moderate program was, however, soon to be challenged by the more radical wing under the leadership of **Lenin** (Vladimir I. Ulianov). Lenin was the son of a school inspector and the brother of a prominent terrorist who was executed in 1887 for plotting against the life of the tsar. Lenin himself spent several years in exile in Siberia, but after his escape became one of the most energetic and uncompromising champions of the worker. The socialists were obliged to operate from abroad (especially from Switzerland). **Split in the Social Democratic Party** (1903) at the party congress in London: *Mensheviks* (moderates) and *Bolsheviks* (extremists).

1901. Organization of the **Social Revolutionary Party,** which took its inspiration from the earlier Populist movement. This party, to which many of the students adhered, was concerned chiefly with the peasant problem and advocated the nationalization of the land. Its methods were those of **terrorism** and the years following its birth were marked by an increasing number of assassinations.

1903. Formation of the **Union of Liberation,** the third of the opposition parties and at the time the most important. This group consisted largely of intellectuals, members of the liberal professions, and zemstvo workers. Its program called for a liberal constitution.

The development of popular opposition to the government was greatly facilitated by the outbreak and course of the

1904-1905. RUSSIAN-JAPANESE WAR. This was the direct result of the Russian forward policy in the Far East: construction of the **Trans-Siberian Railway** (1891-1903); intervention after the **Sino-Japanese War** (1895); **treaty with China** (1896) and penetration of northern **Manchuria;** interference in **Korea;** lease of **Port Arthur** (1898); occupation of **Manchuria** after the Boxer Insurrection (1900-1903); activity of Russian interests in **northern Korea,** etc. (see pp. 793 f., 922). Repeated efforts of the Japanese to reach an agreement were treated with disdain by the Russians, so that long-drawn negotiations ended in the outbreak of hostilities (Feb. 8, 1904). The Russians were consistently defeated (**battles of Liaoyang,** August; **Sha-ho,** October; **fall of Port**

Arthur, January 1905; **battle of Mukden,** February 23–March 10; **naval disaster at Tsushima,** May 27). The government was wholly discredited and popular pressure became ever greater.

1904, July 28. Assassination of Viacheslav Plehve, the ruthless but able minister of the interior. This event induced the government to attempt a policy of conciliation, represented by **Prince Sviatopolk-Mirsky,** but it proved to be too late for halfway measures and the relaxation of repression only gave the opposition better opportunities for organization and expression.

Nov. A great **zemstvo congress** met at St. Petersburg and demanded the convocation of a representative assembly and the granting of civil liberties. Similar demands were advanced by numerous other groups and by the professional classes.

1905, Jan. 22. Bloody Sunday, marked by the first bloodshed and by the emergence of the workers as a factor in the movement. A procession of workers, led by **Father Gapon,** while proceeding to the palace to lay its demands before the tsar, was fired on by the troops: 70 killed and 240 wounded. Growing indignation and unrest; epidemic of strikes.

Mar. 3. The tsar announced his intention to convoke a **"consultative" assembly.** Further concessions: edict of religious toleration, permission to use the Polish language in Polish schools, relief for the Jews, cancellation of part of the redemption payments.

May 8. Organization of the **Union of Unions,** under the chairmanship of **Professor Paul Miliukov.** This brought together all the liberal groups in a renewed demand for parliamentary government and the institution of universal suffrage.

June-Aug. Increasing unrest and disorder throughout the country: strikes, agrarian outbreaks, national movements in the border provinces, mutinies in the army and navy (*Potemkin* episode). Yielding to the popular pressure,

Aug. 19. The tsar published a **manifesto creating the imperial duma,** or assembly, to be elected by a limited franchise and with deliberative powers only. This concession was far too modest to meet the popular demand and the revolutionary movement became ever more widely spread until it culminated in the

Oct. 20-30. The **GREAT GENERAL STRIKE,** a spontaneous movement in which the whole country joined.

Oct. 26. The St. Petersburg workers formed the **first soviet** (council) to direct the strike. This was essentially a moderate socialist organization and had relatively little influence on the course of events. The strike soon paralyzed the government and forced the tsar to yield. Pobiedonostsev and other reactionary ministers were obliged to resign, and Nicholas, advised by Witte (who had been disgraced in 1903, but had been restored to favor after the conclusion of the **treaty of Portsmouth** with Japan), issued the

Oct. 30. OCTOBER MANIFESTO, granting Russia a constitution: the projected duma was to have real legislative power, the franchise was to be greatly extended, civil liberties were guaranteed, etc. **Witte was appointed prime minister.**

The manifesto satisfied all the more moderate liberal groups, but appeared inadequate to those who had called for a constituent assembly. The immediate effect of the government's capitulation was, therefore, to split the liberal group; the moderates became known as the **Octobrist Party,** while the progressives took the name **Constitutional Democratic Party** (abbreviated to K.D. = *Cadet*). The Social Democrats rejected the whole program of the government and the St. Petersburg soviet (with branches opened in many cities) attempted several times to organize another strike. The sole effect of this policy was to drive more of the liberals into the government ranks. At the same time Witte made every effort to bring back the troops from the Far East. When he felt sufficiently strong,

Dec. 16. The members of the St. Petersburg soviet (about 190) were arrested. This move led to

Dec. 22.-Jan. 1. INSURRECTION OF THE WORKERS IN MOSCOW. Severe street fighting, and much bloodshed. But the troops remained loyal to the government and the uprising was finally suppressed. Vigorous action by the army during the winter to restore order in the provinces (**Black Hundreds**—punitive raids, etc.). Meanwhile Witte arranged to float a huge loan ($400,000,000) in France and Britain, so that, when the duma met, the government might not be dependent on the representatives of the people for funds.

1906, May 2. Dismissal of Witte, who was never popular with Nicholas and who was no longer needed. In his place the tsar appointed **Ivan Goremykin,** a conservative bureaucrat of the old school.

May 6. Promulgation of the **Fundamental Laws,** issued on the very eve of the meeting of the duma. These extensive regulations decided in advance many of the questions left open by the October Manifesto. The tsar was proclaimed autocrat, and retained complete control over the executive, the armed forces, and foreign policy. Changes in the fundamental laws could be made only with his consent. The legislative power was to be divided between the duma and an upper chamber, the imperial council, half the members of which were to be appointed by the tsar, the other half to be elected by various privileged bodies throughout the country. The government reserved the right to legislate by decree when the duma was not in session. The budgetary powers of the duma were closely restricted.

May 10. Meeting of the **FIRST DUMA,** elected by what amounted to universal suffrage. But the radical parties had, for the most part, boycotted the elections and the Cadets formed the largest party. Profoundly disappointed by the fundamental laws, the Cadets criticized the government violently and this first representative assembly ended in a deadlock.

July 21. Dissolution of the first duma. The Cadet leaders adjourned to Viborg and issued the **Viborg manifesto,** calling upon the country to refuse taxes. The manifesto found but little response in the country, where the revolution was already a thing of the past.

Nov. Agrarian reform act of Peter Stolypin, who had become prime minister in June. Though a conservative, Stolypin was far from being a reactionary. He was eager to maintain the constitutional system, and hoped gradually to wean the country from revolutionary sentiment by well-planned reforms. The Agrarian Law put an end to the communal (*mir*) system of landholding and enabled each peasant to withdraw from the commune at will, receiving his own share of the land in private ownership. Any commune was able to end the old system by majority vote. This law was later approved by the third duma.

1907, Mar. 5–June 16. The **SECOND DUMA,** more radical than the first because of the active part taken in the elections by the revolutionary parties. The Cadets were now anxious to co-operate with the government to save the constitutional system (though they refused Stolypin's invitation to some of the leaders to join the ministry). But these efforts were frustrated by the radicals. The reactionary groups at court, constantly pressing for a return to the simple autocratic system, finally forced the dissolution of the duma and

June 16. The promulgation of a **new electoral law,** which greatly increased the representation of the propertied classes to the detriment of peasants and workers. At the same time it reduced the representation of the national minorities.

1907–1912. The **THIRD DUMA,** elected on the new basis, returned a conservative majority. Stern suppression of all revolutionary outbreaks and disorders (*Union of True Rus-*

sian Men; League of the Russian Nobility: drumhead courts-martial, etc.). At the same time Stolypin, with co-operation of the duma, continued his **reform activities:** social insurance, zemstvo reform, education, police reorganization, land banks, encouragement of emigration to Siberia, etc. With the restoration of order came the resumption of economic expansion, industrialization, etc.

1907, Aug. 31.   Conclusion of the Anglo-Russian entente (p. 797), an important milestone in Russian foreign policy, which definitely aligned Russia with Britain and France against the Central Powers.

1908–1909.   Tension between Russia and Austria over the annexation of Bosnia and Herzegovina (p. 798). Marked **revival of Panslav or Neoslav agitation.**

1911, Sept. 14.   Stolypin was assassinated by a revolutionary, at Kiev. He was succeeded by **Vladimir Kokovtsev,** an able financier and a statesman of moderate type, lacking, however, the prestige and will power of his predecessor.

1912–1916. The **FOURTH DUMA,** similar to the third in character and purpose. This period was taken up largely with major questions of foreign policy, notably by the crisis of the

1912–1913.   Balkan Wars (p. 801 *f.*), in which Russia played a very prominent rôle.

Meanwhile the reforms inaugurated by the government proved insufficient to quiet the political and social unrest. The national minorities, too, were antagonized by the policy of the government (especially in Poland and Finland). On the eve of the First World War there was growing dissatisfaction, which spread even to more moderate circles. The latter were irritated particularly by the state of affairs at court, where the tsarina, a deeply religious person, had become the center of a group of mystics and magic healers, originally called in to cure the only son of the imperial couple of an incurable disease. Of this group **Gregory Rasputin** was the most remarkable and powerful, and he was to play a most important rôle in the history of Russia during the war.

1914, Aug. 1.   GERMANY DECLARED WAR ON RUSSIA. For the details of the July crisis and Russia's policy in international affairs see p. 803 *f.*   (*Cont. pp. 947, 1028.*)

RUSSIAN CULTURE

The realistic novel reached its height in the middle of the 19th century: **Nikolai Gogol** (1809–1852; *Revizor* [*The Inspector-General*], a comedy, 1835; *Mertriye Dushi* [*Dead Souls*], 1842); **Ivan Goncharov** (1812–1891); **Ivan Tur-**

genev (1818-1883; *Otzi i Deti* [*Fathers and Sons*], 1862); **Fyodor Dostoevsky** (1821-1881; *Prestuplenie i Nakazaniye* [*Crime and Punishment*], 1866; *Bratja Karamazovy* [*The Brothers Karamazov*], 1879-1880); **Leo Tolstoy** (1828-1910; *Voina i Mir* [*War and Peace*], 1869; *Anna Karenina*, 1875-1877; *Vosbreseniye* [*Resurrection*], 1899-1900); **Dmitri Merezhkovsky** (1865-1941); **Maxim Gorki** (1868-1936; also plays, short stories); **Feodor Sologub** (1863-1927; *Melki Bes* [*The Little Demon*]).

Drama: Alexander Ostrovsky (1823-1886); **Anton Chekhov** (1860-1904; also short stories).

Poetry: Theodore Tyutchev (1803-1873); **Nikolai Nekrasov** (1821-1877); **Vladimir Soloviev** (1853-1900); **Alexander Blok** (1880-1921).

Russian music likewise reached its peak, especially in opera and orchestral compositions: **Mikhail Glinka** (1803-1857), **Alexander Borodin** (1834-1887), **Modest Moussorgsky** (1839-1881),

Peter Ilyich Tchaikovsky (1840-1893), and **Nicolai Rimsky-Korsakov** (1844-1908).

POLISH CULTURE

Literature: The leader of the Romantic movement was **Adam Mickiewicz** (1798-1855; epics *Konrad Wallenrod*, 1828; *Pan Tadeusz*, 1834). Other Romantic poets and dramatists: **Count Alexander Fredro** (1793-1876; comedies), **Juljusz Slowacki** (1809-1849), **Zygmunt Krasinski** (1812-1859). Later novels by **Joseph Ignatius Kraszewski** (1812-1887) and **Zygmunt Kaczkowski** (1826-1896); *Quo Vadis* by **Henryk Sienkiewicz** (1846-1916); historical writings by **Joachim Lelewel** (1786-1861) and **Jozef Szujski** (1835-1883; *Dzieje Polski* [*History of Poland*]).

Painting: Jan Matejko (1839-1895); **Stanislaw Wyspianski** (1869-1907), better known as a dramatist and art editor of *Zycie*.

E. THE BALKANS AND THE NEAR EAST, 1762-1916

1. THE BALKAN STATES

(*See p. 769*)

a. GREECE, 1821-1914

1821-1831.   Greek War of Independence (p. 769).

1832-1862.   OTTO I, king. Otto was a Bavarian prince, 17 years of age. During the first three years the country was governed by a regency of three Bavarian advisers, which attempted to establish a centralized, bureaucratic system, wholly unsuited to the conditions of the country. The entire reign was marked by unpopularity, internal dissension, continued brigandage, and economic want.

1843, Sept. 14.   Popular rising in favor of a constitution. Otto yielded and agreed to a fundamental law establishing a bicameral parliamentary régime. This, however, worked but little better than the preceding system.

1850, Jan.-Mar.   British blockade arising out of friction over the unsatisfied claims of British subjects (**Don Pacifico affair,** p. 662).

1854, Jan.-Feb.   Greek bands invaded Thessaly and **Epirus,** to take advantage of the war of Russia against Turkey (p. 773). Relations between Greece and Turkey were severed (Mar. 28), but the Greeks were prevented from making war by the **occupation of the Piraeus** by the British and French (this lasted until February 1857).

1862, Feb. 13.   A military revolt was successful.

Otto deposed (Oct. 23); he left the country (Oct. 27).

1863, Feb. 3.   The Greek assembly proclaimed Prince Alfred of Great Britain king, after a plebiscite. The election was rejected by the British government.

1863-1913.   GEORGE I, a Danish prince (17 years old), who was finally chosen with the consent of the powers.

1864, June 5.   Britain turned over to Greece the **Ionian Islands** (under British protectorate since 1815).

Nov. 28. A new **democratic constitution** was introduced, providing for manhood suffrage and a single-chamber parliament (*Boulé*).

1866-1868.   Cretan revolt; excitement in Greece; rupture of relations with Turkey (December 1868; resumed February 1869).

1878, Jan. 28.   Rising in Thessaly, part of the general upheaval in the Balkans resulting from the war of Russia against Turkey (p. 780). The Greek government declared war on Turkey (Feb. 2), but was constrained by the powers from larger hostilities.

1881, July 2. By a convention with Turkey the Greeks finally acquired **Thessaly** and part of **Epirus,** promised them at the congress of Berlin (p. 780).

1886, Apr. 26.   Ultimatum of the powers to Greece, to prevent Greek action in harmony with the revolution in Eastern Roumelia (p. 784). The Greeks refused to disarm, whereupon **the powers blockaded Greece** (May 10–June 7), forcing compliance.

1893, Aug. 6. Opening of the **canal of Corinth.**

1896, Apr. Revival of the **Olympic Games.**

1896–1897. Cretan Insurrection. Intervention of Greece (Feb. 1896) and resultant **war with Turkey** (Apr. 17, 1897). The Greeks were utterly defeated, but were saved by the powers from the fruits of their folly (p. 789).

1898, Feb. International commission set up to control Greek finance, after the Greek government had defaulted on its obligations.

Nov. Forced evacuation of Crete by Turkish troops, after attacks on British forces. Contingents of Britain, France, Russia, and Italy remained in occupation of the island.

Nov. 26. Prince George of Greece named **high commissioner for Crete.**

1905, Mar. 30. Insurrection in Crete, after the powers had repeatedly rejected appeals for union with Greece. The assembly (leadership of **Eleutherios Venizelos**) decreed union, but the powers, despite attacks upon their troops, remained adamant.

1906, Sept. 25. Prince George resigned as high commissioner for Crete, and was succeeded by **Alexander Zaimis.**

1908, Oct. 7. The **Cretans proclaimed union with Greece,** following the annexation of Bosnia and Herzegovina and the declaration of Bulgarian independence (p. 798).

1909, July. Britain, France, Russia, and Italy withdrew their forces from Crete.

1910, Jan. The **Military League,** an association of officers, forced the Greek assembly to agree to revision of the constitution. Thereupon the league voluntarily dissolved itself (Mar.).

Oct. 18. Venizelos became prime minister. He at once undertook the work of military and financial reform.

1911, June 11. Completion of the revision of the constitution.

1912, May 29. Treaty of alliance with Bulgaria (p. 801).

Oct. 14. Cretan representatives were finally admitted to the Greek assembly.

Oct. 17. THE FIRST BALKAN WAR (p. 801).

1913, Mar. 18. Assassination of King George.

1913–1917. CONSTANTINE I, king.

June. SECOND BALKAN WAR (p. 802).

Dec. 10. Crete officially taken over by Greece.

1914. Crisis arising from Greek claims in **southern Albania** and from the question of the **Aegean Islands** (p. 802).

July–Aug. Outbreak of the First World War. Constantine rejected appeals from Germany to join in the conflict.

Sept. 7. Resignation of Venizelos (p. 954), marking the beginning of the crisis of Greek neutrality in the war.

(*Cont. pp. 953 f., 1024.*)

b. SERBIA, 1804–1914

(*See p. 767*)

1804–1813. First Serbian insurrection, under **Kara George** (p. 767).

1815–1817. Second Serbian insurrection, under **Milosh Obrenovich** (p. 769).

1817. Milosh recognized by the sultan as **prince of Serbia** (the pashalik of Belgrade), which was given a measure of self-government. Cautious policy of Milosh, who, through bribery, gradually secured larger powers from the Porte. During the Greek War, he managed to play a canny game between Russia and Turkey.

1829. The treaty of Adrianople guaranteed the **autonomy of Serbia,** religious liberty, etc.

1830. The sultan recognized **Milosh as hereditary prince,** added some territory to his jurisdiction, obliged the Turkish landlords to sell their holdings, and confined the Turkish troops to a few garrison towns.

1835. Opposition of the notables to Milosh's autocratic and oppressive rule (use of bastinado on his opponents, appropriation of forests, control of the pork business, etc.) forced Milosh to grant a **constitution** providing for a senate of elders with legislative, executive, and judicial powers, and a popular assembly (*Skupshtina*) with control of the budget.

1838. The sultan, supported by Russia, forced the **abrogation of the constitution** and the appointment of a senate of notables with almost complete power.

1839, June 13. Milosh abdicated, in protest against the oligarchic system.

1839. Milan, son of Milosh. He died after a rule of only a few weeks.

1839–1842. MICHAEL, another son of Milosh, only 17 years old. His short rule was marked by constant intriguing on the part of the Karageorgevich faction (*Defenders of the Constitution*) who demanded the convocation of the Skupshtina. Michael was finally forced to flee.

1842–1858. ALEXANDER KARAGEORGEVICH, elected by the Skupshtina. Loud protests of Russia, which forced the banishment of the popular leaders. Alexander's reign was the quietest in Serbian history, marked by a cautious foreign policy, spread of Western influence, growth of trade (especially with Austria), and development of education (**Academy of Sciences,** 1841; **University of Belgrade,** 1844). Politically it was a period of factional trouble

The BALKANS
1878~1914

Area of Turkey in Europe before Treaty of Berlin, 1878

Area of Turkey in Europe before the Balkan Wars 1912~1913

Boundaries before the Balkan Wars

Boundaries after the Balkan Wars

Dniester R.

BESSARABIA

Prut R.

MOLDAVIA

Drave R.

Save R.

BANAT

ROUMANIA

Bucharest

Belgrade

BOSNIA
Occupied by Austria
1878; Annexed, 1908

Sarajevo

SERBIA

Danube R.

Area Ceded
by Bulgaria
to Roumania
1913

HERZEGOVINA

BULGARIA

DALMATIA
(AUS.)

MONTE-
NEGRO

Sofia

Black Sea

Scutari

Adrianople

Constantinople

Bosporus

Albania created
from former Turkish
territory
1913

MACEDONIA

Vardar R.

THRACE

ITALY

ALBANIA

Saloniki

Sea of
Marmora

Dardanelles

Smyrna

THESSALY

to GREECE
1881

Aegean
Sea

IONIAN ISLANDS

GREECE

Athens

MOREA

DODECANESE
to ITALY
1912

RHODES

Mediterranean
Sea

to GREECE
1913

CRETE

Kings of Greece: Danish Line (1863–   )

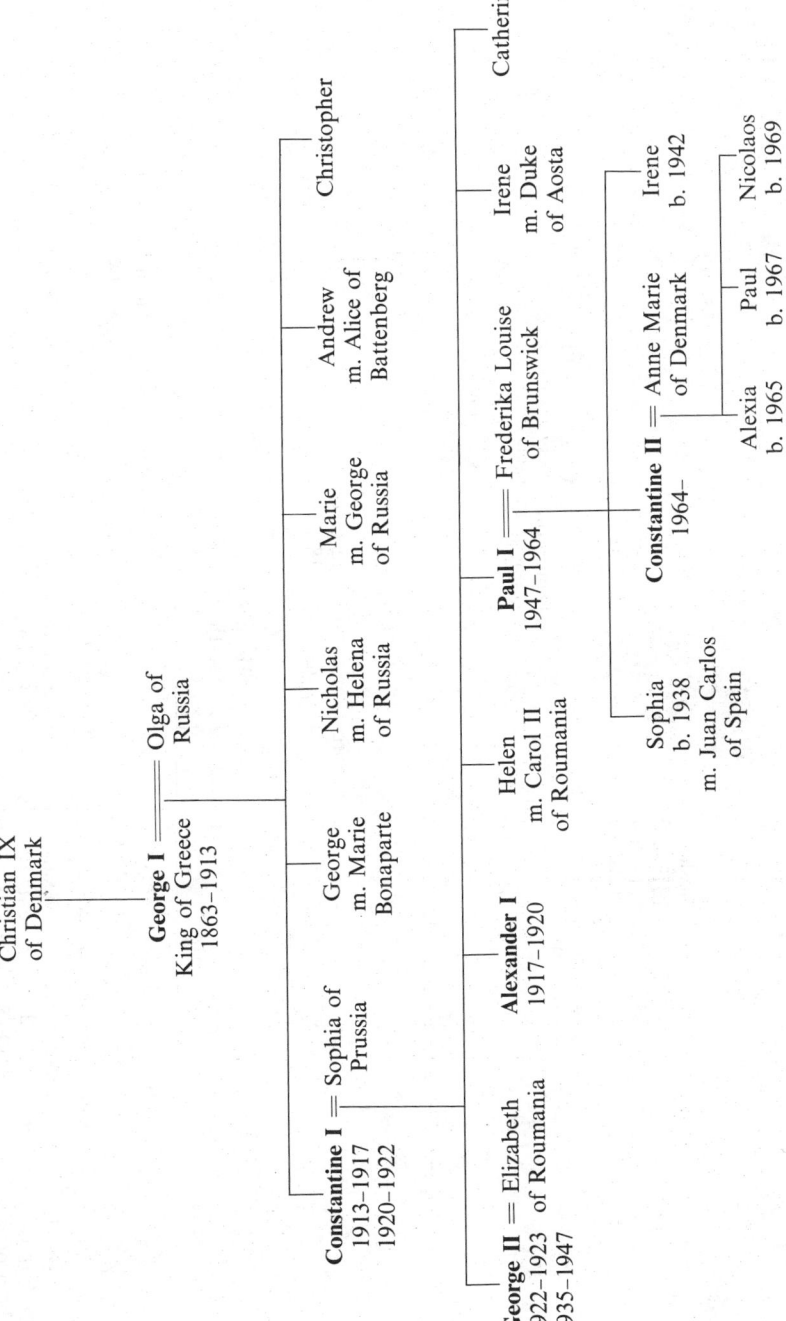

Christian IX
of Denmark

George I = Olga of
King of Greece   Russia
1863–1913

Constantine I = Sophia of
1913–1917   Prussia
1920–1922

George
m. Marie
Bonaparte

Nicholas
m. Helena
of Russia

Marie
m. George
of Russia

Andrew
m. Alice of
Battenberg

Christopher

George II = Elizabeth
1922–1923   of Roumania
1935–1947

Alexander I
1917–1920

Helen
m. Carol II
of Roumania

Paul I = Frederika Louise
1947–1964   of Brunswick

Irene
m. Duke
of Aosta

Catherine

Sophia
b. 1938
m. Juan Carlos
of Spain

Constantine II = Anne Marie
1964–   of Denmark

Irene
b. 1942

Alexia
b. 1965

Paul
b. 1967

Nicolaos
b. 1969

Rulers of Serbia (Yugoslavia, 1804–1945)

(1) *OBRENOVICH FAMILY*

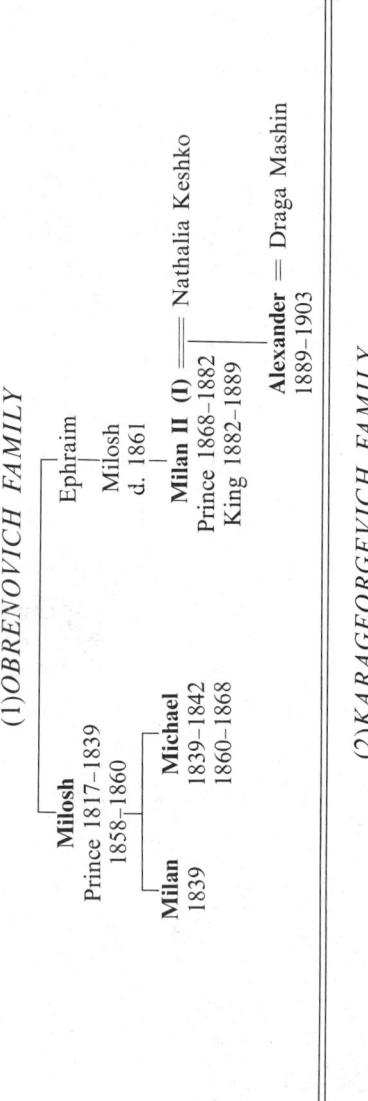

Milosh
Prince 1817–1839
1858–1860

Ephraim

Michael
1839–1842
1860–1868

Milosh
d. 1861

Milan
1839

Milan II (I)
Prince 1868–1882
King 1882–1889 ═ Nathalia Keshko

Alexander ═ Draga Mashin
1889–1903

(2) *KARAGEORGEVICH FAMILY*

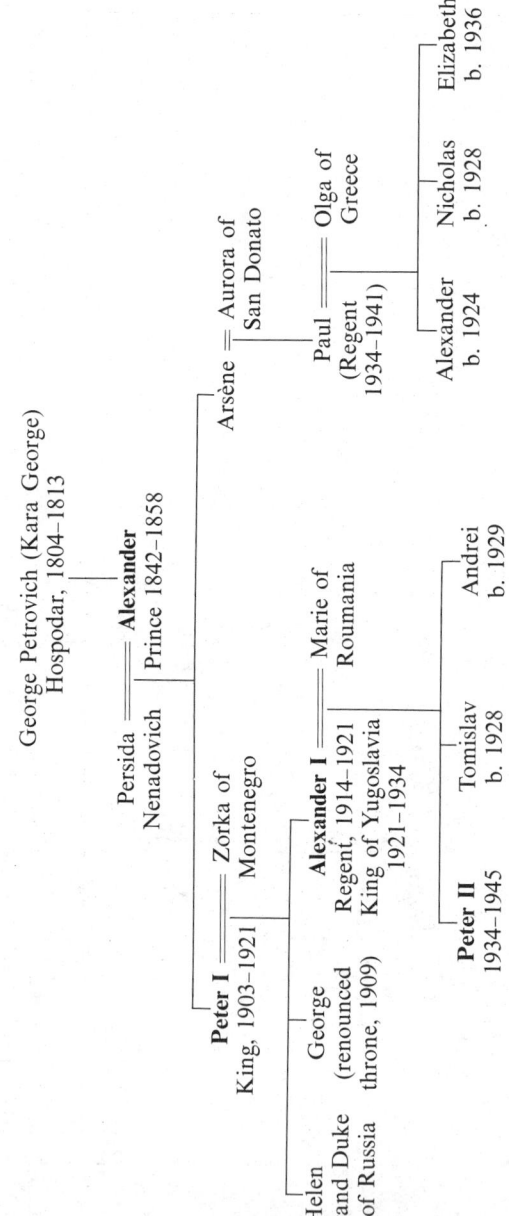

George Petrovich (Kara George)
Hospodar, 1804–1813

Persida ═ **Alexander**
Nenadovich   Prince 1842–1858

Peter I ═ Zorka of
King, 1903–1921   Montenegro

Arsène ═ Aurora of
San Donato

George
(renounced
throne, 1909)

Alexander I ═ Marie of
Regent, 1914–1921   Roumania
King of Yugoslavia
1921–1934

Paul ═ Olga of
(Regent   Greece
1934–1941)

Helen
m. Grand Duke
Ivan of Russia

Peter II
1934–1945

Tomislav
b. 1928

Andrei
b. 1929

Alexander
b. 1924

Nicholas
b. 1928

Elizabeth
b. 1936

and corruption, the senate being in complete control.

1856. By the **treaty of Paris** (p. 774), Serbia was placed under the **collective guaranty of the powers.**

1858, Dec. 23. Alexander forced to abdicate by an opposition faction, supported by the Obrenovichs and by Turkey and Russia.

1858–1860. Restoration of Milosh Obrenovich, now 79 years old. He died after wreaking vengeance on his enemies.

1860–1868. MICHAEL, son of Milosh, reascended the throne. He was a well-educated and intelligent prince, whose great aim was to unite the Balkans in a crusade against the Turks. Introduction of compulsory service in the army and gradual development of an efficient administration.

1862, June 15. Bombardment of Belgrade by Turkish troops, after clashes between the garrison and the populace. Michael appealed to the powers and the sultan was induced to concentrate his forces in three or four places.

1866. Michael appealed again for the **withdrawal of Turkish troops.** The powers induced the sultan to yield, and the last troops left Serbian territory in April 1867.

1866, Sept. 23. Secret offensive and defensive **alliance between Serbia and Montenegro.**

1867, May 26. Secret Serbian-Roumanian treaty, with the object of securing independence.

Aug. 26. Secret treaty between Serbia and Greece (treaty of Voeslau): Serbia was to get Bosnia and Herzegovina, Greece Thessaly and Epirus. Action was to be taken against Turkey in 1868. A **Balkan confederation** was envisaged as the ultimate goal. Michael organized a far-reaching propaganda in Bosnia and Macedonia, and established close contact with the Bulgarian revolutionary leaders. Widespread nationalist agitation (**United Serbian Youth** or *Omladina,* founded 1867).

1868, June 10. Michael assassinated by conspirators aiming at the restoration of Alexander Karageorgevich. But Michael's chief adviser, **Iliya Garashanin,** anticipated them, roused the garrison, and had the assassins arrested.

1868–1889. MILAN, cousin of Michael, appointed prince, with a regency, which undertook the **revision of the constitution** (1869) in a liberal sense, to meet the growing demands of the nationalist organizations.

1876, July. Declaration of **war on Turkey,** following the insurrection in Bosnia and Herzegovina. Rampant nationalism of the government (**Jovan Ristich**) and of the country. Complete **defeat of the Serbs** (p. 779).

1878, July 13. The **TREATY OF BERLIN**

made Serbia completely independent, but Serbia received but slight increase of territory and the coveted provinces of Bosnia and Herzegovina were occupied by Austria (p. 780).

1881, June 28. Secret treaty with Austria, giving the latter practically a protectorate over Serbia (p. 782).

1882, Mar. 6. Milan proclaimed himself king, with Austrian support.

1883, Nov. Serious revolt against the government by the newly formed **Radical party (Nicholas Pashich,** leader), a violently nationalist group.

1885, Nov. 13. War with Bulgaria, after the union of Eastern Roumelia. The Serbs completely defeated at **Slivnitza** (Nov. 17), but saved from invasion by the intervention of Austria (p. 783).

1888, Aug. Milan divorced his Russian wife, **Nathalia,** who left the country. Growing split between the Austrian party and the pro-Russian, nationalist factions.

Dec. 16. The Radicals won a victory in the elections.

1889, Jan. 3. Despite warnings from Milan, the assembly passed a **revision of the constitution** in a liberal sense.

Mar. 6. Abdication of Milan.

1889–1903. ALEXANDER I, son of Milan, 13 years old at the time of his accession. A regency under Ristich was established.

1893, Apr. 14. *Coup d'état* of Alexander, who abolished the regency.

1894, May 21. Restoration of the constitution of 1869.

1899, Aug. 5. Alexander married Draga Mashin, a lady of questionable position. This and his ruthless persecution of the Radicals led to increased opposition to him.

1901, Feb. 11. Death of Milan, who had spent the last ten years of his life intriguing behind the throne and further discrediting the rule of his house.

1903, June 10. Alexander, Draga, and some twenty members of the court, **murdered** by a group of conspirators, mostly military men.

June 15. The **assembly elected Peter Karageorgevich** to the throne, and restored the constitution of 1889.

1903–1921. PETER I, a well-intentioned ruler who was, however, wholly at the mercy of the conspirators.

1904, Dec. 10–1905, May 22. First ministry of Nicholas Pashich. Serbian policy became outspokenly nationalist and anti-Austrian.

1905–1907. "Pig War" with Austria, a tariff conflict which did much to embitter relations.

1906, May 1–1908, July 6. Second ministry of Pashich.

1908–1909. Bosnian annexation crisis (p. 798).

Acute danger of war between Serbia and Austria. Serbia was obliged to back down, but the crisis left a legacy of hate. Foundation of propagandist societies (*Narodna Odbrana*, 1908; *Union or Death* [Black Hand], 1911).

1912, Mar. 13. **Treaty of alliance with Bulgaria** (p. 800).

Sept. 12. **Pashich** again premier.

Oct. 18. Outbreak of the **First Balkan War** (p. 801).

1913, June 1. Offensive and defensive **treaty of alliance with Greece,** concluded for ten years (p. 802).

June 29. Outbreak of the **Second Balkan War** (p. 802).

1914, June 24. **Prince Alexander,** heir to the throne, proclaimed regent for the deranged king.

June 28. **Assassination of the Archduke Francis Ferdinand** at Sarajevo.

July 28. **Declaration of war on Serbia** by Austria-Hungary (p. 805).

(*Cont. pp. 947 f., 1021.*)

c. MONTENEGRO, 1782-1914

1782-1830. **PETER I,** vladika (i.e. *prince-bishop*). He was a regular ally of Russia in the wars against the Turks.

1799. Selim III recognized the complete **independence of Montenegro.**

1830-1851. **PETER II,** national poet of the Southern Slavs.

1851-1860. **DANILO I.** He abolished the office of prince-bishop and established himself as a secular ruler. His efforts to reform and modernize the state led to opposition which ended in **Danilo's murder** (Aug. 12, 1860).

1852-1853. One of the numerous clashes between the Montenegrins and the Turks threatened to lead to disaster for the former when **Omar Pasha** invaded the little state. The Turks were obliged to withdraw (Feb. 1853) under threats from Austria **(Leiningen mission).**

1860-1918. **NICHOLAS I,** who, during his long reign, effected many military, administrative, and educational reforms and modernized the state. Montenegro definitely assumed a position among the lesser European powers.

1861. Following a **revolt in Herzegovina,** supported by the Montenegrins, the country was again invaded by Omar Pasha, who forced the **recognition of Turkish supremacy.**

1876, July 2. **War against Turkey,** resulting from the great insurrection in Bosnia and Herzegovina. Successes of the Montenegrins (p. 779).

1878, July 13. **TREATY OF BERLIN,** recognizing the **complete independence of Montenegro,** which received some increase of territory.

1905, Dec. 19. Nicholas finally granted a **constitution,** with an assembly elected by universal suffrage. Since the advent of the Karageorgevich dynasty in Serbia (1903) there was growing rivalry for leadership of the Southern Slavs, resulting in conspiracy against the life of Nicholas.

1910, Aug. 28. **NICHOLAS** proclaimed himself king.

1912, Oct. 18. **First Balkan War.** Montenegro, though not bound to the other states by formal alliance, was the first power to declare war (p. 801).

1913, Apr. 10. **Blockade of the Montenegrin coast** by the powers, to raise the **siege of Scutari.** Nicholas took Scutari (Apr. 22), but was forced by Austrian threats to evacuate it (May 5).

1914, Aug. 5. **Montenegro** declared war on Austria. (*Cont. pp. 973, 1021.*)

d. BULGARIA, 1762-1915

1762. The monk **Paisi** wrote his *History of the Bulgarian People,* generally taken to mark the beginning of the Bulgarian national renaissance.

1840. **Translation of the Bible** into Bulgarian by the monk **Neophytos,** aided by the American missionary, **Elias Riggs.**

1858. Opening of the first **American mission** (1861, **Samokov Seminary** founded by **James F. Clarke).** Rapid growth of Bulgarian national movement, with revolutionary committees at Bucharest and Odessa. Connection of the revolutionaries (**George Rakovski** and **Christo Botev)** with Prince Michael of Serbia.

1870. Establishment of the **Bulgarian exarchate,** a national branch of the Greek Orthodox Church. The exarch was given jurisdiction over large parts of Macedonia and Thrace, as well as Bulgaria.

1875, Sept. **Abortive rising** of the Bulgarians against Turkish rule.

1876, Apr.-Aug. **Great insurrection in Bulgaria,** put down by Turkish irregulars (*Bulgarian Horrors*).

1878, Mar. 3. **TREATY OF SAN STEFANO,** with provision for a large Bulgarian state to include most of Macedonia (p. 780).

July 13. **TREATY OF BERLIN** (p. 780) establishing a small Bulgarian principality north of the Balkan Mountains and an Eastern Roumelia, south of the mountains. Macedonia left under Turkish rule, with promises (Art. XXIII) of reform.

1879, Feb. 22. A **constitution** granted the new Bulgarian state, under Russian auspices.

Apr. 29. **Alexander of Battenberg** elected prince. He was a favorite nephew of the tsar

Montenegro: The Petrovich–Njegosh Dynasty.

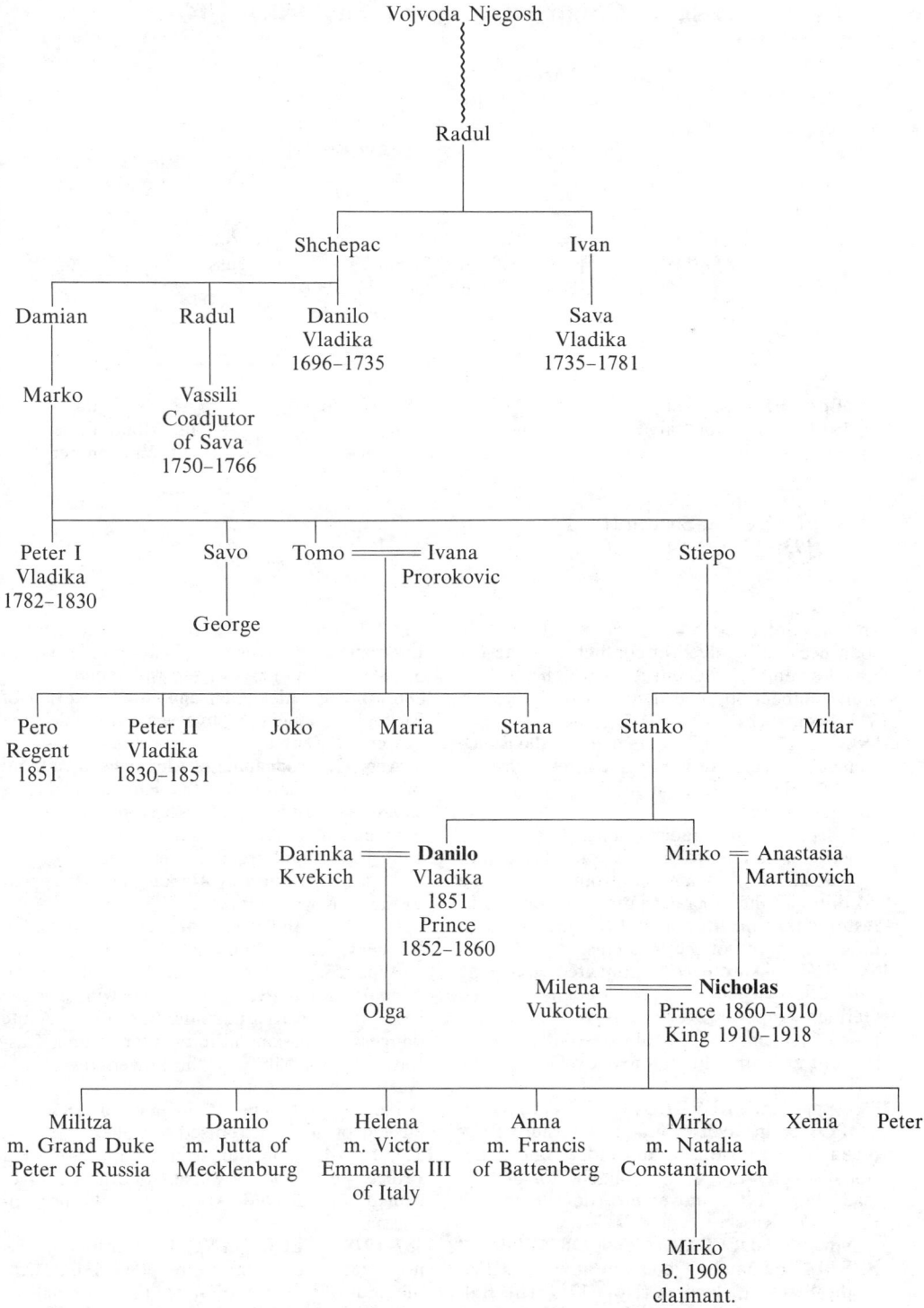

This chart is based upon that by Michael Petrovich in Milovan Djilas: *Njegoš* (N.Y. 1966), courtesy of Harcourt, Brace and World, Inc.

Rulers of Bulgaria
(Saxe–Coburg–Gotha Family, 1887–1946)

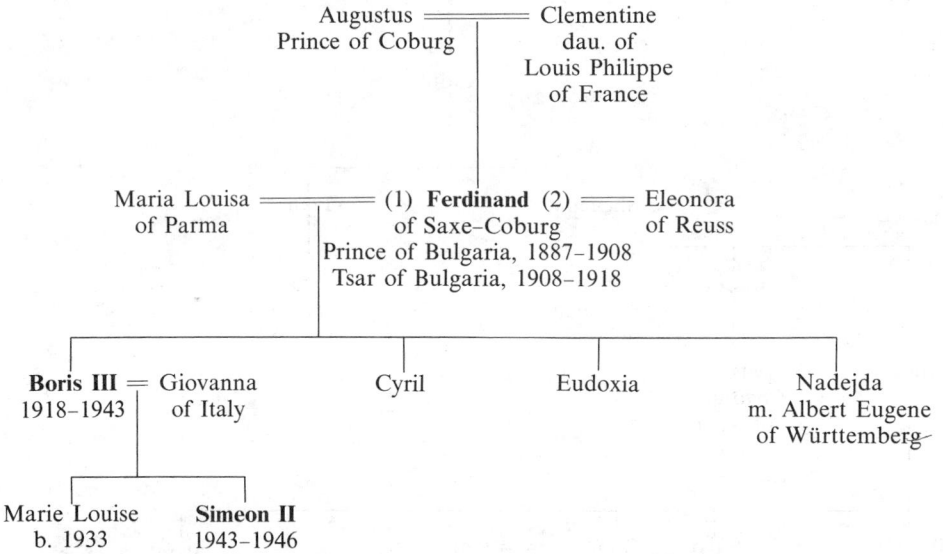

Augustus ═══ Clementine
Prince of Coburg   dau. of
Louis Philippe
of France

Maria Louisa ═══ (1) **Ferdinand** (2) ═══ Eleonora
of Parma   of Saxe–Coburg   of Reuss
Prince of Bulgaria, 1887–1908
Tsar of Bulgaria, 1908–1918

Boris III ═ Giovanna   Cyril   Eudoxia   Nadejda
1918–1943   of Italy   m. Albert Eugene
of Württemberg

Marie Louise   **Simeon II**
b. 1933   1943–1946

and was intended to serve as a satrap. He soon became involved in conflict with the national assembly (*Sobranye*), of which the Liberal members opposed dictation by Russia.

1879–1886. ALEXANDER I, prince.

1881, July 13. With Russian consent **the prince changed the constitution** to give himself greater power. He appointed a ministry headed by Russian officers.

1883, Sept. 30. **Alexander,** hounded by Russian concession-hunters (demands for a Rustchuk-Küstendil railway) and confronted with the hostility of the liberal, nationalist elements, **restored the constitution of 1879,** thereby winning the enmity of the Russians.

1883–1884. Alexander's projected marriage with Princess Victoria, granddaughter of the German emperor. This was vigorously opposed by Bismarck, fearful of estranging Russia, but ardently championed by Queen Victoria.

1885, Sept. 18. REVOLUTION AT PHILIPPOPOLIS, in favor of union of Eastern Roumelia with Bulgaria. Alexander, under nationalist pressure, was obliged to assume leadership of the movement, despite violent protests of Russia (page 783).

Nov. 13. DECLARATION OF WAR BY SERBIA, demanding compensation. Defeat of the Serbs at **Slivnitza** (Nov. 17). The Bulgarians invaded Serbia and took **Pirot** (Nov. 27), but were forced to withdraw as a result of intervention by Austria. Peace made March 3, 1886, on the basis of the *status quo.*

1886, Apr. 5. Alexander appointed governor of Eastern Roumelia for five years, to which the powers consented.

Aug. 21. Kidnaping of Alexander by a band of officers, inspired by the Russians. Provisional government of **Stephen Stambulov,** energetic nationalist leader, who arrested the conspirators and recalled Alexander.

Aug. 29. Return of Alexander. His appeal to the tsar, who replied coldly.

Sept. 4. Abdication of Prince Alexander. Regency, led by Stambulov.

Sept. 25. Mission of the Russian general, **Nicholas Kaulbars,** who tried to win over the country to the Russian side, but failed. Acute danger of Russian military intervention, frustrated by opposition of the powers (especially Austria and Britain).

Nov. 10. Prince Waldemar of Denmark elected prince, but refused the offer.

1887, July 4. The Bulgarian assembly elected **Prince Ferdinand** of Saxe-Coburg, who accepted and arrived August 14. Protests of Russia.

1887–1918. FERDINAND I. Ferdinand was not recognized by any of the powers, but, with the aid of Stambulov and the nationalists, managed to maintain himself, though the first ten years of his reign were punctuated by plots against him, assassinations of ministers, etc.

1890, July. The Turkish government appointed three Bulgarian bishops to Macedonian dioceses.

1892, Aug. Visit of Stambulov to Constantinople. His policy throughout was one of friendship with Turkey and the extraction of concessions in regard to Macedonia. Suggestions by **Charilaos Tricoupis,** the Greek statesman, for formation of a **Balkan league,** were rejected (1891).

1893. Formation of the **Internal Macedonian Revolutionary Organization** (*I.M.R.O.*) to work for an autonomous Macedonia.

1894, June 12. Dismissal of Stambulov, due in part to Prince Ferdinand's desire to pave the way for reconciliation with Russia, partly to pressure of Macedonian elements, dissatisfied with Stambulov's cautious policy.

1895. Formation of the **External Macedonian Revolutionary Organization,** with headquarters in Sofia.

June. Beginning of **raids into Macedonia,** from Bulgaria (**Boris Sarafov,** leader).

July 15. Brutal **murder of Stambulov** by Macedonian revolutionaries.

1896, Feb. Reconciliation of Russia and Bulgaria, on the occasion of the conversion of the crown prince, **Boris,** to the Orthodox faith.

Feb. 19. Prince Ferdinand recognized by Russia and the other powers.

1901. Arrest of Macedonian leaders, after the assassination of certain Roumanians and acute tension between Bulgaria and Roumania. They were tried, but acquitted.

1902–1903. Great **insurrection in Macedonia,** accompanied by raids from Bulgaria. Danger of war between Bulgaria and Turkey. Bulgarian government helpless in the face of the Macedonian agitation and revolutionary bands. The situation was cleared by the introduction of the **Mürzsteg reform program** by the powers (p. 794).

1908, Oct. 5. DECLARATION OF INDEPENDENCE by Ferdinand, who assumed the title of *tsar.* Beginning of the Bosnian annexation crisis, which overshadowed the action of Bulgaria (p. 798).

1909, Feb. 21. Visit of Ferdinand to St. Petersburg, where he was received with royal honors.

Apr. 19. Convention with Turkey, which recognized Bulgarian independence. Agreement with Russia, which assumed responsibility for the financial settlement.

Nov. Draft treaty of alliance between Russia and Bulgaria. Ferdinand avoided committing himself, preferring to balance between Russia and Austria. Efforts of the Serbs to effect an alliance were evaded, because of Ferdinand's unwillingness to abandon claim to all of Macedonia.

1911, Mar. 22. Ivan Gueshov cabinet. Beginning of negotiations with Serbia (Oct.) as a result of the Tripolitan War (p. 800).

1912, Mar. 13. CONCLUSION OF THE ALLIANCE WITH SERBIA (p. 800).

May 29. TREATY OF ALLIANCE WITH GREECE (p. 801).

Oct. 18. OUTBREAK OF THE FIRST BALKAN WAR. Bulgarian victories (p. 801).

1913, May 7. Bulgaria agreed to cede Silistria to Roumania, in compensation for Bulgarian gains elsewhere.

June 14. Stojan Danev cabinet. Effort to arbitrate the conflict with Serbia regarding division of the spoils (p. 802).

June 29. OUTBREAK OF THE SECOND BALKAN WAR, following the attack of General Michael Savov and the Bulgarians on the Serbian and Greek positions (p. 802).

July 15. Formation of the Vasil Radoslavov cabinet.

Aug. 10. Disastrous treaty of Bucharest, following Bulgaria's defeat (p. 802).

Sept. 29. Treaty of Constantinople, concluding peace between Turkey and Bulgaria.

1914, July 29. Bulgaria declared **neutrality in First World War.**

1915, Oct. 14. BULGARIA ENTERED THE FIRST WORLD WAR.

(*Cont. pp. 953 f., 1025.*)

e. ROUMANIA, 1774–1916

1774. By the **treaty of Kuchuk Kainarji** (p. 517) **Russia** was given certain rights of intervention in behalf of the Danubian Principalities (**Moldavia** and **Wallachia**), which were still ruled by *hospodars* (usually phanariot Greeks) appointed by the sultan.

1802. Russia forced the sultan to promise to appoint the **hospodars for seven years** and not to remove them without Russian consent.

1812. By the **treaty of Bucharest** (p. 645), **Bessarabia** was detached from Moldavia and ceded to Russia.

1829, Sept. By the **treaty of Adrianople** Russia strengthened her protectorate and secured for the principalities **complete autonomy** (p. 750).

1829–1834. Continued **Russian occupation.** Enlightened rule of the Russian governor, **Count Paul Kisselev,** who took precautions against the plague, organized a militia, reformed the finances, and abolished trade restrictions.

1832. The **ORGANIC STATUTE,** worked out by a group of *boyars* (landed gentry) under

Russian auspices: an **assembly of boyars** was to elect the prince from among their own numbers. He was to be elected for life and irremovable without Russia's consent. The result was an **oligarchic system,** which continued until 1856.

1832-1856. Period of great **economic expansion** (demands of western Europe for Roumanian grain; development of steamboat traffic on the Danube) and the rapid spread of **French influence** (many Roumanian students in France; influence of the Polish emigration). Progressive rule of **Prince Michael Sturdza** in Moldavia, but both principalities continued under strong Russian influence.

1848, June.   REVOLUTION IN WALLA-CHIA, demanding a liberal régime (leaders **Constantine Rossetti, Ion** and **Dmitri Bratianu**). The hospodar accepted a liberal constitution and then fled.

Sept. By agreement with Turkey, **Russia invaded the principalities** and put down the revolution.

1849, May 1.   Convention of Balta Liman between Russia and Turkey: the hospodars were to be appointed for only seven years; assemblies of boyars abolished and replaced by *divans,* appointed by the hospodars. Russia and Turkey were to occupy the country jointly. The Russians stayed until 1851.

1853, July 2.   Occupation of the Principalities by Russia, following the dispute with Turkey which led to the Crimean War (p. 773).

1854, Aug. 8. Evacuation of the country by the Russians and **occupation by the Austrians** (till March 1857) in agreement with Turkey (p. 773).

1856, Feb.-Mar.   CONGRESS OF PARIS (p. 774). **Napoleon III** favored union of the Principalities (influence of **Mme. Cornu** and of **Ion Bratianu**). This was opposed by Turkey and Austria, gradually supported by Britain. Russia sided with France. It was finally decided that the sultan should summon popularly elected divans to ascertain the wishes of the population. At the same time an **international commission** was to investigate and suggest an organization.

1857, Mar.   Evacuation by Austria. In the elections every kind of pressure and corruption was employed to debar the unionists, who were consequently defeated. France at once demanded annulment, which the sultan refused.

Aug. France, Russia, Prussia, and Sardinia broke off relations with Turkey. Acute danger of war between France and Britain, the latter supporting Turkey.

Aug. 9. Visit of Napoleon III to Osborne and **Osborne pact** between France and Britain: Britain agreed to annulment of the elections

and approved of a system of common institutions under separate princes (*broad administrative union*).

Sept. New elections; a great **victory for the unionists.**

1858, Aug. 19. A conference of the powers at Paris decided to establish the **United Principalities of Moldavia and Wallachia,** with separate but identical administrations; delegates from each of the two assemblies to form a central commission for legislation.

1859, Jan. 17.   Colonel Alexander Cuza, a relatively unknown officer, elected prince in Moldavia.

Feb. 5. The Wallachians also elected Cuza. Napoleon recognized him at once and the other powers followed more or less grudgingly.

1862, Feb. 5. The sultan allowed the **fusion of the two legislatures** and the union of the Principalities was recognized, with the new name of *Roumania.*

June 20,   Assassination of Barbu Catargiu, Conservative journalist and politician. Thereafter Cuza, whose sympathy was with the peasant class, appointed a Liberal ministry under **Mikhail Kogalniceanu** and proceeded to a policy of Liberal reform: **expropriation of the monasteries,** etc.

1864, Mar. 28. *Coup d'état* of Cuza, designed to break the Conservative opposition. A plebiscite approved his proposal to strengthen the prince's power by establishing an appointed senate, etc.

Aug. Cuza introduced a great **land reform** by decree: abolition of serfdom and feudal dues, with compensation to the landlords; the peasants were given a small share of the land.

1866, Feb. 23.   Cuza kidnaped and forced to abdicate by a conspiracy of Conservatives and Liberals who desired a foreign prince. The assembly at once offered the position to the **count of Flanders,** son of Leopold II of Belgium, who declined.

Apr. 14. The provisional government (with the secret approval of Napoleon III and Bismarck) proclaimed **Prince Charles of Hohenzollern-Sigmaringen.** A plebiscite approved of the action.

May 22.   Charles arrived at Bucharest, having crossed Austria in disguise.

July. Introduction of a **new constitution,** based upon the Belgian charter of 1831 (liberal, but not democratic).

Oct. 24. The **sultan recognized Charles** and the powers followed suit.

1866-1914.   CHARLES I (Carol). His reign was characterized by rapid economic development (especially petroleum).

1877, Apr. 24.   Invasion of Roumania by the Russians during the war with Turkey, after a convention had been forced upon the government.

May 21. Roumania entered the war on Russia's side and **proclaimed independence.** The Russians rejected active help until they were hard pressed at the **siege of Plevna** (p. 780).

1878, July 13. The **TREATY OF BERLIN** recognized the **full independence of Roumania,** but the Roumanians were obliged to cede **Bessarabia** to Russia in return for the much less desirable **Dobrudja** (p. 780). By Art. XLIV of the Berlin treaty the Roumanian government was obliged to promise **protection to the Jews,** of whom there were many in Moldavia. Actually nothing was done and anti-Semitism became rampant in the country; protests of the powers achieved but little.

1881, May 23. PRINCE CHARLES proclaimed king.

1883, Oct. 30. ALLIANCE BETWEEN ROUMANIA AND AUSTRIA, acceded to by Germany and Italy. This continued in effect until 1914, but was kept a strict secret by the king, so that only a few chosen ministers were ever initiated. The alliance was the result of Roumanian fear of Russia, but it failed to overcome the basic antagonism between Roumania and Hungary over Transylvania.

1888, Apr. Serious **agrarian insurrection,** due to the failure of the government to face the vital land question.

1893, Jan. 10. Marriage of Prince Ferdinand and **Princess Marie of Edinburgh.**

1900–1901. Tension in relations with Bulgaria, arising from conflicting aspirations in Macedonia and the murder of several Roumanians by Macedonian revolutionaries.

1905–1911. Rupture of relations with Greece as the result of friction over the treatment of Kutzo-Vlachs in Macedonia by Greek comitadjis. Large numbers of Greeks were expelled from Roumania.

1907, Mar.–Apr. Great **insurrection of peasants** in Moldavia, which had to be put down by military forces. Martial law proclaimed throughout the country.

1913, May 7. Agreement with Bulgaria by which the latter was to cede **Silistria** as compensation for gains made in the Balkan Wars. The Roumanian government demanded more.

July 10. DECLARATION OF WAR ON BULGARIA, Roumania joining with Serbia and Greece in the **Second Balkan War** (p. 802).

1914, June 14. Visit of Tsar Nicholas and Sazonov to **Constantza,** taken as evidence of Roumania's veering to the side of the Entente powers (p. 803).

Aug. 4. Roumania proclaimed neutrality in the First World War.

Oct. 10. Death of King Charles, heartbroken over the failure of the government to honor the treaty of alliance with Austria.

1914–1927. FERDINAND I, nephew of Charles.

1916, Aug. 27. ROUMANIA DECLARED WAR ON AUSTRIA. *(Cont. pp. 964, 1026.)*

2. THE OTTOMAN EMPIRE

(From p. 521)

1793. The **New Regulations,** providing for the complete reorganization of the military system and the establishment of a corps modeled on European lines, revision of commercial arrangements (to get rid of the abuse of *berats* or licenses by foreign representatives), revision of the tax system, etc. These **reforms of Selim III** were strongly opposed by the Janissaries and the religious leaders. Nothing much came of them, though Selim built up a small and effective military force of a few thousand men, trained on European lines.

1798. Napoleon's Egyptian Expedition (p. 635).

1804, Feb. RISING OF THE SERBS, under George Petrovich **(Kara George),** a well-to-do trader in pork. The Serbs had been aroused to national self-consciousness by the writings of **Rajich** and **Obradovich,** but the movement was directed less against Turkish rule than against the oppression of the Janissary garrison at Belgrade. The Janissaries were driven out in December 1806 and in 1808 the supreme command was made hereditary in the family of Kara George. Encouraged by Russia, the movement took on a much larger aspect.

1806–1812. War with Russia (p. 642).

1807, July. Selim III dethroned as a result of a rising of the Janissaries, who put **Mustapha IV** on the throne. **Bairakdar,** the pasha of Rustchuk, led a strong force to Constantinople in the hope of seizing control. He took the city (1808), but his opponents had Selim strangled before he could be restored. Bairakdar thereupon put upon the throne **Mahmud II,** the cousin and pupil of Selim. Having made the mistake of sending most of his troops to the Danube, Bairakdar was soon faced with a new revolt, in which he lost his life. Mahmud was left on the throne only because he was the last of the Ottoman house.

Rulers of Roumania
(Hohenzollern-Sigmaringen Family, 1866–1947)

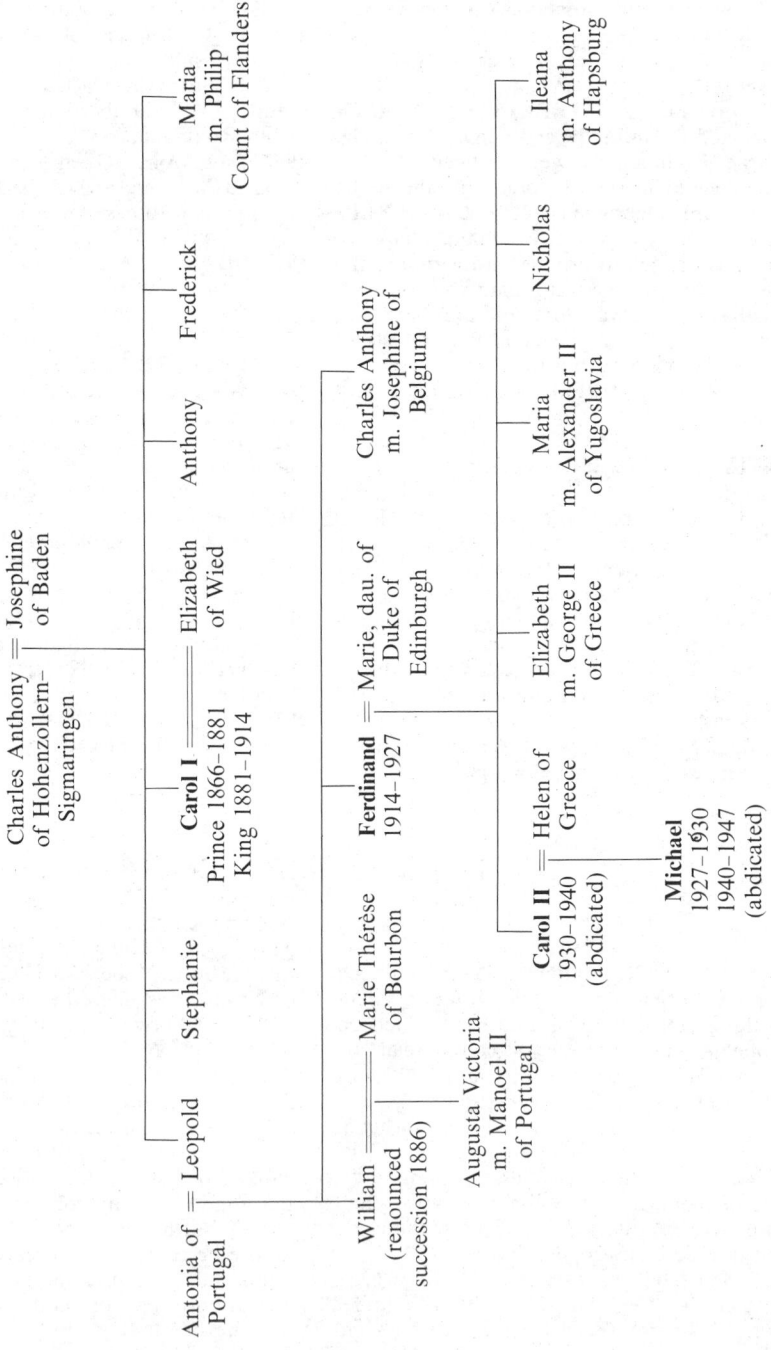

1808–1839. MAHMUD II, a proud and obstinate ruler, whose great object was to put down the rebellious pashas in the provinces and to re-establish the absolute power of the sultan. In the first ten years of his reign he succeeded in displacing most of the derebeys in Anatolia.

1815–1817. Second rising of the Serbs, under **Milosh Obrenovich.** The Serbs had been shamefully deserted by the Russians in the treaty of Bucharest and the first insurrection had been suppressed (1813). Kara George returned from exile in Austria in 1817, but was murdered by his Obrenovich opponents. Beginning of the blood feud between the Obrenovich and Karageorgevich families. Milosh was recognized by the Turks in 1817 as hereditary prince of Serbia, which at that time was only a very small part of present-day Serbia.

1821–1830. GREEK WAR OF INDEPENDENCE. This was the result of growing prosperity of the Greeks in the later 18th century (Black Sea grain trade), the cultural renaissance (Korais, Rhigas), the encouragement of Russia (Catherine's *Greek Scheme*); revolt of 1769–1776, and the influence of the French Revolution and the intrigues of Napoleon. A secret revolutionary society, the *Philiké Hetairia,* was founded at Odessa in 1814 and was in close touch with the Russian government (**Count Giovanni Capo d'Istria,** close friend of Tsar Alexander I). At the head of the movement was **Alexander Hypsilanti,** member of a powerful Greek phanariot family from Moldavia and an officer in the Russian army.

1821, Feb. Outbreak of an **insurrection in Wallachia** against Turkish-Greek rule. This precipitated action by the Greeks.

Mar. 6. Hypsilanti proclaimed the **revolt in Moldavia** and appealed to the tsar for aid. Tsar Alexander, under Metternich's influence, disavowed him and refused to countenance a revolutionary movement. Hypsilanti lost courage, and was defeated by a Turkish force at **Dragashan** (June 26). He fled, but was captured and imprisoned by the Austrians.

At the same time a more imposing insurrection took place in the **Morea,** which was joined by some of the more prosperous islands. The Turks, a small minority, were ruthlessly slaughtered and the movement spread rapidly to the rest of Greece. The Turks retaliated by hanging the Greek patriarch and massacring Greeks in Constantinople. This, in turn, led to protests from Russia and acute danger of war.

July 27. Russian ultimatum to Turkey, demanding restoration of Christian churches, protection of the Christian religion, etc. The Turks rejected this and relations were severed. War was prevented only through the efforts of Metternich and Castlereagh, who reminded the tsar of the dangers of supporting revolution.

Oct. 5. The **Greeks took Tripolitsa,** the main Turkish fortress in the Morea. Massacre of 10,000 Turks.

1822, Jan. 13. A Greek assembly at Epidauros declared **Greek independence** and drew up an organic statute (constitution) providing for a liberal parliamentary system and an executive directory of five.

Feb. 5. A Turkish army finally took Janina and brought to an end the career of **Ali of Janina,** one of the most powerful of the pashas. The Turks were now free to press the campaign against the Greeks.

Apr. A **Turkish fleet,** under Kara Ali, **took the island of Chios** and either massacred or sold into slavery most of the population.

June 19. The Turkish fleet was destroyed by the Greeks under Admiral Constantine Kanaris.

July. **Invasion of Greece** by an army of 30,000, which overran the whole peninsula north of the Gulf of Corinth. The Greek government fled to the islands.

1823, Jan. The **Turks were obliged to fall back,** having been unable to take the key fortress of **Missolonghi,** at the entrance to the Gulf of Corinth. The Greeks failed to take advantage of this respite, but devoted themselves to personal rivalries (**Theodoros Kolokotronis** against **Lazaros Kondouriottis;** conflict between the executive power and the legislature).

1824. First civil war. Kolokotronis was defeated. The government was established at Nauplia. Meanwhile the sultan had appealed for help to his powerful vassal, **Mohammed (Mehemet) Ali,** of Egypt, who possessed a strong army and navy. The Egyptians had already conquered **Crete** (1822–1824).

1825, Feb. Ibrahim, the son of Mohammed, effected a landing in the Morea and quickly subdued the whole peninsula. At the same time the Turks, under Reshid Pasha, invaded from the north and renewed the **siege of Missolonghi** (finally taken by the Turks, April 23, 1826).

The Turkish-Egyptian successes aroused sentiment in Europe, where the Greeks were regarded as descendants of the heroes of old, renewing the struggle against the barbarians. Rapid spread of **Philhellenism** in Germany, Switzerland, France, and England. The governments were obliged to do something and an ambassadorial **conference at St. Petersburg** (1824–1825) discussed projects for establishing Greece as a group of three self-governing but tributary states, but Austria and Britain were unwilling to follow Russia in action against the Turks.

July 26. The Greeks put themselves under **British protection** and after the fall of Missolonghi appealed for British mediation.

1826, Apr. 4.   St. Petersburg protocol, signed by Britain (**Wellington mission** to St. Petersburg) and Russia. The two powers agreed to mediate between the Turks and Greeks on the basis of complete autonomy for Greece under Turkish suzerainty. Canning, who was chiefly concerned with preventing separate action by Russia, tried hard to associate other powers.

Apr. 5.   Russian ultimatum to Turkey: demanded return to the *status quo* in the Danubian Principalities and dispatch of a special envoy to discuss outstanding questions between Russia and Turkey. The Turks yielded, on the advice of Austria and France.

June 15–16.   DESTRUCTION OF THE JANISSARIES. This had been planned by Mahmud ever since his accession. The hopeless inefficiency of the troops gave him an opening and he succeeded in winning over the religious leaders. In May he decreed the formation of a new corps, admission being opened to the Janissaries. But the latter rose in revolt. The small loyal corps of the sultan bombarded the barracks and the mob did the rest. From 6000 to 10,000 Janissaries are said to have been massacred.

1827, Apr. 11. The Greek factions, whose rivalries paralyzed all plans of action, united to elect **Capo d'Istria** president for seven years.

May 17.   Constitution of Trözene, which practically deprived the executive of all power and vested it in a single chamber, the senate. Despite the efforts of the Englishmen, **Lord Thomas Cochrane** and **Sir Richard Church,** united action proved illusory.

June 5. The **Acropolis capitulated** to the Turks.

July 6.   TREATY OF LONDON. France joined Russia and Britain, and it was provided that if the Turks refused an armistice the three powers would threaten to support the Greeks and use their naval forces. In the interval the British made desperate efforts to induce Mohammed Ali to withdraw from the conflict (**Cradock mission**).

Aug. 16.   Note of the three powers to the Porte, demanding an armistice. The Turks refused, whereupon the admirals were instructed to stop all reinforcements and supplies from reaching the forces in Greece.

Sept. 8. A large Egyptian fleet with transports landed at **Navarino,** but Ibrahim was induced, by **Admiral Sir Edward Codrington,** to await instructions from Alexandria before continuing operations. When Ibrahim learned that the Greeks were continuing the fighting at Patras, he disregarded the engagement.

Oct. 20.   BATTLE OF NAVARINO. The British, French, and Russian squadrons entered the harbor, where the Egyptian fleet was crowded together. The battle was an artillery fight at short range and resulted in the sinking or blowing up of most of the Egyptian fleet. Wild enthusiasm in Europe; indignation of the Turks, who demanded reparation.

Dec. 28.   The allied ambassadors left Constantinople.

1828, Apr. 26.   Russia declared war on Turkey. The British disapproved (Wellington ministry, January 1828), but the French were friendly to Russia, and Austria did not dare raise too many objections.

June 8. The **Russians crossed the Danube,** but were held up by the garrisons of the fortresses on the south bank (Shumla, Silistria, Varna).

Aug. 9.   Anglo-French convention with Mohammed Ali, providing for the evacuation of the Egyptian forces from Greece. This was carried out by a **French expeditionary force** under General Maison (winter 1828–1829).

Oct. 12. The **Russians took Varna,** but were too exhausted to continue the campaign that winter.

1829, Mar. 22.   LONDON PROTOCOL, drawn up by an ambassadorial conference: Greece, south of a line from the Gulf of Volo to the Gulf of Arta, with Negroponte (Euboea) and the Cyclades (but without Crete) to be an autonomous, tributary state, under a prince (*not* to be chosen from the ruling families of Britain, France, or Russia).

June 11.   Battle of Kulevcha. The Russians, under General Diebitsch, opened the road to the Balkan Mountains.

July 15.   Diebitsch crossed the mountains (first time a Russian army advanced so far).

Aug. 20.   The Russians took Adrianople. Meanwhile General Paskievich took **Kars** and **Erzerum** on the Asiatic front. The Turkish Empire on the verge of collapse (**scheme of Prince Polignac,** the French prime minister, for the partition of the empire and a complete revamping of the map of Europe).

Sept. 14.   TREATY OF ADRIANOPLE, concluded through the mediation of the Prussian officer, Major von Müffling. The Russians, decimated by disease, were hardly in a position to take Constantinople and decided not to try (fear of foreign intervention). The terms were lenient: Russia abandoned her conquests in Europe, but the frontier on the Pruth was extended from the northern to the southern mouth of the Danube; Russia was to occupy the Danubian Principalities pending the payment of an indemnity of 15,000,000 ducats in ten years; the hospodars of Moldavia and

Walêachia were to be appointed for life and the Turks were to withdraw all Moslems and raze all fortresses in the two provinces; with regard to Greece the Turks agreed to accept the London protocol.

Nov. 30. The **London conference** decided that Greece should be given complete independence, but the frontier was moved back to the line Aspropotamo—Gulf of Lamia, i.e. almost to the Gulf of Corinth. This decision was embodied in a **new London protocol** (Feb. 3, 1830), which the Greeks rejected as inadequate. The powers chose **Leopold of Saxe-Coburg** as prince, but he declined the offer on the grounds that the frontiers of the new state were too restricted. For the time being Capo d'Istria ruled the state in dictatorial fashion.

1831, Oct. Assassination of Capo d'Istria. Civil war between his brother, Agostino, and Joannes Kolettis.

1832, Mar. The powers chose for the throne the Bavarian prince, **Otto,** and extended the frontiers of the state to the Volo–Arta line.

1832–1833. CONFLICT BETWEEN THE SULTAN AND MOHAMMED ALI of Egypt, who demanded all Syria as a reward for his aid in Greece. When the sultan refused to yield, Mohammed picked a quarrel with the pasha of Acre and sent Ibrahim with an army to occupy the country. **Ibrahim took Acre** (May 27, 1832), **Damascus** (June 15), and **Aleppo** (July 16). He defeated a Turkish army near **Alexandretta** (July 29) and began the invasion of Anatolia. The sultan appealed to Britain for aid, but Palmerston was preoccupied with the Belgian situation and did not as yet recognize the threat involved in Mohammed Ali's designs.

1832, Dec. 21. BATTLE OF KONIAH. Ibrahim completely defeated the grand vizir and the main Turkish army. With no further opposition, he pressed the advance to near Brusa and was on the point of overthrowing the Ottoman house. The Russians, however, intervened, offered the sultan aid, and warned Mohammed Ali (**Muraviev mission** to Constantinople and Alexandria, Dec.–Feb.).

1833, Feb. 20. A Russian squadron arrived in the Bosporus. Alarm of Britain and France, which began to mediate.

Apr. 8. Convention of Kutahia. France induced the sultan to grant Mohammed Ali all of **Syria** and **Adana.** But the sultan tried to hold out on Adana and the Russians began to land troops on the Asiatic side of the Bosporus. Great tension: British and French fleets at Smyrna. The sultan finally yielded (May 4).

July 8. TREATY OF HUNKIAR-ISKEL-ESI, (Unkiar Skelessi), between Russia and Turkey, concluded for eight years: each party to come to the other's aid in case of attack; a secret article relieved the Turks of this obligation in return for an engagement to keep the Dardanelles closed to all foreign warships. The Russians then withdrew from the Bosporus (July 10). Vigorous protests of France and Britain, which took the treaty to mean that the Bosporus was to remain open to Russian warships and that Turkey was to be henceforth at the mercy of Russia.

Sept. 18. Münchengrätz agreement, between Russia and Austria. The tsar declared for the maintenance of the Ottoman Empire and agreed that if partition became inevitable he would act only in agreement with Austria. But the meeting was taken in Britain merely as a **reaffirmation of the Holy Alliance.**

1835. Exploration, by **Captain Francis Chesney,** of a possible line of communication from the Syrian coast down the Euphrates to the Persian Gulf. This reflected growing British interest in the routes to the east. Growing tension in relations with Mohammed Ali, who obstructed the British schemes and rejected a proposal for a railway from Cairo to the Red Sea. Mohammed, on the contrary, pushed his conquests in Arabia as far as the Persian Gulf (1838) and the Indian Ocean, while the **British occupied Aden** (Jan. 1839). Palmerston became more and more convinced of the necessity of defending the Ottoman Empire against both Egypt and Russia (violent anti-Russian propaganda of **David Urquhart**), aided the sultan in the construction of a fleet and concluded an advantageous tariff treaty (1838). The French, on the other hand, became increasingly favorable to the Egyptian pasha and encouraged him in plans for a vast Arabo-Egyptian empire.

1838, Dec.–1839, Apr. Mission of Reshid Pasha to London. In view of Mohammed Ali's threat to declare himself independent, the sultan proposed to the British an offensive and defensive alliance. Palmerston flatly refused anything beyond a defensive pact.

1839, Apr. A Turkish army began the **invasion of Syria** from the Euphrates.

June 24. BATTLE OF NESIB. Ibrahim completely defeated the Turkish forces.

July 1. The **Turkish fleet,** having gone to Alexandria, **voluntarily surrendered** to Mohammed Ali, either through treachery or through fear of the admiral that the grand vizir, Chosrew Pasha, was planning to abandon it to the Russians.

July 1. Death of Mahmud II. The new sultan, **Abdul Mejid** (1839–1861), a mere boy, was ready to yield and make Mohammed Ali hereditary pasha of Egypt and Ibrahim pasha of Syria.

July 27. Collective note of the five great powers to Constantinople: they reserved the right to settle with Mohammed Ali. Palmerston from the outset insisted that Mohammed must give up Syria, while the French were sympathetic to him and refused to consider pressure.

Sept., Dec. Missions of Baron Philip Brunnow to London. In order to effect a break between Britain and France, the tsar agreed to pressure on Mohammed Ali to force him to abandon Syria, and promised that Russia would not enter the Bosporus without similar action by the British at the Dardanelles.

Nov. 3. HATT-I SHERIF OF GULHANÉ, a reform decree issued by the sultan under the influence of **Reshid Pasha,** who favored reform on western lines and hoped to increase the popularity of the Turks in Britain. The Hatt was chiefly a declaration of principles, guaranteeing the life, liberty, and property of all subjects and promising military and taxational reform. It was followed, in the next decade, by numerous specific measures resulting in the establishment of a modern, centralized administration, an assembly of notables, provincial councils, mixed tribunals, technical schools, etc.

1840, Feb.–Oct. Ministry of Adolphe Thiers in France. He resolutely rejected all proposals to coerce Mohammed and attempted to mediate between the Turks and Egyptians without intervention by the other powers. This disloyal policy enabled Palmerston to carry a reluctant cabinet for a policy of action with Russia and without France.

July 15. TREATY OF LONDON: Britain, Austria, Prussia, and Russia agreed to force a settlement on Mohammed Ali and to support the sultan if necessary. Mohammed was to be offered Egypt as an hereditary possession and southern Syria for life, but was to give up Crete, northern Syria, Mecca, and Medina, and return the Turkish fleet. Failure to accept these terms in ten days was to mean the withdrawal of the offer of southern Syria; failure to accept the revised offer in ten days would mean the withdrawal of the whole offer and freedom for the sultan to make other arrangements. Mohammed rejected these terms, relying on France. The British induced the sultan to depose him. Panic in Paris when the treaty became known. Violent bellicosity of Thiers and of the press, **danger of war on the Rhine.**

Sept. 9. The British admiral, **Sir Robert Stopford, bombarded Beirut,** and **General Sir Charles Napier** landed troops. Revolt against the Egyptians in Syria. **Capture of Beirut** (Oct. 10); bombardment and **capture of Acre** (Nov. 3); Ibrahim forced to evacuate all Syria.

Oct. 20. Resignation of Thiers, reflecting Louis Philippe's decision against war.

Nov. 27. Convention of Alexandria, concluded by Napier: Mohammed Ali agreed to return the Turkish fleet and to abandon claims to Syria, in return for hereditary rule of Egypt. The sultan was finally induced to accept (firman of February 13, 1841).

1841, July 13. STRAITS CONVENTION, signed by the five great powers and marking France's return to the European concert: the Straits (Bosporus and Dardanelles) were to be closed to all foreign warships in time of peace.

1844. Visit of Tsar Nicholas to London. Discussions with **Lord Aberdeen** about the precarious condition of the Ottoman Empire. The tsar proposed that, in case of Turkish collapse, Russia and Britain should consult as to what should be done. **Gentlemen's agreement** to this effect.

1848, Sept. Rising in the Danubian Principalities, directed chiefly against the Russian influence. In agreement with the Turks, the Russians invaded the provinces and occupied them until 1851.

1849, Oct. International crisis, resulting from the Russian and Austrian demand on Turkey that the **Hungarian refugees** be extradited. The Turks appealed to Britain for aid, and Palmerston promised it. France supported Britain and both powers made a naval demonstration at Besika Bay. On November 1 the British squadron actually entered the Straits, to escape bad weather. It was withdrawn after Russian protests.

1851. Dispute between France and Turkey regarding the privileges of the Roman Catholic monks at the **Holy Places** in Palestine. These had fallen under the control of the Greek Orthodox monks, supported by Russia. Pressure of clerical circles in France induced Napoleon to press the claims of France, traditional protector of the Roman Catholics. In February 1852 the sultan yielded and granted certain privileges to the Latins; these were extended in December. Indignation of the tsar, enhanced by his dislike of the upstart French emperor.

1853, Jan.–Feb. Nicholas' talks with Lord George Seymour, the British ambassador. The tsar envisaged the demise of the "sick man" and made a bid for an agreement with Britain concerning the ultimate disposition of the heritage: Russia did not desire Constantinople, but would not allow any other power to take it; Serbia and Bulgaria might be made independent states; Britain might take Crete and Egypt, etc. Aberdeen, apprehensive of French plans toward Britain, was not unfavorably disposed toward the Russian advances.

Feb.–May. **Mission of Prince Alexander Menshikov** to Constantinople, to secure concessions in the matter of the Holy Places and, in return for a promise of support against a western power (France), to secure a treaty recognizing a **Russian protectorate over Orthodox churches** in Constantinople "and elsewhere." These concessions Menshikov tried to obtain by intrigue, cajolery, and threats.

Apr. 5. Arrival of Lord Stratford de Redcliffe (British ambassador to Turkey, 1842–1858—the *great Elchi*) at Constantinople, with instructions to arrange a settlement of the question of the Holy Places in Russia's interest. This he did, only to learn (May 5) of the wider demands of Menshikov. He advised rejection of these and the Turkish grand council voted them down (May 17). Menshikov left (May 21) after many unfulfilled threats.

May 31. The tsar decided to occupy the Danubian Principalities as a method of pressure on the sultan; on the same day the British and French governments decided to send their squadrons to Besika Bay. Stratford was empowered to call the fleet to Constantinople, if necessary. Division of the British cabinet: **Aberdeen** pro-Russian; **Palmerston** for strong action; **Clarendon,** the foreign minister, attempting to mediate. Strong public feeling in Britain against autocratic Russia.

June 13. The British and French fleets at Besika Bay.

July 2. Occupation of the Principalities by Russian forces. The powers protested, but restrained the Turks in their desire to declare war.

July 28. The **VIENNA NOTE,** drawn up by the French ambassador and submitted to Russia by Austria. This was a formula vaguely worded and designed to give the Russians satisfaction in principle without offending the Turks. The tsar accepted it (Aug. 5), but the Turks insisted (Aug. 19) on an amendment making it clear that the protection of the Christians should depend on the sultan, not on the "active solicitude" of the tsar. The Russians rejected this (Sept. 7), and in a circular revealed the fact that they had intended to derive a virtual protectorate from the original vague phraseology. After a **meeting of Nicholas and Francis Joseph at Olmütz,** the Austrians continued to work for acceptance of the note, but the British and French refused to follow suit.

Sept. 23. After demonstrations and disorders at Constantinople, the **British fleet was ordered to Constantinople.**

Oct. 4. The Turks enthusiastically declared war on Russia.

Oct. 23. The Turks, under **Omar Pasha,** crossed the Danube and in an engagement at **Oltenitza** (Nov. 4) held their own against the Russians.

Nov. 30. A Turkish squadron and transports on the way to the Asiatic front were caught and destroyed by the Russians off **Sinope.** Great indignation in Britain.

1854, Jan. 3. At Napoleon's suggestion the **British and French fleets entered the Black Sea,** to protect the Turkish coasts and transports.

Feb. 6. Russia broke off relations with Britain and France.

Feb. 27. Anglo-French ultimatum to Russia, demanding evacuation of the Principalities by April 30. The tsar did not even reply to this.

Mar. 12. Alliance of Britain and France with Turkey.

Mar. 20. The Russians crossed the Danube.

Mar. 28. Britain and France declared war on Russia and concluded an alliance with each other (Apr. 10).

Apr. 20. Defensive alliance between Austria and Prussia, each guaranteeing the other's territory for the duration of the war, and agreeing to oppose Russia if the latter made an effort to incorporate the Principalities or attempt an advance beyond the Balkan Mountains. Austria began to mass troops in Galicia and Transylvania.

June 3. Austrian ultimatum to Russia: Russia must not carry the war across the Balkan Mountains and must state a date for evacuation of the Principalities.

June 14. Austrian treaty with Turkey: Austria to occupy the Principalities until the end of the war and to intervene in Bosnia, Albania, or Montenegro in case disturbances broke out there.

Aug. 8. The **Russians evacuated the Principalities,** which were occupied by the Austrians (Aug. 22). Beginning of the sharp antagonism between Russia and Austria, which outlasted the century.

Aug. 8. The **VIENNA FOUR POINTS,** agreed to by Britain and France: conditions of peace to be: (1) collective guaranty of the position of the Principalities and Serbia; (2) free passage of the mouths of the Danube; (3) revision of the Straits convention in the interests of the European balance of power; (4) abandonment of the Russian claim to a protectorate over the sultan's subjects and agreement by the five great powers to secure privileges for the Christians without impairing the independence of Turkey. The Russians indignantly rejected these terms.

Sept. 14. Landing of the allied troops at Eupatoria in the Crimea, the campaign in the

Balkans (from Varna) having been cut short by the Russian evacuation of the Principalities. The British were commanded by **Lord Fitzroy Raglan,** the French by **General Armand Saint-Arnaud.** The objective was the strong Russian fortress of **Sevastopol.**

Sept. 20. BATTLE OF THE ALMA RIVER, in which the allies, marching south, defeated an inferior Russian force. Saint-Arnaud died of cholera and was succeeded by General Canrobert.

Oct. 17–19.   First bombardment of Sevastopol. The allies, lacking heavy artillery, were unable to make much impression and had to settle down to a siege.

Oct. 25.   BATTLE OF BALACLAVA, another allied victory (*charge of the Light Brigade*).

Nov. 5.   BATTLE OF INKERMAN, in which the Russians again failed to break through the enveloping forces. In the interval Sevastopol was strengthened through the efforts of **Colonel Franz Todleben,** famous military engineer. Horrible sufferings of the allied forces during the winter (lack of fuel, clothing, and supplies); relief work and nursing organized by **Florence Nightingale.**

Dec. 2.   Offensive and defensive alliance of Austria with Britain and France; the latter powers guaranteed Austria's possessions in Italy for the duration of the war and promised support against an attack by Russia; Austria promised to defend the Principalities and give the allies free hand there. Austria mobilized all her forces, but still abstained from hostilities.

1855, Jan. 26.   Sardinia (Piedmont) **entered the war** on the allied side and sent a force of 10,000 men under General Alfonso La Marmora, to the Crimea.

Mar. 2.   Death of Nicholas I. His successor, **Alexander II,** was more disposed to make peace and engaged in abortive negotiations at Vienna (Mar.–June).

Apr., June.   Violent attacks on Sevastopol failed to break the resistance of the Russians.

Sept. 8. The French forces finally succeeded in taking the **Malakov tower,** a key position; the British took the **Redan,** but were driven out again.

Sept. 11. The **Russians abandoned Sevastopol,** sinking their ships and blowing up the forts.

Nov. 21.   Sweden concluded a treaty with the allies: Sweden to make no cessions or exchanges of territory with Russia and the allies to support Sweden against such demands.

Nov. 28. On the Asiatic front the **Russians captured Kars.**

Dec. 28.   Austrian ultimatum to Russia, threatening war if Russia refused to accept the Vienna four points, plus the neutralization of the Black Sea and the cession of Bessarabia. Russia finally yielded and agreed to preliminary peace terms at Vienna (Feb. 1, 1856).

1856, Feb. 18. The **HATT-I HUMAYUN,** the most important Turkish reform edict of the 19th century, guaranteeing Christian subjects security of life, honor, and property and abolishing the civil power of the heads of the Christian churches. These churches in future were to be governed by a synod of the clergy and a national council of laymen. Full liberty of conscience was guaranteed and all civil offices thrown open to all subjects of the sultan. Christians were technically eligible for military service, but were allowed to buy themselves off. Torture was abolished and prisons reformed. Acquisition of property by foreigners allowed under certain circumstances, etc. These arrangements were opposed by the Turks as too far-reaching, and met with opposition from the Christian communities, but the whole program was worked out by the British, French, and Austrian ambassadors and forced on the Turkish government in order to effect a settlement before Russia could intervene.

Feb. 25–Mar. 30.   CONGRESS OF PARIS (Walewski, French foreign minister, president; for Britain, **Clarendon** and **Cowley;** for Austria, **Buol** and **Hübner;** for Russia, **Orlov** and **Brunnow;** for Turkey, **Ali Pasha** and **Mehmed Jemil;** for Sardinia, **Cavour).** Napoleon had high hopes of using the occasion to effect a general revision of the treaties of 1815, with special reference to Italy and Poland. These schemes were frustrated by Britain, which drew closer to Austria in a policy of preserving the *status quo;* France thereupon began to court Russia. By the **treaty of Paris** (Mar. 30) the powers admitted **Turkey** to the European concert and promised to respect the independence and integrity of the empire; **Russia** ceded the mouths of the Danube and a small part of Bessarabia; in Asia, Russia returned Kars; Russia gave up claims to a protectorate over the Christians in Turkey and the powers "recognized the high value" of the Hatt-i Humayun; the **Danubian Principalities** were placed under the joint guaranty of the powers and the status of the provinces was to be determined later; no change was made in the Straits convention, but Russia agreed to the **neutralization of the Black Sea; an international commission** was established to assure safe navigation of the Danube. Adoption of **four rules of international law:** (1) **privateering** remained abolished; (2) the **neutral flag covers enemy goods,** except contraband; (3) **neutral goods,** except contraband, were **not liable**

to capture under an enemy flag; (4) **blockade,** to be binding, must be effective.

Apr. 15. Anglo-French-Austrian treaty: the three powers agreed to regard any infringement of Turkish independence and integrity as a *casus belli* and to concert measures to meet it.

1856-1858. Settlement of the problem of the Principalities (p. 766).

1858. Definitive abolition of feudal holdings in the Ottoman Empire.

1860. Founding of Robert College, crowning achievement of American missionaries in Turkey (since 1820: **Bebek Seminary** founded by **Cyrus Hamlin,** 1840; **Home School for Girls,** later **Constantinople Women's College,** 1871).

1860-1861. Insurrection in Syria and conflict between the Moslem **Druses** and Christian **Maronites,** many of whom were massacred. The powers gave France a mandate to intervene (1860, Aug. 2) and a French expeditionary force restored order. Evacuation of the French (June 1861); special constitution for the Lebanon region.

1861-1876. ABDUL AZIZ. His reign was distinguished by a rapid **spread of western influence,** resulting from the association with Britain and France during the Crimean War (first loans to Turkey; construction of railroads from the Black Sea to the Danube, etc.), and by striking **development of liberalism (literary revival,** throwing off of the old Persian manner; **Namik Kemal,** radical dramatist and political writer; his history of the Ottomans and translations of Rousseau, Montesquieu, etc.; phenomenal growth of Turkish journalism). The leading statesmen of the period were **Ali** and **Fuad,** both followers of Reshid Pasha and committed to liberal reform. Encouragement of education: **Lycée of Galata Serai** (1868); **University of Constantinople** (1869); **School of Law** (1870).

1863. Foundation of the Banque Impériale Ottomane.

1864. Vilayet Law, establishing larger provinces under governors-general and subdivision into sanjaks, each with mixed councils and tribunals.

1865. Establishment of the **Ottoman National Debt Administration.**

1866-1868. Cretan insurrection. The islanders proclaimed their independence and union with Greece (1866, Sept. 2), but after years of fighting the revolt was put down. The sultan then proclaimed the **Organic Statute,** providing for Christian assessors to assist Turkish officials and for an elective assembly.

1867. Abdul Aziz attended the great exposition at Paris, the first sultan to travel abroad, visiting also London and Vienna.

1868. Concession granted for a **railroad to con-** nect Constantinople with the Hungarian lines (work begun 1872).

1868-1876. Elaboration of the **Code Civil Ottoman.**

1869. OPENING OF THE SUEZ CANAL (p. 867), the effect of which was to put the Ottoman Empire once more on the main trade route to the Far East.

1869. New **law of citizenship.**

1870. Establishment of the **Bulgarian exarchate,** a separate branch of the Greek Orthodox Church; an important stage in the development of the Bulgarian national movement (p. 762).

Oct. 31. Repudiation of the Black Sea clauses of the treaty of Paris by Russia, taking advantage of the Franco-German War. Britain and Austria protested, but Germany supported Russia. A **conference at London** finally (Mar. 13, 1871) accepted the Russian action while declaring against unilateral breaches of international agreements.

1872. A scheme, put forward by Ali Pasha, for the complete **reorganization of the empire.** The Balkan nationalities were to be given a self-governing status like that of Bavaria in the German Empire. This plan was ruined by the opposition of the nationalities and the protests of Russia.

1874. Financial collapse of the empire, due to heavy borrowing abroad and poor management. Half the interest on the debt was repudiated.

1875, July. INSURRECTION IN HERZEGOVINA AND BOSNIA, then in Bulgaria; war with Serbia and Montenegro; Russo-Turkish War of 1877-1878; **congress and treaty of Berlin** (p. 780).

1876, May 10. Midhat Pasha, dominant figure of a new ministry. Midhat was the successor of Reshid, Ali, and Fuad, and an ardent reformer. His brilliant administration of Bulgaria (1861-1869) and of Baghdad (1869-1873). His plans for the establishment of a national state, including the Christians in the **new Ottoman nationality.**

May 30. Midhat and his associates **deposed Abdul Aziz** and proclaimed his nephew, **Murad V,** as sultan. Abdul Aziz died soon after, either by suicide or murder.

June 15. Assassination of several members of the government by a Circassian officer. **Midhat supreme leader** of the victorious reforming party.

Aug. 31. Deposition of Murad V on the plea of insanity.

1876-1909. ABDUL HAMID II.

1876, Dec. 23. PROCLAMATION OF THE CONSTITUTION by **Midhat Pasha:** it declared the indivisibility of the Ottoman Empire, liberty of the individual, freedom of conscience, the press, and education; equality of taxation; irremovability of judges; parliamentary government based on general representation.

1877, Feb. 5. Dismissal of Midhat Pasha, who was banished.

Mar. 19. Opening of the **first Turkish parliament.** It made a serious effort to fulfill its mission, but was soon prorogued by the sultan, who allowed the constitution to lapse and devoted himself to the re-establishment of his absolute power. Midhat and others were tried in 1881 for the murder of Abdul Aziz and convicted. Only intervention by the British government saved them from execution.

1878. Insurrection in Crete. After its suppression the sultan granted (Oct.) the **pact of Halepa,** giving the Christians a majority in the general assembly and allowing the island practical self-government.

1881. French occupation of Tunis (pp. 782, 873).

1882. British occupation of Egypt (pp. 783, 868).

1885-1888. INSURRECTION IN EASTERN ROUMELIA and resultant eastern crisis (pp. 764, 783).

1888, Aug. 12. Opening of the railroad from Hungary to Constantinople.

Oct. 6. Concession to German interests for a railroad to **Angora** (Ankara), the first stage in the **Baghdad Railway project** (p. 794).

1889. Insurrection in Crete, encouraged by Greece. The powers showed little interest and the rising was put down. The sultan thereupon curtailed the pact of Halepa, reducing the power of the assembly and increasing that of the governor.

1890-1897. ARMENIAN REVOLUTIONARY MOVEMENT and subsequent Armenian massacres, resulting from the growth of a national movement since 1840 and the failure of the powers (1879-1883) to secure reforms for the Anatolian provinces (p. 776).

1895. Raids of Bulgar revolutionaries into Macedonia and beginning of the systematic activity of Bulgarian, Greek, and Serbian *komitadjis* (members of revolutionary committees) in that region (p. 765).

1896-1897. CRETAN INSURRECTION, fomented and supported by Greeks and resulting in the Turco-Greek War of 1897 (p. 789).

1896-1908. REVIVAL AND DEVELOPMENT OF THE YOUNG TURK MOVEMENT, harking back to the constitution of 1876. The Young Turks (mostly exiles in France, Switzerland, and Britain) hoped to capitalize the discredit of the sultan; their chief aim was to prevent the disruption of the empire and

to reconstitute it on a liberal, national basis. To some extent they arranged co-operation with the Armenian, Macedonian, and other revolutionary organizations (1903), but the movement throughout was hampered by dissensions between factions and by the drastic repressive measures of Abdul Hamid, which made all activity within Turkey impossible.

1900-1908. Construction of the Hijaz Railway to the Moslem Holy Places in Arabia. The line was built by popular subscription and was intended as a Pan-Islamic project.

1902-1903. Insurrection in Macedonia. Intervention of the powers. **Mürzsteg program** of reforms (p. 794).

1905, Nov., Dec. After prolonged argument between the Turkish government and the powers regarding the number of officers to be employed in the Macedonian gendarmerie, the terms of international control of Macedonian finance, etc., the powers made a naval demonstration and occupied Lemnos, forcing the sultan to yield.

1906, May. Dispute with Britain regarding the frontier between Palestine and Egypt **(Tabah, Akaba).** The sultan yielded to a British ultimatum.

1907, Dec. Meeting of various **Young Turk** and revolutionary groups at Paris. They concerted plans for action in common, and established contact with groups of discontented army officers **(Committee of Liberty,** founded 1905–1906) and **Masonic lodges** at Saloniki and in other towns of the empire.

1908, June 9. Reval meeting between King Edward and Tsar Nicholas. The Russians agreed to a much more extensive British plan of Macedonian reform. Fear that the three Macedonian provinces would be lost to the empire precipitated action by the Young Turk organization, the **Committee of Union and Progress.**

July 5. Niazi Bey, chief organizer of the revolutionary movement in Turkey, raised the standard of revolt at **Resna,** in Macedonia. When the sultan had a number of officers arrested at Saloniki, others, notably **Enver Bey,** joined Niazi (July 8). The Committee of Union and Progress adopted the insurrection (July 13), which was supported also by the Albanians. Government troops sent against the rebels deserted to the movement.

July 24. RESTORATION OF THE CONSTITUTION OF 1876 by Abdul Hamid, after several days of debate in the council of ministers. The sultan now posed as a good father who had been misled by his ministers. The revolutionaries gave up all thought of deposing him. Several weeks of frantic joy and fraternization throughout the empire, all nationalities joining with the Turks in the common celebration.

Oct. 5, 6. Proclamation of Bulgarian independence and annexation of **Bosnia and Herzegovina** by Austria (p. 798).

Dec. 17. First meeting of parliament, which had a large Young Turk majority. Growing rift between the representatives of the subject nationalities **(Liberal Union)** and the Turkish nationalists, who dominated the Committee of Union and Progress: main issue that of decentralization in favor of the nationalities, and introduction of Turkish as the only official language.

1909, Feb. 13. Fall of Kiamil Pasha, the grand vizir. He was a liberal, sympathetic to reform and to the program of the moderates. The committee forced his resignation and had one of its sympathizers, **Hilmi Pasha,** appointed grand vizir.

Apr. 13. REVOLT OF THE FIRST ARMY CORPS, chiefly Albanian, at Constantinople, after violent attacks upon committee rule by the **Mohammedan Union** and other conservative forces. The insurgents took the parliament house and telegraph offices and forced Hilmi Pasha to resign. The committee thereupon appealed to the troops in Macedonia.

Apr. 24. Mahmud Shevket Pasha, with an **army of liberation** numbering some 25,000, reached Constantinople and after five hours of fighting took the city. The leaders of the mutiny were executed and the control of the committee re-established.

Apr. 26. ABDUL HAMID DEPOSED by unanimous vote of the parliament, because of his approval of the counter-revolution. He was sent into exile at Saloniki (d. Feb. 10, 1918).

1909–1918. MOHAMMED V, brother of Abdul Hamid, a weak and helpless ruler.

1909, Apr. Massacre of Armenians at Adana and other places of Little Armenia. These were provoked by Armenian demonstrations which aroused the Moslems.

Aug. Revision of the constitution: the sultan was henceforth to name only the grand vizir, who was to appoint the other ministers; the sultan was deprived of the power to dissolve parliament; the cabinet was made responsible to parliament, which was given equal right to initiate legislation.

1910, Apr.–June. Insurrection in Albania, the result of Albanian demands for autonomy and the repressive policy of the Turkish national-ists. The revolt was put down with much bloodshed by a large Turkish army. In **Arabia,** too, there was constant disorder.

1911, Sept. 28. Outbreak of the **WAR WITH ITALY** (pp. 710, 800).

1912, Jan. 18. The **sultan dissolved the first parliament,** after a phenomenal growth of criticism of government by the committee.

Apr. The **elections** turned out a great victory for the committee, which appears to have used every form of pressure on the electorate.

June 25. Discontented officers at Monastir **(Saviors of the Nation)** joined the Albanians in a new insurrection against the government.

July 21. Cabinet of Ghazi Ahmed Mukhtar Pasha, a non-committee government representing the victory of the moderate groups over the extreme nationalists. The new government dissolved parliament by force (Aug. 5) and proclaimed martial law.

Oct. 8, 18. OUTBREAK OF THE BALKAN WAR (p. 801).

Nov. 28. Proclamation of Albanian independence, by an assembly at Valona which rejected the grant of autonomy made by the Turkish government on August 20.

1913, Jan. 23. *COUP D'ETAT* OF THE YOUNG TURKS (especially **Enver Bey**) against the government, which was prepared to cede Adrianople to the victorious Balkan states. **Mahmud Shevket Pasha** became grand vizir.

May 30. Treaty of London, closing the First Balkan War (p. 802).

June 11. Assassination of Mahmud Shevket Pasha. This led to a period of Young Turk terrorism, which lasted until the World War. The country was, to all intents and purposes, ruled by **Enver, Talaat,** and **Jemal,** a triumvirate which ruthlessly suppressed all opposition.

July 20. The **Turks took Adrianople,** in the course of the Second Balkan War (p. 802). This was retained by the **treaty of Constantinople** (Sept. 29).

Dec. The **Liman von Sanders crisis** (p. 803).

1914, Feb. 8. The Turkish government accepted a program of **reform for the Armenian provinces,** worked out by the powers under the leadership of Russia.

Aug. 2. Secret treaty of alliance with Germany (p. 955).

Nov. 4. RUSSIA DECLARED WAR ON TURKEY (p. 805). (*Cont. pp. 955 f., 1085.*)

F. INTERNATIONAL AFFAIRS, 1870–1914

The period was characterized at first by the power of Germany, the weakness of France, and the aloofness of Britain. In the first decade Bismarck, whose figure dominated the scene, attempted to follow a policy of the free hand, but the constant friction between Austria and Russia with regard to the Near East made it necessary for him to make a choice between them. Thereby he embarked upon the policy of alliances, which ultimately involved most of the European powers in one group or another. The effect of technical and industrial advance on warfare resulted in growing anxiety for security on all sides, and consequently to alignments for the event of war which, in fact, tended to make war more likely. At the same time the expansion of European powers in Africa and Asia greatly extended the field of possible friction.

1871, Aug., Sept. Meetings of Emperor William and Francis Joseph, with their foreign ministers, at Ischl, Gastein, and Salzburg. The Austrians, their hopes of revenge for 1866 blasted by the defeat of France, were ready for better relations with the powerful German Empire. This policy was represented especially by the Magyars (**Count Julius Andrássy,** foreign minister, November 13, 1871).

1872, Sept. 6–12. Meeting of the three emperors in Berlin William, Francis Joseph, Alexander II of Russia, who invited himself, lest Austria and Germany become too intimate. No political agreements were made at the meeting, but Andrássy and Gorchakov, the Russian chancellor, discussed the Near Eastern situation and agreed to work for the *status quo.*

1873, May 6. Military convention between Germany and Russia, concluded during the visit of the Emperor William, Bismarck, and Moltke to St. Petersburg. If either party were attacked by another European power, the other was to come to its assistance with 200,000 men.

June 6. Agreement between Russia and Austria (Schönbrunn convention) providing for consultation and eventual co-operation in case of attack on either. These agreements were loose in nature. Together they formed the **Three Emperors' League,** the main aim of which was to emphasize monarchical solidarity against subversive movements and to secure for Germany support in the event of trouble with France (May 1873, overthrow of Thiers by the French monarchists).

Sept. Visit of King Victor Emmanuel II to Vienna and Berlin. Italy loosely associated with the Three Emperors' League, in order to obtain assurance against action by France in behalf of the pope.

Sept. Completion of the evacuation of French territory by German troops. Activity of the French royalists and clericals. Efforts at alliance with Russia. Friction with Italy and Germany over the question of the Papacy and the *Kulturkampf* (p. 738).

1875, Feb. Mission of Radowitz to St. Petersburg, reflecting Bismarck's anxiety to hold Russia, in view of tension in relations with France.

Apr. 8. The article **"Is War in Sight?"** published in the Berlin *Post.* This referred to the new French army law and concluded that war was in sight. Panic in France, where the article was regarded as an inspired one. The **Duc Decazes,** French foreign minister, appealed to Britain and Russia for support, with the aim of discrediting Bismarck.

May 10. Visit of Tsar Alexander and Gorchakov to Berlin. Warnings of Gorchakov, supported by similar action by the British ambassador, Lord Odo Russell. Acrimonious discussion between Bismarck and Gorchakov. The latter's telegram: "Peace is now assured." Results: Bismarck realized the weakness of the Three Emperors' League and the suspicious jealousy of the other powers. France strengthened by the "moral coalition" that had been formed against Germany and by the knowledge that neither Britain nor Russia would stand idly by if France were attacked by Germany in a preventive war.

July. Outbreak of the **insurrection against Turkish rule** in Herzegovina and then Bosnia (p. 775). This initiated three years of acute Near Eastern tension, which profoundly modified the relations of the powers to each other. The **Serbs** at once supported the insurgents, in the hope of acquiring the two provinces for themselves. **Russia** was extremely sympathetic (religious affinity, racial relationship to the South Slavs, Panslav movement and ambitions, secular aims for the destruction of Turkey, opening of the Straits to Russian warships, etc.).

Nov. 25. Purchase of the khedive of Egypt's shares in the Suez Canal, a master-stroke of British policy (**Benjamin Disraeli**) which indicated Britain's growing interest in the Near East.

Dec. 12. Efforts at mediation by the powers having led to nothing, the sultan, in order to forestall more energetic action, promulgated reforms for the whole Ottoman Empire which were to meet the demands made by the insurgents.

Dec. 30. The **Andrássy note,** communicated to all powers signatories of the treaty of Paris of 1856. It called for complete religious freedom in Bosnia and Herzegovina, abolition of tax-farming, use of local revenue for local needs, and establishment of a mixed Christian-Moslem commission to supervise these reforms. This program was adopted by the powers and by the sultan (Jan. 31, 1876), but failed of its purpose because it was rejected by the insurgents.

1876, Jan.–Feb. Bismarck's advances to Britain, in the hope of meeting a possible Austrian-Russian rupture. This move was ruined by the suspicion of **Lord Derby,** the British foreign secretary.

May 13. The **Berlin memorandum,** drawn up by Andrássy, Gorchakov, and Bismarck after a conference at Berlin. It reflected Andrássy's aversion to any policy of annexations (suggested by Bismarck and Gorchakov) and was an expansion of the Andrássy note. It called for a two months' armistice, resettlement of the insurgents, concentration of the Turkish troops in a few localities, retention of arms by the insurgents, supervision of reforms by the consuls of the powers. The memorandum was accepted by France and Italy, but was rejected by Britain, partly for technical reasons, but chiefly because of Disraeli's resentment of the failure to consult Britain in the drafting of the program.

May–Sept. Insurrection in Bulgaria, suppressed with great severity by Turkish irregular troops (*Bulgarian horrors*); thousands slaughtered.

June 30. Serbia declared war on Turkey, trusting in Russia for support and hoping for the eventual acquisition of the insurgent provinces.

July 2. Montenegro joined Serbia in the war.

July–Aug. The **Serbs,** commanded by the Russian general, Chernaiev, defeated in a series of engagements. Serbia invaded.

July 8. Meeting at Reichstadt of Andrássy and Gorchakov. **Reichstadt agreement:** the two powers to insist on the *status quo ante bellum* in the event of the defeat of Serbia and Montenegro, and on the reforms for Bosnia and Herzegovina laid down in the Berlin memorandum. In the event of Serbian-Montenegrin victory, these two powers to be given parts of Bosnia and Herzegovina, but the larger part of these provinces to be awarded to Austria. Russia to obtain Bessarabia (lost in 1856). In the event of Turkey's collapse, Bulgaria and Roumelia to be autonomous states or independent principalities; Greece to acquire some territory; Constantinople to be a free city.

Sept. 1. Complete defeat of the Serbs at Alexinatz. They appealed to the powers for mediation. The Turks rejected proposals for an armistice, except on very hard terms. Great excitement in Russia and demand for war. Efforts of the Russians to secure assurance of German support in the event of war developing between Russia and Austria. Bismarck's reply: Germany would intervene only to prevent either Russia or Austria being mortally wounded or seriously weakened by the other.

Sept. 6. Gladstone's pamphlet: *The Bulgarian Horrors and the Question of the East.* Tremendous agitation in Britain against Turkish misrule. This greatly hampered the government in a policy of supporting Turkey against Russia.

Oct. 31. Turkey agreed to a six-week armistice, as a result of a **Russian ultimatum** to check the continued successes of the Turks.

Nov. Russian preparations for war against Turkey. Bellicose attitude of Disraeli, determined to frustrate the Russian designs.

Dec. 12. First meeting of the **Constantinople conference,** convoked at the instance of Britain. Negotiations between **Lord Salisbury,** the British plenipotentiary, and **Count Nicholas Ignatiev,** the Russian ambassador. Agreement: Serbia to lose no territory; Montenegro to secure parts of Herzegovina and Albania conquered from the Turks; Bulgaria (i.e. the regions under the Bulgarian exarchate, extending over most of Macedonia) to be divided into an eastern and a western province; Bosnia and Herzegovina to be united as a province, and this, as well as the two Bulgarias, to have a governor-general appointed by the powers with approval of the Turkish government, and a provincial assembly; reforms to be supervised by the powers.

Dec. 23. Midhat Pasha, the grand vizir and leader of the Turkish liberals and nationalists, published the famous **constitution,** introducing a liberal régime for the whole empire and making reforms in special provinces ostensibly unnecessary.

1877, Jan. 18. An **assembly of notables** in Constantinople rejected all demands of the powers. Failure of the Constantinople conference, which closed January 20.

Jan. 15. January convention (Budapest convention) between Russia and Austria, to settle disputes as to the terms of the Reichstadt convention: Austria to remain neutral in an eventual Russian-Turkish war; Austria to occupy Bosnia and Herzegovina when she saw fit; Serbia, Montenegro, and Herzegovina to form a neutral zone. An **additional convention,** signed March 18 but antedated to January 15, reaffirmed the terms of the Reichstadt convention with regard to the disposition of

Turkish territory; no large state, Slavic or otherwise, to be erected in the Balkans.

Feb.–Mar.   Ignatiev mission to western capitals. Efforts of the British to arrange disarmament of both Russia and Turkey.

Apr. 24.   RUSSIA DECLARED WAR ON TURKEY, the government yielding to the pressure of the Panslav circles.

May 6.   British note to Russia, warning against an attempted blockade of the Suez Canal or occupation of Egypt and reaffirming Britain's traditional stand with regard to Constantinople and the Straits. Bismarck's suggestions to the British to take Egypt and other parts of the Ottoman Empire rather than provoke war. Evasive reply of the Russians to the British note (June 8).

July 26, Aug. 14.   Loose and negative **agreement between Britain and Austria,** listing seven points to which they would not agree in the event of a Russian victory. The British cabinet had decided (July 21) to declare war on Russia if the latter occupied Constantinople and did not make arrangements for immediate retirement. The reverses of the Russians at Plevna (July 20 ff.) eased the situation.

Dec. 10.   Fall of Plevna, resumption of the Russian advance.

Dec. 12.   The Turks appealed to the powers for mediation. This was rejected by Bismarck. Disraeli anxious to act, but his schemes were frustrated by members of his own cabinet (especially Derby). Andrássy contented himself with warning the Russians that Austria and the powers would demand a voice in the peace settlement.

1878, Jan. 9.   The Turks appealed to the Russians for an armistice.

Jan. 23.   The **British cabinet decided to send the fleet to Constantinople,** at the sultan's request. Resignation of Lord Derby. The fleet was recalled after reassuring reports had arrived from Constantinople. Derby rejoined the cabinet.

Jan. 28.   Andrássy proposed the convocation of a European conference.

Jan. 31.   Armistice concluded, the Russians to occupy the lines just outside Constantinople. War fever in Britain (*"We don't want to fight, but by jingo, if we do, we've got the men, we've got the ships, we've got the money too."*).

Feb. 8.   Second British decision to send up the fleet. Other powers invited to join. The fleet started to enter the Straits, but returned when the sultan, under pressure from the Russians, failed to give permission.

Feb. 15.   The British fleet finally arrived at Constantinople, having been ordered to proceed even without permission.

Mar. 3.   The **TREATY OF SAN STE-FANO** between Russia and Turkey (ratified March 23): **Montenegro** to be enlarged and given the port of Antivari; both **Montenegro and Serbia to be independent,** the latter also receiving some territory; **Roumania to be independent,** Russia reserving the right to give Roumania the Dobrudja in return for Bessarabia; **Bosnia and Herzegovina** to be granted reforms; **Bulgaria** to be an autonomous state under an elected prince and to be occupied for two years by Russian troops; it was to include most of Macedonia and to have a seaboard on the Aegean; **Russia** to receive **Ardahan, Kars, Batum,** and **Bayazid** on the Asiatic front; **Turkey** to pay a huge indemnity.

Mar. 6.   Andrássy issued invitations to a congress of the powers to meet at Berlin. Long disputes between Britain and Russia as to what subjects might be discussed at the congress.

Mar. 25.   Mission of Ignatiev to Vienna; he failed to reconcile the Austrians to the Russian peace settlement.

Mar. 27.   The British cabinet agreed to call out the reserves and to bring troops from India to occupy one or two stations in the eastern Mediterranean. **Second resignation of Lord Derby. Lord Salisbury became foreign minister.**

Apr. 1.   Salisbury's circular, restating the British position in strong and effective fashion. British efforts to establish common action with Austria. These were met by evasion.

May 8.   Mission of Count Peter Shuvalov, Russian ambassador to London, to St. Petersburg. He there imposed a policy of agreement with Britain. He returned May 23 with the offer to push Bulgaria back from the Aegean, pare it down in the west, and divide it into a north and south part.

May 30.   Secret Anglo-Russian agreement, as arranged by Shuvalov.

June 4.   Secret Anglo-Turkish agreement, reluctantly accepted by the sultan. To meet the Russian advance in Asia Minor, the British promised to defend Turkey against any further attack on the sultan's Asiatic possessions. In return they were to be allowed to occupy **Cyprus.** The sultan promised to introduce reforms in his Asiatic territories.

June 6.   Anglo-Austrian Agreement, following the failure of the Ignatiev mission. The agreement dealt with the future organization of Bulgaria and the length of Russian occupation.

June 13–July 13.   The **BERLIN CONGRESS: Bismarck,** the "honest broker"; **Gorchakov** and **Shuvalov** for Russia; **Andrássy** for Austria; **Disraeli** and **Salisbury** for Britain; **Waddington** for France; **Count Corti** for Italy; **Caratheodory** (a Greek) for Turkey. The main decisions had been made in the preceding secret agreements, but there was much trouble and friction about details, especially after the Anglo-Russian agreement leaked out. **Bulgaria was divided** into three parts: (1) Bulgaria proper, north of the Balkan Mountains, to be tributary and autonomous; (2) Eastern Roumelia, south of the mountains, to have a special organization under the Turkish government; (3) Macedonia, which was to have certain reforms. **Austria** was given a mandate (June 28) to occupy Bosnia and Herzegovina and to garrison the Sanjak of Novi Bazar, a strip lying between Serbia and Montenegro. The territory given to Serbia and Montenegro was reduced. The **Greeks** were put off with promises for the future. **Roumania** was given the Dobrudja, but had to hand over southern Bessarabia to Russia. **Serbia, Roumania,** and **Montenegro** became independent states. **Russia** received Batum, Kars, and Ardahan. Reforms were promised for the sultan's Asiatic provinces. The British occupied Cyprus under the **Cyprus convention** (above). Objections of the **French** were met by promising them permission to occupy **Tunis.** The **Italians** were put off with suggestions of expansion in Albania. The upshot of the treaty was that it left Russian nationalists and Panslavs profoundly dissatisfied and left the aspirations of Serbia, Bulgaria, and Greece unfulfilled. The Ottoman Empire, wholly at the mercy of the powers, was left with a few fragments of territory in Europe which were a constant bait for covetous neighbors. The promise of reforms in Macedonia and Asia Minor led to far-reaching agitation and trouble on the part of the Macedonians and Armenians.

Oct. 11. Agreement between Germany and Austria abrogating the provision of the treaty of Prague (1866) requiring a plebiscite in North Schleswig. This agreement had really been reached on February 13, 1878, but was postdated. Its publication (Feb. 4, 1879) was taken to reflect a German rapprochement with Austria.

Nov. 20. Outbreak of **war between Britain and Afghanistan,** the result of the Russian advance in central Asia and the determination of the British to secure their frontier in India (p. 902). The British drove out the amir, **Sher Ali,** and put **Yakub Khan** on the throne. In September 1879 the British agent, **Major Sir Pierre Cavagnari,** was murdered and the war flared up anew. **Abd ar-Rahman** entered Afghanistan with Russian support, but made an agreement with the British (July 20, 1880): the British recognized him and gave him a pension.

1879, Sept. 4. Establishment of the **Dual Con-**trol (Britain and France) **in Egypt** (p. 867). This grew out of the heavy investments of Europeans in Egypt and the financial difficulties resulting from the construction of the Suez Canal and many other public works by the **khedive Ismaïl.** The dual control was first established in November 1876, but had been suspended in December 1878 when the khedive initiated ministerial government and gave the British and French controllers of finance seats in the cabinet. This plan had not worked, because of the policy of the khedive of retaining power. Britain and France thereupon forced the **abdication of Ismaïl** (1879, June 26) and the succession of **Tewfik,** who restored the dual control.

Oct. 7. ALLIANCE TREATY BETWEEN GERMANY AND AUSTRIA, concluded for five years, but regularly renewed; it remained in force until 1918 and was the foundation stone of Bismarck's alliance system. Provisions: If either party were attacked by Russia, the other should come to its assistance with all forces; if either should be attacked by some other power, its partner should preserve at least neutrality; if some other power should be supported by Russia, then each ally was obliged to aid the other. The alliance was the result of a period of tension between Germany and Russia following the Berlin congress, the Russian nationalists blaming Bismarck for Russia's diplomatic defeat. There had been months of newspaper recrimination culminating in a threatening letter of Tsar Alexander II to William I. Bismarck, always fearful of a coalition built up by Russia against Germany and suspecting that Andrássy would soon be displaced by the pro-Russian party in Vienna, decided on the alliance, which Andrássy welcomed. The negotiations were held up by the obstinate resistance of Emperor William, who yielded only when Bismarck threatened to resign. There was some thought of bringing **Britain** into the combination; Disraeli was friendly, but the German ambassador, Count Münster, misrepresented the projected alliance as one directed chiefly against France and Bismarck allowed the matter to drop. The immediate result of the negotiation was the **mission of Count Pierre Saburov** to Berlin, in the effort to effect a Russian-German alliance or the revival of the Three Emperors' League (Sept.–Oct. 1879). For the moment Bismarck evaded these advances.

1880, June–Nov. Montenegrin troubles. The Albanian League, a union of tribes supported by the sultan, vigorously and successfully resisted the efforts of the Montenegrins to take over the Albanian territory assigned them by the treaty of Berlin. A conference of the powers at Berlin (June) decided that Montenegro should receive Dulcigno in lieu of some of the disputed territory. The Turks resisted. A naval demonstration of the powers at **Dulcigno** (Sept. 28) had no effect. The British government (under Gladstone since April) took a strong line and threatened to occupy the customs house at Smyrna. The Turks finally yielded (Nov. 25).

1881, May 12.   Treaty of Bardo, establishing a French protectorate over Tunis. This went back to the assurances of Salisbury and Bismarck during the congress of Berlin, but the French government had not acted because of the indifference of French public opinion in matters of colonial expansion and because of distrust of Bismarck's motives. The question was precipitated by the activity of the Italians, determined to make good their failure to secure gains at the Berlin congress at Austria's expense. The French prime minister, **Jules Ferry,** an ardent imperialist, took advantage of raids by Krumir tribes into Algeria (Mar. 1881) to secure credits from the chamber. After the invasion of Tunis the bey gave in without much resistance. The affair initiated a long period of **Franco-Italian tension** and modified the Mediterranean situation to Britain's disadvantage. Gladstone protested, but the British government was committed by Salisbury's assurances.

May 24.   The Turks were obliged to cede to Greece a considerable part of **Thessaly** and part of **Epirus.** These territories had been promised Greece at the Berlin congress, but the Turks had temporized. In the autumn of 1880 there was acute danger of war. In the end the Greeks had to content themselves with much less than had originally been envisaged.

June 18.   The ALLIANCE OF THE THREE EMPERORS: term three years, renewed in 1884 for three more years. Provisions: If one of the contracting powers found itself at war with a fourth power (except Turkey), the other two were to maintain friendly neutrality. Modifications of the territorial *status quo* in Turkey should take place only after agreement between the three powers; if any one of them should feel compelled to go to war with Turkey, it should consult its allies in advance as to the eventual results; the principle of the closure of the Straits was recognized; if this principle were infringed by Turkey, the three powers would warn Turkey that they would regard her as having put herself in a state of war with the aggrieved power; Austria reserved the right to annex Bosnia and Herzegovina when it saw fit; the three powers agreed not to oppose the eventual union of Bulgaria and Eastern Roumelia. This treaty, kept rigorously secret, was the outcome of long negotiations between Bismarck and Saburov, the Russians being anxious for an alliance with Germany as protection against Austrian policy in the Balkans, and equally anxious for recognition of the closure of the Straits against possible British action. Bismarck refused an agreement that would not include Austria and the Austrians were hostile to the idea until after the advent of the Gladstone government in Britain, which was unfriendly to Austria. The final conclusion of the agreement was delayed by the assassination of the tsar (Mar. 13, 1881).

June 28.   Secret treaty between Austria and Serbia, the result of Prince Milan's resentment at being deserted by Russia in 1878 and of his chronic need for Austrian financial support. Term ten years. Serbia promised not to tolerate intrigues against Austria. Austria promised to recognize Milan as king. By Art. IV Serbia engaged not to conclude any political agreement with another power without consulting Austria. In case of war with other powers, each promised the other neutrality. Austria promised that in favorable circumstances she would support Serbia in making acquisitions toward the south. The treaty established more or less of a protectorate over Serbia and roused protests from the Serbian ministers. But Milan assumed personal responsibility.

1882, May 20.   TRIPLE ALLIANCE, between Germany, Austria, and Italy, concluded for five years and renewed at intervals until 1915. Terms: If Italy were attacked by France without provocation, Germany and Austria were to come to Italy's aid; Italy to come to Germany's aid if the latter were attacked by France; if one or two of the contracting parties were attacked or involved in war with two or more great powers, the non-attacked member or members of the alliance should come to the aid of the other or others; if one of the allies should be forced to make war on some other great power, the others were to preserve benevolent neutrality. The treaty was the result of Italy's isolation after the French occupation of Tunis and also a reflection of popular demand for security against radicalism and the prospect of intervention by other powers in behalf of the pope. The Italians wanted above all a treaty of guaranty, assuring them of the possession of Rome. This neither Austria nor Germany was willing to consider, though Austria was anxious for an agreement that would put an end to **irredentist agitation** (very active since 1876), and Germany was uneasy about the renewed Panslav agitation (speech of Gen. **Skobelev** in Paris, February 1882) and the possibility of a Franco-Russian alliance. The Italians secured no specific guaranty of Rome, but received assurances against attack by France.

July 11. Bombardment of Alexandria by the British fleet.

Sept. 13. Defeat of the Egyptians by the British in the **battle of Tel-el-Kebir. British occupation of Egypt** (p. 868).

1883, Feb.-Apr. Establishment of the Germans, under Lüderitz, at Angra Pequeña (Southwest Africa), marking the **beginning of German colonialism** (growing agitation from 1875 onward—*German Colonial Society*, 1882) and Bismarck's conversion to imperialism (p. 881). There followed two years of growing **tension between Britain and Germany,** the dispute extending to East African territory, the Cameroons, etc. Bismarck managed to establish a loose **entente with the French** (Jules Ferry), especially in the question of Egypt (financial conference at London, June–August 1884), and thereby to oblige the British to accept Germany as a colonial power.

Oct. 30. Alliance of Roumania and Austria, to which Germany adhered. This was due to Roumanian dissatisfaction with the settlement of 1878 and fear of violation of Roumanian territory in the event of another advance of the Russians into the Balkans. The Roumanians, by the alliance, shelved their irredentist aspirations in Transylvania, but the agreement was kept exceedingly secret and had little effect on public opinion. Terms: Austria to come to the assistance of Roumania in case the latter were attacked without provocation; Roumania to come to Austria's aid if the latter were attacked in a portion of its states bordering on Roumania (i.e. by Russia). The treaty was concluded for five years, but was periodically renewed and remained in force until 1916.

Nov. Battle of El Obeid. General William Hicks and an Egyptian force defeated by the **Mahdi,** religious leader of a movement directed against Egyptian rule in the Sudan (p. 868).

1884, Feb. 26. British agreement with Portugal, recognizing the latter's rights to territory at the mouth of the Congo (p. 878). France and Germany together protested so vigorously that the British abandoned the treaty (June 26).

1884, Nov. 15–1885, Feb. 26. The **Berlin conference on African affairs,** arranged by Bismarck and Ferry. Fourteen nations, including the United States, agreed to work for the suppression of slavery and the slave trade and declared complete liberty of commerce in the basin of the Congo and its affluents and on the adjacent coasts. Freedom of navigation on the Congo and Niger and their affluents was also declared. The Congo basin was declared

neutral. The principle of effective occupation to establish a claim on the coasts was set up. At the same time the various powers recognized the **Congo Free State,** which had developed under Leopold of Belgium from the **International Association for the Exploration and Civilization of Central Africa** (1876), and later the **International Association of the Congo** (1878), financed by Leopold and exploiting the discoveries of **Henry M. Stanley.**

1885, Mar. 31. Fall of Jules Ferry from power, after a minor French reverse at Langson in the course of the **war with China** (p. 912) over Annam and Tonkin· (July 12, 1884–June 9, 1885). **End of the Franco-German entente;** gradual reconciliation of the British and Germans, with recognition of the German acquisitions in Africa and the Pacific.

Apr. Acute **Anglo-Russian crisis,** resulting from an attack by Russian troops on the Afghan forces at **Penjdeh** (Mar. 30). The Russians had gradually absorbed the central Asian khanates (**occupation of Merv,** February 1884) and reached the territory supposedly under the amir of Afghanistan. Efforts to delimit the frontier had been unsuccessful, due largely to the temporizing of the Russians. News of the Penjdeh clash brought the two countries to the verge of war. The British occupied **Port Hamilton,** on the Korean coast (Apr. 26), in view of probable operations against Vladivostok. But the British government ultimately drew back, apparently after abortive efforts to secure the consent of the powers for the passage of British warships through the Straits into the Black Sea. The question was adjusted by compromise (June 18, 1886).

Sept. 18. Revolution in Eastern Roumelia, initiating another period of tension in the Near East. The movement was directed at union with Bulgaria. **Prince Alexander of Battenberg** (elected prince of Bulgaria in April 1879) was obliged to assume leadership or else abandon his position. The Russian tsar at once (Sept. 23) recalled all Russian officers from the Bulgarian army, an expression of the dislike and even hatred for Prince Alexander that had been developing during the preceding years. Bulgaria was saved through the unwillingness of the sultan to send troops, and through the warm sympathy of Britain, which reversed its attitude on the question of union in order to meet the change in Russian policy. Austria was sympathetic to the union, but embarrassed by the clamor of the Serbs, who, like the Greeks, feared the movement might spread to Macedonia, where they too had claims.

Nov. 13. Serbia declared war on Bulgaria, after it had become clear that an ambassadorial conference at Constantinople would not rescind the union of Bulgaria and Eastern Roumelia.

Nov. 17. Complete defeat of the Serbians in the battle of Slivnitza.

Nov. 27. Serb defeat at Pirot. **Bulgarian invasion.** This was stopped only through Austrian intervention to save Serbia **(Khevenhüller mission).**

1886, Jan. 4. Greek note to Turkey demanding the territorial promises of 1878 by way of compensation for Bulgarian claims.

Jan. 24. Note of the powers to Greece warning against attack on Turkey. The Greeks ignored these warnings and prepared for war.

Feb. 1. Agreement between Bulgaria and Turkey. Prince Alexander appointed governor-general of Eastern Roumelia for five years. Russia insisted that Alexander should not be specifically named. The powers accepted this compromise and the agreement was signed on April 5.

Mar. 3. Treaty of Bucharest: "Peace is restored between Bulgaria and Serbia."

May 10–June 7. Pacific blockade of the Greek coast by an international naval force. The Greeks were obliged to disarm.

Aug. 20. Kidnaping and **abdication of Alexander of Battenberg** by a group of officers, supported by Russia. A counter-movement in Eastern Roumelia, led by **Stephen Stambulov,** overthrew the Russian faction and recalled Alexander.

Aug. 29. Arrival of Alexander. He appealed to the tsar for mercy, but received a cold reply.

Sept. 4. Definitive abdication of Alexander of Battenberg. Indignation in Europe generally, but especially in Britain.

Nov. 10. Bulgarian national assembly at Tirnovo. Despite pressure from Russia **(Kaulbars mission)** the Bulgarians elected as prince **Waldemar of Denmark,** who declined the offer. Kaulbars and other Russian agents left the country (Nov. 17). Danger of Russian occupation of Bulgaria.

Nov. 13. Speech of Count Kálnoky, the Austrian foreign minister, warning against Russian action. **Growing Austro-Russian tension,** much deplored by Bismarck, who was constantly urging an agreement based on the division of the Balkans into an Austrian (western) and a Russian (eastern) sphere of influence. Bismarck reminded the Austrians that the alliance of 1879 did not oblige Germany to support a forward policy of Austria in the Balkans, but the Austrians enjoyed the sympathetic support of Britain.

1886–1887. Rapid development of **nationalist and revenge agitation in France,** the reaction to Ferry's policy of understanding with Germany

in colonial expansion. Activity of **Paul Déroulède** and his *League of Patriots* (founded 1882) in behalf of an alliance with Russia. Appointment of **General Georges Boulanger** as minister of war (Jan. 1886). He quickly became the darling of the country and the symbol of revenge on Germany (Longchamps review, July 14, 1886). Corresponding anti-German, pro-French agitation of the Russian nationalists (**Michael Katkov** and the *Moscow Gazette*).

1887, Jan. 11. Great speech of Bismarck, reviewing the international situation, warning the nations against war, redefining the German attitude, and advocating a large increase in the German army.

Feb. 12. FIRST MEDITERRANEAN AGREEMENT, between Britain and Italy, adhered to by Austria (Mar. 24) and Spain (May 4). The agreement took the form of an exchange of notes (Anglo-Italian; Anglo-Austrian; Italian-Spanish, acceded to by Germany and Austria, May 21). Bismarck had encouraged the combination, exploiting the acute Anglo-French tension (over Egypt) and the Italian-French tension (tariff war, etc.). The notes provided for the maintenance of *status quo* in the Mediterranean, including the Adriatic, Aegean, and Black Seas. Italy was to support the British policy in Egypt and Britain the Italian policy in North Africa. The Anglo-Austrian note stressed rather the community of interest of the two powers in the Near East. Spain promised not to make an agreement with France regarding North Africa which should be aimed at Italy, Austria, or Germany. Britain refused to bind herself to any specific action, but the effect of the agreements was to provide a basis for common action in the event of disturbance in the Mediterranean by France or Russia.

Feb. 20. RENEWAL OF THE TRIPLE ALLIANCE for five years. Negotiations had been carried on since November 1886, the Italians demanding more far-reaching support of their interests in North Africa. This Bismarck was willing to concede, in order to be assured of Italy's friendship in case of a clash with France. But Austria objected, her attention being focused on the Balkans. In the end the old alliance was renewed and additional German-Italian and Austro-Italian agreements made. Germany promised that in the event of French efforts to expand in North Africa, if Italy were obliged to take action or even make war on France, Germany would come to the aid of Italy. If France were defeated, Germany would not object to Italy's taking "territorial guaranties for the security of the frontiers and of her maritime position." The Austro-Italian agreement provided for the maintenance of the *status quo* in the Orient. If this became impossible, neither party should occupy territory except in agreement with the other on the principle of reciprocal compensation. This was not to apply to the eventual annexation of Bosnia and Herzegovina by Austria.

Apr. 20. Arrest of Schnaebelé, a French frontier official who had been condemned by a German court for espionage. He was released a week later, when it was shown that he had been invited to a conference by his German colleagues. The affair roused great popular excitement.

May 18. Fall of the French cabinet in which Boulanger was minister of war. He was excluded from the new cabinet of Maurice Rouvier. Beginning of the reaction against him in French government circles.

May 22. The **Drummond-Wolff convention,** by which Britain agreed to evacuate Egypt within three years, but reserved the right to reoccupy in case of disorder. This convention was wrecked by the opposition of France and Russia—the first striking case of Franco-Russian collaboration against Great Britain.

June 18. Signature of a secret **RUSSIAN-GERMAN TREATY** (the *Reinsurance Treaty*) to replace the expiring Alliance of the Three Emperors, which Russia refused to renew. The two powers promised each other neutrality in the event of either becoming involved in war with a third power, but this was not to apply in case of aggressive war of Germany against France, or of Russia against Austria. They were to work for the maintenance of the *status quo* in the Balkans and Germany was to recognize Russia's preponderant influence in Bulgaria. The principle of the closure of the Straits was once more reaffirmed. An additional and very **secret protocol** promised German assistance in re-establishing a regular government in Bulgaria and in opposing the restoration of Battenberg. It also promised moral and diplomatic support "to the measures which His Majesty [the tsar] may deem it necessary to take to control the key of his empire" (i.e. the entrance to the Black Sea). This famous treaty represented Bismarck's effort to keep Russia from France and to buy her friendship by signing away things that he could never get on account of British and Austrian opposition. On the Russian side the treaty reflected the victory of the foreign minister, Nicholas Giers, over the extreme nationalist groups.

July 7. The **Bulgarian assembly elected Prince Ferdinand** of Saxe-Coburg-Kohary as prince, despite the opposition of the Russians. He was not recognized by the powers. Continuance of the Bulgarian crisis and of the danger of Russian intervention.

Dec. 12. SECOND MEDITERRANEAN AGREEMENT (better *Near Eastern Entente*) between Britain, Austria, and Italy (Bismarck having refused to participate—Bismarck-Salisbury correspondence, November). It restated the principle of the *status quo* in the Near East and the importance of keeping Turkey free of all foreign domination. Turkey must not cede its rights in Bulgaria to any other power or allow occupation of Bulgaria by any other power. Neither must it give up any rights in the Straits or in Asia Minor. If it resists efforts at encroachment, the three contracting powers will agree as to measures to support it. If it fails to resist, the three powers will consider themselves justified, jointly or separately, in the provisional occupation of such Turkish territory as may be deemed necessary to secure respect for the treaties.

1888, Jan. 28. Military agreement between Germany and Italy, providing for the use of Italian troops against France in the event of a Franco-German war.

Feb. 3. Publication of the German-Austrian alliance of 1879. This was intended as a warning to Russia, where nationalist agitation against Germany and Austria continued.

Feb. 6. Bismarck's great Reichstag speech, dealing largely with the Russian situation and ending, "We Germans fear God, and nothing else in the world." The main terms of the Triple Alliance and of the Mediterranean Agreements were allowed to leak out at the same time. Taken together they served as a cold douche on the hopes and aspirations of both France and Russia.

Feb. Acute crisis in Franco-Italian relations, Crispi fearing a sudden attack by the French fleet on Spezzia.

May 15. Italy adhered to the alliance of Germany and Austria with Roumania (p. 767).

July. Crisis in the relations of Italy and the Papacy. The pope was on the verge of leaving Rome. The Italians again feared an attack by France, and induced the Germans and British to issue warnings.

1890, Mar. 18. DISMISSAL OF BISMARCK (p. 740), resulting at least in part from the dissatisfaction of the young Emperor William II with Bismarck's policy toward Russia and his desire for closer relations with Austria and Britain.

Mar. 23. A German ministerial conference decided, on the advice of **Baron Fritz von Holstein** (long a collaborator of Bismarck, who had recently drifted from him), not to renew the Reinsurance Treaty with Russia. It lapsed on June 18, despite numerous Russian attempts to reopen the question of renewal.

July 1. Anglo-German colonial agreement (*Heligoland treaty*), by which Germany gave up large claims in East Africa and received in return the island of Heligoland, which Britain had obtained from Denmark in 1815. Since the island at that time was regarded as practically useless, the whole treaty was looked upon as a striking demonstration of German readiness to purchase the friendship of Britain.

Aug. 17–22. Visit of the Emperor William to the Tsar at Narva. Last efforts of the Russians to secure some agreement with Germany, evaded by the Germans.

1891, Feb. 18–27. Visit of the Empress Frederick, mother of William II, to Paris. Anti-German demonstrations and Franco-German tension.

May 6. Premature renewal of the Triple Alliance, the three documents being merged in one and Germany assuming somewhat larger obligations to support the Italian claims in North Africa. The renewal of the treaty was due to German fears lest France might force Italy into her orbit. The contracting parties were to do their utmost to associate Britain in support of Italian aspirations.

July 4. Great state visit of Emperor William to London. Much talk of Britain's association with the Triple Alliance.

July 24. Visit of a French squadron under Admiral Alfred Gervais, to Cronstadt. Frantic demonstrations of Franco-Russian friendship. The tsar listened to the *Marseillaise* played on one of the French warships. The **Franco-Russian agreement,** which had been prepared by French loans, etc., began to loom on the horizon, the result primarily of German rejection of the Reinsurance Treaty, the hasty renewal of the Triple Alliance, and the demonstrations of Anglo-German solidarity.

Aug. 21, 27. The AUGUST CONVENTION between France and Russia, first fruit of the negotiations. The French desired a hard-and-fast agreement, but this was watered down by the Russians until it was hardly more than an agreement to consult as to what measures should be taken by the two powers in case the maintenance of peace were threatened or one of the parties menaced by aggression. All efforts of the French to arrange for mobilization, etc. (especially during Giers' visit to Paris, November), proved abortive.

1892, Aug. 1. Mission of General Le Mouton de Boisdeffre to St. Petersburg, with a draft military convention. He found the Russian military men hesitant and the draft was subjected to many changes. It was finally accepted "in principle," but as such had no force. Further development of the Franco-Russian alliance was delayed by the outbreak of the **Panama**

scandal (p. 690), which upset the French political scene for a year, and by the great **famine in Russia,** which paralyzed the government for an even longer period.

1893, July 13. French ultimatum to Siam, resulting in a short but severe crisis in Anglo-French relations. The French took a strong stand and generally won their point, thereby making a good impression on Russia. The Germans, who were half prepared to back the British, were disgusted by the backdown.

July 15. Passage of the **German military bill,** reducing service in the infantry to two years and increasing the forces. This created much uneasiness in both France and Russia and reminded the Russians of the value of the connection with France.

Oct. 13. Visit of a Russian squadron under **Admiral Feodor Avellan to Toulon.** Wild demonstrations of affection for Russia throughout France. Alarm of the British for their position in the Mediterranean.

1893, Dec. 27, 1894, Jan. 4. Exchange of notes between the **Russian and French governments,** formally accepting the military convention worked out 18 months before. The agreement was really political as much as military, but was classed as a military convention in order to circumvent the French constitution, which required submission of treaties to the chamber of deputies. The convention was to remain in force as long as the Triple Alliance. It provided: (1) that if France were attacked by Germany, or by Italy supported by Germany, Russia would employ all available forces against Germany; if Russia were attacked by Germany, or by Austria supported by Germany, France would employ all available forces against Germany. (2) In case the forces of the Triple Alliance, or of any one power a member of it, mobilized, France and Russia should mobilize without delay. Other articles provided for the number of troops to be employed, for specific plans of the general staffs, for secrecy, etc.

1894, Mar. Resignation of Gladstone and succession of **Lord Rosebery** as British prime minister. Passage of the **Spencer naval program,** providing for a great increase of forces in the next five years. This was the culmination of a severe naval scare and widespread agitation during the winter, the reflection of British anxiety about the Franco-Russian combination as it affected the Mediterranean situation.

Mar. 16. Conclusion of the **Russian-German tariff treaty,** after years of tariff war and negotiations. This agreement demonstrated the Russian desire not to be drawn into hostilities with Germany.

May 12. Treaty between the British govern-

ment and the Congo Free State (p. 879) by which the British leased to King Leopold for the duration of his life a large tract on the left bank of the Upper Nile, and to Leopold and his successors a much larger tract lying to the west of the first. In return Leopold leased to the British a corridor 25 kilometers in width between Lakes Tanganyika and Albert Edward, which was to serve as a connecting link for the **Cape-to-Cairo telegraph and railway system,** under discussion since 1888. Vigorous protests of the French and Germans, on the basis of earlier agreements. Leopold was dragooned into submission and the British obliged to acquiesce in abandonment of the deal (Aug. 1894). The whole episode was of vital importance in the **British struggle to control the Nile.** From the European angle it demonstrated once more the rift between Britain and Germany and the renewed tendency of Germany and France to collaborate in colonial affairs against Britain.

June. Breakdown of efforts by Rosebery and Kálnoky to revitalize the connection between Britain and the Triple Alliance. Negotiations had extended over six months and finally failed because of Germany's unwillingness to assume responsibility for any British interest. Beginning of the Anglo-German estrangement.

Aug. 1. Outbreak of **war between China and Japan,** over Korea (below, and p. 913).

Aug.-Sept. Armenian massacres. These were the result of the failure of the powers (1878-1882) to secure for the Asiatic provinces of Turkey the reforms envisaged by the treaty of Berlin. Armenian nationalists, inspired by the example of Russian Pan-Slavs and terrorists, had organized secret revolutionary groups (leader **Avetis Nazarbek**), which, operating from Geneva, Tiflis, Paris, and other places, followed a policy of provoking troubles in Armenia in the hope of calling forth reprisals by the Turks and so bringing about European intervention. From 1890 on there were constant disturbances, culminating in the Armenian rising of August 1894 in the vicinity of **Sassun.** This was put down with ferocity by the Kurdish irregular cavalry (Hamidié regiments). The result was a great outcry in Europe, particularly in Britain, where ill-informed humanitarians called on the Liberal government to intervene. Ultimately the sultan appointed a **commission of investigation,** which was joined by British, French, and Russian delegates. Lord Rosebery hoped to develop further this **Near Eastern Triplice,** but Russia, threatened in her own territory by the prospect of an Armenian state, was adverse to any action. The commission produced a fairly innocuous program of reform (Apr. 1895).

The sultan, as usual, temporized. Suggestions of the British for the use of pressure were flatly rejected by Russia and nothing was done.

Oct. 6. The British government invited Germany, France, Russia, and the United States to join in **intervention in the Far East,** the Chinese having been repeatedly defeated in battle with the Japanese. The projected intervention failed because of the unwillingness of the United States and Germany to take part.

1895, Apr. 17. Treaty of Shimonoseki between China and Japan (p. 913). Reaction of the powers: **Britain** reasonably well satisfied, especially with the commercial clauses, and ready to abandon defeated China for the rising power of Japan; **Russia** most directly affected since the beginning of Russian activity in the Far East (Trans-Siberian Railway begun 1891) and the development of interest in Manchuria and Korea (important because of its excellent open harbors). The Russians were long undecided whether to oppose the Japanese or to seek an agreement with them. The Tokyo government was quite prepared for a territorial deal, but ultimately the Russians rejected these advances in view of the readiness of the **Germans** to join in action to check Japan (growing German commercial interests in the Far East; above all German anxiety to re-establish close relations with Russia and to divert Russia to the Far East, thus emasculating the Franco-Russian alliance). **France,** though she had extensive interests and aspirations in southwestern China, followed the Russian lead rather reluctantly, simply in order not to be left out of the picture.

Apr. 23. INTERVENTION OF RUSSIA, GERMANY, AND FRANCE at Tokyo. Britain refused at the last moment to join in the action. The Japanese were "advised" to retrocede the Liaotung Peninsula in return for an increased indemnity. After some hesitation the Japanese government yielded. Beginning of the acute antagonism between Russia and Japan in the Far East. Formation of the **Far Eastern Triplice** (Russia, Germany, and France) which, in the following years, exploited the weakness of China.

June 25. Formation of the **Salisbury cabinet** in England, with **Joseph Chamberlain** at the colonial office. Beginning of the most active phase of British imperialism. In view of Britain's isolation and the situation in the Near East, Africa, and the Far East, Salisbury tried at first to throw off the danger of French and Russian advance by reconstituting close relations with Germany and the Triple Alliance.

Aug. 5. FAMOUS INTERVIEW BE-

TWEEN WILLIAM II AND SALISBURY AT THE COWES YACHT RACES. Salisbury hinted broadly at the advisability of partitioning the Ottoman Empire as the best solution of the chronic Near Eastern troubles. His idea was clearly that the Russians should be allowed to take Constantinople, but the Germans misunderstood the premier's design and interpreted it as a move to embroil the Continental powers in the Near East and smash the reviving friendship between Germany and Russia. The emperor therefore rejected all suggestions. When he discovered his mistake, he tried to arrange a further interview with Salisbury, but this came to naught through further misunderstanding. The result was profound distrust between Salisbury and the emperor (encouraged by Baron von Holstein), which only served to aggravate relations between the two countries.

Oct. 1. First Armenian massacres in Constantinople following a great and provocative Armenian demonstration.

Oct. 17. Under pressure from the powers, the sultan finally accepted the **program of reforms for Armenia.** Nevertheless, the massacres continued, taking place in various cities all over Anatolia. A British squadron was assembled outside the Dardanelles and British action was deferred solely because of apprehension as to what France and Russia might do. The Italians supported the British and **Count Agenor Goluchowski** (Austrian foreign minister since June) actually ignored German advice and took the lead in recommending international naval action at Constantinople. During the crisis (Nov.) the Russians planned to send an expeditionary force to the Bosporus (**Nelidov scheme**) and to seize the Turkish capital before the British and their allies could get there. The execution of the scheme was deferred in part because of inadequate preparation, in part because of the unwillingness of the French to become embroiled in war.

1896, Jan. 3. The **KRUGER TELEGRAM,** sent by Emperor William to **President Paul Kruger** of the South African Republic (**Transvaal**) congratulating him on the defeat of the raiders led by Dr. Jameson (p. 889). German interests in the Transvaal were considerable, but not decisive. The Germans made themselves the advocates of the Transvaal because they hoped (this was Holstein's plan) to demonstrate the value of German friendship to Britain by annoying the British into better relations. When news of the Jameson raid reached Berlin, the emperor, assuming that the British government was privy to the scheme, demanded strong measures and even military intervention on behalf of Kruger. His ad-

visers did their utmost to cool his ardor, but in the end agreed to the telegram of congratulations to Kruger. This created a storm of indignation and recrimination in Britain, especially when it became known that the real purpose of the German government was to beat the British into friendship. The governments indeed remained calm, but public opinion on both sides was so stirred up that for the future a policy of friendship became almost impossible. Loud demands for an agreement with France and Russia were met by the British government by an agreement with France (Jan. 15) in which the British abandoned many of their claims in Siam, and by approaches to Russia which, however, led to nothing.

Feb. Reconciliation between Russia and Bulgaria, the new tsar, Nicholas II, desiring to bring the feud to an end, and Prince Ferdinand having expressed his readiness to baptize the Crown Prince Boris in the Orthodox faith. Russia took the initiative in securing the **recognition of Ferdinand by the powers,** but refused to encourage the Bulgarian agitation in Macedonia, which had become very active since the **dismissal of Stambulov** (June 1894).

Feb. Outbreak of the **insurrection in Crete,** fomented by Greeks who were intent on the annexation of the island. Under pressure from the powers the sultan eventually agreed (July 3) to the restoration of the **pact of Halepa** (1878), which had introduced a large measure of self-government in the island and which had been curtailed after the suppression of a rising in 1889. Greek support of the insurgents continued. The Austrian government proposed a blockade of Crete (July 25). This was rejected (July 29) by Britain, where anti-Turkish feeling ran high. The sultan accepted a **new reform scheme** (Aug. 25) drawn up by the ambassadors of the powers (Crete to have a Christian governor, named by the sultan with the approval of the powers; the Cretan Christians to have two-thirds of all offices and the Cretan assembly to have wide powers; a European commission to reorganize the gendarmerie, courts, and finances). This program was accepted by the insurgents (Sept. 12).

Mar. 1. Battle of Adua. Disastrous defeat of the Italians by the Ethiopians (p. 709).

Mar. 12. British decision to begin the **reconquest of the Sudan** by an advance on Dongola. This decision was taken less because of the frantic appeals of Italy and Germany for aid, or because of the reports of dervish misrule, than because of the fact that the Italian collapse in Ethiopia meant the collapse of the British system of protecting the Nile on the east. Danger of French advance in that region, as well as from the west (second **Monteil mission,** July 1895; **Marchand mission,** February 1896), despite the famous **Grey declaration** (Mar. 28, 1895) stating that Britain would regard such action as "unfriendly," obliged the government to re-establish control of the Sudan itself. The French and Russian governments refused their consent to the use of Egyptian funds, but the British circumvented this difficulty by making Egypt a loan.

June 3.   Treaty of alliance between Russia and China, signed by **Li Hung-chang** during his attendance at the coronation of the tsar at Moscow (p. 913).

June 9.   Lobanov-Yamagata agreement between Russia and Japan, regarding Korea (p. 917).

Aug. 26.   Attack on the Ottoman bank by Armenian revolutionaries. They seized the building and threatened to blow it up unless their demands were met. Eventually they were induced to withdraw, but other outbreaks occurred in the capital. This led to the greatest of the **Armenian massacres,** lasting three days and resulting in the slaughter of thousands of humble Armenians. The horror was stopped by the vigorous intervention of the ambassadors. Repetition of the crisis of 1895 as regards the European powers. Britain was anxious to intervene and an effort was made to persuade the tsar (who visited the queen at Balmoral in September) to join in the action, but Nicholas was held back by his advisers (**death of Lobanov,** August 30; ascendancy of Alexander Nelidov, ambassador at Constantinople). The Russian government adopted **Nelidov's scheme** for the seizure of Constantinople and the Straits in the event of action by the British (Nov.). But, as in the preceding year, nothing came of the plan, not so much because of the opposition of Witte, the powerful finance minister, as because of inadequate preparation and the lukewarmness of France. With respect to Armenia the powers were unable to agree on any course of action. The disorders continued more or less until June 1897, after which the revolutionary movement, having attained nothing but the massacre of thousands of Armenians, gradually collapsed.

897, Feb. 2.   Cretan insurrection resumed, supported by the Greek *Cretan Committee* and the *Ethniké Hetairia,* an organization designed for the realization of Greek aspirations in Macedonia. The Greek government was forced by public opinion to send ships and troops to Crete (February 10, following the proclamation of union with Greece, February 6). The powers, in dread of a rising in Macedonia, were eager to check the movement, despite popular sympathy with the Greeks. At the suggestion of **Count Michael Muraviev,** the new Russian foreign minister, the powers (Feb. 15) landed troops in Crete, to hold the island in "escrow" for the time being. But Britain (Feb. 17) rejected a Russian-Austrian proposal that the Piraeus be blockaded. The powers handed in notes to Greece and Turkey (Mar. 2) promising **autonomy for Crete** and demanding withdrawal of the troops on pain of "measures of constraint." The Greek government rejected the note and on March 18 the **blockade of Crete** was proclaimed. The war in Crete went on.

Apr. 17.   WAR BETWEEN GREECE AND TURKEY, the result of the massing of Greek troops on the Macedonian frontier and attacks by the bands of the *Ethniké Hetairia.* The British had refused to take part in a blockade of Volo, which would have made these preparations impossible. Serbia and Bulgaria were eager to join in the assault on Turkey, but were deterred by strong warnings from Russia.

Apr. 30.   Russian-Austrian agreement, concluded during a visit of Francis Joseph and Goluchowski to St. Petersburg. The two powers agreed to maintain the *status quo* in the Balkans, and, if partition became inevitable, to work for the division of the area among the Balkan states, to which was to be added an Albanian state. The joint action of the two powers prevented Serbia and Bulgaria from associating themselves with Greece.

May 10.   The Greeks appealed to the powers, after a series of decisive defeats by the Turks. They had first been obliged to recall their troops from Crete and to accept in advance the decisions of the powers. An armistice was arranged (May 19) and a peace settlement reached (Sept. 18). Turkey was allowed only a small rectification of the frontier in its favor, and an indemnity. The Cretan question remained open until November 1898, when the powers finally agreed to name **Prince George of Greece** as governor of the island.

Nov. 14.   Landing of German forces at Kiaochow Bay, and occupation of Tsingtao, following the murder of two German missionaries (Nov. 1). Ever since 1895 the Germans were determined to secure a port on the Chinese coast as reward for their intervention against Japan. But they had been unable, until 1897, to decide which port was most desirable. Kiaochow had finally been settled on. Despite the fact that the tsar had given his approval (visit of William II to St. Petersburg, August 1897), the Russian foreign minister raised objections and claimed prior rights. There was a period of acute uncertainty, but the Russians gave up their opposition. The Chinese refused the German demands until March 6, 1898, when an agreement was signed giving Germany a lease of the bay for 99 years and permission to construct two railways in Shantung Province and to operate mines.

Dec. 14. The Russian fleet ordered to proceed to Port Arthur. This was the first step in the acquisition of the port, as recommended by Muraviev and approved by the tsar, though opposed by Witte and all the other ministers (council of November 25).

Dec.–1898, Mar. Conflict between Russia and Britain over a loan required by China. Both sides put forward extremely hard conditions. Russia demanded a monopoly of railroad-building in Manchuria and the right to build a railroad from the Trans-Siberian south to the Yellow Sea, where it was to be permitted to construct a port; Britain demanded a concession for a railroad from the Burmese frontier to the Yangtze basin and a promise not to alienate territory in the Yangtze valley, as well as other commercial concessions.

1898, Jan. 25. Salisbury's note to Russia, aiming at a compromise. The British premier in effect proposed that all Asia should be divided by a line from Alexandretta to Peking into a northern (Russian) sphere and a southern (British) sphere. The Russians evaded these advances, feeling no need for abandoning half of Asia (the better half) to Britain. Instead, the Russians pressed on the Chinese a demand for the lease of **Talienwan** and **Port Arthur** (Mar. 3). This brought the Anglo-Russian crisis to a head.

Mar. 8. Britain sounded the United States government regarding possible collaboration in the Far East, but received no encouragement.

Mar. 17. Chamberlain's advances to the Japanese, which were also abortive, as the Japanese did not yet feel ready to act against Russia and were negotiating with Russia an agreement regarding Korea.

Mar. 27. The **Chinese yielded** to Russian pressure and leased to Russia Port Arthur and Talienwan for 25 years. The British government had decided (Mar. 25) that the question was not worth a war with Russia and that the best course would be to lease Weihaiwei as a counterweight. The Chinese agreed to this on March 27.

Mar. 28. Passage of the **first naval law** by the German Reichstag. This was the work of **Admiral Alfred von Tirpitz,** minister of marine, and laid the basis for the naval expansion of Germany. The arguments for a larger fleet were the need for protecting colonies and commerce and the necessity for a fleet if Germany was to make her weight felt in international affairs (especially against Britain). It was therefore decided to build a battle fleet (influ-

ence of the teaching of Mahan) so strong that even the strongest naval power would hesitate before attacking. Tirpitz also hoped that the possession of a fleet would heighten Germany's alliance value in the eyes of Russia and France.

Mar. 29. Beginning of the **discussions between Joseph Chamberlain and the German ambassador,** the object of which was to enlist German support against further Russian encroachments in the Far East. Count Bernhard von Bülow (German foreign minister since June 1897) treated the matter evasively, being unwilling to antagonize Russia. In Britain there was little official or public sentiment for Chamberlain's project. The discussions were complicated by the overeagerness of **Baron Hermann von Eckardstein,** who misled his own government as well as the British. Lord Salisbury, on his return from a vacation, showed little enthusiasm and took the Far Eastern situation less seriously than Chamberlain.

Apr. 10. The **French extorted from China an agreement** not to alienate the three provinces of Yunnan, Kwangtung, and Kwangsi, and to permit the construction of a railroad to Yunnan-fu. France was given a **lease on Kwangchowan** for 99 years. Numerous other concessions were extorted from the Chinese government in the following months, initiating the partition of China.

Apr. 25. The **Nishi-Rosen agreement** between Russia and Japan. This had been under negotiation since February and was meant by the Russians to circumvent Japanese opposition to the advance in Manchuria. The Russians rejected a Japanese offer of a free hand in Manchuria in return for a free hand in Korea, but recognized Japan's preponderant economic interests in Korea and promised not to obstruct them.

May 13. Chamberlain's great speech at Birmingham, extremely anti-Russian and a bid for the friendship of the United States and Germany. This made an unfavorable impression both in England and in the world at large. Neither the United States nor Germany did anything to encourage the colonial secretary.

Aug. 30. Anglo-German agreement regarding the future of the **Portuguese colonies.** The Portuguese government was bankrupt and in urgent need of a loan. This the British government was ready to grant, in return for the cession or lease of **Delagoa Bay,** long coveted as the key to the Transvaal and now of prime importance because of the growing tension in relations between Britain and the Transvaal. The Germans demanded a hand in the matter and the British reluctantly agreed for fear of German collaboration with France (advances of June 1898). The two powers agreed to share in a loan to Portugal, with the colonies as security. The northern half of **Mozambique** and all but a central strip of **Angola** were assigned to Germany as the area of which the revenues should serve for the German share of the loan; the southern half of Mozambique and the rest of Angola were assigned to Britain. In the event of default of the Portuguese government these territories were to pass to the contracting powers. The Germans expected the agreement to bear early fruit. The British did all they could to prevent its coming into effect, and regarded the whole agreement as a piece of blackmail.

Sept. 18. Beginning of the **FASHODA CRISIS,** between Britain and France. Since March 1896 the Egyptian forces, under **General Sir Herbert Kitchener,** had been advancing up the Nile. The dervishes were decisively defeated on the **Atbara River** (Apr. 8, 1898) and at **Omdurman** (Sept. 2). During the same period British expeditions were trying to reach the Nile from Uganda, all with the object of heading off the French, with whom the Congo government co-operated. The **Marchand mission,** sent out in February 1896, succeeded, after countless delays and hardships, in reaching the Nile at Fashoda (now Kodok) on July 10, 1898, and establishing itself there. Just before that, in June, a force of Ethiopians, accompanied by two Frenchmen, had pushed down the Sobat River and reached the Nile just above Fashoda, this being part of a plan to push Ethiopian claims to the right bank of the Nile, while the French established themselves on the left bank. After the battle of Omdurman, Kitchener at once proceeded up the Nile, where he found Marchand. The latter refused to evacuate without orders of his government. There ensued the most acute crisis in Anglo-French relations during the whole pre-war period. The British refused to discuss the *pros* and *cons* of the French claims until Marchand had evacuated territory which the British claimed for Egypt by right of conquest. The French government, harassed by the Dreyfus affair (p. 691), finding itself unprepared for war at sea and securing no support from Russia (visit of Muraviev to Paris, October), yielded to a poorly veiled threat of war. On November 3 the **evacuation of Fashoda** was ordered. The French claims were not settled until March 21, 1899, when they were obliged to renounce all territory along the Nile, in return for worthless districts in the Sahara. The episode made more difficult the pursuit of a policy of friendship with Britain, as advocated by **Théophile Delcassé,** French foreign minister from June 1898 to June 1905.

Nov. 21. Commercial treaty between France and Italy, bringing to an end a long and disastrous tariff war. The treaty marked the beginning of the reconciliation of France and Italy and the gradual **defection of Italy from the Triple Alliance** (tacitly renewed for six years in 1896). This policy was necessitated by the collapse of the Italian colonial policy and the instability of the domestic situation (p. 709).

1899, May 18–July 29. FIRST HAGUE PEACE CONFERENCE, which met at the invitation of the Russian tsar (Aug. 24, 1898). It is now known that the Russian proposal was due chiefly to financial stringency and inability to keep up with the armaments of Austria and other powers. The suggestion was regarded with distrust and dislike by most of the powers, not least by France. Twenty-six states were represented, but little more was achieved than the signature of conventions for the pacific settlement of international disputes and the definition of the laws of war (prohibition for five years of the use of projectiles thrown from balloons, prohibition of gas warfare and dumdum bullets, provision for better treatment of war prisoners and wounded, etc.). Nothing was done about disarmament or limitation of armament; compulsory arbitration was rejected, but a **permanent court of arbitration** was provided for.

Aug. 9. Extension of the Franco-Russian Alliance, during Delcassé's visit to St. Petersburg. In view of the Austrian constitutional crisis (p. 744) and the possibility of the dissolution of the Hapsburg monarchy, the alliance was extended to provide for the maintenance of the balance of power as well as the maintenance of peace, and the term of the military convention was made indefinite.

Sept. 6. Open Door note of the American secretary of state, **John Hay.** In view of the division of China into spheres of influence, it proposed that Britain, Germany, and Russia should not interfere with treaty ports and should not levy higher harbor or railroad dues on foreign goods than on their own within their spheres. This was agreed to by all powers interested, but by Russia only with vague reservations. The note had little immediate importance, but set up an ideal policy often referred to later.

Oct. 9. Outbreak of the Boer War (p. 890). Almost from the beginning there were rumors of the possibility of **Franco-Russian-German intervention** against Britain, and Count Muraviev appears to have made some efforts in that direction, but neither the French nor the Germans showed much desire to become embroiled.

Oct. 14. The so-called **Windsor treaty** between Britain and Portugal. The secret agreement renewed older treaties of 1642 and 1661, involving a guaranty of Portuguese territory, and included a promise by Portugal not to let munitions pass through **Delagoa Bay** to the Transvaal, or to declare neutrality. The agreement was a negation of the spirit of the German-British agreement of August 1898.

Nov. 1. Agreement between Great Britain and Germany regarding the **Samoan Islands.** The disorders in Samoa (p. 939) and the desire of the Germans to acquire the British share of the group had embittered relations between the two countries for almost a year. In view of the war in South Africa the British government finally gave in, though with poor grace. Germany got the islands of **Upolu** and **Savaii,** the British taking in return the **Tonga Islands, Savage Islands,** and lesser islands of the Solomon group, as well as a disputed strip of **Togoland.**

Nov. 25. Baghdad Railway concession granted to a German syndicate. This was the fruit of a decade of German economic activity in the Near East. There had been innumerable schemes for railways in Anatolia, especially from the Syrian coast to Baghdad and the Persian Gulf. The sultan, anxious to increase the income from the more remote provinces and to bind the empire together strategically, had (Oct. 4, 1888) given a German company a concession to build a railroad from opposite **Constantinople to Angora** (Ankara) with the idea of going on through northern Anatolia to Baghdad. This line was completed in 1892, after which there was a scramble for a new concession. The British were obliged to withdraw when the Germans threatened to discontinue support of their policy in Egypt. On February 15, 1893, the German company received a concession to continue the line from **Angora to Kaisarieh** (this was not built) and for another line, through the more promising southern districts, from **Eskishehr to Konia.** This was finished in 1896 and therewith the question of continuing to Baghdad became an immediate one. Countless projects and applications (British, French, Russian) were put forward, but the Germans remained in the ascendent, especially after the **visit of Emperor William II to Constantinople and the Holy Land** (Oct. 1898) and his proclamation of friendship for the 300,000,000 Moslems in the world. The French ultimately gave up their opposition and agreed to co-operate with German interests. The British were taken up with other affairs and had protected their interests in the Persian Gulf by an agreement with the **sheikh of Kuwait** (he promised to cede no territory without British consent) on January 23, 1899. The Russians remained vigorously hostile to the German project, but the Germans obtained a preliminary concession for a line from Konia to Baghdad on November 25, 1899. Though primarily an economic enterprise, the Baghdad Railway project quickly became a vital factor in the relations of Germany with Russia and Britain.

Nov. 20–28. Visit of William II and Bülow to England (the first since 1895). Conversations between Bülow, Chamberlain, and Balfour. Discussion of a possible Anglo-German-American agreement. Bülow suggested that Chamberlain say something publicly of the common interests which bound the two countries. In his **Leicester speech** (Nov. 30) Chamberlain went much further and thereby raised a storm of ill-will in both Britain and Germany, where pro-Boer sentiments were very pronounced. Bülow, in a Reichstag speech (Dec. 11), rejected the advances and even stressed the need of Germany for a stronger fleet. Marked cooling in Anglo-German relations.

1900, Jan. Acute tension in Anglo-German relations resulting from the stopping of the German ship *Bundesrath* on very inadequate suspicion that she was carrying contraband. The British government eventually gave in (Jan. 16).

Feb. 28, Mar. 3. Muraviev suggested to the French and German governments the possibility of joint "amicable" pressure on Britain to bring about peace in South Africa. The Germans rejected the suggestion unless action were preceded by a mutual guaranty of territory between the three powers. There was no serious effort made to intervene against Britain, though the Russians took advantage of Britain's plight to advance their interests in **Persia, Afghanistan,** and **Tibet,** and the French in **Morocco.**

Mar. Russian squadron at Chemulpo. Efforts made to secure a naval base on the southern coast of Korea **(Masampo).** These attempts were frustrated by the vigorous opposition of Japan.

June 12. Passage of the **second German naval law,** providing for a fleet of 38 battleships, to be built in 20 years. This was the basic building program, carried through the Reichstag on a wave of ill-feeling toward Britain, which the government exploited through the Navy League and other organized propaganda.

June 13–Aug. 14. Boxer rising and **siege of the Peking legations** (p. 914). The legations were finally relieved by an international expeditionary force. But the whole episode had given the Russian military men (opposed by Witte and the new foreign minister, **Count Vladimir Lamsdorff**) an opportunity to occupy Manchuria with 100,000 troops. The question of evacuation soon became the key to the whole Far Eastern problem.

Oct. 16. Anglo-German Yangtze agreement, the result of British anxiety because of Russian designs. It provided for the maintenance of the "Open Door" in "all Chinese territory as far as they [the contracting powers] can exercise influence," and disclaimed all territorial designs. Other powers acceded to it.

Nov. 9. The **Alexeiev-Tseng agreement,** between Russia and the Chinese governor of Manchuria. The Chinese civil administration was to be restored and Russian troops concentrated at Mukden and other points along the railroad. This was disavowed by both the Russian and Chinese authorities.

Dec. 14. Franco-Italian agreement, by which Italy gave France a free hand in **Morocco** in return for a free hand in **Tripoli.** This marked the full development of the Franco-Italian entente.

1901, Feb. 8. Russian proposals to China for the evacuation of Manchuria. In return for evacuation, the Chinese government was to agree not to keep more than a police force in Manchuria and to give Russia a monopoly of concessions in Manchuria, Mongolia, and Chinese Central Asia, as well as a concession for a railroad running toward Peking. Appeals of China to the powers. Strong stand of Japan, backed by Britain and, more cautiously, by Germany.

Mar. 15. Bülow's speech in the Reichstag, declaring that the Yangtze agreement did not apply to Manchuria. This brought to an end the first discussions in London on the possibility of an Anglo-German-Japanese bloc directed against Russia. The Germans were unwilling to go beyond a promise of neutrality in a Russian-Japanese or Anglo-Russian war.

Apr. 6. Following new and stronger protests from Japan and Britain, the Russian government dropped the draft convention with China and denied that it had been authentic.

May 29. Lord Salisbury's memorandum on British policy, a confidential document defending a policy of isolation. This rang the death-knell of the Anglo-German alliance discussions, carried on since March by **Eckardstein,** secretary of the German embassy in London. Eckardstein reported the British much more anxious for alliance than they were, which induced the German government to insist on an alliance with the whole Triple Alliance. To this the British would not agree, being lukewarm about the whole matter.

June. Moroccan missions to Paris, London, and Berlin. Discussion of an Anglo-German pact on Morocco. This the Germans rejected except as part of a larger alliance.

July–Aug. Beginning of the negotiations for an **Anglo-Japanese alliance.**

Oct.–Nov. Renewed discussions between Russia and China regarding the conditions for the evacuation of Manchuria.

Oct. 16. Resumption of **Anglo-Japanese discussions** by **Baron Tadasu Hayashi,** the Japanese minister in London. Hayashi made it clear that for Japan Korea was the crux and that Japan was interested in Manchuria only as the approach to Korea. The negotiations hinged on the definition of Japan's interests in Korea and on the question whether the alliance should be extended to include Siam and India.

Nov. 25–Dec. 4. Visit of Prince Itō to St. Petersburg. Contrary to expectation he found Witte and Lamsdorff eager for an agreement and willing to make far-reaching concessions to Japan in Korea. Itō was thereby induced to exceed his instructions and draft an agreement with Russia.

Dec. 7. The Japanese government, feeling committed to Britain, decided to drop the negotiations with Russia and conclude the alliance with Britain.

1902, Jan. 30. The **ANGLO-JAPANESE ALLIANCE,** marking the end of Britain's "splendid isolation." It had been decided, in the later negotiations, to drop the idea of inviting Germany to join. The alliance was concluded for five years and provided for the independence of China and Korea and the recognition of Japan's special interests in Korea; if either party became involved in war with a third party, its ally was bound to maintain neutrality, but if another power or powers should join in the war, the allied power was bound to join in the conflict; neither party was to enter into separate agreements with another power (Russia) without consulting its ally. The treaty was published on February 11.

Mar. 20. Franco-Russian declaration in favor of the principles enunciated in the Anglo-Japanese Alliance and reserving the right to take counsel to safeguard their interests. This was generally taken as a counterblast to the new combination and an extension of the Franco-Russian Alliance to the Far East, but this was probably an exaggeration.

Apr. 8. Russian-Chinese agreement, providing for the evacuation of Manchuria within 18 months.

May 31. Treaty of Vereeniging (p. 891) bringing to an end the South African War and restoring to Britain greater liberty of action.

June 28.   Renewal of the Triple Alliance for six years. The demands of the Italians for greater concessions were evaded, but they were given assurances with regard to Tripoli.

Nov. 1.   Italian note to France assuring it that in the event of its being attacked, Italy would remain neutral; "the same shall hold good in case France, as the result of a direct provocation, should find herself compelled, in defense of her honor or of her security, to take the initiative of a declaration of war." Italy also gave assurance that it was not a party and would not be a party to any military agreement in conflict with this declaration. **Completion of the Italian-French entente,** the work largely of Camille Barrère, the French ambassador at Rome. **Nadir of the Triple Alliance,** the relations between Italy and Austria being badly strained by irredentist agitation.

Nov. 8.   Failure of the French agreement with Spain on Morocco. The French had offered the Spaniards a substantial part of northern Morocco as a sphere, but the Spanish government drew back for fear of antagonizing Britain.

1902–1903.   The Venezuela Crisis (p. 854).

1903, Feb.   Russian-Austrian program of reform for **Macedonia.** The country had for years been the prey of rival Bulgarian, Serbian, and Greek bands and had broken out in insurrection in 1902. Mild reforms introduced by the sultan (Nov. 1902) had failed to pacify the region. The Russian-Austrian program called for a gendarmerie composed of Moslems and Christians according to population, appointment of foreign officers, and reorganization of the financial system. It was accepted by the other powers.

Apr.   Baghdad Railway crisis. The German company had obtained a definitive concession for the road from Konia to Basra (Jan. 17, 1902) and had done its utmost to secure the co-operation of the British and French governments in financing the scheme. The British government was favorably disposed, but the bankers were finally scared off by an organized press campaign against participation. Thereupon the British and French governments refused to become associated. The Russian government, as before, was irreconcilably opposed to the whole project.

May 1–4.   Visit of King Edward VII to Paris. This first move toward reconciliation ended as a great success.

May 15.   Lord Lansdowne's declaration of British interests in the **Persian Gulf:** Britain "would regard the establishment of a naval base or a fortified port in the Persian Gulf as a very grave menace to British interests, and would certainly resist it by all means at her disposal." This was intended primarily as a warning against Russian plans for a railroad across Persia to Bunder Abbas.

July 6–9.   Visit of President Loubet and Delcassé to London. Beginning of the conversations that were to lead to the Anglo-French entente.

Aug. 12.   First Japanese note to Russia, following the failure of the Russians to carry through the evacuation of Manchuria. Earlier conversations had failed through the unwillingness of the Russians to abandon their claims in northern Korea (**Yalu concession,** in which even Tsar Nicholas was interested financially).

Aug. 29.   Dismissal of Count Witte, the Russian finance minister. This was tantamount to the victory of the group favoring Russian expansion in Manchuria and Korea (notably **Bezobrazov**). The **viceroyalty of the Far East** was established to deal with Asiatic affairs independently of the foreign office. The Russians refused to take the Japanese policy seriously. They did not believe that Japan would go the limit and were confident that if she did, Russia would easily defeat her. The notes from Tokyo were treated with disdain and delay.

Oct. 2.   The Mürzsteg program of reform for Macedonia, worked out by Russia and Austria and approved by the powers. This program was to replace the February program, which had been proved inadequate. Austrian and Russian inspectors were to be attached to the inspector-general and a foreign general was to command the gendarmerie. Further administrative and judicial reforms were provided for.

Nov.   Anglo-Russian conversations looking toward an understanding. These broke down because of Russia's unwillingness to agree to a partition of Persia into spheres of influence.

1904, Feb. 8.   OUTBREAK OF THE RUSSIAN-JAPANESE WAR, following the failure of the Russians to give the Japanese satisfaction (p. 922).

Apr. 8.   The ANGLO-FRENCH ENTENTE concluded. This had been under negotiation since July and especially since October. The outbreak of the Russian-Japanese War undoubtedly served to hasten the conclusion. The agreement represented a complete settlement of colonial differences, particularly with regard to Egypt and Morocco: France recognized the British **occupation of Egypt,** but was given guaranties regarding the Egyptian debt; Britain was to make effective the treaty of 1888 providing for the free navigation of the **Suez Canal;** Britain recognized French interests in **Morocco** and promised diplomatic support in realizing them; secret articles envisaged the eventual breakdown of Moroccan independence and the partition of the country between France and Spain; France surrendered ancient rights on the shores of **Newfoundland,** but retained the right to fish; in return France was given territory near **French Gambia** and east of the **Niger;** British and French spheres of influence were delimited on the frontiers of **Siam** and disputes regarding **Madagascar** and the **New Hebrides** were adjusted.

Apr. 24-29. Visit of President Loubet and Delcassé to Rome. Acute crisis in the relations of France and the Papacy (p. 692) and much ill-feeling between Germany and Austria and Italy, because of the failure of Victor Emmanuel III to make mention of the Triple Alliance in the toasts and speeches.

Sept. 7. British treaty with Tibet, signed by **Colonel Francis E. Younghusband** after an expedition to Lhasa. The Tibetan lama agreed not to cede or lease territory to any foreign power or to allow foreign intervention. Thus Britain took advantage of the Russian-Japanese War to destroy the Russian advance in Tibet.

Oct. 3. Franco-Spanish treaty regarding Morocco. The public clauses reaffirmed the independence and integrity of Morocco, but a secret convention provided for eventual partition. Spain was to have the Mediterranean coast of Morocco (but less of the hinterland than was offered her in 1902). Spain was to take no action without the consent of France, and was not to erect any fortifications.

Oct. 21. The Dogger Bank episode. The Russian fleet, under Admiral Zinovy Rodjestvensky, passing through the North Sea on its way to the Far East, fired upon British trawlers, supposed to be Japanese destroyers. One trawler was sunk and several lives lost. The Russian fleet continued on its way and the Russian government evaded giving satisfaction. Acute crisis in Anglo-Russian relations. The British fleet was ordered to stop the Russian fleet off Gibraltar, even by force. The situation was finally saved through the efforts of Delcassé, and the matter was adjusted by an international commission (Feb. 25, 1905).

Oct. 27-Nov. 23. German-Russian negotiations for an alliance. These arose from the tension between Russia and Britain and from British protests against the coaling of the Russian fleet by German companies. The tsar accepted a German draft treaty (Oct. 30) providing for mutual aid in case of attack by another European power. The plan broke down because of Russia's unwillingness to sign before consulting France, which was expected to be drawn in. Ultimately the two powers

agreed merely (Dec. 12) to aid each other in the event of complications arising from the coaling of the fleet.

Dec.-1905, Feb. Mission of Saint-René Taillandier to Fez. He carried to the sultan a program of reforms (police, state bank, communications) that would have given France practically a protectorate over Morocco.

1905, Feb. 3. Speech of Arthur Lee, first lord of the British admiralty, directed against German naval armaments. This reflected the growing anxiety of the British regarding German naval plans.

Mar. 31. VISIT OF THE GERMAN EMPEROR TO TANGIER, initiating the **first Moroccan crisis.** Delcassé had wantonly excluded the Germans from the Moroccan negotiations and had not officially communicated the agreement with Britain. The Germans were uncertain about the Anglo-French entente, but had declared their disinterestedness in Morocco except for the Open Door, regarding which Delcassé had given assurances. The French had thereupon proceeded to capitalize the free hand secured in the agreements with Italy, Britain, and Spain. After the failure of the German-Russian negotiations, Bülow and Holstein decided to make the Moroccan affair a test of the strength of the Anglo-French entente and carried the unwilling emperor along on this course. At Tangier he proclaimed Germany's adherence to the principles of independence and integrity and declared in favor of the policy of equal opportunity for all. His visit at once created a panic in Paris and led to a loud outcry against Delcassé's policy. Delcassé at once offered to make good his mistake and to buy off the German opposition, but the Germans turned a deaf ear.

Apr. 6. The Germans accepted the invitation of the sultan of Morocco to an international conference.

May 1-5. Efforts of **Maurice Rouvier,** the French prime minister, to reach an adjustment with the Germans. He was even ready to concede them a port on the coast of Morocco, but the Germans insisted on a conference.

May 17, 25. British correspondence with France. The British, apprehensive about German designs on the Moroccan coast, proposed "full and confidential discussion . . . in anticipation of any complications." Delcassé took this as the first step toward an alliance and tried to develop the British advance, but Rouvier objected.

June 6. FALL OF DELCASSÉ, who urged the French cabinet to accept the British offers. He argued that the Germans were only bluffing and that a Franco-British front would be invincible. The cabinet voted unanimously against him, fearing that France was poorly prepared for war, that an agreement with Britain would precipitate war at a time when Russia was rendered helpless by her defeat in the Far East, and that France would bear the burden of German hostility. Rouvier took over the foreign office and renewed his efforts to strike a bargain. The Germans stood by their previous attitude.

July 8. The **French government,** assured of American support against unreasonable demands, accepted the idea of a conference.

July 24. **BJÖRKÖ TREATY,** signed by the Emperor William and the tsar during a visit to each other's yachts. The treaty was essentially a return to the draft of October 1904, excepting that it was to be confined to Europe and was to take effect only after the conclusion of peace between Russia and Japan. Bülow objected to its restriction to Europe and threatened to resign, but was persuaded to remain after a pathetic appeal from the emperor. The treaty was warmly opposed by the Russian foreign office and was ultimately wrecked by the refusal of the French government, estranged by the Moroccan crisis, even to consider joining in such a pact (Oct.).

Aug. 12. **Renewal of the Anglo-Japanese alliance** for ten years. The treaty was modified to provide for mutual support in the event of attack by *one* other power, and was extended to include India.

Sept. 5. **Treaty of Portsmouth,** ending the Russian-Japanese War (p. 922). This was effected through the mediation of President Theodore Roosevelt. Russia ceded to Japan the northern part of **Sakhalin,** but paid no indemnity; Russia recognized Japan's predominant interests in **Korea** and agreed not to oppose any steps Japan might take in Korea; Russia's lease of the **Liaotung Peninsula** was transferred to Japan.

Sept. 28. **France and Germany** finally reached an agreement on the agenda for the **Moroccan conference,** which was to meet in January 1906. Most of the French demands were met, in the hope that France would be disposed to accede to the Björkö treaty.

Oct. Beginning of **Anglo-Russian discussions** regarding an eventual entente.

1906, Jan. 10. Beginning of **Anglo-French military and naval conversations,** which had been unofficially initiated in December. The new Liberal government (**Sir Edward Grey, foreign secretary** since December 1905) refused to promise support to France in the event of German attack, but agreed to nonbinding discussions of the modalities of co-operation in case such co-operation should be decided on. Creation of the "moral obligation" of Britain to France. The cabinet as a whole was not informed of these conversations until 1911.

Jan. 16-Apr. 7. **Algeciras conference** on Morocco. France was supported throughout by all the powers except Austria, which sided with Germany. There were countless disputes regarding details, and some danger of war, allegedly favored by Baron von Holstein until his dismissal on April 5. The **act of Algeciras** reaffirmed the independence and integrity of Morocco and "economic liberty without inequality." The French were entrusted with the police on the Moroccan-Algerian frontier. In the rest of the country the police was to be under French and Spanish control. A state bank was to be organized, on which France was to have a larger measure of control than the other powers.

Feb. 10. **Launching of the *Dreadnought*** by the British navy, the first all-big-gun battleship (ten 12-inch guns), which revolutionized the world naval situation.

May. The German government decided to increase the tonnage of battleships in the naval program, to add six cruisers to the program, and to widen the Kiel Canal to allow the passage of projected ships of the *Dreadnought* type.

Aug. 15. **Visit of King Edward to Emperor William at Cronberg;** futile discussion of the naval situation.

Dec. 13. Agreement between Great Britain, France, and Italy regarding **Ethiopia.** It provided for the independence and integrity of Ethiopia and respect for earlier agreements, but divided the country into spheres of influence for the event of Ethiopia's collapse.

1907, May 16. **Pact of Cartagena** between Britain, France, and Spain. It provided for the maintenance of the *status quo* in the Mediterranean and the part of the Atlantic that washes the shores of Europe and Africa. The agreement was directed chiefly at supposed German designs on the **Balearic Islands** and the **Canaries.**

June 10. **Franco-Japanese agreement,** providing for the independence and integrity of China and equality of treatment there.

June 15-Oct. 18. **SECOND HAGUE PEACE CONFERENCE,** called at the suggestion of President Theodore Roosevelt (Oct. 21, 1904), but postponed because of the war in the Far East. All efforts of the British to secure some limitation of armaments were wrecked by the opposition of other powers, for which Germany, fearing a British attempt to check the growth of the German fleet, acted as spokesman. Germany also rejected all proposals for compulsory arbitration. But the conference enlarged the machinery for voluntary arbitration and concluded conventions regulating action to collect debts, rules of war, rights and obligations of neutrals, etc.

July 30. Russian-Japanese agreement, similar to the Franco-Japanese agreement (above).

July. Renewal of the Triple Alliance for six years, despite the complete lack of faith on the part of Germany and Austria in Italy's loyalty.

Aug. 3-5. Meeting of Emperor William and Tsar Nicholas and their foreign ministers **at Swinemünde.** Discussion of the Baghdad Railway; assurances of the Russians that any agreement they made with Britain would not be directed against Germany.

Aug. 31. THE ANGLO-RUSSIAN ENTENTE. This had been discussed at various times since the conclusion of the Russian-Japanese War, and was encouraged by the French. Negotiations had lagged because of opposition in Russian court circles, because of the confusion created by the Russian revolutionary movement (p. 754), and because of the fears of **Alexander Izvolski** (Russian foreign minister since May 1906) lest Germany take offense. The agreement was much less extensive than that between France and Britain: **Persia,** the root of the Russian-British antagonism, was divided into three spheres of influence: a large Russian sphere in the north, covering the most valuable part of the country, a neutral sphere in the center, and a smaller British sphere in the southeast. Russia agreed that **Afghanistan** should be outside her sphere of influence and that she would deal with the amir only through Britain; Britain promised not to change the status of the country or to interfere with its domestic affairs. Both governments recognized the suzerainty of China over **Tibet** and promised to respect its territorial integrity. In a separate note (Apr. 1907) the British government had expressed itself as well disposed toward a change in the **Straits agreements** favorable to Russia. In another separate note (Aug. 29) the Russian government recognized Britain's preponderant position in the **Persian Gulf.**

Sept. 5. Meeting of King Edward and Izvolski at Marienbad, followed by a meeting of Izvolski and **Count Alois Aehrenthal** (Austrian foreign minister since October 24, 1906). Izvolski gave the most explicit assurances regarding the entente with Britain and sounded out Austria with regard to an eventual revision of the Straits convention.

1908, Jan. 27. Aehrenthal announced the intention of the Austrian government to build a **railway through the Sanjak of Novi Bazar** toward Saloniki. The purpose of this was to drive a wedge between Serbia and Montenegro, where anti-Austrian agitation had grown rapidly since the advent of the Karageorgevich dynasty (1903; **Serbian-Austrian tariff war,** 1906-1911). The Austrian move was much resented by Izvolski, who claimed it was a violation of the spirit of the Austro-Russian entente of 1897. He brought forward a rival scheme for a railroad from the Danube to the Adriatic. The British were also much wrought up by the Austrian step, which they regarded as a bribe by Turkey to Austria to induce the latter to oppose further reforms in Macedonia.

Mar. Grey put forward a scheme of **reform for Macedonia** which would have given the three provinces practical autonomy.

Apr. 23. The **Baltic and North Sea conventions,** the first between Germany, Sweden, Denmark, and Russia, the second between Great Britain, Germany, Denmark, France, the Netherlands, and Sweden. They provided for the maintenance of the *status quo* on the shores of the two seas and for consultation between the signatories in case the *status quo* was threatened.

June 9. Reval meeting, between King Edward and Sir Charles Hardinge on the one hand and Tsar Nicholas and Izvolski on the other. The British secured **Russian approval for the Macedonian reform scheme** and discussed the problems presented by German armaments.

June 23. Counter-revolution in Persia, where the shah, **Mohammed Ali,** overthrew the constitution that had been granted (Dec. 30, 1906) as a result of the liberal-nationalist movement of that year. The Russians supported the shah, and the British, bound by the agreement with Russia, were obliged to desert the liberal cause.

July. Mulay Hafid, having defeated his brother, **Abdul Aziz,** sultan of Morocco, in a long civil war, took Fez. The Germans supported Mulay Hafid and the Moroccan question drifted toward another crisis.

July 24. Victory of the **Young Turk Revolution** (p. 776). The whole movement was a reflection of Turkish excitement about the Reval interview (above) and resulted in the collapse of German influence in Turkey and a period of frantic Anglophilism.

Aug. 11. Meeting of King Edward and Sir Charles Hardinge with Emperor William at Friedrichshof. Acrimonious discussion of the naval situation. The emperor flatly refused all suggestions of reduction of the German program, which had been indirectly enlarged by the reduction of the service-term of warships and by the acceleration of German building operations.

Aug. 13. King Edward and Francis Joseph met at Ischl. Reputed efforts of the British to enlist Austrian pressure on Germany.

Aug 27. Austrian reply to a note of Izvolski proposing an agreement regarding Bosnia and Herzegovina on the one hand and the Straits question on the other.

Sept. 16. BUCHLAU CONFERENCE between Aehrenthal and Izvolski. After long discussion an informal agreement was reached: Russia was not to oppose the annexation of Bosnia and Herzegovina by Austria and Austria was not to oppose the opening of the Straits to Russian warships, under certain conditions. An international conference was to put the stamp upon these arrangements and other minor modifications of the Berlin treaty.

Sept. 23. Visit of Prince Ferdinand of Bulgaria to Budapest. Aehrenthal evidently gave his approval to eventual declaration of Bulgarian independence. Both Austria and Bulgaria felt threatened by the determination of the Young Turk régime to summon delegates from Bosnia and Herzegovina and from Bulgaria to the new parliament.

Sept. 25. Casablanca affair. Three German deserters from the French foreign legion were taken by force from a German consular official. Acute tension in Franco-German relations.

Sept. 26. Meeting of Izvolski and Baron Wilhelm von Schön (German foreign minister) at Berchtesgaden. Schön agreed to the Russian Straits program on the understanding that Germany should receive compensation (probably in the Baghdad Railway question).

Sept. 28. Meeting of Izvolski and Tommaso Tittoni (Italian foreign minister) at Desio. The Italian minister evidently accepted the Russian program in return for promises of support in Tripoli and Albania.

Oct. 4. Arrival of Izvolski at Paris, where he received a letter from Aehrenthal announcing the coming annexation decree.

Oct. 5. Proclamation of Bulgarian independence.

Oct. 6. PROCLAMATION OF THE ANNEXATION OF BOSNIA AND HERZEGOVINA BY AUSTRIA, which gave up the right to occupy the Sanjak militarily. Excitement in Turkey, where a boycott against Austrian goods was instituted. Frenzy and rage in **Serbia** and **Montenegro,** where the two annexed provinces had long since been looked upon as a future legacy. Military preparations were at once begun and negotiations were initiated looking toward a Turkish-Serbian-Montenegrin-Greek alliance against Austria. In **Russia** the event caused hardly less consternation in nationalist circles, where nothing was known of Izvolski's bargain with Aehrenthal. The prime minister, Count Peter Stolypin, at once wrote Izvolski

instructing him to oppose the Austrian action and it was this primarily that obliged Izvolski to repudiate his agreement, declare that he had been duped, and take the lead in championing the Serbian claims. The **Germans,** though rather outraged by Austria's failure to give advance notice, supported Austria loyally in order to uphold the alliance. The **French and British,** though they resented Izvolski's underhanded negotiation with Austria, supported Russia and demanded the convocation of an **international conference** to consider the Austrian action.

Oct. 7. Crete proclaimed union with Greece, thereby adding to the crisis.

Oct. 9-14. Izvolski's visit to London, to secure support for his Straits program. The British, unwilling to sacrifice the newly found friendship of the Turks and having sounded and found them ill-disposed to any concession to Russia, made their consent to the opening of the Straits conditional on previous Turkish consent. Russian efforts to secure that consent naturally failed. Complete collapse of Izvolski's scheme. He now became virulent in his denunciation of Aehrenthal and his demand for a conference. Aehrenthal, on his part, would agree only to a conference to register (not discuss) the Austrian action. Negotiations on this question continued through the autumn.

Oct. 27. Izvolski in Berlin. The Germans, recognizing his difficulties, made no objection to his Straits program, provided they were given compensation.

Oct. 28. The *Daily Telegraph* affair (p. 741). The publication of the indiscreet utterances of Emperor William to a British nobleman served to create a crisis in Germany and at the same time to accentuate the Anglo-German antagonism.

Nov. 10. Germany and France agreed to submit the **Casablanca affair** to an arbitral board, which rendered a report on May 22, 1909.

Dec. 4. LONDON NAVAL CONFERENCE, attended by ten naval powers. The conference agreed on certain regulations of naval warfare (blockade, contraband, prizes, convoy, etc.), but the convention was never ratified.

Dec. 25. Izvolski's Christmas speech advocating a league of the Balkan states and Turkey to resist further encroachments. This program was also supported by Britain, but came to nothing because of the difficulty of adjusting the Serbian and Bulgarian claims in Macedonia, and because of Turkey's insistence on an offensive as well as defensive alliance.

1909, Jan. 12. Austro-Turkish agreement (final

form February 26), by which Turkey recognized the annexation and was paid compensation. This agreement greatly strengthened Aehrenthal's position, since Turkey was the power chiefly concerned.

Feb. 8. German-French agreement on Morocco. It reaffirmed the independence and integrity of the country, but Germany recognized France's "special political interests" in return for recognition of Germany's economic interests and a promise to associate German nationals in future concessions.

Mar. 2. The powers intervened to prevent a war between Serbia and Austria. The Serbs had continued to arm and were becoming less and less ready to surrender their claims. The Austrians had also armed and the military party in Vienna (**Conrad von Hötzendorff,** chief of staff) was urging a war in order to clear the situation. The powers advised the Serbs to yield, but the Serbian note to Vienna (Mar. 10) avoided any recognition of the annexation and was generally regarded as unsatisfactory.

Mar. 12. New British naval appropriations, the result of a panic called forth by dubious statements by the first lord of the admiralty regarding German strength.

Mar. 18. Russian-Bulgarian agreement, by which Russian financial claims on Turkey (unpaid since 1878) were cancelled to meet the compensation demanded by Turkey from Bulgaria.

Mar. 21. German note to Russia, calling upon her to abandon support of the Serbs and to recognize the annexation. The Germans asked for a definite reply, failing which they would allow matters to take their course. Izvolski seems to have been glad for a chance to get out of a hopeless impasse (Russia being quite unprepared for war). He yielded, but thereafter set afloat the legend of a German "ultimatum" to Russia. The British were indignant at Russia's "climb-down," which left them in a most embarrassing position.

Mar. 31. Serbian note to Austria, recognizing the annexation, declaring that it did not infringe on Serbian interests, and promising to check anti-Austrian propaganda and maintain good neighborly relations in the future.

Apr. 9. Turkey recognized the independence of Bulgaria.

Apr. 13. Turkish counter-revolution (p. 777). Gradual revival of German influence.

May. Mission of Baron Ferdinand von Stumm to London. He was instructed to offer an agreement on naval affairs in return for a defensive alliance, a neutrality agreement, or at least a general settlement of colonial questions. These suggestions were coolly received in London, where there was no desire to estrange France and Russia or to weaken the entente. The British view was that the naval agreement must come first.

July 14. Resignation of Prince Bülow (German chancellor since 1900). Bülow had come more and more to disapprove of the uncompromising naval policy of the emperor and Tirpitz and his position had been hopelessly weakened by the *Daily Telegraph* episode. His successor, **Theobald von Bethmann-Hollweg,** was, if anything, more conciliatory and eager for an agreement with Britain.

Oct. 24. Racconigi agreement between Russia and Italy. Both powers promised to work for the *status quo* in the Balkans. Italy agreed to support Russian aspirations in the Straits, while Russia agreed not to oppose the Italian designs in **Tripoli.**

Nov.-Dec. Anglo-German negotiations (Gwinner and Cassel) looking toward a general settlement, but dealing chiefly with the **Baghdad Railway.** The Germans were prepared to give up all claims to control the railway from Baghdad to the Persian Gulf, but the British demanded full control (not international) of that section, and were unwilling to act without Russia and France.

1910, Feb. Official **Russian-Austrian reconciliation** based on agreement to maintain the *status quo* in the Balkans, the Russians being in constant dread of a further move by the Austrians.

Nov. 4-5. Visit of Tsar Nicholas and the new foreign minister, **Sergei Sazonov,** to Emperor William at **Potsdam.** Tentative agreement on the Near East. The Germans gave the Russians a free hand in **northern Persia,** while the Russians promised no longer to oppose the **Baghdad Railway** and to arrange for the connection of this line with the Persian railways. Disappointment of the British, who had always refused to negotiate without Russia and who were now deprived of their chief support in the Baghdad Railway matter.

1911, Apr.-May. France advance in Morocco, following anti-foreign disturbances. The French entered Fez on May 21, despite warnings from the Germans that they were violating the Algeciras act.

June-Nov. SECOND MOROCCAN CRISIS, resulting from the forward movement of the French and the general dissatisfaction of the Germans with the working of the 1909 agreement. The French government was not unwilling to make compensation to the Germans, and **Jules Cambon,** the ambassador at Berlin, engaged in conversations with the German foreign secretary, **Alfred von Kiderlen-Wächter,** at Kissingen (June 20-21). But the Germans refused to advance demands and took the stand that the French should make an offer. Kiderlen was genuinely anxious to liquidate the Moroccan affair and pave the way to better relations with France and Britain. Negotiations on the French side were hampered by a cabinet change the result of which was the formation of a **ministry under Joseph Caillaux** (June 28).

July 1. The **German gunboat** *Panther* **arrived at Agadir** on the Atlantic coast of Morocco, ostensibly to protect German interests, but in reality to frighten the French into action. The French foreign minister, **Justin de Selves,** appealed to Britain to join in sending ships. This action was disavowed by Caillaux and rejected by the British (July 4).

July 15. After much fencing, the Germans admitted to the French that they would require the whole of the **French Congo** as compensation for the abandonment of their rights and interests in Morocco. This was regarded by the French as out of the question, but discussions continued, carried on to a large extent irregularly by Caillaux.

July 21. Mansion House speech of Lloyd George, in which he declaimed against Britain's being ignored in the Moroccan matter and used threatening language. Since Lloyd George had been regarded as pacifically minded, the speech caused a great stir and led to much recrimination between the German ambassador and Grey. The crisis now came to a head and elaborate preparations were made on the British side for eventual war. Nevertheless negotiations continued between the Germans and French and by October substantial agreement was reached. By the **convention of November 4,** Germany agreed to leave France a free hand in Morocco and not to object even to the erection of a protectorate; in return France ceded part of the French Congo, with two strips of territory connecting the German Cameroons with the Congo and Ubangi Rivers.

Sept. 28. OUTBREAK OF THE TRIPOLITAN WAR between Italy and Turkey (p. 710). This was due in large measure to the desire of the Italians to realize on the agreements with France and to counterbalance the French gains in Morocco. In one way or another all the great powers were bound not to oppose the Italian action, though they all disapproved of it. The Austrians, however, objected from the outset to all operations that would disturb the *status quo* in the Balkans and thereby prevented attacks upon the Adriatic or Aegean coasts. Numerous attempts at mediation by the powers broke down through the hasty **annexation of Tripoli** by the Italians, which the Turks stoutly refused to recognize.

Oct. 14–Dec. 6. The Charykov kite. Nicholas Charykov, the Russian ambassador at Constantinople and the chief proponent of a Balkan league which would include Turkey and would serve as a bulwark against the dreaded advance of Austria in the Balkans, took matters more or less into his own hands and offered the Turks a guaranty of their territory in Europe in return for accession to such a league and opening of the Straits to Russian warships. The Turks treated the matter in dilatory fashion and, when pressed, appealed to the other powers. Charykov's action was disavowed by Sazonov after a visit to Paris (Dec. 6).

Nov. 11. Russian ultimatum to Persia, followed by an invasion of northern Persia and Russian control of the Russian sphere (p. 897). Despite British protests the Russians made themselves at home in northern Persia. British action was hampered by fear of rupturing the entente with Russia at a time when the Moroccan crisis and the Tripolitan War raised the specter of a general conflagration.

1912, Feb. 8. Haldane mission to Berlin. On the British side this was the outgrowth of dissatisfaction with Grey's policy in the Agadir crisis and discontent with the policy of Russia in Persia, reflected in a demand of the Radicals for better relations with Germany. On the German side Tirpitz and the emperor were determined to increase the fleet beyond the previous program, but Bethmann and Kiderlen were anxious for an agreement with Britain that would weaken the entente. At Berlin Haldane suggested that Britain would be willing to support German colonial aspirations in Africa in return for abstention from increase of the fleet. The Germans were unwilling to make naval concessions without a political agreement. Bethmann demanded a promise of neutrality under certain conditions, while Grey refused more than an assurance not to attack or take part in a hostile combination against Germany.

Mar. 8. Publication of the **new German naval bill,** providing for an increase in the number of ships, an increase in personnel, and the establishment of a third squadron in commission. With this the Anglo-German discussions came to an end, though conversations regarding the Baghdad Railway and colonial affairs continued and an effort was made on both sides to put relations on a better footing.

Mar. 13. Treaty of alliance between Bulgaria and Serbia. This had been under discussion since 1908 and had been warmly supported by the Russians (especially Nicholas Hartwig, the minister at Belgrade). Serious negotiations were initiated in October 1911, in view of the Tripolitan War, but were delayed by the insistence of the Bulgarians that the alliance be directed against Turkey rather than Austria and that Macedonia should receive autonomy. The secret *annexe* of the treaty provided for a possible war against Turkey. In the event of victory Serbia was to receive the Sanjak of Novi Bazar and the territory north of the Shar Mountains; the territory south and east of the Rhodope Mountains was to go to Bulgaria; the rest of Macedonia was to be autonomous, but if partition was decided on later, most of it was to fall to Bulgaria, a disputed area being left to the arbitration of the tsar of Russia. The treaty was supplemented by a **military convention** (May 12). Its general tenor became known to most of the powers at an early date, but it was not taken very seriously. The Russians, who had sponsored it, regarded it chiefly as a defensive bulwark against Austria and relied on their ability to hold back the Balkan states from aggression against Turkey.

Apr. 18. The **Italians bombarded the Dardanelles,** which were thereupon closed by the Turks. After vigorous protests from Russia and other powers, they were reopened on May 4.

May 4-16. The **Italians conquered Rhodes** and other islands of the Dodecanese, thereby establishing a footing in the eastern Mediterranean and causing much uneasiness in Britain and France.

May 29. **Treaty of alliance between Bulgaria and Greece.** This had been proposed by Venizelos a year before, but had been evaded by the Bulgarians for fear of becoming involved in a war concerning Crete. Such a war was not provided for in the treaty, and the definition of claims in Macedonia was postponed. A **military convention** was concluded on October 5.

July 16. **Naval convention between France and Russia,** to supplement the military convention of 1893. This was part of Raymond Poincaré's (French premier since January 14, 1912) policy of strengthening the alliance with Russia.

July 22. Decision of the British admiralty to withdraw battleships from the Mediterranean and concentrate them in the North Sea, in view of the growing naval strength of Germany. The French soon afterward reversed the process and withdrew their battleships from Brest to the Mediterranean, chiefly to face the growing power of Italy and Austria.

Aug. **Visit of Poincaré to St. Petersburg,** where he was first shown the text of the Serbian-Bulgarian alliance. He saw the import of it and warned Sazonov, but at the same time discussed the need for the strength-

ening of Russian military preparations in Poland.

Aug. 14. **Bulgarian note to Turkey,** demanding establishment of autonomy for Macedonia, where outbreaks had become more frequent.

Aug. 14. **Note of Leopold von Berchtold** (Austrian foreign minister since February 1912) to the powers suggesting pressure on the Balkan states to keep the peace and pressure on the Turks to institute far-reaching reforms in Macedonia. This was accepted by the powers, which commissioned Austria and Russia to act for them.

Sept. 18. **Bulgaria and Serbia decided for war** against Turkey, using the demand for reform merely as a blind. The two powers were anxious to take advantage of the Tripolitan War, which was coming to a close.

Sept. 25. The Turks announced maneuvers, to be held at Adrianople.

Sept. 30. **Mobilization of the Balkan states.** Russia announced a trial mobilization in Poland.

Oct. 8. **Austrian-Russian note to the Balkan states,** demanding respect for the *status quo* and promising reforms for Macedonia.

Oct. 8. **Montenegro declared war on Turkey.**

Oct. 18. **OUTBREAK OF THE FIRST BALKAN WAR,** between Bulgaria, Serbia, and Greece on the one hand, and Turkey on the other.

Oct. 18. **Treaty of Lausanne,** between Turkey and Italy. This had been under discussion since July and had been forced by an Italian ultimatum (Oct. 12): Turkey promised to withdraw her forces from Tripoli and the Italians promised to withdraw from the Aegean Islands as soon as the Turkish withdrawal from Tripoli was complete; the Turks were allowed to keep in Tripoli a representative of the sultan as caliph.

Oct. 22. **Bulgarian victory at Kirk Kilissé,** in Thrace, where the Turks had rashly taken the offensive.

Oct. 24-26. **Serbian victory at Kumanovo.**

Oct. 28-Nov. 3. **Great Bulgarian victory at Lulé Burgas.** Advance of the Bulgarians to the Chatalja lines, last line of defense before Constantinople.

Nov. 3-5. **Russian warnings to the Bulgarians** against the occupation of Constantinople, which the Russians would resist by the use of their fleet.

Nov. 10. The **Serbs reached the Adriatic,** after overrunning northern Albania.

Nov. 15-18. **Serb victory at Monastir.**

Nov. 17-18. **Bulgarian attack on the Chatalja lines,** which failed.

Nov. 21–22.   Grey-Cambon correspondence, in which Britain and France agreed to consult in the event of either one being threatened by attack.

Nov. 24.   The Austrians announced their unalterable opposition to territorial access to the Adriatic for Serbia and came out for an independent Albania.   Acute international crisis.   The Serbs remained steadfast and were at first supported by Russia, which was given assurances by France of support in the event of war with Germany.   Austria was supported by Italy, which also opposed the appearance of the Serbs on the Adriatic.   The Germans, after some hesitation, promised Austria support if she were attacked while defending her interests.   Britain was sympathetic to the Austrian position and tried to work with Germany for an adjustment without jeopardizing relations to France and Russia.   The crisis was most acute in late November and early December, when both Austria and Russia began to mobilize.   It was overcome when the Russians, unprepared for war, abandoned the Serb territorial claims.

Dec. 3.   Armistice between Turkey, Bulgaria, and Serbia.   Greece did not join in it. Operations were to continue around **Scutari** (besieged by the Montenegrins), **Janina** (invested by the Greeks), and **Adrianople.**

Dec. 5.   Last renewal of the Triple Alliance, for six years from July 1914.   This reflected the closer relations between Italy and Austria and the friction between Italy and Britain and France growing out of the occupation of the Dodecanese.

Dec. 17.   Opening of the **London peace conference.**   At the same time an ambassadorial conference at London discussed the status and boundaries of Albania, the fate of the Aegean Islands, etc.

1913, Jan. 6.   Breakdown of the London conference, because of the refusal of the Turks to give up Adrianople, the Aegean Islands, and Crete.

Jan. 22.   The powers finally induced the Turks to abandon Adrianople.

Jan. 23.   *Coup d'état* at **Constantinople;** downfall of Kiamil Pasha and victory of the extreme nationalists led by **Enver Bey.**

Feb. 3.   Resumption of the war.

Mar. 5.   The Greeks took Janina.

Mar. 26.   The Bulgarians took Adrianople.

Apr. 16.   The Bulgarians and Turks concluded an armistice, which was accepted by other belligerents.

Apr. 22.   The **Montenegrins took Scutari,** despite protests of the powers, who had assigned it to Albania.

May 3.   Under threat of war from Austria, the **Montenegrins gave up Scutari** and the **Serbs evacuated Durazzo** (May 5).

May 7.   An ambassadorial conference at St. Petersburg awarded to **Roumania the town of Silistria,** without the fortifications, as compensation for the gains of Bulgaria.

May 20.   Reopening of the London peace conference.   The victorious allies were obliged by an ultimatum from Grey to accept the settlement agreed to by the great powers.

May 30.   TREATY OF LONDON, ending the First Balkan War.   Turkey ceded all territory west of a line between Enos and Midia and abandoned all claim to **Crete;** the status of **Albania** and of the **Aegean Islands** was left to the decision of the powers.

June 1.   Treaty of alliance between Serbia and Greece against Bulgaria.   This was the result of Serbia's failure to make good her claims on the Adriatic and the unwillingness of Bulgaria to grant Serbia more of Macedonia than had been envisaged in the treaty of March 13, 1912.   The Bulgarians were willing to leave the matter to the arbitration of the tsar, which the Serbs tried to evade.

June 29–July 30.   SECOND BALKAN WAR.   The Bulgarian commander, General Michael Savov, ordered an attack on the Serbian-Greek positions without informing the prime minister, Stojan Danev, who was just leaving for St. Petersburg.   The government disavowed the action, but the Serbs and Greeks took advantage of the situation to carry out the attack they had long planned.   Roumania and Turkey entered the war against Bulgaria, which was rapidly defeated.

Aug. 10.   TREATY OF BUCHAREST.   The Roumanians were given the northern **Dobrudja,** from Turtukaia on the Danube to Ekrene on the Black Sea; the Serbs and Greeks retained those parts of **Macedonia** they had occupied.   Bulgaria retained only a small part of Macedonia, having lost **Monastir** and **Ochrid** to Serbia and **Saloniki** and **Kavalla** to Greece.   On the Aegean seaboard the Bulgarians kept only the stretch between the Mesta and Maritza Rivers, with the second-rate port of **Dedeagatch.**

Sept. 23.   Invasion of Albania by the Serbs, following Albanian raids into areas assigned to Serbia by the treaty of London.

Sept. 29.   TREATY OF CONSTANTINOPLE between Bulgaria and Turkey; the Turks recovered **Adrianople** and the line of the **Maritza River.**

Oct. 18.   Austria demanded **Serbia** evacuate Albania within eight days.   Serbia yielded.

Oct. 30.   Austro-Italian note to Greece, demanding the evacuation of southern Albania by December 31.

Nov.–Dec. THE LIMAN VON SANDERS CRISIS. Liman had been appointed by the Turkish government to reorganize the army. He was to have command of the First Army Corps, at Constantinople, and other far-reaching powers. The Russians protested when they learned how extensive the authority of the German mission was to be. They demanded that Liman be given a command elsewhere than at Constantinople. The French vigorously supported the Russian stand, but the British were lukewarm. Ultimately a note was sent to the Turkish government (Dec. 13) warning it against too great concessions. The affair was closed (Jan. 1914) when the Germans agreed that Liman should give up the Constantinople command and become inspector-general of the army. The incident left the Russians suspicious of German designs on the Turkish capital and led to much recrimination.

Dec. 13. Grey proposed to the powers the division of disputed southern Albania between Greece and Albania, with compensation to Greece in the Aegean Islands. This was finally accepted, but the Greeks did not evacuate until April 27, 1914, after which the dispute continued with regard to the Aegean Islands. By June 1914 there was an acute danger of war between Greece and Turkey.

1914, Feb. 21. A famous **Russian crown council** discussed the question of the Straits and concluded that Russian aims there could be attained only in case of a European war.

Apr. 22–24. Visit of King George and Grey to Paris. The French, at the request of the Russians, urged the conclusion of an **Anglo-Russian naval convention** (the British refusing to consider an alliance). Discussions were carried on throughout the remaining months of the pre-war period.

June 14. Visit of Tsar Nicholas and Sazonov to Constantza and **Bucharest.** The Russians and Roumanians agreed to co-operate in the event of the closure of the Straits in a Turkish-Greek war, but the Roumanians refused to commit themselves to intervene in the event of an Austrian attack upon Serbia.

June 15. An **Anglo-German agreement** initialed. This settled the **Baghdad Railway** problem, the Germans promising not to construct the line south of Baghdad and recognizing Britain's preponderant interests in the shipping on the Euphrates. The agreement reflected a real desire on both sides to remove many outstanding colonial difficulties.

June 24. Austrian memorandum for Germany, discussing the Balkan situation as it emerged after the treaty of Bucharest. The Vienna government favored an alliance with Bulgaria and Turkey to make impossible a re-constitution of the Balkan League under Russian and French auspices. The Germans had, on the other hand, been urging on Vienna a reconciliation with Serbia and Roumania and Greece. On this basic question the two allies had drifted far apart.

June 28. ASSASSINATION OF THE ARCHDUKE FRANCIS FERDINAND at Sarajevo. The assassin was **Gavrilo Princip.** He and other young Bosnian revolutionaries acted as agents of the Serbian society **Union or Death** (*The Black Hand*), a terrorist organization founded in 1911 for agitation against Austria in behalf of Serbian aspirations. The Serbian government was cognizant of the plot, but did little to prevent its consummation or to warn the Austrian government. The Vienna government, though convinced of the complicity of Serbia, was intent on making out a tight case and sent a legal expert to Sarajevo to collect evidence. The world generally was outraged by the assassination and sympathetic toward Austrian claims for satisfaction.

July 5. Mission of Count Alexander Hoyos to Berlin. He took the memorandum of June 24 on the Balkan situation, to which had been added some remarks on the need for settling, once and for all, the intolerable activity of the Serbs. Both the emperor and Bethmann recognized the justice of the Austrian stand, promised support (the Blank Check) and urged that steps be taken while world opinion was favorable. The Germans evidently regarded a localized settlement as possible, and believed the Russians too unprepared to take an extreme stand.

July 7. Austrian crown council. Most of the members favored war against Serbia, but this course was opposed by the Hungarian premier, **Count Stefan Tisza,** who insisted on diplomatic action to avoid larger European complications.

July 13. Baron Friedrich von Wiesner, sent to collect evidence, reported that he had been unable to find conclusive evidence of Serbian complicity, though the part played by members of the Black Hand Society was clear.

July 14. Austrian crown council. Tisza was won over to a policy of warlike action, on condition that no Serbian territory should be annexed by Austria.

July 20–23. Visit of President Poincaré and Premier René Viviani of France to St. Petersburg. Agreement to invite Britain to join with France and Russia in pressure on Vienna, though the Austrian demands on Serbia were not yet known, except in a vague way. The French apparently disregarded the merits of the case and took the whole matter as a test of the solidarity of the entente in face of action by the Triple Alliance.

July 23. Austrian ultimatum to Belgrade (48 hours). This had been ready on July 20, but had been held back until Poincaré should have left St. Petersburg. It demanded suppression of publications hostile to Austria; dissolution of patriotic organizations engaged in anti-Austrian propaganda; cessation of propaganda in the schools; dismissal of officials accused by Austria of propaganda; collaboration of Austrian with Serbian officials in the inquiry regarding responsibility for the assassination; judicial proceedings against those accessory to the plot; arrest of two Serbian officials known to be involved; explanations and apologies.

July 24. First formulation of **Russian policy:** Serbia must not be attacked and devoured by Austria.

July 25. Austrian assurances to Russia that no Serbian territory would be annexed. A Russian crown council decided on first military measures against Austria, to be followed by war if Serbia were attacked. **French assurances of support** given to Russia.

The **Serbian reply** to the Austrian ultimatum, generally favorable at first sight, was actually evasive. The crucial point VI was rejected. The Serbian reply may have been due to reports from St. Petersburg of Russia's decision to support Serbia. On reception of the Serb reply the Austrian minister at once left Belgrade. Serbia had ordered mobilization against Austria even before making the reply. Austria at once mobilized against Serbia.

July 26. Grey proposed a conference to deal with the Austro-Serb issue. France accepted; Austria refused to submit a question of national honor to the decision of others; Germany also refused an international discussion of the Austrian claims, though ready for a conference to deal with the Austro-Russian tension; Russia accepted the Grey proposal in principle, though preferring direct conversations with Vienna, which had been initiated.

July 27. First French preparatory measures. The **British fleet ordered not to disband** after maneuvers. Grey promised Russia diplomatic support and did nothing to hold Russia back from further steps.

July 28. AUSTRIA DECLARED WAR ON SERBIA. Belgrade was bombarded the next day, though Austria was not ready for real operations until about August 12. The declaration of war was meant to create a *fait accompli*. Rupture of the Austro-Russian pourparlers. Germany urged the **occupation of Belgrade** as a pawn, to be followed by negotiations with Russia regarding the Serbian reply. This course was also favored by Grey,

but was ignored by Berchtold. France renewed assurances of support to Russia.

July 29. Bethmann, resisting pressure from General Helmuth von Moltke, chief of staff, urged the resumption of Austro-Russian negotiations and began to bring **pressure on Vienna.** At the same time he made a bid for **British neutrality:** Germany ready to promise not to take French territory in Europe, or Belgian territory, if Britain promised neutrality. This was rejected.

The **Russian tsar** yielded to pressure from Sazonov and the military men and agreed to **general mobilization.** The order was recalled and mobilization against Austria alone decided on when the tsar received a telegram from Berlin telling of the Emperor William's efforts to bring the Austrians into line.

July 30. Austro-Russian conversations resumed. Due to technical difficulties the Russian government reversed its action of July 29 and decided for **general mobilization,** despite numerous German warnings.

July 31. Germany proclaimed "**state of threatening danger of war**" and sent a **12-hour ultimatum to Russia** demanding cessation of preparations on the German frontier.

German inquiry in Paris as to what attitude France would take in a Russian-German conflict.

Germany refused a British request that the neutrality of Belgium be respected.

5.00 p.m. Austria decreed general mobilization.

Aug. 1. French reply to Germany: France would be guided by her own interests.

3.55 p.m. French mobilization.

4.00 p.m. German mobilization. Germany offered Britain a promise not to attack France if Britain would guarantee French neutrality.

7.00 p.m. GERMAN DECLARATION OF WAR ON RUSSIA, no reply having been received to the German ultimatum.

Aug. 2. The **British cabinet,** after many meetings and much disagreement regarding support of France, **voted to give France assurances** to protect the coast against German attack (the "moral obligation" arising from previous naval arrangements).

The **Germans began the invasion of Luxemburg** and submitted to Belgium a demand for permission to cross Belgian territory, in return for a promise to uphold Belgian integrity. This was rejected.

Aug. 3. GERMANY DECLARED WAR ON FRANCE, on the flimsy pretext of frontier violations. In reality the German action was due to military considerations and to the conviction that France would come to Russia's support in any case.

Beginning of the invasion of Belgium.

Aug. 4. BRITAIN DECLARED WAR ON GERMANY, the invasion of Belgium giving Grey a welcome argument in the cabinet and in parliament.

Aug. 6. AUSTRIA DECLARED WAR ON RUSSIA.

Declarations of War

1914

July 28 Austria on Serbia
Aug. 1 Germany on Russia
Aug. 3 Germany on France
Aug. 4 Germany on Belgium
   Great Britain on Germany
Aug. 5 Montenegro on Austria
Aug. 6 Austria on Russia
   Serbia on Germany
Aug. 8 Montenegro on Germany
Aug. 12 France on Austria
   Great Britain on Austria
Aug. 23 Japan on Germany
Aug. 25 Japan on Austria
Aug. 28 Austria on Belgium
Nov. 4 Russia on Turkey
   Serbia on Turkey
Nov. 5 Great Britain on Turkey
   France on Turkey

1915

May 23 Italy on Austria
June 3 San Marino on Austria
Aug. 21 Italy on Turkey
Oct. 14 Bulgaria on Serbia
Oct. 15 Great Britain on Bulgaria
   Montenegro on Bulgaria
Oct. 16 France on Bulgaria
Oct. 19 Russia on Bulgaria
   Italy on Bulgaria

1916

Mar. 9 Germany on Portugal
Mar. 15 Austria on Portugal
Aug. 27 Roumania on Austria
Aug. 28 Italy on Germany
   Germany on Roumania
Aug. 30 Turkey on Roumania
Sept. 1 Bulgaria on Roumania

1917

Apr. 6 United States on Germany
Apr. 7 Panama on Germany
   Cuba on Germany
Apr. 13 Bolivia severs relations with Germany
Apr. 23 Turkey severs relations with United States
June 27 Greece on Austria, Bulgaria, Germany, and Turkey
July 22 Siam on Germany and Austria
Aug. 4 Liberia on Germany
Aug. 14 China on Germany and Austria
Oct. 6 Peru severs relations with Germany
Oct. 7 Uruguay severs relations with Germany
Oct. 26 Brazil on Germany
Dec. 7 United States on Austria
Dec. 8 Ecuador severs relations with Germany
Dec. 10 Panama on Austria
Dec. 16 Cuba on Austria

1918

Apr. 23 Guatemala on Germany
May 8 Nicaragua on Germany and Austria
May 23 Costa Rica on Germany
July 12 Haiti on Germany
July 19 Honduras on Germany

G. NORTH AMERICA

1. THE UNITED STATES

a. THE UNITED STATES, 1789–1861

(From p. 563)

1789, Mar. 4. First Congress met at New York.
Apr. 30. WASHINGTON INAUGURATED AS PRESIDENT. Creation by congress of three executive departments: state, war, and treasury. The **Judiciary Act** of 1789 provided for a system of federal district and circuit courts. The first ten amendments to the constitution, the so-called *Bill of Rights,* were adopted by congress and sent to the states.

1790, Jan.–1791, Dec. Formulation of **Alexander Hamilton's** fiscal policies. These included the **Funding Bill,** authorizing the treasury to accept old securities at par in payment for new bonds, bearing interest; the **Assumption Bill,** providing for federal assumption of the debts of the states; the **Bank of the United States;** and an excise tax. In his *Report on Manufactures* Hamilton argued cogently for tariff protection, but the tariff, first imposed in 1789, remained primarily a revenue measure.
1791–1814. Economic developments. In 1791 **Samuel Slater** and **Moses Brown** successfully applied power-driven machinery to the spin-

ning of cotton yarn at Pawtucket, Rhode Island. This is commonly taken to date the introduction of the factory system and the beginning of the industrial revolution in the United States. In 1793 **Eli Whitney** introduced the **cotton gin,** which, by rendering profitable the cultivation of short staple cotton in the uplands of the south, had a revolutionizing influence on the south and on the slavery problem.

1792. Political parties made their appearance, largely because of differences of opinion with respect to Hamilton's policies. **Thomas Jefferson,** who became the leader of the **Republican** (later the Democratic) **Party,** felt that Hamilton's policies were designed in the interest of financial and commercial groups and were inimical to the agrarian elements. **Hamilton** and **John Adams** became the leaders of the **Federalist Party.**

1792. Washington and Adams re-elected. With the outbreak of war in Europe between Britain and France, the latter sent **Edmond Genet** as minister to the United States. His efforts to commit the United States to the support of France, even to the point of appealing from the president to the people, forced Washington to ask for his recall. Determined to maintain neutrality in spite of the efforts of Hamilton and Jefferson to influence him in favor of Britain and France respectively, Washington issued his proclamation of neutrality (Apr. 22). The following year (1794) the **Neutrality Act** was passed.

1794. Whiskey insurrection in western Pennsylvania, resulting from opposition to the excise tax on domestic spirits; put down by militia of Pennsylvania and other states.

The **eleventh amendment** proposed by congress as a result of the decision of the supreme court in *Chisholm v. Georgia.* The amendment closed the federal courts to suits instituted against a state by citizens of another state or citizens or subjects of a foreign state.

Since the treaty of 1783 **relations between Britain and the United States** had been far from satisfactory. Britain refused to enter into a commercial treaty and refused to evacuate the posts on the Great Lakes (ostensibly because of failure of the United States to observe the treaty provision with respect to collection of debts owed to British creditors, really in order to obtain control of the fur trade and build up an Indian buffer state in the northwest). Britain was charged with inciting the Indians to hostility, with imprisonment of American seamen, and with capture of American merchant ships. To adjust these differences **John Jay** was sent to Britain and on

Nov. 19. Jay's treaty was concluded. It provided for the evacuation of the border posts in 1796, permitted trade with the British East Indies, placed trade between the United States and Great Britain on a basis of "reciprocal and perfect liberty," and admitted American boats of not more than 70 tons burden to the West Indies. Joint commissions were provided for settling the questions of the debt and the northeast boundary. Claims on behalf of loyalists were dropped, balanced by claims for slaves carried away by the British armies. Claims arising from alleged illegal seizures of ships were referred to commissions. The senate grudgingly ratified, after striking out the clause with respect to the West Indies.

1795, Oct. 27. Treaty of San Lorenzo or **Pinckney's treaty.** Since 1783 there had been constant friction with Spain over the southern boundary of the United States (Britain having retroceded Florida to Spain), over the navigation of the Mississippi, over Spain's machinations with the Indians of the southwest, and over her intrigues with the frontiersmen. In 1786 negotiations between Jay and Diego de Gardoqui came to naught. Finally in 1795 Thomas Pinckney succeeded in negotiating a treaty establishing the southern boundary at the 31st parallel, giving to Americans the right to navigate the Mississippi to its mouth, and granting to them the *right of deposit* at New Orleans for three years.

1796, Sept. 18. Washington's Farewell Address.

1797, Mar. 4. JOHN ADAMS, president, with Jefferson as vice-president.

The conclusion of Jay's treaty with Britain involved the United States in **difficulties with France,** which regarded the treaty as evidence of a pro-British policy by the United States. The difficulties culminated in the attempt of the French Directory to extort money from the three American commissioners Pinckney, Marshall, and Gerry. This is the so-called **X.Y.Z. affair.** Fighting on the sea occurred, a navy department was created, Washington was named commander of the army, and until September 30, 1800, a naval war was carried on. By the **treaty of 1800** the treaty of alliance of 1778 with France was abrogated.

1798. Stung by the criticisms of its opponents (many of them French citizens), the Adams administration enacted a series of repressive measures against them: the **Naturalization Act,** extending the required time of the residence to fourteen years; the **Alien Act;** the **Alien Enemies Act,** and the **Sedition Act.** The last act especially represented an attempt to make a crime of political opposition. These acts led to

1798–1799. The **Kentucky** and **Virginia Resolutions,** penned by Jefferson and Madison

The United States during the Confederation Period

CANADA

Lake of the Woods

Boundary Undetermined

L. Superior

L. Michigan

L. Huron

Quebec

St. Lawrence R.

Montreal

In Dispute with Great Britain

Ontario

L. Erie

Detroit

West Reserve

Cl. by N.Y. to 1790

N.H.

MASS-N.Y. Claims Adjusted 1786

Claimed by Conn. to 1782

CHUSETTS

MASS.

Boston

CONN.

R.I.

NORTH WEST

Claimed by to By Mass.

Virginia 1784 to 1785

Claimed by Va. to 1784 and by Connecticut to 1786

TERRITORY Organized in 1787

Claimed by Virginia to 1784

Claimed by New York to 1781

NEW YORK

New York

PENNSYLVANIA

Philadelphia

N.J.

Missouri R.

St. Louis

Ohio R.

DIST. OF KENTUCKY

Claimed by Virginia until admitted as a State 1792

VIRGINIA

MD.

Baltimore

Washington

DEL.

Richmond

Norfolk

LOUISIANA

Mississippi R.

TERRITORY SOUTH OF THE OHIO

N. Carolina Claims Ceded in 1790

S. Carolina Claims Ceded 1787

NORTH CAROLINA

Claimed by Georgia until 1802, added to MISSISSIPPI TERR. 1804

SOUTH CAROLINA

Wilmington

Savannah R.

Chattahoochee R.

Claimed by Spain until 1795 Organized as MISSISSIPPI TERRITORY in 1798

GEORGIA

Charleston

Savannah

WEST FLORIDA

New Orleans

St. Augustine

EAST FLORIDA

Atlantic Ocean

Gulf of Mexico

BAHAMA

IS.

CUBA

HISPANIOLA

(Fr.) (Sp.)

JAMAICA

The United States during the Confederation Period

0 100 200 300 400

Scale of Miles

respectively, which, in effect, asserted that a state might nullify the force of an act of congress within its confines, if it regarded such act as contrary to the constitution.

1800. In the election, commonly referred to as the **revolution of 1800,** Adams was defeated, but, because Jefferson and Burr had the same number of votes, the election was decided by the house of representatives in favor of Jefferson. The tie led to the movement culminating in the **twelfth amendment** (1804), which altered the method of electing the president and vice-president by requiring that separate ballots be cast for each.

1801. John Marshall, chief justice of the supreme court.

Mar. 4. THOMAS JEFFERSON, the first president to be inaugurated in Washington, the new capital.

1801-1802. Repeal of the internal revenue taxes and of the Judiciary Act of the Adams administration.

1803. Ohio admitted as the seventeenth state, and the first state to be carved out of the Old Northwest. It had been preceded into the union by Vermont (1791), Kentucky (1792), and Tennessee (1796). The first authorized settlement of Americans north of the Ohio was made by the **Ohio Company** at Marietta (1788). A short time later the **Symmes Company** established a settlement in southwestern Ohio, while in 1796 Connecticut settlers established **Cleaveland** in the Connecticut Western Reserve. The planting of these settlements aroused the Indians in opposition. In 1791 General Arthur St. Clair was decisively beaten by them, but in 1794 at **Fallen Timbers** General Anthony Wayne defeated them. By the **treaty of Greenville** (1795), the Indians ceded all but the northwest quarter of Ohio, thereby paving the way for the increased settlement leading to the admission to statehood.

1803. *Marbury* v. *Madison,* the case in which John Marshall established the principle of judicial review of acts of congress by declaring a section of the Judiciary Act of 1789 unconstitutional.

Apr. 30. THE LOUISIANA PURCHASE. In 1800 Spain had retroceded Louisiana to France. Napoleon was then interested in Louisiana because of his ambition to re-establish a French colonial empire in America. This alarmed Jefferson, who feared a strong power at the mouth of the Mississippi. To reassure the west, alarmed at the possible closing of the river to its trade, Jefferson instructed **Robert Livingston,** the American minister to France, to open negotiation for the purchase of a sufficient area at the mouth of the river to guarantee freedom of navigation and trans-

shipment of goods. Monroe was sent to assist Livingston. Meanwhile the failure of Napoleon's army to reconquer Santo Domingo, combined with the ominous turn of events in Europe, caused Napoleon to lose interest in a colonial empire. He therefore sold Louisiana to the United States for 80,000,000 francs, thereby doubling the size of the country. Louisiana included the area between the Mississippi and the Rocky Mountains, plus the island on which New Orleans stands. Uncertainty as to the southern boundary of Louisiana led to prolonged controversy with Spain as to whether it included Texas and West Florida, which was not finally settled until the treaty of 1819.

1803-1804. New England Federalists, believing the accession of Louisiana would so strengthen the agrarian states as to lead to a decline in New England influence, planned the formation of a **northeastern confederacy,** composed of New England and New York. To carry New York with them they approached **Aaron Burr,** vice-president, who was disgruntled with Jefferson, and proposed that he run for the governorship, with Federalist support. The opposition of Hamilton to this plan was followed by the duel between Burr and Hamilton (July 11, 1804), in which Hamilton was killed.

1804-1806. Lewis and Clark expedition. Meriwether Lewis and William Clark were selected by Jefferson to explore the trans-Mississippi country. Leaving St. Louis, they ascended the Missouri to its source, crossed the head-waters of the Snake River, proceeded thence down the Columbia River to the Pacific. The mouth of the Columbia had first been entered in 1792 by Captain Robert Gray of Boston. Explorations of Lewis and Clark gave the United States another claim to the "Oregon country."

1805. The **Tripolitan War,** which had begun in 1801, brought to a close by a treaty.

Mar. 4. Thomas Jefferson began his second term as president, with George Clinton as vice-president.

Decision in the *Essex* case, reversing the decision in the case of the *Polly* (1800), and declaring the American re-export trade a violation of the rule of 1756.

1806, May 16. Fox's order declared the coast of Europe from Brest to the Elbe River to be in a state of blockade, except between Ostend and the mouth of the Seine, where neutral vessels were admitted if not coming from or bound to an enemy port. Napoleon retaliated (Nov. 21) with his **Berlin decree** declaring a paper blockade of the British Isles. A British order in council of January 7, 1807, closed to neutrals the coasting trade between French ports. On November 11, 1807, an order in

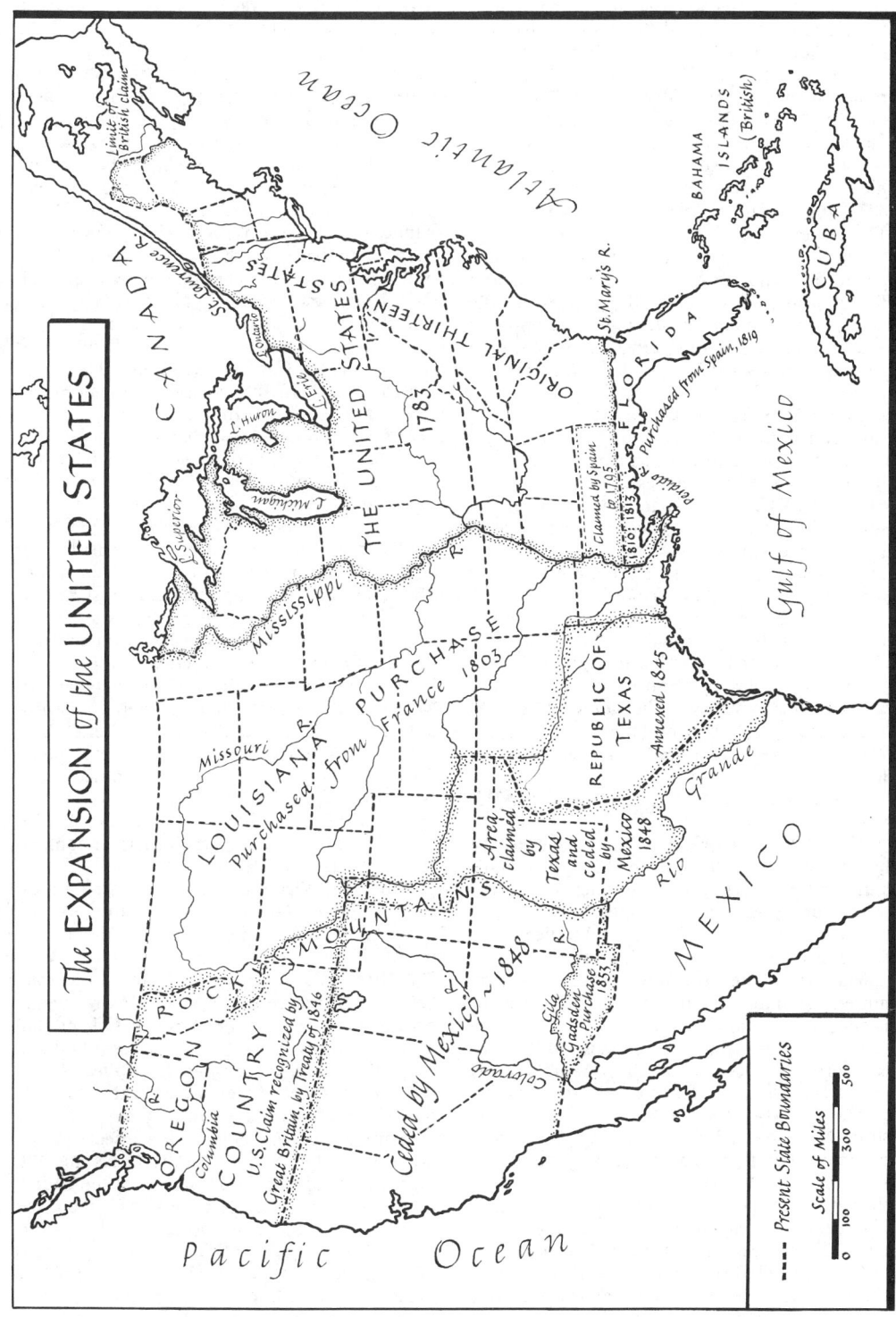

The Expansion of the UNITED STATES

council blockaded the coast from Copenhagen to Trieste against neutrals unless they had first entered or cleared from a British port and paid duties there. In December Napoleon replied with his **Milan decree** which declared that ships lost their neutral character if they obeyed the British order in council of November 11, or if they submitted to search on the high seas by British officers.

1807, June. The *Chesapeake-Leopard* affair. The American ship *Chesapeake* was fired on by the British ship *Leopard* and four deserters taken from her. Although Federalists and Republicans forgot their differences in the face of this national insult, Jefferson, opposed to war, merely ordered British ships of war to leave American waters, and demanded reparation and the abandonment of impressment.

Dec. 22. The Embargo Act. Jefferson, still averse to war, resolved on commercial coercion as a means of forcing France and Britain to withdraw their restrictions on American trade. The act forbade the departure of ships for foreign ports, except foreign vessels in port at the time the act was passed. Coasting vessels were required to give bond to land their cargoes at American ports.

Aaron Burr tried for treason and acquitted. The trial was the outgrowth of Burr's activities in the west after his duel with Hamilton. He planned the creation of an independent state, either at the expense of the United States or Spain, more probably the latter.

1808. African slave trade prohibited after January 1.

1809, Mar. 4-1817, Mar. 4. JAMES MADISON the fourth president.

Mar. 15. The **repeal of the Embargo Act** became effective. It had not brought Britain and France to terms, but had fallen with great weight upon American shipping. New England opposition to the policy was reflected in Federalist gains in the election of 1808.

May 20. The **Non-Intercourse Law** permitted commerce with all countries except France and Britain.

1810, Mar. 23. Napoleon's **Rambouillet decree** ordered the sale of all American ships seized for violation of French decrees.

May 1. Macon's Bill No. 2 repealed all restrictions on trade with the warring powers and provided that if either should remove its restrictions on American trade, the president should renew non-intercourse with the other. Napoleon announced revocation of the Berlin and Milan decrees, effective November 1, whereupon Madison, on November 2, proclaimed the renewal of non-intercourse with Britain within 90 days. Napoleon continued to seize American ships.

1810-1811. Rise of the war party. The election of 1810 resulted in the defeat of many of the old members of pacific views and the choice of younger men, especially from the west, who were impatient with the peace policy. These men, commonly known as the *War Hawks,* were especially aroused by the opposition of the Indians, led by **Tecumseh,** to the advance of white settlement in the northwest. In November 1811 occurred the **battle of Tippecanoe,** which made **William Henry Harrison** a hero in the eyes of the frontiersmen. More and more the west became convinced that British aid and encouragement from Canada stiffened the Indian opposition. The result was a growing demand for war with Britain and the conquest of Canada. Reading the lesson of the election of 1810 aright, Madison adopted a firmer tone toward Britain.

1812, Apr. Ninety-day embargo to insure that American ships would be safely in port when war with Britain began. By this time Britain, fighting the Peninsular War in Spain, needed American supplies. It therefore would have gladly revoked the orders in council if it could have been certain that Napoleon would absolutely withdraw his decrees against American shipping. A new order in council announced that whenever the Berlin and Milan decrees were unconditionally revoked, the British decrees would automatically cease. The French foreign minister thereupon produced a decree, dated a year earlier, which declared that the decrees were non-existent, so far as the United States was concerned, after November 1, 1810. The document was drawn up in 1812 and antedated, but the British accepted it and revoked the orders in council, June 23. Meanwhile,

June 18. War was declared on Britain, on the ground of impressment, violation of the three-mile limit, paper blockade, and orders in council.

1812-1814. WAR OF 1812. In the naval warfare of the first year the Americans were surprisingly successful, the *Essex* capturing the *Alert;* the *Constitution,* the *Guerrière* and the *Java;* the *Wasp,* the *Frolic;* the *United States,* the *Macedonian.* Later in the war, however, the American ships were one by one captured or bottled up. Except for the effect on the morale of the people, the victories on the high seas were without influence on the course of the war. For the operations in Canada, see p. 832. In 1814, the British captured and **burned Washington,** but were repulsed at Baltimore (Sept. 13), whereupon they launched attacks on the Maine coast and on New Orleans. In the southwest **Andrew Jackson** broke the military power of the Creek Indians and dismembered their territory (Aug. 9, 1814), whereupon he proceeded to New Orleans to defend it against the British attack. On January 8, 1815, he won the **battle of New Orleans.**

1814, Dec. 24.   The treaty of Ghent brought the war to a close. The treaty was silent on the questions which had been the chief cause of controversy before the war. It restored the *status quo ante,* and provided for joint commissions to determine disputed boundary questions between the two countries.

Dec.   The Hartford Convention. The New England states, disgruntled since the time of the embargo, had refused the call for militia during the war and had talked freely in terms of state rights. When the federal government stationed no troops in the section and the British invaded the Maine coast in 1814, Massachusetts asked her sister states to join her in a convention to be held at Hartford. The fact that moderates obtained control prevented any possibility of secession, for which the bulk of the New England people were not prepared. The convention contented itself, therefore, with drawing up some proposed amendments to the constitution, designed to safeguard more adequately New England interests. With the conclusion of peace at Ghent the New England states soon forgot their grievances.

1816.   The Second Bank of the United States chartered. The **tariff of 1816** provided increased protection. The conclusion of the War of 1812 was marked by an outburst of national feeling hitherto unknown within the country. While the Madison administration had been unwilling to recharter the First Bank in 1811, it now regarded such an institution as necessary to a uniform circulating medium. The Second Bank, chartered for twenty years, was to have a capital of $35,000,000, one-fifth to be subscribed by the government, which should name a like proportion of the directors. The tariff of 1816 was enacted in response to the demand of young industries for protection against the dumping of British goods, long held back by embargo and war.

1817, Mar. 4-1825, Mar. 4.   JAMES MONROE, the fifth president. An era of good feeling, in which party strife seemed about to disappear, as indicated by the re-election of Monroe in 1820 with but one dissenting electoral vote.

1817, Apr. 28.   The Rush-Bagot agreement between Great Britain and the United States, limiting naval forces on the Great Lakes.

1818, Oct. 20.   A convention between Great Britain and the United States established the 49th parallel as the boundary from the Lake of the Woods to the Rocky Mountains. Being unable to agree on a division of the Oregon country, north of the 42d parallel and west of the mountains, the convention provided for joint occupation for a period of ten years. This was renewed in 1827.

Feb. 22.   Treaty with Spain. Since 1803 Florida had been a source of difficulty between the United States and Spain. In 1810 Madison took advantage of an insurrection in West Florida to annex that province. After 1815 Amelia Island was a base for smugglers and freebooters. Fugitive slaves escaped to Florida, and raids against settlements in Georgia and Alabama led to trouble. In 1817-1818, in the so-called **Seminole War,** Jackson invaded Florida and executed two British subjects. **John Quincy Adams,** secretary of state, demanded that Spain maintain order in Florida or cede it to the United States. Spain chose the latter because of inability to comply with the former demand. The United States agreed to pay an indemnity of $5,000,000 to its citizens for their claims against Spain. The treaty also delimited the western boundary of the Louisiana purchase, and provided for Spain's relinquishment of all claims to territory on the Pacific north of the 42d parallel.

1819-1824. The nationalism of the post-war period was emphasized by a series of notable Supreme Court decisions by John Marshall. In *McCulloch v. Maryland* (1819), *Cohens v. Virginia* (1821), and *Gibbons v. Ogden* (1824) he gave judicial sanction to the doctrine of centralization of power at the expense of the states. In *Dartmouth College v. Woodward* (1819), as in the earlier case of *Fletcher v. Peck* (1810), the court provided judicial barriers against democratic attacks upon property rights.

1820, Mar. 3.   The Missouri Compromise. The admission to statehood of **Louisiana** (1812), **Indiana** (1816), **Mississippi** (1817), **Illinois** (1818), and **Alabama** (1819) had not raised the question of slavery. After the Revolution many southerners had agreed with northerners as to the desirability of the abolition of slavery. Southerners had been prominent in the organization of the **American Colonization Society** (1816) for the purpose of colonizing free blacks in Liberia. With the spread of cotton culture into the interior of the south, following the invention of the cotton gin by Eli Whitney (1793), southern sentiment gradually changed. Meanwhile increasing feeling in the north against the spread of slavery resulted in strong opposition to the admission of **Missouri** as a slave state. The attempt to balance the admission of Missouri as a slave state by admitting **Maine** as a free state having failed, a compromise was arranged whereby Missouri was to be admitted without restriction as to slavery, while in all the remaining portions of the Louisiana purchase north of 36° 30′ slavery was to be forever prohibited. **Maine** was admitted (1820) and **Missouri,** after careful scrutiny of its constitution by congress, was finally admitted as a slave state (Aug. 10, 1821).

Apr. 24. A **land law** was passed abolishing the credit system, established by the law of 1800, which had encouraged overpurchase of land with resulting distress, especially in the period of declining prices following the close of the war in 1815. The act of 1820 established the minimum price of public lands at $1.25 per acre.

1823, Dec. 2. The **MONROE DOCTRINE** enunciated by the president in his annual message to congress. The background of the doctrine is to be found in the threat of intervention by the **Holy Alliance** to restore Spain's revolting American colonies and in the aggressive attitude of Russia on the northwest coast of America. It was, at the same time, an expression of American national sentiment and of distrust of Britain, whose foreign minister, George Canning, had proposed a joint declaration. The message stated that *"the American continents, by the free and independent condition which they have assumed and maintained, are henceforth not to be considered as subjects for future colonization by any European powers,"* and that European intervention in this hemisphere could not be viewed *"in any other light than as the manifestation of an unfriendly disposition toward the United States."* It also disclaimed any intention of the United States to take any part *"in the wars of the European powers"* or *"in matters relating to themselves,"* i.e. the European powers.

1824. Presidential election, in which none of the four candidates, J. Q. Adams, Jackson, Clay, and W. H. Crawford, obtained an electoral majority, although Jackson received a plurality. In the house of representatives Adams was elected president.

1825, Mar. 4–1829, Mar. 4. **JOHN QUINCY ADAMS,** sixth president.

1825. **COMPLETION OF THE ERIE CANAL** begun in 1817. The canal made possible the opening of the west, and assured New York's primacy as a port.

1826. The abortive **Panama Congress** planned by Bolívar and others to present a united American front against Spain and Europe. The senate reluctantly approved the appointment of an American mission to the congress. One delegate died en route while the other arrived after the congress had adjourned.

1828, May 19. The **tariff of abominations,** framed by Jackson men for defeat, to discredit J. Q. Adams and bring about the election of Jackson. To their surprise it passed congress, was signed by Adams, and promptly aroused strong opposition, especially in South Carolina, where Calhoun penned his *South Carolina Exposition* (1828), which gave the classic statement of the nullification doctrine.

The **American Peace Society** founded in New York by **William Ladd. Elihu Burritt** became the chief leader of the American peace movement.

July 4. The **Baltimore and Ohio Railroad begun,** the first public railroad in the United States.

1829, Mar. 4–1837, Mar. 4. ANDREW JACKSON, who defeated Adams in the election of 1828, seventh president. The election of Jackson was a triumph of the frontier democracy of the west.

The **spoils system,** the practice of basing appointments on party service, was nationalized by Jackson. The system was already well-established in certain states of the north and west.

1829–1850. Rise of the common man and era of reform. By 1829 the principle of **white manhood suffrage** was established in most states. Between 1810 and 1826 Maryland, South Carolina, and New York had adopted it. Massachusetts reduced her former suffrage requirement to mere tax payment. The Virginia convention of 1830 removed the chief restrictions on the suffrage. Opposition to reform was strongest in Rhode Island.

1829. The **Workingmen's Party** organized in New York, following the example set in Philadelphia the preceding year. The movement spread to other seaboard states in the north. The program of the movement included social reform, free public schools, banking legislation, abolition of imprisonment for debt, etc.

1830. Organization of the **Mormon Church** at Fayette, New York, by **Joseph Smith.** *Book of Mormon* first printed.

Great debate between **Daniel Webster** and **Robert Hayne** on the nature of the union. The debate was really begun by Thomas Benton, who protested against New England attempts to limit the sale of western lands.

Jackson's veto of the **Maysville Road Bill.**

1831. William Lloyd Garrison established the *Liberator* at Boston to advocate unconditional emancipation of the slaves. This marks the beginning of the abolitionist movement. The **New England Anti-Slavery Society** (1832) and the **American Anti-Slavery Society** (1833). **Oberlin College** opened its doors to Negroes as well as to women (1833).

1830–1834. Controversy between Georgia and the Cherokee Indians and development of Jackson's **Indian policy.** An act of March 10,

1830, authorized the president to locate on lands west of the Mississippi all Indians who surrendered their holdings east of the river. This act was prompted largely by the controversy between the state of Georgia and the Cherokee Indians. It led to the creation of an area west of Arkansas as the final home for the southern Indians. A commission of Indian affairs was created.

1831, July 4. Treaty by which France agreed to pay $5,000,000 in satisfaction of spoliation claims.

1832, July. Tariff Act of 1832, an improvement over the tariff of abominations, but retaining the protective principle which was unsatisfactory to South Carolina and led to

1832–1833. The **nullification episode** in that state, in which a state convention declared the tariff laws of 1828 and 1832 unconstitutional and void within the state. On December 10 Jackson issued his proclamation against the nullifiers, and on January 16, 1833, he asked congress for additional legislation to enable him to enforce the tariff law. On March 1 congress enacted the **Force Bill.** Meanwhile **Henry Clay** brought forward (Feb. 12) his compromise tariff, providing for gradual reduction of the tariff until July 1, 1842, when it should reach the 20 per cent level.

1832. The Bank controversy. The Second Bank of the United States, although capably managed after 1819, had committed certain political indiscretions which, in combination with Jackson's prejudice against the alleged monopolistic tendencies of the bank, aroused his opposition. When Clay and Webster urged the bank to apply for a renewal of the charter in order to embarrass Jackson in the campaign of 1832, Jackson was aroused to the point where he vetoed the measure. Jackson construed his election over Clay as popular approval of his veto of the Bank Bill, and he resolved to crush the institution. In 1833 there began the **removal of the deposits,** or the transfer of government funds to certain state banks known as the *pet banks.*

1833. The **General Trades' Union** linked all the trade societies of New York in one organization. Trade unionism began to supersede the workingmen's parties as the characteristic form of labor activity, until the collapse of the movement in the panic of 1837.

1833–1837. The Whig Party. Southern particularists who were angered by Jackson's handling of the nullification episode, those who feared the leveling tendencies of Jacksonian democracy, the supporters of the bank, and the industrial and financial groups generally formed the Whig Party, largely lacking in constructive principles, but held together by a common

hatred for and distrust of Jackson.

1836. Texan independence. The American colonization of Texas had begun in 1821 when **Stephen Austin** obtained a grant of land on condition that he settle a certain number of families thereon. This was followed by similar grants to other *empresarios* who introduced a substantial number of American settlers. This movement, largely of southerners, was part of the normal westward movement of the American people. Beginning about 1830 difficulties developed. In 1836 the **Republic of Texas** was established. The decisive battle was that of **San Jacinto** (Apr. 21, 1836).

1836. Act for **distribution of surplus revenue** among the states, theoretically as a loan.

1837, Mar. 4–1841, Mar. 4. MARTIN VAN BUREN, eighth president.

1837. Panic of 1837. Fundamentally this crash was due to the wave of speculation and reckless expansion that swept the country in the years of 1833–1837. The situation was complicated by the failure of certain great business houses in Britain which had invested heavily in American securities, by poor crops in the west in 1835 and 1837, and by Jackson's **Special Circular** (July 11, 1836) which required that public lands be paid for in "hard" money.

1837–1840. Struggle between Van Buren and the Whigs over the **independent treasury** proposed by Van Buren for the deposit of government funds. The Whig leaders favored the establishment of a third United States Bank. Independent treasury plan adopted (1840).

1837. Mt. Holyoke Seminary, first women's institution of college rank, opened by **Mary Lyon.**

1837–1842. Difficulties between the United States and Canada. The *Caroline* affair (Dec. 1837) in which an American steamer in the service of Canadian rebels was seized by Canadian militia on the American side of the Niagara River, and in which an American citizen was killed. One **Alexander McLeod,** a Canadian, boasting that he had killed the American, was arrested and tried in New York courts. His acquittal averted the possibility of serious difficulties between the United States and Great Britain.

Difficulty over the northeastern boundary led to the **Aroostook County War** (1838–1839). The boundary was finally adjusted in the **Webster-Ashburton treaty** (Aug. 9, 1842).

1838. The **Underground Railroad** organized.

1838–1839. Congress adopted **gag resolutions** against anti-slavery petitions.

1841. The Pre-emption-Distribution Act. Benton had long advocated the pre-emption policy with respect to public lands, while Clay had advocated the distribution of the proceeds of the sale of public lands among the states. By a compromise the two measures were now combined, with a proviso, insisted upon by the south, which required that distribution should cease if the tariff should rise above the 20 per cent level.

1841, Mar. 4–1845, Mar. 4. WILLIAM HENRY HARRISON and **JOHN TYLER,** the ninth and tenth presidents. Harrison died April 4, 1841.

1842. The **Dorr rebellion** in Rhode Island, occasioned by refusal of conservatives to liberalize the suffrage and to reform representation. It swept away the charter of 1663, which had served as the constitution of the state of Rhode Island, 1776–1842.

The **Whig tariff** restored protective features on the expiration of the compromise tariff of 1833.

1844, Apr. 12. Calhoun's treaty for annexation of Texas signed. Defeated in the senate, June 8, 1844.

Presidential campaign. The Democrats nominated **James K. Polk** on the platform declaring for reannexation of Texas and the reoccupation of Oregon. The Whigs nominated **Henry Clay.** The Liberty Party nominated **James G. Birney** and took enough popular votes from Clay to enable Polk to carry New York and win the election.

1845, Mar. 1. Tyler brought about **annexation of Texas** by joint resolution of Congress.

1845, Mar. 4–1849, Mar. 4. JAMES K. POLK, eleventh president.

1846, June 15. Oregon treaty with Great Britain. The two countries had long claimed the Oregon country, between 42° and 54° 40′, although the region really in dispute was that between the Columbia River and the 49th parallel. The **treaty of joint occupation** of 1818 was renewed in 1827, with provision that it might be terminated by either party upon a year's notice. British interest in the Oregon country centered in the fur trade, dominated, after 1821, by the **Hudson's Bay Company.** American traders had visited the Oregon coast at an early day. Captain Robert Gray had discovered the mouth of the Columbia River (1793), Lewis and Clark had explored the region, and John Jacob Astor had established the post of **Astoria** (1811). A Methodist mission was established in the Willamette Valley (1834) and was followed by others. By the early forties a substantial migration of American farmers to the Willamette Valley was under way, so the Anglo-American rivalry became one of fur trader versus settler. The treaty established the 49th parallel as the boundary on the mainland, and then the middle of the channel to the ocean.

The **Walker tariff** enlarged the free list and established a rate of 26.5 per cent on dutiable imports.

Re-enactment of the **Independent Treasury Act** which the Whigs had repealed in 1841.

1846–1848. WAR WITH MEXICO. The United States had many grievances against Mexico, while Mexico could not forgive the United States for the annexation of Texas. Polk was determined to have New Mexico, preferably by peaceful means, but when **Slidell's mission** to Mexico for the purpose of purchasing that territory failed (Nov. 1845–Mar. 1846), Polk was prepared for war. By sending American troops into the disputed area between the Rio Nueces and Rio Grande, he brought about a skirmish which enabled him to say that Mexico had "shed American blood on American soil." An army under General Zachary Taylor invaded Mexico and won the **battles of Palo Alto** and **Resaca de la Palma** (May 8 and 9), took **Monterey** (May 24), and won a victory at **Buena Vista** (Feb. 22 and 23, 1847). Colonel S. W. Kearny occupied **Santa Fé** (Aug. 18, 1846). Marching inland from Vera Cruz, **Winfield Scott** fought the battles of **Cerro Gordo** (Apr. 17 and 18, 1847), **Churubusco** (Aug. 20), **Chapultepec** (Sept. 12 and 13), and captured **Mexico City** (Sept. 14). On the Pacific an American squadron seized the California ports.

1846, Aug. 8. The **Wilmot Proviso** introduced into the house of representatives, when Polk asked for an appropriation to enable him to treat with Mexico for territorial cessions. It provided that in any territory acquired from Mexico, slavery should be excluded. Although it never passed the senate, it raised the slavery issue and aroused the fears of the south.

1848, Jan. 24. Discovery of gold at Coloma, sixty miles east of Sutter's Fort, California. Beginning of the great gold rush.

Feb. 2. The **treaty of Guadalupe Hidalgo** closed the war with Mexico. Mexico gave up claims to Texas, recognized the Rio Grande as the boundary, and ceded New Mexico and California to the United States in return for $15,000,000 and the assumption of American claims against Mexico.

July 19. First Women's Rights convention, the first in world history, held at Seneca Falls, New York. The movement had started with the visit of **Frances Wright** to America in 1827. Her example aroused to action **Sarah** and **Angelina Grimke, Lucretia Mott,** and **Elizabeth Cady Stanton.**

Presidential campaign, in which the Whig candidate was **Zachary Taylor,** hero of the recent war. The Democrats nominated **Lewis**

Cass, who had recently proposed squatter sovereignty as a solution of the problem of slavery in the territories, raised by the Wilmot Proviso. The **Free Soil Party,** favoring homestead and the exclusion of slavery from the territories, nominated **Van Buren,** who, by splitting the Democratic vote in New York, enabled Taylor to carry the state and win the election.

1849, Mar. 4–1853, Mar. 4. ZACHARY TAYLOR and **MILLARD FILLMORE,** twelfth and thirteenth presidents. Taylor died July 9, 1850.

1850. THE COMPROMISE OF 1850. On January 29, 1850, Clay introduced his compromise resolutions providing that California should be admitted as a free state; that territorial governments should be established in the remainder of the Mexican cession without any action by congress with respect to slavery; Texas should yield her claims in the boundary dispute with New Mexico, in return for which the United States would assume the Texan debt; the slave trade should be abolished in the District of Columbia; and congress should enact a more drastic fugitive slave law. Great debate in which Calhoun spoke (Mar. 4) against the compromise; Webster (Mar. 7) for the compromise; Douglas for, Jefferson Davis, Seward, and Chase against. On April 18 the resolutions were referred to a senate committee of thirteen, with Clay as chairman. Between September 9 and 20 the separate measures, known collectively as the **Compromise of 1850,** were passed: California to be admitted as a free state; the remainder of the Mexican cession to be divided at the 37th parallel into the territories of New Mexico and Utah, to be admitted to the union ultimately as states, with or without slavery as their constitutions might provide at the time of admission; the claims of Texas to a portion of New Mexico to be satisfied by payment of $10,000,000; the slave trade in the District of Columbia to be abolished, and a more effective fugitive slave law enacted.

Land grants to railways adopted by congress. A grant was made to the state of Illinois to help the **Illinois Central Railroad** and another to Mississippi and Alabama in support of the **Mobile and Ohio** line.

Apr. 19. The **Clayton-Bulwer treaty** between the United States and Great Britain with respect to British encroachments in Central America and a future interoceanic canal.

June 3. Nashville convention of nine southern states. Dominated by moderates, it demanded merely the extension of the 36° 30′ line.

1851. Maine prohibition law, sponsored by Neal Dow. It became the model for all similar legislation of the period restricting the sale of alcoholic liquors.

June 2. The **Erie Railroad** reached Dunkirk, on Lake Erie, being the first railway to make connection with the Lakes.

1852. The Democratic Party, committed to finality of the Compromise of 1850 as a solution of the problem of slavery in the territories, elected

1853, Mar. 4–1857, Mar. 4.   FRANKLIN PIERCE, fourteenth president.

1853. Rail connection established between New York and Chicago. By 1860 the region north of the Ohio River and east of the Mississippi had been firmly attached commercially to the North Atlantic seaboard. The movement of internal trade, originally north and south along the Mississippi, now became predominantly a west-east movement, the shift proving of great economic and political significance.

Dec. 30. The **Gadsden purchase** rounded out United States possessions in the Far West.

1854, May 30. The **KANSAS-NEBRASKA ACT,** which repealed the Missouri Compromise of 1820, opened the Nebraska country to settlement on the basis of **popular sovereignty,** and provided for the organization of two territories, Kansas and Nebraska. Stephen A. Douglas was the author of the measure, and he was largely motivated by his desire to pave the way for a Pacific railway. The act undid the sectional truce of 1850 and proved the death-blow to the Whig Party.

Mar. 31. Commodore Matthew Perry negotiated a **treaty with Japan,** opening the country to commercial intercourse with the United States.

Oct. 18. The **Ostend Manifesto.** The American ministers to Britain, France, and Spain, instructed to confer on the best means of acquiring **Cuba,** met at Ostend and drew up the manifesto saying that, if Spain refused to sell Cuba, the United States would be justified in taking it by force. This caused great excitement in the free states.

The **Know-Nothing** and **Republican Parties** appeared, the former as a protest against the Kansas-Nebraska Act.

1855. Opening of **Soo Canal** between Lakes **Superior** and **Huron** provided cheap transportation of iron ore and laid the basis for rapid development of the steel industry.

1854–1858. War for "Bleeding Kansas." The opening of Kansas to settlement under the Douglas doctrine of popular sovereignty precipitated a mad scramble for control between pro-slavery and free-soil elements. In April 1854 the **New England Emigrant Aid Society** was formed to colonize free-soilers in Kansas.

This aroused the pro-slavery people. **Border ruffians** from Missouri interfered in elections in Kansas. A pro-slavery element attacked the town of Lawrence, and in return **John Brown** staged the massacre at **Pottawatomie Creek** (May 24, 1856). The **Lecompton constitution** was formed by pro-slavery forces, but was denounced by Douglas as a fraud upon the people of Kansas and a violation of the popular sovereignty doctrine. This led to a break between Douglas and James Buchanan. The senate accepted the Lecompton constitution, but the house rejected it. The deadlock was broken by the **English Bill,** enacted May 4, 1858, providing for resubmission of the constitution to popular vote in Kansas. If accepted, the state would receive a grant of land; if rejected, statehood must await further growth of population. It was rejected, and Kansas did not become a state until January 1861.

1857, Mar. 4-1861, Mar. 4.   JAMES BU-CHANAN, fifteenth president.

Mar. 7. The **Dred Scott decision,** declaring that the Missouri Compromise was unconstitutional because congress had no right to enact a law which deprived persons of their property in the territories of the United States. Dred Scott, therefore, had not acquired his freedom by being taken into a territory where slavery had been prohibited by the compromise. The decision caused bitter criticism of the court in the north.

Tariff of 1857; reduced duties.

Panic of 1857, following a period of overexpansion and speculation.

Aug.   Lincoln-Douglas debates, seven in number, in the campaign for election to the senate. Douglas was elected, but Abraham Lincoln, by asking Douglas to reconcile his doctrine of popular sovereignty with the Dred Scott decision, forced him to enunciate his **Freeport heresy,** which was deeply distasteful to the southern wing of the party.

Abandonment of the government **ship subsidy policy** (introduced 1845), because of opposition of the southern states.

1859, Oct. 19.   John Brown's raid on Harper's Ferry still further aroused sectional passions.

1860. The **Davis resolutions,** introduced by Jefferson Davis, demanded a federal slave code for the protection of property in slaves in the territories.

Presidential campaign. The Republicans nominated **Abraham Lincoln** on a platform opposing further extension of slavery in the territories and supporting homestead and tariff. The Democrats split at Charleston on the question of slavery in the territories. Two platforms were drawn up, one demanding a federal slave code, the other endorsing the Freeport doctrine of Douglas. Subsequently the northern Democrats nominated **Douglas,** while the southern Democrats named **John C. Breckinridge.** The Union Party nominated **John Bell.** Lincoln was elected, in a purely sectional contest. He received no electoral support in the slave states.

Dec. 20. South Carolina adopted the **ordinance of secession,** as a protest against the election of Lincoln.

1860, Dec.-1861, Feb. 4. Futile efforts to save the union. The **Crittenden compromise resolutions,** proposing the extension of the Missouri Compromise line to the Pacific; conference of governors of northern states; the **peace convention** at Washington, February 4, 1861.

1861, Jan.-May. Mississippi, Florida, Alabama, Georgia, Louisiana, Texas, Virginia, Arkansas, Tennessee, and North Carolina seceded from the union.

Jan. 9. The ship *Star of the West* was fired upon by a battery at Charleston.

Feb. 4. Delegates of the seven seceding states met at Montgomery, Alabama, and formed a provisional government, taking the name **Confederate States of America.**

Feb. 8. **Jefferson Davis** elected president and **Alexander H. Stephens** vice-president of the Confederacy.

1861, Mar. 4-1865, Apr. 15.   ABRAHAM LINCOLN, sixteenth president.

CULTURAL DEVELOPMENTS

Literature: The national literature that began to develop in the early 19th century showed many of the characteristics of the Romantic movement in European literature. Novelists and writers of sketches and tales: **Washington Irving** (1783-1859), **James Fenimore Cooper** (1789-1851), **Nathaniel Hawthorne** (1804-1864; *The Scarlet Letter,* 1850); **Edgar Allan Poe** (1809-1849); **Herman Melville** (1819-1891; *Moby Dick,* 1851). Poets: **William Cullen Bryant** (1794-1878), **Henry Wadsworth Longfellow** (1807-1882), and **John Greenleaf Whittier** (1807-1892). Essayists: **Ralph Waldo Emerson** (1803-1882) and **Oliver Wendell Holmes** (1809-1894, *The Autocrat of the Breakfast Table,* 1858). The best-known novel of the era **Harriet Beecher Stowe's** *Uncle Tom's Cabin* (1852), a most forceful piece of abolitionist literature. **Henry David Thoreau** (1817-1862), also the author of anti-slavery articles, in 1846-47 wrote his best prose in *Walden: or, Life in the Woods* (1854), an account of his solitary life and studies of nature.

Art: The vogue was for landscape painting (Hudson River School; **George Inness,** 1825-1894). The buildings designed by **Charles Bul-**

finch (1763–1844), **Benjamin Latrobe** (1764–1820), and **Thomas Jefferson** bear testimony to a revival of the classical style in architecture.

Music: The songs of **Stephen Foster** (1826–1864) are among the first truly American compositions.

b. THE CIVIL WAR, 1861–1865

MILITARY EVENTS. The Confederates, having seized Federal funds and property in the south, proceeded (Apr. 10) to demand the evacuation of the Federal **Fort Sumter** in Charleston Harbor. Major Robert Anderson, in command, having refused unconditional surrender, Gen. Pierre Beauregard bombarded it April 12–13, just as a relief expedition of the Federalists approached.

Apr. 15. Lincoln called for 75,000 volunteers to serve three months, and summoned congress to meet July 4. May 3 he appealed for 42,000 men to serve three years or for the duration of the war. General expectancy of a short conflict. Immense advantages of the North; 23 states with almost 23,000,000 population against 11 states with 5,000,000 white population; financial strength of the North; manufacturing facilities; more extensive railway communications, etc. South largely dependent on cotton-growing and badly hampered by the blockade of the Confederate ports (proclaimed April 19); from the beginning the South was on the defensive.

May 13. Great Britain recognized the Confederate States as belligerents.

July 21. FIRST BATTLE OF BULL RUN. By July there were some 30,000 raw troops in and around Washington, under command of Gen. **Winfield Scott.** Across the Potomac lay 25,000 Confederates under **Beauregard** near the Manassas railway junction. Another force, under Gen. **Joseph E. Johnston,** lay in the Shenandoah Valley, near Harper's Ferry. Congress, meeting July 4, demanded action. Gen. **Robert Patterson** was sent to contain this latter force, while Gen. **Irvin MacDowell** reluctantly advanced on Beauregard. But part of Johnston's army, under Col. **T. J. (Stonewall) Jackson,** got away and joined Beauregard. At Bull Run the Federal army was routed. It streamed back to Washington in a state of dissolution. The effect of the battle was to open the eyes of the Federalists and to introduce a period of more extensive and systematic preparation.

Nov. 1. Gen. **George B. McClellan** appointed to succeed Scott in command of the Federal forces. McClellan's policy one of cautious, careful preparation and reliance on numbers. He spent the winter training some 200,000 men (Army of the Potomac) for a march on the Confederate capital, Richmond.

Nov. 8. James Mason and John Slidell, commissioners of the Confederate States to Great Britain and France, were taken off the British steamer *Trent* by the Federal steamer *San Jacinto.* Sharp protests of Great Britain and danger of war. War averted by the prudence and skill of **William H. Seward,** secretary of state. The commissioners were given up, in accordance with a principle of international law for which the United States had invariably contended.

1861–1862. NAVAL OPERATIONS. To make the blockade of the southern coasts effective and to prevent privateering, a joint naval and military expedition was sent out in August 1861 to take key positions on the coast.

1861, Aug. 28–29. Attack and capture of **Forts Clark** and **Hatteras** on the North Carolina coast.

1862, Feb. 8. Capture of **Roanoke Island** and **Elizabeth City** (Feb. 10).

Mar. 3–4. Amelia Island, on the Florida coast, taken.

Mar. 8. The Confederate frigate *Merrimac,* made over as an ironclad, appeared in Hampton Roads and sank the *Cumberland.*

Mar. 9. The Federal ironclad *Monitor* (revolving gun-turret) engaged the *Merrimac* and finally obliged her to withdraw. Epoch-making development in naval warfare.

Mar. 12. Jacksonville, Florida, occupied by Federal forces.

Mar. 14. Capture of New Bern, North Carolina. This gave the Federal forces a base from which to threaten Richmond, and obliged the Confederates to keep an army near the capital.

Apr. 24–25. A Federal force (27 ships and 15,000 troops), under command of Flag-officer (later Admiral) **David G. Farragut** and Gen. **Benjamin F. Butler,** ran the forts below New Orleans and bombarded the city. After the landing of troops, the city was taken (May 1).

1862. THE PENINSULA CAMPAIGN. After endless delay, McClellan decided to advance on Richmond, not overland through territory cut by many rivers, but by water to the mouth of the James River, whence he could proceed up the peninsula between the James and the York. The advance began in April. The Confederates, under Johnston and **Robert E. Lee** (Confederate commander-in-chief after June 1, 1862), were greatly outnumbered and fell back. They were saved in part by McClellan's vacillation and by the operations of Jackson, who managed to draw a considerable Federal force into the Shenandoah Valley and ultimately succeeded in joining Lee with substantial reinforcements. Heavy fighting around

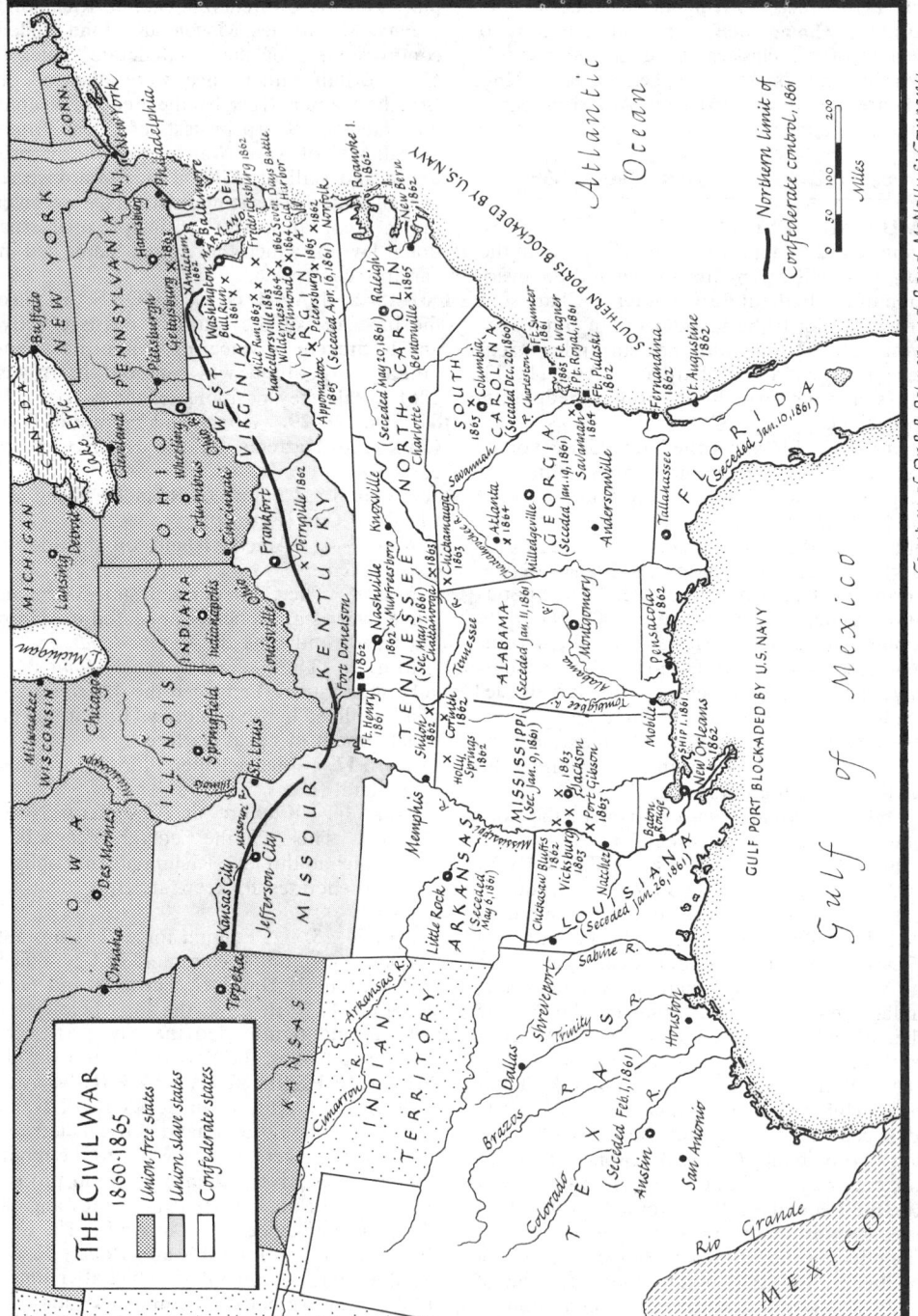

Courtesy of Dr. R.R. Palmer and Rand McNally & Company

THE CIVIL WAR
1860-1865

Union free states

Union slave states

Confederate states

Richmond: **battle of Fair Oaks** (May 31); **Seven Days' battle** (June 25–July 1: **Mechanicsville, Gaines' Mill, White Oak Swamp, Malvern Hill**), resulting in the withdrawal of the Federal forces from the peninsula.

Campaign in Maryland. In the autumn of 1862 Lee began to push on toward Washington. Confederate forces under Jackson defeated the Federal forces under Nathaniel Banks at **Cedar Mountain** (Aug. 9), while the Federal army under Gen. John Pope was defeated by Jackson in the **second battle of Bull Run** (Aug. 30). The Confederates crossed the Potomac (Sept. 4) and invaded Maryland.

Sept. 17. BATTLE OF ANTIETAM, indecisive, but Lee began to fall back into Virginia. McClellan, as usual unable to take advantage of his opportunities, did little to pursue him and did not cross the Potomac until October 26.

Nov. 7. Gen. **Ambrose E. Burnside** was appointed to succeed McClellan. He pushed the advance in Virginia, but was badly defeated by Lee in the **battle of Fredericksburg** (Dec. 13). January 25, 1863, he was succeeded by Gen. **Joseph Hooker.**

CAMPAIGNS IN THE WEST. In western Kentucky and Tennessee there was active campaigning throughout the year 1862. Brig.-Gen. **Ulysses S. Grant,** serving under Gen. **Henry W. Halleck,** in command of the Federal troops, on February 6 forced the **surrender of Fort Henry** on the Tennessee River, and on February 16 he secured the **surrender of Fort Donelson** on the Cumberland. The Confederates abandoned **Nashville** and fell back on the line Memphis–Chattanooga.

Apr. 6–7. Battle of Shiloh. The Confederates, under Gen. **Albert S. Johnston,** attacked Grant's lines at **Pittsburg Landing.** After an initial success the Confederates (Johnston killed, Beauregard in command) were driven back. They evacuated **Corinth** (May 30) and surrendered **Memphis** (June 6). The Federal forces commanded the Mississippi as far south as Vicksburg.

Oct. 8. Battle of Perryville, Kentucky. A Confederate force under Gen. **Braxton Bragg** had advanced into Kentucky in the hope of compelling the withdrawal of the Federal forces to the north. Bragg threatened Cincinnati, but the Kentuckians failed to support him. He was retreating southward when he met the Federal army of Gen. **William Rosecrans** in the battle of **Murfreesboro** on **Stone River** (Dec. 31, 1862–Jan. 3, 1863).

1863. EASTERN CAMPAIGNS. After several months spent in reorganization, Hooker on May 1 ordered an advance from Chancellorsville, Virginia.

May 1–4. BATTLE OF CHANCELLORSVILLE. The Federal forces were defeated by the Confederates (death of Stonewall Jackson). Gen. **George G. Meade** relieved Hooker as commander of the Army of the Potomac (June 28). Meanwhile Lee had begun the invasion of the North by way of the Shenandoah Valley, establishing himself in southern Pennsylvania. Meade took up his position at Gettysburg.

July 1–3. BATTLE OF GETTYSBURG. In three days of heavy fighting Lee was unable to dislodge the Federal forces and was obliged to fall back to the Potomac. Decisive battle of the war. Henceforth the Confederates were obliged to remain on the defensive and the war became a test of endurance.

WESTERN CAMPAIGNS. The operations in the west centered first on the taking of **Vicksburg,** key to the control of the Mississippi. On April 30 **Grant** crossed the river below the fortress, marched east and took Jackson and then doubled back, hemming in the fortress.

July 4. VICKSBURG SURRENDERED, starved out after a short siege. On July 8 **Port Hudson,** farther down the river, surrendered, giving the Federals command of the entire river and cutting off Texas, Arkansas, and Louisiana from the rest of the Confederacy.

Sept. 9. The Federal troops, under Rosecrans, took **Chattanooga** and pursued the Confederates, under Bragg, into Georgia. Defeated in the **battle of Chickamauga** (Sept. 19–20), Rosecrans was obliged to fall back to Chattanooga, where he was hard pressed by the Confederates. Reinforced by troops from Vicksburg under Gen. **William T. Sherman** and from the Potomac under Hooker, Grant, in command of the armies of the west, fought the

Nov. 23–25. BATTLE OF CHATTANOOGA (Lookout Mountain, Nov. 24; **Missionary Ridge,** Nov. 25), driving the Confederates out of Tennessee and opening the road into Georgia.

1864, Mar. 9. Grant made lieutenant-general and commander-in-chief of all the armies; Sherman given command in the west. Grant's plan was to defeat Lee's army. He crossed the Rapidan (May 3) and began the advance from near Chancellorsville through the Wilderness.

May 5–6. BATTLE OF THE WILDERNESS. Grant, attacked by Lee, was unable to defeat him, but maintained his ground and continued the advance toward Spotsylvania Court House.

May 8–18. Battles around Spotsylvania Court House, on the **North Anna River** (May 21–31), and at **Cold Harbor** (June 1–3). Grant was unable to defeat Lee, but crossed the James River and assaulted **Petersburg** (June

15–18), twenty miles below Richmond, which he then besieged. In order to create a diversion, Lee sent Gen. **Jubal Early** to threaten Washington. Early carried through raids into Maryland and Pennsylvania, but was defeated by Gen. **Philip H. Sheridan** in the **battles of Winchester** (Opequan Creek) and **Fisher's Hill** (Sept. 19, 21), after which the Confederates were obliged to withdraw from the Shenandoah Valley (**battle of Cedar Creek,** Oct. 19). Sheridan laid the whole region waste and then rejoined Grant at Petersburg.

SHERMAN'S CAMPAIGN. Sherman started from Chattanooga (May 5) with about 100,000 men to march through Georgia to Atlanta. He was opposed by one of the ablest Confederate commanders, Gen. **Joseph E. Johnston,** with 65,000 men. Johnston did what he could to impede Sherman's advance, but wisely refused a general battle. Sherman, however, crossed the Chattahoochee River (July 17), as a result of which Johnston was removed from his command. His successor, Gen. **John B. Hood,** offered battle, but was defeated (**battle of Atlanta,** July 22).

Sept. 2. Evacuation of Atlanta by the Confederates. Sherman destroyed the factories and stores and urged upon Grant his plan of a march to the sea. Part of the army, under Thomas, was sent north to watch Hood, who was defeated before **Nashville** (Dec. 15–16). Sherman himself, with 60,000 men, started for the southeast (Nov. 16), ravaging the country as he proceeded. He reached the sea (Dec. 12) and the Confederates abandoned **Savannah** Dec. 20). Sherman then turned north into South Carolina. **Columbia** was taken (Feb. 17, 1865) and the advance continued into North Carolina. A Federal fleet took **Charleston** (Feb. 18) and Sherman took **Goldsboro** (Mar. 19).

1865. LAST CAMPAIGNS. The Confederate armies, caught between Grant in the north and Sherman in the south and deprived of food supply, were no longer able to withstand the pressure. Sheridan won the **battle of Five Forks** (Apr. 1) and thus forced the **evacuation of Petersburg** (Apr. 2) and the **surrender of Richmond** (Apr. 3). Grant with all his forces then pursued and surrounded Lee.

Apr. 9. LEE'S CAPITULATION AT APPOMATTOX COURT HOUSE. Johnston, with the southern army, surrendered to Sherman (Apr. 26), and the last Confederate army, under Gen. Kirby Smith, surrendered at Shreveport, Louisiana, on May 26. Jefferson Davis, president of the Confederacy, fled to Georgia, but was captured (May 10) and imprisoned.

POLITICAL AND SOCIAL ASPECTS OF THE WAR PERIOD:

1861, Mar. The **Morrill tariff,** marking the beginning of successive tariff increases which by 1864 reached duties of 47 per cent.

Aug. Income tax of 3 per cent on all income in excess of $800.

1862, Feb. First of the **Legal Tender Acts,** followed by similar acts in 1862 and 1863.

July. The first comprehensive **internal revenue act,** born of the war.

Sept. 22. The president issued a preliminary proclamation declaring that all slaves in states or parts of states which should still be in rebellion on January 1, 1863, should be free from the latter date on. The formal **Emancipation Proclamation** was issued on January 1, 1863.

1863, Feb. 25. National Banking Act passed to create a market for United States bonds, to drive out of circulation the notes of banks chartered by the states, to create a powerful financial support for the government, and to provide for the country a uniform circulating medium. Stockholders obtaining a charter could buy government bonds, deposit them with the treasurer of the United States, and then issue national bank notes up to 90 per cent of the current market value of the bonds. The banks having proved slow to take out charters, state bank notes were driven out of existence by a tax of 10 per cent (1865).

June 20. West Virginia (the loyal part of Virginia) admitted to the union as the thirty-fifth state.

1864, Nov. 8. Re-election of Lincoln. Andrew Johnson, vice-president.

1865, Feb. 1. Resolution in Congress to submit to the states the **thirteenth amendment** to the constitution, prohibiting slavery within the United States. The amendment was ratified by two-thirds of the states by December 18.

1865–1873. Serious and recurring **epidemics** of smallpox, typhus, typhoid, cholera, scarlet fever, and yellow fever in Philadelphia, New York, Boston, Baltimore, Washington, Memphis, and New Orleans led to the realization of the need for improved sanitation. In 1866 a municipal **board of health** was created in New York and in 1869 a state board of health was established in Massachusetts.

1861–1868. New territories. In the years just before the war the discovery of precious metals in the Pike's Peak country and in the Washoe Mountains led to mining rushes to those regions, with the result that the territories of **Colorado** and **Nevada** were organized in 1861. Mining rushes elsewhere in the years of the war resulted in the organization of the territories of **Arizona** (1863), **Idaho** (1863), and **Montana** (1864). **Wyoming** was made a territory in 1868.

1862-1886. Taming of the Plains Indians. The constant pressure of white population, combined with broken promises, led to continued outbreaks of the Indians. The **Homestead Act** (1862) played a prominent part in the settlement of the west. The **Morrill Act** (1862), providing for grants of land to states in order to aid the establishment of agricultural colleges, opened up more areas. In 1862 the **Union** and **Central Pacific Railways** were chartered by congress and given a large grant of land. They formed the first transcontinental railway (completed May 10, 1869).

In 1862 the **Sioux Indians** of Minnesota were defeated by Gen. Henry Sibley at **Wood Lake.** In 1864 the **Cheyennes** went on the warpath, with the aid of the Arapahoe, Apache, Comanche, and Kiowa tribes. Troops under Col. John Chivington staged a massacre of Indians at **Sand Creek,** Colorado (Nov. 1864). Efforts of troops to build an emigrant road from Fort Laramie along the Powder River to the mines of Montana and Idaho led to war with the **Plains Sioux** (1866). A commission authorized by congress persuaded the Apache, Comanche, and Kiowa tribes to locate in **Indian Territory,** and secured the removal of other tribes from the Plains to more remote regions. In 1869 congress created the **Board of Indian Commissioners** to supervise all government expenditures for the Indians. Meanwhile the advance of white settlers, slaughter of the buffalo, and the gold rush to the Black Hills caused an outbreak of the Plains Sioux (1876) under **Sitting Bull,** which resulted in the **massacre of Col. George Custer** and his men at the **Little Big Horn** (June 25). **Nez Percé Indians** under **Chief Joseph** were defeated (Oct. 1877) and removed to Indian Territory. The last important Indian uprising came in the years 1882-1886, when the **Apaches** in Arizona and New Mexico, under **Victorio** and **Geronimo,** resisted efforts to confine them to reservations. By 1886 the Indians had all been removed to Indian Territory or to reservations.

c. THE UNITED STATES, 1865-1917

1865, Apr. 14. ASSASSINATION OF LINCOLN; death April 15. **Andrew Johnson,** vice-president, succeeded.

Cost of the war. National debt in 1860, $64,842,287; in 1866, $2,773,236,173, which great increase was in addition to the debts incurred by the states and municipalities.

May 29. President Johnson issued a **proclamation of amnesty,** granting pardon to all ordinary persons who had participated in the rebellion on taking an oath of allegiance.

Dec. Joint Committee of Fifteen on Reconstruction appointed by congress.

Dec. 18. Ratification of the thirteenth amendment, abolishing slavery.

1866, Feb. Johnson vetoed a measure extending the life of the **Freedmen's Bureau,** thereby increasing tension between himself and congress.

April. Congress passed over Johnson's veto the **Civil Rights Bill,** declaring all persons born in the United States to be citizens of the United States and entitled to equality of treatment before the law. This was designed to guarantee equal treatment to Negroes in southern states.

June 13. FOURTEENTH AMENDMENT sent to states for ratification. Declared ratified July 28, 1868. It incorporated in the constitution the principle of the Civil Rights Act; gave the southern states the choice of Negro enfranchisement or reduced representation in the lower house of congress; barred from office-holding ex-Confederates who had been federal or state officials before the war, until they should be pardoned by a two-thirds vote of congress; provided that the war debt of the south should never be paid or that of the union repudiated; and that former masters should never be compensated for their slaves. In the light of subsequent events, the most significant provision of the amendment was the clause, **"nor shall any state deprive any person of life, liberty, or property, without due process of law."** It was generally assumed at the time that this clause was designed solely to safeguard the freedmen in the possession of their civil rights and it was so interpreted by the supreme court in the **Slaughter House Cases** (1873). In 1886, however, in the case of *Santa Clara County* v. *Southern Pacific Railroad,* the supreme court declared that a corporation was a "person" within the meaning of the amendment and thus entitled to its protection. From this time the **due process clause** of the amendment came to have a new significance. More and more it was applied by the courts to shield business and corporations against hostile legislative action by the states, and by reading into the clause the doctrine of **liberty of contract** the court made it a formidable barrier against the enactment of much-needed social legislation by the states.

1867, Mar. 2. THE BASIC RECONSTRUCTION ACT. Johnson having advised the southern states to reject the fourteenth amendment, all except Tennessee promptly did so, the quarrel over reconstruction thereby becoming the major issue in the congressional election of 1866, in which Johnson was repudiated. This act, as supplemented by regulations of March 23 and July 19, 1867, and March 11, 1868, divided the southern states into five military districts. To be restored to the union, the states must hold state conventions, whose delegates must be elected with the aid of Negro suffrage; these conventions must frame constitutions approved by congress and ratified by the people of the states; and the legislatures elected under the constitution must ratify the fourteenth amendment.

Mar. 2.   Tenure-of-Office Act. On March 4 it was passed over Johnson's veto.

Mar. 30.   Purchase of Alaska for $7,200,000.

1868, Feb. 24–May 26.   Impeachment and trial of Andrew Johnson. Johnson and congress had disagreed over the reconstruction policy. The immediate occasion for the impeachment proceedings was Johnson's alleged violation of the Tenure-of-Office Act. He was acquitted by a vote of 35 to 19, 36 votes (two-thirds of the senate) being required for conviction.

1869, Feb. 26. The **fifteenth amendment** adopted by congress. The radicals, fearing that southern whites might obtain power in their states and repeal the provisions of their state constitutions granting the suffrage to the Negro, sponsored this amendment, providing that the right to vote shall not be abridged because of "race, color, or previous condition of servitude." It was declared ratified, March 30, 1870. Virginia, Texas, Mississippi, and Georgia were forced to ratify this amendment as a condition of restoration to the union.

Sept. The **National Prohibition Party** was organized by a convention in Chicago.

Nov. The **National Woman's Suffrage convention** met at Cleveland (**Rev. Henry Ward Beecher,** president) and organized the **American Woman Suffrage Association,** indicating increased activity of women in regard to the ballot.

1869, Mar. 4–1877, Mar. 4.   ULYSSES S. GRANT, eighteenth president.

1871, May 8.   TREATY OF WASHINGTON with Great Britain, providing (1) for reference to the German emperor of the dispute as to the northwest boundary (decided in favor of the United States, October 21, 1872); (2) for a partial settlement of the fishery dispute (**Halifax award,** 1877, which gave Great Britain $5,500,000)—this part of the treaty was abrogated by the United States, 1883; (3) and for the settlement of the *Alabama* claims by an international commission to sit at Geneva.

1872, Aug. 25. The **Geneva award** of $15,-500,000 to the United States as compensation for direct damages resulting from the depredations of the *Alabama* and other Confederate cruisers.

Nov.   Re-election of Grant, the Republican candidate, over **Horace Greeley,** the Liberal Republican candidate, who was endorsed by the Democratic Party, which abstained from placing a candidate in the field. Increasing dissatisfaction of many Republicans with the Grant administration had led to the organization of the **Liberal Republican Party.** Grant received 286 electoral votes to 62 for Greeley.

1873. *Crédit Mobilier* **scandal,** resulting from the revelation by congressional investigating committees that **Schuyler Colfax,** the outgoing vice-president, and a number of members of congress, including James A. Garfield, held stock, for which they had not paid, in the Crédit Mobilier, the construction company which built the Union Pacific Railway. This was merely one of the numerous instances of corruption in the Grant régime. In 1874 **William A. Richardson,** secretary of the treasury, hastily resigned to escape a vote of censure by congress. Grant's private secretary, **Orville E. Babcock,** was implicated in the **Whiskey Ring,** while **William W. Belknap,** secretary of war, resigned in 1876 to escape impeachment for bribe-taking. **James G. Blaine,** speaker of the house, was compromised through the *Mulligan letters.*

Sept. Panic precipitated by the **failure of Jay Cooke and Company.** Fundamentally the panic was due to inflated currency, unlimited credit, reckless speculation, and overexpansion. As much of the business expansion had been financed from abroad, a panic in Vienna (May 1873), which spread to other European money centers, caused the withdrawal of much of the foreign capital from the United States.

The Great Bonanza. Important discovery of silver in Nevada.

1875, Jan 14. The **Resumption Act** passed by congress, providing for the resumption of specie payment (suspended in 1861), January 1, 1879.

1876.   Johns Hopkins University opened in Baltimore. As the first real graduate school in the United States, it gave great impetus to advanced study.

Feb. 15.   Patent for manufacture of **barbed wire.** This was of the utmost significance in the conquest of the Great Plains.

The Granger decisions. These decisions of the supreme court came as a climax to the first important farmers' movement in American history. In 1867 there had been formed the

Patrons of Husbandry, commonly called the *Grange,* a non-political organization of farmers. At this time the farmers in the Middle Western states were incensed because of the unfair practices of railways and grain elevators. Organizing farmers' parties, they proceeded (1870–1875) to enact legislation in Illinois, Iowa, Wisconsin, Minnesota, and other states, bringing railways and grain elevators under state control. The Granger decisions established the following principles: (1) A state under its police power has authority to regulate a business which is clothed with a public interest. (2) Until Congress acts in the premises, the states may establish rates for interstate shipments. (3) The determination of the reasonableness of rates is a legislative rather than a judicial function. The second of these principles was set aside in 1886 in the case of the *Wabash, St. Louis and Pacific Railroad* v. *Illinois,* while the third was undermined and set aside by a series of decisions between 1889 and 1898, the last being the case of *Smyth* v. *Ames.*

Nov. The disputed election. In the election, **Samuel J. Tilden,** the Democratic candidate, was assured of 184 electoral votes; **Rutherford B. Hayes,** Republican, had 165 electoral votes, with 20 votes in the states of Oregon, Florida, South Carolina, and Louisiana in dispute, with two sets of returns. For election 185 electoral votes were necessary. Since the constitution made no provision for such an eventuality, congress created on

1877, Jan. 29. The electoral commission, composed of five senators, five representatives, and five justices of the supreme court, the fifth justice to be chosen by the four named in the statute. The commission was composed of eight Republicans and seven Democrats, and, deciding all questions by a strict party vote, awarded the 20 electoral votes to Hayes, giving him the 185 necessary for election.

Mar. 3. The **Desert Land Act,** designed to encourage development of irrigation in arid areas by private effort.

1877, Mar. 4–1881, Mar. 4. RUTHERFORD B. HAYES, nineteenth president.

1878, Feb. The Bland-Allison Act. In 1873 congress had omitted the standard silver dollar from the list of authorized domestic coins to be minted in the future. This action synchronized with the demonetization of silver by various European countries, and with a marked increase in silver production, especially in the Comstock Lode in Nevada. As a result the commerical price of silver declined sharply, giving rise to a demand by the silver interests for the coinage of silver, which was precluded by the legislation of 1873, commonly referred to as the *Crime of 1873.* The silver producers were supported by the farmers, who believed the free coinage of silver would bring an upturn in the price of farm products. In 1877, therefore, **Richard P. Bland** of Missouri introduced into the house of representatives a bill providing for the free coinage of silver. Although it passed the house by a sectional vote, it was amended in the senate, and as the **Bland-Allison Act** it was passed over the veto of Hayes. It authorized the secretary of the treasury to purchase from two to four million dollars' worth of silver bullion monthly for coinage.

1879, Jan. 1. Resumption of specie payment. The success of the policy was greatly aided by the unusual demand abroad for American agricultural products, which brought gold into the country in large quantity.

1881, Mar. 4. JAMES A. GARFIELD, twentieth president. Shot July 2 and died September 19, 1881, being succeeded by **Chester A. Arthur,** vice-president.

May 21. The **American Red Cross Society** organized, with **Clara Barton** as president.

1882, May 6. The Chinese Exclusion Act. The increasing immigration of Chinese, especially in California, led to a race riot as early as 1871. The formation of a workingmen's party in that state in 1877 brought the matter into prominence and to the attention of congress. The act of 1882 barred Chinese laborers from entrance into the United States for a period of ten years. In 1902 the exclusion was made permanent and the same act prohibited the immigration of Chinese to the United States from Hawaii and the Philippines. In 1885 an act of congress prohibited the entrance of all laborers under contract.

1883, Jan. 16. The Pendleton Act. After more or less continual discussion since 1865, congress provided in this act for a bipartisan commission to set up and administer a system of **competitive examinations** as a test of fitness for appointment to federal office. It also prohibited the levying of **campaign contributions** upon federal office-holders. Although the plan applied immediately only to the executive departments in Washington, to the customhouses, and to the larger post-offices, the president was authorized, at his discretion, to extend the "classified list."

Tariff Act. Despite a redundant revenue and the recommendation of tariff reductions by a tariff commission, the protective principle, so securely established by the Civil War tariffs, remained intact. Although substantial reductions were made in internal revenue duties, the reductions in import duties averaged less than 5 per cent.

Sept. 8. The **Northern Pacific Railroad** completed (chartered and endowed with an enormous grant of land in 1864). This was the second transcontinental line. The **Southern Pacific** was the third, and by 1893 no less than five were completed. Other lines threaded their way across the prairies and plains to the mountains, letting in the tide of population which brought the frontier to an end.

1883-1890. The problem of the **treasury surplus.** Cleveland would deal with the surplus by reducing the tariff duties, which he urged in his message to congress in 1887 and which he made the leading issue in the campaign of 1888. Republicans attempted to remove the surplus by retirement of Civil War bonds, the building of a new navy, and reckless pension legislation.

1884. Presidential campaign between **James G. Blaine** (Republican) and **Grover Cleveland** (Democrat). The **Mugwumps,** the reforming wing of the party, deserted Blaine in favor of Cleveland. Cleveland was elected, 219 electoral votes to 182.

1885, Mar. 4-1889, Mar. 4. GROVER CLEVELAND, twenty-second president.

1886. The **Presidential Succession Law,** providing that in the event of the death of both president and vice-president, members of the cabinet should succeed to the presidency in definite order.

Dec. The **American Federation of Labor** organized. The Civil War years witnessed the formation of a number of national trade unions, which **William H. Sylvis** attempted to federate into a single nation-wide association known as the **National Labor Union** (1866). In 1869 **Uriah Stephens** formed the **Knights of Labor,** which represented an attempt to combine all labor, skilled and unskilled, organized and unorganized, into one body. Between 1879 and 1885 the organization grew rapidly. In 1885-1886 it became involved in a series of strikes on the Gould railway system, in the last of which the strikers were routed and discredited. In 1886 there occurred a widespread movement in favor of the eight-hour day. May 4, 1886, the **Haymarket Square riot** in Chicago still further discredited the Knights of Labor, who now gave way to the American Federation of Labor as the first permanent national labor movement in American history. The germ of the organization dated from 1881, when disgruntled members of the Knights of Labor, led by **Samuel Gompers,** formed the **Federation of Organized Trades and Labor Unions.**

1887, Feb. 4. INTERSTATE COMMERCE ACT. As early as 1874 the **McCrary Bill,** looking to federal regulation of the railways, passed the house of representatives, but failed in the senate. In 1878 the **Reagan Bill** passed the house, but was defeated in the senate. The growing realization of the shocking practices of the railways led to the appointment by the senate in 1885 of the **Cullom committee,** which conducted hearings in the principal cities of the country. This was followed by the passage of the **act of 1887.** It declared that charges of the railways must be reasonable and just, made pooling illegal, contained a long-and-short-haul clause, declared rebates illegal, and created an **Interstate Commerce Commission** with power to inquire into the management of the carriers, summon witnesses, compel the production of papers, and invoke the aid of the federal courts. Up to 1903 the commission was largely frustrated by the courts. In 1897, in the *Maximum Freight Rate Case,* the supreme court denied the commission's authority to prescribe a maximum rate. The long-and-short-haul clause was rendered ineffective and the commission was left with the duty of collecting railway statistics and requiring the publication of rates by the companies.

Feb. 8. The **Dawes Act,** authorizing the president, at his discretion, to terminate tribal government and communal ownership of land among the Indians and to divide the land at the rate of a quarter section for each head of a family, full ownership to be withheld for 25 years. In 1906 the **Burke Act** authorized the secretary of the interior to bestow full property title whenever convinced of the Indians' fitness.

1888. Presidential campaign. Cleveland (Democrat) against Benjamin Harrison (Republican). The tariff was the dominant issue. Although Cleveland had a popular plurality, he lost the election, receiving 168 electoral votes to 233 for Harrison. Treachery of Tammany in New York cost Cleveland the election.

1889, Mar. 4-1893, Mar. 4. BENJAMIN HARRISON, twenty-third president.

1889, Apr. 22. Oklahoma opened to settlement. The territory of Oklahoma was organized in 1890. The movement into the trans-Mississippi country led to the admission of the last states to the union: **Neveda** (1864); **Nebraska** (1867); **Colorado** (1876); **North Dakota, South Dakota, Washington,** and **Montana** (1889); **Wyoming** and **Idaho** (1890); **Utah** (1896); **Oklahoma** (1907); **New Mexico** and **Arizona** (1912).

June 14. Samoan treaty signed (p. 939).

Oct. 2. FIRST PAN-AMERICAN CONFERENCE convened at Washington. The idea of closer relations among the nations of the western hemisphere, with the United States playing the rôle of an elder sister, had long been in the mind of James G. Blaine, who as Garfield's secretary of state had planned such a congress in 1881. His successor, Frederick T. Frelinghuysen, cancelled the arrangements. As secretary of state in Harrison's cabinet, Blaine carried the idea to fruition. All Latin-American nations except Santo Domingo were represented. The conference rejected Blaine's plan of reciprocity and refused to adopt a convention calling for the promotion of peace by arbitration, but established the **Pan-American Union,** a bureau of information.

1890, June 19. The **Force Bill,** providing for federal control of federal elections, reported in the house of representatives. It aimed to protect Negro voters in southern states against attempts to disfranchise them. It passed the house, but was not adopted by the senate.

June 27. Disability Pension Act, in reality a service pension act, since it provided pensions for all veterans of 90 days' service who could claim physical or mental disability, regardless of origin, which precluded the gaining of a livelihood by manual labor. Pensions were to be granted to widows of soldiers without regard to the cause of the husband's death if the marriage had occurred prior to 1890.

July 2. The **SHERMAN ANTI-TRUST LAW** enacted. After the formation of the Standard Oil Trust in 1879 (revised in 1882), numerous large business combinations made their appearance, thereby raising the specter of monopoly, which led to the demand for legislation by congress. The **Sherman Act** declared illegal *"every contract, combination in the form of trust or otherwise, or conspiracy in restraint of trade or commerce among the several states or with foreign nations."* The act was loosely drawn and left several important questions unanswered: Did it apply to combinations of labor, did it apply to combinations of the railways, and was the word "every" to be construed literally? In the case of *Debs* (1895) the supreme court gave an affirmative answer to the first question, while in the *Trans-Missouri Freight Association Case* (1897) it answered the other two in an affirmative manner.

July 14. The Sherman Silver Purchase Act. The continued decline in the commercial price of silver, plus the strengthening of the silver forces in the senate by the appearance of senators from the newly admitted states of the northwest, led to a demand for further legislation with respect to silver. As the price of their support of new tariff legislation desired by the conservative wing of the Republican Party, the silver group obtained the desired legislation. The act authorized the treasury to purchase 4,500,000 ounces of silver monthly for coinage into dollars and to issue treasury certificates, to be redeemed in either gold or silver at the discretion of the treasury.

Oct. 1. The McKinley Tariff Act. The purpose of the law was such an increase in protective duties as would diminish the revenue from customs duties, thereby relieving the treasury of the surplus. By placing sugar on the free list and providing a bounty on domestic sugar, a substantial decline in revenue was certain. The law made provision for limited reciprocity treaties.

1892, Feb. 29. Treaty with Great Britain regarding the **Bering Sea seal fisheries.** Blaine, as secretary of state, had carried on a long controversy with Great Britain on this question, basing his arguments on faulty law, history, and ethics. The treaty submitted the controversy to an arbitral court, which in 1893 denied the right of the United States to prohibit fishing beyond the three-mile limit. In 1911 an international convention prohibited pelagic sealing for fifteen years.

1892–1895. Labor troubles. A strike of workers in the Homestead Plant of the Carnegie Steel Company was called by the Amalgamated Association of Iron and Steel Workers (June 30, 1892) as a result of disagreement over a wage scale. The use of Pinkerton detectives by the Carnegie Company led to violence, which was followed by the use of state troops to protect the Carnegie properties. Sympathy of the public, at first with the workers, was alienated later. In the end the Amalgamated Association was destroyed. May 11, 1894, a strike occurred in the plant of the Pullman Company, in which the American Railway Union, formed the previous year by **Eugene V. Debs,** participated, with resulting obstruction of the mails and destruction of property. Without consulting Gov. John Altgeld, Cleveland sent federal troops to Chicago, and on the advice of Richard Olney, the attorney-general, an injunction was issued ordering the officials of the union to desist from obstruction of the mails or from injuring the property of the railroads. Upon disregarding the injunction, Debs was arrested for contempt of court and sent to jail. The United States circuit court approved the use of the injunction, sentenced Debs to prison for six months, and approved the use of the Sherman Anti-Trust Act against labor unions where they were engaged in a "conspiracy to hinder and obstruct interstate commerce." The next year the supreme court sustained the judgment of the lower court. The use of the injunction gave capital a formidable weapon against labor.

1892, Feb. 22. The People's Party organized at St. Louis. For a decade there had been a gathering discontent of the farmers, resulting from the depressed condition of agriculture. Organizations of farmers, known as the *South-*

ern Alliance and the *Northwestern Alliance,* had appeared, and held meetings at St. Louis (Dec. 1889), Ocala, Fla. (Dec. 1890), and Cincinnati (May 1891). They now formed the **People's** or **Populist Party.** In July 1892, at their Omaha convention, they nominated **James B. Weaver,** a veteran inflationist, as their candidate for the presidency and drew up a platform declaring for a national currency without the use of banking corporations, free and unlimited coinage of silver, a graduated income tax, postal savings banks, and government ownership of railways and telephone and telegraph lines.

Harrison defeated for re-election by **Cleveland,** who denounced the McKinley Tariff and the Force Bill. Cleveland received 277 electoral votes; Harrison, 145; and Weaver, the Populist candidate, 22.

1893–1898.   Hawaii became of increasing concern to the United States. On January 17, 1893, a provisional government, established with the connivance of the American minister, supplanted the Hawaiian monarchy. On February 14 there was signed a treaty annexing Hawaii to the United States. When the senate failed to ratify before Cleveland came into office, he promptly withdrew the treaty and sent a commissioner to the islands to investigate. Failing in his efforts to bring about a restoration of the monarchy, Cleveland recognized the republic which had in the meantime been established. In June 1897 McKinley arranged a new treaty of annexation, which was defeated in the senate. On July 7, 1898, Hawaii was annexed by joint resolution of the two houses of congress.

1893, Mar. 4–1897, Mar. 4.   GROVER CLEVELAND president for the second time.

1893.   Panic of 1893. Depression had begun to spread over the western world in 1890 when the banking house of Baring collapsed as a result of unfortunate investments in the Argentine. British investors in American securities began to sell, which was largely responsible for the movement of gold from the country. Over-expansion in rails, due to the import of British capital, had created a boom which collapsed when the railways were unable to meet their charges. The situation was complicated by the dissipation of the treasury surplus through reckless pension legislation and the tariff of 1890, which sharply reduced revenue. To Cleveland there was just one cause of the panic: the world-wide fear of American inability to maintain a gold standard was draining off the supply of gold. For this fear he blamed the Sherman Silver Purchase Act. He therefore asked the special session of congress to repeal the act. After bitter debate, on

Oct. 30.   The Sherman Silver Purchase Act was repealed.

The **Anti-Saloon League** founded, a milestone in the development of the prohibition movement. It inaugurated a nation-wide campaign in 1895.

1894–1896.   Sale of government bonds in an effort to maintain the gold reserve. Finding that repeal of the Silver Purchase Act did not stop the outflow of gold, the treasury, to obtain gold, arranged for sale of bonds by banks in January and November 1894. In February 1895 the Morgan-Belmont syndicate sold $60,000,000 bonds at a profit of $7,000,000, causing much criticism. In January 1896 bonds were offered at public subscription.

1894, Aug. 18. The **Carey Act,** granting 1,000,000 acres of land to each of the states of Colorado, Idaho, Montana, Nevada, Oregon, Utah, Washington, and Wyoming to encourage irrigation by state action. In 1908 they each received another million acres.

Aug. 27. The **Wilson-Gorman Tariff Act,** a violation of the Democratic platform, became law without Cleveland's signature. As a result of senate amendments to the original bill, the act retained the protective principle, although duties were lowered to about 40 per cent. It contained a provision for a 2 per cent tax on incomes above $4000. On

1895, May 20. The income tax was declared unconstitutional in the case of *Pollock* v. *Farmers Loan and Trust Co.,* causing much criticism. An income tax was declared a direct tax which, in accordance with the constitution, must be apportioned among the states in proportion to population.

The Venezuela boundary dispute. Upon the refusal of Great Britain to submit to arbitration the disputed boundary between Venezuela and British Guiana, Secretary of State **Olney,** on July 20, 1895, sent a note to Britain, asserting that a forcible rectification of the boundary by Britain would violate the Monroe Doctrine, and declaring that the one way to settle the dispute was by arbitration. He then stated that *"today the United States is practically sovereign on this continent, and its fiat is law upon the subjects to which it confines its interposition."* **Lord Salisbury** replied (Nov. 26), rejecting arbitration and denying the applicability of the Monroe Doctrine to this dispute. On December 17 Cleveland asked congress to authorize a commission to ascertain the facts in the dispute, and asserted the duty of the United States to support the findings. The commission was authorized and appointed, January 4, 1896. On February 2, 1897, Britain and Venezuela signed a treaty, submitting the dispute to arbitration. The awards made in

1899 largely supported the British position.

1896. Election of William McKinley, running on a single gold standard platform, over **William Jennings Bryan,** Democratic candidate, supporting free silver. Because of the Democratic espousal of free silver, the Populists supported Bryan. Silver Republicans supported Bryan. McKinley elected, 271 electoral votes to 176 for Bryan.

1897, Mar. 4–1901, Sept. 14. WILLIAM McKINLEY, twenty-fifth president.

1897–1901. Return of prosperity, to which the increased gold production of the world and the unusual demand abroad for American agricultural products were important contributing factors. Great increase in the gold reserve. A period of great activity in the formation of large combinations in the field of business, despite the Sherman Anti-Trust Act. This movement culminated in the organization of the **United States Steel Corporation** (1901), the first billion-dollar corporation. Great concentration of control by banking interests in the business world.

1897, July 24. The **Dingley Tariff Act,** which, despite McKinley's purpose, was primarily designed to increase protection rather than revenue. It greatly increased the duties and provided for reciprocity treaties with a view to the extension of foreign trade.

1898. THE SPANISH-AMERICAN WAR. The insurrection in Cuba, which broke out in 1895 and toward which Cleveland had maintained an entirely correct attitude, was increasingly attended by inhuman treatment of the rebels, which aroused the sympathy of various elements in the United States and afforded an opportunity for the new "yellow press" of the United States to influence American sentiment against Spain. On February 15, 1898, the *U.S.S. Maine* was mysteriously blown up in Havana harbor, producing strong feeling against Spain in the United States. In the face of the belligerent attitude of the press and various groups in the country, McKinley finally yielded to the war clamor, despite the fact that Spain had agreed to every condition laid down by his ultimatum with respect to Cuba. On

Apr. 11. McKinley sent his war message to congress asking authority for forcible intervention. On

Apr. 20. Congress adopted a resolution authorizing intervention, but disclaiming any intention of annexing Cuba.

Apr. 24, 25. War formally declared. The war consisted of five operations: (1) Defeat of the Spanish fleet at Manila by Commodore **George Dewey** (May 1); (2) the blockade of Cuba; (3) the search for the main Spanish fleet; (4) the land and sea battles (**battles of El Caney**

and **San Juan Hill,** July; and the **naval battle of Santiago,** July 3); and (5) the invasion of Puerto Rico (July 25). On August 12 the **peace protocol** was signed and on August 13 Manila was captured.

Dec. 10. TREATY OF PEACE SIGNED AT PARIS. Spain withdrew from **Cuba** and ceded to the United States **Puerto Rico, Guam,** and the **Philippines** (for the loss of the latter she was paid $20,000,000). The larger effect of the war was to establish the United States as a world power and to extend the sphere of her political interests and contacts.

1899–1902. Philippine insurrection. Although the Filipinos under **Emilio Aguinaldo** had aided the Americans against the Spaniards, and had conquered the island of Luzon, they were deeply disappointed when the conditions of the peace treaty were made known. Hostilities broke out in February 1899. For the next three years an American army of 60,000 was engaged in the islands. Guerrilla warfare, with all its attendant horrors, developed. Although Aguinaldo was captured (Mar. 1901) it was not until April 1902 that the insurrection was finally brought to an end.

1899, Sept. 6. John Hay, secretary of state, sent his **Open Door** note to London, Paris, Berlin, and St. Petersburg (p. 791).

1900, Mar. 14. Currency Act, declaring other forms of money redeemable in gold on demand, and providing for a gold reserve of $150,000,000. This extended the issue of national bank notes from 90 per cent to full face value of the bonds upon which they were issued and reduced capital requirements of banks in small communities.

Boxer uprising in China (p. 914). In June the United States participated in the relief expedition against Peking. Hay made this the occasion for reaffirming the Open Door policy.

Nov. 6. Bryan, running on a platform of free silver and anti-imperialism, defeated by **McKinley,** who received 292 electoral votes, to 155 for Bryan.

1901, Mar. 2. The **Platt amendment** respecting Cuba, added to the Army Appropriation Bill for 1901–1902. The Cuban constitutional convention incorporated the amendment in the Cuban constitution (June 12) as a condition of American withdrawal from the island. Cuba agreed not to impair her independence by treaty with foreign powers; not to assume public debt beyond the ability of her ordinary revenues to liquidate; to permit American intervention for the protection of Cuban independence; to sell or lease to the United States land necessary for naval or coaling stations.

The Insular Cases decided. The supreme court held that territory might be subject to the jurisdiction of the United States without being incorporated into the country. The constitution was not applicable, in every particular, to all lands over which the country exercised sovereignty. This enabled the United States to develop a distinctive colonial policy and to enact legislation for the government of backward peoples, where a degree of paternalism was necessary.

Sept. 14. **McKinley died** from an assassin's bullet.

1901, Sept. 14–1909, Mar. 4. **THEODORE ROOSEVELT,** twenty-sixth president.

1901–1903. **Isthmian Canal diplomacy** (p. 856).

1902, May 12–Oct. 13. **Strike of anthracite coal miners,** demanding union recognition, a nine-hour day, and wage increase. In the face of a threatened coal famine, Roosevelt intervened and threatened to work the mines with federal troops, whereupon the owners accepted his suggestion of a commission to investigate. The miners returned to work, but when the commission made its award, union recognition was withheld. Not until 1916 did the miners receive union recognition, with an eight-hour day.

June 17. The **Newlands Act** providing for the irrigation of the arid lands of the west.

Maryland enacted the first **state workmen's compensation law.** By 1920 all but five states had enacted such laws.

Oregon adopted the thoroughgoing use of the **initiative and referendum.**

1902–1908. **Roosevelt and foreign affairs.** In 1902, because of the refusal of Venezuela to meet her debt obligations, Great Britain, Germany, and Italy blockaded five of her ports. On December 19, upon the urging of the state department and the expressed willingness of **Cipriano Castro,** the Venezuelan dictator, to submit the European claims to a mediator, the European powers agreed to arbitrate. In February 1903 the blockade was lifted and a mixed commission was set up by the Hague Tribunal to pass upon the claims.

On December 2, 1904, Roosevelt enunciated the **Roosevelt corollary of the Monroe Doctrine.** This was occasioned by the debt situation of the Dominican Republic and the pressure of European countries to compel payment. He said that chronic wrong-doing by powers in the western hemisphere might compel the United States under the Monroe Doctrine to exercise an international police power as the only means of forestalling European intervention. Under this doctrine the **United States intervened in Santo Domingo** and unofficially collected the customs. On July 31, 1907, the American administration left Santo Domingo.

In the summer of 1905 Roosevelt offered his services as **mediator between Russia and Japan**

and August 9 the peace conference at **Portsmouth** (N.H.), opened (p. 796).

In Europe, Roosevelt was instrumental in bringing about the **Algeciras conference,** January 16, 1906 (p. 796).

In October 1906 the **segregation of Japanese schoolchildren** in San Francisco schools led to strained relations with Japan, which were adjusted by the intervention of Roosevelt. This school controversy, however, proved to be merely one aspect of the general opposition on the Pacific coast to Japanese immigration. Japan declared it was not her practice to issue passports to laborers to come to the United States, though passports were issued for Hawaii, Canada, and Mexico, the holders of which in most cases came to the United States. Japan expressed her intention of continuing this policy, and, relying on this **gentlemen's agreement,** congress inserted in the Immigration Act of 1907 a clause authorizing the president to exclude from the continental territory of the United States holders of passports issued by any foreign government to its citizens to go to any country other than the United States. By the **Root-Takahira agreement** of November 1908 Japan confirmed *"the principle of equal opportunity for commerce and industry in China"* and agreed to support the *"independence and integrity"* of that empire.

1903, Jan. 24. **Alaskan boundary question** referred to a commission of three Americans, two Canadians, and one Briton. When **Lord Alverstone,** the British member, voted against the Canadians, the dispute was decided in favor of the American contention.

Beginning of effective **state legislation limiting hours of labor of children** and establishing state departments of labor or industrial boards. By 1930, 37 states had established the 48-hour week for children in factories.

Wisconsin enacted the first **direct primary** law.

1903–1913. **Railroad legislation.** In 1903 the **Elkins Act** was passed to strengthen the Interstate Commerce Act of 1887, which had proved so ineffective. The Elkins Act forbade railroads to deviate from published schedules of rates and made railway officers as well as the companies liable in cases of rebating. The **Hepburn Act** of 1906 extended the control of the commission to express companies, sleeping-car companies, pipeline, ferry, and terminal facilities. The commission was given power to reduce a rate found to be unreasonable. Passes were abolished and a commodity clause included. The **Mann-Elkins Act** (1910) extended the commission's jurisdiction to telephone and telegraph lines, cable and wireless companies. The long-and-short-haul clause was made effective. On March 1, 1913, Taft signed the **Physical Valuation Act,** requiring the commission to evaluate the properties of the railways as the basis for the fixing of rates which would enable the companies to earn a fair return on their investments.

1904, Mar. 14. The **Northern Securities Case** decided. The efforts of Edward H. Harriman to gain control, first of the Burlington system and then of the Northern Pacific, had led to the struggle between Harriman and James J. Hill, in which Northern Pacific stock was bid up to fabulous prices, producing the so-called *Northern Pacific Panic* (1901). This was followed by an agreement between the rival groups for the merging of the Northern Pacific, Great Northern, and Burlington systems through the Northern Securities Company. This the supreme court declared to be a violation of the Anti-Trust Act and its dissolution was ordered.

Nov. 8. Roosevelt elected president over **Alton B. Parker,** the Democratic candidate, 335 electoral votes to 133.

1906, June 30. The **Pure Food and Drug Act,** prohibiting the misbranding and adulteration of foods.

1908. Oregon adopted the principle of the **recall** of all elective officials.

The supreme court, in the case of *Muller* v. *Oregon,* upheld the Oregon ten-hour law for women in industry. By 1930 all but five states had laws limiting hours of work of women.

Nov. 3. William H. Taft (Republican) elected president over **William Jennings Bryan,** by 321 electoral votes to 162.

1909, Mar. 4–1913, Mar. 4. WILLIAM HOWARD TAFT, twenty-seventh president.

1909–1912. Foreign relations of the United States. In 1909 Taft and **Philander C. Knox,** his secretary of state, interceded with China to secure the participation of New York bankers with British, French, and German capitalists in the loan for the construction of the Hukuang Railways in China. This gave rise to the charge of **dollar diplomacy.** In May 1910 the American bankers were admitted into the consortium. When in 1912 American bankers were invited to participate in the currency loan to China, Taft gave his approval, but when Wilson in 1913 refused the formal encouragement of the American government, the bankers withdrew.

On September 7, 1910, the **Newfoundland fisheries question** was settled by the international court of arbitration at The Hague. American privileges were affirmed and extended.

The unsettled condition of affairs in **Nicaragua** and **Honduras** in 1911 caused Knox to attempt to emulate the example of Roosevelt in Santo Domingo. He negotiated conventions with the two countries providing for loans from American bankers, with an American receiver of customs and with the customs pledged as security for the loans. When the senate withheld ratification, **American marines** were landed in **Nicaragua** (Aug. 1912), fiscal affairs were turned over to an American collector, the Nicaraguan Bank was controlled by New York bankers, and the Nicaraguan government placed on a monthly allowance. Knox negotiated a **treaty with Nicaragua** giving the United States the right of way for an interoceanic canal, a naval base on the Gulf of Fonseca, and long-term leases over the Great and Little Corn Islands. The senate refused to ratify, but in 1916 the Wilson administration secured the ratification of a similar treaty. During 1912 troops were concentrated on the Mexican border and the revolutionary Madero government of Mexico was warned that it would be held accountable for loss of life and property.

In 1911 the proposed **reciprocity agreement with Canada** came to naught as a result of the Dominion election.

1909, Aug. 5. Payne-Aldrich Tariff, which disregarded party pledges and maintained protection unimpaired. Strongly opposed by the insurgent Republicans from the west. The first step in the downfall of Taft's administration.

The announcement by **Henry Ford** that thereafter his company would manufacture only the **Model T** chassis heralded the advent of the automobile as a universal method of individual transportation by bringing it within the reach of the average man.

1910, Jan. Taft removed **Gifford Pinchot** from the forestry service as a result of the **Ballinger-Pinchot controversy.**

Mar. 19. Insurgent Republicans in the house moved to shear the speaker of his power by supporting a resolution providing for the election of the rules committee and the exclusion of the speaker from its membership. In 1911 the speaker was deprived of the right of appointing other standing committees of the house.

Aug. 31. Theodore Roosevelt's speech at **Ossawatomie,** Kansas, in which he enunciated his doctrine of the **New Nationalism.** This augured ill for Taft.

1911, Jan. 21. National Progressive Republican League organized. Another step in the break in the Republican Party. Robert La Follette the leader of the league.

May 1. The supreme court, under the Sherman Anti-Trust Act, ordered the **dissolution of the Standard Oil Company** and the **American Tobacco Company.** In the Standard Oil case the court enunciated the *rule-of-reason doctrine,* indicating its belief that the government should not attempt to outlaw "every" combination in restraint of trade, but should confine action to those contracts which resulted in an "unreasonable" restraint of trade. The enunciation of this doctrine marked a turning-point in the court's attitude toward the so-called "trusts."

Illinois adopted the first state-wide law for **assistance to mothers with dependent children.** In 1912 Colorado took action, while in 1913 eighteen other states enacted similar laws.

1912. Massachusetts set up a commission to establish **minimum-wage schedules** for women and children. By 1923 fourteen other states and the District of Columbia had taken similar action, setting up either a statutory minimum or giving commissions mandatory powers. All such laws were dealt a severe blow by the supreme court decision of 1923, in the **Adkins case,** in which the court declared unconstitutional the District of Columbia law because it deprived the individual of liberty of contract.

Feb. 24. Theodore Roosevelt announced he would accept the Republican nomination for president. He carried the preferential primaries over Taft in six states, and was successful in four state conventions. In spite of this the Republican machine brought about **June 22. Taft's renomination.** Roosevelt delegates withdrew and August 7 nominated **Roosevelt as the candidate of the Progressive Party.**

July 2. Woodrow Wilson nominated by the Democratic convention on the forty-sixth ballot.

Nov. 5. Wilson elected with 435 electoral votes, with 88 for Roosevelt and 8 for Taft.

1913, Feb. 25. Sixteenth amendment to the constitution, empowering congress to levy income taxes without apportionment among the states and without regard to any census or enumeration, declared in effect.

Mar. 4. Department of Labor created with a seat in the cabinet.

1913, Mar. 4–1921, Mar. 4. WOODROW WILSON, twenty-eighth president.

1913, May 31. The **seventeenth amendment** to the constitution, providing for direct election of senators by the people, declared in effect.

Oct. 3. The **Underwood Tariff Act** reduced the average rate of duty to 26.67 per cent. Based on *ad valorem* rather than specific duties. Reductions covered largely those commodities on which protection had served its purpose or where American goods controlled the markets. Graduated surtax on incomes above $20,000.

Dec. 23. THE FEDERAL RESERVE BANK ACT. The panic of 1907 had emphásized the weakness of the national banking system. The **Aldrich-Vreeland Act** was passed in 1908 as an emergency measure, and provided for the appointment of a national monetary commission to study the problem. Report of the commission submitted (1912). Wilson asked for legislation which would provide an elastic currency, based on commercial assets rather than bonded indebtedness, mobilization of bank reserves, public control of the banking system, and decentralization rather than centralization. These features were embodied in the **act of 1913.** The country was divided into twelve districts, each with a federal reserve bank.

1914, Apr. 21–1921. Relations with Mexico. Wilson's refusal to recognize the Huerta régime in Mexico led to the seizure of the port of **Vera Cruz** by American marines (Apr. 21, 1914). Wilson then accepted the mediation of the **A.B.C. powers,** and at the **Niagara conference** a protocol was signed (June 24), which availed little because Huerta fled the country. In October 1915 an inter-American conference decided to recognize **Carranza,** which prompted Villa to raid Columbus, New Mexico (Mar. 1916). Punitive **expedition against Villa** under command of Gen. **John J. Pershing,** 1916 (see p. 860).

Article 27 of the **Mexican constitution of 1917** led to the demand by American business interests for intervention which Wilson successfully resisted.

Aug. 15. Panama Canal formally opened.

Sept. 26. Federal Trade Commission Act, abolishing the Bureau of Corporations (1903) and establishing a bipartisan commission of five members, with investigative and regulatory powers in regard to business and corporate practices.

Oct. 15. Clayton Anti-Trust Act, an amendment of the Sherman Act (1890), prohibiting price discrimination, exclusive selling or leasing contracts, intercorporate stockholdings, and interlocking directorates in large corporations. It sought to restrict the use of the injunction in labor difficulties, and exempted labor, agricultural, and horticultural organizations from the operation of the anti-trust laws.

Arizona adopted an **old-age pension system** which was declared unconstitutional by the state supreme court. In the 1920's, however, under the intelligent propaganda of the **American Association for Old-Age Security,** many states took up the principle of public responsibility for the aged, and began enactment of old-age pension laws.

1915, Feb. 15–1916, Dec. 18. American neutrality. On February 15 the American government protested against the German war-zone proclamation. On May 7 the sinking of the *Lusitania,* with loss of American life, led to Wilson's warning to Germany of May 13. He dispatched a second note June 9 and a third July 21. In February 1916 the McLemore resolution to warn Americans to refrain from traveling on armed merchant ships defeated. In April 1916 Wilson delivered an ultimatum to Germany as a result of the sinking of the *Sussex* March 24. German concession May 4, with respect to submarine warfare. On December 18, 1916, Wilson called upon the belligerent powers to state their war aims. (See p. 969.)

1915–1917. Wilson's policies in the Caribbean (pp. 861, 862).

On January 17, 1917, the purchase of the **Virgin Islands** from Denmark was ratified.

1916, July 17. Federal Farm Loan Bank Act passed to improve the agricultural credit situation; established a federal land bank to conduct the lending business, provided for farm loan associations of borrowing farmers, and a federal farm loan board for administrative purposes.

Aug. 29. The **Jones Act,** granting to the Philippines what was practically a territorial status. Declared purpose of the United States to grant independence "as soon as a stable government can be established therein."

Sept. 3. The **Adamson Act** establishing the eight-hour day on interstate railways.

Sept. 7. The **United States Shipping Board** formed to acquire merchant vessels for sale or charter to United States citizens. A corporation formed with capital up to $50,000,000 to purchase, lease, or operate the vessels.

1917, Jan. 18. Wilson before the senate made a plea for termination of the war and outlined the principles necessary thereto.

Jan. 31. Unrestricted submarine warfare renewed by Germany, in violation of the agreement of May 4, 1916.

Feb. 3. Diplomatic relations with Germany severed.

Mar. 1. State department released the **Zimmerman note** showing German efforts to enlist Mexico in support of Germany.

Mar. 12. Presidential order authorizing the **arming of merchantmen.**

Mar. 16 and 17. Three American ships, homeward bound, attacked without warning and sunk by German submarines.

Mar. 21. Wilson called congress to meet in special session, April 2.

Apr. 2. Wilson asked congress to recognize the existence of a state of war between the United States and Germany.

Apr. 6. WAR DECLARED ON GERMANY. (*Cont. p. 970 f., 1046.*)

CULTURAL DEVELOPMENTS

Literature: Novelists and writers of short stories came more and more to show strong local color in their stories: **Francis Bret Harte** (1836–1902); **Joel Chandler Harris** (1848–1908); Samuel Langhorne Clemens **[Mark Twain]** (1835–1910; *Tom Sawyer,* 1876; *Huckleberry Finn,* 1884; *Life on the Mississippi,* 1883). A greater realism characterized the novels of **William Dean Howells** (1837–1920) and **Henry James** (1843–1916). American poets of the second half of the 19th century: **James Russell Lowell** (1819–1891), **Walt Whitman** (1819–1892), **James Whitcomb Riley** (1849–1916), **Sidney Lanier** (1842–1881), **Emily Dickinson** (1830–1886).

Art: Painters of sea- and landscapes: **Winslow Homer** (1836–1910), **Childe Hassam** (1859–1935). American-born was **James McNeill Whistler** (1834–1903), renowned for his portraits, as were **Thomas Eakins** (1844–1916), and **John Singer Sargent** (1856–1925). **Mary Cassatt** (1845–1926) painted figures, especially mothers and children. **Frederic Remington** (1861–1909) was a regional painter and depicted in great detail and with animation the life and struggles of the West.

The finest monuments of the period were carved by **Augustus St. Gaudens** (1848–1907) and **Daniel Chester French** (1850–1931).

Music: One of the first American symphonic composers was **John Knowles Paine** (1839–1906). **Edward MacDowell** (1861–1908) is remembered chiefly for his piano music. **Victor Herbert** (b. Ireland 1859, d. New York 1924) composed numerous operettas (*Babes in Toyland,* 1903; *Naughty Marietta,* 1910).

2. BRITISH NORTH AMERICA

a. THE DOMINION OF CANADA, 1783–1914

1783–1787. Settlement of the loyalists from the United States. Thousands of these established themselves in New Brunswick (separated from Nova Scotia, August 16, 1784) and in Upper Canada. The British government assigned lands to them (100 acres to each head of a family and 50 acres to each member) and spent some $30,000,000 in equipping them. Effect of the immigration to give Canada a more English composition, and to arouse sentiment of the English settlers against the Quebec act.

1791, June 10. PASSAGE OF THE CANADA ACT through the British parliament. It went into effect December 26. Canada divided at the Ottawa River into Upper Canada (chiefly English) and Lower Canada (predominantly French). Each part had a governor, a legislative council appointed by him, and an elected assembly. Colonial laws could be disallowed by the home government within two years of passage. One-seventh of all land granted to be reserved for the maintenance of the Protestant clergy. All rights of the Catholic Church reaffirmed.

1783— EXPLORATION OF THE WEST. In 1783 the **Northwest Company** was organized in competition with the **Hudson's Bay Company.** In 1788 **Captain John Meares** sailed along the Pacific coast and established a fur post at Nootka. In 1789 a Spanish expedition from Mexico took possession of the northwest coast on the basis of discovery in 1775. Several British ships were seized, but in 1790 Spain made reparation for them and abandoned claims to the region **(treaty of October 28).** In 1792 **Captain George Vancouver** explored the Pacific coast and circumnavigated Vancouver Island. In 1793 **Alexander Mackenzie** reached the coast after the first overland journey from the east. Meanwhile (1785–1795) **David Thompson** had traversed much of the territory along the coast of Hudson Bay north to Fort Churchill, as well as the regions about Lake Winnipeg and along the Saskatchewan and Athabasca Rivers. **Jay's treaty** between the United States and Great Britain (Nov. 19, 1794) provided for a boundary commission to determine the frontier west of the Lake of the Woods. In 1797 Thompson, in the service of the Northwest Company, pushed west along the 49th parallel and to the upper Missouri; in 1798 he explored the region about the headwaters of the Mississippi. During the following years he continued his travels in what are now

Manitoba, Saskatchewan, and Alberta, and in 1807 founded **Fort Kootenay,** the first post on the Columbia River. At the same time (1805–1807) **Simon Fraser** and **James Stuart** explored the Fraser River region to the ocean. Thompson continued his work on the Columbia. By 1810 much of the southern half of present-day Canada had been gone over by various explorers and traders. In 1811 **Lord Selkirk** bought from the Hudson's Bay Company 116,000 square miles for settlement in Manitoba, Minnesota, and North Dakota. Scottish settlers arrived there on the Red River in 1812. In 1815 an attack was launched on the colony by agents of the rival Northwest Company; colonists were driven out in 1815 and 1816. An investigation in 1817 upheld the claims of Lord Selkirk and the colony was re-established.

1812, June 18. UNITED STATES DECLARED WAR ON GREAT BRITAIN. Among the causes of conflict were the continued trouble with the Indians, supposedly instigated and equipped by the British in Canada, and the American desire to conquer Canada. A triple attack was planned: on Montreal; on the region opposite Niagara; and on the region opposite Detroit. On the Montreal front and at Niagara the offensive failed to materialize. At Detroit a short advance was made, followed by retreat. The British, under General Isaac Brock, secured the **surrender of Detroit** (Aug. 16, 1812). Brock then turned to Niagara and fought the successful engagement of **Queenston Heights** (Oct. 13), in which he was killed.

1813. The Americans captured **York** (Toronto) April 27, but abandoned it soon afterward (May 2). In Ohio the Americans were vigorously attacked by the British, supported by the Indians (**Tecumseh**). On September 10 **Lieutenant Oliver Hazard Perry** with an improvised fleet won the naval **battle of Lake Erie** and forced the British to abandon Detroit. The Americans, under **General William Henry Harrison,** crossed into Ontario and fought the successful engagement on the **Thames River** (Oct. 5), but were unable to follow up the advantage. The campaign against Montreal was begun October 17, but the Americans were defeated by a greatly inferior force (**battle of Crysler's Farm,** November 11) and the advance abandoned. On December 10 an American force burned **Newark,** in retaliation for which the British and Canadians, after taking **Fort Niagara** (Dec. 18), burned **Buffalo** (Dec. 29–31).

1814, July 5. The Americans, advancing from Niagara, took **Fort Erie** and won the engagement at **Chippewa Plains.** They advanced to

Queenston, but then fell back again.

July 25. Battle of Lundy's Lane, which was indecisive, but the Americans blew up Fort Erie and recrossed the river (Nov. 5).

Meanwhile 16,000 British troops had been sent to Canada and an invasion was begun by way of Lake Champlain.

Sept. 11. An American naval force under **Lieutenant** (later Captain) **Thomas Macdonough** won the **battle of Plattsburg** and forced the retirement of the British.

Sept. 21. The British, having invaded Maine, declared all territory east of the Penobscot annexed to New Brunswick.

Dec. 24. The **treaty of Ghent** brought the war to a close. All captured territory was returned and a commission to delimit the northeastern frontier provided for.

1817, Apr. 28. Exchange of notes between the United States and Great Britain, by which they agreed to **restrict naval forces on the Lakes** to one each on Lake Champlain and Lake Ontario and two on the upper lakes.

1818, Oct. 20. Treaty between the United States and Great Britain giving Americans the right to fish on the coasts of Newfoundland and Labrador and dry fish in unsettled bays. Boundary between the United States and Canada west of the Lake of the Woods fixed on the 49th parallel to the Rocky Mountains. Territory west of the Rockies to be jointly occupied for ten years.

1821, Mar. 26. The **Northwest Company** merged with the Hudson's Bay Company under the latter's name. Rights of exclusive trade to the company in the territory allotted to it renewed for 21 years.

1836, July 21. First Canadian railroad opened, from Laprairie on the St. Lawrence to St. Johns on the Richelieu.

1837. REBELLION IN UPPER AND LOWER CANADA. This had been brewing ever since 1815 and was the result of constitutional conflict between the governors and the appointed legislative councils, representing bureaucratic and vested interests (*family compact* in Upper Canada, *château clique* in Lower Canada) on the one hand and the popularly elected assemblies on the other. Popular leaders in Upper Canada, **Robert Gourlay** (expelled 1818), **William Lyon Mackenzie, Egerton Ryerson;** in Lower Canada, **Louis Joseph Papineau.** Grievances: control of judiciary, control of revenue, supply bills, clergy reserves, established churches, executive council. The situation was worst in Lower Canada, where the British minority, represented by the governor and the council, was opposed by the French majority in the assembly. In 1822 it had been proposed to reunite Upper and Lower Canada,

but the project roused a storm of protest in Lower Canada. A British parliamentary investigation was made in 1828 and led to various administrative reform proposals, but nothing came of them. In 1834 the assembly of Lower Canada adopted the 92 resolutions, a declaration of rights. By 1837 affairs had reached a deadlock and the popular leaders decided to resort to force.

In Lower Canada the rebellion was confined to an area around Montreal. There were a number of riots and some fighting at **St. Denis** and **St. Charles.** Most of the population remained passive, the rebels were easily defeated, and the leaders fled to the United States. In Upper Canada the rebels, under Mackenzie, attacked **Toronto** (Dec. 5), but were driven off. Mackenzie fled across the border and on December 13 seized **Navy Island** in the Niagara River, where he proclaimed a provisional government.

Dec. 29. A Canadian government force crossed the river and burned the American steamer *Caroline,* which had been supplying the rebels; a famous case in international law.

1838, Jan. 13. Mackenzie abandoned Navy Island and was arrested in the United States.

During the year 1838 the rebels, supported by American sympathizers (*Hunters' Lodges*), staged several invasions from the United States, but none of these assumed large proportions.

May 29. Lord Durham arrived at Quebec as governor-in-chief of all the British North American provinces. His lenient treatment of the rebels led to disavowal by the home government. On October 9 he resigned.

1839, Feb. 11. Durham's famous *Report on the Affairs of British North America.* He proposed the union of Upper and Lower Canada and the grant of responsible government. The imperial government was to retain control only of foreign relations, regulation of trade, disposal of public lands, and determination of the colonial constitution.

June 20. Lord John Russell introduced in the British parliament a resolution based on the *Durham Report.*

Oct. 19. Poulett Thomson (Lord Sydenham) arrived at Quebec as governor-in-chief, to prepare the provinces for union.

1840, July 23. THE BRITISH PARLIAMENT PASSED THE UNION ACT. This united Upper and Lower Canada into one government, with one governor, one appointed legislative council, and one popularly elected assembly, in which the former two provinces had equal representation. Various administrative reforms were carried through. The issue of responsible government was evaded, and the principle was not firmly established in practice

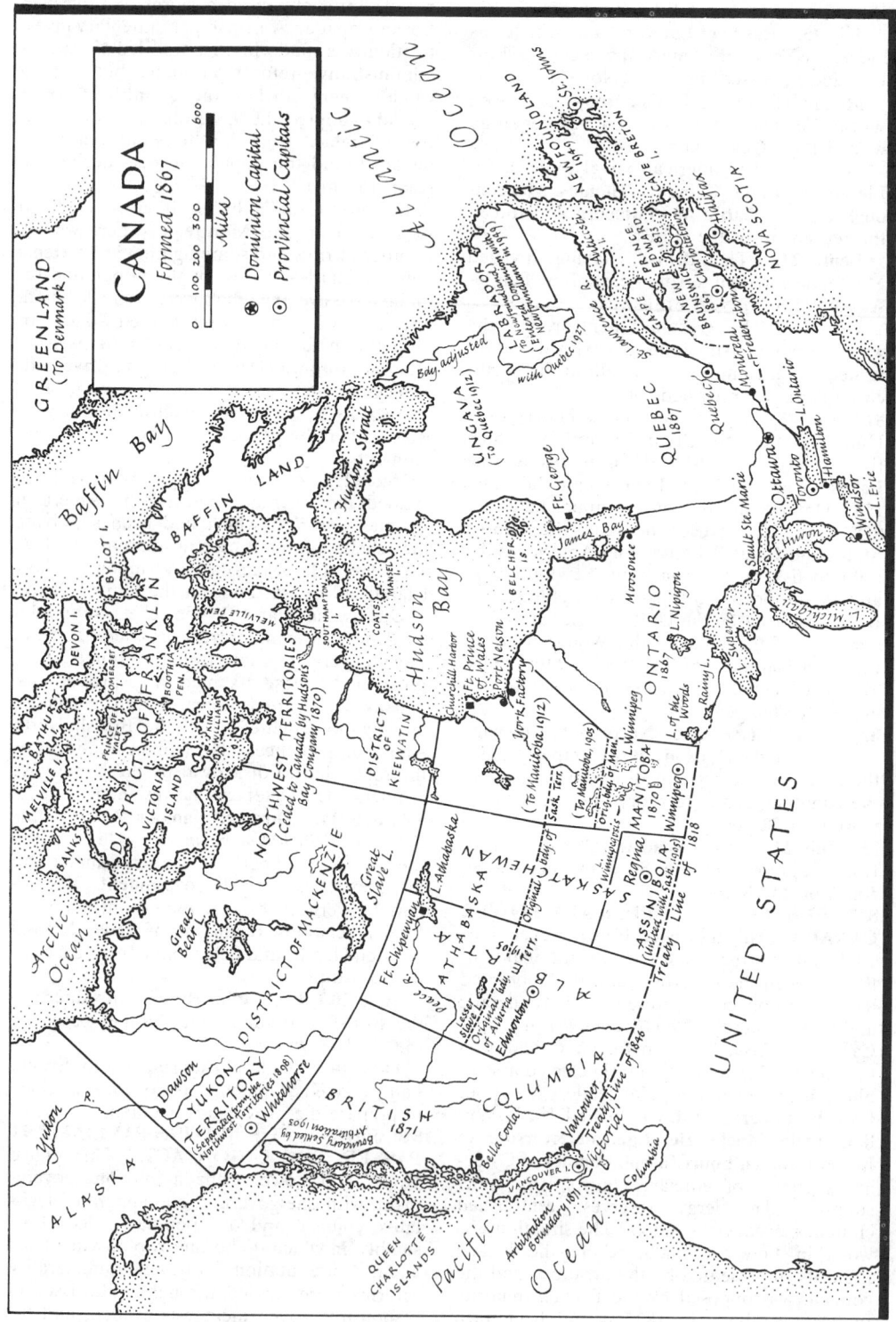

CANADA
Formed 1867

Miles

0 100 200 300   600

⊛ Dominion Capital
⊙ Provincial Capitals

until the time of **Lord Elgin's governorship** (1847-1854), in the course of the crisis arising from the **Rebellion Losses Bill** (1849).

1842, Aug. 9. **Ashburton treaty** between the United States and Great Britain. Great Britain abandoned more than half of the territory claimed on the northeast frontier.

1846, June 15. **Oregon boundary treaty** between the United States and Great Britain, following a period of acute tension.

Aug. 28. **British Possessions Act** gave Canada the right to fix tariffs.

1849, June 26. Abolition of the British **Navigation Acts,** removing restrictions on foreign shipping. This, following on the abolition of the Corn Laws in 1846, led to an acute economic depression in Canada and to a short-lived agitation for annexation to the United States (*Annexation Manifesto,* October 10, 1849).

1854, June 5. **Elgin treaty,** establishing reciprocity between Canada and the United States. This was abrogated by the United States in 1866.

Sept.-Dec. Law converting **clergy reserves** into a special fund to be distributed to counties and cities for secular purposes. Another law abolished **seignorial tenure,** feudal dues being converted into cash rents.

1856, June 24. The legislative council, hitherto appointive, was made elective.

1858, Aug. 2. **British Columbia,** having been withdrawn from the jurisdiction of the Hudson's Bay Company, was given separate administration.

1866. Beginning of the **Fenian** (Irish-American) **raids,** designed to bring pressure on the British government in favor of Ireland. Fenians from Buffalo seized **Fort Erie** (June 1), but were driven out. Other raids took place from Vermont and Fenian troubles continued to some extent until 1871.

1867, Mar. 29. **BRITISH NORTH AMERICA ACT** united Ontario, Quebec, New Brunswick, and Nova Scotia in the **Dominion of Canada** (effective July 1). The movement for confederation was the result of growing difficulty in the government of United Canada (religious and racial differences, problems of representation), as well as of economic (especially railway) considerations and military (defense) problems in the Civil War period. The movement began in the Maritime Provinces (**Charlottetown conference,** September 1864), but expanded almost at once (**Quebec convention,** October 10-28, 1864, in which all provinces were represented). The 72 **Quebec resolutions** became the basis for the act of confederation. They provided for a federal government and provincial governments, a federal parliament

of two houses (senate consisting of 24 members each from Ontario, Quebec, and a third division comprising Nova Scotia and New Brunswick; and an elected lower house). Representatives of the provinces conferred with imperial authorities in London (Dec. 1866) and drew up the **London resolutions,** which were transformed into the final act.

1867-1868. **Lord Monck,** first governor-general. (Sir) **John A. Macdonald** first premier of the Dominion.

1868, Dec. 29. **Sir John Young** (Lord Lisgar) appointed governor-general (1868-1872).

1869, Nov. 19. **PURCHASE OF NORTH-WEST TERRITORIES** from the old Hudson's Bay Company for $1,500,000, the company retaining one-twentieth of the land. Taken over, 1870.

1869-1870. **RED RIVER REBELLION.** Half-breeds, led by **Louis Riel** about Fort Garry (Winnipeg), irritated chiefly by the belief that surveys being made were to rob them of their land, set up a provisional government (Nov. 1869) with Riel president; expedition from Portage Laprairie defeated and captured (Feb. 1870); **Thomas Scott** (Orangeman) executed (Mar.) and great indignation aroused in Ontario. The rebels dispersed without a blow before the advance of an expedition under **Col. Garnet** (later Lord) **Wolseley.**

1870, July 15. **Manitoba** constituted a province of the Dominion.

1871, July 1. **British Columbia** joined the Dominion; a transcontinental railroad to be commenced within two and completed within ten years.

1871. **Sir John Macdonald** a member of the British commission to Washington to settle outstanding difficulties with the United States.

1872, May 22. **Marquess of Dufferin** appointed governor-general (1872-1878).

1872. General elections; government victory.

1873, June 1. Death of **Joseph Howe;** Howe had opposed Nova Scotia's entrance into the union, but later accepted it rather than agree to radical proposals for annexation to the United States.

July 1. **Prince Edward Island** joined the Dominion; the Dominion to assume railway debt.

Nov. 7. Resignation of Macdonald owing to pressure of public opinion following **transcontinental railway scandal** and charges of corruption in last elections. Alexander Mackenzie formed a Liberal cabinet; overwhelming victory at general elections.

1874. Introduction of **ballot voting;** elections on a single day.

1876. Opening of the **Intercolonial Railway** connecting Ontario with the Maritime Provinces; government-owned and operated.

1878, Oct. 5.   Marquess of Lorne, governor-general (1878–1883).

Oct.   General elections on **tariff issue.** Conservatives victorious in support of protection; Macdonald premier (Oct. 17), and protective tariff instituted.

1881.   Charter given to newly formed **CANADIAN PACIFIC RAILWAY COMPANY** for construction of a transcontinental railroad, following financial difficulties of old companies. Government grant of $25,000,000 with 25,000,000 acres of land and 670 miles of track already laid; loan of $20,000,000 in 1884 (repaid 1887). Last spike driven, November 7, 1885, and formally opened May 1887, with 2905 miles of rail joining coast to coast. Marked results in Canadian development; steamship lines established; flow of immigrants to the west accelerated.

1883, Aug. 18.   Marquess of Lansdowne, governor-general (1883–1888).

1885, Mar. 26.   Outbreak of the **Northwest Rebellion;** quickly suppressed by the Dominion government with troops from all the provinces transported over the new Canadian Pacific Railway. **Riel** surrendered (May 15); executed (Nov. 16).

1886.   Canadian and Bering Sea fisheries dispute with the United States.

1888, May 1.   Lord Stanley (Earl of Derby), governor-general (1888–1893).

1890.   Liberals urged policy of "unrestricted reciprocity" to remedy the depression following the United States McKinley tariff. **Continental Union Association** formed. The **Imperial Federation League** (formed 1885) urged preferential trade with the mother country.

1891, June 6.   Death of **Sir John A. Macdonald;** succeeded by **Sir John J. C. Abbott** (June 16).

1892, Nov.   Resignation of Abbott; succeeded by **Sir John S. D. Thompson** (Dec. 5).

1892–1893.   Bering Sea arbitration (p. 825).

1893, May 22.   Earl of Aberdeen appointed governor-general (1893–1898).

1894, June 23–July 10.   Second colonial conference held at Ottawa.

Dec. 12.   Death of **Thompson. Mr.** (later Sir) **Mackenzie Bowell** succeeded (Dec. 21).

1896.   The offer of Newfoundland to enter the Dominion was refused through financial disagreement.

Apr. 27.   Resignation of **Bowell; Sir Charles Tupper,** premier (Jan. 15, 1895).

July 11.   Mr. (later Sir) **Wilfrid Laurier** became premier (1896–1911) as a result of a Liberal victory in the general elections (June).

1897.   British preferential tariff instituted. In 1898 the preference was increased to 25 per

cent and in 1900 to 33⅓ per cent. Germany retaliated (July 7, 1899) by depriving Canada of most-favored-nation treatment.

1898.   Canadian Northern Railway chartered.

July 30.   **Lord Minto** appointed governor-general (1898–1904).

1899, Oct. 29.   South African War. The first Canadian contingent sent to South Africa. A second contingent sent in 1900; but the official contingents were withdrawn before the end of the war owing to dissatisfaction in Quebec.

1902, Oct. 31.   Cable from Vancouver to Brisbane completed.

1903.   Alaskan boundary arbitration with the United States (p. 828).   High dissatisfaction with the award.

1904, Sept. 26.   Earl Grey appointed governor-general (1904–1911).

1905, Sept. 1.   Formation of the provinces of **Alberta** and **Saskatchewan.**

1908.   Civil Service Commission appointed for the selection of civil officials.

1910.   Formation of a small Canadian navy.

1911, Jan. 26.   Publication of a **reciprocity agreement** with the United States; ratified by the United States senate (July 22). But in the general elections (Sept. 21) the Liberals were defeated on the issue and reciprocity was dropped. **Mr.** (later Sir) **Robert L. Borden** formed a Conservative ministry (Oct. 10).

Mar. 21.   **Duke of Connaught** appointed governor-general (1911–1916).

1913, May 30.   Defeat in the senate of a navy bill providing for the contribution of three dreadnoughts to the imperial navy.

1914, Apr. 7.   Completion of the **Grand Trunk Pacific Railway.**

May 21.   *S.S. Komagatu Maru* in Vancouver harbor; 300 Hindus refused entrance to British Columbia and sent back to India.

May 29.   *S.S. Empress of Ireland* sunk in collision in the Gulf of St. Lawrence; 1023 lives lost.

Aug. 4.   Entrance of Great Britain into the **First World War.**   (*Cont. p. 1054.*)

b. NEWFOUNDLAND, 1855–1909

1855.   Responsible government granted; bicameral legislature, legislative council (15), appointed by the governor-in-council, house of assembly (36), elective, and a responsible cabinet.

1864.   Copper discovered in the north and mining operations begun.

1873.   Direct steam communication with England and America established.

1880.   Government loan of £1,000,000 to a **railway from St. John's to Hall's Bay;** completed to Harbor Grace (1884); after financial difficulties, construction was taken over by Mr. R. G. Reid (1893) and built to Port-aux-Basques.

1888.   Bait Act took effect, after considerable controversy and protests of the French government, prohibiting capture in Newfoundland waters, for exportation or sale, of bait fish except under special license. French retaliations followed until a *modus vivendi* was enacted (1890). Finally settled in the Anglo-French convention of 1904.

1894–1895.   Bank failures and insolvency; Canadian banks replaced former government institutions; followed by renewed prosperity.

1895–1896.   Severe financial depression. Delegation to Ottawa regarding union with Canada. Canada objected to assuming all of the $16,000,000 debt and negotiations were broken off.

1900.   Resignation of Sir James Winter; succeeded by **Mr.** (later Sir) **Robert Bond.**

1906, Oct.   *Modus vivendi* with the United States following difficulties with fishing rights under the treaty of 1818. Referred to the Hague tribunal and award (Sept. 1910) allowed Great Britain (Newfoundland) the right to make regulations subject to the treaty of 1818, and defining the "three-mile limit" in bays as from a line across the bay at a point where distance of ten miles is not exceeded.

1909.   Resignation of premier Sir Robert Bond; succeeded by **Sir Edward P. Morris.**

(*Cont. p. 1057.*)

3.   ALASKA, 1728–1912

1728.   Vitus Bering, a Dane, sailed through the straits now bearing his name.

1741.   Bering explored the Alaskan coast. From this time on the Russians were active in the region, establishing sealing and fishing stations.

1776.   Captain James Cook made the first British explorations on the coast. He was followed by **Captain George Vancouver.**

1793.   Alexander Mackenzie crossed the continent from the east to the Pacific coast, and returned.

1799.   The Russian-American Fur Company organized by the Russian government and given a trade monopoly for twenty years (later renewed). A most active period of Russian enterprise under the governorship of **Alexander Baranov** (1790–1819).

1804.   Baranov founded **Sitka.**

1821.   Russian decree claiming the coast south to latitude 51 and forbidding all foreign ships approaching within 100 miles of the coast. Protests of the United States and Great Britain. The matter was settled by treaties between Russia and the United States (Apr. 17, 1824) and between Russia and Great Britain (Feb. 28, 1825), by which Russia was given the territory north of 54° 40′ and west of 141°.

1867, Mar. 30.   The United States purchased Alaska from Russia for $7,200,000. The formal transfer was made October 18.

1884, May 17.   The Organic Act applied the laws of Oregon to Alaska, after a period of government by the war department.

1903.   Passage of a homestead law for Alaska.

Oct. 20.   Settlement of the boundary dispute between the United States and Canada by a board of three American, two Canadian, and one British jurist. The Canadian case was lost and Canada was debarred from the ocean inlets.

1906.   Alaska permitted to elect a delegate to congress.

1912.   Alaska given territorial status. A bicameral legislature was established under a governor appointed by the president of the United States. The legislature was not permitted to pass laws dealing with excise, game, or fur, and the American congress reserved the right to veto Alaskan legislation.

The population of Alaska increased from 30,000 in 1867 to 55,000 in 1920. The population engaged chiefly in fishing (halibut, cod, herring) and in the fur trade. A treaty between the United States, Britain, Russia, and Japan in 1911 prohibited pelagic killing of seals. The value of the furs taken between 1867 and 1925 was over $100,000,000. Mining (especially gold—**Klondike gold rush,** August 1896) was also an important industry, the value of the product between 1880 and 1927 having been almost $600,000,000.

H. LATIN AMERICA
1. THE WARS OF INDEPENDENCE

a. CAUSES

(From p. 537)

Political, economic, and social factors inherent in the Spanish colonial system were the fundamental causes that led to the separation of the American colonies from the mother country. The creoles (Spaniards born in America) and mestizos (mixed Spanish and Indian) increasingly desired participation in government. The virtual exclusion from more important civil and ecclesiastical offices, the economic policy of Spain, and the exploitation of the colonies, fully revealed by the reforms of Charles III, and certain aspects of religious policy created discontent. The freedom enjoyed during the long periods when Spain was at war, and the successful revolution of the North American colonies of Great Britain, engendered a desire for independence. The doctrines of the French philosophers and the French Revolution created a demand for reform among intellectuals. Geographical influences, lack of communication, the administrative division of the colonies, and traditional Spanish separation and individualism aided in creating sentiment for independence.

In **South America** the movement for separation was fundamentally liberal. From the first it was led by creoles and originated in the *cabildos,* later expanding to national proportions. In **Mexico** the earliest and unsuccessful phases, led by certain creoles, developed into a servile revolt as well as a movement for independence. Separation was finally achieved by a reactionary movement after the revolution of 1820 in Spain (p. 694).

The **Wars of Liberation** were also civil conflicts within New World administrative districts. The royal government and the Church, until the Spanish revolution of 1820, constituted the basis of Spanish resistance. The ignorant masses frequently became a source of manpower for the Spanish régime as well as for the creole movement. In the region of the Río de la Plata and New Granada provincial separatist tendencies led to internecine strife among proponents of independence from Spain.

The **immediate cause** of the movement which led to the independence of the South American colonies was the domination of Spain by **Napoleon Bonaparte** and his establishment of his brother **Joseph** on the throne (p. 642). The American colonies opposed French control and refused to recognize Joseph, proclaiming allegiance to the deposed **Ferdinand VII.** Certain areas declared their independence when it appeared that Napoleon had established complete control over Spain. The restoration of the absolute rule of Ferdinand in 1814 and his determination to restore the old system (despite the liberal policies that had been adopted by the Spanish agencies representing his authority during the Napoleonic period) turned the movements into a definitely separatist channel. Internal strife and disturbed political conditions in Spain after 1814 contributed to the success of the colonists.

The **Wars of Independence** passed through two phases, that between 1809 and 1816, during which movements for separation failed everywhere except in the area of the Río de la Plata, and that between 1816 and 1825, during which independence was achieved.

b. EARLIER INSURRECTIONS, 1721–1806

The first serious insurrectionary movements occurred in the 18th century, the gravest taking place in **Paraguay** (1721–1735), **Peru** (1780–1782), and **Colombia** (1781).

1721–1735. The comuneros of Paraguay. José de Antequera, appointed by the audiencia of Charcas to resolve a controversy between the cabildo of Asunción and the governor of Paraguay, supported the cabildo and was chosen governor (1721). An autonomous commune was created, and Antequera, speaking of the sovereignty of the people, refused to relinquish office on demand of the higher Spanish authorities. Open warfare between the forces of the commune and royal forces ensued. After maintaining their cause for a considerable period, Antequera and the Paraguayans were overcome (1731). Antequera was executed, but a follower, **Fernando Mompó de Zayas,** revived the organization and continued the struggle, which was finally completely suppressed (1735).

1780–1782. The revolt of Tupac Amarú. Abuses in connection with forced labor under the *mita* and *repartimiento* and with administration caused the natives of the Peruvian highlands to revolt under leadership of **Tupac Amarú,** descendant of the Inca rulers, who proclaimed himself liberator of his people.

Two attacks were made on Cuzco by Tupac Amarú at the head of a horde of ill-armed Indians, but the Spaniards crushed the native forces and executed the leader. The revolt was continued and La Paz was twice subjected to siege before the movement was definitely crushed.

1781. The comuneros of New Granada. Attempts to increase royal revenues in New Granada led to a widespread revolt under the leadership of two creoles, **Berbeo** and **José Antonio Galán.** Moving on Bogotá, the insurrectionary forces compelled the authorities to consent to their conditions, whereupon they dispersed. The viceroy, receiving reinforcements, suppressed the movement, although later (1784) representatives of New Granada, declaring themselves allies of Tupac Amarú, fruitlessly sought British and French aid for the liberation of South America.

1790–1806. The early efforts of Francisco de Miranda. The greatest of the early leaders who planned the independence of the Spanish colonies was **Francisco de Miranda.** A Venezuelan creole, Miranda served in the Spanish army and became a general in the French revolutionary forces. He early formulated plans for liberation and long but fruitlessly sought the aid of the British, French, and United States governments. Organizing a filibustering expedition in the United States, Miranda captured **Coro,** but Venezuela was not prepared for revolt and the movement failed (1806). Support of the British government was at length secured and an expedition for the liberation of northern South America was being organized under command of Wellington when developments in the Iberian Peninsula caused abandonment of the project.

c. THE RÍO DE LA PLATA, 1806–1817

The period of independence in the region of the Río de la Plata was introduced by a British attempt to gain possession of at least a portion of the area.

1806. On his return from the occupation of Cape Colony (p. 884), **Sir Home Popham,** acquainted with the projects of Miranda, on his own initiative occupied **Buenos Aires.** The viceroy fled and **Santiago de Liniers,** at the head of the colonial militia, forced the British to capitulate. Upon his return the viceroy was deposed by a *cabildo abierto* and Liniers was elected to the office, an act of sovereignty which the crown approved.

1806–1807. Although the action of Popham had not been authorized, the British govern-ment dispatched an expedition of 10,000 men under **Gen. John Whitelocke.** This force occupied **Montevideo** and moved against Buenos Aires, the defenders of which, under Liniers, forced Whitelocke to capitulate and withdraw from the area of the Río de la Plata. These events stimulated national feeling in the region.

1809–1810. Liniers was replaced by a viceroy appointed by the central junta of Spain, but in view of the apparent success of Napoleon he was removed by the cabildo of Buenos Aires and a provisional junta of the **provinces of the Río de la Plata** was established in the name of Ferdinand VII (1810, May 25). Direct Spanish authority was never restored.

1810–1811. The provisional junta, dominated by **Mariano Moreno,** soon rejected the authority of the provisional government of Spain representing Ferdinand VII and sought to extend control over the **Banda Oriental** (Uruguay) and **Paraguay.** An army was dispatched to liberate upper Peru (Bolivia), but was disastrously defeated. Paraguay refused to adhere to the provinces of the Río de la Plata. Forces were sent against the province by Buenos Aires, but were defeated by the royal governor, supported by the majority of Paraguayans (1811). Moreno was forced from office and a triumvirate replaced the provisional junta.

1812–1813. Manuel Belgrano, placed in command of the northern forces, defeated the royalists near **Tucumán** and at **Salta,** and prevented the invasion of the southern portion of the region of the Río de la Plata. A second attempt to invade upper Peru failed.

1813. Authority was vested in a director, the former viceroyalty was divided into provinces, and a congress was convened at Tucumán (1816).

1816, July 9. JUAN MARTIN DE PUEYRREDON was named supreme director and the **congress declared the independence of the United Provinces.** Meanwhile **José de San Martín,** one of the two great figures of the period of independence, who was born in the Misiones territory while his father was governor of the province and who had served in the Spanish army in Africa, Portugal, and Spain, was given command of the army of the north (1814).

1814–1817. Comprehending the geographical difficulties of a campaign in upper Peru, San Martín formulated a plan to organize an army in western Argentina, liberate Chile, and move by sea to attack Peru, the center of Spanish authority. San Martín established himself at **Mendoza** and prepared to carry his plans into effect.

d. PARAGUAY, 1811-1816

1811. After the defeat of the forces of Buenos Aires, the **Paraguayans** overthrew the royal governor, and a revolutionary junta was established at Asunción.

1811, Aug. 14. PARAGUAY PROCLAIMED INDEPENDENCE FROM SPAIN, and later from Buenos Aires (1813). A republican government with two consuls at its head was created (1813).

1814. The First Consul **José Rodríguez de Francia** was declared *Dictator,* and was soon made *Perpetual Dictator* (1816).

e. THE BANDA ORIENTAL (URUGUAY), 1811-1821

1811-1814. Spanish control in the Banda Oriental, territory claimed by the Portuguese crown and by the provinces of the Río de la Plata, was brought to an end by forces of Buenos Aires and by Uruguayan revolutionaries led by **José Artigas.** Artigas, who favored a federal system of government, at first maintained allegiance to Buenos Aires, but controversy concerning federal and unitary forms led to conflict and he advocated independence.

1816-1820. After establishing control over an extensive area, Artigas was driven from Uruguay by Brazilian troops, who occupied the province (1816-1820).

1821. The Banda Oriental was incorporated into Brazil.

f. CHILE, 1810-1820

1810. Upon the apparent triumph of Napoleon in Spain the captain-general of Chile was deposed and a junta assumed authority in the name of Ferdinand VII. A **general congress** convened at **Santiago,** from which, after controversy concerning reforms and separation from Spain, the radical elements withdrew. The remaining groups constituted themselves into an executive power.

1811-1812. José Miguel Carrera overthrew the government and sanctioned a republican organization, at the same time acknowledging the sovereignty of the king. A constitution was framed which assigned supreme authority to a junta of three under the control of Carrera, whose rule aroused strong opposition headed by **Bernardo O'Higgins.**

1814. This dissension enabled the viceroy of Peru to crush the Chilean armies, despite the ultimate co-operation of O'Higgins and Carrera. Santiago was taken and royal government was re-established.

1817. San Martín, having completed his preparations at Mendoza (above), crossed the Andes with some 5200 men, defeated a Spanish army at **Chacabuco** (Feb. 12) and occupied **Santiago.** O'Higgins was made supreme director after San Martín had refused the post.

1818, Feb. 12. THE INDEPENDENCE OF CHILE WAS PROCLAIMED. A royal army from Peru was defeated by San Martín at **Maipú** (Apr. 5). With these events the independence of Chile was definitely achieved.

1818-1820. San Martín prepared for the liberation of Peru, receiving support from Buenos Aires and aid from O'Higgins. A navy was organized under **Admiral Lord Thomas Cochrane,** an able British naval officer, and an army of 4000 men was formed.

g. PERU AND BOLIVIA, 1809-1825

1809. The inhabitants of **Chuquisaca** deposed the president and established a junta, while those of **La Paz** deposed the intendant and also created a junta, declaring loyalty to Ferdinand VII. Royal troops soon crushed the movements. Another unsuccessful revolutionary movement occurred at **Cuzco** (1813). Peru long remained a bulwark of royal authority.

1820. After completing preparations in Chile, **San Martín** transported his forces to Peru by sea, where he resorted to propaganda rather than immediate military action on a large scale, and opened negotiations with the viceroy. Negotiations failed, but efforts to influence opinion met with success. The viceroy abandoned Lima, and San Martín, invited by the people, entered the capital.

1821, July 28. He proclaimed the **INDEPENDENCE OF PERU,** and assumed supreme authority as protector.

1823. A factional quarrel among the proponents of independence in Lima led to the establishment of a new government, which invited **Bolívar** to Peru. A force under **Andrés Santa Cruz** was dispatched into Charcas (Bolivia), but was defeated by the royalists. **Sucre** moved to Lima with Colombian troops and Bolívar followed, being proclaimed dictator.

1824. Carrying the war to the royalists, under the viceroy, **José de La Serna,** and José **Canterac,** Bolívar and Sucre moved into the highlands and defeated the Spaniards at **Junín** (Aug. 24). Bolívar returned to Lima to assume the government. Sucre continued the campaign, and with some 5800 men defeated La Serna and Canterac, with 9300 men, in the decisive **battle of Ayacucho** (Dec. 9). The Spanish leaders were forced to sign a capitulation which included the withdrawal of the

23,000 royal troops which remained in Peru. With these events the independence of Peru was achieved. Invading Charcas, Sucre liberated the presidency and convened a **congress at Chuquisaca.**

1825, Aug. 6. CONGRESS PROCLAIMED INDEPENDENCE and designated the new state the **republic of Bolívar (Bolivia).**

h. VENEZUELA, 1808–1822

1808. Upon the intervention of Napoleon in Spain the cabildo of **Caracas,** proclaiming Ferdinand VII king of Spain and the Indies, proposed the establishment of a junta. Two years later an extraordinary cabildo deposed the captain-general and created a junta in the name of the sovereign (1810).

1811. The junta soon disavowed the Spanish regency and claimed for Venezuela a place among free states, inviting other colonies to take similar action. A commission, which included **Simón Bolívar** (cf. below), was sent to England to secure aid. **Miranda** returned to Venezuela to assume leadership.

July 5. A general congress proclaimed **VENEZUELAN INDEPENDENCE** and a constitution was adopted. Miranda was given command of the revolutionary forces and Bolívar became one of his lieutenants. **Simón Bolívar,** born in Caracas of distinguished creole parents, educated in his native city and widely traveled in Europe, deeply read in the French philosophers and strongly influenced by his republican tutor, Simón Rodríquez, had dedicated himself to the liberation of the Spanish colonies, and became one of the two greatest figures of the independence movement.

1811–1812. Spanish forces under **Juan Domingo Monteverde** achieved marked success in a campaign of reconquest, and internal strife developed.

1812, Mar. 26. An earthquake wrought great destruction and created demoralization in the area controlled by the revolutionists, but spared that held by the royalists. The clergy proclaimed the catastrophe to be divine retribution for disloyalty, with detrimental effect upon the revolutionary cause.

July 25. **Miranda was made dictator** to organize further resistance, but the royal forces made rapid progress and he was forced to capitulate by the **treaty of San Mateo,** which provided clemency for the revolutionists. Monteverde, notwithstanding, dealt with Venezuela as a conquered province. Bolívar and other leaders, indignant at the capitulation, permitted Miranda to fall into Spanish hands, and he was sent a prisoner to Cadiz, where he died (1816).

i. GREAT COLOMBIA (NEW GRANADA, VENEZUELA, AND QUITO), 1808–1822

1808. Ferdinand VII was proclaimed king at Bogotá upon the invasion of Spain by Napoleon, and in the following year the president of Quito was driven from office. A junta, in the name of Ferdinand VII, and a senate, vested with the powers of the audiencia, as well as secretaries for war and foreign affairs, were created. The viceroy of New Granada was compelled to call an advisory junta to consider action with respect to the movement in Quito. This body displayed dissatisfaction with Spanish rule, and with its authority a memorial of grievances was drawn up, to be sent to the central junta of Spain. An extraordinary cabildo at Bogotá, in the name of the king, established a junta for the viceroyalty and named the viceroy its president. The junta soon expelled the viceroy and broke with the Spanish regency, but again proclaimed loyalty to Ferdinand VII. Principal towns of New Granada, while affirming loyalty to the sovereign, also overthrew the Spanish officials and created provincial juntas, certain of which drew up constitutions. Meanwhile the movement in Quito was crushed by the Spanish authorities (1809).

1811, Nov. 11. Cartagena later declared its independence, and was followed by Cundinamarca (1813). A congress drew up an *Act of Federation of the United Provinces of New Granada,* but the provinces displayed marked separatist tendencies and conflict between them weakened the revolutionary cause. **Bolívar** took service with Cartagena and drove the Spanish forces from the lower Magdalena valley.

1813. Commissioned by the congress of New Granada to carry the war into Venezuela, **Bolívar** regained Caracas and **became virtual dictator** under authority of the cabildo of the capital.

1814. A savage war to the death ensued in which the royalists, under **José Tomás Boves,** triumphed and re-established Spanish control throughout Venezuela.

Returning to New Granada, Bolívar under authority of the congress of New Granada undertook to conquer the separatist provinces of Cundinamarca, Cartagena, and Santa Marta. He brought Cundinamarca under control of the central government, which then established itself in Bogotá, and besieged Cartagena, preparatory to a campaign against Santa Marta.

1815. While the siege of Cartagena was progressing, an army of 10,000 Spanish veterans under **Pablo Morillo** landed in Venezuela, the close of the Napoleonic wars having made the dispatch of troops possible. Morillo, leaving a portion of his forces in Venezuela, moved into New Granada and everywhere defeated the revolutionary armies. Bolívar, recognizing the hopelessness of the situation, departed for Jamaica. Acting ruthlessly, Morillo restored royal authority virtually throughout New Granada.

1816. After dispatching a commissioner to England to secure support, **Bolívar returned** to the area of Orinoco.

1818–1819. With the aid of **José Páez,** Bolívar secured control over the lower basin of the Orinoco and established headquarters at Angostura. A congress convened at Angostura elected **Bolívar president** and he presented a constitution to that body.

1819. Leaving Páez to contain Morillo, Bolívar, his army augmented by British volunteers, moved up the valley of the Orinoco, crossed the Andes, defeated a superior royalist army at the **Boyacá River** (Aug. 7), and **occupied Bogotá** (Aug. 10). **New Granada was definitely liberated** by this campaign.

Dec. 17. The **congress of Angostura,** including representatives of New Granada, proclaimed **Great Colombia,** to be constituted of New Granada, Venezuela, and Quito. A constitution was adopted and Bolívar was made president and military dictator.

1820. The **Spanish revolution of 1820** caused Ferdinand VII to adopt a conciliatory policy and Morillo was instructed to conclude peace on condition that the revolutionists accept the constitution of 1812, which accorded the colonies representation in the cortes. A six months' truce was concluded (Nov. 25) and Bolívar dispatched emissaries to Spain under instructions to uphold the independence of Colombia. As the crown refused to acknowledge Colombian independence, war was soon resumed. Morillo meanwhile departed, placing **Miguel de la Torre** in command.

1821. Bolívar dispatched his able lieutenant, **Antonio José de Sucre,** to liberate Quito, moved into Venezuela, uniting with Páez, defeated the royalist army at **Carabobo** (June 24), and occupied Caracas (June 29). The battle of Carabobo assured Venezuelan independence.

Aug. 30. A **congress at Cucutá** framed a republican constitution and named **Bolívar president.** Bolívar placed Páez in command of the army in Venezuela.

1821–1822. Moving by sea to Guayaquil, **Sucre,** aided by forces sent by San Martín, achieved the liberation of Quito through the decisive **battle of Pichincha** (1822, May 24).

Bolívar meanwhile, placing authority in the hands of the vice-president, **Francisco de Paula Santander,** moved to aid Sucre. He persuaded the provinces of Quito to unite with Great Colombia (May 29).

1822, July 26–27. San Martín, who had been advancing on Quito, and Bolívar met at Guayaquil to consider prosecution of plans for liberation. Comprehending the ambitions of Bolívar, realizing the impossibility of co-operation, and fearing detriment to the cause of independence, San Martín withdrew in favor of Bolívar.

j. NEW SPAIN (MEXICO), 1808–1822

1808. Events in Spain following the intervention of Napoleon caused creole elements to desire a greater share in government. With support from the viceroy, **José de Iturrigaray,** who hoped to advance his own interests, a general junta was convened, despite opposition of the audiencia, which, composed of Spaniards, mistrusted the creole elements. Within a short time a group of Spaniards, instigated by the audiencia, expelled the viceroy. Four viceroys followed in rapid succession (1808–1813).

The first direct action against Spanish rule was led by **Miguel Hidalgo y Costilla,** a creole priest steeped in French philosophy and interested in the welfare of the native masses.

1810. Hidalgo, his object being separation and social reform, initiated a revolt in the province of **Guanajuato** with the support of certain creoles (Sept. 16). Joined by Indians, mestizos, and an increasing number of creoles, Hidalgo captured Guanajuato, Guadalajara, and Valladolid and reached the vicinity of the capital, from which his ill-armed horde of 80,000 was forced to retreat by a small Spanish force under **Felix Calleja** (Nov. 6). The movement headed by Hidalgo rapidly assumed the character of a servile revolt, with resultant alienation of the upper classes of the creoles.

1811. Assuming the offensive, **Calleja,** with 6000 men, crushed the revolutionary forces at the **bridge of Calderón,** near Guadalajara (Jan. 17). Hidalgo and a small remnant fled northward, but the leader fell into Spanish hands, was tried, and executed (July 31).

The revolt was continued by **José María Morelos,** a mestizo priest, who, as a lieutenant of Hidalgo, had been operating west of Mexico City.

1812. Moving southeast, Morelos secured control of a wide area and captured **Oaxaca** (Nov. 25). Turning westward, he took **Acapulco** (1813, Apr. 12).

1813. A congress was convened at **Chilpancingo** (Sept. 14), Morelos was made head of the government, **independence was declared** (Nov. 6), and administrative, social, and fiscal reforms were adopted.

1814, Oct. 22. The **constitution of Apatzingan** was promulgated.

Morelos failed in an attempt to take Valladolid and was forced to retreat by **Agustín de Iturbide,** a creole in Spanish service. The revolutionary cause became increasingly hopeless, reinforcements reached the royalists from Spain, and the government was forced to move frequently.

1815. Morelos, having relinquished executive authority though retaining military command, was captured while escorting the government to Tehuacán and was shortly thereafter executed (Dec. 22). The revolutionary congress was dissolved.

1816–1821. The viceroy, **Juan Ruíz de Apodaca,** instituted a conciliatory policy and secured the surrender of the majority of the revolutionary leaders. Spanish authority was again firmly established, and only certain guerrilla leaders among them **Vicente Guerrero,** continued resistance.

1817. An expedition raised in Britain and the United States under **Francisco Xavier Mina** landed on the Gulf Coast and penetrated to Guanajuato, but was defeated. Xavier Mina was executed (Nov. 11).

1821. The **revolution of 1820 in Spain** and the restoration of the constitution of 1812 menaced the position of the clergy and the upper classes, and reactionary and conservative elements determined upon separation. These groups found an instrument in **Iturbide,** who concluded with Guerrero the *plan of Iguala.*

Feb. 24. This proclaimed the **INDEPENDENCE OF MEXICO,** declared that the government should be a constitutional monarchy under Ferdinand VII or another European prince, guaranteed maintenance of the Roman Catholic religion and the preservation of the position and property of the Church, and urged the union of all classes to support the instrument. The royalists, higher clergy, and prominent creoles supported the movement, an army was formed, and the viceroy Apodaca was deposed.

Aug. 24. The newly arrived viceroy, **Juan O'Donojú,** accepted the plan of Iguala by the **convention of Córdoba.** The revolutionary army occupied Mexico City (Sept. 27). A **regency under Iturbide** was formed pending choice of a sovereign. A constituent congress was convened.

1822. The Spanish government refused to accept the convention of Córdoba.

May 19. ITURBIDE induced a section of the congress to elect him **emperor.** He was crowned **Agustín I** (July 25).

k. GUATEMALA AND CENTRAL AMERICA, 1811–1823

1811–1814. Several revolutionary movements occurred in the **captaincy-general of Guatemala** (Guatemala, San Salvador, Honduras, Nicaragua, Costa Rica, and Chiapas), but were speedily suppressed.

1821, Sept. 15. Influenced by events in Mexico a junta convened by the captain-general in Guatemala City declared for the independence of the provinces with the royal executive as administrative head. **Iturbide** invited the new state to become a part of Mexico.

1822, Jan. 5. Guatemala accepted, but the other provinces, tending toward republicanism, opposed union.

1822. After coronation Iturbide demanded that he be proclaimed emperor in the former captaincy-general and dispatched troops under **Vicente Filísola** to force acceptance of his authority. In **San Salvador,** where opposition to union was especially strong, a congress proposed incorporation into the United States of America (1822, Dec. 2). The other states accepted **inclusion in the Mexican Empire** and coercive action was taken against San Salvador.

1823. Upon the abdication of Agustín I (p. 858), Filísola convened a general constituent assembly in Guatemala City (Feb. 21) in which all provinces except Chiapas, which remained incorporated with Mexico, were represented.

July 1. This body declared the provinces of Guatemala, San Salvador, Nicaragua, Honduras, and Costa Rica sovereign as the confederated **United Provinces of Central America.** Mexico recognized the independence of the United Provinces (Aug. 20).

1. BRAZIL, 1820–1823

1820–1822. The immediate causes of **Brazilian independence** arose from a complex combination of circumstances in Portugal and Brazil. The administrative system of the court, the position accorded the Portuguese, and the spread of republican theories, evidenced by a revolt in Pernambuco (1817), created discontent among Brazilians, while in Portugal there was growing dissatisfaction with the British-dominated regency (p. 698), the transfer of government to Brazil, and the opening of Brazil to free trade.

1820. Following the example of Spain, the **Portuguese overthrew the regency** and provisionally adopted the Spanish constitution of 1812. The cortes, convened for the first time in more than a century, summoned the king to return and invited Brazil to send representatives to a constituent assembly.

1821, Feb.–Apr. Vacillating and fundamentally an absolutist, **John VI** was forced by a military rising to accept the **Portuguese constitution** yet to be promulgated, and to appoint a liberal ministry. Upon the demand of the assembly, convened to select representatives to the Portuguese constituent convention, he later adhered to the provisional Spanish constitution. After excesses on the part of the Brazilian assembly, the king dispersed it by military action and reversed his position.

    Apr. 22–26. Convinced of the ultimate necessity of returning to Portugal, John VI designated his son **Pedro** as prince-regent and departed, thoroughly discredited.

1821–1822. Eventual separation of Brazil from Portugal was hastened by the determination of the cortes to reduce Brazil once again to the status of a dependency. That body, over the protest of Brazilian representatives, created in Brazil directly responsible provisional administrative councils, ordered the regent to visit Europe to study constitutional forms, subordinated the tribunal of Rio de Janeiro to the supreme court of Portugal, and finally, in effect, re-established the commercial monopoly of Portugal.

1822. Meanwhile **Brazilian national sentiment** crystallized about the regent, who, upon petition of his subjects, declared his determination to remain in Brazil (Jan. 9). A design of the Portuguese commander in Rio de Janeiro to carry the regent to Portugal failed and the garrison was later forced to withdraw. Dom Pedro formed a new ministry (Jan. 16) and decreed that no law of the cortes be put into effect without his assent (Feb. 21). A Portuguese squadron which arrived to convey the regent to Portugal was forced to withdraw.

1822. Having gained the support of Minas Gerães (Mar.), **Dom Pedro** was declared **perpetual defender of Brazil** (May 13). He soon convoked a Brazilian constituent assembly (June 3). A visit to São Paulo secured that province.

    Sept. 7. The *Grito de Ypiranga* (Cry of Ypiranga). While en route to the city of São Paulo, the regent received dispatches from Portugal which offered concessions but made clear the determination of the cortes to subordinate Brazil. He therefore **proclaimed Brazilian independence.**

    Oct. 12. The regent, upon initiative of the senate, was proclaimed at Rio de Janeiro **constitutional emperor of Brazil.** Dom Pedro pledged acceptance of the constitution to be formulated by the already summoned convention. His coronation as **Pedro I** followed (Dec. 1). Armed resistance by Portuguese garrisons and Brazilian elements opposed to separation in certain northern provinces and the Cisplatine Province was overcome by the close of 1823, due in large part to the Brazilian navy, organized by **Lord Cochrane.**

2. LATIN AMERICA, 1825–1914

The movement for independence in the Spanish colonies produced ephemeral co-operation between the states of South America and between Mexico and Central America, and there existed the ideal of union, which was one of the objectives of Bolívar. The individualism of the Spaniard, the separatist traditions inherited from Spain, the influence of administrative division during the colonial period (which created rudimentary nationalism and in certain instances cultural entity within the upper classes), geographical and climatic factors, lack of communications, and the personal ambition of individual leaders prevented the achievement of union and co-operation between states.

Orderly progress within nations was rendered difficult by these same factors, by ethnic differences, and by class distinctions and vested interests, which independence from Spain did not eliminate. The Church was determined to maintain its vast influence, interests, and privileged position, and wealth and political power remained the possession of a small minority. Of the peoples of Spanish America some 19 per cent were whites, 31 per cent mestizos, 45 per cent Indians, and 4 per cent Negroes. The vast bulk of the population was abjectly ignorant, and large native groups had scarcely been touched by European culture in other than its religious aspects. The educated upper classes had no experience in government other than that afforded by the municipal cabildos and the governmental agencies created during the period of liberation. Military influence, resulting from the long period of wars, was strong.

As there existed no community of interest,

political, economic, social, and religious dissension and division into bitterly opposed conservative and liberal reforming groups were inevitable. Conditions after independence demanded firm government and capable administrators. San Martín favored monarchical forms and Bolívar, a man of theoretical democratic and republican beliefs, comprehending the problems involved, advocated compromise between monarchy and republicanism. The majority of the intellectual leaders of the independence movement were impractical, idealistic, and doctrinaire republicans. As a result republican forms, for which the peoples were least prepared, were adopted. Republican leaders were divided among themselves on the question of the unitary as opposed to the federal system.

The conflict of forces within the newly formed states made inevitable a long period of instability and adjustment.

a. ARGENTINA

At the achievement of independence, there existed little feeling of unity in Argentina and a fundamental issue at once arose concerning the adoption of a unitary or federal form of government. Buenos Aires favored a unitary system, while the provinces, controlled by local leaders (*caudillos*) and fearing the preponderance of the capital, favored a federal system. The Argentine provinces wished to include Paraguay and Uruguay within the nation, and this laid the basis for foreign complications.

1825. Hoping to achieve the incorporation of Uruguay, **Argentina** aided in a revolt of that state against **Brazil** and made war on the empire.

1827. Argentine and Uruguayan forces defeated the Brazilians, gaining the decisive **battle of Ituzaingó** (Feb. 20).

1828. Through the **mediation of Great Britain** Uruguay was made an independent buffer state.

1829. Almost constant rebellion in the provinces reduced Argentina to anarchy until **Juan Manuel de Rosas,** a provincial leader and a federalist, became governor of Buenos Aires (Dec. 8) after a victory over its forces in the field (Apr.).

1835. Rosas assumed complete authority in Buenos Aires and twelve provinces recognized him as chief executive. The **Argentine confederation** thus became a reality. Rosas governed with absolute authority. He sought to raise Argentine prestige abroad, and desired to bring Uruguay and Paraguay into the confederation.

1831–1841. Controversies arose with the United States and Great Britain concerning the **Falkland Islands,** which Britain claimed, and with France concerning treatment of French subjects. This led to a blockade of the Argentine coast (1838).

1845–1850. Further disputes arose with France and Great Britain concerning **intervention in Uruguay** and the closing of the Paraná to foreign commerce, and resulted in a **blockade of the Río de la Plata** by British and French naval forces. From these controversies Argentina emerged with credit, although the position of Rosas was weakened thereby.

1851. The tyrannical rule of Rosas caused internal opposition, led by **Justo José de Urquiza,** and his intervention in Uruguay aroused the enmity of Brazil.

1852. In alliance with Uruguay and Brazil, Urquiza overthrew Rosas in the **battle of Caseros** (Feb. 3). Despite its drawbacks, the arbitrary régime of Rosas constituted a necessary period of transition between anarchy and constitutional organization. Argentine designs on Uruguay were henceforth relinquished.

1853. Urquiza became chief executive and a **federal constitution,** to which Buenos Aires refused to adhere, was promulgated (May 1). A president with a six-year term, a bicameral congress, and an independent judiciary were provided by the instrument.

1854. **Buenos Aires** drew up a separate constitution (Apr. 12). Both Buenos Aires and the provinces of the federation progressed materially, but basic antagonism led to war between the federation and Buenos Aires (1859).

1859. The latter was speedily defeated (Oct. 22) and agreed to union with the federation under constitutional amendments (Nov. 10).

1862. Efforts to adjust differences failed and **Bartolomé Mitre,** governor of Buenos Aires, upon the withdrawal of Urquiza from politics after the indecisive engagement of **Pavón** (1861, Sept. 17), became head of the national government (1862, Aug. 27).

These events gave Buenos Aires ascendancy over the remainder of the nation, and the city was made the national capital for a period of five years. Under Mitre administrative reforms were carried out, material progress continued, and education was promoted. Insurrections in several provinces were suppressed.

1865, May 1. **Argentina** concluded an **alliance with Uruguay and Brazil.**

1865–1870. **WAR WITH PARAGUAY.** Dictator López declared war after Argentina refused to permit passage of Paraguayan troops across national territory (p. 848). Mitre commanded the allied forces during the first two years of the war.

San Francisco

MEXICO

Rio Grande

Mississippi

Gulf of
Mexico

Mexico

CUBA

BELIZE

CENTRAL AMERICA

HAITI

PUERTO
RICO

Caribbean Sea

PANAMA

Caracas

VENEZUELA

NEW GRENADA

Bogota

COLOMBIA

GUIANA

Quito

QUITO

Amazon R.

P
E
R
U

Lima

BRAZIL

BOLIVIA

Sucre

PARAGUAY

Asunción

Rio de Janeiro

UNITED PROVINCES of LA PLATA

Paraná R.

CISPLATINE PROVINCE

Santiago

CHILE

Montevideo

Buenos
Aires

Atlantic
Ocean

Pacific

Ocean

Atlantic

Ocean

LATIN
AMERICAN
STATES
after the
REVOLUTIONS

0   500   1000   1500

Scale of Miles

1868-1880. During the administrations of **Domingo Sarmiento** (1868–1874) and **Nicolás Avellaneda** (1874–1880) education, commerce, and immigration were encouraged and the southern frontiers were advanced through subjugation of Indian groups. The first census indicated a population of over 1,700,000 (1869).

1880. The ascendancy of Buenos Aires, the province including 30 per cent of the population, created dissatisfaction in the provinces and they formed the **league of Córdoba,** supporting **Julio Roca** for the presidency. Buenos Aires resorted to civil war to maintain its position, but was defeated (July 20–21). The city of Buenos Aires was erected into a federal district and made the national capital, and the province was made co-ordinate with the remainder. Roca became president (Sept. 21). Thus the problem of the relation of the city and province of Buenos Aires to the remainder of the nation was solved.

1880-1886. Under Roca economic progress continued, and the Indian frontiers were pushed forward.

1886-1890. Excessive speculation and corruption, for which President **Miguel Juárez Celman** was largely responsible, aroused demands for reform. A new party, the *Unión Cívica,* was formed (1890) to achieve this and secure a wider franchise.

1890. An unsuccessful revolt occurred (July 26–27), but **Celman resigned** (Aug. 5) and the vice-president, **Cárlos Pellegrini,** assumed office.

1890-1904. Pellegrini (1890–1892), **Luis Sáenz Peña** (1892–1895), **José Uriburu** (1895–1898), and **Julio Roca** (1898–1904) carried on the task of economic rehabilitation. **Boundary disputes** with Brazil (1895) and Chile (1899, 1902), the latter leading the two nations to the verge of war, were adjusted by arbitration.

1904-1910. The administrations of **Manuel Quintana** (1904–1906) and **José Figueroa Alcorta** (1906–1910) were characterized by labor difficulties and a demand on the part of Radicals for increased suffrage.

1910-1913. **Roque Sáenz Peña,** president. Secret voting and universal suffrage were instituted (1912). (*Cont. p. 1059.*)

b. CHILE

1818-1823. Supreme Director **Bernardo O'Higgins** (p. 840) laid the foundations of the Chilean state and established a highly centralized government.

1823-1827. Opposition developed and **Ramón Freire** became chief executive. A federalist form of government was adopted (1826).

1827. In face of discontent Freire resigned in favor of Vice-President **Francisco Antonio Pinto.** A second federalistic constitution was promulgated (1828). A Liberal Party, advocating democracy and local autonomy, and a Conservative, supported by the upper classes and clergy, advocating a centralized system with a strong executive authority, developed.

1829-1830. Civil war ensued. The Conservatives, under leadership of **Diego José Victor Portáles,** were victorious (1830, Apr. 17), and entered into a long period of power (to 1861).

1833. A highly centralized constitution, which accorded great powers to the president, was adopted. Roman Catholicism remained the state religion.

1836. Chile opposed the formation of the preponderant **Peruvian-Bolivian Confederation** by Santa Cruz, and declared war (Nov. 11).

1839. Chilean troops under **Manuel Búlnes** overthrew the confederation through the decisive **battle of Yungay** (Jan. 20).

1841-1851. During the two **administrations of Búlnes** great internal development took place and steps were taken to extend Chilean sovereignty over the area of the Straits of Magellan. A new Liberal Party, opposed to Conservative oligarchical control and advocating curtailment of presidential powers, developed.

1851-1861. Manuel Montt succeeded Búlnes and served two terms. Material progress continued, education was promoted, and certain liberal reforms, which alienated reactionaries, were adopted. Two Liberal revolts were suppressed.

1861-1871. With the support of Montt, **José Joaquín Pérez,** acceptable to the Liberals, was elected. This marked a movement toward greater democracy and a shift of power in favor of the commercial and intellectual elements. Pérez held office for two terms, during which internal development increased and Chilean capital was invested in Peru and Bolivia for exploitation of guano and nitrate. The lands of the Araucanian Indians were made part of the national domain following their final subjugation.

1865. Chile united with Peru in war against Spain (p. 851), and Valparaiso was bombarded (1866).

1871-1876. During the administration of the Liberal **Federico Errázuriz** education was promoted, anti-clerical reforms were adopted, administrative reforms tending toward increased democratization were introduced, and material progress continued.

1876-1881. Financial problems and **war with Peru and Bolivia** (pp. 850, 851) developed during the term of **Aníbal Pinto** (1876–1881), who was followed by **Domingo Santa María** (1881–1886).

1879–1884. Chile was completely victorious in the **War of the Pacific** because of superior governmental efficiency and military and naval supremacy, and emerged unquestionably the dominant power of western South America.

1883, Oct. 20. By the **treaty of Ancón,** Peru ceded the province of **Tarapacá,** and Chile was to occupy **Tacna** and **Arica** for ten years, after which a plebiscite was to be held.

1884, Apr. 4. By the **treaty of Valparaiso** Chile retained possession of the **Bolivian littoral.** Chile thus gained rich nitrate territories of vast importance to the national economic structure. After termination of the war religious and administrative reforms were adopted, but efforts to separate Church and State failed. The reforms of Santa María aroused much Conservative opposition, and the Liberal Party became divided.

1886. José Manuel Balmaceda followed in the presidency. Parliamentary principles had been evolved (although not envisaged in the constitution) by which a ministry might not remain in office without the support of a majority in congress. Balmaceda maintained full presidential prerogatives.

1891. Civil war ensued (Jan.) in which the congressional forces were victorious and the parliamentary principle was established. Balmaceda, driven from office, committed suicide (Sept. 19). Congressional elements were incensed by supposed sympathy of the United States for Balmaceda and when an attack on members of the crew of the *U.S.S. Baltimore* occurred (Oct. 16) at Valparaiso an acrimonious controversy arose. This was adjusted upon agreement by Chile to pay an indemnity.

1891–1896. Jorge Montt, head of the Congressional Party, was made president, and financial and administrative reforms, including the establishment of a large degree of local autonomy, were adopted.

1896–1901. Federico Errázuriz, son of the former president, succeeded Montt. Efforts to solve the territorial question arising out of the War of the Pacific failed. Boundary disputes with Argentina were submitted to arbitration, although war was but narrowly averted.

1901. The Liberal Party, which had lost prestige as a result of the civil war of 1891, regained strength and secured the election of **Germán Riesco.** The Conservative Party declined thereafter.

1906–1920. During the administrations of **Pedro Montt** (1906–1911), **Ramón Barros Lucco** (1911–1915), and **Juan Luis Sanfuentes** (1915–1920) internal progress took place. The population reached 3,000,000 by 1907.

(*Cont. p. 1060.*)

c. PARAGUAY

1816–1840. José Rodríguez de Francia, perpetual dictator of Paraguay (1816) (p. 840), assumed absolute governmental authority and made himself head of the Paraguayan Church. Fearing Argentina, he isolated the country, developed a strong army, and created an intense national feeling. The power of the Church and the influence of the upper classes were broken, and Francia readily established his unlimited control over the docile Guaraní, who constituted the vast bulk of the population. Agriculture (into which state socialism was introduced) and industry were encouraged.

1844–1862. After the death of Francia the government was reorganized and commercial relations were established with other nations. Paraguayan independence was reaffirmed (1842). **Cárlos López** became president (1844) and remained in office with dictatorial powers for the remainder of his life (d. 1862). He asserted Paraguayan territorial claims against Argentina and Brazil and peacefully adjusted **disputes with the United States, France, and Great Britain.** After the fall of Rosas (1852) the danger of incorporation into Argentina disappeared. Commerce, agriculture, and industry were encouraged, and a system of primary schools was established. The first railway was constructed. The population increased to over 1,000,000.

1862–1870. Francisco Solano López, son of Cárlos López, was made president (1862) and immediately established absolute control. López desired territory and perhaps envisaged a **Greater Paraguay** which would include Uruguay and the Argentine provinces of **Corrientes** and **Entre Ríos.** He also feared Argentina and Brazil. The army was made the largest and most efficient in South America, and a system of defenses was erected.

1865–1870. The ambitions of López, Brazilian intervention in Uruguay in support of the *Colorados* while López supported the *Blancos* (p. 849), and unsettled territorial claims led to overt acts by the Paraguayan dictator that brought about **war with Brazil, Argentina, and Uruguay** under the Colorado government of Flores (Mar. 18). Brazil, Argentina, and Uruguay concluded an alliance, and a large army, of which the greatest part was Brazilian, supported by a Brazilian fleet, invaded Paraguay. After five years of large-scale operations, the Paraguayan nation, despite its valiant resistance, was virtually annihilated and the war terminated when López was killed (1870, Mar. 1). The population was reduced to some 28,000 men and slightly over 200,000 women.

After the **occupation of Asunción** by the allies (1868, Dec. 31), a provisional government was established, a treaty of peace was concluded (1870, June 20), and a centralized constitution was adopted (Nov. 25). Paraguay lost some 55,000 square miles of claimed territory, and was saved from greater losses only by Brazilian support against Argentine claims (1872–1876).

1878. Argentina and Paraguay submitted certain territorial claims to arbitration of President Hayes of the United States, who decided in favor of the latter. Heavy indemnities imposed on Paraguay by the treaty of peace were never paid, and the allies did not press for action.

1879. Attempts of Bolivia and Paraguay to adjust territorial claims failed.

1872–1912. The close of the Paraguayan War was followed by a long period of political instability. The *Colorado* or Radical Party, without clearly defined principles, was in control throughout the greater part of this period.

(*Cont. p. 1061.*)

d. URUGUAY

1828, Aug. 27. Uruguay became a sovereign nation under the treaty which terminated the war between Brazil and Argentina over the status of the **Banda Oriental.** A constitution was framed for the Banda Oriental del Uruguay, and in accord with the treaty this instrument was approved by Brazil and Argentina (1830, May 26).

1836–1843. Factional strife developed and two parties, *Blancos* and *Colorados,* evolved, headed respectively by **Manuel Oribe** and **Fructuoso Rivera.** Rosas, dictator of Argentina, with his expansionist policy (p. 849), supported Oribe, and Rivera was aided by French forces.

1843–1851. Upon withdrawal of the latter, following agreement between the French consul and Rosas, Oribe began an eight years' **siege of Montevideo.** During the period of the blockade of the Río de la Plata, French and British troops occupied Uruguayan territory as a check to Rosas (1845–1849). Efforts to resolve the situation in the Banda Oriental by negotiation were fruitless.

1851. After the conclusion of an alliance between Urquiza, the Colorado government, and Brazil (May 29), Urquiza forced Oribe to abandon the siege of Montevideo and concluded a treaty which terminated the war and permitted the Colorado government to remain in power (Oct. 8). The overthrow of Rosas (1852) removed a serious menace to Uruguayan independence.

1851. Seeking to expand its influence, **Brazil** secured a portion of the **Misiones** territory from Uruguay and intervened to maintain order at the request of the Colorado president, **Venancio Flores** (1854).

1863. Internal disorders continued and evolved into a prolonged civil war between the Blanco president, **Anastasio Aguirre,** and **Flores.** Brazil pressed claims for injuries to her nationals and when Aguirre proved intransigent an agreement was reached with Flores. Brazilian forces occupied certain Uruguayan frontier towns (1864–1865).

1865. Flores occupied Montevideo and assumed the government (Feb. 22). As **Francisco Solano López,** dictator of Paraguay, had an understanding with Aguirre, these events did much to bring on the **Paraguayan War** (pp. 848, 855), in which Uruguay under a Colorado government was allied with Brazil and Argentina (1865–1870).

1870–1872. A protracted civil conflict between Blancos and Colorados, in which the latter were victorious, followed the war.

1872–1907. Political instability, with many changes of executive, continued through the first decade of the 20th century. During this entire period the Colorados remained in power. Despite political instability, great material progress took place: agriculture became highly developed, commerce expanded, and an extensive railway system was built. The foundations of a system of public education were laid. The population, estimated at 70,000 in 1830, increased to 224,000 by 1860, and almost 1,000,000 by 1900. (*Cont. p. 1062.*)

e. BOLIVIA

1825–1826. Bolívar and **Sucre** organized the government of Bolivia and launched the nation on its career as a sovereign state. Peru recognized the independence of Bolivia (1826) and Bolivian claims to territory on the coast from Cape Sama to the Loa River (1828).

1828. Antonio José de Sucre, president after the departure of Bolívar for Colombia, was forced to withdraw as a result of discontent in Bolivia and an invasion of Peruvian troops.

1829. Andrés Santa Cruz became president, and, with the collaboration of Orbegosa of Peru, **united Bolivia and Peru** (divided into North and South Peru) into a confederation (1835–1836).

1839. Argentina and Chile opposed the creation of a preponderant confederation, and Chilean troops under Búlnes defeated the forces of Santa Cruz at **Yungay** (Jan. 20) and brought the union to an end.

1841. An attempt of **President Gamarra** of Peru to annex Bolivian territory during the presidency of **José Ballivián** was thwarted when his invading army was defeated at **Ingavi** and he himself was killed (Nov. 20).

1841–1847. Ballivián sought to promote economic development. He was forced from office by **Manuel Belzu,** who was succeeded by **Jorge Córdova** (1855).

1857. José María Linares drove Córdova from the presidency and took office. Linares introduced many governmental reforms. He was forced to relinquish office and was succeeded by **José de Achá** (1861), who was unable to preserve order and gave way to **Mariano Melgarejo** (1864).

1866. A **treaty was concluded with Chile** by which Bolivia ceded the territory between the Salado River and parallel 24° from the Andes to the Pacific and accorded economic privileges. Bolivia also recognized Brazilian claims to a large area on the Madeira and Paraguay Rivers (1867).

1870. Melgarejo was forced from office. **Agustín Morales** became president, but was killed, and **Adolfo Ballivián** took office (1872). Ballivián sought to reform finances and concluded an alliance with Peru (1873, Feb. 6).

1874–1876. During the administration of **Tomás Frías** the **boundary between Bolivia and Chile** was fixed at parallel 24° (1874). Bolivia agreed that Chileans might engage in mining industry for twenty-five years without additional taxation.

1876–1880. Hilarión Daza became president after a *coup d'état* (1876). An additonal tax was placed on nitrate exported from the Bolivian littoral (1878) and the **Chilean Nitrate Company** of Antofagasta appealed to the Chilean government. Despite negotiations Bolivia decided temporarily to rescind the contract of the nitrate company.

1879, Feb. 14. Chilean troops occupied Antofagasta and Bolivia proclaimed a state of war. Peru refused to guarantee neutrality and Chile declared war on the allies (Apr. 5).

1879–1884. WAR OF THE PACIFIC. Chilean troops, everywhere successful, occupied the entire Bolivian littoral, Tarapacá, Tacna, and Arica (1879). **Daza was overthrown** (1880) and **Narciso Campero** took office. Hostilities between Bolivia and Chile were terminated by the **treaty of Valparaiso** (1884, Apr. 4), which provided for an indefinite truce, Chilean control of Atacama for the life of the agreement, and tariff concessions by Bolivia. Bolivia thus ceded territory rich in nitrate and lost access to the sea.

1888–1892. During the period of office of **Aniceto Arce** a railway was opened between Antofagasta and Oruro, affording Bolivia access to the coast by rail.

1892–1896. Mariano Baptista succeeded Arce. Two agreements with Chile envisaging the granting to Bolivia of access to the sea sea were ratified (1895, May 18, Dec. 9), but not put in effect.

1898. Following an attempt of Conservatives to erect Sucre into a permanent capital, a **revolt headed by José Pando** occurred in La Paz (Nov. 6), which had shared the status of the seat of government with Sucre and other cities. **Pando became president** (1899).

1899. Brazilians who had entered the rubber-producing **Arce district** proclaimed a separate state (July).

1903. By the **treaty of Petropolis** (Nov. 17) Bolivia ceded the territory to Brazil and the latter undertook to provide Bolivia with rail and water outlet eastward through construction of a railway around the cataracts of the Madeira.

1904–1909. During the presidency of **Ismael Montes** education and railway construction were encouraged and finances were improved. Public worship of religions other than Roman Catholicism was permitted.

1904, Oct. 20. A **treaty between Bolivia and Chile** formally terminated the **War of the Pacific,** recognized Chilean possession of the littoral, and provided for the construction by Chile of a railway to connect Arica and La Paz, the Bolivian portion to be turned over to Bolivia fifteen years after completion. In a **supplementary protocol** (Nov. 15), **Bolivia recognized Chilean sovereignty** over the territory between parallels 23° and 24°.

1909–1913. Eleodoro Villazón promoted economic development. In the administration of Montes, again president (1913–1917), material progress continued.

1913. The **boundary between Bolivia and Argentina** was adjusted, and efforts were made to determine the limits with Paraguay.

(*Cont. p. 1062.*)

f. PERU

1825–1826. Bolívar as head of the state aided in the governmental organization of Peru and upon completion of his task departed for Colombia.

1827. José de Lamar as president adopted an expansionist policy, intervened in the affairs of Bolivia, despite recognition of Bolivian independence, and sought to annex southern Colombian provinces. Invading Peruvian troops aided in forcing Sucre to withdraw from Bolivia (1828). A Peruvian fleet took **Guayaquil** (1829, Jan. 21), but the Peruvian army of invasion was defeated by Sucre at **Tarqui** (Feb. 27) and Guayaquil was soon retaken (Feb. 28). The plans of Lamar for northern expansion were thus thwarted.

1835–1839. During civil strife, while **Luis Orbegosa** was president, **Santa Cruz** with the collaboration of Orbegosa established the Peruvian-Bolivian Confederation, which was brought to an end by the **battle of Yungay** (p. 849).

1841. Expansionist aims caused President **Agustín Gamarra** to invade Bolivia, but he was defeated and killed at **Ingavi** (Nov. 20).

1842–1845. Civil war followed, from which **Ramón Castilla** emerged as head of the state, remaining virtual dictator for fifteen years.

1845–1862. Castilla established order, sought to stabilize finances, promoted internal development, including exploitation of guano and nitrate, and adopted administrative, religious, and social reforms.

1863–1865. During the administration of **Juan Antonio Pezet** a long-standing controversy with Spain, which had not acknowledged Peruvian independence, came to the fore. After unsuccessful negotiations a **Spanish fleet seized the Chincha Islands** (1864, Apr. 14). Pezet concluded a treaty (1865, Jan. 27) by which Spain virtually recognized the independence of Peru, but which contained provisions which aroused the resentment of his countrymen. He was consequently driven from office.

1865. **Mariano Prado** became president and **declared war on Spain** (1866, Jan. 14). Alliances were concluded with Chile, Bolivia, and Ecuador. After blockading allied ports and attacking Valparaiso and Callao, the Spanish fleet abandoned hostilities (May 9). An armistice was later arranged through mediation of the United States (1871), and separate treaties of peace were signed.

1868, Jan. 7. While the war with Spain was in progress **Prado was overthrown** and **Pedro Díaz Campero** became president. He was followed by **José Balta** (1868–1872), who undertook an extensive program of internal developments, but created a serious financial situation through heavy expenditures and the contracting of large foreign loans.

1872. Balta was driven from office and murdered (July 26) and was succeded by **Manuel Pardo** (1872–1876). Education was promoted and governmental reforms were adopted. The financial situation created by Balta led to governmental bankruptcy.

1873, Feb. 6. **Peru and Bolivia concluded a secret treaty of alliance,** and when the conflict over Atacama arose between Chile and Bolivia (pp. 847, 850), Peru, under the presidency of **Mariano Prado,** unsuccessfully sought to medi-

ate. After Peru refused to proclaim neutrality, Chile declared war.

1879–1884.   WAR OF THE PACIFIC. Chile was completely victorious: Tarapacá, Tacna, and Arica were occupied, the navy gained undisputed control of the sea, and **Lima** was taken by an army landed on the coast (1879–1881). The United States sought in vain to mediate between the belligerents.

1883, Oct. 20. Chile concluded the **treaty of Ancón** with the government of **Miguel Iglesias.** By this treaty Peru ceded the nitrate province of **Tarapacá** and Chile was to remain in possession of **Tacna** and **Arica** for ten years, after which a plebiscite was to be held to determine final disposition. The war brought Peru to the verge of national collapse and a long period of attempted readjustment followed.

1885–1890. Under the administration of **Andrés Cáceres** the foreign debt was funded and assumed by the **Peruvian Corporation,** a society of bondholders, in return for the cession of railways and guano deposits for a period of sixty-six years. Attempts to adjust the question of Tacna and Arica failed, and the ten-year period elapsed without a plebiscite.

1895–1899. **Nicolás de Piérola** became president after a period of instability, and during his administration monetary reforms were initiated and unsuccessful attempts made to determine the question of Tacna and Arica.

1899–1903. Under his successor, **Eduardo de Romaña, boundary disputes with Ecuador and Brazil** developed, and **American interests** began development of the copper deposits of Cerro de Pasco. A vigorous stand was taken against possible loss of Tacna and Arica, and this was continued by succeeding presidents.

1908–1912. During the administration of **Augusto Leguía,** Chile having adopted an intransigent attitude, diplomatic relations between Peru and Chile were severed (1910, Mar. 21). While Leguía was in office Peru acknowledged Brazilian sovereignty over a portion of the Arce region and concluded a boundary treaty with Bolivia (1911), which established the basis of a permanent adjustment.   (*Cont. p. 1063.*)

g. ECUADOR

1822–1830. After the liberation of **Quito** (p. 842), the territory, in accord with the plans of Bolívar, was incorporated into Great Colombia. A movement for independence developed before the death of Bolívar.

1830, May 13. The **Republic of Ecuador** was created, with **Juan Flores** as president (1830–1835). Opposition to separation in **Guayaquil** was overcome, and by treaty **Cauca,** which had adhered to Ecuador, was restored to New

Granada and the Carchi River was declared the boundary (1832, Dec. 8). **Flores** became the leader of the Conservative element and **Vincente Rocafuerte** of the Liberal.

1834, July. After **civil war** a compromise political arrangement was reached by the two leaders.

1835–1843. During the administrations of **Rocafuerte** (1835–1839) and **Flores** (1839–1843) administrative and social reforms were adopted and material progress was fostered. Upon the re-election of Flores under a new constitution (1843, Apr. 1), Rocafuerte went into exile.

1845, Mar. 6. **Flores** was overthrown by a Liberal revolt. A period of political instability and foreign complications ensued (1845–1860).

1856, July 9. During this period a portion of the **boundary between Ecuador and New Granada** was fixed, and Peruvian naval forces blockaded Guayaquil (1860).

1860. After the revolutionist leader **Rafael Franco** had been driven from Guayaquil (Sept. 24), **Gabriel García Moreno,** an extreme conservative, who was convinced of the supremacy of the Roman Church over all earthly powers, became president (1861).

1861–1875. He dominated Ecuador until his assassination. A new constitution according wide powers to the president was promulgated (1861, Apr. 10). Moreno governed with absolute authority. Order was restored and insurrections were ruthlessly suppressed, internal improvements were carried out, and financial, military, and administrative reforms were introduced.

1862, Sept. 26. **A concordat was concluded** with the Papacy by which the Church was granted great authority, influence, and wide privileges.

1863. President **Tomás Mosquera** of New Granada (p. 853) invited Ecuadorians to overthrow Moreno, and **Flores** led an army into New Granada, but was defeated (Dec. 6). A treaty restored the *status quo.*

1865–1866. **Ecuador united with Peru and Chile against Spain** (pp. 847, 851).

1869. A new constitution granting extensive powers to the executive and assuring the position of the Church was adopted (June 9). Toward the close of his career Moreno became increasingly proclerical and Ecuador became virtually a theocracy.

1875–1895. A period of political instability, characterized by strife between Liberals, who sought to restrict the influence of the Church, and Conservatives followed the death of Moreno.

1895–1916. During the administrations of the Liberals **Eloy Alfaro** (1895–1901; 1907–1911) and **Leonidas Plaza Gutiérrez** (1901–1905;

1912–1916) relatively liberal constitutions were adopted (1897, 1906) and the authority, privileges, and influence of the Church were greatly restricted.

1904, May 6. **Ecuador recognized Brazilian claims** over territory between the **Caquetá** and **Amazón,** but efforts to adjust the boundary with Peru were but partially successful.

1908. A railway between Guayaquil and Quito was completed.

1916–1924. Comparative tranquillity existed during the second term of Plaza Gutiérrez and the **administration of Alfredo Baquerizo Moreno** (1916–1920). (*Cont. p. 1064.*)

h. COLOMBIA (NEW GRANADA)

Great Colombia as established by Bolívar comprised the viceroyalty of New Granada, the captaincy-general of Venezuela, and the presidency of Quito.

1829–1830. **Separatist movements** in Venezuela (1829–1830) and Quito (1830) brought the confederation to an end despite the efforts of Bolívar, who, the center of controversy, retired to Santa Marta and soon died (1830, Dec. 17).

1831, Nov. 17. New Granada was declared a separate state, and a centralized constitution was adopted (1832, Feb. 29). Political dissension in New Granada had developed with independence.

1832. Colonial traditions caused reactionary tendencies, the Church was powerful, and sectional rivalry and geography made difficult the attainment of unity. Two parties, almost equal in strength, arose, the Conservative, favoring a centralized administration, the Church, and class privilege, and the Liberal, advocating federalism, secularization, disestablishment, religious toleration, and extended suffrage.

1832–1837. **Francisco de Paula Santander,** a Conservative, executive while Bolívar was engaged in the liberation of Quito, Peru, and Bolivia, and president of New Granada after the disruption of Great Colombia, was confronted by forces of disunity which he was unable to control.

1837–1842. During the administration of his successor, **José de Márquez,** a period of **civil wars** began. Order was temporarily restored by **Pedro Herrán,** who followed Márquez, and a new centralized constitution was adopted (1843).

1845–1849. During the administration of **Tomás Mosquera,** a Conservative, a commercial treaty was concluded with the United States granting that government right of transit across the Isthmus of Panama and guaranteeing the neutrality of, and New Granadan sovereignty over, that area (1846, Dec. 12).

1849-1853. José López, a Liberal, succeeded Mosquera. Slavery was abolished with compensation for the owners (1851–1852) and Colombian rivers were opened to foreign commerce (1852). A liberal and federalistic constitution was adopted (1853, May 28) during the term of **José María Obando** (1853–1854), a Liberal, and laws were enacted to separate Church and State (June).

1854, Apr. As the result of a conservative movement **Obando was removed** and the vice-president, **Manuel Mallarino,** assumed office. A **railway across Panama** was completed (1855).

1855, Feb. 27. Panama was given a **federal status** by a constitutional amendment, which also provided that other provinces might establish that form.

1858. Certain provinces assumed a federal organization and, during the presidency of **Mariano Ospina** (1857–1861), a federal constitution, which failed to define the powers of the central government, was adopted (Apr. 1), the republic being designated the **Granadan Confederation.**

1860. Opposing legislation which assigned the central government certain powers in local affairs, **Mosquera,** who had become a Liberal and governor of Cauca, declared that state independent. Other states took similar action.

1861. Civil war ensued, and Mosquera occupied **Bogotá** and assumed the presidency (July 18).

1861-1863. Religious reforms were adopted, a congress proclaimed the union of seven sovereign states as the **United States of Colombia,** and a new federal constitution was promulgated (1863, May 8).

1867. Mosquera quarreled with the Liberal Party and his policies became dictatorial. He was exiled.

1867-1880. The ensuing administrations were characterized by civil war, impotent central government, disorganized finances, and increasing opposition of the Conservatives, who became a clerical and traditionalist party.

1878, May 18. A concession for ninety-nine years was granted a French company to construct **a canal across Panama.**

1880-1898. With Liberal support **Rafael Núñez** became president (1880–1882) and introduced economic reforms. After the administration of **F. J. Zaldúa** (1882–1884) **Núñez** again became president (1884). He advocated complete reorganization of the nation and became the head of a new group, the **Nationalists,** composed of Conservatives and Independents. A Liberal revolt (1885, Jan.–Aug.) was suppressed. These events marked a triumph for conservatism, centralized government, and clericalism.

1886, Aug. 4. A **centralized constitution** was adopted and a **concordat** was concluded with the Papacy (1887, Dec. 31) which accorded the Church a privileged position. **Núñez** was re-elected (1892), but the vice-president, **Miguel Caro,** actually exercised authority. Upon the death of Núñez (1894), **Caro became president.**

1898-1900. During the presidency of **Miguel Sanclemente,** a Liberal revolt occurred (1899–1900). Vice-President **José Marroquín,** a Conservative, forced Sanclemente from office (1900, July 31) and assumed authority.

1900-1903. A **prolonged civil war** ended with a victory of the Conservatives.

1902. The **French company,** headed by **Ferdinand de Lesseps,** had begun work on the canal across Panama (1881), but had become bankrupt (1891) and a new company sought to sell the assets (1902).

1903, Jan. 22. Freed from the Clayton-Bulwer treaty (p. 856), the United States and Colombia negotiated the **Hay-Herrán treaty** according to the United States canal rights and lease of territory. Colombia delayed ratification.

Nov. 3. The **Panamanian elements,** fearing choice by the United States of the alternate Nicaraguan route and assured of American support, **proclaimed an independent republic.** American warships prevented Colombian forces from landing to quell the movement, and the **United States recognized the independence of Panama** (Nov. 6). These events aroused Colombia, which was unsuccessful in an attempt to secure redress. Colombia refused to recognize the independence of Panama.

1904-1909. Rafael Reyes succeeded Marroquín and governed dictatorially. Efforts were made to reorganize the finances.

1907, Apr. 24. Colombia relinquished to **Brazil** disputed territory about the mouth of the **Caquetá River** and the headwaters of the **Río Negro.**

1909, Jan. 9. The conclusion of a **convention with the United States** which involved recognition of Panama and abrogation of the treaty of 1846 aroused resentment, and **Reyes was forced to resign** (July 8).

1910-1914. During the administration of **Carlos Restrepo** educational and governmental reforms, including minority representation in congress and the cabinet (provided for by a law of 1906), were placed in effect and efforts were made to rehabilitate the finances.

1914-1918. José Concha succeeded Restrepo.

1914, Apr. 6. The **Thomson-Urrutia treaty,** by which the United States expressed regret for the differences which had arisen with Colombia, accorded transportation privileges on the Isthmus, and agreed to pay Colombia

$25,000,000, and by which Colombia recognized the independence of Panama, was ratified by Colombia, but not by the United States senate. (*Cont. p. 1064.*)

i. VENEZUELA

1830, Sept. 22. Separatist sentiment increased rapidly in Venezuela after the creation of Great Colombia, and under the leadership of **José Páez** the state was made sovereign.

1830-1846. As president, Páez maintained order, stimulated internal development and commerce, and promulgated religious and administrative reforms. The oligarchic group which controlled Venezuela during the early period became known as the Conservative Party and about 1840 a Liberal opposition made its appearance. The Conservatives advocated a centralized system of government and the Liberals a federal.

1846-1850. **José Tadeo Monagas,** a Conservative elected with support of Páez, appointed a Liberal ministry and became involved in difficulties with congress, whereupon Páez led an unsuccessful revolt and was driven into exile (1850).

1851-1855. Under the presidency of **José Gregorio Monagas,** who succeeded his brother José Tadeo, slavery was abolished with recompense to owners (1854).

1855-1858. **José Tadeo Monagas** again became president. The issue of centralized government as opposed to federal led to civil strife.

1861, Mar. **Páez,** invited to return, became dictator.

1863-1864. The Federalists gained the ascendancy and an agreement was reached under which Páez relinquished office, a Federalist constitution was promulgated, and the leader of the Federalists, **Juan Falcón,** became president.

1870-1888. After a further period of civil war **Antonio Guzmán Blanco,** a Liberal, assumed authority and controlled Venezuela, directly or through delegates, for eighteen years. During this period he was upon several occasions absent in Europe. Internal development was encouraged, administrative and religious reforms were adopted, and two constitutions were promulgated (1874, 1881), the second of which provided for a president elected for two years by a federal council constituted of state representatives.

1889. Reaction against his rule while he was in Europe led to the elimination of Guzmán Blanco from Venezuelan affairs (Oct.).

1892. The attempt of president **Raimundo Anduza Palacio** (1890-1892) to prolong his term beyond the constitutional period led to his overthrow by **Joaquín Crespo** (June 17), who became president under a new constitution (1894).

1895-1896. A serious **boundary dispute with Great Britain** concerning the limits of British Guiana caused the United States to protest vigorously to London under the Monroe Doctrine, and, after a serious crisis had arisen, the dispute was submitted to arbitration (p. 828). The award was largely favorable to Great Britain, but Venezuelan sovereignty over territory at mouth of the Orinoco was confirmed (1899, Oct. 3).

1899. After a successful revolt (May 23–Oct.) against the successor of Crespo, **Cipriano Castro** assumed authority (Oct. 23).

1902, Dec. Claims of nationals because of injuries during revolutionary disturbances caused **Great Britain, Germany, and Italy to institute a naval blockade** of Venezuelan ports (p. 828).

1908. Refusal of Castro to give compensation for injuries to American citizens caused the **United States to suspend diplomatic relations** (June 23). Charges that political refugees were being harbored on the island of Curaçao caused Castro to dismiss the Dutch minister (July 22). The **Netherlands thereupon blockaded** Venezuelan ports (Nov. 7).

1909. While Castro was absent in Europe the vice-president, **Juan Vicente Gómez,** made himself president (Dec. 19). (*Cont. p. 1065.*)

j. BRAZIL

1822-1831. THE REIGN OF PEDRO I. Dissension and opposition arose in the constituent assembly convoked before the declaration of independence.

1823. Dom Pedro dissolved the assembly and promulgated a constitution (1824, Mar. 25).

1824, July 2. Discontent with the acts of the emperor caused the formation of the **Confederation of the Equator** by certain northern provinces, with republican intent, but this movement was suppressed (Sept. 17).

1825. **Opposition to Brazilian rule** had never disappeared from the **Cisplatine Province** (Banda Oriental), and Argentina desired its incorporation.

1825-1828. War between Brazil and Argentina resulted from an independence movement in the Banda Oriental (1825) and the desire of Argentina to annex that territory. Brazil was decisively defeated in the **battle of Ituzaingo** (1827, Feb. 20). Through the mediation of Great Britain the Banda Oriental, or **Uruguay,** became independent (1828, Aug. 27).

Opposition to Pedro I arose from his autocratic tendencies, his preference for Portuguese advisers, and, most important, his attempts to secure his daughter, **Maria da Gloria,** on the Portuguese throne and his consequent interest in the affairs of Portugal. The loss of the Cisplatine Province increased his unpopularity.

1831, Apr. 7. In face of this opposition he was forced to abdicate in favor of his five-year-old son, **Pedro de Alcántara, Pedro II.**

1831-1840. The regency. During this period anarchy reigned because of factional quarrels and provincial revolts, the most serious of which was a separatist movement in **Rio Grande do Sul** (1835-1845). To re-establish direct monarchical government Pedro II was proclaimed of age (1840).

1840-1889. THE REIGN OF PEDRO II. The provincial revolts were brought to a close and a period of order and progress was initiated, control alternating constitutionally between the Liberal and Conservative Parties.

Great **material progress** took place after 1850. Agriculture, commerce, and industry expanded, railway construction, encouraged by the government, was carried on (about 650 miles in 1870 and over 6000 miles in 1889). Coffee production greatly increased, stock-raising remained important in the south, and sugar production in the north. Rubber production in the Amazon basin became important after 1880. In 1850 the estimated population was 8,000,000, including 2,500,000 slaves; in 1872 over 10,000,000, including 1,500,000 slaves; and in 1889 over 14,000,000.

In **foreign affairs,** Brazil sought to extend her influence to the west and southwest. She intervened in the affairs of Uruguay, opposed the expansionist policies of Rosas, dictator of Argentina, and aided in his overthrow (1851-1852) (p. 845), and, allied with Argentina and Uruguay, conducted a major **war against Paraguay** (1865-1870) (p. 848). During this period Brazilian prestige increased greatly.

1870-1888. A movement for **emancipation of Negro slaves** developed rapidly after 1850. After the enactment of a law stipulating that children of slaves should be free (the **Río Branco Law,** 1871), after the freeing of slaves by the provinces of Ceará and Amazonas, and the freeing of all slaves of over sixty years (1885), a Liberal ministry provided for **complete emancipation** with no recompense for owners (1888, May 13).

1870. Republicanism, originally a movement of intellectuals, at first spread gradually. A Republican Party was formed (1870). The movement grew rapidly. The monarchy was gradually undermined by a number of forces: the dissatisfaction of the army with the peaceful policies of Pedro II after 1870, friction with the clergy, the rapid growth of republicanism,

the alienation of the landed aristocracy through the emancipation of the slaves, the virtual extinction of provincial autonomy, and the unpopularity of the French husband of Princess Isabella, Gaston d'Orléans, Comte d'Eu.

1889, Nov. 15. The army, headed by General **Manoel Deodoro da Fonseca,** revolted and **deposed the emperor.** A republic was immediately proclaimed and a provisional government was established.

CULTURAL DEVELOPMENTS

The contribution of Brazil to the cultural development of Latin America in this period is characterized by the foundation of such institutions as the National Library (1808); the Brazilian Historical Geographical Society (1838), the oldest natural history society in the western hemisphere; the Rio de Janeiro conservatory of music (1841); and the National Academy of Fine Arts, founded in the reign of Dom Pedro II.

Two Brazilian composers also gained renown in the 19th century: Carlos Gomes (1839-1896) and Alberto Nepomuceno (1846-1920).

1889- THE REPUBLIC. During this period trade, cattle-raising, mining, agriculture, and forestry were greatly expanded and there was some development of manufacturing (cotton textiles). Railway mileage increased greatly. Coffee production came by 1925 to comprise four-fifths of the world supply. Overproduction of coffee led São Paulo, Rio de Janeiro, and Minas Geraes in 1906-1907 and the central government somewhat later to establish a valorization system. Rubber production reached its height in 1910, after which it declined, because of the introduction of plantation systems in the East Indies. The problems of coffee and rubber production played an important part in creating economic difficulties.

The **population** in 1920 reached a total of over 30,000,000, and in 1935 of over 47,500,000. During this period there was extensive **immigration,** especially of Spaniards and Italians.

The proper functioning of the national government under the republic was, from the very beginning, rendered difficult by the existence of **illiteracy** (estimated at 80 per cent in 1910 and at 75 per cent in 1920), by **political inexperience** and intolerance, by the absence of real political parties, and by the prevalent tendency toward **military rule.** The southern states, especially São Paulo and Minas Geraes, sought to control the country. Presidential candidates were chosen by caucuses representing controlling political groups of the more important states.

1891, Feb. 24. A constitution which provided

for a federal republic, the **United States of Brazil,** a president elected for four years, a bicameral legislature, and the separation of Church and State was promulgated, and **Deodoro da Fonseca** was elected president.

Nov. 23. The dictatorial policies of the president caused a naval revolt and he was forced from office. Vice-President **Floriano Peixoto** assumed authority and governed arbitrarily.

1893–1895. A **rebellion** occurred in **Rio Grande do Sul,** and the navy revolted under **Admiral Custodio de Mello,** but the movements were suppressed after serious fighting.

1894–1910. Presidents **Moraes Barros** (1894–1898), **Manoel de Campos Salles** (1898–1902), **Rodriquez Alves** (1902–1906), **Affonso Penna** (1906–1909), and **Nilo Peçanha** (1909–1910) sought to stabilize finances, secured loans, and adopted fiscal reforms. **Boundary controversies** with Argentina (1895), France (1900), Bolivia (1903), Britain (1904), and Holland (1906) were adjusted by arbitration or direct negotiations.

1910–1920. The political campaign of 1910 was of unusual significance because it involved the question of militarism in politics. **Hermes da Fonseca,** the candidate of the conservative and army elements, was elected and governed arbitrarily. A financial crisis resulting from a drop in the prices of rubber and coffee and the resultant need of unity caused the withdrawal of the anti-militarist candidate in the campaign of 1914, and **Wenceslau Braz** was elected.

(*Cont. p. 1066.*)

k. PANAMA AND THE PANAMA CANAL ZONE

Prior to the revolution of 1903, Panama was part of Colombia. The district had long been of interest because of the numerous **projects for an interoceanic canal** which were put forward from time to time from the 16th century onward. Schemes of this kind, involving complicated engineering problems, became practicable only in the later 19th century.

1850, Apr. 19. CLAYTON-BULWER TREATY, between Great Britain and the United States, by which both powers agreed not to obtain or maintain any exclusive control of a proposed canal, and guaranteed its neutrality.

1878, May 18. The Colombian government granted a French company under **Ferdinand de Lesseps** exclusive rights to construct a canal. The French **Panama Canal Company** was organized August 17, 1879, and began construction of a sea-level canal (Jan. 1, 1880). The company failed in 1889 and a second company was

organized in 1894. Work continued until 1899.

1899, June 10. The United States congress appointed a **canal commission** to report on possible routes through Panama.

1900, Feb. 5. The **first Hay-Pauncefote treaty,** between Great Britain and the United States. This treaty, by which Britain renounced the right to joint construction and ownership, was rejected by parliament.

1901, Nov. 18. SECOND HAY-PAUNCEFOTE TREATY, giving the United States sole right of construction, maintenance, and control.

1903, Jan. 22. Hay-Herrán Treaty, between the United States and Colombia, providing for the acquisition by the United States of a canal zone. The senate of Colombia failed to ratify this treaty.

Nov. 3. **REVOLUTION IN PANAMA; independence from Colombia** (p. 853).

Nov. 18. **HAY-BUNAU-VARILLA TREATY** between the United States and the new Panaman government: Panama granted the United States in perpetuity the use of a zone five miles wide on either side of the future canal, with full jurisdiction. The United States guaranteed the neutrality of the canal, in return for the right to fortify it. The United States paid $10,000,000 and thereafter paid $250,000 annually. The treaty was ratified February 26, 1904.

1904, Feb. 13. Adoption of the Panaman constitution; president, unicameral legislature, etc. The constitution also stipulated that if by treaty the United States guaranteed the independence and sovereignty of Panama, that power should also have the right to intervene to maintain order.

1904–1908. Manuel Amador Guerrero, first president of the republic.

1904, Apr. 23. The United States acquired the property of the French canal company for $40,000,000. At this time American engineering opinion still favored a sea-level canal.

1906, Feb. 5. The Isthmian Canal Commission reported in favor of a lock canal. On June 29 the United States congress passed an act providing for such a canal.

1907, Apr. 1. Lieut.-Col. George W. Goethals appointed chief engineer.

1914, Aug. 15. THE PANAMA CANAL WAS OPENED. Its use during the first years was limited, because of constant landslides. The official and formal opening was postponed until July 12, 1920.

Sept. 2. The **boundaries of the Canal Zone** were defined and further rights of protection were conceded to the United States by treaty.

(*Cont. p. 1067.*)

1. CENTRAL AMERICA

(1) General

1824, Nov. 22. After separation from Mexico (p. 843) the assembly of the **United Provinces of Central America** promulgated a federal constitution and **Manuel José Arce** was elected president. Guatemala City was made the capital. A Conservative Party (Servile), favoring centralized government and the Church, and a Liberal, advocating the existing federalism and reform, developed.

1826. Discontent with the preponderance of Guatemala, dissension concerning religious questions, and political discord soon developed, and **civil war** ensued. Arce supported the Conservatives and **Francisco Morazán** became the Liberal leader.

1829. Morazán was victorious, occupied Guatemala City (Apr. 12), and became dictator, later assuming the presidency (1830).

1829-1835. Anti-clerical reforms were adopted, control of the Church was assumed, religious freedom was established, measures were taken against Spaniards and members of religious orders, and the capital was transferred to Salvador.

1837-1838. Political and religious tension led to **civil strife,** and **Rafael Carrera,** of mixed blood, placed himself at the head of the revolt, gaining clerical support.

1839-1840. The **Liberals were defeated** and Morazán was forced into exile. Congress meanwhile had adjourned, and with the defeat of Morazán the confederation dissolved into its component states: **El Salvador, Honduras, Nicaragua,** and **Costa Rica.**

1840-1865. **Carrera** became **dictator of Guatemala,** in which he established an extremely conservative régime, and dominated a large part of Central America.

1842-1852. **Honduras, Nicaragua,** and **El Salvador** formed a short-lived union (1842-1844), El Salvador and Guatemala sought to establish co-operation (1845), Honduras, El Salvador, and Nicaragua attempted to form a union (1847), and Honduras, Nicaragua, and El Salvador formed a confederation which was to include Costa Rica and Guatemala (1849-1852), but no permanent results were achieved because of friction or open hostilities.

1855-1862. An attempt by **William Walker,** an American, to establish control over Nicaragua (which he achieved for a short period) and perhaps extend his authority over a wider area, produced political and military co-operation between the Central American states. As a result of this and the antagonism of **Cornelius Vanderbilt,** who desired control of the transit route across Nicaragua, which became important after acquisition of California by the United States, **Walker was defeated** (1855-1860).

1862. **Nicaragua,** supported by Honduras and Salvador, sought to form a Central American union, but with no results.

1876-1885. **Justo Rufino Barrios,** president of Guatemala, attempted without success to form a union (1876). Later he sought to establish a confederation by force. Honduras alone supported Rufino Barrios, while Costa Rica, Nicaragua, and El Salvador placed forces in the field to oppose him. **Barrios invaded Salvador,** but was defeated and killed at **Chalchuapa** (1885, Apr. 2).

1886-1887. Upon the initiative of Guatemala the Central American states framed a constitution and concluded a **treaty of peace and amity.**

1888-1889. Under this organization congresses met at **San José, Costa Rica,** and **San Salvador.** Definite union was decided upon by the latter congress, but controversy between Guatemala and Salvador prevented consummation.

1895-1898. Representatives of Nicaragua, El Salvador, and Honduras at **Amapala** concluded a **treaty of union** which created a governing commission (1895, June 20). A constitution for a confederation, the **Greater Republic of Central America,** was framed and an executive council met, but opposition in El Salvador brought the union to an end (1898, Nov. 25).

1893-1909. **President José Santos Zelaya** of Nicaragua appears to have projected the establishment of a confederation by force.

1907. In a **war with Honduras** he placed a president of his choice in power in that country and openly aided a **revolution in El Salvador.** Zelaya prepared to invade El Salvador, which was supported by Guatemala, and a general war threatened. In this situation, through the mediation of the United States and Mexico, a **conference of Central American states** to promote peace, unity, and eventual federation was held in Washington (Nov. 13-Dec. 20). Treaties were concluded providing for unification of currency, communications, tariffs, and similar matters, non-interference in internal affairs, neutralization of Honduras, and the creation of a Central American court of justice to determine all disputes. Honduras proposed confederation, but without result. The court of justice was established at Cartago (1908). When Nicaragua ignored its adverse decisions concerning the conclusion of the Bryan-Chamorro canal treaty between that country and the United States, the court lost influence and provision for its continuance was not made.

(2) Territorial Adjustments

1823–   **Great Britain** maintained a **protectorate over the Mosquito Indians** of Nicaragua and Honduras, acquired during the colonial period, and the British from **Belize** expanded southward. Desiring a weak Central America, Great Britain was opposed to reunion after dissolution of the confederation.

1841. The **Bay Islands,** occupied by British, were placed under jurisdiction of the superintendent of Belize, and claim was laid to the mouth of the San Juan River.

1848. After acquisition of California by the United States, and with the prospect of canal construction, Great Britain took possession of the mouth of the **San Juan River** in the name of the ruler of the Mosquito Indians.

1850, Apr. 19. Opposition of the United States to British domination of a canal route across the Isthmus led to the conclusion of the **Clayton-Bulwer treaty,** by which the United States and Great Britain agreed to neutralization of the proposed canal and pledged not to occupy or exercise sovereignty over any part of Central America. Britain at first refused to withdraw from the Bay Islands and the Mosquito Coast under this treaty, but eventually agreed to do so upon vigorous American representations.

1859, Nov. 28. A **treaty between Great Britain and Honduras** gave the latter control of the appropriate portion of the Mosquito Coast and recognized the sovereignty of Honduras over the Bay Islands.

1860, Jan. 28. Great Britain recognized Nicaraguan sovereignty over the Mosquito territory within its boundaries by a similar treaty, although Nicaragua did not gain full control until the presidency of Zelaya (1894).

1859, Apr. 30. A **treaty between Guatemala and Great Britain** fixed the southern limits of Belize.

(3) Nicaragua

1909. The **United States opposed President José Santos Zelaya** of Nicaragua because of his bellicose policies and interference in other states (p. 829), and American pressure together with a Conservative revolt forced him from office (1909, Dec. 16).

1911, June 6. As Nicaraguan finances were unsatisfactory, a treaty was concluded between the **United States and Nicaragua** providing for a loan to be secured by customs, these customs to be collected by a collector-general approved by the United States. **President Taft** appointed

a commissioner-general and created a claims commission, and loans were extended. The United States senate refused to ratify the treaty, and loans were thereupon restricted.

1912. Upon the outbreak of **civil war** (July) the United States intervened to protect the Conservative government. An election was held under supervision of American forces and **Adolfo Díaz,** a Conservative, was elected (Nov.). A legation guard of American marines was established at Managua. (*Cont. p. 1068.*)

(4) Honduras

1907, Feb.–Dec. **War between Honduras and Nicaragua.** The Hondurans were defeated and the capital occupied by President Zelaya of Nicaragua. **President Bonilla** of Honduras captured. He was replaced by **Gen. Miguel Dávila.**

1909, Dec. **Outbreak of a revolt** against Dávila, led by former President Bonilla. The ensuing civil war lasted until 1911.

1911, Feb. 8. **Armistice:** both factions agreed to abide by the forthcoming elections.

     Oct. 29. **Bonilla elected president.**

1912, Jan. 9. **American marines landed** in Honduras to protect American property.

1913, Mar. 21. **Death of Bonilla.** He was succeeded by the vice-president, **Francisco Bertrand.** (*Cont. p. 1069.*)

m. MEXICO

1823, Mar. 19. **AGUSTÍN I** (p. 843), confronted by financial difficulty and political discontent, was forced from the throne by a revolt of which one of the leaders was **Antonio López de Santa Anna.**

1824, Oct. 4. A federal republic was established and **Guadalupe Victoria** was made president. Controversy arose between Liberal and Conservative elements, and upon the conclusion of the term of Guadalupe Victoria (1828) a period of disorder was initiated.

1829. During this period, while **Vicente Guerrero** was in office, a Spanish expedition from Cuba took **Tampico** (Aug. 18), but was forced to capitulate (Sept. 11).

1833, Apr. 1. **Santa Anna** was elected president by the Liberals and for over twenty years dominated Mexican affairs directly or indirectly. Santa Anna alternated in office with Vice-President **Valentín Gómez Farías** (1833–1834), who undertook political and religious reforms. Gómez Farías was driven from office by Santa Anna (1834, Apr. 24).

1835, Dec. 15. A highly **centralized government** was established.

1836, Mar. 2. Americans who had colonized **Texas** opposed direct Mexican control, **pro-**

claimed a republic, and maintained their independence, defeating and capturing Santa Anna at **San Jacinto** (Apr. 21).

1838, Apr. 16. In enforcement of claims a **French expedition** occupied **Vera Cruz** and withdrew when Mexico agreed to indemnities (1839, Mar. 9).

1841, Oct. 10. After further civil strife **Santa Anna** again assumed **dictatorial power** and promulgated a highly centralized constitution (1843, June 12).

1844. A revolt forced him into temporary exile (1845).

1846–1848. THE EXPANSIONIST POLICY OF THE UNITED STATES. Boundary disputes, the question of Texas, and unsettled claims had created strained relations between the United States and Mexico, and the annexation of Texas by the United States (1845, Mar. 1) led to **war between the two nations** (p. 814). Mexico was totally defeated, and its capital occupied (1847, Sept. 14).

1848, Feb. 2. By the **treaty of Guadalupe Hidalgo,** Mexico ceded **Upper California, New Mexico,** and the northern portions of **Sonora, Coahuila,** and **Tamaulipas,** the United States paying $15,000,000 and assuming payment of claims against the Mexican government.

1848–1853. Following the war Presidents **José Joaquín de Herrera** and **Mariano Arista** sought unsuccessfully to rehabilitate finances and restore order.

1853. Santa Anna again became president and established a dictatorship which tended toward monarchy. A Liberal revolt drove him from office and ended his control of Mexican affairs (1855, Aug. 9).

1855. A program of **religious and political reform** was undertaken by the Liberal government, including an attempt to release from mortmain the great holdings of the Church (**Ley Juarez,** Nov. 23), and a federal constitution was adopted (1857, Feb. 5).

1857–1860. These reforms led to civil war between Conservatives and Liberals, the **War of the Reform.**

1858. The Liberal government, with **Benito Juárez** as president, established its capital at **Vera Cruz** (May 4), being recognized by the United States (1859, Apr. 6). The Conservative capital was Mexico City. Laws providing for separation of Church and State, confiscation of ecclesiastical property except churches, and suppression of religious orders were promulgated by the Liberal government.

1860, Dec. 22. The **Liberal forces triumphed** in the field and Juárez placed the reform laws in effect throughout Mexico. The war disorganized Mexican finances and created friction with other powers.

1861. Upon suspension of payment on foreign debts by the Mexican government (May 29, July 17), **France, Great Britain, and Spain,** by the **treaty of London** (Oct. 31) undertook joint intervention to protect their interests. Napoleon III desired to create in Mexico a Catholic empire under French hegemony, which would provide markets and raw materials and check the expansion of the United States. French designs, supported by Mexican reactionaries, became clear after **allied occupation of Vera Cruz** (Dec. 17), and Spain and Great Britain withdrew (1862, Apr. 8).

1863. French troops occupied Mexico City (June 7), and the **Archduke Maximilian of Austria** was made **emperor** (1864, Apr. 10). The Mexican Liberal government continued resistance and the liberal policies of Maximilian alienated certain conservative elements.

1865–1867. After the close of the Civil War the United States (which refused to recognize Maximilian and supported Juárez) insistently demanded withdrawal of French troops, as the Monroe Doctrine was definitely involved. In view of the attitude of the United States and the delicate European situation, **Napoleon III withdrew** support from Maximilian (1867, Mar. 12).

1867, May 14. The emperor was forced to **capitulate at Querétaro,** and was executed (June 19). **Juárez** restored order, and was re-elected to the presidency (Dec. 19).

1872. Upon the death of Juárez, **Sebastián Lerdo de Tejada** became president. Constitutional amendments were enacted to safeguard the liberal reforms earlier adopted (1873, May 29).

1876. **Porfirio Díaz** overthrew Lerdo de Tejada (Nov. 20) and became president (1877, May 2).

1876–1911. DIAZ CONTROLLED MEXICO with absolute authority until 1911, remaining in office constantly with the exception of the period 1880–1884. Under Díaz order was established, Mexican prestige was raised, finances were stabilized, and vast material progress was achieved. Railways were built, public works were promoted, industry was developed, and commerce increased. Much foreign capital, especially American, was invested. A mining code was promulgated which, contrary to Spanish law, provided that title to land carried ownership of subsoil products (1884, Nov. 22). A census of 1895 indicated a population of 12,500,000 and that of 1910 a population of 15,150,000 (1,150,000 white; 8,000,000 mestizos; 6,000,000 Indians). The government of Díaz favored the upper classes. Lands of the Indians and mestizos and communal lands (*ejidos*) were permitted to come into possession of large landowners. Concessions to foreigners acted to the detriment of the Mexican middle class, exploitation of the working classes was general, and peonage developed. Education was neglected and Mexicans, with the exception of a small group, were denied participation in government. By 1910 all elements of political and social revolt had developed.

1911, May 25. **Díaz was overthrown** by a movement begun in 1910 and headed by **Francisco Madero,** who became president (Nov. 6), and an era of revolution was initiated. Madero, whose objectives were largely political, had an imperfect understanding of the fundamental issues involved and the forces he unleashed soon passed beyond his control.

1913, Feb. 18. Madero was overthrown by **Victoriano Huerta** and shot (Feb. 22). **Venustiano Carranza** headed a movement against Huerta, whom the United States refused to recognize.

1914, Apr. 21. As a result of overt acts, **United States forces occupied Vera Cruz,** and war was narrowly averted.

July 15. **Huerta** was forced from office by Carranza. Civil war soon broke out between the latter and his lieutenant, **Francisco Villa,** and complete disorder followed.

1915, Oct. 19. The United States and eight other American nations recognized Carranza as *de facto* president.

1915-1916. Injury to life and property of foreigners created a delicate international situation and a demand for intervention arose in the United States.

1916, Mar. 9. A raid by Villa on Columbus, New Mexico, caused the United States to dispatch **punitive expeditions** into Mexico under **Gen. John J. Pershing** (Mar. 15). Carranza opposed this action.

1917, Feb. 5. American troops were withdrawn after having failed in their objective. These developments greatly stimulated Mexican anti-interventionist sentiment. The Carranza government was sympathetic to Germany during the World War. (*Cont. p. 1069.*)

n. THE WEST INDIES

(1) Cuba

During the wars of liberation **Cuba** and **Puerto Rico** remained loyal to Spain and served as bases of operations for Spanish forces. Many royalists from revolutionary areas established themselves in Cuba. Arbitrary government and an economic policy which reacted detrimentally upon the expanding Cuban sugar industry over a long period created discontent among Cubans.

1868-1878. The **TEN YEARS' WAR** ensued when reforms were not adopted by the Spanish government (p. 696). This revolt, in which the Cubans had the sympathy of the United States (which had earlier sought to purchase Cuba for strategic reasons), was terminated by the **convention of El Zanjón** (1878, Feb. 10), by which Spain promised administrative reforms. The spirit of the convention of El Zanjón was not observed by Spain, although slavery was eventually abolished (1880, 1886).

1895-1898. Political and economic unrest and a desire for independence led to a new **revolutionary movement** (Feb. 24, 1895). The Cubans were supported by American opinion, which was further aroused by the ruthless measures adopted by the Spanish authorities.

1897, Nov. 25. The Liberal Spanish premier, **Práxedes Sagasta,** offered the Cubans a large measure of self-government, but they were determined upon complete independence.

1898. THE SPANISH-AMERICAN WAR. The Cuban situation rapidly became a direct issue between the United States and Spain, which, after the **destruction of the** *U.S.S. Maine* in Havana harbor (Feb. 15), led to war (Apr. 25). Spain was decisively defeated (p. 827). By the **treaty of Paris** (Dec. 10), which terminated the war, Spain relinquished sovereignty over **Cuba** and ceded **Puerto Rico** to the United States, and the United States undertook to maintain order in Cuba during the period of occupation. Thus ended Spanish dominion in the Americas.

1899-1900. Upon termination of the Spanish-American War **Gen. John R. Brooke** as military governor promulgated administrative reforms. **Gen. Leonard Wood** succeeded Brooke (Dec. 13) and under his direction the civil government was organized, steps were taken to establish a Cuban administration, sanitation and public health measures were initiated (notable among them efforts which led to eradication of yellow fever), legal reforms were instituted, schools were standardized, municipal elections were held, and elections for a constituent assembly were called.

1901, Feb. 21. The **constituent assembly** adopted a **constitution,** providing for a president and bicameral congress, into which, at the insistence of the United States, was inserted the **Platt Amendment** (June 12) to the American army appropriation bill. This provided that Cuba might not enter into any treaty with a foreign power which impaired her sovereignty, that excessive foreign debts might not be contracted, that the United States might intervene to maintain Cuban independence and a government capable of preserving life, property, and personal liberty, and that lands be leased to the United States as coaling stations.

1902-1906.   Tomás Estrada Palma was chosen president and continued the policies initiated by Wood. American forces were withdrawn. A Liberal Party formed in opposition to Estrada Palma, who became leader of conservative elements.

1906. A **Liberal revolt** (August) followed the re-election of Estrada Palma and upon his appeal President Theodore Roosevelt dispatched **William H. Taft** and **Robert Bacon** to adjust the situation. They were unable to do so and Estrada Palma resigned (Sept. 25). As congress was unable to agree upon a successor, Taft established a provisional government and American forces occupied the island. **Charles E. Magoon** succeeded Taft (Oct. 3). Order was re-established, electoral reforms were adopted, and further public improvements were carried out (1906-1908).

1908, Nov. 14.   Elections were held and **José Miguel Gómez,** a Liberal, became president (1909-1913), whereupon Magoon and the occupation forces were withdrawn (1909, Feb. 1). But the Liberal Party divided into factions and disorders occurred (1912) which brought threat of American intervention. Increasing opposition to the Platt Amendment developed.

1913-1917. Presidency of the Conservative **Mario García Menocal.**

1916-1917. The elections of 1916, in which Menocal was opposed by the Liberal **Alfredo Zayas,** were disputed, and the Liberals, led by ex-President Gómez, revolted (1917, Feb. 9). The United States proclaimed that a government established by force would not be recognized and American forces were landed at Santiago (Mar. 8). **Gómez** was defeated and **Menocal** took office (May 20). (*Cont. p. 1072.*)

(2) Puerto Rico

Puerto Rico was discovered by Columbus on his second voyage (1493) and colonization was begun in 1506. During the period of Spanish rule it was several times attacked (by the English under Lord George Clifford, 1598; by the Dutch, 1625; by the English under Abercromby, 1797). Slavery was abolished in 1873, after which a number of reforms were promulgated. In 1897 the Spanish government introduced an autonomous régime.

1898, May 12. During the Spanish-American War, **Admiral William Sampson** appeared off San Juan and landed troops (July 25). Fighting continued until August 13.

   Oct. 18.   Gen. John R. Brooke took possession for the United States. A military government was established.

   Dec. 10. By the **treaty of peace** Spain ceded the island to the United States. Under the leadership of **Eugenio M. de Hostos,** agitation for "self-determination" began at once.

1899, Jan. An insular police force replaced the Spanish civil guard. This "state constabulary" constituted the sole police force after 1902: some 800 men preserved order for a population of 1,000,000.

   Mar. 24. A Puerto Rican regiment was organized to serve as garrison. It was composed entirely of white inhabitants. In 1918 it served as part of the garrison of Panama. In 1920 it became the 65th Infantry, U.S. Army.

   Aug. 8.   San Ciriaco hurricane, the most destructive in the history of the island; 3369 persons killed; coffee plantations destroyed.

1900, Apr. 12.   Foraker Act, by which Congress established civil government for the island and introduced free trade with the United States.

1901, May 27, Dec. 2. The United States supreme court decided (*De Lima* v. *Bidwell*) that Puerto Ricans were not, *ipso facto,* United States citizens.

   Features and results of civil government: Manhood suffrage was established and proved a stimulant to popular education. Duties collected in Puerto Rico on foreign products were devoted to island affairs. The foreign trade increased between 1900 and 1924 from $16,602,004 to $177,650,164. A corresponding increase of population took place, from 952,243 in 1898 to 1,299,809 in 1920, of which 948,709 were whites. During the American period there was a rapid extension of the school system, and a reduction of illiteracy from 90 per cent to less than 50 per cent. There was also much progress in sanitation, the death rate falling from 41 per 1000 in 1898 to 18.6 in 1922. Less commendable was the gradual concentration of wealth in fewer hands. Small holdings decreased by more than 30 per cent.

1909. Two half-mile tunnels were opened through the mountains, providing irrigation for the south side of the island, which is a trade-wind desert.

   Growing agitation, under the leadership of **Luis Muñoz Rivera,** for the extension of American citizenship to Puerto Ricans.

(*Cont. p. 1073.*)

(3) The Dominican Republic

1808-1809. A **revolt in Santo Domingo,** aided by British naval forces, established freedom from Haiti and France.

1814. Santo Domingo was again assigned to Spain by the treaty of Paris.

1821, Dec. 1.   Santo Domingo proclaimed independence following the action of other Spanish colonies, and unsuccessfully sought incorporation with Colombia.

1822.   Haiti under President Jean Boyer **conquered Santo Domingo,** which remained incorporated until independence was established by a revolution (1844, Feb. 27).

1861, Mar. 18. Because of internal disorder and fear of conquest by Haiti, **Santo Domingo** at its own request was **annexed to Spain.**

1865, May 1. A nationalist revolution caused **Spain to relinquish sovereignty.**

1868–1870. An effort to secure **annexation to the United States failed** when the United States senate refused approval.

1882–1899. During the presidency of **Ulises Heureaux** comparative tranquillity and prosperity existed, although heavy debts were contracted abroad.

1899–1904. After a period of turbulence, the government was bankrupt. Heavy loans had been contracted abroad and the possibility of intervention by European powers existed.

1905. Concerned as to the Monroe Doctrine, President Theodore Roosevelt, after rejection by the senate of a treaty providing for supervision of Dominican finances, arranged by a *modus vivendi* for administration of Dominican customs and appointed a customs receiver (Mar. 31).

1907, Feb. 8. A treaty was later concluded by which the United States was accorded control of customs for fifty years. Under American control Dominican finances were rehabilitated. Loans were floated in New York to aid stabilization.

1916, May. Despite supervision of elections by the United States, disorder developed and **American naval forces were landed** to preserve order. As the result of the refusal of the provisional president, **Francisco Henríquez y Carvajal,** to sign a new treaty providing American financial control, the United States withheld customs revenues. (*Cont. p. 1073.*)

(4) Haiti

1697. In the 17th century the French gained control of the western extremity of **Española,** Saint-Domingue, or Haiti, and by the **treaty of Ryswick** Spain ceded the western part of the island to France. **Saint-Domingue** became a prosperous plantation colony.

1795. In the **treaty of Basel** Spain ceded the eastern part of Española to France. At this time the population of Saint-Domingue consisted of some 40,000 whites, 28,000 freedmen, and 500,000 Negro slaves.

1794, May 6. The mulattoes and Negroes, desiring equal rights and independence, during the French Revolution revolted, and under leadership of **Toussaint L'Ouverture, Jean-Jacques Dessalines,** and **Henri Christophe** achieved independence after forcing capitulation of a large French army dispatched by Napoleon (1804, Jan. 1). All slaves were freed. The whites were either killed or forced to flee during the revolution.

1804, Dec. 8. Dessalines made himself emperor, Jacques I. After his assassination (Oct. 17, 1806) **Christophe proclaimed himself king** of all Haiti, as **Henri I** (1811), though the southern part was controlled by **Alexandre Pétion** as president of a republic. A long civil war ended with the death of Pétion (1818).

1818, Mar. 20. Jean Pierre Boyer succeeded Pétion as president and, on the **suicide of Christophe** (1820) established control of all Haiti.

1822. Santo Domingo, which had again come under control of Spain (1814), was conquered by Boyer and the island was united as the **republic of Haiti,** to which France accorded recognition (1838, Feb. 12).

1843, Mar. 13. Boyer was forced from office.

1844, Feb. 27. Santo Domingo established its independence through a revolution.

1847. Faustin Soulouque became president and soon proclaimed himself **Faustin I** (1849).

1859, Jan. 15. After oppressive rule he was overthrown and **Fabre Geffrard** assumed power. Fabre Geffrard governed for eight years before being forced from office (1867).

1867– . An **era of instability** followed. Haitian finances became disorganized and obligations were contracted abroad.

1914, June 14. France and Germany demanded control of Haitian customs to secure payment, and the United States, with interests in Haiti, also desired control.

1915, July 3. After a series of disorders the **United States landed forces** to restore order. Under American supervision **Philippe Dartiguenave** was named president (Aug. 12). A treaty was concluded by which the United States established a political and financial protectorate for ten years (Sept. 16). This was later renewed for a second ten-year period to end in 1936. (*Cont. p. 1072.*)

I. AFRICA

1. GENERAL: EXPLORATION, 1795–1895

(From p. 564)

1795–1796. **MUNGO PARK** explored the **Gambia** and reached the **Niger** at Segu, finally establishing the fact that the great river flowed east.

1798–1799. The Portuguese **Francisco de Lacerda** traveled from Tete on the Zambezi northward to **Lake Mweru.**

1801. **Pieter Jan Truter** and **William Somerville** explored **Bechuanaland** and penetrated the interior almost as far as **Lake Ngami.**

1802–1811. The Portuguese, **Pedro Baptista** and **A. José, crossed the continent** from Angola to Tete on the Zambezi.

1805. **MUNGO PARK EXPLORED THE NIGER** as far as the **Bussa Rapids,** where he was drowned.

1807, 1811. **The British government abolished the slave trade.**

1812–1814. A Swiss, **Johann L. Burckhardt,** advanced up the **Nile** and crossed to the Red Sea.

1815. **France abolished the slave trade.** Other countries (notably Spain and Portugal) followed suit.

1818. **Gaspard Mollien** discovered the **sources of the Gambia** and **Senegal.**

1822–1825. **Walter Oudney, Dixon Denham,** and **Hugh Clapperton** journeyed from Tripoli across the desert to **Lake Chad** and thence westward to the **Niger,** proving that the river had no connection with the lake.

1825. **Alexander G. Laing** crossed the desert from Tripoli to **Tuat** and thence to **Timbuktu,** the first modern to visit the latter city.

1827. **René Caillé** reached **Timbuktu** from French Guinea and proceeded thence to Fez.

1827. **Linant de Bellefonds** ascended the **Nile** to lat. 13° 6′ N.L.

1830–1834. **Richard Lander** explored the **lower Niger** from Bussa to the sea.

1831–1833. **Edouard Rüppell** explored northern **Ethiopia.**

1837–1848. Extensive researches of **Antoine T. d'Abbadie** in Ethiopia.

1839. An **Egyptian force,** accompanied by **G. Thibaud,** ascended the **Nile** to lat. 6° 30′ N.L.

1840–1843. **Charles T. Beke** mapped much of **Ethiopia.**

1848–1863. **John Petherick** carried on extensive investigations in the **Niam-Niam country.**

1849. **DAVID LIVINGSTONE** crossed the Kalahari Desert and advanced to **Lake Ngami,** returning (1850) to the upper Zambezi.

1849–1853. **Heinrich Barth** and **Adolf Overweg** crossed from Tripoli to the Niger and Lake Chad, thoroughly studying the country for the first time.

1853–1856. **LIVINGSTONE CROSSED THE CONTINENT** from the Zambezi to Loanda and return, discovering the **Victoria Falls.**

1853. The Portuguese, **Silva Porto, crossed the continent** from Benguella to the mouth of the Rovuma River.

1858–1859. **Richard Burton** and **John Speke** discovered **Lake Tanganyika** and **Victoria Nyanza,** Speke concluding that Victoria Nyanza was the source of the White Nile.

1858–1861. **THIRD EXPEDITION OF LIVINGSTONE,** from the Zambezi to the interior. He discovered **Lake Nyasa** (1859).

1860–1863. **SPEKE AND JAMES GRANT** passed through Uganda, **reached the Nile** and descended it to **Gondokoro,** where they met **Sir Samuel Baker** (1863), who had ascended the river to that point.

1864. **Baker,** continuing up the Nile, **discovered Albert Nyanza,** whence he returned to Gondokoro.

1865. Extensive exploration of the **Benuë-Niger region** by **Gustav Rohlfs.**

1866–1871. **Livingstone** traveled from the mouth of the Rovuma inland to Lake Nyasa and thence to Lake Tanganyika and Bangweolu, whence he returned to Tanganyika.

1868. **St. Vincent Erskine** explored the region of the **Limpopo River.**

1868–1871. **GEORG SCHWEINFURTH** went from Khartum to the Niam-Niam country and discovered the **Welle River,** flowing west.

1870. **Gustav Nachtigal** explored the **Chad region** and crossed from there to Egypt.

1871. **HENRY M. STANLEY,** searching for Livingstone, found him on Lake Tanganyika. Death of Livingstone (May 1, 1873).

1874. **Verney L. Cameron crossed the continent** from Lake Tanganyika to Benguella, mapping large territories.

1874–1877. **STANLEY CIRCUMNAVIGATED VICTORIA NYANZA,** proceeded thence to Lake Tanganyika, crossed to the **Lualaba,** which he **descended to the Congo,** ultimately reaching the Atlantic coast.

1874. **Charles Chaillé-Long** traced the course of the **Somerset Nile** and discovered **Lake Kioga.**

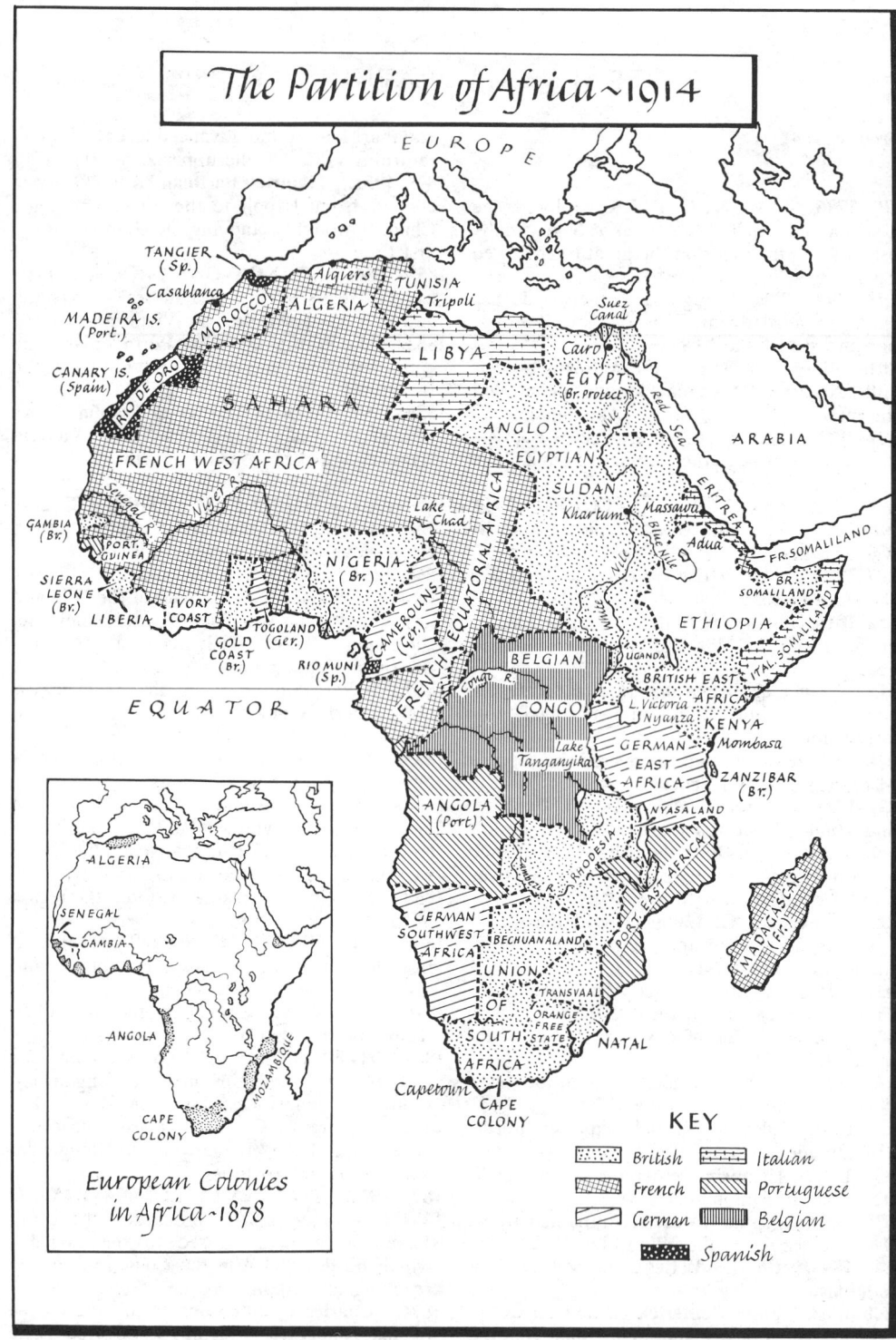

The Partition of Africa ~ 1914

EUROPE

TANGIER (Sp.)
Casablanca
Algiers
TUNISIA
Tripoli
Suez Canal
MADEIRA IS. (Port.)
MOROCCO
ALGERIA
LIBYA
EGYPT (Br. Protect.)
Cairo
CANARY IS. (Spain)
RIO DE ORO
SAHARA
ANGLO EGYPTIAN SUDAN
ARABIA
Red Sea
FRENCH WEST AFRICA
Lake Chad
Khartum
Massawa
ERITREA
GAMBIA (Br.)
Senegal R.
NIGER R.
PORT. GUINEA
NIGERIA (Br.)
Adua
FR. SOMALILAND
SIERRA LEONE (Br.)
IVORY COAST
TOGOLAND (Ger.)
CAMEROUNS (Ger.)
FRENCH EQUATORIAL AFRICA
Blue Nile
BR. SOMALILAND
LIBERIA
GOLD COAST (Br.)
RIO MUNI (Sp.)
BELGIAN
ETHIOPIA
ITAL. SOMALILAND
Congo R.
CONGO
UGANDA
BRITISH EAST AFRICA
L. Victoria Nyanza
KENYA
Mombasa
EQUATOR
ANGOLA (Port.)
Lake Tanganyika
GERMAN EAST AFRICA
ZANZIBAR (Br.)
NYASALAND
GERMAN SOUTHWEST AFRICA
BECHUANALAND
Zambesi R.
RHODESIA
PORT. EAST AFRICA
MADAGASCAR (Fr.)
UNION OF SOUTH AFRICA
TRANSVAAL
ORANGE FREE STATE
NATAL
Capetown
CAPE COLONY

ALGERIA
SENEGAL
GAMBIA
ANGOLA
MOZAMBIQUE
CAPE COLONY

European Colonies in Africa ~ 1878

KEY

British	Italian
French	Portuguese
German	Belgian
Spanish	

1875. **Pierre Savorgnan de Brazza** explored the region of the **Ogowe** and **lower Congo.**

1876. **Foundation of the International Association for the Exploration and Civilization of Africa,** under the auspices of **Leopold II** of Belgium.

1877. The Portuguese, **Serpa Pinto,** crossed from Benguella to Natal.

1879-1886. **Wilhelm Junker** demonstrated that the Welle River was part of the Congo system and carried on extensive researches about Lake Albert.

1879-1884. **Stanley,** in the service of Leopold, ascended the Congo and established posts in the basin.

1878-1881. **Joseph Thomson** explored the region between Lakes Nyasa and Tanganyika.

1880-1886. **HERMANN VON WISSMANN** explored the **Congo Basin** and twice crossed the continent.

1882. The Italians, **Pellegrino Matteucci and Alfonso Massari,** crossed the continent from **Suakin** on the Red Sea to the **Niger River.**

1882. **Junker** explored the **Ubanghi River** system.

1887-1890. **STANLEY'S EXPEDITION TO RELIEVE EMIN PASHA** (Eduard Schnitzer, Egyptian governor of Equatoria, 1877-1888). Stanley ascended the Congo, crossed to the great lakes, traced the **Semliki River** to **Lake Edward,** which he discovered. He found Emin on the upper Nile and induced him to leave for the east coast.

1888. **Count Samuel Teleki,** a Hungarian scientist, discovered **Lakes Rudolf** and **Stephanie.**

1892-1895. **Vittorio Bottego** explored the **Juba River.** Later explorations have been chiefly of a scientific nature with the object of filling out the map and supplementing the work of earlier travelers.

2. EGYPT AND THE SUDAN, 1805-1914

1805. **Mohammed Ali** appointed **governor of Egypt** by the Ottoman sultan. Mohammed (b. 1769) was a tobacco merchant from Kavalla, who had come to Egypt in 1799 in command of an Albanian contingent. By intervening freely in the intrigues of the Turkish officials and the Mamluks and supporting the latter, he succeeded in driving out the Turkish governor and establishing his own power, which the sultan recognized only with reluctance.

1807. **British invasion** and occupation of Alexandria. The British failed to make further progress and withdrew (p. 642).

1811, Mar. 1. **Massacre of the Mamluks** in the citadel of Cairo. They had obviously been intriguing against Mohammed and were probably supported by the sultan. Mohammed invited them to a banquet and had them treacherously slaughtered. Only a few escaped to upper Egypt. Thereafter **Mohammed was supreme.** Though illiterate, he was a firm believer in western technology and reorganized the country administratively on the French model. In time he built up a powerful army (organized by **Col. Joseph Sèves,** or Soliman Pasha) and a substantial fleet. In order to secure the necessary funds, he gradually took over most of the land, organized **state monopolies** of trade, introduced the **culture of cotton and hemp,** and developed the **irrigation system** (Delta Barrage).

1815. **Revolt of the Albanian regiments,** which resented Mohammed's efforts at Europeanization. Mohammed was forced to flood Cairo,

but the revolt was ultimately repressed and the mutinous troops sent to upper Egypt.

1818. Conclusion of seven years of **war against the Wahabis** in Arabia, who had occupied Mecca and Medina and threatened Syria. The campaign was undertaken at the behest of the sultan. The result was the subjection of the eastern coast of the Red Sea to Egyptian rule.

1820-1822. **CONQUEST OF THE SUDAN** (Nubia, Senaar, Kordofan) by Egyptian forces under Mohammed's son Hussein. The primary object of the campaign was to find gold supplies and slaves. **Khartum founded** (1823).

1823-1828. **Mohammed Ali's intervention** in behalf of the sultan against the insurgents **in Greece.** As a result Mohammed acquired the governorship of **Crete** (p. 769).

1832-1833. **WAR BETWEEN MOHAMMED AND THE SULTAN** (p. 771). As a result Mohammed acquired control of all **Syria** and **Adana.** In the subsequent years he expanded his influence as far as the Persian Gulf, arousing the distrust and opposition of Britain.

1833. Arrival of a group of **Saint-Simonians in Egypt.** Their aim was the development of the country on western lines and above all the construction of a **canal at Suez.** This latter project was opposed by Mohammed Ali for fear of its international implications.

1839-1841. **SECOND WAR BETWEEN MOHAMMED ALI AND THE SULTAN** (p. 771). Due to the intervention of the powers, **Mohammed lost Crete and Syria,** but secured the **hereditary tenure of Egypt,** paying tribute to the sultan and accepting a reduction of the

Rulers of Egypt (1811–1953)

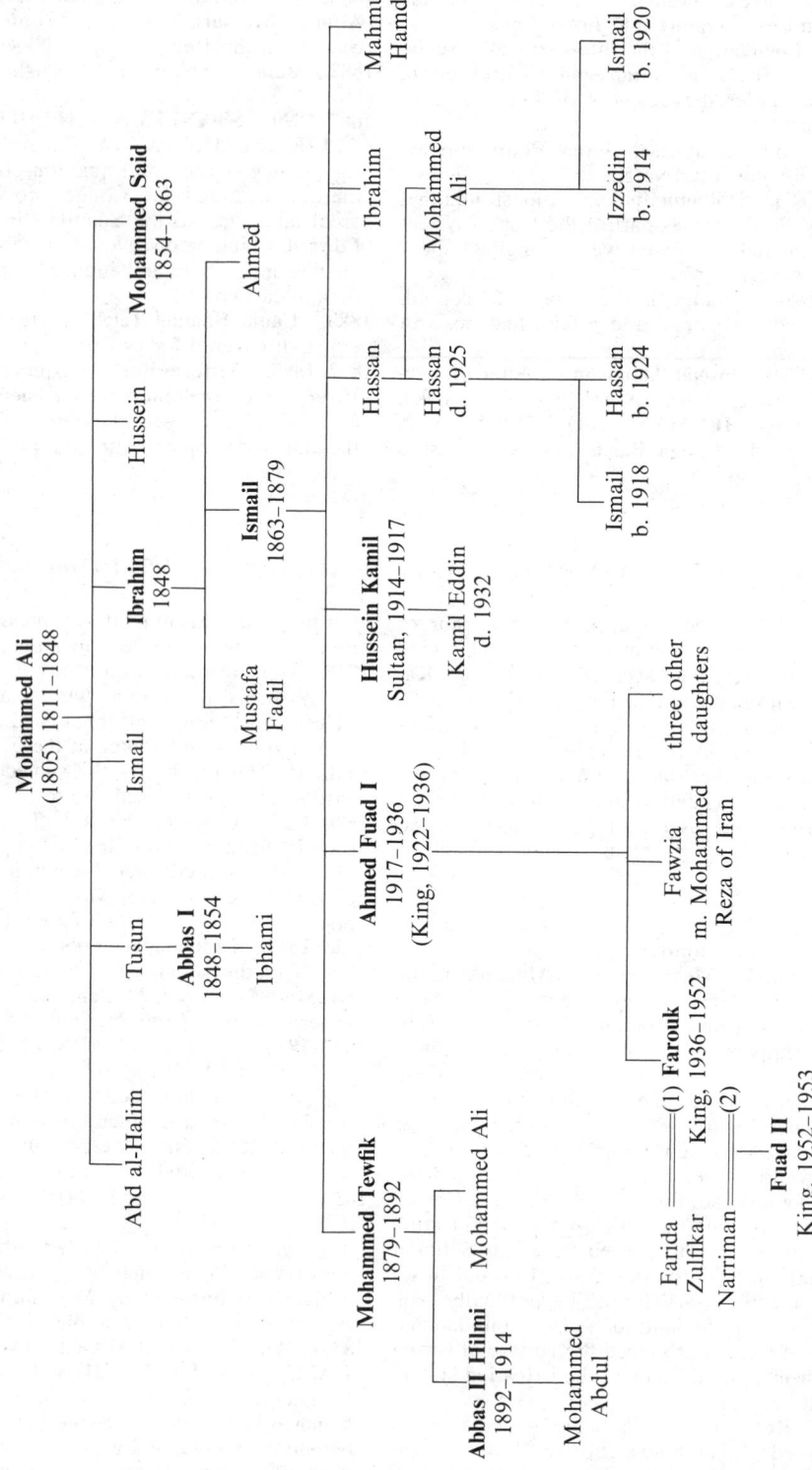

army to 18,000 men (firmans of February 13 and June 10, 1841).

1847. Regency of Ibrahim, following the mental derangement of Mohammed Ali in his later years. In July 1848 Ibrahim was formally invested as khedive.

1848, Nov. 10. Death of Ibrahim.

1849, Aug. 2. Death of Mohammed Ali.

1848-1854. ABBAS I, khedive. He was a grandson of Mohammed Ali and was born in 1816. His reign was characterized by hostility to European and especially French influence and by a more subservient attitude toward the sultan. He was assassinated by his opponents at court (July 13, 1854).

1854-1863. MOHAMMED SAID, khedive. He was the youngest son of Mohammed Ali (b. 1822), an enlightened ruler friendly to western penetration. He took **steps to suppress slavery,** abandoned the state ownership of land, ended the system of monopolies, and reorganized the administration along liberal lines. During his reign the **first foreign loan** was contracted (£3,000,000, floated by British bankers).

1854, Nov. 30. Suez Canal concession granted to **Ferdinand de Lesseps,** a French diplomat and promoter and a friend of Said's of long standing.

1857. Completion of the **railroad from Alexandria to Cairo.** This was later extended to Suez.

1858. Organization of the Suez Canal Company, which raised a loan of 200,000,000 francs.

1859, Apr. 29. Work was begun on the **Suez Canal.** The project had been vigorously opposed by the British (Lord Palmerston) at every step, because of its French connections and because of the supposed threat to India.

1863-1879. ISMAIL, khedive. He was the son of Ibrahim and was born in 1830. Partly educated in France, he had traveled widely in Europe and set himself to complete the **modernization of Egypt.** In his first years the Civil War in America created a great demand for Egyptian cotton and resulted in widespread prosperity. Ismail took advantage of this and of the readiness of European interests to lend huge sums of money (at usurious rates of interest) to carry through immense **public works**—Suez Canal, irrigation canals, railroads, telegraphs, harbor works, bridges, etc. Most notable was the development of **primary schools,** which increased from 185 to 4685 during his reign. On the other hand, Egypt was confronted with a tremendous public debt.

1865. Ismail induced the sultan to put under Egyptian control the ports of **Suakin** and **Massawa** on the Red Sea, the beginning of a sys-

tematic expansion in that direction.

1869, Nov. 17. OFFICAL OPENING OF THE SUEZ CANAL; presence of the Empress Eugénie, Emperor Francis Joseph, and many other European celebrities. First performance of Verdi's opera, *Aïda.*

1870-1873. Sir Samuel Baker, in Egyptian service, completed the **conquest of the upper Nile region,** as far as Unyoro, and initiated the **suppression of the slave trade,** which had seriously depopulated the country.

1872-1875. Occupation of the Red Sea coast and Harrar. The Egyptian control was extended as far as Cape Guardafui and cut off Ethiopia from access to the sea.

1874. Zobeir, a powerful former slave-trader of the Sudan, **conquered Darfur** for the khedive.

1874-1879. Gen. Charles George Gordon governor-general of the Sudan. He completed the work of Baker, established posts on the upper Nile, and dealt the slave-traders a mortal blow.

1875, Nov. The khedive, in financial stringency, **sold his 176,000 shares in the Suez Canal Company to the British government** for 100,000,000 francs. The British government thereupon became the largest single shareholder.

1875-1879. War with Ethiopia. The Egyptians were at first defeated, but won a crushing victory in February 1876.

1876, Apr. 4. Publication of the **report of Mr. Stephen Cave** on the finances of Egypt. Some measure of European supervision was declared indispensable.

May 2. Establishment of the *Caisse de la Dette* to manage the service of the debt.

Nov. 18. Appointment of a British and a French controller, following reduction of the debt and of interest. **Anglo-French condominium.**

1878, Aug. 15. Appointment of a **ministry under Nubar Pasha,** with an Englishman (**Sir Rivers Wilson**) as minister of finance, and a Frenchman (**André de Blignières**) as minister of public works. A vigorous effort was made to meet the demands of the European creditors, with resulting hardship on the country and much discontent and hatred of foreigners.

1879, Feb. 18. Fall of the Nubar ministry after a demonstration of army officers, possibly encouraged by Ismail, who resented the curtailment of his own power.

June 25. Deposition of Ismail by the sultan, under pressure from the European powers.

1879-1892. TEWFIK, khedive.

1879, Sept. 4. The **European controllers were reappointed** and henceforth were to be irremovable without the consent of Britain and France.

1880, July 17. The **Law of Liquidation,** promulgated after another international investigation. It rearranged the finances and provided that all surplus should go to the service of the debt.

1881, Feb. 1. Rising of Egyptian officers, following the dismissal of one of their number. The officers forced the appointment of **Mahmud Sami,** a nationalist, as minister of war. The movement was led by **Ahmed Arabi** and was the first definite expression of the new **nationalist movement,** inspired by **Jamal ud-Din el-Afghani,** famous Moslem teacher (at Cairo after 1871) who preached resistance to the West and adoption of Western political methods for purposes of defense. The national movement in Egypt was primarily directed against foreign control and against the Turkish influence, but also aimed at constitutional government.

Sept. 9. A **second rising,** led by Arabi, forced the khedive to revoke the dismissal of Mahmud Sami.

1882, Jan. 8. The **Gambetta Note,** handed to the Egyptian government by France and Britain. It pronounced in favor of the khedive and was intended to strengthen him against nationalist pressure. Its effect was merely to discredit him, since the British refused to follow up the note by concrete action.

Feb. 5. The khedive was obliged to appoint **a nationalist ministry** under Mahmud Sami, in which Arabi became war minister. The ministry began discussion of a constitution.

Apr. 12. A **conspiracy of Circassian officers** against the government was discovered.

May 2. Forty of the conspirators were condemned to exile in the Sudan. The khedive thereupon appealed to the powers for support and the ministry summoned the chamber, evidently with the idea of deposing Tewfik.

May 20. British and French squadrons appeared **at Alexandria** as a demonstration in behalf of the khedive.

May 25. An **ultimatum from Britain and France** forced the resignation of the nationalist government.

May 28. The **khedive,** unable to form another government, was **obliged to recall Arabi** and the nationalists.

June 12. Outbreak of riots at Alexandria, in which some fifty Europeans were killed. These riots have been attributed by some to the khedive, as part of a scheme to force intervention in his behalf.

June 23. Opening of an **ambassadorial conference at Constantinople,** to discuss the modalities of Turkish intervention under the supervision of the powers.

July 11. BOMBARDMENT OF ALEXANDRIA by the British under **Adm. Sir Beauchamp Seymour.** The ostensible object was to destroy the earthworks which the nationalists were throwing up. The French government refused to take part in the action, fearing international complications. The British thereupon began to land troops and to send a force to protect the Suez Canal. The French and also the Italians refused invitations to participate.

Sept. 13. The British under **Sir Garnet Wolseley, defeated the Egyptian forces** of Arabi **at Tel el-Kebir.**

Sept. 15. THE BRITISH OCCUPIED CAIRO. Arabi surrendered; he was later tried and banished to Ceylon.

Nov. 9. The **dual control** of Britain and France **was abolished.**

1883, Jan. 3. Granville Circular to the powers, declaring Britain's desire to withdraw her forces from Egypt *"as soon as the state of the country and the organization of proper means for the maintenance of the khedivial authority will admit of it."*

Feb. 6. Dufferin report, proposing the reorganization of the Egyptian government.

May 1. The **ORGANIC LAW,** embodying the Dufferin proposals, went into effect: in addition to the cabinet there was to be a **legislative council** composed of nominees of the khedive and members elected by the provincial assemblies; a **general assembly** was to include the ministers and legislative council and additional members chosen by the provincial and town governments. Neither the council nor the assembly had more than advisory power, the real authority resting with the khedive and through him with the British representative.

1883–1907. SIR EVELYN BARING (1892— **Lord Cromer) resident and consul-general.** Cromer's rule was that of a strong man, who ordered the finances, developed the economic power of the country, revised taxation, abolished the corvée, etc., though doing little for popular education or for the development of self-government. British advisers were appointed for all important native officials and exercised an ill-defined but effective control.

1883, Nov. 5. Battle of El Obeid. Gen. **William Hicks,** with an Egyptian force, was completely defeated and his army wiped out by the forces of the **Mahdi Mohammed Ahmed** of Dongola, who set himself up as a prophet and organized a movement throughout the Sudan directed against the Egyptian rule. Throughout 1882–1883 he had fought with varying success against the Egyptians until his victory at El Obeid gave him control over Kordofan. **Slatin Bey** and **Lupton Bey,** governors of Darfur and Bahr-el-Ghazal respectively, were soon obliged to surrender, only **Emin Pasha** retaining his position in Equatoria. **Osman Digna,** ablest of the lieutenants of the Mahdi, carried on a vigorous offensive against the Red Sea ports.

1884, Jan. 6. The British obliged the reluctant Egyptian government to decide on the **evacuation and abandonment of the Sudan.**

Jan. 18. Gen. Gordon was sent out to effect the evacuation of the Egyptian garrisons. He reached Khartum on February 18 and offered remission of taxes, non-interference with the slave trade, and recognition of the Mahdi as sultan of Kordofan, his idea being to re-establish the local chiefs in their positions under Egyptian suzerainty. These offers were rejected by the Mahdi, who continued his conquests.

June 28–Aug. 2. International conference on Egyptian finance at London. The British proposed the reduction of interest on the debt and the use of the surplus revenue to meet the heavy charges of the Sudan campaigns. The powers rejected these suggestions, Bismarck working closely with Jules Ferry to frustrate the British (p. 783).

Sept. 18. The **British suspended the sinking-fund payments,** but were obliged by protests of the powers and a decision of the mixed tribunals to give up this course of action.

1885, Jan. 26. The **MAHDI TOOK KHARTUM,** massacring Gordon and the garrison. A relief force, sent out from Wadi Halfa (Aug. 1884), reached the city just too late.

Mar. 27. An **international conference at Paris** accepted the French proposals regarding the financial problem—reduction of interest and a loan under international guaranty. Thus **international control** was in some measure retained, giving France in particular ample opportunity to impede the British policy.

June 21. Death of the Mahdi, who was succeeded by the **Khalifa Abdullah el Taashi.** On July 30 the dervishes (followers of the Mahdi) took the key position of **Kassala,** completing their control of the whole Sudan except for the Red Sea fortresses. There and along the new Egyptian frontier at Wadi Halfa, fighting continued throughout the next ten years.

1887, May 22. Drummond-Wolff Convention between Turkey and Great Britain. The British promised to evacuate Egypt within three years provided conditions were favorable, but retained the right to reoccupy the country if it were menaced by invasion or internal disorder. Under pressure from France and Russia the sultan refused to ratify this convention and the British became more and more convinced that they must remain in the country for some time.

1888, Oct. 29. SUEZ CANAL CONVENTION (treaty of Constantinople) signed by Great Britain, France, Germany, Italy, Austria, Spain, the Netherlands, Russia, and Turkey, after an international conference at Paris in 1885 had failed to establish a régime for the canal. The **convention of 1888** declared the canal free and open to merchant and war vessels of all powers in time of war as in time of peace; the canal was not to be blockaded and no acts of hostility were to be committed within its confines, but the sultan and khedive were to be free to take such measures as they *"might find necessary for securing by their own forces the defense of Egypt and the maintenance of public order."* The British government **reversed the application of the convention** in so far as *"they might fetter the liberty of their government during the occupation of Egypt by their forces."*

1892–1914. ABBAS HILMI II, son of Tewfik, khedive. He was a headstrong young man who resented the tutelage of the British and, relying on French support, attempted to shake off the domination of Lord Cromer. This led to much friction and an acute **crisis in January 1893,** in which Cromer asserted British authority to the full and increased the forces of occupation.

1896–1898. RECONQUEST OF THE SUDAN by **Gen. Herbert Kitchener.** This was due less to indignation at the conditions under dervish rule than to a growing realization of the importance of the Sudan to assure and increase the Egyptian water-supply, and further to the constant advance upon the Sudan of forces of the Belgian Congo and of France. For the international aspects of the Nile problem see p. 788.

1896, Sept. 21. Kitchener took Dongola. He proceeded with the greatest caution, building a railroad as he advanced.

1897, Aug. 7. The Anglo-Egyptian forces took Abu Hamed.

1898, Apr. 8. Kitchener's **victory at the Atbara River.**

Sept. 2. BATTLE OF OMDURMAN, decisive defeat of the khalifa, who fled. Kitchener's forces took Khartum.

Sept. 19. Kitchener reached Fashoda and found the French under **Maj. Jean-Baptiste Marchand** in occupation. For the **Fashoda crisis** see p. 791.

1899, Jan. 19. An **Anglo-Egyptian convention** established a condominium in what became known as **the Anglo-Egyptian Sudan.**

Mar. 21. Convention between Britain and France ending the Fashoda crisis. The French were definitely excluded from the Bahr-el-Ghazal and from all contact with the Nile.

Nov. 24. **Defeat and death of the khalifa,** who had been pursued into Kordofan by **Sir Reginald Wingate.**

1902, May 15. Treaty between Britain and Ethiopia, by which the latter accepted a frontier with the Sudan well removed from the Nile.

Dec. Opening of the **Aswan Dam,** first of the great storage reservoirs on the upper Nile.

1904, Apr. 8. The **Anglo-French entente cordiale** finally brought to an end the French obstruction of British policy in Egypt. Great Britain recognized the Suez Canal convention as in full force.

1906, May 3. A British ultimatum to Turkey obliged the latter to renounce claims to the **Sinai Peninsula,** which became Egyptian territory.

May 9. Agreement between Britain and King Leopold as sovereign of the Congo. After years of friction, Leopold gave up his claims to the Bahr-el-Ghazal (under the treaty of 1894), but was given the **Lado Enclave** on the upper Nile for the duration of his life.

June 13. The Denshawi affair. Several British officers, on a pigeon-shooting expedition, were attacked by natives and one officer was killed. The episode revealed popular hatred of foreign rule, and the punishment of the culprits, which was made a demonstration, served to arouse Egyptian national feeling.

1907-1911. SIR ELDON GORST, resident and British consul-general, on the retirement of Cromer (d. 1917). Gorst attempted a more lenient policy, established friendlier relations with the khedive and encouraged popular education.

1907, Dec. 7. First Nationalist congress and organization of a Nationalist Party under leadership of **Mustapha Kamel.** The program was a liberal, pacific and cultural one.

1908, Feb. 10. Death of Mustapha Kamel, aged only thirty-four, a great loss to the reviving nationalist movement.

Nov. 12. The **khedive,** possibly to counteract the nationalist movement, appointed as premier a Christian Copt, **Butros Ghali.** This led to violent Islamic agitation.

1909, Mar. 25. The government instituted a system of **press censorship** and supervision to check the extravagances of the Nationalists.

July 4. A law of **police supervision** enabled the government to exile undesirable agitators.

1910, Feb. 20. Assassination of Butros Ghali by a Nationalist fanatic. The trial and execution of the assassin brought the unrest to a new pitch.

June 16. On the death of Leopold II, the **Lado Enclave reverted to the Sudan.**

1911-1914. LORD KITCHENER, resident and consul-general on the death of Sir Eldon Gorst. He proceeded vigorously against disorderly agitation, but at the same time attempted to satisfy Egyptian opinion by liberal concessions.

1913, July 21. The government introduced a **new electoral law and a new constitutional system:** the old general assembly was abolished and all popular authority vested in a new legislative assembly, largely elective, which was given the power to initiate legislation and wide powers of supervising the budget, etc.

1914, Jan. 22-June 17. Meeting of the first assembly, which was then suspended during the First World War.

Nov. 6. Proclamation of a **state of war with Turkey.**

Dec. 18. Declaration of a British protectorate over Egypt.

Dec. 19. Deposition of Abbas II, who was accused of intrigue with the sultan of Turkey and of anti-British designs.

1914-1917. HUSSEIN KAMIL (uncle of Abbas II), proclaimed sultan. (*Cont. p. 1075.*)

3. ETHIOPIA AND THE RED SEA AREA, 1855-1918

1855. Ras Kassa succeeded in deposing **Ras Ali of Gondar** and thereupon conquered the rulers of Tigré, Gojjam, and Shoa, making himself king of kings, under the throne name of *Theodore.*

1855-1868. THEODORE, emperor. He was supported by the Englishmen **Walter Plowden** and **John Bell** in suppressing his rebellious subordinates.

1862, Mar. The **French** acquired the port of **Obock** from the sultan of Tajura.

Oct. After Plowden's death Theodore, through the new British consul, **Charles D.** Cameron, proposed an **alliance with Britain** against the Turks. Through an oversight no reply was made to this proposal, and Theodore, deeply offended, threw Cameron and other European traders and missionaries into prison at Magdala (Jan. 1864).

1866, Jan. Theodore received Hormuzd Rassam, a British envoy, but threw him also into prison. Several ultimata from the British government failed to reach him.

1868. EXPEDITION OF SIR ROBERT NAPIER and an Anglo-Indian force to Ethiopia. Napier proceeded with great caution, but found much support from local chiefs, estranged by Theodore's boundless vindictiveness and cruelty.

Apr. 10. **Battle of Arogee.** Theodore was defeated and committed suicide.

Apr. 13. The **British stormed Magdala** and released the prisoners, after which Napier withdrew from the country, which relapsed into anarchy.

1869. The Italian **Rubattino Company** bought the port of **Assab** on the Red Sea, to be used as a station on the new Suez-Red Sea route.

1872–1889. **JOHANNES IV** (ruler of Tigré), king of kings.

1875–1879. **War between Ethiopia and Egypt,** in which the Egyptians were successful, cutting off Ethiopia from the sea.

1882. **Johannes,** having defeated **Menelek,** king of Shoa, made a pact with him and designated him as his successor.

1882. The **Italian government took over Assab,** which became the kernel of the colony of **Eritrea** (1890).

1884. Following the Egyptian withdrawal from the Sudan and the Red Sea coast, **Britain established a protectorate** over part of the **Somali coast,** with **Zeila** as the chief port. The French at the same time expanded their station at Obock into a **French Somali protectorate.**

1885, Feb. 6. The **Italians,** encouraged by the British, established themselves at **Massawa,** whence they at once began a policy of expansion into the highlands.

1887–1889. **War of Johannes against the Italians.** The Ethiopians attacked Massawa and on January 26 annihilated an Italian force in the **battle of Dogali.** The Italians were saved by the attacks of the Mahdist forces in northern Ethiopia, which diverted Johannes.

1887. The French transferred the seat of their protectorate from Obock to **Jibuti,** commanding the chief caravan route to Ethiopia.

1888, Feb. The British and French made an agreement regarding their spheres in Somaliland and engaged not to expand into **Harrar.**

Dec. **Revolt of Menelek** of Shoa against Johannes. He was supported by the Italians, to whom he promised parts of northern Ethiopia in return for munitions.

1889, Mar. 12. **Death of Johannes,** killed in the **battle of Metemma** against the Mahdists. Menelek's succession was disputed by **Ras Mangasha,** son of Johannes. The Italians supported Menelek and took over Keren and Asmara by way of reward.

1889–1911. **MENELEK,** emperor.

May 2. **TREATY OF UCCIALLI** between Italy and Menelek, from which the Italians derived a claim to a protectorate over all Ethiopia.

Aug. 3. The **Italians secured** from the sultan of Zanzibar **the entire Benadir coast** from Kismayu to Cape Guardafui.

1891, Feb. 9. **Menelek,** having subdued Ras Mangasha, **denounced the Italian claims** to a protectorate, which were unjustified, according to the Amharic text of the treaty of Uccialli.

Mar. 24, Apr. 15. Two **Anglo-Italian agreements** defined the frontiers of their Red Sea colonies. Great Britain recognized the Italian protectorate over the whole of Ethiopia to within 100 miles of the Nile and Italy agreed not to interfere with the water-supply of the Atbara River.

Apr. 10. **Menelek's circular** to the powers, claiming all territory to the Nile and to Lake Victoria.

Dec. The **Italians defeated** and threw back the **Mahdists** who had attacked Eritrea.

1894, Mar. 9. Menelek granted to his Swiss adviser, **Alfred Ilg,** a concession for a **railway from Jibuti** to the new capital, **Addis Ababa,** and thence westward to the Nile.

May 5. **Another Anglo-Italian agreement** abandoned **Harrar** to Italy (despite the Anglo-French agreement of 1888), but gave Britain the freedom to act there until Italy should take it over.

July 17. The **Italians took Kassala** from the dervishes.

1895, Mar. 25. The **Italians began their advance** into Ethiopia and took **Adigrat.**

Sept. **Menelek declared war** against the Italians.

Dec. 8. Defeat of the Italians at **Amba Alagi.**

1896, Mar. 1. **BATTLE OF ADUA.** An Italian force of some 20,000 was annihilated by some 80,000 Ethiopians under Menelek (p. 709).

Oct. 26. **Treaty of Addis Ababa** between Ethiopia and Italy, the Italians recognizing the independence of Ethiopia and restricting themselves to their coastal possessions.

1897, Mar. 20. **Treaty between Ethiopia and France,** defining the Somali frontier. The French influence at Addis Ababa was at its height at this time and the French hoped to use Ethiopia as a base for the advance on the Nile.

May 14. Treaty of Ethiopia with Great Britain **(Rodd mission);** the British abandoned much of the territory claimed in Somaliland, but failed to get Menelek to surrender his claims toward the Nile.

Dec. 25. The **Italians,** hard pressed by the dervishes, **ceded Kassala** to the Egyptians.

1898, June 22. An **Ethiopian force,** accompanied by a French mission, **reached the Nile,** but was unable to effect contact with Marchand coming from the west. Other Ethiopian armies pushed to the north and south and brought all the highland territory under Menelek's control, thus founding the **modern Ethiopian Empire.**

1899, Sept. Rise of the "Mad Mullah," Mohammed ben Abdullah, a Somali chief who proclaimed himself Mahdi and began systematic raids on the British and Italian possessions.

1900, July 10. An **Ethiopian-Italian agreement** defined the frontier of their respective territories.

1901, Dec. 7. Anglo-Italian agreement defining the frontier of the Sudan and the Italian possessions. There were many supplementary agreements.

1902, Feb. 6. The French government agreed to subsidize the **Jibuti-Addis Ababa railroad** enterprise. This led to strong protests from Britain and Italy, which demanded the internationalization of the line.

Mar. 18. Agreement between Britain and Ethiopia regarding the **Nile water-supply,** and an eventual dam at Lake Tana.

May 15. Anglo-Ethiopian agreement regarding the **Sudan frontier;** Menelek gave up all claim to territory bordering the Nile.

1905, Mar. 5. After years of campaigning by Britain, Italy, and Ethiopia against the Mad Mullah, an agreement was reached with him allowing him territory in Italian Somaliland.

1906, July 4. TRIPARTITE PACT between Great Britain, France, and Italy: they declared for the independence and integrity of Ethiopia and engaged not to interfere, but for the event of the situation becoming untenable they defined **spheres of influence** (Lake Tana region to Britain; the railway zone to France; a crescent-shaped belt of territory connecting Eritrea with Italian Somaliland to the west of Addis Ababa to Italy). Britain and Italy were given seats on the board of the railway company. Menelek protested against the implications of the treaty and reserved his sovereign rights (Dec. 10).

1907, Oct. 26. Menelek, stricken by partial paralysis, organized a cabinet to assist him.

Dec. 6. An agreement between Britain and Ethiopia defined the frontier with **Uganda** and **East Africa.**

1908, June. Menelek named his grandson, **Lij Yasu** (twelve years old), as his heir, with **Ras Tessama** as regent. As Menelek became more and more helpless, a three-cornered struggle for influence developed between the supporters of Lij Yasu, the Empress Taitu, and Ras Tessama. For several years the empress was supreme. **Growing influence of the Germans** during this period.

1908. Resumption of the **raids of the Mad Mullah.** The British withdrew to the coast, but sporadic fighting continued until 1920, when the Mullah died (Nov. 23).

1911, May 15. LIJ YASU PROCLAIMED EMPEROR, on the death of Ras Tessama.

July 15. An Anglo-Italian agreement defined the boundary of **Italian Somaliland** and **British East Africa** at the mouth of the Juba River.

Dec. 12. Death of Menelek.

1916, Apr. Lij Yasu announced his conversion to Islam. This aroused a storm of opposition among the local chiefs, supported by the British, French, and Italian representatives, who regarded Lij Yasu as a tool of the Germans and his conversion as a step in the direction of an alliance with Turkey and Germany.

Sept. 27. Lij Yasu was deposed by the head of the Ethiopian Church and fled to the Danakil country.

1916–1926. The **EMPRESS ZAUDITU** (Judith), a daughter of Menelek, was proclaimed queen of kings, with Ras Tafari as heir. The internal struggles in Ethiopia continued for several years.

1918, May 21. Completion of the railroad from Jibuti to Addis Ababa (begun in 1897).

(*Cont. p. 1078.*)

4. NORTH AFRICA, 1816–1914

(Morocco, Algeria, Tunisia, Libya)

At the beginning of the 19th century these territories were all (except Morocco) more or less under the suzerainty of the Ottoman Porte, but the local rulers were to all intents and purposes independent. They engaged freely in **piratical enterprises** against European and American commerce in the Mediterranean and made the coast towns veritable slave emporia. Their territories were organized on a tribal basis and their authority did not run far from the coast. Disorder, poverty, and general backwardness were characteristic of the entire area.

1816. Commissioned by the congress of Vienna, the **British bombarded Algiers** and obliged the dey to put an **end to Christian slavery.**

1827. The French consul at Algiers was slapped in the face by the dey, who ignored repeated French demands for satisfaction.

1830, July 5. A FRENCH EXPEDITIONARY FORCE, after a short campaign, **took Algiers** and deposed the dey. A few other coast towns were occupied, but the French seem to have been uncertain of their own further plans.

1832–1834. Attacks upon the French by **Abd el-Kader** of Mascara, proclaimed dey by the native chiefs. After suffering several setbacks, the French recognized him as **dey of Mascara.**

1835. A Turkish force landed at Tripoli, put an end to the independence of the country, and replaced the last Karamanli ruler by a Turkish governor.

1835–1837. Second war of the French with Abd el-Kader. The French were repeatedly defeated.

1837, May 30. By the **treaty of Tafna,** the French abandoned most of the hinterland of Algeria to Abd el-Kader.

1840, Dec. Outbreak of the **third war with Abd el-Kader.** The French sent a large expeditionary force under **Marshal Thomas Bugeaud,** who began the systematic subjugation of the interior.

1841. Abd el-Kader was **driven across the frontier** into Morocco, where he secured the aid of the sultan.

1844, Aug. 6. The French, under the duke of Joinville, began **hostilities against Morocco,** bombarding **Tangier** and occupying **Mogador.**

Aug. 14. Battle of Isly. Bugeaud completely defeated Abd el-Kader and the Moroccans.

Sept. 10. Treaty of Tangier, concluding the war of the French against Morocco. The French withdrew.

1845, Mar. 18. Convention of Lalla Maghnia, fixing the boundary between Algeria and Morocco on the Mediterranean coast.

1847, Dec. 23. Abd el-Kader surrendered to Gen. Christophe Lamoricière. Contrary to promise, he was sent a prisoner to France. He was released in 1852 by Napoleon III and died at Damascus in 1883.

1848. Algeria was organized as three departments, represented in the French parliament. This system was revoked by Napoleon III, who restored military rule. Continued insurrections in the interior obliged the French to continue operations. By 1870 they had subjugated the central part of present-day Algeria.

1863. An important **land law** recognized private ownership in Algeria and did much to break up the tribal organization. The French made staunch attempts to settle the country with military colonists, but with indifferent success.

1869. The **bey of Tunis,** having borrowed heavily in Europe and having failed to meet his obligations, was obliged to accept an **international financial control** of Britain, France, and Italy.

1879. Algeria was definitively put **under civil government.**

1879–1881. Acute rivalry between the **French and Italians in Tunis,** both sides struggling and intriguing for key concessions (railroad, telegraph, land grants, etc.).

1880, July 3. MADRID CONVENTION, signed by the leading European powers and the United States, by which the status and privileges of foreigners in Morocco were regulated and the independence and integrity of the country recognized.

1881, Mar. Raids of Krumir tribes from Tunisia across the frontier into Algeria. Though there was nothing unusual about these raids, they gave the French a convenient excuse for settling the score with the bey and concluding the competition with Italy.

Apr. 30. A French naval force seized **Bizerte,** while a land force invaded Tunis from Algeria.

May 12. TREATY OF BARDO (Kasr es-Said), by which the bey of Tunis accepted a **French protectorate.** Loud protests from the Turkish government, from Italy and from Britain led to nothing, since Bismarck gave the French steady support.

June 30. Outbreak of a serious **insurrection against the French** under **Ali ben Khalifa.** The French were obliged to subdue southern Tunisia in a regular campaign.

July. At the same time a major **uprising against the French in Algeria** was led by **Bou Amama.** This was not suppressed until 1883.

1883, June 8. The **convention of Marsa,** between the French and the bey of Tunis, gave the French effective control (through a resident-general) of Tunisian affairs.

1893. Attacks of the Riff tribes of Morocco upon the Spanish possessions on the coast. The Spaniards had great difficulty in maintaining themselves.

1894. ABDUL AZIZ (a boy of thirteen) became sultan of Morocco. He was intelligent and well-intentioned, but was unable to control his powerful ministers or to keep within bounds the growing forces of European penetration. By 1900 the country had fallen into complete anarchy.

1896, Sept. 28. A Franco-Italian agreement brought an end to the long-drawn dispute about the **status of Italian residents in Tunis.** Their nationality and that of their descendants was to be regulated by Italian law.

1898. Reorganization of the government of Algeria; decentralization of the administration;

establishment of an assembly with elected members.

1899, Mar. 21. Anglo-French convention defining the hinterland of Tripoli, after the Fashoda crisis. The Italians protested loudly against the large concessions to France in the Sahara.

1900–1903. French occupation of the oases (Igli, Gourara, Timmimun, Tidikelt, Tuat) to the southwest of Algeria. These had belonged to Morocco, though the effective control of the sultan had broken down.

1900, Dec. 14. Secret Franco-Italian agreement gave France a free hand in Morocco, Italy a free hand in Tripoli.

1901, July 20. French agreement with Morocco giving France considerable control of the police on the frontier.

1902–1903. Growing disorder in Morocco: **rising of the pretender Omar Zarhuni.**

1904, Apr. 8. The ENTENTE CORDIALE between Britain and France (p. 794). This gave France a free hand in Morocco and assured her of the diplomatic support of Britain.

May 18. Kidnaping of Ion Perdicaris, an American citizen, by the Moroccan chieftain **Raisuli.** He was released for a ransom on June 24, but Raisuli continued for years to terrorize the country behind Tangier.

Oct. 3. Franco-Spanish agreement on Morocco: the northern, Mediterranean belt was reserved to Spain as a zone of influence.

1905, Jan.–Feb. Mission of Saint-René Taillandier to Fez, to induce the sultan to accept a far-reaching scheme of reform under French guidance.

Mar. 31. Spectacular **visit of the Emperor William II** to Tangier. Beginning of the **first Moroccan crisis** between France and Germany (p. 795).

June 3. The sultan of Morocco invited the powers to a conference to arrange for reform.

1906, Jan. 16–Apr. 7. The ALGECIRAS CONFERENCE and the **act of Algeciras** (p. 796), giving France and Spain substantial control of Moroccan reform, but reaffirming the independence and integrity of Morocco and equality of economic opportunity. This was accepted by the sultan on June 18.

1907, July 30. The **French occupied Ujda** (northwest Morocco) following continued disorders and the **murder of Dr. Emile Mauchamp.**

Aug. 4. The **French bombarded Casablanca** and then occupied the whole Shawia region on the Atlantic coast, following serious anti-foreign outbreaks.

Nov. 24. Mulay Hafid (brother of Abdul Aziz), who had been proclaimed sultan at Marakesh (May 5), was defeated by the sultan's troops.

1908, Jan. 4. Mulay Hafid was proclaimed sultan at Fez.

Aug. 23. Abdul Aziz was defeated at Marakesh.

Sept. 3. The German government notified its intention of recognizing Mulay Hafid. The other powers reluctantly followed suit (Dec. 17) after Mulay Hafid had agreed to respect the act of Algeciras and other international obligations.

Sept. 25. The **Casablanca affair,** arising from the seizure of German deserters from the French foreign legion. The matter was adjusted by the Hague Court in May 1909 (p. 798).

1909, Feb. 8. FRANCO-GERMAN AGREEMENT on Morocco. Germany recognized France's special political position, in return for economic concessions (p. 799).

July–Oct. Attacks of the Riff tribesmen upon the Spaniards at Melilla. Despite heavy losses the Spaniards began to spread in the zone reserved to them.

Oct. 24. Russian-Italian agreement at Racconigi (p. 799). The Russians gave the Italians a free hand in Tripoli.

1910, Mar. 4. Agreement between France and Morocco. The French evacuated Udja and the sultan accepted the program of reform.

1911, Apr. 2. Attack of Berber tribemen on Fez.

May 2. A **French force occupied Fez** on the plea of protecting foreigners.

July 1. Arrival of the **German gunboat** *Panther* at Agadir. Beginning of the **second Moroccan crisis** between France and Germany (p. 800).

Sept. 28. Outbreak of **war between Italy and Turkey,** following a short-term ultimatum demanding guaranties for the protection of Italians and Italian enterprises in Tripoli. The war reflected Italy's determination to secure compensation for the French advance in Morocco (p. 710).

Nov. 4. Franco-German agreement regarding Morocco. In return for compensation in the French Congo, the Germans gave the French a free hand in Morocco (p. 800).

Nov. 5. The Italians proclaimed the **annexation of Tripoli and Cyrenaica,** though only a few coastal towns had been taken.

1912, Mar. 30. TREATY OF FEZ. The sultan of Morocco was obliged to accept a **French protectorate.**

May 24. Gen. Louis Lyautey appointed resident-general in Morocco. By his judicious policy rapid strides were made in the restoration of order and the recognition of French authority.

Aug. 11. Mulay Hafid abdicated rather than rule as the client of France. He was succeeded by **Mulay Yusuf.**

Oct. 18.   The **treaty of Lausanne** brought the Tripolitan War to a close. The Turkish sultan abandoned Tripoli, but retained religious authority (p. 801).

Nov. 27.   **Franco-Spanish agreement,** defining the position of the Spanish zone in Morocco in relation to the French protectorate and establishing a **special status for Tangier.**

1913.   **Italian subjugation of the interior of Tripoli** (Libya).

1914, Sept.   Outbreak of a formidable **insurrection among the Arabs** (Senussi) of Libya. On the entry of Italy into the First World War (May 1915) the movement assumed ever larger dimensions. The Italians were obliged to withdraw from the interior and during the war held only the towns of **Tripoli** and **Homs** on the coast.   **Misurata** and other ports were used as German submarine bases.

(*Cont. p. 1079.*)

5. WEST AFRICA AND THE FRENCH SUDAN, 1799-1914

(French West Africa, Gambia, Sierra Leone, Gold Coast, Togoland, Nigeria, Cameroons, Río de Oro, Portuguese Guinea)

At the beginning of the 19th century the Portuguese, Spanish, French, British, Dutch, Danes, and Swedes all had forts or posts on the coasts of West Africa, engaged in the slave trade and in trade in gold, ivory, and oil. With the abolition of the slave trade many of these stations languished and were abandoned. The interior of the country had to a large extent been conquered by **Tukulor chiefs** with the aid of the pastoral Fulani tribes. Various Tukulor sultans (Moslem) ruled from the Senegal to Lake Chad, the populations of these regions remaining to a large extent pagan. South of the Niger lay a number of strong Negro kingdoms, **Mandingo, Ashanti, Dahomey.** Farther to the east were the empires of **Bagirmi** (dating from the 16th century), which was subjected by Wadai in 1808; and **Wadai** (dating from the 17th century), which was almost chronically at war with the sultans of Darfur. In the eastern Sudan there arose (1805) the power of the **Senussi,** a puritanical sect of Islam (later centered at Kufra) which made a special point of keeping the infidel Christians from Moslem territory.

1799.   Foundation of the **British Church Missionary Society,** which carried on extensive work in West Africa.

July 5.   **Sierra Leone** (acquired 1787 and used for the settlement of freed slaves) was made a separate British colony.

1807.   The British settlement on the **Gambia** was put under the government of Sierra Leone, which became a crown colony (1808).

1809.   The British captured the French settlements on the Senegal.

1817.   The British returned Senegal to the French.

1821.   Sierra Leone, the **Gold Coast,** and the **Gambia** were joined as the **British West African Settlements.**

1822.   **Foundation of Liberia** as a colony for freed American slaves (first colonists had arrived in 1820).

1824-1827.   First war of the British on the Gold Coast with the powerful rulers of the **Ashanti.**

1828.   The **Basel Mission** (Swiss) began active missionary work on the Gold Coast.

1829.   The **British Slave Trade Commissioners** took over the administration of the island of **Fernando Po,** with Spanish consent.

1842-1843.   The French made the first treaties with the native chiefs of the **Ivory Coast.**

1843.   **Fernando Po was returned** to Spanish rule.

1843.   **Gambia** was separated from Sierra Leone and made a separate crown colony.

1845.   **Edward Saker** and the Baptist Mission established themselves at **Ambas Bay,** on the coast of the Cameroons.

1846.   The **British Presbyterian Mission** began its activities on the Nigerian coast. By this time numerous other missionary societies (British, Swiss, German) had begun to operate. Their success among the Moslem inhabitants of West Africa was limited.

1847, July 26.   Establishment of the **FREE AND INDEPENDENT REPUBLIC OF LIBERIA.** It was recognized first by Great Britain, and then by other countries.

1849, Apr. 5.   The French proclaimed a **protectorate over French Guinea.**

1850, Aug. 17.   Denmark sold her four posts on the Gold Coast to Great Britain.

1854-1865.   **GOVERNORSHIP OF GEN. LOUIS FAIDHERBE** in Senegal. He carried on successful campaigns against **El Hajj Omar,** the powerful Tukulor chieftain, who was ultimately defeated and driven eastward to the upper Niger. He died in 1864, but his sons succeeded to his kingdom, which was rent by dynastic wars until its conquest by the French in 1890. Faidherbe extended and consolidated the Senegal colony.

1860. German traders (Woermann and Company) opened a factory on the **Cameroons coast.**

1861, Aug. 6. Britain got possession of the **Lagos coast** through treaties with the chiefs.

1862, June 3. The **United States** recognized the republic of Liberia.

1863, Feb. 25. The French established a **protectorate at Porto Novo** on the Dahomey coast.

1871, Feb. 21. The **Dutch sold El Mina** and other posts on the Gold Coast to Great Britain.

1873–1874. SECOND ASHANTI WAR; campaigns of **Sir Garnet Wolseley,** who entered the Ashanti capital, **Coomassie,** February 4, 1874.

1878. The **Mission of the White Fathers** (under Cardinal Lavigerie) was given charge by the pope of the Catholic missions in Africa.

1874, July 24. The **British West African colonies** were separated.

1879. Foundation of the **United African Company** (National African Company after 1881) by **Sir George Goldie.** This brought together a number of small British firms trading on the Nigerian coast since 1832 and made possible British expansion in this area.

1882, June 28. An **Anglo-French agreement** delimited the boundary between Sierra Leone and French Guinea.

1883. Re-establishment of the French on the coast of **Dahomey** and beginning of expansion into the interior.

1883–1888. French conquest of the upper Niger region, from Senegal. A key fort was built at **Bamaku.**

1884, July 5. Gustav Nachtigal proclaimed a German protectorate over the coast of **Togoland** and

July 12. Over the **Cameroons coast,** five days before the arrival of the British representative dispatched for the same purpose. The British resigned their rights and recognized the German protectorate May 7, 1885.

1885, Jan. 9. The Spanish proclaimed a **protectorate over Río de Oro** and **Spanish Guinea.**

June 5. The British proclaimed a **protectorate over the Niger River** region.

Nov. 11. The boundary between **Sierra Leone and Liberia** was defined by agreement.

1885–1886. Campaigns of the French against the powerful Mandingo ruler, **Samori,** in the Ivory Coast hinterland.

1886, Jan. 13. Lagos, on the west coast of Nigeria, was set up as a separate British colony.

May 12. A **French-Portuguese agreement** defined the frontier between French and Portuguese Guinea.

July 10. The **ROYAL NIGER COMPANY** was chartered and given full control of the British sphere in Nigeria. This company succeeded the National African Company.

July 14. An **Anglo-German agreement** delimited the frontier between the **Gold Coast** and **Togoland.**

1889, Jan. 10. France established a formal **protectorate over the Ivory Coast.**

Aug. 10. An **Anglo-French agreement** defined their respective spheres on the **Gold** and **Ivory Coasts** and on the **Senegal** and **Gambia.**

1890. French war with the **king of Dahomey,** who was defeated and forced to recognize the French protectorate. Beginning of the French expansion into the interior.

Aug. 5. An important **Anglo-French agreement** defined their possessions in northern Nigeria by a line running from **Say** to **Lake Chad.**

1892. Second Dahomey War. The French deposed the king, but were confronted with further risings of the warlike natives in 1893–1894.

1892. Further **conquests of the French on the upper Niger.** Col. Louis Archinard took Segu and broke the powers of the Fulani.

Dec. 8. A **French agreement with Liberia** defined the boundary between the Liberian Republic and the Ivory Coast.

1893. Further advance of the **French on the Niger.** They took Jenné and Timbuktu, defeating the Tuaregs (Dec. 16).

Mar. 10. The colonies of **French Guinea** (hitherto Rivières du Sud) and the **Ivory Coast** formally established.

Nov. 15. An **Anglo-German agreement** defined the **Nigerian-Cameroons boundary,** leaving the region east of Lake Chad to Germany to within 100 miles of the Nile.

1893–1894. THIRD ASHANTI WAR. The natives were defeated and a British protectorate set up.

1894–1895. Abortive campaign of the French under Maj. P. L. Monteil against the forces of **Samori.**

1894, Mar. 15. Franco-German agreement on the boundary between the Cameroons and the French Congo. The French were given the basin of the Shari River and the Bagirmi region, and therewith an open road to the eastern Sudan and the Nile.

June 22. Dahomey was made a French colony.

1895, Jan. 1. The Royal Niger Company proclaimed a **protectorate over Busa** on the middle Niger and **Nikki** in the hinterland of Dahomey.

June. The **French possessions in West Africa were united** under a governor-general.

1895-1896. FOURTH ASHANTI WAR. Sir Francis Scott took **Coomassie** (Jan. 18, 1896), made the king a prisoner, and proclaimed a British protectorate (Aug. 16).

1897, July 23. A **Franco-German agreement** defined the boundary between Dahomey and Togoland.

1897-1898. Acute tension in Anglo-French relations arising from competition for the possession of western Nigeria. The French, eager to connect their territories on the Niger with those in Dahomey, dispatched numerous expeditions into the disputed area, which took **Busa** (Feb. 13, 1897) and **Nikki** (Nov. 30). The British protested vigorously and by the spring of 1898 the two countries were on the verge of war.

1898, June 14. The **ANGLO-FRENCH CRISIS** was ended by an agreement defining the frontier from the coast (between Dahomey and Lagos) to the Niger. The French retained Nikki, while the British were awarded Busa.

Sept. 29. The **French** finally defeated and **captured Samori,** thus breaking the Mandingo power. Samori was exiled to Gabun and died in 1900.

1898-1899. The French, under **Émile Gentil,** organized the entire region along the Shari and Lake Chad. This expedition united near Lake Chad with other missions from the Senegal and Niger and from Algeria, thus establishing the **connection of all the French possessions.**

1899, Mar. 21. Following the **Fashoda crisis** (p. 791), an **Anglo-French agreement** excluded the French from Bahr-el-Ghazal and Darfur, but left them a free hand in Wadai, Borku, and Tibesti in the western Sudan.

Aug. 9. The **British government took over Nigeria** from the Royal Niger Company and made it a British protectorate (Jan. 1, 1900).

Nov. 14. An **Anglo-German agreement** settled the Togoland-Gold Coast frontier and abolished the neutral zone previously established on the upper Volta River.

1900, Mar.-Nov. Rising of the Ashantis, who besieged Coomassie. The rebellion was ultimately suppressed and the capital relieved.

Apr. 22. In the **battle of Lakhta** or **Kusseri** the French defeated and killed **Rabah Zobeir,** who since 1878 had been ravaging Wadai, Bagirmi and Bornu.

May. The **French conquest of Tidikelt, Tuat, Insalah,** and other oases south of Morocco and Algeria, gave them control of the northern Sahara.

June 27. A **Franco-Spanish agreement** defined the frontier of Río de Oro and of Spanish Guinea.

1900-1903. British conquest of northern Nigeria: Kano and Sokoto taken (Feb. 3, Mar. 15, 1903) and subdued.

1901, Sept. 26. The kingdom of **Ashanti** was definitely **annexed** and joined to the British Gold Coast colony.

1904. Reorganization of the French possessions (Mauretania, Senegal, French Guinea, Ivory Coast, Dahomey, Upper Senegal, and Niger) as **French West Africa,** with capital at Dakar.

1904. Insurrection of the Ekumekus, a fanatical sect, in southern Nigeria.

1904-1905. Serious **insurrection in the Cameroons.**

1906. Native rising in Sokoto.

Feb. 18. The British colony **Lagos** was incorporated with southern Nigeria.

1908-1909. French conquest of Mauretania by Gen. Henri Gouraud.

1909. An **American commission investigated** the finances of **Liberia,** which was bankrupt. The United States supported the government against native insurrections and gave financial aid until an international loan was arranged for (June 1912).

1909-1911. French conquest of Wadai.

1911, Nov. 4. By the **Franco-German agreement** settling the second Moroccan crisis (p. 799) about 100,000 sq. miles of the French Congo were added to the German Cameroons colony.

1914. The **French occupied Tibesti,** but owing to the exigencies of the First World War, were obliged to abandon the eastern Sudan in 1916. The region was reoccupied in 1920.

Jan. 1. Southern and northern Nigeria were joined under one administration.

1914, Aug. CONQUEST OF THE GERMAN COLONIES, Togoland and Cameroons, by French and British forces from the neighboring colonies. (*Cont. pp. 968, 1081.*)

6. THE CONGO REGION, 1839-1914

(French Equatorial Africa, Spanish Guinea, Belgian Congo, Angola)

This area is inhabited by the **Bantu,** who, because of the thick tropical jungles and the consequent difficulty of communication, never built large empires comparable to those of West Africa. In the 19th century the chief "kingdoms" were those of the **Congo** (on the lower reaches of the great river), the **Ansika** (on the Congo plateau, above Brazzaville), **Lounda** (on the border between the present-day Congo State and Angola), **Manyema** (to the west of Lake Tanganyika), and **Balouba** (to the south of Manyema).

1839-1845. The **French** acquired land by treaty on both sides of the **Gabun River.**

1840. The **Portuguese** extended their possessions in Angola south to **Mossamedes.**

1849. The **French founded Libreville,** using freed slaves as settlers.

1857-1859, 1863-1865. **Explorations of Paul du Chaillu** (a Franco-American) in the region of the Gabun and Ogowe Rivers.

1875-1878. **Explorations of Pierre Savorgnan de Brazza** in the region north of the Congo.

1876, Sept. 12. **King Leopold** of Belgium, an ardent imperialist, summoned to Brussels an international congress of geographers, explorers, and scientists and founded the **International Association for the Exploration and Civilization of Central Africa,** one of the chief purposes of which was to suppress the slave trade. Each national group was to establish a national committee to carry on the work in special areas. The Belgian committee was most active, and in the years 1877-1879 began to found posts on Lake Tanganyika.

1878, Nov. 25. The Belgian committee was transformed into the **Comité d'Études du Haut-Congo.** **Henry M. Stanley,** recently returned from his crossing of Africa by the Congo route, was engaged to establish stations in the Congo area. This he did in the years 1879-1884.

1880. The French, alarmed by Stanley's activity, sent out **Savorgnan de Brazza,** who made treaties with the chiefs on the north side of the Congo, **founded Brazzaville** and organized a protectorate.

1882. The Comité d'Etudes du Haut-Congo was transformed into the **International Association of the Congo,** with trade as a main objective. A number of companies were organized to exploit the Congo region.

1884, Feb. 26. An **ANGLO-PORTUGUESE TREATY** gave Portugal both sides of the lower Congo from 5° 12′ to 8° S. Lat. and inland to Noki. Portugal agreed to freedom of navigation on the Congo and promised a low tariff. The treaty was intended primarily to check the French advance. Owing to vigorous parliamentary opposition and to protests from France and Germany, it had to be abandoned (June 26).

Apr. 22. The **United States recognized the International Association** as a territorial power.

Apr. 23. By treaty France secured the **right of pre-emption** in the event of the International Association alienating its territory.

Nov. 8. **Germany recognized the International Association.**

Nov. 15-1885, Feb. 26. BERLIN CONFERENCE on Congo affairs, arranged by Germany and France. It provided for freedom of navigation on the Congo and Niger, free trade in the Congo Basin, abolition of slavery and the slave trade, effective occupation of territory claimed, etc.

Dec. 16. Britain recognized the International Association. France and Russia followed on February 5, 1885, and the Association took the name **Independent State of the Congo.**

1885, Feb. 5. An **agreement,** concluded between **France and the Congo State** in connection with the recognition of the latter, defined the frontier between the Congo State and the French Congo at the Congo River and the Ubanghi, a northern confluent.

Feb. 14. An **agreement between the Congo State and Portugal** gave the latter the Kabinda Enclave to the north of the river, and the south bank as far up as Noki.

Apr. **King Leopold assumed sovereignty** of the Congo State, which became his personal possession. The character of the state became less and less international and the king's objective became more and more the exploitation of the country. Concessionaires were granted large areas, but much of the country (the central portion) was set aside as state land (*domaine de la couronne*) and as the king's private domain (*domaine privé*).

Aug. 1. Leopold proclaimed the **neutrality of the Congo State** and announced its territorial claims.

Nov. 22. A **treaty between France and the Congo State** defined the boundary in the Manyanga region.

Dec. 24. An **agreement between France and Germany** defined the frontier between the French Congo and the Cameroons in the southern part.

1886, Apr. 27. **Savorgnan de Brazza** was made

commissioner-general of the French Congo.

May 12. A **Franco-Portuguese agreement** fixed the boundary of the Kabinda Enclave.

Dec. 30. A **German-Portuguese agreement** fixed the frontier between Angola and German Southwest Africa.

1887, Apr. 29. A **new Franco-Congolese treaty** defined the frontier as the Ubanghi River and the 4th parallel N. Lat.

1888. The French explorer, **Paul Crampel,** opened up the region from the French Congo to Lake Chad. He was followed by others **(Ian Dybowski, Casimir Maistre).**

Dec. 11. The French colony of **Gabun was united with the French Congo.**

1888–1889. **"RESCUE" OF EMIN PASHA,** the governor of Equatoria, by Henry M. Stanley. The relief expedition had been largely financed by King Leopold and his friend Sir William MacKinnon, chairman of the Imperial British East Africa Company. Its real purpose was to secure Equatoria and thereby an outlet to the upper Nile for the Congo State.

Aug. 2. Leopold designated the **Belgian State as the heir of the Congo.**

1890, May 24. The **MacKinnon treaty,** concluded between Leopold and the Imperial British East Africa Company. In return for a strip of territory between Lake Albert Edward and Lake Tanganyika (important for the project of an all-British Cape-to-Cairo route), the company recognized as Leopold's sphere the western bank of the upper Nile as far as Lado. This agreement, while not officially recognized by the British government, was not disavowed by it.

July 2. The **BRUSSELS ACT,** concluding an international conference at Brussels. It arranged for the systematic extirpation of the slave trade, prohibition of the sale of firearms, etc.

July 3. Leopold gave the Belgian State the right to annex the Congo State after ten years.

July 11. In return the Belgian State granted the Congo a loan without interest and a subsidy for ten years.

Nov. 14. An **agreement between Britain and Portugal** defined the frontier of Angola and South Africa.

1891, Apr. 15. The **Katanga Company** formed under Leopold's auspices to exploit the rich copper deposits of Katanga, after the defeat of the native king, **Msidi.**

May 25. By treaty the Congo State and Portugal divided Lounda between them.

June 11. A further **Anglo-Portuguese agreement** assigned Barotseland to Great Britain. Later disagreements were arbitrated by the king of Italy (May 30, 1905).

1892, May 8. The natives of the Congo were forbidden to collect ivory and rubber excepting for the state.

May 15. Beginning of a great **rising of the Arab slaveholders** and traders on the upper Congo and in the Tanganyika region. The Belgians proceeded against them. The Arabs were defeated by Baron Francis Dhanis (Nov. 22) and then by Col. Louis Chaltin, who took their chief centers, **Nyangwe** (Mar. 4, 1893) and **Kasongo** (Apr. 22).

Dec. 5. **Forced labor of the Congo natives** was introduced in the guise of taxes in kind and labor.

Oct. A Belgian force, under **Guillaume Van Kerckhoven, reached the Nile** at Wadelai and proceeded to take over the region assigned the Congo by the MacKinnon treaty.

1893, June. The **French,** alarmed by the advance of the Belgians, sent out **P. L. Monteil** and Lieut. Decazes to occupy the country from the M'Bomu River to the Nile, after futile attempts to reach an agreement with Leopold.

1894, Mar. 15. A **Franco-German agreement** regarding the Cameroons frontier left the French free to advance through the Sudan to the Nile.

May 12. The **CONGO TREATY,** between Britain and the Congo State. In order to frustrate the French advance, the British leased to Leopold for the duration of his life the entire region west of the upper Nile from Lake Albert to Fashoda and west to 30° E. Long. The region west of this (to 25° E. Long.) and north of the Congo-Nile watershed was leased to Leopold and his successors. In return Britain was to have a lease of a corridor 25 kilometers wide from Lake Tanganyika to Lake Albert Edward. Violent protests of the Germans forced the abandonment of the lease of the strip (June 22) while the threatening attitude of the French obliged Leopold to make an agreement with them.

Aug. 14. FRANCO-CONGOLESE AGREEMENT, fixing the frontier on the M'Bomu River and the Nile-Congo watershed along the parallel 5° 30′ N. Lat. Leopold was thus obliged to give up his claim to the northern part of the lease, but retained the region known as the **Lado Enclave.**

Sept. **Victor Liotard** was made French commissioner of the upper Ubanghi and was sent out to establish posts in the Bahr-el-Ghazal region. The French had visions of occupying the southern part of the former Egyptian Sudan and thereby forcing the British to evacuate Egypt by a threat of interference with the Nile water-supply. Some even dreamed of extending the French belt from West Africa across the Nile and Ethiopia to French Somaliland.

1895–1897. The **Gentil mission** opened up the Bagirmi country, the hinterland of the French Congo.

1895, Mar. 28. **Statement of Sir Edward Grey** in the British parliament, that any French expedition to the upper Nile would be regarded as an *"unfriendly act."*

Sept. Visit of King Leopold to Paris. He made an agreement with the French to cooperate on the upper Nile, and during visits to England (Oct., Jan.) attempted to bring about an adjustment of rival claims. His aim was to secure the agreement of Britain to a lease of the upper Nile region to the Congo State.

1896, Mar. 13. Beginning of the **Egyptian reconquest of the Sudan,** under Gen. Kitchener. The main object of the reconquest was to prevent the Sudan falling into the hands of France.

June. The **Marchand expedition** left France, with instructions to advance to Fashoda and claim the country for France.

1897, Feb. The Belgians, under Chaltin, reached the Nile at Rejaf, and, after defeating the Sudan dervishes, occupied Loda and Wadelai.

Aug. Marchand reached the Bahr-el-Ghazal region, but was unable to proceed because of the low water of the rivers.

Sept. Great mutiny and **rising of the Batetelas** on the upper Congo. Baron Dhanis proceeded against them in force, but the insurrection was not finally suppressed until October 1900.

1898, July 10. Marchand reached the Nile at Fashoda and established a post.

Aug. 30. Secret Anglo-German agreement for the eventual partition of the Portuguese colonies. Germany was to get the larger part of Angola (p. 790).

Sept. 19. Arrival of Kitchener at Fashoda. Acute crisis in the relations of France and England (p. 791).

Nov. 4. The French government ordered the **evacuation of Fashoda.**

1899. Granting of **concessions in the French Congo** to a number of rubber companies. Through rubber taxes and forced labor a form of slavery was introduced not much different from that of the Congo State.

1900, June 27. An **agreement between France and Spain** defined the boundary of Spanish Guinea.

1902. Great **native uprising in Angola,** suppressed with difficulty.

July 5. The French possessions on the Congo were divided into two colonies: Lower Congo-Gabun, Chad.

1903, May. Beginning of a large-scale agitation, first in Britain, then in the United States, Germany, and other countries, directed against the **conditions in the Congo.** The writings of **Edward D. Morel** and the reports of the British consul, **Sir Roger Casement,** aroused great indignation. In July 1904 Leopold sent out a commission of three to investigate. Its report (Nov. 1905) was unfavorable. The agitation continued until the annexation of the Congo by Belgium.

Dec. 29. The **French Congo was divided** into four colonies: Gabun, Middle Congo, Ubanghi-Shari, Chad.

1905. A serious **insurrection** broke out **in the French Congo.** An investigating commission under Savorgnan de Brazza was sent out.

1906, May 9. After years of friction the **British** finally **obliged Leopold to accept a compromise** settlement of his claims on the upper Nile. He was given the **Lado Enclave,** but only for the duration of his life.

1907. Another **insurrection in Angola,** connected with the Herrero rising in German Southwest Africa.

1908, Oct. 18. By act of the Belgian parliament, the **Congo State was annexed to Belgium.** Thenceforth the parliament exercised effective control and began the removal of abuses.

Dec. 23. A **Franco-Belgian agreement** definitively fixed the boundaries of the French and Belgian Congos.

1910, Jan. 15. The French Congo was renamed **French Equatorial Africa,** and was redivided into three colonies: Gabun, Middle Congo, Ubanghi-Shari.

May 2. The **labor tax was abolished** in the Belgian Congo.

May 14. An **Anglo-Belgian agreement** gave the Belgian Congo the west shore of Lake Albert.

June 16. The **Lado Enclave reverted to the Anglo-Egyptian Sudan** on the death of Leopold.

July 1. An extensive **program of reform** was introduced in the **Belgian Congo.** At much the same time the French government thoroughly revised the concessions to the companies operating in the French Congo.

Aug. 11. A **German-Belgian agreement** fixed the frontier between the Belgian Congo and German East Africa.

1911, May 4. An **Anglo-Belgian agreement** defined the boundary between the Belgian Congo and Uganda.

Nov. 4. The **FRANCO-GERMAN AGREEMENT** ending the **second Moroccan crisis** (p. 799) involved the cession by France to Germany of about 100,000 square miles of the French Congo.

1912, July 1. Freedom of trade in the entire

Belgian Congo was declared.
1913, Jan. 31. The **liquor trade was forbidden** in the Belgian Congo.
1914, Feb. 3. An **Anglo-Belgian agreement** fixed the boundary between the Belgian Congo and British East Africa.

July. The **Belgian Congo was divided** into four provinces and a general program of administrative decentralization was introduced.
Aug. 15. Angola was given autonomy.

(*Cont. p. 1082.*)

7. EAST AFRICA, 1823–1914

(Kenya, Uganda, Tanganyika, Nyasaland, Mozambique)

East Africa is inhabited almost exclusively by Negroes of the **Bantu race.** At the beginning of the 19th century the only European settlements were those of the **Portuguese,** and of these only the more southerly ones remained after the **conquests by the Arabs of Muscat** (Oman) in the late 17th century. From Cape Delgado northward to Cape Guardafui the coast was under the rule of the sultan of Muscat, who was represented by a viceroy (*Sayyid*) residing first at Mombasa, later at Zanzibar. The Arabs carried on a lively trade in slaves, and in the course of time the slave-raiders penetrated farther into the interior, reaching the region of the great lakes. When the European powers, intent on the suppression of the slave trade and on the expansion of their commerce, began to interest themselves in this region, they were confronted first with the claims of the Arab ruler and then with the pretensions of Portugal.

1823. Adm. William Owen, commanding a British squadron, raised the British flag on the south shore of **Delagoa Bay,** but this was removed after his departure, by the Portuguese.
1824–1828. Owen occupied Mombasa, the region being in dispute between the sultan of Muscat and his local representative.
1840. Sayyid Said, representative of the sultan of Muscat, established his capital at **Zanzibar.**
1841. The first British consul-general was appointed to Zanzibar.
1860–1865. Explorations of the German discoverer, **Karl von der Decken,** in East Africa. He first outlined schemes for a German dominion in this region.
1861. Under pressure from the British, the **dominions of the sultan of Muscat were divided,** Zanzibar becoming the seat of the **Sultan Majid,** who claimed control over some thousand miles of the coast.
1862, Mar. 10. The British and the French recognized the independence of the sultan of Zanzibar.
1866–1887. Sir John Kirk, British consul-general at Zanzibar. Under his influence the sultan was induced to take measures against the slave trade. British interests became predominant and Kirk to a large extent determined the policy of the sultan.
1870–1888. Barghash Sayyid, sultan of Zanzibar.
1873, June 5. Under British pressure, the **sultan prohibited the export of slaves** and closed the public slave markets of Zanzibar.
1875. Following the explorations of Livingstone (p. 863), the first **British missionaries** appeared on the **Shiré River** and about Lake Nyasa. **Blantyre** was founded in 1876.
July 24. An arbitral award of President MacMahon of France assigned the south shore of **Delagoa Bay to Portugal,** rejecting the British claims.
1876. The sultan of Zanzibar offered his continental possessions to **Sir William MacKinnon,** chairman of the British India Steam Navigation Company. MacKinnon appealed to the British government for support and, failing this, declined the offer.
1877. The first **Protestant missions** arrived in **Uganda,** following an appeal from King Mtesa, transmitted through Stanley.
1878. The **German African Society,** as a branch of the International Association for Exploration and Civilization of Africa, established a number of posts in the region between Bagamoyo and Lake Tanganyika.

British missionary and trading interests organized the **African Lakes Trading Company** on Lake Nyasa.
1879. Catholic French missionaries of the **White Fathers** arrived in **Uganda.**
1884, Oct. 10. Death of King Mtesa of Uganda. He was succeeded by his young and headstrong son, **Mwanga,** who soon became involved in struggles with the various religious factions (Moslem-Arab; Protestant-British; Catholic-French).
Nov. 19. Karl Peters, moving spirit of the German colonial movement, signed the first of a long series of treaties with the native chiefs of the regions behind Bagamoyo.
1885, Feb. 12. The **German East Africa Company** was chartered, to take over the claims established by Peters.

Feb. 17. The German government established a **protectorate over East Africa** from the Umba River in the south to the Rovuma in the north.

Apr. 8. The **Denhardt brothers**, Germans, secured the Witu region from the local sultan, for the newly formed **Witu Company**.

May 27. The German government established a **protectorate over Witu**.

Aug. 14. The sultan of Zanzibar was obliged to recognize the German protectorate over Witu, following a naval demonstration and an ultimatum.

Oct. Murder of Bishop James Hannington at the command of Mwanga of Uganda. Beginning of a period of persecution of the Christians and general chaos in that region.

1885-1896. Prolonged **wars of the British in Nyasaland** against the Arab slave-traders and their allies.

1886, May 12. France recognized the **Portuguese claims** to all territory between Angola in West Africa and Mozambique in East Africa, without prejudice to the claims of others. On December 30 the German government likewise recognized the Portuguese claims.

Oct. 29, Nov. 1. After an investigation of claims by a British-German-French commission (report June 9), the British and German governments concluded an agreement defining the possessions of the sultan of Zanzibar: the islands of Zanzibar, Pemba, and Lamu; the northern towns of Kismayu, Brava, Merka, Magdoshu, and Warsheikh; and the coastal strip (ten miles wide). The **German and British spheres of interest** were defined by a line from the mouth of the Umba River northwest around the northern base of Mt. Kilimanjaro and thence northwest to the point where the first parallel S. Lat. strikes the east coast of Lake Victoria. In the north the British sphere extended to the Tana River, leaving Witu to the Germans.

1887, May 24. The **British East Africa Company** (Sir William MacKinnon, chairman) secured from the sultan of Zanzibar a fifty-year lease of his coastal strip between the Umba and the Tana Rivers.

1888, Mar. 26. Death of Barghash; **Sayyid Khalifa,** sultan of Zanzibar.

Apr. 28. The Germans secured from the sultan a fifty-year lease of that part of the coast between the Rovuma and the Umba Rivers.

Sept. 3. The **British East Africa Company** was given a charter to develop the territory in the British sphere.

Sept. Victory of the Moslem-Arab faction in Uganda; deposition and flight of Mwanga.

1888-1890. Great **insurrection of the coast**

Arabs in the German sphere, under **Bushiri**. In December 1888 the British joined the Germans in a blockade of the coast. The rising was ultimately mastered by the German explorer and administrator, **Hermann von Wissmann.**

1888-1890. Portuguese expeditions into the regions west of Lake Nyasa and into the Manica district, with the object of establishing Portuguese claims to the whole of the interior, which had been assigned by the British government to the newly founded South Africa Company (p. 888).

1889, Sept. 21. The British proclaimed a protectorate over the Shiré River region.

Oct. 4. Mwanga, supported by the Christians, defeated the Moslems in Uganda. Ascendency of the Catholic faction.

Dec. Emin Pasha, the governor of Equatoria, having been "rescued" by Stanley (p. 879), arrived at Bagamoyo. He soon took service with the Germans and set out for the region west of Lake Victoria, where he was killed (1892) by Arab slave-traders.

1890, Jan. 10. The British sent to the Portuguese government a stiff **ultimatum** protesting against the expeditions into the interior.

Mar. 4. The British East Africa Company secured from the sultan of Zanzibar the concession of the **Benadir coast.**

Mar. Karl Peters, having entered Uganda by way of the Tana River country, induced Mwanga to sign a treaty, by which it was hoped that the German position in Uganda might be established.

Apr. 14. A mission of the British East Africa Company, under **Frederick Jackson,** arrived in Uganda. Peters withdrew to the south side of Lake Victoria and Jackson induced Mwanga to recognize the protection of the company.

May 24. The so-called **MacKinnon treaty,** concluded between the British East Africa Company and King Leopold as ruler of the Congo. The company recognized Leopold's rights on the west bank of the upper Nile, in return for the cession of a strip of territory between the south tip of Lake Albert Edward and the north tip of Lake Tanganyika. This agreement was not officially sanctioned by the British government (p. 879).

June 14. The British established a **protectorate over Zanzibar.** This was recognized by Germany in the agreement of July 1 and by France (in return for recognition of the protectorate over Madagascar) on August 4.

July 1. An **ANGLO-GERMAN AGREEMENT** disposed of conflicting claims and aims in East Africa: in return for the cession of Heligoland (p. 786) the Germans gave up all claims to Uganda and abandoned their position in Witu. The frontier between British and German East Africa was extended on the west side of Lake Victoria as far as the frontier of the Congo State.

Oct. 28. Following the suppression of the Arab rising, the **German East Africa Company ceded all its territorial rights to the German government.**

Nov. 19. The British proclaimed a **protectorate over Witu** and the coastal area as far as the Juba River.

Dec. 18. Arrival of Sir Frederick Lugard with a British force in Uganda. He induced the king to sign a new treaty (Dec. 26) and attempted to restore peace between the religious factions. In 1891 he moved to the western areas, establishing posts and enlisting remnants of the Sudanese forces which had been in the service of Emin Pasha.

1891, Mar. 24. An **Anglo-Italian agreement** fixed the Juba River as the boundary between British East Africa and Italian Somaliland.

June 11. An **ANGLO-PORTUGUESE AGREEMENT** brought to an end the long-standing dispute about claims in East Africa: Portugal was to have both banks of the Zambezi to a point ten miles west of Zumbo; the Rovuma River was to be the northern boundary; British claims in Nyasaland were recognized, as also in Manicaland.

July 30. The Portuguese government chartered the **Mozambique Company,** which was financed to a large extent by British capital, to develop the region behind Beira.

1891-1893. The **Wahehe War** in German East Africa.

1892, Jan. Outbreak of new **religious conflicts in Uganda.** Lugard intervened energetically and secured the victory of the Protestant faction.

1892-1898. Pacification of Nyasaland through the suppression of Angoni and Arab risings, chiefly by **Sir Harry H. Johnston.**

1893, Mar. Arrival of **Sir Gerald Portal** in Uganda. The British East Africa Company had announced its intention of withdrawing and had been induced to stay on only through the intervention and financial support of the missionary interests. The government of Lord Rosebery was eager to take over the country in order to protect the approach to the head-waters of the Nile, but the anti-imperialist element in the cabinet objected. Portal raised the British flag and recommended retention of control by Britain.

Feb. 22. The name of **Nyasaland** was changed to **British Central African Protectorate.**

1894, Feb. 4. Major Douglas Owen, sent out to counteract Belgian expeditions along the Nile, reached the river from Uganda and raised the British flag at Wadelai.

May 12. The **Congo treaty** between King Leopold and Great Britain, along the lines of the MacKinnon treaty (p. 879). The protests of the German government led to the cancellation of the lease, by the Congo State, of a narrow strip of territory adjacent to the German East African frontier, thus frustrating the hope of a Cape to Cairo connection through Africa.

June 18. The British government formally announced a **protectorate over Uganda.**

Sept. 1. A **German-Portuguese agreement** defined the boundaries between German East Africa and Mozambique.

1895-1899. Native risings in Mozambique greatly hindered the development of the colony.

1895, July 1. Following the dissolution of the British East Africa Company, the British government organized its sphere as the **East Africa Protectorate.**

1896, June 30. The kingdom of **Unyoro** was added to the Uganda Protectorate.

Aug. A disputed succession in Zanzibar led to a dangerous Arab movement against British rule and to a **bombardment of Zanzibar** by a British squadron.

1897, Apr. 6. Slavery was abolished in Zanzibar, by decree of the sultan.

July-Aug. New troubles in Uganda, provoked by King Mwanga. He was forced to flee and surrendered to the Germans.

Sept. Outbreak of a great **mutiny of the Sudanese troops in Uganda,** which was not suppressed until 1898, after a regular campaign by **Maj. James MacDonald.**

Nov. **Daudi Chwa** was made king of Uganda. Being a child, the country was ruled, under the British, by a regency (until 1914).

1898, Sept. Maj. Cyril G. Martyr took Wadelai and Rejaf on the Nile, as part of the reconquest of the Sudan.

1899, June. Capture of Mwanga and his ally, **Kabarega of Unyoro.** These two troublesome opponents of British rule were exiled to the Seychelles.

Sept. 13. First ascent of Mt. Kenya, by Halford J. Mackinder.

1900, Mar. 10. A definitive **treaty between Uganda and Great Britain** regulated the form of government: the country to be ruled by the king (*kabaka*) with the advice and assistance of the British commissioner.

1901, Feb. 23. An **Anglo-German agreement** regulated the boundary between German East Africa and Nyasaland.

Dec. 26. The first railroad train reached

Lake Victoria by the **Uganda Railway,** from Mombasa (surveyed 1891–1892; constructed 1896–1901, and since then the most important single factor in the opening up of the country).

1902, Apr. 1. The eastern province of Uganda was joined to British East Africa.

1902. A land grant of five hundred square miles in British East Africa to the **East African Syndicate** initiated white settlement in the upland region (regulated by the **First Crown Lands Ordinance,** September 27).

1905. A serious **rising of Moslems and pagans** in the southern part of German East Africa led to the practical extermination of the Angonis, a powerful native tribe.

1906, Oct. 22. Executive and legislative councils were established in British East Africa, the latter composed exclusively of nominated members.

1907, May 23. The government of **Mozambique was organized,** with the establishment of a legislative council on which the European elements were represented.

July 6. The name of British Central Africa was changed back to **Nyasaland Protectorate.**

Sept. 4. Nominated executive and legislative councils were established in Nyasaland.

1908, Mar. 31. Opening of the **Shiré Highlands Railway** to Blantyre.

1912, Feb. 26. Opening of the **railroad from Dar-es-Salaam to Tabora,** the main line in German East Africa.

1914, Feb. 1. The Dar-es-Salaam Railroad reached the shore of Lake Tanganyika.

(*Cont. p. 1082.*)

8. SOUTH AFRICA, 1795–1914

(Cape of Good Hope, Orange Free State, Natal, South African Republic, Rhodesia, German Southwest Africa)

At the end of the 18th century the Dutch were still in possession of Cape Colony, where they had established themselves in 1652. The settlement was originally designed exclusively as a refreshment station for the ships of the **Dutch East India Company** en route to the Spice Islands, but the need for supplies had led to the establishment of **free burghers** (1657) who were to grow grain and make wine. To provide the necessary farm labor, **slaves** were introduced from West Africa and from Asia (1657). The neighboring native tribes (**Bushmen** and **Hottentots**) were primitive, but early efforts to prevent contact and conflict could not be maintained. The need for fresh meat resulted in trade with the Hottentot cattlemen and in gradual expansion of the burghers beyond the immediate vicinity of Capetown. The population was increased (1688–1694) by the arrival of several hundred **French Huguenot settlers** who had taken refuge in Holland after the revocation of the edict of Nantes and whose passage to the Cape was financed by the Dutch East India Company. By 1700 there were about a thousand free burghers at the Cape. Progress during the 18th century continued to be modest. The stiff regulations of the company served as a deterrent and European immigration was almost insignificant. Nevertheless, the tendency toward expansion remained strong. Cattle farmers continued to push the frontier of settlement eastward along the coast and northward into the veld. The Orange River was reached in 1760

and the Great Fish River in 1776. Graaff Reinet was founded in 1786. In the last years of Dutch rule there developed also a **demand for burgher representation** and a more liberal régime. By 1795 this movement had reached the point where local magistrates were driven out and projects for a national assembly brought forward.

1795, Sept. 16. By the **capitulation of Rustenburg,** the Dutch garrison at the Cape surrendered to Adm. George Elphinstone and a British fleet. The British acted under mandate from the exiled prince of Orange, but the chief purpose of the seizure was to prevent the Cape, like Holland, from falling into the hands of the French.

1803, Feb. 21. Under the terms of the **treaty of Amiens** (p. 638) the **British returned the Cape** to the Dutch (Batavian Republic).

1806, Jan. 10. By the **capitulation of Papendorp** the Dutch garrisons once more surrendered to a powerful British fleet.

1807. Abolition of the slave trade throughout the British Empire. This created a serious labor problem in South Africa and brought to the fore the question of drafting the Hottentots.

1809. Legal restrictions on the free movement of the Hottentots were introduced, with the object of forcing them into service.

1814, May 30. By the **TREATY OF PARIS** (p. 650) the British secured definitive possession of the Cape. By an agreement of August 13 the Dutch were paid £6,000,000 funds, ostensibly by way of compensation. Until 1825 the new possession was ruled autocratically by the British governor.

1816. Great influx of **British missionaries** (Moravian missions, 1792; London Missionary Society, 1794; Wesleyans, 1816). The missionaries undertook to convert the natives in the eastern areas and to improve their lot. Through their exertions (especially **Dr. John Philip**) the problem of native protection was brought to the fore. Philip proposed segregation of the Hottentots and their settlement on the land. All such proposals roused strong opposition among the farmers.

1820. About four thousand **British colonists** (*Albany Settlers*) settled in the eastern coastal region by the British government, giving the colony for the first time a noticeable English tinge.

1822. A proclamation provided for the gradual establishment of English in place of Dutch as the official language.

1824, Aug. 27. **Francis G. Farewell** and a group of merchants from the Cape declared **Natal** British, but this step was not recognized by the government. The settlement was renamed **Durban** in 1835.

1825. After an investigation, the British government established an **advisory council** at the Cape (three official members; three nominated) to assist the governor. Two years later provision was made for an **independent judiciary.**

1826. The Cape colony was extended northward to the Orange River.

1828. Through the efforts of John Philip an ordinance (the **Fiftieth Ordinance**) was passed, allowing Hottentots to buy and hold land, and abolishing earlier restrictions on free movement.

The old Dutch magistracy (*Landdrosts, Heemraden*) was replaced by the **English judiciary system.**

1833. In Cape Colony the advisory council was replaced by a **legislative council,** similarly constituted, but with expanded powers.

1834. **Abolition of slavery** throughout the British Empire, with compensation to the owners. In South Africa, where 35,000 slaves were freed, there was much complaint about the inadequacy of the compensation.

Great invasion of the eastern regions **by the Bantu** (Kaffirs), irritated by the constant encroachment of the Dutch cattlemen and farmers. The natives were driven back with some difficulty.

1835. British territory was extended eastward to the Kei River **(province of Queen Adelaide),** but the region between the Keiskamma and the Kei (Kaffraria) was left to friendly natives

under supervision, as well as to white settlers. The British government, under pressure from philanthropic and missionary interests, disavowed the extension of Cape authority and the province had to be abandoned, much to the disgust of the settlers.

1835-1837. The **GREAT TREK** of the Dutch (Boer) cattlemen and farmers to the north and the east of the Orange River. Irritated by the restrictions on slavery and by the sympathetic native policy of the government, they sought new lands and freedom from interference. About 10,000 moved northward, seriously depopulating the eastern parts of the Cape Colony. Under **Andries H. Potgieter** they passed beyond the Vaal River and settled in what became the Transvaal. Those under **Piet Retief** crossed the Drakensberg and began to occupy Zululand and Natal, regions largely depopulated by the ravages of **Chaka,** the great military leader of the Zulus.

1838, Feb. **Retief** and sixty followers were treacherously **slain by Dingaan,** the powerful king of the Zulus, who massacred the immigrants and thereupon destroyed Durban.

Dec. 16. In the **battle of Blood River** Dingaan was defeated by the Boers, now led by **Andreas Pretorius.** The Boers thereupon settled in Natal **(Republic of Natal),** founding **Pietermaritzburg** (1839).

1840. **Dingaan was defeated** by his rival, Umpanda, who became king of the Zulus and accepted the rule of the Boers. Immigration of the Zulus from Zululand into Natal continued unchecked.

1842. **War between the Boers and the British** in Natal. The Boers were repulsed and British authority established.

1843, Aug. 8. **Natal was made a British colony,** with the object of protecting the natives against exploitation. Thereupon many of the Boers departed, moving northward over the Vaal River.

Dec. 13. By **treaty with Moshesh,** powerful leader of the Basutos, **Basutoland** became a native state under British protection. A similar treaty was made with **Adam Kok,** the Griqua chief. Thus many Voortrekkers were put under native jurisdiction.

1844, May 31. **Natal was combined with Cape Colony** for administrative purposes.

1846-1847. **War of the Axe,** between the British and the Kaffirs. The latter were defeated and **British Kaffraria** (between the Keiskamma and the Kei Rivers) was set up as a native preserve (1847).

1846. In Natal the first **location commission** set up preserves for the immigrant Zulus, under a revived tribal system. Beginning of the policy of **native segregation.**

1848, Feb. 3. Sir Harry Smith, the British governor of the Cape, proclaimed as British territory all the region between the Orange and Vaal Rivers and the Drakensberg. The Boers were disunited but some, under Pretorius, opposed the British. They were defeated by Smith at **Boomplaats** (Aug. 29) and the **Orange River Sovereignty** became a reality.

1850-1853. Great Kaffir War on the eastern frontier of Cape Colony.

1852, Jan. 17. By the **SAND RIVER CONVENTION** the British government recognized the **independence of the Transvaal.**

1853, July 1. A **new constitution** was introduced in the Cape Colony, after years of agitation. It provided for an elected legislative council of 15 members and an elected house of assembly with 46 members. The parliament was to be summoned annually by the governor, but the executive was not made responsible to it. The franchise was extended to all British subjects (white and black alike) on fulfillment of certain conditions as to employment, property, or salary.

1854, Feb. 17. By the **convention of Bloemfontein** the British government withdrew from the territory north of the Orange River, despite the protests of some of the settlers. This was the final step in the policy of withdrawal initiated by the Sand River convention. The settlers thereupon organized the **Orange Free State,** with a president and a volksraad.

1854-1861. SIR GEORGE GREY, governor of the Cape Colony. His administration was distinguished by an active policy of native protection, under white magistrates, the ultimate object being the civilization of the blacks.

1856, July 12. Natal was made a **separate colony** with an elected assembly.

Dec. 16. Organization of the South African Republic (*Transvaal*), after years of confusion. **Marthinus Pretorius** became president, and Pretoria (founded 1855) the capital. Dissenting groups stood aloof and continued their separate state organizations in **Zoutpansberg, Lydenburg,** and **Utrecht.**

Self-destruction of the Kaffirs, who slaughtered their cattle in the hope, encouraged by their prophets, that the heroes of old would return and drive out the white man. The population, deprived of food, died of starvation and in the end was reduced to about one-third of the original number. This tragedy did much to end the long-standing Kaffir problem.

1857, June 1. The South African Republic and the Orange Free State recognized each other's independence.

1858. Zoutpansberg joined the South African Republic, while Lydenburg and Utrecht united as one state.

1858. Sir George Grey recommended the **federation of the colonies,** including the Orange Free State, but not the South African Republic. The idea was at once repudiated by the home government.

1860. The **first laborers were imported from India** to work (under three-year indenture) on the sugar plantations of Natal. Large numbers were imported in the course of the next generation, many of whom remained in the country after expiration of the indenture. "Free" Indians also immigrated and soon became an important factor in trade and small industry.

Opening of the **first railway in Cape Colony.** In 1864 it reached Wellington.

Lydenburg joined the South African Republic.

1860-1864. Pretorius was at the same time president of the South African Republic and of the Orange Free State, thus establishing a close bond between the two Boer states.

1861. The British occupied islands in **Delagoa Bay,** in order to keep this strategic harbor from falling into the hands of the Transvaal.

1864-1888. Jan Brand, president of the Orange Free State.

1865-1866. War of the Boers of the Orange Free State **against Moshesh,** the chieftain of the Basutos. Moshesh, defeated, was obliged to cede large tracts of his territory and open them to white settlement.

1866. Kaffraria was joined to Cape Colony.

1867. DISCOVERY OF DIAMONDS near Hopetown, on the Orange River. By 1870 a considerable diamond industry grew up in the region between the Vaal and Orange Rivers.

1867-1868. The Orange Free State defeated the Basutos, who had risen in protest against the cession of territory in 1866.

1868, Mar. 12. The **British annexed Basutoland,** following a petition by Moshesh. His lands were returned to him, despite the protests of the Orange Free State.

Forces from the **Transvaal attempted to occupy Delagoa Bay,** but withdrew under protest from the British. The question was ultimately arbitrated by President MacMahon of France, who awarded it to Portugal (1875).

1869, July 29. An agreement between the Transvaal and Portugal fixed the boundary in southeast Africa.

1871. The town of **Kimberley was founded** and soon became the center of the great diamond industry. By 1890 some six tons of diamonds had been mined, valued at £39,000,000. The opening up of this great wealth completely changed the economic set-up in South Africa.

Oct. 27. The **British government annexed the diamond region** (Griqualand West), which had been under the rule of the Griqua (half-breed) chief, **Nikolaas Waterboer,** under the authority of the Orange Free State since 1854. The Orange Free State vigorously protested against this action, which had much to do with stimulating Boer distrust of the British.

1871–1872. The efforts of the British colonial secretary, **Lord Carnarvon,** and his special agent, the historian **James Froude,** to bring about federation of the South African colonies were frustrated by the opposition of the Cape government (under **John Molteno).**

1871. The government of **Basutoland was taken over by the Cape Colony.**

1872. Thomas Burgers, a learned Dutch minister from Cape Colony, became president of the South African Republic.

1872. Responsible government was established in Cape Colony.

1875. Lord Carnarvon, continuing his efforts toward federation, arranged for an informal conference at London (Aug.). As a result the claims of the Orange Free State to the diamond country were settled by a money payment of £90,000.

1876. The Cape government extended its influence up the west coast of Africa, concluding treaties with native chiefs as far as the frontier of Angola, but this policy was disavowed by the home government.

1877–1880. Sir Bartle Frere, governor of Cape Colony. His purpose was to push forward the work toward federation.

1877, Apr. 12. ANNEXATION OF THE SOUTH AFRICAN REPUBLIC by the British under **Sir Theophilus Shepstone.** This was intended as a step toward federation, but was a flagrant violation of the Sand River convention. The Boers, under the leadership of **Paul Kruger,** protested vigorously, but without avail.

1877–1878. Kaffir War. As a result the British annexed all of Kaffraria, and in the following years (1879–1886) extended their authority to the northeast as far as Pondoland.

1877, Mar. 12. The **British annexed Walfish** (Walvis) **Bay** on the coast of Southwest Africa. German missionaries had been active on that coast since 1842 **(Bethany Mission),** and had, in 1868, appealed to the British government for annexation. This appeal had been rejected.

1879. The **ZULU WAR,** against **Cetywayo** (king since 1872). Cetywayo had built up again the military power of the Zulus. On January 22 he defeated the British in a **battle at Isandhlwana.** Reinforcements were rushed to the front, and on July 4 Sir Garnet Wolseley won a decisive **victory at Ulundi.** Cetywayo was captured on August 28 and peace was made with the Zulu chiefs on September 1.

1879. Foundation of the **Afrikander Bond,** a Dutch group designed to work for recognition of the Dutch language. Under the influence of **Jan Hofmeyr** it soon rallied most of the Dutch elements in the Cape Colony, but with a much larger program of South Africa for the South Africans, with gradual elimination of interference from the British government.

1880–1881. REVOLT OF THE TRANSVAAL BOERS against the British. On December 30 a Boer republic was proclaimed by Kruger, Joubert, and Pretorius. On January 28, 1881, the Boers repulsed a British force under Sir George Colley at **Laing's Nek,** and on February 27 they again defeated and killed Colley at **Majuba Hill.** The British government, under Gladstone, was unwilling to contest the desire of the Boers for freedom, and on April 5 concluded the **treaty of Pretoria,** by which the South African Republic was given independence, but under the suzerainty of Great Britain.

1880. Organization of the diamond industry. Two great corporations were founded: the **Barnato Diamond Mining Company** (by Barney Barnato, an English Jew), and the **De Beers Mining Corporation** (by Cecil Rhodes and Alfred Beit).

1880–1881. The **"Gun War"** in Basutoland, resulting from the refusal of the natives to surrender their arms. As a result of this war, the British government in 1883 resumed the government of Basutoland as a crown colony.

1882. Cetywayo was restored as king of the Zulus, but was opposed by the native chiefs. The troubles were ended by Cetywayo's death in 1884.

1882. Establishment of Stellaland and Goshen, two Boer states in Bechuanaland. This was part of the Boer expansion to the westward as far as the Kalahari Desert.

1883, Apr. 16. Kruger became president of the South African Republic.

Aug. Franz A. E. Lüderitz, a German merchant, purchased from the natives a large tract of territory north of the Orange River. A short time before (Feb.) the German government had inquired in London whether the British government exercised any authority in this region. The reply was evasive, but when Lüderitz hoisted the German flag at **Angra Pequena** there was much excitement in London as well as at Capetown. The British government now announced that it regarded any claim to sovereignty in the region between Cape Colony and Angola as an infringement of Britain's legitimate rights. There followed a rather acrimonious discussion between London and Berlin. The Cape government, in the interval, urged the home government to annex all territory north as far as Walfish Bay. But the attempt was frustrated by the **proclamation**

of German protection over the region (Apr. 24, 1884), which was extended over all Namaqualand and Damaraland (Oct. 15, 1884). Sovereignty was vested in the Deutsche Kolonial Gesellschaft until it was assumed by the German government (1892).

1884, Feb. 27. The **convention of London** further defined the relations of the South African Republic to Great Britain. The Transvaal was deprived of Stellaland and Goshen, but the British government agreed to the omission of definite reference to suzerainty, though the Transvaal government was precluded from making treaties without submitting them for approval to the British government.

May. Fearful of German expansion eastward as far as the Transvaal and obstruction of the route to the north, the British, under the influence of **Cecil Rhodes,** concluded treaties of protection with the native chiefs of **Bechuanaland.**

Aug. The Boers, under Joubert, attempted to establish a republic in **Zululand** and thus secure themselves access to the sea on the east.

Dec. 18. In order to frustrate this move, the **British government annexed St. Lucia Bay** to Natal.

1885, Sept. 30. The **Bechuana territory was organized** as British Bechuanaland (the region between the Orange and the Molopo Rivers) and as the Bechuanaland Protectorate (north of the Molopo).

Nov. 28. The **railroad from the Cape** was opened as far as Kimberley.

1886, Dec. 30. An agreement between Germany and Portugal fixed the frontier between German Southwest Africa and Angola.

1886. DISCOVERY OF GOLD on the Witwatersrand in the southern Transvaal. Gold had been found in various parts of the Transvaal before this, but the rich reefs were opened up only at this time. There was a wild rush to the Rand from all parts of the world. **Johannesburg** was laid out (Sept. 1886) and before long had a population of 100,000, of whom half were native workers. By 1890 there were 450 mining companies on the Rand (capitalized at £11,000,000). The output was almost 500,000 ounces in 1890, and 1,210,865 ounces in 1892. Rhodes and his associates took an active part in the financing and organization of the industry and his company **(Consolidated Goldfields)** soon controlled a large share of the business.

1887, June 21. The **British annexed Zululand,** in order to block the effort of the Transvaal government to establish territorial connection with the sea.

1888. Amalgamation of the De Beers and Barnato diamond interests, giving the De Beers corporation, under Rhodes, practically a monopoly of the industry.

Feb. The **project of a customs union** between the Cape, Natal, and the Orange Free State was much discussed, but the Transvaal, under Kruger, remained unalterably opposed to all schemes of federation.

Feb. 11. John S. Moffat, a missionary and agent of Rhodes, concluded a **treaty with Lobengula,** king of the Matabele, by which the latter accepted British protection and promised to cede none of his extensive territories without the consent of the governor of the Cape.

Oct. 30. In a further treaty Lobengula gave the Rhodes interests **exclusive mining rights** in Matabeleland and Mashonaland.

1889. The Cape Colony and Orange Free State concluded a **customs union.** At the same time the Free State and the Transvaal (South African Republic) concluded a defensive alliance.

Oct. 29. The British government granted a charter to the **British South Africa Company,** headed by Rhodes. It was given almost unlimited rights and powers of government in the huge area north of the Transvaal and west of Mozambique, without northern limit. The effect was to hedge in the Transvaal on the north, Rhodes cherishing the hope that gradually the Boer Republic would be forced into closer economic and political relations with the other states.

1890, July 17. Cecil Rhodes became prime minister of the Cape Colony. He enjoyed the support of the Afrikander Bond, under Homeyr, the British and Dutch elements co-operating in a policy of South Africa for the South Africans.

Sept. 12. The town of **Salisbury was founded** in Mashonaland, part of the dominion of the British South Africa Company.

Dec. The railroad from Capetown through the Orange Free State reached the Vaal River.

1891, June 10. Leander Starr Jameson, a close friend of Rhodes's, was made administrator of the South Africa Company's territories.

Dec. By an **agreement between the Cape government and the Transvaal,** the Cape advanced money to finance the building of the railway from Pretoria to the Portuguese frontier, there to join the line (completed in 1889) to Delagoa Bay. In return the Transvaal government agreed to construct a short line from Johannesburg to the Vaal River and to bridge the river to connect with the line to Capetown. The Cape government was to have the right to fix rates on this short line until December 31, 1894.

1892, Sept. The first trains from the Cape arrived at Johannesburg. An immense traffic developed and the income from the railways came to be a vital factor in the finance of Cape Colony.

In Johannesburg **Charles Leonard** organized the foreign (*Uitlander*) element in the **National Union,** to agitate for better educational advantages, better police, easier franchise requirements, etc.

1893, Apr. 22. Kruger was elected president of the South African Republic for another term of five years.

May 12. Responsible government was introduced in **Natal.**

July. War of Lobengula against the Mashonas. The South Africa Company interfered, defeated the Matabeles, and took Bulawayo (Nov. 4). The chiefs submitted (Jan. 1894) and the danger passed with the death of Lobengula (Jan. 23).

Nov. 13. By the **Pretoria convention** Great Britain agreed that the Transvaal should have **Swaziland,** which, however, did not give the Boers access to the sea.

1894, Sept. 25. The **British annexed Pondoland,** thus connecting the Cape Colony with Natal.

Aug. Passage of the **Glen Grey Act** by the Cape parliament. This provided for a new native policy in the region east of the Kei River: the natives were to be given self-government under native councils, together with a general council, under the British magistrate. Individual landholding was made possible. At the same time the property qualification for black voters in Cape Colony was raised and an educational test introduced.

Nov. Rhodes paid a visit to Kruger and renewed his efforts to induce the Transvaal government to join the other states in a customs union. Having failed once more, Rhodes began to support the Uitlander agitation in Johannesburg and ultimately financed a **revolutionary movement against Kruger's government.**

1895, May 3. The territory of the South Africa Company south of the Zambezi was named **Rhodesia,** in honor of Rhodes.

June 11. The **British annexed Tongáland** in order to block the last possible access of the Transvaal to the sea (through Swaziland).

July 8. Opening of the Delagoa Bay Railway from Johannesburg and Pretoria to the sea. This gave the Transvaal at least an economic outlet free of all British influence. The Delagoa Bay route being much shorter than that to the Cape, traffic began to be diverted. This process was hastened by the imposition of prohibitive rates on the short line from Johannesburg to the Vaal River. In order to circumvent this move, the shippers began to use ox-wagons, crossing the fords (*drifts*) of the Vaal and proceeding thence to the Rand.

Kruger then ordered the drifts closed, but the British government interfered vigorously and Kruger yielded to an ultimatum (Nov. 8).

Nov. 11. British Bechuanaland was attached to the Cape Colony. Northern Bechuanaland became the Bechuanaland Protectorate, but a narrow strip of it, along the Transvaal frontier, was turned over to the South Africa Company on Rhodes's plea that it was needed for the extension of the railway from Mafeking north into Rhodesia. In reality the strip was desired so that the company could station a force at Mafeking, the nearest point on the frontier to Johannesburg. When the revolution, planned for December, should have broken out on the Rand, Jameson was to ride in and take control of the situation. Actually the conspirators in Johannesburg decided to postpone action and Rhodes warned Jameson not to proceed. But the latter, convinced that all that was needed was a little encouragement, disregarded orders and set out on his famous raid.

1895, Dec. 29–1896, Jan. 2. THE JAMESON RAID. With 660 men Jameson tried to cover the 140 miles to Johannesburg, but the Boers, who had learned of his plans, closed in on him, defeated him at **Krugersdorp** (Jan. 1), and forced his surrender at **Doorn Kop** (Jan. 2). At the demand of the British government Jameson was handed over for trial in England. He was convicted, but given a light sentence. The Johannesburg leaders were arrested and several condemned to death by the Transvaal courts. They were ultimately released in return for a large money payment.

1896, Jan. 3. The **Kruger telegram,** in which the German emperor congratulated Kruger on his success in supressing the movement. This step created an acute crisis in the relations of Britain and Germany (p. 788).

Jan. 6. Because of his part in the Jameson raid episode, **Rhodes was obliged to resign** as prime minister of the Cape Colony. He did not re-enter politics until 1898.

Mar. In Rhodesia there was another **rising of the Matabele** and (June) Mashona tribes. This was not suppressed until October.

Mar. 17. The Transvaal and the Orange Free State concluded an offensive and defensive treaty, a direct reaction to the Jameson raid.

Sept. 26. Aliens Expulsion Act passed in the Transvaal. This, and

Nov. 26. The **Aliens Immigration Restriction Act,** and various restrictions on the press and on public meeting resulted in continuous friction between Great Britain and the Transvaal, culminating in a **dispute about British suzerainty** over the republic.

1897, Aug.   Sir Alfred Milner became high commissioner in South Africa.

Nov. 4.   The railroad from the Cape reached Bulawayo, in southern Rhodesia. This line was intended by Rhodes ultimately to connect the Cape with Cairo.

Dec. 1.   Zululand was annexed to Natal. In Natal the growing feeling of opposition to immigration of Indians led to the prohibition of entry of "free" (i.e. unindentured) Indians and the closing of many occupations to those already in the country.

1898, Feb. 10.   Kruger was re-elected president of the South African Republic for five years. This meant a defeat for the more progressive element among the Transvaal Boers, which favored a more generous policy toward the immigrant foreigners and an agreement with the other South African states. The result was a marked revival of the **Uitlander agitation,** which met with the fullest sympathy from Milner. By the end of the year Milner was already convinced that the only solution of the problem would be through war, and that the war would amount to little more than a slap in the face. This forward policy, however, had little response in England. The cabinet, confronted with several serious international problems, was eager to avoid an unpopular war, and so resisted Milner's prodding.

1899, Mar. 24. The Uitlanders sent a petition with 20,000 names to Queen Victoria, recounting their numerous grievances.

May 31–June 5.   The Bloemfontein conference between Milner and Kruger, arranged through the efforts of President Martinus Steyn of the Orange Free State. Milner insisted on the immediate grant of the franchise to foreigners who had been five years resident in the Transvaal. This Kruger refused and the conference broke down. But on July 11 the Transvaal government passed a law granting the franchise on completion of seven years' residence. The British government thereupon proposed a joint inquiry as to the working of this law, but Kruger countered with the suggestion of reducing the term to five years in return for an abrogation of suzerainty. When Britain rejected this, Kurger took back his offer. By this time (Sept.) both sides had begun to make military preparations. Kruger, ever since the Jameson raid, had been convinced that the British were intent on the acquisition of the rich Transvaal, while the British had gradually come to believe that Kruger was actively furthering a plan to drive the British out of South Africa and set up a confederation of Boer republics. Feeling that further negotiation was futile, and wishing to take advantage of the small forces which the British

yet had in South Africa, Kruger sent an ultimatum (Oct. 9), which the British rejected. The Orange Free State joined the Transvaal (Oct. 11) and war broke out on October 12.

1899, Oct. 12–1902, May 31.   THE SOUTH AFRICAN (BOER) WAR. At the outset the British had only about 25,000 men available, the Boers having a distinct advantage in numbers. In addition the Boer forces were admirably equipped with small arms and with Krupp and Creusot artillery. The commander-in-chief, **Gen. Petrus Joubert,** hoped to push through Natal and capture Durban, thus gaining access to the sea. He brushed aside Sir George White at **Laing's Nek** (Oct. 12), suffered a temporary reverse at **Elandslaagte** (Oct. 21), but won a battle at **Nicholson's Nek** (Oct. 30) and invested **Ladysmith** (Nov. 2). In the west the Boers invested **Mafeking** (Oct. 13; valiant defense by Colonel Robert Baden-Powell) and besieged **Kimberley** (Oct. 15). The British, under Gen. Paul Methuen, drove back Gen. Piet Cronje and the Boers on the **Modder River** (Nov. 28), but there soon followed the **Black Week** (Dec. 10–15), when Cronje's victory at **Magersfontein** (Dec. 10–11) frustrated Methuen's efforts to relieve Kimberley and when Gen. Sir Redvers Buller, commanding in Natal, failed (**battle of Colenso,** Dec. 15) to effect the crossing of the Tugela River in the advance on Ladysmith.

Buller was thereupon relieved of the supreme command, and his place was taken by **Gen. Lord Frederick Roberts,** with **Gen. Herbert Kitchener** as his chief-of-staff. They arrived in South Africa on January 10, 1900. Meanwhile the fighting about Ladysmith had continued indecisive. On January 18 Buller finally managed to cross the Tugela and capture **Spion Kop** (Jan. 25), but was again forced back. A third attempt to establish himself beyond the river also met with failure (Feb. 6–7). But Gen. John French began a vigorous advance to relieve Kimberley, which was successful (Feb. 15). Cronje was defeated at **Paardeberg** (Feb. 18) and obliged to surrender (Feb. 27). At the same time Buller, having finally crossed the Tugela (Feb. 18), **relieved Ladysmith** (Feb. 28).

The British, now heavily reinforced, were henceforth able to maintain the offensive. Roberts took **Bloemfontein** (Mar. 13), and, advancing up the railroad, arrived at **Kroonstad** (May 12), while in Natal Buller drove the Boers back from Glencoe and Dundee (May 15). The **Orange Free State** having been overrun, it was annexed to the British possessions as the **Orange River Colony** (May 24). **Mafeking was relieved** (May 17–18) and the invasion of the Transvaal begun. **Johannesburg was** taken (May 31) and **Pretoria occupied** (June 5). Buller then forced the passes of the Drakensberg and began the invasion from Natal (June 10). On July 4 the forces of Roberts and Buller effected a junction at **Vlakfontein.** On September 3, the **Transvaal was annexed** as the Transvaal Colony. Kruger fled to Delagoa Bay and went thence to Europe. All efforts to interest other powers and provoke intervention failed. But the Boer leaders, defeated in regular warfare, now adopted **guerrilla tactics,** thereby prolonging the war by another eighteen months. Small forces repeatedly raided into the Cape Colony, harassed the lines of communication, attacked the railway lines, etc. Ultimately Kitchener (commander-in-chief since November 1900) was obliged to erect a line of **blockhouses** and organize **concentration camps,** into which some 120,000 Boer women and children were brought (about 20,000 of this number died of disease and neglect). The Boer farms were ruthlessly destroyed and the *guerrilleros* finally harried into submission. At the end of the war Britain had 300,000 troops in South Africa to deal with the 60,000 to 75,000 Boers. By the **treaty of Vereeniging** (May 31, 1902) the Boers accepted British sovereignty, but were promised representative institutions as soon as circumstances should permit; the British government promised a grant of £3,000,000 to enable them to rebuild their farms.

1903, Feb. Visit of Joseph Chamberlain, secretary for the colonies, to South Africa. He convinced himself of the hopelessness of the policy initiated by Milner of establishing British supremacy throughout the conquered areas. Gradually the government swung back to a conciliatory policy of Anglo-Dutch equality.

Dec. The Transvaal government, under pressure from the mining interests, agreed to the **importation of Chinese coolies.** In a short time over 50,000 of them were brought in, but their disorderliness, marked by several outbreaks and much terrorism, soon brought about vigorous agitation for their repatriation.

1904, Jan.-1908. The great **HERERO INSURRECTION in German Southwest Africa,** which was suppressed only after many systematic campaigns, by a force of some 20,000 men.

1905, Jan. Gen. Louis Botha formed the organization called *Het Volk,* to agitate for the introduction of responsible government in the Transvaal. A similar organization, *Orangia Unie,* sprang up in the Orange River Colony.

Mar. 1. The **earl of Selborne** succeeded Milner as high commissioner in South Africa.

1906, Dec. 6. By a new constitutional instrument, the **Transvaal was granted responsible government.**

1907, Feb. 26. In the first Transvaal elections, Botha's party, *Het Volk,* won 37 seats, as against 21 for the Progressive Party. Botha thereupon became premier (Mar. 4) and control passed to the conquered Boer element.

Mar. 22. The Transvaal government passed an **Asiatic registration bill** and provided for the restriction of immigration of Indians. The Indian population, led by an Indian lawyer, **Mohandas Gandhi,** later to become leader of the nationalist movement in India, began a long campaign of passive resistance.

June 14. The Transvaal government decided to repatriate the Chinese coolies imported a few years previously.

July 1. A **new constitution,** with responsible government, was established in the **Orange River Colony.**

1908, Oct. 12–1909, Feb. 3. Meeting of a **CONSTITUTIONAL CONVENTION,** first at Durban, then at Capetown. The purpose of the meeting was to discuss the relationship of the Cape Colony, Natal, Orange River Colony, and Transvaal to each other. The older ideas of federation were now brushed aside and the sentiment spread rapidly in favor of union. The convention agreed on a scheme for a **Union of South Africa,** at the head of which was to be the king, represented by the governor-general. There was to be a two-chamber parliament: the **senate,** composed of eight members from each state (province), elected by the representatives of that province in the house of assembly, sitting with the provincial council of the province; the governor-general was to appoint eight additional members of the senate; the term of the senate was fixed at ten years; the **house of assembly** was to be composed of about 150 members, popularly elected, roughly on the basis of population, but in each province under the electoral arrangements in existence there; the term of the house was to be five years; it was to have complete budgetary control and the ministry was to be responsible to it. The English and Dutch languages were both established as official languages. Each province was to be governed by an **administrator** appointed by the Union government; he was to be assisted by an **executive committee,** consisting of himself and four members elected by the provincial council; the **provincial council** was to be popularly elected, have a term of three years, and be indissoluble before the completion of the term. The powers of the provincial governments were distinctly limited, and they were clearly subordinated to the Union government. The **seat of the legislature** was at Capetown, the **seat of government** at Pretoria; Bloemfontein was the seat of the court of appeal.

1909, Sept. 20. The draft constitution was approved by the British parliament as the **South Africa Act.** It went into effect on May 31, 1910.

1910, Apr. 27. Botha and James Hertzog founded the **South African Party** as the successor to the old *Afrikander Bond* in the Cape Colony, *Het Volk* in the Transvaal, and *Orangia Unie* in the Orange Free State (this name was restored at the time of union). The party was a moderate nationalist party, aiming at equality of British and Boer and at independent status for South Africa within the British Empire.

May 24. Jameson founded the **Unionist Party,** a British-imperialist group.

Sept. 15. In the **first Union elections,** the South African Party won a decided victory (67 seats as against 37 for the Unionists). **Botha became prime minister** of the Union.

1911, Aug. 17. Northeastern and northwestern Rhodesia, were united as **Northern Rhodesia,** under the administration of the South Africa Company.

1913, June 14. An **Immigration Act** restricted the entry and free movement of Asiatics. This measure was followed by extensive agitation and rioting on the part of the Indians, led by Gandhi.

June 16. The **Natives Land Act** restricted the purchase or lease of land by natives and set aside further areas as reserves, thus extending the policy of segregation.

1914, Jan. Gen. Hertzog founded the **Nationalist Party** in opposition to Botha's South African Party. It drew its strength almost exclusively from the rural, Boer areas and became the organ of Boer separatism.

June 30. The **Smuts-Gandhi letters,** in which Jan Smuts, as colonial secretary in the Botha cabinet, promised Gandhi that the law regarding Asiatics would be enforced in a just manner and with due regard to vested interests. So much having been gained, Gandhi departed for India (July 20).

Sept. Botha, despite Hertzog's opposition, secured approval for a policy of supporting Great Britain in the First World War and for sending an expedition against German Southwest Africa. (*Cont. pp. 968, 1083.*)

9. MADAGASCAR, 1500–1904

Little is known of the original inhabitants of Madagascar, but the island was subjected to several waves of invasion from outside. **Arabs** came in before the 9th century and settled on the northwest and southeast coasts, where remnants are to be found today. There was evidently also an influx of **Africans,** probably slaves of the Arabs. But the bulk of the population, speaking one language of many dialects, is of **Malayo-Polynesian** and **Melanesian** stock. The most advanced group, which probably arrived from overseas in the 8th to 10th centuries, is the **Hova,** light in color and of distinct Mongoloid features. They moved from the east coast onto the central plateau, but not until the early 19th century were they able to establish predominance over other tribes.

Madagascar was first discovered by the Portuguese **Diego Diaz** in 1500. The first Frenchmen landed in 1527, without settling. **Portuguese missionaries** attempted, though unsuccessfully, to convert the natives (1600–1619). During the 17th and 18th centuries both the Dutch and the French attempted to establish posts along the coasts. The **French took Diego Suarez** on the northern tip of the island in 1638 and settled on the Bay of Antongil in 1642. They founded **Fort Dauphin** (southeast coast) in 1643. In 1664 the French posts were turned over to the **Société des Indes Orientales** and the island was successively called *La France Orientale* and *Ile Dauphine.* But in 1672 the natives drove the French out of Fort Dauphin, which was destroyed. In the following century the French once again established a foothold, this time on the island of **Ste. Marie,** off the east coast (1750–1761). In 1774 a Slovak nobleman, **Maritius Benyowski,** who had escaped from Siberia, was given a commission for a French settlement. He founded **Louisbourg** on the Bay of Antongil and set himself up as ruler of the whole northeast coast. Having returned to France in 1776 to ask for formal protection, he was repudiated. Ultimately he received a subsidy from the United States government, returned to Madagascar, and proclaimed himself an independent ruler. He was attacked and slain by a French expedition in 1786.

1787–1810. ANDRIAN AMPOINMERINA, king of the Hovas. He reunited the territory and extended the Hova authority over much of the island.

1803. Under orders from Napoleon, **Sylvain Roux** and a French force established itself at **Tamatave.**

1810–1811. The British, under **Sir Robert Farquhar,** seized Mauritius, Réunion, and the French stations in Madagascar. Réunion was returned by the treaty of Paris (1814), but Farquhar's efforts to maintain the British position in Madagascar were not encouraged by the home government.

1810-1828. RADAMA I, king of the Hovas. He was a vigorous ruler, intent on modernizing his kingdom. From the British at Mauritius he secured firearms and military trainers. In other ways, too, he encouraged the spread of British influence.

1818. The **London Missionary Society** established its first posts in the country, meeting with unusual success. By the end of the century almost half a million of the natives had been converted to Christianity.

1818-1819. The French began to occupy posts, notably Fort Dauphin. But in 1825 Radama, allegedly instigated by the British, ejected them.

1828-1861. RANAVALONA I, queen of the Hovas. She showed herself hostile to European influence (British as well as French) and also to missionary enterprise.

1829, Oct. A **French squadron bombarded Tamatave** in protest against the hostile policy of the government, but without real effect.

1830. The new French government of Louis Philippe ordered the withdrawal from all French stations except Ste. Marie.

1835. The Hova government forbade the practice of the Christian religion and forced the British missionaries to leave.

1840-1841. By treaties with the local chiefs, the French acquired a number of the islands off the northwest coast.

1845, May 13. By order of the Hova government, all foreigners were made subject to native law, including trial by ordeal. By way of protest the **French and British together bombarded Tamatave** in 1846, but again without making any impression upon the government. European influence was reduced to almost nothing.

1859. A number of chiefs on the west coast accepted the French protectorate.

1861-1863. RADAMA II, son of Ranavalona. The new king was a Christian, and at once reopened the country to the Europeans.

1862. The Hova government concluded **treaties with both France and Great Britain.**

1863, May 13. The Hova aristocracy (*Andriana*) revolted against the policy of the king, who was taken and strangled.

1863-1868. RASOHERINA, queen of the Hovas.

1865-1870. Exploration of Madagascar by the French scientist, **Alfred Grandidier,** whose exhaustive researches are still authoritative.

1865, June 27. By **treaty with Great Britain,** Christians were again tolerated and missions protected.

1868-1883. RANAVALONA II, queen. During her reign and that of her successor (i.e. till 1896) the real ruler of the country was the first minister, **Rainilaiarivony,** who was married to the last three queens in succession. Rainilaiarivony was a Christian, but distinctly suspicious of French designs. His policy, therefore, was to rely upon the British to resist French encroachment.

1868, Aug. 8. TREATY OF FRIENDSHIP AND COMMERCE WITH FRANCE. The French recognized Hova supremacy over the entire island, but in return were given consular jurisdiction over French nationals.

1869. Protestantism was proclaimed the state religion.

1877, Oct. Treaty of commerce with the British, who induced the Hova government to proclaim the **liberation of slaves.**

1879. Beginning of **friction with France,** growing directly from a dispute as to the inheritance of extensive lands which had been granted to the French consul, **Jean Laborde.**

1882. The **French government claimed a protectorate** over the entire northwestern part of the island, on the basis of the treaties of 1840. The Hova government took its stand on the treaty of 1868.

1883, June 1-1885, Dec. 17. WAR WITH FRANCE. The French government submitted a stiff ultimatum, which was rejected. French squadrons thereupon bombarded **Majunga** and **Tamatave,** which was taken June 13. The war dragged on inconclusively until 1885, when the downfall of the colonialists (Jules Ferry) in France led to the conclusion of

1885, Dec. 17. The **treaty with France** which gave France control of Madagascar's foreign affairs; **Diego Suarez,** at the northern tip of the island, was ceded to France outright; a heavy **indemnity** was to be paid, and **Tamatave occupied** until the obligation had been met; France was permitted to send a resident to the court of Tananarive, but with the understanding that there should be no interference with domestic affairs.

1886. The **French occupied the Comoros Islands** (Mayotte had been taken in 1841).

1890. Great Britain (Aug. 5) and Germany (Nov. 17) recognized the **French protectorate over Madagascar,** as part of the larger general colonial settlements made at that time.

1893. Further friction between the French and the Hova government, which resented the French claims to a protectorate.

1894, Nov. 10-1896, Jan. 16. THE FRENCH CONQUEST. The Hova government rejected a French ultimatum embodying extensive claims. The French thereupon occupied **Tamatave** (Dec. 12) and sent an expeditionary force of about 15,000 men under Gen. **Jacques Du-**

chesne to conquer the country. Duchesne landed at Majunga (Feb. 1895), but was delayed for months by fever and transportation difficulties. Finally a small column was organized to push on to the capital, **Tananarive.** The town was bombarded (Sept. 30) and surrendered at once. The queen agreed to accept the French protectorate on condition that she retain sovereignty, but a treaty along these lines (Oct. 1) was rejected by the French government.

1896, Jan. 16. The **French proclaimed possession** of the island, after forcing the queen to accept. The immediate result of this step was the outbreak of a widespread anti-foreign and anti-Christian insurrection.

Aug. 6. MADAGASCAR WAS PRO-

CLAIMED A FRENCH COLONY. **Gen. Joseph Gallieni** was sent out to pacify the island and organize the government. He remained as governor-general until 1905, which time order had been restored, administration set up, roads built, native tribunals organized, and some schools opened.

1897, Feb. 28. Gallieni deposed the queen and put an **end to the Hova dynasty.** Ranavalona was exiled first to Réunion, then to Algeria (d. 1917). The French thenceforth ignored the primacy of the Hovas and dealt with all tribes on an equal basis.

1904, Apr. 8. By the general settlement between Great Britain and France (p. 794) all British claims in Madagascar were disposed of.

(*Cont. p. 1085.*)

J. ASIA

1. PERSIA, 1794–1911

(*From p. 568*)

1794–1925. The **KAJAR DYNASTY,** founded by

1794–1797. AGA MOHAMMED (crowned 1796), a brutal, avaricious, and ambitious chieftain. He managed to suppress a revolt in Georgia and also to reduce Khorasan, but his successful military operations were cut short by his assassination.

1797–1835. FATH ALI SHAH, the nephew of Aga Mohammed, a ruler fond of wealth and splendor, but no general. His reign was marked by the involvement of Persia in the conflicts of Europe, by the rapid infiltration of foreign influence, and by the beginning of Russia's successful advance in Central Asia.

1798. The **British,** fearful for India, **induced the Persians to attack Afghanistan,** thus initiating a long struggle by the Persians to recover their eastern provinces.

1800. Russia annexed Georgia, the last king of which, George XII, appealed for Russian support against Persia.

1800. The **first Malcolm mission** to Persia. Sir John Malcolm, representing the East India Company, concluded a political and commercial treaty; the shah was to make no peace with the Afghans unless the latter renounced their designs on India. The British were to supply arms and money in the event of an attack on Persia by Afghanistan or France.

1804. War with Russia. The Russians advanced on Erivan, but were forced to retire. Indecisive fighting continued in Gilan.

1806. Arrival of a **French mission under Pierre Jaubert.** Napoleon offered to support the Persians in the reconquest of Georgia and in an attack on India.

1807, May. Treaty of Finkenstein, between France and Persia. The French government sent out **Gen. Claude Gardanne** with 70 officers to reorganize the Persian army, but after the conclusion of the treaty of Tilsit (p. 642) the French lost interest.

1808. Mission of Sir Harford Jones. He induced the Persians to dismiss Gardanne, in return for a subsidy and the aid of British officers.

1810. Another mission under Malcolm succeeded in definitely establishing the British influence.

1812. Russian victory over the Persians in the **battle of Aslanduz.**

1813, Oct. 12. Treaty of Gulistan, between Russia and Persia. The latter ceded Derbent, Baku, Shirvan, Shaki, Karabagh, and part of Talish, and also gave up claims to Georgia, Daghestan, Mingrelia, Imeritia, and Abkhasia.

1814, Nov. 25. Definitive treaty with Britain. Persia was to cancel all treaties with European powers hostile to Britain and to exclude all European armies hostile to Britain. Mutual aid was to be given in case of attack, and Britain was to pay a subsidy of £150,000.

1821–1823. The **last war with Turkey** brought Persia some successes, but ended in the **treaty of Erzerum,** which involved no territorial changes.

1825–1828. War with Russia resulting from the

Russian seizure of Gokcha, disputed territory. The Persians were defeated by Paskievich in the **battle of Ganja** (1826), after which the Russians took Erivan and Tabriz (1827).

1828, Feb. 22. TREATY OF TURKMAN-CHAI: Persia ceded to Russia the provinces of Erivan and Nakhchivan, and paid a huge indemnity.

1835-1848. MOHAMMED SHAH, who ascended the throne with the support of both Britain and Russia. His general policy, however, was less friendly to Britain, and a military mission (1834-1838) which tried to modernize the army had ultimately to withdraw.

1837-1838. The **Persians besieged Herat,** which was valiantly defended (Eldred Pottinger). Finally the shah yielded to British pressure and gave up the operation.

1847. Confirmation of the treaty of Erzerum (1823), providing for delimitation of the Turkish-Persian frontier. This was not actually completed until October 1914, Britain and Russia acting as arbitrators.

1848-1896. NASIR UD-DIN, the son of Mohammed, and on the whole the ablest ruler of the Kajar dynasty. In his early years (till 1852) his energetic minister, **Mirza Taki Khan,** undertook extensive financial and military reforms, which promised well for the country, but which came to an end with Taki's downfall. The shah himself on three occasions visited Europe (1873, 1878, 1889).

1849-1854. Russian conquest of the Syr Darya Valley, beginning the advance of Russia to the Persian frontier in Central Asia.

1850. Execution of Sayyid Ali Mohammed, the *Bab* (Gateway), and founder of **Babism,** a new mystical movement in Islam. In the succeeding years the numerous followers of the Bab were ruthlessly persecuted and finally (1864) expelled, most of them finding refuge in Turkey. The Bab's successor, **Baha Ulla** (*Splendor of God*), gave the movement a new turn and founded **Bahaism,** a less strictly Islamic version of the new doctrine.

1856. The **Persians took Herat,** whereupon the **British declared war** on Persia. A British force took Kharak Island and occupied Bushire and (1857) Mohammerah. By the **treaty of Paris** (1857) the shah was obliged to evacuate Afghan territory and to recognize the independence of the country. In case of dispute he was to make use of British good offices.

1864. Opening of the **first telegraph** in Persia (Baghdad-Tehran-Bushire) constructed by British interests as part of the line to India. The line from Europe (Odessa-Tiflis-Tehran) was opened in 1870.

1872. The boundary between Persia and Afghanistan was defined.

1872. The **Reuter concession,** granted to Baron Paul von Reuter, a British subject, envisaged the economic development of the country in many directions and pledged the customs by way of payment. The concession proved impracticable and was cancelled by the government.

1878. Establishment of the **Cossack Brigade,** a force trained by Russian officers and an important instrument for the spread of Russian influence.

1884. The **Russian conquest of Merv** completed the subjection of Turkmenistan and brought Russia to the frontier of Persia. From this time the **growth of Russian influence** in northern Persia was rapid and almost irresistible.

1888. Opening of the lower Karun River to navigation by British interests (Lynch Brothers).

1889. Baron de Reuter secured a concession for the **Imperial Bank of Persia,** with the right to exploit the mineral wealth of Persia (except gold and silver). The bank became the focal point of British interests.

1890. The government granted a concession for the production, sale, and export of tobacco, but aroused thereby so much popular and religious opposition that the concession was cancelled.

1892. The British government granted Persia a loan, with the customs of the Persian Gulf coast as security.

1896. Assassination of the shah, who was succeeded by his son,

1896-1907. MUZAFFAR UD-DIN, an incompetent and weak ruler, constantly in need of money for his own purposes. His reign marked the **acute phase of the rivalry of Russia and Britain.**

1900, Jan. Russia, through the Banque d'Escompte de Perse (practically a branch of the Russian finance ministry) granted Persia a loan of $22\frac{1}{2}$ million rubles, with the customs of all Persia, excepting the Gulf coast, as security. Persia was to liquidate the earlier British loan and to accept no other offers for ten years. In March 1902 the Russian government added another loan, receiving in return the **concession for a road from Julfa to Tabriz and Tehran.**

1900. Russian ships appeared at Bunder Abbas and plans were being considered for the construction of a railroad across Persia to the Gulf coast. The British government made no secret of its opposition, and finally, in 1903, Lord Curzon made a grand tour of the Persian Gulf to refresh the British ascendancy there.

1901. William K. d'Arcy, a New Zealander, secured a 60-year **concession to exploit for oil** through most of the country. The government was to receive £20,000 and the same amount in paid-up shares, and was to have 16 per cent of

The Kajar Dynasty in Iran (1794–1925)

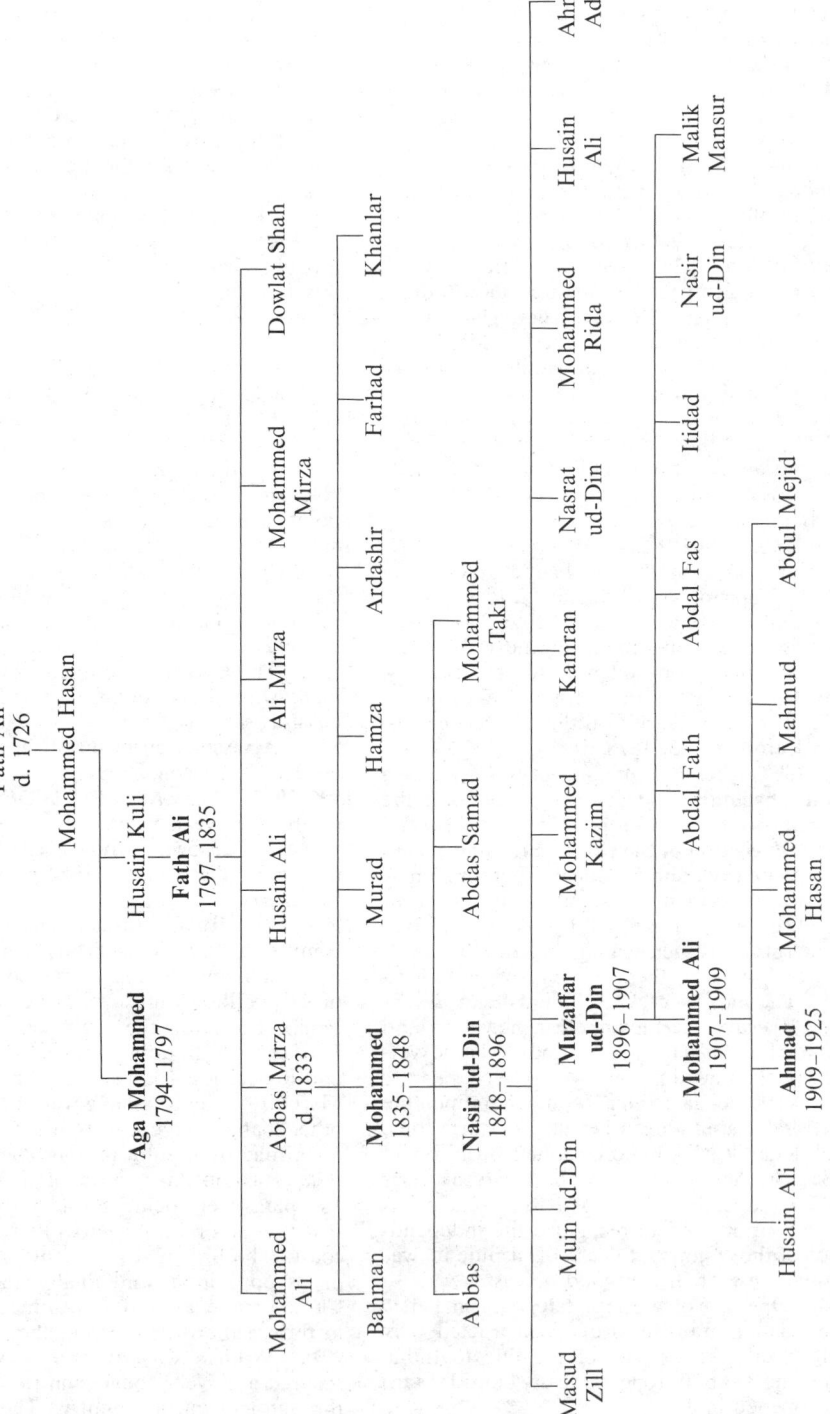

the annual profits. The concessionaire spent much time and money in futile operations, until, in 1908, the field at Masjid Sulaiman was discovered.

1902, Dec. 13. Russia induced Persia to promulgate a **new tariff,** very favorable to Russian goods and equally unfavorable to the British.

1903. The Persian customs were put under the administration of **M. Naus,** a Belgian national.

1905, Dec. Beginning of the **PERSIAN REVOLUTION.** Opposition to the incompetent rule of the shahs went back at least until 1890, and was centered in the commercial classes and the religious leaders. Inspiration of **Jamal-ud-Din el Afghani,** the eminent teacher of Pan-Islamic ideas, who was a Persian by birth (b. near Hamadan, 1838) and was at times closely associated with Shah Nasir ud-Din. In 1905 the movement was directed at the spread of foreign interests and control and at **Ayn ud-Dola,** the powerful and corrupt minister (1903–1906), who was held chiefly responsible.

1906, July. The **Great** *Bast* at the British legation. Several thousand revolutionaries took refuge on the legation grounds. The shah was obliged to yield to the popular demand. He dismissed Ayn ud-Dola and (Aug. 5) agreed to the convocation of a national assembly (*majlis*).

Oct. 7. The **first majlis** met at Tehran and drew up a constitution of the accepted liberal type. The shah died just after signing it (Dec. 30) and was succeeded by his son

1907–1909. MOHAMMED ALI SHAH, who from the outset was hostile to the new movement and attempted to circumvent the majlis. The result was

1907, Aug. The **assassination of** his reactionary minister, **Atabegi-Azam,** and the establishment of a liberal ministry under **Nasir ul-Mulk.**

Aug. 31. Conclusion of the **ANGLO-RUSSIAN ENTENTE** (p. 797), by which these two powers, both uneasy about German policy in the Near East, compromised their interests in Persia. Russia recognized Britain's preponderant interest in the Persian Gulf. The southeastern part of the country was reserved as a British sphere, while the entire northern half of the country became a Russian sphere. A central belt was to be left open to concessions for either party. The Persians were in no way consulted, but were not misled by the reaffirmation, in the agreement, of the principle of the independence and integrity of Persia.

Dec. 15. The shah attempted a *coup d'état* and imprisoned the liberal prime minister. This led to a **popular uprising** in various parts of the country, and the shah was obliged to yield.

1908, June 23. Successful *coup d'état* of the shah. With the secret support of the Russian legation and the aid of the Cossack Brigade, the shah shut down the assembly and had many of the liberal leaders killed. Martial law was established in Tehran, but at Tabriz the **populace revolted** and seized control. The shah sent an army against the city, but a deadlock ensued.

1909. Formation of the **Anglo-Persian Oil Company** to exploit the d'Arcy concession. A pipe line was constructed from the oil fields of southwestern Persia to Abadan Island in the mouth of the Shatt el-Arab and Persia soon became a leading producer of oil.

Mar. 26. A **Russian force invaded northern Persia** and raised the siege of Tabriz. Brutal action of the Russians in occupying the city for the shah.

June. **Ali Kuli Khan,** a leader of the Bakhtiari tribe, began the march on Tehran to defend the constitutional régime.

July 12. He took the city and deposed the shah (July 16).

1909–1925. SULTAN AHMAD SHAH, the twelve-year-old son of Mohammed Ali. He was wholly under the control of the more radical elements, who set up a regent to govern the country.

1911, May 12. Arrival of **W. Morgan Shuster,** an American, who had been invited to order the finances of Persia. Shuster was given almost dictatorial power by the majlis, and began to organize a treasury gendarmerie. The Russians, already suspicious, frustrated his attempt to secure the services of **Maj. Claude Stokes,** a British officer, and in other ways opposed the constructive efforts of the reformer.

July 18. The **ex-shah,** evidently with the connivance of the Russians, left his retreat in Russia and **landed at Astrabad.** His force was defeated by the government (Sept. 5).

Nov. 5, 29. Two **Russian ultimata,** aiming at the dismissal of Shuster, were rejected by the majlis. Thereupon **the Russians began to invade northern Persia.** Acute tension in Anglo-Russian relations.

Dec. 24. The **majlis was suddenly closed** and locked by the action of a group of politicians, who then formed a **directory.** From this time until the outbreak of the First World War, Persia was pretty much under the domination of Russia. (*Cont. pp. 965, 1097.*)

2. AFGHANISTAN, 1793–1907

(*From p. 569*)

1793–1799. ZAMAN SHAH, the son of Timur. His reign marked the beginning of a prolonged period of dynastic conflict and tribal strife, during which the **Punjab was definitively lost** to the Sikhs. Zaman at first defeated his brothers, but finally fell into the hands of his brother Mahmud, who blinded him.

1799–1803. MAHMUD SHAH, who was supported by Persia.

1803–1810. SHAH SHUJA, a brother of Mahmud, who seized control. His reign is memorable chiefly for the beginning of **relations with the British East India Company.**

1809, June 17. First **agreement with the British.** The latter, fearful of a Persian or French attack on India, induced the Afghans to oppose such a move and promised to support them if necessary.

1810–1818. MAHMUD SHAH, having escaped from captivity and having defeated Shah Shuja, resumed the throne. His main support was the vizir **Fath Ali Khan** of the Barakzai tribe, an able and energetic soldier and statesman.

1816. The **Persians captured Herat,** but were soon driven out by the Afghans.

1818. Revolt of the tribes after Fath Ali's dismissal by the shah. Mahmud was unable to stay the tide and was driven out of all his territory excepting Herat, where he ruled until 1829. The rest of the country fell to the various brothers of Fath Ali, who established practically **independent khanates** such as Kabul, Kandahar, Ghazni, etc.

1819. Conquest of Kashmir by Ranjit Singh, who took advantage of the confusion in Afghanistan.

1826. Dost Mohammed, brother of Fath Ali and ruler of Ghazni, **captured Kabul** and began gradually to extend his influence over much of the country.

1834. Dost Mohammed took over Kandahar after defeating the local ruler. In the same year **Ranjit Singh conquered Peshawar.**

1835–1839. DOST MOHAMMED became ruler of all Afghanistan and took the title of *Amir,* founding the **Barakzai dynasty.**

1837. The Persians, supported by the Russians, launched an **attack on Herat.** This offensive led to the conclusion of

1838, July 25. The **tripartite treaty** between the British East India Company, Ranjit Singh and Shah Shuja, the object of which was to restore the latter to the Afghan throne and block the advance of the Persians and the Russians.

1839–1842. The **FIRST AFGHAN WAR** of the British against Dost Mohammed. A British force advanced to Kandahar and thence to Ghazni and Kabul. Dost Mohammed was captured, deposed, and sent to India.

1839–1842. SHAH SHUJA ascended the throne again. Great discontent in the country and agitation against British influence.

1841. Rising against the British. Murder of **Sir Alexander Burnes** and **Sir William Macnaghten,** the British envoys.

1842, Jan. The British were obliged to fall back from Kabul. In the course of the retreat they were attacked by the Afghans under **Akbar Khan** (son of Dost Mohammed). With few exceptions the entire force of over 3000 men was massacred. Shah Shuja was murdered.

Sept. 14. Gen. Sir George Pollock and a punitive force from India **reoccupied Kabul** and punished the guilty, but the British government insisted on withdrawal from so exposed a position (Oct.).

1842–1863. DOST MOHAMMED again ascended the throne and re-established his power, though he secured Kandahar only in 1855.

1855, Mar. 30. Treaty of Peshawar, between Dost Mohammed and the British. The treaty was directed against Persian designs on Herat.

1856. The **Persians seized Herat** on the death of the local ruler. This move led to the declaration of war by Britain (p. 895) and

1857, Mar. 4. The **treaty of Paris,** between Britain and Persia. The latter power gave up its claim to Herat and recognized the independence of Afghanistan.

1863. Dost Mohammed finally took Herat, after a ten months' siege, from the khan who had been set up after the evacuation.

1863–1870. Civil war following the death of Dost Mohammed. His third son, **Sher Ali,** who was recognized by the British, had a hard time asserting his claim against his brothers, who for years held the upper hand.

1870–1879. SHER ALI, amir. His general policy was to lean on Russia as a counterweight to the British. The result was growing tension in relations with India.

1878, June. Arrival of a Russian mission under Gen. Nicholas Stolietov at Kabul and conclusion of a treaty of mutual support (Aug.). The Indian government thereupon insisted upon the reception of a British mission, which Shir Ali refused. The result was

1878–1879. The **SECOND AFGHAN WAR,** in the course of which Sher Ali died (Feb. 1879).

1879. YAKUB, the son of Sher Ali, became

The Barakzai Dynasty in Afghanistan (1747–1929)

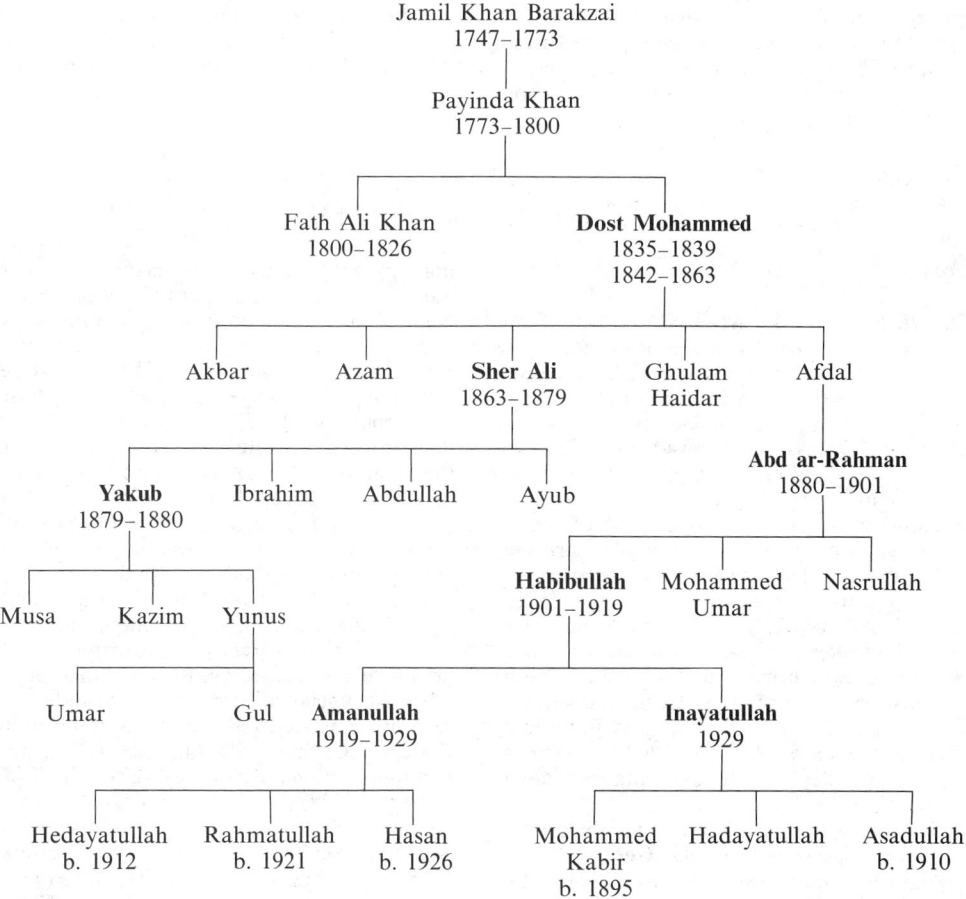

amir. The British having overrun much of the country, he was forced to accept

May 16. The **treaty of Gandamak,** by which the British were to occupy the Khyber Pass, but to pay the amir an annual subsidy of £60,000. The amir was to conduct his foreign relations only through the Indian government. British trade was to have full freedom.

Sept. 3. Native outbreak against the British. Murder of **Sir Louis Cavagnari** and his escort. The British thereupon advanced and took Kabul once more (Oct. 12).

Oct. 19. Yakub abdicated and surrendered to the British.

1880–1901. ABD AR-RAHMAN, nephew and opponent of Sher Ali, who had been in retirement in Russia, then became amir. In a general way he accepted the treaty of Gandamak, but throughout his reign he succeeded in play-

ing off the British and the Russians and thereby protecting his country. At the same time he subdued many of the tribes and established his authority as ruler. The reign was noteworthy also for the gradual fixing of the Afghan frontiers.

1885, Apr. The **Penjdeh incident,** a clash between Russian and Afghan troops on the disputed border. A severe Anglo-Russian crisis ensued (p. 783), but the matter was finally settled by negotiations (June 18, 1886).

1893, Nov. 12. The **Durand agreement,** with Britain, fixed the frontier with India from Chitral to Baluchistan.

1895, Mar. 11. Settlement of the Pamir boundary, after years of friction with Russia. Afghanistan retained a narrow strip which separated the Russian and British possessions.

1901–1919. HABIBULLAH KHAN, son of

Abd ar-Rahman, amir. He was a much less effective ruler and fell more and more under harem and religious influences. Gradual penetration of European ideas.

1905, Mar. 21. **A new agreement with Britain** reaffirmed earlier engagements. This was a reply to renewed Russian activity since about 1900 (mission of commercial agents, etc.).

1907, Aug. 31. The **Anglo-Russian entente,** which involved compromise of Russian and British interests in Persia, included recognition by Russia of Britain's predominant position in Afghanistan. Russia agreed once more to abstain from interference in Afghan affairs.

(*Cont. p. 1099.*)

3. INDIA, 1798–1914

(*From p. 574*)

1798–1805. **LORD MORNINGTON** (later **marquis of Wellesley**) governor-general. He developed the system of subsidiary alliances (map p. 570) by which Britain supplied troops and protection in exchange for territory or monetary grants, was allowed control of the state's foreign affairs, but pledged non-intervention in internal government, and secured exclusion of every other foreign power from the state's service. The fourth **Anglo-Mysore War** (Tipu d. 1799) led to a protectorate over Mysore; various annexations extended British control over nearly all southern India. The **Maratha leaders,** angered by the **treaty of Bassein** (1802) which made the Peshwa a subsidiary ally, opened hostilities. Costly but successful warfare (defeat of Sindhia and Bhonsle at **Assaye,** September 23, 1803) led to alarm at home, Wellesley's recall, and temporary abandonment of his policy.

1805. **Lord Cornwallis** again governor-general (d. Oct.), succeeded by **Sir George Barlow** (1805–1807), and **Lord Minto** (1807–1813).

1809. **Treaty of Amritsar fixed the river Sutlej as northwestern boundary** of the company's territories, checking the advance of a Sikh confederacy under **Ranjit Singh** (d. 1839).

1808–1810. To curb French expansion in Asia, Minto made **treaties with Sind, Persia, and Afghanistan,** and captured the French islands in the Indian Ocean and Java, which was under French control (Bourbon was later restored to France and Java to the Dutch).

1813–1823. **LORD MOIRA** (later **marquis of Hastings**) governor-general, followed by John Adam (acting) and Lord Amherst (1823–1828).

1813. Parliament **renewed the company's charter** for another twenty years, but under pressure of free trade interests **abolished its monopoly of trade with India,** and extended the sovereignty of the British crown over the East India Company's possessions. Missionaries were for the first time allowed to evangelize in the company's territories.

1814–1816. **Border dispute with Nepal,** provoking hard-fought war, British acquisition of the Kumaun Division, and permanent peace with Nepal, which retained its complete independence.

1816–1818. The marauding **Pindari tribes,** after raiding British territory, were suppressed and broken up by Hastings; hostile Maratha leaders were also defeated, leaving only Nepal, the Sikh state, and Afghanistan independent of direct or indirect British control.

In Bengal, the introduction by the British of **printing** (Wilkins, 1778) stimulated a growing volume of publishing in English, Bengali, Persian, Sanskrit, and Hindustani, and made possible the establishment of schools imparting both modern and traditional learning. In the field of **higher education,** the combined efforts of British officials and private British and Indian philanthropists led to the founding of the Hindu College (Calcutta, 1816), the Elphinstone Institution (Bombay, origins 1827), the Delhi College (1827), and the Madras University High School (1841), the nuclei of the later universities. **Newspapers** made their appearance in the 1780's in Calcutta, Madras, and Bombay (government controls imposed sporadically, and licensing required 1823–1835).

These developments, and the discoveries by British **orientalists** active in the Asiatic Society (founded 1784 by **William Jones**), the **College of Fort William** (founded 1800 by Wellesley), and the **Serampore Baptist Mission** (founded 1800 by **William Carey**), stimulated an intellectual renaissance among Bengali Hindu scholars. **Rammohun Roy** published Vedic texts in five languages, condemned idolatry and *satī* as corrupt practices, espoused Christian ethics but ridiculed Christian theology, and established the **Brahmo Samaj** (1828–1830), open to monotheists of every persuasion. An opposing movement, led by **Radhakanta Deb,** organized the **Dharma Sabha** (1830), sponsoring educational change but not social or religious reform. Bengali prose developed rapidly as a literary medium from this time on.

1824–1826. Following Burmese aggression the **first Anglo-Burmese War** led to British acquisition of Assam, Arakan, and Tenasserim.

1827. Pretense of subordination to the Delhi emperor abandoned; his name removed from the coinage (1835).

1828-1835. LORD WILLIAM BENTINCK, governor-general. Relative peace favored reform measures: *satī* was made a criminal offense (1829); bands of *thags* began to be suppressed; inland transit duties were abolished (1835); tea and coffee production were added to that of indigo; roads and canals were planned (Grand Turk Road begun 1839) and river and ocean steamship lines encouraged. Administrative costs were cut; revenue settlement inaugurated in the northwest provinces; more responsibility given to Indian subordinate officials; and law revision and codification undertaken by **Thomas B. Macaulay** (law member, 1834-1838), whose **Minute on Education** (1835), along with the pressure of Hindu demands and administrative convenience, prompted the momentous decision to subsidize primarily education along Western lines through the medium of English.

1820-1831. The Muslims of northern India, generally resentful of the new order, and hostile to secular education in English as subversive of their faith, responded in large numbers to the appeal of **Sayyid Ahmad Shahid** of Rae Bareilly (influenced by the reformism of Shah Wali-Ullah and the puritan ideas of Ibd 'Abd-ul-Wahhab of Arabia) for a return to the ways prescribed in the Koran, and a restoration of Muslim government in India. Mindful of the strength of the British, Sayyid Ahmad preached and organized a *jihad* (holy war) against the Sikh rulers of the Punjab (1826-1831) and was killed in battle against them (1831). His followers, although dispersed, developed a well-knit organization and continued his movement until the 1870's, when by assassinations of British officials they provoked their suppression by the government.

In Bengal, **Titu Mir** led a Muslim uprising against oppressive Hindu *zamindars* and was killed by government troops (Nov. 19, 1831). The *Fara'izi* (obligationist) reform movement launched early in the century by **Haji Shari' at-Ullah** became a radical sect under his son **Dudhu Miyan.** The moderate reforms of **Karamat 'Ali,** a disciple of Sayyid Ahmad Shahid, meanwhile attracted widespread support among Bengali Muslims.

1831-1881. Mysore state taken under direct British control owing to misgovernment.

1833. Parliament renewed the company's charter for twenty years, **abolishing its trade** in India and China, and restricting its functions to the administration of its Indian territories. European settlements in India were allowed,

and funds for education (first provided 1813) were substantially increased.

1835-1836. Sir Charles Metcalfe, governor-general, followed by **Lord Auckland** (1836-1842), **Lord Ellenborough** (1842-1844), and **Sir Henry Hardinge** (1844-1848).

1837. Persian abandoned as the language of record and the courts, replaced by English and regional languages, a decision welcomed by the Anglicized Bengali Hindus but deplored by the Muslims, whose numbers in the administration steadily declined. British officials, now trained initially in England (Haileybury College established 1805), and increasingly accompanied by their wives, gradually became socially and intellectually more aloof from their Indian subjects.

1839-1842. The **FIRST ANGLO-AFGHAN WAR,** a fiasco precipitated by Auckland's exaggerated fear of Russian influence in Afghanistan. Although 16,000 British and sepoy troops succeeded in occupying Kabul (1839-1841), popular revolt brought on their evacuation (Jan. 6, 1842) and massacre (121 survivors).

1843. Annexation of Sind, following provocation of hostilities by **Sir Charles Napier,**

1845-1848. FIRST AND SECOND ANGLO-SIKH WARS, arising from disorders after Ranjit Singh's death (1839), led to **annexation of the Punjab,** modernization of its government, and permanent loyalty of the Sikhs. **Kashmir** was sold (1846) to a Hindu chieftain, who accepted British paramountcy.

1848-1856. LORD DALHOUSIE, governor-general, accelerated public works, developing roads, irrigation canals, and **railways** (first line opened 1853), introducing telegraph service (Calcutta-Agra line opened 1854), and fixing uniform postal rates.

Dalhousie adhered consistently to the **doctrine of lapse** (disavowed 1859), whereby dependent states with no heirs in the ruling line fell to the paramount power; seven principalities were annexed in this manner.

1851. British Indian Association with branches in Madras and Avadh (Oudh) and **Debendranath Tagore,** the Brahmo Samaj leader, as secretary, founded in Calcutta to press for administrative and political reforms in the forthcoming renewal of the company's charter. The **Bombay Association** (1852), under Parsi leadership, had similar aims but was short-lived.

1853. Company's charter renewed.

1854. Education dispatch of Sir Charles Wood, president, board of control, laid down the pattern for future government-aided expansion of elementary and secondary schools, and affiliating universities (founded 1857 at Calcutta, Madras, and Bombay).

1856. Annexation of Avadh (Oudh), on grounds of misgovernment, aroused deep resentment, especially among the 40,000 Avadhi sepoys in the Bengal army.

1856-1862. EARL CANNING, governor-general and (from 1858) first viceroy, was confronted by a short war with Persia (1856-1857) and

1857-1858. REBELLION in northern India, comprising mutinies (beginning at Meerut, May 10) by sepoy troops, popular **uprisings,** and scattered **revolts** by Hindu and Muslim chiefs seeking restoration of cancelled privileges. The recapture of Delhi by loyal forces from the Punjab (Sept. 20) marked the turning of the tide, but three expeditions were required to retake Lucknow (Mar. 5, 1858) and guerrilla warfare continued for some months. Although British losses were small, the memory of atrocities committed by both sides (notably the massacre of 211 British women and children at Cawnpore, July 15, 1857) embittered social relations between Indians and Europeans for the next ninety years. The last of the Mughal rulers, **Bahadur Shah II,** having been declared emperor of India by the Delhi rebels, was deposed, tried, exiled, and died in Rangoon (1862).

1858, Aug. 2. By the **GOVERNMENT OF INDIA ACT,** parliament transferred the government of India from the East India Company (dissolved 1874) to the crown. The governor-general received the additional title of viceroy, and was made directly responsible to the secretary of state for India in the British cabinet.

Nov. 1. Proclamation by the queen renounced the policy of annexation of princely states, promised non-interference in religious belief or worship, and opened higher administrative offices to qualified Indians.

1859-1862. Paper currency, license, and income taxes, and a 10 per cent tariff were introduced to meet the **heavy debt** left after suppression of the rebellion.

1859-1862. Administrative reforms undertaken to strengthen the government: cabinet system introduced; civil service appointments regulated (competitive since 1853); army reorganized, recruited increasingly from the Punjab and Nepal; code of civil procedure (1859), penal code (1860), code of criminal procedure (1861), and high courts (1862) regularized administration of justice; **legislative councils** appointed (governor-general's 1853, reorganized and enlarged 1861; provincial, 1862), containing a small proportion of Indian members.

Public works were pressed energetically: the railway network embraced all major cities by 1875; telegraph service to Europe was opened (1865). Archeological survey (1861), famine relief (1861), forestry (1861), agriculture and sanitation (1864) began to be fostered by official measures.

1862-1863. Lord Elgin, viceroy, succeeded by **Lord Lawrence** (1864-1869), **Lord Mayo** (1869-1872), **Lord Northbrook** (1872-1876), and **Lord Lytton** (1876-1880).

1866. Collapse of the cottom boom which had arisen from increased production during the American Civil War.

1868. Security of land tenure granted to peasants by Oudh and Punjab Tenancy Acts, following precedent of Bengal Rent Act (1859), which applied also to Agra and Central Provinces.

Hindu reform movements broadened their influence among the English-speaking middle class: **Keshab Chunder Sen** formed the **Brahmo Samaj of India** (1865), stimulating the establishment of the **Prarthana Samaj** in Bombay (1867); annual mettings of the **Hindu Mela** at Calcutta (1867-1880) propagated neo-Hindu and proto-nationalist ideas; **Arya Samaj** founded by **Swami Dayananda** (Bombay, 1875), and its headquarters fixed at Lahore (1877).

Muslim reform given momentum: in north India by the educational and journalistic work of **Sayyid Ahmad Khan,** who founded the **Muslim Anglo-Oriental College** at Aligarh (1877); in Bombay by the **Aga Khan;** in Calcutta by **'Abdul Latif (Muslim Literary Society,** 1863) and **Sayyid Amir Ali (National Muslim Association,** 1877).

1869. Opening of the Suez Canal eliminated the overland Suez link (regular service opened 1843), greatly cheapening freight shipments. Both India's overseas trade and the percentage of manufactured goods in her total exports nearly tripled in the following four decades.

1872. Assassination of Lord Mayo by a Muslim fanatic.

1876. Occupation of Quetta as a safeguard against the Russian southward advance toward Afghanistan (p. 898).

1876-1878. Great famine in the Deccan and adjacent areas took over 5,000,000 lives.

1877. On Disraeli's initiative, the **queen was proclaimed empress of India** at a Delhi ceremony (*durbar*) at which the Indian princes were assembled to offer their homage.

1878-1881. The **SECOND ANGLO-AFGHAN WAR,** provoked by Lytton, led to his recall, increased the public debt, but established British control over Afghanistan's foreign relations.

1880-1884. LORD RIPON, viceroy, a Gladstonian liberal, introduced local self-government but fierce opposition by British residents in India defeated the **Ilbert Bill** (1883) by which Indian judges in outlying areas could try Europeans. These developments spurred the growth of nationalist sentiment. Concurrently the spread of higher education, the rise of the daily press, and the ease of travel created by the railway network facilitated the establishment of regional and all-India associations by the English-speaking middle class: **Indian Association** (1876), **Poona Sarvajanik Sabha** (1876), **National Conference** (1883), **Madras Mahajana Sabha** (1884), **Bombay Presidency Association** (1885), many of whose leaders joined in founding

1885, Dec. 27. The **INDIAN NATIONAL CONGRESS**, fathered by **A. O. Hume.** At successive annual meetings (held at different cities in the last week of each year), the congress demanded expansion and reform of the legislative councils and more rapid Indianization of the civil service. Sayyid Ahmad Khan, fearing Hindu domination of representative institutions, led conservative Muslim opposition to the congress, organizing the Muslim Education Conference (meeting annually from 1887), the Indian Patriotic Association (1888), and the Upper India Muslim Defence Association (1893). The viceroy, **Lord Dufferin** (1884–1888), originally encouraging, grew cooler to the congress as its agitation assumed a more aggressive character.

1885–1886. **Third Anglo-Burmese War,** ending in **annexation of Upper Burma.**

1888–1894. **Lord Lansdowne,** viceroy, followed by **Lord Elgin** (1894–1898).

1892. **Dadabhai Naoroji,** Parsi business and political leader resident in England, was elected to parliament on the Liberal ticket. His example of selfless service to India inspired many younger compatriots (notably **Mohandas K. Gandhi** and **Mohammad A. Jinnah**) during their visits to London.

Legislative councils were enlarged and their powers increased. The provision that the non-official (European and Indian) members were to be nominated by local bodies gave tacit recognition to the principle of election.

1893. The **Durand Line** demarcated by mutual agreement the border between India and Afghanistan, but bisected the area inhabited by the Pathan tribes.

In this same year the Bengali **Swami Vivekananda,** a disciple of the mystic **Sri Ramakrishna,** became a hero in India by his well-received speeches at the World Parliament of Religions in Chicago; **Mrs. Annie Besant** arrived at Madras to take charge of the growing Theosophist movement; and in the Punjab **Mirza Ghulam Ahmad** was attracting a growing

following (later known as the **Ahmadiyas**) by his claims to prophethood. Anti-Christian sentiment and its corollaries, Hindu and Muslim revivalism, grew more pronounced from this time onward, all contributing to the increasingly popular character of the nationalist movement.

1895. The **Indian Social Conference** (founded 1887 by **Mahadeo G. Ranade**) was forced by the orthodox agitation of **Bal G. Tilak** to separate its venue from that of the congress.

1896–1900. Two widespread famines in western, central, and northern India took an estimated 2,000,000 lives.

1897. Assassination of two British plague inspectors at Poona, and subsequent trial and imprisonment of Tilak, marked the rise of the extremist school of nationalism, deeply imbued with Hindu orthodoxy (in Maharashtra) and neo-Hindu ideas (in Bengal).

1898–1905. **LORD CURZON,** viceroy, put through vigorous reforms in the administration, sent an **expedition to Tibet** (1903–1904), but alienated educated Indians by deciding on

1905. The **PARTITION OF BENGAL** (effective October 16), detached East Bengal (preponderantly Muslim) and Assam from the rest of the province. **Nationalist opposition,** organized by the congress, provoked the founding of the **All-India Muslim League** (Dec. 30, 1906), whose leaders affirmed their loyalty to the government and asked for separate communal representation as part of any future constitutional reforms.

1906, Dec. The congress demanded that "the system of government obtaining in the self-governing British colonies" be extended to India.

1907, Dec. 27. **Split at Surat between moderates and extremists** in the congress over methods of agitation.

1908, Apr. 30. A terrorist bomb at Muzaffarpur killed two Englishwomen. The government seized the occasion to imprison prominent extremists.

1909, May 25. **INDIAN COUNCILS ACT** passed (operative November 15), evolved by John Morley (secretary of state for India) and **Lord Minto,** viceroy (1905–1910). The legislative councils were again greatly enlarged and given increased power, six (seven from 1913) provincial ones having elected majorities, with **separate electorates** for Muslims and other special groups, a provision condemned as divisive by congress moderates, led by **Gopal K. Gokhale.**

1911, Jan. Congress and Muslim League leaders held a conference to work for Hindu-Muslim unity.

Dec. 12. Coronation durbar at Delhi.

King-Emperor George V announced **transfer of the capital from Calcutta to Delhi, and reversal of the partition of Bengal.**

1912, Dec. 23. Lord Hardinge (viceroy, 1910–1916) wounded by a terrorist bomb in Delhi.

1913, Nov. 13. The Bengal poet **Rabindranath Tagore** was awarded the Nobel prize for literature.

Dec. At the annual meeting of the Muslim League, Muslim leaders, alienated by the reversal of the Bengal partition and suspicious of British policy toward the Ottoman Empire, carried a resolution calling for the eventual "attainment of self-government for India."

1914, May 21. *Komagatu Maru* **incident:** 300 Indians arrived at Vancouver to test Canadian immigration laws, but were not admitted; resentment in India and some rioting in Calcutta on return of vessel (Oct. 2); 16 killed.

(*Cont. p. 1101.*)

4. INDO-CHINA

a. BURMA, 1753-1900

(*From p. 580*)

The modern Burmese state was built upon the conquests of **Alaungpaya** (1752–1760), whose successors managed to repulse **invasions by the Chinese** (1766–1769), but were unable to maintain themselves in Siam (1771).

1781–1819. Bodawpaya, king. Conquest of Arakan (1784) and further encroachments on Indian territory. **Peace with Siam** (1793). Acquisition of the Tenasserim coast (1793).

1819–1837. Bagyidaw, king. He continued the advance toward India, seizing Manipur and Assam (1822) and invading Kachar (1824). This policy of expansion soon brought him into conflict with the British East India Company.

1824–1826. FIRST BURMESE WAR. Despite vigorous resistance the Burmese were unable to withstand the force of a modern army. The British, under **Sir Archibald Campbell,** took Rangoon, and then Syriam, Tavoy, Mergui, Martaban, and Pegu. An attempt by the Burmese to recapture Rangoon failed (1825). The British advanced up the Irrawaddy and at the same time overran Arakan. February 24, 1826: by the **treaty of Yandabu** (near Ava) the British secured Assam, Arakan, and the Tenasserim coast, as well as an indemnity and the right to send a resident to Ava (discontinued 1837).

1837–1846. Tharawaddi Min, king.

1846–1852. Pagan Min. Under these reigns the friction with the British continued. The Burmese rulers continued to treat the British with contempt and to hamper the development of British trade.

1852–1853. SECOND BURMESE WAR. Rangoon was again taken, by Gen. Henry Godwin. Pegu was also occupied and annexed (Jan. 20, 1853). A revolution in the capital led to the deposition of the king and the elevation of

1853–1878. Mindon Min, described as the best king of Burma in modern times. He accepted the British gains without concluding a formal treaty, and attempted, throughout his reign, to maintain friendly relations with his neighbor.

1857. Mandalay, built by the king, **became the capital** of the country.

1862. Conclusion of a **commercial treaty with Great Britain.** The customs duty was fixed at 5 per cent and the British were given the right to trade throughout the country.

1875. A **British expedition** to explore the route from Bhamo into Yunnan was checked by the murder of the British interpreter.

1878–1885. THIBAW, king. He proved himself an apathetic and unwise ruler. From the beginning of his reign he caused trouble by his interference with British trade. At the same time he established contact with French interests and negotiated with them for the organization of a royal bank and for the construction of a railroad from Mandalay to the Indian frontier. This anti-British attitude resulted in

1885. THE THIRD BURMESE WAR. The British (Oct. 22) sent an ultimatum demanding that Thibaw receive a British envoy and that his interference with trade be stopped; furthermore, that in future the foreign relations of Burma be conducted in accordance with the advice of the Indian government. On the rejection of this ultimatum, a British steamer expedition, commanded by **Gen. Sir Harry Prendergast,** occupied Mandalay (November 28). Thibaw surrendered and was sent to India.

1886, Jan. 1. UPPER BURMA WAS ANNEXED by the British, but desultory guerrilla warfare continued for years. The **Shan States** were not reduced until 1887 and the **Chin Hills** not until 1891.

July 24. An **Anglo-Chinese convention** recognized the British position in Burma. Chinese prestige was saved by a continuation of Burmese decennial tribute missions.

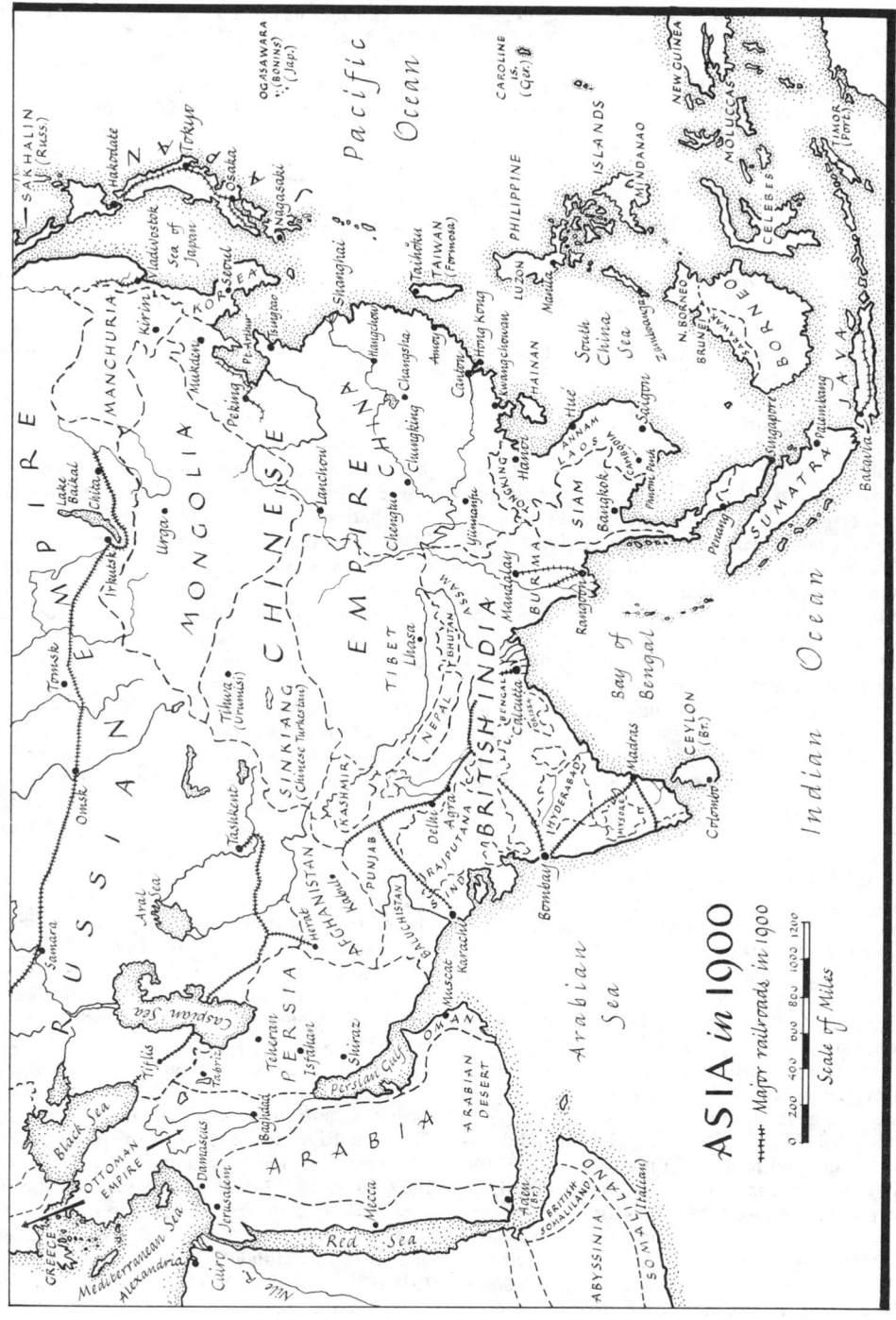

ASIA in 1900

++++ Major railroads in 1900

0 200 400 600 800 1000 1200
Scale of Miles

1893. **Siamese boundary** set by convention.
1895. **Agreement with France** on the boundary with Cochin China.
1900. **Agreement with China** finally fixed the Burmese frontier on that side. (*Cont. p. 1103.*)

b. SIAM, 1782–1917

(*From p. 580*)

1782–1809. **RAMA I** (Phra Buddha Yod Fa Chulalok), first of the new line. He finally brought to an end the long conflict with Burma (1793), re-established control over the local potentates throughout the country, and secured part of Cambodia through division of that state with Annam.
1809–1824. **RAMA II** (Phra Buddha Loes Fa Nobhalai).
1824–1851. **RAMA III** (Phra Nang Klao), whose reign was distinguished by the reopening of **contact with the western nations.**
1826, June 20. Conclusion of a **treaty of commerce with Great Britain.** This was followed (Mar. 20, 1833) by a similar treaty with the United States. Both agreements left much to be desired, as they did not even provide for the establishment of consuls.
1844. Cambodia passed under the protection of Siam.
1851–1868. **RAMA IV** (Phra Chom Klao Mongkut), who, as a monk, had made a study of western governments and who began the work of modernizing Siam.
1855, Apr. 18. **A NEW TREATY WITH GREAT BRITAIN,** modeled on the Anglo-Chinese treaty. **Opening of Siam:** consuls to be established; extra-territorial system introduced; right to trade throughout the kingdom. Similar treaties were concluded with the United States (1856, May 29) and with France (1856, Aug. 15), and thereafter with many other powers.
1863. The French established a protectorate over Cambodia. After long negotiations, the Siamese gave up their claims (1867).
1868–1910. **RAMA V** (Phra Maha Chulalongkorn), the real founder of modern Siam. After attaining his majority (1873) he devoted himself almost entirely to the reform of his government and the improvement of his country: feudal system abolished; slavery reduced and stamped out; administrative reform (central bureaucracy); taxation and finance reform; postal service; modernization of the army; introduction of the telegraph (1883); opening of the first railway (1893).
1885. Failure of a French **proposal to neutralize Siam** resulted in ever-increasing friction

and continuous border disputes, culminating in
1893, May–Aug. **THE SIAMESE CRISIS.** The French had been trying for years to extend their dominions westward to the Mekong River, a policy that met with opposition not only from Siam but from Britain, which desired to preserve Siam as buffer between Burma and the French possessions. Border clashes in May 1893 led to the mission of two gunboats to Bangkok in July. The Siamese fired upon them, whereupon the French submitted a stiff ultimatum (July 13). This was rejected and the French then instituted a blockade (July 31), which led to a short but acute **Anglo-French crisis** (p. 786). The Siamese were obliged to yield and ultimately accepted the
Oct. 3. Franco-Siamese treaty, by which the Siamese abandoned all claim to territory east of the Mekong and paid an indemnity of three million francs. The French remained in occupation of Chantabun until 1905.
1896, Jan. 15. An **Anglo-French agreement** ended the long friction between the two countries on the Siamese question. The British recognized the gains made by France in 1893 and abandoned the demand for a buffer between Burma and the French colonies. Both sides guaranteed the independence of Siam.
1897. The king of Siam paid an extended visit to the European capitals.
1904, Feb. 13. A **further treaty with France** replaced the agreement of 1893. France returned Chantabun, while Siam ceded Bassac, Melupré, and that part of Luang Prabang which lay on the right (west) bank of the Mekong; also Krat on the coast.
1907, Mar. 23. By agreement **France retroceded to Siam Battambong, Siemrap, and Sisophon** on the Cambodian frontier, and received in return the region of **Krat and Dansai.** France agreed to **modification of the extra-territorial system,** giving Siam jurisdiction over French Asians.
Apr. 8. An **Anglo-French convention** confirmed the independence of Siam, but established **spheres of influence;** territory west of the Menam River to be the British sphere, that to the east the French sphere.
1909, Mar. 10. Great Britain gave up the system of extra-territoriality, in return for the cession of Kedah, Kelantan, Trengganu, and Perlis to the Malay States.
1910–1925. **RAMA VI** (Vajiravudh). Educated in England, he continued the policy of modernization and westernization: irrigation projects, education, calendar reform, reduction of compulsory labor, etc.
1917, July 22. Siam declared war on Germany and Austria. (*Cont. p. 1104.*)

c. FRENCH INDO-CHINA, 1802–1902

At the beginning of the 19th century most of what became French Indo-China was ruled by the **emperor of Annam.** The region was predominantly Chinese in culture and the empire acknowledged the suzerainty of the Chinese emperor. After a long period of **dynastic struggle and civil war** (1772–1802) the imperial domain was reunited by

1802–1820. GIA LONG (Nguyen Anh), emperor, who had been supported in his struggles by the French missionary, **Pigneau de Béhaine.** Catholic missions had been active in the country since 1615 and had worked with considerable success. The emperor, who was a great organizer as well as a soldier, gave the French Catholics free rein.

1820–1840. MINH-MANG, emperor. A strict Confucian and a great admirer of all things Chinese, Minh-Mang was decidedly hostile to Christians, whom he suspected of supporting the rebellious provincial lords. He therefore ordered them expelled (1824 and on many later occasions).

1840–1847. THIEU-TRI, emperor. He continued the persecution of the Christians and refused flatly to receive foreign missions. During his reign the French naval commanders intervened several times to save the lives of the Christians.

1847–1883. TU DUC, emperor. He was a learned, simple, and pious ruler, who, like his predecessors, attempted to keep his country closed to outsiders. Persecution of Christians continued.

1858. A joint French and Spanish expedition under **Adm. Rigault de Genouilly,** in order to put a stop to the exclusive and unfriendly attitude of the Annamite court, bombarded Tourane on the coast. Unable to proceed to the capital, Hué, the expedition turned south and **occupied Saigon** in Cochin China. The operations were interrupted by the war of the French against China, but they led ultimately to the

1862, June 5. Treaty of Saigon, by which the emperor abandoned to the French the three eastern provinces of Cochin China and agreed to pay an indemnity of 20,000,000 francs in ten years. Free exercise of the Catholic religion was to be allowed and three ports (Tourane, Balat, and Kuang-An) were to be opened to French trade.

1863–1868. Adm. Pierre de La Grandière, governor of Cochin China. He organized the system of government through admirals, so called, which continued until 1879. Actual adminis-

tration was left largely to native mandarins.

1863, Aug. 11. King Norodom of Cambodia, a Hindu state dependent on both Annam and Siam and constantly threatened by these neighbors, **accepted a French protectorate.**

1867. France occupied the three western provinces of Cochin China, after an insurrection.

1868. French exploration of the Mekong River, as far as Yunnan. It was hoped that this would prove a useful route into southwestern China, but the river was shown to be unnavigable in the upper reaches and the French therefore began to turn their attention to the Red River of Tonkin.

1873. Exploration of the Red River by Jean Dupuis, a French merchant active in China. The Annamites objected to French activity in Tonkin, but

1873–1874. FRANCIS GARNIER, with a handful of men, attacked and **took Hanoi** and conquered most of the Red River delta.

1874, Mar. 15. By a **TREATY SIGNED AT SAIGON,** the emperor was obliged to promise to conform his foreign policy to that of France and to recognize the French possession of Cochin China. Freedom of the Christian religion was once again promised. In return France promised protection and offered to supply gunboats and officers to help suppress piracy. The French returned Hanoi, but the treaty was systematically evaded by the emperor, who now began to appeal to the Chinese for aid against the French.

1882. Insurrection in Tonkin. Death of **Henri Rivière** and a small force (1883).

1883, Aug. 25. TREATY OF HUÉ. Tu Duc was forced once more to recognize the French protectorate, which was now extended to Tonkin and Annam itself. But the French still had to deal with the pirates and guerrilla Black Flags in Tonkin, who were supported by the Chinese. The result was **war with China** (p. 912), in the course of which the French suffered a setback at **Langson** (Mar. 28, 1885) which in turn led to the overthrow of Jules Ferry, the prime mover for expansion in France. But by the **treaty of Tientsin** (June 9, 1885) China was obliged to recognize the French protectorate over Tonkin.

The year 1883 was marked by severe **internal strife,** following the death of Emperor Tu Duc. The regents elevated and deposed several emperors in succession, but after the French control was established the native ruler was subject to French orders.

1884, June 6. The **TREATY OF HUÉ** gave France the right to occupy militarily any place in Annam. Thereby effective French control was established.

June 17. A **new treaty with Cambodia** gave the protecting power much more extensive control than theretofore.

1885-1895. Pacification of Tonkin and Indo-China generally. There were many revolts in the interior, those in Tonkin being led by the formidable insurgent **De Tham.**

1887. Cochin China, Cambodia, Annam, and Tonkin were administratively united as the *Union Indo-Chinoise.*

1893. FRANCE ACQUIRED A PROTEC-TORATE OVER LAOS, the interior region along the Mekong which had long been in dispute between Annam and Siam.

1897-1902. Paul Doumer, governor-general. He first inaugurated the far-reaching reforms and administrative arrangements which modernized the region. (*Cont. p. 1105.*)

d. BRITISH MALAYA, 1790-1914

1795. The **British took Malacca** to hold for the Dutch, who were under French domination at the time.

1800. The **British secured Province Wellesley** from the sultan of Kedah.

1802. Malacca was restored to the Dutch under terms of the **treaty of Amiens.**

1811. The **British retook Malacca,** which was used as a base for the expedition against Java.

1818. The **Dutch recovered Malacca,** under terms of the **treaty of Vienna.**

1819. FOUNDING OF SINGAPORE by **Sir Stamford Raffles.** The place had been practically abandoned for centuries, but was soon to become the strategic and commercial center of the region, completely overshadowing Malacca.

1824, Mar. 17. The **Dutch ceded Malacca** to Britain, in return for Bengkulen in Sumatra.

1826. British treaty with Siam (p. 906). Under terms of this agreement the sultanates of Perak and Selangor were recognized as independent, while Siamese control of Kedah was acknowledged. At the same time Perak ceded to Britain **Pangkor Island** and the **Sembilan Islands** for use as bases in the fight against piracy.

1850- Steady influx of Chinese laborers into the peninsula. These were employed chiefly in the tin mines, though many also turned to piracy on the coast. Their presence created disturbance in many states and ultimately provoked British interference.

1867, Apr. 1. End of the rule of the British East India Company. The Straits Settlements thenceforth had the status of a crown colony.

1873, June 20. TREATY OF PANGKOR. After serious Chinese disorders in Perak and a prolonged dynastic conflict, the British obliged the Perak chiefs to accept a British resident and to take his advice on all matters excepting religion and custom. The introduction of this system soon outraged the native chiefs, who in

1875. Rose in revolt. Murder of the British resident, **J. W. W. Birch.** The insurrection was suppressed by a British force and in the ensuing years further treaties were concluded with the other Malay states.

1885, Dec. 11. British treaty with Johore, regulating relations.

1889. Nine of the smaller states were federated and became **Negri Sembilan.**

1896, July 1. TREATY OF FEDERATION of Perak, Selangor, Negri Sembilan, and Pahang. Together they were to have one British resident-general (the governor of the Straits Settlements), while retaining their separate residents.

1909, Mar. 10. By **treaty with Siam,** Britain secured suzerainty and protection over **Kelantan, Trengganu, Kedah,** and **Perlis.** Protection was proclaimed July 14, 1909, and treaties concluded with these states in 1910. Together with Johore they comprised the Unfederated Malay States.

1914, May 12. The **sultan of Johore** accepted a general adviser and a further measure of British supervision and control.

British Malaya was entirely under British rule or control. The different states were organized as follows:

Straits Settlements (crown colony) comprised Singapore, Penang, Province Wellesley, the Dindings, Malacca;

The Federated Malay States: Perak, Selangor, Negri Sembilan, Pahang.

Unfederated Malay States: Johore, Kedah, Perlis, Kelantan, Trengganu. (*Cont. p. 1105.*)

e. THE MALAYAN ARCHIPELAGO, 1798-1908

(*From p. 580*)

1798. End of the Dutch East India Company.

1808. The **Dutch subdued Bantam** in western Java. Mission of **Marshal Herman Daendels,** who reorganized the Dutch possessions and began the systematic curtailment of the powers of the princes and feudal lords.

1811. A **British expedition captured Batavia** and took over **Java.** Under the administration of **Stamford Raffles** (1811-1816) much of the old system was swept away: extension of European control while retaining native administration; land leases to natives, etc.

1814, 1816. Sumatra and then Java were restored to the Dutch, in accordance with the peace treaties.

1824, Mar. 17. The **British ceded Bengkulen**

(Sumatra) to the Dutch in return for Malacca: end of British hold in the island.

1825-1830. REVOLT OF THE JAVANESE against the Dutch, led by **Dipo Negora.** The rising was suppressed only with great difficulty. The ultimate effect was to oblige the Dutch to conquer the interior and to extend their control. Later revolts (1849, 1888) had the same effect.

1830. Introduction of the **forced culture system** by the Dutch. This involved government contracts with the natives, crop control, and fixed prices—a system very lucrative to the Dutch.

1839. Native chiefs of **Bali acknowledged Dutch control,** but disorders continued until 1849.

1841. The **sultan of Brunei,** in northern Borneo, **ceded to Sir James Brooke** the region of **Sarawak,** in return for aid against enemies. Brooke became rajah of the region and ruled until 1868, when he was succeeded by his nephew Charles (1868–1917) and the latter's son, Vyner (1917–1946). He induced the British government to take an active part in the work of suppressing piracy in the China Sea.

1847. The British secured from the sultan of Brunei the island of **Labuan,** off the northwest coast of Borneo, which it was expected would become an important naval base.

1859, Apr. 20. The **Dutch and Portuguese** by agreement **divided Timor** and the neighboring islands between them.

1865. The American government concluded a treaty with the sultan of Brunei and the **American Trading Company of Borneo** acquired title to lands, but the effort to exploit the region proved abortive.

1870. The Dutch introduced a **new sugar law and a new agrarian law in Java,** which involved a relaxation of the culture system and the gradual extension of private agriculture.

1881. The British government issued a **charter to the North Borneo Company.** This company took over the assets of the American company and secured new concessions from the sultans of Brunei and Sulu. Protests of the Dutch and Spaniards were of no avail (Spanish claims renounced in 1885).

1888, Mar. 17. Great Britain established a protectorate over Sarawak.

May 12. British protectorate over North Borneo, which, however, continued to be held and administered by the North Borneo Company.

1891, June 20. The British and Dutch by treaty defined their respective **domains in Borneo,** the Dutch retaining by far the larger part.

1907, Dec. The **Dutch,** after many years of warfare, finally **subdued the Achinese** in northern Sumatra (Atjeh), thus completing the pacification of Sumatra.

1908. Direct Dutch rule was established **in Bali,** after a series of native insurrections.

(*Cont. p. 1105.*)

5. CHINA, 1796-1914

(*From p. 579*)

1796-1820. The **CHIA CH'ING REIGN OF JEN TSUNG** was filled with revolts which had been postponed only by the prestige of his father.

1796-1804. Suppression of **revolt of the White Lotus Society** impoverished the three provinces of Hupei, Szechwan, and Shensi.

1805. Christian literature was proscribed, and a Catholic priest strangled for presence in China without permission (1815).

1813. An attempt by the **Heavenly Reason Society** to seize Peking failed.

Scholarship profited by labors of three brilliant critical editors: **Sun Hsing-yen, Yen K'o-chün,** and **Juan Yüan.** The last prepared the best edition of the *Thirteen Classics with Commentary* and gathered in 360 volumes the best *Classical Comment of the Reigning Ch'ing Dynasty.* **Robert Morrison,** the first Protestant missionary. translator of the Bible, and author

of the first Chinese-English dictionary, arrived in Canton (1807).

1816. British ambassador, **Lord Amherst,** sent away from Peking without being received.

1821-1850. THE TAO KUANG REIGN OF HSÜAN TSUNG.

1821. The illicit **trade in Indian opium,** 5000 chests annually despite imperial prohibition (1800), was transferred to Lintin Island off the Canton River. The conditions of trade at Canton became intolerable through official arbitrariness and venality, recurrent conflict of principles of individual as against collective responsibility under criminal law, restrictions on personal freedom, and denial of appeal to the central government.

1825-1831. Kashgaria was with difficulty defended against Jehangir of the Khoja family and Mohammed Ali of Khokand.

1830-1834. American missionary, medical, and sinological work begun in southern China.

1834. The **end of the East India Company's**

The Manchu (Ta Ch'ing) Dynasty (1795–1912) (From p. 577)

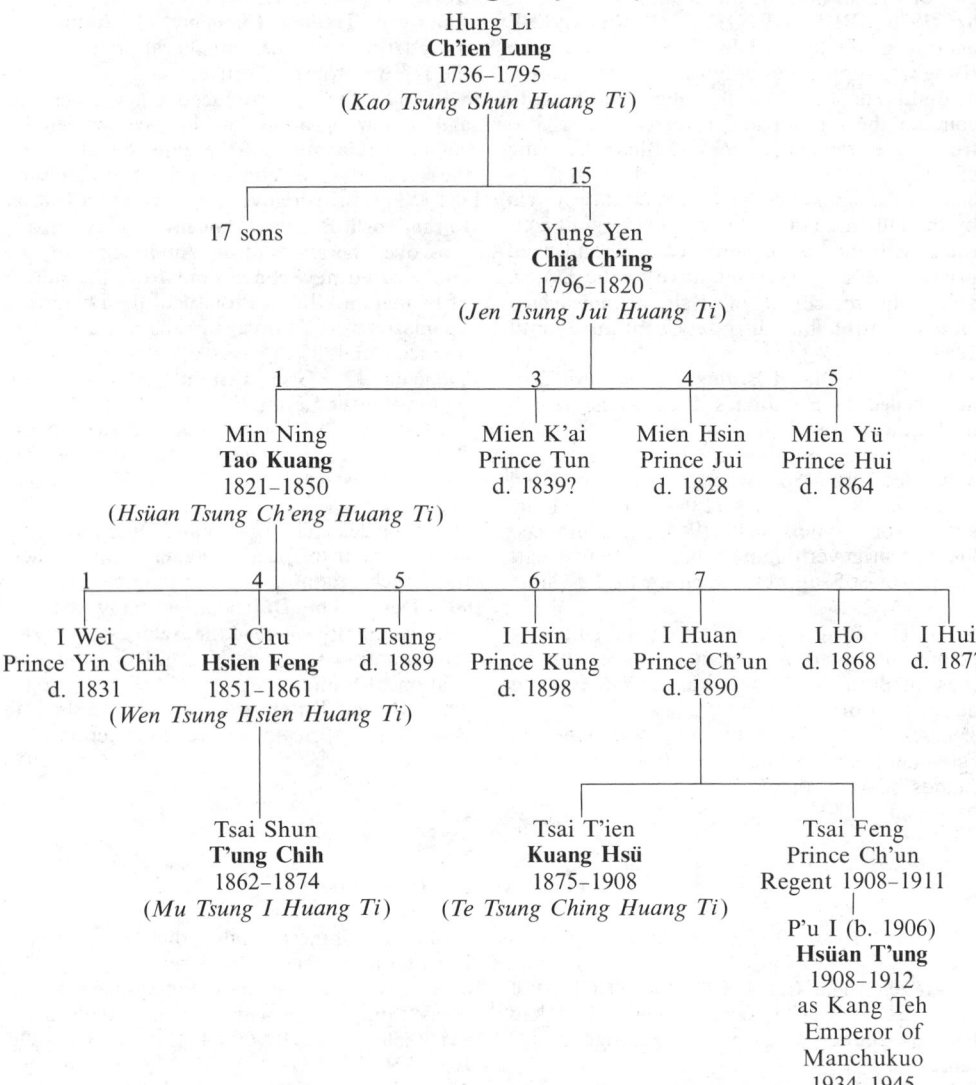

Hung Li
Ch'ien Lung
1736–1795
(*Kao Tsung Shun Huang Ti*)

15

17 sons

Yung Yen
Chia Ch'ing
1796–1820
(*Jen Tsung Jui Huang Ti*)

1

Min Ning
Tao Kuang
1821–1850
(*Hsüan Tsung Ch'eng Huang Ti*)

3
Mien K'ai
Prince Tun
d. 1839?

4
Mien Hsin
Prince Jui
d. 1828

5
Mien Yü
Prince Hui
d. 1864

1
I Wei
Prince Yin Chih
d. 1831

4
I Chu
Hsien Feng
1851–1861
(*Wen Tsung Hsien Huang Ti*)

5
I Tsung
d. 1889

6
I Hsin
Prince Kung
d. 1898

7
I Huan
Prince Ch'un
d. 1890

I Ho
d. 1868

I Hui
d. 1877

Tsai Shun
T'ung Chih
1862–1874
(*Mu Tsung I Huang Ti*)

Tsai T'ien
Kuang Hsü
1875–1908
(*Te Tsung Ching Huang Ti*)

Tsai Feng
Prince Ch'un
Regent 1908–1911

P'u I (b. 1906)
Hsüan T'ung
1908–1912
as Kang Teh
Emperor of
Manchukuo
1934–1945

Note: Names in plain type are personal names, taboo after a ruler ascended the throne.

Names in boldface type are reign titles, or year names, adopted for reckoning time, but often applied by westerners to the emperor himself.

Names in italic type are dynastic titles, or temple names, conferred posthumously to refer to the ruler. *Huang Ti* means simply "emperor."

monopoly of British trade with China removed an important element in the Canton system of commercial regulation. The assertion of diplomatic equality by the first superintendent of British trade in China, **Lord Napier,** was followed by the temporary stoppage of trade; Napier died October 11; his successors followed a "quiescent policy."

1836. Chinese proposals to legalize the importation of opium, and concern over the "drain of silver" to pay for it, led to heated discussions at Peking. Chinese policy remained weak and lawlessness grew until

1839. Imperial Commissioner **Lin Tse-hsü arrived at Canton** (Mar. 10), forced surrender of opium (annual import 30,000 chests, 1835–

1839), and burned it. Hostilities followed (Nov.).

1840. British occupation of Chusan and **Canton River forts** led to an agreement **(Ch'uanpi convention)** between Capt. Charles Elliot and Ch'i-shan (Jan. 1841), which was repudiated by both governments.

1841-1842. The **FIRST BRITISH WAR,** with seizure of several coastal ports and Chinkiang on the Grand Canal, ended in dictation by **Sir Henry Pottinger** of the

1842, Aug. 29. TREATY OF NANKING, which ended the tributary status and Canton monopolistic system of maritime trade. China ceded **Hong Kong** (occupied January 1841) to Britain; opened **Canton, Amoy, Foochow, Ningpo,** and **Shanghai** to trade under consular supervision; established **uniform import tariff** of about 5 per cent, *ad valorem;* paid £21,000,-000 indemnity.

1843, Oct. 8. Supplementary treaty, also negotiated by Pottinger and Imperial Commissioner Ch'i-ying, conceded "most-favored-nation" status (later extended to other powers) and amplified the details of the new commercial system. Opium traffic continued. The

1844, July 3. Treaty of Wanghsia signed by **Ch'i-ying** and by **Caleb Cushing** for the United States placed American (ultimately all foreign) residents under extra-territorial criminal and civil jurisdiction of consular and mixed courts. The study of Chinese became legal for foreigners. The French **treaty of Whampoa** (Oct. 24) secured **toleration of Roman Catholicism,** extended (1845) to **Protestantism.**

1846-1849. Popular opposition to foreign entrance into the city of Canton increased Anglo-Chinese friction.

1851-1861. The **HSIEN FENG REIGN** revealed approaching dissolution of the dynasty. Agrarian unrest due to official exactions, to natural calamities, and to absentee landlordism which centered especially in Kiangsi, found expression in the

1850-1864. T'AI P'ING REBELLION. The *Heavenly Kingdom of Great Peace* was founded in Kwangsi by a mystic, **Hung Hsiu-ch'üan,** who borrowed certain forms of Protestant doctrine. With help of an able strategist, **Yang Hsiu-ch'ing,** he led disciplined forces through Hunan to Wuch'ang (1852) and down the river past Nanking, his capital (1853-1864), to the Grand Canal. An advance toward Peking was deflected through Shansi by floods of the Yellow River, which shifted its bed north of Shantung (1853). The rebels were repelled (1855). Neglect of the rebels to provide conquered territory with either protection or constructive administration foredoomed their régime to ꜰailure.

1853-1868. Nien Fei, organized bandits of Anhuei, N. Kiangsu, and Shantung, later also Shansi, profited by preoccupation of imperial troops with the T'ai P'ing and foreign invaders to plunder. They were suppressed (1865-1868) by the same men who put down the T'ai P'ing rebellion.

1854, July 12. Capture of Shanghai city by rebels (Sept. 7, 1853) led to inauguration of **foreign inspectorate of customs.**

1855-1873. Muslims (Panthays) in **Ynnan** revolted and set up an independent state at Tali, the ancient capital of Nan-chao.

1855-1881. Miao tribesmen in Kweichow seized the opportunity to revolt.

1856, Oct. 8. Lorcha *Arrow* incident at Canton precipitated Anglo-Chinese hostilities.

1857-1858. Anglo-French seizure of Canton and military threat in the north forced the

1858, June 26-29. TREATIES OF TIENTSIN between China and Great Britain (Lord Elgin), France, the United States, and Russia. China opened eleven more ports, permitted legations at Peking and trade and Christian missions in the interior; subsequent tariff and rules of trade (Nov.) established a maritime customs service with foreign inspector-general (Horatio N. Lay) and staff, and legalized the importation of opium. The **treaty of Aigun** signed by I-shan and Nicholas Muraviev gave the north bank of the Amur to Russia. Khabarovsk founded.

1859. Refusal of British demands for admission of foreign diplomats to Peking and repulse of attack on the Taku forts (June 25) before Tientsin led to

1860, Oct. 12. Occupation of Peking by 17,000 British and French troops. **Burning of the Summer Palace** to punish the court for seizure of envoys (Harry Parkes) under a flag of truce suggested unfortunate parallels with conduct of earlier barbarian invaders. **Peking conventions** (Oct. 24 with Britain, Oct. 25 with France) increased indemnities, and the French secured right of Catholic missions to hold land. The Russian envoy, **Gen. Nicholas Ignatiev,** secured cession (Nov. 14) of the **Maritime Province.** Vladivostok was founded. Eruption of the T'ai P'ing rebels from Nanking desolated Kiangsu and Chekiang.

1861. The **Tsungli Yamen was created** to handle foreign affairs.

1861-1864. Tseng Kuo-fan with able help, including Tseng Kuo-ch'üan, Li Hung-chang, Tso Tsung-t'ang, and the Ever-Victorious Army (1862-1863) of **Frederick T. Ward** and **Charles G. Gordon** near Shanghai, suppressed the immensely destructive T'ai P'ing rebellion by recapture of Anking (1861), Soochow (1863), and Nanking (1864).

1862-1874. THE T'UNG CHIH REIGN OF MU TSUNG. The dowager empress Tzu Hsi ruled as co-regent for her son until 1873. Under leadership of **Tseng Kuo-fan** and his protégés reform and study of the west was begun.

1862-1873. Muslim rebellions were suppressed by **Tso Tsung-t'ang** in Shensi (1868-1870) and Kansu.

1863-1908. (Sir) Robert Hart built up the Maritime Customs Service as mainstay of government revenue and credit, with collateral services to train men, light the coast, improve rivers and harbors, and organize a postal service (1896, independent 1911).

1864-1889. Protestant missionaries in China increased from under 200 to nearly 1300, and introduced western medicine and ideas. Communicants numbered 55,000 in 1893.

1868-1870. Anson Burlingame, with two Chinese associates, was sent on a good-will mission to western states.

1870, June 21. The **Tientsin massacre,** by a mob, of a French consul and missionaries led to a mission of apology to France by Ch'ung-hou (1871-1872).

1871. Cables were laid from Vladivostok via Nagasaki to Shanghai, Hong Kong, and Singapore. A land line was built, Shanghai-Tientsin in 1881.

1872-1881. One hundred and twenty Chinese students were brought to the United States by **Yung Wing** (Yale 1854), and thirty sent to England and France for technical training (1876).

1874. A **Japanese expedition to occupy Formosa** to punish murder by natives of Liu Ch'iu islanders and Japanese (1871) was withdrawn in return for indemnity; but by revelation of Chinese military weakness served to strengthen demands (since 1867) by **Tseng Kuo-fan, Li Hung-chang,** and a small group of liberal Chinese statesmen that China undertake reform and establish representatives abroad.

1875-1908. THE KUANG HSÜ REIGN OF TE TSUNG. As the late emperor was childless, an infant cousin (born 1871), a nephew of the dowager empress Tzu Hsi, was adopted as second son of Wen Tsung to carry on dynastic sacrifices, and his prospective offspring was destined to be adopted son of the late emperor. An uncle, **Prince Kung,** was named regent under supervision of the two dowager empresses. Personal rule 1889.

1875-1878. Tso Tsung-t'ang suppressed (1875-1876), the Tungans of the northern T'ien Shan, in revolt since 1862, and reconquered Kashgaria (1877-1878), which had become independent under **Yakub Beg** in 1866. Both areas

were organized as one province, the **New Territory,** Sinkiang (Hsin-chiang), with capital at Urumtsi (Tihwa).

1876. The **Chefoo** (or Yentai) **convention** forced by Britain on occasion of the murder of interpreter Augustus Margary on the Burmese border (1875) opened ten additional ports, and improved the status of foreigners in China. Ratified by Great Britain in 1885 with additional article relating to opium, importation of which reached an annual average (1875-1885) of 82,000 chests, an amount greatly exceeded, however, by production in China.

1877-1878. Diplomatic missions, determined in 1875, established legations in London and Berlin (1877), Paris, Washington, and Tokyo (1878), Madrid and St. Petersburg (1879), and Lima (1880).

1879, Sept. 15. The **unratified treaty of Livadia** gave Russia much of Ili (occupied by it 1871), strategic passes, and indemnity; but after Chinese threat of war

1881, Feb. 24. The **treaty of St. Petersburg** negotiated by Tseng Chi-tse, returned to China most of the Ili Valley and the passes in return for more money.

1883, Aug. 25. Treaty of Hué (p. 907), by which Annam accepted a French protectorate with administration of Tonkin by French residents in disregard of Chinese suzerainty and protests (1881-1882).

1884. Prince Kung and the grand council were **dismissed by the dowager empress Tzu Hsi** for failure to repel the French. A preliminary convention signed by Li Hung-chang with Capt. Fournier (May 11) resulted in misunderstanding, and a French defeat at Baclé (June 23) led to **undeclared war.** French naval destruction of the new Foochow arsenal (Aug. 23) and attacks on Formosa were balanced in part by reverses on the Tonkin border (**Langson** March 28, 1885).

1885, June 9. The **treaty of Tientsin,** facilitated by negotiations of Robert Hart, recognized the French protectorate in Tonkin in return for a reciprocal promise to respect the southern frontier of China. Tso Tsung-t'ang in a dying memorial urged modernization and foreign study.

In **Korea,** a tributary to the Manchus since 1637, China evaded responsibility for persecution of Christians and for the French punitive expedition which was repulsed from Seoul (1866). China did not protest a **Japanese treaty** (1876) recognizing Korean independence, nor a Korean embassy to Japan. Li Hung-chang, however (1882), sent as resident to Seoul **Yüan Shih-k'ai** who was thereafter active in intrigue against Japan, uninterrupted by the

1885, April 18. Li-Itō convention for withdrawal of troops of both powers from Korea (p. 917).

1886, July 24. British protectorate in Burma was recognized in return for continuance of decennial tribute.

1887, Dec. 1. Portugal secured cession of Macao on promise not to alienate it.

1888. The **first imperial railway** (Tangshan-Tientsin, 80 miles) was opened and extended to Shanhaikuan (1894) and to Fengt'ai outside Peking (1896). **Chang Chih-tung,** governor-general of Hupei, opened **coal mines,** the great Ta-yeh **iron mines,** and the Han-yang **steel works,** as necessary preliminaries to interior railway construction.

1890. Abolition of the board of admiralty and subsequent neglect of the new and promising navy, as a result of the resignation of Capt. William Lang (British) and the death of Prince Ch'un and Marquis Tseng Chi-tse.

1894. Sun Yat-sen (Sun Wen) organized at Canton the first of several **secret revolutionary societies** with which he tried ten times before 1911 to overthrow the Manchu dynasty. After his first failure (1895), he organized the Chinese in Honolulu and America, and was kidnaped and held for ten days by the Chinese legation in London (1896).

1894-1895. The **SINO-JAPANESE WAR,** the outcome of ten years' rivalry and intrigue in Korea. **Rising of the Tonghak** (*Eastern Learning*) **Society** in southern Korea led to seizure by the Japanese of the Korean queen and appointment of a regent. The British ship *Kowshing* (July 25, 1894), carrying Chinese troops to Korea, sunk by the Japanese; the Korean regent declared war on China (July 27); China and Japan declared war on each other (Aug. 1). Vain efforts of the European powers and the United States to mediate. Easy victories of the Japanese at **Ping-yang** (Sept. 16), off the **Yalu River, at Port Arthur** (Nov. 21), **and at Wei-haiwei** (Feb. 12) destroyed the Chinese army and navy and forced the Chinese to accept

1895, Apr. 17. THE TREATY OF SHIMO-NOSEKI. *Terms:* China recognized the independence of Korea and ceded to Japan the island of Formosa, the Pescadores Islands, the Liaotung Peninsula; China was to pay an indemnity of 200,000,000 taels, and to open four more ports to foreign commerce.

China's helplessness in the face of a despised Asiatic neighbor equipped with modern instruments of war was clearly revealed to all. It awakened the majority of the educated Chinese, much as the bombardments of 1863-1864 had roused the Japanese. Chinese demands for reform were further stimulated by the rush of the European powers for political and economic concessions and by their efforts

to set up exclusive spheres of influence. Dilemma of the Chinese government: native capital not available for military, railway, and industrial development; foreign capital could be secured only at the expense of further extension of foreign control within the empire. Revenue from the customs was limited by interlocking agreements to about 5 per cent in 1858, and to an effective 2-3 per cent in the later 19th century.

Apr. 23. Russia, Germany, and France intervened and obliged Japan to return the **Liaotung Peninsula** to China in consideration of a further indemnity of 30,000,000 taels. For reasons for the intervention see p. 787. All three intervening powers expected to be well repaid by the Chinese.

June 20. France secured extensive territorial and commercial concessions in the southern provinces.

July 6. Franco-Russian loan to China (400 million francs at 4 per cent, to run for 36 years, with the Chinese customs as security).

1896, May 23. An **Anglo-German loan** (£16,000,-000 for 36 years at 5 per cent, secured by the customs revenues, the administration of which was meanwhile to continue as then constituted).

June 3. RUSSIAN-CHINESE TREATY, secretly concluded at the coronation of Nicholas II at Moscow by **Li Hung-chang.** In return for a defensive alliance for fifteen years, China granted Russia the right to build and operate the **Chinese Eastern Railway** across northern Manchuria, as a link in the Russian Trans-Siberian line to Vladivostok.

July 21. A commercial treaty with Japan, imposed as part of the peace settlement, gave Japan most-favored-nation status and granted all the treaty powers the right to operate industrial enterprises in treaty ports.

1897, Feb. 4. Great Britain was permitted by treaty to extend the Burmese railways into Ynnan (later proved impracticable), and gained further rights in southwest China to offset the French penetration.

Nov. 14. The **GERMANS OCCUPIED KIAOCHOW** (Chiao-chou) **Bay** with Tsingtao, following the murder of two missionaries in Shantung. The move had been long under consideration and was looked upon by the Germans as the logical sequence to the intervention in favor of China in 1895. But it precipitated the

1898. SCRAMBLE FOR CONCESSIONS, in which most of the great European powers took part.

Feb. Britain secured agreements to open inland waters to foreign steamers, not to alienate any part of the Yangtze River valley to any other power, and to employ a British inspector-general of customs so long as British trade remained preponderant.

Mar. 6. **Germany** extracted a convention giving her a **99-year lease on Kiaochow Bay,** with exclusive right to build railways and develop mines in Shantung (the Tsingtao-Tsinan Railway opened in 1904). A **second Anglo-German loan** of £16,000,000 for 45 years at $4\frac{1}{2}$ per cent was secured by certain likin and salt revenues, as well as the customs.

Mar. 27, May 7. **Russia** extorted from China a **25-year lease of** the southern part of the Liaotung Peninsula, including **Talienwan** (Dairen, Dalny) and **Port Arthur,** with the right to construct a railroad from Harbin in the north to the newly leased ports.

Apr. 10. **France** received a **99-year lease of Kwangchowan** (Kuang-chou) **Bay** and the vicinity, with the right to extend a railway to Yunnan-fu (completed 1910) and a promise not to alienate to any other power any part of the provinces bordering Tonkin.

Apr. 26. **Japan** secured a promise from China not to alienate any part of **Fukien.**

June 9. **Britain** secured a **99-year lease of Kowloon** (Chiu-lung) opposite Hong Kong, and (July 1) a **lease of Weihaiwei** to run as long as the Russian occupation of Port Arthur.

June 11–Sept. 16. The **HUNDRED DAYS OF REFORM,** embarked upon by the emperor under the guidance of the radical reformer **K'ang Yu-wei** and a Cantonese faction of students of foreign education, and of **Chang Chih-tung,** who wrote *Learn,* a classic appeal for reform (a million copies sold). The reformers aimed at hastening the construction of the **Peking-Hankow Railway** (1898–1905), to give western arms to the Manchu Banners, to prepare for naval training, to establish schools and a **University of Peking.** These measures met with general approval, but the decrees of August 30–September 16 struck boldly at vital interests of the civil and military officials by abolishing sinecures and the Green Banner provincial armies, and by introducing a budget system. To prevent seizure of her own person, **Sept. 22.** The **empress dowager** Tzu Hsi, supported by Jung-lu, **seized the emperor** and imprisoned him. Reforms contrary to interests of the Manchus and official classes were revoked. Reactionary officials were placed in control of the central government.

1899, Feb. **Italian demand for a port** and concession in Chekiang was rejected with a show of force and vigorous efforts to strengthen imperial defense.

In response to notes of September and November **John Hay,** American secretary of state, secured assurances from the great powers that the **open door** to equal commercial opportunity would be maintained in spheres of special interest in China (p. 791).

Boxers, militia forces organized in Shantung and southern Chihli in response to imperial decrees, showed hostility to aggressive foreign powers by persecution of their visible representatives, Christian missionaries and converts, with encouragement of **Yü-hsien,** Manchu governor of Shantung until he was replaced by Yüan Shih-k'ai (Dec. 6).

1900. The **BOXERS,** driven from Shantung into Chihli, were encouraged by an anti-foreign Manchu clique at court, which hoped to use them as auxiliaries to expel all foreigners from China. Identic notes of foreign diplomats at Peking (Jan.–May) by demanding suppression increased resentment. A **mob attack on Feng-t'ai railway station** (May 28) was followed by admission of legation guards to Peking (total 458), but repulse to Tientsin of a joint naval column of 2066 men (June 10–26). Foreign **seizure of the Taku forts** (June 17) was cited in an imperial declaration of war (June 20), disregarded as a forced document both by foreign powers and by Chinese officials outside Chihli and Shansi. Murder of the German minister, **Baron Klemens von Ketteler** (June 20), opened a **siege of the legations** which would have succeeded but for Jung-lu's protection. An **international expedition** took Tientsin (July 14) and relieved the legations (Aug. 14). Elsewhere, especially in Shansi, where Yü-hsien was now governor, at least 231 foreign civilians, chiefly missionaries, were killed by imperial order (June 24–July 24). The **court fled** (Aug. 15) to Sian, whence a rescript (Dec. 26) promptly accepted a joint note embodying the allied demands. Russians at Blagovestchensk, in retaliation for Chinese bombardments across the Amur (July 14–15) and in fear of attack by the local Chinese, drove thousands of civilians to death in the river. Russia quickly seized possession of southern Manchuria (Sept. 4–Oct. 10), without being able to secure ratification of a secret convention extorted at Port Arthur (Nov. 11). German troops, which had arrived late at Peking, alone carried out 35 of 46 punitive missions (Dec. 12–Apr. 30, 1901). After eight months' haggling between the allies, the

1901, Sept. 7. **Boxer protocol,** signed by twelve powers, provided for expressions of regret, punishment of 96 officials, payment over 40 years of 450,000,000 taels with interest (or a total value of gold $738,820,707, which became more burdensome as silver depreciated), revision of the tariff to an effective 5 per cent, fortification of an enlarged legation quarter, the razing of all forts, and establishment of foreign garrisons along the railway to Shanhai-kuan. The indemnity was to be met from maritime customs surplus, native customs, and salt monopoly, the maritime customs under Hart being given charge of the native customs within 50 *li* of all treaty ports.

1902, Jan. The **dowager empress** with the emperor **returned to Peking** by rail. Educational, economic, and military reform immediately undertaken. **Death of Li Hung-chang** (1901), **Liu K'un-i,** and **Jung-lu** (1903) left Chang Chih-tung and Yüan Shih-k'ai her ablest advisers. Intermarriage of Manchus with Chinese was for the first time sanctioned. The most distinguished Chinese jurist, **Shen Chia-pen,** was ordered to revise the legal code. A new code was promulgated (1910).

Sept. 5. **Anglo-Chinese commercial treaty,** with American and Japanese treaties of October 8, provided for changes in the treaty system and internal reform (largely ineffective).

1904-1905. **Defeat of Russia by Japan** (p. 922) again revealed to the Chinese the advantages of learning the lessons of the west. The treaty of Portsmouth returned Manchuria from Russian to Chinese administration (1907). Japan retained only the leasehold in southern Liaotung which had already been definitively conceded to Russia, together with the South Manchurian Railway. Hitherto a Manchu preserve under military government, the three eastern provinces were now (1907) reorganized on a civilian basis and thrown open to Chinese settlement.

1905. **Boycott of American goods** as a protest against further exclusion of Chinese from the United States reflected growing national consciousness.

On Chang Chih-tung's recommendation of Japanese education, a **ministry of education** was created and Chinese students swarmed to Japan (15,000 there at one time).

Sun Yat-sen organized in Japan the *T'ung Meng Hui,* a union of societies which constantly strove to eject the Manchus from China.

1906. **Preparation for constitutional government** proclaimed, following the report of a mission sent in 1905 to study foreign states. But **reorganization of the ministries** (Nov. 6) was followed by the appointment of Manchu princes to direct them (1907-1909).

Provision for progressive 10-year **suppression of opium cultivation and consumption** was supplemented by an agreement with Britain which cut imports from 48,530 chests (1907) to 4136 chests in 1915. At the suggestion of the United States (1909) a series of conferences began at Shanghai and later (1912) at The Hague to establish international control over the world drug traffic.

1908, Jan. 13. **Foreign loans for a railway from Tientsin to P'u-k'ou** (opposite Nanking) were contracted on the basis of construction, control, and operation exclusively by the Chinese government. The line was completed and opened in January 1912.

May 13. **Remission by the United States of half her share in the Boxer indemnity** made possible the establishment of **Tsing Hua College** (1911) and the sending of about 1100 graduates to America for advanced study (1911-1927).

Nov. 14-15. **Death of the emperor and of the dowager empress.** Power passed to the reactionary **Prince Ch'un,** regent for the

1908-1912. **HSÜAN T'UNG REIGN OF THE EMPEROR P'U-I.**

1908, Dec. 3. A **draft constitution** was published, providing for election of a parliament after nine years. This signified little, for

1909, Jan. 2. The **dismissal of Yüan Shih-k'ai** and the **death of Chang Chih-tung** (Oct. 4) placed the whole administration in Manchu hands. Consequently, when provincial assemblies and a national assembly met (1910), they insisted on early convocation of parliament, which was finally promised for 1913.

Scholarship of a high order continued without break through the last reign of the dynasty. The state papers of **Tseng Kuo-fan** and of **Chang Chih-tung** are regarded as models of the classical style. **Wang Hsien-ch'ien** compiled a supplement in 320 volumes (1886-1888) to the *Classical Comment of the Reigning Dynasty,* the best critical edition of the two Han histories with collected modern comment, and the *Tung Hua Lu,* a judicious selection from the official archives of the dynasty through 1874 (284 volumes, 1879-1887). Baron Iwasaki Koyata purchased and took to Tokyo (1907) the library of **Lu Hsin-yüan,** an active critic, archaeologist, and editor of the *Shih Wan Chuan Lou Ts'ung Shu.* **Miao Ch'üan-sun,** bibliographer and archeologist, thereupon persuaded governor-general Tuan Fang to buy the library of the Ting family for Nanking as the **first public library in China. K'o Shao-min** prepared a new standard *History of the Yüan Dynasty.* **K'ang Yu-wei's** *Study of the Classics Forged in the Hsin Era* (1891) and *Study of Confucius as a Reformer* (1897) together served to focus upon early texts historical criticism of a type which had fallen in abeyance since the time of Ts'ui Shu. Chinese envoys to Japan, **Yang Shou-ching** and **Li Shu-ch'ang,** found there many early editions which they reproduced in the *Ku I Ts'ung Shu* (1884). A profusion of other early documents, both Chinese and Central Asiatic, was recovered in 1907-1908 by **Aurel Stein** and **Paul Pelliot** from a temple library immured (c. 1000 A.D.) at Tun-huang, the point of bifurcation of medieval caravan routes north and south of the T'ien Shan Mountains. Discovery in 1899 of a deposit of oracular inscriptions on bone and tortoise-shell from the Shang dynasty was followed quickly by their decipherment by paleographers already trained in the archaic script of ritual bronzes.

1911, Oct. OUTBREAK OF THE CHINESE REVOLUTION, precipitated by discovery of the headquarters of the revolutionary organization at Hankow. The movement, fed by provincial distrust of the central railway administration of Sheng Hsüan-huai, spread rapidly through the west and south, without causing much bloodshed.

Nov. 8. Yüan Shih-k'ai, who had been recalled to military command (Oct. 14) was elected premier by the national assembly.

Dec. 4. Yüan signed a truce with the rebel general Li Yüan-hung, and sent T'ang Shao-i to represent him in negotiations at Shanghai.

Dec. 30. Sun Yat-sen, recently returned from Europe, was **elected president of the United Provinces of China** by a revolutionary provisional assembly at Nanking.

1912, Feb. 12. Abdication of the boy emperor.

Feb. 15. Yüan Shih-k'ai elected provisional president of the Chinese Republic by the national assembly. **Sun Yat-sen resigned** in order to unite the country.

Mar. 10. The **Nanking provisional constitution,** which aimed at making the bicameral assembly supreme. Yüan Shih-k'ai soon came into conflict with the assembly through his efforts to strengthen his own power. **Formation of opposition parties:** the *Harmony* or *Progress Party* **of Liang Ch'i-ch'ao,** advocating a strong executive; the *Kuomintang* or *Nationalist Party* **of Sun Yat-sen,** championing the system of parliamentary government.

1913, April 8. Convocation of the elected parliament.

Apr. 21. Yüan obtained from Great Britain, France, Russia, and Japan **a loan for £25,000,000,** secured by the salt tax. Fearing that this would strengthen him even more, his opponents started the

July 10. "Second Revolution" in the southern provinces. This movement was soon suppressed (Nanking taken, September 1).

Oct. 6. Yüan Shih-k'ai was elected president, and Li Yüan-hung vice-president of the republic. In order to prevent adoption of the constitution, Yüan

Nov. 4. Purged the parliament of its Kuo Ming Tang members, and soon afterward dissolved it (Jan 10, 1914).

Nov. 5. The Chinese government recognized the **autonomy of Outer Mongolia,** which had been secured by treaty between Outer Mongolia and Russia a year before (Nov. 7, 1912).

1914, May 1. A "constitutional compact" promulgated by Yüan Shih-k'ai gave him a ten-year term of office, with ample powers.

(*Cont. p. 1106.*)

6. KOREA, 1777–1910

(*From p. 581*)

1777. Introduction of Christianity, evidently by Chinese converted by the Jesuits at Peking. The new religion made considerable progress, and by the mid-19th century there were some 10,000 converts in the kingdom. Despite all prohibitions, Catholic missionaries, mostly French, stole into the country in the early 19th century.

1797. Exploration of the east coast of Korea by Capt. William R. Broughton.

1800–1834. Sunjo, king.

1835–1849. Hŏn-jong, king.

1850–1863. Ch'ŏlchong, king.

1864–1907. Kojong (usually known as I T'aewang [the reign title was changed in 1896 and again in 1897]), the twelve-year-old grandson of King Sunjo, succeeded. His father, **Hŭngsŏn,** generally known as **Tai Wen Kun** (or Taewŏngun), became regent, ruled directly until 1873, and was the dominant political figure until his death in 1898. From the outset he was extremely hostile to all foreign influence and especially to Christianity.

1865–1870. Systematic **persecution of the Christians.** A number of French missionaries were executed.

1866. A **French expedition** under Adm. Pierre Roze, occupied and burned Kanghwa at the mouth of the Han River, but was unable to proceed to the capital, Seoul; after some reverses at the hands of the natives, it was obliged to withdraw.

1867, Oct. Expedition of the German, **Ernst Oppert,** assisted by an American, Jenkins, with the object of rifling the royal tombs (supposedly of pure gold). The landing force reached the tombs, but was unable to open them. Attacks by the natives forced withdrawal.

1871, May 16. An **American naval force,** under

Capt. **Robert Shufeldt** and the minister to Peking, Frederick Low, tried to open Korea to foreign trade. Marines were landed at the mouth of the Han, but hostilities ensued and the project had to be given up.

1876, Feb. 26. OPENING OF KOREA, through a **treaty with Japan.** Japan recognized Korean independence without eliciting a protest from China. Three ports were opened to Japanese trade and Japan was permitted to have a resident at Seoul.

1882, May 22. TREATY WITH THE UNITED STATES, negotiated by Shufeldt and by Viceroy Li Hung-chang (in charge of Chinese-Korean relations): no mention of Korean independence, but the United States secured extra-territorial rights and permission to trade. Similar treaties were concluded with Great Britain (Nov. 26, 1883), Russia (July 7, 1884), and other powers.

July 23. An **attack by the Koreans on the Japanese legation** in Seoul led to **intervention by the Chinese.** The Japanese were given compensation and the right to keep a legation guard. **Yüan Shih-k'ai** became Chinese resident at Seoul and during the ensuing decade devoted himself to strengthening the Chinese influence as against Japan. In Korea the regent returned to power and there soon developed between him and the energetic **Queen Min** a struggle for control of the government.

1884, Dec. 5-7. The **reform party,** supported by the Japanese, hatched a conspiracy, assassinated a number of ministers, and secured control of the king. The Chinese thereupon dispatched troops to Seoul, recaptured the king and the palace, but provoked further intervention by Japan. The two powers were on the very verge of war, but finally concluded the

1885, Apr. 18. CONVENTION OF TIEN-TSIN (*Li-Itō Convention*): both agreed to withdraw their troops and to notify each other if it became necessary in future to intervene.

Apr. 26. The **British occupied Port Hamilton** in the course of the Anglo-Russian crisis, for fear lest Russia seize a port on the Korean coast. (Despite Chinese protests the British remained until February 27, 1887.)

1894-1895. The **SINO-JAPANESE WAR,** which was the direct outcome of the rivalry of the two powers for control of Korea. Following an insurrection by the Tonghak Society in southern Korea in the spring of 1894, the king called upon the Chinese for aid (June 10). Several thousand men were dispatched and Japan notified. Thereupon the Japanese sent twice as many men and occupied Seoul (June 25). On the suggestion of the Chinese that both forces be withdrawn, the Japanese in-

sisted first on the introduction of extensive reforms. Hostilities soon broke out and war was declared on August 1 (for the course of the war see p. 913). Korea was obliged to conclude an alliance with Japan (Aug. 26) and the Japanese soon took over control of the government.

1895, Apr. 17. Treaty of Shimonoseki, ending the Sino-Japanese War. By this treaty the independence of Korea was recognized by China. The Japanese, still in substantial control, pushed through far-reaching and for the most part unpopular reforms. Opposition of the queen and the court led to the

Oct. 8. Murder of the queen, with the connivance of the Japanese resident, Viscount Miura. The commanding position of Japan was, however, at once challenged by popular outbreaks and anti-reform riots. The country became divided into a conservative, anti-Japanese, and a progressive, pro-Japanese party (the latter represented by the **Independence Club,** founded 1896),

1896, Feb. 10. The **king fled to the Russian legation** in the course of another insurrection. He remained under Russian protection for a year and during this period the Russians quickly supplanted the Japanese as the dominant influence. Mission of Russian advisers and instructors; foundation of the Russian-Korean Bank; timber and mining concessions to Russia, etc. The situation became so dark for the Japanese that they were glad to conclude with Russia

June 9. The **LOBANOV-YAMAGATA AGREEMENT,** which established a type of condominium: Russia and Japan to co-operate in the reform of army and finances. In practice the agreement proved almost worthless and the Russian penetration continued unabated.

1897, Feb. 20. The king left the Russian legation and moved into the new palace. **The king took the imperial title** (Oct. 17).

Dec. An **Anglo-Russian crisis,** arising from efforts of the Russians to replace the financial adviser, **M'Leavy Brown** (since 1895), by a Russian. A British naval demonstration at Chemulpo made the Russians draw back.

1898, Apr. 25. The **ROSEN-NISHI AGREEMENT** between Russia and Japan. Russia, involved in the international crisis following the occupation of Kiaochow and Port Arthur (p. 789), was eager to avoid friction with Japan and withdrew many of the advisers and officers. By the new convention both sides engaged not to interfere with the internal affairs of Korea, but Japan was given a free hand in economic matters.

Nov. Dissolution of the Independence Club

and arrest of many of the leaders resulted in widespread riots and disorders. The conservative (pro-Russian) and progressive (pro-Japanese) groups were now almost at open war with each other.

1900, Mar. 18. The Russians attempted to secure a **concession at Masampo** for a naval station, but were foiled by the stiff opposition of Japan. Despite all previous agreements, the two powers were gradually moving toward a crisis. The Japanese, determined to exclude Russia from Korea, concluded with Britain

1902, Jan. 30. The **Anglo-Japanese alliance,** which again affirmed the independence of Korea. The Japanese then entered upon negotiations with Russia, which was trying to exploit a great **timber concession on the Yalu River** in northern Korea (first secured in 1896). The negotiations bringing no results, the Japanese embarked on

1904, Feb. 8. THE RUSSIAN-JAPANESE WAR (p. 922). The Japanese at once occupied Seoul, and Korea was obliged to annul all concessions made to the Russians. Once again Korea fell entirely under Japanese control,

and was forced to accept Japanese diplomatic and financial advisers.

1905, Sept. 5. The **treaty of Portsmouth,** between Russia and Japan, provided for Russian recognition of the preponderant interest, political, military, and economic, of Japan in Korea and provided further that Russia should not oppose any measures for the government of Korea or its protection and control which the Japanese government might deem necessary.

1906-1908. **Prince Itō,** Japanese resident-general. He regulated the relations between Japan and Korea and set the Korean government on the road to reform and modernization.

1907, July 19. **Abdication of the emperor** under Japanese pressure. His successor was a mere figurehead.

July 25. The administration was placed almost entirely under **Japanese control** and the Korean army was ordered disbanded. This at once led to widespread insurrection and a **war of independence,** which was suppressed only with great difficulty after years of fighting.

1910, Aug. 22. KOREA WAS FORMALLY ANNEXED TO JAPAN, and renamed *Chōsen.*
(*Cont. pp. 1111, 1347*)

7. JAPAN, 1793–1914

(*From p. 587*)

1793. **Adam Laxman,** a Russian lieutenant, arrived at Hakodate in Hokkaidō but failed to establish friendly relations.

1793-1838. The **PERSONAL RULE OF IENARI** as *shōgun* was characterized by increasing extravagance and inefficiency and by signs of the breakdown of isolation and the collapse of military rule. During this period lived **Ninomiya Sontoku,** a famous peasant-philosopher and economic reformer; **Kyokutei** (or Takizawa) **Bakin,** an author of adventure novels; and **Katsushika Hokusai** and **Andō** (or Utagawa) **Hiroshige,** two of the best known ukiyo-e woodblock artists.

1795. **Capt. William Broughton,** a British explorer, visited Hokkaidō, charting parts of the coast.

1797-1809. **American ships traded with Japan** nearly every year, on behalf of the Dutch.

1798. The *Kojikiden,* a commentary to the *Kojiki,* was completed after thirty-five years' labor by **Motoori Norinaga,** the greatest of the Shintō scholars. This achievement was an important event in the revival of Shintō and of the imperial cause. Influential in these movements were also **Kamo Mabuchi** and **Hirata Atsutane.**

1804. A Russian ambassador, **Nicholas Rezanov,** representing the Russian-American Company, reached Nagasaki, but after six months failed to obtain a treaty. In 1806-1807 his subordinates raided Sakhalin.

1814. **Kurozumi Munetada** founded the **Kurozumi sect,** the first of the modern popular Shintō sects which on the whole stress patriotism and sometimes faith-healing. This and twelve similar sects founded in the course of the next century counted over 17,000,000 believers.

1837. The *Morrison,* an American ship with merchants and missionaries from Macao, visited Napa in the Ryūkyū (Chinese *Liu-ch'iu*) Islands, was bombarded at Edo and Kagoshima and failed to open relations. This was but one of some half a hundred efforts to establish more extensive intercourse with Japan before 1854. One reason for these efforts was that since about 1820 the northern Pacific whaling industry had developed greatly, and more humane treatment of crews of whalers wrecked in Japanese waters was desired, particularly by the United States.

1838-1853. **IEYOSHI** as *shōgun.* The question of opening the country to foreign trade in compliance with the demands of the occidental nations became pressing. Sentiment in favor of an imperial restoration was growing, and economic ills were impoverishing many warriors who became *rōnin,* masterless warriors.

1838. Nakayama Miki, a woman, founded the faith-healing **Tenri sect,** the most popular of the modern Shintō sects.

1839-1840. Conservative scholars in an effort to check the rapid growth of occidental learning had restrictive measures instituted and imprisoned two leading scholars of the occidental school (*Rangaku,* "Dutch Learning"), who favored opening of Japan, **Watanabe Kazan** and **Takano Chōei.**

1841-1843. Mizuno Tadakuni carried through misguided and ineffectual reforms.

1844. William II of Holland warned the *shōgun* by letter of the futility of the exclusion policy.

1846. American **Commodore James Biddle visited Edo Bay,** but trade was refused.

1849. Commodore James Glynn succeeded in liberating American castaways at Nagasaki.

1851. American **Commodore John H. Aulick** was commissioned to open relations with Japan, but was removed from his command (Nov.); **Commodore Matthew C. Perry** appointed as his successor (Mar. 1852). The Perry expedition was sent to improve treatment in Japan of American castaways and to open one or two ports for trade and supplies, especially coal for California-Shanghai steamship service; instructions pacific in nature.

1853, July 8. PERRY with four ships anchored off Uraga in Edo Bay and remained ten days, delivering the president's letter, which was referred to the emperor and to the *daimyō,* an unprecedented course which aroused the whole nation and elicited a largely anti-foreign response.

1853-1858. IESADA as *shōgun.* The feudatories increasingly criticized the action of Edo, and the public became divided into two camps —(1) those in favor of the expulsion of the foreigners (*jōi*), led by emperor-honoring **Tokugawa Nariakira,** ex-lord of Mito, and (2) the realists who saw that concessions to the foreigners were necessary, led by **Ii Naosuke** (Kamon-no-kami). The two groups also divided over proposed heirs for the childless Iesada. Naosuke favored **Tokugawa Iemochi,** lord of Kii. **Nariakira** favored his own son, **Hitotsubashi Yoshinobu** (Keiki), and resorted to the unprecedented stratagem of seeking imperial backing for his candidate.

1854, Feb. 13. Perry returned to Edo Bay with more ships, hastened by fear of Russian and French efforts to get treaties, and secured the **treaty of Kanagawa** (Mar. 31), which opened two ports, permitted trade under regulations, provided better treatment of American castaways, and included a most-favored-nation clause, but omitted extra-territoriality. This was followed by treaties with Britain (Oct. 1854), Russia (Feb. 1855), and the Netherlands (Nov. 1855, Jan. 1856), which gave further privileges. Japan was not yet really open to trade. All these treaties were signed by the *shōgun* (called by foreigners *tycoon* [*tai-kun*], and wrongly regarded by them as the "secular emperor").

1854-1855. The Dutch aided the Japanese in laying the foundations for a future navy.

1856, Aug. American consul-general **Townsend Harris** arrived at Shimoda with instructions to procure a commercial treaty.

1858, Mar.-May. Growing imperial prestige was seen in an extraordinary Edo appeal to the emperor for approval of further foreign intercourse, which was refused. The strong anti-foreign spirit in Kyōto became linked with a pro-emperor movement (*sonnō*).

June. Ii Naosuke appointed *tairō* and soon all-powerful at Edo. He secured the appointment of Iemochi as the *shōgun's* heir and the signature (July 29) without imperial approval of the important commercial treaty previously arranged with Harris, which provided for unsupervised trade and permanent residence at five ports, residence at Edo and Ōsaka, an envoy at Edo, extra-territoriality, a conventional tariff, the prohibition of the import of opium, revision in 1872 or later. Treaties followed with the Netherlands (Aug. 18), Russia (Aug. 19), Britain (Aug. 26), France (Oct. 7), all on the model of the Harris treaty.

1858-1866. IEMOCHI as *shōgun.* The antiforeign sentiment continued unabated, and desire for the restoration of the emperor's direct rule increased rapidly.

1859, Feb. Kyōto informed Edo that foreigners were to be expelled as soon as possible.

1859. Foreign merchants settled at Yokohama. A series of attacks upon foreigners followed and resulted in foreign pressure upon Edo for redress. Silver-gold exchange rate of 5 to 1 led to outflow of gold.

Nov. Yoshida Shōin, a leading anti-foreign, pro-imperial spirit of Chōshū (W. Hondō), was executed for anti-Edo activities, but his teachings continued to influence the Chōshū warriors.

1860, Mar. 24. Ii Naosuke was assassinated by former Mito men.

May 17. First Japanese embassy to the United States exchanged treaty ratifications in Washington.

Sept. 17. Nariakira died, and leadership of anti-foreign, pro-imperial movement passed to **Satsuma** (*Kyūshū*), **Chōshū,** and **Tosa** (*Shikoku*) fiefs.

1861, Mar.-Sept. Russia occupied Tsushima.

1862, Jan.   Mission to European governments.
Agreement signed in London (June) postponing
until 1868 opening of Niigata and Hyōgo and
residence in Edo and Ōsaka.

Sept. 14.   An Englishman, **C. L. Richardson,** murdered by Satsuma men near Yokohama. This was but one of many murderous
attacks on foreigners or their employees by
anti-foreign warriors.

Oct.   The forced residence of *daimyō* in
Edo was greatly curtailed and the western
daimyō began to congregate around the court in
Kyōto.

1863, Apr.   Iemochi went to Kyōto in response
to a summons from the emperor. This unprecedented step signified that the political center
of the empire had already shifted back to
Kyōto. On June 5 a date (June 25) was chosen
for expulsion of foreigners.

June 24.   Edo paid indemnity to the British
for Richardson and others and announced
negotiations would be begun for closing of ports.

**June 25.   Chōshū forts at Shimonoseki fired
on an American vessel** and later on French and
Dutch vessels; direct reprisals by American and
French warships.

**Aug. 15–16.   A British squadron bombarded
Kagoshima,** thereby convincing Satsuma that
expulsion of foreigners was impracticable.

Sept.   *Coup d'état* at Kyōto; extremist
Chōshū forces expelled.

1864.   Internecine strife in Mito robbed it of all
leadership in national affairs.

Aug.   Chōshū men defeated in pitched
battle at Kyōto in effort to regain influence at
court.

Sept. 5–8.   Allied expedition (British, Dutch,
French, American) silenced Chōshū forts at
Shimonoseki, thereby breaking back of antiforeign movement. Edo agreed to pay indemnity for Chōshū (Oct.).

1865, Nov.   Allied naval demonstration at Osaka
secured imperial ratification of treaties.

1866, June 25.   Tariff convention signed with
United States, Britain, France, and the Netherlands. Five per cent duty on almost all imports and exports (in force until 1899).

July–Oct.   Edo engaged in **unsuccessful
expedition to punish Chōshū** for its extremist
activities.

Sept.   Iemochi died and was succeeded by
1867.   KEIKI (Hitotsubashi Yoshinobu) as
shōgun. Young leaders, like **Saigō** and **Ōkubo**
of Satsuma, plotted to undermine Edo rule; a
vigorous young ruler, **Mutsuhito** (Meiji emperor), came to the throne (Feb.); Keiki, who
as a Mito scion was predisposed to surrender
to Kyōto, resigned (Nov.), bringing almost
seven hundred years of feudal military government to an end.

**1868, Jan. 1.   Hyōgo (Kobe) and Ōsaka opened
to foreign trade.**

Jan. 3.   The **EMPEROR assumed direct
control of the nation;** western clans seized power
at Kyōto; remaining Tokugawa forces defeated
in civil war (July 4, **battle of Ueno** in Edo).

**Mar.   The emperor received French, Dutch,
and British representatives.**

Apr. 6.   Charter oath by the emperor promised a deliberative assembly, decision of public
affairs by public opinion.

Nov.   Capital moved to Edo, renamed
Tōkyō (*Eastern capital*). Meanwhile the year
period was changed to Meiji marking the
beginning of

1868–1912.   THE MEIJI PERIOD. The antiforeign policy of the imperial party was dropped as soon as it came to power, and Japan
entered upon a period of great borrowing from
the Occident comparable only to the period of
the imitation of China. The remnants of military rule and feudalism were abolished, a strong
centralized bureaucratic government fashioned
along occidental lines was built up under the
able leadership of the Meiji emperor, and Japan
became a modern world power. **Rapid industrialization** on western models took place, and,
as a consequence, the wealth and population
of the land multiplied. In the fields of science,
education, philosophy, and even art and literature great transformations were wrought by
the impact of occidental civilization, and for a
few decades many of the native traits and
institutions were somewhat discredited if not
completely superseded.

1869, Mar.   The *daimyō* of Satsuma, Chōshū,
Tosa, and Hizen offered their lands to the
emperor as a step toward the abolition of
feudalism; others followed this example.

July.   *Daimyō* were appointed governors of
their former estates with one-tenth their former
revenue. Representatives of the 276 fiefs,
appointed by their lords, met in an assembly
(*kogishō*); this body lacked legislative power,
was prorogued in 1870 and abolished in 1873.

**1871, Aug. 29.   Imperial decree abolished the
fiefs** and substituted prefectures (*ken,* at first
71, later 44, with three prefectural cities [*fu*]).
First regular government **postal service established** (Tōkyō to Osaka). **Ministry of education
reorganized** to promote universal education.
First daily newspaper.

Sept. 3.   Treaty of Tientsin with China
signed as between equals. Japan did not gain
extra-territorial and commercial rights equal to
those of the West, nor a most-favored-nation
clause.

Oct.   The **Iwakura mission** (including
Ōkubo and Itō) departed to seek treaty revision from the West and to prepare for reforms

necessary to that end. It failed to secure revision and returned in September 1873.

1872. **Universal military service introduced;** the army was modeled at first on the French, later on the German. **First railway opened** (Tōkyō-Yokohama, 18 miles). National bank regulations issued on American model.

1873, Jan. 1. Solar **Gregorian calendar adopted** in place of lunar calendar. British officers employed to reorganize the navy. Policy of **religious toleration** permitted the propagation of Christianity once more.

Oct. A **peaceful policy toward Korea** was chosen rather than a warlike policy.

1874, April. Expedition sent via Amoy to **Formosa** to redress murder by natives of Ryūkyū sailors in December 1871; Japan having claimed suzerainty over Ryūkyū and China having avoided responsibility. In October Japan agreed to recall the expedition, China to pay indemnity.

1875. **Assembly of prefectural governors** convened (not a representative nor a legislative body). A **senate** (*Genrōin*), convened in 1876, likewise had advisory duties only (abolished 1890). Agitation for representative institutions continued, led by **Itagaki** of Tosa.

1876, Feb. 26. Japanese naval demonstration secured **treaty with Korea,** recognizing the latter as independent of China and granting extraterritorial and commercial privileges to Japan.

Aug. Compulsory commutation of the pensions which had been granted the warrior class, and which were a heavy financial burden, and the prohibition of the wearing of two swords signified the **end of the warrior class** as a separate group. Natural resentment over this led to several disturbances including

1877, Jan.–Sept. The **SATSUMA REBELLION** led by **Saigō,** a leader in the restoration movement. It was crushed by the modern trained army of commoners. A large issue of inconvertible paper money was used to defray expenses.

1878, May. **Ōkubo was assassinated.**

1879. **Prefectural assemblies,** elected by males over 25 who paid a land tax of five yen or more, were convened with powers to determine local budgets.

1880, July. Promulgation of **revised penal code** and **code of criminal procedure,** based largely on French models, in order to remove necessity for extra-territoriality.

1881. Imperial decree promised to convene a **national assembly** in 1890; fostered organization of political parties (*Jiyūtō* or **Liberal Party** by Itagaki; *Kaishintō* or **Progressive Party** by Ōkuma) in opposition to Satsuma-Chōshū bureaucracy.

1882, Jan.–July. In treaty revision conference at Tōkyō foreign minister Inoue failed to secure revision.

Mar. Itō was appointed to draft a constitution and visited the Occident, being particularly impressed by the German political system (returned in September 1883).

Oct. **Bank of Japan** established as central bank of European type.

1883, Apr. 16. **Revision of the press law** with drastic libel regulations.

1884. **Creation of a newly organized peerage** of 500 members to provide a basis for an upper house.

Dec. *Coup d'état* by pro-Japanese liberal party in Korea; the Japanese envoy and troops were forced out by Chinese; this led to

1885, Apr. 18. **CONVENTION BETWEEN ITŌ AND LI HUNG-CHANG:** both powers to withdraw their troops and to inform each other of any intention to send them back to Korea; really a victory for Japan. An attempt by Russia to gain a protectorate over Korea prevented. Great Britain occupied Port Hamilton (Apr.), but withdrew (Feb. 27, 1887).

Reorganization of the cabinet on German lines with a premier (Count Itō) and nine departmental ministers responsible to him.

1886, May 1–1887, July 29. **Treaty revision conference** in Tōkyō, conducted by Inoue as foreign minister, failed to obtain the abolition of extra-territoriality; individual negotiations were then carried on by Inoue's successor, Ōkuma.

Period of **rapid economic expansion** with government paper-making and cotton-spinning plants (200 steam factories in Japan by 1890); extension of railroads (959 miles of government lines by 1901 and 2905 of private); increase in steamship tonnage (15,000 by 1893, 1,522,000 by 1905); and unification of telegraph and postal systems (1886).

1888, Apr. **Privy council created** as an advisory body to the emperor. **Kuroda** succeeded Itō as premier.

1889, Feb. 11. **NEW CONSTITUTION PROMULGATED.** The emperor's powers were carefully guarded, including the right to declare war and make peace, and power to issue ordinances having the force of laws. **Bicameral diet;** upper house of peers and representatives of merit and wealth (363 members); lower house elected through limited suffrage (463 members); the diet had restricted control of finances.

Dec. **Count Yamagata became premier.**

1890. The emperor formally approved the new civil, commercial, and criminal **codes of law** based on western models, in order to eliminate necessity for extra-territoriality. Mexico had already in 1888 granted Japan judicial autonomy over Mexicans in Japan. The civil code was put in force, 1892 and 1898, and the commercial code, 1899.

July. First general election, by males aged 25 who paid direct national taxes of 15 yen or more (460,000 qualified voters out of 42,000,-000).

1891, May. Resignation of Premier Yamagata, Count Matsukata succeeding.

1892, June. Resignation of the cabinet following defeats in the diet; **Count Itō became premier.**

1894, Mar. Rising of the anti-foreign **Tonghak Society in southern Korea** led China and Japan to send troops to Korea.

July 16. Aoki-Kimberley treaty, signed in London, revised British treaty of 1858, abolished extra-territoriality in 1899, prepared the way for similar treaties with other powers. By August 4, 1899, all occidentals were subject to Japanese courts; a new international status for Japan.

1894–1895. SINO-JAPANESE WAR—primarily a struggle for control of Korea (p. 913).

1895, Apr. 17. TREATY OF SHIMONOSEKI signed by Count Itō, Count Mutsu, minister of foreign affairs, and Li Hung-chang, Chinese ambassador extraordinary. China recognized the full independence of Korea, ceded to Japan the Pescadores, Formosa, and the Liaotung Peninsula, paid an indemnity of Tls. 200,000,000, opened four more treaty ports, and negotiated a new commercial treaty.

Nov. Japan yielded to **tripartite intervention of Russia, France, and Germany** and gave up the Liaotung Peninsula, receiving instead from China Tls. 30,000,000 additional indemnity.

1896. Japanese domination and reorganization of the **Korean government,** following the murder of Queen Min (Oct. 8, 1895) (p. 917).

June 9. Lobanov-Yamagata protocol, signed in St. Petersburg, recognized Russia's position in Korea (p. 917).

Sept. Matsukata again premier.

1897, Mar. 29. Japan adopted the gold standard; ratio, 32⅓ to 1.

1898, Jan. Itō again premier.

Apr. 25. Nishi-Rosen protocol signed, by which Russia agreed to Japanese economic penetration of Korea; both powers were to refrain from interference with internal affairs.

Apr. 26. Japan assured by the Tsungli Yamen at Peking respecting the **non-alienation of Fukien province** to any other power.

June. Ōkuma-Itagaki ministry of Kenseitō party formed.

Nov. Yamagata ministry formed.

1899, July 17. Revised treaties with foreign nations took effect. France and Austria retained consular jurisdiction until August 4.

1900, June 6. Boxer uprising in China. Japan joined the international relief expedition (p. 914).

Oct. Itō formed a Kenseitō ministry.

1901, June 2. Viscount Katsura formed a ministry.

Aug. Plans of naval and military reorganization adopted; cabinet ministers for these departments might be civilians, but direct responsibility to the emperor was retained.

1902, Jan. 30. ANGLO-JAPANESE ALLIANCE signed (negotiated by Hayashi in London) (p. 793).

1904. Continued Russian penetration of northern Korea and failure to withdraw from Manchuria, together with breakdown of Russo-Japanese negotiations, led to Japanese severance of diplomatic relations (Feb. 6) and

1904–1905. THE RUSSO-JAPANESE WAR.

Feb. 8. Japan attacked Port Arthur (*Ryojun*), bottling up Russian fleet.

Feb. 10. War declared.

Feb. 23. Treaty between Japan and Korea by which the latter virtually became a protectorate of Japan in return for guaranties of integrity.

May 1. Russians defeated at the **Yalu River** by Kuroki.

May 30. Japanese occupied **Dalny** (Dairen). Nogi began **siege of Port Arthur,** Ōyama advanced northward, and

Aug. 25–Sept. 4. Defeated Russians at **Liaoyang.** The latter withdrew to Mukden.

1905, Jan. 2. Port Arthur surrendered.

Feb. 20–Mar. 9. Russians defeated at **Mukden** by five combined Japanese armies under **Ōyama.**

May 27–29. In **naval battle of Tsushima Straits** the Russian fleet of 32 vessels, come from European waters, was annihilated by Japanese under **Tōgō.**

Aug. 12. Anglo-Japanese alliance renewed for ten years; *casus belli* redefined as attack by a single power on either party.

Sept. 5. TREATY OF PEACE signed at **Portsmouth,** after a conference which began August 5 through President Roosevelt's mediation. Russia acknowledged Japan's paramount interest in Korea, transferred to Japan the lease of the Liaotung Peninsula and the railroad to Ch'angchun, and ceded the southern half of Sakhalin. Manchuria to be evacuated by both powers and restored to China. Because of failure to obtain an indemnity the treaty was unpopular in Japan and riots occurred in Tōkyō.

Nov. 17. Japan secured by treaty control of the foreign relations of Korea.

1906, Jan. Resignation of Premier Katsura

because of popular dissatisfaction with Portsmouth treaty. **Kenseitō ministry formed by Marquis Saionji.**

Mar. 16. Bill passed lower house for **nationalization of all railways** at estimated cost of $250,000,000. By 1921 there were 6481 miles of state railways and 1993 of private.

1907, June 10. Franco-Japanese treaty guaranteeing the "open door" and integrity of China, *status quo* in the Far East, and a most-favored-nation agreement; mutual promise regarding security of Chinese territory in which each had special interests (for Japan, Fukien and parts of Manchuria and Mongolia).

July 25. Japan obtained a protectorate over Korea by treaty, with complete control by Japanese resident-general.

July 30. Russo-Japanese treaty similar to the Franco-Japanese treaty (1907), with an agreement about the Chinese Eastern and Southern Manchurian railroads and spheres in Manchuria.

1908, Feb. 18. Plans handed to American minister at Tōkyō for Japanese **restriction of labor emigration to the United States** (*Gentlemen's agreement*) to settle existing difficulties between the two countries.

July. Katsura succeeded Saionji as premier.

Nov. 30. Exchange of notes with the United States (*Root-Takahira agreement*) on the common policy of the *status quo* in the Pacific and "open door" and integrity of China.

1909, June. Prince Itō resigned after confessed failure to reform Korean administration.

Oct. 26. Itō assassinated by a Korean fanatic.

1910, July 4. Russo-Japanese agreement demarcated spheres in Manchuria, in joint opposition to American proposals (Knox scheme of November 1909) and for common action in defense of their interests.

Aug. 22. KOREA ANNEXED by treaty, and a program of development and attempted assimilation begun.

1911, Feb. 24. New treaty with the United States, continued restriction of emigration of Japanese laborers.

July 13. Anglo-Japanese alliance renewed for ten years without reference to Korea. Neither party to be drawn into war with a nation with which it had a general arbitration treaty.

Aug. Saionji succeeded Katsura as premier.

1912, Feb. 3. Heavy naval program submitted to the diet, involving eight dreadnoughts and eight armored cruisers to be commenced in 1913.

July 8. Secret Russo-Japanese treaty further delimited spheres in northeastern Asia.

July 30. The **Meiji emperor died** and was succeeded by his son, **Yoshihito.** The year period was changed to **Taishō,** marking the beginning of

1912–1916. THE TAISHŌ PERIOD. The movements begun in the Meiji Period continued with no startling new developments. The personal weakness of the Taishō emperor almost eliminated the direct control of the throne over practical politics. The First World War and natural economic advance made Japan one of the great world powers.

1912, Dec. 20. Prince Katsura became premier without a majority when Saionji resigned because of opposition to his retrenchment policy in Korea.

1913, Feb. 12. Adm. Yamamoto succeeded Katsura as premier.

May 9. Formal **protest sent the United States** against proposed anti-alien land legislation in California. The bill nevertheless was signed (May 19), and Japan assured that treaty rights were not infringed.

1914, Apr. Count Ōkuma formed a ministry after Yamamoto resigned because of defeat of a heavy naval budget.

Aug. 15. Japanese ultimatum to Germany demanding withdrawal of German fleet from Far East and the surrender of Kiaochow within a week. Since no reply was received

Aug. 23. WAR DECLARED ON GERMANY. (*Cont.* pp. 969, 1111.)

K. THE PACIFIC AREA

1. GENERAL: EXPLORATION AND ANNEXATION, 1513–1906

(*From p. 391*)

1513, Sept. 25. Vasco Nuñez de Balboa first sighted the Pacific from the coast of Panama.

1520, Nov. 28. MAGELLAN (Fernão de Magalhaes) with three ships passed from the Straits of Magellan into the Pacific, which he crossed to the Ladrone and Philippine Islands in the course of 110 days. Only a couple of deserted islands were sighted. Magellan was killed on the island of Cebu, but one of his ships, under **Juan Sebastián del Cano,** returned to Europe by the Cape of Good Hope, discovering **New Amsterdam Island** on the way (1522).

1527. Portuguese traders to the Spice Islands

seem to have touched on the northwest coast of Australia.

1542. The Spaniard **Lopez de Villalobos** crossed from Mexico to the Philippines, discovering some of the **Caroline** and **Palau Islands** on the way.

1545. The Spaniard **Ortiz de Retes** touched on the north coast of **New Guinea,** which he named. The island seems to have been sighted by the Portuguese **Antonio de Abrea** in 1511.

1565. The Spaniard **Andres de Urdaneta** discovered the **northern seaway** from the Philippines to New Spain, thus making the return voyage relatively easy. For the **Spanish settlement of the Philippines** and the connection with Latin America see p. 580.

1567. **Alvaro de Mendaña** (Spanish) discovered the **Solomon, Marshall,** and **Ellice Islands.**

1578. **Francis Drake crossed the Pacific,** east to west, the first Englishman to make the voyage.

1595. **Mendaña,** on a second voyage, discovered the **Marquesas** and **Santa Cruz Islands.**

1606. **Pedro Fernandez de Quiros,** one of Mendaña's captains, continuing the search for new lands and a southern continent (*Terra Australis*), discovered **Tahiti** and the **New Hebrides.** One of his captains, **Luis Vaez de Torres,** sailed through **Torres Straits,** between Australia and New Guinea. In the same year the Dutchman, **Willem Janszoon,** entered Torres Straits from the west side and coasted along the west coast of York Peninsula.

1616, Oct. 25. The Dutchman **DIRK HARTOG** landed on the island named for him on the coast of **West Australia.** During the next ten years Dutch mariners explored the west coast and part of the north coast, and in 1627 part of the south coast.

1616. The Dutchmen **Willem Cornelisz van Schouten** and **Jacob Lemaire,** seeking a route to the Indies not under control of the East India Company, first rounded Cape Horn and crossed the Pacific, discovering the **Bismarck Archipelago** and exploring the north coast of New Guinea.

1642-1644. **ABEL JANSZOON TASMAN,** in the service of the East India Company, sailed east from Mauritius, discovered the west and south side of **Tasmania** (Van Diemen's Land), touched on the west coast of **New Zealand,** and on the way back to Batavia discovered **Tonga** and **Fiji.** He proved that Australia was not part of a great Antarctic continent, though in circumnavigating Australia he did not even sight it.

1699. **William Dampier,** an Englishman, coasted along the northwest and west coasts of Australia.

1722. **Jacob Roggeveen** (Dutch), sailing from

east to west across the Pacific, discovered **Easter Island** and **Samoa.**

1766-1767. **Samuel Wallis** and **Philip Carteret** rediscovered **Tahiti** and explored the Solomon Islands and the New Guinea coasts.

1767-1769. **Louis Antoine de Bougainville,** a French nobleman seeking new lands for France, explored Tahiti, Samoa, and the New Hebrides.

1768-1771. **FIRST VOYAGE OF CAPT. JAMES COOK,** the greatest explorer of the Pacific. Cook's party set out to observe the transit of Venus, from Tahiti. Having achieved this end, Cook sailed around New Zealand, proving its insularity, and thence discovered the east coast of Australia. He passed thence to Java and home by the Cape of Good Hope.

1772-1775. **COOK'S SECOND VOYAGE,** this time west to east. He attempted to find the Terra Australis (see p. 621) and explored the New Hebrides, New Caledonia, and Norfolk Island.

1772. The Frenchman **Yves de Kerguelen-Trémarec** discovered **Kerguelen Island.**

1776-1779. **COOK'S THIRD VOYAGE,** in search of a passage from Hudson Bay to the Pacific. Cook discovered **Christmas Island** and (1778) **Hawaii** (Sandwich Islands), after which he passed through Bering Strait and explored the Arctic coasts of America and Asia (p. 614).

1785-1788. **Jean François de La Pérouse,** one of the greatest explorers of the period, made extensive discoveries in the northwest part of the Pacific, about Japan and Siberia.

1788, Jan. 18. The **first shipload of British convicts was landed at BOTANY BAY,** Australia, and **Britain claimed Australia** east of 135° E. Long. For the further development of Australia see p. 925.

1790. Mutineers from the British ship *Bounty* settled on little **Pitcairn Island,** the first British settlers on a Pacific island. Their descendants, by native women, still occupy the island, which was annexed by Britain in 1838.

1796. **Fanning Island** and **Gilbert Island** were discovered.

1797. The **first British mission** was established on Tahiti, and soon afterward on the Marquesas and Friendly Islands. The British Protestants were soon followed by **French Catholics,** and, although at first the missions were rather unsuccessful, in the course of the 19th century the islands were for the most part converted.

1798. **George Bass** and **Matthew Flinders** discovered **Bass Strait,** separating Australia and Tasmania.

1802-1803. **Flinders** completed the exploration of the south coast of Australia and (1803) circumnavigated the continent and suggested the name **Australia.**

During the 19th century the **development of European trade** ran parallel to the expansion of missionary activity. Sandalwood, trepang, and coconut oil the chief products. Ruthless treatment of the natives (**Kanaka traffic** to Australia, i.e. kidnaping and selling into slavery). Phenomenal **decline of the native populations,** due in part, no doubt, to practice of infanticide and to the **ravages of disease** brought in by the Europeans. The traders, and especially the whalers, completed the exploration of the ocean, while European expeditions extended scientific study.

1818-1819. The Frenchman **Claude de Freycinet** explored the coasts of New Guinea, the Mariannes, and Hawaii.

1823-1824. Another Frenchman, **Louis Duperry,** visited and studied the Gilbert, Marshall, and New Britain Islands.

1826-1829. **Jules Dumont d'Urville,** next to Cook the greatest explorer of the Pacific, investigated New Zealand, New Guinea, New Hebrides, Fiji, and the Marianas.

1828. **The Dutch annexed western New Guinea.**

1833-1835. **Capt. Robert Fitzroy,** with **Charles Darwin,** made a famous scientific voyage in the *Beagle* to Tahiti and New Zealand.

1837-1840. **Dumont d'Urville,** in a second voyage, explored the Louisiades, Fiji, the Solomons, Marquesas, and Tuamotus. He established the **division of the island world into** *Melanesia, Micronesia,* and *Polynesia.*

1842. The French initiated a policy of annexation by taking the **Marquesas** and establishing a **protectorate over Tahiti and the Society Islands.** In 1844 they took over **Gambier Island** in the Tuamotus, claiming a protectorate over the entire group, which was formally annexed in 1881. In 1853 the French annexed **New Caledonia.**

1857-1859. The Austrian *Novara* expedition, one of the most fruitful scientific voyages.

1864. **The French annexed the Loyalty Islands.**

1874-1875. The British *Challenger* expedition, under **Sir George Nares.**

1874, Oct. 10. The **British government annexed Fiji,** inaugurating an extensive annexationist policy which had been previously rejected by the government, but now appeared necessary in view of French and German activity and because of clamor from Australia and New Zealand.

1880. **Tahiti was made a French colony.**

1884. **Britain annexed the southeast part of New Guinea,** while the Germans appropriated the northeast as well as the islands of the Bismarck Archipelago.

1885. **Germany annexed the Marshall Islands** and the **Solomons.**

1887. Britain and France established a **condominium over the New Hebrides.**

1888. The British established a **protectorate over the Cook Islands.**

1889. Britain, Germany, and the United States arranged for joint **supervision of the affairs of Samoa** (p. 939).

1892. The British proclaimed a **protectorate over the Gilbert and Ellice Islands** (annexed 1915).

1898, Aug. 12. **The United States annexed Hawaii** (p. 938). By the war with Spain the United States secured the **Philippines** (p. 937) and **Guam.**

1899. By purchase, the Germans secured from Spain the **Marianas** (Ladrone) and the **Palau Islands.**

1899. **Settlement of the Samoan dispute** (p. 939). The United States retained **Tutuila** and the rest of the islands went to Germany. As compensation the British secured a number of the Solomon Islands from Germany.

1900. **British protectorate over the Friendly Islands (Tonga) and Savage Island.**

1901. The **Cook Islands** were turned over to New Zealand for administration.

1906. **British New Guinea** was turned over to Australia. (*Cont. p. 1114.*)

2.   AUSTRALIA, 1788-1914

The **Dutch,** who discovered and explored the western and parts of the northern and southern coasts of Australia (1613-1627), called the land **New Holland. Capt. James Cook,** who discovered and explored the east coast during his first voyage (1768-1771), called that part **New South Wales.** His favorable reports led the British government, after 1783, to consider it for possible settlement by the loyalists from America, but ultimately, after failure of convict settlements

in West Africa, it was decided to use New South Wales for the deportation of criminals and offenders who crowded the British prisons after it became impossible to send them to America. The plan was merely to set up a convict colony that would support itself.

1788, Jan. 26. Capt. Arthur Philip arrived at **Port Jackson** (Sydney) **with the FIRST CONVICT TRANSPORTS** and convoy, 11 ships with 717 convicts, of whom about 520 were men. In the following month 15 convicts and escort were sent to organize another settlement on **Norfolk Island** (till 1803). Philip remained governor until 1792, during the most critical period of the colony: scarcity of food; uncertainty of supplies; laziness, incompetence, and quarrelsomeness of the convicts; prevalence of vice of every kind. The colony was protected by the **New South Wales Corps,** raised in England and itself an unimpressive and insubordinate body. The governor enjoyed absolute power and alone formulated policy. The convicts were supplied from government stores, but on expiration of their terms they were given 30 to 50 acres of land. Discharged soldiers were given grants of 80 to 100 acres. The officers were more richly endowed, and some of them, like **John Macarthur,** soon became wealthy and influential.

1792-1795. Francis Grose and then **William Paterson** acted as vice-governors. As members of the New South Wales Corps, they provided richly for their comrades. The officers were given the service of convicts and were allowed to establish a monopoly of cargoes brought to the settlement. **Importation of rum** was permitted and rum soon became currency, much to the detriment of the settlement.

1793. Arrival of the first free settlers (11 in all), who received free passage, tools, convict service, and land grants.

1794. Macarthur first began **sheep-raising and breeding,** which soon became a most profitable venture for himself and for the colony.

1795-1800. John Hunter, governor. A mild, well-intentioned administrator, he was soon at loggerheads with the officers of the corps, through whose influence at home he was ultimately recalled.

1800-1806. Philip King, governor. His main ambition was to break the power of the officers, wherefore he forbade their trading and prohibited the importation of spirits. Neither policy proved much of a success, and so King, like his predecessor, was in constant conflict with the officers, of whom Macarthur was the leader.

1803-1804. Settlement of Tasmania, carried through by the governor for fear that the French might seize it. Settlements were established near present-day **Hobart** and near **Launceston.** In 1808 the convicts on Norfolk Island were transferred to Tasmania. From the outset the settlers had much trouble with aborigines and bushrangers, i.e. escaped convicts turned bandits and freebooters.

1804. Insurrection of the Irish convicts, who had been sent in large numbers after the suppression of the revolution in Ireland in 1798. The rising was put down with ruthless vigor.

1806-1809. William Bligh, governor. He was appointed in the hope that, as a well-known disciplinarian, he would be able to end the domination of the officer clique and stop the disastrous liquor traffic. But his drastic methods and fiery temperament resulted merely in the

1808, Jan. 26. Rum Rebellion. The officers, outraged by the arrest of Macarthur, induced the commander, **Maj. George Johnston,** to arrest Bligh as unfit for office and to hold him captive until the arrival of a new governor (1809). Though the home government condemned this action, it accepted it and removed Bligh.

1809-1821. COL. LACHLAN MACQUARIE, governor. His appointment marked the **end of rule by the naval commanders.** Macquarie took his Highland regiment to Australia and obliged the members of the New South Wales Corps to enlist in the regular force or return home, which about one-half of them did. For the rest the new governor devoted himself to the systematic building-up of Sydney, to road construction, establishment of orphanages, and to unrelenting war on the vice prevalent throughout the colony. **Civil courts** were established (1814) and a bank opened (1817). In 1816 the home government removed all restrictions on free emigration to Australia, thus preparing the way for a change in the character of the colony. But by 1810 there were already 3000 free settlers, endowed with large blocks of land. These freemen objected violently to **Macquarie's efforts to secure social equality for the emancipists** (i.e. pardoned convicts or those who had served their time) and to discourage free immigration. As a result, Macquarie, like earlier governors, was engaged in constant struggle, though on a different basis.

1813. Gregory Blaxland with two companions (William Lawson and William C. Wentworth) first succeeded in penetrating the confused mass of mountains along the coast, thus paving the way for the advance to the plateau of the interior.

1815. Bathurst, the first town in the interior, was founded and a road built to it from Sydney.

1817-1818. John Oxley began the exploration of the interior, following the Lachlan and Macquarie Rivers. He found the country more or less flooded, but the discovery of great grassy regions stimulated settlement. The government granted land freely to immigrants and to emancipists, in addition to whom large numbers of squatters began to occupy grazing lands. Brutal and rapid **extermination of the natives,** who had become aggressive after many outrages by the whites (kidnaping of women and

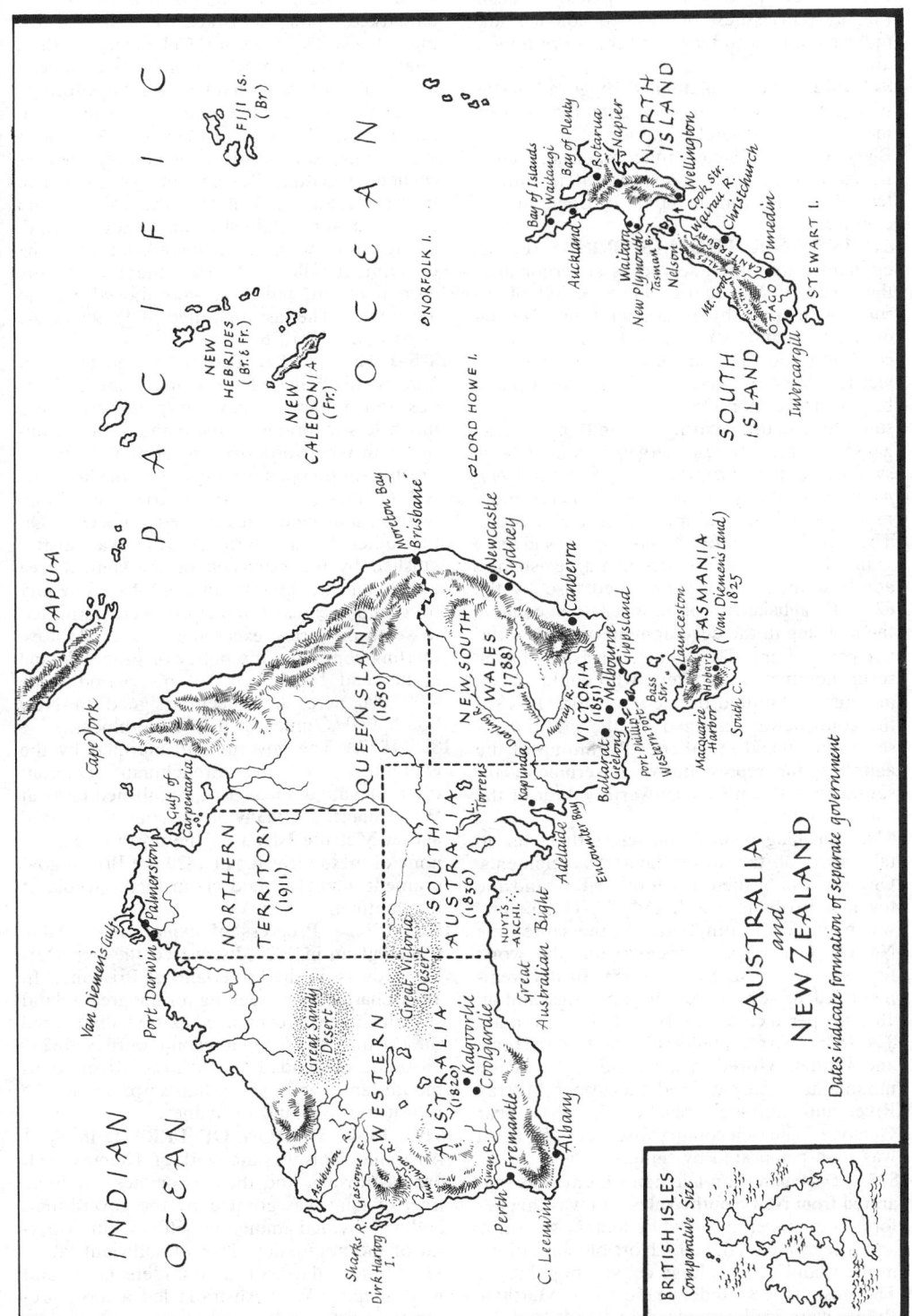

AUSTRALIA
and
NEW ZEALAND

Dates indicate formation of separate government

INDIAN OCEAN

PACIFIC OCEAN

PAPUA

FIJI IS. (Br.)

NEW HEBRIDES (Br. & Fr.)

NEW CALEDONIA (Fr.)

NORFOLK I.

LORD HOWE I.

NORTH ISLAND

Bay of Islands
Bay of Plenty
Waikanagi
Rotorua
Napier
Wellington
Auckland
Waitara
New Plymouth
Tasman B.
Nelson
Cook Str.
Christchurch
Dunedin

SOUTH ISLAND

Mt. Cook
OTAGO
Invercargill
STEWART I.

Van Diemen's Gulf
Cape York
Gulf of Carpentaria
Port Darwin, Palmerston

NORTHERN TERRITORY (1911)

QUEENSLAND (1859)

Moreton Bay
Brisbane

Newcastle
Sydney
Canberra

NEW SOUTH WALES (1788)

Great Sandy Desert
Great Victoria Desert

WESTERN AUSTRALIA (1829)

SOUTH AUSTRALIA (1836)

NUYTS ARCHL.

Great Australian Bight

Kalgoorlie
Coolgardie

Sharks R.
Dirk Hartog I.
Gascoyne R.

Perth
Fremantle
C. Leeuwin
Albany

Torrens
Kapunda
Adelaide
Encounter Bay

Darling R.
Murray R.

VICTORIA (1851)
Gippsland
Ballarat
Geelong
Melbourne
Port Phillip
Western Port
Bass Str.

Launceston
Hobart
Macquarie Harbor
South C.

TASMANIA (Van Diemen's Land) 1825

BRITISH ISLES
Comparative Size

children, etc.). Rapid **development of bush-ranging** (lawlessness of escaped convicts and other bandits, who terrorized the more remote areas).

1819–1821. Inquiry of John T. Bigge, a London barrister sent out to investigate the government and the general condition of the colony. Bigge, having collected much material, recommended liberal land grants to settlers and extensive use of convict labor to open up the country.

1821–1825. SIR THOMAS BRISBANE, the eminent astronomer, served as governor after the recall of Macquarie. The period of his rule was marked by an acceleration of development. Land was granted generously on condition that the grantee take over one convict for every 100 acres. **Sale of crown lands,** but not more than 4000 acres to any one person. Systematic clearing of lands by convict gangs, at fixed prices. Organization of large syndicates: the *Australian Agricultural Company* received a grant of 1,000,000 acres and a monopoly of the coal mining near Newcastle. The *Van Diemen's Land Company* was given a grant of 400,000 acres in Tasmania. Brisbane's administration was distinguished also by the **1823. Establishment of a legislative council,** the first step in the development of representative government. The council consisted of five–seven nominated members, who could act on measures submitted by the governor. In 1828 the council was enlarged by the addition of seven nonofficial members. Beginning of the **agitation for representative government,** inspired by **William C. Wentworth,** editor of the *Australian* (1824).

1824. Opening of new convict settlements, to take care of the most dangerous elements. One was established at **Moreton Bay** and the town of Brisbane was founded. This colony was maintained until 1842. At the same time **Norfolk Island** was reopened and the worst felons were transported thither. Brutal treatment led to several serious uprisings and in 1855 the penal colony on Norfolk was given up.

1824–1825. Explorations of Hamilton Hume and **William Hovell** in the region west of the mountains. They crossed the upper Murray River and ultimately reached the coast near Geelong. The rich country discovered by them was soon penetrated by settlers.

1825. Tasmania (Van Diemen's Land) **was separated from New South Wales** and was thenceforth administered by a lieutenant-governor and a legislative council. Horrible conditions in the island with its large convict population. The bushrangers, under leaders like **Matthew Brady,** were well organized in bands and attacked settlers and natives. The natives, driven

to desperation by the treatment of the whites, embarked upon the **Black War,** which cost many lives. The governor, **Col. George Arthur,** finally managed to track down the bushrangers, many of whom were hanged, but his efforts to corral the natives (the *Black Line*) met with failure. Finally **George Robinson,** a Methodist settler, offered to serve as conciliator. He succeeded in getting the remnants of the native tribes to submit and in 1835 the 200–300 who remained were established on Flinders Island, where efforts were made to civilize them. The experiment failed. By 1844 there were only 44 natives left, and these were moved back to Tasmania. The last man died in 1869 and the last woman in 1876.

1825–1831. RALPH DARLING, governor of New South Wales. He was much more vigorous and autocratic than his predecessor and much less favorable to the emancipists. Conflict with Wentworth over freedom of the press; drastic suppression of disorder; **Bushranging Act** (1830)—suspects to be arrested without warrant and held until proved innocent. On the other hand, Darling's rule was distinguished by the extension of the council (see above) and by the introduction of **trial by jury** for criminal cases. Emancipists were permitted to serve on juries, excepting in special cases. Darling continued the policy of **generous land grants** and by the end of his period some 4,000,000 acres had been assigned in New South Wales, much of it in large blocks.

1825–1827. The government, alarmed by the explorations of the Frenchman, Dumont d'Urville, along the coasts, established **posts at Westernport, at Albany** on the southwest coast, **and at Melville Island** on the north coast, but none of these thrived. In 1829 the British government, however, laid claim to the whole of the continent.

1827–1830. Progress of exploration. Allan Cunningham in 1827 discovered the rich Darling Downs, in the hinterland of Brisbane. In 1828 **Charles Sturt,** seeking for the great inland sea which he was convinced existed, discovered the Darling River. On a second journey (1829–1830) he descended the Murray River to its mouth and, with great hardship, made the return trip overland to Sydney.

1829. FOUNDATION OF PERTH, in West Australia. This was the work of **Thomas Peel, James Stirling,** and their associates. A huge tract of land was granted by the government and was divided among the settlers, but dispersal of the population, lack of sufficient labor, etc., led to collapse of the founders' hopes and investments. West Australia led a most precarious existence for many years.

1831–1838. Sir Richard Bourke, governor. The

British government fixed the minimum price of land at five shillings per acre, thus bringing to an end the unrestricted granting of land. Half of the proceeds from land sales was to be devoted to financing of immigration, the other half to public works. In 1832 the New South Wales government began the encouragement and financing of free immigration.

1834-1836. FOUNDING OF SOUTH AUSTRALIA. Whalers and sealers from Tasmania and America had for some time maintained stations on the coast, but the establishment of the colony was due to the efforts of **Edward Gibbon Wakefield,** the famous colonial theorist. Wakefield argued that land must be sold at a "sufficient price," which meant a price sufficient to oblige the laborer to work for several years before being able to acquire land for himself. In the interval the proceeds from land sales could be devoted to the importation of further labor, and thus a perpetual turnover of capital, land, and labor could be effected. On August 2, 1834, Wakefield's followers, supported by the duke of Wellington, George Grote, and others, secured for their *South Australia Association* a charter to found a colony. The first settlers were landed at Kangaroo Island in 1836, but were soon moved to the mainland, where **Adelaide was founded.** Wakefield's theory was not closely adhered to, but the land sales resulted in widespread speculation, which ruined the beginnings of the enterprise. **Sir George Grey** (lieutenant-governor 1841-1845) finally succeeded in clearing up the financial muddle and re-established the colony on the basis of cultivation and grazing.

1834-1837. SETTLEMENT OF VICTORIA. This was begun by colonists from other parts of Australia and Tasmania. In 1834 **Edward Henty** and his brothers from West Australia began farming and ranching at Portland Bay and in the following year **John Batman** and his associates from Tasmania (the *Port Philip Association*) concluded a treaty with the natives at Port Philip and began to open the country. A rival group from Tasmania, led by **John Fawkner,** established itself close by. The Sydney government, ill disposed to extension of its responsibilities, warned the squatters off, but in the end could do nothing more than dissolve the association and add the region to New South Wales (1837). Batman and his friends were the **founders of Melbourne.**

1837. A British parliamentary committee investigated the whole question of **transportation of convicts** and reached conclusions unfavorable to the system. Beginning of the movement to abolish it.

1838. The **minimum price of land** was raised to 12 shillings per acre (in 1840 to £1 per acre).

The government, however, issued **grazing licenses** for a small fee, thereby facilitating the occupation of large tracts in the interior. Between 1840 and 1850 the Darling Downs were opened up and New South Wales entered upon the golden age of the grazing and wool-raising industry.

1840, Nov. 18. The **LAST CONVICTS** were landed in New South Wales. Since 1788 between 60,000 and 75,000 had been brought in, but in 1840 there were perhaps less than 25,000 under sentence. The free population already greatly outnumbered the convicts and emancipists.

1840-1841. Edward J. Eyre explored the barren region north of Spencer Bay as far as Lake Torrens. Thence he made his way, alone with one native, across the huge deserts to Albany (West Australia).

1842. Reconstruction of the legislative council, which henceforth was to consist of 36 members, of whom 24 were to be elected by the propertied classes. Emancipists were given the vote provided they could meet the property qualifications.

1844-1845. Charles Sturt, starting from Adelaide, pushed his way north into the great **Stony Desert** as far as the Diamantina. At the same time (1845) the German scientist **Ludwig Leichhardt** explored the region from Darling Downs to the Gulf of Carpentaria and as far as Port Essington (post founded 1831).

1847. By order in council the great pastoralists who had occupied land on grazing licenses were transformed into **lease-holders,** thus securing fixity of tenure. The measure reacted favorably on the sheep industry, but accentuated the conflict of pastoralists and small farmers.

1848. The **British government resumed transportation of convicts** on the new Pentonville (conditional pardon) system. Convicts who had proved their good behavior for a couple of years in England were transported to Australia and set free on condition that they should not return to England until their sentence was completed. The new plan roused a howl of protest in New South Wales.

1850-1855. Construction of the first railway (Sydney to Goulburn).

1850. Convicts were for the first time sent to **West Australia,** in response to a request from the settlers, who were desperately in need of laborers.

1850, Aug. The **AUSTRALIAN COLONIES GOVERNMENT ACT** passed by the British parliament. The colonies were given the right to constitute their own legislatures, fix the franchise, alter their constitutions, determine their own tariffs, all subject to royal confirmation. Thus the Australian states, in conformity with the new colonial policy of the British government after 1837, were given self-government. A committee headed by **William Wentworth** worked out a **constitution of New South Wales** which was adopted in November 1855. It provided for a legislative council appointed for life and a legislative assembly elected on a restricted franchise, together with cabinet government on the British model. At the same time the other states (excepting West Australia) adopted similar constitutions, though for the most part they provided for an elective upper house.

1851. The legislative council of New South Wales unequivocally forbade the landing of further convicts on any system, and the British government yielded.

1851, July 1. VICTORIA was separated from New South Wales and became a distinct colony.

Aug. 9. DISCOVERY OF GOLD in large nuggets at Ballarat (Victoria), then at Bendigo and other places. Isolated finds had been made ever since 1839, but the government had discouraged the search for fear of the diversion of labor from grazing. From the Victoria fields about £80,000,000 worth of gold was taken in the first decade. Tremendous **influx of workers and adventurers** from all over the world. The population of Victoria rose from 77,000 in 1851 to 333,000 in 1855. Recrudescence of bushranging. Efforts of the government to secure some part of the new wealth, in the form of mining licenses. Growing discontent on the gold fields culminated in November-December 1854 in **open rebellion,** led by German and Irish revolutionaries who proclaimed the **Republic of Victoria.** The insurrection was put down by government troops without much trouble.

1852. Foundation of the University of Sydney, followed in 1853 by that of Melbourne and later other state capitals.

1852. Arrival of the first steamship at Sydney. In 1856 the Peninsula and Oriental Steamship Company opened regular service, at first in competition with the fast clipper ships which had greatly reduced the time of passage from England.

1853. Discontinuance of transportation to Tasmania. Since 1803 about 67,000 convicts had been landed in the island (about 4000 a year after 1841). The name *Tasmania* now definitively replaced that of *Van Diemen's Land,* and a constitution not unlike that of New South Wales was adopted.

1855. The **convict colony on Norfolk Island was abandoned,** after several serious and bloody insurrections.

1855. The Victoria government passed an **act to restrict Chinese immigration** (33,000 had come to the gold fields since 1851). The new law provided for a poll tax of £10 on every Chinese immigrant. In 1859 a residence tax of £4 per annum was added. Similar measures were adopted by South Australia (1857) and New South Wales (1861) despite pressure from the British government. The effect was to check Chinese immigration almost completely.

1855. New South Wales, having first adopted a railway guage of 5 ft. 3 in., changed to the 4 ft. 8½ in. gauge, leaving Victoria with the broader gauge. South Australia and West Australia and Queensland, for reasons of economy, adopted the 3 ft. 6 in. gauge, thus producing complete **confusion in the continental railway systems.** In all the colonies the railways soon came under the control of the state.

1859. QUEENSLAND was established as a separate colony, following agitation against government from Sydney. **Brisbane** became the capital.

1860. Robert O. Burke and **William J. Wills** headed a lavishly financed and well-equipped expedition across the desert from Melbourne, using camels for the first time. The expedition first **succeeded in crossing Australia** from south to north (Gregory River on the Gulf of Carpentaria), but the leaders lost their lives on the return journey.

1861. In New South Wales the **Land Occupation Act** limited the tenure of leases and permitted **selection of small holdings** for purchase. The measure was intended to help the small farmer (*selector*), but gave rise to much abuse (selecting of the best part of a large sheep run, e.g., and "dummying" or purchase by selectors who were mere agents of the large holders). Greater and greater efforts were made in most colonies to restrict and break up the large holdings (resumption of crown lands on expiration of leases, compulsory resale, etc.) culminating (1910) in a heavy tax on unimproved estates of over £5000 value. But none of these measures proved entirely successful.

1862. M'Duall Stuart, on his third attempt to cross the continent from Adelaide to Port Darwin, succeeded. This expedition was of far greater scientific importance than that of Burke and Wills.

1863. Administration of the Northern Territory (i.e. central as well as northern Australia), which, since the separation of Queensland, was no longer contiguous to New South Wales, was **assigned to South Australia,** where there was high hope of fertile territory.

1864. Beginning of the **importation of native (Kanaka) laborers** into Queensland from the Solomon and other islands. The system was intended to meet the labor shortage on the sugar plantations. Though officially a system of contract labor, it soon degenerated into something closely akin to slave-raiding, until regulated, to some extent, by the government.

1866. The Victoria parliament, influenced by the writing of **David Syme,** an influential Melbourne editor, gave up free trade and **introduced protection.** The measure led to a great constitutional conflict between the assembly and the council, which was dominated by the squatter oligarchy. Similar struggles continued until finally the farmer and industrial labor groups secured control of the political situation. The other colonies followed the example of Victoria in adopting protection, with the sole exception of New South Wales, which contented itself with a tariff for revenue only.

1867. The **Public Schools Act** in New South Wales laid the basis for the modern system of compulsory education for the young.

1867. The **last convicts were landed in West Australia,** which, since 1853, had received about 10,000. Thus ended the transportation system to any part of the continent.

1870. The **British government withdrew imperial forces** from Australia, after which the different colonies established militia systems of their own.

1872. **Opening of the telegraph line across the continent** from Adelaide to Port Darwin, which was soon afterward connected with Java and so with the lines to India and Europe.

1873. **Introduction of compulsory, secular schooling in Victoria.** At the same time the Victoria government passed the **first factory act,** aimed at protection of children and women and at the maintenance of sanitary and safe working conditions. This pioneer move was improved upon in 1884 and was imitated by the other colonies.

1873. **The New Guinea problem.** Already in 1867 the New South Wales government had appealed to London for action in the non-Dutch part of New Guinea, but the government had turned a deaf ear. In 1873 **Capt. Fairfax Moresby** raised the British flag on the south coast, but the home government, still cool, refused to act unless the colonies agreed to assume responsibility for the administration of the territory. This some of the colonies were unwilling to do, so that Moresby's action was disavowed.

1874. Crossing of the western half of the continent by **John Forrest,** who made his way from the Murchison River across the desert to the newly constructed south-north telegraph line and thence to Adelaide.

1878. The **Queensland government annexed the islands in Torres Strait.**

1879. Organization of the **first trade-union congress.** Unions had existed for some years previously and had embarked upon a widespread **agitation for the eight-hour day** (one of many points borrowed from the Chartists who had come to Australia after 1848). The unions became powerful factors in New South Wales, Victoria, and South Australia.

1880. Meeting of the **first federal conference at Sydney,** to consider the possibility of federation of the colonies. The idea had been put forward long before by William C. Wentworth and was ardently championed by **Sir Henry Parkes,** the eminent statesman of New South Wales. Homogeneity of race, common tradition, the needs of defense, etc., favored some sort of union, but the colonies were jealous of their independence and in many respects downright hostile to each other.

1883-1884. THE NEW GUINEA CRISIS. The Queensland government, uneasy about German designs, offered to assume the administration of the island if the home government would annex it. On April 4, 1884, the Queensland government, exasperated by delay in London, proclaimed possession, but was disavowed by London. Other colonies joined in the agitation for action. Ultimately, when the home government decided to act, the Germans had already laid claim to the northeastern part, leaving to the British (annexation November 6, 1884) only the southeastern part. This danger at the door appears to have had much to do with furthering the sentiment for federation in Australia.

1883. **Opening of the Sydney-Melbourne railway line.**

1885. The British parliament authorized the **establishment of a federal council** to meet every two years for the discussion of intercolonial problems. The first meeting was held at Hobart (1886), after which New Zealand no longer attended. Since the council had merely consultative power it was regarded as inadequate by Parkes and other federalists, who renewed their demands for real union.

1885. **Victoria established wages boards,** empowered to fix wages in sweated industries. These boards, composed of employers and employees, with a neutral chairman, were given extensive powers to regulate entire industries. A daring experiment in labor relations, the system was gradually adopted by other colonies (1908–) under pressure of the labor parties.

1888. The British privy council upheld the **exclusion of the Chinese** as practiced in Victoria. Thereafter the policy was enforced by all the colonies and the idea of a "White Australia" met with general acceptance. As a matter of fact, there was growing hostility to any immigration, especially on the part of labor, and the influx of new settlers rapidly declined to a mere trickle.

1890. The Australian colonies and New Zealand agreed to support financially a British naval squadron, to be maintained in Australasian waters.

1890. Responsible government was at last established **in West Australia.**

1890. A great shipping, mining, and shearing strike resulted in failure, but thereby came to mark an important turning-point in the **development of the labor movement.** In several colonies the trade unions embarked upon political activity and soon became crucial factors in the political situation.

1891, Mar.-July. The **FIRST AUSTRALASIAN FEDERAL CONVENTION** met at Sydney, under the presidency of **Sir Henry Parkes.** The members were chosen from the colonial parliaments and included most of the outstanding political figures of Australia and New Zealand. The convention worked out a draft constitution, which later served as a basis for the federal system, but the scheme had to be dropped because of the **opposition of New South Wales.** The result was renewed agitation for federation, especially by popular societies and leagues (1893-). The great **financial crisis of 1893,** the growth of the White Australia sentiment, and the emergence of Australian nationalism contributed further to the desire for union.

1894. South Australia introduced woman suffrage, which was later adopted by the other states (West Australia, 1899; New South Wales, 1902; Tasmania, 1903; Queensland, 1905; Victoria, 1909). At the same time South Australia established **compulsory arbitration of industrial disputes,** another experiment in the settlement of labor problems.

1897-1900. THE ACHIEVEMENT OF UNION. A federal convention met at Hobart in January 1897 (ten members from each colony except Queensland). This assembly reconsidered the draft constitution of 1891 and finally evolved the arrangement which was later accepted. The federation was modeled in large measure upon the United States system, though with the responsible government characteristic of Great Britain. The united states were to be called the *Commonwealth of Australia,* and the new federal government was to be established in a new capital city to be determined later. The federal government was to have control of foreign affairs, defense, trade, tariffs, posts and telegraphs, currency, naturalization, marriage and divorce, pensions, etc. At the head was to be a **govenor-general,** appointed by the crown. The **executive council, or cabinet,** was to be composed of members of parliament and responsible to parliament. Parliament was to be bicameral: the upper house **(senate)** was to consist of six members from each state, elected directly for a six-year term, one-half renewable every three years; the **house of representatives** was to be directly elected on the basis of populational districts. A high or **supreme court** was provided for as guardian of the constitution.

The draft constitution was submitted to the colonies for popular vote. Victoria, South Australia, and Tasmania were overwhelmingly in favor, but in New South Wales the proposal was lost by a fairly small vote. In 1898 a **conference of prime ministers,** in which Queensland joined, arranged for amendments (chiefly financial) to meet the objections of New South Wales. In a new election in New South Wales (1899) the amended draft was adopted. After some discussion of the limitation of appeals to the British privy council, the British government and parliament accepted the project, which was given royal assent on July 9, 1900. West Australia then decided to join the federation (July 31) and on

1901, Jan. 1. The **COMMONWEALTH OF AUSTRALIA came into being.** The first cabinet was led by **Edmund Barton,** ardent federationist and protectionist. The opposition, led by **George H. Reid,** favored a tariff for revenue only. The **Labor Party** formed the third group. Led by **John C. Watson** and better disciplined than the other parties, it was able, from the outset, to control the balance, and thus to carry into the commonwealth field the program of state socialism already introduced in the states. In 1901 New South Wales introduced conciliation and arbitration courts and adopted a scheme for old-age pensions. The Labor Party was particularly determined in the matter of immigration restriction, to which all parties, indeed, were committed.

1902. The **Immigration Restriction Act** (federal) provided that an immigrant, on demand, must demonstrate ability to pass a test in a European language (changed in 1905 to "a prescribed language" to spare Japanese susceptibilities). In this way Orientals and, if desired, Europeans could be excluded at will. The federal government at the same time put a stop to the importation of Kanakas into Queensland (they were repatriated in 1906). A high tariff on sugar protected the sugar-growers from competition from outside.

The **federal tariff** established in 1902 placed the whole continent on the protectionist system.

Woman suffrage was established (1902) for all federal elections.

1902–1904. Alfred Deakin, leader of the opposition, became premier, dependent on support of the Labor Party. When the latter abandoned him

1904. Watson formed the first Labor cabinet, which, however, was able to maintain itself for only a few months. Watson was succeeded by

1904–1905. Reid, who governed with support of the non-Labor representatives. The combination did not work very smoothly and the Reid cabinet was followed by a

1905–1908. Deakin ministry, which enjoyed the support of the Labor Party, now led by **Andrew Fisher.**

1905. British New Guinea became an Australian federal possession, and was renamed *Papua* (the Portuguese name). The territory had been but little developed (white population c. 600), but was regarded as vital for defense, especially in view of the rise of Japan and its victory over Russia.

1908–1909. Second Labor cabinet (Fisher). The government was much preoccupied by foreign affairs and defense. The new tariff (1908) gave British goods a 5 per cent preference, and other efforts were made to draw closer the bonds to Great Britain, chiefly in view of the rising naval power of Germany and the gradual withdrawal of British naval forces from the Pacific. The Australian colonies had all taken part with the mother country in the South African War, and contributions had been made since 1890 to the maintenance of a naval squadron in the South Pacific. In 1908 the Australian government decided on the **construction of a naval force** of its own and began work on a 22-year program.

1909. The **commonwealth capital was finally fixed at Canberra** (New South Wales), the state government ceding the necessary territory, with a strip of land to the sea.

1909–1910. Another Deakin government, based on fusion with the following of Reid and his successor, **Joseph Cook.**

1909. Federal old-age pensions were established for those over 65 years of age and resident in Australia at least 25 (later 20) years.

1909–1910. Defense Acts. After a visit and recommendations by Lord Kitchener, the Australian government introduced a system of **compulsory military training** and began to organize a regular military force.

1910. The **Northern Territory,** administered by South Australia, **became a federal possession.**

Apr. In the general election the **Labor Party** for the first time **won a clear majority** of seats in the house of representatives, thus ending the system of three minority parties working in combination. Fisher formed his second government, which lasted until 1913. **Continuation of the social program** (heavy tax on large and absentee properties, etc.). In order to make the White Australia more secure, the government resumed the **system of assistance to desirable white immigrants,** especially with the view of settling the Northern Territory.

1913. In the general election the **Fusion Party** (Joseph Cook) **secured a majority** of one. Cook formed a ministry, but legislation was effectively blocked by the Labor Party, which still had a majority in the upper house. To break the deadlock the governor-general dissolved both houses, and in the

1914. General election the **Labor Party recovered its majority.** Fisher formed his third government, which in 1915 was taken over by his successor, **William M. Hughes.**

(*Cont. p. 1115.*)

3. NEW ZEALAND, 1814–1914

New Zealand was discovered by the Dutch captain, **Abel J. Tasman,** in 1642. But the islands were not rediscovered until **Capt. James Cook,** on his first voyage, landed (Oct. 7, 1769) and later circumnavigated the group. The inhabitants, numbering perhaps 100,000, were located chiefly in the warmer, north island. They were **Maoris,** a people of the Polynesian family, who had probably occupied the country between 900–1400 A.D. Their culture was Neolithic and the practice of cannibalism was general. Tasman and Cook both had occasion to note their fighting qualities.

Though several other explorers touched New Zealand in the last quarter of the 18th century, it was only after 1792 that **whalers, sealers, and traders** began to arrive more frequently. Merchants from Sydney were interested in the fine **timber** and in the native **flax,** which was bought from the Maoris in exchange for firearms. After securing muskets, native chiefs near the coast began to attack and exterminate tribes of the interior. There followed, especially after 1821, the **depredations of Hongi,** of **Te Rauparaha** (*Satan*), who carried his wars into the South Island, and of **Tu Hawaiki** (*Bloody Jack*), who dominated Otago. By this time the bay whalers were establishing **permanent shore settlements** on the coast of the South Island and in Cook Strait. Escaped convicts from New South Wales and beachcombers of all descriptions made these early settlements by-words for lawlessness and depravity. In the meanwhile

1814. SAMUEL MARSDEN, chaplain of the New South Wales penal colony, who had become acquainted with Maoris serving on whaling ships, established the **first Church of England mission** at the Bay of Islands. He himself did not remain in the islands, but opened a seminary for Maori chieftains in his New South Wales home. In 1822 a **Wesleyan mission** was opened, and in 1823 the first Anglican clergyman, **Henry Williams,** arrived and initiated a period of greater activity and success. **William Colenso** translated the Bible into Maori (1827–) and in 1842 **George Selwyn** was named first Anglican bishop of New Zealand. The missionaries did much to teach the natives and their influence spread far and wide in a relatively short period. In general the missionaries were opposed to settlement by Europeans, desiring to keep the islands for the Maoris. The **first Catholic mission** was opened at Kokianga in 1838.

1826. The **first New Zealand Company** was founded in England. It enjoyed powerful support and at once dispatched colonists. These, arriving at the height of the native wars, were unfavorably impressed and insisted on going on to Australia.

1833. In order to combat the spread of lawlessness, the British government appointed **James Busby as resident** in the islands. Since the British government did not claim sovereignty, Busby had no real standing and was unable to achieve much.

1837. Baron Charles de Thierry, a Belgian-British adventurer, arrived on the northwest coast and attempted to set up a kingdom of New Zealand on land he claimed to have bought from the natives. His venture was only one of many in these years. Missionaries, traders, speculators in Australia and England began to buy land in large blocks and under frequently suspicious circumstances, so that by 1840 land claims amounted to 56,000,-000 acres.

1837. Foundation of the NEW ZEALAND ASSOCIATION by Edward Gibbon Wakefield, who had been chiefly instrumental in the colonization of South Australia (p. 929). The association agitated for annexation and settlement, but met with no favorable response from the colonial office which, like the missionaries, opposed further settlement. Thereupon Wakefield and his followers organized the **New Zealand Company** (May 1839), bought out the rights of the earlier company, and began to sell land at £1 per acre to prospective colonists and investors. The government still opposing,

the company, fearful of action by a rival French enterprise **(Capt. Langlois and the Nanto-Bordelaise Company),** sent out colonists without securing permission of the government.

1840, Jan. 22. The **FIRST BRITISH COLONISTS landed at Port Nicholson** in Cook Strait. A huge tract of land was acquired from the Maori chiefs and the town of **Wellington was founded.** In the interval the British government, also exercised by French designs, proclaimed

Jan. 30. British sovereignty. Capt. William Hobson had been sent out as governor, and, with aid of the missionaries, concluded with the native chiefs

Feb. 6. The **TREATY OF WAITANGI,** which was subscribed to by some five hundred chiefs in the course of the next six months. By the treaty the native leaders ceded their sovereignty to Britain, and in return were guaranteed their lands and other possessions. On May 21 Hobson proclaimed British sovereignty and established the **capital at Auckland.** On August 10 a British force landed at Akaroa (Banks Peninsula), only a day before the arrival of the French colonials. The latter settled for a time, but all danger of French possession was obviously past.

1840–1842. Capt. William Hobson, governor. He made desperate efforts to regulate the confused land claims, and by ordinance of June 9, 1841, voided all claims until investigated and approved by the government. This brought him into **conflict with the New Zealand Company,** which had claims to some 20 million acres and which was sending out colonists in large numbers. While the government tried to sell lands at £1 per acre, the company sold at 5s. Ultimately the company's rights to about 283,000 acres were recognized, but in London as in New Zealand the conflict between government and company continued for years.

1840. The company established **settlers at New Plymouth,** renamed *Taranaki* in 1859.

1841. The company settled the south side of Cook Strait, founding the **town of Nelson.**

1843–1845. Capt. Robert Fitzroy, governor. In his eagerness to bring in settlers, he permitted purchase of land direct from the natives on payment of 10s. (soon reduced to 1d.) per acre to the government. This measure was disallowed by the home government and Fitzroy was recalled. By that time

1843–1848. The **FIRST MAORI WAR** had broken out. It originated from a dispute about land in the Nelson district, where the settlers took the offensive and were cut down **(massacre of Wairau).** There followed anti-foreign outbreaks in the north. Many of the tribes remained loyal and the movement at all times lacked cohesion. To meet the emergency the home government sent

1845-1854. Capt. (later Sir) **GEORGE GREY** from South Australia as governor. With his usual vigor he suppressed the traffic in arms and while putting down disorders asserted his personal authority and gained the confidence of many Maori leaders. He cancelled his predecessor's land ordinances and forbade direct purchase on penalty of heavy fine (1846).

1846, Dec. 23. The **British government conferred a constitution** on New Zealand (named *New Munster* and *New Ulster*). Each province was to have its own governor, appointed council, and elected assembly. This system, obviously premature, was rescinded in 1848. Meanwhile the Maori wars in the North Island had deterred settlers from colonizing the disaffected regions, but

1846. The advent of the Russell ministry in Britain introduced an element friendly to the company. The government granted loans and allowed a very liberal land settlement. Under the auspices of the company other organizations took up colonization.

1848. A Scottish Free Church association settled Otago (capital Dunedin), and in

1850. An organization of **Church of England members settled Canterbury** (Christchurch). In the open regions of the South Island, where there were few natives, **sheep-raising** soon established itself (the industry was inaugurated in 1843-1844 and operated on grazing licenses issued by the government).

1851. The government began to issue **grazing leases** for 14 years, thus facilitating the **organization of large holdings.** Wool-raising became the most important industry. By 1871 there were in New Zealand 10 million sheep and wool was exported to the value of £2,700,000.

1851. The New Zealand Company was dissolved. By the terms of the settlement the members received £268,000, which became a charge on the New Zealand government.

1852. A NEW CONSTITUTION WAS PROMULGATED. It provided for six provinces, each under a superintendent and each with a provincial (district) council elected on the basis of a property franchise. For the colony as a whole there was to be a governor assisted by a nominated legislative council and a house of representatives elected on the provincial franchise. The regulation of native affairs was reserved to the home government (colonial office). Since the district councils were organized and functioned before the colonial assembly met, the provincial governments secured control over most affairs and until 1875 New Zealand was essentially disunited **(period of provincialism).**

1853. Grey reduced the price of crown lands to 10s. per acre, making possible the establishment of the small farmer.

1856. Responsible government was established in New Zealand. At the same time the provincial councils were authorized to dispose of the crown lands within their districts.

1858. The **new province of Hawke's Bay** was established. There followed the provinces of **Marlborough** (1859), **Southland** (1861-1870), and **Westland** (1873).

1860-1870. THE SECOND MAORI WAR. Like the first, this was a series of outbreaks, confined almost entirely to the North Island. The main cause was the rapid acquisition of native land by the government and the growing feeling of the natives that they were doomed. Development of the **king movement,** which aimed at union of the Maori tribes under a king. This was never more than partially successful. There followed (1865-) the **Hau-Hau movement,** a religious movement compounded of native mythology and Judaeo-Christian lore, the basic idea being opposition to Christianity as well as to European domination. Like the first war, the second, concentrated particularly in the Taranaki and Waikato country, was a matter of guerrilla warfare, and therefore difficult to deal with. Australian troops were sent to aid the government, but the **campaigns of Generals Thomas Pratt and Trevor Cameron** were indecisive.

1861-1867. SIR GEORGE GREY, governor for the second time. He did what he could to restore order and introduced the system of **confiscating the lands of rebels.** At the same time he made concessions to the Maoris (four chiefs being admitted to the legislative assembly in 1867). By 1870 the native disorders had been for the most part suppressed. During the remainder of the century the Maoris declined rapidly in numbers.

1861. Discovery of gold in Otago and (1865) in **Westland.** The result, as in similar cases elsewhere, was a great inrush of miners, so that the population rose from 100,000 in 1861 to 250,000 in 1870. The South Island became by far the most populous and rich and so it remained throughout the rest of the century.

1862. The **government abandoned its right to pre-emption of native lands** and established free trade in such lands. In 1865 a **native land court** was established to investigate titles before sale. Under this system the Maoris were quickly separated from their lands, so that by 1892 most of the good land was in the hands of the settlers.

1863. Opening of the first railroad (Christchurch to Ferrymead). The railways were from the start state-owned and operated.

1865. The **capital was transferred from Auckland to Wellington,** removing a longstanding grievance.

1870. The **British government withdrew its troops** from New Zealand, following the conclusion of the Maori War.

1870–1890. The **"continuous ministry" of Sir Harry Atkinson,** representing primarily the large pastoral, landed interests, was in power during most of twenty years. The period was one of deep depression, following the gold rush boom. To meet the situation the government, inspired by **Sir Julius Vogel,** embarked upon a policy of heavy borrowing, extensive railroad building, and public works construction generally. In 1873 the **ownership of native land was individualized,** which made purchase from the natives easier. Extensive program of **assisted immigration** for settlers carefully selected in England by an agent of the New Zealand government. The population rose from 256,000 whites in 1871 to about 772,000 in 1901.

1870. **Steamship connection** was established with San Francisco. The **New Zealand Shipping Company** (1873) also contributed to improvement of communications.

1875. The **district councils were abolished** (effective November 1, 1876), thus ending the period of provincialism. New Zealand was thenceforth under one government.

1876. **Opening of the transoceanic cable to Australia.**

1881. **Chinese Immigrants Act,** similar to the regulations introduced in Australia to restrict the influx of Orientals.

1882. Successful **introduction of meat refrigeration** on transoceanic steamers. For New Zealand this invention was epoch-making. Sheep thenceforth were raised not merely for wool, but for food. Furthermore, refrigeration made possible the **development of a great dairy industry** to supply the British market.

1887. **Annexation of the Kermadec Islands** to New Zealand. Already in 1871 the New Zealand government had appealed to Britain to annex Samoa, but these appeals proved fruitless. The New Zealanders throughout took a frankly imperialist view of southern Pacific affairs.

1888. **Adoption of a protective tariff,** under pressure from Labor groups. One effect of this change was that the Atkinson party began to divide and disintegrate.

1889. **Introduction of manhood suffrage,** another concession to popular agitation.

1890. In the general election the **Liberal-Labor Party,** led by **John Ballance,** defeated the Conservatives. For more than twenty years the progressive elements controlled policy. Under **Richard Seddon** (prime minister 1893–1906) an energetic social program was realized, which gave New Zealand a world reputation for state socialistic experiment. In the land question the government acted to restrict and break up large holdings through taxes on unimproved values and absentee estates. Every effort was made to establish small farmers on the land. Stringent **factory laws** (1894, 1901) and **progressive income tax.** The Labor Department, under **W. Pember Reeves** (1891–1896) instituted many other measures, some of which are listed below.

1893. **Adoption of woman suffrage.**

1894. Establishment of **industrial conciliation and arbitration boards,** with obligatory clauses. In practice the result was rapid **growth of trade-unionism** and regulation of all industrial conditions by the arbitration courts (wages, hours, factory conditions, etc.). This was the key measure in the New Zealand social program.

1897. The **eight-hour day** established by law.

1898. Introduction of **old-age pensions.**

1899. **Further restriction of oriental immigration:** an educational test was introduced, as in Australia.

1900. The **Cook Islands,** as well as **Savage Island** and **Suvorov Island,** were **annexed to New Zealand.**

1903. New tariff arrangements provided for **preferential treatment of British goods.** New Zealand was extremely loyal to the empire and, like Australia, contributed to the upkeep of the British Pacific squadron. New Zealand sent a contingent to participate in the South African War.

1906–1911. **Joseph Ward became prime minister** on the death of Seddon. During these years New Zealand enjoyed great prosperity, but politically the governing Liberal-Labor Party began to disintegrate and in 1909 the **Labor Party** organized separately. Rapid spread of a strike movement, inspired by the **Federation of Labor** (founded 1907).

1907, Sept. 26. NEW ZEALAND WAS GIVEN THE STATUS OF A DOMINION within the British Empire.

1909. The government decided to pay for a battleship to be added to the British navy.

1911. **A system of universal military training** for those between 14 and 41 was established to meet the growing tension in international affairs.

Oct. **Defeat of the Liberals** in the election. After an interim cabinet

1912. **William F. Massey,** leader of the Reform (Conservative) Party, became prime minister. The **Reform Party** drew its support from the small farmers and dairymen, chiefly in the North Island, which, since 1906, had again passed the South Island in population and which became ever more influential. One of the first acts of the new government was to transform the crown leaseholders into free-holders.

1913. Foundation of the United Federation of Labor and of the Social Democratic Party, designed to protect the interests of the industrial workers. (*Cont. p. 1117.*)

4. THE PHILIPPINES, 1892–1913

(*From p. 581*)

1892. Organization of native secret societies directed against Spanish rule.

1896, Aug. 26. Beginning of the native insurrection, led by **Emilio Aguinaldo.** Execution (Dec. 30) of **Dr. José Rizal,** one of the most prominent native leaders.

1897, Dec. 14. Pact of Biac-na-bato between the governor-general, Primo de Rivera, and Aguinaldo, bringing the insurrection to an end. Reforms to be introduced within three years; Aguinaldo and other leaders left the islands in return for a money payment.

1898, Apr. 21. Outbreak of the **Spanish-American War.**

May 1. Commodore George Dewey's victory over Spanish fleet in Manila Bay.

May 19. Arrival of Aguinaldo in the Philippines. He proceeded to organize a native army under American auspices.

June 12. Aguinaldo proclaimed independence and organized a provisional government, with himself as president.

Aug. 13. Manila captured by American forces, assisted by Aguinaldo.

Dec. 10. By the **treaty of Paris** Spain ceded the islands to the United States for $20,000,000. Government of the islands put in the hands of Gen. **Elwell S. Otis.**

1899, Jan. 5. Aguinaldo protested against American sovereignty and called on the Filipinos to declare independence.

Jan. 20. The **Malolos constitution** proclaimed. Aguinaldo named president of the rebel government. The insurrection against American rule began February 4.

Mar. 4. Arrival of the **first Philippine commission,** under **Jacob G. Schurman.** On April 4 it promised "the amplest liberty of self-government," but the revolt went on.

1900, Feb. 6. Second Philippine commission, headed by **Judge William H. Taft.** It reached Manila (June 3) and began to take over the administration and organize a government.

Dec. 23. Formation of the Filipino **Federal Party,** aiming at peace under the sovereignty of the United States.

1901, Mar. 2. The **Spooner amendment** to the army appropriation bill authorized the president of the United States to establish civil government in the Philippines.

Mar. 23. Capture of Aguinaldo by **Gen. Frederick Funston** as a result of a stratagem. Aguinaldo took the oath of allegiance to the United States (Apr. 2) and issued a proclamation advising submission. Guerrilla warfare continued to some extent until April 1902.

July 4. Taft inaugurated as first civil governor of the islands.

Sept. 1. Three Filipinos were added to the Philippine commission.

1902, Jan. 21. Bureau of Education established.

June 12. Judicial system established: supreme court of seven justices, and sixteen courts of first instance.

July 1. Philippine Bill passed by Congress, the first organic law for the government of the islands: bicameral legislature, consisting of appointive upper house and elected assembly, with veto power reserved to United States congress.

1903, Mar. 2. Coinage established (silver peso = 50¢).

Dec. 22. "**Friars' Lands**" (c. 400,000 acres) purchased from the Catholic Church for $7,237,000.

1904, Feb. 1. Gen. **Luke E. Wright** inaugurated as governor.

1906, Apr. 2. Henry Clay Ide inaugurated as governor.

Sept. 20. James F. Smith, governor.

1907, Jan. 9. Election law, providing for 80 delegates to the assembly.

Mar. 12. Formation of the **Partido Union Nacionalista,** advocating independence.

July 30. Election for the first assembly. 105,000 voters elected 32 Nationalists, 20 Independents, and 16 Progressives. The assembly met on October 16 and became the lower house of the legislature, of which the Philippine commission formed the upper house.

1908, May 12. The number of members of the commission was increased to nine, of whom four were to be Filipinos.

1909, Oct. 6. The **Payne-Aldrich Tariff,** allowing free importation into the United States of limited quantities of Philippine products (sugar and tobacco) and of unlimited quantities of hemp.

Nov. 11. W. Cameron Forbes appointed governor-general. Extensive program of education, economic development, and general modernization.

1913, June 1. English became the official language, but the use of Spanish was to be permitted until 1920.

Aug. 21. Francis B. Harrison, governor-general.

Oct. 3. The **Underwood Tariff** removed restrictions on the free import of Philippine sugar and tobacco into the United States.

(*Cont. p. 1118.*)

5. HAWAII, 1778–1919

1778, Jan. 18. The islands were discovered by **Capt. James Cook** and were named the *Sandwich Islands.* Cook was killed there by the natives (Feb. 14, 1779).

1810. Kamehameha I (1795–1819) conquered most of the islands and established his dynasty.

1820. Arrival of the **first American missionaries.**

1826. Treaty of friendship and commerce with the United States. Treaties were signed with Great Britain (1836) and with France (1839).

1842, Dec. 19. The United States recognized the independence of the islands.

1843, Nov. 28. In a convention, Britain and France recognized the independence of the islands and promised not to annex them. A representative form of government had been introduced in 1840 and the king appointed a number of Americans to administrative and judicial office.

1851. In reply to French demands on the island government, the American government warned France and took the stand that annexation by a European power would not be permitted.

1875, Jan. 30. Reciprocity treaty with the United States. Hawaiian sugar admitted to the United States free of duty. The United States was given the use of Pearl Harbor for a coaling and naval station in 1887 when the treaty was extended.

1891, Jan. 20. Lydia Liliuokalani became queen. Growing constitutional unrest.

1893, Jan. 14. *Coup d'état* and new constitution promulgated by the queen. American residents organized a **committee of safety.** American marines landed (Jan. 16) to protect life and property.

Jan. 17. Provisional government organized. Monarchy declared abolished.

Feb. 1. The American minister proclaimed a protectorate.

Feb. 14. Treaty of annexation by the United States signed. This was withdrawn by President Cleveland (Mar. 9), and a special commissioner sent out. The commissioner, **James H. Blount,** reported the revolution engineered by Americans supported by the American minister. Efforts of American government to restore the queen were wrecked by the opposition of the provisional government.

1894, July 4. Republic of Hawaii proclaimed (**Sanford B. Dole,** president). This was recognized by the United States (Aug. 7).

Dec. 8. A royalist revolt broke out, but was soon suppressed.

1897, June 16. Treaty of annexation signed with the United States. This was ratified by the Hawaiian senate (Sept. 9) and by the United States congress July 7, 1898 (**Newlands' Joint Resolution).**

1898, Aug. 12. Formal transfer of the islands to the United States.

1900, April 30. The islands organized as a territory of the United States. Unlike Puerto Rico, Hawaii paid its tariff duties, internal revenue collections, and income tax to the federal treasury.

An acute labor shortage existed on the islands, resulting in considerable **immigration of Japanese.** The government encouraged immigration of Spanish, Portuguese, and Filipino laborers and excluded Japanese, Chinese, and Koreans. In 1910 the total population was 192,000, of whom only 26,000 were Hawaiians and 12,500 part-Hawaiians; on the other hand there were 80,000 Japanese and 21,500 Chinese.

1919. Pearl Harbor fortifications and drydock completed.

The population increased rapidly (426,654 in 1940) and the sugar and pineapple industries were further expanded. The islands have also become a center of tourist traffic and an important station on the trans-Pacific air route.

(*Cont. p. 1120.*)

6. SAMOA, 1722–1900

1722. The Samoan Islands were discovered by the Dutchman, **Jacob Roggeveen.** American and European activity dates from about 1790.

1872, Apr. 9. A number of chiefs petitioned for annexation by the United States.

1878, Jan. 16. Treaty of friendship and commerce with the United States, which secured the harbor of **Pago Pago** as a coaling and naval station.

1879, Jan. 24. Similar treaty with Germany, which secured the harbor of **Apia.**

1880, Mar. 24. Agreement between United States, Great Britain, and Germany, recognizing **Malietoa Talavou** as king and providing for an executive council consisting of one American, one German, and one Briton.

Nov. 8. Death of the king. Civil war between rival factions. The three powers recognized (July 12, 1881) **Malietoa Laupepa** as king.

1887, June 25–July 26. Conference on the affairs of Samoa at Washington, the United States, Britain, and Germany taking part.

July 24. Demanding satisfaction of claims, the Germans landed troops and proclaimed **Tamasese** king. Malietoa surrendered and was exiled.

1888, Sept. 4. Native revolt under **Mataafa** directed against the Germans.

1889, Mar. 15–16. Terrific hurricane in Apia Harbor. Three American and three German warships driven ashore.

Apr. 29–June 14. New Samoan conference of the three powers at Berlin.

June 14. The Samoa Act. The three powers recognized **Malietoa** as king and provided for joint supervision of the administration.

1898, Aug. 22. Death of Malietoa. Mataafa and other chiefs landed by a German warship. Mataafa was elected king (Nov. 12), but was rejected by the American and British consuls. Civil war broke out between Mataafa and **Malietoa Tana,** son of the dead king. Mataafa was successful (Jan. 1899) and a provisional government was set up.

1899, Mar. 15. British and American warships bombarded Apia as a protest against Mataafa and his German supporters.

May 13. Arrival of a combined American-British-German commission. This declared the monarchy abolished.

Nov. 14. Anglo-German treaty, by which Britain relinquished rights to Savaii and Upolu in favor of Germany, and rights to Tutuila and other islands in favor of the United States. The three powers signed this treaty on December 2 and it was ratified February 16, 1900.

The American islands, of which **Tutuila** was the most important, were put under the control of the navy department. Pago Pago became a naval base.

VI. THE FIRST WORLD WAR AND THE INTER-WAR PERIOD, 1914–1939

VI. THE FIRST WORLD WAR AND THE INTER-WAR PERIOD, 1914–1939

A. THE FIRST WORLD WAR

1. THE WESTERN FRONT, 1914–1915

GERMAN STRATEGY was based on the **Schlieffen Plan,** which provided for the concentration of the main German forces on the French front, the passage through Belgium, and a huge wheeling movement to encircle Paris. This plan required a massing of forces on the German right flank, but even before the outbreak of war the German chief of the general staff, **Gen. Helmuth von Moltke** (1906–Sept. 14, 1914), had transferred some divisions from the right to the left (Lorraine) wing, in order to block an invasion of South Germany. The German forces on the eastern (Russian) frontier were relatively few in number and were intended merely to delay the invaders until a decisive victory could be won in the west.

The **French plan of campaign** (Plan 17) had been drawn up in 1913 by **Gen. Joseph Joffre** (chief of the general staff, July 28, 1911–Dec. 12, 1916), under the influence of the teaching of **Gen. Ferdinand Foch.** The plan ignored the danger of a great German advance through Belgium and depended entirely on a vigorous French offensive on the right wing and center. The French reckoned on a Russian advance in the east with about 800,000 men on the eighteenth day of mobilization. **Britain** was expected to contribute about 150,000.

The Germans concentrated about 1,500,000 men, organized in seven armies as follows: 1st **(Alexander von Kluck)** and 2nd **(Karl von Bülow)** on the Belgian front; 3rd **(Max von Hausen)** opposite Liège; 4th **(Prince Albrecht of Württemberg);** 5th **(Crown Prince Wilhelm)** at Luxemburg; 6th **(Prince Rupprecht of Bavaria)** at Metz; 7th **(Josias von Heeringen)** at Strassburg.

Aug. 4. In the night the **Germans crossed the frontier** of Belgium. Armies I and II were obliged to pass through a narrow strip between the Netherlands and the Ardennes, heavily guarded by the fortifications of **Liège.** August 5–6 the Germans **(Gen. Otto von Emmich)** by a night attack got past the forts, which were then reduced by heavy artillery (Aug. 6–17). The Belgians fell back on Brussels and then Antwerp, destroying the bridges of the Meuse.

Aug. 20. Kluck entered Brussels, after driving the Belgians back in the **battle of Tirlement** (Aug. 18–19).

Meanwhile the **French offensive** (five armies) had been developing in the region between Mézières and Belfort, Joffre hoping for a break-through on either side of Metz.

Aug. 14–25. Battle of the Frontiers (Lorraine). The French invasion was checked almost at once and the French armies driven out of Lorraine with heavy losses. The 3rd and 4th armies were also driven back from Luxemburg, the western wing **(Gen. Charles Lanrezac)** being defeated in the **battle of Charleroi** (Aug. 21–24). **Namur** taken by the Germans (Aug. 25); **Longwy** (Aug. 27); **Montmédy** (Aug. 30); **Soissons** (Sept. 1); **Laon** (Sept. 2); **Rheims** (Sept. 3); **Maubeuge** (Sept. 7).

Aug. 23. Battle of Mons. First contact between Germans and British. The latter were obliged to fall back with the French 5th army. Further delaying action fought by the British **(Gen. Horace Smith-Dorrien)** at **Le Cateau** (Aug. 26).

Spectacular German advance, as the French and British fell back to the **Marne River.** The French government moved to Bordeaux (Sept. 3–Dec. 1914). Joffre hastily formed a 6th army on his left, to outflank the German 5th army. Meanwhile Moltke, believing a decision had already been reached by August 25, detailed six corps from the 2nd and 3rd armies to serve on the Russian front. Two of these were actually dispatched, later being sadly needed on the German flank, and arriving too late in the east to be of much use.

Aug. 30. Kluck gave up his advance to the west of Paris, in order to keep contact with Bülow's 2nd army. By September 4 Kluck realized the danger threatening him from the 6th French army before Paris. On the same day Moltke ordered Kluck and Bülow to turn southwest to meet this danger. In the course of the operation a gap was allowed to open between the 1st and 2nd German armies.

Sept. 5–12. BATTLE OF THE MARNE. The opposing armies tried to outflank each other **(battle of the Ourcq).** Strongly urged by **Gen. Joseph Gallieni** (military governor of Paris), Joffre decided to order a general counter-offensive (Sept. 5) in the hope of breaking

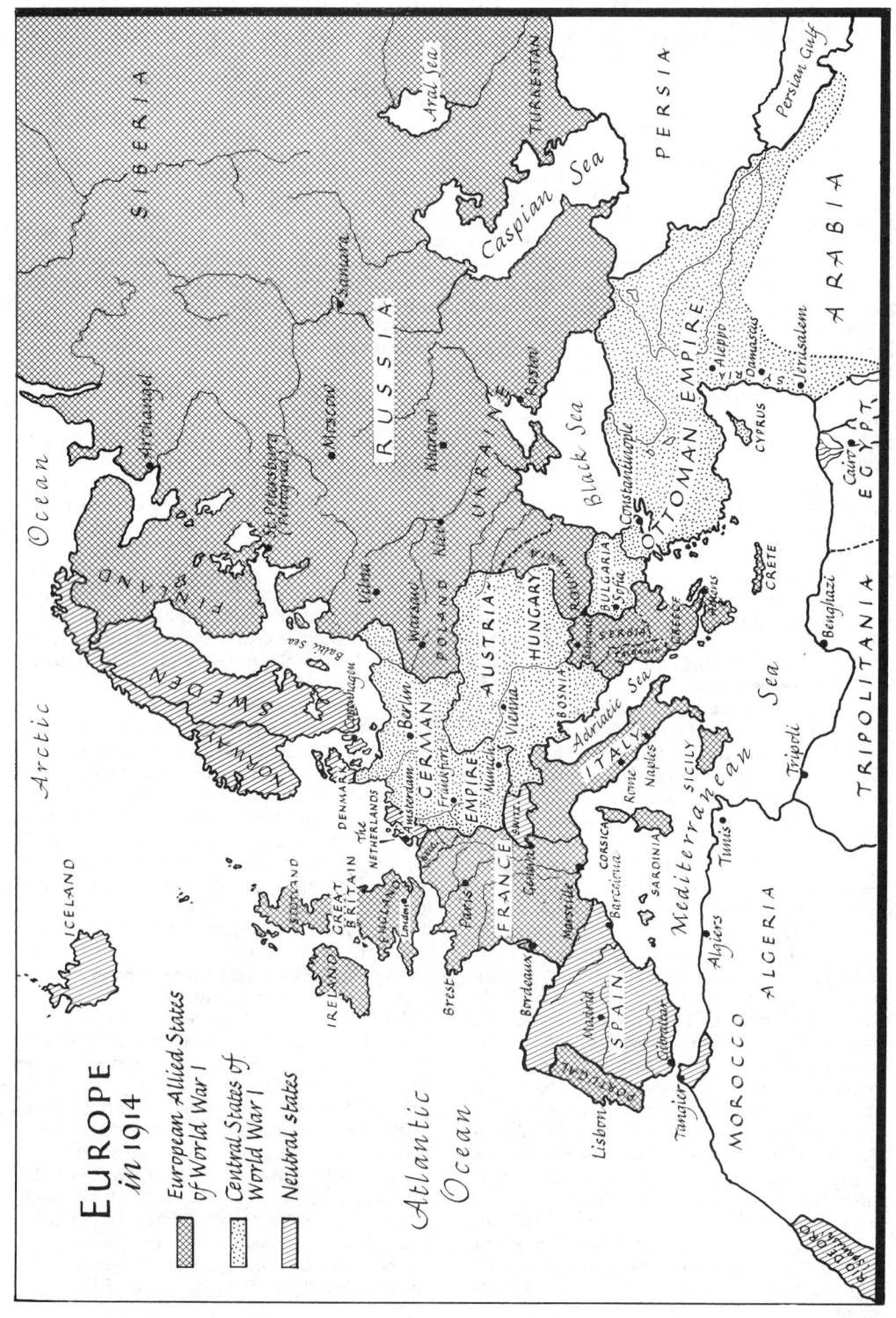

EUROPE
in 1914

European Allied States of World War I

Central States of World War I

Neutral states

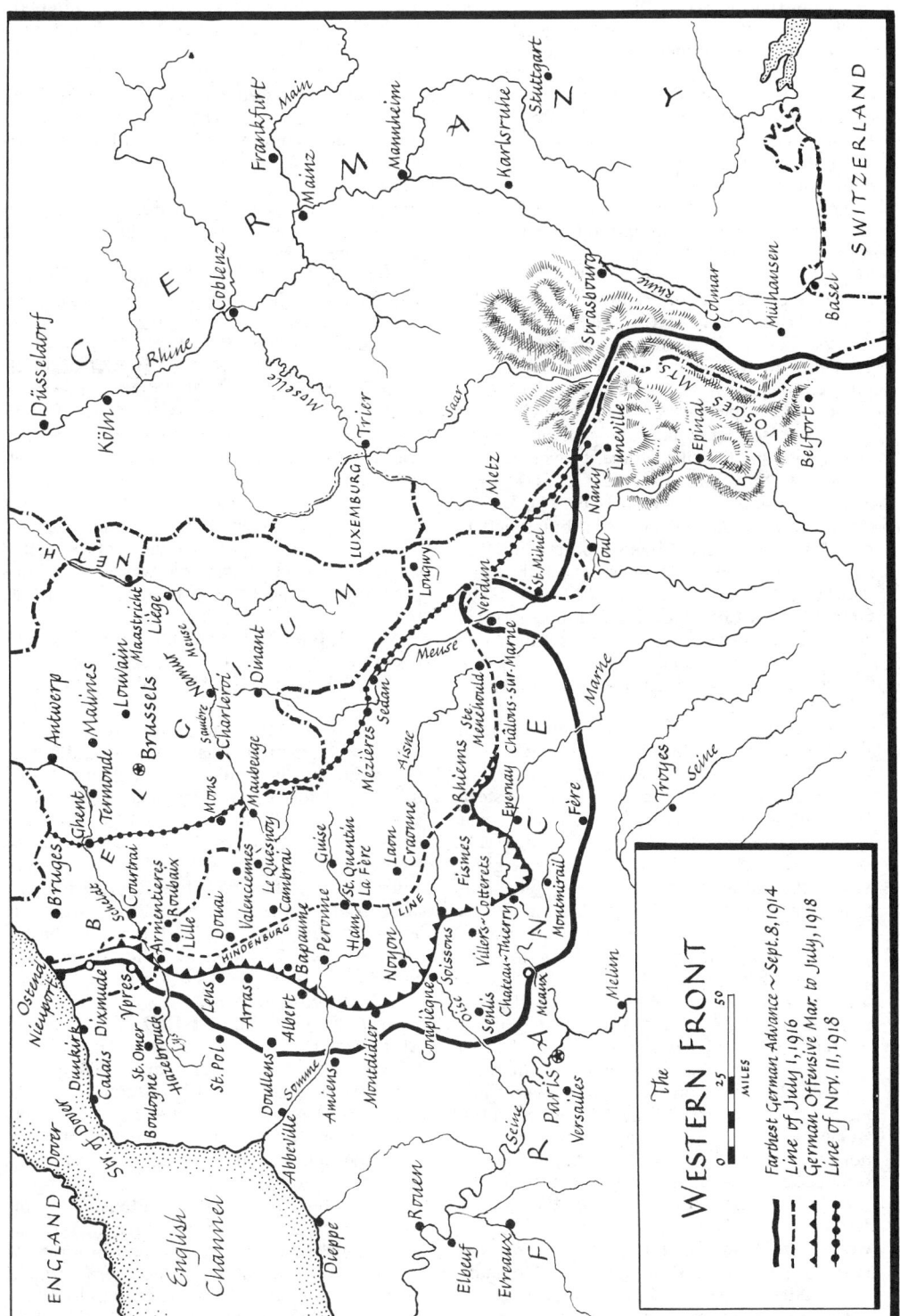

The
WESTERN FRONT

MILES
0   25   50

Farthest German Advance ~ Sept. 8, 1914
Line of July 1, 1916
German Offensive Mar. to July, 1918
Line of Nov. 11, 1918

in on the right and rear of Bülow's 2nd army. September 6–9, no decision. Kluck's efforts to outflank the French increased the gap between the German 1st and 2nd armies, but the British and French failed to take full advantage of this. September 9, Kluck and Bülow began to fall back (oral instructions of **Col. Hentsch,** from German headquarters). The whole German line began to withdraw west of Verdun. Cautious advance of the British and French.

Sept. 13. The Germans stood, north of the Aisne River. All efforts of the Allies to dislodge them ended in failure (**battles of the Aisne,** Sept. 15–18; of **Picardy,** Sept. 22–26; and of **Artois,** Sept. 27–Oct. 10).

Sept. 22–25. Repeated German assaults at **Verdun. St. Mihiel,** on the left bank of the Meuse, taken.

Oct. 1–9. Operations at **Antwerp.** Germans (**Hans von Beseler**) finally obliged the Belgian army, with small British force, to evacuate.

Oct. 10–Nov. 10. THE RACE FOR THE SEA. Germans took **Ghent** (Oct. 11), **Bruges** (Oct. 14), and **Ostend** (Oct. 15), but failed to push through to the **Channel ports,** the Belgians having flooded the district of the Yser (**battle of the Yser,** Oct. 18–Nov. 30). The Germans took **Lille** (Oct. 12) and massed great numbers of troops for an attack southeast of **Ypres,** but failed to take the town or wipe out the salient at that point (**first battle of Ypres,** Oct. 30–Nov. 24).

Dec. 14–24. The Allies launched a general attack along the whole front from Nieuport to Verdun, but made no substantial gains.

By the end of 1914 the line on the western front had become fairly well fixed and the war had become a **war of position,** confined largely to trench warfare. All but a tip of Belgium was in the hands of the Germans. The Belgian government was established at **Le Havre,** while the occupied area was governed successively by **Gen. Colmar von der Goltz** (to Nov. 1914), **Gen. Moritz von Bissing** (to Apr. 1917), and **Gen. Ludwig von Falkenhausen** (to the end of the war). The Germans also retained about one-tenth of the territory of France (21,000 square kilometers), including many of the most valuable coal and iron mines and several important industrial areas. The line, which in the course of the next three years did not vary by more than ten miles, left to the Allies **Verdun, Rheims,** and **Soissons** and thence turned northward between **Noyon** (Ger.), **Montdidier** (Fr.), **Peronne** (Ger.), **Albert** (Fr.), **Bapaume** (Ger.), **Arras** (Fr.), **Lens, La Bassée** (Ger.), **Armentières, Ypres** (Brit.), **Passchendaele, Dixmude** (Ger.), **Nieuport** (Brit.), **Ostend** (Ger.).

The operations in France in 1915 were de-void of broader interest. The commanders on both sides persisted in the belief that a decision was to be won in this area, and consequently devoted as many men and guns as possible to renewed efforts to break through the opponents' line. None of these "offensives" had a notable effect. All were characterized by appalling loss of life.

1915, Feb. 16–Mar. 30. After terrific bombardments of the German positions in eastern **Champagne,** the French attacked, with but insignificant results.

Mar. 10–13. The British launched a vigorous attack in the vicinity of **Neuve Chapelle** and succeeded in breaking through the German line for a short distance.

Apr. 22–May 25. SECOND BATTLE OF YPRES. The original Allied plans for a major offensive were more or less frustrated by the **use of gas** (chlorine) by the Germans (Apr. 22). Though the French had advance information of what was coming, they had made no preparation for it. The troops fled, leaving Ypres exposed. The Germans gained some ground at first, but were apparently themselves skeptical of the effect of the new weapon and unprepared to take full advantage of the situation.

May 9–June 18. SECOND BATTLE OF ARTOIS. After an unprecedented bombardment, the French (**Gen. Henri-Philippe Pétain**) succeeded in breaking through on a six-mile front north of Arras and facing Douai.

The western front was unusually quiet during most of the summer, the Allies utilizing this period for preparation of a "great offensive" for the autumn.

Sept. 22–Nov. 6. SECOND BATTLE OF CHAMPAGNE. This was the key operation in Joffre's great offensive. The French attacked on a front between Rheims and the Argonne. The Germans, however, held their own on the heights between Rheims and Ste. Menehould, so that after many weeks of desperate fighting Joffre had little to show.

Sept. 25–Oct. 15. THIRD BATTLE OF ARTOIS. This was the British contribution to the great offensive in Champagne. The British here first used gas. Greatly outnumbering the Germans, they succeeded in driving the enemy back toward Lens and Loos (**battle of Loos,** Sept. 25–Oct. 8), but then failed to realize on this advantage.

The failure of the great offensive of the French and British, which Joffre had hoped would work like a pair of pincers to force the German withdrawal from northern France, left the situation in the west substantially where it was a year previous. (*Cont. p. 959.*)

2. THE EASTERN FRONT, 1914-1915

The Russian plan of campaign (**Grand Duke Nicholas Nicolaievich** commander-in-chief, August 3, 1914–September 5, 1915) was concerned primarily with Austria; large forces were therefore concentrated on the Galician frontier. The Austrians (**Archduke Frederick** commander-in-chief, **Gen. Conrad von Hötzendorff**, chief of staff, 1912–1917, commander-in-chief, 1917–July 16, 1918) on their part had drawn plans which depended on German support through an advance on the **Narev River**. Pressure elsewhere prevented the Germans from keeping this engagement, but the Austrians, unable to abandon eastern **Galicia**, with its valuable oil-wells, decided to advance from **Lemberg** toward **Lublin** and **Cholm**, to cut the railways to Warsaw.

Aug. 26–Sept. 2. The Austrians under **Gen. Moritz von Auffenberg-Komarow** won a great victory over the Russians (**battle of Zamosc-Komarov**), but at once the Russians (**Gen. Alexei Brusilov**) with much larger forces began to drive back the Austrian right wing.

Sept. 13. The Russians took Lemberg. The battle of **Lemberg** (Sept. 8–12) obliged the Austrians to abandon eastern Galicia. The Russians took **Czernowitz** in the Bukovina (Sept. 15) and **Jaroslav** (Sept. 21). At the same time the Russians invested the key fortress of **Przemysl** (Sept. 16) and launched an attack upon the passes of the Carpathians leading into northern Hungary (Sept. 24).

On the **Serbian front** the Austrians were able to concentrate fewer forces than originally intended. They bombarded **Belgrade** (July 29), and crossed the **Drina River** (Aug. 13) to begin the invasion of Serbia. The Serbs, however, repulsed them (**battle of the Tser and the Jadar**, August 17–21) and obliged the Austrians to withdraw from Serbian territory. In September the Serbs invaded **Syrmia**, while the Austrians again crossed the Drina (Sept. 8). The Serbs took **Zemlin** (Zemun) September 10, but were unable to continue the advance into Austrian territory. The two opponents fought the long-drawn **battle of the Drina** (Sept. 8–17), which was followed by a long series of desultory engagements on the heights along the river. The Serbs were ultimately forced to retreat, and the Austrians were able to take **Belgrade** (Dec. 2).

The decisive battles on the eastern front in 1914, however, were won by the Germans. In response to French appeals for action against the Germans, the Russians formed two armies to invade **East Prussia** from the east and the south. The 1st army (**Gen. Paul Rennenkampf**) defeated the German 8th army (**Gen.**

Friedrich von Prittwitz) in the **battle of Gumbinnen** (Aug. 19–20). The German commander decided on a retreat to the Vistula, despite the objections of his chief of staff, **Colonel** (later General) **Max Hoffmann**, one of the few geniuses of the war. On learning of Prittwitz' decision, the German high command at once dismissed him and sent to the eastern front **Gen. Erich von Ludendorff**, who had distinguished himself at Liège and was recognized as an outstanding staff officer. Ludendorff, a junior officer, was to serve as chief of staff to **Gen.** (later Field Marshal) **Paul von Hindenburg**, a retired officer of no great distinction.

Aug. 23. Hindenburg and Ludendorff arrived at Marienburg, only to find that their arrangements had been anticipated by Hoffmann. The essence of this joint plan was to withdraw the German army from in front of Rennenkampf and concentrate it against the second Russian army (**Gen. Alexander Samsonov**), which was beginning the invasion of East Prussia from the southeast. Throughout these and later operations the Germans were aided greatly by the interception of unciphered Russian messages, and by the unreadiness of Rennenkampf to do much to relieve Samsonov.

Aug. 26–30. BATTLE OF TANNENBERG. The Germans completely defeated Samsonov's army. Brilliant work of **Gen. Hermann von François**, who managed to surround the Russian forces from the west. The Germans took over 100,000 prisoners. Samsonov, in desperation, shot himself.

The Germans then turned on Rennenkampf's army, which was obliged to fall back.

Sept. 6–15. BATTLE OF THE MASURIAN LAKES. The Germans (**Gen.**, later Field Marshal, **August von Mackensen**) drove the enemy into the difficult lake country and succeeded in capturing 125,000 men. Completely demoralized, the Russians fell back, while the Germans advanced to the lower Niemen River and occupied the *gouvernement* of Suvalki. Early in October most of the German troops on this front had to be withdrawn for operations farther south, so that the Russians were able to invade **East Prussia** for the second time.

Meanwhile it was necessary for the Germans to do something to relieve the Austrians. **Hindenburg**, who now enjoyed an immense if somewhat fictitious prestige, was made **commander-in-chief of the German armies in the East** (Sept. 18). The plan, as worked out by the German and Austrian staffs, was for a great combined attack on Poland. The Aus-

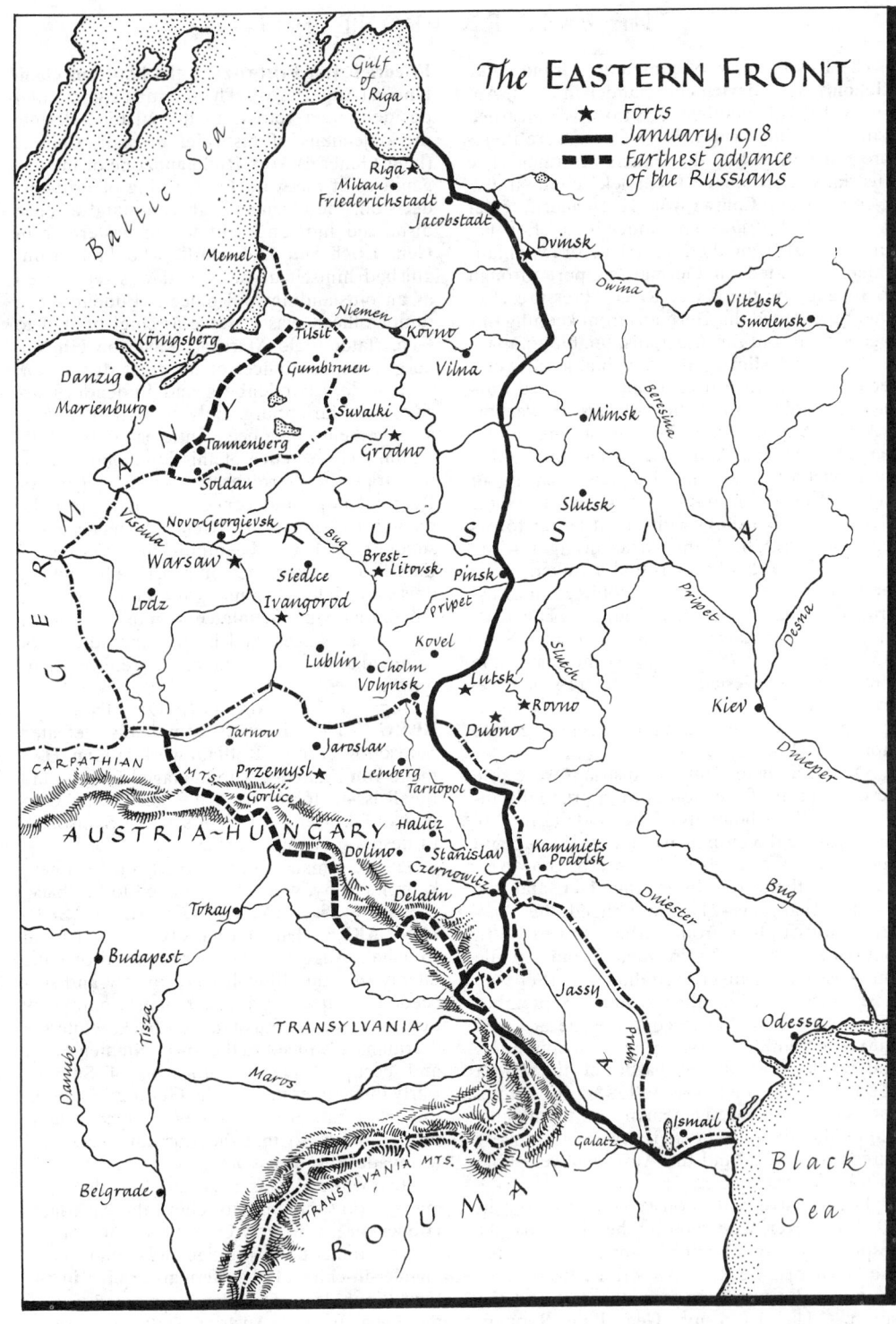

The EASTERN FRONT

★ Forts
━━━ January, 1918
┅┅┅ Farthest advance
of the Russians

Baltic Sea

Gulf of Riga

Riga ★
Mitau
Friederichstadt
Jacobstadt
Dvinsk
Dwina
Vitebsk
Smolensk
Memel
Niemen
Kovno
Tilsit
Vilna
Königsberg
Gumbinnen
Danzig
Marienburg
Suvalki
Tannenberg
Grodno
Soldau
Minsk
Berezina
Vistula
Novo-Georgievsk
Bug
Slutsk
Warsaw ★
Siedlce
Brest-Litovsk
Pinsk
Pripet
Lodz
Ivangorod
Pripet
Desna
Kovel
Lublin
Cholm
Volynsk
Lutsk
Rovno
Kiev
Tarnow
Dubno
Dnieper
CARPATHIAN MTS.
Jaroslav
Przemysl ★
Lemberg
Tarnopol
Gorlice
AUSTRIA-HUNGARY
Halicz
Dolino
Stanislav
Czernowitz
Kaminiets Podolsk
Tokay
Delatin
Dniester
Bug
Budapest
TRANSYLVANIA
Jassy
Odessa
Maros
Pruth
Tisza
Galatz
Ismail
Danube
TRANSYLVANIA MTS.
Black Sea
Belgrade
ROUMANIA

GERMANY
RUSSIA

trians took the offensive in Galicia (Oct. 4), relieved **Przemysl,** and forced the Russians to withdraw from the Carpathians. Meanwhile the Germans **(Mackensen),** advancing on the Austrian left, pushed on toward the Vistula.

Oct. 9-20. BATTLES OF WARSAW AND IVANGOROD. Mackensen advanced as far as **Warsaw** (Oct. 12), but was obliged to fall back when the Russians counter-attacked against the Austrians farther east. The Austrians retreated to **Cracow,** while the Russians commenced the second investment of **Przemysl** (Nov. 10) and renewed the invasion of **northern Hungary** (Nov. 15). Farther west, heavy fighting **(battle of Cracow,** November 16–December 2).

To relieve the pressure in the south, Hindenburg and Ludendorff planned a great offensive, which, it was hoped, would knock the Russians out before the onset of winter. They appealed to the high command for the transfer of large forces from the west, but the demand was rejected by **Gen. Erich von Falkenhayn** (minister for war, 1906–January 21, 1915; chief of the general staff, September 14, 1914–August 29, 1916), whose attention at this time was concentrated on the drive for the Channel ports.

Nov. 16-25. THE BATTLES OF LODZ AND LOWICZ. A confused and bloody conflict in mud and snow. For a time the Russians, having brought up reinforcements, threatened to surround the Germans, but in early December the Germans were themselves strengthened by the arrival of new divisions from the west front. **Lodz** fell to the Germans (Dec. 6).

On the **Galician front** the Austrians attempted an offensive to coincide with the German advance.

Dec. 5-17. BATTLE OF LIMANOVA. The Austrians failed to break the Russian position before Cracow. Throughout the winter the Russians were within thirty miles of the city.

In **Serbia** the Austrians met with even less success. Having taken Belgrade (Dec. 2), they were soon confronted with a formidable Serbian force on the **Morava River.**

Dec. 3-6. Battle of Kolubara. The Austrians were forced to recross the frontier. **Belgrade** retaken by the Serbs (Dec. 15). End of the second invasion of Serbia.

During the winter months the fighting on the Russian front was inconclusive.

1915, Feb. 4-22. Winter battle in Masuria. The Germans advanced and took **Memel** (Feb. 17). Further German offensive in East Prussia **(battle of Augustovo Forest,** March 9-10). But in this area the Russians resisted stoutly.

The idea of Hindenburg and Ludendorff was to concentrate more and more troops in the east, in the hope of enveloping the Russians by an advance from East Prussia. But Falkenhayn insisted on the attempt to reach a decision in the west. This difference of view led to acute tension and a threat by Hindenburg to resign. Ultimately the emperor decided that the newly formed 10th army should be sent to the east, but Falkenhayn had it sent to the Galician front, partly to relieve the Austrians, partly to act as the southern shear in a movement to force the further withdrawal of the Russians from Poland.

Mar. 22. The Russians had at last taken **Przemysl** and were in a position to break through the Carpathian passes into northern Hungary.

Apr. 2-25. Austrians, with the aid of a **German South Army** (Gen. Alexander von Linsingen), drove the Russians back from the Carpathians. An 11th army, under Mackensen, was then formed to co-operate with the Austrian forces from the region southeast of Cracow, in the direction of Przemysl.

May 2. Beginning of the great **Austro-German offensive in Galicia.** The Russians, already suffering severely from lack of rifles, artillery, ammunition, and clothing, gave way at once **(battle of Gorlice-Tarnow).** The Austro-German armies crossed the Dunajec (May 3–5) and took **Jaroslav** (May 14). By May 15 they had reached the San and forced a crossing **(battle of the San,** May 15–23). **Przemysl** was retaken (June 3) and gradually the whole Russian south front collapsed. **Lemberg** fell (June 22) and farther east **Zuravno** (June 5) and **Stanislav** (June 8). The Dniester River was crossed June 23–27. By the end of June the Austro-German forces had advanced almost 100 miles, had liberated **Galicia** and **Bukovina,** and had taken huge numbers of prisoners. The Russian armies on this front were completely demoralized.

The failure of the British at the Dardanelles (p. 957) enabled the Germans to postpone a projected campaign in Serbia designed to make direct contact with the Turks, and to exploit further their great successes against Russia. It was now planned to organize a much greater movement in northern Poland as part of a pincers movement to trap the Russians.

July 1. Beginning of the **second great offensive. The Austrians** (Archduke Joseph Ferdinand) took **Lublin** and **Cholm** (July 31) and stormed **Ivangorod** (Aug. 4). In Courland the **Germans** took **Windau** (July 18) and **Mitau** (Aug. 1), while in northern Poland they (Gen. Max von Gallwitz with the 12th army) advanced to the Narev and took **Warsaw** (Aug. 4–7). The Germans took **Kovno** (Aug. 18) and stormed the key fortress of **Novo-Georgievsk** (Aug. 20). **Brest-Litovsk** fell into their hands (Aug. 25) and **Grodno** (Sept. 2). In the south the Austrians took **Lutsk** (Aug. 31) and **Dubno** (Sept. 8). The capture of **Vilna** (Sept. 19) marked the end of the great offensive. When the German advance came to a stop in September the Russians had lost all of Poland, Lithuania, and Courland, along with almost a million men. The line in September ran from west of Riga and Dvinsk almost due south to Baranovici (German) and Pinsk (Russian) and thence farther south to Dubno (Austrian), Tarnopol (Russian), and Czernowitz (Austrian).

Sept. 5. The **Grand Duke Nicholas Nicolaievich** was relieved of the supreme command and sent as viceroy to the Caucasus. The supreme command was taken over by the tsar in person. (*Cont. p. 961*.)

3. THE WAR AT SEA, 1914–1915

The **British Grand Fleet (Adm. Sir John Jellicoe,** commander, August 4, 1914–November 29, 1916) consisted of twenty dreadnoughts and a corresponding number of battle cruisers, cruisers, destroyers, and other craft. The fleet was based on **Scapa Flow, Cromarty,** and **Rosyth,** with **Harwich** as the base for destroyers and submarines. A second fleet, consisting largely of pre-dreadnought types, guarded the Channel. The **Germans** had a **High Seas Fleet** of thirteen dreadnoughts, based on the North Sea ports. The Germans remained in port, despite the efforts of **Adm. Alfred von Tirpitz** to bring about a more active policy.

1914, Aug. 28. British cruisers, supported by battle cruisers **(Adm. Sir David Beatty),** raided **Heligoland Bight.** The German cruisers came out and drove the British off, but Beatty was able to sink three enemy ships.

The Germans now devoted their attention to mine-laying and **submarine work.** The *U.9* sank the three old cruisers, *Hogue, Cressy,* and *Aboukir* (Sept. 22). After an attempted German submarine raid on **Scapa Flow** (Oct. 18) the Grand Fleet was withdrawn from that base and concentrated, for a time, on the west coast of Scotland.

Apart from occasional sinkings, the war in the North Sea was restricted to raids, chiefly by German battle cruisers **(Adm. Franz von Hipper),** on the English coast (November 3— **raid on Yarmouth;** December 16—**bombardment of Scarborough and Hartlepool).**

1915, Jan. 24. Naval action off the **Dogger Bank** between the British and German battle-cruiser squadrons. Hipper, though outnumbered, did much damage to the British flagship and ultimately got away, losing only his poorest ship, the *Blücher.*

When the war broke out, there were eight German cruisers on foreign stations, mostly on the China station. When **Japan** declared war (see p. 923), the commander, **Adm. Maximilian von Spee,** left for the South American coast with the cruisers *Scharnhorst, Gneisenau,* and *Nürnberg.* He bombarded **Papeete** (Sept. 22) and destroyed the British cable station at **Fanning Island.** At **Easter Island** (Oct. 12–18) Spee was joined by the cruisers *Dresden* (from the West Indies) and *Leipzig* (from the California coast). Together they proceeded to the Chilean coast.

Meanwhile **Adm. Sir Christopher Cradock,** with three old ships, had been ordered to hunt down Spee.

1914, Nov. 1. NAVAL ACTION OFF CORONEL. Spee destroyed two of Cradock's ships (the *Monmouth* and the *Good Hope;* the *Glasgow* escaped).

To meet the danger from the German squadron, all available Allied warships were assembled off the southeast coast of South America. Three battle cruisers were hastily dispatched from the Grand Fleet to the South Atlantic.

Dec. 8. BATTLE OF THE FALKLAND ISLANDS. Spee made the fatal decision to attack the **Falklands** on his way homeward. The British squadron **(Adm. Sir Frederick Sturdee)** came upon the Germans unexpectedly and sank four of their five ships (*Scharnhorst, Gneisenau, Leipzig,* and *Nürnberg*). Only the *Dresden* escaped. Heroic death of Spee, his two sons, and 1800 men.

German cruisers still abroad caused great damage to Allied shipping. The *Emden* **(Capt. Karl von Müller)** left the China station for the Indian Ocean. Between September 10 and November 9 she bombarded **Madras** (Sept. 22) and captured several ships before she was sunk at Cocos Island. The German cruiser *Königsberg* was also very destructive until located and shut into the mouth of the Rufigi River. The *Dresden,* having escaped from the Falklands, engaged in commerce-destroying until cornered at Juan Fernandez, where she was blown up by her own crew (Mar. 14, 1915).

From the very beginning of the war the

question of **neutral shipping** had arisen. Both the British and French governments issued new and more rigorous **interpretations of contraband** (Aug. 20, 25, 1914), adding greatly to the list of contraband goods. To this the United States government replied (Oct. 22) stating that it would insist on the observance of the existing rules of international law. Nevertheless the British continued to revise the list of contraband and to modify the declaration of London of 1909. On November 2 they declared the North Sea a military zone, and on January 30, 1915, the British admiralty ordered British merchant ships to fly neutral ensigns or none in the vicinity of the British Isles.

1915, Feb. 4. The German government announced that a submarine **blockade of Great Britain** would begin February 18. To this the London government replied with an order in council (Mar. 11) ordering the seizure of all goods presumably destined for the enemy. Cotton was declared contraband March 18.

Mar. 28. First passenger ship sunk by German submarine (*S. S. Falaba*).

May 1. First American ship (*Gulflight*) sunk without warning.

May 7. *LUSITANIA* SUNK off the coast of Ireland, with a loss of 1198 lives, including 139 Americans. Before the ship left New York a warning against sailing on her had been inserted in the newspapers by the German embassy, but it is not true that a submarine was sent out specially to sink her. The captain failed to observe instructions to zigzag his course, and so came within range of the submarine. The *Lusitania* carried a part-cargo of small arms and munitions.

The sinking of the *Lusitania* brought the United States and Germany to the verge of war and created much greater tension than had developed between the American and Allied governments over questions of contraband and blockade. In a speech of May 9 **President Wilson** publicly denounced the sinking, but the note of protest to Berlin (May 13) was somewhat milder in tone, demanding reparation and abstinence from such practices in the future.

June 8. William J. Bryan resigned as American secretary of state, because of unwillingness to follow the president in his policy. Bryan was succeeded by **Robert Lansing.**

On the very next day a much stronger note was dispatched to Berlin, without eliciting a disavowal or assurance for the future. A third note was sent on July 21.

Aug. 19. Sinking of the *Arabic*, with the loss of two American lives. This new offense resulted in a second period of acute tension, but the German ambassador at Washington, **Count Johann von Bernstorff,** finally convinced his government of the real danger of war.

Sept. 1. The German government gave assurances that no liners would be sunk in future without warning and without some provision for the safety of noncombatants, provided the ship made no effort to offer resistance or to escape. These assurances were reasonably well observed during the remainder of the year, and so the first phase of the submarine crisis came to an end. (*Cont. p. 966.*)

4. THE INTERVENTION OF ITALY, 1915

On the plea that the Austrian action against Serbia was an offensive action and therefore incompatible with the terms of the **Triple Alliance,** the Italian government in July 1914, refused to join the Central Powers, and declared neutrality (Aug. 3). But almost from the outset the Italian government maintained that, under Art. VII of the Triple Alliance, Italy was entitled to some compensation to counter-balance the Austrian gains in the Balkans. These claims were advanced the more persistently when the foreign ministry was given to **Baron Sidney Sonnino** (Nov. 3), following the sudden demise of **Marquis Antonio di San Giuliano** (Oct. 16).

The necessity for making some concession to Italy in order to keep her neutral was fully recognized in Berlin, but the Austrian foreign minister **(Baron Leopold von Berchtold)** refused to entertain suggestions of territorial cessions.

1914, Dec. 20. Prince Bernhard von Bülow, former German chancellor, arrived in Rome on special mission. He admitted the Italian claim to the Trentino and the German government made every effort to persuade the Austrians to give in (mission of Count Betho von Wedel to Vienna, Jan. 16, 1915).

1915, Jan. 13. Count Stephen Burian appointed Austro-Hungarian foreign minister to replace Berchtold. Burian finally agreed to the cession of territory (Mar. 9), but was willing to cede the **Trentino** only after the conclusion of peace. This was not enough to satisfy the Italians, who were already negotiating with the Entente powers. Sonnino demanded of Austria the immediate cession of the **South Tyrol,** the district of **Gorizia** and **Gradisca,** the establishment of **Trieste** and its neighborhood as a free state, the cession to Italy of the **Curzolari Is-**

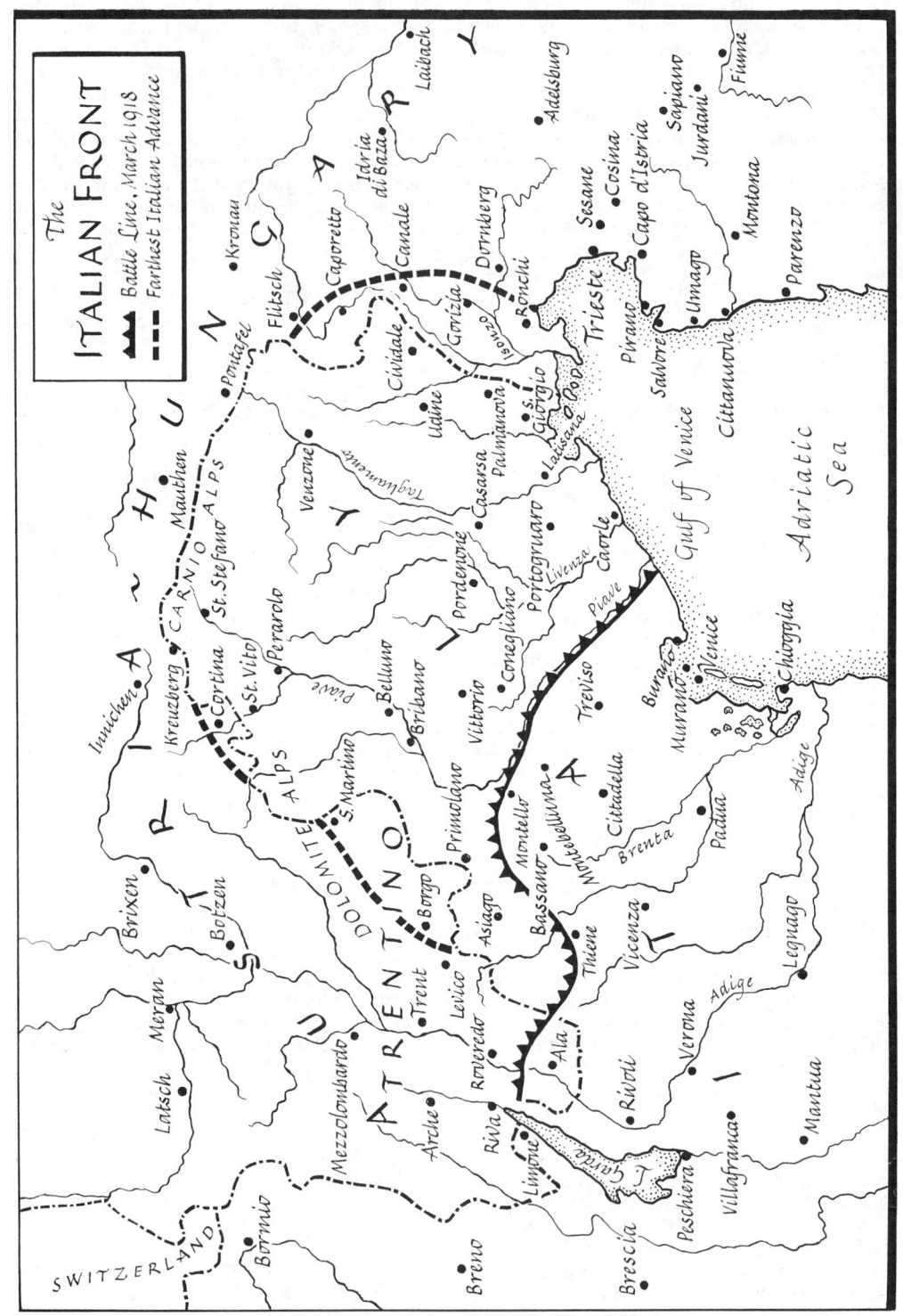

The
ITALIAN FRONT

Battle Line, March 1918
Farthest Italian Advance

lands off the Dalmatian coast, full sovereignty over the island of **Saseno** and over **Valona** on the Albanian coast (Italian occupation of Saseno, October 30, 1914; "provisional" occupation of Valona, December 26, 1914). These demands were exorbitant, from the Austrian point of view, but the Germans finally (May 10) induced their allies to agree to substantially all the Italians held out for. As it turned out, the Austrians yielded too late.

Apr. 26. Britain, France, Russia, and Italy concluded the **secret treaty of London. Antonio Salandra,** the Italian prime minister, had envisaged Italian intervention on the Entente side almost since the beginning of war, but the non-interventionists, led by **Giovanni Giolitti,** were too strong to make that at first a practicable policy. During the winter, however, the interventionist movement gathered strength (**Mussolini** broke with the Socialist Party and became an active proponent of intervention). The western powers, meeting with failure on the western front, were ready to offer much. Negotiations were embarked upon in February 1915, but were delayed by the opposition of the Russian foreign minister, Sazonov, to the assignment of the Dalmatian coast to Italy, in view of the Serbian aspirations in that region. Under the terms of the treaty as finally concluded, a military convention was to be drawn up to protect Italy against the full force of Austrian attack. The political clauses promised Italy the **South Tyrol** and **Trentino, Gorizia, Gradisca, Trieste, Istria,** the most important **Dalmatian islands,** and the southern part of the province of **Dalmatia; Saseno** and **Valona,** full sovereignty over the **Dodecanese Islands** (occupied since 1912); in the event of the partition of Turkey, Italy was to have the province of **Adalia;** in the event of Britain and France enlarging their empires by the addition of German colonies, Italy was to receive extensions of her territory in **Libya, Eritrea,** and **Somaliland.** Italy was further to receive a loan, and ultimately part of the war indemnity.

The Entente powers were to support Italy in preventing the Holy See from taking diplomatic steps for the conclusion of peace. Italy was to commence hostilities within a month of the signature of the treaty.

May 3. The Italian government denounced the Triple Alliance.

May 10. Conclusion of a **naval convention** between Britain, France, and Italy.

May 23. Italy mobilized and declared war on Austria-Hungary. Germany at once severed diplomatic relations (May 24), but for various financial reasons Italy did not declare war on Germany until August 28, 1916.

May 29. The Italian government "formally" occupied **Valona. Albania** being in a state of anarchy (flight of Prince William von Wied, September 3, 1914; provisional government of Essad Pasha at Durazzo, October 4, 1914), this little state, the independence of which had been guaranteed by the powers (Dec. 20, 1912), now became a prey to its neighbors.

June 26. The **Montenegrins** occupied **San Giovanni di Medua.**

July 4. The **Serbians** occupied **Durazzo,** which they evacuated again July 17, under pressure from the Italian government.

Dec. 20. Durazzo occupied by the **Italians. 1915. FIRST FOUR BATTLES OF THE ISONZO.** The first two years of Italy's participation in the war were taken up with the fighting of eleven successive battles on the Isonzo, along a front of only about sixty miles. The Austrians (commander **Archduke Eugene**) held the two important bridgeheads at **Gorizia** and **Tolmino.** The Italians (**Gen. Luigi Cadorna,** commander-in-chief, May 23, 1915– November 7, 1917) tried to force the passage, but their total advance never exceeded ten or twelve miles. The Isonzo battles of 1915 were the first (June 29–July 7); second (July 18– Aug. 10); third (Oct. 18–Nov. 3); and fourth (Nov. 10–Dec. 10). (*Cont. p. 961.*)

5. THE BALKAN SITUATION, 1914–1915

The three Balkan states, Greece, Bulgaria, and Roumania, all exhausted by the Balkan Wars of 1912–1913, proclaimed neutrality at the beginning of the European conflict. The Russians entertained high hopes of securing the aid of **Roumania,** which would have been an important factor in the Galician campaign. On various occasions (July 30, Sept. 16) they attempted to bait the Bucharest government with promises of Transylvania, but so long as **King Carol** lived

(d. Oct. 10, 1914) there was no hope of Roumanian intervention, since the king strongly regretted Roumania's failure to side with her Austrian and German allies. **King Ferdinand** felt morally less bound, but the prime minister, **Ion Bratianu** (premier and foreign minister January 14, 1914–February 6, 1918), was determined to drive a hard bargain.

1914, Dec. 6. Bratianu rejected allied suggestions that Roumania guarantee Greece against

Bulgarian attack or make concessions in the Dobrudja to secure Bulgarian support.

1915, Jan. 25. He refused to join Greece in support of Serbia.

May 3. The Roumanians asked not only for **Transylvania,** but also for part of **Bukovina** and the **Banat.**

July. The Russians were prepared to concede most of these demands, but Bratianu was then unwilling to act unless the Allies had 500,000 men in the Balkans and the Russians 200,000 in Bessarabia (Nov. 1915).

The **POSITION OF BULGARIA** became crucial after the entry of Turkey into the war in November 1914.

1914, Nov. 9. In order to secure Bulgarian help the Allies offered Bulgaria the **Enos-Midia line** in eastern Thrace and, after the war, the (1912) **uncontested zone of Macedonia,** this territory being in the possession of Serbia.

It was clear almost from the outset, however, that such an offer would not prove attractive, since the Bulgarians aspired not only to part of **Thrace,** but to most of **Macedonia,** the **Kavalla-Drama-Seres** region of western Thrace, and also that part of **Dobrudja** lost to Roumania in 1913.

1915, Jan. As the Dardanelles campaign was being decided on, the Allies offered to **Greece** the Turkish city of **Smyrna** and its hinterland, on condition that the Greeks cede the **Kavalla** region to Bulgaria and join a Balkan bloc in support of Serbia. **Venizelos** favored this policy strongly, but **King Constantine** preferred the sparrow in the hand to the pigeon on the roof (Jan. 24, 29).

Mar. 6. **Venizelos** fell from power when the king refused to adopt his policy of aiding the Allies at the Dardanelles (see p. 957). His successor, **Demetrios Gounaris** (Mar. 9–Aug. 22), was less favorable toward the Entente.

Apr. 12. He rejected a second offer of the Smyrna region, on the plea that the Allies would not guarantee Greek territory (i.e. against Bulgaria).

May 7. The **Allies,** more eager than ever to secure the aid of Bulgaria in view of their failure at the Dardanelles, gave **Serbia** a conditional guaranty of the eventual acquisition of Bosnia and Herzegovina and "a wide access to the Adriatic," as compensation for the part of Macedonia required to bring in Bulgaria.

May 29. A definite offer along these lines was made to **Bulgaria.** The Sofia government treated these advances dilatorily, and was already leaning to the Central Powers, which were prepared to promise whatever Bulgaria wanted, in view of the fact that Bulgarian aspirations were directed chiefly to Serbian and Greek territory.

July 22. The **Germans** persuaded the **Turks** to cede to Bulgaria a strip of territory along the **Maritza River** (definitive agreement September 22). On August 8 the Bulgarian government secured from Germany and Austria a loan of 400 million francs.

Sept. 6. Bulgaria concluded an alliance and military convention with Germany and Austria, providing for mutual aid against attack by a neighboring state, for a German-Austrian campaign against Serbia within 30 days, and for Bulgarian participation five days later. Bulgaria was to receive **Macedonia,** and, if Roumania joined in the war, **Dobrudja** also; if Greece proved hostile, Bulgaria was to receive the **Kavalla** region as well.

Sept. 21. The **Bulgarians began to mobilize.** The Serbs, being directly threatened, appealed to Greece for aid, under the terms of the treaty of May 1913. **Venizelos,** who had returned to power August 22, was as eager as ever to intervene, but made it a condition that the Allies furnish the 150,000 troops which Serbia was required to supply under the treaty terms.

Sept. 24. The British and French governments gave a promise to this effect. Venizelos then secured the secret consent of the king to the landing of the Allied forces at **Saloniki,** but publicly the request of the Allies to land was rejected (Sept. 28).

Oct. 3–5. One **British** and one **French** division were **landed at Saloniki,** followed by two more French divisions at the end of the month. King Constantine now refused to support Venizelos to the extent of joining in the war; the prime minister resigned (Oct. 5, 1915) and was succeeded by **Alexander Zaimis** (Oct. 6–Nov. 5, 1915).

Oct. 6. Beginning of the **great Austro-German campaign in Serbia (Gen. von Mackensen). Belgrade** fell (Oct. 9) and **Semendria** (Oct. 11).

Oct. 14. Bulgaria and Serbia declared war on each other. Britain and **France** declared war on Bulgaria (Oct. 15, 16), and so did Russia and Italy (Oct. 19). The Allies made great efforts to induce Greece to join, the British offering them the island of **Cyprus** (Oct. 16), but this offer too was rejected (Oct. 20).

Oct. 22. The **Bulgarians** (Gen. Jekov) took **Üskub** (Skoplje), and then (Oct. 28) **Pirot.** Nish fell (Nov. 5). An attempt of the British and French from Saloniki to block the Bulgar advance on the Strumitsa (Nov. 3–5) and on the Cerna (Nov. 12) was brushed aside. The Allies were again repulsed on the lower Vardar (Dec. 4–10) and forced to retreat to Greek territory. The British were, by this time, prepared to give up the whole Saloniki adventure, but the French, under **Gen. Maurice Sar-**

rail, persisted in staying. The result was that ever greater forces were tied up at Saloniki.

Nov. 5. Zaimis resigned and was succeeded by **Stephanos Skouloudis** (Nov. 6, 1916–June 21, 1916). The Greek government then declared its benevolent neutrality (Nov. 8) and agreed not to interfere with the Allied forces at Saloniki, in return for a guaranty of the eventual restoration of Greek territory (Nov. 24).

Nov. 16. The **Bulgarians** took **Prilep**, then **Pristina** (Nov. 23), **Prizrend** (Nov. 29), and **Monastir** (i.e. Bitolje, Dec. 2). The **Serbs** were now in full flight into **Albania**, the Bulgars pursuing them and taking **Dibra** and **Okhrid** (Dec. 8) and ultimately **Elbasan** (Feb. 2, 1916).

Dec. 2. The **Austrians** took **Plevlje**, and then **Ipek** (Dec. 6). **Mt. Lovchen**, guarding Montenegro, was stormed (Jan. 10, 1916) and **Cettinje** taken (Jan. 13). **King Nicholas** laid down his arms and retired to Italy.

1916, Jan. 11. The **French occupied Corfu** as a refuge for the Serbian troops. The Greek government refused its consent, but the Serbs were landed nevertheless (Jan. 15).

Jan. 23. The **Austrians took Scutari**, then **San Giovanni di Medua** (Jan. 25) and **Berat** (Feb. 17). The **Albanian provisional government**, under Italian protection at Durazzo, left for Naples (Feb. 24), and the town was taken by the Austrians from the Italians (Feb. 27). Mountain warfare between the Austrians and the Italians in Albania continued until the end of the war. (*Cont. p. 962.*)

6. THE OTTOMAN FRONT, 1914–1915

At the outbreak of the war, the policy of **Turkey** was determined primarily by **Enver Pasha,** the minister of war, whose pro-German inclinations were well known. At the height of the July crisis (July 27) the Turks themselves proposed to the Germans the conclusion of an alliance directed against Russia. The Germans accepted, and the treaty, which was known only to a few of the Turkish ministers, was concluded August 2. The Turks were to enter the war as soon as hostilities were opened by Russia against Germany or Austria (which adhered to the pact). Actually the Turkish government, with the assent of its allies, remained neutral for some time, in order to complete the necessary military preparations.

1914, Aug. 11. The German cruisers *Goeben* and *Breslau* arrived at the Dardanelles, and were allowed to pass through. These two cruisers, stationed in the Mediterranean, had bombarded **Bône** and **Philippeville** in French Africa (Aug. 3) and had then gone on to Messina. The British **Adm. Sir Berkeley Milne** watched for them at the northern end of the Straits of Messina, but the German **Adm. Wilhelm Souchon** left by the southern end (Aug. 6). A small British squadron **(Adm. Ernest Troubridge)** followed the German ships, but did not dare attack. Milne failed to prevent the ships from reaching the Dardanelles. Their presence at Constantinople not only served to reveal the trend of Turkish policy, but also helped the Germans to establish a firm influence over that policy. The ships were officially bought by the Turkish government to take the place of two battleships that were building in Britain and had been taken over by the British government.

Aug.–Oct. Many efforts were made by the British government to secure the neutrality of Turkey, by offering a guaranty of independence and integrity and by promising concessions in the matter of the capitulations. The Turkish government, in the interval, declared the **capitulations abolished** (Sept. 7), but probably never seriously considered either neutrality or alliance with the western powers. Longdrawn negotiations for an alliance with Russia were probably meant only as a blind.

Oct. 29. Turkish warships, including the two German cruisers, suddenly bombarded **Odessa, Sevastopol,** and **Theodosia** on the Russian Black Sea coast. Britain and her allies at once severed relations and sent an ultimatum. **Russia declared war** (Nov. 2) and **Britain** and **France** followed (Nov. 5), Britain on the same day proclaiming the **annexation of Cyprus** (occupied since 1878, see p. 781).

Nov. 14. The sultan, as caliph, proclaimed a Holy War (*Jihad*) against all those making war on Turkey or her allies. This move proved to be of slight importance.

Dec. 18. The British proclaimed a **protectorate over Egypt** (occupied since 1882, see p. 868), and hastily began to concentrate troops for the defense of this strategic area. (December 1—first units of the Australian and New Zealand expeditionary force **[Anzac]** arrived in Egypt.)

Gen. Liman von Sanders, head of the German military mission in Constantinople, urged the Turks to attempt the invasion of the Ukraine from Odessa, evidently in the hope of bringing Roumania in on the side of the central powers. But **Enver Pasha** insisted on a campaign against the Russians in the **Caucasus.**

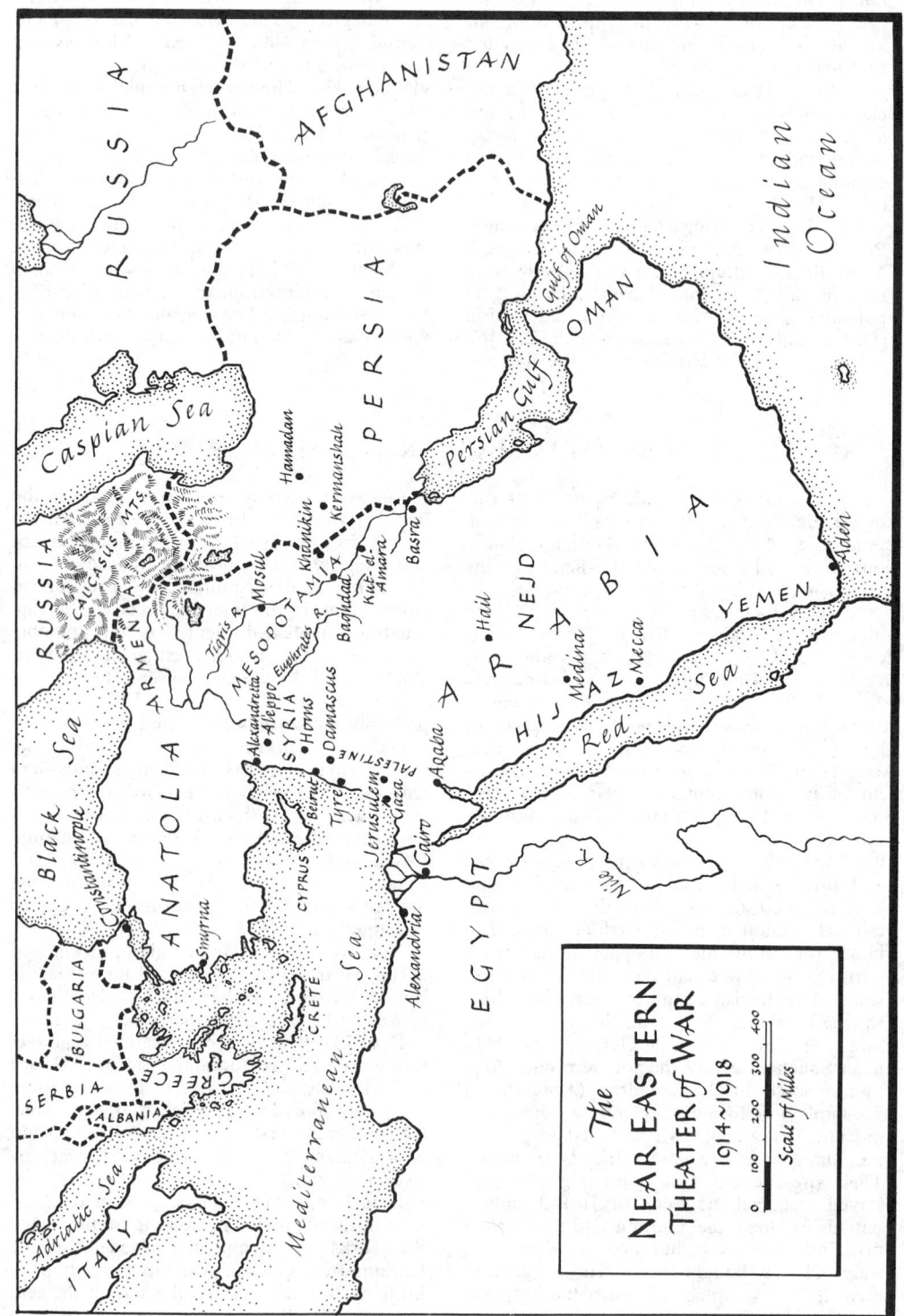

The
NEAR EASTERN
THEATER of WAR
1914~1918

Scale of Miles
0   100   200   300   400

Dec. 17. The Turks began their offensive against **Kars.**

Dec. 29-1915, Jan. 2.   Battle of Sarikamish. The Turks took **Tabriz** (Jan. 8), but this important town was retaken by the Russians (Jan. 30) and the whole Turkish offensive gradually ran out. The Caucasus front remained quiet until April (1915) when the Turks began the deportation and **massacre of the Armenians,** whom they accused of aiding the Russian invader. The Armenians rose in revolt at **Van** (Apr. 20) and held the fortress until relieved by a Russian force (May 19). After months of desultory fighting the Russians were finally obliged to abandon Van (Aug. 3, 1915), which was then reoccupied by the Turks (Aug. 5).

In the interval the Turks had initiated **operations against Egypt.** They attacked the **Suez Canal** (Feb. 3-4, 1915), but were easily repulsed. Nevertheless, the constant threat of another such attack obliged the British to keep large numbers of troops in Egypt throughout the war.

The entry of Turkey into the conflict had extended tremendously the area of possible operations. In view of the deadlock on the west front, the idea was soon advanced in England (notably by **Winston Churchill,** supported by **Lloyd George** and by **Lord Kitchener**) that it would be wiser to allow the French armies to hold the western front, while Britain should devote her newly raised armies to attacking the enemy in some more vulnerable spot, preferably in the Near East, where success might serve to bring in the Balkan states on the side of the Entente. This idea was received sympathetically by a few French generals (**Gallieni, Franchet-d'Esperey**), but on the whole met with the most vigorous opposition from **Joffre** and the other commanders in France, who stuck to the idea that a decision could be reached only in the main theater of war, and that all available forces must be massed there for another attempt at a break-through.

The exponents of an eastern campaign (**Easterners**) continued to press the issue and advanced three different courses of action: (1) to land a force in the **Gulf of Alexandretta,** cut the railway between Syria and Anatolia, prevent a Turkish campaign against Egypt, and encourage the Arabs to break with the Constantinople government; (2) to send a force to **Saloniki,** strong enough to bring Greece and Bulgaria into the war on the Allied side; this force to march either up the Vardar to relieve the Serbs, or else to Constantinople and thence by way of the Danube against Austria; (3) to launch an attack on the **Dardanelles,** land a force and thus capture the Turkish capital. All

these schemes, however, had to be shelved because of the insistence of the generals that the newly raised forces be sent to France.

1915, Jan. 2. The Russians appealed to Britain for a diversion to relieve the pressure of the Turks in the Caucasus. The war council, after much debate, finally (Jan. 13) decided on a naval action against the Dardanelles, with Constantinople as the objective. Later (Feb. 16) it was decided to send one division of troops, which was to be reinforced from Egypt.

The Greek government offered to aid the Allied operations with a number of divisions (Mar. 5), but this policy was rejected by **King Constantine,** whereupon **Venizelos resigned** (Mar. 6).

Mar. 4. The Russian foreign minister, **Sazonov,** handed to the French and British representatives a note claiming for Russia, in the event of success, **Constantinople** and a strip along the northern side of the Bosporus, Sea of Marmora, and Dardanelles, as well as **Thrace** to the Enos-Midia line, and the Asiatic side of the Bosporus to the **river Sakarya.** To this Britain and France agreed, the latter reluctantly, on condition that Constantinople be made a free port and that merchant ships should be free to pass through the Straits. British and French claims in Asiatic Turkey were to be defined later (Mar. 12).

Feb. 19. The British began the naval action against the Dardanelles, and occupied the island of **Lemnos** as a base (Feb. 23). The forts were soon silenced and several companies of marines were landed, suggesting that more extensive military operations at this time would have been relatively easy.

Mar. 18.   Adm. John de Robeck and eighteen warships tried to force the Narrows. Four ships struck mines, whereupon Robeck gave up the attempt, perhaps prematurely.

The interval of more than a month that followered was used by the Turks (**Gen. Liman von Sanders** put in command) to strengthen the defenses and to concentrate about 100,000 men. The British sent out about 75,000 men, under the command of **Sir Ian Hamilton.**

Apr. 25.   LANDING OF THE BRITISH at several places at the tip of the peninsula, while Australian troops made a feint farther north and a French force landed on the Asiatic side. Poor co-ordination between the different parties; heroic resistance of the Turks, who managed to keep the various landing parties off the heights and prevented their coalescence (distinguished work of **Mustapha Kemal,** later leader of the Turk national revival, see p. 1085).

Several months of futile fighting ensued, during which the troops suffered from heat, lack of water, flies, etc.

May 12. Hostile submarines began to appear off the Straits. British warships *Goliath, Triumph,* and *Majestic* sunk. Allied submarines ultimately penetrated to Constantinople on a raid (Aug. 1), but for the most part the British squadron was withdrawn to **Mudros** excepting when needed for attack.

Aug. 6. **LANDING AT SUVLA,** after many additonal divisions had been sent out from England. The plan was to cut in behind the Turkish position and so reach the Narrows. Four days of heavy fighting (**battle of Sari Bahr,** Aug. 6–10). Timid and confused leadership on the British side; staunch resistance of the Turks, who succeeded in holding the heights.

This second failure turned opinion in England against the whole project. Hamilton was replaced by **Sir Charles Munro** and preparations were made for evacuation (Oct. 16).

Dec. 19–20—1916, Jan. 8–9. The British forces were withdrawn from **Gallipoli** without loss, much to the astonishment of the British command. With the failure of the effort at the Dardanelles, the Straits remained closed and Russia was effectively cut off from supplies which her allies might have furnished her.

(*Cont. p. 964.*)

7. THE MESOPOTAMIAN CAMPAIGN, 1914–1916

This campaign began very modestly when a British force from India occupied **Basra** (Nov. 22, 1914) in order to protect the oil pipeline from Persia. Then, for the sake of greater security, the British began to extend the sphere of their occupation.

1914, Dec. 4–8. Fighting about **Qurna,** which was taken by the Anglo-Indian forces (Dec. 9).

1915, Apr. 11–13. **Sir John Nixon** repulsed Turkish attacks on Basra.

June 3. **Gen. Charles Townshend** took the town of **Amara** on the Tigris, and then **Nasiriya** on the Euphrates (July 25).

Sept. 28. **BATTLE OF KUT-EL-AMARA.** Townshend defeated the Turks and drove them as far as Aziziya.

Nov. 11. Beginning of the **advance on Baghdad.**

Nov. 22–24. **BATTLE OF CTESIPHON.** The engagement was indecisive, but both armies began to fall back, Townshend retreating as far as Kut.

Dec. 7–Apr. 29, 1916. **SIEGE OF KUT-EL-AMARA.** Three attempts were made by the British to relieve the garrison (Jan. 18–21, Mar. 8, Apr. 1–9), but the armies were hampered by floods and mud. Efforts were made to buy off the Turks, but these too led to no result.

1916, Apr. 29. **CAPITULATION OF KUT-EL-AMARA,** with 10,000 men.

In the effort to divert the Turkish forces and to establish contact with the British, the **Russians** in November 1915 had begun an advance into **western Persia,** which was followed by an offensive in **Armenia.** They took **Kasvin** (Nov. 2), **Hamadan** (Dec. 14), **Kirmanshah** (Feb. 26, 1916), **Karind** (Mar. 12), and, turning westward toward the flank of the Turkish force in Mesopotamia, took **Khanikin** (May 15) and **Rowanduz** (May 15), a detachment actually joining hands with the British on the Tigris. The **British** had occupied **Bushire** (Aug. 8, 1915).

1916, Jan. 11. Russian offensive in Armenia. The **Russians** took **Koprikoi** (Jan. 18), and, after a battle of three days, **Erzerum** (Feb. 16) and **Mush** (Feb. 18). **Bitlis** fell (Mar. 2), and then **Trebizond** (Apr. 17) and **Erzinjan** (July 25).

June 5. The **Turks began a counter-offensive** in western Persia. They drove the Russians out of **Khanikin** (June 5), and retook **Kirmanshah** (July 1) and **Hamadan** (Aug. 10).

Aug. 15. In **Armenia** the Turks also took the offensive, taking **Bitlis** and **Mush** (Aug. 15), but losing them again to the Russians (Aug. 24).

IN EGYPT during this period large numbers of troops were kept concentrated to meet the double threat of trouble from the Senussi tribes in the west and from the Turks advancing on the Suez Canal. (*Cont. p. 964.*)

8. THE WESTERN FRONT, 1916–1917

(*From p. 946*)

Both **Joffre** and **Falkenhayn** were still convinced, at the end of 1915, that a military decision could be reached only on the French front. Joffre planned for a great Anglo-French offensive to begin in the summer, to be supported by simultaneous Russian and Italian offensives. **Sir Douglas Haig** (who succeeded Sir John French as commander-in-chief of the British forces December 19, 1915) would have preferred to arrange for an offensive in Flanders, but Joffre insisted on operations in the Somme area, where the British and French could collaborate more easily.

Meanwhile Falkenhayn, having disposed of the threat from the east, was able to bring almost half a million men to the west front and to carry out his long-cherished plan for a crushing blow. The plan was not so much for a break-through as for mere attrition. The French were to be bled white at Verdun, a salient with poor communications and hard to hold and yet a place which for sentimental reasons if for no other would have to be fought for to the end. The French, having lost faith in forts, had taken away most of the guns about Verdun, and Joffre, intent on preparations for the Somme offensive, ignored the warnings of danger in that area.

1916, Feb. 21. THE BATTLE OF VERDUN. The **Germans** (Crown Prince William in command) concentrated 1400 guns on a short front of eight miles on the right bank of the Meuse. After a devasting bombardment they took **Fort Douaumont** (Feb. 25). French reinforcements (Gen. Pétain) were rushed to this sector, but the defense was hampered by the bottle-mouth of the salient.

Mar. 6–Apr. 10. Renewal of the attack, this time on both sides of the salient. **Gen. Robert Nivelle** replaced Gen. Pétain and the French began a series of vigorous counterattacks (May).

June 2. The **Germans** finally took **Fort Vaux**, and before the end of the month the works of **Thiaumont** (June 23). Heavy attacks continued until July 11, when the Germans went over to the defensive. The French losses have been estimated at about 350,000, the German at somewhat less.

The immediate effect of the assault on Verdun was felt in the preparation for the Somme offensive. The French were obliged to reduce their contribution from 40 divisions to 16 and their front of attack from 25 miles to 10, so that the operation was in the main a British one.

July 1–Nov. 18. THE BATTLE OF THE SOMME. After a long and intensive bombardment the British advanced on a front of 15 miles toward Bapaume, while the French objective was Péronne. Though the Germans were outnumbered at least six to one at first, the British had but little success. The heavily laden infantry was unable to move fast enough to keep up with an extraordinarily rigid time schedule. British losses on one day were 60,000, heavier than in this or any other war.

Sept. 15. First use of tanks by the British. These had been suggested long before, but the military authorities had been hostile to the idea, and even when they were finally used there were far too few (only 18 on the field) to gain the fullest advantage.

The **battle of the Somme** gradually ran out in rain and mud. The Allies had conquered about 125 square miles of territory, but nothing of prime strategic importance. The maximum advance was about seven miles. British losses were over 400,000 and French almost 200,000. The German losses were between 400,000 and 500,000.

Oct. 24–Dec. 18. The **French** (Gen. Charles Mangin) **counter-attacked at Verdun,** retaking Forts Douaumont and Vaux (Nov. 2) and making a total advance of about two miles.

The operations of 1917 were prefaced by important changes in the German and French high commands. On August 29, 1916 **Hindenburg succeeded von Falkenhayn** as chief of staff of the German field armies, with **Ludendorff** as quartermaster-general. Despite their constant advocacy of a concentration of forces on the eastern front, both Hindenburg and Ludendorff now came to share the opinion of Falkenhayn, that a decision could be reached only on the French front.

On December 12 **Nivelle succeeded Joffre** as commander-in-chief of the French armies. Nivelle had distinguished himself in the fighting at Verdun. His energy and dash made a profound impression, and it was hoped that his appointment would lead to a more fruitful campaign.

Nivelle, like his predecessor, hoped to effect a break-through and planned a great French offensive in the direction of Laon, to be introduced by a preliminary Franco-British advance on both sides of the Somme. The execution of this plan was delayed by **disagreement between Nivelle and Haig,** who himself would have preferred an offensive in Flanders and resented being put more or less under Nivelle.

In the interval **Ludendorff** had decided that the western front could be made stronger and more defensible if some of the bulges were eliminated. A strong new position was therefore constructed, which became known as the *Hindenburg Line.* After completely destroying the area between, and after mining the roads **1917, Feb. 23–Apr. 5.** The Germans abandoned **Bapaume, Péronne, Roye, Noyon, and Chauny.**

Though this move on the part of the Germans dislocated the French plans, Nivelle was still optimistic. The new **cabinet of Alexandre Ribot** (succeeded Briand, March 20) and Paul Painlevé (minister of war) brought pressure upon him to give up the plan but yielded when Nivelle threatened to resign.

Apr. 9–May 4. BATTLE OF ARRAS. The British 3rd army **(Gen. Edmund Allenby)** began the advance after a heavy gas attack (use of the gas projector). **Canadian troops took Vimy Ridge** and the British made a total advance of about four miles, without, however, effecting a break-through. On the Somme they advanced to near St. Quentin.

Apr. 16–20. SECOND BATTLE OF THE AISNE and **THIRD BATTLE OF CHAMPAGNE.** Nivelle's plans had been so well advertised that the Germans had been able to concentrate large forces in the area of attack. The French took only the **Chemin des Dames,** and this with very heavy losses. Discontent and mutiny became widespread in the weary army, till 16 corps were affected (May–June).

May 15. Nivelle was dismissed and his place taken by **Pétain,** who did what he could to redress the grievances of the troops and wisely decided to stand on the defensive until American reinforcements could make themselves felt. At the same time the government proceeded with the greatest rigor against socialist and pacifist agitators. Twenty-three leaders were executed.

The collapse of the Nivelle offensive gave **Haig** greater freedom to act. In view of the great destructiveness of the submarines, based on the Belgian coast, Haig was more determined than ever to start an **offensive in Flanders** and to roll up the German right flank. The French command was not enthusiastic about the plan, and pointed out that it could co-operate only to the extent of launching lesser attacks on the Verdun and Champagne fronts.

June 7. Battle of Messines (till June 14). The British 2nd army **(Gen. Herbert Plumer)** launched a surprise attack on **Messines Ridge,** and was entirely successful in straightening the Ypres salient.

July 31–Nov. 10. THIRD BATTLE OF YPRES. Despite the opposition of Lloyd George and the skepticism of some of his subordinates, Haig proceeded hopefully to the main offensive. The third battle of Ypres (or **Passchendaele**) was a series of eight heavy attacks, carried through in driving rain and fought over ground water-logged and muddy. No break-through was effected and the total gain was about five miles of territory, which made the Ypres salient more inconvenient than ever and cost the British about 400,000 men. The British forces were almost as demoralized by this operation as the French by the Nivelle offensive.

Aug. 20–Dec. 15. Second battle of Verdun. Intended to serve as relief for the British in Flanders. The French gained several key positions, even on the east bank of the Meuse.

Oct. 23–Nov. 1. Battle of Malmaison. The French, attacking along the Chemin des Dames, cut off a German salient northeast of **Soissons.** The Germans fell back to the Oise-Aisne Canal.

Nov. 20–Dec. 3. Battle of Cambrai. First great tank raid. Without preliminary bombardment the British launched a surprise attack with 380 tanks. They penetrated the three German lines and were on the point of breaking through into open country, but the exhausted troops were unable to take advantage of the situation. The British advanced five miles in the direction toward **Cambrai** on a six-mile front, but November 30 the Germans suddenly counter-attacked on both flanks of the salient and forced the British to give up much of the ground they had conquered. (*Cont. p. 974.*)

9. THE EASTERN FRONT, 1916–1917

(*From p. 950*)

1916, Mar. 19–Apr. 30. Battle of Lake Naroch. This inconclusive Russian offensive was intended solely to relieve the pressure of the Germans at Verdun.

June 4. The great **BRUSILOV OFFENSIVE,** initiated somewhat prematurely in order to meet the Italian appeals to distract the Austrians in the Trentino. Brusilov (appointed to the command of the Russian southern front, April 4) had planned the offensive for June 15, to coincide with Joffre's great offensive on the Somme. But the Brusilov offensive was meant to be followed by an even larger operation farther north. The objective in the south was **Kovel,** an important railway center, but the advance extended over a front of 300 miles. The Austrians, taken by surprise, fell back, leaving many prisoners in Russian hands. The **Russians took Lutsk** (June 8) and **Czernowitz** (June 18). Heavy fighting continued about Kovel, Tarnopol, and Baranovici (**battles of the Strypa,** June 11–30; **Baranovici,** July 2–9; **Kovel,** July 28–Aug. 17) until September. The Russians advanced from 25 to 125 kilometers in the region from Pinsk south to Czernowitz and took half a million prisoners, but the offensive was stopped by the arrival of 15 divisions of Germans from the west front. The Russians had failed to take either Kovel or Lemberg. Their losses were about a million men, and the whole operation left the army demoralized and discontented.

The situation in the east was dominated, in 1917, by the developments of the **Russian Revolution** (see p. 1029). The provisional government (**Paul Miliukov,** foreign minister, March 15–May 16, 1917) was strongly in favor of prosecution of the war in the hope of realizing the national aspirations. The same was true of **Alexander Kerensky** (minister of war, May 16, prime minister, July 16), who hoped to combat disruptive tendencies and galvanize the country by a new military effort.

1917, July 1. Brusilov began a **great offensive on the Galician front.**

July 18–28. Battle of East Galicia. The Germans and Austrians drove the Russians back and retook **Halicz, Tarnopol, Stanislav** (July 24–26), and **Czernowitz** (Aug. 3).

Aug. 1. Brusilov was succeeded by Gen. Lavr Kornilov.

Sept. 3–5. Battle of Riga. The Germans took Riga (Sept. 3).

Sept. 8–14. Kornilov marched on Petrograd as leader of a counter-revolutionary movement, which failed.

Oct. 11–20. The **Germans,** having overrun much of Latvia, **conquered the Baltic Islands.**

Nov. 7 (Oct. 25 O.S.). Bolshevik *coup d'état* **in Russia.**

Nov. 28. The new Bolshevik régime offered the Germans an armistice and peace.

Dec. 15. Armistice concluded on the eastern front. (*Cont. p. 971.*)

10. THE ITALIAN FRONT, 1916–1917

(*From p. 953*)

1916, Feb. 15–Mar. 17. The **fifth battle of the Isonzo,** which, like the previous engagements, led to no substantial change.

The Austrian chief of staff, **Conrad von Hötzendorff,** had for some time been urging upon the German high command the desirability of massing troops in the Trentino for an attack upon the Italian rear and flank, but **Falkenhayn** had flatly refused to contribute forces which he needed for the operations at Verdun. The Austrians decided to make the try alone. As many troops as possible were withdrawn from the Russian front and prepared for an advance on the Asiago plateau.

May 15–June 3. The Austrian offensive in the Trentino. The Italians were taken by surprise and yielded **Asiago** and **Arsiero** (May 31). But the Austrians lacked sufficient forces to break through, the more so as the Italians hastily brought up reserves from the Isonzo front. The Italian lines held and by June 17 a counter-offensive was launched. When this came to a close (July 7) most of the territory had been recovered, but the Italian losses were about 150,000 men.

Aug. 6–17. Sixth battle of the Isonzo. The Italians finally took **Gorizia** (Aug. 9).

Sept. 14–18. Seventh battle of the Isonzo.

Oct. 9–12. Eighth battle of the Isonzo.

Oct. 31–Nov. 4. Ninth battle of the Isonzo. During the first part of 1917 the Italian effort continued to center on the Isonzo.

1917, May 12–June 8. Tenth battle of the Isonzo.

Aug. 17–Sept. 12. Eleventh and last battle of the Isonzo. As a result of two years of operations the Italians had advanced only about ten miles, or halfway to Trieste.

In part the Italian failure was due to inadequate artillery and ammunition. **Gen. Luigi Cadorna** had urged Britain and France to send supplies and men in large numbers, so that a knock-out blow might be delivered against war-weary Austria. Foch and Lloyd George were favorable to this plan, but Haig had his way and proceeded to the offensive in Flanders.

Meanwhile **Ludendorff** decided to follow the annihilation of Serbia and Roumania with a similar assault on Italy. Six divisions of German troops were sent to reinforce the nine Austrian divisions on the Isonzo front. It was decided to attack on the Upper Isonzo, near Caporetto, in the hope of breaking through and advancing as far as the Tagliamento River.

Oct. 24–Dec. 26. The **CAPORETTO CAMPAIGN** (sometimes called the **twelfth battle of the Isonzo**). The German-Austrian forces attacked after a short bombardment, but in heavy fog. The Italian forces, worn down by long and inconclusive fighting, broke at once. The Austro-German advance on the first day was fully ten miles. In three days they were through the hills and almost prevented the completely demoralized enemy from crossing the Tagliamento. **The Italians fell back to the Piave.** French and British troops were rushed to Italy to help hold the front (Nov. 3, 4). The Austro-German forces, outrunning their supply system, were obliged to slow down. The line became fixed on the Piave River, after the Italians had lost almost 300,000 men taken prisoner and even more than that in deserters.

Nov. 7. **Cadorna was replaced by Gen. Armando Diaz,** who devoted himself to establishing a defensive position and above all to restoring the morale of the troops.

(*Cont. p. 973.*)

11. THE BALKAN FRONT, 1916–1917

(*From p. 955*)

Throughout the summer and autumn of 1916 the **Greek situation** continued to be most unsatisfactory from the Entente viewpoint.

1916, May 26. A **Bulgarian-German** force occupied **Fort Rupel** in Greek Macedonia, this action enhancing the suspicion that King Constantine was secretly bound to the Central Powers.

June 6–22. The **"pacific blockade"** of **Greece** by the Entente Powers. France and Britain sent Greece an ultimatum (June 21) demanding demobilization of the Greek army and the institution of responsible government. The Greek government yielded. The **Skouloudis ministry resigned** and a Zaimis cabinet was organized. The army was put on a peace footing (June 27) and new elections were arranged for.

July 25. The reconstituted Serbian army, which had been shipped from Corfu to Saloniki, came into action on that front. Russian troops from France and an Italian contingent also arrived (July 30, Aug. 11).

Aug. 2–21. Battle of Doiran. The Allies began to advance against the Bulgarians on the Saloniki front.

Aug. 17–19. Battle of Florina. The Bulgars and Germans counter-attacked and pushed back the Saloniki forces. They took **Seres** (Aug. 19), **Drama,** and **Kavalla** (Sept. 18), where the fourth Greek army corps voluntarily surrendered.

Aug. 30. A Venizelist, pro-Ally movement, fostered by Gen. Sarrail, took place at Saloniki.

Sept. 29. **Venizelos** and Adm. Paul Condouriotis **established a provisional government** in Crete. Venizelos then (Oct. 9) went to Saloniki, where the **provisional government declared war on Germany and Bulgaria** (Nov. 23).

Oct. 10. The **Entente Powers,** incensed by the surrender of the Greek forces at Kavalla, **submitted an ultimatum** to Athens demanding the surrender of the Greek fleet. The Athens government (**Lambros ministry,** Oct. 10–May 3, 1917) yielded (Oct. 11), whereupon the Entente Powers demanded (Nov. 19) the dismissal of the representatives of the Central Powers at Athens and the surrender of war matériel. These demands were rejected (Nov. 30) and in consequence **French and British** landing parties **debarked at Piraeus.** They withdrew again December 1 after conflicts with the Greeks.

Dec. 8. Blockade of Greece. The Allies demanded (Dec. 14) the complete withdrawal of Greek forces from Thessaly. The Athens government once more gave in (Dec. 15), but December 19 the British government decided to recognize the provisional government of Venizelos.

Oct. 5–Dec. 11. The Allied forces under Sarrail began a great offensive in Macedonia **(first battle of Monastir).** Monastir (Bitolje) was taken (Nov. 19) and the Allies pushed forward as far as Lake Okhrid. On the Bulgarian frontier no advance was made.

The Macedonian front was quiet during the winter of 1916–1917.

NORWAY

SWEDEN

FINLAND

Baltic Sea

ESTONIA

LATVIA

LITHUANIA

SOVIET

UNION

North Sea

GREAT BRITAIN

DENMARK

NORTH-SCHLESWIG

MEMEL

Danzig

EAST PRUSSIA

'CORRIDOR'

POLAND

NETHERLANDS

GERMANY

BELGIUM

LUXEMBURG

EUPEN-MALMÉDY

SAAR

UPPER SILESIA

GALICIA

BESSARABIA

ALSACE-LORRAINE

CZECHOSLOVAKIA

SWITZER-LAND

AUSTRIA

HUNGARY

TRANSYLVANIA

ROUMANIA

FRANCE

SOUTH TYROL

ISTRIA

YUGOSLAVIA

BULGARIA

Black Sea

SPAIN

ITALY

ALBANIA

GREECE

TURKEY

Mediterranean

Sea

TERRITORIAL CHANGES
following WORLD WAR I

Territory lost

by Germany   by Russia

by Bulgaria   by Austria-Hungary

1917, Mar. 11–19. Second battle of Monastir and battle of Lake Presba.

May 5–19. Battle of the Vardar (or Doiran). These engagements were inconclusive, but served to convince the Allied powers that success on this front hinged on the Athens government.

June 11–12. The newly arrived French envoy **(Charles Jonnart)** presented an Allied ultimatum, demanding the abdication of King Constantine and the renunciation of the claims of the Greek crown prince. At the same time Allied troops invaded Thessaly and a French force occupied the Isthmus of Corinth.

June 12. Constantine abdicated in favor of his second son, Alexander.

June 26. Venizelos became premier, replacing Zaimis.

June 27. The **Greek government** severed relations with the Central Powers and **entered the war on the Allied side.**

ROUMANIA

Since the spring of 1916 the Russian government had been redoubling its efforts to bring Roumania into the war. The success of the Brusilov offensive and the readiness of the Russian government and its allies to recognize the Roumanian claims to the Bukovina and Banat as well as to Transylvania resulted in the conclusion of a political and military agreement (Aug. 18).

1916, Aug. 27. ROUMANIA DECLARED WAR ON AUSTRIA-HUNGARY. Germany declared war on Roumania, and Italy finally declared war on Germany (Aug. 28). Turkey and Bulgaria declared war on Roumania a few

days later (Aug. 30, Sept. 1 respectively).

Aug. 28. The Roumanians began the **invasion of Transylvania** and took **Kronstadt** (Brasov) and **Hermannstadt** (Sibiu).

Sept. 27–29. The **Austro-German forces,** hastily assembled in Transylvania and commanded by Falkenhayn, counter-attacked and surrounded the Roumanians at Hermannstadt **(battle of Sibiu).**

Sept. 26–Nov. 23. Operations of a Bulgarian-German force under Gen. August von Mackensen, in the **Dobrudja. Silistria** was taken (Sept. 10), then **Constantza** (Oct. 22) and **Cernavoda** (Oct. 25).

Oct. 7–9. Battle of Kronstadt (Brasov). The Austro-German forces retook the city and advanced to the Carpathian passes.

Nov. 10–14. Falkenhayn forced the Vulcan Pass into Roumania and began the invasion of Wallachia.

Nov. 23. Mackensen's troops crossed the Danube at Sistova and advanced toward Bucharest, as did Falkenhayn coming from Craiova.

Dec. 1–5. The Roumanians tried to counterattack on the Arges River, but were completely defeated **(battle of Argesul).** The Roumanian government was hastily moved to Jassy, and the capital, **Bucharest, fell into the hands of the enemy** (Dec. 6).

1917, Jan. The Austro-German forces continued the advance both in the Dobrudja and in Moldavia. **Braila** was taken (Jan. 5) and **Focsani** (Jan. 8). By the middle of January the Roumanians had reached the Sereth River, where the campaign came to a stop. Most of Roumania, with important wheat- and oil-producing areas, was in the hands of the Central Powers. *(Cont. p. 1026.)*

12. CAMPAIGNS IN ASIATIC TURKEY, 1916–1917

(From p. 958)

1916, Apr. 26. Anglo-Russian-French agreement with regard to the future partition of Asiatic Turkey. This agreement had been maturing ever since March 1915, when France and Britain promised Russia Constantinople and the Straits. It provided that in the independent Arab state that was to be formed, **Britain** should have as a sphere of influence Mesopotamia and in Syria the ports of Haifa and Acre. The **French sphere** was to include the coastal strip of Syria, the Adana vilayet, Cilicia and southern Kurdistan, with Kharput. **Palestine** was to be under an international administration. **Russia** was to receive Armenia and part of Kurdistan and northern

Anatolia westward from Trebizond to a point to be determined later.

May 9. The **SYKES-PICOT AGREEMENT** between Britain and France. This made the French and British claims more specific. The territories mentioned in the above agreement were to be the French and British administrative zones, while the rest of Arabia was to be divided into French and British spheres of influence, though organized as an Arab state or federation of states.

1917, Apr. 19–21. The St. Jean de Maurienne agreement. In return for recognition of the Sykes-Picot agreement, Italy was given further concessions in the regions of Adalia and Smyrna.

These agreements were not entirely compatible with other agreements made with Arab chieftains, agreements which, indeed, were not compatible with each other.

a. ARABIA

1914, Oct. 31. Lord Kitchener had offered **Hussein,** the grand sherif of Mecca, a conditional guaranty of independence. Negotiations between the sherif and the British government were embarked upon in July 1915.

1915, July 14. Hussein submitted his terms for entering upon a campaign against the Turks. Britain was to recognize the independence of the Arab countries south of 37° N. L.

Oct. 24. The **British reply** took exception to the Arab claims to the Mersina-Alexandretta region and to Syria west of Damascus, Hama, Homs, and Aleppo. For the rest the boundaries of the future Arab state were accepted with respect to "those portions of the territories therein in which Great Britain is free to act without detriment to her ally, France."

Nov. 5. Hussein accepted the British proposals with regard to Mersina and Alexandretta, but held out for Beirut and Aleppo, as well as Baghdad and Basra.

Dec. 21. The **French government accepted** the idea of Arab administration of western Syria, but only under French influence.

1916, Jan. 30. The **British accepted Hussein's terms,** leaving the exact status of Baghdad and Basra, and of the sphere of French influence in Syria, undetermined.

b. NEJD

1915, Dec. 25. The **government of India,** after long negotiations with **Ibn Saud,** king of Nejd, concluded an agreement with him (ratified July 18, 1916) by which it recognized Nejd, Qatif, Jubail, and territories along the Persian Gulf coast of Arabia as the independent possessions of Ibn Saud, despite the obvious contradiction between these concessions and those offered to Hussein.

c. THE ARAB REVOLT

1916, June 5. Beginning of the **Arab revolt in the Hijaz.** Attack on the Turkish garrison at Medina.

June 7. Hussein proclaimed the **independence of the Hijaz.** The garrison of Mecca surrendered (June 10).

Oct. 29. Hussein proclaimed king of the Arabs. He summoned all Arabs to make war on the Turks.

Dec. 15. The **British government recognized Hussein** as king of the Hijaz.

It was largely in order to strengthen the Arab insurrection that **Sir Archibald Murray** (commander in Egypt, since March 19, 1916) decided on a cautious offensive in Sinai and Palestine.

Dec. 21. The **British took El Arish,** after building a railway and pipeline across the desert. They then took the fortified posts of **Magdhaba** (Dec. 23) and **Rafah** (Jan. 9, 1917).

1917, Mar. 26-27. First battle of Gaza. The cavalry had surrounded the town, but through a misunderstanding was recalled.

Apr. 17-19. Second battle of Gaza. The Turks, in the interval, had strengthened their position and had been reinforced by German troops (*Asienkorps,* under Falkenhayn). The British were forced back with heavy losses.

June 28. Murray was replaced by **Sir Edmund Allenby.**

July 6. Emergence of the spectacular war hero, **Col. Thomas E. Lawrence,** who galvanized the Arab movement and took **Aqaba,** thus beginning the brilliant thrusts against the Turkish garrisons and especially against the guards of the Hijaz railway, the most important link in the Turkish communications.

d. MESOPOTAMIA

Operations on the Mesopotamian front were also resumed in the autumn of 1916, with **Sir Stanley Maude** in command. After troops and supplies had been collected in large numbers **1916, Dec. 13.** The **advance** was begun **toward Kut-el-Amara.**

1917, Jan. 9-Feb. 24. Battle of Kut. The city was taken February 23. The victorious British then pursued the Turks toward Baghdad.

Mar. 11. BAGHDAD OCCUPIED BY THE BRITISH.

The British campaign in Mesopotamia was accompanied by a new **Russian advance in western Persia.**

1917, Mar. 2. The **Russians took Hamadan,** then **Kirmanshah** (Mar. 12), **Karind** (Mar. 17), and **Khanikin** (Apr. 4).

Apr. 23. The **British reached Samarra,** 80 miles north of Baghdad.

July 8. The **Russians began to retreat** from western Persia: one of the effects of the Russian Revolution.

Sept. 29. The **British captured Ramadi** on the Euphrates, and then (Nov. 6) **Tikrit** on the Tigris, the farthest extent of the advance in Mesopotamia in 1917.

e. PERSIA (IRAN)

The war sealed the fate of the old régime in Iran (Persia until 1935). The government

1914, Nov. 1. Proclaimed neutrality, but was far too weak to enforce it. The only troops available were the Cossack Brigade, under Russian officers, and the gendarmerie (since 1911) under Swedish officers who tended to sympathize with the Germans. Russian forces were still in occupation of important towns in the north, while the British established themselves on the Gulf coast.

1915, Jan. 7. The **Turks,** campaigning against the Russians in the Caucasus, **took Tabriz,** which, however, was soon retaken by the Russians (Jan. 30). Persian territory was freely violated by both sides. At the same time the British, to strengthen their Russian allies, granted them a free hand in their zone under the 1907 agreement, while the neutral zone was added to the British sphere.

Jan. Arrival in Persia of Wassmuss, former German consul at Bushire. Wassmuss organized a number of tribes around Bushire and harassed the British, who were in occupation of the town. At the same time other German agents **(Niedermayer, Zugmayer)** established themselves in other towns of the interior, with the purpose of opening a route to Afghanistan and preparing a Turkish-German advance on India. One mission reached Afghanistan, but the amir evaded any commitment. For a time, however, the German influence was predominant.

Nov. The **Russians invaded northern Persia** to break the German influence at Tehran.

1916. The **Turks,** having defeated the British in Mesopotamia, **twice invaded Persia,** but were stopped by the Russians.

Mar. Sir Percy Sykes arrived at Bunder Abbas and began the organization of the **South Persia Rifles,** with which it was hoped that southern Persia could be protected from German influence and Turkish invasion. He marched to Kerman (May), Yezd (Aug.), Isfahan (where the Russians were already in occupation), and Shiraz (Nov.). His force ultimately numbered some 11,000 men, with which the British position was reinforced as against the Persian gendarmerie and the fractious tribesmen.

1917. Mar. The **Turks,** defeated at Baghdad, **fell back from Persia.**

Nov. The **Russians,** following the Bolshevik Revolution, also **began to withdraw** from the country. By this time the country was in a state of complete anarchy.

1918, Jan. Arrival of Gen. Lionel Dunsterville and a small British force, the object of which was to stiffen the Georgians and Armenians against the Turks and establish a Caucasus front against possible German advance from the Ukraine. Dunsterville reached Enzeli from Baghdad, but, under threat from the Bolsheviks at Baku, was obliged to fall back on Hamadan. His force was gradually increased, and another, under **Gen. Sir Wilfrid Malleson,** was sent to northeastern Persia to block a possible Bolshevik attempt on India from that direction.

(*Cont. p. 1097*)

13. THE WAR AT SEA, 1916–1917

(*From p. 951*)

The second half of 1915 and the first half of 1916 were not marked by any striking events of naval warfare. The Germans continued their efforts to reduce British preponderance by submarine and mine destruction, and at the same time extended their operations against merchant shipping.

1916, Feb. 21. The German government notified the United States government that thenceforth armed merchantmen would be treated as cruisers. The "extended" submarine campaign began March 1.

Mar. 24. The *Sussex* sunk by torpedo in the English Channel with the loss of American lives. Acrimonious debate between Washington and Berlin, culminating in an American ultimatum. The Germans agreed to give up unrestricted submarine warfare for the time being (May 10).

Meanwhile (Jan. 1916) **Adm. Reinhardt Scheer** had succeeded Adm. Hugo von Pohl in the command of the German High Seas Fleet. The famous minister of marine, **Adm. von Tirpitz, resigned** (Mar. 14) in protest against the emperor's unwillingness to make full use of German sea-power. He was succeeded by **Adm. Eduard von Capelle.**

Apr. 24–25. A German squadron raided and bombarded **Yarmouth** and **Lowestoft.** Submarines appeared off the Scottish naval bases.

May 31–June 1. BATTLE OF JUTLAND (SKAGERRAK). May 30 **Adm. Franz von Hipper** with the German battle-cruiser squadron had been sent to show himself off the Norwegian coast. May 31 he came into contact with **Adm. Sir David Beatty** and the British battle-cruisers, running southeast before the Grand Fleet. Though decidedly outnumbered, Hipper and the Germans, through superior marksmanship, sank two of Beatty's ships. Beatty, sighting the German High Seas Fleet (Scheer) in battle order, turned north to join Jellicoe and the Grand Fleet. The German fleet, having been sucked in, met the Grand Fleet just before 6 P.M. **Jellicoe** tried to deploy across Scheer's line of retreat, but **Scheer** turned about suddenly and made away to the south and then to the east, coming up on the flank of the British, in pursuit. Scheer turned again, launching a torpedo attack, which obliged Jellicoe to fall back. Scheer then sent Hipper and the battle-cruisers to attack while the High Seas Fleet effected its escape. Night fell, leaving the two fleets steaming southwest about six miles apart. But at 9 P.M. Scheer turned east and made for Horns Reef, forcing his way through the tail end of Jellicoe's forces, still steaming south. The German fleet reached Horns Reef in safety at 3:30 in the night. Each fleet lost six ships in the Jutland engagement, but the British ships lost totaled almost twice the tonnage of the Germans. Scheer had to yield to the superiority of the British in capital ships, but in battle-cruiser warfare the Germans were completely victorious. They showed themselves brilliant in maneuver and marksmanship.

Aug. 19, Oct. 26-27. German raids on the English coast. At the same time German light cruisers slipped through the blockade and ravaged commerce in the Atlantic. The German commercial submarine *Deutschland* made a trip to America and back (July 10, 1916, at Norfolk, Virginia).

The German high command reckoned confidently on winning the war through the destruction of the British food-supply. The prospects were indeed, excellent. Already in the last months of 1916 German submarines had destroyed 300,000 tons of shipping a month. By the beginning of 1917 the Germans had about 120 submarines, the number being increased to 134 by October 1917.

1917, Apr. Submarine warfare reached the high point. In this month alone 875,000 tons of shipping were destroyed, more than half of it British. This figure exceeded the German estimates (600,000) and brought the British admiralty to the point of despair. Finally, owing largely to the insistence of Lloyd George, the admiralty agreed to try **convoying** merchant ships (first convoy, May 10). The system proved to be an unqualified success. At the same time the British increased the numbers of their destroyers and submarine chasers, developed the depth bomb and the system of scouting with hydroplanes. Ship-building was pushed to the very limit.

By October 1917 the Germans had destroyed about 8,000,000 tons of shipping, but they had lost 50 submarines and their campaign was becoming less and less effective. By the beginning of 1918 the Allies were building more new tonnage than was being destroyed. The German gamble on the submarine had failed.

Naval operations during the years 1917–1918 were confined largely to submarine and destroyer activities. The **Germans** repeatedly **raided the English coast** (Apr. 20, 26, 1917; Jan. 14, Feb. 15, 1918) and **attacked British convoys** in the North Sea (Oct. 17, Dec. 12, 1917). But there were no larger engagements, excepting for a British **light cruiser attack off Heligoland,** which was beaten back (Nov. 17, 1917).

In order to meet the constant menace from the submarine, Adm. Sir Roger Keyes of the Dover Patrol had long urged an operation against the submarine bases, Zeebrugge and Ostend, on the Belgian coast.

1918, Apr. 23. Attack on the mole at Zeebrugge while three old cruisers were run in and sunk in the canal entrance. A similar operation at Ostend was unsuccessful, and even at Zeebrugge the blocking was not complete.

Oct. 17–20. The British, in their advance, took Zeebrugge, Ostend, and the other Channel ports.

14. THE WAR IN THE AIR, 1914-1918

Although only France had done much before the war to develop the military use of the airplane, throughout the war the British and the Germans were the main antagonists.

1914, Aug. 30. The first German airplane raid on Paris.

Sept. 22, Oct. 8, Nov. 21. British airplanes raided the German flying-fields at **Düsseldorf, Köln,** and **Friedrichshafen.**

Dec. 21. The first German air raid on England (Dover).

On the western front, and on other fronts to a less extent, the airplane was used for reconnaissance, but almost immediately (Sept. 1914) experiments were made by the British in wireless communication between airplanes and artillery, in aerial photography, and in bomb-dropping. There was not much aerial combat until the middle of 1915.

1915, Oct. The Germans began the use of the **Fokker** plane, equipped with a device allowing the pilot to shoot through the propeller. This plane was so superior that, for the better part of a year, it gave the Germans **mastery of the air,** though the British, with a greater number of planes, kept carrying the fight over the German lines. Great German fighters of this period were **Oswald Boelcke** (d. Oct. 28, 1916) and **Max Immelmann** (d. June 1916).

1916, April. Battle of Verdun, including heavy air fighting between Germans and French. The French, with the **Nieuport 3** and the **Spad 3,** succeeded in securing mastery of the air. Great French fighters were **René Fonck** and **George Guynemer** (d. Sept. 1917).

July. Battle of the Somme. The British, with the new **De Havilland** and **Farman Experimental** planes, definitely put an **end to German Fokker supremacy.** Great British fighters: **Albert Ball** (d. May 7, 1917), **J. T. B. McCudden** (d. July 1918), **W. A. Bishop,** and **Edward Mannock** (d. July 1918).

Sept. The Germans introduced the **Albatross and Halberstadt planes** and developed formation flying. This re-established something like a balance on the British front, though the British had a distinct superiority in numbers and continued to take the offensive.

1917. The British began to use the **Scouting Experimental** and **Bristol Fighter.** This period was marked by the spectacular achievements of **Manfred von Richthofen** (d. Apr. 21, 1918) and by the development of ever larger formations and more intricate tactics.

1918. The Allied superiority became more marked, and American air squadrons began to take part (Apr.). The British did much in the development of large-scale bombardment, especially of munitions centers. At sea much use was made of the airplane for scouting and submarine-chasing.

During these years the Germans continued their raids on England, first with **Zeppelins,** then with airplanes, with the object of drawing back British air forces from France, of interrupting industry, and of demoralizing the civil population.

1915, Jan. 19. First German airship raid on England.

Oct. 13. The worst of the **Zeppelin raids** on eastern England and London. There were 19 such raids in 1915 and 41 in 1916. On September 2, 1916, London was raided by 14 Zeppelins at once. But by the end of 1916 the British had elaborated a fairly good defense against airships (fighting planes, anti-aircraft guns, searchlights, sirens, etc.). The Germans used 80 Zeppelins in the course of the war, of which only seven remained at the time of the armistice.

1916, Nov. 28. First German airplane raid on London. There were a great many of these in the course of 1917–1918, first by daylight, then by night. There was a considerable loss of life and property, but the raids do not appear to have achieved any marked results.

15. THE WAR IN THE COLONIES, 1914–1918

Most of the German colonies were seized by the British and French during the first months of the war.

1914, Aug. 26. Togoland defense force capitulated to an Anglo-French force. The colony was divided between the British and the French in agreements of August 26, 1914, and December 27, 1916.

Aug. 30. A New Zealand expeditionary force occupied **Samoa.**

Sept. 11. An Australian force landed on the **Bismarck Archipelago.** German forces in **New Guinea** surrendered to Australians (Sept. 21).

Sept. 7. A British force from Nigeria invaded the **Cameroons** and took **Duala** (Sept. 27). The French invaded the colony from the south and east. The Germans were obliged to fall back, and ultimately crossed into Spanish territory (Feb. 9, 1916).

Sept. 19. A British force landed at **Lüderitz Bay,** German Southwest Africa. The Union of South Africa decided to prosecute

the war in the German colony, and **Gen. Louis Botha** crossed the Orange River, taking **Swakopmund** (Jan. 14, 1915). He defeated the German forces at **Riet** and **Treckkopje** (Apr. 26, 1915), took **Windhoek** (May 12, 1915), and finally forced the 3500 German and colonial troops to capitulate at **Otawi** (July 9, 1915).

1914, Aug. 8. The British opened hostilities in German East Africa by bombarding the coast towns of **Bagamoyo** and **Dar-es-Salaam.** Indian forces were then brought to East Africa for the campaign. But the German commander **(Gen. Paul von Lettow-Vorbeck)** defeated a greatly superior landing force in the **battle of Tanga** (Nov. 2–5, 1914). The campaign remained desultory until in November 1915 the British secured naval control of **Lake Tanganyika,** and landing forces took **Tanga** (July 7, 1916) and **Bagamoyo** (Aug. 15, 1916). **Gen. Jan Smuts,** with a force of Afrikanders and Portuguese, now began to push the operations. **Dar-es-Salaam** fell (Sept. 4); **Lindi** (Sept. 16) and **Tabora** (Sept. 19). Lettow-

Vorbeck and his troops were obliged to fall back to the southeast corner of the colony. The campaign was resumed in 1917, when the Germans defeated their enemies at **Mahiwa** Oct. 15–18, 1917) and began the invasion of Portuguese East Africa. Lettow-Vorbeck advanced almost to the mouth of the Zambezi, but then fell back to **Lake Nyasa.** On November 2, 1918, he began the invasion of **Rhodesia.** The armistice went into effect November 14, 1918, at which time the Germans were still in the field.

1914, Aug. 23. Japan declared war on Germany and began to land forces in Shantung for an attack on the German position at **Tsingtao.** The Japanese were joined by a British detachment. The bombardment of **Tsingtao** was begun in October, and was accompanied by an attack from the land side. On November 7 the fortress was obliged to capitulate. During this same period the Japanese naval forces occupied a number of the German islands **(Marshall Islands, Marianas, Palau, Carolines).**

16. PEACE NEGOTIATIONS, 1916–1917, AND THE INTERVENTION OF THE UNITED STATES, 1917

From the very outbreak of the war, **President Wilson** appears to have felt that ultimately the opportunity would present itself for the United States government to step in as mediator. The president himself regarded the work of peacemaking as his great mission, and was prepared to act at once when the moment was opportune. **1916, Jan.-Feb.** The president's close friend and intimate adviser, **Col. Edward M. House,** visited Europe and consulted with leading statesmen. His conferences with Sir Edward Grey resulted in the so-called **House memorandum** of February 22, which stated that the president was ready, whenever Britain and France thought the time opportune, to propose a peace conference. If the proposal was accepted by the Allies but rejected by Germany, the United States would *probably* enter the war on the Allied side. The terms on which the United States would mediate would include the restoration of Belgium and Serbia, the retrocession of Alsace-Lorraine to France, the acquisition of Constantinople by Russia, and the transfer of the Italian-speaking parts of Austria to Italy. Poland was to be independent. Germany would retain some colonies and perhaps be given more. The offer illuminates the sympathies of Wilson, House, Page, and other American statesmen.

Public opinion in the United States was still distinctly divided, but sentiment for peace was prevalent, excepting in the eastern states where there was some feeling for intervention on the Allied side (influence of British propaganda, etc.). The president was re-elected (Nov. 7, 1916) very largely on a platform of peace, but he applied himself almost at once to the resumption of his mediatory efforts.

Dec. 12. The **German government** appealed to the United States to inform the Entente governments that the Central Powers were **prepared to negotiate peace.** This offer appears to have been designed to anticipate any move by Wilson and may have been intended to divide the Allies or prepare the way for the introduction of unrestricted submarine warfare. In any event, the military situation, after the wiping-out of Roumania, could hardly have been more favorable, a fact which was not overlooked in the drafting of the German note. Failure of the Germans to mention any specific terms, and the fact that all the advantages were on their side, made it relatively easy for the Allied governments to reject the German advances (Dec. 30).

Dec. 18. President Wilson transmitted his own proposals to the warring powers. He suggested that the belligerents state their terms for peace and for arrangements to guarantee the world against renewal of conflict. The German, Austrian, and Turkish governments replied (Dec. 26) in an appreciative way, but reiterated their opinion that the best method would be to call a meeting for exchange of views. No definite terms were mentioned. The Allied powers in their reply (Jan. 10, 1917) named specific terms. These included the restoration of Belgium, Serbia, and Montenegro; the evacuation of French, Russian, and Roumanian territory, with just reparation; the reorganization of Europe on the basis of nationalities; the restoration of territory previously taken from the Allies; the liberation of Italians, Slavs, Roumanians, and Czechoslovaks from foreign rule; the freeing of subject nationalities under Turkish rule, and the expulsion of the Turks from Europe.

The far-reaching nature of the Allied terms, at a moment when the military situation was by no means in their favor, estranged even Wilson, who still stuck by the idea of **"peace without victory"** (speech to the senate, January 22). The first step, however, was to elicit from the Germans a concrete statement of aims. These were confidentially communicated to the president on January 29: restitution of the part of Alsace occupied by the German forces; acquisition of a strategical and economic zone between Germany and Poland on the one hand and Russia on the other; return of colonies and the granting to Germany of colonial territory in accord with her population and economic needs; restoration of occupied France; renunciation of economic obstacles to normal commerce; compensation for German enterprises and civilians damaged by the war; freedom of the seas, etc.

Though this program was anything but hopeful, the president and the German ambassador, **Count Johann von Bernstorff,** continued to negotiate. It was felt that the Allies were rapidly coming to the point where they would be unable to continue the war without American aid and that, when that time came, they would have to accept American mediation and a compromise peace without victory. But these discussions were cut short by the decision of the Germans to begin unrestricted submarine warfare.

1917, Jan. 8. A **meeting** of the highest military and civil officials of Germany, **at Pless,** finally concluded that the unrestricted use of the submarine was the only method by which Britain could be brought to its kness. It was calculated that shipping could be sunk at the rate of 600,000 tons a month and that in six months Britain would have to yield. It was understood that the decision would probably mean war with the United States, but it was felt that the conflict would be over before the full weight of America could be thrown in. The chancellor, Bethmann-Hollweg, and men like Helfferich were not convinced of the soundness of the policy, but offered no other solution. To counterbalance the hostility of the United States, the foreign minister, Arthur von Zimmermann, sent instructions to the German minister in Mexico to work for an **alliance with Mexico and Japan** directed against the United States (Jan. 19).

Jan. 31. The United States were notified that **unrestricted submarine war** would begin on February 1.

Feb. 3. The **United States government severed relations** with the German government. In response to an appeal from Wilson, Brazil, Bolivia, Peru, and other Latin-American states followed suit. So did China (Mar. 14).

The president had decided not to declare war until the Germans had committed an overt act. Several American ships were in fact sunk during February and March. At the same time the British secret service intercepted and deciphered the **Zimmermann note,** revealing German plans against the United States.

Apr. 6. The **UNITED STATES DECLARED WAR ON GERMANY,** following the president's war message to the senate (April 2). War was not declared on Austria-Hungary until December 7, 1917.

1917, Feb.–June. Secret negotiations between **the Emperor Charles** of Austria and his foreign minister, Count Ottokar Czernin, **and the French and British governments.** The emperor seems to have been determined, from the time of his accession (Nov. 1916), to make peace, even without Germany. The negotiations were carried on through his brother-in-law, **Prince Sixtus of Bourbon,** who was serving in the Belgian army. After several secret meetings in Switzerland, Prince Sixtus went to Vienna, with the full knowledge and approval of the French foreign office, and had a conference with the emperor and Czernin. He returned to Paris with a letter from Charles (dated March 24) in which the writer promised to use his influence with his allies to support "the just French claims relative to **Alsace-Lorraine.**" Belgium was to be restored, with compensation for her losses; so also Serbia, which was to have access to the Adriatic. The emperor was also not opposed to Russia's acquisition of Constantinople.

This offer was well received by **Poincaré** and **Briand** and also by **Lloyd George.** The one flaw was the failure to offer adequate gains to Italy. In the ensuing negotiations, which continued till June (second visit of Prince Sixtus to Vienna, May 6–8), it became clear that the Austrians were willing to turn over the **Trentino** to Italy, but not **Trieste,** and that the Italians (statement of Sonnino at the **St. Jean de Maurienne conference,** April 19–21) were unwilling to accept anything short of the full terms of the treaty of London (see p. 953). Efforts continued to be made by Poincaré and Lloyd George, but the French prime minister, **Alexandre Ribot** (succeeded Briand, March 20), took a hopeless attitude and indeed the Italians made no move in the direction of concessions.

Aug. 1. Outline **proposals for peace** submitted to the warring parties by the pope. These included disarmament, arbitration, freedom of the seas, renunciation of indemnities, evacuation and restoration of occupied territories, examination of conflicting territorial gains. Prolonged negotiations proved futile.

17. THE SETTLEMENTS IN EASTERN EUROPE, 1917–1918

(From p. 961)

While discussion of peace between the western powers led to an impasse, the winter of 1917–1918 produced a settlement in the east.

1916, Nov. 5. The **Germans,** in occupation of Poland, announced the formation of an **independent Polish state.** The object of this move, inspired by the military men, was to win over the Poles and induce them to enlist on the German side. This hope was sadly disappointed.

1917, Mar. 30. The Russian provisional government recognized the independence of Poland.

Apr. 5. The British government adhered to the principle of an independent and united Poland.

Sept. 12. The Central Powers granted a constitution to what was formerly Russian Poland, and appointed a regency council (Oct. 15).

Nov. 7. The **Bolshevik Revolution in Russia** (see p. 1030). **Lenin** and his followers, who regarded the war as a capitalist and imperialist venture, were in favor of a peace without annexations or indemnities, and were determined to make peace, which the Russian people yearned for. The old Russian Empire, indeed, was already dissolving.

Nov. 20. The Ukrainians proclaimed the **Ukrainian People's Republic.**

Nov. 21. The Bolshevik government, having invited all belligerents (Nov. 8) to make peace on the basis of no annexations and no indemnities, and having elicited no reply, opened separate discussions with the Central Powers.

Nov. 28. The local diet proclaimed the **independence of Estonia.**

Dec. 3. Opening of peace conference at Brest-Litovsk. Germany (Kühlmann), Austria (Czernin), and their allies negotiated an armistice with Russia (represented by **Leon Trotsky**).

Dec. 6. Finland proclaimed its independence.

Dec. 23. Proclamation of the Moldavian (i.e. Bessarabian) **Republic.**

Dec. 25. The Central Powers accepted the principle of no annexations and no indemnities on condition that the Allied powers accept it within ten days. Trotsky's appeals brought no response and there was nothing to moderate the German demands (these were laid down by the German general staff, and were regarded as too extreme by Kühlmann).

1918, Jan. 4. Beginning of the peace discussions at Brest, after a suspension of ten days. Trotsky refused to recognize the new Baltic states without a plebiscite, and much acrimonious discussion ensued.

Jan. 12. Latvia declared its independence.

Feb. 1. The Central Powers recognized the independence of the Ukraine.

Feb. 9. TREATY OF PEACE between the Central Powers and the Ukraine signed at Brest-Litovsk.

Feb. 10. Trotsky declared the war ended, without peace having been made.

Feb. 18. The Germans at once resumed hostilities. They took **Dvinsk** (Feb. 18), **Dorpat** (Feb. 24), **Reval** (Feb. 25), **Pskov** (Feb. 25), and **Narva** (Mar. 4), advancing to within 100 miles of Petrograd.

Feb. 28. The Russians, at the insistence of Lenin, renewed negotiations at Brest.

Mar. 2. At the request of the Finnish government the **Germans occupied the Aaland Islands.**

Mar. 3. The **Russians signed the TREATY OF BREST-LITOVSK,** abandoning Poland, Lithuania, the Ukraine, the Baltic provinces, Finland, and Transcaucasia.

Mar. 3. In order to clear the Bolsheviks out of the Ukraine the Germans and Austrians sent an expeditionary force. They occupied **Kiev** (Mar. 3), **Odessa** (Mar. 13), **Nicolaiev** (Mar. 17), **Kharkov** (Apr. 8), and then invaded the Crimea, taking **Sevastopol** (May 1). The Ukraine henceforth became an important granary for the Central Powers, though the returns were never as great as anticipated. Under German direction **Gen. Paul Skoropadski was proclaimed hetman of the Ukraine** (Apr. 29).

Apr. 3. German forces landed in Finland itself. They took **Helsingfors** (Apr. 13) and **Viborg** (Apr. 30). After a five-day battle the **Whites,** supported by the Germans, **defeated** the **Reds** and the Finnish civil war came to an end (May 7).

June 4. The Lithuanian assembly elected Duke William of Württemberg king.

Oct. 8. The Finnish assembly proclaimed Prince Frederick Charles of Hesse king. German troops remained in Finland until December 16, 1918.

ROUMANIA was likewise obliged to make peace in the winter of 1918.

1917, Aug. 6–Sept. 3. Battle of Putna. After

the failure of the Brusilov offensive (see p. 961) the Germans and Austrians began the **invasion of northern Moldavia.** Though it had been reorganized by the French general **Henri Berthelot,** the Roumanian army was forced to fall back.

Dec. 6.   Truce of Focsani. Hostilities between the Central Powers and Roumania ceased.

1918, Feb. 6. A German ultimatum demanded the opening of peace negotiations at once. **Bratianu resigned** and was succeeded by

Alexander Averescu as premier and foreign minister.

May 7.   TREATY OF BUCHAREST. Roumania was obliged to cede **Dobrudja** to Bulgaria and to turn over the Carpathian passes to Austria-Hungary. The Germans took a 90-year lease of the Roumanian oil-wells.

Apr. 9. The **Moldavian Republic** (Bessarabia) proclaimed its union with Roumania. The Russian government protested against this (Apr. 23), but the union was recognized by the Central Powers in the treaty of Bucharest. (*Cont. p. 979.*)

18. THE COLLAPSE OF BULGARIA AND TURKEY

(*From p. 964*)

The Bulgarian front was the first to break down. Under **Gen. Louis Guillaumat** (succeeded Sarrail December 22, 1917) the forces at Saloniki had been reorganized and greatly strengthened. Guillaumat did much to convince the British and French authorities of the desirability of a great attack in the Balkans. There were then 29 divisions (over 700,000 men) available at Saloniki, with **Gen. Franchet d'Esperey** in command.

1918, Sept. 15–24.   Battles of Dobropolje or **Monastir-Doiran.** The Allies (Italians on the left, Serbs in the center, French, British, and Greeks on the right) began a great offensive all the way from Albania to the Struma River. The Serbs advanced almost forty miles in a week and threatened to drive a wedge into the German-Bulgarian forces. On the right the British were less successful, but the Bulgarians, who had been taking soundings for peace since June (June 18, Germanophile Radoslavov cabinet succeeded by **Malinov government**), were unable to hold out longer. They appealed for an armistice.

Sept. 30.   ARMISTICE CONCLUDED WITH BULGARIA AT SALONIKI: the Bulgarian army was to be demobilized at once and its equipment put into Allied custody; Greek and Serb territory still occupied was to be evacuated; all means of transport to be put at the disposal of the Allies; Bulgarian territory to be available for Allied operations.

Gen. Franchet d'Esperey's plan was to break the communication between Germany-Austria and Turkey, and to attack the Turks in Thrace and force the opening of the Straits. A force was indeed sent into Thrace, and reached the **Maritza River** (Oct. 30). Other forces took over strategic positions in Bulgaria, crossed the whole country, and effected the **passage of the**

Danube at Rustchuk (Nov. 10).

Oct. 4.   Tsar Ferdinand of Bulgaria abdicated and was succeeded by his son Boris.

Nov. 10. The Allies having entered **Roumania,** that government now **re-entered the war** on the Allied side (November 8, resignation of the **Marghiloman ministry**).

TURKEY

On the Palestine front the new British commander, **Gen. Edmund Allenby,** had begun his advance in October 1917.

1917, Oct. 31. After a month of heavy fighting between Gaza and Beersheba, the British took the latter town and began rolling up the enemy line, thus forcing the **evacuation of Gaza** (Nov. 7) and **Jaffa** (Nov. 16).

Dec. 9.   ALLENBY TOOK JERUSALEM. The British advance was delayed by the fact that Allenby was obliged to send large contingents to France to meet the crisis of March 1918. The operations of the spring of 1918 were confined to Transjordania.

1918, Sept. 18. Beginning of the great British offensive in Palestine. **Battles of Megiddo.** The British broke the Turkish lines near the Mediterranean and began to roll up the enemy forces, which were surrounded by cavalry. The German corps managed to escape into Transjordania, and thence to Damascus and Aleppo. The British, assisted materially by the Arabs under Lawrence, were now able to push northward.

Oct. 1–2.   British and Arabs took Damascus, then **Beirut** (taken by French naval forces, Oct. 7), **Homs** (Oct. 15), **Aleppo** (Oct. 26).

Oct. 13. The new Turkish sultan, **Mohammed VI** (succeeded Mohammed V July 3, 1918), **dismissed his Young Turk ministers** (Talaat and Enver) and appointed **Izzet Pasha grand vizir.** The Turks then (Oct. 14) appealed to President Wilson to arrange an armistice. Having received no reply, they liberated **Gen. Townshend** and sent him to the British naval commander in the Aegean, **Adm. Sir Somerset Calthorpe.**

Oct. 30. ARMISTICE CONCLUDED AT MUDROS to take effect the next day. The Turks were obliged to open the Straits, repatri-

ate Allied prisoners, demobilize their armies, sever relations with the Central Powers, and place Turkish territory at the disposal of the Allies for military operations.

Nov. 12. The **Allied fleet passed the Dardanelles** and arrived at Constantinople (Nov. 13). (*Cont. p. 979.*)

19. THE END OF THE HAPSBURG MONARCHY

By the summer of 1918 the **Hapsburg Monarchy** was already in full process of dissolution. Disorders were common in the larger centers, parliamentary government had had to be given up, and desertions from the army had reached a large scale. In Russia, in France, and in Italy there had been formed Czech, Polish, and Yugoslav legions which were fighting for the Allies, while national councils of these subject nationalities were springing up not only in the provincial capitals, but in Paris and London.

1918, Apr. 10. Meeting of the **Congress of Oppressed Austrian Nationalities** in Rome. Here the Czech, Yugoslav, Polish, and Roumanian representatives proclaimed the right of self-determination, denounced the Hapsburg government as an obstacle to free development of the nations, and recognized the need for fighting against it.

Apr. 21. The Italian government recognized the Czechoslovak National Council as a *de facto* government.

May 29. Secretary **Lansing** declared the sympathy of the United States for the Czechoslovaks and Yugoslavs.

June 3. Allied declarations were made supporting the national aspirations of Poles, Czechoslovaks, and Yugoslavs.

June 30. Italy and France officially recognized the **independence of Czechoslovakia.** Britain followed suit August 13, and the United States September 3.

In view of the rapid disintegration of the monarchy the Austrians made a last bid for military victory.

June 15-24. Battle of the Piave. The Austrians crossed the river, but were unable to maintain their position. They withdrew again after losing some 100,000 men. From this time on there was steady demoralization of the army.

Sept. 15. The Austrian government appealed to President Wilson to call an informal conference to discuss peace. This plea was rejected by Wilson.

Oct. 4. The Austrians joined the Germans in appealing for an armistice (see p. 976).

Oct. 16. The **Emperor Charles proclaimed** the reorganization of the non-Hungarian part of **the monarchy as a federal state,** with complete self-government for the subject nationalities. This move was patently belated.

Oct. 21. THE CZECHOSLOVAKS DECLARED THEIR INDEPENDENCE.

Oct. 24-Nov. 4. BATTLE OF VITTORIO VENETO. Diaz attacked the Austrian front all the way from the Trentino to the Adriatic. The Austrians held out for a week on the Monte Grappa but on the lower Piave they collapsed completely. The Italians advanced to **Vittorio Veneto** (Oct. 30), by which time the Austrian armies were in a state of dissolution, several hundred thousand men being captured and the remainder streaming back toward home. The **Italians took Trieste** (Nov. 3) and **Fiume** (Nov. 5).

Oct. 27. Count Julius Andrássy (succeeded Burian as Austrian foreign minister, October 25) notified Wilson that Austria was willing to recognize the rights of the subject nationalities and to make a separate peace.

Oct. 29. The **YUGOSLAV NATIONAL COUNCIL** at Agram (Zagreb) **proclaimed the independence of the Yugoslavs.**

Oct. 29. The Austrians offered to surrender unconditionally to the Italians.

Meanwhile disorders in both Vienna and Budapest had resulted in revolutionary changes.

Oct. 30. Formation of a **German National Council in Vienna,** for the German provinces.

Nov. 1. Establishment of an independent Hungarian government, under **Count Michael Károlyi.**

Nov. 3. CONCLUSION OF AN ARMISTICE between the Allied powers and Austria-Hungary: complete demobilization of the armies and withdrawal of troops fighting with the Germans; surrender of half the equipment; evacuation of territories still occupied and of territory in dispute between Austrians, Italians, and Slavs; Allied occupation of strategic points; surrender of the fleet, etc.

Nov. 7. A Yugoslav conference at Geneva decided for the **union of Croatia and Slovenia**

with Serbia and Montenegro.

Nov. 12. Abdication of the Emperor Charles.

Nov. 1ɔ. PROCLAMATION OF THE AUSTRIAN REPUBLIC.

Nov. 16. PROCLAMATION OF THE HUNGARIAN REPUBLIC.

Nov. 24. PROCLAMATION OF THE UNITED KINGDOM OF THE SERBS, CROATS, AND SLOVENES at Zagreb. King

Peter of Serbia became king, with Prince Alexander as regent.

Dec. 1. King Nicholas of Montenegro, having opposed union, was declared deposed by the parliament, which then voted for union with the new kingdom.

Dec. 1. A national assembly of the Roumanians of **Transylvania** and the Banat at Alba Julia **voted for union** of these regions with **Roumania.** (*Cont. p. 978.*)

20. OPERATIONS IN THE WEST, JANUARY TO JULY 1918

(*From p. 960*)

The tremendous gains made by the Germans in the east did not serve to improve the situation with respect to the western powers. On the contrary, it was generally felt that the terms imposed on Russia and Roumania were irrefutable proof of Germany's expansionist aims. In the west the demands for peace died away and the governments were able to take a stronger line than ever.

1918, Jan. 5. Lloyd George, in an address to the Trades Unions Congress, **formulated the British war aims.** These included the restoration of Belgium, Serbia, Montenegro, and the occupied parts of France, Italy, and Roumania. In addition, a "reconsideration" of the great wrong done to France in 1871; the establishment of an independent Poland "comprising all those genuinely Polish elements who desire to form part of it"; genuine self-government of the nationalities in the Austro-Hungarian Monarchy; satisfaction of the Italian national claims, and of Roumanian aspirations; "recognition of the separate national conditions" of Arabia, Armenia, Mesopotamia, Syria, and Palestine. Lloyd George envisaged further some future organization to limit armaments and prevent war.

Jan. 8. In an address to congress **President Wilson outlined** a peace program consisting of **Fourteen Points,** as follows: (1) Open covenants openly arrived at. (2) Absolute freedom of navigation alike in peace and war, except as the seas might be closed by international action to enforce international covenants. (3) The removal, so far as possible, of all economic barriers. (4) Adequate guaranties that armaments would be reduced to the lowest point consistent with domestic safety. (5) An impartial adjustment of all colonial claims on the principle that the interests of the population must have equal weight with the claims of the government. (6) The evacuation of Russian territory and the free determination of her

own political and national policy. (7) Evacuation and restoration of Belgium. (8) Evacuation and restoration of French territory and righting of the wrong done to France in the matter of Alsace-Lorraine. (9) Readjustment of the frontiers of Italy along clearly recognizable lines of nationality. (10) Opportunity for autonomous development for the peoples of Austria-Hungary. (11) Evacuation and restoration of Roumanian, Serbian, and Montenegrin territory, together with access to sea for Serbia. (12) The Turkish parts of the Ottoman Empire to be given a secure sovereignty, but the other nationalities to be given an opportunity for autonomous development, and the Dardanelles to be permanently opened to the ships of all nations under international guaranties. (13) An independent Poland, to include territories indisputably Polish, with free and secure access to the sea. (14) A general association of nations to be formed to afford mutual guaranties of political independence and territorial integrity to great and small states alike.

The Allied war aims could be realized only through military victory, and prospects for this were not very good at a time when the Germans were able to transfer troops from the east to the west and when the American forces were not yet numerous enough to make much difference. Some efforts had been made, however, to establish greater co-ordination of effort among the Allies, and after the Italian disaster at Caporetto

1917, Nov. 27. The **Supreme War Council** had been established, consisting of the leading statesmen, with their military advisers (first Sir Henry Wilson, Foch, Cadorna, and Bliss). Even this new board was unable to establish harmony.

The **Germans,** now disillusioned about the submarine campaign, fully cognizant of the war-weariness of their allies, and feeling acutely the pinch of the blockade, decided to stake everything on a decision in the west, which it was hoped could be reached before the Americans arrived in great force. **Ludendorff** planned a series of crushing blows to be delivered against the British on a 60-mile front south of Arras, by which he hoped to break through, roll up the opposing forces, and drive them westward to the sea.

The British expected an attack, but not along the southern part of their front, so that the 5th army (Gen. Sir Hubert Gough) was left holding an extensive front with relatively few forces.

1918, Mar. 21–Apr. 5. THE GREAT MARCH OFFENSIVE. After cleverly concealed preparations, the Germans began with a bombardment of 6000 guns and a heavy gas attack. They advanced from **St. Quentin** in a thick fog, which recurred for several days. In a few days the Germans drove in the British line to a depth of about 40 miles, taking **Péronne, Ham, Bapaume, Chauny, Noyon,** and even **Montdidier.** The hasty and generous supply of reserves by the French helped to check the advance.

Mar. 26. In the midst of the crisis a **conference at Doullens** named **Gen. Ferdinand Foch** to co-ordinate operations on the west front.

Apr. 14. Foch named commander-in-chief of the Allied armies in France. In practice the national commanders (Haig, King Albert, Pershing) retained extensive control.

Apr. 9–29. Battles of the Lys. The second great German blow, delivered south of Ypres on a short front. The **Germans stormed Messines Ridge** and took **Armentières,** opening up a wide breach in the British front. Lack of reserves made it impossible for them to take full advantage of the situation.

May 27–June 6. (THIRD) BATTLE OF

THE AISNE. Ludendorff, in order to draw the French reserves from Flanders preparatory to the main offensive there, arranged an attack upon the French between Soissons and Rheims, along the strong and therefore weakly held **Chemin des Dames.** The French were taken by surprise and driven back 13 miles on the first day. The Germans took **Soissons** (May 29) and May 30 reached the Marne River, only 37 miles from Paris. The new salient was 40 miles deep.

June 9–14. Battle of the Matz. Ludendorff, astounded at his own success in Champagne, gave up the idea of an offensive in Flanders and undertook to join up the Soissons and Noyon salients by an attack toward Compiègne. The Germans advanced about six miles, but the move had been hastily prepared and the French were able to contain it.

June 4. The American forces at Château-Thierry. The 2nd division, collaborating with the French, managed to break the German advance. In this engagement the Americans first played a substantial rôle.

July 15–Aug. 7. (SECOND) BATTLE OF THE MARNE. Ludendorff threw his weary troops into yet another attack. East of Rheims no progress was made, and west of the city, though the **Germans crossed the Marne,** they made but little progress against strong French and American forces. **July 18 Foch ordered a counter-attack,** in which nine American divisions took part. The Germans were forced back over the Marne to the Vesle River, while the French retook **Soissons** (Aug. 2). The Allied counter-offensive was of importance chiefly because it frustrated Ludendorff's plan for a great attack in Flanders, and because it enabled Foch to take the initiative in the months to come.

21. THE ALLIED VICTORY IN THE WEST

After the **second battle of the Marne** the Allied forces, together with the Americans, gradually went over to a sustained offensive, consisting at first of a series of local attacks, but later merging into a general movement.

1918, Aug. 8–11. Battle of Amiens. The British attacked with 450 tanks. They advanced about eight miles the first day, after which the German lines tightened.

Aug. 21–Sept. 3. Second battles of the Somme and of Arras. The British and French gradually extended their attacks. They took **Roye** (Aug. 27), **Bapaume** (Aug. 28), **Noyon** (Aug. 28), and **Péronne** (Aug. 31), and obliged

the Germans to fall back to the Hindenburg Line.

Sept. 12–13. The **American forces,** attacking on both sides of the **St. Mihiel** salient, pinched out that area, capturing some 15,000 of the enemy.

Sept. 26–Oct. 15. BATTLES OF THE ARGONNE AND OF YPRES (Sept. 28–Oct. 2). Foch's plan was to execute a pincer movement with an American thrust north through the Argonne and a British thrust eastward toward Cambrai and farther north toward Lille. If successful this would have cut the main lateral German railway and forced a general withdrawal. But at both ends the advance was much slower than expected. By mid-October the Americans had got through part of the Argonne, while the British had taken **St. Quentin, Lens,** and **Armentières** (Oct. 1–2).

These blows, together with the news of the surrender of Bulgaria, shook the nerve of Gen. Ludendorff, who, in something of a panic, demanded (Sept. 29) that the government initiate armistice and peace negotiations while the army could still hold out.

Sept. 30. Hertling and his fellow ministers resigned.

Oct. 4. Prince Max of Baden, a Liberal, named chancellor and foreign minister, with support of the Center, Progressive, and Socialist Parties. On the same day the **German and Austrian governments appealed to President Wilson for an armistice,** accepting the **Fourteen Points** (see p. 974) as a basis for peace. There followed an exchange of notes between Berlin and Washington extending over several weeks, Wilson demanding evacuation of occupied territories, insisting that the Allies could negotiate only with a democratic government, etc. In the interval Ludendorff regained some of his composure and began to talk of resistance, renewal of the war in the spring, etc. The home situation, however, was bad and the democratic tide strong. The government (Oct. 27) accepted **Ludendorff's resignation.** He was succeeded as quartermaster-general by **Gen. Wilhelm von Gröner.**

During October the British continued to advance in the north. They took **Ostend, Zeebrugge, Roubaix, Lille,** and **Douai** (Oct. 18), **Bruges** (Oct. 19), and **Valenciennes** (Nov. 1). By that time the American troops also resumed the advance. The Germans began to withdraw rapidly, and by November 10 the Americans were at **Sedan.** Foch was then planning still another thrust east of Metz, and arranging for the mission of a force through Austria to attack Bavaria.

Oct. 28. Mutiny broke out **in the German fleet** at Kiel, the crews refusing to put to sea on a series of cruiser raids planned by Adm. Scheer. The mutiny spread rapidly to Hamburg, Bremen, and Lübeck and thence to the whole of northwestern Germany.

Nov. 7–8. Revolution broke out in Munich. The king abdicated. In Berlin the ministry convinced itself that the abdication of William II was imperative if the monarchy was to be preserved. The emperor, who was at Spa, resisted the suggestion, but Prince Max, feeling that he was unable to wait,

Nov. 9. ANNOUNCED THE ABDICATION IN BERLIN. Philipp Scheidemann, the Socialist leader, then **proclaimed the German Republic.**

Nov. 10. William II, having been told by Hindenburg and Gröner that they were unable to guarantee the loyalty of the army, took their advice and **fled to Holland.** Meanwhile

Nov. 8. The **German armistice commission,** headed by **Matthias Erzberger,** the leader of the Center Party, was received by Foch in his railway coach near Compiègne. The terms submitted by the Allies were designed to make Germany helpless and to ensure the acceptance of the peace terms. The armistice provided for immediate evacuation of occupied territory on the west front and of all territory west of the Rhine, which was to be occupied by Allied forces. The **treaties of Brest-Litovsk** and **Bucharest** were to be renounced and German troops were to be withdrawn from Roumania, Austria-Hungary, Turkey, and eventually Russia. Germany was to surrender 5000 locomotives, 5000 motor lorries, and 150,000 freight cars. She was to turn over 160 submarines and a large number of other warships. The armistice, harsh though the terms were, had to be accepted. It was concluded for a period of 30 days, but was periodically renewed until peace was signed.

Nov. 11. AT 11 A.M. HOSTILITIES CEASED ON THE WEST FRONT. The Allies at once began to take over the occupied and western German territories. French troops occupied Strassburg November 25, while British and American troops began the occupation of Germany December 1.

FIRST WORLD WAR LOSSES

The number of known dead has been placed at about 10,000,000 men, the wounded at about 20,000,000, distributed among the chief combatants as follows (round numbers):

	Dead	Wounded	Prisoner
Great Britain	947,000	2,122,000	192,000
France	1,385,000	3,044,000	446,000
Russia	1,700,000	4,950,000	2,500,000
Italy	460,000	947,000	530,000
United States	115,000	206,000	4,500
Germany	1,808,000	4,247,000	618,000
Austria-Hungary	1,200,000	3,620,000	2,200,000
Turkey	325,000	400,000	

The total direct cost of the war has been figured at $180,500,000,000, and the indirect cost at $151,612,500,000.

22. THE PEACE SETTLEMENTS

a. THE TREATY OF VERSAILLES

1919, Jan. 18. The **peace conference** was formally opened at Paris, with 70 delegates representing 27 of the victorious powers. The Germans were excluded until the terms were ready for submission. The German request for a peace on the basis of Wilson's **Fourteen Points** had been granted by the Allied note of November 5, 1918, with two reservations, but the Fourteen Points receded into the background as the conflict of views and interests developed at the conference. **President Wilson,** received with the wildest enthusiasm when he arrived in Europe in mid-December, represented the new idealism in international relations and was intent primarily on securing the adoption of a plan for a **League of Nations,** to be included in the peace treaty. **Lloyd George,** the chief representative of Great Britain and the empire, was disposed to make a moderate peace, but was deeply committed by promises made in the general election recently held, to the effect that the war criminals would be brought to justice and that Germany would be made to pay for the war. **Clemenceau,** in turn, was frankly the exponent of the old diplomacy, being intent on revenge, on the interests of France, and on provisions for the security of France. Both Britain and France were bound further by their agreements with Italy, by commitments in the Near East, etc. The Italian prime minister, **Vittorio Orlando,** played a secondary rôle, but the foreign minister, **Sidney Sonnino,** stood forth as an unbending champion of Italian claims against Austria and against the new Yugoslav state.

The plenary sessions of the conference were of little significance, for the decisions rested from the start with the **Supreme Council,** the **Big Ten,** composed of President Wilson and the prime ministers and foreign ministers of the five chief powers (Wilson, Lansing, Lloyd George, Balfour, Clemenceau, Pichon, Orlando, Sonnino, Saionji, Makino). Russia was not represented, though the **Russian situation** was of vital import. The wars of the counter-revolution were in full swing and the fate of the new states on Russia's western frontiers depended on the outcome. Clemenceau having refused to invite delegates of the warring parties to Paris, a conference was arranged for at the Prinkipo Islands. The Bolshevik government was apparently anxious for some kind of adjustment, but **Kolchak** and **Denikin,** the two leading generals of the counter-revolution, refused to enter upon discussion and the whole project fell flat. Public opinion in both France and Britain was violently anti-Bolshevik and it seems hardly likely that an agreement could have been reached.

Jan. 25. The conference unanimously adopted a resolution for the **creation of a League of Nations.** A committee was appointed to draft a constitution, and other committees were organized to deal with reparations and various territorial questions.

Feb. In the middle of the month **President Wilson returned** for a time **to America** and Lloyd George to London.

Mar. 25. After the return of Wilson and Lloyd George to Paris, the statesmen devoted themselves to the working out of the German treaty. The Council of Ten was replaced by the **Council of Four,** for the expedition of business.

Apr. 28. The **Covenant of the League of Nations** (worked out by a committee consisting of Wilson, House, Cecil, Smuts, Bourgeois, and Venizelos) was presented in final form. The League was to consist of the signatory states and others admitted by two-thirds vote. The members were to afford each other mutual protection against aggression, to submit disputes to arbitration or inquiry, to abstain from war until three months after an award. All treaties between members which were incompatible with these obligations were declared abrogated; all subsequent treaties were to be registered with the League. The League was to devote itself to problems of disarmament, labor legislation, health, international administration, etc. A permanent secretariat was provided for, to be located at Geneva (**Sir Eric Drummond,** first secretary-general). All member states were to be represented by one vote in a **General Assembly,** while a **Council,** consisting of representatives of the five great powers and four others chosen periodically by the Assembly, was to fill the position of executive. The League, the covenant of which was an integral part of the peace treaty, came into effect in January 1920.

The drafting of the peace terms was marked by violent conflict between the members of the Council of Four. Clemenceau insisted on the separation of the **left bank of the Rhine** from Germany, and desired also the annexation of the **Saar Basin** to France. These demands were opposed by Wilson and Lloyd George, and French security was finally arranged for otherwise, Wilson having ordered preparations for his return home (Apr. 7). Other disputes arose from the demands of Britain and France that

Germany be required to meet the **costs of the war,** a proposition to which Wilson objected. The **Polish claims,** supported by France, also caused friction, as did the **Japanese pretensions** in Shantung and the **Italian claims** in Dalmatia, neither of which Wilson was prepared to recognize. All these questions were finally settled by compromise in order to keep the conference together (the Italian delegates left the conference April 23 and did not return until May 6).

May 7. The **treaty was submitted to the German delegation,** which had arrived April 29. The Germans (**Count Ulrich von Brockdorff-Rantzau,** chief of the delegation) protested vigorously that the terms were not in keeping with the conditions on which Germany had laid down her arms and that many of the clauses were impossible of fulfillment. Nevertheless the victorious powers made only slight modifications in the draft and the Germans, after an acute domestic crisis, decided that they were unable to resist and that their only possible course was to sign.

June 21. The **German fleet** (10 battleships, nine armored cruisers, eight smaller cruisers, 50 torpedo boats, 102 submarines, totaling about 500,000 tons) **was scuttled** by the crews under command of Adm. Ludwig von Reuter, **at Scapa Flow,** where the fleet had been interned. This act of defiance made the victors more determined to enforce the terms of the treaty draft.

June 28. SIGNATURE OF THE TREATY OF VERSAILLES at Versailles. The treaty provided for the **League of Nations** and for the following territorial cessions by Germany (*see map on p. 963*): **Alsace-Lorraine** to France; **Moresnet, Eupen,** and **Malmédy** to Belgium, with a plebiscite in Malmédy after cession; **the Saar** area to be under international administration for fifteen years, after which a plebiscite was to be held, France exploiting the coal mines in the meanwhile; northern and central **Schleswig** were to decide their allegiance by plebiscite; in the east, Germany was to cede the larger part of **Posen** and **West Prussia** to Poland; a plebiscite was to be held in **Upper Silesia; Danzig** was to be a free state within the Polish customs union; plebiscites were to be held in parts of **East Prussia** to decide whether they should go to Poland or remain with Germany; **Memel** was ceded to the Allies; the **German colonies** were also ceded to the Allies, to be organized as mandates under supervision of the League. Germany, in **Article 231,** accepted sole responsibility for causing the war. She was henceforth to keep an **army of not more than 100,000 men,** was to have no large guns and only a limited number of

smaller ones. The **navy** was limited to six warships and a corresponding number of other craft; Germany was to have **no submarines or military aircraft;** the fortifications of **Heligoland** were to be dismantled; the Allies were to occupy the **Rhineland** for 15 years, and longer if necessary, and a belt 30 miles wide on the **right bank of the Rhine** was to be **demilitarized.** The **Kiel Canal** was opened to the warships and merchant shipping of all nations, and the **German rivers** were internationalized. The former **emperor** and other offenders were to be tried. The Germans were required to pay for all **civilian damage** caused during the war, the final bill to be presented by May 1, 1921; in the interval Germany was to pay five billion dollars, the rest to be paid in 30 years. Germany was to hand over all **merchant ships** of more than 1600 tons, half of those between 800 and 1600 tons, and a quarter of her **fishing fleet.** She was to build 200,000 tons of shipping for the victors annually for five years. Large quantities of **coal** were to be delivered to France, Belgium, and Italy for ten years. Germany was to bear the **cost of the armies of occupation.** She bound herself further to agree to the sale of German property in Allied countries.

July 7. The **German government ratified the treaty,** as did France (Oct. 13), Great Britain (Oct. 15), Italy (Oct. 15), and Japan (Oct. 30). The United States government never ratified it, the senate having first proposed amendments, which failed of the necessary votes. The United States government also refused to ratify the **treaty of alliance signed with Great Britain and France** (June 28) providing for assistance in case of attack by Germany. This treaty thus also failed of effect.

(*Cont. p. 1004.*)

b. THE TREATY OF SAINT-GERMAIN

1919, Sept. 10. **Austria signed the treaty** which had been submitted July 20. This merely registered the break-up of the Hapsburg Monarchy, at the same time penalizing the new Austrian Republic as the representative of the old régime. Austria recognized the **independence of Czechoslovakia, Yugoslavia, Poland, and Hungary,** these states being obliged to give guaranties of protection of minorities. **Eastern Galicia, the Trentino, South Tyrol, Trieste,** and **Istria** were ceded by Austria. The **army** was limited to 30,000 men and Austria, like Germany, was to pay **reparations** for 30 years. The **union of Austria with Germany** was forbidden, except with consent of the Council of the League.

(*Cont. p. 1013.*)

c. THE TREATY OF NEUILLY

1919, Nov. 27. The **Bulgarians signed the treaty of peace,** which deprived them of a seaboard on the Aegean and gave them only an economic outlet. Bulgaria recognized the **independence of Yugoslavia.** She agreed to pay **reparations** of $445,000,000. Her **army** was reduced to 20,000 men, and she was obliged to surrender most of her war materials.

(*Cont. p. 1025.*)

d. THE TREATY OF TRIANON

1919, Mar. 21. The Hungarian government headed by **Count Károlyi** was overthrown by a **Bolshevik coup,** headed by Alexander Garbai and **Béla Kun.** This government became involved in war with most of Hungary's neighbors when it became known that territory was to be assigned to them. Ultimately the **Roumanians invaded and took Budapest** (Aug. 4) just after the Bolsheviks had been overthrown (Aug. 1). The monarchists then regained control and appointed **Adm. Nikolaus Horthy as regent** (Mar. 1, 1920). The Roumanians were finally induced to withdraw (Nov. 14, 1919), under pressure from the Allies, but only after they had carried away most of what was movable.

1920, June 4. The **Hungarians signed the treaty of Trianon,** by which the old Hungary was shorn of almost three-quarters of its territory and two-thirds of its inhabitants. Czechoslovakia was given **Slovakia,** Austria received **western Hungary,** Yugoslavia took **Croatia-Slavonia** and part of the **Banat of Temesvar,** and Roumania received the rest of the **Banat, Transylvania,** and part of the **Hungarian plain.** Hungary agreed to pay **reparations,** to keep an **army** of only 35,000 men, to assume part of the old Austro-Hungarian debt, to hand over war criminals, etc.

(*Cont. p. 1019.*)

e. THE TREATY OF SÈVRES

In the settlement of the Turkish question the Allies were much hampered by the downfall of the tsarist régime in Russia, the withdrawal of Russian claims to Constantinople, and the publication by the Bolsheviks of the **secret treaties** revealing the Allied plan of partition. President Wilson in particular opposed the former program, while American opinion showed little interest in assuming responsibility for either the Straits area or Armenia. The question dragged on through 1919, while in Turkey a nationalist movement under **Mustapha Kemal** (see p. 1085) was building up a strong opposition to the Allied plans.

1919, May 15. The **Greeks,** with the support of the Allies, **landed troops at Smyrna,** acting as agents for Allied interests. The Italians also landed troops in southwestern Anatolia.

1920, Apr. 18. At a **conference** of the Allied prime ministers **at San Remo** the main lines of the Turkish treaty were agreed upon.

Aug. 10. The feeble and helpless government of the sultan, protected by an international force of occupation at Constantinople, signed the **treaty of Sèvres.** By this treaty the sultan's government renounced all claims to non-Turkish territory. **The kingdom of the Hijaz was recognized as independent.** Syria became a mandate of France, and **Mesopotamia** (with Mosul), as well as **Palestine,** became British mandates. **Smyrna** and its hinterland were to be administered by Greece for five years, after which a plebiscite was to be held. The **Dodecanese** and **Rhodes** went to Italy, while **Thrace** and the remainder of the **Turkish islands** in the Aegean were assigned to Greece. **Armenia** was recognized as independent. The **Straits** were to be internationalized and the adjoining territory demilitarized. **Constantinople** and the strip of territory to the Chatalja lines remained Turkish, as did the remainder of **Anatolia.** This treaty was not recognized by the Turkish nationalists who, under Mustapha Kemal's leadership, continued to build up a military force in Anatolia and to organize a government in defiance of the sultan and the victorious Allied powers. As a result of nationalist successes the treaty of Sèvres was ultimately replaced by the **treaty of Lausanne** (p. 1086). (*Cont. pp. 1085, 1120.*)

B. EUROPE, 1914-1939

1. THE BRITISH ISLES

a. GREAT BRITAIN

(From p. 671)

1915, May 25. The **Asquith ministry** (since 1908) was reorganized as a coalition. Churchill resigned as first lord of the admiralty (May 27) and was succeeded by Arthur Balfour. An inner group of the cabinet, first called the **War Committee** and then (June 7) the **Dardanelles Committee,** took over the conduct of operations. A ministry of munitions was set up (July 2).

June 3. An **Allied conference met in Paris** to establish concerted action in economic matters. This was followed (Nov. 25) by arrangements for inter-Allied munitions control, and by numerous measures designed to restrict trade with Germany, even by the method of rationing the supply of raw materials, etc., to neutrals (December 23, introduction of the Black List; January 27, 1916, establishment of the **Shipping Control Commission;** February 23, 1916, organization of a **ministry of blockade** in Britain).

1916, Jan. 6. The British parliament passed the **compulsory military service bill,** despite the opposition of Labour groups.

Apr. 20. **Sir Roger Casement,** the Irish leader, landed on the Irish coast from a German submarine, to start a rebellion.

Apr. 24. Beginning of the great **Easter Rebellion in Ireland.** After a week of fighting the insurrection was suppressed (May 1). Several of the leaders, including Casement, were tried and executed (Aug. 3).

June 5. **Field Marshal Lord Kitchener,** on secret mission to Russia, was lost when *H.M.S. Hampshire* was sunk off the Orkneys.

July 7. **David Lloyd George** became secretary of state for war to succeed Kitchener.

Dec. 4. The Asquith cabinet resigned. Lloyd George formed a **war cabinet** (Dec. 7-10), in which Balfour took the place of Sir Edward Grey at the foreign office.

Great Britain's losses in the First World War were almost 1,000,000 killed and over 2,000,000 wounded. The total expense exceeded £8,000,000,000 and the burden of domestic and foreign debt was ten times what it had been in 1914. Britain was faced with the problem of returning soldiers to industry and introducing social reforms loudly demanded by the laboring classes, and was confronted at the same time with increased competition in foreign trade in a world generally disorganized and impoverished. In Ireland, India, Egypt, and Palestine it was confronted with almost insoluble problems. Even the self-governing Dominions demonstrated enhanced national feeling and reluctance to be committed to any share in future European wars.

1918, Dec. 14. The **Khaki election,** with an electorate increased by the granting of suffrage to all men of 21 and over and to women over 30. The coalition government won a huge majority on a platform promising punishment of the German "war criminals," full payment by the defeated powers of the costs of war, and the prevention of dumping of foreign goods in Great Britain. These promises greatly hampered Lloyd George's freedom of action at the Paris peace conference (p. 977).

1919-1922. COALITION GOVERNMENT OF DAVID LLOYD GEORGE.

1920, Dec. 9. Milner report on the government of Egypt (p. 1075).

Dec. 23. GOVERNMENT OF IRELAND ACT passed, providing for the division of Ireland (p. 984).

1921, Mar. 3. The **Emergency Unemployment Act** increased unemployment payments to 20s. a week for men and 18s. for women. There were at this time almost 1,000,000 unemployed.

Mar. 31. Great coal strike begun as government control of the mines ended and proposals for nationalization had been rejected. The strike ended July 1 when the miners accepted a government offer of subsidy and increase of wages.

Dec. 6. TREATY WITH IRELAND (p. 984).

1922, Feb. 28. End of the British protectorate over Egypt (p. 1075).

Oct. 19. The Unionists decided to withdraw their support from the Lloyd George government, which thereupon resigned.

Oct. 23-1923, May 20. CABINET OF A. BONAR LAW.

Nov. 15. General election. The Conservatives (Unionists) won a majority of the seats. The Liberals split between the followers of Asquith and Lloyd George. The Labour Party (142 seats) became for the first time His Majesty's Opposition.

1923, May 22-1924, Jan. 22. CABINET OF STANLEY BALDWIN.

Oct. 1-Nov. 8. Imperial Conference. This recognized the right of the Dominions to make treaties with foreign powers.

Dec. 6. A **general election** to pass upon

Baldwin's scheme for a protective tariff to relieve unemployment resulted in heavy loss for the Conservatives and a decided gain for Labour.

1924, Jan. 22–Nov. 4. FIRST LABOUR CABINET, under **Ramsay MacDonald; Philip Snowden,** formerly a clerk, became chancellor of the exchequer, and **Arthur Henderson,** formerly an iron worker, became home secretary.

Feb. 1. *De jure* **recognition of Soviet Russia.**

Aug. 8. Commercial treaty with Russia, giving British goods most-favored-nation treatment and promising Russia a British loan if and when the debt of the former tsarist government should have been settled.

Oct. 29. The **general election** turned out a great victory for the Conservatives, owing largely to the so-called **Zinoviev letter** (Oct. 25), by which the Third International allegedly instructed British subjects to provoke revolution.

1924, Nov. 7–1929, June 4. SECOND BALDWIN MINISTRY.

Nov. 21. The new government **denounced the treaties with Russia.**

1925, Mar. 12. Rejection of the Geneva protocol by Great Britain (p. 1123).

May 1. Cyprus (annexed in 1914) **made a crown colony.**

Dec. 3. Signature of the Irish boundary agreement, fixing the frontier between Northern Ireland and the Irish Free State.

1926, May 1. Strike of coal miners, after a commission report adverse to continuation of government subsidy.

May 3–12. GENERAL STRIKE, in sympathy with coal miners. It involved about 2,500,000 of the 6,000,000 trade-union members in Great Britain. Volunteers, largely from the upper classes, maintained essential transport and other services. The Trade-Union Council called off the strike May 12 with an understanding that negotiations on wages and hours would be resumed. But the miners' union continued to strike until November 19, when it surrendered unconditionally

Oct. 19–Nov. 18. Imperial Conference. Its report declared that Great Britain and the Dominions "are autonomous communities within the British Empire, equal in status, in no way subordinate one to another in any aspect of their domestic or external affairs, though united by a common allegiance to the crown and freely associated as members of the British Commonwealth of Nations."

1928, July 2. An act of parliament extended the **franchise to women** on the same terms as men.

Dec. 20. Treaty with China, recognizing the Nanking government and Chinese tariff autonomy, China to abolish coast and interior duties.

1929, May 30. In the **general election** the Labour Party was victorious, securing 288 seats against 260 for the Conservatives.

June 5–1931, Aug. 24. SECOND MACDONALD CABINET.

Oct. 1. Diplomatic relations with Russia resumed.

1930, Jan. 21. Opening of the **London Naval Conference** (p. 1125).

June 10. Publication of the **Simon Report** on the government of India.

1931, July. Report of the **May Committee** of financial experts. They claimed the deficit for the fiscal year would be over £100,000 sterling and suggested drastic economies, including a cut in the dole to the unemployed. This report caused a **split in the cabinet,** the majority rejecting the proposals as too burdensome to the workers. There were, at this time, over 2,000,000 unemployed.

Aug. 24. Resignation of the MacDonald cabinet, the result of the financial crisis and disagreement as to remedies.

Aug. 25–Oct. 27. A NATIONAL COALITION GOVERNMENT formed to include Conservatives, Liberals, and Labour members, with MacDonald as prime minister. The Labour Party opposed this coalition and expelled those of its leaders who favored it. MacDonald, Snowden, Thomas, and others formed a new **National Labour group.** Henderson became leader of the old Labour Party.

Sept. 21. England forced to abandon the gold standard. The pound sterling fell from par ($4.86) to $3.49.

Oct. 27. A **general election** gave the coalition government a majority of almost 500 seats over the combined opposition.

1931, Oct. 27–June 7, 1935. NATIONAL COALITION CABINET under MacDonald.

Dec. The **STATUTE OF WESTMINSTER** passed by parliament, giving force of law to the changes in empire relations worked out by the Imperial Conference in 1926.

1932, Feb. 29. Protective Tariff Acts, including a new "corn law" which guaranteed British farmers about $1 a bushel for a specified quantity of home-grown wheat. Abandonment of free trade.

July 21–Aug. 20. Ottawa Imperial Economic Conference. A series of agreements for a carefully limited measure of imperial preference led to the resignation (Sept. 28) of the free-trade Liberal members of the cabinet, who went into opposition under the lead of **Sir Herbert Samuel.** The Liberals who remained in the government were led by **Sir John Simon.**

1933, June 12–July 27. World Economic Con-

ference at London (p. 1127). The failure of this conference led the British government to extend its neo-mercantilist policy of economic nationalism. Campaign to "buy British." Managed paper currency; control of foreign exchanges through an exchange equalization fund. Gradual but slow recovery took place.

1935, Feb. 1–3. Anglo-French conference at London regarding action to be taken with reference to Germany's announcement of rearmament.

June 7. Reconstruction of the cabinet, following a general election which continued the majority of the coalition government. **Stanley Baldwin succeeded MacDonald as prime minister** and Sir Samuel Hoare became foreign secretary.

June 18. Conclusion of the **Anglo-German naval agreement** (p. 1011).

Aug. 2. The **Government of India Act** passed by parliament (p. 1103).

Sept. The Ethiopian crisis (p. 1000). The British government, especially after the failure of the Hoare-Laval plan to victimize Ethiopia, gave way to a strong current of British opinion. Under the lead of **Anthony Eden,** who now became foreign secretary, Britain assumed the guidance of the League of Nations in the **imposition of sanctions,** etc. The result was acute danger of war in the Mediterranean.

Nov. In a **general election** the Labour Party gained 95 seats, but the Unionists retained a majority of 385.

1936, Jan. 20–Dec. 10.   EDWARD VIII.

Mar. 25. The **London naval agreement,** signed by Britain, France, and the United States after Japan and Italy had abandoned the conference.

Apr. 30. The government announced plans for the construction of 38 warships, the largest building program since 1921.

Aug. 27. Conclusion of the **Anglo-Egyptian treaty** on terms very favorable to the Egyptian Nationalists (p. 1078).

Dec. 10. Abdication of Edward VIII, the first voluntary abdication in British history. The Baldwin ministry and the Dominion governments had refused to consent to a morganatic marriage between the king and **Mrs. Wallis Warfield Simpson,** an American-born lady whose second divorce had not yet become final. Edward, apparently at odds with his ministers on other matters also (social policy, etc.), insisted on his right to shape his own life and abdicated rather than abandon his plan. He became **Duke of Windsor** and in June 1937 married Mrs. Simpson in France.

1936–1952.   GEORGE VI, brother of Edward VIII, became king.

1937, Jan. 2. Signature of the **Anglo-Italian**

Mediterranean agreement, which, it was hoped, would bring to an end the dangerous antagonism in that sea (p. 1128).

May 28. Neville Chamberlain became prime minister on the retirement of Stanley Baldwin. Chamberlain had been chancellor of the exchequer. He was confronted at the outset with a most difficult and dangerous European situation, which overshadowed all issues of purely domestic character. Abandoning the rather aimless, opportunist policy of Baldwin, Chamberlain held that in order to secure peace, it must be definitely worked for. He therefore sought to reach agreements with Germany and Italy, even at the expense of considerable concessions. This became known as the **policy of appeasement.**

July 8. Publication of the Peel Report recommending the ending of the **Palestine mandate** and the division of the country into Arab and Jewish states, Britain to retain a mandate only over Jerusalem, Bethlehem, and a corridor to the sea. Parliament refused to commit itself to this scheme and the opposition to it on the part of both Jews and Arabs resulted in its reconsideration (p. 1091).

July. Outbreak of hostilities in China. Though British interests were deeply involved and suffered enormous damage, the government avoided challenging Japan in any way, even when the British ambassador was badly injured in an attack of Japanese planes upon the ambassadorial party (p. 1109).

Nov. 17. Visit of Lord Halifax to Chancellor Hitler at Berchtesgaden. This was the first concrete step in the policy of appeasement.

1938, Feb. 20. Resignation of Anthony Eden, British foreign secretary and outstanding champion of the system of collective security and action. He resigned in protest against the prime minister's determination to seek an agreement with Italy without waiting for a settlement of the Spanish problem. Lord Halifax became foreign secretary in his place.

Mar. In the **Austrian annexation crisis** (p. 1016) the British government played but a small part, having apparently reconciled itself to this development after Halifax's visit to Hitler.

Apr. 16. Conclusion of the **Anglo-Italian agreement,** for which Chamberlain had been working for some time. (For terms see p. 1128.)

Apr. 25. Conclusion of a three-year **agreement with Ireland,** bringing to an end a feud which had continued for years (p. 985).

Sept.   THE GERMAN-CZECH CRISIS AND THE MUNICH AGREEMENTS (p. 1129).

Nov. 17. Conclusion of **trade agreements between Great Britain, Canada, and the United**

States. These had been under negotiation for a long time and involved substantial sacrifices on all sides.

Dec. 1. Opening of a "national register" for war service. This was entirely voluntary, but was looked upon as an important item of preparedness. After the crisis of 1938 the British government pushed its preparations to the utmost, going so far as to buy large numbers of planes in the United States.

1939, Jan. Visit of Chamberlain and Lord Halifax to Rome.

Mar. 31. British-French pledge to Poland (p. 1039), marking the end of the policy of appeasement. After the Italian conquest of Albania (p. 1023) guarantees were given to Greece and Roumania, a mutual assistance pact was concluded with Turkey, and the British government finally embarked on the arduous task of bringing Russia into the *"peace front."*

Apr. 27. The **British government introduced conscription** for men of 20–21 years, in order to increase the forces by 300,000 men.

Apr. 28. Hitler, in a major Reichstag speech, denounced the Anglo-German naval agreement of 1935.

May 17. The British published a **new plan for Palestine** (p. 1092), after abortive negotiations with both Arabs and Jews.

King George and Queen Elizabeth **arrived in Canada** for an extended visit, followed (June 8–11) by a **visit to the United States** obviously intended to strengthen Anglo-Saxon ties in the face of threatening war in Europe.

Aug. 20–Sept. 1. The **Danzig-Polish crisis** (p. 1132) and the

Sept. 3. OUTBREAK OF WAR BETWEEN GREAT BRITAIN AND GERMANY.

CULTURAL DEVELOPMENTS

Literature: Among the novelists of the late 19th and early 20th centuries, the most popular were **Thomas Hardy** (1840–1928), **Joseph Conrad** (1857–1924), **Arthur Conan Doyle** (1859–1930), **James M. Barrie,** a Scotsman (1860–1937), **Rudyard Kipling** (1865–1936), **H. G. Wells** (1866–1946), **John Galsworthy** (1867–1933), **Arnold Bennett** (1867–1931), **Virginia Woolf** (1882–1941), **Hugh Walpole** (1884–1941), **D. H. Lawrence** (1885–1930), and **Katherine Mansfield** (1888–1923). Short story writers: **Saki** [H. H. Munro], **C. E. Montague, Sir A. P. Herbert, W. Somerset Maugham.** Other writers of prominence: **E. M. Forster, J. B. Priestley, Evelyn Waugh, Aldous Huxley.**

Interest in history and biography is apparent in the publication of the final volume of the *Dictionary of National Biography* (1900); of the

first volume of the *Cambridge Modern History* (1902); of the *Cambridge Ancient History* (1923). Authors devoting themselves chiefly to historical writing: **Arnold J. Toynbee, G. M. Trevelyan, Sir J. G. Frazer** (*The Golden Bough*), **Lytton Strachey** (*Eminent Victorians,* 1918).

Poets: Robert Bridges (1844–1930) and **John Masefield** (1878–1967), Poets Laureate; also **A. E. Housman** (1859–1936), **Francis Thompson** (1859–1907); **Rupert Brooke** and **Siegfried Sassoon** during the First World War; **Edith Sitwell, Walter de la Mare,** and **T. S. Eliot.**

Essayists: Sir Max Beerbohm, G. K. Chesterton, Maurice Baring, Hilaire Belloc, Robert Lynd, E. V. Lucas.

Critics: William Empson, I. A. Richards, Sir Desmond McCarthy.

Drama: See under Ireland, p. 985.

Music: Edward Elgar (1857–1934), **Frederick Delius** (1862–1934), **Ralph Vaughan Williams** (1872–1962), **Gustav Holst** (1874–1934), **William Walton** (1902–   ), **Benjamin Britten** (1913–   ; composer of opera as well as instrumental music).

Painting and sculpture: Roger Fry (1866–1934), painter and critic; **Graham Sutherland** (1903–   ); **Ben Nicholson** (1894–   ), and **John Piper** (1903–   ). Of the sculptors, **Henry Moore** (1898–   ) has exerted the greatest influence.

(*Cont. p. 1171.*)

b. IRELAND

1916, Apr. 24–29. The **EASTER REBELLION,** led by Patrick H. Pearse and the Irish Republican Brotherhood, despite failure of German aid. The rebellion was suppressed by the British (p. 980).

1917, June 15. Amnesty granted the rebels of 1916.

July 11. Release of Eamon de Valera, Sinn Fein leader, who was re-elected to parliament.

Oct. 25–27. A Sinn Fein convention at Dublin adopted a constitution for the Irish Republic and elected **De Valera president.**

1918, Mar. 6. Death of John Redmond, leader of the Irish Nationalist group in the British parliament.

Apr. 17. Adoption of **conscription for Ireland.** The Irish Nationalists thereupon deserted the British parliament and organized opposition to the measure, forcing its abandonment (June 25).

May 18. De Valera and other Sinn Fein leaders again arrested.

Dec. 14. Great victory of the **Sinn Fein** candidates in the elections for the British parliament.

1919, Jan. 21. The **Sinn Fein members** of parliament, having decided not to attend, **organized a parliament** of their own for Ireland (the *dail Eireann*) and declared Irish independence.

Feb. 3. Escape of De Valera from prison; he took refuge in the United States.

Sept. 12. The **dail was suppressed** and the headquarters of the Sinn Fein party raided.

Nov. 26. Suppression of the Sinn Fein movement; **beginning of war** between the Sinn Fein and the British forces: attacks on the constabulary, arson, etc.

1920, May 15. Arrival of British reinforcements (*Black and Tans*) and initiation of a **policy of reprisal.** There followed several months of ferocious conflict.

Dec. 23. PASSAGE OF THE GOVERNMENT OF IRELAND ACT by the British parliament: **Northern Ireland** and **Southern Ireland** each to have its own parliament, and each to retain representatives in the British parliament. A **Council for Ireland,** representing the two parts, was to attempt to effect common action in common affairs.

1921, May 13. Elections: in the north the Government of Ireland Act was generally accepted and the new system went into effect. In Southern Ireland the **Sinn Fein won 124 out of 128 seats.**

June 28. The parliament for Southern Ireland was opened, but only the four delegates not members of the Sinn Fein attended. The Sinn Feiners declared themselves the dail Eireann and rejected the settlement proposed.

July 14–21. Conferences of De Valera and **Sir James Craig** (representing Northern Ireland) with Lloyd George and other British representatives. De Valera rejected offers of Dominion status for Ireland.

Oct. 11–Dec. 6. Second conference with the British leaders; De Valera did not attend and the negotiations for the Sinn Fein were conducted by **Arthur Griffith** and **Michael Collins.**

Dec. 6. The **IRISH REPRESENTATIVES SIGNED A TREATY** with the British government which granted Ireland **Dominion status** as the **Irish Free State** (Northern Ireland retaining the right of keeping the existing arrangement).

Dec. 8. De Valera denounced the settlement made by Griffith.

1922, Jan. 7. The **dail Eireann accepted the settlement,** 64–57.

Jan. 9. Resignation of De Valera. Griffith became president of the executive council and Collins prime minister. The dail ratified the treaty (Jan. 14).

Mar. 15. De Valera organized a new Republican Society and began an **insurrection** against his former colleagues; irregular forces

resumed the methods of assassination and arson formerly used against the British.

June 16. The government forces won a great victory in the elections.

Aug. 12. Death of Arthur Griffith.

Aug. 22. Assassination of Michael Collins by the Republicans.

Sept. 9. WILLIAM T. COSGRAVE BECAME PRESIDENT of the executive council and, aided by **Kevin O'Higgins,** began a policy of rigorous repression of the Republicans.

Oct. 25. The **DAIL ADOPTED A CONSTITUTION,** providing for a two-chamber parliament (a senate, with 12-year term, one-fourth renewable annually, with suspensive veto; a chamber of deputies, popularly elected and with exclusive power in financial affairs; the lower chamber to elect the president).

Dec. 6. The constitution went into effect and the **Irish Free State was officially proclaimed.**

1923, Aug. 14. De Valera was captured by government forces, and imprisoned.

Sept. 10. Ireland was admitted to the League of Nations.

1924, July 16. De Valera was liberated. He and his Republicans continued to refuse to take their seats in the dail, rejecting the necessary oath of loyalty to the king.

1925, Dec. 3. Boundary with the state of Northern Ireland fixed after long negotiations.

1926, Mar. 11. De Valera resigned as head of the Sinn Fein.

1927, July 10. Assassination of Kevin O'Higgins, dominant figure of the government. Popular condemnation of the tactics of the Republicans. A drastic **public-safety law** enacted.

Aug. 12. De Valera and other Republican leaders **agreed to take the oath** and assume their seats in the dail.

Sept. 15. Elections. The government party had 61 seats against 57 for the Republicans, but failed to secure a clear majority and had to rely on support of the Independents.

1930, Mar. 27. Resignation of Cosgrave, who was soon re-elected (April 2: 80 votes against 65 for De Valera).

1931, Oct. Passage of a **new public-safety law** to meet the revival of Republican agitation and activity, stimulated by economic stress. The Republican army was declared illegal and military tribunals set up to deal with sedition, illegal drilling, etc.

1932, Feb. Elections. The **Republicans won** 72 seats against 65 for the government. The Labour deputies supported the Republicans, thus giving them a majority.

Mar. DE VALERA ELECTED PRESIDENT, with a program of abolishing the oath to the king.

July. Outbreak of tariff war with Great Britain, following long abortive negotiations.
1933, Jan. 2. De Valera dissolved the dail and in the ensuing elections (Jan. 24) secured for his party a clear majority of one.

May 3. The dail abolished the oath of loyalty and soon afterward voted that the approval of the governor-general should no longer be necessary to put legislation into effect; appeals to the British privy council were made illegal.

July 23. Formation of the National Guard (*Blue Shirts*) in opposition to De Valera's Republican army.

Sept. 3. Union of the National Guard and the Center (Cosgrave Party) to form the *United Ireland Party,* under **Gen. Owen O'Duffy.** There followed a period of disorder and conflict between the two groups.

Sept. 22. Resignation of O'Duffy, a reflection of disapproval of his methods by the more moderate opposition elements. Cosgrave became leader of the United Ireland Party.

1934-1935. Continuation of the tariff war with Great Britain. Ireland suffered tremendously from the loss of her export markets, and much discontent developed.

1935, Jan. Conclusion of a coal and cattle agreement with Great Britain which enabled the Irish to get rid of at least some of their meat.

1936, Feb. 17. Conclusion of an Anglo-Irish trade pact, bringing to an end the disastrous tariff war.

Nov. 3. The NEW CONSTITUTION re-established the senate (abolished in June), but as a functional body. The relationship to Great Britain was ignored.

1937, July 16. The elections resulted in a stalemate, the De Valera party winning exactly one-half of the seats.

1938, Feb. 9. The elections in Northern Ireland resulted in an overwhelming victory for the Unionists, thus blasting any hope of merger of the Free State and Northern Ireland.

Apr. 25. CONCLUSION OF AN AGREE-MENT WITH GREAT BRITAIN for three years. The Ulster (Northern Ireland) problem had to be shelved, but other outstanding questions were adjusted. All recent tariff barriers were thrown down. Great Britain turned over to the Free State (*Eire* or *Ireland* in the new constitution) the coast defenses of Cobh, Bere Haven, and Lough Swilly. This agreement, restoring close friendly relations between Ireland and Britain, was approved by the Irish opposition, which also joined the government party in electing

May 4. DOUGLAS HYDE FIRST PRESIDENT under the new constitution. Hyde was one of the leaders of the Gaelic cultural revival, and a Protestant. His election was taken as a persuasive gesture toward Northern Ireland.

June 17. The elections resulted in a great victory for De Valera, who became prime minister under the new system.

CULTURAL DEVELOPMENTS

Literature: The playwright and poet **William Butler Yeats** (1865-1939) produced his plays at the Abbey Theater in Dublin. His successors in Irish tragedy were **J. M. Synge** and **Sean O'Casey.** The greatest Irish-born playwright was **George Bernard Shaw** (1856-1950), for many years a critic of art and music, drama and literature: *Arms and the Man* (1894), a satire popular in England and abroad, was followed by *The Devil's Disciple* (1897), *The Man of Destiny, Candida* (1895), *Man and Superman* (1903), *Pygmalion* (1912), *Saint Joan* (1923), *Back to Methusaleh* (1921).

Oscar Wilde (1854-1900), Irish-born dramatist and poet, belonged to the English literary scene (*Picture of Dorian Gray; Salome; Lady Windermere's Fan*), and was quickly accepted in the United States. **James Joyce,** the Irish novelist (1882-1941), created a stir with his use of language, first in *Ulysses,* even more in *Finnegans Wake* (1939).   (*Cont. p. 1176.*)

2. THE LOW COUNTRIES

a. BELGIUM

(*From p. 674*)

Of all the countries involved in the First World War, **Belgium** suffered most. The total damage was estimated at over $7,000,000,000, but the country showed extraordinary recuperative power and soon returned to a peace basis. Politically the country was ruled by the Catholic and Socialist parties. One of the major questions at issue was the demand of the Flemish for recognition of their language.

1919, May 9. A new electoral law introduced **universal suffrage** and gave the franchise to certain classes of women.

May 30. By agreement with Great Britain, later confirmed by the League of Nations, Belgium was given the **mandate over part of German East Africa** (Ruanda and Urundi).

June 28. By the treaty of Versailles, Belgium acquired the German districts of **Eupen, Malmédy,** and **Moresnet.**

1920, Sept. 7. Military convention with France. In the following years Belgium acted closely with France in most questions of international import.

1922, Jan. 1. A law went into effect putting **Flemish on a par with French** as an official language.

1923, Jan. 11. Invasion of the Ruhr, by French and Belgian troops (p. 1123).

1925, Apr. 3. A treaty with the Netherlands settled a long-standing dispute regarding the **navigation of the Scheldt.**

Oct. 16. Belgium was a party to the **Locarno treaties** (p. 1124).

1926, May 22. A **treaty with Britain and France** formally abrogated the treaty of 1839.

July. Financial crisis. The king was given dictatorial powers for six months to solve the problem. Devaluation and stabilization of the Belgian franc.

1932, July 18. Enactment of **new language regulations.** Henceforth French was to be the administrative language only of the Walloon provinces, while in Flanders the Flemish language was to be official.

July 19. Conclusion of the **Ouchy convention** between Belgium, Luxemburg, and Holland. The three parties agreed to gradual reduction of economic barriers between them.

Sept. 14. The **government was granted extraordinary power** to deal with the alarming budget deficits. The worldwide depression struck Belgium very hard in view of the cessation of German reparations payments.

1933, Mar. 16. The victory of the National Socialists in Germany obliged the government to take precautionary measures. 150,000,000 francs were devoted to **fortifications along the Meuse** and Belgium thenceforth constantly increased appropriations for defense. In December 1936 the term of service for the infantry was extended from seven to eighteen months.

1934, Feb. 17. Death of King Albert I.

1934–1944. LEOPOLD III.

July 12. The government prohibited the formation of military units and the wearing of uniforms by political organizations. This law was directed at the **growing fascist movement,** and also at the **Labor Defense Militia.** Both organizations were dissolved.

1935, Mar. 25. Paul Van Zeeland, eminent financier, formed a **Government of National Unity,** which was given decree powers for a year to cope with the desperate financial situation.

1936, May 24. Parliamentary elections. The

fascists, led by **Léon Degrelle,** and generally called *Rexists,* won 21 seats.

June 24. Social improvement program, roughly the equivalent of the Popular Front program in France.

Oct. 14. BELGIUM DENOUNCED THE MILITARY ALLIANCE WITH FRANCE AND RESUMED LIBERTY OF ACTION. This step resulted from the German reoccupation of the Rhineland and was generally taken as a reflection of Belgium's determination not to become embroiled with Germany through connection with the Franco-Russian alliance.

1937, Oct. 13. GERMANY, in a note to Brussels, **guaranteed the inviolability and integrity of Belgium** so long as the latter abstained from military action against Germany.

Oct. 24. Resignation of Van Zeeland, following charges of corruption in connection with the National Bank. After a prolonged cabinet crisis, **Paul Janson** (Liberal) formed a new coalition government, which

1938, May 13. Gave way to a coalition headed by **Paul Spaak** (Moderate Socialist).

1939, Feb.–Mar. A prolonged **cabinet crisis** resulted from failure to construct a parliamentary majority.

Apr. 2. The **elections** brought no great change, though the Rexist deputies dropped from 21 to only 4.

Apr. 18. Hubert Pierlot formed a **Catholic-Liberal government.**

Aug. 23. King Leopold issued an **appeal for peace** on behalf of Belgium, the Netherlands, and the Scandinavian states. This proved of no avail. Belgium mobilized but proclaimed neutrality in the European war that broke out on September 3 (p. 1132). (*Cont. p. 1177.*)

b. THE KINGDOM OF THE NETHERLANDS

(*From p. 677*).

Though the Netherlands took no part in the First World War, the nation suffered considerably through interference with trade. Toward the end of the war the government was obliged to submit to stringent regulations by the Allies and to permit the requisitioning of Dutch shipping.

1919, Aug. 9. A **new electoral law** provided for direct election of deputies by all men and women 23 years of age or older.

1920, Jan. 23. The Dutch government refused the Allied demand for the surrender of the **former German Emperor William.** He lived in retirement, first at Amerongen, then at Doorn.

1926, Nov.–1927, July. A great **communist revolt** in the East Indies was suppressed only with difficulty.

1928, Apr. 4. **Palmas Island,** near the Philippines, in dispute between the Netherlands and the United States, assigned to the Netherlands by arbitration.

1930, Dec. 22. Conclusion of the **Oslo agreements** between the three Scandinavian countries, the Netherlands, Belgium, and Luxemburg. The contracting parties promised not to raise tariffs without notification and consultation. July 19, 1932, the Netherlands, Belgium, and Luxemburg concluded the **Ouchy convention** arranging for more specific reduction of tariffs. The Oslo agreements were renewed in 1937, but on July 1, 1938, the trade agreement had to be dropped.

1931, Dec. 22. The **Dutch government began to increase the tariff** and to set up import quotas, in order to help the agricultural and dairying interests, hard hit by the world depression.

1933, Apr. 26. Following the elections, **Hendryk Colijn constructed a crisis cabinet** which attempted to deal with the serious financial situation and to check the growth of extremist movements on both Right and Left.

1934, May. The government was granted **emergency powers** to regulate trade and industry. **Drastic measures against extremists:** National Socialists, Revolutionary Socialists, and Socialists debarred from holding office. Despite these measures, the National Socialists continued to increase their numbers and influence throughout 1935.

1936. In view of developments in Germany, the government felt obliged to strengthen its defenses.

1937, Jan. 7. **Marriage of Princess Juliana** (heiress to the throne) to **Prince Bernhard of Lippe-Biesterfeld.**

May 26. The elections proved to be a **setback for the National Socialist movement.** The Liberal Democratic Party showed a marked gain.

1939, June 30. **Resignation of the Colijn government,** which was reformed amidst much party dissension. (*Cont. p. 1178.*)

3. FRANCE

(*From p. 693*)

1914, Sept. 3. **Fearing that Paris might fall** to the advancing German armies, the **French government moved to Bordeaux.** This temporary withdrawal made it more difficult for the civilian ministers to control the army commanders and the French general staff displayed a spirit of independence that sometimes verged on insubordination.

Although French political parties relaxed their feuds in a *union sacrée,* discontent and division brought down successive cabinets. The second ministry of **René Viviani** (August 1914–October 1915) was followed by the fifth ministry of **Aristide Briand** (to December 1916) and his sixth (to March 1917).

In the spring of 1917 the inability of both sides to win a decision on the battlefield and the victory of the revolution in Russia led to a wide spread of defeatism, pacifism, and socialism.

1917, Mar. 17. The **Briand cabinet** was obliged to resign, and was succeeded by a ministry in which **Alexandre Ribot** was premier and **Paul Painlevé** minister of war. It was this cabinet, led by a tired septuagenarian, that had to bear the full brunt of the discontent arising from Nivelle's ill-starred offensive. Deserted by the Socialists, Ribot resigned (Sept. 9).

Sept. 12. **Painlevé formed a cabinet,** in which Ribot became foreign minister. This proved to be merely a transition government.

Oct. 23. **Jean Louis Barthou succeeded Ribot** as foreign minister.

Nov. 16. **The Painlevé cabinet fell.** Formation of the great **ministry of Georges Clemenceau,** in which the prime minister was also minister of war, while **Stephen Pichon** was given the foreign office. Clemenceau's policy was one of victory *sans phrase.* He set out at once to hunt down the preachers of disaffection **(Malvy, Humbert, Bolo Pasha, Caillaux)** and to organize the country for victory.

Under the leadership of Clemenceau (second ministry, November 1917–January 1920), France survived the final year of the war. Clemenceau took a leading part in shaping the peace that followed.

WAR LOSSES. The acquisition of Alsace-Lorraine and of mandates in Africa and Syria (pp. 1081, 1088) did not compensate victorious France for her losses in the war, which had been fought largely on French soil. The 1,385,000 French soldiers known to be dead; 700,000 seriously wounded; 2,344,000 other wounded; 446,000 prisoners or missing meant a loss of man-power proportionately greater than that suffered by any other belligerent. Of Frenchmen who in 1914 were aged 20 to 32, more than half were killed. Property damage in the war zone in the north and east of France included 300,000 houses destroyed, and as many more damaged; 6,000 public buildings and 20,000 workshops and factories destroyed or badly damaged; 1,360,000 head of livestock killed or confiscated; thousands of acres of farm land and forest ravaged by shell fire. These figures explain the intensity of the postwar demand for security and reparation. Since most Frenchmen believed Germany solely responsible for the war, these losses, which brought suffering to almost every French household, stood in the way of any compromise or cooperation between France and post-war Germany.

1919, July 12. A new electoral law introduced the *scrutin de liste* and a measure of proportional representation. The effect of this was to make it more difficult than ever for any one party to secure a majority.

Nov. 16. Elections. The coalition which had governed under Clemenceau split into a Right *Bloc National* (Clemenceau, Millerand, Poincaré, Briand) and a *Cartel des Gauches,* led by Herriot. The Royalists, Socialists, and Communists were not included in either group. The elections gave a majority to the *Bloc National,* which was also victorious in the senatorial elections of January 1920.

1920, Jan. 17. Presidential election. Clemenceau was defeated by Paul Deschanel, a reflection of public opinion which held the treaty of Versailles too lenient.

Jan. 19-Sept. 24. Cabinet of Alexandre Millerand.

Feb. 18-Sept. 15. PRESIDENCY OF PAUL DESCHANEL.

Apr. 23. Joseph Caillaux, former prime minister, sentenced to three years' imprisonment and other penalties after conviction of dealings with the enemy.

Sept. 15. Resignation of President Deschanel on account of ill health.

1920, Sept. 23-1924, June 11. PRESIDENCY OF ALEXANDRE MILLERAND,

Dec. 30. The **Socialist Party,** at the Tours Congress, voted to join the **Third International.**

1921, Jan. 13. The **General Confederation of Labor dissolved** by court order. This organization (C.G.T.) was the center of the syndicalist movement, which was supported by many unions.

Jan. 16-1922, Jan. 12. Cabinet of Aristide Briand.

Feb. 19. Defensive treaty with Poland.

Mar. 9. Peace treaty with Turkey ending hostilities in Cilicia (p. 1086).

May 28. Diplomatic relations with the Vatican resumed (ruptured in 1904).

1922, Jan. 15-1924, June 1. Cabinet of Raymond Poincaré, with a program of forcing reparations payments from Germany, chiefly to meet the expense of restoration of the devastated regions, on which 20 milliard francs had already been spent.

1923, Jan. Invasion of the Ruhr (p. 1123).

Apr. 1. Compulsory military service reduced to one and one-half years.

1924, Jan. 6. The **Catholic Church** was given the right to reoccupy its former property under a system of *"diocesan associations."*

Jan. 25. Treaty with Czechoslovakia, providing for mutual aid in the event of unprovoked attack.

May 11. The **elections** gave the *Cartel des Gauches* a majority in the chamber, as a result of the failure of Poincaré's policy of coercing Germany. Poincaré resigned.

June 11. Resignation of President Millerand. This was forced by Édouard Herriot, leader of the Radical Socialist Party, the strongest group in the chamber, who refused to form a government while Millerand was president, charging that the president had abandoned the traditional neutrality and had openly sided with the Right.

1924, June 13-1931, June. PRESIDENCY OF GASTON DOUMERGUE.

June 14-1925, Apr. 10. Édouard Herriot, prime minister.

Oct. 28. *De jure* **recognition of Soviet Russia.**

1925, Apr. Beginning of the insurrection in Morocco (p. 1080).

July. Rising of the Druses in the Lebanon against French rule (p. 1090).

July 26. Agreement with Spain for common action in Morocco.

Oct. 16. The **Locarno treaties** (p. 1124).

Nov. 27-1926, July 15. Three **ministries of Aristide Briand.**

1926, June 10. Treaty with Roumania.

July 15. Fall of the Briand ministry as a result of the financial crisis. The franc had declined to the value of 2¢ and the budget could not be balanced, despite the imposition of new taxes and increases of income and other taxes. War debts, post-war extravagance, and the failure of reparations payments made a partial repudiation of the debt inevitable.

1926, July 28-1929, July 26. National Union ministries of Poincaré. Briand remained as minister for foreign affairs. The new government voted new taxes and drastic economies which balanced the budget.

Aug. 10. The two chambers, sitting as a national assembly, incorporated a **sinking-fund measure** in the constitution. Income from the tobacco monopoly and from inheritance taxes was to be used to redeem part of the national debt.

1927, July 13. The system of *scrutin d'arrondissement* restored for the elections.

Nov. 11. **Treaty with Yugoslavia** (p. 1022).

1928, Mar. 28. **Military service** reduced to one year.

June 24. The **franc was devalued** from 19.3¢ to 3.92¢, this being a disguised repudiation of about four-fifths of the national debt. The measure hit the *rentier* class hardest and explains later opposition to further devaluation.

Aug. 27. The **Kellogg-Briand pact** (p. 1124).

1929, July 27. **Resignation of Poincaré,** on account of ill health. There followed a series of short-lived cabinets, based on shifting parliamentary blocs rather than on genuine party groupings.

1930, Apr. 30. A **National Workmen's Insurance Law** passed after years of discussion. It insured 9,000,000 workers against sickness, old age, and death. Workers contributed 3 per cent of wages, employers an equal amount. The state contributed in some cases.

June 30. **End of the evacuation of the Rhineland.**

1931, June–1932, May. **PRESIDENCY OF PAUL DOUMER.** Briand was passed over, since his efforts at international conciliation had estranged the Right. Death of Briand (Mar. 7, 1932).

1932, May 6. **President Doumer assassinated** by a Russian *émigré*.

1932, May–1940, July 11. **PRESIDENCY OF ALBERT LEBRUN.**

May. The **elections** gave the Left parties a majority.

June–Dec. Second **ministry of Édouard Herriot.** He resigned because the government proposal to pay the scheduled debt installment to the United States was voted down by the chamber. There followed five short-lived ministries in the next thirteen months. All were concerned with keeping France on the gold standard and with balancing the budget without resorting to inflation.

1933, Dec. The **Stavisky case.** Alexandre Stavisky, a Russian promoter, involved in the floating of a fraudulent bond issue by the municipal pawnshop of Bayonne, fled to escape arrest and when cornered was alleged to have committed suicide. Royalists and fascists stirred up an agitation against the republic which recalled the Dreyfus case. It was believed that important officials and politicians were involved and that their guilt was being concealed. The full facts were never made known.

1934, Feb. 6–7. **SERIOUS RIOTS IN PARIS** and other cities, resulting from the Stavisky case.

Feb. 8. **Coalition cabinet** under ex-President **Doumergue,** including leaders of all parties except Royalists, Socialists, and Communists, formed to avert civil war (general strike February 12–13).

Oct. 9. **Assassination, at Marseilles,** of **King Alexander of Yugoslavia** and foreign minister **Barthou** (p. 1022), who had been engaged (Apr.–June) in a grand tour of European capitals in the hope of building up a strong alliance system against the new Nazi Germany.

Nov. **Fall of the Doumergue ministry,** Doumergue having proposed a constitutional reform by which change of ministry should, as in Britain, necessitate a new election. The coalition was reorganized under **Pierre Flandin.**

1935, Jan. 7. **Agreement between France and Italy** with regard to Africa. In this accord France made a number of concessions to Italy (status of Italians in Tunisia, frontier rectifications, part ownership in the Ethiopian Railway, etc.), in the hope of establishing a strong front against the growing German menace.

May. The **Flandin cabinet was overthrown** when it demanded quasidictatorial powers to save the franc. A **Laval ministry** followed.

May 2. Conclusion of the **alliance treaty with Soviet Russia.** For some time the French government had labored not only to resuscitate its alliances with the Little Entente powers and Poland, but to bring Germany and Poland and Russia into an eastern pact which would serve to maintain the *status quo*. Both Germany and Poland evaded this suggestion and, after the announcement of German rearmament (p. 1011), the French government hurried into the alliance with Russia, an arrangement by no means popular with the more conservative elements in France.

Nov. 3. **Merger of various Socialist groups** to form a *Socialist and Republican Union*. This group soon established close relations with the Communists and with the Radical Socialists, to form a **Popular Front,** the main objective of which was to counteract the agitation of the reactionary groups (**Col. François de La Roque** and his *Croix de Feu*, etc.). To meet this new pressure from the Left,

Dec. 28. The government ordered **political leagues dissolved.** Most of them promptly re-emerged as political "parties."

1936, Jan. 22. **Downfall of the Pierre Laval government,** which was thoroughly discredited by its half-and-half attitude toward Italy during the Ethiopian crisis (p. 1000) and further suspected of supporting the reactionary currents. There followed a **cabinet under Albert**

Sarraut which was nothing more than a stop-gap.

May 3. The **parliamentary elections gave the Popular Front a majority** in the chamber of deputies and led to the formation of the

June 5.   FIRST POPULAR FRONT MINISTRY, under **Léon Blum,** leader of the Socialist Party. The cabinet was composed of Radical Socialists and Socialists, and enjoyed the support of the Communists. A great **wave of sit-down strikes** (300,000 workers out) accompanied this important change and led at once to the introduction of a far-reaching **program of social reform:** establishment of the 40-hour week (June 12); reorganization and ultimately nationalization of the Bank of France; suppression of fascist groups (June 30); nationalization of the munitions industry (July 17); compulsory arbitration of labor disputes, vacations with pay, etc. These measures, hailed by the workers as marking the dawn of a new era, at once aroused the hostility of the employing classes. Rapidly rising costs of production brought with them rising prices. The franc began to sink steadily and capital started to flee the country in large amounts. To the increasing financial difficulties was added the **enhanced tension in international affairs** following the German reoccupation of the Rhineland, the Italian victory in Ethiopia, the collapse of the League system (on which France had depended so much), and the outbreak of civil war in Spain. The government was obliged to expend huge sums on further rearmament and, after Belgium's resumption of neutrality, to undertake the **fortification of the Belgian frontier.** In the Spanish affair Blum felt impelled to follow the British lead and adopt a policy of non-intervention. **Anglo-French relations** had grown so cool as a result of Laval's Italian policy that Blum looked upon revival of close relations as worth any cost.

Oct. 2. A **bill devaluing the franc,** but not definitely fixing its gold content, was finally passed. Co-operation of Great Britain and the United States averted violent fluctuations in the foreign exchanges.

1937, Mar.   Blum was obliged to announce a "breathing spell" in the work of social reform, in order to reassure capitalist groups and make possible the flotation of huge defense loans.

June 19. The senate refused Blum's demands for emergency fiscal powers, whereupon **the cabinet resigned.** The government was reformed with **Camille Chautemps** (Radical Socialist) as premier and Blum as vice-premier. The new government secured the necessary powers and devoted itself to the Herculean task of financial reconstruction. At the same time

the foreign minister, **Yvon Delbos,** embarked upon an extended visit to France's eastern allies (Dec.), without finding much prospect of active collaboration against Germany.

Nov. 18. Discovery of a **royalist plot** against the republic. The *Cagoulards* (Hooded Ones) appear to have been a terrorist group within a larger revolutionary (fascist) movement. Secret plans, fortified dugouts, caches of weapons and munitions were discovered.

1938, Jan. 14. The **Socialists deserted the cabinet,** which was reorganized by Chautemps as a Radical Socialist ministry. This the Socialists at first tolerated, but

Mar. 10.   Chautemps's government fell when the Socialists rejected a demand for full powers.

Mar. 13–Apr. 10.   Léon Blum, after trying in vain to organize a national coalition cabinet to face the acute international situation, formed a **new Popular Front government.** Like its predecessor it was frustrated by the senate, which refused Blum all confidence. Forced out of office, Blum made way for

Apr. 10. The **cabinet of Édouard Daladier** (Radical Socialist), who stood farther to the Right. Daladier was given decree powers until July 31, and proceeded to devalue the franc and end a new strike movement. Blum and the Socialists supported him.

July 19–21. State visit of **George VI** of Great Britain to Paris; a striking demonstration of Anglo-French solidarity in the face of the Berlin-Rome Axis.

Sept.   THE GERMAN-CZECHOSLOVAK CRISIS (p. 1017).

Oct. 4. The **Daladier government broke definitely with the Socialists and Communists** when the former abstained from the vote of confidence on the Munich agreements and the Communists voted in opposition. **End of the Popular Front.**

Nov. 12. The government promulgated a large number of decrees aimed at improvement of the desperate financial situation. Among other things the 40-hour week, retained in principle, was to be much modified in practice. This departure created much ill-feeling, especially in the ranks of the C.G.T. (*Confederation of Labor*) with its 5,000,000 members. A new strike epidemic was launched by the workers and this culminated in

Nov. 30. A **general strike of protest,** called for 24 hours. The government had prepared to meet the threat, had put railway workers under military orders, and had otherwise requisitioned services. Under threats of punishment the whole movement collapsed, relatively few workers going on strike.

Dec. 6.   Conclusion of the Franco-German

pact (p. 1130). This made but a slight impression in France, the more so as it coincided with a new

Dec.-1939. Franco-Italian crisis, arising from Italian demands for French colonies and other concessions. The government took an uncompromising attitude toward any cessions of territory and

1939, Jan. Daladier paid a demonstrative visit to Corsica and Tunisia. On the other hand the conquest of Catalonia by the Spanish fascists, supported by the Italians, brought France face to face with a new dictatorship on its frontiers.

Mar. The continued expansion of Germany to the east produced ever greater tension. Daladier asked for and received from parliament power to govern by decree without express limitations, a situation unprecedented under the Third Republic. The premier used his power to speed up rearmament, to effect partial mobilization, etc. France assumed an attitude of quiet determination, but at the same time joined with Britain in guarantees to Poland, and Greece, and used all her influence to draw Russia into the non-aggression system (p. 1132).

June 23. Conclusion of a **treaty with Turkey** providing for cession of Alexandretta to Turkey.

Aug. 20-Sept. 1. The Danzig-Polish crisis (p. 1132). The French government throughout stood shoulder to shoulder with Britain and

Sept. 3. Declared **WAR ON GERMANY** (p. 1132).

CULTURAL DEVELOPMENTS

Marcel Proust (1871–1922) is best known for his psychological novel in seven parts (*À la recherche du temps perdu,* 1913–1928); **André Maurois** (1885–   ) for his biographies (*Disraeli,* 1927). Other novelists: **André Gide** (1869–1951); **Romain Rolland** (1866–1944; *Jean Christophe,* in 10 volumes), **André Malraux** (1901–   ), **Jules Romains** (1885–   ), **Georges Duhamel** (1884–   ), **Sidonie Colette** (1873–1954), **Albert Camus** (1913–1960). **Jean-Paul Sartre** (1905–   ; *Nausea,* 1938) is also known for his plays; other popular playwrights have been **Jean Cocteau** (1892–   ), **Jean Anouilh** (1910–   ), **Sacha Guitry** (1885–   ), **Eugène Brieux** (1858–1932), and **Henri Bernstein** (1876–1953). Among modern French poets **Paul Valéry** (1871–1945) and **Louis Aragon** (1897–   ) are the foremost.

Modern French music was introduced in the 1920's by "Les Six," a group of composers including **Darius Milhaud** (1892–   ), **Arthur Honegger** (1892–1955), **François Poulenc** (1899–1963), **Louis Durey** (1888–   ), **Georges Auric** (1899), and **Germaine Taillefere** (1892–   ). The structures of the architect **LeCorbusier** (Charles Jeanneret, 1887–1965) belong to the "international style" of European architecture. **Painters: Georges Braque** (1881–1963) and **Georges Rouault** (1871–1958); **André Derain** (1880–1954); **Raoul Dufy** (1877–1953); the "Intimistes" **Pierre Bonnard** (1867–1947) and **Jean Édouard Vuillard** (1868–1940).

(*Cont. p. 1180.*)

4. THE IBERIAN PENINSULA

a. SPAIN

(*From p. 698*)

Though Spain was spared the horrors of the First World War, the effects of the conflict made themselves felt. The demands of the combatants for iron, munitions, and other goods led to a striking **development of Spanish industry,** centering in Catalonia. The growth of industry in turn resulted in increased tension between the semi-feudal upper classes, supported by the Church and the army, and the new forces of **socialism** and **anarchism.** The movement for **autonomy for Catalonia,** which had survived the centralizing policies of the 19th century, flared up anew, and the government was throughout confronted with the additional **problem of Morocco,** where constant native risings required a great military effort and the expenditure of

much money. Politically the pre-war system extended through the First World War and immediate post-war periods, with repeated changes of ministry and the rotation of Liberals and Conservatives in power.

1917, July 5. The **Catalan deputies and senators** in the cortes **demanded the convocation of a constituent assembly** to consider home rule for Catalonia.

1919, Jan. 24. A **Catalonian Union** met at Barcelona and drafted a program for home rule. The government appointed a commission to consider the question, but its carefully circumscribed report was rejected by the Catalonians as inadequate.

1921, July 21. DISASTER AT ANUAL, Morocco, culmination of the troubles there. **Gen. Fernandez Silvestre** and 20,000 Spaniards were defeated by the Riffians under **Abd-el-Krim** and some 12,000 killed. Silvestre committed suicide. The disaster precipitated a political crisis and a widespread demand for an investigation of responsibility. A parliamentary commission was established, but its report, when submitted to the cabinet in 1922, was at once suppressed.

1923, Sept. 12. Mutiny of the garrison at Barcelona and outbreak of a separatist movement.

Sept. 13. MILITARY COUP OF GEN. MIGUEL PRIMO DE RIVERA, who acted with the approval of the king. He took Barcelona, formed a military directorate, proclaimed martial law throughout the country, dissolved the cortes, suspended jury trial, and instituted a rigid press censorship. Liberal opponents were imprisoned or harried out of the land (Miguel de Unamuno, Blasco Ibáñez).

1924, Feb. 7. The **Tangier convention** (Britain, France, Spain) providing for permanent neutralization of the Tangier zone and government by an international commission.

Nov. 19–28. Visit of Alfonso XIII and Primo de Rivera to Rome, in return for a visit of the king and queen of Italy (June). This exchange of visits marked the dictator's efforts to establish a close understanding with fascist Italy, culminating in the **treaty of friendship** of August 7, 1926.

1925, July 26. Agreement with France for co-operation in the war against the Riffs.

Dec. 3. End of the dictatorship, because of widespread and increasing popular discontent. But Primo de Rivera was at once named prime minister, with a predominantly military cabinet.

1926, June 10. Spain resigned from the League of Nations, but the resignation was later withdrawn (Mar. 22, 1928).

Nov. 2. Attempted **coup in Catalonia** by conspirators operating from France.

1927, Feb. 9. International conference at Paris to consider the Spanish demand that Tangier be included in the Spanish zone.

July. End of the Franco-Spanish campaign in Morocco.

1928, Mar. 3. France agreed to give Spain somewhat larger share in the government of Tangier.

1929, Jan. 29. Military revolt at Ciudad Real, indicating spread of dissatisfaction to military groups.

Mar. 17. The University of Madrid and other universities were closed in order to put an end to the agitation of the students and intellectuals.

1930, Jan. 28. RESIGNATION OF PRIMO DE RIVERA, discouraged and in ill health (death Mar. 16).

Jan. 30. Government of Gen. Damaso Ber-

enguer, who attempted a policy of conciliation. An amnesty was granted, Primo de Rivera's assembly was dissolved, local government organs restored, juridical rights recognized. The government promised early elections for a national parliament. But the students continued their agitation and **Republican leaders openly denounced the monarchy** as responsible for national disasters and dictatorship. After the removal of the censorship (Sept.) criticism and demonstrations became the order of the day.

Dec. 12–13. Mutiny of the garrison at Jaca, demanding a republic. This was suppressed only with difficulty.

1931, Feb. 8. The king announced the **restoration of the constitution** and fixed parliamentary elections for March. Popular demand for a constituent assembly. **Berenguer resigned.**

Mar. The government called for municipal and provincial elections and promised a constituent assembly.

Apr. 12. The **municipal elections** resulted in an overwhelming victory for the Republicans. Niceto Alcalá Zamora, the Republican leader, called for the king's abdication.

Apr. 14. KING ALFONSO LEFT SPAIN without abdicating, stating that he would await the expression of popular sentiment. Alcalá Zamora at once set up a provisional government, with himself as president.

June 28. Elections for the constituent assembly gave the Republican-Socialist coalition a huge majority.

Nov. 12. A committee of the assembly declared **Alfonso XIII guilty of high treason** and forbade his return to Spain. The royal property was confiscated.

Dec. 9. The **new constitution** was adopted. It provided for universal suffrage and a single-chamber parliament (cortes), to be elected for four years. The president of the republic was to be chosen by an electoral college consisting of parliament plus an equal number of electors chosen by popular vote. His term was to be six years. No army officer or member of the clergy was to be eligible. The ministry was to be responsible to parliament. The constitution proclaimed complete religious freedom and separated Church and State; education secularized; church property nationalized; Jesuit Order dissolved (1932, Jan.) and its property taken over. Catalonia was given a measure of local autonomy. The government was granted power to expropriate private property, to socialize large estates, and to nationalize public utilities.

Dec. 10. Alcalá Zamora elected first president. He had resigned in October in protest against extremist anti-clerical legislation, and had been succeeded by **Manuel Azaña,** who became first prime minister under the constitution. The national assembly continued to function as the first regular parliament.

1932, Aug. 10. Revolt of Gen. José Sanjurjo, who seized Seville. The movement was quickly suppressed by loyal troops, but was indicative of conservative opposition to the radical legislation of the new régime.

Sept. 25. CATALAN CHARTER OF AUTONOMY. The home rule leaders had drawn up the charter soon after the revolution and had secured Catalan approval by a plebiscite (Aug. 1931). After much agitation and disorder in the province, the Republican government was obliged to accept it. Catalonia was given its own president, parliament, and government, with extensive taxing and other powers. The Catalans were to have their own flag and Catalan was made the official language. The Catalan parliament met for the first time in December. Success of the movement led to similar demands by the Basques and other regionalists.

1933, Jan. 8. Great radical rising (anarchists and syndicalists) in Barcelona, which spread to many other large cities. It was successfully suppressed by government troops, but indicated the impatience of the lower classes at the social reform movement.

Apr. 23. Municipal elections reflected a distinct veering of opinion to the Right.

May 17. An **Associations Law** required that heads of all religious orders be Spaniards; members of religious orders were forbidden to engage in industry or trade; church schools were abolished and all secular education by religious orders prohibited; church property nationalized, though left in the custody of the clergy. Vigorous protests of the pope (encyclical *Delectissimi nobis*).

Sept. 8. Elections for the Tribunal of Constitutional Guaranties (a body to test the constitutionality of legislation and protect civil liberties) showed a further trend toward the Right.

Nov. 19. The **first regular elections** for the cortes gave the Right parties 44 per cent of the seats, the Left parties only 21 per cent. There followed a series of coalition ministries, all of them more or less helpless and unpopular.

Dec. 9. Syndicalist-anarchist rising in Barcelona, put down only after ten days of fighting.

1934, Jan. 14. Catalan elections, resulting in a victory for the moderate Left groups; a protest against the swing to conservatism in Spain generally. **Luis Companys president** of Catalonia.

Apr. A **great strike in Barcelona,** led by Socialists, created further tension with Madrid and was suppressed only with difficulty.

Oct. 4. Cabinet of Alejandro Lerroux, in which the Catholic *Popular Action Party* of **Gil Robles** was represented. This party was allied with the monarchists, was outspokenly clerical.

Oct. 5. The Left parties called a **general strike** in protest against the rising opposition to the democratic, social republic.

Oct. 6. President Luis Companys of Catalonia proclaimed the **independence of Catalonia.** This separatist uprising was suppressed by government troops, as was also an **insurrection of the miners in the Asturias** where a communist régime had been proclaimed. As a result of the rising in Catalonia, the Catalan statute was suspended preparatory to revision (Dec. 15).

1935, Sept. The **Lerroux cabinet fell,** and was succeeded by several ephemeral ministries, all more or less at the mercy of the Right.

1936, Jan. 6. The cortes was dissolved.

Feb. 16. Elections. The Left parties (Republicans, Socialists, Syndicalists, Communists) combined in a *Popular Front* and won a decisive victory over Conservative Republicans, Clericals, and Monarchists. **Manuel Azaña formed a new cabinet** (Feb. 19), which at once proclaimed an amnesty and undertook the **restoration of Catalan autonomy.** The social reform program (distribution of land, development of schools, etc.) was resumed, as was the anti-clerical policy.

Apr. 10. The **cortes voted to remove President Alcalá Zamora** for exceeding his powers.

May 10. Manuel Azaña was regularly elected president.

July 18. THE SPANISH CIVIL WAR. The conflict began with a revolt of the army chiefs at Melilla in Spanish Morocco. It spread rapidly to the garrison towns of Spain (Cadiz, Seville, Saragossa, Burgos, etc.). In Madrid and Barcelona the government held its own, thus making early success of the Insurgents impossible. All the parties of the Left united in resistance and the government declared the **confiscation of all religious property** (July 28). The Insurgent leaders, **Gen. Francisco Franco** and **Gen. Emilio Mola** (Gen. Sanjurjo was killed at the very outset in an airplane accident), were supported by the bulk of the army and air force, and had at their disposal large Moorish contingents. July 30 they set up a **Junta of National Defense** at Burgos. At an early stage in the war **foreign powers began to intervene and Spain became the battle-ground of rival ideologies.** Italian and German "volunteers" joined the Insurgents, while Russia supplied the government with equipment and advisers.

Aug. 15. The **rebels captured Badajoz** and began a great advance eastward up the Tagus Valley through Talavera and **Toledo** (relieved September 28 after a ten weeks' siege of the famous Alcazar fortress by the Loyalists).

Sept. 4. The **rebels captured Irun** in the north. On the same day a Popular Front government was formed in Madrid under **Largo Caballero,** with Catalan and Basque Nationalists represented. In November anarchist-syndicalists were included. On September 12 the Insurgents took **San Sebastian.**

Oct. 1.   GEN. FRANCISCO FRANCO was appointed by the Insurgents as *Chief of the Spanish State.*

Oct. 8. The government adopted **home rule for the Basque provinces,** which established the first autonomous Basque government under **President José Aguirre.**

Nov. 6.   Beginning of the siege of Madrid by the Insurgents. The government moved to Valencia. Despite heavy fighting in the suburbs of the city and appalling air bombardments, the Loyalist troops held the capital and the Insurgent assault ended in deadlock.

Nov. 18.   Germany and Italy recognized the government of Gen. Franco. Great Britain and France continued their ban on supplies to the legitimate government and attempted to unite the powers on a **policy of non-intervention,** for fear lest the war expand into a general conflict. Twenty-seven nations, including Germany and Italy, agreed to participate in a **non-intervention committee,** sitting at London. A scheme for supervision was introduced, but this, like other methods adopted, failed to prevent participation by those powers which cared to intervene. The Italian government came out more and more openly in support of Franco, and ultimately had from 50,000 to 75,000 troops in Spain.

1937, Feb. 8. The **rebels captured Malaga** with Italian aid, but failed to cut the road from Madrid to Valencia.

Mar. 18.   Loyalist forces defeated Italian troops at Brihuega, capturing large stores. The Insurgents, frustrated in the effort to cut off Madrid, turned to the north and concentrated on Bilbao.

May 17.   A new government, under Juan Negrin, replaced that of Largo Caballero. Negrin represented the Socialists, but took in members of other Left parties (except the Anarcho-Syndicalists). The new cabinet took the view that the war must be won before the social revolution could be carried further. All defense ministries were unified under **Indalecio Prieto.**

May 31. Four **German warships bombarded Almeria** by way of reprisal for an air attack by the Loyalists upon the *Deutschland.*

June 18.   Bilbao fell to the Insurgents after weeks of heavy fighting and countless air bombardments. Basque resistance soon collapsed and the rebels pushed on to Santander.

June 23.   Germany and Italy quitted the neutrality patrol off the Spanish coast in protest against the unwillingness of the other powers to secure satisfaction for the attack on the *Deutschland.* At the same time they refused to accept patrol by Britain and France. Acute international tension, the French being held back from opening the frontier to supplies for the Loyalists only by pressure from Britain. Meanwhile "piracy" became rife in the western Mediterranean, mysterious submarines attacking British ships and even warships. Thereupon the British government convoked the **Nyon conference,** and, with French support, organized a new and drastic anti-piracy patrol (p. 1128).

Oct. 21.   Franco's troops finally captured Gijon, breaking the resistance in the Asturias and **completing the conquest of the northwest.**

Oct. 28. The Spanish government moved from Valencia to Barcelona, having taken over control of the Catalan government (Aug. 12).

Nov. 28. Franco announced a **naval blockade** of the entire Spanish coast, using the island of Majorca as a base.

Dec. 5. Beginning of a great **Loyalist counter-offensive around Teruel,** which was taken December 19. This move served to divert the Insurgents from operations to the northeastward. But the government forces, much less adequately supplied and equipped than their opponents, were unable to sustain the offensive.

1938, Feb. 15.   Franco's forces recaptured Teruel and made a spectacular drive toward the sea.

Apr. 15. The **Insurgents took Vinaroz,** on the seacoast, thus severing Loyalist territory in Castile from Barcelona and Catalonia. A tremendous battle developed along the Ebro River, where the contestants were deadlocked during most of the summer. In accordance with the **Anglo-Italian agreement** (p. 1128), Mussolini withdrew some troops from Spain, but there still remained a substantial force estimated at 40,000.

Dec. 23. Beginning of the great **Insurgent drive in Catalonia.** Despite valiant resistance, the Loyalists forces were gradually driven back toward Barcelona.

1939, Jan. 26.   BARCELONA WAS TAKEN BY FRANCO'S TROOPS, with Italian aid. The Loyalist resistance now collapsed and within a couple of weeks the Insurgents had overrun all of Catalonia, some 200,000 Loyalist troops crossing the French frontier, where they were disarmed.

Feb. 27. Britain and France finally recognized the government of Gen. Franco, without conditions. Thereupon

Feb. 28. President Azaña, who had taken refuge in Paris, **resigned** his position. Efforts of Britain and France to bring the civil war to an end met with the opposition of Premier Negrin, who enjoyed the support of the more radical elements in Republican Spain, but

Mar. 6. A military coup in Madrid, led by **Gen. Segismundo Casado,** resulted in the removal of Negrin and his colleagues. They fled to France by air, while at Madrid a new *National Defense Council* was organized, with **Gen. José Miaja** (defender of Madrid in 1936–1937) at the head. The Republican fleet escaped from Cartagena and took refuge in the Tunisian port of Bizerte, where it was interned by the French authorities. The new Madrid régime was committed to a policy of "peace with honor," but this policy at once led to **conflict with the Communists** in the capital, producing a civil war within the larger civil war. The Communists were finally defeated and Miaja then devoted himself to the task of reaching a compromise with Franco. Failing to secure assurances of leniency, the national defense council was finally obliged to accept unconditional surrender.

Mar. 28. END OF THE CIVIL WAR came with the **SURRENDER OF MADRID** and Valencia. Members of the defense council fled. The war had cost about 700,000 lives in battle, 30,000 executed or assassinated, 15,000 killed in air raids. Franco and his government at once set up special tribunals which convicted hundreds of Loyalist leaders, despite efforts of Britain and France to ensure moderation. The United States recognized the new régime (Apr. 1) and on

Apr. 7. Spain announced **adhesion to the German-Italian-Japanese anti-Communist pact** (p. 1011).

May 20–June. Withdrawal of Italian and German forces from Spain after an imposing victory parade in battered Madrid. As it turned out, the Germans had some 10,000 men in Spain, mostly in the aviation and tank services. Together with the Italian "volunteers" they had aided Franco greatly in transporting troops from Morocco in the early days of the war, and had played a major rôle in many later engagements.

Sept. 3. Spain indicated her intention of remaining neutral in the great European conflict over Danzig and Poland (p. 1132).

CULTURAL DEVELOPMENTS

Spain's foremost artist of the 20th century is **Pablo Picasso** (b. 1881), a founder of the school of Cubism and still a leader in the world of painting. **Manuel de Falla** (1876–1946) gained recognition for his orchestral works, especially ballet music. In the field of literature, the leading poet was **Juan Ramon Jiménez** (1881–1958); the dramatist, **Jacinto Benavente y Martinéz** (1866–1954; Nobel prize, 1922); the novelist, **Vicente Blasco Ibáñez** (1867–1928); the chief essayists, **Miguel de Unamuno y Jugo** (1864–1936) and **Ortega y Gasset** (1873–1955).

(Cont. p. 1185.)

b. PORTUGAL

(From p. 699)

1914, Nov. 23. The **Portuguese national assembly voted to join Great Britain** and France in the war against Germany, but action in accord with this vote was delayed by

1915, Jan. 28–May 14. The insurrection and **dictatorship of Gen. Pimenta de Castro,** representing a pro-German faction in the army. He in turn was overthrown by a democratic revolt May 14.

1915–1917. Bernardino Machado became president on the resignation of President Arriaga.

1916, Mar. 9. GERMANY DECLARED WAR ON PORTUGAL after the seizure of German ships in the harbor of Lisbon. The Portuguese organized an expeditionary force, which arrived in France February 3, 1917, and took over a small sector of the front.

1917, Dec. 5. Gen. Sidonio Pães led another pro-German uprising, arrested and deported the president, and **made himself president-dictator.**

1918, Dec. 14. Pães was assassinated by a radical, whereupon the democratic régime was re-established. The situation in the country continued to be utterly confused. In a land which was still 65 per cent illiterate the democratic system could hardly be expected to function well. One cabinet relieved another, the average duration of governments being about four months. Insurrections and coups were hardly less numerous. The financial condition of the country, long parlous, went from bad to worse. Multiplication of offices, widespread political corruption, appalling inefficiency characterized the decade from 1918 to 1928.

1919, Jan. 19–Feb. 14. A **royalist uprising** in the north assumed substantial proportions, but was ultimately suppressed.

May 6. The Allied supreme council assigned to Portugal the **mandate for part of German East Africa,** known as the *Kionga Triangle.*

Aug. 5.   Antonio José de Almeida became president.

1920, Apr. 8.   Portugal joined the League of Nations.

1923, Aug. 6.   Teixeira Gomes succeeded as **president.**

1925, Apr. 18–19.   An attempted military coup directed against the democratic régime led to some shooting and bloodshed in Lisbon, but then collapsed from want of leadership.

Dec. 16.   Bernardino Machado was again elected **president.**

1926, May 28.   OVERTHROW OF THE EXISTING RÉGIME by an army movement inspired by **Mendes Cabeçadas** and led by **Gen. Gomes da Costa.** The revolt broke out in the north and was supported by most of the army. Gomes da Costa, an audacious, vain, and politically innocent leader, became a national hero. Machado and the cabinet of Antonio Mara da Silva were overthrown, parliament was dissolved, and parties broken up.

July 9.   Gen. Antonio de Fragoso Carmona deposed the utterly incompetent Gomes da Costa, who was honorably exiled to the Azores.

1927, Feb. 3–13.   Insurrection against the military dictatorship broke out at Oporto and then (Feb. 7) at Lisbon. This was described as "communist," but was really inspired by a group of intellectual reformers (group about the *Seara Nova*). After some severe fighting the movement was defeated.

1928, Mar. 25.   Gen. Carmona was elected president. The new régime, which had no very specific program, proved itself not much different from its predecessors, excepting that the spoils were in the hands of the military clique rather than in those of the parliament.

Apr. 27.   ANTONIO DE OLIVEIRA SALAZAR became minister of finance, with extraordinary powers. Born 1889, he had been educated for the priesthood, had then turned to law, and had finally become a professor of economics. In a remarkably short time he solved the long-standing financial muddle (using old-fashioned methods of economy and strict accountancy). Before long he became the dominant figure in Portugal, a retiring, studious statesman, proponent of a national renaissance.

1930, July 30.   Foundation of the National Union, a political-social party of a fascist type.

This was the only party permitted by the government and was designed to prepare the way for the *Estado Novo.*

1932, July 5.   OLIVEIRA SALAZAR BECAME PREMIER and to all intents and purposes dictator. He ruled with a strong hand, but opposition to fascism and dictatorship continued to smolder, as shown by occasional uprisings and attempts on the life of the dictator.

1933, Feb. 22. The government promulgated a **NEW CONSTITUTION,** which was approved by plebiscite March 19. Provisions: a **president** elected for seven years; a **cabinet** appointed by the president and responsible to him alone; a **national assembly** elected by heads of families possessing a certain degree of education; a **corporative chamber** representing occupations (on the Italian model), but with only advisory power.

1934, Jan. 18. A **revolutionary movement** led by the General Confederation of Labor and by the Communists was suppressed and the leaders imprisoned.

Dec. 16. In the **elections** the voters were allowed to choose among candidates put forward by the National Union; no others were permitted. The first national assembly of the new régime met January 10, 1935.

1935, Feb. 17.   President Carmona was elected for another term.

1936, July–1939. With the **outbreak of the civil war in Spain** (p. 993) the Portuguese dictatorship at once sided with the Insurgents against the republican government. Portugal became one of the main routes by which supplies reached Franco from Germany and elsewhere. This continued until in April 1937 the British government persuaded the Portuguese to permit a British border control. By that time Franco was able to get his supplies through the north Spanish coast towns. The British were obliged to strain themselves to the utmost to uphold the traditional alliance with Portugal, the latter country having become of immense strategic importance because of its location athwart the routes from Africa to Britain and France.

1939, Mar. 18. Portugal concluded a non-aggression pact with fascist Spain, but at the same time

May 22, 26. Portugal and Britain reaffirmed their traditional alliance, Portugal thereby demonstrating the desire to stand well with both fascist and democratic powers.

(*Cont. p. 1186.*)

5. ITALY AND THE PAPACY

a. ITALY

(*From p. 711*)

When World War I commenced in August 1914, the Italian cabinet, headed by **Antonio Salandra**, chose neutrality despite Italy's membership in the Triple Alliance. After weighing offers from both camps, the Italian government turned against the **Central Powers** and joined the **Allies** on May 23, 1915 (see p. 951).

1916, Dec. 12. The **Salandra cabinet** resigned and was succeeded by a new ministry led by **Paolo Boselli.**

1917, Oct. 29. The **Boselli cabinet** fell as a result of the **Caporetto disaster** (see p. 962). A new cabinet under **Vittorio Orlando** took office and remained in power until June 1919.

Italy had entered the war primarily to gain territory and wrest control of the Adriatic from Austria-Hungary. Her military achievement proved far below Allied expectations and as a result Italy was given but little say at the peace conference. President Wilson took a hostile stand toward the provisions of the **treaty of London** (p. 953) and Italy, in return for 600,000 lives lost, received only 9000 square miles of territory with a population of 1,600,000. None of the former German colonies was assigned to her as a mandate. The war, then, left Italy loaded with debt, suffering from high costs of living, and generally restless and discontented. The governments enjoyed no prestige. The political situation was complicated by a rapid spread of communism and by the emergence of an organized clerical party. Efforts of the government to meet the situation by social legislation had little success.

1919, Jan. 19. Formation of the *Partito Popolare*, a Catholic party.

Mar. 23. Formation of the first *Fascio di Combattimento* by **Benito Mussolini** (b. 1883), former socialist and editor of *Avanti*, who had turned violently interventionist and nationalist.

Apr. 24. The Italian delegation left the Paris peace conference after the public appeal of President Wilson against the Italian territorial claims on the Adriatic. The Italian delegation returned May 5.

Apr. 29. Italian troops landed at Adalia to make good Italian claims to a share in the Turkish spoils (p. 1085).

June 19. The Orlando cabinet resigned. A new ministry was formed by **Francesco Nitti**, with **Tommaso Tittoni** at the foreign office.

July 29. Treaty signed with Greece: Italy to support Greek claims in Thrace and Epirus, Greece to support an Italian protectorate over Albania and Italian claims in Anatolia. Italy was to keep Rhodes for fifteen years and the **Dodecanese Islands** were to be ceded to Greece.

Sept. 2. A new electoral law introduced universal suffrage and the French system of *scrutin de liste* (election by departmental lists) and proportional representation.

Sept. 12. Gabriele d'Annunzio, eminent writer, ardent nationalist, and World War hero, **seized Fiume** with a band of volunteers (p. 1121).

Oct. 5–8. The Socialist Congress at Bologna voted for adherence to the Third International.

Nov. 11. The pope definitely lifted the prohibition against participation by Catholics in Italian political life.

Nov. 16. Elections for parliament. The Socialists secured 160 seats; Catholics 103; Liberals 93; Radicals 58.

1920, Apr. 26. The **San Remo conference** decided to leave the Fiume question to settlement by Italy and Yugoslavia.

June 9. Fall of the Nitti cabinet, after it had been twice reconstructed. A new government was formed by the veteran, **Giovanni Giolitti,** with **Count Carlo Sforza** at the foreign office.

Aug. 2. Agreement with Albania to evacuate the country, with the exception of the island of Saseno. The Albanians had attacked the Italian forces and made their position untenable.

Aug. 10. Treaty with Greece, confirming cession of the Dodecanese; Rhodes to be given to Greece after fifteen years if Great Britain ceded Cyprus to Greece, and a plebiscite in Rhodes resulted in favor of Greece.

Aug. 31. A general lockout in the metallurgical factories led to the **occupation of the factories** by the workers, the beginning of a far-reaching movement.

Nov. 12. Treaty of Rapallo with Yugoslavia; Fiume to be an independent state, as envisaged by the peace treaties; Italy renounced claims to Dalmatia, except Zara; Istria divided; Yugoslavia to have Susak.

Dec. 1. D'Annunzio declared war on the Italian government.

Dec. 27. Italian troops bombarded Fiume and forced D'Annunzio to evacuate. Disorders continued in the city between the autonomists and the nationalists.

1921, Jan. 13–22. Congress of the Socialist Party at Livorno. The party split into a moderate and a radical wing, the latter frankly communist.

Feb. 27. Communist and Fascist riots at

Florence, inaugurating a period of repeated clashes which ultimately approximated civil war between the two factions.

May 15. Elections, the first held under a system of universal suffrage. The Liberals and Democrats won a resounding victory and secured 275 seats, as against 122 for the Socialists and 107 for the Popular (Catholic) Party. The Communists had only 16, the Fascists 22.

June 26. Fall of the Giolitti cabinet, the result of dissatisfaction with its foreign policy. A new ministry was organized (July 5) by **Ivanhoe Bonomi.**

1922, Feb. 9. The Bonomi cabinet resigned. The new government (Feb. 25) was led by **Luigi Facta,** supported by Liberals and Democrats.

Mar. 3. A Fascist coup overthrew the Fiume government. The town was then occupied by Italian troops (Mar. 17).

May. Fascists drove out the communist city government of Bologna. The conflict between the factions extended to all the larger cities.

Aug. 3–4. Fascists seized control of the Milan city government. The government seemed quite unable to cope with the aggressive action of the bands.

Oct. 8. Italy denounced the agreement with Greece on the Dodecanese Islands, despite protests from Britain.

Oct. 16. Formation of a quadrumvirate under Mussolini (Michele Bianchi, Italo Balbo, Gen. Emilio De Bono, Dino Grandi).

Oct. 23. Treaty of Santa Margherita with Yugoslavia, reaffirming the treaty of Rapallo (independence of Fiume).

Oct. 24. Fascist congress at Naples. Mussolini, having refused a seat in the cabinet, demanded the resignation of Facta and formation of a Fascist cabinet. Facta refused, apparently underestimating the power of the Fascist movement which was, to be sure, a minority movement, but one led aggressively and supported by nationalist elements and by business interests which feared communism.

Oct. 28. The **"MARCH ON ROME"** by the Fascists. The king refused Facta's demand for the proclamation of martial law, whereupon Facta resigned. The Fascists occupied Rome.

Oct. 31. Mussolini, summoned by the king from Milan, **formed a cabinet** of Fascists and Nationalists.

Nov. 25. Mussolini was granted by the king and the parliament **dictatorial powers** until December 31, 1923, to restore order and introduce reforms. He then appointed prefects and subprefects of Fascist sympathies and, with the support of the army, gradually established control of the government machinery. He still professed the intention of governing constitutionally and the constitution remained technically in force.

1923, Jan. 14. A voluntary **Fascist militia** authorized by the king.

Mar. 24. Reform of the judicial system.

May 16. The Popular (Catholic) Party voted to support the Fascist régime, but the leader, **Don Luigi Sturzo,** resigned. Fascists continued their attacks on the Catholics.

July. Initiation of a rigid policy of **Italianization in South Tyrol** (Upper Adige).

Aug.–Sept. THE CORFU INCIDENT. Gen. Enrico Tellini and four members of his staff were assassinated (Aug. 27) while engaged in delimiting the Greek-Albanian frontier. The Italian government sent a stiff ultimatum to Greece (Aug. 29) and August 31 bombarded and occupied Corfu. Greece appealed to the League of Nations and agreed to accept the decision of the council of ambassadors. The latter sent a note to Greece embodying most of the Italian demands. Under considerable pressure from Britain and other powers the Italians evacuated Corfu (Sept. 27), the first Fascist reassertion of power in international affairs having resulted in something of a *débâcle.*

Nov. 14. A new electoral law. Before the expiration of his dictatorial powers, Mussolini forced through parliament a law providing that any party securing the largest number of votes in an election (provided it had at least one-fourth of the total) should receive two-thirds of the seats. The remaining seats were to be divided according to proportional representation. This arrangement would avoid the difficulty of coalitions and blocs in a parliament where no party had a majority.

1924, Jan. 27. Treaty with Yugoslavia regarding Fiume. The town was ceded to Italy, Yugoslavia receiving Porto Barros and special facilities at Fiume.

Apr. 6. In the **elections** the Fascists, through government control of the machinery and through liberal use of "squad" methods, polled 65 per cent of the votes and were given 375 seats in the chamber (as against the 35 they had previously had).

June 10. MURDER OF THE SOCIALIST DEPUTY GIACOMO MATTEOTTI, who had written a book, *The Fascisti Exposed,* containing detailed case histories of hundreds of acts of violence illegally carried out by Fascists. The murderers were Fascists, some of them prominent in the party. When tried in 1926 they were either acquitted or given light sentences.

June 15. Most of the non-Fascist third of the new chamber seceded (*Aventine Secession*) and vowed not to return until the Matteotti affair had been cleared up and the complicity of the government disproved. The opposition demanded the disbandment of the Fascist militia and the cessation of violence. Mussolini, faced by a major crisis (the most serious during his rule), disavowed all connection with the affair and dismissed all those implicated. A rigid **press censorship** was introduced (July 1) and meetings of the opposition group were forbidden (Aug. 3). The support of part of the Liberal group, under Salandra, helped to break the force of the opposition, which never returned to parliament.

1925. Continuation of the crisis, marked by revival of Liberal and Communist demonstrations in various parts of the country. Mussolini twice reorganized the cabinet (Jan. 5; Aug. 30) and extended the work of repression through the *Legge Fascistissime,* which tightened control of the press, forbade **Freemasonry** and similar secret organizations (May 19), and established government control of local government through the appointed *podestàs.* Many political opponents of the régime arrested and transported to the Lipari Islands.

1926, Feb. Acute tension in relations with Germany, arising from the ruthless policy of Italianization in the South Tyrol.

Apr. 3. Recognition of a number of **labor syndicates** and establishment of compulsory arbitration in industrial disputes. Lockouts and strikes made illegal.

Apr. 3. Organization of the *Ballilla,* a Fascist youth association to train the rising generation.

Apr. 7. Mussolini wounded in the nose by Violet Gibson, a deranged Irish noblewoman. Two other attempts were made to assassinate the *Duce* (Sept. 11, Oct. 31).

Aug. 7. Treaty of friendship with Spain.

Sept. 25. Beginning of the **campaign against the *Mafia,*** a loose criminal organization which had dominated Sicilian politics and life for fifty years.

Nov. 27. Treaty with Albania, establishing what amounted to an Italian protectorate.

1927, Apr. 5. Treaty of friendship with Hungary, beginning of the Fascist policy of rallying the "revisionist" states against the Little Entente and its supporter, France.

Nov. 22. Second treaty with Albania.

1928, May 12. A new electoral law. Universal suffrage abolished and franchise restricted to men of 21 and over who paid syndicate rates or taxes of 100 lire. Electorate reduced from almost 10,000,000 to about 3,000,000. Four hundred candidates for election to be submitted to voters by the Fascist grand council, to be voted for or rejected *in toto* by the electorate.

Aug. 2. Treaty of friendship with Ethiopia.

Sept. 23. Treaty of friendship with Greece.

Nov. 15. The **Fascist grand council** made an official organ of the state and charged with the duty of naming candidates for the chamber and/or co-ordinating all government activities.

1929, Feb. 11. The **LATERAN TREATIES** with the Papacy (ratified June 7) (p. 1002).

Mar. 24. Elections. The four hundred official candidates received almost 100 per cent of the votes.

Apr. 21. National Council of Corporations established to adjust disputes between various groups in the interest of national production. The council was composed of representatives from the syndicates and from the government. Despite much official oratory about the *Corporate State* it does not appear that much actual power was entrusted to the syndicates or corporations.

1930, Feb. 6. Treaty of friendship with Austria. Mussolini began to come out more openly as the champion of revision of the peace treaties.

Apr. 30. Great naval program, the result of failure to secure recognition of Italian parity from France.

Oct. 25. Marriage of Princess Giovanna to King Boris of Bulgaria. Bulgaria brought more and more within the orbit of Italian influence.

1930–1935. The **economic depression,** aggravated for Italy by lack of basic raw materials and constant adverse trade balance. Great efforts were made to increase the production of food (battle of wheat) and to reclaim swamp areas for agricultural exploitation (Pontine marshes, etc.), as well as to develop hydroelectric power. Industrial production was increased and cost of production reduced by cuts in wages and other devices. Italy, like many other countries, tried to stave off the worst effects of the depression by the conclusion of **trade pacts,** rigid control of foreign exchange, conversion of the public debt, etc. The result was almost complete government control of finance and industry.

1933, Jan. The advent of the National Socialist government in Germany at once raised the **prospect of Italo-German co-operation,** which would have involved an immeasurable strengthening of Italy's position with respect to Great Britain and France. Goering and Papen visited Rome at an early date (Apr. 11–19), but the sole result of the *rapprochement* appears to have been the agreement of Germany to join in the

July 15. Signature of the Four-Power Pact

between Britain, France, Italy, and Germany. This was a favorite idea of Mussolini, who aimed at replacing the influence of the small states in the League of Nations by a bloc of major powers. In actual practice the Four-Power Pact proved of almost no significance.

1934, Mar. 17. Conclusion of the Rome protocols between Italy, Austria, and Hungary. Dollfuss and Gömbös had come to Rome for conferences, at which the agreements were worked out. They provided for closer trade relations, consultation, and common policy, and in general represented the organization, under Fascist auspices, of a Danubian bloc to counter-balance the Little Entente and the French influence.

June 14–15. First visit of Chancellor Hitler to Italy. He and Mussolini made a poor impression on each other and made no progress toward establishing a common policy. Quite the contrary, considerable tension developed between Germany and Italy, especially with regard to Austria.

July. The **abortive Nazi coup in Vienna** (p. 1015), which resulted in the death of Dollfuss, was solved in favor of Austria largely through the energetic action of Mussolini, who mobilized a huge army on the Brenner Pass and made clear his determination to intervene to frustrate the German designs.

Nov. 10. Establishment of the **Central Corporative Committee,** a type of economic parliament intended to complete the structure of the corporative state.

Dec. 5. CLASH OF ITALIAN AND ETHIOPIAN TROOPS AT UALUAL, on the disputed Ethiopian-Somaliland frontier. This was seized upon by the Italian government as the point of departure for the conquest of Ethiopia. After the great disaster at Adua in 1896 (p. 709), the Italian designs on Ethiopia had been more or less dormant. By **agreement with Britain and France in 1906,** Italy had been obliged to accept a relatively unpromising slice of Ethiopia as a sphere of interest. In the post-war period there had been negotiations with Britain, but these had no concrete results. The Italian government had, indeed, adopted a policy of friendship with Ethiopia and had supported the admission of Ethiopia to the League of Nations. Now, however, this policy was reversed and the old policy of imperialist expansion was resumed.

1935, Jan. 7. AGREEMENT BETWEEN FRANCE AND ITALY, negotiated by Laval during a visit to Rome. In the hope of winning Italian support against Germany, Laval made large concessions to Italian claims in Africa (p. 1079), including more or less of a free hand in Ethiopia. Mussolini at once took advantage of the situation and sent to Eritrea **Generals De Bono** and **Rodolfo Graziani** with large forces (Feb. 23).

Apr. 11–14. The **Stresa conference,** called by France to consider action against German rearmament and provide further guaranties for Austrian independence. Italy joined in the declarations and protests, which were of no avail because of the complications that soon arose from the Ethiopian affair.

June 23–24. The British minister for League affairs, **Anthony Eden, visited Rome** and offered Mussolini concessions which the latter rejected as inadequate.

July 25. The League council set September 4 as the date when it would itself begin to investigate the situation. By that time the Italian preparations were complete and Mussolini no longer concealed the fact that only the annexation of Ethiopia would satisfy him. While the League made belated efforts at adjustment,

Oct. 3. THE ITALIAN FORCES BEGAN THE INVASION OF ETHIOPIA. They took **Adua** on October 6.

Oct. 7. The **LEAGUE COUNCIL DECLARED ITALY THE AGGRESSOR** in the Ethiopian affair and began to arrange for sanctions.

Nov. 8. After a rather slow advance the Italians finally took the fortress of **Makallé.** The command was then taken over by **Marshal Pietro Badoglio,** who reorganized the forces and prepared for the difficult advance through the mountainous country.

Nov. 18. The League of Nations voted the **application of sanctions** against Italy (prohibition of import of Italian goods; arms embargo, financial embargo, etc.). Italy thereupon ended all economic relations with the sanctionist powers and adopted a system of rigid control of food and raw materials to meet the emergency. Britain and France continued their efforts to effect a compromise settlement, but the famous **Hoare-Laval proposals** (very favorable to Italy) were wrecked by public indignation over the suggested reward to a nation branded as the aggressor.

By the end of 1935, the **international tension** had reached a high pitch and Britain and Italy were coming close to a collision in the Mediterranean. Britain concentrated a huge naval force at Alexandria and secured promises of support from France, Yugoslavia, Greece, and Turkey. But the British forces were poorly prepared, especially with respect to air power, and therefore avoided all provocative action. Italy weathered the sanctionist storm, the more so as the nations could not agree to apply the **oil sanction** (Feb. 1936), which might have proved decisive, but which might also have involved armed conflict. The reoccupation of the Rhineland by Germany (Mar. 1936) diverted the attention of Britain and France and made all prospects of further action against Italy illusory.

1936, May 5. The Italian forces finally occupied **Addis Ababa** and the resistance of the Ethiopians collapsed (p. 1079).

May 9. The **ITALIAN GOVERNMENT FORMALLY PROCLAIMED THE ANNEXATION OF ALL ETHIOPIA,** the king of Italy assuming the title *Emperor of Ethiopia*. Gradual pacification of the country (p. 1079).

July 4. The League council voted to discontinue sanctions.

July. OUTBREAK OF THE CIVIL WAR IN SPAIN (p. 993). From the very outset Mussolini took an active part in supporting the Insurgents with men and equipment, on the theory that Italy could not permit the establishment of a "communist" government in the Mediterranean. The expense of sending 50,000 to 75,000 "volunteers" to Spain, added to the cost of the Ethiopian campaigns and the demands for ever greater armaments, necessitated the **devaluation of the lire** (Oct. 5) and the introduction of various forms of levy on capital. At the same time the Italian action in Spain aroused the apprehensions of Great Britain and France and served to increase the tension in the Mediterranean. Mussolini, under these circumstances, was obliged to draw closer to Germany and to conclude

Oct. 25. The **Italian-German agreement regarding Austria** (p. 1011), which served as a foundation for Italo-German co-operation, and may be taken as the beginning of the **Rome-Berlin Axis.**

Nov. 9–12. **Vienna conference** between the representatives of the Rome protocol states, marking the gradual consolidation of the Italian position in the Danube Basin.

1937, Jan. 2. Conclusion of a "gentlemen's agreement" between Italy and Great Britain (p. 1128).

Mar. 16. Imposing visit of Mussolini to Libya (p. 1081), in the course of which he declared his interest and **friendship for Moslems** everywhere and permitted himself to be hailed as their protector. This was taken as a move directed against British and French dominance over Arab countries, and the Italians were accused of subversive propaganda throughout North Africa, Egypt, Palestine, and Syria.

Mar. 25. Conclusion of an **Italian-Yugoslav treaty,** guaranteeing the existing frontiers and the maintenance of the *status quo* in the Adriatic (p. 1022).

Nov. 6. Italy adhered to the anti-Communist

pact between Germany and Japan (p. 1011).

Dec. 11. The withdrawal of Italy from the League of Nations.

1938, Jan. 7. The Italian government announced a huge **naval construction program,** to supplement the great rearmament plan introduced a year previous.

Mar. The German annexation of Austria (p. 1016). The world was astounded at Mussolini's calm acceptance of a situation which involved the breakdown of the Rome protocol system and brought the powerful German Nazi state to the Brenner Pass.

Apr. 16. Conclusion of the **Anglo-Italian pact** (p. 1128).

Aug. 3. The Italian government, despite past policy and assurances, introduced a "**racial" program** directed against the Jews, who were few in Italy. Various regulations barred foreign Jews from Italian schools, ordered all Jews who had taken up residence in Italy since 1919 to leave within six months, discharged Jewish teachers and students from schools and universities, prohibited marriage between Italians and non-Aryans, etc.

Sept. In the **Czechoslovak crisis** (p. 1017) Mussolini remained in the background until the tension reached the breaking point. He delivered himself of a series of threatening speeches, but in the last resort did his utmost to bring about the Munich meeting.

Oct. 8. The Fascist grand council abolished the chamber of deputies, last vestige of the old constitution, and replaced it with a **chamber of fasces and corporations.**

Nov. 16. Ratification of the Anglo-Italian pact.

Nov. 30. A great **demonstration in the Italian chamber,** with loud demands for the cession of Corsica and Tunisia by France (p. 991).

1939, Jan. 20–23. Count Ciano, the Italian foreign minister, **paid a visit to Belgrade** and arranged for closer political, economic, and cultural relations between Italy and Yugoslavia.

Apr. 7. Italian invasion and **conquest of Albania,** which voted personal union with Italy (p. 1023).

May 22. Conclusion of a political and **military alliance with Germany.** The closest co-operation was now established, with much coming and going of military men and technical experts.

Aug. **Conferences of Count Galeazzo Ciano with the German leaders** were kept extremely secret, but were taken to presage the international crisis which broke on August 20 (p. 1132). Throughout Germany's dispute with Poland the Italian press strongly supported the German position, though Mussolini used his influence to effect a pacific solution. When the storm broke on September 1–3, Italy surprised the world be maintaining **neutrality.**

CULTURAL DEVELOPMENTS

The outstanding literary figures of Italy in this period were **Luigi Pirandello** (1867–1936), novelist, dramatist (*Sei personaggi in cerca d'autore,* 1921) and winner of the Nobel prize for literature (1934), and **Benedetto Croce** (1866–1952), founder of the periodical *La Critica.*

(*Cont. p. 1188.*)

b. THE PAPACY

(*From p. 714*)

1914, Sept. 3.   BENEDICT XV (Giacomo della Chiesa) was elected pope on the death of Pius X (Aug. 20). The new pontiff was confronted with the world conflagration, which he did his utmost to terminate. After various appeals to the warring governments,
1917, Aug. 1.   The pope put forward outline proposals to serve as a basis for peace (p. 970).
1922, Feb. 6.   PIUS XI (Achille Ratti) was elected pope on the demise of Benedict XV (Jan. 22). His reign proved to be one of the most critical in the whole modern history of the Papacy. Although the long-standing quarrel with the French government was gradually adjusted by compromise (May 13, 1923, Jan. 18, 1924), in Russia the Bolshevik campaign against religion appalled all Christendom. From the outset the pope took a strong **stand against communism,** which he condemned publicly on many occasions (most recently in the encyclical of March 19, 1937). In the same way the
1926.   Anti-clerical policy of the Mexican government (p. 1070) called from the pope the strongest protests. With the **Fascist government in Italy** there was constant friction, marked by much bitterness, especially in view of the suppression of the Popular (Catholic) Party, which had been formed after the revocation of the papal prohibition of participation in Italian politics (Nov. 11, 1919). Ultimately, however, the two parties to the dispute managed to reach agreement, and the conflict which dated back to 1870 was disposed of by
1929, Feb. 11.   The LATERAN TREATIES, which were ratified June 7. Of these agreements the **Lateran treaty** proper restored the temporal power of the pope, who was to rule over **Vatican City,** a small section of Rome (108.7 acres) about St. Peter's and the Vatican, in full sovereignty. A **concordat with the Italian government** defined the position of the

Church in the Fascist state, while a **financial agreement** involved the payment by the Italian government of an indemnity of 750,000,000 lire in cash and 1,000,000,000 lire in government bonds. Under the new conditions, the pope gave up his status of voluntary prisoner, and July 25 for the first time left the Vatican. Unfortunately the agreements by no means ended friction between the Church and the government. Much dispute arose regarding the activities of the Catholic youth organization, the *Azione Cattolica.*
1931. The **revolution in Spain** (p. 992) ushered in a policy of anti-clericalism on the part of the Spanish government and so added yet another problem to those already weighing on the Papacy. Here again the pope issued protests and, in order to make clear the sympathy of the Church with the needs and aspirations of the lower classes, published
May 15. An important **encyclical,** *Quadragesimo anno,* to supplement the famous encyclical *Rerum novarum* of Leo XIII (1891). The pope called for social and economic reform, condemned the maldistribution of wealth, and strongly urged fundamental changes to give the worker a fairer share in the product of his labor. At the same time he once more condemned communism and socialism.
1933, July 20. Conclusion of the **concordat with the National Socialist government of Germany.** Although the position of the Church was carefully defined, the anti-clericalism, not to say the atheism and neo-paganism of the new régime in Germany was so strong that conflict was almost inevitable. The Nazi threat to the Church was seen to be no less serious than that from communism. The Church fought for its position as well as it could, but there was no real amelioration of the situation, and the German annexation of Austria, a purely Catholic state, in March 1938, made conditions if anything even worse.
1936, July. The outbreak of the **civil war in Spain** appeared to promise a reaction against the anti-clericalism of the republican régime. The pope therefore supported Franco and recognized the Insurgent régime (Aug. 27, 1937). But when Pius XI died (Feb. 10, 1939) the Spanish situation was as yet undecided and the world was rent by the conflict of fascism and democracy and communism. In the midst of this confusion the position of the Church had become extremely precarious, but the pontiff had earned world-wide respect for the firmness of his stand against any régime threatening religion or the fundamental rights of the individual (i.e. his **condemnation of the racial**

policies of Germany and Italy).

1939, Mar. 2. PIUS XII (Eugenio Pacelli) was elected pope. He had served for years as papal secretary of state and chief adviser to Pius XI and was generally recognized as a man of strong will, great astuteness, and diplomatic skill. He devoted himself at once to efforts for the pacification of Europe, but for the rest introduced no basic change of policy.

(*Cont. p. 1190.*)

6. SWITZERLAND

(*From p. 715*)

1914, Aug. 1. The **Swiss Confederation mobilized** its forces in view of the international crisis and remained on a war footing throughout the conflict. August 4 the government announced its **neutrality,** and its readiness to defend it no doubt had something to do with respect for Swiss territory on both sides. The war resulted in ever-increasing authority of the federal as against the cantonal governments (the federal council was given exceptional powers August 3, 1914). Switzerland suffered much from food shortage and was obliged to establish highly **centralized control of economic activity.** The demands of the combatants and the need for food resulted in a striking **development of Swiss industry,** with a corresponding growth of industrial labor and a spread of socialist and radical thought.

1918, Dec. 8. Switzerland broke off relations with Soviet Russia, which was suspected of subversive propaganda.

1919, Apr. 11. Geneva was chosen as the seat of the League of Nations. The Swiss, though long interested in international collaboration, were nevertheless primarily concerned with maintenance of their neutrality, and were anxious to avoid dangerous commitments. When,

Apr. 11. The people of **Vorarlberg voted** by a large majority **for union with Switzerland,** the federal government ignored the opportunity to extend the confederation. By the

June 28. Treaty of Versailles the powers recognized the **perpetual neutrality of Switzerland,** while the Swiss gave up their treaty right to occupy northern Savoy in the event of war (this right or obligation had not been exercised). The intricate **problem of the free zones** of Upper Savoy and Gex, so important for the defense of Geneva, was left to direct Franco-Swiss negotiations.

Nov. 19. The Swiss parliament voted to join the League of Nations, but the federal government first secured from the League council

1920, Feb. 13. The **declaration of London,** by which the League council agreed that Switzerland should not be obliged to take part in military sanctions under the terms of the covenant. Thereupon

Mar. 8. Switzerland formally joined the League. Nevertheless, a plebiscite arranged to decide the issue, on

May 16. Showed a vote of only 416,000 in favor as against 323,000 opposed.

1921, Aug. 7. Agreement with France with respect to the free zones. Switzerland gave up former treaty rights, but this arrangement was repudiated by a Swiss plebiscite (Feb. 18, 1923). Thereupon the French government took unilateral action, moving its customs stations forward to the political frontier (Nov. 10, 1923). The Swiss government protested and it was finally decided to investigate the legal aspects of the problem and to arbitrate the dispute (Oct. 30, 1924, Mar. 18, 1925).

1923, Mar. 29. Conclusion of a **customs union between Switzerland** and the little principality of **Liechtenstein,** which before the war had been closely associated with Austria-Hungary.

May 10. Vaslav Vorovsky, Russian delegate to the Lausanne conference (p. 1086), **was assassinated by Maurice Conradi,** a Swiss who had suffered under the Soviet régime in Russia. Conradi was acquitted by the courts (Nov. 16) and the incident brought Switzerland and Russia to a state of extreme tension.

1930, Apr. 13. The Swiss and French governments having failed to reach agreement on the **free zones,** the Permanent Court of International Justice was appealed to.

1932, June 7. The court decided the question in favor of Switzerland. The French government was directed to withdraw its customs stations by January 1, 1934.

Nov. 9. Serious labor disturbances at Geneva resulted from the growing pressure of the world crisis. The government proceeded with vigor against all extremists.

1933, May 12. The wearing of party uniforms was forbidden.

1934. The **Swiss government bitterly opposed the admission of Russia to the League of Nations,** and voted against it in the League council.

1935, Feb. 24. By plebiscite the people voted to extend the period of military training. The

Swiss embarked upon an **extensive armament program** (June 5, 1936) which involved thorough modernization of frontier defenses, mechanization of army units, development of air defense, etc.

1936, Feb. 4.   Assassination of the National Socialist leader **Wilhelm Gustloff** by a Jew, at Davos. The government at once forbade continuation of a national organization of National Socialists.

Sept. 26. The **government decided to devalue the Swiss franc,** in keeping with the policy of France.

1937, June 15. The government, though it had taken part in economic sanctions against Italy during the Ethiopian crisis (p. 1000), decided to recognize the Italian conquest.

Dec. 7.   Romansch was recognized as a fourth national (though not official) **language.** This was a step designed to win renewed support from the cantons most directly exposed to Italian designs.

1938, Apr. 30. The **government appealed to the council of the League of Nations to recognize Switzerland's unconditional neutrality,** pointing out the great change that had come over Europe since 1919 and stressing the particularly exposed position of Switzerland between the League powers and those of the Rome-Berlin Axis. The **League council accepted the Swiss view** (May 14), thus freeing Switzerland from all obligation to take part even in economic sanctions against a future aggressor.

(*Cont. p. 1178.*)

CULTURAL DEVELOPMENTS

Francesco Chiesa (b. 1871) has been the foremost writer in Italian Switzerland.

The foremost Swiss-born composer, **Arthur Honegger** (1892–1955), and the foremost Swiss-born artist, **Paul Klee** (1879–1940), are associated with French and German rather than Swiss schools.

7. GERMANY

(*From p. 978*)

Theobald von Bethmann-Hollweg, chancellor since 1909, remained in office until July 1917, but German policies were increasingly influenced by the military leaders.

1916, Nov. 20. The foreign minister, **Gottlieb von Jagow,** resigned and was replaced by **Arthur Zimmermann.**

1917, Jan. 8. The German government decided to resume **unrestricted submarine warfare.** Bethmann-Hollweg opposed but was unable to prevent this decision. (See p. 970.)

By 1917 growing unrest led to certain important promises by the government.

Apr. 7. The Emperor William, as king of Prussia, in an **Easter message** announced the end of the famous three-class system of voting in Prussia. The introduction of a system of equal, direct, and secret suffrage was announced somewhat later (July 11).

July 14.   Bethmann-Hollweg, having lost the support of the Conservatives, National Liberals, and Center, and having long since become objectionable to the military men, **was allowed to retire.**

July 14–Oct. 30.   Chancellorship of George Michaelis, an almost unknown official, who was the appointee of the high command and served chiefly as a cloak for the **power of Ludendorff.**

July 19. Under the leadership of **Matthias Erzberger** and his Catholic Center Party, the Reichstag passed a resolution in favor of a **peace of understanding,** without annexations (212 Centrists, Majority Socialists, and National Liberals against 126 Conservatives, National Liberals, and Independent Socialists). The new chancellor declared that his aims were attainable within the limits of the resolution as "he understood it."

Aug. 5.   Richard von Kühlmann succeeded Zimmermann as German secretary for foreign affairs.

Oct. 30.   Count Georg von Hertling replaced Michaelis as chancellor.

1918, Sept. 30.   Hertling resigned after a year in office and **Prince Max of Baden** was named chancellor (Oct. 4).

Oct. 28.   Mutiny of sailors at Kiel, caused by orders from the admiralty to go to sea and fight the British. "Further than Heligoland we will not go."

Oct. 29. Emperor William II, alarmed at demands in the Reichstag for his abdication, left Berlin for army headquarters at Spa.

Nov. 4 and 5. The revolt at Kiel spread to other seaports. **Councils of workers and soldiers formed.**

Nov. 7.   Revolt at Munich, led by **Kurt Eisner,** an Independent Socialist, led to the proclamation of a republic in Bavaria (Nov. 8).

Nov. 8. The emperor rejected advice from the cabinet of Prince Max of Baden that he abdicate to save the nation from civil war.

Nov. 9.   ABDICATION OF THE EM-

PEROR announced in Berlin by Prince Max. **REPUBLIC PROCLAIMED.** Government turned over to Majority Socialists, led by **Friedrich Ebert** and **Philipp Scheidemann.** The emperor fled to Holland in his special train. His abdication was not signed until November 28, by which time all other German rulers had abdicated.

Nov. 10. A joint **ministry of Independent and Majority Socialists** took control in Berlin. Struggle between the extreme Left, or **Spartacist,** group, led by **Karl Liebknecht** and **Rosa Luxemburg,** who favored a communist régime, and the Social Democrats (Majority Socialists), who wanted a gradual and not a violent abandonment of a capitalism.

Nov. 25. A conference of representatives of the new state governments met at Berlin and agreed that a **national constituent assembly** should be elected. The Spartacists opposed the plan for a national assembly.

1919, Jan. 5–15. **Spartacist revolt** in Berlin, crushed by the provisional government with the aid of the regular army. The Independent Socialists sided with the Spartacists, now avowed communists. Rosa Luxemburg and Karl Liebknecht were killed while under arrest (Jan. 15).

Jan. 19. **Election of a national assembly,** to draw up a constitution. The Communists refused to take part, but all other groups both Right and Left were represented. Majority Socialists won 163 seats, Center 88, Democrats 75, Nationalists 42, Independent Socialists 22, others 31.

Feb. 6. National assembly met at Weimar.

Feb. 11. **Friedrich Ebert chosen as first president of the German Republic,** by the national assembly.

Feb.–Mar. Further **communist uprisings** in Berlin, Munich, etc., suppressed by **Gustav Noske,** acting for the government.

Feb. 21. **Assassination of Kurt Eisner,** by a conspiracy to re-establish the monarchy.

Apr. 4–May 1. **Soviet Republic established in Bavaria.** This was overthrown by armed forces of the federal government.

June 1. **Proclamation of a Rhineland Republic,** instigated and supported by France. After some months the movement collapsed because of the hostility of the inhabitants.

June 20. The **Scheidemann ministry** resigned rather than sign the peace treaty dictated by the Allies.

June 21. The **German fleet was scuttled at Scapa Flow,** by its crews.

June 23. The new cabinet, under **Gustav Bauer** (**Matthias Erzberger,** vice-chancellor; **Count Ulrich von Brockdorff-Rantzau,** foreign minister), **accepted the peace treaty uncondi-**tionally after the Weimar assembly had voted 237 to 138 for conditional acceptance, in order to avoid invasion of the country.

July 12. The **Allied blockade** was finally lifted, after a large part of the population had been reduced to the verge of starvation.

July 31. **ADOPTION OF THE WEIMAR CONSTITUTION.** The president, elected for a seven-year term, was to appoint a chancellor who in turn chose a cabinet which could command a majority in the Reichstag. By Articles 25 and 48 the president was empowered to suspend constitutional guaranties and dissolve the Reichstag in periods of national emergency. The Reichsrat, composed of delegates from 18 states (no one of which was to have more than two-fifths of the seats), could delay but not prevent legislation. The members of the Reichstag were elected, not as individuals or as representatives of districts, but by party lists for all Germany. A system of proportional representation insured the representation of minority parties, but also necessitated coalition governments.

Sept. 22. The government was obliged by the Allies to strike out provision for the **representation of Austria** and to promise to respect Austrian independence.

Oct. 6. The government ordered the **evacuation of Latvia** by **Gen. Colmar von der Goltz** and his corps, at the command of the Allies.

1920, Feb. 10. **Plebiscite in** the northern zone of **Schleswig** resulted in a vote for Denmark. The plebiscite in the southern zone (Mar. 14) was in favor of Germany.

Feb. 12. French troops and the Allied commission of control took charge in Upper Silesia.

Mar. 13–17. **KAPP PUTSCH,** a monarchical coup, led to seizure of government buildings in Berlin. The government fled to Stuttgart, but the movement collapsed as result of a general strike of the trade unions.

Mar. 19. A great **Spartacist rising** took place in the Ruhr mining districts.

Mar. 26. **Resignation of the Bauer cabinet.** A new ministry was formed by **Hermann Müller.**

Apr. 3. Government troops, having entered the Ruhr, put down the revolt with great severity.

Apr. 6–May 17. **French troops occupied Frankfurt** and some of the Ruhr towns as a reply to invasion of the Ruhr by German government troops.

Apr. 30. Union of eight central German states to form the **new state of Thuringia.**

June 6. **General elections,** to replace the national assembly by a regular Reichstag. The Weimar coalition lost its majority and a new coalition was formed of the People's Party

(Liberal), Center, and Democrats. The Müller cabinet resigned (June 8) and a new government was formed by **Konstantin Fehrenbach,** leader of the Center Party (June 25). The Socialists were excluded.

July 5-16. Spa conference (p. 1121). The Germans signed a protocol of disarmament and arranged for reparations payments.

July 11. A plebiscite in Allenstein and Marienwerder resulted in a large majority for Germany.

Sept. 20. By decision of the League, **Eupen and Malmédy were turned over to Belgium.** Five-sixths of the 600,000 inhabitants were German-speaking.

Nov. 9. Danzig proclaimed a free city, as provided for in the peace treaty. It was placed under protection of the League.

1921, Mar. 8. Allied occupation of Düsseldorf, Duisburg, and **Ruhrort,** because of alleged German default in reparations payments.

Mar. 20. Plebiscite in Upper Silesia, in favor of Germany (p. 1121).

May 4. Resignation of Fehrenbach. A new ministry was formed by **Joseph Wirth** (May 10).

May 11. Germany accepted the Allied **reparations terms** (p. 1122).

July 16. Trial of war criminals at Leipzig.

Aug. 29. Assassination of Matthias Erzberger by reactionary conspirators, who escaped.

Oct. 12. Award of the League of Nations in the **Upper Silesian question** (p. 1121).

1922, Apr. 16. Treaty of Rapallo with Russia (p. 1122).

June 24. Assassination of Walther Rathenau, Jewish industrialist and cabinet minister, by reactionary nationalists. The assassins committed suicide and their accomplices were mildly dealt with by the government.

June 30. Membership in monarchist organizations made a criminal offense.

Aug. Beginning of the **collapse of the mark,** due to heavy reparations payments.

Nov. 14. Resignation of the Wirth cabinet. A new government was formed by **Wilhelm Cuno,** an influential industrialist.

1923, Jan. 11. OCCUPATION OF THE RUHR by French and Belgian forces, after Germany had been declared in default (p. 1123). The government suspended all deliveries to the Allies, but the Franco-Belgian commission arrested the recalcitrant mine-owners and took over mines and railroads. The government supported the population in a policy of passive resistance.

Aug. 12. Resignation of Cuno. A new cabinet was formed by **Gustav Stresemann,** leader of the People's Party. He was supported by the Socialist, Center, and Democratic Parties.

Sept. 26. The government ended passive resistance.

Oct. 21. A Rhineland Republic was proclaimed at Aachen, with Belgian and French support. The government was faced also with communist troubles in Saxony and with monarchist plots in Bavaria.

Nov. 8-11. "BEER HALL PUTSCH" in Munich, occasioned by the general crisis resulting from the Ruhr occupation and the financial collapse. **General Erich Ludendorff** and **Adolf Hitler,** leader of a growing National Socialist Party, attempted to overthrow the Bavarian government. The rising was poorly organized and was easily put down. Hitler was arrested and sentenced to five years in prison. While serving his term he wrote *Mein Kampf,* a book outlining his career, his theories, and his program. He was released after serving less than a year, and at once resumed his propaganda and organizing activity.

Nov. 15. Opening of the *Rentenbank*. Hjalmar Schacht, appointed special currency commissioner, undertook the difficult task of substituting a new monetary unit for the worthless paper currency. The new *Rentenmark,* theoretically secured by a blanket mortgage on all land and industry to the amount of 3,200,-000,000 gold marks, was exchangeable for one trillion of the old marks. **Hans Luther,** as minister of finance, tried by drastic economies, including the dismissal of more than 700,000 government employees, to balance the budget. But the Dawes Plan and the foreign loan that went with it were what really made it possible for Germany to emerge from bankruptcy. In the process most of the internal debt, public and private, was wiped out. The business men, who tended to dominate the various coalition governments, were, however, convinced that Germany, in need of raw materials, markets, and new capital, must remain on good terms with Britain, the United States, and possibly France. Hence the **policy of fulfillment** represented by **Gustav Stresemann,** who remained in every cabinet until his death in 1929. The policy made possible the flotation of large bond issues, largely in the United States, which helped pay reparations and brought on a fictitious prosperity.

Nov. 23. Fall of the Stresemann ministry. It was succeeded by a government under **Wilhelm Marx** (Center), in which Stresemann became minister for foreign affairs.

1924, Jan. 31. Collapse of the separatist movement in the Rhineland, after the assassination (Jan. 9) of **Heinz,** the president of the autonomous Palatinate government.

Apr. 9. The Dawes Plan (p. 1123). It was accepted by the German Reichstag August 28.

May 4. Reichstag elections. Gain of Nationalists and Communists at the expense of the moderate parties.

Dec. 7. **Reichstag elections,** in which the Socialists regained some of their losses.

1925, Jan. 15. Cabinet formed by Hans Luther. A Nationalist for the first time was included.

Feb. 28. **Death of President Ebert.**

Mar. 29. **Presidential election.** None of the seven candidates received the needed majority, but the Nationalist candidate, **Karl Jarrès,** was in the lead, with 10,416,655 votes against 7,802,496 for **Otto Braun** (Socialist). The constitution provided for a second election, in which the candidate receiving the largest number of votes should be elected. The Socialists and Democrats supported **Wilhelm Marx,** leader of the Center, while the Right parties abandoned Jarrès in favor of Field Marshal **Paul von Hindenburg,** in retirement since 1919. The Communists put forward **Ernst Thälmann.**

Apr. 26. **HINDENBURG ELECTED PRESIDENT,** with 14,655,766 votes against Marx's 13,751,615. Thälmann polled almost 2,000,000 votes, which, if they had gone to Marx, would have been sufficient to defeat Hindenburg.

Oct. 16. **Locarno treaties** (p. 1124). The Reichstag voted for ratification November 27.

Nov. 29. The Prussian government settled the **Hohenzollern claims,** leaving the former emperor large tracts of land and many estates.

Dec. 5. **Resignation of the Luther cabinet.** This caused a deadlock which was broken only by Hindenburg's threat to invoke Article 48. Luther ultimately reformed his cabinet.

1926, Feb. 10. Germany applied for admission to the League, in accord with the Locarno treaties. Her admission was postponed because of a dispute regarding seats on the council (p. 1124).

Apr. 24. **Treaty of friendship and neutrality with Russia,** extending the Rapallo treaty of 1922.

May 12. **Resignation of the Luther cabinet,** following its instructions that the old imperial colors should be used in the diplomatic service.

May 17. **Second cabinet of Wilhelm Marx.**

Sept. 8. **Germany admitted to the League,** with a permanent seat on the council.

1927, Sept. 18. President von Hindenburg, in a memorial speech dedicating the Tannenberg monument, **repudiated German responsibility for the war** (Article 231 of the Versailles treaty).

1928, Jan. 29. Treaties with Lithuania, regarding the frontiers and the status of **Memel,** and providing for arbitration.

May 20. **Reichstag elections.** The Socialists so strengthened their number that they had to be included in the government. The Nationalists lost heavily.

June 13. **Resignation of the Marx ministry.**

Hermann Müller (Socialist) formed a new government.

1929, Feb. 6. Germany accepted the Kellogg-Briand pact (p. 1124)

Sept.–1930, June. **Evacuation of the Rhineland.**

Oct. 3. **Death of Gustav Stresemann.**

Dec. 22. A referendum upheld the decision to adopt the **Young Plan.** This marked a defeat for the Nationalists, led by **Alfred Hugenberg.**

1930, Mar. 27. Resignation of the Müller cabinet. A new coalition was formed by **Heinrich Brüning** (Center), in which parties of the Right replaced the Socialists.

July 16. The Reichstag having rejected a **budget bill,** President Hindenburg authorized it by decree. This act was condemned by the Reichstag, which was thereupon dissolved, the budget being put into effect by decree.

Sept. 14. **Reichstag elections. Emergence of Hitler's National Socialists** as a major party (107 seats as against their previous 12). The Communists returned 77 candidates. The Socialists retained 143 seats, but all the moderate parties lost heavily. This was probably a reflection of the world economic situation and the cessation of loans by the United States. The election ushered in a period of disorder, with numerous **clashes between National Socialist (*Nazi*) and Communist bands.**

Dec. 12. **Completion of the evacuation of the Saar** by Allied troops.

1931, Mar. 21. Publication of a **project for a German-Austrian customs union.** This met at once with vigorous protest from the French government and its satellites, the protest resting on the claim that a customs union involved infringement of Austrian sovereignty, and was therefore contrary to earlier obligations assumed by the Austrian government. Under pressure, Germany and Austria voluntarily renounced the project (Sept. 3) on the eve of an adverse decision by the World Court (Sept. 5).

May 11. **The failure of the Austrian Credit-Anstalt** marked the beginning of the financial collapse of central Europe, including Germany. With the financial collapse came a great economic crisis and depression. By the beginning of 1932 the number of unemployed was already more than 6,000,000. Economic hardship brought greater social tension: rapid growth of communism and of its opponent, national socialism.

1932, Mar. 13. Presidential election. Hindenburg secured 18,651,497 votes as against 11,-300,000 for Hitler and 4,983,341 for Thälmann (Communist). Hindenburg fell just short of the required majority. In the second election (April

10) he secured a plurality of only 6,000,000 out of a total vote of 36,000,000.

May 30. Brüning, who had been obliged to govern largely by emergency decrees issued by the president, **resigned** when the president refused to sanction a decree which would have divided bankrupt East Prussian estates into allotments for small farmers. Hindenburg, himself of the Junker class, seems to have felt that the Brüning régime was no longer popular with the public or with the army.

May 31. Franz von Papen was asked by the president to form a ministry responsible to the executive alone. This *ministry of barons* included **Constantin von Neurath** (foreign minister) and **Gen. Kurt von Schleicher** (minister of defense). Brüning had refused the foreign office. National Socialists were excluded.

June 16. The **government lifted a ban on Nazi storm troops,** which had been imposed by Brüning (Apr. 13). The National Socialist movement now gained great momentum. Disorders and clashes of rival groups became the order of the day.

July 20. *Coup d'état* **in Prussia.** Papen removed the Socialist prime minister and other officials. Berlin and Brandenburg were put under martial law, because the activities of Nazi storm troops had made it difficult for civil authorities to maintain order.

July 31. Reichstag elections, following a dissolution (June 4). The National Socialists returned 230 candidates; Socialists 133; Center 97; Communists 89. Since neither the Nazis nor the Communists would enter a coalition, no majority was possible.

Aug. 13. Hitler refused Hindenburg's request that he serve as vice-chancellor under Papen. He demanded "all or nothing."

Sept. 12. The Reichstag dissolved. After a presidential decree had been read, a vote was taken, contrary to rules, on a Communist motion of "no confidence." This was passed by 512 votes to 42, indicating the impossibility of securing popular support for the Papen ministry.

Nov. 6. An election failed to break the Reichstag deadlock. The National Socialists lost some seats, while the Communists gained.

Nov. 17. Resignation of Papen.

Nov. 24. Hitler rejected the proffer of the chancellorship on certain conditions. His demand for full powers was refused by Hindenburg.

Dec. 2. Gen. Kurt von Schleicher formed a new presidential cabinet.

1933, Jan. 28. Schleicher forced to resign after his efforts to conciliate the Center and Left had failed and Hindenburg had rejected a demand for another dissolution.

Jan. 30. ADOLF HITLER, CHANCELLOR. Papen, vice-chancellor; **Hermann Goering** (Nazi), without portfolio; **Wilhelm Frick** (Nazi), interior; **Gen. Werner von Blomberg,** defense; **Constantin von Neurath,** foreign affairs. **Hugenberg** and **Franz Seldte,** Nationalists, were included. The ministry, regarded as a coalition of National Socialists and Nationalists, with important posts assigned to non-party men of the old governing class, lacked a majority so long as the Center stood aloof. But Hitler refused to compromise with **Mgr. Ludwig Kaas,** the Centrist leader, and the Reichstag was dissolved. The new elections were set for March 5.

The **National Socialist German Workers' Party** appealed to prejudices widely held in Germany against Jews, intellectuals, pacifists, communists, socialists, and liberals. Hitler exacted unquestioning obedience from his followers, but promised in return to make Germany strong, self-sufficient, respected—an Aryan nation purified of Jewish elements, able to revive the traditions of early Teutonic heroism. His denunciations of the Versailles treaty had brought him much support. The middle classes, ruined by inflation and economic depression, were offered the elimination of Jewish competition in business and the professions. Thousands of unemployed and hopeless young men were put into uniform as storm troops, with the support of which the lieutenants of Hitler, such as Goebbels, were able to organize an unusually effective propaganda and imposing demonstrations. To what extent the movement was financed by well-to-do classes and big business interests cannot be definitely ascertained, but by many such people the movement was regarded as the last bulwark against communism. On the other hand, many radical workingmen believed Hitler's rather vague denunciations of "interest slavery" and of the evils of bourgeois capitalism in general. Hitler's fanatical patriotism and extreme nationalism, combined with asceticism, and his extraordinary powers as a popular orator, secured him the backing of many who were moved by a dark discontent with things as they were. At this stage the movement was still pretty much all things to all men.

Feb. 27. A violent **election campaign** culminated in **a fire which partly destroyed the Reichstag building.** Hitler denounced this as a Communist plot and President von Hindenburg issued emergency decrees suspending the constitutional guaranties of free speech and free press, as well as other liberties. The Nazi storm troops were able to intimidate and bully their opponents with impunity.

Mar. 5. The **Reichstag elections** gave the

Nazis only 44 per cent of the votes, and their Nationalist allies (party of big business and of the old aristocracy) only 8 per cent. The Center Party elected 74, the Socialists 120, the Communists 81, and other non-Nazi parties 23 members. There were 288 Nazis and 52 Nationalists. The vote cast exceeded all preceding ones.

Mar. 23. Passage of the Enabling Act by the Reichstag and Reichsrat. The National Socialists and the Nationalists found support among deputies of the Catholic Center. The Communist Party had already been outlawed after the Reichstag fire. Only 94 votes (all Social Democratic) were cast against the crucial **Enabling Bill,** which gave the government dictatorial powers until April 1, 1937. Thereby the **Nazi dictatorship** was firmly established.

The **Nazi revolution** proved to be one of the greatest overturns in German and European history. It affected almost every phase of life. The policies and achievements of the first years may be briefly summarized as follows:

(1) *CONSTITUTIONAL CHANGES.* The German states were allowed to continue, but the state governments were gradually shorn of effective power. *Statthalter* were appointed for all the states (Apr. 7, 1933), and the Reichsrat, representing the states, was abolished (Jan. 30, 1934). Thereby the sovereignty of the states came to an end and **Germany became a national rather than a federal state.** Relations between the state governments and the local party organizations (*Gaue*) were not clearly defined, but the tendency was to identify them more and more.

(2) *ADMINISTRATIVE.* By the **Civil Service Law** of April 7, 1933, all non-Aryan (i.e. Jewish) officials of national, state, and municipal governments could be retired, as also notaries, teachers, and other semi-public servants. Thenceforth no opponent of the Nazi régime could hope to retain his position.

(3) *JUDICIAL.* The entire legal system was overhauled, all traditional concepts of law being discarded and the welfare of the state and the Nazi régime becoming the sole deciding considerations. The **People's Court** (May 3, 1934) was set up to try cases of treason (which was given an extremely wide definition); the proceedings were made secret and there was no appeal except to the *Führer.* Summary execution of sentences became the usual thing. **Concentration camps,** in which thousands of opponents were detained without trial, became standing institutions.

(4) *POLITICAL.* All opposing parties were liquidated under government pressure. Socialist parties were prohibited on May 10,

1933; the Nationalist Party dissolved itself (June 27, 1933); the Catholic parties were obliged to dissolve (July 5, 1933); all monarchist organizations were forbidden (Feb. 2, 1934). In the same way such non-political organizations as the *Stahlhelm* were incorporated with the Nazi party (June 21, 1933) and ultimately disbanded (Nov. 11, 1935). The **National Socialist Party was declared the only political party** July 14, 1933.

(5) *RACIAL.* From the very outset the new régime aroused indignation throughout the world by the ruthless **persecution of the Jews.** A national boycott of all Jewish businesses and professions (Apr. 1, 1933) introduced a long series of outrages. As quickly as possible Jewish businesses were liquidated and lawyers and doctors barred from practice. By the famous **Nürnberg Laws** (Sept. 15, 1935) the Jews (including all those of one-quarter Jewish extraction) were deprived of rights of citizenship and all intermarriage with Jews was strictly forbidden. Many Jews left the country, though they were required to sacrifice almost all of their property in so doing. After the annexation of Austria the same measures were extended to the new state, and, June 16, 1938, the Jews were required to register all their property, at home and abroad, within a couple of weeks. Early in November 1938 the persecution came to a head when, following the assassination of a German diplomat by a Jew in Paris, well-organized attacks upon synagogues and Jewish property took place throughout the Reich. The government levied a fine of one billion marks upon the Jewish community, which amounted to a capital levy of 20 per cent on property above 5000 marks. No secret was made of the determination of the government to drive all Jews out of the country. In view of this desperate situation an **international refugee committee** was organized to arrange ways and means of effecting the emigration of so large a number as soon as possible. One great obstacle to a satisfactory arrangement was the unwillingness of the German government to allow the emigrants to take money or property with them.

(6) *RELIGIOUS.* Though both Catholics and Protestants gave the Nazis considerable support at the outset, it soon became evident that the new régime was bent on co-ordinating all religious organizations with the state machinery. **Neo-pagan movements,** which were many, were countenanced and even encouraged by the government, while the Christian churches were exposed to great pressure. The Protestant state churches amalgamated to form a new **Evangelical Church** (July 11, 1933), but when the government appointed as national

bishop **Ludwig Müller,** many pastors who objected to him broke away and formed the **German Confessional Church,** which soon found itself in conflict with the authorities. September 28, 1935, the Protestant Church was placed under state control and **Hans Kerrl** was made minister of Church affairs with decree powers. The opposition was led by Pastor **Martin Niemoeller,** who was finally arrested (July 1, 1937). Though acquitted after trial (Mar. 1938), he was at once re-arrested by the secret police and returned to a concentration camp. How many other recalcitrant pastors suffered the same fate can only be guessed at. The **Catholic Church** had an equally hard time. July 20, 1933, the government signed a new **concordat** with the Vatican, replacing the older agreements with separate German states. The Catholic clergy was forbidden to take part in politics and future diocesan appointments were to be made by the Holy See only after consultation with the German government. On the other hand Catholic schools and societies were to be permitted so long as they did not meddle in public affairs. Despite this agreement the government brought pressure to bear to prevent parents from sending children to confessional schools (Catholic or Protestant), and furthermore brought children into the **Youth Movement,** where doctrines wholly objectionable to many Christian parents were freely taught. The policy of the government led to many protests by Catholic leaders (notably **Card. Faulhaber** of Munich). But these proved futile. On the contrary, the government took the offensive (1937), brought many monks to trial on charges of immorality, etc., and in general did its utmost to discredit and break the influence of the Catholic Church.

(7) *ECONOMIC.* The workers' parties, after dissolution, were replaced by the **Nazi Labor Front,** which was given a new constitution (Oct. 24, 1934). Strikes and lockouts had already been forbidden (May 17, 1933), and under the new constitution the employers (as leaders in their respective factories and industries) were given extensive control. On the other hand the new régime succeeded, within a remarkably short time, in **eliminating all unemployment** (chiefly through opening of labor camps for young men and even women, by public works and rearmament, etc.). Many of the workers were won over to the Nazi Party by the establishment of the organization *Kraft durch Freude* **(Strength through Joy)** which provided for cheap entertainment, vacations, etc. In the larger sphere the government brought to an end the reparations problem and embarked upon a **policy of self-sufficiency** (autarchy) which would make the country independent (especially in raw materials) in the event of war. This underlay the famous **Four-Year Plan** of October 19, 1936. Germany suffered greatly from the parlous condition of world trade, and considerably also from the boycott of German goods resulting from the anti-Jewish policies. The great costs of government and rearmament were met by internal loans, more forced than voluntary. Industry was more and more brought under government control, just as the peasants were more and more attached to their land.

(8) *MILITARY.* The government restored **universal compulsory military service** March 16, 1935, and from that time on made rapid progress in rearmament. By 1938 Germany not only had an impressive land army, equipped with the latest weapons, but an air fleet superior to that of any other country. In the course of 1938 the western frontier was heavily fortified, giving the country further assurance against attack from France.

1933, May 28. The **elections in the free city of Danzig** a victory for the National Socialists (led by **Albert Forster**), who captured 39 out of 72 seats in the senate. June 20 the Nazis took over the government and thenceforth exerted themselves in the work of conforming with developments in Nazi Germany. The Polish government for a time served as a check, as did also the commissioner of the League of Nations. But after the **German-Polish agreement** of January 1934 the Polish government concerned itself more exclusively with protection of Poles in Danzig. In the elections of April 7, 1935, the Danzig Nazis secured 43 seats. There soon developed a conflict with the League representative, whom the government boldly defied (July 1936). The League, discredited by the Ethiopian débâcle, was unable to assert its authority, so that during 1937 the Nazis, by one device or another, gradually got rid of their opponents in the senate. On May 14, 1937, the Nationalist Party dissolved itself and a number of its representatives joined the Nazis. The Socialist Party was prohibited October 14, 1937. By 1938 the Nazis had 70 seats in the senate, the other two going to Poles. The government then began to introduce legislation against the Jews and indeed to follow step by step the lead of Berlin. To all intents and purposes, Danzig was part of the German Reich.

Oct. 14. WITHDRAWAL OF GERMANY FROM THE DISARMAMENT CONFERENCE AND FROM THE LEAGUE OF NATIONS. This marked the beginning of an independent policy in foreign affairs.

Nov. 12. Election of a new Reichstag.

Ninety-three per cent of the voters approved the government's action in withdrawing from the League; 92 per cent voted for the Nazi list of candidates. There were no opposition candidates, but opponents of the régime, despite intimidation, cast about three million invalid ballots, the only way of registering disapproval. The Reichstag itself, under the new system, lost all importance and became little more than an assembly of Nazi leaders occasionally convoked to hear addresses by the Führer.

1934, Jan. 26. Conclusion of the German treaty with Poland. This followed a period of extreme tension, and provided for non-aggression and respect for existing territorial rights for ten years. It was the first breach in the French alliance system in eastern Europe.

June 14. Hitler paid a visit to Mussolini at Venice. This move, designed to pave the way for closer relations between the two Fascist states, proved to be only a prelude to a clash of interests in the Danube Valley.

June 30. The GREAT BLOOD PURGE, in which, according to Hitler's own admission in the Reichstag (July 13), 77 persons, many of them leaders high in the party, were summarily executed because of an alleged plot against Hitler and the régime. In reality this dramatic move was directed against representatives of the more radical, social revolutionary wing of the party, which aimed at incorporation of the storm troops (i.e. party forces) in the army, and at far-reaching property changes. Outstanding among the victims were **Gen. von Schleicher** and his wife (later said to have been shot by mistake); **Ernst Roehm,** one of the ablest organizers in the movement; **Gregor Strasser,** one of the earliest and most energetic, but also one of the most radical of the Nazis; **Erich Klausener,** prominent Catholic leader.

July 25. Nazi putsch in Vienna, in the course of which Chancellor Dollfuss was assassinated. The coup was the culmination of Nazi propaganda and pressure on the Austrian government (p. 1015).

Aug. 1. Law concerning the head of the state, combining the presidency and chancellorship.

Aug. 2. Death of President von Hindenburg (aged 87), followed by

Aug. 19. A plebiscite which approved **Hitler's assumption of the presidency** and of sole executive power (88 per cent of the votes affirmative). Hitler, however, preferred to retain the title *Der Führer.*

1935, Jan. 13. PLEBISCITE IN THE SAAR BASIN, conducted by the League of Nations in accordance with the treaty of Versailles. Ninety per cent of the electors voted for reunion of the territory with Germany as against union with France or continuation of League administration. The return of the Saar to the Reich (Mar. 1) marked the beginning of German expansion under the Hitler régime.

Mar. 16. Hitler startled the world by denouncing the clauses of the Versailles treaty providing for German disarmament. Under French lead, Great Britain and Italy joined in a strong protest against the German action (p. 1127).

June 18. Anglo-German naval agreement, by which Germany promised not to expand her navy beyond 35 per cent of that of the British. By this pact Hitler did much to reassure the British and drive a wedge into the Anglo-French entente.

1936, Mar. 7. The **GERMAN GOVERNMENT DENOUNCED THE LOCARNO PACTS** of 1925 **and reoccupied the Rhineland** (p. 1127).

July 11. German-Austrian agreement, ending a period of great bitterness (p. 1015).

Oct. 25. Formation of the Berlin-Rome Axis, which resulted from a visit of the Italian foreign minister, Count Ciano (Oct. 25-27). This agreement strengthened the position of both Germany and Italy with respect to France and Great Britain, setting up a league of "have-nots" (i.e. revisionist powers) against a league of the "haves."

Nov. 14. Hitler denounced the clauses of the Versailles treaty providing for international control of German rivers.

Nov. 18. The German government recognized the Insurgent government of Gen. Franco in Spain. From the beginning of the civil war in Spain, the Germans had openly sided with the rebels, supplying Franco with armaments and technical experts, as well as with some troops (p. 993).

Nov. 25. Conclusion of the German-Japanese pact, ostensibly directed against communism, but in reality an extension of the Berlin-Rome combination (p. 1128).

1937, Nov. 24. Walther Funk replaced Schacht as minister of economics, Schacht remaining president of the Reichsbank. Schacht had done much to develop German trade through **bartering agreements** with the Balkan and Near Eastern countries. But his methods, however clever, were not in accord with the more extreme theories of Nazi circles. In October 1936 the **Four-Year Plan** had been introduced and Goering had been made economic dictator. Funk's advent marked a further advance of the more extreme Nazi elements.

1938, Feb. 4. Reorganization of the military

and diplomatic command. **Werner von Blomberg** (minister of war) and **Werner von Fritsch** (commander-in-chief of the army) were removed. Hitler assumed the ministry of war, while Gen. Wilhelm Keitel became his representative at the supreme command and Gen. Heinrich von Brauchitsch became commander-in-chief of the army. In the foreign office the place of **Constantin von Neurath** was taken by **Joachim von Ribbentrop.** Definitive subordination of both the army and the foreign service to the Nazi Party. The new men were known to be exponents of a bolder, forward policy.

Feb. 12. Visit of Chancellor Schuschnigg of Austria to Chancellor Hitler **at Berchtesgaden.** Harshly taken to task for his policy of opposition to National Socialism in Austria, Schuschnigg was obliged to promise amnesty to imprisoned Nazis, greater scope for their activity, and inclusion of Nazis in the cabinet. This ushered in the Austrian and indirectly the Czechoslovakian crisis (pp. 1015, 1017).

Mar. 12–13. GERMAN INVASION AND ANNEXATION OF AUSTRIA (p. 1016). Thereby over 6,000,000 Germans were added to the Reich and the way paved for future expansion in the Danube Valley.

May 7. Visit of Hitler to Rome, a state affair of great magnificence. Politically it demonstrated that the Berlin-Rome Axis continued to function despite the Austrian affair.

May 19–20. The first Czech crisis (p. 1017). The strong stand taken by France and Britain led to the hurried fortification of the western frontier of Germany, carried out by half a million men working day and night.

Sept. 12–29. The **GREAT CZECHOSLOVAK CRISIS** (p. 1018), as a result of which Hitler annexed to Germany over 3,000,000 Germans of the Sudeten region. Politically the German success reduced the Little Entente to ruins, broke down the French alliance system in eastern Europe, and made Germany easily the dominant power on the Continent.

1939, Jan. 20. Dismissal of Schacht, whose place as president of the Reichsbank was taken by Walther Funk. Schacht had supposedly warned that the huge armament program must be curtailed if catastrophic inflation was to be averted. Germany's adverse trade balance in 1938 was 432,000,000 marks, and by standards of bourgeois capitalism the country had been bankrupt since 1931.

Mar. 15. German occupation of rump Bohemia and Moravia, and extinction of the Czechoslovak state (p. 1018). Bohemia-Moravia became a German protectorate, Slovakia remained nominally independent.

Mar. 21. German annexation of Memel.

At the same time extensive demands were made on Poland with regard to Danzig and Pomorze. The firmness of the Poles and the alarm of Britain and France, which guaranteed Poland against attack (p. 1039), induced the German government to hold back.

Apr. 28. Hitler's Reichstag speech, in reply to President Roosevelt's appeal (p. 1131). He denounced the Anglo-German naval convention of 1935 and the German-Polish agreement of 1934 because of the new policy of "encirclement" supposedly followed by Britain and Poland. At the same time he renewed his demands on Poland and offered any state assurance against aggression. Specific offers of **bilateral non-aggression pacts** were made to the Scandinavian and Baltic states, but only Denmark, Latvia, and Estonia accepted.

May 22. Conclusion of a political and **military alliance with Italy,** an obvious reply to the British "peace front" and British efforts to reach an agreement with Russia. With European alignments gradually reverting to the pre-war situation, Germany's position was somewhat weakened, though she was clearly dominant on the Continent and more or less mistress of Central Europe.

During the summer the **dispute with Poland** over Danzig and Pomorze rapidly came to a head. Despite repeated warnings from Britain and France, the Germans reiterated their demands and their determination to secure satisfaction at any cost. At the end of June German "volunteers" began to arrive in Danzig and a "free corps" was organized. Border incidents became frequent and finally, on

Aug. 20, 21. The crisis broke when the German government succeeded in arranging a **pact with Russia** that marked a complete reversal of the anti-Communist policy which had underlain National Socialist theory. Throughout two weeks of tension (p. 1132) the Berlin government refused to negotiate directly with Poland and on

Sept. 1. War between Germany and Poland began, without formal declaration. This brought in its train almost at once the

Sept. 3. DECLARATION OF WAR BY GREAT BRITAIN AND FRANCE.

CULTURAL DEVELOPMENTS

Literature: Expressionist dramas of **Georg Kaiser** (1878–1945; *Die Bürger von Calais,* 1914; *Gas,* 1918–1920) and **Ernst Toller** (1893–1939); novels of **Jakob Wasserman** (1873–1934), **Thomas Mann** (1875–1955; *Buddenbrooks,* 1901; *Der Zauberberg,* 1925); **Franz Werfel** (1890–1945; *Die vierzig Tage des Musa Dagh,* 1934).

Music: **Paul Hindemith** (1895–1963).

Art: Painters **Otto Dix** (b. 1891) and **Emil Nolde** (1867–1956); sculptors **Ernst Barlach** (1870–1938) and **Wilhelm Lehmbruck** (1881–

1919); architects **Ludwig Mies van der Rohe** (b. 1886) and **Walter Gropius** (b. 1883), leader of the Bauhaus school of design.

(*Cont. p. 1192.*)

8. AUSTRIA

(*From p. 978*)

The strain of war intensified the divisions and weaknesses of the Hapsburg Empire and prepared the way for its dissolution.

1916, Oct. 21. The Austrian prime minister, **Count Karl Stürgkh**, was assassinated. His place was taken (Oct. 28) by **Ernst von Körber.**

Nov. 21. The old emperor, **Francis Joseph, died,** and was succeeded by his grand-nephew, **Charles, emperor** to November 11, 1918.

Dec. 14. The Körber ministry was followed by a cabinet under **Count Richard Clam-Martinitz. Count Ottokar Czernin** took the place of Count Burian as Austro-Hungarian foreign minister.

1917, May 23. The Hungarian ministry of Count Tisza resigned.

June 15–Aug. 9. Count Maurice Esterhazy's ministry in Hungary.

Aug. 21–1918, Oct. 24. Count Alexander Wekerlé's ministry in Hungary.

1917, June 18. The cabinet of Count Clam-Martinitz in Austria resigned, being succeeded by **Ernst von Seidler,** who continued in office until June 21, 1918.

1918, Apr. 15. Count Czernin, the Austrian foreign minister, was **replaced by Baron Stephen Burian,** who continued in office until October 25, 1918.

THE REPUBLIC OF AUSTRIA

German Austria, with a population almost entirely German, was the most unfortunate creation of the peace conference. Of less than 8,000,000 population, 2,000,000 lived in Vienna, a great industrial center, which was cut off from the former territories of the monarchy and shut in by the high tariff walls of the new neighbors. The economic viability of the country was in question from the outset. Despite the principle of self-determination, Austria was forbidden to unite with Germany for political reasons. The history of the country since the peace treaty centered upon the conflict between the countryside (conservative and clerical) and the metropolis, controlled by the Socialists; upon the question of union with Germany (*Anschluss*); and upon the question of subsistence.

1918, Nov. 11. Abdication of the Emperor Charles.

Nov. 12. A provisional government was established.

1919. The larger part of the year was one of confusion, marked particularly by **communist disorders.**

Feb. 16. Election of a constituent assembly. The Socialists secured 72 seats, the Christian Socialists (agrarian, clerical) 69, the German Nationalists 26.

Mar. 12. The assembly voted Austria an integral part of the German Reich. **Karl Renner** (Socialist) became the first chancellor.

Sept. 10. Austria signed the **treaty of Saint-Germain** (p. 978) in which union with Germany was expressly forbidden. The name of the state had to be changed from German Austria to *Republic of Austria.*

1920, June 11. The **Renner cabinet resigned** and was followed by a ministry of all parties under **Michael Mayr.**

Oct. 1. A new constitution created a federal state on the Swiss model with eight provinces (Vienna a separate province) and a two-chamber legislature.

Oct. 10. A dispute with Yugoslavia over the **Klagenfurt** area was decided by plebiscite in favor of Austria.

Dec. 9. Michael Hainisch elected first president of the republic.

1921. Acute food shortage, leading to much suffering and unrest.

Apr. 24. Plebiscite in the Tyrol, which voted for union with Germany.

May 29. Salzburg voted for union with Germany. The movement of separation was stopped by Allied threats.

June 21. New cabinet of **Johann Schober,** supported by Christian Socialists and German Nationalists.

July–Dec. The **Burgenland dispute** with Hungary (p. 1121).

1922, May 31. CABINET OF IGNAZ SEIPEL (Christian Socialist).

Oct. 4. The **League of Nations** took over the problem of Austrian reconstruction, following the earnest appeal of the chancellor. An international loan, under guaranty of the League, was accorded and a League commissioner appointed to supervise Austrian finance.

1923, Oct. 20. In the elections the **Christian Socialists won a victory** over the Socialists.

1924, Nov. 17. Resignation of Seipel because of ill health. His place was taken by his follower, **Rudolf Ramek.**

1925, Sept. 10. The League voted to discontinue control of Austrian finance in July 1926, the reconstruction scheme having put Austria on its feet.

1926, Oct. 15. The Ramek cabinet gave way to a new **Seipel ministry.** During this period there was a marked recrudescence of agitation in favor of union with Germany, and a growing antagonism between the Christian Socialist government and the Socialist government of Vienna, which carried on a policy of "soaking the rich" in order to carry through socialist experiments in housing, relief, etc.

1927, July 15. The acquittal of three Nationalists of the murder of two Socialists led to riots and a **general strike in Vienna.** The mob burned the beautiful palace of justice, destroying many valuable records. The disorders were put down with some bloodshed. In the succeeding years clashes between the factions became more and more frequent in various parts of the country, each organizing private armies (the Christian Socialists the *Heimwehr*, the Socialists the *Schutzbund*).

1928, Dec. 5. Wilhelm Miklas elected second president.

1929, Sept. 26. Second Schober cabinet, supported by Christian Socialists and Nationalists, with a program of restoring order.

1930, Feb. 6. Treaty of friendship with Italy. Beginning of the systematic support of the fascist elements by Italy.

Sept. 30. Cabinet of Karl Vaugoin.

Nov. 9. The elections gave the Socialists 72 seats as against 66 for the Christian Socialists.

Dec. 3. Cabinet of Otto Ender (Christian Socialist), including Schober and Vaugoin.

1931, Mar. 20. The Anschluss problem culminated in a projected **customs union with Germany** (p. 1007).

May 11. Collapse of the Austrian Credit-Anstalt, due in part to the withdrawal of short credits by France to force the abandonment of the customs union with Germany. The Austrian government attempted to save the bank, but was ultimately obliged to appeal for aid abroad. France refused support excepting on the most burdensome terms, but at the last moment (June 16) the British government offered a necessary loan. On the same day the **Ender cabinet resigned** and

June 21. Karl Buresch (Christian Socialist) **formed a new government,** concerned primarily

to save the desperate financial situation.

Sept. 13. The Fascist Heimwehr attempted **a coup in Styria** and proclaimed **Walter Pfrimer** "dictator."

Oct. 9. President Miklas was re-elected.

1932, May 20. A CABINET UNDER ENGELBERT DOLLFUSS (Christian Socialist) replaced that of Buresch. Like its predecessor, the new government represented a coalition of Christian Socialists and Agrarians.

July 15. The **League of Nations finally agreed to a loan** of 300,000,000 schillings, Austria engaging not to enter into political or economic union with Germany before 1952.

1933, Mar. Growing anti-governmental agitation in Austria, following the victory of the National Socialists in Germany. To meet the situation, **Dollfuss suspended parliamentary government** (Mar. 4) and prohibited parades and assemblies; freedom of the press was also curtailed (Mar. 8). Nevertheless the Austrian Nazis staged a great demonstration and riot in Vienna March 29, and the Styrian branch of the Heimwehr became frankly Nazi. The government (May 4) forbade the wearing of uniforms by all political parties. Nazi agitators were harried from the land and relations with Germany became tense. June 1, Hitler imposed a charge of 1000 marks on Germans desiring to visit Austria, thereby completely ruining the Austrian tourist business.

June 14. The **Austrian government expelled Theodor Habicht,** Hitler's "inspector for Austria." The Germans retaliated with a series of **terrorist outrages.**

June 19. The **Nazi Party** in Austria **was dissolved.** Agitation and terrorism continued, encouraged by a virulent Nazi radio campaign. On October 3 an attempt was made to assassinate Dollfuss.

1934, Feb. 11–15. DESTRUCTION OF THE AUSTRIAN SOCIALISTS. This followed a decree dissolving all political parties except Dollfuss' *Fatherland Front.* Raids by government forces and Heimwehr on Socialist headquarters led to an uprising and the bombardment of the Karl Marx Hof, Socialist housing unit, where the leaders had concentrated. These leaders were either captured or forced to flee. By this drastic action Dollfuss and the Christian Socialists permanently antagonized the working classes of Vienna and deprived themselves of what might have been the most effective support against the Nazi threat.

Mar. 17. Signature of the Rome protocols, effecting close relations between Austria, Hungary, and Italy. Dollfuss was obliged to rely more and more upon Italian support against a hostile Germany.

Apr. 1. Promulgation of a **new constitution**

for **Vienna,** which deprived the capital of most of its powers of self-government.

Apr. 30. A complicated **constitution for Austria** was accepted by the national assembly. It set up a **dictatorship under Dollfuss,** who (July 10) reconstructed his cabinet along Fascist lines.

May 1. A concordat with the Vatican gave the Church in Austria wide control of education.

July 25. NAZI COUP. A band of Nazis seized the radio station in Vienna and forced the staff to broadcast Dollfuss' resignation. They then entered the chancellery and (probably unintentionally) **shot and killed Dollfuss.** The whole affair was badly mismanaged and the conspirators were routed by Heimwehr troops. Action by Germany in behalf of the Nazis was made impossible by the strong stand of Italy and Yugoslavia, which concentrated large forces on the frontier. Thereupon the German government disavowed all connection with the affair and recalled its ambassador to Vienna.

July 30. Kurt Schuschnigg, close collaborator of Dollfuss, **formed a new cabinet** committed to the same policies. Twice in the course of the autumn he visited Mussolini. Economic agreements with Italy and Hungary led to some improvement in the situation, and political agitation also died down somewhat.

1935, July 4. Repeal of the anti-Hapsburg laws and restoration of part of the imperial property. This move was symptomatic of increased **sentiment for return of the Hapsburgs,** advocated by Prince Rüdiger von Stahremberg and supposedly encouraged by Mussolini. The opposition of the Little Entente and of France served, however, as an effective damper.

1936, Apr. 1. Reintroduction of conscription, in violation of the provisions of the treaty of Saint-Germain. The Austrian step followed similar action by Germany (p. 1010) and was intended to give the Austrian dictatorship an armed force more reliable than the Heimwehr. On May 14 Schuschnigg forced **Prince Stahremberg,** commander of the Heimwehr, out of the offices of vice-chancellor and leader of the Fatherland Front, thus removing his only serious rival.

July 11. German-Austrian agreement, ending the feud between the two countries at least temporarily. Germany engaged to respect the independence of Austria and Schuschnigg promised to pursue a policy befitting a German state. The agreement was evidently inspired by Mussolini during a visit by Schuschnigg to Rome (June 1), Mussolini being anxious, on the eve of the Ethiopian campaign, to secure the good-will of Germany.

Oct. 10. Schuschnigg disbanded the Heimwehr and had the members absorbed into the Fatherland Front militia. He dropped the remaining Heimwehr members from his cabinet, and October 18 had himself proclaimed *Front Führer.*

1937, Feb. 14. Schuschnigg publicly claimed the right to decide the **question of Hapsburg restoration.** All indications were that he was veering more and more in that direction. This was highly objectionable to Hitler and to the entire Nazi party, and probably accounts for the **recrudescence of Nazi demonstrations** and mutual recrimination (Feb.). Schuschnigg's position was further weakened by the conclusion of the Rome-Berlin Axis (p. 1011) and by Mussolini's preoccupation with the Spanish civil war.

Apr. 22. Schuschnigg visited Mussolini at Venice, where he was warned that Italy could not be counted on to give armed support against Germany. Mussolini seems further to have opposed the projected restoration of the Hapsburgs and to have objected to a suggested alliance between Austria and Czechoslovakia for common defense. His advice was that Schuschnigg make his peace with Hitler and admit Nazis to the government. Schuschnigg rejected this advice, but continued throughout the year to further **negotiations with Czechoslovakia** and the Little Entente. Indications were that, deserted by Italy, he was seeking and finding a measure of support from France and its allies. This policy, on the other hand, led to much dissatisfaction in Germany and to ever more outspoken demands on the part of the Austrian Nazis and Pan-Germans.

1938, Feb. 12. Schuschnigg paid a visit to Hitler at Berchtesgaden, and under pressure was obliged to promise an amnesty to Austrian Nazis who had been imprisoned, and furthermore to agree to take certain Nazis into the cabinet. On February 16 **Arthur Seyss-Inquart** (Nazi) became minister of the interior. **Full amnesty** was granted and (Feb. 19) the Fatherland Front was opened to Nazis.

Feb. 24. Schuschnigg, replying to a speech of Hitler (Feb. 20) promising protection to 10,000,000 Germans outside the Reich, **reaffirmed the independence of Austria** and appealed for support against further demands. This speech called forth a good deal of enthusiasm in Austria, but the Nazis, confident of success, assumed the offensive. On March 1 serious **disorders broke out at Graz** and soon all Styria, as well as other places, were in a state of revolution. The government was unable to cope with the situation without offending Nazi Germany. Last-minute efforts of Schuschnigg to arrange a reconciliation with the Socialist working classes came to nothing. As a last resort, Schuschnigg suddenly announced (Mar. 9) that a plebiscite would be held on the following Sunday on the question of Austrian independence; only *Yes* ballots were to be distributed (those who desired to vote *No* would have to supply their own ballots, of specified form). This announcement drove the Nazis to extremes and plunged the country into chaos. Hitler seized the opportunity, and

Mar. 11. Germany submitted an ultimatum demanding postponement of the plebiscite and the resignation of Schuschnigg. German troops began to concentrate on the frontier. Unable to resist, **Schuschnigg resigned and Seyss-Inquart became chancellor.**

Mar. 12. The German army began the **invasion of Austria.** No resistance was offered. **President Miklas resigned** and

Mar. 13. SEYSS-INQUART PROCLAIMED THE UNION WITH GERMANY. Hitler arrived in Vienna March 14 and took formal possession. He had already decreed a plebiscite to be held April 10. Meanwhile the most ruthless revenge was taken on all opponents of the Nazis, many of whom committed suicide and most of whom, unable to get away,

were thrown into concentration camps. Schuschnigg allowed himself to be arrested and was kept in confinement without trial. The Jews suffered assault and humiliation of all kinds.

Apr. 10. The **plebiscite in Austria** revealed a vote of 99.75 per cent in favor of the union with Germany. Austria was incorporated with the Reich as a new state, and was divided into seven districts (*Gaue*). The union was carried through with such speed and energy on the part of the Germans that no international complications ensued. Britain and France protested, but these powers were too deeply involved in Mediterranean and Far Eastern problems to be able to take further action, the more so as Italy refused to join in protest. Mussolini, though his ally's success brought a powerful state to the Brenner Pass, could only acquiesce as gracefully as possible.

(*Cont. p. 1201.*)

CULTURAL DEVELOPMENTS

Prominence of Austria in the field of **music: Arnold Schoenberg** (1874–1951) and his 12-tone system, and his followers, **Alban Berg** (1885–1935) and **Anton von Webern** (1883–1945).

9.　CZECHOSLOVAKIA

(*From p. 978*)

The new state, with a population of about 15,000,000, inherited the most valuable part of the old Austro-Hungarian Monarchy, with most of the industrial areas. Its political life after the war was dominated by the racial problem and the resulting multiplication of political parties.

1918, Oct. 14. The Czechoslovak national council in Paris organized a **provisional government,** with **Thomas Garrigue Masaryk** as president, and **Eduard Beneš** as foreign minister.

Oct. 28. DECLARATION OF INDEPENDENCE, by the national council.

Oct. 30. The **Slovak national council voted for union with the Czechs.**

1919, Jan. The **dispute with Poland** regarding the Teschen area (p. 1121).

Apr. 16. The **Land Reform Bill.** This involved the confiscation, with compensation, of the large estates and their partition among the peasants in lots of about 25 acres, with state aid.

1920, Feb. 29. Adoption of the constitution, closely modeled on that of France.

Apr. 18. The **first regular elections.** There were numerous parties, representing racial groups and social strata. The country had to

be ruled by various coalitions, representing chiefly the bourgeois, democratic elements.

Aug. 14. Treaty with Yugoslavia, the basis of the **Little Entente** (p. 1121).

1921, Apr. 23. Treaty with Roumania, completing the Little Entente.

1924, Jan. 25. Treaty of alliance with France.

1927, May 27. President Masaryk re-elected. Eduard Beneš remained foreign minister in all cabinets and took an active part in the work of the League of Nations.

July 1. An **administrative reform** gave a greater measure of self-government to the provinces. This was designed to meet the constant complaints of the Slovaks and Ruthenians that their districts were ruled from Prague by Czechs. In both areas there was an active movement demanding autonomy.

1928, Dec. The arrest and **conviction of Voitech Tuka,** a Slovak deputy accused of irredentist agitation in favor of Hungary, caused much ill-feeling in Slovakia.

1931, Mar. The government, in association with France, offered strenuous **opposition to the projected German-Austrian customs union** (p. 1007).

1932, Apr. 6–8. A conference, attended by representatives of Great Britain, France, Germany, and Italy, met at London to discuss the **Danube problem.** The French (Tardieu) plan, which would have excluded Germany and Italy from the projected regional understandings, was wrecked by the opposition of those two countries.

1933, Feb. 14–16. The powers of the **Little Entente,** meeting at Geneva, **concluded a pact of organization,** providing for a standing council and a permanent secretariat, as well as for co-ordination of policies and for economic collaboration. This step toward greater solidarity was provoked partly by revival of irredentist agitation in Hungary, in part by the advent of Hitler's National Socialist government in Germany. In the course of the year **Nazi agitation** spread rapidly among the more than 3,000,000 Germans living along the frontiers of the republic. These areas, largely industrial, were particularly hard hit by the depression, so that economic grievances were added to the earlier cultural and political ones.

Oct. 4. The **Sudete National Socialist Party dissolved itself,** on the eve of a government order prohibiting it. Led by **Konrad Henlein,** the party soon emerged again as the *Sudetendeutsche Partei,* Nazi in its program but officially not directed at the disruption of the state.

1934, Apr. 26. Visit of the French foreign minister, **Louis Barthou,** to Prague. His purpose was to discuss the Danubian situation as it appeared after the conclusion of the Rome protocols (p. 1000) and generally to revivify the Franco-Czech alliance.

May 24. **President Masaryk was once again re-elected.**

1935, May 16. Conclusion of a **pact of mutual assistance with Russia,** together with an air convention. By the terms Russia was obliged to come to the aid of Czechoslovakia in case of attack, provided that France did likewise. The agreement followed the breakdown of French efforts to engineer an eastern pact, and the conclusion of the Franco-Russian alliance (p. 989). It aroused much opposition in Germany and exposed the republic to German wrath.

May 19. In the **general elections** the government coalition secured 149 out of 300 seats in the chamber. The Sudete Party won a sweeping victory in the German areas and, with 44 seats, became the strongest single party, with the exception of the Czech Agrarians.

Nov. 5. **Milan Hodža,** a Slovak and the leader of the Agrarian Party, **formed a new cabinet.**

Dec. 13. **Resignation of President Masaryk,** who had reached the age of 85. He was succeeded by his close friend, the foreign minister,

1935–1938. EDUARD BENEŠ, president. He continued to guide the republic's foreign policy, though on February 29, 1936, **Kamil Krofta,** well-known Czech historian, became foreign minister.

1936, Mar. 9–10. Premier Hodža visited Vienna. On April 2 a trade treaty was concluded between Czechoslovakia and Austria. This rapprochement reflected the Austrian desire for support in the face of German hostility and Italian uncertainty, as well as the hope of the Czechs, backed by France, to bring Austria, and perhaps Hungary, into association with the Little Entente. The Czech government had already embarked upon an extensive **program of armament** and had undertaken the construction of a strong line of fortifications along the German frontier.

Sept. 10. **Joseph Goebbels,** the German minister of propaganda, publicly **accused Czechoslovakia of harboring Soviet army planes** and permitting Soviet airdromes on Czech soil. Despite Czech protests, these accusations were repeated and there developed a Nazi campaign of denunciation and recrimination reminiscent of the Nazi campaign against Austria.

1937, Sept. 14. Death of President Masaryk.

Oct. 16. The Czech police suppressed a meeting of the Sudete German Party at Teplitz. Some violence having occurred, **Henlein** protested against the government's methods and **demanded complete autonomy** for the Germans in the republic. In view of the general excitement and tension, the government postponed the elections scheduled for November 14. All political meetings were forbidden.

Nov. 29. The **Sudete German deputies left parliament,** declaring that they had been beaten by the police.

1938, Mar.–May. The first German-Czech crisis. Hitler's speech of February 20 promising protection to German minorities outside the Reich was answered by Premier Hodža (Mar. 4) by a firm declaration that Czechoslovakia would defend itself against outside interference. But the **German annexation of Austria** (Mar. 13) completely changed the position of the Czechoslovak Republic, now surrounded on three sides by the new German Empire. The German government gave Prague assurances of its desire to improve German-Czech relations (Mar. 14) and both the French and Russian governments categorically declared their intention to honor their treaty obligations. Nevertheless the situation rapidly grew worse. The **German Activists** (i.e. German parties which had joined the cabinet) **all withdrew** (Mar. 22–25), and Hodža's announcement of a forthcoming **Nationality Statute** made but little impression on the German elements. On April 24 the Sudete leader, Henlein, put forward his demands (the

Carlsbad program: *eight points:* full equality of status for Germans and Czechs; delimitation of the German areas; full autonomy; removal of all injustices and reparation for damages suffered by the Germans since 1918; full liberty for the Germans to proclaim their Germanism and their adhesion to "the ideology of Germans"; furthermore, Henlein demanded complete revision of Czech foreign policy). These demands were rejected by the Prague government, despite strong urging by France and Britain that the utmost concessions be made. Henlein then paid visits to London and Berlin where he posed as the soul of moderation. On his return disorders began to break out in the German districts. This situation and rumors of German troop concentration on the frontier led the Czech government to mobilize 400,000 men. France and Britain took a strong stand and the crisis blew over. Shortly afterward Henlein began negotiations with the Czech government with regard to the Nationality Statute, but Hitler, with feverish haste, began the fortification of the German-French frontier and ordered a huge increase in the German air forces.

July–Aug. The summer was filled with **negotiations between the government and the Sudete leaders,** but little progress was made. On July 26 the government finally published a draft Nationality Statute, based on the principle of proportionality, but falling short of Henlein's Carlsbad program. At the same time it was announced that a British mediator, **Lord Walter Runciman,** would come to Prague. He arrived August 3 and held many conferences with Sudete leaders. Meanwhile (Aug. 12) the German government announced huge maneuvers which involved calling 750,000 men to the colors, and August 28 Hitler began a demonstrative tour of the new fortifications in the west. At the same time (Aug. 26) the British government announced the concentration of most of the fleet for early September. British statesmen on various occasions warned publicly that British abstention in a crisis should not be counted on. By the beginning of September the situation was clearly critical; various Czech proposals for cantonal organizations, etc., were flatly rejected by Henlein after visits to Hitler. The Carlsbad program was insisted on as a minimum. The French government (Sept. 7) began to call up reservists, so that about 1,000,000 men were under arms.

Hitler's demands on Czechoslovakia (Nürnberg speech, September 12) produced an international crisis in **September 1938,** which eased only after Britain and France yielded to the German chancellor's belligerence in a final gesture of appeasement. For the Munich conference and the subsequent dismemberment of Czechoslovakia see pp. 1129–1130.

CZECH LOSSES THROUGH THE DISMEMBERMENT: In all the republic lost 5,000,000 inhabitants (retaining 10,000,000), distributed as follows: Germans, 2,850,000; Hungarians, 591,000; Poles, 77,000; Jews, 60,000; Ruthenians, 37,000; Czechs and Slovaks, 1,161,000. In territory Czechoslovakia lost 16,000 square miles (retaining 38,500).

Oct. 5. Resignation of President Beneš, who had been the target of German attack throughout the crisis. He left the country almost at once, going eventually to the United States. His departure was the signal for a violent campaign directed against him and Masaryk and the policies that had led to Munich.

Oct. 6. Slovakia was given the full autonomy which Slovak leaders had demanded for a long time. **Mgr. Joseph Tiso** became premier of Slovakia.

Oct. 8. Ruthenia was given full autonomy and was renamed *Carpatho-Ukraine.* This remote region of Europe at once assumed a crucial importance as the base for Ukrainian agitation, supposedly inspired from Berlin. The Polish government made every effort to arrange for its partition between Poland, Hungary, and Roumania, but all such plans were frustrated by German opposition.

Oct. 20. The **Communist Party was outlawed** in Czecho-Slovakia (so spelled after the federal reorganization). This was merely one move in the direction of the new policy planned in conformity with Germany. **Persecution of Jews,** etc., soon followed.

Nov. 30. EMIL HACHA, judge of the high court, **was elected president. Rudolf Beran** (Agrarian), an opponent of Beneš, became prime minister.

1939, Mar. 10–16. THE ANNIHILATION OF THE CZECHOSLOVAK STATE. The crisis began when the Prague government deposed Mgr. Tiso, premier of Slovakia, for allegedly working for separation, with support of the Fascist *Hlinka Guards.* Tiso appealed to Hitler and during a visit to Berlin was given assurances of support. Hitler summoned President Hacha and foreign minister František Chvalkovsky to Berlin and induced them to "place the fate of the Czech people . . . trustingly in the hands of the Führer," who guaranteed "an autonomous development of its national life corresponding to its peculiarities." **Slovakia and Carpatho-Ukraine declared independence.** On March 15 Bohemia and Moravia became a German protectorate, which was promptly occupied by German forces, the Czechs offering no resistance. On March 16 Tiso put Slovakia also under German protection. **Constantin von**

Neurath, former German foreign minister, became **protector of Bohemia and Moravia,** Hacha continuing as "head of the state." The disappearance of Czechoslovakia was momentous, inasmuch as it demonstrated Hitler's readiness to extend his claims beyond German racial areas and base them on German needs for "living area" (*Lebensraum*). The small states were thrown into a panic, and Britain and France promptly adopted a policy of guarantees to prevent further German expansion (p. 1039). (*Cont. p. 1203.*)

10. HUNGARY

(*From p. 979*)

Hungary, left a country of some 8,000,000 population by the peace settlements, was predominantly agricultural, socially still organized on a semi-feudal basis. Much of the political history after 1918 had to do with the successful efforts of the landholding classes to secure and retain control and with the agitation for revision of the peace treaties and the restoration of the monarchy. The antiquated political arrangements effectively kept the lower classes from exerting much influence.

1918, Oct. 17. The **Hungarian parliament,** in reply to the Emperor Charles's declaration of reorganization of the monarchy, declared **complete independence from Austria,** except for the personal union.

Oct. 31. REVOLUTION IN HUNGARY. Count **Michael Károlyi,** grand seigneur of liberal, republican, and pacifist views, made prime minister in the hope of securing satisfactory peace terms and maintaining the unity of the monarchy.

Nov. 16. The national council proclaimed **Hungary a republic.**

1919, Jan. 11. Károlyi appointed president of the republic. The government at once proceeded to the work of dividing the large estates among the peasants.

Mar. 21. Károlyi resigned in protest to the Allied decision to assign Transylvania to Roumania.

Mar. 21. Formation of a **Socialist-Communist government** under **Alexander Garbai** (president) and **Béla Kun** (foreign affairs). The Socialists were soon crowded out and a communist dictatorship established under Béla Kun, henchman of Lenin, who had come from Russia in November 1918 but had been imprisoned for communist agitation.

Mar. 28. Hungary declared war on Czechoslovakia and proceeded to the reconquest of Slovakia.

Apr. 10. Roumanian troops began to invade Hungary to forestall reconquest of Transylvania. A provisional government was set up by **Count Julius Károlyi** (brother of Michael), **Count Stephen Bethlen, Admiral Nikolaus Horthy,** and **Archduke Joseph** at Szeged (under French occupation). **Beginning of the counter-revolution.**

June 24. Communist constitution.

Aug. 1. Béla Kun fled to Vienna in the face of the Roumanian advance.

Aug. 4. The **Roumanians occupied Budapest** (until November 14).

Aug. 6. Archduke Joseph took control as state governor, but was forced by Allied protests to resign.

1920, Feb. 25. Final evacuation of the country by the Roumanians, who took with them all that was moveable.

Mar. 1. Admiral Nikolaus Horthy, commander-in-chief of the forces, appointed **regent and head of the state.**

Mar. 23. He proclaimed **Hungary a monarchy,** with the throne vacant.

June 4. SIGNATURE OF THE TREATY OF TRIANON, consecrating the immense losses of territory and population involved in the establishment, of Czechoslovakia, Roumania, and Yugoslavia.

1921, Mar. 27. King Charles returned to Hungary and called on Horthy to give up his powers. Owing to the threatening attitude of the neighboring states, the national assembly voted against restoration and Charles was obliged to return to Switzerland.

Apr. 14. CABINET OF COUNT STEPHEN BETHLEN, who remained in power until 1931.

July–Dec. The **Burgenland dispute** with Austria (p. 1121).

Oct. 21. Second arrival of King Charles, at Ödenburg. With an improvised force he marched on Budapest. Czechoslovakia and Yugoslavia began to mobilize and a government force was obliged to turn back and capture the king, who was exiled to Madeira (d. Apr. 1, 1922).

Nov. 4. A **Dethronement Act** abrogated the rights of Charles.

1922, June 2. Elections, held under a system of carefully restricted suffrage and open voting, gave the government a strong majority. Bethlen proceeded on a conservative policy designed to maintain the *status quo*. Efforts of the extreme royalists and fascists (*Awakening Mag-*

yars, etc.) to overthrow the government were summarily dealt with.

Sept. 18. Hungary was admitted to the League of Nations.

1923, Dec. 20. The League of Nations adopted a **plan for economic reconstruction** of Hungary, not unlike the one successfully applied in Austria. This continued until June 1926.

1926, Nov. 11. Re-establishment of an upper house, representing the landed aristocracy.

1927, Apr. 5. Treaty of friendship with Italy, initiating a period of close relations. This was reflected in the growing **agitation for treaty-revision,** which was ardently supported in Britain by the Rothermere press.

1928, Jan. Austrian customs officials discovered five freight cars loaded with machine-gun parts, shipped from Italy and destined for Hungary. The Little Entente powers protested to the League, which held an investigation.

1930, Nov. 20. Archduke Otto, pretender to the throne, **reached his majority.**

1931, Aug. 15. France granted a loan to Hungary, evidently on condition that revisionist agitation should cease.

Aug. 19. Resignation of Count Bethlen, officially because of ill health, actually because of inability to cope with the financial situation. His friend, **Count Julius Károlyi,** took his place, but

1932, Oct. 4. Julius Gömbös, former reactionary and anti-Semite, took his place. Gömbös was not averse to a measure of agrarian and electoral reform, but was above all an ardent nationalist and revisionist. He opposed the restoration of the Hapsburgs, but sought to further realization of Hungary's territorial claims by **close co-operation with Fascist Italy.**

1933, Jan. Discovery of another shipment of arms from Italy to Hungary threw some light on the subterranean aspects of European politics. Once again the Little Entente countries took a strong stand.

The advent of Hitler and the National Socialists in Germany led to the **rapid spread of Nazi agitation** to Hungary, where there were large-scale demonstrations already in April.

June. Gömbös visited Berlin, and in July journeyed to Rome. His hope was that Germany and Italy could both be brought to support the Hungarian claims. It was only natural, then, that he should reject the Franco-Czech plans for a Danube Federation (Dec.).

1934, Mar. 17. SIGNATURE OF THE ROME PROTOCOLS, establishing close political and economic ties between Italy, Austria, and Hungary and forming a bloc in opposition to the Francophile Little Entente.

Oct. 9. Assassination of King Alexander of Yugoslavia (p. 1022). The assassins had operated from Hungary. Acute danger of conflict developed, but the matter was finally adjusted by the League of Nations which, in a masterpiece of diplomatic circumlocution, mildly rebuked the Hungarian government (Dec. 10).

1935, Apr. 11. In the **parliamentary elections** the opposition groups polled 1,041,000 votes as against 908,000 for the government, but the intricate electoral system enabled the government to retain 166 seats in the chamber as against 25 for the Agrarians, 14 for the Christian Socialists, and 12 for the Social Democrats.

June 1. Count Bethlen and his followers joined the most important opposition group, the **Agrarian Party** of **Tibor Eckardt.** This party resented the dictatorial methods of Gömbös and suspected him of designs against the constitution. At the same time it advocated land reform in behalf of the 3,000,000 landless peasants, and electoral reform as a stage on the road toward real democracy. Only by timely reform along national lines could the threat of Nazism and Fascism be removed.

Oct. 6. Death of Premier Gömbös, who was succeeded by **Koloman Darányi.** Darányi tried to follow a somewhat more conciliatory course. Hungary's position became steadily worse through international developments. The German government showed but little interest in Hungarian revisionism and was downright hostile to all proposals of a Hapsburg restoration. The attention of Italy, too, was diverted by the Ethiopian crisis and the Mediterranean situation. The formation of the **Rome-Berlin Axis** (Oct. 1936) involved the sacrifice of Austria by Mussolini. In the same way the **Italo-Yugoslav agreement** of March 1937 was tantamount to desertion of Hungary in favor of its neighbor. Under the circumstances, Darányi, during 1937, drew closer to Austria and both Austria and Hungary began to seek contact with the nations of the Little Entente. This policy of necessity estranged Germany (Hungary's most important customer) and was vigorously opposed by the Hungarian Nazis.

1937, Mar. 5. The existence of a widespread **Nazi plot** was revealed. The Nazi leader, **Ferenc Szálasi,** and other conspirators were arrested, but treated rather mildly. The Nazi elements had a most effective weapon against the government, viz. the promise of land reform and relief for the agrarian proletariat. The government resorted to strenuous methods to repress agitation, but without avail.

Oct. 11. Eckardt and his Agrarian Party **joined the Legitimists.** Even the Social Democrats became friendly to the idea of Hapsburg restoration as the most effective way to block the Fascist elements.

Oct. 16. Various Fascist groups united to form the **Hungarian National Socialist Party,** under the leadership of Szálasi. Efforts were made to glorify the regent, Admiral Horthy, and to further his candidacy for the throne. Horthy himself discountenanced these efforts. **1938, Feb. Szálasi was again arrested,** with 72 associates. He was sentenced to prison and drastic steps were taken to stamp out the Fascist-Nazi movement. But

Mar. 13. The **annexation of Austria** by Germany brought the powerful Reich to the Hungarian border. The idea of a bloc consisting of Austria, Hungary, and the Little Entente states was exploded and the scheme of a Hapsburg restoration likewise. The large German element in Hungary (c. 500,000) became more and more restless.

May 13. A **new cabinet was formed by Béla Imredy,** eminent financier, who was regarded by the ruling classes as the strong man needed to manage the situation. Imredy did, indeed, rule with a strong hand. At the same time, however, he initiated certain **political and economic reforms** (a part of all large estates to be distributed to the peasantry, etc.) and undertook the **limitation of Jewish activity** in business and the professions. In this way he hoped to steal the thunder of the Nazi agitators. For the rest he tried to maintain good relations with Germany. In August Admiral Horthy paid a visit to Germany, where he was received with great ceremony.

Nov. 2. ACQUISITION OF SOUTHERN SLOVAKIA, as a result of the dismemberment of Czechoslovakia (p. 1130). The Hungarian claims were valiantly championed by both Germany and Italy, two powers which served as arbitrators after the Czech and Hungarian governments had failed to agree. Hungary was given 5000 square miles of territory, with 1,000,000 inhabitants.

1939, Jan. 20–23. The Italian foreign minister, Ciano, devoted himself to the **adjustment of Hungarian-Yugoslav relations,** but Yugoslavia's unwillingness to consider any cessions of territory to Hungary made any reconciliation difficult.

Feb. 15. Resignation of Premier Imredy. The Nazis, whom he had tried to outdo in his anti-Semitic policy, had taunted him with his own Jewish ancestry.

Feb. 24. The **new government of Count Paul Teleki** suddenly suppressed the leading Fascist organization, yet at the same time, to placate Germany, **joined the anti-communist pact** of Germany, Japan, and Italy.

Mar. 15. HUNGARY OCCUPIED CARPATHO-UKRAINE and annexed it after heavy fighting with the inhabitants, who had driven out the Czechs and, under Augustin Volosin, had enjoyed independence for one day.

Apr. 11. Hungary withdrew from the League of Nations, revealing further influence of German pressure.

May 3. Introduction of drastic **anti-Jewish laws** providing for rigorous limitation of Jews in professions and business, expulsion from government service, and eventual emigration within five years.

May 28. In the **elections** the government secured 180 seats out of 260, but the Nazis increased their representation from 6 to 53, while the Agrarians had 14 seats as against a previous 23. (*Cont. p. 1187.*)

11. THE BALKAN STATES

a. YUGOSLAVIA

The history of the new state, composed of Serbia, Montenegro, Croatia, Slovenia, and Dalmatia, was marked chiefly by the efforts of the Serbs to establish a centralized Serb state and by the vigorous resistance of the Croats and Slovenes (Roman Catholic and much more westernized than the Serbs) to secure some type of autonomy.

1917, July 20. The **PACT OF CORFU,** signed by Serbian, Croatian, Slovenian, and Montenegrin representatives, declared that the Serbs, Croats, and Slovenes formed a **single nation,** to be organized under the Serbian dynasty.

1918, Apr. 8–10. Congress of Oppressed Nationalities (chiefly under Hapsburg rule) at Rome. Italy recognized the unity and independence of the Yugoslav nation.

Oct. 19. The **national council** at Zagreb proclaimed itself the authoritative body for the Yugoslavs and declared for union.

Nov. 26. A **national assembly in Montenegro proclaimed union** with Serbia and declared **King Nicholas,** who had resisted previous efforts at union, **deposed** (d. Mar. 1, 1921, in exile).

Dec. 1. Prince Alexander of Serbia accepted the **regency** of the new state.

Dec. 4. THE KINGDOM OF THE SERBS, CROATS, AND SLOVENES FORMALLY PROCLAIMED.

1919, Feb. Dispute with Italy regarding the allocation of **Fiume** and territory on the **Dalmatian coast** (p. 1121).

June 13. The peace conference decided that the **Banat of Temesvar,** in dispute between Yugoslavia and Roumania, should be divided between them.

1920, Aug. 14. TREATY OF ALLIANCE WITH CZECHOSLOVAKIA laying the foundation for the **Little Entente** (p. 1121).

Nov. 12. Treaty of Rapallo with Italy, settling the **Fiume question.**

1921, Jan. 1. The **new constitution** provided for a centralized form of government. Nicolas Pashich became premier of a coalition of Serbian Radicals and Democrats. The Croats continued in opposition.

June 7. TREATY WITH ROUMANIA, second link in the Little Entente.

Aug. 16. Death of King Peter.

1921–1934. ALEXANDER I. He was a hardworking, intelligent ruler, whose aim was to consolidate the kingdom despite opposition from Croats and other groups.

1924, Jan. 27. Treaty of friendship with Italy for five years, following settlement of the Fiume problem. This was not renewed in 1929.

1926, Aug. 17. Treaty with Greece, which settled the question of the Yugoslav **free zone at Saloniki.**

Sept. 18. Treaty of friendship with Poland.

Dec. 10. Death of Pashich, veteran leader of the Radical Party.

1927, June. Rupture of relations with Albania, following repeated frontier incidents (p. 1023).

Nov. 11. Treaty of friendship with France, intended as a reply to the Italian advance in the Balkans.

1928, June 20. Stephen Radich, leader of the Croatian Peasant Party, and his associates were **fired upon** in parliament by a Radical deputy. **Radich died** August 8. The Croat deputies withdrew from parliament.

Aug. 1. The **Croats** once more demanded the institution of a federal régime as the price of their co-operation. They then set up a separatist "parliament" at Zagreb and refused to have anything more to do with the Belgrade government (Oct.). All efforts of the king to effect a compromise ended in failure.

1929, Jan. 5. KING ALEXANDER PROCLAIMED A DICTATORSHIP.

Jan. 21. The Croat and all other parties were dissolved.

Feb. 17. A **legislative council,** with only advisory powers, was set up to replace parliament.

Mar. 27. Treaty of friendship with Greece.

Oct. 3. The **name of the kingdom** was officially changed to *Yugoslavia,* another indication of the king's effort to wipe out the old historic divisions. The traditional provinces were divided into nine new *banats,* with purely geographical names.

1931, Sept. 3. The king announced the **end of the dictatorship** and introduced a **new constitution** (two-chamber parliament). The **electoral law** left no place for purely local parties; two-thirds of the seats were to go to the party receiving the largest number of votes; voting to be open.

Nov. 9. Farcical **elections.** The government named most of the candidates and therefore won a great victory; most of the opposition groups abstained.

1932, Nov. 14. The Croat Peasant Party denounced the régime and again demanded autonomy, following the imprisonment of the Croat leader, Vladko Machek (Oct. 17).

1933, Feb. 15. Reorganization of the Little Entente, the treaties becoming indefinite in duration and a permanent secretariat being set up (p. 1127).

1934, Feb. 9. CONCLUSION OF THE BALKAN PACT between Yugoslavia, Greece, Roumania and Turkey (p. 1127).

June 1. Conclusion of a **trade agreement with Germany;** fears that Yugoslavia might veer to the German side, especially in view of the Italian-Austrian-Hungarian rapprochement.

Oct. 9. ASSASSINATION OF KING ALEXANDER and **Louis Barthou** at Marseilles. The assassin was a Macedonian revolutionary, working with Croat revolutionists having headquarters in Hungary. The assassination led to **danger of war between Yugoslavia and Hungary** (deportations on both sides), which was finally avoided (Dec. 10) through the good offices of the League of Nations.

1934–1945. PETER II (b. 1923). **Prince Paul** (cousin of Alexander) chief regent.

1935, May 5. In the **elections** the coalition of the Croats and a new party of Serbian peasants polled two-fifths of the votes.

1936, May. Conclusion of a **barter agreement with Germany.** This was made necessary by the falling-off of trade with Italy subsequent to Yugoslavia's imposition of sanctions during the Ethiopian crisis. Ever closer trade relations with Germany brought in their train a political rapprochement.

1937, Jan. 24. Signature of the **BULGARIAN-YUGOSLAV TREATY OF FRIENDSHIP AND PERPETUAL PEACE,** bringing to an end the long antagonism between the two states.

Mar. 25. CONCLUSION OF A NON-AGGRESSION AND ARBITRATION PACT WITH ITALY for five years. Both parties guaranteed each other's frontiers; the Yugoslav minority in Italy was to be given language and school concessions; economic collaboration was envisaged. This new agreement associated Yugoslavia more closely than ever with the Berlin-Rome Axis, and was therefore warmly denounced by the opposition groups in Yugoslavia itself.

1939, Aug. 26. DEMOCRATIC GOVERN-MENT WAS RE-ESTABLISHED in Yugoslavia and new elections by secret ballot arranged for. The state was to be reorganized on a federal basis, the Croats receiving complete autonomy in all cultural and economic matters. Machek became vice-premier and five other Croats joined the cabinet.

(*Cont. p. 1207.*)

b. ALBANIA

(*From p. 802*)

1912, Nov. 28. Proclamation of independence by a national assembly at Valona; provisional government under **Ismail Kemal.**

1913, May 30. The **treaty of London** (p. 953) recognized the independence of Albania and set up a commission to determine the boundaries.

1914, Jan. 15. The government of Ismail Kemal gave way to one under **Essad Pasha.**

Feb. 21. Prince William of Wied, a German officer and close relative of Queen Elizabeth of Roumania, was offered the crown by Essad and accepted.

Sept. 4. William left the country, after the outbreak of the First World War.

Sept. 13. The Italians landed at Valona. During the war the Italians gradually occupied most of southern Albania and the Serbs and Montenegrins the northern part. Both were driven out by the Austrians. The **government of Essad fled** to Italy (Feb. 24, 1916).

1918, Dec. 25. A national assembly elected **Turkhan Pasha president.** The government had to deal with the incursions of the Yugoslavs in the north and the Italians on the coast.

1920, Aug. 2. Italy agreed to evacuate Valona, while retaining the island of **Saseno.** The Italians left September 2.

Dec. 17. Albania was admitted to the League of Nations.

1925, Jan. 21. The **NATIONAL ASSEMBLY PROCLAIMED ALBANIA A REPUBLIC,** with Ahmed Zogu as first president.

Mar. 2. A constitution was promulgated, providing for parliamentary government, but granting the president almost dictatorial powers.

1926, July 30. A final act fixing the frontiers was signed by Great Britain, France, Italy, Greece, and Yugoslavia.

Nov. 27. TREATY OF TIRANA, between Italy and Albania. The two powers promised each other support in maintaining the territorial *status quo,* and Italy promised not to interfere in Albania except by request.

1927, May–July. A rupture of Albanian-Yugoslav relations was finally patched up by the powers.

Nov. 22. SECOND TREATY OF TIRANA, taken as a reply to the French treaty with Yugoslavia (Nov. 11): the treaty established a defensive alliance for twenty years and provided for military co-operation. It marked the beginning of what became practically an Italian protectorate. The Italians granted Albania substantial loans and in return secured valuable concessions (notably oil), supervision of military affairs, construction of roads, educational privileges, etc.

1928, Sept. 1. Ahmed Bey Zogu was proclaimed king as

1928–1939. ZOG I. Throughout he acted as the champion of the modernization of the country (building of Tirana as a modern capital, language reform, educational development, religious independence, etc.).

Nov. 22. The assembly adopted a **new monarchical constitution.**

1931, June. An **Italian loan,** spread over ten years and subject to Italian supervision, established Italian economic control of the country.

1932. King Zog rejected a proposal for a customs union with Italy; beginning of Albanian opposition to too great extension of Italian influence.

1933, June. Further friction with Italy, resulting from the closing of Italian schools.

1934, June 23. After further disputes an **Italian fleet** suddenly appeared **at Durazzo** and frightened the government into submission. The Italian control of the army was strengthened, Italians were given the right to colonize certain areas, etc.

1936, Mar. 19. Further agreements between Italy and Albania provided for even closer financial and trade relations.

1937, May 15–19. Insurrection of the Moslems in the southern sections. The immediate cause was the government's decree forbidding the veiling of women, but in the larger sense it was another expression of discontent with King Zog's dictatorial rule.

1939, Apr. 7. END OF ALBANIAN INDE-PENDENCE. The Italians, long irritated by Albanian resistance to their direction (prohibition of a Fascist party, etc.) took advantage of the confusion produced by German absorption of Czechoslovakia. They bombarded the coast towns and landed an army which, after some resistance by the natives, overran the whole

country. **King Zog and his queen fled to Greece
and then Turkey.** On April 12 an Albanian
constituent assembly voted **personal union with
Italy** and King Victor Emmanuel graciously
accepted the crown. On June 3 Albania was
given a constitution providing for a superior
Fascist corporative council over which the
king, however, retained extensive control.
(*Cont. p. 1209.*)

c. GREECE

(*From p. 964*)

1917–1920. ALEXANDER I, king.
1919, April 29. The **Dodecanese,** in a plebiscite, voted for **union with Greece.**
    May 15. Landing of the Greeks at Smyrna
(p. 979).
    July 29. Venizelos-Tittoni agreement: the
Dodecanese to be ceded to Greece when the
treaty of Sèvres went into effect.
1920, May 14. Agreement with Italy providing
for the immediate cession of the Dodecanese,
except Rhodes, which was to have a plebiscite
at the end of fifteen years.
    June 22. Beginning of the **Greek offensive
in Anatolia** (p. 1085).
    Aug. 10. The **TREATY OF SÈVRES:**
Greece obtained Smyrna, the Dodecanese
(except Rhodes), eastern Thrace, Imbros, and
Tenedos.
    Oct. 25. Death of King Alexander. Re-
gency of Queen Olga.
    Nov. 14. Defeat of the Venizelists in the
election, due to dissatisfaction with the Anatolian adventure. **Venizelos resigned.**
    Dec. 5. A **plebiscite,** held despite Allied
warnings, showed an almost unanimous vote
for King Constantine. The Allies thereupon
withdrew all support from Greece.
1920–1922. CONSTANTINE I, restored. He
announced continuation of the war with Turkey.
1921, Aug. Battle of the Sakarya. The Greeks
failed to reach Ankara (p. 1086).
1922, Aug. 18. Turkish counter-offensive. Taking
of **Smyrna,** September 9 (p. 1086).
    Sept. 26. The **Venizelists took Saloniki** and
demanded the abdication of the king.
    Sept. 27. Abdication of Constantine (d.
Jan. 11, 1923).
1922–1923. GEORGE II, a mere puppet in the
hands of the military men.
    Oct. 8. Italy denounced the agreement
regarding the Dodecanese, pleading the collapse of the Sèvres treaty.
    Nov. 13. Trial for treason of the ministers
and commanders of Constantine. **Demetrios
Gounaris and five others convicted and shot.**
1923, May 10. Yugoslavia granted a small free

zone at Saloniki for fifty years beginning 1925.
    July 24. TREATY OF LAUSANNE
(p. 1086). Exchange of populations: in the
period till 1930 some 1,250,000 Greeks repatriated, with the help of the League and of the
Near East Relief Commission; great financial
and other problems connected with this great
transfer, but Greece enriched by influx of
artisans and farmers.
    Aug. 31. Italian bombardment and **occupa-
tion of Corfu.** Settlement of the incident by
the League of Nations in December (p. 998).
    Dec. 16. Great victory of the Venizelists in
the elections.
    Dec. 18. George II left Greece, under
pressure from the military junta.
1924, Jan. 11. Venizelos premier. He opposed
the deposition of the king, but, failing to convince the military men, resigned (Feb. 3) and
retired from Greece.
    Apr. 13. A plebiscite resulted in an over-
whelming **vote for a republic.**
    **May 1. GREECE PROCLAIMED A RE-
PUBLIC. Adm. Paul Kondouriottis** made provisional president.
1925, June 25. *Coup d'état* of Gen. Theodore
Pangalos.
    **Oct. 22–23. Clash of Greek and Bulgarian
forces** on the frontier, followed by the invasion
of Bulgaria. The matter was settled by the
League of Nations (Dec. 14), which fined Greece.
1926, Jan. 3. Pangalos made himself dictator,
voiding the republican constitution of September 30, 1925.
    Mar. 19. President Kondouriottis resigned.
    Apr. 11. Pangalos, president.
    **Aug. 22. Pangalos overthrown by Gen.
George Kondylis,** who recalled Kondouriottis.
    Sept. 24. The **new constitution promulgated.**
    Nov. 7. The Republicans won a bare ma-
jority in the elections. A **coalition government**
formed by **Alexander Zaimis.**
1928, May 31. Return of Venizelos, who formed
a cabinet (July 4).
    Sept. 23. Pact of friendship with Italy, first
step in Venizelos' policy of restoring Greece's
international position.
**1929, Mar. 17. Settlement of the free zone
controversy** with Yugoslavia, which was given
more extensive privileges at Saloniki than in
an agreement of 1926.
    **Mar. 27. Pact of friendship with Yugo-
slavia.**
    May 16. Venizelos restored the **senate**
(abolished 1862) in the hope of adding stability
to the republican régime.
    **Dec. 10. Retirement of President Kon-
douriottis. Zaimis** provisional **president.**
1930, Oct. 5–12. First Balkan conference at
Athens, called by Venizelos in the hope of es-

tablishing better relations between the Balkan states and improving the economic situation.

Oct. 30. TREATY OF ANKARA with Turkey, following Venizelos' visit to Ankara (p. 1087).

1932, Sept. 25. The Venizelists failed to secure a majority in the election. **Growing power of the royalists,** strengthened by general economic stringency.

Oct. 31. Venizelos resigned and was followed (Nov. 4) by a moderate royalist cabinet under **Panyoti Tsaldaris,** who declared his loyalty to the republic and was therefore tolerated by the Venizelists.

1933, Jan. 13. Fall of the Tsaldaris cabinet, defeated on its financial policy.

Jan. 16. Venizelos became premier again, but, after dissolving parliament, suffered

Mar. 5. Defeat in the elections. **Nicolas Plastiras,** an ardent republican general, attempted a *coup d'état,* which failed.

Mar. 10. Tsaldaris premier again, despite Venizelist opposition.

Sept. 15. Ten-year non-aggression pact with Turkey. The two countries agreed to close co-operation in foreign policy.

1934, Feb. 9. CONCLUSION OF THE BALKAN PACT between Greece, Turkey, Yugoslavia, and Roumania (p. 1127).

Oct. 19. Zaimis elected president for five years.

1935, Mar. 1. Rising of the Venizelists in Athens, Macedonia, and Crete, as a protest against royalism. The movement was put down, after some fighting, by **Gen. George Kondylis.** Venizelos fled to France.

June 9. In the elections the followers of Tsaldaris and Kondylis secured most of the seats, the Republicans having abstained from voting.

Oct. 10. By a coup, **Kondylis ousted Tsaldaris** and induced parliament to vote for the **recall of the king.**

Nov. 3. A farcical plebiscite resulted in an almost unanimous call for restoration of the monarchy.

Nov. 24. Return of George II, from exile in England. The king was supported by Britain (Ethiopian crisis), but was at the mercy of Kondylis.

1935–1947. GEORGE II, RESTORED. He insisted on a general amnesty (Dec. 1).

1936, Jan. 26. The elections were a **victory for the Venizelists,** who, however, failed to secure a majority.

Apr. 13. Gen. John Metaxas, premier.

Aug. 4. *COUP D'ÉTAT* OF METAXAS, who made himself dictator, proclaimed martial law, and dissolved the parliament. Institution of a régime of rigid repression (parties abol-

ished; censorship; persecution of opponents). The Metaxas régime rested squarely on the army, but real efforts were made to conciliate the population by wage increases, social security legislation, artificially low bread prices, etc., as well as by cancellation of agricultural debts. A huge **public works program** (especially rearmament) necessitated a substantial increase of taxation and domination of business by government. In **foreign affairs** Metaxas drew closer to Germany (barter agreements), but at the same time attempted to retain the good-will of Britain and France. **Relations with Turkey** continued to be close.

1938, July 29. A **revolt in Crete** was quickly suppressed. Despite widespread dissatisfaction with the dictatorship, the régime became more and more firmly entrenched, and

July 30. Metaxas became premier for life.

1939, Apr. 13. Britain and France guaranteed Greek independence and integrity following the Italian conquest of Albania (p. 1023).

(*Cont. p. 1210.*)

d. BULGARIA

(*From p. 979*)

Defeated in the First World War, Bulgaria not only failed to recover any of the territory lost in the Second Balkan War, but was also deprived of some further areas on the Serbian frontier and of all access to the Aegean. The country was flooded with **thousands of refugees** from Thrace and Macedonia, whom the government, loaded with debt and heavy reparations payments, was unable to settle. They formed a huge mobile element, easy converts to the revolutionary program of the **Macedonian committees** or to **Bolshevik agitators.** The drastic policy of nationalization pursued by the Yugoslav and Greek governments in Macedonia stimulated the unrest in Bulgaria, which the government was unable to control. **Raids of revolutionary bands** across the frontiers became the order of the day, creating a state of chronic tension between Bulgaria and her neighbors.

1918, Oct. 4. Abdication of **Tsar Ferdinand.**

1918–1943. BORIS III, son of Ferdinand, tsar.

1919, Aug. 17. In the elections the **Peasant Party won a great victory.**

Oct. 6. Alexander Stamboliski, leader of the Peasant Party, became premier.

Nov. 27. Bulgaria signed the treaty of Neuilly (terms, p. 979).

1920, Dec. 16. Bulgaria became a member of the League of Nations.

1923, June 9. STAMBOLISKI WAS OVERTHROWN by a conspiracy of officers, Macedonians, and others affected by his class policies.

June 10. A cabinet was formed by **Alexander Zankov.**

June 14. Stamboliski was shot and killed, allegedly in an effort to escape. Zankov and the new government proceeded with great vigor in a policy of revenge.

1924, Aug. 31. Assassination of Todor Alexandrov, the Macedonian leader, by members of a rival faction. The Internal Macedonian Revolutionary Organization then broke into two mutually hostile groups, one led by **Alexander Protoguerov** and the other by **Ivan Mihailov.**

1925, Apr. 16. Bomb outrage in Sofia Cathedral. The bomb, which killed 123 persons, was set off by communists; it only served to heighten the terrorist policy of the government.

May 4. Communists outlawed in Bulgaria.

Oct. 22. Greek invasion of Bulgaria, following serious frontier incidents. The matter was settled by the League (p. 1024).

1926, Jan. 4. A cabinet of **Andrew Liapchev** followed that of Zankov and attempted a more conciliatory policy.

1929, Mar. 6. Treaty of friendship with Turkey.

Sept. 26. Agreement with Yugoslavia for the establishment of a frontier régime.

1930, Jan. 20. The Hague agreement greatly reduced the Bulgarian **reparations payments.**

Oct. 5–12. First Balkan conference at Athens. Bulgaria sent delegates, but from the outset made further co-operation dependent on a settlement of the **minorities question.**

Oct. 25. Marriage of Tsar Boris and Princess Giovanna, daughter of Victor Emmanuel III of Italy. Gradual **rapprochement between Italy and Bulgaria.**

1931, June 21. In the elections the **Peasant Party won a victory** over the Democratic Entente, which had supported Zankov and Liapchev. A new cabinet was formed (June 29) by **Alexander Malinov,** Democrat, in alliance with the peasants.

1932, Feb. 8. Bulgaria denounced further reparations payments.

Sept. 25. Striking success of the Communists in the Sofia municipal elections. But in the communal elections (Nov.) the Democrats and Agrarians won an overwhelming victory.

1933, June 24. The government arrested over a thousand Communists and Macedonians.

1934, Feb. 8. Conclusion of the Balkan pact, without Bulgaria, the government having refused, even by indirection, to recognize the *status quo* established by the peace treaties.

May 19. *Coup d'état* of army officers under Gen. **Kimon Gueorguiev,** who set up a **dictatorship** for one year. The policy of reconciliation with Yugoslavia was continued.

1935, Jan. 22. Gueorguiev was forced out and his place taken by **Gen. Petko Zlatev.**

Apr. 18. A purely **civilian cabinet** was formed by **Andrew Tochev,** the officers' group having been weakened by factional dissension.

Nov. 23. A **new cabinet** was formed by George Kiosseivanov.

1936, Feb. Trial and conviction of a number of military men, including **Damyon Veltchev,** supposed to be the leader of the military party.

1936, Mar. The Military League was dissolved. To all intents and purposes Tsar Boris was master of the situation.

1937, Jan. 24. CONCLUSION OF THE PACT OF FRIENDSHIP WITH YUGOSLAVIA, bringing to an end the long period of hostility and opening the way for closer relations between Bulgaria and the other Balkan powers.

Oct. 13. More than forty political leaders petitioned the tsar for free elections and a return to constitutionalism. Thereupon the tsar promulgated a **new electoral law** providing for free voting by men and married women, but forbidding candidates to run as representatives of the old parties.

1938, Mar. The **elections** resulted in victory for a number of opponents of the government.

May 22. Parliament met for the first time since the military coup of 1935. Its powers were merely consultative.

July 31. AGREEMENT WITH GREECE (acting for the Balkan Entente) **recognized Bulgaria's right to rearm.** By this time Bulgarian rearmament (in contravention of the treaties) had already made considerable headway, Germany supplying much of the material. This did not, however, imply acceptance of National Socialism by the Bulgarian government. On the contrary, the National Socialist organization was disbanded (Apr. 30) and the government readily accepted an **Anglo-French loan** of $10,000,000 to support the rearmament program (Aug.). In the growing international tension of 1938–1939 Bulgaria, like most of the lesser states, was pulled this way and that. Great efforts were made to bring her into the Balkan Entente, but this courting merely enabled the government to demand more insistently a revision of the treaties. Claims to the Dobrudja created rather tense relations between Roumania and Bulgaria in the spring of 1939. (*Cont. p. 1211.*)

e. ROUMANIA

(*From p. 964*)

1914–1927. FERDINAND I.

1916, Aug. 27. Roumania declared war on Austria-Hungary, but the Roumanian armies were decisively defeated before the end of the year.

1918, May 7. **Treaty of Bucharest** (p. 972).

Nov. 10. **Roumania** re-entered the war and Roumanian forces occupied **Transylvania.**

Dec. 2. A government, headed by **Julius Maniu,** Transylvanian peasant leader, was soon (Dec. 14) obliged to give way to a cabinet under **Ion Bratianu,** leader of the Liberal Party, representing the industrial, commercial, and professional classes of the old kingdom.

1919, Apr. Beginning of the **Roumanian advance into Hungary.** The Roumanians ultimately occupied Budapest (Aug. 4) and did not evacuate until November 14 (p. 979).

May 18. **Russia declared a state of war.**

May 28. The **Jews were emancipated** and given full citizen rights, but **anti-Semitism** continued to be rampant, especially in the universities, which had to be closed repeatedly because of anti-Semitic riots.

1920, Mar. 2. **Armistice with Russia.**

Sept. 14. **Roumania joined the League of Nations.**

Oct. 28. Britain, France, Italy, and Japan recognized the Roumanian possession of Bessarabia. This treaty was not ratified by Britain and France until 1924, and not by Italy until 1927.

1921, Mar. 3. **Defensive treaty with Poland and Hungary,** directed against Russia.

Apr. 23. **ALLIANCE WITH CZECHO-SLOVAKIA,** part of the **Little Entente treaties.**

June 7. **ALLIANCE WITH YUGO-SLAVIA,** completing the Little Entente.

1923, Mar. 27. The **new constitution** abolished the three-class system of voting and introduced the direct, secret ballot.

1924, Apr. **Conference with Russia** on the Bessarabian question broke down when Roumania refused to hold a plebiscite.

1925, Dec. 28. **Prince Charles (Carol) renounced his right of succession** to the throne and preferred to live in exile with his mistress, **Magda Lupescu.** Bratianu and the Liberals were actively hostile to the prince.

1926, Mar. 25. A **new electoral law** provided that the party polling 40 per cent of the votes should have one-half of the seats in parliament.

Mar. 26. **Treaty of alliance with Poland.**

June 10. **Treaty of friendship with France.**

Sept. 16. **Treaty of friendship with Italy,** which made a large loan in return for oil and other concessions.

Oct. Fusion of the peasant parties to form the new **National Peasants' Party,** under Maniu's leadership.

1927, July 20. **Death of King Ferdinand.**

1927-1930. **MICHAEL** (b. 1921). Principal regent **Prince Nicholas,** brother of Prince Charles, the father of Michael.

1928, May 6. **Congress of the National Peasants' Party** at Alba Julia, demanding representative government, decentralization, and reform.

Nov. 9. **JULIUS MANIU became premier.** He set out to purge the administration, make easier the influx of foreign capital, improve the lots of the peasants, etc.

1930, June 6. **Prince Charles arrived by airplane** and was accepted by Maniu. The parliament (June 8) revoked the law excluding him from the throne. Michael was put aside in favor of his father.

1930-1940. **CAROL (CHARLES) II.** He soon fell out with Maniu, brought back Mme. Lupescu, and attempted to establish his personal rule.

1931, Apr. 18. The king appointed a coalition **(National Union)** cabinet under **Nicholas Iorga,** his former tutor. This was regarded as a prelude to a royal dictatorship.

1932, Jan.-May. **Negotiations with Russia,** held under Polish auspices at Warsaw, failed to effect a settlement of the Bessarabian question.

May 31. **Iorga resigned,** after failure to secure a loan from France.

June 6. A **new cabinet** was formed **by Alexander Vaida-Voevod,** Peasant leader.

July 17. The **Peasants won** a great victory in the elections. But their position was weakened by the inability of Maniu to get along with the king and by rivalry between Maniu and Vaida-Voevod. On October 20 Maniu took over the premiership (until Jan. 5, 1933).

1933, Jan. A system of **League supervision of Roumanian finances** was introduced for four years.

July. A **PACT OF NON-AGGRESSION** was finally concluded **with Russia;** this involved tacit recognition of Roumania's possession of Bessarabia, and was the direct result of the victory of Hitler in Germany and of Russia's preoccupation with the Far Eastern situation.

1934, Feb. 9. **CONCLUSION OF THE BALKAN PACT** between Roumania, Yugoslavia, Greece, and Turkey. The consummation of the plan was largely the work of **Nicholas Titulescu,** the Roumanian foreign minister.

1936, Feb. The anti-Semitic **Christian League,** headed by A. C. Cuza, and the **National Christian Party,** led by the poet Octavian Goga, united with one wing of the Peasants' Party, under Vaida-Voevod, to form a reactionary bloc not much different from the fascist Iron Guard.

Aug. 29. Foreign minister **Titulescu,** representing close connections with France, Russia, and the Little Entente against Germany, **was forced out** by the groups of the Right, which were favorable to Germany.

1937, Dec. 21. The elections, to the surprise of the whole world, resulted in a **defeat for the government.** Thereupon the government resigned (Dec. 26) and King Carol, once more astounding the world, appointed

Dec. 28. OCTAVIAN GOGA prime minister, despite the fact that his National Christian Party had gained only 10 per cent of the votes in the election. Goga at once embarked upon an orgy of **anti-Semitic legislation,** forbidding Jews to own land, depriving those naturalized after 1920 of their citizenship, barring Jews from the professions, etc. At the same time Goga aimed at the establishment of a dictatorship by sending his party troops into all localities.

1938, Jan. 18. King Carol dissolved the parliament, which had not yet met. New elections were arranged for March. This unconstitutional procedure led to protests from the non-fascist parties, while the anti-Semitic policy quickly brought the country to the verge of business collapse.

Feb. 10. The **king dismissed Goga,** using as a pretext the fact that the courts had invalidated several of the anti-Semitic laws. Goga and the fascists had thoroughly discredited themselves and had really strengthened the position of the king, who now assumed complete control of the situation. A new "concentration" cabinet, containing seven former premiers, was established under the leadership of the patriarch, **Miron Cristea. The constitution was suspended and all political parties** were suppressed. Rigid censorship was instituted. These moves were violently opposed both by the fascist Iron Guard and by the Peasants' Party of Maniu, but

Feb. 24. A **plebiscite,** properly managed by the government, **approved Carol's action** by an overwhelming vote (only 5300 opposed).

Apr. 19. Corneliu Codreanu, Fascist leader, **was condemned** to six months' imprisonment for libel, and then (May 27) to ten years at hard labor for treason. The government's **attack upon the Fascists** now assumed major proportions, hundreds of Iron Guardists being arrested and imprisoned after discovery of an alleged plot against the king.

Nov. 30. DEATH OF CODREANU. He and thirteen other Iron Guardists were reported shot by their guards while being moved from one prison to another.

1939, Mar. 6. Armand Calinescu became premier on the death of Patriarch Cristea.

Apr. 13. Great Britain and France guaranteed Roumanian independence and integrity following the German annihilation of Czechoslovakia and rumors of a German ultimatum to Roumania. But the Bucharest government nevertheless concluded a **commercial agreement with Germany** giving the latter broad scope for expansion of Roumanian industry. In short, the government attempted to straddle the two groups of powers in Europe.

(*Cont. p. 1213.*)

12. RUSSIA

(UNION OF SOVIET SOCIALIST REPUBLICS)

(*From p. 755*)

On Germany's declaration of war (Aug. 1, 1914), the opposition parties in Russia declared their readiness to put aside domestic quarrels and support the government. Since the government failed to respond, political discontent developed rapidly. Public opinion was deeply stirred by

1915, May. The great **Russian defeat in Galicia** (p. 949), and openly accused the government of inefficiency in failing to supply the armies.

June 25. The tsar was obliged to dismiss Gen. Vladimir Sukhomlinov, the minister of war (tried and convicted by the provisional government in 1917), and to admit representatives of the duma and other public bodies (the Union of Zemstvos and Municipalities, the War Industry Committee, etc.) to direct participation in the work of army supply and the mobilization of industry. Nicholas refused, however, to comply with the demand of the progressive bloc in the duma for an entirely new ministry enjoying the confidence of the country and committed to a more liberal policy. The situation was aggravated when

Sept. 5. The tsar decided to dismiss the popular commander-in-chief, **Grand Duke Nicholas,** and to assume the command himself. The tsar's absence from the capital opened the way for **domination of the Empress Alexandra,** known to be bitterly hostile to the duma and under the influence of the notorious adventurer, **Gregory Rasputin.** The government was completely discredited in the eyes of the public when

1916, Feb. 3. Boris Stürmer, arch-conservative and allegedly pro-German, replaced Ivan Goremykin as **chief of the cabinet.** On July 23 Stürmer took charge of the foreign office. Rumors of treason in high places undermined the morale of the army and the population generally. To all this was added a **grave economic problem:** shortage of labor, due to repeated mobilizations; disorganization of railroad transport, failure of food and fuel supplies in the cities.

Nov. 18.   Meeting of the duma. In a turbulent session the leaders denounced the "dark forces" in the government and warned the country of impending disaster unless there was an immediate change of policy.

Nov. 24.   Alexander Trepov replaced Stürmer as president of the council of ministers and the government embarked upon a policy of repression of dissatisfaction. But opposition continued, and

Dec. 30.   Rasputin was assassinated by Prince Felix Yusupov and other aristocrats. Even these drastic measures were barren of results, and in some political and military circles there was discussion of a palace revolution. Before any plans could materialize

1917, Mar. 8.   Strikes and riots broke out in St. Petersburg (named *Petrograd* at the beginning of the war). These were followed by

Mar. 10.   A general mutiny of the troops in the capital, which sealed the fate of the old régime.

Mar. 11. The duma refused to obey an imperial decree ordering its dissolution, and established

Mar. 12.   A PROVISIONAL GOVERNMENT, headed by **Prince George Lvov** (chairman of the Union of Zemstvos and Municipalities). The new government included **Paul Miliukov,** leader of the Constitutional Democrats (as minister for foreign affairs); **Alexander Guchkov,** leader of the Octobrists (minister of war); and **Alexander Kerensky,** the only Socialist (minister of justice).

Mar. 15.   Nicholas II abdicated for himself and his son in favor of his brother Michael, who in turn (Mar. 16) abdicated in favor of the provisional government pending election by a constituent assembly.

Mar.–Nov.   THE RULE OF THE PROVISIONAL GOVERNMENT. At the outset the new régime proclaimed **civic liberties** and recognized equality of all citizens without social, religious, or racial discrimination. **Finland** recognized as independent within a Russian federation (Mar. 21); **Poland's** complete independence accepted (Mar. 30); **Estonia** granted autonomy (Apr. 12). At the same time the government announced a program of far-reaching **social reforms,** including distribution of land among the peasants (confiscation of imperial and monastery lands, March 30). But the decision on these and other matters was reserved for the **constituent assembly.** From the outset the provisional government, essentially liberal and bourgeois, found itself in

Conflict with the Petrograd Soviet (*Council of Workers' and Soldiers' Deputies*), which had been organized by the Socialists (Mar. 12). The government pledged itself (Mar. 18, May 1) to continuation of the war against the Central Powers, in common with the Allies, until the attainment of a "victorious end." It attempted to maintain the efficiency of the army and proceeded but cautiously toward its democratization. The Soviet leaders, on the other hand, insisted on a radical revision of war aims, renunciation of secret diplomatic agreements concluded by the tsarist government (and promising Russia Constantinople), and the speedy conclusion of a "general democratic peace," without annexations or indemnities. Suspecting the generals of counter-revolutionary tendencies, the Soviet issued (Mar. 14) **Order No. 1,** which deprived the officers of all authority excepting for strategic operations, and entrusted the administration of the army to committees elected by both officers and men. The counter-order of the provisional government was virtually ignored and the committee system was subsequently introduced in all army detachments. The antagonism of the Soviet to the government became more outspoken when

Apr. 16.   Lenin, Gregory Zinoviev, Karl Radek, Anatoli Lunacharski, and other **Bolshevik leaders arrived at Petrograd** from Switzerland, having been transported through Germany in a sealed carriage, the German high command having calculated that these extremists would soon undermine the pro-Allied provisional government. **Lenin's program** was: (1) transfer of power from the "bourgeois" provisional government to the Soviets; (2) immediate cessation of the war, if necessary by the acceptance of a separate peace with the Central Powers; (3) immediate seizure of land by the peasants, without awaiting the decision of the constituent assembly; (4) control of industry by committees of workers. Lenin was ably supported by **Leon Trotsky** (Bronstein), who returned from the United States and England early in May, but his program was not accepted by the more moderate (Menshevik) wing of the Social Democratic Party, nor by the Social Revolutionaries. Consequently much difference of opinion and considerable friction was generated within the Soviet.

May 14, 16.   Guchkov and Miliukov were obliged to resign from the provisional government as a result of agitation over war aims and army organization. The government was remade, and now accepted a policy of no annexations and no indemnities, though still declaring against a separate peace. Several Socialists were included in the cabinet, and **Kerensky became minister of war.** He undertook to revive the war spirit and the fighting power of the army on the basis of the new "revolutionary discipline." After a spectacular visit to the front and a stirring appeal to the soldiers, he ordered the

June 29–July 7. Russian offensive against the Austro-German forces. After a brief initial success the offensive collapsed and the disorganized Russian troops were completely defeated (p. 961). The radicals now took the initiative.

July 16–18. The **Bolsheviks attempted to seize power** in Petrograd, but the effort proved premature. The movement was suppressed by the government and many of the leaders (including Trotsky) were arrested. Lenin went into hiding in Finland. This coup, as well as disagreement between ministers regarding the burning question of land reform and the status of national minorities (assumption of power in the Ukraine by the local rada, June 26; establishment of Gen. Alexis Kaledin as hetman of the Don Cossacks, June 30; Finnish declaration of complete independence, July 20), resulted in

July 20. The **resignation of Prince Lvov,** whose place was taken by Kerensky. The position of the government, however, remained precarious in view of the growing restlessness of the masses, who suffered from war-weariness and material privations, and were all too ready to listen to Bolshevik propaganda. On the other hand, the conservative elements opposed the government because of its alleged weakness in dealing with the Bolsheviks. The advocates of a strong line found a champion in **Gen. Lavr Kornilov,** recently appointed commander-in-chief. A rift between Kerensky and Kornilov finally led to

Sept. 9–14. The **Kornilov attack** upon the government. Kerensky had dismissed Kornilov, who refused to obey and ordered his troops to advance on Petrograd, his avowed aim being to destroy the Soviet and liberate the provisional government from Socialist domination. The movement broke down because of defection on the part of many soldiers and because of mobilization of the radical elements in the capital, to whom Kerensky appealed for support against the "counter-revolution" (Trotsky and some other Bolshevik leaders were released from prison).

Kornilov was defeated, but Kerensky now found himself under the domination of his Bolshevik allies. The masses had come to suspect not only the army command, but the provisional government also, of counter-revolu-

tionary designs. Bolshevik influence made rapid progress among the factory workers and soldiers of the Petrograd garrison. In October the Bolsheviks secured a majority in the Soviet, Trotsky becoming its chairman. Thereupon Lenin decided to attempt a coup.

Nov. 6. (O.S. Oct. 24.) **THE BOLSHEVIK REVOLUTION.** The Bolsheviks, led by the military revolutionary committee, the soldiers of the Petrograd garrison, the sailors from Kronstadt, and the workers' Red Guards, captured most of the government offices, took the Winter Palace by storm, and arrested the members of the provisional government. **Kerensky managed to escape,** and, after a futile attempt to organize resistance, went into hiding and subsequently into exile abroad.

Nov. 7. The **Second All-Russian Congress of Soviets,** from which the moderate Socialists bolted, approved the coup and handed over power to the Bolsheviks.

The history of Russia (*Union of Soviet Socialist Republics*) from 1917 to 1941 may be conveniently divided into **three periods:** (1) the **Period of Militant Communism** (1917–1921); (2) the **Period of the New Economic Policy** (1921–1927); (3) the **Period of the New Socialist Offensive** (1928–1941).

The new government (organized Nov. 7) assumed the name *Council of People's Commissars.* It was headed by **Lenin,** and included **Trotsky** (commissar for foreign affairs), **Joseph Stalin** (commissar for national minorities). To protect itself and to crush opposition, the council organized (Dec. 20) the *Extraordinary Commission to Combat Counter-Revolution* (the *Cheka,* later known as the *G.P.U.*).

Nov. 25. The **elections to the constituent assembly** returned 420 Social Revolutionaries as against only 225 Bolsheviks. When the assembly met in Petrograd (Jan. 18, 1918) it was dispersed at once by the Red troops. Therewith one of the most influential elements of the opposition was disposed of. Some of the Social Revolutionaries joined in the anti-Bolshevik movements which soon began to take form.

1917–1921. SOCIAL AND ECONOMIC POLICY. The victorious Bolsheviks at once undertook the reorganization of society along collectivist lines. A **Land Decree** (Nov. 7) ordered immediate partition of the large estates and distribution of the land among the peasants. But February 19, 1918, the **nationalization of the land** was proclaimed (all land to be the property of the state, and only those willing to cultivate it themselves to be permitted to use it). No further efforts were made in the direction of collectivization, but when the civil war brought the cities and the armies into danger of starvation, the peasants were ordered (Dec. 14, 1920) to turn over to the government their entire surplus (the **food levy**). As they were reluctant to do so, and saw no prospect of any return in consumer goods, the government was driven to adopt **forcible requisitioning,** which created widespread discontent.

On their advent to power the Bolsheviks at once declared all **banks nationalized,** confiscating private accounts. The **national debt was repudiated** (Jan. 28, 1918). The workmen were given **control over the factories** (Nov. 28, 1917), and by the summer of 1918 all the larger plants (and subsequently the smaller ones also) were nationalized (law of June 28, 1918). The workers were instructed to join **government-controlled trade unions,** and were denied the right to strike. In emergencies the government resorted to a system of **compulsory labor.** Private trade was gradually suppressed and the government undertook the distribution of food and other commodities among the urban populations, introducing a **rationing system** and making use also of the co-operatives. All **church property was confiscated** (Dec. 17, 1917) and all religious instruction in the schools was abolished. Only civil marriages were thenceforth to be recognized. The **Gregorian calendar** was introduced on January 31, 1918.

1917–1918. CONCLUSION OF PEACE WITH THE CENTRAL POWERS (p. 971).

Mar. 9. The government moved the capital from Petrograd (renamed Leningrad, January 26, 1924) **to Moscow.** This was partly due to the exposed position of Petrograd with relation to the Germans and their satellites, and partly to the threat of counter-revolution emanating from the borderlands. Monarchists and members of the propertied classes, who favored political and economic restoration, as well as Liberals and Moderate Socialists who were opposed to the Communist dictatorship, were all more or less united in their refusal to accept the disastrous Brest-Litovsk treaty. The British and French, who regarded the Bolsheviks as tools of the German general staff and were eager to keep supplies and munitions from falling into the hands of the Germans, encouraged and supported movements among the opponents of the Bolsheviks. **Independent governments** were established all along the Russian frontiers (**Lithuania,** Dec. 11, 1917; **Moldavia,** Dec. 15; **Republic of the Don,** Jan. 10, 1918; **Ukraine,** Jan. 28; **Transcaucasia,** Apr. 22, etc.). The revolt of the Don Cossacks, led by **Gens. Kornilov** and **Kaledin,** December 9, 1917, may be said to mark the beginning of the

1918–1920. GREAT CIVIL WAR. The Bolshevik government was at first faced with the prospect of war without anything like an ade-

quate trained force. During the first period of the war it suffered one reverse after another, but gradually a new **Red Army** of volunteers was organized. Under the leadership of Trotsky (who had become commissar for war) it developed into a regular army based on conscription and subject to strict discipline. The Bolsheviks had the advantage of fighting on the inside lines and derived a certain measure of support from the fact that they were defending Russian territory. At the same time the lack of cohesion among the counter-revolutionary movements and the fitful attitude of the Allied powers constantly hampered the operations of the Whites.

(1) **The war with the Cossacks.** Operations began with the new year. **Kaledin** committed suicide after a defeat (Feb. 13) and **Kornilov** was killed in battle (Apr. 13). The command in the south was taken over by **Gen. Anton Denikin,** supported by **Gen. Peter Krasnov** (hetman of the Don Cossacks, May 11).

(2) **The struggle for the Ukraine.** The Ukraine had declared its independence of Russia (Jan. 28, 1918) and the Moderate Socialist government at Kiev had concluded a separate peace with the Germans and Austrians (Feb. 9). Thereupon the Bolsheviks attacked and took **Kiev** (Feb. 18), but they were soon ejected by the Germans (Mar. 2), who then took also Odessa (Mar. 13) and overran the whole Ukraine, from which they tried, rather unsuccessfully, to secure much-needed food supplies. With German aid a more conservative government, under **Gen. Paul Skoropadsky,** was set up, but after the end of the World War, Skoropadsky was overthrown (Nov. 15) by the Ukrainian Socialists, under **Gen. Simon Petliura.** The French occupied **Odessa** (Dec. 18), but the Bolsheviks, having assumed the offensive, took Kiev (Feb. 3, 1919) and expelled the Allied forces from Odessa (Apr. 8). The **Ukraine became a Soviet Republic,** which was conquered by the White armies of Gen. Denikin (Aug.–Dec. 1919) only to be retaken by the Bolsheviks (Dec. 17) and then invaded by the Poles (May 7, 1920). The Bolsheviks managed to drive the Poles back and December 28 concluded a treaty with the Ukrainian Soviet government, recognizing the latter's independence. On December 30 the Ukraine joined with the other Soviet Republics to form the Union of Soviet Socialist Republics.

(3) **The war in White Russia and the Baltic region.** Most of this area continued to be occupied or dominated by the Germans down to and beyond the conclusion of the World War armistice. In the autumn of 1919 a White army under **Gen. Nicholas Yudenitch** advanced on Petrograd (Oct. 19), but was forced back by

the Bolsheviks. The Soviet government recognized the **independence of Estonia** (Feb. 2, 1920), **of Lithuania** (July 12), **of Latvia** (Aug. 11), **and of Finland** (Oct. 14). White Russia continued to be a Soviet Republic until its union with the other Soviet Republics in 1922.

(4) **Allied intervention in northern Russia.** The British landed a force at Murmansk June 23, 1918, primarily with the object of holding German forces in the east and protecting Allied stores from falling into hostile hands. On August 2 the **British and French took Archangel** and began to support a puppet **government of Northern Russia.** The Americans also sent a force, and during the spring of 1919 there was considerable fighting between the Allies and the Bolsheviks. The French were the most ardent advocates of more extensive intervention against the Bolsheviks, but neither the British nor the Americans were willing, after the armistice, to go beyond financial and other support for the anti-Bolshevik movements. On September 30, 1919, the Allies abandoned Archangel and then (Oct. 12) Murmansk. These territories were quickly taken over by the Bolsheviks.

(5) **Campaigns of Denikin and Wrangel in the Caucasus and southern Russia.** The Caucasian states (**Georgia, Armenia,** and **Azerbaijan**) declared their independence April 22 and May 26, 1918. After the withdrawal of the Germans and Austrians from southern Russia, the Bolsheviks made an effort to reconquer this territory, so valuable for its oil, but **Denikin** defeated them (Jan. 1919). After a rather spectacular advance northward, Denikin was himself driven back to the Black Sea coast (Apr.), where he maintained himself until the autumn. In another swift offensive he then captured Odessa (Aug. 18) and took Kiev (Sept. 2), only to be forced to retreat again (Dec.). By March 27, 1920, his last base fell to the Bolsheviks and he turned over the command to **Gen. Peter Wrangel.** The Bolsheviks meanwhile advanced into the Caucasus and took Baku (Apr. 28), but Wrangel, starting from the region north of the Sea of Azov, began to overrun much of southern Russia (June–Nov.). Finally, however, the Bolshevik forces, freed by the conclusion of the war with Poland (see below), were able to concentrate against Wrangel, who was forced back to the Crimea (Nov. 1) and then obliged to evacuate his army to Constantinople (Nov. 14). Early in 1921 **Soviet governments were set up in Georgia** (Feb. 25) **and in Armenia** (Apr. 2). By the treaty with Turkey (Oct. 13) **Batum was restored to Russia.** On March 12, 1922, the Soviet governments of Georgia, Armenia, and Azerbaijan were combined to form the **Trans-**

caucasian Soviet Socialist Republic, which on December 30 became part of the larger Union of Soviet Socialist Republics.

(6) **The war in Siberia and eastern Russia. Japanese forces** were landed at **Vladivostok** December 30, 1917, at a time when the **Czech legions** (organized before the revolution out of large numbers of Austrian war prisoners) had already started their march toward Vladivostok with the purpose of ultimately joining the Allied forces in Europe. Disagreement between them and the Soviet government led to armed conflict (June 1918), in the course of which the **Czechs seized control of the Trans-Siberian Railway** and formed an alliance with local anti-Bolshevik forces. An **autonomous Siberian government** had already been formed at Omsk. This government later merged with the directory organized in Ufa by former members of the constituent assembly (mostly Moderate Socialists). Meanwhile the Czechs extended their operations to the Volga region, taking Ekaterinburg (July 26) and other places. At Omsk the military and conservative elements executed a coup (Nov. 18) by which the Socialists were forced out of the government and **Adm. Alexander Kolchak was proclaimed** *Supreme Ruler of Russia.* His Siberian White army then staged an **advance into eastern Russia,** capturing Perm (Dec. 24) and Ufa. But the Bolsheviks initiated a vigorous counter-offensive, taking Orenburg and Ekaterinburg (Jan. 25, 27, 1919) and gradually forcing Kolchak back into Siberia. They recaptured Omsk (Nov. 14) and drove the White army back on Irkutsk. Kolchak gave way to **Gen. Nicholas Semenov** (Dec. 17) and was subsequently captured and executed by the Bolsheviks (Feb. 7). The Bolsheviks attempted to take Vladivostok by a coup (Jan. 30), but were obliged to yield to the greater power of the Japanese. In order to avoid conflict, the Soviet government of Russia set up a buffer state in eastern Siberia (Apr. 6). This was known as the **Far Eastern Republic,** with capital at Chita. When the Japanese finally evacuated Vladivostok (Oct. 25, 1922), the city was occupied by troops of the Far Eastern Republic, which was itself annexed to Soviet Russia November 19, 1922.

Other important developments of this confused and crucial period were:

1918, July 10. PROMULGATION OF THE SOVIET CONSTITUTION, which was adopted by the Fifth All-Russian Congress of Soviets. The main lines of the soviet system were these: (1) **local soviets** elected representatives to the **provincial congresses of soviets,** which in turn sent delegates to the **All-Russian** (subsequently **All-Union**) **Congress of Soviets;**

(2) the latter elected the **executive committee,** a permanent body which acted in the intervals between sessions of the congress; the congress also elected the **council of people's commissars;** (3) elections were held on an occupational, and not on a territorial basis: the factory workers were more generously represented than the peasants, while the "non-toiling" bourgeois classes (including the clergy) were disfranchised; (4) all elections were open, with no provision for secret ballot. In practice this system of "soviet democracy" was dominated by a **dictatorship of** (or for) **the proletariat,** and this in turn was exercised by the Bolshevik Party (renamed the **Communist Party** in March 1918). No other parties were permitted, and the press and other channels of expression were put under sweeping government control. The Communist Party was governed by a **central committee,** within which there was a smaller group called the **political bureau** (*Politburo*). This latter was the real governing body of the country. Lenin's authority remained supreme in both party and government until his death.

July 16. Murder of Nicholas II, Tsarina Alexandra, and their children in a cellar at Ekaterinburg, where they had been kept in captivity. On the outbreak of the revolution the imperial family had been confined first in the palace of Tsarskoe Selo. Thence it had been moved to Tobolsk and finally (Apr. 1918) to Ekaterinburg. The murder was perpetrated by local Bolsheviks who feared the imminent capture of the city by the advancing Czechs and Whites.

Aug. 30. An attempt was made by a Social Revolutionary to assassinate Lenin. Coming at the time of severe crisis, this move inaugurated a systematic **reign of terror** by the Bolsheviks, in the course of which huge numbers of intellectuals and bourgeois of all types were wiped out.

1919, Mar. 2. Foundation of the Third International (Communist), an organization for the propagation of communist doctrine abroad with the purpose of bringing about the world revolution, on which Lenin and his associates reckoned with confidence in the stormy period following the end of the war.

1920, Apr. 25–Oct. 12. WAR WITH POLAND which, in agreement with Petliura, attempted to wrest the Ukraine from the Bolsheviks. The Poles quickly overran the country, taking Kiev (May 7), but the Bolsheviks launched a vigorous counter-attack, and drove the Poles out of Kiev (June 11) and Vilna (July 15). By August 14 the Russians were on the outskirts of Warsaw. But the Poles, vigorously aided by the French **(Gen. Maxime Weygand)** made a

stand and were soon able to turn the tables. The Bolsheviks were forced to fall back and abandon their Polish conquests. The preliminary treaty of Riga (Oct. 12) was followed by the definitive **treaty of Riga** (Mar. 18, 1921), which defined the frontier between the two countries.

The effects of the Allied blockade and of the devastating civil war, together with the revolutionary economic policy of the government, led to an almost complete **collapse of the Russian economy** by 1921. There was a sharp decline in production in both industry and agriculture, widespread disorganization of transport, acute shortage of food and fuel, especially in the cities. Popular discontent found expression in numerous **peasant uprisings** during 1920 and in rioting of the factory workers in Petrograd, culminating finally in

1921, Feb. 23–Mar. 17. The mutiny and uprising of the sailors at Kronstadt, which was put down only with difficulty and after much bloodshed. This situation finally forced the Communist Party to adopt

Mar. 17 *et seq.* The **NEW ECONOMIC POLICY** (often spoken of as the *NEP*), sponsored by Lenin himself. To placate the peasants, the **food levy was abolished,** and in its place there was introduced a limited **grain tax,** thus leaving the peasants at least part of the surplus. To enable them to dispose of this surplus, **freedom of trade** within the country was partially restored. Subsequently (1922) a **new land statute** was passed which made possible reconstruction of small individual farms and even permitted, under certain conditions, limited use of hired labor and lease of land. In industry some of the small plants were returned to former owners and licenses were given to private persons to start new enterprises.

Private commercial establishments were also permitted in the cities. In course of time the **financial system** was recast on a semi-capitalistic basis: the state bank was given the right to issue bills backed either by goods or by foreign bonds; attempts were made to stabilize the currency (the devaluated paper money was replaced by the new *chervonets* bills). Large industry and transport, however, remained nationalized, and foreign trade continued to be a government monopoly.

The *NEP* was declared to be a "temporary retreat" from communism, necessary for purposes of economic reconstruction. After the **great famine** of 1921–1922 (caused by drought, but aggravated by the economic collapse that preceded it), the national economy recovered at a rapid pace. Production in industry and agriculture reached the pre-war level and there was marked improvement in living standards both in the cities and in the countryside. Along with this recovery went an **abatement of the Red terror** and a slight relaxation of governmental censorship and repression. With the end of the civil war, more attention could be given to cultural work, and the government introduced an ambitious **educational program** aiming at a speedy elimination of illiteracy.

1922, Apr. 10-May 19. Russia took part in the **economic conference at Genoa** (p. 1122), thus for the first time indicating a readiness to collaborate with non-Bolshevik countries for common ends.

Apr. 16. The **TREATY OF RAPALLO** between Germany and Soviet Russia. The agreement provided for economic co-operation and established close political connections. Despite the indignation of the other powers, Russia and Germany, as outcast powers, held steadfastly to the pact, which was supplemented by a commercial treaty (Oct. 12, 1925), and a treaty of friendship and neutrality (treaty of Berlin) of April 24, 1926, which remained technically in effect until Hitler's attack in 1941. During the 1920's the German high command made secret agreements with its Russian counterpart which enabled it to manufacture munitions and carry out training in violation of the treaty of Versailles.

Dec. 30. The **Union of Soviet Socialist Republics** was organized, bringing together Russia, the Ukraine, White Russia, and Transcaucasia in one federation. The member states retained a large measure of cultural autonomy, but political control was exercised from Moscow through the All-Union Communist Party organization.

1924, Jan. 21. THE DEATH OF LENIN. This important event marked the beginning of a **struggle for power** within the inner councils of the party and the government. The chief contestants were **Trotsky** and **Stalin.** The latter at first allied himself with **Leo Kamenev** (Rosenfeld) and **Gregory Zinoviev,** but these two soon quarreled with Stalin and adhered to the opposition bloc of Trotsky. Open conflict of the factions broke out in 1926.

Feb. 1. Great Britain recognized the Bolshevik régime, and was soon followed by most of the other European and some extra-European powers (Italy, February 7; France, October 28).

1925, Jan. 21. Japan recognized the Soviet government and agreed to withdraw from northern Sakhalin (evacuation April 4).

May 12. Revision of the federal constitution. A number of new republics were added to the federation (**Uzbekistan, Turkmenistan, Kazakhstan,** etc.).

1926, July-Oct. Victory of Stalin over the Leftist opposition bloc led by Trotsky. This bloc insisted on discontinuation of the *NEP* policy, the speeding-up of "socialist construction," and the active resumption of work for the world revolution. Trotsky held that a communist régime in one country was an anomaly and that the proletarian revolution could be safe only when the whole world had been directed into the same channel. Trotsky, Zinoviev, Radek, and other leaders were now expelled from the political bureau of the party.

1927, May 26. Great Britain severed relations with Soviet Russia because of continued Bolshevik propaganda in contravention of treaty agreements.

Dec. 27. Definitive victory of the Stalin faction over the Trotsky group, when the fifteenth All-Union Congress of the Communist Party condemned all "deviation from the general party line" as interpreted by Stalin. Trotsky and his followers were banished to the provinces after expulsion from the party. In January 1929 **Trotsky was expelled from the Union** and was obliged to take refuge in Constantinople. Later he moved to Norway and ultimately to Mexico. The same party congress made several decisions which signified the end of the *NEP* and the inauguration of a

1928- NEW SOCIALIST OFFENSIVE. A program of speedy industrialization was introduced in the form of several successive **five-year plans** (beginning October 1, 1928). Considerable success was achieved in the **development of heavy industries** (primarily for purposes of national defense). But production of manufactured products still lagged far behind the needs of the population and the government was constantly faced with inefficiency, to say nothing of ill-will (1930-: a series of **trials of technicians** for mismanagement and sabotage). In the field of agriculture the government now returned to a policy of socialization by pooling individual peasant farms in large concerns, such as the **collective farms** (*kolkhoz*) and the **state farms** (*sovkhoz*). The collectivization campaign in the villages was carried out by means of both propaganda and coercion (drastic measures against the recalcitrant peasants and especially against the well-to-do farmers or *kulaks,* who were completely wiped out). The objectives of the government were substantially achieved, and within a few years the great majority of the peasants were collectivized, the government controlling the output of the new farms.

1929, Nov. 17. Expulsion of Bukharin and other members of the Rightist opposition. This group had advocated further concession to the peasants along the lines of the *NEP.* Stalin was now undisputed master of the situation and dictator of Russia.

Dec. 22. An **agreement with China** brought to an end a prolonged dispute over the conflicting claims to the **Chinese Eastern Railway.**

1932–1933. Another **severe famine** swept over Russia, due in part, at least, to the excesses of the government's agrarian policy. The famine centered in the Ukraine and the northern Caucasus and the government did its utmost to conceal it from the world. The desperate situation resulted in a reduction of the amount of foodstuffs taken by the state and in permission to the collective farms to sell at least part of their surplus produce.

1932, July 25. Conclusion of **non-aggression pacts with Poland, Estonia, Latvia, and Finland,** followed by a similar **agreement with France** (Nov. 29). These pacts reflected the government's uneasiness about developments in the Far East, notably the establishment of the Manchukuoan state under Japanese auspices. Relations between Russia and Japan degenerated rapidly and considerable tension developed with regard to the **Chinese Eastern Railway.** This particular issue was settled by the sale of the Soviet interest for 140,000,000 yen (Mar. 23, 1935), but Japanese activity on the border of **Outer Mongolia** (allied to Russia and really under Soviet protection) gave rise to a series of "incidents" of a dangerous nature. As a result of Japanese expansion in eastern Asia and the growing threat to the Soviet position, the Moscow government not only attempted to stabilize relations with its European neighbors, but began to take an active part in the **disarmament conference** (p. 1126) and in general international co-operation. This new departure was signalized by a notable lull in the activities of the Third International.

1933. Purge of the Communist Party. About one-third of the members (1,000,000) were expelled for one reason or another. In April a number of British engineers were put on trial for sabotage. The British government protested and put an embargo on Soviet goods. Though convicted, the engineers were permitted to leave the country, but Anglo-Soviet relations continued to be distant.

Nov. 17. Recognition of the Soviet government by the United States brought to an end a long period of estrangement. Trade relations were opened and the Soviet government promised to abstain from propaganda in the United States.

1934, May 5. The **non-aggression pacts** with Poland and the Baltic states were extended into ten-year agreements. In view of the National Socialist victory in Germany (p. 1008) and the openly expressed hostility of the new German régime to communism, the Soviet Union felt more than ever endangered. Trade relations with Germany continued and even expanded for a few years, but the Moscow government at once embarked upon an extensive **program of armament** on land, sea, and air. Within a few years the Soviets had a formidable air fleet and had made considerable progress toward the construction of a powerful navy (especially submarines). In accord with the effort to secure support in Europe, Russia made

June 9. Agreements with Czechoslovakia and Roumania, at long last recognizing the **loss of Bessarabia.** Above all the government

Sept. 18. JOINED THE LEAGUE OF NATIONS, which before it had roundly denounced. Russia now took an active part in all work for the furtherance of collective security and supported France in the scheme for an eastern European pact along the lines of the Locarno agreements.

Dec. 1. The **assassination of Serge Kirov,** a close collaborator of Stalin, revealed the existence of a strong and desperate opposition to the régime within the ranks of the Communist Party itself. The incident was followed by another **outbreak of terror** and by repeated "purges" of the party and the administration. In several spectacular trials many of the most prominent of the older communist leaders were convicted.

1935, Jan. 15–17. Zinoviev, Kamenev, and several other leaders were **tried for treason** and conspiracy. They were convicted and imprisoned for terms of five to ten years.

May 2. CONCLUSION OF THE FRANCO-RUSSIAN ALLIANCE (p. 989).

May 16. An **alliance between Russia and Czechoslovakia** (p. 1017) obliged the Russians to come to the assistance of Czechoslovakia in the event of attack, provided France decided to act.

July 25–Aug. 20. At a **meeting of the Third International** it was decided that Soviet Russia, in view of the growing tension between the democratic and fascist states, should throw its weight on the side of the democracies against the common enemy. Henceforth communists in other countries were to give up their opposition to military appropriations and to support the governments, even though these were bourgeois.

1936, Aug. 19–23. Zinoviev, Kamenev, and a group of their followers were put on trial again, this time as Trotskyists, accused of plotting with enemy powers against the existing régime. They openly confessed to most of the charges brought against them, much to the astonishment of the world. On conviction, sixteen of them were at once executed.

July. On the outbreak of the **civil war in Spain** (p. 993) the Russian government at once took the side of the Madrid government and sent airplanes and other supplies to the Loyalists.

Nov. 17. Conclusion of the **Anti-Comintern Pact** by Germany and Japan, an agreement actually directed against Russia.

Dec. 5. ADOPTION OF A NEW "DEMO-CRATIC" CONSTITUTION. The Soviet Federation was recast and the Union thenceforth was composed as follows: (1) **Russia;** (2) **Ukraine;** (3) **White Russia;** (4) **Azerbaijan;** (5) **Georgia;** (6) **Armenia;** (7) **Turkmenistan;** (8) **Uzbekistan;** (9) **Tadjikistan;** (10) **Kazakhstan;** (11) **Kirghistan.** Russia and subsequently all other states of the Union adopted an **electoral system** from which no elements in the country were any longer debarred: all votes were to be equal; elections to the higher assemblies were made direct; votes were to be cast on a territorial, not on an occupational basis; the secret ballot was introduced. The place of the congresses of soviets was taken by a two-chamber parliament (the **Supreme Soviet**), consisting of a **Council of Nationalities** (i.e. a federal chamber) and a **Union Council.** This parliament was to appoint a **Presidium** to act while the council itself was not in session. All civic rights were guaranteed, but the Communist Party continued to be the only political group permitted in the country.

1937, Jan. 23–30. **Georgei Piatakov, Karl Radek,** and other leaders were put on trial and convicted, thirteen of them suffering the death penalty. The various "purges" continued throughout the year and extended through the entire administration, ultimately reaching also the army and the diplomatic service. Political commissioners were appointed to watch over the army commands. On May 31 **Marshal Ian Gamarnik** was reported to have committed suicide, and

June 12. Marshal **Michael Tukhachevski** and seven other generals of the highest rank were executed after a secret court-martial. They were accused of conspiracy with the Germans and the Japanese. There followed further purging, in the course of which all "Trotskyists" and others objectionable to Stalin were "liquidated." These trials and executions did much to discredit Russia as a reliable factor in international relations.

Dec. 12. The **first elections** under the new constitution were held. Most of the candidates elected were those of the Communist slate, so that no significant change resulted from the new system. The supreme soviet met for the

first time January 12, 1938, and appointed to the key positions those who were already dominant in the government.

1938, Mar. 2–15. **Nicolai Bukharin, Alexei Rykov, Genrikh Yagoda,** and other prominent Bolsheviks were put on trial, accused of wanting to restore bourgeois capitalism and of joining with Trotsky in treasonable conspiracy. They were **convicted and executed.** More and more Stalin trusted to the younger generation, which had never known anything but the Bolshevik régime and which was therefore less apt to criticize.

July 11–Aug. 10. Open warfare broke out between the **Russians and the Japanese** on the frontier of eastern Siberia and Manchukuo (p. 1110).

Sept. The great **Czech crisis** (p. 1018). The Russian government publicly announced its readiness to come to the assistance of the Czechs if France did so. But neither Britain nor France appeared to relish the idea of communist support and followed a policy of yielding. As a result the Franco-Russian alliance lost most of its significance and Russia was almost completely isolated in Europe. Indeed the supposed **German designs on the Ukraine** seemed to presage a conflict between Germany and Russia in the not too distant future.

1939, Mar.–June. The **extinction of Czechoslovakia** and the German annexation of Memel threw Europe into consternation and produced a revolution in British policy (p. 1039).

May 3. **Maxim Litvinov** was suddenly dismissed from the post of commissar for foreign affairs, after eighteen years of service. Premier Vyacheslav Molotov took his place.

Aug. 20, 21. A **trade pact** was concluded with Germany and announcement was made of a forthcoming **non-aggression pact** (concluded August 23) (p. 1012). When Germany made war on Poland (p. 1039) Bolshevik Russia stood by as a benevolent neutral.

CULTURAL DEVELOPMENTS

Poetry flourished for a time immediately after the revolution: **Boris Pasternak** (1890–1960, also prose writer, *Dr. Zhivago*, 1957; declined Nobel prize for literature, 1958); **Marina Tsvetayeva, Sergius Esenin** (1895–1925). Among "proletarian" novels, *Rossiya* (1926) by **Artem Vesely** (b. 1899) is the best.

Composers: **Igor Stravinsky** (1882–1971), ballet, operas, symphonic works; **Serge Prokofiev** (1891–1953), operas, symphonic music; **Dmitri Shostakovich** (1906–1975), symphonies.

(*Cont. p. 1214*)

13. POLAND

During the First World War Poland was a pawn in the conflict between Russia and the Central Powers. On the one hand the Russian government, to hold the loyalty of the Poles, **1914, Aug. 14.** Promised that Poland should be **restored as an autonomous kingdom.** This policy secured the support of an important faction of Polish nationalists, led by **Roman Dmowski,** who November 25, formed the Polish National Committee at Warsaw. On the other hand,

Aug. 16. Gen. Joseph Pilsudski (a Russian Pole by birth and several times convicted and imprisoned in Russia for radical, revolutionary activity) founded the **Supreme National Committee** at Cracow, under Austrian protection. The Austrian government permitted the formation of Polish legions to fight against Russia. In the course of 1915 most of Poland was conquered by the Germans and Austrians, who for a time divided the administration of the territory between them. Ultimately, however, the German high command took almost complete control of the country.

1916, July 25. Pilsudski resigned from his command in protest against the failure of the Central Powers to establish a Polish kingdom. The Polish legions were incorporated with the Austro-Hungarian army.

Nov. 5. The German and Austrian governments joined in the proclamation of an **"independent" Polish kingdom** and set up a council of state, which adopted a constitution (Jan. 30, 1917). On this council Pilsudski accepted a seat.

1917, Mar. 30. The **Russian provisional government declared in favor of an independent Poland,** to include all lands in which the Poles comprised a majority of the population.

July 2. Pilsudski resigned from the council of state in protest against continued German control. He was thereupon arrested and imprisoned at Magdeburg (until November 2, 1918).

Aug. 15. Dmowski established the Polish national committee at Paris, the French government having given permission (June 4) for the formation of a Polish army in France.

Oct. 15. The Germans set up a regency council in Poland which exercised effective control under German supervision. On the collapse of the Central Powers in

1918, Oct. 12. The **regency council took charge** of affairs. But the Ukrainians had already begun the invasion of Galicia and before long

Nov. 1. Poland made war on the Ukraine, reconquering Galicia for the new Polish state.

Nov. 3. The **POLISH REPUBLIC WAS PROCLAIMED** at Warsaw. This soon fell under the control of Pilsudski, who returned from his German captivity November 10 and was granted full military power by the regency council, which thereupon resigned (Nov. 14). Under Pilsudski's direction the Poles continued their advance in Galicia, taking Lemberg (Nov. 23). At the same time they attempted to realize their aspirations in the west, and

Dec. 27-28. Occupied Posen (*Poznania*) with their troops. Pilsudski succeeded in reaching agreements with other provisional governments (that of **Ignace Daszynski** at Cracow and that of **Dmowski** and **Ignace Jan Paderewski** at Paris), so that

1919, Jan. 17. Paderewski could form a coalition cabinet, Pilsudski acting as provisional president. A constituent assembly was elected (Jan. 26) and worked out a temporary constitutional system. Meanwhile the entire effort of the government was devoted to the conquest of the territories belonging to Poland at the time of the first partition of 1772. This brought the Poles into conflict with the Bolsheviks in White Russia and Lithuania (p. 1031).

June 28. TREATY OF VERSAILLES established the Polish frontier in the west, Poland receiving a **corridor along the Vistula** to the sea (the **city of Danzig** to be a free city under supervision of the League of Nations, but economically connected with Poland), and large parts of **West Prussia** and **Posen.** A plebiscite was to determine the frontier in Upper Silesia. Poland was obliged to accept a **minority treaty** guaranteeing full rights and numerous religious, educational, linguistic, and other privileges to the minority peoples.

Dec. 7. Paderewski resigned as premier. Pilsudski, now marshal of Poland, remained as chief of the state.

Dec. 8. The supreme council laid down the so-called **"Curzon Line"** for Poland's eastern frontier. This line deprived Poland of Vilna.

1920, Mar. 27. The Poles demanded of the Russians the **boundaries of 1772** with a plebiscite in the region west of that boundary. This the Bolsheviks would not accept, though they made many efforts to effect a compromise. Breakdown of negotiations led to

Apr. 25–Oct. 12. THE RUSSIAN-POLISH WAR (p. 1033).

1921, Feb. 19. Conclusion of the **Polish alliance with France,** followed shortly by a similar

Mar. 3. Alliance with Roumania. For many years Polish foreign policy was based on these agreements (supplemented with less extensive pacts with Czechoslovakia and Yugoslavia as well as with the Baltic states). Poland had a hostile Germany and a hostile Russia on its frontiers and for that reason was bound to France and the French system. The French supplied large sums of money for armaments and for reconstruction of the country.

Mar. 17. ADOPTION OF THE CONSTITUTION, which provided for a president, elected for seven years by a two-chamber parliament (**senate** and **sejm**) chosen by popular vote. The whole system was modeled closely on that of France.

Mar. 20. The **plebiscite in Upper Silesia** resulted in a victory for the Germans, but

May 4. The Poles under **Adalbert Korfanty** occupied some of the disputed areas. The matter was referred to the League of Nations, which finally decided, on the plea of economic necessity, to partition the region (Oct. 12).

1922, Jan. 8. The **Vilna plebiscite** showed a majority in favor of Poland, and the city and district were incorporated April 18. The result was a bitter **feud with Lithuania.**

Mar. 17. Poland concluded **treaties with Latvia, Estonia, and Finland** which provided for maintenance of the treaty settlements and neutrality in case one of these powers should be attacked.

Nov. 5. The elections resulted in a victory of the Rightist parties. Pilsudski resigned as chief of state and became chief of the army staff. The parliament elected

Dec. 9. Gabriel Narutowicz president, but he was assassinated December 18 and

Dec. 20. STANISLAS WOJCIECHOWSKI became president.

The next few years were devoted to the work of reconstruction. The finances were in bad condition, the parliamentary system was characterized by bitter strife between the more conservative and nationalist parties and the socialists and peasants. At the same time there was much friction with the minorities (especially the Ukrainians and the Germans). Cabinets changed with the greatest suddenness until

1923, Dec. 19. Ladislav Grabski formed a non-parliamentary ministry of experts, which managed to stabilize the currency, made some concessions to the demands of the minorities (including Jews), and regulated Polish relations with some of the neighboring states. On Grabski's downfall (Nov. 13, 1925) there followed another period of political confusion, during which

1925, Dec. 28. An important **land law** was passed, providing for the distribution of about 500,000 acres of land to the peasants annually for ten years.

1926, May 10. Vincent Witos, the leader of the Peasant Party, formed a government, but

May 12–14. PILSUDSKI LED A MILITARY REVOLT against the government. After two days of fighting Pilsudski took the capital, forcing Witos to resign. President Wojciechowski also resigned (May 15), whereupon Pilsudski was elected to take his place. Pilsudski declined the honor, but his friend

June 1. IGNACE MOSCICKI became president. Pilsudski was the real ruler of the country, though he acted through the president, who, by

Aug. 5. A revision of the constitution, was given much greater power.

Oct. 2. Pilsudski assumed the premiership, which he retained until June 27, 1928. His coup and practical dictatorship had aroused great resentment and opposition among the parties of the Left. Under Pilsudski the government resorted to the most **drastic methods of repression.** The sejm was dissolved and 54 opposition deputies arrested (Nov. 28, 1927) but new elections indicated the continuance of strong opposition to the rule of the military (**rule of the "colonels"**).

1930, Aug. 25. Pilsudski again took over the premiership (until November 28) in order to break the Leftist opposition. Many of the radical leaders were tried and imprisoned (including Witos), and finally

Nov. 16. The elections returned a majority of deputies supporting the government bloc. Pilsudski's control was complete, but the country began to suffer severely from the world depression, and the unrest attending general want produced an ever greater tendency on the part of the ruling group to turn to more conservative policies.

1932, Mar. Parliament granted the president **decree powers** for a period of three years, and these were later extended.

1933, May 8. Moscicki was re-elected for a second term of seven years.

Aug. 5. An **agreement with the city government of Danzig** (which had recently fallen under National Socialist control) assured the Poles in Danzig fair treatment, while guaranteeing to Danzig a certain percentage of Poland's seaborne trade. By this time the new Polish **port of Gdynia** (constructed after 1920 because of the constant friction between Poland and Danzig) had already outstripped its older German neighbor as a trade center.

1934, Jan. 26. Conclusion of a ten-year **NONAGGRESSION PACT WITH GERMANY** (p. 1011), which gave Poland at least some assurance against a Nazi attempt to recover the Polish corridor by force of arms.

May 5. The Poles extended to ten years a

non-agression pact with Russia which had been first concluded July 25, 1932.

1935, Apr. 23. A NEW CONSTITUTION was adopted after years of planning and discussion. The new régime, railroaded through the sejm while the opposition stayed away, brought to an end the democratic, parliamentary system.

May 12. Death of Marshal Pilsudski. He was succeeded as head of the army by **Gen.** (later Marshal) **Edward Smigly-Rydz,** the new power behind the presidential system.

Sept. 8. The **elections,** in which only 45 per cent of the electorate took part, produced a sejm dominated by the deputies of the government bloc. The Socialists and Peasant Party persisted in demanding a return to genuine democracy. The Ukrainians became bolder and bolder in their claims for autonomy or independence.

1937, Mar. 1. Col. Adam Koc organized the *Camp of National Unity,* intended to be an all-inclusive union of those supporting the government. Its program called for maintenance of the constitution of 1935, popular support for the army as the shield of national existence, anti-communism, distribution of land to the peasants, Polonization of minorities, etc. In reply to this move the workers and peasants in the same month joined in a *Workers', Peasants', and Intellectuals' Group,* opposed to Koc and his camp. Peasant strikes became widespread and led to some bloodshed.

1938, Jan. 11. Col. Koc resigned leadership of the camp to **Gen. Stanislas Skwarczynski,** who represented a somewhat more conciliatory wing of the government group. On April 21 the camp broke definitely with the *Union of Young Poland,* an out-and-out fascist and violently anti-Semitic organization founded by Koc.

Mar. 16–19. The Polish government, taking advantage of the international situation created by the German annexation of Austria, sent an **ultimatum to Lithuania** demanding an end to hostility and an early regulation of relations between the two countries.

Sept. 29. A POLISH NOTE was sent **to Czechoslovakia** demanding the cession of the Teschen area (seized by the Czechs during the Polish-Russian War of 1920). The Czechs, face to face with the threat of German invasion and deserted by their friends, were obliged to yield. On October 2 **Polish forces occupied**

Teschen. In the discussions following the **Munich agreement** (p. 1129) the Poles ardently championed the Hungarian claims in Slovakia and Ruthenia and tried to secure a common frontier with Hungary, but these schemes were frustrated by the opposition of Germany.

1939, Mar.–Apr. A **Polish-German crisis** ensued after the German action in Czechoslovakia and the annexation of Memel (p. 1018). At the end of March the German government submitted extensive demands to Warsaw, including the cession of Danzig to Germany and the right to construct an extra-territorial railway and automobile highway across Pomorze (the "corridor"), in return for a guarantee of Polish frontiers and a non-aggression pact. The demands were rejected, but resulted directly in the

Mar. 31. Anglo-French guarantee of aid to Poland in the event of aggression (expanded April 6 into a mutual pact of assistance "in the event of any threat, direct or indirect, to the independence of either"). In reply

Apr. 28. Hitler denounced the agreement of 1934 with Poland. Relations continued to be tense, with much friction in Danzig. In view of this situation the Poles gave up opposition to a proposed guaranty by Russia and approved the British efforts to bring the Soviet government into the new "peace front."

The Danzig problem developed rapidly during the summer and frontier incidents became frequent. The Germans began to send troops into Danzig and the Poles began to take counter measures, while reiterating their determination to oppose any effort to change the *status quo* by force. Finally the crisis broke on August 20 (p. 1132). The British and French stood by Poland while the Germans refused to engage in direct negotiations. Two weeks of tension ended with

Sept. 1. The **GERMAN ATTACK ON POLAND,** followed by the European war (p. 1135).

CULTURAL DEVELOPMENTS

Prominent literary figures were the lyric poet **Jan Kasprowicz** (1860–1926) and the novelist **Wladyslaw S. Reymont** (1868–1925), winner of the Nobel prize in 1924 (*Chlopi* [*The Peasants*], 1904–06). (*Cont. p. 1219.*)

14. THE BALTIC STATES

a. GENERAL

The development of the three Baltic states after the First World War was more or less along a common line. All were originally part of Russia; they were, during the war, occupied by the Germans, who ruled them through puppet régimes; after Germany's collapse, efforts were made by the Bolsheviks to recover these territories, which gave access to the Baltic. Through German and Allied aid, and by their own efforts, the Baltic forces drove out the Bolsheviks and established independent governments. In all three states there was a German minority of landed wealth and influence, against which **agrarian legislation,** involving the breakup of large estates, was directed. The democratic systems set up after the war gave rise to considerable confusion, with much party wrangling between Social Democrats, Agrarians, etc. **Communism** was an ever-present danger, against which all the governments took vigorous measures. But after the victory of National Socialism in Germany the Baltic states hastened to improve their relations with Soviet Russia in order to forestall German intervention in behalf of the German minorities. An entente between the various states had often been discussed, but had been frustrated by Lithuania's demand for recognition of her claims to Vilna. Finally

1934, Sept. 12. The **TREATIES OF THE BALTIC ENTENTE** were signed between the three states, the Vilna problem being passed over. The **Baltic Pact** provided for common action in defense of independence and in foreign affairs, with semi-annual meetings of foreign ministers.

By 1939 all three of the Baltic states had gone over to some form of **dictatorship,** not from deference to the German system, but rather to forge a stronger régime for ultimate resistance to Germany.

b. LITHUANIA

After the victory of the revolution in Russia, **1917, Sept. 23.** A Lithuanian conference at Vilna led to the **establishment of a national council** and a demand for independence from Russia. The movement was encouraged by the Germans and resulted in

1918, Feb. 16. A FORMAL DECLARATION OF INDEPENDENCE. The new state was at once invaded by the Bolsheviks, but by

Mar. 3. The treaty of Brest-Litovsk (p. 971). Russia was obliged to recognize Lithuanian independence. The Germans also recognized the new state (Mar. 23), and drew it into alliance with Germany (May 14). The Lithuanian government was obliged to elect

June 4. Duke William of Urach as king. But when German power collapsed in November this election was rescinded and

Nov. 11. Augustine Voldemaras formed a national government, the first of many short-lived cabinets. The Germans were obliged to withdraw, whereupon the Bolsheviks again invaded the country and

1919, Jan. 5. Took Vilna, which they lost soon afterward to the Poles (Apr. 4).

Dec. 8. The Allied powers defined the Polish-Lithuanian boundary by the Curzon Line, which left **Vilna to Lithuania.**

1920, July 12. The **treaty of Moscow** brought to an end Russian-Lithuanian hostilities. The Bolsheviks, at war with Poland, hastened to recognize Lithuania and the latter's possession of Vilna, which was taken over by the Lithuanians on the evacuation by the Bolsheviks (Aug. 24).

Oct. 9. Gen. Lucien-Zeligowski and his Polish freebooters seized Vilna by surprise. The Lithuanians refused to give up their claims and the League of Nations arranged for a plebiscite. Meanwhile the Lithuanian capital was fixed at **Kaunas** (Kovno).

1921, Sept. 22. Lithuania joined the League of Nations.

1922, Jan. 8. The **Vilna plebiscite,** supervised by Zeligowski and his Poles, resulted in a majority vote for union with Poland. The Lithuanians refused to accept this as a valid vote and all intercourse between Lithuania and Poland was cut off.

Aug. 1. Adoption of the constitution which had been worked out by a constituent assembly convoked in May 1920. Lithuania became a democratic republic, recognized by the United States July 27, and by Britain, France, and Italy December 20.

Dec. 21. Antanas Stulgenskis became president of the republic.

1923, Jan. 11. INSURRECTION IN MEMEL, engineered by Lithuanians. The city, which was predominantly German, had been under inter-Allied control since 1918. Lithuanian troops now occupied it, obliging a French garrison to withdraw. An inter-Allied commission was sent out to investigate, and thereupon

Feb. 16. The council of ambassadors decided to grant Lithuania sovereignty but to constitute **Memel an autonomous region** in the Lithuanian state. Lithuania accepted

(Mar. 16) and the *Memel Statute* was signed by Britain, France, Italy, and Japan on May 8, 1924.

1926, Dec. 17. *COUP D'ÉTAT* OF ANTANAS SMETONA, who arrested the president and cabinet and had himself made president, with Augustine Voldemaras as premier. The constitution was suspended and the diet dissolved, Smetona becoming virtual dictator with the support of the **Nationalist Union.**

1929, Sept. 19. Voldemaras forced to resign. He was later (May 1930) tried for high treason, exiled to a village, and ultimately convicted and imprisoned for a term of twelve years (June, 1934).

1931, May 6. A treaty of friendship with Russia (first concluded in 1926) was renewed for another five-year term.

Dec. 11. Smetona was re-elected for another seven-year term.

1932, Feb. 6. The **arrest of Herbert Boettcher,** head of the Memel directorate, for alleged treasonable correspondence with Germany, ushered in a period of continued German protests and recrimination. Britain, France, and Italy periodically made efforts to hold Lithuania to respect the spirit as well as the letter of the Memel Statute, but with little success.

Dec. 16. The **Nationalist Union,** supporting Smetona, frankly adopted a fascist (of course not German fascist) program.

1934, Sept. 12. CONCLUSION OF THE BALTIC PACT (see above).

1935, Mar. 25. Conviction of almost a hundred Memallanders on a charge of plotting the return of Memel to Germany.

1936, Feb. 6. The government suppressed all political parties excepting the Nationalist Union.

June 9–10. Elections were held for a new parliament along fascist lines. Only Nationalist candidates were presented, and these were elected by local authorities. The parliament met September 1.

1938, Mar. 16. The **Polish government sent a stiff ultimatum to Lithuania** demanding reopening of the frontier and regularization of relations. After a short crisis the Lithuanian government yielded (Mar. 17).

Dec. 11. The **elections in Memel** brought a vote of more than 90 per cent for the National Socialists. In view of the resurgent power of Germany, the Lithuanian government was obliged to leave the Nazis practically a free hand in Memel.

1939, Mar. 23. The **Germans took Memel** after extorting an agreement from Lithuania. In return they guaranteed Lithuanian independence and integrity and concluded a commercial treaty.

Mar. 28. Gen. Jonas Cernius, the chief of the general staff, formed a new **National Coalition cabinet** in which the outlawed opposition parties were represented. On April 8 Cernius resigned so that the government might not have a military character. Lithuania, practically at Germany's mercy, made efforts to draw closer to Poland, the old enemy.

c. LATVIA

1917, Oct. 29. Formation of the **Latvian national council,** following the Soviet seizure of power in Russia. Since German forces remained in the country, the national council was unable to assert its authority or build up an effective national army. For more than a year German efforts to organize a **Baltic duchy** continued, especially since by

1918, Mar. 3. The **treaty of Brest-Litovsk** (p. 971) the Bolsheviks were obliged to accept loss of the Baltic States. After the defeat of Germany, the Latvians set up

Nov. 17. A people's council, with **Karlis Ulmanis** as prime minister. The council on

Nov. 18. Proclaimed the independence of the **state of Latvia.** Almost immediately, however,

1919, Jan. 3. A Bolshevik army invaded the country and took **Riga** (Jan. 4). A Soviet government was set up, but German-Latvian forces, with the approval of the Allies, drove the Soviet troops back (March).

June 28. The **treaty of Versailles** (p. 977) required the Germans to withdraw from the Baltic States. Gen. von der Goltz was recalled (Aug. 16) at Allied insistence, but fighting between Germans and Latvians continued (German attack on Riga, October 8) until about November 20, when the country was finally cleared of German forces. By

1920, Jan. The last of the Bolshevik troops had also been expelled.

Feb. 1. An **armistice** was concluded between the Latvian and Soviet governments.

May 1. The Latvian **constituent assembly** met and drafted a constitution. By the

Aug. 11. Treaty of Riga the Soviet government recognized Latvian sovereignty and renounced all rights to the territory.

1921, Jan. 26. The Allied powers recognized the new state and on **September 22** Latvia joined the **League of Nations.**

1922, May 1. The new constitution went into effect. It provided for a single-chamber parliament **(saiema)** and ministerial responsibility.

Oct. 8. The elections resulted in a victory for the **Social Democrats.**

Nov. 14. Jan Chakste became president.

1927, Apr. 8. Gustav Zemgalis, president.

1928, Jan. 14. The conservative parties for the first time formed a government.

1930, Apr. 9. Albert Kviesis, president.

1932, July 25. Conclusion of a **non-aggression pact with Soviet Russia.**

1934, May 15. *COUP D'ÉTAT* OF KARLIS ULMANIS, the prime minister, assisted by Gen. Francis Balodis.

Sept. 12. Latvia joined the Baltic pact with Lithuania and Estonia (see p. 1040).

1936, Apr. 11. Ulmanis succeeded Kviesis as **president.**

1939, May. Latvia, directly exposed to the German advance to the east, became an object of great concern to Russia. In the negotiations for an Anglo-Russian pact (p. 1132) the Moscow government insisted on a guaranty of the independence of all the Baltic States, but the Latvian government, as ever suspicious of the Soviets, accepted the German offer of a mutual non-aggression pact (June 7).

d. ESTONIA

1917, Nov. 28. The **Estonians,** taking advantage of the Bolshevik revolution in Russia, **proclaimed their independence,** but the Soviet government at once undertook the reconquest of this strategically important area. To block the Russian advance, the Germans occupied the country (Dec.) and

1918, Feb. 24. The independence of Estonia was again proclaimed, under German protection. A provisional government was formed by **Konstantin Paets,** who was to play a prominent rôle throughout the entire post-war period.

Mar. 3. By the treaty of Brest-Litovsk (p. 971) Russia was obliged to recognize Estonian independence.

Nov. 11. The Germans began the withdrawal from the country, following the end of the First World War. They ceded complete power to Paets.

Nov. 22. The **Russians began a second invasion** of the country. The Estonians put up a valiant resistance and were supported by a British fleet.

1919, Jan. The **Bolsheviks were finally driven out** and the Estonian government was able to establish its control throughout most of the land.

June 15. Adoption of a constitution drafted by a national assembly. Estonia, like Latvia, became a democratic republic, with Reval as the capital. One of the first acts of the government was to pass an

Oct. 10. Agrarian law which inaugurated the breaking up of the large estates of the (German) Baltic barons and distributing the

land among the peasants.

1920, Feb. 2. The **treaty of Tartu** (Dorpat) with Russia brought Estonia definitive recognition as an independent state.

1921, Sept. 22. Estonia joined the League of Nations.

1923, Nov. 1, 2. Conclusion of **defensive treaties with Latvia and Lithuania** which paved the way for close relations and the ultimate construction of a Baltic bloc (1934).

1924, Nov. 27. Trial of 150 **communists,** most of whom were convicted and imprisoned. Estonia continued to be particularly exposed to communist agitation, which finally culminated in

Dec. 1. A **communist uprising,** which, however, was suppressed.

1933, Oct. 14–16. A **plebiscite in favor of constitutional revision,** providing for the election of a president (thus far the premier had acted as head of the state), to whom wide powers were to be assigned.

1934, Jan. 24. The **new constitution** went into effect. The Liberators at once attempted a *coup* in order to secure control of the government, but this was suppressed and

Mar. 12. KONSTANTIN PAETS, aided by **Gen. John Laidoner, set up a virtual dictatorship.**

Sept. 12. Estonia joined in the Baltic pact (p. 1040).

1936, Feb. 23–25. In a plebiscite, the nation voted 3 to 1 in favor of abolishing the **constitution of 1934** and returning to the democratic system. In December a national assembly was convoked to work out a new constitution.

May 6. About 150 leaders of the Liberators were put on trial for attempting another *coup* in December 1935. Only seven of them were acquitted. Paets continued to be irreconcilably opposed to fascism and national socialism, as he was to communism.

1937, July 29. The **new constitution,** providing for a president and a two-chamber parliament, was adopted. Restoration of civil liberties was provided for, as were democratic elections. But under the new system the president (to be elected for six years) was to enjoy great authority, with power to appoint and dismiss the cabinet, dissolve both houses of parliament, and rule by decree in national emergencies.

1938, Feb. 24. The **election** resulted in a chamber containing 63 deputies of Paets' National Front and 17 of opposition groups.

Apr. 24. Paets was elected president.

1939, May. Estonia concluded a mutual **non-aggression pact with Germany,** acting together with Latvia (see above).

15. THE SCANDINAVIAN STATES

a. GENERAL

The Scandinavian states were all able to preserve neutrality during the First World War, though they were obliged to accept various Allied regulations and restrictions made necessary by the Allied blockade of Germany. After 1918 they all took an active part in the development of collective security, in which obviously they had a great interest. For the rest they all became thoroughly democratic states, outstanding for their progressiveness and enlightenment. In politics the situation in most cases was rather unstable, due to the relative strength of conservative, liberal, agrarian, and social democratic parties and the difficulty of establishing majority government. In foreign policy efforts were made consistently to develop a program of close co-operation and solidarity, which became all the more necessary after the resurgence of Germany as a powerful military state. Efforts at collaboration go back to the

1914, Dec. 18–19. Meeting of the kings of the three Scandinavian states at Malmö. They discussed various problems of the war, neutrality, etc.

1926, Jan. 14, 15, 30. Agreements were made between Denmark, Sweden, Norway, and Finland providing **for the pacific settlement of all disputes.** Ultimately, when these countries began to suffer severely from the world economic crisis,

1931, Sept. 6. Prime ministers of the Scandinavian states met for discussion of economic problems, and there finally came into force the

1932, Feb. 7. Oslo convention, by which the Scandinavian states joined with the Netherlands and Belgium in a scheme of economic co-operation, albeit on a modest scale. More recently Scandinavian solidarity was celebrated by the institution of

1936, Oct. 27. Scandinavia's Day. In view of the collapse of the League system for security and the imposing rearmament of Germany and Russia,

1938, Apr. 5–6. The four Scandinavian foreign ministers met for a discussion of the **defense problem.** In view of the unwillingness of Denmark to challenge Germany, the specific question of armament and defense had to be left to the individual governments.

July 1. The Oslo mutual trade agreements came to an end. Nevertheless, relations between the so-called Oslo powers continued to be cordial and even close.

1939, June 17. Sweden, Norway, and Finland declined the **German offer of a mutual non-aggression pact,** an offer provoked by President Roosevelt's suggestion, in his letter to Hitler, that Germany's neighbors felt threatened by aggression. (*Cont. p. 1221.*)

b. DENMARK

(*From p. 747*)

1912–1947. CHRISTIAN X, king.
1916, Aug. 4. Sale of the Danish West Indies to the United States. The transaction was approved by a Danish plebiscite December 14.
1918, Apr. 21. Complete **universal suffrage** (male and female) went into effect. In the
Apr. 22. Elections under the new system the Conservatives secured 23 seats, the Left (Liberals) 45, the Radicals 33, and the Socialists 39. The government was formed by a coalition of Radicals and Socialists.
Nov. 30. By the Act of Union, **Iceland was recognized as a sovereign state,** united with Denmark only in the person of the ruler. But until 1944 certain affairs were to be handled jointly.
1920, Feb. 10, Mar. 14. By the plebiscites provided for in the treaty of Versailles, **a northern zone of Schleswig** went to Denmark by popular vote. It was officially incorporated July 9.
Mar. 8. Denmark joined the League of Nations.
1924, Apr. 11. In the elections the Socialists increased their representation from 39 to 55. Thereupon **Theodor Stauning** (Socialist) formed a government.
1926, Mar. 12. The Danish parliament voted for almost complete **disarmament,** which was subsequently carried through.
Dec. 2. A Liberal government was formed by **Thomas Madsen-Mygdal** after a severe setback to the Socialists in the elections.
1929, Apr. 24. Stauning organized another government after Socialist successes at the polls. His party acted in coalition with the Radical Left.
1931, July. A serious **dispute with Norway** developed over the problem of sovereignty over East Greenland (see below).
1933. Agitation of the Germans in North Schleswig followed on the victory of the National Socialists in Germany. National Socialism itself made but little progress in Denmark, although Denmark, practically disarmed, remained more or less at the mercy of her powerful neighbor. (*Cont. p. 1222.*)

c. NORWAY

(From p. 749)

1905–1957. HAAKON VII, king. Norway, much more dependent on trade and fishing than either Denmark or Sweden, alone among the Scandinavian powers revealed a tendency toward expansion overseas.

1919, Sept. 25. The Allied supreme council awarded Norway the sovereignty over **Spitsbergen,** which was thereupon annexed (Feb. 9, 1920). Other acquisitions are mentioned below.

1920, Mar. 5. Norway joined the League of Nations.

1924, Oct. 20. In the **elections** the Conservatives emerged victorious, with 54 seats as against 34 for the Radicals, 22 for the Agrarians, 24 for the Labor Party, and eight for the Socialists. But in the next

1927, Oct. 17. Elections the Labor Party for the first time became the strongest group (59 seats as against 31 for the Conservatives and 31 for the Liberals). The **first labor government** was organized by **Christopher Hornsrud,** but was soon forced out by its opponents (Feb. 10, 1928). Thereupon **Johan Mowinckel** (Liberal) formed a cabinet.

1928, Jan. 18. Annexation of Bouvet Island and of

1929, Feb. 2. Peter Island, both in the South Atlantic and both important as whaling stations.

    May 8. Annexation of Jan Mayen Island in the Arctic.

1929–1930. Explorations of Capt. Hjalmar Riiser-Larsen in the Antarctic continent (p. 626).

1931, May 8. Peter Kolstad (Farmers' Party) formed a government.

    July 10. Annexation of the East Greenland coast between 71° 30′ and 75° 40′ N.L. Norwegian fishermen had settled along the coast and there was some fear lest Denmark, which claimed sovereignty, attempt to make its control effective. Denmark at once protested against the Norwegian action and both parties agreed to refer the matter to the Permanent Court of International Justice. While the case was pending the Norwegian government (July 12, 1932) proclaimed annexation also of part of the more southern coast (60° 30′ to 63° 40′ N.L.), but finally (Apr. 5, 1933) the Permanent Court decided against the Norwegian claims. The Oslo government accepted the decision without demur.

1932, Mar. 5. On the death of Premier Kolstad, his place was taken by **Jen Hundseid,** but

1933, Jan. 25. Mowinckel organized another Liberal cabinet, which continued in power even after the elections of October 16 gave the Labor Party 69 seats (Right 30; Left 24; Farmers 23).

1935, Mar. 20. A **second Labor government** was formed by **Johan Nygaardsvold,** with **Halvdan Koht,** an eminent historian, at the foreign office. This government was successful in overcoming the economic crisis, and became noteworthy for its extension of social security legislation (1937, Jan.: **Workers' Security Law** and **Seamen's Security Law**).

1939, Jan. 14. Norway laid claim to 1,000,000 square miles of **Antarctic territory** extending from 20° W. Long. to 45° E. Long. (Coats Land to Enderby Land, about one-fifth of the entire Antarctic coast, see p. 627).

(Cont. p. 1222.

d. SWEDEN

(From p. 749)

1907–1950. GUSTAVUS V, king.

1917, Dec. 29. The **Aaland Islands,** following the Bolshevik Revolution in Russia, **voted to join Sweden,** but later (June 24, 1921) the League of Nations council assigned them to Finland, with the proviso that they should be demilitarized.

1919, May 26. The introduction of **woman suffrage** completed the democratization of the franchise.

1920, Mar. 4. Sweden joined the League of Nations.

    Mar. 10. Hjalmar Branting formed the first purely Socialist cabinet, but he was forced to resign after the defeat of his party in the elections of October 22.

1921, Oct. 13. Branting formed a second government, which remained in office until April 6, 1923, and was followed in

1924, Oct. 18. By the **third Branting government.** The prime minister died February 24, 1925, and his place was taken by **Rickard Sandler,** the cabinet continuing in power until June 1, 1926. These Socialist cabinets enacted a large body of **social reform legislation** for both workers and peasants, and greatly reduced the military establishment. After the downfall of the Socialist government in June 1926, there followed a number of Liberal and Conservative governments:

1926, June 7. Carl Ekman (Liberal), premier.

1928, Oct. 2. Arvid Lindman (Conservative) premier.

1930, June 1. Ekman again assumed power but the elections of September 1932 revealed substantial gains by the Social Democrats and Farmers and

1932, Sept. 24. **Per A. Hansson** became premier of a Socialist government, with Sandler as foreign minister. This government did much to combat the evils of the depression by introducing large-scale public works, drastically economizing in administration, and passing a long-term unemployment insurance act (May 1934). The government also undertook a **program of rearming** which appeared essential after the rise of Hitler and the rapid deterioration of German-Russian relations.

1936, June 13. **Axel Pehrsson** (Agrarian) formed a cabinet, but after the elections of September 20 (Socialists 112 seats; Conservatives 44; Agrarians 36; Liberals 27),

Sept. 28. **Hansson again became premier,** his government representing a coalition of Socialists and Agrarians. (*Cont. p. 1223.*)

e. FINLAND

1917, Mar. 21. The Russian provisional government recognized Finland as an **independent state** within the proposed Russian federation, but the

Dec. 6. **FINNS PROCLAIMED THEIR COMPLETE INDEPENDENCE** of Russia, and this was recognized by the Soviet government (Jan. 2, 1918) as well as by Sweden (Jan. 4), France, and Germany (Jan. 6). In Finland itself there ensued a period of

1918, Jan. 28. **CIVIL WAR.** Finnish communists (*Reds*), supported by the Russian Bolsheviks, seized Helsingfors (Helsinki) and overran much of southern Finland, but in

Apr. The *Whites* (i.e. opponents of Bolshevism), led by **Baron Karl Gustav Mannerheim** and supported by a German force under **Gen. Rüdiger von der Goltz,** retook the capital (Apr. 13) and drove the Reds out of the country (**battle of Viborg,** April 30).

Oct. 8. **The Finnish diet elected Prince Frederick Charles of Hesse as king.** After the defeat of the Central Powers, Frederick Charles renounced the crown (Dec. 31). In the interval

Dec. 11. **Baron Mannerheim** had become **head of the state,** and the last German forces had departed (Dec. 17).

1919, June 6. **War with Russia** broke out again, over conflicting claims to Karelia. After desultory fighting, hostilities were concluded by the **treaty of Dorpat** (Tartu) of October 14, 1920, by the terms of which the independence of Finland was reaffirmed and Finland was given a narrow strip of territory between Murmansk and the eastern frontier of Norway, with the ice-free port of **Pechenga.**

July 17. A **democratic constitution** was adopted and

July 25. **KARL J. STAHLBERG was elected president** for six years.

1920, Dec. 16. **Finland joined the League of Nations,** and

1921, June 24. The League council assigned to Finland **sovereignty over the Aaland Islands,** on condition that the islands be given an autonomous régime.

1922, Oct. 14. Passage of an **agrarian law** which inaugurated the breakup of the large estates and the distribution of the land to the peasants.

1925, Feb. 16. **LAURI RELANDER** succeeded Stahlberg as **president.**

1930, Oct. 14. **Attempted coup of Gen. Kurt Wallenius** and his fascist *Lapua* organization.

1931, Feb. 16. **PEHR SVINHUFVUD** became president. During his term of office he threw his influence in the direction of conservatism, encouraging the fascist elements to attempt

1932, Feb. 27–Mar. 7. **Another Lapua uprising.** Once again the movement failed. Wallenius was arrested and November 21 more than fifty leaders were convicted. The organization was disbanded, but in 1933 there emerged the *Patriotic National Movement,* similar to the Lapuan.

1933, May 4. The government forbade the military organization of political parties and groups, and

1934, Apr. The wearing of uniforms and political emblems was prohibited.

1935, Aug. 28. The Finnish foreign minister for the first time joined in the meeting of ministers of the other Scandinavian states. Thereafter Finland regularly participated in these meetings. In view of the changed conditions in the Baltic after Hitler's rise to power, Finland attempted to form a **bloc of Scandinavian and Baltic states** to hold a balance between Germany and Russia. In close collaboration with these states Finland proceeded to **refortification of the Aaland Islands,** despite the opposition of the inhabitants.

1937, Feb. 15. **KYOSTI KALLIO,** premier and leader of the Agrarian Party, **was elected president,** with support of the Social Democrats.

1938, Nov. 22. The **government dissolved the Patriotic National Movement,** which was the spearhead of fascism.

1939, May 17. Finland, together with Norway and Sweden, declined the German offer of a mutual non-aggression pact, but at the same time made known its opposition to the Soviet suggestion of a joint Russian-British-French guarantee of the independence of all the Baltic States. Relations with Russia continued cool, the more so as the Soviet delegate blocked League approval of the refortification of the Aaland Islands.

CULTURAL DEVELOPMENTS

The novelists **Selma Lagerlöf** (1858-1940) of Sweden and **Sigrid Undset** (1882-1949) of Norway won Nobel prizes for literature (1909 and 1928 respectively). **George Brandes** (1842-1927) of Denmark was the foremost literary critic. In Finland **Frans Eemil Sillanpää,** also a novelist, won the 1939 Nobel prize. Finland's greatest contribution to the arts has been the symphonies and songs of **Jan Sibelius** (1865-1957). Finland was also the birthplace of the modern architects of international renown, **Eliel** (1873-1950) and **Eero** (1910-1961) **Saarinen.** (*Cont. p. 1223.*)

C. NORTH AMERICA, 1914-1939

1. THE UNITED STATES

(*From p. 831*)

1917, Apr. 6. WAR DECLARED ON GERMANY (see above, p. 970). Diplomatic relations with Austria-Hungary were terminated April 8, but war was declared only December 7. Diplomatic relations with Turkey were severed April 20, but war was never formally declared on either Turkey or Bulgaria.

May 18. Selective Service Act passed, providing for the registration of those between 21 and 31 years inclusive. On June 5 local draft boards registered 9,586,508 men. On June 5, 1918, another million (those who had come of age during the year) were added. On September 12, 1918, a third registration, of those between 18 and 48 years, added another 13,228,-762 men.

June 13. First division embarked for France.

June 15-1918, May 6. The **Espionage Act,** the **Trading-with-the-Enemy Act** (Oct. 6, 1917) and the **Sedition Act** (May 6, 1918).

July. War Industries Board created and placed in complete charge of all war purchases.

Aug. 10. The **Lever Act,** establishing control over food and fuel. **Herbert Hoover,** food administrator.

Sept. 1. Grain Corporation inaugurated, which fixed price of grain and financed the 1917, 1918, and 1919 crops.

Oct. 3. War Revenue Act, greatly increasing income tax and imposing an excess profits tax on business earnings of corporations and individuals.

Nov. 2. Lansing-Ishii agreement, reaffirming the assurances of the Root-Takahira agreement (1908), with the admission by the United States that "territorial propinquity" gave Japan special interests in China.

Dec. William G. McAdoo, secretary of the treasury, made director-general of the railroad administration.

Dec. 18. Under stress of war conditions and the need of food conservation congress had in August 1917 prohibited the use of food products in the making of distilled beverages. Ownership of large numbers of breweries and distilleries by persons of German origin accentuated popular resentment against liquor traffic. As a result, congress adopted the **eighteenth amendment,** prohibiting the manufacture, sale, and transportation of alcoholic liquors, and sent it to the states for ratification. It became part of the constitution January 29, 1919.

1918, Jan. 8. Fourteen Points set forth by President Wilson in an address to congress defining war aims of the United States (p. 974).

Apr. 5. War Finance Commission created with fund of $500,000,000 for financing essential industries.

Apr. 10. Webb-Pomerene Act exempting export associations from the restraints of the anti-trust laws, with a view to encouraging export trade.

July 18-Nov. 11. American troops participated in six prolonged assaults upon German positions. Two of these were conducted wholly by American forces: **battle of St. Mihiel** (Sept. 12-16) and that of the **Meuse-Argonne** (Sept. 26-Nov. 11), in which 1,200,000 men were engaged (p. 975).

Nov. 11. Armistice signed (see First World War).

Dec. 13. Arrival of President Wilson in France, for the peace conference.

1919, Mar. 2. Senate round-robin, declaring the opinion of 39 senators that only after the establishment of peace should the League of Nations concern the negotiators.

July 10-1920, Mar. 19. Treaty of Versailles before the senate. Strong objection developed to the treaty. Wilson refused to accept amendments or reservations. On November 19 the senate defeated the treaty with and without reservations. Finally, on March 19 (1920) the treaty with reservations was rejected by a vote of 49 to 35. Wilson then vetoed a joint resolution of congress declaring war with Germany at an end. A similar resolution was passed

July 1921, and signed by Harding.

Sept. 22–1920, Jan. 8. Steel strike. Although the public sympathized with the steel workers, the strikers were defeated.

Oct. 28. The **National Prohibition Act,** commonly known as the **Volstead Act,** passed over President Wilson's veto. It defined as intoxicating all beverages containing more than one-half of 1 per cent of alcohol; provided several regulations for the manufacture and sale of alcohol for industrial, medicinal, and sacramental purposes. Strengthened by amendments of 1921 and 1929.

1920, Feb. 28. Transportation Act signed by President Wilson, giving the Interstate Commerce Commission power to establish and maintain rates which would yield a "fair return upon the aggregate value of the railway property of the country," and power to prescribe minimum rates. Prosperous roads were to share profits with the less prosperous. The commission was empowered to draw up a plan for the consolidation of the railway lines into a limited number of systems, such combinations to be exempt from operation of the anti-trust laws.

Mar. 1. The railroads were returned to their owners.

1920, June 5–1928. Merchant Marine Acts. Under the act of 1920 the Shipping Board was to dispose of the wartime merchant fleet to private parties, and to operate those ships which it could not sell; to establish new shipping routes and to keep ships in these services until private capital could be attracted to them. These measures failing to interest private capital, the Merchant Marine Act of 1928 established a revolving fund from which construction loans up to three-fourths of the costs of building were to be made to private operators, and private owners were to be given, as an inducement to shipbuilding and operation, long-term mail-carrying contracts. In effect the act of 1928 provided for subsidies to the merchant marine.

1920, June 20. Water-Power Act passed, creating a federal Power Commission composed of the secretaries of war, interior, and agriculture and subordinate appointive officers. Its authority extended to all waterways on public lands, to all navigable streams, including falls and rapids. It might license power companies to utilize appropriate dam sites for periods not exceeding fifty years.

Aug. 28. Nineteenth amendment, providing for woman suffrage.

Sept. 8–11. Transcontinental air mail service established between New York and San Francisco, 16,000 letters being carried.

Nov. 2. The Westinghouse Electrical Company arranged the **first general radio broadcast** for the national election. On November 31 the same company broadcast the first regular evening program.

Nov. 2. Warren G. Harding (Republican) elected president over **James M. Cox** (Democrat), 404 electoral votes to 137.

1921, Mar. 4–1923, Aug. 2. WARREN G. HARDING, twenty-ninth president.

Apr. 20. Colombian treaty ratified by the senate; the United States was to pay Colombia $25,000,000 for the loss of Panama and to grant free access to the Panama Canal.

May 19. Immigration Act signed, limiting the immigrants from a given country to 3 per cent of the number of foreign-born persons of such nationality resident in the United States according to the U.S. Census of 1910.

May 27. Emergency Tariff Act, raising duties on agricultural products, wool, and sugar. It placed an embargo on German dyestuffs; those products that could not be made in the United States were put on a licensing basis.

Aug. 24. Treaty of peace signed with Austria.

Nov. 12–1922, Feb. 6. WASHINGTON CONFERENCE. Aug. 11 President Harding issued a call to Great Britain, France, Italy, and Japan to meet for discussion of naval limitation, and to the same powers plus Belgium, Netherlands, Portugal, and China for discussion of questions affecting the Pacific and the Far East. For the agreements concluded see p. 1122.

1922, Feb. 11. By the **Yap treaty** (Feb. 11) the United States secured equality with Japan and other nations in the use of cable and wireless facilities in Yap and other Japanese mandates.

Mar. 24. Four-power treaty ratified by the senate.

Mar. 29. Five-power naval treaty ratified.

Apr. 1–Sept. 4. Strike of coal miners in protest against wage reductions and in support of the check-off system by which the unions require employers to deduct union fees from wages. **Herrin riots** in Illinois.

July 1–Sept. 13. Railway shopmen's strike in protest against wage reductions set by Railway Labor Board.

Sept. 19. Fordney-McCumber Tariff Act passed. Contained highest rates in American tariff history. *Ad-valorem* duties were to be assessed on the foreign value of the goods. The act explicitly stated that the principle underlying American protection was to be that of equalizing the cost of American and foreign production.

Nov. 20. An American observer sent to the Lausanne conference. This break with the administration's policy of non-interference in European affairs was largely due to the concern of American oil interests over the oil situation in the Near Eastern fields, where a British monopoly was feared.

1923–1930. Refunding of debts owed the United States by Allied Powers. During and immediately following the war the United States lent to foreign powers a total of $10,350,000,000. The first refunding agreement was with Great Britain, which was to pay over a period of 62 years, with interest at 3.3 per cent. The settlement with Italy came in November 1925, with interest rate fixed at 0.4 per cent. That with France was in April 1926, with interest at 1.6 per cent over a period of 62 years. By May 1930 seventeen nations had come to terms with the United States.

Aug. 2. CALVIN COOLIDGE became thirtieth president upon death of Warren G. Harding.

1924, Jan. 14. Gen. Charles G. Dawes chosen chairman of reparation commission expert committee. **Conference of London** (July 16–Aug. 16) used the report as a basis of agreement (p. 1123).

Feb.–Mar. Teapot Dome oil scandal. On April 7, 1922, **Albert Fall,** secretary of the interior, leased the Teapot Dome oil reserve to Harry F. Sinclair, and by agreements of April 25 and December 11, 1922, he leased the Elk Hills reserve to Edward L. Doheny. Secrecy attending the leases, combined with the sudden opulence of Fall, led to senate investigation under direction of Senator Thomas J. Walsh. It was shown that Sinclair had personally befriended Fall, while Doheny had "loaned" $100,000 to Fall without security or interest. As a result, Edwin Denby, secretary of the navy, resigned (Fall had previously resigned), and in 1927 the supreme court ordered the reserves returned to the government.

May 19. Soldiers' Bonus Bill for veterans of the First World War passed over the president's veto.

May 26. Immigration Bill signed, limiting annual immigration from a given country to 2 per cent of the nationals of the country in the United States in 1890. A further provision of the law stipulated that from July 1, 1927 (later deferred to 1929) the annual immigration should be limited to 150,000, to be apportioned among the different countries in proportion to the relative strength of the various foreign elements represented in the American population in 1920. The bill provided for the total exclusion of the Japanese, thereby abrogating the gentlemen's agreement. Protest from Japan and resulting ill feeling.

May 27. Rogers Bill signed consolidating the diplomatic and consular services.

Nov. 4. Calvin Coolidge elected president over John W. Davis (Democrat) and Robert M. La Follette (Progressive) by 382 electoral votes to 136 for Davis and 13 for La Follette.

1925 Mar. 4–1929, Mar. 4. CALVIN COOLIDGE president.

1925–1929. Agricultural legislation. In February 1922 the **Capper-Volstead Act** granted to agricultural associations and co-operatives the right to process, prepare, handle, and market their goods in interstate commerce. In March 1923 the **Federal Intermediate Credit Act** provided for the creation of a system of federal intermediate credit banks for the purpose of handling agricultural paper exclusively. Agriculture continuing in a depressed state, legislation was shortly introduced into congress with a view to its rehabilitation. The **McNary-Haugen Bill,** a measure designed to make the tariff on agricultural products effective, was defeated in the house in June 1924 and again in May 1926. In June 1926 it was defeated in the senate, but in February 1927 it passed both houses, only to be vetoed by Coolidge. In April and May 1928 it again passed both houses but was again vetoed by the president. This measure, as well as the export debenture plan, was opposed largely because of price-fixing and subsidy features. In June 1929 the **Agricultural Marketing Act** of the Hoover administration was enacted with its plan for the redemption of agriculture through voluntary co-operation and self-discipline under governmental auspices. Producers were to be encouraged to form effective marketing corporations, owned and controlled by themselves. A **Federal Farm Board** was created with a revolving fund of $500,000,000 for loans to co-operatives and with power to create stabilization corporations. Grain and cotton stabilization corporations bought extensively with a view to sustaining prices of farm products, but to little avail.

1925, June. Secretary of state Frank B. Kellogg charged the Calles government in Mexico with failure to protect American lives and property rights, creating tension between the two countries which was increased by the enactment of the Mexican Petroleum Law and the Alien Land Law in December 1925 (p. 1070).

May 20–21. Charles A. Lindbergh made the **first non-stop New York to Paris flight,** alone in the monoplane *Spirit of St. Louis.* His time was 33 hours 39 minutes.

1927, Oct. Dwight W. Morrow appointed ambassador to Mexico. By his tact and understanding he secured

Dec. The amendment of the **Mexican Petroleum Law,** improving markedly the relations between the two countries.

1928, Aug. 27. The **pact of Paris** (Kellogg pact) signed (p. 1124).

Nov. Herbert Hoover (Republican) elected president over **Alfred E. Smith** (Democrat) by 444 electoral votes to 87.

1929, Jan. 15. Pact of Paris ratified by the senate, with the declaration that it did not curtail the country's right of self-defense; that the treaty was not inconsistent with the Monroe Doctrine; and that it did not commit the United States to engage in punitive expeditions against aggressor states.

1929, Mar. 4–1933, Mar. 4. HERBERT HOOVER, thirty-first president.

1929, Oct. STOCK MARKET CRASH, the culmination of the boom market and unrestrained speculation of the Coolidge era. It ushered in prolonged depression which gradually settled upon the country with increasing unemployment, bank failures, and business disasters.

1930, Jan. 21–Apr. 22. London naval conference, resulting in a three-power treaty by the United States, Great Britain, and Japan (p. 1125).

Mar. CLARK MEMORANDUM ON THE MONROE DOCTRINE made public by the state department. Written by J. Reuben Clark, undersecretary of state two years before, the memorandum declared: 1. The Monroe doctrine is unilateral. 2. *"The Doctrine does not concern itself with purely inter-American relations."* 3. *"The Doctrine states a case of the United States versus Europe, not of the United States versus Latin America."* 4. The United States has always used the doctrine to protect Latin-American nations from the aggressions of European powers. 5. The Roosevelt corollary is not properly a part of the doctrine itself, nor does it grow out of the doctrine.

June 17. Smoot-Hawley Tariff Act signed by Hoover in spite of protest of more than 1000 trained economists. Duties higher than ever. In many instances the duties on raw material were 50 to 100 per cent greater than in 1922 schedules. This led to widespread reprisals and retaliation by other countries. By the end of 1931 some 25 countries had taken steps to retaliate.

July 21. London naval treaty ratified by the senate.

1931, June. Debt and reparations moratorium (p. 1125).

June. Wiley Post and **Harold Gatty** circumnavigated the globe by air in eight days, 15 hours 51 minutes.

1932, Jan. 7. Stimson doctrine enunciated by the secretary of state. Stimson, in notes to Japan and China, stated that the United States would not *"recognize any situation, treaty, or agreement which may be brought about by means contrary to the covenants and obligations of the*

pact of Paris." This was in protest against Japanese occupation of Manchuria.

Feb. 2. Reconstruction Finance Corporation created with a fund of $500,000,000 and the right to borrow more money, for the purpose of making available government credits to release the frozen assets of financial institutions and to provide aid for the railways.

Feb. Norris Anti-Injunction Act, declaring "yellow-dog" contracts unenforcible before the federal courts and providing that certain types of activity in labor conflicts should be immune from injunctions. It provided that *"no person participating in, or affected by, such disputes shall be enjoined from striking, or from striving for the success of the strike by customary labor-union effort, short of fraud or violence."* The immunity extended to all persons *"in the same industry, trade, or occupation"* rather than merely to employers and their own employees.

Nov. Franklin D. Roosevelt (Democrat) elected president over Herbert Hoover (Republican) by 472 electoral votes to 59.

Dec. 15. Default of various European governments in payment of war debts owed to the United States.

1933, Feb. 6. Twentieth amendment to the constitution proclaimed. It provided that after October 15, 1933, senators and representatives should take office January 3 following the election and that congress should convene annually on that date. The president and vice-president were to take office January 20, after election.

Feb. 14. Closing of all banks in the state of Michigan gave warning of an impending **banking crisis.** Bank holidays spread from state to state until the climax was reached on the night of March 3.

Mar. 4. FRANKLIN D. ROOSEVELT, thirty-second president. Banks closed and business virtually at a standstill.

Mar. 6. Banks closed for four days by proclamation of the president and an embargo placed on the export of gold in order to protect the gold reserve.

Mar. 9. Congress convened in special session, legalized the president's action with respect to banks and authorized the comptroller of the currency to take charge of insolvent banks. Within a week after the president's proclamation the sound banks began to reopen.

1933–1936. NEW DEAL AGRICULTURAL LEGISLATION: May 12, 1933, the **Agricultural Adjustment Act** became law. Its aim was the establishment of that parity for farm products which had existed in the period 1909–1914. This was to be achieved through removal of the agricultural surplus by means of compensated crop curtailment, financed through the licensing and taxing of the processors of farm products. Provision was also made for the refinancing of farm mortgages.

The **Farm Credit Act** (approved June 16, 1933) authorized the **Farm Credit Administration** to centralize *"all agricultural credit activities."*

The **Farm Mortgage Refinancing Act** (approved January 31, 1934) created the **Federal Farm Mortgage Corporation** to aid further in the refinancing of farm debts and guaranteed both as to principal and interest federal bonds exchanged for consolidated farm loan bonds.

The **Farm Mortgage Foreclosure Act** (approved June 12, 1934) extended the lending authority of the land bank commissioner to permit him to make loans to farmers for the purpose of enabling them to redeem farm properties owned by them previous to foreclosure regardless of when foreclosure took place.

Frazier-Lemke Farm Bankruptcy Act (approved June 28, 1934) facilitated agreements between distressed farmers and their creditors and granted extension of time to farmers during which they might remain in possession of their farms.

The **Crop Loan Act** (approved February 23, 1934) permitted the Farm Credit Administration to make loans to farmers in 1934 for crop production and harvesting.

The **Cotton Control Act** (approved April 21, 1934) placed the production of cotton on a compulsory rather than a voluntary basis.

The **Jones-Costigan Sugar Act** (approved May 9, 1934) included among the basic crops of the original Agricultural Adjustment Act sugar beets and sugar cane.

Tobacco Control Act (approved June 28, 1934) placed the production of tobacco on a compulsory basis.

The Frazier-Lemke Farm Bankruptcy Act was subsequently declared unconstitutional, while January 6, 1936, the **Agricultural Adjustment Act** met a similar fate. The objective of the latter act was then achieved by the **Soil Conservation Act** by which farmers were paid for planting soil-conserving crops in lieu of the ordinary staples.

1933-1934. NEW DEAL BANKING LEGISLATION: the **Emergency Banking Relief Act** (approved March 9, 1933) gave the president power to regulate transactions in credit, currency, gold and silver, and foreign exchange. It also authorized the secretary of the treasury to require the delivery of all gold and gold certificates; provided for the appointment of conservators of national banks in difficulties.

The **Banking Act of 1933** (approved June 16, 1933) extended federal reserve open-market activities; created the **Federal Bank Deposit Insurance Corporation** to insure deposits; regulated further the operations of member banks and separated security affiliates.

The **Bank Deposit Insurance Act** (approved June 19, 1934) amended deposit features of the Banking Act and raised the amount eligible for insurance of each depositor to $5000.

1933-1934. NEW DEAL HOME FINANCING: the **Home Owners' Refinancing Act** (approved June 13, 1933) created the **Home Owners' Loan Corporation** to refinance home mortgages.

The **Home Owners' Loan Act** (approved April 27, 1934) guaranteed the principal of the HOLC's bond issues and permitted loans for repair of dwellings.

1933-1934. NEW DEAL MONETARY LEGISLATION: the **Gold Repeal Joint Resolution** (approved June 5, 1933) cancelled the gold clause in all federal and private obligations and made them payable in legal tender.

The **Gold Reserve Act** (approved January 30, 1934) authorized the president to revalue the dollar at 50 to 60 cents in terms of its gold content; set up a $2,000,000,000 stabilization fund.

The **Silver Purchase Act** (approved June 19, 1934) authorized the president to nationalize silver.

1933-1935. NEW DEAL RELIEF LEGISLATION: the **Federal Emergency Relief Act** (approved May 12, 1933) authorized the RFC to make $500,000,000 available for emergency relief to be expended by the **Federal Emergency Relief Administration** created by the act.

The **Civil-Works Emergency Relief Act** (approved February 15, 1934) appropriated an additional $950,000,000 available until June 30, 1935, for continuation of the civil-works program and for direct relief purposes under the FERA.

The **Emergency Relief Appropriation Act** of April 8, 1935, was designed to provide relief and work relief and to increase employment by providing for useful projects; it appropriated $4,000,000,000 to be used nominally at the president's discretion. It further appropriated unexpended balances of several earlier appropriations aggregating about $880,000,000.

1933-1934. NEW DEAL SECURITIES LEGISLATION: the **Securities Act of 1933** (approved May 27, 1933) provided for filing with the federal trade commission and for transmission to prospective investors of the fullest possible information, accompanied by sworn statements, about new security issues sold in interstate commerce or through the mails.

The **Securities Exchange Act** (approved June 6, 1934) provided for the regulation of securities exchanges and established a securities and exchange commission.

1933-1935. NEW DEAL LABOR LEGISLA-TION: the **Labor Disputes Joint Resolution** (approved June 19, 1934) abolished the national labor board and created a federal agency for the investigation and mediation of labor disputes growing out of the **National Industrial Recovery Act** (NIRA).

The **Railway Pension Act** (approved June 27, 1934) provided a comprehensive retirement system for railway employees based on employer and employee contributions. This act was subsequently declared unconstitutional.

The **Crosser-Dill Railway Labor Act** (approved June 27, 1934) provided for the settlement of labor disputes on the railroads and outlawed company unions.

The **Wagner-Connery Labor Relations Act,** of July 5, 1935, was designed to satisfy the complaints of labor organizations against provisions of the Recovery Act of 1933 as it affected them, and also to remedy their disappointment at losing the advantage of these provisions by the invalidation of that act. It declared it the policy of the United States to encourage collective bargaining and to protect employees' freedom of self-organization, and their negotiating as to their employment through representatives of their own choosing. New **National Labor Relations Board** created.

1933-1936. FOREIGN POLICIES of the New Deal: November 17, 1933, diplomatic **relations with Russia** were resumed, ending policy of non-recognition which had prevailed since the overthrow of the Kerensky government in 1917.

The **Johnson Debt Default Act** (approved April 13, 1934) prohibited financial transactions with foreign governments in default in payment of obligations to the United States.

The **Cuban Treaty** (ratified May 31, 1934) abrogated the Platt amendment.

Pan-American Conference convened at Buenos Aires, December 1, 1936, addressed by President Roosevelt in person, who outlined his program for an American peace program. Secretary Hull presented the plan for a neutrality pact for American nations.

1933-1935. OTHER NEW DEAL LEGISLA-TION: the **Beer-Wine Revenue Act** (approved March 22, 1933) levied a tax of $5 on every barrel of beer and wine manufactured; re-enacted portions of the Webb-Kenyon Act as a protection to states whose laws prohibited liquors with alcoholic content in excess of 3.2 per cent. The states were left in control of the sale and distribution of liquor.

1933, May 18. The **Tennessee Valley Authority Act** created the Tennessee Valley Authority to maintain and operate Muscle Shoals and to develop the water-power resources of the Tennessee Valley. Also to improve the economic and social status of the valley population.

June 16. The **Emergency Railroad Transportation Act** created a federal co-ordinator of transportation.

June 16. The **National Industrial Recovery Act** created a national recovery administration to supervise the preparation of codes of fair competition and to guarantee to labor the right to organize and bargain collectively; also made provision for a program of public works. The act was declared unconstitutional by the supreme court, May 27, 1935.

Dec. 5. Ratification of the twenty-first amendment, repealing the eighteenth or prohibition amendment.

1934, June 12. Reciprocal Tariff Act, authorizing the president, for a period of three years, to negotiate trade agreements with foreign countries without the advice and consent of the senate; gave the president the power to raise and lower tariff rates by not more than 50 per cent.

June 19. The **Communications Act** created a federal commission to regulate interstate and foreign communications by telegraph, telephone, cable, and radio. It abolished the Federal Radio Commission and transferred its functions, and those of the Interstate Commerce Commission, with respect to telephone and telegraph, to the new commission.

1935, Aug. 9. The **Motor Carrier Act** placed interstate bus and truck lines under control of the Interstate Commerce Commission.

Aug. 14. Social Security Act. Its primary objects were: (1) to provide, in co-operation with each of the states, systems in the states for the payment of support to the needy aged; (2) to pay sums to persons during limited periods after their loss of employment. Provision was also made for federal aid toward states' aid for needy, dependent children, for crippled children, for neglected children, for the vocational rehabilitation of the disabled, for health-service agencies, and for the blind. The purpose as to old-age pensions was to be effected in the first place by the government's matching states' allowance to needy persons over the age of 65 years, up to $15 a month for each case. A tax on employees and a tax at an equal rate on the payrolls of employers was to be levied, starting in 1937 at 1 per cent and rising by steps to 3 per cent in 1949, to provide a fund out of which, not before January 1, 1942, qualified employees retiring at 65 would receive to the end of their life payments of from $10 to $15 per month.

To help states pay allowances to persons losing employment, the act created a separate tax of 1 per cent the first year, 2 per cent the second, and 3 per cent the third, and thereafter on employers' payrolls, starting with the payrolls of 1936.

Aug. 26. Public Utility Holding Company Act. Purpose: (1) doing away with holding companies among the public-utility enterprises serving communities with electricity except where such companies might be needful; (2) regulating the relations of remaining holding companies and their relations with the subsidiary companies that they controlled. The **Federal Power Commission** was made the administrative agency for these purposes. It was charged to proceed, after January 1, 1938, to limit each holding company system to "a single, integrated public-utility system," save for minor and appropriate transgressions of the exact limit. It was to make exceptions in favor of a holding company's plural system or systems if these would suffer loss of economies by segregation, if systems were all in one state or in adjoining states, and where the combination of systems was not too great to admit of localized management, efficiency of operation, and effective regulation.

Aug. 30. Guffey-Snyder Bituminous Coal Stabilization Act. Provisions of the act followed in great measure those of the bituminous coal code under the NRA. A national Bituminous Coal Commission created to administer the act, particularly to establish a code for the industry, embodying mandatory features detailed in the law. These included price-fixing features and a re-enactment of section 7-b of the Recovery Act, obliging employers to accept labor organizations and negotiate with representatives of the employees' own choosing. A tax of 15 per cent on the selling price or market value of soft coal produced was imposed on producers, but nine-tenths of this was remitted to producers filing acceptance of the code. Thus producers were at liberty to stay out, but must pay heavily for non-conformity. Declared unconstitutional, May 1936.

Aug. 30. Wealth-Tax Act. Use of federal power of taxation as a weapon against "unjust concentration of wealth and economic power." Increased surtaxes on individual yearly incomes of $50,000 and over.

1936, Nov. 3. Franklin D. Roosevelt re-elected president over **Alfred M. Landon** (Republican) by 524 electoral votes to 7. He carried every state except Maine and Vermont.

1937, Jan. 20. FRANKLIN D. ROOSEVELT inaugurated for second term.

Jan.–June. Widespread labor troubles resulting from efforts of the C.I.O. to organize the workers in the automobile and steel industries on the basis of industrial unionism. The **sit-down strike** made its appearance in the General Motors strike as a weapon of labor. The strike spread to Chrysler Corporation employees and to those of the Republic Steel Corporation, the Youngstown Sheet Steel and Tube Company, the Inland Steel Company, and the Bethlehem Steel Corporation. A strike among workers of the United States Steel Corporation was avoided when the company signed a contract with the C.I.O. on March 2. The strike of the employees of the Republic Steel Corporation resulted in bloodshed. Although the sit-down strikes and the aggressiveness of the C.I.O. in this period seriously divided public opinion, labor, through the application of the collective-bargaining provisions of the Wagner Labor Relations Act by the National Labor Relations Board, made substantial progress in the unionization of the mass-production industries, where the principle of collective bargaining had never before been admitted by employers.

Feb. 5. President Roosevelt in a special message to congress recommended the enactment of legislation empowering him to appoint *"additional judges in all federal courts without exception, where there are incumbent judges of retirement age who do not choose to resign."* This proposal aroused widespread opposition in and out of congress as an attempt on the part of the president to "pack" the **Supreme Court,** whose adverse decisions on various items of New Deal legislation had greatly displeased Mr. Roosevelt. After months of debate and controversy the bill failed of enactment, due largely to opposition of members of the president's own party in the senate.

Apr. 26. The president signed the **Guffey-Vinson Act,** successor to the Bituminous Coal Act of 1935, largely invalidated by the supreme court. The act created a **Bituminous Coal Commission,** to administer a code covering "unfair" practices, fixing minimum and, in some cases, maximum prices for coal, and dealing with arrangements for marketing.

May. Neutrality Act, reaffirming and somewhat enlarging statutes of August 1935 and February 1936. Whenever the president proclaimed a state of war outside of the Americas, the export of arms and munitions to the belligerents was to be prohibited. Certain materials designated by the president must be paid for before leaving the United States, and must be carried in foreign ships. All other trade with the combatants was subject to the cash, but not to the carry, restriction. In addition the act prohibited American citizens from traveling on belligerent ships and barred loans to warring powers.

Sept. 2. President Roosevelt signed the

Wagner-Steagall Act, declaring a federal policy of employing government funds and credit to help states and their subdivisions to remedy the housing shortage.

Oct. A **business recession,** the gradual onset of which had been evident for several months, brought sharp declines in the stock market. By November the recession had become general throughout the country.

Nov. 15. Congress assembled in special session, with earnest recommendation of the president that it carry forward his legislative program. A bill to regulate wages and hours passed the senate, but was recommitted in the house by a combination of Republicans and southern Democrats. Congress adjourned December 21, having accomplished little of a constructive nature.

1938, Oct. 24. Wages and Hours Law became operative. It provided for minimum wages and maximum weekly hours in industries affecting interstate commerce; it also prohibited child labor.

Nov. 8. State and congressional elections, showing substantial Republican gains for first time since 1928.

Dec. 24. The **declaration of Lima** adopted by 21 American states at the session of the Pan-American conference (p. 1130).

1939, Jan. 12. President Roosevelt asked congress for $552,000,000 for defense. Preparations were made for extensive fortifications in the Pacific and in the Caribbean (Puerto Rico and Virgin Islands). More and more openly the president expressed the sympathies of the United States for the European democracies. France was permitted to buy large numbers of military planes and the United States government itself embarked upon construction of 600 additional airplanes. After German annexation of Czechoslovakia the United States refused recognition of the change and imposed countervailing duties on imports from Germany. The danger of a German-Polish conflict led to

Apr. 15. Roosevelt's letter to Mussolini and Hitler asking for assurances that they would refrain from aggression on 31 named nations (p. 1130).

June. King George VI and Queen Elizabeth paid a four-day visit to the United States, the first reigning European sovereigns to set foot on American soil.

Despite all efforts of the administration, congress refused to modify the **Neutrality Act** which provided for an embargo on arms to belligerents. The president publicly stated that, indirectly at least, the Neutrality Act constituted an encouragement to a would-be aggressor. When, in August, the German-Polish conflict came to a head (p. 1132), Roosevelt appealed to Victor Emmanuel, Hitler, and Moscicki, but without avail. The American government secured from the belligerents a promise not to bombard open cities, and

Sept. 5. The **United States proclaimed neutrality** in the European war.

CULTURAL DEVELOPMENTS

Literature: Poetry flourished as never before in the United States, with its emancipation from traditional stereotypes. Some of the major "new" poets were: **Edwin Arlington Robinson** (1869–1935); **Edgar Lee Masters** (1869–1950); **Amy Lowell** (1874–1925); **Robert Frost** (1874–1963); **Carl Sandburg** (1878–1967); **Vachel Lindsay** (1879–1931); **Ezra Pound** (1885–1968); **Thomas S. Eliot** (1888–1965), though American born, is commonly considered with British authors.

Novelists were primarily concerned with social and psychological problems: **Theodore Dreiser** (1871–1945; *An American Tragedy,* 1925); **Sherwood Anderson** (1876–1941; *Winesburg, Ohio,* 1919); **Upton Sinclair** (1878–1968; *The Jungle,* 1906; Lanny Budd series beginning with *World's End,* 1940); **Sinclair Lewis** (1885–1951; *Main Street,* 1920; *Babbitt,* 1922; Nobel prize, 1930); **Ernest Hemingway** (1898–1961; *A Farewell to Arms,* 1929; *For Whom the Bell Tolls,* 1940; Nobel prize, 1954); **William Faulkner** (1897–1962; *The Sound and the Fury,* 1929; Nobel prize, 1950); **John Steinbeck** (1902–1968; *The Grapes of Wrath,* 1939; Nobel prize, 1962). Authors of less problematic novels were **Edith Wharton** (1862–1937), **Booth Tarkington** (1869–1946), **Willa Cather** (1874–1947).

The first notable American dramatist was **Eugene O'Neill** (1888–1953; Nobel Prize for Literature 1936); chief among his experimental plays are *Anna Christie* (1922), *Strange Interlude* (1928), *Mourning Becomes Electra* (1931). Later successful dramatists have been **Maxwell Anderson, Tennessee Williams, William Saroyan.**

Art: The paintings of **Thomas Hart Benton** (b. 1889), **Grant Wood** (1892–1942), and **John Steuart Curry** (1897–1946) show strong regional characteristics. Illustrations were the major output of **Charles Dana Gibson** (1868–1945), **Albert Sterner** (1871–1918), and **Rockwell Kent** (b. 1882). **Frank Lloyd Wright** (1869–1959) was a pioneer in the field of modern architecture. The sculptor **Sir Jacob Epstein** (1880–1959) was American born.

Music: Charles Ives (1874–1954) was one of the early experimenters in unconventional modern music in all media. **Ernest Bloch** (b. Switzerland 1880; d. 1959) wrote for orchestra and strings. **Wallingford Riegger** (1885–1961) was the first significant American composer to use the Schoenberg twelve-tone method. Composers of orchestral works are **Walter Piston** (b. 1894), **Henry Cowell** (b. 1897), **Aaron Copland** (b. 1900), **Samuel Barber** (b. 1910). **Gian-Carlo Menotti** (b. 1911) is the leading operatic composer, and musicals have been the major contribution of **Irving Berlin** (b. Russia 1888), **Cole Porter** (1893–1965), **Richard Rodgers** (b. 1902; with librettist **Oscar Hammerstein,** 1895–1960). **George Gershwin** (1898–1937) also composed successful operettas or musicals (*Of Thee I Sing,* 1933; *Porgy and Bess,* 1935).

(*Cont. p. 1225.*)

2. THE DOMINION OF CANADA

(*From p. 836*)

1914, Aug. 4. Entrance of Great Britain into the First World War. Message of Canada to the mother country: *"If unhappily war should ensue, the Canadian people will be united . . . to maintain the honor of the empire"* (Aug. 2). Special session of parliament called (Aug. 18) and a war budget voted. 30,000 volunteers embarked for England by the end of September.

1914. Nationalization of the Canadian Northern Railway forced by fear of imminent failure and a collapse of national credit. The **Grand Trunk Railway** was nationalized in 1920. The government operated about 23,000 miles of railway representing a capital of $1,652,000,000, known as **Canadian National Railways.** Gradual co-ordination of lines. Sir Henry Thornton appointed in 1922 as the non-political head of the system.

1915, Dec. 3. Internal war loan of $50,000,000 subscribed twice over; others for $100,000,000 (1916) and $150,000,000 (1917) were also oversubscribed.

1916, Feb. 3–4. The parliament buildings at Ottawa were destroyed by fire.

Nov. 11–1921. The DUKE OF DEVONSHIRE, governor-general.

1917, Sept. 26. Compulsory Military Service Act became law, conscripting men between ages of 20 and 45.

Oct. 6. Parliament dissolved and a **coalition cabinet** formed. The Liberal Party was split, with **Sir Wilfrid Laurier** opposing conscription; **French-Canadians** were dissatisfied with conscription and with English language requirements in the schools and failed to enlist. The elections (Dec. 17) resulted in a sweeping victory for the coalition; Quebec unrepresented in the cabinet.

Dec. 6. Explosion in Halifax Harbor with heavy loss of life and destruction of property.

1918, Mar. Woman Franchise Bill passed extending the federal vote to all women over 21 years of age.

Apr. Riots in Quebec due to enforcement of conscription; several civilians killed.

Nov. 11. Armistice declared (see First World War). Canada had supplied 640,886 men for the war; cost to Canada, over $1,500,-000,000.

1919, Feb. 17. Death of Sir Wilfrid Laurier.

1920, May 10. Official announcement that Canada would be represented at Washington by a Canadian resident minister; **new international status;** no appointment made until 1926, but treaties with the United States on North Pacific halibut fisheries (Mar. 1923), and for mutual assistance to prevent smuggling (June 6, 1924), both signed by a Canadian official (Ernest La Pointe).

July 10. Resignation of Sir Robert Borden. **Arthur Meighen** prime minister.

1921, Aug. 11. Arrival of **Lord Byng of Vimy** as governor-general (1921–1926).

Dec. 6. General elections resulting in Liberal (opposition) victory. **Mr. W. L. Mackenzie King** prime minister.

1923. Redistribution Bill increasing seats in house of commons from 235 to 245, with the loss of two seats by the eastern provinces and the gain of 12 by the western.

1924, Mar. 21. A liquor treaty between Great Britain and the United States was ratified by the Dominion house of commons and April 4 by the senate.

1925, Oct. 29. National elections. Liberal platform called for an adequate but moderate tariff, the reform of the senate, a strong immigration policy, government steps to develop the foreign trade of the Dominion, completion of the Hudson's Bay Railway, and the reduction of grain rates. Conservatives advocated higher tariff. Liberals had 101 seats in the house of commons, Conservatives, 118, Progressives, 23, Labor, 2, Independent, 1. The Progressives held the balance of power.

1926. King maintained a precarious hold on the government to June 28, when he resigned because of customs scandal. **Arthur Meighen** then organized a cabinet which was defeated on the first government measure placed before parliament.

Sept. 14. National elections. Liberals had 119 seats, but not a majority.

Sept. 25. Liberal cabinet, with **King** as prime minister.

Oct. 2. **Lord Willingdon**, new governor-general, came into office.

Nov. 10. **Vincent Massey** appointed first **Canadian minister to Washington.**

1927, Feb. **William Phillips** appointed American minister to Ottawa.

Nov. 15. **Election of Canada** to a seat on the **council of the League of Nations.**

1928. Appointment of **Canadian diplomatic representatives to Japan** and **France,** another evidence of Canadian nationhood. Proposal made that a British diplomatic representative to Ottawa be appointed since the governor-general is merely the personal representative of the king.

1929, Apr. 9. Canadian minister at Washington protested the sinking of the Canadian ship *I'm Alone* in the Gulf of Mexico by a United States coast guard prohibition patrol boat. On April 25 it was announced the case would be settled by arbitration.

Growing irritation in Canada at threat of hostile American tariff legislation against Canadian agricultural products.

Dec. 15. Agreement between Dominion government and the governments of **Alberta** and **Manitoba,** subject to ratification by Dominion parliament and provincial legislatures, providing for return of natural resources to the two provinces and for continuation of the annual subsidies previously received by the provinces.

1930, May 2. **Dunning Tariff** became effective; most drastic tariff revision since 1907. Gave expression to uneasiness and resentment aroused in Canada by the high duties on Canadian articles in the Smoot-Hawley Tariff of the United States. Imports from Great Britain given preferential treatment.

July 28. **National election.** Basic issue the economic depression and the failure of the Liberal government to provide a policy for relief of unemployment. Conservatives had 139 seats, a clear majority. **Richard B. Bennett** and Conservative cabinet took office on August 7.

Sept. 8–22. **Special session of Parliament** to enact emergency unemployment and tariff legislation. Public works appropriation of $20,000,000 voted as an unemployment relief measure, supplemented by a similar amount from the provinces, substantial contributions by the municipalities and $21,000,000 by the railways, making a total of between 80 and 90 million available for expenditure within the next 12 to 18 months. Tariff duties increased on about 125 classes of goods, including textiles, shoes, paper, agricultural implements, cast-iron pipe, fertilizers, electrical apparatus, jewelry, and meats.

Oct. 1. **Transfer of natural resources to Alberta** and **Manitoba.**

1931. In accordance with the decision of the federal-provincial conference held at Ottawa, April 7 and 8, the **statute of Westminster** stipulated that the British North America Act should remain unchanged. The statute of Westminster, providing that laws of the United Kingdom do not apply to any dominion unless that dominion so requests, was adopted by parliament without a division.

June 18. **Tariff of 1930 revised upward.** It was estimated that the new duties would cut off two-thirds of the goods previously imported from the United States.

1932, July 21–Aug. 21. **IMPERIAL ECONOMIC CONFERENCE IN OTTAWA.** Seven bilateral treaties signed by Great Britain, one of them being with Canada, gave raw material of the Dominion a preference of about 10 per cent in the British market. The United Kingdom imposed new duties on wheat and other imports in order to give Dominions this preference. British preferential tariffs also imposed on foreign meat, butter, cheese, fruit, and eggs. For Canada's benefit Great Britain removed the restriction on Canadian live cattle, placed a tariff of four cents on copper, and promised that the 10 per cent *ad-valorem* tariff on foreign timber, fish, asbestos, zinc, and lead would not be reduced unless Canada agreed. In return, Great Britain received concessions on manufactured goods entering Canada. Canada also signed new treaties with South Africa, Rhodesia, and the Irish Free State, and began the revision of existing treaties with Australia and New Zealand.

1933. **Railway legislation** embodying the recommendations of the royal commission in report of September 1932. Three trustees for C.N.R. and co-operation between it and the Canadian Pacific.

May 12. **Trade agreement with France** signed, and went into effect June 10. It provided for reciprocal tariff preferences on 1148 items.

Aug. 25. Canada joined in **wheat agreement** with United States, Argentina, Australia, and Soviet Union. The countries agreed to export a maximum of 560,000,000 bushels for 1933–1934, and, except for the Soviet Union and Danubian states, promised to reduce either acreage or exports by 15 per cent.

1934, July 3. The **Natural Products Marketing Act** assented to. It provided for the creation of a Dominion marketing board with powers to form local boards and to co-operate with marketing boards created by the provinces, and authorized the regulated marketing of any natural products, control by license of the export of any regulated products, and control of interprovincial marketing.

Aug. 4. Henry H. Stevens, minister of trade and commerce, in a privately printed pamphlet, made revelations which transformed widespread popular demand for governmental action to alleviate the depression into a demand for regulation of big business in Canada. Stevens resigned his cabinet position on October 27.

Oct. 1. The **Dominion Companies Act** went into force. Repealed the Companies Act of 1927 and established stringent regulations safeguarding the security of investors, shareholders, and creditors.

1935, Mar. 11. The **Bank of Canada** opened its doors, making effective the **Bank of Canada Act of 1934.** This privately owned but government-supervised institution served as a central bank.

Prime Minister Bennett early in the year proposed a **platform of social legislation** as the only means of escaping defeat in the face of growing popular dissatisfaction. Before adjourning July 5, parliament enacted a comprehensive series of laws designed to cope with the economic situation. Among them were: the **Wheat Board Act,** establishing a board to buy wheat at a fixed minimum price, the government to absorb the loss if the board failed to sell the wheat at a profit over the fixed minimum; an act providing for a **Dominion trade and industry commission** to administer the **Combines Investigation Act,** prohibiting monopolies operating to the detriment of the public; a **Fair Wages and Hours of Labor Act,** guaranteeing fair wages on public works and a 44-hour week; an **Employment and Social Insurance Act,** providing for contributory unemployment insurance for workers receiving less than $2000 per year, with certain industries excepted, equal premiums to be paid by employers, employees, and federal government; the **Minimum Wage Act,** authorizing the establishment of a federal agency to fix minimum wages in manufacturing and commerce; the **Limitation of Hours of Work Act** providing for eight-hour day and 48-hour week for industrial workers.

Aug. 14. Dissolution of parliament and call for general election.

Aug. 22. Victory of the Social Credit Party in Alberta, under leadership of **William Aberhart,** promising to every adult citizen of the province a regular income of $25 per month, funds for which were to be provided by a turnover tax of about 10 per cent on domestic products. Death-blow to Alberta's credit.

Oct. 14. General election. A Liberal landslide gave Liberals 171 seats, with eight seats

held by independent Liberals who would ordinarily support the party.

Oct. 23. King prime minister for third time.

Nov. 15. Prime Minister King signed at Washington the **reciprocal trade agreement with the United States.** The treaty granted Canada lower rates or other concessions on two-thirds of her exports by volume to the United States. The United States, in turn, received concessions on three-fourths of her dutiable exports to Canada.

Dec. 9-13. Conference of federal and provincial governments agreed unanimously that it was "imperative" to amend the constitution, and that Canada should have the power to amend its own constitution.

1936, June 17. Supreme court of Canada invalidated most of "New Deal" legislation enacted by the Bennett government in 1935.

1937, Jan. 28. The judicial committee of the privy council in London, England, declared unconstitutional the bulk of the "New Deal" legislation of the Bennett government, sustaining the decision of the supreme court of Canada.

Apr. The **demand of the C.I.O. for the recognition of the local branch** of the National Automobile Workers Association (an affiliate of the C.I.O.) in the Oshawa, Ontario, plant of the General Motors Corporation led to a **sit-down strike.** Premier Hepburn of Ontario intervened, denounced the C.I.O., and brought about an agreement (Apr. 23) granting concessions to workers on wages and working conditions, but withholding recognition of the N.A.W.A.

The Dominion minister of justice announced (Mar. 24) that the sit-down strike was wholly illegal in Canada and that all the powers of the government would be used to prevent its use in the Dominion.

Aug. 15. Prime Minister Mackenzie King appointed a royal commission (Rowell commission) to study **amendment of the British North America Act,** which now seemed imperative in view of the court decisions on social and economic legislation. The commission was charged specifically to consider the economic and financial relations between the federal and provincial governments, but was given wide powers to investigate all phases of the confederation.

1939, May. Visit of King George VI and Queen Elizabeth to Canada. They were the first reigning sovereigns to visit the Dominion and were given an enthusiastic reception.

Sept. 3. Britain's declaration of war on Germany (p. 1132) brought forth expressions of solidarity in Canada and the government at once took steps to aid the mother country in the great conflict. (*Cont. p. 1237.*)

3. NEWFOUNDLAND

(*From p. 837*)

1914, Aug. 4. Declaration of war by Great Britain. Newfoundland, like the other members of the empire, supported the mother country and sent troops.

1917. Resignation of Premier Sir Edward Morris, who was succeeded by **Sir William F. Lloyd.**

1919, May 23. Michael P. Cashin, premier. Elections (Nov. 1) resulted in the overthrow of the Cashin ministry and **Sir Richard A. Squires** became premier.

1923. William R. Warren, premier.

Dec. 26. Grave **charges of misappropriation of funds** brought against Sir Richard Squires and others (later acquitted) by Premier Warren. The latter was defeated in the assembly following the arrest of Squires (Apr. 22, 1924) and resigned. He was succeeded by **Walter Munroe.**

1933. NEWFOUNDLAND LOST ITS STATUS AS A DOMINION, and reverted to that of a crown colony, because of debt resulting from incompetence and corruption. A **royal commission** (appointed in March) reported

(Nov.) the following **recommendations:** (1) Replacement of the existing form of government by a special commission consisting of three British and three Newfoundlanders, with the governor as president. This commission was to have legal and executive authority subject to the supervisory control of the British government. (2) Readjustment and lowering of tariffs. (3) Assumption by the United Kingdom of responsibility for Newfoundland finances until the island should have become self-supporting. These recommendations were approved by the Newfoundland parliament November 29 and received the royal assent December 21.

1934. Substantial progress toward economic and financial recovery.

Oct. 1. The commission announced that on January 1, 1935, import duties would be revised, generally downward.

1936–1937. The commission continued to devote itself to the problem of **economic rehabilitation,** giving particular attention to the development of alternative sources of employment, to the encouragement of subsistence farming, to the relief of poverty, and to the improvement of medical and educational facilities.

D. LATIN AMERICA, 1914–1939

1. GENERAL

THOUGH MOST Latin American states, at the suggestion of the United States government, either declared war on Germany or broke off diplomatic relations, they played no part militarily in the First World War. Nevertheless the war period was of utmost importance for the entire region for the demand for raw materials made possible a **phenomenal expansion of trade.** Excepting for the slump of 1920–1921 this expansion continued from 1916 to 1929. It was accompanied by **great capital investments,** especially by the United States after the war, and by the emergence in the more advanced countries of a local industry. The **growth of the urban middle classes** enabled them to dispute with the great landholders the control of the government. At the same time the **agrarian proletariat** (on coffee, sugar, and other plantations) was reinforced by **workers in the oil-fields and mines,** as well as in the factories. The result was increased **demand for social legislation** (carried out, however imperfectly, in several states), together with political organization of

the lower classes (in many instances in alliance with the middle classes, at least for a time). These basic social changes created a ferment throughout the continent, the world depression adding its share to stimulate unrest.

Between the different Latin American states and between Latin America and the United States co-operation along various lines increased, despite periods of profound distrust between Latin America and the great neighbor in the north.

1915, May 24. The **first Pan-American financial conference** met at Washington.

May 25. Conclusion of an **arbitration treaty between Argentina, Brazil, and Chile** (the A.B.C. Powers).

1916, Apr. 3. A **Pan-American high commission,** meeting at Buenos Aires, worked out a scheme for improvement of telegraph and railway communication. A permanent high commission was created to elaborate uniform commercial laws.

1923, Mar.–May. The **fourth Pan-American**

Caribbean Sea

Atlantic Ocean

PANAMA

Panama R.

Caracas

Orinoco R.

VENEZUELA

Georgetown

Paramaribo

Cayenne

BRITISH GUIANA

DUTCH GUIANA

FRENCH GUIANA

Bogota

COLOMBIA

Rio Negro

Quito

ECUADOR

Amazon

River

B R A Z I L

Araguaya R.

Madeira R.

São Francisco R.

Salvador

PERU

Lima

BOLIVIA

Sucre

CHACO

TACNA ARICA

Pilcomayo R.

Paraguay R.

PARAGUAY

Paraná R.

Rio de Janeiro

São Paulo

Pacific

Asuncion

Paraná R.

Uruguay R.

URUGUAY

Ocean

A R G E N T I N A

Santiago

CHILE

Buenos Aires

Montevideo

Atlantic Ocean

Ocean

SOUTH AMERICA
in 1930

Shaded areas show territories in dispute

0 200 400 600 800

Miles

conference at Santiago resulted in various agreements providing for fact-finding commissions in cases of disputes, for trademark regulations, publication of documents, etc., in addition to many resolutions touching health, education, etc.

May 3.   Signature of the Pan-American treaty for the pacific settlement of disputes.

1928, Jan.-Feb.   The sixth Pan-American conference met at Havana. The Pan-American Union was placed on a treaty basis and various conferences arranged for matters of common interest. The United States, however, opposed a resolution directed against intervention in the internal affairs of other states.

Dec.-1929, Jan.   The Pan-American conference on conciliation and arbitration met at Washington, revised the treaty of May 3, 1924, declared for conciliation and arbitration of all disputes, and set up commissions to deal with cases as they should arise.

1930, Sept.   Meeting of the **first Pan-American conference on agriculture** at Washington.

1933.   President Roosevelt declared publicly against a policy of intervention in Latin America and made consistent efforts to demonstrate his policy of the "good neighbor." At the

1933.   Seventh Pan-American conference, at Montevideo. Secretary of state Hull did his utmost to remove distrust of the United States and impress upon the American states the need for confidence and collaboration.

1936, Dec. 1-23.   Pan-American conference for the maintenance of peace, in session at Buenos Aires. The American governments for the first time accepted the **principle of consultation** in case the peace of the continent should be threatened. A convention was drawn up to provide for a **common policy of neutrality** in the event of conflict between American states.

1938, Dec. 24.   The Pan-American conference, meeting at Lima (21 states represented) adopted the *Declaration of Lima,* which reaffirmed the absolute sovereignty of the various American states, but also expressed their determination to defend themselves against *"all foreign intervention or activities that may threaten them."* It provided further for consultation in case *"peace, security, or territorial integrity"* of any state should be menaced. The declaration, less outspoken than Washington desired, was a reflection of growing uneasiness, especially in the United States, over possible designs of the fascist powers of Europe upon Latin American territory.   (*Cont. p. 1239.*)

CULTURAL DEVELOPMENTS

In the realm of letters, Chile claims the poet **Gabriela Mistral** (1889-1957), winner of the 1945 Nobel prize in literature. Among contemporary artists Mexico's **José Clemente Orozco** (b. 1883) and **Diego Rivera** (1886–1965) are best known; likewise the composer **Carlos Chavez** (b. 1889). Prominent among modern South American composers are the Brazilian **Heitor Villa-Lobos** (1881–1959) and the Argentine-born **Alberto Williams** (1862–1952) and **Alberto Ginastera** (b. 1916).

2.   ARGENTINA

(*From p. 847*)

1916–1922.   HIPÓLITO IRIGOYEN, leader of the Argentine radicals, was **elected president** after an electoral reform (1912) made possible the expression of popular (mass) sentiment. During his administration he carried through a **program of social reform** (factory acts, regulations of hours, pensions, etc.). Irigoyen refused to give up neutrality during the First World War, although diplomatic relations with Germany were strained after the sinking of Argentine ships by German submarines (1917). Argentina supplied huge quantities of wheat and meat to the Allied powers.

1920.   Argentina became an original member of the League of Nations, but withdrew from the assembly in 1921 on rejection of an Argentine resolution that all sovereign states be admitted to the League.

1922–1928.   MARCELO ALVEAR, president. In general he continued the policies of his predecessor in the sphere of social legislation.

1928.   Irigoyen was again elected to the presidency, but

1930, Sept. 6.   JOSÉ URIBURU forced him from office. Irigoyen's assumption of wide personal powers had aroused much criticism, while the distress created by the world depression had provoked a demand for further relief measures. With Uriburu the landowning and big business and other **conservative groups returned to power.** After a temporary dictatorship

1932–1937.   AGUSTÍN JUSTO was regularly elected **president.** Political and social unrest continued and culminated in an unsuccessful **radical revolt** in the northeastern provinces (1933–1934).

1932, Nov. 17.   Carlos Saavedra Lamas, the foreign minister, published a proposed South American **anti-war pact,** which had already been accepted by several states. Argentina also (1933) resumed full membership in the League of Nations, taking an active part in the negotiations concerning the war between Bolivia and Paraguay (p. 1061).

1933. The government launched a **program of national economic recovery,** which achieved marked success. A commercial treaty with Great Britain made possible the shipment of large quantities of beef and wheat.

1935. Conflict between the Conservative government of Justo and the opposition Radical and Socialist Parties, which represented the majority of voters. **Fascist organizations** also opposed the government and formed a common front of the extreme Right (Oct.).

1936, Mar. In congressional elections, the Radical Party, under the leadership of former president Alvear, triumphed. A Leftist **Popular Front was organized** (May 1), but fascist groups continued to gain ground. The Rightist elements supporting the government formed a **National Front,** favoring a conservative dictatorship (May 31). The **Communist Party was declared illegal** (Nov. 10).

1937, Sept. 5. Presidential elections, bitterly contested. **Roberto M. Ortiz,** candidate of the government, was elected over the nominee of the Radical Party, Alvear. Efforts of the Leftist parties to prevent a quorum in a joint session of congress to confirm the election failed when a majority was declared sufficient, and Ortiz was proclaimed elected. He was inaugurated February 10, 1938.

1938-1940. Roberto M. Ortiz, president.

1939, Sept. 4. Argentina proclaimed neutrality in the Second World War. (*Cont. p. 1251.*)

3. CHILE

(*From p. 848*)

Chile remained neutral in the First World War despite violation of her neutrality by both German and British warships. The export of nitrate in large quantities to the Allied powers created a period of great prosperity.

1920, Jan. 10. Chile became a member of the League of Nations.

1920-1921. Chile suffered severely from the general world slump and the cessation of the demand for nitrate. The lower classes demanded a more democratic régime and extensive social legislation.

1920-1924. ARTURO ALESSANDRI, elected president after a disputed election. He was the candidate of the **Liberal Alliance Party** and advocated wide political, religious, and social reforms. His election represented a **victory for the middle classes,** supported by labor elements. But during his term Alessandri was unable to achieve much, partly because of the stagnation of the parliamentary system. In 1924 he was forced from office. After control by a military junta under **Gen. Luis Altamirano,**

1925, Jan. 23. A *coup d'état* engineered by **Maj. Cárlos Ibañez** resulted in the recall of Alessandri and the promulgation of a

Sept. 18. New constitution, providing for responsibility of the cabinet to the president, broader suffrage, separation of Church and State, provincial autonomy, etc.

Oct. 1. Alessandri resigned, in view of the continued disorder and uncertainty. He was succeeded by

1925-1927. EMILIANO FIGUEROA, who was, in turn, forced out by

1927-1931. GEN. CÁRLOS IBAÑEZ, who made himself **dictator-president,** and then promulgated many of the social reforms that Alessandri had advocated.

1929, June 3. SETTLEMENT OF THE TACNA-ARICA QUESTION, which had embittered the relations of Chile and Peru for many years (diplomatic relations severed 1910). Efforts of the United States (1922-1926) to mediate a settlement through a plebiscite led to no result, but served to bring about direct negotiations and the final agreement, by which **Chile received Arica** and **Peru was awarded Tacna,** Chile agreeing to accord Peru port and transportation facilities at Arica. Chile retained all territory taken from Bolivia (despite appeals of that country to the United States and Argentina), but accorded Bolivia a railway outlet to the Pacific. Thenceforth Chile and Bolivia drew closer.

1931. Ibañez resigned because of the general discontent with his measures of economy (made necessary by the world depression).

1931. JUAN MONTERO, representative of the conservative elements, was elected in opposition to Alessandri. Political and social unrest continued, and

1932, June 4. Montero was overthrown. A junta headed by **Cárlos Dávila** assumed power and adopted a socialistic policy, but

Sept. 13. **Dávila was overthrown** by a military coup and Alessandri became president once more, after an election (Dec. 24).

1932-1938. The **GOVERNMENT OF ALESSANDRI,** supported by a coalition of Conservative and Liberal Parties, assumed ever greater control of economic activity, enacting far-reaching social reforms. Marked improvement of economic conditions after 1933 did not, however, relieve the political tension. The government was opposed on the one hand by **fascist groups,** on the other by **Communists.**

1938, Sept. 5. A **fascist** (*Nacista*) **uprising** proved abortive, but in the ensuing elections the parties of the Left elected

1938-1941. PEDRO AGUIRRE CERDA, president. The Popular Front comprised Radicals, Socialists, and Communists, as against the combination of Conservative, Agrarian, and Liberal Parties which supported **Gustavo Ross.** The new régime promptly embarked on a policy of helping the worker (low bread prices, housing, education), despite strong protests from the agrarian groups.   (*Cont. p. 1253.*)

4. PARAGUAY

(*From p. 849*)

1912-1916. The **presidency of Edward Schaerer** was an era of progress and relative political stability. Trade, industry, grazing, and agriculture expanded, transportation and communications were improved, and foreign capital was invested. **Paraguay remained neutral during the First World War,** and in 1920 became an **original member of the League of Nations.**

1916-1919. Manuel Franco, president. On his death

1919-1920. José Montero, the vice-president, succeeded.

1920-1921. Manuel Gondra, president. He was forced to resign by a revolutionary group. After the short presidencies of **Eusebio Ayala** (1921-1923), **Eligio Ayala** (1923-1924), and **Luis Riart** (1924),

1924-1928. ELIGIO AYALA was **elected president.** Representing the Liberal groups, he inaugurated a policy of social legislation.

1928-1931. JOSÉ GUGGIARI, president. During his administration

1928-1930. The **dispute with Bolivia over the Chaco** territory came to a head. Despite earlier agreements (1913, 1915) the respective claims were still unsettled. On December 6, 1928, the forces of the two states clashed and war seemed inevitable. Diplomatic relations were severed and Paraguay appealed to the League of Nations, but the Pan-American conference at once offered to mediate. An **arbitration convention** was drafted (Aug. 31, 1929), but was rejected by both parties. Direct negotiations were agreed to, but skirmishes in the contested area continued until a **temporary arrangement** (return to *status quo ante*) was arrived at (Apr. 4, 1930).

1932-1935. THE CHACO WAR. The League of Nations and the Pan-American Union both called upon the two parties to desist from hostilities and accept neutral arbitration, but the numerous efforts to preserve peace resulted chiefly in added confusion. The Paraguayans, after a series of major campaigns, occupied the larger part of the Chaco, but failed in their attempts to invade Bolivian territory. During the war the **relations between Paraguay and Chile** became badly strained because of service of Chilean officers with the Bolivian army and employment of Chilean workmen by Bolivia.

1935. At the suggestion of the League of Nations, some twenty nations lifted the embargo on arms in favor of Bolivia, while retaining it against Paraguay. Thereupon **Paraguay announced withdrawal from the League.**

June 14. **Paraguay and Bolivia concluded a truce,** at the instance of the United States and five of the South American governments. A peace conference at Buenos Aires met in July. **Definitive peace** was not signed until July 21, 1938 (approved by plebiscite August 10). The treaty provided for arbitration of boundaries between American states. The territorial award, made by six American presidents (Oct. 10), assigned the **greater part of the Chaco to Paraguay,** but provided Bolivia with an outlet to the sea by way of the Paraguay River.

1936, Feb. 17. A **military revolt,** provoked by opposition of the army to the supposed weakness of the government in the peace negotiations, led to the **overthrow of President Ayala. Rafael Franco** became provisional president. Supported by a junta of officers, and by radical and nationalist elements, he made himself a military dictator.

Mar. 11. **Franco proclaimed a totalitarian state,** and introduced economic, social, and financial reforms. These policies antagonized Paraguayan and foreign interests, which resented the heavy taxation.

1937, Aug. 15. Franco was forced to resign as a

result of a bloodless *coup d'état*. **Felix Pavia,** of the Liberal Party, became provisional president and suppressed a number of counter-revolutionary movements.

Oct. 11. **Pavia** was elected **constitutional president.**

1939, Apr. 30-1940. **José Félix Estigarribia** was elected president.   (*Cont. p. 1254.*)

5. URUGUAY

(*From p. 849*)

Uruguay has, in the 20th century, enjoyed comparative stability and prosperity. During the administrations of
1907-1911. **Claudio Williman,**
1911-1915. **José Batlle y Ordóñez,**
1915-1919. **Feliciano Viera,**
1919-1923. **Baltasar Brum,** and their successors, many **social and administrative reforms** were initiated and the internal development of the country was rapid.

On the entry of the United States into the First World War, Uruguay expressed moral solidarity and later **severed relations with Germany.**
1919, Mar. 1. A **NEW CONSTITUTION** curtailed the powers of the president, created a **national council of administration** (nine members elected on proportional basis by popular vote and endowed with important functions), and **disestablished the Roman Catholic Church.**
1920. **Uruguay joined the League of Nations.**
1923-1927. **José Serrato, president.** He, and his successor,

1927-1931. **Juan Compisteguy,** continued and accelerated the policy of social reform until Uruguay, like the rest of the world, began to feel the pinch of the depression.
1931-1938. **GABRIEL TERRA, president.** He represented the more advanced wing of the Liberal Party, and soon found himself in conflict with the national council of administration concerning the division of executive authority. In view of the political and social unrest and the consequent threat of civil war,
1933. **Terra established a temporary dictatorship.**
1934, Apr. 19. A **new constitution** provided for a strong executive, restricted the powers of parliament, and established compulsory voting. **Terra was re-elected president** and
1935. A revolt against him was crushed.
1935-1938. The **Terra government** continued the work of social and economic reform, and Uruguay gradually experienced economic improvement.
1938-1943. **Alfredo Baldomir elected president** to succeed Terra.   (*Cont. p. 1255.*)

6. BOLIVIA

(*From p. 850*)

1913-1917. **Ismael Montes** president for his second term in office.
1917, Apr. 13. **Bolivia severed relations with Germany,** but did not declare war.
1917-1920. **José Gutiérrez Guerra, president.**
1920, Jan. 10. **Bolivia became an original member of the League of Nations.**
      Mar. 16. In the **Tacna-Arica dispute,** the Bolivian government took the stand that neither Chile nor Peru was entitled to the provinces. The Bolivian government claimed access to the Pacific, preferably through the port of Arica. On November 1 Bolivia appealed in vain to the League of Nations to secure such access.
      July 11. A *coup d'état* led to the overthrow of Gutiérrez Guerra, and
1921-1925. **JUAN BAUTISTA SAAVEDRA became president.** His administration was

marked by industrial development, public improvements, encouragement of agriculture and mining, flotation of large loans in the United States, etc. The **exploitation of oil** added greatly to the national resources.
1925, May 2. **José Cabino Villanueva, president.** His election was annulled (Sept. 1) by congress, because of fraud. Villanueva fled the country and
1926-1930. **HERNANDO SILES became president.**
1928-1929. **Dispute between Bolivia and Paraguay over the Chaco** region (p. 1061).
1929. **Settlement of the Tacna-Arica question** (p. 1060). Bolivia definitely lost Atacama, but obtained the right to use the Chilean-built railway between La Paz and Arica.
1930, May 28. **Overthrow of President Siles,** whose régime had become unpopular through economic depression, fall in the price of tin, closing of the mines, and resultant labor un-

rest. After a temporary government by a military junta, led by **Gen. Carlos Blanco Galinda,
1931. DANIEL SALAMANCA** was elected **president.**
1932-1935. The **CHACO WAR,** between Bolivia and Paraguay (p. 1061).
1934, Dec. President Salamanca was overthrown by a military coup, following serious defeats of the Bolivian forces. The vice-president, **Luis Tejada Sorzano,** assumed the presidency.
1936, May 17. Another coup led to the **fall of Tejada Sorzano,** who was replaced by a joint civil and military junta under **David Toro,** who established a dictatorship. Measures to promote economic revival were adopted (virtual government monopoly over the petroleum industry; confiscation of Standard Oil Co. properties, March 1937; efforts to control mining and banking). Toro's policies aroused much opposition and
1937, July 14. Toro was driven from office by fellow army officers.
1938-1939. GERMÁN BUSCH succeeded as **president.**
1939, Apr. 24. Busch assumed dictatorial powers, dissolving congress and suspending the constitution. All connection with European totalitarianism was, however, denied.
   Aug. 22. Death of President Busch. **Gen. Carlos Quintamilla** assumed power.

(*Cont. p. 1255.*)

7. PERU

(*From p. 851*)

1914, Feb. 4. A military revolt led to the **overthrow of President Guillermo Billinghurst.**
1914-1915. Col. Oscar Benavides served as provisional president.
1915-1919. José Pardo, president.
1917, Oct. 5. Peru severed relations with Germany, after attacks on Peruvian ships.
1919, July 4. A *coup d'état* led to the resignation and imprisonment of President Pardo, who was succeeded (Aug. 24) by
1919-1930. AUGUSTO LEGUÍA as president. Leguía's administration was noteworthy for **great material progress.** An extensive program of internal reform was undertaken, **large loans** were secured in the United States (1924, 1927, 1928), **education** was expanded, relations of Church and State revised, **social and labor legislation** enacted. For the rest, Leguía's régime was notorious for corruption.
1919, Dec. 27. A **new constitution** (went into effect January 18, 1920) introduced compulsory primary education, compulsory labor arbitration, income tax, etc.
1920, Jan. 10. Like most Latin-American states, **Peru joined the League of Nations** at the very outset.
1921-1929. The long-drawn **dispute with Chile over Tacna and Arica** (p. 1060), when finally settled, assigned Tacna to Peru.
1924, June 21. Signature of a **protocol with Ecuador,** envisaging negotiations concerning the old boundary dispute, and providing for arbitration in the event of failure of direct discussion.
1930, Aug. 25. . RESIGNATION AND FLIGHT OF LEGUÍA, following a revolt led by **Col. Luis Sánchez Cerro.** Leguía was captured and tried, but was acquitted. Sánchez Cerro became provisional president, but
1931, Feb.-Mar. A series of revolts obliged Sánchez Cerro to give way to **David Samanez Ocampo.**
   Oct. 11. Sánchez Cerro was elected president.
1932-1933. Threat of war with Colombia, over the disputed territory of **Leticia.** Peru took a strong line and prepared for war, though accepting proffered mediation of the League. The question was finally settled by agreement November 2, 1934.
1933, Apr. 9. A **new constitution** was introduced.
   Apr. 30. Assassination of Sánchez Cerro. He was succeeded at once by
1933-1939. OSCAR BENAVIDES, as president. Social and political unrest continued, despite the gradual recovery of the country from the depression. Benavides, supported by conservative and clerical elements, was opposed by the radical *Apra* (**Alianza Popular Revolucionaria Americana),** an organization in which the student element was strong. The Aprista opposition was held down with an iron hand.
1936, Oct. 11. The elections resulted in the **defeat of Benavides' candidate** by the Leftist groups, a Socialist being chosen president. Thereupon Benavides had the elections declared null and had his own term prolonged for three years.
   Dec. 8. The constituent assembly was dissolved and **Benavides became virtually a dictator.** The radical opposition was suppressed (**Public Security Law** of February 21, 1937) and efforts were made to counteract radicalism by the extension of social reform activities.
1938, June. The **boundary dispute with Ecua-**

dor threatened to end in war when the troops of the two states clashed on the frontier. On October 12 Ecuador appealed to several American presidents to mediate, but Peru took an uncompromising attitude toward Ecuadorean demands for cession of territory.

1939-1945. Manuel Prado Ugarteche president. *(Cont. p. 1256.)*

8. ECUADOR

(*From p. 852*)

1916-1920. Alfredo Baquerizo Moreno, president.

1917, Dec. 7. Ecuador severed relations with Germany because of the submarine campaign, but did not, like most other Latin American states, join the League of Nations at the conclusion of the war. During the war and immediate post-war period much progress was made in education, social legislation, and above all sanitation (work of the American **Col. William Gorgas** at Guayaquil, long a center of bubonic plague).

1920-1924. José Luis Tamayo, president. He was succeeded by

1924-1925. Gonzalo Córdova, who was driven from office by a military revolt led by **Gen. Francisco Gómez de la Torre** (July 9, 1925).

1926-1931. ISIDRO AYORA, president. He introduced

1929, Mar. 28. A **new constitution** which ended the military régime set up in 1925, but paved the way for endless disputes between the executive and the legislature. Ayora had elaborate social and labor laws enacted and adopted many financial reforms.

1931, Aug. 25. Ayora resigned. Col. Luis Alba became provisional president, but was forced to flee after a *coup d'état* (Oct.). There followed a period of utter confusion, marked by conflict between the executive and legislature and between the conservative and liberal groups. After the suppression of a revolt (Aug. 1932), **Martínez Mera** became president,

only to be replaced in December 1933 by **José M. Velasco Ibarra.**

1932-1934. The **Leticia dispute** between Peru and Colombia (p. 1063) gave Ecuador an opportunity to assert claims to portions of the Amazon Basin. In part motivated by these desires,

1934, Sept. 28. Ecuador entered the League of Nations.

1935, Aug. 20. President Ibarra was overthrown by a military junta, after he had attempted to assume dictatorial powers. He was replaced by **Antonio Pons,** who, in turn, was forced to resign.

Sept. 26. A **military dictatorship** under **Federico Páez** was set up, to prevent the election of a conservative (the dominant Liberal Party was split by dissensions).

1935-1937. DICTATORSHIP OF PÁEZ. He suppressed a number of movements directed against his régime, but after a conflict with a constituent assembly, convened to promulgate a new constitution,

1937, Oct. 22. Páez was obliged to resign.

1937-1938. Gen. G. Alberto Enríquez became provisional president. With support of the army he adopted strong measures to maintain his authority. At the same time he liberated many political prisoners, abrogated objectionable repressive legislation, and embarked upon the work of financial and legal reform.

1938, June-Oct. Growing tension in relations with Peru, due to the long-standing dispute about the boundary (p. 1063).

Dec. 2. The congress elected **Aurelio Mosquera Narváez president.** *(Cont. p. 1257.)*

9. COLOMBIA

(*From p. 854*)

1914-1918. José V. Concha, president. He represented the conservative groups which had been in power since 1884 and continued to rule the country until 1930. But even the conservative administrations of Colombia were obliged to initiate a measure of **social legislation** to meet growing pressure from the lower classes.

Colombia remained neutral during the First World War, but joined the League of Nations (Feb. 16, 1920).

1918-1921. Marco Fidel Suárez, president.

1919, Aug. 15. Signature of a contract with the **Tropical Oil Company** for exploitation of the Colombian oil-fields, one of the most important sources of national wealth.

1921, Apr. 20. The United States senate finally ratified the **Thomson-Urrutia treaty** (concluded

1914) with certain modifications, thus ending the long dispute with regard to Panama. The Colombian congress ratified it December 22.

1922–1926. PEDRO NEL OSPINA, president.

1922, Mar. 24. An award by the Swiss federal council ended a long-standing **boundary dispute with Venezuela** in favor of Colombia. A boundary treaty with Peru settled the frontier on that side.

1926–1930. MIGUEL ABADIA MENDEZ, president. During his administration the growing social tension found an outlet in a number of **major strikes,** in the course of which many were killed by the police and government forces.

1930–1934. The **election of ENRIQUE OLAYA HERRERA,** a moderate liberal, brought to an end the long domination of the conservative groups. The world depression brought with it a rapid decline in coffee prices, and necessitated heavy borrowing.

1932–1934. The **LETICIA DISPUTE** with Peru (p. 1063). Occupation of the town of Leticia by armed Peruvians brought the two countries to the verge of war. Under pressure from the Latin-American powers and the United States the disputants finally permitted supervision of the area by a League of Nations commission. By the final settlement (1934) Peru and Colombia proclaimed peace and amity and renounced armed action.

1934–1938. ALFONSO LÓPEZ became president, continuing the rule of the Liberal Party. The government now embarked upon far-reaching **social reforms,** aiming at government control of sub-soil riches, agrarian reforms, etc. **Primary education** was made free and compulsory, and the Catholic Church was disestablished. All these policies called forth the opposition of the conservatives and clericals, who were further aided by the **split in the Liberal ranks** into moderate and progressive or even radical wings. Nevertheless, in the

1938. Election the Liberals were able to maintain a majority, and

1938–1942. EDUARDO SANTOS, a moderate Liberal, **became president.** The Liberals won in the elections of March 19, 1939.

(*Cont. p. 1257.*)

10. VENEZUELA

(*From p. 854*)

1909–1935. Dictatorship of JUAN VICENTE GÓMEZ, who served during this period as either president or chief of the army. Gómez pursued a policy of nepotism and took care to have a congress entirely subservient to him. For the rest, the period of his rule was marked by striking **material progress:** administrative reforms were adopted, finances stabilized (national debt liquidated 1930), commerce and industry encouraged. After the opening of the **Venezuela oil-fields** (1918), the country soon became one of the leading oil producers, thus adding greatly to its wealth. On the other hand, the industrial development implied a growth of a proletarian class and a **spread of radicalism** which found much support among the students. The latter became active opponents of the dictatorship.

Venezuela maintained neutrality during the First World War, but

1920, Mar. 3. Joined the League of Nations.

1929, 1931. Revolts led by Gen. Arévalo Cedeño were put down, as were other opposition movements directed against the Gómez régime.

1935, Dec. 18. Death of President Gómez ended the dictatorship. **Gen. Eleazar López Contreras** became provisional president and succeeded in suppressing the disorders that broke out after the death of the strong man.

1936, Apr. 25–1941. Gen. Eleazar López Contreras was elected president, and

July 16. A **new constitution** provided that the president's term should be limited to five years, with no eligibility for re-election.

1937, Jan. Elections were held for about one-third of the seats in congress. These turned out to be a decisive **victory for the Left parties,** whereupon (Feb. 4) the government arrested many of the leaders of the Left (including newly elected congressmen) on the charge of communism. Most of these leaders were exiled, and most of the radical organizations (including the **Federation of Students**) were dissolved. The president then undertook to suppress radicalism, but at the same time embarked on a far-reaching **program of social reform** designed to meet the needs and demands of the lower classes and to check the spread of subversive tendencies.

(*Cont. p. 1258.*)

11. BRAZIL

(*From p. 856*)

1914-1918. Wenceslau Braz Pereira Gomes, president.
1915, May 25. Agreement with Argentina and Chile (*A.B.C. treaty*) providing for arbitration of disputes.
1917, Oct. 26. BRAZIL DECLARED WAR ON GERMANY. Relations had been severed April 11 after sinking of Brazilian ships. During the war Brazilian warships co-operated with the Allies and Brazil furnished large stocks of food and raw materials.
1918. Rodrigues Alves, president. He died (1919) before assuming office, and was succeeded by
1919-1922. EPITACIO PESSOA as president.
1920, Jan. 10. Brazil joined the League of Nations as an original member.
1922-1926. ARTURO DA SILVA BERNARDES, president. Widespread discontent with the governmental system led to a
1924, July. Formidable revolt in São Paulo and Rio Grande do Sul, led by **Gen. Isidor Lopes.** After suppression of the insurrection, the government undertook certain economic reforms.
1926, June 14. Brazil announced withdrawal from the League of Nations (effective 1928), after failure to secure a permanent seat on the council.
1926-1930. WASHINGTON LUIS PEREIRA DE SOUZA, president. He maintained order and tried, without much success, to improve the finances. Social unrest developed rapidly during this period and resulted in drastic **measures against strikes and communism** (strikes illegal, August 13, 1927).
1930. The **election of** the Conservative **Julio Prestes as president** provoked
Oct. A GREAT REVOLT IN THE SOUTHERN PROVINCES, led by **Getulio Vargas,** governor of Rio Grande do Sul. Vargas accepted the presidency (Oct. 26) and forced Pereira de Souza to resign (Oct. 30).
1931. Establishment of the National Coffee Department, which year after year supervised the destruction of large quantities of coffee, in the hope of maintaining a good price in the world market. Coffee being Brazil's chief export article, the collapse of prices during the depression created much financial difficulty.
1932, July-Oct. A **revolt broke out in São Paulo,** which was successfully mastered by the government. The movement was the result of rivalry between São Paulo and Minas Gerães for control of the federal government.
1933. The government introduced a **program of economic rehabilitation,** with numerous social and political reforms, including
1934, July 16. A **new constitution** which involved greater centralization of control. The president was henceforth to be elected by congress and was not to be eligible for re-election.
1934-1937. VARGAS was elected president under the new system. Economic conditions gradually improved, but social and political unrest increased. Among the industrial and plantation workers radical and communist propaganda made marked progress, while among the middle classes a strong fascist (*Integralista*) **green shirt movement** gained many adherents. The **communist movement** was said to be supported from Moscow, while the new Nazi government in Germany, whether connected with the Integralista group or not, unfolded an active and rather successful propaganda among the many Germans in the southern provinces. Barter arrangements with Germany resulted in a huge increase of trade between the two countries.
1935, Nov. A **communist revolt** broke out in Pernambuco and then in Rio de Janeiro. Though suppressed within a week, the revolt gave the government an excuse for the introduction of martial law. The president was granted almost dictatorial powers, a strict censorship was inaugurated and special tribunals were set up to try communist leaders.
1937, Nov. 10. VARGAS PROCLAIMED A NEW CONSTITUTION, after months of heated rivalry respecting the succession to the presidency. The new constitution gave the president full **dictatorial powers** and established a system of corporative nature (organization of a **national economic council**). The president announced that the new régime was not fascist, but the distinction was not obvious.
1938, May 11. An **Integralista rising** was put down by the government without much difficulty.
1939, Mar. 9. Brazil concluded a series of **agreements with the United States,** thereby obtaining financial aid and support in the work of general economic development.

(*Cont. p. 1259.*)

12. CENTRAL AMERICA

a. GENERAL

After the declaration of war on Germany by the United States, the states of Central America severed relations with Germany and ultimately declared war, mostly in 1918 (**Panama,** Apr. 7, 1917; **Costa Rica,** Mar. 23, 1918; **Nicaragua,** May 8, 1918; **Honduras,** July 19, 1918; **Guatemala,** Apr. 23, 1918). After the war almost all of them became **members of the League of Nations (Salvador** joined in 1924, the others in 1920).

In the political sphere most of these states continued in unstable conditions, with numerous insurrections and overturns. Common to all of them was the growing class consciousness of the laborers on banana, coffee, and sugar plantations, which came to constitute an ever more formidable challenge to the ruling groups. Despite representative machinery, the governments in many states were essentially dictatorships. During the 1920's the United States government intervened frequently to protect American lives and property. This policy, among other things, aroused much hostility toward the United States throughout Latin America, and was later replaced by the "good neighbor policy," which eschewed intervention.

1918, Mar. 10. The **Central American court was dissolved** after denunciation by Nicaragua and failure of the members to renew the arrangements.

1921–1922. The **PACT OF UNION** between **Costa Rica, Guatemala, Honduras,** and **Salvador,** signed at San José (Jan. 19, 1921). The agreement set up an indissoluble and perpetual union, to be called the **Federation of Central America.** A provisional federal council was organized (June 17) and **Vicente Martínez** of Guatemala became president. On October 10 the federal constitution was completed, but once again the project of union was to be frustrated. On December 8 a revolution broke out in Guatemala, directed against the government's policy of federation. With its success the whole scheme fell through and the **federation was dissolved** (Jan. 29, 1922). In the ensuing years there was chronic trouble about frontiers between the different states, with occasional danger of war.

1922, Dec. 4–1923, Feb. 7. A **Central American conference** met at Washington at the instance of the United States government, which hoped to terminate the dangerous friction between Nicaragua and Honduras. A general **treaty of neutrality** was drawn up, provision was made for the creation of a Central American court

of justice, and measures to limit armaments and to further economic development were envisaged. The majority of the states ratified the treaties by 1926, but little was done to put them into effect.

b. PANAMA

(*From p. 856*)

1921. A **boundary dispute with Costa Rica,** inherited from the period of Colombian sovereignty, threatened to provoke war when Panamanian troops occupied disputed territory and armed clashes ensued (Feb.–Mar.). The United States government induced Panama to evacuate the area involved, which was then occupied by Costa Rica (Aug.).

Apr. 20. By the **THOMSON-URRUTIA TREATY** (p. 1064), Colombia recognized the independence of Panama. The boundaries, hitherto disputed, were adjusted, diplomatic relations established, and various accords signed (1924–1925).

1926, July 28. TREATY WITH THE UNITED STATES, designed to protect the canal in time of war. It provided that Panama consider itself at war when the United States was belligerent, and that Panama permit peacetime maneuvers by American forces on Panamanian territory. Opposition by the Panamanian assembly because of infringement of sovereignty prevented ratification (Jan. 26, 1927). The question of sovereignty over the Canal Zone then arose, Panama denying that the United States possessed such sovereignty. Panama virtually appealed to the League of Nations to determine the question, but the League took no action and the president of Panama disavowed the appeal.

1931. President Florencio Harmodio Arosemena was forced to resign as a result of revolution (Jan. 2). A military government was set up and

1932–1936. HARMODIO ARÍAS became president.

1933, Oct. 17. President Arías conferred with President Roosevelt in Washington regarding the treaty relations between the two countries. The result was a declaration that Panama should be permitted all the commercial rights of a sovereign nation in the Canal Zone, and that there should be no American economic enterprise detrimental to Panama in the Canal Zone. The Panamanians having become more and more nationalistic,

1934–1935. Panama opened negotiations with

the **United States** to secure modification of the treaty of 1903, so as to eliminate the American guaranty of Panama's independence and the American right to intervene.

1936–1939. JUAN AROSEMENA, president. The negotiations with the United States finally eventuated in

Mar. 2. A new treaty with the United States which met many of the objections raised by Panama to the earlier treaty.

1939–1940. Augusto S. Boyd, president.

(*Cont. p. 1242.*)

c. COSTA RICA

(*From p. 858*)

1917, Jan. 27. President Alfredo Gonzales Flores was overthrown by a military coup led by **Federico Tinoco.** The United States refused recognition to the new régime and

1919, May 6. Tinoco was deposed by the Flores party. American marines were landed (June 4) to protect American interests. After the

Dec. 9. Election of Julio Acosta as president, the United States government granted recognition (1920).

1921. Conflict with Panama over the boundary (p. 1067).

1924–1928. Ricardo Jiménez, president.

1924, Dec. 24. Costa Rica withdrew from the League of Nations.

1928–1932. Cleto Gonzáles Viquez, president.

1932–1936. Ricardo Jiménez, again president.

1936–1940. Léon Cortes Castro, president.

(*Cont. p. 1243.*)

d. NICARAGUA

(*From p. 858*)

1914, Aug. 5. Conclusion of the Bryan-Chamorro treaty with the United States, giving the latter the right to construct a canal across Nicaragua and lease sites for naval bases on both coasts. Costa Rica and Salvador at once protested against what they claimed was an infringement of their sovereignty.

1916, Apr. 13. The treaty was ratified by the United States, with the inclusion of a declaration that its provisions were not intended to affect the rights of other states.

1916–1921. EMILIANO CHAMORRO, president.

1917, Mar. 2. Salvador submitted the question of the Bryan-Chamorro treaty to the Central American court of justice, which declared the treaty to be a violation of the treaties of 1907. Nicaragua ignored the decision and the efficacy of the court was thereby destroyed.

1917–1924. An American financial commission, in collaboration with the collector-general of customs, stabilized Nicaraguan finances.

1921–1923. Diego Chamorro, president.

1923–1925. Martínez Bartolo, president.

1925, Aug. 3. CÁRLOS SOLÓRZANO elected president. Like his predecessors he was a Conservative, but the new vice-president, **Juan Sacasa,** was a Liberal.

Oct. 25. A revolt, led by Emiliano Chamorro, forced Sacasa and other Liberals out of the government.

1926, Jan. 14. Solórzano resigned and **Chamorro became president.** The United States refused him recognition and when

May 2. A Liberal insurrection was started by **Gen. Agustino Sandino,** the American government hastily landed forces. An armistice was effected by the United States (Sept. 23); Chamorro resigned and the Nicaraguan congress elected

Nov. 11. Adolfo Díaz (Conservative) **president.** But

Dec. 2. Sacasa returned from exile in Mexico and set up a Liberal government of his own, which was recognized by Mexico. During the civil war which ensued, the United States government supported Díaz.

1927, May 4. Henry L. Stimson, representing the United States, succeeded in bringing the two factions together. President Díaz was to complete his term of office, the opposition was to disarm, and the United States was to supervise the forthcoming elections.

1928, Nov. 4. José Moncada (Liberal) **was elected,** the United States government supervising the polling. **Sandino,** who had been continuing the fighting on his own account and who had gone so far as to attack the American troops, withdrew to Mexico, but in 1931 resumed the struggle.

1933. The Sandino insurrection was suppressed. Sandino was killed (1934), but sporadic outbreaks of his followers continued for some years.

1933–1936. JUAN SACASA, president.

1936, June 2. Sacasa was deposed by the National Guard, led by **Gen. Anastasio Somoza.**

1937–1947. ANASTASIO SOMOZA, president. He made himself virtually dictator and proceeded with the utmost vigor against communists and other radicals. The introduction of rigid exchange control was designed to help the country economically, but met with indifferent success.

1939, Mar. 23. A constituent assembly approved a **new constitution** and re-elected Somoza to the presidency. (*Cont. p. 1243.*)

e. HONDURAS

(*From p. 858*)

1916, Mar. Francisco Bertrand became president following a successful revolution.

1919, Aug. Insurrection of Rafael López Gutiérrez, a Liberal. President Bertrand was obliged to flee, and American marines were landed (Sept. 11). Through American mediation a civil war was avoided and

1920–1923. Gutiérrez became president. When the elections of 1923 proved to be indecisive,

1924, Feb. 1. GUTIÉRREZ ESTABLISHED A DICTATORSHIP. The Conservatives, under Tiburcio Carías, rose in revolt and marched on the capital. The United States severed relations with Gutiérrez and landed more troops. Gutiérrez was killed (Mar. 10), and

Mar. 31. The insurgents occupied the capital. Through United States mediation **(mission of Sumner Welles)** agreement was reached between Honduras and its neighbors, depriving insurgent bands of their bases **(pact of Amapala,** May 3). **Vicente Tosta** became provisional president and suppressed an attempt at further revolution by **Gregorio Ferrara** (Aug.–Oct.). A new constitution was then framed and

1925. MIGUEL PAZ BARAHONA became president, the United States forces having prevented revolutionary leaders from becoming candidates. The United States supported Barahona against further attempts at revolt by Ferrara.

1928. Vicente Mejía Colindres, president.

1933. Gen. TIBURCIO CARÍAS president. He assumed practically dictatorial powers.

1936, Apr. 15. The **constitution was amended** to enable the president to retain power until 1943. The growing unrest in the country led to numerous outbreaks and revolts.

1937, Jan.–Feb. A serious uprising, led by **Gen. Justo Umana,** was crushed. The government drove all opponents of the régime into flight or else imprisoned them.

1939, Dec. 23. Parliament extended Carías' term to 1949. (*Cont. p. 1243.*)

f. EL SALVADOR

(*From p. 858*)

The recent history of El Salvador has been much less spectacular than that of the neighboring states. The constitutional system operated without much friction until

1931, Dec. 2. A *coup d'état* **enabled Maximiliano H. Martínez** to make himself **president.**

1932. Martínez established a dictatorship. Like near-by dictators, he devoted himself to the suppression of communism and other radical movements.

1937, Aug. 10. El Salvador withdrew from the League of Nations.

1939, Jan. 20. A constitutional congress abrogated the constitution of 1886 and adopted a new régime, headed by **Gen. Andrés I. Menéndez.** (*Cont. p. 1244.*)

g. GUATEMALA

(*From p. 858*)

1920, Apr. 8. ESTRADA CABRERA, president since 1898, was deposed by the assembly because of his opposition to the scheme of Central American federation (p. 1067).

1920–1921. Cárlos Herrera, president. He was overthrown by a revolution (1921, Dec. 5) led by **Gen. José Orellana,** who rejected the Central American federation scheme.

1922–1926. Orellana, president.

1926–1930. Lázaro Chacón, president.

1930. Bautillo Palma, president. He was overthrown (Dec. 16) by **Gen. Manuel Orellana,** who was not recognized by the United States and who soon resigned.

1930–1931. José M. Andrade, president, until

1931–1944. GEN. JORGE UBICO made himself president-dictator. He established close contact with the dictators of Honduras and Salvador for the suppression of all opposition.

1935, June. By "plebiscite" **Ubico's term was extended** until 1943 and subsequently (1941) a constitutional convention extended it to 1949, but he was expelled in 1944. (*Cont. p. 1244.*)

13. MEXICO

(*From p. 860*)

The revolution that convulsed Mexico after the downfall of Díaz in 1911 (p. 860) had reduced the country to a state of utter confusion by 1914. Numerous leaders (Huerta, Carranza, Obregón, Villa, Zapata, etc.) held various parts of the territory, installing their own presidents, fighting each other, and creating difficulties with Mexico's neighbors.

1914, Apr. 9. A group of American marines was arrested at Tampico. The United States government demanded satisfaction (especially a salute). On the refusal of Huerta to meet

American demands, **United States troops occupied Vera Cruz** (Apr. 21). Huerta broke off relations with the United States. The major South American states attempted to mediate, and November 23 the American forces evacuated Vera Cruz.

July 5. Victoriano Huerta was elected president. He resigned almost at once (July 15), admittedly because of the refusal of the United States government to recognize him, which made his position impossible.

Aug. 15. Gen. Alvaro Obregón and a Constitutionalist army took Mexico City and **Venustiano Carranza became president.** As yet the Constitutionalists controlled only part of the country. In the north **Francisco Villa** was practically dictator. He at once declared war on the Carranza régime, installing **Eulalio Gutiérrez** as president (deposed again January 17, 1915). For a time Villa held Mexico City, but

1915, Jan. 27. Obregón recaptured the capital for the Constitutionalists.

Oct. 19. The **United States government** and a number of Latin American states **recognized Carranza** as de facto president. Great Britain followed suit (Nov. 16).

1916, Mar. 9. Forces of **Villa's party raided** across the frontier **into New Mexico.** Thereupon American troops pursued him (Mar. 15). Carranza at once protested against the violation of Mexican territory and began to offer resistance. Clash of Americans and Mexicans at **Carrizal** (June 21). Ultimately conferences were arranged to arrive at some settlement. **American troops departed** February 5, 1917.

1917, Jan. 31. The **NEW CONSTITUTION** was adopted by the Mexican congress (promulgated February 5). This instrument had been worked out by a constitutional convention, in session since November 21. Representing advanced nationalist and radical social views, the constitution of 1917 at once became the **charter of the new Mexico.** It provided for universal suffrage, the curbing of foreign ownership of lands, mines, and oil-fields, restriction of the power and property of the Church and monastic orders, the eight-hour day, a minimum wage, arbitration of labor disputes, agrarian reform (breakup of large estates and distribution among the landless), housing reform, etc.

Mar. 11. CARRANZA was elected president, for a four-year term. By the constitution he was ineligible for re-election, in 1921.

1918, Feb. 19. By decree, **oil was declared an inalienable national resource** and a tax was levied on oil lands and contracts made before May 1, 1917. Titles to oil lands were to be transformed into concessions. American and British companies, supported by their govern-

ments, at once protested. The matter was settled by compromise, but the episode was only the first move in a long campaign to break the power and wealth of foreign companies.

1918. Formation of the Confederation of Labor (*Confederación Regional Obrera Mexicana,* popularly called the *CROM*). The confederation was the counterpart of the American Federation of Labor, and before long was to be challenged by a more radical organization. For the time being, however, it was an important factor in the furtherance of the constitutional and social reform movement.

1920, Apr. 9. Three of the leading generals (Adolfo de la Huerta, Alvaro Obregón, and Plutarco Elias Calles) **joined forces against Carranza,** who was accused of attempting to dictate the presidential succession. The opposition proclaimed the **Republic of Sonora** and took the field. May 8 Obregón took Mexico City and thereafter many of the cities on the east coast. **Carranza was killed** (May 21) and **Villa surrendered** to the victorious insurgents (July 27; he was endowed with a handsome estate, which he enjoyed until his assassination in 1923).

Sept. 5. OBREGON was elected president. He was recognized by the United States (Aug. 31, 1923) upon agreement to respect titles to land acquired before 1917 and to accept an adjustment of American claims.

1923, Dec. 6. Adolfo de la Huerta led a revolt against the government of Obregón and the latter's candidate for the presidency, Calles. The United States government supported Obregón, who was able to crush the insurrection (1924).

1924–1928. PLUTARCO CALLES, president. After a long and serious controversy with the United States regarding the application of the constitution to foreign properties, an adjustment was finally arrived at (1927, **Calles-Morrow agreement**), due to the conciliatory attitude of the United States government and the mission of Dwight Morrow as ambassador.

Calles continued the work of **agrarian and educational reform** initiated in 1917, but soon came into **conflict with the Roman Catholic Church** over the application of constitutional provisions.

1927, Feb. The Church publicly repudiated the constitution of 1917, but the government (Feb. 11) ordered **nationalization of Church property** and began to close Church schools. Foreign priests, monks, and nuns were deported.

Oct. A **great insurrection** broke out and soon covered a dozen provinces. Calles proved himself the strong man of Mexico by proceeding at once and with great vigor against the rebels. Within a couple of months most of the leaders had been defeated, captured, and executed.

1928, July 1. Obregón was re-elected president, but was assassinated a few weeks later (July 17). Thereupon

1928–1930. EMILIO PORTES GIL served as provisional president. Calles remained the real power in the government and put down another

1929, Mar.–Apr. Insurrection, provoked by political and religious discontent and led by Gens. **Jesus María Aguirre** and **Gonzalo Escobar.**

June 21. A **compromise agreement** was reached **with the Church,** which relieved the tension for the time being.

Aug. 11. Promulgation of an **extensive labor code,** in accordance with the constitution of 1917: eight-hour day, six-day week, right to strike, minimum wage, compulsory insurance, etc.

1930–1932. PASCUAL ORTIZ RUBIO, president. Calles remained the dominant figure, and the new administration simply continued the policy of its predecessors.

1931, Sept. 9. Mexico joined the League of Nations.

1932, Sept. 3. President Ortiz Rubio resigned after a difference with Calles, who had (1931) assumed the ministry of war.

1932–1934. Gen. Abelardo Rodríguez served as provisional president.

1933. Adoption of a **six-year plan** of social legislation and economic development, which really signified a move toward the Right on the part of Calles and the National Revolutionary Party, in so far as it deferred some of the more extreme measures earlier envisaged.

1934, July 2. GEN. LAZARO CÁRDENAS, the choice of Calles, was **elected president** after the constitution had been amended to extend the presidential term to six years. Conflict soon developed between Calles and the new president, who, though young, at once demonstrated strong will-power. Representing the more advanced wing of the party, Cárdenas regarded Calles as too conservative. In 1935 he forced Calles into exile and, on the latter's return to Mexico (1936), had him arrested and sent off to the United States. Thereafter Cárdenas, undisputed master of the country, embarked upon an **accelerated program of reform,** in which he was supported by the new **Confederation of Mexican Workers** (Feb. 1936), led by **Vicente Lombardo Toledano,** next to the president the most outstanding figure on the political scene. Within a couple of years as much land was expropriated as in the years 1917–1934. This was distributed to the peasants on the communal (*ejido*) basis. With regard to the Church, Cárdenas adopted a somewhat more conciliatory attitude, though he insisted on the elimination of the Church from politics and upheld the nationalization of Church property.

1936, Nov. 23. A **new expropriation law** empowered the government to seize private property when necessary for the "public or social welfare," Thereupon

1937, June 23. The **National Railways of Mexico were taken over** by the workers, and

Nov. 1. The **sub-soil rights** of the Standard Oil Company and other companies were **declared nationalized.** These steps inaugurated a new phase of the conflict with foreign interests. The Federal Labor Board ordered American and British oil interests to increase the wages of workers by one-third, which the companies declared to be impossible.

1938, Jan. 19. A **new tariff** raised the rates from 100 to 200 per cent on articles imported chiefly from the United States.

Mar. 1. The Mexican courts decided for the government and against 17 oil companies, in the wages dispute.

Mar. 18. The **GOVERNMENT TOOK OVER THE PROPERTIES OF THE AMERICAN AND BRITISH OIL COMPANIES,** valued at $450,000,000. The governments at once protested against such action. The United States government, securing no encouragement to hope for settlement, discontinued silver purchases from Mexico, as a retaliatory measure. The British government suspended diplomatic relations. The issue raised tremendous excitement throughout Mexico, the people vigorously supporting the government.

May–June. Cárdenas proceeded against Gen. **Saturnino Cedillo,** former minister of agriculture and "boss" of the province of San Luis Potosí, who was reported on the verge of revolt in the interest of conservative groups. The movement was easily broken.

July 21. The United States government proposed arbitration of claims against Mexico for expropriation of lands held by Americans (valued at $10,000,000). The American government did not dispute the right of Mexico to expropriate, but insisted on full compensation. The Mexican government refused both arbitration and compensation (except in very general statements). On the contrary, it proceeded to conclude

Sept. 5. Oil barter agreements with Germany, Italy, and other nations, by which the oil should be exchanged for manufactured goods (previously imported chiefly from the United States and Britain). Nevertheless the United States government showed great reluctance to abandon the "good neighbor" policy. Finally

Nov. 12. The United States and Mexico reached an agreement on the land question. Commissioners were to appraise the value of the properties and the Mexican government

was to pay compensation at the rate of $1,000,000 per annum until the claims were liquidated. Repeated efforts to reach an agreement on the oil issue (spring, 1939) failed to produce results. *(Cont. p. 1241.)*

14. THE WEST INDIES

a. CUBA

(From p. 861)

1917, Apr. 7. Cuba declared war on Germany. The war period was one of great prosperity for the sugar industry, large quantities being shipped to the United States. But after the war the market collapsed with serious results for Cuba.

1920, Mar. 8. Cuba joined the League of Nations.

Nov. 1. Dr. Alfredo Zayas, candidate of the coalition National League, was elected by what his opponent, **José Gómez** (Liberal), declared to have been fraudulent methods. To prevent conflict the United States government sent **Gen. Enoch Crowder,** who arranged for new elections (1921, Mar. 15), which resúlted in another victory for Zayas.

1921–1925. ALFREDO ZAYAS, president. Crowder was recalled (1923) and the Cuban government gradually adopted a policy of opposition to American influence.

1925–1933. GERARDO MACHADO (Liberal), **president.** He attempted to solve the problems of the sugar industry by restricting production, stimulated industrial development (higher tariffs), and promoted public improvements and health. The term of the president was extended to six years and **Machado was re-elected.** He made himself virtually dictator, but thereby aroused much opposition that was enhanced by economic difficulties arising from the world depression.

1930–1931. A revolt led by Marío Menocal was suppressed and various restrictive measures were introduced, but unrest and disorders continued (1931–1933). The United States had, at the outset, declared its intention not to intervene except in case of extreme anarchy. But it attempted to mediate, thereby arousing the resentment of Machado.

1933, Aug. 12. An **army revolt** forced Machado out of office. **Cárlos Manuel de Céspedes became president,** but disorder continued and the United States felt obliged to send warships to Cuba.

Sept. 5. Céspedes was driven from office

by another army coup, led by **Fulgencio Batista,** who became practical dictator, though he eschewed political office.

Sept. 10. Grau San Martín became president and formed an extremely radical government, which was not recognized by the United States.

1934, Jan. 20. Overthrow of Grau San Martín. Cárlos Mendieta became president and succeeded in concluding with the United States

May 29. An agreement by which the PLATT AMENDMENT (p. 860) **WAS ABROGATED** and limitations on Cuban sovereignty were removed. Somewhat later (Aug. 24) the United States and Cuba signed a reciprocal trade agreement favorable to the latter.

1935, Dec. 10. Mendieta resigned, and

1936, Jan. 10. Miguel Mariano Gómez was elected. Before the year was out,

Dec. 23. Gómez was forced from office by Batista, and

1936, Dec. 24–1940. FEDERICO LAREDO BRÚ became president. Batista remained the real dictator, and his régime, after 1933, embarked on a policy which apparently aimed at a corporative state along fascist lines. All political and social opposition was dealt with in drastic fashion. At the same time the government threw itself into radical social legislation and adopted (July 25, 1937) a **three-year plan** which involved state control of the sugar and mining industries, the reorganization of agricultural schools, the distribution of land, etc. In

1940, Feb., a convention assembled to draft a new constitution which came into force October 10, with **Gen. Fulgencio Batista** as head of the government (July 14). *(Cont. p. 1245.)*

b. HAITI

(From p. 862)

1914–1915. Haiti was wracked by **revolutionary movements,** one president following another in rapid succession and the country in chaos. **American marines were landed** to protect foreigners and foreign property, and finally to supervise an election in the hope of re-establishing ordered government.

1915–1922. PHILIPPE DARTIGUENAVE, president. He concluded

Sept. 16. A TREATY WITH THE UNITED STATES which gave the latter a practical protectorate. United States marines remained in occupation, and the United States government was given supervision of the customs offices and the power to organize a constabulary.

1918, June 19. A new constitution was introduced.

July 12. Haiti declared war on Germany.

1918–1919. A revolt directed against the American occupation and, led by **Charlemagne Perlate,** caused much trouble, but was finally suppressed.

1920, June 30. Haiti joined the League of Nations.

1922–1930. LUIS BORNO, president. Opposition to his rule led to

1929, Dec. Serious disorders. Larger American forces were sent to the island, where they were attacked by the mobs. In view of the widespread anti-American feeling, the Washington government sent out

1930, Feb.–Mar. A commission of investigation, headed by **W. Cameron Forbes.** This commission recommended administrative reforms, the replacement of the military high commissioner by a civilian, and the continuation of the treaty relationship until 1936. It persuaded Borno to relinquish office, and

1930–1941 STENIO VINCENT became president. With American aid order was restored, finances and administration were reformed, public improvements introduced, and education was developed. At the same time a series of agreements were made providing for eventual termination of American control. These were blocked by the Haitian assembly, which insisted on immediate withdrawal. After the advent of the Roosevelt administration arrangements were quickly made for complete termination of American control and liquidation of the Haitian foreign debt.

1934, Aug. 6. The American forces were withdrawn. After a plebiscite and under executive pressure, the Haitian assembly approved the agreements with the United States and adopted

1935, June 17. A new constitution, which endowed the president with wide executive powers. Vincent's term was extended to 1941.

1937, Oct. An acute crisis developed in **relations between Haiti and the Dominican Republic,** because of maltreatment of Haitians. The Vincent government sought a peaceful solution and requested the good offices of the United States, Mexico, and Cuba. An agreement was finally reached January 31, 1938.

(*Cont. p. 1248.*)

c. THE DOMINICAN REPUBLIC

(*From p. 862.*)

Chronic revolution and widespread disorder in Santo Domingo led to

1914, June 26. Intervention by the United States, which restored peace between the warring factions.

1916, May. Further outbreaks resulted in further intervention and

Nov. 29. PROCLAMATION OF AMERICAN MILITARY OCCUPATION. This step called forth opposition in the republic and in the United States also, with the result that from 1920 onward the American government sought to arrange for withdrawal.

1922, June 30. Agreement between the Dominican government and the United States. American rule ended October 21 and the last marines were withdrawn September 18, 1924. A provisional government was set up and

1924–1930. HORACIO VASQUEZ became president.

1924, Sept. 29. The **Dominican Republic joined the League of Nations** as soon as the last American forces had left.

1929, Apr. An **American commission,** headed by **Charles G. Dawes,** at the request of the Dominican government investigated the finances and made recommendations.

1930, Feb. 23. President Vásquez was forced to resign as a result of a revolt.

1930–1938. RAFAEL LEONIDAS TRUJILLO, president. He adopted a policy of social reform and public works, developing communications, introducing sanitation, encouraging agriculture, and distributing lands. Opposition to his rule was dealt with harshly, so that members of opposition parties were obliged to flee abroad.

1937, Oct. The Dominican government drove a large number of immigrant Haitians back over the border, killing many in the process. This led to protests and demands for reparation from the Haitian government, which invoked American conciliation treaties for settlement of the dispute. By this method an agreement was arrived at (Jan. 31, 1938).

1938, May 17. Jacinto B. Peynardo was elected president after Trujillo had announced his forthcoming retirement. (*Cont. p. 1248.*)

d. PUERTO RICO

(*From p. 861*)

1917, Mar. 2. The **JONES ACT,** making Puerto Rico a territory and granting American citizenship to its inhabitants. Voting was made compulsory. Proportional representation was established by means of a "limited vote" for certain senators and representatives. It was further provided that United States internal revenue collections on the island should be paid into the Puerto Rican treasury. (Subsequently permission was accorded the island, practically, to collect United States income taxes for the benefit of the local treasury.) With such assistance, the budget of the insular government increased from about $2,000,000 in 1901 to $11,000,000 in 1924. More than half of these funds were derived from what would normally be federal taxation.

May. The United States having declared war on Germany, the **selective draft was extended to Puerto Rico** by request of the insular government. Some 18,000 men were inducted into service.

1918, June 2. The war, thus far rather distant, was suddenly brought home to the Puerto Ricans when a German submarine sank the *Carolina* near the end of her voyage from San Juan to New York.

1924, Mar. A delegation, including Gov. Horace Towner, came to the United States with the request that Puerto Rico be granted the **rights of statehood** without representation in congress.

1928. The **Puerto Rican legislature petitioned President Coolidge for the grant of autonomy** without statehood. Autonomy was desired to provide homesteads for the peasantry, to free the island from American tariff restrictions, and to deal with the problem of absentee landlordism.

1930. Gov. Theodore Roosevelt was forced to appeal to congress and to private philanthropy to aid the depressed population, of whom 60 per cent were without employment.

1933. The Democratic administration in the United States took a greater interest in the Puerto Rican situation and extended a **large measure of relief,** along lines followed in the United States itself. Nevertheless, there developed in the island an ever stronger demand for redefinition of status. Apart from a widespread sentiment in favor of statehood, there emerged a strong **nationalist movement** aiming at complete independence.

1936-1937. The **Nationalists provoked demonstrations and riots,** which in turn resulted in serious clashes with the police, arrest of many leaders, outbreaks of terrorism, etc.

1939, June 4. A committee of the legislature brought forth a demand for statehood and in the interval "demanded" an elective governor with power to appoint officials.

(*Cont. p. 1250.*)

e. VIRGIN ISLANDS

1916, Aug. 4. AMERICAN-DANISH TREATY, by which Denmark agreed to cede the Danish West Indies (about 100 islands with a total area of 132 square miles) to the United States for $25,000,000. The treaty was ratified January 17, 1917, and formal possession was taken March 31 of the same year. Danish laws were allowed to remain in effect.

The population (c. 26,000 in 1917) suffered much from economic distress. The **sugar industry** of St. Croix had been in process of concentration and many small sugar mills had been abandoned. Ultimately all grinding was done in three large "centrals." Many laborers were thereby thrown out of employment. The loss of the free port status, which had existed under Danish rule, reduced the trade of the islands, especially of St. Thomas. The American prohibition law (1919) further destroyed the market for sugar products, though bay rum continued to be manufactured. The main achievement of the American administration was the **development of education.**

1931, Feb. After a succession of governors from the U.S. Navy, the United States established a **civil government** for the islands, making St. Thomas the capital. **Paul M. Pearson** became the first civil governor.

Mar. The **depression** became so pronounced in the islands that President Hoover was able to refer to them as "an effective poorhouse" with 90 per cent of the population dependent upon the bounty of the United States.

1933. The **Roosevelt administration** began **relief measures** in the islands. Development of the **tourist trade,** expansion of the **rum industry,** etc., did much to ameliorate economic conditions.

1936, June 22. The **Organic Act** revised the political arrangements of government. The governor was to be assisted by a territorial legislative assembly, composed of the elected municipal councils of St. Thomas and St. Croix.

1938, Jan. 1. Universal suffrage went into effect under the new arrangements.

E. AFRICA, 1914–1939

1. GENERAL

1915, Mar. Completion of a railroad and steamer **route from east to west** from Dar-es-Salaam to Lake Tanganyika and thence to the Congo River.

1918, May. The **Cape to Cairo Railroad** reached Bukama on the Lualaba River, making possible travel from the Cape to Cairo by rail and water with two short breaks (Tabora to Mwanza and Nimule to Rejaf).

1919, Sept. International agreement prohibiting the **manufacture and importation of liquor** into Africa and controlling the **arms and munitions trade.**

1920, Feb.–Mar. 20. Sir Helperus A. van Ryneveld and Sir Christopher J. Brand first flew from Cairo to the Cape.

Feb.–Mar. Maj. Joseph Vuillemin flew from Algiers to Gao on the Niger and thence to Dakar.

Dec. The **Courtot expedition** crossed the Sahara to Lake Chad by motor.

1921, Jan. 14. Rosita Forbes and Hassanein Bey visited the oasis of **Kufra** and traveled thence to Alexandria.

1922, Dec.–1923, Mar. The **Haardt expedition** crossed the **Sahara to the Niger** and back again with caterpillar motors.

1924, Feb.–Mar. Lieuts. Paul Arrachard and Henri Lemaitre flew across the desert to **Timbuktu and back.**

Nov.–1925, July. Capt. Alfred Delingette and his wife first crossed Africa by motor from **Oran to Capetown.**

1926, Sept. 25. An **international slavery convention** was signed by 20 states.

Nov.–1927, Mar. Alan Cobham flew from London to Cairo and thence to Capetown.

1929, Jan.–Apr. Prince Sixtus of Bourbon opened a **motor route** from Algiers to Lake Chad.

Mar. Capt. Richard Crofton and Owen Tweedy went by motor from Rejaf on the upper Nile to Lake Chad, the Niger River, and thence to Algiers.

1935, Jan. 14. The **first train crossed the lower Zambezi bridge,** one of the longest in the world.

(*Cont. p. 1260.*)

2. EGYPT AND THE SUDAN

(*From p. 870*)

1914, Dec. 18. Egypt proclaimed a British protectorate.

Dec. 19. Khedive Abbas Hilmi deposed.

1914–1917. SULTAN HUSSEIN KAMIL, uncle of Abbas.

1917, Oct. 9. Death of the sultan.

1917–1936. AHMED FUAD, brother of Hussein Kamil, became sultan, then king.

1919, Mar. 8. Saad Zaghlul Pasha and other Nationalist leaders deported to Malta to prevent their going to the Paris peace conference. The Nationalist Party (*Wafd*) had grown tremendously during the war as a result of Egyptian resentment at British methods (forced labor conscription, requisition of materials, etc.). Its program was one of independence. The deportation of Zaghlul was followed by a serious **national insurrection,** which had to be put down by the British military.

Oct. 17. Gen. Edmund Allenby appointed high commissioner for Egypt.

Dec. 7.–Mar. 6, 1920. Milner commission to inquire into the disorders and recommend the future organization of Egypt.

1920, Mar. 10. A legislative assembly passed a **resolution in favor of independence.**

Dec. 9. Publication of the **Milner report,** proposing independence with guaranties for British interests.

1921, Apr. 5. Return of Zaghlul to Egypt. Attacks of the Nationalists on the government.

July 12–Nov. 20. Further **negotiations at London,** conducted by the Egyptian premier, Adli Pasha. These broke down on the question of the retention of British troops in Egypt.

Dec. 22. Zaghlul and other Nationalists again deported.

1922, Jan. 23. The Wafd proclaimed a policy of **passive resistance.**

Feb. 28. TERMINATION OF THE PROTECTORATE by unilateral action on the part of Britain. **Egypt declared independent,** but the decision on security of communications, defense, protection of foreigners, and the future of the Sudan reserved for further negotiation.

Mar. 15. Fuad I assumed the title of *king.*

1923, Apr. 4. Zaghlul released by the British.

Apr. 19. PROMULGATION OF THE CONSTITUTION: it provided for a **senate** and a **chamber,** three-fifths of the former and the whole of the latter to be elected by **universal suffrage;** ministers to be responsible to the chamber alone.

Sept. 27. Great victory of the Wafd in the elections.

1924, Jan. 28. Saad Zaghlul, premier.

Sept. 25–Oct. 3. Conferences between Zaghlul and Ramsay MacDonald failed to produce an agreement on the reserved questions.

Nov. 20. Death of Sir Lee Stack, sirdar of the Egyptian army and governor-general of the Sudan, assassinated by a fanatic. The Egyptian government at once expressed regret and promised punishment of those responsible.

Nov. 22. BRITISH ULTIMATUM, demanding punishment, apology, indemnity, suppression of political demonstrations, and **withdrawal of Egyptian forces from the Sudan.** Zaghlul agreed to these terms, excepting those relating to the Sudan. When the British insisted, he resigned in protest. His successor yielded (Nov. 24).

1925, Feb. 26. Sir George Lloyd, high commissioner.

Mar. 12. The **Wafd again victorious** in the elections; Zaghlul became president of the chamber. The Nationalists blocked all measures of the government, which repeatedly dissolved parliament only to find a new Nationalist majority at the next elections.

1926, Jan. 21. Opening of the **Makwar** (Senaar) **Dam,** an important stage in the utilization of the Nile water. The Egyptians were much exercised by the development of cultivation in the Sudan, which might deprive Egypt of necessary water.

1927, Apr. 18. Sarwat Pasha, premier.

July 18. New draft treaty with Great Britain, envisaging British military occupation for ten years.

Aug. 23. Death of Zaghlul Pasha; Mustafa Nahas Pasha became leader of the Wafd.

1928, Mar. 4. The **Egyptian parliament rejected the British draft as** incompatible with Egyptian independence.

Mar. 16. Nahas Pasha, premier.

Apr. 29. British ultimatum, forcing the Egyptian government to give up a bill providing for freedom of public assembly.

June 25. Dismissal of Nahas Pasha; Mohammed Mahmud (Liberal) became premier.

July 19. Parliament dissolved for three years; freedom of press and assembly suspended.

1929, Mar. 8–May 1. Resumption of **discussions at London,** the Egyptians hoping for concessions from the Labour government.

May 7. Agreement on Nile water: only Blue Nile water to be used for the Sudan, the water of the White Nile being reserved to Egypt.

Aug. 6. New draft treaty with Great Britain: British occupation to be replaced by a military alliance and British troops to be restricted to a few points on the Suez Canal; Egypt to join the League of Nations; the Sudan to be returned to an Anglo-Egyptian condominium.

Aug. 8. Sir Percy Loraine, high commissioner.

Oct. 31. Restoration of the constitution.

Dec. 21. The Wafd again swept to victory in the elections.

1930, Jan. 1. Nahas Pasha premier again.

Mar. 27–May 8. Negotiations in London regarding the British draft. These broke down chiefly on the issue of the Sudan.

June 21. ISMAIL SIDKY PASHA, premier. He was the appointee of the king, who chose him as an able administrator to deal with grave internal problems arising from the general world depression. The settlement with Britain was to be postponed, until the Wafd Party could be weakened.

June 26. The Wafd adopted a **policy of non-co-operation** with the government and advocated non-payment of taxes. Nationalist outbreaks became common throughout the country.

Oct. 22. INTRODUCTION OF A NEW CONSTITUTION: the senate to be three-fifths appointive; elections to the chamber to be indirect. Loud Nationalist protests and riots. **Union of the Liberal Constitutional Party with the Wafd** in common opposition to the king and Sidky.

Dec. 8. Sidky Pasha organized a party of his own, the **People's Party.**

1931, Apr. 22. Treaty of friendship between Egypt and Iraq, the first link in the chain binding Egypt to the other Arab states.

May. Elections. Through prohibition of Wafd meetings and other repressive measures, the government party won a victory.

1933, June. Anti-missionary and **anti-Christian outbreaks;** formation of the *Committee for the Defense of Islam.*

Sept. 21. Sidky obliged to resign because of ill health. After the failure of a "palace" cabinet, the king accepted a

1934, Nov. Cabinet of Mohammed Tewfik Nessim, who attempted a policy of reconciliation and allowed Wafd activity. He insisted on the

Nov. 30. Suspension of the constitution of 1930. Agitation of the Nationalists for restoration of the constitution of 1923. This was not done, on British advice.

1935, Nov. Ethiopian crisis. This was made the occasion of a violent outbreak of Nationalist agitation (Nov. 13–Dec. 2) and a union of parties, designed to extract concessions from the British in their hour of need.

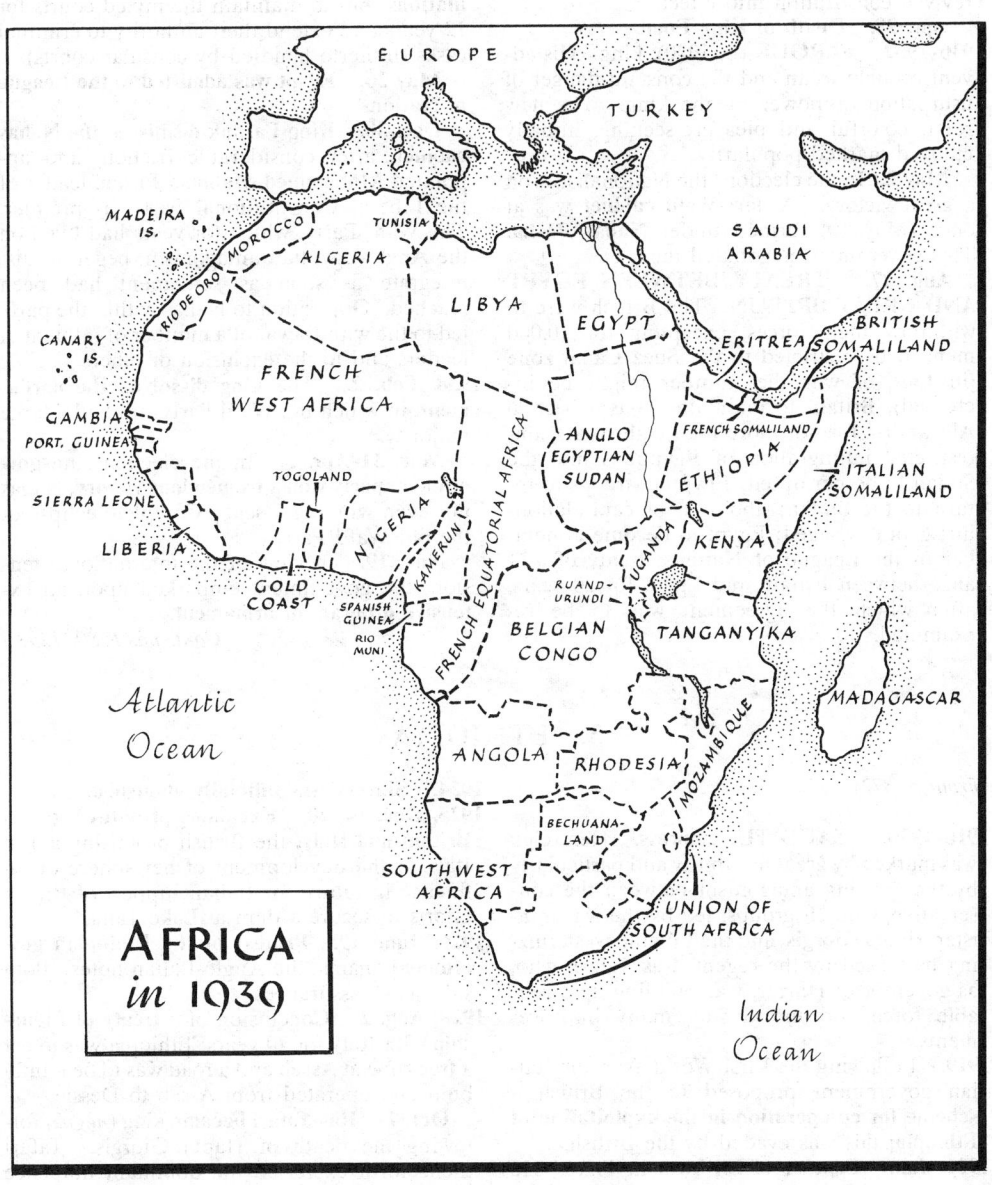

EUROPE

TURKEY

MADEIRA IS.

TUNISIA

MOROCCO

ALGERIA

LIBYA

EGYPT

SAUDI ARABIA

RIO DE ORO

CANARY IS.

FRENCH WEST AFRICA

ERITREA

BRITISH SOMALILAND

GAMBIA
PORT. GUINEA

FRENCH SOMALILAND

ANGLO EGYPTIAN SUDAN

ETHIOPIA

ITALIAN SOMALILAND

SIERRA LEONE

TOGOLAND

LIBERIA

NIGERIA

KAMERUN

FRENCH EQUATORIAL AFRICA

UGANDA

KENYA

GOLD COAST

SPANISH GUINEA
RIO MUNI

RUANDA-URUNDI

BELGIAN CONGO

TANGANYIKA

Atlantic Ocean

MADAGASCAR

ANGOLA

RHODESIA

MOZAMBIQUE

BECHUANA-LAND

SOUTHWEST AFRICA

UNION OF SOUTH AFRICA

Indian Ocean

AFRICA
in 1939

Dec. 12. RESTORATION OF THE CONSTITUTION OF 1923, long demanded by the Nationalists.

1936, Jan. 22. Cabinet of Ali Maher Pasha, a non-partisan government designed to put the revived constitution into effect.

Apr. 28. Death of King Fuad.

1936–1952. FAROUK (b. 1920), king. His advent brought to an end the constant danger of usurpation of power by the king. The new ruler, colorful and pleasure-seeking, initially enjoyed marked popularity.

May 2. In the elections the Nationalists won a great victory. A **new Wafd cabinet** was at once (May 10) formed under **Nahas Pasha.** This government negotiated the

Aug. 27. TREATY BETWEEN EGYPT AND GREAT BRITAIN. The British were to withdraw their forces, excepting for 10,000 men, to be restricted to the Suez Canal zone (in time of war the number might be increased); Britain to maintain a naval base at Alexandria for not more than eight years; unrestricted immigration of Egyptians into the Sudan to be permitted; Egyptian troops to return to the Sudan; abolition of capitulations in Egypt envisaged; Egypt to become a member of the League of Nations; treaty of alliance between Britain and Egypt for 20 years, after which the agreement was to be re-examined.

Dec. 22. Ratification of the treaty by the Egyptian parliament.

1937, Apr. 12–May 8. Conference of Montreux between the powers enjoying capitulatory rights in Egypt. **Agreement to abolish the capitulations,** but to maintain the mixed courts for 12 years and extend their authority to criminal cases (hitherto handled by consular courts).

May 26. Egypt was admitted to the League of Nations.

Dec. 30. King Farouk dismissed the Nahas cabinet, after considerable friction, and appointed **Mohammed Mahmud Pasha,** leader of the Liberal Constitutional Party, as premier. The Wafd Party, which for years had lived on the Anglo-Egyptian antagonism, began to disintegrate as soon as settlement had been reached. Opposition to Nahas within the party led to the withdrawal of a number of influential leaders and to the exclusion of others.

1938, Feb. 2. The **king dissolved the parliament,** in which the Wafd Party still had a large majority.

Mar. 31–Apr. 2. In the elections the **government party won a tremendous victory,** Nahas not even winning a seat. Complete eclipse of the old Wafd Party.

Nov. 19. In view of the international tension, the government embarked upon an **extensive program of armament.**

(*Cont. pp. 1280, 1293.*)

3. ETHIOPIA

(*From p. 872*)

1916–1930. ZAUDITU, empress. Her reign was marked by great instability and particularly by the growing antagonism between the conservative, Church groups, led by the war minister, **Hapta Giorgis,** and the Liberal, westernizing party, led by the regent, **Ras Tafari,** who, as governor of Harrar, was building up a reliable force and introducing many improvements.

1919. Following the First World War, the Italian government proposed to the British a **scheme for co-operation in the exploitation of Ethiopia;** this was evaded by the British.

1921, Jan. Capture of Lij Yasu in Tigré. He was handed over to the custody of Ras Kassa, the powerful governor of the province.

1923, Sept. 28. Ethiopia was admitted to the League of Nations. Britain had opposed the admission but it had been advocated by Italy and France, and Ethiopia was ready to accept the international arms traffic convention and to take steps against slavery.

1924. Slavery was officially abolished.

1925, Dec. 14, 20. Exchange of notes between Britain and Italy, the British promising aid to Italy in the development of her sphere of influence in return for Italian support of British efforts to secure a dam at Lake Tana.

1926, June 19. Protest of the Ethiopian government against the Anglo-Italian notes. Both sides gave assurances.

1928, Aug. 2. Conclusion of a **treaty of friendship with Italy** for 20 years: Ethiopia was to get a **free zone at Assab** and a road was to be jointly built and operated from Assab to Dessié.

Oct. 7. Ras Tafari became king (*negus*) following the death of Hapta Giorgis. Tafari thenceforth exercised the dominant influence and began to initiate his policy of modernization.

1930, Mar. 1. The negus granted a **concession for a dam at Lake Tana** to the American J. G. White Corporation, which had the support of the British and Egyptian governments.

Mar. 31. A dangerous **revolt of Ras Gugsa,** the husband of Zauditu, was put down.

Apr. 2. Death of the Empress Zauditu.

Nov. 2. Coronation of Ras Tafari as king of kings with the title of

1930–1936. HAILE SELASSIE I.

1931, July 16. Haile Selassie introduced a constitution providing for a parliament chosen by the provincial governments. This was part of his policy of governmental reorganization: appointment of younger men who had visited Europe to important governorships; establishment of schools; progressive measures to end slavery, etc.

1934, Dec. 5. Clash of Ethiopian and Italian forces at Ualual, in a disputed zone on the frontier of Italian Somaliland. The Italians demanded apology and reparation; the Ethiopian government insisted on an investigation of responsibilities.

1935, Jan. 7. Franco-Italian agreement (p. 1000), including a cession of part of French Somaliland to Italy and the sale to Italy of shares in the Ethiopian railway.

May. The council of the League of Nations arranged for an **arbitral tribunal** to deal with the Ualual dispute.

July. The tribunal having been unable to agree on procedure, the League arranged for a fifth arbitrator, but only to establish responsibility for the clash, not to determine the possession of Ualual.

Aug. 16. After a meeting of British, French, and Italian delegates at Paris, **Italy was offered wide opportunities for the development of Ethiopia,** subject to Ethiopian agreement. These offers were rejected, and it became more and more evident that Italy was bent on conquest.

Sept. 3. The **arbitral board reported** neither side to blame in the Ualual incident, since each side regarded the place as within its territory.

Oct. 3. BEGINNING OF THE ITALIAN INVASION OF ETHIOPIA (p. 1000).

Nov. 18. The Italians advanced slowly in the north and south. The Ethiopians avoided a pitched battle, but finally, in the spring of 1936, the Italians brought into full play their **air power** and began the use of **poison gas.** Unable to cope with these methods the Ethiopian defense broke down.

1936, May 5. The **Italians occupied Addis Ababa,** the emperor having fled to the coast and thence to Palestine and England.

May 9. ETHIOPIA WAS FORMALLY ANNEXED TO ITALY, and, with Eritrea and Italian Somaliland, was organized as **Italian East Africa.** The king of Italy assumed the title *Emperor of Ethiopia.* The conquest was recognized by Italy's friends (Germany, Austria, and Hungary), but only after considerable delay by some of the other powers (Britain, France, 1938).

Pacification of Ethiopia. The Italians established posts and forts throughout the occupied territory, linking them up by roads. The great and immediate problem, however, was to defeat what native forces remained in the field and to disarm the Ethiopians. Isolated attacks on the Italians continued and

1937, Feb. 19. An **attempt was made to assassinate the viceroy,** Gen. Rodolfo Graziani, at Addis Ababa. He and a number of his staff were wounded. Wholesale arrests and executions in the capital, designed to intimidate the population.

Feb. 21. Ras Desta Demtu, the most formidable opponent of the Italians, was defeated outside the capital, and captured (executed February 24). (*Cont. p. 1281.*)

4. NORTH AFRICA

(Morocco, Algeria, Tunisia, Libya)

(*From p. 875*)

1919, Feb. 4. In Algeria French citizenship was extended to all those who had served in the First World War, to those who owned land, to literates, etc.

May 17. Civil government was re-established in **Libya,** which was divided into **Tripolitania** and **Cyrenaica.** Citizenship was granted to natives and a system of self-government with elected assemblies was established (July–Nov.).

July 11. Beginning of the **attacks of Raisuli** upon the Spanish possessions in **Morocco.**

Sept. 12. A **Franco-Italian agreement** led to the cession of several important oases in **southeast Tunisia** to Italy; Italian nationals were given the same status as Frenchmen in Tunisia.

1920, Oct. 25. The **Italian government recognized Sheikh Sidi Idriss** as head of the **Senussi,** with wide authority over Kufra and other oases.

1921, July 21. The **ANUAL DISASTER,** in which a large Spanish force under Gen. Fernandez Silvestre was destroyed by the Riff leader, **Abd-el-Krim** (p. 991).

Nov. 8. A **new nationality law** decreed that children of foreign parents, if the latter were born in **Tunisia,** should be French subjects. Great Britain protested and brought the matter before the Permanent Court, which found that the French legislation went beyond ordinary national powers. A **Franco-British agreement** (May 24, 1923) provided that the children in question might elect their nationality, but that the same should not hold for their own children.

1922, May 22.   Gen. Pietro Badoglio began the **offensive against the Arabs in Libya.** The operations dragged on for years, though pressed more insistently after Mussolini's rise to power. By 1930 the conquest of the country by the Italians was at last completed.

July 13.   Reorganization of the government of Tunisia, where the **Young Tunisians** (nationalists) had developed an extensive agitation for self-government. A complicated **system of councils,** composed of French and natives, was organized, but was given power only in economic matters.

Sept. 28.   Submission of Raisuli; end of the war in the western part of the Spanish zone of Morocco.

1924, Feb. 7.   Tangier convention signed by Spain, France, and Great Britain. Tangier was to be governed for the sultan by a mixed commission, on which the French had the major influence.

Dec.   After repeated reverses, the **Spaniards were obliged to withdraw** from the interior of Morocco and concentrate on the coast.

1925, Jan. 27.   Abd-el-Krim captured Raisuli, who died soon afterward.

Apr. 13.   Abd-el-Krim began to attack the French, who were busy subduing the regions on the Riffian frontier.

July 26.   A **Franco-Spanish agreement** provided for full co-operation against Abd-el-Krim. The French gradually concentrated an army of 150,000 men against the Riffians.

Sept. 9.   Under command of **Marshal Henri Pétain,** the French and Spanish **began a major offensive,** driving back the Riffians.

Sept. 24.   Resignation of Louis Lyautey as French resident, after a long and brilliant career as pacifier of Morocco.

Dec. 6.   An **Anglo-Italian agreement** (the **Milner-Schialoja agreement)** provided for the cession of the **Jarabub Oasis** and other parts of western Egypt to Italy.

1926, May 26.   ABD-EL-KRIM SURRENDERED. He was exiled to the island of Réunion and the Riffian war came to an end.

1927, Mar. 9.   The system of **self-government in Libya was revoked.**

Nov. 17.   Death of Mulai Yusuf, sultan of Morocco. He was succeeded by his son, **Sidi Mohammed III.**

1928, Jan. 3.   The Senussi leader in Cyrenaica surrendered, bringing to an end the war in eastern Libya.

July 25.   The **Tangier statute** was revised and Spain given somewhat larger measure of control. Italy became a signatory of the convention.

1929, Jan. 24.   Tripoli and Cyrenaica were once more united under one government.

1930.   The **world economic crisis** made itself acutely felt in North Africa, Morocco in particular suffering from drought, locusts, and general falling-off of the demand for phosphate. Despite relief offered by the French government in various forms, the prevalent distress led to rapid **spread of native unrest.**

1931, Oct.   Founding of a League of Ulemas at Constantine, Algeria. The purpose of this was to further the work of Moslem reform as outlined by the Moslem congress at Jerusalem.

Dec. 29.   Spanish Morocco was reorganized under a high commissioner with civil and military authority.

1932–1934.   Completion of the pacification of French Morocco. On January 15, 1932, the French occupied the **oasis of Tafilet,** headquarters of the restless tribesmen. With the submission of the Atlas and Anti-Atlas regions, the conquest was completed.

1933, Nov. 28.   Opening of the **Moroccan-Tunisian railway,** which united the French possessions and which, in time of war, would enable the government to send troops from Tunisia to Moroccan Atlantic ports and thus obviate the dangerous Mediterranean route.

1934, Jan. 1.   Libya was divided into four provinces (Tripoli, Misurata, Bengasi, and Derna).

Aug.   Violent **attacks upon the Jews** at Constantine and in other Algerian towns. Anti-Semitism was one of the main planks in the program of the Arab nationalists.

Nov.   A group of young Moroccans, many of them educated in Europe, presented a *Plan of Moroccan Reforms* which may be taken as marking the **birth of Moroccan nationalism,** as distinct from the tribal opposition to foreign rule. The Moroccan nationalists drew much of their inspiration from Egypt.

1936.   The electoral victory of the Left parties in Spain and France (February and May) served as a great stimulus to radicalism and nationalism throughout North Africa. The French colonists, alarmed by concessions made by the home government to the lower classes, became extremely hostile to the Popular Front in France.

July 18.   The **Spanish civil war** (p. 993) broke out when the Spanish troops in Morocco (under **Gen. Francisco Franco)** rebelled and seized Melilla.

1937, Jan. Acute tension resulted from **rumors of the landing of German forces** in Spanish Morocco.

Mar. Spectacular visit of Mussolini to Libya, where he opened a new military road running the entire length of the colony. Mussolini proclaimed **protector of Islam** and presented with a sword of Islam.

Sept.–Oct. Nationalist uprising in French Morocco. The French government rushed troops and airplanes and snuffed out the movement as quickly as possible. Many nationalist leaders were arrested. **Albert Sarraut,** eminent French colonial administrator, was appointed to head a new **Commission of Co-ordination for**

North Africa with the objective of strengthening the French position.

1938, Dec. Tunisia began to focus world attention after vociferous demonstrations in the Italian chamber and throughout Italy calling for cession of Tunisia and Corsica to Italy (p. 991).

1939, Jan. The French premier, **Édouard Daladier, paid a visit to Corsica and Tunis.** His enthusiastic reception in North Africa appeared to demonstrate that the Arabs, whatever their grievances against France, had no desire to exchange French rule for Italian. Tension between France and Italy continued as the French government flatly declined to discuss any cession of French territory. (*Cont. p. 1230.*)

5. WEST AFRICA AND THE FRENCH SUDAN

(*From p. 877*)

The partition of Africa having been completed before the First World War, the period after the war was devoted to the **consolidation of European rule.** In most French and British colonies some form of **representative government** (councils, predominantly composed of officials, but with representation of economic and native groups) was established and the inhabitants were given some control over economic affairs. Consistent efforts were made to put an end to slavery, to introduce primary and vocational education for the natives, to organize justice, and to further economic development. Railroads were built in most colonies and motor roads were opened. In accordance with international agreements, the importation of "trade spirits" (i.e. liquors not usually consumed by Europeans) and of arms and munitions was prohibited. Land legislation aimed at the prevention of a landless native proletariat.

1916, Mar. 4. An **Anglo-French agreement** defined respective spheres in the conquered **Cameroons** and **Togoland.** To France was assigned by far the larger part.

Aug. 21. The French part of **Togoland** was **attached to French West Africa.**

1917, July 8. **French Cameroons** was attached to French Equatorial Africa.

Aug. 4. Liberia declared war on Germany.

1919, Mar. 1. The French organized a separate **colony of the Upper Volta.**

May 6. The supreme council assigned the **German Cameroons and Togoland** as **mandates to Great Britain and France.**

July 10. Britain and France made an agreement defining the frontier of their mandates in the Cameroons.

1920, June 30. Liberia became a member of the League of Nations.

Dec. 4. The name of the French colony Upper Senegal-Niger was changed to the **French Sudan.** A superior council (partly elective) was created for French West Africa.

1921, Jan. 1. Mauretania was created a **French colony.**

Oct. 13. The French created a separate **colony of the Niger.**

Nov. 21. Establishment of the **legislative council in Nigeria.**

1923, Oct. 11. British Togoland was put under the government of the **Gold Coast.**

1924, Jan. 21. An **Anglo-French agreement** fixed the frontier between the French Sudan and the Anglo-Egyptian Sudan.

1925, Sept. 16. Agreement between the Liberian government and the Firestone Rubber Plantation Company provided for the lease to the company of one million acres of land for 99 years, and for a loan by the company of $5,000,000 (for 40 years at 7 per cent).

Oct. 21. The city of **Dakar** (capital of French West Africa) was made an **autonomous area.**

1927, Sept. 22. Slavery declared abolished in Sierra Leone.

1930, Mar. 8. A joint American-League of Nations investigation **(Johnson-Christy Commission) to Liberia** investigated the conditions of native labor and reported (Sept. 8) that slavery actually existed.

1932, Dec. 23. Liberia was forced to suspend payment of interest and amortization of the Firestone debt, which in 1931 had absorbed 55 per cent of the revenue.

1935, June. The Liberian legislature ratified an **agreement with American interests,** by which interest on the 1926 loan was reduced to 5 per cent and all payments were made dependent on the state of revenue. The United States government resumed diplomatic relations with Liberia (broken off in 1930), and the British government followed suit (1936). Rapid development of the Firestone plantations secured the government greater revenue and enabled it to resume interest and amortization payments. (*Cont. p. 1288.*)

6. THE CONGO REGION

(French Equatorial Africa, Spanish Guinea, Belgian Congo, Angola)

(*From p. 881*)

1914–1918. Troops of the Belgian Congo assisted the British and French colonial forces in the **defense of Rhodesia** and the conquest of the **Cameroons.**

1916. Belgian forces occupied the districts of **Ruanda** and **Urundi,** part of German East Africa. Other German posts on the shores of Lake Tanganyika were taken, including **Tabora** (Sept. 19).

1919, May 30. An **Anglo-Belgian agreement** assigned Ruanda and Urundi to Belgium as a prospective mandate, but without the district of Kisaka. This was conceded to Belgium by agreement of August 3, 1923, after which **Belgium accepted the mandate** (Oct. 20, 1924). The mandated territory was united administratively with the Belgian Congo (Aug. 21, 1925).

June 28. By the treaty of Versailles, Germany retroceded to France that part of the **French Congo** (French Equatorial Africa) which had been ceded to Germany by the agreement of November 4, 1911.

1921–1924. Administration of **Gen. Norton de Mattos** in Angola. He attempted to open up the country by improved communications and other methods of encouragement, but met with great financial difficulties.

1921, Aug. 21. The Belgian government voted a credit of 300,000,000 francs for the **development of the Belgian Congo** through the construction of railways, etc.

1922, July 6. The Belgian Congo was given a wide **measure of autonomy.**

1924. An **Anglo-French agreement** defined the frontier between French Equatorial Africa and the Sudan (Wadai and Darfur).

1926, July 1. An **Anglo-Portuguese agreement** defined the frontier between Angola and Southwest Africa at the Kunene River.

1927, July 27. By an **agreement between Portugal and Belgium,** the latter ceded to the former 480 square miles on the southwest frontier of the Congo in return for one square mile of territory near Matadi, required for the reconstruction of the Matadi-Stanleyville Railway.

1928, June. **King Albert** of Belgium **visited the Congo** and formally opened the new **railway from the Katanga Province to the Kassai River** (Bukama-Ilebo), providing direct communication by rail and water between Leopoldville and the rich Katanga copper mines.

1931, July 1. Opening of the **Benguella-Katanga Railway,** from Lobito Bay on the Angola coast to Katanga in the Belgian Congo, thus completing the **first trans-African railway** (Benguella-Beira, via Katanga and northern Rhodesia).

1934, May. **Angola was reorganized,** with division into five provinces.

June 18. Opening of the **air line from Algiers to Brazzaville.**

July 10. Opening of the **railway from Brazzaville to the coast** at Pointe Noire.

1935, Apr. 16. **Spanish Guinea** (Rio Muni) **was divided,** Fernando Po being given separate administration. (*Cont. p. 1269.*)

7. EAST AFRICA

(Kenya, Uganda, Tanganyika, Nyasaland, Mozambique)

(*From p. 884*)

1919, May 7. **The supreme council assigned German East Africa to Great Britain.**

July 22. The legislative council of British East Africa was enlarged to eleven elected members for the Europeans, two nominated members for the Asiatics (Anglo-Indians), and one for the Arabs.

Sept. 23. The supreme council assigned the **Kionga Triangle** (part of German East Africa) to Portugal.

1920, Jan. 10. The **BRITISH MANDATE OVER GERMAN EAST AFRICA** went into effect. The name of the territory was changed to *Tanganyika;* the German settlers were sent home, and their estates were sold.

July 23. British East Africa was renamed *Kenya* and was made into a crown colony. The coastal strip, leased from the sultan of Zanzibar in 1887, became the **Kenya Protectorate.**

June 5. A nominated **legislative council** was established **in Uganda.**

1922, July 1. Opening of the **railway from Beira to the south bank of the Zambezi,** thus connecting Nyasaland with a good port.

1924, July 15. An **Anglo-Italian agreement** provided for the cession to Italy of a strip of territory from 50 to 100 miles wide on the British side of the **Juba River,** in fulfillment of the provisions of the treaty of London of 1915 (p. 953).

1925, Jan. 1. New immigration regulations for Tanganyika permitted the return of German settlers.

1926. A **conference of East African governors,** at Nairobi, discussed the possibility of an East African federation, much desired by the white settlers of Kenya.

Mar. 19. A nominated **legislative council** was established **for Tanganyika.**

1928, Jan. 11. Opening of the **Nakuru-Mbula-muti-Jinja railway** line in Kenya, giving access to some of the most valuable territory for white settlement.

Feb. 13. Junction of the railway lines from Katanga and from Beira provided an outlet to the east for the rich mineral resources of Katanga.

Aug. 15. Opening of the **railway line from Tabora** (in Tanganyika) **to Mwanza** on the south shore of Lake Victoria.

Sept. 11. An important **convention between Portugal and the South African Union** regulated questions of transportation from the Transvaal to the coast, problems of labor recruitment, etc.

1929, Jan. 18. The **Hilton-Young commission** recommended closer union of the East African and Central African colonies.

1935, Jan. 14. Opening of the **Lower Zambezi bridge** (12,064 feet long and one of the longest bridges in the world), providing for uninterrupted rail connection between Beira and Nyasaland.

Sept. 10. A "parliament" of white settlers in Kenya met and denounced the government policy, especially on its financial side, and demanded closer union of Kenya, Uganda, and Tanganyika (rejected by a British parliamentary committee in 1931 as inopportune).

Oct. 7. The colonial office announced the appointment of **Sir Alan W. Pym** to inquire into the financial problems of the colony.

(*Cont. pp. 1274, 1278.*)

8. SOUTH AFRICA AND SOUTHWEST AFRICA

(*From p. 892*)

1919, Apr. Gen. James Hertzog and a delegation of his Nationalist Party appeared at the Paris peace conference and asked for the recognition of complete independence for South Africa. During the war the party had become more pronounced in its **secessionist** and **republican** views. Since Hertzog represented a minority party in South Africa, nothing was done about the petition.

May 7. The supreme council of the Allied powers assigned **German Southwest Africa as a mandate** to the South African Union. Botha had tried in vain to have it ceded outright.

Aug. 28. Death of Gen. Louis Botha. He was succeeded as prime minister and leader of the South African Party by **Gen. Jan Christiaan Smuts.**

1920, Mar. 10. In the **elections** the Nationalist Party won the largest number of seats (45, as against 40 for the South African Party, 25 for the Unionists, and 21 for the Labor Party). The Unionists now began to support the South

African Party but the Laborites tended to join the Nationalists, thus creating a most delicate balance.

July 28. A **native affairs commission** was set up and the council system was extended to all native reservations. But the native question continued to be a burning one, partly because the reservations were wholly inadequate and partly because a large part of the native population had become detribalized and settled as laborers on the farms of the whites, or as mine and industrial workers in the larger towns.

1921, Feb. 8. In **new elections** the South African Party (with which the Unionists had merged) secured 76 seats, as against 47 for the Nationalists and 10 for Labor.

1922, Oct. 27. A popular **referendum in Southern Rhodesia** resulted in a heavy vote against joining the Union of South Africa, despite very attractive terms offered by Smuts.

1923, July 25. The claims of the South Africa Company in Southern Rhodesia were finally settled along the lines laid down by the **Cave**

commission report (Jan. 1921).

Sept. 1. SOUTHERN RHODESIA BE-CAME A CROWN COLONY, with a system of responsible government.

1924, Apr. The South Africa Company abandoned its administrative powers in **Northern Rhodesia,** which also became a crown colony.

June 17. ELECTIONS: victory of a coalition of the **Nationalists** and the **Labor Party** (resentful of the government's labor policy on the Rand and of the association of Botha's party with the Unionist mineowners) over the South African Party (53 seats as against 63 for the Nationalists and 18 for Labor).

June 30. Hertzog, leader of the Nationalists, **became prime minister.** In return for the support of the Labor Party he was, however, obliged to shelve the projects for secession and republicanism. The definition of Dominion status as laid down by the imperial conference of 1926 served further to meet the claims of the Nationalists.

1925, July 27. German Southwest Africa was given a constitution, providing for a legislative assembly. The German population became British citizens, but German was recognized as an official language.

1927, Feb. 21. A conference with representatives of the government of India finally led to arrangements for aid to those **Indians** who were willing to return home.

Nov. 11. The **Nationality and Flag Act** was passed after acrimonious discussion. The inclusion of the Union Jack in the South African flag was finally decided upon.

1929, June 12. In the elections the Nationalists renewed their victory of 1924.

1930, May 19. The franchise was extended to all white women.

1931, Aug. The reconstituted Labor Party repudiated its arrangements with the Nationalist Party and the coalition began to break down.

1932, Apr. In Southwest Africa the **Farmers' and Labor Party** was organized and began a drive for abolition of the mandate and establishment of the territory as a separate province with responsible government.

Dec. 27. The **Union government went off the gold standard,** last of the British Dominions to take this step.

1933, Jan. 24. Smuts called upon the government to resign in favor of a national government pledged to empire co-operation on non-racial lines.

Mar. 30. ESTABLISHMENT OF A NATIONAL GOVERNMENT. The two Labor members of the government dropped out, Hertzog remained prime minister, but Smuts and two other members of the South African Party joined the cabinet.

May 17. In the **elections** the national government won a great victory.

Aug. In **Southwest Africa** the victory of the National Socialists in Germany provoked an immediate response. The English settlers, by a narrow majority, put through a measure forbidding National Socialist "cells" and the wearing of uniforms. The English and Dutch settlers (a majority, owing to emigration of Germans and immigration from the Union after 1919) became more insistent on incorporation in the Union, which the Germans naturally opposed.

1934, June 5. Formal fusion of the South African Party (Smuts) **and the Nationalist Party** (Hertzog) under the new name of *United South African National Party* (United Party). The non-fusion element in the Nationalist Party re-formed under the same name and became a group representing republican and anti-native policies (leader **Daniel F. Malan**).

June 12. Status of the Union Act, passed to define the position of the Union after the Westminster Statute. It established the Union as "a sovereign independent state" in every respect, though it left the field open for endless discussion regarding the "right of secession" from the British Commonwealth.

Nov. 29. The legislative assembly of **Southwest Africa petitioned** the Union parliament **for admission to the Union** as a fifth province. A commission was sent out which reported (June 1936) that the existing government was a failure and that there was no obstacle in the mandate to the incorporation of Southwest Africa. But in December the government announced that it had no intention of changing the status of the territory, much less any intention of abandoning the mandate.

1936, Apr. 7. The **REPRESENTATION OF NATIVES ACT** finally clarified the native policy of the government. The natives retained the right to register as voters in Cape Province, but they were to be put on a separate electoral roll and were to be permitted to elect three Europeans to represent them in the Union parliament. A native representative council (22 members, 12 of whom elective) was to be established, but with purely advisory powers.

1937, Apr. 2. The Union government by decree prohibited **political activity by foreigners in Southwest Africa** (including non-naturalized German residents). Strong protests by the German government were of no avail. In September a new German Party replaced the forbidden German *Bund.*

1937, Nov. A **royal commission** was appointed to visit Northern and Southern Rhodesia and Nyasaland, to investigate the possibility of closer union between them.

1938, May 18. The **South African elections** resulted in a victory for the United Party and Hertzog remained premier.

(*Cont. pp. 1265, 1276, 1280, 1281.*)

9. MADAGASCAR

(*From p. 894*)

1916. During the First World War a **secret anti-French society** was organized among native officials. This was discovered and suppressed with great severity.

1918. Opening of the railway from Tamatave to Tananarive.

1923. Opening of the railway from Tananarive to Antsirabe, first section of a line to the south.

1924, May 7. **Reorganization of the administrative system,** in the direction of decentralization and increase of the number of native officials. The governor-general was henceforth to be assisted by economic and financial councils, composed of an equal number of Europeans and natives, to advise him on public works and general budgetary matters.   (*Cont. p. 1278.*)

F. ASIA, 1914–1939

1. TURKEY

(*From p. 777*)

1914, Oct. 29. Turkey entered World War I on the side of the Central Powers (p. 805).

1918, July 3–1922, Nov. 1. **MOHAMMED VI,** sultan.

Oct. 4. **Collapse of Turkish armies; flight of Talaat and Enver.**

Oct. 30. Armistice of Mudros (p. 973).

Dec. 8. Allied military administration of Constantinople.

1919, Mar. 7. **Cabinet of Damad Ferid Pasha,** with a policy of co-operation with the victorious powers.

Apr. 29. **Landing of the Italians at Adalia,** first step in the taking over of southwestern Anatolia.

May 15. **Landing of the Greeks at Smyrna,** with approval of the Allies.

May 19. **MUSTAPHA KEMAL PASHA** (hero of the battle at the Dardanelles and of the last battles in Syria; ardent Nationalist) arrived at Samsun as inspector of the 3rd army. He began organization of resistance to the further dismemberment of Turkey and was officially dismissed by the sultan (July 8), and outlawed (July 11).

July 23–Aug. 6. **Nationalist congress at Erzerum,** under Mustapha's lead.

Sept. 4. **NATIONALIST CONGRESS AT SIVAS** and **DECLARATION OF SIVAS** (Sept. 9): affirmed unity of Turkish territory and declared against Allied occupation and the formation of an Armenian state.

Sept. 13. The **National Pact:** enunciation of six principles, including self-determination, security of Constantinople, opening of the Straits, rights of minorities, abolition of capitulations.

Oct. **Victory of the Nationalists** in the elections to parliament.

Oct. 5. **Cabinet of Ali Riza,** who attempted conciliation with the Nationalists.

1920, Jan. 28. The **National Pact was adopted by the parliament** at Constantinople.

Mar. 16. To check the spread of the Nationalist agitation, Gen. Sir George Milne and an Allied force occupied Constantinople, while repudiating any idea of depriving the Turks of it. The announced object of the move was to keep open the Straits and to protect the Armenians. The Nationalists were denounced and many sent into exile. A **new cabinet under Damad Ferid** was set up. **Parliament was dissolved** (Apr. 11).

Apr. 23. A **provisional government** was set up by the Nationalists at **Ankara,** with **Mustapha Kemal as president.**

Apr. The Nationalists concluded a **military agreement with Soviet Russia,** by which they secured necessary supplies.

June 10. The **TREATY OF SÈVRES** presented to the Turkish government at Constantinople (terms, p. 979). Vigorous protests of the sultan and uncompromising opposition of the Nationalists, who received more and more popular support.

June 22. **Beginning of the Greek advance**

against the Nationalists. The Greeks were encouraged by Lloyd George, who meant to use them to force the peace terms on the Turks.

June 24. The Greeks defeated the Turks at Alashehr.

July 9. The Greeks took Bursa.

July 25. Adrianople surrendered to the Greeks.

Aug. 10. THE CONSTANTINOPLE GOVERNMENT SIGNED THE TREATY OF SÈVRES. Definitive break between the Nationalists and the sultan's government.

Oct. 21. In a campaign against the Armenian Republic, the **Turks took Kars.**

Dec. 3. Turco-Armenian peace treaty: Turkey got Kars and Ardahan, and Armenia (now a Soviet republic) was reduced to the province of Erivan.

1921, Jan. 20. The **Fundamental Law** adopted by the Ankara assembly: provided for sovereignty of the people; a parliament elected by manhood suffrage; responsible ministry; a president with extensive power.

Feb. **London conference** of the Allied powers, with both the Constantinople and the Ankara governments represented, as well as the Greeks. Efforts to reach an adjustment broke down.

Mar. 9. The **Franklin-Bouillon agreement** between France and Mustapha Kemal. This followed months of hostility in Cilicia, which France now agreed to evacuate, in return for economic concessions.

Mar. 13. **Agreement between Mustapha Kemal and the Italians.** The latter agreed to evacuate Anatolia in return for promises of extensive economic concessions. The last Italian forces left in June.

Mar. 16. TREATY OF MUSTAPHA KEMAL WITH SOVIET RUSSIA: Turkey was to retrocede Batum; in return Russia recognized the Turkish possession of Kars and Ardahan.

Mar. 23. Beginning of the **new Greek offensive.** The Greeks took **Afiun-Karahissar** and **Eskishehr** (Mar. 28–30), but were thrown back by the Turks (Apr. 2).

July 16–17. Battle of Kutahia. The Greeks took the town, as well as Afiun-Karahissar and Eskishehr.

Aug. 24–Sept. 16. BATTLE OF THE SAKARYA. Desperate defense of the Turks. The Greeks failed to reach Ankara. Though the Allied powers proclaimed neutrality in the war and attempted to mediate, Lloyd George nevertheless encouraged the Greeks in their aggressive policy.

Oct. 13. **Treaty of Kars:** Turkey formally recognized the Armenian Soviet Republic.

1922, Mar. 26. The Allied powers agreed to some revision of the Sèvres treaty and attempted a settlement of the Greek-Turkish conflict. The Turks refused to grant an armistice until the Greeks had evacuated Anatolia. Further efforts at mediation (June) again failed.

July 29. The Allied powers, in an ultimatum to Greece, forbade the occupation of Constantinople.

Aug. 18. Beginning of the **Turkish counteroffensive** against the Greeks. The Turks took **Afiun-Karahissar** (Aug. 30) and **Bursa** (Sept. 5). The Greek armies broke and fled in confusion to the coast.

Sept. 9–11. The **TURKS TOOK SMYRNA,** which was to a large extent destroyed by fire (Sept. 13–14).

Sept. 15. **Lloyd George appealed to the Allied powers** and the British Dominions to join in defense of the Straits against the Turks. The French took a negative stand, as did the Italians. Of the Dominions only Australia and New Zealand showed any interest.

Sept. 16. **A British force under Gen. Sir Charles Harington landed at Chanakkale.**

Oct. 3–11. **Conference and convention of Mudania** between the Allies and **Ismet Pasha**, representing the Turkish Nationalists. The Allies agreed to the return of Eastern Thrace and Adrianople to the Turks, and the Turks accepted the neutralization of the Straits under international control.

Nov. 1. Mustapha Kemal proclaimed the **ABOLITION OF THE SULTANATE.** Mohammed VI fled from Constantinople on a British ship.

Nov. 18. **Abdul Mejid,** cousin of Mohammed VI, **proclaimed caliph.**

Nov. 20. **Lausanne conference,** to conclude peace between the Allies and the Turks. The conference broke up temporarily February 4, 1923, after heated disputes about the abolition of capitulations and the status of Mosul. It resumed sittings April 23 and concluded its work July 24.

1923, July 24. TREATY OF LAUSANNE: Turkey gave up all claims to the non-Turkish territories lost as a result of the First World War, but recovered **Eastern Thrace** to the Maritza River, with **Karaagach;** Turkey received **Imbros** and **Tenedos,** but the rest of the Aegean Islands went to Greece; Italy retained the **Dodecanese** and Britain **Cyprus;** the **capitulations** were abolished in return for a promise of judicial reforms; Turkey accepted **treaties to protect minorities;** Turkey paid no reparations, the **Straits** were demilitarized, with a zone on either bank; they were to be opened to ships of all nations in time of peace and in time of war if Turkey remained neutral; if Turkey was at war, enemy ships, but not neutrals, might be excluded. A separate **Turkish-Greek agreement** provided for **compulsory exchange of populations.**

Aug. 23. Evacuation of Constantinople by the Allies. The Turks took possession October 6.

Oct. 14. Ankara was made the capital of the Turkish national state.

Oct. 29. FORMAL PROCLAMATION OF THE TURKISH REPUBLIC: Mustapha Kemal president, **Ismet Pasha** prime minister.

1924, Mar. 3. ABOLITION OF THE CALIPHATE; all members of the house of Osman banished.

Apr. 20. Adoption of the constitution, an elaboration of the Fundamental Law.

Aug. 6. The **Anglo-Turkish dispute** about the status of **Mosul** (left open by the treaty of Lausanne) was submitted to the League of Nations.

Oct. 29. The **League council fixed a provisional line** (*Brussels line*) assigning most of Mosul to Iraq.

1925, Feb.-Apr. Great insurrection in Kurdistan, directed against the religious policy of the government and aiming at autonomy. The suppression of the revolt cost much effort and blood. The leaders were executed.

Aug. Polygamy was abolished and **divorce introduced.**

Sept. 2. Religious orders suppressed; a severe blow at the conservative opposition.

Nov. Wearing of the fez forbidden. The use of the veil by women was made optional, but discouraged.

Dec. 16. Mosul award by the League council; most of the territory, with rich oil-fields, was assigned to Iraq. Strong protests of the Turks.

Dec. 17. ALLIANCE WITH SOVIET RUSSIA, establishing close political and economic collaboration.

1926, Jan.-Feb. Introduction of the new civil, criminal, and commercial **law codes,** based respectively on Swiss, Italian, and German systems.

June 5. Treaty with Britain, disposing of the Mosul issue according to the League's decision.

Sept. 1. Civil marriage made compulsory.

1927, Sept. 2. Elections. Mustapha was empowered to name all candidates, so that his party (*The People's Party*) had a monopoly.

Oct. 15. Historic speech of Mustapha Kemal to the national assembly, reviewing the whole course of the national revival and movement.

Nov. 1. Mustapha Kemal unanimously elected **president for four years.**

1928, Apr. 9. Abolition of the article of the constitution declaring Islam the state religion.

May 30. Conclusion of a non-aggression pact with Italy for five years.

June 15. Pact with Persia.

Nov. 3. Decree introducing the Latin alphabet, to be in universal use within 15 years. It was applied first to newspapers and then to books. All Turks under 40 years were obliged to attend schools to learn it. Arabic and Persian words were gradually rooted out.

1929, Mar. 6. Treaty with Bulgaria, settling many outstanding questions.

June. Introduction of a high protective tariff, in the effort to encourage Turkish industry.

June. Suppression of communist propaganda making clear the limits placed by Mustapha Kemal on friendship with Russia.

Dec. 17. Treaty with Russia, extending and amplifying the treaty of 1925.

1930, Mar. 28. The **name of Constantinople** was changed to *Istanbul;* **Angora** to *Ankara;* **Smyrna** to *Izmir;* **Adrianople** to *Edirne,* etc.

May. Formation of an opposition party (*Liberal Republican Party* under **Ali Fethi Bey**) permitted, in the effort to enliven political life. The new party favored a more moderate nationalism and greater co-operation with the west. After an extremely weak showing in the elections, Ali Fethi dissolved it, but an independent group of deputies continued to exist in the assembly.

June-July. Kurd revolt in the region about Mt. Ararat.

Oct. 30. TREATY OF ANKARA between Turkey and Greece, following the settlement of property claims of repatriated populations and other outstanding questions. The two parties recognized the territorial *status quo* and agreed to **naval equality** in the eastern Mediterranean.

Oct. The Turks attended the **first Balkan conference,** at Athens, and took an active part in the work of Greek-Bulgarian reconciliation and the formation of a Balkan pact.

Dec. 23. Dervish rising near Smyrna. This led to further measures to break the Moslem opposition, 28 leaders being executed.

1931, Mar. 8. Naval agreement with Russia: neither party was to add to its Black Sea fleet, excepting after six months' notice to the other.

May 4. Mustapha Kemal unanimously **re-elected president** for four years.

Oct. 20-26. Meeting of the **second Balkan conference at Istanbul.**

1932, Jan. 23. Settlement of the Turkish-Persian frontier dispute.

July 18. Turkey accepted the invitation to **join the League of Nations.**

1933, Apr. 22. New arrangement for payment of the **Ottoman debt.** The total was reduced from £T107,000,000 to £T8,000,000.

1934, Jan. **Five-year plan** for the development of industry, most of which was to be government-owned. The great depression necessitated a policy of rigid economy, but the encouragement of agriculture, opening of mines, construction of railroads and roads, etc., was continued.

Feb. 9. CONCLUSION OF THE BALKAN PACT, between Turkey, Greece, Roumania, and Yugoslavia (p. 1127).

May. Beginning of an active **policy of rearmament,** occasioned chiefly by distrust of Italian policy in the eastern Mediterranean.

Dec. 14. Women were given the vote and were permitted to sit in the assembly (17 women elected in March 1935).

1935, Jan. 1. **Introduction of family names.** Mustapha Kemal, at the suggestion of the assembly, adopted the name *Kemal Atatürk* (father of the Turks).

Mar. 1. Kemal Atatürk re-elected president for four years.

1936, Apr. 11. The Turkish government appealed to the signatories of the Lausanne treaty for **permission to refortify the Straits** (effect of the Ethiopian crisis, p. 1000, and Turkish support of the League action).

July 20. The **international conference at Montreux** approved the Turkish request, Italy not voting. The Straits thereby were returned to Turkish control.

1937, May 29. The League of Nations council, after acceptance by France and Turkey, adopted a **fundamental law for the sanjak of Alexandretta.** Despite acceptance of the new régime, which called for demilitarization, autonomy, and special rights for the Turkish population, disorders continued in connection with the forthcoming election.

July 9. SIGNATURE OF A NON-AGGRESSION PACT between Turkey, Iraq, Iran (Persia), and Afghanistan, securing the Turks

on the Asiatic side as the Balkan pact did on the European.

Oct. 25. Resignation of Ismet Inönü, close collaborator of Kemal Atatürk and since 1925 prime minister. He was succeeded by **Jelal Bey Bayar,** whose economic training made him especially suited for the management of the extensive industrial and agricultural program of the government.

Dec. 7. Beginning of the **Alexandretta crisis.** The Turkish government denounced the treaty of friendship with Syria (of May 30, 1926), whereupon the French government sent a military mission to Ankara. After bitter recriminations and threat of war

1938, July 3. The **French and Turks came to an agreement:** each to send 2500 troops into the sanjak to supervise the elections. In the elections of September the Turks secured 22 deputies out of a total of 40.

Sept. 2. The **REPUBLIC OF HATAY** (i.e. Alexandretta), a new autonomous state, was voted by the new assembly. The Turks were evidently in complete control and the republic existed only *pro forma.*

Nov. 10. DEATH OF KEMAL ATATÜRK. On the next day the national assembly unanimously elected

1938–1950. ISMET INÖNÜ, president.

1939, May 12. Conclusion of a **British-Turkish agreement of mutual assistance** in case of aggression or war in the "Mediterranean area." Despite close economic relations with Germany, the Turkish government identified itself with the British bloc designed to check German expansion into the Balkans. Negotiations for a similar pact between Turkey and France gave promise of success since the French indicated readiness to abandon Hatay (Alexandretta) completely to the Turks.

June 23. France and Turkey concluded a **non-aggression pact,** and France agreed to the **incorporation of the republic of Hatay** into Turkey. The Turkish Republic thereupon took its stand squarely by the western powers.

(*Cont. p. 1297.*)

2. SYRIA

1918, Oct. 5. The **French took Beirut,** which was entered by British troops soon afterward. **A Syrian state was proclaimed by Emir Faisal.**

1919, July 2. A **national congress at Damascus** asked for **complete independence** for Syria, or, failing that, a mandate by the United States or Great Britain.

Sept. 15. The British gave over control to the French.

Oct. 9. Gen. Henri Gouraud, high commissioner.

Dec. Fighting between the Arabs and the French.

1920, Mar. 8. A **Syrian national congress** again declared for complete independence.

Mar. 11. FAISAL PROCLAIMED KING. Britain and France refused to recognize him.

Apr. 25. The supreme council assigned

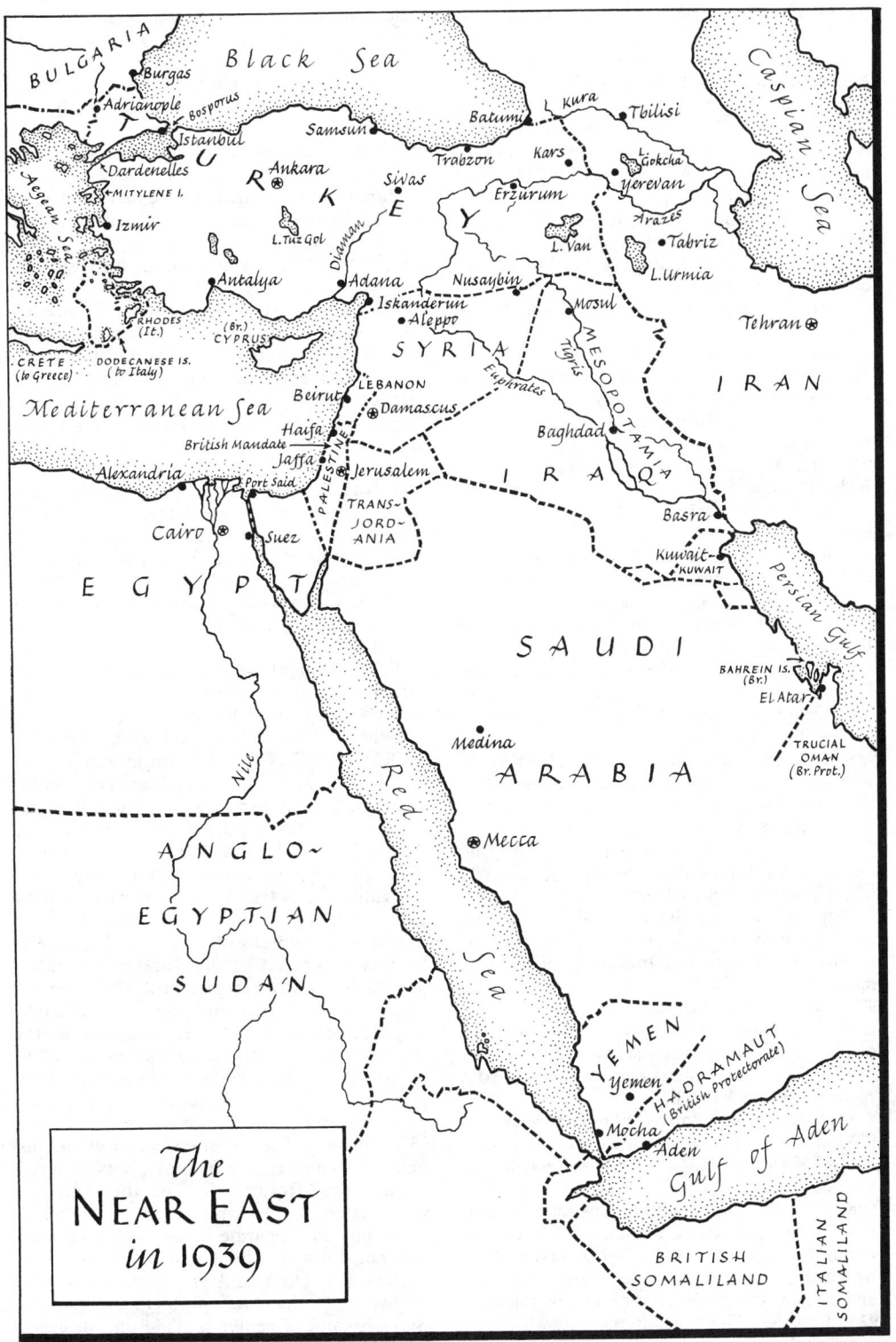

The
NEAR EAST
in 1939

the **mandate for Syria to France** (approved by the League, July 24, 1922).

July 25.   The French took Damascus. Faisal was dethroned and forced to flee.

Sept. 1. Organization of the territory by the French: states of **Aleppo, Damascus, Alaouite,** loosely federated (1922) autonomous units, under one French commissioner; **Great Lebanon** (Christian) given a separate status.

Dec. 23.   Anglo-French agreement on frontiers with Palestine and Iraq.

1921, Mar. 4. A fifth state, **Jebel Druse,** recognized as autonomous.

Mar. 9.   Agreement with Mustapha Kemal and the Turkish Nationalists, ending hostilities (p. 1086).

1923, Mar. 4. The **sanjak of Alexandretta** was separated and given autonomy.

Apr. 20.   Gen. Maxime Weygand, high commissioner.

1925, Jan. 1.   Damascus and Aleppo united to form the state of *Syria.*

Jan. 2.   Gen. Maurice Sarrail, high commissioner.

Feb. 9. Organization of the **People's Party,** a nationalist group demanding unity of the Syrian states and independence.

Apr. 2.   Agreement with Turkey regarding the autonomy of Alexandretta.

July 11.   Arrest of Druse notables who had been invited to a conference at Damascus. The Druses accused the French of favoritism toward the Christians.

1925, July 18–1927, June.   GREAT INSURRECTION OF THE DRUSES, under Sultan Pasha. They soon controlled the countryside and attacked even the larger cities.

Oct. 14.   Rising of Damascus, after the exposure of rebels' corpses by the French. The French withdrew from the city.

Oct. 18 Two-day **bombardment of Damascus,** followed by tank and airplane attacks.

Nov. 6.   Henri de Jouvenel, high commissioner.

1926, May 7. Second attack of the Druses on Damascus, followed by a **second bombardment** of the city by the French (May 8–19).

May 23.   The Great Lebanon proclaimed a republic by the French.

Oct. 12.   Henri Ponsot, high commissioner.

1927, June.   End of the Druse insurrection, after a large-scale campaign. The leaders fled to Transjordania.

1928, June 9. A **constituent assembly,** summoned by the French, contained a large Nationalist majority. It drafted a **constitution** which did not recognize the French mandate and which the high commissioner rejected.

1929, Feb. 5. The constituent assembly was indefinitely adjourned.

1930, May 22. The high commissioner introduced a constitution of his own: **Syria to be a republic,** with a parliament elected for four years; this was to elect a president, with a five-year term. **Latakia** was also established as a republic.

1932, Jan.   Elections; through French pressure the majority turned out to be moderate.

June. The parliament elected **Ahmed Ali Bey el-Abed president,** and he was approved by the French.

1933, July.   Damien de Martel, high commissioner.

Nov. 16.   Treaty with France, following the lines of the Anglo-Iraqi treaty: France to support Syria's admission to the League within four years; Syria to remain in alliance with France for 25 years, during which France would enjoy extensive control of foreign relations, army, and finance. The treaty was not to apply to the other Syrian states.

1934, Nov. 3.   Parliament was indefinitely prorogued because of opposition to the treaty (objection to separate treatment of the Syrian states and tó continued French control).

1936, Jan. The **Nationalist Party** (founded 1935) **was dissolved.** Violent street-fighting in most cities, followed by proclamation of martial law.

Feb.   General strike in Syria. The French administration was obliged to permit the formation of a **Nationalist cabinet** (Feb. 23).

Sept. 9.   SIGNATURE OF THE FRENCH-SYRIAN TREATY of friendship and alliance (ratified December 26); mandate to end within three years and Syria to be admitted to the League of Nations; Jebel Druse, Alaouite, and Alexandretta to be included in the Syrian state, with special status; the Lebanon to retain its individuality. A **treaty between France and the Lebanon** was concluded November 13.

Oct. 6. Outbreak of **rioting in Alexandretta** by way of protest of the Turkish population against the new arrangements. The problem, aggravated by Turkey's interference, was finally disposed of through League action and a separate **Franco-Turkish agreement** (p. 1088).

Nov. 30. The **elections** resulted in a huge Nationalist victory, whereupon (Dec. 21) a new president and premier took office.

1937, Jan. 4. The **Lebanon constitution,** suspended some years previously, was restored.

July–Aug.   Insurrection of the Kurds in northeastern Syria, who advanced claims to autonomy and separate status. The movement was put down by liberal use of air power.

Sept. 8. The **Pan-Arab congress at Bludan** to deal with the Arab problem in Palestine. Syria became a center of Palestine insurgent activity during the Arab revolt. (*Cont. p. 1298.*)

3. PALESTINE AND TRANSJORDANIA

1916, Apr. 26. Secret Anglo-French-Russian agreement providing that Palestine should be placed under **international administration.**

1917, Nov. 2. BALFOUR DECLARATION, stating that the British government favored *"the establishment in Palestine of a national home for the Jewish people and will use their best endeavors to facilitate the achievement of that object, it being clearly understood that nothing shall be done which may prejudice the civil and religious rights of existing non-Jewish communities in Palestine."*

Dec. 9. British armies took Jerusalem (p. 972).

1920, Apr. 25. The supreme council assigned the **mandate for Palestine and Transjordania to Great Britain** (approved by the League of Nations, July 24, 1922), on the terms set forth in the Balfour declaration, excepting that provisions for a Jewish national home were not to apply to Transjordania.

July 1. Civil government instituted: **Sir Herbert Samuel, high commissioner.**

1921, May 1–6. Serious anti-Jewish riots by the Arabs, who objected to the sudden influx of Jewish immigrants and to the acquisition of lands by Jewish interests.

Sept. 1. A **constitution** was promulgated by the high commissioner: there was to be an appointive executive council and a partly elective legislative council. The Arabs refused to vote for the council and therefore the constitution could not be put into effect.

1923, May 26. Transjordania was organized as an **autonomous state,** ruled (since April 1, 1921) by **Emir Abdullah ibn Hussein,** son of the sherif of Mecca.

1925, Apr. 1. The **Hebrew University** at Jerusalem was opened by Lord Balfour.

July 1. Field Marshal Herbert Plumer, high commissioner.

1928, Feb. 20. Transjordania was recognized as independent, the British retaining military and some financial control.

July 6. Sir John Chancellor, high commissioner.

1929, Aug. FIRST LARGE-SCALE ATTACKS UPON THE JEWS, of whom many were killed. The conflict followed a dispute concerning Jewish use of the **Wailing Wall** in Jerusalem.

1930, Mar. 31. Report of an **investigating commission under Sir Walter Shaw.** It attributed the conflict to Arab hatred of the Jews and disappointment of the Arab hopes for independence.

May 17. A **decree restricting Jewish im-**migration led to a Jewish strike of protest.

Aug. 25. Report of the League of Nations mandates commission on the clashes in Palestine, containing harsh condemnation of the British administration for having supplied inadequate police protection.

Oct. 20. The **PASSFIELD WHITE PAPER,** following the report of **Sir John Hope-Simpson.** It stressed the plight of the landless Arab proletariat and the increasing land-hunger, and suggested that Jews be forbidden to acquire more land while Arabs were landless, and that Jewish immigration be stopped so long as Arabs were unemployed.

Nov. Acrimonious debate in the British parliament on the Passfield paper. The British government denied that any change of policy was envisaged. Nevertheless the confidence of the Jews was badly shaken.

1931, July 14. Sir Arthur Wauchope, high commissioner.

1932. Restrictions on Jewish immigration were somewhat relaxed, but this move simply led to more and more outspoken protests from the Arabs.

1933, Feb. 25. The high commissioner rejected an Arab demand that sale of Arab lands be forbidden and immigration restricted. Thereupon the Arab executive announced a policy of non-co-operation with the British and boycott of British goods.

Dec. Jewish protests and riots against restriction of immigration (this problem having become crucial in view of the persecution of Jews in Germany).

1935, Jan. 4. Opening of the great **British oil pipeline from Mosul to Haifa.**

1936, Apr. Formation of the Arab High Committee with the aim of uniting all Arabs in opposition to the Jewish claims. By this time the demonstrations and riots of the Arabs had reached the dimensions of open war against the Jews. Conciliatory efforts made by the four Arab rulers (Aug.) were of no effect. The Arabs called a **general strike** which continued until October 12. To meet the situation the British government, somewhat belatedly, sent additional troops and appointed a commission of investigation and recommendation **(Peel Commission),** which took evidence in Palestine during the autumn. The Arabs boycotted it until just before its departure in January 1937.

1937, July 8. Publication of the **Peel Commission report.** Convinced that Arabs and Jews could not get along together, the commission recommended a **scheme for partitioning** the mandate, making three states: (1) A

Jewish state (about one-third of the whole) embracing the coastal territory from the northern boundary to just south of Jaffa. This state would contain about 300,000 Jews and about 290,000 Arabs; most of the land would be held by Arabs. (2) A **British mandated territory** comprising a strip from Jaffa along the railway to Jerusalem, both cities, as well as Bethlehem, to be included in it. (3) The rest was to be an **Arab state,** united with Transjordania.

Aug. 2. The Peel scheme was adopted by the **World Zionist Congress,** conditional on revisions in favor of the Jews. A minority voted against it and Jewish non-Zionist opinion throughout the world denounced the plan as a violation of the Balfour declaration.

Aug. 23. The mandates commission of the League of Nations, and later the assembly, accepted the plan in principle.

Sept. 8. The **PAN-ARAB CONGRESS AT BLUDAN** (Syria), composed of some 400 non-official representatives from all the Arab countries. The congress was called to deal with the Palestine situation and voted overwhelmingly against the Peel plan. **Demands of the Arabs** were: termination of the mandate and establishment of Palestine as an independent state in alliance with Great Britain; abandonment of the Jewish national home and cessation of Jewish immigration; the Jews to have merely the status of a guaranteed minority within the Arab state; partition unreservedly rejected. The congress arranged for a permanent executive, for economic support of the Palestine Arabs, and for extensive propaganda. Boycott of Jewish goods and enterprises, and eventually of the British, was provided for.

Sept. 26. **Assassination of Yelland Andrews,** British district commissioner for Galilee, brought on the most acute phase of the great Arab insurrection.

Oct. 1. The **British administration arrested the members of the Arab High Committee** and deported many of them to the Seychelles. The most influential Arab leader, the grand mufti of Jerusalem, **Haj Amin el Husseini,** took refuge in a mosque and later (Oct. 16) fled to Syria, which became the headquarters of the insurgents. The more radical elements (terrorist) secured ever greater control of the movement, and in Palestine outrages against the Jews multiplied to the point of pitched battles (Jerusalem, November 14).

Nov. 11. The British commissioner set up **special military courts** to deal with terrorists: the mere carrying of firearms or bombs made an offense punishable by death.

1938, Jan. 4. The British government announced the **postponement of the partition** scheme and the appointment of a **new commission under Sir John Woodhead** to study the boundaries of the new states and to investigate economic and financial aspects. The commission took evidence in Palestine from April until August, but was systematically boycotted by the Arabs.

Mar. 3. **Sir Harold MacMichael** arrived to replace Sir Arthur Wauchope **as high commissioner.** This was taken to presage more drastic repression of disorders. Before the end of the year the British had from 25,000 to 30,000 troops in Palestine.

June 29. **Execution of Solomon ben Yosef,** a young Jewish terrorist, representing the revisionist wing of Jewry, which advocated retaliation on the Arabs. During July and August Palestine was immersed in an undeclared war, with **bombings in the Jerusalem, Haifa, and Jaffa Arab markets,** with considerable loss of life. By many it was claimed that these outrages were not the work of Jewish extremists, but of Arab terrorists who dominated the whole Arab population.

Oct. 2. **Massacre of twenty Jews at Tiberias.** The Arab extremists seized several towns, which were retaken by the British only with some difficulty (Bethlehem retaken, October 10; the old city of Jerusalem, October 18).

Nov. 9. **Report of the Woodhead commission.** After analyzing various schemes of partition, the commission concluded that they were all impracticable. Thereupon the British government abandoned the plan and decided to convoke a **conference of Jews and Arabs,** the latter not only from Palestine but from the other Arab countries, all of which had demonstrated complete solidarity with the Palestinians.

1939, Feb.–Mar. The **Palestine conference** in session at London. Neither Jews nor Palestine Arabs were ready to accept a British proposal, despite efforts of non-Palestine Arabs to effect a compromise. The conference closed (Mar. 17) without reaching a settlement. Thereupon,

May 17. The **British plan** was published. It provided for an independent Palestine state in ten years, in treaty relationship with Great Britain. Arabs and Jews were to share in the government *"in such a way as to ensure that the essential interests of each community are safeguarded."* During a transition period Arabs and Jews were to serve as heads of departments (but with British advisers), and to take part in an advisory executive council according to population. After five years a representative body was to draft a constitution, which must provide for the different communities and for a Jewish home. In the matter of Jewish immigration the principle of absorptive capacity of the country was given up. Immigration was to stop after five years unless the Arabs agreed to its continuance. In that period 75,000 might be admitted, giving the Jews one-third of the population in 1944. The government was henceforth to prohibit or regulate transfer of land.

The British parliament approved this plan by a majority of only 89 as against the usual 200 or more (May 23), but it was violently denounced by the Jews throughout the world as making a "territorial ghetto" of the homeland. The Palestine Arabs also rejected it. Clashes and outrages again broke out in many parts of the mandate. The situation continued very unsatisfactory but was soon overshadowed by the crisis in Europe (p. 1132). When Britain declared war on Germany (Sept. 3), the Zionist organizations at once proclaimed solidarity with Britain against persecuting Germany.

(*Cont. p. 1298.*)

4. SAUDI ARABIA AND YEMEN

1915, July-Dec. Correspondence of Sherif Hussein of the Hijaz and the British regarding the terms of Arab intervention in the war against Turkey (p. 965).

1916, June 27. Hussein proclaimed the establishment of the Arab state.

Oct. 29. HUSSEIN PROCLAIMED KING OF THE ARABS.

Nov. 6. Britain, France, and Russia recognized Hussein as head of the Arab peoples and king of the Hijaz.

1919, May. Hijaz forces defeated by Abd al-Aziz ibn Saud, leader of the **Wahabis of Nejd,** a puritanical sect of Moslems (rose about 1740 and extended rapidly over interior Arabia; the Wahabis took Mecca and Medina, 1803–1806, and threatened Damascus, 1808; they were defeated and suppressed by Mohammed Ali of Egypt, 1812–1820). Ibn Saud, by 1913, had conquered much of eastern Arabia and had also made a treaty of friendship with Great Britain (Dec. 26, 1915). His claims were in direct competition with those of Hussein.

1920, Aug. Ibn Saud conquered and annexed **Asir.**

1921, Nov. 2. Ibn Saud took **Hail** and put an end to the Rashid dynasty.

1922, July. Ibn Saud took **Jauf** and ended the Shalan dynasty.

Dec. 2. Agreement between Ibn Saud and Iraq defining the frontier.

1924, Aug. 24. The Wahabis of Ibn Saud attacked **Taif,** in the Hijaz, and took it (Sept. 5).

Oct. 3. HUSSEIN WAS FORCED TO ABDICATE by his subjects, in favor of his son **Ali.** Ali was obliged to evacuate Mecca.

Oct. 13. Ibn Saud took **Mecca.**

1925, Jan.-June. Siege of Jidda by the Wahabis.

Nov. 1. Agreement of Ibn Saud with **Iraq** regarding the frontier tribes.

Nov. 2. Agreement of Ibn Saud with **Great Britain,** regarding the frontiers of Transjordania.

Dec. 5. Medina surrendered to Ibn Saud.

Dec. 19. Sherif Ali abdicated.

Dec. 23. Ibn Saud took **Jidda.**

1926, Jan. 8. IBN SAUD PROCLAIMED KING OF THE HIJAZ and **sultan of Nejd** (changed February 1927 to *king of the Hijaz and Nejd*).

Sept. 2. Treaty of friendship between Italy and the imam of Yemen; beginning of Italian efforts to establish influence on the east coast of the Red Sea.

1927, May 20. Treaty between Ibn Saud and Great Britain, which recognized the complete independence of the kingdom.

1929, Aug. 3. Treaty of friendship with Turkey.

Aug. 24. Treaty of friendship with Persia (Iran).

1930, Feb. 24. Treaty of friendship with Iraq.

1932, May-July. Invasion of rebels from Transjordania and subsequent insurrection in Nejd, evidently due to opposition to the westernizing and centralizing policy of the king (road-building, telegraph construction, aviation, etc.).

Sept. 22. The **kingdom of Hijaz and Nejd** was renamed *Saudi Arabia.*

1933, July 27. Treaty of friendship with Transjordania, ending years of hostility and tension between the two states.

1934, Feb. 11. Treaty of Sanaa concluded for 40 years with Great Britain.

Mar.-June. Campaign against the Yemen, after numerous border troubles and continued rivalry. Ibn Saud was completely successful, but the final peace (June 23), mediated by Great Britain, left **Yemen independent,** Ibn Saud acquiring only a rectification of the frontier.

1936, Apr. 2. Conclusion of a **treaty of non-aggression and Arab brotherhood between Arabia and Iraq.** This became the basis of a whole series of pacts between the Arab states, all of which were united in their stand on the Palestine question. General prevalence of the **Pan-Arab idea** and talk of an Arab federation. **Yemen adhered to the treaty** in April 1937.

Saudi Arabia: The Wahabi Dynasty (1735–   )

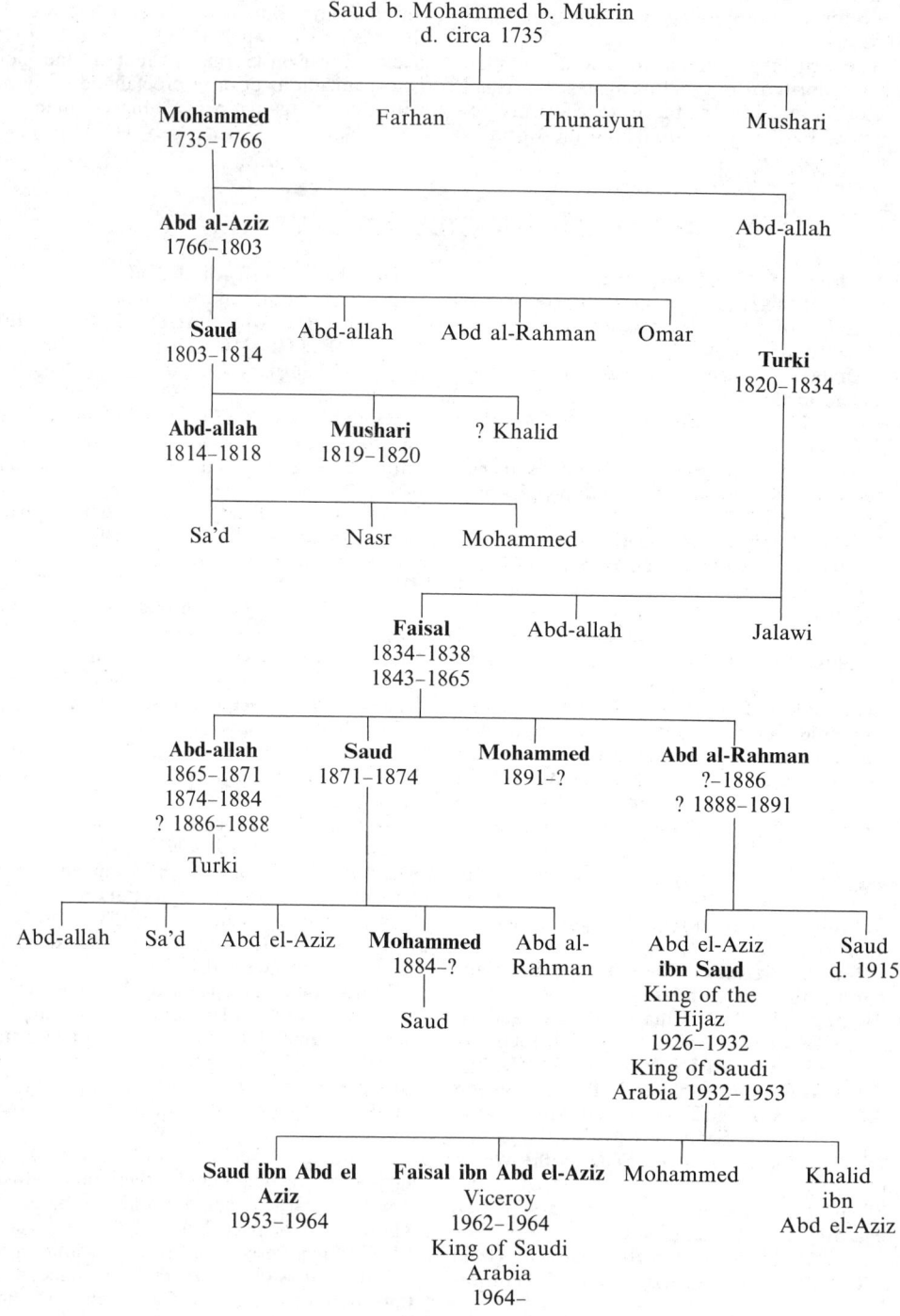

Saud b. Mohammed b. Mukrin
d. circa 1735

Mohammed
1735–1766   Farhan   Thunaiyun   Mushari

Abd al-Aziz
1766–1803   Abd-allah

Saud
1803–1814   Abd-allah   Abd al-Rahman   Omar

Turki
1820–1834

Abd-allah   **Mushari**   ? Khalid
1814–1818   1819–1820

Sa'd   Nasr   Mohammed

Faisal   Abd-allah   Jalawi
1834–1838
1843–1865

Abd-allah   **Saud**   **Mohammed**   **Abd al-Rahman**
1865–1871   1871–1874   1891–?   ?–1886
1874–1884   ? 1888–1891
? 1886–1888

Turki

Abd-allah   Sa'd   Abd el-Aziz   **Mohammed**   Abd al-   Abd el-Aziz   Saud
1884–?   Rahman   **ibn Saud**   d. 1915
King of the
Saud   Hijaz
1926–1932
King of Saudi
Arabia 1932–1953

Saud ibn Abd el   **Faisal ibn Abd el-Aziz**   Mohammed   Khalid
Aziz   Viceroy   ibn
1953–1964   1962–1964   Abd el-Aziz
King of Saudi
Arabia
1964–

May 7.   **Agreement between Arabia and Egypt,** the latter recognizing the annexation of the Hijaz by Arabia.

1937, Oct. 15.   Renewal of the 1926 **treaty between Italy and the Yemen,** for a period of 25 years.   The imam of Yemen, occupying a crucial position on the Red Sea, tried hard to maintain an independent status between Arabia, Britain, and Italy. (*Cont. pp. 1305, 1306.*)

5. IRAQ

1919, Jan. 10.   The British occupied Baghdad.

1920, Apr. 25.   The supreme council assigned the **mandate for Iraq** to Great Britain, which accepted (May 5).

July–Dec.   Great Arab insurrection against the British.   Several British garrisons were besieged for weeks before the movement could be suppressed.

Oct. 1.   Sir Percy Cox named high commissioner.

1921, June 23.   Emir Faisal, former king of Syria, arrived at Basra.

Aug. 23.   Cox proclaimed **FAISAL KING OF IRAQ,** after a plebiscite had turned out 96 per cent in favor.

1921–1933.   FAISAL, king.

1922, Mar. 25.   A **military agreement** was concluded with Great Britain, giving the latter a large measure of control.

June 18.   Insurrection of the Kurds under **Sheikh Mahmud.**   The movement aimed at independence or autonomy, and was not suppressed until July 1924.

Oct. 10.   An **agreement with Britain** transformed the mandate into an alliance relationship.

Dec. 2.   Treaty with Nejd regarding the frontiers.   Nevertheless the following years were marked by constant border raids and clashes between tribes.

1923, Apr. 30.   Protocol to the treaty of October 10: Iraq was to become free when it joined the League of Nations and in no case later than four years after the conclusion of peace with Turkey.

July 24.   Treaty of Lausanne.   The decision regarding the **Mosul area,** rich in oil, was left to negotiation and led to a long-drawn dispute (p. 1086).

Sept. 25.   Sir Henry Dobbs, high commissioner.

1924, Mar. 27.   The **constituent assembly** met and ratified the agreement with Great Britain.

July 10.   The assembly adopted the **Organic Law** (constitution), introducing a liberal, parliamentary system of government.

1925, Nov. 1.   Agreement with Nejd regarding the assignment and rights of the border tribes.

1926, Jan. 13.   In accordance with the League recommendation that the relationship with Britain should be extended if Mosul was to be assigned to Iraq, a **new treaty** was signed extending the connection to 25 years, or until Iraq joined the League.

June 5.   Settlement of the Mosul question, by agreement between Britain and Turkey. Most of the area went to Iraq.

1927, Nov.   Visit of King Faisal to London, in an attempt to secure Iraq's admission to the League immediately.

Dec. 14.   New treaty with Great Britain, which recognized the independence of Iraq and promised to support Iraq's admission to the League in 1932.   In return Iraq granted Britain three new **air bases** and agreed that British officers should train the army.

1929, Mar. 2.   Sir Gilbert Clayton, high commissioner.

Aug. 11.   Treaty of friendship with Iran.

Oct. 3.   Sir Francis Humphreys became high commissioner on the death of Clayton (Sept. 11, 1929).

1930, Feb. 24.   Treaty of friendship with Nejd.

Sept. 11.   New Kurd outbreak under Sheikh Mahmud.   The sheikh surrendered in April 1931.

Nov. 16.   The **Iraqi parliament ratified the treaty** with Britain, providing for admission to the League in 1932.   The treaty confirmed Iraq's complete independence and sovereignty.

1931, Jan. 22.   The Anglo-Iraqi treaty was presented to the League.

1932, Apr.–June.   Third rising of the Kurds. The rebels were driven over the Turkish frontier by Iraqi forces aided by the British air patrol.

Oct. 3.   IRAQ WAS ADMITTED TO THE LEAGUE OF NATIONS after a favorable though somewhat dubious report of the mandates commission.

Nov.   The **frontier with Syria,** long in dispute, **was finally settled** through the aid of the League of Nations.

1933, Aug.   Massacre of the Christian Assyrians as they tried to recross the frontier from Syria, to which they had migrated earlier.   The League took up the matter and tried to arrange for resettlement elsewhere, but with no success.

Sept. 8.   Death of King Faisal at Berne.

The Hashimite Dynasty (1921–   )

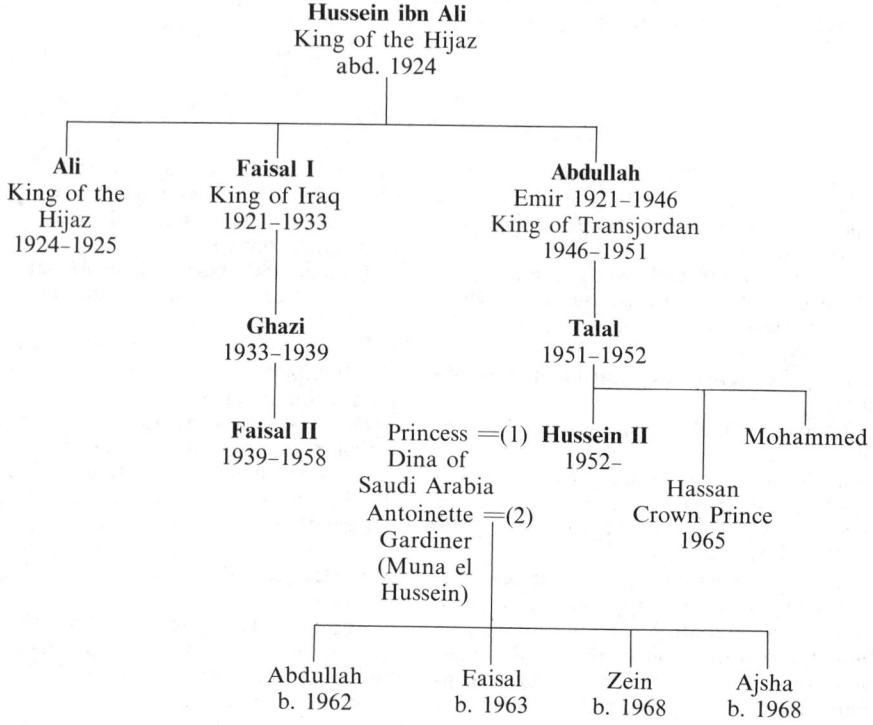

Hussein ibn Ali
King of the Hijaz
abd. 1924

Ali
King of the
Hijaz
1924–1925

Faisal I
King of Iraq
1921–1933

Abdullah
Emir 1921–1946
King of Transjordan
1946–1951

Ghazi
1933–1939

Talal
1951–1952

Faisal II
1939–1958

Princess ═(1) **Hussein II**
Dina of   1952–
Saudi Arabia
Antoinette ═(2)
Gardiner
(Muna el
Hussein)

Mohammed

Hassan
Crown Prince
1965

Abdullah
b. 1962

Faisal
b. 1963

Zein
b. 1968

Ajsha
b. 1968

1933–1939. KING GHAZI, son of Faisal.
1934, July 14. Opening of the great **oil pipeline** from Mosul to Tripoli in Syria. The line to Haifa was opened January 14, 1935.
1935, Mar. Formation of a **national government under Gen. Yasin Pasha el Hashimi.** Incipient revolts were put down, and compulsory military training was introduced (June 19). The new government won a decisive victory in the elections of August 6.
1936, Apr. 12. Conclusion of a **treaty of non-aggression and Arab brotherliness with Saudi Arabia.** This agreement became the basis for a general Arab alliance, the aim of the **Pan-Arab movement.** Other Arab states were invited to join.

    Oct. 29. *Coup d'état* of Gen. Bakr Sidqi, a prominent Pan-Arab leader. The king was a party to the movement, which was followed by the dissolution of parliament and a practical dictatorship of Gen. Sidqi.

    Nov. 26. Formation of a new party, the So-ciety for **National Reform,** an organ of the governing group. Vigorous prosecution of road and railroad construction, irrigation, and other schemes of development.
1937, July 9. Conclusion of the **Turkish-Iraqi-Iran-Afghan non-aggression pact,** forming a loose **Oriental entente** of Moslem states able to offer effective resistance against imperialist designs of outside powers.

    Aug. 11. Assassination of **Gen. Sidqi** by a Kurd. Formation of a new Pan-Arab cabinet. The Iraqi government took an active part in defense of the claims of the Palestine Arabs and became one of the prime movers in the cause of Arab solidarity.
1939, Apr. 4. Death of Ghazi in an automobile accident at Baghdad. In the ensuing disorders the British consul, supposed to have plotted the accident, was stoned to death. Ghazi was succeeded by his three-year-old son,
1939–1958. FAISAL II, as king.

(*Cont. p. 1308.*)

6. IRAN (PERSIA)

(*From p. 966*)

1918, Nov. A **British flotilla,** organized on the Caspian, **drove the Turks out of Baku.**

1919, May 21. Comm. **David T. Norris** of the British flotilla **defeated the Bolshevik naval force** at Alexandrovsk. In August the British ships were handed over to the White Russians.

1919. The Persian government sent a **delegation to the Paris peace conference** and demanded abrogation of the 1907 agreement, abolition of the capitulations and consular guards, restoration of Transcaspia, Merv, and Khiva, the Caucasus and Derbent, including Erivan and Baku, Kurdistan, and everything to the Euphrates River. This delegation, at the instigation of the British, was not officially recognized.

Aug. 9. The **ANGLO-PERSIAN AGREEMENT,** negotiated by **Sir Percy Cox.** Once again Britain reaffirmed the independence and integrity of Persia. Britain further engaged to furnish advisers and officers and to supply munitions for a force to preserve order. A loan was to be granted to Persia and aid to be given in railroad and road construction. The tariff was to be revised. This agreement was to seal the British ascendancy, and there was widespread opposition in Persia. The assembly (*majlis*) refused to convene to ratify it.

1920, Jan. 10. Persia became one of the original members of the **League of Nations.**

May 18. The **Bolshevik fleet,** having defeated the counter-revolutionary forces, **took Enzeli and Resht,** and occupied most of Gilan (**Soviet Republic of Gilan,** to October 1921). The British forces in northern Persia fell back on Kazvin.

Aug. 24. The **Persian Cossack Brigade,** commanded by Col. Peter Storroselski, **took Resht** from the Bolsheviks, but was later defeated and driven back from Enzeli, after which the British helped to reorganize it.

1921, Jan. 18. The **British began to withdraw from northern Persia.**

Feb. 21. THE *COUP D'ETAT* OF REZA KHAN. The latter was born in Mazandaran in 1878 and was an officer of the Cossack Brigade. Energetic and patriotic, he engineered the dismissal of the Russian officers after the defeat at Enzeli and then entered into negotiations with **Sayyid Zia ud-Din,** an eminent writer and reformer. With 3000 Cossacks Reza marched on Tehran and established a new government in which Zia ud-Din was prime minister and Reza himself minister of war and commander-in-chief.

Feb. 26. The first act of the new government was to drop the unratified British agreement and conclude a **treaty with the Bolsheviks.** The latter, in order to break down the British ascendancy, agreed to evacuate Persia, abrogate the capitulations, cancel all debts and concessions, and turn over, without indemnity, all Russian property in Persia.

Dec. 12. **Persian-Turkish treaty of peace and friendship.**

1922-1927. **Financial mission of Dr. Arthur C. Millspaugh,** an American expert. He was given wide powers and enjoyed the firm support of Reza Khan, though the finances of the army were kept beyond his control. With a new and enlarged army Reza suppressed a serious revolt in Gilan and (1922) subjected Azerbaijan.

1923, Oct. 28. **Reza Khan took over the premiership.** The shah, unable to approve the dictatorship, left for Europe, from which he never returned (died 1930).

1924, Mar. Rumors of the shah's return provoked a widespread **agitation for a republic.** Supposedly inspired by the Bolsheviks and by the events in Turkey, the movement was opposed by the religious leaders, who persuaded Reza of their view. Reza's threat of resignation brought the popular excitement to an end.

Oct. **Campaign against Sheikh Khazal of Mohammerah** and the Bakhtiari chiefs of southwestern Persia who, with the support of the Anglo-Persian Oil Company and the British government, had made themselves practically independent. They were all subdued and government control established throughout most of Persia.

1925, Feb. The majlis invested Reza Khan with dictatorial powers.

Oct. 31. The majlis declared the absent shah deposed.

Dec. 13. Reza Khan proclaimed shah by the assembly.

1925-1941. **REZA SHAH PAHLAVI.** The new shah consistently followed a policy like that of Mustapha Kemal in Turkey, excepting for the anti-religious aspect. He continued the work of restoring order, built up the army, developed roads, began the construction of a railway from the Caspian to the Persian Gulf, encouraged aviation, etc.

1926, Apr. 22. **Persian-Turkish-Afghan treaty** of mutual security, concluded under Russian auspices. Nevertheless, friction between Persia, Turkey, and Iraq over the Kurdish populations in the boundary regions continued.

1927, Feb. The Junkers Company (German) opened regular **air service** to Baku, Tehran,

Iran: The Pahlavi Dynasty (1925–)

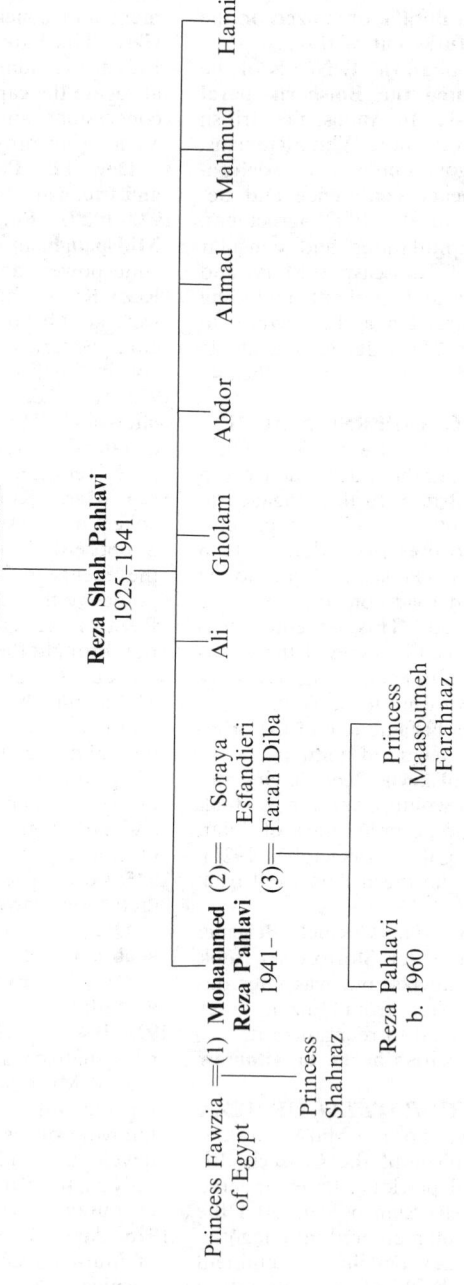

Isfahan, and Bushire. This continued until 1932.

Nov. 22. The Persian government advanced its **claims to the Bahrein Islands,** the Arab sheikh of which was under British protection. Discovery of oil gave the islands a new value.

1928, May 10. The Persian government, having introduced a **new judicial system** based on the French (1927), declared the **capitulations abolished.** New minimum tariff rates were offered to nations concluding treaties. Britain, followed by other powers, accepted the new system.

1929, Aug. 11. Persia recognized the Iraqi state and thus paved the way for better relations.

1930, June–July. A **great rising of the Kurds** on the Persian-Turkish frontier strained relations between the two countries, but led to renewed efforts to establish a satisfactory frontier.

1931, Feb. The government took over the Persian lines of the **Indo-European Telegraph Company.** At the same time the government established close **control over all foreign trade,** though private enterprise was permitted as before.

1932, Jan. 23. The **Persian-Turkish boundary was revised** in the vicinity of Mt. Ararat, thus obviating a constant source of trouble with Turkey.

Apr. 26. King Faisal of Iraq visited Tehran, paving the way for friendly relations.

Oct. Founding of the **Persian fleet** on the Gulf. The nucleus was a number of gunboats built in Italy for the Persian government.

Nov. 26. The **Persian government cancelled the concession granted to d'Arcy** in 1901 and taken over by **the Anglo-Persian Oil Company** in 1909. The British government, the largest single shareholder, brought the matter before the council of the League of Nations, which urged further efforts at direct negotiation. The result was the **new concession of May 29, 1933,** which extended the original contract from 1961 to 1993, but restricted the area from 500,000 square miles to 250,000 and after 1938 to 100,000. The company was to pay £225,000 annually in taxes for 15 years and £300,000 annually for a second period of 15 years. The minimum royalty was to be £750,000 annually.

1934, May. A concession granted to the Standard Oil Company of California to exploit for oil in the Bahrein Islands raised once again the Persian claim to ownership.

June 16–July 2. Visit of Reza Shah to Ankara. Persia and Turkey drew ever closer.

1935, Mar. 21. PERSIA BECAME OFFICIALLY *IRAN.*

1937, July 9. Conclusion of a **NON-AGGRESSION PACT** between **AFGHANISTAN, TURKEY, IRAQ, AND IRAN.** These four nations now formed an **Oriental Entente** comparable to the Balkan Entente.

1939, Jan. Opening of the **Trans-Iranian Railway** from the Caspian to the Persian Gulf. This important line, begun in 1927, was constructed entirely with Iranian capital.

(*Cont. p. 1309.*)

7. AFGHANISTAN

(*From p. 900*)

Afghanistan remained neutral throughout the First World War, despite German and Turkish missions and despite widespread religious agitation for participation on the Turkish side. Heavy subsidies from the government of India no doubt played a considerable rôle in holding the amir to the policy of his father.

1919, Feb. 19. Assassination of Habibullah near Jelalabad, evidently because of his subservience to the British. His brother **Nasrullah was proclaimed amir** by the conservative, religious parties, but his son **Amanullah,** governor of Kabul, not only held the capital, but enjoyed the support of the army. Nasrullah therefore yielded.

1919–1929. AMANULLAH, amir. Borne upon a wave of anti-British sentiment he took advantage of the war-weariness in India to proclaim a religious war and appeal to the Indian Moslems to rise against British rule. The Afghans began to invade India, but after a few initial successes were thrown back and threatened with invasion themselves. Neither side being prepared for a long struggle, they negotiated

1919, Aug. 8. The **treaty of Rawalpindi,** by which Britain recognized for the first time the complete independence of Afghanistan and the right to direct relations with other powers. The British subsidies were discontinued.

1921, Feb. 28. Conclusion of a **treaty of friendship with Soviet Russia,** similar to the Turkish-Russian treaty. There followed a period of several years during which Amanullah leaned rather heavily on the Bolsheviks as a protection against the British.

Mar. 1. Treaty of friendship and alliance with Turkey, laying the basis for a close rela-

Rulers of Afghanistan (1929–   )

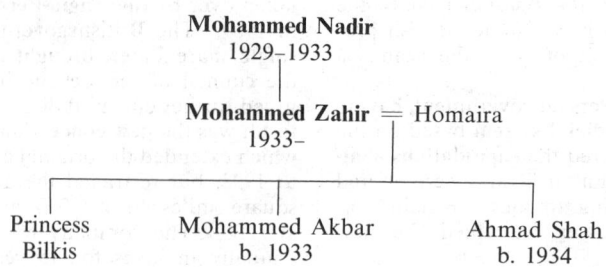

Mohammed Nadir
1929–1933

Mohammed Zahir ═ Homaira
1933–

Princess   Mohammed Akbar   Ahmad Shah
Bilkis   b. 1933   b. 1934

tionship between the two powers.

June 22. Treaty with Persia (non-aggression), another link in the Oriental combination under the aegis of Russia.

1923, Apr. 9. PROMULGATION OF THE FUNDAMENTAL LAW, or constitution, modeled on the Turkish and representing Amanullah's desire to modernize his country. The amir retained extensive powers, but the new assembly (council of state), which was one-half appointed and one-half elected, had certain powers over legislation. The constitution was followed by a landslide of reform edicts, aiming at the establishment of an effective central administration, development of education, encouragement of trade and industry, opening of the country through roads, etc. Amanullah played the rôle of a Peter the Great, hastily overturning everything in his desire to modernize the country.

1926, June 10. Amanullah assumed the title of *king.*

Aug. 31. A neutrality and non-aggression pact was signed **with Russia,** supplementing the earlier agreement.

1927, Nov. 27. Conclusion of a **second treaty** of friendship and security **with Persia.**

1928, Jan.–July. Amanullah and his queen paid an extended visit to India, Egypt, and Europe, arranging for further contacts and for financial and advisory support.

May 25. Second treaty with Turkey.

Nov. Outbreak of a **great revolt** directed against the king and his revolutionary reforms.

1929, Jan. 14. Amanullah abdicated in favor of his older brother, **Inayatullah,** an easygoing and ineffectual person.

Jan. 17. Bacha-i-Saquao, a bandit leader with a small but determined following, captured Kabul and had himself proclaimed

1929. HABIBULLAH GHAZI. His position was challenged by many other claimants, among others by Amanullah, who collected

an army at Kandahar but was defeated in his advance on Kabul.

Mar. Arrival from Europe of **Gen. Mohammed Nadir Khan,** an outstanding Afghan officer. He managed to collect an army and

Oct. 8. Took Kabul. Thereupon he was proclaimed (Oct. 16)

1929–1933. MOHAMMED NADIR SHAH. Habibullah Ghazi, having been captured, was executed, but the new ruler was faced with a large number of pretenders and followers of Amanullah, who were only gradually subdued. The general policy of Nadir was to continue the work of modernization, but in a less ostentatious and provocative way.

1932, Feb. A **new constitution** (*Fundamental Rules*) was issued. Its general tenor was much like that of the 1923 constitution, but it provided for a two-chamber assembly, an appointed chamber of notables, and an elected council of state.

1933, Nov. 8. Assassination of Nadir Shah. The murder had no political significance, and the shah was succeeded without trouble by his son

1933– MOHAMMED ZAHIR SHAH, who, with the aid of his uncles, continued the wisely moderate but progressive policy of his father.

1936. The government granted to the **Inland Exploration Company** of New York a 75-year concession for the exploitation of oil.

1937, July 9. Afghanistan joined with Turkey, Iraq, and Iran in forming an Oriental Entente, designed as a bulwark against pressure from any of the great European powers.

1938, June 20–24. Revolt of Shami Pir, a religious leader who operated from Waziristan. His movement was directed against the dynasty and its policy. After his defeat, Shami Pir fled to India, where he was arrested and transported to Syria.

(*Cont. p. 1311.*)

8. INDIA

(*From p. 904*)

1914, Aug. 4. Britain at war with Germany, making India automatically a combatant. Indian leaders responded loyally, and during the first two years of the war the political situation in India was comparatively quiet. The imperial legislative council voted a gift of £100,000,000 towards Britain's war effort. British India and the Indian states provided about 1,200,000 troops (combatants and laborers), who took part in the campaigns in Europe, Mesopotamia, Palestine, Egypt, and East Africa. During the second half of the war unrest became more and more prevalent, with rising prices and heavy taxation adding to popular discontent.

1915. Annie Besant, the Theosophist leader, founded the Benares Hindu University and organized the Home Rule League outside the Indian National Congress. The return from imprisonment (since 1908) of **Tilak,** and the deaths of **Gokhale** and **Pherozeshah Mehta** opened the way for a reunion of the moderate and extremist groups in the Congress. Meanwhile the Muslim leaders **Abul Kalam Azad** and **Mohammed Ali** were interned for opposing Muslim participation in the war against the Ottoman Empire.

1916–1921. Baron Chelmsford, viceroy. He was met at once with a demand for increased self-government made by 19 Indian elected members of the imperial legislative council. This was elaborated in the scheme, approved in December by the Indian National Congress and the All-India Muslim League meeting simultaneously at Lucknow, calling for dominion status, extension of the franchise, 80 per cent of legislative councillors to be elected rather than government-appointed, and half the members of executive councils to be responsible to the legislatures. The efforts of Tilak and **M. A. Jinnah** produced the **Lucknow pact** between the Congress and the League, recognizing separate electorates for the Muslim minority, giving them more seats in the legislatures than their numbers required ("weightage"), and allowing three-fourths of the Hindu or Muslim legislators to veto any measure affecting their communal interests.

1917. Tilak and Besant carried on a vigorous agitation for home rule. To forestall serious trouble, and embarrassed by the revelation of maladministration of the Indian forces in Mesopotamia, the British government, through the new secretary of state for India, Edwin Montagu,

Aug. 20. Announced a policy of developing **self-governing institutions** in India, with a view to introduction of responsible government. Montagu visited India in 1918 and together with Lord Chelmsford worked out a report (1918, Apr. 22) for limited self-government, presented to parliament in July, which was denounced by the Congress as "disappointing and unsatisfactory" and similarly condemned by the Muslim League. The moderate members of the Congress seceded and formed the **National Liberal Federation** (Nov. 1918), pledged to co-operate with reforms.

1918–1919. Influenza epidemic caused 5,000,-000 deaths.

1919, Mar. 18. The **ROWLATT ACTS,** two anti-sedition measures which enabled the government to intern agitators without trial and entitled judges to try cases without juries, became law despite the united dissent of the Indian members of the imperial legislative council. Angered at this, **Mohandas K. Gandhi** (1869–1948), saintly leader of the Indians in South Africa (1893–1913), having loyally supported the war effort, now proclaimed a day of fasting and work stoppage (*hartal*) throughout India, but ignorance of his pacifist program led to rioting. At Amritsar in the Punjab, five Englishmen were killed and an Englishwoman beaten (Apr. 10).

Apr. 13. THE AMRITSAR MASSACRE. General Reginald Dyer, aiming to terrorize the populace, ordered his Gurkha troops to fire on an unarmed assembly until their ammunition was exhausted; 379 persons were killed and 1200 left wounded. Gandhi (Apr. 18) suspended his civil disobedience (*satyagraha*) campaign, calling it a "Himalayan miscalculation." Mounting agitation throughout India followed, aggravated by belated and mild official censure of Dyer's action.

May 3–Aug. 8. The **third Anglo-Afghan War** (p. 1099), begun by the new **Amir Amanullah,** who appealed to India's Muslims to rise against the British.

Dec. 23. The **GOVERNMENT OF INDIA ACT** introduced the **Montagu-Chelmsford reforms.** The Indian parliament (opened at Delhi in February 1921), was to consist of the viceroy, **council of state** (60 members, of whom 26 were to be officials), and **legislative assembly** (140 members, of whom 100 were to be elected). The **provincial governments** were to have Indian as well as British ministers.

Under the "dyarchy" principle, important matters were "reserved" for the governor and the appointed British members of his executive council; the less important (sanitation, education, agriculture, etc.) were to be "transferred" to the Indian members. **Provincial legislative councils** were to be 70 per cent elective, with an extended franchise limited by property qualifications. The Indian National Congress rejected the new system but members of the National Liberal Federation cooperated with the government and in many places worked the new system with considerable success.

1920. Seeking to unite Hindus and Muslims, Gandhi joined the **Ali** brothers and **Azad** in organizing the **Khilafat movement** to protest the treatment of the Turks by the victorious Allies.

Aug. 1. Death of Tilak, who had been pressing for further constitutional advances. On the same day, Gandhi, accompanied by the Ali brothers, began a nation-wide speaking tour to enlist support for a great **non-co-operation movement,** involving boycott of foreign goods, schools, law courts, official functions, legislatures, and overseas military service. A special session of the Congress at Calcutta (Sept. 4–9) approved Gandhi's program, and the regular session at Nagpur (Dec.) reaffirmed it, converted the Congress into a mass organization under a hierarchy of full-time leaders, and defined its aim as "the attainment of *swaraj* [self-rule] by peaceful and legitimate means."

1921–1926. LORD READING, viceroy.

1921. Height of the non-co-operation movement. Despite Gandhi's insistence on non-violent action, terrorist outbreaks were frequent, and in some parts of the country serious peasant risings against landlords and moneylenders took place: **rising of the Akalis** (Sikh peasant puritans) in the Punjab, March 1921; **rising of the Moplahs** (Muslim peasants of Malabar) August 1921, with forced conversions and slayings of Hindu landlords. The latter episode set off a decade of chronic clashes between Hindus and Muslims, with much bloodshed.

Nov. 2. The Ali brothers were convicted and sentenced to two years in prison for calling on Muslim troops to desert.

Dec. 24. The Indian National Congress gave Gandhi sole executive authority. Gandhi denounced all violence and introduced a **campaign of civil disobedience** toward the law. Despite his great authority, violence continued to spread, culminating in

1922, Feb. 4. The Chauri Chaura affair. Insurgent peasants, led by Indian nationalists, attacked the police station at Chauri Chaura (United Provinces) and killed 22 policemen. Gandhi at once ordered suspension of non-co-operation and civil disobedience, but the government took drastic measures.

Mar. 10. Gandhi was arrested and sentenced to six years' imprisonment.

1923, Sept. 25. Victory of the moderate element in the Indian National Congress. This group (the **Swaraj Party**), led by **Chitta R. Das,** favored participation in the elections with the aim of using its representatives in the legislature to obstruct government and so force the granting of home rule. In the elections the nationalists did, in fact, win an impressive victory, but many of the elected deputies soon forgot about obstruction and began co-operating with the government (tariff autonomy bill passed, 1923). The leaders, Das and **Motilal Nehru,** began to advocate the granting of **dominion status** to India.

1924, Feb. 4. Gandhi was released from prison because of his precarious health. A **united conference at Delhi** (Sept. 26) brought together representatives of the Hindus, Muslims, Parsis, Sikhs, and Christians, who agreed to set up local committees to prevent religious clashes. The militant activities of the Hindu Mahasabha (founded 1915) and the Arya Samaj (Swami Shraddhanand murdered by a Muslim, December 23, 1926), nevertheless continued to aggravate Hindu-Muslim relations.

1925, Sept. 7. The nationalists in the Indian legislative assembly called for the establishment of round-table conferences to frame a scheme for responsible government.

1926–1931. LORD IRWIN, viceroy.

1926, Nov. 8. The British parliament appointed the **statutory** (Simon) **commission,** with members from all British parties, to study the situation in India and the working of the Montagu-Chelmsford system. Most Indian parties voted to boycott the commission because no Indians were included. The total effect of the move was to revive agitation and call forth further disorder during the commission's tour of India (1927–1928).

1928. India was swept by a **great series of strikes** among the Bombay textile workers, railway employees, etc., marking the emergence of the industrial proletariat as an important factor (All-India Trade Union Congress founded 1920), and the growing influence of the Communist Party of India (origins 1923).

Aug. 28. All-parties conference at Lucknow adopted the **Nehru report,** a proposed constitution which would give India dominion status under a representative government. Muslim leaders, although divided, disliked the omission of the safeguards for minorities agreed on 12 years earlier. Extremists, led by **Jawaharlal Nehru** (son of Motilal Nehru, chairman of the constitutional committee), **Subhas Chandra Bose** of Bengal, and **Srinivasa Iyengar** of Madras, rejected the dominion status provision and organized

Aug. 30. The Independence of India League, calling for complete independence. Their demand beclouded the central issue of Hindu-Muslim co-operation, which broke down at the

Dec. 22–1929, Jan. 1. All-parties national convention at Calcutta and the concurrent **Calcutta session of the Congress** (Dec. 29–1929, Jan. 1), at which Gandhi emerged from virtual retirement to heal the extremist-moderate rift with a compromise resolution calling on the government to grant dominion status within one year, failing which the Congress goal would become complete independence and another non-co-operation campaign would be inaugurated.

1929, Mar. 15. Thirty-one Communist leaders arrested for sedition; their trial, the **Meerut conspiracy case,** lasted four years and aroused the sympathy of the nationalists.

Oct. 31. The viceroy announced that a **round-table conference** would be opened with the objective of dominion status, but Conservative opposition in Britain prevented his making a firm pledge. Accordingly,

1930, Jan. 1. The Congress declared the Nehru report to have lapsed and empowered Gandhi to begin civil disobedience.

Mar. 12–Apr. 6. The **salt march** inaugurated the campaign. Gandhi marched to the Gujarat seacoast to make salt illegally as a symbol of defiance. The government remained inactive until violence broke out.

Apr. 18. Chittagong armory raid, eight guards killed.

Apr. 23–May 4. Peshawar in revolt after government troops fired on an unarmed crowd, killing at least thirty.

May 5. Gandhi arrested and imprisoned without trial, but his followers continued the movement: altogether 60,000 were jailed in this year, 103 killed and 420 injured by police firings.

Nov. 12–1931, Jan. 19. The **first round-table conference** held in London, attended by representatives of the Indian princes, the Liberals and the Muslim League.

Dec. 29. Muhammad Iqbal, president of the Muslim League, proposed the formation of a separate state for the Muslims of northwestern India.

1931, Jan. 26. Gandhi was released from prison, and, at Lord Irwin's request, entered upon discussions with the government. These resulted in

Mar. 4. The Delhi pact. Gandhi agreed to discontinue civil disobedience and promised that the Congress would recognize the round-table conferences; in return Lord Irwin agreed to release political prisoners who had not been guilty of violence.

Sept. 7–Dec. 1. Second round-table conference. Gandhi went to London as sole representative of the Congress, but the conference broke up without reaching agreement on the representation of religious and other minorities.

1931–1936. Earl of Willingdon, viceroy, whose unwillingness to negotiate led Gandhi to resume civil disobedience soon after his return to India (Dec. 28).

1932, Jan. 4. Gandhi was again arrested, the Congress declared illegal, and repressive measures were instituted to crush the non-violent demonstrations which followed.

Aug. 16. The round-table conference having failed to settle the question of minority representation under a new constitution, Prime Minister MacDonald announced the **communal award,** retaining the principle of separate communal electorates and extending it to embrace the depressed classes (untouchables). Gandhi, in prison, condemned the latter provision and embarked on a "fast unto death" (Sept. 20–26), ended when he and the untouchable leader **B. R. Ambedkar** agreed on the **poona pact,** giving the depressed classes a larger number of representatives, chosen by themselves in a primary election but elected by the general Hindu electorate. Gandhi's fast, and a second one (May 8–29, 1933) did much to arouse public sentiment against caste restrictions.

Nov. 15–Dec. 24. Third round-table conference, confined to minor matters.

1933, Apr.–1934, Nov. 22. A **parliamentary joint committee,** reviewing the material of the Simon commission and of the round-table conferences, worked out a draft constitution.

1933, May–1934, May. Gradual suspension of the civil disobedience movement. Gandhi now devoted all his efforts to raising the status of the depressed classes, whose members he renamed *Harijans* ("children of God").

1934, Oct. 21. All-India Congress Socialist Party founded.

Oct. 24. To free the hands of its younger leaders, **Gandhi resigned from the Congress,** but remained the supreme arbiter of its policies.

1935, Aug. 2. The **GOVERNMENT OF INDIA ACT** passed by the British parliament. **Burma and Aden were separated from India.** British India was divided into 11 provinces, each under an appointed governor and an appointed executive council. Each province was to have an elected legislature (bicameral in six provinces and unicameral in five), with a ministry responsible to it. Representation was to be based on the communal award. The **provincial governments** were to enjoy wide autonomy, though the governors retained certain emergency powers. The ultimate objective was the establishment of an **All-India Federation,** to include the Indian states as well as the provinces of British India, but this arrangement was doomed by the fierce opposition of the Congress and the states' refusal to join. A **central legislature** at Delhi consisted of an upper house (*council of state*) composed of 34 elected members and 26 appointed members, and a lower house (*legislative assembly*) of 105 members elected by the provincial assemblies and 40 appointed members. The governor-general retained control of defense, foreign affairs, etc.

1936-1943. MARQUESS OF LINLITHGOW, viceroy and governor-general.

1937, Jan.-Feb. Elections for the provincial assemblies. The **All-India Congress** (chiefly Hindu and demanding complete independence) was the only well-organized party and so won absolute majorities in six provinces and pluralities in three others. The objective of the party having been to force the abrogation of the new constitution and secure the convocation of an Indian constituent assembly, the leaders were now confronted with the problem whether or not to make use of such power as had been gained in the elections.

July. After prolonged negotiations, the Congress agreed to form ministries in six provinces (and in two more by 1938).

1937-1939. Deepening conflict between the Muslim League and the Congress, touched off by a Congress ultimatum to the United Provinces League to disband, which was rejected.

Once in power, the Congress ministries liberated many political prisoners and restored civil liberties. Attention began to turn more and more toward extensive social and agrarian reform. The war in China and the revelation of Japanese imperial designs contributed to the greater cordiality and collaboration between the nationalists and the British authorities.

1938, Feb. 19-21. At the Congress session in Haripura the radical leader **Subhas Chandra Bose** was elected president.

Apr. 28. After a lengthy correspondence, Gandhi met Jinnah in Bombay to discuss the Muslim League's demand that it alone represent India's Muslims. Gandhi and the Congress executive rejected this demand, and further attempts to reach an understanding were finally abandoned by both parties (Oct. 1938).

1939, Jan. 29. Bose was re-elected Congress president, defeating Gandhi's candidate. The delegates to the ensuing Congress session (Tripuri, March 10-12) rejected Bose's proposal to send the British government an ultimatum demanding independence within six months and reiterated their faith in Gandhi's non-violent policy and program. Unable because of Gandhi's opposition to form a working committee (the Congress executive), Bose resigned (Apr. 29) and formed his own party, the Forward Bloc (May 3), outside the Congress.

During the great depression the peasantry was adversely affected by the fall of prices on the world market, but business interests were able to expand in areas left vacant by the shortage of investment capital from abroad. The standard of living remained pitifully low for the vast mass of the people, 85 per cent of whom lived in rural areas, and 90 per cent of whom were illiterate. By 1940 the total population had grown to about 385,000,000 from an estimated 160,000,000 in 1800.

(*Cont. p. 1311.*)

9. INDO-CHINA

a. SIAM (THAILAND)

(*From p. 906*)

1917, July 22. Siam declared war on Germany and Austria-Hungary, and in the summer of 1918 sent a small expeditionary force to Europe. The war enabled the government to inaugurate the work of freeing the country of extra-territoriality and tariff restriction. By the peace treaties Germany, Austria, and Hungary were obliged to abandon their claims in these matters.

1920, Jan. 10. Siam became an original member of the League of Nations.

Sept. 1. A **TREATY WITH THE UNITED STATES** did away with American extra-territorial rights and granted Siam tariff autonomy.

1924, Mar. 10. By **treaty with Japan** the latter power also gave up extra-territorial and tariff rights.

1925, Feb. 14. TREATY WITH FRANCE. France followed the example of the United States and Japan, gave up all special rights, arranged for arbitration of disputes, and finally agreed (Aug. 25, 1926) to the establishment of a demilitarized zone along the Indo-Chinese frontier. Britain concluded a similar treaty July 14, and the other European powers followed suit, so that by 1926 Siam had secured full jurisdiction and tariff autonomy.

1925–1935. RAMA VII (Prajadhipok), king, succeeding his brother. He appointed a council of state, composed of five royal princes, to aid him in government, and at once initiated a policy of economy.

1927, Mar. 25. With the ratification of the last treaties with the powers, the **consular courts came to an end** and the Siamese government established a new tariff.

1932, June 24. A *coup d'état* put an **END TO ABSOLUTE GOVERNMENT** in Siam. The movement was organized by a group of young radicals, educated in Europe or imbued with European democratic theory, who formed a **People's Party.** The king, held captive for a short time, at once agreed to a constitution and the organization of a senate. The definitive **constitution** was adopted December 10: provision for popular sovereignty; the council of state, though appointed by the king, to be responsible to a national assembly, half the members of which were to be appointed while the other half were to be elected by universal (male and female) suffrage.

1933, Apr. 3. The king, convinced that the country would support him against the radicals, **suspended the new constitution** and set up a new council of state. This led to a new

June 20. *Coup d'état,* led by Col. **Phya Bahol Sena** and other army officers. While affirming their loyalty to the king, they forced the resignation of his council of state and recalled the national assembly. Phya Bahol Sena became prime minister.

Oct. 11. Attempted counter-revolution by a number of princes and nobles, led by **Prince Bovaradet,** failed; several of the leaders were captured and the others fled the country.

1934, Jan. 12. The king left for a prolonged visit to Europe, from which he did not return.

1935, Mar. 2. Abdication of King Prajadhipok, who was dissatisfied with the new régime and disagreed with the government over the execution of the counter-revolutionary leaders.

1935–1946. ANANDA MAHIDOL, the ten-year-old nephew of Prajadhipok, became king, and a council of regency, headed by **Prince Aditya Dibabha,** was set up in his behalf. The young ruler was being educated in Europe and did not even visit his kingdom until November 1938. Meanwhile the country was governed by a **triumvirate** consisting of the prime minister (Phya Bahol Sena), the minister of defense **(Col. Luang Pibul Songgram),** and the foreign minister **(Luang Pradit).** (*Cont. p. 1324.*)

b. OTHER STATES

(*From p. 909*)

The situation after the First World War in Indo-China and Malaysia was comparatively quiet, marked by rapid expansion of administrative control, development of sanitation and education, and above all by increase of population and productivity. The extension of rubber plantation in particular had a profound effect on the economic setup in many of the states. Some progress was made toward the introduction of a popular element in government, and in all parts of the region (least in the Malay States) there was a growing demand for national recognition. The great depression after 1930 struck all states equally hard, led to the adoption of economic control measures by the governments, and called forth a considerable amount of labor agitation, with some communistic tinges. The great Far Eastern crisis after 1931 revealed the exposed position of the whole area, and in all states measures were taken to strengthen defenses. The completion of the harbor works, dry-dock, air-field, and fortifications of Singapore (June 1937) made that crucial port what was considered to be one of the strongest places in the world.

FRENCH INDO-CHINA. In 1922 a number of elected members were added to the colonial council which assisted the governor-general, and in 1927 a government council (60 members, of whom 35 were Frenchmen) was established and given advisory powers. The year 1930–1931 was marked by rather serious outbreaks in Tonkin, which were put down with considerable rigor. But agitation against French rule revived and grew steadily stronger.

NETHERLANDS EAST INDIES. A legislative council (*Volksraad*) was created in 1916 and met in 1918. It was composed of 24 nominated and 24 elected members, the latter chosen by local councils. Racially there were 30 Dutchmen, 25 East Indians, and 5 members of other races (Chinese, e.g.). This body was given advisory powers in budgetary, military, and other matters. In 1922 the Volksraad became a genuinely legislative body when its assent was made obligatory for all government ordinances. In 1925 the entire administrative system was overhauled, and in 1929 it was decreed that in future the Volksraad should have 30 East Indian members (out of the 60). Despite the vigorous and efficient rule of the Dutch, there developed a movement for independence, represented by the **National Indonesian Party.** In 1937 the Volksraad unanimously petitioned the Dutch government to grant Dominion status within ten years. (*Cont. pp. 1320, 1322, 1334.*)

10. CHINA

(*From p. 916*)

1914, Aug. 23. The Japanese declaration of war against Germany was followed by **violation of China's neutrality** (Sept. 2) and capture of Tsingtao (Nov. 7).

1915, Jan. 18. JAPAN PRESENTED 21 DE-MANDS in secrecy. An ultimatum extracted from the Chinese government (May 8) modified acceptance of the first **four groups:** (1) Japanese succession to German rights in Shantung; (2) extension to 99 years of the leases in southern Manchuria with commercial freedom for Japanese there; (3) a half interest in the Han-yeh-p'ing Company which operated iron and steel mills at Han-yang, iron mines at Ta-yeh, and a colliery at P'ingshan; and (4) a declaration that no part of China's coast should be leased or ceded to any power. The **fifth group,** calling notably for Japanese advisers in political, financial, and military affairs, and railway concessions in the Yangtze River Valley (Britain's sphere of interest), was set aside.

Dec. 9. **Yüan Shih-k'ai,** following a monarchist campaign by the **Ch'ou An Hui** (Aug. 14), and election by a hand-picked national convention, **accepted imperial office** for the ensuing January 1, and adopted the reign title **Hung Hsien;** but in face of immediate successful **rebellion in Yünnan** led by **Ts'ai Ao** (Dec. 25),

1916, Mar. 22. **Yüan cancelled his imperial plans** and organized a republican cabinet under **Tuan Ch'i-jui,** senior general of the Pei Yang clique. Yüan died June 6 and was succeeded by **Li Yüan-hung,** who promptly restored the constitution of 1912 and convoked the original parliament of 1913.

1917, Jan. 23. **Special rights were exacted by Japan in Manchuria and Inner Mongolia.**

May 23. **Dismissal of Tuan** led to a rising of northern military governors. **Chang Hsün,** called to intervene, declared in Peking, with help of **K'ang Yu-wei,**

July 1. The **restoration of the Manchu dynasty,** which was again overthrown (July 12) by Tuan, who resumed the premiership. Resignation of Li left the presidency to the vice-president, **Feng Kuo-chang** (elected October 1916). **Sun Wen** headed a secession government at Canton (Sept.).

Aug. 14. **WAR WAS DECLARED AGAINST GERMANY AND AUSTRIA-HUNGARY,** and labor battalions were sent to France, Mesopotamia, and Africa. China secured termination of German and Austrian extra-territoriality and Boxer indemnity payments, and return of their concessions at Tientsin and Hankow. The Allies postponed their Boxer payments five years.

1918, May 16. **Japanese defensive alliance** against any Communist Russian threat provided for action by Japanese-trained Chinese troops in Siberia under Japanese direction (notes March 25, treaty May 16, clarified September 6). Loans of perhaps 250,000,000 yen for Manchurian projects were contracted, about half through Premier Terauchi's agent, Nishihara, with Premier Tuan and his clique, now called the **An-Fu** (Anhui-Fukien) **Club.**

Aug. 12. **A newly selected parliament convened,** and elected **Hsü Shih-ch'ang president** (Sept. 4–June 1922). Chinese politics continued, however, to be dominated by personal ambitions and the schism between the governments of Peking and Canton.

1919. Refusal of the Versailles peace conference to return the **former German concessions** in Shantung to China aroused violent resentment, refusal to sign the treaty (June 28), and (rather ineffective) boycott of Japanese goods.

Nov. 16. The Hutuktu of Urga placed **Mongolia again under Chinese suzerainty,** in recognition of a new Chinese garrison, but expulsion of the garrison by Mongols, led by White Russian Baron Ungern von Sternberg (Jan. 1921), and his expulsion by forces of the Far Eastern Republic, resulted in formation of the **Mongolian People's Revolutionary Government** (July 6), under Soviet auspices.

1920-1926. **CIVIL WAR** between local military dictators left no real power to the national government, which struggled to maintain its envoys abroad. Revenues from customs and salt were already pledged and administered for service of foreign loans. Those from railways and land taxes were absorbed by local armies for which the civilian population felt no concern since they supported no local interests. Since the death of Yüan Shih-k'ai there was no personality, no concrete cause strong enough to direct or to claim the loyalty of all Chinese.

1922, Feb. 4. The **WASHINGTON CONFERENCE** (p. 1122) resulted in a **nine-power treaty** to respect China's sovereignty, independence, territorial and administrative integrity, to maintain the "open door," and to afford China opportunity to develop stable government; a **nine-power treaty** (Feb. 6) to grant an immediate customs revenue increase to an effective 5 per cent, and to call a conference to prepare for

Chinese tariff autonomy; and a **Sino-Japanese treaty** (Feb. 4) to evacuate Japanese troops from Shantung, and to restore to China all former German interests in Tsingtao and the railway to Tsinan, in return for their assessed value plus Japanese improvements. The mines were to be operated by a joint company. Britain announced (Feb. 1) **return of Weihaiwei** (actually effected October 1, 1930). Joint resolution by eight powers (Dec. 10, 1921) called for re-examination of Chinese law and its administration in relation to extra-territoriality.

1924, Jan. 21. The **first Kuomintang national congress** at Canton (**Sun Yat-sen** president) admitted Communists to the party, and accepted Russian advisers, notably **Michael Borodin** (arrived September 1923) who reorganized the party for offense. **Chiang K'ai-shek** (Chiehshih, b. 1887), himself trained in Japan, headed Russian and German instructors in a new **Whampoa Military Academy** (June). **Sun Wen** presented his platform in a series of lectures on the *San Min Chu I,* "Three Principles of the People" (Nationalism, Democracy, and Social Progress), which he had already defined in 1907. Upon the death of Dr. Sun (March 12, 1925), he and his doctrine were promptly canonized as a focus for Chinese loyalty.

May 31. Soviet Russia, in fulfillment of repudiation (July 1919 and September 27, 1920) of the tsar's ill-gotten gains, **gave up extra-territoriality, concessions** at Tientsin and Hankow, and the rest of the **Boxer indemnity,** to be used for education under Russian veto. The Chinese Eastern Railway was placed under joint management.

Despite Japanese objection to competition with the South Manchurian Railway, the Chinese built two lines, Ta-hu-shan to Tungliao and Kirin to Hailung.

Remission by the United States of the $6,000,000 Boxer indemnity balance (May 21) created the

Sept. 17. China Foundation for Promotion of Education and Culture which made annual grants for scientific education, and housed and built up the national library beyond any Chinese precedent.

1925. Sentiment against the "unequal treaties" and against the British, who used gunfire to disperse dangerous student demonstrations at Shanghai (May 30) and Canton (June 23), found effective expression in a strike and **boycott of British goods and shipping,** until October 1926.

1926, July–Oct. Chiang K'ai-shek's northern campaign, with aid of Russian **Gen. Vasili Blücher** (then called Galen), followed the T'ai P'ing route from Canton through Hunan

to Hankow (Sept. 6) and Wuch'ang (Oct. 10).

1927, Feb. 19–20. From the British, tired of boycott, and hopeful of wooing the Chinese from the Russians, the Nationalists extracted **rendition of concessions at Hankow and Kiukiang.**

Mar. 24. Seizure of Nanking gave the Communists a chance to foment trouble for Chiang by attacking foreigners (six killed). An international force of 40,000 men protected Shanghai.

Apr. 18. Chiang and the conservative members of the Kuo Min Tang split with the radicals at Hankow and set up a **new government at Nanking.** Surface harmony was restored by a purge of Russians and Communists from Hankow in return for (temporary) retirement of Chiang from public life (Aug. 8). Advance to Peking was partly blocked by Japanese troops, sent to protect residents of Tsinan.

1927–1934. A considerable body of the landless were organized on the Communist model in Kiangsi and adjacent Fukien, where they seized the land. Under **Mao Tse-tung** and **Chu Teh** they defended themselves against all attacks from Nanking. When dislodged they effected an orderly **long march** (1934–1935) through Kueichou and Szechwan into northern Shensi.

1928, Apr. 7. Chiang was recalled to lead a fresh northern campaign, in co-operation with **Yen Hsi-shan,** model governor of Shansi since 1912, **Feng Yü-hsiang,** a magnetic but erratic northern war lord since 1920, and two Kwangsi strategists, **Li Tsung-jen** and **Pai Ch'ung-hsi.** Despite conflict (May 3–11) with Japanese troops, again in Tsinan (withdrawn May 1929), **Peking was occupied** (June 8), renamed *Peip'ing,* and the capital transferred to Nanking. Chihli province was renamed *Hopei.* The Chinese indicated their resentment at Japanese intrusion by a vigorous boycott (1928–1929). **Chang Tso-lin,** military governor in Manchuria since 1911 with Japanese approval, was forced to return there; and, since he now rejected Japanese advice, was assassinated (June 4). His son **Chang Hsüeh-liang** completed unification by recognizing the Nanking government (Nov.).

Oct. 10. The central executive committee of the Kuo Min Tang promulgated a **temporary organic law** which provided for a council of state headed by the president (who is also the highest military authority), presiding over **five administrative divisions:** executive, legislative, judicial, civil service, and censorial. All appointments to these offices were to emanate from the central executive committee and the party congress.

A series of **treaties with twelve states** (July 25–Dec. 22) **recognized the Nanking govern-**

ment and its right to **complete tariff autonomy** provided it practiced no national discrimination.

1929-1930. Japanese concern over the certainty of rapid loss of a large market for her cotton goods if the Chinese textile industry should receive protection dragged out treaty negotiations until May 6, 1930. Tariff autonomy, a substantial revenue source, was regained May 16. By 1930 nine nationalities had lost **extra-territorial privilege** in China, and several more had by treaty agreed to its end when it should be universally abolished; but it was still (1939) retained by France, Great Britain, Japan, and the United States.

1930, Oct. 1. **Weihaiwei restored** to China by Great Britain.

1931, May 5. A **People's National Convention** in Nanking adopted a **provisional constitution** which confirmed separation of five branches within the government, transferred power of executive appointment to the state council chairman, established autonomy of the (*hsien*) districts under provincial authority, and guaranteed personal freedom. The government pledged itself to free education and social insurance. A national congress to inaugurate full constitutional government should be called when autonomous district organization should be completed in a majority of provinces.

July 1. Serious **anti-Chinese riots in Korea,** stimulated by false report of a minor affair at Wanpaoshan in Manchuria, resulted in re-newal of the boycott against Japanese goods. Report (Aug. 17) of murder by Chinese soldiers of a Japanese officer (Nakamura) in West Manchuria (June) inflamed Japanese opinion.

1931-1932. THE JAPANESE OCCUPATION OF MANCHURIA. The Kuantung army, en-gaged in night maneuvers at Mukden (Sept. 18), alleged an explosion on the railway as ex-cuse for the preconcerted seizure before morn-ing of the arsenal and of Ant'ung, Yingk'ou, and Changchun, leaving to the Chinese troops no option save withdrawal. Amid for-eign-office statements of intention to localize the incident, **Kirin was seized** (Sept. 21) and the whole of the **three eastern provinces** pres-ently occupied (Harbin, February 5, 1932). Floods in the Yangtze River Valley added to Communist pressure, prevented any Chinese military effort to save Manchuria; but an im-mediate and more intense Chinese boycott cut Japanese exports (Nov.-Dec.) to one-sixth their usual figure.

1932, Jan. 7. United States secretary of state **Stimson notified all signatories of the nine-power treaty of February 4, 1922 that the United States would recognize no gains achieved through armed force** contrary to the pact of Paris of August 27, 1928.

Jan. 28-Mar. 4. To compel the Chinese to abandon their economic war, 70,000 **Japanese troops landed at Shanghai** and drove the Chi-nese 19th Route Army from the vicinity of the international settlement, destroying Chapei. An agreement (May 5) established a demili-tarized zone about the settlement and termina-tion of the boycott.

Feb. 18 INDEPENDENCE OF MAN-CHUKUO (Manchuria), to consist of the for-mer three eastern provinces with Jehol, was proclaimed at Hsin-ching (*New Capital*) the former Changchun. **Henry P'u-i,** who abdi-cated the throne of China (1912), was installed as regent (Mar. 9), and promoted (Mar. 1, 1934) as **emperor of the K'ang Te reign.** Jap-anese advisers and secretaries controlled from the first all important activities.

Sept. 15. A protocol established a close **protectorate of Japan over Manchukuo.**

Oct. 2. **Report of a League of Nations com-mission of inquiry** under the **earl of Lytton** (signed September 4) found that Japanese ac-tion on September 18-19, 1931, was not self-defense, and that creation of Manchukuo did not flow from a "genuine and spontaneous in-dependence movement." It recommended establishment in Manchuria of an autonomous administration under Chinese sovereignty with international advisers and police, and recogni-tion of Japanese economic interests.

1933, Feb. 24. Approving this report, the **League assembly adopted the Stimson formula of non-recognition,** and indicated that Japanese military pressure should cease.

Jan.-Mar. **Japanese occupation of Jehol** and advance south of the great wall (Apr.) forced

May 31. The **T'ang-ku truce,** which re-quired Chinese troops to evacuate the Tientsin area.

1935, Mar. 23. **Russia sold to Manchukuo her interest in the Chinese Eastern Railway** after negotiations begun in May 1933.

Apr. The government decreed one year of **military training for all male high-school and college students** to provide 100,000 reservists each year.

June 9. The Japanese army extracted the **Ho-Umezu agreement** for withdrawal from Hopei of troops objectionable to the Japanese.

Continuing excessive cost of occupation of Manchukuo, in which bandits and irregular guerrillas prevented any durable pacification, led the Japanese army to attempt to force, without actual invasion, formation of a local Chinese government willing to afford Japan opportunity for exploitation of resources and markets of North China. Efforts to secure secession of five provinces (Shantung, Hopei, Shansi, Chahar, and Suiyüan) having failed, **Nov. 24.** An **East Hopei autonomous régime** was set up between T'ung-chou (outside Peip'ing) and the sea. Japanese goods were smuggled wholesale into China through this area, and narcotics were poured from it upon the world market.

Dec. 18. A **Hopei-Chahar political council** was established at Peip'ing under **Gen. Sung Che-yüan,** who rendered lip service to the Japanese but made no vital concessions.

1936, July 19. Chiang succeeded in gaining control of Kwangtung, in spite of Japanese aid to his adversaries, and of Kwangsi (Sept. 6), where the local leaders loudly demanded war against Japan, for which Chiang was still unprepared. The same demand was constantly voiced by the Chinese Communists, who had set up (Oct. 1935) orderly government in northern Shensi.

Sept. Japan presented seven secret demands (known October 1) under threat of immediate invasion of both north and central China. Most serious were: brigading of Japanese with Chinese troops against Communists everywhere (ground for action in any part of China), employment of Japanese advisers in all branches of government, autonomy for five northern provinces, and reduction of tariff to the level of 1928. Although Japan sent troops to Shanghai, Nanking stood firm.

Dec. 12–25. Gen. Chang Hsüeh-liang kidnapped Chiang K'ai-shek at Si-an to force him to declare war on Japan. Demonstration of loyalty to Chiang throughout China, even by the Reds, who now effected his release.

1937, Jan. 28. Negotiations terminated the long anti-Communist campaign, and brought the Shensi government into harmony with Nanking.

The **Hankow-Canton Railway was completed** with help from British Boxer indemnity funds, and a new Hangchow-Nanch'ang Railway was opened.

June 1. Szechwan was brought into the new national union, made effective by telegraph, long-distance telephone, and radio communication; Sino-American and Sino-German **airlines;** 75,000 miles of new **motor roads;** and a uniform stabilized paper currency. Achievement of **political unity and stability** (1927–1937) supplemented and accelerated fundamental changes which had been in progress since 1912 in many departments of life, often led by students returned from study abroad. Vital to China's clearly approaching struggle with Japan was introduction of **modern finance and banking.** Finance minister T. V. Soong in 1932 announced a balanced budget, conversion of domestic debt, and abolition of *likin* transit

dues which had been a vexation ever since the T'ai P'ing rebellion. Substitution (Nov. 1934) of paper silver certificates for the new standard silver dollars (minted March 1, 1933) operated to concentrate in the treasury large deposits of silver bullion. These the United States treasury under the Pitman Act agreed (July 9, 1937) to exchange for gold, thus affording a large volume of credits abroad just when they were urgently required for purchase of arms.

Scholarship was immensely stimulated by close contact with western thought and literature. An official commission (1914–1928) drafted from the archives a *History of the Ch'ing Dynasty* to complete the standard series. **Wang Kuo-wei** (1877–1927) was a traditional scholar brilliant in decipherment of Shang oracular inscriptions as in textual and historical criticism. His elder friend **Lo Chen-yü** noted for his archaeological publications. Younger men carried modern methodology into every domain of the humanities and sciences. **Hu Shih** led (since 1917) in developing a completely successful *pai hua* "**plain speech**" **style of writing** closely allied to colloquial speech and far easier to use and read than the terse classical style. It won general acceptance for scholarly, literary, and practical purposes. Introduction of punctuation facilitated understanding of both ancient and modern texts, and preparation of indexes made their content accessible to a greater degree than ever before. A flood of periodicals, quarterly, monthly, and weekly, afforded a medium for scholarly publication and interchange of current views almost totally lacking in 1912. **Education** was altered as much in content and method as in diffusion. Elementary pupils increased (1912–1935) from 2,793,633 to 11,667,888, and high-school students from 52,100 to c. 500,000. In place of four colleges in 1912 there were (in 1933) 40 universities, 40 colleges, and 23 technical schools, with 43,000 students, libraries totaling 4,500,000 volumes, and a budget of over $40,000,000 silver.

1937–1945. The **JAPANESE CAMPAIGNS IN CHINA** (no declaration of war, for technical reasons of international law). The conflict had been long in the offing, and the evidence would seem to indicate that Japan decided to act before the renaissance of China had gone too far.

July 7. The **incident at Lukouchiao** (near Peip'ing): Japanese troops, on night maneuvers, clashed with Chinese. The fighting spread rapidly and led to the **seizure of Peip'ing** (July 28) and **Tientsin** (July 29) by the Japanese. A large-scale campaign was begun in northern China. Without meeting much resistance, the **Japanese took Kalgan** (Sept. 3), **Paoting**

(Sept. 24), **Shihchiachuang** (Oct. 10), **Kweisui** (Oct. 14), **and T'ai-yüan** (Nov. 9). By this time the Chinese had become better organized and managed to slow down the advance, though inferiority in equipment told heavily against the Chinese throughout.

Aug. 8–Nov. 8. THE SHANGHAI CAMPAIGN. The killing of two Japanese marines at a Chinese military airdrome led to the landing of a Japanese naval force (Aug. 11) which soon found itself endangered by vastly superior Chinese forces. The Japanese were obliged to send an army which, after dogged resistance by the Chinese and very severe fighting, ultimately forced the Chinese back from the city (Nov. 8). The **fall of Shanghai** was followed immediately by the **taking of Suchow** (Nov. 20) and by an energetic drive up the Yangtze River. Merciless **bombing of Chinese cities** by the Japanese outraged world opinion.

Aug. 25. The **Japanese naval blockade** of South China was extended (Sept. 5) to the entire coast, but Tsingtao, Hong Kong, Macão, and Kwangchowan were excepted, out of consideration for foreign powers.

Aug. 29. Conclusion of a **non-aggression treaty between China and Soviet Russia.** This led to the sale of military aircraft to China and to shipment of large quantities of munitions after

Oct. 5–6. The League of Nations and the United States condemned the action of Japan. A conference of the powers at Brussels (Nov. 15) failed to effect mediation.

Nov. 20. The **Chinese capital was moved from Nanking to Chungking** (Ch'ung-ch'ing), though the executive power was, for the time being, established at Hankow.

Dec. 12. The *Panay* incident: attack of Japanese bombers upon American and British ships near Nanking produced acute tension between the powers. The United States government ultimately accepted Japanese explanations, but the Japanese government continued a high-handed policy toward foreign property and rights in China and evaded all protests from the United States, Great Britain, and France. The tense situation in Europe enabled the Japanese to pursue their aims without running serious risk of intervention.

Dec. 13. FALL OF NANKING, after heavy fighting. Atrocities committed by the Japanese troops. The Chinese fell back, denying the Japanese a decision. The first six months of the war had demonstrated to an astonished world the **moral unity of the Chinese people.** All factions, including the Communists, acted on the orders of the central government. Chiang had the country behind him in the announced purpose of making no compromise at the ex-

pense of Chinese territory or independence.

Dec. 24. The **Japanese took Hangchow** and, advancing from the north, occupied **Tsinan** (Dec. 27).

1938, Jan. 10. Capture of Tsingtao by the Japanese, after the Chinese had destroyed the Japanese mills in that area. The Japanese then began the advance south along the Hankow Railway and through Shansi. They reached the Yellow River (Mar. 6), but mobile Chinese forces restricted the Japanese to the railway zone. More and more it became evident that the Japanese could capture the large cities and important communications, but that the countryside would remain in the hands of the Chinese guerrillas. During the spring of 1938 the Japanese forces suffered several reverses at the hands of the Chinese.

Mar. 28. The Japanese installed a **Reformed Government of the Republic of China** at Nanking, thus repeating the technique employed earlier in Manchukuo.

May. Resumption of the Japanese advance. They took **Amoy** (May 10), **Suchow** (May 20), **Kaifeng** (June 6), and **Anking** (June 12).

July 11–Aug. 10. Clash of Russian and Japanese forces at Changkufeng Hill, on the border between Siberian, Manchukuan, and Korean territory. After severe fighting a truce was finally arranged for, the Russians retaining their position.

Sept. 22. Creation of a **United Council for China at Peip'ing,** under Japanese auspices. The Japanese made less and less of a secret of their intention to overthrow Chiang and his Nationalist régime and transform China into a Japanese protectorate, as part of the projected "new order" in the Far East.

Oct. 12. The **Japanese landed** forces at Bias Bay, **near Hong Kong,** evidently intending to realize on the acute crisis in Europe arising from the Czechoslovak affair (p. 1129). They advanced inland and on

Oct. 21. The **JAPANESE TOOK CANTON,** almost without a struggle. The city had been mercilessly bombed for months and a large part of the population had already fled. Capture of the city enabled the Japanese to cut the Canton-Hankow Railway, the most important line for transportation of supplies from abroad to the Chinese forces in the interior.

Oct. 25. FALL OF HANKOW to the Japanese. The Chinese government and army withdrew up the Yangtze to Chungking. Japanese control over the Yangtze below Hankow became ever more rigid, leading to repeated and insistent **protests on the part of the western powers.** The American secretary of state, Cordell Hull, reasserted the validity of the nine-power treaty (Nov. 4) and was supported in his attitude by the British government. But protests made only the slightest impression in Tōkyō.

1939. The fighting continued in an inconclusive fashion over a large area. There was no indication of any slackening of Chinese determination, and the government of Chiang continued to receive supplies from Russia and other powers, even by the most devious routes. Both the United States and Britain made substantial loans to the Nationalist government. The Japanese, unable to force a decision, developed an indirect attack on the position of foreign powers in China, demanding larger share in the Shanghai international concession and challenging foreign rights everywhere.

June 14. The Japanese established a **blockade** of the British concession **at Tientsin** (and incidentally also of the French), following refusal of the British authorities to surrender four Chinese accused of terrorism. Japanese spokesmen publicly announced that Britain must give up support of the Chinese Nationalist régime and must co-operate with Japan in establishing the "new order" in the Far East.

(*Cont. p. 1338.*)

11. JAPAN

(*From p. 923*)

1914–1918. THE FIRST WORLD WAR. During the war Japan manufactured and sent to Europe large quantities of munitions (especially to Russia). At the same time Japanese merchants took advantage of the conflict to supplant German commerce in eastern Asia.

1914, Nov. 7. Kiaochow surrendered to the Japanese after a two months' siege (p. 969).

1915, Jan. 18. JAPAN SUBMITTED TO CHINA TWENTY-ONE DEMANDS (p. 1106), initiating the policy of subordinating China and establishing Japanese preponderance in the Far East.

Oct. 19. Japan formally joined the pact of London (Sept. 5, 1914) binding herself not to conclude a separate peace.

1916, July 3. Russo-Japanese convention, by which Russia accepted the extension of Japanese influence in China under agreements of 1915, and Japan recognized the Russian advance into Outer Mongolia.

Sept. 3. Fresh demands on China, increasing Japanese rights in South Manchuria and Inner Mongolia, followed a clash between Japanese and Chinese troops at Chêng-chia-tun (Aug.). Agreed to by China (Feb. 1917).

Oct. 9. Count Juichi Terauchi succeeded Ōkuma as premier, with a slight minority in the lower house.

1917, Apr. 20. The **general election** proved a victory for the government.

Nov. 2. Notes were exchanged with the United States **(Lansing-Ishii agreement)** by which the latter recognized the special interests of Japan in China and Japan gave pledges of good faith in the maintenance of Chinese integrity, independence, and the "open door."

1918, Apr. 5. British and Japanese marines landed at Vladivostok.

May 16. Sino-Japanese treaty (p. 1106).

July 6. Allied commanders took command of Vladivostok. An announcement of intervention (Aug. 3) was issued.

Sept. 29. The **Terauchi ministry resigned** because of inability to cope with unrest caused largely by high prices resulting from war boom. **Takashi Hara** (first commoner premier) **succeeded.**

1919, Jan. 18. Peace conference opened. Japan was favorable to the League of Nations, but her demand for a statement as to racial equality was refused.

Feb. 14. Acrimonious **debate on universal suffrage** in the diet. The franchise then was limited to men over 25 paying a direct tax of three yen, thus excluding agricultural and industrial labor. Organized demonstrations in Tōkyō and dissolution of the diet (Feb. 26) followed.

Apr. Rioting and open **rebellion in Korea** was mercilessly suppressed. There followed a **revision of the Korean government** substituting civil for military control and promising larger powers of self-government when the Koreans abandoned their independence movement.

Mar. 25. A reform act increased the electorate from 1,500,000 to 3,000,000.

May 10. A general election with the universal suffrage issue dominant resulted in 283 seats for the government party (*Seiyūkai*), which was opposed to it, 108 for the *Kenseikai*, and 68 for other parties.

1920, Jan. 10. Formal **peace with Germany** by exchange of ratifications. Japan, after initial satisfaction, became chagrined over the failure to secure recognition of its special position in the Far East.

Dec. 17. Japan received as mandates from the League of Nations the former German islands of the Pacific north of the equator

Japanese Emperors (1867–   )

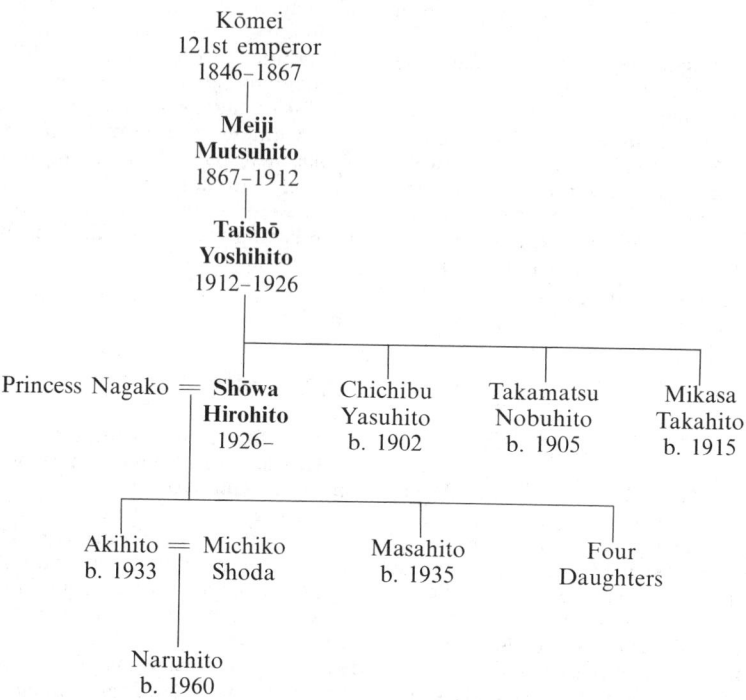

Kōmei
121st emperor
1846–1867

**Meiji
Mutsuhito**
1867–1912

**Taishō
Yoshihito**
1912–1926

Princess Nagako = **Shōwa
Hirohito**
1926–

Chichibu
Yasuhito
b. 1902

Takamatsu
Nobuhito
b. 1905

Mikasa
Takahito
b. 1915

Akihito = Michiko
b. 1933   Shoda

Masahito
b. 1935

Four
Daughters

Naruhito
b. 1960

(Caroline, Marshall, and Marianas [Ladrone] archipelagoes).

Dec. 31. The first **imperial census** revealed population of 55,961,140 (including Sakhalin, Formosa, and Korea, 77,005,112).

1921, Mar.–Aug. The **world tour of the crown prince, Hirohito,** marked the first time a member of the imperial family had been abroad.

Nov. 4. **Murder of Premier Hara** by a political fanatic.

Nov. 12. **Viscount Korekiyo Takahashi** premier.

Nov. 12–1922, Feb. 6. **Washington conference** (p. 1122). Prince Tokugawa, Adm. Katō, and Baron Shidehara were the Japanese delegates.

Nov. 25. **Crown Prince Hirohito regent** because of illness of the emperor.

1922, Feb. 11. **Yap treaty** signed with the United States (p. 1047).

Feb. 23. Serious **riots over universal suffrage.**

June 2. **Ratification of the Sino-Japanese agreement on Shantung,** resulting in more friendly relations with China and **return of Kiaochow** (Dec. 10).

June 11. Baron Tomosaburo Katō suc-

ceeded Takahashi as premier.

July 6. **Washington treaties** ratified by Japan; naval budget reduced by 117,000,000 yen.

Sept. 6–24. The **Changchun conference with Russia** was a failure and Japan continued to occupy North Sakhalin.

Oct. The last of **Japanese troops embarked from Siberia.**

1923, Mar. 2. **Universal suffrage bill defeated.**

Aug. 28. **Count Gombei Yamamoto** succeeded Katō as premier.

Sept. 1. **Great Tōkyō earthquake** followed by great fires in Tōkyō, Yokohama, and neighboring cities, tidal waves, and repeated shocks. 200,000 estimated killed; $1,000,000,000 estimated losses. Relief sent from abroad, particularly the United States.

Dec. 29. **Resignation of the ministry** following an attack on the life of the prince regent; **Viscount Keigo Kiyoura premier.**

1924, Apr.–June. High feeling aroused by the **American abrogation of** the gentlemen's agreement and total exclusion of Japanese. Demonstrations and boycotts of American goods.

May 10. **General election** held; defeat for Kiyoura ministry; **Katō premier** and Baron

Kijouro Shidehara foreign minister (June 1924–Apr. 1927), with **conciliatory policy toward China.**

1925, Jan. 20. **Russo-Japanese convention** reestablished diplomatic relations: Russia recognized the treaty of Portsmouth of 1905; the fisheries convention of 1907 was to be revised; Japan received oil and coal concessions in North Sakhalin and agreed to evacuate her troops. This and subsidiary agreements formed a general settlement of issues between the two countries.

Mar. Bill passed granting **universal male suffrage;** voters increased from three to fourteen million.

1926, Jan. 28. **Premier Katō died** and was succeeded by the new leader of the *Kenseikai*, **Reijiro Wakatsuki,** the second commoner to become premier.

Dec. 25. The **Taishō emperor died,** and the prince regent succeeded. The year period was changed to **Shōwa,** marking the beginning of

1926– **THE SHŌWA PERIOD.** After a few more years of the liberalism and internationalism of the Taishō period, a sudden strong **militaristic and imperialistic reaction** set in after the Mukden incident (p. 1108). There was a partial repudiation of the intellectual and cultural aspects of Occidental civilization and a revival of older Japanese ideologies. Politicians lost their influence, and the army and, to a lesser extent, the navy became the dominant forces in the government, with the peasantry supporting the military against the city bourgeoisie and the capitalists. Under this leadership the nation embarked on a daring program of territorial expansion on the continent. Meanwhile, Japanese industry was growing rapidly, and Japanese manufactured goods began to flood the world market.

1927, Apr. 17. **Fall of Wakatsuki ministry; Baron Giichi Tanaka,** leader of the *Seiyūkai,* **became premier** and foreign minister (until July 2, 1929), pursuing a "positive" policy toward China.

May–June. **Japanese intervention in Shantung** blocked the northward advance of Chinese Nationalist forces upon Peking.

1928, Apr. **Japan again intervened in Shantung,** leading to

May 3–11. **Sino-Japanese clashes at Tsinan:** Japan temporarily seized control of railways in Shantung; Chinese boycott movement against Japan lasted for over a year; incident settled March 28, 1929; China to pay damages but not indemnity; Japanese troops withdrawn May 20, 1929.

1929. Growth of **labor unions,** begun particularly during 1915–1920, reached a total of 600 associations with a third of a million members;

increase of labor disputes (576 in 1929).

July 2. **Fall of the Tanaka ministry; cabinet formed under Yūkō Hamaguchi** of *Minseitō;* Shidehara returned as foreign minister.

1930. The **population,** which had been estimated at 26.5 million in 1726 and 34.8 million in 1872, doubled in following 63 years (69.2 million in 1935), the rate of increase accelerating steadily to a peak of 15.3 per thousand in 1930 before beginning to decline (14.4 in 1935). This rate of increase (c. one million a year by 1930) created a problem because of the high density of Japanese population already in the late Tokugawa period. Public concern over the population question after 1922 and failure of emigration to provide a solution (total of all emigrants in modern period up to 1930 estimated to have been less than annual increase in 1930) led to emphasis on manufacturing and foreign trade as means to provide employment.

May 6. **Sino-Japanese tariff agreement** signed at Nanking by which Japan recognized China's tariff autonomy and received certain commercial safeguards and recognition of Japanese loans to former Chinese governments.

Oct. Japanese ratification of the **London naval treaty** (signed April 22) following acrimonious debate in which the *Seiyūkai* attacked the policy of Hamaguchi and Shidehara.

Nov. 14. **Premier Hamaguchi shot by an assassin** in Tōkyō and succeeded by

1931, Apr. **Reijiro Wakatsuki,** new leader of the *Minseitō*, as premier.

Sept. 19. **MUKDEN INCIDENT** (p. 1108).

Dec. **Fall of the Wakatsuki ministry; cabinet formed by Ki Inukai,** leader of the *Seiyūkai;* Gen. Sadao Araki war minister.

1932, Jan. 28–Mar. 2. **Sino-Japanese hostilities at Shanghai** (p. 1108).

Feb. 18. **Independence of Manchukuo** (p. 1108).

May 15. **Assassination of Premier Inukai** by military reactionaries. A ministry chiefly of non-party members was formed under **Viscount Makoto Saitō;** Araki war minister, **Korekiyo Takahashi** finance minister. This marked the **end of party government** in Japan.

1933, May 27. Following the report to the League of Nations of the Lytton commission (p. 1126), Japan announced its **withdrawal from the League** (to take effect in two years).

May 31. **Japanese invasion of Jehol** (Jan.–Mar.) led to a **truce signed at T'ang-ku** which created a demilitarized zone in eastern Hopei under Japanese domination.

1934, Apr. 18. Foreign office statement asserting **virtual Japanese protectorate over Chinese relations with western powers.**

July 7. **Saitō ministry succeeded by that of**

Adm. **Keisuke Okada.** Koki Hirota continued as foreign minister.

1935, June 9.   Ho-Umezu agreement (p. 1108).

Oct. 28.   Enunciation of foreign minister **Hirota's three points:** establishment of a Japan-China-Manchukuo bloc, suppression of anti-Japanese activities in China, organization of a joint Sino-Japanese front against communism.

Nov.   Failure of Japanese effort to create an autonomous North China. Instead, an "East Hopei Autonomous Council" was created (Nov. 25). This led to student demonstrations in Peip'ing (Dec.).

1936, Feb. 20.   In the election, the Liberal *Mineseitō* regained the leading position in the diet.

Feb. 26.   Assassination of Viscount Saitō, finance minister **Takahashi,** and others in an **uprising of young army officers** at Tōkyō aiming at military dictatorship. Seventeen of the rebels were sentenced to death (July 7) by a military court.

Mar. 9.   Hirota became premier, forming a cabinet dominated by the military **(Gen. Juichi Terauchi);** budget greatly increased; development of heavy industry pushed.

Nov. 25.   German-Japanese anti-Communist pact (p. 1011).

1937, Jan. 23.   Fall of the Hirota cabinet; Gen. Ugaki prevented by army leaders (Terauchi, Sugiyama) from forming a cabinet; on February 2 **Gen. Senjuro Hayashi formed a cabinet.**

Apr. 30.   General election went in opposition to the Hayashi ministry, which resigned May 31. **Prince Fumumaro Konoye** formed a "national union" cabinet with Hirota foreign minister, Sugiyama war minister (June 3).

July 7.   SINO-JAPANESE HOSTILITIES (p. 1109).

Establishment of **cabinet advisory council** (Oct.) and **imperial headquarters** (Nov.) centralized the conduct of the war in the hands of the military and naval leaders, acting under direct authority of the emperor. Persons suspected of liberal or radical tendencies were arrested (371 on December 14).

Nov. 3.   Opening of the **Brussels conference.**

1938, Mar. 26.   Passage of the **National Mobilization Bill** allowing state dictation of almost all phases of economic life.

May 26.   Reorganization of the cabinet, military and naval officers taking six portfolios.

Sept. 29.   Resignation of Gen. Ugaki as foreign minister.

Oct. 29.   Hachiro Arita appointed Japanese foreign minister.

1939, Jan. 4.   Resignation of Prince Konoye as premier; he was succeeded by **Baron Kiijiro Hiranuma,** who formed a cabinet including Konoye.

Apr. 2.   A sharp dispute between Russia and Japan over fishing rights was settled by agreement for one year, Japan to participate on Soviet terms in auction of the fishing areas.

May.   Outbreak of serious **fighting between Manchukuan and Mongolian forces** on the Mongolian frontier. The conflict, really one between Russia and Japan, assumed considerable dimensions in the course of the summer.

Aug. 23.   Conclusion of the **German-Russian pact** (p. 1012) proved a tremendous shock to Japan, which at once scrapped the anti-Communist pact and resumed freedom of action.

Aug. 28.   The Hiranuma cabinet resigned and a **new ministry under Gen. Noboyuki Abe** was formed to put the new policy into effect.

(*Cont. p. 1344.*)

G.   THE PACIFIC AREA, 1914–1939

1.   GENERAL

(*From p. 925*)

IN THE EARLY months of the First World War, British ships with Australian and New Zealand forces conquered the **German island colonies** south of the equator, while in October 1914 the Japanese took possession of those north of the equator (the Marianas, Carolines, and Marshalls). At the war's end Japan, Australia, and New Zealand favored outright annexation of these territories, but because of American objections, they were finally classified as *C* mandates.

1919, May 7.   The supreme council assigned **German New Guinea** and the neighboring German islands (Bismarck Archipelago) as a mandate to Australia; **German Samoa** (West Samoa) became a New Zealand mandate; the rich phosphate island of **Nauru** was mandated to the British Empire and by agreement the administration was divided between Great Britain, Australia, and New Zealand: Japan received the **German islands north of the equator** as a mandate. These arrangements were confirmed by the League December 17, 1920.

1920–1922. The **dispute about Yap** between the United States and Japan (p. 1047).

1921, Dec. 13. The **PACIFIC TREATY,** concluded by Great Britain, the United States, France, and Japan during the Washington conference (p. 1122).

1922, Feb. 6. The **naval treaty** between the five great powers included an engagement to maintain the *status quo* with regard to fortifications and naval bases in the Pacific (the American and Alaskan coasts not included).

Apr. The Japanese government established civil government in the mandated islands (1400 islands with a total area of only 836 square miles, scattered over an immense area). The capital was set up at Korror Island (Palau group) and six branches of government were established in the major island groups. Much was done for sanitation, etc. For the rest the Japanese ruled through appointed native headmen. Economically the development of the sugar industry was most important. It brought with it a considerable **influx of Japanese immigrants** (1933: native population 50,000; Japanese 32,000).

1933, May 27. Japan announced **withdrawal from the League of Nations,** to become effective in two years' time. At the same time the Japanese government made it clear that it had no intention of abandoning the mandate.

1936, Jan. 1. With the **expiration of the international naval limitation treaties,** the provisions for the maintenance of the *status quo* of fortifications in the Pacific fell to the ground. Since 1932 there had been rumors of Japanese fortifications and submarine bases. After 1935 Australia and New Zealand were very active in coastal preparations and the United States government projected a great scheme of fortifications extending from the Alaskan coast and the Aleutian Islands to Midway Island, Guam, and Samoa. (*Cont. p. 1153.*)

2. AUSTRALIA

(*From p. 933*)

The outbreak of the First World War revealed all Australian parties united in loyalty to the mother country and in readiness to contribute to its defense. During the war Australia sent 329,000 men overseas, who took a prominent part in the Dardanelles campaign, the Palestine campaign, and the fighting in France (after 1916). In May 1918 the five Australian divisions in France were organized as an **Australian army corps,** under the command of **Sir John Monash,** an Australian. The war was financed chiefly by borrowing and was accompanied, in Australia as elsewhere, by a great extension of government control, economic as well as political. Rising prices together with decline in real wages led to much **labor unrest** and a very extensive strike in August–September 1917. The failure of this strike resulted in stricter organization of the trade unions and greater concentration on economic rather than political aims. In the military field the Australian government took advantage of the opportunity to seize the German island colonies south of the equator.

1914, Sept. 5. The general elections resulted in a great **victory for the Labour Party** and in the formation (Sept. 17) of the **third Fisher cabinet.** In 1915 Fisher became high commissioner in London and his place was taken by

1915, Oct. 27. William M. Hughes as premier and leader of the Labour Party. Hughes became the embodiment of Australian and British patriotism, and, after a visit to England in the summer of 1916, began to advocate **conscription** of men for service overseas. The suggestion roused much opposition and

1916, Oct. 28. Conscription was defeated by a narrow margin in a popular referendum. The result was an open **rift in the Labour Party,** which ejected Hughes and several of his colleagues. The cabinet was reconstructed and ultimately

1917, Feb. 17. Hughes organized a national war government, relying on the new **Nationalist Party,** which was composed of Labour leaders who followed Hughes and by a large section of the Liberal opposition. The new party received a popular mandate in the elections of May.

Oct. 17. Completion of the **railroad from Port Augusta to Kalgoorlie,** thus first attaching West Australia by rail to the other states.

In order to meet the steady decline in voluntary enlistment, the prime minister, unwilling to enforce conscription by parliamentary action, decided to refer the matter once more to popular vote, but

1918, Jan. 10. Conscription was again defeated by referendum. Through the exertions of influential leaders voluntary enlistment was increased to some extent, but not enough to satisfy Hughes and his associates. In the summer of 1918 Hughes went to England and in the spring of 1919 took part in the Paris peace conference. There, with the support of the other Dominion statesmen, he succeeded in excluding from the covenant of the League of

Nations any recognition of the principle of race equality. At the same time he intervened actively in the problem of the German colonies, so that on

1919, May 7.   THE SUPREME COUNCIL ASSIGNED TO AUSTRALIA THE MANDATE FOR THE GERMAN COLONIES SOUTH OF THE EQUATOR, excepting Nauru Island and Samoa (which went to New Zealand). This arrangement was confirmed by the League December 17, 1920. By agreement with Britain and New Zealand (July 2, 1919) Australia was given the administration of Nauru Island, which the three held together as mandatories.

Dec. 10.   Sir Ross Smith arrived at Port Darwin by air, completing the flight from England in 27 days.

Dec. 23. The elections resulted in a victory for the Nationalist Party and the Hughes government continued in power.

1920, Jan. 10.   Australia became an original member of the League of Nations with the full status of an independent nation.

1920. In a famous decision **(Engineers' case)** the Australian high court gave the commonwealth Conciliation and Arbitration Court authority to regulate the conditions of labor of state employees.

1921, Dec. 15.   Adoption of a higher tariff, chiefly to protect the industries that had been born of the war. All parties were more or less united on the tariff issue.

1922. By the **Empire Settlement Act,** the British government undertook to assist in the promotion of emigration to Australia and in the settlement of emigrants on the land.

Dec. 10. The elections resulted in 27 seats for the Nationalist Party, 29 for Labour, and 14 for the **Country Party** (founded 1919), led by **Earle Page** and representing the farmer element. The Country Party held the balance of power and, being hostile to Hughes, finally forced the

1923, Feb. 3.   Resignation of the Hughes government. The Nationalist Party began to disintegrate and

Feb. 9.   Stanley Bruce, together with Page, formed a coalition cabinet composed of Nationalists and Country Party men.

1925, Sept. 23.   A new immigration restriction act gave the governor-general authority to prohibit the entrance of aliens of any specified nationality, class, race, or occupation, either for economic or racial reasons. This act was never systematically applied, but it made possible restriction of Italian immigration, which had begun to arouse objections, especially among the labor groups.

1926. The **Northern Territory was divided** along 20° S.L. into **Northern Australia** and **Central Australia,** and a commission was set up to study possibilities of development.

1927, May 9.   Parliament House was officially opened at **Canberra.** Thus far parliament had sat at Melbourne while numerous schemes for the new capital were under debate. In a competition among architects, **Walter B. Griffin** of Chicago received first prize and his plan became the basis for the new city.

June 8.   Financial agreement between the commonwealth government and the state governments, following years of dispute concerning continued federal support to the states (the federal government having gradually appropriated most of the best springs of revenue).

1928, June 9.   Capt. Charles Kingsford-Smith arrived at Brisbane after his trans-Pacific flight from California.

1929, Oct. 12. The Labour Party won in the elections, whereupon

Oct. 22.   James H. Scullin formed a Labour cabinet. For the most part Labour had remained moderate in its policy, though in 1921 the party had adopted a program of socialization, and in 1927 the Council of Trade Unions had been organized as a left-wing group associated with Moscow.

1930-1936 The **great depression** made itself acutely felt in Australia, where the government tried to combat it by drastic economy and other obvious devices. The rising price of gold and (after 1933) of wool, however, enabled Australia to recover more readily than many other countries.

1931. Foundation of the **United Australia Party,** composed of a number of dissident Labourites together with remnants of the Nationalist Party. The leader of the group was **Joseph A. Lyons.**

Dec. 19. The Labour Party was badly defeated in the elections, and a new **Lyons cabinet** was formed.

1932. The **Financial Agreement Enforcement Act** further strengthened the power of the federal government as against the states.

1933, Apr. 8.   West Australia voted 2-1 to secede from the commonwealth. Together with South Australia and Tasmania, the other agricultural states, West Australia had long protested against the "incidence of federation" and had demanded abatement of taxes or some form of federal relief. The government thereupon appointed a **grants commission** to investigate the claims of aggrieved states and to decide on compensation. Meanwhile (1934, Mar.) West Australia sent a petition to the king asking for legislation to effect secession. The

British parliament, however, refused to accept the petition without the previous approval of the Australian people as a whole.

May 26. The **Australian government assumed authority over about one-third of the Antarctic continent** (an area roughly the size of Australia itself).

1934, July 25. The government adopted a three-year **defense program** which involved the development of an air force, increase of naval power, mechanization of forces, etc.

Nov. 7. The Lyons cabinet was replaced by a **Lyons-Page combination,** representing a coalition between the United Australia Party and the Country Party.

Dec. 8. Inauguration of a **weekly airmail service** between England and Australia.

1936–1945. **Baron Gowrie,** governor-general.

1936, May 23. A new and **higher tariff** was introduced, to replace the more modest tariff of 1932. The new schedule led to considerable **friction with Japan,** whose textiles were hard hit, but by an agreement of December 27 the Australian government agreed to take as many Japanese textile products as in 1934, in return for Japanese purchase of a specified amount of Australian wool.

1937, Oct. 23. The **Lyons-Page government** won a sound victory in the elections (United Australia Party 28 seats; Country Party 17; Labour 29). The outstanding issue of the elections was the **defense problem,** the government advancing a program of naval construction, Labour calling for emphasis on air-armaments and less dependence on Great Britain. Establishment of the first airplane factory. Appointment of an Australian counsellor at the British embassy in Washington.

1939, Apr. 7. Death of Premier Lyons, who was succeeded by Sir Earle Page.

Apr. 24. **Robert G. Menzies** formed a new government which devoted itself wholeheartedly to the problem of defense. When (Sept. 3), **Britain declared war on Germany,** Australia unhesitatingly joined the mother country and arranged for assistance of all kinds.

(*Cont. p. 1351.*)

3. NEW ZEALAND

(*From p. 937*)

New Zealand, like Australia, supported Great Britain enthusiastically throughout the First World War. Though **conscription was introduced** (Aug. 1, 1916), the great majority of men sent overseas (117,000) were volunteers. Together with the Australian forces they formed the **Anzac divisions** at Gallipoli and later took part in the French and Palestine campaigns. At home the war led to increased government control, both political and economic.

1914, Aug. 29. German Samoa surrendered to an expeditionary force from New Zealand.

1915, Aug. 12. The cabinet of William F. Massey (Reform Party) was reorganized as a **national war cabinet** through association of the Liberal Party (Joseph Ward, leader).

1919, May 7. The Supreme War Council assigned **Samoa as a mandate** to New Zealand, which shared with Great Britain and Australia the mandate for the rich phosphate island of **Nauru** as well. The New Zealanders would have preferred to have Great Britain assume the Samoan mandate, if only to avoid the problem of further colored populations.

Aug. 25. End of the coalition government. Massey and the Reform Party resumed the government, and in the elections of December 17 secured a substantial majority in the legislature. The elections of 1922 and 1925 produced essentially the same results.

1920, Jan. 10. New Zealand became an original member of the League of Nations.

1925, May 10. Death of the prime minister. He was succeeded by **Joseph G. Coates.**

1927, July–Oct. Troubles in Samoa, where the native chiefs complained against the administration. An investigating commission vindicated the government and reported that the natives were instigated by Europeans. The government then proceeded to repatriate objectionable Europeans (Germans), whose properties were taken over.

1928, Nov. 14. In the elections the **Reform Party was defeated** by the United (i.e. Liberal) Party: Reform 28 seats; United 29; Labour 19.

Dec. 10. Sir Joseph G. Ward, leader of the United Party, formed a cabinet.

1930, May 28. George W. Forbes (United Party) became premier on the retirement of Ward for reasons of health.

New Zealand suffered severely from the **world depression,** being essentially a producer of primary materials. The fall of prices and unemployment drove the government to a policy of drastic curtailment of expenditure (including salaries), restriction of imports, exchange control, conversion of the debt, etc. During the most critical years much of the famous social machinery was allowed to fall into disuse (notably wage and hour provisions, etc.). As a result the Labour Party withdrew its support from the government.

1931, Sept. 18. A **coalition** was effected **between the United and Reform Parties,** Coates entering the government. In the elections of December 2 the government won a pronounced victory.

1935, Nov. 27. The Labour Party for the first time won a majority in the elections (Labour 53 seats; United and Reform Parties 20; Independents 7). Thereupon **Michael J. Savage** formed the first Labour cabinet (Dec. 5). The Labour Party came into power with an elaborate **program of socialization and social reform.** During the years 1935-1938 the major part of the program was translated into legislation. The chief measures were:

Nationalization of the Reserve Bank. All share capital was abolished and private shareholders paid off.

By the **Primary Products Marketing Act** the government arranged to buy farm produce at a guaranteed price and dispose of it in London at the best available figure. Deficits were to be made up from reserve bank credit.

The **State Advances Corporation Act** re-modeled the mortgage corporation as a state institution designed to liberalize government lending activities.

The **Industrial Conciliation and Arbitration Amendment Act** restored the compulsory arbitration system in disputes about wages and hours.

The **Government Railways Amendment Act** restored the railroads to complete government control and regulated road transport companies to prevent competition with railroads.

The arbitration court in 1936 fixed the **basic wage** for a man with wife and three children at £3 16*s.* per week.

1937, May 13. Formation of the National Party, a merger of the old Reform and United Parties, under leadership of **Adam Hamilton.** The new party was opposed primarily to the socializing policy of the government and presented a program of private enterprise and initiative.

1938, Oct. 15. In the elections the Labour government managed to retain its majority intact (Labour 54 seats; National Party 24).

1939, Sept. 3. British declaration of war on Germany. New Zealand, like Australia, at once decided on full support of the home country. (*Cont. p. 1352.*)

4. THE PHILIPPINES

(*From p. 938*)

1916, Feb. 4. National Bank of the Philippines chartered and made the depository of public funds. A **council of state** was created, composed of the governor-general, the presidents of both houses of the legislature, and the heads of executive departments.

Aug. 29. JONES ACT, abolishing the Philippine Commission and creating an **elective senate** of 24 members; greater powers vested in the Philippine government. Ultimate independence was promised as soon as stable government was established. As interpreted by Gov. Harrison, this act gave the islands practical autonomy.

1917, Apr. 25. A Filipino **national guard** was organized and its services offered to the United States.

1918, Nov. 20. A **Filipino division** was taken into federal service.

1919, Mar. 6. Use of the Spanish language in the courts was continued until 1930.

May. A delegation of forty prominent Filipinos, including **Manuel Quezon,** arrived in the United States and asked for the fulfillment of promises of independence.

1921, May 4, Sept. 12. The **Wood-Forbes mission,** sent to investigate conditions in the islands. Its report declared that an immediate grant of independence would be "*a betrayal of the Philippine people*" and that "*under no circumstances should the American government permit to be established in the Philippines a situation which would leave the United States in a position of responsibility without authority.*"

Oct. 5. Gen. Leonard Wood, governor-general.

1923, July 2. Manuel Quezon, president of the senate, accused the governor of undue interference. On July 17 the Filipino members of the council of state resigned for the same reason. The United States government, however, upheld the official acts of the governor.

1924, Mar. 6. President Coolidge stated by letter: "*The Philippine people are by no means equipped, either in wealth or experience, to undertake the heavy burden which would be imposed upon them with political independence.*"

May 6. A **special mission,** under Quezon, arrived in Washington and the Philippine legislature (Nov. 19) adopted a resolution demanding full and complete independence.

1925, Dec. 7. A **petition** from the legislature,

demanding **independence,** presented to congress.

1926, July 26. The legislature adopted a resolution calling for a plebiscite on independence. This was vetoed by the governor.

Dec. 7. Report of Carmi Thompson, sent to investigate conditions. He recommended that independence be postponed, but that the policy of home rule be extended and that the Philippine government should continue to liquidate its business enterprises.

1927, Aug. 7. Death of Gov. Wood. Henry L. Stimson appointed to succeed him (Dec. 13) and adopted a conciliatory policy.

1929, May 17. Dwight F. Davis, governor-general.

Earlier American opinion in favor of independence gradually became reinforced by **economic considerations:** (1) American economic conquest of the islands had not made great headway; (2) the American stake in the islands remained small; (3) the American sugar interests desired to be freed from competition of Philippine sugar. When the Smoot-Hawley tariff was under consideration, Senator King of Utah and Senator Broussard of Louisiana introduced amendments calling for Philippine independence. These were defeated, however.

1931, Oct. President Hoover declared that *"economic independence of the Philippines must be attained before political independence can be successful."*

1933, Jan. 13. The **HOWES-CUTTING BILL** passed over the president's veto. It provided for a **transitional commonwealth** for a period of twelve years, under a Filipino executive. The United States was to retain the right to military and naval bases and decisions of the Philippine courts were to be subject to review by the United States supreme court. During the probationary period tariffs were to be imposed on Philippine sugar, coconut oil, and fibers when introduced into the United States in excess of specific quotas. The Philippine legislature was to accept the independence measure within one year.

Oct. The **Philippine legislature rejected the proposed plan** on the ground that it was not an independence bill, but a tariff against Philippine products and an immigration bill against Philippine labor.

1934, Mar. 2. President Roosevelt urged congress to revive the Howes-Cutting Bill, with removal of the provision for American military reservations on the islands, and naval bases made subject to further negotiations.

Mar. 24. The **TYDINGS-McDUFFIE ACT** adopted. It was essentially the Howes-Cutting Bill modified in accordance with the president's recommendations. The Philippine legislature, with misgivings, accepted the measure (May 1).

July 30. A constitutional convention convened to frame a constitution for the commonwealth. It completed its task February 8, 1935, and President Roosevelt approved the document March 23.

1935, May 14. The **constitution was accepted** by the voters of the islands.

Sept. 17. Elections to choose a president, vice-president, and national assembly. **Manuel Quezon, first president.**

Nov. 15. COMMONWEALTH GOVERNMENT FORMALLY ESTABLISHED. The **president** (elected for six years) enjoyed most of the powers of the governor-general. The **legislature** (national assembly) was unicameral. The United States retained control of defense and foreign relations, exercised supervision over important phases of finance, and reserved the right to intervene to preserve the commonwealth government. Appeals from decisions of the Philippine courts might be carried to the United States supreme court.

Growth of opposition to President Quezon and his policy, linked with loud demands for immediate independence, in

1937, Feb.–Mar. Brought President Quezon to the United States for conferences on the working of the independence act. He suggested independence in 1938 or 1939 in order to prevent the economic difficulties bound to arise from prolonged uncertainty. The United States government agreed to the establishment of a **joint preparatory committee,** composed of six Americans and six Filipinos. While this committee pursued its investigations, the outbreak of the Sino-Japanese conflict produced a reversion of feeling among the more conservative groups in the Philippines. Growing discussion of permanent Dominion status under American sovereignty as the only effective method of defense. President Quezon was rather favorable to this view, which was opposed by various groups.

1938, May 20. Report of the joint committee. It recommended that the American tariff should be gradually extended to the Philippines, to become completely effective only in 1960 (instead of 1946).

Nov. 8. In the elections President Quezon's Nationalist Party won a decisive victory over the united opposition groups **(Popular Front).** The opposition, while bitterly criticizing Quezon for his dictatorial methods and infringements of civil rights, demanded independence in 1946, but no longer called for "immediate" independence, for which most Filipinos seemed to have lost the taste. (*Cont. p. 1353.*)

5. HAWAII

(From p. 938)

Hawaii became more and more the key to the American strategic position in the Pacific. The naval base at **Pearl Harbor,** one of the finest deep-water basins in the world, was steadily developed after the channel was cleared and straightened in 1908–1910. On August 21, 1919, the great drydock was finally completed and every facility for supplying and repairing warships was provided.

Sugar and pineapple plantations comprised the main wealth of the islands, though the **tourist trade** was of great economic importance. The population was extremely mixed, the figures for 1940 being: Hawaiian and part Hawaiian, 64,310; Caucasian, 103,791; Chinese, 28,774; Filipinos, 52,569; Japanese, 157,905; Korean, 6,851; Puerto Rican, 8,296.

1923, Apr. 26. "Bill of Rights" by which the territorial legislature defined and declared the claims of the territory concerning its status in the Union and provided for appointment of a commission to secure recognition of such claims by the federal government.

1927, June. Lt. Lester Maitland and Lt. Albert Hegenberger first flew from California to Hawaii.

1937. Samuel King, the Hawaiian delegate in the United States congress, introduced a bill to change the status of the islands from that of territory to that of state. A congressional committee, however, reported against the project, the mixed character of the population and the strategic position of the islands making it appear inadvisable.

1937. Regular air connection was established with California with the introduction of the trans-Pacific line to Manila.

1939. The **Hawaii Equal Rights Commission** created by act of the territorial legislature to further claims for equal treatment and to oppose federal legislation discriminatory to the territory.

H. INTERNATIONAL AFFAIRS, 1919–1939

(From p. 979)

International affairs between the two World Wars involved the following **major problems:** (1) the attempt to establish collective security by means of new international bodies, the League of Nations, and the World Court, without creating any form of superstate; (2) the unwillingness of the non-European powers, the United States, Japan, and the British Dominions in particular, to assume responsibility for anything outside their respective spheres of interests; (3) the efforts of Japan to dominate the Far East by force and of the United States to organize the Americas by a "good neighbor policy"; (4) the competition between French efforts to maintain the position of leadership on the continent of Europe established by the peace settlements and German endeavors to evade or revise the terms imposed in 1919; (5) the problem of restoring world trade and general prosperity in a war-impoverished world; (6) the attempts to attain security and prosperity by neo-mercantilist ideas imposed dictatorially as emergency measures.

The era between the wars may be divided chronologically into three phases: (1) the period of settlement (from the peace treaties to the Dawes plan, 1924); (2) the period of fulfillment (1924 to the evacuation of the Rhineland, 1930); (3) the period of repudiation and revision (1930–1939).

1. THE PERIOD OF SETTLEMENT, 1919–1924

1919, June 28. Conclusion of **defensive treaties between France, Britain, and the United States.** Britain and the United States were to come to France's assistance in case of aggression by Germany. The United States senate refused to ratify this agreement and also rejected the Versailles treaty (Nov. 19), thus knocking out one of the keystones in the international peace structure established at Paris.

1919–1922. The **Vilna dispute,** between Poland and Lithuania. **Gen. Joseph Pilsudski** took the town from the Bolsheviks (Apr. 19, 1919). The **Curzon line** (Dec. 8) established a boundary depriving Poland of the city, which was retaken by the Bolsheviks (June 15, 1920). The Lithuanians took it when the Russians evacuated (Aug. 24), but were driven out by Polish freebooters under **Gen. Lucien Zeligowski** (Oct. 9). By decision of the League a plebiscite was to be held to decide the fate of the city, but this was later abandoned (Mar. 3, 1921). A **plebiscite** (Jan. 8, 1922) held by Zeligowski decided for Poland and the Vilna diet voted for union. On April 18 it was incorporated with Poland, though Lithuania refused to recognize this disposition of the question.

1919–1920. The **Teschen conflict** between Poland and Czechoslovakia. The Czechs had occupied the disputed area (Jan. 1919) and serious clashes took place (May). The supreme council decided for a plebiscite (Sept. 27), but disorders continued (Mar., May, 1920) until the conference of ambassadors divided the territory (July 28).

1919–1920. The **Polish-Russian War,** resulting from the effort made by the Poles to push their frontier east to the frontier of 1772 (p. 1033).

1919–1921. The **Burgenland dispute** between Austria and Hungary. The strip of territory had been assigned to Austria by the peace treaties, it being only 15 miles from Vienna. The population, too, was predominantly German. But Hungarian irregulars were in occupation and refused to evacuate (Aug. 1921). Through Italian mediation a plebiscite was arranged for. This was held (Dec. 1921) and gave Austria most of the area, though Ödenburg went to Hungary.

1919–1922. The **Greek invasion of Anatolia** (see p. 1085).

1919–1924. The **Fiume question.** President Wilson had rejected the Italian claim to the town and the coast south of it (Apr. 14, 1919), whereupon the Italians had withdrawn from the peace conference. A compromise, suggested by **André Tardieu,** which would have created a buffer state of Fiume (May 30), was rejected by Yugoslavia. **Gabriele d'Annunzio** led a filibustering expedition which occupied the town and set up a visionary government (Sept. 12). The matter was finally left to Italy and Yugoslavia to settle (Mar. 6, 1920). The **treaty of Rapallo** (Nov. 12) made Fiume an independent city and gave Italy Zara and a number of Dalmatian islands. But a Fascist coup (Mar. 3, 1922) overthrew the local government, and government troops took control (Mar. 17). By a treaty of January 27, 1924, Yugoslavia abandoned claims to Fiume, but received **Porto Barros** in return.

1919–1922. The **Upper Silesian question.** The peace treaties had provided for a plebiscite in this valuable area. It was held March 20, 1921 (see p. 1038) and returned 717,122 votes for

Germany as against 483,154 for Poland. But an armed rising under the Polish commissioner **Adalbert Korfanty** (May 3, 1922) was acquiesced in by the French commander acting for the League. In August 1922, the council of ambassadors referred the matter to the League and the League council accepted a **scheme of partition** by which a majority of the population and more than half of the territory were awarded to Germany, while Poland was given the principal mining and industrial districts.

1920, Jan. 10. Official **birth of the League of Nations.** The assembly met for the first time November 15. In its first years the League was entrusted with many territorial questions and with a host of other problems.

Jan. 23. The Dutch government refused to surrender the **former Emperor William,** though it later agreed to intern him.

Feb.–Mar. The **plebiscites in North Schleswig** gave the northernmost zone to Denmark and the remainder to Germany.

Apr. 19–26. The **San Remo conference** of the Allied powers, to discuss various territorial problems and to assign the Class *A* mandates.

June 19–22. **Conferences of Hythe and Boulogne,** to discuss the Near Eastern situation and the reparations problem.

July 5–16. The **Spa conference,** where the Germans submitted a scheme of reparations payments and signed a disarmament engagement. The Allies decided to apportion reparations money as follows: France, 52 per cent; British Empire, 22 per cent; Italy, 10 per cent; Belgium, 8 per cent; the smaller powers to receive the rest.

Aug. 14. **Treaty between Czechoslovakia and Yugoslavia,** which became the foundation of the **Little Entente.** Its purpose was to enforce observance of the peace treaty by Hungary and to forestall a possible restoration of the Hapsburgs.

Nov. 12. **Treaty of Rapallo** between Italy and Yugoslavia, regarding Fiume and other Adriatic issues (p. 997).

1921, Jan. 24–30. **Paris conference,** to discuss reparations.

Feb. 19. **Treaty between Poland and France,** providing for mutual assistance in case of attack.

Feb. 21–Mar. 14. **London conference,** dealing with reparations. Schedules of payment were worked out for the Germans and the latter made counter-proposals.

Mar. 3. Offensive and defensive **treaty between Poland and Roumania.**

Mar. 8. The **French occupied Düsseldorf, Duisburg,** and **Ruhrort,** after an ultimatum to Germany had been evaded.

Mar. 24. The reparation commission declared **Germany in default,** though the Germans, reaching other figures on payments already made, denied the default.

Apr. 23.   Roumania joined Czechoslovakia in the Little Entente.

Apr. 27. The reparations commission announced that Germany should pay a **total of 132,000,000,000 gold marks.**

Apr. 29–May 5. London conference on reparations. It sent an ultimatum to Germany demanding one billion gold marks by the end of the month on penalty of occupation of the Ruhr. The Germans raised the money by borrowing in London, and accepted the payment schedules.

June 7. Treaty between Yugoslavia and Roumania, completing the Little Entente.

Aug. 24, 25. By separate treaties the **United States made peace with Austria and Germany.**

Oct. 6. The **Loucheur-Rathenau agreement,** arranging for payments in kind.

Oct. 20. The **Aaland Islands convention** signed at Geneva. It provided for the neutralization and non-fortification of the group.

Oct. 20. The former **King Charles arrived in the Burgenland** by airplane and began a march on Budapest (p. 1019). Czechoslovakia and Yugoslavia mobilized and the Hungarians, unable to face another war, did not dare restore their Hapsburg king.

Nov. 12–1922, Feb. 6. The **WASHINGTON CONFERENCE,** which met at the invitation of the United States government to consider naval armaments and Far Eastern questions. Great Britain, France, Italy, Belgium, the Netherlands, China, Japan, and Portugal were represented. Russia, not yet recognized by the United States, was not invited, despite its great interests in the Far East. The conference resulted: (1) in the **four-power Pacific treaty,** December 13 (United States, Great Britain, France, and Japan), by which the signatories guaranteed each other's rights in insular possessions in the Pacific and promised to consult if their rights were threatened. The Anglo-Japanese alliance came to an end; (2) **the Shantung treaty** (Feb. 4) by which Japan returned Kiaochow to China; (3) two **nine-power treaties** (Feb. 6) guaranteeing the territorial integrity and administrative independence of China and reiterating the principle of the "Open Door"; (4) the **naval armaments treaty** (Feb. 6) providing for a ten-year naval holiday during which no new capital ships (defined as ships over 10,000 tons with guns larger than eight-inch) were to be built, and establishing a ratio for capital ships of 5-5-3-1.67-1.67. This meant that Great Britain and the United States were each allowed 525,000 tons, Japan 315,000, and France and

Italy each 175,000. Total tonnage of aircraft carriers was restricted and a maximum size fixed for capital ships, aircraft carriers, and cruisers.

1922, Feb. 15. The **Permanent Court of International Justice** was opened at The Hague.

Mar. 13–17. Conference at **Warsaw** of the Baltic states and Poland, provided for arbitration and a defensive league in the event of attack by another power.

Apr. 10–May 19. GENOA CONFERENCE, including Germany and Russia, called to consider the Russian problem and the general economic questions of the world. The conference broke down on the insistence of France that Russia recognize its pre-war debt.

Apr. 16.   Rapallo treaty of alliance between Germany and Russia, in which both renounced reparations, etc.

May 31. The reparations commission, despite protests from France, granted Germany a moratorium for the remainder of the year, it having become clear that payments were resulting in the collapse of the mark and creating an impossible transfer problem.

June 30. The new **Danube statute** went into effect.

Aug. 1.   Lord Balfour, the British foreign secretary, sent a note to the Allied powers indebted to Great Britain offering to abandon all further claims for payment and all claims to reparations, provided a general settlement could be made which would end "the economic injury inflicted on the world by the present state of things." If the United States, which had not demanded a share of reparations payments, should refuse to cancel the debts owed by European governments, then Great Britain would have to insist on receiving enough from her debtors to pay its own obligations to the United States. The American attitude was that reparations and inter-Allied debts were not connected problems, so that German default on reparations would not excuse default on Allied payments to the United States.

Aug. 7–14.   London conference. Poincaré demanded, as conditions for a moratorium, a series of "productive guaranties," among them appropriation of 60 per cent of the capital of the German dyestuff factories on the left bank of the Rhine, and exploitation and contingent expropriation of the state mines in the Ruhr. British and French policy now diverged sharply, as the former refused Poincaré's scheme and Poincaré refused to grant a moratorium.

Nov. 20–1923, Feb. 4.   First Lausanne conference, to conclude peace between Turkey and Greece (p. 1086).

Dec. 9–11.   Second London conference. Bonar Law offered to cancel Allied debts to

Great Britain even if Great Britain had to continue to pay the United States. Poincaré remained adamant, since the reparations expected from Germany were theoretically much larger than the French debt to Great Britain.

Dec. 26. The reparations commission again declared **Germany in default** on the motion of Louis Barthou, the French representative. The point at issue was a minor delay in deliveries of timber.

1923, Jan. 2–4. Paris conference. British and Italian schemes for bond issues, etc., were rejected by the French.

Jan. 9. Germany declared in default on coal deliveries.

Jan. 11. French and Belgian troops began the **OCCUPATION OF THE RUHR DISTRICT.** The British government refused to take part in it and in a note of August 11 declared that the "Franco-Belgian action . . . was not a sanction authorized by the treaty." The Italian government, though technically associated, took no active part. The activities of the *M.I.C.U.M. (mission interalliée de contrôle des usines et des mines),* sent into the heart of Germany to supervise business enterprises under military protection, were not, according to the Franco-Belgian note (Jan. 10), to disturb the normal life of the civilian population. But the German government urged **passive resistance** on the people of the Ruhr and recklessly inflated the currency to defray the expense of supporting idle workers and compensating their employers. The French fomented a **separatist movement** in the Rhineland, which failed, after some bloodshed, to establish an independent buffer state.

Apr. 23–July 24. Second Lausanne conference, on the Near East (p. 1086).

July 24. Treaty of Lausanne, replacing the abortive treaty of Sèvres (p. 979).

Aug. 29. The **Corfu incident;** Italian ultimatum to Greece (p. 998).

Sept. 26. End of passive resistance in the Ruhr. German paper marks had sunk to the point of being worth less than the paper they were printed on. The effect of the financial collapse could not be confined to Germany. The French franc fell about 25 per cent and by November the French were willing to make an agreement directly with the Ruhr mine operators to secure deliveries. **Stanley Baldwin,** British prime minister, secured a promise of American co-operation to avert the complete economic and financial collapse of the world.

Nov. 30. Two committees were organized to investigate the German economic problem as it touched reparations.

1924, Apr. 9. THE DAWES PLAN. The committee under the chairmanship of the American, **Charles G. Dawes,** presented its report. Based on the slogan, "Business, not politics," this Dawes plan provided for a reorganization of the German Reichsbank under Allied supervision. Reparation payments of one billion gold marks were to be made annually, increasing by the end of five years to two billion five hundred thousand. Germany was to receive a foreign loan of 800,000,000 gold marks.

Apr. 16. The Germans accepted the Dawes plan.

July 16–Aug. 16. A conference at London adopted the Dawes plan. The Reichstag promptly passed the necessary legislation. Of the loan, $110,000,000 was taken up in the United States, the rest in Europe.

2. THE PERIOD OF FULFILLMENT, 1924–1930

1924, Oct. 2. The **Geneva protocol** (protocol for the pacific settlement of international disputes). This was the product of continued efforts to strengthen the international machinery and to overcome the weakness in the League structure resulting from the absence of Russia, Germany, and the United States. A **draft treaty of mutual assistance,** based on proposals made by Lord Robert Cecil and Col. Edouard Réquin, had attempted a definition of the aggressor and had submitted an ingenious scheme for combining the advantages of a general guaranty and a local system of alliances. The objection of Great Britain and the Dominions to the regional and continental character of the plan had led to its rejection by the League assembly (Sept. 1923).

The Geneva protocol, brought forward by **Ramsay MacDonald,** British prime minister, and drafted by Eduard Beneš and Nicholas Politis, was unanimously recommended to the governments members of the League. It provided for compulsory arbitration of all disputes and defined the aggressor as the nation unwilling to submit its case to arbitration. The decisive factor in the rejection of the scheme was the **opposition of the British Dominions,** which regarded the risks in this mutual insurance scheme as too unequal: "We live in a fireproof house, far from inflammable materials" (Raoul Dandurand for Canada). The newly elected Conservative government in Britain therefore rejected the protocol (Mar. 1925).

1925, Feb. 9. The German government proposed a **Rhineland mutual guaranty pact.** The idea was taken up by the British, who were seeking some European arrangement to replace the Geneva protocol. **Aristide Briand,** who became French foreign minister in April 1925, accepted the suggestion on condition that Germany join the League.

Feb. 11, 19. **International opium conventions** providing more effective control of production and trade in opium.

June 17. **Arms traffic convention,** dealing with international trade in arms and munitions. A protocol was also signed, prohibiting use of poison gas.

Aug. 25. The French **evacuated Düsseldorf, Duisburg,** and **Ruhrort.**

Oct. 5–16. **LOCARNO CONFERENCE AND TREATIES** (signed December 1). The treaties included: (1) a **treaty of mutual guaranty** of the Franco-German and Belgo-German frontiers (signed by Germany, France, Belgium, and by Great Britain and Italy as guarantors); (2) **arbitration treaties** between Germany and Poland and Germany and Czechoslovakia; (3) **arbitration treaties** between Germany and Belgium and Germany and France; (4) a **Franco-Polish** and a **Franco-Czechoslovakian treaty for mutual assistance** in case of attack by Germany. The effect of the treaties was far-reaching. For some years the "spirit of Locarno" gave the European powers a sense of security, though Britain had guaranteed only the western frontiers of Germany and Germany had not specifically bound itself to refrain from aggression to the east and south. Realizing this, France secured itself by alliances with Poland and the states of the Little Entente and proceeded with a program of fortifying the German frontier (Maginot line) and reorganizing the army.

1926, Mar. 17. The **admission of Germany to the League** was postponed because of complications raised by Spain and Brazil regarding seats on the council.

May 18–26. **First meeting of the Preparatory Commission for a Disarmament Conference.** This had been appointed by the League in 1925 to tackle the problem of disarmament, foreshadowed in the treaty of Versailles. The United States was represented, but not Russia (until 1927). The commission held many sessions during the next years.

June 10. **Spain announced withdrawal from the League,** but later rescinded this decision.

Sept. 8. **Germany admitted to the League** and given a permanent seat on the council.

1927, Jan. 31. End of the **inter-Allied commission of military control** in Germany. Problems of German armament were henceforth

put under jurisdiction of the League.

May 4–23. **International economic conference at Geneva,** some fifty countries being represented.

June 20–Aug. 4. Great Britain, the United States, and Japan met in a **three-power naval conference at Geneva** in an effort to reach an agreement on cruisers, destroyers, and submarines. The conference failed to reach agreement.

Nov. 30–Dec. 3. At a meeting of the preparatory commission on disarmament, **Maxim Litvinov,** for Russia (now admitted to the meetings), **proposed complete and immediate disarmament,** but this was rejected as a communist trick.

1928, Apr. 13. **Frank B. Kellogg,** American secretary of state, submitted to the Locarno powers a **plan for the renunciation of war,** the suggestion flowing out of American-French negotiations.

Apr. 21. **Aristide Briand,** for France, put forward his draft for a treaty outlawing war.

June 23. **Explanatory note** on the **Kellogg-Briand pact** sent to Britain, Germany, Italy, and Japan and to the allies of France and to the British Dominions. There was almost immediate and universal adherence, since the pact only involved renunciation of aggressive war and made no provision for sanctions.

Aug. 27. The **KELLOGG-BRIAND PACT** signed at Paris (pact of Paris).

Sept. 3–26. The ninth assembly of the League implemented the Kellogg-Briand pact by a general act providing for conciliation and arbitration and an **optional clause** like that of the World Court, acceptance of which involved compulsory arbitration. This was accepted by 23 nations, in some cases with reservations.

Dec. 6. Outbreak of hostilities between Bolivia and Paraguay over the **Chaco region** (p. 1061).

1929, Jan. 5. **General act of inter-American arbitration,** analogous to the above optional clause, signed at the Pan-American conference in Washington.

Jan. 19. **Appointment of the Young committee** to re-examine the reparations problem and make final disposition of it.

Feb. 9. **Litvinov protocol,** an eastern pact for renunciation of war, signed at Moscow by Russia, Poland, Roumania, Estonia, and Latvia.

Apr. 12. **Report of the Young committee,** to which the Germans made some counter-proposals.

June 7. **THE YOUNG PLAN.** Responsibility for transferring payments from German marks into foreign currency was to be undertaken by Germany and was to be made under a new institution, the **Bank for International Settlements** at Basel. On the directorate of this bank all the principal central banks were to be represented. Germany was to pay annuities ending in 1988 and increasing gradually for the first 36 years. But only Rm. 660,000,000 were unconditionally payable annually. The transfer of the rest of the annuity might be postponed for two years. These safeguards were meant to cover any possible crisis in transfer. The unconditional annuity was secured by a mortgage on German state railways. The total annuity of Rm. 1,707,000,000 was less than Germany had been paying with apparent ease under the Dawes plan, so that experts and diplomats had no doubt that the Young plan was a permanent settlement.

June 3. Settlement of the dispute between Chile and Peru over the districts of **Tacna and Arica** (p. 1060).

Aug. 6–31. Hague conference on the Young plan. The Germans accepted it and were rewarded by **evacuation of the Rhineland,** before June 1930.

Sept. 5–9. Briand proposed a European federal union. The plan was discussed by the League, but nothing came of it.

1930, Jan. 21–Apr. 22.   LONDON NAVAL CONFERENCE. It led to a treaty, signed by Great Britain, the United States, France, Italy, and Japan, regulating submarine warfare and limiting the tonnage and gun-caliber of submarines. The limitation of aircraft carriers, provided for by the Washington treaty, was extended. Great Britain, the United States, and Japan also agreed to scrap certain warships by 1933 and allocated tonnage in other categories. An "escalator clause," permitting an increase over specified tonnages if national needs of any one signatory demanded it, was included. The agreements were to run until 1936.

Oct. 5–12. First Balkan conference at Athens. These conferences met annually for several years and were the basis for the **Balkan Entente.**

Nov. 6–Dec. 9. Final meeting of the Preparatory Commission on Disarmament. It adopted by majority vote a draft convention to be discussed at a disarmament conference called by the League council for February 1932. This draft was not approved by the German and Russian representatives, and was much criticized by the Swedish and American delegates. The most obnoxious clauses preserved rights and obligations secured by previous treaties, which France interpreted as including strict maintenance of the military clauses of the treaty of Versailles, thus barring the way to German equality in armament and to revision in general.

3. THE PERIOD OF REPUDIATION AND REVISION, 1930–1939

The years following 1930 were dominated by the great international **economic depression,** which almost ruined world trade and brought many nations to the verge of bankruptcy. The tension in domestic affairs led to a marked turn toward dictatorial forms of government and to widespread repudiation of financial and moral obligations in the effort to solve domestic problems. A number of less favored nations embarked frankly upon a policy of territorial expansion.

1931, May 11. The **failure of the Austrian Credit-Anstalt,** caused largely by the artificial and impracticable restrictions on commerce and finance imposed by the succession states of the old monarchy, precipitated an alarming financial and diplomatic crisis in central Europe which threatened to involve the whole continent. A guaranty of the Credit-Anstalt's foreign debts by the Austrian government, backed by a foreign exchange credit from ten of the largest central banks (arranged through the Bank for International Settlements), failed to check the panic. Foreign funds were rapidly withdrawn from Germany. The Bank of France, actuated by the purely political motive of forcing the abandonment of a proposed customs union between Austria and Germany, refused financial support for the Austrian bank.

June 16. The Bank of England, despite difficulties at home, advanced 150,000,000 schillings to the Austrian National Bank. Everywhere, from Austria to Australia, governments, banks, and corporations were exposed to immediate bankruptcy and were in terror of fascist or communist uprisings.

June 20. President Hoover, persuaded by expert opinion that one factor in the crisis was the always difficult problem of transferring sums due as reparation and war-debt payments from one currency to another, **proposed a moratorium** of one year on all intergovernmental debts. French opposition, chiefly political, caused disastrous delay.

July 6. Hoover announced **acceptance of**

the **moratorium** by all important creditor governments. The moratorium showed that there was, in fact, a close connection between inter-Allied debts and reparations, though Hoover continued to deny it. European governments regarded the moratorium as an American acknowledgment that inter-Allied debts and reparations would stand or fall together.

Aug. 19.   Layton-Wiggin report, from an international committee of bankers which had met at Basel. It called for a six months' extension of all foreign credits to Germany, expressed in terms of foreign currencies, so that these were "frozen." Germany never after became fully solvent in international transactions, i.e. it remained unable to pay promptly and in full principal and interest on long- and short-term foreign obligations.

Sept. 21. The **Bank of England was forced off the gold standard,** in spite of credits of £25,000,000 each from the Federal Reserve Bank of New York and the Bank of France, and the formation of a National Coalition ministry which was to balance the budget. Great Britain then experimented with a managed paper currency, while the fluctuations of sterling exchange were followed by numerous currencies, such as the Scandinavian, which had been tied to sterling. The depreciation of these currencies, in terms of those of countries which remained on the gold standard and did not devalue, amounted to an export subsidy which temporarily stimulated trade and eventually forced devaluation by almost all other countries. But trade was greatly contracted in the absence of any fixed medium of exchange. Capital showed a tendency to flee from one country to another and back again, in a vain attempt to escape the shrinkage of assets involved in devaluation.

Sept. 18.   Japanese army leaders took advantage of the hopeless world situation and of recurrent disorders in China to **occupy Mukden, Changchun,** and **Kirin,** important Manchurian towns. The result was the opening of an unofficial war between China and Japan that completely changed the complexion of affairs in the Far East (p. 1108).

1932-1935. The **Chaco War** between Bolivia and Paraguay (p. 1061).

1932, Jan. 4.   Occupation of Shanhaikwan by Japanese troops completed Japanese military control of South Manchuria.

Feb. 2-July. Meeting of the **DISARMA-MENT CONFERENCE** at Geneva, 60 nations represented, including the United States and the Soviet Union. The session led to nothing chiefly because of the divergence of view between France and the other powers. The French proposed a system of international

police and insisted that security must precede disarmament. The Germans demanded equality. In June President Hoover suggested the division of national forces into "police components" and "defense components," the latter to be reduced by one-third. This plan also failed of acceptance.

June 16-July 9.   LAUSANNE CONFERENCE. Representatives of Germany, France, Belgium, Great Britain, Italy, and Japan reached an agreement which set aside the German reparation debt and substituted for it 5 per cent bonds for Rm. 3,000,000,000, to be deposited with the Bank for International Settlements and issued when and if it became possible to market them at a price of 90 per cent or better, within the ensuing 15 years. Ratification of this agreement was made conditional on a satisfactory agreement between the associated powers and their creditors (i.e. United States). This agreement became impossible when the American congress (Dec.) passed a resolution that "it is against the policy of congress that any of the indebtedness of foreign powers to the United States should in any manner be cancelled or reduced." Technically, then, the failure of the Lausanne agreement meant a return to the Young plan. Actually Germany made no payments and the National Socialist government repudiated the international form of "interest slavery." Britain and several other European debtors made small "token payments" to the United States until congress ruled against such payments. Thereafter only Finland paid her installments in full. (The total sum borrowed from the United States was $10,338,000,000, of which $3,261,-000,000 was borrowed after November 11, 1918. Between 1923 and 1930 separate agreements were negotiated by a **World War Foreign Debt Commission,** created by congress, which decided each debtor's capacity to pay and arranged principal and interest payments for a period of 62 years. The original 5 per cent interest was reduced for each debtor, thus cancelling a varying portion of the debt. Payments actually came chiefly from Great Britain—almost $2,000,000,000—and France—almost $500,000,000. The total actually paid by all debtors remained under $3,000,000,000).

Oct. 4.   Lytton report, drawn by a commission appointed by the League on motion of the Japanese member (Dec. 10, 1931) to investigate the situation in Manchuria (p. 1108).

1933, Feb. 25. The **Lytton report** was adopted almost *in toto* by the League, despite its rejection by Japan. Japan gave notice of withdrawal from the League (May 27). The whole episode proved to be the **first serious blow at**

the **League structure** and Japan's example proved a stimulus to aggression elsewhere.

Feb. 2–Oct. 14. Meeting of the disarmament conference, after the United States government had engineered (Dec. 11, 1932) a **No Force Declaration,** by which Germany, France, Great Britain, and Italy promised "not in any circumstances to attempt to resolve any present or future differences between them by resort to force." The conference discussed a plan put forward by **Édouard Herriot** along familiar French lines, but this was nullified by German opposition (advent of Hitler, January 30). **Ramsay MacDonald** put forward (Mar. 16) a scheme by which European armies would be reduced by almost half a million men, and France and Germany would be given equality. Despite strong American support, this proposal also failed because of German insistence that storm troops should not be counted as effectives. The conference adjourned in June, to meet again in October. In the interval desperate attempts were made to reach an agreement. Great Britain, France, Italy, and the United States were ready not to increase armaments for four years and at the end of that time to allow Germany all such armaments as the other powers had. The Germans insisted on having at least "defensive" weapons at once.

Feb. In view of the danger from the new nationalist Germany, the **Little Entente was reorganized** and given a permanent council.

Mar. Mussolini proposed a four-power pact between Britain, France, Germany, and Italy.

June 12–July 27. INTERNATIONAL ECONOMIC CONFERENCE at London. It disregarded war debts and reparations and tried to secure an agreement on currency stabilization. This was blocked by President Roosevelt's repudiation of it in his message to the conference (July 3). The conference failed.

July 15. Conclusion of the four-power pact between Britain, France, Germany, and Italy (p. 999).

Oct. 14. Germany announced her withdrawal from the disarmament conference and from the League of Nations (Oct. 23).

1934, Jan. 26. Conclusion of the **German-Polish non-aggression pact,** the first break in the French alliance system.

Feb. 9. Conclusion of the Balkan pact between Turkey, Greece, Roumania, and Yugoslavia. It was the counterpart of the Little Entente and was designed to protect the Balkans from encroachment by other powers. The great weakness of the pact was the absence of Bulgaria.

May 29–June 11. The **disarmament conference** met for a brief session, but last-minute efforts to reach an accommodation were wrecked by the stiff French attitude.

Sept. 18. The Soviet Union joined the League of Nations, another reflection of fear of the new Germany.

Dec. 19. Japan denounced the naval agreements of 1922 and 1930.

1935, Jan. 7. Franco-Italian agreement (p. 1000), dealing with conflicting interests in Africa, but meant to pave the way to Franco-Italian co-operation in the event of action by Germany.

Jan. 13. Plebiscite in the Saar Basin, resulting in an overwhelming vote for union with Germany (p. 1011).

Mar. 16. GERMANY FORMALLY DENOUNCED THE CLAUSES OF THE TREATY OF VERSAILLES CONCERNING HER DISARMAMENT, reintroduced conscription, and announced that her army would be increased to 36 divisions. This step was based on the failure of the other powers to disarm as provided in the peace treaties and on the steady growth of French and Soviet military establishments.

Apr. 11. Stresa conference between Britain, France, and Italy establishing a common front in view of the German action.

Apr. 17. The League formally condemned Germany's unilateral repudiation of the Versailles treaty.

May 2. Franco-Russian Alliance concluded for five years (p. 989). Each promised the other aid in case of unprovoked aggression.

June 18. Anglo-German naval agreement (p. 1011).

Sept. BEGINNING OF THE ETHIOPIAN CRISIS (p. 1000).

Oct. 3. The League council declared that Italy had "resorted to war in disregard of her obligations under Art. XII," though neither Italy nor Ethiopia had declared war.

Oct. 11. Representatives of 51 nations voted in the League to impose sanctions on Italy, under Article XVI (p. 1000).

1936, Mar. 7. DENUNCIATION OF THE LOCARNO PACTS AND GERMAN REOCCUPATION OF THE RHINELAND. The Germans took advantage of the Ethiopian crisis and pleaded the danger from the Franco-Russian combination. Acute international crisis, influenced by the British attitude not to resort to military action in defense of the treaties.

Mar. 12. Great Britain, France, Belgium, and Italy denounced the German violation of the Locarno treaties. The League also recognized this violation, but, despite acute danger of war between Germany and France, the crisis blew over, due largely to Britain's unwillingness to invoke sanctions. Hitler's vague proposals for a new agreement came to naught through his refusal to consider the extension of the agreement to eastern Europe.

Mar. 25. London **naval agreement** between Britain, France, and the United States.

May 5. The **Italian army occupied Addis Ababa,** bringing to an end the Ethiopian war (p. 1079). **Complete collapse of the League as a political instrument.** Ethiopia, though a member of the League, was abandoned to its fate and Italian aggression, like the Japanese in Manchuria, proved successful in the face of world opinion and even the application (though incomplete) of sanctions.

July 18.   BEGINNING OF THE CIVIL WAR IN SPAIN (p. 993). The Spanish war divided Europe into fascist and non-fascist groups.

July 20. The **Montreux conference** approved the Turkish request for permission to fortify the Straits.

Oct. 25. A **German-Italian pact** established the Berlin-Rome Axis, marking the division of Europe into contending groups (p. 1011).

Nov. 14. Germany denounced international control of her waterways. Only France, Czechoslovakia, and Yugoslavia protested.

Nov. 25. A **German-Japanese agreement,** followed by an Italian-Japanese agreement (Nov. 6, 1937), directed against communism and the Third International (the Anti-Comintern pact).

1937, Jan. 2. An **agreement between Great Britain and Italy** for mutual respect of interests and rights in the Mediterranean and the maintenance of the independence and integrity of Spain. This failed to affect the situation materially.

Mar. 25. Conclusion of a **non-aggression and neutrality pact** for five years **between Italy and Yugoslavia.** The latter agreed to recognize Italian possession of Ethiopia, while Italy made extensive trade concessions. The agreement brought to an end the long-standing feud between the two powers and reflected Premier Stoyadinovich's anxiety to establish a middle position between the French and the Italians.

July 7. Beginning of **hostilities between Japan and China,** initiating an acute international crisis (p. 1109).

Sept. 10-14. The **Nyon conference and agreement,** to deal with piracy in the Mediterranean in connection with the Spanish civil war. Nine powers adopted a system of patrol zones, though Britain and France assumed the chief burden. Italy, unable to obstruct this action, belatedly joined in the scheme.

Nov. 3-15. Conference of the powers at Brussels, in vain effort to settle the war in China.

Nov. 17. Visit of Lord Halifax, member of the British cabinet, **to Hitler,** with the aim of discovering the German objectives and, if possible, striking some peaceful settlement. Halifax returned deeply impressed with the magnitude of the German program, especially in central and eastern Europe.

Dec. 1-17. The French foreign minister, **Yvon Delbos,** paid an extended visit to France's allies (Poland, Roumania, Yugoslavia, and Czechoslovakia) in the hope of reanimating the French alliance system and preparing for any German moves in central and eastern Europe. He found but little readiness to take a strong stand against so formidable an opponent as Germany. Poland and Yugoslavia, at least, hoped to maintain a free hand policy.

1938, Mar. The **AUSTRO-GERMAN CRISIS** and the annexation of Austria by Germany (p. 1016) created remarkably little tension in international relations. Italy, which might have been expected to offer stiff opposition, was so bound up with Spanish and Mediterranean affairs that Mussolini had to accept the inevitable as graciously as possible. France, at the moment, was in the midst of a cabinet crisis. The British appear to have been reconciled to the German move from the outset. Beyond a few half-hearted attempts to revive the Stresa front of 1935, the powers acquiesced and accepted the *fait accompli.*

Mar. 16-19. The **Polish-Lithuanian crisis,** following on the heels of the German action. The Poles demanded establishment of normal relations. Since Lithuania capitulated at once to the Polish ultimatum (p. 1039), the affair had no broader effects.

Apr. 16. Conclusion of the **Anglo-Italian pact,** which had been under negotiation for some time. The British being eager to free themselves of Italian hostility in the Mediterranean and Near East and Mussolini apparently desiring some counter-weight to the oppressive friendship of Hitler, the two parties succeeded in liquidating their differences. Great Britain was to recognize Italian sovereignty over Ethiopia and use her influence to induce other states to do likewise. Italy was to respect Spanish territory and withdraw her "volunteers" at the end of the war (at that time regarded as very near). Italy was to desist from hostile propaganda in the Near East, and both powers were to collaborate in maintaining the *status quo* in the Red Sea. The provisions of the agreement were to come into force as soon as the Spanish affair had been settled.

May 3-9. Visit of Hitler to Rome, a great and impressive state function evidently designed to demonstrate the solidarity of the Rome-Berlin Axis.

May 19-20. First **Czech crisis** (p. 1017).

July 19-21. State visit of King George VI

and Queen Elizabeth to Paris, clearly meant as a counter-demonstration of Anglo-French solidarity.

Aug. 21-23. Meeting of the Little Entente statesmen at Bled (Yugoslavia). The three powers **recognized Hungary's right to rearm** and arranged for the conclusion of non-aggression pacts.

Relations between Germany and Czechoslovakia grew seriously strained again in August and produced a **second crisis in September** that brought the powers to the verge of war.

Sept. 7-29. Height of the **GERMAN-CZECH CRISIS.** The Sudete leaders broke off negotiations with the government (Sept. 7) after an affray at Moravska Ostrava. Discussions were resumed (Sept. 10), but disorders, provoked by extremists, became more and more frequent. On September 12 Hitler, in a speech at Nürnberg, first demanded in no uncertain terms that the Sudete Germans be given the **right of self-determination.** This address was the signal for widespread disorders and the proclamation of martial law by the government (Sept. 13). Henlein and other leaders fled across the frontier (Sept. 15). To meet this dangerous situation, Prime Minister Chamberlain, in agreement with the French government, proposed a personal conference to Hitler.

Sept. 15. CHAMBERLAIN-HITLER CONFERENCE AT BERCHTESGADEN. The German chancellor baldly stated his demand for annexation of the German areas of Czechoslovakia on the basis of self-determination, and did not conceal his readiness to risk a war to attain his end. Chamberlain returned to London, as did Runciman from Prague. On September 18 Premier Édouard Daladier and Georges Bonnet (French foreign minister) arrived in London. Decision reached to advise and urge the Czech government to accept Hitler's terms, promising an international guaranty of the rump state. After long deliberations the **Czech government** (Sept. 20) **suggested arbitration** on the basis of the German-Czech Locarno treaty of 1925. This proposal was at once rejected by Britain and France as inadequate. After further pressure and threats of desertion by France and Britain, the **Prague government finally yielded** (Sept. 21), despite the fact that Poland and Hungary had both put in additional claims for territory. The **Hodza cabinet resigned** (Sept. 22) and a new government was formed by **Gen. Jan Sirovy,** popular military leader.

Sept. 22-23. CHAMBERLAIN'S SECOND VISIT TO HITLER AT GODESBERG. Further demands of the German chancellor: surrender of the predominantly German territories at once, without removal or destruction of military or economic establishments; plebiscites to be held in areas with large German minority by November 25, under German-Czech or international supervision. These terms were regarded by Chamberlain as quite inacceptable, and as an unwarranted extension of the original German demands.

Sept. 24-29. ACUTE INTERNATIONAL CRISIS, the most serious since 1918. The Czech government ordered full mobilization and the great powers took precautions of every kind. **Italy,** however, came out more and more definitely on the German side. Daladier and Bonnet again came to London (Sept. 26) and the decision was evidently reached to support Czechoslovakia in resisting the extended German demands. Chamberlain appealed to Hitler for a conference, so that the cession of Sudete territory, already agreed on by all, might be effected by discussion, not by force. **President Roosevelt** also appealed to Hitler and urged a conference (Sept. 27). Finally (Sept. 28) Hitler, apparently persuaded by Mussolini (to whom both Chamberlain and Roosevelt had appealed), agreed to a conference.

Sept. 29. The **MUNICH CONFERENCE AND AGREEMENT.** Hitler, Ribbentrop, Mussolini, Ciano, Chamberlain, and Daladier conferred during the afternoon and evening, Czechoslovakia being unrepresented. The agreement (dated September 29) was actually signed just after midnight. Hitler secured about all that he had demanded: evacuation to take place between October 1 and October 10, under conditions arranged by an international commission, which should also determine the plebiscite areas. Britain and France undertook to guarantee the new frontiers of Czechoslovakia against unprovoked aggression. When the Polish and Hungarian minorities questions should have been solved, Germany and Italy would give a like guaranty. The Czech government felt impelled to acquiesce in this settlement September 30.

The statesmen, returning from Munich, received warm ovations from their peoples and there could be no doubt that the will to peace was strong, not only in Britain and France, but also in Italy and Germany. The crisis, however, soon led to much dispute. Many felt that the democratic powers had not only deserted the one democratic outpost in central Europe, but that they had suffered a tremendous defeat, which might have been avoided if the strong stand taken just before the Munich conference had been maintained. Others believed that the German case in Czechoslovakia was too strong to justify war against Germany, and that Hitler, far from bluffing, was deter-

mined to march. In any event, the final outcome established **German hegemony in central
Europe** and opened the way to domination of
the entire Danubian area.

THE SETTLEMENTS:

(1) *GERMAN.* The occupation was carried
through as scheduled at Munich, taking over
all the vital Czech frontier fortresses. The predominantly German regions were determined
by the Austrian census of 1910. The international commission caused Germany no trouble,
and in the end there were no plebiscites. Germany acquired about 10,000 square miles of
Czech territory, with about 3,500,000 inhabitants, of whom about 700,000 were Czechs.
By agreement with the Czechoslovak government (Nov. 20, 1938) Germany was given
**rights to a highway across Moravia to Vienna,
and to a canal connecting the Oder and the
Danube Rivers.** The truncated Czechoslovak
state, without defensible frontiers, became of
necessity a satellite of the Reich.

(2) *POLISH.* During the crisis the Polish
government had renewed its long-standing
claims to the Teschen region. On September 29 a virtual ultimatum was submitted to
Prague, to which the Czech government
yielded. On October 2 Polish forces occupied
the Teschen area and Czechoslovakia lost
about 400 square miles of territory with some
240,000 inhabitants (less than 100,000 Poles).

(3) *HUNGARIAN.* The Hungarian **claims
to Slovakia** were to be settled by negotiation,
and delegates of the two countries met October 9. Agreement proved impossible and serious clashes took place on the frontier. Ultimately the matter was adjusted by joint
decision of Germany and Italy. Hungary received a broad strip of southern Slovakia and
Ruthenia, almost 5000 square miles, with
1,000,000 population. The Hungarian claim,
supported by Poland, for a common frontier
with Poland, was denied.

As a result of Hitler's immense victory the
**Little Entente disappeared as an important
factor** in international relations. What remained of Czechoslovakia fell entirely under
German influence. Much the same was true of
Hungary and the other Danubian countries.
The Czech alliances with Russia and France
became all but valueless, and the Franco-Russian alliance of 1935 lost most of its significance.
Germany now emerged as the strongest power
on the Continent.

Nov. 16. The **Anglo-Italian agreement of
April 16 was put into force,** despite the fact
that the conditions of enforcement had been
only very imperfectly fulfilled.

Nov. 26. **Poland and Russia suddenly renewed their non-aggression pact.** Poland,

directly exposed to the German advance eastward, now required closer relations with Russia
and, indeed, made efforts to build up a barrier of Baltic and Balkan states to join with
Poland in the interest of the *status quo.*

Nov. 30. **Anti-French demonstrations in
the Italian chamber of deputies** (demands for
Corsica and Tunisia, which were then taken up
by the government-controlled press) ushered
in a period of acute **tension between France
and Italy,** which became even more accentuated with the fascist victories in Spain.

Dec. 6. **France and Germany concluded a
pact** by which they guaranteed the inviolability of the existing frontier and provided for
consultation with the aim of settling any disputes pacifically.

Dec. 17. An Italian note to France declared
the agreement of 1935 invalid because ratifications had not been exchanged. France rejected
this argument.

Dec. 24. The **declaration of Lima** was
adopted by 21 American republics. It reaffirmed their solidarity and decision to oppose
any foreign intervention or activity threatening
their sovereignty. The United States favored
an even stronger statement, underlining hemisphere solidarity as against the totalitarian
states of Europe.

1939, Mar. The **SLOVAK CRISIS** and the
**ANNIHILATION OF THE CZECHOSLO-
VAK STATE** (p. 1018). None of the great
powers made a move to check the German
annexation of the rump Czech state or the
Hungarian conquest of Ruthenia (Carpatho-
Ukraine). Yet Hitler's action served to disil-
lusion those who held that his aims were restricted to German territories.

Mar. 21. **German annexation of Memel**
(p. 1012).

Apr. 7. **Italian invasion and conquest of Albania** (p. 1023).

Apr. 15. **Letter of President Roosevelt to
Hitler and Mussolini** asking assurances against
agression on 31 named nations and suggesting
discussions on reduction of armaments.

May 12. Announcement of an **Anglo-Turkish mutual assistance pact.**

May 22. Conclusion of a political and **military alliance between Germany and Italy** marking the full development of the Rome-Berlin
Axis.

June 17. Sweden, Norway, and Finland
rejected a German offer of a bilateral non-
aggression pact, preferring to maintain a rigid
neutrality. Denmark, Estonia, and Latvia,
however, accepted the German proposal.

June 23. **Treaty between France and Turkey** by which the republic of Hatay was abandoned to Turkey in return for a promise of

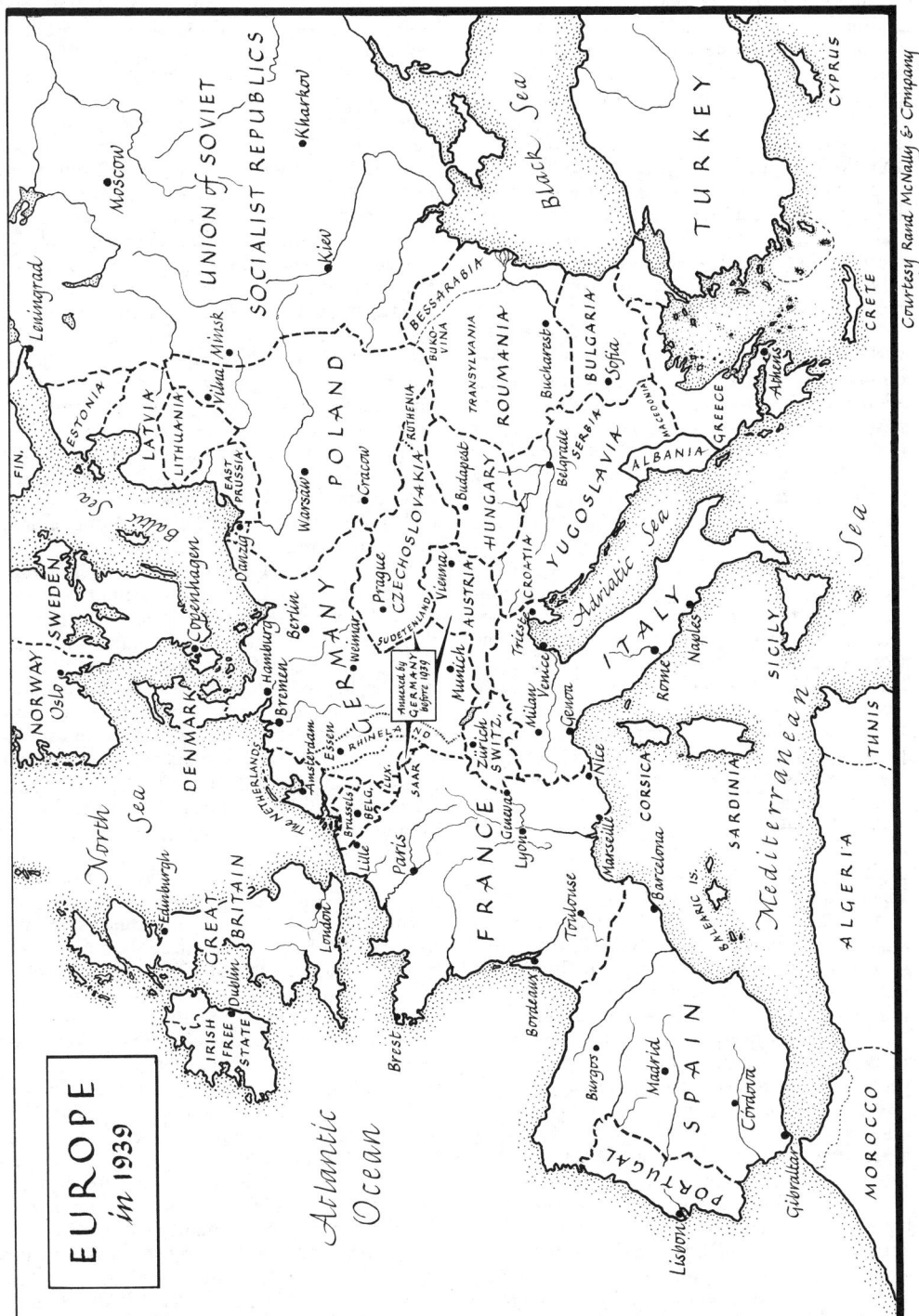

EUROPE
in 1939

mutual aid in case of aggression.

June–Aug. Triangular negotiations between Britain, France, and the Soviet Union for a "peace front" to block further Nazi expansion. The Soviets insisted on a complete alliance and military convention, in addition to clear guarantees for the Baltic states. Negotiations dragged on through the summer and were marked by growing Soviet distrust. Eventually the Soviets insisted on the right to send troops through Poland in the event of German aggression. Since the Poles themselves objected violently to such an arrangement, a deadlock ensued.

Aug. 20–Sept. 1. The DANZIG-POLISH CRISIS. After months of agitation and recrimination, punctuated by incidents on the Danzig-Polish frontier, the long-anticipated crisis broke when Albert Forster, Nazi leader in Danzig, announced publicly that the hour of deliverance was near. At the same time the world was startled by the conclusion of a trade treaty between Germany and Soviet Russia, followed by

Aug. 21. The announcement that Germany and Russia were about to conclude a non-aggression pact. Coming after months of negotiation, this move was regarded in the west as a demonstration of Soviet perfidy. Discussion of Russia's inclusion in a peace front was at once dropped. In Britain and France as well as in Germany military preparations were initiated, the Germans concentrating forces in Slovakia as well as along the Corridor.

Aug. 22. The British government reiterated its pledges to Poland, but at the same time appealed to Germany for a truce in eastern Europe and negotiation of German claims.

Aug. 23. The **German-Russian pact** was signed at Moscow by the German foreign minister Ribbentrop, artisan of the anti-Comintern pact of 1936. It provided not only for abstention by either party from attack on the other, but for neutrality by either party if the other were attacked by a third power. Each signatory promised not to join any group of powers "which is directly or indirectly aimed at the other party." As a result of this amazing agreement the anti-Comintern pact at once collapsed, Japan resuming freedom of action.

Aug. 24. President Roosevelt appealed to King Victor Emmanuel, to Hitler, and to President Moscicki of Poland, suggesting direct negotiations between Germany and Poland, arbitration, or conciliation. Poland agreed to conciliation by a third party.

The British parliament met in special session and voted the government practically dictatorial powers; at the same time **Britain and Poland signed a pact of mutual assistance.** Poland began to call up reserves.

Aug. 25. In discussion with the British ambassador, Hitler renewed his demand for a free hand against Poland. Roosevelt again appealed to Hitler to seek a peaceful solution.

Aug. 26. Premier Daladier of France appealed to Hitler, receiving in reply (Aug. 27) a plea for German-French peace but also a reiteration of the German demands on Poland.

Aug. 28. The British government replied to Hitler, again urging a truce and repeating former warnings of British action in case of German aggression. British shipping was recalled from the Baltic and Mediterranean. In Germany emergency rationing was introduced. On all sides military preparations were accelerated.

Aug. 29. Hitler reiterated to Britain his extreme demands on Poland and refused to negotiate until these demands were met. He called for arrival of a Polish plenipotentiary in Berlin within 24 hours.

Aug. 30. The **Poles decreed partial mobilization,** while in Germany a six-man "cabinet council for defense of the Reich" was set up under the presidency of Hermann Goering.

Aug. 31. The German government published a **16-point proposal to Poland.** This was of rather moderate tenor, but before it could be transmitted to Warsaw, communications were cut off. On this same day the Russian supreme soviet ratified the pact with Germany and Hitler, claiming his proposals to Poland had been rejected, gave the order to march.

Sept. 1. GERMAN ATTACK ON POLAND on land and in the air. Forster proclaimed the **reunion of Danzig and Germany.** Britain and France mobilized but expressed readiness to negotiate if German forces were withdrawn from Poland. Italy declared its intention of remaining neutral.

Sept. 2. Italy proposed a five-power conference to discuss the situation, but Britain refused negotiation so long as the Germans remained on Polish soil. Hitler having failed to reply to the Anglo-French notes, these two powers sent an ultimatum, to which Hitler replied by a note blaming Britain for encouraging the Poles in a policy of persecution and provocation. The German government having rejected the Anglo-French demands for withdrawal from Poland,

Sept. 3. BRITAIN AND FRANCE DECLARED WAR ON GERMANY, thus initiating the second great war of the twentieth century.

VII. THE SECOND WORLD WAR AND ITS AFTERMATH 1939–1970

VII. THE SECOND WORLD WAR AND ITS AFTERMATH 1939–1970

A. THE SECOND WORLD WAR

1. THE CAMPAIGNS IN POLAND AND FINLAND, 1939–1940

1939, Sept. 1. POLAND WAS INVADED by German forces estimated at 1,700,000 men. Headed by mechanized divisions and supported by overwhelming air power, the German thrusts disorganized and defeated the poorly equipped Polish armies. Though the latter had a numerical strength of 600,000 men, they were unable to mobilize effectively or concert their resistance. The rapidity of the German convergence, from East Prussia, Silesia, and Slovakia alarmed the Soviet government.

Sept. 17. Russian troops therefore **invaded Poland** from the east, meeting the advancing Germans near Brest-Litovsk two days later.

Sept. 27. After heroic resistance and destructive bombing, **Warsaw surrendered** and Polish organized opposition came to an end. The *Blitzkrieg* had lasted less than four weeks and the outcome had been determined in the first ten days.

Sept. 29. The German and Russian governments divided Poland. Germany annexed outright the Free City of Danzig (population 415,000) and 32,000 square miles between East Prussia and Silesia. In addition an area of 39,000 square miles, known as *Gouvernement Général,* remained under German protection. The total German gains were estimated at 72,866 square miles with a population of 22,140,000. The Russians occupied 77,620 square miles of eastern Poland, with a population of 13,199,000. Lithuania and Slovakia received small cessions of Polish territory.

The Germans lost no time in putting their **racist doctrines** into effect. Many thousands of Polish officers, professional men, and intellectuals were rounded up and executed out of hand, and many more were sent off to Germany to work in factories or perform menial tasks. At the very least large numbers of Poles, as an inferior race, were moved from their homelands into less desirable areas so as to make room for German settlers, who were to inherit the new territory for the Reich.

Extermination of the Jews. German conquests in the east made possible for the Nazi leaders the "final solution" of the Jewish question, a case of genocide such as the modern world had never seen nor indeed had ever imagined. The numerous Jewish population of Poland (and later of the Ukraine and western Russia) was herded into cities and concentrated in ghettoes, where large numbers, deprived of means of livelihood, perished of hunger or disease. Presently special Nazi formations were employed to massacre the Jews in mass executions. Still later (1941–1944) the Jews, rounded up in all parts of Nazi-occupied Europe, were sent to concentration camps, of which Auschwitz, near Cracow, was only the most notorious, to be slain—men, women, and children—in huge gas chambers, of which there were four in Auschwitz alone, with a capacity of 6000 victims a day. Human monsters then ripped out the gold teeth and plundered the corpses of rings and other jewelry before cremating them. It has been estimated that during the war no less than five to six million Jews were "liquidated" under these appallingly brutal circumstances.

Sept. 29. The Soviet government concluded a **treaty with Estonia** which gave Russia naval and air bases in Estonian territory.

Oct. 5. A similar **pact with the Latvian government** allowed the Russians to establish fortified bases in Latvia.

Oct. 10. Russia and Lithuania concluded a mutual assistance pact. The Russians acquired the right to occupy stations of military importance in Lithuania and ceded Vilna and surrounding territory to Lithuania in return. The assistance pact was to run for 15 years.

Nov. 26. The **Finnish government rejected Soviet demands** similar to those accepted by the lesser Baltic states. The Soviet government demanded the withdrawal of Finnish troops mobilizing on the frontier.

Nov. 30, 1939–Mar. 12, 1940. RUSSO-FINNISH WAR. Russian armies attacked on three fronts: below Petsamo on the Arctic Sea, in central Finland, and on the Karelian Isthmus.

Dec. 14. Russia was expelled from the League of Nations for acts of aggression against Finland.

1940, Mar. 12. After three months of varying success but increasing pressure, the Russians breached the Mannerheim Line. **Finland accepted peace,** negotiated at Moscow, ceding to the Union of Soviet Socialist Republics the Karelian Isthmus, the city of Viipuri (Viborg), a naval base at Hangoe, and territories totaling 16,173 square miles with a population of 450,000. Most of the Finns in the ceded areas were to be resettled in Finland.

2. THE INVASION OF DENMARK AND NORWAY, 1940

1940, Feb. 16. **British naval forces entered Norwegian waters** to rescue 299 prisoners of war from the German ship *Altmark.* The Norwegian government protested.

Apr. 8. The French and British governments announced that Norwegian waters had been mined to prevent the passage of German ships.

Apr. 9. **German sea and airborne forces descended on Norway.** Oslo, Bergen, Trondheim, Stavanger, and Narvik were rapidly invaded. At the same time German forces entered and occupied Denmark without more than formal resistance.

Apr. 9. A German destroyer squadron landed at Narvik and held the town even after destruction of the German ships by the British (Apr. 13). On May 28 a British force recovered the town but was withdrawn on June 10 in view of the German attack in the West.

Apr. 11. Rallying from the surprise attack, Norwegian forces offered growing resistance.

Three German cruisers and four troopships were lost in the invasion.

Apr. 16–19. **Anglo-French expeditionary forces** landed in southern Norway, but were compelled to withdraw after two weeks (May 3).

Apr. 30. The Germans, reinforced steadily, captured Dombas, a key rail center, and **Norwegian resistance was broken,** though military operations were carried on until June 10. Haakon VII and his cabinet escaped to London to continue resistance.

Sept. 25. The German Reich-Commissar for Norway set aside the legal administration, dissolved all political parties except the *Nasjonal Samling,* and entrusted the government to thirteen commissars.

1942, Feb. 1. The German commissar, Joseph Terboven, appointed **Vidkun Quisling** "minister president" of the German-dominated régime. Disowned by the Norwegian government in London, Quisling abolished the constitution and made himself dictator (Feb. 7).

3. THE CONQUEST OF THE LOW COUNTRIES AND THE FALL OF FRANCE, 1940

1940, May 10. **German armies,** without warning, **invaded the Netherlands, Belgium, and Luxemburg.**

The French and British governments dispatched expeditionary forces into Belgium to co-operate with the Belgian army in its resistance. The Germans captured Fort Eben Emael, key Belgian defense position.

May 12. The **Germans crossed the Meuse** at Sedan.

May 13. **Rotterdam surrendered** to the Germans after part of the city had been blasted by an exterminating air attack. The Netherlands government, headed by Queen Wilhelmina, escaped to London. The **Netherlands army capitulated** May 14.

May 17–21. **German mechanized divisions drove deep into northern France,** racing down the Somme valley to the English Channel at Abbeville. The British and Belgian forces in Flanders were thus separated from the main French armies. **Gen. Maxime Weygand** replaced Gen. Gustave Gamelin as French commander-in-chief, but he was unable to arrest the French collapse. The **fall of Brussels** and Namur forced the British and Belgian armies back upon Ostend and Dunkirk.

May 26. **Boulogne fell** to the Germans. The Belgian armies, disorganized and short of supplies after eighteen days of fighting, could not sustain further attacks, and Leopold III ordered them to capitulate.

May 28. Exposed by the capitulation of the Belgians, the British expeditionary force of some 250,000 had to be withdrawn, chiefly from the beaches of **Dunkirk.**

June 4. By heroic efforts some 200,000 British and 140,000 French troops were rescued, but were forced to abandon almost all equipment. British losses including prisoners totaled 30,000.

June 5. Having secured their right wing, the German invaders launched a wide attack against the French on an arc from Sedan to Abbeville.

June 10. ITALY DECLARED WAR AGAINST FRANCE AND GREAT BRITAIN. Italian forces invaded southern France.

June 13. Paris was evacuated before the continued German advance.

June 15. The French fortress of **Verdun was captured.**

June 16. Marshal Henri-Philippe Pétain replaced Paul Reynaud as head of the French government.

June 17. Pétain asked the Germans for an armistice.

June 22. The **armistice was signed at Compiègne.** It provided that the French forces be disarmed, and that three-fifths of France be surrendered to German control.

June 23. Gen. Charles de Gaulle, at the head of a French National Committee in London, pledged continued French resistance to Germany. The British government supported de Gaulle and severed relations with the régime of Marshal Pétain.

June 24. An armistice was concluded between France and Italy.

July 3. Battle of Mers-el-Kebir. The British, to prevent the battle cruisers *Dunkerque* and *Strasbourg* and other naval forces, called upon the French commander to join the British or sail to British or West Indian ports to be disarmed. The French commander, on orders from Vichy, resisted, whereupon the British opened fire, destroyed or damaged three battleships. The *Strasbourg* escaped to Toulon.

The *Dunkerque* (26,000 tons), the *Provence* (22,000), the *Bretagne* (22,000), and an aircraft carrier (10,000) were damaged and French losses in men were 1300 dead.

July 4. All French ships in ports under British control were seized.

July 5. The **French government** at Vichy **severed relations with the British government.**

July 9. At **Vichy,** where the French government established its seat July 2, the parliament voted to give the Pétain régime the power to establish an **authoritarian government.** The vote was almost unanimous (395 to 3 in the chamber of deputies, 225 to 1 in the senate). Pétain designated **Pierre Laval** as his vice-premier (July 12). On November 11, 1942, German forces entered unoccupied France, following the Anglo-American invasion of North Africa.

Nazi rule in France and other western countries was not as barbarous as in the east. Nonetheless it was government by terror, thousands of persons being shot as hostages in reprisal for attacks on Germans. Eventually all these countries, even allied Italy, were obliged to enact anti-Semitic legislation and to send off Jews to Nazi concentration camps for disposition. As the war progressed and the labor shortage in Germany became acute, hundreds of thousands of French, Belgians, and Dutch were rounded up and sent to work in German factories, living frequently under the most appalling conditions. Much the same fate befell the several million Russian prisoners of war, if they were lucky enough to escape with their lives at all. By the end of the war there were about seven million foreign "slaves" serving their Nazi masters in one way or another. (For the liberation of France see p. 1150 *f.*)

4. THE BATTLE OF BRITAIN, 1940

1940, June. The **fall of France** and the loss of war matériel in the evacuation from Dunkirk led the British prime minister, Winston Churchill, to appeal to the United States government for military supplies. These were released by the war department (June 3), and three weeks later a first shipment, including 500,000 rifles, 80,000 machine guns, 900 75-mm. field guns, and 130,000,000 rounds of ammunition, reached Britain.

July. On the fall of France the Germans occupied islands in the English Channel and intensified their air attacks on British cities, communications, and shipping.

Aug. 8. German bombers opened an **offensive designed to destroy British air strength** by blasting the airfields and vital industries.

Aug. 15. One thousand German planes ranged as far north as Scotland. Croydon airfield was bombed. The British retaliated with heavy raids on Berlin, Düsseldorf, Essen, and other German cities.

Aug. 17. The German government proclaimed a **total blockade** of the waters around Great Britain.

Sept. 2. An important **defense agreement** was concluded **between Great Britain and the United States.** Fifty American destroyers were transferred to Britain to combat the air and submarine menace. In exchange the United States received a 99-year **lease of naval and air bases** in Newfoundland, Bermuda, the Bahamas, Jamaica, Antigua, St. Lucia, Trinidad, and British Guiana.

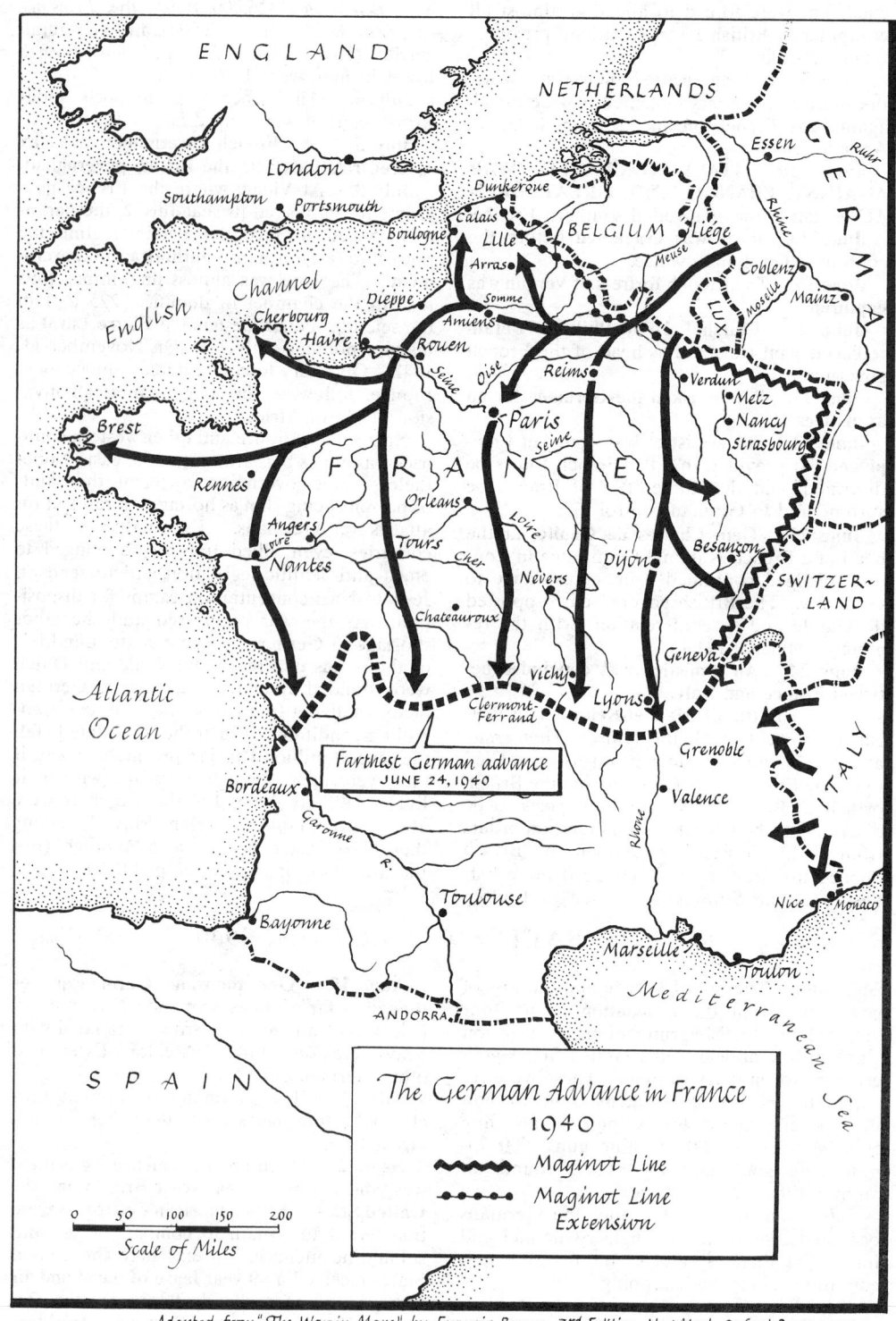

Farthest German advance
JUNE 24, 1940

The German Advance in France
1940

〜〜〜 Maginot Line
•••••• Maginot Line
Extension

Scale of Miles
0   50   100   150   200

Adapted from "The War in Maps" by Francis Brown. 3rd Edition. New York, Oxford Press, 1944.

Sept. 7. **Intensified bombing of London** raised the casualties to 300–600 a day killed and 1000–3000 injured.

Sept. 11. The **British bombed Continental ports,** including Antwerp, Ostend, Calais, and Dunkirk, to frustrate German invasion preparations.

Sept. 16. Improved British defense measures inflicted heavy losses on German air raiders, 185 invading planes crashing in one day.

Sept. 27. A **GERMAN-ITALIAN-JAPANESE PACT** was concluded at Berlin providing for a ten-year military and economic alliance. The three contracting powers further promised each other mutual assistance in the event that any one of them became involved in war with a power not then a belligerent.

Oct. 10. Resuming the **air assault** with full intensity, the German Luftwaffe raided London heavily. Some Italian air squadrons joined in the attack. But shorter days, stormy weather, and improved defenses diminished the effectiveness of the air arm.

Nov. 10. In a supreme effort at crushing British industrial resources and demoralizing the population, the Germans blasted the industrial city of **Coventry** with destructive effect. Thereafter the air attacks became more sporadic. The British had survived the worst of the aerial Blitzkrieg and after November the winter weather made any attempt at invasion less likely. German losses in aircraft had been heavy: an official estimate placed them at 2375 German to 800 British planes destroyed in the period August 8–October 31. But many British cities had been severely shattered and burned, and 14,000 civilians had been killed in London alone. British losses at sea had also been heavy. On November 5 Churchill declared that the **submarine boat** had become a greater menace than the bombing plane. (See p. 1146 *ff.*)

Nov. 20. The **Stimson-Layton agreement,** arranged between Sir Walter Layton, for the British ministry of supply, and Henry L. Stimson, United States secretary of war, provided for a partial **standardization of military weapons and equipment** and initiated a general policy of pooling British and American technical knowledge, patents, and formulas in armament production.

1941. Great Britain became increasingly dependent for arms, food, and raw material upon the United States as the German sea and air blockade was extended. President Roosevelt had proposed (Nov. 1940) an equal division of the American arms output between the United States and Britain. British credit in dollar exchange, which had amounted to $6,500,000,000, was exhausted by January 1941, however, and British purchases had to be curtailed. This situation was eased by the signing (Mar. 11, 1941) of the **LEND-LEASE ACT.** The first shipments of food for Britain (Apr. 16) came just in time to avert a critical shortage there. Between April and December 1941 one million tons of foodstuffs reached Britain from the United States.

May. **Intensified German air attacks,** facilitated by longer days and clearer skies, culminated in a shattering assault on London (May 10) which damaged the houses of parliament and the British Museum. Thereafter, however, secret German preparations for the invasion of Russia (June 22) reduced the number of bombers available for raids on Britain. Enormous damage had been endured by the British with remarkable courage. One home in every five was damaged or destroyed, factories shattered, and transport, gas, and water systems disrupted.

June 22. The **battle of Britain subsided** with the opening of the Russian front in June 1941. But the German submarine blockade remained a grave menace to British supply services throughout 1941 and 1942. It was gradually curbed by air and sea patrols, improved detection devices such as radar, and the extension of the convoy system. (See p. 1146 *ff.*)

5. THE BALKAN CAMPAIGNS, 1940–1941

1940, June. The **fall of France** and the desperate position of Great Britain in the summer of 1940 caused a shift in the European balance. In the Balkans Roumania, which had won territory from all its neighbors in the 20th century, was particularly menaced.

June 26. The **Union of Soviet Socialist Republics** demanded of Roumania the return of **Bessarabia** and the cession of northern **Buko-**vina. The disputed territory, 19,300 square miles with a population of 3,500,000, was occupied by Soviet troops June 28.

Aug. 30. Under pressure from Berlin and Rome, the Roumanian government agreed to yield an area of 16,642 square miles with a population of 2,392,603 to Hungary (**Vienna conference**).

Sept. 5. These reverses caused a political

overturn in Roumania. **Gen. Ion Antonescu** became premier.

Sept. 6. King Carol fled and was replaced by his son as **Michael V.**

Sept. 8. A further territorial cession of some 3000 square miles **(southern Dobrudja)** was demanded by, and yielded to, Bulgaria **(treaty of Craiova).** These cessions cost Roumania in all about 40,000 square miles and 4,000,000 population.

Oct. 4. Hitler and Mussolini conferred at the Brenner Pass. The failure to break British resistance and increasing activity in the Balkan and Mediterranean areas forecast a shift in Axis strategy. Hitler also conferred with the French vice-premier, **Pierre Laval** (Oct. 22), with **Gen. Francisco Franco** of Spain (Oct. 23), with **Marshal Henri-Philippe Pétain,** head of the Vichy French government (Oct. 24), and again with Mussolini, in Florence (Oct. 28).

Oct. 8. German troops entered Roumania to "protect" the oil fields.

Oct. 28. Greece rejected a demand of the Italian government for the use of Greek bases. Thereupon the Italians invaded Greece from Albania.

Oct. 30. British reinforcements were landed on Crete and other Greek islands. The Russian government delivered 134 fighter planes to Greece in accord with existing agreements.

Nov. 12. Vyacheslav Molotov, Soviet commissar for foreign affairs, **conferred with Hitler** in Berlin. Soviet troops were massed on the Roumanian border.

Nov. 13. British bombing planes destroyed or damaged half of the Italian fleet anchored in the inner harbor at **Taranto.** At the same time Churchill announced the addition of five 35,000-ton battleships to the British navy.

Nov. 20. Hungary joined the Berlin-Rome-Tokyo pact.

Nov. 23. Roumania joined the Berlin-Rome-Tokyo pact.

Dec. 3. The **Greeks broke through the Italian defenses** in Albania, captured Porto Edda, and claimed a total of 28,000 prisoners. Agyrokastron was likewise captured five days later, and the Greeks overran one-fourth of Albania. The Germans dispatched 50,000 troops to reinforce the Italian armies. Combined with temporary successes of the British against the Italians in Africa, the Greek victories marked a blow to Axis prestige.

1941, Jan. 10. German air squadrons, transferred to Italy, attacked British naval forces off Sicily.

Feb. 10. The British government severed diplomatic relations with Roumania.

Mar. 1. Bulgaria joined the Rome-Berlin Axis and German troops occupied Sofia. The British delegation had left February 24, and the Soviet government warned the Bulgarians not to expect Soviet aid.

Mar. 25. Yugoslav envoys signed the Rome-Berlin-Tokyo pact at Vienna.

Mar. 26–28. A political coup at Belgrade overthrew the regency of Prince Paul, and **Peter II** was proclaimed king. A new cabinet under **Gen. Dushan Simovich** announced that Yugoslavia would follow a policy of neutrality.

Apr. 6. German troops, which had been massing on the Hungarian, Roumanian, and Bulgarian borders, **poured into Yugoslavia and Greece.** In Moscow official journals laid the responsibility for the spread of war upon the Germans.

Apr. 13. RUSSIAN AND JAPANESE DIPLOMATS SIGNED A MUTUAL NON-AGGRESSION PACT AT MOSCOW.

Apr. 17. The **Yugoslav government capitulated** after a campaign of twelve days. Resistance against the Germans and Italians was maintained by guerrilla forces.

Apr. 23. Greek resistance was broken and an **armistice signed.** King George II fled to Crete.

Apr. 27. The Germans entered Athens. Of the British expeditionary force in Greece 48,000 of the 60,000 men were evacuated, but much valuable equipment was abandoned.

May 2. In **Iraq** a pro-Axis régime under **Premier Rashid Ali** invited German aid, whereupon British forces entered the country.

May 20. German parachute troops invaded Crete and superior German air power inflicted serious losses and damage on the British cruisers and destroyers in Cretan waters.

May 31. Surviving **British forces in Crete were evacuated** to Cyprus and Egypt. The Axis position in the eastern Mediterranean was greatly strengthened by the possession of Greece and Crete, which made the Aegean Sea unsafe for British ships. **Rebellion in Iraq** ended when British troops entered Baghdad after Iraqi airfields had been bombed. Mosul was occupied June 4. An armistice was concluded and a government friendly to Great Britain installed. Iraq later declared war on Germany, Italy, and Japan (Jan. 16, 1943).

July 12. Confused **fighting in Syria** ended with an armistice after British and Free French forces moved on Beirut and Damascus. British naval units landed troops on the Lebanon coast. This occupation terminated the authority of the French Vichy government over Syria and Lebanon and defeated the attempts of the Germans to obtain control of these territories. Possession of Syria and Iraq enabled the British to exert increased **pressure upon Iran,** the government of which was persuaded to co-operate (Aug. 28) after British and Soviet forces entered the country. The danger that the German successes in the Balkans would bring Constantinople and the Straits under Axis con-trol was fully realized in Moscow and the pos-sibility that a Soviet offensive might threaten the German flank explains in part why Hitler attacked Russia on June 22.

6. THE CAMPAIGNS IN RUSSIA, 1941-1944

1941, June 22. GERMAN ARMIES INVADED RUSSIA, opening hostilities on a front of 2000 miles, from the White to the Black Sea. The German invaders, with their allies, Italians, Roumanians, Hungarians, and Finns, were estimated at over 3,000,000 men. The Russians were credited with 2,000,000 men under arms, and an indefinite reserve. Churchill promised that Great Britain would extend all possible aid to the Russians.

June 29. The Germans reached Grodno, Brest-Litovsk, and Vilna.

July 1-2. Riga, capital of Latvia, **was occu-pied by German troops,** and the Russian re-treat continued with heavy losses, especially around Bialystok.

July 13. A pact promising mutual aid was concluded between Great Britain and Russia.

July 16. The Germans captured Smolensk.

Aug. 1. Britain severed relations with Fin-land, which the Germans were using as a base for their invasion of Russia.

Aug. 19. The **Germans claimed all Ukrain-ian territory** west of the Dnieper except Odessa.

Aug. 25-29. British and Soviet forces in-vaded Iran (Persia).

Sept. 4. The Germans commenced the **in-vestment of Leningrad,** a state of partial siege which was not ended until January 1943.

Sept. 19. Kiev and Poltava were stormed by the Axis forces, which continued their vic-torious advance to Orel (Oct. 8), Bryansk (Oct. 12), Viazma (Oct. 13), Odessa (Oct. 16), Tanganrog (Oct. 19), and Kharkov (Oct. 24). By the end of October the Germans had **entered the Crimea** on the southern end of the vast front and had commenced the **siege of Moscow** in the north. The Soviet government transferred its headquarters to Kuibyshev.

Oct. 1. The **FIRST SOVIET PROTO-COL,** signed at Moscow, provided that Great Britain and the United States would supply materials essential to the Russian war efforts for nine months. Purchase of American sup-plies was speeded by extending the Soviet government a credit of one billion dollars (Oct. 30). This was supplemented (June 11, 1942) by a **master lend-lease agreement** whereby the United States promised to supply the Soviet Union with such materials and serv-ices as the president might authorize. In re-turn the Soviet government pledged that such articles or information would not be trans-ferred to a third party without the consent of the president. The arrangement was to con-tinue until a date agreed upon by the two gov-ernments and materials unconsumed were to be returned to the United States at the end of the emergency.

Nov. 15. The **siege of Sevastopol,** an heroic epic of the war on the eastern front, com-menced.

Nov. 16. The **Germans captured Kerch.** Rostov, entered by the invaders (Nov. 22), was retaken by the Russians a week later (Dec. 1). A counter-thrust temporarily re-lieved the pressure on Moscow (Dec. 6) and the Russians were also able to retake Kalinin (Dec. 16).

1942, Jan. 20. Continuing their **winter offen-sive** the Russians recaptured Mozhaisk. Doro-gobuzh also fell to them (Feb. 23) and Rzhev (Mar. 20). In addition they scored advances toward Kursk (Apr. 29) and Kharkov (May 12).

May 26. The **mutual aid pact** between Great Britain and Russia was extended to a **twenty-year treaty.**

July 2. The Germans, who had opened a new **summer offensive** in southern Russia, cap-tured Sevastopol, which had sustained a siege of eight months. Driving powerfully toward the Caucasus, the Germans claimed Voronezh (July 7), Millerovo (July 15), and Rostov (July 24).

Aug. 9. Maikop fell to the invaders, who crossed the Don River (Aug. 20) and opened a vital **offensive against Stalingrad** (Aug. 22). This city was important as a communications center through which Volga River traffic, espe-cially oil from the Caspian region, reached Russian distribution points. The Germans hoped not only to obtain needed supplies of petroleum for themselves, but to cripple the Soviet war effort by cutting a major line of supply.

Sept. Russian agricultural supplies also were seriously reduced by the loss of the Ukraine and North Caucasus regions, for these

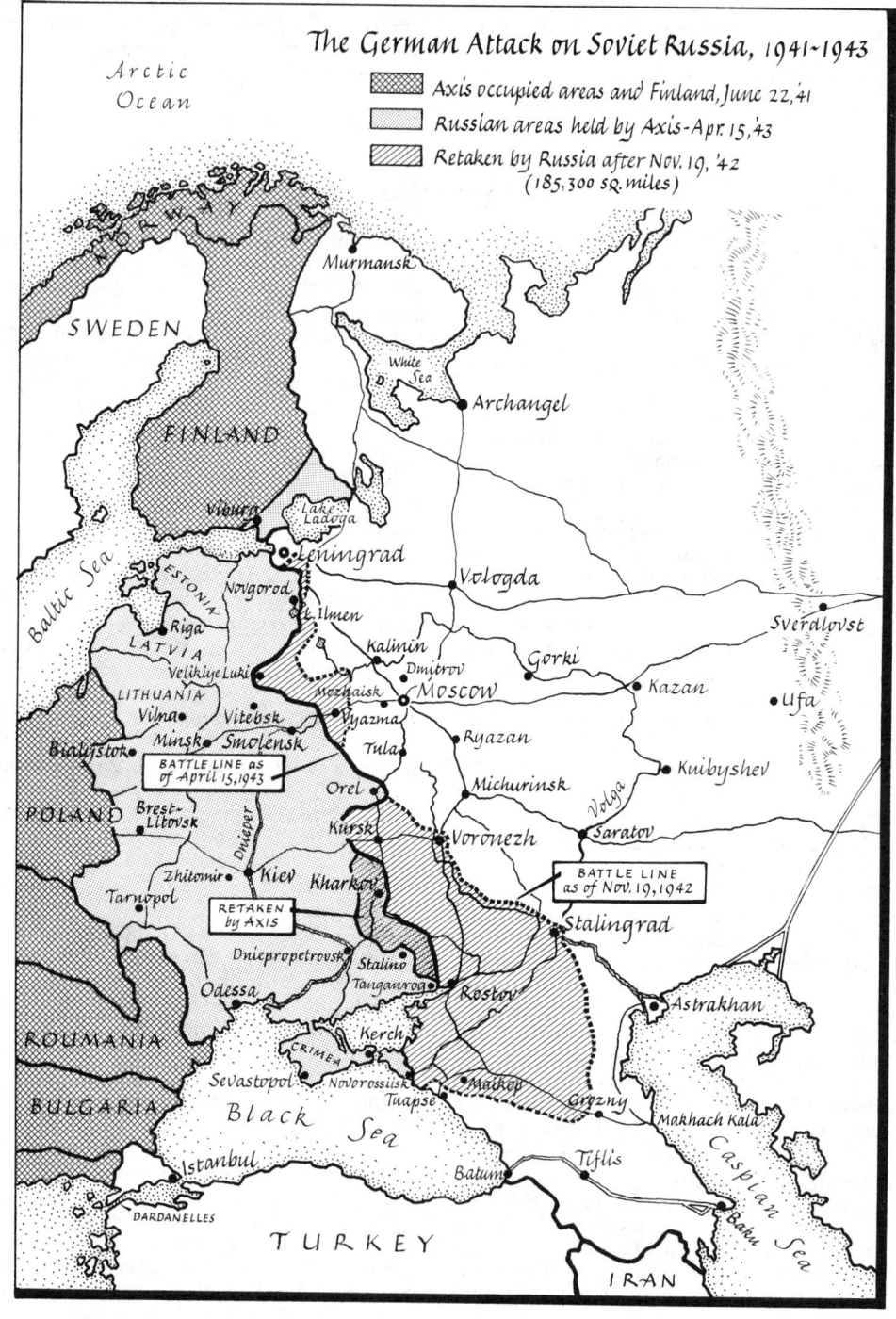

The German Attack on Soviet Russia, 1941-1943

Axis occupied areas and Finland, June 22, '41
Russian areas held by Axis - Apr. 15, '43
Retaken by Russia after Nov. 19, '42
(185,300 SQ. miles)

areas had produced half the Soviet wheat and pork output. The grave deficiency was met in part after September 1942 by increasing the shipments of canned meats, butter, fats, oils, dehydrated fruits and vegetables from the United States. By July 1943 the Soviet Union had received 1,5000,000 tons of foodstuffs under this arrangement.

Sept. 1. The **Germans crossed the Kerch Straits** and captured Novorossiisk (Sept. 6). Farther north, a week later, they penetrated the city of Stalingrad (Sept. 14). Their summer offensive appeared on the point of succeeding, but they had overstretched their lines. **Soviet forces counter-attacked** northeast of Stalingrad (Sept. 21) and ten days later (Oct. 1) opened a second thrust from southeast of the city.

Nov. 19. Without permitting the Germans time to entrench or to withdraw, the Russians intensified their pincer attack on the **Stalingrad front** while opening new drives toward Rzhev (Nov. 25) and Kharkov (Dec. 16).

1943, Jan. 1–18. The list of **German defeats** mounted to a **debacle.** Soviet forces recaptured Velikiye Luki (Jan. 1), entered Mozdok (Jan. 3), and relieved **Leningrad** from a 17-month siege. Twenty-two German divisions, cut off at Stalingrad, and reduced to 80,000 men, were forced to capitulate by February 2. This second Soviet winter offensive then rolled on, with the capture of Kursk (Feb. 8), Belgorod (Feb. 9), Rostov (Feb. 14), Kharkov (Feb. 16), Rzhev (Mar. 3), and Viazma (Mar. 12). The losses of the Germans and their allies, in killed and captured, exceeded 500,000 for three months of winter fighting.

Mar. 15. Despite these casualties the Germans were able to open a **spring drive,** wresting Kharkov from the Russians once more (Mar. 15), and retaking Belgorod (Mar. 21). This checked the Russian tide of conquest temporarily and the lines were more or less stabilized. The Axis armies had been driven back halfway from the Don to the Dnieper. When they attempted to open a summer offensive in July, they found that the Russians had also been gathering men and material for a renewal of the struggle.

July. **Military supplies from Great Britain and the United States** helped materially to arm the Soviet forces for the campaigns of 1943. The United States shipped 4100 planes, 138,000 motor vehicles, shiploads of steel, and industrial machinery for Soviet arms factories. Part of the equipment went by northern **convoy routes** to Archangel, part in Russian ships to Vladivostok, part via the Persian Gulf. Shipments through Iran increased to 100,000 tons a month by July 1943.

July. **The Soviet summer campaign of 1943.** The Germans and their allies had 240–260 divisions, the Soviet armies had grown to 250–275, and the advantage in matériel had passed to the Russians. Anglo-American bombing was crippling German industry, greatly reducing the output of German planes, and this unhinged the plane-tank combination of mechanized warfare which had won earlier successes for the Wehrmacht. The output of Russian factories had increased greatly, and the United States shipments of planes to Russia, mounting to a total of 6500 by the autumn of 1943, deprived the Germans of their superiority in the air.

July 5. The **Germans opened an offensive** in the Orel-Belgorod sector, but were checked after a week's fighting.

Aug. 23. Broadening and gathering momentum the Soviet drive swept on to **Kharkov.** In the south, Taganrog fell (Aug. 30), in the center, Bryansk was recaptured (Sept. 17) and Smolensk (Sept. 25). By October the **Russians had reached the Dnieper** at several points, capturing Kiev (Nov. 6). The year closed with the reconquest of Zhitomir (Dec. 31).

1944. In January Novgorod in the north fell to the Russians (Jan. 20) and by February they had penetrated Estonia and were on the borders of prewar Poland.

Feb. 17. **Ten German divisions,** trapped in a pocket near Cherkassy, were largely destroyed, and the survivors made prisoner.

Mar. 26. The **Ukrainian drives** carried the Russians to the Roumanian border. Odessa fell to them on April 10 and Tarnopol on April 15. By May 9 they had taken Sevastopol, and the Crimea, like the Ukraine, was cleared of invading forces.

June 20. An **offensive against the Finns** delivered Viborg into Soviet hands. Farther south Vitebsk fell to them (June 26) and Minsk (July 3). The opening of an Allied front in the west, following the **invasion of Normandy** (June 6), prevented the Germans from strengthening the eastern front, and July and August brought an almost unbroken series of Soviet triumphs. By the end of August they had reached the borders of East Prussia and were invading Poland and Roumania.

Aug. 24. The **ROUMANIAN GOVERNMENT SURRENDERED** when Soviet troops reached the mouth of the Danube, and captured Jassy and Kishinev. The capitulation of Roumania trapped major units of the German Black Sea naval forces, although some of the smaller craft escaped up the Danube before the Russian advance closed that route of escape. Soviet domination of the Black Sea opened a new and important supply route whereby cargoes could reach the Soviet Union.

Sept. 5. The Soviet Union declared war on Bulgaria. Three days later the Bulgarian government asked for an armistice (Sept. 8) and Soviet columns moved into Sofia (Sept. 16).

Oct. 20. German forces of occupation in Yugoslavia were harassed increasingly by the Partisans and failed to halt the advance of the Russians, who entered Belgrade (Oct. 20). Two weeks later they were at the gates of Budapest, but the Hungarian capital resisted savagely for

over two months and was not conquered until February 13, 1945.

Victorious in the Balkans, with their central armies pressing into Poland, and their northern (right) end of the line anchored on the Baltic after the **capture of Tallinn** (Sept. 22) **and Riga** (Oct. 13), the Russians opened their final drives into Germany (Jan. 1945). These maneuvers, synchronized with the Allied drives across the Rhine, merged into the **battle of Germany** (p. 1151).

7. DEFENSE OF THE WESTERN HEMISPHERE, 1939–1945

1939, Oct. 2. A **Pan-American conference at Panama** declared that the waters surrounding the Western Hemisphere for a distance of 300 miles from shore and as far north as Canada constituted "sea safety zones" and must be kept free from hostile acts by non-American belligerent nations. The conference also issued a **general declaration of neutrality** of the American republics.

Nov. 4. President Roosevelt signed an **amendment to the neutrality act** which repealed the embargo on the sale of arms and placed exports to belligerent nations on a *cash-and-carry* basis.

Dec. 13. Three British cruisers attacked the German battleship *Graf Spee* and drove it into the harbor of Montevideo. When forced to leave harbor, it was scuttled by the German crew. In the name of the American republics the president of Panama protested to Great Britain, France, and Germany at this and other belligerent acts committed in American waters.

1940, May 16. President Roosevelt asked the congress to appropriate $2,500,000,000 for **expansion of the army and navy** and proposed a productional goal of 50,000 airplanes a year. This program of expansion was to be supervised by a **defense advisory commission.**

June 16. Congress authorized the sale of munitions to the government of any American republic. This measure, known as the **Pittman Act,** was extended by provisions authorizing the Export-Import Bank to lend the American republics up to $500,000,000 (Sept. 26) and permitting them to procure munitions of a total value of $400,000,000 for their defense. These programs were taken over by the **lend-lease administration** after its creation in March 1941.

June 17. The **United States department of state notified European governments that it**

would not recognize the transfer of any geographic region of the Western Hemisphere from one non-American power to another non-American power.

July 20. President Roosevelt signed a bill providing for a **two-ocean navy** as part of a vast defense plan for the United States in particular and the Western Hemisphere in general.

July 30. The republics of the Pan-American Union approved a convention setting up an **Inter-American commission on territorial administration** to guard the sovereignty of the states of the Western Hemisphere. At this meeting the delegates also approved an **act of Havana** providing that the American republics, jointly or individually, should act as their own defense and that of the continent required.

Aug. 18. President Roosevelt and **Prime Minister Mackenzie King** of Canada agreed to set up a **joint board of defense.**

Sept. 2. The **United States obtained naval and air bases** in Newfoundland, Bermuda, the Bahamas, Jamaica, St. Lucia, Trinidad, Antigua, and British Guiana on 99-year leases from Great Britain. In exchange Britain acquired 50 overage destroyers from the United States. The facilities at these bases were extended to the Latin American governments in conformity with understandings reached at the conferences of Lima, Panama, and Havana.

Sept. 16. The United States congress passed the **Selective Service Act** providing for the registration of all men between 21 and 36 years of age, and for the training, for one year, of 1,200,000 troops and 800,000 reserves.

Dec. 20. The president named a defense board headed by **William A. Knudsen** to prepare defense measures and speed armament production.

1941, Feb. 1. The **United States patrol force** in the Caribbean area was raised to fleet status. Naval bases at Guantanamo Bay, Cuba; San Juan, Puerto Rico; and St. Thomas, Virgin Islands, were developed rapidly. A third set of locks was designed for the Panama Canal.

Mar. 11. The **LEND-LEASE ACT** was signed by President Roosevelt. It had passed the senate by a vote of 60 to 31 and the house of representatives by 317 to 71. Under this enactment "any country whose defense the president deems vital to the defense of the United States" became eligible to receive any defense article by sale, transfer, exchange, or lease.

Mar. The **Republic of Panama** granted the United States the right to extend its air defenses outside the limits of the Canal Zone. A **Pan-American highway,** to extend ultimately from Mexico City through Central America to Santiago, Chile, and thence across the Andes to Buenos Aires, and up the Atlantic coast to Rio de Janeiro, was two-thirds completed by December 1941. A highway from the state of Washington to Alaska was also undertaken.

Apr. 10. The United States concluded an **agreement with Denmark,** undertaking to defend Greenland against invasion in return for the right to construct air and naval bases there.

July 7. **United States forces landed in Iceland** at the invitation of the Icelandic government, to relieve British troops in defending the island. Plans were completed (Sept. 25) for air and naval base facilities in Iceland.

Nov. 24. The United States sent forces to occupy **Dutch Guiana,** to protect the resources and prevent possible activities by agents of the Axis powers.

Dec. 7. THE JAPANESE ATTACKED HAWAII AND THE PHILIPPINES.

Dec. 8. THE CONGRESS OF THE UNITED STATES DECLARED WAR ON JAPAN.

1942, Jan. 15. Representatives of the American republics met for an **Inter-American conference at Rio de Janeiro.** It was convoked to concert measures for defending the Western Hemisphere against aggression.

Jan. 21. The representatives of 21 American republics, assembled at Rio de Janeiro, adopted unanimously a resolution calling for severance of relations with the Axis powers.

Mar. An **Inter-American defense board** was established to promote working co-operation among the American states in defense of the Western Hemisphere.

June 28. Eight German agents who had landed from a submarine on the shore of Long Island were captured by agents of the Federal Bureau of Investigation.

Sept. **Ecuador** granted the United States naval bases in the Galápagos Islands and the Santa Elena peninsula.

1943, Jan. 29. President Roosevelt visited President Getulio Vargas of Brazil. They announced the joint determination of the governments of the United States and Brazil to safeguard the sea lanes of the Atlantic Ocean.

Mar. 11. The **Lend-Lease Act was extended** for one year by a vote of 82 to 0 in the senate and 407 to 6 in the house of representatives.

Apr. 21. President Roosevelt visited President Avila Camacho of Mexico. They emphasized the good relations existing between the United States and Mexico as an example of the Good Neighbor policy.

Oct. 13. The government of Portugal conceded to Great Britain the right to use **bases in the Azores Islands** for air and naval patrol. This privilege was shared by United States ships and planes.

1944, Sept. 29. President Roosevelt called attention to the "growth of Nazi-Fascist influence" in **Argentina** and the failure of the Argentine government to fulfill its inter-American obligations. United States ships were forbidden to call at Argentine ports.

The **Mexican government** agreed to pay $24,000,000 with interest at 3 per cent for the property of United States oil companies expropriated in 1938.

1945, Feb. 21-Mar. 8. **Inter-American conference on problems of war and peace** met in Mexico City. The United States offered an "economic charter for the Americas," to promote orderly reconversion and raise the standards of living. In addition, the United States government guaranteed for the duration of the war to aid any American state if its political independence or territorial integrity were attacked by a neighbor.

Mar. 3. The "**Act of Chapultepec**" was approved by the delegates of 19 American republics, providing for joint action to guarantee each American state against aggression. The states of the Western Hemisphere were to act collectively in their own defense unless and until the world security council should take effective measures to deal with an attack.

Mar. 27. The **Argentine Republic declared war on Germany and Japan.** One week later (Apr. 4) the governing board of the Pan-American Union admitted Argentina to membership and the Argentine régime was recognized (Apr. 9) by the United States, Great Britain, and France.

8. NAVAL WARFARE AND BLOCKADE, 1939–1944

The gross tonnage of the merchant fleets of the leading nations in 1939 reflected the overwhelming advantage that Great Britain and its subsequent allies enjoyed on the sea. The ships of Norway, the Netherlands, and Belgium, most of which escaped when these countries were overrun by the Germans in 1940, took service with the British and helped to build up the pool of **United Nations** shipping.

Merchant tonnage, 1939.

Great Britain	21,001,925	Japan	5,629,845
United States	11,470,177	Germany	4,482,662
Norway	4,833,813	Italy	3,424,804
Netherlands	2,969,578		
France	2,933,933		
Belgium	408,418		
Total	43,617,844		13,537,311

In 1939 the **world tonnage** for merchant ships of 100 tons or over was 68,509,432. More than half of this was destroyed, largely by submarine or air attack, in the course of the next five years. Yet, so energetic was the shipbuilding program, carried out largely in American yards immune to air attack, that by May 1945, Britain and the United States, through the **war shipping administration,** disposed of over 4000 ships with a deadweight tonnage of 43,000,000. The Germans, Italians, and Japanese, on the other hand, found it increasingly difficult to make good their losses, and by 1945 their fleets, merchant and naval, had been almost completely eliminated.

1939, Sept. 3. The British government proclaimed a **naval blockade of Germany.**

Nov. 21. The British tightened the blockade on German imports and announced that German exports likewise would be halted.

Dec. 1. From this date neutral shippers were advised to obtain a *"navicert"* or certificate from British consular officials. These navicerts enabled a cargo to be passed through the patrols established by the British government in concert with its allies. Italy, the Netherlands, Belgium, and Japan protested against the British blockade measures.

Dec. 8. The United States department of state questioned the British practice of seizing German goods on neutral vessels, and challenged (Dec. 14) the diversion of United States ships to British and French control bases. The state department also protested (Dec. 27) against the British **examination of neutral mail** in the search for contraband.

Dec. 13. The German battleship *Graf Spee,* damaged by British cruisers in the South Atlantic, sought refuge at Montevideo. When forced to depart, it was blown up by order of the commander (Dec. 17).

1940, Feb. 16. A **British destroyer invaded Norwegian coastal waters** to attack the German ship *Altmark,* which was attempting to reach Germany with British prisoners of war aboard. The Norwegian government protested to London.

Apr. 8. The British and French governments announced that Norwegian waters had been mined to prevent the transit of German ships.

July 3. BATTLE OF ORAN. British naval forces destroyed part of the French fleet stationed at Oran to make certain the ships would not be available for the Germans. The French crews had refused to surrender.

July 20. The United States congress passed a bill calling for the creation of a **"two-ocean" navy.**

Sept. 2. The United States acquired the use, on a 99-year lease, of **naval and air bases** in Newfoundland, Bermuda, the Bahamas, Jamaica, Antigua, St. Lucia, Trinidad, and British Guiana. In exchange, fifty overage destroyers were transferred to Great Britain.

Sept. 6. The United States congress passed a **defense measure** appropriating $5,246,000,000 and providing for 201 ships of war, seven to be battleships of 55,000 tons each.

Sept. 22–25. British naval forces aided a "Free French" expedition, under **de Gaulle,** in an attempt to take possession of **Dakar** in French West Africa. The forces holding Dakar for the Vichy government of France resisted and the attack was abandoned.

1941, Mar. 30. Battle of Cape Matapan. Three Italian cruisers and two destroyers were sunk by British naval forces in the waters between Crete and Greece.

Apr. 10. The United States declared **Greenland** under its protection and arranged with the Danish government to establish naval and air bases there.

May 24. The giant battleship *Bismarck* escaped into the Atlantic, where it sank the British dreadnought *Hood,* but was itself destroyed by combined British air and naval attack (May 27).

July 7. United States troops landed in Iceland to relieve British occupying forces, provide for the defense of the island, and develop air and naval bases.

Sept. 16. The United States navy assumed protection of all shipments as far as Iceland.

Oct. 17. The United States destroyer *Kearny* was torpedoed off Iceland, but reached port. The destroyer *Reuben James,* likewise torpedoed in the Atlantic, was lost (Oct. 31).

Dec. 7.   THE JAPANESE OPENED A SURPRISE ATTACK ON HAWAII, THE PHILIPPINES, MALAYA, AND HONG KONG. (For developments in the Pacific area see p. 1153.)

1942, Apr. 18.   Sixteen bombing planes from the United States carrier *Hornet,* led by **Col. James H. Doolittle,** bombed **Tokyo.**

Nov. 8.   American and British expeditionary forces landed in French North Africa in the greatest amphibious invasion hitherto attempted (p. 1148).

Nov. 27.   The greater part of the **French navy,** which had been rated the fourth largest in the world in 1939, was scuttled by the crews in **Toulon** harbor to prevent the Germans obtaining the ships.

1943, Mar. 17.   The United States, Britain, and Canada issued official assurances that their governments agreed on the most effective methods for combating the **U-boat menace.**

July 10.   American, British, and Canadian forces invaded Sicily in the second mass amphibious invasion of the war. Over 2500 vessels were involved.

July 16.   President Roosevelt created a new **Board of Economic Warfare.**

Aug. 24.   At the **Quebec conference,** which ended on this date, Prime Minister Churchill and President Roosevelt announced important progress in curbing German submarine activity. "In the first six months of 1943 the number of ships sunk by U-boats was only half that of the last six months in 1942 and one-quarter that of the first six months of 1942." Figures subsequently released by the **Office of War Information** (Nov. 29, 1944) revealed that the tonnage of Allied and neutral merchant ships lost through enemy action between September 1939, and January 1, 1944, aggregated 22,161,000 gross tons. This was replaced by the output of United States shipyards alone, which launched 4308 ships with a deadweight tonnage of 44,082,000 in the same period.

Aug. 29.   When the Germans attempted to seize the Danish naval vessels anchored in the navy yard at Copenhagen, the crews scuttled 29 of the 48 ships. Some of the smaller craft, 13 in all, escaped to Sweden, and six fell into German hands.

Sept. 3.   With air and naval support **ALLIED FORCES CROSSED THE STRAITS OF MESSINA AND LANDED IN SOUTHERN ITALY.** This marked the first successful amphibious invasion of continental Europe in the course of the war.

Sept. 12.   The major part of the **Italian fleet** escaped to the Allies after the Italian government of Marshal Pietro Badoglio surrendered.

Oct. 13.   Portugal granted Great Britain the use of the **Azores Islands** as an Allied naval and air base.

1944.   By 1944 the Allied nations had achieved a position of **naval supremacy** which increased monthly and could no longer be seriously challenged. Despite improvements in submarine construction, 500 U-boats had been destroyed and merchant-ship losses from this cause sharply reduced. The Germans no longer had any capital ships in fighting condition and had all but ceased to build or repair shipping. What warships survived of the Italian and French navies were wrecked or in Allied control, part of the French fleet having been repaired at a cost of $200,000,000. The Japanese still possessed a respectable navy, including 17 capital ships, but it was inadequate to protect the long route to the East Indies and Malaya, threatened increasingly by American and British aircraft and submarines. **Japanese air power** in particular was seriously reduced, and less than ten Japanese carriers survived, a fatal deficiency when the British carrier list had risen to 40 and the United States navy possessed over 100. Inability to maintain air protection for warships even in harbor was to doom the remnants of the Japanese navy in 1945.

1944, Jan. 23.   The **Allies landed forces on the Italian coast south of Rome** in a second amphibious invasion of the Italian mainland (p. 1149).

June 6.   ALLIED FORCES LANDED AT SEVERAL POINTS ON THE COAST OF NORMANDY, with strong naval support, an armada of 4000 ships, and over 10,000 aircraft (p. 1150). For naval activities in the Pacific areas see the war in the Pacific (p. 1153 *ff.*).

9.   THE CAMPAIGNS IN AFRICA, 1940–1943

1940, June 10.   ITALY DECLARED WAR ON FRANCE AND GREAT BRITAIN.

Aug. 6.   Italian forces invaded British Somaliland from Italian East Africa, completing their conquest by August 19.

Sept. 13–15.   An **Italian army invaded Egypt** from Libya.

Sept. 22–25.   British naval forces and Free French troops under **de Gaulle** tried unsuccessfully to occupy **Dakar** in French West Africa.

Oct. 9. Free French forces under de Gaulle took possession of **Duala** on the Kamerun Coast, West Africa.

Dec. 8. The British opened a **surprise drive against the Italians** in North Africa. From Mersa Matruh in Egypt, to which they had retreated, Imperial troops outflanked the Italians, captured 1000 prisoners, and advanced so rapidly that they were in **Sidi Barrani** and had begun the invasion of Libya by December 12.

1941, Jan. 5. The **Italian garrison at Bardia surrendered** to the Imperial forces, which took 25,000 prisoners and valuable war material.

Jan. 15. British forces from the Anglo-Egyptian Sudan and Kenya opened **drives into Italian East Africa** (Ethiopia) and also penetrated **Eritrea** (Jan. 19).

Jan. 22. **Tobruk fell** to the Imperial forces invading Libya. **Derna** surrendered (Jan. 24), **Bengasi,** capital of Cyrenaica, was entered (Feb. 7), and advance units reached **El Argheila** (Feb. 8). In a campaign of two months the Imperial divisions, commanded by **General Sir Archibald Wavell,** had captured over 114,-000 prisoners at a cost of 3000 casualties.

Feb. 26. **Mogadiscio,** capital of Italian Somaliland, fell to the Imperial forces.

Mar. 22. **Neguelli** in southern Ethiopia was occupied by the British and Ethiopian forces, and the capital, **Addis Ababa,** capitulated (Apr. 6). Italian resistance in Eritrea collapsed by June, and before the end of 1941 all Italian East Africa was under British control.

Apr. 3. The Italians, reinforced by German divisions trained for desert fighting, and brilliantly commanded by **Gen. Erwin Rommel,** opened an attack against the Imperial outposts in Libya. Weakened by the dispatch of 60,000 troops to Greece, the British were forced to abandon their recent conquests in a costly retreat.

Apr. 14. **The Germans reoccupied Sollum and Bardia.**

Apr. 20. **Tobruk was encircled,** but the Imperial garrison held out with naval support. The drive of Axis mechanized divisions stopped at the Egyptian frontier (May 29). Through the summer the British prepared for a counteroffensive.

Dec. 11. **Second British drive into Libya.** After relieving Tobruk, Imperial troops reached **Benghasi** for the second time (Dec. 25), but stopped short of **El Argheila** (Jan. 18, 1942). Rommel's reserves in Africa had been depleted because of the opening of the German drive on Russia (p. 1141).

1942, May 27. **Second Axis drive on Egypt.** Reinforced, Rommel opened a powerful drive which captured **Tobruk** once more (June 21)

and swept on to **Bardia** and **Bir-el-Gobi.** The victorious advance of the Axis troops was finally checked at **El Alamein,** only seventy miles from Alexandria. A four months' lull followed.

Oct. 23. **Third British offensive in North Africa.** The British 8th Army under **Gen. Bernard L. Montgomery** drove from **El Alamein** and expelled Rommel's divisions from Egypt by November 12.

Nov. 8. **INVASION OF FRENCH NORTH AFRICA.** An Anglo-American invasion force, commanded by **Gen. Dwight D. Eisenhower,** disembarked in French Morocco and Algeria. This amphibious operation, on a scale hitherto unequaled in history, required 850 ships. The French garrisons at Casablanca, Oran, and Algiers were overcome after brief fighting, and an armistice arranged (Nov. 11) by **Adm. Jean-François Darlan,** who was in Algiers. Darlan, whose rôle as representative of the Vichy government was ambiguous, aided the Anglo-American forces to assume control of French North Africa and West Africa.

Nov. 11. **The Germans entered and took over control of unoccupied France.**

Nov. 27. The greater part of the **French fleet** was scuttled by the crews in **Toulon** harbor to frustrate the attempt of the Germans to obtain possession of the ships.

Dec. 1. **Darlan** retained his post as chief of state in North Africa with Anglo-American approval. On his assassination (Dec. 24), **Gen. Henri Giraud** was designated to succeed him.

1943, Jan. 24. **Tripoli was occupied by the British 8th Army,** which pursued the retreating Axis forces into Tunisia.

Jan. 17–27. **Conference at Casablanca,** Morocco, with President Roosevelt, Prime Minister Churchill, Gen. Giraud, and Gen. de Gaulle attending. The relationship between **Giraud** and the **de Gaulle** "Fighting French" party remained undefined, and Eisenhower took command of the unified North African operations. Plans for reducing the Axis powers to "unconditional surrender" were discussed at Casablanca but not disclosed.

Feb. 22. The Germans, who had rushed reinforcements to Tunisia, sought to hold this protectorate, and seized **Kasserine Pass.** The Americans reoccupied it four days later.

Mar. 15. Giraud at Algiers restored representative government in French North Africa, declared legislation introduced there since 1940 void, and promised that after victory the French nation should decide its own form of government.

Mar. 19. American forces, striking east from Algeria, captured **El Guettar** in Tunisia.

Mar. 30. The British 8th Army broke

through the **Mareth Line** into southern Tunisia, meeting the advancing American 2nd Army Corps between Gabès and El Guettar on April 8.

May 8–12. **End of Axis resistance in North Africa.** British and United States forces captured the cities of **Tunis** and **Bizerte.** Possession of the whole North African coast opened the central Mediterranean to Allied shipping and exposed Italy to invasion. The threat to Egypt and the Suez Canal was ended and the Italian dream of a great African empire had proved a costly failure. Fighting in Africa was estimated to have drained the Axis powers of 950,000 men, killed or captured, 8000 airplanes, and 2,400,000 tons of shipping.

10. THE INVASION OF ITALY, 1943–1944

1943, July 10. United States, British, and Canadian forces invaded Sicily under the command of Gen. Dwight D. Eisenhower. Over 2000 vessels were employed to convoy 160,000 men, and landings were effected along the southern coast. The Americans seized Gela; the British 8th Army and Canadian troops, disembarking at Cape Passaro, drove along the east shore.

July 14. **Port Augusta was captured.**

July 19. Allied **bombing planes wrecked Naples,** and, after repeated warnings, attacked railway terminals and military objectives in Rome (July 20).

July 22. **Half of Sicily was occupied,** the Allied front stretching from Catania to Mazzara. Palermo fell July 24.

July 25. **BENITO MUSSOLINI WAS FORCED TO RESIGN** with his cabinet and his place was taken by **Marshal Pietro Badoglio.** This coup was virtually a revolution, breaking the 21-year period of fascist rule. Badoglio declared the Fascist Party dissolved (July 28) and opened negotiations for an armistice.

Aug. 18. **Resistance in Sicily collapsed** with the fall of Messina. The campaign had cost the Allied armies an estimated 22,000 casualties, the Axis forces 167,000. At a loss of 274 planes the Allied airmen accounted for 1691 enemy aircraft.

Sept. 2. **British and American forces crossed the Straits of Messina and landed in southern Italy.**

Sept. 3. An **armistice was signed** at Algiers, ending hostilities between the Anglo-American forces and those of the Badoglio régime. It was announced (Sept. 8) that the Italian surrender was unconditional. The actual terms were not disclosed.

Sept. 15. Ex-Premier Mussolini, who had been held a prisoner near Rome, was rescued by German troops (Sept. 12) and proclaimed the establishment of a **Republican Fascist Party** (Sept. 15) in alliance with the German army of occupation. The Italian people were confused and divided, and the German divisions in the country seized the leading cities, including Rome.

Oct. 1. After **landing near Salerno** (Sept. 9) American troops entered Naples. Thereafter, however, winter weather, the mountainous countryside, and stubborn German resistance stopped the Allied advance on a line south of Cassino.

1944, Jan. 22. **Allied forces landed at Anzio** in an attempt to outflank the German lines. The beachhead proved costly to hold and changed the situation little.

Feb. 11. Part of southern Italy, with Sicily and Sardinia, were returned to the jurisdiction of the Italian government. After occupation these areas had been administered with the aid of an **Allied Control Commission,** an **Allied Military Government** (A.M.G.), and an **Advisory Council** for Italy composed of representatives of the United States, Great Britain, the Soviet Union, and the French Committee of National Liberation.

Mar. 15. The Allied armies launched a heavy **assault against Cassino,** which fell May 18.

June 4. **Anglo-American troops entered Rome.**

Aug. 12. **Florence was captured** after bitter fighting and the Allies controlled Italy north to a line running from Livorno to Ancona. Thenceforth the Italian front remained a tense but unprogressive field of action until the final collapse of Germany in April and May 1945. The German divisions in Italy were forced to capitulate (Apr. 29–May 1, 1945), and the Fascist Republican Party dissolved. **Mussolini** was seized when he attempted to escape to Switzerland and was shot by his anti-Fascist captors without formal trial (Apr. 28, 1945).

11. THE LIBERATION OF FRANCE AND BELGIUM, 1944

1944, June 6. INVASION OF NORMANDY. For many months careful and elaborate plans had been matured by the supreme headquarters of the Allied expeditionary forces (SHAEF) for invading France. Command of this greatest amphibious operation in history was entrusted to **Gen. Dwight D. Eisenhower.** The British Isles provided the chief base for the concentration of men and war matériel, and the plan of campaign to follow the invasion date (D-Day) was rehearsed in exhaustive detail. **Air control** was to be maintained by the United States 8th and 9th Air Forces and the British royal air force, with a combined strength of over 10,000 planes. An American naval task force and a British naval task force were assembled to support the assault, and the invasion was planned to proceed under cover of an intense and accurately directed bombardment by 800 guns on 80 warships. To convey the troops and supplies across the Channel, 4000 other ships were utilized, and the lack of port facilities for disembarkation was overcome by a dramatic improvisation in engineering. **Artificial harbors** were to be constructed on an exposed coast by sinking lines of blockships and concrete caissons to form breakwaters, with floating pierheads and pontoon causeways to serve as wharves and docks.

June 6. United States and British forces succeeded in **landing on the Normandy coast** between St. Marcouf and the Orne River. Within a week a strip of beach 60 miles long had been occupied and the artificial harbors constructed.

June 18. An unusually **severe gale** with high waves delayed landing operations for three days and wrecked the major causeways of one artificial harbor. It was abandoned and traffic diverted to a British-built harbor which was less exposed and had suffered less severely.

June 27. The **capture of Cherbourg** placed a major port in Allied control. During the first hundred days following D-Day 2,200,000 men, 450,000 vehicles, and 4,000,000 tons of stores were landed. This extraordinary achievement was rendered possible by perfecting the services of supply, on the basis of experience gained in the First World War, and in the amphibious landings in Africa and Italy. The enormous output of Allied factories and shipyards, which made it possible to duplicate all wrecked or damaged equipment, was also an important factor.

July 9. British and Canadian troops captured Caen. Allied tanks broke through German defenses near **St. Lô** and fanned out disorganizing enemy resistance. Persistent bombing of all bridges and railways severely crippled the German attempts to bring up adequate forces to halt Allied drives.

Aug. 15. In another amphibious operation the Allies effected successful **landings on the French Mediterranean coast** between Marseille and Nice.

Aug. 24. The citizens of **Paris** rioted against German forces of occupation as Allied armed divisions crossed the Seine and approached the capital. **French Forces of the Interior (FFI),** which had been organized for underground resistance and supplied with arms, rose against the retreating Germans.

Sept. 2. Allied forces, which had penetrated into Belgium, **liberated Brussels.**

Sept. 12. The **American 1st Army crossed the German frontier** near Eupen, and American armored forces entered Germany north of Trier. The Germans, however, manning their **Westwall** defenses, offered firm resistance and the Allied advance was halted. An Allied attempt to outflank the Westwall through the flat Dutch territory to the north (Sept. 17–26) failed, and survivors of an Allied airborne division which was dropped at **Arnhem** had to be withdrawn.

Sept. 15. The American 7th and the French 1st Armies, sweeping up the Rhone Valley from beachheads won (Aug. 15) on the Riviera, joined the American 3rd Army at Dijon. The American, British, and French forces were then reorganized in liberated France for a projected assault on Germany.

Dec. 16–25. BATTLE OF THE BULGE. The German supreme commander in the west, **Gen. Karl von Rundstedt,** under orders from Hitler, dislocated Allied preparations by a sudden drive against thinly held American lines in the Belgian and Luxemburg sector. Suffering heavy losses, the Allied forces were driven back to the Meuse, but they rallied to attack strongly on both sides of the "bulge" and the Germans were checked before the close of December.

With the opening of 1945, the American, British, and French drives into Germany from the west, co-ordinated with the rapid and powerful Russian thrusts from the Danube Valley, Poland, and East Prussia, fused into one vast combined operation.

12. THE BATTLE OF GERMANY, 1945

THE RÔLE OF AIR POWER. In 20th-century warfare the assembly line became as important as the battle line and consequently an equally vital target for attack. The strategy of blockade adopted by the Allied governments was designed primarily to starve, not the German population, but German industrial and military machines, chiefly by cutting off fuel and essential raw material. This aim could best be achieved by supplementing the naval blockade with a systematic **bombing of German factories, power plants,** and **transportation centers.**

At the commencement of the Second World War, in 1939, the Germans possessed the strongest air force in the world. By the close of 1943, however, their bombing squadrons were depleted, though they still had a peak force of 3000 first-line fighters. In 1944 the Allied air offensive was sharply intensified and German air strength declined decisively. Over 1000 Luftwaffe planes were destroyed in January and February and vital machine plants in **Essen** and **Schweinfurt** were crippled. **Gen. Henry H. Arnold,** commanding general of the United States army air forces, later characterized the week of February 20–26, 1944, as "probably the most decisive of the war" because of the shattering damage inflicted upon German installations in six days of favorable flying weather. By the end of hostilities the Germans had received 315 tons of explosive in retaliation for every ton of aerial bombs they had launched against Britain. Their loss in planes, by January 1, 1945, had passed 50,000, in comparison with a total loss of 17,790 suffered by the United States air forces on all fronts. During the last four months of fighting, Allied air squadrons roamed Germany almost at will, destroying communications, obliterating plants and stores, and wrecking many of the remaining German aircraft on the ground, where they lay helpless for lack of fuel and repairs.

1945. The **military collapse of Germany** was consummated in four months by simultaneous drives launched by Soviet armies in the east and south and American, French, and British Imperial forces in the west.

Jan. 12. Opening a powerful **drive into Poland,** the Russians took **Warsaw** (Jan. 17), swept into **Tarnow, Cracow,** and **Lodz** two days later (Jan. 19), and forced the Germans to abandon the whole **Vistula defense line.** By February 20 Russian mechanized units, spearheads of the encroaching Soviet host that numbered 215 divisions, were within 30 miles of Berlin.

Feb. 7. Yalta conference. While President Roosevelt, Prime Minister Churchill, and Marshal Stalin met at Yalta in the Crimea, to plan the final defeat and occupation of Germany (p. 1178), the United States 3rd Army crossed the German frontier at ten points. British and Canadian divisions opened an offensive southeast of **Nijmegen** (Feb. 8).

Feb. 22. The 3rd Army continued its progress, crossing the **Roer River.** American advance forces drove toward the **Ruhr Valley** (Feb. 23) and entered **Trier** (Mar. 2) and Köln (Mar. 5). Supreme headquarters announced that 954,377 German prisoners had been taken since D-Day (June 6, 1944).

Mar. 7. The United States 1st Army **crossed the Rhine at Remagen,** and the German defense system on the east bank collapsed. By April 11 the United States 9th Army had reached the **Elbe River;** eight days later the Russians fought their way into **Berlin** (Apr. 20); and advance units of the **American and Soviet armies met on the Elbe at Torgau** (Apr. 25).

Apr. 28. German resistance in northern Italy broke as American and British forces swept into the Po Valley. The **Fascist Republican régime disintegrated,** and Benito Mussolini, attempting to escape to Switzerland, was captured and shot by Italian anti-Fascist partisans. **The German divisions in Italy surrendered unconditionally.**

May 1. BATTLE OF BERLIN. Soviet forces continued to shell Berlin and fight their way into the capital. A German radio announcement from Hamburg declared that **Adolf Hitler had died** defending the Reichschancellery, and that **Admiral Karl Doenitz** had succeeded him.

One million German and Italian soldiers in Italy and Austria laid down their arms.

May 4. The **dissolution of the German National Socialist régime** continued, with local military commanders making their own offers of capitulation. German divisions in northwestern Germany, the Netherlands, and Denmark surrendered.

May 7. A group of **German army leaders** sent envoys to Reims, where they **signed terms of surrender.**

May 8. President Truman for the United States and Prime Minister Churchill for Great Britain proclaimed the **end of the war in Europe (V-E Day).**

May 9. Marshal Stalin announced the end of the war to the Russian people. German army chiefs completed the formula of surrender in Berlin.

May 9-23. While German forces were being disarmed, the Allied governments transmitted orders through a **provisional German government** headed by Doenitz. After two weeks this provisional régime was superseded. Doenitz, with several colleagues, and members of the German high command and the general staff, were taken into custody.

June 5. An **Allied Control Committee,** including **Gen. Dwight D. Eisenhower, Field Marshal Sir Bernard L. Montgomery,** and **Marshal Gregory K. Zhukov,** assumed full control throughout Germany. German territory, as of December 31, 1937, was delimited in four **zones of occupation** under American, British, Soviet, and French military administration.

13. THE WAR IN ASIA, 1939–1941

1939. **Economic penetration** and **military intervention** enabled the Japanese to bring a widening area of China under their control after 1931, and especially after 1937. By the capture of Hankow in 1938, they forced the Chinese Nationalists to establish a new capital at **Chungking** (p. 1110). At the same time, the outbreak of war in Europe compelled the British, French, and Soviet governments to concentrate their forces in that quarter, and left the United States the only great power in a position to oppose Japanese expansion.

Dec. 31. **Russia and Japan reached an accord** concerning the renewal of fishing rights and the settlement of debt claims between Russia and Manchukuo.

1940, Jan. 14. **Admiral Mitsumasa Yonai** formed a new Japanese cabinet.

Jan. 26. The **trade treaty between the United States and Japan,** first negotiated in 1911, expired. The state department informed the Japanese government that commercial arrangements would continue on a day-to-day basis.

Mar. 30. The Japanese supported the establishment of a **puppet government under Wang Ching-wei** at Nanking to administer the areas of China under their control.

Apr. 17. Secretary of State **Cordell Hull** warned the Japanese that the United States would oppose any attempt to change the *status quo* of the **Netherlands East Indies** by other than peaceful means.

June 9. **Russia and Japan reached an accord** regarding the disputed frontier of Manchukuo.

June 25. With the **collapse of France,** the Japanese demanded the right to land forces in **French Indo-China.** Japanese warships arrived at several ports there.

July 16. **Prince Fumumaro Konoye** became Japanese premier with a mandate to organize the government on totalitarian lines.

July 18. The British government closed the **Burma Road.** This was the main route by which the Chinese Nationalist armies under Gen. **Chiang Kai-shek** could obtain foreign war matériel. The Japanese agreed to discuss peace terms with the Chinese Nationalist government.

Aug. 9. British garrisons at Shanghai and in northern China were withdrawn.

Sept. 4. Secretary of State Hull warned the Japanese government that aggressive moves against Indo-China would have an unfortunate effect upon public opinion in the United States.

Sept. 26. After the French government at Vichy had conceded the use of three airfields and several ports in Indo-China, Japanese forces began the **occupation of Indo-China** and crossed into China 120 miles from Hanoi. The United States government placed an embargo on the export of iron and steel scrap after October 15 to countries (except Great Britain) outside the Western Hemisphere. The Japanese ambassador at Washington described this (Oct. 8) as an "unfriendly act."

Sept. 27. **JAPAN JOINED ITALY AND GERMANY** in a ten-year tripartite pact "for the creation of conditions which would promote the prosperity of their peoples." The pact also contained mutual pledges of total aid in the event any of the partners became engaged in war with a country not yet a belligerent.

Oct. 18. **Great Britain reopened the Burma Road.**

1941, Jan. 31. Under Japanese auspices an armistice was arranged to end hostilities which had broken out between **Thailand and French Indo-China.** The Japanese obtained rice, rubber, coal, and minerals from Indo-China, and confirmed their military occupation.

Mar. 11. **France and Thailand concluded a convention,** later signed at Tokyo (May 9) whereby Thailand acquired the section of Laos province west of the Mekong River, three-fourths of the Campong-Thom province, and territory in northern Cambodia.

Apr. 13. **JAPAN AND SOVIET RUSSIA CONCLUDED A NEUTRALITY PACT.**

July 26. **All Japanese credits** in the United

States were "frozen" by a presidential decree. Great Britain took similar action regarding Japanese assets in that country. All armed forces in the Philippine Islands were placed under the control of the United States, with **Gen. Douglas MacArthur** as commander-in-chief in the Far East.

Aug. 17. President Roosevelt warned the Japanese ambassador, Adm. Kichisaburo Nomura, that any further policy of military domination in Asia by the Japanese would force the United States "to take immediately any and all steps necessary" to safeguard legitimate American rights and interests. **Prime Minister Churchill** declared a week later (Aug. 24) that Great Britain would support the United States if negotiations with Japan failed.

Oct. 17. Prince Konoye resigned as Japanese premier and was replaced by **Gen. Hideki Tojo.**

Nov. 17. Ambassador **Joseph C. Grew** at Tokyo cabled a warning to the United States that the Japanese might make a sudden attack.

Nov. 20. At Washington **Nomura** and a special Japanese envoy, **Saburo Kurusu,** proposed that the United States and Japan reopen trade relations and co-operate in securing the commodities of the Netherlands East Indies.

Nov. 26. Secretary Hull proposed as a **basis of agreement** that the Japanese withdraw

their forces from China and Indo-China, recognize the territorial integrity of these countries, and accept the Chinese Nationalist government. The United States and Japan could then negotiate a liberal trade treaty. Kurusu declared such proposals practically "put an end to the negotiations." Three days later (Nov. 29) Hull informed the British ambassador that diplomatic conversations between the United States and Japan had virtually broken down.

Dec. 6. President Roosevelt cabled a personal message to the emperor of Japan urging him to use his influence to preserve peace.

Dec. 7. JAPANESE ATTACK ON PEARL HARBOR (below).

After December 7, when Japan was at **war with the United States and Great Britain,** the conflict in China was overshadowed by developments in the Pacific and the East Indies. Japanese **conquest of Burma** (1942) closed the Burma Road, the last practicable route by which military supplies could reach Chungking, for only a few tons a month could be flown in by air. Chinese armies remained in the field, and the Japanese kept an army of 1,000,000 men as an occupying force to protect towns and railway lines. The ultimate fate of these Japanese armies in Asia, and their communications with the Japanese home islands, depended upon the outcome of the war at sea.

14. THE WAR IN THE PACIFIC, 1941–1945

1941, Dec. 7. The **JAPANESE SEA AND AIR FORCES LAUNCHED A SURPRISE ATTACK ON THE UNITED STATES BASE AT PEARL HARBOR, HAWAII, ON THE PHILIPPINES,** and against British forces in **Hong Kong** and **Malaya.** The United States forces were caught unprepared. At Hawaii five battleships and three cruisers were sunk or seriously damaged, three battleships less severely damaged, many smaller vessels sunk or crippled, and 177 aircraft destroyed. The casualties included 2343 dead, 876 missing, and 1272 injured.

Dec. 8. THE UNITED STATES DECLARED WAR ON JAPAN. Japanese air and naval forces attacked **Guam** and **Wake Island.** Resistance on Guam ended December 13 and on Wake Island December 20. **Great Britain declared war on Japan.**

Dec. 10. The British battleship *Prince of Wales* and the battle-cruiser *Repulse,* which had been dispatched to Singapore, were sunk by Japanese aircraft off the Malay coast.

Dec. 11. GERMANY AND ITALY DE-

CLARED WAR ON THE UNITED STATES.

Dec. 21. A ten-year treaty of alliance was signed at Bangkok **between Japan and Thailand.** The Thai government agreed to aid Japan and declared war (Jan. 25, 1942) against Great Britain and the United States.

Dec. 25. British forces at **Hong Kong surrendered** to the Japanese.

1942, Jan. 2. Manila and Cavite were captured by the Japanese. United States and Philippine forces fortified their position on **Bataan Peninsula** and held out until April 9. The island fort of **Corregidor** at the entrance to Manila Bay did not fall until May 6.

Jan. 11. Japanese forces commenced an **occupation of the Netherlands East Indies,** landing on Celebes, at Rabaul (Jan. 23), New Ireland (Jan. 25), the Solomon Islands (Jan. 26), and Amboina (Jan. 31).

Jan. 24–27. Allied forces sank five Japanese transports in a naval engagement in the **Macassar Straits.**

Feb. 15. Japanese forces, which had penetrated Malaya, captured **Singapore** from the north by land, taking 60,000 prisoners.

Feb. 27–Mar. 1. Battle of the Java Sea. Naval units of the Allied powers were largely destroyed, opening the way for the Japanese conquest of the East Indies. Batavia fell on March 6.

Mar. 7. The **British evacuated Rangoon** and the Japanese rapidly occupied Burma. **Lashio** was taken (Apr. 30), closing the Burma Road at that point, and **Mandalay** fell on May 2.

Mar. 9. The **conquest of Java** was virtually completed by the Japanese, who had won **Timor** (Feb. 20) also. The growing threat to Australia was checked in the jungles of New Guinea, and **Gen. Douglas MacArthur** assumed command of the combined Allied forces in the southwest Pacific (Mar. 17).

Apr. 18. United States carrier-based bombers, commanded by **Col. James H. Doolittle**, raided Tokyo and landed on Chinese bases.

May 5. To avert possible Japanese penetration, British forces landed at **Diego Suarez**, naval base on the north end of Madagascar, and proceeded to occupy this French colony, entering the capital, Tananarive, on September 23.

May 7. BATTLE OF THE CORAL SEA. Allied naval and air power frustrated a possible Japanese invasion of Australia or the New Hebrides by destroying 100,000 tons of Japanese shipping between New Guinea and the Solomon Islands.

June 4–7. A Japanese naval force attacked **Midway Island** and was dispersed with heavy losses by United States naval and air units.

June 12. Japanese invaders occupied Attu in the Aleutian Islands and later landed on **Kiska.** The Japanese tide of conquest was at its height, coinciding with the German drive for the Caucasian oil fields.

July 9. The Chinese Nationalist armies won a major success over the Japanese in Kiangsi Province.

Aug. 7. United States marines landed in the Solomon Islands. Tulagi and Japanese airfields on **Guadalcanal** were captured.

Nov. 12. A three-day **naval battle in the Solomon Islands** ended in a victory for United States forces. One Japanese battleship and five cruisers were reported sunk, and twelve transports destroyed.

1943, Mar. 4. Allied air squadrons destroyed a Japanese convoy approaching New Guinea.

July 1. Opening a **concerted offensive** in the South Pacific, Allied forces captured **Rendova Island** (July 2) while Australian troops linked up with American troops at **Salamaua** (July 3). The Japanese base and airfield at **Munda** on New Georgia Island fell August 7.

In September a Japanese force of 20,000 was encircled near **Lae** (Sept. 6–7), the airfield at Salamaua was captured (Sept. 13), and **Finschhafen** occupied (Oct. 3). Allied forces disembarked on **Bougainville Island** (Oct. 31). Landing on the **Gilbert Islands** (Nov. 22), United States forces crushed Japanese resistance in three days' fighting, and marines captured the important air base at **Cape Gloucester** on December 31.

1944, Feb. 2. Invasion of the Marshall Islands. **Roi** was seized by the United States troops (Feb. 3), **Kwajalein** (Feb. 6), and an air base in **Eniwetok** (Feb. 20). On March 1 American troops landed on the **Admiralty Islands**, and new landings were achieved in **New Guinea** (Apr. 24) at **Hollandia** and **Aitape**. The **Schouten** group was invaded (May 28) and the **Marianas** (June 16).

June 16. United States superfortress bombing planes raided the Japanese home island of Kyushū, opening a campaign of destructive attacks on Japanese cities which ended only with the Japanese capitulation.

Aug. 11. The **reconquest of Guam** was completed. On the Indian frontier the last Japanese invaders were driven back to Burma.

Sept. 14. American forces disembarked on **Morotai** in the Molucca Islands, and on the **Palau Islands** in the Carolinas (Sept. 15).

Oct. 19. United States invasion groups, commanded by MacArthur, **landed on the island of Leyte**, opening the campaign for the **reconquest of the Philippines.**

Oct. 21–22. SECOND BATTLE OF THE PHILIPPINE SEA. The Japanese fleet, having failed to halt the invasion, withdrew from Philippine waters (Oct. 25). It had suffered 40 ships sunk, 46 damaged, and 405 planes destroyed. More United States forces were promptly landed on the island of **Samos** (Oct. 26).

Nov. 26. A new phase of the Pacific war opened with the initiation of **raids on Japan** by United States land-based B-29 bombers operating from **Saipan** in the Marianas.

1945, Feb. 19–Mar. 17. The stubborn and protracted **battle for Iwo Jima** gave the United States air forces a base 750 miles from Yokohama, at a cost of 19,938 American casualties.

Mar. 21. United States carrier aircraft, penetrating Japanese inland waters, attacked principal units of the Japanese fleet, damaged 15 warships and destroyed 475 planes. No United States ship was lost.

Apr. 30. In Southeast Asia the 14th British Imperial army **(Admiral Lord Louis Mountbatten)**, with support from United States and Chinese forces, completed the destruction in fifteen months of the Japanese 15th, 28th, and

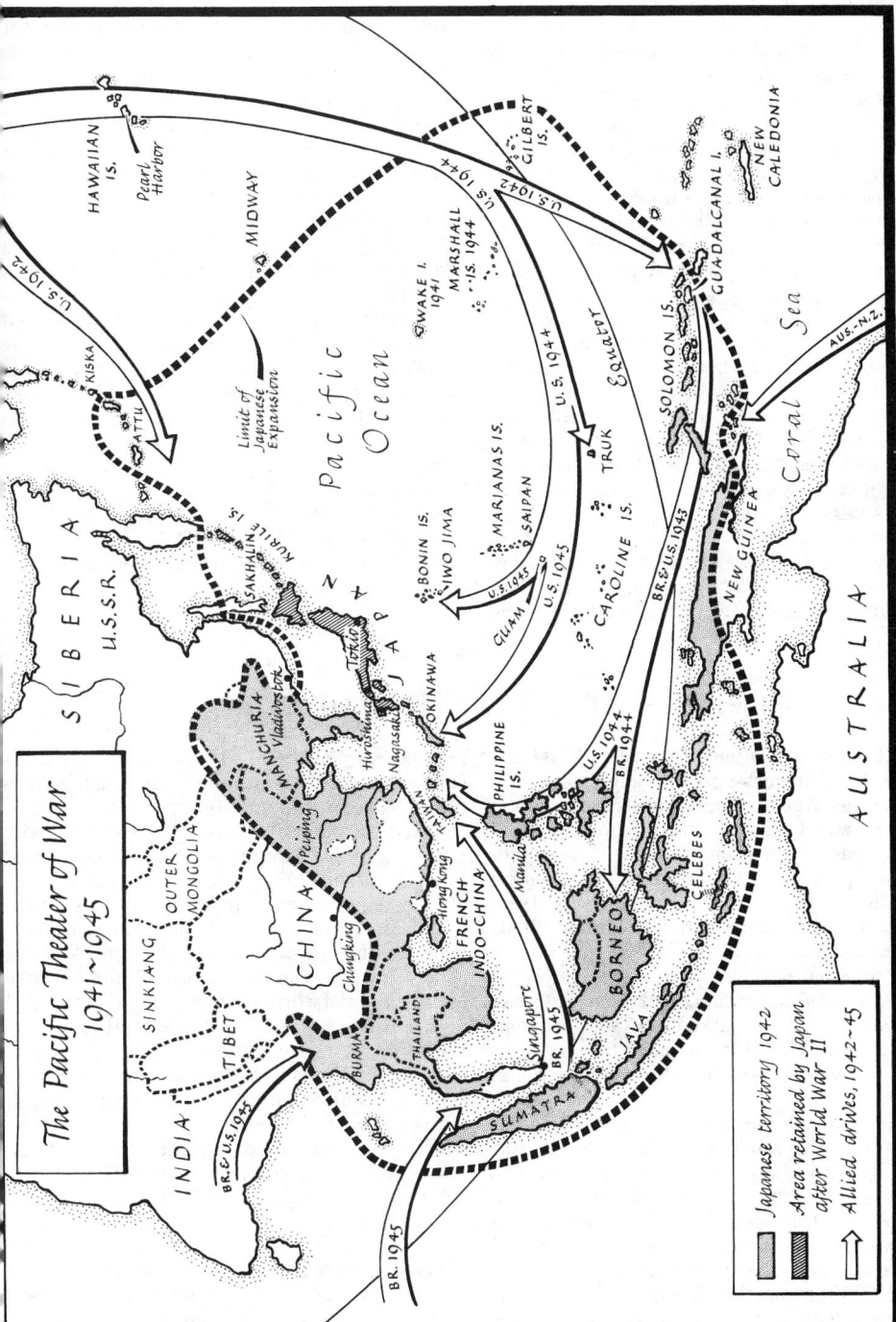

The Pacific Theater of War
1941~1945

Japanese territory 1942
Area retained by Japan after World War II
Allied drives, 1942~45

HAWAIIAN IS.
Pearl Harbor
MIDWAY
U.S. 1942
KISKA
ATTU
Limit of Japanese Expansion
Pacific Ocean
WAKE I. 1941
MARSHALL IS. 1944
GILBERT IS.
U.S. 1944
U.S. 1942
U.S. 1942
GUADALCANAL I.
NEW CALEDONIA
Coral Sea
SOLOMON IS.
AUS.-N.Z.
Equator
TRUK
CAROLINE IS.
MARIANAS IS.
SAIPAN
GUAM
BONIN IS.
IWO JIMA
U.S. 1945
U.S. 1945
OKINAWA
BR.&U.S. 1943
NEW GUINEA
U.S. 1944
BR. 1944
SIBERIA
U.S.S.R.
KURILE IS.
SAKHALIN
Vladivostok
MANCHURIA
Peiping
TOKYO
Hiroshima
Nagasaki
JAPAN
PHILIPPINE IS.
Manila
CELEBES
BORNEO
JAVA
AUSTRALIA
OUTER MONGOLIA
SINKIANG
TIBET
CHINA
Chungking
Hong Kong
FRENCH INDO-CHINA
THAILAND
BURMA
Singapore
BR. 1945
SUMATRA
BR.&U.S. 1945
INDIA
BR. 1945

33rd armies. Total Japanese casualties were set (May 5) at 347,000.

Apr. 1. United States marines and army troops invaded Okinawa. An attempt by the Japanese fleet to check this amphibious operation resulted in the sinking by American aircraft (Apr. 7) of the Japanese battleship *Yamato,* two cruisers, and three destroyers. The last bitter resistance on Okinawa did not end until June 21, but the island provided an airbase 325 miles from Japanese cities.

May–Aug. In the **greatest air offensive in history** United States land-based and carrier-based aircraft destroyed or immobilized the remnants of the Japanese navy, shattered Japanese industry, and curtailed Japanese sea communications by submarine and air attack and extensive minefields. United States battleships moved in to shell densely populated cities with impunity and the **20th Air Force** dropped 40,000 tons of bombs on Japanese industrial centers in one month.

After the collapse of Germany in May (p. 1151) the Japanese were left without allies, and the British and American resources in men and material were redirected toward the Pacific theater of war. Japanese strength was already half-broken and Japanese morale was beginning to disintegrate when three terrible strokes within one week hastened the conclusion of the war.

Aug. 6. An **ATOMIC BOMB,** secretly prepared by American and British scientists, was dropped on the Japanese city of **Hiroshima** with obliterating effect. The city was more than half destroyed.

Aug. 8. SOVIET RUSSIA DECLARED WAR ON JAPAN and commenced **invasion of Manchuria.**

Aug. 9. A **second atomic bomb** was dropped by the Americans on **Nagasaki.**

Aug. 10. The Japanese cabinet decided to make an **offer of surrender.** The Allied terms of capitulation were communicated to Tokyo and accepted four days later (Aug. 14). **United States forces of occupation landed in Japan on August 26.**

Sept. 2. The **FORMAL TERMS OF SURRENDER WERE SIGNED** by the Japanese officials and military leaders on board the *U.S.S. Missouri* in Tokyo Bay (p. 1157).

15. THE ORGANIZATION OF PEACE

The **League of Nations,** formed at Versailles in 1919, failed to curb powerful aggressors or to protect its weaker members from attack. It was never a well-balanced, truly supra-national league, and proved itself unfitted to deal with economic problems or to enforce its decisions. When the Second World War opened in 1939, the League of Nations had lost almost all its prestige and influence.

The **international anarchy,** repudiation of treaties, acts of aggression, and final outbreak of a general war that marked the 1930's brought home to peaceful nations the need for an organization better adapted to adjust international tensions and disputes.

Three **projects for international federation** took form in the war years 1939–1945. In Europe, Germany, Italy, and their satellite states forged an anti-Comintern, anti-democratic bloc which Adolf Hitler called his **"New Order."** In Asia and the East Indies the Japanese extended their power over a widening area, which they termed a **"Co-prosperity Sphere"** and in which they promulgated the doctrine of Asia for the Asians. Both the German and the Japanese hegemony had contracted and finally collapsed in defeat by the summer of 1945.

The third international federation formed in the war years came to be known as the **United Nations Organization.** It was based ideologically upon the foundations of the **Atlantic charter** (p. 1205), structurally upon the wartime solidarity of the "Big Three," Britain, the Soviet Union, and the United States, and financially upon the credits (43 billion dollars) made available to nations which opposed the Axis by the lend-lease policy of the United States government. The victory of the United Nations, achieved in large measure through the effective mobilization of world resources, left their leaders in a position to write the peace treaties.

1942, Jan. 1. Declaration by the United Nations at Washington to co-operate, on the basis of the Atlantic charter, in employing their full forces against Germany, Italy, and Japan. The declaration was signed by the United States, Great Britain, Soviet Russia, and 23 other nations at war. Subsequently 19 other nations adhered.

1943, Oct. 19–Nov. 1. Moscow conference of British, United States, and Soviet foreign ministers, who agreed (China adhering) to establish an international organization for peace and security, to set up a European advisory commission on terms of German surrender, to separate Austria from Germany, and to destroy the Italian Fascist régime.

Nov. 9. The **United Nations Relief and**

Rehabilitation Administration (UNRRA) was established by agreement signed at Washington. This international body was to aid countries which had been subjugated by the Axis powers.

Nov. 28–Dec. 1. Tehran Conference (Roosevelt, Churchill, Stalin): discussion of landing in France and of co-operation in the peace settlements. Agreement to set up a **European Advisory Commission** to study European problems.

1944, Apr. A United Nations Organization for **Educational and Cultural Reconstruction** was proposed by the ministers of education from the Allied countries, meeting in London.

July 1–22. A **United Nations Monetary and Financial Conference** (Bretton Woods Conference) met for three weeks of discussion. To improve world economic conditions, the delegates of the United Nations proposed to create an **International Monetary Fund** and an **International Bank for Reconstruction and Development,** the first with a credit of $8,800,000,000, the second with a capital of $10,000,000,000. The major purpose was to avert currency disorders and stabilize exchange rates, and the plans, worked out by the financial experts of 44 nations, were referred to the governments concerned for approval.

Sept. 16–26. The **council of the United Nations Relief and Rehabilitation Administration** held its second session, at Montreal. The allotment of $50,000,000 to Italy, partly for medical supplies, marked the first extension of aid by the United Nations to a former enemy country. Plans were laid to provide for a budget of $11,500,000 for 1945, by assessing member states. Whether UNRRA supplies and administrators would be admitted to countries liberated by the Soviet armies remained undecided.

Oct. 9. Dumbarton Oaks conference. Delegates representing the United States, the British Commonwealth, and the Soviet Union, after meeting from August 21 to September 27, published proposals for a permanent international organization to be known as the **United Nations.** The aim of the new society of nations was the preservation of world peace and security.

1945, Apr. 25–June 26. SAN FRANCISCO CONFERENCE. Delegates of 50 nations met at San Francisco to complete a **charter for the United Nations Organization.** A preliminary draft was submitted to the conference on June 22 by the United States secretary of state **Edward R. Stettinius.** It provided for four organs in the new body: (1) a **general assembly** as the major policy-shaping forum; (2) a **security council** to supervise military and political problems; (3) an **economic and social** council to deal with problems of economic and social conflict; and (4) an **international court of justice** for the adjustment of international disputes. The administrative work of the United Nations Organization was to be handled by a general **secretariat** directed by a secretary general.

July 17–Aug. 2. POTSDAM CONFERENCE. President Harry S. Truman for the United States, **Prime Minister Winston Churchill** for Great Britain, and **Generalissimo Joseph V. Stalin** for the Union of Soviet Socialist Republics met in Potsdam to confer on plans for re-establishing peace. After July 28, **Clement R. Attlee,** head of the new British Labour cabinet, replaced Churchill at the conference. An agreement was reached to establish a **council of foreign ministers,** representing the United States, Great Britain, the Soviet Union, France, and China, to continue the drafting of peace settlements. Its first session was held in London (Sept. 11).

For **Germany** the decisions reached at the Potsdam conference implied: (1) disarmament and demilitarization; (2) dissolution of National Socialist institutions; (3) trial of war criminals; (4) encouragement of democratic ideals; (5) restoration of local self-government and democratic political parties; (6) freedom of speech, press, and religion, subject to the requirements of military security.

Economic restrictions drafted by the conference for Germany included: (1) prohibition of the manufacture of war materials and implements of war; (2) controlled production of metals, chemicals, and machinery essential to war; (3) decentralization of German cartels, syndicates, and trusts; (4) emphasis upon agriculture and peaceful domestic industries; (5) control of exports, imports, and scientific research. The methods whereby the victors would enforce these conditions were to be worked out in detail later.

The **conference further ordained** "that Germany be compelled to compensate to the greatest possible extent for the loss and suffering that she caused to the United Nations. . . ." The members of the conference agreed in principle on the disposal of the German navy and merchant marine, but in this matter likewise the details were not worked out.

Peace treaties with Finland, Bulgaria, Hungary, Roumania, and Italy were to be drawn up as promptly as possible.

Sept. 2. FORMAL TERMS OF SURRENDER were signed by the Japanese civil and military envoys aboard the *U.S.S. Missouri* in Tokyo Bay. The Japanese home islands were placed under the rule of a United States army of occupation, but the emperor remained as the head of the state and the Japanese political and police officials continued to fulfill their functions. The high command and the military organizations were progressively disbanded. American forces also occupied island possessions regained or newly captured in the Pacific Ocean.

Korea was placed under Soviet and United States occupation, pending establishment of a Korean democratic government. The **Kurile Islands** and the southern part of **Sakhalin** were ceded to Russia, **Outer Mongolia** was recognized as part of the Soviet sphere of control, and Russia shared with China the facilities and supervision of **Port Arthur** and the Manchurian railroads.

Sept. 9. Capitulation terms for Japanese forces in China (estimated at 1,000,000 men) were signed at Nanking by Japanese commanders and representatives of Chiang Kaishek.

China regained sovereignty over **Inner Mongolia** and **Manchuria**, as well as the islands of **Formosa** and **Hainan**. **Hong Kong** was reoccupied by the British, who likewise accepted the formal surrender at Singapore (Sept. 12) of all Japanese forces (585,000 men) in Southeast Asia and the East Indies.

1946, July 29–Oct. 15. A PEACE CONFER ENCE of the 21 nations which waged wa against the Axis in Europe met at Paris t discuss the draft treaties for peace with **Italy Roumania, Hungary, Bulgaria,** and **Finland** These treaties had been prepared by the for eign ministers' council of Great Britain France, the United States, and the Sovie Union.

1947, Feb. 10. The **peace treaties were signe** in Paris. **Italy** lost four small border region to France, her Adriatic islands and most o Venezia Giulia to Yugoslavia, and the Dode canese Islands to Greece. It also renounce sovereignty over its North African colonie and agreed to the creation of the **Free Terri tory of Trieste.** Its armed forces were reduce to 300,000 men and it agreed to pay $36(million in reparations. **Roumania** lost Bes sarabia and northern Bukovina to the Sovie Union, but received back all of Transylvania **Hungary** was left with her 1938 borders, excep for a minor frontier rectification in favor o Czechoslovakia. **Bulgaria** retained the south ern Dobrudja. **Finland** ceded the port o Petsamo to the Soviet Union and granted th Russians a fifty-year lease of a naval base a Porkkala.

B. THE UNITED NATIONS AND GENERAL INTERNATIONAL AFFAIRS

(For a complete list of the members of the United Nations and the dates of their admission se Appendix IX.)

1945, Apr. 25–June 26. The **SAN FRANCISCO CONFERENCE** setting up the United Nations (see p. 1157).

Oct. 24. The **United Nations came into formal existence** when the twenty-ninth government ratified the charter. Its permanent seat was to be in New York City.

1946, Jan. 10. The first session of the U.N. general assembly took place in London. **Paul-Henri Spaak** of Belgium was elected president.

Feb. 1. Trygve Lie of Norway was elected secretary general of the U.N. for a five-year term.

Apr. 18. The **League of Nations,** after a final meeting at Geneva, dissolved itself and **transferred its assets to the United Nations.**

Dec. 11. The **general assembly voted to bar**

Spain from all U.N. activities and recommended that members sever diplomatic relations with Madrid.

Dec. 30. The **U.N. atomic energy commis sion,** with Soviet Russia and Poland abstaining voted to approve the United States plan fo extensive control and regulation of atomic de velopments.

1947, Feb. 18. The Soviet government, in series of amendments, objected to the degree of international control. Subsequent efforts o the U.N. security council to devise an alternat plan foundered on Soviet vetoes.

Oct. 21. The general assembly called on the Balkan states to compose their differences b peaceful means and established a **Balkan com mittee** to supervise developments.

1948, Dec. 10. The general assembly adopted

the **Convention on the Prevention of Genocide** and the **Universal Declaration of Human Rights.**

1949, Apr. 9. The **international court of justice,** in its first decision, held Albania responsible for explosions in the Corfu Channel and awarded damages to Great Britain.

July 29. The **atomic energy commission** voted to end its deliberations until the great powers should have found a basis for agreement.

Dec. 5. The general assembly adopted recommendations of the **commission on conventional armaments** that members of the U.N. submit full information on their armed forces.

Dec. 9. The general assembly reiterated its proposal that **Jerusalem** be placed under a permanent U.N. régime.

1950. The U.N. adopted an **expanded program of technical assistance** to developing nations.

1950–1953. In the **Korean crisis** (p. 1348) the U.N. established a **unified command** (July 7, 1950) to which sixteen members contributed forces.

1950, Nov. 3. The **"UNITING FOR PEACE" RESOLUTION,** by which the general assembly provided for emergency action in the event that the security council, for lack of unanimity, should fail to function.

1951, Mar. 5–June 21. A **meeting of the deputy foreign ministers** of the Soviet Union, the United States, Great Britain, and France at Paris became deadlocked on the question of disarmament and failed in its effort to draft an agenda for a full foreign ministers conference.

Apr. 30. The security council appointed **Frank P. Graham** as mediator in the **Kashmir dispute** (p. 1313).

Nov. 6. At a meeting of the general assembly in Paris the Western powers offered Soviet Russia broad **proposals for disarmament.** After weeks of proposals and counter-proposals the discussions ended in stalemate.

Dec. 7. The **special committee on the Balkans** was dissolved.

1952. The U.N. set up a **disarmament commission** on which all members were to be represented.

Sept. 18. The **Soviet Union,** by its fifty-second veto, **blocked the admission of Japan** and then (Oct. 10) of three Indo-Chinese states.

Nov. 10. Resignation of Trygve Lie as secretary general.

953, Apr. 7. ELECTION OF DAG HAMMARSKJÖLD as secretary general.

May 11. Proposal of Prime Minister Churchill for a big-power meeting to discuss East-West issues. The United States declined (May 13) failing more indications of the Soviet

Union's desire for peace.

July 10–14. United States, British, and French foreign ministers, meeting in Washington, proposed a meeting with their Soviet colleague to discuss German reunification, the Austrian peace treaty, etc. They threatened to reopen the war in Korea in the event of violation of the truce or of further Communist aggression in Asia.

Sept. 21. The Soviet delegate to the U.N. general assembly submitted a proposal for a one-third reduction in the armed forces of the great powers and for a ban on all atomic weapons.

1954, Feb. 18. The **Berlin conference of Big Four foreign ministers** adjourned until Apr. 26, when they were to reassemble at Geneva to discuss settlement of the Korean and Indo-Chinese questions. Communist China was to be invited to participate.

May 13–June 22. A five-power subcommittee of the U.N. disarmament commission met and discussed the problem of an **inspection system,** possible methods of preventing **surprise attacks,** and a possible ban on **nuclear testing.** The discussions registered but little progress.

Nov. 4. The general assembly approved an East-West proposal for further negotiations on disarmament and the banning of nuclear weapons.

Dec. 4. The general assembly unanimously endorsed a plan, advocated by President Eisenhower, for agreement on the **peaceful uses of atomic energy.**

1955, Apr. 18–24. The **BANDUNG CONFERENCE OF ASIAN-AFRICAN NATIONS,** of whom 29 attended. The conference adopted resolutions on world peace and self-determination for all nations.

July 18–23. A **BIG FOUR SUMMIT MEETING** at Geneva discussed various European problems (p. 1196). **President Eisenhower** proposed a Soviet-U.S. exchange of blueprints on their respective military establishments and also proposed mutual aerial inspection. **Premier Bulganin** in turn called for a non-aggression treaty between the North Atlantic Treaty Organization and the Warsaw pact.

Oct. 27–Nov. 16. A conference of the Big Four foreign ministers at Geneva failed to implement the "summit" directives of July.

Nov. 25. The French delegation returned to the general assembly when the latter voted to terminate debate on the **Algerian question.**

Dec. 13. A "package deal" for the admission of **eighteen nations** failed when Nationalist China vetoed the application of the Mongolian People's Republic. The assembly nonetheless admitted sixteen new members.

Dec. 16. The general assembly voted approval of the Eisenhower **plan for aerial inspection** and exchange of military blueprints.
1956, Nov. 2. The general assembly, in emergency session, called for a **cease-fire in the Suez Canal zone** (p. 1283) and condemned the **Soviet assault on Hungary** (p. 1206).
1957. Establishment of the **U.N. International Atomic Energy Commission,** which thereafter held periodic conferences (1958, 1964).

Establishment of the **U.N. emergency force** to supervise the truce provisions in the **Gaza Strip** and **Sinai Peninsula** (p. 1283).

June 30. The **International Geophysical Year** began. Scientists from 64 countries participated in a vast program of study and research.

Sept. 17. The **general assembly** unanimously **re-elected Hammarskjöld** for a second term.

Dec. 26–Jan. 1. A "**solidarity conference**" of the Asian and African peoples met at Cairo and established a permanent council.
1958, Jan. 9. Soviet Premier Bulganin, in letters to 19 Western governments, called for a summit conference to discuss major international issues. The United States (Jan. 12) agreed provided profitable preliminary discussions take place.

Jan. 13. The U.N. secretary general received a petition from more than 9000 scientists in 43 countries asking for international agreement banning the testing of nuclear weapons.

Mar. **Soviet Russia announced the suspension of nuclear tests,** reserving the right to resume if other powers failed to take similar action. Great Britain and the United States followed suit.

June 13. The U.S.S.R. agreed to discussions at Geneva of technical problems of **nuclear test detection.**

July–Aug. The U.N. security council failed in its efforts to stabilize the **situation in Lebanon and Jordan** (p. 1284).

Oct. 20. The French delegate to the U.N. announced that France would not be bound by an eventual nuclear test ban agreement.

Oct. 31. **Geneva conference on discontinuance of nuclear weapons tests** opened with the United States, the Soviet Union, and Great Britain represented, but after two years of discussion the issue of controls remained unresolved.
1959, Dec. 1. **THE ANTARCTIC TREATY,** signed by the United States, the Soviet Union, and ten other nations. It reserved the Antarctic for scientific and other peaceful activities and marked an important event in international co-operation.

Dec. 12. The general assembly adopted a resolution, drafted by the United States and the Soviet Union, to renew efforts to promote and regulate the **peaceful use of outer space** and to establish a permanent committee on this issue.

Establishment of a **permanent committee on the peaceful uses of outer space.**

Dec. 19–21. **Conference in Paris** of Eisenhower, Macmillan, de Gaulle, and Adenauer. They announced their invitation to Premier Khrushchev to attend summit talks in Paris early in 1960. The Soviet premier accepted (Dec. 30).
1960. Employment of a **U.N. peace-keeping force in the Congo.** This force, consisting of contingents from several smaller states, proved highly effective until withdrawn in 1964 (p. 1270).

Mar. 15. **Convocation of a disarmament conference,** agreed upon by the Big Four, at Geneva. Though outside the U.N., this conference was to report periodically to it.

May 1. **The U-2 incident,** creating acute tension in relations between the U.S. and the U.S.S.R. (p. 1217).

May 16. Khrushchev refused to continue with the Paris summit conference and canceled the invitation to President Eisenhower to visit the Soviet Union.

July 27. The Soviet delegate, supported by four East European colleagues, broke up the **Geneva armaments talks** and the U.S.S.R. requested the U.N. general assembly to consider international disarmament at its September meeting.

Sept. 19. After a resolution reaffirming support for **Hammarskjöld's Congo policy** had been defeated in the security council by a Soviet veto, the general assembly was called in emergency session.

Sept. 20. The U.N. general assembly, with Khrushchev, Tito, Castro, and other heads of state present, approved the Congo policy by a vote of 70–0. The Soviet bloc and France abstained.

Sept. 23. **Khrushchev,** in an assembly speech, **demanded the removal of Hammarskjöld** and the replacement of the general secretary's office by a three-man body representing the Eastern, Western, and neutral powers (**troika** plan).

Dec. 14. Signature of the convention setting up the **Organization for Economic Co-operation and Development.**

Dec. 18. The general assembly voted to hold a **plebiscite in Western Samoa** in May 1961 on the question of independence.
1961. Establishment of the **World Food Program** for the relief of hunger and famine.

Feb. 14. The **Soviet Union withdrew recog-**

nition of Hammarskjöld, charging him with being an "accomplice" in the murder of the former Congolese Premier Lumumba (p. 1270).

Mar. 21. Resumption of the Geneva talks on the banning of nuclear tests.

June 3-4. CONFERENCE OF PRESIDENT KENNEDY AND PREMIER KHRUSHCHEV AT VIENNA. A joint communiqué stated that the two leaders reaffirmed support for the neutrality of Laos and discussed a nuclear test ban, disarmament, and the German problem.

Sept. 1-6. CONFERENCE OF NON-ALIGNED NATIONS at Belgrade, attended by 25 nations. The conference called for immediate Kennedy-Khrushchev talks to avert war and halt the armaments race.

Sept. 5. Resumption by the United States of nuclear weapons tests without radioactive fallout.

Sept. 18. Death of Secretary General Dag Hammarskjöld in an airplane accident *en route* to meeting with Tshombe, the governor of Katanga (p. 1270).

Nov. 3. The **general assembly unanimously elected U Thant of Burma** as acting secretary general.

Dec. 21. The general assembly authorized the issue of bonds totaling $200 million to meet the **financial crisis** deriving from the expenditures for the Congo and other forces.

1962, Jan. 18, 20. The Netherlands and Indonesia accepted **U Thant's offer to act as mediator in the New Guinea dispute** (p. 1337).

Mar. 14. Opening of the seventeen-nation **DISARMAMENT CONFERENCE** at Geneva. France had declined the invitation to participate. The conference sat under joint U.S. and U.S.S.R. chairmanship, and had as its objective general and complete disarmament.

June 21-28. A **"World without the Bomb" conference met at Accra** under the auspices of **President Nkrumah** of Ghana. Among those attending were representatives of the U.S. and the U.S.S.R. The conference called on the U.N. to train teams of experts for inspection purposes and exhorted the African states to achieve continent-wide disarmament.

July 16. Closing of the tariff conference at Geneva, after discussions extending over almost two years. The forty-five nation conference announced 4400 concessions involving some $4.9 billion in world trade.

Nov. 30. U Thant was elected to a four-year term as secretary general of the U.N.

1963, May 22. The U.S.S.R. notified the U.N. that it would not pay its share of any U.N. expenses "unlawfully voted" by the general assembly. Beginning of a prolonged **dispute**

about **U.N. peace-keeping forces** to which certain members objected.

July 15. Opening of United States, Soviet Union, and British **negotiations for a nuclear test ban treaty.**

Aug. 5. The three powers signed a limited **TEST BAN TREATY** at Moscow. The treaty went into effect on Oct. 10, with over 100 signatories. It prohibited nuclear testing in the atmosphere and space, and underwater, but not underground.

Aug. 29. The Geneva **disarmament conference adjourned** without reaching any agreements.

Oct. 10. The general assembly adopted, by acclamation, a **resolution banning nuclear weapons in space** (p. 000).

1964. U.N. peace-keeping action in the Cyprus crisis (p. 1296).

Jan. 21. The **disarmament conference reconvened.** On Feb. 11 the American delegate rejected a Soviet proposal for the abolition of submarine-based missiles, since to do so would weight the nuclear balance in favor of the Soviet Union. On Mar. 5 the United States delegate offered to permit international inspection of one of the largest American reactors and appealed to the Soviet Union to follow this example. A few days later (Mar. 19) the United States offered to destroy 480 B-47 bombers if the U.S.S.R. would scrap an equal number of its TU-16 bombers.

Mar. 22-27. Sixth meeting of the **Afro-Asian solidarity council** at Algiers.

Mar. 23-June 15. U.N. CONFERENCE ON TRADE AND DEVELOPMENT at Geneva, attended by 120 nations. It set up a permanent **trade and development board.**

Apr. 20. President Johnson and Premier Khrushchev announced an agreement to reduce the production of materials used in nuclear weapons.

June 30. Withdrawal of U.N. forces from the Congo. In the four years of their operations they had contributed heavily to the prevention of civil war.

Sept. Refusal of certain U.N. members to pay their share of expenses of peace-keeping operations, on score of illegality. U.S. insistence that two years in arrears should lead to loss of voting power in the assembly. Issue deferred.

Sept. 4. Termination of the U.N. observation mission in Yemen (p. 1307).

Oct. 5-11. CONFERENCE OF NON-ALIGNED NATIONS IN CAIRO, with 47 nations represented. Declarations against Western colonialism and the retention of foreign bases.

Nov. 30. Special **U.N. committee report on**

South Africa, calling for total economic sanctions, etc. (p. 000).

Dec. 30. Adoption of a security council resolution on the Congo (p. 1271).

1965, Jan. 1, 21. Resignation and **withdrawal of Indonesia** from the U.N. in protest against election of Malaysia to a non-permanent seat on the security council.

Feb.–Aug. Vain efforts of the **special committee on peace-keeping operations** to resolve the conflict of views between the U.S. and the U.S.S.R. on Article XIX of the charter. The committee recommended continuance of operations, depending on voluntary contributions of members to defray expenses. Eventually (Aug. 16) the U.S. dropped its demand that the U.S.S.R., France, and certain other members be deprived of their vote in the assembly for failure to meet assessments.

Apr. 9. Security council support of **British oil blockade of Rhodesia,** but rejection of proposal to call on Britain to apply force (p. 1275).

May 6. Further security council resolutions (Oct. 12, Nov. 5, 12, 20) on the **Rhodesian issue** (p. 1275).

May 22. Action of U.N. representative in effecting a cease-fire in the **Dominican civil war** (p. 1249).

July 27–Sept. 16. Resumption of the U.N. committee on disarmament sessions at Geneva. On Aug. 17 the U.S. delegate proposed a treaty to prevent the spread of nuclear weapons.

Aug. 31. **Charter amendments** in effect: membership of security council raised from 11 to 15 (with 9 as the effective vote) and the economic and social council from 18 to 27.

Aug. 31–Sept. 10. Second World Population Conference, in session at Belgrade.

Sept. 4. U.N. action in the India-Pakistan conflict. U Thant personally visited the area and the security council was enabled to effect a cease-fire (Sept. 20) and eventually secure withdrawal to the Aug. 5 lines (p. 1314).

Nov. 5. Disorders in Aden. General assembly calls on Britain to close its military base immediately (p. 1307).

Nov. 22. The general assembly voted to establish a **United Nations development program** merging various existing activities and organizations, with **Paul G. Hoffman** as administrator.

Dec. 15. After reports of special committees the general assembly recommended mandatory, universally applied **sanctions against the South African Republic** (p. 1277).

Dec. 21. The general assembly called for a **boycott of Portugal** and the severance of diplomatic relations (p. 1187).

1966, Apr. 9. Rhodesia. The security council

authorized British use of force if necessary to stop arrival of tankers at Beira with oil intended for Rhodesia (p. 1275).

July 18. General assembly votes to terminate the **mandate of South Africa for Southwest Africa** (Namibia) (p. 1277).

Nov. 25. Security council **censure of Israel** for large-scale reprisal action against Jordan (Nov. 13).

Dec. 2. U Thant unanimously elected to a second term as secretary general.

1967, Jan. 27. TREATY OF PRINCIPLES GOVERNING THE ACTIVITIES OF STATES IN THE EXPLORATION AND USE OF OUTER SPACE. The treaty, negotiated by the U.S. and U.S.S.R., prohibited the orbiting of weapons of mass destruction and forbade all claims to celestial territories. It was signed by 62 nations.

May 15. General Agreement on Tariffs and Trade arrived at by 53 nations after years of negotiation. It provided for reductions of tariffs over a five-year period on both agricultural and industrial products. The treaty was signed by 46 nations at Geneva on June 30, 1967.

May 19. The general assembly voted to set up a special council to administer Namibia. On May 24 the South African government announced its refusal to have any dealings with the council (p. 1277).

June 5. Outbreak of the Israeli-Arab war. Efforts of the U.N. to secure a cease-fire, etc. (p. 1285).

Aug. 24. Draft treaty on non-proliferation of nuclear weapons, submitted by the U.S. and U.S.S.R. as sponsors to the U.N. disarmament committee.

Nov. 3. Assembly resolution calling on Britain to use force against Rhodesia, since sanctions had proved inadequate.

Nov. 7. Status of women: assembly declaration on the elimination of discrimination against women unanimously adopted.

Nov. 17. Assembly condemnation of war being waged by Portugal against its colonial peoples.

Nov. 22. Basic **resolution** of the security council **on terms of a just and lasting peace between Israel and the Arab states. Dr. Gunnar Jarring** of Sweden appointed special representative of the U.N. with headquarters in Cyprus (p. 1286).

Nov. 24–25. Cyprus crisis. Successful efforts of U Thant to secure withdrawal of some of Greek and Turkish troops (p. 1297).

Dec. 5. Assembly resolution approving **treaty for prohibition of nuclear weapons in Latin America.**

1968, Jan. 31. The **Nauru trust territory became an independent state.**

Apr. 22. Agreement on the rescue of astronauts, etc.

Apr. 22–May 13. International conference on human rights in session at Tehran.

May 29. Unanimous security council resolution imposing **mandatory sanctions on Rhodesia** (p. 1275).

June 4. The general assembly approved the **NUCLEAR NON-PROLIFERATION TREATY** submitted by the U.N. disarmament committee. By July 1, 62 nations had ratified the agreement.

Nov. 29. The general assembly by overwhelming vote condemned **Portuguese policies in Africa.**

Dec. 2. The general assembly denounced South African *apartheid* and called on all countries for greater support for African liberation movements.

Dec. 18. By resolution the general assembly declared the **situation in Gibraltar** incompatible with the U.N. charter and called for termination of the British base by Oct. 1, 1969 (p. 1187).

969, Mar. U.N. action in bringing about the **withdrawal of Spanish troops and nationals from Equatorial Guinea** (p. 1269).

Mar. 20. The security council called on South Africa to withdraw its administration immediately from Namibia. The demand was repeated on Aug. 12, and South Africa's persistent refusal was condemned by the assembly (Oct. 31).

July 3. A security council resolution censured in the strongest possible terms measures changing the **status of Jerusalem** and deploring Israel's failure to respect previous resolutions.

July 28. The **security council censured Portugal** for attacks on Zambia, and successively (Dec. 9) for violating the sovereignty of Senegal, and (Dec. 22) for violating that of Guinea.

Aug. 2. In **West Irian, representative councils,** voting under U.N. supervision, decided to remain with Indonesia.

Nov. 17–Dec. 22. STRATEGIC ARMS LIMITATION TALKS (SALT) between the United States and the Soviet Union began with preliminary discussions at Helsinki. Thereafter the discussions were resumed at intervals, alternately at Helsinki and Vienna, without producing concrete results in more than a year.

Nov. 19. The general assembly approved the Aug. 2 decision.

Nov. 24. Ratification of the non-proliferation treaty by both the U.S. and the U.S.S.R.

Nov. 25. Unilateral pledge by the United States never to engage in **germ warfare** or use **chemical weapons** in anything but self-

defense. Germ weapons, exclusive of tear gas and defoliants, were to be destroyed.

1970, Sept. 8–10. CONFERENCE OF NON-ALIGNED NATIONS AT LUSAKA (Zambia) attended by several heads of state and by delegates of 54 nations. Resolutions were passed for drastic action against the South African states and in favor of liberation movements everywhere. U.S. policy in Vietnam was roundly denounced and sanctions against Israel approved.

Sept. 14. The **Lusaka declaration on peace, independence, development, co-operation, and democratization of international relations.** A chief objective was to be the admission of Communist China to the U.N.

Oct. 24. The **general assembly,** ending the **observance of its twenty-fifth birthday,** unanimously adopted a declaration condemning colonialism and racism in South Africa. It also adopted a ten-year program of development for poorer nations: U.N. members, including the U.S., pledged themselves to devote 1% of their GNP to such assistance, if possible by 1975. By a simple majority the assembly adopted a resolution condemning colonialism in every form as a crime and calling on members to give material aid to liberation movements. The U.S., Great Britain, and several other governments either abstained from this vote or cast negative votes.

Nov. 17. The security council voted unanimously to call on Great Britain to take urgent and effective measures to end the illegal rebellion in Rhodesia and to enable the Rhodesian population to exercise their right of self-determination.

The **political committee** of the U.N. approved a treaty prohibiting the placing on the ocean floor outside the twelve-mile coastal limit of any installations for storing, testing, or utilizing nuclear weapons.

Nov. 22. General assembly vote on the **admission of Communist China to the U.N.** This issue had been before the assembly year after year, and during recent sessions the vote in favor of admission had been steadily rising. Since the issue had been classed as an important one, a favorable decision would have required a two-thirds vote. The Peking government made it clear that it would not in any case accept membership unless Nationalist China, which held one of the permanent seats on the security council, should resign that position in favor of Communist China, and that Nationalist China, furthermore, should be expelled from membership in the U.N., on the theory that there was only one legal China. This solution was unacceptable to the U.S. and to many other members of the U.N. The vote on Nov. 22 was 57 in favor of admission, 49 opposed, and 25 abstaining.

Dec. 1. The **social committee** of the assembly adopted a resolution, sponsored by the U.S., calling for regular **inspection of prisoner of war camps** and the treatment of inmates. The U.S.S.R. and other Communist governments were opposed.

C. EUROPE

1. INTERNATIONAL RELATIONS

1947, Mar. 10–Apr. 24. The **council of foreign ministers,** meeting at Moscow, failed in its effort to draft peace treaties for Germany and Austria (p. 1193).

July 12–15. The **MARSHALL PLAN,** a program for European recovery proposed by U.S. secretary of state George Marshall, was discussed by delegates of 16 European nations meeting at Paris. A committee was set up to draft a **European Recovery Program.** The Soviet Union and its satellites refused to participate in a program of European reconstruction.

Oct. 5. The **COMMUNIST INFORMATION BUREAU** (*Cominform*) was established by the Communist parties of the Soviet Union, Yugoslavia, Bulgaria, Roumania, Hungary, Poland, France, Italy, and Czechoslovakia. With headquarters in Belgrade, the bureau was to co-ordinate the activities of European Communist parties.

Oct. 29. Ratification of the **customs union between Belgium, the Netherlands, and Luxemburg.**

Nov. 25–Dec. 16. A conference of the Big Four foreign ministers at London again failed to agree on solution of the German problem (p. 1194).

1948, Mar. 17. The **BRUSSELS TREATY,** signed by Great Britain, France, Belgium, the Netherlands, and Luxemburg. It constituted a fifty-year alliance against attack in Europe, and provided for economic, social, and military co-operation.

Apr. 16. The subscribers to the European Recovery Program met at Paris and set up the permanent **Organization for European Economic Co-operation** (OEEC).

May 7. The first **Congress of Europe** convened at The Hague under the honorary chairmanship of Sir Winston Churchill to discuss **plans for European Union.**

June 28. **Yugoslavia was expelled from the Cominform** for alleged doctrinal errors and hostility to the Soviet Union.

July 30–Aug. 18. The future **status of the Danube River** was discussed by a ten-nation conference at Belgrade. The Soviet delegate introduced a new statute, to replace that of 1921, restricting membership on the Danubian Commission to the riparian states, thus excluding Great Britain, France, and the United States. Such a commission was set up (Nov. 11, 1949) despite the protest of the three Western powers.

1949, Jan. 25. A **COUNCIL FOR MUTUAL ECONOMIC ASSISTANCE** (COMECON) set up by the Communist governments.

Mar. 13. Belgium, the Netherlands, and Luxemburg agreed to organize full economic union at an early date. France and Italy made a similar agreement (Mar. 26).

Apr. 4. The **NORTH ATLANTIC TREATY ORGANIZATION (NATO)** founded by signature of the **North Atlantic Treaty** at Washington, by the foreign ministers of the United States, Great Britain, France, Belgium, the Netherlands, Luxemburg, Italy, Portugal, Denmark, Iceland, Norway, and Canada. The treaty provided for withdrawal at the end of 20 years, on one-year notification. It provided further for mutual assistance against aggression within the North Atlantic area and for co-operation in military training, arms production, and strategic planning. The **North Atlantic council,** consisting of the foreign ministers of all members, was to meet semi-annually and to serve as the directing body. A **defense committee,** consisting of the ministers of defense, and a **military committee,** consisting of the chiefs of staff, was to deal with military problems. A **standing group** (U.S., Britain, and France) was to provide general guidance. This organization was completed in Sept. 1949.

May 5. The **statute of the Council of Europe** was signed in London. It provided for an executive committee of ministers and a consultative assembly. Headquarters were fixed at Strasbourg.

Sept. 27. **The Soviet Union denounced its treaty of friendship with Yugoslavia** and other Communist governments presently did likewise. For some time there seemed acute danger of attack on Yugoslavia by its former allies, despite the Tito government's firm adherence to Communism (p. 1207).

1950, Jan. 6. The NATO council approved the "master defense plan" prepared by the defense committee.

Jan. 29. In a series of bilateral agreements the United States contracted to supply arms and other equipment to the members of NATO.

Mar. 30–Apr. 1. The **Council of Europe** decided to invite West Germany and the Saar to be associate members.

May 9. The **SCHUMAN PLAN** for the integration of the Western European coal and steel industries was proposed by French foreign minister **Robert Schuman.**

Sept. 12–19. A three-power conference in New York agreed on a **more liberal policy toward Western Germany** (p. 1195).

Oct. 20–21. The foregoing decision was denounced by a Communist conference at Prague.

Nov. 16–22. The second **world peace congress** (Communist-inspired and directed) met in Warsaw, with 60 countries represented.

Dec. 18. **General of the Army Dwight D. Eisenhower was named supreme allied commander, Europe,** with headquarters near Paris.

Dec. 20. The Brussels treaty powers decided to merge their military resources with those of NATO.

1951, Feb. 21. The British government indicated opposition to a U.S. suggestion that **Spain** be associated with NATO. The hostility of labor governments and organizations against Spain continued generally unabated through the years.

Apr. 18. France, West Germany, Italy, Belgium, the Netherlands, and Luxemburg signed a treaty embodying the Schuman Plan and set up a **single market for coal and steel.** An important first step in the direction of European economic union.

May 2. **West Germany became a full-fledged member of the Council of Europe.**

Sept. 6. The **Azores** became integrated with the NATO defense plan, by agreement between the U.S. and Portugal.

Sept. 15–20. Meeting at Ottawa, the **NATO council decided to invite Greece and Turkey** to become members of NATO.

Dec. 31. The **Marshall Plan** came to an end as the Economic Co-operation Administration was replaced by the **Mutual Security Agency.**

1952, Jan. 18. Prime Minister Churchill and President Truman agreed on the appointment of an **American admiral as supreme commander of NATO naval forces in the Atlantic.**

Feb. 20–25. **Greece and Turkey were formally admitted to NATO** at a meeting of the council in Lisbon. The council also voted to provide 50 divisions for the defense of Western Europe by the end of 1952. Actually, this figure was never attained.

Apr. 4. **General Lord Hastings Ismay took office as secretary general of NATO.**

Apr. 15. The British government aligned Britain with the **European Army project** and accepted extension of its commitments under the Brussels treaty to cover military assistance to West Germany and Italy.

Apr. 28. **General Matthew B. Ridgway succeeded General Eisenhower** as supreme allied commander, Europe.

May 27. A **EUROPEAN DEFENSE COMMUNITY** (EDC) was created by a Paris conference to establish a single unified command and bind West Germany to the Atlantic defense plan. The charter of EDC was signed by Italy, the Netherlands, Belgium, Luxemburg, France, and West Germany. These six countries signed a treaty with Great Britain by which the latter agreed to aid any EDC member if attacked. A NATO protocol extended that alliance's guarantees to West Germany. In a declaration signed by Britain and the U.S. these powers agreed to regard any threat to the EDC as a threat to their own security.

Aug. 1. French-German negotiations on the **question of the Saar Valley.** The French desired it to be "Europeanized" and made the seat of the Schuman Plan.

Aug. 10. The first session of the high authority of the **European Coal and Steel Community** took place at Luxemburg.

Sept. 10. The members of the Coal and Steel Community, meeting in a supra-national assembly, voted unanimously to establish a **European federal political community.**

Nov. 14. **Control of Tangier.** The U.S., Britain, and France agreed to set aside the 1945 agreement and restore police powers in the Tangier zone to Spain.

1953, Feb. 23. Meeting at Rome, the members of the Coal and Steel Community voted unanimously to support ratification of the EDC and gave tentative approval to a Dutch proposal to create a single market through tariff reductions.

Mar. 10. A "constituent assembly" voted 50–0 to approve that draft of a **charter for a European Union.**

Apr. 23–25. By the regular ministerial council of NATO it was agreed that Soviet policy had not changed, despite the launching of a "Peace Offensive." It was therefore decided to add six more divisions to the NATO forces by the end of 1953.

May 13. General Alfred M. Gruenther succeeded General Ridgway as supreme allied commander, Europe.

Oct. 8. The **Trieste Problem.** The U.S. and Britain, abandoning their 1945 promise to restore all of Trieste to Italy, announced plans to withdraw their forces from Zone A, which was to be returned to Italy, while leaving Yugoslavia in control of Zone B. Italy favored the plan, but Yugoslavia denounced it. Tito threatened to send his troops into Zone A the minute the Italians attempted to occupy it (Oct. 11).

Oct. 12-15. Tito called for an international conference on Trieste, while the Soviet Union sought action by the U.N. On Oct. 18 the foreign ministers of Britain, France, and the U.S. proposed a conference with Italy and Yugoslavia.

Nov. 1. The **Trieste crisis was averted** when Yugoslavia and Italy agreed (Nov. 21) to attend such a conference and (Dec. 5) to withdraw their troops from the disputed area.

Dec. 14. U.S. **secretary of state Dulles,** irked by the failure of some NATO members to meet their military commitments, warned a NATO conference at Paris that unless a European army were established "soon," his government would be forced to undertake **"an agonizing reappraisal"** of its own basic policies.

1954, Jan. 25-Feb. 18. A Big Four foreign ministers conference at Berlin discussed the **German and Austrian problems** and considered a Soviet proposal for a European security organization. The conference ended in deadlock, but decided to hold a further conference at Geneva to discuss East Asian questions, and to invite Communist China to attend.

Jan. 31. The **Yugoslav government** declined the invitation of the Cominform to "restore the ancient bonds" with Soviet Russia, arguing that political and economic decentralization had reached such a point that restoration of centralized Communist control would lead to "convulsion."

Aug. 30. The **FRENCH NATIONAL ASSEMBLY REJECTED THE EDC** treaty of 1952, thus sounding the death knell of hope for establishment of an integrated European army.

Sept. 30. Pierre Mendès-France, speaking before the European assembly at Strasbourg, announced French agreement to link West Germany with West European defense arrangements, provided Britain joined the alliance.

Oct. 3. Nine powers (Britain, France, Italy, Belgium, the Netherlands, Luxemburg, West Germany, the United States, and Canada) reached agreement on an alternative to the EDC.

Oct. 5. The **Trieste issue was settled** by agreement between Italy and Yugoslavia. Italy was accorded Zone A, including the city of Trieste, and Yugoslavia, Zone B. American and British troops were to be withdrawn shortly.

Oct. 20-23. A **NATO ministerial conference** at Paris **voted to terminate the occupation of West Germany** but provide for the retention of foreign troops there; to admit West Germany into NATO; and to expand and revise the Brussels treaty so as to create a **Western European Union** (WEU) by adding West Germany and Italy and by providing control of armaments of the member states.

Nov. 13. The **Soviet Union, Poland, and Czechoslovakia invited the European nations and the United States to a conference on European security,** to open in Moscow Nov. 29. Washington denounced the proposal as an attempt to forestall ratification of the Paris agreements.

Nov. 29. At a conference of Communist nations in Moscow **Foreign Minister Molotov** declared that the rearmament of West Germany required the Communist governments to take common measures for defense.

1955, May 9. At a conference of NATO foreign ministers in Paris **West Germany was formally admitted to membership in NATO.**

May 14. The **WARSAW PACT,** signed by eight European Communist governments, was the reply to the integration of West Germany with NATO. **Marshal Ivan S. Koniev** became chief of the joint military command. A **political consultative committee** was to serve as the directing organ.

1956, Jan. 27-28. Meeting of the Warsaw pact consultative committee in Prague. It called for immediate agreement among the great powers to prohibit the placement of nuclear weapons in Germany. A new **East German army** was to be added to Koniev's command.

Apr. 17. The **Cominform was officially dissolved.**

May 4. "Three Wise Men," a subcommittee of NATO, were appointed to "advise the Council on ways and means to improve and extend NATO co-operation in non-military fields and to develop greater unity within the Atlantic Community." The members were **Lester Pearson,** Canadian secretary of state for external affairs, **Gaetano Martino,** the Italian foreign minister, and **Halvard Lange,** the Norwegian foreign minister.

Nov. 20. General Lauris Norstad succeeded General Gruenther as supreme allied commander, Europe.

Dec. 14. Paul-Henri Spaak succeeded Lord Ismay as secretary general of NATO.

1957, Feb. 7. General Hans Speidel, of West Germany, was appointed **commander of NATO land forces in Central Europe.**

Mar. 25. The **ROME TREATY** established the **European Economic Community,** better known as the **Common Market.** Its members were France, West Germany, Italy, Belgium, the Netherlands, and Luxemburg. Another treaty set up a **European Atomic Community** (Euratom). Both organizations were to come into effect on Jan. 1, 1958.

Nov. 14–16. Meeting of delegates from 13 Communist countries in Moscow. It called for unity in opposing imperialism and capitalism abroad and for the elimination of deviationism at home. Mao Tse-tung, for Communist China, recognized Soviet Russia as the head of the "socialist camp."

Dec. 19. Establishment of **missile bases in Europe** was decided on by a top-level meeting of NATO in Paris. The United States was to retain basic control of the weapons, but assured its allies of its readiness to discuss "any reasonable proposal" for "comprehensive and controlled disarmament."

1958, Mar. 19. Opening meeting of the **European Economic Assembly** (the deliberative body of the Coal and Steel Community, of the Common Market, and of Euratom). **Robert Schuman** was elected president.

May 21–23. The **Communist COMECON,** meeting in Moscow, pledged increased economic co-operation. Four Asian nations (Communist China, North Korea, North Vietnam, Mongolia) agreed to integrate their economies with COMECON.

May 24–27. Meeting of the **Warsaw pact countries** in Moscow. They agreed on early **withdrawal of Soviet forces from Roumania and of one Soviet division from Hungary.**

July 31–Aug. 3. Meeting of Soviet Premier Khrushchev and Mao Tse-tung in Peking. In a communiqué they called for "summit talks" on the Middle East and especially for the immediate withdrawal of American and British troops from Lebanon and Jordan (p. 1284).

Sept. 3. The **European Court of Human Rights** came into existence when Austria and Iceland completed the necessary ratifications.

Dec. 2. The **Benelux** (Belgian, Dutch, Luxemburg) foreign ministers decided that their three countries should become a single economic unit early in 1959.

Dec. 13–16. The NATO council, meeting in Paris, supported the **determination of the United States, Britain, and France not to abandon West Berlin,** and to reject the Soviet contention that it could withdraw unilaterally from the international agreements concerning Berlin.

1959, Jan. 27–28. The **twenty-first congress of the Soviet Communist Party** ended in agreement for common opposition to the Tito-led "revisionist" movement.

Mar. 14. Beginning of **French defection from NATO** precipitated by President De Gaulle's refusal to put one-third of France's naval forces in the Mediterranean under NATO command. Disagreement between the United States and France on the **stockpiling of nuclear weapons.** The U.S. decided to transfer 200 airplanes from French to British and West German bases.

Sept. 9. Soviet neutrality in the conflict between Communist China and India. Khrushchev, on a visit to Peking (Sept. 29), warned publicly against a test of force with the capitalist world.

1960, May 3. The **European Free Trade Association** (EFTA) of Great Britain, Sweden, Norway, Denmark, Switzerland, Austria, and Portugal (the *"Outer Seven"*) was established as a counterpart to the Common Market.

May 14. Beginning of the **ESTRANGEMENT OF SOVIET RUSSIA AND COMMUNIST CHINA** (p. 1341). This important departure, based in part on ideological differences and rivalry for leadership, but also on long-standing territorial claims, soon became a public scandal and profoundly influenced the further course of international relations.

Sept. 23. NATO members agreed to establishment of a unified **West European air defense command** and related measures to strengthen the alliance.

Nov. 19. Twenty nations agreed on a charter for the **Organization for Economic Co-operation and Development** (OECD) to replace the Organization for European Economic Co-operation (OEEC). The United States and Canada joined the older organization to form the new, the objective of which was to expand trade, provide aid to underdeveloped countries, etc. The convention was signed Dec. 14.

Dec. 5. A manifesto, signed by leaders of 81 Communist parties, meeting at Moscow since Nov. 7, pledged a world Communist victory by peaceful means and reaffirmed the leadership of the Soviet Party as against Chinese claims.

1961, Jan. 31. Dirk U. Stikker, of the Netherlands, **succeeded Paul-Henri Spaak** as secretary general of NATO.

Apr.–May. Recall of Soviet technicians from Albania and termination of all aid to that country, in response to Albania's support of the Chinese position.

Oct. 27. At the **twenty-second congress of the Soviet Communist Party** Khrushchev abused the Albanians and called for the ouster of Hoxha and Shehu (p. 1209).

Dec. 7. Agreement between the Common Market members to admit eighteen African states as "associates."

1962, June 6–7. The **COMECON conference** at Moscow adopted the principle of the "internationalist socialist division of labor."

June 14. Ten Western European governments set up a **European Space Research Organization,** devoted to space experiments.

July 25. General Lyman L. Lemnitzer was appointed to **succeed General Norstad** as supreme allied commander, Europe.

Aug. 5. Negotiations for **British entry into the Common Market** foundered on the relationship of the Commonwealth to the European market, but Prime Minister Macmillan and President De Gaulle agreed (Dec. 15) to continue examination of the problem.

Dec. 12. State visit of Marshal Tito to Moscow, during which Premier Khrushchev, addressing the Supreme Soviet, angrily attacked the Chinese Communists, who in reply began to call on Communists the world over to revolt against Soviet domination.

1963, Jan. 29. FRANCE VETOED BRITAIN'S APPLICATION FOR MEMBERSHIP IN THE COMMON MARKET.

Feb. 5. Walter Hallstein, the executive head of the Common Market, castigated De Gaulle's plan for transforming Europe into a "Third Force" and sharply criticized French obstruction of British entry into the Common Market.

May. The seven members of the European Free Trade Association voted to eliminate all tariffs on non-farm products by the end of 1966.

June 21. The French government announced its intention to withdraw its Channel and Atlantic naval forces, except for some submarines, from the NATO North Atlantic command.

July 24–26. A **Communist inter-party conference** at Moscow shelved a Soviet plan for integration of the Communist states and reaffirmed the principles of "equality, strict observance of sovereignty, and mutual comradely assistance."

Oct. 11. Delegates from the United States, Britain, West Germany, Italy, Belgium, Greece, and Turkey began discussions looking toward an **integrated atomic fleet** for the defense of Europe.

Oct. 14–24. The COMECON decided to establish among Communist states a **multination payments system** and an **International Bank of Economic Collaboration.**

1964, Jan. The Chinese Communist Party began to recognize **pro-Chinese factions** in countries such as Belgium and Switzerland as well as in those of Asia, Africa, and Latin America.

Mar. 3–10. A high-level Roumanian delegation arrived in Peking, in the effort to bridge the Soviet-Chinese rift.

Apr. 22. The Roumanian Communist Party asserted in the strongest terms its claims to full equality and independence.

May 4. France withdrew its officers from the NATO naval commands.

May 13. Manlio Brosio of Italy was **elected to succeed Dirk Stikker** on Aug. 1 as secretary general of NATO.

June 12. Signature of a twenty-year **treaty of friendship and mutual assistance between the Soviet Union and East Germany.** The treaty included a guarantee of the frontiers of the German People's Republic.

July 22. Celebration of the **twentieth anniversary of the Polish Republic.** Khrushchev, Ulbricht, and Novotny joined in aspersions on Roumanian nationalism.

Nov. Visit of Chou En-lai to Moscow, following the dismissal of Khrushchev, the *bête noir* of the Chinese Communists.

Dec. 15. Members of the **Common Market,** after prolonged debate, agreed on a **common price for wholesale wheat.** German farmers were to be compensated for substantial losses in behalf of their French counterparts.

Dec. 16. Prime Minister Wilson's counterproposal for a broader **Atlantic nuclear force.** The U.S. proposal for a **NATO multilateral nuclear force** of 25 mix-manned surface ships, equipped with Polaris missiles, had met with a favorable response only from West Germany.

1965, Feb. 21. De Gaulle announced his intention to modify the arrangements between France and its NATO partners.

Mar. 2. Decision of the Common Market countries to merge the Common Market, the Coal and Steel Community, and the Atomic Energy Community, with headquarters in Brussels.

July 27. Reconvening of the U.N. disarmament committee at Geneva.

1966, Mar. 11. De Gaulle, describing NATO as outmoded yet desiring to retain membership, stated the **decision of the French government to withdraw all French troops from the integrated NATO command** and requested that all NATO bases and headquarters be removed from French soil by Apr. 1, 1967.

Apr. 21–27. Visit of Soviet Foreign Minister **Gromyko to Italy** and reception by the pope. Beginning of closer economic and cultural relations between the two countries.

June 20–July 1. Visit of President De Gaulle to Russia, following visits of French Foreign Minister **Couve de Murville** to other East European capitals. The French envisioned a "Europeanized Europe" free from both American and Soviet domination.

July 1. Supreme headquarters allied powers Europe moved from Paris to Casteau, Belgium.

July 4–6. Meeting of the Warsaw Pact powers at Bucharest. Roumanian **Premier Ceauşescu** proposed the dissolution of both the North Atlantic alliance and the Warsaw pact, as well as withdrawal of all foreign troops from the territory of other nations.

1967, Jan. 15–Mar. 8. Prime Minister Wilson's tour of Common Market countries and extensive discussions of the conditions of British membership.

Jan. 31. Establishment of **diplomatic relations between West Germany and Roumania,** the initial move in the development of better relations between Central and Eastern Europe.

Feb. 9. Soviet premier Kosygin, addressing the House of Commons during a visit to England, called for a treaty of friendship and non-aggression, the dissolution of NATO and of the Warsaw pact, the denial of nuclear weapons to Germany, and a declaration that the European frontiers were to be regarded as unalterable and inviolable.

May 2. Prime Minister Wilson announced the **British government's decision to apply for membership in the Common Market.** The Commons supported him, 487–26 (May 8).

May 11. The **British government formally applied for admission to the Common Market.** Denmark, Ireland and Norway did likewise.

May 15. General agreement on tariffs and trade (GATT) arrived at by 53 nations after years of negotiation. The agreement provided for progressive reductions in tariffs over a five-year period, varying in amount from 30% to 50% on both industrial and agricultural products. The agreement was signed at Geneva by 46 nations (June 30).

May 16. De Gaulle once more vetoed the British application on grounds of British insularity, ties to the United States, etc.

July 5. The new **European Community,** consolidating former entities, went into effect. **Jean Rey** (Belgium) became president.

July 7. Marshal Ivan I. Yakubovsky became supreme commander of the Warsaw pact forces.

June 18–20. A visit of Prime Minister Wilson to Paris failed to move De Gaulle, who called upon Britain to undergo a **"profound transformation"** before attempting to enter the Common Market. On the other hand, the council of ministers of the Common Market voted (June 27) five to one (France) in favor of the British application.

1968, Jan. 19. British-Soviet agreement to cooperate in applied science and technology.

Mar.–June. A new period of **harassment and obstruction of traffic between West Ger-**

many and West Berlin, by the East German authorities.

June 15. Extensive **Soviet and Warsaw pact maneuvers** in Poland, East Germany, and Czechoslovakia.

July 1. The **European Community became a single trading area** for all industrial produce, with a common external tariff.

Aug. 20–21. Occupation of Czechoslovakia by Warsaw pact forces, creating an acute international crisis (p. 1204).

Sept. 12. Albania formally withdrew from the Warsaw pact.

Oct. 16. Soviet agreement with the new Czech government permitting the stationing of troops in Czechoslovakia.

1969, Mar. 17. The Warsaw pact powers proposed a European security conference, a proposal reiterated by Foreign Minister Gromyko on July 10. The Western powers, shocked by the Czech affair, exhibited little enthusiasm.

May 6. General Andrew J. Goodpaster became supreme allied commander, Europe, **replacing General Lemnitzer.**

May 28. The **NATO defense planning committee** decided to organize an "on call" naval force in the Mediterranean, in response to the constant strengthening of Soviet naval forces in the eastern Mediterranean.

June 3. Conclusion of a **British-Soviet trade treaty.**

Aug. 2–3. Visit of United States President Nixon to Roumania.

Dec. 4–5. The NATO council endorsed the idea of a security conference provided it were carefully prepared and that the United States and Canada be included.

1970, Feb. 6. Conclusion of a **trade agreement between the Common Market and Yugoslavia,** the first such agreement with an East European country.

May 27. The NATO council, meeting in Rome, called for discussions with the Soviet Union and the Warsaw pact governments looking to the reduction of forces in Central Europe.

Aug. 12. West German Chancellor Willy Brandt in Moscow for the signing of a **TREATY BETWEEN WEST GERMANY AND THE SOVIET UNION** recognizing the **inviolability of all post-war European boundaries,** including specifically the **Oder-Neisse line.** The Soviet Union disclaimed opposition to the reunification of Germany provided it was achieved by peaceful means. West Germany reserved all its ties with the West, but agreed to develop economic, scientific, and cultural ties with the Soviet Union. **Ratification of the treaty,** which could prove a milestone in East-West relations, was made conditional on suc-

EUROPE in 1970

- ☐ U.S.S.R. in 1938
- ▦ Acquired by U.S.S.R. 1939~1945
- ▨ Soviet Satellites
- ▩ Communist, but not a Satellite
- ⸬ North Atlantic Treaty Organization★

Arctic Ocean

Atlantic Ocean

NORWAY
SWEDEN
FINLAND

IRELAND
GREAT BRITAIN
DENMARK
NETHER-LANDS
London
BELGIUM
Bonn
Paris
LUXEMBURG
FRANCE
SWITZER-LAND
ITALY
SPAIN
PORTUGAL
Madrid
Rome

GER. DEM. REPUB.
GERMAN
FEDERAL
REPUBLIC
Berlin
Danzig
POLISH ADMIN.
ESTONIA
LATVIA
LITHUANIA

UNION of
SOVIET SOCIALIST REPUBLICS

Moscow

Boundary of
U.S.S.R. in 1938

POLAND
CZECHOSLOVAKIA
Vienna
AUSTRIA
HUNGARY
YUGOSLAVIA
ROUMANIA
BULGARIA
Black Sea
TURKEY
GREECE
ALBANIA

Mediterranean Sea

★ Plus Canada, Iceland, and the United States.

cessful conclusion of negotiations regarding the status of West Berlin.

Nov. 19. Members of the European Community adopted measures aimed at the co-ordination of their foreign policies. A newly created **political committee** was to hold monthly meetings.

Dec. 1–4. The **NATO council and defense ministers** meeting at Brussels announced plans by which the European members should contribute over $1 billion during the ensuing five years to improve bases, forces, and weapons so as to counter-balance increases in the strength of the Warsaw pact forces. The United States disclaimed any intention of reducing its own forces in Europe. In a concluding statement the conference declared that even the first steps toward a European security conference depended on satisfactory improvements in the **status of West Berlin,** about which talks had been initiated in March.

Dec. 7. Visit of West German Chancellor Brandt to Warsaw for signature of a **treaty with Poland.** Both sides renounced the use of force in settling disputes and West Germany conditionally recognized the Oder-Neisse line as the western frontier of Poland. In return Poland was to allow some 90,000 ethnic Germans to leave for Germany. This treaty, too, was to be ratified only after settlement of the problem of West Berlin.

2. THE BRITISH ISLES

a. THE UNITED KINGDOM AND THE COMMONWEALTH

(From p. 983)

1939, Sept. 3. GREAT BRITAIN DECLARED WAR ON GERMANY. The French declaration followed within a few hours, and these events marked the **commencement of World War II.**

1940, Apr. 4. Winston S. Churchill was assigned general direction over the **British defense program,** indicating a declining confidence in Neville Chamberlain's cabinet.

May 10. Chamberlain resigned as British prime minister and **Churchill headed a coalition cabinet** which included Conservatives and Labourites.

Dec. 23. Anthony Eden was appointed foreign secretary and **Viscount Halifax** was sent to the United States as ambassador.

1941, July 13. Great Britain and Soviet Russia concluded a mutual aid treaty.

Aug. 14. Prime Minister Churchill and President Franklin D. Roosevelt issued the ATLANTIC CHARTER, a joint declaration of British and American peace aims (p. 1226).

Aug. 24. Churchill pledged British aid to the United States if the latter should become involved in war with Japan.

1942, May 26. Great Britain and Russia agreed to a twenty-year **mutual aid treaty.**

June 9. Great Britain and the United States agreed to pool all resources of food and production to assure victory.

June 18. Churchill and Roosevelt opened a series of **Anglo-American conferences** in Washington.

Aug. 12. Churchill visited Moscow to discuss with **Marshal Stalin** the opening of a **second front** in Europe.

1943, May 12. Churchill and Roosevelt conferred in Washington on the problem of opening a **second front in Europe.** These discussions of Allied war aims and Allied strategy were resumed at the

Aug. 11–24. QUEBEC CONFERENCE (p. 1147), followed by the

Nov. 28–Dec. 1. TEHRAN CONFERENCE (p. 1157), the

1945, Feb. 7–12. CRIMEA (OR YALTA) CONFERENCE (p. 1151), and the

July 17–Aug. 2. POTSDAM CONFERENCE (p. 1157).

July 26. The **British Labour Party** won 388 seats out of 640 in a **national election** of July 5. A **Labour cabinet,** with **Clement R. Attlee** as prime minister. Attlee replaced Churchill for the later sessions of the Potsdam conference. The new government immediately embarked on an ambitious **program of socialization,** the ultimate aim of which was to make Britain a socialist state. A brief period of post-war optimism was followed by an extended régime of **economic austerity,** due chiefly to the profound dislocation of Britain's economy as a result of the war. To facilitate reconversion to peace-time production, demobilization of manpower and industry was carried out only gradually. On

Oct. 15. The house of commons voted to extend the government's **wartime emergency powers** for five years. To make up for the **cessation of lend-lease,** which came as a deep shock to Britain's economy,

Dec. 6. The **United States** granted a **loan** of $3.75 billion to Great Britain. **Canada** subsequently provided a loan of $1.25 billion. Both these loans became exhausted, however, by the end of 1947, due to high prices on the American market.

1946, Feb. 13. Parliament repealed the **Trades Disputes Act of 1927,** which had made certain strikes illegal and had hampered the political activities of labor unions.

Feb. 14. The **Bank of England** was brought under public ownership.

May–July. In a burst of socialist legislation, parliament passed a bill providing for the **nationalization of the coal industry,** a **National Insurance Bill** (consolidating existing schemes of social insurance and extending them to a larger section of the population), a **National Health Service Bill** (to make free medical services available to everyone) and a **Cable and Wireless Act,** nationalizing imperial communications.

July 21. Britain's export difficulties and the world shortage of wheat combined to necessitate **bread rationing.** This was followed by restrictions on most other staple foods.

Oct. 30. Parliament approved the coordination of the three armed services under a **defense committee,** headed by a minister of defense **(Albert V. Alexander).**

1947, Jan. 1. The **nationalization of the coal mines** went into effect.

Jan.–Apr. A serious **coal shortage,** made worse by severe weather conditions, led to drastic **fuel restrictions** and curtailment of industrial production. At the same time, parliament continued its socialization program by adopting the **Transport Act,** affecting railroads, road transport, and inland waterways, the **Electricity Act,** nationalizing the electricity supply industry, and the **Town and Country Planning Act,** which set up a new planning system to regulate the growth of communities.

Mar. 4. An **Anglo-French treaty of alliance** was signed at Dunkirk.

Nov. 20. **Princess Elizabeth** and **Philip Mountbatten,** duke of Edinburgh, were married in Westminster Abbey.

1948, Jan. 1. The British railways passed into public ownership.

Mar. 17. A 50-year **treaty of mutual assistance** between **Britain, France, Belgium,** the **Netherlands,** and **Luxemburg** was signed at Brussels.

Apr. 1. The **British Electrical Authority** took over the electricity industry.

July 30. The **British Nationality Act** received royal assent. It gave each Dominion the right to determine who were its citizens, while at the same time conferring the status of British subjects upon all citizens of the Commonwealth.

Dec. The **National Service Act** conscripted all men between the ages of eighteen and twenty-six.

1949, Feb. 1. Rationing of clothing was discontinued, while meat, dairy products, and sugar continued to be on the list of restricted items.

June–July. A major **dock strike,** which, according to the government, was Communist-inspired, led to the proclamation of a state of emergency before it was finally settled.

Sept. 18. To meet the rapid decline of British exports and to remedy the growing dollar deficit, the **British government devalued the pound sterling** from $4.03 to $2.80. This set in motion a widespread devaluation of other European currencies.

Nov. 24. The **Iron and Steel Bill,** calling for the nationalization of these key industries, passed both houses of parliament, after raising considerable opposition. It was not to go into effect until 1951.

Dec. 16. Despite opposition from the house of lords, the **Parliament Bill,** restricting the powers of the upper house to veto legislation, was enacted into law.

1950, Feb. 13. PARLIAMENTARY ELECTIONS reduced the Labour Party's majority from 148 in 1945 to 7 in 1950. The final count gave Labour 315 seats, the Conservatives and their allies 297, and the Liberals 9. The government of Prime Minister **Clement Attlee** remained in office, although its position was precarious. As a result, few controversial measures were introduced into parliament.

June 25. The outbreak of **war in Korea** found Great Britain on the side of the United States and the United Nations against the North Korean aggressors. It subsequently contributed naval and ground forces to the United Nations cause and embarked on increased defense production and expansion of the armed services.

Nov. 28. The **Columbo plan** to aid India, Pakistan, Ceylon, Sarawak, and Borneo was presented to the British Commonwealth parliaments; it envisaged an eight billion pounds economic program over six years from July 1, 1951.

Dec. 13. The **Marshall Plan aid to the United Kingdom,** it was announced, would be **suspended** on January 1, 1951.

1951, Jan. 29. Prime Minister Attlee announced a **three-year armament program** costing 4.7 billion pounds.

Mar. 9. **Herbert Morrison** succeeded **Ernest Bevin** as foreign secretary.

Apr. 22. **Aneurin Bevan,** Labour minister since January 17, resigned in protest against a decision to give defense priority over social service needs.

June 26. Defense ministers of the British Commonwealth discussed the **situation in the Middle East.** The Egyptian foreign minister announced (Aug. 6) that the **Anglo-Egyptian treaty of 1936 would be abrogated.** Formal abrogation followed October 27.

Sept. 12. After the failure of earlier discussions (Aug. 22) the **Iranian government sent an ultimatum to Great Britain** and subsequently (Sept. 27) **occupied Abadan.** The British appealed to the United Nations security council without result and then completed the evacuation of Abadan (Oct. 4).

Oct. 25. The **Labour Party was defeated** in a general election and the **Conservatives** won a majority of sixteen seats in the house of commons. **WINSTON CHURCHILL BECAME PRIME MINISTER** and minister of defense (Oct. 27), with **Anthony Eden as foreign secretary** and **Richard Austen Butler** as chancellor of the exchequer.

Dec. 10. The government of **Iran** agreed to submit its oil dispute with Britain to the **International Court of Justice.**

1952, Feb. 6. **KING GEORGE VI DIED.** His daughter **Elizabeth,** who was on a visit to East Africa, flew back to take the oath as **QUEEN ELIZABETH II** (Feb. 8).

Feb. 26. **Churchill** announced that the British had produced an **atom bomb.** It was tested successfully in the Monte Bello Islands near Australia on October 2.

Apr. 15. The government announced Great Britain's willingness to agree to **a mutual defense treaty** with the **European Defense Community.**

1953, Jan. 5–9. On a visit to Washington and New York, **Churchill** conferred with **President Truman** and **President-elect Eisenhower** on European defense, the Korean war, and Anglo-American relations. Two months later (Mar. 4–7) **Foreign Secretary Eden** visited Washington to discuss United States **air bases** in Britain, British relations with **Iran,** and other problems.

June 2. **Coronation of Elizabeth II.**

Dec. 5. The governments of **Great Britain** and **Iran** announced that they would renew diplomatic relations and seek a negotiated settlement of their **dispute over Iranian oil.**

Dec. 4–7. **Prime Minister Churchill, President Eisenhower,** and **Premier Joseph Laniel** of France met in Bermuda to discuss the **relations of the Big Three with Soviet Russia,** the problem of Germany and Austria, and the defense of the free world.

1954, Apr. 13. **Great Britain** completed an agreement to associate itself with the **European Defense Community.**

July 28. The **British government offered**

Cyprus **limited self-government** but refused to consider a change in its sovereignty.

Dec. 21. An agreement signed in London defined **Great Britain's relations with the European Coal and Steel Community.**

1955, Apr. 5. **CHURCHILL RESIGNED** for reasons of age and health, and **Anthony Eden** succeeded him.

May 26. A national election returned the **Conservative government** to power with **a majority of 67** seats in the house of commons.

June 15. **Great Britain and the United States** concluded an accord in Washington to co-operate in **the peaceful use of nuclear power.**

Dec. 7. **Hugh Gaitskell** replaced **Clement R. Attlee** as leader of the **Labour Party.**

1956, July 26. President **Gamal Abdel Nasser** of Egypt announced that the **Suez Canal would be "nationalized."** This threat to British communications with the East produced a critical situation in which the cabinet considered **military intervention.**

Oct. 30. Following the **Israeli attack on Egypt** (Oct. 29), **Britain and France intervened,** but on November 6 accepted the U.N. general assembly order to cease fire (p. 1282).

1957, Jan. 9. Discredited by the failure of his policy in the Suez Canal crisis, **Eden resigned** and was replaced by **Harold Macmillan** (Jan. 10).

Mar. 21–24. To mend the strain in Anglo-American relations that resulted from the Suez debacle and other disagreements, Prime Minister Macmillan and Foreign Secretary Selwyn Lloyd conferred with President Eisenhower and Secretary Dulles in Bermuda. The British announced their intention to reduce their armed forces and to rely on a higher measure of mechanization. The United States promised to supply them with intermediate-range guided missiles.

Apr. 11. By an **agreement with Singapore,** the latter was to attain internal self-government on January 1, 1958.

May 15. British scientists exploded a **hydrogen bomb** at Christmas Island in the Pacific Ocean. Further tests were carried out on May 31 and June 19, and in Australia from September 14 to October 9.

Oct. 17–20. Queen Elizabeth II and her husband paid a state visit to Washington.

Oct. 23–25. Macmillan and Lloyd visited Washington to discuss the new situation created by the Russian success in orbiting a manned space vehicle, Sputnik I. The conference closed with a "Declaration of Common Purpose."

1958, Feb. 22. The United States agreed to supply Britain with 60 "Thor" missiles carrying atomic warheads.

Aug. 4. An agreement for Anglo-American **co-operation on nuclear defense** projects went into effect.

1959, Jan. 17. Britain and Egypt agreed on a **settlement of the financial problems arising from the Egyptian seizure of the Suez Canal** in 1956.

Feb. 19. An agreement, signed in London, provided for the **independence of Cyprus** (p. 1296).

Feb. 21–Mar. 3. Macmillan conferred with Khrushchev in Moscow but failed to reach any definite agreement. Subsequent discussions at Washington (Mar. 19 and 22) likewise failed to achieve a significant Anglo-American accord.

May 24. An **Anglo-Russian trade agreement** to last five years was signed in Moscow.

June 3. A **new constitution for Singapore** ended its status as a crown colony.

1960, Mar. 28–30. Macmillan visited Washington to urge a modification in the American position on limiting nuclear tests. In a joint declaration, Macmillan and Eisenhower announced their willingness to proclaim a joint moratorium on smaller tests as soon as a treaty had been concluded that outlawed larger tests.

July 27. In a cabinet reorganization, Lord Home was named foreign secretary, succeeding Selwyn Lloyd, who became chancellor of the exchequer.

Sept. 25–Oct. 5. Macmillan, after attending the United Nations general assembly and consulting with President Eisenhower, returned with somewhat indefinite assurances that the British **demand for prior consultation** would be respected.

Nov. 1. Macmillan announced that Britain had agreed to allow the United States to use Holy Loch on the Firth of Clyde as a base for nuclear-powered and nuclear-armed submarines.

Nov. 4. Hugh Gaitskell retained his leadership of the Labour Party over an opposition which favored unilateral nuclear disarmament.

1961, Feb. 2. Forty thousand persons petitioned parliament protesting British possession of nuclear weapons.

Mar. 15. At the **Commonwealth conference in London,** South Africa withdrew its application for readmission to the Commonwealth when it became a republic on May 31, 1961.

July 25. Selwyn Lloyd, chancellor of the exchequer, introduced his **"austerity" program** to combat excess of imports over exports.

Aug. 10. The British government formally applied **for membership in the Common Market** after the house of commons, by a vote of 313–5 (Aug. 3), had approved the move.

Sept. 26. Secretary of state for Common- wealth relations Duncan Sandys declared a the Commonwealth parliamentary conference that if "vital Commonwealth interests" were not safeguarded, Britain would not accep membership in the Common Market.

1962, Apr. 10. Edward Heath, leading Britain's negotiations on the Common Market declared that Britain planned to play its "ful part" in the political as well as economic future of the Common Market.

Aug. 16. An agreement was reached to merge Aden with the **Federation of South Arabia** no later than March 1963.

Sept. 11–12. The prime ministers of Australia, New Zealand, Canada, Nigeria, and Tanganyika expressed **opposition to British membership in the Common Market,** at the 15-nation Commonwealth conference.

Dec. 21. Prime Minister Macmillan and President Kennedy, at the end of a four-day meeting in the Bahamas, announced plans to replace Britain's Skybolt missiles project with U.S. Polaris missiles.

1963, Jan. 29. Entry into the Common Market was vetoed by France at a Brussels meeting of the EEC.

Feb. 14. The British Labour Party elected Harold Wilson as leader, succeeding Hugh Gaitskell, who had died on January 18.

May 20. In London, a communiqué issued at the end of constitutional discussions promised internal **self-government for the Bahamas** early in 1964 if possible.

June 5. **John Profumo** resigned as secretary for war, after admitting that he lied (Mar. 22) in his denial of any impropriety with Christine Keeler.

July 31. The bill permitting peers to disclaim their titles and relinquish membership in the house of lords went into effect.

Oct. 19. **PRIME MINISTER MAC-MILLAN RESIGNED** because of ill health. **Sir Alec Douglas-Home** (formerly the earl of Home) was named to succeed him.

1964, Jan. 24. The government declared its readiness to go to war if necessary to uphold its **commitments to Malaysia** (p. 1321).

Feb. 6. Anglo-French agreement was reached for the construction of a railroad **tunnel under the English Channel.**

Feb. 13. In a white paper, the government reported its decision to maintain an independent nuclear deterrent, and announced a record peace-time $5.5 billion defense budget.

Apr. 1. The government created a new **ministry of education and science** to replace previous separate ministries.

Oct. 15. In the elections the **Labour Party** won a four-seat majority in the house. **Harold Wilson** formed a new cabinet.

Nov. 19. Establishment of a **secretary of state for Wales.**

Dec. 7–8. Visit of Prime Minister Wilson to Washington for general discussions of European and world problems.

1965, Jan. 24. Death of Sir Winston Churchill after a stroke. Impressive state funeral Jan. 30.

May 6. Decision of the Labour government to nationalize 85% to 90% of the **steel industry.**

June 17–25. An important **meeting of Commonwealth prime ministers,** among whom African and Asian statesmen had by now become a majority. The conference decided at long last to set up a **Commonwealth secretariat.** It approved in principle a Commonwealth **peace mission to Vietnam** (which never materialized). There was extended discussion of the **problem of Rhodesian independence** and general approval of the British position that independence should be granted only under guarantees of future constitutional development toward majority rule.

July 28. Edward Heath elected leader of the Conservative Party in succession to Sir Alec Douglas-Home (resigned July 22).

1966, Feb. 21–24. Visit of Prime Minister Wilson to Moscow in a futile effort to enlist Soviet aid in bringing about peace in Vietnam.

Feb. 22. Economy measures of the Labour government: reduction of defense expenditures; resignation of the secretary for the navy and the first sea lord in protest against the decision to abandon aircraft carriers as the main strike force and to put future emphasis on shore-based F-111A planes, to be purchased from the United States.

Mar. 23. Visit of the archbishop of Canterbury, Arthur M. Ramsey, **to Pope Paul VI:** agreement on efforts to bring the Anglican and Roman Catholic churches together.

Mar. 31. The **elections** greatly strengthened the position of the Labour Party, which thenceforth had a majority of 97 in the house and was freer to embark on economic planning and the development of social services.

May 16–July 1. Strike of the National Union of Seamen, the most serious labor dispute since 1926. The government declared a state of emergency (May 23), but finally agreed to a compromise settlement.

July 1. Introduction of a **freeze on wages, salaries, and prices** for one year in the effort to check inflation and improve the balance of payments situation.

July 6–8. Conference of Prime Minister Wilson and French Premier Pompidou: decision to proceed with construction of the **Channel tunnel** and to collaborate in the design and development of a **supersonic airliner,** the Concorde.

July 14. A **Welsh nationalist** for the first time defeated all other candidates in a by-election, a reflection of the growing spirit of nationalism in both Wales and Scotland.

July 16–18. Second visit of Wilson to Moscow, equally unsuccessful. Growing pressure in the United Kingdom to abandon support of the U.S. in the Vietnamese war.

July 31. Abolition of the Colonial Office, whose responsibilities for the remaining dependencies were to be taken over by the Commonwealth Office.

Sept. 6–15. A **conference of Commonwealth prime ministers** agreed to wait another year before submitting the Rhodesian issue to the U.N. (p. 1275).

Oct. 5. The **Gibraltar issue** became acute when the Spanish government closed the customs facilities at La Linea and rejected the British offer to submit the question of sovereignty to the International Court of Justice (Dec. 14).

1967, Feb. 6–13. Soviet Premier Kosygin's visit to Britain. Despite discussions of a possible British-Soviet treaty of friendship and cooperation, the Soviet statesman still refused to support a move to promote peace in Vietnam.

Apr. 10–15. The Conservatives won a large majority of the seats on the Great London Council, reflecting rapidly developing dissatisfaction with the Labour Party.

May 11. Formal application of the British government for membership in the European Common Market again vetoed by President de Gaulle (May 16).

Nov. 18. Devaluation of the pound sterling, from $2.80 to $2.40, in the hope of checking the decline in balance of payments.

1968. Continuance of **economic stringency,** and consequently of austerity measures.

Jan. Government **plans for progressive withdrawal of military forces** and liquidation of commitments everywhere **east of Suez** by the end of 1971. Profound uneasiness in the Commonwealth and the U.S.

Apr. 23. The **Race Relations Bill,** prohibiting discrimination in employment, housing, etc., on the basis of color, race, or national origin. Growing popular resentment at the **influx of Asians, Africans, and Caribbeans,** with resulting protests and demonstrations.

Mar. 1. Drastic **restriction of immigration** of Asians holding British citizenship—applying chiefly to Kenyan businessmen who were being expelled by the Kenyan government and were arriving in Britain by the thousands (p. 1280).

Oct. 5. Growing **crisis in Northern Ireland,** marked by civil rights riots in Londonderry, where the Catholic majority claimed rank discrimination of the Protestant-controlled local government in matters of employment, housing, etc. Tension had been rising since the summer of 1966 when the **Reverend Ian Paisley** and his ultra-Protestant **"Free Presbyterian Church"** had denounced any concessions to Roman Catholics and had staged a riot in Belfast.

Oct. 16. The **Commonwealth Office** was merged with the Foreign Office to form the new **Foreign and Commonwealth Office.**

Oct. 27. Proliferation of **student demonstrations** and disorders, directed mostly against antiquated university requirements and practices, but also against war and support of United States policy in Vietnam.

Nov. 22. The Belfast government's program of moderate reforms again aroused the opposition of Paisley and his extremists.

1969, Jan. 7–15. Meeting of Commonwealth prime ministers in London: sharp discussions of British immigration restrictions, as well as of the Rhodesian and Nigerian situations (pp. 1275, 1268).

Jan. 17. A new **Trade Union Bill,** designed to check wildcat striking. The government proposed a Permanent Commission on Industrial Relations, but after long and acrimonious discussions yielded to the pressure from the trade unions and (June 18) abandoned the bill in return for a promise of the Trade Union General Council to set up machinery to forestall and control strikes.

Feb. 27. Northern Ireland. Victory of the Unionists, but with a heavy vote for Reverend Paisley and the Protestant extremists.

Apr. 20. Major **religious conflicts in Belfast and Londonderry,** following the election to parliament of **Bernadette Devlin,** fiery twenty-two-year-old Catholic leader. On the request of the Belfast government the British government decided to send troops to help guard key utilities.

Apr. 23. The Northern Ireland government accepted the demand for universal adult suffrage in local elections, thus breaking the power of Protestant minorities in some localities.

Apr. 28. Resignation of Prime Minister O'Neill of Northern Ireland, who was succeeded (May 1) by **Major James Chichester-Clark.**

Aug. 2–4. Northern Ireland: huge **riots in Belfast,** followed by similar disturbances in Londonderry and other towns. Further British troops sent (Aug. 12–16).

Aug. 18. Conferences between British Prime Minister Wilson and Major Chichester-Clark. It was decided that a British commander should take over control of security and that the largely Protestant part-time security forces should be phased out. The British government was to

have a voice in Northern Ireland's affairs and press for further reforms.

Dec. 18. The British parliament voted the permanent **abolition of the death penalty.**

Dec. 22. Miss Devlin was convicted of incitement to riot and sentenced to six months in prison.

1970, Jan. 18. DEFEAT OF THE LABOUR PARTY in the elections. The Conservatives won a majority of 30 in the house of commons, and **Edward Heath became prime minister,** with Sir Alec Douglas-Home as foreign secretary.

June 26–28. Northern Ireland: further violent outbreaks between Protestants and Catholics, resulting in the dispatch of yet further British forces. These disturbances, frequently involving loss of life as well as widespread destruction of property, continued spasmodically to the end of the period.

b. IRELAND (EIRE)

(From p. 985)

1939, Sept. 3. The **republic of Ireland (Eire) remained neutral** throughout the Second World War and refused Great Britain the use of its ports and airfields for naval and military purposes.

1944, Mar. 11. Eamon de Valera, prime minister, declined a request from the United States government that he **close the German and Japanese ministries** in Dublin to curb the possible transmission of military intelligence by Axis agents. Great Britain **suspended all travel** between the United Kingdom and Ireland (Mar. 13), and limited the privileges of foreign diplomats except those of Soviet Russia and the United States (Apr. 19).

1945, May 3. De Valera expressed official condolences to the German minister in Dublin upon Hitler's death.

June 4. Elections in Northern Ireland favored continued Irish partition.

June 25. Douglas Hyde retired and **SEAN T. O'KELLY BECAME SECOND PRESIDENT OF EIRE.**

1948, Feb. 4. In a **general election** de Valera's **Fianna Fail Party lost its majority.**

Feb. 18. James A. Costello of the Fianna Gael Party was nominated prime minister.

Dec. 21. President O'Kelly signed the **Republic of Ireland Bill** calling for complete independence of Ireland at an early date.

1949, Feb. 8. The Irish government declared that participation in the **North Atlantic pact** was impossible so long as Ireland remained divided.

Feb. 10. Elections in Northern Ireland

showed that at least two-thirds of the population favored continued union with Great Britain.

Apr. 18. The **REPUBLIC OF IRELAND** was officially proclaimed in Dublin on the anniversary of the Easter Rebellion of 1916. King George VI sent his good wishes.

May 17. The British house of commons adopted the **Ireland Bill,** recognizing the independence of the republic, but affirming the position of Northern Ireland within the United Kingdom. This provision met with protest from the republic of Ireland.

1950, Jan. 26. Ireland concluded a **treaty of friendship, commerce, and navigation** with the **United States.**

1951, May 4. The cabinet headed by **James A. Costello** resigned. An election (May 30) gave a majority to the **Fianna Fail Party** and a new cabinet with **Eamon de Valera** as prime minister took office on June 13.

1954, May 18. After de Valera's defeat in national elections, Costello formed a coalition government.

1955, Dec. 14. The **admission of Ireland to the United Nations.**

1959, June 17. **Eamon de Valera** was elected **president of Ireland** and resigned the post of prime minister.

June 23. Deputy Prime Minister **Sean Lemass** was elected prime minister by the **dail** (parliament).

1960, Sept. 20. **Frederick H. Boland,** the representative from Ireland, was elected president of the fifteenth session of the general assembly of the United Nations.

1961, Oct. 11. The new parliament (chosen on October 4) elected **Sean Lemass prime minister.**

1965, Jan. 14. **Meeting of the prime ministers of Northern Ireland and the Irish Republic** at Belfast and later (Feb. 9) at Dublin. Efforts of the two governments to improve relations at least in the economic and cultural spheres.

Mar. 1. **State funeral of Sir Roger Casement** (executed in 1916 for participation in the Easter Rebellion). His remains were returned by the British government.

1967, Dec. 11. **Visit of Prime Minister John Lynch to Northern Ireland:** further discussions on trade, tourism, etc. The visit was returned (Jan. 1968) by Prime Minister Terence O'Neill of Northern Ireland.

1970, Oct. 23. **Charles Haughey,** former finance minister of the Irish Republic, was acquitted of secret dealings to supply arms to the Catholics of Northern Ireland. Haughey was an outspoken opponent of Prime Minister Lynch and of the policy of peaceful rapprochement between the two Irelands.

Dec. 4. The Irish government threatened to invoke the **Offenses against the State Act** if necessary to forestall plans of radicals and nationalist extremists to assassinate or kidnap officials to force the reunion of the two Irelands. The activities of the outlawed **Irish Republican Army** in Northern Ireland were hardly more than an open secret.

3. THE LOW COUNTRIES

a. BELGIUM

(*From p. 986*)

1940, May 10. **GERMAN ARMIES INVADED BELGIUM** (p. 1136).

May 28. **Leopold III** ordered the Belgian forces to **cease fighting.** Leaders of the Belgian government on French territory declared **Leopold deposed.**

1944, Sept. 2. **Brussels was liberated** from German occupation by the 2nd British Army.

Belgium, after its liberation, was governed by coalitions of the main political parties, with **Prince Charles** as regent. Its major domestic issue was the return of **King Leopold,** which the Catholics favored and the Socialists opposed. On July 17, 1945, parliament passed a bill making Leopold's return dependent upon parliamentary approval.

1946, Feb. 17. A **general election** gave the Catholic **Christian Socialists** the largest number of votes; but continued disagreement over the future of the monarchy prevented the formation of a coalition cabinet.

1947, Mar. 19. **Paul-Henri Spaak** was able to form a coalition government of Catholics and Socialists, thus assuring greater stability in the handling of pressing economic problems.

Nov. 1. A **customs union** with Holland and Luxemburg (**Benelux**) became effective.

1949, June 26. In a **general election** the Christian Socialists came within two seats of an absolute majority.

Aug. 10. **Gaston Eyskens** (Christian Socialist) formed a coalition cabinet with Liberal support. The Socialists refused to join.

1950, Mar. 12. A **popular referendum** voted 57.7 per cent in favor of King Leopold's return.

June 4. **General elections** gave the Catholics an absolute majority, thus upholding the verdict of the referendum.

June 8. The first all-Catholic government in 30 years was formed by **Jean Duvieusart.**

July 22. KING LEOPOLD RETURNED after six years of exile, greeted by violent protests from the Left, notably the Socialists. To avoid violence, Leopold decided to abdicate when his son, **Prince Baudouin,** came of age in September 1951.

Aug. 11. **Prince Baudouin** was invested with the royal powers as prince royal.

Aug. 18. **Julien Lahaut,** head of the Communist Party, was **assassinated.**

1951, July 16. LEOPOLD III ABDICATED and his son **Baudouin** became king the following day.

1952, Jan. 9. **Premier Joseph Pholien** resigned and a new cabinet, likewise **Christian Socialist** in composition, was formed (Jan. 15) under **Jean van Houtte.**

1954, Apr. 23. After an indecisive election (Apr. 11) a Socialist-Liberal coalition cabinet took office with **Achille van Acker.**

1958, Feb. 3. A **50-year treaty,** signed at The Hague, united Belgium, the Netherlands, and Luxemburg in a **Benelux Economic Union.** The Union came into force November 1, 1960.

June 1. The Christian Socialist Party won 104 out of 212 seats in the chamber of deputies and a senate majority. **Gaston Eyskens** established a minority government (June 2) and a stronger Social-Liberal government November 6.

1959, Jan. 13. **Premier Eyskens** and **King Baudouin** both announced that the **Belgian Congo** would be granted **independence** but no date was set for this.

1960, Mar. 16. Parliament approved a bill for a general election in the Congo to be held prior to independence on June 30.

Sept. 2. **Premier Eyskens** organized a new coalition cabinet to deal with the **crisis in the Congo.** The Belgian Congo, granted independence too precipitately the previous June, had been plunged into disorder (p. 1269).

Dec. 15. King Baudouin and Dona Fabiola de Mora y Aragon of Spain were married.

Dec. 20. **Socialist-led strikes** broke out to protest the government's austerity program. **1961, Feb. 17.** **Liberal members** of the coalition

government of Premier Eyskens **resigned** in disagreement over the application of a new economic reform measure. King Baudouin, on February 20, refused to accept their resignation, but dissolved parliament and scheduled new elections, March 26. Premier Eyskens resigned (Mar. 27) and on April 25 **Theo Lefevre,** president of the Christian Social Party, was installed as premier and Paul-Henri Spaak as vice-premier and foreign minister.

1962, Oct. 14. **Demonstrations by Flemish-speaking Belgians,** to protest the denial of their cultural and political equality by the French-speaking (Walloon) community, and to demand that Dutch replace French as the language of business.

1963, July 3. King Baudouin rejected Premier Lefevre's resignation, offered on July 2, following a **renewed outbreak of the Flemish-Walloon** language dispute.

On July 6 Lefevre announced a settlement of the dispute and, on July 12, the lower house of parliament approved a **new boundary line between the Walloon and Flemish areas,** to take effect September 1.

1964, Apr. 1–18. **Physicians went on strike** protesting a new national health insurance law which established a fixed low fee schedule.

Renewed agitation for the reorganization of Belgium as a federal state. Conferences of the government with representatives of both nationalities broke down over the demand of the Walloon minority for a veto over any future legislation in the field of nationality.

1966, July 11. **Language riots,** focusing on the insistence of the Flemings that the Walloon section of the **University of Louvain** be moved to some location on Wallonia.

1968, Feb. 7. **Resignation of the Vanden Boeyants** government over continued agitation on the issue of Louvain University.

Mar. 31. In the **national elections** the traditional parties managed to hold their own against the extremist groups, the Flemish **Volksunie** and the **Rassemblement Walloon.**

June 18. A **new coalition** of Center-Left parties was formed by **Gaston Eyskens,** who embarked upon a program of expanded regional autonomy, especially in cultural matters, between the Flemish and the Walloon areas. The new government was committed also to a gradual division of the University of Louvain between the two nationalist factions.

b. THE KINGDOM OF THE NETHERLANDS

(*From p. 987*)

1940, May 10. GERMAN ARMED FORCES INVADED THE NETHERLANDS (p. 1136).

1941, Aug. 18. The **German commission** in the Netherlands **suppressed all representative bodies** in the country.

1942, June 17. A consultative board for the affairs of the **Netherlands East Indies** was set up at London to assist the minister for the colonies of the Netherlands government in exile.

The damage suffered by the Netherlands during the war was especially heavy, and large-scale famine was averted only by Allied aid.

1945, May 3. QUEEN WILHELMINA RETURNED.

June 24. Willem Schermerhorn formed a coalition government.

1946, May 17–30. Parliamentary elections gave first place to the Catholic People's Party, with Socialist Labor running a close second. **Louis J. M. Beel** formed a new coalition cabinet.

1948, Mar. 17. Signing of the **treaty of Brussels** between Great Britain, France, and the Benelux countries (p. 1172).

July 7–8. General elections lost the government some support and a new coalition was formed under Labor's leader, **Willem Drees.**

Sept. 4. Queen Wilhelmina abdicated for reasons of health and was succeeded on September 6 by **QUEEN JULIANA.**

1949, Aug. 3. Holland's upper chamber ratified the **North Atlantic treaty.**

Dec. 27. Formal transfer of sovereignty to the **United States of Indonesia** (p. 1335).

1951, Jan. 24. A proposal offered by Foreign Minister **Dirk Stikker** that the Netherlands share **Western New Guinea** with the republic of Indonesia brought on a prolonged cabinet crisis (Mar. 14).

Oct. 31. A treaty creating the **European Coal and Steel Community** was accepted by the lower chamber of the Netherlands parliament.

1952, June 25–26. Elections for parliament gave the **Labor Party** and the **Catholic Party** equal strength in the second chamber.

Sept. 1. Willem Drees of the Labor Party formed a coalition cabinet.

1953, July 23. The **European Defense Community** treaty was approved by the second chamber of the Netherlands parliament, 75 to 11.

1954, Aug. 10. THE UNION OF THE NETHERLANDS AND INDONESIA WAS DISSOLVED.

Dec. 15. Surinam and the **Netherlands Antilles won autonomy** in a statute signed by Queen Juliana.

1956, June 13. The **Labor Party** won a small margin in the second chamber in a general election.

After the longest cabinet crisis in Netherlands history Willem Drees of the Labor Party formed **a new coalition cabinet.**

1957, Dec. 1. Netherlands citizens in Indonesia and property owned by Netherlands nationals there suffered because of **Indonesian indignation** over the status of **Netherlands New Guinea,** which the Dutch refused to surrender.

1958, Dec. 11. The coalition cabinet headed by Willem Drees resigned and was succeeded (Dec. 22) by a coalition cabinet under the leadership of **Louis J. M. Beel** of the People's Party.

1959, May 19. The 68-day government crisis ended with the swearing in of **Jan Eduard de Quay,** the new premier, and his coalition cabinet. For the first time since World War II, the Labor (Socialist) Party was excluded from the government.

1961, Jan. 2. A 12-day cabinet crisis ended when Premier Jan de Quay withdrew his resignation after Queen Juliana asked him to remain in office.

1962, Nov. 28. Queen Wilhelmina died at the age of 82.

1963, May 15. Premier de Quay's **Catholic People's Party** won the general elections to parliament with 50 seats in the 150-member lower house. The Labor Party won 43 seats, the Protestants 26, and the Liberals 11.

May 20, Queen Juliana asked Catholic party member, **Carl P. M. Romme** to form a coalition government.

1964, Apr. 29. Marriage of Princess Irene and Prince Carlos Hugo of Bourbon-Parma in the Basilica of St. Mary Major in Rome.

1966, June 13–15. The Netherlands, like many other countries, was confronted with serious **youth demonstrations and riots.**

1967, Feb. 15. General elections.

Apr. 5. Petrus de Jong, of the Catholic party, formed a new government.

c. LUXEMBURG

1940, May 10. GERMAN ARMED FORCES TOOK POSSESSION OF LUXEMBURG (p. 1136).

1942, Aug. 30. The German gauleiter announced the **annexation of Luxemburg to the German Reich,** and the introduction of military conscription. Luxemburg workers responded with a **general strike;** a number were shot and others deported.

1948, Jan. 1. After suffering German occupation in two world wars, the **grand duchy of Luxemburg** abandoned its policy of unarmed neutrality and joined in a **customs union with Belgium and the Netherlands.** Ten years later (Feb. 3, 1958) the accord was expanded into the **Benelux Economic Union.**

1952, July 2. **Pierre Dupong** organized a new cabinet. On his death

1953, Dec. 22, his place was taken by **Joseph Bech** (Christian Social Party).

1954, May 30. The Christian Social Party won 26 seats and the Socialist parties 17 seats in the 52-member chamber of deputies. **Bech remained in power** as head of a new coalition cabinet that took office on June 29.

1958, Mar. 26. **Bech** resigned with his cabinet but became foreign minister in a new cabinet headed by **Pierre Frieden,** also of the Christian Social Party. The Frieden government resigned December 10.

Dec. 18. **Grand Duchess Charlotte** dissolved parliament and scheduled elections for

1959, Feb. 1. After the elections, **Pierre Werner** became premier.

1964, Nov. 12. **ABDICATION OF GRAND DUCHESS CHARLOTTE** in favor of her son, who ascended the throne as **Grand Duke Jean.**

1964–1968, Oct. Pierre Werner continued as prime minister supported by a coalition of the Christian and Socialist parties.

1968, Dec. 15. Following the elections Werner retained the premiership, but with a coalition of Christian and Democratic parties.

4. FRANCE

(From p. 991)

1939, Sept. 3. **FRANCE AND BRITAIN DECLARED WAR ON GERMANY.**

1940, Mar. 20. **Édouard Daladier resigned** and **Paul Reynaud** formed a new French cabinet.

May 10. **GERMAN FORCES INVADED THE NETHERLANDS, BELGIUM, AND LUXEMBURG and** (May 12) **crossed the Meuse at Sedan, opening the battle of France** (p. 1136).

June 10. **ITALY DECLARED WAR ON FRANCE AND BRITAIN.**

June 14. **German forces occupied Paris.** The French government moved to Tours and then to Bordeaux.

June 16. **Marshal Henri-Philippe Pétain replaced Paul Reynaud** as head of the government and sued **for peace** (June 17).

June 22. **FRANCE AND GERMANY CONCLUDED AN ARMISTICE.**

July 5. The **French government of Marshal Pétain,** now established at Vichy, **severed relations with Great Britain.** Despite assurances from the Pétain régime (June 18) to the United States that the Germans would never obtain the French fleet, the British had attacked French naval vessels at Oran on July 3.

July 9. The **French legislature** voted to establish an **authoritarian government,** granting Marshal Pétain almost dictatorial powers.

Oct. 27. **Gen. Charles de Gaulle,** who had escaped to Britain on the fall of France, **formed a free government** for France in exile.

Dec. 14. **Marshal Pétain excluded Pierre Laval** from the French council of ministers. Laval favored a closer working arrangement between Vichy and Berlin.

1941, Oct. 21. The **assassination** of a German officer at Nantes was punished by the execution of **fifty French hostages.**

Dec. 23. **Free French forces** took possession of **St. Pierre and Miquelon,** small islands off the coast of Newfoundland, which had been administered by officials loyal to the Vichy government of France.

1942, Apr. 14. **Marshal Pétain reinstated Laval** under German pressure.

Sept. 14. The Vichy government decreed **compulsory labor** for men between 18 and 65 and for unmarried women between 20 and 35. This move was regarded in France as an enforcement of German demands for labor collaboration.

Nov. 11. In retaliation for the Anglo-American invasion of French North Africa, **German forces moved into the hitherto unoccupied portions of France.** At Toulon, where most of the surviving ships of the French navy were stationed, the **ships were sunk by their crews** (Nov. 27) to prevent German efforts to seize them.

Nov. 17. **Marshal Pétain appointed Laval** his successor and assigned him the power to make laws and issue decrees. This step reflected the increased German control over the Vichy régime.

Dec. 1. **Adm. Jean-François Darlan** assumed authority as **chief of state in French North Africa,** with the approval of the British and United States governments. He was assassinated three weeks later (Dec. 24).

1943, Mar. 15. **Gen. Henri Giraud,** successor to Darlan as head of the French government in North Africa, declared that legislation passed there since 1940 was without effect, restored representative government, and promised that France itself would regain the right of self-determination after victory.

June 4. A **Committee of National Liberation** was formed, including both **Gen. Charles de Gaulle** and **Gen. Henri Giraud.** The committee pledged itself to support the Allied nations in their war against the Axis.

Nov. 11. In **Lebanon** French authorities arrested the president, **Sheikh Bishara al-Khoury,** and his ministers, after the Lebanese chamber of deputies had proclaimed the **independence of the Lebanese republic** (p. 1300).
1944, June 6. **INVASION OF NORMANDY BY ALLIED EXPEDITIONARY FORCES. The liberation of France had commenced** (p. 1150).

July 11. The **United States recognized the French Committee of National Liberation,** headed by **de Gaulle,** as the *de facto* civil government of France in the liberated areas of that country. **Gen. Dwight D. Eisenhower** warned the German government that French "underground" forces aiding in the fight to liberate their country were to be regarded as combatants.

Aug. 23–24. **German forces in Paris were compelled to capitulate** as Allied armies approached and armed citizens liberated the city. The administration was turned over to **de Gaulle** with the approval of the Allied commanders.

Nov. 7. A **consultative national assembly,** summoned by **de Gaulle,** held its first session. Municipal and departmental elections for the 89 *départements* were set for February 1945, with the franchise extended to all citizens, male or female, over 21.

Dec. 10. A **Franco-Soviet treaty of alliance** and mutual security was negotiated. It was to run for 20 years.
1945, Jan. 1. **France joined the United Nations** in full partnership three years after the Free French government in exile had offered its adherence.

May 21. The governments of **Syria** and **Lebanon broke relations** with the French (p. 1298). The French denied (June 2) that they were using lend-lease equipment against the Syrians and Lebanese.

June 30. The **French Communist Party** voted for union with the **Socialist Party.**

The main tasks facing liberated France were the liquidation of her Vichy past and the establishment of the Fourth Republic.

Aug. 15. **Henri-Philippe Pétain,** head of the Vichy régime, was sentenced to death for treason, but his sentence was commuted to life imprisonment.

Oct. 9. **Pierre Laval** was sentenced to death for collaborating with the Germans. He was executed on October 15.

Oct. 21. **Elections for the constituent assembly** showed a swing to the Left, the Communists receiving 152 seats, the Socialists 151, and the *Mouvement Républicain Populaire* 138.

Nov. 16. **Gen. Charles de Gaulle** was unanimously elected **president of the provisional government** by the assembly and on

Nov. 21. Formed a **cabinet of National Union.**
1946, Jan. 20. **DE GAULLE RESIGNED** abruptly because of continued Leftist opposition.

Jan. 22. Socialist **Félix Gouin** was elected **president.**

May 5. A **popular referendum rejected** the draft constitution which the assembly had approved on April 19.

June 2. **Elections** for a new **constituent assembly** resulted in a victory for the M.R.P., with the Communists in second and the Socialists in third place.

June 19. **Georges Bidault** was elected **president of the provisional government.**

Oct. 13. The revised **draft constitution** was **adopted** by 9,120,576 to 7,980,333 votes, with 7,938,884 abstentions. The new constitution closely resembled that of the Third Republic, except that the senate was replaced by the council of the republic and France's relations to her overseas possessions were revised by creating the **French Union.**

Nov. 10. **Elections for the national assembly** gave the Communists 186 seats, the M.R.P. 166, and the Socialists 103. The resulting deadlock between Communists and M.R.P. left a Socialist premier as the only choice.

Dec. 16. After vainly trying to form a coalition, **Léon Blum** formed an **all-Socialist cabinet.**
1947, Jan. 16. **PRESIDENCY OF VINCENT AURIOL.** Blum resigned as premier for reasons of health and

Jan. 21. **Paul Ramadier** formed a **coalition cabinet.**

Mar. 4. **Anglo-French treaty of alliance** was signed at Dunkirk.

Apr. 14. **Gen. de Gaulle** assumed control of the nation-wide *Rassemblement du Peuple Français* to rally non-Communists to the cause of unity and reform.

May 9. The growing split between Communist and non-Communist members of the government, increased by economic difficulties and a wave of strikes, led to the **exclusion of the five Communist ministers** from the cabinet. An unbalanced budget, a poor harvest, and refusal of many peasants to deliver their grain further aggravated the situation in the summer and early fall.

Oct. 19–26. De Gaulle's R.P.F. emerged as the strongest group in the **municipal elections,** with the Communists in second place. In face of this growing extremism, the government and middle parties decided to co-operate and created a new *Third Force.*

Nov. A **series of strikes,** affecting nearly two million workers, was overcome by firm governmental action and a growing realization on the part of many workers that the leadership of their unions (C.G.T.) was Communist-dominated. The non-Communist members of the C.G.T.'s executive committee, on December 19, seceded and formed the *Force Ouvrière*.

Nov. 19. At the height of the crisis, **Ramadier resigned.**

1947, Nov. 23–1948, July 19. Cabinet of Robert Schuman, supported by a Third Force coalition of Socialists, M.R.P., and Radicals. After a brief period of economic stability, a renewed rise in prices and corresponding demands for higher wages temporarily deprived the government of Socialist support and thus led to its fall. André Marie and Schuman both tried unsuccessfully to form a lasting cabinet.

1948, Sept. 10. The Radical leader **Henri Queuille** formed a government with Schuman as foreign minister.

Oct.–Nov. To exploit the country's economic difficulties, the C.G.T. initiated another **wave of strikes.** Its cause was weakened however, as the political, pro-Communist motivation of the strikes became obvious and the government took strong counter-measures.

Nov. 7. Elections to the council of the republic continued the swing to the Right, as de Gaulle's R.P.F. gained the largest number of seats.

1949, Feb. 22. Communist leader **Maurice Thorez** stated that French Communists would refuse to defend France against a Soviet army.

Oct. 5. Economic difficulties led to the **resignation of Henri Queuille.** After unsuccessful efforts of Jules Moch and René Mayer to form a cabinet,

Oct. 28. The assembly approved a **coalition under Georges Bidault.**

Dec. 30. Transfer of **sovereignty to Vietnam** (Indo-China, p. 1324).

1950, Mar. 8. The chamber adopted a strict **anti-sabotage bill,** primarily directed against Communist-inspired activities.

June 24. The **Bidault government** was **defeated.** After a short-lived cabinet under Henri Queuille,

July 11. René Pleven succeeded in forming a coalition based on economic compromise with the Socialists.

Aug. 6. The French government announced that it planned to create **15 new and fully equipped army divisions** within the following three years. After conversations in Washington, **Jules Moch,** minister of defense, and **Maurice Petsche,** minister of finance, declared (Oct. 15) that the United States would furnish over **two billion dollars** in aid to France and that this would include aid for the war in Indo-China.

Oct. 26. Premier Pleven recommended the creation of a **European ministry of defense** rather than the rearmament of (West) Germany.

1951, Jan. 31. In Washington **Premier Pleven** and **President Truman** declared that the French and American views were in agreement.

Feb. 28. The cabinet of **René Pleven** resigned and **Henri Queuille** formed a coalition cabinet (Mar. 10).

Apr. 18. France signed the **Schuman plan treaty** (see p. 1165).

May 24. The **French national assembly was dissolved** and a general election held June 17 gave the **Communist Party** 26.5 per cent of the popular vote and the **Rally of the French People** 21.7 per cent. In the chamber of deputies, however, the Rally of the French People won 118 seats to 103 for the Communists.

July 10. The **Queuille cabinet resigned** and **René Pleven** again constructed a ministry (Aug. 11).

Dec. 13. The **French assembly** approved the **Schuman plan treaty.** Five days later (Dec. 18) Premier Pleven and Prime Minister Churchill announced that France and Britain would support the Schuman plan, the proposals for a European army, and the ideal of European unity.

1952, Jan. 7. The **Pleven cabinet was overthrown** and supplanted by a new coalition cabinet headed by **Edgar Faure** (Jan. 22). The Faure cabinet lasted only five weeks, and that of **Antoine Pinay,** which won approval from the assembly on March 11, resigned on December 23.

1953, Jan. 7. A two-weeks' cabinet crisis ended with **René Mayer** organizing a new cabinet.

May 20. France and the Saar concluded an accord that gave the Saar autonomy but provided for its economic union with France.

May 21. The **Mayer cabinet resigned** and **Joseph Laniel** won approval for a new cabinet on June 26.

Aug. 6–28. Public services were disrupted by a **wave of strikes.**

Dec. 23. RENÉ COTY WAS ELECTED PRESIDENT of the French Republic to succeed **Vincent Auriol** and assumed office January 17.

1954, June 12. The cabinet headed by Joseph Laniel suffered defeat and **Pierre Mendès-France** formed a new cabinet June 18.

Aug. 27. The national assembly approved a government plan to grant a greater measure of **self-rule to Tunisia and Morocco** (p. 1292).

Aug. 30. The **national assembly rejected the European Defense Community** treaty.

1955, Feb. 5. Pierre Mendès-France alienated many of his fellow deputies by his attempts to solve the conflict between France and the insurgent forces in **French North Africa.** The national assembly overthrew the **Mendès-France** cabinet (Feb. 5) and approved a cabinet led by **Edgar Faure** (Feb. 23). The Faure cabinet lasted until November 29, and when it fell Faure ordered the assembly dissolved (Nov. 30).

1956, Jan. 2. In the resulting elections the Left (Communists) and Right **(Poujardists)** gained strength.

Jan. 24. **Faure's** cabinet resigned and a Socialist, **Guy Mollet,** organized a new one that lasted until

1957, May 21. It was succeeded by a coalition government of Socialists and Radicals under **Maurice Bourgès-Maunoury** which carried through a 20 per cent **devaluation of the franc** but suffered defeat (Sept. 30) over the Algerian issue. After more than five weeks' delay **Félix Gaillard** organized (Nov. 6) a combination of the center parties to form the 23rd cabinet France had seen since the Second World War. The war in North Africa, following the long struggle in Indo-China (pp. 1324–1325), had placed a heavy strain on French government finances. The national economy, however, benefited from the **creation of a Common Market,** promoted by the treaties concluded at Rome (Mar. 25, 1957).

1958, Jan. 30. France was promised over 655 million dollars in aid from the United States, the European Payments Union, and the International Monetary Fund.

Jan. 31. The national assembly voted an **Algerian Reform Bill** which failed to satisfy the Algerians.

Apr. 16. The cabinet of Félix Gaillard was overthrown (again over the North African deadlock) and **Pierre Pflimlin** of the *Mouvement Républicain Populaire* **headed a new cabinet** on May 13. During the month-long cabinet crisis a **committee of public safety,** headed by **Brig. Gen. Jacques Massu** and **Commander-in-Chief Raoul Salan,** seized control in Algeria and faced France with the **threat of civil war.** The Pflimlin cabinet resigned after two weeks in office which witnessed a virulent pro-Gaullist movement, and President Coty named **GEN. CHARLES DE GAULLE PREMIER** (May 31).

June 1. De Gaulle headed an emergency régime with the approval of the assembly (329–244), rallied the people of Metropolitan France to his support, and prepared to reorganize the French government.

Sept. 28. The **CONSTITUTION FOR A FIFTH FRENCH REPUBLIC** was approved by more than four to one in a popular referendum and the Fifth Republic was inaugurated October 5. Elections (Nov. 23 and 30)

gave the Gaullist Union control of the assembly and a special college (Dec. 21) named **DE GAULLE PRESIDENT OF THE REPUBLIC** for a seven-year term, commencing January 8, 1959. The new constitution granted French overseas possessions six months to decide whether to remain as they were, to become *départements* closely integrated with France, or to become autonomous member states of a French Community.

1959, Jan. 10. **Michel Debré became premier.**

Feb. 3–4. Premiers of the twelve African autonomous republics of the French Community conferred with President de Gaulle in Paris in the first meeting of the Community's executive council.

1960, Feb. 13. France exploded its **first atomic bomb** in the Saharan area of southwestern Algeria.

Apr. 25. The Gaullist Union for the New Republic ousted one of its founders, **Jacques Soustelle,** who was a strong believer in Algeria's integration with France.

1961, Jan. 8. In a national referendum, 75.3 per cent of French voters approved de Gaulle's plan to grant Algeria eventual self-determination.

Apr. 11. President de Gaulle announced his government's unwillingness to take part in any **U.N. activities,** and reiterated his refusal to pay the French share of U.N. costs in the Congo (p. 1161).

Apr. 23. French leaders alerted the nation to a possible invasion by Rightist military **insurgents from Algeria;** President de Gaulle assumed full powers to deal with the crisis.

1962, Mar. 5. The government announced its refusal to send a representative to the **Geneva disarmament conference.**

Mar. 23. After a peace agreement with the Algerian rebels (Mar. 18) de Gaulle instructed the French army to wage all-out war against OAS resistance.

Apr. 8. In a national **referendum on the Algerian settlement** of March 18, 90 per cent of the valid ballots cast approved.

Apr. 14. Upon the resignation of Michel Debré, de Gaulle named **Georges Pompidou** to succeed to the premiership.

May 20. French authorities organized an airlift to evacuate Europeans from Algiers.

May 23. As OAS terrorism continued in Algeria, OAS leader **Raoul Salan was sentenced** by a military tribunal in Paris **to life imprisonment.**

Oct. 5. Parliament censured the proposal, announced on September 20, to elect the president by popular vote, but a national referendum (Oct. 28) approved it. Pompidou's cabinet resigned, but he was re-appointed premier (Nov. 25).

1963, Jan. 14. De Gaulle declared his **opposition to Britain's entry into the EEC,** and rejected proposals for a **multilateral nuclear force** within NATO (p. 1174).

Jan. 22. A **Franco-German treaty of reconciliation** was signed in Paris by de Gaulle and West German Chancellor Adenauer.

July 29. De Gaulle declared that France would not sign the limited nuclear test ban treaty.

1964, Jan. 27. Establishment of diplomatic **relations with the government of Communist China** was agreed upon. The French denied that this step implied disruption of relations with Taiwan (Jan. 28) or recognition of East Germany (Feb. 4).

Jan. 28. France and the U.S.S.R. agreed to negotiate a five-year trade agreement to increase French-Soviet trade.

Feb. 10. Nationalist China broke diplomatic relations with France.

Mar. 14. Twenty-one **administrative regions** were established, each headed by a "coordinating prefect" presiding over a "commission of regional economic development" to stimulate economic growth.

Mar. 15–24. De Gaulle visited Mexico and the French territories in the Western Hemisphere.

Apr. 16. In a radio-TV address, de Gaulle declared that France would build its own **nuclear striking force,** and that he favored continued French economic **aid to the poorer nations,** thus providing an alternative to United States and Soviet aid.

Apr. 28. The government ordered the **removal of French naval staff officers from NATO commands** in the Mediterranean and the English Channel.

June 9. The French government, retaliating against Tunisia's nationalization of foreign-owned farmlands, announced that beginning October 1 Tunisian products would no longer enter France on preferential terms, thus abrogating the 1959 trade agreement.

Sept. 20–Oct. 16. President de Gaulle, in an unprecedently long absence, **visited ten South American countries** in an effort to strengthen economic and cultural relations.

1965, Dec. 19. In a run-off election **President de Gaulle defeated François Mitterand** and began his second term as president.

1966, June 20–July 1. Visit of Pres. de Gaulle to the Soviet Union. Discussion of a program for co-operation in the exploration of space and in general technological development.

Sept. Tour of Asia by Pres. de Gaulle. In a speech at Pnom-Penh he called upon the U.S. to withdraw from Vietnam.

1967, Mar. 5, 12. In the **national elections** the Gaullists lost 25 seats and were left with a majority of one in the assembly. They could usually count on the support of **Giscard d'Estaing's** Independent Republican Party.

May 16. President de Gaulle for the second time vetoed the admission of Great Britain to the Common Market (p. 1175).

1968, May–June. Violent **student outbreaks** at the University of Nanterre quickly spread to the Sorbonne and other institutions. After widespread street-fighting and occupation of buildings the **universities were closed,** but the crisis was aggravated by a **series of strikes** by workers in various industries. In a truly revolutionary atmosphere Pres. de Gaulle in a radio address appealed to the country for restoration of order (May 24) and promised the drafting of reforms which would be submitted to popular referendum. On May 30 **parliament was dissolved** and new elections proclaimed.

June 23, 30. The Gaullist party won an outright majority of seats in the elections, while the Communists and other radicals suffered losses. It was obvious that the country at large was opposed to revolution and desired an end to disorder.

July 11. Couve de Murville succeeded Georges Pompidou as **premier.**

1969, Apr. 28. RESIGNATION OF PRES. DE GAULLE after an unexpected defeat in the popular referendum (Apr. 27) on various proposed administrative reforms. **Alain Poher,** president of the senate, acted as interim president.

June 1, 15. In a run-off election **Pompidou defeated Poher** and became president (June 20). **Jacques Chaban-Delmas** was appointed premier.

Aug. 18. The new administration undertook a limited **devaluation of the franc,** long resisted by de Gaulle. In other respects, too, an effort was made to soften the previous French position, notably with regard to NATO and to the problem of Britain's admission to the Common Market.

1970, Oct. 13. Visit of Pres. Pompidou to Russia and conclusion of an agreement "to extend and deepen political consultations on major international problems of mutual interest," though without prejudice to the commitments of either party to other nations.

Nov. 3. Administrative reform in the direction of further decentralization: local authorities were thenceforth to decide on local projects without reference to Paris ministries.

Nov. 11. DEATH OF FORMER PRESIDENT CHARLES DE GAULLE.

5. THE IBERIAN PENINSULA

a. SPAIN

(*From p. 995*)

1939, Sept. 3. Spain remained neutral during the **Second World War** despite its close ties with Germany and Italy.

1940, June 14. Spanish troops took over the **International Zone** in Morocco on the pretext of guarding its neutrality.

1942, July. The **cortes,** the national representative body of Spain, was re-established by **Gen. Francisco Franco,** but on fascist lines. It was to form the supreme organ of the state and to be composed of 438 members, almost all selected by virtue of the fact that they had qualified for administrative or juristic posts.

1944, May 3. The Spanish government agreed to restrict the **shipment of minerals to Germany** and to limit the **activities of Axis agents** in Spain. The United States thereupon cancelled its embargo on oil shipments to Spain.

1945, Mar. 22. Don Juan, the Bourbon claimant to the Spanish throne, called for the resignation of General Franco and **the restoration of the monarchy.**

May 8. Spain broke off diplomatic relations with Germany.

May 12. Falangist officials attended **a requiem mass for Adolf Hitler.** Spain continued to give refuge to large numbers of Germans, despite Allied demands for their repatriation.

June 20. The **San Francisco conference excluded Spain from** membership in the **United Nations.** A similar exclusion was contained in the report on the Potsdam conference (Aug. 2).

July 20. General Franco made changes in his cabinet, filling several government posts with reputedly royalist sympathizers, and stated that the **monarchy would be restored** at a future date.

Aug. 22. José Giral became premier of a Republican government-in-exile at a meeting of the cortes in Mexico City.

1946, Mar. 4. The **United States, Britain, and France appealed to the Spanish people to oust the Franco régime** and prepare the way for democratic elections.

Oct. 12. President Perón of Argentina presented General Franco with the highest Argentine decoration. This was followed on

Oct. 30. By a very advantageous **Spanish-Argentine commercial agreement.** Señora Perón paid a state visit to Spain in 1947.

Dec. 11. The **United Nations Assembly** voted to bar Spain from all U.N. activities and urged its members to break off diplomatic relations with Spain.

1947, Feb. 9. Rodolfo Llopis formed a new coalition government-in-exile.

Mar. 31. General Franco announced a **bill of succession** (ratified, on July 6, by national referendum), according to which Spain again became a monarchy, the choice of the monarch being left to General Franco as head of the state.

Apr. 2. Don Juan condemned the bill of succession and maintained his opposition to Franco.

Aug. 27. The **Rodolfo Llopis** government-in-exile **resigned** because of growing collaboration between Republican and Monarchist opposition groups. A new government was formed by **Alvaro de Albornoz.**

1948, Aug. 28. The exiled **Monarchists** and the anti-Franco **Republicans** (except the Communists) issued a "statement of accord."

Sept. 20. The **treaty of friendship and non-aggression,** concluded with **Portugal** in 1939, was extended for ten years.

1949, Sept. King Abdullah of Jordan was the first head of state to visit Franco Spain.

Oct. 22–27. General Franco paid a visit to Lisbon, demonstrating the **close relations between Spain and Portugal.**

1950, Sept. 6. The United States congress recommended, with certain restrictions, a $62.5 million **Marshall Plan loan for Spain.**

Nov. 4. The **United Nations** adopted a resolution, sponsored by several Latin American states, and supported by the United States, which **rescinded** the proposals of the earlier **resolution of December 11, 1946,** thus opening the door to Spain's admission into the Western, anti-Communist camp.

1951, Apr. 23. Some 250,000 workers went on strike against rising living costs.

1953, Sept. 26. In agreements with the United States, Spain gave the right to establish **naval and air bases** on its territory in return for military and economic aid.

1954, Jan. 28. Anti-British **demonstrations over Gibraltar** forced the cancellation of plans for the British fleet to visit Spanish ports.

Dec. 29. At a meeting of Don Juan of Bourbon, pretender to the throne, and General Franco, the future régime of Spain was discussed.

1956, Apr. Spain terminated its Moroccan protectorate (p. 1288).

1959, Feb. 1. Liberal and Rightist foes of the Franco régime joined to organize the **Spanish Union,** an illegal action, since all political parties excepting the Falange had been forbidden.

May 14. A liberal Catholic group organized the **Christian Democratic Left Party** in opposition to the ban upon political parties.

1960, June 13. In a letter to their bishops, 342 Basque priests protested police brutality toward political prisoners and violation of civil rights.

1963, Aug. 10. The government announced plans to grant some **autonomy** to the two provinces of **Rio Muni** and **Fernando Po,** comprising Spanish Guinea (p. 1289).

1964, Jan. 8. The United States Air Force announced plans to close one of its three bases in Spain.

Dec. 14. A **new constitution,** mildly liberal, was approved by an overwhelming vote in national elections.

1964–1970. Evolution of the Gibraltar issue, growing out of Spain's claim to the base as part of its territory, despite the fact that the permanent Spanish population there was a minority (see p. 1187).

1969, July 22. PRINCE JUAN CARLOS DE BORBON, son of the pretender to the throne, named by Generalissimo Franco as his eventual legal successor and heir to the Spanish throne.

Oct. 2. Visit of President Nixon to Spain, in the course of his Mediterranean tour. Relations between the U.S. and Spain had remained close in view of the **use of Spanish bases by American air and naval units,** in return for which the United States had provided large sums of money for economic and military development. President Nixon assured Generalissimo Franco that Spain was vital to the security of the Mediterranean basin.

1970, Aug. 6. Renewal of U.S.-Spanish agreements on bases, for a period of five years.

Dec. THE BASQUE PROBLEM. On Dec. 1 the honorary West German consul at San Sebastian was kidnaped by a Basque nationalist group demanding independence for the Basque provinces. The kidnaping was in protest to the court martial at Burgos of 15 Basque nationalists charged with having assassinated a hated police official in 1968. The incident led to widespread protests on the part of Spanish intellectuals and church authorities.

Dec. 4. On opening the court martial the government proclaimed a three-month **state of emergency** in Guipúzcoa province which permitted search without warrant and indefinite detention of suspects. Emergency measures were extended to all Spain on Dec. 14.

Dec. 28. The court martial sentenced six of the Basque prisoners to death and nine others to unusually long prison terms. The **wide-spread unrest** in the country induced Franco to commute the death sentences and to reduce the prison terms (Dec. 30).

b. PORTUGAL

(From p. 996)

1939, Sept. 3. Portugal remained technically neutral during the Second World War but helped the Allied nations substantially by allowing them to use naval and air **bases in the Azores.**

1945, May 3. The **government** ordered official flags at half-mast because of Hitler's death, but on May 5 **severed diplomatic relations with Germany.** The defeat of the Axis, however, gave rise to demands for greater political freedom, and on

Oct. 7. Premier Antonio de Oliveira Salazar permitted the formation of opposition parties. Censorship was removed on October 12, and a **political amnesty** was granted. Yet on October 14, because of immediate attacks against his government, Salazar reimposed the censorship of the press.

Nov. 18. The first **general election** in twenty years, because of a boycott by the opposition, brought victory for the **National Union Party** and the paternalist régime of Premier Salazar.

1946, June 2. The United States and Great Britain returned the bases they had held in the Azores during the war.

1949, Feb. 13. President Antonio Carmona, 79, was re-elected after the single opposition candidate had withdrawn.

Apr. 4. Portugal signed the North Atlantic treaty. It still was excluded from the United Nations, however, by Soviet veto.

1950, Sept. 26–27. General Franco and **Premier Salazar** discussed questions of Peninsular strategy and emphasized the solidarity of their two countries.

1952, Apr. 14–15. Premier Salazar and General Franco of Spain agreed upon an intensification of their political and military collaboration to defend their countries, "within the general framework of Western defense," against Soviet aggression.

1954, Dec. 28. The government reminded Britain of its obligations under the treaty of 1373 and subsequent agreements in relation to **India's sealing off of Daman** and the likelihood of an Indian invasion of the Portuguese enclaves.

1957, Nov. 15. The 1951 **Azores common defense pact** with the United States was extended to 1962.

1959, June 18. The national assembly approved government-sponsored legislation to abolish the system of direct presidential elections by universal suffrage.

1961, Jan. 24. At the request of the Portuguese government, United States and British planes and ships searched for the Portuguese cruise ship *Santa Maria,* seized on January 22 by Portuguese exiles in the name of **Lt. Gen. Humberto Delgado,** the defeated presidential candidate in 1958.

Feb. 2. The Portuguese liner *Santa Maria* disembarked 607 captive passengers and crew at Recife, Brazil; the next day **Henrique Galvao,** rebel leader, surrendered the liner to Brazil, which returned it to Portugal.

1962, Jan. 3. Premier Salazar severely condemned Britain and the United States for not strongly supporting Portugal in the U.N. when **India seized three of its enclaves.**

1964-1970. The Portuguese government was exposed to increasing and more threatening protests against **continuance of its colonial rule** in Africa, both by the United Nations and the Organization of African Unity. **Liberation movements** of various kinds were organized in various places and obliged the government to keep huge armed forces in Africa at great expense. Nonetheless the government refused to yield, maintaining that the African colonies were simply *"overseas territories"* of Portugal, represented in the Portuguese parliament just as were the European territories (pp. 1273).

1968, Sept. 16. Premier Salazar was stricken by brain hemorrhage and sank into a coma.

Sept. 27. Dr. Marcello Caetano was named to succeed Salazar in the premiership.

1970, July 27. Death of former Premier Antonio de Oliveira Salazar.

Dec. 2. Caetano announced plans to accord the **African colonies** additional seats in the legislature and extensive autonomy in planning and administration of their local and social affairs, but all within a system of complete racial equality.

Dec. 8. The U.N. security council voted to condemn the **invasion of Guinea** (p. 1264) by Portuguese forces and demanded compensation for the loss of life and property. It urged all nations to abstain from giving Portugal military or other material aid.

Dec. 9-11. The ministerial council of the **Organization of African Unity,** meeting at Lagos, condemned "those states, particularly the NATO powers, who sustain Portugal in her colonial aggression by their continued assistance to her." The council directed its **liberation committee** to afford substantially increased financial and material aid to **Amilcar Cabral** and his **Party for Independence of Guinea and Cape Verde.**

c. GIBRALTAR

1964, Sept. Further **tension over Gibraltar.** Spanish protests against the new constitution promulgated for the base, followed by restrictions on vehicular traffic and on the free movement of workers to and from the mainland to Gibraltar.

1965, July 8. A new **coalition government** on Gibraltar proclaimed its desire for free association with Great Britain.

1966, May-Oct. Anglo-Spanish discussions of the Gibraltar situation at London. On Oct. 5 the Spanish government ordered the **closing of the customs post** at La Linea.

Dec. 14. Spain rejected the British proposal to submit the question of sovereignty over Gibraltar to the International Court of Justice.

1967, Sept. 10. A plebiscite on Gibraltar registered 12,762 votes. Of these, 12,138 favored remaining a British possession, while 44 voted for union with Spain.

1968, May 5. The Spanish government **closed the frontier** to all but residents and daily workers employed on Gibraltar.

1969, May 30. A new **Gibraltar constitution** declared the city "part of Her Majesty's dominions" until parliament should decide otherwise, but in no case contrary to the wishes of the inhabitants.

June 5. By **further measures of closure** the Spanish government threw 4800 Spanish workers on Gibraltar out of employment.

June 27. The **ferry service** from Algeciras to Gibraltar was terminated.

July 30. Gibraltar elections. Formation of a government of the Integration with Britain Party together with the Independents, with **Major Robert Peliza** as chief minister (Aug. 6).

Sept. 29. Spanish naval demonstration off Gibraltar.

6. THE ITALIAN PENINSULA

a. ITALY

(*From p. 1002*)

1939, Sept. 2. Italy proclaimed neutrality at the outbreak of war despite its **"pact of steel"** with Germany.

1940, June 7. Italy ordered its ships to neutral ports.

June 10. ITALY DECLARED WAR ON FRANCE AND BRITAIN.

June 12. The **British government** announced a **complete blockade** of Italy.

Sept. 27. Italy, Germany, and Japan concluded a **three-power pact.**

1941, June 22. ITALY DECLARED WAR ON SOVIET RUSSIA.

Dec. 11. ITALY DECLARED WAR ON THE UNITED STATES.

1943, July 25. Mussolini resigned and was placed under arrest. **Marshal Pietro Badoglio replaced him and declared the Fascist Party dissolved** (July 28).

Sept. 9. The **Badoglio cabinet accepted terms of surrender for Italy,** whereupon German forces in Italy seized control of the leading cities, including Rome, Milan, Trieste, Genoa, Bologna, Verona, and Cremona.

Sept. 15. Mussolini, rescued from his captivity by German troops, **proclaimed a Republican Fascist Party** and achieved some authority in the areas of Italy still under German control.

Oct. 5. The British government announced that the **Italian fleet had been surrendered.**

Oct. 13. The **Badoglio government of Italy declared war on Germany.**

1944, June 4. The United States 5th Army entered Rome. Marshal Badoglio resigned as Italian premier and was succeeded by **Ivanoe Bonomi.**

1945, Apr. 28. MUSSOLINI WAS CAPTURED AND EXECUTED by Italian anti-Fascist forces.

May 12. Bonomi requested the Allied governments to send troops to occupy Trieste. Marshal Tito of Yugoslavia was warned by Britain and the United States that Trieste must remain under Allied control.

June 17. Ferrucio Parri succeeded Bonomi as premier.

Nov. 24. The coalition cabinet of **Ferrucio Parri resigned.**

Nov. 30. The leader of the Christian Democrats, **Alcide de Gasperi,** formed a new government supported by all major parties.

1946, Jan. 1. With the **transfer of Bolzano** province by the Allies, the whole country, except for Venezia Giulia (claimed by both Italy and Yugoslavia), was under Italian sovereignty.

May 9. KING VICTOR EMMANUEL III ABDICATED. His son proclaimed himself **King Umberto II.**

June 2. Elections to the **constituent assembly** gave 207 seats (out of 556) to the Christian Democrats, 115 to the Socialists, and 104 to the Communists. At the same time a referendum rejected the monarchy by 12,717,923 to 10,719,284 votes, thus making **ITALY A REPUBLIC.**

June 11. The prime minister, **Alcide de Gasperi,** was made temporary head of state.

June 13. King Umberto, while refusing to accept the popular verdict against the monarchy, **left the country** to prevent the outbreak of violence.

June 27. The foreign ministers of Great Britain, the United States, Soviet Russia, and France transferred the **Dodecanese Islands** from Italy to Greece and awarded the **Briga** and **Tenda** areas of northern Italy to France.

June 28. ENRICO DE NICOLA was **elected PRESIDENT OF THE REPUBLIC** by the assembly.

July 12. Alcide de Gasperi formed a new coalition government.

1947, Feb. 10. The **PEACE TREATY** with Italy was signed at Paris. Besides confirming earlier territorial changes, it made **Trieste** a Free Territory. A final decision on the future of **Italy's colonies** was postponed. Italian **reparation payments,** after the Western allies had waived their claims, were set at $360 million.

May 13. De Gasperi resigned because of friction with the Left-Wing members of his coalition.

May 31. De Gasperi formed a new government of Christian Democrats and Independents.

Dec. 22. The constituent assembly adopted the **new constitution,** which called for far-reaching decentralization of government, a chamber of deputies and a popularly elected senate. Relations between Church and State remained unchanged.

Dec. 28. Ex-King **Victor Emmanuel died** in exile.

1948, Feb. 2. With the United States, Italy signed a treaty of friendship, commerce, and navigation.

Mar. 26. A **Franco-Italian customs union** was concluded to become effective within one year.

Apr. 18. In the crucial first **national elections** under the new constitution, with Communist control as the main issue, the **Christian Democrats won an absolute majority.** The Popular Front of Socialists and Communists received 30.7 per cent of the votes cast.

May 11. Senator **LUIGI EINAUDI** was elected **PRESIDENT OF THE REPUBLIC.**

May 23. Prime Minister **de Gasperi** formed a new government, which was severely hampered by Communist-inspired unrest, such as the **general strike** proclaimed by the Communist-dominated Federation of Labor (C.G.I.L.) in protest against an attempt on the life of Communist leader **Palmiro Togliatti** (July 14), who was shot and seriously wounded by a student.

June 28. Italy was allocated $601 million under the **Marshall Plan** to aid her economic rehabilitation.

Oct. 18. The non-Communist elements in the C.G.I.L. seceded and formed a separate trade union.

1949, Apr. 4. Italy signed the **North Atlantic treaty** despite strong opposition from the Left.

Nov. 21. The U.N. Assembly decided for **eventual independence of Italy's former colonies.** Until such time they were to remain under U.N. supervision.

1950, Jan. The government announced a ten-year economic plan, designed to wipe out Italy's large-scale unemployment. Some progress was made during 1950 with plans for much-needed agricultural reform, especially in the South.

Apr. 1. Italy assumed **trusteeship** under the United Nations over **Somaliland,** although it remained barred from U.N. membership by veto of the Soviet Union.

1951, May 1. A new **"Socialist Party"** emerged as a result of the union (Apr. 4) of the right-wing Socialists, led by **Giuseppe Saragat,** and the Unitarian Socialists, led by **Giuseppe Romita.**

July 26. Premier Alcide de Gasperi's seventh cabinet was sworn in, following a decision on July 3 that the government needed more liberal members.

1953, Jan. 1. **Civil rights were restored** to several thousand former fascists, previously barred from voting or holding office.

July 28. Following a vote of no confidence, **Premier de Gasperi resigned.**

Aug. 15. Veteran financial expert **Guiseppe Pella became premier** as fears spread that a Yugoslav seizure of Trieste was imminent. (p. 1166).

1954, Jan. 5. An extended cabinet crisis began with the resignation of the Pella cabinet.

Feb. 10. **Mario Scelba became premier** of a government of Christian Democrats, right-wing Socialists, and Liberals.

Aug. 19. **Alcide de Gasperi died.**

Oct. 5. The signature of an **agreement with Yugoslavia** ended the Trieste dispute (p. 1160).

1955, Apr. 29. Parliament elected **Giovanni Gronchi,** a left-wing Christian Democrat, to the presidency.

June 26. **Antonio Segni,** Christian Democratic Party, **became premier,** following Scelba's resignation (June 22).

1956, Apr. 23. A **constitutional high court,** similar to the supreme court of the United States, was inaugurated as the nation's supreme judicial body.

1957, May 15. **Adone Zoli became premier** after Segni's cabinet resigned (May 6) when the Social Democrats withdrew.

Oct. 11. The twelve-year rule of **San Marino** by Communists ended with the inauguration of **Federico Bigi** as the head of the government.

Nov. 14. The left-wing Socialists, led by **Pietro Nenni,** approved "unity of action" with the Communists.

1958, May 25–26. The center parties, led by the Christian Democrats, were victorious in the national elections.

June 25. **Amintore Fanfani,** secretary of the Christian Democratic Party, **became premier.**

1959, Feb. 16. **Antonio Segni became premier** in a Christian Democratic cabinet, ending a three-week impasse after Fanfani's resignation (Jan. 26).

1960, Apr. 25. After two months of governmental crisis, President Gronchi ordered Signor Tambroni, Christian Democrat, who had resigned (April 11), to continue in office.

July 27. Amintore Fanfani headed a new Christian Democratic government.

1961, Sept. 12. The government formally protested to Austria over terroristic acts by persons demanding autonomy for the **German-speaking populace of Alto Adige** province (formerly Austrian South Tyrol).

1962, Feb. 2. Premier Fanfani and his cabinet resigned to prepare for a **Center-Left government** with outside support from Pietro Nenni's left-wing Socialists.

Feb. 21. Fanfani government formed, composed of Christian Democrats, Democratic Socialists and Republicans, with left-wing Socialist parliamentary support.

May 7. After five days of voting, former premier and Christian Democrat **Antonio Segni was elected president.**

1963, May 16. The Fanfani cabinet resigned following the results of parliamentary elections, April 28, in which the Christian Democrats lost 13 seats and the Communists gained 25.

June 22. Giovanni Leone became premier in a completely Christian Democratic cabinet.

1964, Jan. 11. The left wing of the Socialist Party, representing about 40 per cent of the membership, announced that it would form a new group, the **Italian Socialist Party of Proletarian Unity.**

Dec. 28. GUISEPPE SARAGAT WAS ELECTED PRESIDENT in succession to Antonio Segni, who resigned for reasons of health.

1964–1968. A period of **political instability** and **social unrest.** The Center-Left cabinets, of which **Aldo Moro** headed three in this period, were unable to attack and solve major problems because of conservative opposition even within Moro's dominant Christian Democratic Party and because of continuing dissension in socialist ranks.

1968, May. Following significant losses in the elections, the Socialists refused to participate further in the Center-Left alliance.

June 5. Resignation of the Moro cabinet following withdrawal of the Socialists.

June–Nov. Giovanni Leone headed an interim minority Christian Democratic cabinet.

Dec. 13. Mariano Rumor (Christian Democrat) managed to reconstruct the Center-Left combination and formed a cabinet with a program of sweeping reforms. It seemed impossible, however, to attain political stability. Despite growing unrest in student and worker circles, the government fell (July 5, 1969) following a split in the Socialist Party and desertion of the cabinet by the Socialist ministers.

1969, Aug. Mariano Rumor tried to carry on with a purely Christian Democratic government.

Nov. 20. Agreement between Italy and Austria on a system of self-government for **Alto Adige** (South Tyrol).

1970, Feb. 7–Mar. 27. Another prolonged cabinet crisis, following the **resignation of the Rumor government** and various vain attempts to construct a new coalition. Such a new government was announced by Rumor on Mar. 27, but lasted only until July 6.

Aug. 6. Emilio Colombo (Christian Democrat) presented a new coalition cabinet, renewing the Center-Left combination. Meanwhile **student riots, strikes, and demonstrations** of all kinds had become almost endemic in several of the large cities (Dec.), making early action for reform all but imperative.

Dec. 1. After long and heated debates, the chamber of deputies passed the **first Italian divorce law,** despite vigorous opposition by the Catholic hierarchy and conservative organizations of many kinds.

b. THE VATICAN

(From p. 1003)

Throughout the Second World War the papal chair was occupied by **Pius XII** (1939–1958) who sought to promote peace but maintained a neutral position. He failed to speak out vigorously against the policy of extermination by which Hitler proposed to solve the Jewish problem.

1946, Feb. 18. Pope Pius XII ordained thirty-two new cardinals.

May 3. Myron C. Taylor was appointed personal representative of President Truman at the Vatican. He resigned in 1950.

1949, July 13. A **Vatican** decree **excommunicated all Catholics who followed** and taught the **Communist doctrine** and denied the sacraments to those who "consciously and freely" supported Communist activities.

1950, June 30. A papal decree excommunicated all plotters against legitimate ecclesiastical authorities.

Nov. 1. As climax of the twenty-fifth Holy Year, **Pope Pius XII pronounced the dogma of the corporeal Assumption of the Virgin Mary.**

1954, May 29. Pope Pius XII officiated at a ceremony canonizing **Pope Pius X.**

1958, Oct. 9. Pope Pius XII died at Castel Gandolfo at the age of 82.

Oct. 28. The college of cardinals elected **Angelo Giuseppe Cardinal Roncalli as supreme pontiff.** Taking the name **John XXIII,** he was enthroned November 4.

1961, July 14. Pope John XXIII issued the encyclical *Mater et magistra,* stressing the need to search for social justice and condemning materialism. He appealed for aid to underdeveloped areas and asked that workers be given a greater voice in industry at all levels.

1962, Oct. 11. Pope John XXIII opened the **twenty-first Ecumenical Council** of 2700 Roman Catholic prelates at Vatican City.

1963, April 10. The pope issued the encyclical *Pacem in terris,* which called for a world community of nations to ensure the peace.

May 11. The **pope called on Italian President Segni,** the first pope to visit a president of the Italian Republic.

June 3. Pope John XXIII died in Vatican City at the age of 81 after one of the most notable pontificates in the history of the papacy.

June 22. The sacred college of cardinals elected **Giovanni Battista Montini** pope (**Paul VI**). He was crowned on June 30 as the 262nd Roman Catholic pope.

Sept. 29. Pope Paul VI reopened the ecumenical council with an **appeal for the unity of all Christians.**

Dec. 4. The Vatican council ended its second session after authorizing the **use of vernacular languages** in the mass and sacraments.

1964, Jan. 4. Pope Paul VI and Ecumenical **Patriarch Athenagoras** of the Eastern Orthodox Church conferred in Jerusalem, during the Pope's **visit to the Holy Land.**

Sept. 14. Opening of the **third session of the Ecumenical Council** (*Vatican II*). It ended on Nov. 21 with the constitution (*De ecclesia*) providing for the sharing of power in the Catholic Church between pope and bishops. It furthermore pronounced in favor of eventual Christian unity and recognition of autonomy for the Eastern churches.

Dec. 2-6. Visit of Pope Paul to India, to attend the Eucharistic Congress in Bombay.

1965, Sept. 14. Opening of the **fourth** and last **session of Vatican II.** The pope announced that a synod of bishops would collaborate in the governance of the Church.

Oct. 4. Visit of the pope to New York to address the United Nations general assembly and to throw the weight of his authority into the struggle for peace.

Oct. 28. The pope declared the decrees of Vatican II to be Church doctrine. He denounced **anti-Semitism** and **absolved the Jews of the charge of collective guilt** for the crucifixion of Christ.

1966, Mar. 23. Visit of the Archbishop of Canterbury to the pope, the first step in the attempt to reconcile the Anglican and the Roman Catholic churches.

1967, Jan. 9-12. Meeting of Roman Catholic and Anglican delegations at Gazzoda, Italy, to explore the possibilities of unity.

July 25-26. Visit of Pope Paul to Istanbul, where he conferred with **Patriarch Athenagoras I** of the Greek Orthodox Church. The pope's efforts in behalf of ecumenism were rewarded by the return visit of the patriarch to the Vatican (Oct. 26).

1968, July 29. The pope, in an encyclical (*Humanae vitae*) condemned all **artifical methods of birth control,** despite the fact that a papal commission, after long deliberations, had recognized the threat of overpopulation to the world and had recommended approval of certain methods of birth control. The papal encyclical came as a great shock to world opinion and caused considerable consternation in Roman Catholic circles.

1969, July 31. Visit of Pope Paul to Uganda, to do honor to missionary martyrs of earlier days.

1970, June 5. Henry Cabot Lodge named President Nixon's **personal envoy to the Vatican,** reviving a connection established by President Roosevelt.

Sept. 12-17. The World Congress on the Future of the Church brought some 700 theologians to Brussels. Demands were advanced for a more democratic organization of the Church and Church procedures, a greater role for women, etc. In general it was felt that the Church needed a fundamental restructuring in the direction of great decentralization.

Oct. 12. The pope, in a message to the convention of Roman Catholic physicians, declared **legal abortion** the equivalent of infanticide and called for "absolute respect for man, from the first moment of his conception to his last breath of life."

Oct. 25. Canonization of forty English martyrs of the 16th and 17th centuries. The occasion gave the pope an opportunity to reiterate his hope for reunion of the Catholic and Anglican churches.

Nov. 23. By a *Motu Proprio* the pope decreed that officials of the Curia should resign voluntarily on reaching the age of seventy-five and that cardinals on passing the age of eighty should no longer have a vote in the papal elections.

Nov. 26-Dec. 6. Lengthy journey by air took Pope Paul on **visits to Southeast Asia, the Philippines, Samoa, and Australia.** In Manila an attempt to assassinate him was unsuccessful.

Dec. 1. The pope protested vigorously against the **divorce law** enacted by the Italian parliament.

c. MALTA

1947. Malta, a British base since Napoleonic times, was granted self-government.

1964, Sept. 21. The island became a **completely independent monarchical state,** at the request of the local government. By a ten-year **mutual defense pact** Britain retained the right to station armed forces there.

1966, Mar. 26-28. In the elections the **Nationalist Party** was victorious over the **Malta Labour Party.** The Nationalist leader, **Dr. Borg Olivier,** was prime minister.

1967, Jan.-Mar. Anglo-Maltese crisis, deriving from the decision of the British government to accelerate the withdrawal of military forces, as a matter of economy. Since this was a major threat to the economy of the island, which depended largely on the British defense system, the Maltese government protested. Agreement was eventually reached (Mar. 12) by which the British government slowed down its withdrawals and promised larger grants to cushion the rate of unemployment.

1968. Establishment of a **standing consultative group of NATO** to deal with any eventual threat to Maltese security.

June 13–16. Visit to Malta of the Prince and Grand Master of the Sovereign Military Hospitaller Order of St. John of Jerusalem, Rhodes, and Malta, to renew the ties forcibly severed by Napoleon's conquest of the island in 1798.

7. SWITZERLAND

(From p. 1004)

1939, Sept. 1. Switzerland proclaimed its neutrality and successfully preserved it throughout the Second World War as it had done throughout the First World War.

1940, Nov. 19. The **Swiss government dissolved the Swiss Nazi Party** on the ground that the activities of the party were "of a nature to endanger public order and create conflict."

1946, Mar. 19. Switzerland resumed **diplomatic relations with the Soviet Union.**

Mar. 25. An agreement between Switzerland and the Allied powers provided for the disposal of **German assets** in Switzerland.

Apr. 2. Switzerland announced her decision to stay outside the **United Nations,** so as not to endanger her traditional neutrality.

1947, Oct. 28. General elections brought no important changes in the lineup of parties. The Progressive Democrats received 51, the Social Democrats 48, the Catholic Conservatives 44, and the Labor Party (Communist) seven of the total 194 seats.

1950, Feb. Switzerland embarked on a **five-year plan of military preparedness** and announced that she would fight to defend her neutrality.

Sept. The **federal council expelled all Communists from government service.**

1952, Nov. 28. The federal council directed the finance ministry to draft a **constitutional amendment providing for a direct federal tax.**

1953, Dec. 6. After the chamber of deputies (Mar.) and the council of estates (June) had modified a finance ministry's draft, the voters rejected the federal direct tax constitutional amendment.

1956, Dec. 12. Reviewing Swiss foreign policy, **Foreign Minister Max Petitpierre** told parliament that the Swiss could best secure the world and themselves by maintaining their traditional neutrality, and by keeping their armed services strong.

1958, July 11. The federal government decided to equip the Swiss army with **nuclear weapons** as the most effective way "to maintain our independence and protect our neutrality."

1959, Feb. 1. Male voters defeated a **constitutional amendment to allow women to vote** in national elections and to run for national offices.

1960, Mar. 6. Geneva citizens voted to give women the ballot in local elections.

Mar. 23. Parliament ratified **Swiss membership in EFTA** (European Free Trade Association).

1962, Sept. 24. Formal application was made for **membership in the Common Market,** with the right to withdraw if Swiss neutrality were prejudiced.

1965, Feb. 28. A national referendum approved the continuance of the **anti-inflationary regulations** of the government.

Sept. The federal parliament voted to continue for five years the **ban on the holding of land** and other property **by foreigners.** There was much concern over the fact that there were over 800,000 foreigners, chiefly Italian workers, in Switzerland, and systematic efforts were made to effect a gradual reduction in their numbers.

1968, June. Agitation of the Catholic, French-speaking **population of the Jura** (part of the canton of Berne) for the establishment of the area as a separate canton. A federal special commission was set up to seek a solution of the problem (Aug.).

8. GERMANY

(From p. 1013)

1939, Sept. 1. GERMAN ARMIES INVADED POLAND, an act that brought on the Second World War (p. 1135).

Sept. 30. Germany notified Britain that **British armed merchantmen would be sunk** without warning.

1940, July 1. Germany warned the United States that the Monroe Doctrine could be legally valid only if the American nations did not interfere in the affairs of the European continent.

1941, Jan. 30. Hitler promised a historic year for the **new European order** that he and Mussolini had inaugurated.

1943, Feb. 3. A broadcast from Hitler's headquarters conceded that the **battle of Stalingrad** had ended in a German defeat.

1944, July 20. An unsuccessful **attempt to assassinate Hitler** by a group of German officers and officials was followed by **savage reprisals** against the conspirators.

1945, Apr. 30. HITLER COMMITTED SUICIDE IN BERLIN as Soviet forces captured the city.

May 8. Terms of **unconditional surrender, signed at Rheims** on the previous day, became effective and **ended the European phase of the Second World War.** Surrender terms were also signed in Berlin between German and Soviet commanders.

With the total defeat of the Hitler régime, no German government remained. Instead supreme authority was vested in an **Allied Control Council of Great Britain, France, the United States,** and the **Soviet Union.** Each of these powers administered its own occupation zone, with the Soviet Union holding the region east of the Elbe. The former capital, **Berlin,** was likewise divided into four sectors. The future policy toward Germany had been outlined at the **Potsdam conference** (p. 1157), though its implementation varied in the different occupation zones. The most immediate measures of the victors were concerned with the liquidation of the Nazi system, the transformation of Germany's economy to peacetime production, and the transfer of administrative functions into German hands. On November 20 the **trial of major Nazi leaders** opened at Nürnberg before an inter-Allied tribunal. In addition, thousands of lesser Nazis were removed from office and held for trial. Germany's industrial power was drastically reduced by **dismantling of war plants** and the removal of equipment for reparations purposes. At the same time large stores of food were imported to maintain a minimum ration. In all occupation zones **political parties** were authorized by the end of 1945. In the Soviet zone administrative authority was vested in the provincial councils, which immediately initiated far-reaching land reforms. In the three western zones, **German self-government** was initiated on local and provincial levels. On November 20 the Control Council approved the **transfer of 6,500,000 Germans** from Austria, Hungary, Czechoslovakia, Poland, and the German region beyond the **Oder-Neisse line,** which had been handed to Poland at the Potsdam conference, pending a peace settlement.

1946, Jan. 27. Local elections in the U.S. zone resulted in victory for the **Christian Democrats,** with the **Social Democrats** in second place.

Mar. 26. The Allied Control Council limited the future **level of German production** to half its 1938 volume, with German steel capacity set at 7.5 million tons. The limitations soon proved unworkable, since they seriously hampered German recovery.

Apr. 21. The **Social Democrats** and **Communists** in the **Soviet zone** merged into the Communist-directed **Socialist Unity Party (S.E.D.),** which received majorities in all subsequent elections. The Liberal Democrats and the Christian Democrats remained merely for purposes of democratic window-dressing.

June 30. Elections for constituent assemblies in the American zone brought victories for the **Christian Socialists** in Bavaria, the **Christian Democrats** in Wuerttemberg-Baden, and the **Social Democrats** in Greater Hesse.

July 2. The first of several **political amnesties** was declared by the Americans, to help overcome some of the difficulties of large-scale denazification.

Sept. 6. U.S. Secretary of State **James F. Byrnes,** in a speech at Stuttgart, announced a more lenient American policy toward Germany and called for a unified German economy.

Sept. 30. The **International Tribunal at Nürnberg** announced its decisions. The Nazi Leadership Corps, the S.S., the Security Police, and the Gestapo were found criminal organizations, while the S.A., the cabinet, and the general staff were acquitted. Of the 22 defendants, Schacht, Fritzsche, and Papen were acquitted, the rest received sentences ranging from ten years' imprisonment to death. Shortly before his scheduled execution, on October 15, **Hermann Goering** committed suicide.

Dec. 2. James F. Byrnes and **Ernest Bevin** signed an agreement for the **economic fusion of the U.S. and British zones (Bizonia),** inviting France and Soviet Russia to join.

1947, Mar. 10–Apr. 24. The **Moscow conference** of the **Big Four foreign ministers** revealed considerable **disagreement on the German question** between the Soviet Union and the West. Notably the Soviet demand for $10 billion in German reparations, to be paid from current production, ran counter to U.S.-British policy of making Western Germany economically self-supporting. The only agreement reached was on the formal **abolition of the state of Prussia.**

June 2. A **German economic council** was created to direct bizonal economic reconstruction.

Aug. 29. A revised **plan for Western German industry** set the 1936 production level as an ultimate goal and raised the yearly figure of steel production.

Oct. 5.   Elections in the Saar brought victory to the **Christian People's Party** and the **Socialists,** which was seen as a popular endorsement of the new **Saar constitution** adopted previously by these parties. Its first article proclaimed the Saar an autonomous territory, joined economically to France.

Nov. 25–Dec. 15.   In another **unsuccessful meeting** of the **council of foreign ministers** at **London,** the Soviet demand for $10 billion in German reparations from current production again proved the main obstacle to a general German settlement.

1948, Feb. 6.   A new **bizonal charter** further perfected German administration of "Bizonia."

Feb. 13.   As a counter-move, Soviet authorities conferred extensive powers on a **German economic commission** in the Soviet zone.

Mar. 20.   The **Soviet delegates walked out of the Allied Control Council,** after charging the Western powers with undermining the quadripartite administration of Germany.

Apr. 1.   The Soviets began interfering with traffic going between Berlin and Western Germany.

June 1.   A **six-power agreement** of the three Western powers and the Benelux countries was reached, calling for **international control of the Ruhr,** German representation in the **European recovery program,** closer integration of the three western zones, the drafting of a **federal constitution** for Western Germany, and the creation of an **Allied military security board.**

June 18.   The Western powers announced the introduction of **currency reform in Western Germany,** establishing the stable *Deutsche Mark,* and initiating a process of **rapid economic recovery.**

June 23.   Soviet authorities introduced a **currency reform for the Soviet zone.**

July 24.   Disagreement between the Soviet Union and the West over the latter's program of economic and currency reforms brought complete Soviet **stoppage of rail and road traffic between Berlin and the West.** To circumvent this blockade, the Western powers began a large-scale **air lift** of vital supplies.

Nov. 30.   After ousting the democratic majority of the Berlin municipal assembly, the **Communists set up a new administration,** claiming authority **over the whole of Berlin.** In reply,

Dec. 5.   **Elections in the western sectors of Berlin** gave the Socialists 64.6 per cent of the vote, and Socialist **Ernst Reuter** became lord mayor.

Dec. 28.   The United States, Great Britain, France, and the Benelux countries constituted themselves (and eventually Germany) as an **International Ruhr Authority** with far-reaching powers of control.

1949, Jan. 17.   The **Western allies** established a **military security board** to supervise German disarmament and demilitarization.

Mar. 19.   The Soviet-sponsored **people's council** in Eastern Germany **approved a draft constitution** for a **Democratic Republic** of Germany and called for the election of a people's congress.

Apr. 8.   The three **Western powers** agreed on an **Occupation Statute** for Western Germany, which assured the Germans of considerable self-government, while reserving far-reaching powers to the occupation authorities. Simultaneously dismantling provisions were eased and numerous industrial restrictions were removed, to meet German demand for greater economic freedom.

Apr. 23.   Thirty-one minor **rectifications of the West German frontier** were carried out.

a. THE GERMAN FEDERAL REPUBLIC (WEST GERMANY)

1949, May 8.   The Western parliamentary council adopted the **basic law** for the **FEDERAL REPUBLIC OF GERMANY.** While following in many respects the Weimar constitution, the basic law tried to avoid the main shortcomings of its predecessor. It was subsequently ratified by all states except Bavaria. The **Federal Republic,** with Bonn as capital, **came into existence on May 23.**

May 12.   The **Berlin blockade** was officially lifted.

Aug. 14.   **Elections for the Bundestag** (lower house) in **Western Germany** gave the Christian Democrats a small lead over the Socialists, with the Free Democrats holding the balance. A **United States court at Nürnberg** concluded the last of its **war crimes trials** with the sentencing of 19 German government officials and diplomats.

Sept. 12–15.   **THEODOR HEUSS** (Free Democrat) was **ELECTED PRESIDENT** and **KONRAD ADENAUER** (Christian Democrat) **CHANCELLOR** of the **Federal Republic.**

Sept. 21.   The **Allied occupation statute came into force.** The functions of military government were transferred to the **Allied high commission.**

Sept. 30.   The **Berlin air lift ended** its operation after 277,264 flights.

Nov. 24.   In the **Petersberg agreement** the Allied high commission made further economic concessions to Western Germany, in return for German membership in the International Ruhr Authority. Despite the fact that industrial production had reached 93 per cent of the 1936 level, the influx of more than eight million Germans from the East had caused widespread unemployment. To speed economic recovery,

Dec. 15. **Western Germany** received the first allotment of funds from the Economic Co-operation Administration, and thus **became a full participant in the Marshall plan.**

1950, Jan. 16. The last rationing restrictions were ended in Western Germany.

Mar. 3. A **French agreement with the Saar,** confirming the region's autonomy and its economic union with France, created consternation in West Germany and led Chancellor Adenauer to demand (May 30) that the Saar be allowed freely to choose between France and Germany.

May 9. The **Schuman plan** was welcomed by the Bonn government.

Largely as a result of the Korean War, the status of **Western Germany during 1950 underwent a rapid change from that of a former enemy into that of a future ally.** This became clear when on

Sept. 19. The **Western powers** announced that they would consider any attack against the Federal Republic or against Berlin as an attack upon themselves and that they would strengthen their military forces in Germany. At the same time they **agreed to revise the occupation statute,** to relax economic controls, to lift the limit on steel production, and to permit the Bonn government to establish diplomatic relations with foreign countries. A special security police was authorized to meet the threat of the much larger Soviet-sponsored "People's Police" of Eastern Germany. At the same time the Western allies began considering possible **German participation** in a Western army under the **North Atlantic treaty.** This growing collaboration in matters of military security between the Bonn government and the West, however, met with violent criticism from the **Socialist opposition** and its leader, **Kurt Schumacher,** whose opposition to remilitarization found strong popular support, as was shown in the **Landtag elections** of the American zone (Nov. 19–26), which resulted in noticeable **Socialist gains.**

1951, Jan. 20. In notes to Britain and France, the U.S.S.R. reaffirmed with forcefulness and detail its charge that Germany's remilitarization was a prime threat to peace and security in Europe.

Jan. 25. Industrialists agreed to trade-union demands for a **"co-determination" law** giving labor a share in the management of the coal and steel industries.

Sept. 10. The foreign ministers of Great Britain, France, and the United States met in Washington, D.C., for a two-day conference on measures to contain Soviet aggression. They agreed on plans for a **German "peace contract"** to replace the occupation statute and on the use of West German troops in a European army.

Sept. 24. The three Allied high commissioners, meeting with Chancellor Adenauer, informed him that the occupation statute would be abrogated and the Allied high commission abolished only after Germany agreed to contribute to the defense of Europe.

Dec. 6. Both the East and West German governments agreed to send representatives to the United Nations to discuss the holding of free elections in Germany. On December 19 a five-nation commission was approved to inquire into the possibility of such elections. Soviet opposition made the prospect unlikely.

1952, Jan. 11. The West German Bundestag ratified the **Schuman plan** by a vote of 232 to 143. The Communists and Socialists voted against it.

Jan. 25. The French government decided to substitute a diplomatic mission for the **High Commissariat of the Saar.** This action created a furor in West Germany where on February 4 Chancellor Adenauer demanded that the Western powers consult German wishes on the Saar question.

Mar. 10. The U.S.S.R. in notes to the United States, Great Britain, and France called for a four-power conference to discuss the **unification and rearmament of Germany.** On March 23 the Western powers replied that they would consider the establishment of an all-German government only on the basis of **free elections,** that such a government should not be empowered to rearm, but could enter security agreements with other powers, that the German borders drawn at the 1945 Potsdam conference were to be subject to revision.

Apr. 10. The U.S.S.R. continued the exchange of notes on Germany which began on March 10. The new note proposed that all-German elections be held under a four-power commission rather than United Nations supervision. It rejected Western views on the rectification of Germany's 1945 frontiers.

May 26. Nine months of negotiations with Britain, France, and the United States ended in the **signature at Bonn of the contractual agreement giving West Germany internal independence.**

Nov. 18. Objecting to the alleged political domination of the Saar by France, the Bundestag's major parties supported a Bundestag declaration denying the **legality of the Saar elections** to be held on November 30 and refusing to recognize any Saar government so elected.

Nov. 26. The French cabinet approved terms for revising the French-Saar conventions to permit an enlargement of the Saar's economic independence. Saar Premier **Johannes Hoffmann** praised the step as a concession by France of equal rights to the Saar.

Nov. 30. The **Saar elections** resulted in a victory for the autonomists and for the French, as most voters rejected German appeals to boycott the polls or invalidate their votes.

1953, Mar. 4. The combined steel group of the Allied high commission lifted its controls from the **Krupp industrial empire,** in exchange for Alfred Krupp's pledge to liquidate his iron, steel, and coal holdings, and not to return to those industries.

Aug. 16. The U.S.S.R. proposed a **Big Four conference** within six months on a German peace treaty. Moscow suggested that East and West Germany meet first to set up a provisional all-German régime.

Sept. 6. In **general elections,** Chancellor Adenauer's coalition won a sweeping victory.

1954, Jan.–Feb. The **Berlin conference of foreign ministers** failed to agree upon peace terms (p. 1166).

Mar. 26. **President Heuss** signed the constitutional amendment permitting **rearmament as a member of the EDC,** if established.

July 30. The United States senate unanimously authorized the president to take direct action for the restoration of German sovereignty if France did not ratify the EDC treaty.

Oct. 3. A **nine-power conference in London** agreed upon alternatives to EDC (p. 1173).

Oct. 6. Soviet Foreign Minister Molotov urged immediate four-power talks regarding German unification, neutralization, and evacuation, but British Prime Minister Churchill firmly rejected the proposal (Oct. 26).

Oct. 23. After France and Germany reached agreement on the Saar question, Premier Mendès-France joined the other Allies in signing **protocols to make West Germany a sovereign and equal member of the Western alliance** (p. 1166).

1955, May 3. The Free Democratic Party broke with Chancellor Adenauer over the issue of German unification.

May 5. The **WEST GERMAN FEDERAL REPUBLIC GAINED SOVEREIGN STATUS** as the final instruments of ratification of the Paris treaties were deposited at Bonn; it joined NATO four days later.

June 6. Adenauer resigned from his post as foreign minister, and **Heinrich von Brentano** succeeded him.

July 18–23. The **Geneva conference**

(p. 1159) discussed German unification among European and world problems, and provided for a Big Four foreign ministers' conference, which failed to agree on the German problem (Oct. 27–Nov. 16).

July 22. A **rearmament bill** was enacted which authorized the immediate enlistment of 6000 officers and men to form the nucleus of a future half-million-man army.

Sept. 9–13. During **Chancellor Adenauer's visit in Moscow,** West Germany and the U.S.S.R. decided to establish diplomatic relations, and the U.S.S.R. promised to release German war prisoners.

Oct. 23. **Saarlanders voted overwhelmingly to reject Europeanization,** agreed upon by France and Germany (Oct. 5), and in parliamentary elections (Dec. 18) gave a majority to pro-German parties.

1956, July 25. **Compulsory military service** became law.

Oct. 27. A Franco-German agreement was signed for the **transfer of the Saar Basin to West Germany.** Also France, Germany, and Luxemburg agreed to canalize the Moselle River, connecting the Lorraine steel industry with the Ruhr Valley.

1957, Jan. 1. The **Saar returned to Germany,** becoming the Federal Republic's tenth state.

July 1. The first three of twelve West German divisions formally joined the NATO command.

July 28. The **Berlin declaration,** signed by the United States, Britain, France, and West Germany, called for a free and reunited Germany as a requisite in a European settlement.

Sept. 15. In parliamentary elections, Chancellor Adenauer's Christian Democratic Union obtained an absolute majority in the Bundestag.

1958, Mar. 28. The Bundestag, after a heated debate, approved the government's **atomic armament policy,** and rejected a Soviet offer of a peace treaty and reunification through a confederation with East Germany.

Nov. 27. Soviet **Premier Khrushchev's demand that the four-power occupation of Berlin terminate** created tension, eased by the visit of Deputy Premier Mikoyan to Washington (Jan. 4–19, 1959) and Prime Minister Macmillan to Moscow (Feb. 21–Mar. 3, 1959).

Dec. 14. The foreign ministers of Britain, France, and the United States reasserted their determination to maintain their **rights and duties in West Berlin,** including the "right of free access," and rejected Soviet proposals for the demilitarization of the city. On December 31 they called for talks on Berlin within the context of German unity and European security.

1959, Jan. 10. The Soviet government rejected the Allied proposal of December 31, 1958, and proposed, instead, a **draft peace treaty** providing for a demilitarized Germany and East German control over all access points to a free Berlin. It also recommended that 28 nations meet within two months in Prague or Warsaw to establish a peace treaty with a neutralized but divided Germany.

Mar. 26. Britain, France, and the United States invited Soviet participation in a foreign ministers' conference on the question of a German peace treaty and the ending of Berlin's occupation. The U.S.S.R. accepted on March 30.

Apr. 30. The United States revealed its decision to halt flights to Berlin above the 10,000-foot ceiling, as the Soviet Union had earlier requested.

May 11–Aug. 5. The **foreign ministers conference at Geneva** on Berlin made no progress toward narrowing the gap between the Soviet demand for a peace treaty with both West and East Germany and the Western insistence upon the reunification of Germany upon the basis of free elections.

July 1. **Heinrich Luebke,** the CDU candidate and minister of agriculture since 1953, was **elected president,** succeeding Theodor Heuss.

Sept. 28. At the end of Khrushchev's tour of the United States, President Eisenhower reported that the Soviet premier had promised not to set a deadline for the solution of the Berlin problem.

1960, Apr. 25. Khrushchev stated that a **separate peace treaty with East Germany** would terminate Allied entry rights into West Berlin "by air, land or water." He warned that any Allied attempt to maintain its rights in Berlin by force would be matched by Soviet force.

Apr. 27. President Eisenhower reaffirmed that western troops would not evacuate West Berlin.

1961, June 4. A **Soviet memorandum** called for a peace treaty with East and West Germany and the demilitarization of Berlin as a free city; and Khrushchev declared (June 15) that the U.S.S.R. would conclude a treaty by the end of the year, and "rebuff" any Western move to enforce its right of access to West Berlin.

July 17. Britain, France, and the United States rejected Soviet proposals to hold a peace conference on Germany and make Berlin a free city, and a month later a U.S. force of 1500 troops entered West Berlin to reinforce the Western garrison.

July 25. President Kennedy spoke on **United States preparedness in the Berlin crisis** (p. 1232).

Sept. 17. In **parliamentary elections** Adenauer's Christian Democratic Union lost its majority with 241 seats while the Free Democratic Party, with 66 seats, greatly gained, and the Social Democrats won 190 seats.

Oct. 26–28. A **crisis arose over the right of U.S. civilians to enter East Berlin** when the East German government demanded that they must submit identity papers to East German border guards. Both the Soviet Union and the United States moved tanks to the Friedrichstrasse crossing point while United States officials in civilian dress crossed the border under military escort. Both governments withdrew their tanks on the 28th.

Nov. 4. After two-week-long negotiations the CDU and the Free Democratic Party agreed upon a **coalition government.** After the Bundestag approved **Adenauer as chancellor** (Nov. 7), the new government took office (Nov. 14) with **Gerhard Schroeder** as foreign minister in place of Heinrich von Brentano who had resigned at the insistence of the Free Democrats.

Nov. 7. Premier Khrushchev declared his willingness to postpone a settlement of the Berlin issue.

1962, Aug. 8. Foreign Minister Schroeder indicated that Bonn would break diplomatic relations with any country endorsing a peace treaty between East Germany and the U.S.S.R.

Nov. 2–28. A prolonged government crisis arose over Free Democratic Party demands for changes in the cabinet, ending with Adenauer's agreement to drop Defense Minister **Franz Josef Strauss** from a reconstructed government. **Kai-Uwe von Hassel** replaced him on December 14.

1963, June 24. United States **President Kennedy,** during a **four-day visit to West Germany,** pledged with Adenauer joint efforts to reunify Germany, achieve European unity, and defend West Berlin from Communist encroachment, and on the 26th electrified West Berlin with his statement in a public address: "I am a Berliner."

Oct. 16. Adenauer stepped down as chancellor and **Ludwig Erhard** succeeded him.

1964, Feb. 16. West Berlin **Mayor Willy Brandt** became leader of the Social Democratic Party.

Mar. 31. The United States Air Force announced that training flights in a 70-mile zone along the East-West German border would be prohibited in the future. The three airmen (shot down on March 10) had been released earlier by the Soviet Union.

Apr. 29–May 12. **President Luebke toured Chile, Argentina, and Brazil** to promote trade and cultural relations.

May 26. The **Moselle Canal** was opened by President de Gaulle of France, Grand Duchess Charlotte of Luxemburg, and President Luebke of Germany.

June 9–12. Chancellor Ludwig Erhard officially visited Canada and the United States.

July. **Agreement with Yugoslavia** on trade and cultural relations, the first step in a policy of improving and developing relations with East European countries.

July 1. Re-election of Dr. Heinrich Luebke as president of the German Federal Republic.

Sept. **Agreement between West Germany and East Germany** allowing West Berliners to visit their relatives in East Berlin at four specified seasons of the year. Before long this agreement was restricted to Christmas and New Year's and presently it became an additional bone of contention between the two Germanies.

Dec. **Negotiations within the Common Market** in the effort to establish an acceptable price for grain finally led to agreement on a low price to meet French requirements, which however involved government subsidies to the West German farmers.

1965. The **Statute of Limitations,** which fixed July 1965 as the final date for the trial of Nazi war criminals, was extended to Dec. 31, 1969, in view of the large number of cases still to be tried.

German policy in the Middle East. On Feb. 12, the West German government, in order to avoid estrangement of the Arab states, terminated the arms supply agreement with Israel secretly concluded in 1960. However, after the visit of the East German leader Walter Ulbricht to Cairo (Feb. 24) the Bonn government demonstrated its displeasure by ending all development aid to the United Arab Republic. Furthermore, it **officially recognized Israel** (May 12) with the result that in May the **UAR and nine other Arab states broke off diplomatic relations** with West Germany.

Apr. 7. The West German parliament held a one-day session in West Berlin, despite East German and Soviet protests and harassments.

May 18–25. Visit of Queen Elizabeth and Prince Philip to West Germany, where they were warmly greeted. The Queen in one of her speeches pleaded for co-operation.

Sept. The **national elections** once again proved a victory for the Christian Democrats and the Christian Social Union, despite a substantial gain by the Social Democrats. **Erhard remained chancellor** and a new coalition of the Christian Democrats and Free Democrats assumed power.

Dec. Visit of Chancellor Erhard to Washington. Discussion of the knotty problem of the possible role of West Germany in the NATO program of nuclear defense.

1966, Oct. Defection of the Free Democrats from the government left Erhard and the Christian Democrats in a minority in parliament.

Nov. 8. The Christian Democrats and the Christian Social Union chose **Dr. Kurt Kiesinger,** prime minister of Baden-Württemberg, as their leader. Thereupon **Erhard resigned** (Nov. 30).

Dec. 1. Kiesinger was named chancellor and undertook the formation of a **GRAND COALITION GOVERNMENT,** combining the Christian Democrats, the Christian Social Union, and the Social Democrats. **Franz Josef Strauss** of the Christian Social Union became minister of finance, and **Willy Brandt,** former mayor of West Berlin and leader of the Social Democrats, became minister for foreign affairs.

Dec. 13. In a programmatic speech Kiesinger emphasized his intention to revivify the **relationship with France** and to attempt improvement of relations with eastern European countries, all, however, without prejudice to West Germany's position in NATO.

1967, Jan. 13–14. Visit of the chancellor to Paris and discussions with President de Gaulle.

Jan. 31. Establishment of **diplomatic relations with Roumania,** the first achievement of the new *Ostpolitik*.

Apr. 19. Death of former Chancellor Konrad Adenauer, aged 91.

June. Serious **student outbreaks** growing out of protests against the visit of the shah of Iran. The **Socialist Student League** was particularly radical and violent and soon paralyzed work in many of the universities.

Aug. Visit of Kiesinger to Washington.

Oct. 23–25. Visit of the chancellor to London, where he counseled patience with respect to British entry into the Common Market.

Nov. Rise of conservative nationalism in Germany. The **National Democratic Party,** under **Adolf von Thadden,** gained consistently in various state elections and gave rise to fears of a recrudescence of Nazism in Germany.

1968, Apr. 11. An attempt to assassinate **Rudi Dütschke,** the leader of the Socialist Students' League, resulted in widespread violence, with demands for university reforms rapidly growing into demands for abolition of the existing democratic régime and establishment of student and worker soviets.

May. Parliament at last passed an **emergency powers bill** which, among other things, provided for use of the armed forces in support of the police in the event of insurrection.

Sept. Formation of a **new Communist Party.** The old one had been banned in 1956 and the new one was obliged to conform to requirements of the security laws.

The **Soviets claimed,** following the Czech invasion, that reactionary forces in Germany were becoming a threat to European peace and that, eventually, the Soviet Union might exercise a right of intervention. The Western powers, in notes to Moscow, roundly denied the existence of such a right.

1969, Mar. 5. DR. GUSTAV HEINEMANN (Social Democrat) **elected president** of the Federal Republic by the Bundestag meeting in West Berlin, despite protests and threats and obstructions to travel on the part of East German and Soviet authorities, who steadfastly maintained that West Berlin was not a part of the Federal Republic.

Sept. 28. In the **national elections** the Social Democrats registered substantial gains (42.7% of the total vote cast).

Oct. 21. Foreign Minister **Willy Brandt** (Social Democrat) succeeded in arranging a coalition with the Free Democrats and **became chancellor** in succession to Kurt Kiesinger. The largest party, the Christian Democrats, were out of office for the first time since the war.

Oct. 24. Revaluation of the German mark upward by 8.5%, a step that had been resisted by the Kiesinger government.

Oct. 28. The new chancellor outlined an extensive program of **domestic reforms** and spoke at length on the new government's **objectives in foreign policy.** For the first time he recognized that **two German states actually existed,** even though West Germany did not and would not officially recognize the East German state. He indicated his readiness to discuss ways and means of improving relations between them and also indicated his intention to push on with the West German *Ostpolitik,* while safeguarding West Germany's position in NATO.

Nov. In notes to Moscow and Warsaw the West German government suggested the initiation of discussion looking toward an agreement. The Soviet government responded at once and a start was made before the end of the year.

Nov. 28. West Germany signed the nuclear **non-proliferation treaty.**

Dec. **Walter Ulbricht,** the East German Communist Party leader, **sent proposals to Bonn** for improving relations. Discussions were to be embarked upon soon.

Dec. 16. The United States, Britain, and France, in identical notes to Moscow, proposed talks reviewing the **status of West Berlin** with the objective of improving and stabilizing the situation of the disputed city.

1970, Mar. 19. First meeting of Chancellor Willy Brandt and the East German prime minister

Willi Stoph at Erfurt. Though inconclusive, they marked an important departure.

Mar. 26. First meeting of delegates of the four great powers (U.S., Britain, France, and U.S.S.R.) to canvass possible improvements in the West Berlin situation.

Apr. 11. Visit of Chancellor Brandt to Washington, where he found approval for his *Ostpolitik.*

May 21–22. Second conference of Brandt and Stoph at Kassel. Discussions still failed to overcome West Germany's refusal to recognize formally East Germany as a state, and East Germany's refusal to accept the notion of West Berlin as part of the German Federal Republic.

Aug. 12. SIGNATURE OF THE WEST-GERMAN-SOVIET TREATY of friendship and co-operation, a possible landmark in the development of the European international situation. The negotiations had been long and difficult, but agreement was evidently much desired by both sides. By it the West German government recognized the **inviolability of all post-war European boundaries,** including specifically the **Oder-Neisse line** as the western boundary of Poland. The Soviet Union undertook not to oppose the **reunification of Germany,** provided it could be achieved by peaceful means. Other provisions touched on co-operation in economic, scientific, and cultural matters, but the **ratification** of the entire treaty was made, by the West German government, **dependent on the achievement of substantial improvements in the status of West Berlin.** Chancellor Brandt went personally to Moscow for the signing of this epochal document.

Dec. 7. Chancellor Brandt went to Warsaw for the signature of a **SIMILAR PACT BETWEEN WEST GERMANY AND POLAND.** The two parties renounced the use of force, and West Germany conditionally recognized the Oder-Neisse line as Poland's western frontier. They further pledged to respect each other's territorial integrity and to settle all differences by peaceful means.

b. THE GERMAN DEMOCRATIC REPUBLIC (EAST GERMANY)

1948, May 16. Elections for a people's congress in Eastern Germany, despite official pressure, gave only 66.1 per cent backing to the single list of Communist-approved candidates. On May 30 the congress adopted the draft constitution of the **Democratic Republic.**

1949, Oct. 7. As a counter-move to developments in the West, the **GERMAN DEMOCRATIC REPUBLIC** was established in Eastern Germany without an election and with **WILHELM PIECK** as **PRESIDENT** and **OTTO GROTEWOHL** as **MINISTER PRESIDENT** of a predominantly Communist cabinet. The Soviet military government was replaced by a **Soviet control commission.** Politically and economically the new East German state was merely another Soviet satellite.

1950, June 6. An **agreement between East Germany and Poland** recognized the **Oder-Neisse line** as the final German-Polish frontier and evoked protests from Western Germany.

Oct. 15. **Elections to the East German legislature** brought the expected "victory" for the official list of candidates.

1952, May 1. President Pieck announced that **East Germany would be forced to rearm** if West Germany became integrated with Western Europe. On May 7 the government announced plans to form an army to defend the Soviet zone "against aggression."

May 26–June 5. Increased pressure on West Berlin coincided with the signing of the **Bonn agreement** (p. 1195) as the East German government ordered new restrictions on communications between East and West Germany.

1953, May 28. The Soviet Union abolished the **Soviet control commission** in East Germany and created the post of **high commissioner,** to which **Vladimir Semyenov** was appointed.

June 16. The lifting of Communist curbs on protests enabled East Berlin workers to demonstrate, shouting anti-government slogans and demanding a general strike.

June 17. The Soviet Union sent tanks and troops against the 30,000 East Berlin rioters.

June 22. As arrests continued, the Communist government offered a **ten-point reform program,** including provisions for pay increases, reduced work, and improved living conditions.

1954, Mar. 7. **Walter Ulbricht** emerged as the new strong man, when President Pieck and Premier Grotewohl were relieved of their chairmanship positions on the Communist Party's central committee.

Mar. 25. The U.S.S.R. granted **"full sovereignty"** to East Germany, and announced the end of its occupation, although Soviet troops would remain "temporarily" for security reasons.

1955, Sept. 20. **East German-Soviet agreements** were signed conferring sovereignty on East Germany as well as control over civilian traffic between Berlin and West Germany.

1956, July 17. Premier Otto Grotewohl and Soviet Premier Bulganin, meeting in Moscow, declared that **German unification** must proceed by East-West German negotiations.

1957, Nov. 14. East and West Germany reached an **agreement to trade** $260 million of goods in 1958.

1959, Nov. 24. East and West Germany agreed upon $545 million in trade in 1960.

1960, Sept. 8. East Germany announced that **travel by West Germans to East Berlin** was under permanent restriction; West Germans would henceforth have to obtain a Communist police pass before entering East Berlin. The Allied powers declared that this was the most serious infringement to date of the four-power agreement on Berlin.

Sept. 30. The West German cabinet decided to break off trade relations with East Germany after January 1, 1961, unless East Germany lifted its travel restrictions, but later (Nov. 25) announced that it would reopen trade talks despite the restrictions, and finally (Dec. 29) agreed to extend the current trade pact.

1961, Aug. 13. The **East German government closed the border between East and West Berlin** and began (Aug. 15) to build a wall between the two. These actions followed publication of a communiqué of the Warsaw pact nations, appealing to the East German parliament to halt the **mass flights of refugees** to the West.

1962, Aug. 22. The U.S.S.R. abolished the office of Soviet commandant in East Berlin. The United States declared that the action would not affect the rights of Western commandants in Berlin.

1963, Dec. 19. Upon permission of the East German government, over 500,000 West Berliners visited relatives in East Berlin during the holidays, ending January 5, 1964.

1964, June 12. A **treaty of friendship, mutual aid, and co-operation** was signed with Soviet Russia. This treaty fell short of the peace treaty desired by Walter Ulbricht.

Sept. Ulbricht, in a parliamentary speech, asked for East German membership in the U.N. and **proposed a treaty between NATO and the Warsaw pact,** general reduction of forces in Germany, etc.

Sept. 21. Death of Otto Grotewohl, who was succeeded as prime minister by **Willi Stoph.**

1965, Feb. 24–Mar. 2. Visit of Ulbricht to Cairo. The UAR still withheld full recognition of the German Democratic Republic.

Apr. 7. Closure of the autobahn between West Germany and West Berlin in protest against the meeting of the West German parliament in Berlin. Higher tariffs were also imposed on rail and water traffic from West Germany to Berlin.

June 13. Visit of Marshal Tito to East Germany.

1966, Feb. Ulbricht suggested talks between the

West German Social Democratic Party and the East German Communist Party. The plan for exchange of views finally broke down over legal details.

Apr. Professor Robert Havemann, a critic of the Ulbricht régime, was dismissed from membership in the Academy of Science in East Berlin, a clear warning that the East German régime would allow no more free expression than the Soviet Union.

1967. East German treaties of friendship with Poland, Czechoslovakia, and Hungary, involving promises on the part of these powers not to open diplomatic relations with West Germany unless the latter were prepared to recognize the existence of two German states.

Apr. Chancellor Kiesinger of West Germany submitted suggestions for improving relations with East Germany. Ulbricht responded by proposing a meeting between Kiesinger and Stoph and the negotiation of a treaty "between the two German states."

May 10. Stoph formally proposed talks, which the West German government accepted, but only on condition that formal recognition

of the German Democratic Republic should not be involved (June 13).

Sept. 18. Stoph sent the Bonn government a detailed **draft treaty** setting forth such extreme demands that the draft was ignored by the West German government.

1968, Apr. A **new constitution** for "the Socialist State of the German Nation" approved by referendum. It claimed East Berlin as its capital.

Aug.–Sept. Soviet intervention against the Czech régime of Alexander Dubček (p. 1204). The East German attitude was harshly anti-Czech and East German troops participated in the occupation of Czechoslovakia.

1969, Mar. Further **obstruction of access to West Berlin,** in reply to the insistence of the West German parliament on holding the election of the new federal president in West Berlin.

Dec. 18. New **Ulbricht proposals** to Bonn, asking full diplomatic relations, the recognition of West Berlin, and an independent unit, etc. (For the further development of the relationship between West and East Germany, see pp. 1169, 1199.)

9. AUSTRIA

(*From p. 1016*)

From 1938 to 1945 Austria formed part of the German Reich.

1945, Apr. 28. The **occupation of Austria by Allied armies** was followed by the proclamation of a **new provisional Austrian government.**

As a "liberated" rather than defeated country, Austria after the war was treated with leniency by the Western allies, who did everything in their power to hasten its recovery. The Soviet Union, on the other hand, after initial requisitions of livestock and industrial equipment, made far-reaching demands for reparations from former German assets, thus seriously hampering Austria's economic reconstruction. Under these circumstances, the Austrian government was eagerly awaiting the conclusion of a final peace settlement and the withdrawal of the occupation forces.

1945, Apr. 25. A **provisional government** was set up with Socialist **Karl Renner** as **chancellor.**

May 14. THE DEMOCRATIC REPUBLIC OF AUSTRIA was **re-established.**

Aug. 8. The division of Austria and Vienna into **four occupation zones** was completed. The **Allied Council for Austria** assumed authority over matters affecting the whole of Austria.

Nov. 25. The first **general election** since 1930 gave the **People's Party** a majority over the Socialists and Communists.

Dec. 18. Leopold Figl (People's Party) formed a coalition cabinet with the Socialists.

Dec. 20. KARL RENNER was unanimously elected **PRESIDENT OF THE REPUBLIC** by the national assembly.

1946, Jan. 7. The **occupying powers officially recognized the Austrian Republic** within its 1937 frontiers.

June 28. The Austrian government was given a large measure of authority by the Allied Council.

July 6. The **Soviets claimed,** as German assets, important **industrial establishments** in their zone.

Sept. 6. An **Austro-Italian agreement** gave considerable autonomy to the **South Tyrol.**

1948–50. Repeated **attempts to reach a peace settlement for Austria failed** because of Soviet and Yugoslav demands against Austria. To facilitate negotiations, the Western allies renounced their own claims for German assets in Austria and made far-reaching concessions to Soviet claims for such assets, but the **deadlock continued through 1949 and 1950.**

1949, Oct. 9. General elections brought losses to both the **People's Party** and the **Socialists,** as many former Nazis rallied behind the new **Union of Independents.** Communist strength remained negligible. The coalition government of People's Party and Socialists remained substantially unchanged, despite their basic disagreement on economic questions.

1950, Dec. 31. President Karl Renner died.

1951, May 27. Theodore Koerner, Socialist mayor of Vienna, was **elected president.**

1952, June 14. After seven years, the Soviet government agreed to the **reopening to Austrian shipping** of that part of the Danube running through the Soviet zone.

1953, Feb. 6. A **deputy foreign ministers' conference** on an Austrian peace treaty was quickly deadlocked.

Feb. 22. In general elections the extreme right and left suffered serious losses, while the militant anti-Communist Socialists made substantial gains.

Apr. 2. Julius Raab, formerly president of the chamber of commerce, formed a People's Party–Socialist coalition government.

June 8. The Soviet Union lifted its control measures along the border between the Soviet and Western zones.

July 30. The Soviet government announced it would pay its own **costs of occupation** in Austria after August 5, as the United States had been doing since July 1947.

Aug. 17. The three Western powers withdrew their **proposal for a "short" Austrian treaty** and proposed a London meeting, August 31, to prepare a full peace treaty for Austria, but the U.S.S.R. rejected the invitation (Aug. 29).

1955, Apr. 11. Chancellor Raab arrived in Moscow to discuss Soviet proposals for a treaty, and agreed upon terms (Apr. 15) calling for the withdrawal of all occupation forces from Austria by December 31.

May 15. After a fortnight of negotiations a **peace treaty** with Austria was agreed upon by the four-power foreign ministers conference at Vienna.

July 27. AUSTRIA FORMALLY REGAINED ITS SOVEREIGNTY, and the Allied Council for Austria held its final meeting in Vienna.

1956, May 13. Chancellor Julius Raab's People's Party won the national elections.

1957, Feb. 8. The government gave Italy assurances of its intention to abide by the 1946 **agreement on the Southern Tyrol.** Italy offered a continuation of talks with Austria on the problem.

May 5. Adolf Schaerf, leader of the Socialist Party and vice-chancellor, was **elected** as Austria's third post-war **president.**

1959, July 10. The People's Party and the Socialists agreed to form a coalition government, thus ending a nine-week rift over the division of ministries within the cabinet. The coalition government, under Chancellor Julius Raab, was sworn in on July 16.

Sept. 13. Demonstrations in the Austrian Tyrol protested Italian violation of the rights of Austrian Tyrolese, as guaranteed in the Italian-Austrian Tyrol agreement of 1946.

1960, Sept. 21. Foreign Minister **Bruno Kreisky** asked the U.N. general assembly to discuss the status of the German-speaking minority in South Tyrol.

1961, Apr. 11. Alfons Gorbach, head of the People's Party, was sworn in as chancellor, succeeding Julius Raab who had resigned for reasons of health.

1963, Apr. 28. Adolf Schaerf was re-elected president.

Sept. 20. The People's Party elected ex-finance minister **Josef Klaus** chairman, to succeed Gorbach.

1964, Feb. 26. Chancellor Gorbach resigned and on April 2 Josef Klaus succeeded him at the head of a People's Party-Socialist coalition government.

1965, Feb. 28. Death of President Adolf Schaerf.

Mar.–Dec. Intermittent **negotiations with the Common Market** with a view to Austria's admittance were systematically opposed by the Soviet Union and made no progress because of uncertainty on the side of the market.

May. Dr. **Franz Jonas,** former mayor of Vienna, was **elected president.**

Oct. 23. Resignation of the government as a result of recurring party wrangles.

1966, Mar. The **national elections** resulted for the first time in an **absolute majority for the People's Party.**

Apr. 19. End of the coalition government. Josef Klaus became chancellor with a strictly People's Party cabinet. He at once introduced an extensive program of economic, educational, and other reforms.

Continued negotiations with the Common Market.

Aggravation of the **situation in the South Tyrol,** where Austrian terrorists engaged in numerous bombings and other outrages.

1967, Mar. Visit of Chancellor Klaus to Moscow. The Soviet government refused to abandon its opposition to Austrian membership in the Common Market, but signed a cultural agreement with Austria. During the year the chancellor visited a number of Balkan countries and established better relations, even with Hungary.

1968, Nov. 13. A **constitutional amendment** reduced the voting age from 21 to 19.

1969, Nov. The South Tyrol People's Party accepted the **Italian proposals for autonomy** of the province of Bolzano, hence to be known as the South Tyrol. Official approval was given to this settlement by the Italian government (Dec.) and the Austrian government (Dec. 16).

1970, Mar. 1. Victory of the Socialist Party in the national elections. **Bruno Kreisky** replaced Klaus as chancellor and restored the traditional coalition between the Socialist and People's Parties.

10. CZECHOSLOVAKIA

(*From p. 1019*)

1939, Sept. 3. The **republic of Czechoslovakia had already been dismembered and had fallen under German domination** before the outbreak of the **Second World War.**

1945, Apr. 3. President Eduard Beneš appointed a national front government with **Zdenek Fierlinger** as **prime minister.**

May 10. The new **government moved to Prague.** In a sweeping political purge many collaborators were tried and executed. **Ex-President Hacha** died in prison, **Konrad Henlein** committed suicide.

June 29. Czechoslovakia ceded Ruthenia to the Soviet Union.

Aug. 3. All **Germans and Hungarians** in Czechoslovakia were **deprived of their citizenship** and subsequently **expelled from the country.**

Oct. 14. A **provisional national assembly** was elected by indirect suffrage.

Oct. 18. The government embarked on a far-reaching program of **industrial nationalization and agricultural reform.**

1946, May 26. Elections to the constituent assembly gave the **Communists** 2.7 million of the total 7.1 million votes and 114 out of 300 seats. As a result, Communist leader **Klement Gottwald** formed a new coalition cabinet.

June 19. The assembly unanimously **re-elected President Beneš.**

1947, Apr. 16. Josef Tiso, former president of Slovakia, was condemned to death and **executed.**

July 7. Czechoslovakia first accepted, but later, under Soviet pressure, **rejected an invitation** to participate in the **Marshall Plan conference** in Paris.

1948, Feb. 25. COMMUNIST COUP. The **Communists,** having infiltrated most government services and trade unions, and enjoying Soviet support, **threatened a** *coup d'état* and thus secured President Beneš's signature to a **predominantly Communist government under Klement Gottwald.** In a drastic purge, lasting several months, democratic **Czechoslovakia was transformed into a Communist-run people's democracy and a Soviet satellite.**

Mar. 10. Foreign Minister **Jan Masaryk** was killed in a fall from his office window, reported as suicide.

May 9. The **constituent assembly adopted the new constitution.**

May 30. The **national elections resulted in a victory** for the single list of the Communist-dominated **national front.**

June 7. President Beneš resigned on grounds of ill health. He died on September 3.

June 14. KLEMENT GOTTWALD was elected **PRESIDENT.**

Oct. 25. Forced labor camps were set up to punish reactionaries and saboteurs.

1949, Jan. 1. A **five-year plan** of industrial development was started to make Czechoslovakia economically independent of the West.

June. In an **attempt to destroy the influence of the Catholic Church,** the government founded its own **Catholic action committee** to take the direction of Church affairs away from **Archbishop Beran** and the Catholic hierarchy.

June 20. The **Vatican,** as a counter-measure, **excommunicated all active supporters of Communism in Czechoslovakia.**

Oct. 14. The **government assumed full control over Church affairs** and required all clergy to swear an oath of loyalty to the state. Most of the lower clergy complied.

1950. In an uninterrupted **series of political trials,** the government not only prosecuted its foes, but also some of its own members, who were accused of anti-Soviet, pro-Western leanings. In addition, several **Western diplomatic representatives were charged with espionage** and most Western correspondents were barred from Czechoslovakia.

April. The **new minister of defense,** Če-pička, after dismissing several leading officers, announced a thoroughgoing **reorganization of the army along Soviet lines.**

1951, Mar. 2. Reports indicated that the Czech Communist Party was undergoing a **purge of "Titoist" elements.**

July 4. The state court convicted an American correspondent, **William Oatis,** of espionage. After an official request for his release was refused on July 21, the United States prepared to take diplomatic reprisals.

1952, June 7. Premier Zapotocky announced a "**desperate coal shortage**" and the complete failure of the state farms.

Nov. 20. A **mass treason trial** opened in Prague, with **Rudolf Slansky,** former secretary general of the Czechoslovakia Communist Party, pleading guilty of treason, espionage, and sabotage.

Nov. 27. Slansky and ten other prominent Communists were sentenced to be hanged; their execution took place on December 3.

1953, Jan. 1. President Gottwald announced a lag in industrial production and a scarcity of food.

Mar. 21. Following President Gottwald's death, March 14, Premier **Antonin Zapotocky** was unanimously **elected president** by parliament. He was succeeded as premier by **Viliam Siroky.** Antonin Novotny retained his earlier post of deputy premier and assumed leadership of the Communist Party secretariat.

June 7-8. Rioting occurred against currency reform designed to stop inflation.

1954, Dec. 13. Viliam Siroky formed a new government.

1957, Nov. 17. Following the **death of President Antonin Zapotocky** on November 13, parliament elected Antonin Novotny to replace him. Novotny retained his post as first secretary of the Communist Party.

1958-1968. For a decade Czechoslovakia to a large extent disappeared from the international scene, being an obedient satellite of the Soviet Union and a key member of COMECON, whose important industries contributed greatly to the economy of the Communist bloc.

1960, July 11. In a new thorough-going **Communist constitution** Czechoslovakia was designated a "Socialist Republic," in recognition of the progress it had made in the direction of Communism. Nonetheless, **forces of discontent** were rapidly developing and pressure rose for relaxation of the repressive system imposed by the Soviets. The first break came in

1968, Jan. 25. When **President Novotny was replaced as First Secretary of the Communist Party by Alexander Dubček,** a young and attractive Slovak leader.

Mar. 22. **Resignation of President Novotny** at behest of the National Assembly, the first important move along the road to democratization.

Apr. 6. **General Ludvik Svoboda** was elected president and **Oldrich Černik** appointed premier. The reorganization of the Communist Party was undertaken and a **new party program** published, pledging freedom of speech, press, assembly, and religion. Slovakia was to be given a greater measure of autonomy. These changes evoked widespread enthusiasm throughout the country but were viewed with much concern and distrust by Moscow and some other Communist capitals.

July. Increasing **Soviet pressure on Dubček** to check the liberalizing tendencies of his régime. Dubček declined invitations to attend conferences in Warsaw or Moscow (July 15), whereupon the Soviet government announced the **mission of the entire Soviet politburo** to Prague (July 22). At the same time Soviet forces were concentrated on the Czech frontiers, ostensibly for maneuvers (July 23–Aug. 10). The Soviet politburo arrived at the border town of Cierna on July 29.

Aug. 9-11. **Visit of President Tito and** (Aug. 15–17) of **President Ceauşescu** to Prague in demonstration of support for Dubček and his party and if possible to forestall Soviet intervention.

Aug. 20-21. **THE INVASION OF CZECHOSLOVAKIA** by 200,000 Soviet and satellite troops (Roumania abstaining). Popular protests and demonstrations threatened to lead to revolution and the invading forces were soon raised to 650,000. Dubček disappeared for several days, evidently summoned to Soviet headquarters. On Aug. 23 President Svoboda was called to Moscow.

Aug. 27. **Dubček and Svoboda returned to Prague** and announced the annulment of several important reforms.

Sept. 6. Soviet **Deputy Foreign Minister Kuznetsov** arrived in Prague, whereupon political clubs were banned, a preventive censorship system introduced (Sept. 13), and Czech foreign minister **Jiri Hajek,** who had presented the Czech case at the U.N., was forced to resign (Sept. 19).

Oct. 3-4. The **Czech leaders were summoned to Moscow** and obliged to promise abandonment of reforms as well as to accept Soviet military occupation "temporarily."

Oct. 27. A **new federal constitution** was introduced giving **Slovakia complete autonomy** as an equal partner with Bohemia-Moravia. Each partner was to have its own institutions and only foreign affairs, defense, and foreign trade were to be dealt with in common.

1969, Apr. The **central committee** of the Czech Communist Party **removed Dubček, Smrkovsky,** and other liberal leaders from office.

Sept. 28. **Dubček was ousted from the presidium** of the central committee and forced to resign as chairman of the federal assembly. These were merely discreet steps in the process of eliminating him entirely from Czech public life. On Dec. 15 he was appointed Czech ambassador to Turkey, the remaining steps being resignation as a member of the central committee (Jan. 28, 1970), expulsion from the Communist Party (June 26, 1970), and finally deprivation of his seat in the assembly (July 8, 1970).

1970, Jan. 28. The central committee replaced Černik as premier with **Lubomir Strougal.** Černik was presently (Dec.) expelled from the Communist Party.

The attempt of the Czechoslovak leaders to bring about a relaxation of the repressive Communist system was watched with keen anticipation throughout the world and the Soviet-Warsaw pact invasion and occupation of the country once again revealed the determination of Moscow to maintain that system. The Soviet charge was that the Czech leaders were flirting with the West Germans and their "imperialist" allies and thereby endangering the entire Communist bloc. But such charges carried little conviction to the vast majority of mankind.

11. HUNGARY

(From p. 1021)

1944, Mar. 22.   German troops occupied Hungary and a pro-German puppet régime was set up the following day, with **Doeme Sztojay** as prime minister and minister for foreign affairs.

A provisional Hungarian government, established under **General Miklos** in 1944, concluded an **armistice** with the United Nations on

1945, Jan. 20.   Hungary henceforth co-operated in the war against Germany.

Nov. 3.   The first **general election** gave an absolute majority to the anti-Communist **Smallholders' Party,** whose leader, **Zoltan Tildy,** formed a coalition cabinet.

The economic situation of the country was desperate as a result of the war, with serious food shortages and an unprecedented currency inflation. Large-scale Soviet requisitions further aggravated the situation.

1946, Feb. 1.   A republic was proclaimed with Zoltan Tildy as president. Ferenc Nagy of the Smallholders' Party became **premier** on February 4.

1947, Feb. 10.   The **HUNGARIAN PEACE TREATY** was signed at Paris. It called for the **return of Transylvania to Roumania,** a small frontier rectification in favor of Czechoslovakia, reparations, and the reduction of armed forces.

Feb. 25.   The **arrest of Béla Kovács,** secretary general of the Smallholders' Party, for alleged plotting against the occupation forces, ushered in the gradual purge of the party's anti-Communist wing.

May 31.   Premier Nagy, accused of conspiracy by the Communists, **resigned** and was replaced by Smallholder **Lajos Dinnyes.**

Aug. 1.   A **three-year plan** went into effect, calling for a planned economy and nationalization of the banks.

Aug. 31.   A general election gave the Communists the largest number of seats. **Premier Dinnyes** continued in office at the head of a coalition cabinet of fifteen members, including five Communists.

1948, Jan. 12.   A fusion of Communists and Social Democrats into the **United Workers' Party** was engineered by the Communists.

July 30.   President Tildy was forced to resign and was replaced by the chairman of the United Workers' Party, ex-Socialist **Arpád Szakasits.**

Dec. 9.   After completing its purge of anti-Communist members, the Smallholders' Party called for **Premier Dinnyes'** resignation and put pro-Communist **István Dobi** in his place. The real power, however, was in the hands of the Communist Deputy Premier **Mátyás Rákosi.**

Dec. 27.   The refusal of the Catholic Church to make concessions to the government led to the arrest of **Josef Cardinal Mindszenty** and other dignitaries on charges of conspiracy to overthrow the government. Cardinal Mindszenty was found guilty and sentenced to life imprisonment (Feb. 8, 1949). He sought asylum in the American embassy.

1949, May 15.   A **general election** with open voting **gave complete victory** to the Communist-controlled **National Independence Front.**

June 16.   The **arrest of Communist Foreign Minister Laszlo Rajk** on charges of conspiracy **set off a wholesale purge of Hungarian Communists** accused of deviating from the pro-Soviet line.

Aug. 7.   A new constitution was proclaimed, **following very closely that of the Soviet Union.**

Dec. 28.   The government decreed the **nationalization of all major industries** and announced the start of a **five-year plan.**

1950, May–June.   The remaining ex-Socialists, among them **Arpád Szakasits,** were **dismissed** from the government. Hungary, in its domestic and foreign affairs, had come completely under Communist and Soviet domination.

1951, June 28.   Archbishop Josef Groesz was convicted of conspiring to overturn the government.

July 21. The **Roman Catholic bishops** took an oath of allegiance to the "people's republic," after having refused to do so for two years.

1952, Aug. 14. István Dobi formally resigned as premier and was succeeded by **Mátyás Rákosi.**

1953, Feb. 21. A purge, reportedly dictated by a visiting Soviet group, took a toll of thirty Jewish Communist leaders.

July 2. Following a shakeup of top Communist leadership, the government resigned. The next day parliament re-elected István Dobi to the presidency and Daniel Nagy to the vice-presidency. On July 4 **Prime Minister Rákosi resigned,** as a concession to the farmers and consumers, to make way for the new premier, **Imre Nagy.**

1955, Apr. 18. Parliament, endorsing Communist Party action, named **Andras Hegedus** to the premiership, replacing Imre Nagy, accused (Apr. 14) of right-wing deviationism.

Dec. 14. Hungary entered the U.N. as part of a "package deal" involving sixteen nations.

1956, Mar. 29. Laszlo Rajk, who was executed in 1949 after being prosecuted, along with other leaders, for treason and Titoism, had been posthumously cleared, according to an announcement by Mátyás Rákosi.

July 18. Mátyás Rákosi was replaced as first secretary of the Hungarian Workers (Communist) Party by **Erno Gero,** a first deputy premier.

Oct. 21. With the threat of university students to strike if their demands for freedom were not met, a revolutionary situation rapidly developed.

Oct. 24. Imre Nagy, who had been re-admitted to the Communist Party (Oct. 13), **became premier,** as anti-Russian rioting developed in Budapest and Soviet forces sought to quell the uprising.

Oct. 25. Anti-Russian rioters won a concession with the replacement of Stalinist Erno Gero as head of the Hungarian Communist Party by **János Kádár;** the rioters pressed for further concessions.

Oct. 27. As the revolt began to spread throughout the country, the central committee of the Hungarian Communist Party promised to work for the withdrawal of Soviet troops as soon as the rioting ended, and Nagy appointed leaders of the illegal Smallholders' Party to his cabinet.

Oct. 30. Soviet forces withdrew from Budapest, and Premier Nagy, in a radio speech, promised Hungarians free elections and a prompt ending of one-party dictatorship.

Nov. 2. Nagy denounced the Warsaw pact and requested the U.N. to take up the Hungarian situation; it had already voted (Oct. 28) to discuss the Hungarian problem.

Nov. 4. Soviet forces reversed their withdrawal and moved in to smash the revolt. Nagy was ousted as premier and replaced by János Kádár. The **U.N. general assembly adopted a resolution condemning the Soviet assault on Hungary** and calling for an investigation.

Nov. 14. Soviet forces crushed the last rebel stronghold on Csepel Island, and later (Nov. 22) **seized Nagy** as he left the Yugoslav embassy in Budapest.

Dec. 12. While a general strike protested the Kádár régime, the U.N. general assembly adopted a resolution which condemned Soviet repression in Hungary, called on the U.S.S.R. to withdraw its forces, and urged that Hungarian independence be re-established.

1957, Feb. 10. The government initiated measures to restore the *status quo ante,* by making Russian compulsory in the schools, by giving workers piece-work payment rather than fixed wages, and by repudiating the promised religious education.

Mar. 28. Premier Kádár signed **agreements in Moscow,** providing for Soviet economic aid and the continued presence of Soviet troops in Hungary to guard against a repetition of the 1956 uprising.

Sept. 13. The **U.N. general assembly** approved a resolution condemning for the second time Soviet intervention in Hungary in 1956. The resolution also included appointment of Thailand's Foreign Minister **Prince Wan** as the U.N.'s "special representative on the Hungarian problem." Hungary announced on September 14 its refusal to admit Prince Wan.

1958, Jan. 27. János Kádár resigned as premier, but kept his post as first secretary of the Hungarian Socialist Workers Party. He took a post in the cabinet as minister without portfolio. On January 28, First Deputy **Ferenc Muennich** succeeded Kádár as premier.

June 17. Budapest announced the **execution,** after a secret trial, **of former Premier Imre Nagy, General Pal Malater,** and two other leaders of the 1956 revolt. Others received prison terms.

1959, Nov. 30. János Kádár, Hungarian Communist Party secretary, said Soviet troops would remain in Hungary as long as the international situation required.

1962, Aug. 19. An official announcement disclosed that twenty-five **"Stalinists,"** including Erno Gero and Mátyás Rákosi, had been **expelled from the Socialist Workers party.**

1964, Apr. 1–10. Khrushchev visited Hungary. In a joint statement Hungary declared its support of the Soviet Communist Party in its dispute with the Chinese.

1965, June. Kádár resigned as premier but remained as First Secretary of the Socialist Workers' Party. Though **Gyulla Kállai** became premier, Kádár remained the effective ruler of the country, following the Soviet lead in all matters of foreign policy, accepting the presence of Soviet troops on Hungarian territory, but trying in return to lighten the repression

characteristic of Communist rule.
1966, Oct. A new electoral law gave the voters a somewhat larger measure of choice as between candidates on the official list.
1967. Jenö Fock succeeded Kállai as premier.
1968, Aug. Hungarian troops participated with other Warsaw pact countries **in the invasion of Czechoslovakia.**

12. THE BALKAN STATES

a. YUGOSLAVIA

(*From p. 1023*)

1939, Sept. 3. On the outbreak of the Second World War Yugoslavia remained neutral.
1941, Mar. 25. The Yugoslav government, under the regent, **Prince Paul,** announced the **adherence of Yugoslavia to the Axis pact.**
Mar. 27. The **government was overthrown** by a military coup and the young king, **Peter II,** was installed. This defiant move led to an **invasion of Yugoslavia** (Apr. 6) **by German forces.** Belgrade was occupied by the Germans on April 20.
1943, Oct. 9. Yugoslav guerrilla forces commanded by **Marshal Tito** (Josip Broz) **opened an offensive** against Axis troops in the region of Trieste.
1944, Oct. 20. Belgrade was occupied by Soviet and Yugoslav forces.
1945, May 20. Marshal Tito agreed to withdraw Yugoslav forces from **Carinthia** after United States troops were withdrawn from **Trieste.**

As the war ended, Yugoslavia was still theoretically a monarchy. The actual power, however, was wielded by **Marshal Tito** and his **National Liberation Movement.**
Nov. 11. Elections for a constituent assembly gave a substantial **majority to Tito's Communist-dominated National Front.**
Nov. 29. The assembly proclaimed a **FEDERAL PEOPLE'S REPUBLIC OF YUGOSLAVIA,** and on
1946, Jan. 31. A **new constitution** was adopted, closely resembling that of the Soviet Union. The new government was recognized by the Western powers, though its leanings, from the start, were decidedly pro-Soviet.
Mar. 10. General Drazha Mihailovich, wartime resistance leader, was captured, tried for collaboration with the enemy, and despite Western protests, was **shot on July 17.**
Sept. 18. Archbishop Stepinac, Catholic leader of Croatia, was arrested on similar charges and **sentenced to sixteen years' hard labor.**

1946–47. Yugoslavia concluded a series of **political and economic agreements with Poland, Czechoslovakia, Albania, Bulgaria, and Hungary.** She also became one of the founding members of the **Cominform.**
1947, Apr. 27. Marshal Tito announced a **five-year plan** of industrial development.

Despite Yugoslavia's close outward association with the Soviet Union, Marshal Tito had repeatedly asserted Yugoslavia's own interests. Differences between the two countries became more frequent, so that finally, on
1948, Mar. 18. The **Soviet Union recalled its military and technical advisers from Yugoslavia,** and on
June 28. The **COMINFORM EXPELLED YUGOSLAVIA** from membership for doctrinal errors and hostility to the Soviet Union.
July 21–29. Marshal Tito denied the Cominform charges before a congress of the Yugoslav Communist Party and received a vote of confidence. The party was later purged of Cominform supporters.
1949, June–July. The Soviet Union's eastern satellites broke off all economic relations with Yugoslavia. As a counter-move, Marshal Tito concluded a series of economic agreements with the West, notably the United States.
Sept. 27. As a final gesture the **Soviet Union denounced its treaty of friendship with Yugoslavia.** Its satellites subsequently followed the Soviet example.
1950, Mar. 25. General elections, in methods and results, differed little from those in other Communist-controlled countries and **brought an overwhelming endorsement** of the single list of **People's Front candidates.** Still, the rapprochement between Yugoslavia and the West spread from the economic to the political sphere, as Yugoslavia opposed Chinese intervention in the Korean War, resumed diplomatic relations with Greece, and improved its relations with Italy, which had been disturbed by conflicting claims over Trieste. In the ideological field, Marshal Tito continued to adhere to his own brand of anti-Russian Communism or **"Titoism."**
1951, Sept. 10. Tito offered to negotiate a gen-

eral settlement of all outstanding problems with the Italian government.

Nov. 14. The government signed an **agreement with the United States,** which undertook to supply military equipment, materials, and services to the armed forces of Yugoslavia.

1952, July 6. Tito declared his government's willingness to co-operate with Greece, Turkey, and Austria, but ruled out pacts and alliances.

July 13. The United States announced its decision to equip the Yugoslav armed forces with tanks, heavy artillery, and jet aircraft.

Dec. 17. The government broke **diplomatic relations with the Vatican** to protest the latter's refusal to settle the church-state conflict in Yugoslavia.

1953, Jan. 14. Parliament, in joint session, formally appointed **Marshal Tito as president** of the Federal People's Republic.

Jan. 20. Turkey's foreign minister arrived in Belgrade for talks regarding the formation of a formal **Balkan defense alliance.**

Mar. 31. After a five-day **visit to Britain** (Mar. 16–21), President Tito announced that Prime Minister Churchill had promised to protect Yugoslavia, and the latter had pledged resistance to any aggression.

June 14. President Tito disclosed that the **U.S.S.R. had requested a resumption of normal diplomatic relations,** a "great victory" for Yugoslavia.

Dec. 22. Agreement in principle was reached by Yugoslavia, Greece, and Turkey to arrange a **defense alliance,** providing that an attack by or through Bulgaria on any one of the three would be regarded as an attack on all.

1954, Jan. 17. The Communist Party condemned Vice-President **Milovan Djilas** for criticizing party policy and stripped him of his party position.

Apr. 16. A joint **statement with Turkey** reaffirmed their objectives of a Balkan military alliance, but gave Greece assurances that its approval would be sought on "all questions of principle."

June 3. President Tito and Greek **Premier Papagos** were reported in "complete agreement" on a **tripartite alliance with Turkey.**

Aug. 9. Yugoslavia, Greece, and Turkey **signed a twenty-year "treaty of alliance,** political co-operation and mutual assistance."

Oct. 5. The **agreement with Italy,** ending the dispute over **Trieste,** was signed (p. 1166).

1955, May 26. Khrushchev arrived in Belgrade with an apology for Soviet treatment of Yugoslavia in 1949 and called for a renewal of close ties.

June 2. A joint communiqué, issued at the end of the Khrushchev-Tito meeting in Belgrade, called for a European collective security treaty, banning of nuclear weapons, and U.N. membership for Communist China.

1956, Jan. 3. An agreement with the Soviet provided for Soviet construction of an **experimental reactor** in Yugoslavia.

June 20. **President Tito concluded a three-week Moscow visit.**

June 24. In his first official visit to a Soviet satellite since 1948, President Tito journeyed to Roumania for **talks with Roumanian leaders,** concluding agreements (June 26) for closer Yugoslav-Roumanian ties.

Sept. 19. Khrushchev began an unofficial visit, followed September 30 by a meeting at Yalta of Bulganin, Khrushchev, Tito, and Hungarian Communist leader Gero.

1957, Feb. 19. **Khrushchev confirmed the rift** which had developed since the previous autumn by stating that Yugoslavia could not expect any more economic favors from the Soviet Union.

Mar. 20. Representatives of Yugoslavia, Greece, and Turkey met to discuss "activation" of the Balkan alliance.

July 29. **Reconciliation talks** in Moscow resulted in an agreement providing for the restoration of $250 million in Soviet aid.

Aug. 3. At a secret meeting in Roumania, Yugoslav and U.S.S.R. leaders agreed upon closer co-operation.

Oct. 7. **Tito recognized East Germany.**

1958, Dec. 22. An **agreement with the United States** provided for the Yugoslav purchase of $95 million of surplus agricultural goods.

1962, July 23. Speaking at the close of a two-day meeting of the Communist Party's central Committee, Tito declared that liberalism and deviation from official ideology would no longer be tolerated in politics, economics, or literature.

1963, Apr. 7. The federal parliament unanimously approved a **new constitution** permitting President Tito to remain in office for life. Future presidents, however, would be elected by parliament for a maximum of two consecutive four-year terms. The new constitution, naming the country **"The Socialist Federal Republic of Yugoslavia,"** provided for a Communist-controlled state, and created the post of premier.

Nov. Roumanian Communist leader **Gheorghiu-Dej visited Yugoslavia** and signed an agreement with Tito on the construction of an "Iron Gate" hydro-electric navigation system on the Danube.

1965. Relaxation by the government **of various controls over the economic life** of the country. This tendency to abandon the system of strict regulation and approach the principles and practices of a free economy has been continued, though with deliberation and caution.

1966, July. Ouster of Vice-President Aleksandar Ranković, alleged to have opposed the liberalizing tendencies. The office of vice-president was abolished and its function assigned to the president of the national assembly.

1967, Apr. Constitutional amendments tended to strengthen the parliamentary system and expand the powers of the six local republics which constituted the federal state.

1968, Dec. Further constitutional changes laid greater emphasis on the chamber of nationalities and the federal structure of the country.

1969, Jan. A new electoral law permitted voters to reject the candidates on the official party list and to propose candidates of their own. This was simply the latest evidence of the gradual evolution of Yugoslavia in a somewhat more pronounced liberal, democratic direction. In the world at large Marshal Tito had over the years made himself a **leader of the non-aligned and anti-colonial states.** He traveled widely and established close relations with President Nasser of the UAR and with India, while enjoying much prestige throughout Africa.

1970, Dec. 29. Death, in exile, of former King Peter.

b. ALBANIA

(From p. 1024)

After its **occupation by Italian forces** in April 1939, Albania remained under the **control of the Axis powers** until their defeat in 1945.

1945, Nov. 10. The Communist-dominated government of **Premier Enver Hoxha was recognized** by the Soviet Union and the Western powers. It was upheld in

Dec. 2. General elections, which **returned the single list of official candidates.**

1946, Jan. 11. The **constituent assembly** proclaimed the **PEOPLE'S REPUBLIC OF ALBANIA.** Its domestic and foreign policy followed closely the Communist, pro-Soviet line taken by other Russian satellites. Relations with the West, and notably Great Britain, rapidly deteriorated.

May–Oct. Two naval incidents in the Corfu Channel, caused by Albanian coastal batteries and mines, and resulting in the loss of British lives, further **increased British-Albanian tension.**

1948–49. Relations between Albania and Yugoslavia, which had been particularly close, **were broken as a result of the latter's exclusion from the Cominform.**

1949, June 10. Koci Xoxe, former Communist vice-premier, and a number of other high officials, were convicted as Yugoslav agents. Xoxe was executed on June 11. As arrests for sabotage and espionage continued, large numbers of Albanians fled the country.

1950, May 28. A general election confirmed the Hoxha régime. Albania fell completely under Soviet domination as she **joined the Cominform and concluded a treaty of friendship with the U.S.S.R.**

1953, July 24. A government shuffle stripped Marshal Enver Hoxha of his posts of minister of defense and of foreign affairs but left him as premier. **Lt. Gen. Mehmet Shehu,** Hoxha's rival, remained as interior minister and head of the police, but lost his post as secretary of the central committee of the Labor (Communist) Party.

Dec. 22. Resumption of **diplomatic relations between Albania and Yugoslavia,** disrupted since 1948.

1954, July. The principle of **collective leadership** was adopted, involving a separation of the premiership (government) from the post of first secretary (party). General Hoxha, the prime minister, resigned to become the first secretary of the central committee, and the interior minister, **Shehu, formed a new government.**

1956, Jan. 11. The government announced an **amnesty for all Albanian exiles,** to expire December 31, 1957.

1958, Feb. 8. The government signed an **agreement with the Greek government** for the joint removal of mines between Corfu and the Albanian mainland. On July 30 the two governments signed a joint declaration that the straits were safe for navigation.

1961, Apr.–May. The **U.S.S.R. withdrew all Soviet technicians,** terminated economic aid, and recalled Soviet naval units from Vlore, as a result of **Albanian support of the Chinese.**

Dec. 10. According to Albanian sources, the U.S.S.R. recalled its diplomatic mission from Albania and ordered the Albanian embassy in Moscow closed.

1962, Jan. 19. A one-year **trade pact was signed with Poland,** the only European Communist state which had not recalled its ambassador from Albania.

July 16. Parliament unanimously reelected Mehmet Shehu as premier.

1964, Jan. 3. Communist Chinese Premier **Chou En-lai completed a four-day official visit.**

1964–1970. There were no significant internal changes in Albania during the period. It remained a Communist dictatorship, ruled by the same politicians who had emerged after 1945.

Only in foreign relations did it occupy a notable position, one of uncompromising **opposition to Soviet Russian policies** and complete **devotion to Communist China.** The latter's protection insured it not only against attack by neighboring powers but also provided the economic and technical aid needed for the gradual development of the country.

1968, Sept. Albania formally withdrew from the Warsaw pact, thus terminating all official identification with the Soviet bloc.

c. GREECE

(*From p. 1025*)

1939, Sept. 3. **Greece remained neutral on the outbreak of the Second World War.**

1940, July 1. The **Italian government** threatened to take **action against Greece** on the ground that British warships were using Greek territorial waters in their attack on Italian ships.

Oct. 28. **Italian forces attacked Greece,** creating a state of war. The Greeks offered a stout defense.

1941, Apr. 6. **Germany attacked Greece.**

Apr. 23. The **Greek army surrendered unconditionally** to the Germans and Italians. The **British forces** which had been landed in Greece to aid in its defense were withdrawn May 1.

1944, Oct. 13. **Athens was occupied by Allied forces.**

Dec. 25. The British prime minister, **Winston Churchill,** and his foreign secretary, **Anthony Eden,** arrived in Athens to arrange a **settlement in the civil war** that had developed between Greek factions. A **regency government** was proclaimed and **Archbishop Damaskinos** sworn in as regent after his appointment (Dec. 30) by the Greek king, **George II.**

1945, Jan. 11. The **Greek civil war** ended with a truce between the British forces and the leftist factions opposing British intervention.

The war left Greece a legacy of economic ruin, starvation, and domestic strife. The end of the **civil war** did not bring political stability. The regent, **Archbishop Damaskinos,** supported by British occupation authorities, appointed six different ministries during 1945, none of which was able to bridge the gap between moderate and left-wing resistance groups.

1946, Mar. 31. The first **general election** won an **overwhelming majority** for the Royalist **Popular Party.** The EAM and other leftist groups refused to participate in the voting.

1946, May–1949, Oct. Several thousand Communists, supported by Greece's Communist neighbors, engaged in extensive guerrilla activities, which soon developed into a regular **civil war.**

Apr. 18. Populist leader **Panyoti Tsaldaris** formed a cabinet.

Sept. 1. **A plebiscite decided** 69 per cent **in favor of the monarchy, and**

Sept. 28. **King George II returned to Athens.**

1947, Mar. 12. President Truman announced a far-reaching program of economic aid to Greece and Turkey **(TRUMAN DOCTRINE).**

Mar. 31. The **Dodecanese Islands were returned to Greece.**

Apr. 1. **King George II died and was succeeded by his brother, Prince Paul.**

Sept. 7. **Themostokles Sophoulis** formed a **coalition government** of Liberals and Populists.

Oct. 21. The **U.N. General Assembly called upon Greece, Yugoslavia, Albania, and Bulgaria** to settle their disputes by peaceful means, and set up a Balkan Committee to observe compliance with the resolutions.

Dec. 24. "General Markos," leader of an estimated 20,000 guerrillas, proclaimed the establishment of the "**First Provisional Democratic Government of Free Greece.**"

Dec. 27. The Greek government dissolved the Communist Party and EAM.

1949, June 30. **Prime Minister Sophoulis died and was succeeded by Alexander Diomedes.**

Oct. 16. After three years of fighting, the civil war ended with the **defeat of the rebel forces.** This was made possible partly by American aid and partly by the closing of the Yugoslav frontier as a result of Tito's quarrel with the Cominform.

1950, Mar. 5. A **general election** gave the largest number of votes to the Populists, but the majority went to the Center and moderate Left. This distribution of forces, together with the aftermath of the civil war, greatly contributed to the instability of the government, as shown in a rapid succession of five cabinets during the remainder of 1950.

Nov. 28. Full **diplomatic relations with Yugoslavia** were restored.

1951, Feb. 15. In a speech to parliament, **Premier Venizelos** called on Britain to permit **Cyprus** to unite with "Mother Greece."

Sept. 24. The result of **general elections** held on September 9 gave the conservative **Greek Rally Party** of **Field Marshal Alexander Papagos** a clear plurality. But a parliamentary deadlock ensued because no party had an absolute majority.

Sept. 29. King Paul broke the political deadlock by appointing **General Nicholas Plastiras,** of the Progressive Union of the Center, to head a coalition cabinet with the Liberals.

1952, Nov. 16. Papagos' conservative Greek

Rally Party won a sweeping victory in **general elections,** with at least two-thirds of the members of the new parliament.

1954, June 3. Premier Papagos and Yugoslav President Tito reportedly agreed upon a **tripartite alliance with Turkey** (p. 1208).

Dec. 14. United States resistance to Greek efforts in the U.N. to establish the "principle of self-determination" for Cyprus touched off anti-American riots in Athens.

1955, Oct. 4. **Premier Papagos died** at 71.

1956, Feb. 19. The **National Radical Union,** led by **Premier Constantine Karamanlis,** won a narrow victory in parliamentary elections.

1958, Mar. 3. King Paul named former minister of education **Constantine Georgakopoulos** to head a caretaker government following the resignation of Karamanlis.

May 17. A new government of Constantine Karamanlis was installed following the victory of his National Radical Union in the chamber of deputies.

1959, June 4. **Greece rejected a Soviet note** urging that no missile bases be established on Greek soil.

1961, Nov. 4. Karamanlis, whose National Radical Union was victorious in the October 29 elections, again headed the government.

1962, Nov. 1. Greece became an associate **member of the Common Market.**

1963, June 11. Premier Karamanlis resigned, and King Paul on June 17 asked **Panayoti Pipinelis,** a member of the National Radical Union, to form a caretaker government.

1964, Feb. 19. After the Center Union Party won the national elections (Feb. 16), its leader, **George Papandreou,** became premier.

Mar. 6. **King Paul died,** and was succeeded by **Crown Prince Constantine.** During the spring and summer acute tension developed in the relations between Greece and Turkey as a result of the renewed Cyprus question (p. 1296).

1965, July 15. Forced **resignation of Premier Papandreou,** believed by the court to be planning to take over the ministry of defense and purge the army of conservative elements. The fall of the Left-Center coalition led to popular riots (July 19–21) and to a general strike (July 27).

Aug. Papandreou's **Center Union Party,** still commanding a majority in parliament, rejected the king's nominations to the premiership.

Sept. 25. Following the defection of a number of Papandreou's followers, parliament voted approval of a **cabinet headed by Stephanos Stephanopoulos.**

1967, Apr. 21. **COUP BY A GROUP OF RIGHTIST ARMY OFFICERS,** led by Colonel **George Papadopoulos** and **Brigadier General Styliano Patakos.** The cabinet was overthrown and leftist leaders, such as Papandreou and his son Andreas, were arrested. The constitution was suspended and strict censorship enforced. The United States imposed an **embargo on military supplies** to the new régime.

Oct. 7. **Release of George Papandreou** and several other political leaders, but Andreas Papandreou and hundreds of others remained under arrest.

Dec. 13. **Failure of King Constantine's appeal** for popular support in restoring democratic institutions. On Dec. 14 **the king fled to Rome,** while the military junta appointed a new cabinet with George Papadopoulos as premier.

Dec. 25. **Andreas Papandreou was freed** by a Christmas amnesty. He went into exile in Paris, whence he denounced the Greek dictatorship and called on democratic countries to aid in its overthrow. The Greek dictatorship was regarded with much aversion throughout most of the Western world.

1968, Sept. 29. **A new constitution,** drafted by the military government, was approved by an overwhelming popular vote. It greatly reduced the royal power, though still defining Greece as a "crowned democracy." Parliament was to be deprived of most authority, which was vested in the military. Civil rights and political rights, though recognized, were kept in abeyance.

Oct. The United States partly lifted the embargo on military supplies, chiefly because of Greece's importance in the developing naval tension in the eastern Mediterranean.

Nov. 24. The **right to form trade unions** and the **right to assembly** were restored, to demonstrate the intention of the dictatorship to reestablish representative institutions eventually. Additional rights were restored in Apr. 1969.

1970, Sept. 22. **Termination of the U.S. embargo** on shipment of heavy armaments and equipment.

d. BULGARIA

(*From p. 1026*)

1939, Sept. 3. **Bulgaria remained neutral on the outbreak of the Second World War.**

1940, Feb. 15. A new cabinet was organized under **Bogdan Philov.**

June 18. **Bulgaria demanded Dobrudja** and an outlet to the Aegean Sea. A Bulgarian-Roumanian agreement whereby Roumania ceded this territory was concluded September 7.

1941, Apr. 6. **Bulgaria joined Germany and Italy in attacking Yugoslavia.** It annexed parts of Yugoslavia (July 31).

Sept. 12. Bulgaria received a **warning from**

the Soviet government that its activities did not reflect a friendly attitude.

Nov. 25. **Bulgaria joined the Rome-Berlin-Tokyo alliance,** and

Dec. 13. **Declared war on the United States.**

1943, Aug. 29. King Boris III died suddenly and was succeeded by his six-year-old son **Simeon II.** A **council of regency,** including the young king's uncle, **Prince Cyril,** the statesman **Bogdan Philov,** and **Gen. Nikola Michov** was established and approved by the Bulgarian parliament (Sept. 9).

1944, Sept. 8. **Bulgaria accepted armistice conditions laid down by the Soviet government** in accord with other Allied nations.

Post-war developments in Bulgaria were decisively determined by the **Soviet invasion** of the country in 1944 (p. 1144). The Soviet-sponsored coalition government under **Premier Kimon Gueorguiev (Sept. 9, 1944)** contained only few Communists, though in key positions. **Bulgaria formally capitulated on October 28, 1944,** and remained occupied by Soviet forces, which proved most advantageous to the Communists.

1945, Nov. 18. The first **general election gave overwhelming support** to the single list of the **Fatherland Front,** a wartime coalition of major parties, by now under Communist control.

1946. In a sweeping purge, more than 1500 high-ranking and ten times as many minor figures of the old régime were killed.

Mar. 31. **Premier Gueorguiev formed a Communist-dominated government.**

Sept. 8. **A referendum decided against the monarchy,** and on

Sept. 15. **Bulgaria was proclaimed a PEOPLE'S REPUBLIC.** Young **Tsar Simeon II** went into exile.

Oct. 27. **General elections** for a constituent assembly, carried on with considerable governmental interference, **resulted in a Communist majority.**

Nov. 21. Veteran Communist **Georgi Dimitrov returned from Moscow to become premier.**

1947, Feb. 10. The **BULGARIAN PEACE TREATY** was signed in Paris. Bulgaria retained the Southern Dobrudja, but had to pay reparations and reduce her armed forces.

Apr. 1. A **two-year plan** was announced, followed by **nationalization of banks and industries** (Dec. 26).

June 6. **Nikola Petkov,** leader of the Agrarian Party, was arrested. He was convicted of treason and executed (Sept. 23).

Aug. 26. An extended campaign against the opposition culminated in the **dissolution of the Agrarian Party.**

Nov. 27. **Bulgaria and Yugoslavia signed a treaty of friendship and mutual aid.**

Dec. 15. **Soviet occupation forces left Bulgaria.**

1948. The standard "treaties of friendship" were signed with the Soviet Union and her East European satellites.

1949, Jan. 1. **A five-year plan was inaugurated.**

June 25. Communist Deputy Premier **Traicho Kostov was arrested and charged with ideological deviation and treason.** Together with ten associates he was later found guilty and was **executed on December 16.**

July 2. **Premier Dimitrov,** who earlier had gone to Russia for medical treatment, **died in Moscow.** He was succeeded by **Vassil Kolarov.**

Oct. 1. **Bulgaria denounced her treaty of friendship with Yugoslavia.**

1950, Jan. 23. **Premier Kolarov died and was succeeded by Vulko Chervenkov,** head of the Communist Party. A **large-scale purge of government officials,** charged with complicity in the Kostov conspiracy, continued throughout the year.

Feb. 21. Similar charges of complicity against U.S. diplomatic representatives in Bulgaria led to a **break in U.S.-Bulgarian diplomatic relations.**

Apr. 1. The Communist Party revealed that **92,500 of its members had been expelled** during the previous twelve months.

1951, April. The government announced a **six-year plan** for the collectivization of the Dobrudja in order to turn the area into a vast collective farm.

1953, Feb. 13. The government decreed that all persons who left the country without permission were subject to the death penalty and their families to internment in concentration camps.

1955, Dec. 14. **Bulgaria entered the U.N.** in a sixteen-nation "package deal."

1956, Apr. 17. **Vulko Chervenkov,** a protegé of Stalin, was **succeeded as premier by Anton Yugov.**

1959, Feb. 16. First secretary of the Bulgarian Communist Party **Todor Zhivkov** issued new directives calling for a 100 per cent increase in industrial production and providing for decentralization of the administration and the economy.

1960, Mar. 7. U.S. Minister **Edward Page, Jr.,** arrived in Sofia, terminating a nine-year break in diplomatic ties.

1964–1970. **Bulgaria** might be described as **the perfect Soviet satellite.** Its governmental system remains essentially Stalinist and it follows the Soviet lead in all matters of importance. Its economy is closely integrated with that of the Soviet Union and the latter supplies the financial support to implement the development plans.

1968, Aug. **Bulgarian troops took part** with

other Warsaw pact forces in the invasion and occupation of Czechoslovakia.

e. ROUMANIA

(From p. 1028)

1939, Sept. 21.   Premier Armand Calinescu was assassinated by members of the **Iron Guard,** a pro-fascist group. **General George Argeseanu** succeeded him, was replaced (Sept. 28) by **Constantine Argetoianu,** and the latter followed in turn by **Jorge Tatarescu** (Nov. 24).

1940, July 1.   Roumania renounced Anglo-French guarantee of its integrity.

Sept. 6.   King Carol fled and was replaced by his son, **Michael.**

Nov. 23.   Roumania joined the Rome-Berlin-Tokyo tripartite pact.

Nov. 27.   The Iron Guard executed 64 for-mer officials of King Carol's government while rioting spread throughout Roumania.

1941, Dec. 12.   Roumania declared war on the United States.

1942, Sept. 18.   Roumania concluded a trade accord with Turkey.

1944, Aug. 23–24.   King Michael of Roumania dismissed the cabinet of **Gen. Ion Antonescu** and **accepted armistice terms** from the United Nations.   The **Russians occupied Bucharest** (Aug. 31).

Although Roumania had surrendered, it took several months before a workable government could be established. Constant agitation of the Communist-controlled **National Democratic Front,** combined with direct Soviet pressure, finally brought results, when

1945, Mar. 2.   King Michael asked Petru Groza, leader of the left-wing Plowman's Front, **to form a government.** Based largely on the National Democratic Front, the new government from the start showed its Communist, pro-Russian leanings. It was only due to British and American pressure that

1946, Jan. 7.   Representatives of the opposition parties were included in the government, although the important posts continued to be in Communist hands.

May 17.   General Ion Antonescu, war-time premier, was **condemned to death.**

Nov. 19.   The general election, preceded by a campaign of violence against the opposition, **resulted in a majority for the government.**

1947, Feb. 10.   The ROUMANIAN PEACE TREATY was signed in Paris. It called for reparations, reduction of armaments, and the **return of Transylvania** to Roumania.

July 15.   Julius Maniu, leader of the National Peasant Party, was **arrested,** together with some hundred members of the opposi-

tion, on charges of espionage and treason. He was sentenced to solitary confinement for life.

July 28.   The National Peasant Party was dissolved.

Nov. 5.   Foreign Minister Tatarescu, non-Communist, resigned and was **succeeded by veteran Communist Anna Pauker.**

Dec. 19.   Roumania and Yugoslavia signed a treaty of friendship and mutual aid.

Dec. 30.   KING MICHAEL ABDICATED under Communist pressure.

1948, Mar. 28.   In a general election the official **People's Democratic Front** received 91 per cent of the votes. **Petru Groza** continued as premier.

Apr. 13.   A new constitution was adopted, modeled on that of Soviet Russia.

1949.   The transformation of Roumania into a full-fledged Soviet satellite made further progress. An uninterrupted **series of trials** purged the country of all political opponents and the Communist Party of "deviationists." All **religious organizations** were **subjected to state control.** Catholic opposition led to the arrest of the remaining bishops and the **dissolution of all Roman Catholic congregations.** There was **collectivization of agriculture, nationalization of industry,** and the death penalty was imposed for even minor offenses against the state. **Relations with the Western powers** further deteriorated as several Western diplomats were accused of espionage.

Oct. 21.   Roumania denounced its treaty of friendship with Yugoslavia.

1950, July.   The Roumanian Communist Party announced the expulsion of 192,000 members over the previous two years.

1952, May 29.   Foreign Minister Anna Pauker was removed from the Politburo and the secretariat of the central committee.

1955, Aug. 12.   Premier Gheorghe Gheorghiu-Dej announced that Soviet troops would stay in Roumania until United States forces pulled out of Western Europe and NATO was abolished.

1956, Jan. 3.   A trade agreement was completed with Communist China.

Aug. 25.   Diplomatic relations were resumed with Greece, for the first time since the war.

1958, July 26.   The government announced the withdrawal of Soviet occupation forces.

1960, Sept. 30.   First secretary of the Communist Party in Roumania, Gheorghiu-Dej, affirmed the continued possibility of creating a **neutral buffer zone** in the Balkans composed of Roumania, Hungary, Bulgaria, Albania, Yugoslavia, Greece, and Turkey.

1961, Mar. 21.   Bucharest radio announced a new government structure, under which the·

presidium would be replaced by a seventeen-man **state council.** Gheorghiu-Dej was elected council president.

1964, Apr. 22. The Communist Party issued a declaration bluntly insisting upon the full equality and independence of all Communist parties and nations, and non-interference in Roumania's industrialization program. In the sequel the Roumanian government, while half-heartedly supporting the U.S.S.R. in the ideological dispute with Communist China, embarked upon economic negotiations with the U.S., France, and other countries.

1965, Mar. Death of Premier Gheorghiu-Dej, who was succeeded by **Nicolae Ceauşescu** as chief of the party.

Ceauşescu became president of the council and thus head **of state.** He continued his predecessor's policy of maintaining strict internal controls, but in international affairs insisting on the full sovereignty of all nations, which meant full independence within the Communist bloc.

1966, May 10-13. Visit of the secretary of the Soviet Communist Party, **Brezhnev, to Bucharest.** Ceauşescu stood firm by Roumanian claims and even argued for the withdrawal of Soviet troops from Poland, East Germany, and Hungary. Roumania regularly objected to having Warsaw pact maneuvers taking place on its territory.

1967. Roumania established diplomatic relations with West Germany, the first country of the bloc to do so.

1968, Aug. Roumania, alone among the Warsaw pact countries, **refused to contribute troops to the invasion and occupation of Czechoslovakia.** It firmly rejected the Soviet doctrine of the "limited sovereignty" of the Communist countries.

1969, June. At the meeting of the Communist parties in Moscow, the Roumanian representative voted against the condemnation of Communist China, stressing again the full sovereignty of all countries.

Aug. 2-3. Visit of President Nixon to Bucharest, a demonstration of Western interest in Roumania. The visit was later returned to Washington by President Ceauşescu (Oct. 1970).

1970, Oct. 19. President Ceauşescu, in his address to the U.N. general assembly, reiterated his demand for the abolition of military blocs, the dismantling of bases on the territory of other nations, and the withdrawal of armed forces from foreign territories.

13. RUSSIA

(UNION OF SOVIET SOCIALIST REPUBLICS)

(*From p. 1036*)

1939, Aug. 20-21. CONCLUSION OF A RUSSO-GERMAN PACT at Moscow marked a reversal of Hitler's policy and prepared the way for his attack on Poland (Sept. 1).

Sept. 17. Soviet troops moved into Poland (p. 1135).

Sept. 29. By agreement, **Russia and Germany divided Poland** between them (p. 1135).

Nov. 26. The government of **Finland rejected Soviet demands.**

Nov. 30-Mar. 12, 1940. RUSSO-FINNISH WAR (p. 1135).

1940, July 21. Incorporation of **Estonia, Latvia,** and **Lithuania** in the Soviet Union after Moscow, with German connivance, had secured military bases in those countries (ultimatums of June 15, 16, charging hostile activities), had occupied them militarily, and had arranged for pro-Soviet administrations to request admittance to the Soviet union.

1941, Apr. 13. RUSSIA AND JAPAN CONCLUDED A NEUTRALITY PACT.

June 22. GERMAN ARMIES INVADED RUSSIA WITHOUT WARNING (p. 1141).

1942, Jan. 29. Russia and Great Britain agreed to respect the sovereignty and political independence of Iran.

Aug. 12. Prime Minister Churchill visited Moscow (p. 1171).

1943, May 6. Marshal Stalin declared that Soviet Russia would hope to maintain friendly relations with a **strong, independent Poland** after the war.

May 23. The **Third International** (Communist) **was dissolved.** Moscow announced that **Communist parties** in other countries would be **autonomous** henceforth.

1944, Feb. 1. An **amendment to the constitution** of the Union of Soviet Socialist Republics granted **separate commissariats for defense and for foreign affairs** to each of the constituent republics. Each could thus maintain its own army (which would form, however, a component element in the army of the U.S.S.R.) and could conduct its own negotiations with foreign countries and conclude treaties with them.

July 24. Soviet forces drove the Germans from the last large Russian city by **liberating**

Pskov. This opened the way for a Soviet drive against the German divisions holding Estonia.

Sept. 8. The Soviets imposed **peace terms on Bulgaria** (p. 1212).

Oct. 20. In Yugoslavia partisan forces and Soviet troops **occupied Belgrade.**

Dec. 10. The U.S.S.R. and France concluded a **twenty-year treaty of alliance and mutual security.**

1945, Apr. 5. The **Soviet Union denounced** its five-year non-aggression pact with Japan.

May 7. Surrender of Germany. Formal ratification was signed in Berlin May 9.

June 29. The **Soviet Union acquired Ruthenia** from Czechoslovakia.

Aug. 8. THE SOVIET UNION DE-CLARED WAR ON JAPAN (p. 1156).

Aug. 14. Surrender of Japan.

The ability of Soviet Russia to withstand the terrific shock of German invasion and its decisive contributions to Germany's defeat were generally recognized as signs of its great inherent strength. Yet with close to 25 million people rendered homeless by the war, and large areas in complete devastation, the Soviet government was faced with a tremendous task of reconstruction. Despite these domestic difficulties, the Soviet Union, in its foreign policy, was able with considerable skill and initial success, to use the inevitable international confusion of the post-war period for the advancement of Communist (and hence Soviet) influence.

1946, Feb. 10. The first **general elections** since 1937 for the **supreme soviet** returned the official list of approved candidates.

Mar. 15. The fourth **five-year plan,** designed to increase pre-war industrial output by more than 50 per cent, was adopted by the supreme soviet. Much of the necessary industrial equipment was collected from regions under Soviet occupation.

Mar. 19. In a series of governmental changes, **President Michael Kalinin** resigned because of ill health and was **succeeded by** the former trade-union leader **Nikolai Shvernik.** A **council of ministers** (with **Stalin** as chairman and Foreign Minister **Molotov** as deputy chairman) **replaced** the former **council of people's commissars.**

June 28. The **ministry of state control** announced widespread dismissals in the industrial field for incompetence and dishonesty. This was followed in August by a similar purge of agricultural offenders.

Nov. 18. Marshal **Koniev** replaced **Marshal Zhukov** as **commander-in-chief** of Soviet armed forces.

1947, Mar. 3. Stalin was succeeded as minister of defense by General **Bulganin.**

Mar. 5. The **Soviet Union rejected** the report of the U.N. Atomic Energy Commission on **atomic control.**

July. The **Soviet Union** and her satellites refused to participate in European economic reconstruction under the **Marshall Plan** (p. 1164).

Oct. According to official reports of the Soviet **state planning commission** (Gosplan), Russia's industrial output under the **five-year plan,** while failing to reach its yearly goal in 1946, surpassed it in 1947. Shortage of manpower continued to be the main economic drawback. A severe food shortage, resulting from drought and crop failures in 1946, was relieved by an excellent harvest in 1947, and on

Dec. 15. The government was able to abolish food rationing. At the same time, on

Dec. 16. A drastic **currency devaluation,** at the rate of ten to one, brought renewed hardships to most people, but served to strengthen further the Soviet economy.

1948, Feb.–Mar. The U.S.S.R. concluded treaties of friendship and mutual assistance with **Roumania, Hungary,** and **Bulgaria.**

Feb. 10. The **central committee of the Communist Party** accused Soviet composers, including **Dmitri Shostakovich, Sergei Prokofief,** and **Aram Khachaturian,** of losing touch with the masses by showing bourgeois influences in their works. The accused confessed and repented.

Apr. 6. The U.S.S.R. concluded a military assistance pact with **Finland.**

Aug. A further ideological shake-up occurred when the biologist, **Trofim Lysenko,** backed by the central committee, condemned the generally accepted "formal genetics," based on the findings of **Gregor Mendel** (p. 601), and substituted the outmoded teachings of **Michurin,** as in complete accordance with Marxian doctrine.

Aug. 31. Andrei Zhdanov, deputy premier and one of the party's leading ideologists, died.

1949, Mar. 4. A series of governmental changes was initiated with the replacement of Foreign Minister **V. M. Molotov** by **A. Vishinsky** and of Minister of Defense Marshal **N. A. Bulganin** by Marshal **A. M. Vassilievsky.** Both Molotov and Bulganin continued as members of the politburo.

Sept. 27. The **U.S.S.R. repudiated** her 1945 treaty of friendship with **Yugoslavia.**

Dec. 31. Stalin's seventieth birthday was the occasion for world-wide Communist celebrations. The announcement of several Stalin peace prizes was seen as a move in the Soviet **"peace offensive,"** which had become the main Communist propaganda weapon in the "cold war."

1950, Jan. 12. The **death penalty,** abolished after the war, was **reintroduced** for espionage, treason, and sabotage.

Feb. 14. **The U.S.S.R.** and the **Chinese People's Republic** signed a thirty-year **treaty of alliance.**

Oct. 20–21. **Molotov and the foreign ministers of East Germany, Poland, Bulgaria, Hungary, and Roumania, meeting at Prague,** denounced the agreement of the Western Big Three to liberalize their German policy (see West Germany, p. 1194), and called for German unification and a German peace treaty.

1951, Jan. 5. After a two-year stalemate the U.S.S.R. agreed to reopen talks with the United States on January 15 for a settlement of its $11 billion **lend-lease aid account** in accord with the 1942 agreement, but negotiations were suspended indefinitely on January 31.

Feb. 22. The Soviet press announced that in recent elections for the supreme soviet, the Stalinist bloc had won a popular majority of 99.76 per cent.

Apr. 16. The Moscow radio announced the **successful completion of the fourth five-year plan;** production had increased by 73 per cent over 1940.

1952, Oct. 5–14. The nineteenth party congress gave special attention to outlining the **transition from socialism to communism;** the presidium replaced the politburo and assumed the functions of the ogburo.

1953, Jan. 31. A *Pravda* announcement of the "Doctors' Plot" to kill leading Soviet commanders presaged a purge, especially of Jews, which ended with Stalin's death (Mar. 5), and the release of doctors arrested (Apr. 4).

Mar. 5. **STALIN DIED** and was interred in the Lenin mausoleum, March 9.

Mar. 6. **Georgi M. Malenkov** became head of the Soviet government with the following first deputy chairmen of the council of ministers: **Laurentia Beria, Vyacheslav Molotov** (also foreign minister), Marshal **Nikolai Bulganin,** and **Lazar Kaganovich.** Vishinsky, formerly foreign minister, became permanent Soviet representative at the U.N.

Mar. 20. **Nikita Khrushchev** succeeded Malenkov as first secretary of the Communist Party's central committee.

June 22. The government lifted most of its **curbs on travel by foreigners,** including diplomatic personnel.

July 10. **Beria's expulsion from the party** and dismissal as minister of internal security was announced. His execution, along with six associates, December 23, followed conviction of treason by the Soviet supreme court.

Aug. 8. Premier Malenkov declared that "the United States no longer possesses a monopoly of the hydrogen bomb."

Nov. 16. The **International Labor Office** rejected a Soviet application for membership.

1954, Feb. 26. The government decreed a change in the **status of the Crimea,** making it a part of the Soviet Ukraine.

May 3. The government, with one reservation, ratified the **genocide convention,** making illegal the destruction of religious, racial, ethnic, or national groups.

Nov. 22. **Andrei Y. Vishinsky,** chief Soviet delegate to the U.N., **died.**

1955, Jan. 15. The Soviet Union recognized the **sovereignty of West Germany.**

Feb. 8. **Malenkov resigned** as chairman of the council of ministers and was succeeded by **Marshal Bulganin.**

Feb. 9. In his inaugural address, Premier Bulganin emphasized the Sino-Soviet tie. **Marshal Gregory K. Zhukov** was appointed minister of defense.

Mar. 2. The government decreed a **decentralized system of agricultural planning** to provide the farmer with greater initiative and independence.

May 7. The presidium of the supreme soviet annulled the **treaties of friendship with Britain and France.**

Aug. 12. The government announced a **reduction** by December 15 **of its armed forces** by 640,000 men because of the post-Geneva conference "relaxation of international tension" (p. 1159).

Oct. 10. The government announced a plan to offer industrial and agricultural equipment and technical assistance to any underdeveloped Arab or Asian nation.

Nov. 18. **Bulganin and Khrushchev arrived in New Delhi** to begin their visit to India, Burma, and Afghanistan.

Dec. 29. In addresses in Moscow, Bulganin and Khrushchev denounced western "colonialism," and Khrushchev criticized the **aerial inspection plan** proposed by President Eisenhower.

1956, Feb. 14. At the opening of the twentieth congress of the Communist Party of the U.S.S.R., Khrushchev launched an **attack on Stalin** and the **"cult of personality";** he also declared that **coexistence** was now the goal of Soviet foreign policy. The congress, sitting till February 25, adopted the **sixth five-year plan.**

Apr. 23. **Khrushchev,** on a ten-day **visit to England,** April 18–27, announced that the U.S.S.R. would produce an **H-bomb guided missile.**

May 14. The government announced a **reduction** by 1.2 million men **in the armed forces** by May 1, 1957.

June 1. **Foreign Minister Molotov resigned**

his post, and was succeeded by **Dmitri T. Shepilov,** editor of *Pravda.*

July 17. Despite its friendship with Arab countries, the Soviet government signed an **agreement to step up its oil deliveries to Israel.**

Oct.–Nov. U.S.S.R. forces were involved in the **Hungarian revolt** (p. 1206).

Dec. 26. The state of **war with Japan was ended.**

1957, Feb. 11. A January 9 decree was revealed, providing for the **rehabilitation of five minority groups:** the Balkars, Chechens, Ingush, Kalmyks, and Karachais, who had been accused of disloyalty and exiled to Central Asia and Kazakhstan during World War II.

Feb. 15. Foreign Minister Dmitri T. Shepilov was replaced by **Andrei Gromyko.**

May 7. Khrushchev presented a plan to the supreme soviet for a sweeping **reorganization of industrial production,** including the establishment of 92 economic regions.

July 3. *Tass* reported the **ouster of Vyacheslav Molotov, Georgi Malenkov, and Lazar M. Kaganovich** from the central committee and from its presidium because of anti-party activities; **Dmitri Shepilov** was ousted on the 4th.

Sept. The overly optimistic sixth five-year plan was replaced by a **seven-year plan** (1959–1965), the goals of which were to be worked out by mid-1958.

Oct. 5. THE SOVIET UNION FIRED AN EARTH SATELLITE, *Sputnik I,* into orbit, which circled the globe at 18,000 m.p.h. (p. 1357).

Oct. 26. Marshal Gregory K. Zhukov was dismissed as defense minister and succeeded by **Marshal Rodion Y. Malinovsky.** Later (Nov. 2) Zhukov was ousted from the presidium and central committee for promoting his own "cult of personality" in the army.

Nov. 3. With a live dog aboard, *Sputnik II,* the second earth satellite, was fired into outer space.

1958, Mar. 27. NIKITA S. KHRUSHCHEV SUCCEEDED MARSHAL BULGANIN AS PREMIER. On March 31 the supreme soviet approved all of Khrushchev's political appointments, including those of **Anastas I. Mikoyan** and **Frol R. Kozlov,** who were both given the title of first deputy premier.

Mar. 31. Foreign Minister Gromyko announced Soviet **suspension of nuclear weapons tests.**

Oct. 29. Boris Pasternak, Soviet writer, informed the Swedish Academy of his "voluntary refusal" to accept the **Nobel prize** in literature, which was awarded him on October 23 for his novel, *Doctor Zhivago.*

1959, Jan. 27–Feb. 5. The twenty-first party congress in Moscow adopted a new **seven-year economic plan.**

Feb. 21–Mar. 3. British **Prime Minister Macmillan visited Russia** (p. 1174).

June 6. Khrushchev stated that unless the Western powers agreed to a **nuclear free zone** in the Balkans, Soviet rocket bases would be set up in Albania, Bulgaria, and Roumania.

July 24. U.S. **Vice President Nixon** opened the American national exhibition in Moscow, engaging in informal debate with Khrushchev.

Sept. 15–27. Khrushchev visited the United States (p. 1231).

1960, Jan. 14. Khrushchev announced that the Soviet Union would **reduce its standing armed forces** by a third in 1960–1961.

Jan. 14. Talks reopened with the United States, after a lapse of seven years, **on lend-lease debts,** but again broke off without agreement, February 23.

Feb. 13–Mar. 5. Khrushchev toured Asia.

Mar. 29. A **trade pact with China** provided for an exchange of goods totaling 7.9 billion rubles.

May 1. A high altitude United States reconnaissance plane, a **U-2, was shot down over Soviet Russia.** Khrushchev used this incident to break up the **Paris summit conference** (p. 1160).

May 30. The Soviet defense minister announced that Soviet rockets had been ordered to fire on any foreign base from which an Allied plane took off for a flight over the U.S.S.R.

Aug. 17. United States U-2 pilot **Francis Gary Powers** pleaded guilty before a high Soviet military tribunal to charges of having flown an intelligence mission over the Soviet Union. On August 19 he was found guilty of espionage for the United States and sentenced to ten years' loss of liberty.

1961, April 12. Major Yuri A. Gagarin, in spaceship *Vostok I,* became the first man successfully to **orbit the earth;** he circled the earth for 108 minutes at a maximum altitude of 203 miles (p. 1357).

July 8. Khrushchev announced the **suspension of planned Soviet reductions in the armed forces** and an increase in defense expenditures as a result of the Berlin crisis (p. 1200).

Aug. 31. The **resumption of nuclear testing** was announced.

Oct. 17. Khrushchev, in an address opening the Soviet Communist Party's twenty-second congress in Moscow, offered to delay the year-end deadline for signing a **German peace treaty;** declared the U.S.S.R. would "probably" test a 50-megaton hydrogen bomb; and attacked Albania for pursuing Stalinist policies.

Oct. 30. An **explosion of a 50-plus megaton bomb** occurred in the Arctic.

1962, Feb. 10. The Soviet Union released **Francis Gary Powers,** United States pilot of the U-2 aircraft which crashed in the U.S.S.R. in May 1960, in exchange for **Col. Rudolf Abel,** Soviet spy convicted of espionage by the United States in 1957.

Mar. 21. Khrushchev accepted President Kennedy's proposal for Soviet-American **co-operation in outer space exploration** and research. Discussions regarding the possibility of such co-operation began on March 27.

July 13. Khrushchev told a group of United States newspaper editors that the U.S.S.R. possessed an **anti-missile missile** that could hit "a fly in space."

Aug. 5. The U.S.S.R. resumed its **nuclear tests** with a high altitude blast thought to be in the 40-megaton range.

Nov. 21. The government announced the **end of the state of alert** which called for Warsaw-pact and Soviet forces because of the Cuban crisis (p. 1246).

1963, Mar. 8. Khrushchev declared that de-Stalinization policies did not permit individual **political liberties** or artistic **deviations from socialist realism.**

Aug. 5. A limited **nuclear test ban** treaty was signed in Moscow (p. 1161).

Nov. 1. The government announced the launching and successful performance of *Polyot I,* the first **maneuverable unmanned satellite.**

1964, Jan. 1. In a message to the world capitals, the Soviet Union proposed the **renunciation of force in all territorial disputes.**

Feb. 10-15. A meeting of the Communist Party's central committee called for the use of more scientific and technological methods to increase **agricultural production.**

Apr. 3. *Pravda* confirmed the **expulsion of Malenkov, Molotov, and Kaganovich from the Communist Party** for "anti-party" activity directed against Khrushchev.

Apr. 12. Khrushchev called on all Communist governments to join in a "resolute rebuff" to Chinese claims to a special place in the Socialist world. He insisted on the **equality of all Communist countries.**

May 11-25. Visit of Khrushchev to Egypt and inspection of work on the projected Aswan Dam. He promised Soviet aid and support of Egypt in times of crisis.

June 16-July 4. Khrushchev's visits to the Scandinavian countries, with suggestions that they resign from NATO.

Oct. 12-13. Three men in a Soviet spacecraft completed 16 orbits of the earth.

Oct. 14-15. DEPOSITION OF KHRUSHCHEV, charged by his opponents with hasty decisions, phrase-mongering, personality cult, etc. The new first secretary of the Communist Party was **Leonid I. Brezhnev** and the new premier **Aleksei N. Kosygin.**

1965. Efforts to revitalize the Soviet economy. In the industrial sphere more freedom of decision was given to management and a system of profit-sharing was introduced. More emphasis was placed on increased production of consumer goods. In agriculture too the collective farmers were assured of a monthly wage and of old-age pensions. Expanded use of fertilizers and introduction of improved varieties of seed.

Feb. 11-15. Visit of Kosygin to North Vietnam and North Korea: proclamation of Soviet support to strengthen the defenses of North Vietnam.

Mar. 1-15. A meeting of representatives **of Communist parties** was boycotted not only by the Chinese, but by the North Vietnamese, the North Koreans, the Indonesians, the Japanese, and the Roumanians and Albanians. All efforts to bridge the rift between the U.S.S.R. and Communist China proved unavailing.

Mar. 18-19. Lieutenant Colonel Aleksei A. Leonov in the Soviet spacecraft *Voskhod II* became the **first human being to walk in space** (p. 1357).

1966, Feb. 14. Conviction and imprisonment of Andrei Sinyavsky and Yuli Daniel for arranging the publication of anti-Soviet writings in the West. In the entire sphere of literature and art the Soviet authorities frowned upon extension of freedom of expression. Neither **Pasternak** nor **Solshenitzyn** was able to go to Stockholm to accept the Nobel Prize awarded him. On the other hand prominent scientists such as **Sakharov** and even **Kapitsa,** being essential to the Soviet military effort as well as the space program, went unpunished despite their repeated pleas for greater freedom of thought and expression and improved relations with the West.

Mar. 29-Apr. 8. Twenty-third Soviet Communist Party congress. The Chinese Communists not only rejected an invitation to attend, but also seized the occasion for a new blast against Soviet policies.

Apr. 21-27. Visit of Foreign Minister Gromyko to Italy and to the Vatican. His visit led to conclusion of an agreement for the construction of a Fiat automobile factory in Russia (May 4).

June 20-July 1. Visit of President de Gaulle to Russia: agreement on improved trade and cultural relations (p. 1184).

Dec. 1-19. Visit of Premier Kosygin to

France, followed (Dec. 20–27) by an extended visit to Turkey.

1967, Jan. 27. Signature of the **treaty for the exploration and uses of outer space** (p. 1358).

Feb. 6–13. **Visit of Premier Kosygin to London,** where he resisted all British efforts to enlist Soviet support for attempts to arrive at peace in Vietnam.

June. **Outbreak of the Arab-Israeli war.** The U.S.S.R., which had for years supplied the UAR with military equipment and training, immediately began the replacement of the matériel (esp. planes) which had been wiped out in the Israeli surprise attack. At the same time the Soviet government began to strengthen its **naval units in the eastern Mediterranean** and even in the **Indian Ocean,** presaging a fundamental change in the balance of power in the Middle East and Indian Ocean areas.

July 7. **Marshal Ivan I. Yakubovsky** named supreme commander of the Warsaw pact forces.

1968, June 3. Conclusion of a **Soviet-British trade treaty.**

June 4. Signature of the **treaty for non-proliferation of nuclear weapons,** ratified Nov. 24, 1969 (p. 1163).

Aug. **Invasion and occupation of Czechoslovakia** by Soviet and other Warsaw pact forces (p. 1204).

1969, Mar. 2, 15. Serious **border clashes** between Soviet and Communist Chinese troops threatened the possibility of major conflict.

June 15–17. **Conference of Communist Parties in Moscow,** with 75 parties represented. Chief subject of debate was the deepening division in the Communist world, but the final outcome was refusal of the conference to condemn and outlaw Communist China. The conference revealed much criticism of the Soviet action in Czechoslovakia.

Sept. 11. Brief **conference of Premier Kosygin** (returning from North Vietnam) **and Premier Chou En-lai** at the airport in Peking.

1970, Aug. 12. Signature of the important **SOVIET TREATY WITH THE GERMAN FEDERAL REPUBLIC.** It reflected, among other things, the keen desire of the Soviet government to secure more technical aid from Germany (p. 1199).

Oct. 6–14. **Visit of President Pompidou of France to Russia:** discussions of ways and means for increasing trade and for collaboration in the exploitation of Soviet mineral resources. An agreement was concluded for closer political and cultural consultation (p. 1184).

Nov. 17. Beginning of **Strategic Arms Limitation Talks** (SALT) between the United States and the Soviet Union, at Helsinki (p. 1163).

Nov. 23. Signature of a new **trade pact with Communist China,** reviving a trade which had become all but non-existent. There were indications of slight improvement in relations as China emerged from the Cultural Revolution and began to re-establish its position in the world.

14. POLAND

(*From p. 1039*)

1939, Sept. 1. **POLAND WAS INVADED by the German armed forces,** and seventeen days later **Soviet troops marched in** from the east (p. 1135).

Sept. 28. **GERMANY AND RUSSIA** agreed to divide Poland between them.

Sept. 30. Polish exiles formed a provisional **government-in-exile** at Paris.

1940, June 19. The government-in-exile transferred from Paris to London.

1941, Dec. 11. The government-in-exile **declared war on Japan.**

1943, April 16. The government-in-exile asked the **International Red Cross** to investigate a German report that **10,000 Polish officers,** allegedly slain by the Russians, had been **found near Smolensk.**

April 18. **Soviet radio** declared the slaughter and burial of **Polish officers** near Smolensk could be traced to the **German Gestapo,** and

(Apr. 27) suspended relations with Poles in London.

1944, Aug. 1. **Polish underground forces in** Warsaw **under General Tadeo Bor attacked the German forces of occupation.** Soviet troops, although they had almost reached Warsaw, failed to support the uprising, which was suppressed by October 2.

1945, Apr. 21. The **Soviet government** and a **Polish provisional government** set up in Moscow agreed on a **twenty-year treaty** of mutual aid.

June 12. The British and French, who favored the Polish government-in-exile at London, persuaded the U.S.S.R. to agree to a **tripartite commission** which would aid in the **organization of a Polish government.** At the Yalta conference (p. 1151), Poland's eastern territories were reduced approximately to the "Curzon line" of 1919 (p. 1037), while its western border, pending a final peace settlement, was extended to the **Oder-Neisse line** in eastern Germany. The leadership of post-war Poland was claimed by two rival groups, the Soviet-sponsored **provisional government at Lublin,** and the Polish **government-in-exile in London.** After lengthy negotiations,

June 28. A **government of national unity** was formed, under Socialist **Premier Eduard Osobka-Morawski** of the Lublin administration. It was recognized by the Western powers, though its leanings turned out to be decidedly pro-Soviet. For this reason many Polish citizens, who, as displaced persons or members of Poland's armed forces, were still in western Europe, refused to be repatriated.

1946, Jan. 6. The government announced the **nationalization of all industries** employing more than fifty workers.

June 30. A **popular referendum** approved the government's program of nationalization and land reform, and the establishment of a one-house parliament, as advocated by the Communists.

1947, Jan. 19. The first **general election,** preceded by repressive measures against Deputy Prime Minister **Stanislaw Mikolajczyk's Peasant Party,** gave the government bloc 394 seats and the Peasant Party 28. Both Great Britain and the United States charged that the Yalta provisions for free and honest elections had been violated.

Feb. 4. **Boleslaw Bierut** was elected **president of the republic** and **Josef Cyrankiewicz** formed a new coalition cabinet.

Feb. 19. The diet approved an **interim constitution** and proclaimed liberty and equality for all citizens.

Sept. 14. Poland **denounced its concordat** and entered upon a series of conflicts with the Catholic Church.

Oct. 24. A campaign among pro-government members of the Peasant Party for his dismissal led to **Mikolajczyk's flight to London** and the purge of his followers from the ranks of the Peasant Party.

1948. The **transformation of Poland into a Communist-dominated Soviet satellite** made further headway as the Socialist Party was fused with the Communists, the Peasant Party joined the government bloc, a compulsory youth organization was set up, and the judiciary was changed along Communist lines.

June 26. A five-year **trade agreement** was signed with the **Soviet Union** to counterbalance the Marshall Plan, in which Poland had refused to participate.

Sept. 5. The secretary general of the Communist Polish Workers' Party, **Wladyslaw Gomulka,** was forced to resign because of ideological deviation from the Soviet line.

1949, Jan. 25. Poland joined the **Council for Mutual Economic Assistance.**

Sept. 30. **Poland** again showed its adherence to Soviet and Cominform policy when it **denounced its treaty of friendship with** Yugoslavia.

Nov. 7. Soviet **Marshal Konstantin Rokossovsky** was appointed **minister of defense and commander-in-chief of the Polish army.** The latter was thoroughly reorganized along Soviet lines.

Nov. 11–13. The **central committee of the United Workers' Party** expelled a number of prominent members for "Titoist" leanings.

1950. **Poland's relations with the western powers,** which had deteriorated steadily since the war, **came close to the breaking point** as several western diplomats and correspondents were accused of hostile acts against the Polish government.

Mar. 20. Hostility between church and state led to the **confiscation of church lands** and other restrictions on Catholic activities.

June 6. The **East German Democratic Republic recognized the Oder-Neisse line as final.** Most Germans east of this line had been expelled and the region had been thoroughly Polonized.

1951, May 22. The deputy prime minister met with Soviet Foreign Minister Vishinsky and signed an **agreement to cede territory in the Lublin area** to the U.S.S.R. in return for part of Drohobycz province, reportedly containing enough oil wells to increase Polish oil production by 20 per cent.

1952, Nov. 20. With the abolition of the presidency by the **new constitution,** President Boleslaw Bierut stepped down to become premier. The **council of state** became the nation's highest political organ.

1953, Dec. 18. The Warsaw radio reported that all **Roman Catholic bishops** in Poland had taken an oath of loyalty to the state.

1954, Mar. 19. **Josef Cyrankiewicz** succeeded Boleslaw Bierut as prime minister.

1956, Apr. 6. **Wladyslaw Gomulka,** who had been arrested in 1951, and other Polish Communists were reported to have been **freed and rehabilitated.**

June 28. **Rioting,** leading to more than one hundred deaths, broke out **in Poznan** after workers had demonstrated for better social and economic conditions.

Oct. 10. Signs of an approaching storm occurred when the **trials of Poznan rioters** ended abruptly and (Oct. 16) several Communist leaders urged that Soviet officers be removed from the Polish army.

Oct. 20. Wladyslaw Gomulka re-entered the central committee of the Communist

Party. While Khrushchev and other Soviet leaders hastily arrived to plead for the continuation of pro-Soviet policies, Defense Minister and Commander-in-Chief Konstantin K. Rokossovsky, a former Soviet officer, ordered troops to take positions near Warsaw. **Polish and Soviet frontier troops exchanged fire.**

Oct. 21. Gomulka became first secretary of the Polish Communist Party. By not electing Marshal Rokossovsky to the new politburo, the Polish Communist Party gained some **independence from interference by the Soviet Union.**

Oct. 24. Gomulka announced the **return of Soviet troops** stationed in Poland **to their regular bases** "within two days." But the Soviet troop removal, which began on October 25, did not include the three or four Soviet divisions from East Germany, which had entered Poland a few days earlier. Polish militia used tear gas to quell **Polish attacks on Soviet army installations** at Liegnitz.

Oct. 28. Marshal Rokossovsky returned to the U.S.S.R. when an investigation unearthed evidence of his plot to stage a military coup against Gomulka.

Oct. 29. Cardinal Wyszinski was released from custody.

Oct. 30. The Gomulka government decided to present the Soviet Union with a bill for Poland's fair share (15 per cent) of the **German reparations payments** to the Soviet Union.

Nov. 18. Gomulka and Premier Cyrankiewicz signed an **agreement** in Moscow with Khrushchev and Bulganin **for equality in Soviet-Polish relations.**

Dec. 17. A Polish-Soviet agreement limited the **role of Soviet troops** in Poland.

1957, Jan. 20. The **National Front,** led by Gomulka, was victorious in the national elections.

Feb. 27. Parliament approved the new government of Premier Josef Cyrankiewicz.

May 1. Subject to **United States** congressional authorization, the United States formally agreed to provide $95 million aid in the form of commodities and mining machinery, and a month later (June 7) arranged two loans to Poland amounting to $48,900,000.

1958, Dec. 6. The government revealed plans for building an **oil pipeline** from Russian fields to Poland and East Germany.

1959, Mar. 31. The **repatriation of Poles from the Soviet Union** to East Poland, under the agreement of November 1956, ended, after some 250,000 Poles had been repatriated.

1960– While the Polish government remained a reliable partner of the Soviet government, especially in the ideological conflict between Moscow and Peking, growing unrest among intellectuals and artists obliged the government to relax measures of repression and to accept greater academic and business contacts with the West.

1964, Aug. 12. Edward Ochab, a veteran Polish Communist, elected president by the Sejur, to replace Aleksander Zawardzki, deceased.

1966, May 3. Celebration of 1000 years of Polish Christianity. The projected attendance of Pope Paul was vetoed by the Polish government.

1968. Growing **dissatisfaction with the Gomulka régime:** student demonstrations and outbreaks, accompanied by much factional struggle in government ranks. This led to a **purge of** "Zionist" elements and the emigration of many Jews. Gomulka, however, retained the support of the Soviet authorities.

Aug. The invasion and occupation of Czechoslovakia. Golmulka supported the Soviet position 100% and Polish troops participated in the military operations (p. 1204).

Nov. 11-16. The **Polish Communist Party Congress** failed to shake Gomulka's position.

1970, Dec. 7. Signature of the **TREATY WITH THE GERMAN FEDERAL REPUBLIC,** by which the latter at least provisionally recognized the Oder-Neisse line as Poland's western frontier and the Polish government assented to the repatriation of Germans still living in the area east of that line (p. 1199).

Dec. 14. Outbreak of serious **RIOTS IN GDAŃSK AND OTHER PORT CITIES** resulting from food shortages and increased prices on food and other commodities. Police and troops were able to quell the disturbances only with difficulty and with considerable loss of life. The Gomulka régime was so badly shaken that on

Dec. 20. Gomulka and other members of the politburo were obliged to resign. Edward Gierek, chief of the party in Upper Silesia, succeeded to Gomulka's offices.

15. THE SCANDINAVIAN STATES

(From p. 1043)

The chief concern of the Scandinavian countries during the post-war period was with military security. Negotiations between Denmark, Norway, and Sweden in 1948–1949 for a joint defense pact broke down as Denmark and Norway (together with Iceland) decided to join the North Atlantic pact, while Sweden was determined to do nothing that might impair its traditional neutrality. Finland likewise tried to maintain a middle course. But while it avoided carefully any association with the West, it could not very well refuse Soviet overtures for more cordial relations.

In economic and cultural matters, however, the Scandinavian states drew ever closer. On Feb. 12, 1953, all of them except Finland joined in organizing the **Nordic Council,** which Finland joined two years later. The council consisted of members of the various parliaments, meeting annually for discussion of common problems and for general consultation. Presently committees were set up to deal with economic, social, financial, and cultural matters. In 1967 the council set up the **Nordic Cultural Foundation,** and in 1969 it endorsed plans for a **Nordic Economic Union.** Various other foundations were established for scientific and other purposes.

a. DENMARK

(From p. 1043)

1940, Apr. 9. GERMAN ARMED FORCES OCCUPIED DENMARK.

1941, Apr. 9. The people of **Greenland,** while affirming their loyalty to Christian X of Denmark, **accepted the protection offered by the United States.**

May 17. The **Icelandic parliament announced that Iceland would separate from Denmark.**

1945, May 5. Vilhelm Buhl, Social Democrat, formed the first post-war cabinet.

Oct. 30. General elections for the first time gave 18 of the 148 seats in the lower house to the Communists. The Social Democrats lost an equal number, but still emerged as the strongest party. Since no coalition was possible, **Knud Kristensen** formed a Liberal minority government.

1947, Apr. 20. King Christian X died and was succeeded by his son, as **KING FREDERICK IX.**

Oct. 28. General elections brought an increase of Socialist strength and a corresponding decline of the Communists.

Nov. 13. Hans Hedtoft formed a Social Democratic minority cabinet.

1949, Apr. 4. Denmark signed the North Atlantic treaty.

1950, Sept. 5. In a **general election** the Socialists showed further gains.

Oct. 28. The leader of the Liberal Agrarians, **Erik Eriksen,** formed a coalition cabinet of Liberals and Conservatives.

1951, Apr. 27. A twenty-year **agreement with the United States** was signed, providing for the joint **defense of Greenland** against the threat of attack or invasion.

1953, Apr. 21. Following a setback in the April 21 elections, Premier Eriksen's coalition Agrarian-Liberal-Conservative government announced its resignation. King Frederick asked the Social Democratic Laborites to form a new cabinet.

June 5. King Frederick signed a **new constitution** which abolished the upper house of parliament and enlarged the lower house *(Folketing).*

Sept. 30. Hans Hedtoft formed a new Social Democratic minority cabinet.

1955, Jan. 29. Prime Minister Hedtoft died, and was succeeded by **Hans Christian Hansen.**

1957, May 15. After losing their parliamentary majority in the May 14 elections, Premier **Hansen** and his Social Democratic government **resigned.**

May 27. Hansen formed a **coalition government** of nine Social Democrats, four Radical Liberals, and three Single Taxers.

1960, Feb. 19. Prime Minister Hansen died, and Finance Minister **Viggo Kampmann,** also a Social Democrat, succeeded him.

Nov. 19. Premier Kampmann formed a new minority coalition government made up of Social Democrats and Radicals.

1962, Aug. 31. Premier Kampmann resigned for reasons of health. The majority Social Democratic party named Foreign Minister **Jens Otto Krag** as his successor.

1964, Feb. 21. Premier Krag, on a **state visit to the Soviet Union,** stated that he hoped to increase trade with the U.S.S.R.

June 16. Khrushchev arrived in Denmark to begin an 18-day Scandinavian tour.

1968, Jan. 23. In the **elections** Premier Krag and the Social Democrats retained their lead, but more conservative parties made significant gains and a **new government was formed by Hilmar Baunsgaard** (Radical Liberal), supported by a coalition of Conservatives, Agrarian Liberals, and Radical Liberals.

b. NORWAY

(From p. 1044)

1940, Apr. 9. GERMAN ARMED FORCES INVADED NORWAY (p. 1136).

1942, Feb. 1. The German commissioner for Norway, **Joseph Terboven,** appointed **Vidkun Quisling "minister-president"** of a puppet régime. Quisling abolished the Norwegian constitution (Feb. 7) and made himself **virtual dictator.**

1945, June 26. The leader of the Labor Party, **Einar Gerhardsen,** formed the first post-war coalition government.

Sept. 10. Vidkun Quisling was sentenced to death and **executed** on October 24.

Oct. 7. The first **general elections** since 1936 gave a majority to the Labor Party, and **Einar Gerhardsen** formed a Labor government.

1947, Mar. 3. Parliament rejected a Soviet request for military bases in **Spitsbergen.**

1949, Apr. 4. Norway signed the North Atlantic treaty.

Oct. 10. General elections increased the majority of the Labor Party, while the Communists lost all their seats in the lower house.

1950, Jan. 6. A serious imbalance of imports over exports necessitated shelving the **project of a customs union with Sweden and Denmark.**

1951, Nov. 13. Resignation of Labor Prime Minister Gerhardsen; and on

Nov. 19. Oscar Torp, the Labor Party's leader in parliament, **formed a government.**

1955, Jan. 14. Prime Minister Torp resigned, to be succeeded (Jan. 21) by Gerhardsen.

1957, Sept. 21. Crown Prince Olaf succeeded to the throne as **KING OLAF V,** following the death of his father, King Haakon VII.

1960, Sept. 28. An **agreement with Britain** was signed in Oslo allowing British trawlers to fish within six miles of the Norwegian coast for ten years; thereafter the limit would be twelve miles offshore.

1962, Apr. 28. Parliament approved the government's decision to apply for full **membership in the EEC.**

1963, Aug. 2. For the first time in 28 years the **Labor party was ousted** when parliament voted no confidence in the government of Premier Einar Gerhardsen. King Olaf V asked **John Lyng,** leader of the Conservative Party in parliament, to form a government. On August 27 a four-party coalition government led by Premier Lyng took office.

1965. The long rule of the **Labor Party was supplanted** by a coalition of four non-socialist parties under **PER BORTEN.**

c. SWEDEN

(From p. 1045)

1939, Sept. 3. Sweden preserved its neutrality throughout the **Second World War** as it had done throughout the First World War.

1941, June 25. In response to a demand from Germany and Finland the Swedish government allowed the **passage of one division of German troops** from Norway to Finland.

1942, Nov. 7. The Swedish foreign minister announced that **Sweden was determined to maintain neutrality** but regarded a free Finland and a free Norway as essential for the survival of a free Sweden.

1945, July 31. The coalition government of **Per A. Hansson** was replaced by a Social Democratic cabinet under Hansson.

1946, Oct. 5. Premier Hansson died and was succeeded by **Tage Erlander.**

1948, Sept. 19. General elections maintained the Social Democrats as the strongest party, while the Communists lost seven of their fifteen seats.

1950, Oct. 29. King Gustav V died. He was succeeded by his son as **KING GUSTAV VI ADOLF.**

1954, July 1. The inauguration of a **common labor market** with Norway, Denmark, and Finland placed workers on the same footing with respect to employment.

1957, Oct. 26. Premier Tage Erlander's Social Democratic and Agrarian government resigned, following the withdrawal of the Agrarians on October 24. On October 26, Erlander's **all-Socialist minority government** took office.

1961, Aug. 22. Premier Erlander said his government could not join the **Common Market** because the views of that organization could not be reconciled with Sweden's policy of neutrality, but

Aug. 28. He declared Sweden's willingness to negotiate with Common Market countries as long as any compromises did not affect Swedish neutrality.

1968, Sept. 15. In the **elections** the Social Democrats won an absolute majority of the seats in the lower house for the first time since 1946. **Tage Erlander** remained premier.

1969, Jan. Sweden established **diplomatic relations with North Vietnam** and became an asylum for deserters from the United States forces. On account of the Vietnam war sentiment against American "imperialism" ran high.

Parliament approved a **constitutional reform** establishing a unicameral Riksdag as of 1971.

Oct. 1. Resignation of Premier Erlander, chief of the Social Democratic Party.

Oct. 14. Olof Palme became premier.

1970, Sept. 20. The elections brought substantial losses to the dominant **Social Democratic Party,** while the Communists and the Center Party registered gains. Premier Palme, though his party was now in a minority, continued in office, with the approval of the Communists. He was faced with widespread discontent, despite the prosperity of the country, because of drastic legislation grievously affecting the status and income of the educated and upper classes.

d. FINLAND

(From p. 1046)

1939, Sept. 1. Finland announced its neutrality in the impending war.

Oct 5. The **Soviet government invited Fin-**

land to enter political discussions. The Finns mobilized (Oct. 9) and replied to Soviet proposals to garrison certain positions in Finland by offering counter proposals (Oct. 23). The talks were broken off (Nov. 13) and the U.S.S.R. denounced the Soviet-Finnish non-aggression treaty, which had been renewed April 7, 1934.

Nov. 30. SOVIET FORCES INVADED FINLAND, and Finland appealed to the League of Nations (Dec. 3) which responded (Dec. 14) by expelling the Soviet Union from the League. The SOVIET-FINNISH WAR lasted from November 30, 1939 to March 12, 1940, when Finland yielded territory and concessions to the Soviet Union.

1941, June 22. Finland attacked the Soviet Union in collaboration with the surprise attack launched by the Germans.

Sept. 22. Requests from Great Britain and subsequently (Oct. 3) from the United States that Finland cease its war with the U.S.S.R. were rejected by the Finns.

1944, Aug. 1. Risto Ryti, president of Finland, resigned his office and the Finnish parliament voted that Marshal Karl Gustav Mannerheim should succeed him.

Nov. 10. Juho Paasikivi formed a new cabinet. The Finnish Communist Party, having secured recognition, prepared to contest the elections.

1945, Mar. 3. FINLAND DECLARED WAR AGAINST GERMANY.

Mar. 17–18. The general election brought a swing to the Left.

Apr. 17. Paasikivi formed a new coalition cabinet.

1946, Feb. 21. A number of wartime leaders, among them ex-President Risto Ryti, were sentenced to prison for involving Finland in the war or preventing the conclusion of peace. They were pardoned, over Soviet protests, in 1949.

Mar. 4. President Mannerheim resigned for reasons of health.

Mar. 9. JUHO PAASIKIVI was elected president.

Mar. 24. Mauno Pekkala formed a new coalition government.

1947, Feb. 10. The FINNISH PEACE TREATY was signed at Paris. The Soviet Union received the Petsamo area, a fifty-year lease of a naval base at Porkkala, and substantial reparations.

1948, Apr. 6. The U.S.S.R. and Finland concluded a treaty of friendship and mutual assistance, directed primarily against Germany.

July 1–2. In the general election the Communists lost one-fourth of their parliamentary seats.

July 29. Karl-August Fagerholm formed a Social Democratic cabinet.

1949, Aug.–Sept. A wave of Communist-instigated strikes was defeated by firm government action and the loyalty of the non-Communist workers.

1950, Jan. 16–17. Parliamentary elections gave a majority to the parties supporting President Paasikivi, who was re-elected on February 15 for a term of six years.

Mar. Urho K. Kekkonen became premier and also minister of the interior (till January 1951). His government, with some changes, lasted until

1954, May 5. The leader of the Swedish People's Party, Ralph Törngren, formed a coalition government with the Social Democrats and the Agrarians. Kekkonen became foreign minister.

Oct. 14. Törngren resigned in the face of a threatened general strike protesting the high cost of living. On October 20 Kekkonen formed a coalition government of Social Democrats and Agrarians.

1955, Sept. 19. A treaty signed with the Soviet Union provided for the return to Finland of the Porkkala naval base. The Soviet government also agreed to permit all Finnish nationals, including war prisoners, to leave Russia if they wished. Porkkala was restored to Finland, January 26, 1956.

1956, Feb. Urho Kekkonen became president.

1957, Nov. 29. President Kekkonen ended a 43-day crisis with the appointment of Rainar von Fieandt, chairman of the Bank of Finland, to head a business government.

1958, Aug. 29. A four-week crisis ended with the approval of a new coalition cabinet, led by Social Democrat Karl-August Fagerholm.

Dec. 4. The resignation of five Agrarian party members of the cabinet touched off a crisis, resulting in the collapse of Premier Fagerholm's coalition Socialist government. On December 10 President Kekkonen, in a broadcast to his people, declared that "the overriding question" for Finnish foreign policy was good relations with the Soviet Union.

1961, July 14. Martti J. Miettunen, governor of Lapland, was named premier of a new Agrarian minority government. He succeeded Vieno Sukselainen, who resigned after being found guilty of administrative irregularities.

Oct. 30. The U.S.S.R., in a note to Finland, declared that the threat of aggression by West Germany was grounds for invoking the Soviet-Finnish mutual defense treaty of 1948. Consultations were requested.

Nov. 23–25. A communiqué, issued after a two-day meeting of Kekkonen and Khrushchev in Novosibirsk, Siberia, declared the Soviet Union's willingness to postpone military talks.

On November 26 Kekkonen reported to the Finnish people on his talks with Khrushchev, stating that all political opposition leaders who had earned Moscow's enmity should leave politics.

1962, Jan. 15–16. President Kekkonen received an overwhelming majority of the popular vote in the two-day presidential election. His Agrarian party received 145 seats in the 300-man electoral college, scheduled to meet on February 15 to select the president.

Feb. 4–5. In parliamentary elections, President Kekkonen's Agrarian Party replaced the Communists as the largest single parliamentary group.

Mar. 1. President Kekkonen was inaugurated for his second six-year term.

Apr. 13. Ahti K. Karjalainen formed a new coalition government.

1963, Aug. 30. Karjalainen's coalition government resigned following a cabinet disagreement on how to finance increases in farmers' incomes, but President Kekkonen requested the cabinet to remain in office.

Dec. 18. Reino R. Lehto was appointed to head a caretaker government.

1970, July 14. A **new coalition government** of socialists and non-socialists was formed by former **Premier Karjalainen.**

e. ICELAND

1939, Sept. 3. Iceland, as a dependency of Denmark, **remained neutral** when the Second World War commenced.

1940, May 9. British troops occupied Iceland to forestall the possibility that the Germans, who had seized Denmark a month earlier, might attempt to claim Iceland also.

1941, July 7. After an exchange of letters between Iceland and the United States concerning the defense of Iceland, the **United States landed troops** to supplement and ultimately to replace the British troops there. Iceland had formally **separated itself from Denmark** seven weeks earlier (May 17).

1944, July 17. ICELAND ESTABLISHED AS AN INDEPENDENT REPUBLIC.

1950, April. The Danish parliament passed a law annulling the Act of Union between Denmark and Iceland.

1951, Apr. 7. At the government's request, the **United States sent a contingent of its armed forces** to aid in Iceland's defense.

May 5. A **United States-Iceland agreement** was signed providing for the use by NATO nations of defense facilities in Iceland.

1952, July 1. Asgeir Asgeirsson was elected president.

1956, Mar. 28. Parliament called for the **withdrawal of foreign forces** from the country.

July 21. A new coalition was formed by the Progressive Party, the Social Democrats, and the Communist People's Alliance, with the latter filling two cabinet posts.

Dec. 6. The United States government revealed Iceland's **cancellation of its request for the withdrawal of United States forces.**

1958, Dec. 4. Premier Hermann Jonasson's coalition government of Progressive, Social Democratic, and Labor Alliance parties collapsed, in disagreement over economic policy.

1959, Nov. 19. Premier Emil Jonsson resigned, and Independence Party leader **Olafur Thors** formed a coalition government.

1963, June 11. Returns from the **parliamentary elections** (June 9) revealed that the coalition of Premier Thors' Independence Party and the Social Democratic Party had won 32 seats in the 60-seat parliament.

D. NORTH AMERICA

1. THE UNITED STATES

(*From p. 1054*)

1939, Sept. 5. On the outbreak of the Second World War the United States announced its neutrality.

Nov. 4. The **Neutrality Act** of May 1, 1937 (p. 1052) was amended, repealing the embargo on arms and placing **exports to belligerents on a cash and carry basis.**

1940, June 22. The congress passed a **National Defense Tax Bill** to produce $994,300,000 a year, and raised the national debt limit from $45 billion to $49 billion.

June 28. The Republican national convention at Philadelphia nominated **Wendell L. Willkie** and **Charles L. McNary** as candidates for the presidency and vice-presidency.

July 18. The Democratic national convention at Chicago nominated **Franklin D. Roosevelt** as presidential candidate for a third term, and **Henry A. Wallace** as candidate for vice-president.

July 20. President Roosevelt signed a bill providing for a **"two-ocean" navy** as part of a vast defense plan.

Sept. 16. The **Selective Training and Service Act** was adopted. The act provided for the **registration of all men between the ages of 21 and 36 years** of age, and for the training, for one year, of 1,200,000 troops and 800,000 reserves. On October 16, 16,400,000 men were registered, and the draft lottery commenced October 29.

Sept. 26. President Roosevelt placed an **embargo on the export of scrap iron and steel.**

Nov. 5.   FRANKLIN D. ROOSEVELT WAS RE-ELECTED PRESIDENT for a third term.

Dec. 20. President Roosevelt named a four-man **Defense Board** headed by **William A. Knudsen** to prepare defense measures and to hasten aid to Great Britain. The German government denounced this action as "moral aggression" on December 21.

1941, Jan. 8. President Roosevelt appointed a four-man **Office of Production Management** to coordinate defense activities.

Mar. 11. The congress passed the **LEND-LEASE ACT, empowering the president to provide goods and services to those nations whose defense he deemed vital to the defense of the United States.**

May 27. President Roosevelt proclaimed an unlimited state of national emergency.

June 16. The government ordered German consulates throughout the country closed. Three days later the German and Italian governments asked that United States consulates in Axis-controlled areas of Europe be closed.

Aug. 14.   THE ATLANTIC CHARTER. President Roosevelt and Prime Minister Churchill, representing the United States and Great Britain, issued a joint declaration of peace aims. They announced that their countries sought no aggrandizement, desired no territorial changes contrary to the wishes of the people concerned, respected the right of nations to choose their form of government, and wished to see sovereign rights and self-government restored to peoples who had been forcibly deprived of them. They likewise favored equality of economic opportunity with access to essential raw materials for all nations, they sought to promote friendly collaboration among the peoples of the world, fair labor standards, social security, freedom from fear and want, free traverse on the high seas, the abandonment of force, and the disarmament of aggressor nations.

Aug. 18. President Roosevelt signed a bill permitting the army to keep men in service eighteen months longer.

Sept. 20. A revenue measure, designed to provide for **defense expenditures** of $3,553,400,-000 became law.

Sept. 24.   Fifteen governments (nine in exile) **endorsed the Atlantic Charter.**

Nov. 6.   The United States extended a one billion dollar lend-lease credit to the Soviet Union.

Nov. 10. The **National Defense Mediation Board** ruled against **John L. Lewis** and the United Mine Workers of America in the captive coal-mine dispute. Lewis accepted arbitration (Nov. 22).

Dec. 2.   President Roosevelt asked the government of Japan for a definition of its aims in Indo-China, and appealed (Dec. 6) to **Emperor Hirohito** to help in preserving peace.

Dec. 7.   THE JAPANESE OPENED HOSTILITIES with a surprise attack on Hawaii, the Philippines, Guam, Midway Island, Hong Kong, and Malaya.

Dec. 8.   THE UNITED STATES CONGRESS DECLARED A STATE OF WAR WITH JAPAN.

Dec. 11.   GERMANY AND ITALY DECLARED WAR ON THE UNITED STATES.

Dec. 15.   Congress voted an appropriation of $10,077,077,005 for the defense of the United States and for lend-lease aid. Four days later it **extended the draft** for military service to men from 20 to 44 years of age.

1942, Jan. 13.   Donald M. Nelson became chief of the **War Production Board,** created to speed the armament program.

Jan. 30.   President Roosevelt signed the **Price Control Act** which was intended to limit inflation.

Apr. 4. The **War Production Board** halted all non-essential building in order to conserve materials.

Apr. 27.   President Roosevelt proposed that the American people **combat inflation** by a seven-point program: (1) heavier taxes, (2) a ceiling on prices, (3) wage stabilization, (4) price control on agricultural products, (5) increased purchase of war bonds, (6) the rationing of essential commodities if scarce, (7) reduction of installment buying.

June 30. The congress voted a **record appropriation of forty-two billion dollars** for the defense of the United States.

July 16. The **War Labor Board** decreed that, in the interest of **wage stabilization,** wage increases would be granted equivalent to the rise in living costs between January 1, 1941, and May 1942. This was known as the **Little Steel Award.**

Oct. 3.   James F. Byrnes was appointed **Director of Economic Stabilization.**

Oct. 12.   Attorney General Francis Biddle

announced that 600,000 **unnaturalized Italians** in the United States would no longer be classed as enemy aliens.

Nov. 8. UNITED STATES FORCES LANDED IN FRENCH NORTH AFRICA (p. 1148).

Dec. 16. The **seventy-seventh congress** adjourned after the longest session in United States history.

1943, Jan. 14–24. President Roosevelt attended the Casablanca conference (p. 1148).

Feb. 10. President Roosevelt established as a wartime measure a **minimum 48-hour work week** for areas where there was a labor shortage.

May 29. The **Office of War Mobilization**, directed by **James F. Byrnes**, became the supreme federal agency for the prosecution of the war effort on the home front.

June 26. The **Smith-Connally Anti-Strike Bill** made anyone who instigated or aided in promoting strikes in government-operated plants or mines subject to criminal penalties.

July 16. The **Office of Economic Warfare** superseded the Board of Economic Warfare and assumed some functions of the Reconstruction Finance Corporation. Later (Sept. 25) it was consolidated with the Lend-Lease Administration, the Office of Foreign Relief and Rehabilitation, the foreign procurement division of the Commodity Credit Corporation, and some sections of the Office of Foreign Economic Co-ordination. The new organ was named the **Foreign Economic Administration**.

Aug. 11–24. **Quebec conference** of Prime Minister Churchill and President Roosevelt (p. 1147).

Nov. 28–Dec. 1. TEHRAN CONFERENCE (p. 1157).

1944. June 6. INVASION OF NORMANDY (p. 1150).

July 21. Franklin D. Roosevelt was nominated for a **fourth term** as president of the United States by the Democratic national convention at Chicago. **Harry S Truman** was named candidate for vice-president. They won the subsequent election of November 7.

Nov. 27. Cordell Hull resigned as secretary of state and was succeeded by **Edward R. Stettinius**.

1945, Feb. 7–12. YALTA CONFERENCE (p. 1151).

Apr. 12. PRESIDENT ROOSEVELT DIED SUDDENLY at Warm Springs. Vice-President Truman became president.

May 18. President Truman informed the French ambassador that the United States would relinquish part of the American zone of occupation in Germany to the French.

June 9. The department of state an-

nounced that **Venezia Giulia, including Trieste,** would be placed under a temporary military administration established by the United States, Great Britain, and Yugoslavia.

Aug. 6–14. The **war in the Pacific ended** in a week of disaster for Japan (p. 1344). **The Japanese accepted terms August 14.**

1945, Nov.–1946, Mar. **Large-scale strikes** in several leading industries, after seriously curtailing production, led to a first round of wage increases.

Dec. 4. The senate approved **United States participation in the United Nations.**

1946, Apr.–May. A **second wave of strikes** hit the soft coal mines and the railroads. Before they were settled, the government had taken control of the railroads (May 17) and the coal mines (May 20).

June 25. The senate passed a measure extending **Selective Service** until March 31, 1947. Prior to this, public pressure had brought about the **hasty demobilization** of close to nine million men.

July 1–25. Experiments conducted at **Bikini** demonstrated the effect of an atomic explosion on warships and under water.

July 15. President Truman signed a bill extending a **credit of** $3.75 billion to Great Britain.

Sept. 20. Secretary of Commerce **Henry A. Wallace** was **asked to resign** following his criticism of the government's increasingly firm policy toward the Soviet Union.

Nov. 5. Congressional elections gave the **Republicans substantial majorities** in both houses.

Nov. 9. Following a futile battle with congress to maintain price and wage controls, **President Truman removed virtually all controls** except those on rent and some foods.

1947, Jan. 7. James F. Byrnes resigned as secretary of state and was succeeded by **General George C. Marshall**.

Feb. 2. The **United States and Canada** announced the continuation of their defense cooperation under the **Permanent Joint Defense Board** of 1940.

Mar. 12. President Truman, in a message to Congress, outlined the **TRUMAN DOCTRINE** of economic and military aid to nations threatened by Communism. He specifically requested urgently needed aid for **Greece** and **Turkey.** The Greek-Turkish Aid Bill went into effect on May 22.

June 5. Secretary Marshall, in a speech at Harvard University, called for a **European Recovery Program**, initiated by the European powers and supported by American aid (**MARSHALL PLAN**) (p. 1164).

June 23. Congress, over the president's

veto, passed the **Taft-Hartley Act,** which prohibited the use of union funds for political
purposes, introduced a 60-day notice before a
strike or lockout, outlawed the closed shop,
and empowered the government to serve injunctions against strikes likely to cripple the
nation's economy.

July 26. Congress approved the **unification
of the armed services** under a secretary of defense **(James V. Forrestal).**

1948, Mar. 14-31. Congress passed the **Foreign
Assistance Act (Marshall Plan)** and authorized
an initial $5.3 billion for European recovery.
Paul G. Hoffman was appointed chief of
the **Economic Co-operation Administration
(E.C.A.)** on Apr. 6.

Apr.-July. Strikes in the coal, railway, and
steel industries were stopped by government
action and a third round of wage increases,
to meet the constantly rising cost of living.

June 19. Congress passed a peace-time **Selective Service Bill** for men between 19 and 25.

Aug. 25. The **Soviet Union broke off all
consular relations with the United States** when
the latter refused to surrender a Soviet citizen
against her will.

Nov. 2. Contrary to most predictions,
**HARRY S TRUMAN WAS RE-ELECTED
president** over **Thomas E. Dewey** (Republican)
by 303 electoral votes to 189. At the same time
the Democrats gained a majority in both houses.

1949. Growing fear of Communism. The spread
of Communism in eastern Europe and the Far
East created a growing awareness among many
Americans of a possible Communist danger at
home. The trial and conviction for espionage
of Judith Coplon, employee of the Justice Department, the revelations made in connection
with the trial of Alger Hiss, formerly of the
State Department, and the trial of the leaders
of the American Communist Party were only
the more prominent among a large number of
investigations and restrictive measures conducted by federal, state, and local authorities
to uncover or prevent Communist infiltration,
espionage, and sabotage.

Jan.-Oct. In one of its longest peace-time
sessions, **congress,** largely because of the opposition of the southern Democrats, **failed to give
support** to the major points of **President Truman's "Fair Deal" program**—the repeal of the
Taft-Hartley Act and the enactment of federal
civil rights legislation. In the field of foreign
affairs, on the other hand, congress, on the
whole, shared the administration's international orientation.

Jan. 7. Secretary of State Marshall resigned for reasons of health and was succeeded
by **Dean Acheson.**

Jan. 20. HARRY S TRUMAN was inaugurated for his second term. In his inaugural
address he presented a four-point plan for
American foreign policy, **Point Four** of which
called for "a bold new program" of assistance
to economically underdeveloped areas.

Mar. 3. Secretary of Defense **Forrestal** resigned, worn out by his futile efforts to bring
about the unification of the armed services.
He was succeeded by **Louis A. Johnson.**

Apr. 4. The **NORTH ATLANTIC TREATY**
(p. 1164) was ratified by the senate on July 21
and signed by the president on July 25.

Aug. 10. President Truman signed a bill
establishing a **Department of Defense,** with
broader and more definite powers for the secretary of defense. **General Omar N. Bradley**
was appointed chairman of the joint chiefs
of staff (Aug. 11).

Sept. 15. Congress extended the **Reciprocal Trade Agreement Act** for two years.

Oct. 6. President Truman signed the **Mutual Defense Assistance Act** appropriating
more than one billion dollars for military aid
primarily to members of the Atlantic pact.

Oct. 14. The leaders of the **American Communist Party** were convicted of conspiracy to
advocate the violent overthrow of the United
States government and sentenced to fines and
imprisonment.

1950, Jan. 25. Alger Hiss was found guilty of
perjury for having denied his Communist
affiliations and his rôle in the transfer of State
Department secrets to the U.S.S.R. prior to the
war.

Jan. 31. President Truman instructed the
Atomic Energy Commission to proceed with
its work on the **hydrogen bomb.**

June 5. President Truman signed the third
Foreign Aid Bill, appropriating close to $3
billion for the European Recovery and Point
Four programs.

June 25. The **invasion of South Korea** by
North Korean forces led to

**June 27. UNITED STATES INTERVEN-
TION IN THE KOREAN WAR,** described as
"police action" to support the United Nations
(p. 1348).

June–Sept. The administration's policy
found immediate support in congress. Selective service was extended, the military budget
was almost doubled, and far-reaching military
aid was appropriated under the Mutual Defense Assistance Program.

July 8. General Douglas MacArthur was
appointed **commanding general of United Nations forces in Korea.**

July 20. The charges made by **Senator Joseph McCarthy** of large-scale Communist infiltration into the State Department were found
to be untrue by a senate committee. The

senator's careless accusations brought great hardships to a number of people.

Sept. 12. Secretary of Defense **Louis A. Johnson** resigned and was replaced by **General George C. Marshall.**

Sept. 23. Congress, over the president's veto, adopted the **Internal Security Bill,** which called for the registration of Communists and Communist "front" organizations.

Oct. 15. A meeting at **Wake Island** between **President Truman** and **General MacArthur** tried to clarify differences between the administration and its Far Eastern commander over America's policy in eastern Asia. MacArthur, on several occasions, and without authorization, had openly advocated a pro-Nationalist and anti-Communist policy in China. While such views were applauded by critics of the government's Far Eastern policy and of Secretary of State Acheson, the general's interference in matters outside his military sphere had caused considerable embarrassment to the administration's conduct of foreign policy.

Nov. 7. **Congressional elections** reduced the Democratic majority in both houses.

Dec. 16. Reversals suffered by United Nations troops in Korea led to the **proclamation of a state of national emergency** by President Truman. **Charles E. Wilson** was made head of the newly created **Office of Defense Mobilization.**

1951, Jan. 4. President Truman told his weekly news conference that the United States probably would not bomb China without a formal congressional declaration of war.

Jan. 5. The senate opened the **"great debate" on American foreign policy** with an attack on the administration by **Senator Robert A. Taft.**

Jan. 6. Washington revealed that United States **arms and ammunition** were being sent **to Nationalist China** to strengthen the defenses of Taiwan.

Feb. 26. The **twenty-second constitutional amendment,** limiting the presidency to two terms, came into force.

Mar. 12. The senate committee to investigate organized crime in interstate commerce **(Kefauver committee)** held its first public hearings in New York City. Two weeks of sensational disclosures followed.

Mar. 28. The commander of the U.S. 7th Fleet declared that any attempted invasion of the mainland or commando raids by the Chinese Nationalists would be blocked by the U.S. navy.

Apr. 4. After three months of debate, the senate approved (69–21) a resolution expressing the "sense" of its members on the **issue of sending troops to Europe.** It affirmed the

president's plan to send four divisions to Europe, but served notice that no additional divisions should be sent without further congressional approval.

Apr. 11. **General Douglas MacArthur was relieved of all his commands** in the Far East, to be succeeded by **General Matthew B. Ridgway.** In an address to a joint session of congress on April 19 MacArthur presented his arguments against the administration's policies. On April 24 the senate voted to conduct an investigation of the U.S. Far Eastern policy and the dismissal of MacArthur. Hearings, May 3–June 25, ended in approval of a limited war in Korea.

Apr. 25. Secretary of State Acheson revealed a U.S. commitment, undertaken ten weeks earlier, to give **military aid to the Chinese Nationalist government** for "the legitimate self-defense of Formosa."

June 3. **John Foster Dulles,** U.S. ambassador-at-large, arrived in London to try to dissuade Britain from its position that Communist China should participate in the negotiation of a **Japanese peace treaty** and sign the treaty as well. His mission failed, June 5.

June 4. The Supreme Court upheld (6–2) the Smith Act and the conviction of eleven Communists.

June 19. President Truman signed a **military manpower bill** extending the draft until July 1, 1955, lowering the draft age to $18\frac{1}{2}$ and authorizing universal military training to take effect at some unspecified date.

July 6. The State Department informed the U.S.S.R., Roumania, Bulgaria, Hungary, and Poland that **tariff rates** for them would revert to the levels of 1930, as required by the Trade Agreements Act of 1951. Tariff reduction benefits were formally suspended on August 1.

Oct. 5. The house of representatives approved a $56.9 billion **armed forces appropriation bill.** Senate approval followed on October 12.

Oct. 19. President Truman signed a **joint resolution formally ending the war between Germany and the United States.**

1952, Jan. 5. **Prime Minister Winston Churchill began talks with President Truman** in Washington on exchange of raw materials, support for the European Army plan, and measures to strengthen the North Atlantic Treaty Organization. On January 17 Churchill addressed a joint session of congress.

Mar. 20. The **senate ratified the Japanese peace treaty,** and approved Pacific security agreements contracted with Japan, the Philippines, Australia, and New Zealand.

Apr. 8. The president ordered **government seizure of the nation's steel industry** to avert a strike. On April 29 the district court of Washington, D.C., ruled that the seizure was unconstitutional. On June 2 the Supreme Court upheld the ruling.

May 23. The **government returned the railroads** to private owners after twenty-one months of government management.

June 26. The **McCarran-Walter Immigration and Nationality Act,** passed over the president's veto, permitted naturalization of Asiatics and established a quota for further admission, but also provided for exclusion and deportation of aliens and control of citizens abroad.

July 24. A White House agreement ended the 54-day **strike of steel workers.**

Nov. 5. **Dwight D. Eisenhower** (Republican) carried thirty-nine states to defeat **Adlai Stevenson** (Democrat) for the presidency. The Republicans also won a slight majority in congress.

Dec. 2. General Eisenhower visited Korea, and on his return declared that the Korean problem was not susceptible of an easy solution.

1953, Jan. 20. DWIGHT D. EISENHOWER WAS INAUGURATED as the thirty-fourth president. **Richard M. Nixon** became vice-president.

May 22. The **Submerged Lands Act** was signed, providing for state ownership of submerged coastal lands within "their historic boundaries," but federal jurisdiction beyond them.

July 7. **J. Robert Oppenheimer,** former director of Los Alamos Laboratory, was barred from access to classified material in the continuing McCarthy-led campaign against Communism.

Dec. 4-7. **President Eisenhower met with British and French leaders** in Bermuda (p. 1173).

1954, Jan. 12. **Secretary of State Dulles** declared that the basis of U.S. defense policy was **"a great capacity to retaliate"** against an aggressor "instantly by means and at places of our own choosing."

Feb. 25-26. The senate rejected the Bricker and all other proposals to limit by constitutional amendment the presidential treaty-making power.

Mar. 1. A **hydrogen bomb** was exploded in the Marshall Islands testing grounds.

Mar. 16. Secretary of State Dulles declared that the NATO and Rio treaties empowered the president, without consulting congress, to order **instant retaliation in Europe and the Western Hemisphere** if an ally were attacked.

May 7. Secretary of State Dulles declared that a distinct possibility existed that the United States might be forced to intervene militarily in Indo-China, in association with other free nations.

May 17. The supreme court, in *Brown* v. *Board of Education of Topeka,* unanimously held that **public school segregation was unconstitutional** under the fourteenth amendment.

May–June. **Senator Joseph McCarthy climaxed his campaign against Communism** with 35 days of televised hearings before his subcommittee on "investigations" of government operations.

June 1. The AEC's **personnel security board** unanimously found **Dr. J. Robert Oppenheimer** "loyal" and "discreet" in handling atomic secrets, but recommended, in a 2–1 decision, that he not be reinstated as a government consultant.

June 25-29. President Eisenhower and Secretary of State Dulles conferred with Sir Winston Churchill and Foreign Secretary Eden on Anglo-American differences, particularly over **Communist action in Southeast Asia.** The British agreed not to approve or condone Communist conquests, nor to press at this time for the admission of Communist China to the United Nations. The results of the talks were announced in a **"Potomac charter."**

Aug. 9. The senate passed an **Agriculture Act** which set up a flexible scale of price supports for farm products.

Aug. 24. President Eisenhower reluctantly signed the **bill outlawing the Communist Party.**

Sept. 9. The **Agricultural Trade Development and Assistance Act** went into effect; it authorized sale or gift of surplus farm products to needy foreign nations and American families.

Nov. 2. **Congressional elections** returned a Democratic majority of one in the senate and 29 in the house.

Dec. 2. **The senate passed a resolution, 67-22, condemning some of Senator McCarthy's actions.** The November elections, by returning a Democratic majority, deprived him of his chairmanship of the senate internal security committee.

Dec. 20. Defense Secretary Wilson announced an **accelerated reduction of military manpower,** cutting the armed forces from 3,218,000 men to 2,815,000 men over a period of 18 months.

1955, Jan. 25. President Eisenhower asked congress to authorize the **use of armed force to defend Taiwan,** the Pescadores, and certain "closely related localities." Congress granted his request by large majorities.

Feb. 9. A joint **AFL-CIO unity** committee announced agreement on unification which was formally consummated the following December.

Mar. 23. President Eisenhower declared that the United States would not use nuclear weapons in a "police action."

May 31. The **Supreme Court** ruled that STATES MUST END RACIAL SEGREGATION IN THE PUBLIC SCHOOLS within a "reasonable" time.

June 15. An accord with Great Britain on **peaceful use of nuclear power** was concluded.

July 11. The **United States Air Force Academy** near Denver, Colorado, was dedicated.

Nov. 25. The Interstate Commerce Commission issued an order to end, after January 10, 1956, **racial segregation** on those buses and trains which crossed state lines.

1956, Jan. 28. President Eisenhower rejected Soviet Premier Bulganin's proposal for a friendship pact.

May 4. A new **series of atomic tests** began in the Pacific. On May 21 the **first airborne H-bomb** was exploded.

May 9. Secretary of State Dulles explained that the United States had refused to supply **arms to Israel** in order to avoid a U.S.–U.S.S.R. war-by-proxy.

May 28. The president signed the **Agriculture Act** which embodied the "soil bank" plan in an effort to reduce surpluses.

June 29. The **Federal Aid Highway Act** authorized a 42,500-mile network linking major urban centers, 90 per cent of the cost to be borne by the federal government.

Aug. 14. The government established a **Middle-East Emergency Committee** to assure Western Europe of U.S. oil supplies if the Suez crisis interrupted shipments.

Nov. 6. The **Eisenhower-Nixon Republican ticket** won the presidential elections by a landslide, but the Democrats won a majority in both houses of congress. President Eisenhower was inaugurated January 21, 1957.

1957, Mar. 9. A joint congressional resolution empowered the president to use up to $200 million for **economic and military assistance to any Middle Eastern nation** desiring it; it asserted vital U.S. interest in the integrity and independence of all Middle East countries ("**Eisenhower Doctrine**").

Mar. 21-24. President Eisenhower talked with Prime Minister Macmillan in Bermuda (p. 1173).

Sept. 3. At **Little Rock, Arkansas,** national guards blocked Negro students from entering Central High School. A federal court injunction required **Governor Orval Faubus** to remove the national guards (Sept. 20), and on September 24 President Eisenhower sent federal troops to prevent "mob rule."

Sept. 9. A **CIVIL RIGHTS ACT** set up a bipartisan **Civil Rights Commission** to investigate infringements of voting and other rights, and strengthened executive and court procedures. The commission was appointed November 7.

Oct. 17-20. **British Queen Elizabeth II and her husband visited Washington.**

1958, Jan. 27. **The United States and the U.S.S.R. signed an agreement to expand cultural, educational, technical, and sports exchanges.**

Apr. 28. **Nuclear tests** began at Eniwetok in the Pacific.

July 15-19. **Eight thousand U.S. troops landed in Lebanon** (p. 1301).

Aug. 3. The U.S.S. *Nautilus* completed the **first undersea crossing of the North Pole.**

Aug. 16. An **Agriculture Act,** signed by the president, provided for a gradual lowering of price supports.

Sept. 2. The president signed the **National Defense Education Act** which provided loans to college students, grants to schools for facilities in the sciences and foreign languages, and fellowships for graduate students intending to teach.

Nov. 4. The Democrats enlarged their majorities in congress; 64 to 34 in the senate and 283–153 in the house.

1959, Jan. 3. President Eisenhower signed the document making **Alaska the forty-ninth state** in the union.

Jan. 4. Soviet First Deputy Premier **Anastas I. Mikoyan arrived in Washington** on a two-week visit to the U.S. On January 19 he suggested a reduction of U.S. barriers to Russian trade, but the State Department rejected the suggestion.

Apr. 15. John Foster Dulles resigned as secretary of state because of illness. His successor, **Christian A. Herter,** took office on April 22.

Aug. 21. **President Eisenhower proclaimed Hawaii the fiftieth state.**

Aug. 26. **President Eisenhower** began a 12-day **visit to Germany, Britain, and France.**

Sept. 14. The **Labor-Management Reporting and Disclosure** (Landrum-Griffith) **Act** to end corruption and place new limitations on labor unions became law.

Sept. 15-27. Premier Khrushchev toured the United States. During the last three days he talked with President Eisenhower at Camp David and agreed to hold further discussions on the **Berlin issue** and to expand the U.S.–U.S.S.R. exchange program ("*The Spirit of Camp David*").

Dec. 3-22. President Eisenhower, on a 22,370-mile goodwill tour of three continents, **visited Italy, Turkey, Pakistan, Afghanistan, India, Iran, Greece, Tunisia, France, Spain, and Morocco.**

1960, Jan. 5. Steel companies and unions, after six months in which President Eisenhower had invoked the Taft-Hartley Act to end the steelworkers' strike, came to an agreement on wages, benefits, and work rules.

Feb. 1. First of the **"sit-in" demonstrations,** inspired by the **Rev. Martin Luther King, Jr.,** to end segregation in restaurants and stores, occurred at Greensboro, North Carolina.

Mar. 28–30. Prime Minister Macmillan discussed **nuclear tests** in Washington.

Apr. 21. Congress passed the **Civil Rights Act** of 1960, providing for voting referees in areas where Negroes were barred from the polls by state barriers. President Eisenhower signed it, May 6.

June 12–21. President Eisenhower made a 23,000-mile **trip to the Far East,** visiting the Philippines, Taiwan, Okinawa, and Korea.

July 20. A Polaris missile was launched from a submerged submarine.

Nov. 8. JOHN F. KENNEDY DEFEATED RICHARD M. NIXON for the presidency. The Democratic party enlarged its majority in the house (260 to 172) and the senate (65–35). Kennedy was inaugurated, January 20, 1961.

1961, Mar. 1. President Kennedy issued an executive order creating the **Peace Corps.**

May 4. "Freedom rides" by Negro and white citizens sought to break down "Jim Crow" restrictions in buses and terminals. At Montgomery, Alabama (May 20) mob action against the riders led to the despatch there of several hundred federal marshals.

June 3–4. President Kennedy conferred with Premier Khrushchev in Vienna (p. 1161).

July 25. President Kennedy, in a national address on the **Berlin crisis,** proposed an increase in armed forces by 217,000 men and in defense spending to $3.4 billion to meet the Soviet "world-wide" threat.

Sept. 22. The Interstate Commerce Commission ordered the **desegregation of all interstate bus and railroad terminals,** effective November 1.

1962, Jan. 11. In his state of the union message to congress, President Kennedy called for a **reduction of tariff barriers,** expansion of welfare programs, and measures to help the economy.

Feb. 20. Lt. Col. John H. Glenn, Jr., became the **first U.S. astronaut to make an orbital flight,** circling the earth three times (p. 1357).

Apr. 25. The United States resumed **nuclear testing** by exploding a nuclear device at the Christmas Island test site in the Pacific Ocean.

July 10. Telstar, a 170-pound communications rocket, was **put into orbit** in a joint effort by the government and the American Telephone and Telegraph Company.

Oct. 22. President Kennedy announced a **"quarantine" of Cuba** (p. 1247).

Oct. 23. President Kennedy signed the $3.9 billion **foreign aid bill,** clauses of which forbade aid to eighteen Communist nations and to any country shipping arms to Cuba.

Nov. 6. Congressional elections returned a majority of Democrats to congress; in the senate 67 to 33, and in the house 258 to 176.

1963, May 15–16. Astronaut **Major L. Gordon Cooper, Jr.,** orbited the earth 22 times in Mercury capsule *Faith VII.*

June 17. The Supreme Court ruled that local governments could not require **recitation of the Bible or prayers in the public schools.**

June 20. The **agreement with the U.S.S.R.** was signed to set up an **emergency communications link** ("hot line") to reduce the risk of accidental war. The Soviet Union had accepted the proposal on April 5.

Aug. 28. In Washington, D.C., some 200,000 persons marched in an orderly **demonstration in support of the civil rights bill** requested by President Kennedy (June 19).

Nov. 22. Upon the **ASSASSINATION OF PRESIDENT KENNEDY** in Dallas, Texas, Vice-President **LYNDON BAINES JOHNSON** was sworn in as the thirty-sixth president of the United States.

Dec. 28–29. German **Chancellor Erhard met with President Johnson.** They pledged themselves to explore ways to ease cold war tensions.

1964, Jan. 10. Export licenses increased **wheat sales to the U.S.S.R.,** first approved by President Kennedy on October 9, 1963.

Feb. 13. At the end of a two-day conference, **President Johnson and British Prime Minister Alec Douglas-Home** issued a joint communiqué endorsing each other's **policies in Malaysia and South Vietnam.**

Feb. 25. To end the 90-day-old longshoremen's ban on loading Russian-bound wheat, President Johnson ordered that the government must honor its commitment to ship 50 per cent of the wheat in U.S. vessels.

Apr. 28. President Johnson asked Congress for a $228 million program for fiscal 1965 to wipe out poverty in the ten Appalachian states.

May 28. A consular agreement was completed with the U.S.S.R. to protect tourists and other travellers.

June 12. Visit of West German Chancellor Erhard to Washington. President Johnson reaffirmed American policy with respect to Berlin.

June 15. The Supreme Court ruled that both bodies of a bicameral legislature must be

apportioned on the basis of population.

June 19. The senate passed the **Civil Rights Bill** (73–27) which greatly increased federal powers to combat racial discrimination. Previously (June 10) the senate had voted cloture to end the filibuster carried on since March 30.

July 18–21. Major **race riots in Harlem,** with several dead and large-scale destruction.

July 26. James R. Hoffa, president of the International Brotherhood of Teamsters, convicted of fraudulent use of union funds and efforts to bribe a jury. He was sentenced to 15 years in prison (Aug. 17).

July 28–31. U.S. spacecraft Ranger VII relayed numerous close-up pictures of the moon's surface before plunging into it.

Aug. 2–4. Racial riots in Jersey City and Elizabeth, followed by similar outbreaks in Paterson (Aug. 11–14), Chicago (Aug. 16–17), and Philadelphia (Aug. 28–30).

Sept. 3. The **Wilderness Preservation Act,** by which over a million acres of wilderness were put under federal jurisdiction.

Sept. 27. Voluminous **report of the Warren Commission** investigating the assassination of President Kennedy. The report held Lee Oswald solely responsible for the act. Oswald had been shot and killed (Nov. 24, 1963) while being transferred from one jail to another. His assassin was Jack Ruby.

1965, Jan. 18–23. Disturbances at Selma, Alabama, over registration of blacks as voters. Thousands of protesters arrested (Feb. 1–9).

Jan. 20. LYNDON B. JOHNSON AND HUBERT H. HUMPHREY INAUGURATED as president and vice-president.

Feb. 21. Assassination of Malcolm X, former Black Muslim leader, in New York City.

Mar. 9–25. Second **civil rights march from Selma to Montgomery,** Alabama, led by **Reverend Martin Luther King.** The march was temporarily halted by a federal restraining order, but following Governor Wallace's statement of inability to protect the marchers, President Johnson federalized the Alabama national guard and ordered federal troops to the scene. From Mar. 21–25 King with over 3000 blacks and some white marchers coming from all over the country, completed the march to Montgomery. Governor Wallace finally agreed (Mar. 30) to meet with a delegation demanding equal civil rights.

Mar. 11. Death of Reverend James J. Reeb, who with two other white ministers had been attacked and beaten during the Selma demonstrations. His death led to wild protests and clashes in Montgomery. On Mar. 25 Mrs. Viola Liuzzo, a civil rights worker, was murdered by Ku Klux Klansmen on the road from Selma to Montgomery.

Mar. 13. Conference of President Johnson and Governor Wallace of Alabama. The president insisted on protection of the civil rights of all people. On Mar. 17 the president called on congress for legislation to end discrimination in registration and voting.

Apr. 14–15. Visit of Prime Minister Wilson to Washington. He reiterated British support of U.S. policies in Vietnam. The deepening involvement of the United States in the Vietnam war led to growing opposition and protest not only at home but abroad.

July 1. Civil rights demonstrations and counter-demonstrations at Bogalusa, Louisiana.

July 30. Passage of the **MEDICARE LEGISLATION,** which involved medical care for the aged, to be financed from the funds of Social Security.

The **Water Quality Act,** providing for federal co-operation with the states in the struggle against pollution.

Aug. 6. The **Voting Rights Act.** It suspended literacy and other tests designed to exclude undesirables from voting.

Sept. 29. Establishment of the **National Foundation of the Arts and Humanities,** designed to encourage and aid both the arts and the artists.

Oct. 3. New **immigration laws** fixed the annual quota of immigrants at 120,000 from the Western Hemisphere, without establishing national quotas, and at 170,000 from the rest of the world, not more than 20,000 to come from any one country.

Oct. 20. The **Higher Education Act** for the first time provided federal scholarship aid for undergraduates.

1966, Apr. 14–15. Visit of President Johnson to Mexico City; reaffirmation of the Alliance for Progress.

Apr. 27. Approval of the **merger of the Pennsylvania Railroad and the New York Central Railroad.**

May. Involvement of the U.S. in the **civil war in the Dominican Republic** (p. 1249).

May 5. Beginning of the attacks of **Senator J. W. Fulbright,** chairman of the Senate Foreign Relations Committee, on the administration's Vietnam policy.

June 5–26. Great Negro **march on the capitol at Jackson,** Mississippi, in a drive to induce Negroes to register.

July. A veritable **epidemic of race riots** in Chicago, Brooklyn, Cleveland, and other cities.

July 1–4. Convention of the **Congress of Racial Equality** (CORE) at Baltimore. It endorsed the objective of "black power," rejected the doctrine of non-violence, demanded the withdrawal of U.S. forces from Vietnam, and supported resistence to the draft.

July 4–9. The **National Association for the Advancement of Colored People** (NAACP) in its Los Angeles convention, rejected the notion of black power as being a separatist movement.

Aug. 11–16. Great **racial riot at Watts**, a poor Negro section of Los Angeles. Twenty-eight Negroes were left dead and the destruction of property by burning and looting reached the figure of $200,000,000.

Sept. 23. The **minimum wage** was raised from $1.25 per hour to $1.40 per hour by Feb. 1, 1967, and to $1.60 per hour by Feb. 1, 1968.

Oct. 15. Creation of the **Department of Transportation,** to exercise control over air, rail, and highway transportation.

Oct. 19–Nov. 2. **President Johnson's visit to New Zealand, Australia, Philippines, South Vietnam, Thailand, Malaysia, and South Korea.** At a conference in Manila (Oct. 24–25) leaders of the allied nations pledged support for the war in Vietnam.

1967, Feb. 10. Ratification by the thirty-eighth state of the **twenty-fifth amendment** to the U.S. constitution, concerned with the problem of presidential infirmity and succession.

Feb. 13. Furor in academic circles over the revelation of the fact that the **Central Intelligence Agency** had secretly financed the **National Student Association** in certain of its activities. The fact that this was done to counter-act the efforts of European Communists to secure control of the international student movement was soon lost from sight.

Feb. 18. **Report of the president's Commission on Law Enforcement,** containing detailed proposals for reducing crime.

Mar. 16. Conclusion of a **consular agreement with the Soviet Union.**

Apr. 15. Huge **marches** in New York City and San Francisco **protesting the war in Vietnam** and demanding peace.

June 23–25. **Conferences of President Johnson and Soviet Premier Kosygin at Glassboro,** New Jersey: inconclusive discussions of the Middle East crisis and the Vietnam war.

July 1. Conclusion of the **treaty restricting the proliferation of nuclear weapons** (p. 1162).

July 12–17. Renewed destructive **race riots in Newark.**

July 15. Initiation of **direct air service between the United States and the Soviet Union.**

July 18–22. The **American Medical Association** in convention adopted a resolution favoring liberalization of the various state **laws on abortion.**

July 23–30. **Race riots in Detroit** cost forty persons their lives. Federal paratroopers had to be brought in to help restore order.

Aug. 15–16. **Visit of West German chancellor George Kiesinger** to Washington.

Sept. 18. Announcement of the decision to construct, over the ensuing five years, a "light" **anti-missile network** to counter an eventual Chinese Communist missile attack. The proposal at once aroused great popular opposition to such escalation of the armaments race.

Oct. 2. **Justice Thurgood Marshall** became the first Negro to serve as an associate justice of the Supreme Court.

Oct. 21–22. A huge **peace march on Washington** from all over the country, culminating in clashes between demonstrators and army troops protecting the Pentagon.

Nov. 7. Inauguration of the **Corporation for Public Broadcasting,** a non-profit public corporation for the allocation of funds to non-commercial radio and television stations to assist them in improving programs.

Dec. 1–8. **Stop the Draft Week** organized by 40 anti-war groups. Huge demonstration in New York City followed by many arrests.

1968, Jan. 7–8. Israeli **premier Levi Eshkol in Washington** seeking military supplies to counter-balance Soviet supplies to the Arab countries.

Jan. 19. **Nomination of Clark Clifford** to succeed Robert McNamara as secretary of defense. He was confirmed by the senate on Jan. 30.

Feb. 8–9. **State visit of Prime Minister Wilson,** following his visit to the U.S.S.R. on Jan. 22–24.

Feb. 29. Voluminous report of the president's **National Advisory Commission on Civil Disorders.** It held white racism primarily responsible for the riots of the summer of 1967 and made numerous detailed recommendations for dealing with racial antagonisms, warning that American society threatened to divide into separate and unequal white and black sections.

Mar. 31. President Johnson, in a moving speech, announced that he would neither seek nor accept nomination for a second term.

Apr. 1. The **Open Housing Law.** It forbade discrimination in the sale or rental of about 70% of all the housing in the country.

Apr. 4. **ASSASSINATION OF REV. MARTIN LUTHER KING, JR.,** the influential leader of the non-violent civil rights movement, in Memphis. This lamentable act led at once to an epidemic of riots affecting some 125 cities, including Washington. In many places the national guard and even army troops had to be called out.

Apr. 11. A **Civil Rights Act** banned racial discrimination in housing and made it a federal crime to injure civil rights workers or even to cross state lines with the intention of inciting to riot.

Apr. 23–May 6. A crisis at Columbia University brought the unrest in academic circles to a head. The radical **Students for a Democratic Society** protested the building of a gymnasium in an area needed for low-class housing, and denounced ·also the Institute of Defense Analysis as an agency of the military establishment and of American imperialism. Protesting students eventually occupied the university library and sacked the president's office. After much hesitation the administration called on the police to clear the protestors from the buildings (Apr. 30). Hundreds were arrested and allegedly abused by the police. Presently similar disturbances took place at many other institutions.

May 3–June 23. Poverty march on Washington. Thousands of indigents, of various races, attempted to set up a Resurrection City on the Potomac. **Reverend Ralph D. Abernathy,** successor to Dr. King, hoped to impress congress with the needs of millions of Americans for food, clothing, and jobs.

June 5. ASSASSINATION OF SENATOR ROBERT F. KENNEDY, brother of the late president, at Los Angeles. The assassin was a young Arab, **Sirhan Beshara Sirhan,** evidently outraged by the pro-Israeli utterances of the senator.

July 23–24. Cleveland riots resulting from sniper attacks on the police, which were becoming an important part of the revolutionary tactic. The disorders led to some loss of life and heavy property losses through looting.

Aug. 8. The **Republican national convention** at Miami nominated **Richard M. Nixon** and **Spiro T. Agnew,** the governor of Maryland, for president and vice-president.

Aug. 26–29. The **Democratic national convention** at Chicago nominated **Hubert H. Humphrey** and **Senator Edward S. Muskie** of Maine for president and vice-president. The convention, extremely disorderly itself, was accompanied by violent street demonstrations and fighting.

Oct. 4. Nomination of Justice Abe Fortas to be Chief Justice of the Supreme Court was withdrawn by President Johnson in view of the vigorous and widespread opposition to his confirmation by the senate.

Nov. 5. NATIONAL ELECTIONS, resulting in a narrow margin of **victory for Nixon** and the Republicans. Nixon's popular vote was 31,770,237 against Humphrey's 31,270,533. The third-party candidate, Governor Wallace of Mississippi, polled 9,906,141. The Democrats, however, retained control of both houses of congress.

Dec. 24–25. Colonel Frank Borman and two companions orbited the moon ten times before returning to earth (p. 1358).

1969, Jan. The **unrest in the universities** and other schools continued unabated, centering on violent opposition to the Vietnam war, but including various other demands.

Feb. 4. Heated debate in congress and outside on the government's anti-ballistic missile (ABM) program.

Feb. 23–Mar. 2. President Nixon visited Europe to strengthen and revitalize NATO. His visit included the Vatican.

Mar. 28. Death of former President Dwight D. Eisenhower.

Sept. 10. Oil leases on the newly discovered Alaskan North Slope fields netted over $900,000,000.

Sept. 24. Beginning of the **trial of eight radicals** (the *"Chicago Eight"*) charged with conspiring to incite riots in Chicago during the democratic convention in Aug. 1968. The trial produced so much disorder in the courtroom that ultimately **Bobby Seale,** the Black Panther leader, was ordered bound and gagged. On Nov. 5 Seale was cited for contempt of court and sentenced to four years in prison.

Oct. 15. Moratorium Day: nationwide opposition to the Vietnam war and demands that the troops be brought back immediately. There was, however, no agreement as to the best and quickest road to peace.

Oct. 30. The Supreme Court ordered that an immediate end be put to separate school systems for blacks and whites.

Nov. 13, 20. Attacks of Vice-President Agnew on television networks and newspapers, charging them with biased versions of the news and with misrepresentation of the government's policies.

Nov. 15. Second Vietnam Moratorium. 250,000 war protesters marched in Washington and about 100,000 in San Francisco.

Nov. 21. Agreement between the United States and Japan for the **return of Okinawa to Japan** in 1972 (p. 1347).

The senate refused to confirm **Clement F. Haynsworth, Jr.,** as associate justice of the Supreme Court.

Nov. 26. Amendment of the Selective Service Act of 1967, providing for selection by lottery.

Dec. 4. Death of Black Panther leader Fred Hampton in a Chicago police raid.

Following a White House conference on food, nutrition, and health, President Nixon ordered **extension of the food-stamp program** and substantial increases in allowances.

Dec. 9. Secretary of State Rogers' **proposals for settlement of the Arab-Israeli war** (p. 1287).

Dec. 12. Final report of the **National Commission on the Causes and Prevention of Violence.** It warned of the rising tide of violence and called for massive expenditures on social reform programs.

Dec. 16. President Nixon endorsed a senate amendment prohibiting the **use of combat troops in Thailand and Laos,** part of a military appropriations bill.

1970, Jan. 1. Establishment of a three-man **Council on Environmental Quality,** a crucial step in the fight against pollution.

Jan. 14. Tension in the southern states as the **Supreme Court ordered immediate desegregation of schools** in Georgia, Mississippi, Alabama, Florida, Louisiana, and Texas by Feb. 1.

Jan. 26. President Nixon vetoed a $19 billion appropriation for health, education, and anti-poverty on the score that such expenditure would aggravate inflation. The house of representatives failed to override the veto.

Feb. 20. Five of the "Chicago Eight" were convicted of crossing state lines to incite riots and were sentenced to five years in prison.

Feb. 23–Mar. 1. Visit of President Pompidou of France to Washington, where he addressed a joint session of congress.

Mar. 6. The president signed a revised appropriations bill for the Health, Education, and Welfare, and Labor Departments.

Mar. 8. A White House task force declared direct U.S. aid to individual nations no longer politically desirable and recommended action through international programs.

Apr. 8. The senate refused to confirm **G. Harrold Carswell** as an associate justice of the Supreme Court.

Apr. 13. The president signed an **education bill** providing over $24 billion for elementary and secondary education over a period of three years.

Apr. 30. The president announced the commitment of U.S. troops in the **war in Cambodia** against the Vietnamese Communists. This announcement, involving an escalation of the war which he had promised to liquidate, caused a storm of indignation in the country and brought the peace movement to a head.

May 4. At **Kent State University** in Ohio four students were killed when the national guard opened fire on an unruly student demonstration. Added to the outrage felt over Cambodia, the Kent State incident, regarded by most people as indefensible in any case, produced such disorder in academic circles that many universities and colleges were temporarily closed.

May 8. Attack by construction workers on anti-war demonstrators in New York City.

May 9. Huge **anti-war protest demonstration** by students in Washington. Visits by faculty members and students to congressmen, seeking an explanation of the Cambodia episode.

May 11–12. **Rioting in Augusta,** Georgia, following the death of a black prisoner by beating.

May 12. The senate finally confirmed a presidential nomination for the Supreme Court, **Justice Harry A. Blackmun.**

May 14. **Two black students were killed** and nine wounded when police opened fire on a dormitory at **Jackson State College,** Mississippi.

June 10. Creation of the new **Office of Management and Budget,** to replace the Bureau of the Budget.

June 13. Appointment of a **Commission on Campus Unrest,** with former governor of Pennsylvania **William W. Scranton** as chairman.

June 15. The Supreme Court ruled that exemption from the draft on grounds of **conscientious objection** need not be based on religious belief but may be granted for moral or ethical reasons.

June 22. The **Voting Rights Act** was extended to 1975 and the voting age reduced to 18, beginning in 1971.

June 24. The senate voted overwhelmingly a **repeal of the Gulf of Tonkin Resolution** of 1965, on which the government's involvement in the Vietnam war was largely based.

June 30. Completion of the **evacuation of Cambodia** by American troops, as promised by the president.

July 9. Creation of an independent **Environmental Protection Agency** and of a **National Oceanic and Atmospheric Administration.**

July 24. A new law provided for the construction of 1,300,000 new housing units.

Aug. 12. A **United States Postal Service** established as an independent government agency to take over the Post Office and operate the postal service as a business enterprise.

Aug. 18. Congress overrode the president's veto of the $4.4 billion **appropriation for the Office of Education.**

A government ship loaded with nerve gas was scuttled in the Atlantic 280 miles off Florida.

Aug. 24. Bombing of the **U.S. Army Mathematical Research Center** at the University of Wisconsin, with the loss of one life. The building was wrecked and many neighboring buildings badly damaged. Responsibility was assumed by the **Weathermen,** a radical, violent faction of the Students for a Democratic Society. This incident was followed by many less serious bombings in various parts of the country and led eventually to punitive legislation.

Sept. 3–7. A congress of African people,

meeting at Atlanta, studied problems of culture and ideology (pp. 1233–1234).

Oct. 12. The U.S. **Commission on Civil Rights,** in a comprehensive report, concluded that due to a lack of inter-agency co-ordination and adequate supervision there had been a "major breakdown" in the implementation of the voluminous legislation designed to ensure equal rights for all.

Sept. 27–Oct. 6. **Visit of President Nixon to five European countries,** with emphasis on U.S. interests in the Mediterranean. Important discussions with Marshal Tito of Yugoslavia.

Oct. 15. The **Organized Crime Control Act** established federal jurisdiction over major gambling operations, control over the interstate sale of explosives, etc. The death penalty was made mandatory for bombings resulting in loss of life.

Oct. 22. The **Merchant Marine Act** provided for the construction of 300 ships over the next ten years and the extension of operating subsidies so as to restore the United States to the position of a first-rate maritime power.

Oct. 24. President Nixon "totally repudiated" the **report of the National Commission on Obscenity and Pornography,** declaring "morally bankrupt" its conclusion that pornography was not a contributing factor to crime and social deviation and that recommended that pornographic literature be made freely available to adults. On many sides it was charged that this was a partial interpretation of a generally sound report.

Nov. 4. In the **national elections** the Democrats made no notable gains in congressional seats, though they won a number of governorships.

2. CANABA

(From p. 1056)

1939, Sept. 10. **Canada followed the British action of September 3 and DECLARED WAR ON GERMANY.**

1940, Mar. 26. The **Liberal Party** won a decided victory in the Canadian elections.

1941, Dec. 8. **CANADA DECLARED WAR ON JAPAN.**

1942, Nov. 8. **Canada severed relations with the French Vichy régime** on the grounds that there no longer existed in France any government with "effective independent existence."

1945, June 11. National elections held a majority for Prime Minister Mackenzie King's Liberal Party, thus endorsing the government's conduct of the war. The Progressive Conservatives came out second and the Co-operative Commonwealth Federation (Socialist) third.

1946, Apr. 12. **Field Marshal Sir Harold Alexander** succeeded the earl of Athlone as **governor-general.**

July 1. Proclamation of the **Canadian Citizenship Act,** clarifying the definition of Canadian citizenship, but retaining the status of British subjects for Canadians. It went into effect on January 1, 1947.

July 15. A royal commission, investigating the activities of a **Soviet spy ring** in Canada, reported on the disclosure of important secret information by Canadian officials and the existence of a Communist fifth column in Canada, directed by Soviet agents. Among the Canadians involved was the one parliamentary delegate of the Labor-Progressive (Communist) Party.

Aug. 3. An **Anglo-Canadian wheat agreement** provided for British purchases of large amounts of Canadian wheat at prices considerably below the world market.

1947, Feb. 12. Prime Minister King announced continued **military co-operation between Canada and the United States.**

1948, July 22. A referendum in **Newfoundland** to decide between future self-government and confederation with Canada, by a narrow margin of 78,408 to 71,464 voted in favor of confederation. On March 31, 1949, Newfoundland joined Canada as a tenth province.

1949, Apr. 4. **Canada signed the North Atlantic treaty.**

June 27. **National elections** gave the Liberal Party an overwhelming majority of 193 out of 262 seats in the house of commons.

Nov. 22–Dec. 2. The British parliament passed a **British North America Bill** granting the parliament of Canada the right to amend Canada's constitution.

1950, June–Dec. Upon the outbreak of the Korean War, Canada immediately rallied to the support of the United Nations. The first Canadian troops arrived in Korea on December 19. Earlier in the year the Canadian government had placed three destroyers at the disposal of the United Nations for action in Korean waters. Defense appropriations were more than doubled, and a 40 per cent increase of Canada's armed forces was authorized by parliament. The **Essential Materials Act,** adopted in September, gave the government extensive control over defense industries.

1952, Jan. 24. **Vincent Massey** was **appointed**

governor-general of Canada to succeed Viscount Alexander. His was the first appointment of a Canadian to that post.

Aug. 13. The government announced its decision to provide about $150 million in 1952 as a **mutual aid gift to Britain.**

1953, Aug. 10. In **national elections,** the Liberal Party, under **Prime Minister Louis S. St. Laurent,** won its fifth straight victory.

1955, Oct. 11. An **agreement with the U.S.S.R.,** negotiated by **Secretary Lester B. Pearson** in Moscow, granted most-favored-nation trade privileges and **co-operation in arctic research.**

1956, May 23. **Sir Saville Garner** was appointed to succeed **Sir Archibald Nye** as British high commissioner.

Dec. 14. The national convention of the Progressive Conservative Party elected **John Diefenbaker** as its new leader, succeeding **George Drew.**

1957, June 17. Following the Conservatives' victory in the June 10 parliamentary elections, **John Diefenbaker formed a new cabinet,** the first Conservative government in twenty-two years.

1958, Jan. 16. Lester B. Pearson succeeded St. Laurent as leader of the opposition Liberal Party.

Mar. 31. Prime Minister Diefenbaker and the Conservative Party won the **greatest election victory in Canada's history,** securing 202 seats out of 265 in the federal house of commons.

July 10. President Eisenhower and Prime Minister Diefenbaker agreed in Ottawa to establish a **Canada-United States Committee on Joint Defense.**

1959, June 26. United States President Eisenhower and Queen Elizabeth II officially opened the **St. Lawrence Seaway,** linking the Great Lakes with the Atlantic Ocean.

1961, May 2. The government announced that Canada and Communist China had negotiated a **grain sale agreement.**

Jan. 17. President Eisenhower and Prime Minister Diefenbaker signed a treaty in Washington for the **joint development of the Columbia River Basin.**

1962, June 18. The ruling Conservative Party lost its parliamentary majority in national elections.

1963, Jan. 31. Prime Minister Diefenbaker denounced as an "unwarranted intrusion" the U.S. state department criticism (Jan. 30) of Canada for not having made "practical arrangements to equip its defense forces with nuclear weapons."

Feb. 6. Following a **defeat of the Diefenbaker government** on its **nuclear weapons policy** (Feb. 5) parliament was dissolved and elections scheduled.

Apr. 8. The Liberal Party won the **general elections** by receiving a plurality of 129 seats in the house of commons. **Lester B. Pearson** took office on April 22 as Liberal **prime minister.**

May 11. President Kennedy and Prime Minister Pearson agreed to **equip Canadian missiles with U.S.-supplied nuclear warheads.**

1964, Jan. 22. An agreement signed with the United States provided for a multimillion dollar **power and flood control development of the Columbia River Basin.**

Sept. 18. **Columbia River treaty** signed by British Columbia, Canada, and the United States, providing for the development and distribution of hydroelectric power.

Oct. 5–13. **Visit of Queen Elizabeth and Prince Philip.** They were greeted in Quebec by deserted streets, a form of protest by the advocates of autonomy for French-speaking Quebec.

1965, Aug. 11. Huge Canadian **sales of wheat to the Soviet Union and to Communist China.**

Nov. 8. **National elections.** The Liberal Party failed to secure a majority of seats in parliament and the government of Lester Pearson became dependent on the **New Democrats,** who had polled 18% of the vote, for support.

1966. In the **Quebec provincial election Daniel Johnson's** *Union Nationale* defeated **Jean Lesage's Liberal Party,** which held power. The *Union Nationale* favored the concept of two nations in the Canadian confederation.

1967, Apr. Consolidation of the navy, army, and air force to form the **Canadian Armed Services.**

Abolition of the death penalty for a five-year trial period, except for the murder of a policeman or prison guard.

Apr.–Oct. Celebration of the **centennial of dominion status.** The great world exposition (*Expo 67*) brought millions of visitors to Montreal.

July 24–26. **State visit of President de Gaulle.** He openly promised French support for Quebec's efforts to become master of its own destiny, and in a speech at Montreal shouted, *"Vive le Québec libre."* For this amazing outburst he was rebuked by Premier Pearson, and abruptly canceled his projected visit to Ottawa, returning directly home. There seems no doubt that de Gaulle's interference in Canadian affairs encouraged the **growth of a separatist movement** in the province of Quebec, despite the disapproval of the principal parties. The separatist leader was **René Levesque.**

Nov. Confederation for Tomorrow. In conferences of federal and provincial officials Premier Johnson of Quebec opposed separatism but called for greater provincial autonomy and complete equality within the confederation for Quebec.

1968, Feb. The former African French colony of **Gabon invited the Quebec minister of education** to attend a conference and treated him as representative of a sovereign state. The Canadian government broke off relations with Gabon and blamed France for using Gabon as a front.

Further **conferences on constitutional questions,** attended by premiers of all ten provinces. Discussion of linguistic rights for French-speaking minorities outside Quebec Province.

Apr. 6. Pierre Elliott Trudeau elected leader of the Liberal Party following the resignation of Pearson.

Apr. 20. TRUDEAU BECAME PRIME MINISTER.

June 25. Decisive victory of the Liberal Party in the national elections indicated tremendous popular appeal of Trudeau.

July 5. Trudeau organized an all-Liberal Party cabinet.

1969, Feb. 10–12. The federal-provincial conference on constitutional reform grappled with the question of the **allocation of revenues** as between the federal and the provincial governments.

Apr. 3. The Canadian government announced its intention of carrying out a phased **reduction of its forces in Europe,** while remaining faithful to its obligations under NATO.

May. The **Criminal Code Amendment Act,** liberalizing laws on abortion, homosexuality, lotteries, etc.

July 9. The **Official Languages Act.** The English and French languages were made equally official in federal administration. **Bilingual districts** were to be established anywhere in Canada where the English or French population exceeded 10% of the total.

Sept. 19. The government announced that the forthcoming **reduction of forces in Europe** would be almost 50% and that its nuclear role would be ended by 1972.

Oct. 7. Strike of police and firemen in Montreal demanding higher pay. The city soon became the prey of criminals and arsonists and the Canadian army forces had to be brought in. On Oct. 8 the Quebec provincial parliament ordered the strikers back to work.

1970, Oct. 5. Kidnaping of James R. Cross, a British trade official, and (Oct. 10) of **Pierre Laporte,** Quebec minister of labour, by terrorists of the **Front for Liberation of Quebec.** The men were held hostage to force the liberation of 23 political prisoners and payment of a large ransom. The governments of Quebec and of Canada rejected the demands.

Oct. 13. Establishment of diplomatic relations with Communist China and severance of relations with Nationalist China. Canada recognized the People's Republic as "the sole legal government of China," but without recognizing its claim to the possession of Taiwan.

Oct. 16. Prime Minister Trudeau invoked, for six months, the **War Measures Act** to meet the threat of insurrection in Quebec. While army units were assigned to preserve order in the province of Quebec, police forces pressed the search for Cross and Laporte, arresting hundreds of members of the outlawed front and other suspects.

Oct. 18. The murdered **body of Mr. Laporte was found** in the trunk of an abandoned automobile.

Oct. 19. The house of commons approved Trudeau's invocation of emergency legislation by 190–16.

Dec. 1. The house of commons passed the **Public Order** (Temporary Measures) **Act** to replace the more stringent War Measures Act. The new law still outlawed the secret Quebec nationalist society and authorized the police to arrest without warrant and hold suspects for as long as a week without bringing charges.

Dec. 3. Mr. Cross was rescued after 59 days in captivity, but only after the government had provided three kidnapers and four relatives with a Canadian army plane on which to escape to Cuba.

Dec. 28. Arrest of three additional suspects in the Laporte murder.

E. LATIN AMERICA

1. GENERAL

(*From p. 1059*)

1939, Oct. 2. The Pan-American conference proclaimed a **safety zone** around the Western Hemisphere.

1940, July 27. Meeting at Havana, the conference adopted plans for a **joint trusteeship of European colonies** in the Western Hemisphere.

1942, Jan. 15. In Rio, the conference discussed possible joint action against aggression.

1945, Feb. 21. The Inter-American conference, at a meeting in Mexico City, agreed to strengthen the inter-American system and work out a general defense treaty.

1947, Sept. 2. THE INTER-AMERICAN MUTUAL ASSISTANCE TREATY, adopted by the Inter-American conference meeting at Rio. It provided for mutual assistance against aggression within a defense zone from Greenland to the Antarctic.

1948, Apr. 30. The ninth Pan-American conference, at Bogotà, established the **ORGANIZATION OF AMERICAN STATES** (OAS) as a regional grouping under the United Nations. The Inter-American conference became the supreme authority of the OAS, and the Pan-American Union its secretariat.

1951, Oct. 14. The **Organization of Central American States** founded by Costa Rica, El Salvador, Guatemala, Honduras, and Nicaragua to further regional integration.

Dec. 13. The **OAS charter went into effect** on ratification by Colombia, the fourteenth state.

1954, Mar. 12. The Inter-American conference, meeting at Caracas, adopted a United States resolution calling for **action to exclude Communism** from the Western Hemisphere. Guatemala dissented. The conference (Mar. 19) called also for the **ending of European colonies** in the Americas (the United States abstaining).

1956, July 21. Conference of the presidents of the American republics at Panama. President Eisenhower urged the OAS to establish an **atomic commission.**

1959, Aug. 12–18. The **Declaration of Santiago,** signed by the foreign ministers of 21 American states, condemning dictatorial régimes, but also efforts by other governments to overthrow them.

Sept. 30. A **South American free trade zone** was agreed to by Brazil, Argentina, Bolivia, Chile, Paraguay, Peru, and Uruguay.

1960, Aug. 20. A foreign ministers conference at San José condemned the **Dominican Republic** for "acts of aggression and intervention" against Venezuela and called for sanctions against the Dominican Republic.

Aug. 28. The **declaration of San José,** in which the foreign ministers condemned the efforts of the Soviet Union and Communist China to spread Communism in the Western Hemisphere. The Cuban delegation walked out of the meeting.

Sept. 5–12. Conference on economic aid at Bogotá. The United States delegate revealed (Sept. 6) a program for liberal aid in social development. Nineteen delegates voted (Sept. 11) support for the **Act of Bogotá,** embodying the program. Cuba refused to join.

Nov. 16. In response to appeals from Nicaragua and Guatemala, President Eisenhower ordered **U.S. naval units to patrol Central American waters** to forestall possible Communist-led invasion forces from Cuba. These units were recalled (Dec. 7).

Dec. 13. The **Central American Common Market** founded by five states. Within the next decade it eliminated interstate tariffs and vastly increased reciprocal trade.

1961, Jan. 4. The OAS council voted 14 to 1 (6 abstaining) to impose an **economic boycott on the Dominican Republic.**

Mar. 13. An **Alliance for Progress** to aid Latin American countries proposed by President Kennedy.

Aug. 17. THE ALLIANCE FOR PROGRESS CHARTER signed by the United States and all Latin American governments except Cuba, at the meeting of the inter-American economic and social conference at Punta del Este (Uruguay). A ten-year program involving expenditure of $20 billion of public and private investment was designed to raise the per capita income of Latin American populations by 2.5% annually.

1962, Jan. 23–31. A conference of OAS foreign ministers at Punta del Este voted that **Cuba** had in effect **excluded itself from OAS activities,** though it retained its membership.

1963, Mar. 19. President Kennedy and the presidents of six Central American states signed the **declaration of San José,** pledging economic co-operation and a common front against Communist aggression.

Oct. 4. The U.S. government announced the withholding of economic and military aid from Honduras and the Dominican Republic, following military coups in those countries.

1964, July 21–26. The OAS conference of foreign ministers voted to **invoke sanctions against Cuba** and called on all members to sever diplomatic and trade relations. Only Mexico and Jamaica failed to do so.

Dec. At the fourth annual meeting of the **Latin American Free Trade Association** agreement was reached on a list of products to be traded duty-free.

1965, Apr.–1966, Oct. OAS intervention in Dominican civil war (p. 1249).

1965–1970. A period of **increasing crisis,** arising largely from an exceedingly high rate of population increase, lack of adequate employment possibilities, steadily mounting inflation, and general prevalence of poverty. Governments attempted to meet the crisis by encouraging development of industry and diversification of production, by nationalization of foreign properties, and by the formation of regional economic blocs. But Communism of various stripes continued to make headway, soon to be accompanied by the **emergence of urban terrorist groups** or cells, which aimed to attain their ends by kidnaping and holding hostage high officials and particularly foreign diplomats.

1966, Jan. Tricontinental conference of Asian, African, and Latin American **Communists** at Havana to discuss ways and means of combating imperialism and promoting revolution. Decision to found the **Organization of Latin American Solidarity,** which held its first meeting at Havana in 1967 (July 31–Aug. 10).

Aug. 14–16. DECLARATION OF BOGOTÁ: presidents or representatives of Colombia, Chile, Ecuador, Peru, and Venezuela discussed economic integration and planned eventual establishment of a **Latin American common market.**

1967, Feb. 14. Fourteen nations of Central America, South America, and the Caribbean signed a **treaty prohibiting the manufacture,** **use, or possession of nuclear weapons** on their territory.

Apr. 12–14. MEETING of nineteen American chiefs of state **AT PUNTA DEL ESTE** (Uruguay) to discuss economic problems. Plans for a Latin American common market to absorb the Latin American Free Trade Association and the Central American Common Market. Absent were Cuba and Bolivia. Ecuador alone among those present declined to sign the declaration.

July 5. Meeting at San Salvador of five **Central American presidents,** presently joined by President Johnson of the U.S. to plan speedier integration and economic and social development.

1968, Oct. 8. Death of Ché Guevara, Cuban revolutionary, in clash with Bolivian troops.

1969, May 26. Agreement for **ANDEAN INTEGRATION** signed at Cartagena by Colombia, Ecuador, Bolivia, Peru, and Chile.

June–July. OAS intervention in the Salvadorian-Honduran war (p. 1244).

2. MEXICO AND CENTRAL AMERICA

a. MEXICO

(*From p. 1072*)

1940, July 7. Avila Camacho elected president.

1942, Feb. 27. A Mexican-United States **defense commission** planned to coordinate defense.

May 22. Mexico declared war on Germany, Italy, and Japan.

Nov. 19. Mexico re-established **diplomatic relations with the Soviet Union.**

1946, July 7. MIGUEL ALEMAN ELECTED PRESIDENT, the first civilian to attain that office. He named a cabinet of economic experts and embarked on an extensive **program of internal development,** including industrialization, electrification, irrigation, and transportation. Foreign capital was welcomed, though under government control. **Relations with the United States** were cordial and for the first time an exchange of presidential visits took place in 1947.

1947, Sept. 30. A final settlement was made by the Mexican government for the 1938 expropriation of **United States oil properties.**

1952, July 6. The government party's candidate, **Adolfo Ruiz Cortines,** was **elected president** of Mexico.

1958, July 6. Adolfo Lopez Mateos, candidate of the Party of Revolutionary Institutions and minister of labor and social security, was **elected president.**

1959, Feb. 19–20. President Mateos and U.S. President Eisenhower, conferring in Acapulco, Mexico, agreed on construction of the Diablo Dam and on **United States-Mexico economic collaboration.**

1963, July 18. The United States and Mexico reached a **settlement of the** 50-year-old **dispute over the border zone** of El Chamezal, which the United States agreed to cede to Mexico.

1964, Mar. 18. President Mateos and French **President de Gaulle,** in a joint communiqué, agreed to promote **closer French-Mexican trade relations and cultural ties.**

July. Election of Gustavo Diaz Ordaz as president.

1967, Oct. 28. Meeting of President Johnson and President Diaz Ordaz on the bridge at El Paso for formal **transfer of El Chamezal** to Mexico.

1968, Sept. Monster **STUDENT DEMONSTRATIONS** on the eve of the international Olympic Games. Students occupied the National University and proclaimed a strike. Intervention of the army (Oct. 2), followed by fighting and considerable loss of life. Over a thousand students, professors, and other intellectuals arrested and over a hundred held without trial until Nov. 1970, when, despite widespread agitation for amnesty, 68 were sentenced to prison terms of 3 to 17 years.

1969, Sept.–Oct. Recrudescence of student dis-

orders, punctuated by bombings of public offices. Further large-scale arrests.

1970, Aug. 20. President Nixon, on a visit to Mexico, concluded an **agreement** with President Diaz Ordaz **for the peaceful settlement of** all future border and other **disputes.**

b. PANAMA

(From p. 1068)

1941, Oct. 9. In **Panama** a political overturn deposed **Arnulfo Arias** and installed as president **Ricardo Adolfo de la Guardia,** who was more friendly toward the United States than his predecessor.

1948, Feb. 15. The **United States** announced the final **withdrawal of troops** from their wartime bases, thus settling a burning issue between the two countries.

May 9. Presidential elections brought a close and contested decision between former president **Arnulfo Arias** and the Liberal **Domingo Diáz Arosemena.** The latter finally won out, and on October 1 succeeded **Enrique Jiménez** as president of Panama.

1949, Aug. 25-Nov. 24. The death of **President Arosemena** on August 23 touched off a struggle for his succession, from which **Arnulfo Arias,** with the aid of the national police, emerged victorious. He immediately began to suppress the opposition.

1951, May 9. Rioting in Panama City followed the dissolution of the national assembly and the **suspension of the constitution** by President Arias. Next day the **president was impeached** and replaced by First Vice-President Arosemena.

1952, May 11. The government's candidate, former police chief **José A. Ramón Guizado,** won the presidential elections, described by the opposition candidate as a "dangerous burlesque of democratic principles."

1955, Jan. 15. Following the national assembly's dismissal of President José Ramón Guizado for being implicated in former president Ramón's assassination (Jan. 2), **Ricardo Arias Espinosa** was installed as **president.**

1956, June 15. The returns from the May 13 election were announced. They indicated that **Ernesto de la Guardia** had won the presidency.

1960, May 8. Roberto F. Chiari, the Liberal Party candidate, won the presidential election.

Sept. 17. U.S. President Eisenhower ordered that the **Panama flag** be flown with the **United States flag in the Canal Zone.**

1961, Oct. 1. President Chiari announced that he had formally requested the United States to revise the **Panama Canal Zone treaty,** and give Panama rights over the Zone.

1964, Jan. 9. Rioting erupted when U.S. students in the Canal Zone ignored the agreement that United States and Panamanian flags should fly side by side. On the following day the **government broke relations with the United States and denounced the Canal Zone treaties.** Both Panama and the United States agreed to let the Inter-American peace committee use its good offices to settle the dispute. In the following days President Chiari demanded that the United States give assurance of a revision of the canal treaties, and U.S. President Johnson refused to commit himself, although he later (Jan. 23) declared that the United States would engage in a "full and frank" review of all controversial issues.

Feb. 4. The **OAS council** voted to act as an "organ of consultation" and established (Feb. 7) a seventeen-member committee to investigate and find a solution of the United States-Panamanian crisis.

Mar. 17. An OAS five-nation subcommittee ended its efforts to mediate the United States-Panamanian dispute without reaching agreement.

Apr. 3. After U.S. President Johnson, in a public statement to the OAS council (Mar. 21), expressed U.S. willingness to "review every issue" involved in the rift with Panama, **diplomatic relations were resumed.**

Mar. 10. Marco A. Robles, government candidate and advocate of a tough policy toward the United States, was elected president by a substantial majority.

1965, Sept.-1967, June. Negotiation of new agreements with the United States. Final drafts provided for abrogation of the 1903 treaty, recognition of Panamanian sovereignty over the Canal Zone and of Panama's right to a share in the management of the canal, as well as the right of the United States to ensure defense and to build a second canal on Panamanian territory.

1968, Mar. 14. The national assembly voted to impeach President Robles on charges of misuse of public funds. Robles called on the national guard for support. Clashes between the guard and the populace followed (Mar. 24-29).

May 12. In presidential elections **David Samudio,** Robles' candidate, was defeated by former president **Arnulfo Arías.**

Oct. 11-12. Arías was ousted by the national guard following his attempted shakeup. Colonel **José Maria Pinilla** proclaimed chief of a **provisional junta,** which was actually controlled by **Colonel Omar Torrijos,** commander of the guard.

1969, Feb. All political parties were declared

abolished by the junta.

Dec. 15-16. A coup, though abortive, led to the replacement of two military members of the junta by civilians.

1970, Sept. 1. **Panama rejected the 1967 draft agreements** with the United States as falling short of complete integration in control of the canal.

c. COSTA RICA

(*From p 1068*)

1941, Dec. 8. **Costa Rica declared war on Japan** as a consequence of the Japanese attack on the United States.

1948, Feb. 8. **Otilio Ulate** of the National Union Party was elected president to succeed **Teodoro Picado.** When the government declared the election invalid a civil war broke out, which was won by Ulate's followers under **José Figueras.**

May 8. **Figueras headed a military junta** which broke relations with the U.S.S.R., outlawed the Communist Party, and embarked on a program of political and economic reforms.

Dec. 10. **Costa Rica was invaded from Nicaragua** by Costa Rican exiles. Charges of Nicaraguan complicity were examined by a commission of the **Organization of American States** and dismissed as unfounded.

1949, Feb. 21. **Costa Rica and Nicaragua signed a pact of friendship.**

Nov. 8. Twenty-one months after his election, **Otilio Ulate** was inaugurated as president.

1953, July 26. Socialist **José (Pepe) Figueres** won a sweeping victory over his Conservative opponent in presidential elections.

1955, Jan. 11. Rebels in Costa Rica seized the northern border town of **Villa Quesada.** Figueres accused Nicaragua of aggression.

Jan. 20. Costa Rica and Nicaragua accepted the OAS plan to set up a **buffer zone.**

Feb. 17. The OAS investigating committee indicated some **Nicaraguan responsibility for the recent revolt** in Costa Rica, but did not accuse Nicaragua of outright aggression.

1962, Feb. 4. **Francisco José Orlich Bolmarcich** was elected president.

1966, Feb. José Joaquín Trejos elected president.

d. NICARAGUA

(*From p. 1068*)

1941, Dec. 11. **Nicaragua declared war on Japan, Germany, and Italy,** and subsequently (Dec. 20) on **Roumania, Hungary, and Bulgaria.**

1947, Feb. 2. **Leonardo Arguello** was elected president to succeed dictator **Anastasio Somoza.** The latter had supported Arguello as a possible figurehead, but when the new president showed signs of independence, he was immediately removed (May 27). In September, a puppet of Somoza's, **Victor Román Reyes,** was made president.

1950, Mar. 25. **General Somoza resumed the presidency** and in subsequent "elections" had his return endorsed by the people.

1956, Sept. 29. **President Somoza died** of gunshot wounds, inflicted on September 22. He was succeeded by his son, **Luis,** who was unanimously elected to serve until May 1957, and then was re-elected for a six-year term.

1963, Feb. 3. **René Schick Gutierrez,** the candidate selected by retiring President Somoza, defeated **Diego Chamorro** in the presidential election.

1966, Aug. 3. **Election of Lorenzo Guerrero** as president.

1967, Jan. 22-25. Civil strike between opposing factions in the forthcoming presidential elections. Followers of Dr. **Fernando Aguero Rochas** subdued by the national guard.

Feb. **General Anastasio Somoza Debayle elected president,** thus assuring dominance of the Somoza dynasty.

e. HONDURAS

(*From p. 1069*)

1941, Dec. 8. **Honduras declared war on Japan** and four days later (Dec. 12) on **Germany and Italy.**

1948, Oct. 10. **President Tiburcio Carías,** after fifteen years of dictatorship, supported the election of Nationalist candidate **Juan Manuel Gálvez** to become his successor. This did not keep the new president from adopting a program of moderate constitutional, social, and economic reform.

1954, Dec. 5. Unable to secure a quorum, parliament dissolved, and control of the country was taken over by acting-president **Julio Lozano Dias.**

1956, Oct. 21. The first **bloodless coup** in the nation's history took place as a group of military officers forced the **resignation of Lozano Dias** as chief of state. On October 22 all political parties endorsed the military junta, led by **Col. Hector Caraccioli,** and pledged themselves to the formation of a democratic government.

1957, Sept. 22. In elections for a constituent assembly, the Liberal Party, led by **Ramón Villeda Morales,** won a majority.

Nov. 15. The constituent assembly elected **Villeda Morales president.**

1960, Nov. 18. The International Court of Justice awarded **border areas, claimed by Nicaragua,** to Honduras.

1963, Oct. 3. Armed forces, led by **Col. Osvaldo Lopez Arellano,** overthrew the government of President Ramón Villeda Morales.

1965, June 5. Return to a constitutional régime, under the presidency of **General Osvaldo López Arellano,** and a new constitution worked out by a constituent assembly.

1969, July. Undeclared war between **Honduras and El Salvador,** precipitated by popular demonstrations against Salvadorian migrant workers in Honduras following the defeat of Honduras in a football match with El Salvador. Of the 300,000 Salvadorian workers some 10,000 were expelled, with the result that Salvadorian forces invaded Honduras (July 14). The OAS succeeded in bringing about an armistice (July 18) and inducing the Salvadorian forces to withdraw (July 30). Despite the fact that the council of foreign ministers of the Central American states agreed on a formula for settlement of the dispute (Dec. 5) and the opening of peace negotiations in Costa Rica (Jan. 26, 1970), hostilities continued to break out sporadically.

f. EL SALVADOR

(From p. 1069)

1941, Dec. 8. El Salvador declared war on **Japan** and (Dec. 13) on **Germany and Italy.**

1948, Dec. 14. President Salvador Castaneda (who had succeeded **Maximiliano Martínez** in 1944) was forced to resign. A provisional revolutionary government restored full constitutional liberties and called for

1950, Mar. 26–28. The first completely free elections since 1931. **Major Oscar Osorio** was elected president.

1956, Sept. 14. Lt. Gen. José Maria Lemus became president.

1961, Jan. 26. After a three-months-old junta was overthrown on January 25, a new five-member junta, entitled the **Military-Civilian Directorate,** took control.

Feb. 15. U.S. President Kennedy announced recognition of the junta.

1962, Jan. 5. The constituent assembly approved a **new constitution** to replace the 1950 constitution, and on January 25, **Eusebia Rodolfo Cordón** was inaugurated as provisional president.

Apr. 29. With opposition parties boycotting the presidential election, **Lt. Col. Julio Adalberto Rivera** ran unopposed, and on July 1

was inaugurated for a five-year term.

1967, Mar. 5. Election of Colonel Fidel Sánchez Hernández, of the ruling National Conciliation Party, as president (inaugurated July 5).

1969, July. War with Honduras (see Honduras, p. 1244).

g. GUATEMALA

(From p. 1069)

1941, Dec. 8. Guatemala declared war on Japan, "thus expressing the solidarity of the Guatemalan government and people with the United States." On December 11 Guatemala also declared war on **Germany and Italy.**

1944, Dec. 17–19. In Guatemala's first free elections, **Juan José Arévalo,** a university professor, was chosen president to succeed dictator **Jorge Ubico,** who had been expelled. The new president followed a program of socialization and economic reform, which met with growing opposition from large landowners, foreign investors, and the military.

1950, Nov. 10–12. Colonel Jacobo Arbenz Guzmán, a consistent supporter of Arévalo's liberal program, was elected president.

1951, Mar. 15. Jacobo Arbenz Guzmán was sworn in as president of Guatemala.

1952, June 17. The president signed a **Communist-supported land reform bill,** just passed by congress.

1953, Feb. 25. In accordance with the government's agrarian reform, the agrarian department informed the **United Fruit Company** of a plan to expropriate 225,000 of the company's 300,000-acre holdings.

Oct. 14. U.S. assistant secretary of state **John Cabot** declared that Guatemala, "openly playing the Communist game," could expect no United States help or co-operation.

1954, Jan. 29. The government officially charged that **Nicaragua,** with the support of several Latin American states and the "tacit assent" of the United States, was **planning a land, sea, and air invasion** of Guatemala.

Mar. 17. The U.S. state department, reporting a major **shipment of Communist-made arms** to Guatemala, expressed grave concern with the strong Communist movement developing there.

May 21. Foreign Minister Toriello declared that his country had been forced to buy arms elsewhere because the United States boycott had left Guatemala defenseless.

June. Internal and external uneasiness over Communist influence in Guatemala came to a head when the United States sought to stop arms shipments, and army officers under **Col. Carlos Castillo Armas rebelled against the**

Arbenz government. The U.N. security council, seeking to bring about a cease-fire between rebel and government forces, at last (June 25) postponed further action pending the completion of an **OAS investigation.**

June 28. A **military junta,** headed by Col. Castillo Armas, ousted **President Arbenz,** but on the following day yielded power to a government under **Col. Elfego Monzon,** which arranged a cease-fire and ordered the **arrest of all Communist leaders** in the country.

July 8. Col. **Castillo Armas was chosen president** of the ruling military junta.

1957, July 26. **Castillo Armas was assassinated,** and on July 27 **Vice-President Luís Arturo Gonzales** was installed as provisional president.

Oct. 24. Charges of fraud in the presidential election of October 20, won by **Miguel Ortiz Passarelli,** touched off a **national crisis** which brought a three-man junta to power. On October 26 the military junta annulled the October 20 election and ordered congress to install a provisional president and arrange for new elections. **Guillermo Flores Avendano** took office as interim president on October 27.

1958, Mar. 2. **General Miguel Ydigores Fuentes** was inaugurated as president for a six-year term.

1963, Mar. 30. The **government** of President Ydigores Fuentes was **overthrown by a rightist anti-Fidelista rebel group,** led by **Defense Minister Col. Enrique Peralta Azurdia.**

Apr. 10. The new military government issued an interim **basic government law** giving public power to the army. The United States recognized the new government on April 17.

July 24. The **government broke diplomatic relations with Britain,** because of the latter's announcement, on July 22, of plans for giving limited autonomy to British Honduras, claimed by Guatemala.

1966, July 1. Inauguration of **Julio César Méndez Montenegro,** a civilian, as president. The **CONSTITUTION OF SEPT. 15, 1965,** restored a democratic régime, but led to further polarization between the radical (mostly Communist) elements and the conservative groups associated with the army.

1966, Nov. 2. Proclamation of a state of siege, due to the rapid **spread of terrorist activity.**

1968, Jan. 16. Two U.S. military attachés were slain by Communist terrorists. On Aug. 28 the U.S. ambassador, **John G. Mein,** was kidnaped and slain by a Communist guerrilla organization. Urban terrorism became widespread.

1970, Feb. 26. Kidnaping of the Guatemalan foreign minister, **Alberto Fuentes Mohr,** for whose release (Mar. 1) the government freed the guerrilla leader **Giron Cavillo.** Kidnapings continued.

Mar. 31. The **kidnaping of the West German ambassador,** for whose release the terrorists demanded release of 17 political prisoners. On refusal by the government, the ambassador was murdered, whereupon the West German government broke off diplomatic relations (Apr. 6).

July 1. **Carlos Arana Osorio,** a conservative, inaugurated as president, following his election on Mar. 1.

Nov. 13. In the struggle against terrorists a **state of siege** was again imposed, all party activities were suspended, and the president was given dictatorial powers for a period of ten days.

3. THE WEST INDIES

a. CUBA

(From p. 1072)

1940, July 14. Col. **Fulgencio Batista was elected president** of Cuba.

1941, Dec. 9. **Cuba declared war on Japan** and also (Dec. 11) on **Germany and Italy.**

1942, Oct. 16. Cuba established **diplomatic relations with the U.S.S.R.**

1944, May 31. **Ramón Grau San Martín was elected president** for a four-year term.

1948, June 1. **Carlos Prío Socarras** was elected president to succeed **Grau San Martín,** who

finished his four-year term. Both were members of the Auténtico Party and anti-Communist.

1952, Mar. 10. **General Fulgencio Batista** overthrew President Prío Socarras. Batista assumed the titles of chief of state and premier. The presidency was left vacant pending elections.

1954, Oct. 30. On the eve of **presidential elections,** Gen. Batista's only rival for the presidency, Ramón Grau San Martín, withdrew from the contest, charging that the election was completely rigged. November 2, Batista was declared elected.

1957, May 20. Rebel leader **Fidel Castro,** from

his mountain hideout, appealed to the United States to stop sending arms to Batista.

May 30. The army declared an intensified **war against rebel troops** in Oriente Province.

1958, Mar. 17. Rebel leader Fidel Castro issued a manifesto calling for "total war" against the Batista régime, beginning April 1.

1959, Jan. 1. After Castro's **capture of Santa Clara,** capital of Las Villas province (Dec. 31, 1958), President Batista resigned and fled. On the same day **Castro forces took Santiago, and two days later Havana.**

Jan. 5. **Manuel Urrutia, named provisional president** by Castro (Jan. 3), named **José Miro Cardona** premier, and the following day announced rule by decree for eighteen months. The United States recognized the new régime, January 7.

Feb. 16. Castro took office as premier following the sudden **resignation of Cardona** and his cabinet.

Apr. 15. **Castro arrived in Washington** for an unofficial visit. On April 17 he declared that his régime was not Communist, and characterized his revolution as "humanistic."

June 4. An **agrarian reform law** was promulgated, providing for state appropriation of large landholdings. Under this law, United States sugar companies were expected to lose 1,666,000 acres of land within a year.

July 17. President Urrutia resigned in a dispute with Premier Castro over **Communist influence** in the government. **Osvaldo Dorticos Torrado** succeeded to the presidency.

Nov. 3. The U.S. State Department declared it would not tolerate the establishment, by Cuban refugees, of an exiled, provisional government in the United States.

1960, Feb. 13. Premier Castro and Soviet first deputy premier **Anastas I. Mikoyan** signed an agreement in Havana for the **Soviet purchase of five million tons of sugar** and for $100 million of Soviet credit to Cuba.

June 23. Castro threatened to meet "economic aggression" by the United States with the seizure of all American-owned property and business interests in Cuba.

July 6. **President Eisenhower,** citing Cuba's policy of hostility to the United States, **cut Cuba's sugar quota** by about 95 per cent. On July 9 Eisenhower declared that the United States would never allow the establishment in the Western Hemisphere of a régime "dominated by international communism."

July 9. **Soviet Premier Khrushchev,** in a Moscow address, **threatened Soviet use of rockets** if the U.S. intervened militarily in Cuba. At a news conference on July 12, Khrushchev declared that the United States' **Monroe Doctrine** had died a "natural death."

On July 14 the U.S. state department reaffirmed the Monroe Doctrine, and charged Khrushchev with seeking to set up a "Bolshevik doctrine" for world-wide Communist expansion.

Oct. 14. **The Cuban government nationalized all banks and all large industrial and commercial enterprises.**

Oct. 19. The United States imposed an **embargo on all exports to Cuba** except for medical supplies and most foodstuffs.

Oct. 28. The United States, in a note to the OAS, charged that Cuba was receiving substantial **arms shipments from the Soviet bloc.**

1961, Jan. 3. The **United States severed diplomatic relations with Cuba,** after Castro demanded that the United States cut its embassy personnel in Havana to eleven persons.

Mar. 22. In New York, the **Democratic Front** and the **Revolutionary Movement of the People,** the two major Cuban opposition groups, announced agreement on setting up a **revolutionary council** with ex-Premier **José Miro Cardona** as president. He urged (Apr. 9) all Cubans to revolt against the Castro régime.

Apr. Rumors became rife of anti-Castro forces, under the leadership of the Cuban revolutionary council, stationed in Guatemala, Louisiana, and Florida. At the U.N., April 15, Cuban **Foreign Minister Raul Roa** accused the United States and Latin American nations of preparing an invasion.

Apr. 17-20. A **CUBAN REBEL FORCE** of about 1600 men **INVADED SOUTHERN CUBA** and established a beachhead near Bahia de los Cochinos **(Bay of Pigs),** but was driven off with heavy losses.

Apr. 18. Soviet **Premier Khrushchev** demanded that the United States halt its invasion of Cuba and **promised aid to the Castro government,** to which President Kennedy replied that the United States would not permit outside military intervention. Two days later he asserted that the United States would take steps, if necessary for its security, to halt Communist expansion.

May 17. Castro declared his willingness to **exchange Cuban rebel prisoners** taken in April for 500 United States bulldozers. On May 22 a Tractors for Freedom Committee was set up in the United States. Negotiations broke down, however, June 30, over the total sum to be involved.

Dec. 2. **Premier Castro declared himself a Marxist-Leninist** and announced the formation of a united party to bring Communism to Cuba.

1962, Aug. 18. Following disclosure on August 14 that Cuba would have no sugar to sell on the world market in 1963 or 1964 because of production failures, Castro announced that henceforth agriculture would be based completely on collectives and that the co-operatives owned by peasants would be turned into state farms.

Sept. 2. The **U.S.S.R.** announced an agreement **to supply arms and technical specialists** to Cuba.

Sept. 11. The U.S.S.R. accused the United States of preparing aggression against Cuba, and warned that this would mean war. Khrushchev declared that Soviet arms were being sent to Cuba "exclusively for defensive purposes."

Sept. 13. President Kennedy declared that United States military action was not "required or justified" at this time, but said that the United States would act if its security were imperiled.

Oct. 10. The United States government agreed to help pay the $60 million **ransom** set by Castro **for the release of 1113 Cuban prisoners.**

Oct. 22. A **CUBAN CRISIS** came to a head in a U.S.-U.S.S.R. confrontation over the **installation in Cuba of Soviet offensive missile and bomber bases.** President Kennedy announced a U.S. air and naval "quarantine" to prevent arms shipments, and asked the U.N. security council to meet at once to discuss the crisis. On October 23 the OAS authorized the use of armed force to impose the quarantine, which went into effect on October 24.

Oct. 25. The proposal of U.N. acting secretary general U Thant to conduct negotiations between the principals involved in the Cuban crisis was accepted by President Kennedy and Premier Khrushchev.

Oct. 28. **President Kennedy and Premier Khrushchev reached agreement,** substantially on terms proposed by President Kennedy the previous day: (1) the Soviets to halt construction of missile bases in Cuba and remove weapons under U.N. supervision; and (2) the United States to end the quarantine and give assurances that it would not invade Cuba, as soon as Soviet forces and weapons were withdrawn.

Nov. 1. Fidel Castro, after a failure of U Thant's effort in conference with him to arrange a **U.N. inspection of missile bases** (Oct. 30–31), rejected proposals for international inspection of Soviet missile sites.

Nov. 7. Following an announcement that all Soviet rockets had been removed from Cuba, a U.S.-U.S.S.R. agreement revealed that U.S. naval vessels would verify the missile withdrawals by counting them at sea. The following day, the U.S. Department of Defense reported that all known offensive missile

bases in Cuba had been dismantled.

Nov. 16. After Castro, November 15, threatened to shoot down **U.S. reconnaissance planes,** the United States announced that it would continue the flights and defend the planes, until a better method was devised for checking upon Cuba's offensive military buildup.

Nov. 20. President Kennedy announced the **end of the United States blockade of Cuba,** since Khrushchev had agreed to withdraw Soviet jet bombers from the island within thirty days.

Dec. 23–24. The remaining 1113 **Cuban rebels,** who had been captured in the invasion attempt of April 1961, were **returned to the United States** in exchange for foods and medicines valued at $53 million.

1963, Jan. 7. The United States and the Soviet Union announced that their negotiations on the Cuban crisis were ended and that the matter was closed.

Feb. 18. The Soviet Union informed the United States that "several thousand" of its 17,000 troops in Cuba would be withdrawn by March 15.

Mar. 30. The U.S. departments of state and justice announced that the United States would "take every step necessary" to see that U.S. territory was not used as a base for Cuban refugee raids on Cuba or on Soviet shipping.

1964, Jan. 11. The Castro government purchased $11 million worth of buses from Great Britain.

Jan. 22. Concluding a **visit by Castro to Moscow,** Cuba and the Soviet Union signed a long-term **trade agreement** calling for increased Soviet purchase of Cuban sugar. Castro agreed to support the limited test ban treaty.

Feb. The **seizure of four Cuban fishing boats** in U.S. territorial waters (Feb. 3) led to the announcement (Feb. 6) that the water supply to the U.S. Guantanamo naval base would be limited to one hour a day. The United States took countermeasures against Cubans working in the base and to insure its own water supply (Feb. 7).

Feb. 26. Minister of Industry **Ché Guevara** announced a reduction in industrial investments to allow for more production of consumer items.

July 21–26. **Isolation of Cuba,** following condemnation by the Organization of American States for supplying pro-Communist Venezuelan guerrillas with arms. The OAS voted to invoke sanctions and called on members to sever diplomatic and trade relations. Only Mexico and Jamaica refused to do so (Aug. 3).

1965, Oct. Castro announced that Cubans were

free to leave. On Nov. 6 an agreement was reached with the U.S. government to air-lift 3000–4000 Cuban refugees monthly. In the next five years several hundred thousand, including many members of the educated classes, left the island.

Oct. 3. Departure of Major Ernesto (Ché) Guevara, former Cuban minister of industry, for unspecified South American destination. Guevara, who renounced Cuban citizenship, was to lead the revolutionization of Latin America. He was killed on Oct. 8, 1967, by Bolivian troops while operating in the field.

1966, Feb. A new trade agreement was signed with the U.S.S.R. Cuba, with an economy based largely on the sugar crop, was unable to overcome the economic handicap created by the boycott of the American states, and was therefore dependent on Soviet Russia for both direct and indirect aid.

1967, June 27–29. Visit of Soviet Premier Kosygin to Cuba, followed by the cancellation (Oct.) of President Dorticos' projected visit to Moscow. Serious friction had developed between the two countries, which was reflected in a savage attack in *Pravda* on the Cuban ideology.

1968, Jan. Eleven old-guard **Communist leaders tried for treason** and sentenced to long prison terms, apparently because of their objections to Cuban revolutionary activity abroad.

b. HAITI

(From p. 1073)

1941, Dec. 8. Haiti declared war on Japan and later (Dec. 12) on **Germany and Italy.**

1946, Jan. 11. A military group under **Col. Paul Magloire** ousted **President Elie Lescot,** took over the government, and installed **Dumarsais Estimé** as president.

1948, Feb. 11. The Communist Party was outlawed.

1950, May 10. President **Estimé** was overthrown by a military junta under **Col. Paul Magloire,** who was subsequently elected president.

1956, Dec. 12. Under the pressure of a general strike, Magloire gave up the presidency.

1957, Feb. 7. The legislature elected **Franck Sylvain provisional president,** and invalidated a constitutional provision under which a presidential vacancy was filled by the ranking member of the supreme court. Sylvain's predecessor, **Joseph Nemours Pierre-Louis,** had assumed the presidency in accord with this provision.

Apr. 2. Under accusations of trying to "fix" the elections scheduled for April 28, provisional

President Sylvain resigned. On April 26 a provisional executive council took over, to rule until after the presidential election, postponed for three months.

May 26. Following a flareup of civil war between the executive council and the forces of army chief of staff **Cantave, Daniel Fignola** took over as provisional president.

June 14. The army, led by **Brig. Gen. Antonio Kebreau,** quietly ousted provisional President Daniel Fignola, and proclaimed a state of emergency.

Sept. 22. The presidential election resulted in victory for **François Duvalier.**

Oct. 22. Amidst a **crisis with the United States** over the fatal beating of an American citizen by police, Duvalier became president and the military junta resigned.

1963, May 2. An OAS commission began investigating the **Haitian-Dominican conflict** which concerned the violation of diplomatic immunity after armed soldiers surrounded the Dominican embassy in Port-au-Prince in April. Haiti refused to grant safe conduct exits for some of the twenty-two foes of Duvalier who had taken refuge in the Dominican embassy.

May 15. President Duvalier's constitutional right to office ended, as his legal term expired.

May 17. United States suspension of diplomatic ties with Haiti.

Aug. 5–7. An invasion by a small force of Haitian exiles attempting to overthrow President Duvalier failed.

1964, Apr. 1. François Duvalier became president for life.

June. A **new constitution,** while it provided for universal suffrage and an elected one-chamber legislature, concentrated all executive power in a president elected for life. Duvalier's power could not be seriously threatened, since he posed as the champion of the poverty-stricken Negro masses, had broken the power of the army, and was loyally protected by a personal guard.

1968, May. Another attempt to invade Haiti, staged by opposition elements in exile, was easily defeated, as had been previous efforts.

1969, June 2. A **bombing raid on Port-au-Prince** resulted in wholesale arrests and numerous disappearances.

c. THE DOMINICAN REPUBLIC

(From p. 1073)

1941, Dec. 8. The **Dominican Republic declared war on Japan** and shortly after (Dec. 11) on **Germany and Italy.**

1947, May 16. Rafael Leonidas Trujillo, who had controlled the country, directly or indirectly, since 1930, was re-elected president.

1947–50. The Dominican Republic repeatedly accused its neighbors, notably **Cuba** and **Guatemala,** of abetting subversive activities (such as the so-called "Caribbean League") directed against the Trujillo régime. The council of the **Organization of American States** finally considered the matter and condemned the Dominican Republic as well as Cuba and Guatemala for engaging in conspiracies and attempted invasions.

1960, Aug. 3. Vice-President Joaquin Balaguer was sworn in as president, succeeding **Hector Trujillo Molina,** who resigned August 2. Popular unrest continued and the OAS maintained sanctions throughout August and September.

1961, May 30. Generalissimo Trujillo was assassinated in Ciudad Trujillo by a group led by **General Juan Tomas Diaz.**

July 17. A four-nation OAS investigatory commission reported to the OAS sanctions committee that **surveillance of the Dominican Republic** should be maintained.

Sept. 21. Yielding to popular pressure President Balaguer assembled delegates from opposition parties to initiate steps toward more democratic government.

Nov. 18–19. General **Rafael L. Trujillo, Jr.,** and other members of the Trujillo family left the country amid reports of a threatened military coup. U.S. navy warships were patrolling the Dominican coast.

Dec. 19–20. After prolonged strikes and demonstrations, President Balaguer and the opposition **National Civic Union** reached a political agreement. Balaguer announced the creation of a governing council of state, headed by himself, until the OAS lifted its sanctions against the Republic. The council would schedule elections for a constituent assembly by August 16, and would hold general elections no later than December 20, 1962. United States President Kennedy praised the settlement on December 20 and promised United States support.

1962, Jan. 1. A seven-man **council of state** was inaugurated; it pledged to restore civil liberties. **Rafael Bonnelly** became vice-president.

Jan. 4. The OAS removed sanctions against the Dominican Republic imposed in August 1960. The **United States resumed diplomatic ties** with the country on January 6.

Jan. 18. A military counter-coup deposed the military junta which had overthrown the ruling council of state on January 16. The council was reinstated and elected Rafael Bonnelly president.

Dec. 20. Juan Bosch Gaviño was elected president.

1963, Feb. 27. Bosch took office as the country's first constitutionally elected president since 1924.

Sept. 25. Military leaders overthrew the government of President Bosch in a bloodless coup. The United States suspended diplomatic ties and economic aid to the country.

1965, Apr. 24–25. Overthrow of the ruling junta by a coup in favor of ex-president Bosch. Opposition to Bosch was organized by conservative **General Elías Wessín y Wessín.** Factional fighting led to defeat of the Bosch forces and the former junta resumed control. But the struggle between rightist and leftist elements was soon resumed and led to the **landing of U.S. Marines** to protect American lives (Apr. 27–28). Though a truce was arranged by the OAS (May 5), fighting continued and more American forces were landed. These were eventually merged with the **INTER-AMERICAN ARMED FORCE,** voted by the OAS (May 6), which went into operation on May 23, with contingents from Brazil, Paraguay, Honduras, and Costa Rica.

May 7. Meanwhile, the Wessín forces formed a **National Government of Reconstruction,** headed by **General Antonio Imbert Barreras.** In the ensuing heavy fighting the Imbert forces made considerable gains.

Aug. 30. The Imbert junta resigned and leaders on both sides agreed to the OAS **RECONCILIATION ACT,** which provided for a provisional government, to be followed by gradual withdrawal of foreign forces.

Sept. 3. Hector Garcia-Godoy, former foreign minister, was accepted by both factions as president of the provisional government.

Sept. 25. Return of Juan Bosch from abroad. He called at once for withdrawal of the OAS forces.

1966, Feb. 9–13. Outbreak of riots and proclamation of a general strike by leftist elements which demanded that rightist army officers accept diplomatic appointments and leave the country.

June 3. Presidential elections. **Victory of Joaquín Balaguer,** a moderate, over Juan Bosch.

June 24. Decision of the OAS to withdraw the armed forces. Withdrawal was completed by Oct.

July 1. INAUGURATION OF PRESIDENT BALAGUER, whose régime was supported by the United States in a program of urgently needed economic and social reform.

1969, Jan. Return of Gen. Wessín y Wessín, the rightist leader, from exile.

1970, Mar. 24–26. Kidnaping of a U.S. air at-

taché by radical terrorists. He was released when the government agreed to free twenty political prisoners.

May 17. **Election of President Balaguer** to a second four-year term.

Aug. 16. Inauguration of President Balaguer, who now undertook **drastic action against radical elements,** including Bosch's Dominican Revolutionary Party.

d. PUERTO RICO

(From p. 1074)

1948, Nov. 2. Popular Party candidate **Luis Muñoz Marín** became the first elected governor of Puerto Rico.

1950, July 3. An act of the United States congress permitted Puerto Rico to draft its own constitution.

Nov. 1. The **attempt on President Truman's life** by two Puerto Ricans led to the arrest of large numbers of Communists and Nationalists on the island. The latter were accused of plotting to overthrow the Puerto Rican government.

1952, Mar. 3. Puerto Rico, by popular vote, ratified its **new constitution.**

July 4. Governor Muñoz Marín proclaimed the **Commonwealth of Puerto Rico,** one day after U.S. President Truman had signed a congressional resolution approving its constitution, which came into force on July 25.

1960, Nov. 8. Governor Muñoz Marín and his **Popular Democratic Party** won all but one of 83 precincts, despite the order to Catholic voters by the three Roman Catholic bishops (Oct. 23, 28) not to vote for him. The **Republican Statehood Party** increased its share of the vote to 32 per cent, but the **Independence Party** was reduced to 3.1 per cent of the votes cast.

1964, Feb. 24. U.S. President Johnson signed a bill creating a thirteen-member committee to study the political future of Puerto Rico. The island continued to make great progress, though still afflicted by population pressure.

1967, July 23. In a **popular referendum** on the future status of the island over 60% voted for continuance as a commonwealth associated with the United States, and 39% for attainment of full statehood in the United States. The vote for independence was negligible.

1968, Nov. 5. **Luis A. Ferré,** leader of the New Progressive Party and advocate of statehood, was **elected governor.** He was inaugurated on Jan. 2, 1969.

e. BRITISH CARIBBEAN TERRITORIES AND GUIANA

1953, Oct. 6. Britain dispatched troops and warships to Guiana to handle a suspected **attempt to set up a Communist régime** there.

1956, Feb. 23. Delegates from Jamaica, Trinidad, Tobago, Barbados, the Windward Islands, and the Leeward Islands came to a preliminary agreement for a **Caribbean federation.**

1957, Aug. 12. **Cheddi Jagan's left-wing** party won nine of the fourteen elective seats in the Guiana legislative council. On August 16 **Governor Patrick Renison** invited Jagan to participate in, but not to form, a new cabinet.

1958, Jan. 3. The **Federation of the West Indies** came into being. The 77,000-square-mile federation, with a population of three million, was composed of ten units: Trinidad, Tobago, Jamaica, Barbados, St. Lucia, St. Vincent, Grenada, Montserrat, St. Kitts-Nevis-Anguilla, Dominica, and Antigua.

Mar. 26. In **West Indies Federation elections** to the 45-member house of representatives, the Socialist-oriented Labor Party won a majority of seats over the opposition Democratic Labor Party.

1960, Mar. 31. The British colonial office announced that if a new constitution were accepted for British Guiana, it would go into effect in August 1961. Two years after the first general election, full independence would be considered.

Aug. 21. The **People's Progressive Party** in Guiana, headed by Cheddi Jagan, won 20 of the 35 seats in the legislative council.

Sept. 19. **Jamaica voted to withdraw** from the West Indies Federation.

1962, Jan. 15. The **People's National Movement** announced that the colony of Trinidad and Tobago would seek independence outside the West Indies Federation.

Feb. 6. The British government announced its **decision to dissolve the West Indies Federation,** in view of the withdrawal of Jamaica and Trinidad-Tobago.

Apr. 10. Legislative **elections in Jamaica** gave **Sir Alexander Bustamente's** Labor Party a majority. He took office as premier April 24.

May 24. Eight small colonies in the West Indies announced **plans for a new federation** without Jamaica and Trinidad-Tobago.

Aug. 6. **Jamaica became an independent dominion** within the British Commonwealth.

Aug. 31. The **independence of Trinidad-Tobago** within the Commonwealth was celebrated.

1963, July 22. The colonial office announced that **British Honduras** would attain internal self-government on January 1, 1964.

1964, May 24. More British troops arrived in Guiana to help preserve order in the face of continuing **race riots between Indians and Negroes.**

June 14. Governor Sir Richard Luyt of British Guiana assumed full **emergency powers** for an indefinite period in order to end violence over Indian-Negro racial conflicts. Prime Minister Jagan refused to resign, although members of his cabinet and party were detained by the governor.

Dec. 7. Elections by proportional representation gave Dr. Jagan's People's Progressive Party 24 seats in the legislature, Forbes Burnham's People's National Congress 22 seats, and Peter D'Aguair's United Force 7 seats. Burnham and D'Aguair joined to form a coalition government, despite Jagan's protests that the coalition represented only a minority of the population.

1965, Dec. British government proposals that Antigua, Dominica, St. Lucia, St. Vincent, Grenada, St. Kitts-Nevis-Anguilla each become a state associated with the United Kingdom, with complete autonomy and indeed the power to declare for independence. The British government was to provide defense and control foreign relations. Conferences in London in 1966 culminated in agreement on establishment of Associated States of the United Kingdom, with the various islands to attain this status on specified dates between Feb. and June 1967.

1966, May 26. BRITISH GUIANA BECAME AN INDEPENDENT STATE within the British Commonwealth, assuming the name **Guyana.** Forbes Burnham, the Negro leader, became the first prime minister.

1967, Apr. 11. Death of prime minister Sir Donald Sangster, of Jamaica. He was succeeded by **Hugh Shearer.**

May 30. Under the leadership of **Ronald Webster** the island of **Anguilla declared its in-**dependence of the Associated Territories of St. Kitts-Nevis. Though this act was supported by a popular vote (July 11) it was disapproved by the British government.

Oct. Meeting of heads of Commonwealth Caribbean governments at Barbados, reinforced by representatives of the United Kingdom, the United States, and Canada. Agreement on establishment of a **Regional Development Bank,** a **Caribbean Population Research Centre,** and adoption of measures to further freedom of trade.

1968, Jan. The new Guyana government was confronted by **Surinam claims** to the Corentyne area, rich in bauxite, and (July) by **Venezuelan claims** to frontier areas rich in oil.

June 27. Jamaica joined the **Caribbean Free Trade Area,** which provided for early abolition of interstate tariffs among members of the British Commonwealth.

Dec. In the **Guyana elections** Burnham's National Congress Party won 30 of the 53 seats in the assembly. Jagan's party was reduced to 20 seats.

1969, Mar. In **Anguilla,** temporarily administered by a British official, the British undersecretary for foreign and Commonwealth affairs, was driven out while trying to find a solution. British paratroopers and police forces then took over. Webster was deposed as acting president and a British commissioner appointed.

Apr. 5. Webster demanded withdrawal of British forces, but the situation was relieved when a commissioner was appointed.

1970, Feb. 23. Guyana proclaimed a Co-operative Republic within the British Commonwealth, by Prime Minister Burnham.

Apr. 21–24. An attempted **rebellion in Trinidad-Tobago** was defeated. All political activities were then banned.

Nov. 24. On lifting of the ban, there was a renewal of black militancy.

4. SOUTH AMERICA

a. ARGENTINA

(From p. 1060)

1942, July 6. President Ramón S. Castillo announced that the republic would maintain its **policy of neutrality.**

1943, June 5. The isolationist régime of **President Castillo** was **overthrown by a military junta.** The congress was dissolved and a new government formed by **Gen. Pedro P. Ramirez** (June 8).

1944, Jan. 27. The discovery of an **espionage plot** involving agents of the Axis powers led the Argentine government to sever **relations with Germany and Japan.**

1946, Feb. 24. Colonel JUAN D. PERÓN was elected president, and his supporters won a majority in both houses. During the campaign the United States, on the basis of captured German documents, accused Argentina and Perón of collaboration with the Axis.

1947, Jan. 1. A **five-year plan** of economic reform and industrialization went into effect.

1948, Mar. 4. Argentina and Chile agreed on the joint defense of their rights in the Antarctic and the **Falkland Islands** against British claims.

Aug. 13-14. The chamber of deputies gave **unlimited powers** to Perón in case of a national emergency and voted to reform the constitution. **Elections** for a constituent assembly **(Dec. 5)** gave the **Perónista** Party a substantial majority.

1949, Mar. 8. The **new constitution,** which was approved by the assembly, largely confirmed Perón's policy of land reform, nationalization of industries, regulation of foreign trade, etc., and made the president eligible for re-election.

1950. Argentina had by now become a thinly disguised dictatorship under Perón, actively and ably seconded by his wife, Eva. In domestic affairs, censorship of the press and far-reaching powers of arrest helped stamp out public criticism. In its foreign relations, the Perón régime claimed an intermediary position between Eastern Communism and Western capitalism.

1951, Apr. 13. Perón suppressed the newspaper *La Prensa.*

Sept. 28. The government easily put down a minor **military uprising** led by **General Benjamin Menendez.**

Nov. 11. In **national elections** President Perón won another six-year term of office.

1952, July 26. The president's wife, Eva Perón, died.

1954, Feb. 17. A secretly promulgated law established **employer groups,** and agreements with labor obligatory for all.

1955, May 17. Supporters of Perón introduced a bill in the senate to deprive the Roman Catholic Church of its tax exemption. On May 13 the house of deputies had prohibited **religious instruction in the schools,** and the minister of education had suspended the teaching of the Catholic religion in all schools.

May 26. On independence day, demonstrations by Roman Catholics resulted in a wave of arrests.

June 16. Climaxing several days of clashes between demonstrators and the police, the **pope excommunicated President Perón;** naval officers seized outlying towns, and planes bombed government buildings in the capital.

June 23. After several days of maneuvering in which President Perón had given control of security forces to the army, and the army had returned control to him, the cabinet and other high officials resigned.

July. Perón called for a political truce (July 5), but the strongest opposition party, the Radicals, rejected his plea. On July 18 Perón promised to give up all dictatorial powers.

Sept. 19. A **four-man military junta,** which had led a revolt on the 16th, **ousted Perón.** On September 23 **General Eduardo Lonardi** became provisional president.

Oct. 5. The position of the provisional president was strengthened by his **dismissal of the supreme court** and the attorney-general, and by an **anti-Perón revolt** among the rank and file of the General Confederation of Labor, whose leadership had been one of the chief supports of Perón.

Nov. 13. Following a **bloodless military coup,** which ousted the Lonardi régime, **General Pedro Aramburu** was installed as president.

1956, June 10. Loyal forces smashed a **Perónist revolt.** Twenty-six of the rebels were executed.

1957, Sept. 24. The constituent assembly voted to **restore the 1853 constitution.** The provisional government, earlier, had annulled the 1949 constitution of exiled President Perón.

1958, Feb. 22. **Arturo Frondizi** was elected president, the first to be elected in twelve years. He took office, May 1.

1962, Feb. 8. The government severed diplomatic ties with Cuba.

Mar. 18. **Perónist parties** polled 35 per cent of the votes and won ten governorships. This showing brought growing dissatisfaction with President Frondizi's moderation and his encouragement of foreign investments to a head, and on

Mar. 28. Military leaders **deposed President Frondizi** and seized control of the government. On March 30 president of the senate **José Maria Guido** became Argentine president with the endorsement of the armed services.

Apr. 24-25. Under pressure from some extreme anti-Perónist military leaders, **Guido** **nullified the recent** provincial and legislative **elections.** A month later, the cabinet decreed a recess of congress and **rule by decree** for the time being.

July 24. The government issued four decrees banning the Perónist and Communist parties, providing controls over the internal affairs of all parties, and installing a system of proportional representation.

Sept. 6. Agreeing to the demands of the three military secretaries, **President Guido dissolved the rump congress,** and signed a decree scheduling presidential and congressional elections for October 27, 1963.

Sept. 18. The dismissal by War Secretary Savaria of three generals sparked an **army revolt** which led to the seizure of Buenos Aires, September 23.

1963, May 12. Eleven cabinet members resigned in protest against the interior minister's demands for authority to purge Perónistas and followers of ex-president Frondizi. The minister resigned on the 13th.

May 17. A presidential decree forbade the **Union Popular** (Perónista front) **Party** to nominate candidates for the presidency or provincial governorships; it could seek only legislative posts.

July 7. Dr. **Arturo Illia** and his Popular Radical Party won a major **election victory** over Perónist groups. The electoral colleges in the provinces formally elected Illia president on July 31. He took office October 12.

1964, Dec. 2. The **attempt of Perón to return** from exile in Spain was thwarted when Brazil refused him passage and obliged him to return to Spain.

1966, June 28. A **military coup,** backed by the chiefs of the armed services, obliged President Illia to resign and named **General Juan Carlos Onganía,** former commander in chief of the army, to be president. Congress and all political parties were disbanded, the judges of the Supreme Court replaced, new governors of the provinces appointed. All executive and legislative power was concentrated in the office of the president, who pursued a frankly anti-Communist course. Unrest in the universities was ruthlessly suppressed (July 31).

July 15. The U.S. government recognized the Onganía régime.

Sept. Creation of state councils, one for economic development and one for national security. The new régime encouraged foreign investment and made marked progress in development, but suffered from the severe inflation and from discontent prevalent in working circles.

1967, Mar. Devaluation of the peso from 250 to 350 to the U.S. dollar. Foreign exchange controls abolished and more liberal economic policies adopted.

1968. Stabilization of the economy; control of trade unions and regulation of strikes; freezing of wages.

1969, May 13. Major **student outbreaks,** followed by labor demonstrations and strikes. A limited state of siege proclaimed (May 28).

Aug. General strike in Córdoba, followed (Sept.) by a railway strike and a student "week of struggle and agitation." The government reluctantly granted certain wage increases.

1970, May 29. KIDNAPING OF FORMER PRESIDENT PEDRO EUGENIO ARAMBURU by terrorist radicals, in revenge for the suppression of radicalism under Aramburu's régime. Aramburu was later found murdered.

June 8. President Onganía deposed by military leaders, who appointed Brig. Gen. **Roberto Marcelo Levingston** president.

Aug. 27. Assassination of José Varela Alonso, prominent labor leader and Perónist, apparently by rightist terrorists.

b. CHILE

(From p. 1061)

1943, Jan. 20. Chile severed diplomatic relations with Germany, Italy, and Japan.

1946, Sept. 4. Gabriel González Videla was elected president by a left bloc to succeed **Don Juan A. Rios** (1942–1946). He formed a coalition cabinet, including Communists, who later dropped out, as the régime moved to the right.

1947, Oct. Communist-led strikes brought the arrest of 200 Communists, the expulsion of two Yugoslav diplomats, and the **break of diplomatic relations with the Soviet Union and Czechoslovakia** (Oct. 21).

1948, Sept. 2. The **Communist Party was outlawed,** but the Communist-inspired strikes and disorders continued.

1949, Mar. Parliamentary elections gave the government coalition a majority.

1952, Sept. 4. Voters gave an overwhelming victory to **General Cárlos Ibañez** in presidential elections. He had been forced out of office twenty-one years before.

1955, May 21. As inflation mounted, President Ibañez blamed the problem on political opposition, with only one of the nineteen parties in congress consistently supporting him, and called for fundamental **constitutional reform** to strengthen the executive power. On August 12 Ibañez appointed his eleventh cabinet since taking office.

Aug. 24–Sept. 4. Sixty thousand government workers struck for higher pay, forcing the government to promise substantial salary increases.

1957, Mar. 3. General elections revealed dissatisfaction with the president's economic program.

Apr. 11. In the face of increasing protests against the rising cost of living, congress voted **special powers to the president** to impose censorship, arrest without warrants, and prohibit public meetings.

1958, Aug. 5. The **Communist Party was legalized** after a ten-year ban.

Sept. 4. In presidential elections, a former finance minister, **Senator Jorge Alessandri,** won a plurality of the vote, and took office on November 3.

1959, May. In view of growing opposition to

President Alessandri's **austerity program,** a Conservative-Liberal-Radical coalition of congressmen voted special powers to him for one year to direct the economy and reorganize the bureaucracy.

1961, Mar. 5. In **congressional elections** the Communists and Socialists made significant gains, the Radicals of the center retained their strength, and the Liberals and Conservatives of the right suffered substantial losses.

1964, Sept. 4. In the **presidential elections EDUARDO FREI MONTALVA,** candidate of the Christian Democratic Party, secured 55.7% of the popular vote, while Senator **Salvador Allende Gossens,** candidate of a Socialist-Communist coalition, polled 38.5%. Frei became president, with a policy of non-violent, gradual economic and social reform.

1966, Jan. Establishment of a **National Copper Corporation,** an independent agency to control the production and sale of copper, where possible in partnership with foreign-owned copper mining corporations.

1967, July. Passage of an **Agrarian Reform Act,** involving progressive distribution of land to needy peasants.

1969, Mar. The **congressional elections** revealed serious losses on the part of the Christian Democrats, who lost their majority in both houses, while the National Party on the Right and the Communists on the Left registered substantial gains. The results reflected growing dissatisfaction with the gradual reform program of the Frei administration and the continuing steep rise in the cost of living.

June. Large-scale **student and worker demonstrations** led the government to cancel the projected visit of Governor Nelson A. Rockefeller.

July–July. **Nationalization** of the holdings of the Anaconda Company and renegotiation of agreements with the Kennecott Corporation.

1970, Aug. 26. **Seizure of land** near Santiago by organized Marxist groups (*Revolutionary Junta of the Homeless*). Political tension made the government hesitant to interfere.

Sept. 4. **Presidential elections.** Senator Allende, supported by the Socialist-Communist coalition, won 36.3% of the popular vote, while former president **Jorge Allesandri Rodríguez,** of the National Party, secured 34%. Since no candidate had a majority, it was left to the congress to choose between the two leaders. After much political maneuvering and bargaining the Christian Democratic Party agreed to support Allende in return for his promise to amend the constitution so as to guarantee civil liberties. Allende was profuse in assurances that while he intended drastic reforms, he would adhere to strictly non-violent methods.

Oct. 22. General **René Schneider Chereau,** commander in chief of the army, was attacked and fatally wounded, supposedly by Right-wing extremists hoping to block the election of Allende. Schneider died on Oct. 25.

Oct. 24. **ALLENDE WAS ELECTED** by a joint session of congress, the vote being 153–35. He was inaugurated Nov. 3.

Nov. 12. Re-establishment of diplomatic relations with Cuba, the first breach in the Pan-American front and the first step in Allende's policy of rapprochement with the Communist countries. Allende was the first overtly Marxist president popularly elected in an American state. His avowed policy was to remake Chilean society along Cuban lines, with nationalization of all industries and far-reaching agrarian reform.

c. PARAGUAY

(*From p. 1062*)

1940, Feb. 14–18. The cabinet and parliament resigned and the president, **General José Félix Estigarribia,** who had been elected the preceding April, took over the functions of government.

1946, July 26. **General Higenio Morínigo,** after revoking his 1940 ban on political activity, formed a two-party cabinet, thus ending his six-year dictatorship.

1947, Mar.–Aug. **Civil war** between the government and left-wing forces under former president **Rafael Franco** ended with the latter's defeat.

1948–1949. The retirement of **President Morínigo** ushered in a veritable procession of presidents: **Manuel Frutos** (June 6, 1948), **Natalicio González** (Aug. 5, 1948), **Raimundo Rolón** (Jan, 30, 1949), **Molás López** (Feb. 27, 1949), and **Federico Chávez** (Sept. 12, 1949).

1954, May 6. A **revolution** led to the installation of a **government junta.**

1957, Dec. 27. An **agreement with Japan** provided for acceptance of 150,000 Japanese immigrants in return for a loan of $12 million.

1963, Feb. 10. **General Alfred Stroessner,** president since 1955, met only token opposition in his bid for re-election.

Aug. 15. Stroessner was sworn in for a third term as president.

1967, May. **Elections for a constituent assembly** resulted in a victory for the ruling Colorado Party. A new constitution, which went into effect on Aug. 25, provided for a popularly elected, two-chamber parliament, and the possibility of overriding a presidential veto by a two-thirds vote. The new régime represented a distinct liberalization of the former authoritarian system.

1968, Feb. President Stroessner was re-elected for his fourth term.

1969, Sept. Growing liberal and church opposition to government restrictions led to increasing tensions. Asunción was placed under interdict by its archbishop (Oct. 26).

d. URUGUAY

(From p. 1062)

1942, Feb. 23. General Alfredo Baldomir, president, dissolved both chambers of the legislature and created a **state council** of members drawn from all parties except Communists and Herreristas.

1946, Nov. 24. Tomás Barreta was elected president. He died on August 2, 1947, and was succeeded by Vice-President **Luiz B. Berres.** Both belonged to the Liberal Colorado Party.

1950, Nov. 26. Andres Martinez Trueba was elected president to succeed Berres.

1952, Mar. 1. The inauguration of a nine-man **federal council** replaced the presidency, from which Trueba had resigned. The new system called for elections to the council every four years.

1959, Mar. 1. The defeated **Colorado Party,** after 93 years in office without interruption, handed over the governmental powers to the **Nationalist Party,** which had won its first election victory in November 1958.

1963, Mar. 1. A new government took office following the victory of the **Blancos** (the more Conservative of the two big parties) in the latest national election. **Daniel Ferandez Crespo** became president of the executive body, the nine-man national council.

1966, Nov. 27. The **election of General Oscar Diego Gestido** as president signified the renewed victory of the Colorado Party. He was inaugurated on Mar. 1, 1967, at which time a constitutional amendment marked the abandonment of the council system and return to the presidency.

1967, Nov. Devaluation of the currency.

Dec. 6. Death of President Gestido, who was succeeded by Vice-President **Jorge Pacheco Areco.** The new administration took a strong line in the face of economic crisis resulting from fantastically high inflation, strikes, and agitation by Communists and other radical groups.

1968, June. Conflict with trade unions. State of emergency proclaimed and wage and price freeze imposed.

1969, Mar. Removal of security restrictions.

However, the growth of terrorist activities (*Tupamaros,* directed against authoritarianism and corruption) led to reimposition of security measures (June 24).

Apr. 23. Signature of the five-nation **treaty for the joint development of the Rio de la Plata Basin.**

1970, July 31. The *Tupamaros* kidnaped one Brazilian and two American officials, whom they held hostage pending release by the government of 150 political prisoners. The government in contrast to many other governments, refused absolutely to negotiate under conditions of blackmail.

e. BOLIVIA

(From p. 1063)

1943, Dec. 21. The government of **President Enrique Peñaranda** was unseated by a group headed by **Major Gualberto Villarroel.** The new régime was not recognized diplomatically except by Argentina (Jan. 4, 1944). The **United States refused recognition** (Jan. 25, 1944).

1946, July 21. President Gualberto Villarroel was killed and his régime overthrown by rebellious workers, soldiers, and students. A provisional government promised a liberal régime and was recognized by Argentina and the United States.

1947, Jan. 5. Enrique Hertzog, leader of the Republican Socialist Union Party was **elected president.** Several subsequent attempts by the **National Revolutionary Movement (M.N.R.)** to overthrow the government were unsuccessful.

1949, May 1. Congressional elections gave a continued majority to the government. A strike in the tin mines in May and a rebellion by the outlawed M.N.R. in September were put down by the army, leaving the country on the verge of bankruptcy.

Oct. 19. President Hertzog resigned because of ill health and was succeeded by **Vice-President Mamerto Urriolagoita.** Disturbances from the Right and Left continued, and on

1950, Apr. 10. The Communist Party was outlawed.

1951, May 16. The **president resigned** and delivered governmental power to a **military junta** led by **General Hugo Ballivan.**

1952, Apr. 11. A **revolt** overthrew the junta of General Ballivan. The leader of the National Revolutionary Movement, **Victor Paz Estenssoro,** was sworn in as president on April 16. He promised to nationalize the tin industry.

1956, June 17. The candidate of the ruling National Revolutionary Movement. **Vice-Presi-**

dent **Herman Siles Zuazo,** was elected president.
1960, June 5. Victor Paz Estenssoro succeeded Siles Zuazo as **president.**
1962, Apr. 16. Bolivia cancelled **diplomatic ties with Chile** over a 23-year fight on the use of the waters of the Lauca River. On April 20 the dispute was placed before the OAS.
June 3. Elections gave President Estenssoro's National Revolutionary Movement control of both houses of congress.
1963, June 17. Bolivia formally withdrew from the OAS council because of its "mishandling" of the border dispute with Chile.
1964, May 31. Victor Paz Estenssoro was re-elected to a third term as president.
Nov. 3. President **PAZ ESTENSSORO OVERTHROWN** by a military faction which set up a junta under the presidency of Gen. **René Barrientos Ortuño.**
1965, May 17-24. Strike of the tin miners against the government; occupation of government-owned mines by the workers. The government thereupon sent in troops and began to draft insurgent workers into the army.
1966, July 3. Elections resulted in the victory of President Barrientos, whose Bolivian Revolutionary Front controlled congress. Barrientos also enjoyed strong support in the army, while being bitterly opposed by the mine workers.
1967, Mar.–Oct. A formidable **guerrilla movement** broke out in southeast Bolivia, led by the Cuban revolutionary **Ché Guevara.** Bolivian forces, with U.S. training, captured Guevara and managed to suppress the movement. Guevara died of his wounds (Oct. 8).
1968, July. Violent rioting, following revelation that a former minister of the interior had maintained contacts with Castro. The cabinet was obliged to resign and the government suspended constitutional rights and canceled the elections.
1969, Apr. 27. Death of President Barrientos in a helicopter accident. He was succeeded by Vice-President **Adolfo Siles Salinas.**
Sept. 26. President Siles was overthrown by a military coup and was followed by **President Alfredo Ovando Candia,** commander in chief of the armed forces, who at once introduced a more liberal policy: political prisoners were released, troops were withdrawn from the mines, and restrictions on trade unions were rescinded.
Oct. 17. The government nationalized the U.S.-owned Bolivian Oil Company, whereupon the company stopped refining operations at Arica and halted construction of the pipeline to Argentina (Nov. 12).
1970, Aug. 27. Major **student demonstrations**

and labor protests against the allegedly increasing conservative policies of the government.
Oct. 4. An **army coup forced Pres. Ovando to resign** (Oct. 6). **General Rogelio Miranda,** army chief of staff, then appointed a ruling junta. But air force officers, led by the leftist **GENERAL JUAN JOSÉ TORRES** and supported by students and workers, claimed the presidency and began to attack army posts. Thereupon the junta capitulated and **Torres became president** (Oct. 7).
Oct. 14. Workers began to seize the properties of the state mining corporation and to expel the officials and the police guards.

f. PERU

(From p. 1064)

1942, Jan. 24. Peru severed diplomatic relations with Germany, Italy, and Japan.
1945, June 10. José Luis Bustamente was elected president, supported by Liberal and Aprista forces, to succeed **Manuel Prado Ugarteche.**
1948, Oct. 29. President Bustamente's government was overthrown and replaced by a military junta under **General Manuel Odría.** The Apra and Communist Parties were outlawed.
1950, July 2. General Odría was **elected president** by a large majority and transformed his junta into a cabinet.
1951, Aug. 13. Peru asked the United States, Argentina, Brazil, and Chile to investigate **border incidents with Ecuador.** Fighting began on August 11 over the old issue of access to certain Amazon tributaries.
1956, June 17.. Manuel Prado Ugarteche was elected **president.**
1962, July 18. A **military junta** overthrew and imprisoned the president. It also barred congress from convening and **suspended constitutional guarantees.** The United States suspended diplomatic relations and on July 19–20 halted all economic and military aid.
Aug. 17. The **United States resumed diplomatic relations** with Peru.
1963, July 28. Fernando Belaúnde Terry was inaugurated as **president,** ending one year of military rule.
1964, May. AGRARIAN REFORM LAW provided for the distribution among Indian communities and landless tenant farmers of virtually all state lands and church-owned agricultural property.
1967, Aug. Devaluation of the currency by 50% in the effort to alleviate the economic crisis which was assuming threatening proportions.
1968, Aug. A **compromise settlement** was ar-

rived at **with the U.S.-owned International Petroleum Company.**

Oct. 3. President Belaúnde overthrown by a military coup, following widespread discontent with the government's economic policies. Congress was dissolved and a revolutionary government formed with Gen. **Juan Velasco Alvarado,** chief of staff of the army, as president. The new régime promised to retain previous reforms and to continue further development, but along strictly nationalist lines.

1969, Feb. 6. Seizure of the properties of the International Petroleum Company, after long disputes as to ownership of the La Brea oilfields and repudiation by the government of the earlier compromise agreement.

Feb. Establishment of **diplomatic and trade relations with the U.S.S.R.** and other Communist bloc countries.

Feb. 13. Expropriation of the International Petroleum Company's properties. Far from offering compensation, the government claimed that since 1924 $690 million in oil had been taken out. The expropriated properties were turned over to a new agency, **Petróleos Peruanas** (Aug.).

June. Announcement of a far-reaching **program of land distribution.**

g. ECUADOR

(From p. 1064)

1942, Jan. 29. Ecuador severed diplomatic relations with Germany, Italy, and Japan. On the same date an agreement was signed to settle boundary disputes between Ecuador and Peru.

1946, Aug. 11. President José Velasco Ibarra was re-elected by the assembly.

1947, Aug. 23. Colonel Mancheno, in a successful revolt, **ousted President Ibarra,** only to be overthrown himself on September 3 by a Conservative counter-revolution. **Carlos Arosemena** became acting president.

1948, June 6. In the first popular elections since 1940, **Galo Plaza Lasso** was elected president.

1949, Aug. 5. An earthquake in central Ecuador killed more than 4000 persons.

1952, June 1. Voters gave the Liberal candidate, **Velasco Ibarra,** an upset victory over the Conservative candidate in presidential elections.

1961, Nov. 6–9. The government resigned as a result of riots and military unrest. **Carlos Julio Arosemena** was installed as **president.**

1962, Aug. 24. The cabinet of **President Arosemena resigned** after congressional leaders suggested reorganization to meet labor and economic problems.

1963, July 11–12. A military junta, headed by **Captain Ramón Castro Jijon,** overthrew the government, outlawed the Communist Party, and promised to wipe out pro-Castro terrorist bands.

1966, Mar. 29. The military junta was overthrown and a civilian government established under **Clemente Yerovi Indaburu.**

Oct. 16. Election of a **constituent assembly,** which named **Otto Arosemena Gómez** as president *pro tem.*

1967, May 25. The **new constitution** was essentially a return to that of 1946.

1968, June 2. In the elections **Dr. José María Velasco Ibarra,** four times formerly president, led the field with about one-third of the popular vote. He assumed the presidency (Sept. 1).

1969, Mar. Establishment of **trade relations with the U.S.S.R.**

1970, Oct. 27. Kidnaping of General César Rohan Sandoval, chief of the air force, by terrorists. Martial law was proclaimed, and Gen. Rohan was released a few days later (Nov. 1).

h. COLOMBIA

(From p. 1065)

1941, Dec. 8. Colombia broke diplomatic relations with Japan, citing the Havana resolution.

1942, Nov. 26. Colombia severed diplomatic relations with (Vichy) France.

1946, May 4. Conservative leader **Mariano Ospina Pérez** became president. Because of a continued Liberal majority in congress, he formed a coalition government.

1948, Apr. 9. The assassination of left-wing Liberal **Jorge Gaitán** touched off a major revolt which interrupted the ninth **Pan-American conference in Bogotá** and caused 1400 deaths. Careful investigation failed to reveal the instigators of the upheaval.

1949, June 5. Congressional elections gave the Liberals a reduced majority.

Nov. 27. Following a violent campaign costing over 1000 lives, the Conservative **Lauriano Gómez** was elected president. The Liberals boycotted the election.

1953, June 14. General Gustavo Rojas Pinilla seized power, ousting President Gómez.

1957, May 8. Despite a constitutional provision that a president could not succeed himself, **General Rojas Pinilla** was **re-elected** by 76 members of the legislative assembly, meeting under military protection.

May 9. The Roman Catholic Church accused the Rojas régime of murder in its suppression of student riots. On May 10 **Rojas resigned,** before the completion of his first term, and a military junta took control.

July 26. Amid popular demonstrations and rioting, the ruling **military junta dissolved the constituent assembly** and announced presidential and congressional elections for May 4, 1958.

Dec. 1. Colombians voted to **amend their 1866 constitution** to provide for joint rule by Conservatives and Liberals for twelve years.

1958, May 4. **Alberto Lleras Camargo** was elected president, and was inaugurated on August 7.

1959, Mar. 24. President Lleras Camargo announced a new cabinet composed of six Liberals and six Conservatives and one military figure in accordance with a national policy of bipartisan government.

1962, Mar. 18. The ruling **Liberal-Conservative coalition** government won the congressional elections.

May 6. **Guillermo Leon Valencia,** endorsed by the National Union Coalition, won the presidential election.

1964, Apr. 16. The government made an **agreement with the United States** to investigate the practicality of a **sea-level canal** through Colombia to connect the Atlantic and Pacific Oceans.

1965, May—1969, Dec. **State of siege** was in effect, due to student unrest and disturbances resulting from the economic crisis.

1966, May. In the presidential elections the candidate of the National Front, **Dr. Carlos Lleras Restrepo,** was successful. He took office on Aug. 7.

1968, Jan. Resumption of **diplomatic relations with the U.S.S.R.**

Dec. Adoption of constitutional reforms which provided in detail for the progressive termination of joint-party rule.

1969, May 26. Signature of the agreements for **establishment of ANDEAN INTEGRATION,** between Colombia, Ecuador, Bolivia, Peru, and Chile.

Sept. Alarming spread of student unrest and guerrilla activities.

1970, Apr. 26. Misael Pastrana Borrero declared victor in the presidential election. The result was contested by former president Rojas Pinilla, but was confirmed after a recount (July 15). Pastrana was inaugurated Aug. 7.

i. VENEZUELA

(From p. 1065)

Venezuela ranked third among the nations of the world in **petroleum production** when the Second World War commenced, but the result-

ing wealth was concentrated in too few hands. A large majority of the people remained impoverished, while a high birthrate caused a rapid rise in population.

1945, Oct. 18. **President Isaias Medina** was overthrown by a revolt of army officers and **Rómulo Betancourt** was made provisional president on October 22.

1946, Oct. 27. **Elections** for the constituent assembly gave a majority to the Democratic Action Party.

1947, Dec. 14. **Rómulo Gallegos,** well-known literary figure, was elected president, and his Democratic Action Party maintained an overwhelming majority.

1948, Nov. 24. The government was overthrown and a military junta under **Colonel Carlos Delgado Chalbaud** took control. Its program called for close relations with the new government of Peru and with Franco Spain.

1950, May 13. The Communist Party was outlawed.

Nov. 13. **President Delgado Chalbaud** was assassinated, and **Suarez Flammerich** became president of the junta (Nov. 27).

1951, Oct. 13. The government quelled a **revolt in Caracas** which was alleged to have been fomented by members of the illegal Communist and Democratic Action Parties.

1954, Jan. 9. In the wake of suspicion and charges of fraud in the announcement of the November 30 election results, **Col. Marcos Perez Jimenez** was named provisional president by the national assembly to serve "until constitutional government is re-established."

1957, Nov. 4. Perez Jimenez cancelled the presidential election scheduled for December 15 and announced a **plebiscite** instead. On November 8 the government announced its readiness to initiate its own aid program for Latin America.

Dec. 31. A revolt against President Perez Jimenez broke out.

1958, Jan. 23. A military junta, led by **Admiral Wolfgang Larrazabal ousted President Perez Jimenez.** The junta assumed power after army units defeated the secret police in Caracas.

May 13. During U.S. **Vice-President Richard Nixon's goodwill tour** of South America, mobs in Caracas stoned his car. President Eisenhower demanded that Nixon's safety be assured by Venezuela, and ordered marines and paratroopers to Caribbean bases as a "precautionary measure."

Dec. 7. **Rómulo Betancourt was elected president.** He was inaugurated February 13, 1959.

1960, Aug. 15. A **five-nation investigating committee** reported to the OAS that it had conclusive evidence that the attempted June 24 assassination of President Betancourt was linked to high officials of the Dominican Republic.

1963, Feb. 13. Nine Communists were reported to have hijacked a Venezuelan freighter in the Caribbean, as part of a **terrorist campaign** against the Betancourt government. After docking in Brazil on February 18, the captors were granted asylum.

Dec. 1. Voters elected **Raúl Leoni** of the ruling Democratic Action Party to succeed Rómulo Betancourt as president despite acts of terrorism by leftists. President Leoni took office, March 11, 1964.

1964–1969. PRESIDENCY OF RAÚL LEONI. The formation of a coalition government by the Democratic Action, Republican Democratic Union, and National Democratic Front provided a majority in congress and insured a measure of stability. Nonetheless the country continued to be plagued by incursions by **Cuban-trained guerrillas** and by various **urban terrorist organizations.** Economically, however, great strides were made as exports of oil, iron, and other products provided the government with foreign exchange unique in amount for Latin American countries.

1968, Dec. 1. The **presidential elections** resulted in a narrow victory for **Dr. Rafael Caldera Rodríguez,** the leader of the opposition Social Christian Party. He was inaugurated on Mar. 11, 1969, and continued the policies of development and social reform of the preceding administration.

j. BRAZIL

(From p. 1066)

1942, Jan. 28. Brazil broke off diplomatic and trade relations with the Axis nations.

Aug. 11. The **United States and Brazil** agreed to set up a **joint defense board,** similar to those established with Canada and Mexico.

1943, Feb. 6. Brazil announced its formal **acceptance of the declaration of the United Nations.**

1945, Oct. 25. General demand for a more liberal government led to the forced resignation of **President Getulio Vargas** after almost fifteen years of dictatorship. He was succeeded by **Chief Justice José Linhares.**

Dec. 2. General Enrico Dutra was elected president. His Social Democratic Party won 40 per cent and the National Democratic Union 33 per cent of the vote. The new government pledged co-operation with the United States abroad and the elimination of totalitarianism at home.

1946, Sept. 17. A **new constitution** authorized the government to outlaw any anti-democratic party.

1947, May 1. The Communist Party was outlawed.

Oct. 20. Brazil broke off diplomatic relations with the Soviet Union.

1950, Oct. 3. Economic difficulties and a rising inflation paved the way for the re-election of **Getulio Vargas** as president of Brazil.

1954, Aug. 24. Compelled to resign by the armed forces, President Vargas turned his office over to the vice-president, **João Cafe Filho,** and committed suicide.

1955, Oct. 3. In national elections, Social Democrat **Juscelino Kubitschek** and Laborite **João Goulart** won the presidency and vice-presidency, respectively. They were inaugurated January 31, 1956.

1960, Apr. 21. Brasilia was declared the new capital.

Oct. 3. Presidential elections resulted in victory for **Janio da Silva Quadros,** an independent moderate. He took office January 31, 1961.

1961, Aug. 25. President Quadros resigned, saying that the forces of reaction blocked his attempt to achieve economic and social progress.

Sept. 7. Vice-President **João Goulart succeeded Quadros** as president, after initial opposition by Brazil's three top military chiefs. On September 8 the congress accepted Goulart's nominee for the premiership, **Tancredo Neves,** and his coalition cabinet.

1962, May 23. The council of ministers approved a decree authorizing the government to **nationalize public utilities** in Brazil.

June 26. Premier Tancredo Neves and his ten-month-old cabinet **resigned.** On June 28 the chamber rejected the nomination of **Francisco Dantros,** outgoing foreign minister, as premier.

July 10. The chamber of deputies confirmed **Francisco Brochado da Rocha** as premier.

Sept. 13. Premier da Rocha and his cabinet **resigned.** On September 15 the chamber of deputies approved the senate bill for a **national plebiscite,** on January 6, 1963, to choose between a parliamentary and a presidential form of government. On September 17 President Goulart named **Hermes Lima,** former labor minister, as premier.

Nov. 30. Hermes Lima was confirmed as premier by the chamber of deputies.

1964, Feb.–Mar. President Goulart ordered **distribution of federal lands** to landless peasants, doubled the minimum wage scale, and expropriated land adjacent to federal highways.

His actions aroused conservative opposition, and

Mar. 31–Apr. 2. Military leaders and several state governments **revolted** against him. He fled to Uruguay. An anti-Communist purge followed.

Apr. 11. Congress elected army chief of staff **General Humberto Castelo Branco** president to serve for the remainder of Goulart's term.

1965, Oct. 27. PRESIDENT CASTELO BRANCO ASSUMED DICTATORIAL POWERS, abolishing the thirteen political parties, packing the Supreme Court, suspending constitutional rights, and in general suppressing radicalism in all forms. Henceforth popular election of the president was to be replaced by a majority vote in congress.

1966, Oct. 3. Marshal Arthur da Costa e Silva, former minister of war, was **elected president** by the congress.

Nov. 15. In general elections the government-sponsored **Aliança Renovadora Naçional** won a resounding victory and was transformed into a political party. Only one opposition party, the **Movimento Democrático Brasiliero,** was permitted.

1967, Jan. 22. Congress approved a **new constitution** greatly strengthening the presidential power and federal control over state governments.

Mar. 15. Inauguration of President Costa e Silva.

July. Former president **Castelo Branco was killed** in a plane accident.

1968, Mar.–Apr. Violent **student demonstrations** against the repressive policies of the government. These demonstrations were forbidden (June), but outbreaks occurred nevertheless.

In Aug. police invaded the University of Brasília in an effort to arrest student leaders.

Dec. 13. ESTABLISHMENT OF UNDISGUISED AUTHORITARIAN REGIME. The president suspended congress indefinitely, assumed power to rule by presidential decree, instituted drastic censorship. A new **Institutional Act** gave the president power to proclaim state of siege, to suspend the political rights of individuals for ten years, to annul parliamentary mandates, etc.

1969, July 13. Destruction of the TV station in São Paulo by terrorist bombing. Rapid development and spread of **guerrilla** and **terrorist movements,** marked by kidnapings and bombings.

Aug. 31. President Costa e Silva incapacitated by a stroke. A triumvirate of military chiefs assumed control.

Sept. 4. C. Burke Elbrick, the U.S. ambassador, kidnaped by terrorists and threatened with execution unless the Brazilian government released 15 political prisoners within 48 hours. The ambassador was released when the government complied (Sept. 7).

Oct. 7. The military junta named **General Emilio Garrastazú Médici president.**

1970, Mar. 11. Nobuo Okuchi, Japanese consul general in São Paulo, kidnaped by terrorists and released only when the government agreed to free five political prisoners.

June 11. Kidnaping of the West German ambassador **Ehrenfried von Holleben,** who was released (June 16) in exchange for 40 political prisoners.

Dec. 7. Kidnaping of the Swiss ambassador **Giovanni Bucher,** by terrorists who demanded release of 70 political prisoners.

F. AFRICA

[*For the Arab states of North Africa see section G: The Arab World and Middle East.*]

1. GENERAL

(*From p. 1075*)

In Africa the political picture changed after the Second World War as colonies and protectorates won independence and emerged as sovereign states. Since the North African peoples are more closely identified with the Mediterranean region than with the rest of Africa, they have been

listed under G., *The Arab World and Middle East.*

1947, Apr. 10. The first **Pan-African Trade Union Congress** met at Dakar, Senegal, and decided to organize two million European and African workers.

1952, Mar. 30. The **International Zone of Tan-**

gier was torn by violently anti-French riots.

Apr. 7. The Spanish government formally demanded control over the police force of the international zone of Tangier.

1956, Oct. 20. Tangier became a part of independent Morocco.

1958, Nov. 23. Ghana's **Prime Minister Kwama Nkrumah** and Guinea's **Premier Sékou Touré** issued a declaration in Accra, Ghana, calling for a **Ghana-Guinea confederacy.**

1959, May 1. President Touré and Prime Minister Nkrumah signed a **draft agreement** in Conakry, Guinea, **for a union of independent African states.**

June 6. Seven states of French West Africa —Senegal, French Sudan, Ivory Coast, Mauritania, Niger, Volta, and Dahomey—agreed to form a **customs union,** establishing a free trade area.

1960, Dec. 24. The presidents of Guinea, Ghana, and Mali, meeting in Conakry, Guinea, agreed on a **union of the three republics.**

1961, Jan. 7. Heads of state of Morocco, Ghana, Guinea, Mali, and the UAR, meeting in Casablanca, Morocco, proclaimed the African **charter of Casablanca,** announcing their decision to set up a NATO-like organization of African states.

1962, Jan. 30. Leaders of twenty African nations, at a six-day conference in Lagos, Nigeria, agreed to establish an **organization of African states.** This conference was boycotted by the "Casablanca states," Ghana, Guinea, Mali, Morocco, and the UAR, because the rebel Algerian provisional government was not invited.

Apr. 2. A meeting at Casablanca of the Casablanca bloc nations (including Morocco, Ghana, Guinea, Mali, and the UAR) agreed to set up an **African common market,** an **African payments union,** and an **African development bank** with a capital of $30 million.

June 16. The leaders of the **Casablanca bloc,** meeting in Cairo, agreed to establish a **high military command,** with headquarters in Ghana and under an Egyptian general. On June 17 they proceeded to establish the common market, effective on January 1, 1963.

Sept. 11. Gabon **President Léon Mba** was elected president of the **African-Malagasy Union.** On the 13th the twelve members agreed to support U.N. policies in the Congo.

1963, May 25. At a **meeting in Addis Ababa,** leaders of thirty African nations signed a charter for the **Organization of African Unity.**

June. Kenya, Tanganyika, and Uganda agreed to form a federation and set up a group to prepare a constitution.

Aug. 5. At the end of a five-day **meeting in Khartum,** delegates from thirty-two African states signed an agreement setting up an **African development bank** with a capitalization of $250 million. The Economic Commission for Africa had been working on this project for two years.

1964, Feb. 12. An **emergency session of the Organization of African Unity** met in Tanganyika to consult on restoring internal security there and to discuss the **Ethiopian-Somali border conflict.**

July 17–21. First meeting of African heads of state under the **Organization of African Unity** at Cairo. Resolutions to tighten boycotts against Portugal and South Africa.

Aug. Senegal River development: agreement between Guinea, Senegal, Mali, and Mauritania for co-operation in developing power, industry, and agriculture.

Dec. Projected **Central African Customs Union** between Cameroon, Central African Republic, Gabon, Congo (Brazzaville), and Chad, to be inaugurated in Jan. 1966.

First meeting of the **Eurafrican Parliament** at Dakar. Parliamentarians from the European Common Market countries conferred on economic problems with 18 associated African governments.

1965, Feb. Meeting of heads of state of French-speaking African states at Nouakchott and formation of the **Afro-Malagasy Common Organization** (*Organisation Commune Africaine et Malgache*), in competition with the OAU.

Oct. 21–26. Third meeting of the OAU at Accra. Vote to urge Britain to prevent Rhodesian declaration of independence and, in the event of failure, to introduce sanctions.

Dec. 17. Nine members of the OAU severed diplomatic relations with the United Kingdom in response to the latter's failure to suppress the Rhodesian régime.

1966, Feb. 28–Mar. 6. Meeting of the OAU at Addis Ababa. Much disagreement on recognition of the new Ghana government. Resolutions calling on Britain to use force against Rhodesia and on the United Nations to impose sanctions on South Africa.

June. Meeting at Tananarive of the heads of state of 14 countries comprising the **Afro-Malagasy Common Organization.** Signature of a convention for political and economic co-operation between the French-speaking states of Africa.

Nov. 5–19. Meeting of the OAU at Addis Ababa, clouded by Ghana's detention of the Guinean foreign minister and his staff at Accra (Oct. 26) as hostages for return of Ghanaians held in Guinea. Mediation by the OAU and threat of boycott led to release of the Guineans.

1967, Feb. 27–Mar. 4. The **OAU council of ministers** called for use of force to overthrow

North
Atlantic
Ocean

EUROPE

Black Sea

Mediterranean Sea

MOROCCO

SPANISH SAHARA

TUNISIA

ALGERIA

LIBYA

Cairo

UNITED
ARAB
REP.

A R A B I A

MAURITANIA

SENEGAL

PORT.
GUINEA

GUINEA

SIERRA
LEONE

LIBERIA

M A L I

UPPER
VOLTA

IVORY
COAST

GHANA

TOGO

DAHOMEY

NIGER

NIGERIA

CHAD

CAMEROUN

CENTRAL
AFRICAN REPUBLIC

S U D A N

ERITREA

Red Sea

Nile

Gulf of Aden

TERRITORY OF
THE AFARS
AND ISSAS

ETHIOPIA

SOMALI REP.

BATA

GABON

CONGO (REP.)

CONGO

RWANDA

BURUNDI

KENYA

TANZANIA

South
Atlantic
Ocean

ANGOLA

S. WEST
AFRICA

ZAMBIA

MALAWI

RHODESIA

MOZAMBIQUE

MADAGASCAR
(Malagasy Rep.)

BOTSWANA

SWAZILAND

REP. OF
SOUTH
AFRICA

LESOTHO

Cape
Town

Indian
Ocean

AFRICA in 1970

Independent in 1945

Gained independence 1945-1970

Under European control in 1970

the Rhodesian régime and also to end the South African mandate over Southwest Africa.

June 6. Establishment of the **East African Community** and common market between Kenya, Tanzania, and Uganda. Decision to abolish internal tariffs, coordinate development, etc.

Sept. 11–14. Meeting of OAU heads of state at Kinshasa. Condemnation of the British policy in South Africa and demand for economic boycott of South Africa and Rhodesia. Unanimous resolution demanding the departure of white mercenaries from the Congo, with threat of united action in the event of refusal.

1968, Jan. 20–23. Meeting of the heads of the **Afro-Malagasy Common Organization** at Niamey, with 14 members present.

Mar. Organization of the Senegal River states, going beyond questions of development in economic, social, and even political issues.

Sept. 13–16. OAU heads of state meeting at Addis Ababa. **Swaziland** and **Mauritius** admitted as members (making 42). **Appeals to Biafra** to co-operate with the Nigerian federal government and restore unity.

1969, Jan. 27–29. Meeting of heads of state of the **Afro-Malgasy Organization** at Kinshasa. Mauritius became a member. The discussions hinged on economic matters and technical co-operation.

Sept. 6–10. Heads of state of OAU meeting at Addis Ababa. **Convention on refugees** (850,000 in number) created by disorders and conflicts in various areas.

1970, Feb. Tour of ten African countries by U.S. Secretary of State Rogers, together with conference of U.S. diplomats in Kinshasa. Expression of support for greater political freedom for blacks in South Africa and Rhodesia, as well as in the Portuguese colonies.

2. WEST AFRICA

a. MAURITANIA

1958, Nov. 28. Mauritania became an autonomous republic within the French Community.

1960, Nov. 28. Mauritania proclaimed an independent **Islamic republic** with **Moktar Ould Daddah** as president.

1961, May 23. The **constitution,** while it provided for a national assembly elected by universal suffrage, vested most of the power in the president, supported by a single political party.

Dec. 4. The U.S.S.R. vetoed Mauritania's application for membership in the United Nations.

1966. Growing **tension between the Arab and African populations** led to repeated closing of the schools.

1967, Oct. President Daddah visited China and North Korea, reflecting increased **Chinese influence** in Mauritanian affairs.

1969, Sept. Attendance of Pres. Daddah at the Islamic Conference at Rabat marked the **reconciliation of Mauritania and Morocco,** following chronic tension over frontier questions.

b. SENEGAL

1958, Nov. 25. Senegal became an autonomous state within the French Community.

1959, Apr. 4. Union with the French Sudan to form the **Federation of Mali,** which became fully independent with **Modibo Keita** as premier.

1960, Aug. 20. Senegal withdrew from the Mali

Federation following a dispute as to the powers of the Senegalese premier.

Sept. 5. The **republic of Senegal was proclaimed,** with **Leopold S. Senghor** as president and **Mamadou Dia** as premier.

1962, Dec. After an abortive coup by the premier, Pres. Senghor assumed full power.

1963, Mar. 3. A constitution recognized the **presidential system,** supported by a single party, the Senegalese Progressive Union.

1965, Mar. Discovery of an alleged **Communist plot.** The leaders were tried and sentenced to prison terms. A new anti-sedition law (June) was directed at all subversive organizations.

1968, May–June. Serious **student disturbances** led to the closing of the University of Dakar and other schools. A general strike was proclaimed, and troops were brought on the campus to suppress disorders. The government yielded to the extent of promising university reform and making concessions to the workers.

1969, Mar. Further student strikes. The university was again closed (May).

c. THE GAMBIA

1963, Oct. 3. Gambia, a British colony, was granted full autonomy.

1965, Feb. 18. The Gambia became a fully independent **constitutional monarchy** under the British crown. A referendum (Nov.) on the issue of becoming a republic was narrowly defeated.

1966, May 26. In the elections the prime minister, **Dawda K. Jawara,** and his People's Progressive Party won a resounding victory.

1967, Apr. A visit by Pres. Senghor of Senegal led to the conclusion of a **treaty of association** for further co-operation in all areas. Under a permanent secretariat visas were to be abolished and work to be initiated to develop the Gambia River Basin.

1969, Aug. Premier Jawara proposed a republican constitution with a president to assume the powers of the Queen and the prime minister. This proposal was approved by parliament, but was still subject to popular referendum.

1970, Apr. 23. The Gambia was proclaimed a republic, within the British Commonwealth. Jawara became the first president.

d. PORTUGUESE GUINEA

Portuguese Guinea remained a Portuguese colony, but chronically afflicted by insurgency. The **Front for the Liberation of Portuguese Guinea and the Cape Verde Islands** was supported by Guinea and other African states. Under the leadership of **Amilcar Cabral** guerrilla forces were able to secure control of the entire eastern part of the colony, and the Portuguese government was obliged to keep large numbers of troops in the field.

1970, Dec. 2. Portuguese premier Caetano announced plans to accord the African colonies additional seats in the national parliament and a substantial degree of autonomy in local economic and social affairs, but at the same time reasserted the intention of his government to retain control of Portugal's African empire.

e. GUINEA

1958, Oct. 2. Following a popular referendum (Sept. 28) Guinea became the only French African colony to decline the invitation to become a member of the French Community. Instead it became an **independent republic,** with Sékou Touré as president.

Nov. 12. The **constitution** provided for a presidential system and a single party.

1959, Jan. 15. France recognized the republic.

1960, Mar. 1. Guinea withdrew from the French franc zone and accepted a large **Soviet credit.** Sékou Touré's policy was generally socialistic and politically modeled on that of the Soviet Union. Soviet and later Chinese influence was strong.

1965, Nov. 15. Diplomatic relations with France were severed after the discovery of a plot, supposedly involving France and various neighboring states, to assassinate Sékou Touré and overthrow the existing régime.

1966, Mar. Sékou Touré championed the cause of the deposed **President Nkrumah** of Ghana, offered him asylum, named him co-president of Guinea and threatened to use Guinean forces to restore him to his former position.

1967, Feb. Acute tension in **relations with the Ivory Coast,** following seizure of an Ivory Coast trawler. The Ivory Coast government thereupon seized the Guinean foreign minister and other Guinean officials on their way to the United Nations meeting (June). Through the good offices of the OAU the trawler and the hostages were ultimately released (Sept. 23).

Mar. A campaign directed against Western influences led to deportation of French and other clerics.

1968. Nonetheless the government succeeded in associating United States aluminum interests with the extraction of bauxite, one of the country's most valuable resources.

1970, Nov. 22-23. INVASION OF GUINEA from the sea by some 350–500 filibusters, who burned the summer palace and destroyed other buildings, while engaging the small Guinean army in hostilities. Sékou Touré appealed to the U.N. and to other powers for help and the United Arab Republic and Nigeria actually sent token forces. Sentiment of the African governments was overwhelmingly in support of the Guinean régime, suspecting an effort by Portugal to destroy the base of the organization attempting to liberate Portuguese Guinea.

Dec. 4. A five-man **United Nations mission** to investigate the situation reported: that the invaders had landed from ships, probably coming from Portuguese Guinea, commanded by white Portuguese officers and men; and that the invading troops were mostly Africans from Portuguese Guinea, commanded by white officers, but which included also some Guineans opposed to Sékou Touré and intent on his destruction. The main aim of the invasion appears to have been the assassination or capture of Amilcar Cabral, the leader of the Front for the Liberation of Portuguese Guinea. The Portuguese government from the outset disclaimed knowledge or responsibility for the coup, but the U.N. security council (Dec. 8) nevertheless condemned Portugal, demanded compensation for loss of life and property, and urged all nations to abstain from giving Portugal either military or material assistance.

Dec. 9-11. The **ministerial council of the OAU,** meeting at Lagos, went even further and condemned "those states, particularly the NATO powers, who sustain Portugal in her colonial aggression by their continued assistance to her." The council directed the liberation committee of the OAU to increase substantially its aid to Cabral and the Front for the Liberation of Portuguese Guinea.

f. MALI

1958, Nov. 28. Mali (the French Sudan) became an autonomous state within the French Community.

1959, Apr. 4. Mali became federated with Senegal to form the independent **Federation of Mali.**

1960, Aug. 20. Mali withdrew from the federation and became the **Republic of Mali,** under the presidency of **Modibo Keita,** who introduced a one-party dictatorship leaning strongly in the Soviet and Chinese Communist direction.

1968, Nov. 19. President **Modibo Keita was overthrown** by a group of young officers who set up a Military Committee of National Liberation, under **Lieutenant Moussa Traoré** as chief of state and **Captain Yoré Diakité** as premier. The new régime quickly undid the collectivist policies of Keita, attempted to bring in Western capital, and envisaged restoration of democratic rule.

g. UPPER VOLTA

1959, Mar. Upper Volta became an autonomous state within the French Community.

1960, Aug. Full independence under **Maurice Yaméogo,** who established a one-man rule based on repression of opposition.

1965, Oct. 3. Yaméogo was re-elected for a second term.

1966, Jan. 3. The president was forced to resign and was later tried by a group of young officers. **Colonel Sangoulé Lamizana** became president and premier, and undertook a liberalizing policy envisaging return in 1970 to a democratic régime.

h. NIGER

1960, Aug. 3. Niger became an independent republic, after having been granted complete autonomy by France in 1958. Under the presidency of **Hamani Diori** it has maintained close relations with France and has to a degree assumed leadership of the states of French Africa.

1969, Feb. The capital, Niamey, was the seat of the conference of heads of state of the French-speaking countries.

i. CHAD

1960, Aug. 11. The **republic of Chad** became fully independent but remained within the French Community and maintained close relations with France. **François Tombalbaye,** of the pro-French Progressive Party, became president and established one-man rule. The government has been faced from the beginning with the opposition of the nomadic tribes of the north, who are in more or less chronic state of rebellion.

1966, Aug. Hostilities with the Sudan were eventually mediated by Pres. Diori of Niger (Oct.).

1968, Aug. The government requested the **aid of French troops** to deal with disturbances in the north. The **Force d'Intervention** was recalled in Nov., but was obliged to intervene again in 1969, when 900 Foreign Légionnaires went into action at the request of Pres. Tombalbaye.

j. SIERRA LEONE

1961, Apr. 27. Sierra Leone became an independent monarchical state within the British Commonwealth. For some years the country was governed by **Sir Milton Margai** (d. 1963) and his half-brother **Sir Albert Margai,** leaders of the Sierra Leone **People's Party,** which drew its strength from the Mende, the dominant people of the southern areas.

1967, Mar. 17. In the elections the opposition party **(All People's Congress)** won a surprising success and its leader, **Siaka P. Stevens,** became prime minister (Mar. 21).

Mar. 23. A coup by younger military men overthrew the Stevens government. Lieutenant-Colonel **Andrew Juxon-Smith,** leader of the **National Reformation Council,** suspended the constitution and dissolved all political parties in a campaign to purge the administration and forestall tribal conflict.

1968, Apr. 18. Another coup by young officers put an end to the existing régime and restored **civilian rule,** with Siaka Stevens as prime minister, supported by the All People's Congress and the Temne peoples of the northern sections. The country continued to be troubled by tribal and social strife.

1970, Sept. 14. A state of emergency was proclaimed, the opposition People's Party was banned and many leaders arrested in response to an alleged plot to overturn the government.

k. LIBERIA

(From p. 1082)

1943, May 4. William V. S. Tubman of the **True Whig Party** was elected president for an initial term of eight years and since 1951 has been repeatedly re-elected for additional four-year terms, usually unopposed. The country has enjoyed political stability and considerable economic prosperity, due to American investments in rubber production and more recently in iron mining.

l. IVORY COAST

1958, Dec. 4. The French colony became an **autonomous state** within the French Community, of which **Félix Houphouet-Boigny** of the Democratic Party became premier (1959).

1960, Aug. 7. The Ivory Coast became a completely independent republic, associated for a time with the French Community. Houphouet-Boigny became president (Nov. 27) after he had polled 98% of the votes in the election. He has remained in power since that time, pursuing an essentially Western policy in close collaboration with France. Production of coffee and cocoa has insured a reasonable prosperity, but has not prevented the rise of opposition elements demanding a more progressive and democratic system.

1969. Student strikes at the University of Abidjan led to suppression by armed forces and closure of the university for some months.

m. GHANA

1957, Mar. 6. The British colony of the **Gold Coast,** united with the U.N. trust territory of **British Togoland,** became the **independent state of Ghana,** with **Kwama N. Nkrumah** as prime minister and the Convention People's Party as the ruling organization.

1960, July 1. Ghana became a republic within the British Commonwealth, with Nkrumah as the first president.

1962, May 5. Nkrumah declared a general amnesty for refugee Ghanaians and ordered the release of many prisoners detained under the Preventive Detention Act.

1964, Jan. 16. At the end of a visit by the Communist Chinese premier Chou En-lai, Pres. Nkrumah joined him in calling for an **"anti-imperialist conference"** of African, Asian, and Latin American peoples.

Feb. 2. The national referendum revealed 99.9% of the voters in favor of the government proposal to make **Ghana a one-party state** and to give the president power to dismiss judges at his discretion.

July 17–22. At the second meeting of the Organization of African Unity Pres. **Nkrumah urged the formation of an African union government.**

Oct. 5–11. At the conference of non-aligned powers at Cairo Nkrumah denounced the intervention of Belgians in the Congo. More and more Nkrumah assumed the role of leader of African nationalism and champion of libera-

tion movements, all in the spirit of anti-imperialist Communism.

1965, Oct. 21–26. The meeting of the OAU at Accra was boycotted by eight of the French-speaking states.

Dec. 3. Ghana severed relations with the British government on the Rhodesian issue and threatened to leave the Commonwealth.

1966, Feb. 24. While Pres. Nkrumah was absent on a visit to Peking a group of army and police officers staged a coup that put an **END TO THE 15-YEAR RULE OF NKRUMAH.** A **National Liberation Council,** with **General Joseph A. Ankrah** as head of state, promptly purged the administration of Nkrumah's appointees, dissolved the Convention People's Party, and suspended the constitution. Nkrumah, threatening military action, took refuge in Guinea, where Pres. Sékou Touré generously named him co-president.

Mar. Re-establishment of relations with Britain and expulsion of the Soviet and Communist Chinese advisers. Severance of diplomatic relations with Communist China and Guinea.

1967, Apr. 17. An abortive coup led by two lieutenants, who were promptly tried and executed. Many members of the former Convention People's Party arrested or detained.

July 1. Establishment of an **Executive Council of Ministers,** most of whom were civilians, to administer the country.

1969, Apr. 2. Resignation of President Ankrah, following charges of corruption. He was succeeded by **General Akwasi A. Afrifa.**

May 1. The ban on political parties was lifted in preparation for return to civilian government.

Aug. 29. National elections; victory of the **Progress Party.** Three-man presidential commission to govern pending assumption of power by Prime Minister **Kofi A. Busia** (Sept. 3).

Sept. 30. Resumption of civilian rule.

Nov. 19. Aliens, estimated to number 500,000, were ordered to leave Ghana in the absence of regular residence permits.

1970, Aug. 31. Edward Askufo-Addo, former chief justice, **was elected president,** to replace the presidential commission set up in 1969.

n. TOGO

1956. Togo, the French-administered eastern part of the U.N. trust territory, was declared an **autonomous republic,** following a U.N. plebiscite.

1960, Apr. 27. France, in agreement with the U.N., **granted Togo complete independence** and

Sylvanus Olympio became the first chief of state.

1963, Jan. 13. Olympio was assassinated by political rivals, one of whom, **Nicholas Grunitzky,** succeeded him as president and attempted to establish a multi-party system (constitution of May 5, 1963).

1967, Jan. 13. Pres. Grunitzky was overthrown by an army coup led by **Lieutenant Colonel Etienne Eyadema,** the chief of staff. Eyadema suspended the constitution and instituted direct military rule.

Apr. 14. Eyadema declared himself president and embarked on a policy of road building, trade expansion, and industrial development. Although he promised from time to time to restore constitutional rule, no specific date was ever named or adhered to.

o. DAHOMEY

1958, Dec. 4. Dahomey was declared a republic by its territorial assembly.

1960, Aug. 1. With French consent **Dahomey became completely** independent, with **Hubert Maga** as president.

1961, Aug. 1. Dahomey seized the Portuguese territory of **Ajuda.**

1963, Oct. 27-29. A period of political instability was ushered in when **Colonel Christophe Soglo,** the chief of staff, assumed power as head of a three-man provisional government, of which former President Maga became premier.

1964, Jan. The government was revamped and **Sourou Migan Apithy** became president.

1965, Dec. 22. General Soglo took over as president of a **military government.** The constitution was suspended and all political parties banned.

1967, Dec. 17. President Soglo was in turn ousted by a military coup and a **provisional government** was set up under **Major Maurice Kouandété. Lieutenant Colonel Alphonse Alley** was named president.

1968, July 17. Dr. Emile-Derlin Zinsou, former foreign minister, was installed as president as a move toward restoration of civilian government.

1969, Dec. 10. Zinsou was overthrown by a military coup, and **Lieutenant Colonel Paul de Souza** became head of a military junta.

1970, May 2. The military junta was replaced by a three-man **presidential council** under chairmanship of former president Hubert Maga.

p. NIGERIA

1947, Jan. 1. Nigeria was given a new constitution, with a measure of self-government.

1950. A new constitution greatly expanded the area of self-government.

1954. Nigeria was organized as **a self-governing federation.**

1957. Abubakr Tafawa Balewa, leader of the northern Congress Party, became the first prime minister of the Federation of Nigeria.

1960, Oct. 1. NIGERIA BECAME COMPLETELY INDEPENDENT. Nnamdi Azikiwe, of the southern Ibo people, became the first governor-general (Nov. 16).

1961, Feb. 11. Northern Cameroon voted for union with Nigeria in a U.N. plebiscite.

1963, Oct. Nnamdi Azikiwe became the first president of Nigeria, proclaimed a republic.

1964, Dec. 29. Growing tension between the largely Moslem north and the more advanced, largely Christian south and east. In the national elections a southern coalition (**United Progressive Grand Alliance**) opposed a similar northern grouping (the **Nigerian National Alliance**) and then boycotted the elections, charging corruption and fraud.

1965, Jan. 7. In a revamped cabinet, still under Sir Abubakr Tafawa Balewa, the northerners retained their preponderance.

Oct. 11. In regional elections in the west there was much racial and factional strife, with the result that the opposition parties boycotted the elections.

1966, Jan. 15-17. Insurrections by junior officers in several regional capitals led to the abduction and **assassination of Sir Abubakr Balewa** and the premiers of the western and northern regions. A **military government** was set up by **General J. T. U. Aguiyi-Ironsi,** an Ibo, who persuaded the rebels to surrender, abolished the existing institutions of government, and appointed military governors in place of the former regional administrations.

May 29. In the northern provinces Moslem mobs, fearing domination by the better-educated and more prosperous southerners, attacked and killed large numbers of the latter, while thousands fled.

July 28-29. Mutiny of northern troops, who disarmed and slew their eastern officers. **General Aguiyi-Ironsi was kidnaped** and found dead. Power was assumed by **General Yakubu Gowan,** a northerner but a Christian, who induced the rebels to return to their home regions. Meanwhile **Lieutenant Colonel Odumegwu Ojukwu,** governor of the eastern region, set up a *de facto* independent régime. Efforts at reconciliation on the basis of autonomy failed (Sept. 12).

1967-1970. THE NIGERIAN CIVIL WAR.

1967, May 30. General Ojukwu proclaimed the eastern region as the **republic of Biafra** and seceded from the Nigerian Federation. The federal government denounced this act as rebellion and federal troops began to attack Biafra. A federal war cabinet was set up (Aug.) and arms were purchased in Britain, Italy, and the Soviet Union. The Biafran government, on the other hand, secured supplies from France. The African governments unanimously took their stands by the federal government and opposed the disruption of the most important of the native African states.

July–Oct. Federal forces advanced on Biafra from the northwest, while the Biafrans counter-attacked westward and threatened Ibadan. The Biafrans were held at Ore (Aug.) and thrown back across the Niger River (Sept.). Eventually the federal forces took **Enugu,** the Biafran capital (Oct. 4).

1968. Concentric federal attacks reduced Biafran-held territory to a mere fraction. Port Harcourt fell (May 19) and **Owerri** (Sept. 16). The Biafrans, faced by the threat of starvation, organized an effective propaganda campaign and arranged to have considerable supplies of food flown in, despite obstruction by the federal authorities.

1969, Mar. 27–31. Visit of British Prime Minister Wilson to Nigeria, the latest of several efforts to bring about a solution of the problem.

Apr. 24. The Biafrans succeeded in recapturing Owerri and crossing the Niger.

Dec. A massive concentric federal attack with modern weaponry forced the Biafrans back across the Niger.

1970, Jan. 11. Flight of General Odumegwu Ojukwu, the Biafran leader.

Jan. 13. Surrender of Biafra and pledge of loyalty to the federal government.

Oct. 1. President Gowan, in an independence day address, announced that 1976 had been set as the target date for the restoration of constitutional government.

3. CENTRAL AFRICA

a. CENTRAL AFRICAN REPUBLIC

1958, Dec. 1. The territorial assembly of the French colony of **Ubangi Shari** proclaimed itself the **Central African Republic.**

1960, Aug. 13. The republic proclaimed its independence of France, and named **David Dacko** first president.

1964. President Dacko, ruling dictatorially, was re-elected president with a majority of over 99%.

1966, Jan. 1. A military coup, led by **Colonel Jean-Bédel Bokassa,** ousted Dacko, dissolved the assembly, and abolished the constitution of 1959. A **revolutionary council** took over executive power. Bokassa became president and commander of the armed forces. Putting an end to the pro-Communist orientation of his predecessor, he strengthened relations with France and the West. Nonetheless, his position continued to be precarious. Both in 1967 and 1969 he was obliged to call on French troops (*Force d'Intervention*) to forestall coups by opposition elements which continued to pose a threat to the régime.

1968, Apr. 3. The republic joined in a loose confederation with Chad and the Congo Republic (Kinshasa) for purposes of economic development and defense, but withdrew again from this combination within a few months (Dec. 1968) in favor of closer relations with France.

b. CAMEROUN

1942, Apr. 4. The United States government recognized **French Cameroun,** a League of Nations mandate which comprised the major part of the former German colony of Kamerun.

1957. French Cameroun was given autonomous status within the French Community.

1960, Jan. 1. French Cameroun became an independent republic.

Apr. 10. In the first national election the Cameroun Union Party, led by premier **Ahmadou Ahidjo,** won 60 of the 100 seats in the assembly.

1961, Feb. 11–12. A United Nations plebiscite resulted in the union of the southern part of British Cameroon with the republic of Cameroun, which became a federal republic.

1965, Mar. 20. President Ahidjo was elected to a second five-year term.

1966, Sept. The political parties of East (formerly French) Cameroun and West (formerly British) Cameroon were merged to form the **Cameroun National Union,** while the pro-Chinese Cameroun People's Union was banned. Under the leadership of President Ahidjo the country enjoyed a degree of stability rare among the states of Africa.

c. EQUATORIAL GUINEA

1959–1964. Negotiations of the Spanish government with the native leaders of the colonies of

Rio Muni and Fernando Po, widely separated possessions of different tribal compositions and stages of development.

1964. Fernando Po was given an autonomous status.

1968, Aug. 11. In a referendum supervised by the U.N. a majority voted for a **republican form of government,** with safeguards for the interests of the various divisions.

Sept. 29. Francisco Macías Nguema was elected president.

Oct. 12. The republic was granted complete independence by Spain.

1969, Mar. Following an acute political crisis, President Macías assumed **emergency powers** and arrested a number of his opponents.

d. GABON

1958, Nov. 28. The territorial assembly of the French Congo proclaimed the **Gabon Republic** as a self-governing member of the French Community.

1960, Aug. 17. Gabon became an independent republic, with **Léon M'Ba,** leader of the **Gabon Democratic Bloc,** as the first president. M'Ba's efforts to establish a conservative, one-party régime were opposed by **Jean-Hilaire Aubaume** and the Democratic and Social Union.

1964, Feb. 18–19. A bloodless **coup by army officers** forced M'Ba to resign, but the rebel régime was promptly ousted by French troops, acting under terms of the pact of May 1961. M'Ba was restored to power on promising France to permit opposition candidates in the forthcoming elections.

Apr. The elections resulted in a victory of M'Ba's Democratic Bloc, which was then joined by several former opposition groups.

1967, Mar. 19. President M'Ba was elected to another seven-year term, but died on the following Nov. 28. He was succeeded by the vice-president, **Albert-Bernard Bongo.**

1968, Mar. Bongo declared **Gabon a one-party state** under a new national grouping, the **Gabon Democratic Party,** which won an overwhelming victory in the elections of Feb. 16, 1969.

1968–1969. Gabon, closely tied to France, recognized Biafra and became an important entrepôt for French supplies and relief to the Biafran forces.

e. CONGO (BRAZZAVILLE)

1958, Nov. 28. The French colony of **Middle Congo** proclaimed itself the **republic of the Congo,** with Brazzaville as the capital.

1960, Apr. 15. President **Fulbert Youlou** proclaimed the **independence of the republic from France.**

1963, Aug. 15. Youlou resigned in the face of labor disturbances and rioting. On the following day a group of army officers and labor leaders appointed a provisional government, headed by **Alphonse Massamba-Débat,** who attempted to introduce a socialist, one-party system.

1964, Feb. 7. Anti-government riots resulted from attempts to free Youlou from prison, but were suppressed by the police.

1965– Massamba-Débat continued his pro-Communist policy by concluding a ten-year **treaty of friendship with Communist China** and suspending diplomatic relations with the United States.

July. An **invasion of commandos** from Congo (Kinshasa) reflected the tension between the two Congos and induced the Brazzaville parliament to authorize the formation of vigilantes to repel revolutionary movements.

1968, Aug. 3. A military coup led by **Major Marien Ngouabi** resulted in the formation of a **National Council of the Revolution.**

Sept. 4. Massamba-Débat was forced to resign after weeks of rioting and fighting between army units and Cuban-trained insurgents.

1969, Jan. 1. Ngouabi was named head of state, amid continued unrest and plotting, allegedly supported by Congo (Kinshasa).

f. CONGO (KINSHASA)

1959, Jan. 4–5. Anti-European rioting in Leopoldville by Africans demanding independence resulted in 71 persons killed.

Jan. 13. The Belgian government announced a **program for the evolution of independent rule** in the Congo. The plan included the extension of voting rights and better economic conditions. On January 14 the leader of the Congolese national movement, **Patrice Lumumba,** declared the plan was acceptable.

Dec. 20. Local elections, boycotted by some of the nationalist parties, resulted in **defeat for the moderate Party of National Progress** in five major cities.

Dec. 25. At a **nationalist congress** in Kisantu, five nationalist parties demanded immediate and unconditional independence.

1960, June 30. The Belgian Congo became the **INDEPENDENT CONGO REPUBLIC,** with **Joseph Kasavubu** as president and **Patrice Lumumba** as premier.

July. Troop mutinies and **separatist movements** threw the Congo into chaos. **Premier Lumumba appealed** (July 12) **to the U.N. for aid,** and the security council voted (July 14) to send a U.N. force and called for the withdrawal of Belgian forces. **Moise Tshombe**

proclaimed the **independence of Katanga** province and **Albert Kalonji** that of **Kasai** province.

Aug. 12. U.N. Secretary General Hammarskjöld led the **U.N. forces** into Katanga province to replace Belgian forces and pledged neutrality in Congolese internal quarrels.

Sept. 5. President Kasavubu ordered the **dismissal of Lumumba** as premier, and named **Joseph Ileo** to the post. Lumumba, challenging Kasavubu's action as illegal, called the cabinet into session on September 6 and relieved Kasavubu of his presidential duties.

Sept. 11. Premier Lumumba was rebuffed by U.N. troops when he tried to take over the Leopoldville radio station. On September 12 he was **arrested** by Congo army troops. A joint session of both houses of parliament on September 13 voted Lumumba "special powers."

Sept. 14. Col. Joseph Mobutu, commander of the Congo army, took over control of the Congo government. The U.N. security council refused to recognize either of the two delegations representing opposing Congolese leaders Kasavubu and Lumumba.

Sept. 16. President Kasavubu ordered the **withdrawal of the Soviet and Czech diplomatic delegations** for backing Lumumba.

Nov. 22. The U.N. general assembly voted to seat President Kasavubu's delegation in preference to Lumumba's.

Nov. 25. While Premier Ileo sought to convene a conference of all Congolese leaders, **Mobutu's troops captured Lumumba,** who had escaped detention.

Dec. Differences concerning U.N. policy were reflected in the announcement, December 7, that Yugoslavia, Ceylon, and the UAR were withdrawing their troops from the U.N. Congo force. Morocco and Guinea followed suit. Hammarskjöld asked the U.N. assembly for new directives (Dec. 19) but the debate ended in an impasse (Dec. 21).

1961, Jan. 17. President Kasavubu and Moise Tshombe agreed to hold a **round-table conference on constitutional reform** in February.

Feb. 13. Katanga's government reported that Congolese ex-Premier **Lumumba** had been **killed by hostile tribesmen.** The following day the U.S.S.R. accused Hammarskjöld of being an "accomplice" in the murder and demanded the withdrawal of U.N. forces. President Kennedy (Feb. 15) warned that the United States would oppose any attempt to intervene unilaterally in the Congo.

Feb. 21. The U.N. security council adopted a resolution calling for the U.N. force in the Congo to use force if necessary to prevent civil war. Congolese Premier Ileo declared (Feb. 22) that the resolution violated

Congolese sovereignty.

Feb. 28. Meeting in Elizabethville, President Tshombe of Katanga, President Kalonji of South Kasai, and Premier Ileo signed an **agreement to co-operate** in resolving their nation's conflict without "outside" assistance; they agreed to unite to fight both "Communist tyranny" and U.N. "tutelage."

Mar.–Apr. Efforts to establish a confederation of sovereign states in the Congo were thwarted by armed forces under **Antoine Gizenga** at Stanleyville who later, April 17, recognized Major General Mobutu as commander-in-chief, paving the way for President Kasavubu and the U.N. command to agree upon a **reorganization of the Congo army** and the removal of foreign advisers.

Apr. 24–May 31. A meeting of Congo leaders at Coquilhatville failed at first to agree upon the structure of the Congo state because of Tshombe's withdrawal. He and his aides were arrested and accused of treason. At length the conference agreed upon a federal republic of twenty states.

June 19. Gizenga's Stanleyville régime agreed with Kasavubu upon a **Congolese national parliament** to meet under U.N. protection.

June–July. Tshombe, released from detention (June 22) promised to co-operate with the central government, but on July 28 declared he would defend an **independent Katanga,** even though he would send delegates to the national parliament. Katanga's parliament had refused (July 4) to send delegates to Leopoldville; the interior minister had announced (July 24) acceptance of U.S.S.R. offers to help Katanga.

Aug. 1. After the first formal session of the Congo parliament (July 21), President Kasavubu appointed **Cyrille Adoula,** a socialist labor leader, premier, and (Aug. 2) parliament approved him.

Aug. 5. Gizenga's Stanleyville **régime "dissolved."**

Aug. 14. Hammarskjöld assured Premier Adoula that the U.N. recognized his government to be the only legitimate one in the Congo.

Sept. 13. Efforts by the Leopoldville government to bring Katanga back into the federation led to **fighting between the U.N. force** attempting to disarm the Katanga army **and Katanga troops** until a cease-fire was agreed upon, September 20.

Sept. 18. U.N. Secretary Hammarskjöld, en route to a meeting with Tshombe, **died in an airplane crash.**

Nov.–Dec. A **mutiny in Eastern Province** involved the death of thirteen Italians of the U.N. Congo force and fighting again erupted in Katanga during which **acting Secretary General U Thant** ordered U.N. commanders to take whatever action was necessary to restore the U.N. position in Elizabethville, the Katanga capital. A cease-fire went into effect, December 21.

Dec. 21. By the **Kitona agreement** Tshombe accepted the **Fundamental Law** of May 1960 which had set up a provisional Congo constitution, and recognized President Kasavubu as chief of state, although two weeks later (Jan. 4, 1962) he repudiated the Fundamental Law.

1962, Jan. 13. When **fighting erupted in Stanleyville,** U Thant ordered U.N. troops to prevent "civil war" there.

Jan. 15. The chamber of deputies dismissed and censured Vice-Premier Antoine Gizenga following the attempt by his forces to seize Stanleyville. On January 20 **Gizenga** returned to Leopoldville and was **placed under U.N. guard** until his transfer to the custody of the central government on January 23.

Feb. 15. The Katanga assembly agreed to end Katanga's secession.

May–July. Negotiations between Premier Adoula and Tshombe resulted in agreement (July 30) upon a **new constitution** which would provide for provincial autonomy in some areas of government.

Aug. In response to U Thant's plea that all U.N. members exert economic pressure to restore Congolese unity, the United States submitted a plan (Aug. 9), backed by Britain and Belgium, to persuade Katanga, by measures short of economic sanctions, to accept federal union. On August 24 Katanga was given ten days to accept the plan.

Sept. 3. Tshombe announced his approval of the U.N. plan for uniting the Congo "as the basis of an acceptable settlement."

Oct. 20. Fighting again broke out between central government forces and Katanga troops.

1963, Jan. 15. Tshombe proclaimed the **end of Katanga's secession** from the Congolese central government, following successful military operations by the U.N. force in Katanga.

Apr. 17. Premier Adoula announced that a new **Government of National Reconciliation** had been formed and included a large number of opposition members.

June 14. Moise Tshombe fled from the Congo, as parliament took action to abolish his state of Katanga.

1964, Mar. 20. Belgian **Foreign Minister Paul-Henri Spaak** and Premier Cyrille Adoula announced an **agreement on financial problems** and other matters pending since independence in 1960.

June. Rebel forces, including the Comité National de Libération which was allegedly backed by Communist China, threatened to throw the country into chaos again.

June 30. Premier Adoula resigned on the eve of the fourth anniversary of independence and as the last U.N. troops left the country.

July 10. Moise Tshombe, who had returned from exile two weeks earlier, **became premier,** and attempted to form a government of reconciliation. He was faced by major uprisings, especially in the eastern provinces, where the insurgents were supported by the Chinese Communists.

Aug. 30. Government forces took **Albertville** and put an end to the revolutionary government of Katanga.

Sept. A **People's Republic** proclaimed at Stanleyville (Kisangani) by rebels headed by **Christophe Gbenye.**

Sept. 10. Failure of efforts of the **Organization of African Unity** to restore peace in the Congo through a conciliation commission headed by Premier Kenyatta of Kenya.

Nov. 24. Rescue of American and other nationals held hostage by eastern rebels and Belgian paratroopers using U.S. Air Force planes.

Dec. 30. U.N. security council resolution calling for the cessation of foreign intervention and withdrawal of all foreign mercenaries. Nonetheless, insurrectionary movements continued to break out in various areas.

1965, Feb. The Belgian government agreed to turn over to the Congo its shares in companies operating in the Congo.

Mar.–Apr. National elections left the coalition supporting Tshombe with a majority of only 15 in parliament.

Oct. 13. President Kasavubu dismissed Tshombe as premier and named **Evariste Kimba** as his successor.

Nov. 24–25. Bloodless army coup. **General Joseph D. Mobutu deposed Kasavubu** and himself assumed the presidency and proceeded to legislate by decree. The elections were canceled.

1966, June 2. Execution of former Premier Kimba and three other former ministers convicted of plotting to overthrow the régime.

July. Nationalization of two mining companies, followed (Dec. 23) by suspension of exports of copper by the key Union Minière du Haut Katanga and formation of a new Congolese company.

July 23. Mutiny of gendarmerie forces at Kisangani led to serious fighting before its suppression by government forces (Oct. 4). Tshombe, a refugee in Europe, charged with treason *in absentia*.

Oct. 5. Severance of diplomatic relations with Portugal, charged with harboring hostile mercenaries in Angola.

1967, Mar. 13. Former premier Tshombe tried *in absentia* by a military court, convicted of inciting to rebellion, and **sentenced to death.**

June. **New constitution** approved by popular referendum: increase of presidential power, single-chamber assembly, abolition of provincial assemblies, centralization of administration.

June 30. Tshombe's plane hijacked over the Mediterranean and flown to Algeria, where he was held captive.

July. **Revolt of pro-Tshombe European mercenaries** at Kisangani. Rebels driven over Rwanda frontier (Nov. 4) with help of U.S. transport planes.

1968, Jan. 11. Congo broke diplomatic relations with Rwanda on latter's refusal to surrender white mercenaries driven out of eastern Congo. The **mercenaries were evacuated to Europe** (Apr.) and relations between the Congo and Rwanda restored in Sept.

Apr. The Congo government took the initiative in the formation of the short-lived **Union of Central African States,** of which the Central African Republic and the Chad republic were the other members.

June 8. Visit of President Mobutu to Brussels and lengthy negotiations culminating in a decision to co-operate. Gradual return of Belgian specialists to the Congo.

1969, Mar. Death of former president Joseph Kasavubu.

June 4. Serious **student outbreaks,** resulting in numerous fatalities and many arrests. Universities closed and student organizations forbidden.

June 29. Death of Moise Tshombe, while still in detention in Algiers.

1970, Aug. 4. Visit of President Mobutu to Washington.

g. RWANDA

1959, Nov. In a great and bloody **uprising of the Hutu** (Bahutu) tribes against the minority Tutsi (Batutsi) aristocracy, the monarchy was abolished and thousands of Tutsi fled across the frontiers into the Congo, Uganda, and Tanzania. Though the country was a U.N. mandated territory under Belgian administration, the victorious **Party for Hutu Emancipation** on

1961, Jan. 28. Proclaimed a republic. The U.N. refused to recognize this action and called for new elections.

Sept. The result was another victory for the Hutu party and on Oct. 26 **Grégoire Kayibanda was proclaimed president.**

1962, July 1. The U.N. formally terminated the mandate, after acceding to the request of delegates from both Rwanda and Burundi for separation of the two parts of the former mandate.

1963, Dec. An attempted invasion of the country by Tutsi emigrés was defeated and led to large-scale reprisals and flights.

1964, Feb. 6. Another invasion of Tutsi from the Congo was turned back by government forces.

1967, Mar. 20. General **reconciliation between Rwanda and Burundi:** all refugees were to be disarmed and repatriated.

1968, Jan. 11. Rupture of relations with the Congo following the refusal of the Rwanda government to surrender the white mercenaries that had been driven from the Congo. After the evacuation of the mercenaries to Europe relations with the Congo were restored and improved steadily over the ensuing period.

h. BURUNDI

1961. Urundi or Burundi, the southern part of the U.N. Belgian mandated territory, was granted limited autonomy, but joined with Rwanda in petitioning the U.N. for termination of the mandate and the establishment of separate independent states.

1962, July 1. Burundi attained full independence. Unlike Rwanda it remained under the **domination of the Tutsi** (Batutsi, Watusi) minority and under monarchical rule.

1965, Jan. 15. Assassination of Premier Pierre Ngendandumwe, followed by

July 17. King Ntare V's assumption of personal rule.

Oct. 18–19. Attack on the royal palace by army officers supported by Hutu tribesmen. The coup was defeated and the leaders executed (Dec.).

1966, July 8. Prince Charles proclaimed himself head of state and set up a **military government under Captain Michel Micombero** as premier.

Nov. 28. Micombero, in a bloodless coup, **deposed the king and established a republic,** with himself as president. The continued domination of the Tutsi tribe was assured by the **Uprona,** the only legal political party.

1967, Mar. 20. Reconciliation of Burundi and Rwanda: all Tutsi refugees (numbering thousands) were to be repatriated and thereby prevented from further attacks on Rwanda.

4. SOUTH AFRICA

a. PORTUGUESE TERRITORIES

1960– Both Portuguese "overseas territories" have felt the full impact of **African nationalism** and the hostility of world opinion. Though both **Angola** and **Mozambique** were in 1951 given a measure of local autonomy and the African populations in 1961 were accorded full Portuguese citizenship, the Portuguese government continued to regard these possessions as integral parts of the Portuguese state and refused to yield to pressure in behalf of independence. As a result the territories have been exposed to constant liberation raids and Portugal has been obliged to keep some 150,000 men in Africa to defend its position.

1961, Feb. Beginning of **insurgency in Angola,** directed by the **Angolan National Liberation Front,** founded in 1962, with headquarters at Kinshasa. Under the leadership of **Roberto Holden,** the front in 1963 established a **government-in-exile.** A rival and more radical **Angola Popular Liberation Movement** was organized in Zambia by **Agostino Neto.** Competition between these and other lesser groups tended to hamper operations.

1964. Outbreak of **revolt in Mozambique,** led by the **Mozambique Liberation Front** under **Eduardo Mondlane** and operating from Dar-es-Salaam.

July 3. The **U.N. committee on colonialism** passed a resolution calling for independence. At the same time a meeting of heads of government of the **Organization of African Unity** proclaimed a boycott against Portugal. In Oct. the **Conference of Non-Aligned Nations** urged financial and military support for the liberation movements by all members.

1965, Oct. Meeting of representatives of opposition groups at Dar-es-Salaam as the **Conference of Nationalist Organizations of the Portuguese Colonies.** Nonetheless, the liberation movements continued to suffer from lack of planning and coordination.

1966. Severe fighting in Angola against insurgents coming from the Congo (Kinshasa) and Zambia. At the same time repeated invasions of northern Mozambique from Tanzania.

1967, Nov. 17. The **U.N. general assembly called for mandatory sanctions** against Portugal.

1968. The Organization of African Unity recognized **three insurgent liberation movements:** the African Party for the Independence of Guinea; the Popular Front for the Liberation of Angola; the Front for the Liberation of Mozambique. By this time insurgents controlled a large part of Guinea as well as substantial sections of east-central Angola and northern Mozambique.

1969, Feb. 3. Assassination of Mondlane, followed by some disintegration of the Mozambique front.

Apr. Visit of Portuguese premier Caetano to the African possessions. While promising reforms and improvements, he left no doubt of Portugal's determination to maintain possession of its territories.

b. ZAMBIA

1953–1964. Zambia (Northern Rhodesia) was united with Southern Rhodesia and Nyasaland in the **FEDERATION OF RHODESIA AND NYASALAND** (see Rhodesia, p. 1274).

1961, Feb. 21. A British white paper proposed constitutional changes in Northern Rhodesia to make possible an African-dominated government. Federal prime minister **Sir Roy Welensky** succeeded in having these proposals modified.

1962, Oct. 30. In Northern Rhodesian elections Welensky's **United Federal Party** won 15 seats in the assembly, while **Kenneth Kaunda's United National Independence Party** won 14, and the African National Congress, 5. After new elections (Dec. 10) failed to resolve the deadlock, the two African parties joined forces in a coalition giving the Africans a majority in the assembly.

1963, Apr. 1. Northern Rhodesia was granted the right to secede from the federation.

1964, Jan. 1. The Federation of Rhodesia and Nyasaland was dissolved.

Jan. 20–21. In the elections Kaunda's national Independence Party won by a wide margin and he became the country's first prime minister.

Oct. 23. By agreement the British South African Company released mineral rights in Zambia in return for compensation to be paid jointly by the British government and the government of Zambia.

Oct. 24. Northern Rhodesia, with Barotseland, became the independent state of Zambia, with Kenneth Kaunda as first president.

1965, Apr. The government assumed control of the trade unions and thereafter of radio and television facilities, thus inaugurating a socialist program.

Nov.–Dec. Involvement of Zambia in the **Southern Rhodesian crisis.** Since Zambia was largely dependent on Rhodesia for import facilities, Britain and the United States did what they could to maintain coal, oil, and power supplies.

1966, July. Problems raised by the Rhodesian crisis led to adoption of the **Four-Year National Development Plan,** providing for the development of new routes through Tanzania and Malawi, and for the construction of a hydroelectric plant on the Kafue River.

1967. The imposition of **sanctions against Rhodesia** resulted in constant violations of Zambian airspace, guerrilla activities, etc.

June 21-25. Visit of President Kaunda to Communist China, and Chinese offer to build a thousand-mile railway from Zambia through Tanzania to Dar-es-Salaam.

1968, Dec. 19. President Kaunda and his party won the national elections by an overwhelming vote, despite factional wrangling within the party and among its tribal constituents.

1969, Aug. President Kaunda, in an effort to head off serious tribal conflicts, dissolved the central committee of the National Independence Party and **took personal control** as secretary general.

Aug. 11. Pressures for increasing "Zambianization" of the economy led to **nationalization of two major copper-mining** companies, compensation to be paid over 12 years. Mineral rights were placed under state control (Dec. 31).

1970, Oct. 26. Formal **inauguration of the Tanzam Railway,** financed and constructed by the Communist Chinese.

c. MALAWI

1953-1964. Malawi (British Nyasaland) formed part of the Federation of Rhodesia and Nyasaland, but from the outset resented the discriminatory policies of the white elements controlling the federal government.

1959, Mar. 2-3. Nationalist riots followed the banning of the **African National Congress** and the temporary imprisonment of **H. Kamuzu Banda** and other Nyasaland leaders.

1961, Aug. 15. An African majority emerged for the first time from the Nyasaland elections.

1962, Nov. 12-24. A constitutional conference in London resulted in agreement giving **Nyasaland autonomy** within the federation, with Banda the first prime minister.

Dec. 19. Nyasaland was given the right to secede from the federation.

1964, Jan. 1. The Federation of Rhodesia and Nyasaland was dissolved.

July 6. Nyasaland became the independent state of Malawi, remaining within the British Commonwealth. Kamuzu Banda remained prime minister.

Sept. Factional strife led to the **breakup of** the ruling Congress Party and to the flight of six cabinet members.

1965, Feb.-May. Outbreak of rebellion in behalf of refugee minister **Chipembere.** Suppression led to many arrests and trials.

1966, July 7. Malawi abandoned the monarchical form of government and **became a republic,** with Banda as president.

1967, Mar. 13. Trade agreement with South Africa, in defiance of African nationalist feeling. The geographical position of Malawi obliged it to maintain relations with white-controlled governments surrounding it.

Aug. Agreement with South Africa permitting 85,000 Malawi laborers to work in South Africa at any time.

1968, Jan. 1. Resumption of diplomatic relations with South Africa.

Sept. 22. President Banda advanced claims to parts of Tanzania, Zambia, and Mozambique, allegedly parts of the 17th-century Maravi Empire.

1969, Apr. Establishment of diplomatic relations with Portugal.

d. RHODESIA

1953, Oct. 23. The British colony of Southern Rhodesia became the key member of the new **Federation of Rhodesia and Nyasaland.** It had a population of some 4,500,000 Africans, but also some 250,000 white settlers who controlled the political and economic life of the self-governing colony.

1956, Oct. 31. Sir Roy Welensky became prime minister of the federation.

1958, Nov. 12. Welensky's racially moderate **United Federal Party** won a two-thirds majority in the federal elections.

1960-1962. Welensky opposed various African demands and British proposals for constitutional changes, including the right of secession from the federation.

1962, Mar. 8. The prime minister declared he would seek a "mandate to prevent the breakup of the Federation." He dissolved parliament (Mar. 9).

Apr. 27. Welensky held new **elections** which resulted in a 10-1 victory for the whites.

Dec. 15. In Southern Rhodesian elections **Winston J. Field's** extremist white supremacy **(Rhodesian Front)** party won out and he became prime minister.

1963, Apr. 11. The British government rejected the request of the all-white government of Southern Rhodesia for early independence.

1964, Jan. 1. The Federation of Rhodesia and Nyasaland was dissolved.

Apr. 13. Finance minister **Ian D. Smith succeeded Field as prime minister** and leader of the Rhodesian Front.

Apr. 16. The new government banished, without trial, four African leaders, including **Joshua Nkomo,** head of one of the leading nationalist movements.

July 8-15. Meeting of 18 British Commonwealth members. Unanimous pledge not to recognize a unilateral declaration of independence by Rhodesia. The African members pressed the British government to take steps to protect the rights of the African majority.

Aug. 26-27. Suppression of African parties and creation of new **restricted areas** for Africans. Many native leaders under detention.

Sept. 7-10. Prime Minister **Smith in London.** He assured the British government that he could show majority support for the demand for independence. On his return home he revealed that African support would be demonstrated by traditional tribal consultation. At such a meeting (secretly held, Oct. 21-26) the chiefs were allegedly unanimous in favor of immediate independence. The British government regarded this evidence as inadequate and inconclusive.

Oct. 27. British Prime Minister Wilson warned, in a public speech, against a unilateral declaration of independence and threatened sanctions.

Nov. 5. In a referendum, almost exclusively white, 90% voted for independence, though not necessarily immediate or unilateral.

1965, May 7. Overwhelming victory of Smith's Rhodesian Front over the Rhodesian Party in the elections.

Oct. 4-8. Prime Minister **Smith in London** demanded immediate independence. Refusal of the British government unless Rhodesian government first agreed to expanded representation for Africans as prelude to eventual majority rule.

Oct. 25. Visit of Prime Minister Wilson to Salisbury.

Nov. 11. UNILATERAL DECLARATION OF INDEPENDENCE by the Rhodesian government, with reaffirmation of loyalty to the Queen. **Sir Humphrey Gibbs,** governor of Rhodesia, declared Smith and his cabinet deposed and made himself a prisoner in Government House. The British government denounced the declaration as illegal and treasonable. It proclaimed the imposition of **economic sanctions.**

Nov. 12. The **U.N. security council** called on all nations to withhold recognition and aid to the Rhodesian régime.

Dec. 5. The **Organization of African Unity** threatened to sever relations with Britain unless it applied force to suppress the Rhodesian rebellion by Dec. 15.

Dec. 17. The British government announced an **international oil embargo,** supported by the United States. On Apr. 9 the U.N. security council called on all governments to divert oil tankers bound for Mozambique and authorized the British government to use force to prevent such ships reaching Beira.

1966- Continuance of the Rhodesian crisis. Negotiations at various levels went on uninterrupted at Salisbury and London, culminating in

Dec. 1-3. The **first meeting of Prime Ministers Wilson and Smith** on a warship off Gibraltar. Tentative agreement on arrangements for majority rule in Rhodesia within 10 or 15 years was ultimately refused by the Rhodesian government (Dec. 5).

Dec. 6. The British government appealed to the U.N. for imposition of **mandatory sanctions,** which were voted by the U.N. security council on Dec. 16. South Africa and Portugal refused to participate.

1967- Further abortive efforts at agreement on a compromise formula. Meanwhile **African guerrillas,** based in Zambia, embarked on raids across the frontiers. Rebellion was suppressed by the Rhodesian forces aided by South Africa.

1968, Mar. 6, 11. The world was shocked by the **execution of five nationalist leaders** in defiance of a reprieve granted by Queen Elizabeth.

Sept. 13. In defiance of the British privy council, the appellate division of the Rhodesian high court ruled that the existing régime had achieved *de jure* status.

Oct. 9-13. A **second meeting of the prime ministers** off Gibraltar ended in the rejection of the British proposals by Rhodesia (Oct. 18).

1969, June 20. In a **national referendum,** participated in by only some 80,000 whites and 6600 Africans, approval was given to a **new constitution** breaking the connection with Britain and **establishing a republic,** with more than adequate guarantees for the continuance of white supremacy. By a new **land apportionment act** an equal amount of land was assigned to the 250,000 whites and to the 4,500,000 Africans. The new constitution went into effect on Sept. 11.

June 24. Great Britain severed the last ties to Rhodesia, while retaining all claims to the territory.

1970, Mar. 1. PROCLAMATION OF THE RHODESIAN REPUBLIC.

Apr. 10. In the elections Smith's Rhodesian Front secured all the seats reserved for the whites (50 of a total of 66).

Apr. 14. Clifford Dupont was named first president.

e. BOTSWANA

1966, Sept. 30. Botswana, the former British Bechuanaland protectorate, became an independent republic within the British Commonwealth. **Sir Seretse Khama** was the first president.

1968, Oct. 18. In the first elections Khama's ruling party was victorious, but was faced by the Botswana National Front, an opposition party representing the interests of the tribal chiefs.

f. SOUTH AFRICA

1939, Sept. 6. The Union of South Africa declared war on Germany.

1941, Dec. 8. South Africa declared war on Japan.

1942, Apr. 23. South Africa severed diplomatic relations with France.

1945, Oct. The end of the war also meant the end of the coalition government. The Labor Party and the Dominion Party withdrew, leaving **Prime Minister Smuts** at the head of a cabinet composed entirely of members from the United Party.

1946, June 3. The **Asiatic Land Tenure and Indian Representation Bill** was enacted into law. It restricted land tenure for Asiatics and gave direct representation to Indians in the Natal provincial council. The Indian government, in protest, withdrew its high commissioner and broke off trade relations with South Africa.

Dec. 14. The assembly of the United Nations rejected the proposal of South Africa for the incorporation of **Southwest Africa** into the Union.

1947, Jan. 21. Prime Minister Smuts informed parliament that his government would not place **Southwest Africa** under United Nations trusteeship. He later proposed to continue arrangements as they had been under the mandate system.

1948, May 26. In the **general election** the coalition (United and Labor Parties) under Smuts was defeated by the Nationalist-Afrikaner bloc.

June 3. Daniel F. Malan, Nationalist leader, who had campaigned on a platform of racial segregation (*apartheid*), formed a new government with himself as prime minister and minister for external affairs.

1949, Jan. 13. Race riots between Zulus and Indians at Durban left more than 100 dead and 1000 injured.

May 14. The **U.N. general assembly** invited India, Pakistan, and South Africa to discuss alleged discrimination against nationals of Indian origin.

June. The **South African Citizenship Act** discontinued the automatic granting of citizenship to British and Commonwealth immigrants, who now had to wait five years before receiving citizenship at the discretion of the government. At the same time the program of *apartheid* was put into effect as mixed marriages between Europeans and non-Europeans were forbidden and other measures of segregation were introduced.

1950, Apr. 27. The government announced a **Group Areas Bill** which assigned separate areas to the different races of South Africa. This and other segregation measures led to demonstrations and interracial riots and to protests from the Native Representative Council.

July 11. The International Court of Justice ruled that **Southwest Africa** was still a mandate, and that the Union of South Africa was obliged to submit reports on its administration. This decision did not stop the South African government from further integrating Southwest Africa into the Union by giving representation to the territory in the Union parliament.

Sept. 1. Jan Christiaan Smuts died.

1951, Dec. 11. South Africa drew criticism from the **U.N. trusteeship committee** for refusing to place Southwest Africa under international authority.

1952, Mar. 20. The **supreme court invalidated the race legislation** of Prime Minister Malan.

May 29. Parliament approved a government-sponsored bill to restrict the powers of the supreme court.

June 26. A **non-white campaign** began to defy "unjust laws." Demonstrations and arrests continued through July, as the movement's leaders said deliberate violations would continue until all the jails were filled.

1953, Feb. 24. Parliament enacted the **public safety legislation** to give the government dictatorial powers in its fight against the Negro and Indian movements.

Apr. 15. Malan's Nationalist Party won the elections with a considerably increased majority in parliament.

May 10. The solid front of whites cracked with the launching of two new anti-"Malanism" parties: **Alan Paton's** Liberal Party favored full rights of citizenship for all civilized people; and the Federal Union Party favored a federated state.

July 10. The decision of the **United Party opposition** to block Malan's plan to segregate the mixed-blood voters on a register of their own deprived Malan of the opposition votes he would need to amend the constitution.

1954, June 14. For the second time, the legislature rejected legislation sponsored by Prime Minister Malan to separate Cape colored voters from the rolls.

Oct. 29. Prime Minister Malan went into virtual retirement, turning the government over to **Nicolass C. Havenge.**

Nov. 30. Johannes G. Strydom, leader of Afrikaner nationalism, became **prime minister.**

1956, Jan. 13. The Nationalist government revealed plans to tighten its control on the government, by removing 60,000 persons of mixed blood ("Coloreds") from the common roll of voters in Cape Province, and by establishing parliament as the supreme governing body in the country, i.e., denying the right of courts to pass judgment on the validity of parliamentary acts.

Aug. 25. The government ordered over 100,000 non-whites to leave their homes in Johannesburg within a year, in order to make room for whites.

1958, Apr. 16. Elections resulted in victory for the Nationalist Party, led by Prime Minister Strydom.

Sept. 3. Hendrik F. Verwoerd was installed as **prime minister,** succeeding Strydom, who died August 24.

1960, Oct. 5. A referendum approved a proposal to establish a **republican form of government** and to end allegiance to the British crown.

1961, May 31. SOUTH AFRICA BECAME A REPUBLIC and severed ties with the **British Commonwealth. Charles R. Swart** had been elected **president** of the new South African Republic on May 18.

1963, Aug. 7. The U.N. security council voted 9–0 to ask all U.N. members to ban **military equipment shipments** to South Africa until that state ended its racist policies.

1964, Apr. 20. A panel of experts, established by the U.N. security council, issued a report urging immediate steps toward "non-racial" democracy. On the 29th the government abandoned its plan to impose apartheid in the **Southwest Africa trust territory.**

May 6. By the **Bantu Laws Amendment Act** a number of the laws on *apartheid* were consolidated and expanded. The minister of Bantu administration was empowered to declare "prescribed" areas in which the number of Bantus (Africans) to be employed could be specified and regulated.

June 12. Nelson Mandela and seven other native leaders were sentenced to life imprisonment for sabotage and subversion.

July. Numerous arrests under the **General Laws Amendment Act** which permitted police to hold suspects for as much as six months without as much as announcing their detention.

1965, Jan. 11. Release of most detainees, but the minister of justice was empowered to im-

prison for as long as 180 days potential state witnesses, on the plea of their own protection.

1966, Jan. 25. Declaration of policy with respect to the Rhodesian crisis: South Africa will not interfere and will not join in any effort to overthrow the Rhodesian régime by imposition of sanctions. In the sequel South Africa was the chief supporter of Rhodesia through government policy and private aid.

Mar. 30. Unprecedented victory of the Nationalist Party in the elections. It secured 126 of the 170 assembly seats.

July. The **International Court of Justice** rejected the complaint of Ethiopia and Liberia against South African policies in Southwest Africa, on the ground that the mandate did not give individual members of the United Nations the right to supervise the administration.

Sept. 6. Assassination of Prime Minister Verwoerd by a deranged worker. **Balthazar J. Vorster** was named to succeed him (Sept. 13).

Sept. 27. The U.N. general assembly voted to terminate the South African mandate in Southwest Africa (named *Namibia*), and itself to assume responsibility for the administration. The South African government declared this action illegal and ignored it. The U.N. administrative commission was refused entry into the mandate.

Oct. 27. Actual **termination of the mandate.**

1967, Dec. Establishment of **diplomatic relations with Malawi,** the first step in a policy of improving relations (political and economic) with neighboring African states.

Dec. 3. Dr. Christiaan Barnard and his associates performed the first successful **heart transplant operation,** the patient surviving for 18 days before dying of an infection.

1968. Prohibition of Political Interference Act: members of any of the four population groups (white, Bantu, colored, Asian) prohibited from joining in each other's political organizations or activities. The **Separate Representation of Voters Amendment Act** abolished, as of 1971, the existing representation of the colored in the Cape provincial council.

1969, Apr. 14. Parliamentary speech of **Dr. Albert Hertzog,** leader of the more conservative (*verkramptes*) wing of the Nationalist Party called **Reconstituted Nationalists,** criticizing the government's laxity and rapprochement with the non-Afrikaner (mostly English) elements. Hertzog declared only Afrikaners were spiritually equipped to uphold the white man's position in South Africa. This speech increased tension between the conservative and less conservative (*verligtes*) factions in the ruling party. Hertzog and other conservative deputies were expelled from the party (Oct.).

Aug. 12. The U.N. security council again

called for relinquishment of the Southwest African mandate by Oct. 4, only to be again ignored by the South African government.

Sept. 24. First elections of the new Colored Persons Representation Council, designed to give those of mixed blood limited legislative and administrative powers. Only about 50% of the eligibles voted and the anti-*apartheid* Labour Party won a decisive victory. Members nominated by the government were also of a "co-operative" character.

g. SWAZILAND

1968, Sept. 6. Swaziland, almost entirely embedded in South Africa, became independent within the British Commonwealth. With King Sobhuza II it retained the monarchical form of government and attempted to maintain a non-racial system of government.

h. LESOTHO

1966, Oct. 4. Lesotho, the former British Basutoland, became an independent state within the British Commonwealth. Like Swaziland it remained a monarchy, under King Moshoeshoe, with the leader of the Basuto National Party, Chief Leabua Jonathan, as prime minister.

Dec. 28. The king's attempts to establish truly effective control led to conflict with the prime minister and to imprisonment of the ruler, which ended when he promised to abide by the constitution.

1968. Lesotho co-operated closely with South Africa in the so-called struggle against Communism and subversion.

1970, Jan. 31. Prime Minister Jonathan invalidated the results of the election of Jan. 27 and arrested the opposition leader Mokhehle.

i. MADAGASCAR (MALAGASY)

1942, May 5. British forces landed in Madagascar to forestall possible Japanese intervention.

1947, May 29. A nationalist revolt against French rule, which had been restored after World War II. It was finally suppressed in July, after reinforcements had arrived from France.

1958, Oct. 14. The territorial assembly proclaimed the Malagasy Republic as a semi-autonomous unit within the French Community.

1960, June 26. The Malagasy Republic became fully independent within the French Community. Philibert Tsiranana became president and, with the support of the Social Democratic Party (non-Marxist), maintained the political control of the coastal tribes, while attempting to reconcile the anti-French tribes of the interior plateau.

5.   EAST AFRICA

a. TANZANIA

1961, Dec. 9. Tanganyika, a British mandated territory, was given independent status within the British Commonwealth under pressure of the Tanganyika African National Union, led by Julius K. Nyerere.

1962, Dec. 9. Tanganyika became a republic, with Nyerere as president, following an overwhelming victory of the National Union Party in the Nov. elections.

1963, June 24. Zanzibar, a British protectorate, was granted self-government, with Mohammed Shamte as prime minister.

June 30. Death of the ruling sultan of Zanzibar, who was succeeded by his son Seyyid Jamshid bin Abdullah bin Khalifa.

Dec. 10. Zanzibar became an independent monarchy within the British Commonwealth.

1964, Jan. 12. The predominantly Arab government of Zanzibar was overthrown by African nationalists, who set up (Jan. 14) a new cabinet under Abdullah Kassim Hanga, which included three Communist-trained ministers. Zanzibar became a People's Republic, with Abeid A. Karume as president.

Apr. 26. On the proposal of President Nyerere of Tanganyika, Zanzibar merged with that state.

Oct. 29. The two states assumed the name of United Republic of Tanzania, with Nyerere as president. The new state was definitely Communist-oriented, though officially non-aligned. Nyerere visited Peking in Feb. 1965, and Chou En-lai returned the visit in June of the same year.

1965, July 5. By a new constitution, Tanzania became a one-party state, with the African National Union in control on the mainland, and Karume's Afro-Shirazi Party on Zanzibar, which remained semi-independent.

Dec. 15. Tanzania severed diplomatic relations with Britain (till 1968) because of the latter's refusal to apply strong measures to Rhodesia. The Tanzanian government assumed a leading role in the struggle against colonialism and in behalf of African liberation.

1967, Feb. 5. The **Arusha Declaration,** defining the Tanzanian form of socialism or "self-reliance." This involved nationalization of banks, import-export firms, etc.

June. Tanzania joined Uganda and Kenya in signing the **TREATY OF KAMPALA,** establishing an **East African Community** which aimed at gradual amalgamation of government services. Arusha was named as the capital and seat of the overall cabinet.

Dec. 1. Formal **inauguration of the community,** with applications for membership from Zambia, Ethiopia, and eventually Somalia, Congo (Kinshasa), and Burundi.

1969, Aug. The arbitrary régime of Karume in Zanzibar led to treason trials and the execution of four high officials.

Oct. Six officers and other officials were charged with plotting the overthrow of the Tanzanian government.

1970, Oct. 26. FORMAL INAUGURATION OF THE TANZAM RAILWAY, a 1000-mile line from Zambia to Dar-es-Salaam, financed and constructed by the Chinese Communists as their major foreign-aid project.

b. UGANDA

1962, Mar. 1. **Uganda,** a British protectorate, was granted self-government. In the first elections **Milton Obote's Uganda People's Congress** proved victorious, and on

Oct. 9. **Uganda became an independent state** within the British Commonwealth with Obote as prime minister. The federal form of government was adopted to overcome the reluctance of the king or kabaka of Buganda, **Sir Edward Mutesa II,** to abandon the privileged position of his tribe and country.

1963, Oct. 9. Mutesa was elected president. However, friction developed between Buganda and the national government controlled by Obote, who aimed at establishment of a centralized, one-party state.

1966, Feb. 22. Prime Minister Obote took full powers and (Mar. 2) **deposed President Mutesa.**

Apr. 15. A new constitution ended the special position of Buganda and three other kingdoms. Obote was proclaimed president.

May 23–24. An attempted **separatist movement in Buganda** was suppressed by government troops and Mutesa was impelled to flee the country.

June. President Obote declared the end of Mutesa's rule and announced the division of Uganda into four districts.

1967, June. By the **TREATY OF KAMPALA,** Uganda joined with Kenya and Tanzania in the East Africa Community (see Tanzania, p. 1279).

Sept. 8. A **new constitution,** adopted after prolonged debate, made **Uganda a republic,** abolished all kingship, and recognized the division into districts.

1969, Oct. 8. Announcement of the **Common Man's Charter,** designed to close the gap between rich and poor. This involved increasing government control over economic life and giving a larger measure of control to peasant co-operatives.

Dec. 19. An abortive **attempt to assassinate President Obote** led to declaration of a national emergency and resulted in aggravated tribal tensions.

1970, May. "Acquisition" or **nationalization** of 60% of the banks, insurance companies, plantations, and industries, mostly owned by foreigners, presaged a progressively socialist régime, despite government promises of "reasonable" compensation.

c. KENYA

1948, Apr. 6. A new **central legislative assembly** for all of British East Africa held its first session at Nairobi.

1952–1956. The **Mau Mau insurrection** began on Oct. 20, 1952, as a terrorist movement directed against the white settlers. The British government declared a state of emergency and dispatched a cruiser and a battalion of troops.

1961, Aug. 21. Jomo Kenyatta, suspected of being the leader of the Mau Mau, was released from prison after a nine-year term.

1963, May 27. Kenyatta's **Kenya African National Union Party** was successful in the elections and he was sworn in as prime minister as self-government was inaugurated (June 1).

Dec. 12. Kenya became completely independent within the British Commonwealth, with Kenyatta as prime minister.

1964, Dec. 12. Kenya became a republic and essentially a one-party state, with **Kenyatta as president.** The opposition **Kenya African Democratic Union,** led by **Ronald G. Ngala,** merged with Kenyatta's African National Union Party.

1966, Mar.–Apr. The efforts of the vice-president **Ajuma Oginga Odinga** to organize a leftist, pro-Communist party, led to his resignation and the expulsion of his followers from parliament.

1967, Oct. 28. A meeting of the **Kenyan and Somali leaders** at Arusha, under the chairmanship of President Kaunda of Zambia, led to agreement to normalize relations and to end propaganda and guerrilla activities.

1968, Feb. The Kenyan government, in its effort to break the economic control of the Indian and Pakistani element (some 100,000 in number), began to withhold work permits and refuse trading licenses to non-citizens. Beginning of the **exodus of many Asians**, holding British citizenship, to Great Britain.

Mar. 1. Immigration of Asians limited to about 7000 a year.

1969, July 5. Assassination of Tom Mboya, the minister of economic planning and generally regarded as the probable successor to Kenyatta. Mboya, a member of the Luo tribe, was unacceptable to the dominant Kikuyu tribe. His assassination led to acute tribal tensions.

Oct. 27. Opposition leaders, including Odinga (also a Luo) **arrested** and the Kenya People's Union banned (Oct. 30).

1970, Jan. 10. Government orders directed about 1000 **Asian business enterprises to close** by June 1970.

d. SUDAN

The Sudan, under British-Egyptian control since 1898, became a subject of contention between Great Britain and Egypt after the Second World War.

1948, July 15. A British ordinance introduced **governmental reforms** over the protests of the Egyptian government, and on

1951, Oct. 27. The legislative assembly rejected the **Egyptian decision to restore the Sudan to Egyptian rule.**

Nov. 15. Elections for a legislative assembly resulted in a **majority for the anti-Egyptian Independence Front.**

1952, Apr. 2. Britain offered a **draft constitution** providing for limited self-government. The Egyptian government, which had proclaimed King Farouk ruler of the area, protested the British offer.

Oct. 22. Britain approved a new constitution under which the **Anglo-Egyptian Sudan gained self-government** in its internal affairs.

1953, Feb. 12. A compromise agreement, signed at Cairo, provided that the Sudanese could decide whether they preferred a union with Egypt or complete independence. A majority voted for **complete independence,** to become effective January 1, 1956.

1954, Jan. 9. As a result of elections November 29, 1953, **Ismail al Azhari,** leader of the victorious National Unionist Party, formed a government.

1955, Aug. Revolts in the southern provinces emphasized Sudanese **demands that both British and Egyptian troops be withdrawn.**

1956, Jan. 1. Upon the **termination of the Anglo-Egyptian condominium,** a council of state of five members was sworn in, to be

followed (Feb. 2) by the appointment of a cabinet.

Jan. 19. The Sudan joined the Arab League.

July 5. The house of representatives elected **Abdullah Khalil,** leader of the Nationalist (*Umma*) Party, to the premiership.

1958, Mar. 11. A **general election** gave the Umma Party 68 seats in the legislature and the People's Democratic Party 26.

Nov. 17. Gen. Ibrahim Abboud, head of the army, overturned the coalition parliamentary government and made himself **premier.** He suspended the constitution, dissolved the parliament, and abolished all political parties.

1959, Nov. 8. The Sudan and the UAR reached an **agreement on the distribution of the Nile waters.** The UAR agreed to give the Sudan $43 million compensation for the Sudanese lands flooded by the Aswan high dam.

1964, Feb. 27. The government announced the **deportation of 300 missionaries** allegedly responsible for unrest in the southern Sudan.

Oct. Growing opposition to the military régime led (Nov.) to the deposition of Gen. Abboud as chief of state. He was succeeded by a five-man, all-party council, which was confronted by a major insurrection in the southern, non-Arab and non-Moslem provinces, which resented the domination of the north.

1965, Mar. A meeting of northern and southern party leaders at Khartoum led to rejection of an offer of autonomy by the southern leaders. Military operations were resumed (July) and the government forces gained control of most of the towns. Meanwhile tens of thousands of refugees fled across the borders into Uganda, Kenya, and Ethiopia. Rebellion continued to flare up from time to time over a period of years.

1968, Apr.–May. Elections led to the formation (June) of a **coalition government** under **Mohammed Ahmed Mahgoub.**

1969, May 25. A coup by junior officers, led by **Colonel Jaafar al-Nimeri,** overthrew the government, set up a revolutionary council, dissolved the assembly, and forbade all political parties. Former ministers and senior officers were arrested and detained. Thereupon the revolutionaries set up a civilian cabinet under former Chief Justice **Abubakr Awadallah,** which included several Communist ministers. The new régime was extremely nationalist and supported Egypt enthusiastically in the war against Israel. It was also decidedly leftist, aiming at the establishment of a democratic socialist republic.

Oct. Al-Nimeri took over as prime minister, and in

Nov. He paid a **visit to Moscow.**

e. ETHIOPIA

1942, Jan. 31. Great Britain, having played a leading role in the liberation of Ethiopia from Italian rule, recognized the independence of the country and promised various kinds of aid.

1950, Dec. 2. The U.N. general assembly voted the **union of Eritrea with Ethiopia** on a federal basis.

1952, Sept. 11. Eritrea was formally transferred from British administration to Ethiopian.

1960, Dec. 17. Emperor Haile Selassie resumed control after an abortive coup by intellectuals dissatisfied with the absolute rule of the emperor.

1962. Eritrea became an integral part of the Ethiopian state.

1964. Border disputes with the Somalis and growing opposition among the Moslem Eritreans, supported by Syria and other Arab nations, became increasingly serious matters of Ethiopian policy.

Apr. 1. A cease-fire between Ethiopians and Somalis was arranged by the Organization of African Unity. Nonetheless, border conflicts continued to occur.

1967, Sept. Agreement between Ethiopia and the Somali government to suppress border disturbances. However, the activities of the Eritrean Liberation Front continued.

1969, Mar. Ethiopia, like most other countries, was confronted with **student protests,** demonstrations, and disorders, reflecting growing discontent with the failure of the government to introduce political reforms. The schools were closed and hundreds if not thousands of students arrested. Despite the establishment of a national committee on education to hear complaints, renewed outbreaks took place in Dec.

1969. The **Eritrean Liberation Front** began the practice of hijacking Ethiopian Airlines planes as a means of bringing pressure on the government.

1970, Oct. 18. Revelation of an **agreement between the United States and Ethiopia,** concluded in 1960, by which the United States government undertook to supply instructors and materiel to strengthen the Ethiopian army in its defense of national integrity.

Nov. In a renewed flare-up of **Eritrean insurgency,** thousands of refugees were reported to have fled to the Sudan.

f. SOMALIA

1949, Nov. 21. The former Italian colony of Somaliland was placed under **U.N. trusteeship,** with Italy as trustee and on the understanding that the area should become independent in 10 years.

1956, May 19. The first Somali assembly elected **Abdullah Issa** as premier.

1960, May. The British government arranged for the union of British Somaliland with the Italian sector and on

July 1. The two Somalilands were proclaimed an independent republic under the name of Somali Republic. **Aden Abdullah Osman** became the first president.

1964–1967. Widespread **fighting on the borders** with Ethiopia and Kenya, in the Somali nationalist hope of uniting the Somalis in those countries with the mother state. In the struggle Somalia was given **extensive support,** including MIG fighter planes, **by the Soviet Union.**

1967, June. The national assembly elected **Abdi Rashid Ali Shermarke** to replace President Osman. **Mohammed Ibrahim Egal** became prime minister. The new régime, while not renouncing the claim of Somalis in Ethiopia and Kenya to self-determination, arranged to reduce the Communist influence and to that end made **peace with Ethiopia** (Sept.) **and Kenya** (Oct.).

1969, Oct. 15. Assassination of President Shermarke. Military and police officers took over control (Oct. 21) and set up a Supreme Revolutionary Council, with **General Mohammed Said Bare** as head of government (Nov. 3). The assembly was dissolved and the constitution abrogated.

1970, May 7. The new government declared all banks and oil companies nationalized.

g. FRENCH TERRITORY OF THE AFARS AND ISSAS

1958, Sept. 28. Alone among the French possessions in Africa, **French Somaliland,** at the mouth of the Red Sea, chose to remain a French overseas territory rather than become an autonomous republic within the French Community. However, the **Issa** (Somali) majority soon began to agitate for union with Somalia and in

1966, Aug. During a **visit of President de Gaulle** popular demonstrations for independence decided him to hold a referendum.

1967, Mar. 19. A majority (mostly **Afars** and pro-French) voted to remain an "Overseas Territory" under the new name of *The French Territory of the Afars and the Issas,* represented in the French parliament. Since France retains control of foreign policy, defense, and internal security, the efforts of the **Somali Front for Liberation of the Somali Coast** have been held in check.

G. THE ARAB WORLD AND MIDDLE EAST

1. GENERAL

THE **Arab League** of Egypt, Iraq, Jordan, Lebanon, Saudi Arabia, Syria, and Yemen, created in March 1945, the repercussions from the creation of Israel, the ambitions of Egypt to lead the Arab world, and the geographical location of the region between Europe, Africa, and Asia, all combined to make events there widely significant especially in the context of the cold war.

1947. A **central bureau** to coordinate the activities of the North African independence movements and work closely with the Arab League was created in Cairo.

1951, Sept. 3. The Arab League's political committee appealed to the seven member-states to tighten their **economic blockade of Israel** and, especially, to shut off oil supplies, since the growing power of that state constituted a security threat to the area.

Sept. 13. The **United Nations conciliation commission** opened talks with Israeli and Arab delegates in Paris to effect a peaceful settlement in Palestine. The talks ended in failure on November 21.

Nov. 9. France, Great Britain, the United States, and Turkey announced plans for a **security program in the Near East.**

1953, Mar. 28. **Libya joined the Arab League.**

Nov. 14. Jordan rejected the U.S. **plan for a Jordan Valley authority.** But on November 17 the United States representative, **Eric Johnston,** reported that Israel, Jordan, Syria, and Lebanon had promised to give "most careful study" to the United States proposal.

1954, Mar. 30. The Israeli-Jordanian mixed armistice commission, boycotted by Israel, used the "strongest terms" in condemning Israel for a March 29 **attack on a Jordanian village.**

June 11. In accord with the collective security pact, adopted by the Arab states and in effect from August 23, 1952, **Egypt and Saudi Arabia** agreed to place their military forces under a **unified command.**

July 6. Israel, Syria, Lebanon, and Jordan reportedly accepted the principle of the unified development and **international sharing of the waters of the Jordan River.**

1955, Feb. 18. The **BAGHDAD PACT,** a defensive alliance of Turkey and Iraq, was signed at Baghdad. Great Britain, Pakistan, and Iran soon adhered to it, but the United States, which supported it, did not join.

Aug. 22. **Israeli-Egyptian fighting** flared up in the Gaza Strip.

Oct. 20. Egypt made **defensive alliances** and joint military arrangements with Syria and Saudi Arabia.

Nov. 21-22. The first **meeting of the Baghdad pact council** was held in Baghdad and attended by the British foreign minister and the premiers of Iraq, Turkey, Iran, and Pakistan.

1956, Jan. 13. Following an Israeli attack (Dec. 11) on Syrian positions along the Sea of Galilee, **Lebanon and Syria signed a defense pact,** providing for joint retaliation if either were attacked by Israel.

Jan. 19. The **United Nations security council** unanimously voted to censure Israel for its attack on Syria, December 11, 1955, as a "flagrant violation" of the Palestine armistice.

Jan. 19. The **Sudan became the ninth member of the Arab League.**

Feb. 17. The United States government announced a **suspension of all arms shipments to Israel and the Arab nations,** but on the following day lifted the ban on a shipment of tanks to Saudi Arabia.

Apr. 9. In an official statement of policy, the United States pledged opposition to Middle East aggression "within constitutional means," and declared that it would give the fullest measure of support for the United Nations mission.

Apr. 18. The **Israeli-Egyptian cease-fire,** which U.N. Secretary General Hammarskjöld had arranged, went into effect.

Apr. 19. The Baghdad pact council ended a four-day meeting in Tehran, with United States agreement to establish economic and other ties with the organization.

June 13. The 74-year **British occupation of the Suez Canal ended,** with the withdrawal of the last British forces from the Suez Canal Zones, leaving Egypt with full responsibility for the defense of the canal.

July 26. Egyptian President Nasser's **NATIONALIZATION OF THE SUEZ CANAL** (p. 1294) immediately led to feverish attempts to thwart him.

Aug. 1. After talks in London, Britain, France, and the United States called a **conference of most-interested nations** to discuss Egypt's action on the Suez Canal. Although Egypt refused to attend, the conference opened in London, August 16, with twenty-two nations represented.

Aug. 13. The nine members of the Arab League declared that an attack on Egypt would be interpreted as an attack on all members of the League.

Aug.–Sept. Efforts of the **London conference** to negotiate an agreement with Nasser failed (Sept. 9) and Great Britain and France agreed to apply **economic pressure on Egypt** to accept international control of the canal (Sept. 11), while the United States declared that it was opposed to the use of force (Sept. 11).

Sept. 12. British Prime Minister Eden announced a British-French-United States agreement to establish an **association to operate the canal,** but Nasser dubbed this an attempt to provoke war.

Sept. 21. The London conference ended with the announcement of a draft plan for a **Suez Canal Users' Association,** which five participants, however, had opposed.

Sept. 23–26. The **U.N. security council** received British-French claims and Egyptian counter-claims concerning the Suez Canal and decided to discuss them.

Oct. 13. After the U.S.S.R. and Egypt had reaffirmed their rejection of international operation of the Suez Canal, a **Soviet veto** prevented a U.N. security council compromise resolution.

Oct. 29. SUEZ CRISIS. ISRAELI FORCES SUDDENLY INVADED EGYPT, driving toward the Suez Canal.

Oct. 30. Rejecting a United States suggestion, supported by the U.S.S.R., for an Israeli-Egyptian cease-fire, **Britain and France issued an ultimatum** to Cairo and Tel Aviv to end fighting, withdraw from a ten-mile strip along the canal, and permit a Franco-British occupation of key points.

Oct. 31. France and Britain vetoed U.N. **security council resolutions** to refrain from the use of force and opened **bombardments of Cairo and the canal area.**

Nov. 6. The **Soviet Union threatened action** to end the Suez fighting and President Eisenhower ordered a global **alert of U.S. armed forces.** The British government accepted the **cease-fire,** followed by Israel and France, and the U.N. created an **emergency force** (UNEF) to supervise the cease-fire.

Nov. 15. The first units of UNEF arrived in the Suez Canal Zone to enforce the cease-fire.

Dec. 22. British-French evacuation of forces from Egyptian territory was completed. On December 29 U.N. salvage crews began clearance operations in the Suez Canal. On January 22 **Israel completed evacuation of**

Egyptian territory, excepting the Gaza Strip and the area of Aqaba.

1957, Jan. 5. In a message to congress, President Eisenhower requested authorization to **use United States armed forces in the event of Communist aggression** in the Middle East (the **Eisenhower Doctrine**). It was approved by the senate, March 5.

Jan. 18. Premier **Bulganin** and Premier **Chou En-lai** announced their **support of the Middle East** against aggression.

Jan. 19. Egypt, Saudi Arabia, Syria, and Jordan signed a **ten-year pact** in Cairo to provide a $36 million subsidy to Jordan.

Feb. 2. The **U.N. approved resolutions** calling on Israel to withdraw its troops from Egyptian territory still occupied, and broadening the function of UNEF as a buffer between Israel and Egypt. Israel refused, on February 3, to begin the withdrawal until the U.N. provided greater assurance that Israel would be protected.

Feb. 5. The United States indicated its readiness to apply **economic sanctions against Israel** if the U.N. required such measures. On February 11 the United States assured Israel of its willingness to "support free passage" through the Gulf of Aqaba.

Feb. 11. U.N. **Secretary General Hammarskjöld,** after unsuccessful attempts to get Israel out of the Gaza Strip, called on the U.N. general assembly for instructions on how to proceed.

Mar. 1. Israel announced the withdrawal of its troops from the Gaza Strip and the Gulf of Aqaba area, on the "assumption" that free navigation in the Gulf of Aqaba would continue, and that, until a peace settlement was arranged, **UNEF would administer the Gaza Strip.**

Mar. 29. Israel found acceptable the **U.N. proposal to erect a mined fence** along the Gaza border, provided that U.N. troops and not Egyptians patrolled the barrier on the Gaza side.

May. Controversy continued over Israel's right, denied by Egypt, to use the Suez Canal and over the terms set by Egypt for the use of the canal by others. Britain accepted them on May 13, and France on June 13.

June 3. The United States formally joined the military committee of the Baghdad pact.

Aug.–Sept. SYRIAN CRISIS. Cold war tension mounted in the Arab world as Syria and the United States each ousted some of the other's embassy officials (Aug. 13–14) over alleged "plots." President Eisenhower accused the U.S.S.R. of seeking to take over Syria (Aug. 21) and reaffirmed the "Eisenhower Doctrine" (Sept. 7). Meanwhile Syrian **President**

Shukri al-Kuwatly conferred with Nasser in Cairo (Aug. 21), and efforts to establish Arab solidarity led to a **conference in Syria** (Sept. 25) of **King Saud and Iraqui Premier Ali Jawdat** with the Syrian president.

Sept. 5. The United States announced **plans to airlift arms to Jordan,** to make special shipments of arms to Lebanon, and to accelerate past commitments to Turkey and Iraq. On September 7 Syria protested the projected airlift of arms to Jordan by declaring that Syria would not suffer a threat to its security.

Sept. 19. In response to Syrian charges of United States intervention in Jordanian affairs, Jordan accused Syria of meddling in its domestic affairs. U.S. Secretary of State Dulles, speaking in the U.N., declared that the **Soviet arms build-up in Syria** endangered Turkey.

Oct. The **Syrian-Turkish crisis** (p. 1298) aroused international concern. Egyptian President Nasser told the U.N. (Oct. 3) that Egypt would not permit a violation of Syria's integrity; **Syria charged Turkey with aggressive action** (Oct. 10); Lebanon sided with Syria (Oct. 11), and Nasser sent **Egyptian troops to Syria** (Oct. 14). The United States declared that a Soviet attack on Turkey would warrant **U.S. military action,** and Syria called upon the U.N. to investigate the border situation (Oct. 16). King Saud offered his mediation (Oct. 20) which Syria rejected, but the crisis simmered down as the Arab League (Oct. 31) pledged its support of Syria.

1958, Jan. 17–30. At a **meeting of Baghdad pact members** in Ankara, Turkey, Iraq, Iran, and Pakistan agreed upon closer **customs cooperation,** and U.S. **Secretary of State Dulles** declared that the United States would supply a "mobile power of great force" and that the Eisenhower Doctrine committed the country as effectively to the Middle East as membership in the pact (Jan. 30).

July. In a reaction to the **Iraqi coup** of the 14th (p. 1308), **King Hussein of Jordan called for United States and Turkish aid;** Lebanese **President Chamoun** also asked for military assistance. **Landing of U.S. forces** on the Lebanese coast. **British forces** dispatched to Lebanon. U.S. President Eisenhower asked for an emergency meeting of the U.N. security council; and on July 19 Soviet **Premier Khrushchev proposed a five-power summit meeting** to prevent war in the Middle East.

Aug. 8. An emergency session of the U.N. general assembly, called at the request of the United States, met to consider the situation in the Middle East.

Aug. 21. The U.N. general assembly passed an Arab **resolution** designed **to enable the United States and Great Britain to withdraw from Lebanon and Jordan** (done by November).

Oct. 1. The Arab League admitted Tunisia and Morocco to membership.

1959, Jan. 2. There were growing rumors of a **split between Egypt and Iraq** over Syria, with Egypt conducting a campaign against Syrian Communists, and Iraq supporting the Syrian Communist Party.

Mar. 5. The United States signed **bilateral defense pacts** with Iran, Pakistan, and Turkey.

Mar. 11. President Nasser initiated an exchange of critical remarks with Premier Khrushchev by charging that Iraq and foreign Communist agents were trying to create a split in the Arab world, particularly in the UAR. Khrushchev called Nasser "hot-headed" (Mar. 19) and again Nasser lashed out at **Soviet interference in Arab affairs** (Mar. 20).

Apr. 4. At a **meeting of the Arab League** called by the Sudan to discuss the rift in Iraqi-UAR relations, the six nations present (Sudan, UAR, Saudi Arabia, Morocco, Lebanon, and Yemen) agreed that **Iraq's pro-Communist government** might be a threat. Iraq, Jordan, and Tunisia boycotted the meeting and Libya failed to attend.

Aug. 19. After the **withdrawal** (Mar. 24) **of Iraq from the Baghdad pact,** the alliance was re-created as the **Central Treaty Organization** (CENTO) with headquarters at Ankara. The United States supported it, but did not join.

1960, July 28. The Arab League put **Iran under economic boycott** for having extended recognition to Israel on July 23.

1961, Feb. 1. At a meeting in Baghdad, all Arab League member states agreed to send **arms to aid the Algerian rebels.**

July 20. Accusing the **Arab League** of aiding "British imperialism," Iraq walked out of a meeting of that organization when it **voted to admit Kuwait** to membership.

1962, Aug. 16. Algeria was admitted to the Arab League, bringing the total number to thirteen.

1963, Mar. 2. Ralph J. Bunche arrived in Yemen as the U.N. representative to study the situation arising from the involvement of Saudi Arabia and the UAR in the **Yemeni civil war** (p. 1306). Tension lessened between the UAR and Saudi Arabia as the U.N. sought a settlement.

June 7. U.N. **Secretary General U Thant** announced that the head of the U.N. truce supervision organization in the Middle East was being sent to Yemen, and that the UAR, which supported the republic, and Saudi Arabia, which supported the royalists, had agreed to help finance a **peace mission in Yemen.**

1964, Jan. 13–17. The chiefs of state of the nations comprising the Arab League met in Cairo to formulate strategy in opposing **Israel's projected diversion of the Jordan River waters.**

May 5. Opening of the **Israeli oil pipeline** from the Sea of Galilee to the Negev. Vigorous protests of the Arab governments against this tapping of the Jordan River waters for purely Israeli needs.

May 28. A **Palestine National Congress** opened in Arab Jerusalem. Decision to set up a **Palestine Liberation Organization,** open training camps for Palestinians (mostly boys who had grown up in the refugee camps), and to put all Palestine forces under unified Arab command. On June 2 the **Palestine National Charter** was proclaimed, and from this time on the Palestinian organizations (eventually some ten in number, varying in their radicalism and tactics) became ever more active. Raiding and terrorism against Israeli targets became common, and Israeli reprisals constantly more severe.

Aug. 13. The UAR, Kuwait, Iraq, Syria, and Jordan agreed to organize a **common market.**

Sept. 5–11. Arab League Summit at Alexandria. Discussion of possible ways to divert Jordan waters before they came under Israeli control. Establishment of a **United Arab Command,** to include a Palestine army. **Ahmed Shukairy,** the Palestine representative to the Arab League, was made chairman of the Palestine Liberation Organization.

Nov. 16. Serious **clashes between Syrian and Israeli forces** north of the Sea of Galilee. The U.N. truce supervision organization blamed both countries for the troubles.

1965, May 26–30. Arab League meeting in Cairo: failure to agree on a common policy toward Israel, the more so as **President Bourguiba** of Tunisia had **urged recognition of Israel** and a compromise territorial settlement (Apr.).

Sept. Islamic meeting at Casablanca. Further inconclusive discussion of divergence of Jordan waters.

1966. Increasing **guerrilla war on the Jordan and Syrian frontiers** of Israel leading to massive retaliation by the Israelis (July 14, Aug. 15). The situation led to long debates in the U.N.

Nov. 13. Severe reprisal of the Israelis on the Hebron area of Jordan, for which Israel was censured by the U.N.

Dec. 10. The defense council of the **Arab League voted to send Saudi Arabian and Iraqi troops into Jordan** to support that country in defense against Israel. Jordan forbade the entry of Syrian or Palestine liberation forces, suspected of aiming to overthrow Hussein's régime and make Jordan the base for all anti-Israeli liberation activities.

1967, Apr. 7. Massive **Israeli attack on Syria,** following Syrian **guerrilla raids on Israeli settlements.** Iraq and Jordan offered aid, but the UAR was reluctant to act.

May 11. An Israeli note to the U.N. asserted the right of self-defense against commando raids from Syria. Syria, UAR, and Israel all began to mobilize (May 16–17).

May 18. Nasser demanded the withdrawal of the U.N. emergency force, a demand to which U Thant complied at once (May 19), seeing no alternative. Egyptian forces then occupied the Gaza Strip and Sharm el Sheikh, commanding the entrance to the Gulf of Aqaba.

May 22. Nasser announced the **closure of the Strait of Tiran** to Israeli shipping. On both sides leaders began to make threatening and bellicose speeches.

May 24–26. Mission of Israeli foreign minister **Abba Eban to Paris, London, and Washington.** Discussion of the possibility of running the Egyptian blockade into the Gulf of Aqaba. Reluctance of the great powers to take action that might lead to war.

June 5. BEGINNING OF THE ARAB-ISRAELI WAR. In a surprise operation the Israeli air force attacked twenty-five Arab airfields and destroyed just about all the Egyptian, Jordanian, Syrian, and Iraqi planes, mostly on the ground. At the same time armored forces executed a victorious sweep over the entire Sinai Peninsula, reaching the Suez Canal (June 8) and occupying the base at Sharm el Sheikh. All of Jordan west of the Jordan River was overrun (June 7) and on the Syrian front the all-important Golan Heights were taken after some sharp fighting (June 9).

June 6. Egyptian claims that British and American planes had participated with the Israelis in the attack led most Arab states to break off relations with the two powers, despite their vehement denials. Oil shipments also were to be banned.

June 8. Nasser appealed to the U.N. to arrange a cease-fire, which was accepted also by the Israelis and went into effect June 10. The Egyptians had lost about 10,000 men dead and 15,000 prisoners, including some 5000 officers. At the same time the war greatly aggravated the Arab refugee problem. To the more than a million refugees remaining from the 1948–1949 war there were now added some 450,000 from the west bank of the Jordan and 250,000 from the Gaza Strip. The Israeli government made an agreement with Jordan for return of the refugees from the west bank (Aug. 6) but the applications required were complicated and only a few (some 15,000) actually returned.

An **Israeli attack** by torpedoes and planes **on the U.S.S. Liberty,** 15 miles north of the Sinai coast, led to the death of 34 American seamen and the wounding of 75 others. Israel apologized at once for this grievous error and offered compensation.

June 17. Emergency session of the U.N. general assembly voted a resolution rejecting the unification of Arab Jerusalem (taken by the Israelis June 7). This resolution was rejected by the Israeli government (July 10, 14).

June 21–July 4. Mission of Soviet President Podgorny to Egypt, Syria, and Iraq. He promised the Arab states all necessary military aid in replacing their losses and Soviet equipment did in fact begin to arrive almost immediately. Within the next two years most of the Arab losses had been retrieved.

June 28. The Israeli government proclaimed the **union of both parts of Jerusalem,** despite the resolution of the U.N. and the declared opposition of the United States government.

Aug. 14. Speech of Israeli foreign minister Eban rejecting the mediation of any third power and insisting on face-to-face negotiations and conclusion of formal peace treaties with the Arab states.

Aug. 29–Sept. 1. Meeting of Arab leaders at Khartoum (Syria, Algeria, and Tunisia being absent). Discussion of a common position with regard to Israel ("no peace with Israel, no recognition of Israel, no negotiation with it, and insistence on the rights of the Palestinian people in their own country"). The rich oil-producing states of Saudi Arabia, Kuwait, and Libya undertook to subsidize the UAR and Jordan to compensate for their losses.

Oct. 21. Sinking of the Israeli destroyer *Elath* by Egyptian attack. Thenceforth hostilities became more and more frequent. The Suez Canal had been blocked by sunken ships (June 8) and now became the firing line for artillery duels. The oil refining and storage facilities of the town of Suez were destroyed by Israeli fire.

Nov. 22. RESOLUTION OF THE U.N. SECURITY COUNCIL, which was to be the basic document governing the negotiation of peace. It called on Israel to return the territories occupied since June 5. The Arab states were to negotiate permanent, guaranteed frontiers for all Middle East states. Israel was to negotiate a settlement of the Arab refugee problem. **Ambassador Gunnar V. Jarring** was named personal representative of U Thant and U.N. negotiator, with headquarters in Cyprus. During the period Dec. 1967 to Apr. 1969 he made numerous visits to the Middle East capitals and carried on endless conversations, but

to no avail. On the Arab side as on the Israeli the U.N. resolution evoked little popular enthusiasm. It was bitterly attacked by the Syrian authorities and by the Palestine Liberation Organization, whose leader, Shukairy, was so violent in his language that he had to resign.

1968, Mar. Israeli raids into Jordan to destroy commando bases. This move, too, was condemned by the U.N. security council (Mar. 24).

May 21. The U.N. security council declared **Israeli proceedings in Arab Jerusalem invalid.**

July 23. First **hijacking of an Israeli airliner** by members of the **Popular Front for the Liberation of Palestine,** a Marxist, terrorist wing of the Palestine liberation movement. The plane was *en route* from Rome to Tel Aviv and was diverted to Algeria, where 12 Israeli passengers were held hostage until Israel released 16 Arab commandos.

Dec. Agreement of the United States government to deliver 50 Phantom jet fighters to Israel over the ensuing three years in order to ensure continued Israeli air superiority in the area.

1969, Jan. 1–2. Severe **clashes on the Israeli-Lebanese borders** following an Israeli air **attack on the airport at Beirut** (Dec. 28).

Jan. 6. President de Gaulle banned the shipment of arms to Israel, despite the fact that a number of Mirage planes had already been paid for.

Jan. 7. U Thant urged the adoption of a French proposal for four-power (U.S., Britain, France, U.S.S.R.) intervention to work for peace on the basis of the U.N. resolution of Nov. 22, 1967.

Feb. 4. Meeting of Palestine guerrilla (fedayeen) organizations at Cairo. Yasir Arafat became chairman of the Palestine Liberation Organization, a combination of some lesser organizations, but the radical Popular Front for the Liberation of Palestine refused to join.

Feb. 5. Opening of the Big Four talks.

Feb. 18. An Arab terrorist attack on an Israeli plane at Zürich. By this time terrorist attacks as well as artillery duels along the Suez Canal were of almost daily occurrence and the war had at least been unofficially resumed.

Apr. The four-power talks and later separate U.S.–U.S.S.R. discussions **failed to produce a compromise plan** that had any chance of acceptance by the belligerents.

Aug. 21. A fire in the Al Aqsa Mosque in Jerusalem was set by an Australian fanatic, soon arrested by the Israeli authorities. Its effect, however, was to evoke loud protests throughout Islam and renewed demands for a Holy War to liberate Jerusalem.

Sept. An **Islamic conference at Rabat,**

called by King Faisal of Saudi Arabia, led to no result. The division of the Arab world between the rich oil-producing states and the less endowed states led to much disagreement and dissension.

Sept. 4. The **Palestine National Congress at Cairo** condemned terrorist activities abroad and called for concentrated action against Israeli-occupied Palestine.

Sept. 9. An **Israeli force crossed the Suez Canal** and remained in hostile territory for ten hours, during which it destroyed UAR installations.

Sept. 18. President Nixon, addressing the U.N. general assembly, **declared that the U.S. stood by the U.N. resolution** of Nov. 22, 1967, as the best road to Middle East peace: "We are convinced that peace cannot be achieved on the basis of substantial alterations in the map of the Middle East."

Dec. 9. Secretary of State Rogers' speech proposing terms for a Middle East settlement: withdrawal of the Israelis from occupied territories in return for a binding peace treaty, as set forth in the U.N. resolution. Only "insubstantial" territorial changes to be envisaged.

Dec. 21–23. **Arab summit meeting at Rabat.** Plans to renew the war if peace efforts failed. But Saudi Arabia and Kuwait refused to provide funds for massive purchases of arms.

1970, Feb. 2. Renewed **heavy fighting in the Golan Heights** area.

Feb. 10. **Terrorist bomb attacks** on Israeli planes at Munich airport. Effort to hijack an El Al plane (Feb. 13). Explosion of a Swiss aircraft bound for Israel (Feb. 21).

Mar. **Increased Arab attacks** from Egypt, Jordan, and Syria, with infiltration of guerrillas from Lebanon. Drastic Israeli reprisals.

Apr. 6. The Israeli government refused to allow **Naoum Goldmann,** eminent Zionist leader but avowed advocate of a compromise peace, to engage in discussions with UAR officials.

Apr. 28. Israeli charges that **Soviet pilots** were flying MIG-21's in defense of anti-aircraft missile bases being installed by Soviet technicians. Israeli appeals to the U.S. for more planes.

May 12. A major **Israeli raid on Lebanon,** in response to guerrilla operations from Lebanese territory.

June 19. Official **United States letter** to the governments of the Middle East states **proposing a cease-fire** of at least 90 days and the initiation of negotiations on the basis of the U.N. resolution of Nov. 22, 1967. After prolonged conferences with Soviet authorities in Moscow, President Nasser accepted (July 23), followed by Jordan and Lebanon (July 26), and

eventually by Israel (July 31). Iraq, Syria, and Algeria, as well as the Palestine Liberation Organization, refused to be associated with peace negotiations.

Aug. 7. The **cease-fire went into effect,** but negotiations through Ambassador Jarring (begun Aug. 25) were almost immediately broken off by Israel (Sept. 6), which charged that the Egyptian government was taking advantage of the cease-fire to move Soviet anti-missile bases to the very banks of the Suez Canal. The Egyptian government in reply asserted that it had never done more than move missile sites within the cease-fire zone from one place to another, a necessary defense measure. While the argument on this matter continued, the Israelis built formidable bunkers and other installations on their side of the canal, making eventual raids from Egypt impossible. Meanwhile the Israeli government refused to resume negotiations until the situation as of Aug. 7 should have been restored and the Egyptian missile bases removed.

Aug. 27. **Meeting of Arab guerrilla** (fedayeen) **organizations** at Amman. The Palestine National Council declared for continued war against Israel, while delegates from Iraq and Syria proclaimed full support.

Sept. 7. **Hijacking of four international airliners** *en route* to New York from European airports. The hijackers were members of the radical, terrorist Popular Front for the Liberation of Palestine. One plane was flown to Cairo and blown up after the passengers had been removed. Two others were flown to an airstrip outside Amman where, with several hundred passengers, they stood in the desert heat while desperate international efforts were made to secure the release of the hostages. For this the fedayeen demanded the release of members of their organization held prisoner by foreign governments. Eventually the hostages were liberated by Jordanian forces (Sept. 27), whereupon Britain, West Germany, and Switzerland voluntarily released seven commandos captured in earlier hijacking attempts.

Sept. 16–26. **THE CIVIL WAR IN JORDAN** (p. 1305).

Oct. 15. The U.S. State Department, reacting to the events in Jordan, recognized that Palestinians would have to be given a voice in the peace negotiations.

Nov. 4. The **U.N. general assembly** by a large majority **called for a three-month extension of the cease-fire** and unconditional resumption of the peace negotiations through Dr. Jarring. The resolution was opposed by Israel and the United States, which insisted on "rectification" of the military situation in the cease-fire zone.

Nov. 18. After the revelation that the Israelis had built powerful bunkers and revetments along the canal, and after assurances of continued U.S. military support, the Israeli government dropped its demand for the roll-back of the Egyptian missile sites and agreed to resume negotiations (Dec. 28).

2. NORTH AFRICA

a. MOROCCO

(From p. 1081)

1945, Oct. 11. The United States, Great Britain, France, and the Soviet Union set up a new **international administration in Tangier.** This marked a **return to the 1924 convention** which had been modified by the pressure of the Spaniards.

1948, June–Oct. In a series of decrees, the absolute monarchy of **Sultan Sidi Mohammed** in French Morocco was liberalized through the creation of **consultative chambers** elected by Moslems and native Jews.

1953, Aug. 14. Three hundred Moroccan leaders **deposed the sultan,** Sidi Mohammed III and, over French objections, **enthroned Moulay Mohammed ben Arafa,** but he was deposed (Aug. 16) by rebellious Berbers. Bloody rioting followed.

Aug. 20. The **French exiled Sultan Sidi Mohammed III** to Corsica, as Berber tribesmen marched on Rabat. **Sidi Mohammed ben Arafa was proclaimed sultan** (Aug. 21).

1954, Jan. 21. Arab political and religious leaders, meeting in Tetuan, called for the **separation of the Spanish zone** from the rest of Morocco, and condemned the French appointment of Sidi Mohammed ben Arafa to be sultan, as a "machination" which resulted in "the dethronement of the legitimate sultan."

1955, Aug. 21. In view of widespread violence in Algeria and Morocco, French **Premier Faure** went to Aix-les-Bains for a **conference with Moroccan leaders** in an attempt to restore peace. On August 27 they worked out a compromise, providing for the resignation of both the pro-French sultan and the resident general of Morocco, **Gilbert Grandval.**

Aug. 29. The French cabinet, after prolonged and angry debate, accepted Premier Faure's program to establish peace in North Africa by September 12.

Aug. 30. **Boyer de Latour** became the new resident governor-general of Morocco. The pro-French sultan, however, stood firm in his refusal to resign.

Oct. The conflict over who was rightful sultan reached a climax. At first France continued to support Sidi Mohammed ben Arafa, while the Istiqlal party and an increasing number of religious and political leaders demanded the return of the exiled Sidi Mohammed III. On October 30 **Sidi Mohammed ben Arafa abdicated.**

Nov. 5. The **French government granted recognition to Sidi Mohammed III as sultan** of Morocco.

Dec. 7. Morocco's first representative cabinet, led by **Premier M'barek Bekkai,** took office.

1956, Mar. 2. A protocol on **MOROCCAN INDEPENDENCE** was signed in Paris by French **Foreign Minister Christian Pineau** and Moroccan **Premier M'barek Bekkai.**

Apr. 4. The **Spanish government declared the termination of its protectorate over part of Morocco,** and recognized Moroccan independence and unity. The official Spanish-Moroccan protocol was signed on April 7.

Oct. 20. A **nine-power conference** on the status of Tangier agreed to **end international rule in the Tangier zone,** to go into effect on October 29.

1957, Mar. 30. Morocco and Tunisia signed a **treaty of friendship and alliance.**

Aug. 11. Upon the change of name from the Sherifian Empire to **Kingdom of Morocco,** the sultan abandoned his traditional title and became **King Mohammed V.**

Aug. 19. The king announced his decision to begin negotiating with Spain for the acquisition of **Ifni.**

1958, Apr. 1. Spain and Morocco made an agreement providing for the **return of the Southern Protectorate of Morocco** to Morocco.

May 8. Morocco moved toward a **constitutional monarchy** with King Mohammed V's decree giving the deliberative assembly a share in legislative power, and delegating some of the monarch's executive power to ministers. On March 12 a new cabinet, with **Ahmed Balafrej** as premier, was invested.

Oct. 1. **Morocco joined the Arab League.**

Dec. 16. **Abdullah Ibrahim** was asked to form a non-political government, following the resignation of Premier Ahmed Balafrej on December 3.

1959, Dec. 22. U.S. President Eisenhower, in talks with King Mohammed V in Casablanca, agreed to the **evacuation of U.S. military bases**

by the end of 1963.

1960, Mar. 6. U.S. forces evacuated the base at Ben Slimane under the terms of the agreement of December 1959.

Apr. 19. Tangier was integrated economically with Morocco.

May 20. King Mohammed V dismissed Premier Abdullah Ibrahim and his cabinet, and asked party leaders to support his efforts to establish a **government of national union** around the throne. On May 26 the king installed his new cabinet with his son, **Crown Prince Moulay Hassan,** as deputy premier.

1961, Feb. 26. King Mohammed V died in Rabat, and Crown Prince Moulay Hassan was proclaimed **King Hassan II.**

May 3. King Hassan delegated the powers of the premiership to **Ahmed Reda Guedira,** director of the royal cabinet.

Aug. 20. King Hassan II promised to "liberate" territory to the north and to the south which, according to him, belonged to Morocco. The territories to which he referred belonged to Spain, Algeria, and Mauritania.

Sept. 1. Morocco took control of the last Spanish bases, evacuated by Spain the day before. On September 30 France turned over the last **French air base at Marrakesh.**

1962, Jan. 23. King Hassan II announced an **agreement with the Algerian provisional government** leaders to set up a Moroccan-Algerian commission to lay the groundwork for a "United Arab Maghrab," i.e., a North African Union.

Nov. 18-19. King Hassan II announced the draft of a **new constitution,** to be presented to the voters on December 7, 1962. The draft constitution declared Morocco to be "a democratic, social monarchy," and provided for a bicameral parliament and a premier responsible to the king.

1965, June 7. In the midst of student riots and other disturbances **King Hassan declared a state of emergency** and assumed both executive and legislative power. The **constitution and the parliament were suspended** and the king undertook to act as prime minister (till 1967).

Oct. 29. Mehdi Ben Barka, an opposition leader in exile in France, **was kidnaped and slain in Paris,** supposedly by Moroccan enemies. King Hassan at once denied any implication on the part of the Moroccan government.

1966, Feb. 21. President de Gaulle charged the Moroccan minister of the interior, **General Oufkir,** with responsibility for the kidnaping. French aid to Morocco was suspended and for some time relations between the two countries remained tense.

1967, Feb. Visit of King Hassan to the United States, where he was given promises of economic and military support.

June. A French court sentenced Gen. Oufkir (*in absentia*) to imprisonment for life.

1969, June 30. Spain, under pressure from the U.N., **ceded Ifni to Morocco.**

Sept. 22-23. The **Islamic conference at Rabat** (p. 1286).

Dec. 16. Restoration of diplomatic relations with France.

1970, July 25. End of the absolute rule of King Hassan. By a new constitution the parliament was restored, though the king retained a veto power over legislation.

b. ALGERIA

(*From p. 1081*)

1945, May 8. Clashes between Algerian Nationalists and the French in Algeria caused the death of 88 French and over 1000 Algerians. A manifesto issued before the riots called for an autonomous Algeria, federated with France.

1947, Sept. 1. A new statute for Algeria granted French citizenship to all Algerians, created an Algerian assembly, and gave financial autonomy to the region. The nationalist movement continued to mount, however, and on

1954, Oct. 31. Open **revolt against France** broke out. The rebels were organized and led by the **Front de Libération National** (FLN).

1955, Oct. 1. France protested against U.N. discussion of the Algerian situation, and (Oct. 19) passed reform legislation which, Premier Faure argued, would justify **French refusal to accept U.N. intervention.**

1957, July 9. French **President Coty** emphatically restated the French government's refusal to grant Algeria independence. On July 18 the national assembly voted **special powers to Premier Bourgès-Maunoury** to suppress the activities of agents of the Algerian rebels operating in France.

1958, May 15. The day on which General de Gaulle agreed to take office, an **Algiers committee of public safety,** led by **General Jacques Massu,** announced its intention to act as a governing body.

June 6. General de Gaulle informed the Algiers committee of public safety that he was leaving control of Algeria in the hands of **General Raoul Salan,** on orders solely from Paris, but acts of defiance of de Gaulle's government continued throughout June.

July 13. In a radio message to overseas possessions, de Gaulle offered Algeria a key vote in a **new federal system** to link France and her overseas possessions.

Sept. 19. Algerian rebel leaders in Cairo

proclaimed a **provisional government** for the **republic of Algeria,** with **Ferhat Abbas** as premier.

Oct. 25. The Algerian provisional government rejected de Gaulle's offer (issued on October 24) to negotiate a cease-fire, but kept open the possibility of French-Algerian negotiations anywhere but in Paris.

Dec. 12. **Paul Delouvrier** replaced General Raoul Salan as delegate-general in Algeria, responsible only to the French premier. Air Force **General Maurice Challe** was named commander-in-chief of the armed forces in Algeria, and General Salan was appointed inspector-general of national defense, a newly created post.

1959, June 12. **Premier Ferhat Abbas** declared that his rebel government was willing to meet with French officials on neutral ground to discuss the Algerian situation.

Sept. 16. President de Gaulle, in a Paris address, **offered Algerians the right to choose independence, integration with France, or an autonomous federal régime** associated with France. He stated that the referendum on which Algerians decided their own fate would take place within four years after peaceful conditions were restored in Algeria.

Sept. 28. The Algerian provisional government, in a communiqué, declared its willingness to discuss a cease-fire and de Gaulle's plan of self-determination for Algeria, but the French government refused to reply to the communiqué.

1960, Jan. 25–Feb. 1. **French ultranationalists raised an insurrection** which soon collapsed.

June 14. President de Gaulle renewed and clarified his offer to seek an "honorable" peace with the Algerian rebel leaders. On June 20 the Algerian nationalists agreed to send a **peace mission to Paris.** Secret talks began on June 25 as representatives of France and the Algerian rebels faced each other in Paris for the first time since 1954. The preliminary peace talks ended on June 24 without a formal conclusion.

Dec. 9. **President de Gaulle began a five-day tour of Algeria** to promote his plan for steps toward Algerian independence. On December 11 French paratroopers clashed with Europeans in Algiers and more than sixty persons were killed. On December 16 Premier Ferhat Abbas of the Algerian provisional government urged Moslems to work against the referendum.

1961, Apr. 21–22. **French army troops in Algeria staged an insurrection** and seized control of Algiers, but were defeated (Apr. 26) and Algiers reoccupied by loyal French army forces.

May 20. France and Algerian Moslem rebels opened **peace talks in Évian-les-Bains,** France. The delegation of the Algerian provisional government-in-exile was headed by its foreign minister and vice-premier, **Belkacem Krim.** Louis Joxe led the French delegation. France suspended negotiations, June 13.

July 5. Moslem nationalists staged a **general strike in Algeria** to protest the possible partition of the country by France, although earlier (June 12) Tunisian **President Bourguiba** and Mali **President Keita** had called the Sahara "an integral part of African territory" and not Algerian.

July 28. French-Algerian peace negotiations, resumed on July 20 in Lugrin, France, were suspended following France's refusal to recognize the **rebels' claims to the Algerian Sahara.**

Aug. 27. **Ben Youssef ben Khedda** was named the new premier of the provisional government, replacing the more moderate Ferhat Abbas.

Sept. 5. President de Gaulle declared his willingness to yield **sovereignty over the Sahara** to an independent Algeria that would cooperate with France.

1962, Jan. 4. As violence continued to sweep Algerian cities, **Raoul Salan,** head of the illegal **Secret Army Organization** (OAS), issued a manifesto calling for the mobilization of Algerians to prevent an Algerian cease-fire between France and Algerian rebel leaders.

Mar. 18. French and Algerian rebel representatives in Évian-les-Bains, France, signed a **cease-fire agreement** (effective March 19) ending the seven-year war in Algeria.

Mar. 23. After a renewal of violence in Algeria, de Gaulle instructed the French army to wage all-out war to suppress an OAS revolt, to which the OAS replied in kind (Mar. 28).

Apr. 7. The **provisional executive** to govern Algeria through the transition to independence was officially installed.

Apr. 20. French forces in Algiers seized Raoul Salan, French ex-general and commander of the OAS, but the **French-OAS conflict** continued in May and June.

July 1. Algerians, voting in a **national referendum,** approved independence (5,975,581 to 16,534), and on July 3 **FRANCE FORMALLY PROCLAIMED ALGERIA'S INDEPENDENCE.**

July. As Algeria gained independence, leaders of the provisional government fell out, **Deputy Premier Mohammed Ben Bella** impugning the legality of Premier Ben Khedda's government.

Aug. 2. Leaders of the provisional government and the rival Nationalist faction compromised their differences by agreeing that Vice-Premier Ben Bella's **political bureau** should supplant the provisional government until elections could be held. On August 7 the provisional government formally divested itself of its powers in favor of the political bureau.

Aug. 25. The political bureau announced that the **resistance of local military leaders** (especially in Algiers and the Kabylie Mountains) necessitated an indefinite postponement of the elections to the constituent assembly.

Sept. 13. After a **cease-fire** between the political bureau and Algiers military leaders (Sept. 5), a new list of candidates for election to the first national assembly was published which excluded ex-Premier Ben Khedda and fifty-two others who had appeared on an August 20 slate.

Sept. 25. The **national assembly,** elected on September 20, met and chose **Ferhat Abbas** as speaker. On September 26 it voted to ask **Mohammed Ben Bella** to form a government. On September 29 the national assembly voted approval of Ben Bella's eighteen-member cabinet.

Oct. 8. The U.N. admitted Algeria to membership.

1963, Mar. 19. The government protested a French underground **test of a nuclear device** in the Sahara, and on March 20 Premier Ben Bella demanded France negotiate a ban on tests in the Sahara.

Oct.–Nov. An **Algerian–Moroccan frontier war,** in which Egypt participated on the side of Algeria, ended with an agreement to arbitrate the frontier dispute.

1964, Feb. 20. President Ben Bella announced a **cease-fire agreement** with Morocco terminating the border war.

Apr. 16–21. The first **congress of the National Liberation Front** (the only legal party in Algeria) met and elected President Ben Bella secretary-general. The congress also approved a central committee, which, on April 23, selected a new seventeen-member political bureau.

May 7. President Ben Bella ended a visit to Moscow with a long-term loan of $128.5 million to be used to construct a Soviet-designed and equipped steel mill.

June 15. **Withdrawal of the last French troops,** except from the naval base at Mers el Kébir.

July 13. Formation of a **People's Militia,** under Ben Bella, to deal with local insurrections.

1965, June 19. DEPOSITION OF PRESIDENT BEN BELLA by **Colonel Houari**

Boumédienne, the minister of defense, who set up a National Council of the Algerian Revolution to replace the national assembly. **Boumédienne became president** (July 5).

1966, May 8. Nationalization of mines. A national bank was established (May 23) and insurance companies were made a state monopoly (May 27). Boumédienne made no secret of his socialist program and, in the war with Israel, of his intense nationalism.

1967, June. Visit of President Boumédienne to Moscow, where he was promised Soviet aid.

July 26. The armed forces were mobilized and (Oct.) compulsory military service introduced.

Aug. 7. Algeria refused to associate itself with the cease-fire in the Arab-Israeli war (p. 1285).

1968, Apr. An abortive attempt was made on the life of President Boumédienne.

1969, Jan. Visit of Boumédienne to Morocco and gradual settlement of frontier and other issues troubling the relations of the two neighbors.

c. TUNISIA

(*From p. 1081*)

1943, May 15. Sidi Lamine Bey was appointed ruler by General Henri Giraud, French military and civil commander in North Africa.

1951, Feb. 8. The French government announced an agreement with Tunisia giving that protectorate **increased autonomy** within the French Union.

1952, Jan. 14. The government of Tunisia appealed to the United Nations security council for a hearing on its **demands for autonomy.** The appeal was denied. **Anti-French riots** and disorders continued to shake the protectorate.

Mar. 28. The bey of Tunis yielded to French pressure and removed **Premier Mohammed Chenik,** who had supported the views of the **New Independence Party. Salah Eddine ben Mohammed Baccouche** was appointed premier.

Mar. 15. The bey of Tunis, yielding to a threatened French crackdown, called on his people to end their month-long **campaign of violence.** Meanwhile, the United States was strongly urging France to speed the execution of its home-rule reform program for Tunisia.

June 23. Nationalists rejected the recent French offer of reforms to provide greater **home rule for Tunisia,** and, instead, demanded an international conference to settle the dispute.

Dec. 20. Under pressure by France, the bey of Tunis signed two decrees, which he

had earlier rejected, to begin a French program of administrative reform.

1954, July 30. A proposal by **Premier Mendès-
France** to give Tunisia **complete internal independence** was approved by the French cabinet.

Aug. 7. A new government was formed by
Tahar ben Ammar.

Dec. 10. Premier Mendès-France announced his government's **opposition to complete independence** for any of the French territories in North Africa, including Tunisia.

1955, Apr. 21. French **Premier Faure** and Tunisian nationalist leader **Habib Bourguiba** concluded an **agreement on autonomy** for the
protectorate.

June 3. French Premier Faure and Tunisian **Premier Tahar ben Ammar** signed, in Paris,
conventions providing for Tunisia's **internal
autonomy.**

1956, Mar. 20. French **Foreign Minister
Pineau** and Tunisian **Premier Tahar ben Am-
mar**, meeting in Paris, signed a **protocol on
Tunisian independence.**

Mar. 25. The national front, led by Habib
Bourguiba's **Neo-Destour Party,** was victorious
in elections for a constituent assembly.

Apr. 10. At the invitation of the bey of
Tunis, **Sidi Mohammed el-Amin, Habib Bour-
guiba** accepted his appointment as **premier** of
Tunisia.

1957, July 25. The **national constituent assembly deposed the bey of Tunis,** Sidi Mohammed el-Amin, **and proclaimed a republic.
Premier Bourguiba was elected president.**

Sept. 12. After declaring, on September
9, a state of emergency along the Tunisian-
Algerian frontier due to **border clashes** involving French troops and Algerians, President
Bourguiba appealed to the United States for
arms.

Nov. 14. Despite French protests, the
**United States and Britain agreed to supply
small arms** to Tunisia. On November 18 the
government disclosed that it had rejected a
Soviet offer of arms.

1958, Feb. 8. French planes bombed the Tunisian village of Sakiet-Sidi-Youssef, killing
seventy-nine Tunisians.

May 24–25. French and Tunisian troops
clashed at Remada and Gabès, Tunisia.

June 17. A **French-Tunisian agreement**
provided for the withdrawal of French troops
from Tunisia (excepting **Bizerte**) and for the
negotiation of a special arrangement for
French forces in Bizerte.

Oct. 1. Tunisia joined the Arab League.

1959, June 1. President Habib Bourguiba
signed a **new constitution** establishing a presi-
dential-type republic.

Nov. 8. President Bourguiba was over-
whelmingly re-elected.

1961, July 19–20. Tunisian forces besieging the
French military base at Bizerte were defeated
and **Tunisia severed relations with France.**

July 22. The U.N. security council
adopted a resolution calling for a cease-fire in
Tunisia; French and Tunisian forces ordered a
cessation of hostilities.

Sept. 18. French and Tunisian delegates
reached agreement on a French troop withdrawal from the city of Bizerte and its surrounding territory. On September 29 they
signed an agreement providing for the **evacuation of French troops from Bizerte city.**

**1962, July 20. France and Tunisia resumed dip-
lomatic relations.**

1964, Jan. 10. One day after Premier **Chou-
En-lai** arrived in Tunis, Tunisia recognized the
government of Communist China.

May 11. The government announced the
nationalization of all foreign-owned farmlands,
abrogating an agreement with France of March
1963.

1967, June. In the **Arab-Israeli war** President
Bourguiba attempted to play the role of mod-
erator, advising recognition of Israel as a state
and agreement on a compromise settlement of
territorial issues. This position brought him
into ill repute among Arab nationalists.

1969, Nov. 2. President Bourguiba was re-
elected for a third five-year term.

Nov. 6. Bahi Ladgham, the secretary-general
of the ruling Destourian Socialist Party, became
the new premier.

d. LIBYA

(From p. 1081)

Libya was conquered by the Italians before
the First World War and lost by them in the
Second.

1949, Nov. 21. The general assembly of the
United Nations voted to grant **independence to
Libya** to take effect on January 1, 1952.

1950, Dec. 3. The constituent assembly
adopted a resolution formally proclaiming
Mohammed Idris el-Senussi as **King Idris I** of
Libya.

1951, Dec. 24. The **constitution,** prepared by
the constituent assembly, came into force
with the formal **declaration of independence.**
It provided for a federation of Cyrenaica, Tripolitania, and the Fezzan, and a bicameral
federal legislature.

1964, Mar. 16. The chamber of deputies, by
unanimous vote, ordered the government to
negotiate the **liquidation of British and United
States bases** on Libyan soil.

1966, Mar. Departure of the last British troops from Tripolitania.

1967, June. The Libyan government requested the British and United States governments to withdraw their remaining forces at the earliest possible date.

1968. The **Libyan oil production** passed that of Kuwait and became second only to that of Saudi Arabia. In the **Arab-Israeli war** (p. 1285) the Libyan government made a generous financial contribution to the governments of Egypt, Jordan, and Syria to compensate them for the losses they had suffered.

1969. Libya actually overtook Saudi Arabia as **the largest oil producer in the Middle East.**

Apr. Treaty of friendship and co-operation signed with Algeria.

Sept. 1. KING IDRIS WAS DEPOSED by a military coup led by the young **Captain Muammar el-Qaddafi.** Parliament was dissolved and a **revolutionary council** set up in its place. The new **LIBYAN ARAB REPUBLIC** was fanatically anti-Israeli and wholly devoted to the Arab and Palestinian causes.

1970, Jan. 7. The French government agreed to sell Libya $400 million in armaments, including 200 tanks and 50 Mirage jets.

Jan. 16. Muammar el-Qaddafi became premier on the resignation of Mahmud Soliman al-Maghreby.

Mar. 31. Departure of the last British troops.

June 11. Closure of the United States air base at Wheelus Field, which was taken over by Libya.

July 5. Nationalization of oil-distributing companies.

July 21. Confiscation of Italian and Jewish properties.

e. EGYPT
(THE UNITED ARAB REPUBLIC)

(*From p. 1078*)

1939, Sept. 3. Although **Egypt strove to remain neutral** in the Second World War it became a battle ground between British and Axis forces. For the military campaigns fought there, see p. 1147.

1945, Jan. 8. A **general election** (boycotted by the Wafd party) secured a majority for the government of **Prime Minister Ahmed Pasha.**

Feb. 24. The **premier was assassinated** after announcing that Egypt would declare war against the Axis powers. His successor was **Nokrashy Pasha.**

Sept. 23. The **Egyptian government demanded that the Anglo-Egyptian treaty of 1936** (p. 1078) be **revised,** that British military occupation of Egypt be terminated, and that the Sudan be transferred to full Egyptian control.

1946, May 9. In face of growing anti-British agitation, the British government announced its readiness to withdraw its forces from Egypt.

1947, Jan. 25. Great Britain informed Egypt of its intention to prepare the **Sudan** for self-government.

Jan. 26. After breaking off negotiations with Great Britain for revision of the 1936 treaty, the Egyptian government decided to refer the question to the **United Nations.** The matter came before the security council on August 5, but no decision was reached.

1948, May 15. Egyptian forces moved into **Palestine** to intervene on the Arab side against the Israelis (p. 1302).

Dec. 28. Premier Nokrashy Pasha was assassinated and replaced first by **Abdul Hadi Pasha** and subsequently (July 26, 1949) by **Hussein Sirry Pasha.**

1950, Jan. 3. A **general election** returned an overwhelming majority for the **Wafd** (Nationalist) Party, thus ending five years of government by minorities.

Jan. 12. Mustafa el-Nahas Pasha became prime minister and reopened negotiations with Great Britain for revision of the 1936 treaty.

Nov. 16. Mustafa el-Nahas Pasha demanded before parliament the withdrawal of Britain from the Suez Canal zone and the Sudan.

Nov. 20. Great Britain reiterated its intention to work toward a self-governing Sudan.

1951, Sept. 1. The U.N. security council, with the U.S.S.R., China, and India abstaining, approved a resolution calling on Egypt to end its **restrictions preventing ships bound for Israel** from using the Suez Canal. Egypt charged that the resolution was illegal and violated Egypt's rights.

Oct. 27. Egypt formally abrogated the 1936 treaty of alliance with Great Britain and their 1899 condominium agreement covering the Sudan.

1952, Jan. 18. The British cruiser *Liverpool* fired on Port Said as **British troops clashed with Egyptian guerrillas** there. Two days later British troops entered Ismailia. A climax of violence frightening to the Egyptian government was reached on January 26 when **riots in Cairo** brought death to over twenty people and wholesale destruction of foreign properties. Next day King Farouk named **Ali Maher Pasha** to succeed Mustafa el-Nahas Pasha as premier.

Mar. 1. Premier Ali Maher Pasha resigned, and was replaced by **Naguib al Hilaili Pasha,** a former member of the Wafd Party.

May. Efforts of Great Britain to compose differences over the Suez Canal and the Sudan were fruitless.

July 23. KING FAROUK WAS OVERTHROWN in a military coup, led by **Major General Mohammed Naguib Bey.** The next day Ali Maher Pasha became premier and **King Farouk abdicated** and went into exile while his infant son was proclaimed **Fuad II,** king of Egypt and the Sudan.

Sept. 7. Consolidating his power as both military and political ruler, Gen. Naguib removed the premier, imprisoned forty-seven Egyptian leaders, and took over the posts of premier, minister of war, and minister of marine.

Oct. 6. Yielding to intensified government pressure, the **Wafd Party's executive committee** ousted its leader, former Premier Mustafa el-Nahas, and six other officers.

Oct. 29. Premier Naguib signed a final **agreement with the Sudanese independence parties,** providing for a joint program for the Sudan's further political development.

Dec. 10. Naguib **cancelled the constitution** and announced the transfer of authority to "a transitional government."

1953, Jan. 17. The cabinet decreed the **extension of Naguib's absolute powers** for one year, and formally dissolved all political parties because of their "unco-operative attitude."

1954, Jan. 13. The government ordered the dissolution of the fanatical **Moslem Brotherhood** because of its interference in political affairs, and arrested seventy-eight of its leaders.

Apr. 17. Colonel Gamal Abdel Nasser replaced Naguib as premier as a result of maneuvering among the military leaders in the revolution council.

Oct. 19. A **treaty with Britain** provided that the latter give up its rights to the Suez base and **evacuate the Canal Zone** within twenty months. Egypt promised to keep the base in combat readiness and to permit British reentry in case of an attack by an outside power upon Turkey or any Arab state.

1955. Sept. 27. Nasser announced an **agreement with the Communist bloc** pledging rice and cotton in return for Czechoslovak arms.

1956, Jan. 16. Nasser presented a **new constitution** to Egypt, subject to popular approval in a June plebiscite. The constitution provided for a republic headed by a president, elected for a six-year term by the national assembly. All political parties were to be suppressed until the national assembly enacted legislation to regulate their formation. In the meantime, a **National Union** would nominate all candidates for the national assembly.

May 20. Poland agreed to supply arms to Egyptian forces.

May 30. Following **recognition of Communist China,** diplomatic relations were established.

June 23. Egyptians voted approval of the new constitution, and elected **GAMAL ABDEL NASSER PRESIDENT.**

July 19–20. The United States and Britain announced the **withdrawal of their aid offers to Egypt** for construction of the **Aswan high dam.**

July 26. Nasser nationalized the Suez Canal Company in order to provide revenue for the Aswan high dam. For the Suez Canal crisis, see p. 1282.

Sept. 14. Egypt assumed complete control of the Suez Canal's operation.

1957, Apr. 28. U.N. clearance of the Suez Canal, obstructed by sunken vessels since November, was completed.

July 3. The first **parliamentary elections** since the revolution returned a government-picked slate.

1958, Feb. 1. President Nasser and Syrian President Shukri al-Kuwatly signed a proclamation in Cairo forming the **UNITED ARAB REPUBLIC** which voters in both countries approved, February 21.

July 13. A final settlement was reached in Geneva determining the amount of UAR **compensation to shareholders of the Universal Suez Canal Company.** The UAR agreed to pay $64.8 million, in sterling or French francs.

Oct. 23. The U.S.S.R. agreed to lend $100 million toward the construction of the Aswan high dam.

1960, Jan. 9. Nasser inaugurated construction of the Aswan high dam on the Nile River.

July 19. Nasser named **Nureddin Kuhalla** to be Syrian vice-president, the highest Syrian governmental post.

On July 21 the first **parliament of the UAR** opened in Cairo with 400 Egyptian and 200 Syrian deputies.

1961, Sept. 29. Syria withdrew from the UAR (p. 1299).

1962, May 21. At the opening of the 1750-member Egyptian **National Congress of Popular Forces,** President Nasser read his "National Charter of Socialist Principles," providing for future parliamentary elections. The charter outlined ideal "Arab socialism" and the "model Arab state."

Sept. 19. Egyptian involvement in the Yemeni civil war (p. 1306).

Sept. 24. Nasser announced a **reorganization of the government** along "group leadership" lines. He named **Aly Sabry premier.**

1963, Apr. 17. The UAR, Iraq, and Syria signed an agreement to form a new tripartite Arab state.

July 22. Nasser renounced the proposed union of the UAR with Syria and Iraq so long as the Baath Party held power in Syria.

1964, May 9. Khrushchev was warmly welcomed on his **first visit to Egypt.**

May 15. The first stage of the Aswan high dam was completed.

Dec. 20. The UAR and Iraq agreed on the establishment of a high political authority, headed by the two presidents.

1965, Feb. 24. Discontinuance of West German aid to Egypt in protest against the visit of East German President Ulbricht to Cairo. Much friction had developed earlier as a result of West German arms supplies to Israel (p. 1198).

Aug. 24. Agreement of Nasser and King Faisal of Saudi Arabia for an immediate cease-fire in Yemen (p. 1306).

Sept. 29. Resignation of Premier Aly Sabry, who was succeeded by vice-president **Zacharia Mohieddin.**

1966, Aug. 21–Sept. 22. Trial and conviction of several hundred members **of the Muslim Brotherhood** for allegedly plotting against Nasser and the existing régime.

Sept. 10. Sidki Suleiman became premier.

Nov. 7. Agreement with Syria for mutual defense and economic coordination, ending a period of mutual recrimination.

1967, June 5. OUTBREAK OF THE ARAB-ISRAELI WAR (p. 1285).

June 6. Severance of diplomatic relations with Britain and the United States, powers charged with having participated in the Israeli air attack on Egypt.

June 9. Nasser offered to resign and named Zacharia Mohieddin as his successor. Great popular demonstrations induced him to change his mind. He thereupon undertook a thorough **purge of the army and air force. Marshal Sidki Mahmud** and his aides were arrested and tried (Oct. 29). Marshal **Abdel Hakim Amer** committed suicide (Sept. 14). Many other officers were imprisoned.

June 21–23. Visit of Soviet President Podgorny to Cairo with assurances of large-scale Soviet military and economic assistance to aid in the recovery of Egyptian power.

July 10. Visit of a Soviet naval squadron to Egypt, the beginning of the expansion of Soviet naval power in the eastern Mediterranean.

Oct. 24. Destruction of the Suez refineries and pipeline by Israeli attack.

Dec. 12. Resumption of diplomatic relations with Britain.

1968, Sept. 17. First meeting of the **Arab Socialist Union** and appointment of a central committee and higher executive committee. Government thenceforth was to be by the party, overshadowing the cabinet and the national assembly.

1968–1970. For the **Egyptian intervention in the Yemeni civil war** see pp. 1307–1308.

1970, June 29–July 17. Prolonged visit of Nasser to the U.S.S.R.

Sept. 28. DEATH OF PRESIDENT GAMEL ABDEL NASSER, of heart attack. His funeral was attended by Soviet Premier Kosygin and by high officials of many countries, including the U.S.

Oct. 5. Anwar es-Sadat, vice-president under Nasser, was chosen by the United Socialist Union to succeed as president, subject to approval of the national assembly and of a public plebiscite (Oct. 16).

Oct. 18. Foreign Minister Riad, at the U.N. general assembly, flatly rejected suggestions that Egypt withdraw at least a token number of missile bases, so as to make possible the resumption of peace talks. He repeated his earlier denial that new missile sites had been established after the proclamation of the cease-fire.

Oct. 20. Mahmud Fawzi, veteran diplomat and former foreign minister, **was appointed prime minister.**

Nov. 8. Announcement of plans for the **eventual federation of the UAR, the Sudan, and Libya.** These three powers had signed an alliance in Dec. 1969, but the problems of closer union were still under consideration.

3. THE MIDDLE EAST

a. CYPRUS

After 1945 agitation mounted in Cyprus among the Greek population for *Enosis,* **union with Greece,** but the Turkish population, about 20 per cent of the whole, opposed it. **Anti-British demonstrations,** sometimes bloody, and the conflicting views of Greece and Turkey made Great Britain's position extremely difficult.

1955, Aug. 29. British, Turkish, and Greek representatives began a **London conference** on the problem of Cyprus. The conference became deadlocked, September 7.

1956, Feb. 2. With control of internal security the prime issue, **Archbishop Makarios,** who had become the spokesman for the Greek Cypriotes, turned down the British proposal for gradual independence, demanding immediate internal sovereignty.

Mar. 9.   Britain deported Makarios to the Seychelles.

July 2. Turkey rejected a British plan for the eventual self-determination of Cyprus.

1957, Mar. 28. Following his compliance with a British demand that he call for an end to terrorist activities in Cyprus, **Makarios was released** from detention, with permission to go anywhere except to Cyprus. On March 29 he announced his refusal to participate in British negotiations on the Cyprus issue until he was free to return to Cyprus.

1958. Throughout the year **fruitless negotiations** continued, but after the Greek Cypriote underground, led by **Colonel George Grivas,** declared a truce in its anti-Turkish and anti-British violence (Aug. 4), slow progress toward a solution began.

1959, Feb. 19. British Prime Minister Macmillan, Greek Premier Karamanlis, Turkish Premier Menderes, Greek Cypriote leader Archbishop Makarios, and Turkish Cypriote leader Fazil Kutchuk signed an **agreement** in London **to establish Cyprus as an independent republic.** The British would retain sovereignty over two military enclaves; Cypriote independence was scheduled for a date prior to February 19, 1960; the president of the new republic was to be an ethnic Greek Cypriote and was to be elected by the ethnic Greek Cypriote community, while the vice-president was to be an ethnic Turkish Cypriote elected by the ethnic Turkish community; the legislature was to be 70 per cent Greek Cypriote and 30 per cent Turkish Cypriote. "Protecting forces" from Greece, Turkey, and Britain would safeguard the island.

Dec. 13. ARCHBISHOP MAKARIOS, who had returned to the island on March 1, was **ELECTED PRESIDENT OF CYPRUS.**

1960, Aug. 16. CYPRUS BECAME AN INDEPENDENT REPUBLIC. Makarios was sworn in as president and **Fazil Kutchuk** as vice-president. Great Britain, Greece, and Turkey signed the **treaty of guarantee.**

1963, Dec. 21.   Fighting erupted between Greek and Turkish Cypriotes when Turkish Cypriotes interpreted Greek attempts to amend the Cypriote constitution as a threat to Turkish minority rights.

1964, Jan. 1.   President Makarios announced his decision to abrogate the treaties of guarantee with Britain, Greece, and Turkey.

Jan. 15. Delegates from Turkey, Greece, the Greek and Turkish elements on Cyprus, and Great Britain opened **talks in London.**

Feb. 7.   Khrushchev warned NATO members that interference in internal Cypriote affairs might threaten "general peace."

Feb. 14. Great Britain, supported by the United States, requested the U.N. security council to consider establishing an **international peace force** to restore order in Cyprus. The Cypriote government, on the 18th, asked for a guarantee of its independence and territorial integrity, to replace the British-Greek-Turkish agreement.

Mar. 4. The **U.N. security council** adopted a resolution to establish a peace-keeping force in Cyprus.

Mar. 25. U Thant named Finnish Ambassador to Sweden, **Sakari S. Tuomioja,** to serve as the U.N. mediator in Cyprus. Two days later, U.N. troops from Ireland, Sweden, and Canada began their peace-keeping operation.

Apr.–May. Efforts of the U.N. security council, Premier Papandreou of Greece, and Makarios of Cyprus to find a solution to Cypriote problems failed, while sporadic Greek-Turkish fighting continued despite the U.N. peace force.

June 4. In anticipation of a possible Turkish attack on Cyprus, **President Johnson warned the Turkish government** against any attempt to invade the island and sent Gen. Lyman Lemnitzer to Ankara to underline the U.S. position. On June 5 the Turkish government announced the abandonment of plans for landings on the island.

June 20. The U.N. security council voted to continue the **U.N. peacekeeping operation** in Cyprus, consisting of some 6000 men, financed by voluntary contributions of U.N. members, for another three months. In the sequel the operation was renewed again and again for specified periods.

June 22–23. Visit successively to Washington of Turkish Premier Inönü and (June 24–25) of Greek Premier Papandreou. Efforts of U.S. officials to mediate proved abortive.

July. Fighting between Greek and Turkish Cypriots continued unabated, each faction receiving men and supplies from its home country. All efforts at compromise having failed, on

Aug. 7–9.   Turkish planes attacked Greek Cypriot positions, following a Greek Cypriot attack on the Turkish beachhead. Makarios appealed to the Soviet Union and to Egypt for support, but the U.N. was able eventually to effect a cease-fire (Aug. 10).

Sept. The Cypriot government finally lifted the blockade of the Turkish Cypriot areas.

1965.   Sporadic factional strife continued, but most incidents were successfully dealt with by the U.N. representative.

Mar. 31. The report of the U.N. mediator, **Dr. Galo Plaza,** rejected both annexation to Greece and annexation of Turkish sections to Turkey as acceptable solutions.

1966, May 17. Beginning of discussions between the Greek and Turkish governments, which continued throughout the year.

Dec. 4–16. **A new crisis** threatened when it was learned that the Cypriot government was purchasing arms from Czechoslovakia. The Turkish government demanded that they be put under U.N. control and (Dec. 13) threatened to use force to halt further deliveries. The Cypriot government rejected the Turkish demands (Dec. 16).

1967, Nov. 14–Dec. 8. **ACUTE DANGER OF WAR** developed when Greek Cypriot police began to patrol Turkish areas, with resulting fighting. The Turkish government thereupon sent an **ultimatum to Greece** threatening war and the invasion of Cyprus. It demanded the recall of General Grivas and the Greek army forces (some 20,000) that had been sent to Cyprus over the years. **The Greek government thereupon recalled Grivas** (Nov. 19), while both U Thant for the U.N. and President Johnson for the U.S. dispatched special envoys to Athens, Ankara, and Nicosia. Nonetheless, the Turkish president declared (Nov. 24) the determination of his country to settle the Cyprus question once and for all. The American envoy finally succeeded in arranging an agreement, and on Dec. 7 the **Greek government began the withdrawal of its forces.**

1968, Mar. The Cypriot government lifted all economic restrictions on the Turkish community and removed the roadblocks.

May 23. Greek and Turkish Cypriot leaders met for **communal talks** under U.N. auspices.

June 24–July 25. **Formal talks** followed at Nicosia and were resumed in the autumn (Aug. 29–Dec. 9).

1969, Aug. 28. A terrorist **national front** was outlawed after a series of bombings and assassinations.

Dec. 11. **The U.N. security council voted once again to maintain the peacekeeping force in Cyprus,** and then (June 9, 1970) extended it to Dec. 15, 1970.

b. TURKEY

(*From p. 1088*)

1939, Sept. 3. **Turkey preserved neutrality** on the outbreak of the Second World War.

Oct. 19. **Britain and France** offered and Turkey accepted **a fifteen-year mutual assistance pact.**

1940, Nov. 1. **President Ismet Inönü** declared it to be the Turkish policy to remain a nonbelligerent while maintaining friendship with Britain and Soviet Russia.

1943, Feb. 28. The **People's Party** elected all 455 deputies of the national parliament (*kamutay*). **Gen. Ismet Inönü** was re-elected president of the republic (Mar. 8).

1945, Jan. 6. **The Turkish government broke off diplomatic relations with Japan.**

Mar. 19. The Soviet Union denounced the **Turco-Soviet non-aggression pact of 1925.** Turkey subsequently rejected Soviet demands for territorial concessions and a revision of the Montreux convention by the Black Sea powers.

1946, Jan. 8. Following repeated demands for an opposition party, the government admitted the **Democratic Party** under former Premier **Jelal Bayar.** The new party won 66 seats (against the official People's Party's 395) at the **general election** on July 21.

Aug. 3. **Recep Peker** of the People's Party succeeded **Saracoglu** as prime minister.

Aug. 5. **ISMET INÖNÜ** was re-elected president.

1947, Mar. 12. President Truman announced a program of military and economic aid to Turkey **(Truman Doctrine).**

Sept. 10. **Hassan Saka** formed a new cabinet.

1948. As might be expected, Turkey's progress toward democracy was slow. Repeatedly President Inönü had to act as mediator between his own People's Party, reluctant to abandon its monopoly of power, and the Democratic Party, impatient to share that power. Gradually, however, the electoral system was reformed, the power of the police was restricted, and civil rights were restored. In May religious teaching, banned since 1923, was again permitted in primary schools. In foreign affairs the **non-aggression pacts with Britain and France** were reaffirmed, while relations with the Soviet Union continued cool.

1950, Mar. 24. Turkey signed a **treaty of friendship and conciliation** with Italy.

May 14. The **general elections** testified to the democratization of Turkey, as the **Democratic Party won an overwhelming majority,** with 407 seats against 69 for the People's Party. Democratic leader **JELAL BAYAR** became president, and **Adnan Menderes** prime minister.

Sept. 20. Turkey sent a contingent of 4500 men to join the U.N. forces in Korea.

1954, Mar. 7. **Turkey's oil industry was denationalized** in an effort to attract foreign capital.

Apr. 2. Turkey signed a **treaty of friendship with Pakistan.**

Apr. 16. A joint statement with Yugoslavia declared the objective of a **Balkan alliance** (p. 1208).

May 2. President Bayar's Democratic Party

won an overwhelming victory in national elections.

1955, Feb. 24. Turkey and Iraq signed the **Baghdad pact** for mutual defense and co-operation. On Iraq's withdrawal (1959) this became the Central Treaty Organization, of which Britain and Pakistan had become members.

Sept. 6. Anti-Greek riots in the cities of Istanbul and Izmir heightened tension between Turkey and Greece, already mounting over Cyprus (p. 1295).

1957, May 1. Turkish troops moved toward the Syrian border causing Syria (May 7) to issue a warning against the massing of Turkish forces.

Sept. 13. The Soviet Union warned Turkey not to prepare an attack on Syria.

Oct. 27. Premier Menderes' Democratic Party was victorious in parliamentary elections, set by the previous parliament upon dissolution (Sept. 11).

Nov. 1. President Jelal Bayar was re-elected by parliament for another four-year term.

1959, Oct. 10. The United States and Turkey announced agreement on the establishment of an **intermediate range ballistic missile base** in Turkey.

1960, May 27. Lt. General Jemal Gürsel, leading a group of high-ranking military officers, seized control of the government and ousted Premier Menderes. They established a military junta, called the **Turkish National Union Committee,** to organize free, fair elections.

Sept. 29. A civil court **abolished the Democratic Party,** which had ruled Turkey from 1950 to May 27, 1960.

1961, Sept. 12. Ex-premier **Adnan Menderes was executed,** following conviction for violating the Turkish constitution.

Oct. 15. Elections for the new Turkish parliament were held, signaling the transfer of government control from military to civilian hands. On October 23–24 the leaders of four major parties agreed to form a coalition government. On October 26 **General Gürsel was elected president** by parliament and sworn in.

Nov. 20. General Ismet Inönü, named premier on November 10, completed a cabinet composed of his own Republican People's Party and of Justice Party members.

1964, June 22–23. Premier Inönü conferred with U.S. President Johnson in Washington, in an effort to overcome the crisis in Cyprus (p. 1296).

Aug. 7. Turkish air raid on the west Cypriote coast, in reaction to campaign of the Cypriote Greeks against the Turkish minority.

Sept. 16. Expulsion of Greek nationals from Turkey, following the Turkish government's denunciation of the treaty of 1930 on rights of residence.

1965, Feb. 13. Fall of the Inönü cabinet, which was replaced by a caretaker government.

Oct. 10. The Justice Party (successor to the Democratic Party, 1961) **won a majority of seats** in parliament and formed a new cabinet with **Süleyman Demirel** as premier.

Dec. 7. A loan agreement with the Soviet Union reflected the improved relations of the two countries following Soviet support of the Turkish position on Cyprus.

1966, Mar. 28. GENERAL CEVDET SUNAY, the chief of staff, **WAS ELECTED PRESIDENT** to succeed Gen. Gürsel, incapacitated by a stroke (died Sept. 14).

1967, Sept. Meeting of the Turkish and Greek prime ministers in an effort to forestall further aggravation of the Cyprus issue.

Nov.–Dec. ACUTE DANGER OF WAR WITH GREECE, over Cyprus (p. 1297).

1968, Mar. Further **agreement with the Soviet Union** providing for aid in the construction of industrial plants.

Apr.–June. Violent **student demonstrations** and anti-American outbreaks. The universities accepted most of the student demands for examination reform, participation in administration, etc.

1969, Jan. Continuance of student and other radical protests, with resulting clashes with rightist groups and the police.

Oct. 12. The **elections** enabled the Justice Party to retain control.

Nov. 6. The senate approved the **restoration of political rights** (of which they had been deprived by the constitution of 1961) **to leaders of the defunct Democratic Party.**

c. SYRIA

(From p. 1090)

1939, Sept. 3. When the Second World War commenced a **Franco-Syrian treaty** of September 9, 1936, which promised that the French mandate over Syria would end in three years, was due to come into effect. The war delayed application of the treaty.

1940, June 28. After the fall of France and the conclusion of an armistice (June 22), the French announced a **truce in Syria.**

1941, June 8. British and Free French troops entered Syria and Lebanon to eliminate German influence.

Sept. 16. Syria was proclaimed an independent nation. The Free French leaders approved the decision.

1945, Feb. 26. Syria joined the United Nations.

May 21. The governments of **Syria and**

Lebanon broke relations with the French when the latter sent troops into these countries without asking consent. When rioting and resistance spread, the French troops were confined to barracks. The **French army shelled Damascus** in an attempt to assert control.

May 31. **Prime Minister Churchill** of Britain demanded that **Gen. de Gaulle** order the French forces in Syria and Lebanon to cease fire.

June 1. **De Gaulle** accused the British of meddlesome interference and **fighting continued in Damascus.** The British declared that the French were making use of lend-lease equipment to repress the Syrians and Lebanese. The French denied the charge.

Dec. 13. A **Franco-British agreement** pledged the **evacuation** of their troops from Syria. This was accomplished by April 15, 1946.

1947, July 2. The first election under universal manhood suffrage gave only a minority of seats to the government. At the request of **President Shukri al-Kuwatly, Prime Minister Jamil Mardam Bey** remained in office.

1948, Apr. 18. **Shukri al-Kuwatly** was re-elected president.

1949, Mar. 30. In a bloodless **coup,** the government was overthrown by **Chief of Staff Husni Za'im,** who was elected president on June 23.

Aug.–Dec. In a **second coup** (Aug. 14), **President Husni Za'im** was arrested and executed. **Hashim al-Atasi** was elected president on December 14. In a **third coup** (Dec. 19) a number of government members, accused of plotting a union with Iraq, were arrested.

1950, Sept. 4. A new constitution was adopted, limiting the powers of the president.

1951, May. 9. The **U.N. security council ordered a cease-fire** in the border skirmishes of several weeks with Israel (p. 1302).

Nov. 29. A **military coup** led to the arrest of pro-Soviet **Maarouf Dawalibi,** who had become prime minister the day before. The coup was executed by the army chief of staff, **Col. Adib Shishakli,** who on December 2 took over all government authority, with **Col. Fawzi Silo** as premier and defense minister.

1952, Oct. 24. Col. Adib Shishakli inaugurated his **Arab Liberation Movement** as Syria's sole political organization to replace the political parties he had dissolved during the summer.

1954, Feb. 25. An **army revolt** forced President Shishakli to resign. A threat of civil war ended, February 28, when former President **Hashim al-Atasi returned to office.**

1957, Aug.–Sept. **Syrian-United States tension** developed when Syria (Aug. 13) ousted three

U.S. embassy officials on a charge that they were plotting to overthrow President Shukri al-Kuwatly (p. 1283).

Oct. A **Syrian-Turkish crisis** arose (p. 1302).

1958, Feb. 1. An agreement in Cairo created the **United Arab Republic** (p. 1294).

Sept. 28. President Nasser issued a decree for **land reform,** according to which no one was to be permitted to own more than 300 hectares of land (741 acres).

1961, Sept. 28–29. **Syrian troops revolted.** The Syrian revolutionary command set up a civilian government for Syria and proclaimed **independence from the UAR.** Nasser withdrew the order sending Egyptian forces to quell the revolt. **Mahmoun al-Kuzbari,** the new premier and minister of foreign affairs and defense, named a ten-man cabinet, empowered by the rebels to rule by decree.

Dec. 1. In **parliamentary elections** conservative right-wing groups won a small majority. On December 14 the new parliament elected **Nazem el-Kodsi president,** who, on December 20, named **Maarouf Dawalibi premier.**

1962, Mar. 28. Syrian army leaders, in a bloodless coup, ousted the government elected after the Syrian break with Egypt in 1961.

Apr. 13. **Major-General Abdel Karim Zahreddin** announced that President Nazem el-Kodsi, ousted in March, had been returned to office. On April 14 President Kodsi declared that he would try to organize a union of "liberated Arab states, beginning with Egypt." **Bachir al-Azmah formed a cabinet.**

Sept. 14. The assembly named **Khaled el-Azm premier.** On September 20 Premier el-Azm and his cabinet dissolved parliament, and announced they would rule by decree until new elections, planned within a year.

1963, Mar. 8. A group of pro-Nasser and of Baath Party followers overthrew the Syrian government. The UAR and Iraq threatened war if anyone interfered in the Syrian revolt. On March 9 **Salah el-Bitar,** a Baath Party leader, was declared prime minister, and **Louai el-Attassi** the head of the **National Revolutionary Council.**

May 3. The coalition between Baathists and three Nasserite groups ended when five pro-Nasser cabinet ministers resigned. On May 8 **pro-Nasser riots** were staged in Damascus and North Syria.

May 11. Premier Salah el-Bitar (Baathist) resigned, and a pro-Nasser supporter, **Sami el-Jundi,** was named to form a new government. Following his failure, Premier el-Bitar returned to office on May 13 at the head of a cabinet led by the Baath Socialist Party.

July 10. The Baath Party's National Revolutionary Council named **General Amin el-Hafez** defense minister and army chief of staff. He was also interior minister, vice-premier, and deputy military governor. After an **unsuccessful pro-Nasser coup** on July 18, **Major General Amin el-Hafez,** on July 27, succeeded Lt. General Louai al-Attassi as army commander-in-chief and chairman of the ruling Revolutionary Council.

Aug. 4. Premier Salah el-Bitar formed a new cabinet evenly divided between Baathists and Independent Unionists.

1964, Feb. 10. Major General Amin el-Hafez was elected secretary-general of the Baath Party after a purge, on February 6, of Salah el-Bitar, former Baathist premier.

Apr. 17. The chairman of the Revolutionary Council, Major General Amin el-Hafez, ordered the **nationalization of three textile factories** and decreed that workers in "nationalized" and state-run economic establishments manage the companies themselves.

Apr. 28. The Revolutionary Council terminated its military treaty with Iraq.

May 11. **Salah el-Bitar,** veteran Baathist, was **named premier** under an interim constitution which transferred executive powers from the National Revolutionary Council to a five-member presidential council assisted by a cabinet.

Oct. 3. **Premier el-Bitar was replaced by General Amin el-Hafez,** former president of the Revolutionary Council.

1965. Far-reaching **nationalization of business,** indicating the pronounced socialist character of the Syrian régime.

1966, Feb. 23. Left-wing officers, led by **Major-General Salah al-Jadad** of the Baath Party, overthrew the government and (Mar. 2) set up a new cabinet under **Yussef Zayyin.** The new orientation was pro-Communist and fanatically Arab nationalist. **Nureddin al-Atassi** became the new head of state.

Apr. 25. **Zayyin paid a visit to Moscow** and returned with Soviet promises of further military aid and equipment, along with technicians to build a huge dam on the Euphrates.

1967. THE ARAB-ISRAELI WAR. Syria lost the strategically important Golan Heights, yet remained unalterably opposed to any peace settlement with Israel, calling for destruction of that state by a popular all-Arab war.

1968, Mar. Inauguration of work on the Euphrates dam.

1969, Feb. Military pressure, led by **Defense Minister Hafez al-Assad,** forced Nureddin al-Atassi to remake the government (May 29).

Military missions to Communist China, along with the diplomatic recognition of East Germany and of North Vietnam, clearly aligned Syria with the Communist world.

1970, Nov. 13. OUSTING OF NUREDDIN AL-ATASSI BY GEN. HAFEZ AL-ASSAD, following a Pan-Arab Baathist congress at Damascus. Al-Assad was reputed to be less uncompromising in his attitude toward the Israeli war.

Nov. 18. **Ahmed al-Khatib,** former head of the Teachers' Union, named head of state, while (Nov. 19) **Gen. al-Assad assumed the premiership.**

Nov. 27. Syria joined the UAR, Libya, and the Sudan in preparation for eventual federation. The government declared itself ready to join in pooling military, economic, and political resources for a renewed war against Israel.

d. LEBANON

(From p. 1090)

1941, Nov. 26. The Lebanese government proclaimed Lebanon an independent sovereign state.

1943, Nov. 11. French authorities arrested the president, **Sheikh Bishara al-Khoury,** and his ministers, after the Lebanese chamber of deputies had proclaimed the independence of the republic. Strikes and rioting broke out and the prisoners were released (Nov. 22). On November 27 the French yielded and the French Committee of National Liberation transferred all powers exercised by France under the terms of the mandate to the Lebanese and Syrian governments.

1946, Mar. 10. France and Great Britain agreed to **evacuate Lebanon.** The evacuation was completed by August 31.

1947, May 25. **Parliamentary elections** gave the government 49 out of 55 seats in the chamber of deputies. The fairness of the election was questioned.

1948, May 27. President **Bishara al-Khoury** was re-elected for another six years.

1949, Mar. 23. Lebanon concluded an **armistice with Israel,** ending the invasion of Lebanon by Israeli forces.

1952, Sept. 18. In the face of a general strike, President Bishara al-Khoury resigned and was succeeded by **Gen. Fuad Chehab.** On September 23 parliament elected as president **Camille Chamoun,** former foreign minister.

1958, May 9–13. **Riots and street fighting,** allegedly provoked by the UAR, occurred in Tripoli and Beirut, protesting the régime of President Chamoun.

June 6. Foreign Minister Charles Malik called upon the U.N. security council to halt "unprovoked aggression" by the UAR; on **June 11.** The security council voted to send **U.N. observers** to Lebanon to guard against illegal movement of troops or arms into Lebanon.

June 16. The leader of the anti-Western opposition, ex-premier **Saeb Salaam,** warned that civil war would result if President Chamoun refused to resign.

July 15–19. U.S. troops from the 6th Fleet **landed near Beirut.** President Eisenhower stated their purpose to be the protection of American lives and aid in the defense of Lebanese sovereignty and independence.

July 31. Parliament elected **General Fuad Chehab president** to succeed Chamoun. He took office, September 23.

Sept. 24. Rebel leader **Rashid Karumi became premier** in a cabinet of four Christians, three Moslems, and one Druze. The United States announced its support of the new government, September 27.

Oct. 25. The last **U.S. troops withdrew** from Lebanon.

1961, Dec. 31. The government crushed a **right-wing military coup.**

1964, Aug. 18. CHARLES HELOU ELECTED PRESIDENT.

1967, June. OUTBREAK OF THE ARAB-ISRAELI WAR. Lebanon was at first not directly involved, but popular sympathy for Arab nationalism ran strong and guerrilla attacks on Israel from Lebanese territory became increasingly frequent.

1968, May. First serious **border clashes** between Lebanese and Israelis.

Oct. 19. President Helou resigned, but soon resumed office in the midst of factional strife.

Dec. 28. Israeli attack on the Beirut airport, in reprisal for guerrilla attacks on an Israeli plane at Athens and for terrorist attacks from Lebanese territory. Thirteen Arab airliners were destroyed.

1969, Jan. 16. A strong **coalition government** was formed by **Rashid Karami,** following the resignation of Abdullah al-Yaffi.

Apr. 23–25. Major demonstrations and clashes between the pro- and anti-commando factions.

Aug. 11. Beginning of systematic **Israeli attacks on commando bases** in south Lebanon.

Oct. 22. The Karami cabinet resigned after its failure to resolve the commando problem, which was complicated by commando raids from Syria.

Nov. 2. Karami formed a new government after agreement had been reached with the **Palestine Liberation Organization:** the commandos were permitted to take over control of the Palestine refugee camps in Lebanon and to operate against Israel from a few specified bases.

1970, May 12. Heavy fighting by Lebanese troops and commandos in response to Israeli raids against commando bases in Lebanon.

Aug. 17. SULEIMAN FRANJIEH, minister of justice, **ELECTED PRESIDENT** by a narrow majority in parliament.

e. ISRAEL

(From p. 1093)

The immigration of Jews into Palestine had risen sharply during the war. In May 1942, a conference of American Zionists had adopted the **Biltmore program,** which repudiated the **British plan of 1939** for an independent Palestine (p. 1092) and instead demanded a Jewish state and a Jewish army. As the war ended, both Jews and Arabs maintained military organizations in the Holy Land, in a state of uneasy truce.

1945, Aug. 13. The **World Zionist congress** demanded that Palestine be opened to 1,000,000 Jews. President Truman (Aug. 31) requested the immediate admission of 100,000 Jewish displaced persons from Europe.

Oct. 20. Egypt, Iraq, Syria, and Lebanon warned the United States that creation of a Jewish state in Palestine would lead to war.

1946, Apr. 29. An **Anglo-American committee of inquiry** advised against the partition of Palestine and instead recommended an independent state with local and provincial autonomy. This solution satisfied neither side.

July 22. Illegal Zionist activities reached a climax as British headquarters in the **King David Hotel** in Jerusalem were blown up, causing the death of 91 persons.

Sept.–Dec. At a **London conference** on Palestine, boycotted by the Zionists, the Arab states proposed an Arab-dominated Palestinian state. The **Zionist congress** at Basel, on the other hand, called for a Jewish state. Both Jews and Arabs favored the withdrawal of Britain from the Palestine mandate.

1947, Feb. 7. A final British proposal for the division of Palestine into Arab and Jewish zones and its administration as a trusteeship was rejected by Arabs and Jews.

Apr. 2. The British government referred the Palestine problem to the **United Nations.**

Nov. 29. Following the majority recommendation of its committee on Palestine, the **U.N. general assembly voted the partition** of the country into Jewish and Arab states. Jerusalem was to be under a U.N. trusteeship. This was approved by the Jews, but rejected by the Arabs, and on

Dec. 17. The **Arab League council** announced it would stop the proposed division of the Holy Land by use of force and began raids on Jewish communities in Palestine.

1948. Terrorist activities, especially by the Jewish **Irgun, "Stern Gang,"** and (to a lesser extent) **Haganah,** took on war-like proportions and thousands of Arabs fled the country. The British government, unable to solve the Palestine problem, decided to withdraw its forces.

May 14. The **British mandate came to an end.** The same day, a Jewish provisional government under **David Ben-Gurion** proclaimed the **STATE OF ISRAEL,** with **Chaim Weizmann** as president. Within two days it was recognized by the **United States** and the **Soviet Union.**

1948, May–1949, July. **WAR BETWEEN ISRAEL AND THE ARAB LEAGUE.** Starting out on the defensive, Israeli forces soon gained the upper hand, due to superior equipment and fighting ability. **United Nations efforts at mediation** led to an uneasy **truce** (July–Oct.), during which the U.N. mediator, **Count Folke Bernadotte,** who was appointed on May 20, was assassinated by Zionist terrorists (Sept. 17). Continued U.N. efforts finally led to a series of armistices between Israel and the Arab League nations.

1948, Dec. 1. A Palestine Arab congress at Jericho proclaimed **King Abdullah of Transjordan** as king of Palestine.

1949, Jan. 25. **Israel's first elections** brought victory to the Mapai Party of Premier Ben-Gurion.

May 11. **Israel joined the United Nations.**

Dec. 14. Ignoring a resolution of the U.N. general assembly for the **internationalization of Jerusalem,** the Israeli government moved to the city from Tel Aviv.

1950, May 25. Britain, France, and the United States pledged to uphold the armistice lines previously agreed upon.

As a result of the war and the continued immigration of unlimited numbers of Jews, Israel was faced with grave economic difficulties. These were increased by constant friction between the new state and its Arab neighbors. Efforts of the U.N. Palestine conciliation commission to reach a final peace settlement remained unsuccessful.

1951, Apr. 5. The Israeli air force **bombed Syrian military positions** in retaliation for an alleged violation of the Israeli frontier. Border incidents continued until both sides heeded a U.N. security council **cease-fire** order on May 9.

May 24. Israel charged that Jordanian national guardsmen had invaded Israel twice within a week.

Oct. 9. After eight months of **cabinet crisis**

in Israel, Prime Minister Ben-Gurion formed a coalition government which commanded a firm majority.

1952, Sept. 10. After nearly nine months of negotiation, an **agreement** was signed **with West Germany** which undertook to pay $822 million in reparations.

Dec. 8. The knesset chose **Itzhak Ben-Zvi president,** to succeed Chaim Weizmann, who died November 7.

1955, Feb. 17. Former premier David Ben-Gurion ended a 15-month retirement to take the post of defense minister.

Aug. 3. The announcement of parliamentary election results showed that the middle-of-the-road government of **Moshe Sharett** had gained a bare majority, 61 of the 120 seats, in the knesset.

Oct. 11. Israel appealed to the United States for armaments equaling the amount Egypt was receiving from the Soviet bloc.

Nov. 3. David Ben-Gurion formed a new cabinet.

1956, May 12. France, with the tacit approval of the United States, released twelve additional **jet planes** for delivery to Israel, to complement an April shipment.

Oct. 25. Israel promised the U.N. security council that she would never initiate a war but neither would she "sit back and suffer the consequences of a unilateral Arab belligerency." (For Israeli participation in the Suez Canal crisis, see p. 1283.)

1957, Mar. 29. The government accepted the U.N. plan for sealing the **Gaza border** with Egypt (p. 1283).

July 9. **Israeli and Syrian forces battled** for nearly ten hours before U.N. intervention finally stopped the fighting. Accepting (July 16) U.N. "lookout posts" on its side of the border for a 30-day trial period, Israel (July 22) at the U.N. charged Syria with violation of the armistice agreement.

Dec. 30. A series of **government crises** began over the issue of selling arms to West Germany.

1958, Nov. 3. Parliamentary elections gave a victory to Premier Ben-Gurion's Mapai Party which formed a majority in the new cabinet of December 17.

1961, Jan. 31. **Premier Ben-Gurion resigned.** He was asked on February 16 to form a new government, but he declared, on February 28, his inability to do so.

Apr. 11. **Adolf Eichmann** went on trial before an Israeli tribunal in Jerusalem on a 15-count indictment charging crimes against Jews and others during World War II.

Sept. 6. A prolonged government crisis began. It ended on October 31 when leaders of four parties agreed to a coalition under Ben-Gurion.

Dec. 15. Eichmann was sentenced to death by an Israeli court, following his conviction for war crimes. He was executed May 21, 1962.

1963, Apr. 23. President Itzhak Ben-Zvi died at the age of 78, seven months after his election to a third term (Oct. 30, 1962). On May 21 **Schneor Zalman Shazar** succeeded him.

June. Upon the resignation of Premier Ben-Gurion (June 16), **Finance Minister Levi Eshkol formed a government,** approved by the knesset, June 26.

Aug. 20. After Israeli and Syrian forces battled for several hours along the demilitarized zone north of the Sea of Galilee, the government asked the U.N. security council to meet and consider Israeli charges against Syria. On August 25 U.N. truce observers persuaded both sides to agree to a cease-fire.

1964, May 5. Opening of an **Israeli pipeline** from the Sea of Galilee to the Negev, making possible the irrigation of the southern desert. Loud **protests of the Arab states** against unilateral tapping of Jordan waters.

June 1–2. Visit of Premier Eshkol to Washington. President Johnson reaffirmed earlier assurances and approved plans for a huge desalinization plant.

Nov. Serious differences of opinion between Premier Eshkol and Ben-Gurion weakened the Mapai Party.

1965, May 12. Acceptance of the West German offer to re-establish diplomatic relations.

Nov. 2. In the **elections** a coalition of the Mapai and Labour parties won 45 seats of a total of 120. The remainder went to splinter groups, Ben-Gurion's Rafi Party winning on 10 seats.

1966. Increasing hostilities on the Israeli frontiers. For the background and course of the Arab-Israeli war see pp. 1285–1288.

May. Visit of Chancellor Konrad Adenauer of West Germany, marking completion of the payment of reparations by Germany to Israel.

June 1. Formation of a government of national unity. General Moshe Dayan became minister of defense.

1967, June 5. OUTBREAK OF THE ARAB-ISRAELI WAR (pp. 1285–1288).

June 7. The Israelis took Arab **Jerusalem** and presently proclaimed its incorporation with the rest of the city (June 27), with guarantees of freedom of access to the Holy Places for all religions. The U.N. called on Israel to rescind this action (July 4), which the Israeli government refused to do (July 14).

June 10. The Soviet Union severed diplomatic relations with Israel.

1968, Jan. Formation of the **Israel Labour Party**

through merger of three smaller parties.

May 21. The U.N. security council again declared **Israeli actions in Arab Jerusalem invalid.**

Dec. The U.S. government agreed to provide Israel with 50 **Phantom jet fighters** over the ensuing three years, in response to increasing Soviet supplies to the UAR.

1969, Jan. 6. President de Gaulle of France banned the further delivery of arms and planes to Israel.

Feb. Death of Premier Eshkol. He was succeeded as premier by **Mrs. Golda Meir** (Mar. 17) who, after the knesset elections (Oct. 30), formed a broad coalition government.

Sept. 25–26. Visit of Mrs. Meir to Washington in an effort to secure further American help, especially in the form of planes.

1970, Apr. 6. The Israeli government refused to allow **Naoum Goldmann,** eminent Zionist leader but advocate of a compromise peace, to enter into discussions with Egyptian authorities at Cairo.

Aug. 4. The nationalist **Gahal faction** withdrew from the government coalition in protest against the Israeli acceptance of the cease-fire.

Sept. 18. Another visit of Mrs. Meir to Washington to discuss Egyptian cease-fire violations and plead for more support.

f. JORDAN

(*From p. 1093*)

1946, Mar. 22. Great Britain recognized the **independence of Transjordan** and concluded a close alliance with the new state.

May 25. The **KINGDOM OF TRANS-JORDAN** was officially proclaimed, with **Emir Abdullah** as king. Its admission to the **United Nations** was vetoed by the Soviet Union.

1947, Jan. 11. Transjordan and **Turkey** signed a pact of friendship.

Apr. 14. Treaty of alliance concluded with **Iraq.**

Oct. 20. Elections to the national assembly gave almost all seats to the official **Revival Party.**

1948, Mar. 15. A new **treaty of alliance with Great Britain** set up a joint defense board.

May 15. The British-trained **Arab Legion** of Transjordan invaded Palestine and entered Jerusalem.

Dec. 1. A conference of Palestine Arabs proclaimed **Abdullah sovereign of all Palestine,** and on December 13 the parliament of Transjordan approved a future union with Arab Palestine. This was criticized by the Arab League, since it acknowledged the partition of Palestine and presented a step toward Abdullah's scheme for a **"Greater Syria"** under his leadership.

1949, June 2. Transjordan was renamed **"The Hashimite Kingdom of Jordan."**

1950, Apr. 24. Final **incorporation of Arab Palestine into Jordan** over the protest of most of the Arab League.

1951, July 20. King Abdullah was assassinated in Jerusalem. His heir, **Emir Talal,** was proclaimed king by the national assembly on September 5.

1952, Aug. 11. Parliament, declaring King Talal unfit to rule, proclaimed the succession of the 17-year-old Crown Prince Hussein.

1953, May 2. KING HUSSEIN I, on his 18th birthday, began his reign.

1954, May 2. When Britain and the United States objected to Jordan's refusal to participate in armistice talks with Israel, the Jordanian cabinet resigned, to be succeeded on May 3 by a more moderate government.

1955, Dec. 19. Hazza al-Majali's cabinet resigned when riots broke out to protest Jordan's proposed membership in the **Baghdad pact.**

1956, Jan. 9. Samir el-Rifai headed a new cabinet, committed to oppose participation in the Baghdad pact. The new government took immediate and severe steps to quell rioting and the premier, on January 26, declared that Arab unity was the cornerstone of Jordan's security.

Mar. 2. King Hussein dismissed the British commander of the Arab Legion, **Lt. General John Bagot Glubb.**

May 21. Following the resignation (May 20) of Premier Samir el-Rifai and his government, **Said el-Mufti** formed a new government and announced his decision to request a revision of the British-Jordanian defense treaty.

May 26. The government announced the **abolition of the Arab Legion** as a separate force, and its merger with the Jordanian national guard.

June 30. King Hussein accepted the resignation of Premier Said el-Mufti and his cabinet to permit the formation of a caretaker government.

Oct. 22. Amid continuing **border clashes with Israel,** Jordan elected a parliament made up of anti-Western and pro-Egyptian members, including at least three Communists.

1957, Jan. 19. Jordan was promised a **subsidy by Arab states** (p. 1283) to replace Britain's financial support.

Mar. 13. Great Britain agreed to **terminate the 1948 treaty of alliance.** British forces were scheduled to withdraw from Jordan within six months, and actually left the country July 13.

Apr. King Hussein took vigorous action to oust Premier Nabulsi's pro-Egyptian government (Apr. 10) and to purge the army and government of Egyptian-Syrian sympathizers, while ruling under martial law. Anti-Western leaders accused the United States, which ordered the 6th Fleet to the eastern Mediterranean (Apr. 25), of causing Jordan's crisis, but King Hussein reaffirmed (Apr. 25) his resolve to avoid commitments to the United States.

1958, Feb. 14. An **Arab federation,** merging Jordan and Iraq, was proclaimed at Amman.

July 14. Upon news of the **Iraqi coup** (p. 1308) King Hussein asked for aid, while assuming headship of the Arab federation and of the Arab army of Jordan and Iraq. British paratroops began landing at Amman, July 17.

Aug. 2. King Hussein decreed the **dissolution of the Arab federation** with Iraq.

Oct. 20. British troops began to withdraw.

1960, Aug. 29. Premier Hazza Majali, in office since May 6, 1959, and eleven other persons were killed in bomb explosions in Amman.

1962, Aug. 29. King Saud of Saudi Arabia and **King Hussein,** in a joint communiqué, following a three-day meeting, announced their agreement on merging their military troops and economic policies.

1964, Apr. 14. King Hussein, conferring with President Johnson in Washington, declared that no compromise was possible on **Arab plans to dam two tributaries of the Jordan River,** thus blocking Israeli diversion of Jordan waters to irrigate the Negev desert.

1965, May. Massive **Israeli reprisal attack** on the village of Qalqiliya. Jordan, with a population composed largely of Palestinian refugees, was the natural base for many guerrilla organizations and activities. In view of the traditional hatred of many Arabs for the Hashemite dynasty, King Hussein was a marked man not only for Palestinians, but also for Syrians and Egyptians, whose radios were constantly calling for his elimination. Hussein, in turn, did what he could to keep the guerrillas in check, relying on the United States for military equipment, and on Saudi Arabia for general support.

1966, July. The Jordanian government suspended relations with the Palestine Liberation Organization, but was not able to prevent constant raiding across the Jordan.

Nov. 13. The Israelis, in reprisal, **attacked the Jordanian village of Sammu** with tanks and aircraft. The undeclared war continued into 1967, with growing agitation by the Palestinians for Hussein's overthrow.

1967, June 5. OUTBREAK OF THE ARAB-ISRAELI WAR (pp. 1285–1288). Jordan, with only 56,000 men, 250 tanks, and 28 planes, was quickly defeated, despite the valor of its resistance. By losing Arab Jerusalem and all of its territory west of the Jordan it lost one-half its population and one-half of its economic resources. Furthermore, several hundred thousand additional refugees fled across the Jordan River to the vicinity of Amman. Faced with so desperate a situation, Hussein, though opposed to a separate peace with Israel, favored a compromise political settlement, which brought him only more obloquy and hostility on the part of the Palestine liberation movement and neighboring Arab governments. This situation continued and worsened during 1968 and 1969, Hussein's one consolation being the support of the United States and Britain, both of which sent tanks and planes to make good the war losses (Feb.–Apr., 1969).

1970, May. Long conferences between government officials and commando chiefs proved abortive and ended (May 2) in open hostilities between troops and commandos.

June 9. Further **fighting in Amman.** The king was obliged to appoint a new cabinet more acceptable to the liberation leaders (June 27). A joint police force was to be set up to maintain order in the capital.

Sept. 15–26. THE JORDANIAN CIVIL WAR. Despite the compromise of June 9, desultory fighting alternating with further attempts at agreement continued until (Sept. 15) King Hussein proclaimed martial law, dismissed his civilian cabinet, and named a new government of army officers, with **Brigadier Daoud** as premier and **Marshal Habes al-Majali** as commander. Thereupon the Palestinian commandos revolted, gained control of several northern towns where they expected Syrian reinforcements, and battled for control of Amman. Syrians driving Soviet tanks did in fact invade northern Jordan, only to withdraw again when Israel and the United States threatened to intervene. Gradually the government troops gained the upper hand.

Sept. 25. The efforts of Arab leaders and the resignation of Premier Daoud paved the way to a settlement. **King Hussein** arrived in Cairo (Sept. 25) and **signed an agreement with ten Arab leaders,** including Yasir Arafat, the chief of the Palestine Liberation Organization. Both commando and government forces were to be withdrawn from Amman and a **supervisory committee of three,** under chairmanship of the Tunisian premier, was to "ensure the continuance of the Palestinian resistance and respect for the sovereignty of Jordan with the exception of the needs of resistance activity."

Sept. 27. The airplane passengers being held as hostages by the terrorist wing of the liberation movement were liberated by Jordanian forces and commando troops (p. 1287).

Oct. 28. A new **cabinet under Wasfi al-Tal,** was reportedly hostile to commando pretensions and to Syrian interference.

Dec. 4–8. Fighting broke out anew between the Jordanian forces and the commandos as the army tried to clear the guerrillas from Jarash and open the northern route to army control. At year's end the difficult situation in Jordan was as yet unresolved. The king, the target of many and varied enemies, was anxious for a compromise settlement with Israel, while the liberation forces were uncompromisingly opposed to such a settlement and insistent on continued attacks upon Israel in the hope of ultimately reconquering their homeland.

g. SAUDI ARABIA, KUWAIT, AND THE TRUCIAL STATES

(From p. 1095)

Saudi Arabia became a charter member of both the Arab League and the United Nations. Its Arab character and its dependency for approximately 90 per cent of its revenues upon the **American-Arabian Oil Company** have created difficulties whenever tensions arose between the Arab world and the West. **Yemen** became increasingly active in Middle East affairs after it became a charter member of the Arab League. The **Trucial States,** of which the most important is the sultanate of Muscat and Oman, and the British **protectorate of Aden** have likewise been drawn into Middle Eastern politics.

1953, Nov. 9. Upon the **death of Ibn Saud,** the founder of the Saudi Arabian kingdom, his son, **Saud ibn Abdel Aziz,** became king, and another son, **Prince Faisal,** was proclaimed crown prince. Faisal acted as both prime minister and foreign minister for his brother.

1956, Apr. 21. Egyptian Premier Nasser, Saudi Arabia's King Saud, and Imam Ahmed of Yemen signed a **tripartite military pact** in Jidda to set up a unified command under an Egyptian leader for a five-year period.

1957, Feb. 8. At the close of his **ten-day visit to Washington,** King Saud joined President Eisenhower in a communiqué announcing an agreement for the renewal of the United States **lease on the Dhahran air base** in exchange for U.S. arms deliveries.

May 20. The Saudi government informed Egypt of its view that the Gulf of Aqaba was in "Arab territorial waters" and declared its support for any attempt to prevent Israeli shipping from passing through it.

July 19–Aug. 26. Under British leadership, the forces of the **sultan of Muscat and Oman** sought to suppress a tribal revolt under the spiritual leader or Imam of Oman, **Sheikh Ghalib bin Ali,** whose followers at length recognized the sultan's authority, but whose envoy at Cairo voiced his determination not to make peace as long as a single Briton remained in Oman.

1960, Dec. 21. In Saudi Arabia, Crown Prince Faisal resigned his offices, and King Saud assumed complete control of the government.

1961, June 19. Kuwait gained its independence and the end of the British protectorate. Britain signed a treaty of friendship and assured the country of British protection if requested.

July 1. British forces moved into Kuwait, at the request of its ruler, to protect the sheikdom against Iraqi claims, but began to withdraw, September 19, to be replaced by troops of the Arab League.

Nov. 2. Sheik Sulman bin Hamad al-Khalifa of Bahrein died. His son, **Sheik Isa bin Sulman al-Khalifa,** succeeded his father.

1962, Sept. 19. Saudi Arabian involvement in the Yemeni civil war (p. 1306).

Oct. 17. King Saud of Saudi Arabia dissolved his cabinet and appointed Prince Faisal premier.

1964, Mar. 28. King Saud signed a decree giving Prince Faisal full powers and reducing his own role to that of a figurehead. On March 31 **Faisal assumed the title of viceroy.**

Nov. 2. Faisal became king of Saudi Arabia following the deposition of his incompetent brother Saud.

1965, July. A conference of the rulers of the various Persian Gulf states and formation of the **Trucial States Development Council** by which the oil-rich states undertook to aid the less endowed members.

Nov. 24. Kuwait: death of Emir Abdullah al-Salem al-Sabah. He was succeeded by the crown prince Sabah al-Salem al-Sabah.

1966, Aug. 6. Sheik Shakbut bin Sultan of the Trucial State of Abu Dhabi **was deposed** by his brother Sheik Zaid.

Nov. 13. Meeting of the **Islamic World League** in Mecca. Faisal, essentially conservative in his outlook, made great efforts in behalf of Islamic unity in contrast to Arab nationalism.

1967, June 5. Outbreak of the Arab-Israeli war. Saudi Arabia, though it had dispatched 20,000 troops to Jordan (May 24), took no part in the fighting, though in the sequel it contributed regularly to Egypt, Jordan, and Syria to compensate them for their losses.

1968, Jan. Faisal declared his support of Bahrein against Iranian claims to sovereignty and favored (Apr.) a **federation of Persian Gulf states** under the leadership of the state of Qatar.

Jan. 17. The **decision of the British government to withdraw all forces** from areas east of Suez by the end of 1971 led to a complete change in the Persian Gulf situation.

Feb. 27. Formation of the **Federation of Emirates of the Arab (Persian) Gulf** after several meetings of the nine rulers. Emir Sheik Sabah al-Salem of Kuwait declared his support.

May 13. Britain and Kuwait terminated their 1961 defense agreement, but Britain undertook to supply armaments in the future.

July 7. The rulers of the Persian Gulf states decided to form a supreme council of rulers and a federal council to work out the details of the federation.

Oct. Agreement between Saudi Arabia and Iran as to the sovereignty of the two Gulf islands of Al-Arabi and Farsi, the former to be assigned to Saudi Arabia and the latter to Iran.

Oct. 22. A further decision to establish a common defense force.

1969, Oct. 24. The Persian Gulf rulers agreed to name Sheik Zaid of Abu Dhabi president and Sheik Khalifa bin Hamad of Qatar as premier of the federation. Abu Dhabi was to be the temporary capital and each state was to send four delegates to a federal assembly.

1970, July 23. Sultan Said bin Taimur of Oman overthrown by a palace coup led by his son Qaboos bin Said, Oxford educated and advocate of modernizing reforms.

Aug. 10. The name of the sultanate was changed from Muscat and Oman to **Sultanate of Oman.**

h. YEMEN AND SOUTHERN YEMEN

1958, Mar. 8. Crown Prince Saif al-Islam Muhammad al-Badr of Yemen and President Nasser of Egypt agreed to the creation of a **Federation of Yemen and the United Arab States** (later Southern Yemen).

1959, Feb. 3. The British Colonial Office announced that the six western Aden states had agreed to the **Federation of Arab Emirates of the South.** Britain promised them future independence.

1961, Dec. 26. The UAR terminated its federation with Yemen.

1962, Sept. 19. The death of Imam Ahmed of Yemen triggered a rebellion and the **proclamation of the Free Yemeni Republic** by the insurgent troops (Oct. 31). **Colonel Abdullah al-Salal became president.** However, the claimant to the imamate, **Muhammad al-Badr,** found refuge in Saudi Arabia and organized the royalist tribes against the new régime.

Nov. 6. Saudi Arabia broke relations with the UAR, charging that Egyptian planes aiding the Yemeni rebels had bombed Saudi Arabian border villages.

Nov. 11. The UAR and the Yemeni Republic concluded a military defense treaty.

1964, Mar. 3. After prolonged discussions the UAR and Saudi Arabia declared for independence for Yemen.

Mar. 24. Visit of President Abdullah al-Salal of the Yemeni Republic **to Moscow** resulted in a five-year pact of friendship and continuing aid.

Mar. 28. British planes destroyed a Yemeni fort in retaliation for an attack on the Federation of South Arabia.

June 9–July 4. London conference of delegates of 14 federated South Arabian states. The British government promised independence not later than 1968, Britain to retain a base at Aden and aid in defense of the federation.

Sept. 14. At an Arab summit meeting **Prince Faisal** of Saudi Arabia **and President Nasser** of the UAR **agreed to work for a settlement of the Yemeni problem.** A cease-fire was arranged (Nov. 8), but peace efforts failed. Meanwhile 40,000 Egyptian troops were sent to Yemen to support the republican régime.

1965, Aug. 24. The UAR and Saudi Arabia once again agreed to end the Yemeni civil war. Both sides were to withdraw troops and terminate aid. A plebiscite in 1966 was to decide the form of government.

Sept. 25. The British government suspended the Aden constitution because of the failure of the local authorities to deal with the terrorism of the **National Liberation Front,** a radical organization supported by Cairo.

Nov. 5. The U.N. trusteeship committee called on Britain to give up its military base at Aden.

Nov. 23. A **Yemeni peace conference** at Haradh soon became deadlocked on the question of a constitution, the republicans insisting that the royal family be explicitly excluded.

1966, Feb. Nasser declared that the UAR troops would remain in Yemen indefinitely until a plebiscite could be held. By this time factional strife had been resumed.

Feb. 22. The British government announced its intention to abandon the Aden base as soon as South Arabia became independent in 1968.

Mar. 2. A **revolutionary command** was set up at Taiz (Yemen) by the Front for the Liberation of Occupied South Yemen. Supported by the UAR the new front began terrorist operations, especially in Aden.

Apr.–Aug. Futile efforts of the Sheik of Kuwait to mediate in the Yemeni war. The Saudi Arabian government insisted on immediate withdrawal of the Egyptian forces and the establishment of an interim government composed equally of royalists and republicans. Nasser, on the other hand, insisted that the republicans have three-quarters of the seats and

refused to recall the Egyptian troops until his demand was met.

Aug. 12. Return of President Abdullah al-Salal after a year's absence in Cairo. Dissension in republican ranks.

Sept. 30. Deposition and **arrest of Prime Minister Hassan al-Amri** and other officials accused of being anti-Egyptian. Al-Salal became premier as well as president and executed a thorough purge of the republican ranks.

1967, Apr. The South Arabian states were rent by **factional conflict.** A U.N. mission failed entirely to effect agreement. Gradually the left-wing National Liberation Front emerged as the strongest and most ruthless faction.

June. British withdrawal from tribal areas behind Aden. The National Liberation Front took over.

June 18. Beginning of the **withdrawal of Egyptian forces** from Yemen as a result of the Arab-Israeli war (p. 1285).

June 19. Britain promised the South Arabian states independence by Jan. 9, 1968.

Aug. Nasser and King Faisal agreed to a mediated settlement of the Yemeni issue.

Sept. 5. Official dissolution of the Federation of South Arabian States.

Oct. 7. Conference of party leaders at Cairo. **Agreement on a new government for South Arabia** (Nov. 1). Nonetheless sporadic fighting continued in Aden.

Nov. 5. In Yemen **al-Salal was ousted,** in his absence, by a military coup. Many detainees returned from Egypt, while royalists staged an offensive against Sanaa. Presently Russian planes arrived to support the republicans. **Abdul Rahman al-Iryani** assumed the presidency and **Gen. Hassan al-Amri** became premier.

Nov. 29. INDEPENDENCE OF THE SOUTH ARABIAN STATES, henceforth officially the **People's Republic of Southern Yemen,** with **Qahtan a-Shaabi** president.

1968, Jan.–Aug. Repeated **royalist attacks on Sanaa** beaten back by the republicans, who now had the active support of the Soviets and the Syrians, as well as of the republican faction in Southern Yemen.

May. The royalist **Imam Muhammad al-Badr of Yemen was deposed** and succeeded by his cousin Muhammad bin Hussein.

Aug. The republican premier of Yemen, Hassan al-Amri, succeeded in putting down an attempted military coup after considerable fighting.

Sept. 30. Imam Muhammad al-Badr returned from Saudi Arabia and **seized control** of the premiership and the army.

1969, June 22. In Southern Yemen the president and the premier were deposed and **Ali**

Salem Rubai emerged as chairman of a presidential council. The economic situation in southern Arabia became critical as the British withdrew, depriving some 25,000 men of work. At the same time the blocking of the Suez Canal reduced the bunkering trade to almost nothing.

July. In Yemen, **resignation of Hassan al-Amri** and establishment of a new cabinet under **Abdullah al-Karshumi** (Sept.).

Nov. Resumption of fighting between the republican and royalist factions in Yemen.

Nov. 26–Dec. 16. Outbreak of **hostilities between Southern Yemen and Saudi Arabia.** By use of air power the Saudi Arabians were able to drive the Yemenis back from the borders.

i. IRAQ

(From p. 1096)

1941, May 2. Pro-Axis sympathizers attempted to gain control of the government of **Iraq,** but were defeated by **British intervention.**

May 31. The arrival of British reinforcements ended internal disturbances and an armistice between the factions was concluded under British supervision.

1946, Mar. 29. Iraq concluded a treaty of friendship with **Turkey,** calling for joint control over the upper Tigris and Euphrates.

1947, Apr. 14. Treaty of alliance concluded with **Transjordan.**

Oct. 26. Great Britain announced the withdrawal of its army from Iraq, except for a military mission of two R.A.F. detachments.

1948, Jan. 15. The treaty with Britain providing for continued presence of British troops failed of ratification because of popular opposition.

1950, Nov. 27. Premier Nuri as-Said declared that the alliance with Britain had become obsolete.

1952, Nov. 23. Mounting agitation against British troops in Iraq culminated in the **outbreak of anti-British and anti-U.S. rioting.** The regent named army chief of staff **Gen. Nur al-Din Mahmoud** to form a new civilian cabinet. He declared martial law, and on November 24 ordered the dissolution of all political parties, the closing of twelve newspapers, and a ban on demonstrations.

1953, Jan. 17. In the nation's first direct **parliamentary elections,** the supporters of former premier Nuri as-Said were victorious.

May 2. The fourteen-year regency of Emir Abdul Illah ended when **King Faisal II,** on his 18th birthday, **acceded to the throne.**

1955, Feb. 24. Iraq signed with Turkey the

Baghdad pact, for mutual defense and cooperation. Britain and Pakistan joined.

1958, Feb. 14. An **Arab Federation,** merging Iraq and Jordan, was proclaimed at Amman, Jordan.

Mar. 3. General Nuri as-Said became premier, in a move designed to strengthen the newly created Arab Federation. On March 26 parliament approved a constitutional amendment giving King Faisal authority to enter into union with another country.

May 27. King Faisal opened the first parliament of the Arab Federation.

July 14. GENERAL ABDUL KARIM AL-KASSEM LED AN ARMY COUP, ASSASSINATING KING FAISAL AND PROCLAIMING A REPUBLIC. A new cabinet under **General Najil al-Rubai** took office July 16.

July 19. Iraq and the UAR agreed "to stand together as one nation" against aggression.

Aug. 1. Great Britain recognized the new government and the United States followed (Aug. 2).

1959, Mar. 24. Premier Abdul Karim al-Kassem announced **Iraq's withdrawal from the Baghdad pact** (p. 1284).

June 26. Premier Kassem restricted the activities of the pro-Communist civilian militia, the Popular Resistance Forces.

1961, June 25. Premier Kassem claimed newly independent **Kuwait as an "integral part"** of Iraq (p. 1306).

1963, Feb. 8. A coup d'état led by the air force overthrew the government of Premier Kassem. The National Revolutionary Council announced that he was dead. A Nasserite, **Colonel Abdel-Salam Arif,** was named provisional president, and another Nasserite became premier (Feb. 9).

Feb. 16. As Iraqi army troops continued rounding up Communists, the government declared its intention "to crush absolutely the Communist Party."

Mar. 1. The Revolutionary Council broadcast a statement guaranteeing "the rights of the Kurds." The **Kurdish rebel leader Mustafa al-Barzani** had threatened to go to war again if the new government did not honor its promise to grant Kurdish autonomy.

Apr. 17. Iraq agreed with Syria and the UAR to form a tripartite state.

May 11. Upon the resignation of the cabinet, **Premier Ahmed Hassan el-Bakr** proceeded to form a new government presumably more in favor of Arab unity under Nasser. But on May 13 it was announced that Baathists held the key jobs in the new government.

June 10. The government announced **war against the Kurdish troops** under al-Barzani, who was seeking autonomy.

1964, Feb. 10. President Arif and al-Barzani announced a **cease-fire agreement** ending the Kurds' fight for autonomy. A government proclamation recognized "the national rights of the Kurds within one Iraqi national union."

Mar. 11. Kurdish leader al-Barzani conferred with Iraqi officials on transforming the February cease-fire agreement into a permanent peace settlement.

July 14. **Nationalization of banks,** insurance companies, and certain industries served to underline the socialist character of the Iraqi régime.

Oct. 4. The National Revolutionary Council approved President Abdel-Salam Arif's **plan for union with the UAR.**

1965, Apr. Renewed **Kurdish revolt,** the rebels demanding autonomy in a clearly defined area and the maintenance of a Kurdish army.

Sept. 16. **Attempted coup by Prime Minister Arif Abdel Razzak** during the absence of President Arif at Casablanca. Razzak was obliged to flee to Cairo, while **Abdul Rahman al-Bazzaz** became premier in his place.

1966, Mar.–May. Large-scale **offensive against the Kurds,** who accepted a cease-fire (June) in return for a renewed promise of regional autonomy. Since the Kurds retained their arms, the situation continued to be precarious.

Apr. 13. **President Arif was killed** in a helicopter accident. His brother, **Gen. Abdul Rahman Arif,** was chosen to succeed him (Apr. 16).

Aug. 9. **Resignation of Premier Bazzaz,** who was replaced by a new premier and cabinet under **General Naji Taleb,** definitely more nationalist and more radical.

1967, May. In the growing tension between the Arab states and Israel, **Iraqi troops were sent to Jordan, Syria, and the UAR.** They took an active part in the fighting in Jordan and remained in the country thereafter. Iraq took an uncompromising stand on the question of peace negotiations with Israel.

1968, July 17. **President Arif was overthrown** by officers of the right-wing Baathist party, who set up a five-man Revolutionary Command Council under **General Ahmed Hassan al-Bakr** as president and premier. However, acute tension persisted between the two wings of the Baathist Party, with much plotting and subversive activity, followed by large-scale arrests and wholesale executions of "spies and saboteurs," including a number of Jews.

1969, Mar. Continued **operations against the Kurds** and tension in relations with Iran over border incidents and alleged aid to the Kurds.

Nov. 10. By a constitutional change the **office of premier was abolished** and all power vested in the president, who was elected by a 15-man National Council of the Revolutionary Command.

1970, Jan. 21–24. **Execution of 44 alleged plotters** against the government outraged world opinion.

Mar. 11. **The Kurds were once more granted autonomy.**

Oct. **Dismissal of General Hardan Takriti,** member of the Revolutionary Command and reputed leader of the extremist supporters of the Palestine commandos.

j. IRAN

(*From p. 1099*)

1941, Aug. 25–29. **British and Soviet forces entered Iran** (Persia) and established a régime that would co-operate with them. **Reza Shah abdicated** (Sept. 16) and was succeeded by his son, **Mohammed Reza Pahlavi.**

1942, Jan. 29. Great Britain and Soviet Russia agreed to respect the territorial integrity, sovereignty, and political independence of Iran.

1943, Sept. 9. **Iran declared war on Germany** and joined the United Nations.

1945, May 10. The government of Iran requested the United States, Great Britain, and the Soviet Union to withdraw their forces from the country.

Sept. 13. The Iranian government received assurances that evacuation would be completed by March 2, 1946.

Nov. 18. The **Tudeh Party** (Communist) **organized a rebellion** in the province of **Azerbaijan.** When government intervention against the rebels was prevented by the Soviet Union and Soviet troops failed to evacuate Iran,

1946, Mar. 19. The government protested to the **U.N. security council** against Soviet activities.

Apr. 5. Iran and the **Soviet Union** agreed on the **withdrawal of Soviet troops** (completed by May 9), the introduction of reforms in **Azerbaijan,** and the creation of a **Soviet-Iranian oil company** for northern Iran.

June 13. **Azerbaijan** returned to Iranian control, maintaining some autonomy. Unrest in the province continued for some time.

Sept. 22. Rebellion in the province of **Fars** brought reforms and greater local autonomy to the southern tribesmen.

1947, Jan.–Feb. **Parliamentary elections** supported the government.

Oct. 6. An agreement with the United States arranged for an **American military mission** and the purchase of American military equipment.

Throughout the year, resentment had been growing against the oil concessions granted to the Soviet Union in April 1946. Finally, on

Oct. 22. The majlis (parliament) nullified the Soviet oil agreement. Soviet protests against this action, as well as against American military assistance, were rejected.

1949, Feb. 5. The **Tudeh Party** was outlawed, following an attempt on **Shah Mohammed Reza Pahlavi's** life.

May 9. A revision of the constitution gave the shah power to dissolve parliament.

May 10. Announcement of a **seven-year plan** for the economic development of Iran, under the direction of American technicians.

July 18. A new agreement with the **Anglo-Iranian Oil Company,** calling for a larger share in the company's profits, was subsequently rejected by the majlis.

1951, Apr. 29. The senate and majlis named the leader of the extremist National Front, **Mohammed Mossadegh,** as premier. The new government hastened **legislation to nationalize the Iranian oil industry.** The decree of nationalization took effect on May 2, retroactive to March 20. Great Britain at once contested the legality of this unilateral abrogation of a 1933 concession treaty.

May 26. Britain asked the **International Court of Justice** to rule that Iran was obligated to arbitrate its oil nationalization dispute with Britain. On May 28 Iran served notice that it did not recognize the court's competence to act in the dispute.

July 3. The British management of the Anglo-Iranian Oil Company reached a decision to transfer to the Iranians all field operations and to send British personnel from the fields to Abadan for possible evacuation.

July 5. The International Court of Justice at The Hague ruled against Iran in her dispute with Great Britain. President Truman sent a personal message (July 9) and a special emissary, **W. Averell Harriman** (July 15), to urge a compromise settlement on Iran.

Sept. 12. The government sent an **ultimatum to Great Britain** and (Sept. 27) occupied Abadan. After appeal to the U.N. security council, Britain completed evacuation of Abadan, October 4.

Dec. 10. Iran agreed to submit the oil nationalization issue to the International Court of Justice.

1952, Jan. 12. The government ordered the closure by January 21 of all British consulates. On January 13 the British government refused to comply.

Apr. 25. After almost four months of suspension, the United States agreed to resume military aid to Iran.

July 17. Premier Mossadegh resigned and was succeeded by pro-western **Ahmad Ghavam**

for five days until the latter was overthrown in bloody rioting and **Mossadegh was returned to power.**

July 22. The International Court of Justice ruled that it lacked jurisdiction in the British-Iranian oil nationalization dispute.

Aug. 11. Parliament approved full **dictatorial powers for Premier Mossadegh** for six months. On August 21 the premier ordered the collection of unpaid back taxes for the past ten years. If rich Iranians refused to pay, they were to be jailed and have their property confiscated.

Oct. 22. Since Britain had formally rejected Premier Mossadegh's conditions for a settlement of the oil dispute (Oct. 2), **Iran broke off diplomatic relations with Britain.**

1953, Jan. 8. Premier Mossadegh asked the majlis to extend his special dictatorial powers for one year. Despite strong opposition, the request was granted on January 19.

May 11. As a result of an "accord" reached by the shah and the Mossadegh régime after they had clashed in March, the shah issued a decree to transfer his privately held estates to Premier Mossadegh's government.

June 29. President Eisenhower informed Mossadegh that no additional aid would be granted until settlement of the oil dispute with Britain.

Aug. 16. After an attempt to dismiss Premier Mossadegh, **the shah fled to Iraq** for sanctuary, but returned to his country on August 22, after Royalists and loyal troops deposed the premier on August 19. **Major General Fazollah Zahedi,** as designated by the shah earlier, assumed the premiership.

Sept. 5. The United States made a grant-in-aid of $45 million to Iran.

Dec. 5. The government, along with Great Britain, announced an agreement to renew diplomatic relations and negotiate a settlement of their dispute over oil.

Dec. 19. The shah ordered the **dissolution of parliament** and new elections.

1954, Feb. 2. With a new outbreak of rioting, police and troops were used to quell the anti-government demonstrations. On February 20 the government published the returns from the recent elections showing that General Zahedi's government had won overwhelmingly in the senate contests.

Aug. 5. The government reached **agreement with the Western oil companies** for a resumption of work in the Iranian oil industry. Parliament ratified the agreement on October 21.

1955, Oct. 12. The U.S.S.R. informed Iran that the Soviet government considered Iran's plan to join the Baghdad pact "incompatible with the interests of consolidating peace and security" in the Middle East.

1957, Nov. 12. Shah Reza Pahlavi asked the cabinet to prepare a bill designed to bring **Bahrein,** the British oil protectorate, under Iran's jurisdiction.

1959, Mar. 3. Iran announced that it no longer recognized as valid the clauses in the 1921 pact with the U.S.S.R. which gave the Soviet Union the right to move troops into Iran if forces threatening the U.S.S.R. entered Iran.

1963, Apr. 23. After ruling for two years without parliament, Premier Assadollah Alam announced that **general elections** would be held in June 1963.

1964, June 20. Trade agreement signed with the U.S.S.R., marking a distinct improvement in relations between the two countries. Direct **air service** from Moscow to Tehran was opened on Aug. 17 and the U.S.S.R. began to play an increasing role in aid to Iran, both military and economic.

1965, Jan. 21. Assassination of Premier Ali Mansur by religious reactionaries. He was succeeded (Jan. 27) by **Abbas Hoveida.**

1966, Jan. 13. Agreement with the U.S.S.R. for construction of a **steel mill** near Isfahan. Despite more active co-operation with the Soviet Union, the shah continued close relations with the United States and Great Britain and frequently paid visits to Western capitals.

Aug. Agreement with Great Britain for the **supply of destroyers and other naval vessels** to strengthen the position of Iran in the Persian Gulf.

1968, Mar. A new **five-year plan** carried further the shah's policy of reform and modernization.

The Iran government, with various claims to territories in the Persian Gulf, **opposed the federation of the Trucial States.**

1969, Apr. 19. Controversy with the Iraq government on border questions and on the navigation of the Shatt al Arab. Both sides began the mobilization of troops and engaged in a lively propaganda war.

k. AFGHANISTAN

(From p. 1100)

1939, Sept. 3. Afghanistan remained neutral on the outbreak of the Second World War.

1941, Oct. 19. In response to requests from Britain and Soviet Russia, the government consented **to expel citizens of the Axis countries** from Afghanistan.

1946, May. Prime Minister Sirdar Mohammed Hashim Khan, after 17 years in office, resigned and was succeeded by his brother **Sirdar Mahmud Shah Khan,** who inaugurated a program of reform.

1949–50. In a **border dispute with Pakistan,** the government of Afghanistan demanded autonomy for the Pathan border tribes on the Pakistan side of the **Durand line** of 1893 (p. 899).

1955, Dec. 18. Premier Mohammed Daud and Soviet Premier Bulganin signed a protocol in Kabul extending the 1931 nonaggression pact and providing a Soviet loan of $100 million.

1956, Mar. The government made an agreement with the U.S.S.R. providing **Soviet economic aid.**

1964, Oct. 1. Promulgation of a constitution, demonstrating Afghanistan's gradual progression toward modernization. While large powers were reserved for the king, the constitution provided for a two-chamber parliament (House of Elders and House of the People), elected by universal suffrage and exercising control over the cabinet.

1965, Oct. 14. Elections for parliament were held for the first time.

1967, Oct. 15. Establishment of a supreme court.

Afghanistan remains a country in which both Western and Eastern states share amicably the work of development and modernization. However, the opening of roads and the expansion of education have led to growing unrest among the literate classes and there have been serious disturbances at the university.

H. ASIA

1. INDIA

(From p. 1104)

a. BRITISH INDIA

1939, Sept. 3. India declared war on Germany.

1940, Aug. 8. Great Britain offered India partnership and a new constitution after the war.

1942, Apr. 11. The Indian Nationalist leaders rejected a **British offer of autonomy** for India after the war, with the right to secede, conveyed to them by **Sir Stafford Cripps** as emissary of the British government. Instead, they demanded **immediate independence.** Disturbances developed in India, and **Mohandas K. Gandhi, Jawaharlal Nehru,** and **Abdul Kalam**

Azad, leaders of the independence movement, were arrested, but were released later in the year.

July 3. The British government announced a **reorganization of the government,** giving the Indians a large majority on the viceroy's council.

1943–47. FIELD MARSHAL VISCOUNT WAVELL, viceroy.

1945, June 29. The **All-India Congress** failed to agree on a common list of ministers for the new government and the **deadlock between the Moslem leaders and the Hindu leaders** continued.

Sept. 19. The new British Labour government proposed to discuss with Indian representatives the offer for Indian autonomy made in 1942.

Sept. 20–23. The **All-India Congress,** meeting in Bombay, declared this plan to be unsatisfactory, and called on Great Britain to "quit India."

Dec. 27. Elections to the **central legislative assembly** gave the largest number of seats to the **Congress Party** and the **Moslem League.**

1946. **Hindu-Moslem differences** over the future of India, combined with a serious food shortage, led to frequent riots, causing thousands of deaths.

Mar. 14. The British government offered **full independence to India.**

Mar.–June. **Negotiations between Britain and Indian leaders** failed to draw up a plan that satisfied both the Congress Party and the Moslem League. The latter, under **Mohammed Ali Jinnah,** insisted on a separate Moslem state of **Pakistan** and decided on "direct action" to achieve its goal.

Aug. 24. A new **executive council** (boycotted by the Moslem League) was formed as an interim government, including seven Congress members and five non-League Moslems. The Moslem League finally decided to join on October 25.

Dec. 9. The **constituent assembly, elected** earlier, began its deliberations on the future of India. The Moslem League refused to participate.

1947, Feb. 20. To hasten developments, the British government declared its intention to transfer power into Indian hands not later than June 1948.

Feb. 20–Aug. 15. VISCOUNT MOUNT-BATTEN, viceroy.

May 29. The constituent assembly outlawed "untouchability."

June 3. Following negotiations with Hindu and Moslem leaders, the British government announced the new constitutional plan which called for **partition between India and Pakistan.** This plan was endorsed by the Moslem League on June 9 and the All-India Congress on June 16.

July 5. The **Indian Independence Bill** was introduced into parliament. It called for two Dominions, **India** and **Pakistan,** and the termination of British authority over the remaining **Indian states.** Both India and Pakistan were to remain members of the British Commonwealth. The bill became law on July 18, and on

Aug. 15. THE INDEPENDENCE OF INDIA went into effect. The process of partition was accompanied by terrible acts of violence, notably in the Punjab region, between Moslems and Hindus. By the end of September, close to two million refugees had been exchanged between India and Pakistan. On

Sept. 21. The two new governments issued a joint statement stressing their readiness to remove all causes of conflict.

b. THE REPUBLIC OF INDIA

1947, Aug. 15. The **Dominion of India was inaugurated** in Delhi, with **Pandit Nehru** as prime minister and **Lord Mountbatten** as governor-general. Most of the **Indian States** (princely and chiefly), notably excepting Hyderabad, Kashmir, and Junagadh, acceded to the new Dominion for defense, external affairs, and communications, while retaining their internal sovereignties.

Oct. 26. The government of India admitted **Kashmir** into the Indian Union, thus precipitating a crisis with Pakistan, since Kashmir contained a majority of Moslems.

Nov. 9. The Indian government assumed control over the administration of the state of **Junagadh.**

Dec. 30. After vain attempts to solve the conflict over **Kashmir,** the dispute was referred to the **United Nations.** Sporadic fighting continued in Kashmir between Indian and Moslem forces.

1948–1949. The **Integration of States** began. The rulers, in response to an appeal to consolidate the country, agreed to form regional unions of states or to merge their states with the Dominion. While renouncing their ruling powers, they retained their personal privileges, private properties, and privy purses.

1948, Jan. 30. **Mahatma Gandhi was assassinated** by a Hindu for his part in the partition of India.

June 21. **Chakravarti Rajagopalachari** succeeded Earl Mountbatten as governor-general.

Sept. 7. The continued refusal of **Hyder-**

abad to join India or to grant parliamentary government provoked an ultimatum from Prime Minister Nehru, who threatened war unless Hyderabad joined the Dominion. In reply

Sept. 11. The Hyderabad government appealed to the United Nations.

Sept. 13. Indian forces invaded Hyderabad.

Sept. 17. Hyderabad surrendered and accepted India's demands.

1949, Jan. 1. Following the mediation attempts of a United Nations Commission set up by the security council, January 20, 1948, India and Pakistan agreed on a **cease-fire order for Kashmir.** India rejected a subsequent arbitration scheme, submitted by the United Nations.

Nov. 26. The Indian constituent assembly adopted a new **constitution** which made **India a federal republic.** The king continued to be recognized, however, as symbol of the free association of Commonwealth members.

1950, Jan. 26. INAUGURATION OF THE REPUBLIC OF INDIA and election of **Rajendra Prasad** as its first president.

Apr. 8. Mounting tension between India and Pakistan was eased by an agreement **(Delhi pact)** between Prime Ministers Pandit Nehru and Liaqat Ali Khan promising fair treatment to each other's minorities. The continued deadlock over **Kashmir,** on the other hand, made any really close relations between the two countries impossible.

June–Dec. India followed an independent course toward events in **Korea.** While condemning North Korean aggression, India was equally opposed to the crossing of the 38th parallel by U.N. forces. India also advocated the admission of **Communist China** to the United Nations.

Nov. 20. Nehru declared that India accepted the 1941 McMahon **boundary with Tibet,** and not the line indicated on Chinese maps.

1951, Feb. 24. A trade block, existing since 1949, was broken when India and Pakistan reached agreement on a full trade pact.

June 3. After months of famine the Indian Socialist Party staged a giant demonstration in Delhi to protest the government's failure to solve the **food and housing problems.**

July 3. Prime Minister Nehru lodged a formal **complaint against Pakistan** with the U.N. security council. He charged repeated violations of the cease-fire agreement in Kashmir.

1952, Jan. 5. India and the United States signed a five-year **"Point Four" agreement,** whereby each would contribute an equal amount of money to develop the Indian economy.

Mar. 1. Final results of the **first national elections** gave Prime Minister Nehru's Con-

gress Party 364 of 489 seats in the national assembly. Pro-Soviet parties won only 28 seats, but showed surprising strength in the local assemblies.

May 13. Formal installation of Rajendra Prasad as the first president elected under the republican constitution.

Aug. 7. Parliament approved legislation to give **Jammu and Kashmir** greater autonomy than other Indian states.

1953, Dec. 2. The government signed with the U.S.S.R. a five-year trade agreement.

1954, Mar. 1. Prime Minister Nehru, denouncing United States policies, informed parliament of his **rejection of a U.S. military aid offer.** He also demanded the withdrawal of U.S. observers from the Kashmir cease-fire team.

Oct. 14. A two-year **trade agreement with Communist China** was signed.

Oct. 21. France agreed to transfer its four settlements in India to Indian control.

1955, June 7–22. During a **visit of Nehru to Moscow,** the U.S.S.R. and India concluded an agreement for Soviet economic and technical assistance to India.

July 25. The government ordered the **closure of the Portuguese legation** in New Delhi because of Portugal's unwillingness to negotiate on Goa's integration into the Indian republic. On August 15 **Indian demonstrators marched on Goa and Damao.** Portuguese police killed 21 and wounded over 100. India broke relations with Portugal, August 19.

Nov. 18. Marshal Bulganin and Nikita Khrushchev arrived in New Delhi for a visit to India.

1956, May 28. France, in a treaty with India, renounced sovereignty over four Indian territories, held by France for 140 years.

1957, Apr. 5. Kerala, a coastal state in southwest India, installed its recently elected **Communist government.**

July 11. The **Aga Khan,** the spiritual and temporal leader of 20 million Ismailis, died and was succeeded by his oldest grandson, Prince Karim Khan, with the title **Aga Khan IV.**

1958, Jan. 10. Former Kashmiri Prime Minister **Sheikh Mohammed Abdullah,** who was released on January 8 after four and a half years of detention, charged that India had set up an illegal régime in Kashmir. On January 13 he asked for a plebiscite to settle the Indian-Pakistani dispute over Kashmir.

Sept. 11. After two-day talks in New Delhi, Nehru and Pakistani **Prime Minister Malik Firoz Noon** issued a communiqué revealing an **agreement to exchange some territory** along their disputed frontier "with a view to removing causes of tension."

1959, June 30. The government refused to rec-

ognize Tibet's **Dalai Lama** as heading a "separate" government of Tibet functioning in India (p. 1341).

July 31. President Rajendra Prasad issued a **proclamation taking over the state government of Kerala** and ousting its Communist régime.

Oct. 26. Indian border police and a Chinese Communist force clashed in Ladakh.

1961, Feb. 14. The government maintained that China was in "unlawful occupation of about 12,000 square miles of Indian territory," and (May 2) charged China with intrusion on the Indian border and fomenting tensions among Asian nations.

Dec. 18-19. Indian troops invaded and conquered the Portuguese territories of Goa, Damao, and Diu.

1962, Aug. 17. Defense Minister V. K. Krishna Menon disclosed that India had entered into an **agreement with the U.S.S.R.** for the manufacture of engines for Indian jet aircraft.

Oct. 20. INVASION OF INDIA BY CHINESE COMMUNIST TROOPS. On October 29 Prime Minister Nehru asked for U.S. military aid.

Oct. 31. Nehru dismissed V. K. Krishna Menon as minister of defense, in the wake of a Chinese military advance, and assumed the post himself.

Nov. 19. Since Indian troops were retreating in the face of a massive Chinese attack, **Nehru asked U.S. President Kennedy for further military aid.** Two days later the United States responded by sending India transport planes with U.S. crews.

Nov. 21. Communist China unexpectedly ordered a **cease-fire along the Indian border,** and offered to draw its troops back of the "lines of actual control" that existed as of November 7, 1959. Fighting ceased the next day.

Dec. 14. Although Nehru had rejected the Chinese offer of a cease-fire and negotiations, India announced the beginning of a **massive Chinese troop withdrawal** from the northeastern frontier area.

1964, Apr. 8. Sheikh Mohammed Abdullah, the "Lion of Kashmir" (again in detention since April 1958), was released from prison. Upon his release, he denounced the Indian policy toward Kashmir, but on April 29 arrived in Delhi to discuss the future of Kashmir with Nehru.

May 27. Jawaharlal Nehru died suddenly.

June 1. The National Congress Party chose **Lal Bahadur Shastri** to succeed Nehru.

Aug. Sheik Abdullah's talks with Shastri, after consultations with President Ayub Khan of Pakistan.

Oct. 12. Meeting of Shastri and Ayub at Karachi, ending in agreement to work for better understanding.

Nov. 15. According to a government statement 775,000 refugees had entered India from East Pakistan since Jan.

Dec. 30-31. Arrest of members of the pro-Chinese wing of the Communist Party, charged with plotting a violent revolution to be timed with another Chinese attack on India.

1965, Jan. 26. Hindi became India's official language, despite violent opposition in southern India. On Feb. 24 it was decided that English should be an associate language in dealings between the central government and non-Hindi speaking states.

Mar. Dispute with Pakistan over the boundary in the **Great Rann of Kutch.** Spasmodic fighting ensued until a cease-fire was arranged by the British government (July 1).

May 8. Arrest and confinement of Sheik Abdullah for agitation in behalf of self-determination for Kashmir.

May 12-19. Visit of Prime Minister Shastri to Moscow in the interest of further Soviet economic aid.

Aug.-Dec. India suffered an **acute food shortage,** which was relieved only by huge shipments from the United States and Australia.

Aug. 5. NEW KASHMIR CRISIS. Indian forces, charging infiltration of Kashmir by Pakistani irregulars, crossed the cease-fire line (Aug. 16) and launched an offensive in the direction of Lahore. An undeclared war ensued. Britain banned arms supplies to India (Sept. 8) and the United States terminated military aid to both sides. On Sept. 20 the U.N. security council called for a cease-fire, which both sides accepted (Sept. 22). Nonetheless, truce violations occurred frequently in the following months.

Sept. 15. Communist China demanded the immediate dismantling of installations on the Indian side of the Sikkim-Chinese border, a demand which was refused.

1966, Jan. 4-10. Conferences at Tashkent between the Indian and Pakistani prime ministers, under the auspices of Soviet Premier Kosygin. Agreement to restore normal relations, withdraw troops to the lines of Aug. 1965, but without a settlement of the Kashmir issue.

Jan. 11. Death of Prime Minister Shastri, of heart attack.

Jan. 19. Mrs. Indira Gandhi, daughter of Nehru, elected leader of the Congress Party and prime minister.

Mar. 28-29. Mrs. Gandhi's visit to Washington, London (Apr. 1), **and Moscow** (Apr. 2). She continued the policy of non-alignment and

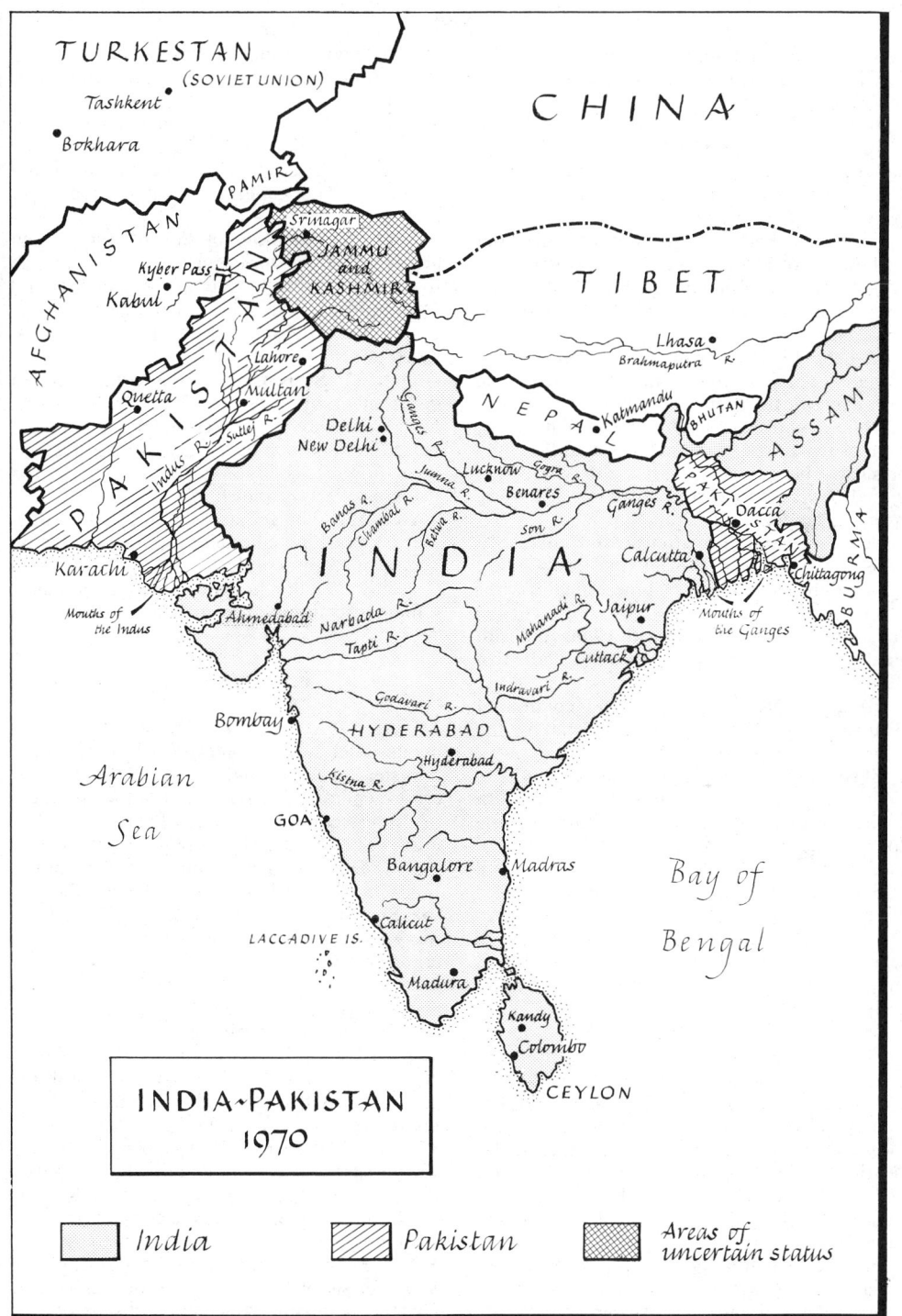

TURKESTAN
(SOVIET UNION)
Tashkent
Bokhara
CHINA
AFGHANISTAN
PAMIR
Kyber Pass
Kabul
Srinagar
JAMMU
and
KASHMIR
TIBET
Lhasa
Brahmaputra R.
PAKISTAN
Lahore
Quetta
Multan
Indus R.
Sutlej R.
Karachi
Mouths of
the Indus
Delhi
New Delhi
Ganges R.
Banas R.
Jumna R.
Chambal R.
Betwa R.
Son R.
Lucknow
Benares
Gogra R.
Ganges R.
NEPAL
Katmandu
BHUTAN
ASSAM
PAKISTAN
Dacca
BURMA
Calcutta
Chittagong
INDIA
Ahmedabad
Narbada R.
Tapti R.
Mahanadi R.
Indravari R.
Jaipur
Cuttack
Mouths of
the Ganges
Arabian
Sea
Bombay
Godavari R.
HYDERABAD
Kistna R.
Hyderabad
GOA
Bangalore
Madras
Calicut
LACCADIVE IS.
Madura
Bay of
Bengal
Kandy
Colombo
CEYLON

INDIA·PAKISTAN
1970

India   Pakistan   Areas of
                             uncertain status

acceptance of economic aid wherever possible. The acute food shortage continued throughout the year.

June 5. Devaluation of the rupee by 36.5%.

July 9–19. Visits of Mrs. Gandhi to Egypt and Yugoslavia. She called for a cessation of U.S. bombing of North Vietnam and the reconvening of the Geneva conference.

Oct. An epidemic of **student riots and strikes.** Several universities were closed.

Nov. 1. Creation of two Sikh states, one Punjabi-speaking, the other (Hariana) Hindi-speaking.

1967, Feb. 15–21. National elections. The Congress party secured a small majority in the lower house, but lost in many of the state assemblies, while the Communists gained. In nine of the sixteen Indian states **coalition governments** became necessary. Growth of regional parties, in part the reflection of tension over the language question.

Sept. Tension in relations with China: Chinese troops crossed the Sikkim frontier and fighting ensued until the Chinese finally withdrew.

1968, Jan. Further tension with China and with Pakistan over their support of Naga and Mizo rebels.

Great increase in student and communal disturbances. In some areas efforts by the Communists to start peasant revolts.

Sheik Abdullah was again released.

Jan. 25–31. Visit of Premier Kosygin to India. Joint Indian-Soviet declaration calling for unconditional cessation of U.S. bombing of North Vietnam.

Feb. Disintegration of the non-Congress Party coalition in West Bengal and (Apr.) in Uttar Pradesh and other states. In these areas, where the Congress Party did not control a majority in the assembly, presidential rule had to be instituted.

Mar. Agreement with Burma for co-operation against insurgents in the border areas supported by China and Pakistan.

1969, May 3. Death of President Zakir Husain.

July 9. The Congress Party accepted Mrs. Gandhi's program for nationalization of banks, restrictions on foreign capital, ceiling on incomes, etc., representing a policy of socialization to forestall further gains by the Communists.

Aug. 16. Election of V. V. Giri as president, by a narrow margin. He was the candidate of Mrs. Gandhi and the left wing of the Congress Party.

Nov. 12. Congress Party leaders of the right wing (the *Syndicate*) expelled Mrs. Gandhi for indiscipline, but the lower house of parliament gave her overwhelming support. The syndicate

then formed a **Congress Parliamentary Party** under **Ram Subhag Singh** as opposition to Mrs. Gandhi.

1970, Aug. "Land Grab" campaigns by Communist and Socialist parties as symbolic seizure of large holdings and distribution to the needy peasants. The leaders of the movement were arrested.

Sept. 2. Abolition of the allowances and privileges of the former princes voted by the lower house with the support of Socialists and Communists. The bill was then rejected by the upper house, but put into effect by presidential fiat (Sept. 6).

Oct. 2. Suspension of the Uttar Pradesh government by decree of the prime minister. Under pressure and criticism Mrs. Gandhi reversed her decision (Oct. 17) and permitted the formation of a coalition government under old Congress Party leadership.

Dec. 15. The Indian Supreme Court ruled that the presidential orders abolishing the privileges of former rulers were illegal. Mrs. Gandhi stated that her government nonetheless remained committed to their abolition.

c. PAKISTAN

1947, Aug. 15. The **Dominion of Pakistan was inaugurated** with **Liaqat Ali Khan** as prime minister and **Mohammed Ali Jinnah** as governor-general. Pakistan, the Islamic provinces of India, consists of West Pakistan on the northwest side of India, and East Pakistan, with only 15% of the territory, but 55% of the population, at the mouths of the Ganges.

1948, Sept. 11. Mohammed Ali Jinnah died and was succeeded by **Khwaja Nazimuddin** as governor-general.

1950, Apr. 8. The **Delhi pact** between India and Pakistan substantially reduced friction between the two dominions.

June–Dec. Pakistan supported the United Nations cause in the **Korean War,** profiting economically from the sudden demand for her raw materials, brought on by the war.

1951, Oct. 16. Prime Minister Liaqat Ali Khan was assassinated while addressing a public meeting. Next day Governor-General Khwaja Nazimuddin assumed leadership of the dominion.

1953, Apr. 17. In the face of a growing **economic crisis** of famine proportions, **Governor-General Ghulam Mohammed** dismissed the cabinet and Prime Minister Nazimuddin, and named **Mohammed Ali,** leader of the progressives in the Moslem League Party, to be prime minister.

Nov. 2. The constituent assembly voted to

make Pakistan a republic within the Commonwealth.

1954, Mar. 19. In elections, voters in East Pakistan turned the administration of the large province over to the opposition, a major setback for the Moslem League Party.

Apr. 2. A Turkish-Pakistani mutual defense pact was signed in Karachi.

May 19. The government signed an **agreement with the United States** for American military and technical assistance, specified for defensive purposes only.

May 30. The central government dismissed East Pakistan's chief minister for having engaged in "treasonable activities," and sent 10,000 troops to the province to suppress labor riots and restore order.

1956, Mar. 23. As the **new constitution** went into effect, Pakistan officially became the **ISLAMIC REPUBLIC OF PAKISTAN.**

Sept. 12. **Hussein Shaheed Suhrawardy** became prime minister, succeeding Mohammed Ali, who had resigned on September 8.

1958, Oct. 7. President Iskander Mirza dismissed the prime minister, annulled the constitution, and declared martial law. He appointed the commander-in-chief of the army, **General Mohammed Ayub Khan** as administrator of martial law.

Oct. 27. GENERAL MOHAMMED AYUB KHAN PRESIDENT (to 1970), after forcing the resignation of Iskander Mirza.

1959, Dec. 3. As **Sino-Indian border clashes** continued, Pakistan protested to the U.N. against a possible partition of **Ladakh,** a province of Indian-held Kashmir, which was claimed by both India and Pakistan, and much of which was under Chinese occupation.

1960, Aug. 1. By presidential order, **Rawalpindi,** an industrial center and military station, was **declared to be Pakistan's only capital,** thus replacing Karachi.

Sept. 19. Indian Prime Minister Nehru and Pakistani President Mohammed Ayub Khan signed **agreements on the joint use of Indus River waters.**

1962, June 7. The cabinet of the military government resigned after 44 months. On June 8 President Ayub Khan announced a **return to constitutional government.** On July 16, when he signed legislation permitting the re-establishment of political parties, the Jamaat-i-Islami, the strongest orthodox Moslem party, and later the Moslem League announced their revival.

Nov. 29. India and Pakistan agreed to discuss a settlement of their 15-year dispute over Kashmir.

1963, Mar. 12. The foreign office published the text of a provisional **Pakistani-Chinese agreement** revealing the tentative cession to Pakistan of 750 square miles of territory held by China. There was to be no corresponding territorial loss to Pakistan.

Aug. 29. The government signed a treaty to provide scheduled **air service with Communist China.** Pakistan was the first Western-oriented nation to sign such a pact.

1964, Jan. 6. The government outlawed **Jamaat-i-Islami** and jailed 60 of its leaders. The ban was lifted by order of the supreme court (Sept. 25).

Jan. 20. Pakistan called for an immediate meeting of the U.N. security council to consider the worsening **situation in Kashmir.** India, January 24, blamed Pakistan for stirring up trouble, and asked for direct negotiations.

Feb. 17. The security council suspended debate on Kashmir at the request of Pakistani Foreign Minister Bhutto, who left for Pakistan.

Feb. 23. In a joint communiqué, at the end of Chinese Premier **Chou En-lai's** eight-day visit, **China supported Pakistan's proposal** that Kashmir choose its own allegiance in a referendum.

1965, Mar. **Elections to the national assembly** gave the government party (Pakistan Muslim League) more than a two-thirds majority.

Aug. **Undeclared war with India,** over Kashmir (p. 1314).

Loan agreement with Communist China, which thenceforth became the chief source of Pakistani military supplies.

Dec. 14–15. **Visit of President Ayub Khan to Washington.**

1966. Growing **agitation in East Pakistan for autonomy.**

Dec. 23. Agreement with the United States for huge grain shipments to relieve the food shortage.

1967. Continuance of the drought and food shortage obliged the government to revise its economic plan and give greater emphasis to development of agriculture. The introduction of new and greatly improved strains of wheat and rice was to prove of great value.

Apr. Emergence of the **Pakistan Democratic Movement** working for direct elections and the extension of provincial autonomy. The movement was supported by most opposition groups.

1968. **Non-renewal of the United States communications base at Peshawar.**

Oct. **Student outbreaks,** culminating in the arrest of Mr. Bhutto, leader of the Pakistan People's Party, and other leftist leaders.

1969, Jan. Formation of the **Direct Action Committee,** composed of eight parties of the Right and Center, under **Nasrullah Khan:** demand for release of political prisoners and return to parliamentary government.

Feb. 21. President Ayub Khan announced that he would not stand for re-election. The news was met with widespread student riots and strikes.

Mar. 25. RESIGNATION OF PRESI-DENT AYUB KHAN. He was succeeded by **General Agha Mohammed Yahya Khan.** Martial law was proclaimed as a result of student and worker unrest.

Nov. 28. The new president announced **constitutional reforms.** West Pakistan was to be divided into provinces and maximum autonomy was to be given local government in both parts of the state.

1970, Nov. 12–13. A **southwest cyclone** with winds of 100–150 miles per hour struck the Ganges-Brahmaputra deltas in East Pakistan, raising the tides as much as 25 feet and sweeping over thickly populated delta islands. The dead numbered in the hundreds of thousands in what was probably the worst natural disaster of the century.

Dec. 7. In the **national elections Sheik Mujibur Rahman** and his East Pakistani **Awami League** won an absolute majority of the 300 seats in the assembly. In West Pakistan **Zulfigar Ali Bhutto's Pakistan People's Party** (Marxist) dominated with 82 seats. There could then be no further question that fundamental changes in the state would be undertaken, chiefly in favor of East Pakistan.

d. CEYLON

1946, May 15. **Ceylon** was granted a **new constitution** which gave it almost complete self-government in domestic affairs.

1947, Sept. 26. The first cabinet under the new constitution took office, with **Stephen Senanayaki** as prime minister. The new parliament opened on November 24. A series of agreements with the United Kingdom (Nov. 11) further reduced British influence in Ceylon, and finally, on

1948, Feb. 4. CEYLON BECAME A SELF-GOVERNING DOMINION in the British Commonwealth, the first non-European colony to achieve this status.

1950, Nov. 7. Ceylon was the second to sign an **agreement with the United States** providing assistance under the Point 4 program.

1952, May 24. Despite vigorous Marxist efforts to win control, the Conservative government won a majority in parliamentary elections.

1956, Apr. 12. After the neutralist **People's United Front** was victorious in parliamentary elections, **Sirimavo Bandaranaike** was appointed to head a leftist coalition cabinet,

made up of Democratic Socialists, Trotsky-Marxists, and orthodox Buddhists.

June 15. Parliament approved the **Sinhalese Language Bill** to make Sinhalese the sole official language of Ceylon, despite rioting by the Tamil-speaking minority. The senate, on July 6, approved the language bill.

1957, June 7. An agreement, concluded in Colombo, provided for Ceylon's payment of $50 million to Britain over a five-year period for **British bases in Ceylon.** The Trincomalee naval base was scheduled for transfer October 1; the Katunayaka base November 1.

July 26. Negotiations from both the government and from the Federal Party successfully compromised the language problem by agreeing to the use of both the Tamil and Sinhalese languages.

Sept. 16. Israel and Ceylon announced plans to establish diplomatic relations.

Sept. 19. Ceylon and Communist China concluded a five-year trade pact.

1959, Sept. 26. Prime Minister Bandaranaike died in Colombo of wounds inflicted by an assassin. Education Minister Wijayananda Dahanayake was named to replace him.

1960, July 20. In **parliamentary elections,** the opposition **Sri Lanka Freedom Party** and its allies won an overwhelming victory over the ruling United National Party. On July 21 **Mrs. Sirimavo Bandaranaike** was sworn in as prime minister.

1961, Apr. The Tamil Federal Party touched off an emergency situation because of its disobedience **campaign for a separate Tamil-speaking state.**

1963, May 1. Emergency rule ended after 743 days.

1964, Feb. 27. Chinese Premier **Chou En-lai** began a three-day visit to discuss the Chinese-Indian border dispute.

Oct. 30. Agreement with India providing for the **repatriation of 525,000 Indians** over the next 15 years; Ceylon to grant citizenship to 300,000 others of Indian origin.

1965, Mar. 22. Elections. The ruling **Freedom Party** of Mrs. Bandaranaike was **defeated by the National United Party,** which formed a new coalition government under **Dudley Senanayake.**

July. A consortium of powers (Britain, the U.S., Canada, Australia, and Japan) extended a credit of $50 million to help meet the cost of import requirements.

1966, Jan. 11. An act was passed allowing more extensive **use of the Tamil language** in the northern and eastern provinces. Violent opposition of the Sinhalese factions.

July. World Buddhist Congress in Colombo.

1967, June 5. Indo-Ceylonese agreement providing for repatriation of Indian plantation workers.

Nov. 22. Devaluation of the rupee, following the devaluation of the British pound sterling.

1969, Dec. Widespread **student unrest:** effort to open a "free" university in Colombo. The universities were closed after a general student strike.

1970, May 28. Resignation of premier Senanayake following a setback in the elections. **Mrs. Sirimavo Bandaranaike** formed a new coalition government.

e. MALDIVES

1953-1954. The islands, a British protectorate, temporarily replaced the sultanate with a re-publican form of government.

1954-1968. The sultanate was restored.

1960. The islands were granted **local self-government.**

1965, July 26. The British government accorded the islands **complete independence,** on condition of retaining an air base on Gan Island until 1986.

Sept. 21. Maldives was admitted to the United Nations.

1968, Mar. A referendum decided for a republican form of government.

Nov. 11. The Republic of Maldives was proclaimed. **Ibrahim Nasir,** former premier, became president.

2. BURMA

(From p. 906)

1942, Mar. 8. The **Japanese occupied Rangoon.** For the campaigns in Burma during the Second World War see p. 1152.

1945, May 17. A British white paper promised Burma **dominion status** after the war.

1946, Dec. 20. The British government invited a Burmese delegation to meet in London and discuss the early achievement of **self-government** for Burma.

1947, Jan. 28. An agreement between British and Burmese leaders called for the

Apr. 9. Election of a constituent assembly. The **Anti-Fascist People's Freedom League** (A.F.P.F.L.), headed by **U Aung San,** received an overwhelming majority.

June 17. The constituent assembly unanimously adopted a resolution calling for an **"independent sovereign republic** to be known as the **Union of Burma."**

July 19. U Aung San and several members of his provisional government were **assassinated** by political opponents under the direction of former premier **U Saw.** The assassins were tried and executed (May 8, 1948).

July 20. Thakin Nu, vice-president of the A.F.P.F.L., formed a new government.

Sept. 24-25. The **new constitution was adopted** by the **constituent assembly,** and **Sao Shwe Thaik,** the sawbwa (ruler) of Yawnghwe (one of the largest of the Shan states), was elected provisional president.

1948, Jan. 4. The **UNION OF BURMA,** an independent republic free from any ties with the British Commonwealth, was officially proclaimed. **Sao Shwe Thaik** continued as president, and **Thakin Nu** as prime minister. The new state immediately embarked on a program of radical nationalization of resources and industries. Its program was not radical enough, however, to satisfy the two Communist parties of Burma, and in late

March. A **Communist rebellion broke out in Southern Burma.** The situation was further aggravated when in

Aug. The **Karens started a rebellion** to achieve an autonomous Karen state. Both Karens and Communists succeeded in occupying large parts of southern and central Burma. At the same time an element of the **"People's Volunteer Organization"** (part of the A.F.P.-F.L.'s old army) ravaged central Burma.

1949, June 14. The Karen rebels proclaimed a separate state, with headquarters at Toungoo.

1950, Mar. 19. Government forces captured **Toungoo.**

May 19. The main center of Communist resistance at **Prome** was taken by the army. The government was thus able to regain some control over the major towns and means of communication. **Rebel activity,** however, continued, and elections, already postponed several times, had to be postponed for another year. In the meantime the economic condition of the country, already seriously affected by the war, was steadily growing worse.

1953, Mar. 3. The army announced a **major offensive** in northern Burma to suppress a strong force of **Chinese Nationalists** in operation there since 1949. On March 25 the government called on the U.N. to condemn Nationalist China for aggression.

Apr. 22. The U.N. political committee adopted, 58-0, a resolution which called for the **removal or internment of "foreign troops"**

in operation in Burma. Burma and Nationalist China abstained.

1954, Nov. 5. A peace treaty with Japan officially ended the Japanese-Burmese war.

1956, Apr. 27. In parliamentary elections, **Premier U Nu's** Anti-Fascist People's Freedom
League and allied parties were victorious.

June 5.   Former defense minister **U Ba Swe**
became premier, after Premier U Nu resigned
for one year in order to reorganize his party,
the Anti-Fascist People's Freedom League.

Oct. 2.   Premier U Ba Swe announced
**Communist Chinese agreement to withdraw the
troops** that had penetrated Burma in July, and
to respect the boundary established by treaty
in 1941.

1957, Feb. 28. Parliament voted unanimously
to approve **U Nu's assumption of the premiership.**

1958, May.   Split in the ruling A.F.P.F.L. Party,
ushering in a period of political instability.

July 23.   More than 1100 insurgents of the
minority Mon racial group surrendered in a
mass ceremony which marked the **end of a
ten-year rebellion.**

Sept. 26.   **The army took over power in
Burma,** as **General Ne Win** agreed to head a
new government, at the request of Premier
U Nu, who resigned in favor of Ne Win,
October 28.

**1960, Jan. 28.   Communist China and Burma
signed a ten-year non-aggression treaty** and
border agreement.

Feb.–Mar.   In the elections U Nu's faction,
now called the **Union Party,** won a decisive
victory.

Apr. 4.   Parliament elected **U Nu premier,**
succeeding General Ne Win.

1961, Oct. 13. Communist China and Burma
signed a protocol, as an annex to their boundary agreement of 1960, stating that a joint
border committee had successfully defined and
marked off the boundaries.

1962, Mar. 2. Ne Win led an **army coup** that
deposed U Nu's civilian government. U Nu
and other leaders of the Union Party were
arrested. Parliament was abolished and a
small **Revolutionary Council** put in its place.
The council on Mar. 8 named **Ne Win chief
of state.**

July 4.   The new régime sponsored the
Burmese Socialist Program Party, committed
to "the Burmese Way to Socialism." All other
parties were banned.

1964, Feb. 14. Chinese premier **Chou En-lai
arrived in Rangoon** on a visit.

Despite the military régime, troubles continued especially in the north, where the Chinese Communists were suspected of encouraging and supporting the rebellious Karen,
Kachin, and Shan tribes.

**1966, Oct.   Release of U Nu and U Ba Swe from
captivity.**

1967, June.   Serious anti-Chinese riots in Rangoon, in response to greatly increased insurgency in the north.

Oct.   **Recall of Chinese technicians** by the
Peking government.   Relations between the
two countries became strained.

1968, Apr. First **Central People's Workers'
Council** met in Rangoon. This was an attempt
to stimulate economic life by the appointment
of agricultural and industrial workers' councils.

1969. Growing dissatisfaction with the government's socialist policy and one-party rule.
U Nu, from London, **called for overthrow of the
régime,** by force if necessary, and the restoration of parliamentary democracy (Aug. 29).

June 2.   Report of an advisory body on the
drafting of a new constitution and return to
civilian rule.

Aug.   U Nu announced plans to set up a
revolutionary movement in Thailand.

1970, Mar.   Communist guerrillas, supported by
Peking, seized the northern town of Kyokuk.
Government troops at first won a victory over
them at **Lushio,** but this was followed by severe
fighting and heavy casualties (July 21).

Aug. 15.   **Further battles** between Nankham
and Kutbai.   The government felt obliged to
set up an independent **Strategic Command
Headquarters** at Lushio to coordinate large-
scale operations.

3.   SOUTHEAST ASIA

(*From p. 1105*)

a. MALAYA (MALAYSIA)
AND SINGAPORE

The **Malay States** had come under British
rule or control in the 19th and early 20th centuries (pp. 908–909).   **Singapore,** founded in
1819, was a British crown colony and one of
Britain's most important naval bases.   As elsewhere in the region, the development of a
nationalist movement was greatly accelerated
by World War II.

1955, July 27. The first **national elections in
Malaya** resulted in victory for the **Alliance
Party.**

1956, Feb. 8. A **British-Malayan agreement** was signed in London, transferring to Malaya control of internal security and defense.

1957, Aug. 3. In preparation for Malayan independence, a conference of rulers elected **Sir Abdul Rahman,** ruler of the Negri Sembilan state, to be the first supreme head of the federation for a five-year term.

Aug. 15. The federal legislative council ratified the constitution of the **federation of Malaya.**

Aug. 31. The British protectorate ended and **Malaya became an independent member of the Commonwealth.**

Oct. 7. Malaya became a **member of the Colombo plan** (p. 1172).

Oct. 12. A **British-Malayan treaty** of mutual assistance and external defense was signed.

1958, May 27. British colonial authorities and an all-party delegation from Singapore agreed to transform Singapore into a self-governing state before March 1959.

1959, June 3. Singapore became a self-governing state as the constitution came into effect, and **Sir William Goode,** the British governor, became "head of state."

Aug. 19. Malayan elections resulted in **victory for the Alliance Party,** the pro-Western group led by Tengku (Prince) Abdul Rahman.

Dec. 3. The first Malayan-born head of the Singapore state, **Inche Yusof bin Ishak,** was installed.

1961, Oct. 16. Malayan Prime Minister Prince Abdul Rahman told parliament that Britain would not be allowed to use Singapore as a SEATO defense base after the merger of Malaya and Singapore.

1962, July 31. The agreement to establish the **federation of Malaysia,** comprising Malaya, Singapore, Sarawak, Brunei, and British Borneo, was signed in London.

1963, June 11. Foreign ministers of Malaya, Indonesia, and the Philippines announced a **proposed mutual defense treaty** to protect their countries from subversion; they urged a "confederation of nations of Malay origin"; and they expressed agreement on their conflict over the projected federation of Malaysia.

Aug. 12. In accordance with a request by the presidents of Indonesia and the Philippines and the prime minister of Malaya, Secretary General U Thant named a **U.N. fact-finding mission** to survey the wishes of the people of North Borneo and Sarawak. But on August 29 the Malayan government proclaimed that the federation of Malaysia would be formed regardless of the United Nations mission report, which was expected to be issued on September 14.

Sept. 16. THE FEDERATION OF MALAYSIA, comprising Malaya, Singapore, Sarawak, and North Borneo, was **formally established.**

Sept. 17. Malaysia severed ties with Indonesia and the Philippines because of their **opposition to the new federation.**

1964, Jan. 20. U.S. Attorney General **Robert Kennedy** arrived to discuss the Indonesia-Malaysia dispute.

Feb. 5-10. The foreign ministers of the Philippines, Indonesia, and Malaysia conferred in Thailand on the Malaysian situation. On the 6th they advised U.N. Secretary General U Thant that they had asked Thailand to police a cease-fire along the Malaysian-Indonesian border.

Feb. 17. Indonesia's **Foreign Minister Subandrio** declared that Indonesian guerrillas, who had infiltrated into the Malaysian territories of Saba and Sarawak, would not be withdrawn until the Malaysian question was settled. Efforts to reach a settlement continued without success, while guerrilla warfare went on.

June 20. The **Tokyo "summit conference"** of Malaysia, Indonesia, and the Philippines broke up without result, and renewed Indonesian guerrilla attacks in Sarawak followed.

July, Sept. Repeated outbreaks of **hostilities in Singapore** between the Chinese and Malays.

July 22. Visit of Prince Abdul Rahman to Washington: assurances of U.S. support of Malaysia in the dispute over Saba and Sarawak.

Aug.-Sept. Indonesian landings and paratrooper **attacks on the coast of mainland Malaysia.** These were successfully contained by Malaysian troops, assisted by British, Australian, and New Zealander contingents. These raids diminished in the course of 1965 as the revolution developed in Indonesia.

1965, Aug. 7. Agreement between the governments of Malaysia and **Singapore** for the latter's **withdrawal from the federation.** The initiative came from the Malaysian government, which was disturbed by the efforts of the Singapore Chinese organization (**the People's Action Party,** led by **Lee Kuan Yew**) to extend its influence elsewhere in Malaysia.

Aug. 9. SINGAPORE BECAME AN INDEPENDENT NATION. It was admitted to the United Nations (Sept. 21) and became a member of the British Commonwealth (Oct. 16).

Sept. 20. The **sultan of Trengganu** succeeded the raja of Perlis as **Paramount Ruler** of Malaysia, chosen by the Conference of Rulers for a term of five years.

Dec. 22. Singapore adopted a republican form of government.

1966, June 1. Agreement between Malaysia and Indonesia to end hostilities. Details were worked out in conferences at Bangkok (Aug.) and the final agreement signed at Jakarta (Aug. 11).

Oct. The Chinese People's Action Party was victorious in the Singapore elections.

1967, Aug. 8. Malaysia, Singapore, Thailand, Philippines, and Indonesia joined in forming the **Association of Southeast Asian Nations** (ASEAN) for economic and cultural co-operation and general support in the face of advancing Chinese influence.

Sept. 1. Malay was declared the only official language in mainland Malaysia.

Nov. Strikes and racial conflicts involving considerable loss of life, growing out of economic and other grievances.

1968, Apr. 13. In Singapore the People's Action Party was again successful in the elections.

June. Revival of Communist guerrilla activity in northern Malaysia.

June–July. Malaysian-Philippine discussions at Bangkok dealing with **Philippine claims to Saba** on historical grounds. These talks having proved abortive, the Philippine government on Sept. 18 passed a law incorporating Saba. Thereupon Malaysia broke off diplomatic relations.

1969, May 10. The **elections in Malaysia** revealed losses to the ruling Malay Alliance and a growing threat to Malay dominance. Communal riots broke out in Kuala Lumpur and lasted for five days. To meet the emergency a para-military **National Operations Council** took over executive power.

July. Appearance of guerrillas on the Thai frontier.

Nov. Agreement of the Malaysian and Thai governments to set up an anti-guerrilla command.

1970, Sept. 6. Abdul Razak designated successor to Prime Minister Prince Abdul Rahman on the latter's retirement (Sept. 21). The new premier announced a future policy of non-alignment.

Sept. 20. Abdul Halim Muazzam, Sultan of Kedah, became Paramount Ruler for a five-year term.

Sept. 22. Abdul Razah succeeded Prince Abdul Rahman as prime minister, with a program of rapprochement to Communist China and other Communist states.

b. THAILAND (SIAM)

(From p. 1105)

1941, Dec. 21. Siam concluded a ten-year treaty of alliance with Japan.

1942, Jan. 25. Siam declared war on Great Britain and the United States.

1946, Jan. 1. The state of war between **Great Britain** and **Siam** was officially ended. The **United States** resumed diplomatic relations with Siam on January 4.

June 9. King Ananda Mahidol was found dead from a bullet wound. His brother, **Phumiphon Aduldet,** succeeded him.

Oct. 13. The Siamese government accepted the United Nations verdict to return to **Indo-China** the provinces acquired in 1941 (p. 1152).

1947, Nov. 8. In a bloodless *coup d'état,* an army group under **Marshal Luang Pibul Songgram** overthrew the government.

1948, Jan. 29. A **general election** resulted in a victory for the new government and on April 8 **Luang Pibul Songgram** became premier. There was considerable resistance, however, notably from the followers of **Nai Pridi Panomyang,** wartime resistance leader.

1949, May. 11. Siam henceforth was to be known again as **Thailand.**

1950. The **rise of communism** in Southeast Asia found Thailand on the anti-Communist side. On March 1 she recognized the **South Korean government,** and later sent a contingent to participate in the **Korean war** on the U.N. side.

Mar. 24. King Phumiphon Aduldet returned from Switzerland, where he had been studying, and was crowned as

May 5. King RAMA IX.

1951, June 30. A **naval revolt** against the government of Premier Pibul Songgram was suppressed by loyal army and air force units.

1954, May 29. The government requested action by the U.N. security council to prevent the Indo-Chinese war from spreading to Thailand, and to send observers.

June 18. The Soviet Union vetoed the **plan for a U.N. peace-observation team** in Thailand.

Oct. 5. A **conference in Canada of the Colombo plan nations admitted Thailand to membership.**

1955, Aug. 6. Premier Pibul Songgram ousted some of the country's most powerful men in a successful attempt to regain exclusive control of the government.

1957, Sept. 17. In a military, but bloodless, coup, **Commander-in-Chief Sarit Thanarat took control of the country.** On September 18 King Phumiphon Aduldet appointed Sarit military governor of Bangkok. Dissolving parliament, the king appointed 123 members pending new elections within 90 days. On September 21 SEATO's **Secretary General Pote Sarasin** was unanimously chosen premier.

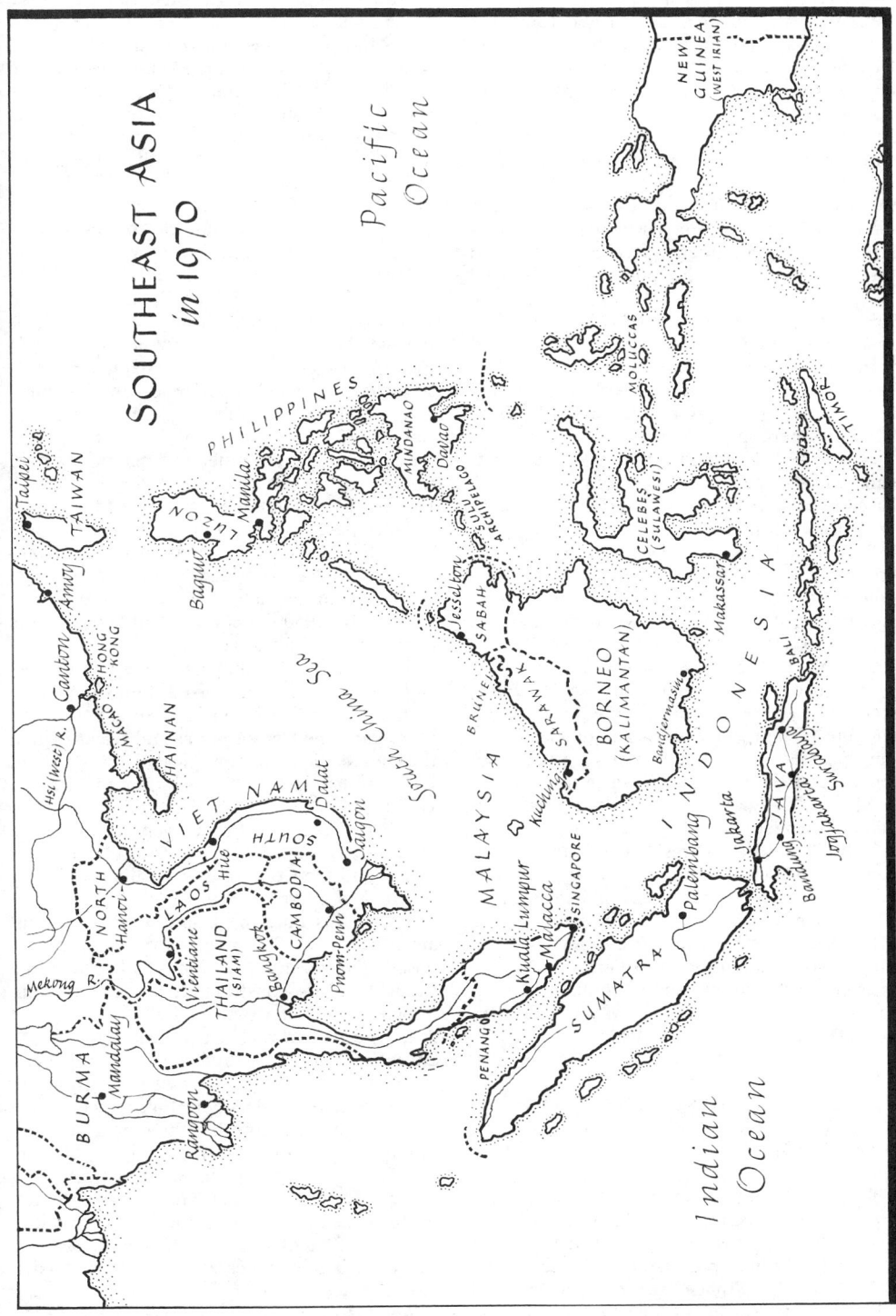

SOUTHEAST ASIA
in 1970

Pacific
Ocean

PHILIPPINES

NEW
GUINEA
(WEST IRIAN)

MOLUCCAS

MINDANAO

Davao

CELEBES
(SULAWESI)

Makassar

TIMOR

Manila

Baguio

LUZON

Taipei

TAIWAN

Amoy

Canton

Hsi (West) R.

HONG KONG

MACAO

HAINAN

South China Sea

VIET NAM

Dalat

Saigon

NORTH

SOUTH

Hue

Hanoi

LAOS

Vientiane

THAILAND
(SIAM)

Bangkok

CAMBODIA

Pnom-Penh

BURMA

Mandalay

Mekong R.

Rangoon

Jesselton

SABAH

BRUNEI

SARAWAK

Kuching

BORNEO
(KALIMANTAN)

Bandjermasin

SULU
ARCHIPELAGO

MALAYSIA

Kuala Lumpur

Malacca

SINGAPORE

PENANG

SUMATRA

Palembang

INDONESIA

Jakarta

JAVA

Surabaja

Bandung

Jogjakarta

BALI

Indian
Ocean

1958, Oct. 20. Field Marshal Sarit Thanarat, supreme commander of the armed forces, in a quiet coup, established **military rule.** On October 21 Sarit abolished political parties and began arresting persons engaged in Communist activity.

1962, Nov. 24. The United States began the **withdrawal of** 2,300 **United States soldiers** from Thailand.

1963, Dec. 8. Marshal Sarit Thanarat, premier, died. **General Thanom Kittikachorn,** former senior deputy premier, succeeded him and promised to follow the policies of Marshal Sarit.

1965– In the **Vietnam war** (p. 1327) the Thai government took its stand with the United States and the anti-Communist governments.

1967, Mar. 22. Agreement with the United States allowing the **use of Thai bases** by B-52 bombers operating in Vietnam.

Sept. A **Thai contingent was sent to Vietnam,** while some 35,000 **American troops were based in Thailand,** mostly to service air attacks on North Vietnam.

1968, June 20. A **new constitution** provided limited parliamentary government. An appointed senate (composed largely of military and police officers) was to wield power until election of a house of representatives.

1969, Feb. 11. The **first general election** in 10 years. The ruling **United Thai People's Party** secured 75 of the 219 seats in the lower house, and the related **Independents** another 72, but the opposition **Democratic Party** garnered all the seats in Bangkok and other cities.

Mar. 7. Marshal Kittikachorn was reappointed premier.

July 28. Visit of President Nixon. There were now 48,000 U.S. troops in Thailand. The president repeated assurances of U.S. support in the event of an attack on Thailand.

1970, Aug. 18. The Thai government notified the U.S. of its **intention to withdraw its 11,000-man contingent from South Vietnam,** in consonance with the U.S. policy of withdrawal. But no date was set for the Thai move.

c. INDO-CHINA

(From p. 1105)

1940, June 19. On the eve of the Franco-German armistice (June 22) Japan announced that it would oppose any change in the status quo of the French possessions in Indo-China.

1941, July 21. France was obliged to yield military control of Indo-China to the Japanese.

1945, Sept. 2. Ho Chi Minh, Nationalist Communist leader of the native resistance to Japan in Tonkin, proclaimed the **independence of the Vietnam Republic.**

1946, Mar. 6. France recognized Vietnam as a free state within the French Union, but this did not deter Ho Chi Minh and his faction from carrying on hostilities aimed at driving out the French and uniting all Indo-China in one Vietnamese state. In retaliation the French had an "autonomous Republic of Cochin China" proclaimed at Saigon (June 1).

July–Sept. In protracted **conferences at Fontainebleau** Ho Chi Minh was unable to persuade the French to accept his program.

Nov. 23. The French **bombardment of Haiphong,** leaving 6000 dead, may be taken as marking the beginning of the long-drawn French struggle to retain Indo-China.

1949, Mar. 8. The French made an agreement with the non-Communist Nationalists under **Bao Dai** (former emperor of Annam) by which they recognized the independence of Vietnam (including Cochin China) within the French Union. France retained the right to maintain military bases in the country. This move only strengthened the determination of the Communists, who drew added encouragement and support from the victory of the Communists in China. By 1950 the conflict had taken on the appearance of a regular war.

1950, Jan.–Feb. Communist China and the Soviet Union both recognized the Communist régime of Ho Chi Minh in Vietnam. On the other hand **the United States and Great Britain recognized Vietnam,** along with Cambodia and Laos, as associated states within the French Union.

1951, Jan.–Feb. The French general **De Lattre de Tassigny,** repulsed Communist attacks on Hanoi and the Communists for the time being reverted to guerrilla tactics.

1953. By this time the Communists had built an army of 125,000 men, to whom were opposed 230,000 French troops. In Nov. the French began construction of a huge **entrenched camp at Dienbienphu.**

1954, Mar. 13–May 7. BATTLE OF DIENBIENPHU. The French, gradually surrounded and cut off, appealed for help to the United States, but President Eisenhower, while he declared (Mar. 24) that the defeat of Communist aggression in Indo-China, Burma, Thailand, or elsewhere in Southeast Asia was of crucial importance to the United States, declined to use American air forces to relieve the siege of Dienbienphu. Meanwhile (Mar. 9) the French had indicated a readiness to discuss a peace settlement.

Apr. 26–July 21. THE GENEVA CONFERENCE was in session. It debated the Korean situation and in addition the problems of Cambodia and Laos as well as those of Vietnam. Much of the time the conference was deadlocked, especially on the questions of a cease-fire, a truce line, and an enforcement commission.

June 19. The new French premier, **Pierre Mendès-France,** who was intent on making peace, conferred with the Chinese Communist **premier Chou En-lai,** at Berne (June 23) and came to agreement with him on the basic lines of a settlement.

July 20. The Geneva conference agreed to an armistice in Indo-China which divided Vietnam into northern and southern parts, with the 17th parallel as the dividing line.

July 21. THE GENEVA AGREEMENTS. In addition to the division of Vietnam, they provided for elections to be held within two years under international supervision (Poland, Canada, India). The Soviet Union, Great Britain, and Communist China signed the accords, but President Eisenhower refused to accept responsibility for the armistice, to be bound by its terms or to try to upset them.

Sept. 8. THE MANILA PACT or **Southeast Asia Collective Defense Treaty** and Organization (SEATO), engineered by the United States in the effort to forestall further Communist gains after the defeat of France. The United States was joined by Great Britain, France, Australia, New Zealand, Philippines, Thailand, Pakistan, with the objective of contributing to peace and security in Southeast Asia through mutual aid in resisting armed attack and countering subversion. Cambodia, Laos, and South Vietnam, precluded by the Geneva accords from formally joining, signed a protocol bringing them within the scope of the treaty's military and economic terms. The treaty became effective Feb. 19, 1955.

d. VIETNAM

At the 1954 Geneva conference **Vietnam was divided** at the 17th parallel between the Communist north (the "Democratic Republic" under Ho Chi Minh) and the south, which had already begun to organize a state early in 1953. The north was supported by the Soviet Union and Communist China, the south by the United States and Great Britain. From the outset the Communist north was determined to subvert or conquer the south and establish a united Vietnamese state. It still had guerrilla units scattered through the country and was prepared to use every means, including terrorism, to gain its end.

1954, June 4. Prince Bau Loa and French **Premier Laniel** signed treaties providing for South Vietnam's "complete independence" in "free association" with France.

June 14. In a government reorganization, **Ngo Dinh Diem** replaced Prince Bau Loa as premier.

1955, Mar. 21. Three armed **opposition religious groups** gave Premier Ngo Dinh Diem a five-day ultimatum to reorganize the government to suit them. Diem rejected the ultimatum on March 24, and on March 29 heavy fighting broke out between government forces and well-armed private religious groups. A cease-fire was negotiated on March 30 and on March 31 one of the private groups switched to the government's support.

Apr. 28. Civil war broke out in Saigon. Premier Diem declared all-out war against the Binh Xuyen rebels.

May 1. Premier Diem won a fifteen-hour **struggle for power** with the supporters of **Bao Dai,** chief of state, over the control of the army.

May 2. After five days of heavy fighting, **government troops forced the Binh Xuyen forces out of the capital.**

May 5. Premier Diem gained backing when a political congress in Vietnam called for the ousting of Bao Dai and establishment of a republic. Another congress urged that all Bao Dai's powers be transferred to the premier until the national assembly decided on a government.

On May 8, Diem indicated that the **French plan**—for Bao Dai's return under a reorganized system of government—would be unacceptable.

May 12. The government asked France either to move her troops to where the Vietminh threat existed, i.e., the northern frontier, or withdraw them completely. On May 20 **France agreed to move her troops to the northern frontier.**

July 7. President Ho Chi Minh of **North Vietnam concluded an agreement with Chinese Communist leaders,** providing for $338 million worth of Chinese economic aid.

Oct. 18. Chief of State Bao Dai dismissed Premier Diem, but Diem refused to resign. The October 23 referendum was held as scheduled, with an overwhelming vote for Diem and against Bao Dai. On October 26 **NGO DINH DIEM PROCLAIMED A REPUBLIC.** As South Vietnam's first president, he promised early elections for a national legislature.

1956, Jan. 23. The cabinet, meeting with President Diem, gave final approval to ordinances setting up new electoral rules and creating an assembly to discuss and approve a new constitution.

Oct. 26. The **new constitution** was promulgated.

1960, Nov. 12. President Ngo Dinh Diem was restored to power by the army, following a coup on November 11 by the paratroop brigade in Saigon.

Dec. 20. In a secret meeting various dissident groups, called collectively **Vietcong** (Vietnamese Communists) formed the **National Front for the Liberation of South Vietnam.**
1961, Apr. 9. Ngo Dinh Diem was re-elected president.

June 16. South Vietnam's chief cabinet minister, **Nguyen Dinh Thuan,** and United States officials completed three days of **conferences in Washington.** The United States agreed to increase the 685-man United States military advisory group, to assign training specialists, and to send United States officers into the field to observe troops in action. In addition to the $40 million in arms previously promised, the United States agreed to pay salaries and supply arms for 20,000 troops to be added to the army of 150,000.
1962, Mar. 22. Troops began "Operation Sunrise" to eliminate **Vietcong guerrillas.**

June 2. The international control commission on Indo-China (composed of Canada, India, and Poland) reported that North Vietnam was supplying the Vietcong rebels in the south in violation of the Geneva agreement on Indo-China. Poland did not sign the report.
1963, May 9. South Vietnam agreed to pay for all the costs ($17 million) of the "strategic-hamlet program," deemed essential to its fight against the Vietcong rebels.

Aug. 21. South Vietnamese **security forces occupied Buddhist pagodas** and arrested many Buddhist priests. A U.N. mission to investigate charges of persecution arrived on October 24.

Nov. 1-2. OVERTHROW OF THE DIEM GOVERNMENT by **General Duong Van Minh** and other anti-Communist officers. Diem and his security chief were killed.
1964, Jan. 6. A power realignment placed the country under the **rule of three generals,** Major General Minh, Major General Tran Van Don, and Major General Le Van Kim.

Jan. 30. General Nguyen Khanh led a bloodless coup against the ruling junta and proclaimed himself chief of state, replacing General Duong Van Minh.

Jan. 31. De Gaulle suggested that in co-operation with Communist China the **former French possessions in Indo-China should be neutralized** under international guarantee.

Feb. 25. *Tass* released an "authorized statement" warning the United States not to carry the war into North Vietnam.

Mar. 7. Premier Khanh announced a one-**year reform program** to improve the standard of living, increase government stability, and strengthen the anti-Communist military effort.

Mar. 8-12. U.S. **Defense Secretary McNamara,** at the head of a fact-finding mission, declared that the United States would aid Vietnam as long as necessary to defeat the Vietcong.

Mar. 18. Premier Khanh declared his willingness to restore **diplomatic relations with Laos,** and named a mission to Cambodia to discuss border problems.

Mar. 26. Secretary McNamara, in a speech, outlined **United States goals in South Vietnam:** to support its independence and prevent a Communist takeover. He rejected neutralization as opening the door to communism.

Apr. 15. The council of the **Southeast Asia Treaty Organization** (SEATO), meeting at Manila, affirmed support of the South Vietnamese struggle against the Vietcong.

May 21. Statement of Ambassador Adlai Stevenson in the U.N. security council: "As long as the peoples of that area are determined to preserve their independence and ask for our help in preserving it, we will extend it."

June-July. Further Vietcong successes brought increased United States efforts to help the Khanh government stem the tide. Growing agitation for extension of the war to North Vietnam, in order to destroy the supply bases of the Vietcong.

July 8. Proposal of U Thant to reconvene the Geneva conference to end the war.

July 24. U.S. rejected de Gaulle's proposal for international neutralization of Vietnam, Cambodia, Laos. DeGaulle doubted possibility of military victory.

Aug. 2. Following South Vietnamese coastal raids on July 30-31, three North Vietnamese torpedo boats pursued and attacked the U.S. destroyer *Maddox* in international waters. The *Maddox,* supported by U.S. airplanes from the carrier *Ticonderoga,* returned fire, disabling one attacker.

Aug. 4. Second North Vietnamese naval attack, on the *Maddox* and the *Turner Joy.* In retaliation, U.S. planes attacked and destroyed oil and naval installations on the North Vietnamese coast. The matter was brought to the U.N. security council, which invited both North and South Vietnam to appear to present evidence.

Aug. 5. THE TONKIN GULF RESOLUTION. At the president's request, congress voted overwhelmingly (only two senators opposing) a resolution authorizing him to "take all necessary measures to repel any armed attack against forces of the United States and to prevent further aggression." Congress also approved "all necessary steps, including the use of armed force, to assist any member or protocol state of the Southeast Asia Collective Defense Treaty requesting assistance in defense of its freedom."

Aug. 16. Adoption of a **new constitution** for South Vietnam. **Premier Khanh was elected president** with near-dictatorial powers. Riots by students and Buddhists (Aug. 19) led the government to withdraw the new constitution (Aug. 25). Khanh then joined **Gen. Duong Van Minh** and **Gen. Tran Thieu Khiem** in a **Committee of Unification** (Aug. 27). But on Sept. 3 **Khanh resumed the premiership,** dissolved the triumvirate, and restored Minh as chief of state.

Sept. 13. An **abortive military coup** directed against Khanh.

Sept. 26. A **High National Council** of civilians began to draft a new constitution. It provided (Oct. 20) for civilian rule, with the cabinet responsible to the assembly.

Nov. 4. Tran Van Huong succeeded Khanh as premier, Khanh remaining commander-in-chief of the army. The new arrangements were supported by the United States ambassador, Maxwell Taylor, but led to much Buddhist protest and army intrigue.

Dec. 11. Announcement of vastly **increased U.S. aid** "to restrain the mounting infiltration of men and equipment by the Hanoi régime in support of the Vietcong."

Dec. 19. A **military coup,** associated with Khanh, overthrew the High National Council and canceled certain provisions of the constitution. An **Armed Forces Council** was now in control, despite the disapproval of the U.S. authorities and their demand for a return to civilian government.

1965, Jan. 26. The government of **Tran Van Huong was forced out** by the military, following Buddhist demonstrations. **Gen. Khanh returned to power.**

Feb. 7, 8, 11. Air bombardment of North Vietnam was inaugurated by U.S. forces in retaliation for a Vietcong attack on the barracks at Pleiku. The Soviet government warned that it would take further measures to strengthen North Vietnam's defense capability. Premier Kosygin visited Hanoi.

Feb. 16. Khanh supported a civilian government under **Phan Huy Quat,** which enjoyed the favor also of the Buddhists.

Soviet Russia proposed a new conference on Indo-China, as suggested by President de Gaulle (Feb. 10). U Thant made heroic efforts to get talks started, but President Johnson (Feb. 25) rejected negotiations so long as North Vietnam failed to respect the independence and security of South Vietnam.

Feb. 20. The Armed Forces Council, led by **Gen Nguyen Cao Ky** and **Gen. Nguyen Van Thieu,** deposed Khanh as commander of the armed forces. Thieu presently became the leader in the Armed Forces Council.

Mar. 2. BEGINNING OF THE NON-RETALIATORY (*Rolling Thunder*) **BOMBING CAMPAIGN** against North Vietnam.

Mar. 7–9. Two battalions of U.S. Marines, the first combat troops to land in Vietnam, arrived to defend the air base at Danang.

Mar. 13. In a press conference President Johnson repeated that "to any in Southeast Asia who ask our help in defending their freedom, we're going to give it . . ."

Mar. 22. Five-point manifesto of the Vietcong: no negotiations until after the withdrawal of U.S. troops.

Mar. 30. Bombing of the U.S. embassy in Saigon by Vietcong, demonstrating their all-pervasive power.

Apr. 7. In a **Baltimore speech,** President Johnson declared the readiness of the U.S. government to embark on "unconditional discussions of peace." At the same time he outlined a vast plan for the economic development of all Southeast Asia.

Apr. 13. As though in reply to the president, the **North Vietnamese** government stated its **terms for peace,** which were basic to all later developments: withdrawal of all U.S. troops from South Vietnam; cessation of U.S. hostilities against North Vietnam; settlement of South Vietnamese affairs in accordance with the Vietcong program; peaceful reunification of North and South Vietnam by the people of both zones, without foreign interference.

Apr. 15–29. Mission of Henry Cabot Lodge to New Zealand, Philippines, Taiwan, South Korea, Japan, and India to explain the U.S. position and solicit support.

June 12. Premier Quat forced out of office by Generals Ky and Thieu, who (June 18) became respectively premier and president of the **"National Leadership Committee."**

July. Arrival in South Vietnam **of Australian and New Zealander detachments.** A South Korean contingent had arrived earlier. On July 28 President Johnson announced that American forces would be increased to 125,000 and that the draft would be doubled. He appealed to the U.N. (July 30) for aid in arriving at a settlement.

July 8. Henry Cabot Lodge succeeded Gen. Maxwell Taylor as ambassador.

Oct. 15–16. In the United States the **National Coordinating Committee to End the War in Vietnam** staged mass anti-war demonstrations in many cities, where there were numerous instances of draft-card burnings.

Nov. 28–29. Secretary of Defense

McNamara in Saigon. Military leaders argue the need of 350,000 to 400,000 men to bring the war to a victorious end.

Dec. 15. U.S. bombing of a power plant on the very outskirts of Haiphong, a port which thus far had been spared in view of the heavy Soviet shipping there.

Dec. 24. Christmas truce began. Suspension of bombing of North Vietnam. Efforts of U.S. to initiate peace talks summarily rejected by Ho Chi Minh.

1966, Jan. 31. Resumption of U.S. bombing of North Vietnam.

Feb. 6-8. Honolulu conference between President Johnson and Generals Ky and Thieu. Discussions of needed social reforms in South Vietnam. Vice-President Humphrey and several U.S. cabinet members sent to non-Communist governments of Asia to explain U.S. policy and advise on domestic problems.

Mar. 10-Apr. 5. Widespread Buddhist protests and demonstrations against the Ky régime and its dismissal of General Tri as commander of the First Corps. The unrest ended when the government (Apr. 14) promised early elections for a constituent assembly.

May 15-June 23. Armed intervention against Buddhist rebels in Danang and Hué, where Buddhists had burned the American consulate (May 31). Arrest of Thich Tri Quang, the Buddhist leader (June 19), followed by seizure of the Secular Affairs Institute, the last Buddhist stronghold, in Saigon (June 23).

June 29-July 5. Repeated U.S. air attacks on oil storage tanks in the environs of Hanoi and Haiphong.

July 12. North Vietnamese threat to try U.S. prisoner pilots as war criminals. Warnings by President Johnson (July 20).

July 25. Ky urges the invasion of North Vietnam even at the cost of Communist Chinese intervention. This risk the U.S. government was never willing to take, though at the time the air war was carried right up to the Vietnamese-Chinese frontier.

Sept. 1. President de Gaulle, on a visit to Cambodia, insisted that the U.S. must withdraw its forces before a negotiated settlement could become possible. Actually Hanoi rejected a U.S. proposal for mutual withdrawal (Sept. 11).

Sept. 11-12. Elections for a constituent assembly. Despite Vietcong threats and pressures, over 80% of the eligible voters went to the polls.

Oct. 24-25. Manila conference. The powers allied in support of South Vietnam pledged to withdraw as their opponents withdrew and stopped infiltration. Hanoi and

Peking scorned the suggestion (Oct. 27).

Dec. 2-5. Intensive bombing of targets around Hanoi.

Dec. 31. U.S. troop strength in South Vietnam had reached 389,000.

1967, Jan. 3. Hanoi offered to negotiate in return for unconditional cessation of bombing.

Feb. 8. Exchange of letters between President Johnson and Ho Chi Minh proved fruitless.

Feb. 8-14. Bombing pause during the Tet holidays. Efforts of Prime Minister Wilson and Premier Kosygin to persuade the U.S. to cease bombing as the prelude to negotiations.

Mar. 15. Ellsworth Bunker succeeded Lodge as U.S. ambassador.

Mar. 18. The constituent assembly unanimously approved the draft of a new constitution.

Mar. 20-21. Meeting of President Johnson with South Vietnamese leaders on Guam.

Mar. 22. Thailand agrees to the use by the U.S. bombers of bases from which to attack targets in Vietnam.

Apr. 1. The new constitution, approved by the government, went into effect. It introduced representative, democratic institutions.

May 18-19. U.S. troops moved into the demilitarized zone dividing North and South Vietnam. Heavy bombing of the power plant at Hanoi.

June. As of mid-year the American forces numbered 463,000, to which the allied powers added another 54,000. The South Vietnamese army counted 600,000. Against this formidable array the North Vietnamese had 50,000 regulars in addition to 294,000 Vietcong and other irregulars. The North had also the support of some 50,000 Chinese coolies who repaired the damage done by the bombing. They had the further advantage of the terrain (infiltration of troops over the jungle Ho Chi Minh trail in eastern Laos), and of the reluctance of the U.S. to provoke Chinese or Soviet intervention through the invasion of North Vietnam or through outright attack on Haiphong or Hanoi. Despite the acute antagonism that had developed between Soviet Russia and Communist China, the Chinese throughout the Vietnamese conflict allowed Soviet supply trains to cross Chinese territory to reach their destination.

July 6-11. Secretary McNamara in Vietnam. Request of General Westmoreland for an additional 70,000 troops.

July 22-Aug. 5. Mission of Gen. Maxwell Taylor and Clark Clifford to solicit more troops from the allied powers. They reported general approval of U.S. bombing and other tactics.

Sept. 3. ELECTIONS IN SOUTH VIETNAM. Generals Thieu and Ky were elected president and vice-president with about 35% of the popular vote.

Dec. 26. Threat of the South Vietnamese government to pursue Communist troops into Cambodia if they used that country as a base for infiltration of South Vietnam. In reply the Peking government (Dec. 29) promised Cambodia support if the U.S. extended hostilities to that country.

1968, Jan.-June 27. The siege of Khesanh by the Communists. This base, commanding an important road juncture and infiltration route, was finally evacuated without serious loss.

Jan. 30. THE GREAT TET OFFENSIVE. During the religious holiday pause in operations the Vietcong and North Vietnamese forces suddenly launched well-planned **attacks on some thirty South Vietnamese cities.** Saigon and Hué were scenes of desperate fighting, the enemy evidently hoping to topple the government and create chaos. Operations continued until Feb. 24, when the South Vietnamese troops finally recaptured the palace grounds at Hué, only to find that during the enemy occupation there had been a mass slaughter of opponents. The Tet offensive, while it failed to attain its objective, made a profound impression on U.S. and world opinion, which was astounded by the power of the Communist forces.

Feb. 24. U Thant, returning from an extended mission in the interest of peace, reported his conviction that a cessation of the bombing would lead soon to meaningful peace negotiations.

Mar. 9. General Westmoreland was reported to be asking for 206,000 additional men.

Mar. 31. President Johnson announced the **CESSATION OF AIR AND NAVAL BOMBARDMENT north of the 20th parallel,** which meant relief for some 90% of the North Vietnamese population.

Apr. 3. The North Vietnamese government offered to meet to discuss unconditional cessation of bombing.

May 5-June. Renewal of Communist attacks on South Vietnamese cities. Shelling and fighting about Saigon, leaving heavy civilian casualties and thousands of refugees.

May 10. PEACE TALKS initiated at Paris, with **W. Averill Harriman** the chief U.S. delegate and **Xuan Thuy** the North Vietnamese. The North Vietnamese at once demanded unconditional cessation of bombing.

June 10. General Creighton W. Abrams assumed command of the U.S. forces in South Vietnam, in succession to Gen. Westmoreland.

July 18-20. Meeting of President Johnson and President Thieu at Honolulu. President Johnson promised that in peace negotiations the U.S. would not impose a coalition government on the Saigon government.

Oct. 31. President Johnson announced the **COMPLETE CESSATION OF U.S. NAVAL, AIR, AND ARTILLERY BOMBING OF NORTH VIETNAM.** The U.S. government later claimed that this was part of an unwritten understanding that the North Vietnamese would respect the demilitarized zone, abstain from bombing southern cities, and embark on meaningful negotiations. Hanoi denied that there was any such understanding.

Nov. The **Paris peace talks,** conceivably meant by the North Vietnamese simply as a means to secure the cessation of bombing or to gain time, made no progress, due to squabbles over procedural matters and over the status of the Vietcong in the negotiations.

1969, Jan. 5. Lodge replaced Harriman as the chief U.S. negotiator at Paris.

Jan. 25. First plenary session of the expanded Paris conference, with both the Saigon government and the Vietcong represented. After further tiresome arguments agreement was finally reached on seating arrangements and other procedural matters.

Mar. 6. It was announced that **U.S. troops in South Vietnam had been increased to 541,000,** in addition to 72,000 allied forces.

May 8. Heavy enemy attacks, with many casualties. Rapidly growing unrest and **criticism of the war** in the United States, where the demand arose for immediate withdrawal, regardless of the consequences.

May 14. President Nixon outlined peace proposals involving the withdrawal of the major part of all foreign forces from South Vietnam within a year. The basic American peace requirement, he said, was a guarantee of freedom for South Vietnam.

June 8. Meeting of President Nixon and President Thieu at Midway. Nixon announced the beginning of U.S. withdrawal and the new policy of *"Vietnamization,"* that is, helping the Vietnamese in every way to deal with their own problems.

Sept. 3. DEATH OF HO CHI MINH, the venerable Vietnamese nationalist and revolutionary.

Nov. 3. Policy statement by President Nixon, announcing that 60,000 American troops would be withdrawn from South Vietnam by Dec. 15. More precipitate withdrawal, he said, would allow the Communists to massacre their opponents as they did recently at Hué. It would mean also the collapse of American leadership in Southeast Asia and indeed in the whole world. The United States had offered repeatedly to negotiate: "We have declared that anything is negotiable except the right of the people of South Vietnam to determine their future." But Hanoi had thus far refused even to discuss terms.

Nov. 15. In the United States, a **huge moratorium demonstration** to impress the administration and congress with the determination of the people to see the war closed out.

Nov. 20. Resignation of Henry Cabot Lodge as chief delegate at Paris, meant in part as a protest against the lack of progress in the talks. Presently the North Vietnamese delegate went on extended and indefinite leave, so that the talks remained stagnant for months.

1970, Jan. 29. Bombing of a North Vietnamese anti-aircraft missile base, as a warning against attacks on U.S. reconnaissance planes.

Apr. 22. President Nixon promised to withdraw 150,000 more troops over the ensuing year.

Apr. 30. THE CAMBODIAN CRISIS, precipitated when the president announced that U.S. combat troops would participate with South Vietnamese troops in invading Cambodia to destroy important enemy supply bases and concentrations. This renewed "escalation" of the war created a furor of opposition in the United States and led to countless student protests.

June 24. The senate voted to repeal the ill-fated Tonkin Gulf resolution (p. 1236) which had given the administration a free hand to conduct its policies in Vietnam.

June 30. The senate passed the **Cooper-Church Amendment,** barring the use of U.S. troops in Cambodia. At the same time the president announced the end of combat operations in Cambodia and promised that in the future the U.S. would provide only air support for South Vietnamese operations.

July 1. Former ambassador **David Bruce appointed to be chief negotiator at Paris.**

Aug. 31. The Buddhist faction won ten seats in the election for partial renewal of the senate.

Sept. 17. Eight-point statement of terms submitted to the Paris conference by the Vietcong delegate. Mostly a repetition of familiar demands, the statement seemed designed to commit the U.S. to withdrawal of all foreign troops from South Vietnam by June 30, 1971, and to replacement of the existing South Vietnamese government by a coalition in which the Vietcong would share.

Oct. 7. President Nixon's **"major new initiative for peace":** a general cease-fire throughout all Indo-China, with international supervision; an international conference to settle Indo-Chinese problems; negotiation of a timetable for complete withdrawal of forces from South Vietnam; a South Vietnamese settlement reflecting the will of the people and the existing relationships of political forces; immediate and unconditional release of all prisoners of war.

Oct. 14. Hanoi rejected the Nixon proposals as "fraud."

Nov. 21. Heavy U.S. bombing of North Vietnamese anti-aircraft and other targets in retaliation for attacks on unarmed, though escorted, American reconnaissance planes.

A United States **helicopter raid on a prisoner of war camp** 23 miles from Hanoi failed when the camp was found to be empty.

e. CAMBODIA

In March 1945 **King Norodom Sihanouk,** with the approval of the Japanese, who had earlier taken over the government, **proclaimed Cambodia's independence** and set up a government under **Premier Son Ngoc Thanh,** a leader in the movement for independence. In October **British, Indian, and French troops occupied Pnom-Penh,** the capital, and sentenced Son Ngoc Thanh to house arrest in Paris. Early in the following year **France accorded Cambodia internal autonomy,** and finally in the autumn of 1949 granted *de jure* **independence** while retaining control of defense, foreign affairs, and internal security.

1951, Oct. Son Ngoc Thanh returned, but he fled the capital when his virulent anti-French campaign led King Sihanouk to close his newspaper.

Oct. 29. The French commissioner in Cambodia, **Jean de Raymond, was assassinated** by a Vietminh rebel.

1952, June 15. King Sihanouk dismissed the cabinet and national assembly and led the government himself, promising a plebiscite at the end of three years.

1953, May 9. French-Cambodian protocols were signed to assure Cambodia of "full sovereignty" in military, judicial, and economic matters.

June 14. King Sihanouk left for voluntary exile in Thailand as a dramatization of his country's demands for complete independence. He returned suddenly, on June 20. Amid mounting tension with France, Cambodian army units seized control of all government buildings.

1954, July 20. The **Geneva conference** (p. 1324) **confirmed Cambodian complete independence,** previously promised by France (Nov. 1953).

1955, Feb. 7–9. A national referendum approved King Sihanouk's rule.

Mar. 2. King Norodom Sihanouk abdicated in favor of **Norodom Suramarit,** his father.

Sept. 11. In elections to the national assembly the People's Socialist Community, founded by Sihanouk, won all 91 seats.

1956, Jan. 4. **Oun Cheeang Sun** was installed as premier, succeeding former King Norodom Sihanouk. The new premier had been elected by the People's Socialist Community.

May 18. The U.S.S.R. announced that diplomatic relations with the kingdom had been established.

1957, Apr. 7. Prince Norodom Sihanouk, of the **People's Socialist Community,** became premier, following the **deposition** by the national assembly **of Premier San Yun** over a budget dispute.

1958, Mar. 23. In elections for the national assembly, the People's Socialist Community won all 61 seats.

July 10. The national assembly invested a new cabinet headed by Prince Norodom Sihanouk. On July 18 Sihanouk notified Peking of the **decision to recognize the Communist Chinese government.**

1960, Apr. 12. Premier Norodom Sihanouk and his cabinet resigned following the **death of King Norodom Suramarit** on April 3.

June 5. A nation-wide referendum gave an overwhelming vote of confidence to Prince Sihanouk.

1963, May 5. Communist Chinese chief of state Liu Shao-chi signed a declaration of friendship with Prince Norodom Sihanouk.

Nov. 20. **Prince Sihanouk demanded that the United States end military, economic, technical, and cultural aid.**

1964, Jan. 5. **French Defense Minister Pierre Messmer,** conferring in Pnom-Penh with Prince Sihanouk, offered French tanks, trucks, and combat aircraft to Cambodia to help defend its neutrality.

Feb. 8. Prince Sihanouk charged the United States with "great responsibility" for the **South Vietnamese attack on a Cambodian village** on February 4, and asked the United States to finance truce observation posts along the Cambodian-South Vietnamese border.

Feb. 11. Prince Sihanouk proposed an international conference to guarantee Cambodia's neutrality, and on February 19 suggested that Thailand, South Vietnam, and the United States sign an agreement to neutralize Cambodia.

Mar. 10. A delegation left for Peking and Moscow to negotiate arms purchases.

Mar. 11. Cambodians attacked the British and United States embassies and information offices. Prince Sihanouk offered his regrets, and withdrew his demand for a four-power conference to guarantee Cambodia's borders.

Mar. 23–25. **Cambodia and South Vietnam formally ended their border talks,** and Prince Sihanouk reiterated his demand for an international conference. The British government rejected a Soviet request that their two nations, as co-chairmen of the 1954 Geneva conference on Indo-China, call an international conference on Cambodian neutrality. In a letter to Prince Sihanouk, **President de Gaulle promised to use his influence** with the United States and Britain to effect the calling of an international conference.

1965, Mar. 1–9. **Indo-Chinese People's Conference** at Pnom-Penh, dominated by Laotian and Vietnamese Communist delegations. No progress was made toward Sihanouk's plan for the neutralization of the whole Indo-Chinese region.

May 3. **Severance of relations with the United States.**

1966, Sept. 11. In the elections Sihanouk's People's Socialist Community captured four-fifths of the seats.

Oct. 18. **A new cabinet** was formed **under General Lon Nol,** who gave indications of desiring better relations with the West.

1967, May 2. **Sihanouk assumed special powers** as head of a provisional government, which at once accorded full recognition to the Vietnamese National Liberation Front (Vietcong) and to North Vietnam.

1969, July 2. **Resumption of diplomatic relations with the United States,** which recognized the sovereignty, independence, neutrality, and territorial integrity of Cambodia.

Aug. 8. **Lon Nol again became premier.**

Oct. 8. Sihanouk permitted the **invasion of 40,000 North Vietnamese forces** and their advance even into central Cambodia.

1970, Mar. 13. The Cambodian government requested the North Vietnamese to withdraw their troops. Conferences followed.

Mar. 18. **PREMIER LON NOL TOOK CONTROL OF THE GOVERNMENT** in the absence of Prince Sihanouk in Peking.

Mar. 21. **Cheng Heng made chief of state.** He promised to expel the Communists from the country.

Mar. 23. Sihanouk, in Peking, proclaimed the **formation of a national liberation army.**

Mar. 25. The North Vietnamese and the Vietcong promised to withdraw their forces from Cambodia.

Apr. 27. **The North Vietnamese government proclaimed its support of Sihanouk.** Communist forces began to press their advance into Cambodia and threatened Pnom-Penh.

Apr. 30. **President Nixon,** in a television address, **announced that U.S. troops would join South Vietnamese forces in an invasion of Cambodia** to destroy North Vietnamese and Vietcong bases near the border of South Vietnam. This news caused a furor in the United

States, where opinion ran strong against any escalation of the war.

May 5. President Nixon promised that U.S. troops would not advance further than 21 miles and (May 8) that they would be withdrawn from Cambodia by June 30.

Prince Sihanouk, in Peking, announced the **formation of a Cambodian government-in-exile.**

May 25. Announcement of the U.S. supply of arms to Cambodia.

June 4. Communist forces were reported to be within 10 miles of Pnom-Penh.

June 29. Withdrawal of the last of the U.S. troops.

July 5. **A military tribunal** in Pnom-Penh **convicted Sihanouk of treason** and corruption and sentenced him to death *in absentia.*

Aug. 20. Fighting continued on the very outskirts of the capital.

Aug. 28. Visit of U.S. Vice-President Agnew to Pnom-Penh. He assured the Cambodian government of U.S. economic and military support in defense of Cambodian independence, but warned that no U.S. troops would be committed. Despite the withdrawal of the U.S. ground forces, however, the war in Cambodia was still in progress at the end of the year. Cambodian and South Vietnamese forces managed to cut some of the important Communist supply lines, but the enemy continued to threaten the capital.

Oct. 9. PROCLAMATION OF THE KHMER REPUBLIC as the new name for Cambodia.

f. LAOS

Like the other Indo-Chinese states, **Laos was occupied by the Japanese** (1945), who supported a declaration of independence on April 15. Following Japan's capitulation, Chinese troops, allotted the task of disarming the Japanese north of the 16th parallel, occupied most of the country. Concurrently a **rebel Laotian government,** acting in collaboration with Vietminh, deposed the king. In 1946, however, the French slowly reoccupied the country and on August 27 signed an agreement with the king providing for the unity and independence of Laos. A **national constituent assembly** met in January 1947 and on May 11 the king proclaimed a constitution providing for a parliamentary constitutional monarchy.

1949, July 19. By a treaty signed in Paris **Laos became an Associated State within the French Union.**

1953, Oct. 22. France and Laos signed a treaty making **Laos "fully independent and sovereign"** within the French Union.

1954, Feb. 1. Vietminh forces, after launching an invasion from the Dienbienphu region, **crossed the Laotian border** and moved thirty-five miles into the country.

Forbidden by the Geneva terms of July 1954 to join regional alliances or seek military aid from either Communist or Western powers, the Laotian government sought to pacify the pro-Communist **Pathet Lao,** which was receiving aid from the Vietminh of North Vietnam.

1956, June 30. The U.S.S.R. recognized Laos.

1957, Aug. 25. A government crisis, which began June 4, ended when the national assembly invested **Prince Souvanna Phouma** as premier.

Nov. 1. Premier Souvanna Phouma's cabinet decided to take the Communist-backed Pathet Lao movement into the government. On November 19 the central government assumed control of the administration of two Pathet Lao provinces in northern Laos.

1958, July. Neutralist Premier Prince Souvanna Phouma brought **Pathet Lao leaders into the national government;** he then resigned (July 23) and was replaced by **Phoui Sananikone,** whose cabinet was approved August 19.

1959, Jan. Premier Phoui Sananikone, aided by an expanded **United States program of military and economic aid,** began an attempt to wipe out the Pathet Lao which had continued to receive Communist help.

Feb. 11. Premier Phoui Sananikone declared that the **government renounced the Geneva agreement** of 1954 terminating the Indo-China war. The premier declared that Laos would rely on the U.N. to arbitrate conflicts. The decision was directed against North Vietnam, whose troops, in January, had occupied a strip of Laotian territory along the frontier.

Aug. 27. The United States promised to increase its aid within the limits of the Geneva accord of 1954.

Sept. 2. The rebels, aided by regular troops from North Vietnam, opened a **major offensive** and captured eighty northern villages.

Sept. 4. The government asked the U.N. to send an emergency force to help defend Laos against "aggression" by North Vietnam. On September 16 the U.N. subcommittee on Laos began its investigation in Vientiane.

Nov. 4. Prince Regent Savang Vathana was named king, succeeding King **Sisavang Vong,** who died October 29.

Nov. 6. A **U.N. investigating subcommittee** revealed that it had found no clear evidence indicating direct participation by North Vietnamese troops in Laotian fighting.

Dec. 15. Premier Phoui Sananikone, in a cabinet shuffle, eliminated eleven members of a young reform group. On December 31 King Savang Vathana finally accepted Sananikone's resignation and placed the country under army control. **General Phoumi Nosavan** headed the new government.

1960, Aug. 9. After several cabinet shifts since January 1959, a **military coup**, led by **Captain Kong Le** ousted the current pro-western government and on August 15 the king asked Prince Souvanna Phouma to form a new government.

Sept. 2–Dec. 16. **Civil strife** over the composition of the government involved the Communist Pathet Lao, the neutralists around Prince Souvanna Phouma, and anti-Communists under **Prince Boun Oum** and General Phoumi Nosavan.

Dec. 16. After defeating Kong Le, General Nosavan installed a **pro-western government under Prince Boun Oum;** Souvanna Phouma had fled into exile in Cambodia (Dec. 9) and Kong Le joined the Pathet Lao. War with the Pathet Lao continued.

1961, Feb. 19. King Savang Vathana asked for an impartial three-man commission of Cambodia, Burma, and Malaya to help restore peace in Laos. He affirmed Laos' neutrality and declared that Premier Boun Oum would effect a policy of non-alignment.

On February 20 the United States voiced approval and urged the U.S.S.R. to support the king's neutrality statement and co-operate with the three-man commission.

Mar. 31. Prince Souvanna Phouma, on a world tour to win support for his proposed fourteen-nation commission to restore peace in Laos, declared in London that if the United States would stop supplying military aid to Laos, he would ask for the cessation of Soviet military aid.

Apr. 19. The Laotian government announced that a **United States military assistance advisory group** had been established. The advisory group, made up of United States forces in uniform, would provide tactical advisers to Laotian army forces and train Laotian soldiers and offer logistical advice.

Apr. 24. Britain and the U.S.S.R. issued a **joint appeal for a cease-fire** in Laos, urged reactivation of the international control commission to verify the end of hostilities, and called for a fourteen-nation conference on the future of Laos to convene in Geneva May 12.

May 3. The Laotian **cease-fire agreement** between the government and the pro-Communist rebels went into effect.

May 16. A **fourteen-nation conference on Laos,** under the joint chairmanship of Britain and the U.S.S.R., met in Geneva. The most troublesome issues were: (1) the establishment of an effective cease-fire, for frequent reports

revealed continuing advances of the Pathet Lao; (2) the formation of a Laotian government acceptable to the three factions.

June 22. The three rival princes—rightist **Boun Oum,** neutralist **Souvanna Phouma,** and leftist **Souphanouvong,** meeting in Zurich, announced **agreement upon a coalition government** without revealing details.

July 30. The national assembly amended the constitution to empower the king to name a government without assembly approval.

1962, Jan. 6. Britain and the U.S.S.R., co-chairmen of the fourteen-nation Geneva conference on Laos, sent a conference-approved message to the three rival princes in Laos, requesting them to go to Geneva to negotiate a new coalition government. The three rival princes accepted the proposal on January 11.

Jan. 19. Neutralist Prince Souvanna Phouma announced that the three princes had agreed on a **coalition government,** but Prince Boun Oum denied it upon his return to Laos on January 21.

May 7. After Pathet Lao took Nam Tha in northern Laos on May 6, the United States called for an investigation by the international control commission for Laos of the invasion as a violation of the May 1961 cease-fire. By May 11 Pathet Lao troops had traveled 100 miles beyond the cease-fire line. On May 12 U.S. President Kennedy ordered **U.S. naval ships** and 1800 marines **to the Gulf of Siam,** and 2000 American soldiers to Thailand, where 2000 Royal Lao soldiers had fled.

May 15. Prince Boun Oum agreed to a coalition government headed by Souvanna Phouma on his terms, i.e., that he would name the ministers of interior and defense. On May 16 pro-Communist leader Souphanouvong agreed to meet with Phouma and Boun Oum to establish a coalition government. On May 26 Phouma met with the international control commission and set June 15 as the deadline for negotiations on a new government.

June 11. Laotian leaders, meeting at Khangkhayi, announced the **formation of a nineteen-member coalition cabinet** headed by neutralist **Prince Souvanna Phouma** as premier.

June 22. King Savang Vathana installed the new coalition government, and the new premier, Souvanna Phouma, declared that Laos no longer recognized the protection of SEATO.

July 23. Delegates to the fourteen-nation conference on Laos, in Geneva, signed **agreements guaranteeing Laotian independence and neutrality.**

Sept. 17–Oct. 5. The **United States withdrew its military personnel** from Laos in accord with the Geneva agreement upon Laotian neutrality.

1963, Mar.–May. Sporadic fighting between the Pathet Lao and neutralist forces occurred.

1964, Feb. 27. The Pathet Lao captured strategic positions in the Plaine des Jarres.

Mar. 16. Representatives of the neutralist, rightist, and pro-Communist factions agreed to halt "all military activities" in the Plaine des Jarres.

Apr. 19. A **rightist coup,** led by two generals, sought to expand rightist representation in the cabinet. The western powers, the U.S.S.R., and China protested such a modification of the Geneva agreement of 1962. Premier Souvanna Phouma agreed to reorganize and enlarge the coalition government. The Pathet Lao denounced the revolutionary committee as illegal and refused to recognize any agreement between it and the premier.

May 16. Premier Souvanna Phouma announced that the Pathet Lao, with the aid of the North Vietnamese, had opened a **general offensive on the Plaine des Jarres.**

May 25. The United States rejected a Soviet proposal, supported by France, to hold a full-scale conference at Geneva on Laos.

May 26. Red China proposed a foreign ministers conference on Laos in Cambodia.

June 1. The **Pathet Lao** withdrew its government officials from Vientiane, thus **severing its last ties with the neutralist government** of Premier Souvanna Phouma.

June 12. U.S. reconnaissance flights over Laotian territory, approved by the Laotian government, provided photographic proof of the presence of North Vietnamese troops. **Laos,** despite all recognitions of its neutrality, was **deeply involved in the Vietnamese war.** Pathet Lao and North Vietnamese troops occupied much of the northern section of the country and staged advances on the Plaine des Jarres as required. The eastern section of the country contained the network of trails known as the **Ho Chi Minh trail,** over which the North Vietnamese transported most of their supplies to South Vietnam. The United States provided the Laotian army with needed supplies and armed and trained the Meo tribesmen, who offered the most effective resistance to the advance of the Pathet Lao.

Aug.–Sept. 22. Paris conferences between the rightist leader, **Boun Oum,** the neutralist **Souvanna Phouma,** and the leftist **Souphanouvong** proved altogether inconclusive.

1965, Oct. The Pathet Lao (*Land of Lao*) was officially renamed the **Lao People's Liberation Army.**

1968. A new vigorous offensive by the Liberation Army, supported by the North Vietnamese, resulted in a substantial advance.

1969, Dec. 14. Souvanna Phouma admitted the presence of four or five battalions of **Chinese Communists in north Laos,** while the North Vietnamese were also advancing. The Communists were eventually driven back from the Plaine des Jarres by Laotian forces and Meo tribesmen, operating with U.S. air support.

1970, Feb. 13–21. In what was really the **Laotian war,** the North Vietnamese forces drove the Laotians back from the Plaine des Jarres, despite heavy U.S. air bombardment.

Mar. 6. President Nixon requested Britain and the U.S.S.R., as joint chairmen of the Geneva conference of 1962, to start talks looking to restoration of the 1962 agreements. In a public statement the president declared that he had no plans for employing U.S. ground troops in the Laotian campaign.

Apr. In the continued fighting the North Vietnamese invaders succeeded in approaching **Luang Prabang** (May 9). By the end of the year operations were still in progress, in fact it might be said that with the lull in fighting in South Vietnam, the struggle shifted more and more to Laos, where presently large South Vietnamese forces were to be engaged.

4. INDONESIA

(From p. 1105)

1940, Apr. 15. Japan announced that should hostilities in Europe be extended to the Netherlands, Japan wished to see the **status quo in the Netherlands East Indies** preserved.

1941, June 18. Japan broke off negotiations with the Netherlands East Indies for an **economic accord.**

Dec. 8. The **Netherlands government-in-exile** and the **Netherlands East Indies declared war on Japan.**

1942, Jan. 11. Japanese forces invaded the Netherlands Celebes, and presently occupied the entire Indies (p. 1153).

1945, Aug. 17. Two days after the Japanese surrender, the Indonesian leaders **Achmed Sukarno** and **Mohammed Hatta** proclaimed the **INDEPENDENCE OF THE REPUBLIC OF INDONESIA.** The Dutch refused to recognize the new government.

Sept. 29–Oct. 3. British and Dutch troops arrived in Batavia to disarm and repatriate the Japanese. Before long, fighting was under way between these troops and the **"Indonesian People's Army."**

Oct. 12. The Dutch government offered to negotiate with those Indonesians who were ready to agree to a self-governing Indonesia within the Netherlands Kingdom.

Nov. 13. **Soetan Sjahrir,** a young Socialist, became premier of the new republic while **Sukarno** became president.

1946, Feb. 19. **Negotiations** began between **Dutch** and **Indonesian** representatives, while Dutch and British troops slowly pushed back the Indonesian forces into central and eastern Java.

Nov. 15. Following the conclusion of a military truce, the Dutch and Indonesians initialed the **CHERIBON AGREEMENT** providing for **Dutch recognition of the Indonesian Republic** (Java, Sumatra, and Madura), and the establishment of a **United States of Indonesia,** to include, besides the Indonesian Republic, the states of **Borneo** and the **Great East** (Celebes, the Sunda Islands, and the Moluccas). The whole was to be joined with the Netherlands in equal partnership under the Dutch crown. The agreement was signed on March 25, 1947.

Nov. 29. The last **British troops left Indonesia.**

1947, May–July. Attempts to carry out the **Cheribon agreement** revealed far-reaching differences in its interpretation between Dutch and Indonesian authorities. On

June 26. Prime Minister **Sjahrir** resigned, but his successor, **Amir Sjarifoeddin,** was no more successful in solving the deadlock in the negotiations. Both sides continued to violate the cease-fire agreement, and when the republic rejected a Dutch proposal for joint police action against the disruptive Indonesian forces,

July 20. The **Dutch launched a full-scale offensive** in central and eastern Java, making rapid advances.

Aug. 1. A resolution of the **U.N. security council** called for a **cease-fire** and formed a **committee of good offices.** Both sides accepted the action but did not strictly observe the cease-fire.

Dec. 8. Negotiations between Dutch and Indonesian leaders were resumed under the auspices of the **U.N. committee of good offices.**

1948, Jan. 17. The Netherlands and the republic of Indonesia signed a **truce agreement on board the** *U.S.S. Renville,* which laid down the principles to serve as basis for future negotiations. Immediately, however, differences arose as to the interpretation of these principles.

Jan. 31. A new Indonesian cabinet was formed under **Mohammed Hatta.**

Sept. 18. Indonesian Communists, under the leadership of **Muso,** a veteran Communist recently returned from Moscow, **set up a "soviet government" at Madioen (Java).** The government intervened successfully and the Communists withdrew to the jungle.

Dec. 18. After repeated breakdowns in their negotiations with Indonesia, the **Dutch resumed their offensive.** Within a few days they occupied the major Republican cities and **captured the Sukarno government.**

1949, Jan. 28. The **U.N. security council** called for an immediate end of hostilities, release of government leaders, and the transfer of sovereignty to the United States of Indonesia by July 1, 1950. Further United Nations efforts finally led to a **round-table conference at The Hague** between Dutch and Indonesian representatives.

Nov. 2. **Complete agreement was reached** on the transfer of sovereignty to the United States of Indonesia and on its relations with the Netherlands.

Dec. 16. **Sukarno** was elected first president and **Mohammed Hatta** became first prime minister of the United States of Indonesia.

Dec. 27. The **Netherlands** and the **Republic of Indonesia** formally **transferred sovereignty to the UNITED STATES OF INDONESIA,** a federal republic of sixteen states, whose independence was proclaimed simultaneously at its capital of Jakarta (Batavia). The status of **Dutch New Guinea,** which remained outside the new federation, was to be determined in future negotiations.

1950. **Local uprisings and guerrilla warfare continued** in many parts of the new state, notably in East Indonesia.

May 19. A conference between the federal government and the states decided to substitute a **unitary state** for the United States of Indonesia. As a result,

Aug. 17. A provisional constitution was drawn up, establishing the **REPUBLIC OF INDONESIA.**

Sept. 6. **Mohammed Natsir** formed a new cabinet.

Sept. 28. The **Republic of Indonesia was admitted to the United Nations.**

1951, Mar. 19. A government spokesman revealed that 25,000 troops had been sent (Mar. 1) to suppress the **extremist Moslem movement,** *Darul Islam,* and armed bands of Communists and outlaws in Java.

1952, Dec. 31. The government announced its decision to participate in the **Colombo plan** but declared that its decision to join "does not and will not obligate Indonesia either politically or militarily."

1953, Mar. 16. A major outburst of violence occurred when the government attempted to enforce its **land redistribution program,** affecting illegal squatters.

July 30. President Sukarno announced the formation of a primarily leftist government, headed by **Ali Sastroamidjojo.** The Moslem party for the first time since 1949 was not represented in the cabinet.

1954, Aug. 11. The **formal dissolution of the Netherlands-Indonesian union** took place without resolving the problem of New Guinea, which Indonesia referred to the U.N.

1955, Sept. 29. The first national elections began.

1956, May 17. Addressing the U.S. congress in Washington, **President Sukarno** called for greater understanding of Asian peoples' needs, and declared that United States arms aid would not produce liberty and stability.

Aug. 4. The **government repudiated debts** amounting to more than $1 billion owed to the Netherlands.

Sept. 12–17. Sukarno made a **state visit to Moscow.** On September 15 the government announced a Soviet loan of $100 million.

1957, Feb. 21. Sukarno issued an appeal to the people to replace the western democratic method with a **system of mutual help,** which would allow Communist participation in the cabinet.

Mar. 2. A **military coup** occurred in the four provinces of eastern Indonesia when the Celebes army commander and a 51-man council declared a state of war there. The rebels demanded **complete autonomy** for the region, and urged that 70 per cent of the revenues collected there be used for local development.

Mar. 5. Sukarno invited the firm anti-Communist and former vice-president, Mohammed Hatta, to meet with him.

Mar. 9. Another **military coup** occurred, when **Lt. Col. Barlian** took control of South Sumatra. On March 12 **Borneo repudiated the central government,** and set up its own council under **Lt. Col. Hasan Basry.**

Mar. 14. Premier **Sastroamidjojo** and his cabinet **resigned,** and President Sukarno declared a **state of war and siege.** In order to break a deadlock among competing parties in the formation of a new government, Sukarno, on March 25, called for a cabinet composed of non-political experts.

Apr. 9. In the face of continuing rebellion in the outer islands, an emergency **extra-parliamentary cabinet** of experts was installed, under a new premier, **Djuanda Kartawidjaja.** The new cabinet of experts contained no Communists.

June 27. Without consulting the central government, officials of North Celebes established a separate province, with **D. Manopo** as governor.

July 6. **Lt. Col. Ventje Sumual,** on his own authority, assumed military command of the whole of East Indonesia. By July 24 defiance was so widespread that the central government was left in control only of Java.

Aug. 22. In a major move to reunify the country, Indonesia's emergency cabinet invited representatives of the rebellious outer regions to a **round-table conference** with representatives of the central government.

Oct. 28. The **government threatened to seize West New Guinea** from the Netherlands by force if the U.N. refused to take up its appeal.

Dec. 1–9. To protest continued Dutch rule of West New Guinea, the government, on December 1, ordered a 24-hour **strike against Dutch businesses.** On December 5 the government asked the Netherlands to close all consular missions except the one in Jakarta and announced the **expulsion of all Dutch nationals** from the country. On December 9 the government expropriated Dutch agricultural properties.

1958, Jan. 9. The government refused to accept U.N. mediation in its dispute with the Netherlands over the territory of West New Guinea.

Feb. 15. A **rebel régime** was proclaimed **in central Sumatra.**

1959, July 5. President Sukarno decreed the **restoration of the 1945 constitution** and dissolved the constituent assembly. On July 6 Premier Kartawidjaja's cabinet resigned. On July 8 a new ten-man "inner" cabinet with Sukarno in the premiership was announced. On July 22 parliament voted to continue under the 1945 constitution.

Dec. 11. Following the government's **prohibition of trade in rural areas by Chinese,** Communist China protested Indonesia's "most cruel treatment" of Chinese residents, regarded as "nationals of a hostile country." In a formal reply, Indonesia charged Peking's diplomats with inciting Chinese residents to defy presidential regulations.

1960, Feb. 28. President Sukarno and Soviet Premier Khrushchev signed an agreement for a **Soviet credit** of $250 million.

Mar. 28. After dissolving parliament on March 5, Sukarno named a 261-man, **"mutual help" parliament,** and promised parliamentary elections in 1962 if conditions permitted.

1961, Apr. 5. In **Netherlands New Guinea,** after the first elected legislative council was sworn in, the Netherlands government told its 28 members to work out a date and method for self-determination within a year.

1962, May 26. With Dutch troops battling Indonesian paratroopers and guerrillas in West

New Guinea, the Netherlands announced its acceptance of a **United States plan** for settling the dispute. The plan called for a U.S. mediator in further discussions between Indonesia and the Dutch on the question of sovereignty over New Guinea and provided for U.N. administration and a plebiscite to enable Papuans to decide their own future status. On May 29 acting U.N. Secretary General U Thant called for an immediate cease-fire and discussions.

July 31. Indonesian and Dutch negotiators in Washington announced **agreement on the transfer of West New Guinea** to the U.N. and later to Indonesia. The agreement was forwarded to each government for approval.

Aug. 15. Dutch and Indonesian negotiators signed an **agreement in New York to transfer the administration of West New Guinea** (West Irian) from the Netherlands to the U.N. on October 1, 1962, and to Indonesia on May 1, 1963. Indonesia ratified the agreement on September 1, the Netherlands on September 13. The U.N. general assembly approved the settlement on September 31.

1963, Feb. 13. Sukarno announced Indonesia's **opposition to the** British-sponsored **federation of Malaysia,** and voiced support for the rebel troops in British Borneo.

May 18. The 623-man congress unanimously named **Sukarno president for life.** Congress members had been appointed by Sukarno.

1964, Jan. 8. Sukarno, conferring in Manila with **President Macapagal,** was unable to persuade the Philippines to join Indonesia in an **economic boycott of Malaysia.**

Jan. 17. Conferring in Tokyo, U.S. **attorney-general Robert Kennedy** urged Sukarno to curb guerrilla raids against Malaysia and warned that a major conflict might develop.

Jan. 23. Sukarno, conferring with Kennedy at Jakarta, agreed to a **cease-fire with Malaysia** (p. 1321).

Feb. 27. The government news agency reported that business concerns linked to Britain would be seized.

Apr. 1–3. Foreign Minister Subandrio visited the Netherlands for talks with Dutch leaders. Subandrio and the Dutch **foreign minister Joseph Luns** signed a technical cooperation agreement.

Dec. 4, 7. Sack of the United States libraries in Jakarta and Surabaja by Communist-inspired mobs protesting the U.S. policy with regard to the Indonesian-Malaysian dispute. The U.S. government thereupon closed all libraries in Indonesia (Mar. 4, 1965).

1965, Jan. 2. Indonesia withdrew from the United Nations, the first nation to do so.

Mar. 19. Seizure of three U.S. oil companies and the Goodyear Tire and Rubber Company.

Apr. 24. The government seized all remaining foreign-owned properties.

Sept. 30. THE COMMUNIST CRISIS. The army defeated an attempt by the Communists to seize control. The army chief of staff and five generals had been kidnaped. President Sukarno then named **General T. N. J. Suharto** as temporary chief of the army.

Oct. 8. Beginning of a general **assault on Communists,** of whom tens of thousands or more were massacred throughout the country.

1966, Feb. 21. Sukarno, in an effort to regain power, replaced the anti-Communist defense minister **General Abdul Haris Nasution** and other anti-Communist officers and cabinet ministers with Leftists. This move led to vast **student riots** and demonstrations (Feb. 25).

Mar. 11. Sukarno was obliged to surrender the powers of government to Gen. Suharto.

Mar. 12. The Communist Party was banned. Foreign Minister Subandrio and other leftist politicians were taken into custody.

May 29–June 1. Peace conference in Bangkok and **termination of hostilities between Indonesia and Malaysia** (p. 1322).

1967, Feb. 20. Sukarno, who retained the titles of president and supreme commander, was obliged to surrender his remaining powers to Gen. Suharto. The latter dismissed many officials of the old régime and did his utmost to undo Sukarno's **economic policies:** drastic measures were introduced to check the almost fantastic inflation, foreign debts were renegotiated, and foreign-owned properties were restored to their owners. At the same time a drive was launched on every form of corruption, in the army as well as the administration.

1968, Mar. 27. General Suharto was given full presidential powers for five years by the **People's Consultative Congress.**

1969, July–Aug. The U.N.-supervised **referendum in West Irian** (West New Guinea) led to annexation of that territory by Indonesia (approval of U.N. general assembly, Nov. 19, 1969).

Oct. 5. Reorganization and **amalgamation of the military services** to reduce duplication and factional rivalries. At the same time the police forces were demilitarized.

1970, May 26. Visit of President Suharto to Washington. The orientation of his régime, in contrast to his predecessor's, was decidedly Western.

June 21. Death of former president Achmed Sukarno.

5. CHINA

(From p. 1111)

1939, Sept. 3. The outbreak of the Second World War in Europe gave the Japanese a chance to press their **undeclared war in China.** War was not formally declared by China against Japan until December 9, 1941.

1940, Mar. 30. A puppet **Chinese government** headed by **Wang Ching-wei** was established at Nanking with Japanese support.

1942, Mar. 8. The governments of **Great Britain and the United States,** to check the serious inflation in China, provided **credits of £50,000,-000 and $500,000,000.**

Oct. 9. Great Britain and the United States announced their **relinquishment of extra-territorial rights** and special privileges in China. (Ratified by treaties January 11, 1943.)

1943, Sept. 13. Gen. Chiang Kai-shek was elected president of the Chinese Republic by the central executive committee, which also permitted him to retain his post as commander-in-chief of the Chinese army. The committee announced that democratic, responsible government would be established in China as soon as the war ended.

1944, Dec. 31. Gen. Chiang Kai-shek promised the Chinese people that a **constitutional government** would be established before the end of the war.

The end of the war found China still divided between the Nationalist forces of **Chiang Kai-shek** and the Red army of **Mao Tse-tung.** The latter, having taken advantage of the sudden Japanese collapse, had overrun most of the northern provinces, and various efforts for a rapprochement between the two parties remained fruitless.

1945, Aug. 14. T. V. Soong, premier of the Nationalist government, concluded a **treaty of friendship and alliance with the Soviet Union.** In return for Soviet recognition of the Nationalists as "the Central Government of China," the latter agreed to the independence of **Outer Mongolia,** gave the U.S.S.R. joint thirty-year ownership of the **Manchurian railway** and the port of **Dairen,** and agreed to the conversion of **Port Arthur** into an exclusively Chinese and Soviet naval base.

Aug. 26–Oct. 11. Negotiations between **Chiang Kai-shek** and **Mao Tse-tung** failed to settle their differences, and before the end of October heavy fighting was in progress between Nationalists and Communists in North China. Each side aimed at the control of Manchuria, which was being evacuated by the Soviet forces. At this point

Dec. 14. The United States intervened and sent **General George Marshall** as mediator to effect a

1946, Jan. 10. Truce between Nationalist and Communist forces, followed by agreement to create a national army, form a coalition government, and draw up a new constitution. Yet, on

Feb. 17. The Communists demanded joint control with the Nationalists over **Manchuria.** When this was ignored,

Apr. 14. All-out civil war was resumed, interrupted by another uneasy truce (May 12–June 30) and intermittent peace overtures from both sides. During the initial campaigns, the Nationalist government forces advanced all along the line.

May 1. The Nationalist government returned from Chungking to Nanking.

Oct. 10. Chiang Kai-shek was re-elected president of China by the Kuomintang.

Nov. 4. China and the **United States** signed a treaty of friendship, commerce, and navigation.

Nov. 15. A national assembly met (without Communist participation) and on December 25 adopted a **new constitution,** which guaranteed political equality and civil rights to all citizens and vested supreme authority in the national assembly. The government was to consist of a legislative yuan (parliament) and an executive yuan (cabinet). The constitution **went into effect on December 25, 1946.**

1947, Jan. 29. The **United States** officially **abandoned its mediation efforts. General Marshall,** in his final report, criticized both the reactionaries in the Kuomintang and the extremists in the Communist camp, who prevented a compromise.

Mar. 19. Nationalist successes against the Communists culminated in the capture of the Communist capital of **Yenan.** An almost immediate reversal resulted in **Communist control over Manchuria by the end of 1947.**

Nov. 21–23. Elections for the national assembly aroused little popular interest. Most of the candidates belonged to the Kuomintang, since Communists and the Democratic League had been excluded.

1948. In the course of 1948, the **decline of Chiang Kai-shek's forces,** already evident in 1947, **proceeded rapidly,** and by the end of the year most of **northern China** was in Communist hands. The Nationalists by now had lost most of their best troops, and corruption among their provincial leaders had led to the surrender or sale of vast amounts of American equipment to the Communists. The Nationalist economy, badly in need of reform and shaken by growing inflation, had long depended on American aid, which, since V-J Day, was estimated at more than $2 billion. In early 1948 an additional $400 million was allocated, but as time went on and the Nationalist government failed to liberalize and reform itself, American aid was drastically curtailed.

Mar. 29. The **national assembly** convened at Nanking. After severely criticizing the government and its conduct of the war, it re-elected **Chiang Kai-shek** as president of China (Apr. 19) and gave him virtual dictatorial powers during the national emergency.

Sept. 1. The Communists announced the formation of a **North China People's Government.**

1949. The rapid **decomposition of the Nationalist armies,** the fall of Tientsin (Jan. 15) and Peiping (Jan. 21), and the Communist threat to the lower Yangtze Valley brought about a **temporary change in the Nationalist government.** On

Jan. 21. **Gen. Chiang Kai-shek resigned** the presidency, leaving Vice-President **Li Tsung-jen** in charge of peace talks with the Communists. These negotiations broke down when

Apr. 20. **Communist demands,** including the formation of a coalition cabinet under **Mao Tse-tung,** and the punishment of "war criminals" (notably Chiang Kai-shek), proved **unacceptable to the Nationalists.** The Communists thereupon resumed their offensive, and in the course of the year they drove the **Nationalist armies off the Chinese mainland.**

July 16. The **Nationalists** organized a supreme council under **Chiang Kai-shek** and began to prepare for withdrawal to the island of **Formosa** (Taiwan), which was completed by December 8.

Aug. 5. The **UNITED STATES** issued a **WHITE PAPER** announcing the cessation of all aid to **Nationalist China.** The latter's collapse was attributed to the military, political, and economic incapacity of the Kuomintang leaders, who had come to rely on United States help to win the war and keep them in power.

Oct. 1. The Communist **PEOPLE'S RE-PUBLIC OF CHINA** was officially proclaimed at Peking (Peiping), with **Mao Tse-tung** as chairman of the central people's administrative council and **Chou En-lai** as premier and foreign minister. The new régime was immediately recognized by the Soviet Union and its satellites, and later by Burma, India, and (Jan. 6, 1950) Great Britain.

Dec. 8. The **U.N. general assembly** called upon all states to respect the political independence of China and the right of the Chinese people to choose their own political institutions.

a. THE PEOPLE'S REPUBLIC OF CHINA (COMMUNIST)

1950. The unification of the country, together with a program of reconstruction and deflation, brought considerable **economic improvement** to the **Chinese People's Republic.** While some changes were introduced in agriculture as land reform went into effect, there were no radical innovations, outside of over-all state planning in industry. The "People's Liberation Army" carried on continued warfare against anti-Communist guerrillas.

Feb. 14. Mao Tse-tung signed a thirty-year **TREATY OF FRIENDSHIP, ALLIANCE, AND MUTUAL ASSISTANCE WITH SOVIET RUSSIA.** It was followed by a series of economic agreements for the joint exploitation of Chinese resources.

May 2. **Communist forces** completed occupation of **Hainan.**

Oct. Chinese Communist "volunteers" intervened in the **Korean War** on the North Korean side (p. 1348).

Nov. 10. Following a **Chinese invasion, Tibet** appealed to the United Nations to bring about a peaceful settlement of Chinese-Tibetan relations.

1951, Mar. 5. The government reportedly reached an **agreement with Tibet,** under which the latter was granted internal autonomy, with China in control of the defense and foreign affairs of the Dalai Lama's realm.

1952, Dec. 31. In accordance with their 1950 treaty, Communist China and the Soviet Union ended their joint administration of the Chinese Changchun railway, with the U.S.S.R. yielding its rights in the partnership.

1953, Sept. 15. The Chinese Communist radio announced the negotiation of an "unprecedented" **economic aid program** with the U.S.S.R. to enable China to build up its heavy industry.

1954, Aug. 13. The supreme governing body approved Premier Chou En-lai's call for a determined **drive to win Taiwan.**

Sept. 27. **Mao Tse-tung was re-elected** to his top post.

Oct. 11. A Sino-Soviet agreement provided for Russia's **evacuation of the Port Arthur naval base** by June 1955, and arranged for a substantial extension of Soviet credit to help build up Chinese industry. The agreement also called for the "occupation" of Taiwan.

Oct. 15. The Soviet Union called on the U.N. general assembly to condemn the United States for aggression against Communist China by its conversion of the Taiwan area into a "breeding ground for a new war."

Nov. 23. A military court sentenced to long prison terms the thirteen **American airmen** who disappeared on anti-Communist missions during the Korean War.

Dec. 10. The U.N. general assembly, voting 47-5, condemned Chinese Communists' conviction of the American airmen for spying. On December 11 **Secretary General Hammarskjöld** conferred with Premier Chou En-lai in Peking about the release of the prisoners. Chou En-lai accepted the proposal on December 17.

1955, Jan.-Feb. Communist and Nationalist forces battled over the **offshore islands** in the Taiwan Straits. Premier Chou En-lai refused (Feb. 3) a U.N. security council invitation to talk about a cease-fire.

Feb. 5. The **U.S. 7th Fleet** was ordered to help evacuate Nationalist Chinese from the **Tachen Islands** which were taken over by the Communists (Feb. 11).

Apr. 23. Premier Chou En-lai told the **Bandung** conferees (p. 1159) that his country did not want war with the United States, and expressed his willingness to negotiate on Far Eastern issues, including that of Taiwan. The offer was renewed on May 16.

1956, Aug. 6. The government lifted the seven-year **ban on visits from United States newsmen,** but on August 20, the U.S. state department reaffirmed its ban on travel to Red China.

Sept. 15. Mao Tse-tung told the eighth party congress, opening in Peking, that there was "a trend toward relaxation of tension in the international situation." On September 16 Premier Chou En-lai announced a plan to increase by 50 per cent the total national income during the **second five-year plan** (1958-1962).

Sept. 24. A **Chinese-Nepalese treaty** was published, by which Nepal surrendered extraterritorial rights in Tibet, and recognized Chinese sovereignty there.

1957, May 11. The foreign ministry declared that future installations of Matador missile units on Taiwan by the United States were to be interpreted as an "act of war."

June 12. The government press printed the partial texts of two of **Mao Tse-tung's speeches** delivered in February and March. Mao had reported the liquidation of 800,000 persons in Red China from 1949 to 1954. He also stated that, even in a Communist state, "contradictions" exist between rulers and ruled. Calling for freer expression, he declared, "Let a hundred flowers bloom, let a hundred schools

of thought contend."

June 17. The government revealed its tentative decision to withdraw its cadres from Tibet.

1958, May 10. The government notified Japan of the **cancellation of all trade** between the two countries, because of Japanese Premier Kishi's "hostile attitude."

Aug. 23. The Chinese Communists began a heavy **bombardment of the Quemoy** and **Little Quemoy islands.**

Aug. 27. **President Eisenhower** declared that Quemoy and Matsu were more important to the defense of Taiwan than they had been three years earlier. The United States navy announced the dispatch of an aircraft carrier and four destroyers from the Mediterranean to the 7th Fleet in the waters around Taiwan.

Aug. 29. The Communist Party politburo adopted a resolution approving the widespread **formation of "people's communes"** to advance the country's economic development.

Sept. 4. U.S. **Secretary of State Dulles** declared that U.S. forces would come to the aid of Chinese Nationalists defending Quemoy and Matsu, if President Eisenhower considered such action necessary for the defense of Taiwan. He also declared that the United States would not respect the twelve-mile offshore territorial limit claimed by the Communists.

Sept. 7. Ships of the U.S. 7th Fleet escorted a Chinese nationalist convoy carrying supplies to Quemoy. The Chinese Communists withheld their fire.

Sept. 11. President Eisenhower, in an address to the nation, said the United States must be ready to fight, if necessary, to prevent the Chinese Communist capture of Quemoy and Matsu, but he urged negotiations. The British government declared that it was under no obligation to support the United States in the Quemoy-Matsu crisis.

Sept. 15. **United States-Communist Chinese ambassadorial talks** on the Taiwan issue opened in Warsaw, Poland.

Oct. 6. The Chinese Communists began a week-long cease-fire. Communist China's defense minister called for talks between the two Chinese governments to settle their "internal differences." On October 8 the United States announced that convoy operations had stopped but would be resumed if the Communists re-opened fire.

Oct. 17. **Chiang Kai-shek reasserted his determination to keep the offshore islands,** and on October 20 the Chinese Communists renewed their shelling of the offshore islands, thereby breaking the extended cease-fire.

Dec. 18. The central committee passed a resolution ordering a slowdown in the establishment of communes in large cities and improvement in the operation of the 26,000 rural communes.

1959, Mar. 13. Fighting broke out in Lhasa, Tibet, between the populace and Chinese Communist forces.

Mar. 28. Premier Chou En-lai dissolved the Tibetan government headed by the **Dalai Lama,** and put the **Panchen Lama** at the head of a preparatory committee for the Tibetan Autonomous Region. On March 31 the **Dalai Lama crossed the border into India,** seeking asylum.

Apr. 23. The government claimed to have dispersed the rebels in southeast Tibet and sealed the border to India.

Apr. 27. Liu Shao-chi succeeded Mao Tsetung as **chief of state of the People's Republic.** Mao remained chairman of the Communist Party.

Sept. 9. The **Dalai Lama called for U.N. action** against Chinese Communist oppression in Tibet.

Oct. 21. In a letter to President Eisenhower, Premier Khrushchev voiced his support of the Red Chinese claim to the Nationalist islands, which he termed an "internal" Chinese problem.

Dec. 19. In the first instance of aerial activity since November 1958, **Quemoy was shelled** by the Chinese Communists and MIG fighters flew over the island.

1960, Mar. 21. China and Nepal signed an agreement by which they set up a committee to demarcate their common border.

Apr. 26. Shortly before his departure from India, after six days of border talks, Premier Chou En-lai declared that his government would not recognize the **McMahon Line** as the Indian-Chinese border.

May 31. *Hsinhua,* Communist Chinese news agency, reported the signing of a **treaty with Outer Mongolia,** hitherto within the Soviet sphere of influence.

June 10. Reports reached New Delhi that **fierce fighting** had been raging for ten days **between Tibetans and Chinese Communist troops** near the Nepalese frontier. On June 19 the international commission of jurists asserted that Chinese Communists were guilty of genocide in attempting a systematic extermination of the Buddhist religion in Tibet.

Dec. 29. Peking newspapers and radio broadcasts reported that during 1960 some 148 million acres of farm land were affected by disastrous "natural calamities" such as drought and floods.

1962, Oct. 20–Nov. 22. For the **border war with India,** see p. 1314.

1963, Feb. 27. The **Chinese Communist Party harshly criticized the Soviet Union** for supplying planes to India and for having stopped economic and military aid to China in 1960. Differences between the two Communist giants led to continuous acrimonious dispute and divided the entire Communist world (p. 1167).

Dec.–Jan. 1964. For seven weeks Premier **Chou En-lai toured ten African nations,** returning to Peking, February 5.

1964, Feb. 25. Diplomatic sources disclosed that **Sino-Soviet consultations** were in progress regarding their border disputes.

Mar. 1. Premier Chou En-lai returned from a good-will tour in Burma, Pakistan, and Ceylon.

Apr. 19. Agreement with Japan was concluded to exchange foreign correspondents and to establish unofficial trade relations offices.

June 15. China and Yemen signed a ten-year "friendship" treaty.

Oct. 16. Explosion of China's **first atomic bomb.**

Nov. 5–13. Visit of Chou En-lai to Moscow, evidently in the hope of improving relations with the Soviet Union following the downfall of Khruschev. The discussions proved fruitless, if not actually damaging, due to China's territorial claims.

1965, Mar. Dispute with the Soviet government over the proposed convocation of a world congress of Communist parties.

Border conflicts with India on the Sikkim front (p. 1314).

Sept. 1. Tibet became an Autonomous Region of the People's Republic.

1965–1968. THE GREAT PROLETARIAN CULTURAL REVOLUTION, an outgrowth of growing discontent with Mao's handling of relations with Russia, as well as with the pace of agricultural collectivization and industrial expansion. For some years high officials of the bureaucracy had been trying to reduce Mao's dominance and introduce some form of collective leadership. In 1958 they had succeeded in blocking, in the politburo, another term for Mao as chairman of the People's Republic. Tension developed as the economic crisis made itself more generally felt. In 1959 the minister of defense, **P'eng Te-huai** condemned the Great Leap Forward, but was dismissed for his pains and **Gen Lin Piao,** a supporter of Mao, was appointed in his place. Veiled attacks and critical articles continued to appear until

1965, Nov. 10. Mao, from Shanghai, **launched a counter-offensive,** attacking the "reactionary bourgeois ideology" and the bureaucrats whom he described as the "Peking Black Gang." In the ensuing duel, Lin Piao and the army supported Mao, while **Liu Shao-chi** (chairman of the People's Republic) and **Teng To** (deputy mayor of Peking) retained control of the party apparatus.

1966, Mar. 26. Departure of Liu on a visit to Pakistan. On the same day **P'eng Chen** (mayor of Peking and vice-premier) **disappeared,** an early victim of the purge.

Apr. 18. The army newspaper called for a "Great Socialist Cultural Revolution" directed against "persons in authority in the Communist Party who have taken the capitalist road." It was the culmination of a conflict between the anti-Russian Military Affairs Committee of the Party (led by Lin Piao, which supported Mao, emphasized ideology, and believed in popular mass action) and the Party Secretariat (led by **Teng Hsiao-ping** and supported by Liu Shao-chi, who advocated more cautious, traditional approaches to both internal and foreign issues).

June 1. The Maoists seized control of the *People's Daily* and on June 4 took over the Peking Municipal Party Committee. On July 18 **Mao returned to Peking.**

Aug. 1. In the central committee of the Party Mao engineered the **promotion of Lin Piao** to be first vice-chairman and demoted Liu. The Party announced the **FORMATION OF RED GUARDS** for the assault on dissidents throughout the country. Therewith the Cultural Revolution came to fruition. The Red Guards, mostly students, soon got out of hand and brought the country to the verge of chaos. Posters, personal attacks, and blind revenge were taken on educators, experts, and all other exponents of old thought and old culture. Liu was forced to undergo self-criticism and was put under house arrest, ultimately deprived of all power (Oct. 1968). Many other high officials were humiliated, including **Chu Teh,** the founder of the Red Army. Eventually the turmoil and confusion reached such a state that **factional fighting** took place in many parts of the country and steps became necessary to check the disorder.

Nov. 22. Mao's secretary, **Ch'en Po-ta** was appointed chairman of a **Central Cultural Revolutionary Committee,** of which Mao's wife, **Chiang Ch'ing,** was vice-chairman. This committee, together with Lin Piao's **military comittee** and Chou En-lai's **state council,** constituted a ruling triumvirate.

1967, Jan. The armed forces were ordered to give political and military training in schools, that is, to restore discipline. At the same time revolutionary committees, largely under military control, were set up at central and provincial levels. Mao issued orders calling on the Red Guards to desist from attacks on government officials.

June 17. Explosion of China's first hydrogen bomb.

1968. Gradual restoration of order. In the spring and summer there were still many violent clashes between the Red Guards and the workers and peasants organized by local authorities to resist them, but by autumn progress had been made in getting the students back to school or assigning them to farm labor. Everywhere in local government, revolutionary committees, increasingly dominated by the military, made their appearance.

1969, Mar.–June. The internal crisis was supplemented by a whole series of **clashes on the Soviet-Chinese frontiers,** both in the east and in central Asia. The two governments embarked on long controversial debates, culminating in the **interview of Chou En-lai with Soviet Premier Kosygin** at the Peking airport (Sept.) during the latter's return from the funeral of Ho Chi Minh.

Apr. 1–24. NINTH PARTY CONGRESS (the first since 1958) met in secrecy and marked the **end of the Cultural Revolution** and the at least formal victory of Mao over the "revisionists." Of the new central committee about 40% were military men, and it was natural that **Lin Piao,** who reported on the success of the Cultural Revolution in arousing the country for the fight against revisionism, should be **officially designated as Mao's eventual successor.** Lin appropriately celebrated Mao as "the great teacher of the world proletariat of our time." While Mao had indeed, with support of the army, purged the bureaucracy of the more moderate elements, he had done so only at the expense of endless turmoil and murderous struggle, and the end result of the conflict was greatly to enhance the influence of the military, who came to dominate the revolutionary committees which had taken over control.

Oct. 19. Beginning of **Soviet-Chinese border discussions** at Peking.

Dec. 19. United States relaxation of restrictions on trade with Communist China. Beginning of a slow and cautious policy of friendlier relations.

1970, Apr. 28. China launched its first space satellite.

July 22. Reopening of Tsinghua University at Peking, which had been closed by Red Guards in 1966.

b. TAIWAN (FORMOSA)—NATIONALIST CHINA

(*From p. 1339*)

1950. The government in Taiwan at last introduced some of the **reforms** it had promised while still in control of the mainland.

Mar. 1. Chiang Kai-shek resumed the presidency.

1953, Feb. 3. President Eisenhower relieved the 7th Fleet from its duties of "neutralization" around Taiwan.

Feb. 24. The legislative yuan **abrogated the treaty** signed **with the U.S.S.R.** in 1945 and reserved the right to sue the Soviet Union for indemnities.

1954, Mar. 14. K. C. Wu, a former governor of Taiwan, broke with the Nationalist government, for its increasingly dictatorial character.

Sept. 3. The Nationalist government reported heavy artillery fire by the Chinese Communists against the **offshore islands** of Quemoy and Little Quemoy.

Dec. 2. A mutual defense pact with the United States was signed. The treaty was confined to Taiwan and the Pescadores and not the offshore islands in Taiwan's possession.

1955, Feb. 25. Following the **evacuation of Nanki Island,** Nationalist China's **Premier O. K. Yui** declared that his government would retreat no further.

1958, June 30. Premier Yui resigned and was **succeeded by Vice-President Chen Cheng.**

Sept. 30. In response to an adverse public reaction to United States policy toward China, Secretary of State Dulles explained that the **United States had no commitment to defend Quemoy and Matsu.** Chinese bombardments gradually dwindled away over the following months.

Oct. 21–23. Secretary of State Dulles and Chinese Nationalist President Chiang Kai-shek, after conferring in Taiwan, issued a communiqué stating that the **Nationalists would not attempt to return to the mainland by force.** They also indicated that Nationalist forces on the offshore islands might be reduced if Communist aggression ceased.

Oct. 31. The U.S. state department revealed that Chiang Kai-shek had reserved the right to use force, in the event of a "large-scale" anti-Communist revolt on the mainland.

1959, Oct. 7. Under Secretary of State **Douglas C. Dillon** stated that if the Chinese Communists attacked Taiwan and the offshore islands, they would risk "total" world war.

1960, Mar. 21. Generalissimo **Chiang Kai-shek** was re-elected for his third presidential term by the national assembly.

1961, Mar. 19. At the urging of the United States, the Nationalist government announced the opening of **"Operation Hurricane"** to remove Chinese irregulars from the Thailand, Laos, and Burma border areas. These irregulars had fled from China in 1948–49 at the time of the Communist takeover.

1962, June 27. President Kennedy stated that the United States "would not remain inactive" if a Communist Chinese attack on Quemoy and Matsu appeared to threaten Taiwan. On June 10 a large buildup of troops and planes had begun in Fukien province opposite the offshore islands of Quemoy and Matsu.

1962–1970. Nationalist China (the Republic of China), with its 13 million inhabitants, remained throughout the period the representative of China in the United Nations, occupying a permanent seat on the security council and claiming authority over all mainland China, with its 600 million people. Year after year the effort was made to have Communist China elected to the U.N., and indeed the vote in favor grew from year to year. But a solution was all but impossible because Communist China would hear nothing of a "two Chinas" solution. It demanded that Nationalist China (Taiwan) be expelled and the permanent seat assigned to the Peking government. The United States, bound by treaty to the Republic of China, was unwilling to desert an ally, so the situation, while less tense in 1970 than it had been a decade before, remained open.

Because of the rift between the Soviet Union and the Communist Chinese régime, and also because of the Cultural Revolution in China (1965–1969), Nationalist China tended to fade from the international picture. However, great progress was being made along economic and social lines. There were important land reforms, noted advances in popular education, development of industrialization, introduction of family planning, etc. Politically affairs remained basically unchanged.

1969, June. Chiang Ching-kuo, the son of the generalissimo, was appointed vice-premier and so informally designated as the probable successor to his father.

6. JAPAN

(*From p. 1114*)

1939, Aug. 25. The Japanese government protested the Russo-German pact of August 21.
1940, Jan. 14. Admiral Mitsumasa Yonai formed a new cabinet.

Mar. 30. The Japanese supported the establishment of a **puppet régime at Nanking** under **Wang Ching-wei.**

July 16. Prince Fumumaro Konoye was named prime minister of Japan to direct a **program of consolidation and defense.**

Sept. 22. Japanese forces commenced the **occupation of French Indo-China** after the French government yielded consent for the use of three airfields and other concessions.

Sept. 27. Japan joined Germany and Italy in a three-power pact whereby all pledged total aid to each other for ten years.

1941, June 23. The Japanese, who had demanded the concession, obtained the consent of the French government at Vichy for **Japanese military control of French Indo-China.**

Oct. 17. The cabinet of Prince Fumumaro Konoye was forced to resign and **Gen. Hideki Tojo,** who was more pro-Axis in his attitude, became premier and minister of war.

Nov. 29. Prime Minister Tojo declared that the influence of Great Britain and the United States must be eliminated from the Orient.

Dec. 7. JAPAN COMMENCED HOSTILITIES WITH THE UNITED STATES AND GREAT BRITAIN BY SURPRISE ATTACKS ON HAWAII, THE PHILIPPINES, GUAM, MIDWAY ISLAND, HONG KONG, AND MALAYA.

Dec. 8. THE UNITED STATES DECLARED A STATE OF WAR WITH JAPAN.

Dec. 11. GERMANY AND ITALY, in accord with the pact of September 27, 1940, **supported Japan by declaring war on the United States.** (For the war in the Pacific 1941–1945, see pp. 1153–1156.)

Dec. 21. Japan concluded a ten-year **treaty of alliance with Thailand. Thailand declared war on the United States and Great Britain** a month later (Jan. 25, 1942).

1942, Mar. 8. The **Japanese occupied Rangoon** in Burma.

1943, July 5. The Japanese government announced that it had approved the **cession of six Malayan states to Thailand.**

1944, July 18. Gen. Hideki Tojo and his entire cabinet resigned and were replaced by **Gen. Kuniaki Koiso** as premier and **Admiral Mitsumasa Yonai** as deputy premier.

1945, July 10–19. The **Japanese home islands**

were attacked with mounting intensity. Over 1000 carrier planes raided Tokyo (July 10); the United States fleet moved in to shell Honshu and Hokkaido (July 14–15); the British fleet joined in carrier raids against Japanese centers (July 17); and American and British fliers sank some of the last remnants of the Japanese navy in Tokyo Bay (July 19). On July 26 the United States, Great Britain, and China demanded that Japan surrender unconditionally, but the demand was ignored.

Aug. 6–14. The **WAR IN THE PACIFIC ENDED** in a week of disaster for Japan. An **atomic bomb,** the formula for which had been secretly perfected by United States and British scientists, was dropped on the Japanese city of **Hiroshima** (Aug. 6). It killed over 50,000 people, injured as many more, and leveled four square miles of homes and factories. Two days later, the **SOVIET UNION DECLARED WAR ON JAPAN** and Soviet armies swept into Manchuria (Aug. 8). On August 9 a **second atomic bomb** shattered **Nagasaki.** The Japanese government offered to surrender if the Emperor Hirohito were permitted to retain his throne (Aug. 10), and on receiving this assurance the **JAPANESE ACCEPTED TERMS OF SURRENDER (AUG. 14).**

Aug. 28–Sept. 2. UNITED STATES FORCES LANDED IN JAPAN to occupy strategic centers while the disarmament of Japanese military forces and the surrender of naval and aircraft proceeded rapidly. **Formal terms of surrender** were signed by the Japanese envoys on board the U.S.S. *Missouri* in Tokyo Bay (Sept. 2) (p. 1157).

With the formal surrender of Japan, supreme authority passed into the hands of **General Douglas MacArthur,** as supreme commander for the allied powers **(SCAP).** Though aided by an allied control council, and following the very general directions of an 11-nation Far Eastern commission with headquarters in Washington, MacArthur pursued a quite independent policy. To facilitate his task, Japan's governmental structure was left intact and put under the direction of **Premier Kijuro Shidehara** and a non-partisan cabinet. The most immediate task of the occupation authorities was to rid Japan of its imperialist past. In a series of decrees, General MacArthur restored civil liberties, liberated political prisoners, dissolved the secret police, liberalized the educational curriculum, granted the franchise to all adults, encouraged the formation of labor unions and the abolition of feudal land tenure, and ended the compulsory adherence to Shintoism. The climax of these moves to break with the past came on January 1, 1946, when **Emperor Hirohito,** in a New Year's message, disclaimed the divinity that was accredited to him by the Japanese people.

1946, Apr. 10. The first **general election** favored the moderate parties. Communist returns were negligible. A new government under **Shigeru Yoshida** took office on May 16.

A series of **purges,** initiated by SCAP, was directed against all "active exponents" of aggressive nationalism, including intellectuals and businessmen, and ultimately involved more than 1.5 million people. In addition, an **international military tribunal** in Tokyo began the trial of major war criminals, while separate British and Australian tribunals were set up in Southeast Asia and the South Pacific respectively.

Nov. 3. A NEW CONSTITUTION provided for an elected upper house, transferred sovereignty from the emperor to the people, safeguarded individual rights, and introduced a broad measure of local self-government. It became effective on May 3, 1947.

1947-1948. The post-war **economic recovery** of Japan was extremely slow and heavily dependent on American aid. To improve matters, the initial allied policy of dissolving the large industrial combines was abandoned in 1948, and **reparations** from capital equipment were drastically reduced. Japan's future **standard of living** was set at the 1930–1934 level. Beginning in April 1947, a limited resumption of private **foreign trade** was authorized, though by the end of 1948 Japan had regained only a small fraction of her former trade volume. To counteract the economic loss from numerous strikes, General MacArthur repeatedly imposed a ban on strikes. On December 23, 1948, the **diet prohibited all strikes** and collective bargaining **by government employees.** The initiative for Japan's economic revival came from the United States, seconded by Great Britain. It met with opposition from Australia and China, which feared a powerful Japan as a threat to their future security.

1947, April. Elections for both houses of the diet returned a right-wing majority for the **house of councillors.** In the **house of representatives** the Social Democrats received the largest number of seats. On May 23 the diet elected Socialist **Tetsu Katayama** to head a coalition government.

1948, Feb. 7. The **Katayama government resigned** because of friction within the Socialist Party. A new coalition was formed by Democratic Party leader **Hitoshi Ashida** on March 9.

Mar. 15. A new right-wing opposition party, the **Democratic Liberals,** was formed under the leadership of former premier **Yoshida.** When

Oct. 7. Premier Ashida resigned, following a financial scandal involving members of his cabinet, **Shigeru Yoshida** formed a Democratic Liberal government on October 14.

Nov. 12. The **international military tribunal** sentenced **General Hideki Tojo** and six others to death for major war crimes. Sixteen others were given life sentences.

1949, Jan. 23. National elections showed a decided swing to the right, with the Democratic Liberals gaining an absolute majority. Communist strength likewise increased. The diet re-elected **Yoshida** as premier.

May 12. The American representative on the Far Eastern Commission announced the **termination of reparation removals** to aid Japan's economic recovery. The inflationary tendencies of Japan's economy were gradually being overcome through a strict program of economic stabilization imposed by General MacArthur.

1950. Largely under the impact of the Korean War, severe restrictions were imposed on **Japan's Communists,** most of whose overt activities were suppressed. In the economic field, the war brought a much-needed increase in Japanese exports. The creation of a **national police reserve** of 75,000 men, to be used against domestic disturbances, was seen by some as the beginnings of a new Japanese army. In September, more than 10,000 prominent figures who had been dismissed at the beginning of the occupation were re-admitted to public life.

1951, Jan. 29. Premier Yoshida and **John Foster Dulles** opened **talks on a peace treaty,** as the Liberal Party issued a call for the restoration to Japan of the Soviet-held **Kurile Islands,** and the United States-held **Ryukyus,** which include Okinawa.

Mar. 29. The United States completed the draft of a peace treaty with Japan and communicated it to the fourteen co-belligerent powers including the Soviet Union.

May 19. The United States officially rejected a **Soviet proposal for a Japanese peace treaty** to be drawn up by the United States, Britain, the U.S.S.R., and Communist China.

Sept. 4. The Japanese **peace treaty conference opened at San Francisco.** Four days later the treaty was approved and signed by delegates of Japan and forty-eight other powers. Defeated in their efforts at obstruction, the Soviet and other Communist delegates boycotted the final session. The treaty deprived Japan of its overseas possessions but levied no reparations and permitted rearmament. Japan ratified the treaty on November 18.

Sept. 8. Japan signed a **mutual security pact with the United States,** permitting U.S. troops to remain indefinitely in Japan and to assist U.N. action in the Far East. The arrangement required Japan not to permit any other nation to have bases or military authority there without United States consent.

1952, Feb. 25. Deadlock of **peace treaty negotiations with Nationalist China** over Japan's refusal to recognize Chinese Nationalist sovereignty over Communist-held territory and over Chinese insistence that 1937 be acknowledged as the date when hostilities broke out rather than 1941 as Japan claimed.

Apr. 28. A **peace treaty with Nationalist China** was signed, under which Japan renounced title to Taiwan (Formosa), the Pescadores, and its former assets in China. On the same date the **war in the Pacific formally ended** and the United States-Japanese mutual security pact went into effect.

Aug. 5. Diplomatic relations were resumed with Nationalist China.

Oct. 1. In **general elections,** the conservative Liberal Party, led by Premier Shigeru Yoshida, won 240 out of 466 seats in the diet. Not a single Communist Party candidate was elected.

Nov. 12. In the first formal step toward **defensive rearmament,** the United States agreed to lend Japan 18 frigates and 50 landing craft.

1953, Apr. 19. In **national elections,** the Liberals' majority in the diet was substantially narrowed.

July 29. The house of representatives unanimously voted to adopt a resolution favoring an increase of **trade with Communist China.**

Oct. 30. A **United States-Japanese agreement** was concluded for the enlargement of Japan's "self-defense forces," to protect her from possible aggression, and to reduce the U.S. burden in the defense of Japan.

1954, June 7. Liberals overcame a Socialist boycott and pushed through the diet legislation to end autonomous local police forces and to establish centralized controls.

Oct. 5. A **conference of the Colombo plan nations** admitted Japan to membership.

Oct. 12. **Acting Premier Ogata** rejected Communist China's offer of normal relations. He termed it "bait" aimed at weakening Japanese-U.S. ties.

Dec. 9. Parliament elected **Ichiro Hatoyama** of the new Japan Democratic Party as interim premier, pending new elections in the spring.

1955, Feb. 27. Prime Minister Ichiro Hatoyama's government won the elections.

Nov. 15. The two conservative parties, the Liberals and the Democrats, merged to form the Liberal-Democratic Party

1956, May 15. A **Soviet-Japanese fishing and sea-rescue agreement** was signed in Moscow.

Sept. 28. When **Soviet-Japanese peace negotiations** reached an impasse over the disposition of the Kurile Islands, the two powers agreed to postpone discussion of the issue and to proceed with the negotiation of a peace treaty.

Oct. 19. A **Japanese-Soviet peace declaration** ended the eleven-year state of war. The treaty left unresolved the question of the **Kurile Islands.** The U.S.S.R. recognized Japanese sovereignty over the **Habomai and Shikotan Islands.** Other provisions of the settlement were: establishing of diplomatic relations, Soviet support for Japanese application for U.N. membership, repatriation of Japanese prisoners, and the relinquishing of reparations from Japan.

1957, Feb. 25. Foreign Minister and Liberal-Democrat **Nobusuke Kishi** was elected premier, succeeding **Premier Tanzan Ishibashi,** who resigned on February 23, due to poor health.

June 21. The United States agreed to the immediate withdrawal of its ground combat forces and to a reduction in strength of other United States units stationed in Japan.

July 16. The government announced an easing of **trade restrictions with Communist China.**

1958, May 22. Premier Kishi and his Liberal-Democratic Party won in national elections.

1960, Jan. 19. A **United States-Japanese treaty of mutual security** and co-operation was signed in Washington.

June 16. Following three weeks of anti-United States leftist demonstrations, Japanese Premier Kishi requested **President Eisenhower** to postpone his scheduled visit to Japan.

June 19. The **United States-Japanese mutual security treaty** was passed by the Japanese house of representatives despite violent leftist riots protesting against it. The treaty became effective on June 23.

July 18. Election of **Hayato Ikeda** as premier. A pro-western former minister of international trade and industry, Ikeda became Japan's ninth post-war premier.

Mar. 20. Elections to the house of representatives resulted in a clear victory for Premier Ikeda's pro-United States Liberal-Democratic Party.

1962, Apr. 26. Six thousand university students staged a **protest march on the Japanese diet,** where the new Japanese-United States security treaty was being considered for ratification.

July 18. After the governing Liberal-Democratic Party retained its majority in July 1st elections, Premier Hayato Ikeda replaced 13

of his 16 cabinet members. **Foreign Minister Zentaro Kosaka** was replaced by **Masayoshi Ohira,** former chief secretary of the cabinet.

1963, May 14. A new **Franco-Japanese trade agreement** was signed which provided that France would free or liberalize import quotas on over 60 Japanese products.

1964, Mar. 24. U.S. **Ambassador Edwin O. Reischauer** was stabbed by a reportedly deranged young Japanese.

May 27. Soviet **Deputy Premier Mikoyan,** with a 29-member parliamentary mission, ended a two-week visit, made at the invitation of Japanese parliamentary leaders.

Nov. 19. Eisaku Sato became premier in succession to the ailing Premier Ikeda.

1965, Jan. 12-13. Visit of Premier Sato to Washington. Discussion of relations to Communist China and of plans for the return of Okinawa to Japan.

June 22. Establishment of **diplomatic relations with the Republic of Korea,** along with agreements favoring Korea in matters of fishing rights.

1967. Development of **relations with the Soviet Union** and the Communist bloc. A trade protocol (Mar.) provided for a 16% increase in trade. Air service between the two countries was opened in April. An agreement for scientific and technological co-operation was signed on June 22.

At the same time increased agitation and pressure for return of the Bonin and Ryukyu Islands.

Nov. Second visit of Premier Sato to Washington: U.S. promise to return the **Bonin Islands,** which was done in 1968.

1968. Repeated demonstrations and clashes by students and other radical elements agitating against the renewal of the 1960 security treaty with the U.S. and against the visit to Japan by U.S. nuclear powered or equipped vessels.

1969, Oct. 21. Anti-War Day, celebrated by huge student riots and drastic action by the police.

Nov. 19-21. Visit of Premier Sato to Washington. The "reversion" of Okinawa to Japan was promised for 1972, the U.S. base on the island then to have the same status as U.S. bases in Japan. Nuclear weapons were to be removed before "reversion," and the **security treaty to continue in effect indefinitely,** subject to termination on one year's notice.

7. KOREA

(*From p. 918*)

According to decisions reached at the Crimea and Potsdam conferences, the **United States** after the war occupied the southern half of Korea up to the **38th parallel,** while the **Soviet Union** took over the northern half. Each occupying power installed a group of Korean advisers, strongly conservative in the American and pro-Communist in the Soviet zone.

1945, Dec. 27. The **Moscow conference** between Great Britain, the United States, and the Soviet Union called for a **provisional Korean democratic government** under a five-year trusteeship of the three powers and of China. Subsequent attempts of a **joint Soviet American commission** to put this agreement into force failed because of basic differences between the two parties over the definition of democracy. **Korea thus remained divided** into an agricultural south and an industrial north, with disastrous consequences to her economy.

1946, Dec. 12. A **legislative assembly,** half popularly elected, half nominated, was opened in the American zone. Its functions, at the start, were largely advisory.

1947, Sept. Following another futile attempt to settle the future of Korea by negotiations with the Soviet Union, **the United States referred the Korean problem to the United Nations.** The Soviet Union in turn proposed the simultaneous withdrawal of American and Soviet occupation forces.

Nov. 14. The U.N. general assembly recognized **Korea's claim to independence** and laid plans for the establishment of a government and the withdrawal of occupation forces.

1948, Jan. 8. A **United Nations commission** arrived in Seoul (South Korea) to supervise elections for a **national constituent assembly.** It was refused admission to the Soviet zone. The committee then recommended

May 10. Elections in South Korea for a new national assembly. The parties of the Right gained a majority.

May 28. The **national assembly,** meeting at Seoul, invited delegates from North Korea to attend. When this invitation was ignored,

Aug. 15. The **REPUBLIC OF KOREA** was proclaimed, with **Syngman Rhee** as president. United States military government was officially terminated and the new government entered into an agreement with the United States for the training of Korean forces.

Sept. 9. A Korean **PEOPLE'S DEMOCRATIC REPUBLIC,** claiming authority over the entire country, was inaugurated in northern Korea, under the presidency of veteran

Communist **Kim Il Sung.** Its institutions were modeled after those of the Soviet Union.

Dec. 12. The U.N. general assembly endorsed the government of South Korea as the only lawfully elected one and set up a commission to aid in the unification of the country.

Dec. 25. The Soviet Union announced the complete withdrawal of its forces from North Korea.

1949, June 29. The United States completed the withdrawal of occupation forces from South Korea.

Sept. 2. The **United Nations commission,** reporting on its failure to mediate between North and South Korea, **warned of a possible civil war.** There already was sporadic fighting along the 38th parallel, assuming the proportions of major battles.

1950, May 30. Elections for the **national assembly of South Korea** gave the majority of seats to the moderate forces rather than to the extreme right-wing supporters of President Rhee.

June 5. North Korea proposed negotiations for an all-Korean assembly, but refused to deal with the government of Syngman Rhee.

June 25. Start of the **KOREAN WAR,** as North Korean troops crossed the 38th parallel at eleven points. The **United Nations security council** called for an immediate cessation of hostilities and withdrawal of North Korean forces.

June 27. The **security council, in the temporary absence of the Soviet representative, asked members of the United Nations to furnish assistance to the Republic of Korea.** The **United States intervened** immediately, to help stem the North Korean Advance.

July 8. Following a request of the security council, which had set up a Korean command under the United States (July 7), President Truman designated **General Douglas MacArthur** as commanding general of the U.N. forces in Korea.

Sept. 5. At its farthest advance, North Korea held most of the Korean peninsula except for a **U.N. beachhead around Pusan** in the southeast.

Sept. 13. American and South Korean forces launched a counter-offensive, coordinated with an **amphibious landing at Inchon** (Sept. 15). By the end of the month, **U.N. forces had reached the 38th parallel** and General MacArthur asked for the surrender of the North Korean forces, which ignored his demand.

Oct. 7. The U.N. general assembly adopted a resolution for a unified, independent, and democratic Korea, and set up a **commission for the unification and rehabilitation of Korea.**

Oct. 9. General MacArthur ordered the crossing of the 38th parallel, acting on implicit authority of the U.N. general assembly. Within three weeks, **U.N. forces were approaching the Manchurian border,** reaching the Yalu River at several points.

Nov. 1. A North Korean counter-offensive halted, and in places **drove back U.N. forces.** The first Chinese prisoners were taken by MacArthur's forces. As the North Koreans failed to follow up their successes,

Nov. 24. General MacArthur launched a general assault to end the Korean War.

Nov. 26. Substantial **CHINESE FORCES INTERVENED,** and by the end of the year **had driven the U.N. forces back to the vicinity of the 38th parallel.**

1951, Jan. 1. North Korean and Chinese Communist forces attacked and broke through United Nations lines along the 38th parallel. **Seoul fell** to the invaders on January 4.

Jan. 11. The **United Nations truce committee** proposed a five-point peace program for the Far East. After the government of Communist China rejected the proposal (Jan. 17), the United States submitted a resolution that China be found guilty of aggression in Korea. The United Nations general assembly so resolved on February 1.

Jan. 25. U.N. forces opened a "limited" offensive in the western sector.

Feb. 12. Prime Minister Attlee announced Britain's opposition to sanctions against China as long as any possibility of a negotiated settlement remained.

Mar. 14. U.N. forces reoccupied Seoul, with North Koreans and Chinese in full retreat.

Mar. 24. General Douglas MacArthur announced his readiness to meet in the field the commander of the North Korean and Chinese Communist forces for a discussion of means to end the bloodshed. The Peking government rejected his offer on March 29. The governments of India (Mar. 31) and Great Britain (Apr. 2) urged that a truce be arranged.

Apr. 3. United Nations forces, having contained the Communists' first spring offensive, **counter-attacked** across the 38th parallel.

Apr. 10. President Truman replaced General MacArthur by **General Matthew B. Ridgway.**

May 15. Chinese Communist and North Korean armies launched their **second spring offensive.** After one week of heavy losses they were halted and forced into a general withdrawal.

May 18. The U.N. general assembly embargoed arms, munitions, and critical raw materials to Red China.

June 23. On a United Nations radio program Soviet representative **Jacob A. Malik** made a vaguely worded call for a cease-fire and armistice talks in Korea. Two days later President Truman replied that the United States was willing to engage in such talks. On June 29 General Ridgway broadcast to the commander-in-chief of Communist forces in Korea an **offer to negotiate an armistice.** The Communist forces agreed to a meeting to discuss a cease-fire, July 1.

July 8. **Truce negotiations opened at Kaesong.**

Aug. 5. General Ridgway broke off **armistice talks.** He charged that Communist troops had violated the demilitarization regulations in Kaesong. Five days later talks resumed but deadlocked on the question of a truce demarcation line. On August 23 the **Communists suspended negotiations** because of an alleged bombing of Kaesong by United Nations planes.

Sept. 23. United Nations forces in Korea captured "Heartbreak Ridge" after 37 days of hard fighting to secure strategic heights north of Yanggu.

Oct. 8. The high command of the Communist forces in Korea agreed to resume **armistice talks at** a new site—**Panmunjom.** United Nations and Communist liaison officers held a series of meetings from October 10 to October 22 to resolve procedural issues. Formal negotiations were renewed on October 25 for the first time since August.

Nov. 27. Allied and Communist truce delegates, meeting in plenary session, approved a **provisional cease-fire line** to go into effect if armistice terms could be negotiated within 30 days.

Dec. 27. The 30-day armistice "trial period" lapsed in Korea with neither side proposing an extension. **Armistice talks** remained stalled on two issues: prisoner exchange and the building of air-fields in North Korea during the prospective armistice.

1952, Mar. 4. The United States proposed an inquiry into Chinese Communist accusations that American forces were using **germ warfare** in North Korea. On March 14 the Soviets repeated the charges but failed to acknowledge an offer by the International Red Cross to investigate them.

Apr. 4. The Korean armistice talks at staff-officer level recessed for six days as each side moved to break the deadlock on the question of prisoner exchange.

Apr. 28. **General Mark W. Clark** was appointed to succeed General Ridgway as U.N. Far Eastern commander.

June 23. The **South Korean assembly,** boycotted by an aroused opposition, **re-elected President Rhee** for an indefinite term.

July 3. The Soviet Union, in its 49th veto, blocked an investigation by the International Red Cross of charges that U.N. forces in Korea had used germ warfare.

Aug. 5. In the country's first popular presidential election, Syngman Rhee was re-elected for another four-year term.

Oct. 8. The **Communists broke off armistice discussions.**

1953, Jan. 5. **Prime Minister Churchill,** at the beginning of a visit in the United States, declared his government's opposition to any "indefinite extension" of the Korean war into Communist China. The "real center of gravity," he said, was in West Europe.

Feb. 25. The new U.S. delegate to the U.N., **Henry Cabot Lodge,** told the U.N. political committee that the Eisenhower administration firmly accepted **India's truce proposal** for Korea.

Mar. 2. Soviet **Foreign Minister Vishinsky** told the U.N. political committee that no Korean armistice except on the Communists' terms would be acceptable.

Apr. 26. After agreements in March and April on the exchange of prisoners, **truce talks were resumed** at Panmunjon.

June 9. South Korea's assembly, rejecting the impending armistice, adopted a resolution calling for preparation to "advance north to unify Korea," but the government was persuaded (July 11) in talks with the United States to accept the proposed armistice terms.

July 26. The **armistice was signed at Panmunjon,** to go into effect on the 27th. It provided for a demilitarized zone along the North and South Korean boundary, a joint U.N.-Communist **military armistice commission,** and a **neutral nations supervisory commission** to enforce the armistice terms.

July 27. The sixteen nations which fought in Korea under the U.N. signed a declaration made public on August 7 promising to resume fighting in the event of any new aggression there.

Oct. 25. Talks opened in Panmunjon between U.N. delegates **Arthur H. Dean** and Communist representatives to arrange for the time and location of a **Korean peace conference.**

Dec. 12. After the Communists charged his government with "perfidy," Dean broke off, for an indefinite period, the negotiations for a Korean peace conference.

1954, Jan. 19. Despite bitter protests by the Communists, the neutral nations repatriation commission began the transfer of some 22,000 anti-Communist prisoners-of-war to the U.N.

command. The prisoners were then freed on January 22.

Jan. 26. The U.S. senate ratified the **mutual security treaty** with South Korea; the pact obligated the U.S. to support South Korea in the event of attack but not if South Korea attemped Korean unification by force.

May 20. In **parliamentary elections,** voters gave President Rhee's Liberal Party a narrow majority.

June 5. At Geneva, Communist China urged that the neutral nations advisory commission, which supervised the Korean armistice, also supervise the proposed elections in Korea. The United States termed the plan "completely fraudulent."

June 15. Sixteen non-Communist delegations at Geneva declared that since the Communists rejected the two fundamental principles for Korean unification and independence, i.e., the full power of the U.N. to repel aggression and establish peace and "genuinely free elections," further discussion "would serve no useful purpose."

1957, May 15. **Syngman Rhee was re-elected** to a third term as president.

June 21. The U.N. command in Korea declared that it was no longer bound by the 1953 armistice ban against the introduction of new equipment because of the continued disregard by North Korea of the provisions of the armistice.

1958, Oct. 22. Peking reported the **withdrawal of the last Chinese Communist forces.**

1960, Mar. 15. **Syngman Rhee,** running for his fourth term unopposed, was **re-elected president.**

Apr. 19. Police and troops fired on demonstrators protesting "rigged" elections; 127 were reported killed. **Syngman Rhee resigned** as president on April 27.

July 29. In parliamentary elections to replace the government of Syngman Rhee, voters gave a large majority to **John M. Chang's** Democratic Party.

1961, May 16. In South Korea an anti-Communist **military junta,** led by army chief of staff **Lt. General Do Young Chang,** overthrew the government and arrested **President Posun Yun.**

June 6. The military junta decreed an absolute **military dictatorship** with power concentrated in a few officers.

July 3. **Major General Chung Hee Park** became chairman of the military junta, and **Defense Minister Song Yo Chan** became head of the cabinet.

1962, July 10. **Kim Hyun Chui,** chairman of the economic planning board, was named premier by the ruling military junta.

1963, Mar. 22. **Marchers demonstrated in Seoul,** protesting General Park's statement of March 16 in which he withdrew his promise of elections to a new government, claiming the necessity of four more years of military government. On March 26 civilian politicians refused General Park's compromise offer of a civilian-military coalition.

Apr. 1. **Civilian leaders,** insisting that the ruling military junta honor its promise to hold elections, agreed to meet with the junta to discuss a coalition government. General Park agreed, on April 6, to hold elections in the fall and to form an **interim coalition government** of military and civilian leaders to prepare the country for the election.

Aug. 31. The pro-government Democratic-Republican Party nominated General Chung Hee Park, head of the ruling junta, as presidential candidate in the October 15 election. Park retired from the army on August 30.

Oct. 15–18. **Presidential elections** resulted in the naming of General Chung Hee Park.

1964, May 9. In a government reorganization, **Foreign Minister Chung Il Kwon** was named **premier.**

June 3–July 28. **Martial law** was proclaimed in Seoul following a long series of **student demonstrations** and charges of corruption in government. A number of ministers were obliged to resign.

1965, Apr. 13–17. **Further student disorders** in protest against the government policy of improving relations with Japan. Disorders created by the opposition became chronic and were matched by scenes of violence in parliament.

June 22. **Diplomatic relations with Japan were restored** and Japan promised extensive economic aid.

Aug. 26. Martial law was again proclaimed. Hundreds were arrested and the universities occupied by the police.

Sept. 25. Martial law was revoked.

1965–1970. **South Korean involvement in the Vietnam war.** South Korea at an early date sent a contingent and by 1966 had 143,000 troops in Vietnam.

1966, Oct. North Korea, which at first had sided with Communist China in its dispute with the Soviet Union, tended to return to its old allegiance following the deposition of Khruschev and the onset of the Cultural Revolution in China.

1967, May 3. The **presidential elections in South Korea** turned out a victory for President Park.

Growing tension in the relations of North and South Korea. **North Korean border raids and guerrilla operations became common and** often assumed major dimensions.

1968, Jan. 23. North Korean gunboats seized the U.S. intelligence ship *Pueblo* and its crew of 82 outside the twelve-mile limit in the Sea of Japan. Despite U.S. naval and air demonstrations and a momentary danger of war, the ship and crew were held by the North Koreans until Dec. 22, when the crew were released.

Apr. 15. The North Koreans shot down a U.S. intelligence plane 90 miles off the Korean coast. The government made no secret of its hatred of American imperialism nor of its determination to effect the reunification of Korea under Communist auspices in the not too distant future, despite the continued presence in South Korea of some 60,000 U.S. troops.

1969, Aug. 21–22. In a **meeting between Presi-** dent Nixon and President Park the American leader explained the new U.S. policy of letting friendly nations solve their own problems, with U.S. economic and military aid, but without involvement of American forces.

Sept. 13. The South Korean assembly passed an amendment permitting President Park to stand for a third term. This amendment was approved by popular referendum (Oct. 17).

1970, July 8. U.S. announcement of its intention to reduce its forces in South Korea. The South Korean government opposed this decision, in view of the increasing threat from North Korea, and demanded large quantities of modern military equipment and more intensive training of the South Korean army.

I. THE PACIFIC AREA

1. AUSTRALIA

(*From p. 1117*)

1945, Jan. 29. The duke of Gloucester succeeded Lord Gowrie as **governor-general.**

July 5. Prime Minister John Curtin died, after holding office since October 1941. **Joseph B. Chifley** was elected leader of the Federal Labour Party and became **prime minister on July 12.**

Nov. 27–Dec. 15. A strike of coal workers in New South Wales seriously crippled Australian industry before it was settled by arbitration. To counteract absenteeism and strikes, and to improve coal production in general, parliament, in August 1946, adopted the **Coal Industry Bill,** setting up a coal board with wide powers of control over every aspect of the coal industry.

1946, Sept. 28. Parliamentary elections maintained the Labour government's majority in both houses.

Oct. 31. A governmental ordinance called for radical improvements in the working conditions of natives in **Papua** and **New Guinea.**

1947, Jan. 27–Feb. 6. A meeting of representatives from Great Britain, France, the United States, the Netherlands, Australia, and New Zealand at **Canberra** established a **regional advisory commission for the South Pacific** to deal with all common questions concerning the treatment and general improvement of the native peoples.

Mar. 11. Sir William McKell, an Australian citizen and member of the Labour Party, took office as **governor-general.**

July 22. To help alleviate the man-power shortage, Australia agreed to admit 12,000 displaced persons per year from Europe.

Nov. 27. The **Banking Bill,** calling for the nationalization of the banks, was passed after one of the most violent controversies in Australian history. Intended to aid in the prevention of depression and inflation, opponents of the bill branded its adoption as dictatorial and unconstitutional.

1949, June 27–Aug. 15. A **Communist-inspired coal strike** almost stopped all industrial activity. It was settled with the aid of emergency legislation and the use of troops in operating the mines.

Dec. 10. The **general election** brought a decisive victory to the anti-Labour coalition of the Liberal and Country Parties. In pre-election campaigns they had opposed the government's socialist measures, especially the Banking Act, and had promised effective action against Communism. A new coalition government was formed by Liberal leader **Robert G. Menzies** (Dec. 17). The Labour Party did maintain its majority in the senate, where most of the new government's legislation was vetoed.

1950, June. Australia participated in United Nations action against **North Korea** and took measures to strengthen its armed forces.

Oct. 19. A bill dissolving the **Communist Party,** after passing both houses, was appealed in the high court.

1951, Apr. 28. General elections resulted in victory for the Liberal-Country coalition of Prime Minister Menzies.

Sept. 1. The United States, Australia, and New Zealand signed a **tripartite security treaty.**

1954, May 29. Menzies' coalition government won a very narrow victory in **parliamentary elections.**

1955, Dec. 10. Menzies' coalition government was victorious in national elections.

1957, Nov. 6. The government concluded an **agreement with the Netherlands** for a joint policy to promote the eventual self-determination of New Guinea.

1961, Dec. 9. Menzies's coalition won a fifth consecutive term in parliamentary elections, but its majority was sharply reduced.

1963, May 9. The United States and Australia signed an agreement permitting the United States to establish a major **navy communications center** in Western Australia, with the United States gaining sole operational rights for at least 25 years.

Nov. 30. Menzies' Liberal-Country coalition won a large majority in **general elections.**

1964, Nov. 10. Adoption of **compulsory military training,** with liability to service overseas. Australia realized more and more that it would have to make larger military commitments in Southeast Asia. It had sent troops to participate in the Korean war, and in Sept. 1964 had sent supplies and troops to southern Malaysia to help resist the operations of Indonesian guerrillas.

1965, Apr. Decision to send troops to South Vietnam, in collaboration with the U.S. As in the U.S., the policy of involvement in Southeast Asia met with increasing popular protest (Oct.).

Dec. An act was passed, similar to the English, to limit and control monopolies.

1966, Jan. 20. Retirement of Sir Robert Menzies, who was succeeded as prime minister by **Harold Holt.**

Feb. 14. Conversion of the currency from the British system to that of Australian dollars and cents.

Apr. The contingent sent to Vietnam was raised to 4500, despite the opposition of the Labour Party to the use of conscripts overseas.

Oct. 20–23. Visit of President Johnson, the first visit of an American executive. He was met with hostile demonstrations in Sydney, Melbourne, and other places.

Nov. 26. The **national elections** gave the combined Liberal and Country Parties another decisive victory.

1968, Jan. 10. Prime Minister Harold Holt was accidentally drowned and **John. G. Gorton** (Liberal Party leader) was appointed to succeed him.

1969, Apr.–May. Visit of Prime Minister Gorton to Washington, where the new trend of the Nixon administration was explained to him.

Oct. 25. In the **elections** the majority of the Liberal-Country Party coalition was reduced from 36 to 7.

2. NEW ZEALAND

(*From p. 1118*)

1945, Aug. 21. The **war cabinet,** a coalition of the Labour and National Parties, in office since 1940, **was dissolved.**

Nov. As further steps in the **socialization program** of the Labour Party, the government, against strong opposition, provided for the nationalization of the Bank of New Zealand and adopted the New Zealand **National Airways Bill** to set up government-controlled airlines.

1946, June 17. General Sir Bernard Freyberg took office as **governor-general.**

Nov. 26. The Labour Party in the **general elections** maintained a narrow majority with 42 seats against the National Party's 38. **Peter Fraser** continued as Labour prime minister.

1948, Aug. 18. The **British Nationality and New Zealand Citizenship Bill** clarified the citizenship status of New Zealanders, while maintaining their status as British subjects.

1949, Aug. 3. A referendum decided overwhelmingly in favor of **peace-time military service.**

Nov. 30. Parliamentary elections brought Labour its first defeat since 1935. The National Party won 46 and Labour 34 seats. **Sidney G. Holland** formed a new cabinet on December 8, pledged to a program of private enterprise and initiative. In fulfillment of this pledge,

1950. The government ended food rationing, removed wage and most price controls, and reversed many of the Labour government's nationalization measures, while maintaining its social security program.

Aug. 19. Parliament voted to abolish the appointed **legislative council** (upper house) as of January 1, 1951, since it served no real purpose. Plans for a new upper house were to be drawn up.

1951, Sept. 1. General elections confirmed Holland's National Party in power.

1957, Sept. 20. Keith J. Holyoake was appointed to succeed Prime Minister Sidney G. Holland, who resigned because of ill health.

Dec. 12. Walter Nash was sworn in as prime minister, succeeding Keith Holyoake.

1960, Nov. 26. The Conservative Party won in

the general election. Keith J. Holyoake was slated to become prime minister, replacing Labour Party leader Walter Nash.

1962, Jan. 1. Western Samoa, administered by New Zealand, **became an independent state.**

1964, Sept. Decision to send **troops to Malaysia** if needed to defeat incursions of the Indonesians. Like Australia, New Zealand was prepared to increase expenditures on defense and to play a larger military role in the Pacific.

Nov. The **Cook Islands Constitution Act** gave those islands substantial autonomy (proclaimed Aug. 8, 1965). The Cook Islands inhabitants were left free to become independent when and if they so desired.

1965. New Zealand sent a small **contingent to support the U.S. effort in South Vietnam,** although there was much popular opposition to this policy of involvement.

1966, Oct. Visit of President Johnson.

3. THE PHILIPPINE REPUBLIC

(From p. 1119)

1946, Apr. 23. Manuel A. Roxas, head of the Liberal Party, narrowly defeated Nationalist Party leader **Sergio Osmeña** (who had been president of the government-in-exile) to become president of the Philippine Commonwealth.

July 4. The **REPUBLIC OF THE PHILIPPINES** was formally inaugurated at Manila. To aid the devastated economy of the new state, the United States had earlier passed a **Rehabilitation Act** for the payment of war damage claims, and the **Bell Act,** which provided for eight years of free trade between the two countries, after which time tariff restrictions were to be gradually imposed by the United States on Philippine imports. To prepare their economy for these restrictions, the Philippine government drew up a long-range program of industrial expansion.

The economic problems of the new state were intensified by continued conflicts between the government and the **Hukbalahaps** ("Huks"), a wartime, Communist-led, peasant party concentrated in central Luzon. The Huks already had appropriated much of the land from the landlords and now demanded further land reform. Government efforts to subdue these unruly elements were met by armed resistance.

1947, Mar. 11. A national referendum approved a **constitutional amendment granting United States citizens equality with Filipinos** in the exploitation of national resources. The amendment had been made a condition for American aid under the Rehabilitation and Bell Acts.

Mar. 14. The **United States was granted a 99-year lease of Philippine military and naval bases,** and an American military mission was to assist the formation of a Philippine army.

Nov. 11. Elections for the senate and provincial offices showed a marked gain for the Nationalists.

1948, Apr. 16. President Roxas died and was succeeded by Vice-President **Elpidio Quirino.**

July–Oct. To end the civil conflict between the government and the **Hukbalahaps,** a general amnesty was granted on condition that the latter surrender. Their failure to comply brought on a full-scale government offensive, which temporarily helped to check guerrilla activities.

1949, Nov. 8. President Quirino was re-elected over the Nationalist candidate (and puppet president under the Japanese), **José P. Laurel.** Quirino's Liberal Party also won a majority in the lower house. One of the main issues of the extremely violent pre-election campaign had been Laurel's opposition to Quirino's close dependence upon the United States.

1950, Oct. 28. A **United States economic survey mission,** appointed at the request of the Philippine government, painted a dark picture of inefficiency, corruption, economic backwardness, and injustice, and recommended far-reaching economic, financial, and administrative reforms. Such reforms, it was felt, especially in the agricultural field, might also help to defeat the continued strong resistance of Huk guerrillas, notably in central Luzon.

1951, Aug. 30. The United States and the Philippines signed a **mutual defense pact.** This was the first of a series of such security pacts among anti-Communist powers in the Far East.

1953, May 14. Brig. General Carlos P. Romulo resigned as ambassador to the United States and permanent delegate to the U.N. to seek the nomination for the presidency. On May 29 he founded the new Democratic Party.

Nov. 10. In presidential elections, **Ramon Magsaysay,** former minister of defense, and his Nationalist-Democratic coalition won a sweeping 2–1 victory.

1956, May 9. The **Philippines and Japan signed a reparations agreement** providing for Japanese payment of $550 million in goods and services over a twenty-year period. The agreement also included a development loan to the Philippines of $250 million.

1957, Mar. 17. President Magsaysay was killed in an airplane crash. On March 18 **Vice-President Carlos P. Garcia** succeeded to the presidency.

Nov. 12. National elections resulted in victory for President Garcia and his Nationalist Party. Liberal **Diosdado Macapagal** was elected to the vice-presidency. They were installed, December 30.

1959, Oct. 12. The United States and the Philippines signed a "memorandum of agreement" revising the arrangements for United States bases on the islands; four major bases of the former twenty-three were to remain.

1961, Nov. 14. In presidential and legislative elections, Diosdado Macapagal and his Liberal Party defeated the incumbent president and his National Party. **Macapagal** was inaugurated on December 30 as the **fifth president of the Philippines.**

1962, June 22. In an official note, the government claimed **sovereignty over British North Borneo** and asked that talks be held immediately in London or Manila for speedy settlement. Britain rejected the claim on August 7.

July 27. President Macapagal proposed the creation of a **Confederation of Greater Malaya,** including the Philippines, to supercede the British-sponsored federation of Malaysia (p. 1321).

1965, Nov. 9. Ferdinand E. Marcos was elected president. He continued the efforts of his predecessor in the direction of land and other reforms, but the Philippines continued to suffer from overpopulation, unemployment, and administrative corruption.

1968. There was a marked **revival of the Huk guerrilla activity,** which added greatly to the burdens of the government.

In the field of foreign policy the Philippines became involved in **controversy with Malaysia** due to the Philippine **claim to Saba** (p. 1322).

4. FIJI ISLANDS

1970, Oct. 10. Proclamation of **independence by the Fiji Islands.** Chief **Sir Kamisese Mara** became the first prime minister.

VIII. THE RECENT PERIOD

VIII. THE RECENT PERIOD

A. THE EXPLORATION OF SPACE

The exploration of space, based on the early experimentation of **Robert H. Goddard** with rockets (1920's and 1930's) and development of long-range missiles during the Second World War (p. 611), was carried forward with great energy during the 1960's by scientists and technicians of both the United States and the Soviet Union, who shared in thitherto unbelievable achievements. Only the most important of many ventures can be listed here.

1957, Oct. 4. THE SOVIET UNION LAUNCHED THE FIRST MAN-MADE SATELLITE, *Sputnik I.*

Nov. 3. The Soviets launched *Sputnik II,* carrying a dog into space.

1958, Jan. 31. The U.S. mission of *Explorer I* resulted in the discovery of the **Van Allen Radiation Belts.**

Aug. 27. Establishment of the **U.S. National Aeronautics and Space Administration** (NASA), which assumed direction of the American effort in the exploration of space.

Oct. 11. U.S. *Pioneer I* went 70,000 miles into space and returned.

1959, Jan. 2. The Soviet *Lunik I* was put into **orbit around the sun.**

Apr. 1. U.S. *Tiros I* was the **first weather observation satellite.**

Sept. 12. Soviet *Lunik II* was the first earth object to strike the surface of the moon.

Oct. 4. Soviet *Lunik III* sent back to earth the first photographs of the dark side of the moon.

Dec. 12. Establishment by the United Nations of the **permanent committee on the peaceful uses of outer space.**

1960, Aug. 12. U.S. *Echo I* introduced a balloon communications satellite.

Aug. 19–21. The Soviet *Spacecraft II* brought back alive two dogs from outer space.

1961, Apr. 12. YURI GAGARIN, Soviet astronaut, became the **FIRST MAN TO ORBIT THE EARTH,** in *Vostok I.*

May 5. Alan B. Shepard, Jr., was the first American in space.

Aug. 6. In *Vostok II,* **Gherman Titov** orbited the earth seventeen times.

1962, Feb. 20. John Glenn was the first American to orbit the earth, making three orbits in *Friendship VII.*

Apr. 26. In a joint Anglo-American effort, *Ariel* was launched for the **study of cosmic rays.**

July 10. U.S. *Telstar* became the **first communications satellite.**

Aug. 27. The unmanned *Mariner II* (U.S.) was launched for a flight to the planet Venus. On Dec. 14 it reported the first readings of the high temperatures of the planet.

1963, June 16. The Soviet **Valentina Tereshkova,** in *Vostok VI,* became the **first woman astronaut.**

Dec. 13. The **United Nations declaration of principles** that should govern the exploration and use of outer space.

1964, Nov. 28. U.S. *Mariner IV* was launched on a **flight to the planet Mars.** On July 15, 1965, it relayed the first photographs of the planet, taken from altitudes of 10,000 to 17,000 miles. They revealed a dry, crater-pocked surface.

1965, Apr. 6. *Early Bird,* the **first commercial communications satellite,** was launched and operated by the Communications Satellite Corporation. This proved to be a most important step in the development of international telephone, television, and other modes of communication.

Mar. 18. Aleksei Leonov, in *Voskhod II* was the **first man to walk in space.** On June 3 the American **Edward H. White** remained for 20 minutes walking in space.

Aug. 21–29. Lt. Col. L. Gordon Cooper, Jr., and **Lt. Comdr. Charles Conrad, Jr.,** remained eight days in orbit and made 120 orbits of the earth in *Gemini V.*

Nov. 26. The French launched their first satellite.

Dec. 4. U.S. *Gemini VII* remained in orbit for 14 days and on Dec. 15 executed the **first space rendezvous** with *Gemini VI.*

1966, Feb. 3. The Soviet *Lunik IX* made a **first unmanned landing on the moon,** relaying pictures showing a relatively firm surface.

The U.S. Aeronautics and Space Administration launched the **first weather reporting satellite.**

Mar. 16. First successful docking in space by *Gemini VIII* and an Atlas-Agena.

Apr. 3. Soviet *Lunik X* was the **first spaceship to orbit the moon.**

June 2. Landing of U.S. *Surveyor I,* an unmanned craft, on the moon. It sent back numerous photographs of the lunar surface.

Sept. 12. *Gemini XI* docked with an Agena during the first orbit of the earth and later cut loose again.

1967, Jan. 27. Death of three American astronauts by fire in *Apollo I* while still on the ramp.

Signature of the U.N.-sponsored **TREATY ON THE EXPLORATION AND USE OF OUTER SPACE** (p. 1219).

June 14. Launching of *Mariner V* for a flight to the planet Mars.

Oct. 18. The Soviets succeeded in **first landing a capsule on Venus,** revealing that the atmosphere is largely carbon dioxide, with no oxygen.

Oct. 30. Two unmanned Soviet spaceships docked successfully while orbiting the earth.

1968, Dec. 21. The U.S. *Apollo VII* was the **first manned spacecraft to orbit the moon.**

1969, Jan. 15. The Soviet *Soyuz V* succeeded in effecting rendezvous with *Soyuz IV.*

Feb. 14. *Mariner VI* was dispatched on a flight to Mars.

Mar. 3. *Apollo IX* docked in space with a lunar landing module.

July 16. *Apollo XI* (**Neil A. Armstrong** and **Col. Edwin E. Aldrin, Jr.**) landed a lunar module on the moon (July 20), while **Lt. Col. Michael Collins orbited the moon. ARMSTRONG WAS THE FIRST AND ALDRIN THE SECOND MAN TO WALK ON THE MOON.** After a brief stay they were able to launch their lunar module and rejoin *Apollo XI* for a successful return to Earth, bringing specimens of rock and soil.

Nov. 14. *Apollo XII* landed a lunar module within 500 feet of *Surveyor III* (Nov. 19).

1970, Apr. Communist China launched its first space satellite.

Apr. 27. A Soviet rocket fired eight unmanned satellites into orbit.

Sept. 21–22. *Lunik XVI,* an unmanned Soviet spacecraft, landed on the moon in the vicinity of the Sea of Fertility and after a stay of 26 hours blasted off to return to Earth, carrying a small cargo of stones and earth scooped up by an electric device.

Oct. 29. Soviet-United States agreement on the development of mutually compatible rendezvous and docking systems.

Nov. 17. Soviet *Lunik XVII* landed *Lunokhod I,* an eight-wheel unmanned, self-propelled vehicle, in the Sea of Rains for more detailed lunar exploration.

Dec. 15. The Soviet unmanned spacecraft *Venera VII,* launched Aug. 17, 1970, **reached the planet Venus** and landed on the surface, sending back data for 23 minutes after landing.

B. SCIENTIFIC AND TECHNOLOGICAL ADVANCES

1964, Oct. 1. Japan introduced the **first high-speed passenger train.**

Oct. 10. The opening ceremonies of the Olympic Games, held in Japan, were transmitted live by way of **Syncom III.**

Konrad Bloch and **Feodor Lynen** were awarded the Nobel Prize for their studies of the **relationship of cholesterol to heart disease.**

1965. The first transistor microphone.

Richard P. Feynman and **Julius S. Schwinger** won the Nobel Prize for their fundamental **researches in quantum electrodynamics.**

Robert B. Woodward was awarded the Nobel Prize for his **syntheses of organic structures.**

Dr. R. J. Fallon and his co-workers went far in demonstrating that **mycoplasmas in leukemia cells** actually cause the disease.

1966. Discovery of a **vaccine for measles.**

Robert S. Mulliken received the Nobel Prize for studies of **chemical bonds holding atoms together** in a molecule.

Completion of the two-mile, 20-billion-volt **linear accelerator at Stanford University,** Cal.

1967. *The Health Consequences of Smoking,* a publication of the U.S. Public Health Service, reinforced the conclusions of earlier studies as to the deleterious effects of tobacco use.

Haldan K. Hartline, George Wald, and **Ragnar Granit** shared a Nobel Prize for their **researches on the eye.**

Hans Bethe won a Nobel Prize for his **studies of solar energy.**

The Lawrence Laboratories created the **heaviest known nucleus, isotope Mendelevium 258.**

Dec. 3. **Dr. Christiaan N. Barnard** of Capetown performed the **first heart transplant operation,** the patient living for 18 days. The first American operation of this kind was performed on Dec. 7 by **Dr. Adrian Kantrowitz** of New York City, whose patient, however, survived only for a few hours. The most significant heart transplant was that of Dr. Barnard on Jan. 2, 1968, the patient, **Dr. Philip Blaiberg,** surviving for nineteen months. Important progress was made by **Dr. Norman E. Shumway's** establishing of a standard technique and **Dr. Denton A. Cooley's** significant shortening of the operation.

Dec. 4. The French **wheelless aerotrain** traveled 215 mph on an air cushion.

1968. **Luis W. Alvarez** received a Nobel Prize for his work on **subatomic particles.**

Lars Onsager was similarly honored for **equations showing reciprocal reactions** such as the interaction of voltage and temperature.

Robert W. Holley, Marshall W. Nirenberg, and H. G. Khorana shared a Nobel Prize for "breaking the genetic code."

1970, May 20. Dr. Albert V. Crewe, with a 35,000-volt electron microscope, took pictures of individual atoms of uranium and thorium.

July. A team of female aquanauts completed two weeks of observation and study in an underwater device off the Virgin Islands.

Aug. 31. The Bell Laboratories produced a pocket-size laser capable of carrying hundreds of thousands of telephone calls, TV signals, and other communications.

APPENDIX

APPENDIX

I. ROMAN EMPERORS

27 B.C.– 14 A.D.	Augustus (Gaius Julius Caesar Octavianus)
14–37	Tiberius (Tiberius Claudius Nero Caesar)
37–41	Caligula (Gaius Claudius Nero Caesar Germanicus)
41–54	Claudius (Tiberius Claudius Nero Caesar Drusus)
54–68	Nero (Lucius Domitius Ahenobarbus Claudius Drusus)
68–69	Galba (Servius Sulpicius Galba)
69	Otho (Marcus Salvius Otho)
69	Vitellius (Aulus Vitellius Germanicus)
69–79	Vespasian (Titus Flavius Vespasianus)
79–81	Titus (Titus Flavius Vespasianus)
81–96	Domitian (Titus Flavius Domitianus)
96–98	Nerva (Marcus Cocceius Nerva)
98–117	Trajan (Marcus Ulpius Nerva Traianus)
117–138	Hadrian (Publius Aelius Traianus Hadrianus)
138–161	Antoninus Pius (Titus Aurelius Fulvius Boionius Arrius Antoninus Pius)
161(146) –180	Marcus Aurelius (Marcus Annius Aurelius Verus)
161–169	Lucius Aurelius Verus (Lucius Ceionius Commodus Verus)
180(177) –192	Commodus (Lucius Aelius Marcus Aurelius Antoninus Commodus)
193	Pertinax (Publius Helvius Pertinax)
193	Didius Julian (Marcus Didius Salvius Julianus Severus)
193–211	Septimius Severus (Lucius Septimius Severus)
211(198) –217	Caracalla (Marcus Aurelius Antoninus Bassianus Caracallus)
209–211	Geta (Publius Septimius Geta)
217–218	Macrinus (Marcus Opellius Severus Macrinus)
218–222	Elagabalus (Marcus Varius Avitus Bassianus Aurelius Antoninus Heliogabalus)
222–235	Alexander Severus (Marcus Alexianus Bassianus Aurelius Severus Alexander)
235–238	Maximin (Gaius Julius Verus Maximinus "Thrax")
238	Gordian I (Marcus Antonius Gordianus)
238	Gordian II
238	Pupienus (Marcus Clodius Pupienus Maximus)
238	Balbinus (Decimus Caelius Balbinus)
238–244	Gordian III (Marcus Antonius Gordianus)
244–249	Philipp "Arabs" (Marcus Julius Philippus "Arabs")
249–251	Decius (Gaius Messius Quintus Traianus Decius)
251	Hostilian (Gaius Valens Hostilianus Messius Quintus)
251–253	Gallus (Gaius Vibius Trebonianus Gallus)
253	Aemilian (Marcus Julius Aemilius Aemilianus)
253–259	Valerian (Gaius Publius Licinius Valerianus)
259(253) –268	Gallienus (Publius Licinius Egnatius Gallienus)
268–270	Claudius II (Marcus Aurelius Claudius Gothicus)
270	Quintillus (Marcus Aurelius Claudius Quintillus)
270–275	Aurelian (Lucius Domitius Aurelianus)
275–276	Tacitus (Marcus Claudius Tacitus)
276	Florian (Marcus Annius Florianus)
276–282	Probus (Marcus Aurelius Probus)
282–283	Carus (Marcus Aurelius Carus)
283–284	Numerian (Marcus Aurelius Numerius Numerianus)
283–285	Carinus (Marcus Aurelius Carinus)
284–305	Diocletian (Gaius Aurelius Valerius Diocles Jovius)
286–305	Maximian (Marcus Aurelius Valerius Maximianus Herculius)
305(293) –306	Constantius I (Flavius Valerius Constantius Chlorus)
305(293) –311	Galerius (Gaius Galerius Valerius Maximianus)

306–307	Severus (Flavius Valerius Severus)
306–308	Maximian (second reign)
306–312	Maxentius (Marcus Aurelius Valerius Maxentius)
308–313	Maximinus Daia (Galerius Valerius Maximinus Daia)
311(307) –324	Licinius (Gaius Flavius Valerius Licinianus Licinius)
311(306) –337	Constantine I, the Great (Flavius Valerius Constantinus)
337–340	Constantine II (Flavius Valerius Claudius Constantinus)
337–361	Constantius II (Flavius Valerius Julius Constantius)
337–350	Constans (Flavius Valerius Julius Constans)
361–363	Julian, the Apostate (Flavius Claudius Julianus)
363–364	Jovian (Flavius Jovianus)
364–375	Valentinian I (Flavius Valentinianus, in the West)
364–378	Valens (in the East)
375(367) –383	Gratian (Flavius Gratianus Augustus, in the West)
375–392	Valentinian II (Flavius Valentinianus, in the West)
379–395	Theodosius, the Great (Flavius Theodosius, in the East, and, after 392, in the West)
383–388	Maximus (Magnus Clemens Maximus)
392–394	Eugenius

395(383) –408	Arcadius (in the East)
395(393) –423	Honorius (Flavius Honorius, in the West)
421	Constantius III
423–425	Johannes
408(402) –450	Theodosius II (in the East)
425–455	Valentinian III (Flavius Placidius Valentinianus, in the West)
450–457	Marcian (Marcianus, in the East)
455	Petronius (Flavius Ancius Petronius Maximus, in the West)
455–456	Avitus (Flavius Maecilius Eparchus Avitus, in the West)
457–461	Majorian (Julius Valerius Maioranus, in the West)
457–474	Leo I (Leo Thrax, Magnus, in the East)
461–465	Severus (Libius Severianus Severus, in the West)
467–472	Anthemius (Procopius Anthemius, in the West)
472	Olybrius (Anicius Olybrius, in the West)
473	Glycerius (in the West)
473–475	Julius Nepos (in the West)
473–474	Leo II (in the East)
474–491	Zeno (in the East)
475–476	Romulus Augustulus (Flavius Momyllus Romulus Augustus, in the West)

II. BYZANTINE EMPERORS

474–491	Zeno
475–476	Basiliscus
491–518	Anastasius I
518–527	Justin I (Flavius Justinus)
527(518) –565	Justinian the Great (Flavius Justinianus)
565–578	Justin II (Flavius Justinus)
578(574) –582	Tiberius II (Flavius Constantinus Tiberius)
582–602	Maurice (Maurikios)
602–610	Phocas I
610–641	Heraclius I
641	Constantine III (Constantinus)
641	Heracleon (Heracleonas)
641–668	Constans II
668–685	Constantine IV (Pogonatus)
685–695	Justinian II (Rhinotmetus)
695–698	Leontius
698–705	Tiberius II (Apsimar)
705–711	Justinian II (restored)
711–713	Philippicus
713–715	Anastasius II
715–717	Theodosius III

717–741	Leo III (the Isaurian)
741–775	Constantine V (Kopronymos)
775–780	Leo IV
780–797	Constantine VI (Porphyrogenetos)
797–802	Irene (empress)
802–811	Nicephorus I
811	Stauracius (Staurakios)
811–813	Michael I (Rhangabé)
813–820	Leo V (the Armenian)
820–829	Michael II (Balbus)
829(820) –842	Theophilus I
842–867	Michael III
867(866) –886	Basil I (the Macedonian)
886–912	Leo VI (the Wise)
912–913	Alexander II
912–959	Constantine VII (Porphyrogenetos)
920–944	Romanus I (Lekapenos)
959–963	Romanus II
963(976) –1025	Basil II (Bulgaroktonos)
963–969	Nicephorus II (Phocas)

969–976	John I (Tzimisces)
1025(976)–1028	Constantine VIII
1028–1050	Zoë (empress)
1028–1034	Romanus III (Argyropulos)
1034–1041	Michael IV (the Paphlagonian)
1041–1042	Michael V (Kalaphates)
1042–1055	Constantine IX (Monomachos)
1055–1056	Theodora (empress)
1056–1057	Michael VI (Stratioticos)
1057–1059	Isaac I (Komnenos)
1059–1067	Constantine X (Dukas)
1068–1071	Romanus IV (Diogenes)
1071–1078	Michael VII (Parapinakes)
1078–1081	Nicephorus III (Botaniates)
1081–1118	Alexius I (Komnenos)
1118–1143	John II (Komnenos)
1143–1180	Manuel I (Komnenos)
1180–1183	Alexius II (Komnenos)
1183–1185	Andronicus I (Komnenos)
1185–1195	Isaac II (Angelos)
1195–1203	Alexius III (Angelos)
1203–1204	Isaac II (restored)
1203–1204	Alexius IV
1204	Alexius V (Dukas)

Latin Emperors

1204–1205	Baldwin I
1205–1216	Henry
1216–1217	Peter of Courtenay
1217–1219	Yolande
1219–1228	Robert of Courtenay
1228–1261	Baldwin II
1231–1237	John of Brienne (co-emperor)

Nicaean Emperors

1204–1222	Theodore I (Lascaris)
1222–1254	John III (Dukas Vatatzes)
1254–1258	Theodore II (Lascaris)
1258–1261	John IV (Lascaris)
1259–1261 (1282)	Michael VIII (Paleologos)

The Paleologi

1261(1259)–1282	Michael VIII
1282–1328	Andronicus II (the Elder)
1295–1320	Michael IX (co-emperor)
1328–1341	Andronicus III (the Younger)
1341–1347	John V (Paleologos)
1347(1341)–1354	John VI (Kantakuzenos)
1355–1376	John V (restored)
1376–1379	Andronicus IV
1379–1391	John V (restored)
1390	John VII
1391–1425	Manuel II
1425–1448	John VIII
1448–1453	Constantine XI

III. CALIPHS, TO 1256

622(570)–632	MUHAMMAD

The Orthodox Caliphate

632–634	Abu Bakr
634–644	Omar
644–656	Othman
656–661	Ali

The Omayyad Caliphate

661–680	Muawiya I
680–682	Yazid I
683	Muawiya II
684–685	Marwan I
685–705	Abdalmalik
705–715	Walid I
715–717	Sulaiman
717–720	Omar ibn Abdul-Aziz
720–724	Yazid II
724–743	Hisham
743–744	Walid II
744	Yazid III
744	Ibrahim
744–750	Marwan II

The Abbasid Caliphate

750–754	Abu-l-Abbas al-Saffah
754–775	Al-Mansur
775–785	Al-Mahdi
785–786	Al-Hadi
786–809	Harun Al-Rashid
809–813	Al-Amin
813–833	Al-Mamun (Mamun the Great)
833–842	Al-Mu'tasim
842–847	Al-Wathiq
847–861	Al-Mutawakkil
861–862	Al-Muntasir
862–866	Al-Musta'in
866–869	Al-Mu'tazz
869–870	Al-Muqtadi
870–892	Al-Mu'tamid
892–902	Al-Mu'tadid
902–908	Al-Muqtafi
908–932	Al-Muqtadir
932–934	Al-Qahir
934–940	Al-Radi
940–944	Al-Muttaqi
944–946	Al-Mustaqfi
946–974	Al-Muti

974–991 Al-Ta'i
991–1031 Al-Qadir
1031–1075 Al-Qa'im
1075–1094 Al-Muqtadi
1094–1118 Al-Mustazhir
1118–1135 Al-Mustarshid
1135–1136 Al-Rashid
1136–1160 Al-Muqtafi
1160–1170 Al-Mustanjid
1170–1180 Al-Mustadi
1180–1225 Al-Nasir
1225–1226 Al-Zahir
1226–1242 Al-Mustansir
1242–1256 Al-Musta'sim

The Omayyad Caliphate of Córdoba

756–788 Abd ar-Rahman I
788–796 Hisham I
796–822 Al-Hakam I
822–852 Abd ar-Rahman II
852–886 Muhammad I
886–888 Al Mundhir
888–912 Abdallah
912–961 Abd ar-Rahman III
961–976 Al-Hakam II al Mustansir
976–1009 Hisham II al Muayyad
1009–1010 Muhammad II al-Mahdi
1009–1010 Sulaiman al-Mustain

1010–1013 Hisham II (restored)
1013–1016 Sulaiman (restored)
1016–1018 Ali ben Hammud
1018 Abd ar-Rahman IV
1018–1021 Al-Qasim
1021–1022 Yahya
1022–1023 Al-Qasim (restored)
1023–1024 Abd ar-Rahman V
1024–1025 Muhammad III
1025–1027 Yahya (restored)
1027–1031 Hisham III

The Fatimid Caliphate of Egypt

909–934 Al-Mahdi
934–945 Al-Qaim
945–952 Al-Mansur
952–975 Al-Muizz
975–996 Al-Aziz
996–1021 Al-Hakim
1021–1036 Az-Zahir
1036–1094 Al-Mustansir
1094–1101 Al-Mustadi
1101–1130 Al-Amir
1130–1149 Al-Hafiz
1149–1154 Az-Zafir
1154–1160 Al-Faiz
1160–1171 Al-Adid

IV. ROMAN POPES

(Names marked with an asterisk indicate popes sainted by the Church. Names in italics are those of anti-popes.)

33–?67 *Peter
?67–?76· *Linus
?76–?88 *Anacletus I
?88–?97 *Clement I
?97–?105 *Evaristus
?105–?115 *Alexander I
?115–?125 *Sixtus I
?125–?136 *Telesphorus
?136–?140 *Hyginus
?140–?155 *Pius I
?155–?166 *Anicetus
?166–?175 *Soter
?175–189 *Eleuterus
189–199 *Victor I
199–217 *Zephyrinus
217–222 *Calixtus I
222–230 *Urban I
222–235 *Hippolytus*
230–235 *Pontian
235–236 *Anterus
236–250 *Fabian
250–251 (Vacancy)

251–253 *Cornelius
251–?258 *Novatian*
253–254 *Lucius I
254–257 *Stephen I
257–258 *Sixtus II
258–260 (Vacancy)
260–268 *Dionysius
269–274 *Felix I
275–283 *Eutychian
283–296 *Caius
296–304 *Marcellinus
304–308 (Vacancy)
308–309 *Marcellus I
309–310 *Eusebius
311–314 *Miltiades
314–335 *Sylvester I
335–336 *Marcus
337–352 *Julius I
352–366 Liberius
353–365 *Felix II*
366–383 *Damasus I
366–367 *Ursinus*
384–399 *Siricius
399–401 *Anastasius I
401–417 *Innocent I
417–418 *Zosimus

418–422	*Boniface I		767	*Philip*
418–419	*Eulalius*		767–772	Stephen III
422–432	*Celestine I		772–795	Adrian I
432–440	*Sixtus III		795–816	*Leo III
440–461	*Leo I		816–817	Stephen IV
461–468	*Hilarius		817–824	Paschal I
468–483	*Simplicius		824–827	Eugene II
483–492	*Felix III		827	Valentine
492–496	*Gelasius I		827–844	Gregory IV
496–498	*Anastasius II		*844*	*John VIII*
498–514	*Symmachus		844–847	Sergius II
498–505	*Laurentius*		847–855	*Leo IV
514–523	*Hormisdas		855–858	Benedict III
523–526	*John I		*855*	*Anastasius III*
526–530	*Felix IV		858–867	*Nicholas I
530–532	Boniface II		867–872	Adrian II
530	*Dioscurus*		872–882	John VIII
533–535	John II		882–884	Marinus I
535–536	*Agapetus I		884–885	Adrian III
536–537	*Silverius		885–891	Stephen V
537–555	Vigilius		891–896	Formosus
556–561	Pelagius I		896	Boniface VI
561–574	John III		896–897	Stephen VI
575–579	Benedict I		897	Romanus
579–590	Pelagius II		897	Theodore II
590–604	*Gregory I		898–900	John IX
604–606	Sabinian		900–903	Benedict IV
607	Boniface III		903	Leo V
608–615	*Boniface IV		903–904	Christopher
615–618	*Deusdedit		904–911	Sergius III
619–625	Boniface V		911–913	Anastasius III
625–638	Honorius I		913–914	Lando
638–640	(Vacancy)		914–928	John X
640	Severinus		928–929	Leo VI
640–642	John IV		929–931	Stephen VII
642–649	Theodore I		931–935	John XI
649–655	*Martin I		936–939	Leo VII
655–657	*Eugene I		939–942	Stephen IX (VIII)
657–672	*Vitalian		942–946	Marinus II
672–676	Adeodatus		946–955	Agapetus II
676–678	Donus		955–963	John XII
678–681	*Agatho		963–964	Leo VIII
681–683	*Leo II		964	Benedict V
684–685	*Benedict II		965–972	John XIII
685–686	John V		973–974	Benedict VI
686–687	Conon		974–983	Benedict VII
687	*Theodore II*		983–984	John XIV
687–692	*Paschal I*		984–985	Boniface VII
687–701	*Sergius I		985–996	John XV
701–705	John VI		996–999	Gregory V
705–707	John VII		*996–998*	*John XVI*
708	Sisinnius		999–1003	Sylvester II
708–715	Constantine		1003	John XVII
715–731	*Gregory II		1003–1009	John XVIII
731–741	*Gregory III		1009–1012	Sergius IV
741–752	*Zacharias		1012–1024	Benedict VIII
752–757	Stephen II		*1012*	*Gregory VI*
757–767	*Paul I		1024–1033	John XIX
767	*Constantine*		1033–1045	Benedict IX

1045	Sylvester III		1261–1264	Urban IV (Jacques Pantaléon)
1045–1046	Gregory VI (John Gratian Pierleoni)		1265–1268	Clement IV (Guy le Gros Foulques)
1046–1047	Clement II (Suitgar, Count of Morsleben)		1268–1271	(Vacancy)
			1271–1276	*Gregory X (Tebaldo Visconti)
1048	Damasus II (Count Poppo)		1276	Innocent V (Pierre de Champagni)
1049–1054	*Leo IX (Bruno, Count of Toul)		1276	Adrian V (Ottobono Fieschi)
1055–1057	Victor II (Gebhard, Count of Hirschberg)		1276–1277	John XXI (Pietro Rebuli-Giuliani)
			1277–1280	Nicholas III (Giovanni Gaetano Orsini)
1057–1058	Stephen IX (Frederick of Lorraine)			
1058	Benedict X (John, Count of Tusculum)		1281–1285	Martin IV (Simon Mompitie)
			1285–1287	Honorius IV (Giacomo Savelli)
1058–1061	Nicholas II (Gerhard of Burgundy)		1288–1292	Nicholas IV (Girolamo Masci)
1061–1073	Alexander II (Anselmo da Baggio)		1294	*Celestine V (Pietro Angelari da Murrone)
1061–1064	*Honorius II*			
1073–1085	*Gregory VII (Hildebrand of Soana)		1294–1303	Boniface VIII (Benedetto Gaetani)
1080–1100	*Clement III*		1303–1304	Benedict XI (Niccolò Boccasini)
1086–1087	Victor III (Desiderius, Prince of Beneventum)		1305–1314	Clement V (Raimond Bertrand de Got)
1088–1099	Urban II (Odo of Chatillon)		1316–1334	John XXII (Jacques Duèze)
1099–1118	Paschal II (Ranieri da Bieda)		*1328–1330*	*Nicholas V (Pietro di Corbara)*
1100–1102	*Theodoric*		1334–1342	Benedict XII (Jacques Fournier)
1102	*Albert*		1342–1352	Clement VI (Pierre Roger de Beaufort)
1105	*Sylvester IV*			
1118–1119	Gelasius II (John Coniolo)		1352–1362	Innocent VI (Étienne Aubert)
1118–1121	*Gregory VIII*		1362–1370	Urban V (Guillaume de Grimord)
1119–1124	Calixtus II (Guido, Count of Burgundy)		1370–1378	Gregory XI (Pierre Roger de Beaufort, the Younger)
1124–1130	Honorius II (Lamberto dei Fagnani)		1378–1389	Urban VI (Bartolomeo Prignano)
1124	*Celestine II*		*1378–1394*	*Clement VII (Robert of Geneva)*
1130–1143	Innocent II (Gregorio Papareschi)		1389–1404	Boniface IX (Pietro Tomacelli)
1130–1138	*Anacletus II (Cardinal Pierleone)*		*1394–1423*	*Benedict XIII (Pedro de Luna)*
1138	*Victor IV*		1404–1406	Innocent VII (Cosmato de' Migliorati)
1143–1144	Celestine II (Guido di Castello)			
1144–1145	Lucius II (Gherardo Caccianemici)		1406–1415	Gregory XII (Angelo Correr)
1145–1153	Eugene III (Bernardo Paganelli)		*1409–1410*	*Alexander V (Petros Philargi)*
1153–1154	Anastasius IV (Corrado della Subarra)		*1410–1415*	*John XXIII (Baldassare Cossa)*
			1415–1417	(Vacancy)
1154–1159	Adrian IV (Nicholas Breakspear)		1417–1431	Martin V (Ottone Colonna)
1159–1181	Alexander III (Orlando Bandinelli)		*1423–1429*	*Clement VIII*
1159–1164	*Victor IV*		*1424*	*Benedict XIV*
1164–1168	*Paschal III*		1431–1447	Eugene IV (Gabriele Condulmer)
1168–1178	*Calixtus III*		*1439–1449*	*Felix V (Amadeus of Savoy)*
1179–1180	*Innocent III (Lando da Sessa)*		1447–1455	Nicholas V (Tommaso Parentucelli)
1181–1185	Lucius III (Ubaldo Allucingoli)			
1185–1187	Urban III (Uberto Crivelli)		1455–1458	Calixtus III (Alonso Borgia)
1187	Gregory VIII (Alberto del Morra)		1458–1464	Pius II (Aeneas Silvio de' Piccolomini)
1187–1191	Clement III (Paolo Scolari)			
1191–1198	Celestine III (Giacinto Boboni-Orsini)		1464–1471	Paul II (Pietro Barbo)
			1471–1484	Sixtus IV (Francesco della Rovere)
1198–1216	Innocent III (Lotario de' Conti di Segni)		1484–1492	Innocent VIII (Giovanni Battista Cibo)
1216–1227	Honorius III (Cencio Savelli)		1492–1503	Alexander VI (Rodrigo Lanzol y Borgia)
1227–1241	Gregory IX (Ugolino di Segni)			
1241	Celestine IV (Goffredo Castiglione)		1503	Pius III (Francesco Todoeschini-Piccolomini)
1243–1254	Innocent IV (Sinibaldo de' Fieschi)		1503–1513	Julius II (Giuliano della Rovere)
1254–1261	Alexander IV (Rinaldo di Segni)		1513–1521	Leo X (Giovanni de' Medici)
			1522–1523	Adrian VI (Hadrian Florensz)

1523–1534	Clement VII (Giulio de' Medici)	1700–1721	Clement XI (Gian Francesco Albani)
1534–1549	Paul III (Alessandro Farnese)		
1550–1555	Julius III (Giovanni Maria Ciocchi del Monte)	1721–1724	Innocent XIII (Michelangelo dei Conti)
1555	Marcellus II (Marcello Cervini)	1724–1730	Benedict XIII (Pietro Francesco Orsini)
1555–1559	Paul IV (Gian Pietro Caraffa)		
1559–1565	Pius IV (Giovanni Angelo de' Medici)	1730–1740	Clement XII (Lorenzo Corsini)
		1740–1758	Benedict XIV (Prospero Lambertini)
1566–1572	*Pius V (Antonio Michele Ghislieri)		
1572–1585	Gregory XIII (Ugo Buoncompagni)	1758–1769	Clement XIII (Carlo Rezzonico)
1585–1590	Sixtus V (Felice Peretti)	1769–1774	Clement XIV (Lorenzo Ganganelli)
1590	Urban VII (Giambattista Castagna)		
1590–1591	Gregory XIV (Niccolò Sfondrati)	1775–1799	Pius VI (Gianangelo Braschi)
1591	Innocent IX (Gian Antonio Facchinetti)	1800–1823	Pius VII (Barnaba Chiaramonti)
		1823–1829	Leo XII (Annibale della Genga)
1592–1605	Clement VIII (Ippolito Aldobrandini)	1829–1830	Pius VIII (Francesco Saverio Gastiglioni)
1605	Leo XI (Alessandro de' Medici-Ottaiano)	1831–1846	Gregory XVI (Bartolomeo Alberto Cappellari)
1605–1621	Paul V (Camillo Borghese)	1846–1878	Pius IX (Giovanni Mastai-Ferretti)
1621–1623	Gregory XV (Alessandro Ludovisi)		
1623–1644	Urban VIII (Maffeo Barberini)	1878–1903	Leo XIII (Gioacchino Pecci)
1644–1655	Innocent X (Giambattista Pamfili)	1903–1914	Pius X (Giuseppe Sarto)
1655–1667	Alexander VII (Fabio Chigi)	1914–1922	Benedict XV (Giacomo della Chiesa)
1667–1669	Clement IX (Giulio Rospigliosi)		
1670–1676	Clement X (Emilio Altieri)	1922–1939	Pius XI (Achille Ratti)
1676–1689	Innocent XI (Benedetto Odescalchi)	1939–1958	Pius XII (Eugenio Pacelli)
		1958–1963	John XXIII (Angelo Roncalli)
1689–1691	Alexander VIII (Pietro Ottoboni)	1963–	Paul VI (Giovanni Battista Montini)
1691–1700	Innocent XII (Antonio Pignatelli)		

V. HOLY ROMAN EMPERORS

(Names marked with asterisks are those of rulers who were never crowned at Rome and who were, therefore, strictly speaking, only Kings of Germany.)

800–814	Charlemagne	1039–1056	Henry III (the Black)
814–840	Louis I (the Pious)	1056–1106	Henry IV
840–855	Lothair I	1077–1080	*Rudolf (of Swabia)
855–875	Louis II	1081–1093	*Hermann (of Luxemburg)
875–877	Charles II (the Bald)	1093–1101	*Conrad (of Franconia)
877–881	(Vacancy)	1106–1125	Henry V
881–887	Charles III (the Fat)	1125–1137	Lothair II
887–891	(Vacancy)	1138–1152	*Conrad III
891–894	Guido (of Spoleto)	1152–1190	Frederick I Barbarossa
892–898	Lambert (co-emperor with Guido)	1190–1197	Henry VI
896–899	Arnulf	1198–1215	Otto IV
901–905	Louis III (of Provence)	1198–1208	*Philip (of Swabia)
911–918	*Conrad I (of Franconia)	1215–1250	Frederick II
915–924	Berengar	1246–1247	*Henry Raspe
919–936	*Henry I (the Fowler)	1247–1256	*William (of Holland)
936–973	Otto I (the Great)	1250–1254	*Conrad IV
973–983	Otto II	1254–1273	The Great Interregnum, during which the crown was contested between
983–1002	Otto III		
1002–1024	Henry II (the Saint)	1257–1272	*Richard of Cornwall and
1024–1039	Conrad II (the Salian)	1257–1273	*Alfonso X (of Castile)
		1273–1291	*Rudolf I (Hapsburg)
		1292–1298	*Adolf I (of Nassau)
		1298–1308	*Albert I (Hapsburg)
		1308–1313	Henry VII (Luxemburg)

1314–1347	Louis IV (of Bavaria)	1558–1564	*Ferdinand I
1314–1325	*Frederick of Hapsburg (co-regent)	1564–1576	*Maximilian II
1347–1378	Charles IV (Luxemburg)	1576–1612	*Rudolf II
1349	*Günther (of Schwarzburg)	1612–1619	*Matthias
1378–1400	*Wenceslas (of Bohemia)	1619–1637	*Ferdinand II
1400	*Frederick III (of Brunswick)	1637–1657	*Ferdinand III
1400–1410	*Rupert (of the Palatinate)	1658–1705	*Leopold I
1410–1437	Sigismund (Luxemburg)	1705–1711	*Joseph I
1410–1411	*Jobst (of Moravia)	1711–1740	*Charles VI
1438–1439	*Albert II (Hapsburg)	1742–1745	*Charles VII (of Bavaria)
1440–1493	Frederick III (last emperor crowned at Rome)	1745–1765	*Francis I (of Lorraine)
		1765–1790	*Joseph II
1493–1519	*Maximilian I	1790–1792	*Leopold II
1519–1558	*Charles V (last emperor crowned by the pope, at Bologna)	1792–1806	*Francis II

VI. KINGS OF ENGLAND SINCE 1066

1066–1087	William (the Conqueror)	1553–1558	Mary
1087–1100	William II (Rufus)	1558–1603	Elizabeth I
1100–1135	Henry I	1603–1625	James I
1135–1154	Stephen	1625–1649	Charles I
1154–1189	Henry II	1649–1660	(the Commonwealth)
1189–1199	Richard I (the Lion-hearted)	1660–1685	Charles II
1199–1216	John (Lackland)	1685–1688	James II
1216–1272	Henry III	1689–1702	William III and (until 1694) Mary
1272–1307	Edward I	1702–1714	Anne
1307–1327	Edward II	1714–1727	George I
1327–1377	Edward III	1727–1760	George II
1377–1399	Richard II	1760–1820	George III
1399–1413	Henry IV	1820–1830	George IV
1413–1422	Henry V	1830–1837	William IV
1422–1461	Henry VI	1837–1901	Victoria
1461–1483	Edward IV	1901–1910	Edward VII
1483	Edward V	1910–1936	George V
1483–1485	Richard III	1936	Edward VIII
1485–1509	Henry VII	1936–1952	George VI
1509–1547	Henry VIII	1952–	Elizabeth II
1547–1553	Edward VI		

VII. KINGS OF FRANCE SINCE 987

987–996	Hugh Capet	1350–1364	John II
996–1031	Robert II (the Pious)	1364–1380	Charles V
1031–1060	Henry I	1380–1422	Charles VI
1060–1108	Philip I	1422–1461	Charles VII
1108–1137	Louis VI (the Fat)	1461–1483	Louis XI
1137–1180	Louis VII (the Young)	1483–1498	Charles VIII
1180–1223	Philip II (Augustus)	1498–1515	Louis XII
1223–1226	Louis VIII	1515–1547	Francis I
1226–1270	Louis IX (Saint Louis)	1547–1559	Henry II
1270–1285	Philip III (the Bold)	1559–1560	Francis II
1285–1314	Philip IV (the Fair)	1560–1574	Charles IX
1314–1316	Louis X	1574–1589	Henry III
1316	John I	1589–1610	Henry IV
1316–1322	Philip V	1610–1643	Louis XIII
1322–1328	Charles IV	1643–1715	Louis XIV
1328–1350	Philip VI	1715–1774	Louis XV

1774–1792 Louis XVI
1792–1804 (First Republic)
1804–1814 Napoleon I (Emperor)
1814–1824 Louis XVIII
1824–1830 Charles X

1830–1848 Louis Philippe
1848–1852 (Second Republic)
1852–1870 Napoleon III (Emperor)
1870–   (Third and later Republics)

VIII. PRESIDENTS OF THE UNITED STATES

George Washington, 1789–1797
John Adams, 1797–1801
Thomas Jefferson, 1801–1809
James Madison, 1809–1817
James Monroe, 1817–1825
John Quincy Adams, 1825–1829
Andrew Jackson, 1829–1837
Martin Van Buren, 1837–1841
William Henry Harrison, 1841
John Tyler, 1841–1845
James Knox Polk, 1845–1849
Zachary Taylor, 1849–1850
Millard Fillmore, 1850–1853
Franklin Pierce, 1853–1857
James Buchanan, 1857–1861
Abraham Lincoln, 1861–1865
Andrew Johnson, 1865–1869
Ulysses Simpson Grant, 1869–1877
Rutherford Birchard Hayes, 1877–1881
James Abram Garfield, 1881

Chester Alan Arthur, 1881–1885
Grover Cleveland, 1885–1889
Benjamin Harrison, 1889–1893
Grover Cleveland, 1893–1897
William McKinley, 1897–1901
Theodore Roosevelt, 1901–1909
William Howard Taft, 1909–1913
Woodrow Wilson, 1913–1921
Warren Gamaliel Harding, 1921–1923
Calvin Coolidge, 1923–1929
Herbert Clark Hoover, 1929–1933
Franklin Delano Roosevelt, 1933–1945
Harry S Truman, 1945–1953
Dwight D. Eisenhower, 1953–1961
John F. Kennedy, 1961–1963
Lyndon B. Johnson, 1963–1969
Richard M. Nixon, 1969–1974
Gerald R. Ford, 1974–1977
James E. Carter, 1977–

IX. MEMBERS OF THE UNITED NATIONS IN ORDER OF ADMISSION

1. Argentina	24 Oct. 1945	26. United Arab Republic	24 Oct. 1945
2. Brazil	24 Oct. 1945	27. United Kingdom	24 Oct. 1945
3. Byelorussia	24 Oct. 1945	28. United States	24 Oct. 1945
4. Chile	24 Oct. 1945	29. Yugoslavia	24 Oct. 1945
5. China (Nationalist)	24 Oct. 1945*	30. Greece	25 Oct. 1945
6. Cuba	24 Oct. 1945	31. India	30 Oct. 1945
7. Czechoslovakia	24 Oct. 1945	32. Peru	31 Oct. 1945
8. Denmark	24 Oct. 1945	33. Australia	1 Nov. 1945
9. Dominican Republic	24 Oct. 1945	34. Costa Rica	2 Nov. 1945
10. El Salvador	24 Oct. 1945	35. Liberia	2 Nov. 1945
11. France	24 Oct. 1945	36. Colombia	5 Nov. 1945
12. Haiti	24 Oct. 1945	37. Mexico	7 Nov. 1945
13. Iran	24 Oct. 1945	38. South Africa	7 Nov. 1945
14. Lebanon	24 Oct. 1945	39. Canada	9 Nov. 1945
15. Luxemburg	24 Oct. 1945	40. Ethiopia	13 Nov. 1945
16. New Zealand	24 Oct. 1945	41. Panama	13 Nov. 1945
17. Nicaragua	24 Oct. 1945	42. Bolivia	14 Nov. 1945
18. Paraguay	24 Oct. 1945	43. Venezuela	15 Nov. 1945
19. Philippines	24 Oct. 1945	44. Guatemala	21 Nov. 1945
20. Poland	24 Oct. 1945	45. Norway	27 Nov. 1945
21. Saudi Arabia	24 Oct. 1945	46. Netherlands	10 Dec. 1945
22. Syria	24 Oct. 1945	47. Honduras	17 Dec. 1945
23. Turkey	24 Oct. 1945	48. Uruguay	18 Dec. 1945
24. Ukraine	24 Oct. 1945	49. Ecuador	21 Dec. 1945
25. U.S.S.R.	24 Oct. 1945	50. Iraq	21 Dec. 1945

*On October 25, 1971, the General Assembly voted to replace the seat of Nationalist China with the People's Republic of China in both the General Assembly and on the Security Council.

51. Belgium	27 Dec. 1945
52. Afghanistan	19 Nov. 1946
53. Iceland	19 Nov. 1946
54. Sweden	19 Nov. 1946
55. Thailand	16 Dec. 1946
56. Pakistan	30 Sep. 1947
57. Yemen	30 Sep. 1947
58. Burma	19 Apr. 1948
59. Israel	11 May 1949
60. Indonesia	28 Sep. 1950
61. Albania	14 Dec. 1955
62. Austria	14 Dec. 1955
63. Bulgaria	14 Dec. 1955
64. Cambodia	14 Dec. 1955
65. Ceylon	14 Dec. 1955
66. Finland	14 Dec. 1955
67. Hungary	14 Dec. 1955
68. Ireland	14 Dec. 1955
69. Italy	14 Dec. 1955
70. Jordan	14 Dec. 1955
71. Laos	14 Dec. 1955
72. Libya	14 Dec. 1955
73. Nepal	14 Dec. 1955
74. Portugal	14 Dec. 1955
75. Roumania	14 Dec. 1955
76. Spain	14 Dec. 1955
77. Morocco	12 Nov. 1956
78. Sudan	12 Nov. 1956
79. Tunisia	12 Nov. 1956
80. Japan	18 Dec. 1956
81. Ghana	8 Mar. 1957
82. Malaysia	17 Sep. 1957
83. Guinea	12 Dec. 1958
84. Cameroun	20 Sep. 1960
85. Central African Republic	20 Sep. 1960
86. Chad	20 Sep. 1960
87. Congo (capital: Brazzaville)	20 Sep. 1960
88. Congo (capital: Leopoldville)	20 Sep. 1960
89. Cyprus	20 Sep. 1960
90. Dahomey	20 Sep. 1960
91. Gabon	20 Sep. 1960
92. Ivory Coast	20 Sep. 1960
93. Malagasy Republic	20 Sep. 1960
94. Niger	20 Sep. 1960
95. Somalia	20 Sep. 1960
96. Togo	20 Sep. 1960
97. Upper Volta	20 Sep. 1960
98. Mali	28 Sep. 1960

99. Senegal	28 Sep. 1960
100. Nigeria	7 Oct. 1960
101. Sierra Leone	27 Sep. 1961
102. Mauritania	27 Oct. 1961
103. Mongolia	27 Oct. 1961
104. Tanganyika	14 Dec. 1961
105. Burundi	18 Sep. 1962
106. Jamaica	18 Sep. 1962
107. Rwanda	18 Sep. 1962
108. Trinidad and Tobago	18 Sep. 1962
109. Algeria	8 Oct. 1962
110. Uganda	25 Oct. 1962
111. Kuwait	14 May 1963
112. Kenya	16 Dec. 1963
113. Zanzibar	16 Dec. 1963*
114. Malawi	1 Dec. 1964
115. Malta	1 Dec. 1964
116. Zambia	1 Dec. 1964
117. Gambia	21 Sep. 1965
118. Maldives	21 Sep. 1965
119. Singapore	21 Sep. 1965
120. Guyana	20 Sep. 1966
121. Botswana	17 Oct. 1966
122. Lesotho	17 Oct. 1966
123. Barbados	9 Dec. 1966
124. Southern Yemen	14 Dec. 1967
125. Mauritius	24 Apr. 1968
126. Swaziland	24 Sep. 1968
127. Equatorial Guinea	12 Nov. 1968
128. Fiji	13 Oct. 1970
129. Bahrain	21 Sep. 1971
130. Bhutan	21 Sep. 1971
131. Qatar	21 Sep. 1971
132. Oman	8 Oct. 1971
133. United Arab Emirates	9 Dec. 1971
134. East Germany	18 Sep. 1973
135. West Germany	18 Sep. 1973
136. Bangladesh	17 Sep. 1974
137. Grenada	17 Sep. 1974
138. Guinea-Bissau Republic	17 Sep. 1974
139. Cape Verde	16 Sep. 1975
140. Sao Tome & Principe	16 Sep. 1975
141. Mozambique	16 Sep. 1975
142. Papua New Guinea	10 Oct. 1975

*Zanzibar's seat was given up, May 13, 1964, following the union of Zanzibar with Tanzania.

X. LIST OF EUROPEAN UNIVERSITIES FOUNDED PRIOR TO 1900

The beginnings of the oldest universities cannot be dated with accuracy, for corporations of teachers or students often existed long before securing a papal or imperial charter and many universities were initially professional schools before adding other faculties. Thus, organized medical teaching at **Salerno** seems to go back to the 9th century, and the law schools at **Bologna** were flourishing before the end of the 12th century.

c. 1150–1160	Paris
1167	Oxford
1204	Vicenza
1209	Cambridge

1214	Palencia	1576	Warsaw
1222	Padua	1578	Vilna
1224	Naples	1582	Edinburgh
1229	Toulouse	1586	Graz
1243	Salamanca	1591	Trinity College (Dublin)
1244	Rome	1607	Giessen
1247	Siena	1614	Groningen
1248	Piacenza	1621	Strasbourg
1253	Sorbonne	1623	Salzburg
1289	Montpellier	1623	Madrid
1290	Lisbon	1632	Dorpat
1303	Avignon	1634	Utrecht
1305	Orléans	1635	Budapest
1308	Perugia	1648	Bamberg
1308	Coimbra	1657	Durham
1339	Grenoble	1665	Kiel
1343	Pisa	1666	Lund
1346	Valladolid	1677	Innsbruck
1348	Prague	1693	Halle
1361	Pavia	1702	Breslau
1364	Vienna	1722	Dijon
1364	Cracow	1734	Göttingen
1379	Erfurt	1735	Rennes
1385	Heidelberg	1742	Erlangen
1391	Ferrara	1755	Moscow
1402	Würzburg	1769	University of Malta
1409	Leipzig	1771	Münster
1411	St. Andrews	1776	Zagreb
1412	Turin	1779	Palermo
1426	Louvain	1801	Oslo
1431	Poitiers	1804	Kharkov
1437	Caen	1804	Kazan
1441	Bordeaux	1808	Lyons
1450	Barcelona	1810	Berlin
1450	Trier	1816	Ghent
1451	Glasgow	1817	Liége
1455	Freiburg im Breisgau	1818	Bonn
1459	Ingolstadt	1819	St. Petersburg
1460	Basel	1827	Helsingfors
1463	Nantes	1828	London
1465	Bourges	1832	Kiev
1475	Ofen	1832	Zürich
1477	Tübingen	1834	Brussels
1477	Uppsala	1837	Athens
1479	Copenhagen	1850	Manchester
1494	Aberdeen	1860	Jassy
1501	Valencia	1864	Bucharest
1502	Wittenberg	1864	Belgrade
1505	Seville	1865	Odessa
1508	Alcalá	1876	Geneva
1527	Marburg	1877	Amsterdam
1531	Debreczen	1878	Stockholm
1533	Granada	1881	Liverpool
1537	Coimbra	1887	Gothenburg
1544	Königsberg	1888	Sofia
1548	Messina	1891	Lausanne
1558	Jena	1893	Wales
1574	Bern	1896	Marseilles
1574	Oviedo	1896	Nancy
1575	Leyden	1900	Birmingham

XI. SELECT LIST OF UNIVERSITIES AND COLLEGES OF THE NEW WORLD FOUNDED PRIOR TO 1900

Readers consulting this list should remember that many present-day institutions were established under a different name, that some date their origin from a charter, others from the beginning of operations, others yet from their amalgamation with other institutions. So far as possible their beginnings are here dated from the time of the original school.

1551	National University of Mexico
1551	National University of San Marcos de Lima (Peru)
1573	National University of Bogotá (Colombia)
1613	National University of Córdoba (Argentina)
1621	National University of Bolivia
1636	Harvard College
1676	San Carlos University of Guatemala
1693	William and Mary
1696	Saint John's College
1701	Yale College
1725	Central University of Caracas (Venezuela)
1728	Central University of Havana
1738	Central University of Chile
1740	University of Pennsylvania
1746	College of New Jersey (Princeton University)
1754	King's College (Columbia University, 1784)
1764	Brown University
1766	Queen's College (Rutgers University, 1825, 1945)
1769	Dartmouth College
1769	Central University of Ecuador
1773	Dickinson College
1785	University of Georgia
1787	Franklin and Marshall College
1787	University of Pittsburgh
1789	Georgetown University
1791	University of Vermont
1793	Williams College
1793	Hamilton-Oneida Academy (Hamilton College, 1812)
1794	Bowdoin College
1794	University of Tennessee
1795	Union College
1795	University of North Carolina
1800	Middlebury College
1801	University of South Carolina
1802	United States Military Academy
1807	University of Maryland
1809	Miami University (Ohio)
1811	National University of Nicaragua
1813	Colby College
1817	University of Michigan
1818	Saint Louis University
1819	University of Virginia

1819	Norwich University
1819	University of Cincinnati
1819	Colgate University
1820	Indiana University
1821	University of Buenos Aires
1821	Amherst College
1821	McGill University
1821	George Washington University
1822	Hobart College
1823	Trinity College (Hartford)
1824	Kenyon College
1824	Rensselaer Polytechnic Institute
1826	Western Reserve University
1826	Lafayette College
1827	University of Toronto
1831	New York University
1831	Wesleyan University
1831	University of Alabama
1831	Denison University
1833	Haverford College
1833	Oberlin College
1833	National University of the Republic (Montevideo)
1834	Tulane University
1834	Wheaton College
1836	Emory University
1837	Knox College
1837	Indiana Asbury University (DePauw University, 1883)
1837	Mount Holyoke College
1839	Boston University
1839	University of Missouri
1840	Bethany College
1841	Fordham University
1841	Dalhousie University
1842	Ohio Wesleyan University
1842	University of Notre Dame
1843	Holy Cross College
1843	University of Delaware
1845	Baylor College
1845	United States Naval Academy
1846	Beloit College
1846	Bucknell College
1846	University of Buffalo
1846	Grinnell College
1847	Lawrence College
1847	State University of Iowa
1848	University of Mississippi
1849	University of Wisconsin
1850	University of Dayton

1850	University of Utah
1850	University of Rochester
1851	University of Minnesota
1851	Northwestern University
1851	Trinity College (Duke University, 1924)
1852	Tufts University
1852	Mills College
1852	Antioch College
1853	University of Florida
1853	Eliot Seminary (Washington University, 1857)
1855	Berea College
1861	Massachusetts Institute of Technology
1861	Vassar College
1861	University of Washington
1861	University of Colorado
1863	Massachusetts Agricultural College (University of Massachusetts, 1947)
1863	Boston College
1864	Marquette University
1864	University of Denver
1864	Swarthmore College
1864	Bates College
1865	University of Kentucky
1865	Lehigh University
1865	University of Maine
1865	Atlanta University
1865	Cornell University
1866	University of Kansas
1866	Carleton College
1867	Fisk University
1867	West Virginia University
1867	Howard University
1867	University of Illinois
1868	University of California
1869	Purdue University
1870	Syracuse University

1870	Wellesley College
1870	Stevens Institute of Technology
1870	University of Akron
1870	College of the Immaculate Conception (Loyola University, 1912)
1871	University of Arkansas
1872	Vanderbilt University
1872	University of Toledo
1872	University of Oregon
1873	Ohio State University
1874	University of Nevada
1876	Johns Hopkins University
1877	University of Detroit
1880	Case Institute of Technology
1881	University of Connecticut
1881	University of Texas
1882	University of South Dakota
1883	University of North Dakota
1884	Temple University
1885	Stanford University
1885	Rollins College
1885	University of Arizona
1885	Bryn Mawr College
1885	Goucher College
1887	Clark University
1887	Occidental College
1887	Pomona College
1887	University of Wyoming
1889	University of Idaho
1890	University of Chicago
1890	University of Oklahoma
1891	Rice University
1891	California Institute of Technology
1892	University of New Mexico
1892	University of Rhode Island
1893	American University

INDEX

INDEX

Byzantine Crusade, 189

Byzantine Empire, 133–138, 166, 172, 186–196, 204, 239, 267–272, 343, 345–348; Bulgarian campaigns, 195–196, 197–198; 265; collapse of, 266, 313, 322, 326, 348; division of, 280; and Turks, 348, 350. *See also* Empire of the West; Latin Empire of the East

Byzantium, 62, 69, 74, 169, 185; in Social War, 77, 78

Cabal, preceded cabinet system, England, 463

Cabeçadas, Mendes, Portuguese revolutionary, 996

Cabet, Étienne, French radical, 591, 679

Cabeza de Vaca, Alvar Núñez, Spanish colonist, 532, 534, 535

Cabildos, South America, 838

Cable and Wireless Act, England, 1171

Caboche, Simon, 301

Cabochian revolt and Ordinance, 301

Cabot, John, explorer, 390, 548, 612

Cabot, John, U.S. government official, 1244

Cabot, Sebastian, explorer, 390, 532, 548, 612

Cabral, Amilcar, Portuguese politician, 1187, 1264

Cabral, Pedro, Portuguese navigator, 385, 390, 418

Cáceres, Andrés Avelino, president of Peru, 851

Cadamosto (Ca da Mosto), Alvise da, explorer, 385

Cade, John, English rebel leader, 293

Cadet Party, Russia, *see* Constitutional Democratic Party, Russia

Cadillac, Antoine de, founded Detroit, 548

Cadiz, 417, 461, 467

Cadmeia of Thebes, 77

Cadorna, Luigi, Italian commander, 953, 962, 974

Cadoudal, Georges, French royalist conspirator, 640

Caecilius Statius, Roman comedist, 103

Caen, capture of (1944), 1150

Caesar, Gaius, *see* Caligula

Caesar, (Gaius) Julius, 6, 86, 97, 108–110; assassination, 110, 115; his *Commentaries,* 112, 157

Caesar, Lucius Julius, 105, 115

Caesarea, captured by Moslems, 199

Caesarion, son of Cleopatra, 109

Caesar Octavianus, *see* Augustus

Caetano, Dr. Marcello, premier of Portugal, 1187, 1264, 1273

Cafe Filho, João, president of Brazil, 1259

Cagni, Umberto, Arctic explorer, 617

Cagoularas (Hooded Ones), French terrorists, 990

Caillaux, Joseph, premier of France, 693, 800, 987

Caillé, René, explorer in Africa, 863

Cairo, 286, 635, 868, 1160, 1293; conference of non-aligned nations at, 1161, 1266; Ulbricht visits (1965), 1200

Caisse de la Dette, established in Egypt, 867

Calabria, 191, 193, 231, 268, 286

Calais, 288, 290, 293, 297; captured by duke of Guise, 399, 411; in World War II, 1139

Calatafimi, battle of, 707

Calatrava, military order of, 251, 280

Calculating machines, *see* Computers

Calculus, 456, 457

Calcutta, India, 572, 904

Caldera Rodríguez, Rafael, president of Venezuela, 1259

Calderón, battle at bridge of, 842

Calderón, Pedro, Spanish dramatist, 416

Cale Acte, 71

Caledonia (Wales), 134, 179

Calendar: Gregorian reform, 6, 424; Sothic cycle, 37; reformed by Omar Khayyam, 272; Chinese computations for, 367; Mayan, 387; seaman's, 458

Calhoun, John Caldwell, U.S. politician, 812, 814, 815

California, U.S. state, 24, 858, 923; Russian settlements in, 749, 752; discovery of gold in, 814; in Compromise of 1850, 815

Caligula, Roman emperor, 119

Calinescu, Armand, premier of Roumania, 1028, 1213

Caliphate, orthodox, 148, 177, 199–200, 204–206, 259, 284; abolished in Turkey, 1087

Calixtines, moderate Bohemian reformers, 329

Calixtus III, anti-pope, 235

Calixtus II, pope, 222, 234

Calixtus III, pope, 313

Callao, attacked by Spanish fleet, 851

Calleja del Rey, Felix Maria, Spanish general, 842

Calles, Plutarco Elias, Mexican politician, 1070–1071

Calles-Morrow agreement (1927), U.S.-Mexico, 1070

Callias, peace of, 70

Callicrates, king of Sparta, 92

Callicratidas, Spartan admiral, 74

Calligraphy, 147, 148

Callimachus, Greek scholar, 88

Callinicum, battle of, 186

Callistratus, Athenian orator and general, 77

Calonne, Charles Alexandre de, French finance minister, 485–486

Calpurnius Piso, Lucius, *see* Piso, L. Calpurnius

Caltabellotta, peace of, 313

Calthorpe, Sir Somerset, British commander, 973

Calvert, Cecilius, Maryland colony charter, 550

Calvert, George (later Lord Baltimore), colonial proprietor, 550, 553

Calvin, John, French theologian and reformer, 156, 414, 429–430, 438, 594

Calvinism, 399, 429–430, in Holland, 408; in treaty of Westphalia, 437; in Poland, 442; in Transylvania, 449

Calvinist-Catholic coalition, Netherlands, 674

Camacho, Manuel Avila, president of Mexico, 1145, 1241

Cámara de Indias, and Spanish colonial affairs, 538, 540

Camarilla, Spain, 696, 697

Camarina, 71

Cambacérès, Jean, duc de, French consul, 637

Cambert, Robert, French composer, 484

Cambodia, 144, 369, 1236, 1324, 1325; and Dvaravati kingdom, 371; and Siam, 372, 906; French protectorate, 906, 907, 908; and Vietnam war, 1329, 1330; independence, 1330–1332

Cambon, Jules, French diplomat, 799, 802

Cambrai: League of, 409, 421, 423, 425, 426; treaty of (*Paix des dames*), 416, 422, 429; battle of, 960

Cambridge Ancient History, published, 983

Cambridge Modern History published, 983

Cambridge University, foundation of, 216

Cambyses, invasion of, 40, 53

Camden, battle of, 561

Camel, battle of, 200

Camels, domestication of, 43

Cameron, Charles D., British consul in Ethiopia, 870

Cameron, Trevor, British commander, 935

Cameron, Verney L., explored Africa, 863

Cameronians, in England, 464

Chalcedon, 62, 73, 140, 189; council of, 136, 138, 156

Chalchuapa, battle of, 857

Chalcidian League, 77

Chalcidice, 62

Chalcis, 62, 66–67

Chalcocondylas, Laonicus, Byzantine historian, 348

Chalcolithic age, 4, 13, 14, 16

Chaldaea, Zenj rebellion in, 205

Chaldeans, 28, 31, 33, 34, 46; dynasty of Babylon, 34–35

Chaldiran, battle of, 450, 565

Chalgrove Field, English Civil War battle, 404

Challe, Maurice, French commander in Algeria, 1290

Challenger, H. M. S., 601

Châlons, battles at, 130, 135, 157, 158, 161

Chaltalja lines, attacked by Bulgaria, 801

Chaltin, Louis, Belgian soldier in Congo, 879, 880

Chalukya-Chola dynasty of southern India, 362

Chalukya (or Solanki Rajput) clan, Indian rulers, 356, 360

Chamberlain, Joseph, British statesman, 667–668, 787, 790; colonial secretary, 891

Chamberlain, Neville, prime minister of England, 982, 983, 1171; and Munich agreements, 1129

Chamber of fasces and corporations, Italy, 1001

Chambers of Reunion, France, 479

Chambord, Henry d'Artois, count of, claimed French throne, 687, 688

Chambre de comptes, France, 299

Chambre introuvable, 677

Chambres ardentes, France, 411

Chamorro, Diego, Nicaraguan politician, 1068, 1243

Chamorro, Emiliano, president of Nicaragua, 1068

Chamoun, Camille, president of Lebanon, 1284, 1300–1301

Champagne, 172; battles of, 946, 960

Champaubert, battle of, 649

Championnet, Jean, French soldier, 636

Champlain, Samuel de, French explorer, 546

Champlitte, Guillaume de, conquered Achaia, 280

Chams, Malay people, 146, 148, 365

Chan, Song Yo, South Korean premier, 1350

Chanakkale, landing of British force at, 1086

Chancelade man, 13

Chancellor, Sir John, British high commissioner in Palestine, 1091

Chancellor, Richard, British explorer, 447, 612

Chancellorsville, battle in U.S. Civil War, 819

Chandellas, dynasty of, 356, 358

Chandragupta I, king of India, 55, 142, 144

Chandragupta II Vikramaditya, 142

Chang, Do Young, led military junta in South Korea, 1350

Chang, John M., South Korean political leader, 1350

Ch'ang-an, Western Han capital, 145, 363, 364

Chang Ch'ien, mission to Asia and India, 145

Chang Chih-tung, governor-general of Hupei, 913, 914, 915

Changchun, 922, 1126, 1339; became Hsin-ching (New Capital), 1108; Sino-Soviet conference at (1922), 1112

Chang Heng, co-founder of Taoism, 147

Chang Hsüeh-liang, military governor in Manchuria, 1107, 1109

Chang Hsün, Chinese politician, 1106

Changkufeng Hill, battle at, 1110

Chang Ling, co-founder of Taoism, 147

Changsu, king of Korea, 149

Chang Tso-lin, military governor in Manchuria, 1107

Changyang (Hupei), skeletal material found at, 12

Ch'an (Dhyana, Zen) sect, 148, 364

Chanson de Roland, see *Song of Roland*

Chansons de geste, 245

Chante fable, 247

Chanute, Octave, his early glider flights, 609

Chao, Chinese imperial surname, 365

Ch'ao, Chinese state, 57

Chao Chung, Chinese general, 146

Chao dynasty, 57

Ch'ao Hsien, Chinese conquest of, 146

Chao-hui, of Turkish Khoja dynasty, 579

Chao Ju-kua, reported itineraries of Marco Polo, 370

Chao K'uang-yin of (Sung) T'ai Tsu, Chinese emperor, 365

Chao Meng-fu, Chinese artist, 370

Chao Ti, 146

Chao T'o, king of southern Yüeh, 145

Chapas (Chapotkatas), Indian clan, 356

Chapei, China, 1108

Chappe, Claude, developed semaphore, 528

Chapultepec, 1214; battle of, 814; Act of (1945), 1145

Charaka, Hindu scientific work, 204

Charaka, his medical ethical code, 143

Charcas, 840, 841

Charcot, Jean B., French explorer, 624

Chares, Athenian general, 77, 78

Charette de la Contrie, François Athanase, led revolt in Vendée, 631, 633

Charge of the Light Brigade, *see* Balaclava, battle of

Chariots, horse-drawn, 32

Charlemagne, king of the Franks, Roman emperor, 166, 167–170, 192, 229, 303; invaded Spain, 177; canonized by Frederick Barbarossa, 223; recognition of Venice, 239; war of Christian reconquest in Spain, 274

Charleroi, battle of, 633, 651, 943

Charles, archduke of Austria, 634, 636, 637, 640, 643, 644

Charles I, Austrian emperor, 970, 973, 974, 1013, 1019, 1122

Charles, cardinal of Bourbon, 413

Charles (Guise), cardinal of Lorraine, 411

Charles IV, duke of Lorraine, 477, 479

Charles, duke of Maine and Provence, 409

Charles, duke of Mayenne, 413

Charles I, Holy Roman Emperor, *see* Charlemagne

Charles II (the Bald), Holy Roman Emperor, king of Neustria, 166, 167, 170, 172, 173

Charles III, Holy Roman Emperor, *see* Charles (the Fat), king of France

Charles IV (Luxemburg), Holy Roman Emperor, 310, 325, 327, 337

Charles V, Holy Roman Emperor, 398, 399, 418, 426, 448, 452, 483, 501, 529, 532, 580; wars with Francis I, 411, 421–422, 428, 429, 430; wars with Henry II, 411, 530; ruled Spain as Charles I, 415–416, 417, 428, 538, 563; Tunis expedition, 416, 452; and treaty of Cambrai, 416, 422; and Holy League, 421; and League of Cognac, 422; conflict with Pope Adrian VI, 424; accomplishments of reign, 428–430; Algiers expedition, 430, 563

Charles VI, Holy Roman Emperor, 476, 500, in war of the Spanish Succession, 481, 483, 487; and Austrian succession, 476, 489, 501

China (cont'd)
with Russia, 753, 913; scramble for concessions in, 913–914; Hundred Days of Reform, 914; Revolution (1911), 916; Republic, 916, 1110, 1339–1342; and World War I, 970; outbreak of hostilities (1937), 982; and Japanese occupation of Manchuria, 1036, 1108–1109, 1126; civil war (1920–1926), 1106; extraterritoriality in, 1106–1108; economic war against Japan, 1106–1108 passim; Japanese campaigns in (1937–1945), 1109–1111, 1128, 1152, 1338; Nanking government, 1110, 1338; and World War II peace terms, 1158; treaty with Soviets (1945), 1338; civil war resumed (1946), 1338. See also Chinese Nationalists; Chinese People's Republic; Sino-Soviet relations
China Foundation for Promotion of Education and Culture, 1107
Chincha Islands, 696, 851
Chinese (Karayō) architecture, 379
Chinese Communist Party, 1109, 1168
Chinese Eastern Railway, 913, 1034, 1107, 1108
Chinese Exclusion Act, U.S., 823
Chinese Immigrants Act, New Zealand, 936
Chinese-Japanese defensive alliance, see Sino-Japanese relations
Chinese labor: excluded from Transvaal, 670, 891; restricted in Australia, 930–932
Chinese Nationalists, 1107, 1152, 1153, 1159, 1338–1339, 1346; and U.N., 1163–1164, 1343; U.S. arms and ammunition to, 1229; operations in Burma (1953), 1319; driven from mainland, 1339; and offshore islands, 1339, 1343
Chinese-Nepalese treaties, 1340, 1341
Chinese People's Action Party, Singapore, 1321, 1322
Chinese People's Republic (Communist), 1159, 1184, 1209–1210, 1213, 1300, 1338–1342; and U.N., 1163, 1208, 1230, 1313, 1339, 1340, 1343; and COMECON, 1167; and India, 1167, 1313–1316, 1341; and Korean war, 1207, 1339, 1348, 1350; and Canada, 1238, 1239; and African nations, 1263, 1264, 1269, 1271, 1274, 1278, 1279, 1292; and Middle East, 1283, 1294; and Pakistan, 1317; and Ceylon, 1318; and Burma, 1320; and Viet Minh régime, 1324, 1325; and Vietnam war, 1328; and Cambodia, 1331; and Laos, 1333; and Indonesia, 1336; conviction of American airmen, 1340; Hundred Flowers campaign, 1340; Cultural Revolution, 1341–1342; nuclear capability, 1342; space satellite, 1358. See also Sino-Soviet relations
Chinese Republic, see China
Ch'ing dynasty, see Ta Ch'ing dynasty
Ching I K'ao, Chinese classic, 578
Ching-te-chen, Kiangsi, imperial kilns at, 576, 578, 579
Ching Ti, Chinese emperor, 371
Chin Hills, Burma, 904
Chin Khan, title adopted by Nurhachi, 575
Ch'in Kuei, Chinese emperor, 367
Ch'in Shih Huang Ti, see Shih Huang Ti
Ch'in Tsung, Chinese emperor, 366
Chioggia, see War of Chioggia
Chios, Ionian city, 68, 70, 74, 347, 425; in Social War, 77, 92; Turkish massacre at, 769
Chipembere, Henry, refugee minister of Maluoi, 1274
Chippewa Plains, battle of, 832
Ch'i-shan, signed Ch'uanpi convention, 910
Chisholm v. Georgia, U.S. Supreme Court decision, 806
Chita, capital of Far Eastern Republic, 1032

Chitor, 569
Chittagong armory raid, India, 1103
Chivington, John, American commander, 821
Ch'i-ying, Chinese Imperial commissioner, 911
Chkalov, V. P., Russian aviator, 618
Chlodio, Salian Frank king, 161
Chlothar, see Lothair I, king of the Franks
Ch'oe family, Korea, 373
Chōei, Takano, Japanese scholar, 919
Choir of Lincoln, 216
Chokier, Baron Surlet de, regent of Belgium, 672
Chola dynasty, Tamil kings, 141, 361–362
Ch'ŏlchong, king of Korea, 916
Chollet, defeat of Vendéans at, 632
Cholm, 947; battle of (1915), 949
Chopin, Frédéric, composer, 679
Chorotegan culture, 24
Chōsen, see Korea
Chōshū (W. Hondō), 919
Chosŏn (Japanese Chōsen), see Korea
Chosroes, king of Parthia, 124, 137
Chosroes I of Persia, see Anushirwan the Just
Chosroes II, see Khusru Parviz of Persia
Chotusitz, battle of, 502
Ch'ou An Hui, Chinese monarchist society, 1106
Chou dynasty, 145; Western, 56–57; Eastern, 57
Chou En-lai, Chinese Communist premier, 1168, 1219, 1283, 1325, 1339–1341, 1342; Albanian visit, 1209; African visit (1964), 1266, 1292, 1341; Pakistan visit (1964), 1266, 1292, 1341; visit to Ceylon, 1318; Rangoon visit (1964), 1320; Moscow visit (1964), 1341; meeting with Kosygin (1969), 1342
Chou-kou-tien, skeletal material at, 10, 11, 12
Chou-li, Chou Ritual text, 146
Chou Pei Suan Ching, mathematical text, 147
Chou Ta-kuan, Mongol emissary to Cambodia (Chen-la), 369
Chou Tun-i, Chinese philosopher, 367
Chremonidean war, 91, 96
Chrétien de Troyes, French poet, 245, 247
Christ, see Jesus
Christian I (of Oldenburg), king of Denmark, Norway, and Sweden, 336
Christian II, king of Denmark, 438–440
Christian III, king of Denmark, 440
Christian IV, king of Denmark, 402, 433, 435, 440
Christian V, king of Denmark, 509
Christian VI, king of Denmark, 509
Christian VII, king of Denmark, 509
Christian VIII, king of Denmark, 746
Christian IX, king of Denmark, 729, 746
Christian X, king of Denmark, 746, 1043, 1222
Christian, prince of Holstein-Augustenburg, 644
Christian Church, 130, 136, 154–155; and Constantine I, 133; and Justinian I, 188; and William the Conqueror, 207
Christian Democratic Left Party, Spain, 1186
Christian Democratic Party, Italy, 1188–1189
Christian era, 6, 15, 117
Christian Frederick, Danish prince, 747
Christiania, see Oslo
Christianity, 115–117, 126, 155–156; Celtic, 179, 184–185; Slavic, 192; Swedish, 219; in Norway, 219; in Russia, 259; African conversion by Frumentius, 353; suppressed in China, 575; in Japan, 581, 582; in Korea, 916

Dupont de Nemours, Pierre, French economist, 521
Dupuis, Jean, explorer, in Tonkin, 907
Duquesne de Menneville, marquis de, French colonial commander, 556
Durand Line, Indian-Afghan border, 899, 903, 1311
Durando, Giacomo, commander papal forces, 703
Durango, founded, 534
Durani dynasty of Afghanistan, 568
Durazzo, 802, 953, 955, 1023
Durban (previously Natal), 885, 1276
Durben, Teutonic Knights defeated at, 229
Dürer, Albrecht, German graphic artist, 431
Durey, Louis, French composer, 991
Durham, England, 207, 208
Durham, John George Lambton, 1st earl, governor-general of Canada, 657, 833
Dürnkrut, battle of, 265
Duroc, Géraud, duke of Friuli, French general, 648
Düsseldorf, 967, 1006, 1121, 1124, 1137
Dutch East India Company, organ of Dutch imperialism, 474, 476, 550, 580, 908; search for Northwest Passage, 614; and establishment of Cape Colony, 884
Dutch East Indies, 674, 986
Dutch Guiana, 1145
Dutch-Japanese dictionary, production of, 587
Dutch New Guinea, see Netherlands New Guinea
Dutch West India Company, 474, 543, 551
Dutch West Indies, 674
Dütschke, Rudi, German student leader, 1198
Dutra, Enrico, president of Brazil, 1259
Duvalier, François, president of Haiti, 1248
Duvieusart, Jean, Belgian political leader, 1178
Dvaravati, Buddhist kingdom in Siam, 371
Dvinsk, taken by Germans, 971
Dvořák, Antonin, Czech composer, 745
Dwelling-Place culture, 22
Dybowski, Ian, explorer in Africa, 879
Dyer, Reginald, and Amritsar Massacre, 1101
Dynasties, 29–31; Egyptian, 36–40; in ancient Israel, 44–45; Chinese, 56–57; Ptolemaic, 96–97

Eakins, Thomas, American artist, 831
EAM, Greek party, 1210
Eannatum, warrior of Lagash, 29
Eannes, Gil, Portuguese explorer, 385
Earldoms, 182, 207
Early, Jubal, general in U.S. Civil War, 820
Early Bird, communications satellite, 1357
Early Dynastic (Sumerian) period, 16, 29
Earthquakes: at Lisbon, 491; destroyed Reggio and Messina, 710; in Venezuela (1812), 841; in Ecuador (1949), 1257
East Africa, 9, 11, 23, 783, 872, 881–884, 1101; between two World Wars, 1082–1083; post-World War II, 1278–1281
East African agreement, Anglo-German, see Heligoland
East African Community, 1263, 1279
East African Syndicate (British), 884
East Africa Protectorate (British), 883
East Anglia, Anglo-Saxon kingdom, 179
East Berlin, 1197, 1198; Soviet tanks in, 1200. See also Berlin
Easter Island, 924, 950
Eastern Chalukyas of Vengi, 360
Eastern Chin dynasty, 147

Eastern Chou dynasty, see Chou dynasty
Eastern Empire, see Byzantine Empire
Eastern Europe, 254–267; World War I, 947–950, 961; peace settlements in, 961, 971–972. *See also* Communist bloc
Eastern Gangas, southern India, 361
Eastern Orthodox Church, 578
Eastern Province, Congo, 1270
Eastern Roumelia, 756, 761, 764, 776, 783, 784
Eastern Wei dynasty, 147–148
Easter Rebellion, Ireland, 980, 983, 1177
East German-Soviet agreements, 1168, 1200
East Germany (German Democratic Republic), 1166, 1169, 1184, 1194, 1199–1201, 1208, 1220
East Greenland, 1043, 1044
East Hopei, autonomous regime (1935), 1109, 1114
East India Company, English, see English East India Company
East Indies, 372, 580, 806, 855, 1154
Eastman, George, American inventor, 609
East Mark (Austria), 174
East Pakistan, see Pakistan
East Prussia, 334, 947, 978, 1143. *See also* Prussia
Eaton, Theophilus, English colonist in U.S., 550
Eban, Abba, Israeli foreign minister, 1285, 1286
Ebert, Friedrich, president of German Republic, 1005, 1007
Ebroin, mayor in Neustria, 164
Ecclesia, Athenian citizens' assembly, 65, 69
Ecclesiastical Titles Bill, 662
Echo I, balloon communications satellite, 1357
Eck, Johann, German theologian, 428
Eckardstein, Baron Hermann von, German diplomat, 790, 793
Eckardt, Tibor, Hungarian political leader, 1020
Eckener, Dr. Hugo, commanded *Graf Zeppelin,* 620–621
Eckmühl, battle of, 643
Eclipses, 56
Ecloga, codification of Byzantine law, 190
Ecnomus, battle of, 99
Ecole Polytechnique, 526, 528
Economic and social council, United Nations, 1157
Economic Commission for Africa, 1261
Economic Co-operation Administration (E.C.A.), U.S., 1165, 1195, 1228
Ecorcheurs, French anarchists, 302
Ecthesis, Eastern Church doctrine, 166, 189
Ecuador, 851–852, 1063, 1064, 1125, 1145, 1256, 1257
Ecumenical councils, 133, 155, 190, 193, 1190, 1191
Eddas, literature of heathen Scandinavia, 186
Eddington, Arthur S., English astronomer, 598
Eddystone Lighthouse, 526
Eden, Anthony, earl of Avon, British statesman, 982, 1000, 1171, 1173, 1210; and Potomac charter, 1230; and Suez crisis (1956), 1283
Eden, Charles, U.S. colonial governor, 553
Edessa, 139, 140, 275
Edgar I, king of England, 182, 217
Edgehill, battle of, 403
Edict of Boulogne, 411
Edict of Caracalla (*constitutio Antoniniana*), 128
Edict of Milan, 133, 138
Edict of Nantes, 413, 480, 884
Edict of Restitution, Thirty Years' War, 433–434
Edict of tolerance, Emperor Joseph II, 505

Ituzaingó, battle of, 845, 854
Ius auxilii, 84
Ivan I Kalita (Moneybag), grand prince of Moscow, 340, 341
Ivan II Krasnyi (the Red), grand prince of Moscow, 340
Ivan III (the Great), Russian grand duke, 333, 341–342, 442, 444
Ivan IV (the Terrible), tsar of Russia, 442, 444–447, 448
Ivan V, tsar of Russia, 514, 516
Ivan VI, tsar of Russia, 516
Ivangorod, battle of, 949
Ives, Charles, American composer, 1053
Ivory, 353, 384, 879
Ivory Coast, West Africa, 875, 876, 877, 1261, 1264, 1266
Ivry, battle of, 413
Iwakura, Prince Tomomi, Japanese statesman, 920–921
I Wen Lei Chü, Chinese literary encyclopedia, 364
Iwo Jima, battle for, 1154
Iyengar, Srinivasa, Indian nationalist leader, 1103
Izmailov, Lev Vasilievich, his mission to China, 578
Izmir, *see* Smyrna
Izumo, 150
Izvolski, Alexander, Russian foreign minister, 797, 798, 799
Izzet Pasha, Ahmet, Turkish grand vizir, 972

Jabir (Gebir) Arab scholar, 204
Jablochkoff, Paul, Russian electrical engineer, 608
Jaca, mutiny of garrison at, 992
Jackson, Andrew, U.S. president, 810–811, 812–813
Jackson, Frederick George, Arctic explorer, 617
Jackson, Frederick John, British emissary in Uganda, 882
Jackson, Mississippi, civil rights march on, 1233
Jackson, Thomas (Stonewall), U.S. general, 817, 819
Jackson State College, Mississippi, 1236
Jacksonville, Florida, in Civil War, 817
Jacobi, Karl G. J., German mathematician, 595
Jacobins, France, 630, 631, 632, 633, 637. *See also* Dominican monks
Jacobites, Scotland, 468, 470
Jacquard, Joseph M., French inventor, 605
Jacqueline, countess of Holland, 406
Jacquerie, peasant uprising in France, 297–298
Jacques I, emperor of Haiti, *see* Dessalines, Jean-Jacques
Jadad, Salah al-, Syrian military leader, 1300
Jadar, battle of the, 947
Jadwiga (Hedwig), queen of Poland, 333, 337, 340
Ja'far, uncle of Muhammad the Prophet, 202
Jafar Shah, Persian sovereign, 568
Jaffa, 635, 972, 1092
Jagan, Cheddi, Guianan politician, 1250–1251
Jagellon dynasty, Poland, 442
Jagiello (Vladislav V of Poland), grand duke of Lithuania, 333, 337, 340
Jagiello family, rulers of Bohemia, 448
Jagow, Gottlieb von, German foreign minister, 1004
Jahangir, Nur-ud-din, Mogul emperor, 569, 572, 573
Jahn, Friedrich Ludwig, Prussian gymnastic director and patriot, 643
Jahwarids of Córdoba, 249
Jaime I of Aragon, *see* James I, king of Aragon
Jainism, in southern India, 144, 356, 360, 572
Jains, 54, 55, 56, 360, 572
Jaipal, king of Bhatinda, 356

Jakarta, *see* Batavia
Jalandhara, fourth church council at, 141
Jalayr dynasty in Iraq and Azerbaijan, 354
Jalula, 140
Jamaat-i-Islami, Pakistan Moslem party, 1317
Jamaica, 390, 529, 659, 1250, 1251; captured by English, 461, 536; U.S. bases, World War II, 1137, 1144, 1146
Jamal Khan, minister of Ahmadnagar, 572
Jamal ud-Din el-Afghani, Moslem politician, 868, 897
Jamdat Nasr period, southern Mesopotamia, 16
James (Jaime) I (the Conqueror), king of Aragon, 251, 252, 277
James II, king of Aragon, 237, 306, 313
James I, king of England (James VI of Scotland), 399, 400–401, 433, 572
James II, king of England, 464–465, 466, 467, 476, 480; lord high admiral and warden of Cinque Ports, 461, 463, 464, 552
James III, king of England, *see* James Edward (the Old Pretender)
James I, king of Scotland, 296
James II, king of Scotland, 296
James III, king of Scotland, 296
James IV, king of Scotland, 395
James V, king of Scotland, 398
James VI, king of Scotland, *see* James I, king of England
James VIII, king of Scotland, *see* James Edward, the Old Pretender
James, Henry, American novelist, 831
James, William, American psychologist and philosopher, 593
James Edward (the Old Pretender), 465, 467–468, 470, 483
James of Lusignan, 322
Jameson, Sir Leander Starr (*known as* Doctor), Scottish statesman in South Africa, 788, 888, 889, 890, 892
James the Greater Saint, Christian apostle, 178
Jamestown, Virginia, 548, 553
James W. Ellsworth Land, Antarctica, 627
Jammu, 1313
Janet, Pierre, French psychologist, 593
Janiculum, 86
Janina, invested by Greeks, 802
Janissary corps, Ottoman, 350, 450, 518, 767, 770; decline of, 453, 454
Jankau, Imperialist defeat at, 436
Jan Mayen Island, 614, 1044
Jansen, Cornelius, Dutch theologian, 484, 493
Jansenism, 484, 485, controversy, 493, 494
Jansky, Karl, scientist, 598
Janson, Paul, Belgian prime minister, 986
Janszoon, Willem, Dutch navigator, 924
Janus, Roman temple to, 111, 114, 122
Japan, 10, 18, 56, 150–152, 369, 373–383, 815, 917–923, 1344–1347; and ancient Korea, 149; culture, 374, 376, 379, 382, 582, 585, 586; Portuguese expelled from, 580; national unification period, 581–583; Tokugawa period, 583–587; isolationism, 583, 586; -U.S. relations, 828, 1152; Meiji period, 921–923; Taishō period, 923; and World War I, 923, 950, 969, 970; and Vladivostok, 1032, 1111; creation of Manchukuo, 1035, 1036, 1108; occupation of Manchuria, 1049, 1108–1109, 1126; Canadian diplomats in, 1055; treaty with Siam (1924), 1104; demands on China, 1106, 1109, 1111; campaigns in China (1937–1945), 1109–1111, 1128, 1152, 1338; new order in Far East, 1110, 1111, 1120; between

Moors, 251, 253, 306, 696; expelled from Castile, 304, 452

Moplahs (Muslim peasants of Malabar), uprising of, 1102

Moqui indians, 534

Moraes Barros, Prudente José de, president of Brazil, 856

Morales, Agustin, president of Bolivia, 850

Morality plays, 294

Morat, battle of, 303, 330

Moratorium, inter-governmental debts, 1122, 1125-1126

Moratorium Day, anti-Vietnam, 1235

Morava River, battle of, 949

Moravia, 173, 255-257, 327, 343, 426; revolutionary movement (1848), 720; Nazis in, 1012, 1018, 1130

Moravian missions (British), South Africa, 885

Moravska Ostrava, German-Czech skirmish at, 1129

Moray, earl of, see Randolph, Thomas

Morazan, Francisco, president of Central American Confederation, 857

More, Sir Thomas, English humanist, 398, 405

Morea, 239, 345, 347, 348; Ottoman conquest, 352; Venetian conquest, 496; insurrection (1821), 769

Moreau, Jean Victor, French soldier, 634, 636, 637, 640

Morel, Edward D., deplored conditions in Congo, 880

Morelos y Pavón, José Maria, Mexican priest and patriot, 842-843

Moreno, Mariano, sought control of Banda Oriental and Paraguay, 839

Moresby, Fairfax, English naval commander, 931

Moresnet, ceded to Belgium, 978, 986

Moret, Sigismondo, led Spanish Liberals, 697

Moreton Bay, Australia, convict settlement at, 928

Morgagni, Giovanni, Italian pathologist, 524

Morgan, Daniel, U.S. Revolutionary general, 562

Morgan, John Pierpont, American financier, 826

Morgan, Sir Henry, British buccaneer, 536

Morgan, Thomas H., American zoologist, 602

Morgan-Belmont banking syndicate, 826

Morgarten, battle of, 329

Morillo, Pablo, Spanish general, 841-842

Morinaga, son of Daigo II of Japan, 381

Morinigo, Higenio, prime minister of Paraguay, 1254

Moriscos, converted Moslems in Spain, 417

Morley, Edward W., American scientist, 597

Morley, John, British colonial secretary, 667, 903

Mormon Church, organized in U.S., 812

Mornington, Richard Wellesley, lord, Indian administrator, 900

Morny, Charles Auguste Louis Joseph de, duke of, half-brother of Napoleon III, 682

Moro, Aldo, Italian political leader, 1190

Moro, Ludovico, ruler of Milan, 409

Moroccan-Tunisian friendship treaty (1957), 1288

Moroccan-Tunisian railway, opened, 1080

Morocco, 9, 249, 286, 792, 873, 991; early cultures, 22; trade with North Africa, 353; crisis of 1905, 668, 692, 741, 795, 894; crisis of 1911, 693, 710, 742, 799-800, 874, 877, 880; Spanish campaign against Moors in, 696; Franco-Spanish agreement regarding, 698, 794, 795, 988; Franco-Italian agreement (1900) concerning, 793; German-French agreement on, 799; insurrection of 1925, 988; Franco-Spanish campaign in, 992; Spanish Morocco, 993, 1079, 1080, 1081, 1261, 1288; between World Wars, 1079-1081; French Morocco, 1080, 1081, 1148, 1182, 1288; self-rule, 1182;

International Zone, 1185, 1288; withdrawal of Spanish protectorate (1956), 1185; Tangier became part of, 1261; and Arab League, 1263, 1284, 1288; and U.N., 1270, 1288-1289; independent kingdom, 1288-1289

Moronobu, Hishikawa, Japanese artist, 586

Morosini, Francesco, Venetian general, 496

Morosini, Pier, Latin patriarch of Constantinople, 277, 280

Morotai, 1154

Morrill Act (1862), U.S., 821

Morrill tariff (1861), 820

Morris, Sir Edward, premier of Newfoundland, 837, 1057

Morris, William, English poet and artist, 672

Morrison, American ship, visited Japan, 918

Morrison, Herbert, British foreign secretary, 1172

Morrison, Robert, missionary in China, 909

Morrow, Dwight W., U.S. ambassador to Mexico, 1048, 1070

Morse, Samuel F. B., invented telegraph, 608

Mortier, Édouard duc de Trévise, French soldier, 649

Mortimer, Roger de, paramour of Isabelle of France, 287

Mortimer's Cross, battle in War of Roses, 293

Mortmain, statute of, 215, 291

Morton, John, bishop of Ely, 294

Morton, William T. G., used ether in surgery, 600

"Morton's Fork," royal revenue, 395

Morveau, Guyton de, see Guyton de Morveau, Baron Louis

Moscicki, Ignace, president of Poland, 1038, 1053, 1132

Moscoso, Luis de, in conquest of Florida, 535

Moscow, 259, 340, 342, 444, 447; university of, 516, 524; French occupy, Russians burn, 647; workers' insurrection (1905), 754; seat of government (1917), 1031; treaty of (1920), 1040; Russian-Japanese non-aggression pact (1941), 1140, 1152; Germans besiege (1941), 1141; conferences of foreign ministers, (1943) 1156, (1947) 1164, 1193, (1945) 1347; limited test ban treaty signed at (1963), 1161, 1218; conference (1954) of Communist nations, 1166; 81-party conference (1960), 1167; Tito visits, 1168; Chou En-lai visits, 1168, 1341; Harold Wilson visits, 1175; Adenauer visits, 1196; Klaus of Austria visits, 1202; conference of Communist Parties (1969), 1219; Ben Bella visits (1964), 1291; Sukarno visits (1956), 1336

Moselle River, canalization of, 1196, 1197-1198

Moses, Hebrew lawgiver, 39, 42-43

Moshesh, leader of the Basutos, 885, 886

Moshoeshoe, king of Lesotho, 1278

Moslem Brotherhood: Egypt, 1294, 1295

Moslem League, India, 1312, 1317

Moslems, 140, 199-206, 304; at battle of Tours, 164, 166, 177, 202; conquered Sicily, 166, 172, 192, 230; reduced by Charlemagne, 169; dominated Mediterranean, 172, 192, 193; articles of faith, fundamental duties, 199; cultural contributions of, 204-205; in First Crusade, 274; in Egypt and North Africa, 286; in India, 355, 572, 901; in China, 370, 911; commercial operations in Malaysia, 372; and Mussolini, 1001; insurrection in Albania, 1023

Mosquera, Tomás, president of New Granada, 852, 853

Mosquera Narváez, Aurelio, president of Ecuador, 1064

Mosquito Indians (Nicaragua and Honduras), 858

Mossadegh, Mohammed, premier of Iran, 1310

Mossamedes, Africa, 878